P9-CKT-244

NOW BATTING, NUMBER...

NOW BATTING, NUMBER...

The Mystique, Superstition, and Lore of Baseball's Uniform Numbers

JACK LOONEY

PRINCIPAL PHOTOGRAPHER, JOHN TREMMEL

BLACK DOG
& LEVENTHAL
PUBLISHERS
NEW YORK

Published by
Black Dog & Leventhal Publishers, Inc.
151 West 19th Street
New York, NY 10011

Distributed by
Workman Publishing Company
708 Broadway
New York, NY 10003

Manufactured in China

Cover design by Jon Valk
Interior design by Jack Looney

Cover photograph/illustration Getty Images
ISBN-13: 978-1-57912-575-2
ISBN-10: 1-57912-575-1

h g f e d c b a

Library of Congress Cataloging-in-Publication Data available on file.

DEDICATION

TO MY LORETTA
who always sums things up so simply and so humanly

My wife grew up in Brooklyn.
One morning she was remembering summer afternoons
when she was young.

"Baseball was like church.
I remember on a Sunday afternoon we would be playing outside
and all the windows would be open.
The game would be on, floating out into the courtyard
from radios and televisions.
It was like stereo—
the different announcers' voices echoing around the walls of the projects.

"The Dodgers somehow represented us,
our community.
And it was very, very important.

"I was too young to understand why it was so important,
but it was an amazing phenomenon.
Nobody was outside,
they were watching the game.
We knew that we couldn't interrupt our fathers.

"We would play on the monkey bars
and sit in the monkey barrels which was like a concrete tunnel.
When something would happen it would echo in there
and we would cheer along
with all the roars coming from all the windows."

Memories on baseball from
Red Hook, Brooklyn

This book would not have been possible
without my wife Loretta's support.

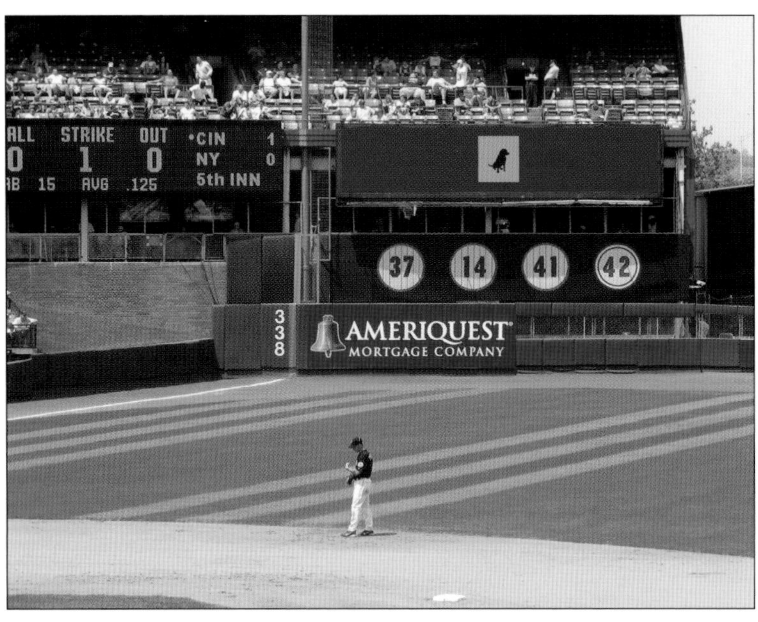

ALL STRIKE OUT
0 1 0
AB 15 AVG .125
CIN 1
NY 0
5th INN
37
14
41
42
338
AMERIQUEST
MORTGAGE COMPANY

NOW BATTING, NUMBER...

TABLE OF CONTENTS

ACKNOWLEDGMENTS

This project has taken many years to put together and in the course of time many people have helped along the way. This is an attempt to acknowledge as many of those people as can be remembered. Forgive me if I have omitted anyone.

Many organizations and individuals have gone out of their way:

Babe Ruth Museum, Baltimore (Greg Schwalenberg)
National Baseball Hall of Fame Library in Cooperstown (Tom Heitz, Bill Guilfoile, Frank Simio, Jim Gates, Bill Francis and staff)
Philadelphia A's Historical Society (Max Silberman)
St. Louis Browns Historical Society (Bill Borst)
St. Louis Cardinals Hall of Fame and Museum (Paula Homan)
Washington Baseball Historical Society

Baseball people who have lent a hand:
Bill Acree, Rob Anthony, Buddy Bates, Mike Burkhalter, Cy Buynak, Joe Cochran, Frank Coppenbarger, Bob DiBiasio, Leonard Garcia, Jay Horwitz, Ralph Kiner, Dennis Liborio, Joe Macko, Doug McWilliams, Phyllis Merhige, Buck O'Neil, Brian Prilaman, Nick Priori, Scott Reifert, John Ricco, Jerry Risch, Jeff Ross, Jim Schmakel, Larry Shenk, John Silverman, George Toma, Joe Torre, Jim Wiesner, Roger Wilson, Butch Yatkeman.

Folks who helped with old scorecards and copying information:
Kevin Andrews, Bob and Pat Bartosz, George Charabowski, Paul Christman, Steve Crawford, Bob Crestohl, Bryan Dec, Bill Diebold, Harold Esch, Joe Esposito, Scot Eyler, Norm Furrow, Scott Gaynor, Doug Goodman, Luke Griffin, Don Hannaford, Craig Hirsch, Patrick Hyde, Kasey Ignarski, Steve Johnson, Herman Kaufman, Don Lancaster, Frank Lhotsky, Lew Lipset, Jeffrey Miller, Doug Ries, Alan Sayarot, Doug Scancarella, Bill Schacht, Todd Schultz, Howard Singer, Lyle Spatz, Jon Springer, Mark Stang, Dave Stephan, Jerry Stern, Fred Taylor, Doug Templeton, Pete Teves, Keith Townsend, Dick Trenery, Steve Verkman, Bob Yahr and a fellow I only know as Phillies Rich.

Some publishing people who have helped from the beginning:
Ian Ballantine, Linda Cunningham, Oscar Dystel, Joe Gonnella, Bill Huelster, Richard Hunt, Tom Lovett, Esther Margolis, Steve Rubin, Polly Schatz, Nan A. Talese.

To those who added creative thinking and general encouragement: Sean, Deb, Jack and Sarah Looney; Jen, Julie and Don Seaman.

To the technical people who kept bailing me out of trouble: Jim Schiuma and my son Doug Looney.

And special thanks to:
John Oats who contributed copies of his vast Houston collection;
Pat Borelli, who gave me the following Cardinals' numbers:
1923: all; 1934: 24,27,29,31; 1937:30,31; 1939: 4,4,18,19; 1940: 2, 7, 17, 28, 31,42; 1942: 34; 1948: 39; 1950: 40; 1956: 38; 1958: 36; 1960: 19; 1968: 14; 1974: 29.
Herm Krabbenhoft gave me the following Tigers' numbers:
1931: 5, 8; 1936: 16; 1941: 17, 34; 1945: 2, 39; 1954: 21; 1956: 33; 1974: 37, 39.
The boys at Retrosheet: Dave Smith, Jim Wohlenhaus and Luke Kraemer. Their concern was constant.
Bill Deane, for his help at the Hall of Fame and afterwards.
John Ziccardi, my agent, who grabbed the project and ran like Rickey—not Branch.
John Tremmel, whose photos make it all work.
JP Leventhal, who has the same inborn enthusiasm for the Game.
And to Becky Koh, my editor, who has fielded everything anywhere near her.

Jack Looney

& COM
York Stock Exchange
Mezzanine
Boatmen's Bank Building
Always as close
s your telephone
Phone DElmar 4720
ST END LAUNDRY
Smack...
others lack
Bavarian Malt
MALT EXTRACTS
SYRUP or POWDER FORM
lumbia Products Co.
2545 W. Dodier Street
BLOCK OF ICE
er Gets Out of Order
We Will Deliver All The
I-C-E
Want...When You Want It!
ION FUEL & ICE
The Browns Wear Raw
FALST
Smoke
a fresh
cigarette
Car
in the ne
WASHINGTON
22 Hayes, 2b
2 S. Rice, rf
3 Manush, lf
4 Cronin, ss
5 West, cf
Kuhel or Jordan, 1b
7 Bluege, 3b
8 Spencer, c
12 Marberry, p
PEVELY
Select
ICE
CREAM
Bricklets
& Eclairs
SERVED
IN PARK
OLD G
NOT A COUGH IN A CAR
NO-JAX
Rawlings
COSTA RICA
★ OFFICIAL BALL ★
NATIONAL LEAGUE
PRES.
★ OFFICIAL BALL ★
AMERICAN LEAGUE
PRES.

INTRODUCTION

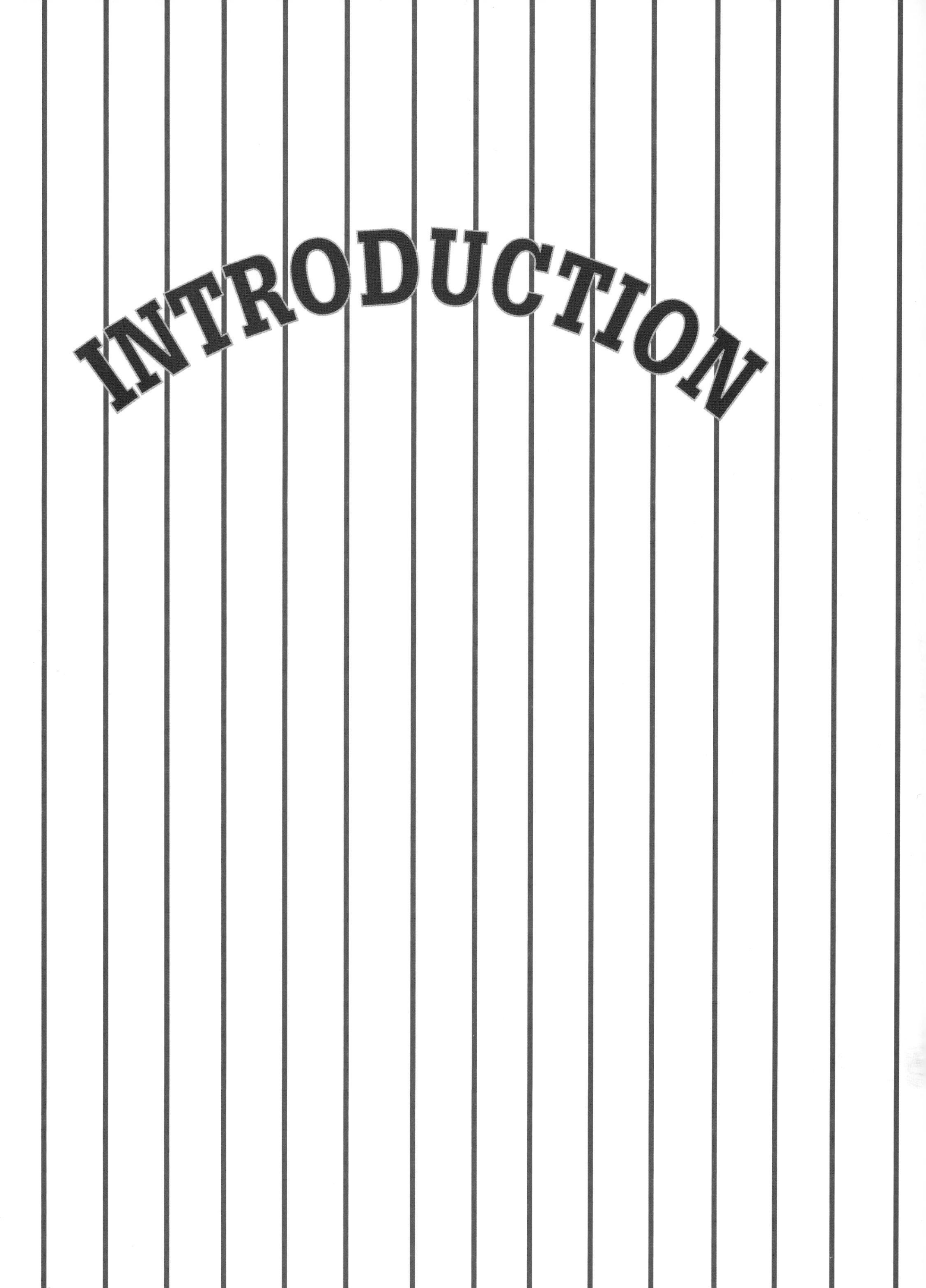

Why would anyone write a book about baseball uniform numbers? Who cares? With a baseball fan, it's a subject about which there are no two-minute conversations. Once you get started with the stories, the superstitions, the guessing games—it goes on and on.

That there is a passion for uniform numbers within the baseball community is very obvious. Roger Clemens paid $16,000 for a beautiful Presidential Rolex watch to help coerce his #21 from Carlos Delgado when he joined the Toronto Blue Jays in 1997. Clemens had worn the number with the Red Sox for his entire 13-year career. But he realized that Delgado had worn it for his revered countryman, Roberto Clemente.

Not taking Delgado's situation lightly, Clemens approached him with respect and admiration for his dedication to his hero.

"I wanted to give him a little memento for the number he passed along. I knew it was special to him, too, because of Clemente," said Clemens. "After I gave it to him, five other guys told me their number was a pretty good one, too."

Delgado was quite philosophical, "It's a seniority thing. He has won Cy Young Awards, MVP Awards. He's going to help us a lot. He could take me to the World Series," he said. "Hopefully, if it is the other way around some day, a young guy will give his number to me."

A player's number is serious business. The mystical qualities, the myths and legends that spring up surrounding numbers in the game of baseball will be explored in the pages ahead. Hundreds of anecdotes and tidbits that flavor the national pastime will be found. We've all heard a great many stories told through the years, but the amazing thing is new tales unfold in the briefest of conversations.

The gathering of accurate data was not an easy task. Some major league ballclubs were extremely helpful. Others did not even keep records that could help.

A young pitcher came in to relieve from the visitor's bullpen at Yankee Stadium back in the forties. Older fans may remember the lanky lefty, Mickey McDermott, who began his career with the Red Sox. The public address system announced him: "Coming in to pitch for the Red Sox, number 36, Maurice McDermott, number 36." And indeed, you could clearly see he was wearing #36 as he took his warm-ups. The scorecard that day listed: #38 McDermott, p. Errors occur quite frequently—especially for the players on the visiting team.

USA Today's *Baseball Weekly* carried Dave Hansen of the Dodgers as wearing #15 until September in 1994, when in fact he had changed to #5 very early in the season. I discovered this fact when I saw a ballgame in Los Angeles that June. Many of the publications are unable to keep up with the frequent roster and number changes. There is a great deal of jockeying among players following spring training to get better numbers, but the results are often missed by publications who continue to show the spring numbers well into the season.

Many of the baseball people approached in putting this book together have expressed a geniuine interest in it and were looking forward to being a part of it.

Mike Burkhalter, the young equipment manager for the Kansas City Royals was happy to see that the EMs were going to be an integral part of a baseball perspective.

"It's about time that the equipment managers are going to have a little of the spotlight on them and be included in a book on baseball," he said.

John Silverman, the Montreal Expos equipment manager said, "You know what I like about this book? It's fun. Nobody's stabbing anybody else in the back. It's just good, clean baseball fun."

Baseball has been seriously hurt by the players and the owners with their continual strikes, lockouts and squabbles with complete indifference to the fan. Nearly one-third of America's baseball fans stopped coming to the ballparks. Attendance at minor leagues games rose sharply indicating the fans would rather see the game played by youngsters on their way up without the bickering and threat of an abrupt end to the season. This became more evident with the failure to play a World Series in 1994. It was the nail in the coffin for many a fan.

But on September 6, 1995 an entire country put aside their chagrin and annoyance toward the feuding adversaries

Roger Clemens holds the ML single 9-inning game strikeout record—20. He did it twice. In one, he struck out 8 in a row, tying a record (April 29, 1986). He's won the Cy Young Award seven times (1986, 87, 91, 97, 98, 01 and 04), the MVP (1986), Pitcher of the Year (1986 and 91). And had an amazing major league batting average prior to Interleague play: 1.000. He got a basehit as a pinch-hitter in 1996 in his only at bat.

to watch Cal Ripken, Jr. be pushed from the dugout to reluctantly take a lap around Camden Yards after playing his 2,131st consecutive major league ballgame. It was a positive step toward filling in the deep crevice between major league baseball and the fan.

The Cinderella saga of Joe Torre and the Yankees the following year brought back a deeper touch of humanity to America's game. Torre's pursuit of his dream to be in a World Series and the personal strife he had to endure during the season: his brother Rocco dying and his brother Frank receiving a new heart, touched the hearts of all of us. Slowly, the fan is returning to the game. It is still a beautiful sport to watch—and considered by no less an authority than the late Ted Williams to be the most difficult to master. It is the sport that is historically linked to our lives and to the lives of our parents and grandparents. The game has grown up with America and we have grown up with it.

This is a look at baseball through the numbers the player's wear with the rich tales surrounding them. It is about the statistics they put up on the board seen from different perspectives. Together they create a look at the sport that is unique and fun.

What better way to celebrate baseball by bringing its fans together with a volume filled with the players and their numbers—uniform and statistics, boyhood idols, birthday babes, history and rosters of uniform numbers, dream teams by the number, all the retired numbers, Hall of Famers and challenging trivia questions. This book bridges the decades and takes you, the reader, through the scorecards of time and through the locker rooms of your favorite eras.

In a more practical vein, it will become an argument-solver as to who wore what when—a shirt collector's dream, and it will help you to look at the game through many different pairs of glasses.

OLIVARES
00
JORDAN
3
ROYER
5
7
JONES
8
11
12
16
18
408 FT.
11
14
37
41
00
13
9 13
2 18
2 34
2
DETROIT

THE MYSTIQUE 0

What is there about numbers?

Iron Man Cal Ripken, Jr. was always a class act. His dedication to the game was exemplified when his work ethic and some luck allowed him to play well past Lou Gehrig's record of 2,130 consecutive games. He returned the admiration of the fans by remaining after ballgames and signing hundreds of autographs. His character has been one of the most uplifting things to happen to baseball in a long, long time.

No one can deny that there is a certain fascination with numbers; the look of them, the feel of them, the power of them. From the earliest ages, we tend to like some numbers more than others. Pretty soon we have "a favorite number." In fact, most people have several numbers they prefer over others.

There's a little game to play when people insist they don't have a favorite. First, find out which group of digits they like better: one through five or six through zero. After some deliberation, people (if they're honest) will be rather definite about one group.

Next, ask if they like the number one better than the five, then if they like the two more than the four, the three better than the one or five and so on. Usually the person will admit that they like the remaining digit better than the others.

It can be more complicated than that, of course. One person asked discovered they liked the double digit 55 while another preferred the fraction 5/8, believe it or not.

Many people afflicted with this fascination of numbers have migrated to the game of baseball. The bookstores abound with volumes spouting figures. *The Sporting News publishes Baseball Guide, Baseball Register, Complete Baseball Record Book, Official Major League Baseball Fact Book* among others—every year! They are stacked with statistics of the past year, the history of the game and the upcoming year.

The Elias Sports Bureau puts out their *Elias Baseball Analyst* annually where you can find out that in 1986 Cal Ripken batted .272 vs. lefties ranking 70th in the AL, his strike out % was 6.14 placing him at 16 in the league, he batted .292 leading off an inning and knocked in runners from third with less than two outs 75% of the time!

Baseballistics, edited by Bert Randolph Sugar, has such entries as "Home Run Leaders by State of Birth" and "Most Times Awarded First Base on Catcher's Interference or Obstruction" and "Pitchers Who Gave Up Most Hits to Pete Rose."

Bill James is the acknowledged guru of baseball statistics having created such ways to analyze hitters as "Offensive Wins and Losses," "Park Adjustments," and "Isolated Power;" to analyze pitchers "Double Play Support" and "Pitcher Run Support" are included and for defense "Range Factor" and "Defensive Spectrum."

On page 2004 in *Total Baseball* by John Thorn and Pete Palmer which lists pitchers Charlie Young to Chris Zachary, there are 1,988 statistical tidbits to browse including the OOBP, the CPI and the SS rate—respectively: opponent's onbase percentage, clutch pitching index and superstat rate which considers player's averages compared to league averages, ballparks, normalized games and run production among other statistical data.

The game of baseball is already filled with numbers. It's 90' from base to base, 127' from home to second, 60'6" from the mound to home plate which is 17" across. A baseball has 216 stitches. It's 355' down the leftfield line in Wrigley, 402' to the centerfield monuments at Yankee Stadium in the Bronx.

It takes a 90-mph fastball (132'/sec.) approximately .40909 seconds to reach the plate from the point of release about 54' away. The batter has about half that time to determine whether or not it is a fastball, if it's in the strike zone, if it's a pitch he can handle and to pull the trigger to hit it.

With a runner on first, the pitcher will use another .5 or .6 seconds with a stretch windup and a slide step toward the plate.

A baserunner leading off firstbase about 7' watching for a combination of heel or shoulder movements by the pitcher to trigger his attempt to steal second should cover the remaining 83' in about 3.5 seconds. The catcher must respond to the situation, receive the ball, convert to a throwing mode and fire a pea 6" in front of the bag about 6-12" above the ground. All this in the 2.5 seconds he has after catching the pitch.

It's a game of inches. It's a game of milliseconds. Players, managers and coaches look for the slightest advantage to tilt games in their direction.

Teams have their groundskeepers grow the infield grass a little longer to slow the ground balls down allowing their speedy players to leg out hits. If the opponents have a slow-footed outfield, the grass is kept short for balls to skip between them.

One of the masters of one-up-manship was Charlie Finley of the A's. He was not a man to let a few feet beat him. His head groundskeeper was George Toma. George is probably the most celebrated man in his business. He is highly sought after for special events. Toma has prepared the playing fields for over 25 Super Bowls and American Bowls. They called in George Toma after the 1989 earthquake in San Francisco to ready the field to resume the World Series. He even made the All-Madden Team!

While the A's were in Kansas City, Finley wanted to boost sagging attendance and add excitement with more homeruns by moving the leftfield fence from 370' to 340'. In spring training, he told Manager Hank Bauer what he intended to do at the home park in Kansas City.

Toma recalls that Bauer was alarmed, "Change the signs to what the fences were before. Our pitchers will get shell-shocked if they see 340' signs out there," said Bauer.

Finley couldn't help staying out of trouble with the League office. He complained that the distances were wrong in Comiskey Park, Chicago. He got a 500' tape measure and paced off the leftfield line finding it a few feet short.

Unfortunately for Charlie, one of the beat writers following the teams, Joe Falls, picked up on the incident and started measuring all the parks.

Finley knew he was in trouble—"We're going to be off 30'," he reminded Toma. Before Falls got to Municipal Stadium in Kansas City, Finley called and admitted "the distances are off in my own ballpark."

During the 1960s, Finley constantly complained about the advantage the Yanks had with their short rightfield porch and their power hitters Mantle, Maris, Berra and Blanchard. He had Toma chalk a line on the outfield grass where the Yankee fence would have been.

On October 18, 1977, Mr. October crunched the second of his three homeruns in the 6th and final game of the World Series between the Yankees and the Dodgers. It took only three seconds (120'/sec.) to bury itself in the right centerfield stands of Yankee Stadium exploding the crowd into a frenzy anticipating victory.

Each time a ball was caught in the "zone," Finley instructed the announcer to say, "That would have been a homer in Yankee Stadium."

While the A's took off on a road trip, Finley actually built an overhanging porch to simulate the short Yankee fence. He called it his "Pennant Porch."

The very first game when the A's returned home, the umpires called Charlie over and asked what that obstruction was in rightfield. He, of course, was delighted to state his case for the "Pennant Porch," but to no avail. The game was held up while welders were brought in to remove it.

Finley needed more than a "Pennant Porch" to help the A's in Kansas City in the '60s. They finished or tied for last place four out of eight years there, not coming in above seventh. They changed their venue and fortunes in 1968 by moving to Oakland.

Numbers mean different things to different people. In the United States there is a preconceived notion that the number 13 is unlucky or even dangerous. Many buildings in cities skip 13 in numbering their floors. *Tridecophobia* they call it. Many ballplayers have a tremendous fear that the number 13 will effect their ability to play.

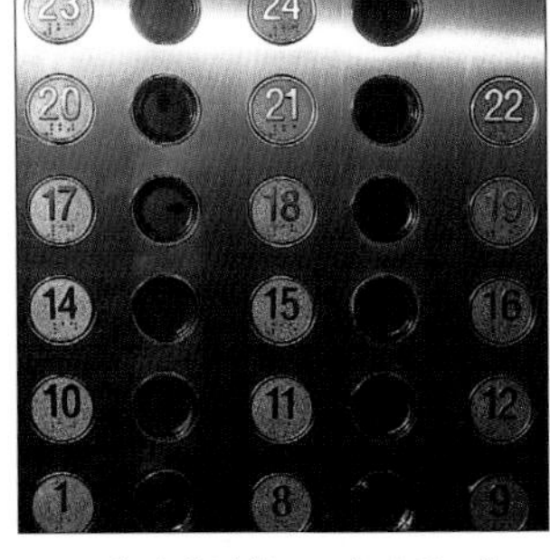

Who's kidding who? Do the people on the 14th floor really think it's not 13?

In Italy, the number 17 carries the same foreboding. Soccer is the national pastime. Superstar Roberto Donadoni missed the final penalty shot for Italy in the 1990 World Cup loss to Argentina while wearing #17. Four years later, Roberto Baggio, the team's top scoring star was to be assigned #17. Fear of a repeat of 1990 prompted team officials to shuffle the order and give #17 to Alberigo Evani. An outstanding midfielder, Evani severly pulled a hamstring and missed the final games.

I asked my Italian-born barber, Mario, about #17—what was all the hocus-pocus? He stopped mid-cut, his eyes bugged, he leaned back and groaned, "Ooooohhh, oooh, Number 17, ooooh no, you don't wanna wear 17, oh no, no, no, no!" Not much light shed on the mystique there.

Many major league clubs won't even assign #13. Players asking for a low number when told #13 is the only one open, will say, "Oh, no! Not 13!" recalled Cy Buynak, Indians former EM. Although the Yankees began wearing numbers permanently in 1929, it was eight years before Red Ruffing became the first Yankee to wear #13 in 1937. Pitcher Lee Stine wore in '38 and then it was another decade until Cliff Mapes switched from #3 when it was retired for Babe Ruth in 1948. The Pirates began numbering uniforms in 1932, but not until pitcher Kirby Higbe got the courage to wear it in 1948 was #13 worn.

Bill Shores, a pitcher for the Philadelphia A's was the first in the AL to wear #13 in 1931. Flint Rhem wore it with the Braves in 1934-35. Tommy Thompson switched to it when Rhem returned to St. Louis the following year. Bob "Fats" Fothergill was an outfielder ending his career when numbers were introduced. He was a .325 career hitter, but had tailed off in his later years. He wore #13 with the Red Sox in his final year of 1933 and batted .344.

After Buck Martinez was released by the Brewers, Jeff Ross, Toronto's EM asked him which number he want-ed in 1981.

"How about 13? I have nothing to lose after being released," said Buck.

He played for the Blue Jays for six more years before calling it quits.

Buddy Bates, the Cardinals EM said, "We always discouraged giving out #13, it's always left on the shelf. Neil Allen asked for it, we tried to talk him out of it. He had a disastrous tour here."

Bobby Valentine finally switched from #13 to #11 while on the Angels after his jaw was broken by a pitch, his leg was broken running into a wall and a ground ball broke his nose.

The Padres EM Brian Prilaman asked all the other players if they were okay with it when he issued #13 to a player. Many EM's secretly fret about the rest of the team if #13 is in circulation.

John Quinn, the Phillies GM, was dead-set against issuing #13. When Dick "Dr. Strangeglove" Stuart (a perennial #7 wearer) came to the Phils in 1965, Bobby Wine wore #7. Wine wore it because his first child was born on the seventh. Stuart felt he would make a stronger contribution to the club, so he should get 7. Wine wanted to switch to #13 because his second child was born on the 13th. The superstitious Quinn finally acquiesced.

"The Shot Heard 'Round the World" was delivered by Ralph Branca in relief. He was wearing #13. His and the Dodgers' season was over instantly in 1951. He switched to #12 for the next year, but returned to #13 in 1953.

Perhaps the most courageous player was John "Blue Moon" Odom who wore #13 for his entire ML career, from 1964 in Kansas City moving to Oakland through 1975. He went to the Indians and the Braves in '75, finishing with the White Sox the following year. Ironically his career spanned 13 years.

Young Bob Beall was miffed because he had to surrender #13 for Odom when he came to the Braves, "It's just another day in the life of a rookie," he said.

For one day in his career, Odom did not wear his beloved #13—it was August 10, 1968 in Washington. Catcher Dave Duncan (#10) was away on military reserves duty for two weeks.

"After three shots at win number 10, I thought I'd wear #10. That way I figured I'd win number 10," said Blue Moon.

He was right, he beat the Senators with his second one-hitter of the year.

"Lot of guys don't like number 13, but I think it's lucky. I've worn it since grammar school," summed up Odom.

Odom wasn't the first pitcher to think that switching his number could influence the outcome of a game. Back in 1942, Mort Cooper who also wore #13 was the ace of the powerful Cardinal staff at the time. He was mired on win number 13. He couldn't buy another victory. After a couple of losses and no decisions, he donned #14 which nobody was wearing then. He won his fourteenth. Next time out he swapped shirts with his brother Walker (#15) and he won his fifteenth. He then switched with Ken O'Dea (#16) and you guessed it. He won again. Mort went on to win 21 games that year for the pennant-winning Cards changing shirts as he went.

The 1933 Cincinnati Reds in their first full year of wearing numbers, finished dead last, a yawning 33 games behind. The majority of the pitching staff switched uniform numbers in an effort to shake things up.

It didn't work. They finished last again in 1934, a whopping 42 games back.

1933	1934
11 ALLYN STOUT	**11**
14 SI JOHNSON	**14** PAUL DERRINGER
15 RAY KOLP	**15** SI JOHNSON
16 BENNY FREY	**16** LARRY BENTON
18 EPPA RIXEY	**18** ALLYN STOUT
19 LARRY BENTON	**19** DON BRENNAN
21 PAUL DERRINGER	**21** RAY KOLP
28	**28** BENNY FREY

The Reds pitching staff before and after swapping numbers.

Blue Moon Odom pitched for 13 years with the number 13. He finished with 84-85 mark. He was an All-Star twice in 1968-69 going 16-10 and 15-6 respectively. He pitched for the great Oakland World Champions of 1972, 1973 and 1974 with dimishing effectiveness—15-6, 5-12, and 1-5 in that order.

Dwight Gooden started his career as a true phenom. After his first five years, he was 91-35, a winning percentage of .722. Whitey Ford leads all lifetime pitchers with .690. But Doc fell on hard times, so much so that in 1993 spring training he went back to wearing #64. That was the original number Doc was assigned in his first spring camp, hoping to bring back the magic that had started him on his sparkling career. He returned to his familiar #16 for the season.

His no-hitter in May of 1996 was with the Yankees while wearing #11.

A mysterious bond develops between a player and his number. It becomes the player. He begins to feel that it is part of him, that he cannot perform at his personal standard without it. He somehow will not be the same player if he's not wearing his number. Nick Priori, the former Yankees EM said, "My theory is that the player makes the number."

So many players will do just about anything to maintain their number. *The Philadelphia Enquirer* reported that Rickey Henderson paid Turner Ward a neat $25,000 to get his number 24 when he was picked up by the Blue Jays in August of 1993.

Bill Acre, the Braves equipment manager and travelling secretary, represents the pragmatic side of the subject. He told John Smoltz when he wanted to change from his 29 in the early '90s, "It's only a number. The person's the one that makes things happen."

The original purpose of numbering the players was for the fans to identify them. When names were sewn across the backs of the uniforms to further identify the players, why weren't the numbers discontinued? It wasn't even considered by anyone; not the teams, not the fans and certainly not the players.

It's clear that numbers go very deep, even into the player's psyche. It is part of his personality. Barry Bonds wanted to continue to wear his #24 in San Francisco even though it was retired for his Godfather, Willie Mays. Jim Kaat wanted to 'unretire' his #36 in Philadelphia, which was retired for Hall of Famer Robin Roberts. David Wells, being a Ruth fan, wanted the Yankees to give him the Babe's retired #3 in 1997. Fat chance! He did wear it in Boston in early 2005. Well-traveled Hall of Famers Joe Medwick and Gaylord Perry always sought out #7 and #36 respectively.

When particular numbers are not available, players will commemorate another player as Joe Torre did in St. Louis where he had his career year in 1971—leading the league in batting (.363), hits (230) and RBI (137). His old number was 15 with the Braves.

"That's what they gave me. I didn't have a choice," said Joe. "In St. Louis, McCarver had it, so I asked for #9. I wore it for Roger Maris. I knew him and I always admired and respected him," Torre stated.

Along with the practice of officially retiring numbers to honor players on a team, individuals will take it upon themselves to honor another. Bobby Knoop, the long-time coach of the Angels, started wearing his friend Deron Johnson's number after Johnson died. When Bob Moose died in 1976, his friend and fellow Pirate pitcher Jim Rooker started wearing his #38. Pitcher Bud Smith, formerly of the Cards, wore Darryl Kile's #57 in the Phillies' 2003 Spring Training camp honoring his sudden death the summer before. "He's out there with me. I love wearing his number out of respect. It's a personal thing that means a lot to me," said Smith.

Equipment managers or the front office also pull numbers out of circulation for a year or two. After that horrible boating accident in spring training 1993 where Tim Crews (#52) and Steve Olin (#31) were tragically killed, the Indians withheld their numbers till 1994 and 1995 repectively. The Yankees held Willie Randolph's #30 from his playing days until he returned as a coach.

Many teams commemorate players who haved passed on by wearing not only the traditional black arm band, but now have begun the practice of wearing the player's number on the sleeve.

The most unusual honoring occurred on the Florida Marlins. Their first president, Carl Barger died while attending the winter baseball meetings in Louisville. The team

Joe Torre began his career in Milwaukee, moved with the team to Atlanta, on to St. Louis and finished with the Mets. He led the league defensively in 1964 and 1968. He never led the league offensively in any department except in 1971 when he almost won the Triple Crown. Joe, a nine-time All-Star, finally made it to theWorld Series as the Yankee manager in 1996.

decided not to issue #5 in his honor. The number belonged to his favorite ballplayer, Joe DiMaggio of the Yankees.

Numbers were not held in universally high regard in the early years. Hall of Famer Bill Terry gave up his #3 when he left the field to manage in 1937. He took #30 (his birthday). In mid-season, Wally Berger came over from the Braves and immediately was issued Terry's #3.

A strong young pitcher named Bobby Munoz was brought up by the Yanks in 1993 in that media-crazed marketplace of New York. He was projected to be their next big closer and was issued #54 to emphasize the point. That was Goose Gossage's number and an awfully big image to live up to.

Before the next season began he was involved in a 5-player deal with the Phillies and he was gone.

When Yankees replacement player Dave Pavlas was assigned number 56 in 1995 it did not escape the attention of Jim Bouton. That was Jim's old number and he's convinced the Yankees have never forgiven him for writing the exposé "Ball Four" revealing some of the players' nighttime escapades. Bouton said, "I'm rooting for this guy like I've never rooted for anyone." He thought Pavlas' luck might change, "I'm 56 this year, so tell Pavlas it's a good omen."

Pavlas switched to #47 in 1996 and had not won or lost a game for the Yanks. He was not voted a World Series share by his teammates although he had pitched in 16 games and saved one.

Myths have sprung up around certain numbers. Tim Wakefield converted to a knuckleball pitcher after failing to make the grade as a third baseman. In AAA he said if he were to make the Pirates, he was going to ask for #49 and join "the knuckleball fraternity."

When he was called up, he found #49 already hanging in his locker—he didn't even have to ask for it.

In recent years, the number 49 has been worn by Charlie Hough and Tom Candiotti. People seem to think that the tradition started with Hoyt Wilhelm. Actually Wilhelm did wear #49 during his first five years with the Giants. He wore many numbers, but

After a modest start with the Yankees, Bobby Munoz was traded to the Phillies where he pitched well in 1994. He was switched to a starting role and went 7-5 with a 2.67 ERA. Injuries the next two years kept him winless with a mushrooming ERA.

Tom Candiotti has worn #49 knuckling down for the Brewers, Indians, Blue Jays, Dodgers and A's since breaking into the ML in 1983. His best year was in 1986 where he was 16-12 with 17 league-leading complete games for Cleveland.

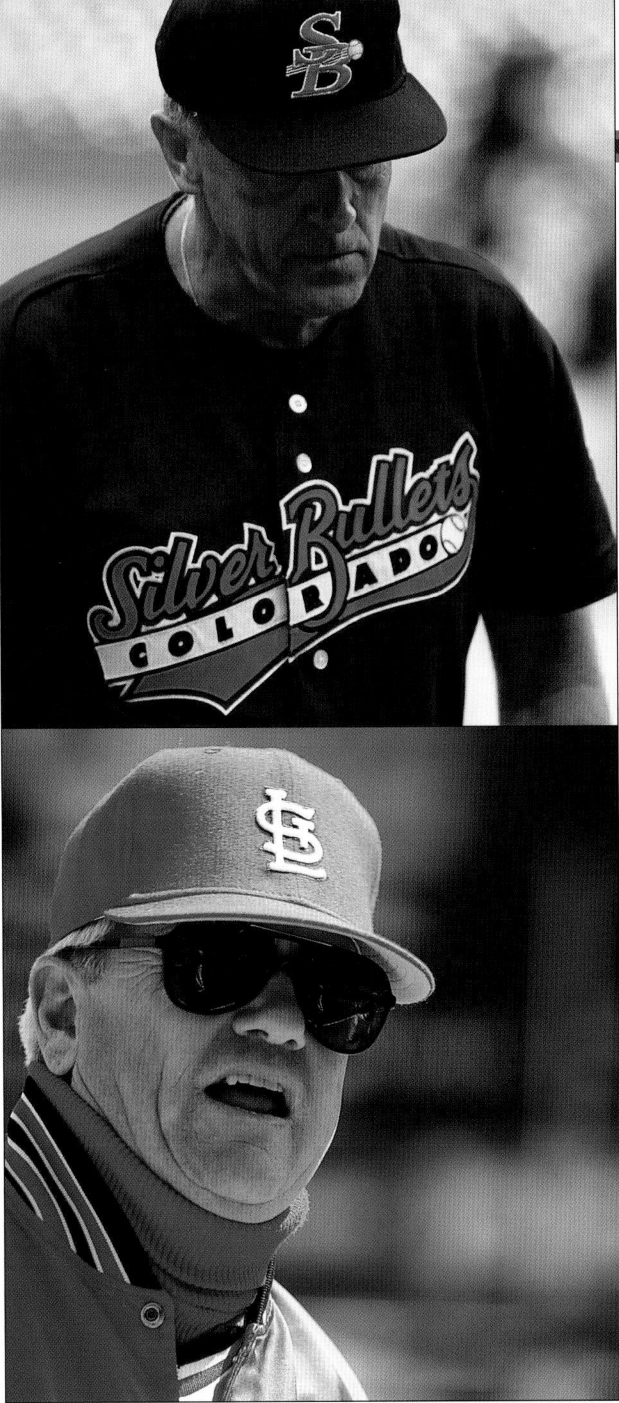

Phil Niekro (Above, top) pitched for 24 years, his knuckler affording him that longevity. The five-time All-Star won 20 or more games three times, led the NL in innings pitched and complete games four times, ERA and strike outs once each. Niekro was elected to the Hall of Fame in 1996. He won 318 games, but also lost 274, that's 29 more than Warren Spahn who won 363. Here he is shown as Manager of the Colorado Silver Bullets, the short-lived pro women's team.

After a modest playing career, Whitey Herzog (Above, bottom) turned to coaching and managing. He won six divisional titles, three pennants and one Championship in 1982 for St. Louis. Player selection and development were his strong suits, nurturing the mix with respect and spirit for team play.

wore #31 longer than any other. He had the opportunity to pick #49 on several occasions, but never wore it again. Incredibly, he retired at the age of 49. Prior to Wilhelm, Pete Alexander spent his whole career numberless. Dutch Leonard tossed his knuckler for the Dodgers, Senators, Phils and Cubs from 1933-1953. He never wore #49.

Johnny Niggeling, Roger Wolff, Mickey Haefner, and Willie "The Knuck" Ramsdell all preceeded Wilhelm and none ever wore #49. There were Barney Schultz and Wilbur Wood who toiled for 29 years between them and never wore #49. Phil Niekro wore #35 for his 24 years. It wasn't until Charlie Hough switched from #31 to #49 in his rookie season of 1970 and kept it for the rest of his career that the number was associated with a knuckler. Tom Candiotti wore it since his debut in 1983. All in all fewer years have seen knucklers wearing the number than not, but the idea is here to stay anyway.

There's also a preconceived notion that the manager wears #1. There are three managers who have retired the #1: Fred Hutchinson (Reds), Billy Martin (Yanks) and Billy Meyer (Pirates).

Martin wore the single digit longer as a manager than anyone else—16 years. But Martin wore the same number as a player. So it was his number anyway. Birdie Tebbetts wore it for a total of 9 years in two stints as manager, but he too wore it as a young catcher for six years with the Tigers. Another catcher turned manager, Del Crandall also wore #1 as both a player and a field leader. The first manager to wear it was Lew Fonseca, a playing manager who was a jack-of-all-trades with the White Sox in 1932-34. He played the outfield, first base and pitched. Lew went on to create his own company that would film the World Series for decades.

John McNamara sought out the number and wore it for 10 years. He never played in the Bigs. Al Dark never wore #1 in his playing days, but sought it out as a manager. Other than the managers mentioned above, no one wore the single digit for more than four years as a manager.

Collectively, since 1929, the #1 was worn by managers under 7% of the time or 108 years out of 1613 total team years through '05.

In Cincinnati the manager wore #1 from 1939-48 and 1954-64 when it was retired for Fred Hutchinson. It's the only team that actually planned to have its manager wear #1. The majority of players to wear #1 were outfielders (16 1/2%). Infielders as a whole wore the digit over 38% of the time with shortstops at nearly 12%.

Leonard Garcia, the Angels EM took it for granted that everyone did things by the numbers. Whitey Herzog while attending one of his many baseball meetings for Gene Autry's Angels was using a new suitcase supplied by Garcia.

Whitey had already left for Arizona when Garcia got a phone call at home. It was Whitey. Leonard was concerned because Whitey never called him at home.

"How the hell do you open this damned suitcase?" groaned an exaspirated Whitey.

"What's your number?" asked Garcia.

There was a pause.

"Your uniform number," said Garcia.

A puzzled answer, "Twenty-four."

"Your combination for the lock is 0-2-4," explained Garcia.

Numbers are everywhere. The players' equipment is all identified by their number in the clubhouse. Jewelry displaying a player's number has become so popular that a recent Spiegel Spring/Summer catalog showed 14K gold pendants—single digit: $79, double digit: $109. 'Prime Time' Deion Sanders, a two-sport pro played outfield for several clubs and was an all-pro cornerback in football. He wore two chains simultaneously—#21 for football and #24 for baseball. A photo of this was used in a Nike ad. Advertisers know how persuasive these images can be. How effective would the photo have been without the numbers?

Many players give their wives pendants with their digits on it. Often it will contain small diamonds shaped into the number. In Palm Springs, California a lot of the Hollywood hopefuls wear chains with #10 on them after the Bo Derek movie "Ten." Stan Musial had given his wife, Lillian, such a piece with his #6 on it. The Musials were having dinner in a restaurant out there when the waitress noticed her necklace. "Are you only a 6?" she asked.

Reggie Jackson has taken to incorporating his #44 into the loop of the J. He also has put "H.O.F. 93" and "Mr. October" on shirts that Upper Deck™ sells. The number with the signature is nothing new. As long ago as 1940 Barney Barnacle of the Braves circled his #27 beneath his signature. Mickey Mantle quite often added his #7 as well. Roberto Alomar squeaks a little 12 under his script. In other sports, big stars also do it. In hockey, the 'Great Gretsky' always includes a #99, Patrick Roy scribes his #33; in football, Dan Marino never signs without his #13. In fact, when he signs a shirt with his numeral 13 on it, he writes his name and #13 anyway. It's become letters in his name.

Footballer Seth Joyner (Top, left) shows his deceased friend and teammate, Jerome Brown, his dedication.

Prime Time (Bottom, left) weighing himself down with his gold pendants for Nike. They're his constant companion and reminder of his versitility and prowess.

Anyone can become a hero now. Pick a number (Top, right) and impress your girlfriend with your stories and your daring.

Reggie Jackson (Bottom, right) neatly squeezes his #44 into the lower loop of the 'J' of his last name. Although he wore #9 for nearly half his career, he elected to be recognized as #44 and entered the Hall as a Yankee where he spent only five years.

The veneration of numbers has spilled over from baseball into just about every sport and on every level. All-Star defensive end Reggie White left the Philadelphia Eagles to help Green Bay win the Super Bowl in 1997. His former jersey, #92, was given to young Bruce Walker out of UCLA. The Eagles new owner, Jeffrey Lurie pulled the shirt back saying, "I don't feel it's appropriate that a superstar like Reggie White's uniform should be worn by someone who hasn't proven their quality of play and quality as a person yet."

Drazen Petrovic, the New Jersey Nets basketball star who was killed in an auto accident while in Europe had his uniform #3 retired in Byrne Arena.

Michael Jordan retired from basketball and his shirt with his famous #23 was retired with him. Michael had turned to baseball where he wore #45. A frustrating year in AA ball saw Jordan returning to the game where he had no peers. Back with the Bulls he continued to wear #45, but Michael did not play well. He had gotten rusty. He decided to go back to his old faithful #23. And of course when Michael got back into playing shape, the Bulls again were the powerhouse of the NBA.

Even the University of Kentucky had retired nearly 30 shirts for their collegiate heroes. Curiously #44 was retired three times—Phil Grawemeyer (1954-56), Cotton Nash (1962-64) and Dan Issel (1968-70).

When Shaquille O'Neal joined Orlando, teammate Terry Catledge refused to give up Shaq's old #33. O'Neal took #32. "I think Shaq should wear 40 with a dollar sign in front of it," said a coy Catledge referring to his $40 million contract.

Advertisers see the power and value in sports' numbers. *Sports Illustrated's* double issue cover of December 27, 1993-January 3, 1994 entitled "93 Things That Went Right in '93" shows dozens of #19's and #93's of various jerseys and such. Nissan ran a large ad in the Sunday *New York Times* touting their dealerships throughout the NY-NJ-CT tri-state area as tops by displaying football jerseys with the twenty towns spelled out above a large #1.

Roma, a first-division hockey club in Sweden, was paid over $1,300 for a player to wear a radio station's frequency on his shirt—100.2.

Players shave numbers on their heads and dangle numbers from their necks. Little toddler's uniforms have pinstripes and authentic-looking numbers. Marge Schott named her dog 'Schottzie 02.' Players and others personalize license plates with numbers; put their numbers in brass on their houses; teams hang numbered-shirts from the rafters and paint numbers on the outfield walls. In some cities buildings have numbers traced in lights to honor players.

Numbers are such a powerful influence today. Sportswear worn by kids from grammar school to college and beyond appear naked or less-desirable if they don't display at least a number or more often a favorite player's name and number.

All in all, multi-billion dollar industries have sprung up merchandising sports and the players in them. Not only are contemporary players' names and numbers featured on shirts, hats, balls, jackets, you name it, but the memorabilia market has seen prices skyrocket. Autographed balls, numbered shirts worn during a memorable game, signed bats, cards, gloves and all the rest have risen so much that the casual collector has been all but pushed out of the marketplace.

The two Roger Maris #9's that were worn when he hit homerun #60 and #61 were removed from the shirts when they were cleaned and replaced by new ones. An industrious worker realized the historical significance of the digits. They were later framed on pinstriped backgrounds. They were sold at auction in 1988 for nearly $5000. Here, Roger hits #60 at the Stadium.

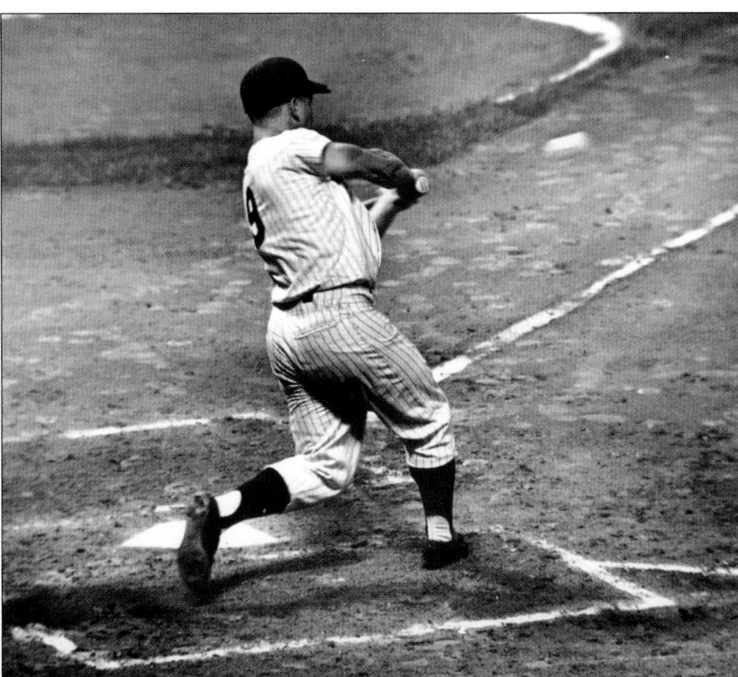

Billy Martin called his book with Peter Golenbock *Number 1*. In the book's foreword, Billy states, "*Number 1* is the story of my life. I hope when you're finished, you will have a better understanding of me as a player, manager, and person."

It's not just a business. It hasn't soley funneled down to dollars and cents. There are some who really care about what their number means, care about the history and tradition of their uniform and about baseball. The mystique is still alive. Just ask Phil. Or Cal. Or Lou who still considered himself "the luckiest man on the face of the Earth."

Billy Martin (Above, right) was considered by many who played for him the best manager they had ever seen. He won five divisional titles, 2 pennants and one World Championship in 1978 with the Yankees.

Phil Rizzuto (Right) was elected to the Hall of Fame in 1994 by the Veterans' Committee. He had a career year in 1950 batting .324, the only time he hit over .300 since his rookie year. He was voted the MVP Award for his outstanding play. Scooter anchored the Yankee infield in an incredible nine World Series during his 13-year career.

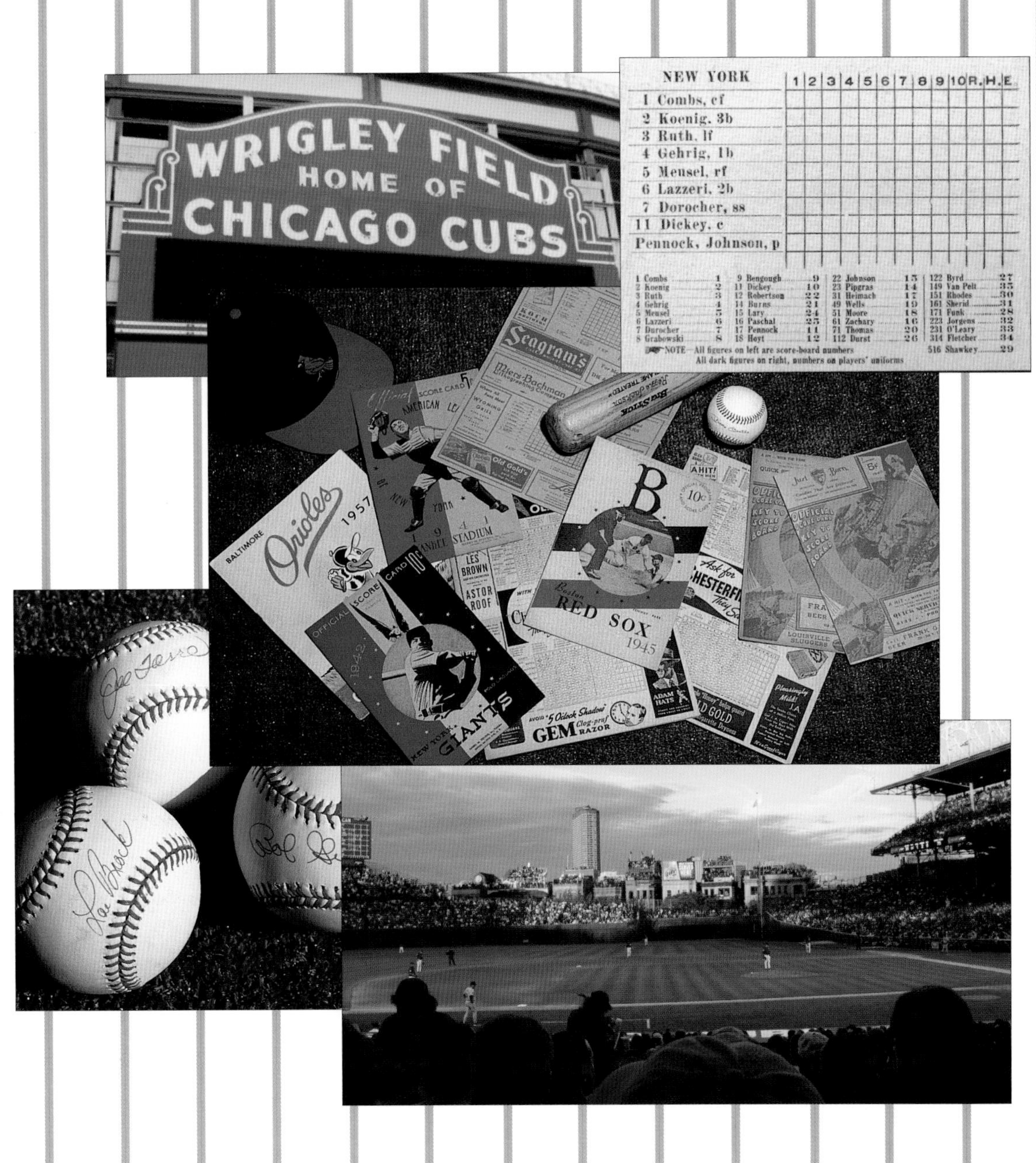
WRIGLEY FIELD
HOME OF
CHICAGO CUBS
NEW YORK
1 2 3 4 5 6 7 8 9 10 R. H. E.
1 Combs, cf
2 Koenig, 3b
3 Ruth, lf
4 Gehrig, 1b
5 Meusel, rf
6 Lazzeri, 2b
7 Dorocher, ss
11 Dickey, c
Pennock, Johnson, p
1 Combs 1
2 Koenig 2
3 Ruth 3
4 Gehrig 4
5 Meusel 5
6 Lazzeri 6
7 Durocher 7
8 Grabowski 8
9 Bengough 9
11 Dickey 10
12 Robertson 22
14 Burns 21
15 Lary 24
16 Paschal 25
17 Pennock 11
18 Hoyt 12
22 Johnson 15
23 Pipgras 14
31 Heimach 17
49 Wells 19
51 Moore 18
61 Zachary 16
71 Thomas 20
112 Durst 26
122 Byrd 27
149 Van Pelt 35
151 Rhodes 30
161 Sherid 31
171 Funk 28
223 Jorgens 32
231 O'Leary 33
314 Fletcher 34
516 Shawkey 29
NOTE—All figures on left are score-board numbers
All dark figures on right, numbers on players' uniforms
Seagram's
Official Score Card
Orioles
1957
BALTIMORE
Boston
RED SOX
1945
GIANTS
GEM
RAZOR
Ask for
CHESTERFIELD
LES BROWN
ASTOR ROOF

EARLY INNINGS

1

A Brief History of Uniform Numbers

In the early days of baseball, going to a ballgame was a challenge for fans. The players did not wear uniform numbers on their backs, nor on their sleeves or chests or legs. There were no name patches sewn above the numbers. Players would swarm the field from the dugouts each half inning with blank uniforms. It was very difficult to identify a favorite player.

The scoreboard listed the players' numbers which were assigned by the club when he became a member of the team. If a player was added to the roster by trade or a new signing, he got the next available number. Each city had their own numbering system too, so members of a visiting team might have different numbers assigned to them than they did at home. Eventually players' numbers reached into the hundreds. For example, on April 29, 1929 in a game featuring the Cleveland Indians at Chicago, two Indians players were listed as such: Porter 123 and Falk 234.

The scoreboard would list the player's number (let's call it the scoreboard number) and his place in the batting order with his position.

For 5¢, the fan could buy a scorecard which would then list the line-ups (with the disclaimer that these line-ups were given by the managers the morning of the game and were subject to change) with their scoreboard numbers and positions. If there was a change, the umpire was to announce that change to the fans. In the days prior to the sophisticated PA systems that we are accustomed to, you can imagine the mass confusion such a method created. Umpires shouting or using megaphones simply didn't cut it. More often than not, the umpire never bothered, so the fan was left in the dark.

The scorecard had become the all important item for the fan. It contained a number listed next to each player with the line-up for the day indicated. These numbers corresponded to the numbers listed on the scoreboard in the outfield. A fan needed to spot a player's name on the scorecard, note his number, check the scoreboard to see if his position was still the same, or if he was in the game. If the player was a shortstop, and he was listed as such, the fan assumed that the player standing at that position was that player. If he batted in the correct position as well, the fan was quite certain.

The programs or scorecards of the 1880s featured beautiful works of art depicting various facets of the relatively new game. But in many of them, the fan had to do all the work on the inside.

Larger and larger crowds were going to ballgames in the 1910s and '20s; bigger and grander stadiums were being built to accommodate them.

The pressure that fans brought to the teams and to the press to number the players for identity grew with each passing season.

The baseball owners were dead set against numbering the players for the most part because they were afraid they would lose revenue from the sale of scorecards. They fought the innovation for many years. Outspoken advocates stepped forward voicing their opinions in the local newspapers championing the cause, but time after time, the move failed. The players themselves did not like the idea either since they felt they became numbers instead of names much like convicts.

It has been reported that the first team to ever try numbering the players was back in 1883. A 1974 New York Yankees Spring Training program and a 1981 Boston Red Sox Yearbook both mention that the Cincinnati Red Stockings wore numbers on their sleeves to identify the players, but the move was short-lived. A book entitled *The Cincinnati Game* by Lonnie Wheeler and John Baskin published by Orange Frazer Press in Wilmington, Ohio, states: "Team president Aaron Stern, who a year earlier *(1882, which was the first year of the American Association in which the Reds resided—author's note)* had identified his players by putting each of them in a uniform of a different color, thought it would be simpler for the fans to recognize the Reds by number. But the players felt a bit dehumanized (they noted that inmates wore numbers), and when they objected, the numbers were removed."

The 1883 season began on May 1: St. Louis at Cincinnati; Eclipse at Columbus; Athletics at Pittsburgh; and the New York Metropolitans at Baltimore. The season closed on September 30. This was the second year of the American Association. *The New York Times*, *The Cincinnati Enquirer* and *The Cincinnati Commerical Gazette* reveal nothing to support that uniform numbers were worn.

There were other claims that say that in 1888 the Reds tried it again. Several beautifully decorated scorecards from those specific years have been reviewed but have not revealed anything concerning uniform numbers. Often the interiors had blank spaces for the players and the fan had to write in the entire line-ups. A team photo of the '88 Reds revealed that no numbers were on the sleeves, but if the practice didn't last long, the photo was obviously taken at another time.

After finding nothing concerning either year, the Reds front office was contacted and could not shed any light on the subject only indicating that the team began wearing numbers permanently in 1932.

Back in 1894, Chicago Cubs owner Jim Hart thought it was a good idea for players to wear numbers. Apparently nothing ever came of it.

In 1911, the Indians tried something a little different using letters in the scorecard in place of numbers to identify the players. It lead to more confusion and was dropped.

The 1916 season began on April 10. The Cleveland Indians wore no uniform numbers on their sleeves at their home opener against St. Louis. The first homestand ended versus Detroit. The second homestand was brief, then the Indians were on the road the entire month of May. Quirky schedules were common in those days due to the slower train transportation.

Their fourth homestand was scheduled to begin on Monday, June 26 against Chicago, but there was a make-up game played the day before between the same two teams. On Monday, the Indians sent Fred Beebe to the mound. They had coaxed him off his farm to return to baseball. He pitched an amazing game—a three-hitter, all singles, and won 2-0. The game lasted one hour and 19 minutes. The Indians wore uniform numbers on their left sleeves corresponding to the scorecard numbers and the scoreboard numbers.

BEEBE BLANKS WHITE SOX.

Former National Leaguer Allows Chicago Three Hits.

CLEVELAND, June 26.—Fred Beebe, former National League pitcher who declined to play with Buffalo this year, made his Cleveland début today and shut out Chicago with three hits, allowing only five men to reach first base and only two to reach second. Cleveland scored its two runs in the first inning on two passes by Danforth and Roth's triple. The score:

CLEVELAND.

	Ab	R	H	Po	A
Graney,lf	3	0	0	2	0
Chapman,ss	4	1	1	4	4
Speaker,cf	3	1	2	1	0
Roth,rf	4	0	1	2	0
Gandil,1b	3	0	1	11	0
Howard,2b	3	0	0	1	6
Evans,3b	3	0	0	1	2
O'Neill,c	3	0	1	5	0
Beebe,p	3	0	0	0	2
Total....	30	2	6	27	14

CHICAGO.

	Ab	R	H	Po	A
Felsch,cf	4	0	1	2	0
Weaver,ss	4	0	0	3	3
E.Collins,2b	4	0	0	0	1
Jackson,rf	3	0	1	1	1
J.Collins,lf	4	0	0	2	0
Fournier,1b	3	0	1	11	0
Schalk,c	2	0	0	5	1
W'fgang,3b	3	0	0	0	1
Danforth,p	0	0	0	0	1
Bens,p	2	0	0	0	2
Russell,p	0	0	0	0	1
aMurphy	1	0	0	0	0
Total....	30	0	3	24	11

a-Batted for Bens in eighth inning.
Error—Wolfgang.

Cleveland ....2 0 0 0 0 0 0 0 .—2
Chicago ....0 0 0 0 0 0 0 0 0—0

Two-base hit—O'Neill. Three-base hit—Roth. Stolen base—Fournier. Double play—Jackson and Fournier. Left on bases—Cleveland, 5; Chicago, 5. First base on error—Cleveland. Bases on balls—Off Beebe, 2; off Danforth, 2. Hits and earned runs—Off Beebe, 3 hits and no runs in 9 innings; off Danforth, 1 hit and 2 runs in 1-3 inning; off Bens, 4 hits and no runs in 6 2-3 innings; off Russell, 1 hit and no runs in 1 inning. Balk—Danforth. Struck out—By Beebe, 4; by Bens, 4. Time of game—One hour and nineteen minutes. Umpires—Messrs. Nallin and Evans.

The boxscore of the ballgame as it appeared in the NYT the following day. Jack Graney was the first man to bat in the 20th Century with a uniform number. He walked, one of 102 for the season. He went on to lead the league in doubles with 41.

INDIANS WEAR NUMBERS.

Players Carry Them on Sleeves for First Time in Baseball History.

CLEVELAND, Ohio, June 26.—Cleveland American League players wore numbers on the sleeves of their uniforms in today's game with Chicago for the first time in the history of baseball so far as known. The numbers corresponded to similar numbers set opposite the players' names on the score cards, so that all fans in the stands might easily identify the members of the home club.

A facsimile of the article that accommpanied the boxscore of the event. This is done for clarity.

How long the numbers lasted is a mystery. Doubtless they only donned them for the home crowd. This particular homestand lasted through a July 4th doubleheader. It's possible that they wore numbers through that homestand and might have done it for the remaining home games.

Again in 1917, there were reports that the Indians wore sleeve numbers, but on the right sleeve. All the homestands were checked and there was no evidence of numbers in the *Cleveland Plain Dealer* or the *Cleveland Press.*

The Cleveland front office knew nothing of any numbering before 1931.

Remember that newspapers in those days did not follow sports the way they do today. Also there were not many action photographs used. The common practice was to use engravings and stock photos sil-houetted of key performers so not much was spontaneous. Rare action photos began creeping into the reports in the late '20s and '30s. But it wasn't until after WWII that the advent of the tabloids and the soon-to-be universal use of the 35mm camera made splashy backpage layouts commonplace. Even *The Sporting News*, though chock full with the previous week's boxscores, in-depth views of baseball events plus tons of odd tidbits rarely showed an action shot of a game relying instead on a stock bust photo or a spring training pose for their story.

Following the game in 1916, there was a renewed interest in the cry for numbers. This editorial out of Philadelphia appeared in *Sporting Life* on July 8.

NUMBER THE BALL PLAYERS

YEARS AGO "Sporting Life" urged the numbering of ball players without, however, producing the slightest impression upon the magnates and the players. It was not expected that the players should seriously consider any innovation, no matter how important or beneficial, but that not one magnate should make any move for a change or system which would cost nothing and be of greatest benefit to patrons, was a matter of geniune surprise and keen disappointment. It was not until the foot ball authorities took up the system that base ball magnates gave even passing consideration to a system obviously pleasing to the public and, therefore, beneficial to the club. Instead, they gave partial relief to the public by way of expensive bulletin boards and equally expensive announcers, which detracted from instead of added to the sale of score cards. But it is a long lane that has no turn. The new and enterprising Cleve-land Club management has taken the bull by the horns and numbered its players... Now that the Cleveland Club has broken the ice, it is only a question of time when all other clubs will fall into line for a system that has everything in its favor and not one sound or even plausible reason against it. But that does not obscure or minimize the fact that but for hidebound conservatism the base ball folks might have been the first to adopt the system instead of tagging along after the foot ball fellows.

A facsimile of the article from July 8.

The St. Louis Cardinals were the first team in the National League to wear numbers in the 20th Century. In 1923, on both June 14 and September 18, the Cards wore numbers on their left sleeves. There's no evidence that they wore them on their away uniforms though. They may have worn them on their home whites for the entire season.

LINCOLN CAR
DAY AND NIGHT SERVICE
AUTHORIZED Ford DEALER
LINCOLN CAR
DAY AND NIGHT SERVICE

CARDINALS	1	2	3	4	5	6	7	8	9	10	R.	H.	P.	A.	E.
1 Smith, lf															
2 Flack, rf															
3 Hornsby, 2b															
5 Stock, 3b															
6 Myers, cf															
15 Toporcer, ss															
11 McCurdy, c															
16 Freigau, 1b															
31 Haines, p															

Board No.		Uniform No.	Board No.		Uniform No.	Board No.		Uniform No.	Board No.		Uniform No.	Board No.		Uniform No.
1	Smith	2	6	Myers	7	11	McCurdy	16	18	North	51	51	Stuart	19
2	Flack	1	7	Lavan	8	14	Mann	12	22	Doak	17	61	Barfoot	21
3	Hornsby	4	8	Clemons	15	15	Toporcer	11	23	Sherdel	23	71	Dyer	20
4	Bottomley	5	9	Ainsmith	14	16	Freigau	61	31	Haines	31	112	Sugden	25
5	Stock	6	12	Blades	3	17	Pfeffer	18	49	Toney	49	122	Shotton	24

JEWETT NEWELL PAIGE 2621 LOCUST ST.

M. A. WILSON
FRANK J. PETELIK
Phone, Olive 2367

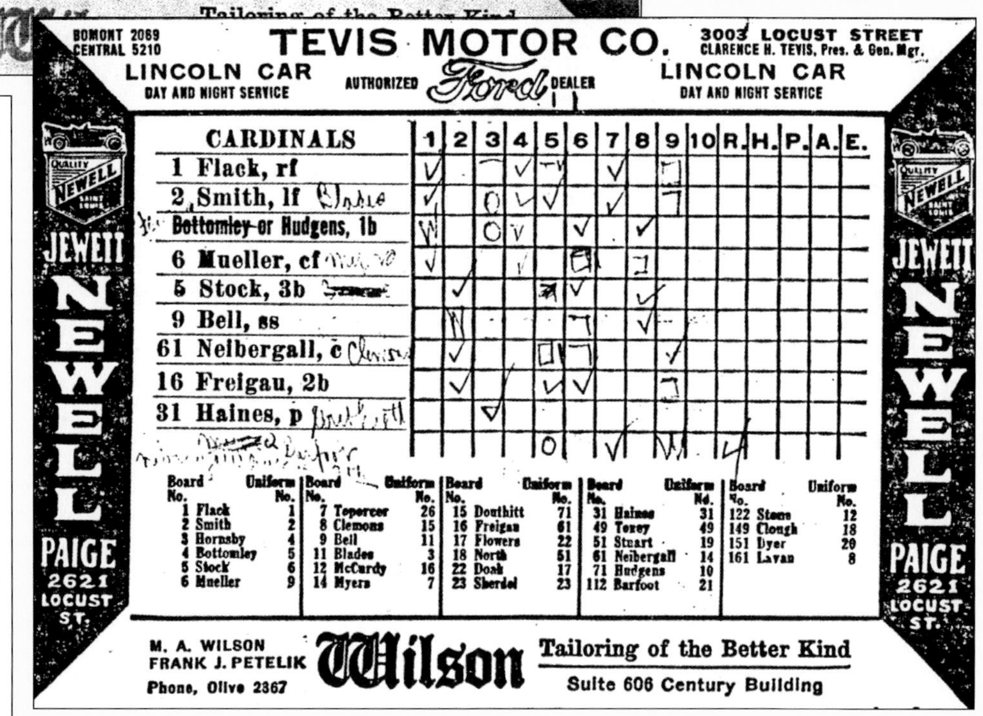
BOMONT 2089
CENTRAL 5210
TEVIS MOTOR CO.
3003 LOCUST STREET
CLARENCE H. TEVIS, Pres. & Gen. Mgr.
LINCOLN CAR
DAY AND NIGHT SERVICE
AUTHORIZED Ford DEALER
LINCOLN CAR
DAY AND NIGHT SERVICE

CARDINALS	1	2	3	4	5	6	7	8	9	10	R.	H.	P.	A.	E.
1 Flack, rf															
2 Smith, lf															
Bottomley or Hudgens, 1b															
6 Mueller, cf															
5 Stock, 3b															
9 Bell, ss															
61 Neibergall, c															
16 Freigau, 2b															
31 Haines, p															

Board No.		Uniform No.	Board No.		Uniform No.	Board No.		Uniform No.	Board No.		Uniform No.	Board No.		Uniform No.
1	Flack	1	7	Toporcer	26	15	Douthitt	71	31	Haines	31	122	Stone	12
2	Smith	2	8	Clemons	15	16	Freigau	61	49	Toney	49	149	Clough	18
3	Hornsby	4	9	Bell	11	17	Flowers	22	51	Stuart	19	151	Dyer	20
4	Bottomley	5	11	Blades	3	18	North	51	61	Neibergall	14	161	Lavan	8
5	Stock	6	12	McCurdy	16	22	Doak	17	71	Hudgens	10			
6	Mueller	9	14	Myers	7	23	Sherdel	23	112	Barfoot	21			

JEWETT NEWELL PAIGE 2621 LOCUST ST.

M. A. WILSON
FRANK J. PETELIK
Phone, Olive 2367
Wilson
Tailoring of the Better Kind
Suite 606 Century Building

The two scorecards pictured here clearly showing scoreboard numbers to the left of the player and the uniform numbers to the right. It seems doubtful that the Cardinals would dip in and out of the numbering game in the same season. It suggests that the Redbirds may have used numbers for the whole season or a major part of it on their home uniforms.

Both scorecards are courtesy of Cardinals expert, Pat Borelli.

On July 17, 1924, Jesse "Pop" Haines of the Cardinals pitched a no-hitter to beat Boston 5-0 in St. Louis. Again they wore uniform numbers on their sleeves. They didn't wear them during games played May 30 in Pittsburgh or June 18 in New York which seems to indicate the numbers were worn only on the home whites. No proof was found that the Cardinals continued the practice into the 1925 or 1926 season despite what Frank Graham wrote in *The New York Yankees* published by Putnam and Sons, 1958. "In St. Louis, Branch Rickey had put small numbers on the Cardinals sleeves in 1924, but since the fans had paid little or no attention to them and none of the other clubs followed his lead, Rickey had the numbers removed two years later."

Apparently this account has the dates wrong as you can see by the scorecards on this and the previous page.

Although the Cards clearly wore numbers that day, the article printed with the boxscore does not mention it. Perhaps they had worn them all year at home as a continuation from 1923.

JESS HAINES HURLS A NO-HIT SHUTOUT

Card Pitcher Passes Qnly Men Who Get on Base—Is First of Year—Final Score Is 5-0.

ST. LOUIS, July 17.—Pitching a no-hit game, the first the season, in the major leagues, Jess Haines of the St. Louis Cardinals shut out the Boston Braves today, 5 to 0, before a crowd of 15,000. This is the first time a Cardinal moundsman has pitched a no-hit game since 1876. Haines fanned five men and walked three. Two Braves died on first base, while another expired on second, reaching there when two passes were issued in the sixth inning. The Cardinal pitcher received excellent support.

Jess Haines's feat in holding the Boston Braves down without a hit or a run today is the sixty-fourth no-hit, no-run game pitched in the National League since the organization of the elder circuit, according to available records of the league. And furthermore, it is the first one to be hurled by a St. Louis pitcher since George Washington Bradley, now a Philadelphia police officer, pitched a no-hit, no-run game against the Hartford Nationals in St. Louis on July 15, 1876, the year the National League was organized.

Haines's game, like Bradley's, cannot be termed a perfect game, as in both contests players of the defeated team reached first and second bases. Despite this imperfection, Haines's name will go down in the league record as the first man to twirl a no-hit, no-run game in 1924.

The score:

ST. LOUIS (N.)	Ab	R	H	Po	A
J. Smith,rf	5	0	2	3	0
Holm,cf	4	1	1	4	0
Hornsby,2b	4	1	3	1	4
Bott'mley,1b	4	1	1	9	0
Blades,lf	4	0	0	3	0
Toporcer,3b	2	1	0	0	0
Gonzales,c	4	0	2	5	0
J. Cooney,ss	4	0	2	2	2
Haines,p	3	1	1	0	3
Total	34	5	12	27	9

BOSTON (N.)	Ab	R	H	Po	A
Felix,cf	4	0	0	3	0
Cun'gham,lf	3	0	0	4	0
Stengel,rf	4	0	0	1	0
McInnis,1b	3	0	0	9	1
Padgett,2b	3	0	0	2	3
Tierney,3b	3	0	0	1	1
R. Smith,ss	3	0	0	0	2
O'Neil,c	3	0	0	3	0
McNamara,p	0	0	0	1	4
J. Cooney,p	0	0	0	0	0
aGibson	1	0	0	0	0
Total	27	0	0	24	11

Errors—St. Louis 0, Boston 2 (Felix, Padgett).

a Batted for McNamara in eighth.

St. Louis .... 1 0 1 0 3 0 0 0 —5
Boston .... 0 0 0 0 0 0 0 0 0—0

Two-base hit—J. Smith. Sacrifices—Haines, Holm. Double plays—Tierney, Padgett and McInnis. Left on bases—Boston 3, St. Louis 9. Bases on balls—Off McNamara 1, Haines 3. Struck out—By Cooney 2, Haines 5. Hits—Off McNamara 12 in 7 innings, Cooney none in 1. Hit by pitcher—By McNamara (Toporcer). Wild pitch—McNamara. Losing pitcher—McNamara. Umpires—O'Day, Sweeney and Quigley. Time of game—1:43.

The boxscore of Haines' no-hitter making his the first one that year. He did walk a man in the third and two more in the sixth. But the Braves never threatened.

CARDINALS	1	2	3	4	5	6	7	8	9	10	R.	H.
1 Smith, rf												
3 Holm, cf												
4 Hornsby, 2b												
Bottomley or [illegible] 1b												
2 Blades, lf												
9 Toporcer, 3b												
8 Gonzales, c												
6 Cooney, ss												
22 Haines, p												

Board No.		Uniform No.	Board No.		Uniform No.	Board No.		Uniform No.	Board No.		Uniform No.	Board No.		Uniform No.
1	Smith	1	6	Cooney	8	14	Niebergall	17	23	Dickerman	19	112	Bell	16
2	Blades	2	7	Mueller	7	15	Vick	20	31	Dyer	61	149	Sherdel	23
3	Holm	71	8	Gonzales	26	16	Freigau	12	40	Pfeffer	49	151	Shotton	21
4	Hornsby	6	9	Toporcer	11	18	Flack	3	51	Sothoron	51	161	Sugden	24
5	Bottomley	4	11	Myers	9	22	Haines	18	61	Stuart	41			

The scorecard of Haines' no-hitter showing the numbers worn in 1924 by the Redbirds. Once again the scoreboard numbers are on the left and the uniform numbers on the right. Courtesy of Paula Homan, Curator, St. Louis Cardinals Hall of Fame and Museum.

The Babe sporting his new #3. Ironically, Ruth is probably the one player who didn't need a number. Everyone knew who he was instantly when they saw the large man with the barrel chest and potbelly over those spindly legs trotting around the bases after one of his towering homeruns.

The New York Yankees announced on January 22, 1929 that they will begin wearing uniform numbers on the backs of their shirts on a permanent basis starting in the coming season.

When Tom Rice, *The Brooklyn Daily Eagle* and *The Sporting News* writer heard this statement, he was overjoyed. He had been the staunchest advocate of numbering players and enthusiastically endorsed the idea for years "in the interests of the players, the fans, the clubs and the United States Treasury, which collects a tax on baseball tickets."

But the Yankees were not the first team to wear numbers that spring. Opening day in New York was Tuesday, April 16—it poured and the game was called to the dismay of the 50,000 fans that were expected. The following day the grounds were so wet that the opening was postponed again. It was not until Thursday, April 18 that the Yanks opened their season by beating the Red Sox 7-3. Waite Hoyt was the Yankee pitcher wearing a large navy-colored #12.

Several hundred miles west of that rainy Tuesday in New York, the Cleveland Indians ran to their positions in the field wearing numbers on their backs. In the bottom of the first inning, a young Earl Averill made his major league debut hitting a homerun while wearing #5. However, the Indians only wore numbers on their home whites while the Yankees made it a permanent feature.

The Yankees arrived in Cleveland to play their first series of the season, Monday, May 13. It would be the first time in the history of baseball that both teams wore numbers on their backs.

Earl Averill as a rookie wearing #5 hitting a HR in Cleveland against the Yankees in May, 1929. He would switch to #3 the following season and the Indians would retire that number for the Hall of Famer.

The box score:

NEW YORK (A.)	ab	r	h	po	a	e
Combs, cf	4	0	0	1	0	0
Koenig, 3b	4	1	1	0	1	1
Ruth, rf	2	1	1	0	0	1
Gehrig, 1b	4	1	1	16	1	0
Meusel, lf	3	0	1	1	0	1
Lazzeri, 2b	3	0	0	2	5	0
Durocher, ss	3	0	0	1	2	0
Dickey, c	4	0	2	3	2	0
Heimach, p	2	0	0	0	2	0
bDust	1	0	0	0	0	0
Johnson, p	0	0	0	0	0	0
cBurns	1	0	0	0	0	0
Total	31	3	6	24	14	3

CLEVELAND (A.)	ab	r	h	po	a	e
Jamieson, lf	4	1	0	2	0	0
Fonseca, 1b	4	1	2	9	1	0
Averill, cf	4	1	2	5	0	0
J. Sewell, 3b	4	0	1	1	1	0
Morgan, rf	3	0	0	1	0	0
Falk, rf	1	0	1	0	0	0
L. Sewell, c	3	0	2	3	0	0
Gardner, ss	2	0	1	3	2	0
aMyatt	1	0	0	0	0	0
Tavener, ss	0	0	0	0	0	0
Lind, 2b	4	1	2	2	4	0
Hudlin, p	1	0	0	1	3	0
Total	31	4	11	27	11	0

a Batted for Gardner in eighth.
b Batted for Heimach in eighth.
c Batted for Durocher in ninth.

New York	000	001	002—3
Cleveland	002	000	20..—4

Runs batted in—Averill (3), Koenig, Lazzeri, Meusel, Fonseca.

Two-base hits—Dickey, Fonseca, Averill, Gehrig. Home run—Koenig. Sacrifices—Hudlin (2), L. Sewell, Lazzeri. Double play—Gardner, Lind and Fonseca. Left on bases—New York 5, Cleveland 7. Base on balls—Off Hudlin 3, Heimach 1. Struck out—By Hudlin 3, Heimach 3. Hits—Off Heimach 10 in 7 innings, Johnson 1 in 1. Wild pitch—Heimach. Losing pitcher—Heimach. Umpires—Owens, Campbell and Geisel. Time of game—1:45.

May 13, 1929
This is the game that quietly made baseball history. It's the first time two teams wore numbers on the field at the same time in the Major Leagues.

John Drebinger reported on the game for *The New York Times*, "The Yankees spent the better part of an afternoon here today sound asleep. It was a gray, murky day of a sort to induce sleep with scarcely an effort."

The Murderer's Row line-up woke up in the ninth inning, but fell one run short, losing to Willis Hudlin 4-3.

The Yankees' numbering system was based on the batting order. Combs led off playing CF wore #1; Koenig batted second, played 3B, wore #2; the Babe batted 3rd and wore his #3; Gehrig batted clean-up and wore #4; Meusel batted 5th, wore #5; Lazzeri batted 6th, wore #6; Durocher batted 7th, wore #7; and Dickey batted 8th but wore #10—he switched to #8 the following year.

Complete List of the Numbers Worn by Yankees This Year

The Yankee players appeared on the field at the Stadium yesterday wearing large numbers on their backs for easier identification. Numbers 13 and 23 have been omitted. Earl Combs was No. 1. Babe Ruth is No. 3. The numbers of all the Yankees follow:

1. Combs, cf.	17. Heimach,p.
2. Koenig, 3b.	18. Moore, p.
3. Ruth, rf.	19. Wells, p.
4. Gehrig, 1b.	20. Thomas, p.
5. Meusel, lf.	21. Burns, i.f.
6. Lazzeri, 2b.	22. Rob'tson, i.f.
7. Durocher, ss.	24. Lary, i.f.
8. Grab'wski, c.	25. Paschal, o.f.
9. Bengough, c.	26. Durst, o.f.
10. Dickey, c.	27. Byrd, o.f.
11. Pennock, p.	28. Funk, o.f.
12. Hoyt, p.	29. Shealy, p.
14. Pipgras, p.	30. Rhodes, p.
15. Johnson, p.	31. Sherid, p.
16. Zachary, p.	32. Jorgens, c.

The list (Above) appeared in the NYT the morning after the Yankees finally opened the season on April 18. (Right) A photo that appeared in the Washington Post on Wednesday, May 14, 1930 showing Ossie Bluege, the Nats third baseman wearing #7.

Drebinger added this about Colonel Ruppert, the Yankees owner— "When he built the Stadium he gave baseball the biggest arena of its kind in the world. And when he decided to number his players he got them the largest numbers that money could buy and still fit on a baseball uniform. The numbers proved an unqualified success. They are clearly discernible to the naked eye."

The Indians apparently followed a different drummer. The line-up used in that game:

1. #7 Jamieson, lf	6. #8 L. Sewell, c
2. #6 Fonseca, 1b	7. #34 Gardner, ss
3. #5 Averill, cf	#9 Myatt, ph
4. #4 J. Sewell, 3b	#1 Tavener, ss
5. #61 Morgan, rf	8. #2 Lind, 2b
#51 Falk, rf	9. #15 Hudlin, p

The following season, 1930, saw the Yanks continuing the numbering. The Indians began the season with numbers at home, but discontinued it before the season ended.

But there was a new club that joined the crusade. The Washington Senators began wearing numbers permanently on opening day: April 14 against the visiting Red Sox.

The Washington Post writes, "One feature which seemed to appeal to the crowd immensely was the numbering of the Nats. Huge black figures adorned the broad backs of the sturdy athletes and it wasn't long until 'No. 3' was identified as Goslin and 'No. 27' as Walter Johnson."

On April 20, 1930, the Yankees played their first series against Washington in the Capital. It is the first time that two teams wearing numbers permanently on their backs played each other.

During the idle winter months prior to the 1931 season, American League president Ernest S. Barnard informed all clubs in the league that the players must wear numbers. He suggested that the regulars wear #1-7, the catchers #8-11, pitchers #12-24 and the utility players the rest. The #13 was to be left to the discretion of each team.

By this time most of the college teams were wearing numbers. In fact, many college football teams had been identifying their players with numbers for over 15 years.

The season opened on April 14, the Indians permanently began wearing numbers as did the White Sox, the Tigers and probably the Browns. They joined the Yankees (beginning their third season) and the Senators (in their second). The Red Sox did not comply until sometime in May. Mark Stang with Linda Harkness, co-authors of *Baseball by the Numbers*, believes it was on or before May 16. They were in the middle of a series in Chicago at the time. It seems more probable and practical that they waited until they finished their road trip and changed to their home whites on the 26th vs. Washington. There is a scorecard dated May 30 that shows the visiting A's and the Red Sox wearing numbers on that date.

Connie Mack's A's handled the situation most bazaarly. He had numbers issued to his ballplayers only at away games. This practice ran from 1931 through the 1936 season. So it wasn't until the home opener in April 1937 that the A's wore numbers permanently throughout the season. Mack believed that numbering the players would eliminate the need for scorecards thus cutting his revenue. He was in the throes of dismantling the powerful A's by selling off his superstars—Lefty Grove, Jimmy Foxx, Mickey Cochrane and Al Simmons—to increase his revenue, not jeopardize it.

Others, of course, argued the opposite. The numbering of players would increase the sale of scorecards, promote more knowledge and goodwill for the game in addition to generating greater enthusiasm which would bring in larger crowds to the ballparks.

The A's at home (Bottom, left) reveals only scoreboard numbers. Although the Yanks had been wearing numbers for a couple of years, Mack saw fit to ignore that. Also he doesn't list all the players. Pitchers and catchers are lumped together, subs are not listed. With this unusual practice, there were actually a few players, playing only home games for the A's, who never wore numbers in their major league careers while everyone else did.

The A's away (Bottom, right) shows both squads wearing uniform numbers. Where the scoreboard number differs, it is to the right.

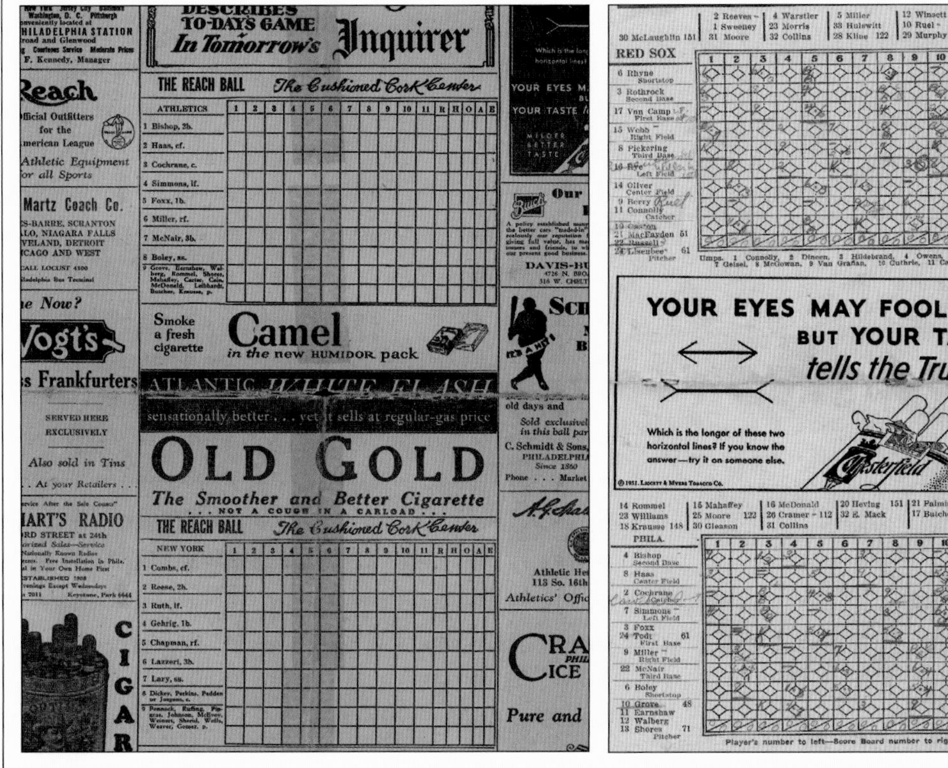

Both scorecards are from 1931. The Red Sox one is for the first game of the May 30 doubleheader.

There is evidence that the A's wore numbers in the Cleveland series (May 15-18). They played in Chicago the three days prior to that (May 12-14), a single date in St. Louis (May 9) and Washington (May 3) sandwiched around a 3-game homestand vs. Boston. They opened the season on the road—four games in Washington (April 14-18) followed by three in New York (April 19-21). They then returned home for five games with those same two clubs (April 22-May 1).

When did Mack begin? If he did not start the season with numbers, he probably would have bypassed the single date in Washington and begun the longer road trip either in St. Louis on the 9th or Chicago on the 12th.

The 1932 National League season began with only one team wearing numbers—the Boston Braves. It wasn't until June that the National League called a special meeting of the owners. *The Sporting News* reported that the group agreed "on June 22 to number all players, both at home and on the road, and thereafter the performers will be as easy to identify as those in the American. An attempt was made last winter to inaugurate the numbering system, but the move failed. Boston took the initiative this season by numbering the players at home, but it is said the Tribe was asked not to use them on the road."

That wasn't the case, however, since Boston began the season using them home and away. They had numbers on their first road trip to New York and Brooklyn (April 12-19). Franchises complained about the numbers on the away uniforms, so they discontinued it until after the league meeting. On their visit to New York, June 30, the Braves wore numbers again.

At the time of the League meeting, the Dodgers were leaving for a three game series at Boston. The numbered uniforms were prepared for their return on June 26 when they were scheduled to meet their arch rivals at Ebbetts Field—the Giants.

The Giants were not wearing numbers for that series. According to the *New York Post*, " the Giants wore their new numbers for the first time" referring to the game of June 30 versus the Braves at home.

Stang places the Cubs' start date specifically at July 1. Why wouldn't they have begun on June 30 at the start of a homestand and a new series with Cincinnati?

The Reds were in Boston when the meeting took place. They continued on to Pittsburgh for a four game set ending with a doubleheader on June 25. As a cruel twist of the schedule, they had another doubleheader at home with the same Pirates the very next day. It may have been this series or a two game set with the Cardinals right afterward that inaugurated their numbering system.

Here again Stang places the start date for the Pirates at July 1. And again a series with the Cardinals began on June 30. Why not then? They definitely did have numbers on at Brooklyn when they arrived on July 10.

Four days after the meeting the Phillies left for a series in Boston where they showed off their new numbers.

The Cardinals were in New York for a four game set with the Giants when the meeting took place. They returned home for a series with their Midwest rivals, the Cubs. "The Cardinal players were numbered, as per the new National League rule," so reports Martin J. Haley in the *St. Louis Globe-Democrat* on the first game of that series, June 25th.

Whether the Cubs and Pirates began on June 30 or July 1, all major league teams wore permanent numbers by July 1, 1932, except for the A's home game permutation.

This is the July 4th ballgame with the Reds showing the Cardinals numbering.

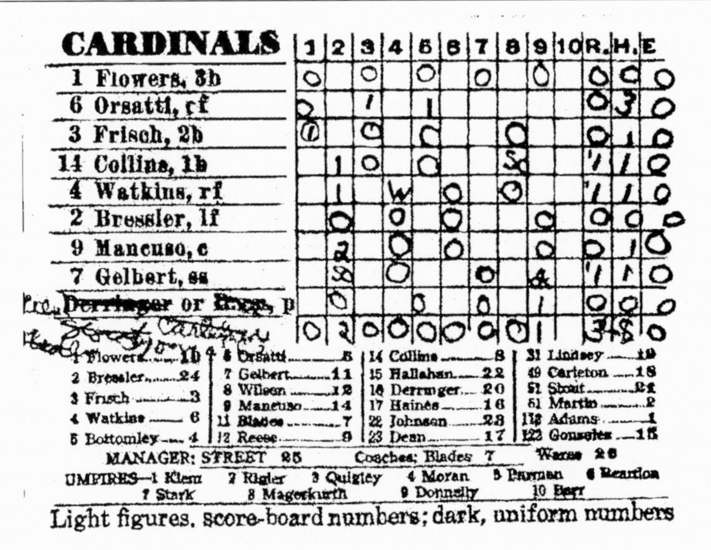
CARDINALS 1 2 3 4 5 6 7 8 9 10 R. H. E.
1 Flowers, 3b
6 Orsatti, cf
3 Frisch, 2b
14 Collins, 1b
4 Watkins, rf
2 Bressler, lf
9 Mancuso, c
7 Gelbert, ss
Derringer or Haines, p

1 Flowers .... 1b | 6 Orsatti .... 5 | 14 Collins .... 8 | 31 Lindsey 19
2 Bressler .... 24 | 7 Gelbert .... 11 | 15 Hallahan .... 22 | 49 Carleton 18
3 Frisch .... 3 | 8 Wilson .... 12 | 16 Derringer .... 20 | 51 Stout 21
4 Watkins .... 6 | 9 Mancuso .... 14 | 17 Haines .... 16 | 61 Martin 2
5 Bottomley .... 4 | 11 Blades .... 7 | 22 Johnson .... 23 | 112 Adams 1
| 12 Reese .... 9 | 23 Dean .... 17 | 122 Gonzales 15

MANAGER: STREET 25 Coaches: Blades 7 Wares 26
UMPIRES—1 Klem 2 Rigler 3 Quigley 4 Moran 5 Pfirman 6 Reardon 7 Stark 8 Magerkurth 9 Donnelly 10 Barr

Light figures, score-board numbers; dark, uniform numbers

Since the advent of permanent numbers in the years spanning 1929-1932, there have been some other innovations worth noting.

In 1952, the Dodgers added numbers to the front of their home whites. Buddy Bates, the Cardinals equipment manager, said that network television pressured the teams into placing numbers on sleeves in the 1970s. It was felt these "TV numbers" could be seen at more angles when televising games. It would make it easier for the announcers and fans alike to identify players.

The truth of the matter is that several teams did shirt fronts in the '50s and many clubs featured it in the '60s. By the time the '70s rolled around only a handful of teams did not do it. Very few clubs used sleeve numbers: White Sox ('71), Cards ('79-'80).

The Kansas City A's (1963-65) not only had numbers on the backs and the fronts of the players, they added it to the sleeves also.

A most unusual treatment was initiated by Houston in 1975—numbers on the front of the pants, on the right leg. This they did for five years. The White Sox, not to be outdone, added the feature to their left leg from 1982-88.

Bill Veeck, while with the White Sox, was the first to add names to the players' backs. Many teams continue the practice today with some notable exceptions. The Yankees have never toyed with this idea. Other teams only do it on the road.

Media guides, the professional baseball reporters' bible, did not exist until after WWII. It was first begun in 1947 by the White Sox and picked up by the Indians a year later.

The next time you go out to a ballgame, close your eyes and imagine that the clock has been turned back; that you are sitting in the stands of a game being played 75-100 years ago. Perhaps there is no public address system, no computer scoreboard and no numbers on the uniforms. Imagine how frustrating that would be in our world today. A world where we are bombarded with such a multitude of visual and commercial concepts every day, every hour, every second, and every millisecond.

Are we able to imagine that?

Opening day, Forbes Field on June 30, 1909. Notice the fans standing around the outfield fence. The foul lines were the longest in the league at that time. It's where Honus Wagner and the Pirates beat Ty Cobb and the Tigers 4 games to 3 in the Fall Classic.

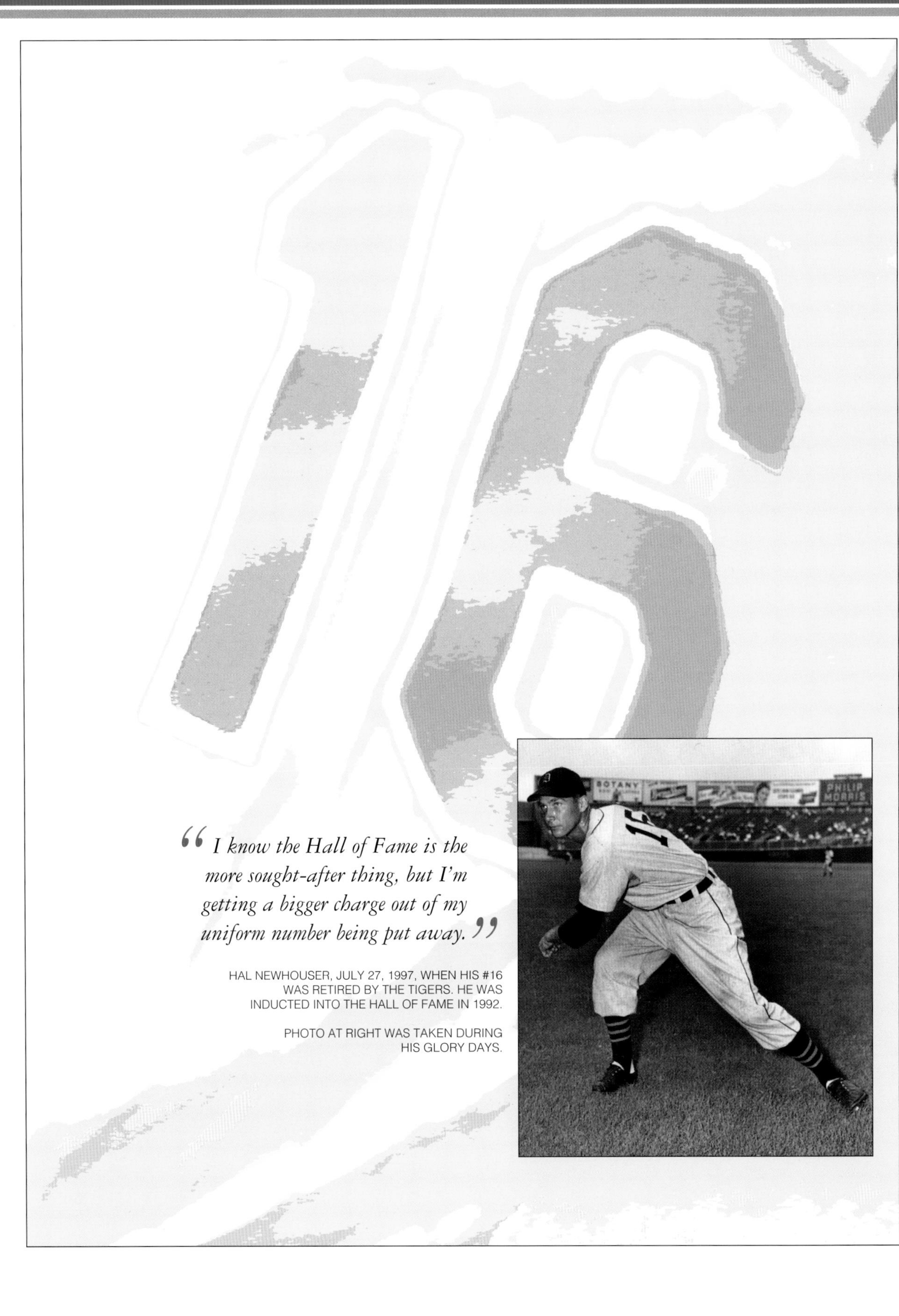

"I know the Hall of Fame is the more sought-after thing, but I'm getting a bigger charge out of my uniform number being put away."

HAL NEWHOUSER, JULY 27, 1997, WHEN HIS #16 WAS RETIRED BY THE TIGERS. HE WAS INDUCTED INTO THE HALL OF FAME IN 1992.

PHOTO AT RIGHT WAS TAKEN DURING HIS GLORY DAYS.

RETIRED NUMBERS

2

When Lou Gehrig sat himself down after 2,130 consecutive games at first base for the New York Yankees, the world of baseball was puzzled. The "Iron Horse" had some sort of strange malady. He constantly felt weak and not himself. The ball no longer jumped off his bat with the customary sting. As captain of the Yanks, he didn't want to hurt the team's ability to win. The fatal disease was diagnosed as amyotrophic lateral sclerosis, ALS. Now,everyone knows it as "Lou Gehrig's Disease."

For fourteen consecutive years, from June 2, 1925 until May 2, 1939, Gehrig slugged his way into the hearts of fans across the country. That was no easy feat with the bigger-than-life Babe Ruth batting in front of him for many of those years.

In 8,001 official trips to the plate he managed to score 1,888 runs. Think about it--that's nearly a run scored every four times up. He rapped 2,721 base hits for a lifetime average of .340.

But the real story is his power. He racked up numbers in those fourteen years that took others many more years to accomplish (Gehrig also played 13 games in 1923, 10 in '24 and 8 in '39). He hit 535 doubles (Tris Speaker had 793 in 22 years), 162 triples, 493 home runs (21st All-Time; (19th place Mel Ott had 511 in 22 years), 1,190 extra base hits puts him 6th All-Time (43.7% of his hits went for extra bases, Hank Aaron had 39.1% extra base hits).

Gehrig knocked in a run every 4.02 AB. Only Ruth topped that (3.79 AB). He was third All-Time in slugging percentage with .632 behind Ruth (.690) and Ted Williams (.634). Larrupin' Lou led the American League in 27 major offensive categories in those fourteen years—averaging 2 per year.

It's no wonder that a special vote was cast electing Gehrig to the Hall of Fame in 1939. The Yankees held a day for Lou on July 4th when he voiced the famous line, "Today, I consider myself the luckiest man on the face of the Earth." It was the day that the first major league baseball jersey number was retired—number 4. No other Yankee would ever wear that number again. The shirt resides in Cooperstown today.

Lou Gehrig on July 4, 1939 saying farewell to baseball at Yankee Stadium in New York. He died two years later.

The mighty Babe's shirt was not retired for another nine years, in August, 1948. As a kid I sat in the Stadium that day and heard Babe's gravelly voice echo into the hushed corners of the "House that Ruth built."

Not only did the Yankees retire the first uniform number, but they have retired the most during their illustrious history.

When Danny Tartabull came to the Yanks before the 1992 season, he wanted to wear his old number with the Kansas City

Royals—4. Sorry, Dan. That was Lou Gehrig's number. He asked about number 3. Sorry, that was Babe Ruth's. Well, how about number 5? Joe DiMaggio's. Tartabull then suggested doubling it to 44. That was Reggie Jackson's number, but the Yankees hadn't retired it yet. Danny thought it might be better to pick another number that wasn't quite as rich in background. He settled for number 45.

In 1972, the year Yogi Berra was elected to the Hall of Fame, the Yankees also retired his number 8. But they had a dilemma. Another Yankee catcher who was also pretty good had worn the number 8 and he was already in the Hall of Fame. So they retired the number 8 twice in 1972, once for Berra and once for Bill Dickey who caught for the pennant-winning teams of the thirties and the early forties.

The Yankees have retired sixteen numbers. The next nearest in the American League is eight, the Chicago White Sox. In the National League the Brooklyn/Los Angeles Dodgers and the New York/San Francisco Giants have retired ten. If you count the #85 retired for owner Augie Busch, Jr., the Cardinals have retired nine.

So far there are two American League teams who have not retired a number yet. You guessed it, the expansion teams who have not had that long a period of history: the Seattle Mariners, and Toronto Blue Jays. Another team, the Oakland A's which, of course, were the Kansas City A's and the Philadelphia A's have retired four numbers—Reggie Jackson, #9, Catfish Hunter, #27, Rollie Fingers, #34 and Dennis Eckersley, #43. Many other names jump to mind that would meet the standards elsewhere. Look at the list: Eddie Collins, Eddie Plank, Lefty Grove, Mickey Cochrane, Al Simmons, Jimmie Foxx, and Frank "Home Run" Baker, naming only the Hall of Famers. That's not to mention the powerful Oakland teams of the early seventies with Campaneris, Rudi, Holtzman, Blue and Odom.

The Milwaukee Brewers have also retired Finger's 34 even though he only pitched four years there and he only registered 28% of his 341 saves leading the AL in 1981 with 28. He missed the 1982 World Series with injury. Brewers fans just know they would have won if he were healthy.

Over in the National League, during the summer of 1993, the expansion Montreal Expos retired #10 for Rusty Staub and #8 for Gary Carter. "The Kid" started his career in Montreal in 1974 and hung it up there as well. That makes theirs the first Canadian numbers retired. Four years later, they retired #10 again for "The Hawk," Andre Dawson. The last Canadian number in the NL to be retired is #30 for Tim Raines in 2004 before the franchise moved to DC.

The lowest number not retired in the AL is 13. The lowest in the NL is 7. The Cards retired Red Schoendienst's number 2 in 1996. Red had been in a Cardinal uniform longer than anyone in their history--as a player from 1945-1956 and 1961-1963; a manager from 1965-1976, 1980, and 1990 (that's four different decades); and as a coach from 1963-1964, 1979-1980, 1981-1990 and 1991-1995 (four different decades, too). That's 45 years. Add being an instructor to this day and you have 55 years.

Uniform shirts with numbers retired by respective ball clubs, from L to R: Roberto Clemente's 21, Pirates; Bob Feller's 19, Indians; Joe DiMaggio's 5, Yankees; Carl Hubbell's 11, Giants; Jackie Robinson's 42, Dodgers; Stan Musial's 6, Cardinals; Ralph Kiner's 4, Pirates and Babe Ruth's 3, Yankees.

On the following two pages the shirts from L to R of: Wade Boggs' 12, Devil Rays; Hank Aaron's 44, Braves; Lou Gehrig's 4, Yankees; Ernie Banks' 14, Cubs; and Dennis Eckersley's 43, Athletics.

AMERICAN LEAGUE

42 ***ALL TEAMS*** APRIL 15, 1997—HONORING JACKIE ROBINSON'S DEBUT 50 YEARS EARLIER

ST. LOUIS BROWNS/ BALTIMORE ORIOLES
4 EARL WEAVER—MGR 1982
5 BROOKS ROBINSON—3B 1977†
8 CAL RIPKEN—SS 2001†
20 FRANK ROBINSON—OF 1971*
22 JIM PALMER—P 1985
33 EDDIE MURRAY—1B 1989*

BOSTON RED SOX
1 BOBBY DOERR—2B 1988
4 JOE CRONIN—SS/MGR 1984
8 CARL YASTRZEMSKI—OF/1B 1989
9 TED WILLIAMS—OF 1960†
27 CARLTON FISK—C 2000

CHICAGO WHITE SOX
2 NELLIE FOX—2B 1976
3 HAROLD BAINES—OF/DH 1989*
4 LUKE APPLING—SS 1975
9 MINNIE MINOSO—OF 1983
11 LUIS APARICIO—SS 1984
16 TED LYONS—P/MGR 1987
19 BILLY PIERCE—P 1987
72 CARLTON FISK—C 1997

CLEVELAND INDIANS
3 EARL AVERILL—OF 1975
5 LOU BOUDREAU—SS/MGR 1970
14 LARRY DOBY—OF 1994
18 MEL HARDER—P/CH 1990
19 BOB FELLER—P 1957
21 BOB LEMON—P 1998

DETROIT TIGERS
2 CHARLIE GEHRINGER—2B 1983
5 HANK GREENBERG—OF/1B 1983
6 AL KALINE—OF 1980
16 HAL NEWHOUSER—P 1997
23 WILLIE HORTON—OF/DH 2000

KANSAS CITY ROYALS
5 GEORGE BRETT—3B 1994
10 DICK HOWSER—MGR 1987
20 FRANK WHITE—2B 1995

LOS ANGELES/CALIFORNIA/ ANAHEIM/LA ANGELS
11 JIM FREGOSI—SS 1998
26 GENE AUTRY—OWNER 1982
29 ROD CAREW—1B 1986
30 NOLAN RYAN—P 1992*
50 JIMMIE REESE—CH 1995

WASHINGTON SENATORS/ MINNESOTA TWINS
3 HARMON KILLEBREW—3B/1B 1974*
6 TONY OLIVA—OF 1991
14 KENT HRBEK—1B 1995
29 ROD CAREW—2B/1B 1987
34 KIRBY PUCKETT—OF 1997

NEW YORK YANKEES
1 BILLY MARTIN—2B/MGR 1986
3 BABE RUTH—OF 1948
4 LOU GEHRIG—1B 1939
5 JOE DIMAGGIO—OF 1952
7 MICKEY MANTLE—OF 1969
8 YOGI BERRA—C 1972
8 BILL DICKEY—C 1972
9 ROGER MARIS—OF 1984
10 PHIL RIZZUTO—SS 1985
15 THURMAN MUNSON—C 1980
16 WHITEY FORD—P 1974
23 DON MATTINGLY—1B 1997
32 ELSTON HOWARD—C 1984
37 CASEY STENGEL—MGR 1970
44 REGGIE JACKSON—OF 1993
49 RON GUIDRY—P 2003

PHILADELPHIA/KANSAS CITY/ OAKLAND A'S
9 REGGIE JACKSON—OF 2004
27 CATFISH HUNTER—P 1990
34 ROLLIE FINGERS—P 1993
43 DENNIS ECKERSLEY—P 2005

SEATTLE MARINERS

TAMPA BAY DEVIL RAYS
12 WADE BOGGS—3B/DH 2000

WASHINGTON SENATORS/ TEXAS RANGERS
34 NOLAN RYAN—P 1996

TORONTO BLUE JAYS

Harmon Killebrew played 22 years in the Bigs with the Washington Senators, the Minnesota Twins, ending up with the Royals in 1975. A career .256 hitter, but he amassed 573 HRs (8th All-Time) while leading the AL in that department 6 times. The Twins retired his number 3 in 1974 and he was elected to the Hall of Fame in 1984.

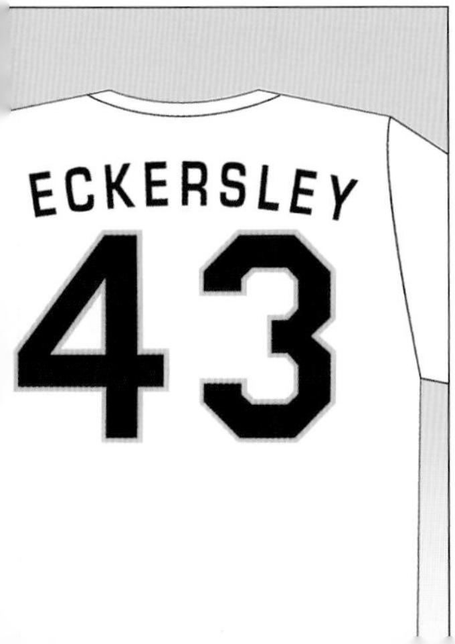

NATIONAL LEAGUE

42 *ALL TEAMS* APRIL 15, 1997—HONORING JACKIE ROBINSON'S DEBUT 50 YEARS EARLIER

ARIZONA DIAMONDBACKS

BOSTON/MILWAUKEE/ ATLANTA BRAVES

3 DALE MURPHY—OF 1994
21 WARREN SPAHN—P 1965
35 PHIL NIEKRO—P 1984
41 EDDIE MATHEWS—3B 1969
44 HANK AARON—OF 1977

CHICAGO CUBS

10 RON SANTO—3B 2003
14 ERNIE BANKS—SS/1B 1982
26 BILLY WILLIAMS—OF 1987

CINCINNATI REDS

1 FRED HUTCHINSON—M 1965
5 JOHNNY BENCH—C/3B 1984
8 JOE MORGAN—2B 1998
10 SPARKY ANDERSON—M 2005
18 TED KLUSZEWSKI—1B 1998
20 FRANK ROBINSON—OF 1998
24 TONY PEREZ—1B 2000

COLORADO ROCKIES

FLORIDA MARLINS

5 CARL BARGER—EXEC 1993

HOUSTON COLT 45s/ASTROS

24 JIMMY WYNN—OF 2005
25 JOSE CRUZ—OF 1992
32 JIM UMBRICHT—P 1965
33 MIKE SCOTT—P 1992
34 NOLAN RYAN—P 1996
40 DON WILSON—P 1975
49 LARRY DIERKER—P/M 2002

BROOKLYN/LA DODGERS

1 PEEWEE REESE—SS 1984
2 TOM LASORDA—M 1997
4 DUKE SNIDER—OF 1980
19 JUNIOR GILLIAM—INF/CH 1978
20 DON SUTTON—P 1998
24 WALTER ALSTON—M 1977
32 SANDY KOUFAX—P 1972
39 ROY CAMPANELLA—C 1972
42 JACKIE ROBINSON—2B 1972
53 DON DRYSDALE—P 1984

SEATTLE PILOTS/ MILWAUKEE BREWERS

4 PAUL MOLITOR—3B/DH 1999
19 ROBIN YOUNT—SS/OF 1994
34 ROLLIE FINGERS—P 1994
44 HANK AARON—OF/DH 1976†

NEW YORK METS

14 GIL HODGES—M 1972
37 CASEY STENGEL—M 1970
41 TOM SEAVER—P 1988

PHILADELPHIA PHILLIES

P PETE ALEXANDER—P 2001
P CHUCK KLEIN—OF 2001
1 RICHIE ASHBURN—OF 1979
14 JIM BUNNING—P 2001
20 MIKE SCHMIDT—3B 1990
32 STEVE CARLTON—P 1989
36 ROBIN ROBERTS—P 1962

PITTSBURGH PIRATES

1 BILLY MEYER—M 1954
4 RALPH KINER—OF 1987
8 WILLIE STARGELL—OF/1B 1982†
9 BILL MAZEROSKI—2B 1987
20 PIE TRAYNOR—3B 1972
21 ROBERTO CLEMENTE—OF 1973
33 HONUS WAGNER—SS 1956
40 DANNY MURTAUGH—M 1977

ST. LOUIS CARDINALS

1 OZZIE SMITH—SS 1996
2 RED SCHOENDIENST—2B/M/ CH—1996
6 STAN MUSIAL—OF/1B 1963†
9 ENOS SLAUGHTER—OF 1996
14 KEN BOYER—3B/M 1984
17 DIZZY DEAN—P 1974
20 LOU BROCK—OF 1979†
45 BOB GIBSON—P 1975†
85 AUGIE BUSCH, JR.—OWNER 1984

SAN DIEGO PADRES

6 STEVE GARVEY—1B 1989
19 TONY GWYNN—OF 2002
31 DAVE WINFIELD—OF 2001
35 RANDY JONES—P 1997

NY/SAN FRANCISCO GIANTS

— CHRISTY MATHEWSON--P 1988
— JOHN McGRAW—M 1988
3 BILL TERRY—1B/M 1985
4 MEL OTT—OF/1B 1949
11 CARL HUBBELL—P 1944
24 WILLIE MAYS—OF 1972*
27 JUAN MARICHAL—P 1975†
30 ORLANDO CEPEDA—1B 1999
36 GAYLORD PERRY—P 2005
44 WILLIE McCOVEY—1B 1975*

MONTREAL EXPOS/ WASHINGTON NATIONALS

8 GARY CARTER—C 1993
10 RUSTY STAUB—OF 1993
10 ANDRE DAWSON—OF 1996
30 TIM RAINES—OF 2004

**NUMBER RETIRED WHILE ACTIVE*
†NUMBER/PLAYER RETIRED SEASON'S END

Few athletes were as beautiful to watch play the game as Roberto Clemente. His galloping stride on the bases and his rifle throws from right field treated the Pirate fans for 18 years. His beauty didn't end on the playing field either. Roberto's brilliant career was tragically cut down on December 31, 1972 when his plane crashed while delivering aid to flood victims. His number was retired in 1973.

The highest retired number of a AL player is 72 which was worn by White Sox catcher Carlton Fisk. The highest National League player's number to be honored is Don Drydale's 53 of the LA Dodgers.

Hank Aaron has the distinction of having his number 44 retired by two teams, the Atlanta Braves as well as the Brewers. Hank played for the Milwaukee Braves from 1954-1965. He moved to Atlanta and played from 1966-1974. His last two years were in the uniform of the Milwaukee Brewers.

"Hammerin' Hank" finished with a .305 lifetime average proving that power hitters can hit for average too. He surpassed the legendary Babe Ruth by hitting his 715th HR in Atlanta on April 8, 1974. Al Downing's (#44) name will live on in baseball trivia as the Dodger pitcher who served up the pitch.

After such an oustanding career you can't blame both cities for joining in the tribute.

Rod Carew's 29 has been retired by two teams as well. Oddly, his teams were named after states rather than cities—Minnesota and California (now Los Angeles of Anaheim).

In 1977, Rod flirted with the .400 mark all season long. Ted Williams, the last player to hit over .400 (.406 in 1941) thought Carew might just be the guy to break into the elite group. He dipped a bit in the last month and finished with .388. He led the league in hits (239), triples (16) and tied his HR best at 14.

Three years after the White Sox retired #72 for Fisk, the Red Sox retired his mirror-image #27. Frank Robinson won MVP Awards in both leagues with teams that retired his #20. He was one of six players who had his number retired while he was active—Harmon Killebrew (1974), Willie McCovey (1975), Eddie Murray (1989), Harold Baines (1989), and Nolan Ryan (1992) were the others.

Another #44 who had his number retired was Reggie Jackson of the Yankees—Mr. October. He played only five years for New York, but was an All-Star four of those years and the Yanks were in the postseason as many times. In 2004, the Oakland A's retired his #9 having played nearly half of his career in the Bay City.

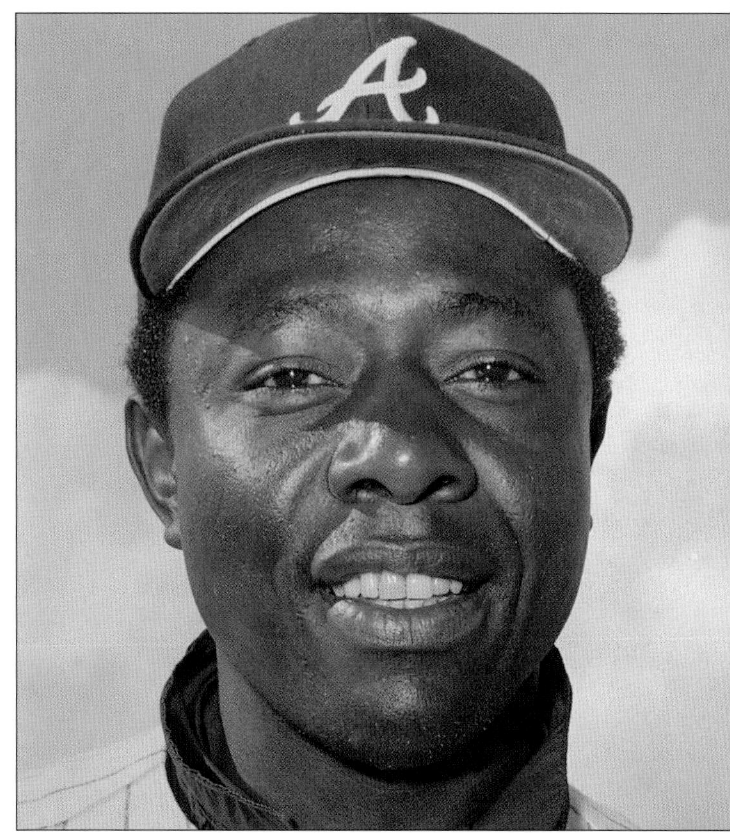

Hank Aaron's numbers are awesome: 3,771 hits (3rd All-Time), 1,477 extra base hits (1st All-Time), 6,856 total bases (1st All-Time), 755 HRs (1st All-Time), 624 doubles (9th All-Time), second to Pete Rose in ABs, struck out only 11% of the time, .555 slugging percentage (23rd All-Time), tied with Ruth at 2,174 runs scored behind Rickey Henderson and Ty Cobb, and the All-Time leader in RBI with 2,297.

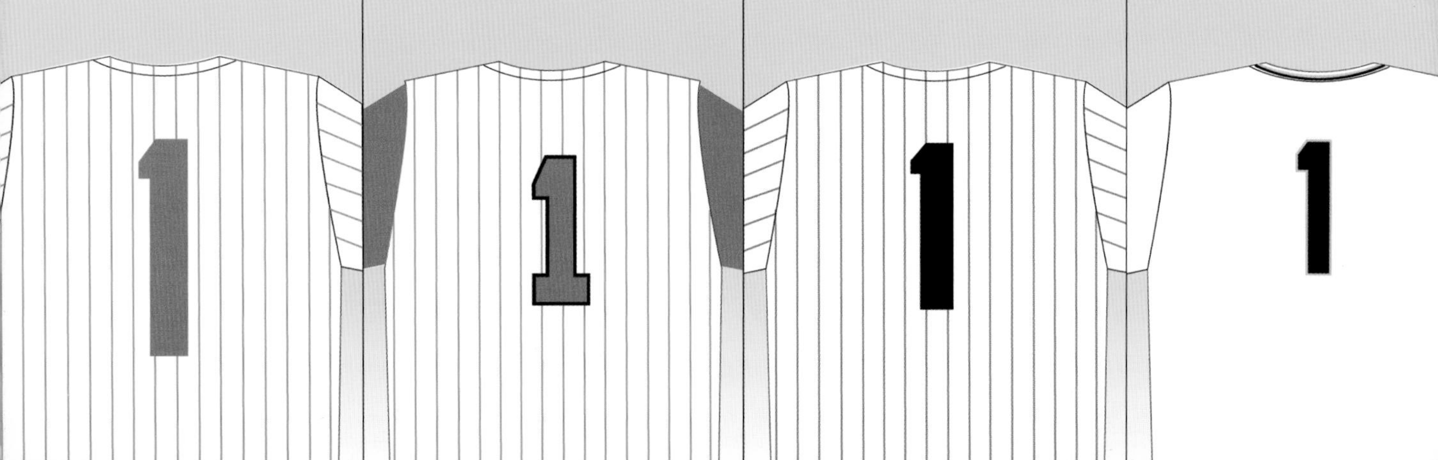

Injury late in the 1993 season forced the retirement of one of baseball's most durable pitchers. Nolan Ryan had 324 wins, 773 starts in 807 games pitched, 5,387 innings, 61 shutouts , 5,714 strikeouts (more than 1 per inning), 2,795 walks, an incredible 7 no-hitters (4 for California, 1 for Houston and 2 for Texas), but alas, Ryan also had 292 loses. That's 13 more than Spud Chandler (109-43) and Ron Guidry (170-91) won combined. He lost 47% of his decisions!

Another individual had the distinction of having his number retired by two different teams. The teams were in the same city—New York. Charles Dillon Stengel—"The Old Professor" had his #37 retired by the Yankees in 1970 and later that same year by the Mets . Casey managed both clubs. Stengel led the powerful Yankees to ten American League pennants and seven World Championships in twelve years, an unprecedented feat. The torch was passed from one powerhouse club to another, from the days of Joe DiMaggio to Mickey Mantle, from Allie Reynolds to Whitey Ford. Stengel retired after 1960.

Old Case was coaxed back to work after a year. He was to take on the "Amazin' Mets," New York's answer to the loss of the Giants and Dodgers to the West Coast. He finished last four years running, (1962-1965) but he drew pretty good crowds with his showmanship. What more could be asked of this collection of over-the-hill cast-offs and raw, inexperienced players.

There were some good, young arms down on the farm though: Tom Seaver, Jerry Koosman, Gary Gentry and a fellow named Nolan Ryan. Four years after Casey had enough, Gil Hodges brought an unbeliev-able pennant and World Series to a New York gone wild for the "Amazin's."

Ryan went on to shatter every record in the book. On June 16, 1992, while still active, the California Angels retired his number 30. Ryan officially retired in October, 1993. The Texas Rangers retired his number 34, so did Houston. That made him the only man to have three different teams retire his number.

Retired players' uniforms from L to R: Richie Ashburn's 1, Phillies; Fred Hutchinson's 1, Reds; Billy Martin's 1, Yankees; Bobby Doerr's 1, Red Sox; Peewee Reese's 1, Dodgers; Billy Meyer's 1, Pirates, Ozzie Smith's 1, Cardinals; and Luis Aparicio's 11, White Sox.

Christy Mathewson (above) was the dominant ML pitcher of his era (1900-1916). "Big Six" had 372 wins, with a remarkable 78 shutouts. He, more than once, won both ends of a doubleheader. John McGraw (below) managed the Giants for 31 years, winning 10 pennants and three World Series. Here, he is seen lecturing the troops in spring.

Managers are notorious for being in and out of jobs and also for retiring, then coming back for one more time. Earl Weaver had his number 4 taken out of circulation in 1982 when he called it quits. However, he couldn't resist thinking that he could pull the Orioles out of the dumps in 1985. He joined the team in 4th place with 105 games to go and they finished up in 4th place. The following year he managed to do no better than seventh place. He quietly retired again.

Billy Martin's stormy playing career and managerial stints ended with the Yankees retiring his number 1 in 1985, but he also came back to manage the Yanks for 68 more games in 1988.

There are three numbers retired for men who are not only not active, they never were professional ballplayers. The California Angels retired the number 26 for owner Gene Autry, the singing cowboy. He was considered the "26th" man. August Busch, Jr. of St. Louis had the #85 retired to commemorate his age in 1984. Carl Barger, an executive, died while attending the winter baseball meetings for the newborn Florida Marlins. They retired the #5 for his favorite ballplayer, Joe DiMaggio.

Several other players so honored didn't have numbers to retire. Before 1929, numbers were not worn on the uniforms regularly. The New York Giants retired the jerseys of two former greats regardless of that fact: Christy Mathewson and John McGraw. Their numberless symbols adorn the outfield walls in San Francisco.

Honus Wagner was numberless during his playing days for the Pittsburgh Pirates too. "The Flying Dutchman" played shortstop from 1900-1917. He led the National League in batting 8 times, finishing with a career

RYAN
34

CARLTON
32

7

37

average of .327. He knocked in over 100 runs nine times, leading the league in 5 seasons. After his playing days, Honus coached for the Bucs from 1933-1951. During that period he wore #33. That's the number the Pirates retired.

The Phillies solved two interesting dilemmas in 2001. Grover Cleveland (Pete) Alexander played for the Phils prior to wearing numbers so they used the 1915 "**P**" as his symbol. Chuck Klein, at the other end of the spectrum wore #1, 3, 8, 26, 29, 32 and 36 while with the Phils. They selected the Old English "𝔓" worn during his first six seasons to represent him.

By 2005, there were 138 baseball men honored by retiring 147 jerseys, 65 American Leaguers and 82 National Leaguers. Forty-two of the one-hundred-thirty-eight names are *not* in the Hall of Fame. Some will be there as soon as they are eligible: Tony Gwynn and Cal Ripken. Others should be in the Hall, but may never get there, such as Tony Oliva, Roger Maris, and Ron Santo.

Some of the others toiled very long and hard for the home team, put up some numbers, helped win pennants and generally exemplified the spirit of the team to the fans. There were Minnie Minoso and Billy Pierce of the '59 pennant-winning "Go-Go Sox". There were Jose Cruz and Jimmy Wynn of the Astros, Ken Boyer of the Cards and Elston Howard, Ron Guidry and Don Mattingly of the Yankees.

Richie Ashburn was finally elected to the Hall of Fame in 1995. He was a premier lead-off hitter for the Philadelphia Phillies. His rookie year, 1948, saw Ashburn batting .333 and leading the league in stolen bases. In his 15 years, he batted over .300 nine times, winning the batting crown twice. He led the NL in hits three times, triples twice, walks four times and on-base percentage four times. The speedy centerfielder had great stats: total chances/game (3.04, 2nd All-Time), putouts (6,089, 6th All-Time) and putouts/game (2.90, 2nd All-Time). Why such a wait?

Retired players' uniforms from L to R: Nolan Ryan's 34, Rangers; Steve Carlton's 32, Phillies; Mickey Mantle's 7, Yankees; Casey Stengel's 37, Mets; Mike Schmidt's 20, Phillies; Eddie Murray's 33, Orioles; Harold Baines' 3, White Sox; and Willie Mays' 24, Giants.

Some players probably would not have been accorded the honor, except for tragic circumstances arising. Jim Umbricht pitched only 194 innings in the majors going 8-3 for Houston and 9-5 overall. He died of cancer at the outset of the 1964 season at the age of 34. Houston retired his uniform #32.

Another horror story hit the Astros on January 5, 1975 when pitcher Don Wilson's body was found in his garage, asphixiated. They retired his number 40.

The entire baseball world was stunned when powerful Gil Hodges suffered a massive heart attack and died April 2, 1972, two days before his forty-eighth birthday. It was just days before the season was to start. The Mets quickly named Yogi Berra to manage. And the team that Hodges was forging won the pennant the following year under Berra. They retired Hodges' 14.

Dick Howser led the underdog Kansas City Royals to their only World Championship in 1985 over the Cardinals. In less than two years he was struck down with brain cancer. The Royals retired his number 10 to pay tribute to the quietly elegant fighter.

Illness struck down the competitive Fred Hutchinson at forty-five. The Reds retired his number 1. He was the first Red so honored. It's hard to believe that more haven't been honored with the parade of stars that have left their mark on that city. Johnny Vander Meer pitched two no-hitters in a row in 1937. Bucky Walters and Duke Derringer brought pennants to Cincy in 1939 and 1940. They finally retired Big Klu's #18 and Frank Robinson's #20. And what about "The Big Red Machine?" One of the most star-laden teams in baseball history: They've retired Bench's #5, Morgan's #8 and Perez's #24. What of George Foster #15, Dave Concepcion's #13, Don Gullett's #35 and yes, Pete Rose's #14. They were awesome!

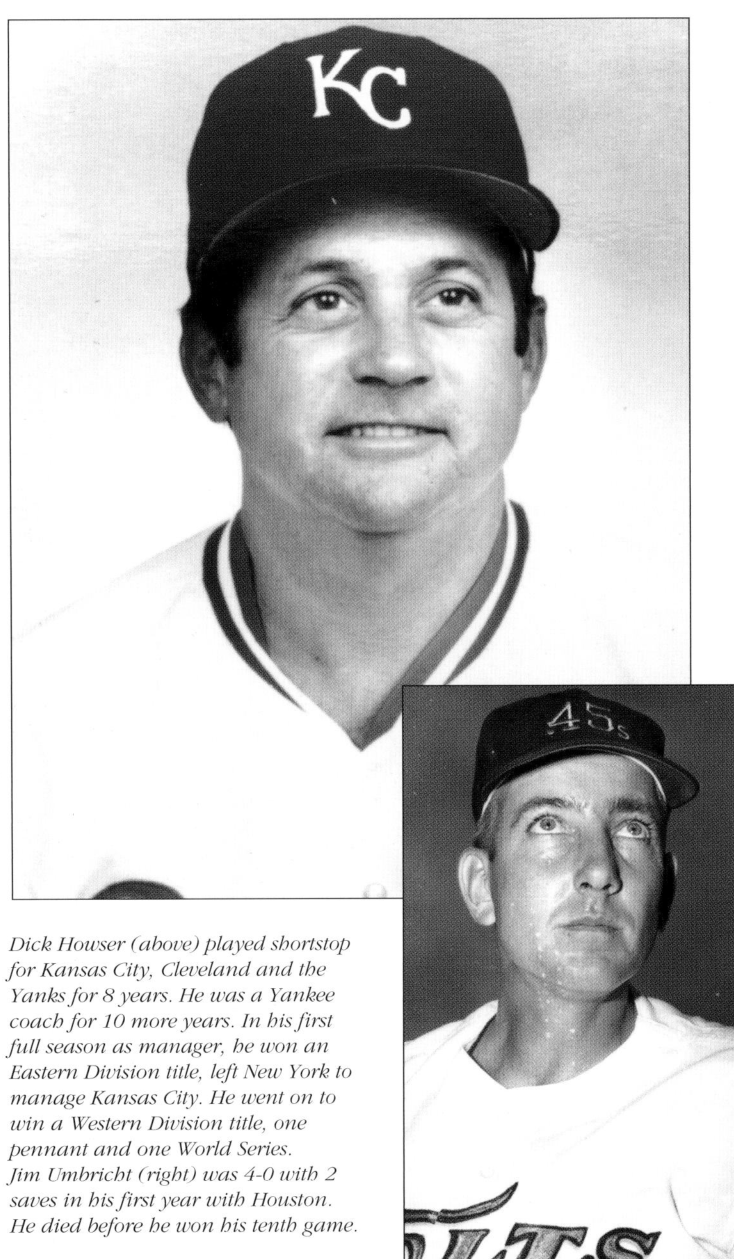

Dick Howser (above) played shortstop for Kansas City, Cleveland and the Yanks for 8 years. He was a Yankee coach for 10 more years. In his first full season as manager, he won an Eastern Division title, left New York to manage Kansas City. He went on to win a Western Division title, one pennant and one World Series.
Jim Umbricht (right) was 4-0 with 2 saves in his first year with Houston. He died before he won his tenth game.

Plane crashes have brutally cut short the careers of two great ballplayers. Clemente's untimely death spurred the Baseball Writer's Association to hold a special election to vote him into the Hall of Fame, waiving the normal five-year waiting period. His number 21 was retired during the upcoming season.

Thurman Munson was piloting his own private plane when he lost control and it went down. Cutting his career short may have kept him out of the Hall. If he had continued at the pace he was going, he surely would have been a strong candidate. The Yankees retired Thurman's number 15 in 1979.

Illness claimed the lives of Junior Gilliam and Ken Boyer. Gilliam was a Dodger coach at the time. Jim had been a sparkplug on seven pennant-winning clubs in his fourteen years. He wore number 19.

Ken Boyer was the National League's MVP in the St. Louis Cardinals' championship year of 1964. His grand slam home run in Game 4 of the World Series turned the tide for the Cards. They went on to beat the mighty Yankees who didn't win another pennant for 13 years. Boyer was a five-time Gold Glove winner at third base. The Cards retired his number 14.

One rainy night in New York in 1958, Roy Campanella's car spun out of control and left one of the all-time great catchers paralyzed and confined to a wheel chair. The Dodgers honored Campy by hanging up his #39.

Retired players' uniforms from L to R: Carl Yastrzemski's 8, Red Sox; Brooks Robinson's 5, Orioles; Roy Campanella's 39, Dodgers; Tony Gwynn's 19, Padres; Johnny Bench's 5, Reds; Lou Boudreau's 5, Indians; Gary Carter's 8, Expos; and Willie McCovey's 44, Giants.

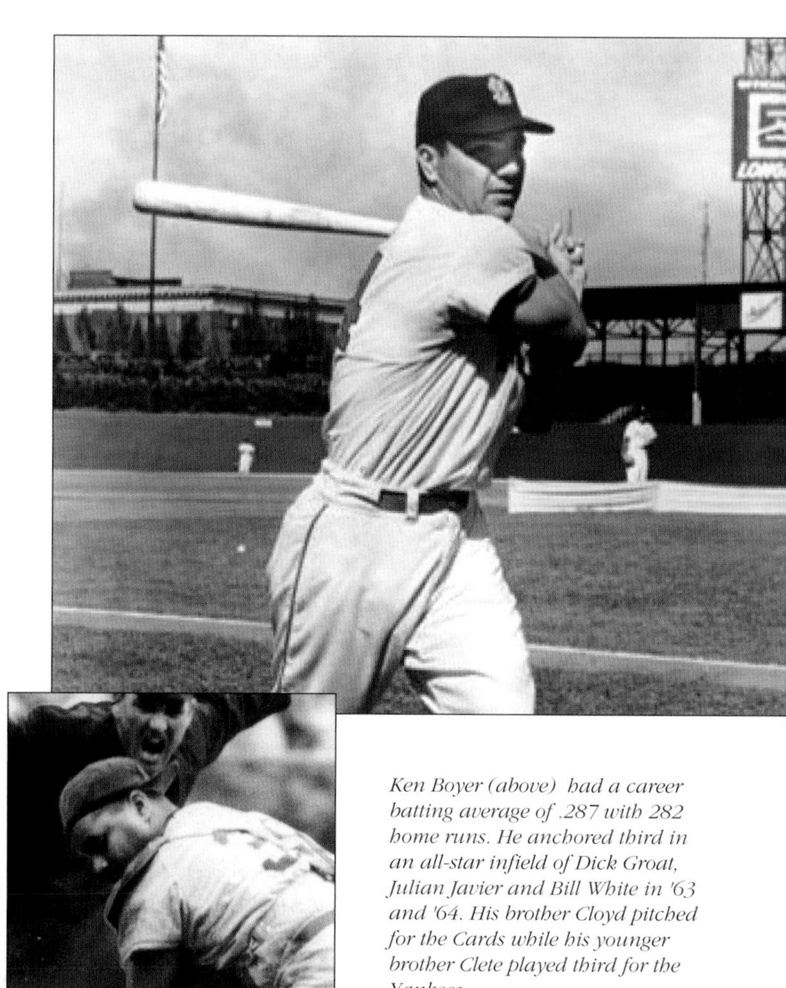

Ken Boyer (above) had a career batting average of .287 with 282 home runs. He anchored third in an all-star infield of Dick Groat, Julian Javier and Bill White in '63 and '64. His brother Cloyd pitched for the Cards while his younger brother Clete played third for the Yankees.

Roy Campanella (left) broke in with the Brooklyn Dodgers in 1948 when he was already 26 years old. His best year was 1953. He had 26 doubles, 41 home runs and led the NL with 142 RBI and the Dodgers won the pennant. But alas, they lost once more to the Yankees in the Subway Series.

RETIRED BY POSITION

LISTED BY PRIMARY POSITION, SECONDARY IN PARENTHESES

FIRST BASE

3 BILL TERRY--GIANTS (MGR)
4 LOU GEHRIG--YANKEES
5 HANK GREENBERG--TIGERS (OF)
6 STEVE GARVEY--PADRES
8 WILLIE STARGELL--PIRATES (OF)
14 KENT HRBEK--TWINS
18 TED KLUSZEWSKI--REDS
23 DON MATTINGLY--YANKEES
24 TONY PEREZ--REDS
29 ROD CAREW--ANGELS
30 ORLANDO CEPEDA--GIANTS (OF)
33 EDDIE MURRAY--ORIOLES
44 WILLIE McCOVEY--GIANTS

SECOND BASE

1 BOBBY DOERR--RED SOX
2 NELLIE FOX--WHITE SOX
2 CHARLIE GEHRINGER--TIGERS
2 RED SCHOENDIENST--CARDS (MGR)
8 JOE MORGAN--REDS
9 BILL MAZEROSKI--PIRATES
19 JUNIOR GILLIAM--DODGERS (3B/CH)
20 FRANK WHITE--ROYALS
29 ROD CAREW--TWINS
42 JACKIE ROBINSON--DODGERS

THIRD BASE

3 HARMON KILLEBREW--TWINS (1B)
4 PAUL MOLITOR--BREWERS (DH)
5 GEORGE BRETT--ROYALS
5 BROOKS ROBINSON--ORIOLES
10 RON SANTO--CUBS
12 WADE BOGGS--DEVIL RAYS
14 KEN BOYER--CARDINALS (MGR)
20 MIKE SCHMIDT--PHILLIES
20 PIE TRAYNOR--PIRATES
41 EDDIE MATHEWS--BRAVES

SHORTSTOP

1 PEEWEE REESE--DODGERS
1 OZZIE SMITH--CARDINALS
4 LUKE APPLING--WHITE SOX
4 JOE CRONIN--RED SOX (MGR)
5 LOU BOUDREAU--INDIANS (MGR)
8 CAL RIPKEN--ORIOLES
10 PHIL RIZZUTO--YANKEES
11 LUIS APARICIO--WHITE SOX
11 JIM FREGOSI--ANGELS (MGR)
14 ERNIE BANKS--CUBS
33 HONUS WAGNER--PIRATES

OUTFIELD

P CHUCK KLEIN--PHILLIES
1 RICHIE ASHBURN--PHILLIES
3 EARL AVERILL--INDIANS
3 HAROLD BAINES--WHITE SOX (DH)
3 DALE MURPHY--BRAVES
3 BABE RUTH--YANKEES
4 RALPH KINER--PIRATES
4 MEL OTT--GIANTS
4 DUKE SNIDER--DODGERS
5 JOE DIMAGGIO--YANKEES
6 AL KALINE--TIGERS
6 STAN MUSIAL--CARDINALS (1B)
6 TONY OLIVA--TWINS (DH)
7 MICKEY MANTLE--YANKEES
8 CARL YASTRZEMSKI--RED SOX
9 REGGIE JACKSON--A's
9 ROGER MARIS--YANKEES
9 MINNIE MINOSO--WHITE SOX (3B)
9 ENOS SLAUGHTER--CARDINALS
9 TED WILLIAMS--RED SOX
10 RUSTY STAUB--EXPOS
10 ANDRE DAWSON--EXPOS
14 LARRY DOBY--INDIANS
19 TONY GWYNN--PADRES
19 ROBIN YOUNT--BREWERS (SS)
20 LOU BROCK--CARDINALS
20 FRANK ROBINSON--ORIOLES, REDS
21 ROBERTO CLEMENTE--PIRATES
23 WILLIE HORTON--TIGERS (DH)
24 WILLIE MAYS--GIANTS
24 JIMMY WYNN--ASTROS
25 JOSE CRUZ--ASTROS
26 BILLY WILLIAMS--CUBS
30 TIM RAINES--EXPOS
31 DAVE WINFIELD--PADRES
34 KIRBY PUCKETT--TWINS
44 HANK AARON--BRAVES
44 REGGIE JACKSON--YANKEES

CATCHER

5 JOHNNY BENCH--REDS (3B)
8 YOGI BERRA--YANKEES
8 GARY CARTER--EXPOS
8 BILL DICKEY--YANKEES
15 THURMAN MUNSON--YANKEES
27 CARLTON FISK--RED SOX
32 ELSTON HOWARD--YANKEES
39 ROY CAMPANELLA--DODGERS
72 CARLTON FISK--WHITE SOX

PITCHER

_ CHRISTY MATHEWSON--GIANTS
P PETE ALEXANDER--PHILLIES
11 CARL HUBBELL--GIANTS
14 JIM BUNNING--PHILLIES
16 WHITEY FORD--YANKEES
16 TED LYONS--WHITE SOX (MGR)
16 HAL NEWHOUSER--TIGERS
17 DIZZY DEAN--CARDINALS
18 MEL HARDER--INDIANS (CH)
19 BOB FELLER--INDIANS
19 BILLY PIERCE--WHITE SOX
20 DON SUTTON--DODGERS
21 BOB LEMON--INDIANS
21 WARREN SPAHN--BRAVES
22 JIM PALMER--ORIOLES
27 CATFISH HUNTER--A's
27 JUAN MARICHAL--GIANTS
30 NOLAN RYAN--ANGELS
32 STEVE CARLTON--PHILLIES
32 SANDY KOUFAX--DODGERS
32 JIM UMBRICHT--COLT 45s
33 MIKE SCOTT--ASTROS
34 ROLLIE FINGERS--BREWERS, A's
34 NOLAN RYAN--RANGERS, ASTROS
35 RANDY JONES--PADRES
35 PHIL NIEKRO--BRAVES
36 GAYLORD PERRY--GIANTS
36 ROBIN ROBERTS--PHILLIES
40 DON WILSON--ASTROS
41 TOM SEAVER--METS
43 DENNIS ECKERSLEY--A's
45 BOB GIBSON--CARDINALS
49 LARRY DIERKER--ASTROS (MGR)
49 RON GUIDRY--YANKEES
53 DON DRYSDALE--DODGERS

DESIGNATED HITTER

44 HANK AARON--BREWERS

MANAGER

_ JOHN McGRAW--GIANTS
1 FRED HUTCHINSON--REDS
1 BILLY MARTIN--YANKEES (2B)
1 BILLY MEYER--PIRATES
2 TOM LASORDA--DODGERS
4 EARL WEAVER--ORIOLES
10 SPARKY ANDERSON--REDS
10 DICK HOWSER--ROYALS
14 GIL HODGES--METS
24 WALTER ALSTON--DODGERS
37 CASEY STENGEL--METS, YANKEES
40 DANNY MURTAUGH--PIRATES

COACH

50 JIMMIE REESE--ANGELS

EXECUTIVE

5 CARL BARGER--MARLINS
26 GENE AUTRY--ANGELS
85 AUGUST BUSCH, JR.--CARDS

RETIRED-- BY THE NUMBERS

— CHRISTY MATHEWSON--P GIANTS*
— JOHN McGRAW--MGR GIANTS*
P PETE ALEXANDER--P PHILLIES*
P CHUCK KLEIN--OF PHILLIES*

1 RICHIE ASHBURN--OF PHILLIES*
1 BOBBY DOERR--2B RED SOX*
1 FRED HUTCHINSON--MGR REDS
1 BILLY MARTIN--2B/MGR YANKEES
1 BILLY MEYER--MGR PIRATES
1 PEEWEE REESE--SS DODGERS*
1 OZZIE SMITH--SS CARDINALS*

2 NELLIE FOX--2B WHITE SOX*
2 CHARLIE GEHRINGER--2B TIGERS*
2 TOM LASORDA--MGR DODGERS*
2 RED SCHOENDIENST--2B/MGR CARDINALS*

3 EARL AVERILL--OF INDIANS*
3 HAROLD BAINES--OF/DH WHITE SOX
3 HARMON KILLEBREW--3B/1B TWINS*
3 DALE MURPHY--OF BRAVES
3 BABE RUTH--OF YANKEES*
3 BILL TERRY--1B/MGR GIANTS*

4 LUKE APPLING--SS WHITE SOX*
4 JOE CRONIN--SS/MGR RED SOX*
4 LOU GEHRIG--1B YANKEES*
4 RALPH KINER--OF PIRATES*
4 PAUL MOLITOR--3B/DH BREWERS
4 MEL OTT--OF GIANTS*
4 DUKE SNIDER--OF DODGERS*
4 EARL WEAVER--MGR ORIOLES*

5 CARL BARGER--EXEC MARLINS
5 JOHNNY BENCH--C REDS*
5 LOU BOUDREAU--SS/MGR INDIANS*
5 GEORGE BRETT--3B ROYALS*
5 JOE DIMAGGIO--OF YANKEES*
5 HANK GREENBERG--OF/1B TIGERS*
5 BROOKS ROBINSON--3B ORIOLES*

6 STEVE GARVEY--1B PADRES
6 AL KALINE--OF TIGERS*
6 STAN MUSIAL--OF/1B CARDINALS*
6 TONY OLIVA--OF TWINS

7 MICKEY MANTLE--OF YANKEES*

8 YOGI BERRA--C YANKEES*
8 GARY CARTER--C EXPOS*
8 BILL DICKEY--C YANKEES*
8 JOE MORGAN--2B REDS*
8 CAL RIPKEN--SS ORIOLES
8 WILLIE STARGELL--OF/1B PARATES*
8 CARL YASTRZEMSKI--OF/1B RED SOX*

9 REGGIE JACKSON--OF A's*
9 ROGER MARIS--OF YANKEES
9 BILL MAZEROSKI--2B PIRATES*
9 MINNIE MINOSO--OF/3B WHITE SOX
9 ENOS SLAUGHTER--OF CARDINALS*
9 TED WILLIAMS--OF RED SOX*

10 SPARKY ANDERSON--MGR REDS*
10 ANDRE DAWSON--OF EXPOS
10 DICK HOWSER--MGR ROYALS
10 PHIL RIZZUTO--SS YANKEES*
10 RON SANTO--3B CUBS
10 RUSTY STAUB--OF EXPOS

11 LUIS APARICIO--SS WHITE SOX*
11 JIM FREGOSI--SS/MGR ANGELS
11 CARL HUBBELL--P GIANTS*

12 WADE BOGGS--3B DEVIL RAYS

14 ERNIE BANKS--SS/1B CUBS*
14 KEN BOYER--3B/MGR CARDINALS
14 JIM BUNNING--P PHILLIES*
14 LARRY DOBY--OF INDIANS
14 GIL HODGES--1B/MGR METS
14 KENT HRBEK--1B TWINS

15 THURMAN MUNSON--C YANKEES

16 WHITEY FORD--P YANKEES*
16 TED LYONS--P/MGR WHITE SOX*
16 HAL NEWHOUSER--P TIGERS*

17 DIZZY DEAN--P CARDINALS*

18 MEL HARDER--P INDIANS
18 TED KLUSZEWSKI--1B REDS

19 BOB FELLER--P INDIANS*
19 JUNIOR GILLIAM--2B/3B DODGERS
19 TONY GWYNN--OF PADRES
19 BILLY PIERCE--P WHITE SOX
19 ROBIN YOUNT--SS/OF BREWERS

20 LOU BROCK--OF CARDINALS*
20 FRANK ROBINSON--OF ORIOLES*
20 FRANK ROBINSON--OF REDS*
20 MIKE SCHMIDT--3B PHILLIES*
20 DON SUTTON--P DODGERS*
20 PIE TRAYNOR--3B PIRATES*
20 FRANK WHITE--2B ROYALS

21 ROBERTO CLEMENTE--OF PIRATES*
21 BOB LEMON--P INDIANS*
21 WARREN SPAHN--P BRAVES*

22 JIM PALMER--P ORIOLES*

23 WILLIE HORTON--OF TIGERS
23 DON MATTINGLY--1B YANKEES

24 WALTER ALSTON--MGR DODGERS*
24 WILLIE MAYS--OF GIANTS*
24 TONY PEREZ--1B REDS*
24 JIMMY WYNN--OF ASTROS

25 JOSE CRUZ--OF/CH ASTROS

26 GENE AUTRY--OWNER ANGELS
26 BILLY WILLIAMS--OF CUBS*

27 CARLTON FISK--C RED SOX*
27 CATFISH HUNTER--P A's*
27 JUAN MARICHAL--P GIANTS*

29 ROD CAREW--1B ANGELS*
29 ROD CAREW--2B/1B TWINS*

30 ORLANDO CEPEDA--1B GIANTS*
30 TIM RAINES--OF EXPOS
30 NOLAN RYAN--P ANGELS*

31 DAVE WINFIELD--OF PADRES

32 STEVE CARLTON--P PHILLIES*
32 ELSTON HOWARD--C YANKEES
32 SANDY KOUFAX--P DODGERS*
32 JIM UMBRICHT--P COLT 45s

33 EDDIE MURRAY--1B ORIOLES*
33 MIKE SCOTT--P ASTROS
33 HONUS WAGNER--SS PIRATES*

34 ROLLIE FINGERS--P BREWERS*
34 ROLLIE FINGERS--P A's*
34 KIRBY PUCKETT--OF TWINS*
34 NOLAN RYAN--P ASTROS*
34 NOLAN RYAN--P RANGERS*

35 RANDY JONES--P PADRES
35 PHIL NIEKRO--P BRAVES*

36 GAYLORD PERRY--P GIANTS*
36 ROBIN ROBERTS--P PHILLIES*

37 CASEY STENGEL--MGR YANKEES*
37 CASEY STENGEL--MGR METS*

39 ROY CAMPANELLA--C DODGERS*

40 DANNY MURTAUGH--MGR PIRATES
40 DON WILSON--P ASTROS

41 EDDIE MATHEWS--3B BRAVES*
41 TOM SEAVER--P METS*

42 JACKIE ROBINSON--1B/2B DODGERS*
42 *ALL TEAMS HONORING ROBINSON*

43 DENNIS ECKERSLEY--P A's*

44 HANK AARON--OF BRAVES*
44 HANK AARON--DH BREWERS*
44 REGGIE JACKSON--OF YANKEES*
44 WILLIE McCOVEY--1B GIANTS*

45 BOB GIBSON--P CARDINALS*

49 LARRY DIERKER--P/MGR ASTROS
49 RON GUIDRY--P YANKEES

50 JIMMIE REESE--CH ANGELS

53 DON DRYSDALE--P DODGERS*

72 CARLTON FISK--C WHITE SOX*

85 AUGIE BUSCH, JR.--OWNER CARDINALS

**HALL OF FAME*

Uniforms of the following retired players, from L to R: Warren Spahn's 21, Braves; Whitey Ford's 16, Yankees; Juan Marichal's 27, Giants; Billy Pierce's 19, White Sox; Sandy Koufax's 32, Dodgers; Jim Palmer's 22, Orioles; Bob Gibson's 45, Cardinals; and Rollie Finger's 34, Brewers.

Dave Concepcion spent his entire nineteen years with the Cincinnati Reds. He had good range at shortstop and a strong throwing arm. He was the first to perfect the one-hop throw from deep in the hole on the artificial carpet. Dave batted over .300 three times, finishing at .267. He knocked in 950 runs in his career and stole 321 bases. He was one of the main cogs in the "Big Red Machine" of the '70s.

Some numbers have never been retired. Since Lou Gehrig's number 4 was taken out of circulation by the Yankees in 1939, no one playing the game wearing 13 was ever honored. That's the lowest number _not_ retired. One can guess why hard-luck Ralph Branca's 13 was not retired, but what about the Reds' Dave Concepcion? He's a bona fide candidate for the Hall of Fame. The highest player's number is Fisk's #72.

NUMBERS NEVER RETIRED

13	47	54-71
28	48	73-84
38	51	86-
46	52	*And on up.*

Don Mattingly's back began to affect his play and shortened his career. The Yankees still retired his #23. And what about the Giants' Bobby Thomson's #23 for one of the most historically exciting moments in baseball—"the shot heard round the world."

Tommy John won 288 games while wearing number 25 for most of his career. His longest stint was with the White Sox for seven years where he was 82-80. He was with the Yankees for two terms adding up to seven years, winning 91 and losing 60. His best percentage was with the Dodgers where he won 87 while losing only 42 (.730). But the first #25 to be retired was Jose Cruz of the Astros, not John's.

Big Dave Winfield is the only number 31 to be retired. It was by the Padres and not the Yankees. The gifted outfielder made the Hall of Fame in 2001. He had 465 homers and drove in 1833 runs.

Dave Dravecky stuns the Candlestick crowd in 1989. He had come back from surgery of his pitching shoulder when he broke his arm and collapsed during a game. Cancer had so weekened him that his arm could not withstand the pressure that pitching created. He retired from baseball and ultimately had to have his pitching arm amputated.

The number 49 was not retired until 2002 when the Astros did so for Larry Dierker. It wasn't until a year later that the Yankees did the same for Ron "Louisiana Lightning" Guidry who's nineteenth on the All-Time percentage list with 170-91 (.651). Hoyt Wilhelm wore that number with one of his nine different clubs over twenty-one years. This Hall of Famer won 143 games and saved another 227, that accounts for 370 games in the win column!

Dave Dravecky wore #43 for the Giants when he struggled against a rare form of cancer. Part of the shoulder muscle of his pitching arm had to be removed. A year later the world watched in horror as his pitching arm snapped and he crumbled to the ground. He's truly a hero. The only 43 retired is for Hall of Famer Dennis Eckersley of the A's.

Others had the misfortune of wearing different numbers everywhere they went. Johnny Mize wore #10 for the Cardinals, #15 for the New York Giants and #36 for the Yankees at the tail-end of his career. "The Big Cat" led the NL in slugging percentage three straight years with the Cards. He led the league in HRs and RBIs three years each.

The Yankees retired #15 for Thurman Munson and not Hall of Famers, pitcher Red Ruffing or second baseman Tony Lazzeri.

Many Hall of Famers have not had their numbers retired. Jimmie Foxx, Lefty Grove, Gabby Hartnett, the Waner brothers, Ducky Medwick, Early Wynn, Monte Irvin, George Kell, Arky Vaughan, and Ferguson Jenkins to name a few.

Retired players' uniforms from L to R: Earl Averill's 3, Indians; Yogi Berra's 8, Yankees; Eddie Mathews' 41, Braves; Don Drysdale's 53, Dodgers; Honus Wagner's 33, Pirates; Dizzy Dean's 17, Cardinals; Hank Greenburg's 5, Tigers; Harmon Killebrew's 3, Twins.

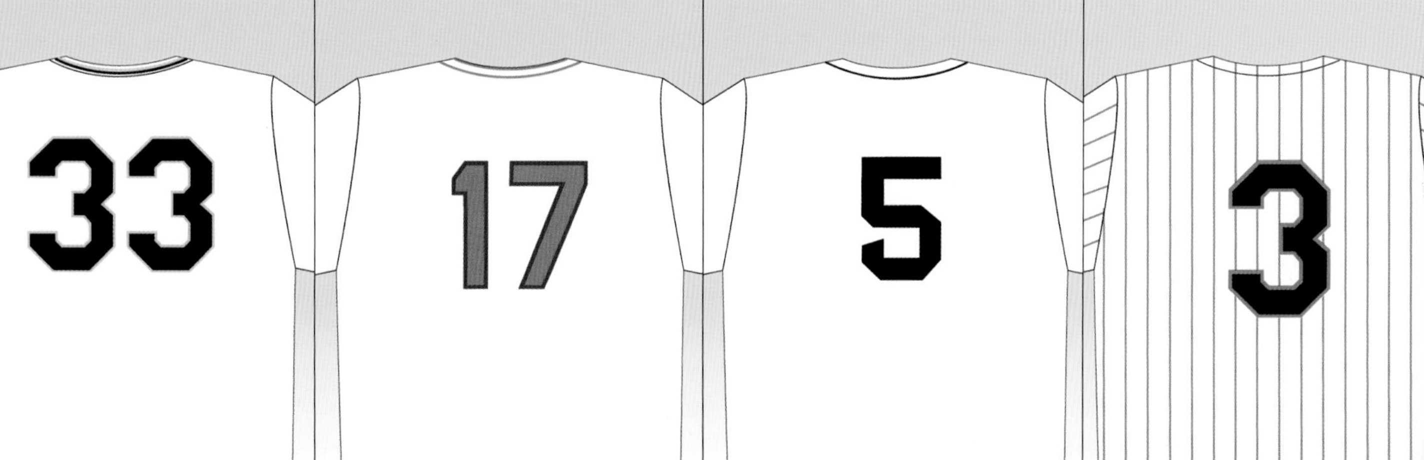

42 The impact was immediate. He was solid (5'11", 204 lbs.), he was strong, he was fast. He danced, he pestered, he instigated. He was smooth, he was aggressive, but he was mute. He had to be. That was the deal.

Play the game hard, play to win, but no matter how much taunting or how many epithets were thrown in your face, stay out of it—don't fight back. For two solid years—don't fight back! That's what Jackie Robinson was asked to do. What he asked of himself to do.

"I think you can play in the major leagues. How do you feel about it?" asked Branch Rickey at their clandestine meeting in his office in Brooklyn in the late summer of 1945. He phrased a sentence that asked if Robinson "had the guts" to play ball in the National League.

Rickey knew there would be explosive situations—racial slurs, excessive taunting from opposing players and fans in each city, perhaps even biased calls on plays, housing problems wherever he went. But he also knew for the color barrier to be broken permenantly the first negro to play ball in the twentieth century would have to hold back, be the shining example of knighthood needed to usher in this new era of baseball. Rickey also knew that the player had to be a superior athlete to overcome the prejudice that was sure to be heaped on Robinson.

Robinson bristled at Rickey's comment, "Mr. Rickey, are you looking for a Negro who is afraid to fight back?"

Rickey knew of Robinson's background; that he had been in many scrapes in his youth, at UCLA, and while he was in the army. He knew he spent time fighting allegations of being a racial agitator, but eventually received his honorary discharge from the miltary.

Jackie Robinson opened the gates for all the talented players that were denied prior to his enduring the initial struggle.

"Robinson, I'm looking for a ballplayer with guts enough not to fight back," said Rickey.

The climate had changed in baseball a little bit. After Judge Kenesaw Mountain Landis' death in 1944, baseball hired Happy Chandler as their new commissioner. The commissioner wasn't the rubber stamp the owners thought they were getting. He freely voiced his opinion, "If a black can make it in Okinawa and go to Guadalcanal, he can make it in baseball."

After Jackie signed to play in Montreal the following year he quietly said, "Of course, I can't tell you how happy I am as the first member of my race in organized ball. I realize how much it means to me, to my race and to baseball. I can only add that I will do my best to come through in every manner."

Robinson excelled in Montreal batting .349 for the year and lead the Royals to victory in their championship series.

April 15, 1947 was D-day. The Dodgers were playing the Boston Braves at Ebbetts Field. Robinson played first base and went 0-for-3. But in the seventh inning he dropped down a sacrifice bunt. As he raced to first the throw hit him in the back and trickled into short right field. He didn't stop until he got to second. Robinson scored the winning run when Pete Reiser singled. A new era was born.

He was quite a picture. Standing at the plate, his bat cocked high, his right hand slapping down at his uniform pants in anticipation of the pitch. His short, compact swing drove his stocky mass through the ball sending stinging line-drives to all parts of the park.

But the place to watch him work was on the basepaths. For a large man, he was surprisingly nimble and quick. He would dance off the base in his pigeon-toed manner, fake moving forward, then back. Pitchers never knew what he was going to do. No baserunner had ever done this kind of dance off a base before. He became the catalyst of a Dodger team that went on to win six National League pennants in his ten-year span. During this time Brooklyn won their only World Series against their perennial adversary, the New York Yankees, in 1955.

Robby, as he quickly came to be known, played in six straight All-Star games. He led the league in batting with .342 in 1949. After switching to second base in 1948, he led the league in fielding three times. He was stolen base champ in '47 and '49. He stole home 19 times in his career, including the controversial 1955 WS one against the Yankees.
In a game on April 23, 1954, he stole second, third, and home. His lifetime on-base average (.410) is higher than Charlie Gehringer's, Joe DiMaggio's or Richie Ashburn's.

He ended with .311 BA, 947 runs, 1518 hits, 273 doubles, 54 triples, 137 HR, 734 RBI, 740 BB and a slugging % of .474.

He was the Rookie of the Year in 1947, the award now bears his name. The MVP of 1949 was elected to baseball's Hall of Fame in 1962 in his first year of eligibility.

The most unprecendented baseball event took place fifty years later, April 15, 1997 when acting Commissioner of Baseball, Bud Selig announced, "No. 42, from this day forward, will never again be issued by a major league club. No. 42 belongs to Jackie Robinson for the ages."

The only exceptions were those players that were midway in their careers while using that number, such as Mo Vaughn in Boston who incidently was wearing it to honor Robinson. When their careers were finished, the team would not reissue the number.

Ralph Branca, a Dodger pitcher and teammate on those pennant-winning clubs perhaps captured the spirit of Robinson better than anyone else. He said, "He had a college education, he was well-spoken, he was very bright, he was a fiery, feisty competitor, and he had enough discipline to turn the other cheek. He was absolutely the only man who could have done it, in my estimation."

Robinson in his own words from his autobiography *I Never Had It Made* said, "I had to deny my true fighting spirit so that the 'noble experiment' could succeed."

And succeed it did.

Uniform shirts with numbers retired by respective ball clubs, from L to R: Ted Williams' 9, Red Sox; Carlton Fisk's 72, White Sox; George Brett's 5, Royals; Jimmie Reese's 50, Angels; Rod Carew's 29, Twins; Carl Barger's 5, Marlins; Dave Scott's 33, Astros and Gil Hodges' 14, Mets.

Getting everything ready from the get-go helps everyone's hopes run high in Spring Training

THE CARETAKERS

3

Equipment Managers

"In those days, 1924, most clubs had batboys from the minor leagues. They would show up one day and not the next," said Butch Yatkeman. "I came from the Northside of St. Louis. Sam Lott was a kid across the street. He was a batboy at the time. Sam would be in school clothes which was white duck pants in the '20s. He would go to the ball park and work like that."

"One day he said, 'How would you like to go to the ball game?' He was the batboy for the Cardinals and he let me do the visiting team."

Butch retired in 1982 as equipment manager of St. Louis. He was recalling that Decoration Day in 1924 when he began his long career.

"They would play two games in one day--not a doubleheader. One game would begin at 10 o'clock in the morning and the other at three in the afternoon. Everyone would leave the ball park after the first game and they would charge admission again for the second one. My friend Sam did the morning game, but had to work in his Dad's furniture store in the afternoon. He asked if I would do the Cards for him at three."

Butch didn't miss a day of work for fifty-nine years! He was a batboy through his teen years, 1924-1931. He traveled with the team to Florida for the first time in 1932.

"I was the first Cardinal equipment manager that traveled with the team, but I wasn't the first in the majors to do it. Danny Cumberford of the Dodgers was. Before that, the trainers handled the equipment."

A conversation with Butch would drift back to a time of woolen uniforms and musty locker rooms. A time where bats would be rolled under the stands to the visiting club in a wheelbarrow.

Butch was the first batboy in old Sportsman Park. He handled the Browns when the Cards were on the road. A fellow named Eddie Bennett handled the visiting clubhouse. On one particular afternoon, the mighty Yankees were in town. Eddie hollered over to Butch, "Hey kid, would you like to batboy for the Yanks, too?" Is the Pope Catholic?

"So I did. There was Ruth and Gehrig and all those great ballplayers," Butch was

Butch Yatkeman handled equipment before numbers were a regular feature of the uniform. He worked with such greats as Dizzy Dean, Pepper Martin, Stan Musial, Wild Bill Hallahan to Keith Hernandez and Bruce Sutter.

still excited when he talked about it more than sixty years later.

"One of my greatest thrills was in the '42 World Series. The Cards were playing the Yanks and we were the underdogs. Even if we won, the Yanks were still the favorites each day," recounted Butch.

"Terry Moore, who was our captain, went out to give the line-up before the fourth game. The Yankee manager was Joe McCarthy and he told the umps that they didn't want me on the bench. Terry got mad and told him, 'With or without Butch, we'll beat you.'"

"Mort Cooper got knocked out, but two pitchers later, Max Lanier came in and shut the door. Our coach, Buzzy Wares, used to kid a lot. He walked up and down and made noise on the bench to stir things up. It worked because we got two runs to break the tie and the Cards went on to beat them 9-6. We won the next game to make it three straight in New York to become champions."

Butch was going to pack it in after fifty years of traveling with the club since 1932. That was the strike-shortened season of 1981.

"I was over in the clubhouse alone when Whitey (Herzog) came in. He said,

'I heard you were going to leave the club after the season. Why don't you think about staying one more year? I might win the pennant and the World Series and you can go out in a blaze of glory.'"

"So I decided to do it and the players started each day with--'*Win one for the Butcher!*'"

"Then Gene Tenace had a birthday in October (the 10th) and it became 'Win one for "The Boat"'--that's what they called him. We won the pennant that day." (The Cardinals won the third game of the play-off to sweep Atlanta.)

"Each day it became someone else. Keith Hernandez had his birthday in October (the 20th) and we won the World Series when we 'Won one for Keith.'" (Hernandez got the key hit to push the Cardinals ahead 4-3. They went on to win that seventh game 6-3 and the Series, 4 games to 3.)

Yatkeman was with the Cards for thirteen of their sixteen World Series appearances. He missed the last three. He was there for all nine World Championships. Maybe they did "Win one for the Butcher!"

On September 12, 1982, the Cardinals had a day for Butch Yatkeman and he did "go out in a blaze of glory." The players presented him with a gold watch and Augie Busch presented him with a Buick Riviera--red, of course.

Bill Acree has been equipment manager of the Atlanta Braves since 1968. He has the added distinction of being the Traveling Secretary of the club as well.

"They used wool uniforms in the old days and the sweatshirts would shrink. Then the player would have to buy new ones. Because of that, the uniforms would hardly ever get washed. It would be done at the beginning of a homestand. A shoe brush was used on the hats.

"The players would be issued only two pairs of shoes a year. They used 'mudders' when the weather looked bad. That was last year's shoes to save the new ones." Bill laughed, "Now they get two pairs a week."

Today, the equipment manager's job is a year-round job. As soon as the season is over, they begin ordering uniforms and other pieces of equipment to be delivered for packing in January. This is all done in preparation for Spring Training. A huge moving van is sent to the training camp a couple of weeks before the players arrive.

In many cases an extra truck is loaded down with boxes, baby carriages and other household items of the veteran players.

Add to that the plight of John Silverman, of the Expos and Jeff Ross of the Blue Jays. They have to clear everything through Canadian and U. S. Customs going to and from training camp.

The Red Sox EM, Joe Cochrane, orders 60 each of the home and away uniforms. He guesses at the sizes and numbers to be assigned for each shirt.

Jim Wiesner of the Twins, assigns his numbers for Spring Training in January in order to prepare the uniforms. Jim handled the visiting clubhouse from 1960-1984 when he took over for the Twins.

After Butch Yatkeman retired in 1982, Buddy Bates switched over from the visiting clubhouse which he handled for 13 years. The Cardinal locker room in training is impressive with their pennant-winning years hanging banner after banner, from the rafters. Buddy assigns the lockers in uniform number order—all the way around the room. He does this regardless of position or personal relationships. "It's just easier to handle with so many people for such a short period of time," says Buddy.

Years earlier, Birdie Tebbetts, then managing the Cleveland Indians, wanted the locker room to be in number order by position. The pitchers in one place, the catchers in another, the infielders together and so on. But you make one trade and it gets all fouled up.

The equipment manager writes the player's number on everything he owns to keep track of it. Batting helmets and gloves, bat knobs, backs of mitts, felt caps, shin guards, shoes, warm-up shirts, sweatshirts, belts—all the way down to the jock strap have the player's number on them.

Hours after a spring practice, three or four washing machines are going full-blast, tumbling the shirts of 60 or 70 players and coaches. All this to be ready for the early birds who show up at 7:00AM for extra batting practice.

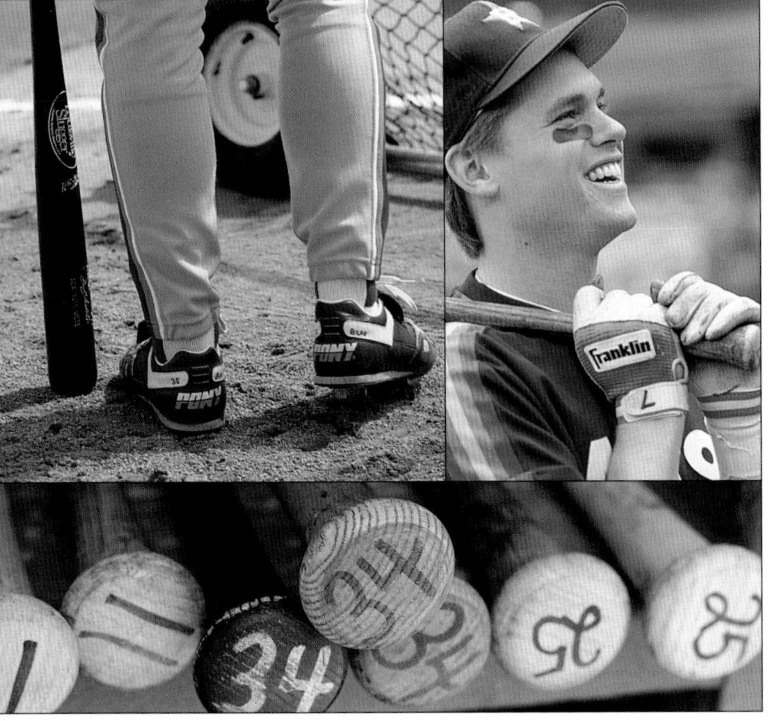

A non-roster invitee to the Mets camp, Dann Bilardello (top, left) can be recognized by his shoes, #35. Dann played 109 games for the Reds in 1983, his strongest season. After eight years in the Bigs, he didn't make the team. (Top, right) Craig Biggio, the feisty catcher-turned-second baseman-turned centerfielder of the Astros sports his #7 on his glove. He made the All-Star team at C and 2B. (Bottom) A by-gone Twins batrack of Knoblauch (#11), Puckett (#34) and Bush (#25).

It's a tough job being laundry steward, father confessor, mother hen and general overall locker room philosopher.

All the EM have funny tales to tell. Practical jokes to relate from the locker rooms. Like the time Don Sutton and Jim Brewer put a live mouse in Al Ferrara's shoe and doubled over with glee when they saw this muscular guy jumping up and down.

Or when the trio of Mike Hargrove, Toby Harrah and Jeff Burroughs would try to one-up each other. One would nail the other's shoes to the locker floor. The next would slit the hat in the back so it would fall over the player's ears. The third would put itching powder in the others' shorts or shaving cream in their hats.

Or the time that they partially cut the seam threads on one guy's pants and the first time he bent over, *split*. That was especially effective in terminals and on commercial flights.

And how about the pennies stuffed into the hotel room key card slot?

Or the time Indian pitcher Jack Kralick shot a jack rabbit and put it in Luis Tiant's bag. In Spring Training, the players tote their own bags. Luis suspected something, because Cy Buynak, the equipment manager, wanted to come along on this particular bus trip. Cy never goes along on those day trips with the team. So the bus arrives for the game, the players enter the clubhouse and Luis opens his bag. There's the rabbit propped up like he's praying with his eyes bugged open. "Luis jumped nine miles," giggled Cy. "To this day, Luis doesn't know who did it."

Cy even became a star, playing in the made-for-TV movie: *Babe Ruth*. A little man, he played the part of the batboy and spoke a couple of lines: "Here's your hot dog, Babe." And "Here's your mail, Gidge."

But the job is much more than funny stories. It attracts an interesting cross-section of men. Many followed the steps of Yatkeman and started out as batboys: Bernie Stowe in Cincinnati, Buddy Bates and Jerry Risch in St. Louis, Charlie Samuels of the Mets, to name a few. Others switched from visiting clubhouse in one city to the head job in another when it opened up.

After spending sixteen years with the Reds' visitors, Roger Wilson moved over to

A notorious low-ball hitter, George Hendrick played for six clubs in his career, twice knocking in over 100 runs. Many felt he should have won the MVP of the 1982 World Series for the Cardinals. He finished up in his native state with the Angels.

Pittsburgh. Joe Cochrane moved into the Red Sox position from the visitors' side. Frank Coppenbarger traded the visitors' clubhouse for the head job in Philadelphia.

Yosh Kimono of the Cubs had the longest streak of service in the NL since Butch Yatkeman before Tom Hellmann took over. Cleveland's Cy Buynak leads the AL with 35 years of service. Mike Burkhalter of the Kansas City Royals wasn't even born yet when Cy began with the Indians. Mike took the job straight out of college in 1989.

Although Joe Macko had been the EM for the Texas Rangers for 23 years in 1998, he had been in baseball for 48. He spent 8 years in the Indians farm system and another 8 with the Cubs system. He amassed the total of 306 minor league home runs, stating it's ninth or tenth all-time! And that doesn't count any post-season play. The last time I saw Joe he looked like he could still knock a few out of the park.

"They auction the uniforms off now," said Joe. "That way they save money. There is a new solution today that lets you change one number—toluene or something like that. It's like a paint thinner and it works on wax or glue. You can get a number right off."

Near the end of the 1974 season, the Indians acquired the great Frank Robinson. For most of his career, Robby wore #20. George Hendrick was wearing #20 for that entire season, but was more than willing to give it up for Frank.

"In those days you couldn't get a number off cleanly," said Buynak. It was pre-toluene. "George switched to #1, but you could see the shadows of the 2 and the 0. It looked like he was wearing #210," chuckled Cy.

Hendrick went to San Diego after Cleveland and then on to the Cardinals. When teams make trades, the equipment managers generally call each other to get the sizes and uniform number of their new man. Butch Yatkeman was told that George wears his pants *very* long. He realized that he didn't have anything that long, so he called Rawlings in St. Louis. They came up with a pair that would do the trick.

Butch recalled, "Hendrick is a great guy and I always want to make them happy.

During warm-ups George is out there shagging fly balls when the General Manager at the time, Bing Divine calls, 'Butch, haven't you got pants that fit Hendrick?'"

"That's the way he likes to wear them and you told me to keep'em pleased," Butch laughed.

Opening Day ceremonies at Fenway Park in Boston against the Yankees saw the Red Sox wearing the letters JRY on their sleeves in honor of Mrs. Tom Yawkey who had recently died.

The Sox had just called up rookie John Flaherty to join the club. EM Joe Cochrane did not have time to get his uniform properly done so they did iron-on numbers and letters for him. During the line-up announcements, both clubs formed up on the foul lines. Flaherty gingerly trotted out when his number 15 was called. "I told him 'As soon as the line-ups are over to put on a jacket because those things are going to pop off,'" said Joe.

Larry Shenk has been with the Phillies since 1963 and is now Vice President, Public Relations. The first thing he thinks of when trading for a player is "What is his number? And do we have a problem right off the bat. It's tough showing around a new member of the ballclub when you know you can't even give him the number he wears to start with," admitted Larry.

Many teams try to follow a numbering scheme when making assignments. The Blue Jays set aside #1-15 for catchers and infielders, 20's for outfielders and pitchers are kept in the 30's and 40's.

The Twins set aside #41-46 for the coaching staff, but Chili Davis wanted #44 and Coach Ron Gardenhire started out as #45, but switched to #35, his old number. In Spring Training the invited coaches wear #60-70.

Orel Hershiser followed the Dodger tradition and picked #55 to wear. He literally followed Don Drysdale into the record books by beating Don's scoreless innings streak by a fraction with 59.

During the season, Wiesner liked to keep all numbers below 60.

Back in the '60s, the Phillies' front office wanted to formularize number assignments much like pro football. The manager could have whatever he wanted. Coaches would be #1-5. Catchers would be single digits, infielders in the teens and outfielders in the 20's. Pitchers were to start at #30 and go up. But along came Jim Bunning who wanted #14 and blew that theory out of the water.

The Red Sox traditionally numbered their coaches #32-36. Manager Butch Hobson wore #4 as a player with the Sox, but as a minor league manager donned #17. He stuck with #17 as the Sox manager. "Rooster" Burleson kept his playing number 7 as a coach to further foul up the system.

The Braves scheme is for catchers and outfielders to be single digits, infielders to be anywhere from 1-15. Pitchers should be anywhere in the 20s, 30s or 40s with the coaches having the high numbers. But there's always one coach who wants to have a low number which is the number from his playing days--the "I did great with that number" syndrome.

Acree prefers not to give out numbers over 50. He thinks it's unnecessary.

By contrast, the Dodgers have a history of pitchers using numbers over 50. Don Drysdale made #53 famous. He first wore it in Brooklyn in 1956. Larry Sherry wore #51, so did Terry Forster, Steve Howe was #57, Orel Hershisher #55, Tim Leary #54. In 1989 and 1990, eight pitchers wore different numbers in the 50's. In 1993, the entire Dodger team wore a black circular patch on their sleeve with #52 to pay tribute to Tim Crews, their former pitcher who was killed in a boating accident in Spring Training.

Joe Macko of the Rangers didn't like to give out numbers under 20 to pitchers. He liked to reserve those numbers for infielders and outfielders. Yet Craig Lefferts wore #11. He had worn it for three years in San Diego.

Whatever the plan, the system is never ironclad. Many other teams keep a loose numbering system knowing full well that a trade or injury might alter that order.

Some teams put the numbers on the brim of the batting helmut. The Astros put them in the rear. Cooling their lids, below, are Casey Candaele (#1), Chris Donnels (#3), Tony Eusebio (#10), Karl Rhodes (#4), Jeff Bagwell (#5) and Craig Biggio (#7) one spring training morn.

"I pretty much give them what they ask for," said Buddy Bates. "Most players ask for a specific number because they wore it in high school, college or the minors. There is sentiment attached to a number--it could be after a father, an uncle or a boyhood idol."

Of course, everything depends on the availability of the number requested. If the player gets the number he has requested, he will keep it if he remains on the 40-man roster, generally speaking. If he is a player of some stature he will retain the number as long as he likes. On some clubs, a fringe or utility player might get bumped if a star joins the team. The player bumped then selects from a list of numbers available.

Other clubs would ask the lesser player to give up the number for the star, but if he refuses the star will have to select another number. "He won't be bumped unless he willingly gives up his uniform number," says Scott Reifert, Assistant Director of Public Relations for the Chicago White Sox.

"Some shuffling does occur if a player has made the Opening Day roster and wants to change to a number that is now available because of attrition," concluded Scott.

Veteran pitcher Bob Kipper was a non-roster player in the Twins camp in 1992. Some young kid already had his number—16. Jim Wiesner told the lefty who pitched seven years for the Pirates, "If you make the club, we'll get you #16." He did make the club and he did wear his old number.

"'Wait till next year,' 'wait until the next homestand' or 'when they reprint the yearbooks' is what I tell them," says Cy Buynak. "Because a lot of the kids no sooner get up there and they're sent back down," he continued. Most young players who are call-ups in September or who fill in a roster slot during an injury don't realize how much printed material is already distributed with the rosters in them.

When multi-talented Brian Jordan was a young player on the Cardinal 40-man roster, he was up and down for two years. In 1992 Spring Training he wore #71, not a hopeful number. But the dual-major league athlete was considered a future star by the Cards. He turned away from pro football and sign-ed an exclusive contract to play baseball. Jordan was hoping to pick his football number—40, but pitching coach Joe Coleman wanted to stick with his old jersey which happened to be #40. Jordan was shown a list of available numbers.

Among the rather slim pickings was #50. He wore that for about a week and asked if #3 were to open up, he would like it. Buddy Bates set aside that number for him, because he knew Jordan would stick.

Cecil Espy moved on from Pittsburgh to Cincinnati for the 1993 season. He found Jeff Kaiser wearing his new image number 56. He wound up taking #22 vacated by Billy Hatcher's move to Boston. He's seen here in his Rangers' #6 prior to joining the Pirates.

"One of my first jobs was to get ready for Spring Training. I assigned #56 to Cecil Espy. Cecil had previously worn #44. (A famous number of Hank Aaron, Willie McCovey and Reggie Jackson.) When Cecil asked about #44, I told him that number was too famous. Take #56 and make it famous," said Roger Wilson, the Pirate equipment manager. "He got off to a great start helping the Pirates with some critical hits and RBI's."

"One day about two or three weeks into the season, I saw a young boy at Three River Stadium during a game with a #56 Pirate shirt on. I had to laugh. When I told Cecil, he smiled. I told him then that I would change his number to whatever and he said, 'No way!'" beamed Roger.

"It does create a problem at times if you get a couple of guys who have some years in, who happen to wear the same number," said Frank Coppenbarger, the equipment manager of the Phillies. "Dale Murphy has worn #3 for many years. When we acquired him, Darold Knowles our pitching coach, was wearing #3. I went to Knowles and asked him to change, which he was more than happy to do. He became #33," said Coppenbarger.

In 1973, Jim Beauchamp was with the Mets. He wore #24 the year before. He was asked to give up the number because none other than Willie Mays was coming back to New York. He couldn't refuse the great Willie and the Mets went on to win the pennant. Again in 1991, Beauchamp was a coach in Atlanta and he was asked to give up his number 26 when Alexandro Pena came over from the Mets.

"Last time I gave up my number with the Mets, we won the championship. Maybe we'll win again," said Beauchamp. So he gave it to Pena and the Braves went on to win the pennant!

Considered one of the classiest guys in the sport, Dale Murphy finally called it quits early in the 1993 season with the expansion Colorado Rockies. His career spanned 15 years with Atlanta and two plus years with the Phillies. Dale was held in such high regard, the Phillies did not announce his release until he was able to hook up with another team--the Rockies. He spent days calling up all his coaches and managers to thank them for their help after he retired.

Dave Winfield reached the 3,000-hit plateau in late 1993. An All-Star 12 times, he amassed figures that were hard for the Hall of Fame to overlook. Winfield had 1,669 runs, 3,110 hits, 540 doubles, 465 HRs, 1,833 RBIs and he walked over 1,200 times. He'd even stolen more than 200 bases and had one of the most respected arms in the game. (Inset, left) Winfield wearing #31 as a Yankee and (right) sporting #32 on the World Champion Toronto Blue Jays.

Dave Winfield was an extraordinary athlete, playing college baseball, football and basketball. He could have played any of them professionally, too. Fortunately for all of us, he chose baseball. Dave always wore #31. When he joined the Padres in 1973, Winfield again took #31. He landed with the Yankees in 1981 and again, Dave took #31. Early in 1990, Dave went to the Angels where Chuck Finley wore #31, so he wound up taking #32.

After the 1991 season, the Angels acquired pitcher Chuck Crim from Milwaukee. Chuck wanted #32, but Winfield still had it. Crim took #33. Both Crim and EM, Leonard Garcia, live in Arizona during the off-season. They were both watching the same sports show when it was announced that Winfield was going to Toronto. No sooner was it announced, when Garcia's phone started ringing. "I had a funny feeling it would be Crim—and it was, asking for #32 again," said an amazed Garcia.

Pitcher Duane Ward had been wearing #31 in Toronto since 1986 and didn't want to give it up, so Winfield wore #32. In Minnesota, Scott Leius wore #31, so Dave again took #32 in 1993. He finished his career in Cleveland wearing his beloved #31.

During Ivan Calderone's last year in Seattle and his five years with the White Sox, he wore #22. He had jewelry with his number forged on it. When he arrived at Spring Training with the Montreal Expos in

1991, he discovered that Nelson Santovenia wore #22 and wanted to keep it. Calderone settled for #27. Catcher Santovenia's playing time was dwindling in the last couple of years and John Silverman, the equipment manager, made up both uniforms for Calderone—#27 and #22.

In late spring, Santovenia was sent down to the minors and subsequently wound up in Chicago. Calderone switched uniforms and finished the season with #22. Ivan moved on to Boston for the 1993 season where Billy Hatcher wore #22. He reluctantly took #23.

"The Brat", Eddie Stanky took over as manager of the 1952 Cards. Tommy "Rabbit" Glaviano was wearing Eddie's number—12. Rabbit jumped to #11. When the boss wants #12, he gets it.

Hall of Famer Duke Snider played his next to last season with the hapless Mets of 1963. His familiar #4 was being worn by another ex-Dodger, Charlie Neal. Charlie wouldn't give it up for the Duke, so Snider settled for #11.

In 1956, Bill Virdon, who wore #9 while with St. Louis, was traded to Pittsburgh. One of the greatest second basemen of all time was wearing #9 when he got there—Bill Mazeroski. Virdon doubled his number to 18 and went on to have a solid career with the Pirates.

Years later Virdon returned to Pittsburgh as a full-time coach only to find another centerfielder whose name also begins with the letter 'V'—Andy Van Slyke, wearing #18. Equipment manager Wilson said, "I told Bill that out of respect for him I would ask Andy to change. Bill, being the type of person he is, told me not to worry about it. Just give him another number." Number 19 was available and he took it.

It's not often that players are accommodating when asked to exchange their number, but sometimes it works out. Utility player Bill Percota asked for #32 when he joined the Braves in 1993. Steve Bedrosian was wearing it. He didn't care, so he switched to #36.

In Houston, Eric Anthony graciously gave up #21 after wearing it for a couple of years to pitcher Greg Swindell. He took #24.

Ace reliever Bruce Sutter joined the 1985 Atlanta Braves and he was such a gentleman that he didn't even ask for his #42. He realized that fellow pitcher Rick Mahler had it, so he took #43. But when Mahler moved

Ivan Calderone (left) wearing his #22 on his leg in 1988 with the Chicago White Sox. In 1987, he had 28 dingers and 83 RBIs. He drove in 87 runs during 1989, but his HR production dropped by half. Andy Van Slyke (right) possessed one of the strongest and most accurate arms in the NL. 'Slick' batted across 100 runs and led the league in triples in 1988. He won the Gold Glove Award five straight years for his outfield play.

on to Cincinnati, Sutter jumped at the chance to get his old #42.

When Bruce was acquired by the Cards in 1981, Bob Sykes of the Willie McGee-trade-fame, wore his #42. He gave it up for Bruce and moved over to #38. Another famous reliever, Kent Tekulve wore #27 for years with the Pirates. When he joined the Phillies, outfielder Glenn Wilson took number 12 so Kent could have his old number.

When Von Hayes came to the Angels, he asked for his #9. First baseman Lee Stevens had been wearing it, but was willing to take his old high school number, #23 and give #9 to Hayes. Hayes didn't last very long with the club and Stevens jumped back to #9. It was just in the knick of time, because a young pitcher, Mike Butcher, was brought up and he wanted #23. It all worked out from Leonard Garcia's point of view.

The poor utility guys are the ones that get bumped around the most. Mick Kelleher was wearing #11 with the Cubs in 1977. From the Dodgers came Ivan DeJesus where he wore #14. But Chicago held out #14 honoring Mr. Cub, Ernie Banks. Ivan decided he'd like #11 and poor Mick moved to #20.

What about Chad Curtis? It seemed whatever he picked, he had to give it up. With the Angels, he selected #30. The club decided to retire it for Nolan Ryan. So he switched to #17 which opened up after Dick Schofield went to the Mets. Kelly Gruber was acquired and he wore #17, Curtis moved to #9. What if Von Hayes made a comeback?

One of the biggest messes involved Joe Morgan when he joined the 1983 Phillies. Pat Corrales, the manager, was wearing his old #8. He moved to #18. Ivan DeJesus had that, so he moved back to his old #11. Ozzie Virgil had that, so he took #17. It was an unusual version of "musical numbers." But it had to be an equipment manager's worst dream. It must have helped though, because the Phillies went on to win the NL East and beat the Dodgers in the play-offs for the pennant.

Some guys are just lucky. Dave Kingman joined the Mets in Spring Training in 1975. He liked #26. Bruce Boisclair wore it in '74, but he didn't stick with the parent club so Dave got his number. Kingman came back to the Mets six years later. Scott Holman had #26 in 1980, but he didn't make the club in '81 either. Dave got his #26 again.

One of the easiest changes ever made occurred in 1987. Cardinal reliever Pat Perry (top) was traded to Cincinnati for Scott Terry who was the same size. All Buddy Bates had to do on uniform #37 was to change the "P" in PERRY to a "T" for TERRY. Reggie (bottom) chose to represent himself in the Hall of Fame as a Yankee wearing #44 even though he spent ten years wearing #9 for the A's and the O's and only five for the Bronx Bombers. Those five years were probably the most impactful of his career where the New York media dubbed him "Mr. October" for his outstanding slugging in post-season play.

When Reggie Jackson came to the Yanks before the 1977 season, he was already a six-time All-Star. He had worn #9 with Oakland and Baltimore. Graig Nettles was wearing #9 at the time. In December of 1976, Jackson wore #42 for some press photos saying he might wear it in honor of Jackie Robinson and what he did for baseball. During the ensuing Spring Training, Reggie changed to #20. It wasn't until Opening Day that he wore his now-famous #44 in pinstripes.

As in Reggie's case, more often than not a player will run into another player unwilling to give up his number. Rusty Staub wore #10 with Houston and then Montreal where he was 'La Grande Orange' to the Expos fans. When he moved on to the New York Mets in 1972, Duffy Dyer wore #10 and wouldn't give it up. Rusty settled for #4. When Dyer was traded, Rusty seized his chance to wear #10.

"I was an iron man with number 10 in Montreal," said Rusty with a twinkle in his eye. "They've been kicking the tar out of me with number 4 for three years in New York. Maybe I'll make a comeback now," mused the redhead. That year his numbers jumped to .282 with 105 RBI, but he was on his way to Detroit. After a few years in Motor City, he briefly came back to Montreal where he asked for #10 again. The Expos had a new 'iron man' though--one Andre Dawson. And Andre wouldn't give it up. Staub finished out his career with the Mets and his beloved #10.

More recently Rob Deer ran into the same problem when he went to the Tigers. He asked for #45, but of course, that was Cecil's number. Cecil Fielder, the leading power hitter in the league had #45 since 1990. Deer took #44 then eventually went back to his old number—28.

Ron Darling had to wait four years until George Foster left the Mets before he could wear #15.

Elliott Maddox had a good year in 1974 with the Yankees, so he didn't want to give his number 27 to the newest member of the club—Jim 'Catfish' Hunter. A number that would eventually be retired for Hunter in Oakland. "It doesn't make any difference," drawled Catfish. "Just give me a number in the twenties." He took #29.

The perennial Phillie All-Star shortstop, Larry Bowa, wore #10 as a player. But Darren Daulton had taken to wearing #10 and was just starting to make a name for himself when Bowa returned as a Phillie coach. Bowa appreciated the situation and took #2.

Imagine the frustration of being traded to a team that is the only team in the league that has your number retired!

Keith Hernandez wore number #37 with St. Louis, but unfortunately the Mets retired that number for Casey Stengel, their beloved original manager. Keith chose #17 for his career in New York and kept it in his final year in Cleveland although #37 was available.

There is only one team in the major leagues that has retired the #36—the Phillies, for Robin Roberts. Gary 'Sarge' Matthews had worn that number for eight consecutive years with the Giants and the Braves. While with the Phils, he wore #34. Three years later he moved on to the Chicago Cubs where he was reunited with #36.

Jim Kaat had fashioned a career worthy of remaining on the Hall of Fame ballot for

New York, with Don Mattingly, already had great defensive play at first, but when Keith Hernandez arrived they had a monopoly. Keith batted over .300 four times and was an All-Star three times while in the Big Apple.

years. When he moved to Philadelphia and learned of his #36 being retired, he was disappointed. Larry Shenk recalled, "He asked us to 'unretire' the number for him. We couldn't do that." Kaat settled for #39. He finished his career with the Yanks and Cards wearing #36.

They officially renamed the newly renovated Yankee Stadium clubhouse 'Pete Sheehy Clubhouse' in 1975. Pete was being honored for his fifty years of service with the club. Pete once said, "When we get a new player now, we don't have that many numbers to choose from. In Spring Training, we should start with 100 and work down."

Since Pete has passed on, the problem has gotten worse for the Yanks. They now have 16 numbers retired, they hold 2 more from circulation out of respect, and there's the manager plus his 6 coaches. That's 24 numbers that are not available. That's nearly an entire roster.

Of the single digits, only the #6 and the #2 are in circulation. Manager Joe Torre wears the inversion of his #9, a 6. That leaves only the #2 available for players. Derek Jeter has been wearing that for a long time.

When Spike Owen joined the Yankees in camp in 1993, he had a dilemma. He's worn #3, #7 and #11 in his 10-year career with Seattle, Boston and Montreal (two stadium heros and a manager: Ruth, Mantle and Showalter). Spike wound up using #17.

Buy-outs or buy-offs occur when all else fails. Rick Manning had been wearing #28 for five or six years with the Indians when Bert Blyleven came along. Bert asked Cy Buynak about #28 and Cy asked Manning if he would give it up. At first, he wouldn't. Cy finally told Blyleven to negotiate directly. This he did and he got his #28. Manning switched to #20. Buynak never found out what a 28 was worth.

Tim Flannery of the Padres was wearing #6 when Steve Garvey was brought in to add some fire power to their line-up. The same situation prevailed. Brian Prilaman, the equipment manager, recalls that it cost Garvey a couple of suits to get his #6. Flannery moved over to #11.

The Cub reliever, Mitch Williams, moved over to the Phillies for the 1991 season. At first he requested #99. The number worn by the 'Wild Thing' played by Charlie Sheen in the Hollywood movie *Major League*. The front office didn't think it was a proper number. Williams then asked for his old Cub number, 28. John Kruk was wearing it.Williams got off easy. It only cost him a couple of cases of beer. Kruk took #29.

Perhaps it was the free spirit of this new Phillies team or the persuasive powers of Williams, whatever it was the front office relented and the 'Wild Thing' came out of the bullpen with #99. Mitch tried #99 again in Houston after being shipped out after his fatal pitch in the 1993 World Series.

Sparky Lyle is said to have paid $1,000 to regain his #28 from Steve Comer when he arrived to play for the Texas Rangers in 1979. Comer wound up with #11.

One of the most off-handed swaps happened in Dunedin, Florida, where the Blue Jays held camp. Alfredo Griffin in a previous stint with the Jays wore #4. Manny Lee had subsequently joined the club and taken #4. Griffin was then assigned #2 when he returned.

Jeff Ross, the equipment manager, was curious because he had a conversation with Griffin about the numbers. He just watched them out of the corner of his eye. "Both were sitting on the bench, chatting, when in a flash they switched workout jerseys. Just like that Lee was #2 and Griffin was #4," marveled Ross. Of course, it never occurred to them that the media guide and all the printed material showed them with their former numbers. Nevertheless, Jeff let it stand. A sometimes difficult problem was easily solved.

On George Washington's birthday, February 22, 1975, the Mets experienced a theft in their locker room in St. Petersburg. Eight uniform jerseys and various pieces of clothing were missing. The thieves took the jerseys numbered 3 (Harrelson), 10 (Staub), 11 (Garrett), 21 (Jones), 28 (Milner), 32 (Matlack), 36 (Koosman) and 41 (Seaver). They were very selective and apparently took the stars of the club.

Herb Norman, the equipment manager at the time, said "The thing that gets me is that they take Harrelson's, and then right across is Joe Torre's shirt hanging there, and they don't touch it."

"Hey Torre," said Jerry Grote, "your shirt is still here."

"Don't get on me," retorted Joe. "They didn't touch yours either."

Spike Owen (top) faced the same problem that every new Yankee has--finding a suitable number to wear. He settled for #41 in camp and took #17 when Andy Stankiewicz was sent down. Andres Galarraga (bottom) had to switch back to #41 with the Cardinals because they had retired #14 for Ken Boyer. He had a very disappointing year. He later joined the Rockies and switched back to #14 where he hit the ball with his former zeal.

"I wonder why they would take Harrelson's," quipped Grote.

"That's simple," said Bud. "They saw pinstripes, and number 3, and they figured it was Babe Ruth."

Granny Hamner wore six different numbers during his playing days with the Phillies. He was among the former players invited back to Philadelphia for an Old-Timers game. The 1973 team vs. the Phils a quarter of a century earlier—1948. Replicas of the 1948 uniforms were made up and Hamner was given his #33 shirt. He complained that he wore #2. He refused to believe that he wore #33. They had to go to the front office and get an old program from 1948 to show him that he wore #33. He didn't wear #2 until the following year.

Another solution for players joining a team with their number already in use is to flip the digits. Andres Galarraga wore #41 for much of his early career. When he got to Montreal, ace reliever Jeff Rearden had it. He turned the digits around to #14. He did so well with it that when Rearden was traded away, EM John Silverman asked if he wanted to change back to #41. Andres said, "No, no, no, I'll stick with #14."

Lou Piniella did just the opposite. Lou wore #14, but in Cincinnati there is only one #14--Pete Rose. Lou became manager of the Reds and out of respect for Rose's abilities, he switched the digits to #41. "Sweet Lou" took over the helm in Seattle in 1993 and promptly moved back to his old number 14.

Wally Joyner had all his success in Anaheim while wearing #21. Joining Kansas City in 1992, he found #21 taken by pitcher Jeff Montgomery. He flipped the digits to #12. Initially, his power numbers were down, but he batted over .300 twice.

The most famous digit-switch of all time was Carlton Fisk when he changed from Red Sox to White Sox. In Boston for eleven years, he wore #27. When joining Chicago, he reversed the digits to #72—that was the year he won the American League Rookie of the Year Award and his son was also born in 1972. Fisk played thirteen more years after they thought he was washed up in Boston. Both numbers are retired for him.

'Wally Ball' moved to the plains, Kansas City to be exact. His production was down somewhat, but he appeared to get back on track in 1993. Joyner moved on to SanDiego in '96 where injury hampered his play while wearing #22. On to Atlanta where he wore #24 and retired with the unfamiliar #5 in Anaheim.

The funniest switch happened in 1992 at Yankee Stadium with Randy Johnson on the mound. Randy normally wears #51 and for some reason, he switched the numbers to #15. "After giving up six unearned runs in the first inning, he wanted to switch them back for the second inning, but wasn't allowed to do it," said Tim Hevly, from the Public Relations office of the Mariners.

In the spring of 1993, pitcher Jim Deshaies, the newest Twin, whispered into GM Andy McPhail's ear that he wanted to reverse his old Astro number from 43 to 34. McPhail laughed, it wasn't quite in the cards to give him Kirby Puckett's number. That would have caused a Minnesota mutiny!

There is one sure way of getting your number, that's by having it written into your contract. The only player that I've found to have done that in all the articles, interviews, questionnaires and letters I've gone through, is Gary Carter. He had it as part of his contract that he must wear number 8 when he signed on with the Mets. Maybe that's why he never played for the Pirates, Yankees or Red Sox--they retired #8!

Other clubs indicate that although the player's number may not be in a contract, it does become a part of negotiations.

Joe Macko of the Rangers reminisced, "Players were happy as long as they got a uniform in the old days. Now they have to have the number they wore in Little League or in college. And they have all kinds of jewelry made up with their number on it, so it's very important to them to get that number."

"Sid Fernandez is from Hawaii and he has always worn uniform number 50 because Hawaii is the 50th state. A few years ago, our pitching staff all wore numbers in the teens but Sid wouldn't switch because of his allegiance to his home state," recalled Jay Horwitz, Director of Public Relations of the New York Mets.

One of the most refreshing spirits in the game was John Kruk, the Phils' first baseman. When he played for the San Diego Padres, he wore #8. Someone asked him if there was any significance to that number and he simply replied, "Yeah, so when I slide my number changes from 8 to infinity."

The foot-loose '93 Phillies were loaded with zany characters: Darren Daulton, Lenny Dykstra, Mitch Williams, Dave Hollins and the most unique, John Kruk (left). John was a pure hitter, batting over .300 seven of his ten years in the majors. He helped gel a free-spirited group into a solid team that was on the brink of deadlocking Game 6 of the World Series before Joe Carter's homerun sent everyone home.

'El Sid'(right), Sid Fernandez was a native of Honolulu. He toiled nine years for the Mets but did not develop into the dominant pitcher many thought he would become. Twice he was an All-Star and three times led the league with the opponent's lowest batting average against a pitcher.

'The Kid' Gary Carter had one of the most positive attitudes in the game of baseball. His love for the game was obviously felt by this youngster in San Francisco where Gary spread his good will in 1990. The ten-time All-Star retired in Montreal, the city where it all began for him. He finished up with 324 HRs, 2,092 hits, 1,025 runs and 1,225 RBIs. His number 8 was retired along with Rusty Staub's #10 in the summer of 1993 making theirs the first Canadian numbers to be so honored.

"That sounds like Johnny!" laughed Brian Prilaman, the Padres ex-equipment manager.

"Jimmy Key wore #21 when he was a kid and in college. It wasn't available, so he got #22," remembered Jeff Ross, Blue Jay EM. "He stuck with the team and had a good year. When #21 opened up, I asked Jimmy if he wanted it. He hemmed and hawed, but decided to stick with #22."

Pete "Inky" Incaviglia wore #29 while in college. He was assigned #5 when he first came up in 1986 with the Texas Rangers. Although he did very well in his rookie year, hitting 30 HRs and knocking in 88 runs, he switched back to his old college number.

Generally speaking, numbers of local heroes who are either traded away or who depart as free agents, are taken out of circulation. They are held back for a year or more out of respect for those players.

The Blue Jays held #37 in honor of long-standing pitching star, Dave Steib, who moved on to the White Sox. The Jays didn't

George Brett (below) already reached the 3,000-hit plateau and ran all the way to Cooperstown. After 14 seasons with the Blue Jays, Dave Stieb (right) joined the White Sox. Injury the last couple of years hampered this workhorse's career. Stieb was an All-Star seven times.

issue his number for a year. Pitchers Randy St. Claire and Tim Crabtree used it in his four-year absence, but he did return in '98 to wear #37 for his last season.

Kansas City did not circulate #5 or #20 when George Brett and Frank White hung up their spikes. They eventually retired both numbers in '94 and '95 respectively.

Jim Schmakel, the Tigers equipment manager, held out Lance Parrish's #13 for six years before he felt comfortable assigning it to Rico Brogna in 1992.

The Atlanta Braves had not assigned #3 to anyone since Dale Murphy left the franchise. It was retired in 1994. Bill Acree said, "Hell, back-to-back MVP's don't happen everyday!" Murphy left baseball in May of 1993 just two home runs short of 400. He began the year with the expansion Colorado Rockies, but did not see much playing time. Rockies manager, Don Baylor didn't think being two homers shy of 400 should detract from Murph's chances of getting in the Hall of Fame, "Al Kaline went into the Hall with 399 home runs," said Baylor.

The Yankees held two numbers out for many years in respect for former players. One of the them was for three-time All-Star, three-time twenty-game winner, Ron Guidry, #49, finally retired in 2003. The other was for Willie Randolph, #30. He played second base for thirteen consecutive years, longer than any other Yankee. He returned in 1994 as a coach and donned #30 again.

Twins did not issue numbers of specific players held in high regard for at least one year. Bert Blyleven's #28 was not worn from 1993 through 1996.

The most unusual reason for not assigning a number took place north of the border. Charles Bronfman was the owner of the Expos and Seagram's Distilleries at the same time. He decreed that no one should wear #7 because it was reserved (no pun intended) for Seagram 7, the whiskey. However, he relented when Bill Virdon became manager in 1982 and 1983. The number went on the shelf again the following year. Hubie Brooks was persuasive enough and of sufficient stature to wear it in the late '80s.

After the 1991 season, Jack Morris left Minnesota after helping the Twins win the pennant and World Series and headed for Toronto to do the same thing. He wore #47 as a Twin. Bill Krueger joined the Twins for 1992. He is exactly the same size as Morris, but refused to wear #47 because he didn't want to be "the Twins answer to Jack Morris" and be deluged by the reporters. He happily wore #22 and went 10-6 with two shutouts for the Twins.

Perhaps that's carrying respect for a number a little bit too far. However, if we turn the clock back to a time when numbers were not held in such high regard, we'll find those worn by stars or soon-to-be stars on the backs of lesser lights. World War II gutted the ranks of the major league teams.

A skinny red-headed rookie from Illinois named Red Schoendienst sported Stan Musial's #6 when Stan was in the Navy. Now it would be considered sacrilegious, but Stan had a good laugh about it. Red, his roommate for many campaigns, took his now-familiar #2 when Musial rejoined the team.

Johnny Lindell, a promising Yankee youngster wore Bill Dickey's #8 in 1944 and 1945 while Bill was away in the service. When Dickey returned in '46, Lindell switched to #27.

Willie Randolph (below) possessed a discerning eye. He struck out only 8% of the time. He led the AL in walks with 119 in 1980, batted .305 in 1987, had a lifetime fielding average of .980 and turned a beautiful pivot on the DP.

Joltin' Joe DiMaggio switched to #5 after his rookie season, but he missed three years during the War. First baseman Nick Etten was reassigned the number while Joe was gone. Some of the magic must have rubbed off because Etten led the AL in homeruns with 22 in 1944. Others might think it was the inferior wartime pitching or the short rightfield porch in Yankee Stadium. When Joe returned in 1946, Etten changed to #9. Etten played only one more major league season with the Phillies after that and hit one HR.

Spud Chandler returned to get his #21 back as he dueled Bob Feller in September of 1945. Yet Red Ruffing wore #15 as the ace of the Yankee staff when he departed for service in 1942. Hank Borowy picked up #15 as he won 56 games for the Yanks from 1942 to midway through 1945. He joined the Cubs and went 11-2 the rest of the way helping the Cubbies to their last pennant. When Ruffing returned, he found that his number was given to Tommy Henrich who had also just gotten out of the service. The Yankees felt Red's better days were behind him and handed him #22.

Many players are superstitious and have been known to change their number hoping it will change their luck with it.

Fred McGriff wore #19 with Toronto. He was traded to San Diego, but #19 belonged to a Padre fixture—Tony Gwynn. During Spring Training, Fred tried out #17. He had a lousy Spring, so he decided to try #29. At least that had part of his old number in it. It seemed to have done the trick.

In 1990, Dick Schofield, the Angel shortstop asked Leonard Garcia if he could change from his #22 to #17. He didn't have one lousy year, he said he had *five* lousy years.

Pitcher Mark Grant wanted to change his luck while with the Padres. Brian Prilaman tried to convince him to take #50. You know, President Grant was on the fifty-dollar bill. Everyone thought it would bring him good luck. Before he was convinced, Grant was traded away. He surfaced in Seattle (1992) after a year in the minors. He wore #50 for the Mariners.

Jack Daugherty of the Rangers, hit over .300 his first two full seasons in the Bigs. He slipped badly to .194 in 1991. Joe Macko accommodated his changing from #8 to #22. Unfortunately for Daugherty, he only improved 11 points on his average.

Scott Cooper of the Red Sox wanted to change his outlook—he switched from #45 to #34. Steve Avery changed to #33 just two months into his major league career. It

Nick Etten (below, left) began and ended his nine-year career in Philadelphia, starting with the A's and winding up with the hapless Phillies in 1947. Sandwiched in between, he was a Yankee. Dick Schofield (below) has led the league four times in fielding percentage. His steady play was overshadowed by the brilliance of the Smiths and Larkins.

Darryl Strawberry (above) raised another cloud of contention around himself when he stated that the Mets had no respect for him because they assigned his old #18 to Bret Saberhagen immediately after his departure. Vince Coleman (below) continued to have his troubles in New York even when he was healthy, which was not often.

apparently helped. Steve went on to win MVP in the 1991 NLCS.

Mark Lewis, an infielder with the Indians, changed from #10 to his old high school #20 but his BA remained exactly the same—.264.

Mlicki had #36. Bielecki wanted #36, but wore #37 in Spring Training for the '93 Indians. Mlicki didn't stay with the club, so Bielicki wore #36.

Back in June of 1982, Frank LaCorte, a temporamental reliever with the Astros, had been known to burn his uniform after a frustrating performance. He ditched his #31 because "I was looking at too many 3 and 1 counts," explained LaCorte. He took #37.

Vince Coleman wore #29 in his better days with the Cardinals. When he arrived in New York to play for the Mets, he found Dave Magadan wearing it. He took Mookie Wilson's old number—1. After some less-than-sparkling years due to injury, the speedy Coleman decided to change his luck and take #11. Ironically, Garry Templeton had to forego wearing his customary #1 because Coleman had it and took #11 the year before.

Tony Gwynn's kid brother, Chris, asked to change his number from #29 to #14. Each year he wore #29, he got hurt and was on the DL for extended periods of time, so he wanted some better luck.

A few years ago, John Smoltz, one of the Braves aces, wanted to switch from #29 to #20. Mark Lemke was wearing it and really didn't want to give it up. Bill Acree stepped in and talked John out of it, saying, "All it is, is a number. The players change—the numbers stay the same." Smoltz has gone on to have a brilliant career as a starter and a closer proving Acree right.

Scooter Rizzuto needed one more hit to reach the coveted 200. The Yanks had already clinched the pennant in 1950, but had a three-game stint in Boston to finish up the season.

Rizzuto remembered, "I received a letter saying that if I played in Boston, I would be shot." Both Rizzuto and Manager Stengel took the threat seriously. But Phil was having the best year of his life and he really wanted that hit.

A young, feisty rookie suggested to Rizzuto, "Let's change uniforms. You wear my shirt and I'll wear yours. I'll take the chance and be the target. Besides I can run faster than you." So Billy Martin wore Phil's #10 shirt and Rizzuto put on Billy's #12.

Stengel liked the idea. "Billy was expendable," laughed Phil. "The only thing I was worried about was that Jimmy Piersall (a rather hyper Red Sox outfielder) would take a swing at me, thinking I was Billy. He and Billy were always fighting," said Phil.

Rizzuto got his hit in the first inning and Stengel took him out immediately. Martin finished the whole game wearing Phil's #10. Scooter lamented, "Poor Billy. He didn't stand still the whole game."

Thank goodness, the crackpot never did carry out his threat.

Some numbers can get a reputation for being jinxed. "Some young players who might bounce up and down from Triple A to the major leagues, might think a certain number has rubber in it," joked EM Roger Wilson of the Pirates.

Jeff Ross, the Toronto EM, was not aware that the players thought #34 was under a spell. It got to the point that they would say, "Oh, that, don't you have something else, that number's jinxed." He went back and checked his records to find that pitcher Jesse Jefferson was traded in 1980. Steve Senteney pitched 22 innings without a decision and was sent down in 1982. Senteney wore it again the next season and didn't make the club. Stan

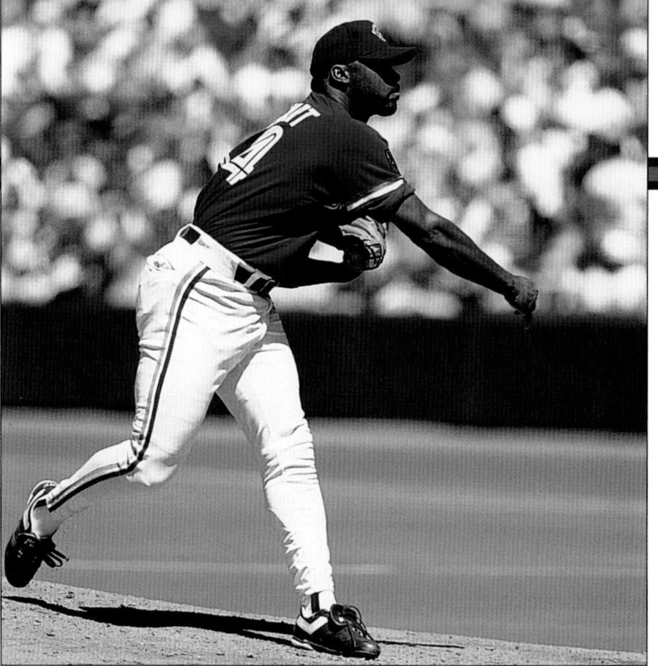

Dave Stewart could stare down adversity, he wouldn't let a little thing like a number get in his way. The first seven years of his career was spent on four teams and he compiled a 39-40 record before he became the ace of the Oakland A's. He moved on to Toronto to bolster a pitching staff depleted by free agency after the 1992 championship season.

Clarke put it on in 1984 and pitched 11 innings with a 1-1 record, then was sent down. The next two years Clarke combined for an 0-1 record, pitching 16+ innings before being sent down each time.

In 1987, Santiago Garcia, an infielder, didn't make the club. Kevin Batiste, an outfielder, got cut in 1988, but managed to play 6 games in 1989 where he collected two hits before he was sent down.

Ross shelved the number at this point and would only assign it if someone asked for it. Jim Acker returned to Toronto from the Braves in mid '89 and asked for it. He went 9-10, with 2 saves and a mushrooming ERA. He was ostracized to Seattle. The spooky #34 was idle until veteran pitcher Dave Stewart donned it in 1993. He won two WS games.

The worst case of a number's influence on a team was recorded between 1948-1950 on the Detroit Tigers. Nash and Zullo call it "The uniform number from HELL" in their book *Believe It Or Else*.

Johnny Gorsica, a relief pitcher who did well for the Tigers in 1947, wore #15 for the first time and developed arm trouble in Spring Training. He was released, never to pitch again.

Art Houtteman, a fine young pitcher, was the next to try it before the '48 season. Houtteman had a 7-2 record in 1947 and the Tigers were expecting good things from him. He lost his first eight games and by June he desperately wanted to change his number.

Goerge Kell, the Tigers' star third baseman, thought it was a hoax. "I'll switch numbers with you, Art. I don't believe in all that stuff about bad luck numbers," said Kell. Kell gave his #21 to Art and took the #15.

Houtteman finally won his first game, however he wound up with an atrocious 2-16 record. To top it off, Joe DiMaggio nailed a wicked one-hop line drive loaded with topspin off Kell's jaw. He was lost for the rest of the season. George refused to wear #15 again, "Too much tough luck goes with it. I don't want any part of it," he said.

Kell got his old #21 back from Houtteman the following spring. You can imagine Houtteman's chagrin when his request for a new number was greeted with #15 again.

He raised cain and insisted on a different number. He was offered the reverse of Kell's number--#12, but new uniforms would take two weeks. So he wore #15 for the time being, against his better judgment.

Exactly nine days later, Houtteman's convertible collided with a tractor-trailer and he fractured his skull. It took him two months to recover from the near-fatal accident.

Paul Campbell, a first baseman, wore #15 for the rest of the season. And after three games in 1950, never played again.

The Tiger trainer stuffed the ill-fated jersey in a forgotten trunk in an effort to break the spell of #15.

"I try to make it as much like their home as possible. Treat everybody the same—like I want to be treated. Each player has the talent to be there, so I respect him as much as the veteran star. That's the way I've been for twenty-eight years," stated Cy Buynak.

Harmony in the clubhouse helps keep the players in a good frame of mind to play their best baseball. To a man, the equipment managers agreed that that was the most important part of their jobs.

"I don't care whatever number they want, they should get. Keep them happy," said John Silverman of the Expos.

When the Toronto Blue Jays became an American League franchise in 1977, there were no superstars. It was a good environment to learn treating all the players equally, felt Jeff Ross.

"You can't help notice the attention the media and the fans pay to a Winfield and other stars. That's why I make sure I treat them all with the same respect," said Ross. "He's a major league ballplayer—he made it. Treat him the same whether he's a rookie or Dave Winfield. I use that philosophy. Then everybody feels part of the team and can contribute," Ross concluded.

"All the things done on the field do not go unnoticed," said Jim Wiesner of the Twins. "We (the Twins) don't throw our helmets," he continued. "'That pitcher is watching you,' we

Art Houtteman came back to have his best year in 1950. He went 19-12, led the AL with 4 shutouts and made his only All-Star appearance. The following year he lost 20 games. He was the fourth starter in the fabled 1954 Indian rotation that combined to win 93 games: Bob Lemon, 23; Early Wynn, 23; Mike Garcia, 19; Houtteman, 15; and Bob Feller, 13. Here's Art sporting the infamous #15.

tell our players. He's trying to get the upper hand psychologically. Why give him that advantage?" said Jim.

"Today's player is bigger, stronger, faster, better," pronounced Wiesner. "He's far better conditioned than players of old."

Some of the players have training facilities at home and work out all year. Terry Steinback of the A's had a quonset hut that's heated. He built official mounds and worked out with friends during the off-season.

Many of the players have rigorous training regimens or play winter ball to stay in shape.

The warm Florida sun reflected brightly on the huge yellow van anchored near the open locker room door. The gleam pierced the humid-laundry air surrounding Jeff Ross as he glided back on his chair and sandwiched his folded hands between his head and the cinder block wall.

"After asking all about the ballplayers' idols, you never asked me who my idol was," puzzled Ross.

I had to ask. "Who?"

"Pete Sheehy," he said with some pride. "He was a great guy. He had lots of stories to tell."

The ghosts of all the Sheehys, the Cobbs, the Ruths, the Gehrigs, the Clementes, the Robinsons, the Hubbs are alive in the kids in all of us. And their tales will be told as long as a raw-boned kid can make a baseball dance.

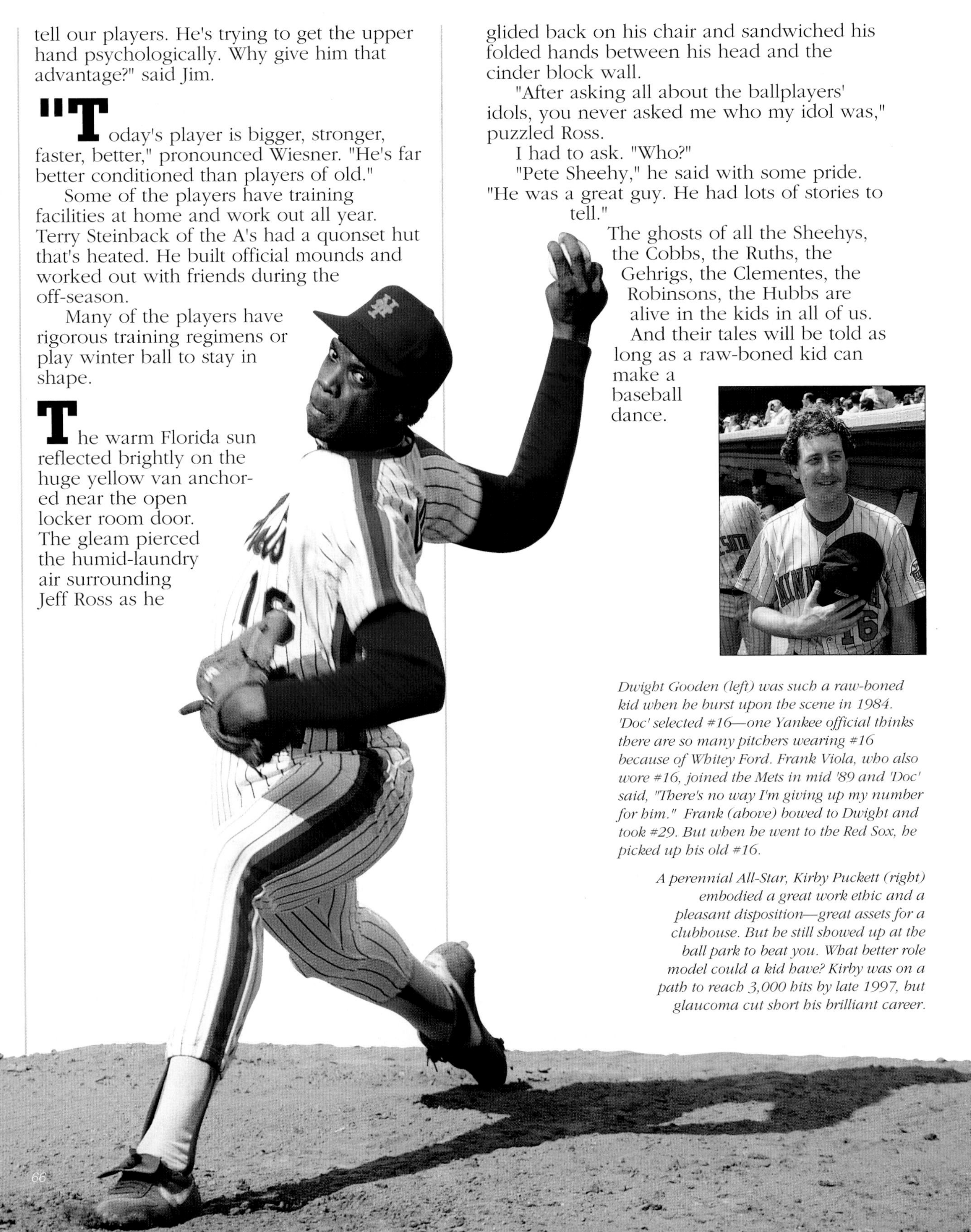

Dwight Gooden (left) was such a raw-boned kid when he burst upon the scene in 1984. 'Doc' selected #16—one Yankee official thinks there are so many pitchers wearing #16 because of Whitey Ford. Frank Viola, who also wore #16, joined the Mets in mid '89 and 'Doc' said, "There's no way I'm giving up my number for him." Frank (above) bowed to Dwight and took #29. But when he went to the Red Sox, he picked up his old #16.

A perennial All-Star, Kirby Puckett (right) embodied a great work ethic and a pleasant disposition—great assets for a clubhouse. But he still showed up at the ball park to beat you. What better role model could a kid have? Kirby was on a path to reach 3,000 hits by late 1997, but glaucoma cut short his brilliant career.

PUCKETT
34
3 NIKE
3 NIKE

"The Birthplace of Baseball"

Softly curls the flag, fanning dreams of kids who play on Doubleday Field throughout the season.

After the induction, the Hall of Fame game is played annually.

Baseball Hall of Fame at Cooperstown, New York..

The bucolic countryside gives way to Main Street where over 350,000 fans visit baseball's shrine year after year.

The moment of glory--the Induction.

THE HALL

4

Cooperstown. The Hall of Fame. Nirvana. Every kid on every lot in America dreams about making the Big Leagues and every Big Leaguer dreams about being a superstar and ultimately being enshrined in the Hall of Fame.

Over 17,000 major league ballplayers have played the game since 1871. How many of them were outstanding enough to be elected to the Hall? —260. That's right, only 260 through 2005. And if we eliminate those members who did not get elected for their playing prowess—the owners, the executives, the umpires, some managers—the numbers become even more amazing.

There are twenty-six who never played Major League ball: Al Barlick, Ed Barrow, Morgan Bulkeley, Alexander Cartwright, Henry Chadwick, Happy Chandler, Nestor Chylak, Tommy Connolly, Billy Evans, Ford Frick, Warren Giles, Will Harridge, Cal Hubbard, William Hulbert, Ban Johnson, Bill Klem, Kenesaw Mountain Landis, Larry MacPhail, Lee MacPhail, Joe McCarthy, Bill McGowan, Frank Selee, Bill Veeck, Earl Weaver, George Weiss, and Tom Yawkey. Twelve others did play, but had rather undistinguished careers until they found their niche as managers or executives.

Branch Rickey played for four years with the Browns and Yankees. His best year was 1906 when he managed to bat .284 and hit his entire major league total of 3 home runs. Had it not been for his brilliant visionary thinking such as initiating the farm system and breaking the color barrier, Rickey would not be in the Hall today.

It's safe to say that if Walter Alston had not had such a brilliant managerial career, he would not be in the Hall either. He appeared in one ball game for the Cardinals, batted once and struck out.

A's Manager Connie Mack, in his business suit, would step up the dugout stairs and wave his outfielders around with a scorecard. He managed fifty-three years and won five World Series. Mack played eleven years as a catcher. He batted .245 with a grand total of 5 home runs. Not the sort of marks to sweep one into the Hall.

Bucky Harris' numbers were rather average (.274 BA, 9 HRs, 166 SB) in playing second base for 12 years. If not for his managerial prowess, he wouldn't be in the Hall.

In eleven years Bill McKechnie batted .251 with 8 HRs. That's hardly the standards for third basemen today. Bill went on to manage for a quarter of a century, won 4 pennants and two World Series.

Jocko Conlan played in 128 games for the White Sox in '34 and '35. He was an outfielder, batting .263 before umpiring.

In Charlie Comiskey's best year, 1887, he batted .335, his only .300+ season. But his career average was only .264, for 13 years.

Al Lopez caught for 19 years, batted over .300 three times. Yet his career average was only .261.

Ned Hanlon played 13 years and batted only .260. He managed for 19 years, winning 5 times with Baltimore and Brooklyn.

The first inductees to the Hall of Fame in 1936 were (L to R): Ty Cobb, Honus Wagner, Babe Ruth, Christy Mathewson, and Walter Johnson. Between them they won 883 and lost 512 (.633), had 1,072 CG, 205 ShO, 67 SV, worked 11,937 innings, gave up 10,128 hits (199 HRs), walked 2,646 with 6,502 Ks while batting .338 with 11,025 hits, 6,397 R, 1,964 2B, 723 3B, 957 HR, 6,130 RBI, 4,378 BB, 2,267 SO and 1,750 SB. Not bad for 5 guys.

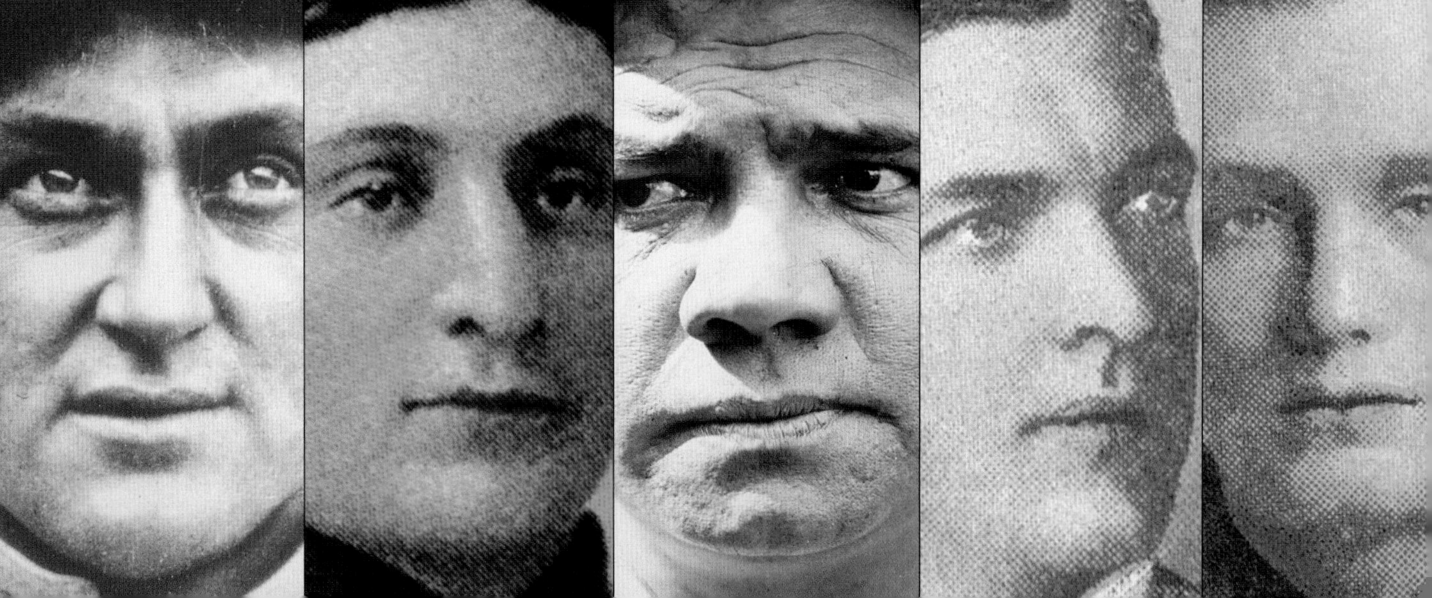

Harry Wright pitched, played outfield and other positions from 1871-1877. He was 4-1 and batted .263 lifetime. A modest career, but fortunately for us his persistence with the Cincinnati Red Stockings helped professional baseball get off the ground.

Tommy Lasorda's pitching career was short and uneventful—no wins, four losses.

Sparky Anderson played one full season at second base for the Phillies in 1959 where he batted a lusty .218 with no HRs.

Four others are more noted for their managing skills than their playing skills: Miller Huggins, Wilbert Robinson, Casey Stengel and Leo Durocher. Hug batted .265 in 13 years with the Reds and Cards. The feisty second baseman had an OBP of .381 and stole 324 bases.

Uncle Robby caught most of his career in Baltimore around the turn of the century. He had a career average of .273 with a total of 18 homers. He did bat over .300 five times and knocked in 98 runs once.

Old Case bounced around the NL for 14 seasons and batted .284 with 60 HRs and a .410 slugging average. His .404 OBP led the league in 1914.

"Lippy" played shortstop for Ruth's Yankees and The Gashouse Gang in the mid-thirties. He hit .247 and won 3 pennants.

Let's assume that these four didn't go on to have illustrious managerial careers. By a stretch, we still might add them to the Hall.

Candy Cummings, was elected as the pioneer of the curve ball. He must have done it pretty well—he won 124 games in four years. He lasted only 6 years, but may have made it into the Hall even without recognition for his new-fangled pitch.

Four members who were inducted into the Hall for making outstanding contributions to baseball, would have made it due to their playing anyway.

There's George Wright, a shortstop who batted .409 in his rookie year (1871) and hit over .300 five other times.

Al Spalding won 52 games in 1874 and 57 in 1875. Sure, the level of play in the beginning of baseball was in its infancy too, but that's 109 games in two years. He went on to win 255 games in 7 short years for a .789 won-lost percentage.

Clark Griffith pitched for twenty years (1891-1914). He won twenty or more games seven times while with the Cubs and White Sox. He finished with 237-146 (.619).

John McGraw was an outstanding third baseman. He batted .334 lifetime and his OBP in 1899 was .547. Try to imagine that!

Of the original 260 members, we will take away the thirty-eight non-players and weaker ones and have 222 remaining players. That means that less than *1.282%* of the players that ever played the game on the major league level are judged good enough to be honored in the Baseball Hall of Fame. This will give you some perspective of the awesome quality of these players.

Honored for being pioneers, executives and managers (L to R): George Wright, Al Spalding, Clark Griffith, and John McGraw would have made it into the Hall on playing performances. Wright was the first great fielding shortstop in the game. He batted .629 for the undefeated Red Stockings in 1869. In addition to winning 24 games in a row while on the mound, Spalding wrote the constitution for the new National League. Griffith pitched (24-7) and managed the White Sox to their first pennant. Later, as Washington's owner, his financial woes helped spur many innovative ideas. McGraw had the highest OBP (.456) of all 1800's players and led his Giants to 10 pennants in 22 years.

Here are the Hall of Fame members listed by the year of their induction. Only their key positions are displayed with the primary one marked with an asterisk. The selecting group is in parentheses and those elected by the Baseball Writers Association of America (BBWAA) show their vote after the slash. A (•) before an entry means playing manager. An M after a year means a non-playing manager; an O is for owner. (CENT) Centennial Commission; (OLD) Old-Timers Committee; (VET) Veteran's Committee; (NEG) Negro Leagues Committee.

1936

VOTES NEEDED:170

TY COBB OF (BBWAA/222)
DETROIT TIGERS 1905-20, •1921-26
PHILADELPHIA A's 1927-28

HONUS WAGNER SS (BBWAA/215)
LOUISVILLE 1897-99
PITTSBURGH PIRATES 1900-17

BABE RUTH P/OF* (BBWAA/215)
BOSTON RED SOX 1914-19
NEW YORK YANKEES 1920-34
BOSTON BRAVES 1935

CHRISTY MATHEWSON P (BBWAA/205)
NEW YORK GIANTS 1900-16
CINCINNATI REDS 1916

WALTER JOHNSON P (BBWAA/189)
WASHINGTON NATIONALS 1907-27

1937

VOTES NEEDED:151

NAP LAJOIE 2B (BBWAA/168)
PHILADELPHIA PHILLIES 1896-1900
PHILADELPHIA A's 1901-02, 1915-16
CLEVELAND INDIANS 1902-04, •1905-09, 1910-14

TRIS SPEAKER OF (BBWAA/165)
BOSTON RED SOX 1907-15
CLEVELAND INDIANS 1916-18, •1919-26
WASHINGTON NATIONALS 1927
PHILADELPHIA A's 1928

CY YOUNG P (BBWAA/153)
CLEVELAND SPIDERS 1890-98
ST. LOUIS CARDINALS 1899-1900
BOSTON RED SOX 1901-08
CLEVELAND INDIANS 1909-11
BOSTON BRAVES 1911

MORGAN BULKELEY EXEC (CENT)
NATIONAL LEAGUE PRESIDENT 1876

BAN JOHNSON EXEC (CENT)
AMERICAN LEAGUE PRESIDENT 1901-27

CONNIE MACK C/MGR* (CENT)
WASHINGTON NATIONALS 1886-89
BUFFALO (PL) 1890
•PITTSBURGH PIRATES 1891-96
PHILADELPHIA A's 1901-50 M

JOHN McGRAW 3B/MGR* (CENT)
BALTIMORE (AA) 1891
BALTIMORE ORIOLES (NL) 1892-98
•BALTIMORE ORIOLES (NL) 1899
ST. LOUIS CARDINALS 1900
•BALTIMORE ORIOLES (AL) 1901-02
•NEW YORK GIANTS •1902-06, 1907-32

GEORGE WRIGHT SS/PIONEER* (CENT)
CINCINNATI RED STOCKINGS 1869-70
BOSTON (NA) 1871-75
BOSTON NATIONALS 1876-78, 1880-81
•PROVIDENCE •1880, 1882

1938

VOTES NEEDED:197

PETE ALEXANDER P (BBWAA/212)
PHILADELPHIA PHILLIES 1911-17, 1930
CHICAGO CUBS 1918-26
ST. LOUIS CARDINALS 1926-29

ALEXANDER CARTWRIGHT FOUNDER (CENT)
NEW YORK KNICKERBOCKERS 1845

HENRY CHADWICK PIONEER (CENT)
NEWSPAPER REPORTER--
CREATED BOX SCORE

1939

VOTES NEEDED:206

GEORGE SISLER 1B (BBWAA/235)
ST. LOUIS BROWNS 1915-22,•1924-26, 1927
WASHINGTON NATIONALS 1928
BOSTON BRAVES 1928-30

EDDIE COLLINS 2B (BBWAA/213)
PHILADELPHIA A's 1906-14, 1927-30
CHICAGO WHITE SOX 1915-24, •1925-26

WEE WILLIE KEELER OF (BBWAA/207)
NEW YORK GIANTS 1892-93, 1910
BROOKLYN 1893, 1899-1902
BALTIMORE ORIOLES (NL) 1894-98
NEW YORK YANKEES 1903-09

LOU GEHRIG 1B (BBWAA/SPEC ELEC)
NEW YORK YANKEES 1923-39

CAP ANSON 1B*/MGR (OLD)
ROCKFORD (NA) 1871
PHILADELPHIA ATHLETICS (NA) 1872-75
CHICAGO WHITE STOCKINGS (NL) 1876-78, •1879-97, 1897M
NEW YORK GIANTS 1898M

CHARLIE COMISKEY EXEC (OLD)
•ST. LOUIS BROWNS (AA) 1882-89,1891
•CHICAGO (PL) 1890
•CINCINNATI REDS 1892-94
CHICAGO WHITE SOX 1901-31 O

CANDY CUMMINGS P/PIONEER* (OLD)
INVENTED CURVE BALL
NEW YORK MUTUALS (NA) 1872
BALTIMORE LORD BALTIMORES (NA) 1873
PHILADELPHIA WHITE STOCKINGS (NA) 1874
HARTFORD DARK BLUES (NA) 1875
HARTFORD (NL) 1876
CINCINNATI REDS 1877

BUCK EWING C (OLD)
TROY 1880-82
NEW YORK GIANTS 1883-89, 1891-92
•NEW YORK (PL) 1890
CLEVELAND SPIDERS 1893-94
•CINCINNATI REDS 1895-97

HOSS RADBOURNE P (OLD)
PROVIDENCE (NL) 1881-85
BOSTON NATIONALS (NL) 1886-89
BOSTON (PL) 1890
CINCINNATI REDS 1891

AL SPALDING P/PIONEER* (OLD)
BOSTON RED STOCKINGS (NA) 1871-75
CHICAGO CUBS •1876-77, 1878

1942

VOTES NEEDED:175

ROGERS HORNSBY 2B (BBWAA/182)
ST. LOUIS CARDINALS 1915-24, •1925-26, 1933
•NEW YORK GIANTS 1927
•BOSTON BRAVES 1928
CHICAGO CUBS 1929, •1930-32
•ST. LOUIS BROWNS 1933-37, 1952M
CINCINNATI REDS 1952-53M

1944

KENESAW MOUNTAIN LANDIS EXEC (OLD)
COMMISSIONER 1920-44

1945

VOTES NEEDED: 186

ROGER BRESNAHAN C (OLD)
WASHINGTON (NL) 1897
CHICAGO CUBS 1900, 1913-14, •1915
BALTIMORE ORIOLES 1901-02
NEW YORK GIANTS 1902-08
•ST. LOUIS CARDINALS 1909-12

DAN BROUTHERS 1B (OLD)
TROY (NL) 1879-80
BUFFALO (NL) 1881-85
DETROIT (NL) 1886-88
BOSTON NATIONALS (NL) 1889
BOSTON (PL) 1890
BOSTON (AA) 1891
BROOKLYN DODGERS 1892-93
BALTIMORE ORIOLES (NL) 1894-95
LOUISVILLE (NL) 1895
PHILADELPHIA PHILLIES 1896
NEW YORK GIANTS 1904

FRED CLARKE OF (OLD)
LOUISVILLE (NL) 1894-96, •1897-99
•PITTSBURGH PIRATES 1900-15

JIMMY COLLINS 3B (OLD)
BOSTON BEANEATERS (NL) 1895, 1896-1900
LOUISVILLE (NL) 1895
BOSTON AMERICANS (AL) •1901-06, 1907
PHILADELPHIA A's 1907-08

ED DELAHANTY 2B (OLD)
PHILADELPHIA PHILLIES 1888-89, 1891-1901
CLEVELAND (PL) 1890
WASHINGTON NATIONALS 1902-03

HUGH DUFFY OF (OLD)
CHICAGO CUBS 1888-89
CHICAGO (PL) 1890
BOSTON (AA) 1891
BOSTON NATIONALS (NL) 1892-1900
•MILWAUKEE (AA) 1901
•PHILADELPHIA PHILLIES 1904-06
CHICAGO WHITE SOX 1910-11M
BOSTON RED SOX 1921-22M

HUGHIE JENNINGS OF (OLD)
LOUISVILLE (AA) 1891
LOUISVILLE (NL) 1892-3
BALTIMORE ORIOLES (NL) 1893-98, 99
BROOKLYN DODGERS 1899-1900, 1903
PHILADELPHIA PHILLIES 1901-02
DETROIT TIGERS •1907, 08, •09, 10-11, •1912, 1913-15, •1918

MIKE KELLY OF (OLD)
CINCINNATI RED STOCKINGS 1978-79
CHICAGO WHITE STOCKINGS (NL) 1880-86
BOSTON NATIONALS •1887, 1888-89, 1891-92
•BOSTON (PL) 1890
•CINCINNATI/MILWAUKEE (AA) 1891
BOSTON (AA) 1891
NEW YORK GIANTS 1893

JIM O'ROURKE OF (OLD)
MIDDLETOWN MANSFIELDS (NA) 1872
BOSTON RED STOCKINGS (NA) 1873-75
BOSTON RED STOCKINGS (NL) 1876-78, 1880
PROVIDENCE (NL) 1879
•BUFFALO (NL) 1881-84
NEW YORK GIANTS 1885-89, 1891-92, 1904
NEW YORK (PL) 1890
•WASHINGTON (NL) 1893

WILBERT ROBINSON C/MGR* (OLD)
PHILADELPHIA (AA) 1886-1890
BALTIMORE/BROOKLYN (AA) 1890
BALTIMORE ORIOLES (AA) 1891
BALTIMORE ORIOLES (NL) 1892-1899
ST. LOUIS CARDINALS 1900
BALTIMORE ORIOLES (AL) 1901, •1902
BROOKLYN DODGERS 1914-1929M

JOHN McGRAW 3B/MGR* (CENT)
BALTIMORE (AA) 1891
BALTIMORE ORIOLES (NL) 1892-98
•BALTIMORE ORIOLES (NL) 1899
ST. LOUIS CARDINALS 1900
•BALTIMORE ORIOLES (AL) 1901-02
•NEW YORK GIANTS •1902-06, 1907-32

GEORGE WRIGHT SS/PIONEER* (CENT)
CINCINNATI RED STOCKINGS 1869-70
BOSTON (NA) 1871-75
BOSTON NATIONALS 1876-78, 1880-81
•PROVIDENCE •1880, 1882

1946

VOTES NEEDED: 198

JESSE BURKETT OF (OLD)
NEW YORK GIANTS 1890
CLEVELAND SPIDERS (NL) 1891-98
ST. LOUIS CARDINALS 1899-1901
ST. LOUIS BROWNS 1902-04
BOSTON PURITANS (AL) 1905

FRANK CHANCE 1B (OLD)
CHICAGO CUBS 1898-1904, •1905-12
NEW YORK HIGHLANDERS (AL) •1913-14
BOSTON RED SOX 1923 M

JACK CHESBRO P (OLD)
PITTSBURGH PIRATES 1899-1902
NEW YORK HIGHLANDERS (AL) 1903-09
BOSTON RED SOX (AL) 1909

JOHNNY EVERS 2B (OLD)
CHICAGO CUBS 1902-12, •1913, 1921 M
BOSTON BRAVES 1914-17, 1929
PHILADELPHIA PHILLIES 1917
CHICAGO WHITE SOX 1922, 1924 M

CLARK GRIFFITH P/EXEC* (OLD)
ST. LOUIS (AA) 1891
BOSTON (AA) 1891
CHICAGO CUBS 1893-1900
CHICAGO WHITE SOX •1901-02
NEW YORK HIGHLANDERS •1903-07, 1908 M
CINCINNATI REDS •1909, 1910-11 M
WASHINGTON NATIONALS (AL) •1912-14, 1915-20 M

TOMMY McCARTHY OF (OLD)
BOSTON (UA) 1884
BOSTON (NL) 1885, 1892-95
PHILADELPHIA PHILLIES 1886-87
ST. LOUIS BROWNS (AA) 1888-89, •1890, 1891
BROOKLYN (NL) 1896

JOE McGINNITY P (OLD)
BALTIMORE ORIOLES (NL) 1899
BROOKLYN DODGERS 1900
BALTIMORE ORIOLES (AL) 1901-02
NEW YORK GIANTS 1902-08

EDDIE PLANK P (OLD)
PHILADELPHIA A's 1901-1914
ST. LOUIS SLOUFEDS (FL) 1915
ST. LOUIS BROWNS (AL) 1916-17

JOE TINKER SS (OLD)
CHICAGO CUBS 1902-12, •1916
•CINCINNATI REDS 1913
•CHICAGO (FL) 1914-15

RUBE WADDELL P (OLD)
LOUISVILLE (NL) 1897, 1899
PITTSBURGH PIRATES 1900-01
CHICAGO CUBS 1901
PHILADELPHIA A's 1902-07
ST. LOUIS BROWNS 1908-10

ED WALSH P (OLD)
CHICAGO WHITE SOX 1904-16, 1924 M
BOSTON BRAVES 1917

1947

VOTES NEEDED: 121

CARL HUBBELL P (BBWAA/140)
NEW YORK GIANTS 1928-1943

FRANKIE FRISCH 2B*/MGR (BBWAA/136)
NEW YORK GIANTS 1919-26
ST. LOUIS CARDINALS 1927-32, •1933-37, 1938 M
PITTSBURGH PIRATES 1940-46 M
CHICAGO CUBS 1949-51 M

MICKEY COCHRANE C*/MGR (BBWAA/128)
PHILADELPHIA A's 1925-33
DETROIT TIGERS •1934-37, 1938 M

LEFTY GROVE P (BBWAA/123)
PHILADELPHIA A's 1925-33
BOSTON RED SOX 1934-41

1948

VOTES NEEDED:91

HERB PENNOCK P (BBWAA/94)
PHILADELPHIA A's 1912-15
BOSTON RED SOX 1915-22, 1934
NEW YORK YANKEES 1923-33

PIE TRAYNOR 3B (BBWAA/93)
PITTSBURGH PIRATES 1920-33, •1934-35, 1936 M, •1937, 1938-39 M

1949

VOTES NEEDED:115

CHARLIE GEHRINGER 2B (BBWAA/159)
DETROIT TIGERS 1924-42

MORDECAI BROWN P (OLD)
ST. LOUIS CARDINALS 1903
CHICAGO CUBS 1904-1912, 1916
CINCINNATI REDS 1913
ST. LOUIS SLOUFEDS (FL) •1914
BROOKLYN (FL) 1914
CHICAGO FEDS (FL) 1915

KID NICHOLS P (OLD)
BOSTON NATIONALS (NL) 1890-1901
ST. LOUIS CARDINALS •1904-05
PHILADELPHIA PHILLIES 1905-06

1951

VOTES NEEDED:170

MEL OTT OF*/MGR (BBWAA/197)
NEW YORK GIANTS 1926-41,•1942-47, 1948 M

JIMMIE FOXX 1B (BBWAA/179)
PHILADELPHIA A's 1925-35
BOSTON RED SOX 1936-1942
CHICAGO CUBS 1942, 1944
PHILADELPHIA PHILLIES 1945

1952

VOTES NEEDED:176

HARRY HEILMANN OF*/1B (BBWAA/203)
DETROIT TIGERS 1914, 1916-29
CINCINNATI REDS 1930, 1932

PAUL WANER OF (BBWAA/195)
PITTSBURGH PIRATES 1926-40
BROOKLYN DODGERS 1941, 1943-44
BOSTON BRAVES 1942-43
NEW YORK YANKEES 1944-45

1953

VOTES NEEDED:198

DIZZY DEAN P (BBWAA/209)
ST. LOUIS CARDINALS 1930-37
CHICAGO CUBS 1938-41
ST. LOUIS BROWNS 1947

AL SIMMONS OF (BBWAA/199)
PHILADELPHIA A's 1924-32, 1940-41, 1944
CHICAGO WHITE SOX 1933-35
DETROIT TIGERS 1936
WASHINGTON SENATORS 1937-38
BOSTON BRAVES 1939
CINCINNATI REDS 1939
BOSTON RED SOX 1943

ED BARROW MGR/EXEC* (VET)
DETROIT TIGERS 1903-04 M
BOSTON RED SOX 1917 EXEC, 1918-20 M/EXEC
NEW YORK YANKEES 1921-45 EXEC

CHIEF BENDER P (VET)
PHILADELPHIA A's 1903-14
BALTIMORE (FL) 1915
PHILADELPHIA PHILLIES 1916-17
CHICAGO WHITE SOX 1925

TOM CONNOLLY UMP (VET)
NATIONAL LEAGUE 1898-1900
AMERICAN LEAGUE 1901-31
AMERICAN LEAGUE CHIEF 1932-54

BILL KLEM UMP (VET)
NATIONAL LEAGUE 1905-41

BOBBY WALLACE SS*/MGR (VET)
CLEVELAND SPIDERS (NL) 1894-98
NATIONAL LEAGUE UMPIRE 1895
ST. LOUIS CARDINALS 1899-1901, 1917-18
ST. LOUIS BROWNS 1902-10, •1911-12, 1913-16
AMERICAN LEAGUE UMPIRE 1915-16
CINCINNATI REDS 1926-28 CH, 1937 M

HARRY WRIGHT P/OF/MGR/PIONEER* (VET)
•BOSTON RED STOCKINGS (NA)1871-75
BOSTON NATIONALS (NL) 1876-77, 1878-81 M
PROVIDENCE 1882-83 M
PHILADELPHIA PHILLIES 1884-93 M

1954

VOTES NEEDED:189

RABBIT MARANVILLE SS (BBWAA/209)
BOSTON BRAVES 1912-20, 1929-33, 1935
PITTSBURGH PIRATES 1921-24
•CHICAGO CUBS 1925
BROOKLYN DODGERS 1926
ST. LOUIS CARDINALS 1927-28

BILL DICKEY C (BBWAA/202)
NEW YORK YANKEES 1928-43, •1946

BILL TERRY 1B*/MGR (BBWAA/195)
NEW YORK GIANTS 1923-31, •1932-36, 1937-41 M

1955

VOTES NEEDED:189

JOE DIMAGGIO OF (BBWAA/223)
NEW YORK YANKEES 1936-42, 1946-51

TED LYONS P (BBWAA/217)
CHICAGO WHITE SOX 1923-42, •1946, 1947-48 M

DAZZY VANCE P (BBWAA/205)
PITTSBURGH PIRATES 1915
NEW YORK YANKEES 1915, 1918
BROOKLYN DODGERS 1922-32, 1935
ST. LOUIS CARDINALS 1933, 1934
CINCINNATI REDS 1934

GABBY HARTNETT C (BBWAA/195)
CHICAGO CUBS 1922-37, •1938-40
NEW YORK GIANTS

HOME RUN BAKER 3B (VET)
PHILADELPHIA A's 1908-14
NEW YORK YANKEES 1916-19, 1921-22

RAY SCHALK C (VET)
CHICAGO WHITE SOX 1912-26, •1927-28
NEW YORK GIANTS 1929

1956

VOTES NEEDED:145

HANK GREENBERG 1B*/OF (BBWAA/164)
DETROIT TIGERS 1930, 1933-41, 1945-46
PITTSBURGH PIRATES 1947

JOE CRONIN SS*/MGR (BBWAA/152)
PITTSBURGH PIRATES 1926-27
WASHINGTON SENATORS 1928-32, •1933-34
BOSTON RED SOX •1935-45, 1946-47 M

1957

SAM CRAWFORD OF (VET)
CINCINNATI REDS 1899-1902
DETROIT TIGERS 1903-17

JOE McCARTHY MGR (VET)
CHICAGO CUBS 1926-30
NEW YORK YANKEES 1931-46
BOSTON RED SOX 1948-50

1959

ZACK WHEAT OF (VET)
BROOKLYN DODGERS 1909-26
PHILADELPHIA A's 1927

1961

MAX CAREY OF (VET)
PITTSBURGH PIRATES 1910-26
BROOKLYN DODGERS 1926-29, 1932-33 M

BILLY HAMILTON OF (VET)
KANSAS CITY (AA) 1888-89
PHILADELPHIA PHILLIES 1891-95
BOSTON BEANEATERS (NL) 1896-1901

1962

VOTES NEEDED:120

BOB FELLER P (BBWAA/150)
CLEVELAND INDIANS 1936-41, 1945-56

JACKIE ROBINSON 2B (BBWAA/124)
BROOKLYN DODGERS 1947-56

BILL McKECHNIE 3B/MGR* (VET)
PITTSBURGH PIRATES 1907, 1910-12, 1918-20, 1922-26 M
BOSTON BRAVES 1913, 1930-37 M
NEW YORK YANKEES 1913
INDIANAPOLIS (FL) 1914
•NEWARK (FL) 1915
NEW YORK GIANTS 1916
CINCINNATI REDS 1916-17, 1938-46 M
ST. LOUIS CARDINALS 1928-29 M

EDD ROUSH OF (VET)
CHICAGO WHITE SOX 1913
INDIANAPOLIS (FL) 1914
NEWARK (FL) 1915
NEW YORK GIANTS 1916, 1927-29
CINCINNATI REDS 1916-26, 1931

1963

JOHN CLARKSON P (VET)
WORCESTER (NL) 1882
CHICAGO CUBS 1884-87
BOSTON NATIONALS (NL) 1888-92
CLEVELAND SPIDERS (NL) 1892-94

ELMER FLICK OF (VET)
PHILADELPHIA PHILLIES 1898-1901
PHILADELPHIA A's 1902
CLEVELAND INDIANS 1902-10

SAM RICE OF (VET)
WASHINGTON SENATORS 1915-33
CLEVELAND INDIANS 1934

EPPA RIXEY P (VET)
PHILADELPHIA PHILLIES 1912-17, 1919-20
CINCINNATI REDS 1921-33

1964

VOTES NEEDED:170

LUKE APPLING SS (BBWAA/189)
CHICAGO WHITE SOX 1930-50
KANSAS CITY A's 1967 M

RED FABER P (VET)
CHICAGO WHITE SOX 1914-33

BURLEIGH GRIMES P (VET)
PITTSBURGH PIRATES 1916-17, 1928-29, 1934
BROOKLYN DODGERS 1918-26, 1937-38 M
NEW YORK GIANTS 1927
BOSTON BRAVES 1930
ST. LOUIS CARDINALS 1930-31, 1933-34
CHICAGO CUBS 1932-33
NEW YORK YANKEES 1934

MILLER HUGGINS 2B/MGR* (VET)
CINCINNATI REDS 1904-09
ST. LOUIS CARDINALS 1910-12, •1913-16, 1917 M
NEW YORK YANKEES 1918-29 M

TIM KEEFE P (VET)
TROY (NL) 1880-82
NEW YORK (AA) 1883-84
NEW YORK GIANTS 1885-89, 1891
NEW YORK (PL) 1890
PHILADELPHIA PHILLIES 1891-93

HEINIE MANUSH OF (VET)
DETROIT TIGERS 1923-27
ST. LOUIS BROWNS 1928-30
WASHINGTON SENATORS 1930-35
BOSTON RED SOX 1936
BROOKLYN DODGERS 1937-38
PITTSBURGH PIRATES 1938-39

MONTE WARD P/SS*/MGR (VET)
PROVIDENCE (NL) 1878-79, •1880, 1881-82
NEW YORK GIANTS 1883, •1884, 1885-89
•BROOKLYN (PL) 1890
•BROOKLYN DODGERS •1891-92
•NEW YORK GIANTS •1893-94

1965

JIM GALVIN P (VET)
ST. LOUIS BROWN STOCKINGS (NA)1875
BUFFALO (NL) 1879-84, •1885
PITTSBURGH (AA) 1885-86
PITTSBURGH PIRATES 1887-89, 1891-92
PITTSBURGH (PL) 1890
ST. LOUIS CARDINALS 1892

1966

VOTES NEEDED:220

TED WILLIAMS OF (BBWAA/282)
BOSTON RED SOX 1939-42, 46-60
WASHINGTON SENATORS 1969-71 M
TEXAS RANGERS 1972 M

CASEY STENGEL OF/MGR* (VET)
BROOKLYN DODGERS 1912-17, 1934-36 M
PITTSBURGH PIRATES 1918-19
PHILADELPHIA PHILLIES 1920-21
NEW YORK GIANTS 1921-23
BOSTON BRAVES 1924-25, 1938-43 M
NEW YORK YANKEES 1949-60 M
NEW YORK METS 1962-65 M

1967

VOTES NEEDED:230

RED RUFFING P (BBWAA/266)
BOSTON RED SOX 1924-30
NEW YORK YANKEES 1930-42, 1945-46
CHICAGO WHITE SOX 1947

BRANCH RICKEY C/MGR/EXEC* (VET)
ST. LOUIS BROWNS 1905-06, 1913 M, •1914, 1915
NEW YORK HIGHLANDERS 1907
ST. LOUIS CARDINALS 1916-42 EXEC, 1919-25 M
BROOKLYN DODGERS 1942-51 EXEC
PITTSBURGH PIRATES 1951-59 EXEC

LLOYD WANER OF (VET)
PITTSBURGH PIRATES 1927-41, 1944-45
BOSTON BRAVES 1941
CINCINNATI REDS 1941
PHILADELPHIA PHILLIES 1942
BROOKLYN DODGERS 1944

1968

VOTES NEEDED:213

JOE MEDWICK OF (BBWAA/240)
ST. LOUIS CARDINALS 1932-40, 1947-48
BROOKLYN DODGERS 1940-43, 1946
NEW YORK GIANTS 1943-45
BOSTON BRAVES 1945

KIKI CUYLER OF (VET)
PITTSBURGH PIRATES 1921-27
CHICAGO CUBS 1928-35
CINCINNATI REDS 1935-37
BROOKLYN DODGERS 1938

GOOSE GOSLIN OF (VET)
WASHINGTON SENATORS 1921-30, 1933, 1938
ST. LOUIS BROWNS 1930-32
DETROIT TIGERS 1934-37

1969

VOTES NEEDED:255

STAN MUSIAL OF*/1B (BBWAA/317)
ST. LOUIS CARDINALS 1941-44, 1946-63

ROY CAMPANELLA C (BBWAA/270)
BROOKLYN DODGERS 1948-57

STAN COVELESKI P (VET)
PHILADELPHIA A's 1912
CLEVELAND INDIANS 1916-24
WASHINGTON SENATORS 1925-27
NEW YORK YANKEES 1928

WAITE HOYT P (VET)
NEW YORK GIANTS 1918, 1932
BOSTON RED SOX 1919-20
NEW YORK YANKEES 1921-30
DETROIT TIGERS 1930-31
PHILADELPHIA A's 1931
BROOKLYN DODGERS 1932, 1937-38
PITTSBURGH PIRATES 1933-37

1970

VOTES NEEDED:225

LOU BOUDREAU SS*/MGR (BBWAA/232)
CLEVELAND INDIANS 1938-41, •1942-50
BOSTON RED SOX 1951, •1952, 1953-54 M
KANSAS CITY A's 1955-57 M
CHICAGO CUBS 1960 M

EARLE COMBS OF (VET)
NEW YORK YANKEES 1924-35

FORD FRICK EXEC (VET)
NATIONAL LEAGUE PRESIDENT 1934-51
BASEBALL COMMISSIONER 1951-68

JESSE HAINES P (VET)
CINCINNATI REDS 1918
ST. LOUIS CARDINALS 1920-37

1971

JAKE BECKLEY 1B (VET)
PITTSBURGH PIRATES 1888-89, 1891-96
PITTSBURGH (PL) 1890
NEW YORK GIANTS 1896-97
CINCINNATI REDS 1897-1903
ST. LOUIS CARDINALS 1904-07

DAVE BANCROFT SS (VET)
PHILADELPHIA PHILLIES 1915-20
NEW YORK GIANTS 1920-23, 1930
•BOSTON BRAVES 1924-27
BROOKLYN DODGERS 1928-29

CHICK HAFEY OF (VET)
ST. LOUIS CARDINALS 1924-31
CINCINNATI REDS 1932-35, 1937

HARRY HOOPER OF (VET)
BOSTON RED SOX 1909-20
CHICAGO WHITE SOX 1920-25

JOE KELLEY OF (VET)
BOSTON NATIONALS (NL) 1891, •1908
PITTSBURGH PIRATES 1892
BALTIMORE ORIOLES (NL) 1892-98
BROOKLYN DODGERS 1899-1901
BALTIMORE (AL) 1902
CINCINNATI REDS •1902-05, 1906

RUBE MARQUARD P (VET)
NEW YORK GIANTS 1908-15
BROOKLYN DODGERS 1915-20
CINCINNATI REDS 1921
BOSTON BRAVES 1922-25

GEORGE WEISS EXEC (VET)
NEW YORK YANKEES 1932-60 EXEC
NEW YORK METS 1961-66

SATCHEL PAIGE P (NEG)
NEGRO LEAGUES 1926-48
CLEVELAND INDIANS 1948-49
ST. LOUIS BROWNS 1950-53
KANSAS CITY A's 1965

1972

VOTES NEEDED:297

SANDY KOUFAX P (BBWAA/344)
BROOKLYN DODGERS 1955-57
LOS ANGELES DODGERS 1958-1966

YOGI BERRA C*/MGR (BBWAA/339)
NEW YORK YANKEES 1946-63, 1964 M, 1984-85 M
NEW YORK METS 1965, 1972-75 M

EARLY WYNN P (BBWAA/301)
WASHINGTON SENATORS 1939-44, 1946-48
CLEVELAND INDIANS 1949-57, 1963
CHICAGO WHITE SOX 1958-62

LEFTY GOMEZ P (VET)
NEW YORK YANKEES 1930-42
WASHINGTON SENATORS 1943

WILL HARRIDGE EXEC (VET)
AMERICAN LEAGUE PRESIDENT 1931-59

ROSS YOUNGS OF (VET)
NEW YORK GIANTS 1917-26

JOSH GIBSON C (NEG)
NEGRO LEAGUES 1930-46

BUCK LEONARD 1B (NEG)
NEGRO LEAGUES 1933-50

1973

VOTES NEEDED:285

WARREN SPAHN P (BBWAA/316)
BOSTON BRAVES 1942, 1946-52
MILWAUKEE BRAVES 1953-64
NEW YORK METS 1965
SAN FRANCISCO GIANTS 1965

BILLY EVANS UMP*/EXEC (VET)
AMERICAN LEAGUE 1906-27
CLEVELAND INDIANS 1927-36 EXEC
DETROIT TIGERS 1947-51 EXEC

GEORGE KELLY 1B (VET)
NEW YORK GIANTS 1915-17, 1919-26
PITTSBURGH PIRATES 1917
CINCINNATI REDS 1927-30
CHICAGO CUBS 1930
BROOKLYN DODGERS 1932

MICKEY WELCH P (VET)
TROY (NL) 1880-82
NEW YORK GIANTS 1883-92

MONTE IRVIN OF (NEG)
NEGRO LEAGUES 1938-48
NEW YORK GIANTS 1949-55
CHICAGO CUBS 1956

ROBERTO CLEMENTE OF (SPEC)
PITTSBURGH PIRATES 1955-72

1974

VOTES NEEDED:274

MICKEY MANTLE OF (BBWAA/322)
NEW YORK YANKEES 1951-68

WHITEY FORD P (BBWAA/284)
NEW YORK YANKEES 1950-67

JIM BOTTOMLEY 1B (VET)
ST. LOUIS CARDINALS 1922-32
CINCINNATI REDS 1933-35
ST. LOUIS BROWNS 1936-37

JOCKO CONLAN OF/UMP* (VET)
CHICAGO WHITE SOX 1934-35
NATIONAL LEAGUE UMPIRE 1941-67

SAM THOMPSON OF (VET)
DETROIT WOLVERINES (NL) 1885-88
PHILADELPHIA PHILLIES 1889-98
DETROIT TIGERS 1906

COOL PAPA BELL OF (NEG)
NEGRO LEAGUES 1922-46

1975

VOTES NEEDED:272

RALPH KINER OF (BBWAA/273)
PITTSBURGH PIRATES 1946-53
CHICAGO CUBS 1953-54
CLEVELAND INDIANS 1955

EARL AVERILL OF (VET)
CLEVELAND INDIANS 1929-39
DETROIT TIGERS 1939-40
BOSTON BRAVES 1941

BUCKY HARRIS 2B/MGR* (VET)
WASHINGTON SENATORS 1919-23, •1924-28, 1935-42 M, 1950-54 M
DETROIT TIGERS •1929, 1930 M, •1931, 1932-33 M, 1955-56 M
BOSTON RED SOX 1934 M
PHILADELPHIA PHILLIES 1943 M
NEW YORK YANKEES 1947-48 M

BILLY HERMAN 2B*/MGR (VET)
CHICAGO CUBS 1931-41
BROOKLYN DODGERS 1941-43, 1946
BOSTON BRAVES 1946
•PITTSBURGH PIRATES 1947
BOSTON RED SOX 1964-66 M

JUDY JOHNSON 3B (NEG)
NEGRO LEAGUES 1921-38

1976

VOTES NEEDED:291

ROBIN ROBERTS P (BBWAA/337)
PHILADELPHIA PHILLIES 1948-61
BALTIMORE ORIOLES 1962-65
HOUSTON ASTROS 1965-66
CHICAGO CUBS 1966

BOB LEMON P (BBWAA/305)
CLEVELAND INDIANS 1941-42, 1946-58
KANSAS CITY ROYALS 1970-72 M
CHICAGO WHITE SOX 1977-78 M
NEW YORK YANKEES 1978-79 M, 1981-82

ROGER CONNOR 1B (VET)
TROY (NL) 188O-82
NEW YORK GIANTS 1883-89, 1891, 1893-94
NEW YORK (PL) 1890
PHILADELPHIA PHILLIES 1892
ST. LOUIS BROWNS (NL) 1894-95,•1896 1897

FRED LINDSTROM 3B (VET)
NEW YORK GIANTS 1924-32
PITTSBURGH PIRATES 1933-34
CHICAGO CUBS 1935
BROOKLYN DODGERS 1936

CAL HUBBARD UMP (VET)
NEW YORK GIANTS (NFL) *(F-HOF)*
GREEN BAY PACKERS (NFL) *(F-HOF)*
AMERICAN LEAGUE UMPIRE 1936-50

OSCAR CHARLESTON OF/M (NEG)
NEGRO LEAGUES 1915-27, •1928-50, 1951-54 M

1977

VOTES NEEDED:288

ERNIE BANKS SS*/1B (BBWAA/321)
CHICAGO CUBS 1953-71

AMOS RUSIE P (VET)
INDIANAPOLIS (NL) 1889
NEW YORK GIANTS 1890-95, 1897-98
CINCINNATI REDS 1901

JOE SEWELL SS*/3B (VET)
CLEVELAND INDIANS 1920-30
NEW YORK YANKEES 1931-33

AL LOPEZ C/MGR* (VET)
BROOKLYN DODGERS 1928-35
BOSTON BRAVES 1936-40
PITTSBURGH PIRATES 1940-46
CLEVELAND INDIANS 1947, 1951-56 M
CHICAGO WHITE SOX 1957-65 M, 1968 (2X)-69 M

MARTIN DIHIGO P/OF (NEG)
NEGRO LEAGUES 1923-45

JOHN HENRY LLOYD SS (NEG)
NEGRO LEAGUES 1905-31

1978

VOTES NEEDED:285

EDDIE MATHEWS 3B (BBWAA/301)
BOSTON BRAVES 1952
MILWAUKEE BRAVES 1953-65
ATLANTA BRAVES 1966, 1972-74 M
HOUSTON ASTROS 1967
DETROIT TIGERS 1967-68

ADDIE JOSS P (VET)
CLEVELAND INDIANS 1902-10

LARRY MacPHAIL EXEC*/OWNER (VET)
CINCINNATI REDS 1934-36 EXEC
BROOKLYN DODGERS 1938-42 EXEC
NEW YORK YANKEES 1946-47 OWNER

1979

VOTES NEEDED:324

WILLIE MAYS OF (BBWAA/409)
NEGRO LEAGUES 1948-50
NEW YORK GIANTS 1951-52, 1954-57
SAN FRANCISCO GIANTS 1958-72
NEW YORK METS 1972-73

WARREN GILES EXEC (VET)
NATIONAL LEAGUE PRESIDENT 1951-69

HACK WILSON OF (VET)
NEW YORK GIANTS 1923-25
CHICAGO CUBS 1926-31
BROOKLYN DODGERS 1932-34
PHILADELPHIA PHILLIES 1934

1980

VOTES NEEDED:289

AL KALINE OF (BBWAA/340)
DETROIT TIGERS 1953-74

DUKE SNIDER OF (BBWAA/333)
BROOKLYN DODGERS 1947-57
LOS ANGELES DODGERS 1958-62
NEW YORK METS 1963
SAN FRANCISCO GIANTS 1964

CHUCK KLEIN OF (VET)
PHILADELPHIA PHILLIES 1928-33, 1936-39, 1940-44
CHICAGO CUBS 1934-36
PITTSBURGH PIRATES 1939

TOM YAWKEY EXEC (VET)
BOSTON RED SOX 1933-77 OWNER
AMERICAN LEAGUE VP 1956-73

1981

VOTES NEEDED:301

BOB GIBSON P (BBWAA/337)
ST. LOUIS CARDINALS 1959-75

JOHNNY MIZE 1B (VET)
ST. LOUIS CARDINALS 1936-41
NEW YORK GIANTS 1942, 1946-49
NEW YORK YANKEES 1949-53

RUBE FOSTER P/MGR* (VET)
NEGRO LEAGUES 1902-26 LEAGUE PRESIDENT, OWNER, M

1982

VOTES NEEDED:312

HANK AARON OF (BBWAA/406)
MILWAUKEE BRAVES 1954-65
ATLANTA BRAVES 1966-74
MILWAUKEE BREWERS 1975-76

FRANK ROBINSON OF (BBWAA/370)
CINCINNATI REDS 1956-65
BALTIMORE ORIOLES 1966-71, 1988-91 M
LOS ANGELES DODGERS 1972
CALIFORNIA ANGELS 1973-74
CLEVELAND INDIANS 1974, •1975-76 , 1977 M
SAN FRANCISCO GIANTS 1981(2X)-84 M

TRAVIS JACKSON SS (VET)
NEW YORK GIANTS 1922-36

HAPPY CHANDLER EXEC (VET)
COMMISSIONER 1945-51

1983

VOTES NEEDED:281

BROOKS ROBINSON 3B (BBWAA/344)
BALTIMORE ORIOLES 1955-77

JUAN MARICHAL P (BBWAA/313)
SAN FRANCISCO GIANTS 1960-73
BOSTON RED SOX 1974
LOS ANGELES DODGERS 1975

GEORGE KELL 3B (VET)
PHILADELPHIA A's 1943-46
DETROIT TIGERS 1946-52
BOSTON RED SOX 1952-54
CHICAGO WHITE SOX 1954-56
BALTIMORE ORIOLES 1956-67

WALTER ALSTON MGR (VET)
ST. LOUIS CARDINALS 1936
BROOKLYN DODGERS 1954-57 M
LOS ANGELES DODGERS 1958-76

1984

VOTES NEEDED:303

LUIS APARICIO SS (BBWAA/341)
CHICAGO WHITE SOX 1956-62, 1968-70
BALTIMORE ORIOLES 1963-67
BOSTON RED SOX 1971-73

HARMON KILLEBREW 1B*/3B/OF (BBWAA/335)
WASHINGTON SENATORS 1954-60
MINNESOTA TWINS 1961-74
KANSAS CITY ROYALS 1975

DON DRYSDALE P (BBWAA/316)
BROOKLYN DODGERS 1956-57
LOS ANGELES DODGERS 1958-69

RICK FERRELL C (VET)
ST. LOUIS BROWNS 1929-33, 1941-43
BOSTON RED SOX 1933-37
WASHINGTON SENATORS 1937-41, 1944-45, 1947

PEEWEE REESE SS (VET)
BROOKLYN DODGERS 1940-42, 1946-57
LOS ANGELES DODGERS 1958

1985

VOTES NEEDED:297

HOYT WILHELM P (BBWAA/331)
NEW YORK GIANTS 1952-56
ST. LOUIS CARDINALS 1957
CLEVELAND INDIANS 1957-58
BALTIMORE ORIOLES 1958-62
CHICAGO WHITE SOX 1963-68
CALIFORNIA ANGELS 1969
ATLANTA BRAVES 1969-70, 1971
CHICAGO CUBS 1970
LOS ANGELES DODGERS 1971-72

LOU BROCK OF (BBWAA/315)
CHICAGO CUBS 1961-64
ST. LOUIS CARDINALS 1964-79

ENOS SLAUGHTER OF (VET)
ST. LOUIS CARDINALS 1938-53
NEW YORK YANKEES 1954-55, 1956-59
KANSAS CITY A's 1955-56
MILWAUKEE BRAVES 1959

ARKY VAUGHAN SS (VET)
PITTSBURGH PIRATES 1932-41
BROOKLYN DODGERS 1942-43, 1947-48

1986

VOTES NEEDED:319

WILLIE McCOVEY 1B (BBWAA/346)
SAN FRANCISCO GIANTS 1959-73, 1977-80
SAN DIEGO PADRES 1974-76
OAKLAND A's 1976

BOBBY DOERR 2B (VET)
BOSTON RED SOX 1937-44, 1946-51

ERNIE LOMBARDI C (VET)
BROOKLYN DODGERS 1931
CINCINNATI REDS 1932-41
BOSTON BRAVES 1942
NEW YORK GIANTS 1943-47

1987

VOTES NEEDED:310

BILLY WILLIAMS OF (BBWAA/354)
CHICAGO CUBS 1959-74,
OAKLAND A's 1975-76

JIM HUNTER P (BBWAA/315)
KANSAS CITY A's 1965-67
OAKLAND A's 1968-74
NEW YORK YANKEES 1975-79

RAY DANDRIDGE 3B (VET)
NEGRO LEAGUES 1933-48

1988

VOTES NEEDED:321

WILLIE STARGELL 1B/OF (BBWAA/352)
PITTSBURGH PIRATES 1962-82

1989

VOTES NEEDED:336

JOHNNY BENCH C (BBWAA/431)
CINCINNATI REDS 1967-1983

CARL YASTRZEMSKI OF (BBWAA/423)
BOSTON RED SOX 1961-83

RED SCHOENDIENST 2B*/MGR (VET)
ST. LOUIS CARDINALS 1945-56, 1961-63, 1965-76 M, 1980 M, 1990 M
NEW YORK GIANTS 1956-57
MILWAUKEE BRAVES 1957-60

AL BARLICK UMP (VET)
NATIONAL LEAGUE 1940-43, 1946-55, 1958-71

1990

VOTES NEEDED:333

JIM PALMER P (BBWAA/411)
BALTIMORE ORIOLES 1965-1984

JOE MORGAN 2B (BBWAA/363)
HOUSTON COLT 45's 1963-64
HOUSTON ASTROS 1965-71, 1980
CINCINNATI REDS 1972-79
SAN FRANCISCO GIANTS 1981-82
PHILADELPHIA PHILLIES 1983
OAKLAND A's 1984

1991

VOTES NEEDED:333

ROD CAREW 2B/1B* (BBWAA/401)
MINNESOTA TWINS 1967-78
CALIFORNIA ANGELS 1979-85

GAYLORD PERRY P (BBWAA/342)
SAN FRANCISCO GIANTS 1962-71
CLEVELAND INDIANS 1972-75
TEXAS RANGERS 1975-77, 1980
SAN DIEGO PADRES 1978-79
NEW YORK YANKEES 1980
ATLANTA BRAVES 1981
SEATTLE MARINERS 1982-83
KANSAS CITY ROYALS 1983

FERGUSON JENKINS P (BBWAA/334)
PHILADELPHIA PHILLIES 1965-66
CHICAGO CUBS 1966-73, 1982-83
TEXAS RANGERS 1974-75, 1978-81
BOSTON RED SOX 1976-77

TONY LAZZERI 2B (VET)
NEW YORK YANKEES 1926-37
CHICAGO CUBS 1938
BROOKLYN DODGERS 1939
NEW YORK GIANTS 1939

BILL VEECK EXEC (VET)
CLEVELAND INDIANS 1946-49 OWNER
ST. LOUIS BROWNS 1951-53 OWNER
CHICAGO WHITE SOX 1959-61 OWNER

1992

VOTES NEEDED:323

TOM SEAVER P (BBWAA/425)
NEW YORK METS 1967-77, 1983
CINCINNATI REDS 1977-82
CHICAGO WHITE SOX 1984-86
BOSTON RED SEX 1986

ROLLIE FINGERS P (BBWAA/349)
OAKLAND A's 1968-76
SAN DIEGO PADRES 1977-80
MILWAUKEE BREWERS 1981-82, 1984-85

HAL NEWHOUSER P (VET)
DETROIT TIGERS 1939-53
CLEVELAND INDIANS 1954-55

BILL McGOWAN UMP (VET)
AMERICAN LEAGUE 1925-54

1993

VOTES NEEDED:318

REGGIE JACKSON OF (BBWAA/396)
KANSAS CITY A's 1967
OAKLAND A's 1968-75, 1987
BALTIMORE ORIOLES 1976
NEW YORK YANKEES 1977-81
CALIFORNIA ANGELS 1982-86

1994

VOTES NEEDED:342

STEVE CARLTON P (BBWAA/436)
ST. LOUIS CARDINALS 1965-71
PHILADELPHIA PHILLIES 1972-86
SAN FRANCISCO GIANTS 1986
CHICAGO WHITE SOX 1986
CLEVELAND INDIANS 1987
MINNESOTA TWINS 1987-88

PHIL RIZZUTO SS (VET)
NEW YORK YANKEES 1941-56

LEO DUROCHER SS/MGR* (VET)
NEW YORK YANKEES 1925, 1928-29
CINCINNATI REDS 1930-33
ST. LOUIS CARDINALS 1933-37
BROOKLYN DODGERS 1938,•1939-41, 1942M, •1943, 1944M, •1945, 1946M, 1947 (SUS), 1948M
NEW YORK GIANTS 1948-55M
CHICAGO CUBS 1966-72M
HOUSTON ASTROS 1972-73M
MINNESOTA TWINS 1987-88

1995

VOTES NEEDED:345

MIKE SCHMIDT 3B (BBWAA/444)
PHILADELPHIA PHILLIES 1972-89

RICHIE ASHBURN OF (VET)
PHILADELPHIA PHILLIES 1948-59
CHICAGO CUBS 1960-61
NEW YORK METS 1962

LEON DAY P (VET)
NEGRO LEAGUES 1934-49

WILLIAM HULBERT EXEC (VET)
FOUNDER NL 1876
PRESIDENT NL 1877-82
PRESIDENT CHICAGO (NL) 1876-81

VIC WILLIS P (VET)
BOSTON NATIONALS 1898-1905
PITTSBURGH PIRATES 1906-09
ST. LOUIS CARDINALS 1910

1996

VOTES NEEDED:353

JIM BUNNING P (VET)
DETROIT TIGERS 1955-63
PHILADELPHIA PHILLIES 1964-67, 70-71
PITTSBURGH PIRATES 1968-69
LOS ANGELES DODGERS 1969

BILL FOSTER P (VET)
NEGRO LEAGUES 1923-37

NED HANLON OF/MGR* (VET)
CLEVELAND NATIONALS 1880
DETROIT NATIONALS 1881-1888
PITTSBURGH NATIONALS •1889, •91
PITTSBURGH PLAYERS •1890
BALTIMORE NATIONALS •1892, 93-98M
BROOKLYN NATIONALS 1899-1905M
CINCINNATI REDS 1906-07M

EARL WEAVER MGR (VET)
BALTIMORE ORIOLES 1968-82, 85-86

1997

VOTES NEEDED:355

PHIL NIEKRO P (BBWAA/380)
MILWAUKEE BRAVES 1964-65
ATLANTA BRAVES 1966-83, 87
NEW YORK YANKEES 1984-85
CLEVELAND INDIANS 1986-87
TORONTO BLUEJAYS 1987

NELLIE FOX 2B (VET)
PHILADELPHIA A's 1947-49
CHICAGO WHITE SOX 1950-63
HOUSTON COLT 45's 1964, ASTROS 65

TOMMY LASORDA P/MGR* (VET)
BROOKLYN DODGERS 1954-55
KANSAS CITY A's 1956
LOS ANGELES DODGERS 1976-96M

WILLIE WELLS SS*/MGR (VET)
NEGRO LEAGUES 1924-49

1998

VOTES NEEDED:355

DON SUTTON P (BBWAA/386)
LOS ANGELES DODGERS 1966-80
HOUSTON ASTROS 1981-82
MILWAUKEE BREWERS 1982-84
OAKLAND ATHLETICS 1985
CALIFORNIA ANGELS 1985-87
LOS ANGELES DODGERS 1988

GEORGE DAVIS SS (VET)
CLEVELAND SPIDERS 1890-92
NEW YORK GIANTS 1893-1901, 03
CHICAGO WHITE SOX 1902, 04-09

LARRY DOBY OF (VET)
CLEVELAND INDIANS 1947-55, 58
CHICAGO WHITE SOX 1956-57, 59
DETROIT TIGERS 1959

LEE MacPHAIL, JR. EXEC. (VET)
BALTIMORE ORIOLES, Pres. 1960-65
AMERICAN LEAGUE, Pres. 1974-84

"Bullet" JOE ROGAN P/ALL (VET)
NEGRO LEAGUES 1917-46

1999

VOTES NEEDED:373

NOLAN RYAN P (BBWAA/491)
NEW YORK METS 1966, 1968-71
CALIFORNIA ANGELS 1972-79
HOUSTON ASTROS 1980-88
TEXAS RANGERS 1989-93

GEORGE BRETT 3B (BBWAA/488)
KANSAS CITY ROYALS 1973-93

ROBIN YOUNT SS/OF (BBWAA/385)
MILWAUKEE BREWERS 1974-93

ORLANDO CEPEDA 1B. (VET)
SAN FRANCISCO GIANTS 1958-66
ST. LOUIS CARDINALS 1966-68
ATLANTA BRAVES 1969-72
OAKLAND A's 1972
BOSTON RED SOX 1973
KANSAS CITY ROYALS 1974

NESTOR CHYLAK UMP (VET)
AMERICAN LEAGUE 1954-78

FRANK SELEE MGR. (VET)
BOSTON NATIONALS 1890-1901
CHICAGO CUBS 1902-05

SMOKEY JOE WILLIAMS P (VET)
NEGRO LEAGUES 1905-32

2000

VOTES NEEDED:375

CARLTON FISK C (BBWAA/397)
BOSTON RED SOX 1969, 1971-80
CHICAGO WHITE SOX 1981-93

TONY PEREZ 1B (BBWAA/385)
CINCINNATI REDS 1964-76, 84-86
MONTREAL EXPOS 1977-79
BOSTON RED SOX 1980-82
PHILADELPHIA PHILLIES 1983

SPARKY ANDERSON 2B/M* (VET)
PHILADELPHIA PHILLIES 1959
CINCINNATI REDS 1970-78M
DETROIT TIGERS 1979-95M

BID McPHEE 2B. (VET)
CINCINNATI RED STOCKINGS (AA) 1882-89
CINCINNATI REDS 1890-99

TURKEY STEARNES OF (VET)
NEGRO LEAGUES 1920-42, 45

2001

VOTES NEEDED:387

DAVE WINFIELD OF (BBWAA/435)
SAN DIEGO PADRES 1973-80
NEW YORK YANKEES 1981-90
CALIFORNIA ANGELS 1990-91
TORONTO BLUE JAYS 1992
MINNESOTA TWINS 1993-1994
CLEVELAND INDIANS 1995

KIRBY PUCKETT OF (BBWAA/423)
MINNESOTA TWINS 1984-1995

BILL MAZEROSKI 2B (VET)
PITTSBURGH PIRATES 1956-72

HILTON SMITH P. (VET)
NEGRO LEAGUES 1932-48

2002

VOTES NEEDED:354

OZZIE SMITH SS (BBWAA/433)
SAN DIEGO PADRES 1978-81
ST. LOUIS CARDINALS 1982-96

2003

VOTES NEEDED:372

EDDIE MURRAY 1B (BBWAA/423)
BALTIMORE ORIOLES 1977-88, 96
LOS ANGELES DODGERS 1989-91, 97
NEW YORK METS 1992-93
TORONTO BLUE JAYS 1992
CLEVELAND INDIANS 1994-96
ANAHEIM ANGELS 1997

GARY CARTER C (BBWAA/387)
MONTREAL EXPOS 1974-84, 92
NEW YORK METS 1985-1989
SAN FRANCISCO GIANTS 1990
LOS ANGELES DODGERS 1991

2004

VOTES NEEDED:380

PAUL MOLITOR DH (BBWAA/431)
MILWAUKEE BREWERS 1978-92
TORONTO BLUE JAYS 1993-95
MINNESOTA TWINS 1996-98

DENNIS ECKERSLEY P (BBWAA/421)
CLEVELAND INDIANS 1975-77
BOSTON RED SOX 1978-1984, 98
CHICAGO CUBS 1984-86
OAKLAND ATHLETICS 1987-95
ST. LOUIS CARDINALS 1996-97

2005

VOTES NEEDED:387

WADE BOGGS 3B (BBWAA/474)
BOSTON RED SOX 1982-92
NEW YORK YANKEES 1993-97
TAMPA BAY DEVIL RAYS 1998-99

RYNE SANDBERG 2B (BBWAA/393)
PHILADELPHIA PHILLIES 1981
CHICAGO CUBS 1982-94, 96-97

Mike Schmidt, rated by most to be "the best all-around third baseman to ever play the game," was inducted into the Hall of Fame in 1995. It was his first year of eligibility and he leaped into the Hall with nearly 100 votes more than necessary. Mike led the NL in HRs eight times, in RBIs four times, in walks four times, OB% three times in a row and in slugging five times. In the field, he was no slouch winning 10 Gold Gloves. He also stole 174 bases in the process.Mike wore his familiar #20 shirt for his entire 18-year career with the Phillies.

Martin Dihigo (Above, top) must have been an incredible athlete. He had batting averages of .386, .391 and .434 in the Negro Leagues. And he had power, leading the league in homeruns several times. He played every position but catcher. His arm was the most feared one in the outfield. Nobody would dare run on him. He also pitched. In 1938, he pitched in both Cuban and Mexican leagues—his record, 32-4. Sounds like Hornsby, Ruth and Feller rolled into one.

Monte Irvin (Above, bottom) batted .361, then .380 before going off to serve in WWII. He came back to hit .401 in 1946 for the Newark Eagles. He came up with the New York Giants in 1949, already 30 years old. He still batted over .300 three times, led the league in RBIs once and batted .458 in the 1951 World Series loss to the Yankees.

Sixty-six members made the Hall of Fame as pitchers. Others such as Babe Ruth, whose bat became more important, entered as an outfielder while curveballer Candy Cummings is recognized as a pioneer. There are sixty-one outfielders.

Many players have played several positions regularly, but recognition has been given to the position played most. Joe Sewell primarily played third base for the Yankees, but earlier in Cleveland he was a shortstop. He is listed as a shortstop.

Harmon Killebrew is listed as a first baseman although he played nearly as many games at third.

When incorporating the players from the Negro Leagues into a listing by position, the toughest decision was Martin Dihigo. I listed him as a pitcher because he has a record of 256-136. But he also played the outfield on his days off. He once led the American Negro League in hitting with a .386 average and he topped the Eastern Colored League in home runs one year.

Adding Gary Carter brings the list of catchers to fourteen.

Rod Carew played 54 more games at first than the 1,130 games he played at second, so he is one of twenty first basemen.

There are sixteen second basemen honored, twenty-two shortstops. Even with adding Ray Dandridge and Judy Johnson from the Negro Leagues plus Wade Boggs, it still leaves the hot corner as the rarest position in the Hall at only twelve players.

There are 16 managers honored for their skills, but many of the players went on to manage—thirty-three others to be exact.

Many became coaches to share their extraordinary skills with younger players coming up. Even the great Babe Ruth was coerced out of retirement briefly in 1938 to coach for the Brooklyn Dodgers. There were a total of 60 players who coached when their careers were finished.

So far, only one player has played more games at DH than any other position and that's Paul Molitor. But there will be others.

THE HALL-- BY POSITION

PITCHERS (66)
PETE ALEXANDER
CHIEF BENDER
THREE-FINGER BROWN
JIM BUNNING
STEVE CARLTON
JACK CHESBRO
JOHN CLARKSON
STAN COVELESKI
LEON DAY
DIZZY DEAN
MARTIN DIHIGO
DON DRYSDALE
DENNIS ECKERSLEY
RED FABER
BOB FELLER
ROLLIE FINGERS
WHITEY FORD
BILL FOSTER
PUD GALVIN
BOB GIBSON
LEFTY GOMEZ
BURLEIGH GRIMES
LEFTY GROVE
JESSE HAINES
WAITE HOYT
CARL HUBBELL
CATFISH HUNTER
FERGUSON JENKINS
WALTER JOHNSON
ADDIE JOSS
TIM KEEFE
SANDY KOUFAX
BOB LEMON
TED LYONS
JUAN MARICHAL
RUBE MARQUARD
CHRISTY MATHEWSON
JOE McGINNITY
HAL NEWHOUSER
KID NICHOLS
PHIL NIEKRO
SATCHEL PAIGE
JIM PALMER
HERB PENNOCK
GAYLORD PERRY
EDDIE PLANK
HOSS RADBOURNE
EPPA RIXEY
ROBIN ROBERTS
BULLET ROGAN
RED RUFFING
AMOS RUSIE
NOLAN RYAN
TOM SEAVER
HILTON SMITH
WARREN SPAHN
DON SUTTON
DAZZY VANCE
RUBE WADDELL
ED WALSH
MICKEY WELCH
HOYT WILHELM
JOE WILLIAMS
VIC WILLIS
EARLY WYNN
CY YOUNG

CATCHERS (14)
JOHNNY BENCH
YOGI BERRA
ROGER BRESNAHAN
ROY CAMPANELLA
GARY CARTER
MICKEY COCHRANE
BILL DICKEY
BUCK EWING
RICK FERRELL
CARLTON FISK
JOSH GIBSON
GABBY HARTNETT
ERNIE LOMBARDI
RAY SCHALK

FIRST BASEMEN (20)
CAP ANSON
JAKE BECKLEY
DAN BROUTHERS
JIM BOTTOMLEY
ROD CAREW
ORLANDO CEPEDA
FRANK CHANCE
ROGER CONNOR
JIMMIE FOXX
LOU GEHRIG
HANK GREENBERG
GEORGE KELLY
HARMON KILLEBREW
BUCK LEONARD
WILLIE McCOVEY
JOHNNY MIZE
EDDIE MURRAY
TONY PEREZ
GEORGE SISLER
BILL TERRY

SECOND BASEMEN (16)
EDDIE COLLINS
BOBBY DOERR
JOHNNY EVERS
NELLIE FOX
FRANKIE FRISCH
CHARLIE GEHRINGER
BILLY HERMAN
ROGERS HORNSBY
NAP LAJOIE
TONY LAZZERI
BILL MAZEROSKI
BID McPHEE
JOE MORGAN
JACKIE ROBINSON
RYNE SANDBERG
RED SCHOENDIENST

SHORTSTOPS (22)
LUIS APARICIO
LUKE APPLING
DAVE BANCROFT
ERNIE BANKS
LOU BOUDREAU
JOE CRONIN
GEORGE DAVIS
TRAVIS JACKSON
HUGHIE JENNINGS
JOHN HENRY LLOYD
RABBIT MARANVILLE
PEEWEE REESE
PHIL RIZZUTO
JOE SEWELL
OZZIE SMITH
JOE TINKER
ARKY VAUGHAN
HONUS WAGNER
BOBBY WALLACE
JOHN MONTE WARD
WILLIE WELLS
ROBIN YOUNT

THIRD BASEMEN (12)
FRANK "HOME RUN" BAKER
WADE BOGGS
GEORGE BRETT
JIMMY COLLINS
RAY DANDRIDGE
JUDY JOHNSON
GEORGE KELL
FRED LINDSTROM
EDDIE MATHEWS
BROOKS ROBINSON
MIKE SCHMIDT
PIE TRAYNOR

OUTFIELDERS (61)
HANK AARON
RICHIE ASHBURN
EARL AVERILL
COOL PAPA BELL
LOU BROCK
JESSE BURKETT
MAX CAREY
OSCAR CHARLESTON
FRED CLARKE
ROBERTO CLEMENTE
TY COBB
EARLE COMBS
SAM CRAWFORD
KIKI CUYLER
ED DELAHANTY
JOE DIMAGGIO
LARRY DOBY
HUGH DUFFY
ELMER FLICK
GOOSE GOSLIN
CHICK HAFEY
BILLY HAMILTON
HARRY HEILMANN
HARRY HOOPER
MONTE IRVIN
REGGIE JACKSON
AL KALINE
WEE WILLIE KEELER
JOE KELLEY
MIKE "KING" KELLY
RALPH KINER
CHUCK KLEIN
MICKEY MANTLE
HEINIE MANUSH
WILLIE MAYS

TOMMY McCARTHY
JOE MEDWICK
STAN MUSIAL
JIM O'ROURKE
MEL OTT
KIRBY PUCKETT
SAM RICE
FRANK ROBINSON
EDD ROUSH
BABE RUTH
AL SIMMONS
ENOS SLAUGHTER
DUKE SNIDER
TRIS SPEAKER
WILLIE STARGELL
TURKEY STEARNES
SAM THOMPSON
LLOYD WANER
PAUL WANER
ZACK WHEAT
BILLY WILLIAMS
TED WILLIAMS
HACK WILSON
DAVE WINFIELD
CARL YASTRZEMSKI
ROSS YOUNGS

DESIGNATED HITTER (1)
PAUL MOLITOR

MANAGERS (16)
WALTER ALSTON
SPARKY ANDERSON
LEO DUROCHER
NED HANLON
BUCKY HARRIS
MILLER HUGGINS
TOMMY LASORDA
AL LOPEZ
CONNIE MACK
JOE McCARTHY
JOHN McGRAW
BILL McKECHNIE
WILBERT ROBINSON
FRANK SELEE
CASEY STENGEL
EARL WEAVER

UMPIRES (8)
AL BARLICK
NESTOR CHYLAK
JOCKO CONLAN
TOM CONNOLLY
BILLY EVANS
CAL HUBBARD
BILL KLEM
BILL McGOWAN

EXECUTIVES/OWNERS (17)
ED BARROW
MORGAN BULKELEY
HAPPY CHANDLER
CHARLIE COMISKEY
FORD FRICK
WARREN GILES
CLARK GRIFFITH
WILL HARRIDGE
WILLIAM HULBERT
BAN JOHNSON
KENESAW MOUNTAIN LANDIS
LARRY MacPHAIL
LEE MacPHAIL
BRANCH RICKEY*
BILL VEECK
GEORGE WEISS
TOM YAWKEY

PIONEERS (7)
ALEXANDER CARTWRIGHT
HENRY CHADWICK
CANDY CUMMINGS
RUBE FOSTER**
AL SPALDING
GEORGE WRIGHT
HARRY WRIGHT

All pictures of grace that exemplified the Hall of Fame, they are (top L) Warren Spahn, the winningest left-hander in history, (top R) Bobby Wallace, the Ozzie Smith of the early 1900's, (bottom L) Brooks Robinson, the quintessential 'hot-corner' gloveman, and (bottom R) Rube Foster, who pitched, managed, presided over and clung to an ideal for the fledgling NNL.

** Rickey was an executive, but an extraordinary one. He definitely brought many innovative ideas to the game and could just as easily be considered a pioneer.*
***Foster is listed by the Hall as a manager, but he was far more than that. He was for all intents "The Father of Black Baseball." He became the President of the Negro National League (NNL) and saved black baseball from going down the tubes.*

Ducky Medwick (Above, top) wore #7 with the Cardinals during his glorious Gashouse days. When he arrived in Brooklyn, Coach Charlie Dressen was wearing it. Ducky thought he could double his luck by taking #77. Infielder Johnny Hudson went to the Cubs in1941 making #6 available. Medwick opted for the #6. His average improved 18 points to .318. In '43 he got his lucky #7 back and promptly dipped to .272 and finished the year with the Giants.

Country Slaughter (Above, bottom) played until he was 43. He only wore #9 as a Cardinal where he was an All-Star ten years in a row. He had two stints with the Yankees where he wore #17, he had a short period in KC wearing #33 and finished in Milwaukee with #25.

The most common number worn by members of the Hall is 4. Twenty-five players wore the number at some time or other in their careers. The numbers 3 and 5 rank next with 20 players wearing them.

Eighteen members wore #2 including two 1997 inductees, Nellie Fox and Tom Lasorda. Sparky Anderson wore it in his short stint at second base. Believe it or not, seventeen members have worn #32, nearly half as managers or coaches. Seventeen members also wore #7.

Oddly, there were 16 members who wore the numbers 21 and 31.

Monte Irvin wore #6 while playing in the Negro League. Mickey Mantle wore it in his rookie year and Stan "The Man" Musial made it famous. A total of fifteen players wore it.

Numbers 8, 9, 11, and 20 were each worn by fifteen players. There were fourteen #1's. Thirteen members wore the numbers 10, 33, and 35. But only four used #33 while playing: Roy Campanella, Eddie Murray, Frank Robinson and Enos Slaughter.

The highest number worn on the shirt of a Hall of Famer was #77 in 1940 by "Ducky" Medwick when he was with the Dodgers.

The lowest number not worn by any member of the Hall is #59. The lowest number not worn by an active player in the Hall is #50. Managers Bucky Harris and Rogers Hornsby have worn it though. Prior to Nolan Ryan's election in 1999, #30 had been worn only by coaches and managers.

Other numbers that have not been worn by Hall of Famers while they were playing are 51, 52, 54, 55, and 59 through to Carlton Fisk's unusual 72.

Besides the previously mentioned 59 not being worn by any member, there are a few of the above that fall into that category: 60-64, 66, 68-71, 73-76, and 78-above.

Only one athlete during his playing days wore the number 13. The courageous one was Roberto Clemente in his rookie year with the Pirates. He rapped 11 triples, 23 doubles, 5 homers, scored 48 runs and drove in 47. This 21-year-old was made of sterner stuff.

Burleigh Grimes wore 13 as manager of the Brooklyn Dodgers in 1938 where he piloted them to a seventh place finish. Judging from the line-up that the Dodgers put on the field, I don't think Burleigh's shirt had anything to do with it.

THE HALL-- BY THE NUMBERS

An M after the team name indicates manager, a CH means coach, a (•) preceding either means a playing manager or coach. NEG is Negro League.

1 SPARKY ANDERSON--PADRES CH
1 RICHIE ASHBURN--PHILS, CUBS, METS
1 JIM BOTTOMLEY--REDS
1 EARLE COMBS--YANKEES
1 BOBBY DOERR--RED SOX
1 TRAVIS JACKSON--GIANTS CH
1 GEORGE KELL--RED SOX, WHITE SOX
1 CHUCK KLEIN--PHILLIES
1 FRED LINDSTROM--DODGERS
1 RABBIT MARANVILLE--BRAVES
1 BILL McKECHNIE--REDS M
1 PEEWEE REESE--DODGERS, CH
1 OZZIE SMITH--PADRES, CARDS
1 PAUL WANER--DODGERS

2 SPARKY ANDERSON--PHILS
2 JIM BOTTOMLEY--BROWNS, •M
2 MICKEY COCHRANE--A's
2 LEO DUROCHER--CARDS, DODGERS •M, M, CH, GIANTS M, CUBS M, ASTROS M
2 RICK FERRELL--RED SOX
2 NELLIE FOX--WHITE SOX, COLT 45s, ASTROS •CH, CH
2 JIMMIE FOXX--A's
2 CHARLIE GEHRINGER--TIGERS
2 GABBY HARTNETT--CUBS, •M
2 BILLY HERMAN--CUBS
2 GEORGE KELLY--REDS CH
2 TOMMY LASORDA--DODGERS M
2 BOB LEMON--PHILS CH, ROYALS CH,M
2 ERNIE LOMBARDI--REDS
2 HEINIE MANUSH--SENATORS
2 SAM RICE--SENATORS
2 RED SCHOENDIENST--CARDS, •CH, CH, M, A's CH
2 EARLY WYNN--INDIANS CH

3 EARL AVERILL--INDIANS, BRAVES
3 JIM BOTTOMLEY--REDS
3 MICKEY COCHRANE--TIGERS •M, M
3 KIKI CUYLER--CUBS
3 JIMMIE FOXX--A's, RED SOX
3 FRANKIE FRISCH--CARDS, •M, M, CUBS M
3 CHARLIE GEHRINGER--TIGERS
3 GOOSE GOSLIN--SENATORS, BROWNS
3 GEORGE KELL--ORIOLES
3 HARMON KILLEBREW--SENATORS, TWINS, ROYALS
3 CHUCK KLEIN--PHILLIES, •CH
3 FRED LINDSTROM--GIANTS
3 HEINIE MANUSH--SENATORS
3 DUCKY MEDWICK--GIANTS,BRAVES
3 JOHNNY MIZE--GIANTS
3 MEL OTT--GIANTS
3 BABE RUTH--YANKEES, BRAVES
3 AL SIMMONS--SENATORS
3 BILL TERRY--GIANTS •M
3 ARKY VAUGHAN--PIRATES

4 LUKE APPLING--WHITE SOX, CH
4 JIM BOTTOMLEY--CARDS
4 LOU BOUDREAU--RED SOX •M, M
4 JOE CRONIN--SENATORS, •M, RED SOX •M, M
4 KIKI CUYLER--REDS
4 LEO DUROCHER--GIANTS M
4 JIMMIE FOXX--PHILLIES
4 LOU GEHRIG--YANKEES
4 GOOSE GOSLIN--TIGERS
4 CHICK HAFEY--REDS
4 BILLY HERMAN--CUBS
4 ROGERS HORNSBY--CARDS, BROWNS, •M
4 GEORGE KELL--ORIOLES
4 RALPH KINER--PIRATES, CUBS
4 CHUCK KLEIN--CUBS
4 BUCK LEONARD--NEG
4 ERNIE LOMBARDI--REDS
4 PAUL MOLITOR--BREWERS, TWINS
4 MEL OTT--GIANTS, •M, M
4 BILL TERRY--GIANTS
4 RED SCHOENDIENST--BRAVES
4 DUKE SNIDER--DODGERS, METS, PADRES CH
4 EARL WEAVER--ORIOLES M
4 BILLY WILLIAMS--CUBS
4 HACK WILSON--DODGERS

5 HANK AARON--BRAVES
5 LUKE APPLING--WHITE SOX
5 EARL AVERILL--INDIANS
5 JOHNNY BENCH--REDS
5 JIM BOTTOMLEY--CARDS
5 LOU BOUDREAU--INDIANS, •M, KC A's M, CUBS M
5 GEORGE BRETT--ROYALS
5 JOE DIMAGGIO--YANKEES, A's CH
5 GOOSE GOSLIN--SENATORS
5 HANK GREENBERG--TIGERS, PIRATES
5 TRAVIS JACKSON--GIANTS
5 JUDY JOHNSON--NEG
5 TONY LAZZERI--YANKEES
5 ERNIE LOMBARDI--BRAVES
5 DUCKY MEDWICK--BRAVES
5 MEL OTT--GIANTS
5 TONY PEREZ--RED SOX
5 BROOKS ROBINSON--ORIOLES, •CH
5 AL SIMMONS--WHITE SOX
5 ARKY VAUGHAN--PIRATES, DODGERS

6 JOE CRONIN--RED SOX •M
6 LARRY DOBY--INDIANS, CH
6 CHICK HAFEY--REDS
6 MONTE IRVIN--NEG
6 TRAVIS JACKSON--GIANTS
6 AL KALINE--TIGERS
6 CHUCK KLEIN--CUBS
6 TONY LAZZERI--YANKEES
6 BOB LEMON--INDIANS
6 ERNIE LOMBARDI--GIANTS
6 MICKEY MANTLE--YANKEES
6 DUCKY MEDWICK--DODGERS
6 STAN MUSIAL--CARDS
6 RED SCHOENDIENST--CARDS
6 AL SIMMONS--TIGERS, A's •CH

7 LEO DUROCHER--YANKEES
7 RICK FERRELL--RED SOX
7 HANK GREENBERG--TIGERS
7 GABBY HARTNETT--CUBS
7 MONTE IRVIN--GIANTS
7 GEORGE KELL--A's, TIGERS
7 TONY LAZZERI--YANKEES
7 FRED LINDSTROM--CUBS
7 ERNIE LOMBARDI--REDS
7 AL LOPEZ--BRAVES
7 MICKEY MANTLE--YANKEES, CH
7 HEINIE MANUSH--RED SOX
7 EDDIE MATHEWS--TIGERS
7 DUCKY MEDWICK--CARDS, DODGERS
7 RED SCHOENDIENST--GIANTS
7 AL SIMMONS--A's, WHITE SOX, SENATORS
7 BILLY WILLIAMS--A's

8 LUKE APPLING--WHITE SOX
8 YOGI BERRA--YANKEES, M, CH, METS •CH, CH, M, ASTROS CH
8 GARY CARTER--EXPOS, METS, GIANTS, DODGERS
8 KIKI CUYLER--REDS
8 BILL DICKEY--YANKEES, M
8 RICK FERRELL--BROWNS, SENATORS
8 BILLY HERMAN--BRAVES CH
8 CHUCK KLEIN--PHILLIES
8 ERNIE LOMBARDI--GIANTS
8 AL LOPEZ--BRAVES
8 JOE MORGAN--REDS, ASTROS, GIANTS, PHILLIES, A's
8 AL SIMMONS--RED SOX
8 WILLIE STARGELL--PIRATES, CH, BRAVES CH
8 PAUL WANER--BRAVES
8 CARL YASTRZEMSKI--RED SOX

9 JOE DIMAGGIO--YANKEES
9 BOBBY DOERR--RED SOX
9 BOB FELLER--INDIANS
9 RICK FERRELL--RED SOX, BROWNS
9 CHICK HAFEY--REDS
9 GABBY HARTNETT--CUBS, GIANTS
9 REGGIE JACKSON--A's, ORIOLES
9 RALPH KINER--INDIANS
9 ERNIE LOMBARDI--GIANTS
9 BILL MAZEROSKI--PIRATES, CH, MARINERS CH
9 ENOS SLAUGHTER--CARDS
9 ARKY VAUGHAN--DODGERS
9 LLOYD WANER--DODGERS
9 PAUL WANER--PIRATES
9 TED WILLIAMS--RED SOX, SENATORS M, RANGERS M

Paul Waner wore seven different numbers with five clubs during his Hall of Fame career. From 1940-45 he was on four teams and wore numbers 9, 31, 8, 1, 24 and 22. All this after wearing #11 for eight years with the Pirates.

10 SPARKY ANDERSON--PADRES CH, REDS M
10 BILL DICKEY--YANKEES
10 LEO DUROCHER--REDS
10 RICK FERRELL--SENATORS
10 LEFTY GROVE--A's, RED SOX
10 CARL HUBBELL--GIANTS
10 WALTER JOHNSON--INDIANS M
10 AL LOPEZ--DODGERS, INDIANS M, WHITE SOX M
10 JOHNNY MIZE--CARDS
10 PHIL RIZZUTO--YANKEES
10 RED SCHOENDIENST--GIANTS
10 AL SIMMONS--RED SOX
10 LLOYD WANER--PIRATES

11 SPARKY ANDERSON--TIGERS M
11 LUIS APARICIO--WHITE SOX, ORIOLES, RED SOX
11 RICK FERRELL--BROWNS
11 LEFTY GOMEZ--YANKEES
11 CHICK HAFEY--REDS
11 BILLY HERMAN--PIRATES •M
11 ROGERS HORNSBY--BROWNS •M
11 WAITE HOYT--YANKEES
11 CARL HUBBELL--GIANTS
11 TONY LAZZERI--DODGERS
11 EDDIE MATHEWS--ASTROS
11 HERB PENNOCK--YANKEES
11 DUKE SNIDER--METS
11 PAUL WANER--PIRATES
11 EARLY WYNN--SENATORS

12 WADE BOGGS--YANKEES, D-RAYS
12 ORLANDO CEPEDA--A's
12 WAITE HOYT--YANKEES
12 HARMON KILLEBREW--SENATORS
12 FRED LINDSTROM--PIRATES
12 AL LOPEZ--PIRATES, INDIANS
12 JOE MORGAN--COLT 45's
12 HERB PENNOCK--YANKEES

13 ROBERTO CLEMENTE--PIRATES
13 BURLEIGH GRIMES--DODGERS M

14 ERNIE BANKS--CUBS, •CH, CH
14 JIM BUNNING--TIGERS, PHILS, PIRATES
14 ORLANDO CEPEDA--WHITE SOX CH
14 LARRY DOBY--INDIANS, WHITE SOX, EXPOS CH, WHITE SOX CH/M
14 BOB FELLER--INDIANS
14 RICK FERRELL--SENATORS CH
14 CHICK HAFEY--REDS
14 WAITE HOYT--TIGERS
14 GEORGE KELLY--DODGERS
14 CHUCK KLEIN--PIRATES
14 TED LYONS--WHITE SOX
14 HEINIE MANUSH--PIRATES

15 JIM BUNNING--TIGERS
15 WAITE HOYT--DODGERS
15 GEORGE KELL--TIGERS
15 TONY LAZZERI--CUBS •CH
15 JOHNNY MIZE--GIANTS
15 SATCHEL PAIGE--NEG
15 RED RUFFING--YANKEES
15 DAZZY VANCE--DODGERS
15 LLOYD WANER--PIRATES
15 HOYT WILHELM--ORIOLES

16 WADE BOGGS--RED SOX
16 WHITEY FORD--YANKEES, •CH, CH
16 JIMMIE FOXX--CUBS
16 BURLEIGH GRIMES--CUBS
16 JESSE HAINES--CARDS
16 BILLY HERMAN--DODGERS
16 ROGERS HORNSBY--BROWNS •M
16 TED LYONS--WHITE SOX, •M, M
16 DUCKY MEDWICK--DODGERS
16 HAL NEWHOUSER--TIGERS, INDIANS
16 HERB PENNOCK--YANKEES
16 WARREN SPAHN--BRAVES

17 COOL PAPA BELL--NEG
17 JIM BUNNING--DODGERS
17 DIZZY DEAN--CARDS
17 LARRY DOBY--EXPOS CH
17 ERNIE LOMBARDI--REDS
17 HERB PENNOCK--RED SOX
17 ENOS SLAUGHTER--YANKEES
17 DAZZY VANCE--REDS

18 RED FABER--WHITE SOX
18 NELLIE FOX--A's
18 BURLEIGH GRIMES--CUBS
18 MONTE IRVIN--NEG
18 JOE MORGAN--ASTROS
18 EPPA RIXEY--REDS
18 RED RUFFING--YANKEES
18 DAZZY VANCE--CARDS

19 RED FABER--WHITE SOX
19 BOB FELLER--INDIANS
19 WHITEY FORD--YANKEES
19 WAITE HOYT--GIANTS
19 FERGUSON JENKINS--RANGERS
19 TONY LAZZERI--GIANTS
19 DUCKY MEDWICK--GIANTS
19 PAUL MOLITOR--BLUE JAYS
19 SATCHEL PAIGE--NEG
19 DAZZY VANCE--CARDS
19 ROBIN YOUNT--BREWERS, D-BACKS CH

20 LOU BROCK--CARDS
20 ORLANDO CEPEDA--BRAVES
20 JOSH GIBSON--NEG
20 LEFTY GOMEZ--YANKEES
20 GOOSE GOSLIN--SENATORS
20 BURLEIGH GRIMES--CARDS, YANKS
20 BILLY HERMAN--BRAVES
20 MONTE IRVIN--GIANTS
20 BOB LEMON--ANGELS CH
20 FRANK ROBINSON--REDS, ORIOLES, CH, M, ANGELS, INDIANS, •M, M, GIANTS M
20 MIKE SCHMIDT--PHILLIES
20 AL SIMMONS--BRAVES
20 DON SUTTON--DODGERS, ASTROS, BREWERS, A's, ANGELS
20 PIE TRAYNOR--PIRATES, •M, M
20 EARLY WYNN--SENATORS

21 WALTER ALSTON--CARDS
21 ROD CAREW--TWINS
21 ROBERTO CLEMENTE--PIRATES
21 BURLEIGH GRIMES--CUBS
21 ROGERS HORNSBY--CUBS •M
21 GEORGE KELL--TIGERS
21 BOB LEMON--INDIANS, CH, ROYALS M, YANKEES CH, M, WHITE SOX M
21 JUAN MARICHAL--RED SOX
21 DUCKY MEDWICK--CARDS
21 BROOKS ROBINSON--ORIOLES
21 RED RUFFING--YANKEES
21 JOE SEWELL--YANKEES
21 WARREN SPAHN--BRAVES, METS •CH, GIANTS, INDIANS CH
21 DON SUTTON--BREWERS
21 DAZZY VANCE--DODGERS
21 ARKY VAUGHAN--PIRATES

22 DIZZY DEAN--CUBS
22 LEFTY GOMEZ--YANKEES
22 BILLY HERMAN--DODGERS CH, ANGELS CH, PADRES CH
22 SATCHEL PAIGE--BROWNS
22 JIM PALMER--ORIOLES
22 GAYLORD PERRY--GIANTS
22 SAM RICE--SENATORS
22 RED RUFFING--YANKEES
22 MIKE SCHMIDT--PHILS
22 PAUL WANER--YANKEES

23 RED FABER--WHITE SOX CH
23 BURLIEGH GRIMES--PIRATES
23 TOMMY LASORDA--A's
23 TONY LAZZERI--YANKEES
23 RYNE SANDBERG--CUBS

24 WALTER ALSTON--DODGERS M
24 EARL AVERILL--TIGERS
24 COOL PAPA BELL--NEG
24 LOU BROCK--CUBS
24 BUCKY HARRIS--PHILS M
24 WILLIE MAYS--GIANTS, METS, CH
24 TONY PEREZ--REDS, CH/M, EXPOS, PHILS
24 RYNE SANDBERG--PHILLIES
24 PAUL WANER--DODGERS, YANKEES
24 EARLY WYNN--INDIANS, WHITE SOX

25 GEORGE BRETT--ROYALS
25 ORLANDO CEPEDA--RED SOX
25 KIKI CUYLER--DODGERS
25 LARRY DOBY--TIGERS
25 WALTER JOHNSON--SENATORS M
25 AL KALINE--TIGERS
25 HARMON KILLEBREW--SENATORS
25 ENOS SLAUGHTER--BRAVES
25 HOYT WILHELM--CARDS

26 WADE BOGGS--RED SOX
26 NELLIE FOX--WHITE SOX
26 JIMMIE FOXX--CUBS, •CH
26 CHUCK KLEIN--PHILLIES, CH
26 HEINIE MANUSH--DODGERS
26 HOYT WILHELM--INDIANS
26 BILLY WILLIAMS--CUBS, CH
26 EARLY WYNN--SENATORS

27 EARL AVERILL--TIGERS
27 CARLTON FISK--RED SOX
27 BUCKY HARRIS--RED SOX M
27 JIM "CATFISH" HUNTER--A's
27 TOMMY LASORDA--DODGERS
27 ERNIE LOMBARDI--REDS
27 JUAN MARICHAL--GIANTS
27 JOE SEWELL--YANKEES
27 DON SUTTON--A's, ANGELS
27 LLOYD WANER--REDS

28 ORLANDO CEPEDA--CARDS
28 NELLIE FOX--A's
28 BUCKY HARRIS--SENATORS M
28 WAITE HOYT--A's
28 WALTER JOHNSON--SENATORS M
28 DUCKY MEDWICK--CARDS
28 GAYLORD PERRY--GIANTS
28 AL SIMMONS--A's •CH, CH
28 DUKE SNIDER--GIANTS
28 BILLY WILLIAMS--A's, CH

29 ROD CAREW--TWINS, ANGELS, CH
29 OSCAR CHARLESTON--NEG
29 JIM "CATFISH" HUNTER--YANKEES
29 CHUCK KLEIN--PHILLIES
29 TOMMY LASORDA--DODGERS
29 SATCHEL PAIGE--INDIANS, BROWNS, A's
29 SAM RICE--INDIANS

30 ORLANDO CEPEDA--GIANTS, CARDS, BRAVES, ROYALS
30 EARLE COMBS--YANKEES CH
30 KIKI CUYLER--RED SOX CH
30 BUCKY HARRIS--SENATORS M
30 FERGUSON JENKINS--PHILS
30 GEORGE KELLY--REDS CH
30 BILL MAZEROSKI--MARINERS CH
30 BILL McKECHNIE--BRAVES M
30 NOLAN RYAN--METS, ANGELS
30 JOE SEWELL--YANKEES CH
30 BILL TERRY--GIANTS M

31 LUKE APPLING--TIGERS CH
31 EDDIE COLLINS--A's CH
31 EARLE COMBS--PHILLIES CH
31 DIZZY DEAN--BROWNS
31 BOBBY DOERR--RED SOX CH, BLUE JAYS CH
31 BOB GIBSON--CARDS
31 LEFTY GOMEZ--SENATORS
31 REGGIE JACKSON--A's
31 TRAVIS JACKSON--GIANTS CH
31 FERGUSON JENKINS--CUBS, CH, RANGERS, RED SOX
31 SATCHEL PAIGE--INDIANS
31 HERB PENNOCK--RED SOX CH
31 CASEY STENGEL--DODGERS CH, M, BRAVES M
31 PAUL WANER--BRAVES
31 HOYT WILHELM--WHITE SOX, DODGERS
31 DAVE WINFIELD--PADRES, YANKS, INDIANS

32 STEVE CARLTON--CARDS, PHILLIES, GIANTS, WHITE SOX, INDIANS
32 MICKEY COCHRANE--A's CH
32 EARLE COMBS--YANKEES CH, RED SOX CH
32 LARRY DOBY--WHITE SOX
32 RICK FERRELL--SENATORS CH
32 ROLLIE FINGERS--A's
32 JESSE HAINES--DODGERS CH
32 BUCKY HARRIS--TIGERS M
32 GEORGE KELLY--BRAVES CH
32 CHUCK KLEIN--PHILS
32 SANDY KOUFAX--DODGERS
32 BUCK LEONARD--NEG
32 AL SIMMONS--A's •CH, CH
32 OZZIE SMITH--PADRES
32 CASEY STENGEL--BRAVES M
32 DAVE WINFIELD--ANGELS, BLUE JAYS, TWINS
32 EARLY WYNN--WHITE SOX

33 LUKE APPLING--A's M
33 ROY CAMPANELLA--DODGERS
33 MAX CAREY--DODGERS M
33 BILL DICKEY--YANKEES CH
33 BURLEIGH GRIMES--DODGERS M
33 GEORGE KELLY--REDS CH, BRAVES CH
33 BOB LEMON--YANKEES CH
33 TED LYONS--TIGERS CH, DODGERS CH
33 BILL McKECHNIE--BRAVES M
33 EDDIE MURRAY--ORIOLES, CH, DODGERS, METS, INDIANS, ANGELS
33 FRANK ROBINSON--INDIANS
33 ENOS SLAUGHTER--A's
33 HONUS WAGNER--PIRATES CH

34 LOU BOUDREAU--INDIANS
34 ROLLIE FINGERS--A's, PADRES, BREWERS
34 BUCKY HARRIS--TIGERS •M
34 WAITE HOYT--DODGERS
34 BILL McKECHNIE--BRAVES M
34 KIRBY PUCKETT--TWINS
34 BROOKS ROBINSON--ORIOLES
34 RED RUFFING--WHITE SOX
34 NOLAN RYAN--METS, ASTROS, RANGERS
34 PIE TRAYNOR--PIRATES M
34 LLOYD WANER--PHILS
34 HACK WILSON--PHILS

35 YOGI BERRA--YANKEES
35 FRANKIE FRISCH--PIRATES M
35 BUCKY HARRIS--SENATORS M
35 BILLY HERMAN--RED SOX CH
35 ROGERS HORNSBY--CUBS CH
35 ERNIE LOMBARDI--REDS
35 JOE MORGAN--COLT 45's
35 PHIL NIEKRO--BRAVES, YANKS, INDIANS, BLUE JAYS
35 GAYLORD PERRY--GIANTS
35 BABE RUTH--DODGERS CH
35 PIE TRAYNOR--PIRATES M
35 HONUS WAGNER--PIRATES CH
35 HOYT WILHELM--CUBS

36 RICK FERRELL--TIGERS •CH, CH
36 CHUCK KLEIN--PHILLIES
36 HEINIE MANUSH--PIRATES
36 JOHNNY MIZE--YANKEES
36 GAYLORD PERRY--GIANTS, INDIANS, RANGERS, PADRES, YANKEES, BRAVES, MARINERS, ROYALS
36 ROBIN ROBERTS--PHILLIES, CUBS
36 FRANK ROBINSON--DODGERS
36 CASEY STENGEL--DODGERS M
36 HONUS WAGNER--PIRATES CH

37 STEVE CARLTON--WHITE SOX
37 LARRY DOBY--INDIANS
37 DENNIS ECKERSLEY--INDIANS
37 RICK FERRELL--SENATORS CH
37 BUCKY HARRIS--YANKEES M
37 TONY PEREZ--PHILS
37 CASEY STENGEL--YANKEES M, METS M
37 LLOYD WANER--BRAVES

38 JIM BUNNING--DODGERS
38 STEVE CARLTON--TWINS
38 YOGI BERRA--YANKEES
38 KIKI CUYLER--CUBS CH
38 ROLLIE FINGERS--TIGERS
38 EARL AVERILL--A's
38 BOB LEMON--INDIANS
38 EARLY WYNN--INDIANS

39 ROY CAMPANELLA--DODGERS
39 MONTE IRVIN--CUBS
39 JOHNNY MIZE--A's CH
39 HOYT WILHELM--ANGELS, BRAVES, CUBS

40 LUKE APPLING--INDIANS CH
40 DENNIS ECKERSLEY--CUBS
40 CARLTON FISK--RED SOX
40 BILL McKECHNIE--RED SOX CH

41 LUKE APPLING--ORIOLES CH
41 JIM BUNNING--TIGERS
41 EARLE COMBS--RED SOX CH
41 CARLTON FISK--RED SOX
41 NELLIE FOX--A's
41 EDDIE MATHEWS--BRAVES, CH, M
41 BILL McKECHNIE--INDIANS CH
41 EDDIE MATHEWS--BRAVES, CH, M
41 BILL McKECHNIE--INDIANS CH
41 TOM SEAVER--METS, REDS, WHITE SOX, RED SOX
41 BILLY WILLIAMS--CUBS

42 KIKI CUYLER--CUBS CH
42 NELLIE FOX--SENATORS CH
42 ROGERS HORNSBY--BROWNS M
42 BOB LEMON--INDIANS
42 AL LOPEZ--WHITE SOX M
42 JACKIE ROBINSON--DODGERS

43 DENNIS ECKERSLEY--RED SOX,CUBS A's, CARDS
43 BURLEIGH GRIMES--A's CH
43 RALPH KINER--PIRATES
43 RED SCHOENDIENST--A's CH

44 HANK AARON--BRAVES, BREWERS
44 LUKE APPLING--A's CH
44 REGGIE JACKSON--YANKEES, ANGELS, A's, CH
44 WILLIE McCOVEY--GIANTS, PADRES, A's
44 JOHNNY MIZE--A's CH
44 RED RUFFING--INDIANS CH
44 AL SIMMONS--INDIANS CH
44 EARLY WYNN--SENATORS

45 SPARKY ANDERSON--PHILS
45 BOB GIBSON--CARDS

46 FERGUSON JENKINS--PHILS
46 JUAN MARICHAL--DODGERS
46 SATCHEL PAIGE--BROWNS
46 GAYLORD PERRY--BRAVES

47 HOYT WILHELM--BRAVES
47 EARLY WYNN--TWINS CH

48 GABBY HARTNETT--A's CH
48 WAITE HOYT--PIRATES

49 HOYT WILHELM--GIANTS

50 BUCKY HARRIS--SENATORS M
50 ROGERS HORNSBY--REDS M

51 HEINIE MANUSH--SENATORS CH
51 BILL MAZEROSKI--MARINERS CH
51 BILLY WILLIAMS--INDIANS CH

52 TOMMY LASORDA--DODGERS CH

53 DON DRYSDALE--DODGERS
53 ROGERS HORNSBY--METS CH
53 EARLY WYNN--TWINS CH

54 RED RUFFING--METS CH

55 LUKE APPLING--BRAVES CH

56 ROY CAMPANELLA--DODGERS

57 GARY CARTER--EXPOS
57 ROGERS HORNSBY--CUBS CH

58 BOB GIBSON--CARDS

65 BILL McKECHNIE--REDS M
65 SATCHEL PAIGE--BRAVES CH

67 EDD ROUSH--REDS CH

72 CARLTON FISK--WHITE SOX

77 DUCKY MEDWICK--DODGERS

If we were to count the Hall of Fame members who as players, coaches and managers wore the uniform of a particular team, some interesting facts would surface.

For instance, of the 260 members, a full sixty of them wore a Giant uniform at one time or another during their careers. That includes the Giants of San Francisco as well as New York. That's far and away the most of any major league franchises. Nearly one-fourth of the membership were Giants!

The Dodgers of Brooklyn and LA added a fiftieth Hall of Famer in 2003. The third most often worn uniform (48) belonged to a National League franchise also—one that hop-scotched around the country from Boston to Milwaukee to Atlanta. That's right—the Braves.

The Chicago Cubs have 44 members and Cincinnati has 40. All of these clubs at least match any American League team.

The Yankees who lead the junior circuit with 40 members passing through the pin-stripes at one time or other while the A's of Philadelphia, Kansas City and Oakland as well as the Boston Red Sox have 39.

The St. Louis Cardinals claim 39 while the Phillies have 36 and the Pirates 35.

The last of the long-established clubs are all in the American League: the Cleveland Indians show 32 members, the Chicago White Sox have 27, while the St. Louis Browns/Baltimore Orioles and the Detroit Tigers have 26. The Washington Senators/Minnesota Twins have 22.

Most of the expansion teams show representation also. Thirteen Hall of Famers have worn the New York Mets colors. The Angels have ten. The Houston Astros have eight. Six members have worn the uniform of the San Diego Padres. There are five Washington Senators/Texas Rangers, Kansas City Royals and Milwaukee Brewers. Hugh Duffy played for and managed the original Milwaukee Brewers who existed for one year (1901), but they moved to St. Louis and became the Browns the next season.

Paul Molitor, Phil Niekro and Dave Winfield represent the Toronto Blue Jays as well as a coach—Bobby Doerr.

When Gaylord Perry was inducted into the Hall, he gave the Seattle Mariners their only representation.

It took the turn of the century for the Expos to gain any Hall members—Tony Perez in 2000 and Gary Carter in 2003. Even the Devil Rays have one—Wade Boggs.

The other expansion teams, the Diamond-backs, Marlins, and Rockies have yet to be honored in the Hall, but they will be of course.

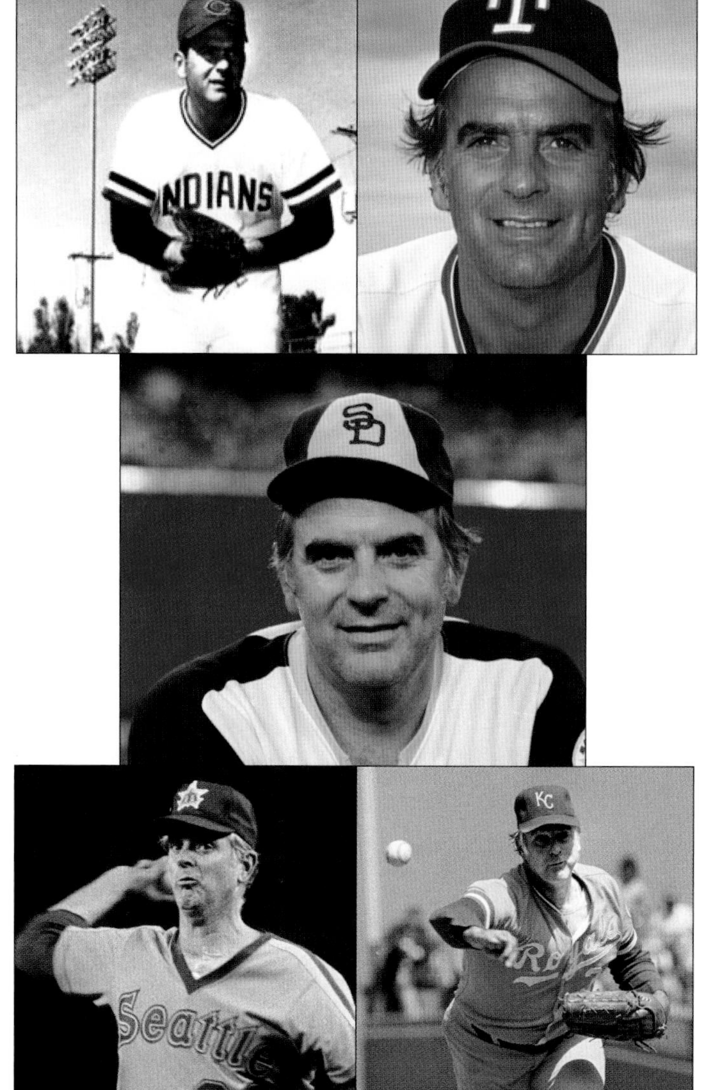

Gaylord Perry wore eight different uniforms while working his way to the Hall of Fame. Here we see five of them. His first club was as one of the 60 Giants in the Hall, then on to the Indians (Top, left), the Rangers (Top, right), Padres (Center), (back to the Rangers), on to the Yankees, the Braves, the Mariners (Bottom, left) and finally the Royals (Bottom, right). He wore #36 with each club. He led the league in wins three times with three different teams, had five 20+ victory seasons and two 19-win years, was tops in complete games two years running, had most shutouts once, most innings twice in a row and finished up with 314-265 lifetime. This Carolina farmboy was quite a workhorse himself.

THE HALL-- BY TEAM

AMERICAN LEAGUE

In the interest of space, only key positions are listed. Particular team in parentheses after entry. If the player followed a franchise move, it is indicated.

ST. LOUIS BROWNS *(15)*
BALTIMORE ORIOLES *(11)* **(26)**
LUIS APARICIO--SS *(BAL)*
LUKE APPLING--CH *(BAL)*
JIM BOTTOMLEY--1B, •CH, •M *(STL)*
JESSE BURKETT--OF *(STL)*
EARLE COMBS--CH *(STL)*
DIZZY DEAN--P *(STL)*
HUGH DUFFY--OF, •M *(STL)*
RICK FERRELL--C *(STL)*
GOOSE GOSLIN--OF *(STL)*
ROGERS HORNSBY--UTIL, •M, M *(STL)*
REGGIE JACKSON--OF *(BAL)*
GEORGE KELL--INF *(BAL)*
HEINIE MANUSH--OF *(STL)*
EDDIE MURRAY--1B *(BAL)*
SATCHEL PAIGE--P *(STL)*
JIM PALMER--P *(BAL)*
EDDIE PLANK--P *(STL)*
BRANCH RICKEY--C, UTIL, •M, M *(STL)*
ROBIN ROBERTS--P *(BAL)*
BROOKS ROBINSON--3B, CH *(BAL)*
FRANK ROBINSON--OF, CH, M *(BAL)*
GEORGE SISLER--1B, •M *(STL)*
RUBE WADDELL--P *(STL)*
BOBBY WALLACE--SS, •M *(STL)*
EARL WEAVER--M *(BAL)*
HOYT WILHELM--P *(BAL)*

BOSTON RED SOX (39)
LUIS APARICIO--SS
ED BARROW--M
WADE BOGGS--3B
LOU BOUDREAU--INF, •M, M
JESSE BURKETT--OF
ORLANDO CEPEDA--DH
FRANK CHANCE--M
JACK CHESBRO--P
JIMMY COLLINS--3B, •M
EARLE COMBS--CH
JOE CRONIN--SS, •M, M
KIKI CUYLER--CH
BOBBY DOERR--2B, CH
HUGH DUFFY--M, CH
DENNIS ECKERSLEY--P
RICK FERRELL--C
CARLTON FISK--C
JIMMIE FOXX--1B
LEFTY GROVE--P
BUCKY HARRIS--M
BILLY HERMAN--M, CH
HARRY HOOPER--OF
WAITE HOYT--P
FERGUSON JENKINS--P
GEORGE KELL--3B
HEINIE MANUSH--OF
JUAN MARICHAL--P
JOE McCARTHY--M
BILL McKECHNIE--CH
HERB PENNOCK--P, CH
TONY PEREZ--1B
RED RUFFING--P
BABE RUTH--P
TOM SEAVER--P
AL SIMMONS--OF
TRIS SPEAKER--OF
TED WILLIAMS--OF
CARL YASTRZEMSKI--OF
CY YOUNG--P, •M

LA/CALIFORNIA/ANAHEIM ANGELS (10)
ROD CAREW--1B *(CAL)*
BILLY HERMAN--CH *(CAL)*
REGGIE JACKSON--OF *(CAL)*
BOB LEMON--CH *(CAL)*
EDDIE MURRAY--1B *(ANA)*
FRANK ROBINSON--OF, CH *(CAL)*
NOLAN RYAN--P *(CAL)*
DON SUTTON--P *(CAL)*
HOYT WILHELM--P *(CAL)*
DAVE WINFIELD--OF *(CAL)*

CHICAGO WHITE SOX (27)
LUIS APARICIO--SS
LUKE APPLING--SS, CH
CHIEF BENDER--P, CH
STEVE CARLTON--P
EDDIE COLLINS--2B, •M
JOCKO CONLAN--OF
GEORGE DAVIS--SS
LARRY DOBY--OF
HUGH DUFFY--M
JOHNNY EVERS--M, CH
RED FABER--P, CH
CARLTON FISK--C
NELLIE FOX--2B
CLARK GRIFFITH--P, •M
HARRY HOOPER--OF
GEORGE KELL--3B
BOB LEMON--M
AL LOPEZ--M
TED LYONS--P, •M, M
EDD ROUSH--OF
RED RUFFING--P
RAY SCHALK--C, •M
TOM SEAVER--P
AL SIMMONS--OF
ED WALSH--P, M, CH
HOYT WILHELM--P
EARLY WYNN--P

CLEVELAND INDIANS (32)
LUKE APPLING--CH
EARL AVERILL--OF
LOU BOUDREAU--SS, •M
STEVE CARLTON--P
STAN COVELESKI--P
GEORGE DAVIS--SS
LARRY DOBY--OF
DENNIS ECKERSLEY--P
BOB FELLER--P
ELMER FLICK--OF
WALTER JOHNSON--M
ADDIE JOSS--P
RALPH KINER--OF
NAP LAJOIE--2B, •M
BOB LEMON--P, CH
AL LOPEZ--C, M
BILL McKECHNIE--CH
EDDIE MURRAY--1B
HAL NEWHOUSER--P
PHIL NIEKRO--P
SATCHEL PAIGE--P
GAYLORD PERRY--P
SAM RICE--OF
FRANK ROBINSON--OF, •M, M
JOE SEWELL--SS
AL SIMMONS--CH
WARREN SPAHN--CH
TRIS SPEAKER--OF, •M
HOYT WILHELM--P
DAVE WINFIELD--OF
EARLY WYNN--P, CH
CY YOUNG--P

DETROIT TIGERS (26)
SPARKY ANDERSON--M
LUKE APPLING--CH
EARL AVERILL--OF
ED BARROW--M
ROGER BRESNAHAN--CH
JIM BUNNING--P
TY COBB--OF, •M
MICKEY COCHRANE--C, •M, M
SAM CRAWFORD--OF
LARRY DOBY--OF
RICK FERRELL--CH, •CH
CHARLIE GEHRINGER--2B, •CH
GOOSE GOSLIN--OF
HANK GREENBERG--1B
BUCKY HARRIS--2B, •M, M
HARRY HEILMANN--OF
WAITE HOYT--P
HUGHIE JENNINGS--OF, •M, M
AL KALINE--OF
GEORGE KELL-3B
TED LYONS--CH
HEINIE MANUSH--OF
EDDIE MATHEWS--3B
HAL NEWHOUSER--P
AL SIMMONS--OF
SAM THOMPSON--OF

KANSAS CITY ROYALS (5)
GEORGE BRETT--3B
ORLANDO CEPEDA--DH
HARMON KILLEBREW--1B
BOB LEMON--M, CH
GAYLORD PERRY--P

MILWAUKEE BREWERS (5)
HANK AARON--DH
ROLLIE FINGERS--P
PAUL MOLITOR--3B/DH
DON SUTTON--P
ROBIN YOUNT--SS, OF

WASHINGTON SENATORS*(17)*
MINNESOTA TWINS *(6)* **(22)**
ROD CAREW--2B *(MIN)*
STEVE CARLTON--P *(MIN)*
JACK CHESBRO--CH *(WAS)*
STAN COVELESKI--P *(WAS)*
JOE CRONIN--SS, •M *(WAS)*
ED DELAHANTY--OF *(WAS)*
RICK FERRELL--C, CH, •CH *(WAS)*
LEFTY GOMEZ--P *(WAS)*
GOOSE GOSLIN--OF *(WAS)*
CLARK GRIFFITH--P, •M, M *(WAS)*
BUCKY HARRIS--2B, •M, M *(WAS)*
WALTER JOHNSON--P, M *(WAS)*
HARMON KILLEBREW--3B, 1B *(WAS/MIN)*
HEINIE MANUSH--OF, CH *(WAS)*
PAUL MOLITOR--DH *(MIN)*
KIRBY PUCKETT--OF *(MIN)*
SAM RICE--OF *(WAS)*
AL SIMMONS--OF *(WAS)*

AMERICAN LEAGUE *(Continued)*

GEORGE SISLER--1B, OF *(WAS)*
TRIS SPEAKER--OF *(WAS)*
DAVE WINFIELD--OF *(MIN)*
EARLY WYNN--P, CH *(WAS)*

NEW YORK YANKEES (40)
HOMERUN BAKER--3B
YOGI BERRA--C, M, CH
WADE BOGGS--3B
FRANK CHANCE--1B, •M
JACK CHESBRO--P
EARLE COMBS--OF, CH
STAN COVELESKI--P
BILL DICKEY--C, M, CH
JOE DIMAGGIO--OF
LEO DUROCHER--SS
WHITEY FORD--P, CH
LOU GEHRIG--1B
LEFTY GOMEZ--P
CLARK GRIFFITH--P, •M, M
BURLEIGH GRIMES--P
BUCKY HARRIS--M
WAITE HOYT--P
MILLER HUGGINS--M
CATFISH HUNTER--P
REGGIE JACKSON--OF
WEE WILLIE KEELER--OF
TONY LAZZERI--2B
BOB LEMON--CH, M
MICKEY MANTLE--OF
JOE McCARTHY--M
BILL McKECHNIE--INF
JOHNNY MIZE--1B
PHIL NIEKRO--P
HERB PENNOCK--P
GAYLORD PERRY--P
BRANCH RICKEY--UTIL
PHIL RIZZUTO--SS
RED RUFFING--P
BABE RUTH--OF
JOE SEWELL--3B, CH
ENOS SLAUGHTER--OF
CASEY STENGEL--M
DAZZY VANCE--P
PAUL WANER--OF
DAVE WINFIELD--OF

PHILADELPHIA *(22)* **/KANSAS CITY** *(8)***/OAKLAND A's** *(11)* **(39)**
LUKE APPLING--CH, M *(KC)*
HOMERUN BAKER--3B *(PHI)*
CHIEF BENDER--P, CH *(PHI)*
LOU BOUDREAU--M *(KC)*
ORLANDO CEPEDA--DH *(OAK)*
TY COBB--OF *(PHI)*
MICKEY COCHRANE--C, CH *(PHI)*
EDDIE COLLINS--2B, CH *(PHI)*
JIMMY COLLINS--3B *(PHI)*
STAN COVELESKI--P *(PHI)*
JOE DIMAGGIO--CH *(OAK)*
DENNIS ECKERSLEY--P *(OAK)*
ROLLIE FINGERS--P *(OAK)*
ELMER FLICK--OF *(PHI)*
NELLIE FOX--2B *(PHI)*
JIMMIE FOXX--1B *(PHI)*
BURLEIGH GRIMES--CH *(KC)*
LEFTY GROVE--P *(PHI)*
GABBY HARTNETT--CH *(PHI)*
WAITE HOYT--P *(PHI)*
CATFISH HUNTER--P *(KC/OAK)*
REGGIE JACKSON--OF *(KC/OAK)*
GEORGE KELL--3B *(PHI)*
NAP LAJOIE--2B *(PHI)*
TOMMY LASORDA--P *(KC)*
CONNIE MACK--M *(PHI)*
WILLIE McCOVEY--1B *(OAK)*
JOE MORGAN--2B *(OAK)*
SATCHEL PAIGE--P *(KC)*
HERB PENNOCK--P *(PHI)*
EDDIE PLANK--P *(PHI)*
RED SCHOENDIENST--CH *(OAK)*
AL SIMMONS--OF, CH *(PHI)*
ENOS SLAUGHTER--OF *(KC)*
TRIS SPEAKER--OF *(PHI)*
DON SUTTON--P *(OAK)*
RUBE WADDELL--P *(PHI)*
ZACK WHEAT--OF *(PHI)*
BILLY WILLIAMS--OF, CH *(OAK)*

SEATTLE MARINERS (1)
GAYLORD PERRY--P

TAMPA BAY DEVIL RAYS (1)
WADE BOGGS--3B

WASHINGTON SENATORS *(2)* **/ TEXAS RANGERS** *(4)* **(5)**
NELLIE FOX--CH *(WAS)*
FERGUSON JENKINS--P *(TEX)*
GAYLORD PERRY--P *(TEX)*
NOLAN RYAN--P *(TEX)*
TED WILLIAMS--M *(WAS/TEX)*

TORONTO BLUE JAYS (4)
BOBBY DOERR--CH
PAUL MOLITOR--DH
PHIL NIEKRO--P
DAVE WINFIELD--OF

PHOTO: DOUG McWILLIAMS OAKLAND A'S

Joe DiMaggio (left) looking somewhat uncomfortable in an Oakland A's uniform, became a coach for their first two years on the West Coast. The Yankee Clipper was asked to make some of his magic rub off on their young star Reggie Jackson.
Bobby Doerr (right) coaching for the Blue Jays from 1977-81, was the first Toronto could claim as a Hall of Famer. Big Dave Winfield, Phil Niekro and Paul Molitor became their first bona fide players.

NATIONAL LEAGUE

BOSTON *(38)* **/ MILWAUKEE** *(7)* **/ ATLANTA BRAVES** *(8)* **(48)**

HANK AARON--OF *(MIL/ATL)*
EARL AVERILL--OF *(BOS)*
DAVE BANCROFT--SS, •M *(BOS)*
DAN BROUTHERS--1B *(BOS)*
ORLANDO CEPEDA--1B *(ATL)*
JOHN CLARKSON--P *(BOS)*
JIMMY COLLINS--3B *(BOS)*
HUGH DUFFY--OF *(BOS)*
JOHNNY EVERS--2B, CH *(BOS)*
BOB GIBSON--CH *(ATL)*
BURLEIGH GRIMES--P *(BOS)*
BILLY HAMILTON--OF *(BOS)*
BILLY HERMAN--INF, CH *(BOS, MIL)*
ROGERS HORNSBY--2B, •M *(BOS)*
JOE KELLEY--OF, M *(BOS)*
GEORGE KELLY--CH *(BOS)*
MIKE KELLY--OF, •M *(BOS)*
ERNIE LOMBARDI--C *(BOS)*
AL LOPEZ--C *(BOS)*
RABBIT MARANVILLE--SS *(BOS)*
RUBE MARQUARD--P *(BOS)*
EDDIE MATHEWS--3B *(BOS/MIL/ATL)* M, CH *(ATL)*
TOMMY McCARTHY--OF *(BOS)*
BILL McKECHNIE--3B, M *(BOS)*
DUCKY MEDWICK--OF *(BOS)*
KID NICHOLS--P *(BOS)*
PHIL NIEKRO--P *(MIL/ATL)*
JIM O'ROURKE--OF *(BOS)*
SATCHEL PAIGE--CH *(ATL)*
GAYLORD PERRY--P *(ATL)*
HOSS RADBOURNE--P *(BOS)*
BABE RUTH--CH *(BOS)*
RED SCHOENDIENST--2B *(MIL)*
FRANK SELEE--M *(BOS)*
AL SIMMONS--OF *(BOS)*
GEORGE SISLER--1B, •CH *(BOS)*
ENOS SLAUGHTER--OF *(MIL)*
WARREN SPAHN--P *(BOS/MIL)*
WILLIE STARGELL--CH *(ATL)*
CASEY STENGEL--OF, M *(BOS)*
ED WALSH--P *(BOS)*
LLOYD WANER--OF *(BOS)*
PAUL WANER--OF *(BOS)*
HOYT WILHELM--P *(ATL)*
VIC WILLIS--P *(BOS)*
GEORGE WRIGHT--SS *(BOS)*
HARRY WRIGHT--OF, •M, M *(BOS)*
CY YOUNG--P *(BOS)*

CHICAGO CUBS (44)

PETE ALEXANDER--P
CAP ANSON--1B, •M
RICHIE ASHBURN--OF
ERNIE BANKS--SS, 1B, CH
LOU BOUDREAU--M
ROGER BRESNAHAN--C, •M
LOU BROCK--OF
THREE-FINGER BROWN--P
FRANK CHANCE--1B, •M
JOHN CLARKSON--P
JIMMY COLLINS--CH
KIKI CUYLER--OF, CH
DIZZY DEAN--P
HUGH DUFFY--OF
LEO DUROCHER--M
DENNIS ECKERSLEY--P
JOHNNY EVERS--2B, •M, M
JIMMIE FOXX--1B
FRANKIE FRISCH--M
CLARK GRIFFITH--P
BURLEIGH GRIMES--P
GABBY HARTNETT--C, •M, •CH
BILLY HERMAN--2B
ROGERS HORNSBY--2B, •M
MONTE IRVIN--OF
FERGUSON JENKINS--P
GEORGE KELLY--1B
MIKE KELLY--OF
RALPH KINER--OF
CHUCK KLEIN--OF
TONY LAZZERI--2B, •CH
FRED LINDSTROM--3B
RABBIT MARANVILLE--SS, •M
JOE McCARTHY--M
ROBIN ROBERTS--P
RYNE SANDBERG--2B
RAY SCHALK--CH
FRANK SELEE--M
AL SPALDING--P, •M
JOE TINKER--SS, •M
RUBE WADDELL--P
HOYT WILHELM--P
BILLY WILLIAMS--OF, CH
HACK WILSON--OF

CINCINNATI REDS (39)

SPARKY ANDERSON--M
JAKE BECKLEY--1B
JOHNNY BENCH--C
JIM BOTTOMLEY--1B
THREE-FINGER BROWN--P
CHARLIE COMISKEY--1B, •M
SAM CRAWFORD--OF
CANDY CUMMINGS--P
KIKI CUYLER--OF
LEO DUROCHER--SS
BUCK EWING--C, •M, M
CLARK GRIFFITH--P, •M, M
CHICK HAFEY--OF
NED HANLON--OF, •M ,M
JESSE HAINES--P
HARRY HEILMANN--OF, •CH
ROGERS HORNSBY--M
MILLER HUGGINS--2B
JOE KELLEY--OF, •M
GEORGE KELLY--CH
MIKE KELLY--OF
ERNIE LOMBARDI--C
RUBE MARQUARD--P
CHRISTY MATHEWSON--P, •M, M
BILL McKECHNIE--3B, M
BID McPHEE--2B
JOE MORGAN--2B
TONY PEREZ--1B
HOSS RADBOURNE--P
EPPA RIXEY--P
FRANK ROBINSON--OF
EDD ROUSH--OF, CH
AMOS RUSIE--P
TOM SEAVER--P
AL SIMMONS--OF
JOE TINKER--SS, •M
DAZZY VANCE--P
BOBBY WALLACE--M, CH
LLOYD WANER--OF

COLORADO ROCKIES (0)

FLORIDA MARLINS (0)

HOUSTON COLT .45s*(2)* **/ HOUSTON ASTROS** *(7)* **(8)**

YOGI BERRA--CH *(ASTROS)*
LEO DUROCHER--M *(ASTROS)*
NELLIE FOX--2B *(COLT 45's)*, 2B, •CH,CH *(ASTROS)*
EDDIE MATHEWS--3B *(ASTROS)*
JOE MORGAN--2B *(COLT 45's/ASTROS)*
ROBIN ROBERTS--P *(ASTROS)*
NOLAN RYAN--P *(ASTROS)*
DON SUTTON--P *(ASTROS)*

BROOKLYN *(43)* **/ LOS ANGELES DODGERS** *(14)* **(50)**

WALTER ALSTON--M *(BKN/LA)*
DAVE BANCROFT--SS *(BKN)*
DAN BROUTHERS--1B *(BKN)*
JIM BUNNING--P *(LA)*
ROY CAMPANELLA--C *(BKN)*
MAX CAREY--OF, M *(BKN)*
GARY CARTER--C *(LA)*
KIKI CUYLER--OF *(BKN)*
DON DRYSDALE--P *(BKN/LA)*
LEO DUROCHER--SS, •M, M, CH *(BKN/LA)*
BURLEIGH GRIMES--P, M *(BKN)*
JESSE HAINES--CH *(BKN)*
NED HANLON--OF, •M, M *(BKN)*
BILLY HERMAN--2B, CH *(BKN)*
WAITE HOYT--P *(BKN)*
HUGHIE JENNINGS--UTIL *(BKN)*
WEE WILLIE KEELER--OF *(BKN)*
JOE KELLEY--OF *(BKN)*
GEORGE KELLY--1B *(BKN)*
SANDY KOUFAX--P *(BKN/LA)*
TOMMY LASORDA--P *(BKN)*, CH, M *(LA)*
TONY LAZZERI--2B *(BKN)*
FRED LINDSTROM--OF *(BKN)*
ERNIE LOMBARDI--C *(BKN)*
AL LOPEZ--C *(BKN)*
TED LYONS--CH *(BKN)*
HEINIE MANUSH--OF *(BKN)*
RABBIT MARANVILLE--SS *(BKN)*
JUAN MARICHAL--P *(LA)*
RUBE MARQUARD--P *(BKN)*
TOMMY McCARTHY--OF *(BKN)*
JOE McGINNITY--P, CH *(BKN)*
DUCKY MEDWICK--OF *(BKN)*
EDDIE MURRAY--1B *(LA)*

NATIONAL LEAGUE *(Continued)*

PEEWEE REESE--SS, CH *(BKN/LA)*
FRANK ROBINSON--OF *(LA)*
JACKIE ROBINSON--2B *(BKN)*
WILBERT ROBINSON--M *(BKN)*
BABE RUTH--CH *(BKN)*
DUKE SNIDER--OF *(BKN/LA)*
CASEY STENGEL--OF, M, CH *(BKN)*
DON SUTTON--P *(LA)*
DAZZY VANCE--P *(BKN)*
ARKY VAUGHAN--3B *(BKN)*
LLOYD WANER--OF *(BKN)*
PAUL WANER--OF *(BKN)*
MONTE WARD--SS, •M *(BKN)*
ZACK WHEAT--OF *(BKN)*
HOYT WILHELM--P *(LA)*
HACK WILSON--OF *(BKN)*

NEW YORK METS (13)
RICHIE ASHBURN--OF
YOGI BERRA--M, CH
GARY CARTER--C
BOB GIBSON--CH
ROGERS HORNSBY--CH
WILLIE MAYS--OF, CH
EDDIE MURRAY--1B
RED RUFFING--CH
NOLAN RYAN--P
TOM SEAVER--P
DUKE SNIDER--OF
WARREN SPAHN--P, •CH
CASEY STENGEL--M

PHILADELPHIA PHILLIES (35)
SPARKY ANDERSON--2B
PETE ALEXANDER--P
RICHIE ASHBURN--OF
DAVE BANCROFT--SS
CHIEF BENDER--P
DAN BROUTHERS--1B
JIM BUNNING--P
STEVE CARLTON--P
EARLE COMBS--CH
ROGER CONNOR--1B
ED DELAHANTY--OF
HUGH DUFFY--OF, •M
JOHNNY EVERS--2B
ELMER FLICK--OF
JIMMIE FOXX--1B
BILLY HAMILTON--OF
BUCKY HARRIS--M
FERGUSON JENKINS--P
HUGHIE JENNINGS--SS
TIM KEEFE--P
CHUCK KLEIN--OF, •CH, CH
NAP LAJOIE--2B
BOB LEMON--CH
TOMMY McCARTHY--OF
JOE MORGAN--2B
KID NICHOLS--P
TONY PEREZ--1B
EPPA RIXEY--P
ROBIN ROBERTS--P
RYNE SANDBERG--2B
MIKE SCHMIDT--3B
CASEY STENGEL--OF
SAM THOMPSON--OF
LLOYD WANER--OF
HACK WILSON--OF
HARRY WRIGHT--M

PITTSBURGH PIRATES (35)
JAKE BECKLEY--1B
JIM BUNNING--P
MAX CAREY--OF, CH
JACK CHESBRO--P
FRED CLARKE--OF, •M
ROBERTO CLEMENTE--OF
JOE CRONIN--INF
KIKI CUYLER--OF
FRANKIE FRISCH--M
PUD GALVIN--P
HANK GREENBERG--1B
BURLEIGH GRIMES--P
BILLY HERMAN--2B, •M
WAITE HOYT--P
JOE KELLEY--OF
GEORGE KELLY--1B
RALPH KINER--OF
CHUCK KLEIN--OF
FRED LINDSTROM--3B
AL LOPEZ--C
CONNIE MACK--C, •M
HEINIE MANUSH--OF
RABBIT MARANVILLE--SS
BILL MAZEROSKI--2B
BILL McKECHNIE--3B, M, CH
WILLIE STARGELL--1B, CH
CASEY STENGEL--OF
PIE TRAYNOR--3B, •M, M
DAZZY VANCE--P
ARKY VAUGHAN--SS
RUBE WADDELL--P
HONUS WAGNER--SS, •M, CH
LLOYD WANER--OF
PAUL WANER--OF
VIC WILLIS--P

ST. LOUIS CARDINALS (39)
PETE ALEXANDER--P
WALTER ALSTON--1B
JAKE BECKLEY--1B
JIM BOTTOMLEY--1B, CH
ROGER BRESNAHAN--C, •M
LOU BROCK--OF
THREE-FINGER BROWN--P
JESSE BURKETT--OF
STEVE CARLTON--P
ORLANDO CEPEDA--1B
ROGER CONNOR--1B, •M
DIZZY DEAN--P
LEO DUROCHER--SS
DENNIS ECKERSLEY--P
FRANKIE FRISCH--2B, •M, M
PUD GALVIN--P
BOB GIBSON--P
BURLEIGH GRIMES--P
CHICK HAFEY--OF
JESSE HAINES--P
ROGERS HORNSBY--2B, •M
MILLER HUGGINS-2B, •M, M
RABBIT MARANVILLE--SS
JOHN McGRAW--3B
BILL McKECHNIE--M, CH
DUCKY MEDWICK--OF
JOHNNY MIZE--1B
STAN MUSIAL--OF
KID NICHOLS--P, •M
BRANCH RICKEY--M
WILBERT ROBINSON--C
RED SCHOENDIENST-2B, M, CH
ENOS SLAUGHTER--OF
OZZIE SMITH--SS
DAZZY VANCE--P
BOBBY WALLACE--SS
HOYT WILHELM--P
VIC WILLIS--P
CY YOUNG--P

SAN DIEGO PADRES (6)
ROLLIE FINGERS--P
BILLY HERMAN--CH
WILLIE McCOVEY--1B
GAYLORD PERRY--P
OZZIE SMITH-SS
DAVE WINFIELD--OF

NEW YORK *(50)* / SAN FRANCISCO GIANTS *(11)* (60)
CAP ANSON--M *(NY)*
DAVE BANCROFT--SS, CH *(NY)*
JAKE BECKLEY--1B *(NY)*
CHIEF BENDER--CH *(NY)*
ROGER BRESNAHAN--C, CH *(NY)*
DAN BROUTHERS--1B *(NY)*
JESSE BURKETT--OF *(NY)*
STEVE CARLTON--P *(SF)*
GARY CARTER--C *(SF)*
ORLANDO CEPEDA--1B *(SF)*
ROGER CONNOR--1B *(NY)*
GEORGE DAVIS--SS *(NY)*
LEO DUROCHER--M *(NY)*
JOHNNY EVERS--CH *(NY)*
BUCK EWING--C, M *(NY)*
FRANKIE FRISCH--2B, CH *(NY)*
BURLEIGH GRIMES--P *(NY)*
GABBY HARTNETT--C, •CH *(NY)*
ROGERS HORNSBY--2B, •M *(NY)*
WAITE HOYT--P *(NY)*
CARL HUBBELL--P *(NY)*
MONTE IRVIN--OF *(NY)*
TRAVIS JACKSON--SS, CH *(NY)*
HUGHIE JENNINGS--M, CH *(NY)*
TIM KEEFE--P *(NY)*
WEE WILLIE KEELER--OF *(NY)*
GEORGE KELLY--1B *(NY)*
MIKE KELLY--OF *(NY)*
TONY LAZZERI--3B *(NY)*
FRED LINDSTROM--3B *(NY)*
ERNIE LOMBARDI--C *(NY)*
JUAN MARICHAL--P *(SF)*
RUBE MARQUARD--P *(NY)*
CHRISTY MATHEWSON--P *(NY)*
WILLIE MAYS--OF *(NY/SF)*
WILLIE McCOVEY--1B *(SF)*
JOE McGINNITY--P *(NY)*
JOHN McGRAW--3B, •M, M *(NY)*
BILL McKECHNIE--3B *(NY)*
DUCKY MEDWICK--OF *(NY)*
JOHNNY MIZE--1B *(NY)*
JOE MORGAN--2B *(SF)*
JIM O'ROURKE--OF *(NY)*
MEL OTT--OF, •M, M *(NY)*
GAYLORD PERRY--P *(SF)*
FRANK ROBINSON--M *(SF)*
WILBERT ROBINSON--CH *(NY)*

EDD ROUSH--OF *(NY)*
AMOS RUSIE--P *(NY)*
RAY SCHALK--C *(NY)*
RED SCHOENDIENST--2B *(NY)*
DUKE SNIDER--OF *(SF)*
WARREN SPAHN--P *(SF)*
CASEY STENGEL--OF *(NY)*
BILL TERRY--1B, •M, M *(NY)*
MONTE WARD--SS, •M *(NY)*
MICKEY WELCH--P *(NY)*
HOYT WILHELM--P *(NY)*
HACK WILSON--OF *(NY)*
ROSS YOUNGS--OF *(NY)*

MONTREAL EXPOS *(2)*/ **WASHINGTON NATIONALS** *(0)* **(2)**
GARY CARTER--C
TONY PEREZ--1B

Yogi Berra (left), another Yankee great wearing his old #8 as a member of the Houston Astros coaching staff. Old Yogi spread his quotable philosophy to any of the young players who would listen.
Gary Carter (above) became the first of the Montreal Expos to be inducted as an Expo into the Hall of Fame. "The Kid" began and ended his career in Montreal. Tony Perez previously made it in 2000 but only played briefly in the Canadian city.

Election to the Hall of Fame is an extremely difficult achievement—as it should be. The onus for such elections falls into the laps of 10-year members of the Baseball Writers' Association of America (BBWAA).

Every year these members vote for up to ten players listed on the ballot. To qualify, players must be retired for five years. A screening committee then nominates players for the ballot. Once on the ballot, players need 5% of the vote to stay on. To be elected, 75% of the vote is needed. If not elected, they may remain on the ballot by maintaining the level of 5% or better for 15 years.

After that they must wait three years to become eligible for selection by the Veterans Committee.

This is tough enough, but add to this the fact that every year another outstanding player or two becomes eligible. In 1993, Reggie Jackson was swept in with 93.6% of the vote. He had 396 of the 423 cast. Phil Niekro was also eligible for the first time, but fell 40 votes short with 278.

In 1994, Steve Carlton was elected on his first try and in '95, Mike Schmidt made it also. This impacted on Niekro's chances to make it despite his 318 wins. A 300-game winner, he finally made it in 1997.

Now let's consider another aspect. A player's last year of eligibility will be twenty years after retirement. His peak years might be twenty-five years ago. A rookie member of the BBWAA may be in his mid-thirties and probably would have been 8-years-old at that time. Disregarding the more obvious selections, the writer will probably only recall the careers of players from his favorite ball club or of the city in which he works.

Let's take a look at some of those players that have failed repeatedly to get elected. Dick Allen had his best year with the Chicago White Sox in 1972 when he batted .308, hit 37 HRs and knocked in 113. Seven times he batted over .300, ten times he hit 20 HRs or more and six times had 90+ RBIs. Pretty awesome bat, but his strong suit was not defense.

In 1957, Ken Boyer moved from third base to center field. He led the NL in fielding. At his own position, he won 5 Gold Gloves, led the league in DPs five times, was a 10-time All-Star, hit over .300 five times and knocked in 90+ runs seven years in a row. His best year was 1964. Ken hit .295, had 24 HRs, with 119 RBIs, won the MVP and the Cards won the World Series with the help of his grand slam.

Before 1990, only one player in baseball history hit at least 30 homers and stole at least 30 bases (30/30 club) five different times. He fell four HRs short of doing it twice more and five HRs short once plus four SBs short another year. Had he accomplished those deeds, he would have done it an amazing nine times. That player was Bobby Bonds. He had 332 home runs and 461 stolen bases. Bonds was a very exciting player, he made things happen. Son Barry has done 30/30 five times since.

"Mr. Clean," Steve Garvey, batted over .300 eight times, led the NL in hits twice, and had five 100+ RBI seasons. He won four Gold Gloves at first base for the Los Angeles Dodgers. He helped the Padres get to the World Series in 1984. They have retired his uniform number.

Amazingly, Jim Kaat pitched on the major league level for 25 years. He won 283 times with some pretty bad clubs. He won 20 three times and had an extraordinary 16 straight Gold Glove Awards for defense. He deserved strong consideration.

A few more years at the rate he was going would have helped Thurman Munson get into the Hall. He batted over .300 five times, was Rookie of the Year in 1970, MVP in 1976 when he batted .302, had 17 HRs and 105 RBIs for the pennant-winning Yankees. They retired his #15 in 1980.

A young Cuban stormed through the AL and finished ahead of everybody in runs (109), hits (217), doubles (43) and batting (.323) where he was named Rookie of the Year in 1964. His name was Tony Oliva and he led the league again the next year with a .321 average. He led in batting a third time while hitting over .300 four other times. Serious knee problems limited him to designated hitting. But despite that, he's had an impressive career.

Ron Santo has run out of time for the BBWAA. He has a long shot to be elected by the Veterans Committee. He has more HRs (342), than Brooks Robinson. He had eight 90+ RBI years, led the NL in walks four times, handled most assists seven years in a row, had most putouts six years in a

How can you win four batting titles and not even make it to the second year on the ballot? Bill Madlock had such a fate.

Tony Oliva had it all. Speed, power, and quick hands. Injuries during two seasons kept Oliva from playing in eight straight All-Star games.

Ron Santo doesn't get credit for his offensive and defensive contributions. He was the spark-plug of the Cubs in the 1960s and early '70s.

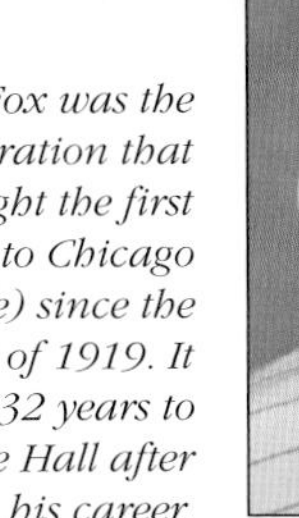

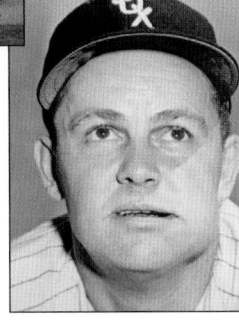

Nellie Fox was the inspiration that brought the first pennant to Chicago (Southside) since the Black Sox of 1919. It took him 32 years to make the Hall after his career.

Joe Gordon was solid around second base. He was selected to nine straight All-Star teams with time out for service in 1944-45.

Roger Maris sitrred up a lot of noise for a quiet guy. Hitting those 61 HRs was one of his greatest days and one of his worst. Not many players can say they won back-to-back MVP Awards. Roger was one of four outfielders to do it.

row, most DPs five times, had 5 Gold Gloves and was an All-Star nine times. The Cubs retired his #10.

Sadly, "Mad Dog," Bill Madlock didn't even muster the 5% vote to remain on the ballot. He's a four-time batting champion with a .305 career average. He batted over .300 nine times. Not considered a power hitter, he managed to hit 163 home runs.

Bobby Grich couldn't hang on the ballot either. As a second baseman, he tied for the lead in HRs in 1981 with 22; hit 30 dingers and had 101 RBIs in 1979. He made only 2 errors in 1985. That's incredible! He had a career fielding mark of .984, a record once.

For years a player had to have 60% of the vote at least once to be eligible for the Veterans Committee. This meant there were only three players whose careers began since 1945 who were eligible: Jim Bunning, Nellie Fox and Gil Hodges.

Bunning won 100 games in each league, pitched a no-hitter in each, but won 20 games only once. He did win 19 games four out of five years in one stretch though. He was selected in 1996.

Nellie Fox missed election to the Hall in 1985 by 2 votes! Fox suffered from being the all-around player without power. He only had 35 HRs in his career. But he batted over .300 six times, finishing with .288. He only struck out every 42.7 times at bat. And he was named MVP in the "Go-Go Sox" pennant-winning year, 1959. He finally was chosen in 1997.

Gil Hodges had his prime years in old Ebbetts Field with the colorful Brooklyn Dodgers, "Da Bums." He hit 370 HRs and batted in 1,274 runs with 1,921 hits. His quiet confidence helped shape the hapless "Amazin'" Mets into World Champions in 1969. Hodges has yet to make it to the Hall.

Many old-timers have been passed by. The further into the past a player's career goes, the more difficult his election. Roger Maris was, quietly, an impact player. Notwithstanding his 61-HR season, he was a solid defensive outfielder. He was on seven pennant-winning teams in 12 years. Only batting .260, he knocked in a run every 5.9 at bats. He deserved a better fate.

Joe Gordon was always being compared to Bobby Doerr during the '40s. Doerr is in the Hall and Gordon is not. Gordon was on five pennant teams in New York and one in Cleveland. Joe had 30 more HRs in three less years. Joe averaged 88.6 RBIs per year and Bobby 89.0. Gordon had no idea of his batting average, fielding average or any personal stats, "he just came to beat you."

Arguably the best fielding shortstop of the '40s was Marty Marion. "The Octopus." "Mr. Shortstop." National League fans always compared Pee Wee Reese and Marion, while American League fans added in Phil Rizzuto. Both Marion and Rizzuto won MVP Awards, Reese did not. Reese played 16 years, three more than the other two.

Marion led the NL in doubles, topped all hitters in the 1943 World Series with a .357 mark and was an All-Star eight times. Using Pete Palmer's stats from "Total Baseball," Marion led the league in clutch hitting in 1949 with 136. His career clutch hitting index (CHI) was 116 compared to 100 for Reese and 93 for Rizzuto. Again, using Palmer's formula FR (fielding runs: above average for position, runs saved) Marion led the NL twice, Reese once and Rizzuto the AL twice. Career FR numbers: Marion 65, Reese -12, Rizzuto 117.

Reese led the league in stolen bases with 30 once, scored 132 runs in 1949 to top the NL, and was tops in walks once. He batted over .300 three times in World Series play. He had most hits for the Dodgers in the '49 and '52 Series.

Rizzuto had the highest BA in the 1942 World Series—.381. He led the AL in fielding average in 1949 and 1950. He collected 200 hits in his MVP season.

PLAYER	BA	R/G	TB/G	RBI/G
MARION	.263	.17	1.35	.478
REESE	.269	.43	1.34	.363
RIZZUTO	.273	.40	1.04	.044

Marion was the picture of grace with his far-ranging skill and he rose up in clutch situations. Reese was a leader and wanted to win. He helped Jackie Robinson get through the tough times while breaking in during 1947. Rizzuto was a feisty little guy who was a fiery competitor. He was an excellent bunter and perfected the delayed steal.

With numbers so similar, it's hard to say why only two would make it. Middle infielders have difficulty sustaining the votes needed to remain on the ballots.

If Henry Chadwick is a pioneer in the Hall of Fame because he spread the word about the young sport of baseball, Curt Flood might be considered a pioneer also. He the person

Marty Marion defined what defense was in the 1940's, much like another Cardinal shortstop has done more recently. Ozzie Smith is probably the greatest defensive ballplayer that ever lived, but Marion covered old Sportsman Park with a fluid grace that was unrivaled in his day. Consider how well he must have played for a .267 hitting middle infielder to win the MVP Award in 1944. Wearing #4, Marty was the antithesis of a slugger. The 6'2", 170 lbs. "Slats" was plagued by back problems as his career worn on.

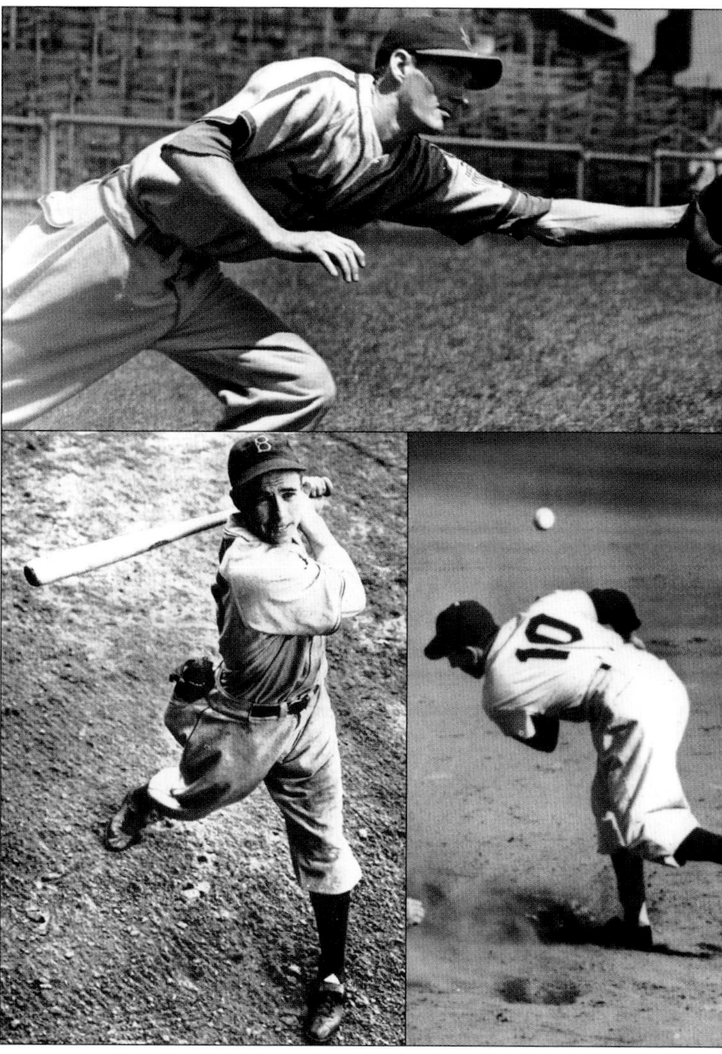

Pee Wee Reese (left), the "Kentucky Colonel", anchored the Dodger infield for 16 years. Seven of those years they went to the World Series—all against the Yankees. Brooklyn only won in 1955.
Phil "Scooter" Rizzuto (right) was one of the smallest men to play big league ball. The peppery infielder ignored all the experts that told him to find another occupation to the tune of election to the Hall of Fame.

might be considered a pioneer also. He is the person most responsible for bringing about the arbitration system and ultimately free agency when he stood against the age-old reserve clause, taking it all the way to the U. S. Supreme Court before losing 5-3. Andy Messersmith and Dave McNally followed in Flood's footsteps and could be considered pioneers also.

You can't have a chapter about the Hall of Fame without mentioning one of the greatest hitters of all time. One who had ten 200-hit seasons, three batting titles, an All-Star at five different positions and drilled more hits than any man alive or dead.

Whether or not Rose's ban will be lifted, remains to be seen. Pete hasn't helped his own cause very much with his admissions on gambling.

What about the "What could have beens?" Every generation there is a player or two who bursts upon the scene and performs superhuman feats. I'm not talking about the flash-in-the-pans like Bobo Holloman who pitched a no-hitter in his first major league game in 1953 for the Browns. He finished his career that same year at 3-7.

Herb Score was a flame-throwing left-hander with a wicked hook. He reminded one of Steve Carlton or Sandy Koufax. In his first two seasons he won 36 games.

His career was never the same after a line-drive accidently struck him in the face. He toiled for several more years but never regained that dominance that would have propelled him toward the Hall.

Pistol Pete Reiser's first full season saw a batting title with .343, most runs (117), most doubles (39), most triples (17) and highest slugging percentage (.558). He batted .310 the following year. He led the league in stolen bases in '42 and '46. Leo Durocher likened young Pete to another young player he knew well—Willie Mays. Reiser played in an era where the outfield walls were not protected. His aggressive style of play senthim headlong into these walls several times. He was never the same. Injury free, who knows what he would have accomplished.

What about Tony C.? At 22 years of age he was the second youngest player ever to reach the 100 home run plateau. Conigliaro was headed for a brilliant career in Boston when a serious beaning cost him his career.

Tommy Davis had back-to-back batting championships early in his career with the Dodgers. Crippling injuries changed his ability to play the game. He went on to play for 18 years, but never quite lived up to the promise of the early years.

Right now there are many bona fide Hall of Fame caliber players. What a list! Bruce Sutter, Cal Ripken, Andre Dawson and Rickey Henderson. And what of those still playing—Randy Johnson, Curt Schilling, Jeff Bagwell, Roger Clemens, Sammy Sosa, Barry Bonds, Mike Piazza, John Smoltz, Greg Maddux, Albert Pujols, Ken Griffey, Jr., Alex Rodriguez.

They may not all make it. The system is extremely arduous. But then, it wasn't supposed to be easy.

Herb Score, Pete Reiser, and Tony Conigliaro (left to right) might have their bronze plaques hanging in the Hall today if career-hampering injuries (a batted ball, a battered wall and a beanball) hadn't riddled their playing years.

BOYHOOD IDOLS

5

Willie Mays played stickball on the streets of New York, from sewer plate to sewer plate. Bob Feller threw strikes behind the barn of an Iowa farm. Other young hopefuls played in schoolyards in Jersey or dusty fields clumped with uneven grass in California, Texas or San Pedro de Macharis.

Imaginery batting orders spawned stances mimicking favorite ballplayers. Every detail was there. Twitching elbows, wagging bats and wiggling rumps were the stuff that boyhood idols were made of.

High leg kicks and distracting glove flips preceeded each delivery, facing those fantasy line-ups.

We were all there, dreaming of making 'The Big Show.' Hoping against hope that we had the stuff that would help us make it. But there are only 1,200 slots on 30 major league 40-man rosters, That's .0000087 of the male population in the U. S.—not counting Canada, Mexico, the Caribbean perimeter or points East.

It's small wonder that we grew up idolizing the lucky few that do dig into a major league batter's box for the first time.

When players finally break through to the majors, many go after the 'hot numbers' as Jeff Ross, the Blue Jays equipment manager calls them.

"Players ask for Yount's, Clemente's or Aaron's numbers," said Jeff. "Or Reggie's number, depending on who they root for."

Rico Carty joined Toronto from Cleveland in 1978 where he wore #9 for several years. Rick Cirone was wearing it when he arrived. Ross offered #21 to Carty, but he was very leary of it until he was told that Roberto Clemente wore that number. He went to Oakland before the season was over only to return for his final season in 1979. He again wore #21. The former batting champ hit over .280 and hit 32 homeruns for the Jays.

Ruben Sierra wore Clemente's #21 to honor his countryman. Both were born in Puerto Rico. Clemente, the ballplayer and the man have reached mythical proportions in his native land.

Three slugging Hall of Famers wore #44: Hank Aaron, Reggie Jackson and Willie McCovey. Eric Davis chose it when he played for the Reds. His buddy, Darryl Strawberry beat him to it when they both joined the Dodgers. Reggie Jefferson wore it while on the Indians, but switched to #18 with the Mariners in 1994.

Ken Landreaux came to Minnesota in the Rod Carew trade in 1979. Ray Crump, the EM at the time said of #44, "It is the lowest available number."

"I might just keep it. It was worn by a pretty capable outfielder," said Ken referring to the great Henry Aaron. He continued to wear it for seven more years with the Dodgers.

Robin Yount spent his entire 20-year career with the Brewers where he cracked 3,142 hits, scored 1,632 runs, drove in 1,406 more, hit 583 doubles, 126 triples, 251 HRs while batting .285. He hit over .300 six times, had a slugging average of .430 while stealing 271 bases. He was also a defensive wonder, leading the league in fielding at both shortstop and outfield.

Yankee officials are convinced that so many pitchers wear #16 because of Whitey Ford. Since his retirement in 1967, seventy pitchers have worn it. Scott McGregor idolized Whitey. He was brought up through the Yankee farm system, but was traded to Baltimore, breaking in with them in 1976. He wore #16 for eleven of his thirteen years with the Orioles.

Among the more notable pitchers that have sported #16 are Frank Viola, Dwight Gooden, David Wells, Mike Norris and Hideo Nomo. Ron Perranoski wore it, but he was a contemporary of Whitey's. Mike Gardner wore #16, not for Ford but revering Viola.

Another number much sought after, especially by outfielders, is #24. Mays' old number was worn by Shane Mack with the Twins, Deion Sanders wore it while a Yankee and a Brave, and Ken Griffey, Jr. used it for the Mariners. He picked his Dad's #30 when he signed with the Reds. Senior was still coaching and moved to #33.

Eric Davis (Below, left) had surprising power for his sinewy frame. Injury prone, much of his career was spent on the DL. Shane Mack (Below, center) quietly averaged over .315 in his first three seasons as a Twin. Lefty Frank Viola's (Below, right) best season was 1988 when he went 24-7 for the Twins. Junior (Right) is on his way to a fabulous career. He and his father were the first father/son tandem to play on the same team in major league baseball history.

Barry Bonds wore #24 during his Pirate days in tribute to his godfather, Willie Mays. The Giants signed him as a free agent before the 1993 season. Barry wanted to wear his old #24, but it was retired for the very man that Bonds wore it—Mays. Willie thought it would be alright for him to wear it, but a bit of a brouhaha was stirred up in the media. Although Barry was a terrific ballplayer, the press suggested that he would have to continue putting up big numbers for many more years to fill Mays' shirt. Many think he has done it already.

"I just decided I'm a fan, I'm not a spoiled brat," said Bonds. "His number belongs to the world; it belongs to the people of San Francisco. I'd rather be in left field looking at that number than wearing it on my back."

Barry held up a jersey with the number 25 on it while meeting the press and said, "It would be a great honor for me to wear this number right here." It was worn by another pretty fair ballplayer, his own father Bobby.

Many players wore numbers to honor family members, many did not. A young Dale Berra fought his way up in the Yankee system. At Columbus, he wore his famous Dad's number 8. After leaving the Yankees' farm, he made it to the Bigs as a Pirate. He wore #4 for eight years there. He caught up to Yogi who managed the Yanks in 1985 and again in Houston where he coached in '87. Dale never did wear #8 as a major leaguer.

Another Yankee, Mel Stottlemyre, wore #30 as a player and continued with it while coaching. Mel, Jr., didn't wear it during his brief career with Kansas City. Son Todd, on the other hand, wore #30 for most of his career. Dad wore #34 more recently coaching.

David "Gus" Bell wore #25 when he roamed the outfield for the Cincinnati Reds from 1953-61. His son, David Gus "Buddy" Bell wore #9 in his rookie year with the Indians, but switched to #25 the following year and kept it for the rest of his career. He played in Cincinnati also for four years.

Another player to break in wearing #9 was Gregg Jefferies of the Mets. He also wore it with the Royals, but when he joined the Cardinals, Mgr. Joe Torre had it. During spring training he took Craig Wilson's #12 after he was traded away. But when the season opened, he chose #25 in honor of his father. It seemed to agree with him; he batted well over .300 and was an All-Star twice with the Cards.

Stan Javier bounced around from the Yankees to the A's, to the Dodgers, Phillies, Angels and back to the A's. He wore #55, #28, #5, #22. But it wasn't until 1993 with the Angels that he wore his father Julian's #25. Julie was an All-Star second baseman with the Cards in the '60s.

Sandy Alomar, Sr. wore several numbers, but wore #2 most often. Sandy, Jr., never wore it, but Roberto did take #2 in his first year with Toronto. He switched to his preferred #12 as soon as he could.

Sandy was a coach with San Diego where his two sons were rookies in 1988.

Not one to stand on his laurels, Barry Bonds (left) continued to tear up the league in San Francisco, winning his seventh MVP (an awesome four in a row!). In his first season in the Bay City, he led the league in HRs (46), RBIs (123) and slugging (.677). He's sure to make Cooperstown after hitting 73 HRs in one season. The Giants might have to retire #25 for Bonds—Barry and Bobby. That would be a first!

In 1986, Robert Paul Wine, Jr. made it to Houston as a catcher. Robbie was the son of Bobby who played shortstop for the Phillies and Expos from 1960-72. For his brief two-year career he wore his Dad's number—7.

"Mark wanted to wear uniform number 45 when he was with the Mets because it was the number worn by his late father, Camilo," said Jay Horwitz, Mets PR Director, in reference to Mark Carreon. Cam was a catcher with the White Sox, Indians and Orioles. Mark moved on to Detroit after the Mets, but a rather dominant player, Cecil Fielder was wearing #45—he took #15. In 1993, Mark joined the Giants where he reverted to his Dad's #45.

Father Mike Tresh spent eleven years as a catcher with the Chicago White Sox with #15 on his back and son Tom Tresh spent nine years with the Yankees wearing the same #15.

He may not be a family member, but what higher tribute could you pay a player than to name your son after him? A teen-ager named after the great "Rajah," Rogers Hornsby McKee pitched during the War for the Phillies. He got in 5 ball games and was a perfect 1-0. He was never heard of after 1944.

Larry Doby was the first African-American to play in the American League. His rookie year was 1947, the same year Jackie Robinson broke the color line in Brooklyn. Larry Doby Johnson was born in Cleveland three years later. He caught for Cleveland in 1972, moved to Montreal in '75 and on to the White Sox in '78. Johnson caught up with Doby who was coaching in all three cities.

Willie Mays Aikens not only was named after the great centerfielder, but wore his #24 also in Kansas City and Toronto.

Number 4 was retired for Duke Snider of the Dodgers, but before it was, a young Dodger hopeful named Kelly Snider (no relation) wore it in spring training. Kelly tried in 1979 and 1980, but never made it.

Hal McRae, then the Royals manager was once asked by a reporter, "How come your son Brian doesn't wear your #11?"

"Look again," laughed Hal. "The 56 is 5 plus 6 equals 11."

Mark Carreon (Left) had a career batting average of .277. His Dad's was .264. However Mark has hit 10 or more HRs in a season three times while Camilo had 11 in his entire career. Willie Mays Aikens (Center) belted 20+ homeruns three times in his eight-year career. He knocked in 98 runs in 1980. His numbers dwindled as did his career when he got involved with substance abuse.
Brian McRae (Right) had some pretty big shoes to fill. His Dad, Hal, was one of the most feared designated hitters in the '70s and '80s with the Royals.

Oddly, the 1994 season saw a young shortstop by the name of Alex Rodriguez in Seattle wearing number 3 and one named Carlos Rodriguez in Boston also wearing #3. They are not related.

An MVP and batting champion in St. Louis in 1979, Keith Hernandez was not in the Cardinal plans by 1983 when he was shipped off to the Mets. In New York, Keith turned his career and his life around which had been sidetracked by drugs. Always regarded as a premier defensive first baseman, he became one of the veteran leaders of the club and helped them bring the World Championship to the Mets in 1986.

1989 was his last season in New York. He finished his career in Cleveland the next year.

"In 1991, David Cone switched his uniform from 44 to 17," said Jay Horwitz, Mets VP, Media Relations, "that was his way of paying respect to Keith for what he accomplished during his career."

Cone was traded to Toronto in 1992, but Kelly Gruber was wearing #17. He took the number Jeff Kent vacated in the trade—#11.

Signing with Kansas City, Cone again took Keith's old number 17 for 1993.

Cone was not the only player whose life Keith Hernandez had impacted. Bret Saberhagen, a close friend of Cone's, switched to #17 with the Mets. Ron Darling, an ex-Met, wore it with the Oakland A's. Reliever Roger McDowell, another ex-Met, adopted #17 with the Dodgers. Still another ex-Met, Bobby Ojeda asked for it when he became a Yankee, but Luis Palonia had it.

Even ex-Met Darryl Strawberry, the player who had a skirmish with Hernandez in training camp some years before, picked 17 on joining the Giants midway through the 1994 season after battling back from drug abuse.

Mark Grace was never a Met, but he idolized Hernandez growing up as a kid and wore #17 his entire Cubs career.

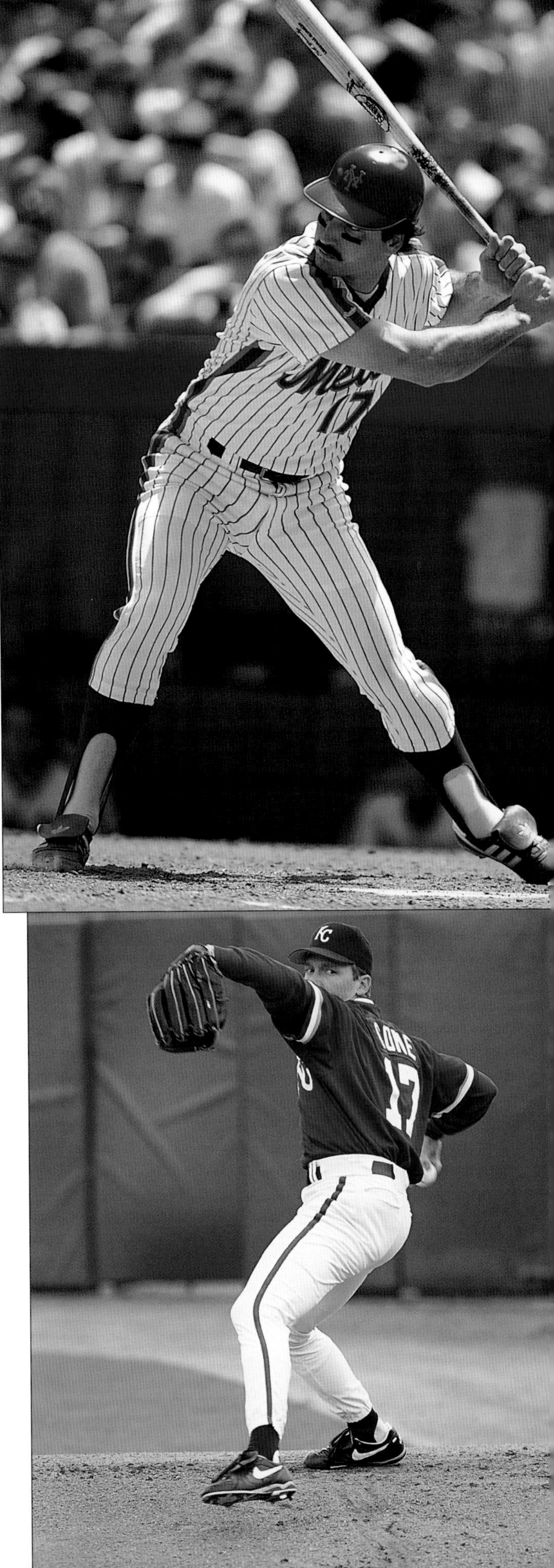

No one was better than Keith Hernandez (Top right) at throwing out a runner going to third in a bunt situation. He won 11 straight Gold Gloves, more than any other first baseman. At 25, David Cone (Right) won 20 while losing only 3 in 1988. He was 41-15 from 1994-96. He returned from injury to win the pivotal third game in the 1996 World Series for the Yanks.

The man that sent Hernandez to the Mets, Whitey Herzog, wanted to wear Casey Stengel's old number (37) when he took over the reigns at St. Louis. But, ironically, Keith himself was wearing it. Whitey first took #3 then settled into #24. He never did wear #37.

Joe Magrane went from number 50 to 41 and finally got the number he wanted—#32. He wore it for his idol, Lefty Steve Carlton. Unfortunately for Joe, he never quite lived up to his promise.

"Franklin Stubbs wore #0 because of Al Oliver, " said Tom Skibosh, Director of Media Relations for the Brewers. Stubbs and Oliver were teammates in 1985 in LA. Stubbs was just beginning his career playing in 10 games and Oliver was in his last season. He obviously left a strong impression.

George Brett was the 18th player in major league history to collect 3,000 hits. He was the franchise in Kansas City during their glory years in the '80s.

"Brooks Robinson was my role model," said George. Brooks was the incredible third baseman for the Orioles. His World Series play against the Reds in 1970 is legendary. He wore Brooks' #5 for most of his career.

Wade Boggs wore #26 in Boston for 11 seasons. Signing on with the Yankees for the 1993 season, Boggs faced a dilemma. Steve Farr had #26, so he decided on #12.

When asked why, he replied, "It's one of the lowest Yankee numbers that isn't retired. I know that 27 and 29 were available, but I decided against them. I thought about 27 into 72, like Pudge did (Carlton Fisk), but that was kind of a copycat antic.

"Then it flooded into my mind that when I was 12 or 13, I once jumped a fence to meet Joe Namath in Tampa. I shook hands with him as he was sitting in a limousine. He was a great hero of mine and I know he wore number 12. Plus my wife and daughter were both born in December, which is the 12th month. This is my 12th year in the big leagues. You might also think I chose 12 because two times six is 12, but that wasn't it."

Brett (Below) won a Gold Glove in 1985. His idol, Brooks Robinson, won 16 straight Gold Gloves 1960-75, a record hard for anyone to measure up to.
Joe Magrane (Right) led the NL in ERA in 1988 with 2.88. He went 18-9 the following year, but nagging injuries took the luster out of his career.

Harvey Haddix came up to the Cardinals in 1952. He was a younger version of another member of the pitching staff, Harry "The Cat" Brecheen. They didn't call him "The Kitten" for nothing. They were about the same size and both were lefthanded. Brecheen wore #31 throughout his career—even as a coach for the Orioles, 1954-67.

When Haddix lost his famous 13-inning perfect game while pitching for Pittsburgh, he wore #31. He wore it from 1959-63. He joined the Orioles in 1964 where Brecheen was the pitching coach. "The Cat" was wearing his #31, "The Kitten" took #30. Later as a coach, Haddix took #31 at the first opportunity wearing it from 1981-84 with the Pirates.

In Cleveland, Charles Nagy idolized 300-game winner Tom Seaver. He wore Tom's old number 41 from 1990-2002.

After leaving Oakland, Catfish Hunter was to be later honored by election to the Hall of Fame and by having his #27 retired. But before these major events took place, a young rookie named Mike Norris joined the A's and asked for Catfish's vacated #27. He wanted to wear it not to honor Hunter, but for his own idol--crosstown rival Juan Marichal. They held it back for a year out of respect for Hunter, so Norris took #16.

Affable Tommy Lasorda wore #52 as a coach for the Dodgers, but switched to #2.

"That was Leo Durocher's number and I always liked Durocher," said Tommy. "Of course, I couldn't take #11, my favorite number, because that is Manny Mota's," said Tom referring to his fabled pinch-hitter.

Teams very often honor a player's passing by issuing sleeve patches with that player's number on them. When Tim Crews was killed in that awful boating accident during spring training in 1993, the Dodgers wore patches with #52 on them in tribute.

Billy Martin was killed on Christmas night in 1989. The Yankees honored Billy the following season by wearing small #1's on their sleeves.

In 1993, the Dodgers lost two more old heroes when Hall of Famers Don Drysdale and Roy Campanella both died. The Dodgers issued a uniform patch that read "39 Roy, Don 53."

The Yankees' Mel Hall (Above) showing Billy Martin's #1 on his sleeve during the 1990 campaign. Martin was hired and fired to manage the Yanks by "Boss" Steinbrenner five times.
Nolan Ryan (Right) pitched 7 no-hitters, 9 one-hitters and 18 two-hitters. He tied Tom Seaver at 7th All-Time shutout leader with 61; was first All-Time in K's with 5,714; first All-Time with 2,795 walks; second All-Time in games started—773; 5th All-Time in innings pitched with 5,386; and tied for thirteenth with Don Sutton at 324 wins, but third All-Time in losses—292.

Individual players will honor a friend who died during the season. Bob Moose died on October 9, 1976, his 29th birthday. His close buddy, Jim Rooker, shelved his own #19 and wore Moose's #38 out of res-pect for him. Off the field, he had associated with him more than any other Pirate.

"Bobby Knoop has worn an Angel uniform longer than anyone in our history," said Leonard Garcia, Angel equipment manager. "His number was 1. He switched to number 2 when his friend Deron Johnson died. Johnson wore #2 during his career and Bobby wanted to pay homage."

Rod Nichols, a former teammate of Steve Olin's, wore his #31 inscribed on the side of his Dodgers hat during the 1993 season.

A page in baseball history was turned on July 13, 1994. Jimmie Reese died at 92. He started in the game in 1917 as a batboy for the Pacific Coast League Los Angeles Angels.

He was a second baseman who played for the Yankees in 1930-31 and finished with the Cardinals in 1932. During his brief stay in pinstripes he was the notorious Babe Ruth's roommate. Reese used to jibe, "I didn't room with Babe. I watched Babe's bags, Babe was never in his room."

Jimmie coached with the Angels from 1972-94. Nolan Ryan thought so highly of Reese that he persuaded the Angels to keep him on permanently as their conditioning coach. He named his second son Nolan Reese Ryan.

The club wore a sleeve patch that read "50 Reese" for the 1994 season to commemorate their great fungo artist. In 1995, they retired his uniform number, a rare honor for a coach.

Randy Johnson became only the twelfth pitcher in major league history to strike out 300 batters in a season. It was September 26, 1993. He needed 10 innings in Seattle's final home game to do it.

Days earlier Nolan Ryan tore a ligament in his throwing elbow to end his career. Ryan had reached the 300 strikeout plateau six times.

Johnson's uniform number was 51, but to commemorate Ryan's great achievements during his long career and to bolster his chances of reaching 300, he wore Ryan's #34.

Another pitcher was wearing #34 in honor of Nolan Ryan. This young hurler was in Class A ball in the New York-Penn League in 1994. He pitched for the Hudson Valley Renegades. His name: Reid Ryan, Nolan's son.

He remarked that everyone kept asking him, "Are you going to be as good as your dad?" His usual response was "No, who is?"

Larry Bird's retirement from the Boston Celtics precipitated some unusual occurrences in the baseball world. Roger Clemens had a #33 inscribed on his cap honoring Bird who wore that number on the basketball court. He was not allowed to continue in the game with that hat. The umpires felt it was too distracting to the opposing hitters.

Gary DiSarcina, the California Angels shortstop wore #11 for over three years. He hails from the Boston area and is a huge fan of Larry Bird's and the Celtics (Isn't it part of Boston law?).

The Angels were on a road trip and when they hit Boston, Bird had just retired. The hooplah was everywhere. As luck would have it, outfielder John Morris had just left the club. His number 33, which happened to be Bird's, had become available. Both DiSarcina and Morris were the same size so Leonard Garcia, the equipment manager had a brainstorm.

"I decided to play a little joke," said Leonard. "At first I was going to use a warm-up jersey, but since Morris' shirt was available I had the name panel taken off and sewed on 'DiSarcina.' I hung it in his locker and didn't say a word.

"He didn't notice it at first, but when he did, he had a good laugh. The rest of the guys loved it."

DiSarcina said, "Yeah, I can do this. I like it. I'll wear it tonight."

He not only wore it for the game, but he got a two-out, two-run single in the ninth inning to beat the Red Sox (of all people) 3-2.

After the game Gary said, "If I never get another chance to play a baseball game in my life, I'll remember this game the rest of my life."

He wore #33 until Eddie Murray became an Angel in 1997. Gary took Ted Williams' old #9.

One of the most unusual displays of using a number to honor another team member was in Cincinnati. Tony Perez was a rookie manager with the club. But the popular Perez was not given much of a chance to prove himself. After only 44 games, the Reds record standing at 20-24, he was fired.

Roger Clemens (Right) had become the dominant pitcher in the American League. He won the MVP in 1986. Combining 1986 and '87, Clemens went 44-13, a .772 record. He averaged a shutout every 8 starts through 1992. In his first nine years, he had the lowest ERA four times in the AL. He went on to win a record-breaking 8th Cy Young Award in 2004 as he pitched his hometown Houston Astros to the NLCS at the age of 42.

The players added #24 to their uniforms in protest to the handling of Perez and they ignored the General Manager, Jim Bowden.

What have you done for me lately? That seemed to be the cry years ago when player's numbers were not held in high regard. Before Babe Ruth's number was retired in 1948, seven players had worn it.

Four players wore Bill Dickey's #8 before Yogi Berra's play forced the Yanks to retire it for both Hall of Fame catchers.

Homerun record holder Roger Maris had #9 retired for him. In the years after he went to St. Louis, his number was reissued to four other Yankees. Nine players wore Phil Rizzuto's number since he first put on #10.

Bobby Doerr was elected to the Hall of Fame in 1986. His #1 was retired by the Red Sox in 1988, but not before 19 assorted players and staff wore it since 1951.

Sixteen players wore Hall of Famer Joe Cronin's number 4 after his playing and managing days until it was retired in 1984. Seventeen wore White Sox Billy Pierce's #19 after his days were over. Twenty three various players used the nearly forgotten Ted Lyons' old shirt #16 before the Pale Hose retired it in 1987. Bill Terry's #3 was used 22 times.

But there were 26 players and/or coaches who wore Pie Traynor's #20, Dizzy Dean's #17 and Gaylord Perry's #36 after they retired and before their uniform numbers were retired.

Tony Perez (Top, left) was always a popular player in Cincinnati. He quietly knocked in over 100 runs six times for the Reds and once for the Red Sox. His 1,652 RBI's lifetime rank him 21st All-Time. He was an All-Star seven times for the Redlegs.

Cliff Mapes (Left) was the last player to wear Babe Ruth's number before they retired it. Mapes was known for his powerful arm in rightfield. I recall him calling off the great DiMaggio on a routine fly ball in right center only to drop it for a three-base error. On the very next play, he caught a fly ball in right and fired home to catch the runner tagging up by ten feet.

Generally speaking, those players whose numbers were retired long after their playing days were over, saw that number reissued year after year. Many teams hold the Hall of Fame as criteria for retiring a player's number. Consequently, when a player is elected by a veteran's committee, many years have passed.

Time gives a better perspective for judging the career of a player. Rated against the players of the past, a club has a much clearer picture of their current players and whether they will retire a number or not.

Below is a list of the star players and the years their numbers were worn before they were retired.

Eddie Murray (Above) was one of a select few who had his number retired while he was still active. Murray had the rare distinction of wearing only one number for his entire career, #33. He was elected to the Hall of Fame in 2003.

AMERICAN LEAGUE

BALTIMORE ORIOLES

4 EARL WEAVER
No one
5 BROOKS ROBINSON
No one
8 CAL RIPKEN
No one
20 FRANK ROBINSON
No one
22 JIM PALMER
No one
33 EDDIE MURRAY
No one

BOSTON RED SOX

1 BOBBY DOERR
Ty LaForest--1945 (WWII)
Ben Steiner--1945 (WWII)
Fred Hatfield--1952
George Kell--1952-54
Grady Hatton--1954-56
Billy Consolo--1957-59
Jim Mahoney--1959
Herb Plews--1959
Don Buddin--1960-61
Eddie Bressoud--1962-65
Joe Foy--1966-68
Joe Azcue--1969
Billy Conigliaro--1969-70
Luis Alvarado--1970
Phil Gagliano--1971-72
Bernie Carbo--1974-78
Jim Dwyer--1979-80
Chico Walker--1981, 83-84
John McNamara--1985-88
4 JOE CRONIN
Sam Mele--1948-49
Ken Keltner--1950
Lou Boudreau--1951-54
Jackie Jensen--1955-59, 61
Lu Clinton--1960-61
Roman Mejias--1963-64
Rudy Schlesinger--1965
Jim Gosger--1965-66
Don Demeter--1966-67
Jim Landis--1967
Norm Siebern--1967-68
Billy Conigliaro--1969
Tom Satriano--1969-70
Tommy Harper--1972-74
Butch Hobson--1976-80
Carney Lansford--1981-82
8 CARL YASTRZEMSKI
No one
9 TED WILLIAMS
Johnny Peacock--1944 (WWII)
27 CARLTON FISK
Mike Brown--1982-86
Jeff Sellers--1985
Pat Dodson--1986-88
Greg Harris--1989-94
Stan Royer-1994
Mark Whiten--1995
Dave Hollins--1995
Butch Henry--1996-98
Kip Gross--1999

CHICAGO WHITE SOX

2 NELLIE FOX
Smoky Burgess--1965-67
Dick Kenworthy--1968
Rich Morales--1969-70
Mike Andrews--1971-73
Jerry Hairston--1973-75
Chet Lemon--1975
3 HAROLD BAINES
No one
4 LUKE APPLING
Grey Clarke--1944 (WWII)
Kerby Farrell--1945 (WWII)
Marty Marion--1955-56
Ron Jackson--1957-59
Gene Freese--1960
Ken Berry--1962
Ron Hansen--1963-69
Tim Cullen--1968
9 MINNIE MINOSO--OF 1983
Al Smith--1958
Johnny Callison--1958-59
Ramon Conde--1962
Charley Smith--1962-63
Danny Cater--1965-66
Wayne Causey--1966-68
Woodie Held--1968-69
Ossie Blanco--1970
Lee Richard--1971-72, 74-75
11 LUIS APARICIO
Dave Nicholson--1963-65
Jerry Adair--1966-67
Sandy Alomar--1967
Jimmy Stewart--1967
Chuck Brinkman--1971-74
Jerry Moses--1975
Jim Essian--1976-77
Don Kessinger--1978-79
Bruce Kimm--1980
Greg Pryor--1980-81
Rudy Law--1982-84
16 TED LYONS
Max Surkont--1949
Gordon Goldsberry--1950
Bob Mahoney--1951
Red Wilson--1951
Marv Grissom--1952
Joe Dobson--1952
Mike Fornieles--1953-54,55-56
Bob Cain--1954
Sammy Esposito--1955
Bob Kennedy--1957
Ted Beard--1957-58
Al Smith--1958-62
Brian McCall--1963
Ken Berry--1965-70
Ken Hottman--1971
Brian Downing--1973-77
Greg Pryor--1978-80
Bruce Kimm--1980
Jim Essian--1981
Marv Foley--1982
Julio Cruz--1983-84
Kenny Williams--1986
Jim Fregosi--1986-87
19 BILLY PIERCE
Dom Zanni--1962-63
Joe Shipley--1963
Bruce Howard--1963-67
Dennis Rybant--1968
Buddy Bradford--1969-70
Barry Moore--1970
Ron Lolich--1971
Steve Huntz--1971
Jim Qualls--1972
Rudy Hernandez--1972
Hugh Yancy--1974
Ken Tatum--1974
Sam Ewing--1976
Mike Squires--1977-78
Mike Colbern--1979
Greg Luzinski--1981-84
Floyd Bannister--1986-87
72 CARLTON FISK
No one

CLEVELAND INDIANS

3 EARL AVERILL
Rusty Peters--1940-44
Bob Rothel--1945
Dutch Meyer--1946
Lyman Linde--1947
Eddie Robinson--1947-48
Mickey Vernon--1949-50
Dale Mitchell--1951-56
George Strickland--1957,63-69
Woodie Held--1958-62
Kerby Farrell--1970-71
Joe Lutz--1972-73
Clay Bryant--1974
Dave Garcia--1975
5 LOU BOUDREAU
Snuffy Stirnweiss--1951-52
Hank Majeski--1952-55
Bobby Young--1955-56
Joe Altobelli--1957
Roger Maris--1958
Ray Webster--1959
Bubba Phillips--1960-62
Steve Demeter--1960
Jim Lawrence--1963
Cal Neeman--1963
Sammy Taylor--1963
Solly Hemus--1964
Ray Mueller--1966
Buddy Booker--1966
Del Rice--1967
Al Dark--1968-70

14 LARRY DOBY
Bill Glynn--1953
Ted Gray--1955
Gene Woodling--1956-57
Tito Francona--1959-62
Jerry Kindall--1963-64
George Banks--1965-66
Tony Martinez--1965
Gordy Lund--1967
Dave Nelson--1968-69, 93-94
Hoot Evers--1970
Chris Chambliss--1971-74
Dwain Anderson--1974
Tommy McCraw--1974-75, 79-82
Larvell Blanks--1976-78
Dave Freisleben--1978
Julio Franco--1983-88
Jerry Browne--1989-91
Jesse Levis--1992
18 MEL HARDER
Russ Christopher--1948
Minnie Minoso--1949
Marino Pieretti--1950
Charlie Harris--1951
Bill Abernathie--1952
Joe Tipton--1952-53
Hal Naragon--1954-59
Billy Moran--1959
Barry Latman--1960-62
Dick Howser--1963-66
Gus Gil--1967
Jack Heidemann--1969-72
Mike Kekich--1973
Ossie Blanco--1974
Duane Kuiper--1974-81
Kevin Rhomberg--1983
Pat Corrales--1983-85
Ken Schrom--1986-87
Ron Tingley--1988-89
Chris James--1990
19 BOB FELLER
No one
21 BOB LEMON
Bob Chance--1963-64
Rocky Colavito--1965-67
Tony Martinez--1966
Jose Vidal--1966
Jim King--1967
Tommy Harper--1968
Frank Baker--1969, 71
Warren Spahn--1972-73
Tony Pacheco--1974
George Hendrick--1975-76
Johnny Grubb--1977
Tom Veryzer--1978-79
Mike Hargrove--1979-85, 92-98
Greg Swindell--1986-91

DETROIT TIGERS

2 CHARLIE GEHRINGER
Dick Wakefield--1943-44
Chief Hogsett--1944
Ed Mierkowicz--1945
Don Ross--1945
Roy Cullenbine--1946-47
Paul Campbell--1948
Johnny Lipon--1949-52
Fred Hatfield--1952
Joe Ginsberg--1952-53
Al Aber--1953
Reno Bertoia--1953
Frank House--1954-57
Frank Bolling--1958-60
Jake Wood--1961-67
Tom Matchick--1967-69
Dalton Jones--1970-72
John Knox--1974-75
Phil Mankowski--1976-79
Richie Hebner--1980-82
5 HANK GREENBERG
Rip Radcliff--1942-43 (WWII)
Don Heffner--1944 (WWII)
Jake Mooty--1944 (WWII)
Billy Pierce--1945 (WWII)
George Vico--1948-49
Vic Wertz--1951-52
Cliff Mapes--1952
Bob Nieman--1953-54
Bill Tuttle--1955-56
Jim Finigan--1957
Gail Harris--1958-60
Sandy Amoros--1960
Dick Gernert--1960-61
Frank House--1961
Purnal Goldy--1962-63
Jim Northrup--1967-74
Mark Wagner--1976-80
Howard Johnson--1982
6 AL KALINE
No one
16 HAL NEWHOUSER
Reno Bertoia--1954-58
Walt Masterson--1956
Ray Narleski--1959
Ray Semprock--1960
Phil Regan--1960-65
Earl Wilson-1966-70
Jim Hannan--1971
Ron Perranoski--1971-72
Gene Michael--1975
Tom Brookens--1979-88
David Palmer--1989
Brian Dubois-1989-90
Dave Haas--1991-93
David Wells--1993-95
23 WILLIE HORTON
Kirk Gibson--1979-87, 93-95
Torey Lovullo--1988-89
Dan Petry--1990
Mark Leiter--1991-92
Gabe Kapler--1999
Hideo Nomo--2000

KANSAS CITY ROYALS

5 GEORGE BRETT
No one
10 DICK HOWSER
No one
20 FRANK WHITE
No one

LA/CALIFORNIA/ ANAHEIM/LA ANGELS

11 JIM FREGOSI
Johnny Stephenson--1973
Bobby Valentine--1975
Billy Smith--1976
Mike Guerrero-1976-77
Joe Ferguson--1981
Doug Decinces--1982-87
Dante Bichette--1988
Jim Eppard--1989
Gary DiSarcina--1990-92
Reggie Williams--1992
Greg Myers--1993-95
Don Slaught--1996
Robert Eenhoorn--1996-98
Justin Baughman--1998
29 ROD CAREW
No one
30 NOLAN RYAN
Tom Brunansky--1981
Gary Pettis--1982
Dave Goltz--1982-83
Dick Schofield--1983-84
Derrel Thomas--1984
Devon White--1985-90
Ruben Amaro--1991
Chad Curtis--1992

WASHINGTON SENATORS/ MINNESOTA TWINS

3 HARMON KILLEBREW
No one
6 TONY OLIVA
No one
14 KENT HRBEK
No one
29 ROD CAREW
No one
34 KIRBY PUCKETT
No one

NEW YORK YANKEES

1 BILLY MARTIN
Bobby Richardson--1958-66
Bobby Murcer--1969-74
Gene Michael--1986
3 BABE RUTH
George Selkirk--1935-42
Bud Metheny--1943-46
Roy Weatherly--1946
Eddie Bockman--1946
Frank Colman--1947
Allie Clark--1947
Cliff Mapes--1948
4 LOU GEHRIG
No one
5 JOE DIMAGGIO
Nick Etten--1943-45 (WWII)
7 MICKEY MANTLE
No one
8 BILL DICKEY
Johnny Lindell--1944-45 (WWII)
Aaron Robinson--1945 (WWII), 47
Frank Colman--1946
Yogi Berra--1948-64, 76-85
8 YOGI BERRA
No one
9 ROGER MARIS
Steve Whitaker--1968
Dick Simpson--1969
Ron Woods--1969-71
Graig Nettles--1973-83
10 PHIL RIZZUTO
Roy Weatherly--1943 (WWII)
Mike Garbark--1944-45 (WWII)
Tony Kubek--1958-65
Dick Howser--1967-68
Frank Fernandez--1969
Danny Cater--1970-71
Celerano Sanchez--1972-73
Chris Chambliss--1974-79
Rick Cerone--1980-84
15 THURMAN MUNSON
No one
16 WHITEY FORD
No one
23 DON MATTINGLY
No one
32 ELSTON HOWARD
No one
37 CASEY STENGEL
No one
44 REGGIE JACKSON
Jeff Torborg--1984-88
John Stearns--1989
Mike Ferraro--1990-91
49 RON GUIDRY
Jeff Johnson--1992

PHILADELPHIA/KC/ OAKLAND A'S

9 REGGIE JACKSON
Rich McKinney--1977
Mike Adams--1978
Joe Wallis--1978-79
Mickey Klutts--1981-82
Garry Hancock--1983-84
Darryl Cias--1983
Mark Wagner--1984
Dan Meyer--1985
Mike Gallego--1985-91
Jamie Quirk--1992
Junior Noboa--1994
Ernie Young--1994-95
Duffy Dyer--1996-98
Olmedo Saenz--1999-02
27 CATFISH HUNTER
Chris Batton--1976
Mark Williams--1977
Matt Keough--1977-83
Lary Sorensen--1984
Don Sutton--1985
Rick Rodriguez--1986-87
Jose Rijo--1987
Ed Jurak--1988
Billy Beane--1989
Ron Hassey--1989-90
34 ROLLIE FINGERS
Bob Lacey--1977-80
Bo McLaughlin--1981-82
Bill Almon--1983-84
Tom Tellman--1985
Dave Stewart-1986-92
43 DENNIS ECKERSLEY
No one

TAMPA BAY DEVIL RAYS

12 WADE BOGGS
No one

WASHINTON SENATORS/ TEXAS RANGERS

34 NOLAN RYAN
No one

NATIONAL LEAGUE

BOSTON/MILWAUKEE/ ATLANTA BRAVES

3 DALE MURPHY
No one
21 WARREN SPAHN
No one
35 PHIL NIEKRO
No one
41 EDDIE MATHEWS
Jim Britton--1967
Mike Thompson-1974
Adrian Devine--1975
Bob Walk--1981
44 HANK AARON
No one

CHICAGO CUBS

10 RON SANTO
Billy Grabarkewitz--1974
Mike Sember--1977
Dave Kingman--1978-80
Leon Durham --1981-88
Lloyd McClendon--1989-90
Luis Salazar--1991-92
Steve Lake-1993
Scott Bullett--1995-96
Terrell Lowery--1997-98
Bruce Kimm--2002
14 ERNIE BANKS
No one
26 BILLY WILLIAMS
Larry Biittner--1976-80

CINCINNATI REDS

1 FRED HUTCHINSON
No one
5 JOHNNY BENCH
No one
8 JOE MORGAN
Joe Amalfitano--1982
Rafael Landestoy--1983
Steve Christmas--1983
Joe Sparks--1984
Bo Diaz--1985
Terry McGriff--1987-90
Alex Trevino--1990
John McLaren--1992
Juan Samuel--1993
Bob Boone--1994
Damon Berryhill--1995
10 SPARKY ANDERSON
Tom Foley--1983-85
Tom Runnells--1985-86
Terry Francona--1987
Leon Durham--1988
Manny Trillo--1989
Luis Quinones--1989-91
Bip Roberts--1992-93
Eddie Taubensee--1994-00
Tim Foli--2001-03
Jason Romano--2004
18 TED KLUSZEWSKI
Steve Bilko--1958
Walt Dropo--1958-59
Cliff Cook--1959
Gordy Coleman--1960-67
Mike de la Hoz--1969
Tim Costo--1993
Davey Johnson--1994
Benito Santiago--1995
Eric Owens--1996-97
20 FRANK ROBINSON
Dick Simpson--1966-67
Ted Savage--1969
Willie Smith--1971
Cesar Geronimo--1972-80
Eddie Milner--1981-86
Danny Jackson--1988-90
Chris Jones--1991
Jeff Branson--1992-97
Chris Stynes--1997
24 TONY PEREZ
Dave Van Gorder--1982-83

HOUSTON ASTROS

24 JIMMY WYNN
Claude Osteen—1974
Ramon de los Santos—1974
Art Gardner—1975, 77
Jimmy Sexton—1978-79
Danny Heep—1981-82
Omar Moreno—1983
Ty Gainey—1985-87
Ed Ott—1989
Mark Davidson—1990
Franklin Stubbs—1990
Chris Jones—1992
Eric Anthony—1993
Orlando Miller—1994-96
Mike Cubbage—1997-00
Glen Barker—2001
Jason Lane—2002-05
25 JOSE CRUZ
Buddy Bell—1988
Denny Walling—1992
32 JIM UMBRICHT
No one
33 MIKE SCOTT
No one
34 NOLAN RYAN
No one
40 DON WILSON
No one
49 LARRY DIERKER
Jeff Calhoun—1984-86
Juan Agosto—1987-91, 93
Rich Scheid—1992
Jim Dougherty—1995-96

BROOKLYN/LA DODGERS

1 PEEWEE REESE
Billy Grabarkewitz--1969-72
Rick Auerbach--1974-76
Derrel Thomas--1979
Gary Weiss--1980-81
2 TOMMY LASORDA
No one
4 DUKE SNIDER
Tommy Hutton--1966, 69
Kevin Pasley--1974, 76-77
Billy North--1978
19 JUNIOR GILLIAM
No one
20 DON SUTTON
Candy Maldonado--1982-85
Ed Amelung-1986
Larry See--1986
Phil Garner--1987
Willie Randolph--1989
Mike Davis--1989
Brian Traxler--1990
Darren Holmes--1990
Mitch Webster--1991-95
Mike Blowers--1996
Darren Lewis--1997
24 WALTER ALSTON
No one
32 SANDY KOUFAX
No one
39 ROY CAMPANELLA
Ken Rowe--1963
Howie Reed--1964-66
Bob Lee--1967
42 JACKIE ROBINSON
Ray Lamb--1969
53 DON DRYSDALE
No one

SEATTLE PILOTS/ MILWAUKEE BREWERS

4 PAUL MOLITOR
Pat Listach--1996
19 ROBIN YOUNT
No one
34 ROLLIE FINGERS
John Henry Johnson--1986
Mark Ciardi--1987
Billy Bates--1989-90
Mark Lee--1990-91
Dennis Powell-1990
44 HANK AARON
No one

NEW YORK METS

14 GIL HODGES
Ron Swoboda--1965
Ken Boyer--1966-67
37 CASEY STENGEL
No one
41 TOM SEAVER
No one

PHILADELPHIA PHILLIES

1 RICHIE ASHBURN
Al Dark-1960
Joe Morgan--1960
Bobby Wine-1960, 72
Al Vincent--1961-63
George Myatt--1964-68
Bob Skinner--1969
Frank Lucchesi--1970-72
Carroll Beringer--1973-77
Jose Cardenal--1978-79
14 JIM BUNNING
Woodie Fryman-1968
Tommy Hutton-1972-77
Bud Harrelson--1978
Pete Rose--1979-83
John Wockenfuss--1985
Jeff Stone--1986-87
Tommy Barrett-1988-89
Denis Menke--1989-96
Rex Hudler--1997-98
Gary Bennett--1998-00
20 MIKE SCHMIDT
Ron Jones--1990
32 STEVE CARLTON
No one
36 ROBIN ROBERTS
No one

PITTSBURGH PIRATES

1 BILLY MEYER
No one
4 RALPH KINER
Sid Gordon--1954-55
Bob Skinner--1956-63, 74-76, 85 85
Rex Johnston--1964
Jerry May--1964
Johnny Pesky--1965-67
Bill Virdon--1968
Larry Shepard--1968-69
Charlie Sands--1971-72
Jim Campanis--1973
Chuck Tanner--1977
Dale Berra--1977-84
Mike Brown--1986
Mike Lavalliere--1987
8 WILLIE STARGELL
No one
9 BILL MAZEROSKI
No one
20 PIE TRAYNOR
Lee Handley--1938-39
Bob Klinger--1940-43
Ray Starr--1944-45
Boom-Boom Beck--1945
Ken Heintzelman--1946-47
Bill Werle--1949
Ernie Bonham--1949
Vern Law--1950-51
Hal Gregg--1950
Jim Dunn--1952
Ron Kline--1952
Paul Pettit--1953
Sam Jethroe--1954
Jim Mangan--1954
Red Swanson--1955
Bill Bell--1955
Red Munger--1956
Hank Foiles--1957-59
Hardy Peterson--1959
Gino Cimoli--1960-61
Walt Moryn--1961
John Gelnar--1964
Frank Carpin--1965
Jesse Gonder--1966-67
Al Luplow--1967
Richie Hebner--1968-71
21 ROBERTO CLEMENTE
No one
33 HONUS WAGNER
No one
40 DANNY MURTAUGH
Dave Wickersham--1968
Dock Ellis--1968-69

ST. LOUIS CARDINALS

1 OZZIE SMITH
No one
2 RED SCHOENDIENST
Whitey Lockman—1956
Hal Smith—1959-60
6 STAN MUSIAL
Red Schoendienst--1945 (WWII)
9 ENOS SLAUGHTER
Bill Virdon—1955-56
Bobby Del Greco—1956
Jim King—1957
Ray Katt—1959-60
Tim McCarver—1960
Hal Smith—1961
Minnie Minoso—1962
Bob Uecker—1964-65
Roger Maris—1967-68
Joe Torre—1969-74, 91-95
Ken Rudolph—1975-76
Vern Rapp—1977-78
Steve Swisher—1979-80
Hub Kittle—1981-83
Jamie Quirk—1984
Terry Pendleton—1984-90
Mark DeJohn--1996
14 KEN BOYER
George Kernek--1966
Steve Huntz--1967, 69
Ron Davis--1968
Joe Hague--1968
Ed Crosby--1970
Terry Hughes--1973
Dave Ricketts--1974-75, 78
Luis Alvarado--1976

Dave Rader--1977
Julio Gonzalez--1981-82
Rafael Santana--1983
Jim Adduci--1983
17 DIZZY DEAN
Joe Stripp--1938
Guy Bush--1938
Hal Epps--1938, 40
Lynn King--1939
Ira Hutchinson--1940
Walker Cooper--1940
Erv Dusak--1942
Frank Demaree--1943
Augie Bergamo--1944-45
Joe Garagiola--1946-51
Wally Westlake--1951
Les Fusselman--1952-53
Sal Yvars--1953
Vic Raschi--1954-55
Mel Wright--1955
Vinegar Bend Mizell--1956-58
Ed Olivares--1960
Jerry Buchek--1961
Fred Whitfield--1962
Jim Beauchamp--1963
Carl Warwick--1964-65
Bobby Tolan--1965-68
Vic Davalillo--1969-70
Matty Alou--1971-72
Bill Voss--1972
Cirilio Cruz--1973
20 LOU BROCK
No one
45 BOB GIBSON
No one

SAN DIEGO PADRES
6 STEVE GARVEY
Keith Moreland--1988
19 TONY GWYNN
No one
31 DAVE WINFIELD
Ed Whitson—1983-84, 87-91
Lamarr Hoyt--1985-86
Dave Staton—1994
Billy Bean—1995
Bob Tewksbury—1996
Trey Beamon—1997
Matt Clement—1998-00
35 RANDY JONES
Luis DeLeon—1982-85
Chris Brown—1987-88
Walt Terrell—1989
Rafael Valdez—1990
Jason Thompson—1996
Al Osuna—1996

NY/SAN FRANCISCO GIANTS
3 BILL TERRY
Mel Ott--1937
Hank Leiber--1937
Wally Berger-1937
Jimmy Ripple--1938
Jo-Jo Moore--1939
Frank Demaree--1940
Harry Danning--1941
Johnny Mize--1942, 46
Johnny Rucker--1943
Joe Medwick--1944-45
Charlie Mead--1945
Jim Mallory--1945
Hank Gowdy--1947-48
Herman Franks--1949-55, 58, 65-68
Bucky Walters--1956-57
Wes Westrum--1959-61
Whitey Lockman--1961-64
Ozzie Virgil, Sr.--1969-72
Mike Sadek--1973, 75-81
Jeff Ransom--1982
John Rabb-1982
Danny Ozark--1983
4 MEL OTT
Leo Durocher-1948
11 CARL HUBBELL
No one
24 WILLIE MAYS
Mario Picone--1952
27 JUAN MARICHAL
No one
30 ORLANDO CEPEDA
Billy Hoeft--1966
Jim Johnson--1970
Don Carrithers--1970-73
John Boccabella--1974
Derrel Thomas--1976-77
John Tamargo--1978-79
Bob Kearney--1979
Chili Davis-1981--87
Rusty Tillman--1988
Donell Nixon--1988-89
Mark Thurmond--1990
Jim McNamara--1992-93
Chris James--1992
Jim Deshaies--1993
Jamie Brewington--1995
Marcus Jensen--1996-97
Dan Peltier--1996
Jacob Cruz--1997-98
Dante Powell--1998
36 GAYLORD PERRY
Sam McDowell--1972
Gary Matthews--1972-76
Skip James--1977-78
Tim Foli--1977
Jim Dwyer--1978
Billy North--1979-81
Dan Schatzeder-1982
Brad Wellman--1982, 84-86
Tom McCraw--1983
Keith Comstock-1987
Dennis Cook--1988
Randy McCament--1989-90
Rafael Novoa--1990
Gil Heredia--1991-92
Steve Reed--1992
Gino Minutelli-1993
Erik Johnson--1993
Tim Layana--1993
Tony Menedez--1994
Kenny Greer-1995
Shawn Estes--1995-96
Jay Canizaro--1996
Wilson Delgado--1997
Joe Nathan-1999-00, 02-03
A. J. Pierzynski--2004
Darren Balsley--2005
44 WILLIE McCOVEY
No one

WASHINGTON NATIONALS/ MONTREAL EXPOS
8 GARY CARTER
No one
10 RUSTY STAUB
Jim Cox--1974-76
Andre Dawson--1976-86
Tom Runnells--1991-92
10 ANDRE DAWSON
Tom Runnells--1991-92
30 TIM RAINES
Cliff Floyd--1993-96, 02
Dustin Hermanson--1997-00

Red Schoendienst's (Above) rookie season was the war year, 1945. The 22-year old redhead was given #6, belonging to a young Cardinal star who was in the Navy, Stan Musial. Something must have rubbed off. Red went on to a Hall of Fame career of his own. He batted over .300 seven times, As a rookie, he led the league in stolen bases with 26. Red never won a Gold Glove Award, but led the NL in fielding 6 times. His career average was .983 . When Stan returned from the service in 1946, he took his #6 back and Red took his familiar #2.

BALL ★
LEAGUE
PRES.
CORK CENTER

BIRTHDAY BABES

6

The gym was dark and silent. Only the soft light that could make it through the glass bricks filtered down the far wall.

The young infielder made the final cut. He made the team. He sneaked out of class early and high-tailed it down the back stairs. The kid wanted a good number.

When he got there, he was the only one. He stood for a moment in the quiet looking at the shirts laid out carefully on the bleacher steps. They didn't appear to be in any order. There were gaps; there were numbers missing. Maybe it was by shirt size.

He looked for number 7. It wasn't there. He looked for number 3. It was gone too. Other kids were coming now—rushing toward the bleachers.

Where's #4? He looked around quickly. What about #6? Nothing.

His mind clogged with frustration and anxiety. All the numbers he dreamed about were not there. The images he had of gliding to his left, fluidly picking up that ball. He saw the #7 as he threw the ball to first. In his other dream, his favorite player's number flashed as he flew over an incoming runner completing a sparkling doubleplay.

Teammates were grabbing shirts. Then he saw it—his birthday, "17." He swooped up the jersey.

Only later did he find out that the returning starters had already taken their old numbers.

One of the relief pitchers from the previous year approached the kid because he had worn the #17. And the mild-mannered kid was very surprised by his own reaction. He refused to give it up. He had become instantly possessive—it was his.

The scene is played out every year in thousands of communities and scores of countries with varying results.

The number of players that live and die for their birthday number or settle on it when they're unable to get the number they want, is surprising.

Many great players wore their birth date their entire careers.

Pete Rose (Right) in happier days when he returned triumphantly to Cincinnati from tours with Philadelphia and Montreal. He rapped out his 4,000th and his Ty Cobb record-beating 4,190th hits in a Reds uniform.

Pete was an All-Star 16 times, playing more positions than any other star: second, third, outfield and first.

The most notable being Pete Rose. He was born on April 14, 1941. Pete chose #14 in 1963 when he broke in with the Reds and wore it his entire career. When Rose left Cincinnati in 1979, the #14 remained on the shelf until he returned near the end of 1984. Should the banishment of Rose be lifted by the Commissioner, the Reds are sure to retire #14. Might they do it anyway?

"Barry Bonds wears number 24," said Roger Wilson, the Pirate equipment manager when Bonds was with the Bucs. "He told me because it was his birthday. He said that was the day the Good Lord chose for him so it must be his lucky number. It was also the number worn by his Godfather, the great player Willie Mays."

Carlos May has been the only major leaguer thus far to wear his entire birthdate on his uniform. The number 17 beneath his last name MAY is the day on which he was born, May 17, 1948. He played for the White Sox for nine years wearing his personal birthday billboard. Ironically, the day after his birth-day in 1976, May was traded to the Yankees for Ken Brett. Mickey Rivers was wearing his number so he took the #38 vacated by Brett.

Gary Carter had his #8 written into his contract—why? It was his birthday.

Luis Tiant arrived at Boston in 1971, he wore his birthday for the first time—#23. He had worn #33 for the first seven years of his career. He became the mainstay of the Red Sox staff and also attached to the number which he'd move on to wear in New York and California.

For nine out of his ten years, Dick Stuart managed to wear his birthday which was one of the most sought after numbers—7. Don Money was also born on the seventh. He wore it for eleven of his 16 years.

Andre Dawson was born on the 10th of July. He began with the Expos wearing #10, but switched to #8 with the Cubs because Leon Durham was wearing #10. Dawson had the opportunity to switch when Durham left, but he didn't bother. Coming to Boston in 1993, he was able to regain his old #10.

Fifteen out of seventeen years in the majors saw Amos Otis wearing his birthday number of 26, plus four years as a coach.

The Yankees have had their share of birthday babes: Jesse Barfield wore his #29 birthday for most of his career, Jimmy Key did the same with his #22, and Pat Kelly's #14 was his birthday.

Terry Harper wore his #19 for 8 years, but wore #17 for the Tigers before moving on to Pittsburgh and #19 to finish his career. Benito Santiago has worn #9 or #09 for 10 of his 20 years. Dwight Gooden wore his #16 for all 11 Mets years, two years with the Indians and in his last year at Tampa Bay and Houston. Only on the Yanks did he not wear it. They retired it for Whitey Ford.

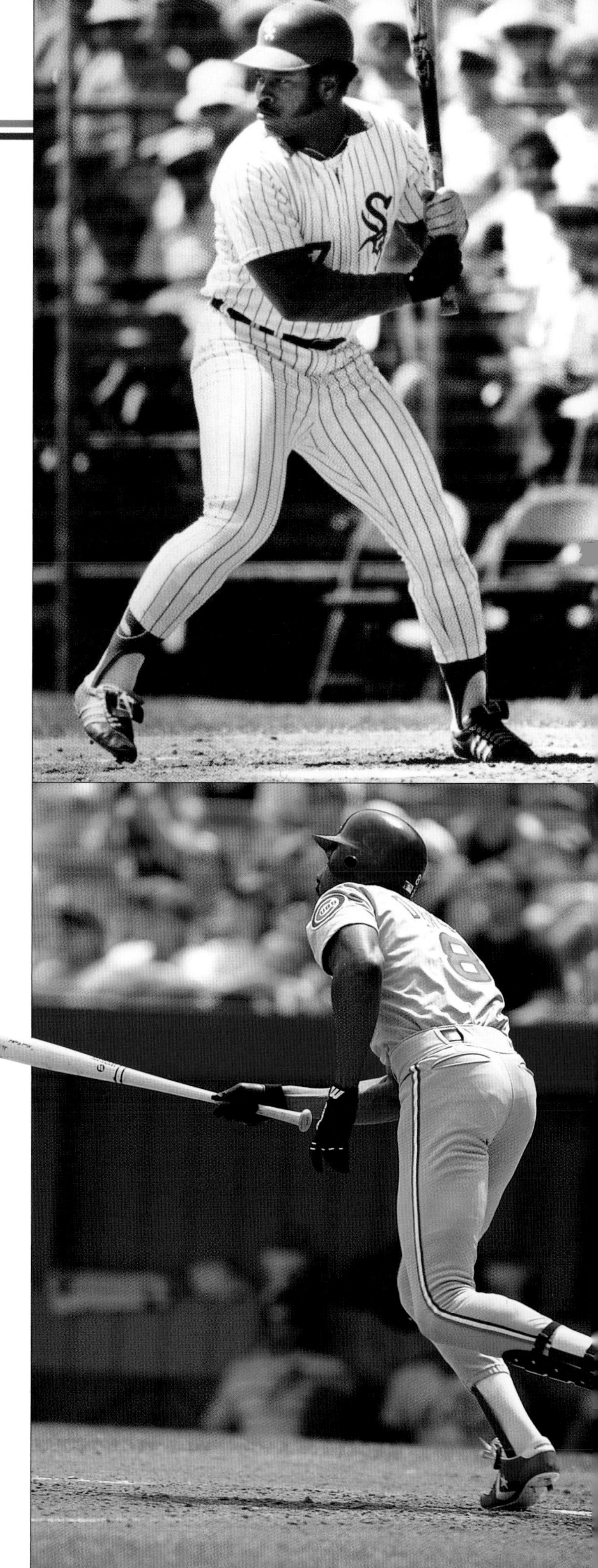

Carlos May (Right, above) was a two-time All-Star with the Chicago White Sox. He knocked in 96 runs while batting .285 in 1970. His highest mark was in 1972 when he batted .308. He ended his career with a very respectable .274.
Andre Dawson (Right) averaged 22.5 homeruns in his ten full seasons with the Expos. Upon moving to the more friendly windswept reaches of Wrigley, Dawson led the league with 49 HRs and 137 RBIs in his first season with the Cubs.

BIRTHDAY NUMBERS

These listings are for players only. If otherwise, parentheses will follow the name. The portion of a player's career that he wore his birthday number follows the name. If a player wore the number for six of his nine years, it is written as 6/9. These are partial lists. For the most part, only the more recognizable players are here.

HALF CAREER OR MORE

2 RED SCHOENDIENST 14/19
5 JIM TABOR 8/9
6 STAN HACK 9/16
7 DON MONEY 11/16
7 DICK STUART 9/10
8 GARY CARTER 18/19
8 ED KIRKPATRICK 11/16
9 PETE O'BRIEN 8/12
9/09 BENITO SANTIAGO 10/20
9 STEVE SWISHER 8/9
10 ANDRE DAWSON 12/21
11 DON SLAUGHT 9/16
12 STEVE FINLEY 15/16
12 MARIO RAMIREZ 5/6
13 ED PELLAGRINI 4/8
14 PAT KELLY 7/9
14 PETE ROSE 24/24
16 DWIGHT GOODEN 14/16
17 CARLOS MAY 8/10
18 JIM CLANCY 13/15
18 LEE MAY 10/18
19 TERRY HARPER 8/8§
19 BOB TURLEY 8/12
22 JIMMY KEY 13/15
22 MIKE MATHENY 12/12•
23 LUIS TIANT 11/19
23 JIM LEMON 8/12
25 CARLOS DELGADO 9/13
25 WHITEY LOCKMAN 13/15
26 AMOS OTIS 15/17
28 PEDRO RAMOS 9/15†
29 JESSE BARFIELD 12/12¶
31 DAVE KOSLO 7/12

§ Wore #17 in early 1987 in Detroit, back to #19 in Pittsburgh that same year.
• Wore #22 every year but also wore #15 and #44.
† Also wore birth year (#35) 2 years in Cleveland.
¶ Wore #28 briefly with Yanks until #29 was available.

FIRST YEARS ONLY

3 CARL EVERETT 7/13
3 BOB SKINNER 1/12
4 MIKE EPSTEIN 1/9
4 TOM GRIEVE 1/9
4 KEN HARRELSON 2/9
4 GIL HODGES 1/18
5 HANK AARON 1/23
6 VINCE DIMAGGIO 2/10
8 ALAN ASHBY 6/17
8 GENE FREESE 4/12
8 JIM PAGLIARONI 1/11
9 JUAN SAMUEL 1/16
9 BILL VIRDON 2/12
11 JERRY MARTIN 2/11
12 CHARLIE LAU 3/11
14 TOMMY HARPER 1/15
14 JOE LAHOUD 3/11
14 JIM MASON 2/9
16 JIM LONBORG 7/15
16 MAX SURKONT 1/9
16 GENE WOODLING 1/17
17 OZZIE VIRGIL, SR. 2/9
18 KEN BRETT 2/14
22 WALT MASTERSON 1/14
22 MOOSE SOLTERS 1/9
25 MICK KELLEHER 2/11
26 ELLIS KINDER 1/12
28 VITA BLUE 1/17

SOMETIME DURING CAREER

3 CESAR TOVAR 2/12
5 MIKE HEATH 1/14
5 JOHN OLERUD 8/17
6 TONY LAZZERI 5/11*
8 RAY MUELLER 2/14
9 NATE COLBERT 1/10
9 RAY KATT 1/8
9 JOE PEPITONE 1/12
11 JIMMY STEWART 3/10
14 FRANK DUFFY 1/10
14 WAYNE GROSS 2/11
15 WILLIE DAVIS 1/18
16 MIKE JORGENSEN 8/17
17 DON ZIMMER 3/12
18 DICK LITTLEFIELD 3/9
19 WOODY WILLIAMS 4/11
20 BOBBY MURCER 2/17
21 KEN CAMINITI 4/15
21 MURRY DICKSON 3/18
21 SCOTT SPIEZIO 3/9
22 GLENN WILSON 1/10
23 BOBBY BONILLA 2/16
23 JULIO FRANCO 3/21
23 TIM LEARY 1/13
23 BOBBY THOMSON 6/15
24 BARRY BONDS 7/20
24 OMAR MORENA 2/12
26 BILL ROBINSON 1/16
29 DAVE LaPOINT 1/12
29 MIKE McCORMICK 3/16
30 CLINT HURDLE 1/10

** Played prior to numbering also.*

Benito Santiago (Below, left) batted .300 in his first full season with the Padres, but has not gotten there since. Darrell Porter (Below, center) quietly faded away in Texas after his glory years in KC and St. Louis. Jesse Barfield (Below, right) wore #29 year after year.

LAST YEARS ONLY

2 MARV THRONEBERRY 2/7
3 CLAY DALRYMPLE 3/12
6 ERNIE LOMBARDI 1/16*
9 ARKY VAUGHAN 2/14
13 JOHNNY ROSEBORO 3/14
13 FRED STANLEY 0/14 (CH) 1/1
14 BILL BUCKNER 2/22
15 BOB SADOWSKI 2/4
17 DARRELL PORTER 1/17
17 BUTCH HOBSON 0/8 (MGR) 3/3
18 ZOILO VERSALLES 1/12
21 GEORGE BELL 2/12
21 MOE DRABOWSKI 0/17 (CH) 1/2
21 ELLIOTT MADDOX 4/11
21 JASON MARQUIS 2/5
22 WALLY BACKMAN 1/14
25 DAVID WEATHERS 2/15
26 RON NORTHEY 1/12
27 BENNIE BENGOUGH 0/4* (CH) 3/18
27 DICK HALL 2/19
28 CHRIS SPEIER 2/19
29 TOM HOUSE 3/8
29 JASON SCHMIDT 5/11
30 KIKI CUYLER 0/8* (CH) 1/3

ONE & ONLY M/L SEASON

2 GARY HARGIS--PIRATES '79
10 JIM CAMPBELL--CARDS '70
15 AUSTIN KNICKERBOCKER--A's '47
17 CHARLIE FRYE--PHILS '40
22 GARY COOPER--BRAVES '80
22 REESE DIGGS--SENATORS '34
24 WALTER WILSON--TIGERS '45
27 DUTCH McCALL--CUBS '48
29 GARLAND LAWING--GIANTS '46†
29 ROBERTO VARGAS--BRAVES '55

** Played prior to numbering also.*
†Wore #28 with Reds same year.

Many players start out their careers wearing their birthday number as a stop-gap measure, being unable to get a desired number. Others are thrilled to get that number, but after being traded away never see it again.

Jim Lonborg began his career wearing his birthday, #16, and wore it for nearly half his career, but never wore it again after leaving Boston in 1972.

Born on February 5, Hank Aaron began his fabulous career wearing #5, but only wore it one year before switching to his much-heralded #44.

Ernie Lombardi wore nine different numbers in his 17 years and the last one was his birthday number—6.

When all else failed, some players have used their birth month or even the year they were born as numbers.

Brooks Robinson was born in May, the 5th month. He wore the #5 for most of his great career. Another famous Oriole wore his birth month—Cal Ripken, #8. He was born in August.

J. R. Richard wore #50 back in the '70s. He was born in 1950. The Cooper boys, Mort and Walker, battery mates for the Cardinals in the '40s wore their birth years—#13 and #15 respectively.

Juan Guzman wore #66 for the Toronto Blue Jays—he was born in 1966. Of the Pirate pitching trio that donned the same #66, one was born in that year—Blas Minor. The Bucs also had a #65, Mark Petkovsek, who was born in 1965. In 2004, two pitchers wore their birth year—Joe Roa of the Twins wore #71 and Ugueth Urbina of the Marlins,Tigers, and Phillies wore #74.

Wally Backman (Left) seen working out in spring training in his penultimate season with the Phillies. He went on to play in ten games with Seattle where he wore his birthdate number—22. In his 14 years, Backman played on three pennant winners. The two years the New York Mets won the NL, 1986 and 1988, he batted over .300, .320 and .303 respectively. He led all NL second basemen in fielding in 1985 with .989.

BIRTH MONTH NUMBERS

Here the player's number coincides with the month in which he was born. The team listed is the team on which he played while wearing that number. The birthday is the last item for easy reference.

1 MIKE ALDRETE--GIANTS 1/29/61
1 CHICO CARRASQUEL--A's 1/23/28
1 ALVIN DARK--INDIANS 1/7/22
1 BILLY MEYER--PIRATES 1/14/1892
1 GEORGE SELKIRK--YANKS 1/4/08
1 DON ZIMMER--GIANTS 1/17/31

2 ROBERTO ALOMAR--BLUE JAYS, D-BACKS 2/5/68
2 SPARKY ANDERSON--PHILS 2/22/34
2 PAUL BLAIR--YANKS 2/1/44
2 SMOKY BURGESS--WHITE SOX 2/6/27
2 TOMMY HENRICH (CH)--GIANTS 2/20/13
2 RED SCHOENDIENST--CARDS, (CH) A's 2/2/23

3 HAROLD BAINES--WHITE SOX, RANGERS, A's, ORIOLES 3/15/59
3 DON BLASINGAME--CARDS 3/16/32
3 RIPPER COLLINS--CUBS 3/30/04
3 WOODIE HELD--INDIANS 3/25/32
3 BRIAN JORDAN--CARDS 3/29/67
3 HOBIE LANDRITH--REDS 3/16/30
3 DALE MURPHY--BRAVES, PHILS, ROCKIES 3/12/56
3 JOHNNY RAY--PIRATES, ANGELS 3/1/57

4 LUKE APPLING--WHITE SOX 4/2/07
4 JIM BOTTOMLEY--CARDS 4/23/00
4 DOLPH CAMILLI--DODGERS 4/23/07
4 JIM EISENREICH--TWINS 4/18/59
4 ALEX GRAMMAS--CARDS 4/3/26
4 RON HANSEN--WHITE SOX 4/5/38
4 SOLLY HEMUS--PHILS 4/17/23
4 ERNIE LOMBARDI--REDS 4/6/08
4 CHARLIE MAXWELL--TIGERS 4/8/27
4 TONY PHILLIPS--TIGERS 4/25/59
4 RUSTY STAUB--METS 4/1/44
4 MICKEY VERNON--SENATORS 4/22/18
4 HACK WILSON--DODGERS 4/26/00

5 JEFF BAGWELL--ASTROS 5/27/68
5 GEORGE BRETT--ROYALS 5/15/53
5 FERRIS FAIN--A's 5/29/21
5 MIKE HIGGINS--A's, RED SOX 5/27/09
5 FELIX JOSE--CARDS 5/8/65
5 BILLY JURGES--CUBS 5/9/08
5 GEORGE McQUINN--BROWNS, A's 5/29/10
5 BROOKS ROBINSON--ORIOLES 5/18/37
5 AL SIMMONS--WHITE SOX 5/22/02

6 FRANK DEMAREE--CUBS, GIANTS 6/10/10
6 BABE HERMAN--REDS 6/26/03
6 TONY PENA--PIRATES, RED SOX, (CH) ASTROS, (M) ROYALS 6/4/57
6 RICO PETROCELLI--RED SOX 6/27/43
6 BRAD WILKERSON--EXPOS 6/1/77

7 LEO DUROCHER--YANKEES 7/27/05
7 HEINIE MANUSH--RED SOX 7/20/01
7 JIM RIVERA--BROWNS, WHITE SOX 7/22/22
7 DARYL SPENCER--DODGERS 7/13/29
7 CHUCK TANNER--(M) WHITE SOX, A's, PIRATES, BRAVES 7/4/29

8 ALBERT BELLE--INDIANS, WHITE SOX 8/25/66
8 ROCKY COLAVITO--ROYALS 8/10/33
8 GARY GAETTI--TWINS, ROYALS, CARDS, CUBS 8/19/58
8 CHARLIE GRIMM--CUBS 8/28/98
8 AL LOPEZ--BRAVES 8/20/08
8 MARK LORETTA--BREWERS, ASTROS, PADRES 8/14/71
8 DALE MITCHELL--DODGERS 8/23/21
8 BOBO NEWSOM--DODGERS 8/11/07
8 CAL RIPKEN--ORIOLES 8/24/60
8 CARL YASTRZEMSKI--RED SOX 8/22/39

9 HARRY DANNING--GIANTS 9/6/11
9 VINCE DIMAGGIO--PIRATES, GIANTS 9/6/12
9 CHARLIE KELLER--YANKEES 9/12/16
9 ROGER MARIS--YANKEES, CARDS 9/10/34
9 BILL MAZEROSKI--PIRATES 9/5/36

10 DAVE COLLINS--BLUE JAYS 10/20/52
10 LENNY HARRIS--MARLINS 10/28/64
10 TONY KUBEK--YANKEES 10/12/36
10 TONY LaRUSSA--A's, (M) WHITE SOX, A's, CARDS 10/4/44
10 BIP ROBERTS--PADRES, REDS, TIGERS 10/27/63
10 RED ROLFE--(CH) TIGERS 10/17/08
10 HARRY WALKER--CARDS 10/22/16
10 MICHAEL YOUNG--RANGERS 10/19/76

11 GARY DISARCINA--ANGELS 11/19/67
11 BILL FREEHAN--TIGERS 11/29/41
11 LEFTY GOMEZ--YANKEES 11/26/08
11 JIMMY ROLLINS--PHILLIES 11/27/78
11 GARY SHEFFIELD--BREWERS, BRAVES, YANKEES 11/18/68

12 RAY JABLONSKI--REDS 12/17/26
12 MIKE MORDECAI--MARLINS 12/13/67
12 BILL NICHOLSON--PHILS 12/11/14
12 A. J. PIERZYNSKI--WHITE SOX 12/30/76
12 TONY TAYLOR--PHILS 12/19/35

Johnny Ray (Left) was a fairly productive second baseman, batting in over 60 runs in six of his ten years in the Bigs. He led the NL in doubles twice and narrowly missed leading in the AL once.

BIRTH YEAR NUMBERS

2 MARK KOENIG--YANKEES 7/19/02
3 MICKEY COCHRANE--TIGERS 4/6/03
3 BABE HERMAN--DODGERS 6/26/03
6 JOE CRONIN--SENATORS, RED SOX 10/12/06
8 ERNIE LOMBARDI--GIANTS 4/6/08

13 MORT COOPER--CARDS, BRAVES, GIANTS 3/2/13
14 HERMAN FRANKS--A's 1/4/14
15 WALKER COOPER--CARDS 1/8/15
15 DIZZY TROUT--TIGERS 6/29/15
16 BILL BEVENS--YANKEES 10/21/16
17 JOE DOBSON--INDIANS, RED SOX 1/20/17
18 JACK KRAMER--RED SOX, YANKS 1/5/18
18 BILL RIGNEY--GIANTS, (M) ANGELS, TWINS 1/29/18

20 DAVE KOSLO--BRAVES 3/31/20
20 BOB LEMON (CH)--ANGELS 9/22/20
20 JOHNNY SCHMITZ--SENATORS 11/27/20
20 FRANK SHEA--YANKEES 10/2/20
20 WALT MASTERSON--RED SOX, SENATORS 6/22/20
21 JIM HEARN--GIANTS 4/11/21
21 WARREN SPAHN--BRAVES, METS, GIANTS 4/23/21
21 ELMER VALO--A's 3/5/21
23 BOB PORTERFIELD--YANKEES 8/10/23
23 PAT SEEREY--INDIANS 3/17/23
23 BOBBY THOMSON--GIANTS 10/25/23
26 DALE LONG--YANKEES 2/6/26
27 TOMMY LASORDA--DODGERS 9/22/27
29 IKE DELOCK--RED SOX 11/11/29
29 WALLY POST--REDS, TWINS 7/9/29

30 VINEGAR BEND MIZELL--PIRATES 8/13/30
31 CHET NICHOLS--RED SOX 2/22/31
33 TED ABERNATHY--REDS 3/6/33
33 BOB SHAW--CUBS 6/29/33
35 PEDRO RAMOS--INDIANS 4/28/35
36 BO BELINSKI--ANGELS 12/7/36
38 MANNY MOTA--GIANTS 2/18/38
39 DAVE GIUSTI--ASTROS, CARDS 11/27/39

40 TONY CLONINGER--BRAVES, REDS, (CH) YANKEES 8/13/40
41 DEAN CHANCE--ANGELS 6/1/41
41 WILBER WOOD--RED SOX 10/22/41
42 CHUCK HARTENSTEIN--CUBS, PIRATES 5/26/42
42 CECIL UPSHAW--WHITE SOX 10/22/42
43 JACK BILLINGHAM--REDS 2/21/43
44 TITO FUENTES--TIGERS, A's 1/4/44
44 CARL MORTON--EXPOS 1/18/44
46 JOE RUDI--(CH) A's 9/7/46
47 AURELIO RODRIGUEZ--ANGELS 12/28/47
49 JERRY REUSS--CARDS 6/19/49

50 RAY BURRIS--(CH) BREWERS 8/22/50
50 J. R. RICHARD--ASTROS 3/7/50
54 STEVE McCATTY--A's 3/20/54
65 MARK PETKOVSEK--PIRATES 11/18/65
66 JUAN GUZMAN--BLUE JAYS 10/28/66
66 BLAS MINOR--PIRATES 3/20/66

71 JEFF GRANGER--DODGERS 12/16/71
71 MIKE HUBBARD--REDS 2/16/71
71 JOE ROA--TWINS 10/11/71
74 UGUETH URBINA--MARLINS, TIGERS, PHILLIES 2/15/74

Tommy Lasorda (Below, left) had to become a manager to win a major league game. He pitched 13 innings in 4 games for the Dodgers without a decision and was 0-4 for the Kansas City A's. Mgr. Lasorda might not have been too happy with pitcher Lasorda's 37 K's and 56 walks either. Blas Minor (Below), a young pitcher, wore #66 for the Pirates, 1993-94.

Amos Otis was born on April 26, 1947 and wore #26 for the Royals from 1970-1983. Nine years later on the Royals, Curtis Wilkerson wore #26. He was born on April 26, 1961.

Eddie Pellagrini was born on Friday the 13th, so it didn't bother him to wear 13 with the Reds, Phils and Pirates in the early '50s.

Charlie Maxwell wore #4 for the Tigers (1955-62), it being his birth month (4/8/27). The following year Whitey Herzog wore it. He was born on exactly the same day.

Some amazing circumstances have occurred with players born on the same day and playing for the same teams although they didn't always wear their birth number.

In 1946, veteran first baseman George McQuinn (born 5/29/10) was playing in his tenth season. It turned out to be his worst full season batting only .225 for the Philadelphia A's while wearing #5. He was shipped off to finish his career with the New York Yankees, making room for a young first baseman who was born on the same day. Ferris Fain born eleven years later to the day, also wore #5.

Billy Champion wore #31 in 1972 for the Phils. He was born on September 18, 1947. Another pitcher, Ken Brett joined the Phils in 1973, wore #31 and was born on September 18, 1948. The #31 on the Phils was worn in successive years by men exactly the same age to the day.

Bill Pecota wore #32 for the Royals in 1991. He was born on 2/16/60. The following year Rico Rossy wore #32 for the Royals and he was born on 2/16/64.

Even more amazingly, in 1958, two pitchers with the same birthday wore the same number with the same team, the Yankees. Sal Maglie (born 4/26/17) wore #21 early in the season to be followed by Virgil Trucks (born 4/26/19).

Two third basemen wore #12 in 1979 for the Chicago White Sox, although they were born a day apart: Eric Soderholm (9/24/48) and Jim Morrison (9/23/52).

The 1994 Reds had consecutive numbers worn by players who had the same birthday —#30 Roberto Kelly born 10/1/64 and #31 Chuck McElroy born three years later on 10/1/67.

Ex-Yankee, Roberto Kelly (Above) was batting at a .319 clip in 1993 for the Reds when he was injured. The two-time All-Star was injured again in 1996 while playing in Minnesota and batting .323. He had uneventful tours in Atlanta, Montreal and Los Angeles in between. He bounced from Seattle to Texas and on to finish with the Yankees, but never quite lived up to the promise he showed.

There have been quite a few occasions where a club will have some players with the same birthday. In 1940, the Boston Braves had outfielder Mel Preibisch born 11/23/14 and first baseman Les Scarsella born 11/23/13.

The 1978 White Sox had pitchers Jack Kucek (6/8/53) and Britt Burns (6/8/59). In 1987, the Pirates also had a couple of pitchers who were born on the same day, Mark Ross on August 8, 1957 and Brett Gideon six years later. The 1991 White Sox had two players a generation apart with the same birthday, Carlton Fisk (12/26/47) and Esteban Beltre (12/26/67).

Again in 1993 the Sox had a pair born on March 3rd: Chuck Cary in 1960 and Scott Radinsky in 1968.

The other Sox in Boston had two utility players who were born on the exact same day, August 26, 1965: Carlos Quintana and Jeff Richardson.

The 1993 and 1994 Astros had two infielders born on April 21, Chris Donnels in '66 and Ken Caminiti in '63.

During the same two years, the Atlanta Braves had an incredible three players with the same birthday—two on the same date. Greg Maddux and David Justice were both born on April 14, 1966 and Steve Avery is four years younger to the day.

The 1966 Boston Red Sox had a player named George Smith who was born on 7/7/37. Smith wore number #14. (7+7=14?) And Johnny Temple, the Reds second baseman who teamed up with Roy McMillan during the '50s was born August 8, 1928. Temple wore #16. (8+8=16?)

Why did Hall of Famer Waite Hoyt who pitched for 21 years, but only wore numbers for eight years, only once wear a number with a 9 in it? He was born on 9/9/99. He wore #11, 12, 14, 28, 19, 48, 34 and 15.

Enough already! You get the idea.

David Justice (Left) was an up-and-coming star with the Atlanta Braves. He added some punch to the lineup, averaging 21.6 homeruns a year ending with 305. Although his career batting average was .279, he slugged at a .500 clip. Injuries slowed him a bit, but he remained a steady bat for the Indians, Yankees and A's.

ARIZONA
ST. LOUIS
PITTSBURGH
NEW YORK
PHILADELPHIA
MONTREAL
ATLANTA
CINCINNATI
FLORIDA
HOUSTON
CUBS
SP RP INNING

From 1916 through 2005

The following pages contain each year that a franchise wore uniform numbers. This includes the Indians of 1916 and 1917 when they wore numerals on their sleeves, and the Indians of 1929 and 1930 who toyed with numbers on the backs of their home jerseys.

In the National League, the Cardinals wore numbers on their sleeves during the 1923 and 1924 seasons.

Each team is listed by the present franchise for the purpose of continuity with the previous incarnations listed chronologically within the present team. For example, the St. Louis Browns (wearing numbers from 1931 until their move to Baltimore in 1954) are listed under the Baltimore Orioles which preceeds Boston alphabetically. The Los Angeles/California/Anaheim Angels are listed under the present Anaheim, thus are first in the American League.

Consequently, the Milwaukee Brewers are listed with the original Seattle Pilots in the National League under M since the franchise was shifted there for the 1998 season.

Teams are designated by a three-letter abbreviation followed by N (National League) or A (American League) except where a two-letter abbreviation fits more naturally such as NY, SF or LA (New York, San Francisco or Los Angeles).

Each roster is headed by the year, under which a line shows their finish, their record, and how many games behind they were to give a sense of the team's quality. Postseason results follow the standing. For example, the Marlins in 2003:

2003
2ND E W/C 91-71 10GB
W NLDS-SFN 3-1
W NLCS-CHIN 4-3
W WS-NYA 4-2
1 LUIS CASTILLO-2B
4 GERALD WILLIAMS-OF
5 *(RET#) CARL BARGER*
6 ANDY FOX-UTIL
7 IVAN (PUDGE) RODRIGUEZ-C
9 JUAN PIERRE-OF
10 JEFF TORBORG-MGR1

They finished second in the NL East (2ND E), capturing the Wild Card (W/C) and were 10 games behind (10 GB) the Braves. They won the NL Divisional Series beating the Giants 3 games to one. They won the NL Championship Series, beating the Cubs four games to three, and finally beat the Yankees four games to two in the World Series.

Duplicate uniform numbers are listed chronologically.

Additional symbols used throughout the teams chapter are shown below:

(BRV) Bereavement leave of absence
(ILL) Illness
(INJ) Injury/on the Disabled List
(MIL) Military duty
(REL) Released
(RET) Retired from play
(SUB) Substance abuse
(SUS) Suspended
(1) after the player's position, indicates that this is the first team for the season
(2) the second team of the year
(3) the third team of the year
(4) the fourth team of the year (very rare)
(PUDGE) nicknames, as in example above, are added in parentheses. If the player is most commonly known by his nickname such as Yogi Berra, that's how he's listed.

(10) A player's number and position in parentheses means he did not play that entire season. When a number was never assigned, the position only will be in parenthesis, ie (OF).

NO# Indicates that a number was not worn.

___ Indicates the number is unknown. (The number of games played and when is shown in parentheses.) *An example of this can be seen on page 128 in the St. Louis Browns section. A player named Showboat Fisher-OF is listed on the 1932 team. Parentheses follow his name:* (18G: 7/3-8/4). *He played in 18 games from July 3 to August 4 of that season.*

[Readers may help identify the player's numbers by sending corroborating evidence to box number BB# in care of the publisher.]

? A question mark after a number shows a fairly apparent guess, but without hard evidence.

9 *(RET#) TED WILLIAMS* Retired numbers are shown with the player in italics beginning with the first season it was done.

5* NAME-P* When a pitcher wears a single digit, it is marked by an asterisk. If a position player pitches and is wearing a single digit, he is also marked.

1 MANAGER'S NAME-MGR2 This indicates that this manager was the second manager for the team that year.

Where to find your favorite team

AMERICAN LEAGUE

NATIONAL LEAGUE

1931
ST. LOUIS BROWNS

5TH 63-91 45GB

1 JIM LEVEY-SS
2 JACK (SLUG) BURNS-1B
3 GOOSE GOSLIN-OF
4 RED KRESS-3B/UTIL
5 OSCAR (SKI) (SPINACH) MELILLO-2B
6 FRED (FRITZ) SCHULTE-OF
7 LIN STORTI-3B/2B
8 RICK FERRELL-C
9 RUSS YOUNG-C
10 JACK (ROXY) CROUCH-C
10 BENNY BENGOUGH-C
12 GEORGE BLAEHOLDER-P
14 LEFTY STEWART-P
15 SAM (SAD SAM) GRAY-P
16 DICK COFFMAN-P
17 CHAD KIMSEY-P
18 RIP COLLINS-P
19 ROLLIE (LENA) STILES-P
20 FRED (LEFTY) STIELY-P
20 JESS DOYLE-P
20 BOB (LEFTY) COONEY-P
21 FRANK (BLACKIE) O'ROURKE-SS/1B
21 BUCK STANTON-OF
22 EARL MCNEELY-OF
23 LARRY BETTENCOURT-OF
24 ED GRIMES-INF
25 FRANK WADDEY-OF
25? NAP KLOZA-OF (3G: 8/16-20)
25 GARLAND BRAXTON-P (2)
26 TOM (TUT) JENKINS-OF
27 WALLY (PREACHER) HEBERT-P
28 JIMMY (PEPPER) AUSTIN-CH
33 BILL KILLIFER-MGR

1932

6TH 63-91 44GB

1 JIM LEVEY-SS
2 JACK (SLUG) BURNS-1B
3 GOOSE GOSLIN-OF/3B
4 RED KRESS-3B/UTIL (1)
4 BRUCE CAMPBELL-OF (2)
5 OSCAR (SKI) (SPINACH) MELILLO-2B
6 FRED (FRITZ) SCHULTE-OF/1B
7 LIN STORTI (INJ)-3B
8 RICK FERRELL-C
9* BUMP HADLEY-P* (2)
10 BENNY BENGOUGH-C
12 GEORGE BLAEHOLDER-P
14 LEFTY STEWART-P
15 SAM (SAD SAM) GRAY-P
16 DICK COFFMAN-P (1)
16 CARL FISCHER-P (2)
17 CHAD KIMSEY-P (1)
18 JOHNNY SCHULTE-C (1)
19 WALLY (PREACHER) HEBERT-P
20 BOB (LEFTY) COONEY-P
21 LOU (CRIP) POLLI-P
22 JIM MCLAUGHLIN-3B
23 LARRY BETTENCOURT-OF
24 ED GRIMES (INJ)-INF
25 NAP KLOZA-OF
26 TOM (TUT) JENKINS-OF
27 JOHNNY SCHULTE-C (1)
28 JIMMY (PEPPER) AUSTIN-CH
29 ALLEN SOTHORON-CH
33 BILL KILLIFER-MGR
__ SHOWBOAT FISHER-OF (18G: 7/3-8/4)
__ DEBS (TEX) GARMS-OF (34G: 8/10-9/25)
__ ART (SCOOP) SCHAREIN-3B/INF (81G: 7/6-9/25)

1933

8TH 55-96 43.5GB

1 JIM LEVEY-SS
2 JACK (SLUG) BURNS-1B
3 CARL REYNOLDS-OF
4 BRUCE CAMPBELL-OF
5 OSCAR (SKI) (SPINACH) MELILLO-2B
6 SAMMY WEST-OF
7 ART (SCOOP) SCHAREIN-3B/INF
8 RICK FERRELL-C (1)
8 MERV SHEA-C (2)
9 MUDDY RUEL-C
10 ROLLIE HEMSLEY-C (2)
12 GEORGE BLAEHOLDER-P
14 LLOYD (GIMPY) BROWN-P (1)
15 SAM (SAD SAM) GRAY-P
16 DICK COFFMAN-P
16 ROGERS (RAJAH) HORNSBY-PH/MGR3 (2)
17 BUMP HADLEY-P
18 JACK KNOTT-P
19 WALLY (PREACHER) HEBERT-P
22 ROLLIE (LENA) STILES-P
24 LIN STORTI-3B/2B
25 JACK (ROXY) CROUCH-C (1)
25? GARLAND BRAXTON-P (5G: 9/7-23)
26 TED GULLIC-UTIL
27 DEBS (TEX) GARMS-OF
28 ED (SATCHELFOOT) WELLS-P
29 ALLEN SOTHORON-CH/MGR2
30 HANK MCDONALD-P (2)
33 BILL KILLIFER-MGR1

1934

6TH 67-85 33GB

1 ALAN STRANGE-SS
2 JACK (SLUG) BURNS-1B
3 BRUCE CAMPBELL-OF
4 ART (SCOOP) SCHAREIN-PH
4 GEORGE (POOCH) (COUNT) PUCCINELLI-OF
5 OSCAR (SKI) (SPINACH) MELILLO-2B
6 SAMMY WEST-OF
7 HARLOND (DARKIE) CLIFT-3B
8 RAY PEPPER-OF
9 FRANK (HANS) GRUBE-C
10 ROLLIE HEMSLEY-C/OF
11 ROGERS (RAJAH) HORNSBY-3B/OF/MGR
12 GEORGE BLAEHOLDER-P
14 EARL CLARK-OF
14 JIM WALKUP-P
(15) SAM (SAD SAM) GRAY (ILL)-(P)
15 DEBS (TEX) GARMS-OF
16 DICK COFFMAN-P
17 BUMP HADLEY-P
18 IVY (POISON) ANDREWS-P
19 ED (SATCHELFOOT) WELLS-P
20 BILL MCAFEE-P
21 BOBO (BUCK) NEWSOM-P
22 OLLIE BEJMA-INF/OF
23 JIM (BIG JIM) WEAVER-P (1)
24 JACK KNOTT-P
25 LEFTY MILLS-P
26 CHARLEY O'LEARY-PH/CH
27 GROVER HARTLEY-C/CH

1935

7TH 65-87 28.5GB

1 ALAN STRANGE-SS (1)
1 LYN (BROADWAY) LARY-SS (2)
2 JACK (SLUG) BURNS-1B
3 BEAU BELL-UTIL
4 JOHN BURNETT-INF
5 OSCAR (SKI) (SPINACH) MELILLO-2B (1)
5 MOOSE SOLTERS-OF
6 SAMMY WEST-OF
7 HARLOND (DARKIE) CLIFT-3B/2B
8 RAY PEPPER-OF
9 FRANK (HANS) GRUBE-C (1)
9 TOMMY HEATH-C
10 ROLLIE HEMSLEY-C
11 ROGERS (RAJAH) HORNSBY-INF/MGR
12 GEORGE BLAEHOLDER-P (1)
12 SUGAR CAIN-P (2)
14 TOM (SCOOPS) CAREY-2B
15 DEBS (TEX) GARMS-OF
15 JIM WALKUP-P
16 DICK COFFMAN-P
16 EARL (TEACH) CALDWELL-P
17 FAY (SCOW) THOMAS-P
18 IVY (POISON) ANDREWS-P
19 RUSS VAN ATTA-P (2)
20 BOB POSER-P
20 MIKE MAZZERA-OF
20 HEINIE MUELLER-1B/OF
21 BOBO (BUCK) NEWSOM-P
21 ED COLEMAN-OF (2)
22 OLLIE BEJMA-INF/OF
24 JACK KNOTT-P
25 HAL WARNOCK-OF
25 BOB (LEFTY) WEILAND-P
25 SNIPE HANSEN-P (2)
26 CHARLEY O'LEARY-CH
27 GROVER HARTLEY-CH

1936

7TH 57-95 44.5GB

1 LYN (BROADWAY) LARY-SS
2 JACK (SLUG) BURNS-1B (1)
2 JIM (SUNNY JIM) BOTTOMLEY-1B
3 TOM (SCOOPS) CAREY-2B/SS
4 ROGERS (RAJAH) HORNSBY-1B/MGR
5 MOOSE SOLTERS-OF
6 SAMMY WEST-OF
7 HARLOND (DARKIE) CLIFT-3B
8 RAY PEPPER-OF
9 ED COLEMAN-OF
10 BEAU BELL-OF/1B
11 ROLLIE HEMSLEY-C
12 TONY GIULIANI-C
14 HARRY (MULE TRADER) (MURPHY) KIMBERLIN-P
15 OLLIE BEJMA-INF
16 CHIEF HOGSETT-P (2)
17 JACK KNOTT-P
18 IVY (POISON) ANDREWS-P
19 SUGAR CAIN-P (1)
19 LES (TOOTS) TIETJE-P (2)
20 EARL (TEACH) CALDWELL-P
21 RUSS VAN ATTA-P
22 JIM WALKUP-P
22 GLENN (SANDY) LIEBHARDT-P
23 SIG (JACK) JAKUCKI-P
23 ROY (POPEYE) MAHAFFEY-P
24 MIKE MEOLA-P
25 TOMMY THOMAS-P
26 CHARLEY O'LEARY-CH
27 GROVER HARTLEY-CH

1937

8TH 46-108 56GB

1 BILL KNICKERBOCKER-SS/2B
2 JIM (SUNNY JIM) BOTTOMLEY-1B/MGR2
3 TOM (SCOOPS) CAREY-2B/INF
4 ROGERS (RAJAH) HORNSBY-2B/MGR1
4 GABBY STREET-CH
5 JOE VOSMIK-OF
6 SAMMY WEST-OF
7 HARLOND (DARKIE) CLIFT-3B
8 ETHAN ALLEN-OF
9* BILL TROTTER-P*
10 BEAU BELL-OF/INF
11 ROLLIE HEMSLEY-C/1B
12 TONY GIULIANI-C
14 SHERIFF BLAKE-P (1)
14? HARRY (MULE TRADER) (MURPHY) KIMBERLIN-P (3G: 9/26-10/1)
14 BILL STRICKLAND-P
15 JERRY (NIG) LIPSCOMB-INF/P
16 CHIEF HOGSETT-P
17 JACK KNOTT-P
18 ORAL HILDEBRAND-P
19 LES (TOOTS) TIETJE-P
19 TOMMY HEATH-C
20 EARL (TEACH) CALDWELL-P
20 ED BAECHT-P
20 EDDIE SILBER-OF
21 RUSS VAN ATTA-P
22 LOU KOUPAL (INJ)-P
23 JULIO BONETTI-P
23 EMIL (HILL BILLY) BILDILLI-P
24 JIM WALKUP-P
25 TOMMY THOMAS-P (1)
25 GEORGE (THREE-STAR) HENNESSEY-P
25 BILL (WILD BILL) MILLER-P
26 CHARLEY O'LEARY-CH
26 RED BARKLEY-2B
27 HARRY (STINKY) DAVIS-1B/OF
28 BEN HUFFMAN-C
29 MIKE (MEL) MAZZERA-PH
37 TOM CAFEGO-OF
__ SAM HARSHANY-C (5G: 9/28-10/3)
__ LEFTY MILLS-P (2G: 9/29-10/3)
__ BOB MUNCRIEF-P (1G: 9/30)

1938

7TH 55-97 44GB

1 DON (JEEP) HEFFNER-2B
2 BILLY SULLIVAN-C/1B
3 RED KRESS-SS
4 GLENN MCQUILLEN-OF
4 SAM HARSHANY-C
5 GEORGE (MAC) MCQUINN-1B
6 SAMMY WEST-OF (1)
6 MEL ALMADA-OF (2)
7 HARLOND (DARKIE) CLIFT-3B
8 ETHAN ALLEN-OF
9 TOMMY HEATH-C
9?* BILL TROTTER-P* (1G: 9/30)
10 BEAU BELL-OF/INF
11 ROY (JEEP) (SAGE) HUGHES-INF
12 BOBO (BUCK) NEWSOM-P
13 GABBY (OLD SARGE) STREET-MGR
14 MIKE (MEL) MAZZERA-OF
15 BUSTER (BUS) MILLS-OF
16 JIM (BIG JIM) WEAVER-P (1)
16 FRED (DEACON) (CACTUS) JOHNSON-P
17 JACK KNOTT-P (1)
17 BILL COX-P (2)
18 ORAL HILDEBRAND-P
19 LES (TOOTS) TIETJE-P
20 VITO TAMULIS-P (1)
20 EMIL (HILL BILLY) BILDILLI-P
20 GLENN (SANDY) LIEBHARDT-P (1)
21 RUSS VAN ATTA-P
22 ED (BABE) LINKE-P
23 HARRY (MULE TRADER) (MURPHY) KIMBERLIN-P (1)
23 JOHNNY LUCADELLO-3B
24 JIM WALKUP-P
25 LEFTY MILLS-P
26 ED COLE-P
27 JULIO BONETTI-P
28 FRED (BOOTNOSE) HOFMANN-CH
29 OSCAR (SKI) (SPINACH) MELILLO-CH
30 JOE GRACE-OF
31 GABBY (OLD SARGE) STREET-MGR
__ SIG GRYSKA-SS (7G: 9/28-10/2)

1939

8TH 43-111 64.5GB

1 DON (JEEP) HEFFNER-SS/2B
2 BILLY SULLIVAN-UTIL
3 RED KRESS-SS (1)
3 JOE GRACE-OF
4 SIG GRYSKA-SS
4 MYRIL HOAG-OF/P
5 GEORGE (MAC) MCQUINN-1B
6 MEL ALMADA-OF (1)
6 MARK CHRISTMAN-SS/2B (2)
7 HARLOND (DARKIE) CLIFT-3B
8 JOHNNY (BERNIE) BERARDINO-2B/INF
8 CHET LAABS-OF (2)
9* EWALD (LEFTY) PYLE-P*
9 SAM HARSHANY-C
10 BEAU BELL-OF (1)
10 JOE (GABBY) GLENN-C
11 ROY (JEEP) (SAGE) HUGHES-2B/SS (1)
11 VERN KENNEDY-P (2)
11 JOHN (SILENT JOHN) WHITEHEAD-P (2)
12 BOBO (BUCK) NEWSOM-P (1)
12 BOB HARRIS-P (2)
12 ROXIE LAWSON-P (2)
13 BOB MUNCRIEF-P
14 JOHNNY (FOOTSIE) MARCUM-P (1)
14 JOHN (SILENT JOHN) WHITEHEAD-P (2)

14 JOHNNY (BERNIE) BERARDINO-2B/INF
15 MYRIL HOAG-OF/P
16 FRED (DEACON) (CACTUS) JOHNSON-P
16 GEORGE GILL-P (2)
17 ROXIE LAWSON-P (2)
17 BILL TROTTER-P
18 MIKE (MEL) MAZZERA-OF
18 JOE (MUSCLES) GALLAGHER-OF (2)
19 BILL COX-P
19 GEORGE GILL-P (2)
19 BOB HARRIS-P (2)
19 MOOSE SOLTERS-OF
20 ED COLE-P
20 LEFTY MILLS-P
21 RUSS VAN ATTA (INJ)-P
21 HARRY (MULE TRADER) (MURPHY) KIMBERLIN-P
22 BILL TROTTER-P
22 GEORGE GILL-P (2)
23 ROXIE LAWSON-P (2)
24 JIM WALKUP-P (1)
24 VERN KENNEDY-P (2)
25 HARRY (MULE TRADER) (MURPHY) KIMBERLIN-P
25 LEFTY MILLS-P
25 HAL SPINDEL-C
26 JOE (GABBY) GLENN-C
26 BOB HARRIS-P (2)
26 FRED (PUDGE) HANEY-MGR
27 LEFTY MILLS-P
27 HARRY (MULE TRADER) (MURPHY) KIMBERLIN-P
28 FRED (BOOTNOSE) HOFMANN-CH
28 JOHN (SILENT JOHN) WHITEHEAD-P (2)
28 JAKE (WHISTLIN' JAKE) WADE-P (2)
29 FRED SHELLENBACK-CH
30 JACK KRAMER-P
31 HAL SPINDEL-C
32 FRED (PUDGE) HANEY-MGR
33 TOMMY THOMPSON-OF (2)
33 VERN KENNEDY-P (2)
35 FRED (BOOTNOSE) HOFMANN-CH
__ EMIL (HILL BILLY) BILDILLI-P (2G: 9/26-10/1)
__ LOY HANNING-P (4G: 9/20-30)
__ JOHNNY LUCADELLO-2B (9G: 9/24-10/1)
__ BOB NEIGHBORS-SS (7G: 9/16-30)
__ EDDIE SILBER-PH (1G: 4/30)

1940

6TH *67-87* *23GB*

1 DON (JEEP) HEFFNER-2B
2 ALAN (INKY) STRANGE-SS/2B
3 LYN (BROADWAY) LARY-SS/2B
3 JOHNNY LUCADELLO-2B
4 JOHNNY (BERNIE) BERARDINO-SS/INF
5 GEORGE (MAC) MCQUINN-1B
6 HARLOND (DARKIE) CLIFT-3B
7 BOB SWIFT-C
8 SAM HARSHANY-C
8 ROY CULLENBINE-OF/1B (2)
9 GEORGE (GOOD KID) SUSCE-C
10 CHET LAABS-OF (2)
11 RIP RADCLIFF-OF/1B
12 WALT (WALLY) JUDNICH-OF
14 MYRIL HOAG-OF
15 JOE GRACE-OF/C
16 JOE (MUSCLES) GALLAGHER-OF (1)
17 BILL TROTTER-P
18 ELDON (SUBMARINE) AUKER-P
19 JACK KRAMER-P
19 MAURY NEWLIN-P
19 WILLIS (ACE) HUDLIN-P (3)
20 ROXIE LAWSON-P
21 JOHNNY NIGGELING-P
22 LEFTY MILLS-P
23 VERN KENNEDY-P
24 BOB HARRIS-P
25 JOHN (SILENT JOHN) WHITEHEAD (INJ)-P
26 EMIL (HILL BILLY) BILDILLI-P
27 BILL COX-P
27 WILLIS (ACE) HUDLIN-P (3)
28 JAKE (WHISTLIN' JAKE) WADE-P
29 FUZZ WHITE-PH
29 BILL COX-P
30 SLICK COFFMAN-P
32 WALTER (UNION MAN) HOLKE-CH
33 FRED (BOOTNOSE) HOFMANN-CH
34 FRED (PUDGE) HANEY-MGR

1941

6TH (TIE) *70-84* *31GB*

1 DON (JEEP) HEFFNER-2B
2 ALAN (INKY) STRANGE-INF
3 GEORGE (MAC) MCQUINN-1B
4 JOHNNY (BERNIE) BERARDINO-SS/3B
5 JOHNNY LUCADELLO-UTIL
6 FRANK (HANS) GRUBE-C
6 VERN (JUNIOR) (BUSTER) STEPHENS-SS
7 HARLOND (DARKIE) CLIFT-3B
8 BOB SWIFT-C
9 JOE GRACE-OF/C
10 CHUCK STEVENS-1B
11 RIP RADCLIFF-OF/1B (1)
11 RICK FERRELL-C (2)
12 WALT (WALLY) JUDNICH-OF
14 BOBBY ESTALELLA-OF
15 GLENN (RED) MCQUILLEN-OF
15 MYRIL HOAG-OF
16 FRITZ OSTERMUELLER-P
17 BILL TROTTER-P
18 ELDON (SUBMARINE) AUKER-P
19 JACK KRAMER-P
20 EMIL (HILL BILLY) BILDILLI-P
21 JOHNNY NIGGELING-P
22 DENNY GALEHOUSE-P
23 MAURY NEWLIN-P
24 BOB HARRIS-P
25 GEORGE (UG) CASTER-P
26 HOOKS IOTT-P
27 VERN KENNEDY-P (1)
28 CHET LAABS-OF
29 BOB MUNCRIEF-P
30 JOHNNY ALLEN-P (1)
30 ARCHIE (HAPPY) MCKAIN-P (2)
32 LUKE SEWELL-MGR2
33 FRED (BOOTNOSE) HOFMANN-CH
34 FRED (PUDGE) HANEY-MGR1
35 JOHNNY BASSLER-CH
36 ZACK TAYLOR-CH
50 ROY CULLENBINE-OF/1B (2)
52 GEORGE ARCHIE-1B (2)

1942

3RD *82-69* *19.5GB*

1 DON (JEEP) HEFFNER-2B/1B
2 ALAN (INKY) STRANGE-INF
3 GEORGE (MAC) MCQUINN-1B
4 DON GUTTERIDGE-2B/3B
5 VERN (JUNIOR) (BUSTER) STEPHENS-SS
7 HARLOND (DARKIE) CLIFT-3B/SS
8 BOB SWIFT-C (1)
8 FRANKIE (BLIMP) HAYES-C (2)
9 RICK FERRELL-C
10 RAY HAYWORTH-PH
10 MIKE (SHOTGUN) CHARTAK-OF (3)
12 WALT (WALLY) JUDNICH-OF
14 TONY CRISCOLA-OF
15 GLENN (RED) MCQUILLEN-OF
16 GEORGE (UG) CASTER-P
17 BILL TROTTER-P (1)
17 STEVE SUNDRA-P (2)
18 ELDON (SUBMARINE) AUKER-P
(19) JACK KRAMER (MIL)-(P)
19 STAN (LEFTY) FERENS-P
20 JOHNNY (BERNIE) BERARDINO (MIL)-INF
20 BOB HARRIS-P (1)
21 JOHNNY NIGGELING-P
22 DENNY GALEHOUSE-P
23 FRITZ OSTERMUELLER-P
23 EWALD (LEFTY) PYLE-P
24 LOY HANNING-P
25 AL (BOOTS) HOLLINGSWORTH-P
26 JOHN (SILENT JOHN) WHITEHEAD-P
27 FRANK (PORKY) BISCAN (MIL)-P
27 PETE (JAKE) APPLETON (AKA JABLONOWSKI)-P (2)
28 CHET LAABS-OF
29 BOB MUNCRIEF-P
32 LUKE SEWELL-C/MGR
33 FRED (BOOTNOSE) HOFMANN-CH
34 ZACK TAYLOR-CH
50 ROY CULLENBINE-OF/1B (1)
__ BABE DAHLGREN-PH (2) (2G:5/16-17)

1943

6TH *72-80* *25GB*

1 DON (JEEP) HEFFNER-2B/1B (1)
2 FLOYD BAKER-SS/3B
2 ELLIS (CAT) CLARY-3B/2B (2)
3 GEORGE (MAC) MCQUINN-1B
4 DON GUTTERIDGE-2B
5 VERN (JUNIOR) (BUSTER) STEPHENS-SS/OF
6 MARK CHRISTMAN-INF
7 HARLOND (DARKIE) CLIFT (ILL)-3B (1)
8 FRANKIE (BLIMP) HAYES-C/1B
9 RICK FERRELL-C
10 MIKE (SHOTGUN) CHARTAK-OF/1B
11 MILT (SKIPPY) BYRNES-OF
12 MIKE KREEVICH-OF
14 TONY CRISCOLA-OF
14 AL (ZEKE) ZARILLA-OF
15 AL (HAPPY) MILNAR-P (2)
15 BOBO (BUCK) NEWSOM-P (2)
15 HAL EPPS-OF
16 GEORGE (UG) CASTER-P
17 STEVE SUNDRA-P
18? HAL EPPS-OF
19 PAUL (DAFFY) DEAN-P
19 AL LAMACCHIA,-P
20 JOE (DODE) SCHULTZ-C
21 JOHNNY NIGGELING-P (1)
22 DENNY GALEHOUSE-P
23 FRITZ OSTERMUELLER-P (1)
23 CHARLIE FUCHS-P (2)
24 NELS (NELLIE) POTTER-P
25 AL (BOOTS) HOLLINGSWORTH-P
27 JACK KRAMER (MIL)-P
27 FRED SANFORD-P
28 CHET LAABS-OF
29 BOB MUNCRIEF-P
30 FRED (BOOTNOSE) HOFMANN-CH
30 AL (HAPPY) MILNAR-P (2)
31 SID PETERSON-P
32 LUKE SEWELL-MGR
33 FRED (BOOTNOSE) HOFMANN-CH
33 BOBO (BUCK) NEWSOM-P (2)
33 FRED (BOOTNOSE) HOFMANN-CH
34 ZACK TAYLOR-CH
36 ARCHIE (HAPPY) MCKAIN-P
36 OX MILLER-P (2)
__ HANK SCHMULBACH-PR (1G:9/27)

1944

1ST *89-65* *0GB*

L WS-STLN 4-2

1 FLOYD BAKER-2B/SS
2 ELLIS (CAT) CLARY-3B/2B
3 GEORGE (MAC) MCQUINN-1B
4 DON GUTTERIDGE-2B
5 VERN (JUNIOR) (BUSTER) STEPHENS-SS
6 MARK CHRISTMAN-3B/1B
7 JOE (DODE) SCHULTZ-C
7 MIKE (SHOTGUN) CHARTAK-1B/OF
8 FRANK MANCUSO-C
9 RED HAYWORTH-C
10 FRANK DEMAREE-OF
10 BABE MARTIN-OF
11 MILT (SKIPPY) BYRNES-OF
12 DENNY GALEHOUSE (WAR)-P
12 MIKE KREEVICH-OF
14 AL (ZEKE) ZARILLA-OF
15 GENE (ROWDY) MOORE-OF/1B
16 GEORGE (UG) CASTER-P
17 STEVE SUNDRA (MIL)-P
17 TOM (HEAVE-O) (THE ARM) HAFEY-OF/1B
17 TOM TURNER-C (2)
18 HAL EPPS-OF (1)
18 LEN SCHULTE-PH
19 JACK KRAMER-P
20 LEFTY WEST-P
21 TEX SHIRLEY-P
22 SIG (JACK) JAKUCKI-P
23 AL LAMACCHIA-P
24 NELS (NELLIE) POTTER-P
25 AL (BOOTS) HOLLINGSWORTH-P
26 SAM (SAD SAM) ZOLDAK-P
27 WILLIS (ACE) HUDLIN (MIL)-P
28 CHET LAABS (WAR)-OF
29 BOB MUNCRIEF-P
30 DENNY GALEHOUSE (WAR)-P
32 LUKE SEWELL-MGR
33 FRED (BOOTNOSE) HOFMANN-CH
34 ZACK TAYLOR-CH

1945

3RD *81-70* *6GB*

1 LEN SCHULTE-INF
2 ELLIS (CAT) CLARY-3B/2B
3 GEORGE (MAC) MCQUINN-1B
4 DON GUTTERIDGE-2B/OF
5 VERN (JUNIOR) (BUSTER) STEPHENS-SS
6 MARK CHRISTMAN-3B/1B
7 JOE (DODE) SCHULTZ-C
8 FRANK MANCUSO-C
9 RED HAYWORTH-C
11 MILT (SKIPPY) BYRNES-OF
12 MIKE KREEVICH-OF (1)
12 CHET LAABS (WAR)-OF
14 PETE GRAY-OF
15 GENE (ROWDY) MOORE-OF/1B
16 GEORGE (UG) CASTER-P (1)
17 EARL (LEFTY) JONES-P
18 BABE MARTIN-OF/1B
18 LOU FINNEY-OF/INF (2)
19 JACK KRAMER-P
20 LEFTY WEST-P
21 TEX SHIRLEY-P
22 SIG (JACK) JAKUCKI-P
23 CLIFF (MULE) FANNIN-P
23 DEE SANDERS-P
24 NELS (NELLIE) POTTER-P
25 AL (BOOTS) HOLLINGSWORTH-P
26 SAM (SAD SAM) ZOLDAK-P
28 CHET LAABS (WAR)-OF
29 BOB MUNCRIEF-P
31 AL LAMACCHIA-P
32 LUKE SEWELL-MGR
33 FRED (BOOTNOSE) HOFMANN-CH
34 ZACK TAYLOR-CH
35 EARL (LEFTY) JONES-P
36 PETE (JAKE) APPLETON (AKA JABLONOWSKI) (MIL)-P (1)
36 OX MILLER-P
37 PETE (JAKE) APPLETON (AKA JABLONOWSKI) (MIL)-P (1)

1946

7TH *66-88* *38GB*

1 LEN SCHULTE-2B/3B
2 BOB (DUKE) DILLINGER-3B/SS
3 BABE DAHLGREN-1B
4 JOHNNY (BERNIE) BERARDINO-2B
5 VERN (JUNIOR) (BUSTER) STEPHENS-SS
6 MARK CHRISTMAN-3B/SS
7 JOHNNY LUCADELLO-3B/2B
8 FRANK MANCUSO-C
9 JOE (DODE) SCHULTZ-C
10 BABE MARTIN-C
10 FRANK (PORKY) BISCAN-P
11 HANK HELF-C
12 KEN (ZIGGY) SEARS-C

12 CHET LAABS-OF
14 AL (ZEKE) ZARILLA-OF
15 GLENN (RED) MCQUILLEN-OF
16 KEN (ZIGGY) SEARS-C
16 RAY SHORE-P
17 WALT (WALLY) JUDNICH-OF
18 LOU FINNEY-OF/INF
18 JEFF HEATH-OF (2)
19 JOE GRACE-OF (1)
19 PAUL (PEANUTS) (GULLIVER) LEHNER-OF
20 AL (ZEKE) ZARILLA-OF
21 ELLIS (OLD FOLKS) KINDER-P
22 GEORGE BRADLEY-OF
23 GEORGE ARCHIE-1B
23 LES MOSS-C
24 CHUCK STEVENS-1B
25 AL (BOOTS) HOLLINGSWORTH-P (1)
25 TOM FERRICK-P (2)
26 SAM (SAD SAM) ZOLDAK-P
27 NELS (NELLIE) POTTER-P
28 TEX SHIRLEY-P
29 BOB MUNCRIEF-P
30 DENNY GALEHOUSE-P
31 STEVE (SMOKEY) SUNDRA-P
32 LUKE SEWELL-MGR1
33 FRED (BOOTNOSE) HOFMANN-CH
34 ZACK TAYLOR-CH/MGR2
35 JACK KRAMER-P
37 OX MILLER-P
37 JERRY WITTE-1B
39 CHET (CHESTY CHET) JOHNSON-P
40 AL (HAPPY) MILNAR-P
41 FRED SANFORD-P
44 AL LAMACCHIA-P (1)
44 FRANK MANCUSO-C
45 STAN (LEFTY) FERENS-P
47 CLIFF (MULE) FANNIN-P

1947

8TH 59-95 38GB

2 BILLY HITCHCOCK-INF
3 RUSTY PETERS-2B/SS
4 JOHNNY (BERNIE) BERARDINO (INJ)-2B
5 VERN (JUNIOR) (BUSTER) STEPHENS-SS
6 BOB (DUKE) DILLINGER-3B
7 JERRY WITTE-1B
7 HANK THOMPSON-2B
8 JAKE EARLY-C
10 LES MOSS-C
11 JOE (DODE) SCHULTZ-PH
14 AL (ZEKE) ZARILLA-OF
15 GLENN (RED) MCQUILLEN-PH
15 WILLARD BROWN-OF
15 PERRY CURRIN-SS
17 PAUL (PEANUTS) (GULLIVER) LEHNER-OF
18 WALT (WALLY) JUDNICH-OF
19 RAY COLEMAN-OF
20 JEFF HEATH-OF
21 JACK KRAMER-P
22 DENNY GALEHOUSE-P (1)
23 GLEN MOULDER-P
24 SAM (SAD SAM) ZOLDAK-P
25 FRED SANFORD-P
26 ELLIS (OLD FOLKS) KINDER-P
27 NELS (NELLIE) POTTER-P
28 CLIFF (MULE) FANNIN-P
30 EARLE (THE KENTUCKY COLONEL) COMBS-CH
31 HOOKS IOTT-P
31 BUD SWARTZ-P
31 DIZZY DEAN-P
33 FRED (BOOTNOSE) HOFMANN-CH
36 WALTER BROWN-P
44 BOB MUNCRIEF-P
51 MUDDY RUEL-MGR

1948

6TH 59-94 37GB

1 SAM (BLACKIE) DENTE-SS/3B
2 JERRY PRIDDY-2B
3 CHUCK STEVENS-1B
3 HANK (BOW WOW) ARFT-1B
4 EDDIE PELLAGRINI-SS
5 WHITEY PLATT-OF
6 BOB (DUKE) DILLINGER-3B
7 ANDY ANDERSON-INF
8 TOM JORDAN-PH
9 JOE (DODE) SCHULTZ-PH
10 LES MOSS-C
11 JOE (DODE) SCHULTZ-PH
11 ROY PARTEE-C
12 ROY PARTEE-C
12 JERRY MCCARTHY-1B
12 KEN WOOD-OF
12 DON LUND-OF (2)
14 AL (ZEKE) ZARILLA-OF
16 AL (LEFTY) GERHEAUSER-P
17 PAUL (PEANUTS) (GULLIVER) LEHNER-OF/1B
19 RAY COLEMAN-OF (1)
19 GEORGE (BINGO) BINKS-OF/1B (2)
19 DICK KOKOS-OF
19 KARL DREWS-P (2)
20 PETE LAYDON-OF
20 BLACKIE SCHWAMB-P
21 BRYAN STEPHENS-P
22 FRANK (PORKY) BISCAN-P
23 CLIFF (MULE) FANNIN-P
24 AL WIDMAR-P
25 FRED SANFORD-P
26 SAM (SAD SAM) ZOLDAK-P (1)
26 BILL (LEFTY) KENNEDY-P (2)
27 NELS (NELLIE) POTTER-P (1)
28 JIM WILSON-P
29 CLIFF (MULE) FANNIN-P
29 RAY SHORE-P
29 KARL DREWS-P (2)
30 AL (LEFTY) GERHEAUSER-P
30 JOE (PROFESSOR) (SPECS) OSTROWSKI-P
31 BRYAN STEPHENS-P
31 NED GARVER-P
32 NED GARVER-P
32 RALPH WINEGARNER-CH
33 FRED (BOOTNOSE) HOFMANN-CH
35 CLEM (STEAMBOAT) DREISEWERD-P (1)
35 AL WIDMAR-P
36 FRANK (PORKY) BISCAN-P
37 RAY SHORE-P
38 BILL (LEFTY) KENNEDY-P (2)
38 ZACK TAYLOR-MGR
39 JOE (PROFESSOR) (SPECS) OSTROWSKI-P
40 KARL DREWS-P (2)

1949

7TH 53-101 44GB

1 JOHN SULLIVAN-INF
2 JERRY PRIDDY-2B
3 HANK (BOW WOW) ARFT-PH
3 GEORGE ELDER-OF
3 FRANKIE PACK-PH
3 AL NAPLES-SS
4 EDDIE PELLAGRINI-SS
5 WHITEY PLATT-OF/1B
6 BOB (DUKE) DILLINGER-3B
7 ANDY ANDERSON-INF
7? OWEN FRIEND-2B (2G: 10/2)
8 STAN SPENCE-OF/1B (2)
9 SHERM LOLLAR-C
10 LES MOSS-C
11 JACK GRAHAM-1B
12 KEN WOOD-OF
14 AL (ZEKE) ZARILLA-OF (1)
15 ROY (SQUIRREL) SIEVERS-OF/3B
17 PAUL (PEANUTS) (GULLIVER) LEHNER-OF/1B
18 IRV MEDLINGER-P
19 DICK KOKOS-OF
20 KARL DREWS-P
21 JOE (PROFESSOR) (SPECS) OSTROWSKI-P
22 JIM BILBREY-P
23 CLIFF (MULE) FANNIN-P
24 TOM FERRICK-P
25 JACK TOBIN-CH
26 RALPH WINEGARNER-P
26 BILL (LEFTY) KENNEDY-P
27 BOB SAVAGE-P
28 DICK STARR (ILL)-P
29 AL PAPAI-P
29 RIBS RANEY-P
30 BILL (LEFTY) KENNEDY-P
30 BOB MALLOY-P
31 NED GARVER-P
32 JOE (DODE) SCHULTZ-CH
33 FRED (BOOTNOSE) HOFMANN-CH
34 RAY SHORE-P
35 RED EMBREE-P
35 ED ALBRECHT-P
36 JIM BILBREY-P
37 AL PAPAI-P
38 ZACK TAYLOR-MGR
40 RALPH WINEGARNER-CH

1950

7TH 58-96 40GB

1 DEMARSBILLY (KID) DEMARS (INJ)-SS/3B
2 LEO (TOMMY) THOMAS-3B
2 SNUFFY STIRNWEISS-INF (2)
3 HANK (BOW WOW) ARFT-1B
4 TOM UPTON-SS/INF
6 FRANKIE GUSTINE-3B
7 OWEN FRIEND-2B/INF
8 BILL SOMMERS-3B/2B
9 SHERM LOLLAR-C
10 LES MOSS-C
12 KEN WOOD-OF
14 DON (FOOTSIE) LENHARDT-1B/UTIL
15 ROY (SQUIRREL) SIEVERS-OF/3B
17 RAY COLEMAN-OF
19 DICK KOKOS-OF
20 AL WIDMAR-P
21 JOE (PROFESSOR) (SPECS) OSTROWSKI-P (1)
21 DUANE (DEE) PILLETTE-P (2)
22 LOU SLEATER-P
22 DON JOHNSON-P (2)
23 CLIFF (MULE) FANNIN-P
24 TOM FERRICK-P (1)
25 LOU (LENA) KRETLOW-P (1)
26 DON JOHNSON-P (2)
27 SID SCHACHT-P
27 JIM DELSING-OF (2)
28 DICK STARR-P
29 CUDDLES MARSHALL-P
30 BILL (LEFTY) KENNEDY-P
31 NED GARVER-P
32 EARLE BRUCKER-CH
33 JACK TOBIN-CH
34 RALPH WINEGARNER-CH
35 ED ALBRECHT-P
35 DUANE (DEE) PILLETTE-P (2)
36 RUSS BAUERS-P
36 CUDDLES MARSHALL-P
37 JACK BRUNER-P (2)
38 ZACK TAYLOR-MGR
40 STUBBY OVERMIRE-P
42 TOMMY FINE-P
46 RIBS RANEY-P
46 HARRY DORISH-P

1951

8TH 52-102 46GB

0 MAX PATKIN-OF/CH
1/8 EDDIE GAEDEL-PH
1 DEMARSBILLY (KID) DEMARS-SS
1 PAUL (PEANUTS) (GULLIVER) LEHNER-OF (3)
2 FREDDIE MARSH-3B/INF
3 HANK (BOW WOW) ARFT-1B
4 TOM UPTON-SS
4 BUD THOMAS-SS
5 BOBBY YOUNG-2B
6 MAX PATKIN-OF/CH
6 BILL JENNINGS-SS
7 BILL JENNINGS-SS
7 JOHNNY (BERNIE) BERARDINO-UTIL
8 JOHNNY BERO-SS/2B
8 BENNIE TAYLOR-1B
9 SHERM LOLLAR-C/3B
10 LES MOSS-C (1)
10 MATT BATTS-C (2)
11 CLYDE KLUTTZ-C
11 JACK MAGUIRE-UTIL (3)
12 KEN WOOD-OF
12 JACK MAGUIRE-UTIL (3)
14 DON (FOOTSIE) LENHARDT-OF/1B (1)
15 ROY (SQUIRREL) SIEVERS (INJ)-OF
15 TOMMY BYRNE-P (2)
16 FRANK SAUCIER-OF
17 RAY COLEMAN-OF (1)
17 EARL RAPP-OF (2)
18 JOE LUTZ-1B
18 BOBBY HOGUE-P (2)
18 FRED SANFORD-P (3)
(19) DICK KOKOS (MIL)-(OF)
19 JIM DYCK-3B
19 BOB NIEMAN-OF
20 AL WIDMAR-P
21 DUANE (DEE) PILLETTE-P
22 DON JOHNSON-P (1)
22 SATCHEL PAIGE-P
23 CLIFF (MULE) FANNIN-P
23 MIKE GOLIAT-2B (2)
23 KERMIT WAHL-3B (2)
24 JIM (HOT ROD) MCDONALD-P
24 DALE LONG-1B/OF (2)
24 JIM DYCK-3B
25 TITO (BOBBY) HERRERA-P
25 BOB MAHONEY-P (2)
26 IRV MEDLINGER-P
26 JIM SUCHECKI-P
26 BOB (BULLET BOB) TURLEY-P
27 JIM DELSING-OF
28 DICK STARR-P (1)
28 FRED SANFORD-P (3)
28 DUKE MARKELL-P
29 SATCHEL PAIGE-P
31 NED GARVER-P
33 JACK TOBIN-CH
34 RALPH WINEGARNER-CH
36 FRED (BOOTNOSE) HOFMANN-CH
38 ZACK TAYLOR-MGR
39 BOB NIEMAN-OF
39 LOU SLEATER-P
40 STUBBY OVERMIRE-P (1)
40 TOMMY BYRNE-P (2)
42 SID SCHACHT-P (1)
42 JIM SUCHECKI-P
42 BOBBY HOGUE-P (2)
44 ED REDYS-CH
46 BILL (LEFTY) KENNEDY-P
46 CLIFF MAPES-OF (2)
47 SATCHEL PAIGE-P

1952

7TH 64-90 31GB

1 JOE (OATS) DEMAESTRI-SS/INF
2 FREDDIE MARSH-INF (1/3)
3 HANK (BOW WOW) ARFT (INJ)-1B
4 MARTY (SLATS) (OCTOPUS) (MR. SHORTSTOP) MARION-SS/MGR2
5 BOBBY YOUNG-2B
6 MIKE GOLIAT-2B
6 CASS MICHAELS-3B/2B (2)
7 JIM (JUNGLE JIM) RIVERA-OF (1)
7 ROY (SQUIRREL) SIEVERS (INJ)-1B
8 LEO (TOMMY) THOMAS-INF (1)
8 GORDON GOLDSBERRY-1B/OF
9 DICK KRYHOSKI-1B
10 LES MOSS-C
11 CLINT (SCRAP IRON) COURTNEY-C
12 DUANE (DEE) PILLETTE-P
14 GORDON GOLDSBERRY-1B/OF
14 AL (ZEKE) ZARILLA-OF (2)
15 TOMMY BYRNE-P
17 EARL RAPP-OF (1)
17 RAY COLEMAN-OF (2)
17 KEN HOLCOMBE-P (2)
18 JIM DELSING-OF (1)
18 DICK LITTLEFIELD-P (2)
(19) DICK KOKOS (MIL)-(OF)
19 BOB NIEMAN-OF
20 CLIFF (MULE) FANNIN-P
20 VIC WERTZ-OF (2)
21 GEORGE (ROCKY) SCHMEES-OF/1B
21 RUFUS (JAKE) CRAWFORD-OF
22 TOM WRIGHT-OF (1)
22 JAY (J.W.) PORTER-OF/1B
23 PETE TAYLOR-P
23 BOB MAHONEY-P
23 DON (FOOTSIE) LENHARDT-OF/1B (3)
24 JOHNNY HETKI-P
24 BOB MAHONEY-P
24 MARLIN STUART-P (2)
24 BOBBY HOGUE-P (2)
25 STUBBY OVERMIRE-P
25 LOU SLEATER-P (1)
26 DAVE MADISON-P (1)
26 MARLIN STUART-P (2)
27 CASS MICHAELS-3B/2B (2)
27 JIM DYCK-3B/OF
28 CLIFF (MULE) FANNIN-P
28 STAN ROJEK-SS
29 SATCHEL PAIGE-P
30 GENE BEARDEN-P
31 NED GARVER-P (1)

ST. LOUIS BROWNS/**BALTIMORE ORIOLES**

33 BOB (SUGAR) CAIN-P
34 HAL (BUD) (LEFTY) HUDSON-P (1)
34 WILLIE MIRANDA-SS (2)
35 EARL (IRISH) HARRIST-P
38 DICK LITTLEFIELD-P (2)
40 DARRELL JOHNSON-C (1)
40 MARLIN STUART-P (2)
42 ROGERS (RAJAH) HORNSBY-MGR1
44 BOB SCHEFFING-CH
47 BILL NORMAN-CH

1953

8TH 54-100 46.5GB

1 WILLIE MIRANDA-SS/3B (1)
2 FRANK KELLERT-1B
3 JOHNNY GROTH-OF
4 MARTY (SLATS) (OCTOPUS) (MR. SHORTSTOP) MARION-SS/MGR
5 BOBBY YOUNG-2B
6 BILLY HUNTER-SS
7 ROY (SQUIRREL) SIEVERS-1B
8 JIM DYCK-OF/3B
9 ED MICKELSON-1B
10 LES MOSS-C
11 CLINT (SCRAP IRON) COURTNEY-C
12 DUANE (DEE) PILLETTE-P
14 DON (FOOTSIE) LENHARDT-OF/3B
15 HANK EDWARDS-OF
16 DICK KRYHOSKI-1B
17 MAX LANIER-P (2)
18 DICK LITTLEFIELD-P
19 DICK KOKOS-OF
20 VIC WERTZ-OF
21 DUANE (DEE) PILLETTE-P
22 VIRGIL (FIRE) TRUCKS-P (1)
22 LOU (LENA) KRETLOW-P (2)
23 MIKE BLYZKA-P
24 BOBO HOLLOMAN-P
24 BOB (BULLET BOB) TURLEY (MIL)-P
25 HAL WHITE-P (1)
26 MARLIN STUART-P
27 DON LARSEN-P
29 SATCHEL PAIGE-P
31 HARRY (THE CAT) BRECHEEN-P/CH
32 BABE MARTIN-C
32 DOC CRANDALL-CH
33 BOB (SUGAR) CAIN-P
34 NEIL BERRY-INF
34 JOHNNY (SKIDS) LIPON-3B/2B (2)
35 BOB (HOBBY) HABENICHT-P
36 DIXIE UPRIGHT-PH
39 BOB (HOBBY) HABENICHT-P
40 BOB (MR. TEAM) ELLIOTT-3B (1)
40 VERN (JUNIOR) (BUSTER) STEPHENS-3B (2)
44 BOB SCHEFFING-CH
47 BILL NORMAN-CH
__ JIM PISONI-OF (3G: 9/25-27)

1954
BALTIMORE ORIOLES

7TH 54-100 57GB

1 CHICO GARCIA-2B
2 NEIL BERRY-SS
2 JIM BRIDEWESER-SS/2B
3 EDDIE WAITKUS-1B
4 VERN (JUNIOR) (BUSTER) STEPHENS-3B
5 BOBBY YOUNG-2B
6 BILLY HUNTER-SS
7 FRANK KELLERT-1B
8 DICK KRYHOSKI-1B
9 RAY (DEACON) MURRAY-C
10 LES MOSS-C
11 CLINT (SCRAP IRON) COURTNEY-C
12 JOE (POP) DURHAM-OF
14 DON (FOOTSIE) LENHARDT-OF/1B (1)
14 RAY (DEACON) MURRAY-C
15 SAM MELE-OF (1)
15 FRANK KELLERT-1B
15 BOB (SARGE) KUZAVA-P (2)
16 GIL COAN-OF
17 JIM (BIG JIM) FRIDLEY-OF
18 DICK LITTLEFIELD-P (1)
18 CAL ABRAMS-OF (2)
19 DICK KOKOS-OF
20 VIC WERTZ-OF (1)
20 BOB (CHICK) CHAKALES-P (2)
21 JIM (BIG JIM) FRIDLEY-OF
21 HOWIE FOX-P
22 DAVE KOSLO-P (1)
23 LOU (LENA) KRETLOW-P
24 VERN BICKFORD-P
24 BILLY O'DELL-P
25 JIMMY DYKES-MGR
26 MARLIN STUART-P (1)
26 RYNE DUREN-P
27 DON LARSEN-P
28 DUANE (DEE) PILLETTE-P
29 TOM (REBEL) OLIVER-CH
30 FRANK SKAFF-CH
31 HARRY (THE CAT) BRECHEEN-CH
32 CHUCK DIERING-OF
33 BOB (BULLET BOB) TURLEY-P
34 MIKE BLYZKA-P
35 JOE COLEMAN-P
36 RYNE DUREN-P
37 HOWIE FOX-P
38 JAY HEARD-P
40 BOB KENNEDY-3B/OF (2)

1955

7TH 57-97 39GB

2 FREDDIE MARSH, (INJ)-2B/INF
3 BILLY COX-INF
3 DAVE POPE-OF (2)
4 VERN (JUNIOR) (BUSTER) STEPHENS-3B (1)
4 KAL SEGRIST-INF
4 DAVE PHILLEY-OF/3B (2)
5 BOBBY YOUNG-2B (1)
5 ANGIE (JUNIOR) DAGRES-OF
5 HANK (HEENEY) (HEINE) MAJESKI-3B/2B (2)
6 BOB HALE-1B
7 WILLIE MIRANDA-SS/2B
8 JIM PYBURN (INJ)-3B/OF
8 KAL SEGRIST-INF
9 EDDIE WAITKUS-1B (1)
9 DON (TIGER) LEPPERT-2B
10 LES MOSS-C (1)
10 TOMMY GASTALL-C
11 GUS TRIANDOS-1B/UTIL
12 PAUL RICHARDS-MGR
13 BILL (LEFTY) (HOOKS) MILLER-P
14 GENE WOODLING-OF (1)
14 WALLY WESTLAKE-OF (2)
14 JIM DYCK-OF/3B
15 BOB (SARGE) KUZAVA-P (1)
15 ED LOPAT-P (2)
16 ERV PALICA-P
17 HOOT EVERS-OF
17 BILL (LEFTY) WIGHT-P (2)
18 CAL ABRAMS-OF/1B
19 DON JOHNSON-P
20 ANGIE (JUNIOR) DAGRES-OF
20 DON FERRARESE-P
20 ART SCHALLOCK-P (2)
21 GIL COAN-OF (1)
21 BROOKS ROBINSON-3B
22 HAL SMITH-C
23 LOU (LENA) KRETLOW-P
23 HARRY DORISH-P (2)
24 HARRY BYRD-P (1)
(24) BILLY O'DELL (MIL)-(P)
24 ROGER (NOONIE) MARQUIS-OF
25 JIM (HOT ROD) MCDONALD-P
25 TED GRAY-P (4)
26 LUM HARRIS-CH
27 SAUL ROGOVIN-P (1)
28 DUANE (DEE) PILLETTE-P
28 HAL (SKINNY) BROWN-P (2)
29 RAY (FARMER) MOORE-P
30 AL VINCENT-CH
31 HARRY (THE CAT) BRECHEEN-CH
32 CHUCK DIERING-OF/INF
33 BOB KENNEDY-3B/OF (1)
33 WAYNE CAUSEY-3B/INF
34 ANGIE (JUNIOR) DAGRES-OF
34 CHARLIE MAXWELL-PH
35 JOE COLEMAN-P (1)
35 GEORGE ZUVERINK-P (2)
36 JIM WILSON-P
37 BOB ALEXANDER-P
37 BOB (TEX) (BABE) NELSON-OF/1B
38 JAY HEARD-P
40 BOB KENNEDY-3B/OF (1)
43 CHARLIE (CHUCK) LOCKE-P
46 DON FERRARESE-P
47 BOB HARRISON-P

1956

6TH 69-85 28GB

1 BOB (THE ROPE) BOYD (INJ)-1B/OF
2 FREDDIE MARSH-INF
2 JOE FRAZIER-OF (3)
3 DAVE POPE-OF (1)
3 BOB NIEMAN-OF (2)
3 GEORGE KELL-3B/INF (2)
4 DAVE PHILLEY-OF/3B (1)
4 GEORGE KELL-3B/INF (2)
4 BOB NIEMAN-OF (2)
5 BOBBY ADAMS-3B/2B
5 GRADY HATTON-2B/3B (3)
6 BOB HALE-1B
7 WILLIE MIRANDA-SS
8 JIM PYBURN-OF
9 BILLY (SHOTGUN) GARDNER-2B/INF
10 TOMMY GASTALL (DIED)-C
11 GUS TRIANDOS-C/1B
12 PAUL RICHARDS-MGR
14 JIM DYCK-OF (1)
14 HOOT EVERS-OF (2)
15 BOB (THE ROPE) BOYD (INJ)-1B/OF
15 GEORGE WERLEY-P
16 ERV PALICA-P
17 BILL (LEFTY) WIGHT-P
18 BILLY O'DELL (MIL)-P
19 MORRIE (LEFTY) MARTIN-P (2)
20 SANDY CONSUEGRA-P (2)
22 HAL SMITH-C (1)
22 JOE GINSBERG-C (2)
23 HARRY DORISH-P (1)
23 DICK WILLIAMS-OF/INF (2)
25 MIKE FORNIELES-P (2)
25 BOB HARRISON-P
26 LUM HARRIS-CH
(27) JOE DURHAM (MIL)-(OF)
27 CHARLIE BEAMON-P
28 HAL (SKINNY) BROWN-P
29 RAY (FARMER) MOORE-P
30 AL VINCENT-CH
31 HARRY (THE CAT) BRECHEEN-CH
32 CHUCK DIERING-OF/3B
32 RON (THE KID) MOELLER-P
33 WAYNE CAUSEY-3B/2B
34 BROOKS ROBINSON-3B/2B
35 GEORGE ZUVERINK-P
36 JIM WILSON-P (1)
36 CONNIE JOHNSON-P (2)
37 BOB (TEX) (BABE) NELSON-OF
38 FRED BESANA-P
38 BILLY LOES-P (2)
39 DON FERRARESE-P
40 MEL (COUNTRY) HELD-P
40 JOHNNY (BEAR TRACKS) SCHMITZ-P (2)
41 BABE BIRRER-P
41 MIKE FORNIELES-P (2)
42 GORDIE SUNDIN-P
43 JIMMY ADAIR-CH
44 TITO FRANCONA-OF/1B
46 DON FERRARESE-P

1957

5TH 76-76 21GB

1 BOB (THE ROPE) BOYD (INJ)-1B/OF
2 AL PILARCIK-OF
3 GEORGE KELL-3B/1B
4 BOB NIEMAN-OF
5 BROOKS ROBINSON (INJ)-3B/2B
6 BOB HALE-1B
7 WILLIE MIRANDA-SS
8 JIM PYBURN-OF/C
8 BUDDY PETERSON-SS
9 BILLY (SHOTGUN) GARDNER-2B/SS
10 TOM PATTON-C
10 BILLY GOODMAN-UTIL (2)
11 GUS TRIANDOS-C
12 PAUL RICHARDS-MGR
16 ART (CHIC) CECCARELLI-P
16 EDDIE MIKSIS-PH
17 BILL (LEFTY) WIGHT-P
18 BILLY LOES-P
21 SANDY CONSUEGRA-P (1)
21 LENNY GREEN-OF
21 ART HOUTTEMAN-P (2)
22 JOE GINSBERG-C
23 DICK WILLIAMS-UTIL (1)
23 MILT PAPPAS-P
23 JIM BUSBY-OF (2)
24 JOE (POP) DURHAM-OF
24 DIZZIE TROUT-P
26 LUM HARRIS-CH
27 CHARLIE BEAMON-P
27 JOE (POP) DURHAM-OF
28 HAL (SKINNY) BROWN-P
29 RAY (FARMER) MOORE-P
30 AL VINCENT-CH
31 HARRY (THE CAT) BRECHEEN-CH
33 WAYNE CAUSEY-2B/3B
34 BROOKS ROBINSON (INJ)-3B/2B
35 GEORGE ZUVERINK-P
36 CONNIE JOHNSON-P (2)
37 BOB (TEX) (BABE) NELSON-OF
37 DON FERRARESE-P
37 EDDIE ROBINSON-PH/CH (3)
38 BILLY O'DELL-P
39 DON FERRARESE-P
39 KEN LEHMAN-P (2)
40 KEN LEHMAN-P (2)
40 JIM BRIDEWESER-INF
41 MIKE FORNIELES-P (1)
41 JERRY WALKER-P
42 CARL (JUG) POWIS-OF
42 FRANK (NOODLES) ZUPO-C
44 TITO FRANCONA-OF/1B
51 DON FERRARESE-P

1958

6TH 74-79 17.5GB

1 BOB (THE ROPE) BOYD-1B
2 AL PILARCIK-OF
3 RON HANSEN-SS
4 BOB NIEMAN (INJ)-OF
5 BROOKS ROBINSON-3B/2B
6 EDDIE MIKSIS-SS (1)
6 JERRY ADAIR-SS/2B
7 WILLIE MIRANDA-SS
8 FOSTER CASTLEMAN-UTIL
9 BILLY (SHOTGUN) GARDNER-2B/SS
11 GUS TRIANDOS-C
12 PAUL RICHARDS-MGR
14 GENE WOODLING-OF
15 HOYT WILHELM-P (2)
17 LEO BURKE-OF/3B
18 BILLY LOES-P
19 LEO BURKE-OF/3B
19 LOU SLEATER-P (2)
20 BERT HAMRIC-PH
20 BOB HALE-1B
21 LENNY GREEN-OF
22 JOE GINSBERG-C
23 DICK WILLIAMS-UTIL
24 ARNIE PORTOCARRERO-P
26 LUM HARRIS-CH
27 CHARLIE BEAMON-P
27 JOE TAYLOR-OF (2)
28 HAL (SKINNY) BROWN (INJ)-P
29 JACK HARSHMAN-P
30 AL VINCENT-CH
31 HARRY (THE CAT) BRECHEEN-CH
32 MILT PAPPAS-P
33 JIM BUSBY-OF/3B
35 GEORGE ZUVERINK-P
36 CONNIE JOHNSON-P
37 EDDIE ROBINSON-CH
38 JERRY WALKER-P
39 KEN LEHMAN-P
40 RON (THE KID) MOELLER-P
40 CHUCK (DUCKY) (SNUFFY) OERTEL-OF
41 BILLY O'DELL-P
42 FRANK (NOODLES) ZUPO-C
43 CHARLIE BEAMON-P
44 JIM MARSHALL-1B/OF (1)
44 WILLIE TASBY-OF
45 JIMMY (CHOPPY) ADAIR-CH

1959

6TH 74-80 20GB

1 BOB (THE ROPE) BOYD-1B
2 AL PILARCIK-OF
3 RON HANSEN-SS
4 BOB NIEMAN-OF
5 BROOKS ROBINSON-3B/2B
6 BILLY KLAUS-INF
7 WILLIE MIRANDA-INF
8 BOBBY AVILA-UTIL (1)
8 JERRY ADAIR-2B/SS
9 BILLY (SHOTGUN) GARDNER-2B/INF
10 BOB HALE-1B
11 GUS TRIANDOS-C
12 PAUL RICHARDS-MGR
14 GENE WOODLING-OF
15 HOYT WILHELM-P
16 GEORGE BAMBERGER-P
17 CHICO CARRASQUEL-SS/INF
18 BILLY LOES-P

21 LENNY GREEN-OF
21 ALBIE PEARSON-OF (2)
22 JOE GINSBERG-C
23 LEO BURKE-2B/3B
24 ARNIE PORTOCARRERO-P
25 WHITEY LOCKMAN-UTIL (1)
26 LUM HARRIS-CH
27 JOE TAYLOR-OF
27 FRED (SQUEAKY) VALENTINE-OF
27 WES STOCK-P
28 HAL (SKINNY) BROWN-P
29 JACK HARSHMAN-P (1)
29 BILLY HOEFT-P (3)
30 AL VINCENT-CH
31 HARRY (THE CAT) BRECHEEN-CH
32 MILT PAPPAS-P
33 JIM FINIGAN-INF
33 BOB (RABBIT) SAVERINE-PR
34 WHITEY LOCKMAN-UTIL (1)
35 GEORGE ZUVERINK (INJ)-P
35 RIP COLEMAN-P (2)
37 EDDIE ROBINSON-CH
37 WALT (MOOSE) DROPO-1B/3B (2)
38 JERRY WALKER-P
40 BARRY SHETRONE-OF
41 BILLY O'DELL-P
44 WILLIE TASBY-OF
45 JIMMY (CHOPPY) ADAIR-CH
46 ERNIE JOHNSON-P
48 JACK (FAT JACK) FISHER-P

1960

2ND 89-65 8GB

1 MARV BREEDING-2B
2 AL PILARCIK-OF
3 RON HANSEN-SS
4 JIM (GENTLEMAN JIM) GENTILE-1B
5 BROOKS ROBINSON-3B/2B
6 BILLY KLAUS-INF
7 JACKIE BRANDT-OF/INF
7 JERRY ADAIR-2B
8 GENE STEPHENS-OF (2)
9 BOB (THE ROPE) BOYD-1B
10 CLINT (SCRAP IRON) COURTNEY-C
11 GUS TRIANDOS (INJ)-C
12 PAUL RICHARDS-MGR
14 GENE WOODLING-OF
15 HOYT WILHELM-P
16 MARV BREEDING-2B
16 JIM BUSBY-OF (2)
17 WALT (MOOSE) DROPO-1B/3B
18 JOHN ANDERSON-P
18 WES STOCK-P
19 GORDON JONES-P
20 JOHNNY POWERS-OF (1)
20 BILLY HOEFT-P
21 ALBIE PEARSON-OF
22 JOE GINSBERG-C (1)
22 DAVE PHILLEY-OF/3B (3)
23 CHUCK ESTRADA-P
24 ARNIE PORTOCARRERO-P
25 JACKIE BRANDT-OF/INF
26 LUM HARRIS-CH
28 HAL (SKINNY) BROWN-P
29 STEVE BARBER-P
30 BOB MABE-P
31 HARRY (THE CAT) BRECHEEN-CH
32 MILT PAPPAS-P
33 DAVE NICHOLSON-OF
35 BOBBY (THE FLYING SCOT) (THE STATEN ISLAND SCOT) THOMSON-OF (2)
35 RIP COLEMAN-P
35 DEL RICE-C (3)
36 GENE GREEN-OF
38 JERRY WALKER-P
40 BARRY SHETRONE-PR
41 VALMY THOMAS-C
44 WILLIE TASBY-OF (1)
44 RAY (BUDDY) BARKER-OF
45 JIMMY (CHOPPY) ADAIR-CH
48 JACK (FAT JACK) FISHER-P
59 STEVE BARBER-P

1961

3RD 95-67 14GB

1 MARV BREEDING-2B
2 CLINT (SCRAP IRON) COURTNEY-C (2)
3 RON HANSEN-SS/2B
4 JIM (GENTLEMAN JIM) GENTILE-1B
5 BROOKS ROBINSON-3B/INF
6 WHITEY HERZOG-OF
7 JERRY ADAIR-2B/INF
8 GENE STEPHENS-OF (1)
8 MARV (MARVELOUS MARV) THRONEBERRY-OF/1B (2)
9 RUSS SNYDER-OF
10 DICK WILLIAMS-OF/INF
10 CHUCK ESSEGIAN-PH
11 GUS TRIANDOS (INJ)-C
12 PAUL RICHARDS-MGR1
13 STEVE BARBER-P
14 EARL ROBINSON-OF
15 HOYT WILHELM-P
16 JIM BUSBY-OF
17 WALT (MOOSE) DROPO-1B
18 WES STOCK-P
19 GORDON JONES-P
20 BILLY HOEFT-P
22 DAVE PHILLEY-OF/1B
23 CHUCK ESTRADA-P
25 JACKIE BRANDT-OF/3B
26 LUM HARRIS-CH/MGR2
28 HAL (SKINNY) BROWN-P
29 DICK HALL-P
30 BOOG POWELL-1B
31 HARRY (THE CAT) BRECHEEN-CH
32 MILT PAPPAS (INJ)-P
36 HANK FOILES (INJ)-C
38 DICK HYDE-P
39 JIM LEHEW-P
39 JOHN PAPA-P
40 BARRY SHETRONE-OF
42 FRANK (NOODLES) ZUPO-C
42 CHARLIE LAU-C (2)
44 CHARLIE LAU-C (2)
45 JIMMY (CHOPPY) ADAIR-CH
48 JACK (FAT JACK) FISHER-P

1962

7TH 77-85 19GB

1 MARV BREEDING-2B
2 JOHNNY TEMPLE-2B (1)
2 BOB (RABBIT) SAVERINE-2B
3 RON HANSEN- (INJ)-SS
4 JIM (GENTLEMAN JIM) GENTILE-1B
5 BROOKS ROBINSON-3B/INF
6 WHITEY HERZOG-OF
7 JERRY ADAIR-2B/INF
8 MARV (MARVELOUS MARV) THRONEBERRY-OF (1)
8 ANDY ETCHEBARREN-C
9 RUSS SNYDER-OF
10 DICK WILLIAMS-UTIL
11 GUS TRIANDOS (INJ)-C
13 STEVE BARBER (INJ)-P
14 EARL ROBINSON-OF
15 HOYT WILHELM-P
16 BOOG POWELL-OF/1B
17 JOHN MILLER-P
18 WES STOCK-P
19 DAVE MCNALLY-P
20 BILLY HOEFT-P
22 JACK (FAT JACK) FISHER-P
23 CHUCK ESTRADA-P
25 JACKIE BRANDT-OF/3B
26 DICK LUEBKE-P
27 ART QUIRK-P
27 NATE SMITH-C
28 HAL (SKINNY) BROWN-P (1)
28 PETE WARD-OF
29 DICK HALL-P
30 BILL SHORT-P
30 HOBIE LANDRETH-C (2)
31 HARRY (THE CAT) BRECHEEN-CH
32 MILT PAPPAS-P
33 DAVE NICHOLSON-OF
34 OZZIE VIRGIL, SR.-PH
34 MICKEY MCGUIRE-SS
36 DARRELL JOHNSON-C/CH (2)
38 JIM LEHEW-P
38 ROBIN ROBERTS-P
39 JOHN PAPA-P
40 BARRY SHETRONE-OF
41 GEORGE (STOPPER) STALLER-CH
42 CAL ERMER-CH
44 CHARLIE LAU-C
45 BILLY HITCHCOCK-MGR

1963

4TH 86-76 18.5GB

1 BOB (RABBIT) SAVERINE-2B
2 BOB JOHNSON-INF
4 JIM (GENTLEMAN JIM) GENTILE-1B
5 BROOKS ROBINSON-3B/SS
6 JOE GAINES-OF
7 JERRY ADAIR-2B
9 RUSS SNYDER-OF
10 DICK BROWN-C
11 LUIS APARICIO-SS
12 JOHN (HORSE) ORSINO-C/1B
13 STEVE BARBER-P
14 IKE DELOCK-P (2)
14 SAM BOWENS-OF
16 AL (FUZZY) SMITH-OF
17 JOHN MILLER-P
18 WES STOCK-P
19 DAVE MCNALLY-P
20 FRED (SQUEAKY) VALENTINE-OF
20 PETE BURNSIDE-P (1)
22 DEAN STONE-P
23 CHUCK ESTRADA (INJ)-P
24 HERM STARRETTE-P
25 JACKIE BRANDT-OF/3B
26 BOOG POWELL-OF/1B
28 GEORGE (LEFTY) BRUNET-P (2)
29 DICK HALL-P
30 HOBIE LANDRETH-C (1)
31 HARRY (THE CAT) BRECHEEN-CH
32 MILT PAPPAS-P
35 BUSTER NARUM-P
35 WALLY BUNKER-P
37 STU MILLER-P
38 ROBIN ROBERTS-P
40 MIKE MCCORMICK-P
41 LUKE (OLD ACHES & PAINS) APPLING-CH
42 HANK BAUER-CH
43 HARRY (THE CAT) BRECHEEN-CH
44 CHARLIE LAU-C (1)
45 BILLY HITCHCOCK-MGR

1964

3RD 97-65 2GB

1 BOB (RABBIT) SAVERINE-SS/OF
2 BOB JOHNSON-UTIL
3 WILLIE KIRKLAND-OF (1)
4 NORM SIEBERN-1B
5 BROOKS ROBINSON-3B
6 JOE GAINES-OF (1)
6 LENNY GREEN-OF (3)
7 JERRY ADAIR-2B
8 BOOG POWELL-OF/1B
9 RUSS SNYDER (INJ)-OF
10 DICK BROWN-C
11 LUIS APARICIO-SS
12 JOHN (HORSE) ORSINO-C/1B
13 STEVE BARBER-P
14 GENE WOODLING-CH
16 SAM BOWENS-OF
17 KEN ROWE-P
18 WES STOCK-P (1)
18 FRANK BERTAINA-P
19 DAVE MCNALLY-P
20 DAVE VINEYARD-P
20 GINO CIMOLI-OF (2)
23 CHUCK ESTRADA (INJ)-P
24 HERM STARRETTE-P
24 LOU PINIELLA-PH
25 JACKIE BRANDT-OF
26 BOOG POWELL-OF/1B
27 WALLY BUNKER-P
29 DICK HALL-P
30 HARVEY (THE KITTEN) HADDIX-P
31 HARRY (THE CAT) BRECHEEN-CH
32 MILT PAPPAS-P
33 PAUL BLAIR-OF
34 EARL ROBINSON-OF
35 SAM JONES-P
37 STU MILLER-P
38 ROBIN ROBERTS-P
39 FRANK BERTAINA-P
40 DAVE VINEYARD-P
40 MIKE MCCORMICK-P
41 SHERM LOLLAR-CH
42 HANK BAUER-MGR
44 LOU JACKSON-OF
44 CHARLIE LAU-C (2)
55 BILLY HUNTER-CH

1965

3RD 94-68 8GB

2 BOB JOHNSON-INF
3 CURT BLEFARY-OF
4 NORM SIEBERN-1B
5 BROOKS ROBINSON-3B
6 DAVEY JOHNSON-INF
6 PAUL BLAIR-OF
7 JERRY ADAIR-2B
8 ANDY ETCHEBARREN-C
9 RUSS SNYDER-OF
10 DICK BROWN (ILL)-C
11 LUIS APARICIO-SS
12 JOHN (HORSE) ORSINO-C/1B
13 STEVE BARBER-P
14 GENE WOODLING-CH
15 DAVEY JOHNSON-INF
16 SAM BOWENS-OF
18 DON LARSEN-P (2)
19 DAVE MCNALLY-P
22 JIM PALMER-P
23 CARL WARWICK-OF (2)
24 HERM STARRETTE-P
25 JACKIE BRANDT-OF
26 BOOG POWELL-1B/OF
27 WALLY BUNKER-P
29 DICK HALL-P
30 HARVEY (THE KITTEN) HADDIX-P
30 ED BARNOWSKI-P
31 HARRY (THE CAT) BRECHEEN-CH
32 MILT PAPPAS-P
33 PAUL BLAIR-OF
35 KEN ROWE-P
35 JOHN MILLER-P
37 STU MILLER-P
38 ROBIN ROBERTS-P (1)
38 ED BARNOWSKI-P
40 FRANK BERTAINA-P
41 SHERM LOLLAR-CH
42 HANK BAUER-MGR
43 DAROLD KNOWLES-P
44 CHARLIE LAU-C
49 MARK BELANGER-SS
55 BILLY HUNTER-CH

1966

1ST 97-63 0GB
W WS-LAN 4-0

2 BOB JOHNSON-INF
3 CURT BLEFARY-OF/1B
5 BROOKS ROBINSON-3B
6 PAUL BLAIR-OF
7 JERRY ADAIR-2B (1)
7 MARK BELANGER-SS
8 ANDY ETCHEBARREN-C
9 RUSS SNYDER-OF
11 LUIS APARICIO-SS
12 WOODIE HELD-UTIL
13 STEVE BARBER (INJ)-P
14 GENE WOODLING-CH
15 DAVEY JOHNSON-2B/SS
16 SAM BOWENS-OF
17 JOHN MILLER-P
18 MIKE (SUPERJEW) EPSTEIN-1B
19 DAVE MCNALLY-P
20 FRANK ROBINSON-OF/1B
22 JIM PALMER-P
23 VIC ROZNOVSKY-C
24 BILL SHORT-P (1)
25 MOE DRABOWSKY-P
26 BOOG POWELL-1B
27 WALLY BUNKER-P
28 EDDIE FISHER-P (2)
29 DICK HALL-P
31 HARRY (THE CAT) BRECHEEN-CH
32 GENE BRABENDER-P
34 LARRY HANEY-C
35 CAM CARREON-C
36 TOM PHOEBUS-P
37 STU MILLER-P
38 ED BARNOWSKI-P
39 ED WATT-P
40 FRANK BERTAINA-P
41 SHERM LOLLAR-CH
42 HANK BAUER-MGR
44 CHARLIE LAU (INJ)-C
55 BILLY HUNTER-CH

1967

6TH (TIE) 76-85 15.5GB

2 BOB JOHNSON-PH (1)
2 MICKEY MCGUIRE-2B
3 CURT BLEFARY-OF/1B
4 MIKE (SUPERJEW) EPSTEIN (1)
5 BROOKS ROBINSON-3B
6 PAUL BLAIR-OF
7 MARK BELANGER-INF
8 ANDY ETCHEBARREN-C
9 RUSS SNYDER-OF
11 LUIS APARICIO-SS
12 WOODIE HELD-UTIL (1)
12 DAVE MAY-OF
13 STEVE BARBER-P (1)
14 GENE WOODLING-CH
15 DAVEY JOHNSON-2B/3B
16 SAM BOWENS-OF
17 JOHN MILLER-P
17 MIKE ADAMSON-P
17 JOHN BUZHARDT-P (2)
19 DAVE MCNALLY-P
20 FRANK ROBINSON (INJ)-OF/1B

ST. LOUIS BROWNS/**BALTIMORE ORIOLES**

21 CURT MOTTON-OF
22 JIM PALMER (INJ)-P
23 VIC ROZNOVSKY-C
24 DAVE LEONHARD-P
24 PETE RICHERT-P (2)
25 MOE DRABOWSKY-P
26 BOOG POWELL-1B
27 WALLY BUNKER-P
28 EDDIE FISHER-P
29 MARCELINO LOPEZ (INJ)-P (2)
30 JOHN BUZHARDT-P (2)
31 HARRY (THE CAT) BRECHEEN-CH
32 GENE BRABENDER-P
33 PAUL (GORILLA) GILLIFORD -P
34 LARRY HANEY-C
36 TOM PHOEBUS-P
37 STU MILLER-P
39 ED WATT-P
40 FRANK BERTAINA-P (1)
41 SHERM LOLLAR-CH
42 HANK BAUER-MGR
44 CHARLIE LAU (INJ)-C (1)
44 JIM HARDIN-P
45 BILL DILLMAN-P
46 TOM FISHER-P
46 PETE RICHERT-P (2)
46 DAVE LEONHARD-P
46 MARCELINO LOPEZ (INJ)-P (2)
47 TOM FISHER-P
49 JOHN BUZHARDT-P (2)
55 BILLY HUNTER-CH

1968
2ND 91-71 12GB
1 CHICO FERNANDEZ-SS/2B
2 BOBBY FLOYD-SS
3 CURT BLEFARY-OF/UTIL
4 EARL WEAVER-CH/MGR2
5 BROOKS ROBINSON-3B
6 PAUL BLAIR-OF/3B
7 MARK BELANGER-SS
8 ANDY ETCHEBARREN (INJ)-C
9 DON BUFORD-UTIL
10 ELLIE HENDRICKS-C
12 DAVE MAY-OF
14 MERV RETTENMUND-OF
15 DAVEY JOHNSON-2B/SS
16 BRUCE HOWARD-P (1)
16 FRED (SQUEAKY) VALENTINE-OF (2)
17 MIKE ADAMSON-P
19 DAVE MCNALLY-P
20 FRANK ROBINSON-OF/1B
21 CURT MOTTON-OF
(22) JIM PALMER (INJ)-(P)
24 PETE RICHERT (MIL)-P
25 MOE DRABOWSKY-P
26 BOOG POWELL-1B
27 WALLY BUNKER-P
28 JOHN O'DONOGHUE-P
30 MIKE FIORE-1B/OF
31 GEORGE BAMBERGER-CH
32 GENE BRABENDER-P
34 LARRY HANEY-C
35 ROGER (SPIDER) NELSON-P
36 TOM PHOEBUS-P
37 JOHN MORRIS-P
39 EDDIE WATT-P
40 DAVE LEONHARD-P
41 VERN HOSCHEIT-CH
42 HANK BAUER-MGR1
44 JIM HARDIN-P
47 MIKE ADAMSON-P
48 RAY SCARBOROUGH-CH
48 GEORGE (STOPPER) STALLER-CH
50 FRED BEENE-P
55 BILLY HUNTER-CH

1969
1ST E 109-53 0GB
W ALCS-MINA 3-0
L WS-NYN 4-1
2 BOBBY FLOYD-INF
3 CLAY DALRYMPLE-C
4 EARL WEAVER-MGR
5 BROOKS ROBINSON-3B
6 PAUL BLAIR-OF
7 MARK BELANGER-SS
8 ANDY ETCHEBARREN-C
9 DON BUFORD-OF/INF
10 ELLIE HENDRICKS-C/1B
12 DAVE MAY-OF
14 MERV RETTENMUND-OF
15 DAVEY JOHNSON-2B/SS
17 MIKE ADAMSON-P
18 AL SEVERINSEN-P
19 DAVE MCNALLY-P
20 FRANK ROBINSON-OF/1B
21 CURT MOTTON-OF
22 JIM PALMER (INJ)-P
23 FRANK BERTAINA-P (2)
24 PETE RICHERT-P
26 BOOG POWELL-1B
29 DICK HALL-P
30 CHICO SALMON-UTIL
31 GEORGE BAMBERGER-CH
32 MARCELINO LOPEZ-P
33 FRED BEENE-P
35 MIKE CUELLAR-P
36 TOM PHOEBUS-P
37 TERRY CROWLEY-1B/OF
39 ED WATT-P
40 DAVE LEONHARD-P
41 CHARLIE LAU-CH
44 JIM HARDIN-P
48 GEORGE (STOPPER) STALLER-CH
55 BILLY HUNTER-CH

1970
1ST E 108-54 0GB
W ALCS-MINA 3-0
W WS-CINN 4-1
2 BOBBY FLOYD-SS/2B (1)
3 CLAY DALRYMPLE (INJ)-C
4 EARL WEAVER-MGR
5 BROOKS ROBINSON-3B
6 PAUL BLAIR (INJ)-OF/3B
7 MARK BELANGER-SS
8 ANDY ETCHEBARREN-C
9 DON BUFORD-OF/INF
10 ELLIE HENDRICKS-C
12 DAVE MAY-OF (1)
12 JOHNNY OATES-C
13 ROGER FREED-1B/OF
14 MERV RETTENMUND-OF
15 DAVEY JOHNSON-2B/SS
16 BOBBY GRICH-INF
19 DAVE MCNALLY-P
20 FRANK ROBINSON-OF/1B
21 CURT MOTTON-OF
22 JIM PALMER-P
23 DON BAYLOR-OF
24 PETE RICHERT-P
25 DON BAYLOR-OF
25 MOE DRABOWSKY-P (2)
26 BOOG POWELL-1B
29 DICK HALL-P
30 CHICO SALMON-INF
31 GEORGE BAMBERGER-CH
32 MARCELINO LOPEZ-P
33 FRED BEENE-P
35 MIKE CUELLAR-P
36 TOM PHOEBUS-P
37 TERRY CROWLEY-OF/1B
38 JOHNNY OATES-C
39 EDDIE WATT-P
40 DAVE LEONHARD-P
41 JIM FREY-CH
44 JIM HARDIN-P
45 FRED BEENE-P
48 GEORGE (STOPPER) STALLER-CH
55 BILLY HUNTER-CH

1971
1ST E 101-57 0GB
W ALCS-OAKA 3-0
L WS-PITN 4-3
2 JERRY DAVANON-INF
3 CLAY DALRYMPLE-C
4 EARL WEAVER-MGR
5 BROOKS ROBINSON-3B
6 PAUL BLAIR-OF
7 MARK BELANGER-SS
8 ANDY ETCHEBARREN-C
9 DON BUFORD-OF
10 ELLIE HENDRICKS-C/1B
11 TERRY CROWLEY-OF/1B
14 MERV RETTENMUND-OF
15 DAVEY JOHNSON-2B
16 BOBBY GRICH-SS/2B
19 DAVE MCNALLY (INJ)-P
20 FRANK ROBINSON-OF
21 CURT MOTTON-OF
22 JIM PALMER-P
23 GRANT JACKSON-P
24 PETE RICHERT-P
25 DON BAYLOR-OF
26 BOOG POWELL-1B
27 ORLANDO PENA-P
28 TOM SHOPAY (INJ)-OF
29 DICK HALL-P
30 CHICO SALMON-INF
31 GEORGE BAMBERGER-CH
32 DAVE BOSWELL-P (2)
35 MIKE CUELLAR-P
36 TOM DUKES-P
37 PAT DOBSON-P
39 ED WATT (INJ)-P
40 DAVE LEONHARD-P
41 JIM FREY-CH
44 JIM HARDIN-P (1)
48 GEORGE (STOPPER) STALLER-CH
55 BILLY HUNTER-CH

1972
3RD E 80-74 5GB
1 AL BUMBRY-OF
2 RICH COGGINS-OF
3 BOBBY GRICH-INF
4 EARL WEAVER-MGR
5 BROOKS ROBINSON-3B
6 PAUL BLAIR-OF
7 MARK BELANGER-SS
8 ANDY ETCHEBARREN-C
9 DON BUFORD-OF/INF
10 ELLIE HENDRICKS-C (1)
10 SERGIO ROBLES-C
11 TERRY CROWLEY-OF/1B
12 JOHNNY OATES-C
12 TOMMY DAVIS-OF/1B (2)
13 DOYLE ALEXANDER-P
14 MERV RETTENMUND-OF
15 DAVEY JOHNSON-2B
16 BOBBY GRICH-INF
16 MICKEY SCOTT-P
19 DAVE MCNALLY-P
20 *(RET #) FRANK ROBINSON*
22 JIM PALMER-P
23 GRANT JACKSON-P
24 DOYLE ALEXANDER-P
24 ENOS CABELL-1B
25 DON BAYLOR-OF/1B
26 BOOG POWELL-1B
28 TOM SHOPAY-OF
30 CHICO SALMON-1B/3B
31 GEORGE BAMBERGER-CH
32 TOM MATCHICK-3B
34 BOB REYNOLDS-P
35 MIKE CUELLAR-P
36 TOMMY DAVIS-OF/1B (2)
37 PAT DOBSON-P
39 EDDIE WATT-P
40 DAVE LEONHARD-P
41 JIM FREY-CH
43 MICKEY SCOTT-P
44 RORIC HARRISON-P
48 GEORGE (STOPPER) STALLER-CH
55 BILLY HUNTER-CH

1973
1ST E 97-65 0GB
L ALCS-OAKA 3-2
1 AL BUMBRY-OF/DH
2 RICH COGGINS-OF/DH
3 BOBBY GRICH-2B
4 EARL WEAVER-MGR
5 BROOKS ROBINSON-3B
6 PAUL BLAIR-OF/DH
7 MARK BELANGER-SS
8 ANDY ETCHEBARREN-C
10 ELLIE HENDRICKS (INJ)-C/DH
11 TERRY CROWLEY-UTIL
12 TOMMY DAVIS-DH/1B
13 DOYLE ALEXANDER (INJ)-P
14 MERV RETTENMUND-OF
15 FRANK BAKER-INF
16 MICKEY SCOTT-P (1)
17 WAYNE GARLAND-P
18 JIM FULLER-UTIL
19 DAVE MCNALLY-P
20 *(RET #) FRANK ROBINSON*
21 LARRY BROWN-3B/2B
22 JIM PALMER-P
23 GRANT JACKSON-P
24 ENOS CABELL-1B/3B
25 DON BAYLOR-OF/UTIL
26 BOOG POWELL-1B
27 ORLANDO PENA-P (1)
30 SERGIO ROBLES-C
31 GEORGE BAMBERGER-CH
32 EARL WILLIAMS-C/UTIL
34 BOB REYNOLDS-P
35 MIKE CUELLAR-P
37 DOUG DECINCES-INF
38 JESSE JEFFERSON-P
39 EDDIE WATT-P
41 JIM FREY-CH
43 CURT MOTTON-OF/DH
44 DON HOOD-P
48 GEORGE (STOPPER) STALLER-CH
55 BILLY HUNTER-CH

1974
1ST E 91-71 0GB
L ALCS-OAKA 3-1
1 AL BUMBRY-OF/DH
2 RICH COGGINS-OF
3 BOBBY GRICH-2B
4 EARL WEAVER-MGR
5 BROOKS ROBINSON-3B
6 PAUL BLAIR-OF
7 MARK BELANGER-SS
8 ANDY ETCHEBARREN-C
9 MIKE REINBACH-OF/DH
10 ELLIE HENDRICKS-UTIL
11 DOUG DECINCES-INF
12 TOMMY DAVIS-DH
13 DOYLE ALEXANDER (INJ)-P
15 FRANK BAKER-INF
17 WAYNE GARLAND-P
18 JIM FULLER-1B/DH
19 DAVE MCNALLY-P
20 *(RET #) FRANK ROBINSON*
21 CURT MOTTON-OF/DH
22 JIM PALMER (INJ)-P
23 GRANT JACKSON-P
24 ENOS CABELL-UTIL
25 DON BAYLOR-OF/UTIL
26 BOOG POWELL-1B/DH
28 JIM NORTHRUP-OF/DH (3)
31 GEORGE BAMBERGER-CH
32 EARL WILLIAMS-C/UTIL
33 BOB OLIVER-1B/DH
34 BOB REYNOLDS-P
35 MIKE CUELLAR-P
38 JESSE JEFFERSON-P
39 ROSS GRIMSLEY, II-P
41 JIM FREY-CH
43 CURT MOTTON-OF/DH
43 TIM NORDBROOK-SS/2B
44 DON HOOD-P
45 DAVE JOHNSON-P
48 GEORGE (STOPPER) STALLER-CH
52 DON HOOD-P
55 BILLY HUNTER-CH

1975
2ND E 90-69 4.5GB
1 AL BUMBRY-UTIL
2 JIM NORTHRUP-OF/DH
3 BOBBY GRICH-2B
4 EARL WEAVER-MGR
5 BROOKS ROBINSON-3B
6 PAUL BLAIR-OF/UTIL
7 MARK BELANGER-SS
8 ANDY ETCHEBARREN (INJ)-C (1)
8 TIM NORDBROOK-SS/2B
9 DAVE DUNCAN-C
10 ELLIE HENDRICKS-C
11 DOUG DECINCES-INF
12 TOMMY DAVIS-DH
13 DOYLE ALEXANDER-P
14 LEE MAY-1B/DH
15 ROYLE STILLMAN-OF
16 TONY MUSER-1B (2)
17 WAYNE GARLAND-P
20 *(RET #) FRANK ROBINSON*
22 JIM PALMER-P
23 GRANT JACKSON-P
24 MIKE TORREZ-P
25 DON BAYLOR-OF/UTIL
28 TOM SHOPAY-UTIL
29 KEN SINGLETON-OF
31 GEORGE BAMBERGER-CH
33 JIM HUTTO-C
34 BOB REYNOLDS-P (1)
34 TONY MUSER-1B (2)
35 MIKE CUELLAR-P
36 PAUL MITCHELL-P
37 DYAR MILLER-P
38 JESSE JEFFERSON-P (1)
39 ROSS GRIMSLEY, II-P
41 JIM FREY-CH
43 TIM NORDBROOK-SS/2B
45 DAVE JOHNSON-P
46 MIKE FLANAGAN-P
48 GEORGE (STOPPER) STALLER-CH
51 LARRY HARLOW-OF
52 BOB BAILOR-SS/2B
55 BILLY HUNTER-CH

1976
2ND E 88-74 10.5GB
1 AL BUMBRY-OF/DH
3 BOBBY GRICH-2B/UTIL
4 EARL WEAVER-MGR
5 BROOKS ROBINSON-3B
6 PAUL BLAIR-OF/DH
7 MARK BELANGER-SS
8 TIM NORDBROOK-2B/SS (1)
9 REGGIE JACKSON-OF/DH
10 ELLIE HENDRICKS-C (1)
10 TERRY CROWLEY-DH/1B (2)
11 DOUG DECINCES-3B/UTIL
12 TOMMY HARPER-UTIL
13 DOYLE ALEXANDER-P (1)
14 LEE MAY-1B/DH

15 ROYLE STILLMAN-DH/1B
16 TONY MUSER-1B/UTIL
17 WAYNE GARLAND-P
20 *(RET #) FRANK ROBINSON*
21 BOB BAILOR (INJ)-SS/DH
22 JIM PALMER-P
23 GRANT JACKSON-P (1)
23 TIPPY MARTINEZ-P (2)
24 RICK DEMPSEY-C/OF
25 DAVE DUNCAN-C
27 ANDRES MORA-DH/OF
28 TOM SHOPAY-OF/C
29 KEN SINGLETON-OF/DH
30 KEN HOLTZMAN-P (1)
30 DAVE PAGAN-P (2)
31 GEORGE BAMBERGER-CH
35 MIKE CUELLAR-P
36TIPPY MARTINEZ-P (2)
37 DYAR MILLER-P
38 TERRY CROWLEY-DH/1B (2)
38 FRED HOLDSWORTH-P
39 ROSS GRIMSLEY, II-P
39 SCOTT MCGREGOR-P
40 KIKO GARCIA-SS
40 DENNIS MARTINEZ-P
41 JIM FREY-CH
43 RUDY MAY-P (2)
44 RICH DAUER-2B
(45) DAVE JOHNSON (INJ)-(P)
46 MIKE FLANAGAN-P
47 CAL RIPKEN, SR.-CH
48 ROSS GRIMSLEY, II-P
53 DAVE PAGAN-P
55 BILLY HUNTER-CH
61 DENNIS MARTINEZ-P

1977

2ND (TIE) E 97-64 2.5GB

1 AL BUMBRY (INJ)-OF
2 BILLY SMITH-2B/INF
3 KIKO GARCIA-SS/3B
4 EARL WEAVER-MGR
5 BROOKS ROBINSON (RET)-3B/CH
5 *(RET#) BROOKS ROBINSON*
7 MARK BELANGER-SS
8 DAVE SKAGGS-C
10 TERRY CROWLEY-DH/1B
11 DOUG DECINCES-3B/UTIL
12 BILLY SMITH-2B/INF
12 KEN RUDOLPH-C (2)
14 LEE MAY-1B/DH
16 TONY MUSER-UTIL
17 ED FARMER-P
18 PAT KELLY-OF/DH
20 *(RET #) FRANK ROBINSON*
21 ELLIOTT MADDOX (INJ)-OF/3B
22 JIM PALMER-P
23 TIPPY MARTINEZ-P
24 RICK DEMPSEY (INJ)-C
27 ANDRES MORA-UTIL
28 TOM SHOPAY-OF/DH
29 KEN SINGLETON-OF/DH
30 DENNIS MARTINEZ-P
31 GEORGE BAMBERGER-CH
32 MIKE PARROTT-P
33 EDDIE MURRAY-DH/UTIL
34 LARRY HARLOW-OF
35 RANDY MILLER-P
35 TONY CHEVEZ-P
36 MIKE DIMMEL-OF
37 DYAR MILLER-P (1)
37 DICK DRAGO-P (2)
38 FRED HOLDSWORTH (INJ)-P (1)
39 SCOTT MCGREGOR-P
40 DAVE CRISCIONE-C
41 JIM FREY-CH
43 RUDY MAY-P
44 RICH DAUER-INF/DH
45 TONY CHEVEZ-P
46 MIKE FLANAGAN-P
47 CAL RIPKEN, SR.-CH
48 ROSS GRIMSLEY, II-P
49 DAVE SKAGGS, C
52 EARL STEPHENSON-P
55 BILLY HUNTER-CH
55 NELSON (NELLIE) BRILES-P (2)

1978

4TH E 90-71 9GB

1 AL BUMBRY (INJ)-OF
2 BILLY SMITH (INJ)-2B/SS
3 KIKO GARCIA-SS/2B
4 EARL WEAVER-MGR
5 *(RET#) BROOKS ROBINSON*
6* LARRY HARLOW-OF/P*
7 MARK BELANGER-SS
8 DAVE SKAGGS-C
9 CARLOS LOPEZ-OF/DH
10 TERRY CROWLEY-UTIL
11 DOUG DECINCES-3B/2B
14 LEE MAY-DH/1B
16 SCOTT MCGREGOR-P
18 PAT KELLY-OF/DH
20 *(RET #) FRANK ROBINSON*
22 JIM PALMER-P
23 TIPPY MARTINEZ-P
24 RICK DEMPSEY-C
25 RICH DAUER-2B/UTIL
26 DON STANHOUSE-P
27 ANDRES MORA-OF/DH
29 KEN SINGLETON-OF/DH
30 DENNIS MARTINEZ-P
31 RAY MILLER-CH
32 JOE KERRIGAN-P
33 EDDIE MURRAY-1B/UTIL
34 NELSON (NELLIE) BRILES (INJ)-P
35 GARY ROENICKE-OF
36 MIKE DIMMEL-OF
37 JOHN FLINN-P
39 MIKE ANDERSON-OF
41 JIM FREY-CH
44 ELLIE HENDRICKS-U/P/CH
46 MIKE FLANAGAN-P
47 CAL RIPKEN, SR.-CH
48 DON STANHOUSE-P
49 TIM STODDARD-P
52 EARL STEPHENSON-P
53 SAMMY STEWART-P
59 DAVE FORD-P

1979

1ST E 102-57 0GB
W ALCS-CALA 3-1
L WS-PITN 4-3

1 AL BUMBRY-OF
2 BILLY SMITH-2B/SS
3 KIKO GARCIA-SS/UTIL
4 EARL WEAVER-MGR
5 *(RET#) BROOKS ROBINSON*
6 LARRY HARLOW-OF/DH (1)
7 MARK BELANGER (INJ)-SS
8 DAVE SKAGGS-C
9 BOB MOLINARO-OF
10 TERRY CROWLEY-DH/1B
11 DOUG DECINCES (INJ)-3B
12 TOM CHISM-1B
12 WAYNE KRENCHICKI-3B/2B
14 LEE MAY-DH/1B
15 MARK COREY-OF/DH
16 SCOTT MCGREGOR-P
18 PAT KELLY-OF/DH
20 FRANK ROBINSON-CH
21 STEVE STONE-P
22 JIM PALMER (INJ)-P
23 TIPPY MARTINEZ-P
24 RICK DEMPSEY-C
25 RICH DAUER-2B/3B
26 DON STANHOUSE-P
27 JEFF RINEER-P
27 BENNY AYALA-OF/DH
29 KEN SINGLETON-OF/DH
30 DENNIS MARTINEZ-P
31 RAY MILLER-CH
32 STEVE STONE-P
33 EDDIE MURRAY-1B/DH
35 GARY ROENICKE-OF/DH
37 JOHN FLINN-P
38 JOHN LOWENSTEIN (INJ)-UTIL
41 JIM FREY-CH
43 JEFF RINEER-P
44 ELLIE HENDRICKS-C/CH
45 WAYNE KRENCHICKI-3B/2B
46 MIKE FLANAGAN-P
47 CAL RIPKEN, SR.-CH
49 TIM STODDARD (INJ)-P
53 SAMMY STEWART-P
59 DAVE FORD-P

1980

2ND E 100-62 3GB

1 AL BUMBRY-OF
2 BOB BONNER-SS
3 KIKO GARCIA-UTIL
4 EARL WEAVER-MGR
5 *(RET#) BROOKS ROBINSON*
6 WAYNE KRENCHICKI-UTIL
7 MARK BELANGER-SS
8 DAVE SKAGGS-C (1)
9 FLOYD RAYFORD-UTIL
10 TERRY CROWLEY-DH/1B
11 DOUG DECINCES-3B/1B
12 LENN SAKATA-INF/DH
14 LEE MAY-DH/1B
15 MARK COREY-OF
16 SCOTT MCGREGOR-P
18 PAT KELLY-OF/DH
20 FRANK ROBINSON-CH
21 DAVE FORD-P
22 JIM PALMER-P
23 TIPPY MARTINEZ-P
24 RICK DEMPSEY-C/UTIL
25 RICH DAUER-2B/3B
26 JOE KERRIGAN-P
27 BENNY AYALA-DH/OF
28 PAUL HARTZELL-P
29 KEN SINGLETON-OF/DH
30 DENNIS MARTINEZ (INJ)-P
31 RAY MILLER-CH
32 STEVE STONE-P
33 EDDIE MURRAY-1B/DH
35 GARY ROENICKE (INJ)-OF/DH
37 DAN GRAHAM-UTIL
38 JOHN LOWENSTEIN (INJ)-OF/DH
41 DRUNGO HAZEWOOD-OF
44 ELLIE HENDRICKS-CH
46 MIKE FLANAGAN-P
47 CAL RIPKEN, SR.-CH
49 TIM STODDARD-P
52 MIKE BODDICKER-P
53 SAMMY STEWART-P

1981

1ST 1/2:2ND E 31-23 2GB
2ND 1/2:4TH E 28-23 2GB
FINAL: 59-46 --GB

1 AL BUMBRY-OF
2 BOB BONNER-SS
4 EARL WEAVER-MGR
5 *(RET#) BROOKS ROBINSON*
6 WAYNE KRENCHICKI-UTIL
7 MARK BELANGER-SS
8 CAL RIPKEN, JR.-SS/3B
10 TERRY CROWLEY-DH/1B
11 DOUG DECINCES-3B/UTIL
12 LENN SAKATA-SS/2B
15 MARK COREY-OF
16 SCOTT MCGREGOR-P
20 *(RET #) FRANK ROBINSON*
21 DAVE FORD-P
22 JIM PALMER-P
23 TIPPY MARTINEZ-P
24 RICK DEMPSEY-C/DH
25 RICH DAUER-2B/3B
27 BENNY AYALA-DH/OF
28 JIM DWYER-UTIL
29 KEN SINGLETON-OF/DH
30 DENNIS MARTINEZ-P
31 RAY MILLER-CH
32 STEVE STONE (INJ)-P
33 EDDIE MURRAY-1B
34 JOSE MORALES-DH/1B
35 GARY ROENICKE-OF
36 STEVE LUEBBER-P
36 JEFF SCHNEIDER-P
37 JOHN SHELBY-OF
38 JOHN LOWENSTEIN (INJ)-OF/DH
39 JOHN SHELBY-OF
39 DALLAS WILLIAMS-OF
40 JIMMY WILLIAMS-CH
41 DAN GRAHAM-UTIL
44 ELLIE HENDRICKS-CH
46 MIKE FLANAGAN (INJ)-P
47 CAL RIPKEN, SR.-CH
49 TIM STODDARD-P
52 MIKE BODDICKER-P
53 SAMMY STEWART-P
54 RALPH ROWE-CH
57 JEFF SCHNEIDER-P
59 WILLIE ROYSTER-C

1982

2ND E 94-68 1GB

1 AL BUMBRY-OF
2 BOB BONNER-SS/2B
3 LEO HERNANDEZ-PH
4 EARL WEAVER-MGR
4 *(RET#) EARL WEAVER*
5 *(RET#) BROOKS ROBINSON*
8 CAL RIPKEN, JR.-SS/3B
9 FLOYD RAYFORD-UTIL
10 TERRY CROWLEY-DH/1B
11 GLENN GULLIVER-3B
12 LENN SAKATA-2B/SS
15 DAN FORD-OF/DH
16 SCOTT MCGREGOR-P
17 JOE NOLAN-C
20 *(RET #) FRANK ROBINSON*
22 JIM PALMER-P
23 TIPPY MARTINEZ-P
24 RICK DEMPSEY-C/DH
25 RICH DAUER-2B/3B
26 DAN STANHOUSE (INJ)-P
27 BENNY AYALA-UTIL
28 JIM DWYER-UTIL
29 KEN SINGLETON-DH/OF
30 DENNIS MARTINEZ-P
31 RAY MILLER-CH
(32) STEVE STONE (INJ/RET)-(P)
33 EDDIE MURRAY-1B/DH
34 JOSE MORALES-PH (1)
34 STORM DAVIS-P
35 GARY ROENICKE-OF/1B
37 JOHN SHELBY-OF
38 JOHN LOWENSTEIN-OF
39 STORM DAVIS-P
40 JIMMY WILLIAMS-CH
43 MIKE YOUNG-DH/OF
44 ELLIE HENDRICKS-CH
46 MIKE FLANAGAN-P
47 CAL RIPKEN, SR.-CH
48 ROSS GRIMSLEY II-P
49 TIM STODDARD (INJ)-P
51 DON WELCHEL-P
52 MIKE BODDICKER-P
53 SAMMY STEWART-P
54 RALPH ROWE-CH
57 JOHN FLINN-P

1983

1ST E 98-64 0GB
W ALCS-CHIA 3-1
W WS-PHIN 4-1

1 AL BUMBRY-OF/DH
2 BOB BONNER-2B/DH
3 LEO HERNANDEZ-3B
4 *(RET#) EARL WEAVER*
5 *(RET#) BROOKS ROBINSON*
6 AURELIO RODRIGUEZ-3B (1)
8 CAL RIPKEN, JR.-SS
9 JOHN STEFERO-C
10 TODD CRUZ-3B/2B (2)
11 GLENN GULLIVER-3B
12 LENN SAKATA-UTIL
15 DAN FORD (INJ) OF
16 SCOTT MCGREGOR-P
17 JOE NOLAN-C
19 DAVE HUPPERT-C
20 *(RET #) FRANK ROBINSON*
21 DAN MOROGIELLO-P
22 JIM PALMER (INJ)-P
23 TIPPY MARTINEZ (ILL)-P
24 RICK DEMPSEY-C
25 RICH DAUER-2B/3B
26 JOE ALTOBELLI-MGR
27 BENNY AYALA-OF/DH
28 JIM DWYER-UTIL
29 KEN SINGLETON-DH
30 DENNIS MARTINEZ-P
31 RAY MILLER-CH
32 DAVE HUPPERT-C
32 BILL SWAGGERTY-P
33 EDDIE MURRAY-1B/DH
34 STORM DAVIS-P
35 GARY ROENICKE-UTIL
36 ALLAN RAMIREZ-P
37 JOHN SHELBY-OF/DH
38 JOHN LOWENSTEIN-OF/UTIL
39 PAUL MIRABELLA-P
39 TITO LANDRUM-OF (2)
40 JIMMY WILLIAMS-CH
43 MIKE YOUNG-OF/DH
44 ELLIE HENDRICKS-CH
46 MIKE FLANAGAN (INJ)-P
47 CAL RIPKEN, SR.-CH
49 TIM STODDARD (INJ)-P
51 DON WELCHEL-P
52 MIKE BODDICKER-P
53 SAMMY STEWART-P
54 RALPH ROWE-CH

1984

5TH E 85-77 19GB

1 AL BUMBRY-OF/DH
4 *(RET#) EARL WEAVER*
5 *(RET#) BROOKS ROBINSON*
6 WAYNE GROSS-3B/UTIL
6 FLOYD RAYFORD-UTIL
8 CAL RIPKEN, JR.-SS
9 JIM DWYER (INJ)-OF/DH
10 TODD CRUZ-UTIL
11RON JACKSON-3B (2)
12 LENN SAKATA-2B/OF
14 WAYNE GROSS-3B/UTIL
15 DAN FORD (INJ)-OF/DH
16 SCOTT MCGREGOR (INJ)-P
17 JOE NOLAN (INJ)-DH/C
18 VIC RODRIGUEZ-2B/DH
18 LARRY SHEETS-OF
20 *(RET #) FRANK ROBINSON*
21 MARK BROWN-P
22 JIM PALMER-P
23 TIPPY MARTINEZ-P
24 RICK DEMPSEY-C
25 RICH DAUER-2B/3B
26 JOE ALTOBELLI-MGR
27 BENNY AYALA-DH/OF
28 JIM DWYER (INJ)-OF/DH
28 JIM TRABER-DH
29 KEN SINGLETON-DH
30 DENNIS MARTINEZ-P

31 RAY MILLER-CH
32 BILL SWAGGERTY-P
33 EDDIE MURRAY-1B/DH
34 STORM DAVIS-P
35 GARY ROENICKE-OF
36 NATE SNELL-P
37 JOHN SHELBY-OF/DH
38 JOHN LOWENSTEIN-OF/UTIL
39 KEN DIXON-P
40 JIMMY WILLIAMS-CH
41 JOHN PACELLA-P
41 ORLANDO SANCHEZ-C (2)
42 TOM UNDERWOOD-P
43 MIKE YOUNG-OF/DH
44 ELLIE HENDRICKS-CH
46 MIKE FLANAGAN-P
47 CAL RIPKEN, SR.-CH
52 MIKE BODDICKER-P
53 SAMMY STEWART-P
54 RALPH ROWE-CH

1985

4TH E — 83-78 — 16GB

2 ALAN WIGGINS-2B (2)
3 LEO HERNANDEZ-UTIL
4 EARL WEAVER-MGR3
5 *(RET#) BROOKS ROBINSON*
6 FLOYD RAYFORD-3B/UTIL
7 CAL RIPKEN, SR.-CH/MGR2
8 CAL RIPKEN, JR.-SS
9 JIM DWYER-OF/DH
10 TERRY CROWLEY-CH
11 FRITZ CONNALLY-INF/DH
12 LENN SAKATA-2B/OF
14 WAYNE GROSS-UTIL
15 DAN FORD (INJ)-DH
16 SCOTT MCGREGOR-P
17 JOE NOLAN (INJ)-C/DH
17 TOM O'MALLEY-3B
18 LARRY SHEETS-DH/UTIL
19 FRED LYNN-OF
20 FRANK ROBINSON-CH
21 KELLY PARIS-2B/DH
21 PHIL HUFFMAN-P
22 *(RET #) JIM PALMER*
23 TIPPY MARTINEZ-P
24 RICK DEMPSEY-C
25 RICH DAUER-INF
26 JOE ALTOBELLI-MGR1
26 AL PARDO-C
27 LEE LACY (INJ)-OF/DH
30 DENNIS MARTINEZ-P
31 RAY MILLER-CH
31 KEN ROWE-CH
31 BRAD HAVENS-P
32 BILL SWAGGERTY-P
33 EDDIE MURRAY-1B/DH
34 STORM DAVIS-P
35 GARY ROENICKE-OF/DH
36 NATE SNELL (INJ) P
37 JOHN SHELBY-UTIL
38 JOHN LOWENSTEIN-DH/OF
39 KEN DIXON-P
40 JIMMY WILLIAMS-CH
41 DON AASE-P
42 KEN ROWE-CH
43 MIKE YOUNG-OF/DH
44 ELLIE HENDRICKS-CH
46 MIKE FLANAGAN (INJ)-P
47 CAL RIPKEN, SR.-CH/MGR2
47 ERIC BELL-P
48 TERRY CROWLEY-CH
52 MIKE BODDICKER-P
53 SAMMY STEWART-P
54 JOHN HABYAN-P

1986

7TH E — 73-89 — 22.5GB

1 REX HUDLER-2B/3B
2 ALAN WIGGINS-2B/DH
3 JUAN BONILLA-2B/UTIL
4 EARL WEAVER-MGR
5 *(RET#) BROOKS ROBINSON*
6 FLOYD RAYFORD-3B/UTIL
7 CAL RIPKEN, SR.-CH
8 CAL RIPKEN, JR.-SS
9 JIM DWYER-UTIL
10 TERRY CROWLEY-CH
11 JACKIE GUTIERREZ (ILL)-INF/DH
12 JUAN BENIQUEZ-UTIL
13 ODELL JONES-P
16 SCOTT MCGREGOR-P
17 TOM O'MALLEY-3B
18 LARRY SHEETS-DH/UTIL
19 FRED LYNN-OF/DH
20 FRANK ROBINSON-CH
21 KELLY PARIS-2B/DH
21 JOHN STEFERO-C/2B
22 *(RET #) JIM PALMER*
23 TIPPY MARTINEZ (ILL/INJ)-P
24 RICK DEMPSEY-C
25 CARL NICHOLS-C
25 TOM DODD-DH/3B
26 AL PARDO-C/DH
27 LEE LACY (INJ)-OF/DH
28 JIM TRABER-UTIL
30 DENNIS MARTINEZ (INJ)-P (1)
30 KELLY PARIS-2B/DH
30 RICKY JONES-2B/3B
31 BRAD HAVENS-P
31 KEN ROWE-CH
32 BILL SWAGGERTY-P
33 EDDIE MURRAY (INJ)-1B/DH
34 STORM DAVIS (INJ)-P
36 NATE SNELL-P
37 JOHN SHELBY-OF/DH
38 KEN GERHART-OF
39 KEN DIXON-P
40 JIMMY WILLIAMS-CH
41 DON AASE-P
42 KEN ROWE-CH
42 RICH BORDI-P
43 MIKE YOUNG-OF/DH
44 ELLIE HENDRICKS-CH
46 MIKE FLANAGAN P
47 ERIC BELL-P
47 BRAD HAVENS-P
48 MIKE KINNUNEN-P
52 MIKE BODDICKER-P
53 RICH BORDI-P
54 JOHN HABYAN-P
57 TONY ARNOLD-P

1987

6TH E — 67-95 — 31GB

2 ALAN WIGGINS (LGL)-UTIL
3 BILLY RIPKEN-2B
4 *(RET#) EARL WEAVER*
5 *(RET#) BROOKS ROBINSON*
6 FLOYD RAYFORD-3B/UTIL
7 CAL RIPKEN, SR.-MGR
8 CAL RIPKEN, JR.-SS
9 JIM DWYER-DH/OF
10 TERRY CROWLEY-CH
11 JACKIE GUTIERREZ-2B/3B
12 PETE STANICEK-INF/DH
14 DAVE VAN GORDER-C
15 TERRY KENNEDY-C
16 SCOTT MCGREGOR (INJ)-P
17 RICK (ROOSTER) BURLESON-2B/DH
18 LARRY SHEETS-OF/UTIL
19 FRED LYNN-OF/DH
20 FRANK ROBINSON-CH
21 JACK O'CONNOR (INJ)-P
22 *(RET #) JIM PALMER*
(23) TIPPY MARTINEZ (INJ)-(P)
23 DOUG CORBETT-P
24 DAVE SCHMIDT-P
25 RAY KNIGHT-3B/UTIL
26 CARL NICHOLS-C
27 LEE LACY-OF/DH
31 MARK WILEY-CH
32 MARK WILLIAMSON-P
33 EDDIE MURRAY-1B/DH
34 JEFF BALLARD-P
36 MIKE HART-OF
37 JOHN SHELBY-OF/DH
37 RON WASHINGTON-UTIL
38 KEN GERHART (INJ)-OF
39 KEN DIXON-P
40 JIMMY WILLIAMS-CH
41 DON AASE (INJ)-P
42 MIKE GRIFFIN-P
42 NELSON SIMMONS-OF/DH
42 TOM NIEDENFUER-P (2)
43 MIKE YOUNG (INJ)-OF/DH
44 ELLIE HENDRICKS-CH
45 ERIC BELL-P
46 MIKE FLANAGAN (INJ)-P (1)
47 LUIS DELEON-P
48 MIKE KINNUNEN-P
49 TOM NIEDENFUER-P (2)
51 JOSE MESA-P
52 MIKE BODDICKER-P
54 JOHN HABYAN-P
57 TONY ARNOLD (INJ)-P
58 KEN DIXON-P
64 MARK WILLIAMSON-P
88 RENE GONZALES-INF

1988

7TH E — 54-107 — 34.5GB

1 JEFF STONE (INJ)-OF/DH
2 DON BUFORD-CH
3 BILLY RIPKEN-2B/UTIL
3 CRAIG WORTHINGTON-3B
4 *(RET#) EARL WEAVER*
5 *(RET#) BROOKS ROBINSON*
6 JOE ORSULAK-OF
7 CAL RIPKEN, SR.-MGR1
7 BILLY RIPKEN-2B/UTIL
8 CAL RIPKEN, JR.-SS
9 JIM DWYER (INJ)-DH/OF (1)
10 TERRY CROWLEY-CH
11 WADE ROWDON-UTIL
12 PETE STANICEK-OF/UTIL
12 MIKE MORGAN (INJ)-P
13 RICK SCHU (INJ)-3B/UTIL
14 MIKE MORGAN (INJ)-P
14 MICKEY TETTLETON-C
15 TERRY KENNEDY-C
16 SCOTT MCGREGOR (INJ)-P
16 BRADY ANDERSON-OF (2)
17 PETE STANICEK-OF/UTIL
18 LARRY SHEETS-OF/UTIL
18 WADE ROWDON-UTIL
19 FRED LYNN (INJ)-OF/DH (1)
20 FRANK ROBINSON-MGR2
21 MARK THURMOND-P
22 *(RET #) JIM PALMER*
23 OSWALD PERAZA-P
24 DAVE SCHMIDT-P
25 RICK SCHU (INJ)-3B/UTIL
25 BUTCH DAVIS-OF/DH
26 CARL NICHOLS-C/OF
27 JOHN HABYAN-P
28 JIM TRABER-UTIL
29 JEFF BALLARD-P
30 GREGG OLSON-P
30 TITO LANDRUM-OF/DH
31 HERM STARRETTE-CH
32 MARK WILLIAMSON-P
33 EDDIE MURRAY-1B/DH
34 JEFF BALLARD-P
35 KEITH HUGHES-OF/DH
37 BILL SCHERRER-P (1)
37 DICKIE NOLES-P
38 KEN GERHART-OF/DH
39 DOUG SISK (INJ)-P
40 MINNIE MENDOZA-CH
41 DON AASE (INJ)-P
42 PETE HARNISCH-P
43 GORDON DILLARD-P
43 CURT SCHILLING-P
44 ELLIE HENDRICKS-CH
47 JOHN HART-CH
48 JOSE BAUTISTA-P
49 TOM NIEDENFUER-P
52 MIKE BODDICKER-P (1)
52 BOB MILACKI-P
53 MARK THURMOND-P
53 JAY TIBBS-P
54 JOHN HABYAN-P
57 MARK THURMOND-P
88 RENE GONZALES-UTIL

1989

2ND E — 87-75 — 2GB

1 JUAN BELL-INF/DH
2 BOB MELVIN-C/DH
3 BILLY RIPKEN-2B/DH
4 *(RET#) EARL WEAVER*
5 *(RET#) BROOKS ROBINSON*
6 JOE ORSULAK-OF/DH
6 KEITH MORELAND-DH (2)
7 CAL RIPKEN, SR.-CH
8 CAL RIPKEN, JR.-SS
9 BRADY ANDERSON-OF/DH
11 CRAIG WORTHINGTON-3B
12 MIKE DEVEREAUX-OF/DH
13 RICK SCHU-2B
14 MICKEY TETTLETON (INJ)-C/DH
15 JAMIE QUIRK-C/OF (3)
16 PHIL BRADLEY-OF/DH
18 BOB MILACKI-P
19 LARRY SHEETS-DH
19 BEN MCDONALD-P
20 FRANK ROBINSON-MGR
21 MARK THURMOND-P
22 *(RET #) JIM PALMER*
(23) OSWALD PERAZA (INJ)-(P)
23 KEVIN HICKEY-P
24 DAVE SCHMIDT-P
26 JOHNNY OATES-CH
27 DAVE JOHNSON-P
28 JIM TRABER-1B/DH
29 JEFF BALLARD-P
30 GREGG OLSON-P
31 AL JACKSON-CH
32 MARK WILLIAMSON-P
33 *(RET #) EDDIE MURRAY*
34 MIKE SMITH-P
34 MICKEY WESTON (INJ)-P
35 DAVE JOHNSON-P
35 FRANCISCO MELENDEZ-1B
36 BOB MELVIN-C/DH
36 TIM HULETT-2B/3B
37 BRIAN HOLTON-P
39 RANDY MILLIGAN-1B/DH
41 MIKE SMITH-P
42 PETE HARNISCH-P
43 FRANCISCO MELENDEZ-1B
43 CURT SCHILLING-P
44 ELLIE HENDRICKS-CH
45 KEVIN HICKEY-P
46 JOHNNY OATES-CH
46 BUTCH DAVIS-OF/DH
47 TOM MCCRAW-CH
48 JOSE BAUTISTA-P
49 STAN JEFFERSON-OF/DH(2)
50 JAY TIBBS (INJ)-P
51 BRIAN HOLTON-P
52 BOB MILACKI-P
52 MARK HUISMANN (INJ)-P
53 JAY TIBBS (INJ)-P
59 CHRIS HOILES-C/DH
88 RENE GONZALES-INF

1990

5TH E — 76-85 — 11.5GB

1 PHIL BRADLEY-OF/DH
2 BOB MELVIN-UTIL
3 BILLY RIPKEN-2B/DH
4 *(RET#) EARL WEAVER*
5 *(RET#) BROOKS ROBINSON*
6 JOE ORSULAK-OF/DH
7 CAL RIPKEN, SR.-CH
8 CAL RIPKEN, JR.-SS
9 BRADY ANDERSON (INJ)-OF/DH
10 STEVE FINLEY-OF/DH
11 JUAN BELL-SS/DH
12 MIKE DEVEREAUX (INJ)-OF/DH
13 JEFF MCKNIGHT-UTIL
14 MICKEY TETTLETON-C/UTIL
15 LEO GOMEZ-3B
15 SAM HORN-DH/1B
17 CHRIS HOILES-UTIL
17 PETE HARNISCH-P
18 BOB MILACKI (INJ)-P
19 BEN MCDONALD (INJ)-P
20 FRANK ROBINSON-MGR
21 DONELL NIXON-OF/DH
21 ANTHONY TELFORD-P
21 DAVID SEGUI-1B/DH
22 *(RET #) JIM PALMER*
23 JOE PRICE-P
24 JOHN MITCHELL-P
25 CRAIG WORTHINGTON-3B/DH
26 JOHNNY OATES-CH
27 DAVE JOHNSON-P
28 MARTY BROWN-UTIL
29 JEFF BALLARD-P
29 BRAD KOMMINSK-OF/DH (2)
30 GREGG OLSON-P
31 AL JACKSON-CH
31 MIKE SMITH-P
32 MARK WILLIAMSON (INJ)-P
33 *(RET #) EDDIE MURRAY*
34 MICKEY WESTON-P
35 DAVE GALLAGHER-OF/DH (2)
35 RON KITTLE-DH/1B (2)
35 GREG WALKER-DH (2)
36 TIM HULETT (INJ)-INF/DH
37 DAN BOONE-P
39 RANDY MILLIGAN (INJ)-1B/DH
40 TOM MCCRAW-CH
41 MIKE SMITH-P
42 PETE HARNISCH-P
43 CURT SCHILLING-P
44 ELLIE HENDRICKS-CH
45 KEVIN HICKEY-P
45 CURT SCHILLING-P
46 JOHNNY OATES-CH
46 DORN TAYLOR-P
46 JAY ALDRICH-P
47 CURT MOTTON-CH
48 JOSE BAUTISTA-P
49 STAN JEFFERSON-OF/DH-(1)
49 BRAD KOMMINSK-OF/DH (2)
50 JAY TIBBS-P (1)
50 ANTHONY TELFORD-P
51 BRIAN HOLTON-P
52 DONELL NIXON-OF/DH
52 JOSE MESA-P
(53) BRIAN DUBOIS (INJ)-(P) (2)
58 JAY ALDRICH-P
88 RENE GONZALES-INF/OF

1991

6TH E — 67-95 — 24GB

1 JUAN BELL-UTIL
2 BOB MELVIN-C/DH
3 BILLY RIPKEN (INJ)-2B
4 *(RET#) EARL WEAVER*
5 *(RET#) BROOKS ROBINSON*
6 JOE ORSULAK-OF/DH
7 CAL RIPKEN, SR.-CH
8 CAL RIPKEN, JR.-SS
9 BRADY ANDERSON-OF
10 LEO GOMEZ-3B/UTIL

11 LEO GOMEZ-3B/UTIL
11 ERNIE WHITT-C/DH
11 LUIS MERCEDES-OF/DH
12 MIKE DEVEREAUX-OF
14 CHITO MARTINEZ-UTIL
15 SAM HORN-DH
17 PAUL KILGUS-P
18 BOB MILACKI-P
19 BEN MCDONALD (INJ)-P
20 FRANK ROBINSON-MGR1
21 DAVID SEGUI-1B/DH
22 *(RET #) JIM PALMER*
23 CHRIS HOILES-UTIL
24 DWIGHT (DEWEY) EVANS (INJ)-OF/DH
25 CRAIG WORTHINGTON (INJ)-3B/DH
26 JOHNNY OATES-CH/MGR2
27 DAVE JOHNSON (INJ)-P
28 ERNIE WHITT-C/DH
28 SHANE TURNER-2B/DH
29 JEFF BALLARD-P
30 GREGG OLSON-P
31 AL JACKSON-CH
32 MARK WILLIAMSON-P
33 *(RET #) EDDIE MURRAY*
34 JEFF ROBINSON-P
36 TIM HULETT-INF/DH
37 GLENN DAVIS-1B/DH
38 JEFF MCKNIGHT (INJ)-UTIL
39 RANDY MILLIGAN-UTIL
40 TOM MCCRAW-CH
41 PAUL KILGUS-P
41 JEFF TACKETT-C
42 MIKE MUSSINA-P
43 ROY SMITH-P
44 ELLIE HENDRICKS-CH
45 KEVIN HICKEY-P
45 JIM POOLE-P (2)
46 MIKE FLANAGAN-P
47 CURT MOTTON-CH
47 PAUL KILGUS-P
48 JOSE BAUTISTA-P
49 JEFF TACKETT-C
49 TODD FROHWIRTH-P
50 ANTHONY TELFORD-P
51 LUIS MERCEDES-OF/DH
51 STACY JONES-P
52 JOSE MESA-P
(53) BRIAN DUBOIS (INJ)-(P)
53 ARTHUR RHODES-P
58 FRANCISCO DELA ROSA-P

1992

3RD E 89-73 7GB

2 MARK MCLEMORE-2B/DH
3 BILLY RIPKEN-2B
4 *(RET#) EARL WEAVER*
5 *(RET#) BROOKS ROBINSON*
6 JOE ORSULAK-OF/DH
7 CAL RIPKEN, SR.-CH
8 CAL RIPKEN, JR.-SS
9 BRADY ANDERSON-OF
10 LEO GOMEZ-3B
11 LUIS MERCEDES-OF/DH
12 MIKE DEVEREAUX-OF
14 CHITO MARTINEZ-OF/DH
15 SAM HORN-DH
15 DAVEY LOPES-CH
17 DICK BOSMAN-CH
18 BOB MILACKI-P
19 BEN MCDONALD-P
20 *(RET #) FRANK ROBINSON*
21 DAVID SEGUI-1B/OF
22 *(RET #) JIM PALMER*
23 CHRIS HOILES-C/DH
24 RICK DEMPSEY-C
25 GREG BIAGINI-CH
26 JOHNNY OATES-MGR
27 MARK PARENT-C
27 STEVE SCARSONE-INF (2)
29 PAT CLEMENTS-P (2)
30 GREGG OLSON-P
31 DICK BOSMAN-CH
31 GREG BIAGINI-CH
31 CRAIG LEFFERTS-P (2)
32 MARK WILLIAMSON-P
33 *(RET #) EDDIE MURRAY*
34 STORM DAVIS-P
35 MIKE MUSSINA-P
36 TIM HULETT-INF/DH
37 GLENN DAVIS-DH/1B
38 SAM HORN-DH
39 RANDY MILLIGAN-1B/DH
40 RICK SUTCLIFFE-P
41 JEFF TACKETT-C/3B
42 DAVEY LOPES-CH
44 ELLIE HENDRICKS-CH
45 JIM POOLE-P
46 MIKE FLANAGAN-P
48 MANNY ALEXANDER-SS
49 TODD FROHWIRTH-P
52 JOSE MESA-P
53 ARTHUR RHODES-P
55 RICHIE LEWIS-P
75 ALAN MILLS-P

1993

3RD (TIE) E 85-77 10GB

2 MARK MCLEMORE-OF/UTIL
3 HAROLD BAINES-DH
4 *(RET#) EARL WEAVER*
5 *(RET#) BROOKS ROBINSON*
6 HAROLD REYNOLDS-2B/DH
6 MIKE (PAGS) PAGLIARULO-3B/1B (2)
6 MIKE PARENT-C/DH
8 CAL RIPKEN, JR.-SS
9 BRADY ANDERSON-OF/DH
10 LEO GOMEZ (INJ)-3B/DH
11 LUIS MERCEDES-OF/DH (1)
11 JEFFREY HAMMONDS (INJ)-OF/DH
12 MIKE DEVEREAUX-OF
13 MIKE PARENT-C/DH
13 MIKE (PAGS) PAGLIARULO-3B/1B (2)
14 CHITO MARTINEZ-OF/DH
15 DAVEY LOPES-CH
17 DICK BOSMAN-CH
18 DAMON BUFORD-OF/DH
19 BEN MCDONALD-P
20 *(RET #) FRANK ROBINSON*
21 DAVID SEGUI-1B/DH
22 *(RET #) JIM PALMER*
23 CHRIS HOILES-C/DH
24 GREG BIAGINI-CH
25 GREG BIAGINI-CH
25 HAROLD REYNOLDS-2B/DH
26 JOHNNY OATES-MGR
27 GLENN DAVIS (INJ/RET)-1B/DH
27 LONNIE (SKATES) SMITH-DH/OF (2)
28 JACK VOIGT-UTIL
30 GREGG OLSON (INJ)-P
31 JERRY NARRON-CH
32 MARK WILLIAMSON-P
33 *(RET #) EDDIE MURRAY*
34 FERNANDO VALENZUELA-P
35 MIKE MUSSINA (INJ)-P
36 TIM HULETT-INF/DH
37 GLENN DAVIS (INJ/RET)-1B/DH
38 MARK LEONARD-OF/DH
40 RICK SUTCLIFFE (INJ)-P
41 JEFF TACKETT-C/P
42 SHERMAN OBANDO (INJ)-DH/OF
43 MIKE FERRARO-CH
44 ELLIE HENDRICKS-CH
45 JIM POOLE-P
46 JOHN O'DONOGHUE-P
47 BRAD PENNINGTON-P
48 MANNY ALEXANDER-DH
48 KEVIN MCGEHEE-P
49 TODD FROHWIRTH-P
50 ANTHONY TELFORD-P
51 JAMIE MOYER-P
53 ARTHUR RHODES (INJ)-P
55 MIKE COOK-P
56 MIKE OQUIST-P
75 ALAN MILLS-P
88 PAUL CAREY-1B

1994

2ND E 63-49 6.5GB

STRIKE NO POST-SEASON

2 MARK MCLEMORE-2B
3 HAROLD BAINES-DH
4 *(RET#) EARL WEAVER*
5 *(RET#) BROOKS ROBINSON*
8 CAL RIPKEN, JR.-SS
9 BRADY ANDERSON-OF/DH
10 LEO GOMEZ (INJ)-3B/DH
11 JEFFREY HAMMONDS (INJ)-OF/DH
12 MIKE DEVEREAUX (INJ)-OF
13 SHEPHERD, ??-CH?
13 DON BUFORD, SR.-CH
14 MARK SMITH-OF
15 DAVEY LOPES-CH
17 CHRIS SABO (INJ)-3B
18 DAMON BUFORD-PR
19 BEN MCDONALD-P
20 *(RET #) FRANK ROBINSON*
21 TOM BOLTON-P
22 *(RET #) JIM PALMER*
23 CHRIS HOILES-C/DH
24 GREG BIAGINI-CH
25 RAFAEL PALMEIRO-1B
26 JOHNNY OATES-MGR
27 DICK BOSMAN-CH
28 JACK VOIGT-UTIL
29 BRAD PENNINGTON-P
30 DWIGHT SMITH-OF (2)
31 JERRY NARRON-CH
32 MARK WILLIAMSON-P
33 *(RET #) EDDIE MURRAY*
34 JERRY NARRON-CH
34 MARK SMITH-OF
35 MIKE MUSSINA-P
36 TIM HULETT-3B/2B
38 MARK (IKE) EICHHORN-P
39 LONNIE (SKATES) SMITH (INJ)-DH/OF
41 JEFF TACKETT-C/P
44 ELLIE HENDRICKS-CH
45 JIM POOLE-P
47 LEE SMITH-P
48 BRUCE DOSTAL-OF
49 ARMANDO BENITEZ-P
50 SID (EL SID) FERNANDEZ (INJ)-P
51 JAMIE MOYER-P
53 ARTHUR RHODES (INJ)-P
55 SCOTT KLINGENBECK-P
56 MIKE OQUIST-P
73 DON BUFORD-CH
75 ALAN MILLS-P
88 PAUL CAREY (INJ)-1B

1995

3RD E 71-73 15GB

144 GAME SEASON

1 AL BUMBRY-CH
2 BRET BARBERIE-2B
3 HAROLD BAINES-DH
4 *(RET#) EARL WEAVER*
5 *(RET#) BROOKS ROBINSON*
6 MANNY ALEXANDER-2B
8 CAL RIPKEN, JR.-SS
9 BRADY ANDERSON-OF/DH
10 LEO GOMEZ (INJ)-3B
11 JEFFREY HAMMONDS (INJ)-OF/DH
12 JEFF MANTO (INJ)-3B
14 LEE MAY-CH
15 CHUCK COTTIER-CH
17 KEVIN BASS-OF
18 ANDY (SLICK) VAN SLYKE (INJ)-OF (1)
19 BEN MCDONALD (INJ)-P
20 *(RET #) FRANK ROBINSON*
21 SCOTT ERICKSON-P (2)
22 *(RET #) JIM PALMER*
23 CHRIS HOILES (INJ)-C
24 MATT NOKES (WAIV)-C (1)
24 GREG ZAUN-C (2)
25 RAFAEL PALMEIRO-1B
26 DAMON BUFORD-OF (1)
26 BOBBY (BOBBY BO) BONILLA-OF/DH (2)
27 PHIL (THE VULTURE) REGAN-MGR
28 JACK VOIGT-1B (1)
28 CURTIS GOODWIN-OF
29 BRAD PENNINGTON-P (1)
29 GENE HARRIS (INJ) P (2)
30 JEFF HUSON-3B
31 DOUG JONES-P
32 JARVIS BROWN-OF
33 *(RET #) EDDIE MURRAY*
34 MARK SMITH-OF/DH
35 MIKE MUSSINA-P
36 TERRY CLARK-P (2)
37 RICK KRIVDA-P
39 MIKE HARTLEY-P (2)
41 KEVIN BROWN (INJ)-P
42 SHERMAN OBANDO-OF
43 STEVE BOROS-CH
44 ELLIE HENDRICKS-CH
45 JOHN DE SILVA-P
46 MIKE FLANAGAN-CH
47 JESSE OROSCO-P
48 GREG ZAUN-C
48 JIMMY MYERS-P
49 ARMANDO BENITEZ-P
50 SID (EL SID) FERNANDEZ (INJ) (WAIV)-P (1)
51 JAMIE MOYER-P
52 MARK LEE-P
53 ARTHUR RHODES (INJ)-P
55 SCOTT KLINGENBECK-P (1)
55 JIM DEDRICK-P
56 MIKE OQUIST (WAIV)-P
58 CESAR DEVAREZ-C
60 JIMMY HAYNES-P
62 RICK KRIVDA-P
75 ALAN MILLS-P
77 JOE BOROWSKI-P

1996

2ND E (W/C) 88-74 4GB

W ALDS-CLEA 3-1

L ALCS-NYA 4-1

1 TONY TARASCO (INJ)-OF
2 SAM PERLOZZO-CH
3 BILLY RIPKEN-2B
4 *(RET#) EARL WEAVER*
5 *(RET#) BROOKS ROBINSON*
6 MANNY ALEXANDER-SS
8 CAL RIPKEN, JR.-SS
9 BRADY ANDERSON-OF
10 MIKE DEVEREAUX-OF
11 JEFFREY HAMMONDS (INJ)-OF
12 ROBERTO ALOMAR-2B
13 ANDY ETCHEBARREN-CH
14 TODD ZEILE-3B (2)
15 DAVEY JOHNSON-MGR
17 B. J. SURHOFF (INJ)-3B
18 JOHN STEARNS-CH
19 SCOTT ERICKSON-P
20 *(RET #) FRANK ROBINSON*
21 KENT MERCKER-P (1)
21 MIKE MILCHIN-P (2)
22 *(RET #) JIM PALMER*
23 CHRIS HOILES-C
24 GREG ZAUN-C (1)
24 MARK PARENT-C (2)
25 RAFAEL PALMEIRO-1B
26 BOBBY (BOBBY BO) BONILLA-OF
27 KEITH SHEPHERD-P
27 ROCKY COPPINGER-P
28 RANDY MYERS-P
29 LUIS POLONIA (REL)-OF (1)
30 JEFF HUSON (INJ)-2B
30 BRENT BOWERS-OF
31 ROGER MCDOWELL (INJ)-P
33 EDDIE MURRAY-DH (2)
34 MARK SMITH (INJ)-OF
35 MIKE MUSSINA-P
36 DAVID WELLS-P
37 PAT DOBSON-CH
38 RICK KRIVDA-P
39 NERIO RODRIGUEZ-P
40 EUGENE KINGSALE-OF
41 ARCHIE CORBIN-P
43 ESTEBAN YAN-P
44 ELLIE HENDRICKS-CH
45 KEITH SHEPHERD-P
46 JIMMY MYERS-P
47 JESSE OROSCO-P
48 RICK DOWN-CH
49 ARMANDO BENITEZ (INJ)-P
50 JIMMY HAYNES-P
51 TERRY MATHEWS-P (2)
52 GARRETT STEPHENSON-P (1)
53 ARTHUR RHODES (INJ)-P
55 PETE INCAVIGLIA-DH (2)
57 BRIAN SACKINSKY-P
59 CESAR DEVAREZ-C
63 NERIO RODRIGUEZ-P
75 ALAN MILLS (INJ)-P

1997

1ST E 98-64 0GB

W ALDS-SEAA 3-1

L ALCS-CLEA 4-2

1 JEROME WALTON (INJ)-OF
2 SAM PERLOZZO-CH
3 TONY TARASCO-OF
3 HAROLD BAINES-DH (2)
4 *(RET#) EARL WEAVER*
5 *(RET#) BROOKS ROBINSON*
6 AARON LEDESMA-3B/1B/2B
8 CAL RIPKEN, JR.-3B
9 BRADY ANDERSON-OF
10 GERONIMO BERROA-OF (2)
10 HAROLD BAINES-DH (2)
11 JEFFREY HAMMONDS-OF
12 ROBERTO ALOMAR (INJ)-2B
13 ANDY ETCHEBARREN-CH
14 MIKE BORDICK-SS
15 DAVEY JOHNSON-MGR
17 B. J. SURHOFF-OF
18 JOHN STEARNS-CH
19 SCOTT ERICKSON-P
20 *(RET #) FRANK ROBINSON*
21 JIMMY KEY-P
22 *(RET #) JIM PALMER*
23 CHRIS HOILES (INJ)-C
24 ERIC DAVIS (INJ)-OF
25 RAFAEL PALMEIRO-1B
26 PETE (INKY) INCAVIGLIA (INJ)-OF/DH (1)
26 DAVID DELLUCCI-OF
27 ROCKY COPPINGER (INJ)-P
28 RANDY MYERS-P
29 PETE (INKY) INCAVIGLIA (INJ)-OF/DH (1)
29 GERONIMO BERROA-OF (2)
30 SCOTT KAMIENECKI-P
31 RAY MILLER-CH
32 SHAWN BOSKIE (INJ)-P
33 *(RET #) EDDIE MURRAY*
34 CHARLIE GREENE-C
35 MIKE MUSSINA-P

ST. LOUIS BROWNS/**BALTIMORE ORIOLES**

46 JEFF REBOULET-2B/SS
47 JEROME WALTON (INJ)-OF
47 TIM LAKER-C
47 DANNY CLYBURN-PH
48 RICK KRIVDA-P
49 MIKE JOHNSON-P (1)
49 NERIO RODRIGUEZ-P
(41) ARCHIE CORBIN-(P)
42 LENNY WEBSTER-C
43 TONY TARASCO-OF
44 ELLIE HENDRICKS-CH
47 JESSE OROSCO-P
48 RICK DOWN-CH
49 ARMANDO BENITEZ-P
50 MEL ROSARIO-C
51 TERRY MATHEWS-P
53 ARTHUR RHODES-P
55 ANDY ETCHEBARREN-CH
55 MIKE JOHNSON-P (1)
55 BRIAN WILLIAMS-P
56 ESTEBAN YAN-P
75 ALAN MILLS (INJ)-P

1998

4TH E 79-83 35GB

1 P. J. FORBES-2B/INF
2 SAM PERLOZZO-CH
3 HAROLD BAINES (INJ)-DH
4 *(RET#) EARL WEAVER*
5 *(RET#) BROOKS ROBINSON*
6 CALVIN PICKERING-DH
8 CAL RIPKEN, JR.-3B
9 BRADY ANDERSON (INJ)-OF
10 RYAN MINOR-3B
11 JEFFREY HAMMONDS (INJ)-OF (1)
11 WILLIE GREENE-3B/OF (2)
12 ROBERTO ALOMAR (INJ)-2B
13 OZZIE GUILLEN (REL)-INF (1)
13 JERRY HAIRSTON, JR.-2B
14 MIKE BORDICK-SS
15 DOUG DRABEK (INJ)-P
17 B. J. SURHOFF-OF
18 JOHN STEARNS-CH
18 RICH BECKER-OF (2)
19 SCOTT ERICKSON-P
20 *(RET #) FRANK ROBINSON*
21 JIMMY KEY (INJ)-P
22 *(RET #) JIM PALMER*
23 CHRIS HOILES-C
24 ERIC DAVIS (INJ)-OF
25 RAFAEL PALMEIRO-1B
26 PETE J. SMITH-P (2)
27 ROCKY COPPINGER-P
28 RADHAMES DYKHOFF-P
28 JOEL BENNETT-P
29 JOE CARTER-1B/DH
30 SCOTT KAMIENECKI (INJ)-P
31 RAY MILLER-MGR
32 BOBBY MUNOZ-P
32 JESUS TAVAREZ-OF
32 LYLE MOUTON-OF
33 *(RET #) EDDIE MURRAY*
34 CHARLIE GREENE-C
35 MIKE MUSSINA (INJ)-P
36 JEFF REBOULET-2B/SS
37 NORM CHARLTON (REL)-P (1)
38 RICHIE LEWIS-P
39 NERIO RODRIGUEZ (INJ)-P (1)
39 JERRY HAIRSTON, JR.-2B
40 EUGENE KINGSALE-OF
41 DANNY CLYBURN (INJ)-OF
42 LENNY WEBSTER-C
43 SIDNEY PONSON-P
44 ELLIE HENDRICKS-CH
45 CARLOS BERNHARDT-CH
46 MIKE FLANAGAN-CH
47 JESSE OROSCO-P
48 RICK DOWN-CH
49 ARMANDO BENITEZ-P
51 TERRY MATHEWS (INJ) (REL)-P
52 WILLIS OTANEZ (INJ)-OF
52 CHRIS FUSSELL-P
53 ARTHUR RHODES (INJ)-P
55 ANDY ETCHEBARREN-CH
55 DOUG JOHNS-P
56 PETE J. SMITH-P (2)
57 JUAN GUZMAN-P (2)
(73) EVERETT STULL (INJ)-(P)
75 ALAN MILLS (INJ)-P

1999

4TH E 78-84 20GB

1 JESSE GARCIA-INF
2 SAM PERLOZZO-CH
3 HAROLD BAINES-DH (1)
4 *(RET#) EARL WEAVER*
5 *(RET#) BROOKS ROBINSON*
6 RICH AMARAL-OF
8 CAL RIPKEN, JR. (INJ)-3B
9 BRADY ANDERSON (INJ)-OF
10 RYAN MINOR-3B
11 DELINO DESHIELDS (INJ)-2B
12 WILL CLARK (INJ)-1B
13 MIKE FIGGA-C (2)
14 MIKE BORDICK-SS
15 JESSE GARCIA-INF
15 JERRY HAIRSTON, JR.-INF
17 B. J. SURHOFF-OF
18 JEFF CONINE-OF/1B
19 SCOTT ERICKSON-P
20 *(RET #) FRANK ROBINSON*
21 CHARLES JOHNSON-C
22 *(RET #) JIM PALMER*
23 TOMMY DAVIS-C
24 WILLIS OTANEZ-3B (1)
25 RICKY BONES-P
25 MATT RILEY-P
27 ROCKY COPPINGER-P (1)
27 JIM CORSI-P (2)
29 DERRICK MAY-DH/OF
30 SCOTT KAMIENECKI (INJ)-P
31 RAY MILLER-MGR
32 AL REYES-P (2)
33 *(RET #) EDDIE MURRAY*
34 MARV FOLEY-CH
35 MIKE MUSSINA-P
36 JEFF REBOULET-2B/SS
37 MIKE FETTERS (INJ)-P
38 EUGENE KINGSALE-OF
39 CALVIN PICKERING-DH
40 MIKE TIMLIN-P
41 JASON JOHNSON-P
42 LENNY WEBSTER (INJ) (WAIV)-C (1)
43 SIDNEY PONSON-P
44 ELLIE HENDRICKS-CH
45 GABE MOLINA-P
47 JESSE OROSCO-P
48 TERRY CROWLEY-CH
49 DOUG LINTON-P
51 HEATHCLIFF SLOCUMB-P (1)
51 BRIAN FALKENBORG-P
52 B. J. RYAN-P (2)
53 ARTHUR RHODES (INJ)-P
54 BRUCE KISON-CH
55 DOUG JOHNS-P
57 JUAN GUZMAN-P (1)
88 ALBERT (JOEY) BELLE-OF/DH

2000

4TH E 74-88 13.5GB

1 JESSE GARCIA-INF
2 SAM PERLOZZO-CH
3 HAROLD BAINES-DH (1)
4 *(RET#) EARL WEAVER*
5 *(RET#) BROOKS ROBINSON*
6 RICH AMARAL-OF
6 MELVIN MORA-INF (2)
8 CAL RIPKEN, JR. (INJ)-3B
9 BRADY ANDERSON-OF
10 MARK LEWIS (INJ)-INF (2)
11 DELINO DESHIELDS-2B
12 CALVIN MADURO (INJ)-P
13 WILLIE MORALES-C
14 MIKE BORDICK-SS (1)
15 JERRY HAIRSTON, JR.-INF
17 B. J. SURHOFF-OF (1)
18 JEFF CONINE-OF/1B
19 SCOTT ERICKSON (INJ)-P
20 *(RET #) FRANK ROBINSON*
21 CHARLES JOHNSON-C (1)
22 *(RET #) JIM PALMER*
23 WILL CLARK (INJ)-1B (1)
23 TRENIDAD HUBBARD-OF (2)
24 BRIAN GRAHAM-CH
25 RYAN MINOR-INF
26 BROOK FORDYCE-C (2)
27 BUDDY GROOM-P
27 TRENIDAD HUBBARD-OF (2)
28 MIKE TROMBLEY-P
29 IVANON COFFIE-INF
29 JAY SPURGEON-P
30 MIKE HARGROVE-MGR
31 JOSE MERCEDES-P
32 AL REYES-P(1)
32 LUIS MATOS-OF
33 *(RET #) EDDIE MURRAY*
34 PAT RAPP-P
35 MIKE MUSSINA-P
36 TIM WORRELL-P (1)
36 DARREN HOLMES-P (2)
36 CARLOS CASIMIRO-INF
37 GREG MYERS-C
38 CHRIS RICHARD-OF (2)
39 MIKE KINKADE-UTIL (2)
40 MIKE TIMLIN-P (1)
40 EUGENE KINGSALE-OF
41 JASON JOHNSON-P
42 *(RET #) JACKIE ROBINSON*
43 SIDNEY PONSON-P
44 ELLIE HENDRICKS-CH
45 GABE MOLINA-P (1)
45 LESLIE BREA-P
47 CHUCK MCELROY-P
48 TERRY CROWLEY-CH
49 SAMMY ELLIS-CH
50 RYAN KOHLMEIER-P
51 FERNANDO LUNAR-C (2)
52 B. J. RYAN-P
53 JOHN PARRISH-P
55 JEFF NEWMAN-CH
57 KARIM GARCIA-OF (2)
60 LUIS G. RIVERA-P (2)
66 SEAN MALONEY-P
75 ALAN MILLS-P (2)
88 ALBERT (JOEY) BELLE-OF/DH

2001

4TH E 63-98 32.5GB

1 BRIAN ROBERTS-SS
2 SAM PERLOZZO-CH
3 LARRY BIGBIE-OF
4 *(RET#) EARL WEAVER*
5 *(RET#) BROOKS ROBINSON*
6 MELVIN MORA-INF
8 CAL RIPKEN, JR. (INJ)-3B
9 BRADY ANDERSON-OF
10 TONY BATISTA-3B (2)
11 DELINO DESHIELDS-2B (1)
11 TIM RAINES, SR.-OF (2)
12 CALVIN MADURO (INJ)-P
14 MIKE BORDICK (INJ)-SS
15 JERRY HAIRSTON, JR.-INF
16 JASON JOHNSON-P
17 MIKE KINKADE (INJ)-OF/3B
18 JEFF CONINE-OF/1B
19 SCOTT ERICKSON (INJ)-P
20 *(RET #) FRANK ROBINSON*
21 MIKE HARGROVE-MGR
22 *(RET #) JIM PALMER*
23 DAVID SEGUI (INJ)-1B
24 GREG MYERS (WAIV)-C (1)
25 JAY GIBBONS-INF
26 BROOK FORDYCE-C
27 BUDDY GROOM-P
28 MIKE TROMBLEY-P (1)
29 JAY SPURGEON-P
30 RYAN KOHLMEIER-P
30 TIM RAINES, SR.-OF (2)
31 JOSE MERCEDES-P
32 LUIS MATOS (INJ)-OF
33 *(RET #) EDDIE MURRAY*
34 MARK WILEY-CH
35 JOSH TOWERS-P
36 LUIS RIVERA-P
36 KRIS FOSTER-P
37 WILLIS ROBERTS-P
38 CHRIS RICHARD (INJ)-OF/1B
39 CHAD PARONTO-P
40 EUGENE KINGSALE-OF
40 WILLIE HARRIS-OF
41 PAT HENTGEN (INJ)-P
42 *(RET #) JACKIE ROBINSON*
43 SIDNEY PONSON (INJ)-P
44 ELLIE HENDRICKS-CH
45 LESLIE BREA-P
45 JOHN WASDIN-P
47 CHUCK MCELROY-P
47 SEAN DOUGLASS-P
48 TERRY CROWLEY-CH
49 JOHN BALE-P
50 JULIO JORGE-P
51 FERNANDO LUNAR-C (2)
52 B. J. RYAN-P
53 JOHN PARRISH-P
55 TOM TREBELHORN-CH
56 RICK BAUER-P
59 JORGE JULIO-P
59 RYAN KOHLMEIER-P
60 GERONIMO GIL-C
61 CASEY BLAKE-3B (2)
63 TIM RAINES, JR.-OF
75 ALAN MILLS (INJ)-P
88 ALBERT (JOEY) BELLE (INJ)-OF/DH

2002

4TH E 67-95 36.5GB

1 BRIAN ROBERTS-2B/DH
2 SAM PERLOZZO-CH
3 LARRY BIGBIE-OF
4 *(RET#) EARL WEAVER*
5 *(RET#) BROOKS ROBINSON*
6 MELVIN MORA-OF/UTIL
9 LUIS GARCIA-OF
9 LUIS LOPEZ-INF/DH (2)
10 TONY BATISTA-3B/DH
11 MIKE MORIARTY-INF
11 EDDIE ROGERS-2B/INF
11 HOWIE CLARK-UTIL
12 CALVIN MADURO (INJ)-P
13 RODRIGO LOPEZ-P
14 MIKE BORDICK (INJ)-SS
15 JERRY HAIRSTON, JR.-2B
16 JASON JOHNSON (INJ)-P
17 GIL GERONIMO-P
18 JEFF CONINE (INJ)-1B/DH
19 SCOTT ERICKSON-P
20 *(RET#) FRANK ROBINSON*
22 *(RET#) JIM PALMER*
23 DAVID SEGUI (INJ)-DH/1B
24 RICK DEMPSEY-CH
25 JAY GIBBONS-OF/1B/DH
26 BROOK FORDYCE-C
27 BUDDY GROOM-P
28 JOHN STEPHENS-P
28 RYAN MCGUIRE-1B
29 CHRIS SINGLETON (INJ)-OF
30 RICK BAUER-P
30 MIKE HARGROVE-MGR
31 IZZY MOLINA-C
31 JOSE LEON-UTIL
32 LUIS MATOS (INJ)-OF/DH
33 EDDIE MURRAY-CH
34 MARK WILEY-CH
35 JOSH TOWERS-P
(36) LUIS RIVERA (INJ)-(P)
36 GARY MATTHEWS, JR.-OF/DH (2)
37 WILLIS ROBERTS-P
38 CHRIS RICHARD (INJ)-DH/1B
39 YORKIS PEREZ (INJ)-P
40 MARTY CARDOVA-OF/DH
41 PAT HENTGEN (INJ)-P
42 *(RET#) JACKIE ROBINSON*
43 SIDNEY PONSON-P
44 ELLIE HENDRICKS-CH
45 CHRIS BROCK (INJ)-P
47 SEAN DOUGLASS-P
48 TERRY CROWLEY-CH
49 TOM TREBELHORN-CH
49 TRAVIS DRISKILL-P
50 JULIO JORGE-P
51 FERNANDO LUNAR-C
51 STEVE BECHLER-P
52 B. J. RYAN-P
55 TOM TREBELHORN-CH
57 ERIK BEDARD-P
57 RAUL CASANOVA-C (2)
59 ERIC DUBOSE-P
(88) ALBERT (JOEY) BELLE (INJ)-(OF)

2003

4TH E 71-91 30GB

1 BRIAN ROBERTS-2B/DH
2 SAM PERLOZZO-CH
3 LARRY BIGBIE (INJ)-OF
4 *(RET#) EARL WEAVER*
5 *(RET#) BROOKS ROBINSON*
6 MELVIN MORA (INJ)-OF/UTIL
8 *(RET#) CAL RIPKEN*
9 GERONIMO GIL-C
10 TONY BATISTA-3B/DH
11 DEIVI CRUZ-SS/DH
12 JOSE MORBAN-INF/DH
13 RODRIGO LOPEZ (INJ)-P
14 OMAR DAAL-P
15 JERRY HAIRSTON, JR. (INJ)-2B/DH
16 JASON JOHNSON-P
17 B. J. SURHOFF (INJ)-DH/UTIL
18 JEFF CONINE-1B/OF (1)
(19) SCOTT ERICKSON (INJ)-(P)
20 *(RET#) FRANK ROBINSON*
21 MIKE HARGROVE-MGR
22 *(RET#) JIM PALMER*
23 DAVID SEGUI (INJ)-DH/1B
24 RICK DEMPSEY-CH
25 JAY GIBBONS-OF/1B
26 BROOK FORDYCE (BRV)-C
27 BUDDY GROOM-P
28 DAMIAN MOSS-P (2)
29 HECTOR CARRASCO-P
29 KURT AINSWORTH (INJ)-P (2)
30 RICK BAUER-P
31 JOSE LEON-3B/1B
32 LUIS MATOS (INJ)-OF
33 *(RET#) EDDIE MURRAY*
34 MARK WILEY-CH
35 RICK HELLING-P (1)
35 MATT RILEY-P
36 GARY MATTHEWS, JR. (WAIV)-OF (1)
36 JOHN PARRISH-P
37 WILLIS ROBERTS (INJ)-P
38 ROBERT MACHADO-C
38 TIM RAINES, JR.-OF
39 JACK CUST-DH
40 MARTY CARDOVA (INJ)-DH/OF
41 PAT HENTGEN-P
42 *(RET#) JACKIE ROBINSON*

43 SIDNEY PONSON-P (1)
44 ELLIE HENDRICKS-CH
46 KERRY LIGTENBERG-P
47 SEAN DOUGLASS-P
48 TERRY CROWLEY-CH
49 TRAVIS DRISKILL-P
50 JORGE JULIO-P
52 B. J. RYAN-P
53 CARLOS MENDEZ-1B/DH
55 TOM TREBELHORN-CH
57 PEDRO SWANN-OF
58 HECTOR CARRASCO-P
59 ERIC DUBOSE-P
71 CARLOS MENDEZ-1B/DH
72 ROBERT MACHADO-C
(79) ERIK BEDARD (INJ)-(P)
(88) ALBERT (JOEY) BELLE (INJ) (RET)-(OF)

2004

3RD E *78-84* *23GB*

1 BRIAN ROBERTS-2B/DH
2 SAM PERLOZZO-CH
3 LARRY BIGBIE-OF
4 *(RET#) EARL WEAVER*
5 *(RET#) BROOKS ROBINSON*
6 MELVIN MORA-OF/UTIL
8 *(RET#) CAL RIPKEN*
9 KEN HUCKABY-C (2)
9 GERONIMO GIL-C
10 MIGUEL TEJADA-3B/DH
11 DARNELL MCDONALD-OF
11 DAVID NEWHAN-DH
12 MATT RILEY-P
13 LEE MAZZILLI-MGR
14 JOSE BAUTISTA-INF
14 JOSE LEON-3B
15 JERRY HAIRSTON, JR. (INJ)-2B
16 DENNY BAUTISTA-P (1)
16 JASON GRIMSLEY-P (2)
16 TIM RAINES, JR.-OF
17 B. J. SURHOFF-OF
18 JAVY LOPEZ-C
19 RODRIGO LOPEZ-P
20 *(RET#) FRANK ROBINSON*
(21) MARTY CORDOVA-(OF)
22 *(RET#) JIM PALMER*
23 DAVID SEGUI (INJ)-DH/1B
24 RICK DEMPSEY-CH
25 RAFAEL PALMEIRO-1B/DH
26 LUIS LOPEZ-INF
27 BUDDY GROOM-P
29 KURT AINSWORTH-P
30 RICK BAUER-P
31 JAY GIBBONS-OF
32 LUIS MATOS-OF/DH
33 *(RET#) EDDIE MURRAY*
34 MARK WILEY-CH
34 RAY MILLER-CH
35 DANIEL CABRERA-P
36 JOHN PARRISH-P
38 TIM RAINES, JR.-OF
38 JASON GRIMSLEY-P (2)
39 JACK CUST-DH
39 DARNELL MCDONALD-OF
39 CHAD MATTOLA-OF
40 KEITH OSIK-C
41 DARNELL MCDONALD-OF
42 *(RET#) JACKIE ROBINSON*
43 SIDNEY PONSON-P
44 ELLIE HENDRICKS-CH
45 ERIK BEDARD-P
47 MIKE DEJEAN-P (1)
47 KARIM GARCIA (REL)-OF (2)
48 TERRY CROWLEY-CH
49 TOM TREBELHORN-CH
49 DARWIN CUBILLAN-P
49 JOHN MAINE-P
50 JORGE JULIO-P
52 B. J. RYAN-P
53 TODD WILLIAMS-P
55 TOM TREBELHORN-CH
61 DAVID BORKOWSKI-P
63 VAL MAJEWSKI-OF
64 BRUCE CHEN-P
72 ROBERT MACHADO-C

2005

4TH E *74-88* *21GB*

1 BRIAN ROBERTS-2B
2 SAM PERLOZZO-CH/MGR2
3 LARRY BIGBIE-OF (1)
3 MIDRE CUMMINGS-OF
4 *(RET#) EARL WEAVER*
5 *(RET#) BROOKS ROBINSON*
6 MELVIN MORA-3B
8 *(RET#) CAL RIPKEN*
9 KEN HUCKABY-C (2)
9 GERONIMO GIL (INJ)-C
10 MIGUEL TEJADA-SS
11 DAVID NEWHAN-OF
12 LEE MAZZILLI-MGR1
13 LEE MAZZILLI-MGR1
13 RODRIGO LOPEZ-P
14 CHRIS GOMEZ-3B/SS
15 RAMON NIVAR-OF
15 ELI WHITESIDE-C
15 ERIC BYRNES-OF (3)
16 JEFF FIORENTINO-OF
16 ELI MARRERO-OF (2)
17 B. J. SURHOFF (INJ)-OF
18 JAVY LOPEZ (INJ)-C
19 RODRIGO LOPEZ-P
19 JAMES BALDWIN-P (1)(3)
20 *(RET#) FRANK ROBINSON*
21 SAMMY SOSA (INJ)-OF
22 *(RET#) JIM PALMER*
23 JAMES BALDWIN-P (1)(3)
23 ALEJANDRO FRIERE-1B
23 JAMES BALDWIN-P (1)(3)
24 RICK DEMPSEY-CH
25 RAFAEL PALMEIRO (SUS:10G)-1B/DH
26 SAL FASANO-C
27 BRUCE CHEN-P
28 ERIC DUBOSE-P
28 KEITH REED-OF
(29) KURT AINSWORTH (INJ)-(P)
30 RICK BAUER-P
30 DAVE CASH-CH
31 JAY GIBBONS-OF/DH
32 LUIS MATOS (INJ)-OF
33 *(RET#) EDDIE MURRAY*
34 RAY MILLER-CH
35 DANIEL CABRERA (INJ)-P
36 JOHN PARRISH-P
37 NAPOLEON CALZADO-OF
37 CHRIS RAY-P
38 JASON GRIMSLEY (INJ)-P
39 STEVE REED-P
40 TIM BYRDAK-P
41 STEVE KLINE (SUS: 4G)-P
42 *(RET#) JACKIE ROBINSON*
43 SIDNEY PONSON (INJ)(REL)-P
44 ELLIE HENDRICKS-CH
45 ERIK BEDARD (INJ)-P
47 AARON RAKERS-P
48 TERRY CROWLEY-CH
49 HAYDEN PENN-P
50 JORGE JULIO-P
52 B. J. RYAN-P
53 TODD WILLIAMS-P
55 TOM TREBELHORN-CH
58 ALEJANDRO FRIERE-1B
61 JOHN MAINE-P
(63) VAL MAJEWSKI(INJ)-(OF)
64 BERNIE CASTRO-2B
67 ED ROGERS-SS
75 WALTER YOUNG-1B
77 ELI WHITESIDE-C

Cal Ripken not only played his entire career with the Baltimore Orioles, he accomplished the very rare thing of wearing only #8 for the entire time! He finally hung up his spikes after the 2001 season. His number was retired at that time. He broke Lou Gehrig's consecutive game record with 2633 games in a row. Cal sat himself out of a game just to end the streak. He played in 17 straight All-Star games and another in his last year. He finished with 3001 games, 1647 runs, 3184 hits of which 603 were doubles, 44 were triples and 431 were homeruns.

BOSTON RED SOX

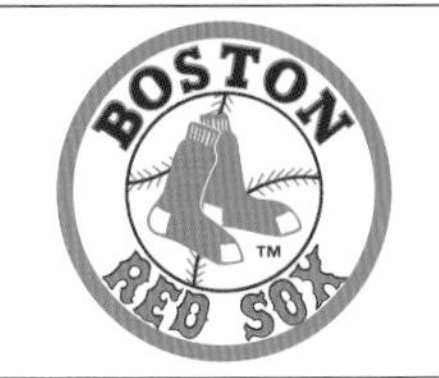

1931
BOSTON RED SOX
6TH 62-90 45GB

1 BILL SWEENEY-1B
2* BOBBY (GUNNER) REEVES (INJ)-2B/P*
3 JACK ROTHROCK-OF/INF
4 RABBIT WARSTLER-2B/SS
5 OTTO MILLER-3B/2B
6 HAL RHYNE-SS
7 BILL MARSHALL-PR
7 OLLIE MARQUARDT-2B/INF
8 URBANE (PICK) PICKERING -3B/2B
9 JOHN SMITH-1B
9 CHARLIE BERRY-C
10 MUDDY RUEL-C (1)
10 MARV (SPARKY) OLSON-2B
11 ED CONNOLLY-C
12 TOM (LONG TOM) WINSETT-OF
14 TOM (REBEL) OLIVER-OF
15 EARL WEBB-OF
16 HOWIE (SPONGE) STORIE-C
16 GENE (HALF-PINT) RYE-OF
17 AL VAN CAMP-OF/1B
19 MILT GASTON (INJ)-P
19 HOWIE STORIE-C
20 MILT GASTON (INJ)-P
21 DANNY (DEACON DANNY) MACFAYDEN-P
22 JACK RUSSELL-P
23 ED (BIG ED) MORRIS-P
23 GEORGE STUMPF-OF
24 HOD LISENBEE-P
25 ED (BULL) DURHAM-P
26 WILCY (CY) MOORE-P
27 JIM BRILLHEART-P
27 BILL MCWILLIAMS-PH
28 BOB (JUNIOR) KLINE (ILL)-P
28 MARTY MCMANUS-3B/2B (2)
29 WALTER MURPHY-P
30 JUD MCLAUGHLIN-P
31 WILCY (CY) MOORE-P
32 SHANO COLLINS-MGR
33 RUDY HULSWITT-CH
NO# PAT (WHOOPS) CREEDEN-2B (5G: 4/14-21)
NO# JOHNNY (BUSTER) LUCAS-OF (3G: 4/15-21)
NO# RUSS SCARRITT-OF (10G: 4/15-5/6)

1932
8TH 43-111 64GB

1* ED GALLAGHER-P*
1 AL VAN CAMP-1B
2 RABBIT WARSTLER-SS
2 ANDY SPOGNARDI-INF
3 MARTY MCMANUS-INF/MGR2
4 HAL RHYNE-INF
5 MARV (SPARKY) OLSON-2B/3B
6* JOHNNY WELCH-P*
7 URBANE (PICK) PICKERING -3B/C
8 OTTO MILLER-PH
8 BENNIE TATE-C (2)
9 CHARLIE BERRY-C (1)
9 SMEAD (GUINEA) (SMUDGE) JOLLEY-OF/C (2)
10 ED CONNOLLY-C
11 HOWIE (SPONGE) STORIE-C
11 HANK PATTERSON-C
12 JACK ROTHROCK-OF (1)
12 JOHNNY (LEFTY) WATWOOD-OF/1B (2)
14 TOM (REBEL) OLIVER-OF
15 EARL WEBB-1B/OF (1)
15 DALE (MOOSE) ALEXANDER-1B (2)
16 JOHNNY (BUSTER) LUCAS-PH
16 GORDON MCNOUGHTON-P
16 JUD MCLAUGHLIN-P
17 GEORGE STUMPF-OF
18 DANNY (DEACON DANNY) MACFAYDEN-P (1)
18 ROY JOHNSON-OF (2)
19 WILCY (CY) MOORE-P (1)
19 GORDON (DUSTY) RHODES-P (2)
20 ED (BULL) DURHAM-P
21 JACK RUSSELL-P (1)
21 PETE (JAKE) APPLETON AKA JABLONOWSKI-P (2)
22 HOD LISENBEE-P
22 ANDY SPOGNARDI-INF
24 BOB (JUNIOR) KLINE-P
25 PETE DONOHUE-P
25 IVY (POISON) ANDREWS-P (2)
25 REGIS LEHENY-P
26 BOB (LEFTY) WEILAND-P
27 JOHN MICHAELS-P
28 JOHNNY REDER-1B/3B
31 SHANO COLLINS-MGR1
31 LARRY BOERNER-P
32 RUDY HULSWITT-CH
ED MORRIS (DIED)-(P)

1933
7TH 63-86 34.5GB

1 RABBIT WARSTLER-SS
2 GREG MULLEAVY-PR
2 MARTY MCMANUS-3B/INF/MGR
3 ROY JOHNSON-OF
4 SMEAD (GUINEA) (SMUDGE) JOLLEY-OF/C
5 JOHNNY HODAPP-2B/1B
6 BERNIE FRIBERG-INF
6 BUCKY WALTERS-3B/2B
7 JOHNNY (LEFTY) WATWOOD-OF
7 DUSTY COOKE-OF
8 JOHNNY GOOCH-C
9 MERV SHEA-C (1)
9 RICK FERRELL-C (2)
10 BOB (SUITCASE BOB) SEEDS-1B/OF
11 TOM WINSETT-OF
11 FREDDIE MULLER-2B
11 GEORGE PIPGRAS (INJ)-P (2)
12 TOM (REBEL) OLIVER-OF
13 BOB (FATS) FOTHERGILL-OF
14 MARV (SPARKY) OLSON-2B
14 CURT FULLERTON-P
15 DALE (MOOSE) ALEXANDER (INJ)-1B
16 IVY (POISON) ANDREWS-P
17 GORDON (DUSTY) RHODES-P
18 HANK JOHNSON-P
18 GEORGE STUMPF-OF
19 BOB (LEFTY) WEILAND-P
20 JOHNNY WELCH-P
21 JUD MCLAUGHLIN-P
21 LOU (DOC) LEGETT-C
21 MEL ALMADA-OF
22 LLOYD (GIMPY) BROWN-P (2)
22 BILLY WERBER-INF (2)
23 MIKE MEOLA-P
23 FREDDIE MULLER-2B
23 JOE JUDGE-1B (2)
24 BOB (JUNIOR) KLINE-P
25 GEORGE STUMPF-OF
25 LOU (DOC) LEGETT-C
26 LLOYD (GIMPY) BROWN-P (2)
31 RUDY HULSWITT-CH

1934
4TH 76-76 24GB

1 MAX (CAMERA EYE) (TILLY) BISHOP-2B/1B
2 BILL CISSELL-INF
3 EDDIE MORGAN-1B
4 ROY JOHNSON-OF
5 CARL REYNOLDS-OF
6 DUSTY COOKE-OF
7 RICK FERRELL-C
8 BUCKY WALTERS-3B/2B (1)
8 DON (RED) KELLETT-INF
9 GORDIE HINKLE-C
10 LEFTY GROVE-P
11 GORDON (DUSTY) RHODES-P
12 BOB (LEFTY) WEILAND-P (1)
12 WES FERRELL-P/PH
14 GEORGE PIPGRAS-P
14? SKINNY GRAHAM-OF (13G: 9/14-30)
14 JOE (BIG JOE) MULLIGAN-P
15 RUBE WALBERG-P
16 HANK JOHNSON-P
17 HERB (THE KNIGHT OF KENNETT SQUARE) PENNOCK-P
18 JOHNNY WELCH-P
19 FRITZ OSTERMUELLER-P
20 BILLY WERBER-3B/SS
21 FREDDIE MULLER-3B/2B
21? MEL ALMADA-OF (23G: 9/1-30)
21 LYN (BROADWAY) LARY-SS (2)
22 MOOSE SOLTERS-OF
23 BOB (SUITCASE BOB) SEEDS-1B/OF (1)
23 DICK (WIGGLES) (TWITCHES) PORTER-OF (2)
24 ED CONNOLLY-C
24 LOU (DOC) LEGETT-C
25 JOE JUDGE-1B
26 JACK ONSLOW-CH
27 BUCKY HARRIS-MGR
28 LOU (DOC) LEGETT-C
28 BIBB FALK-CH
__ GEORGE (LEFTY) HOCKETTE-P (3G: 9/17-30)
__ SPIKE MERENA-P (4G: 9/16-30)
__ AL NIEMIEC-2B (9G: 9/19-30)

1935
4TH 78-75 16GB

1 MAX (CAMERA EYE) (TILLY) BISHOP-INF
2 BILLY WERBER-INF
3 ROY JOHNSON-OF
4 JOE CRONIN-SS/MGR
5 MOOSE SOLTERS-OF (1)
5 SKI (SPINACH) MELILLO-2B (2)
6 CARL REYNOLDS-OF
7 RICK FERRELL-C
8 BABE DAHLGREN-1B
9 DUSTY COOKE-OF
10 LEFTY GROVE-P
11 GORDON (DUSTY) RHODES-P
12 WES FERRELL-P
14 FRITZ OSTERMUELLER-P
14 SKINNY GRAHAM-OF
15 RUBE WALBERG-P
16 JACK (BLACK JACK) WILSON-P
16 HANK JOHNSON-P
17 JOHNNY WELCH-P
18 WALT RIPLEY-P
19 MOE BERG-C
20 JACK (BLACK JACK) WILSON-P
21 MEL ALMADA-OF/1B
22 DOC FARRELL-2B
23 STEW (DOC) BOWERS-P
23 HY VANDENBERG-P
24 LOU (DOC) LEGETT-PR
24 SKI (SPINACH) MELILLO-2B (2)
25 BING MILLER-OF
26 AL SCHACHT-CH
27 DIB WILLIAMS-INF (2)
28 GEORGE (SKEETS) DICKEY-C
28 GEORGE (LEFTY) HOCKETTE-P
35 GEORGE PIPGRAS-P
66 JOE (CROONIN' JOE) CASCARELLA-P (2)
__ JOHN KRONER-3B (2G: 9/29)

1936
6TH 74-80 28.5GB

1 MEL ALMADA-OF
2 RICK FERRELL-C
3 JIMMIE (DOUBLE X) (BEAST) FOXX-1B/UTIL
4 ERIC (BOOB) MCNAIR-SS/INF
5 BILLY WERBER-3B/UTIL
6 JOE CRONIN (INJ)-SS/3B/MGR
7 HEINIE MANUSH (INJ)-OF
8 DOC (FLIT) CRAMER-OF
9 DUSTY COOKE-OF
10 LEFTY GROVE-P
11 JOHNNY (FOOTSIE) MARCUM-P
12 WES FERRELL-P
14 FRITZ OSTERMUELLER-P
15 RUBE WALBERG-P
16 STEW (DOC) BOWERS-P
16 MIKE MEOLA-P (2)
16 BABE DAHLGREN-1B
17 JOHNNY WELCH-P (1)
17 JACK RUSSELL-P (2)
18 JACK (BLACK JACK) WILSON-P
19 EMERSON DICKMAN-P
19 JOE (CROONIN' JOE) CASCARELLA-P
20 JENNINGS (JINX) POINDEXTER-P
21 JIM HENRY-P
22 MOE BERG-C
23 STEW (DOC) BOWERS-P
23 GEORGE (SKEETS) DICKEY-C
23 TED OLSON-P
24 SKI (SPINACH) MELILLO-2B
25 FABIAN GAFFKE-OF
26 JOHN KRONER-3B
27 BING MILLER-OF
30 TOM DALY-CH
31 HERB (THE KNIGHT OF KENNETT SQUARE) PENNOCK-CH
32 AL SCHACHT-CH

1937
5TH 80-72 21GB

1 MEL ALMADA-OF (1)
1 BEN CHAPMAN-OF/SS (2)
2 RICK FERRELL-C (1)
3 JIMMIE (DOUBLE X) (BEAST) FOXX-1B/C
4 JOE CRONIN-SS/MGR
5 MIKE (PINKY) HIGGINS-3B
6 ERIC (BOOB) MCNAIR-2B/INF
7 BUSTER (BUS) MILLS-OF
8 DOC (FLIT) CRAMER-OF
9 BOBBY DOERR-2B
10 LEFTY GROVE-P
11 JOHNNY (FOOTSIE) MARCUM-P
12 WES FERRELL-P (1)
12 BOBO NEWSOM-P (2)
14 FRITZ OSTERMUELLER-P
15 RUBE WALBERG-P
16 DOM (DIM DOM) DALLESANDRO-OF
18 JACK (BLACK JACK) WILSON-P
19 JOE (SMOKEY) GONZALES-P
19 FABIAN GAFFKE-OF
20 ARCHIE (HAPPY) MCKAIN-P
21 JIM HENRY-P
21 BOB (RED) DAUGHTERS-PR
22 MOE BERG-C
23 GENE (RED) DESAUTELS-C
23 JOHNNY PEACOCK-C
24 SKI (SPINACH) MELILLO-INF
25 BOB (RED) DAUGHTERS-PR
27 BING MILLER-CH
28 TED OLSON-P
29 ARCHIE (HAPPY) MCKAIN-P
30 TOM DALY-CH
31 HERB (THE KNIGHT OF KENNETT SQUARE) PENNOCK-CH
32 STEW (DOC) BOWERS-PR
32 TOMMY THOMAS-P

1938
2ND 88-61 9.5GB

1 BOBBY DOERR-2B
2 GENE (RED) DESAUTELS-C
3 JIMMIE (DOUBLE X) (BEAST) FOXX-1B
4 JOE CRONIN-SS/MGR
5 MIKE (PINKY) HIGGINS-3B
6 ERIC (BOOB) MCNAIR-INF
7 JOE VOSMIK-OF
8* DOC (FLIT) CRAMER-OF/P*
9 BEN CHAPMAN-OF/3B
10 LEFTY GROVE (INJ)-P
11 BILL HARRIS-P
11 CHARLIE (BROADWAY) WAGNER-P
12 TED OLSON-P
12 JOHNNY (FOOTSIE) MARCUM-P
14 ARCHIE (HAPPY) MCKAIN-P
15 LEE (BUCK) ROGERS-P (1)
15 AL BAKER-P
16 EMERSON DICKMAN-P
17 J10IM BAGBY-P
18 JACK (BLACK JACK) WILSON-P
19 JOE HEVING-P (2)
19 BILL HUMPHREY-P
19 BILL (LEFTY) LEFEBVRE-P
20 BILL HARRIS-P
21 FRITZ OSTERMUELLER-P

22 MOE BERG-C/1B
23 JOHNNY PEACOCK-UTIL
24 RED NONNENKAMP-OF/1B
25 FABIAN GAFFKE-OF/C
26 JIM (RAWHIDE) TABOR-3B/SS
27 DICK MIDKIFF-P
30 TOM DALY-CH
31 HERB (THE KNIGHT OF KENNETT SQUARE) PENNOCK-CH

1939

2ND 89-62 17GB

1 BOBBY DOERR-2B
2 GENE (RED) DESAUTELS-C
3 JIMMIE (DOUBLE X) (BEAST) FOXX-1B
4 JOE CRONIN-SS/MGR
5 JIM (RAWHIDE) TABOR-3B
6 BOZE BERGER-INF
7 JOE VOSMIK-OF
8 DOC (FLIT) CRAMER-OF
9 TED (THE SPLENDID SPLINTER) (THUMPER) (THE KID) WILLIAMS-OF
10 LEFTY GROVE
11 DENNY GALEHOUSE-P
12 JAKE (WHISTLIN' JAKE) WADE-P (1)
12 ELDON (SUBMARINE) AUKER-P
13 ELDON (SUBMARINE) AUKER-P
14 TOM (SCOOPS) CAREY-2B/SS
15 WOODY RICH (INJ)-P
15 BILL (LEFTY) LEFEBVRE-P
16 EMERSON DICKMAN-P
17 JIM BAGBY-P
17 BILL SAYLES-P
18 JACK (BLACK JACK) WILSON-P
19 JOE HEVING-P
21 FRITZ OSTERMUELLER-P
22 MOE BERG-C
23 JOHNNY PEACOCK-C
24 RED NONNENKAMP-OF
25 MONTY WEAVER-P
25 CHARLIE (BROADWAY) WAGNER-P
26 FABIAN GAFFKE-PH
26 LOU FINNEY-1B/OF (2)
30 TOM DALY-CH
31 HERB (THE KNIGHT OF KENNETT SQUARE) PENNOCK-CH
31 HUGH DUFFY-CH

1940

4TH (TIE) 82-72 8GB

1 BOBBY DOERR-2B
2 GENE (RED) DESAUTELS-C
3 JIMMIE (DOUBLE X) (BEAST) FOXX-1B/UTIL
4 JOE CRONIN-SS/3B/MGR
5 JIM (RAWHIDE) TABOR (ILL)-3B
6 MARV (FRECK) OWEN-3B/1B
7 DOM (THE LITTLE PROFESSOR) DIMAGGIO-OF
8 DOC (FLIT) CRAMER-OF
9 TED (THE SPLENDID SPLINTER) (THUMPER) (THE KID) WILLIAMS-OF/P
10 LEFTY GROVE-P
12 DENNY GALEHOUSE-P
14 TOM (SCOOPS) CAREY-INF
15 WOODY RICH-P
15 CHARLIE GELBERT-INF (2)
15 BILL FLEMING-P
16 EMERSON DICKMAN-P
17 JIM BAGBY-P
18 JACK (BLACK JACK) WILSON-P
19 JOE HEVING-P
20 MICKEY HARRIS-P
20 ALEX MUSTAIKIS-P
20 EARL (LEFTY) JOHNSON-P
21 FRITZ OSTERMUELLER-P
22 MOE BERG-C
23 JOHNNY PEACOCK-C
24 RED NONNENKAMP-OF
24 STAN SPENCE-OF
25 CHARLIE (BROADWAY) WAGNER-P
25 LOU FINNEY-1B/OF
26 HERB HASH-P
26 JOE (GABBY) GLENN-C
27 BILL BUTLAND-P
27 CHARLIE (BROADWAY) WAGNER-P
27 YANK TERRY-P
28 EARL (LEFTY) JOHNSON-P
28 ALEX MUSTAIKIS-P
28 BILL FLEMING-P
28 BILL BUTLAND-P
29 HERB HASH-P
30 TOM DALY-CH
31 HUGH DUFFY-CH
31 FRANK SHELLENBACK-CH
32 TONY LUPIEN-1B

1941

2ND 84-70 17GB

1 BOBBY DOERR-2B
2 FRANKIE PYTLAK-C
3 JIMMIE (DOUBLE X) (BEAST) FOXX-1B/UTIL
4 JOE CRONIN-SS/UTIL/MGR
5 JIM (RAWHIDE) TABOR-3B
6 ODELL (BAD NEWS) HALE-3B/2B (1)
6 AL (BROADWAY) FLAIR-1B
7 DOM (THE LITTLE PROFESSOR) DIMAGGIO-OF
8 LOU FINNEY-OF/1B
9 TED (THE SPLENDID SPLINTER) (THUMPER) (THE KID) WILLIAMS-OF
10 LEFTY GROVE-P
11 JOHNNY PEACOCK-C
12 PETE FOX-OF
14 TOM (SCOOPS) CAREY-INF
15 WOODY RICH-P
15 OSCAR (OSSIE) JUDD-P
15 TEX HUGHSON-P
16 EMERSON DICKMAN (MIL)-P
17 JOE (BURRHEAD) DOBSON-P
18 JACK (BLACK JACK) WILSON-P
19 MICKEY HARRIS-P
20 EARL (LEFTY) JOHNSON-P
21 STAN SPENCE-OF
22 MOE BERG-CH
23 BILL FLEMING-P
24 HERB HASH-P
24 NELSON (NELLIE) POTTER-P (2)
25 MIKE RYBA-P
26 SKEETER NEWSOME-SS/2B
27 CHARLIE (BROADWAY) WAGNER-P
28 DICK NEWSOME-P
29 TEX HUGHSON-P
30 TOM DALY-CH
31 FRANK SHELLENBACK-CH
37 PAUL CAMPBELL-PR

1942

2ND 93-59 9GB

1 BOBBY DOERR-2B
2 ANDY GILBERT-OF
3 JIMMIE (DOUBLE X) (BEAST) FOXX-1B (1)
4 JOE CRONIN-INF/MGR
5 JIM (RAWHIDE) TABOR-3B
6 JOHNNY PESKY-SS
7 DOM (THE LITTLE PROFESSOR) DIMAGGIO-OF
8 LOU FINNEY-OF/1B
9 TED (THE SPLENDID SPLINTER) (THUMPER) (THE KID) WILLIAMS-OF
10 KEN (LEFTY) CHASE-P
11 JOHNNY PEACOCK-C
12 PETE FOX-OF
14 TOM (SCOOPS) CAREY-2B
15 TEX HUGHSON-P
15 PAUL CAMPBELL-OF
16 TONY LUPIEN-1B
17 JOE (BURRHEAD) DOBSON-P
18 YANK TERRY-P
20 MIKE RYBA-P
21 TEX HUGHSON-P
22 LARRY WOODALL-CH
23 BILL CONROY-C
24 BILL BUTLAND-P
25 MIKE RYBA-P
25 MACE BROWN-P
26 SKEETER NEWSOME-INF
27 CHARLIE (BROADWAY) WAGNER-P
28 DICK NEWSOME-P
29 OSCAR (OSSIE) JUDD-P
30 TOM DALY-CH
31 FRANK SHELLENBACK-CH

1943

7TH 68-84 29GB

1 BOBBY DOERR-2B
2 DEE MILES-OF
2 GEORGE (CATFISH) METKOVICH-OF/1B
3 TONY LUPIEN-1B
4 JOE CRONIN-3B/MGR
5 JIM (RAWHIDE) TABOR-3B/OF
6 ROY PARTEE-C
7 EDDIE (SPARKY) LAKE-SS
8 LOU FINNEY (RET)-OF/1B
8 AL (BUCKETFOOT AL) SIMMONS-OF
8 BABE BARNA-OF (2)
10 KEN (LEFTY) CHASE-P (1)
10 AL (BUCKETFOOT AL) SIMMONS-OF
10 PINKY WOODS-P
11 JOHNNY PEACOCK-C
12 PETE FOX-OF
14 JOHNNY LAZOR-OF
15 FORD (ROCKY) (SNAPPER) GARRISON-OF
15 EMMETT O'NEILL-P
15 LOU LUCIER-P
17 JOE (BURRHEAD) DOBSON-P
18 YANK TERRY-P
19 ANDY KARL-P (1)
19 JOE (BURRHEAD) DOBSON-P
20 MIKE RYBA-P
21 TEX HUGHSON-P
22 LARRY WOODALL-CH
23 BILL CONROY-C
24 ANDY KARL-P (1)
24 DANNY DOYLE-C
25 MACE BROWN-P
26 SKEETER NEWSOME-SS/3B
27 LEON (LEE) CULBERSON (INJ)-OF
28 DICK NEWSOME-P
29 OSCAR (OSSIE) JUDD-P
30 TOM DALY-CH
31 FRANK SHELLENBACK-CH
42 BABE BARNA-OF (2)
42 TOM MCBRIDE-OF
81 LOU LUCIER-P
82 JOHNNY LAZOR-OF

1944

4TH 77-77 12GB

1 BOBBY DOERR (MIL)-2B
2 GEORGE (CATFISH) METKOVICHOF/1B
4 JOE CRONIN-1B/MGR
5 JIM (RAWHIDE) TABOR (MIL)-3B
6 ROY PARTEE-C
6* STAN (PARTY) PARTENHEIMER-P*
7 EDDIE (SPARKY) LAKE-INF/P
8 BOB (INDIAN BOB) JOHNSON-OF
9 JOHNNY PEACOCK-C (1)
9 HAL WAGNER (MIL)-C (2)
10 PINKY WOODS-P
11 LEON (LEE) CULBERSON-OF
12 PETE FOX-OF
14 JOHNNY LAZOR-OF/C
14 REX CECIL-P
15 FORD (ROCKY) (SNAPPER) GARRISON-OF (1)
15 EMMETT O'NEILL-P
16 VIC JOHNSON-P
16 LOU FINNEY (RET)-1B/OF
17 JOE WOOD-P
•17 STAN (PARTY) PARTENHEIMER-P
17 FRANK (RED) BARRETT-P
18 YANK TERRY-P
19 FORD (ROCKY) (SNAPPER) GARRISON-OF (1)
19 HAL WAGNER (MIL)-C (2)
20 MIKE RYBA-P
21 CLEM HAUSMANN-P
22 LARRY WOODALL-CH
23 BILL CONROY-C
24 LOU LUCIER-P (1)
24 JIM BUCHER-3B/2B
25 TOM MCBRIDE-OF/1B
26 SKEETER NEWSOME-SS/INF
27 TEX HUGHSON (MIL)-P
28 JOE BOWMAN-P
29 OSCAR (OSSIE) JUDD-P
29 CLEM (STEAMBOAT) DREISEWERD-P
30 BILL BURWELL-CH
31 FRANK SHELLENBACK-CH
32 TOM DALY-CH

1945

7TH 71-83 17.5GB

1 TY LAFOREST-3B/OF
1 BEN STEINER-2B
2 GEORGE (CATFISH) METKOVICH-1B/OF
3 JOHNNY (JACK) TOBIN-3B/UTIL
4 JOE CRONIN-3B/MGR
5 JIM BUCHER-3B/2B
6 SKEETER NEWSOME-2B/INF
7 EDDIE (SPARKY) LAKE-SS/2B
8 BOB (INDIAN BOB) JOHNSON-OF
10 PINKY WOODS (INJ)-P
11 LEON (LEE) CULBERSON-OF
12 PETE FOX-OF
14 JOHNNY LAZOR-OF
15 EMMETT O'NEILL-P
16 BEN STEINER-2B
16 JIM WILSON (INJ)-P
17 FRANK (RED) BARRETT-P
18 YANK TERRY-P
18 OTIE CLARK-P
18 TY LAFOREST-3B/OF
19 RANDY HEFLIN-P
19 NICK POLLY-3B
20 MIKE RYBA-P
21 CLEM HAUSMANN-P
22 LARRY WOODALL-CH
23 BILLY HOLM-C
25 TOM MCBRIDE-OF/1B
26 FRED (WHALE) WALTERS-C
27 BOB GARBARK-C
28 JOE BOWMAN-P (1)
28 DOLPH CAMILLI (MIL)-1B
29 OSCAR (OSSIE) JUDD-P (1)
29 FRANKIE PYTLAK-C
30 DEL BAKER-CH
31 LOU FINNEY (RET)-1B/OF
31 REX CECIL-P
32 TOM DALY-CH
32 CLEM (STEAMBOAT) DREISEWERD (MIL)-P
33 DAVE (BOO) FERRISS (MIL)-P
34 VIC JOHNSON-P
35 LLOYD CHRISTOPHER-OF (1)
37 CLEM (STEAMBOAT) DREISEWERD (MIL)-P
38 DAVE (BOO) FERRISS (MIL)-P
39 OTIE CLARK-P
40 RED STEINER-C (2)
41 RANDY HEFLIN-P

1946

1ST 104-50 0GB

L WS-STLN 4-3

1 BOBBY DOERR-2B
2 GEORGE (CATFISH) METKOVICH-OF
3 RUDY YORK-1B
4 JOE CRONIN-MGR
5 RIP RUSSELL-3B/2B
6 JOHNNY PESKY-SS
7 DOM (THE LITTLE PROFESSOR) DIMAGGIO-OF
8 HAL WAGNER-C
9 TED (THE SPLENDID SPLINTER) (THUMPER) (THE KID) WILLIAMS-OF
10 JIM WILSON-P
10 DON GUTTERIDGE-2B/3B
11 LEON (LEE) CULBERSON-OF/3B
12 EARL (LEFTY) JOHNSON-P
14 TOM (SCOOPS) CAREY-2B
15 JOE (BURRHEAD) DOBSON-P
16 JIM WILSON-P
16 ROY PARTEE-C
17 JIM BAGBY-P
18 EARL (LEFTY) JOHNSON-P
18 TOM MCBRIDE-OF
19 MICKEY HARRIS-P
20 MIKE RYBA-P
21 TEX HUGHSON-P
22 LARRY WOODALL-CH
23 CLEM (STEAMBOAT) DREISEWERD-P
24 FRANKIE PYTLAK-C
24 WALLY MOSES-OF (2)
25 MACE BROWN-P

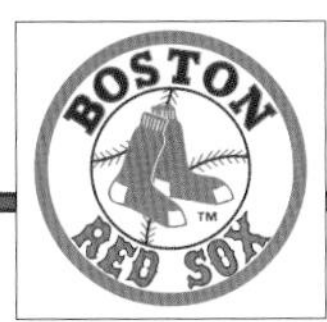

26 RANDY HEFLIN-P
26 BILL (GOOBER) ZUBER-P (2)
27 CHARLIE (BROADWAY) WAGNER-P
28 BILL BUTLAND-P
29 JOHNNY LAZOR-OF
30 DEL BAKER-CH
31 PAUL (VON) SCHREIBER-CH
32 TOM DALY-CH
33 DAVE (BOO) FERRISS-P
34 MEL DEUTSCH-P
35 ERNIE (JUNIE) ANDRES-3B
36 MIKE (PINKY) HIGGINS-3B (2)
37 BOB KLINGER-P
38 ED MCGAH-C
39 EDDIE PELLAGRINI-3B/SS
42 ANDY GILBERT-OF
44 BEN STEINER-3B
44 BILL (GOOBER) ZUBER-P (2)
46 PAUL CAMPBELL-1B

1947

3RD 83-71 14GB

1 BOBBY DOERR-2B
2 ED MCGAH-C
3 RUDY YORK-1B (1)
3 JAKE JONES-1B (2)
4 JOE CRONIN-MGR
5 RIP RUSSELL-3B
5 MATT BATTS-C
6 JOHNNY PESKY-SS/3B
7 DOM (THE LITTLE PROFESSOR) DIMAGGIO-OF
8 HAL WAGNER-C (1)
8 BIRDIE TEBBETTS-C (2)
9 TED (THE SPLENDID SPLINTER) (THUMPER) (THE KID) WILLIAMS-OF
10 DON GUTTERIDGE-2B/3B
10 BILLY GOODMAN-OF
11 LEON (LEE) CULBERSON-OF/3B
12 EARL (LEFTY) JOHNSON-P
14 SAM MELE-OF/1B
15 JOE (BURRHEAD) DOBSON-P
16 ROY PARTEE-C
17 SAM (BLACKIE) DENTE-3B
17 MEL (DUSTY) PARNELL-P
18 TOM MCBRIDE-OF
18 EDDIE SMITH-P (2)
19 MICKEY HARRIS (INJ)-P
20 HARRY DORISH-P
21 TEX HUGHSON (INJ)-P
22 LARRY WOODALL-CH
22 CHUCK STOBBS-P
23 TOMMY FINE-P
24 WALLY MOSES-OF
25 FRANKIE (BLIMP) HAYES-C
25 DENNY GALEHOUSE-P (2)
26 BILL (GOOBER) ZUBER-P
27 BILL BUTLAND-P
27 DOYLE (TEX) AULDS-C
28 BILLY GOODMAN-OF
29 COT DEAL-P
29 STRICK SHOFNER-3B
30 DEL BAKER-CH
31 PAUL (VON) SCHREIBER-CH
32 AL WIDMAR-P
32 MERRILL (MERL) COMBS-3B
33 DAVE (BOO) FERRISS-P
35 SAM (BLACKIE) DENTE-3B
37 BOB KLINGER-P
38 JOHNNY (FORDHAM JOHNNY) (GRANDMA) (FIREMAN) MURPHY-P
39 EDDIE PELLAGRINI-3B/SS
42 CHUCK STOBBS-P

1948

2ND 96-59 1GB

JOE (MARSE JOE) MCCARTHY-MGR
1 BOBBY DOERR-2B
2 STAN SPENCE-OF/1B
3 JAKE JONES-1B
4 SAM MELE-OF/1B
5 VERN (JUNIOR) (BUSTER) STEPHENS-SS
6 JOHNNY PESKY-3B
7 DOM (THE LITTLE PROFESSOR) DIMAGGIO-OF
8 BIRDIE TEBBETTS-C
9 TED (THE SPLENDID SPLINTER) (THUMPER) (THE KID) WILLIAMS-OF
10 BILLY GOODMAN-OF
11 BILLY HITCHCOCK-2B/3B
12 EARL (LEFTY) JOHNSON-P
14 MATT BATTS-C
15 JOE (BURRHEAD) DOBSON-P
16 ELLIS (OLD FOLKS) KINDER-P
17 MEL (DUSTY) PARNELL-P
18 JACK KRAMER-P
19 MICKEY HARRIS-P
20 HARRY DORISH-P
20 MIKE PALM-P
20 EARL (TEACH) CALDWELL-P (2)
21 TEX HUGHSON (INJ)-P
22 CHUCK STOBBS-P
23 NEILL (WILD HORSE) SHERIDAN-PH
23 TOM WRIGHT-PH
24 WALLY MOSES-OF
25 DENNY GALEHOUSE-P
27 JOHNNY OSTROWSKI-PH
27 LOU STRINGER-2B
28 COT DEAL-P
28 TOM WRIGHT-PH
29 LARRY WOODALL-CH
30 DEL BAKER-CH
31 PAUL (VON) SCHREIBER-CH
32 EARLE (THE KENTUCKY COLONEL) COMBS-CH
33 DAVE (BOO) FERRISS-P
34 BABE MARTIN-C
35 WINDY MCCALL-P
35 MICKEY (MAURY) MCDERMOTT-P
36 EARL (TEACH) CALDWELL-P (2)
36 MICKEY (MAURY) MCDERMOTT-P

1949

2ND 96-58 1GB

JOE (MARSE JOE) MCCARTHY-MGR
1 BOBBY DOERR-2B
2 STAN SPENCE-OF (1)
2 AL (ZEKE) ZARILLA-OF (2)
3 WALT (MOOSE) DROPO-1B
4 SAM MELE-OF (1)
5 VERN (JUNIOR) (BUSTER) STEPHENS-SS
6 JOHNNY PESKY-3B
7 DOM (THE LITTLE PROFESSOR) DIMAGGIO-OF
8 BIRDIE TEBBETTS-C
9 TED (THE SPLENDID SPLINTER) (THUMPER) (THE KID) WILLIAMS-OF
10 BILLY GOODMAN-OF
11 BILLY HITCHCOCK-1B/2B
12 EARL (LEFTY) JOHNSON-P
14 MATT BATTS-C
15 JOE (BURRHEAD) DOBSON-P
16 ELLIS (OLD FOLKS) KINDER-P
17 MEL (DUSTY) PARNELL-P
18 JACK KRAMER-P
19 MICKEY HARRIS-P (1)
19 MICKEY (MAURY) MCDERMOTT-P
20 HARRY DORISH-P
20 WALT MASTERSON-P (2)
21 TEX HUGHSON-P
22 CHUCK STOBBS-P
23 TOMMY (OBIE) O'BRIEN-OF
24 MERRILL (MERL) COMBS-3B/SS
25 DENNY GALEHOUSE-P
26 FRANK QUINN-P
27 LOU STRINGER-2B
28 TOM WRIGHT-PH
29 JOHNNY SCHULTE-CH
30 KIKI CUYLER-CH
31 PAUL (VON) SCHREIBER-CH
32 EARLE (THE KENTUCKY COLONEL) COMBS-CH
33 DAVE (BOO) FERRISS (INJ)-P
34 BABE MARTIN-C
35 HARRY DORISH-P
35 WINDY MCCALL-P
35 JOHNNIE (HANS) WITTIG-P
35 WALT MASTERSON-P (2)
36 MICKEY (MAURY) MCDERMOTT-P
37 HARRY DORISH-P
42 TOM DALY-CH
44 JACK ROBINSON-P

1950

3RD 94-60 4GB

JOE (MARSE JOE) MCCARTHY-MGR1
1 BOBBY DOERR-2B
2 AL (ZEKE) ZARILLA-OF
3 WALT (MOOSE) DROPO-1B
4 KEN (BUTCH) KELTNER-3B/1B
5 VERN (JUNIOR) (BUSTER) STEPHENS-SS
6 JOHNNY PESKY-3B/SS
7 DOM (THE LITTLE PROFESSOR) DIMAGGIO-OF
8 BIRDIE TEBBETTS-C
9 TED (THE SPLENDID SPLINTER) (THUMPER) (THE KID) WILLIAMS-OF
10 BOB SCHERBARTH-C
10 BILLY GOODMAN-UTIL
11 BUDDY ROSAR-C
12 EARL (LEFTY) JOHNSON-P
12 JIM ATKINS-P
13 BOB (BUNCH) GILLESPIE-P
14 MATT BATTS-C
15 JOE (BURRHEAD) DOBSON-P
16 ELLIS (OLD FOLKS) KINDER-P
17 MEL (DUSTY) PARNELL-P
18 CHARLIE SCHANZ-P
19 MICKEY (MAURY) MCDERMOTT-P
20 WALT MASTERSON-P
21 BOB (BUNCH) GILLESPIE-P
21 WILLARD NIXON-P
21 JIM SUCHECKI-P
22 CHUCK STOBBS-P
23 TOMMY (OBIE) O'BRIEN-OF (1)
23 CLYDE VOLLMER-OF (2)
24 MERRILL (MERL) COMBS-PH (1)
24 JIM (HOT ROD) MCDONALD-P
24 JIMMY PIERSALL-OF
25 GORDIE MUELLER-P
26 FRANK QUINN-P
26 JIMMY PIERSALL-OF
26 JIM (HOT ROD) MCDONALD-P
26 PHIL (BABE) MARCHILDON-P
27 LOU STRINGER-INF
28 TOM WRIGHT-PH
29 JOHNNY SCHULTE-CH
30 STEVE O'NEILL-CH/MGR2
31 PAUL (VON) SCHREIBER-CH
32 EARLE (THE KENTUCKY COLONEL) COMBS-CH
33 DAVE (BOO) FERRISS-P
34 AL PAPAI-P (1)
34 DICK LITTLEFIELD-P
35 HARRY TAYLOR-P
36 HARRY TAYLOR-P
36 GEORGE SUSCE-CH
37 JIM SUCHECKI-P
37 CHARLIE (SMOKEY) MAXWELL-OF
39 BOB SCHERBARTH-C
39 FRED HATFIELD-3B

1951

3RD 87-67 11GB

1 BOBBY DOERR (INJ)-2B
2 AL EVANS-C
2 MEL HODERLEIN-2B/3B
3 WALT (MOOSE) DROPO-1B
4 LOU BOUDREAU-INF
5 VERN (JUNIOR) (BUSTER) STEPHENS (INJ)-3B/SS
6 JOHNNY PESKY-SS/INF
7 DOM (THE LITTLE PROFESSOR) DIMAGGIO-OF
8 MICKEY (MIKE) GUERRA-C (1)
9 TED (THE SPLENDID SPLINTER) (THUMPER) (THE KID) WILLIAMS-OF
10 BILLY GOODMAN-UTIL
11 BUDDY ROSAR-C
12 HARRY TAYLOR-P
14 MATT BATTS-C (1)
14 LES MOSS-C (2)
15 BILL (LEFTY) WIGHT-P
16 ELLIS (OLD FOLKS) KINDER-P
17 MEL (DUSTY) PARNELL-P
18 RAY SCARBOROUGH-P
19 MICKEY (MAURY) MCDERMOTT-P
20 WALT MASTERSON-P
21 WILLARD NIXON-P
22 CHUCK STOBBS-P
23 CLYDE VOLLMER-OF
24 PAUL (HERKY) HINRICHS-P
24 HARLEY HISNER-P
25 BILL EVANS-P
25 LEO (KIKI) KIELY-P
26 CHARLIE (SMOKEY) MAXWELL-OF
27 FRED HATFIELD-3B
28 TOM WRIGHT-OF
28 KARL (OLE) OLSON-OF
28 AARON ROBINSON-C (2)
29 GEORGE SUSCE-CH
30 STEVE O'NEILL-MGR
31 PAUL (VON) SCHREIBER-CH
32 EARLE (THE KENTUCKY COLONEL) COMBS-CH
33 EDDIE MAYO-CH
34 AL RICHTER-SS
35 NORM ZAUCHIN-1B
36 GEORGE SUSCE-CH
36 BEN FLOWERS-P
38 SAMMY WHITE-C
39 BOB DIPIETRO-OF

1952

6TH 76-78 19GB

1 FRED HATFIELD-3B (1)
1 GEORGE KELL-3B (2)
2 JIMMY PIERSALL (ILL)-UTIL
2 FAYE THRONEBERRY-OF
3 WALT (MOOSE) DROPO-1B (1)
3 DICK GERNERT-1B
4 LOU BOUDREAU-INF/MGR
5 VERN (JUNIOR) (BUSTER) STEPHENS (INJ)-SS/3B
6 JOHNNY PESKY-3B/SS (1)
6 JOHNNY (SKIDS) LIPON-SS/3B (2)
7 DOM (THE LITTLE PROFESSOR) DIMAGGIO-OF
8 HAL BEVAN-3B (1)
9 TED (THE SPLENDID SPLINTER) (THUMPER) (THE KID) WILLIAMS (MIL) -OF
10 BILLY GOODMAN-2B/UTIL
11 GUS NIARHOS-C
12 TED LEPCIO-INF
14 DICK GERNERT-1B
14 HERSH (BUSTER) FREEMAN-P
15 BILL (LEFTY) WIGHT-P (1)
16 ELLIS (OLD FOLKS) KINDER-P
17 MEL (DUSTY) PARNELL-P
18 RAY SCARBOROUGH-P (1)
18 MILT BOLLING-SS
19 MICKEY (MAURY) MCDERMOTT-P
20 WALT MASTERSON-P (1)
20 SID HUDSON-P (2)
21 WILLARD NIXON-P
22 SAMMY WHITE-C
23 HARRY TAYLOR-P
24 RANDY GUMPERT-P (1)
24 DICK BRODOWSKI-P
25 JIM ATKINS-P
25 DIZZY TROUT-P (2)
26 BILL HENRY-P
26 RALPH (BRICK) BRICKNER-P
27 DICK BRODOWSKI-P
27 AL BENTON-P
28 TOM WRIGHT-OF
28 HERSH (BUSTER) FREEMAN-P
29 IKE DELOCK-P
30 CLYDE VOLLMER-OF
31 PAUL (VON) SCHREIBER-CH
31 DON (FOOTSIE) LENHARDT-OF (1)
31 HOOT EVERS (INJ)-OF (2)
32 EARLE (THE KENTUCKY COLONEL) COMBS-CH
32 KEN WOOD-OF (1)
32 ARCHIE WILSON-OF (3)
32 AL (ZEKE) ZARILLA-OF (3)
33 LEN OKRIE-C
33 DEL (BABE) WILBER-C (2)
37 FAYE THRONEBERRY-OF
37 GEORGE (ROCKY) SCHMEES-UTIL/P (2)
37 PAUL (PEANUTS) (GULLIVER) LEHNER-OF
37 CHARLIE (SMOKEY) MAXWELL-1B/OF
38 GENE STEPHENS-OF
39 RALPH (BRICK) BRICKNER-P
40 BILL (DEACON) MCKECHNIE-CH
41 EARLE (THE KENTUCKY COLONEL) COMBS-CH
42 GEORGE (GOOD KID)

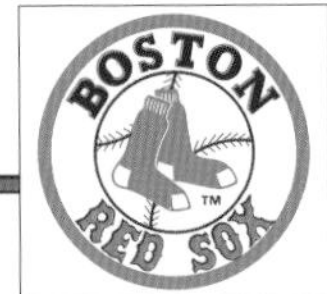

SUSCE-CH
42 SKI (SPINACH) MELILLO-CH
43 GEORGE SUSCE-CH
45 PAUL (VON) SCHREIBER-CH
LEO (KIKI) KIELY (MIL)-(P)
KARL (OLE) OLSON (MIL)-(OF)
NORM ZAUCHIN (MIL)-(1B)

1953

4TH 84-69 16GB

1 GEORGE KELL-3B/OF
2 MILT BOLLING-SS
3 DICK GERNERT-1B
4 LOU BOUDREAU-MGR
5 TED LEPCIO-INF
6 JOHNNY (SKIDS) LIPON-SS (1)
7 DOM (THE LITTLE PROFESSOR) DIMAGGIO-PH
8 BILLY CONSOLO-3B/2B
9 TED (THE SPLENDID SPLINTER) (THUMPER) (THE KID) WILLIAMS (MIL) -OF
10 BILLY GOODMAN-2B/1B
11 GUS NIARHOS-C
12 JACK MERSON-2B
12 IKE DELOCK-P
14 KEN HOLCOMBE-P
15 MARV GRISSOM-P (1)
16 ELLIS (OLD FOLKS) KINDER-P
17 MEL (DUSTY) PARNELL-P
18 BILL (LEFTY) KENNEDY-P
18 FRANK SULLIVAN-P
19 MICKEY (MAURY) MCDERMOTT-P
20 SID HUDSON-P
21 WILLARD NIXON-P
22 SAMMY WHITE-C
23 HERSH (BUSTER) FREEMAN-P
25 BEN FLOWERS-P
27 HAL (SKINNY) BROWN-P
28 BILL (BUGS) WERLE-P
28 BILL HENRY-P
29 IKE DELOCK-P
29 FLOYD BAKER-3B/2B (2)
30 CLYDE VOLLMER-PH (1)
30 FRANK SULLIVAN-P
31 HOOT EVERS (INJ)-OF
32 AL (ZEKE) ZARILLA-OF
33 DEL (BABE) WILBER-C/1B
34 JIMMY PIERSALL-OF
34 KARL (OLE) OLSON (MIL)-OF
35 AL RICHTER-SS
36 GENE STEPHENS-OF
37 JIMMY PIERSALL-OF
38 TOMMY UMPHLETT-OF
40 BILL (DEACON) MCKECHNIE-CH
41 DEL BAKER-CH
42 SKI (SPINACH) MELILLO-CH
43 GEORGE (GOOD KID) SUSCE-CH
45 PAUL (VON) SCHREIBER-CH
DICK BRODOWSKI (MIL)-(P)
LEO (KIKI) KIELY (MIL)-(P)
FAYE THRONEBERRY (MIL) -(OF)
NORM ZAUCHIN (MIL)-(1B)

1954

4TH 69-85 42GB

1 GEORGE KELL-3B/OF (1)
1 GRADY HATTON-3B/INF (3)
2 MILT BOLLING-SS/3B
3 DICK GERNERT-1B
4 LOU BOUDREAU-MGR
5 TED LEPCIO-2B/INF
6 HARRY (THE GOLDEN GREEK) AGGANIS-1B
8 BILLY CONSOLO-INF
9 TED (THE SPLENDID SPLINTER) (THUMPER) (THE KID) WILLIAMS (INJ) -OF
10 BILLY GOODMAN-UTIL
11 MICKEY OWEN-C
12 FLOYD BAKER-3B/2B (1)V
14 BILL (BUGS) WERLE-P
15 JOE (BURRHEAD) DOBSON-P/CH
16 ELLIS (OLD FOLKS) KINDER-P
17 MEL (DUSTY) PARNELL (INJ)-P
18 FRANK SULLIVAN-P
19 LEO (KIKI) KIELY-P
20 SID HUDSON-P
21 WILLARD NIXON-P
22 SAMMY WHITE-C
23 TOM BREWER-P
24 TOM HERRIN-P
24 RUSS (RUSTY) (DUTCH) KEMMERER-P
26 TEX CLEVENGER-P
26 BILL (BUGS) WERLE-P
27 HAL (SKINNY) BROWN-P
28 BILL HENRY-P
28 TOM (WHITEY) HURD-P
29 BILL HENRY-P
29 TOM HERRIN-P
30 JACKIE JENSEN-OF
31 HOOT EVERS-OF (1)
31 SAM MELE-1B/OF (2)
32 JOE (BURRHEAD) DOBSON-P/CH
32 DON (FOOTSIE) LENHARDT-OF/3B (2)
33 DEL (BABE) WILBER-C/1B
34 KARL (OLE) OLSON (MIL)-OF
35 CHARLIE (SMOKEY) MAXWELL-OF
37 JIMMY PIERSALL-OF
39 GUY (MOOSE) MORTON-PH
40 BUSTER MILLS-CH
41 DEL BAKER-CH
(42) DICK BRODOWSKI (MIL)-(P)
43 GEORGE (GOOD KID) SUSCE-CH
45 PAUL (VON) SCHREIBER-CH

1955

4TH 84-70 12GB

1 GRADY HATTON-3B/2B
2 MILT BOLLING (INJ)-SS
3 NORM ZAUCHIN-1B
4 JACKIE JENSEN-OF
5 MIKE (PINKY) HIGGINS-MGR
6 HARRY (THE GOLDEN GREEK) AGGANIS (DIED)-1B
7 SAM MELE-OF (1)
8 SAMMY WHITE-C
9 TED (THE SPLENDID SPLINTER) (THUMPER) (THE KID) WILLIAMS (PER)-OF
10 BILLY GOODMAN-2B/UTIL
11 BILLY CONSOLO-2B
11 FRANK MALZONE-3B
12 TED LEPCIO-3B
14 IKE DELOCK-P
15 WILLARD NIXON-P
16 ELLIS (OLD FOLKS) KINDER-P
17 MEL (DUSTY) PARNELL-P
18 FRANK SULLIVAN-P
19 LEO (KIKI) KIELY-P
20 EDDIE JOOST-INF
21 KARL (OLE) OLSON-OF
22 OWEN (RED) FRIEND-SS/2B (1)
22 JIM (PAG) PAGLIARONI-C
23 TOM BREWER-P
24 PETE DALEY-C
25 HERSH (BUSTER) FREEMAN-P (1)
26 FAYE THRONEBERRY-OF
27 HAL (SKINNY) BROWN-P (1)
27 GEORGE (GOOD KID) SUSCE-CH
28 TOM (WHITEY) HURD-P
29 BILL HENRY-P
30 MICKEY OWEN-CH
31 JACK (SLUG) BURNS-CH
32 DEL BAKER-CH
33 DAVE (BOO) FERRISS-CH
34 PAUL (VON) SCHREIBER-CH
35 BILLY KLAUS-SS/3B
37 JIMMY PIERSALL-OF
38 GENE STEPHENS-OF
39 BOB SMITH-P
40 RUSS (RUSTY) (DUTCH) KEMMERER-P
40 FRANK (THE BEAU) BAUMANN-P
41 GEORGE (GOOD KID) SUSCE-CH
41 DICK GERNERT-1B
42 DICK BRODOWSKI-P
44 JOE TRIMBLE-P
44 HAYWOOD SULLIVAN-C

1956

4TH 84-70 13GB

1 GRADY HATTON-PH (1)
2 MILT BOLLING-INF
3 NORM ZAUCHIN-1B
4 JACKIE JENSEN-OF
5 MIKE (PINKY) HIGGINS-MGR
6 MICKEY VERNON-1B
7 BILLY CONSOLO-2B
8 PETE DALEY-C
9 TED (THE SPLENDID SPLINTER) (THUMPER) (THE KID) WILLIAMS-OF
10 BILLY GOODMAN-2B
11 FRANK MALZONE-3B
12 TED LEPCIO-2B/3B
14 IKE DELOCK-P
15 WILLARD NIXON-P
16 HARRY DORISH-P (2)
16 BOB PORTERFIELD-P
17 MEL (DUSTY) PARNELL (INJ) -P
18 FRANK SULLIVAN-P
19 LEO (KIKI) KIELY-P
20 BOB PORTERFIELD-P
20 MARTY KEOUGH-PH
21 JOHNNY (BEAR TRACKS) SCHMITZ-P (1)
22 SAMMY WHITE-C
23 TOM BREWER-P
24 DON BUDDIN-SS
24 GENE (SKIP) MAUCH-2B
25 DICK GERNERT-OF/1B
26 FAYE THRONEBERRY (ILL)-OF
27 GEORGE (GOOD KID) SUSCE (ILL)-P
28 TOM (WHITEY) HURD-P
29 RUDY (BUSTER) MINARCIN-P
29 HARRY DORISH-P (2)
30 MICKEY OWEN-CH
31 JACK (SLUG) BURNS-CH
32 DEL BAKER-CH
33 DAVE (BOO) FERRISS-CH
34 PAUL (VON) SCHREIBER-CH
35 BILLY KLAUS-3B/SS
(36) JIM (PAG) PAGLIARONI (MIL)-(C)
37 JIMMY PIERSALL-OF
38 GENE STEPHENS-OF
39 DAVE SISLER-P
40 FRANK (THE BEAU) BAUMANN-P

1957

3RD 82-72 16GB

1 BILLY CONSOLO-INF
2 MILT BOLLING-PH (1)
3 NORM ZAUCHIN (INJ)-1B
4 JACKIE JENSEN-OF
5 MIKE (PINKY) HIGGINS-MGR
6 MICKEY VERNON-1B
7 BILLY CONSOLO-INF
7 KEN ASPROMONTE-2B
8 PETE DALEY-C
9 TED (THE SPLENDID SPLINTER) (THUMPER) (THE KID) WILLIAMS-OF
10 BILLY GOODMAN-PH (1)
11 FRANK MALZONE-3B
12 TED LEPCIO-2B
14 IKE DELOCK-P
15 FRANK (THE BEAU) BAUMANN-P
16 HAYWOOD SULLIVAN-C
18 FRANK SULLIVAN-P
19 BOB PORTERFIELD-P
20 RUSS (THE MAD MONK) (MONK) (ROWDY) MEYER-P
20 MIKE FORNIELES-P (2)
21 WILLARD NIXON-P
22 SAMMY WHITE-C
23 TOM BREWER-P
24 GENE (SKIP) MAUCH (INJ)-2B
25 DICK GERNERT-1B/OF
26 FAYE THRONEBERRY-PH (1)
26 MURRAY WALL-P
26 BOB (CHICK) CHAKALES-P (2)
27 GEORGE (GOOD KID) SUSCE-P
28 RUSS (RUSTY) (DUTCH) KEMMERER-P (1)
28 DEAN STONE-P (2)
29 RUDY (BUSTER) MINARCIN-P
31 JACK (SLUG) BURNS-CH
32 DEL BAKER-CH
33 DAVE (BOO) FERRISS-CH
34 PAUL (VON) SCHREIBER-CH
35 BILLY KLAUS-SS
36 JACK SPRING-P
37 JIMMY PIERSALL-OF
38 GENE STEPHENS-OF
39 DAVE SISLER-P
40 BOB (CHICK) CHAKALES-P (2)
41 MARTY KEOUGH-PH

1958

3RD 79-75 13GB

1 BILLY CONSOLO-INF
2 MARTY KEOUGH-OF/1B
3 PETE RUNNELS-2B/1B
4 JACKIE JENSEN-OF
5 MIKE (PINKY) HIGGINS-MGR
(6) JIM (PAG) PAGLIARONI (MIL)-(C)
7 KEN ASPROMONTE-2B (1)
8 PETE DALEY-C
9 TED (THE SPLENDID SPLINTER) (THUMPER) (THE KID) WILLIAMS-OF
11 FRANK MALZONE-3B
12 TED LEPCIO-2B
14 IKE DELOCK-P
15 FRANK (THE BEAU) BAUMANN-P
15 DUANE WILSON-P
15 BUD BYERLY-P (2)
(16) HAYWOOD SULLIVAN (INJ)-(C)
17 LEO (KIKI) KIELY-P
18 FRANK SULLIVAN-P
19 BOB PORTERFIELD-P (1)
19 JERRY CASALE-P
20 MIKE FORNIELES-P
21 WILLARD NIXON (INJ)-P
22 SAMMY WHITE-C
23 TOM BREWER-P
24 DON BUDDIN-SS
25 DICK GERNERT-1B
26 MURRAY WALL-P
27 GEORGE (GOOD KID) SUSCE-P (1)
27 BILL (MOMBO) MONBOUQUETTE-P
28 RIVERBOAT SMITH-P
28 TED BOWSFIELD-P
29 AL (BULL) SCHROLL-P
30 BILL RENNA-OF
31 JACK (SLUG) BURNS-CH
32 DEL BAKER-CH
33 DAVE (BOO) FERRISS-CH
34 PAUL (VON) SCHREIBER-CH
35 BILLY KLAUS-SS
36 LOU BERBERET-C (2)
37 JIMMY PIERSALL-OF
38 GENE STEPHENS-OF
39 DAVE SISLER-P

1959

5TH 75-79 19GB

1 BILLY CONSOLO-SS (1)
1 JIM MAHONEY-SS
1 HERB PLEWS-2B (2)
2 MARTY KEOUGH-OF/1B
3 PETE RUNNELS-2B/INF
4 JACKIE JENSEN-OF
5 MIKE (PINKY) HIGGINS-MGR1
6 VIC WERTZ-1B
7 JIM BUSBY-OF
8 PETE DALEY-C
9 TED (THE SPLENDID SPLINTER) (THUMPER) (THE KID) WILLIAMS-OF
10 GENE STEPHENS (INJ)-OF
11 FRANK MALZONE-3B
12 TED LEPCIO-2B (1)
12 BOBBY AVILA-2B (2)
12 PUMPSIE GREEN-2B/SS
14 IKE DELOCK-P
15 FRANK (THE BEAU) BAUMANN-P
16 HAYWOOD SULLIVAN-C
16 BILLY JURGES-MGR3
17 LEO (KIKI) KIELY-P
18 FRANK SULLIVAN-P
19 JERRY CASALE-P
20 MIKE FORNIELES-P
22 SAMMY WHITE-C
23 TOM BREWER-P
24 DON BUDDIN-SS
25 DICK GERNERT-1B/OF
26 MURRAY WALL-P (1)(3)
26 EARL WILSON-P
27 BILL (MOMBO) MONBOUQUETTE-P
28 TED BOWSFIELD-P
28 TED WILLS-P
28 NELS CHITTUM-P
30 BILL RENNA-OF
30 AL (BULL) SCHROLL-P (2)
31 JACK (SLUG) BURNS-CH
32 DEL BAKER-CH
33 DAVE (BOO) FERRISS-CH
34 RUDY YORK-CH/MGR2/CH
35 HERB MOFORD-P
35 DON (BEAR) GILE-C
37 GARY GEIGER-OF
38 GENE STEPHENS (INJ)-OF
39 DAVE SISLER-P (1)
39 BILLY HOEFT-P (2)
39 JACK HARSHMAN-P (2)
39 JERRY MALLETT-OF

BOSTON RED SOX

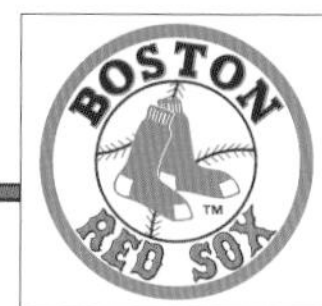

42 HERB MOFORD-P

1960

7TH 65-89 32GB

1 DON BUDDIN-SS
2 MARTY KEOUGH-OF (1)
2 MARLAN COUGHTRY-2B/3B
3 PETE RUNNELS-2B/INF
4 LU CLINTON-OF
5 RON JACKSON-1B
5 RAY (IKE) BOONE-1B (2)
5 MIKE (PINKY) HIGGINS-MGR3
6 VIC WERTZ-1B
7 JIM BUSBY-OF (1)
7 GARY GEIGER (ILL)-OF
8 EDDIE SADOWSKI (INJ)-C
8 JIM (PAG) PAGLIARONI-C
9 TED (THE SPLENDID SPLINTER) (THUMPER) (THE KID) WILLIAMS-OF
10 GENE STEPHENS-OF (1)
10 WILLIE TASBY-OF (2)
11 FRANK MALZONE-3B
12 PUMPSIE GREEN-2B/SS
14 IKE DELOCK-P
15 TOM (SNAKE) STURDIVANT-P
16 BILLY JURGES-MGR1
16 CARROLL HARDY-OF (2)
17 DAVE HILLMAN (INJ)-P
18 FRANK SULLIVAN-P
19 JERRY CASALE-P
20 MIKE FORNIELES-P
21 TOM (SPIKE) BORLAND-P
21 ARNIE EARLEY-P
22 RUSS NIXON-C (2)
23 TOM BREWER-P
25 BOBBY (THE FLYING SCOT) (THE STATEN ISLAND SCOT) THOMSON-OF/1B (1)
25 TED WILLS-P
26 EARL WILSON-P
27 BILL (MOMBO) MONBOUQUETTE-P
28 NELS CHITTUM-P
28 RIP REPULSKI-OF (2)
29 TED BOWSFIELD-P (1)
29 JIM (PAG) PAGLIARONI-C
30 HAYWOOD SULLIVAN-C
31 RAY WEBSTER-2B
31 CHET NICHOLS-P
32 DEL BAKER-CH/MGR2/CH
33 SAL (THE BARBER) MAGLIE-CH
34 RUDY YORK-CH
35 BILLY HERMAN-CH
36 TED WILLS-P
36 BILLY (MUFF) MUFFETT-P
37 GARY GEIGER-OF
38 DON (BEAR) GILE-C
39 AL (RED) WORTHINGTON-P (1)
39 RAY (IKE) BOONE-1B (2)
39 TRACY STALLARD-P
JACKIE JENSEN (RET)-(OF)
SAMMY WHITE (RET)-(C)

1961

6TH 76-86 33GB

1 DON BUDDIN-SS
2 CHUCK SCHILLING-2B
3 PETE RUNNELS-1B/INF
4 LU CLINTON-OF
4 JACKIE JENSEN-OF
5 MIKE (PINKY) HIGGINS-MGR
6 VIC WERTZ-1B (1)
7 GARY GEIGER-OF
8 CARL (YAZ) YASTRZEMSKI-OF
9 *(RET#) TED WILLIAMS*
10 BILLY HARRELL-INF
11 FRANK MALZONE-3B
12 PUMPSIE GREEN (ILL)-2B/SS
14 IKE DELOCK-P
15 GALEN CISCO-P
16 CARROLL HARDY-OF
17 DAVE HILLMAN-P
18 GENE CONLEY-P
19 TOM (SPIKE) BORLAND-P
20 MIKE FORNIELES-P
21 TOM (SPIKE) BORLAND-P
21 ARNIE EARLEY-P
22 RUSS NIXON-C
23 TOM BREWER-P
24 LU CLINTON-OF
24 JOE GINSBERG-C (2)
25 TED WILLS-P
27 BILL (MOMBO) MONBOUQUETTE-P
28 RIP REPULSKI-OF
28 WILBUR WOOD-P
29 JIM (PAG) PAGLIARONI-C
31 CHET NICHOLS-P
32 LEN OKRIE-CH
33 SAL (THE BARBER) MAGLIE-CH
34 RUDY YORK-CH
35 BILLY HERMAN-CH
36 BILLY (MUFF) MUFFETT-P
37 DON SCHWALL-P
38 DON (BEAR) GILE-1B/C
39 TRACY STALLARD-P

1962

8TH 76-84 19GB

1 EDDIE BRESSOUD-SS
2 CHUCK SCHILLING (INJ)-2B
3 PETE RUNNELS-1B
5 MIKE (PINKY) HIGGINS-MGR
6 LU CLINTON-OF
7 GARY GEIGER-OF
8 CARL (YAZ) YASTRZEMSKI-OF
9 *(RET#) TED WILLIAMS*
10 BILLY (SHOTGUN) GARDNER-INF (2)
11 FRANK MALZONE-3B
12 PUMPSIE GREEN-2B/SS
14 IKE DELOCK-P
15 GALEN CISCO-P (1)
15 MERLIN NIPPERT-P
16 CARROLL HARDY-OF
17 DICK (THE MONSTER) RADATZ-P
18 GENE CONLEY-P
19 MERLIN NIPPERT-P
19 DAVE PHILLEY-OF
20 MIKE FORNIELES-P
21 ARNIE EARLEY-P
22 RUSS NIXON (INJ)-C
23 PETE SMITH (MIL)-P
24 LU CLINTON-OF
24 BILLY (SHOTGUN) GARDNER-INF (2)
25 TED WILLS-P (1)
26 EARL WILSON-P
27 BILL (MOMBO) MONBOUQUETTE-P
28 HAL KOLSTAD-P
29 JIM (PAG) PAGLIARONI-C
30 BOB TILLMAN-C
31 CHET NICHOLS-P
32 LEN OKRIE-CH
33 SAL (THE BARBER) MAGLIE-CH
34 RUDY YORK-CH
35 BILLY HERMAN-CH
36 BILLY (MUFF) MUFFETT-P
37 DON SCHWALL-P
38 DON (BEAR) GILE-1B
39 TRACY STALLARD-P
41 WILBUR WOOD-P
42 HAL KOLSTAD-P
47 BILLY MACLEOD-P
49 PETE SMITH (MIL)-P

1963

7TH 76-85 28GB

1 EDDIE BRESSOUD-SS
2 CHUCK SCHILLING-2B
3 GARY GEIGER-OF/1B
4 ROMAN MEJIAS-OF
5 RUSS NIXON-C
6 LU CLINTON-OF
7 DICK (DR. STRANGELOVE) STUART-1B
8 CARL (YAZ) YASTRZEMSKI-OF
9 *(RET#) TED WILLIAMS*
10 BOB TILLMAN-C
11 FRANK MALZONE-3B
12 FELIX MANTILLA-UTIL
14 IKE DELOCK-P (1)
15 BILLY (SHOTGUN) GARDNER-2B/3B
16 DICK WILLIAMS-UTIL
17 DICK (THE MONSTER) RADATZ-P
18 GENE CONLEY (INJ)-P
19 WILBUR WOOD-P
20 MIKE FORNIELES-P (1)
20 BOB HEFFNER-P
21 ARNIE EARLEY-P
22 JOHNNY PESKY-MGR
23 DAVE (MOE) MOREHEAD-P
25 JIM GOSGER-OF
26 EARL WILSON-P
27 BILL (MOMBO) MONBOUQUETTE-P
28 HAL KOLSTAD-P
29 BOB (BULLET BOB) TURLEY (INJ)-P
29 JERRY STEPHENSON-P
31 CHET NICHOLS-P
32 HARRY (SWEDE) MALMBERG-CH
33 AL (MOOSE) LAKEMAN-CH
34 HARRY (FRITZ) DORISH-CH
35 BILLY HERMAN-CH
36 JACK LAMABE-P
38 RICO PETROCELLI-SS
PETE SMITH (MIL)-(P)

1964

8TH 72-90 27GB

1 EDDIE BRESSOUD-SS
2 CHUCK SCHILLING-2B
3 GARY GEIGER (ILL)-OF
4 ROMAN MEJIAS-OF
5 RUSS NIXON-C
6 LU CLINTON-OF (1)
6 LEE THOMAS-OF/1B (2)
7 DICK (DR. STRANGELOVE) STUART-1B
8 CARL (YAZ) YASTRZEMSKI-OF/3B
9 *(RET#) TED WILLIAMS*
10 BOB TILLMAN-C
11 FRANK MALZONE-3B
12 FELIX MANTILLA-UTIL
14 BILL SPANSWICK-P
15 PETE CHARTON-P
16 DICK WILLIAMS-UTIL
17 DICK (THE MONSTER) RADATZ-P
19 WILBUR WOOD-P (1)
19 JAY RITCHIE-P
20 BOB HEFFNER-P
21 ARNIE EARLEY (INJ)-P
22 JOHNNY PESKY-MGR1
23 DAVE (MOE) MOREHEAD-P
24 DAVE GRAY-P
25 TONY (TONY C) CONIGLIARO (INJ)-OF
26 EARL WILSON-P
27 BILL (MOMBO) MONBOUQUETTE-P
28 AL (FUZZY) SMITH-3B/OF (2)
29 ED CONNOLLY-P
30 TONY HORTON-OF/1B
31 CHET NICHOLS-P
32 HARRY (SWEDE) MALMBERG-CH
33 AL (MOOSE) LAKEMAN-CH
34 BOB (BULLET BOB) TURLEY (INJ)-P
35 BILLY HERMAN-CH/MGR2
36 JACK LAMABE-P
39 DALTON JONES-2B/INF
40 MIKE RYAN-C
51 BOBBY GUINDON-1B/OF

1965

9TH 62-100 40GB

1 EDDIE BRESSOUD-UTIL
2 CHUCK SCHILLING-2B
3 GARY GEIGER (ILL) (INJ)-OF
4 RUDY SCHLESINGER-PH
4 JIM GOSGER-OF
5 RUSS NIXON-C
6 LEE THOMAS-1B/OF
7 LENNY GREEN-OF
8 CARL (YAZ) YASTRZEMSKI-OF/3B
9 *(RET#) TED WILLIAMS*
10 BOB TILLMAN-C
11 FRANK MALZONE-3B
12 FELIX MANTILLA-2B/UTIL
14 BOB DULIBA-P
16 JIM LONBORG-P
17 DICK (THE MONSTER) RADATZ-P
18 JERRY STEPHENSON-P
19 JAY RITCHIE-P
20 BOB HEFFNER-P
21 ARNIE EARLEY-P
23 DAVE (MOE) MOREHEAD-P
25 TONY (TONY C) CONIGLIARO-OF
26 EARL WILSON-P
27 BILL (MOMBO) MONBOUQUETTE-P
28 DENNIS BENNETT-P
30 TONY HORTON-1B
31 BILLY (SHOTGUN) GARDNER-CH
32 PETE RUNNELS-CH
33 MACE BROWN-CH
34 LEN OKRIE-CH
35 BILLY HERMAN-MGR
36 JACK LAMABE-P (1)
38 RICO PETROCELLI-SS
39 DALTON JONES-3B/2B
40 MIKE RYAN-C
41 JERRY MOSES-PH
49 LENNY GREEN-OF

1966

9TH 72-90 26GB

1 JOE FOY-3B/SS
2 EDDIE KASKO (INJ)-INF
2 MIKE ANDREWS-2B
3 DALTON JONES-2B/3B
4 JIM GOSGER-OF (1)
4 DON DEMETER-OF/1B (2)
5 GEORGE (BOOMER) SCOTT-1B/3B
6 RICO PETROCELLI-SS/3B
7 LENNY GREEN-OF
8 CARL (YAZ) YASTRZEMSKI-OF
9 *(RET#) TED WILLIAMS*
10 BOB TILLMAN-C
11 TONY HORTON-1B
12 EDDIE KASKO (INJ)-INF
12 JOSE TARTABULL-OF (2)
14 GEORGE SMITH-2B/SS
15 BILL SHORT-P (2)
16 JIM LONBORG-P
17 DICK (THE MONSTER) RADATZ-P (1)
18 JERRY STEPHENSON (INJ)-P
18 GARRY ROGGENBURK-P (2)
19 DAN OSINSKI-P
20 JOE CHRISTOPHER-OF
21 BOB SADOWSKI-P
21 HANK (BULLDOG) FISCHER-P (3)
22 MIKE RYAN-C
23 DAVE (MOE) MOREHEAD-P
24 GEORGE THOMAS-UTIL
25 TONY (TONY C) CONIGLIARO-OF
26 EARL WILSON-P (1)
26 JOHN WYATT-P (2)
27 DARRELL BRANDON-P
28 DENNIS BENNETT (INJ)-P
29 KEN SANDERS-P (1)
30 JOSE SANTIAGO-P
31 BILLY (SHOTGUN) GARDNER-CH
32 PETE RUNNELS-CH/MGR2
33 SAL (THE BARBER) MAGLIE-CH
34 LEN OKRIE-CH
35 BILLY HERMAN-MGR1
36 PETE MAGRINI-P
36 DICK STIGMAN-P
37 GUIDO GRILLI-P (1)
37 LEE STANGE-P (2)
38 HANK (BULLDOG) FISCHER-P (3)
39 GEORGE (BOOMER) SCOTT-1B/3B
40 ROLLIE SHELDON-P (2)
41 REGGIE SMITH-OF
42 DICK STIGMAN-P
44 DON MCMAHON-P (2)
45 PETE MAGRINI-P

1967

1ST 92-70 0GB

L WS-STLN 4-3

1 JOE FOY-3B/OF
2 MIKE ANDREWS-2B/SS
3 DALTON JONES-INF
4 DON DEMETER (ILL)-OF/3B (1)
4 JIM LANDIS-OF (2)
4 NORM SIEBERN-1B/OF (2)
5 GEORGE (BOOMER) SCOTT-1B/3B
6 RICO PETROCELLI-SS/3B
7 REGGIE SMITH-OF
8 CARL (YAZ) YASTRZEMSKI-OF
9 *(RET#) TED WILLIAMS*
10 BOB TILLMAN-C (1)
11 TONY HORTON-1B (1)
12 JOSE TARTABULL-OF
14 JERRY ADAIR-INF (2)
15 SPARKY LYLE-P
15 BILLY ROHR-P
16 JIM LONBORG-P
17 BILLY ROHR-P
17 KEN POULSEN-3B/SS
17 DAVE (MOE) MOREHEAD-P
18 JERRY STEPHENSON-P
18 ELSTON HOWARD-C (2)
19 GARY WASLEWSKI-P
20 LEE STANGE-P
21 HANK (BULLDOG) FISCHER-P
22 MIKE RYAN-C
23 DICK WILLIAMS-MGR
24 GEORGE THOMAS-UTIL
25 TONY (TONY C) CONIGLIARO (INJ)-OF
26 JOHN WYATT-P
27 DARRELL (BUCKY) BRANDON-P
28 DENNIS BENNETT (INJ)-P
28 SPARKY LYLE-P

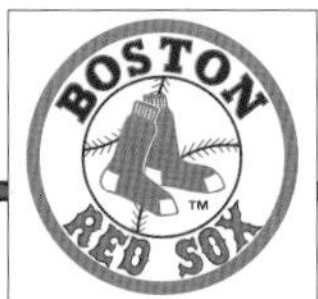

29 BILL LANDIS-P
30 JOSE SANTIAGO-P
31 BOBBY DOERR-CH
32 ED POPOWSKI-CH
33 SAL (THE BARBER) MAGLIE-CH
33 DARRELL JOHNSON-CH
34 AL (MOOSE) LAKEMAN-CH
35 RUSS GIBSON-C
36 KEN BRETT-P
37 DAN OSINSKI-P
37 DAVE (MOE) MOREHEAD-P
38 HANK (BULLDOG) FISCHER-P
38 JERRY STEPHENSON-P
38 GALEN CISCO-P
39 GALEN CISCO-P
39 GARY BELL-P (2)
40 GALEN CISCO-P
40 KEN (HAWK) HARRELSON-OF/1B (3)
44 DON MCMAHON-P (1)
45 GARY BELL-P (2)
45 KEN BRETT-P
46 BILLY ROHR-P
47 GARY WASLEWSKI-P

1968

4TH 86-76 17GB

1 JOE FOY-3B/OF
2 MIKE ANDREWS-2B/INF
3 DALTON JONES-INF
4 NORM SIEBERN-1B/OF (2)
5 GEORGE (BOOMER) SCOTT-1B/3B
6 RICO PETROCELLI-SS/1B
7 REGGIE SMITH-OF
8 CARL (YAZ) YASTRZEMSKI-OF
9 *(RET#) TED WILLIAMS*
10 JERRY MOSES-C
11 FLOYD ROBINSON-OF (2)
12 JOSE TARTABULL (INJ)-OF
14 JERRY ADAIR-INF
15 RUSS NIXON-C
15 JOE LAHOUD-OF
16 JIM LONBORG (INJ)-P
17 DAVE (MOE) MOREHEAD-P
17 GARRY ROGGENBURK (INJ)-P
17 GEORGE THOMAS-UTIL
18 ELSTON HOWARD-C
19 GARY WASLEWSKI-P
20 LEE STANGE-P
21 RAY CULP-P
22 GENE OLIVER-C/OF (1)
23 DICK WILLIAMS-MGR
24 JOE LAHOUD-OF
24 JUAN PIZARRO-P (2)
24 FRED (FIREBALL) WENZ-P
(25) TONY (TONY C) CONIGLIARO (INJ)-(OF)
26 JOHN WYATT-P (1)
26 JUAN PIZARRO-P (2)
26 GARRY ROGGENBURK (INJ)-P
27 DARRELL (BUCKY) BRANDON-P
28 SPARKY LYLE-P
29 BILL LANDIS (MIL)-P
30 JOSE SANTIAGO (INJ)-P
31 BOBBY DOERR-CH
32 ED POPOWSKI-CH
33 DARRELL JOHNSON-CH
34 AL (MOOSE) LAKEMAN-CH
35 RUSS GIBSON-C/1B
36 DICK ELLSWORTH-P
37 DAVE (MOE) MOREHEAD-P
38 JERRY STEPHENSON-P
39 GARY BELL-P
40 KEN (HAWK) HARRELSON-OF/1B
41 LUIS ALVARADO-SS
44 GARRY ROGGENBURK (INJ)-P

1969

3RD E 87-79 22GB

1 JOE AZCUE-C (2)
1 BILLY CONIGLIARO-OF
2 MIKE ANDREWS-2B
3 DALTON JONES-1B/INF
4 BILLY CONIGLIARO-OF
4 TOM SATRIANO-C (2)
5 GEORGE (BOOMER) SCOTT-3B/1B
6 RICO PETROCELLI-SS/3B
7 REGGIE SMITH-OF
8 CARL (YAZ) YASTRZEMSKI-OF
9 *(RET#) TED WILLIAMS*
10 JERRY MOSES-C
11 DICK (DUCKY) SCHOFIELD-UTIL
12 LUIS ALVARADO-SS
14 JOE LAHOUD-OF
15 KEN BRETT-P
15 MIKE NAGY-P
16 JIM LONBORG-P
17 RAY JARVIS-P
18 DON LOCK-OF/1B (2)
19 SYD O'BRIEN-INF
20 LEE STANGE-P
21 RAY CULP (INJ)-P
22 GEORGE THOMAS (INJ)-UTIL/COACH
23 DICK WILLIAMS-MGR1
24 JUAN PIZARRO-P (1)
24 VICENTE (HUEVO) ROMO-P (2)
25 TONY (TONY C) CONIGLIARO-OF
26 JUAN PIZARRO-P (1)
26 RON KLINE-P (3)
26 FRED (FIREBALL) WENZ-P
27 SONNY SIEBERT-P (2)
28 SPARKY LYLE-P
29 BILL LANDIS-P
29 JOSE SANTIAGO (INJ)-P
31 BOBBY DOERR-CH
32 ED POPOWSKI-CH/MGR2
33 DARRELL JOHNSON-CH
34 AL (MOOSE) LAKEMAN-CH
35 RUSS GIBSON-C
36 DICK ELLSWORTH-P (1)
36 GARY WAGNER-P (2)
37 GARRY ROGGENBURK (RET)-P (1)
37 BILL (SPACEMAN) LEE-P
39 MIKE GARMAN-P
40 KEN (HAWK) HARRELSON-1B (1)
40 CARLTON (PUDGE) FISK-P
40 BILLY CONIGLIARO-OF
42 KEN BRETT-P
43 TONY MUSER-1B

1970

3RD E 87-75 21GB

1 BILLY CONIGLIARO-OF
1 LUIS ALVARADO-3B/SS
2 MIKE ANDREWS-2B
3 TOM MATCHICK-INF (1)
3 MIKE FIORE-1B/OF (2)
4 TOM SATRIANO-C
5 GEORGE (BOOMER) SCOTT (INJ)-3B/1B
6 RICO PETROCELLI-SS/3B
7 REGGIE SMITH-OF
8 CARL (YAZ) YASTRZEMSKI-1B/OF
9 *(RET#) TED WILLIAMS*
10 JERRY MOSES-C/OF
10 BOB MONTGOMERY-C
11 DICK (DUCKY) SCHOFIELD-INF
12 LUIS ALVARADO-3B/SS
12 JOHN KENNEDY-3B/2B (2)
14 JOE LAHOUD-OF
15 MIKE NAGY-P
16 JIM LONBORG (INJ)-P
16 BOB BOLIN-P (2)
17 RAY JARVIS-P
17 CAL KOONCE-P (2)
18 KEN BRETT-P
19 DON PAVLETICH-1B/C
20 LEE STANGE-P (1)
20 CHUCK (TWIGGY) HARTENSTEIN-P (3)
20 CARMEN FANZONE-3B
21 RAY CULP-P
22 GEORGE THOMAS (RET)-OF/3B/CH
23 MIKE DERRICK-OF/1B
23 CHUCK (TWIGGY) HARTENSTEIN-P (3)
24 VICENTE (HUEVO) ROMO-P
25 TONY (TONY C) CONIGLIARO-OF
26 RAY JARVIS-P
27 SONNY SIEBERT-P
27 ED PHILLIPS-P
28 SPARKY LYLE-P
29 ROGER MORET-P
30 EDDIE KASKO-MGR
31 DON (FOOTSIE) LENHARDT-CH
32 ED POPOWSKI-CH
33 CHARLIE (BROADWAY) WAGNER-CH
34 DOUG CAMILLI-CH
35 GARY WAGNER-P (2)
36 JOSE SANTIAGO (INJ)-P
36 DICK MILLS-P
37 BILL (SPACEMAN) LEE-P
39 BOB MONTGOMERY-C
40 BILLY CONIGLIARO-OF
42 KEN BRETT-P
42 SONNY SIEBERT-P
43 GARY PETERS-P
44 JOHN (JACK) CURTIS-P
44 CHUCK (TWIGGY) HARTENSTEIN-P (3)
49 ED PHILLIPS-P

1971

3RD E 85-77 18GB

1 PHIL GAGLIANO-UTIL
2 DOUG GRIFFIN (INJ)-2B
3 MIKE FIORE-1B
5 GEORGE (BOOMER) SCOTT-1B
6 RICO PETROCELLI-3B
7 REGGIE SMITH-OF
8 CARL (YAZ) YASTRZEMSKI-OF
9 *(RET#) TED WILLIAMS*
10 BOB MONTGOMERY-C
11 LUIS APARICIO-SS
12 JOHN KENNEDY-INF
14 JOE LAHOUD-OF
15 MIKE NAGY-P
16 JIM LONBORG (INJ)-P
17 CALVIN (CAL) KOONCE-P
17 CECIL COOPER-1B
18 KEN BRETT-P
19 DON PAVLETICH-C
20 JUAN BENIQUEZ-SS
21 RAY CULP-P
22 GEORGE THOMAS-OF (1)
22 JOHN (JACK) CURTIS-P
23 LUIS TIANT-P
24 DUANE JOSEPHSON-C
25 KEN TATUM-P
26 BOBBY BOLIN-P
27 CARLTON (PUDGE) FISK-C
28 SPARKY LYLE-P
29 ROGER MORET-P
30 EDDIE KASKO-MGR
31 DON LENHARDT-CH
32 ED POPOWSKI-CH
33 HARVEY (THE KITTEN) HADDIX-CH
34 DOUG CAMILLI-CH
35 RICK MILLER-OF
37 BILL (SPACEMAN) LEE-P
38 HAROLD (BUDDY) HUNTER-2B
39 MIKE GARMAN-P
40 BILLY CONIGLIARO-OF
41 CARLTON (PUDGE) FISK-P
41 KEN TATUM-P
42 SONNY SIEBERT-P/PH
43 GARY PETERS-P
44 JOHN (JACK) CURTIS-P
45 BEN OGLIVIE-OF

1972

2ND E 85-70 .5GB

1 PHIL GAGLIANO-UTIL
2 DOUG GRIFFIN-2B
3 BOB BURDA-1B/OF
4 TOMMY HARPER-OF
5 DANNY CATER-1B
6 RICO PETROCELLI-3B
7 REGGIE SMITH-OF
8 CARL (YAZ) YASTRZEMSKI (INJ)-OF/1B
9 *(RET#) TED WILLIAMS*
10 BOB MONTGOMERY-C
11 LUIS APARICIO (INJ)-SS
12 JOHN KENNEDY-INF
14 BEN OGLIVIE-OF
15 MIKE NAGY-P
16 LYNN MCGLOTHEN-P
16 RICK MILLER-OF
17 CECIL COOPER-1B
18 LEW KRAUSSE-P
19 KEN TATUM (INJ)-P
20 JUAN BENIQUEZ-SS
21 RAY CULP (INJ)-P
22 JOHN (JACK) CURTIS-P
23 LUIS TIANT-P
24 DUANE JOSEPHSON (ILL)-1B/C
25 MARTY PATTIN-P
25 STAN WILLIAMS-P
26 BOBBY BOLIN-P
27 CARLTON (PUDGE) FISK-C
28 DON NEWHAUSER-P
29 ROGER MORET-P
30 EDDIE KASKO-MGR
31 DON LENHARDT-CH
32 ED POPOWSKI-CH
33 LEE STANGE-CH
33 MARTY PATTIN-P
34 DOUG CAMILLI-CH
35 RICK MILLER-OF
35 LEE STANGE-CH
36 LYNN MCGLOTHEN-P
37 BILL (SPACEMAN) LEE-P
39 MIKE GARMAN-P
40 DWIGHT (DEWEY) EVANS-OF
42 SONNY SIEBERT-P
43 GARY PETERS-P
44 BOB GALLAGHER-PH
44 ANDY KOSCO-OF (2)
48 VIC CORRELL-C
50 STAN WILLIAMS-P
55 BOB VEALE-P (2)

1973

2ND E 89-73 8GB

2 DOUG GRIFFIN (INJ)-2B
4 TOMMY HARPER-OF/DH
5 DANNY CATER-INF/DH
6 RICO PETROCELLI (INJ)-3B
7 REGGIE SMITH-OF/UTIL
8 CARL (YAZ) YASTRZEMSKI-1B/UTIL
9 *(RET#) TED WILLIAMS*
10 BOB MONTGOMERY-C
11 LUIS APARICIO-SS
12 JOHN KENNEDY-INF/DH
14 BEN OGLIVIE-OF/DH
16 RICK MILLER-OF
17 CECIL COOPER-1B
18 MIKE GUERRERO-SS/2B
19 KEN TATUM-P
21 RAY CULP (INJ)-P
22 JOHN (JACK) CURTIS-P
23 LUIS TIANT-P
(24) DUANE JOSEPHSON (ILL)-(C)
24 DWIGHT (DEWEY) EVANS-OF/DH
25 ORLANDO (THE BABY BULL) (CHA CHA) CEPEDA-DH
26 BOBBY BOLIN-P
27 CARLTON (PUDGE) FISK-C/DH
28 DON NEWHAUSER (INJ)-P
29 ROGER MORET (INJ)-P
30 EDDIE KASKO-MGR
31 DON LENHARDT-CH
32 ED POPOWSKI-CH
33 MARTY PATTIN-P
34 DOUG CAMILLI-CH
35 LEE STANGE-CH
36 LYNN MCGLOTHEN (INJ)-P
37 BILL (SPACEMAN) LEE-P
38 BUDDY HUNTER-INF/DH
38 MIKE GARMAN-P
39 MIKE GARMAN-P
40 DWIGHT (DEWEY) EVANS-OF/DH
41 MIKE GUERRERO-SS/2B
42 SONNY SIEBERT-P (1)
44 BOB GALLAGHER-PH
45 DICK POLE-P
49 CRAIG SKOK-P
55 BOB VEALE-P

1974

3RD E 84-78 7GB

1 BERNIE CARBO-OF/DH
2 DOUG GRIFFIN (INJ)-2B/SS
3 DICK MCAULIFFE-INF/DH
4 TOMMY HARPER-OF/DH
5 DANNY CATER-1B/DH
6 RICO PETROCELLI-3B/DH
7 RICK (ROOSTER) BURLESON-INF
8 CARL (YAZ) YASTRZEMSKI-1B/UTIL
9 *(RET#) TED WILLIAMS*
10 BOB MONTGOMERY-C/DH
12 JOHN KENNEDY-2B/3B
14 JIM RICE-DH/OF
16 RICK MILLER-OF
17 CECIL COOPER-1B/DH
18 MIKE GUERRERO-SS
19 FRED LYNN-OF/DH
20 JUAN BENIQUEZ-OF/DH
21 JUAN (MANITO) MARICHAL (INJ)-P
22 DARRELL JOHNSON-MGR
23 LUIS TIANT-P
24 DWIGHT (DEWEY) EVANS-OF/DH
26 REGGIE CLEVELAND-P
27 CARLTON (PUDGE) FISK (INJ)-C/DH
28 DON NEWHAUSER-P
29 ROGER MORET-P
30 DERON JOHNSON-DH (3)
31 DON BRYANT-CH
32 ED POPOWSKI-CH
33 REGGIE CLEVELAND-P
33 TIM MCCARVER-C
34 DON (POPEYE) ZIMMER-CH
35 LEE STANGE-CH
36 DIEGO SEGUI-P
37 BILL (SPACEMAN) LEE-P
38 TERRY HUGHES-3B/DH
39 TIM BLACKWELL-C
40 RICK WISE (INJ)-P
41 DICK DRAGO-P
42 LANCE CLEMONS-P
45 DICK POLE-P

BOSTON RED SOX

46 STEVE BARR-P
48 BOB DIDIER-C
48 CHUCK GOGGIN-2B
55 BOB VEALE-P

1975

1st E 95-65 0GB
W ALCS-OAKA 3-0
L WS-CINN 4-3

1 BERNIE CARBO-OF/DH
2 DOUG GRIFFIN-2B/SS
3 DICK MCAULIFFE (RET)-3B
3 DARRELL JOHNSON-MGR
3 STEVE DILLARD-2B
5 BUDDY HUNTER-2B
5 DENNY DOYLE-2B/INF (2)
6 RICO PETROCELLI-3B/UTIL
7 RICK (ROOSTER) BURLESON-SS/3B
8 CARL (YAZ) YASTRZEMSKI-1B/UTIL
9 *(RET#) TED WILLIAMS*
10 BOB MONTGOMERY-UTIL
11 KIM ANDREW-2B
12 BOB HEISE-INF
14 JIM RICE (INJ)-OF/DH
15 DENNY DOYLE-2B/INF (2)
15 DERON JOHNSON-1B/DH (2)
16 RICK MILLER-OF
17 CECIL COOPER-DH/1B
19 FRED LYNN-OF
20 JUAN BENIQUEZ-UTIL
21 RICK KREUGER-P
22 DARRELL JOHNSON-MGR
23 LUIS TIANT-P
24 DWIGHT (DEWEY) EVANS-OF/DH
25 TONY (TONY C) CONIGLIARO (INJ)-DH
26 REGGIE CLEVELAND-P
27 CARLTON (PUDGE) FISK (INJ)-C/DH
28 DIEGO SEGUI-P
29 ROGER MORET-P
30 DERON JOHNSON-1B/DH (2)
31 DON BRYANT-CH
32 STAN WILLIAMS-CH
33 TIM MCCARVER-C/1B (1)
33 JIM WILLOUGHBY-P
34 DON (POPEYE) ZIMMER-CH
35 JOHNNY PESKY-CH
36 DIEGO SEGUI-P
36 EDDIE POPOWSKI-CH
37 BILL (SPACEMAN) LEE-P
38 JIM WILLOUGHBY-P
39 TIM BLACKWELL-C/DH
40 RICK WISE-P
41 DICK DRAGO-P
43 JIM BURTON-P
45 DICK POLE (INJ)-P
46 STEVE BARR-P
50 ANDY MERCHANT-C
51 BUTCH HOBSON-3B
54 EDDIE POPOWSKI-CH

1976

3rd E 83-79 15.5GB

1 BERNIE CARBO-DH/OF (1)
2 DOUG GRIFFIN-2B/DH
3 STEVE DILLARD-INF/DH
4 BUTCH HOBSON-3B
5 DENNY DOYLE-2B
6 RICO PETROCELLI-UTIL
7 RICK (ROOSTER) BURLESON-SS
8 CARL (YAZ) YASTRZEMSKI-1B/UTIL
9 *(RET#) TED WILLIAMS*
10 BOB MONTGOMERY-C/DH
12 BOB HEISE-3B/SS
14 JIM RICE-OF/DH
17 CECIL COOPER-1B/DH
16 RICK MILLER-OF/DH
17 CECIL COOPER-1B/DH
19 FRED LYNN-OF/DH
21 RICK KREUGER-P
21 JACK BAKER-1B/DH
22 DARRELL JOHNSON-MGR1
22 ERNIE WHITT-C
23 LUIS TIANT-P
24 DWIGHT (DEWEY) EVANS-OF/DH
26 REGGIE CLEVELAND-P
27 CARLTON (PUDGE) FISK C/DH
29 TOM HOUSE (INJ)-P
30 DERON JOHNSON (REL)-DH/1B
31 FERGUSON (FERGIE) JENKINS-P
32 STAN WILLIAMS-CH
33 DON BRYANT-CH
34 DON (POPEYE) ZIMMER-CH/MGR2
35 JOHNNY PESKY-CH
36 EDDIE POPOWSKI-CH
37 BILL (SPACEMAN) LEE (INJ)-P
38 JIM WILLOUGHBY-P
40 RICK WISE-P
42 BOBBY DARWIN-OF/DH (2)
45 DICK POLE-P
46 RICK JONES-P
47 TOM MURPHY-P (2)
50 ANDY MERCHANT-C

1977

2nd (tie) E 97-64 2.5GB

1 BERNIE CARBO-OF/DH
2 DOUG GRIFFIN-2B
3 STEVE DILLARD-INF/DH
4 BUTCH HOBSON-3B
5 DENNY DOYLE-2B
7 RICK (ROOSTER) BURLESON-SS
8 CARL (YAZ) YASTRZEMSKI-OF/UTIL
9 *(RET#) TED WILLIAMS*
10 BOB MONTGOMERY-C
11 RAMON AVILES-2B
12 TOMMY HELMS-UTIL (2)
14 JIM RICE-DH/OF
15 GEORGE (BOOMER) SCOTT (INJ)-1B
16 RICK MILLER (INJ)-OF/DH
18 TED COX-DH
19 FRED LYNN-OF/DH
21 RICK KREUGER-P
22 BILL CAMPBELL-P
23 LUIS TIANT-P
24 DWIGHT (DEWEY) EVANS-(INJ)-OF/DH
26 REGGIE CLEVELAND-P
27 CARLTON (PUDGE) FISK-C
29 TOM HOUSE-P (1)
29 SAM BOWEN-OF
29 RAMON HERNANDEZ-P (2)
30 DAVE COLEMAN-OF
30 BOB BAILEY-PH (2)
31 FERGUSON (FERGIE) JENKINS-P
32 AL JACKSON-CH
33 WALT HRINIAK-CH
34 DON (POPEYE) ZIMMER-MGR
35 JOHNNY PESKY-CH
36 EDDIE (THE WALKING MAN) YOST-CH
37 BILL (SPACEMAN) LEE-P
38 JIM WILLOUGHBY (INJ)-P
39 BO DIAZ-C
40 RICK WISE-P
41 JACK BAKER-1B
42 BOBBY DARWIN-DH/OF (1)
43 JIM BURTON-P
45 DON AASE-P
46 BOB STANLEY-P
47 TOM MURPHY-P (1)
48 MIKE PAXTON-P
49 TOMMY HELMS-UTIL (2)

1978

2nd E 99-64 1GB

1 BERNIE CARBO (INJ)-OF/DH (1)
2 JERRY REMY-2B/UTIL
3 JACK BROHAMER-UTIL
4 BUTCH HOBSON-3B/DH
7 RICK (ROOSTER) BURLESON-SS
8 CARL (YAZ) YASTRZEMSKI-OF/UTIL
9 *(RET#) TED WILLIAMS*
10 BOB MONTGOMERY-C
14 JIM RICE-OF/DH
15 GEORGE (BOOMER) SCOTT (INJ)-1B/DH
16 TOM BURGMEIER (ILL)-P
17 FRANK DUFFY-UTIL
18 FRED KENDALL-UTIL
19 FRED LYNN-OF
21 MIKE TORREZ-P
22 BILL CAMPBELL (INJ)-P
23 LUIS TIANT-P
24 DWIGHT (DEWEY) EVANS-OF/DH
26 REGGIE CLEVELAND-P (1)
27 CARLTON (PUDGE) FISK-C/UTIL
28 JOHN LAROSE-P
28 ALLEN RIPLEY-P
29 SAM BOWEN-OF
30 BOB BAILEY-UTIL
31 ANDY HASSLER-P (2)
32 AL JACKSON-CH
33 WALT HRINIAK-CH
34 DON (POPEYE) ZIMMER-MGR
35 JOHNNY PESKY-CH
36 EDDIE (THE WALKING MAN) YOST-CH
37 BILL (SPACEMAN) LEE-P
38 GARRY HANCOCK-OF/DH
41 DICK DRAGO-P
43 DENNIS ECKERSLEY-P
45 JIM WRIGHT-P
46 BOB STANLEY-P
47 BOBBY SPROWL-P
48 ANDY HASSLER-P (2)

1979

3rd E 91-69 11.5GB

1 JIM DWYER-UTIL
2 JERRY REMY (INJ)-2B
3 JACK BROHAMER (INJ)-2B/3B
4 BUTCH HOBSON-3B/2B
5 GEORGE (BOOMER) SCOTT (INJ)-1B (1)
5 BOB (BULL) WATSON-1B/DH (2)
7 RICK (ROOSTER) BURLESON-SS
8 CARL (YAZ) YASTRZEMSKI-DH/UTIL
9 *(RET#) TED WILLIAMS*
10 BOB MONTGOMERY (INJ)-C
11 TED SIZEMORE-2B/C (2)
12 STAN PAPI-UTIL
14 JIM RICE-OF/DH
15 GEORGE (BOOMER) SCOTT (INJ)-1B (1)
16 TOM BURGMEIER-P
17 FRANK DUFFY-2B/1B
17 TOM POQUETTE-OF/DH (2)
19 FRED LYNN-OF/DH
20 LARRY WOLFE-UTIL
21 MIKE TORREZ-P
22 BILL CAMPBELL-P
24 DWIGHT (DEWEY) EVANS-OF
25 STEVE RENKO-P
27 CARLTON (PUDGE) FISK-(INJ)-C/UTIL
28 ALLEN RIPLEY-P
28 GARY ALLENSON-C/3B
30 JOHN TUDOR-P
31 ANDY HASSLER-P (1)
32 AL JACKSON-CH
33 WALT HRINIAK-CH
34 DON (POPEYE) ZIMMER-MGR
35 JOHNNY PESKY-CH
36 EDDIE (THE WALKING MAN) YOST-CH
39 GARY ALLENSON-C/3B
41 DICK DRAGO-P
42 CHUCK RAINEY (INJ)-P
43 DENNIS (ECK) ECKERSLEY-P
44 JOEL FINCH-P
45 JIM WRIGHT (INJ)-P
46 BOB STANLEY-P
49 WIN REMMERSWAAL-P
50 MIKE O'BERRY-C

1980

4th E 83-77 19GB

1 JIM DWYER-UTIL
2 JERRY REMY (INJ)-2B/OF
3 CHICO WALKER-2B/DH
3 JACK BROHAMER-UTIL (1)
4 BUTCH HOBSON (INJ)-3B/DH
5 TONY PEREZ-1B/DH
7 RICK (ROOSTER) BURLESON-SS
8 CARL (YAZ) YASTRZEMSKI (INJ)-DH/UTIL
9 *(RET#) TED WILLIAMS*
11 TED SIZEMORE-2B
11 DAVE STAPLETON-UTIL
12 STAN PAPI (INJ)-3B (1)
12 JULIO VALDEZ-SS
14 JIM RICE (INJ)-OF/DH
15 JULIO VALDEZ-SS
15 DAVE RADER-C/DH
16 TOM BURGMEIER-P
(17) TOM POQUETTE (INJ)-(OF)
18 GLENN HOFFMAN-3B/INF
19 FRED LYNN (INJ)-OF
20 LARRY WOLFE-3B/DH
21 MIKE TORREZ-P
22 BILL CAMPBELL (INJ)-P
23 DON (POPEYE) ZIMMER-MGR1
24 DWIGHT (DEWEY) EVANS-OF/DH
25 STEVE RENKO-P
26 DAVE STAPLETON-UTIL
27 CARLTON (PUDGE) FISK-C/UTIL
28 STEVE CRAWFORD-P
28 BOB OJEDA-P
28 JACK BILLINGHAM-P (2)
29 KEITH MACWHORTER-P
29 SAM BOWEN-OF
30 JOHN TUDOR-P
31 KEITH MACWHORTER-P
32 TOMMY HARPER-CH
33 WALT HRINIAK-CH
34 JOHNNY PODRES-CH
35 JOHNNY PESKY-CH/MGR2
36 EDDIE (THE WALKING MAN) YOST-CH
37 GARRY HANCOCK-OF/DH
38 SKIP LOCKWOOD-P
39 GARY ALLENSON-UTIL
41 DICK DRAGO-P
42 CHUCK RAINEY (INJ)-P
43 DENNIS (ECK) ECKERSLEY (INJ)-P
45 LUIS APONTE-P
46 BOB STANLEY-P
47 BRUCE HURST-P
49 WIN REMMERSWAAL-P
50 RICH GEDMAN-DH/C
51 REID NICHOLS-OF/DH

1981

1st 1/2:5th E 30-26 4GB
2nd 1/2:2nd (tie) E 29-23 1.5GB
Final: 59-49 --GB

1 CHICO WALKER-2B
2 JERRY REMY-2B
3 RICK MILLER-OF
4 CARNEY LANSFORD-3B/DH
5 TONY PEREZ-1B/DH
6 JOHNNY PESKY-CH
8 CARL (YAZ) YASTRZEMSKI (INJ)-DH/1B
9 *(RET#) TED WILLIAMS*
10 RICH GEDMAN-C
11 DAVE STAPLETON-UTIL
12 JULIO VALDEZ-SS
14 JIM RICE-OF
16 TOM BURGMEIER-P
17 TOM POQUETTE-OF (1)
18 GLENN HOFFMAN-SS/3B
19 BOB OJEDA-P
21 MIKE TORREZ-P
22 BILL CAMPBELL-P
24 DWIGHT (DEWEY) EVANS-OF
25 MARK CLEAR-P
26 JOE RUDI-UTIL
28 STEVE CRAWFORD-P
29 JOHN LICKERT-C
30 JOHN TUDOR-P
32 TOMMY HARPER-CH
33 WALT HRINIAK-CH
34 LEE STANGE-CH
35 RALPH (MAJOR) HOUK-MGR
36 EDDIE (THE WALKING MAN) YOST-CH
37 GARRY HANCOCK-OF/DH
39 GARY ALLENSON (INJ)-C
40 FRANK TANANA-P
42 CHUCK RAINEY-P
43 DENNIS (ECK) ECKERSLEY-P
45 LUIS APONTE-P
46 BOB STANLEY-P
47 BRUCE HURST-P
49 WIN REMMERSWAAL-P
50 DAVE SCHMIDT-C
51 REID NICHOLS-OF/DH

1982

3rd E 89-73 6GB

2 JERRY REMY-2B
3 RICK MILLER-OF
4 CARNEY LANSFORD (INJ)-3B/DH
5 TONY PEREZ-DH/1B
6 JOHNNY PESKY-CH
8 CARL (YAZ) YASTRZEMSKI (INJ)-DH/UTIL
9 *(RET#) TED WILLIAMS*
10 RICH GEDMAN-C
11 DAVE STAPLETON-1B/UTIL
12 JULIO VALDEZ-SS/DH
14 JIM RICE-OF
15 MARC SULLIVAN-C
16 TOM BURGMEIER-P
17 MARTY BARRETT-2B
18 GLENN HOFFMAN-SS
19 BOB OJEDA (INJ)-P
21 MIKE TORREZ-P
22 ED JURAK-3B/OF
23 OIL CAN BOYD-P
24 DWIGHT (DEWEY) EVANS-OF/DH

25 MARK CLEAR-P
26 WADE BOGGS-UTIL
27 MIKE BROWN-P
28 STEVE CRAWFORD(INJ)-P
30 JOHN TUDOR-P
31 BRIAN DENMAN-P
32 TOMMY HARPER-CH
33 WALT HRINIAK-CH
34 LEE STANGE-CH
35 RALPH (MAJOR) HOUK-MGR
36 EDDIE (THE WALKING MAN) YOST-CH
37 GARRY HANCOCK-OF/DH
39 GARY ALLENSON-C
42 CHUCK RAINEY-P
43 DENNIS (ECK) ECKERSLEY-P
45 LUIS APONTE-P
46 BOB STANLEY-P
47 BRUCE HURST-P
51 REID NICHOLS-OF/DH
54 ROGER LAFRANCOIS-C

1983

6TH E 78-84 20GB

1 CHICO WALKER-OF
2 JERRY REMY-2B
3 RICK MILLER-OF/UTIL
5 JEFF NEWMAN-C/DH
6 JOHNNY PESKY-CH
8 CARL (YAZ) YASTRZEMSKI (INJ)-DH/UTIL
9 *(RET#) TED WILLIAMS*
10 RICH GEDMAN-C
11 DAVE STAPLETON-1B/2B
12 JULIO VALDEZ (SUS)-UTIL
12 LEE GRAHAM-OF
14 JIM RICE-OF/DH
16 WADE BOGGS-3B
17 MARTY BARRETT-2B/DH
18 GLENN HOFFMAN-SS
19 BOB OJEDA-P
20 TONY ARMAS-OF/DH
22 ED JURAK-UTIL
23 OIL CAN BOYD-P
24 DWIGHT (DEWEY) EVANS (INJ)-OF/DH
25 MARK CLEAR-P
26 WADE BOGGS-3B
27 MIKE BROWN (INJ)-P
30 JOHN TUDOR-P
32 TOMMY HARPER-CH
33 WALT HRINIAK-CH
34 LEE STANGE-CH
35 RALPH (MAJOR) HOUK-MGR
36 EDDIE (THE WALKING MAN) YOST-CH
39 GARY ALLENSON-C
41 JACKIE GUTIERREZ-SS
42 DOUG BIRD-P
43 DENNIS (ECK) ECKERSLEY-P
45 LUIS APONTE-P
46 BOB STANLEY-P
47 BRUCE HURST-P
48 JOHN HENRY JOHNSON-P
49 AL NIPPER-P
51 REID NICHOLS-OF/DH

1984

4TH E 86-76 18GB

1 CHICO WALKER-OF
2 JERRY REMY (INJ)-2B
3 RICK MILLER-OF/1B
4 *(RET#) JOE CRONIN*
5 JEFF NEWMAN-C
6 JOHNNY PESKY-CH
7 MIKE EASLER-DH/1B
9 *(RET#) TED WILLIAMS*
10 RICH GEDMAN-C
11 DAVE STAPLETON (INJ)-1B/DH
14 JIM RICE-OF/DH
15 MARC SULLIVAN-C
16 BILL (BILLY BUCK) BUCKNER-1B (2)
17 MARTY BARRETT-2B
18 GLENN HOFFMAN-INF
19 BOB OJEDA-P
20 TONY ARMAS-OF/DH
21 ROGER (THE ROCKET) CLEMENS-P
22 ED JURAK-INF
23 OIL CAN BOYD-P
24 DWIGHT (DEWEY) EVANS-OF/DH
25 MARK CLEAR-P
26 WADE BOGGS-3B/DH
27 MIKE BROWN-P
28 STEVE CRAWFORD-P
30 RICH GALE-P
32 TOMMY HARPER-CH
33 WALT HRINIAK-CH
34 LEE STANGE-CH
35 RALPH (MAJOR) HOUK-MGR
36 EDDIE (THE WALKING MAN) YOST-CH
38 CHARLIE MITCHELL-P
39 GARY ALLENSON-C
41 JACKIE GUTIERREZ-SS
43 DENNIS (ECK) ECKERSLEY-P
44 JIM DORSEY-P
46 BOB STANLEY-P
47 BRUCE HURST-P
48 JOHN HENRY JOHNSON-P
49 AL NIPPER-P
51 REID NICHOLS-OF/DH

1985

5TH E 81-81 18.5GB

1 JOHN MCNAMARA-MGR
(2) JERRY REMY (INJ)-(2B)
3 RICK MILLER-OF/DH
4 *(RET#) JOE CRONIN*
6 BILL (BILLY BUCK) BUCKNER-1B
7 MIKE EASLER-DH/OF
9 *(RET#) TED WILLIAMS*
10 RICH GEDMAN-C
11 DAVE STAPLETON (INJ)-UTIL
12 STEVE LYONS-OF/UTIL
13 REID NICHOLS-UTIL (1)
14 JIM RICE-OF/DH
15 MARC SULLIVAN (INJ)-C
16 KEVIN ROMINE-OF/DH
16 DAVE SAX-C/OF
17 MARTY BARRETT-2B
18 GLENN HOFFMAN (INJ)-INF
19 BOB OJEDA-P
20 TONY ARMAS (INJ)-OF/DH
21 ROGER (THE ROCKET) CLEMENS (INJ)-P
22 ED JURAKUTIL
23 OIL CAN BOYD-P
24 DWIGHT (DEWEY) EVANS-OF/DH
25 MARK CLEAR-P
26 WADE BOGGS-3B
27 JEFF SELLERS-P
27 MIKE BROWN-P
28 STEVE CRAWFORD-P
29 BRUCE KISON (INJ)-P
32 TONY TORCHIA-CH
33 WALT HRINIAK-CH
34 BILL FISCHER-CH
35 JOE MORGAN-CH
36 RENE LACHEMANN-CH
38 CHARLIE MITCHELL-P
39 MIKE GREENWELL-OF
41 JACKIE GUTIERREZ-SS
42 ROB WOODWARD-P
43 TOM MCCARTHY-P
44 JIM DORSEY-P
45 MIKE TRUJILLO-P
46 BOB STANLEY (INJ)-P
47 BRUCE HURST-P
48 TIM LOLLAR-P (2)
49 AL NIPPER-P
50 JEFF SELLERS-P
50 KEVIN ROMINE-OF/DH

1986

1ST E 95-66 0GB

W ALCS-CALA 4-2

L WS-NYN 4-3

1 JOHN MCNAMARA-MGR
3 ED ROMERO-UTIL
4 *(RET#) JOE CRONIN*
5 SPIKE OWEN-SS (2)
6 BILL (BILLY BUCK) BUCKNER-1B/DH
7 ED ROMERO-UTIL
9 *(RET#) TED WILLIAMS*
10 RICH GEDMAN-C
11 DAVE STAPLETON (INJ)-INF
12 STEVE LYONS-OF (1)
14 JIM RICE-OF/DH
15 MARC SULLIVAN-C
16 DAVE SAX-C/1B
16 KEVIN ROMINE-OF
17 MARTY BARRETT-2B
18 GLENN HOFFMAN (INJ) (ILL)-SS/3B
19 JEFF SELLERS-P
20 TONY ARMAS-OF/DH
21 ROGER (THE ROCKET) CLEMENS-P
23 OIL CAN BOYD-P
24 DWIGHT (DEWEY) EVANS-OF/DH
25 ED ROMERO-UTIL
25 DON BAYLOR-DH/UTIL
26 WADE BOGGS-3B
27 MIKE BROWN-P (1)
27 PAT DODSON-1B
28 STEVE CRAWFORD (INJ)-P
31 CALVIN SCHIRALDI-P
33 WALT HRINIAK-CH
34 BILL FISCHER-CH
35 JOE MORGAN-CH
36 RENE LACHEMANN-CH
37 MIKE STENHOUSE-OF/1B
37 MIKE GREENWELL-OF/DH
39 MIKE GREENWELL-OF/DH
40 DAVE HENDERSON-OF (2)
41 TOM (TOM TERRIFIC) SEAVER-P (2)
42 ROB WOODWARD-P
43 JOE SAMBITO-P
44 WES GARDNER (INJ)-P
45 MIKE TRUJILLO-P (1)
46 BOB STANLEY-P
47 BRUCE HURST (INJ)-P
48 TIM LOLLAR-P (2)
49 AL NIPPER (INJ)-P
50 DAVE SAX-C/1B
51 REY QUINONES-SS (1)
53 SAMMY STEWART (INJ)-P
55 CALVIN SCHIRALDI-P
55 LASCHELLE TARVER-OF

1987

5TH E 78-84 20GB

1 JOHN MCNAMARA-MGR
4 *(RET#) JOE CRONIN*
6 BILL (BILLY BUCK) BUCKNER-1B (1)
7 SPIKE OWEN-SS
9 *(RET#) TED WILLIAMS*
10 RICH GEDMAN (INJ)-C
11 ED ROMERO-INF
12 DAVE SAX-C/1B
12 ELLIS BURKS-OF/DH
14 JIM RICE (INJ)-OF/DH
15 MARC SULLIVAN-C
16 KEVIN ROMINE-OF/DH
17 MARTY BARRETT-2B
18 GLENN HOFFMAN-INF (1)
19 JEFF SELLERS-P
21 ROGER (THE ROCKET) CLEMENS-P
22 JOHN LEISTER-P
23 OIL CAN BOYD (INJ)-P
24 DWIGHT (DEWEY) EVANS-1B/UTIL
25 DON BAYLOR-DH (1)
26 WADE BOGGS-3B
27 PAT DODSON-1B
28 STEVE CRAWFORD-P
29 DANNY SCHEAFFER-C
30 SAM HORN-DH
31 CALVIN SCHIRALDI-P
32 JOE SAMBITO-P
33 WALT HRINIAK-CH
34 BILL FISCHER-CH
35 JOE MORGAN-CH
36 RAC SLIDER-CH
37 JOHN MARZANO-C
38 TODD BENZINGER-OF/1B
39 MIKE GREENWELL-OF/UTIL
42 DAVE HENDERSON-OF (1)
43 JOE SAMBITO-P
44 WES GARDNER-P
45 ROB WOODWARD-P
46 BOB STANLEY-P
47 BRUCE HURST (INJ)-P
49 AL NIPPER-P
50 TOM BOLTON-P
52 JODY REED-INF
(53) SAMMY STEWART (INJ)-(P)
55 LASCHELLE TARVER-OF

1988

1ST E 89-73 0GB

L ALCS-OAKA 4-0

1 JOHN MCNAMARA-MGR1
1 *(RET#) BOBBY DOERR*
3 JODY REED-SS/INF
4 *(RET#) JOE CRONIN*
5 BRADY ANDERSON-OF (1)
5 RANDY KUTCHER-UTIL
6 RICK CERONE-C/DH
7 SPIKE OWEN-SS/DH
9 *(RET#) TED WILLIAMS*
10 RICH GEDMAN (INJ)-C/DH
11 ED ROMERO (INJ)-UTIL
12 ELLIS BURKS-OF/DH
14 JIM RICE-DH/OF
15 DENNIS LAMP-P
16 KEVIN ROMINE-OF/DH
17 MARTY BARRETT-2B
18 CARLOS QUINTANA-OF/DH
19 JEFF SELLERS (INJ)-P
20 JOHN MARZANO-C
21 ROGER (THE ROCKET) CLEMENS-P
23 OIL CAN BOYD (INJ)-P
24 DWIGHT (DEWEY) EVANS-OF/UTIL
25 LARRY PARRISH-1B/DH (2)
26 WADE BOGGS-3B/DH
27 PAT DODSON-1B
28 STEVE ELLSWORTH-P
30 SAM HORN-DH
32 JERRY MCNERTNEY-CH
33 WALT HRINIAK-CH
34 BILL FISCHER-CH
35 JOE MORGAN-CH/MGR2
36 RAC SLIDER-CH
37 AL BUMBRY-CH
38 TODD BENZINGER-1B/UTIL
39 MIKE GREENWELL-OF/DH
41 MIKE SMITHSON-P
42 JOHN TRAUTWEIN-P
44 WES GARDNER-P
45 JOHN TRAUTWEIN-P
45 ROB WOODWARD-P
46 BOB STANLEY (INJ)-P
47 BRUCE HURST-P
48 LEE SMITH-P
49 DENNIS LAMP-P
50 TOM BOLTON-P
52 MIKE BODDICKER-P (2)
53 STEVE CURRY-P
54 MIKE ROCHFORD-P
55 RANDY KUTCHER-UTIL
56 ZACH CROUCH-P

1989

3RD E 83-79 6GB

1 *(RET#) BOBBY DOERR*
2 LUIS RIVERA-INF/DH
3 JODY REED-SS/UTIL
4 *(RET#) JOE CRONIN*
5 RANDY KUTCHER-UTIL
6 RICK CERONE-C/UTIL
7 NICK ESASKY-1B/OF
8 *(RET#) CARL YASTRZEMSKI*
9 *(RET#) TED WILLIAMS*
10 RICH GEDMAN-C
11 ED ROMERO-INF/DH (1)
12 ELLIS BURKS (INJ)-OF/DH
14 JIM RICE (INJ)-DH
15 DENNIS LAMP-P
16 KEVIN ROMINE-OF/DH
17 MARTY BARRETT (INJ)-2B
18 CARLOS QUINTANA (INJ)-UTIL
19 DANA WILLIAMS-DH/OF
19 JEFF STONE-OF/DH (2)
20 JOHN MARZANO-C
21 ROGER (THE ROCKET) CLEMENS-P
23 OIL CAN BOYD (INJ)-P
24 DWIGHT (DEWEY) EVANS-OF/UTIL
26 WADE BOGGS-3B/DH
27 GREG HARRIS-P (2)
29 DANNY HEEP-UTIL (2)
30 SAM HORN-DH/1B
31 ERIC HETZEL-P
32 RICHIE HEBNER-CH
33 DICK BERARDINO-CH
34 BILL FISCHER-CH
35 JOE MORGAN-MGR
36 RAC SLIDER-CH
37 AL BUMBRY-CH
39 MIKE GREENWELL-OF/DH
40 JOHN DOPSON (INJ)-P
41 MIKE SMITHSON-P
42 GREG HARRIS-P (2)
44 WES GARDNER (INJ)-P
45 ROB WOODWARD-P
46 BOB STANLEY-P
47 ROB MURPHY-P (2)
48 LEE SMITH-P
49 JOE PRICE-P (2)
50 TOM BOLTON-P
52 MIKE BODDICKER-P
54 MIKE ROCHFORD-P

1990

1ST E 88-74 0GB

L ALCS-OAKA 4-0

1 *(RET#) BOBBY DOERR*
2 LUIS RIVERA-SS/INF
3 JODY REED-2B/UTIL
4 *(RET#) JOE CRONIN*
5 RANDY KUTCHER-UTIL
6 TONY PENA-C/1B
7 LUIS RIVERA-SS/INF
7 PHIL PLANTIER-DH/OF
8 *(RET#) CARL YASTRZEMSKI*
9 *(RET#) TED WILLIAMS*
10 RICH GEDMAN-C (1)
10 RICK LANCELLOTTI-1B
11 TIM NAEHRING (INJ)-INF
12 ELLIS BURKS-OF/DH
13 BILLY JO ROBIDOUX (INJ)-1B/DH
15 DENNIS LAMP-P
16 KEVIN ROMINE-OF/DH

OSTON RED SOX

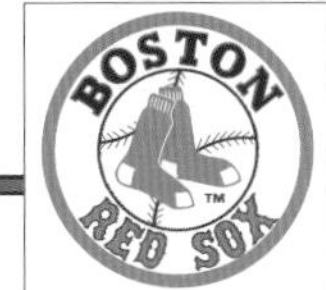

7 MARTY BARRETT-INF/DH
8 CARLOS QUINTANA-1B/OF
9 DANA KIECKER-P
0 JOHN MARZANO-C
1 ROGER (THE ROCKET) CLEMENS-P
2 BILL (BILLY BUCK) BUCKNER-1B
2 MIKE MARSHALL (ILL)-UTIL (2)
3 TOM (BRUNO) BRUNANSKY-OF/DH (2)
4 DWIGHT (DEWEY) EVANS-DH
6 WADE BOGGS-3B/DH
7 GREG HARRIS-P
8 JEFF STONE-DH
9 DANNY HEEP-UTIL/P
1 ERIC HETZEL-P
2 RICHIE HEBNER-CH
3 DICK BERARDINO-CH
4 BILL FISCHER-CH
5 JOE MORGAN-MGR
6 RAC SLIDER-CH
7 AL BUMBRY-CH
8 JOHN LEISTER-P
8 JEFF GRAY-P
9 MIKE GREENWELL-OF
0 JOHN DOPSON (INJ)-P
1 JEFF REARDON (INJ)-P
2 LARRY ANDERSEN-P (2)
2 JOHN PANKOVITS-2B
4 WES GARDNER-P
5 SCOTT COOPER-PH
5 JERRY REED-P (2)
7 ROB MURPHY-P
8 LEE SMITH-P (1)
8 LARRY ANDERSEN-P (2)
0 TOM BOLTON-P
2 MIKE BODDICKER-P
4 MIKE ROCHFORD-P
5 PHIL PLANTIER-DH/OF
5 JOE HESKETH-P (3)
9 DARYL IRVINE-P

1991

2ND (TIE) E 84-78 7GB

1 *(RET#) BOBBY DOERR*
2 LUIS RIVERA-SS/INF
3 JODY REED-SS
4 *(RET#) JOE CRONIN*
6 TONY PENA-C
7* STEVE LYONS-UTIL/P*
8 *(RET#) CARL YASTRZEMSKI*
9 *(RET#) TED WILLIAMS*
0 MIKE BRUMLEY-UTIL
1 TIM NAEHRING (INJ)-INF
2 ELLIS BURKS-OF/DH
5 DENNIS LAMP-P
6 KEVIN ROMINE-OF/DH
6 BOB ZUPCIC-OF
7 WAYNE HOUSIE-OF/DH
8 CARLOS QUINTANA-UTIL
9 DANA KIECKER (INJ)-P
0 JOHN MARZANO-C
1 ROGER (THE ROCKET) CLEMENS-P
2 MIKE MARSHALL-UTIL (1)
2 ERIC WEDGE-DH
3 TOM (BRUNO) BRUNANSKY-OF/DH
5 JACK CLARK-DH
6 WADE BOGGS-3B
7 GREG HARRIS-P
9 PHIL PLANTIER-OF/DH
0 MATT YOUNG (INJ)-P
2 RICHIE HEBNER-CH
3 DICK BERARDINO-CH
4 BILL FISCHER-CH
5 JOE MORGAN-MGR
6 JOHN MCLAREN-CH
7 AL BUMBRY-CH
8 JEFF GRAY (ILL)-P
39 MIKE GREENWELL-OF/DH
40 JOHN DOPSON (INJ)-P
41 JEFF REARDON-P
42 MO VAUGHN-1B/DH
43 KEVIN MORTON-P
44 DANNY DARWIN (INJ)-P
45 SCOTT COOPER-3B
46 DANNY DARWIN (INJ)-P
46 DAN PETRY-P (3)
47 MIKE GARDINER-P
48 TONY FOSSAS-P
50 TOM BOLTON (INJ)-P
51 JOSIAS MANZANILLO-P
54 JEFF PLYMPTON-P
55 JOE HESKETH-P
57 DARYL IRVINE (INJ)-P
59 DARYL IRVINE (INJ)-P

1992

7TH E 73-89 23GB

1 *(RET#) BOBBY DOERR*
2 LUIS RIVERA-SS/UTIL
3 JODY REED-2B
4 *(RET#) JOE CRONIN*
5 HERM WINNINGHAM-OF
6 TONY PENA-C
7 RICK (ROOSTER) BURLESON-CH
8 *(RET#) CARL YASTRZEMSKI*
9 *(RET#) TED WILLIAMS*
10 MIKE BRUMLEY-PH
11 TIM NAEHRING-UTIL
12 ELLIS BURKS-OF
13 JOHN VALENTIN-SS
15 JOHN FLAHERTY-C
16 FRANK VIOLA-P
17 BUTCH HOBSON-MGR
19 STEVE LYONS-UTIL
20 JOHN MARZANO-C
21 ROGER (THE ROCKET) CLEMENS-P
22 BILLY HATCHER-OF
23 TOM (BRUNO) BRUNANSKY-OF/1B
25 JACK CLARK-DH/1B
26 WADE BOGGS-3B
27 GREG HARRIS-P
28 BOB ZUPCIC-OF
29 PHIL PLANTIER-OF
30 MATT YOUNG-P
31 PETER HOY-P
32 GARY ALLENSON-CH
33 TOM BARRETT-2B
34 DON (POPEYE) ZIMMER-CH
35 RICH GALE-CH
36 ERIC WEDGE-C
37 AL BUMBRY-CH
(38) JEFF GRAY-(P)
39 MIKE GREENWELL-OF
40 JOHN DOPSON-P
41 JEFF REARDON-P (1)
42 MO VAUGHN-1B
44 DANNY DARWIN-P
45 SCOTT COOPER-INF
47 MIKE GARDINER-P
48 TONY FOSSAS-P
49 PAUL QUANTRILL-P
50 TOM BOLTON-P
50 KEN RYAN-P
55 JOE HESKETH-P
56 SCOTT TAYLOR-P
57 PETER HOY-P
59 DARYL IRVINE (INJ)-P

1993

5TH E 80-82 15GB

1 *(RET#) BOBBY DOERR*
2 LUIS RIVERA (INJ)-INF/DH
3 BOB MELVIN-C/1B
4 *(RET#) JOE CRONIN*
5 SCOTT FLETCHER-2B/UTIL
6 TONY PENA-C/DH
7 RICK (ROOSTER) BURLESON-CH
8 *(RET#) CARL YASTRZEMSKI*
9 *(RET#) TED WILLIAMS*
10 ANDRE DAWSON-DH/OF
11 TIM NAEHRING (INJ)-INF/DH
12 ERNEST RILES-INF/DH
13 JOHN VALENTIN-SS
15 JOHN FLAHERTY-C
16 FRANK VIOLA-P
17 BUTCH HOBSON-MGR
18 CARLOS QUINTANA-1B/OF
19 JOSE MELENDEZ (INJ)-P
20 JEFF RICHARDSON (INJ)-INF/DH
21 ROGER (THE ROCKET) CLEMENS (INJ)-P
22 BILLY HATCHER-OF/2B
23 IVAN CALDERON-OF/DH (1)
23 ROB DEER-OF/DH (2)
25 JEFF RUSSELL (INJ)-P
27 GREG HARRIS-P
28 BOB ZUPCIC-OF/DH
29 SCOTT BANKHEAD-P
30 STEVE LYONS-UTIL
30 JIM BYRD-DH
32 GARY ALLENSON-CH
33 MIKE EASLER-CH
34 SCOTT COOPER-3B/INF
35 RICH GALE-CH
36 AARON SELE-P
37 AL BUMBRY-CH
39 MIKE GREENWELL-OF/DH
40 JOHN DOPSON-P
42 MO VAUGHN-1B/DH
43 CORY BAILEY-P
44 DANNY DARWIN-P
45 MIKE EASLER-CH
46 JOSE MELENDEZ (INJ)-P
47 GREG BLOSSER-OF/DH
48 TONY FOSSAS-P
49 PAUL QUANTRILL-P
50 KEN RYAN-P
50 JEFF MCNEELY-OF/DH
51 LUIS ORTIZ-3B/DH
55 JOE HESKETH (INJ)-P
56 SCOTT TAYLOR-P
57 NATE MINCHEY-P
58 JEFF MCNEELY-OF/DH
61 JIM BYRD-DH

1994

4TH E 54-61 17GB

STRIKE NO POST-SEASON

1 *(RET#) BOBBY DOERR*
2 OTIS NIXON-OF
3 CARLOS RODRIGUEZ-SS
4 *(RET#) JOE CRONIN*
5 SCOTT FLETCHER (INJ)-2B/UTIL
6 DAMON BERRYHILL-C
8 *(RET#) CARL YASTRZEMSKI*
9 *(RET#) TED WILLIAMS*
10 ANDRE DAWSON (INJ)-DH/OF
11 TIM NAEHRING (INJ)-INF/DH
12 JOHN (DUKE) WATHAN-CH
13 JOHN VALENTIN (INJ)-SS
15 RICK TRLICEK-P
16 FRANK VIOLA (INJ)-P
17 BUTCH HOBSON-MGR
18 RICH ROWLAND-C
19 JOSE MELENDEZ-P
20 FRANK WHITE-CH
21 ROGER (THE ROCKET) CLEMENS-P
22 BILLY HATCHER-OF (1)
22 ERIC WEDGE-DH
23 DAVE VALLE-C (1)
23 TOM (BRUNO) BRUNANSKY-OF (2)
25 JEFF RUSSELL-P (1)
26 WES CHAMBERLAIN-OF (2)
27 GREG A. HARRIS (REL)-P (1)
27 STAN ROYER-3B (2)
28 BOB ZUPCIC-OF (1)
28 GREG LITTON-1B
29 SCOTT BANKHEAD (INJ)-P
30 ANDY TOMBERLIN (INJ)-OF
31 CHRIS HOWARD-P
32 GARY ALLENSON-CH
33 MIKE ROARKE-CH
34 SCOTT COOPER (INJ)-3B/INF
35 TODD FROWIRTH-P
36 AARON SELE-P
38 LEE TINSLEY-OF
39 MIKE GREENWELL (INJ)-OF/DH
40 SERGIO VALDEZ-P
41 STEVE FARR (INJ)-P (2)
42 MO VAUGHN-1B/DH
43 CORY BAILEY-P
44 DANNY DARWIN (INJ)-P
45 MIKE EASLER-CH
46 GAR FINNVOLD (INJ)-P
47 GREG BLOSSER-OF
48 TONY FOSSAS-P
49 PAUL QUANTRILL-P (1)
49 CHRIS NABHOLZ (INJ)-P (2)
50 KEN RYAN-P
51 LUIS ORTIZ-DH/3B
53 TIM VANEGMOND-P
55 JOE HESKETH-P
57 NATE MINCHEY-P

1995

1ST E 86-58 0GB

144 GAME SEASON

L ALDS-CLEA 3-0

1 *(RET#) BOBBY DOERR*
2 TERRY SHUMPERT-2B
3 CARLOS RODRIGUEZ-SS
4 *(RET#) JOE CRONIN*
6 CHRIS DONNELS-3B (2)
7 STEVE RODRIGUEZ (WAIV)-SS (1)
8 *(RET#) CARL YASTRZEMSKI*
9 *(RET#) TED WILLIAMS*
10 LUIS ALICEA-2B
11 TIM NAEHRING-3B
12 RICH ROWLAND-C
13 JOHN VALENTIN-SS
14 JIM RICE-CH
15 MIKE MACFARLANE-C
16 DAVE OLIVER-CH
17 TIM JOHNSON-CH
18 REGGIE JEFFERSON (INJ)-1B
19 MIKE MADDUX-P
20 FRANK WHITE-CH
21 ROGER (THE ROCKET) CLEMENS (INJ)-P
22 CHRIS JAMES (INJ)-DH/OF (2)
23 HERM STARRETTE-CH
25 TROY O'LEARY-OF
26 ALEJANDRO PENA-P
26 LEE TINSLEY (INJ)-OF
27 MARK WHITEN (INJ)-OF (1)
27 DAVE HOLLINS (INJ)-DH (2)
28 DEREK LILLIQUIST-P
28 ERIC GENDERSON-P (2)
29 KARL (TUFFY) RHODES-OF (2)
29 JUAN BELL-2B
30 FRANK RODRIGUEZ-P (1)
30 SCOTT HATTEBERG-C
32 WES CHAMBERLAIN-OF
32 MIKE STANTON-P (2)
33 JOSE CANSECO (INJ)-DH
34 RHEAL CORMIER-P
35 MATT STAIRS-OF
36 AARON SELE-P
37 BILL HASSELMAN-C/DH
38 LEE TINSLEY-OF
38 RICK AGUILERA-P (2)
39 MIKE GREENWELL-OF
40 ERIK HANSON-P
42 MO VAUGHN-1B
43 STAN BELINDA-P
44 KEVIN KENNEDY-MGR
45 JOEL JOHNSTON-P
45 MATT MURRAY-P
46 RON MAHAY-OF
46 DWAYNE HOSEY-OF (2)
47 AL NIPPER-CH
48 ZANE SMITH (INJ)-P
49 MIKE HARTLEY-P
49 TIM WAKEFIELD-P
50 KEN RYAN-P
51 BRIAN LOONEY-P
51 WILLIE MCGEE-OF
52 VAUGHN ESHELMAN (INJ)-P
53 TIM VANEGMOND (INJ)-P
54 KEITH SHEPHERD (INJ)-P
54 JOE HUDSON-P
55 JEFF SUPPAN-P
56 JEFF PIERCE-P
57 BRIAN BARK-P

1996

3RD E 85-77 7GB

1 *(RET#) BOBBY DOERR*
2 ALEX COLE-OF
2 JEFF MANTO-1B (3)
3 JEFF FRYE-2B
4 *(RET#) JOE CRONIN*
5 NOMAR GARCIAPARRA-SS
7 TROT NIXON-INF
8 *(RET#) CARL YASTRZEMSKI*
9 *(RET#) TED WILLIAMS*
10 ESTEBAN BELTRE-3B
10 LEE TINSLEY-OF (2)
11 TIM NAEHRING (INJ)-3B
12 WIL CORDERO (INJ)-2B
13 JOHN VALENTIN (INJ)-SS
14 JIM RICE-CH
15 MILT CUYLER (INJ)-OF
16 DAVE OLIVER-CH
17 TIM JOHNSON-CH
18 REGGIE JEFFERSON-1B
19 MIKE MADDUX (INJ)-P
20 FRANK WHITE-CH
20 PAT MAHOMES-P (2)
21 ROGER (THE ROCKET) CLEMENS-P
22 MIKE STANLEY (INJ)-C
23 PHIL CLARK-3B
23 REGGIE HARRIS-P
24 KEVIN MITCHELL (INJ)-OF (1)
25 TROY O'LEARY-OF
26 AARON SELE (INJ)-P
27 BUTCH HENRY (INJ)-P
28 ERIC GENDERSON-P
29 BILL SELBY-3B
31 BRAD PENNINGTON (WAIV)-P (1)
31 TONY RODRIGUEZ-SS
32 MIKE STANTON-P (1)
32 ALEX DELGADO-C
33 JOSE CANSECO (INJ)-DH
34 RICH GARCES (INJ)-P
35 DAVE CARLUCCI-CH
36 TOM (FLASH) GORDON-P
37 BILL HASELMAN-C
38 JOSE MALAVE (INJ)-OF
39 MIKE GREENWELL (INJ)-OF
41 SAMMY ELLIS-CH
42 MO VAUGHN-1B
43 STAN BELINDA (INJ)-P

44 KEVIN KENNEDY-MGR
45 JOHN DOHERTY-P
45 GREG PIRKL-1B (2)
45 WALT MCKEEL-C
46 DWAYNE HOSEY-OF
47 AL NIPPER-CH
47 LEE TINSLEY-OF (2)
47 SCOTT HATTEBERG-C
48 JIM TATUM-3B (1)
48 JEFF MANTO (INJ)-2B/1B (1)(3)
48 ARQUIMEDES POZO-2B
49 TIM WAKEFIELD-P
50 JAMIE MOYER-P (1)
50 MARK BRANDENBERG-P (2)
51 HEATHCLIFF SLOCUMB-P
52 VAUGHN ESHELMAN-P
53 KERRY LACY-P
54 JOE HUDSON-P
55 JEFF SUPPAN (INJ)-P
56 ALEX DELGADO-C
56 DARREN BRAGG-OF (2)
57 KEN GRUNDT-P
57 RUDY PEMBERTON-OF
58 NATE MINCHEY (INJ)-P
59 BRENT KNACKERT-P
59 PAT MAHOMES-P (2)

1997

4TH E 78-84 20GB

1 *(RET#) BOBBY DOERR*
2 CURTIS PRIDE-OF (2)
3 JEFF FRYE-DH/OF
4 *(RET#) JOE CRONIN*
5 NOMAR GARCIAPARRA-SS
8 *(RET#) CARL YASTRZEMSKI*
9 *(RET#) TED WILLIAMS*
10 SCOTT HATTEBERG-C
11 TIM NAEHRING (INJ)-3B
12 WIL CORDERO-OF
13 JOHN VALENTIN-2B
14 JIM RICE-CH
15 SHANE MACK (INJ)-OF
16 JOE KERRIGAN-CH
17 BRET SABERHAGEN (INJ)-P
18 REGGIE JEFFERSON-DH
19 BRIAN ROSE-P
20 MIKE STANLEY-C (1)
22 JIMY WILLIAMS-MGR
23 HERM STARRETTE-CH
24 SHANE MACK (INJ)-OF
25 TROY O'LEARY-OF
26 AARON SELE-P
27 BUTCH HENRY (INJ)-P
28 MIKE BENJAMIN-SS
29 ARQUIMEDEZ POZO-3B
30 JESUS TAVAREZ-OF
31 WENDELL KIM-CH
32 CHRIS HAMMOND (INJ)-P
33 STEVE AVERY (INJ)-P
34 RICH GARCES (INJ)-P
35 GRADY LITTLE-CH
36 TOM (FLASH) GORDON-P
37 BILL HASELMAN (INJ)-C
38 JOSE MALAVE (INJ)-OF
40 ROBINSON CHECO (INJ)-P
40 HERM STARRETTE-CH
41 JIM CORSI (INJ)-P
42 MO VAUGHN (INJ)-1B
43 RICK TRLICEK-P (1)
43 DEREK LOWE-P (2)
44 RUDY PEMBERTON (REL)-OF
44 MICHAEL COLEMAN-OF
45 WALT MCKEEL-C
46 JOHN WASDIN-P
47 TOBY BORLAND-P (2)
47 JASON VARITEK-C
48 DAVE JAUSS-CH
49 TIM WAKEFIELD (INJ)-P
50 MARK BRANDENBERG-P
51 HEATHCLIFF SLOCUMB-P (1)
52 VAUGHN ESHELMAN-P
53 KERRY LACY-P
54 JOE HUDSON-P
55 JEFF SUPPAN-P
56 DARREN BRAGG-OF
57 RON MAHAY-P
59 PAT MAHOMES-P
59 KEN GRUNDT-P

1998

2ND E (W/C) 92-70 22GB
L ALDS-CLEA 3-1

1 *(RET#) BOBBY DOERR*
2 DAMON BUFORD (INJ)-OF
(3) JEFF FRYE (INJ)-(DH/OF)
4 *(RET#) JOE CRONIN*
5 NOMAR GARCIAPARRA (INJ)-SS
7 TROT NIXON-OF
8 *(RET#) CARL YASTRZEMSKI*
9 *(RET#) TED WILLIAMS*
10 SCOTT HATTEBERG-C
(11) TIM NAEHRING (INJ)-(3B)
12 WENDELL KIM-CH
13 JOHN VALENTIN-2B
14 JIM RICE-CH
15 MARK LEMKE (INJ)-2B
16 JOE KERRIGAN-CH
17 BRET SABERHAGEN-P
18 REGGIE JEFFERSON (INJ)-DH
19 BRIAN ROSE (INJ)-P
20 DARREN LEWIS-OF
22 JIMY WILLIAMS-MGR
23 BILLY ASHLEY-DH/OF/1B (2)
24 MIKE STANLEY-DH/1B (2)
25 TROY O'LEARY-OF
26 ORLANDO MERCED (REL)-OF/1B (2)
26 CHRIS SNOPEK-SS/INF (2)
27 BUTCH HENRY (INJ)-P
28 MIKE BENJAMIN-SS
29 MIDRE CUMMINGS (INJ)-OF
30 KEITH MITCHELL-DH/OF
31 JIM LEYRITZ-C/DH (1)
31 DARIO VERAS-P
32 DEREK LOWE-P
33 STEVE AVERY-P
34 RICH GARCES (INJ)-P
35 GRADY LITTLE-CH
36 TOM (FLASH) GORDON-P
37 GREG SWINDELL-P (2)
39 DAVID WEST (REL)-P
40 ROBINSON CHECO-P
41 JIM CORSI (INJ)-P
42 MO VAUGHN-1B
43 DENNIS (ECK) ECKERSLEY-P
45 PEDRO MARTINEZ-P
46 JOHN WASDIN-P
47 JASON VARITEK-C
48 DAVE JAUSS-CH
49 TIM WAKEFIELD-P
50 LOU MERLONI (INJ)-2B/INF
51 KEITH JOHNS-2B
51 PETE SCHOUREK-P (2)
52 DONNIE SADLER-2B/INF
(53) KERRY LACY (INJ)-(P)
54 MANDY ROMERO-C (2)
55 BRIAN SHOUSE-P
55 CARLOS REYES-P (2)
56 DARREN BRAGG-OF
57 RON MAHAY-P
59 BRIAN BARKLEY-P
61 JIN HO CHO-P
62 DONNIE SADLER-2B/INF
65 CARLOS VALDEZ-P

1999

2ND E (W/C) 94-68 4GB
L ALDS-CLEA 3-1

1 *(RET#) BOBBY DOERR*
2 DAMON BUFORD (INJ)-OF
3 JEFF FRYE (INJ)-2B
4 *(RET#) JOE CRONIN*
5 NOMAR GARCIAPARRA (INJ)-SS
7 TROT NIXON-OF
8 *(RET#) CARL YASTRZEMSKI*
9 *(RET#) TED WILLIAMS*
10 SCOTT HATTEBERG (INJ)-C
12 WENDELL KIM-CH
13 JOHN VALENTIN (INJ)-2B
14 JIM RICE-CH
15 DONNIE SADLER-INF
16 JOE KERRIGAN-CH
17 BRET SABERHAGEN (INJ)-P
18 REGGIE JEFFERSON (INJ)-DH
19 BRIAN ROSE (INJ)-P
20 DARREN LEWIS-OF
22 JIMY WILLIAMS-MGR
23 BRIAN DAUBACH-1B
24 MIKE STANLEY-DH/1B
25 TROY O'LEARY-OF
26 LOU MERLONI-2B/INF
27 KIP GROSS-P
28 PAT RAPP-P
29 BOB WOLCOTT-P
29 JON NUNNALLY-OF
30 JOSE OFFERMAN-2B/INF
31 MARK PORTUGAL-P
32 DEREK LOWE-P
33 KIRK BULLINGER-P
33 JASON VARITEK-C
34 RICH GARCES-P
35 GRADY LITTLE-CH
36 TOM (FLASH) GORDON-P
37 RHEAL CORMIER-P
38 WILTON VERAS-INF
38 LENNY WEBSTER-C (2)
39 CREIGHTON GUBANICH-C
39 BRYCE FLORIE-P (2)
40 MARK GUTHRIE, (INJ)-P (1)
40 MICHAEL COLEMAN-OF
41 JIM CORSI-P
41 KENT MERCKER-P (2)
42 *(RET#) JACKIE ROBINSON*
43 DAVE JAUSS-CH
44 MICHAEL COLEMAN-OF
44 BUTCH HUSKEY-OF (2)
45 PEDRO MARTINEZ (INJ)-P
46 JOHN WASDIN (INJ)-P
47 JASON VARITEK-C
47 ROD (THE SHOOTER) BECK-P (2)
48 RAMON MARTINEZ (INJ)-P
49 TIM WAKEFIELD-P
50 CHAD FONVILLE-INF
52 JOHN CUMBERLAND-CH
53 TOMO OHKA-P
56 TIM HARIKKALA-P
56 STEVE LOMASNEY-C
57 JUAN PENA (INJ)-P
(59) BRIAN BARKLEY (INJ)-(P)
61 JIN HO CHO-P
62 MARINO SANTANA-P

2000

2ND E 85-77 2.5GB

1 *(RET#) BOBBY DOERR*
2 CARL EVERETT-OF
3 JEFF FRYE (INJ)-2B (1)
3 MIKE LANSING-INF (2)
4 *(RET#) JOE CRONIN*
5 NOMAR GARCIAPARRA (INJ)-SS
6 GARY GAETTI-3B
7 TROT NIXON-OF
8 *(RET#) CARL YASTRZEMSKI*
9 *(RET#) TED WILLIAMS*
10 SCOTT HATTEBERG (INJ)-C
11 CURTIS PRIDE-OF
11 RICO BROGNA-1B (2)
12 WENDELL KIM-CH
13 JOHN VALENTIN (INJ)-2B
14 JIM RICE-CH
15 DONNIE SADLER-INF
16 JOE KERRIGAN-CH
17 BRET SABERHAGEN (INJ)-P
18 ANDY SHEETS-SS
18 MIDRE CUMMINGS-OF (2)
19 BRIAN ROSE (INJ)-P (1)
19 ROLANDO ARROJO-P (2)
19 DANTE BICHETTE-OF (2)
20 DARREN LEWIS-OF
22 JIMY WILLIAMS-MGR
23 BRIAN DAUBACH-1B
24 MIKE STANLEY-DH/1B (1)
25 TROY O'LEARY-OF
26 ROB STANIFER-P
26 LOU MERLONI-2B/INF
26 SEAN BERRY-3B (2)
27 *(RET#) CARLTON FISK*
28 BERNARD GILKEY-OF (2)
29 MANNY ALEXANDER-INF
30 JOSE OFFERMAN-2B/INF
31 JEFF FASSERO-P
32 DEREK LOWE-P
33 JASON VARITEK-C
34 RICH GARCES-P
35 HIPOLITO PICHARDO-P
35 TOMMY HARPER-CH
36 TOM (FLASH) GORDON (INJ)-P
37 RHEAL CORMIER-P
38 WILTON VERAS-INF
38 JESUS PENA-P (2)
39 BRYCE FLORIE-P
40 SANG HOON LEE-P
41 DAN SMITH-P
41 STEVE ONTIVEROS-P
42 *(RET#) JACKIE ROBINSON*
43 BUDDY BAILEY-CH
44 MICHAEL COLEMAN (INJ)-OF
44 ED SPRAGUE-3B (2)
45 PEDRO MARTINEZ (INJ)-P
46 JOHN WASDIN (INJ)-P (1)
46 ROLANDO ARROJO-P (2)
47 ROD (THE SHOOTER) BECK-P
48 RAMON MARTINEZ (INJ)-P
49 TIM WAKEFIELD-P
50 PETE SCHOUREK (INJ)-P
51 TOMMY HARPER-CH
52 JOHN CUMBERLAND-CH
53 TOMO OHKA-P
54 MORGAN BURKHART-DH
55 WILLIE ADAMS-P
55 RICK CROUSCHORE-P (2)
56 IZZY ALCANTARA (INJ)-OF
(57) JUAN PENA (INJ)-(P)
58 HECTOR CARRASCO-P (2)
59 TIM YOUNG-P
61 JIN HO CHO-P
63 PAXTON CRAWFORD-P

2001

2ND E 82-79 13.5GB

1 *(RET#) BOBBY DOERR*
2 CARL EVERETT (INJ)-OF
3 MIKE LANSING (INJ)-INF
4 *(RET#) JOE CRONIN*
5 NOMAR GARCIAPARRA (INJ)-SS
7 TROT NIXON-OF
8 *(RET#) CARL YASTRZEMSKI*
9 *(RET#) TED WILLIAMS*
10 SCOTT HATTEBERG-C
11 HIDEO NOMO-P
12 CHRIS STYNES (INJ)-2B/3B
13 JOHN VALENTIN (INJ)-2B
15 CRAIG GREBECK (INJ)-INF
16 JOE KERRIGAN-CH/MGR2
17 BRET SABERHAGEN (INJ)-
18 TOMO OHKA-P (1)
18 WILLIE BANKS-P
19 DANTE BICHETTE-OF
20 DARREN LEWIS-OF
22 JIMY WILLIAMS-MGR1
23 BRIAN DAUBACH (INJ)-1B
24 MANNY RAMIREZ-OF
25 TROY O'LEARY-OF
26 LOU MERLONI-INF
27 *(RET#) CARLTON FISK*
28 MARCUS JENSEN-C (1)
28 DOUG MIRABELLI-C (2)
29 SHEA HILLENBRAND-3B
30 JOSE OFFERMAN-2B/INF
31 GENE LAMONT-CH
32 DEREK LOWE-P
33 JASON VARITEK (INJ)-C
34 RICH GARCES (INJ)-P
35 HIPOLITO PICHARDO (INJ) (RET)-P
35 TOMMY HARPER-CH
36 DAVID CONE (INJ)-P
37 FRANK CASTILLO-P
39 BRYCE FLORIE (INJ)-P
39 JOE OLIVER-C (2)
41 BILL PULSIPHER (WAIV)-P (1)
41 UGUETH URBINA-P (2)
42 *(RET#) JACKIE ROBINSON*
43 CARLOS CASTILLO (REL)-P
44 ROLANDO ARROJO (INJ)-P
45 PEDRO MARTINEZ (INJ)-P
46 BILL PULSIPHER-P (1)
46 ALLEN MCDILL-P
47 ROD (THE SHOOTER) BECK-P
48 RICK DOWN-CH
49 TIM WAKEFIELD-P
50 PETE SCHOUREK (INJ)-P
52 JOHN CUMBERLAND-CH
52 JAMES LOFTON-SS
53 ANGEL SANTOS-SS
54 MORGAN BURKHART-1B
55 TODD ERDOS-P
56 IZZY ALCANTARA-1B
(57) JUAN PENA (INJ)-(P)
57 CALVIN PICKERING-1B (2)
58 NELLIE NORMAN-CH
59 CASEY FOSSUM-P
62 SUN WOO KIM-P
63 PAXTON CRAWFORD-P

2002

2ND E 93-69 10.5GB

1 *(RET#) BOBBY DOERR*
2 SHANE ANDREWS-UTIL
3 GRADY LITTLE-MGR
4 *(RET#) JOE CRONIN*
5 NOMAR GARCIAPARRA-SS
7 TROT NIXON-OF
8 *(RET#) CARL YASTRZEMSK*
9 *(RET#) TED WILLIAMS*
10 CARLOS BAERGA-UTIL
(11) MICHAEL COLEMAN-(OF)
12 CLIFF FLOYD-OF/DH (3)
13 REY SANCHEZ (INJ)-2B/UTIL
15 CASEY FOSSUM-P
16 BOB KIPPER-CH
17 WILLIE BANKS-P
18 JOHNNY DAMON-OF
19 JOHN BURKETT-P
20 MIKE STANLEY-CH
22 TONY CLARK-1B/DH
23 BRIAN DAUBACH-1B/OF/DH
24 MANNY RAMIREZ (INJ)-OF/DH
25 DWIGHT EVANS-CH
26 LOU MERLONI-UTIL
27 *(RET#) CARLTON FISK*
28 DOUG MIRABELLI-C/DH

BOSTON RED SOX

Wade Boggs wore #26 while with the Red Sox for eleven years. When he moved to the Yankees, he wore #12 for five years. He finished up at Tampa Bay where he again wore #12. The Devil Rays retired that number for him although he only played there two years in the twilight of his career.

29 SHEA HILLENBRAND-3B
30 JOSE OFFERMAN-UTIL (1)
31 DUSTIN HOFFMAN (INJ)-P
32 DEREK LOWE-P
33 JASON VARITEK-C
34 RICH GARCES-P
35 RICKEY HENDERSON-OF/DH
36 DARREN OLIVER-P
37 FRANK CASTILLO (SUS:5G)-P
38 KEVIN BROWN-C
39 MIKE CUBBAGE-CH
40 TONY CLONINGER-CH
41 UGUETH URBINA-P
42 *(RET#) JACKIE ROBINSON*
43 ALAN EMBREE (INJ)-P (2)
44 ROLANDO ARROJO (INJ)-P
45 PEDRO MARTINEZ J.-P
(46) CALVIN PICKERING (INJ)-(1B)
46 JUAN DIAZ-1B/DH
46 BOBBY HOWRY-P (2)
47 SUN WOO KIM-P
49 TIM WAKEFIELD-P
50 BENNY AGBAYANI-OF (2)
51 TOMMY HARPER-CH
52 FREDDY SANCHEZ-UTIL
53 JOSH HANCOCK-P
(55) JEFF WALLACE (INJ)-(P)
56 CHRIS HANLEY-P
58 BRYANT NELSON-2B/UTIL
61 WAYNE GOMES-P
(63) PAXTON CRAWFORD (INJ)-(P)

2003

2ND E W/C 95-67 6GB
W ALDS-OAKA 3-2
L ALCS-NYA 4-3

1 *(RET#) BOBBY DOERR*
2 DAMIAN JACKSON-UTIL
3 GRADY LITTLE-MGR
4 *(RET#) JOE CRONIN*
5 NOMAR GARCIAPARRA-SS
7 TROT NIXON-OF
8 *(RET#) CARL YASTRZEMSKI*
9 *(RET#) TED WILLIAMS*
10 DAVID MCCARTY-OF/1B (2)
11 BILL MUELLER-3B/2B
12 TODD WALKER-2B
13 LOU MERLONI-INF (2)
15 KEVIN MILLAR-1B/OF/DH
16 LOU COLLIER-3B
17 ADRIAN BROWN-OF
17 RUDY SEANEZ-P
18 JOHNNY DAMON-OF
19 JOHN BURKETT-P
20 DALLAS WILLIAMS-CH
22 RON JACKSON-CH
23 CASEY FOSSUM (INJ)-P
24 MANNY RAMIREZ-OF/DH
25 JEREMY GIAMBI (INJ)-DH/OF
26 FREDDY SANCHEZ-INF (1)
26 RAMIRO MENDOZA (INJ)-P
27 *(RET#) CARLTON FISK*
28 DOUG MIRABELLI-C
29 SHEA HILLENBRAND-3B/1B (1)
29 GABE KAPLER-OF (2)
30 RYAN RUPE-P
31 ROBERT PERSON (INJ)-P
32 DEREK LOWE-P
33 JASON VARITEK-C
34 DAVID ORTIZ-DH/1B
35 JEFF SUPPAN-P (2)
35 DAVE WALLACE-CH
37 DAVE WALLACE-CH
37 JEFF SUPPAN-P (2)
38 BRANDON LYON-P
39 MIKE CUBBAGE-CH
40 TONY CLONINGER (ILL)-CH
41 JERRY NARRON-CH
42 *(RET#) JACKIE ROBINSON*
43 ALAN EMBREE (INJ)-P
44 CHAD FOX (INJ) (REL)-P (1)
44 BILL HASELMAN-C
45 PEDRO J. MARTINEZ (INJ)-P
46 BOBBY HOWRY (INJ)-P
47 STEVE WOODARD-P
47 SCOTT SAUERBECK-P (2)
48 SCOTT SAUERBECK-P (2)
48 SCOTT WILLIAMSON-P (2)
49 TIM WAKEFIELD-P
50 MIKE TIMLIN-P
51 KEVIN TOLAR-P
51 BYUNG HYUN KIM-P (2)
52 BRUCE CHEN-P (2)
53 ANDY ABAD-1B
54 EUCLIDES ROJAS-CH
55 RAMIRO MENDOZA (INJ)-P
57 JASON SHIELL-P
58 HECTOR ALMONTE-P (1)
59 MATT WHITE (INJ)-P (1)
59 TODD JONES-P (2)
61 BRONSON ARROYO-P

2004

2ND E W/C 98-64 3GB
W ALDS-ANAA 3-0
W ALCS-NYA 4-3
W WS-STLN 4-0

1 *(RET#) BOBBY DOERR*
2 BRAD MILLS-CH
3 POKEY REESE (INJ)-INF
4 *(RET#) JOE CRONIN*
5 NOMAR GARCIAPARRA-SS (1)
7 TROT NIXON (INJ)-OF
8 *(RET#) CARL YASTRZEMSKI*
9 *(RET#) TED WILLIAMS*
10 DAVID MCCARTY-1B
11 BILL MUELLER-3B/2B
12 MARK BELLHORN-2B
13 DOUG MENTKIEWICZ-1B (2)
15 KEVIN MILLAR-1B/OF/DH
16 RICKY GUTTIEREZ-INF (2)
17 DAVE WALLACE-CH
18 JOHNNY DAMON-OF
19 GABE KAPLER-OF
20 KEVIN YOUKILIS-3B/2B
22 RON JACKSON-CH
23 BRIAN DAUBACH-1B
24 MANNY RAMIREZ-OF/DH
25 ELLIS BURKS-DH/OF
26 RAMIRO MENDOZA (INJ)-P
27 *(RET#) CARLTON FISK*
28 DOUG MIRABELLI-C
29 KEITH FOULKE-P
30 CURTIS LESKANIC (INJ)-P (2)
31 CESAR CRESPO-SS
31 DAVE ROBERTS-OF (2)
32 DEREK LOWE-P
33 JASON VARITEK-C
34 DAVID ORTIZ-DH/1B
35 LYNN JONES-CH
36 BOBBY JONES-P
36 ORLANDO CABRERA-SS (2)
36 MIKE MYERS-P (2)
37 FRANK CASTILLO-P
37 EARL SNYDER-1B
37 ADAM HYZDU-OF
38 CURT SCHILLING-P
39 ANDY DOMINIQUE-C
39 PEDRO ASTACIO-P
41 DALE SVEUM-CH
42 *(RET#) JACKIE ROBINSON*
43 ALAN EMBREE-P
44 ORLANDO CABRERA-SS (2)
45 PEDRO J. MARTINEZ-P
46 MARK MALASKA-P
47 TERRY FRANCONA-MGR
48 SCOTT WILLIAMSON (INJ)-P
49 TIM WAKEFIELD-P
50 MIKE TIMLIN-P
51 BYUNG HYUN KIM (INJ)-P
52 JAMIE BROWN-P
53 PHIL SEIBEL-P
53 TERRY ADAMS-P (2)
54 EUCLIDES ROJAS-CH
55 LENNY DINARDO-P
56 JIMMY ANDERSON-P (2)
(57) JASON SHIELL-(P)
57 JOE NELSON-P
58 SANDY MARTINEZ-C (2)
59 ABE ALVAREZ-P
61 BRONSON ARROYO-P
67 ASTACIO MARTINEZ-P

2005

2ND E W/C 95-67 0GB
L ALDS-CHIA 3-0

1 *(RET#) BOBBY DOERR*
2 BRAD MILLS-CH
3* DAVID WELLS-P*
3 EDGAR RENTERIA-SS
4 *(RET#) JOE CRONIN*
7 TROT NIXON (INJ)(SUS:2G)-OF
8 *(RET#) CARL YASTRZEMSKI*
9 *(RET#) TED WILLIAMS*
10 DAVID MCCARTY (WAIV)-1B
10 SHAWN WOOTEN-C
10 TONY GRAFFANINO-2B (2)
11 BILL MUELLER-3B/2B
12 MARK BELLHORN-2B (1)
13 ROBERTO PETAGINE-1B
15 KEVIN MILLAR-1B
16 EDGAR RENTERIA-SS
16 DAVID WELLS (SUS:6G)-P
17 DAVE WALLACE-CH
18 JOHNNY DAMON-OF
19 JOHN OLERUD-1B
20 KEVIN YOUKILIS-3B
22 RON JACKSON-CH
23 RAMON VAZQUEZ-2B (1)
23 ALEX CORA-2B (2)
24 MANNY RAMIREZ-OF
25 ADAM HYZDU-OF (2)
27 *(RET#) CARLTON FISK*
28 DOUG MIRABELLI-C
29 KEITH FOULKE (INJ)-P
30 MATT CLEMENT-P
31 MATT MANTEI (INJ)-P
32 JEREMI GONZALEZ-P
32 JOSE CRUZ, JR.-OF (2)
33 JASON VARITEK-C
34 DAVID ORTIZ (BIG PAPI)-DH
35 LYNN JONES-CH
36 MIKE MYERS-P
37 BILL HASSELMAN-CH
37 MIKE REMLINGER-P (2)
37 MIKE STANTON-P (3)
38 CURT SCHILLING (INJ)-P
39 ADAM STERN (INJ)-OF
40 ALEJANDRO MACHADO-INF
41 DALE SVEUM-CH
42 *(RET#) JACKIE ROBINSON*
43 ALAN EMBREE-P (1)
43 CHAD HARVILLE-P (2)
44 JAY PAYTON-OF (1)
44 GABE KAPLER-OF
46 MATT PERISHO-P (2)
47 TERRY FRANCONA-MGR
48 KELLY SHOPPACH-C
49 TIM WAKEFIELD-P
50 MIKE TIMLIN-P
51 CLA MEREDITH-P
52 WADE MILLER (INJ)-P
53 CHAD BRADFORD-P (2)
54 JOHN HALAMA-P (1)
54 JEREMI GONZALEZ-P
55 LENNY DINARDO-P
56 CRAIG HANSEN-P
57 SCOTT CASSIDY-P (1)
57 MANNY DELCARMEN-P
58 JONATHAN PAPELBON-P
59 BLAINE NEAL-P (1)
59 ABE ALVAREZ-P
60 HANLEY RAMIREZ-INF
61 BRONSON ARROYO (SUS:6G)-P

1931

CHICAGO WHITE SOX

8TH 56-97 51.5GB

1 BILL CISSELL-SS/INF
2* BOB (LEFTY) WEILAND-P*
2 MEL (BUTCH) SIMONS-OF
2 CARL REYNOLDS-OF
3 CARL REYNOLDS-OF
4 SMEAD (GUINEA) (SMUDGE) JOLLEY-OF
5 LUKE (OLD ACHES & PAINS) APPLING-SS/2B
6 JOHNNY (LEFTY) WATWOOD-OF/1B
7 WILLIE KAMM-3B (1)
7 LEW FONSECA-OF/INF (2)
8 BENNIE TATE-C
9 FRANK (HANS) GRUBE-C
12 BUTCH HENLINE-C
12 HANK GARRITY-C
14 TED LYONS (INJ)-P
15 TOMMY THOMAS-P
16 PAT CARAWAY-P
17 HAL MCKAIN (INJ)-P
18 RED FABER-P
19 GARLAND BRAXTON-P (1)
19 GRANT (MOOSE) BOWLER-P
22 DONIE BUSH-MGR
23 JIM MOORE-P
23 LOU GARLAND-P
24 VIC FRASIER-P
25 BIGGS WEHDE-P
26 BILLY SULLIVAN-3B/UTIL
27 LU BLUE-1B
28 IRV JEFFRIES-INF
29 JOHN KERR-2B/INF
33 MIKE KELLY-CH
34 FRED (IKE) EICHRODT-OF
34 BILL NORMAN-2B/INF
35 BOB (FATS) FOTHERGILL-OF
__ BRUCE (SOUPY) CAMPBELL-OF (4G:9/25-27)
23 HAL MCKAIN-P
23 PETE DAGLIA-P
23 FABIAN KOWALIK-P
23 GRANT (MOOSE) BOWLER-P
24 BUMP HADLEY-P (1)
24 RED KRESS-UTIL (2)
25 EVAR SWANSON-OF
25 SAD SAM JONES-P
26 MILT GASTON-P
27 JOHNNY BUTLER-CH
27 BILL NORMAN-OF
28 BILL CUNNINGHAM-CH
29 BOB POSER-P
34 MEL (BUTCH) SIMONS-OF
34 LIZ FUNK-OF
35 LES BARTHOLOMEW-P
35 BOB POSER-P
35 GREG MULLEAVY-2B
35 CHAD KIMSEY-P (2)
36 CHARLIE ENGLISH-3B/SS
36 ART SMITH-P
36 HAL ANDERSON-OF
37 BOB POSER-P
37 BOB (SUITCASE BOB) SEEDS-OF (2)
39 GRANT (MOOSE) BOWLER-P
39 CLARENCE (LEFTY) FIEBER-P
39 PAUL (POP) GREGORY-P
45 PAUL (POP) GREGORY-P
46 JIM MOORE-P
49 BILLY SULLIVAN (INJ)-UTIL
49 GREG MULLEAVY-2B

1932

7TH 49-102 56.5GB

1 FRANK (HANS) GRUBE-C
2 BENNIE TATE-C (1)
3 SMEAD (GUINEA) (SMUDGE) JOLLEY-OF (1)
3 CHARLIE BERRY-C (2)
4 LU BLUE-1B
5 JACKIE HAYES-2B/INF
6 BILL CISSELL-SS (1)
6 JOHNNY HODAPP-UTIL (2)
7 CAREY SELPH-3B/2B
8 LUKE (OLD ACHES & PAINS) APPLING-SS/INF
9 BRUCE (SOUPY) CAMPBELL-OF (1)
9* PETE DAGLIA-P*
12 LEW FONSECA (INJ)-OF/P/MGR
13 BOB (FATS) FOTHERGILL-OF
14 JOHNNY (LEFTY) WATWOOD-OF (1)
14 PHIL GALLIVAN-P
14 ART EVANS-P
14 JACK ROTHROCK-UTIL (2)
15 PAT CARAWAY-P
15 CHARLIE BIGGS-P
15 ARCHIE WISE-P
16 TED LYONS-P
17 TOMMY THOMAS-P (1)
17 BILL CHAMBERLAIN-P
18 VIC FRASIER-P
18 ED WALSH-P
19 RED FABER-P

1933

6TH 67-83 31GB

1 LEW FONSECA (INJ)-1B/MGR
2 JACKIE HAYES-2B
3 RED KRESS-1B/OF
4 LUKE (OLD ACHES & PAINS) APPLING-SS
5 AL (BUCKETFOOT AL) SIMMONS-OF
6 MULE HAAS-OF
7 JIMMY DYKES-3B
8 CHARLIE ENGLISH-2B
8 LIZ FUNK-OF
9 EVAR SWANSON-OF
12 HAL RHYNE-INF
14 FRANK (HANS) GRUBE-C
15 CHARLIE BERRY-C
16 TED LYONS-P
17 JOHN STONEHAM-OF
17 ED (BULL) DURHAM-P
18 RED FABER-P
19 VIC FRASIER-P (1)
19 WHIT WYATT-P (2)
23 MILT GASTON-P
24 PAUL (POP) GREGORY-P
24 HAL HAID-P
25 JOE HEVING-P
27 MILT BOCEK-OF
28 SAD SAM JONES-P
29 CHAD KIMSEY-P
34 IRA HUTCHINSON-P
34 EARL WEBB-OF/1B (2)
35 LES (TOOTS) TIETJE-P
35 GEORGE (SMILER) MURRAY-P
36 BILLY SULLIVAN (INJ)-1B/C
37 JIMMY (PEPPER) AUSTIN-CH
38 JAKE MILLER-P
__ MEM LOVETT-PH (1G: 9/4)

1934

8TH 53-99 47GB

1 LEW FONSECA-MGR1
1 ED MADJESKI-C (2)
2 JACKIE HAYES (INJ)-2B
3 ZEKE BONURA-1B
4 LUKE (OLD ACHES & PAINS) APPLING-SS/2B
5 JIMMY DYKES-3B/INF/MGR2
6 MULE HAAS-OF
7 AL (BUCKETFOOT AL) SIMMONS-OF
8 JOHNNY PASEK-C
8 JOCKO CONLAN-OF
9 EVAR SWANSON-OF
9 RIP RADCLIFF-OF
12 JOE CHAMBERLAIN-SS/3B
14 RED KRESS-2B (1)
14 BOB BOKEN-2B/SS (2)
15 MERV SHEA-C
16 TED LYONS-P
(17) ED (BULL) DURHAM (ILL)-(P)
17 HARRY (SLIM) KINZY-P
18 GEORGE (MOOSE) EARNSHAW-P
19 WHIT WYATT-P
19 HUGO (DUTCH) KLAERNER-P
21 LES (TOOTS) TIETJE-P
22 PHIL GALLIVAN-P
23 MILT GASTON-P
24 MONTY (GANDER) STRATTON-P
24 VERN KENNEDY-P
25 JOE HEVING-P
27 LEE STINE-P
27 MARTY HOPKINS, 3B (2)
28 SAD SAM JONES-P
28 JOHN POMORSKI-P
34 FRENCHY BORDAGARAY-OF
34 CHARLIE UHLIR-OF
36 MARK MAULDIN-3B
36 FRENCHY UHALT-OF
37 JIMMY (PEPPER) AUSTIN-CH
38 LES (TOOTS) TIETJE-P
47 MILT BOCEK-OF
48 PHIL GALLIVAN-P
49 MUDDY RUEL-C
__ GEORGE (SIDEL) CAITHAMER-C (5G: 9/17-30)
__ BILL (DUTCH) FEHRING-C (1G: 6/25)

1935

4TH 74-78 19.5GB

2 JACKIE HAYES-2B
3 ZEKE BONURA-1B
4 LUKE (OLD ACHES & PAINS) APPLING-SS
5 JIMMY DYKES-3B/INF/MGR
6 MULE HAAS (INJ)-OF
7 AL (BUCKETFOOT AL) SIMMONS-OF
8 JOCKO CONLAN-OF
9 RIP RADCLIFF-OF
11 JOHN (SILENT JOHN) WHITEHEAD-P
12 GEORGE (VERN) WASHINGTON-OF
14 LUKE SEWELL-C
15 MERV SHEA-C
16 TED LYONS-P
17 SAD SAM JONES-P
18? GEORGE (MOOSE) EARNSHAW-P (1) (3G: 4/20-5/15)
19 LES (TOOTS) TIETJE-P
20 JOE (SANDY) VANCE-P
22 BILLY WEBB-CH
23 MILT GASTON-P
24 VERN KENNEDY-P
25 LEE STINE-P
25 CARL FISCHER-P (2)
27 MARTY HOPKINS-3B/2B (2)
28 GLENN (BUCKSHOT) WRIGHT-2B
29 RAY PHELPS-P
33 JIMMY (PEPPER) AUSTIN-CH
34 JOHN (SILENT JOHN) WHITEHEAD-P
35 FRANK (HANS) GRUBE-C (2)
36 MONTY (GANDER) STRATTON-P
37 TONY PIET-2B/3B (2)
38 MUDDY RUEL-CH
45 FRED TAUBY-OF
48 JACK SALVESON-P (2)
__ ITALO (CHILLY) (LEFTY) CHELINI-P (2G: 9/12-13)
__ BUD HAFEY-PR (1) (2G: 4/21,5/4)
__ MIKE KREEVICH-3B (6G: 9/24-29)

1936

3RD 81-70 20GB

2 TONY PIET-2B/3B
3 ZEKE BONURA-1B
4 LUKE (OLD ACHES & PAINS) APPLING-SS
5 JIMMY DYKES-3B/MGR
6 MULE HAAS-OF/1B
7 GEORGE STUMPF-OF
7 DIXIE (THE PEOPLE'S CHERCE) WALKER (INJ)-OF (2)
8 MIKE KREEVICH-OF
9 RIP RADCLIFF-OF
12 GEORGE (VERN) WASHINGTON-OF
12 LARRY ROSENTHAL-OF
14 LUKE SEWELL-C
15 MERV SHEA-C
16 TED LYONS-P
17 LES (TOOTS) TIETJE-P (1)
17 SUGAR CAIN-P (2)
18 BILL DIETRICH-P (3)
19 WHIT WYATT-P
19 LES ROCK-1B
20 JOHN (SILENT JOHN) WHITEHEAD-P
22 BILLY WEBB-CH
24 VERN KENNEDY-P
25 MONTY (GANDER) STRATTON-P
26 CLINT BROWN-P
27 JO-JO MORRISEY (INJ)-INF
28 RED EVANS-P
29 RAY PHELPS-P
29 BILL SHORES-P
30 ITALO (CHILLY) (LEFTY) CHELINI-P
32 JIMMY (PEPPER) AUSTIN-CH
34 JOHN (SILENT JOHN) WHITEHEAD-P
35 FRANK (HANS) GRUBE-C (2)
37 JACKIE HAYES-2B
38 MUDDY RUEL-CH
45 DIXIE (THE PEOPLE'S CHERCE) WALKER (INJ)-OF (2)
47 ITALO (CHILLY) (LEFTY) CHELINI-P

1937

3RD 86-68 16GB

2 TONY PIET-3B/2B
3 ZEKE BONURA-1B
4 LUKE (OLD ACHES & PAINS) APPLING-SS
5 JIMMY DYKES-1B/3B/MGR
6 MULE HAAS-1B/OF
7 DIXIE (THE PEOPLE'S CHERCE) WALKER-OF
8 MIKE KREEVICH-OF
9 RIP RADCLIFF-OF
12 LARRY ROSENTHAL (INJ)-OF
14 LUKE SEWELL-C
15 MERV SHEA-C
16 TED LYONS-P
17 SUGAR CAIN-P
18 BILL DIETRICH-P
19 BOZE BERGER-INF
22 BILLY WEBB-CH
24 VERN KENNEDY-P
25 MONTY (GANDER) STRATTON-P
26 CLINT BROWN-P
27 THORNTON LEE-P
28 JOHN (SILENT JOHN) WHITEHEAD-P
29 JOHNNY RIGNEY-P
30 ITALO (CHILLY) (LEFTY) CHELINI-P
32 JIMMY (PEPPER) AUSTIN-CH
34 JOHN (SILENT JOHN) WHITEHEAD-P
35 TONY (PUG) RENSA-C
37 JACKIE HAYES-2B
38 MUDDY RUEL-CH
44 MERV CONNORS-3B
45 GEORGE GICK-P
46 HANK STEINBACHER-OF
66 BILL COX-P

1938

6TH 65-83 32GB

2 MARV (FRECK) OWEN-3B
3 JOE KUHEL-1B
4 LUKE (OLD ACHES & PAINS) APPLING-SS
5 JIMMY DYKES-2B/3B/MGR
6* GENE FORD-P*
6 TOMMY THOMPSON-1B
7 GEE WALKER-OF
8 MIKE KREEVICH-OF
9 RIP RADCLIFF-OF/1B
12 LARRY ROSENTHAL-OF
14 LUKE SEWELL-C
15 MIKE TRESH-C
16 TED LYONS-P
17 SUGAR CAIN-P
17 GEORGE MEYER-2B
18 MERV CONNORS-1B
18 BILL DIETRICH (INJ)-P
19 BOZE BERGER-INF
21 JOHN (SILENT JOHN) WHITEHEAD-P
22 BILLY WEBB-CH
22 BOB (LEFTY) UHL-P
24 BILL COX-P (1)
24 JACK KNOTT-P (2)
25 MONTY (GANDER) STRATTON (INJ)-P
26 CLINT BROWN (INJ)-P
26 HARRY (STRETCH) BOYLES-P
27 THORNTON LEE-P
28 JESSE LANDRUM-2B
29 JOHNNY RIGNEY-P
30 GEORGE GICK-P
33 JIMMY (PEPPER) AUSTIN-CH
34 JOHN (SILENT JOHN) WHITEHEAD-P
35 TONY (PUG) RENSA-C
36 NORM (DUKE) SCHLUETER-C
37 JACKIE HAYES (INJ)-2B
38 MUDDY RUEL-CH

CHICAGO WHITE SOX

45 FRANK (THE GREAT GABBO) GABLER-P (2)
45 JOE (SMOKEY JOE) MARTIN -PR
46 HANK STEINBACHER-OF
47 BOB (LEFTY) UHL-P
47 JOHN GERLACH-SS
48 GEORGE GICK-P

1939

4TH 85-69 22.5GB

2 MARV (FRECK) OWEN-3B
2 BOB KENNEDY-3B
3 JOE KUHEL-1B
4 LUKE (OLD ACHES & PAINS) APPLING (INJ)-SS
5 JIMMY DYKES-3B/MGR
6* EDDIE SMITH-P* (2)
7 GEE WALKER-OF
8 MIKE KREEVICH-OF/3B
9 RIP RADCLIFF-OF/1B
12 LARRY ROSENTHAL-OF
14 VALLIE (CHIEF) EAVES-P
14 JOHNNY (FOOTSIE) MARCUM-P (2)
14 KEN SILVESTRI-C
15 VIC FRASIER (INJ)-P
15 MIKE TRESH-C
16 TED LYONS-P
17 ART HERRING-P
17 JOHN GERLACH-3B
18 BILL DIETRICH-P
19 HARRY (STRETCH) BOYLES-P
22 BILLY WEBB-CH
23 EDDIE SMITH-P (2)
24 JACK KNOTT-P
25 MONTY (GANDER) STRATTON-CH
26 CLINT BROWN-P
27 THORNTON LEE-P
28 OLLIE BEJMA-2B/INF
28 JOHN (SILENT JOHN) WHITEHEAD-P (1)
29 JOHNNY RIGNEY-P
30 JESS DOBERNIC-P
33? JIMMY (PEPPER) AUSTIN-CH
34 JOHN (SILENT JOHN) WHITEHEAD-P (1)
34 JOHNNY (FOOTSIE) MARCUM-P (2)
35 TONY (PUG) RENSA-C
36 NORM (DUKE) SCHLUETER-C
37 JACKIE HAYES (INJ)-2B
37 JOHN GERLACH-3B
38 MUDDY RUEL-CH
45 VIC FRASIER (INJ)-P
46 HANK STEINBACHER-OF
47 ERIC (BOOB) MCNAIR-INF
48 JESS DOBERNIC-P
48 VALLIE (CHIEF) EAVES-P

1940

4TH (TIE) 82-72 8GB

2 JACKIE HAYES (INJ)-2B
3 JOE KUHEL-1B
4 LUKE (OLD ACHES & PAINS) APPLING-SS
5 JIMMY DYKES-MGR
6 TAFT (TAFFY) WRIGHT-OF
7 ERIC (BOOB) MCNAIR-2B/3B
8 MIKE KREEVICH-OF
9 MOOSE SOLTERS-OF
10 PETE (JAKE) (AKA JABLONOWSKI) APPLETON-P
11 ORVAL GROVE-P
12 LARRY ROSENTHAL-OF
14 KEN SILVESTRI-C
15 MIKE TRESH-C
16 TED LYONS-P
17 TOM TURNER-C
18 BILL DIETRICH-P
19 ED WEILAND-P
22 MULE HAAS-CH
23 EDDIE SMITH-P
24 JACK KNOTT-P
25 MONTY (GANDER) STRATTON-CH
26 CLINT BROWN-P
27 THORNTON LEE-P
28 VALLIE (CHIEF) EAVES-P
28 JACK HALLETT-P
29 JOHNNY RIGNEY-P
33? JIMMY (PEPPER) AUSTIN-CH
36 BOB KENNEDY-3B
37 SKEETER WEBB-2B/INF
38 MUDDY RUEL-CH
45 ORVAL GROVE-P
46 EDDIE SMITH-P
47 DON (BUTCH) (CAB) KOLLOWAY-2B
48 PETE (JAKE) (AKA JABLONOWSKI) APPLETON-P
__ DAVE SHORT-PH (4G: 9/16-21)

1941

3RD 77-77 24GB

2 BILL KNICKERBOCKER-2B
3 JOE KUHEL-1B
4 LUKE (OLD ACHES & PAINS) APPLING-SS
5 JIMMY DYKES-MGR
6 TAFT (TAFFY) WRIGHT-OF
7 DARIO LODIGIANI-3B
8 MIKE KREEVICH-OF
9 MOOSE SOLTERS (INJ)-OF
12 LARRY ROSENTHAL-OF (1)
12 BILL KNICKERBOCKER-2B
14 GEORGE (SKEETS) DICKEY-C
15 MIKE TRESH-C
16 TED LYONS-P
17 TOM TURNER-C
18 BILL DIETRICH-P
19 BUCK ROSS-P (2)
20 PETE (JAKE) (AKA JABLONOWSKI) APPLETON-P
21 EDDIE SMITH-P
22 ORVAL GROVE-P
22 MULE HAAS-CH
23 JOE HAYNES-P
23 DAVE SHORT (MIL)-OF
24 MYRIL HOAG-OF (2)
25 MONTY (GANDER) STRATTON-CH
26 JOHNNY HUMPHRIES (INJ)-P
27 THORNTON LEE-P
28 JACK HALLETT-P
29 JOHNNY RIGNEY-P
35 JOE HAYNES-P
36 BOB KENNEDY-3B
37 SKEETER WEBB-INF
38 MUDDY RUEL-CH
42 CHET HAJDUK-PH
45 BEN CHAPMAN-OF (2)
45 ORVAL GROVE-P
46 EDDIE SMITH-P
47 DON (BUTCH) (CAB) KOLLOWAY-2B/1B
48 PETE (JAKE) (AKA JABLONOWSKI) APPLETON-P
49 DAVE PHILLEY-OF
__ STAN (STASH) GOLETZ-PH (5G: 9/9-28)
__ JAKE JONES-1B (3G: 9/20-28)

1942

6TH 66-82 34GB

2 VAL HEIM (MIL)-OF
3 JOE KUHEL-1B
4 LUKE (OLD ACHES & PAINS) APPLING-SS
5 JIMMY DYKES-MGR
6 TAFT (TAFFY) WRIGHT-OF
7 DARIO LODIGIANI-3B/2B
8 MYRIL HOAG-OF
9 WALLY MOSES-OF
12 BUD SKETCHLEY-OF
14 GEORGE (SKEETS) DICKEY (MIL)-C
15 MIKE TRESH-C
16 TED LYONS-P
17 TOM TURNER-C
18 BILL DIETRICH-P
19 BUCK ROSS-P
20 JIMMY GRANT-3B
22 MULE HAAS-CH
24 JAKE (WHISTLIN' JAKE) WADE-P
25 BOB KENNEDY-3B
26 JOHNNY HUMPHRIES (INJ)-P
27 THORNTON LEE-P
29 JOHNNY RIGNEY (MIL)-P
33 BING MILLER-CH
34 SAMMY WEST-OF
34 LEN PERME-P
35 JOE HAYNES-P
36 LEO WELLS-SS/3B
37 SKEETER WEBB-2B
38 MUDDY RUEL-CH
39 ED WEILAND-P
45 ORVAL GROVE-P
46 EDDIE SMITH-P
47 DON (BUTCH) (CAB) KOLLOWAY-2B/1B
48 PETE (JAKE) (AKA JABLONOWSKI) APPLETON-P (1)
__ JAKE JONES (MIL)-1B (7G: 4/26-5/10)
__ BILL (HAWK) MUELLER-OF (26G: 8/29-9/27)
__ THURMAN (JOE E.) TUCKER-OF (7G: 4/14-30)

1943

4TH 82-72 16GB

2 SKEETER WEBB-2B
3 JOE KUHEL-1B
4 LUKE (OLD ACHES & PAINS) APPLING-SS
5 JIMMY DYKES-MGR
6 MOOSE SOLTERS-OF
7 JIMMY GRANT-3B (1)
8 THURMAN (JOE E.) TUCKER-OF
9 WALLY MOSES-OF
12 GUY CURTRIGHT-OF
14 VINCE CASTINO-C
15 MIKE TRESH-C
17 TOM TURNER-C
18 BILL DIETRICH-P
19 BUCK ROSS-P
22 MULE HAAS-CH
24 JAKE (WHISTLIN' JAKE) WADE-P
25 RALPH HODGIN-3B/OF
26 JOHNNY HUMPHRIES (INJ)-P
27 THORNTON LEE-P
28 DICK CULLER-INF
29 FLOYD SPEER-P
29 CASS (AKA KWIETNIEWSKI) MICHAELS-3B
33 BING MILLER-CH
34 DON HANSKI-1B/P
35 JOE HAYNES-P
36 FRANK (FATS) KALIN (MIL)-PH
37 GORDON (MALTZY) MALTZBERGER-P
38 MUDDY RUEL-CH
45 ORVAL GROVE-P
46 EDDIE SMITH-P
47 DON (BUTCH) (CAB) KOLLOWAY (MIL)-2B
47 TONY (COOCH) (CHICK) CUCCINELLO-3B (2)
48 BILL SWIFT-P

1944

7TH 71-83 18GB

2 SKEETER WEBB-SS/2B
4 GREY (NOISY) CLARKE-3B
5 JIMMY DYKES-MGR
6 HAL TROSKY-1B
6 ROY SCHALK-2B/SS
7 ROY SCHALK-2B/SS
7 HAL TROSKY-1B
8 THURMAN (JOE E.) TUCKER-OF
9 WALLY MOSES-OF
12 GUY CURTRIGHT-OF
14 VINCE CASTINO-C
15 MIKE TRESH-C
17 TOM TURNER-C (1)
17 TOM JORDAN-C
18 BILL DIETRICH-P
19 BUCK ROSS-P
22 MULE HAAS-CH
24 EDDIE (LEFTY) CARNETT-OF/1B/P
25 RALPH HODGIN-3B/OF
26 JOHNNY HUMPHRIES-P
27 THORNTON LEE (INJ)-P
28 MYRIL HOAG-OF (1)
28 CASS (AKA KWIETNIEWSKI) MICHAELS-SS/3B
29 CASS (AKA KWIETNIEWSKI) MICHAELS-SS/3B
29 BILL METZIG-2B
33 BING MILLER-CH
34 DON HANSKI-P
35 JOE HAYNES-P
36 JOHNNY (UGLY) DICKSHOT-OF
37 GORDON (MALTZY) MALTZBERGER (INJ)-P
38 MUDDY RUEL-CH
39 FLOYD SPEER-P
45 ORVAL GROVE-P
46 JAKE (WHISTLIN' JAKE) WADE-P
47 TONY (COOCH) (CHICK) CUCCINELLO-3B/2B
48 ED LOPAT-P

1945

6TH 71-78 15GB

2 DANNY (SQUIRREL) REYNOLDS-SS/2B
3 JOE ORENGO-3B/2B
4 KERBY FARRELL-1B
4 LUKE (OLD ACHES & PAINS) APPLING-SS
5 JIMMY DYKES-MGR
6 ROY SCHALK-2B
7 BILL NAGEL-1B/3B
8 FLOYD BAKER-3B/2B
9 WALLY MOSES-OF
12 GUY CURTRIGHT-OF
14 VINCE CASTINO-C
15 MIKE TRESH-C
17 FRANK (PAP) PAPISH-P
18 BILL DIETRICH (INJ)-P
19 BUCK ROSS-P
22 MULE HAAS-CH
23 JOHNNY (SWEDE) JOHNSON-P
25 ORIS (BROWN) HOCKETT-OF
26 JOHNNY HUMPHRIES-P
27 THORNTON LEE-P
28 CASS (AKA KWIETNIEWSKI) MICHAELS-SS/2B
33 BING MILLER-CH
34 BILL (HAWK) MUELLER (MIL)-OF
35 JOE HAYNES (INJ)-P
36 JOHNNY (UGLY) DICKSHOT-OF
37 CLAY TOUCHSTONE-P
38 MUDDY RUEL-CH
45 ORVAL GROVE-P
46 EARL (TEACH) CALDWELL-P
47 TONY (COOCH) (CHICK) CUCCINELLO-3B
48 ED LOPAT-P

1946

5TH 74-80 30GB

2 THURMAN (JOE E.) TUCKER-OF
3 JAKE JONES (INJ)-1B
4 LUKE (OLD ACHES & PAINS) APPLING-SS
5 JIMMY DYKES-MGR1
5 WHITEY PLATT-OF
5 BOB KENNEDY-OF/3B
6 TAFT (TAFFY) WRIGHT (ILL)-OF
7 HAL TROSKY (ILL)-1B
7 CASS (AKA KWIETNIEWSKI) MICHAELS-INF
8 FLOYD BAKER-3B
8 RALPH (BRUZ) HAMNER-P
8 FRANKIE (BLIMP) HAYES-C (2)
9 WALLY MOSES-OF (1)
9 DAVE PHILLEY-OF
12 GUY CURTRIGHT-OF
14 JOE KUHEL-1B (2)
15 MIKE TRESH-C
16 TED LYONS-P/MGR2
17 FRANK (PAP) PAPISH-P
18 BILL DIETRICH (INJ)-P
18 EDDIE SMITH-P
19 GEORGE (SKEETS) DICKEY-C
22 MULE HAAS-CH
22 BUSTER MILLS-CH
23 WHITEY PLATT-OF
23 URBAN FABER-CH
24 RALPH HODGIN-OF
25 ED FERNANDES-C
25 AL HOLLINGSWORTH-P
26 TOM JORDAN (INJ)-C (1)
26 RALPH (BRUZ) HAMNER-P
26 FRANKIE (BLIMP) HAYES-C (2)
27 ED FERNANDES-C
27 THORNTON LEE (INJ)-P
28 CASS (AKA KWIETNIEWSKI) MICHAELS-INF
29 JOHNNY RIGNEY (INJ)-P
33 BING MILLER-CH
34 LEN PERME-P
34 FRANK (HOOKER) WHITMAN-SS
35 JOE HAYNES-P
36 BOB KENNEDY-OF/3B
37 LEO WELLS-3B/SS
38 GORDON (MALTZY)

MALTZBERGER (MIL)-P (2)
38 DAVE PHILLEY-OF
38 EMMETT (PINKY) O'NEILL-P (2)
38 GORDON (MALTZY) MALTZBERGER (MIL)-P (2)
39 DARIO LODIGIANI (INJ)-3B
45 ORVAL GROVE-P
46 EARL (TEACH) CALDWELL-P
47 DON (BUTCH) (CAB) KOLLOWAY-2B/3B
48 ED LOPAT-P
49 EDDIE SMITH-P
59 AL (BOOTS) HOLLINGSWORTH-P
__ JOE SMAZA-OF (2G: 9/18-21)

1947

6TH 70-84 27GB

2 THURMAN (JOE E.) TUCKER-OF
3 JAKE JONES-1B (1)
3 RUDY YORK-1B (2)
4 LUKE (OLD ACHES & PAINS) APPLING-SS/3B
5 BOB KENNEDY-OF/3B
6 TAFT (TAFFY) WRIGHT-OF
7 CASS (AKA KWIETNIEWSKI) MICHAELS-INF
8 FLOYD BAKER-3B/INF
9 DAVE PHILLEY-OF/3B
12 JACK WALLAESA-UTIL
14 JOE KUHEL-PH
15 MIKE TRESH-C
16 TED LYONS-MGR
17 FRANK (PAP) PAPISH-P
18 EDDIE SMITH-P (1)
19 GEORGE (SKEETS) DICKEY-C
22 BUSTER (BUS) MILLS-CH
23 URBAN (RED) FABER-CH
24 LOYD CHRISTOPHER-OF
25 RALPH HODGIN (INJ)-OF
26 JOE STEPHENSON-C
27 THORNTON LEE-P
28 PETE GEBRIAN-P
29 JOHNNY RIGNEY-P
33 BING MILLER-CH
34 RED RUFFING (INJ)-P
35 JOE HAYNES-P
36 BOB (BUNCH) GILLESPIE-P
37 GORDON (MALTZY) MALTZBERGER(MIL)-P
45 ORVAL GROVE-P
46 EARL (TEACH) CALDWELL-P
47 DON (BUTCH) (CAB) KOLLOWAY-2B/INF
48 ED LOPAT-P
49 EARL (IRISH) HARRIST-P
__ HI BITHORN-P (2G: 5/2-4)

1948

8TH 51-101 44.5GB

2 HERB ADAMS-OF
2 JIM DELSING-OF
3 TONY LUPIEN-1B
4 LUKE (OLD ACHES & PAINS) APPLING-3B/SS
5 BOB KENNEDY-OF (1)
5 PAT SEEREY-OF (2)
6 TAFT (TAFFY) WRIGHT-OF
7 CASS (AKA KWIETNIEWSKI) MICHAELS-SS/UTIL
8 FLOYD BAKER-INF
9 DAVE PHILLEY-OF
12 JACK WALLAESA-SS/OF
14 JERRY SCALA-OF
14 MARINO (CHICK) PIERETTI-P (2)
15 MIKE TRESH-C
16 TED LYONS-MGR
17 FRANK (PAP) PAPISH-P
18 AARON ROBINSON-C
18 RANDY GUMPERT-P (2)
19 IKE PEARSON-P
22 BUSTER (BUS) MILLS-CH
23 URBAN (RED) FABER-CH
24 RANDY GUMPERT-P (2)
24 AL GETTEL-P (2)
25 RALPH HODGIN-OF
26 RALPH (WIG) WEIGEL-C/OF
28 AL GETTEL-P (2)
29 BILL (LEFTY) WIGHT-P
33 BING MILLER-CH
35 JOE HAYNES-P
36 BOB (BUNCH) GILLESPIE-P
37 JIM GOODWIN-P
37 MARV (ROTTY) ROTBLATT-P
38 IKE PEARSON-P
38 GLEN MOULDER-P
39 FRED BRADLEY-P
45 ORVAL GROVE-P
46 EARL (TEACH) CALDWELL-P (1)
47 DON (BUTCH) (CAB) KOLLOWAY-2B/3B
47 AL GETTEL-P (2)
48 HOWIE JUDSON-P
49 EARL (IRISH) HARRIST-P (1)
49 MARINO (CHICK) PIERETTI-P (2)
__ FRANK (HOOKER) WHITMAN-SS (3G: 9/22-28)

1949

6TH 63-91 34GB

2 JERRY SCALA-OF
2 BOBBY (ROCKY) RHAWN-3B/SS (3)
2 JOHN OSTROWSKI-OF/3B
3 STEVE (BUD) SOUCHOCK-OF/1B
4 LUKE (OLD ACHES & PAINS) APPLING-SS
5 PAT SEEREY-OF
6 GUS (OZARK IKE) ZERNIAL-OF
7 CASS (AKA KWIETNIEWSKI) MICHAELS-2B
8 FLOYD BAKER-3B/INF
9 DAVE PHILLEY-OF
12 BILLY BOWERS-OF
12 DICK LANE-OF
12 MICKEY HAEFNER-P (2)
14 MARINO (CHICK) PIERETTI-P
15 JOE TIPTON-C
16 MAX SURKONT-P
18 RANDY GUMPERT-P
19 BILLY PIERCE-P
22 BUSTER (BUS) MILLS-CH
23 JACK ONSLOW-MGR
24 ROCKY KRSNICH-2B
24 HERB ADAMS (INJ)-OF
25 GORDON GOLDSBERRY-1B
25 CHARLIE (CHUCK) KRESS-1B (2)
26 EARL RAPP-OF (2)
26 FRED HANCOCK-UTIL
28 AL GETTEL-P (1)
28 EDDIE MALONE-C
29 BILL (LEFTY) WIGHT-P
33 BING MILLER-CH
34 ALEX (MEX) CARRASQUEL-P
35 EDDIE (SPECS) (BABE) KLIEMAN-P (2)
36 ERNIE GROTH-P
36 GEORGE (CATFISH) METKOVICH-OF
38 DON (SCOTT) WHEELER-C
39 FRED BRADLEY-P
39 EDDIE (SPECS) (BABE) KLIEMAN-P (2)
44 RAY BERRES-CH
45 ORVAL GROVE-P
45 CLYDE (HARDROCK) SHOUN-P (2)
46 BOB (SARGE) KUZAVA-P
47 DON (BUTCH) (CAB) KOLLOWAY-3B (1)
47 GEORGE (CATFISH) METKOVICH-OF
48 HOWIE JUDSON-P
49 JACK BRUNER-P
56 BILL EVANS-P
56 BOB (SUGAR) CAIN-P
58 ALEX (MEX) CARRASQUEL-P
58 ROCKY KRSNICH-2B
58 GEORGE YANKOWSKI-C
58 EDDIE MALONE-C
58 JIM BAUMER-SS
59 FRED HANCOCK-UTIL
59 BILL HIGDON-OF

1950

6TH 60-94 38GB

2 JOHN OSTROWSKI-OF (1/3)
2 AL KOZAR-2B/3B (2)
2 MIKE MCCORMICK-OF (2)
2 JOHN OSTROWSKI-OF (1/3)
3 MARV (TWITCH) RICKERT-OF/1B (2)
4 LUKE (OLD ACHES & PAINS) APPLING-INF
5 HANK (HEENEY) (HEINE) MAJESKI-3B
6 GUS (OZARK IKE) ZERNIAL-OF
7 CASS (AKA KWIETNIEWSKI) MICHAELS-2B (1)
7* RAY SCARBOROUGH-P* (2)
8 FLOYD BAKER-UTIL
9 DAVE PHILLEY-OF
12 MICKEY HAEFNER-P (1)
14 ED MCGHEE-OF
15 BILL SALKELD-C
15 JACK BRUNER-P (1)
15 JOE KIRRENE-3B
16 GORDON GOLDSBERRY-1B/OF
17 CHICO CARRASQUEL-SS
18 MICKEY HAEFNER-P (1)
18 RANDY GUMPERT-P
19 BILLY PIERCE-P
22 BUSTER (BUS) MILLS-CH
23 JACK ONSLOW-MGR1
24 HERB ADAMS-OF
24 GUS NIARHOS-C (2)
25 CHARLIE (CHUCK) KRESS-1B
25 GORDON GOLDSBERRY-1B/OF
26 NELLIE FOX-2B
28 EDDIE MALONE-C
28 LOU (LENA) KRETLOW-P (2)
29 BILL (LEFTY) WIGHT-P
33 RED CORRIDEN, SR.-MGR2
34 KEN HOLCOMBE-P
34 BILL WILSON-OF
35 BILL (WILD BILL) CONNELLY-P (1)
35 GUS KERIAZAKOS-P
36 JERRY SCALA-OF
38 PHIL MASI-C
39 JERRY SCALA-OF
44 RAY BERRES-CH
45 JOE (STUBBY) ERAUTT-C
46 BOB (SARGE) KUZAVA-P (1)
46 EDDIE ROBINSON-1B (2)
46 RAY SCARBOROUGH-P (2)
47 JIM BUSBY-OF
48 HOWIE JUDSON-P
49 JACK BRUNER-P (1)
49 CHARLIE CUELLAR-P
49 MARV (ROTTY) ROTBLATT-P
56 BOB (SUGAR) CAIN-P
57 JOHN (PERKY) PERKOVICH-P
57 RANDY GUMPERT-P
58 KEN HOLCOMBE-P
59 LUIS (WITTO) ALOMA-P

1951

4TH 81-73 17GB

2 ZEKE ZARILLA-OF
3 JIM BUSBY-OF
5 HANK (HEENEY) (HEINE) MAJESKI-3B (1)
5 BERT HAAS-UTIL
5 BOB (THE ROPE) BOYD-1B
6 GUS (OZARK IKE) ZERNIAL-OF (1)
6 DON (FOOTSIE) LENHARDT-OF/1B (2)
7 BUD STEWART-OF
8 FLOYD BAKER-INF
9 DAVE PHILLEY-OF (1)
9 MINNIE MINOSO-OF/INF (2)
12 HARRY DORISH-P
14 JOE (OATS) DEMAESTRI-INF
15 PAUL (PEANUTS) (GULLIVER) LEHNER-OF (2)
16 BOB MAHONEY-P
16 RED WILSON-C
17 CHICO CARRASQUEL-SS
18 RANDY GUMPERT-P
19 BILLY PIERCE-P
22 PAUL RICHARDS-MGR
23 LOU (LENA) KRETLOW-P
24 GUS NIARHOS (INJ)-C
25 GORDON GOLDSBERRY-1B
25 BOB (DUKE) DILLINGER-3B
26 NELLIE FOX-2B
27 ROSS GRIMSLEY I-P
27 HAL (SKINNY) BROWN-P
27 SAMMY HAIRSTON-C
28 DOC (FLIT) CRAMER-CH
29 JOE (BURRHEAD) DOBSON-P
33 JIMMY (CHOPPY) ADAIR-CH
34 KEN HOLCOMBE-P
35 SAUL ROGOVIN-P (2)
36 PHIL MASI-C
37 ROCKY NELSON-PH (3)
38 PHIL MASI-C
39 RAY COLEMAN-OF
39 DICK LITTLEFIELD-P
40 LUM HARRIS-CH
44 RAY BERRES-CH
45 BUD SHEELY-C
45 JOE (STUBBY) ERAUTT-C
46 EDDIE ROBINSON-1B
48 HOWIE JUDSON-P
49 MARV (ROTTY) ROTBLATT-P
56 BOB (SUGAR) CAIN-P (1)
59 LUIS (WITTO) ALOMA (INJ)-P

1952

3RD 81-73 14GB

2 ZEKE ZARILLA-OF (1)
3 JIM BUSBY-OF (1)
3 LEO (TOMMY) THOMAS-3B (2)
3 SAMMY ESPOSITO (MIL)-SS
5 GEORGE (TEDDY) WILSON-OF (1)
5 TOM WRIGHT-OF (2)
6 ROCKY KRSNICH-3B
6 BUD SHEELY-C
7 BUD STEWART-OF
8 SAM (BLACKIE) DENTE-UTIL
9 MINNIE MINOSO-OF/INF
12 HARRY DORISH-P
13 MARV GRISSOM-P
14 SAM MELE-OF/1B (2)
15 BUD SHEELY-C
15 BILL (LEFTY) KENNEDY-P
16 MARV GRISSOM-P
16 JOE (BURRHEAD) DOBSON-P
17 CHICO CARRASQUEL (INJ)-SS
18 CHUCK STOBBS-P
19 BILLY PIERCE-P
22 PAUL RICHARDS-MGR
23 LOU (LENA) KRETLOW-P
24 HAL (BUD) (LEFTY) HUDSON-P (2)
25 DON NICHOLAS-PH
26 NELLIE FOX-2B
27 HAL (SKINNY) BROWN-P
28 DOC (FLIT) CRAMER-CH
29 JOE (BURRHEAD) DOBSON-P
33 JIMMY (CHOPPY) ADAIR-CH
34 KEN HOLCOMBE-P (1)
34 KEN (RED) LANDENBERGER-1B
35 SAUL ROGOVIN-P
36 HECTOR RODRIGUEZ-3B
37 BILL (LEFTY) KENNEDY-P
37 AL WIDMAR-P
38 PHIL MASI-C
38 HANK EDWARDS-OF (2)
39 RAY COLEMAN-OF (1)
39 JIM (JUNGLE JIM) RIVERA-OF (2)
40 LUM HARRIS-CH
44 RAY BERRES-CH
45 SHERM LOLLAR-C
46 EDDIE ROBINSON-1B
47 AL WIDMAR-P
47 DARRELL JOHNSON-C (2)
48 HOWIE JUDSON-P
49 WILLIE MIRANDA-INF (1/3)
56 DON NICHOLAS-PH
57 GEORGE (TEDDY) WILSON-OF (1)
59 LUIS (WITTO) ALOMA (INJ)-P
__ RED WILSON-C (2G: 9/24-28)

1953

3RD 89-65 11.5GB

2 NELLIE FOX-2B
3 VERN (BUSTER) (JUNIOR) STEPHENS-3B/SS (1)
3 CONNIE RYAN-3B (2)
5 SAM MELE-OF/1B
6 ROCKY KRSNICH-3B
7 JIM (JUNGLE JIM) RIVERA-OF
8 FERRIS (BURRHEAD) FAIN-1B
9 MINNIE MINOSO-OF/3B
10 SHERM LOLLAR-C
11 LUIS (WITTO) ALOMA-P
12 HARRY DORISH-P
14 SAUL ROGOVIN (INJ)-P
15 BOB (SMILEY) KEEGAN (INJ)-P
16 MIKE FORNIELES-P
17 CHICO CARRASQUEL-SS
18 ALLIE CLARK-OF/1B (2)
18 CONNIE JOHNSON-P
19 BILLY PIERCE-P
20 SAM (BLACKIE) DENTE-SS
20 SANDY CONSUEGRA-P (2)
21 BUD STEWART (ILL)-OF

22 PAUL RICHARDS-MGR
23 LOU (LENA) KRETLOW-P (1)
23 BOB (MR. TEAM) ELLIOTT-3B/OF (2)
23 VIRGIL (FIRE) TRUCKS-P (2)
24 CONNIE JOHNSON-P
25 FREDDIE MARSH-INF
26 RED WILSON-C
27 TOMMY BYRNE-P (1)
27 VIRGIL (FIRE) TRUCKS-P (2)
27 BOB (MR. TEAM) ELLIOTT-3B/OF (2)
28 DOC (FLIT) CRAMER-CH
29 JOE (BURRHEAD) DOBSON-P
30 BUD SHEELY-C
31 BOB (THE ROPE) BOYD-1B/OF
32 TOM WRIGHT-OF
34 HAL (BUD) (LEFTY) HUDSON-P
34 NEIL BERRY-2B (2)
35 EARL (IRISH) HARRIST-P (1)
35 SAUL ROGOVIN (INJ)-P
36 GENE BEARDEN-P
38 BILL WILSON-OF
40 LUM HARRIS-CH
44 RAY BERRES-CH
45 CONNIE JOHNSON-P
48 HOWIE JUDSON-P
SAMMY ESPOSITO (MIL)-(SS)
JOE KIRRENE (MIL)-(3B)

1954

3RD 94-60 17GB

1 GEORGE KELL (INJ)-UTIL (2)
2 NELLIE FOX-2B
3 ED MCGHEE-OF (2)
3 GRADY HATTON-3B/1B (2)
5 JOHNNY GROTH-OF
6 CASS (AKA KWIETNIEWSKI) MICHAELS (INJ)-3B/2B
7 JIM (JUNGLE JIM) RIVERA-OF
8 FERRIS (BURRHEAD) FAIN (INJ)-1B
9 MINNIE MINOSO-OF/3B
10 SHERM LOLLAR-C
11 DICK STRAHS-P
12 HARRY DORISH-P
14 CARL (SWATS) SAWATSKI-C
15 BOB (SMILEY) KEEGAN-P
16 MIKE FORNIELES-P
16 BOB (SUGAR) CAIN-P
17 CHICO CARRASQUEL-SS
18 RED WILSON-C (1)
18 MATT BATTS-C (2)
19 BILLY PIERCE-P
20 SANDY CONSUEGRA-P
21 BUD STEWART (ILL)-OF
22 PAUL RICHARDS-MGR1
23 VIRGIL (FIRE) TRUCKS-P
25 FREDDIE MARSH-INF
26 DON JOHNSON-P
27 WILLARD MARSHALL-OF
28 MARTY (SLATS) (THE OCTOPUS) (MR. SHORTSTOP) MARION-CH/MGR2
29 JACK HARSHMAN-P
31 BOB (THE ROPE) BOYD-OF/1B
32 STAN JOK-3B
33 VITO VALENTINETTI-P
33 JOE KIRRENE-3B
35 DICK STRAHS-P
36 AL SIMA-P (1)
36 MORRIE (LEFTY) MARTIN-P (2)
37 RAY BERRES-CH
37 DON NICHOLAS-PH
38 BILL WILSON-OF (1)
39 TOM FLANIGAN-P
40 LUM HARRIS-CH
42 RON JACKSON-1B
44 RAY BERRES-CH
44 PHIL CAVARRETTA-1B/OF
45 CONNIE JOHNSON-P
46 CONNIE JOHNSON-P
48 HOWIE JUDSON-P
48 RON JACKSON-1B

1955

3RD 91-63 5GB

1 GEORGE KELL-3B/UTIL
2 NELLIE FOX-2B
3 JIM BRIDEWESER-INF
4 MARTY (SLATS) (THE OCTOPUS) (MR. SHORTSTOP) MARION-MGR
5 JOHNNY GROTH-OF (1)
5 JIM BUSBY-OF (2)
6 ED MCGHEE-OF
6 RON (ROLLO) NORTHEY-OF
7 JIM (JUNGLE JIM) RIVERA-OF
8 WALT (MOOSE) DROPO-1B
9 MINNIE MINOSO-OF/3B
10 SHERM LOLLAR-C
11 CLINT (SCRAP IRON) COURTNEY-C (1)
11 BUDDY PETERSON-SS
12 HARRY DORISH-P (1)
12 LES MOSS-C (2)
14 DEL (BABE) WILBER-CH
15 BOB (SMILEY) KEEGAN (INJ)-P
16 MIKE FORNIELES-P
16 SAMMY ESPOSITO (MIL)-3B
17 CHICO CARRASQUEL-SS
18 BOB NIEMAN-OF
19 BILLY PIERCE-P
20 SANDY CONSUEGRA-P
21 SAMMY ESPOSITO (MIL)-3B
21 LEROY POWELL-PR
21 STAN JOK-3B/OF
22 DICK DONOVAN-P
23 VIRGIL (FIRE) TRUCKS-P
24 AL PAPAI-P
24 BOB KENNEDY-UTIL (2)
25 TED GRAY-P (1)
25 BOBBY ADAMS-3B/2B (2)
26 BOB (CHICK) CHAKALES-P (1)
27 WILLARD MARSHALL-OF
27 ED WHITE-OF
28 BOB (CHICK) CHAKALES-P (1)
28 DIXIE HOWELL-P
29 JACK HARSHMAN-P
30 BOB KENNEDY-UTIL (2)
30 LLOYD (CITATION) MERRIMAN-PH
31 DICK DONOVAN-P
32 HARRY BYRD-P (2)
34 GEORGE (MERCURY) (FOGHORN) (STUD) MYATT-CH
35 EARL BATTEY-C
35 VERN (BUSTER) (JUNIOR) STEPHENS-3B (2)
35 GIL COAN-OF (2)
35 ED MCGHEE-OF
36 MORRIE (LEFTY) MARTIN-P
37 RAY BERRES-CH
39 DON GUTTERIDGE-CH
42 RON JACKSON-1B
44 PHIL CAVARRETTA-1B/OF
44 CONNIE JOHNSON-P
45 EARL BATTEY-C

1956

3RD 85-69 12GB

1 GEORGE KELL-3B/1B (1)
2 NELLIE FOX-2B
3 JIM BRIDEWESER-SS (1)
3 FRED HATFIELD-3B/SS (2)
4 MARTY (SLATS) (THE OCTOPUS) (MR. SHORTSTOP) MARION-MGR
5 BUBBA PHILLIPS-OF/3B
6 RON (ROLLO) NORTHEY-OF
6 DAVE PHILLEY-1B/OF (2)
7 JIM (JUNGLE JIM) RIVERA-OF
8 WALT (MOOSE) DROPO-1B
9 MINNIE MINOSO-OF/INF
10 SHERM LOLLAR-C
11 LUIS APARICIO-SS
12 LES MOSS-C
14 LARRY DOBY-OF
15 BOB (SMILEY) KEEGAN-P
16 MIKE FORNIELES-P (1)
18 BOB NIEMAN-OF (1)
18 JIM (BLACKIE) DERRINGTON-P
19 BILLY PIERCE-P
20 SANDY CONSUEGRA-P (1)
(21) LEROY POWELL (MIL)-(PR)
21 GERRY STALEY-P (2)
22 DICK DONOVAN-P
24 HOWIE POLLET-P (1)
24 GERRY STALEY-P (2)
24 DICK MARLOWE-P
25 CAL ABRAMS-OF
25 JIM DELSING-OF (2)
26 EARL BATTEY-C
27 BILL FISCHER-P
27 ELLIS (OLD FOLKS) KINDER-P (2)
28 DIXIE HOWELL-P
29 JACK HARSHMAN-P
30 BOB KENNEDY-3B (1)
30 JIM WILSON-P (2)
31 JERRY (JOE) DAHLKE-P
31 PAUL (LEFTY) LAPALME-P (3)
32 HARRY BYRD-P
32 RON (ROLLO) NORTHEY-OF
33 DEL (BABE) WILBER-CH
34 GEORGE (MERCURY) (FOGHORN) (STUD) MYATT-CH
36 MORRIE (LEFTY) MARTIN-P (1)
36 JIM (HOT ROD) MCDONALD-P
37 RAY BERRES-CH
39 DON GUTTERIDGE-CH
42 RON JACKSON-1B
44 CONNIE JOHNSON-P (1)
44 GERRY STALEY-P (2)
48 SAMMY ESPOSITO (MIL)-INF
66 GERRY STALEY-P (2)

1957

2ND 90-64 8GB

1 JIM LANDIS-OF
2 NELLIE FOX-2B
3 FRED HATFIELD-3B
4 RON JACKSON-1B
5 BUBBA PHILLIPS-3B/OF
6 DAVE PHILLEY-OF/1B (1)
6* STOVER (SMOKEY) MCILWAIN-P*
7 JIM (JUNGLE JIM) RIVERA-OF/1B
8 WALT (MOOSE) DROPO-1B
9 MINNIE MINOSO-OF/3B
10 SHERM LOLLAR (INJ)-C
11 LUIS APARICIO-SS
12 LES MOSS-C
14 LARRY DOBY-OF
15 BOB (SMILEY) KEEGAN-P
16 BOB KENNEDY-PH (1)
16 TED BEARD-OF
17 LEROY POWELL-PR
17 EARL (THE EARL OF SNOHOMISH) TORGESON-1B/OF (2)
18 JIM (BLACKIE) DERRINGTON-P
19 BILLY PIERCE-P
20 BILL FISCHER-P
21 GERRY STALEY-P
22 DICK DONOVAN-P
26 EARL BATTEY-C
26 DON RUDOLPH-P
27 ELLIS (OLD FOLKS) KINDER-P
27 BARRY LATMAN-P
28 DIXIE HOWELL-P
29 JACK HARSHMAN-P
30 JIM WILSON-P (2)???
31 PAUL (LEFTY) LAPALME-P
32 RON (ROLLO) NORTHEY-PH (1)
32 JIM HUGHES-P
33 TONY (COOCH) (CHICK) CUCCINELLO-CH
34 JOHNNY COONEY-CH
36 JIM (HOT ROD) MCDONALD-P
37 RAY BERRES-CH
39 DON GUTTERIDGE-CH
42 AL LOPEZ-MGR
44 BILL FISCHER-P
48 SAMMY ESPOSITO-INF/OF

1958

2ND 82-72 10GB

1 JIM LANDIS-OF
2 NELLIE FOX-2B
3 TITO FRANCONA-OF (1)
3* HAL (HOOT) TROSKY, JR.-P*
4 RON JACKSON-1B
5 BUBBA PHILLIPS (INJ)-3B/OF
6 BILLY GOODMAN-3B/INF
7 JIM (JUNGLE JIM) RIVERA-OF
8 WALT (MOOSE) DROPO-1B (1)
8 RAY (IKE) BOONE-1B (2)
9 AL (FUZZY) SMITH-OF/3B
9 JOHNNY CALLISON-OF
10 SHERM LOLLAR-C
11 LUIS APARICIO-SS
12 LES MOSS-PH
14 SAMMY ESPOSITO-INF/OF
15 BOB (SMILEY) KEEGAN-P
16 TED BEARD-OF
16 AL (FUZZY) SMITH-OF/3B
17 EARL (THE EARL OF SNOHOMISH) TORGESON-1B
18 BARRY LATMAN-P
19 BILLY PIERCE-P
20 BILL FISCHER-P (1)
20 JOHNNY (HONEY) ROMANO-C
21 GERRY STALEY-P
22 DICK DONOVAN-P
24 EARLY (GUS) WYNN-P
26 EARL BATTEY-C
27 DON RUDOLPH-P
27 TURK LOWN-P (3)
28 DIXIE HOWELL-P
28 STOVER (SMOKEY) MCILWAIN-P
29 RAY (FARMER) MOORE-P
30 JIM WILSON-P (2)
31 NORM CASH-OF
31 TOM (MONEY BAGS) QUALTERS-P (2)
31 CHUCK LINDSTROM-C
32 EARLY (GUS) WYNN-P
32 DON (MANDRAKE THE MAGICIAN) MUELLER-OF
32 BOB SHAW-P (2)
33 TONY (COOCH) (CHICK) CUCCINELLO-CH
34 JOHNNY COONEY-CH
35 BOB SHAW-P (2)
36 JIM (HOT ROD) MCDONALD-P
36 TOM (MONEY BAGS) QUALTERS-P (2)
37 RAY BERRES-CH
39 DON GUTTERIDGE-CH
42 AL LOPEZ-MGR
48 JIM MCANANY-OF

1959

1ST 94-60 0GB

L WS-LAN 4-2

1 JIM LANDIS-OF
2 NELLIE FOX-2B
3 JIM MCANANY-OF
3 DEL ENNIS-OF (2)
3 LOU (THE NERVOUS GREEK) SKIZAS-OF
4 RON JACKSON-1B
5 BUBBA PHILLIPS-3B/OF
6 BILLY GOODMAN-3B/2B
7 JIM (JUNGLE JIM) RIVERA-OF
8 RAY (IKE) BOONE-1B (1)
8 HARRY (SUITCASE) SIMPSON-OF/1B (2)
8 TED (BIG KLU) KLUSZEWSKI-1B (2)
9 JOHNNY CALLISON-OF
10 SHERM LOLLAR-C/1B
11 LUIS APARICIO-SS
12 GARY PETERS-P
14 SAMMY ESPOSITO-INF
15 DON RUDOLPH-P (1)
15 KEN MCBRIDE-P
16 AL (FUZZY) SMITH-OF/3B
17 EARL (THE EARL OF SNOHOMISH) TORGESON-1B
18 BARRY LATMAN-P
19 BILLY PIERCE-P
20 JOHNNY (HONEY) ROMANO-C
21 GERRY STALEY-P
22 DICK DONOVAN-P
24 EARLY (GUS) WYNN-P
25 RUDY ARIAS-P
26 EARL BATTEY-C
27 DON RUDOLPH-P (1)
27 TURK LOWN-P
28 JOE HICKS-OF
28 CLAUDE (FRENCHY) RAYMOND-P
29 RAY (FARMER) MOORE-P
32 DON (MANDRAKE THE MAGICIAN) MUELLER-OF
32 J. C. MARTIN-3B
32 LARRY DOBY-OF/1B (2)
33 TONY (COOCH) (CHICK) CUCCINELLO-CH
34 JOHNNY COONEY-CH
35 BOB SHAW-P
36 JOE STANKA-P
37 RAY BERRES-CH
38 NORM CASH-1B
39 DON GUTTERIDGE-CH

42 AL LOPEZ-MGR
44 CAM CARREON-C
49 RUDY ARIAS-P

1960

3RD 87-67 10GB

1 JIM LANDIS-OF
2 NELLIE FOX-2B
3 JIM MCANANY-PH
3 FLOYD ROBINSON-OF
4 GENE (AUGIE) FREESE-3B
5 ROY (SQUIRREL) SIEVERS-1B/OF
6 BILLY GOODMAN-3B/2B
7 JIM (JUNGLE JIM) RIVERA-OF
8 TED (BIG KLU) KLUSZEWSKI-1B
9 MINNIE MINOSO-OF
10 SHERM LOLLAR-C/1B
11 LUIS APARICIO-SS
12 J. C. MARTIN-3B/1B
14 SAMMY ESPOSITO-INF
15 KEN MCBRIDE-P
16 AL (FUZZY) SMITH-OF
17 EARL (THE EARL OF SNOHOMISH) TORGESON-1B
18 HERB SCORE-P
19 BILLY PIERCE-P
20 DICK BROWN-C
21 GERRY STALEY-P
22 DICK DONOVAN-P
23 GARY PETERS-P
24 EARLY (GUS) WYNN-P
25 MIKE (THE BIG BEAR) GARCIA-P
26 ROY (SQUIRREL) SIEVERS-1B/OF
27 TURK LOWN-P
28 DON FERRARESE-P
28 JOE GINSBERG-C
29 RAY (FARMER) MOORE-P (1)
29 BOB RUSH-P (2)
31 JAKE STRIKER-P
31 RUSS (RUSTY) (DUTCH) KEMMERER-P (2)
31 EARL AVERILL, JR.-C (2)
32 JOE HICKS-OF
33 TONY (COOCH) (CHICK) CUCCINELLO-CH
34 JOHNNY COONEY-CH
35 BOB SHAW-P
36 AL (RED) WORTHINGTON-P (2)
37 RAY BERRES-CH
38 FRANK (THE BEAU) BAUMANN-P
39 DON GUTTERIDGE-CH
40 STAN JOHNSON-OF
42 AL LOPEZ-MGR
44 RUSS (RUSTY) (DUTCH) KEMMERER-P (2)
45 CAM CARREON-C

1961

4TH 86-76 23GB

1 JIM LANDIS-OF
2 NELLIE FOX-2B
3 FLOYD ROBINSON-OF
5 ROY (SQUIRREL) SIEVERS-1B
6 BILLY GOODMAN-INF
7 JIM (JUNGLE JIM) RIVERA-PH (1)
7 ANDY CAREY-3B (2)
9 MINNIE MINOSO-OF
10 SHERM LOLLAR-C/1B
11 LUIS APARICIO-SS
12 J. C. MARTIN-1B/3B
14 SAMMY ESPOSITO-INF
15 CAL (BUSTER) MCLISH-P
16 AL (FUZZY) SMITH-3B/OF
17 EARL (THE EARL OF SNOHOMISH) TORGESON-1B (1)
18 HERB SCORE-P
19 BILLY PIERCE-P
20 JOE HORLEN-P
21 GERRY STALEY-P (1)
21 RAY HERBERT-P (2)
23 GARY PETERS-P
24 EARLY (GUS) WYNN (ILL)-P
26 WES COVINGTON-OF (2)
26 DON LARSEN-P (2)
27 TURK LOWN-P
28 JOE GINSBERG-C (1)
28 WARREN HACKER-P
29 AL PILARCIK-OF (2)
30 DEAN LOOK-OF
30 ALAN BRICE-P
31 BOB ROSELLI-C
32 JUAN PIZARRO-P
33 TONY (COOCH) (CHICK) CUCCINELLO-CH
34 JOHNNY COONEY-CH
35 BOB SHAW-P (1)
36 TED LEPCIO-3B (1)
36 MIKE DEGERICK-P
37 RAY BERRES-CH
38 FRANK (THE BEAU) BAUMANN-P
39 DON GUTTERIDGE-CH
40 MIKE HERSHBERGER-OF
42 AL LOPEZ-MGR
44 RUSS (RUSTY) (DUTCH) KEMMERER-P (2)
45 CAM CARREON-C
46 ALAN BRICE-P

1962

5TH 85-77 11GB

1 JIM LANDIS-OF
2 NELLIE FOX-2B
3 FLOYD ROBINSON-OF
4 KEN BERRY-OF
5 JOE CUNNINGHAM-1B/OF
6 AL WEIS-INF
7 BOB FARLEY-1B (1)
7 CHARLIE (SMOKEY) MAXWELL-OF/1B (2)
8 BRIAN (BAM) MCCALL-OF
9 RAMON (WITO) CONDE-3B
9 CHARLEY SMITH-3B
10 SHERM LOLLAR-C
11 LUIS APARICIO-SS
12 J. C. MARTIN-UTIL
14 SAMMY ESPOSITO-INF
15 BOB (SID) SADOWSKI-3B/2B
16 AL (FUZZY) SMITH-3B/OF
18 HERB SCORE-P
19 DOM ZANNI-P
20 JOE HORLEN (INJ)-P
21 RAY HERBERT-P (2)
22 DAVE DEBUSSCHERE-P
23 GARY PETERS-P
23 MIKE JOYCE-P
24 EARLY (GUS) WYNN-P
27 TURK LOWN-P
28 EDDIE FISHER-P
29 FRANK KREUTZER-P
30 JOHN BUZHARDT-P
31 BOB ROSELLI-C
32 JUAN PIZARRO-P
33 TONY (COOCH) (CHICK) CUCCINELLO-CH
34 JOHNNY COONEY-CH
37 RAY BERRES-CH
38 FRANK (THE BEAU) BAUMANN-P
39 DON GUTTERIDGE-CH
40 MIKE HERSHBERGER-OF
41 VERLE TIEFENTHALER-P
42 AL LOPEZ-MGR
44 RUSS (RUSTY) (DUTCH) KEMMERER-P (1)
44 DEAN STONE-P (2)
45 CAM CARREON-C
46 DICK KENWORTHY-2B
47 MIKE DEGERICK-P
50 DEACON JONES-1B

1963

2ND 94-68 10.5GB

1 JIM LANDIS-OF
2 NELLIE FOX-2B
3 FLOYD ROBINSON-OF
4 RON HANSEN-SS
5 JOE CUNNINGHAM (INJ)-1B
6 AL WEIS-INF
7 CHARLIE (SMOKEY) MAXWELL-OF/1B
8 PETE WARD-3B/INF
9 CHARLEY SMITH-SS
10 SHERM LOLLAR-C/1B
11 DAVE NICHOLSON-OF
12 J. C. MARTIN-C/INF
14 SAMMY ESPOSITO-INF
14 TOMMY MCCRAW-1B
16 BRIAN (BAM) MCCALL-OF
17 KEN BERRY-OF/1B
18 FRITZ ACKLEY-P
19 DOM ZANNI-P (1)
19 JOE (MOSES) SHIPLEY-P
19 BRUCE HOWARD-P
20 JOE HORLEN-P
21 RAY HERBERT-P
22 DAVE DEBUSSCHERE-P
23 MIKE JOYCE-P
24 DON BUFORD-3B/2B
25 JIM LEMON-1B (3)
26 GENE STEPHENS-OF
27 JIM BROSNAN-P (2)
28 EDDIE FISHER-P
29 TAYLOR (TAY) PHILLIPS-P
30 JOHN BUZHARDT (INJ)-P
31 HOYT WILHELM-P
32 JUAN PIZARRO-P
33 TONY (COOCH) (CHICK) CUCCINELLO-CH
34 JOHNNY COONEY-CH
35 FRED (BUBBY) TALBOT-P
37 RAY BERRES-CH
38 FRANK (THE BEAU) BAUMANN-P
39 DON GUTTERIDGE-CH
40 MIKE HERSHBERGER-OF
42 AL LOPEZ-MGR
43 GARY PETERS-P
45 CAM CARREON-C
49 FRANK KREUTZER-P
50 DEACON JONES-1B

1964

2ND 98-64 1GB

1 JIM LANDIS-OF
3 FLOYD ROBINSON-OF
4 RON HANSEN-SS
5 JOE CUNNINGHAM (INJ)-1B (1)
5 BILL (MOOSE) SKOWRON-1B (2)
6 AL WEIS-2B/UTIL
7 CHARLIE (SMOKEY) MAXWELL-PH
8 PETE WARD-3B
9 MINNIE MINOSO-OF
10 AL LOPEZ-MGR
11 DAVE NICHOLSON-OF
12 J. C. MARTIN-C
14 TOMMY MCCRAW-1B/OF
15 JERRY MCNERTNEY-C
17 KEN BERRY-OF
18 FRITZ ACKLEY-P
18 JEOFF LONG-1B/OF (2)
19 BRUCE HOWARD-P
20 JOE HORLEN-P
21 RAY HERBERT (INJ)-P
22 DAVE DEBUSSCHERE (MIL)-P
23 DICK KENWORTHY-PH
24 DON BUFORD-3B/2B
26 GENE STEPHENS-OF
27 CHARLEY SMITH-3B (1)
28 EDDIE FISHER-P
29 FRANK KREUTZER-P (1)
29 MARV STAEHLE-PH
30 JOHN BUZHARDT-P
31 HOYT WILHELM-P
32 JUAN PIZARRO-P
33 TONY (COOCH) (CHICK) CUCCINELLO-CH
34 JOHNNY COONEY-CH
35 FRED (BUBBY) TALBOT-P
37 RAY BERRES-CH
38 FRANK (THE BEAU) BAUMANN-P
39 DON GUTTERIDGE-CH
40 MIKE HERSHBERGER-OF
41 DON (THE SPHINX) MOSSI-P
43 GARY PETERS-P
44 JIM HICKS-PR
45 CAM CARREON (INJ)-C
49 FRANK KREUTZER-P (1)
49 SMOKY BURGESS-PH (2)

1965

2ND 95-67 7GB

1 TOMMY AGEE-OF
2 SMOKY BURGESS-C
3 FLOYD ROBINSON-OF
4 RON HANSEN-SS/2B
5 JOHNNY (HONEY) ROMANO-C/UTIL
6 AL WEIS-UTIL
7 DON BUFORD-2B/3B
8 PETE WARD-3B/2B
9 DANNY CATER-OF/INF
10 AL LOPEZ-MGR
11 DAVE NICHOLSON-OF
12 J. C. MARTIN-C/INF
14 BILL (MOOSE) SKOWRON-1B
16 KEN BERRY-OF
17 KEN BERRY-OF
17 FRANK LARY-P (2)
18 JIMMIE SCHAFFER-C (1)
18 GENE (AUGIE) FREESE-3B (2)
19 BRUCE HOWARD-P
20 JOE HORLEN-P
23 BOB LOCKER-P
24 TOMMY MCCRAW-1B/OF
25 TOMMY (T.J.) JOHN-P
26 TED WILLS-P
26 DICK KENWORTHY-PH
28 EDDIE FISHER-P
29 MARV STAEHLE-PH
30 JOHN BUZHARDT-P
31 HOYT WILHELM-P
32 JUAN PIZARRO (INJ)-P
33 TONY (COOCH) (CHICK) CUCCINELLO-CH
34 BILL HEATH-PH
36 CHARLIE METRO-CH
37 RAY BERRES-CH
39 DON GUTTERIDGE-CH
40 FRANK LARY-P (2)
40 BILL VOSS-OF
43 GARY PETERS-P
44 JIM HICKS-PR
46 DUANE JOSEPHSON-C
47 GREG BOLLO-P

1966

4TH 83-79 15GB

1 TOMMY AGEE-OF
2 SMOKY BURGESS-C
3 FLOYD ROBINSON-OF
4 RON HANSEN (INJ)-SS/2B
5 JOHNNY (HONEY) ROMANO-C
6 AL WEIS-2B/SS
7 DON BUFORD-3B/UTIL
8 PETE WARD (INJ)-UTIL
9 DANNY CATER-OF (1)
9 WAYNE CAUSEY-INF (2)
10 J. C. MARTIN (INJ)-C/INF
11 JERRY ADAIR-SS/2B (2)
12 EDDIE (THE BRAT) (MUGGSY) STANKY-MGR
14 BILL (MOOSE) SKOWRON-1B
15 JERRY MCNERTNEY-C
16 KEN BERRY-OF
17 BILL VOSS-OF
18 GENE (AUGIE) FREESE-3B (1)
19 BRUCE HOWARD-P
20 JOE HORLEN-P
23 BOB LOCKER-P
24 TOMMY MCCRAW-1B/OF
25 TOMMY (T.J.) JOHN-P
26 DICK KENWORTHY-3B
27 FRED KLAGES-P
28 EDDIE FISHER-P (1)
29 MARV STAEHLE-2B
30 JOHN BUZHARDT-P
31 HOYT WILHELM (INJ)-P
32 JUAN PIZARRO-P
33 TONY (COOCH) (CHICK) CUCCINELLO-CH
34 KERBY FARRELL-CH
36 JACK LAMABE-P
37 RAY BERRES-CH
39 DON GUTTERIDGE-CH
40 BILL VOSS-OF
40 ED STROUD-OF
41 DENNY HIGGINS-P
43 GARY PETERS-P
44 JIM HICKS-OF/1B
45 JACK LAMABE-P
46 DUANE JOSEPHSON-C
47 GREG BOLLO-P
49 LEE ELIA-SS
50 DEACON JONES-PH
53 BUDDY BRADFORD-OF

1967

4TH 89-73 3GB

1 TOMMY AGEE-OF
2 SMOKY BURGESS-PH
3 WALT (NO-NECK) WILLIAMS-OF
4 RON HANSEN-SS
5 DUANE JOSEPHSON-C
6 AL WEIS (INJ)-2B/SS
7 DON BUFORD-3B/UTIL
8 PETE WARD-OF/INF
9 WAYNE CAUSEY-2B/SS
10 J. C. MARTIN-C/1B
11 JERRY ADAIR-SS/2B (1)
11 SANDY ALOMAR-SS/2B (2)
11 JIMMY STEWART-UTIL (2)
12 EDDIE (THE BRAT) (MUGGSY) STANKY-MGR
14 BILL (MOOSE) SKOWRON-1B (1)
14 KEN BOYER-3B/1B (2)
15 JERRY MCNERTNEY-C
16 KEN BERRY-OF
17 ED STROUD-OF (1)
17 BILL VOSS-OF
17 AURELIO MONTEAGUDO-P
17 RICH MORALES-SS

CHICAGO WHITE SOX

18 JIM KING-OF (2)
18 ROCKY COLAVITO-OF (2)
19 BRUCE HOWARD-P
20 JOE HORLEN-P
21 JIM O'TOOLE (INJ)-P
23 BOB LOCKER-P
24 TOMMY MCCRAW-1B/OF
25 TOMMY (T.J.) JOHN-P
26 DICK KENWORTHY-3B
27 FRED KLAGES-P
28 WILBUR WOOD-P
29 MARV STAEHLE-2B/SS
30 JOHN BUZHARDT-P (1)
30 CISCO CARLOS-P
31 HOYT WILHELM-P
32 BUDDY BRADFORD-OF
33 LES MOSS-CH
34 KERBY FARRELL-CH
35 MARV GRISSOM-CH
36 JACK LAMABE-P (1)
37 GROVER RESINGER-CH
39 STEVE JONES-P
41 DENNY HIGGINS (INJ)-P
42 ED HERRMANN-C
43 GARY PETERS-P
44 DON MCMAHON-P (2)
45 AURELIO MONTEAGUDO-P
46 CISCO CARLOS-P
48 ROGER (SPIDER) NELSON-P
50 COTTON NASH-1B

1968

8TH (TIE) 67-95 36GB

1 SANDY ALOMAR-2B/UTIL
2 DICK KENWORTHY-3B
3 WALT (NO-NECK) WILLIAMS-OF
4 TIM CULLEN-2B (1)
4 RON HANSEN-INF (2)
5 DUANE JOSEPHSON-C
6 BUDDY BOOKER-C
7 RUSS SNYDER-OF (1)
7 LEON WAGNER-OF (2)
8 PETE WARD-3B/UTIL
9 WAYNE CAUSEY-2B (1)
9 WOODIE HELD-UTIL (2)
10 TOMMY DAVIS-OF/1B
11 LUIS APARICIO-SS
12 EDDIE (THE BRAT) (MUGGSY) STANKY-MGR1
14 KEN BOYER-3B/1B (1)
14 BILL MELTON-3B
15 JERRY MCNERTNEY-C/1B
16 KEN BERRY-OF
17 BILL VOSS (INJ)-OF
18 GAIL HOPKINS-1B
19 DENNIS RIBANT-P (2)
20 JOE HORLEN-P
22 JACK (FAT JACK) FISHER-P
23 BOB LOCKER-P
24 TOMMY MCCRAW-1B
25 TOMMY (T.J.) JOHN (INJ)-P
28 WILBUR WOOD-P
29 CARLOS MAY-OF
30 CISCO CARLOS-P
31 HOYT WILHELM-P
32 BUDDY BRADFORD-OF
33 LES MOSS-CH/MGR2
34 KERBY FARRELL-CH
35 MARV GRISSOM-CH
37 GROVER RESINGER-CH
37 RAY BERRES-CH
39 BOB PRIDDY-P
39 DON GUTTERIDGE-CH
40 DAN LAZAR-P
42 AL LOPEZ-MGR3
43 GARY PETERS-P
44 DON MCMAHON-P (1)
45 FRED RATH-P
46 BILLY WYNNE-P
49 JERRY NYMAN-P
52 RICH MORALES-SS/2B

1969

5TH W 68-94 29GB

1 SANDY ALOMAR-2B (1)
1 ANGEL BRAVO-OF
2 RICH MORALES-INF
3 WALT (NO-NECK) WILLIAMS-OF
4 RON HANSEN-INF
5 DUANE JOSEPHSON (INJ)-C
6 TOMMY MCCRAW (INJ)-1B/OF
7 DON PAVLETICH (INJ)-C/1B
8 PETE WARD-UTIL
9 WOODIE HELD-UTIL
10 CHUCK BRINKMAN-C
10 AL LOPEZ-MGR1
11 LUIS APARICIO-SS
12 ED HERRMANN-C
14 BILL MELTON-3B/OF
15 BOB CHRISTIAN-OF
16 KEN BERRY-OF
17 CARLOS MAY (INJ)-OF
18 GAIL HOPKINS-1B
19 BUDDY BRADFORD (INJ)-OF
20 JOE HORLEN-P
21 DAN OSINSKI-P
22 BOB SPENCE-1B
23 BOB LOCKER-P (1)
23 JOSE ORTIZ-OF
24 DANNY MURPHY-P
25 TOMMY (T.J.) JOHN-P
26 BOB PRIDDY-P (1)
26 GARY BELL-P (1)
27 DON SECRIST (INJ)-P
28 WILBUR WOOD-P
29 BOBBY KNOOP-2B (2)
30 CISCO CARLOS-P (1)
32 SAMMY ELLIS-P
32 BART JOHNSON-P
32 DOUG ADAMS-C
32 JACK HAMILTON-P (2)
33 TONY (COOCH) (CHICK) CUCCINELLO-CH
34 KERBY FARRELL-CH
35 LES MOSS-CH
37 RAY BERRES-CH
39 DON GUTTERIDGE-CH/MGR2
40 DAN LAZAR-P
41 PAUL EDMONDSON-P
42 AL LOPEZ-MGR1
42 BART JOHNSON-P
42 DENNY O'TOOLE-P
43 GARY PETERS-P
45 FRED RATH-P
46 BILLY WYNNE-P
47 DENNY O'TOOLE-P
49 JERRY NYMAN-P
50 JACK HAMILTON-P (2)

1970

6TH W 56-106 42GB

1 RICH MCKINNEY-3B/SS
2 RICH MORALES-INF
3 WALT (NO-NECK) WILLIAMS-OF
4 LUKE (OLD ACHES & PAINS) APPLING-CH
5 DUANE JOSEPHSON (INJ)-C
6 TOMMY MCCRAW-1B/OF
7 SYD O'BRIEN-INF
8 JOHN MATIAS-OF/1B
9 OSSIE BLANCO-1B/OF
10 CHUCK BRINKMAN-C
11 LUIS APARICIO-SS
12 ED HERRMANN-C
14 BILL MELTON-3B/OF
15 BOB CHRISTIAN-OF
15 JOSE ORTIZ-OF
16 KEN BERRY-OF
17 CARLOS MAY-OF/1B
18 GAIL HOPKINS-1B/C
19 BUDDY BRADFORD-OF (1)
19 BARRY MOORE-P (2)
20 JOE HORLEN (INJ)-P
21 LEE MAYE-PH
22 BOB SPENCE-1B
23 STEVE HAMILTON-P
23 TOMMIE SISK-P
23 BOB MILLER-P (2)
24 DANNY MURPHY-P
25 TOMMY (T.J.) JOHN-P
26 JERRY JANESKI-P
27 DON SECRIST (INJ)-P
28 WILBUR WOOD-P
29 BOBBY KNOOP-2B
30 JERRY ARRIGO (INJ)-P
30 ART KUSNYER-C
31? CHUCK TANNER-MGR3
32 DON EDDY-P
33 HUGH (LOSING PITCHER) MULCAHY-CH
34 BILL ADAIR-CH/MGR2
35 LES MOSS-CH
39 DON GUTTERIDGE-MGR1
40 JIM MAGNUSON-P
41 FLOYD WEAVER-P
42 BART JOHNSON-P
44 BILL ADAIR-CH/MGR2
44 JERRY CRIDER-P
45 STEVE HAMILTON-P
45 LEE STANGE-P (2)
46 BILLY WYNNE-P
47 GENE ROUNSAVILLE-P
47 DENNY O'TOOLE-P
48 RICHIE MOLONEY-P
52 DENNY O'TOOLE-P

1971

3RD W 79-83 22.5GB

1 LUIS ALVARADO-SS/2B
2 MIKE ANDREWS (INJ)-2B/1B
3 WALT (NO-NECK) WILLIAMS-OF/3B
4 LUKE (OLD ACHES & PAINS) APPLING-CH
5 TONY MUSER-1B
6 ED STROUD-OF
7 CHUCK TANNER-MGR
8 TOM EGAN-C/1B
9 LEE RICHARD (BEE BEE)-SS/OF
10 JAY JOHNSTONE-OF
11 CHUCK BRINKMAN-C
12 ED HERRMANN-C
14 BILL MELTON-3B
15 MIKE HERSHBERGER-OF
16 KEN HOTTMAN-OF
17 CARLOS MAY-1B/OF
18 PAT KELLY-OF
19 RON LOLICH-OF
19 STEVE HUNTZ-INF
20 JOE HORLEN (INJ)-P
21 BART JOHNSON-P
21 LEE MAYE (INJ)-OF
22 BOB SPENCE-1B
23 STEVE KEALEY-P
24 TOM BRADLEY-P
25 TOMMY (T.J.) JOHN-P
26 RICH MCKINNEY-UTIL
27 VICENTE (HUEVO) ROMO-P
28 WILBUR WOOD-P
30 RICH MORALES-UTIL
32 DON EDDY-P
33 JOHNNY SAIN-CH
35 AL MONCHAK-CH
37 JOE LONNETT-CH
40 JIM MAGNUSON-P
42 BART JOHNSON-P
44 PAT JACQUEZ-P
44 STAN PERZANOWSKI-P
46 STAN PERZANOWSKI-P
48 RICK REICHARDT-OF/1B
50 RICH HINTON-P
51 TERRY FORSTER-P
52 DENNY O'TOOLE-P

1972

2ND W 87-67 5.5GB

1 LUIS ALVARADO- INF
2 MIKE ANDREWS-2B/1B
3 WALT (NO-NECK) WILLIAMS-OF/3B
5 TONY MUSER-1B/OF
5 ED SPIEZIO-3B (2)
6 JORGE ORTA-INF
7 CHUCK TANNER-MGR
8 TOM EGAN-C
9 LEE RICHARD (BEE BEE)-OF/SS
10 JAY JOHNSTONE-OF
11 CHUCK BRINKMAN-C
12 ED HERRMANN-C
14 BILL MELTON (INJ)-3B
15 DICK ALLEN-1B/3B
17 CARLOS MAY-OF/1B
18 PAT KELLY-OF
19 JIM QUALLS-OF
19 RUDY HERNANDEZ-SS
21 BART JOHNSON (INJ)-P
22 BUDDY BRADFORD-OF
23 STEVE KEALEY-P
24 TOM BRADLEY-P
25 TONY MUSER-1B/OF
26 JIM LYTTLE-OF
27 VICENTE (HUEVO) ROMO (INJ)-P
28 WILBUR WOOD-P
30 RICH MORALES-SS/INF
31 JIM (MOE) MAHONEY-CH
33 JOHNNY SAIN-CH
34 HUGH YANCY-3B
34 EDDIE FISHER-P (2)
35 AL MONCHAK-CH
36 GLEN ROSENBAUM-CH
37 JOE LONNETT-CH
38 DAN NEUMEIER-P
38 PHIL (THE VULTURE) REGAN-P (2)
39 DAN NEUMEIER-P
41 CY ACOSTA-P
42 HANK ALLEN-3B
43 DAVE LEMONDS-P
44 MOE DRABOWSKI-P (2)
45 STAN BAHNSEN-P
47 KEN FRAILING-P
48 RICK REICHARDT-OF
51 TERRY FORSTER-P
52 DENNY O'TOOLE-P
54 RICH (GOOSE) GOSSAGE-P
55 JIM GEDDES-P

1973

5TH W 77-85 17GB

1 LUIS ALVARADO-INF/DH
2 MIKE ANDREWS-DH/INF (1)
2 JERRY HAIRSTON-UTIL
3 EDDIE LEON-SS/2B
5 BILL SHARP-OF/DH
6 JORGE ORTA-2B/SS
7 CHUCK TANNER-MGR
8 PETE VARNEY-C
10 SAM EWING-1B
11 CHUCK BRINKMAN-C
12 ED HERRMANN-C/DH
14 BILL MELTON-3B/DH
15 DICK ALLEN-UTIL
16 BRIAN DOWNING (INJ)-UTIL
17 CARLOS MAY-DH/UTIL
18 PAT KELLY-OF/DH
20 JOHNNY JETER-OF/DH
21 BART JOHNSON-P
22 BUDDY BRADFORD (INJ)-OF
23 STEVE KEALEY (INJ)-P
24 KEN HENDERSON (INJ)-OF/DH
25 TONY MUSER-1B/UTIL
26 DAVE BALDWIN-P
27 JOHNNY JETER-OF/DH
28 WILBUR WOOD-P
29 JOE KEOUGH-PH
30 RICH MORALES-3B/2B (1)
30 BUCKY DENT-INF
31 JIM (MOE) MAHONEY-CH
32 STEVE STONE-P
33 JOHNNY SAIN-CH
34 EDDIE FISHER-P (1)
35 AL MONCHAK-CH
36 GLEN ROSENBAUM-CH
36 JIM (KITTY) KAAT-P (2)
37 JOE LONNETT-CH
39 GLEN ROSENBAUM-CH
40 JIM (RED) MCGLOTHLIN-P (2)
41 CY ACOSTA-P
42 HANK ALLEN-UTIL
(43) DAVE LEMONDS (INJ)-(P)
45 STAN BAHNSEN-P
46 JOE KEOUGH-PH
47 KEN FRAILING-P
48 RICK REICHARDT-OF/DH (1)
51 TERRY FORSTER-P
52 DENNY O'TOOLE-P
54 RICH (GOOSE) GOSSAGE-P
55 JIM GEDDES-P

1974

4TH W 80-80 9GB

1 LUIS ALVARADO-INF (1)
1 BILL STEIN-3B/DH
2 JERRY HAIRSTON (INJ)-OF/DH
3 EDDIE LEON-INF/DH
5 BILL SHARP-OF
6 JORGE ORTA-2B/UTIL
7 CHUCK TANNER-MGR
8 PETE VARNEY-C
9 LEE RICHARD (BEE BEE)-UTIL
10 RON SANTO-DH/INF
11 CHUCK BRINKMAN-C (1)
12 ED HERRMANN-C
14 BILL MELTON-3B/DH
15 DICK ALLEN (RET)-1B/UTIL
16 BRIAN DOWNING-UTIL
17 CARLOS MAY-OF/DH
18 PAT KELLY-DH/OF
19 HUGH YANCY-DH
19 KEN TATUM-P
20 NYLS NYMAN-OF
21 BART JOHNSON-P
22 BUDDY BRADFORD (INJ)-OF/DH
24 KEN HENDERSON-OF
25 TONY MUSER-1B/DH
26 SKIP PITLOCK-P
28 WILBUR WOOD-P
30 BUCKY DENT-SS
31 JIM (MOE) MAHONEY-CH
33 JOHNNY SAIN-CH
34 BILL (BUGS) MORAN-P
35 AL MONCHAK-CH
36 JIM (KITTY) KAAT-P
37 JOE LONNETT-CH
37 LLOYD ALLEN-P (2)
38 JIM OTTEN-P
39 GLEN ROSENBAUM-CH
40 JOE HENDERSON-P
40 LLOYD ALLEN-P (2)
41 CY ACOSTA (INJ)-P

44 WAYNE GRANGER-P
45 STAN BAHNSEN-P
46 STAN PERZANOWSKI-P
47 FRANCISCO BARRIOS-P
47 WAYNE GRANGER-P
48 LAMAR JOHNSON-1B/DH
50 WAYNE GRANGER-P
51 TERRY FORSTER-P
54 RICH (GOOSE) GOSSAGE (INJ)-P
55 JACK KUCEK-P

1975

5TH W 75-86 22.5GB

1 BILL STEIN-UTIL
2 JERRY HAIRSTON-OF/DH
2 CHET LEMON-UTIL
4 *(RET#) LUKE APPLING*
5 BILL SHARP-OF (1)
5 BOB COLUCCIO (INJ)-OF/DH (2)
6 JORGE ORTA-2B/DH
7 CHUCK TANNER-MGR
8 PETE VARNEY-C/DH
9 LEE RICHARD (BEE BEE)-INF/DH
11 JERRY MOSES-1B/DH (2)
12 LAMAR JOHNSON-1B/DH
12 DERON JOHNSON-DH/1B (1)
14 BILL MELTON-3B/DH
16 BRIAN DOWNING-C/DH
17 CARLOS MAY-1B/UTIL
18 PAT KELLY-OF/DH
18 MIKE SQUIRES-1B
20 NYLS NYMAN-OF/DH
(21) BART JOHNSON (INJ)-(P)
22 BUDDY BRADFORD-OF/DH (1)
22 JERRY HAIRSTON-OF/DH
24 KEN HENDERSON-OF/DH
25 TONY MUSER-1B (1)
25 JESSE JEFFERSON-P (2)
26 SKIP PITLOCK-P
26 LLOYD ALLEN-P
26 DAVE HAMILTON-P (3)
27 KEN KRAVEC-P
28 WILBUR WOOD-P
30 BUCKY DENT-SS
31 JIM (MOE) MAHONEY-CH
32 BILL GOGOLEWSKI (INJ)-P
33 JOHNNY SAIN-CH
34 CECIL UPSHAW-P
35 AL MONCHAK-CH
36 JIM (KITTY) KAAT-P
37 JOE LONNETT-CH
38 JIM OTTEN-P
38 JESSE JEFFERSON-P (2)
39 GLEN ROSENBAUM-CH
40 LLOYD ALLEN-P
40 PETE VUCKOVICH-P
41 CLAUDE OSTEEN-P
42 CECIL UPSHAW-P
42 TIM STODDARD-P
44 RICH HINTON-P
45 STAN BAHNSEN-P (1)
45 CHRIS KNAPP-P
46 OZZIE OSBORN-P
50 OZZIE OSBORN-P
51 TERRY FORSTER (INJ)-P
52 BILL GOGOLEWSKI (INJ)-P
54 RICH (GOOSE) GOSSAGE (INJ)-P
55 JACK KUCEK-P

1976

6TH W 64-97 25.5GB

1 BILL STEIN-UTIL
2 *(RET#) NELLIE FOX*
3 JIM SPENCER-1B/DH
4 *(RET#) LUKE APPLING*
6 JORGE ORTA-OF/UTIL
7 ALAN BANNISTER-UTIL
8 PETE VARNEY-C (1)
8 KEVIN BELL-3B/DH
9 MINNIE MINOSO-DH/CH
10 JACK BROHAMER-2B/3B
11 JIM ESSIAN-C/INF
12 PAUL RICHARDS-MGR
13 BLUE MOON ODOM-P
14 CLEON JONES-OF/DH
14 HUGH YANCEY-2B
15 WAYNE NORDHAGEN-UTIL
15 RICH COGGINS-OF/DH (2)
16 BRIAN DOWNING-C/DH
17 CARLOS MAY-DH/OF (1)
17 PHIL ROOF-C (2)
18 PAT KELLY-DH/OF
19 SAM EWING-DH/1B
20 NYLS NYMAN-OF
21 BART JOHNSON-P
22 JERRY HAIRSTON-OF
22 BUDDY BRADFORD-OF/DH
23 LAMAR JOHNSON-1B/DH
25 JESSE JEFFERSON-P
26 DAVE HAMILTON-P
27 KEN KRAVEC-P
28 WILBUR WOOD (INJ)-P
29 BUDDY BRADFORD-OF/DH
29 GEORGE ENRIGHT-C
30 BUCKY DENT-SS
31 JIM (MOE) MAHONEY-CH
32 JIM BUSBY-CH
33 KEN (HAWK) SILVESTRI-CH
34 KEN BRETT-P (2)
36 CLAY (HAWK) CARROLL (INJ)-P
38 JIM OTTEN-P
40 PETE VUCKOVICH-P
41 LARRY MONROE-P
44 CHET LEMON-OF
45 CHRIS KNAPP-P
46 FRANCISCO BARRIOS-P
48 RALPH (ROAD RUNNER) GARR-OF/DH
50 KEN BRETT-P (2)
51 TERRY FORSTER-P
54 RICH (GOOSE) GOSSAGE-P
55 JACK KUCEK-P

1977

3RD W 90-72 12GB

1 TIM NORDBROOK-INF/DH (1)
1 JOHN FLANNERY-INF/DH
2 *(RET#) NELLIE FOX*
3 JIM SPENCER-1B
4 *(RET#) LUKE APPLING*
5 BOB COLUCCIO-OF
5 BOB MOLINARO-OF (2)
6 JORGE ORTA-2B
7 ALAN BANNISTER-SS/UTIL
8 KEVIN BELL (INJ)-UTIL
9 MINNIE MINOSO-CH
10 JACK BROHAMER-UTIL
11 JIM ESSIAN-C/3B
12 ERIC SODERHOLM-3B/DH
14 LARRY DOBY-CH
15 WAYNE NORDHAGEN-UTIL
16 BRIAN DOWNING-UTIL
17 OSCAR GAMBLE-DH/OF
18 ROYAL STILLMAN-UTIL
19 MIKE SQUIRES-1B
20 NYLS NYMAN-PH
20 BILL NAHORODNY-C
21 BOB LEMON-MGR
22 RICHIE ZISK-OF/DH
23 LAMAR JOHNSON-DH/1B
24 BART JOHNSON-P
25 JERRY HAIRSTON-OF
25 TOMMY CRUZ-OF
26 DAVE HAMILTON-P
27 KEN KRAVEC-P
28 WILBUR WOOD (INJ)-P
29 BOBBY KNOOP-CH
30 DON KESSINGER-INF (2)
31 STAN WILLIAMS-CH
32 STEVE STONE-P
33 DON KIRKWOOD-P (2)
34 KEN BRETT-P (1)
34 CLAY (HAWK) CARROLL (INJ)-P (2)
36 LERRIN LAGROW-P
37 DAVE FROST-P
38 HENRY CRUZ-OF
43 BRUCE DAL CANTON (INJ)-P
44 CHET LEMON-OF
45 CHRIS KNAPP-P
46 FRANCISCO BARRIOS-P
47 SILVIO MARTINEZ-P
48 RALPH (ROAD RUNNER) GARR-OF/DH
50 STEVE RENKO-P (2)
51 LARRY ANDERSON-P
51 JOHN VERHOEVEN-P (2)
52 RANDY WILES-P
55 JACK KUCEK-P

1978

5TH W 71-90 20.5GB

1 HARRY CHAPPAS-SS
2 *(RET#) NELLIE FOX*
3 JIM BREAZEALE-1B/DH
4 *(RET#) LUKE APPLING*
5 BOB MOLINARO-OF/DH
6 JORGE ORTA-2B/DH
7 ALAN BANNISTER (INJ)-UTIL
8 KEVIN BELL (INJ)-3B/DH
9 MINNIE MINOSO-CH
10 RON (BOOMER) BLOMBERG-DH/1B
11 DON KESSINGER-SS/2B
12 ERIC SODERHOLM-3B/UTIL
14 LARRY DOBY-CH/MGR2
15 BILL NAHORODNY-C/UTIL
16 GREG PRYOR-INF
17 ALVIN (JUNIOR) MOORE-UTIL
18 CLAUDELL WASHINGTON (INJ)-OF/DH (2)
19 MIKE SQUIRES-1B
20 WAYNE NORDHAGEN (ILL)-UTIL
21 BOB LEMON-MGR1
21 RUSTY TORRES-OF
22 THAD BOSLEY (INJ)-OF
23 LAMAR JOHNSON-1B/DH
24 MIKE PROLY (INJ)-P
25 BOBBY BONDS-OF/DH (1)
25 BRITT BURNS-P
25 TOM SPENCER-OF/DH
26 JIM WILLOUGHBY-P
26 TONY LARUSSA-CH
27 KEN KRAVEC-P
28 WILBUR WOOD-P
29 BOBBY KNOOP-CH
30 DON KESSINGER-SS/2B
30 MIKE COLBERN-C/DH
31 STAN WILLIAMS-CH
31 JOE GATES-2B
32 STEVE STONE-P
33 STEVE TROUT-P
34 JIM WILLOUGHBY-P
35 PABLO TORREALBA (ILL)-P
36 LERRIN LAGROW-P
37 RON SCHUELER-P
38 JIM WILLOUGHBY-P
38 HENRY CRUZ-OF/DH
40 BRITT BURNS-P
41 ROSS BAUMGARTEN-P
42 MARV FOLEY-C
43 BRUCE DAL CANTON-CH
44 CHET LEMON (INJ)-OF/DH
46 FRANCISCO BARRIOS-P
47 RICH HINTON-P
48 RALPH (ROAD RUNNER) GARR-OF/DH
49 TOM SPENCER-OF/DH
50 BRITT BURNS-P
50 MIKE COLBERN-C/DH
52 RICH WORTHAM-P
54 LARRY DOBY JOHNSON-C/DH
55 JACK KUCEK-P
57 SAM HAIRSTON-CH
65 MIKE EDEN-SS/2B

1979

5TH W 73-87 14GB

1 BOBBY WINKLES-CH
2 *(RET#) NELLIE FOX*
3 JOE SPARKS-CH
4 *(RET#) LUKE APPLING*
5 MILT MAY (INJ)-C (2)
6 JORGE ORTA-DH/2B
7 ALAN BANNISTER-2B/UTIL
8 KEVIN BELL (INJ)-3B/SS
9 MINNIE MINOSO-CH
10 JOE GATES-3B/DH
10 TONY LARUSSA-MGR2
11 DON KESSINGER (RET)-INF/MGR1
12 ERIC SODERHOLM-3B (1)
12 JIM MORRISON-3B/2B
13 HARRY CHAPPAS-SS
14 LARRY DOBY-CH
15 BILL NAHORODNY(INJ)-C/DH
16 GREG PRYOR-SS/INF
17 MARV FOLEY-C
18 CLAUDELL WASHINGTON (INJ)-OF/DH
19 MIKE COLBERN (INJ)-C/DH
20 WAYNE NORDHAGEN-UTIL/P
21 RUSTY TORRES-OF
22 THAD BOSLEY-OF/DH
22 ED FARMER-P (2)
23 LAMAR JOHNSON-1B/DH
24 MIKE PROLY (INJ)-P
25 MIKE SQUIRES-1B/OF
26 RANDY SCARBERY-P
27 KEN KRAVEC-P
28 RICH WORTHAM-P
30 ROSS BAUMGARTEN-P
31 FRED MARTIN-CH
32 DEWEY ROBINSON-P
32 THAD BOSLEY-OF/DH
33 STEVE TROUT-P
34 JOE GATES-3B/DH
34 ALVIN (JUNIOR) MOORE-UTIL
35 PABLO TORREALBA-P
35 DEWEY ROBINSON-P
36 LERRIN LAGROW-P (1)
36 GUY HOFFMAN-P
37 RON SCHUELER (INJ/RET)-P/CH
40 BRITT BURNS-P
41 FRED HOWARD-P
42 MARK ESSER-P
42 LOREN (BEE BEE) BABE-CH
44 CHET LEMON-OF/DH
46 FRANCISCO BARRIOS (INJ)-P
47 RICH HINTON-P (1)
47 RUSTY KUNTZ-OF
48 RALPH (ROAD RUNNER) GARR-OF/DH (1)
49 RICH DOTSON-P
50 LA MARR HOYT-P
55 JACK KUCEK-P (1)
55 GIL RONDON-P
57 JIMMY PIERSALL-ASSOC CH

1980

5TH W 70-90 26GB

1 BOBBY WINKLES-CH
2 *(RET#) NELLIE FOX*
3 HAROLD BAINES-OF/DH
4 *(RET#) LUKE APPLING*
5 BOB MOLINARO-OF/DH
6 RICKY SEILHEIMER-C
7 ALAN BANNISTER-OF/3B (1)
7 RANDY JOHNSON-UTIL
8 KEVIN BELL-3B/UTIL
9 MINNIE MINOSO-PH/CH
10 TONY LARUSSA-MGR
11 BRUCE KIMM-C
11 GREG PRYOR-INF/DH
12 JIM MORRISON-2B/UTIL
13 HARRY CHAPPAS-UTIL
14 ORLANDO (BABY BULL) (CHA CHA) CEPEDA-CH
15 ART KUSNYER-CH
16 GREG PRYOR-INF/DH
16 BRUCE KIMM-C
17 MARV FOLEY-C/1B
18 CLAUDELL WASHINGTON (INJ)-OF/DH (1)
18 RON PRUITT-UTIL (2)
20 WAYNE NORDHAGEN-OF/DH
21 TODD CRUZ-SS (2)
22 ED FARMER-P
23 LAMAR JOHNSON-1B/DH
24 MIKE PROLY-P
25 MIKE SQUIRES-1B/C
26 RANDY SCARBERY-P
27 KEN KRAVEC-P
28 RICH WORTHAM-P
29 NARDI CONTRERAS-P
30 ROSS BAUMGARTEN (INJ)-P
31 LA MARR HOYT-P
32 THAD BOSLEY (INJ)-OF
33 STEVE TROUT-P
34 ALVIN (JUNIOR) MOORE-UTIL
35 DEWEY ROBINSON-P
36 GUY HOFFMAN-P
37 RON SCHUELER-CH
38 GLENN BORGMANN-C
40 BRITT BURNS-P
42 LOREN (BEE BEE) BABE-CH
44 CHET LEMON-OF/UTIL
46 FRANCISCO BARRIOS (INJ)-P
47 RUSTY KUNTZ-OF
48 LEO SUTHERLAND-OF
49 RICH DOTSON-P
50 LA MARR HOYT-P
66 FRAN MULLINS-3B

1981

1ST 1/2:3RD W 31-22 2.5GB
2ND 1/2:6TH W 23-30 7GB
FINAL: 54-52 --GB

1 BOBBY WINKLES-CH
2 *(RET#) NELLIE FOX*
3 HAROLD BAINES-OF/DH
4 *(RET#) LUKE APPLING*
5 BOB MOLINARO-DH/OF
7 MARC HILL-C/INF
8 RON LEFLORE-OF
9 MINNIE MINOSO-CH
10 TONY LARUSSA-MGR
11 GREG PRYOR-INF
12 JIM MORRISON-3B/UTIL
14 TONY BERNAZARD-2B/SS
15 ART KUSNYER-CH
16 JIM ESSIAN-C/3B

CHICAGO WHITE SOX

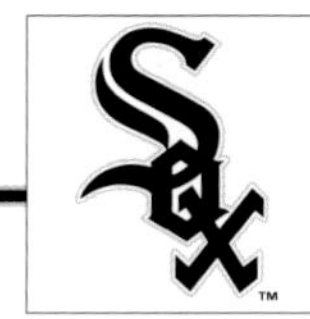

17 JERRY HAIRSTON-OF
19 GREG LUZINSKI-DH
20 WAYNE NORDHAGEN-OF
21 TODD CRUZ (INJ)-(SS)
22 ED FARMER-P
23 LAMAR JOHNSON-1B/DH
24 JERRY TURNER-OF (2)
25 MIKE SQUIRES-1B/OF
27 LYNN MCGLOTHEN-P (2)
28 VADA PINSON-CH
30 ROSS BAUMGARTEN (INJ)-P
31 LA MARR HOYT-P
32 JAY LOVIGLIO-INF/DH
33 STEVE TROUT-P
34 BILL ALMON-SS
35 DEWEY ROBINSON-P
36 JERRY KOOSMAN-P (2)
37 RON SCHUELER-CH
38 DAVE NELSON-CH
40 BRITT BURNS-P
42 LOREN (BEE BEE) BABE-CH
43 DENNIS LAMP-P
44 CHET LEMON-OF
45 KEVIN HICKEY-P
46 FRANCISCO BARRIOS (INJ)-P
47 RUSTY KUNTZ-OF/DH
48 LEO SUTHERLAND-OF
49 RICH DOTSON-P
50 JUAN AGOSTO-P
51 REGGIE PATTERSON-P
53 DENNIS LAMP-P
72 CARLTON (PUDGE) FISK-C/UTIL

1982

3RD W — 87-75 — 6GB

1 JAY LOVIGLIO-2B/DH
2 *(RET#) NELLIE FOX*
3 HAROLD BAINES-OF
4 *(RET#) LUKE APPLING*
5 VANCE LAW-UTIL
6 CHARLIE LAU-CH
7 RON LEFLORE (SUS)-OF
7 MARC HILL-C/INF
8 MARC HILL-C/INF
8 RON LEFLORE (SUS)-OF
10 TONY LARUSSA-MGR
11 RUDY LAW-OF/DH
12 JIM MORRISON-3B/DH (1)
12 STEVE DILLARD-2B
14 TONY BERNAZARD-2B
15 ART KUSNYER-CH
16 MARV FOLEY-UTIL
17 JERRY HAIRSTON-OF/DH
19 GREG LUZINSKI-DH
20 AURELIO RODRIGUEZ-3B/INF
21 JIM LEYLAND-CH
22 STEVE KEMP-OF/DH
23 CHRIS NYMAN-1B/OF
24 CHICO ESCARREGA-P
25 MIKE SQUIRES-1B
27 GREG WALKER-DH
27 LORENZO GRAY-3B
27 EDDIE (BUDDY) SOLOMON-P (2)
28 JIM LEYLAND-CH
28 SPARKY LYLE-P (2)
29 GREG WALKER-DH
30 SALOME BAROJAS-P
31 LA MARR HOYT-P
33 STEVE TROUT-P
34 BILL ALMON-SS/DH
36 JERRY KOOSMAN-P
37 RON SCHUELER-CH
38 DAVE NELSON-CH
40 BRITT BURNS-P
42 RON KITTLE-OF/DH
44 TOM PACIOREK-1B/OF
45 KEVIN HICKEY-P
46 WARREN BRUSSTAR-P (2)
47 RUSTY KUNTZ-OF
49 RICH DOTSON-P
50 JUAN AGOSTO-P
52 RICH BARNES-P
53 DENNIS LAMP-P
58 KEN (HAWK) SILVESTRI-CH
62 JIM SIWY-P
67 JIM KERN-P (2)
72 CARLTON (PUDGE) FISK-C/1B

1983

1ST W — 99-63 — 0GB

L ALCS-BALA 3-1

1 SCOTT FLETCHER-INF/DH
2 *(RET#) NELLIE FOX*
3 HAROLD BAINES-OF
4 *(RET#) LUKE APPLING*
5 VANCE LAW-3B/UTIL
6 CHARLIE LAU-CH
7 MARC HILL-UTIL
8 DAVE STEGMAN-OF
9 *(RET#) MINNIE MINOSO*
10 TONY LARUSSA-MGR
11 RUDY LAW-OF/DH
12 JOEL SKINNER-C
14 TONY BERNAZARD-2B (1)
14 CASEY PARSONS-OF/DH
15 ART KUSNYER-CH
16 JULIO CRUZ-2B (2)
17 JERRY HAIRSTON-OF/DH
18 DAVE DUNCAN-CH
19 GREG LUZINSKI-DH/1B
20 JERRY DYBZINSKI-SS/3B
21 JIM LEYLAND-CH
22 AURELIO RODRIGUEZ-3B (2)
23 CHRIS NYMAN-1B/DH
24 FLOYD BANNISTER-P
25 MIKE SQUIRES-UTIL
27 LORENZO GRAY-3B/DH
28 MIGUEL DILONE-OF/DH (2)
29 GREG WALKER-1B/DH
30 SALOME BAROJAS-P
31 LA MARR HOYT-P
32 TIM HULETT-2B
33 RANDY MARTZ-P
34 RICH DOTSON-P
35 ED BRINKMAN-CH
36 JERRY KOOSMAN-P
38 DAVE NELSON-CH
39 GLEN ROSENBAUM-CH
40 BRITT BURNS (INJ)-P
41 DICK TIDROW-P
42 RON KITTLE-OF/DH
43 STEVE MURA-P
44 TOM PACIOREK-1B/UTIL
45 KEVIN HICKEY (INJ)-P
46 SCOTT FLETCHER-INF/DH
46 LOREN (BEE BEE) BABE-CH
47 RUSTY KUNTZ-OF/DH (1)
47 GUY HOFFMAN-P
49 RICH DOTSON-P
49 AL JONES-P
50 JUAN AGOSTO-P
53 DENNIS LAMP-P
67 JIM KERN (INJ)-P
72 CARLTON (PUDGE) FISK-C/DH

1984

5TH W — 74-88 — 10GB

1 SCOTT FLETCHER-SS/INF
2 *(RET#) NELLIE FOX*
3 HAROLD BAINES-OF
4 *(RET#) LUKE APPLING*
5 VANCE LAW-3B/UTIL
6 CHARLIE LAU-CH
7 MARC HILL-C/1B
8 DAVE STEGMAN-OF/DH
9 *(RET#) MINNIE MINOSO*
10 TONY LARUSSA-MGR
11 RUDY LAW-OF
11 *(RET#) LUIS APARICIO*
12 JOEL SKINNER-C
12 ROY SMALLEY, JR.-INF/DH (2)
13 JAMIE QUIRK-3B (1)
14 JOE NOSSEK-CH
15 ART KUSNYER-CH
16 JULIO CRUZ-2B
17 JERRY HAIRSTON-OF/DH
18 DAVE DUNCAN-CH
19 GREG LUZINSKI-DH
20 JERRY DYBZINSKI-INF/DH
21 JIM LEYLAND-CH
23 CASEY PARSONS-PH
23 RUDY LAW-OF
24 FLOYD BANNISTER-P
25 MIKE SQUIRES-UTIL/P
26 TOM O'MALLEY-3B (2)
28 RANDY NIEMANN-P
29 GREG WALKER-1B/DH
30 SALOME BAROJAS-P (1)
30 GENE NELSON-P
31 LA MARR HOYT-P
32 TIM HULETT-3B/2B
33 DARYL BOSTON-OF/DH
34 RICH DOTSON-P
35 ED BRINKMAN-CH
36 RON REED-P
37 BOB FALLON-P
37 DAN SPILLNER-P (2)
38 DAVE NELSON-CH
40 BRITT BURNS (ILL)-P
41 TOM (TOM TERRIFIC) SEAVER-P
42 RON KITTLE-OF/DH
43 JERRY DON GLEATON-P
43 STEVE CHRISTMAS-C
44 TOM PACIOREK (INJ)-1B/OF
46 LOREN (BEE BEE) BABE-CH
48 RANDY NIEMANN-P
49 AL JONES-P
50 JUAN AGOSTO-P
53 BERT ROBERGE (INJ)-P
54 JIM SIWY-P
58 STEVE CHRISTMAS-C
59 TOM BRENNAN-P
72 CARLTON (PUDGE) FISK-C/DH

1985

3TH W — 85-77 — 6GB

0 OSCAR GAMBLE-DH
0 MARK RYAL-OF
1 SCOTT FLETCHER-INF/DH
2 *(RET#) NELLIE FOX*
3 HAROLD BAINES-OF/DH
4 *(RET#) LUKE APPLING*
5 LUIS SALAZAR-UTIL
7 MARC HILL-C/3B
8 DARYL BOSTON-OF/DH
9 *(RET#) MINNIE MINOSO*
10 TONY LARUSSA-MGR
11 *(RET#) LUIS APARICIO*
12 JULIO CRUZ-2B/DH
13 OZZIE GUILLEN-SS
14 JOE NOSSEK-CH
15 ART KUSNYER-CH
17 JERRY HAIRSTON-DH/OF
18 DAVE DUNCAN-CH
20 JOE DESA-UTIL
20 REID NICHOLS-OF/DH (2)
21 JIM LEYLAND-CH
22 JOEL SKINNER-C
23 RUDY LAW-OF/DH
24 FLOYD BANNISTER-P
25 MIKE SQUIRES-PR
27 BOB FALLON-P
28 MIKE LUM-CH
29 GREG WALKER-1B/DH
30 GENE NELSON-P
31 BRUCE TANNER-P
32 TIM HULETT-3B/UTIL
33 JOHN CANGELOSI-OF/DH
34 RICH DOTSON (INJ)-P
35 ED BRINKMAN-CH
36 BILL LONG-P
37 DAN SPILLNER-P
38 JOE DESA-UTIL
39 DAVE NELSON-CH
39 GLEN ROSENBAUM-BPP
40 BRITT BURNS-P
41 TOM (TOM TERRIFIC) SEAVER-P
42 RON KITTLE-DH/OF
43 BOB JAMES-P
44 TOM PACIOREK-UTIL (1)
44 MARK GILBERT-OF
45 STEVE FIREOVID, P
46 TIM LOLLAR-P (1)
46 JERRY DON GLEATON-P
47 BRYAN (TWIG) LITTLE-INF
48 MIKE STANTON-P (2)
49 AL JONES (INJ)-P
50 JUAN AGOSTO-P
51 DAVE WEHRMEISTER-P
52 JOEL DAVIS-P
56 ED CORREA-P
59 JERRY DON GLEATON-P
72 CARLTON (PUDGE) FISK-C/DH

1986

5TH W — 72-90 — 20GB

1 WAYNE TOLLESON-UTIL (1)
1 KENNY WILLIAMS-OF/DH
2? JOE NOSSEK-CH
2 *(RET#) NELLIE FOX*
3 HAROLD BAINES-OF/DH
4 *(RET#) LUKE APPLING*
7 MARC HILL-C
8 DARYL BOSTON-OF/DH
9 *(RET#) MINNIE MINOSO*
10 TONY LARUSSA-MGR1
10 STEVE LYONS-UTIL (2)
11 *(RET#) LUIS APARICIO*
12 JULIO CRUZ-2B/DH
13 OZZIE GUILLEN-SS/DH
14 RUSS MORMAN-1B
15 ART KUSNYER-CH
15 GEORGE FOSTER-OF/DH (2)
16 KENNY WILLIAMS-OF/DH
16 JIM FREGOSI-MGR3
17 JERRY HAIRSTON-UTIL
18 DAVE DUNCAN-CH
18 BRIAN GILES (INJ)-2B/SS
19 FLOYD BANNISTER (INJ)-P
20 REID NICHOLS (INJ)-UTIL (2)
21 MOE DRABOWSKY-CH
22 JOEL SKINNER-C (1)
22 IVAN CALDERON-DH/OF (2)
23 BRYAN (TWIG) LITTLE-INF (1)
23 TIM HULETT-3B/UTIL
24 DAVE SCHMIDT-P
25 SCOTT BRADLEY-DH/OF (1)
25 RON HASSEY-DH/C (2)
26 BOBBY (BOBBY BO) BONILLA-OF/1B (1)
26 JOSE DELEON-P (2)
27 DICK BOSMAN-CH
28 DOUG (THE RED ROOSTER) (ROJO) RADER-CH/MGR2
29 GREG WALKER (INJ)-1B/DH
30 GENE NELSON-P
32 TIM HULETT-3B/UTIL
32 STEVE CARLTON-P (3)
33 NEIL ALLEN (INJ)-P
34 RICH DOTSON-P
35 ED BRINKMAN-CH
36 RAY SEARAGE-P (2)
37 DAVE COCHRANE-3B/SS
37 STEVE CARLTON-P (3)
38 PETE FILSON-P (2)
39 GLEN ROSENBAUM-BPP
40 BRYAN CLARK-P
40 JOE COWLEY-P
41 TOM (TOM TERRIFIC) SEAVER-P (1)
42 RON KITTLE-DH/OF (1)
42 JACK PERCONTE-2B
43 BOB JAMES (INJ)-P
44 JOHN CANGELOSI-OF/DH
45 BRYAN CLARK-P
46 BILL DAWLEY-P
47 BRYAN (TWIG) LITTLE-INF (1)
47 ROD CRAIG-OF
48 WILLIE HORTON-CH
49 IVAN CALDERON-DH/OF (2)
50 JUAN AGOSTO-P (1)
50 JOEL MCKEON (ILL)-P
51 PETE FILSON-P (2)
52 JOEL DAVIS-P
53 RON KARKOVICE-C
58 BOBBY THIGPEN-P
61 JOEL MCKEON (ILL)-P
72 CARLTON (PUDGE) FISK-C/UTIL

1987

5TH W — 77-85 — 8GB

1 KENNY WILLIAMS-OF
1 JERRY ROYSTER-UTIL (1)
2 *(RET#) NELLIE FOX*
3 HAROLD BAINES (INJ)-DH/OF
4 *(RET#) LUKE APPLING*
5 JERRY ROYSTER-UTIL (1)
5 RON KARKOVICE-C/DH
7 STEVE LYONS-UTIL
7 KENNY WILLIAMS-OF
8 DARYL BOSTON-OF/DH
9 *(RET#) MINNIE MINOSO*
10 FRED MANRIQUE-INF/DH
11 *(RET#) LUIS APARICIO*
12 STEVE LYONS-UTIL
13 OZZIE GUILLEN-SS
14 RALPH CITARELLA-P
15 DONNIE HILL-2B/UTIL
16 JIM FREGOSI-MGR
16 *(RET#) TED LYONS*
17 JERRY HAIRSTON-UTIL
18 JIM FREGOSI-MGR
19 FLOYD BANNISTER-P
19 *(RET#) BILLY PIERCE*
20 BILL LINDSEY-C
21 GARY REDUS-OF/DH
22 IVAN CALDERON-OF/DH
24 FLOYD BANNISTER-P
25 RON HASSEY (INJ)-C/DH
26 JOSE DELEON-P
27 DICK BOSMAN-CH
28 DOUG (THE RED ROOSTER) (ROJO) RADER-CH
29 GREG WALKER-1B/DH
32 TIM HULETT-3B/2B
33 NEIL ALLEN (INJ)-P (1)
34 RICH DOTSON-P
35 ED BRINKMAN-CH
36 RAY SEARAGE-P
37 BOBBY THIGPEN-P
38 PAT KEEDY-UTIL
38 DAVE LAPOINT-P (2)
39 GLEN ROSENBAUM-BPP
40 JIM WINN-P
40 JACK MCDOWELL-P
41 SCOTT NIELSEN-P

CHICAGO WHITE SOX

42 ADAM PETERSON-P
43 ADAM PETERSON-P
43 BOB JAMES (INJ)-P
45 JIM WINN-P
46 BILL LONG-P
47 BRYAN CLARK-P
47 JOHN PAWLOWSKI-P
48 JOHN PAWLOWSKI-P
49 DYAR MILLER-CH
50 JOEL MCKEON-P
51 ART KUSNYER-CH
52 JOEL DAVIS-P
53 RON KARKOVICE-C/DH
53 RALPH CITARELLA-P
54 DERON JOHNSON-CH
72 CARLTON (PUDGE) FISK-C/UTIL

1988

5TH W 71-90 32.5GB

1 LANCE JOHNSON-OF
2 *(RET#) NELLIE FOX*
3 HAROLD BAINES-DH/OF
4 *(RET#) LUKE APPLING*
5 RON KARKOVICE-C
7 KENNY WILLIAMS (INJ)-UTIL
8 DARYL BOSTON-OF/DH
9 *(RET#) MINNIE MINOSO*
10 FRED MANRIQUE-2B/UTIL
11 *(RET#) LUIS APARICIO*
12 STEVE LYONS-3B/UTIL
13 OZZIE GUILLEN-SS
14 RUSS MORMAN-UTIL
15 DONNIE HILL-INF/DH
16 *(RET#) TED LYONS*
17 JERRY HAIRSTON-PH
17 DAVE GALLAGHER-OF/DH
18 JIM FREGOSI-MGR
19 *(RET#) BILLY PIERCE*
20 MIKE WOODARD-2B/DH
•**20** MIKE DIAZ-INF/DH (2)
21 GARY REDUS-OF/DH (1)
22 IVAN CALDERON (INJ)-OF/DH
23 DAN PASQUA-OF/UTIL
24 CARLOS MARTINEZ-3B/DH
25 DONN PALL-P
26 RICKY HORTON-P (1)
27 MARK SALAS-C/DH
28 CARLOS MARTINEZ-3B/DH
28 KELLY PARIS (INJ)-INF/DH
29 GREG WALKER (ILL)-1B
•**30** SAP RANDALL-UTIL
31 JOHN DAVIS-P
32 JEFF BITTIGER-P
33 MELIDO PEREZ-P
34 KEN PATTERSON-P
35 ED BRINKMAN-CH
36 JOSE SEGURA-P
37 BOBBY THIGPEN-P
38 DAVE LAPOINT-P (1)
38 BARRY JONES-P
39 GLEN ROSENBAUM-CH
40 JACK MCDOWELL (INJ)-P
41 JERRY REUSS-P
42 ADAM PETERSON-P
44 JERRY REUSS-P
44 DAN PASQUA-OF/UTIL
45 SHAWN HILLEGAS-P (2)
45 CARL WILLIS-P
46 BILL LONG-P
46 STEVE ROSENBERG-P
47 JOHN PAWLOWSKI-P
47 BILL LONG-P
48 JOHN PAWLOWSKI-P
49 DYAR MILLER-CH
51 WALT (NO-NECK) WILLIAMS-CH
52 JOEL DAVIS-P
53 RON CLARK-CH
54 DON ROWE-CH
55 CAL EMERY-CH
56 RAVELO MANZANILLO-P
57 TOM MCCARTHY-P
58 JOSE SEGURA-P
61 STEVE ROSENBERG-P
72 CARLTON (PUDGE) FISK (INJ)-C

1989

7TH W 69-92 29.5GB

1 LANCE JOHNSON-OF/DH
2 *(RET#) NELLIE FOX*
3 HAROLD BAINES-DH/OF (1)
3 *(RET#) HAROLD BAINES*
4 *(RET#) LUKE APPLING*
5 RON CLARK-CH
6 WALT HRINIAK-CH
7 MATT MERULLO-C
7 SCOTT FLETCHER-2B/SS (2)
8 DARYL BOSTON-OF/DH
9 *(RET#) MINNIE MINOSO*
10 JEFF TORBORG-MGR
11 *(RET#) LUIS APARICIO*
12 STEVE LYONS-2B/UTIL
13 OZZIE GUILLEN-SS
14 FRED MANRIQUE-INF (1)
14 RUSS MORMAN-1B
15 JERRY HAIRSTON-DH
15 JEFF SCHAEFER-INF/DH
16 *(RET#) TED LYONS*
17 DAVE GALLAGHER-OF/DH
18 TERRY BEVINGTON-CH
19 *(RET#) BILLY PIERCE*
20 RON KARKOVICE-C/DH
22 IVAN CALDERON-OF/UTIL
23 ROBIN VENTURA-3B
24 CARLOS MARTINEZ-3B/UTIL
25 EDDIE WILLIAMS-3B
25 SAMMY SOSA-OF (2)
26 RUSS MORMAN-1B
27 GREG HIBBARD-P
27 JACK HARDY-P
28 BILLY JO ROBIDOUX-1B/OF
29 GREG WALKER-1B/DH
30 DONN PALL-P
31 JOHN DAVIS-P
32 JEFF BITTIGER (INJ)-P
32 SAMMY ELLIS-CH
33 MELIDO PEREZ-P
34 KEN PATTERSON-P
34 EDDIE WILLIAMS-3B
34 RICH DOTSON-P (2)
35 JEFF BITTIGER (INJ)-P
36 ERIC KING (INJ)-P
37 BOBBY THIGPEN-P
38 KEN PATTERSON-P
38 BARRY JONES (INJ)-P
39 GLEN ROSENBAUM-CH
41 JERRY REUSS-P (1)
42 RON KITTLE (INJ)-UTIL
43 ADAM PETERSON-P
44 DAN PASQUA (INJ)-OF/DH
45 JACK HARDY-P
45 SHAWN HILLEGAS-P
46 STEVE ROSENBERG-P
47 BILL LONG-P
49 TOM MCCARTHY-P
50 BARRY JONES (INJ)-P
51 JOHN DAVIS???-P???
53 DAVE LAROCHE-CH
54 GREG HIBBARD-P
54 JOSE SEGURA-P
57 SHAWN HILLEGAS-P
57 WAYNE EDWARDS-P
72 CARLTON (PUDGE) FISK (INJ)-C/DH

1990

2ND W 94-68 9GB

1 LANCE JOHNSON-OF/DH
2 *(RET#) NELLIE FOX*
3 *(RET#) HAROLD BAINES*
4 *(RET#) LUKE APPLING*
5 RON CLARK-CH
6 WALT HRINIAK-CH
7 SCOTT FLETCHER-2B
8 DARYL BOSTON-DH/OF (1)
8 PHIL BRADLEY-OF/DH (2)
9 *(RET#) MINNIE MINOSO*
10 JEFF TORBORG-MGR
11 *(RET#) LUIS APARICIO*
12 STEVE LYONS-UTIL
13 OZZIE GUILLEN-SS
14 CRAIG GREBECK-INF/DH
16 *(RET#) TED LYONS*
17 DAVE GALLAGHER-OF/DH (1)
17 DAVE LAROCHE-CH
18 TERRY BEVINGTON-CH
19 *(RET#) BILLY PIERCE*
20 RON KARKOVICE-C/DH
21 MATT STARK-DH
22 IVAN CALDERON-OF/UTIL
23 ROBIN VENTURA-3B/1B
24 CARLOS MARTINEZ-1B/UTIL
25 SAMMY SOSA-OF
26 JERRY WILLARD-C
27 GREG HIBBARD-P
28 RODNEY MCCRAY-OF/DH
29 GREG WALKER-1B/DH (1)
29 JACK MCDOWELL-P
30 DONN PALL-P
31 SCOTT RADINSKY-P
32 ALEX FERNANDEZ-P
32 STEVE ROSENBERG-P
33 MELIDO PEREZ-P
34 KEN PATTERSON-P
35 FRANK (THE BIG HURT) THOMAS-1B/DH
36 ERIC KING (INJ)-P
37 BOBBY THIGPEN-P
38 ERIC KING (INJ)-P
40 JACK MCDOWELL-P
42 RON KITTLE-DH/1B (1)
43 ADAM PETERSON-P
44 DAN PASQUA (INJ)-DH/OF
45 WAYNE EDWARDS-P
46 SAMMY ELLIS-CH
47 BILL LONG-P (1)
47 STEVE ROSENBERG-P
50 BARRY JONES-P
52 JERRY KUTZLER-P
53 DAVE LAROCHE-CH
54 BARRY FOOTE-CH
56 SCOTT RADINSKY-P
57 SHAWN HILLEGAS-P
72 CARLTON (PUDGE) FISK-C/DH

1991

2ND W 87-75 8GB

1 LANCE JOHNSON-OF
2 *(RET#) NELLIE FOX*
3 *(RET#) HAROLD BAINES*
4 *(RET#) LUKE APPLING*
5 MATT MERULLO-UTIL
6 WALT HRINIAK-CH
7 SCOTT FLETCHER-2B/3B
8 BO JACKSON (INJ)-DH
9 *(RET#) MINNIE MINOSO*
10 JEFF TORBORG-MGR
11 *(RET#) LUIS APARICIO*
12 MIKE HUFF-OF/2B (2)
13 OZZIE GUILLEN-SS
14 CRAIG GREBECK-INF
15 JOE NOSSEK-CH
16 *(RET#) TED LYONS*
17 DAVE LAROCHE-CH
18 TERRY BEVINGTON-CH
19 *(RET#) BILLY PIERCE*
20 RON KARKOVICE (INJ)-C/OF
21 JOEY CORA-INF/DH
22 DONN PALL-P
23 ROBIN VENTURA-3B/1B
24 WARREN NEWSON-OF/DH
25 SAMMY SOSA-OF/DH
26 RODNEY MCCRAY-OF/DH
27 GREG HIBBARD-P
28 CORY SNYDER-UTIL (1)
28 ESTEBAN BELTRE-SS
29 JACK MCDOWELL-P
30 TIM (ROCK) RAINES-OF/DH
31 SCOTT RADINSKY-P
32 ALEX FERNANDEZ-P
32 STEVE ROSENBERG-P
33 MELIDO PEREZ-P
34 KEN PATTERSON-P
35 FRANK (THE BIG HURT) THOMAS-DH/1B
36 BARRY FOOTE-CH
37 BOBBY THIGPEN-P
38 WILSON ALVAREZ-P
39 ROBERTO HERNANDEZ,-P
40 WILSON ALVAREZ-P
41 JEFF CARTER-P
42 JEFF CARTER-P
42 RON KITTLE-1B
42 TOM DREES-P
43 RAMON GARCIA-P
44 DAN PASQUA-1B/UITL
45 WAYNE EDWARDS-P
46 SAMMY ELLIS-CH
47 DON WAKAMATSU-C
49 CHARLIE HOUGH-P
50 BRIAN DRAHMAN-P
51 STEVE WAPNICK-P
72 CARLTON (PUDGE) FISK-C/UTIL

1992

3RD W 86-76 10GB

1 LANCE JOHNSON-OF
2 *(RET#) NELLIE FOX*
3 *(RET#) HAROLD BAINES*
4 *(RET#) LUKE APPLING*
5 MATT MERULLO-C/DH
6 WALT HRINIAK-CH
7 GENE LAMONT-MGR
7 STEVE SAX-2B
(8) BO JACKSON (INJ)-(OF)
9 *(RET#) MINNIE MINOSO*
10 STEVE SAX-2B
10 MIKE HUFF-OF/DH
10 SHAWN JETER-OF/DH
11 *(RET#) LUIS APARICIO*
12 MIKE HUFF-OF/DH
13 OZZIE GUILLEN (INJ)-SS
14 CRAIG GREBECK-SS/UTIL
15 JOE NOSSEK-CH
16 *(RET#) TED LYONS*
17 DOUG MANSOLINO-CH
18 TERRY BEVINGTON-CH
19 *(RET#) BILLY PIERCE*
20 RON KARKOVICE-C/OF
21 GEORGE BELL-DH/OF
22 DONN PALL-P
23 ROBIN VENTURA-3B/1B
24 WARREN NEWSON-OF/DH
25 KIRK MCCASKILL-P
26 KIRK MCCASKILL-P
26 MIKE SQUIRES-CH
27 GREG HIBBARD-P
28 JOEY CORA-INF/DH
29 JACK MCDOWELL-P
30 TIM (ROCK) RAINES-OF/DH
31 SCOTT RADINSKY-P
32 ALEX FERNANDEZ-P
33 GENE LAMONT-MGR
34 TERRY LEACH-P
35 FRANK (THE BIG HURT) THOMAS-1B/DH
36 JACKIE BROWN-CH
36 SCOTT HEMOND-UTIL (2)
37 BOBBY THIGPEN-P
38 ESTEBAN BELTRE-SS/DH
38 MIKE SQUIRES-CH
39 ROBERTO HERNANDEZ-P
40 WILSON ALVAREZ-P
41 JACKIE BROWN-CH
42 DALE SVEUM-INF
44 DAN PASQUA-UTIL
45 SHAWN ABNER-OF/DH
48 NELSON SANTOVENIA-C
49 CHARLIE HOUGH-P
50 BRIAN DRAHMAN-P
54 MIKE DUNNE-P
57 CHRIS CRON-1B/OF
72 CARLTON (PUDGE) FISK-C/DH

1993

1ST W 94-68 0GB

L ALCS-TORA 4-2

1 LANCE JOHNSON-OF
2 *(RET#) NELLIE FOX*
3 *(RET#) HAROLD BAINES*
4 *(RET#) LUKE APPLING*
5 MATT MERULLO-DH
6 WALT HRINIAK-CH
7 STEVE SAX-UTIL
8 BO JACKSON-OF/DH
9 *(RET#) MINNIE MINOSO*
10 DAVE STIEB (INJ)-P
10 MIKE (SPANKY) LAVALLIERE-C (2)
11 *(RET#) LUIS APARICIO*
12 MIKE HUFF-OF
13 OZZIE GUILLEN-SS
14 CRAIG GREBECK-INF
15 JOE NOSSEK-CH
16 *(RET#) TED LYONS*
17 DOUG MANSOLINO-CH
18 TERRY BEVINGTON-CH
19 *(RET#) BILLY PIERCE*
20 RON KARKOVICE-C
21 GEORGE BELL (INJ)-DH
22 DONN PALL-P (1)
23 ROBIN VENTURA-3B/1B
24 WARREN NEWSON-DH/OF
25 KIRK MCCASKILL-P
26 ELLIS BURKS-OF
27 IVAN CALDERON-DH (1)
27 RICK WRONA-C
28 JOEY CORA-2B/3B
29 JACK MCDOWELL-P
30 TIM (ROCK) RAINES (INJ)-OF
31 SCOTT RADINSKY-P
32 ALEX FERNANDEZ-P
33 GENE LAMONT-MGR
34 TERRY LEACH (INJ)-P
35 FRANK (THE BIG HURT) THOMAS-1B/DH
36 TIM BELCHER-P (2)
37 BOBBY THIGPEN-P (1)
39 ROBERTO HERNANDEZ-P
40 WILSON ALVAREZ-P
41 JACKIE BROWN-CH
42 RODNEY BOLTON-P
44 DAN PASQUA-UTIL
45 SCOTT RUFFCORN-P
46 CHUCK CARY (INJ)-P
48 JOSE DELEON-P (2)
49 JEFF SCHWARZ-P
50 BARRY JONES-P
50 BRIAN DRAHMAN-P
51 JASON BERE-P
53 NORBERTO (PACO) MARTIN-2B/DH
55 DEWEY ROBINSON-CH
58 CHRIS HOWARD-P
62 DREW DENSON-1B
68 DOUG LINDSEY-C (2)

CHICAGO WHITE SOX

72 CARLTON (PUDGE) FISK (RET)-C
MIKE DUNNE (INJ)-(P)

1994

1st C 67-46 0GB
STRIKE NO POST-SEASON

1 LANCE JOHNSON-OF
2 *(RET#) NELLIE FOX*
3 *(RET#) HAROLD BAINES*
4 *(RET#) LUKE APPLING*
6 WALT HRINIAK-CH
7 NORBERTO (PACO) MARTIN-2B
8 OLMEDO SAENZ-3B
9 *(RET#) MINNIE MINOSO*
10 MIKE (SPANKY) LAVALLIERE-C
11 *(RET#) LUIS APARICIO*
12 CRAIG GREBECK (INJ)-2B
13 OZZIE GUILLEN-SS
14 JULIO FRANCO-DH
15 JOE NOSSEK-CH
16 *(RET#) TED LYONS*
17 DOUG MANSOLINO-CH
18 TERRY BEVINGTON-CH
19 *(RET#) BILLY PIERCE*
20 RON KARKOVICE (INJ)-C
21 SCOTT SANDERSON-P
22 DARRIN JACKSON-OF
23 ROBIN VENTURA-3B/1B
24 WARREN NEWSON-DH/OF
25 KIRK MCCASKILL-P
26 JOE HALL (INJ)-OF
27 DENNIS COOK-P
28 JOEY CORA-2B/3B
29 JACK MCDOWELL-P
30 TIM (ROCK) RAINES-OF
(31) SCOTT RADINSKY (INJ)-(P)
32 ALEX FERNANDEZ-P
33 GENE LAMONT-MGR
34 DANN HOWITT-OF/1B
34 ATLEE HAMMAKER-P
35 FRANK (THE BIG HURT) THOMAS-1B/DH
36 SCOTT RUFFCORN-P
38 DANE JOHNSON-P
39 ROBERTO HERNANDEZ-P
40 WILSON ALVAREZ-P
41 JACKIE BROWN-CH
42 PAUL ASSENMACHER-P
43 BOB ZUPCIC-OF (2)
44 DAN PASQUA (INJ)-UTIL
46 JASON BERE-P
48 JOSE DELEON-P
49 JEFF SCHWARZ-P (1)
49 BOB MELVIN-C (3)
50 PAUL ASSENMACHER-P
55 DEWEY ROBINSON-CH
55 RON TINGLEY (INJ)-C

1995

3rd C 68-76 32GB
144 GAME SEASON

1 LANCE JOHNSON-OF
2 *(RET#) NELLIE FOX*
3 *(RET#) HAROLD BAINES*
4 *(RET#) LUKE APPLING*
5 RAY DURHAM-2B
6 WALT HRINIAK-CH
7 NORBERTO (PACO) MARTIN-2B
8 MIKE DEVEREAUX-OF
9 *(RET#) MINNIE MINOSO*
10 MIKE (SPANKY) LAVALLIERE (INJ)-C
11 *(RET#) LUIS APARICIO*
12 CRAIG GREBECK-SS
13 OZZIE GUILLEN-SS
14 DAVE MARTINEZ-OF
15 KIRK MCCASKILL-P
16 *(RET#) TED LYONS*
17 CHRIS SABO-DH
17 DOUG MANSOLINO-CH
18 TERRY BEVINGTON-CH/MGR2
19 *(RET#) BILLY PIERCE*
20 RON KARKOVICE-C
21 JOE NOSSEK-CH
23 ROBIN VENTURA-3B
24 WARREN NEWSON-OF
24 MIKE CAMERON-OF
25 JIM ABBOTT-P
25 MIKE PAZIK-CH
26 BRIAN KEYSER-P
27 DOUG MANSOLINO-CH
27 CHRIS SNOPEK-3B
28 LYLE MOUTON-OF
29 JOHN KRUK (INJ) (RET)-DH
30 TIM (ROCK) RAINES-OF
31 SCOTT RADINSKY (INJ)-P
32 ALEX FERNANDEZ-P
33 GENE LAMONT-MGR1
33 DOUG BRADY-2B
34 ATLEE HAMMAKER-P
34 ANDREW LORRAINE-P
35 FRANK (THE BIG HURT) THOMAS-1B/DH
36 SCOTT RUFFCORN-P
37 JAMES BALDWIN-P
38 MIKE SIROTKA-P
39 ROBERTO HERNANDEZ-P
40 WILSON ALVAREZ-P
41 JACKIE BROWN-CH
41 BILL SIMAS-P
42 ROD BOLTON-P
45 DAVE RIGHETTI-P
46 JASON BERE (INJ)-P
47 ISIDRO MARQUEZ-P
48 JOSE DELEON-P
48 JEFF SHAW-P
49 RON DIBBLE (WAIV)-P
49 LUIS ANDUJAR-P
50 DON COOPER-CH
50 LARRY THOMAS-P
51 TOM FORTUGNO-P
51 MIKE BERTOTTI-P
52 RON JACKSON-CH
53 CHRIS TREMIE-C
54 BARRY LYONS-C
55 RICK PETERSON-CH
56 ROLY DE ARMAS-CH
60 MATT KARCHNER-P

1996

2nd C 85-77 14.5GB

2 *(RET#) NELLIE FOX*
3 HAROLD BAINES-DH
4 *(RET#) LUKE APPLING*
5 RAY DURHAM-2B
7 NORBERTO (PACO) MARTIN (INJ)-2B
8 TONY PHILLIPS-OF
9 *(RET#) MINNIE MINOSO*
10 DARREN LEWIS-OF
11 *(RET#) LUIS APARICIO*
12 CHAD KREUTER (INJ)-C
13 OZZIE GUILLEN-SS
14 DAVE MARTINEZ-OF
15 KIRK MCCASKILL (REL)-P
15 PAT BORDERS-C (3)
16 *(RET#) TED LYONS*
17 DOUG MANSOLINO-CH
18 TERRY BEVINGTON-MGR
19 *(RET#) BILLY PIERCE*
20 RON KARKOVICE-C
21 JOE NOSSEK-CH
22 BILL (BILLY BUCK) BUCKNER-CH
23 ROBIN VENTURA-3B
24 MIKE CAMERON-OF
25 MIKE PAZIK-CH
26 BRIAN KEYSER-P
27 CHRIS SNOPEK-3B
28 LYLE MOUTON-OF
29 DON SLAUGHT-C (2)
31 GREG NORTON-3B
32 ALEX FERNANDEZ-P
33 MARVIN FREEMAN-P (2)
34 JOE MAGRANE-P
34 DOMINGO CEDENO-INF (2)
35 FRANK (THE BIG HURT) THOMAS (INJ)-1B
36 KEVIN TAPANI-P
37 JAMES BALDWIN-P
38 MIKE SIROTKA-P
39 ROBERTO HERNANDEZ-P
40 WILSON ALVAREZ-P
41 BILL SIMAS-P
42 SCOTT RUFFCORN-P
43 MIKE ROBERTSON-PH
44 TONY CASTILLO-P (2)
45 DANNY TARTABULL-OF
46 JASON BERE (INJ)-P
47 MATT KARCHNER (INJ)-P
48 JEFF DARWIN-P
49 LUIS ANDUJAR-P (1)
49 STACY JONES-P
50 LARRY THOMAS (INJ)-P
51 MIKE BERTOTTI-P
52 RON JACKSON-CH
54 ALAN LEVINE-P
55 ROBERTO MACHADO-C
56 ROLY DE ARMAS-CH
58 MARK SALAS-CH
70 RICH SAUVEUR-P
71 JOSE MUNOZ-2B

1997

2nd C 80-81 6GB

2 *(RET#) NELLIE FOX*
3 HAROLD BAINES-DH (1)
3 *(RET#) HAROLD BAINES*
4 *(RET#) LUKE APPLING*
5 RAY DURHAM-2B
7 NORBERTO (PACO) MARTIN (INJ)-2B/3B
8 ALBERT (JOEY) BELLE-OF
9 *(RET#) MINNIE MINOSO*
10 DARREN LEWIS-OF (1)
11 *(RET#) LUIS APARICIO*
12 CHAD KREUTER (INJ)-C (1)
12 JORGE FABREGAS-C (2)
13 OZZIE GUILLEN-SS
14 DAVE MARTINEZ-OF/1B
15 DOUG DRABEK-P
16 *(RET#) TED LYONS*
17 DOUG (THE RED ROOSTER) (ROJO) RADER-CH
18 TERRY BEVINGTON-MGR
19 *(RET#) BILLY PIERCE*
20 RON KARKOVICE-C
21 JOE NOSSEK-CH
22 BILL (BILLY BUCK) BUCKNER-CH
22 CHAD FONVILLE-INF (2)
23 ROBIN VENTURA (INJ)-3B
24 MIKE CAMERON-OF
25 MIKE PAZIK-CH
26 CHUCK MCELROY-P (2)
27 CHRIS SNOPEK-3B
28 LYLE MOUTON (INJ)-OF
29 TONY PENA (INJ)-C (1)
30 MAGGLIO ORDONEZ-OF
31 GREG NORTON-3B
32 TOM FORDHAM-P
33 MIKE SIROTKA-P
34 MARIO VALDEZ-3B/1B
35 FRANK (THE BIG HURT) THOMAS (INJ)-1B
36 SCOTT EYRE-P
37 JAMES BALDWIN-P
38 JAIME NAVARRO-P
39 ROBERTO HERNANDEZ-P (1)
40 WILSON ALVAREZ-P (1)
41 BILL SIMAS (INJ)-P
(42) ROGER MCDOWELL (INJ)-(P)
42 *(RET#) JACKIE ROBINSON*
43 CARLOS CASTILLO (INJ)-P
44 TONY CASTILLO-P
44 DANNY DARWIN-P (1)
44 KEITH FOULKE-P (2)
45 JEFF ABBOTT-DH/OF
46 JASON BERE (INJ)-P
47 MATT KARCHNER-P
48 JEFF DARWIN-P
49 TONY CASTILLO-P
50 LARRY THOMAS-P
51 MIKE BERTOTTI-P
52 RON JACKSON-CH
53 ART KUSYNER-CH
54 ALAN LEVINE-P
55 ROBERTO MACHADO-C
57 CHRIS CLEMONS-P
58 MARK SALAS-CH
59 BRYAN (TWIG) LITTLE-CH
60 NELSON CRUZ-P
61 CARLOS CASTILLO-P
70 RICH SAUVEUR-P
71 JOSE MUNOZ-2B
72 *(RET#) CARLTON FISK*
73 TONY PHILLIPS-OF (1)

1998

2nd C 80-82 9GB

2 *(RET#) NELLIE FOX*
3 *(RET#) HAROLD BAINES*
4 *(RET#) LUKE APPLING*
5 RAY DURHAM-2B
7 JERRY MANUEL-MGR
8 ALBERT (JOEY) BELLE-OF
9 *(RET#) MINNIE MINOSO*
10 CHRIS SNOPEK-3B (1)
11 *(RET#) LUIS APARICIO*
12 CHAD KREUTER C (1)
12 DOUG (THE RED ROOSTER) (ROJO) RADER-CH
12 WIL CORDERO-1B/OF
15 CHAD KREUTER C (1)
16 *(RET#) TED LYONS*
17 DOUG (THE RED ROOSTER) (ROJO) RADER-CH
17 MIKE CARUSO-SS
18 WALLACE JOHNSON-CH
19 *(RET#) BILLY PIERCE*
20 MIKE CARUSO-SS
20 BRYAN (TWIG) LITTLE-CH
21 JOE NOSSEK-CH
22 CHARLIE O'BRIEN (INJ)-C (1)
23 ROBIN VENTURA-3B
24 MIKE CAMERON-OF
25 MIKE PAZIK-CH
25 JIM ABBOTT-P
26 LOU FRAZIER-OF/DH
27 BRIAN SIMMONS-OF
28 RON JACKSON-CH
28 CRAIG WILSON-OF
29 KEITH FOULKE (INJ)-P
30 MAGGLIO ORDONEZ-OF
31 GREG NORTON-3B
32 TOM FORDHAM-P
33 MIKE SIROTKA-P
35 FRANK (THE BIG HURT) THOMAS-1B/DH
36 SCOTT EYRE-P
37 JAMES BALDWIN-P
38 JAIME NAVARRO-P
40 JIM PARQUE-P
41 BILL SIMAS-P
42 *(RET#) JACKIE ROBINSON*
43 CARLOS CASTILLO-P
44 RUBEN SIERRA-DH/OF
44 CHAD BRADFORD-P
45 JEFF ABBOTT-DH/OF
46 JASON BERE (WAIV)-P
47 MATT KARCHNER (INJ)-P (1)
48 VON JOSHUA-CH
49 TONY CASTILLO-P
50 LARRY CASIAN-P
52 TODD RIZZO-P
53 ART KUSYNER-CH
54 LOU FRAZIER-OF
54 NARDI CONTRERAS-CH (2)
55 ROBERT MACHADO-C
56 BRYAN WARD-P
57 MARK L. JOHNSON-C
58 MARK SALAS-CH
59 BRYAN (TWIG) LITTLE-CH
59 JOHN SNYDER-P
62 BOBBY HOWRY-P
64 MARK L. JOHNSON-C
66 MIKE HEATHCOTT-P
72 *(RET#) CARLTON FISK*
__ BILL (BILLY BUCK) BUCKNER-CH

1999

2nd W 75-86 21.5GB

2 *(RET#) NELLIE FOX*
3 *(RET#) HAROLD BAINES*
4 *(RET#) LUKE APPLING*
5 RAY DURHAM-2B
7 JERRY MANUEL-MGR
8 BROOK FORDYCE-C
9 *(RET#) MINNIE MINOSO*
10 MARK L. JOHNSON-C
11 *(RET#) LUIS APARICIO*
12 CHRIS SINGLETON-OF
14 PAUL KONERKO-1B
15 JOSH PAUL-C
16 *(RET#) TED LYONS*
17 MIKE CARUSO-SS
18 WALLACE JOHNSON-CH
19 *(RET#) BILLY PIERCE*
20 BRYAN (TWIG) LITTLE-CH
21 JOE NOSSEK-CH
22 DARRIN (D.J.) JACKSON (INJ)-OF
25 JEFF ABBOTT-OF
26 MCKAY CHRISTENSEN-OF
(27) BRIAN SIMMONS (INJ)-(OF)
28 CRAIG WILSON-OF
29 KEITH FOULKE-P
30 MAGGLIO ORDONEZ-OF
31 GREG NORTON-3B
32 KIP WELLS-P
33 MIKE SIROTKA-P
34 JASON DELLAERO-INF
35 FRANK (THE BIG HURT) THOMAS-1B/DH
36 SCOTT EYRE-P
37 JAMES BALDWIN-P
38 JAIME NAVARRO-P
39 JEFF LIEFER-OF/1B
40 JIM PARQUE-P
41 BILL SIMAS-P
42 *(RET#) JACKIE ROBINSON*
43 CARLOS CASTILLO-P
44 CHAD BRADFORD-P
45 CARLOS LEE-OF
46 BOBBY HOWRY-P
47 TANYON STURTZE-P
48 VON JOSHUA-CH
49 DAVID LUNDQUIST-P
50 SEAN LOWE-P
51 PAT DANEKER-P
52 DARREN HALL (INJ)-P
52 TODD RIZZO-P
53 ART KUSYNER-CH
54 NARDI CONTRERAS-CH
55 LIU RODRIGUEZ-INF
56 BRYAN WARD-P

58 MARK SALAS-CH
59 JOHN SNYDER-P
60 JOE DAVENPORT-P
61 JESUS PENA-P
62 AARON MYETT-P
72 *(RET#) CARLTON FISK*

2000

1st C 95-67 0GB
L ALDS-SEAA 3-0

2 *(RET#) NELLIE FOX*
3 *(RET#) HAROLD BAINES*
3 HAROLD BAINES-DH (2)
4 *(RET#) LUKE APPLING*
5 RAY DURHAM-2B
7 JERRY MANUEL-MGR
8 BROOK FORDYCE-C (1)
8 CHARLES JOHNSON-C (2)
9 *(RET#) MINNIE MINOSO*
10 MARK L. JOHNSON-C
11 *(RET#) LUIS APARICIO*
12 CHRIS SINGLETON-OF
14 PAUL KONERKO-1B
15 JOSH PAUL-C
16 *(RET#) TED LYONS*
18 WALLACE JOHNSON-CH
19 *(RET#) BILLY PIERCE*
20 BRYAN (TWIG) LITTLE-CH
21 CAL ELDRED (INJ)-P
22 JOSE VALENTIN-INF
23 JOE NOSSEK-CH
24 JOE CREDE-INF
25 JEFF ABBOTT-OF
26 MCKAY CHRISTENSEN-OF
27 BRIAN SIMMONS (INJ)-OF
28 CRAIG WILSON-OF
29 KEITH FOULKE-P
30 MAGGLIO ORDONEZ-OF
31 GREG NORTON-3B
31 J. R. PHILLIPS-INF
32 KIP WELLS-P
33 MIKE SIROTKA-P
34 JASON DELLAERO-INF
35 FRANK (THE BIG HURT) THOMAS-1B/DH
36 SCOTT EYRE-P
37 JAMES BALDWIN-P
38 AARON MYETTE-P
39 JEFF LIEFER (INJ) OF/1B
40 JIM PARQUE-P
41 BILL SIMAS-P
42 *(RET#) JACKIE ROBINSON*
43 HERBERT PERRY-3B (2)
44 KEN HILL-P (2)
44 CHAD BRADFORD-P
45 CARLOS LEE-OF
45 NARDI CONTRERAS-CH
46 BOBBY HOWRY-P
47 TANYON STURTZE-P (1)
47 TONY GRAFFANINO-INF (2)
48 VON JOSHUA-CH
49 LORENZO BARCELO-P
49 DESI WILSON-1B
50 SEAN LOWE-P
52 JIM GARLAND-P
53 ART KUSYNER-CH
54 NARDI CONTRERAS-CH
56 MARK BUEHRLE-P
57 KEVIN BEIRNE-P
58 MARK GINTER-P
60 ROCKY BIDDLE-P
61 JESUS PENA-P (1)
62 ESTEBAN BELTRE-INF
63 YAMIL BENITEZ-OF
64 STEVE GIBRALTER-OF
65 KELLY WUNSCH-P
72 *(RET#) CARLTON FISK*

2001

3rd W 83-79 8GB

2 *(RET#) NELLIE FOX*
3 *(RET#) HAROLD BAINES*
4 *(RET#) LUKE APPLING*
5 RAY DURHAM-2B
7 JERRY MANUEL-MGR
8 MARK L. JOHNSON-C
9 *(RET#) MINNIE MINOSO*
10 ROYCE CLAYTON-SS
11 *(RET#) LUIS APARICIO*
12 CHRIS SINGLETON-OF
13 ANTONIO OSUNA-P
14 PAUL KONERKO-1B
15 SANDY ALOMAR, JR. (INJ)-C
16 *(RET#) TED LYONS*
17 TONY GRAFFANINO-2B
18 WALLACE JOHNSON-CH
19 *(RET#) BILLY PIERCE*
20 GARY PETTIS-CH
21 CAL ELDRED (INJ)-P
22 JOSE VALENTIN (INJ)-INF
23 JOE NOSSEK-CH
24 JOE CREDE-INF
26 MCKAY CHRISTENSEN-OF (1)
27 JOSH PAUL-C
28 JULIO RAMIREZ-OF
29 KEITH FOULKE-P
30 MAGGLIO ORDONEZ-OF
31 JOSE CANSECO-DH
32 KIP WELLS-P
33 DAVID WELLS (INJ)-P
35 FRANK (THE BIG HURT) THOMAS (INJ)-1B/DH
36 BILL PULSIPHER-P (3)
37 JAMES BALDWIN (INJ)-P (1)
38 GARY GLOVER-P
39 JEFF LIEFER-1B
40 JIM PARQUE (INJ)-P
41 BILL SIMAS-P
42 *(RET#) JACKIE ROBINSON*
43 HERBERT PERRY (INJ)-3B
44 AARON ROWAND-OF
45 CARLOS LEE-OF
46 BOBBY HOWRY-P
48 VON JOSHUA-CH
49 LORENZO BARCELO (INJ)-P
50 SEAN LOWE-P
52 JON GARLAND-P
53 ART KUSYNER-CH
54 NARDI CONTRERAS-CH
55 JOSH FOGG-P
56 MARK BUEHRLE-P
57 ALAN EMBREE-P (2)
58 MARK GINTER-P
60 ROCKY BIDDLE-P
61 KEN VINING-P
62 DAN WRIGHT-P
65 KELLY WUNSCH (INJ)-P
66 MARK DELASANDRO-C
72 *(RET#) CARLTON FISK*

2002

2nd C 81-81 13.5GB

1 KENNY LOFTON-OF (1)
2 *(RET#) NELLIE FOX*
3 *(RET#) HAROLD BAINES*
4 *(RET#) LUKE APPLING*
5 RAY DURHAM-2B (1)
7 JERRY MANUEL-MGR
8 MARK L. JOHNSON-C
9 *(RET#) MINNIE MINOSO*
10 ROYCE CLAYTON-SS
11 *(RET#) LUIS APARICIO*
12 WILLIE HARRIS-2B/OF
13 ANTONIO OSUNA-P
14 PAUL KONERKO-1B/DH
15 SANDY ALOMAR, JR.-C (1)
16 *(RET#) TED LYONS*
17 TONY GRAFFANINO (INJ)-INF
18 WALLACE JOHNSON-CH
19 *(RET#) BILLY PIERCE*
20 GARY PETTIS-CH
22 JOSE VALENTIN-2B/SS
23 JOE NOSSEK-CH
24 JOE CREDE-3B
25 JOE BORCHARD-OF
27 JOSH PAUL-C/OF
28 D'ANGELO JIMENEZ-INF (1)
29 KEITH FOULKE-P
30 MAGGLIO ORDONEZ-OF
35 FRANK (THE BIG HURT) THOMAS-DH/1B
36 DANNY WRIGHT-P
38 GARY GLOVER-P
39 JEFF LIEFER-OF/1B/DH
40 JIM PARQUE (INJ)-P
41 MIKE PORZIO-P
42 *(RET#) JACKIE ROBINSON*
43 DAMASO MARTE-P
44 AARON ROWAND-OF
45 CARLOS LEE-OF
46 BOBBY HOWRY-P (1)
47 GARY WARD-CH
48 TODD RITCHIE (INJ)-P
49 LORENZO BARCELO-P
51 JON RAUCH-P
52 JON GARLAND-P
53 MIKE PORZIO-CH
53 ART KUSYNER-CH
54 NARDI CONTRERAS-CH
56 MARK BUEHRLE-P
58 MARK GINTER-P
60 ROCKY BIDDLE (INJ)-P
61 MIGUEL OLIVO-C
63 DON COOPER-CH
65 KELLY WUNSCH (INJ)-P
72 *(RET#) CARLTON FISK*

2003

2nd C 86-76 4GB

1 RAFAEL SANTANA-CH
2 *(RET#) NELLIE FOX*
3 *(RET#) HAROLD BAINES*
4 *(RET#) LUKE APPLING*
5 D'ANGELO JIMENEZ-2B (1)
5 CARL EVERETT-OF (2)
7 JERRY MANUEL-MGR
8 MIGUEL OLIVO-C
9 *(RET#) MINNIE MINOSO*
10 BRUCE KIMM-CH
11 *(RET#) LUIS APARICIO*
12 WILLIE HARRIS (INJ)-OF/2B
12 ROBERTO ALOMAR-2B (2)
12 WILLIE HARRIS (INJ)-OF/2B
14 PAUL KONERKO-1B/DH
15 SANDY ALOMAR, JR. (INJ)-C
16 *(RET#) TED LYONS*
17 TONY GRAFFANINO-INF
19 *(RET#) BILLY PIERCE*
20 JON GARLAND-P
21 ESTEBAN LOAIZA-P
22 JOSE VALENTIN-SS
23 BRIAN DAUBACH-1B/DH/OF
24 JOE CREDE-3B
25 JOE BORCHARD-OF
26 JOE NOSSEK-CH
27 JOSH PAUL-C (1)
27 CARL EVERETT-OF (2)
27 JAMIE BURKE-C
28 ARMANDO RIOS-OF
29 GREG WALKER-CH
30 MAGGLIO ORDONEZ-OF
32 MATT GINTER-P
33 AARON ROWAND-OF
34 DON COOPER-CH
35 FRANK (THE BIG HURT) THOMAS-DH/1B
36 TOM (FLASH) GORDON-P
37 JON ADKINS-P
38 GARY GLOVER-P (1)
38 NEAL COTTS-P
39 AARON MILES-2B
40 BARTOLO COLON (SUS:5G)-P
41 MIKE PORZIO-P
42 *(RET#) JACKIE ROBINSON*
43 DAMASO MARTE-P
44 BILLY KOCH (INJ)-P
45 CARLOS LEE-OF
46 DANNY WRIGHT (INJ)-P
47 GARY WARD-CH
47 SCOTT SULLIVAN-P (2)
48 JOSH STEWART (INJ)-P
50 RICK WHITE (WAIV)-P (1)
50 JOSE PANIAGUA (REL)-P
52 DAVID SANDERS-P
53 ART KUSYNER-CH
56 MARK BUEHRLE-P
60 SCOTT SCHOENEWEIS-P (2)
65 KELLY WUNSCH (INJ)-P
72 *(RET#) CARLTON FISK*

2004

2nd C 83-79 9GB

1 WILLIE HARRIS-2B
2 *(RET#) NELLIE FOX*
3 HAROLD BAINES-CH
3 *(RET#) HAROLD BAINES*
4 *(RET#) LUKE APPLING*
5 JUAN URIBE-2B
7 TIMO PEREZ-OF
8 MIGUEL OLIVO-C (1)
9 *(RET#) MINNIE MINOSO*
10 SHINGO TAKATSU-P
11 *(RET#) LUIS APARICIO*
12 ROBERTO ALOMAR-2B (2)
13 OZZIE GUILLEN-MGR
14 PAUL KONERKO-1B
15 SANDY ALOMAR, JR.-C
16 *(RET#) TED LYONS*
17 RAFAEL SANTANA-CH
18 CLIFF POLITTE-P
19 *(RET#) BILLY PIERCE*
20 JON GARLAND-P
21 ESTEBAN LOAIZA-P (1)
22 JOSE VALENTIN (INJ)-SS
23 JOE NOSSEK-CH
24 JOE CREDE-3B
25 JOE BORCHARD-OF
26 ROSS GLOAD-OF/1B
27 JAMIE BURKE-C
28 JOEY CORA-CH
29 GREG WALKER-CH
30 MAGGLIO ORDONEZ (INJ)-OF
31 BEN DAVIS-C (2)
32 KELLY DRANSFELDT-SS
33 AARON ROWAND-OF
34 DON COOPER-CH
34 FREDDY GARCIA-P (2)
35 FRANK (THE BIG HURT) THOMAS-DH
36 DAN WRIGHT-P
37 JON ADKINS-P
38 GARY GLOVER-P (1)
38 MIKE JACKSON-P
39 WILSON VALDEZ-SS
41 JASON GRILLI-P
42 *(RET#) JACKIE ROBINSON*
43 DAMASO MARTE-P
44 BILLY KOCH-P (1)
45 CARLOS LEE-OF
46 NEAL COTTS-P
48 JOSH STEWART-P
49 ARNIE MUNOZ-P
51 JON RAUCH-P (1)
52 JOSE CONTRERAS-P (2)
53 ART KUSYNER-CH
54 FELIX DIAZ-P
56 MARK BUEHRLE-P
57 VIC DARENSBOURG-P (1)
57 JEFFREY BAJENARU-P
59 EDUARDO VILLACIS-P
60 SCOTT SCHOENEWEIS (INJ)-P
65 KELLY WUNSCH (INJ)-P
72 *(RET#) CARLTON FISK*

2005

1st C 99-73 0GB
W ALDS-BOSA 3-0
W ALCS-LAA 4-1
W WS-HOUN 4-0

1 WILLIE HARRIS (BRV)-2B
2 *(RET#) NELLIE FOX*
3 HAROLD BAINES-CH
3 *(RET#) HAROLD BAINES*
4 *(RET#) LUKE APPLING*
5 JUAN URIBE-SS
7 TIMO PEREZ-OF
8 CARL EVERETT-OF/DH
9 *(RET#) MINNIE MINOSO*
10 SHINGO TAKATSU (REL)-P (1)
11 *(RET#) LUIS APARICIO*
12 A. J. PIERZYNSKI-C
13 OZZIE GUILLEN-MGR
14 PAUL KONERKO-1B
15 TADAHITO IGUCHI-2B
16 *(RET#) TED LYONS*
17 ROSS GLOAD (INJ)-1B
18 CLIFF POLITTE-P
19 *(RET#) BILLY PIERCE*
20 JON GARLAND-P
21 DON COOPER-CH
22 SCOTT PODSEDNIK (INJ)-OF
23 JERMAINE DYE-OF
24 JOE CREDE (INJ)-3B
25 JOE BORCHARD-OF
26 ORLANDO (EL DUQUE) HERNANDEZ-P
27 JAMIE BURKE-C
27 GEOFF BLUM-1B/3B (2)
28 JOEY CORA-CH
29 GREG WALKER-CH
30 TIM (ROCK) RAINES-CH
31 RAUL CASANOVA-C
32 DUSTIN HERMANSON-P
33 AARON ROWAND-OF
34 FREDDY GARCIA-P
35 FRANK (THE BIG HURT) THOMAS (INJ)-DH
36 CHRIS WIDGER-C
37 JON ADKINS-P
38 PABLO OZUNA-UTIL
41 BRANDON MCCARTHY-P
42 *(RET#) JACKIE ROBINSON*
43 DAMASO MARTE (INJ)-P
44 BRIAN ANDERSON-OF
45 BOBBY JENKS-P
46 NEAL COTTS-P
51 LUIS VIZCAINO-P
52 JOSE CONTRERAS-P
53 ART KUSYNER-CH
54 FELIX DIAZ-P
56 MARK BUEHRLE-P
57 JEFFREY BAJENARU-P
58 KEVIN WALKER-P
62 PEDRO LOPEZ-INF
65 DAVID SANDERS-P
72 *(RET#) CARLTON FISK*

CLEVELAND INDIANS

The Indians began wearing numbers on their sleeves in 1916 and 1917. The numbering system followed the scoreboard numbering of the day. However, specific evidence has not identified each player yet. In 1929, the Indians wore numbers on their backs at home before the Yankees began their historic season. Permanent numbering began in 1931. Opening day starters (•) are shown in those early years.

1916
CLEVELAND INDIANS

6TH 77-88 14GB

__ MILO ALLISON-OF
__ WALTER (DINTY) BARBARE-3B
__ AL (DUTCH) BERGMAN-2B
__ JOSH BILLINGS-C
__ JACK BRADLEY-C
__ RAY CHAPMAN (INJ)-INF
__ LARRY CHAPPELL-PH (1)
__ BOB COLEMAN-C
__ TOM DALY-C/OF
__ HANK DEBERRY-C
__ CLYDE (HACK) ENGLE-UTIL
__ JOE (DOC) EVANS-3B
__ CHICK GANDIL-1B•
__ JACK GRANEY-OF•
__ LOU GUISTO-1B
__ IVAN HOWARD-2B•/1B
__ MARTY KAVANAGH-INF (2)
__ JOE LEONARD-2B (1)
__ HOWIE LOHR-OF
__ DANNY MOELLER-OF/2B (2)
__ STEVE O'NEILL-C•
__ BRAGGO ROTH-OF•
__ ELMER SMITH-OF (1)
__ TRIS (THE GREY EAGLE) SPEAKER-OF•
__ TERRY (COTTON TOP) TURNER-3B•/2B
__ BILL WAMBSGANSS-SS•/INF
__ OLLIE WELF-PR
__ JIM (SARGE) BAGBY-P
__ FRED BEEBE-P
__ JOE BOEHLING-P (2)
__ FRITZ COUMBE-P
__ STAN COVELESKI-P
__ SHORTY DESJARDIEN-P
__ AL (PUDGY) GOULD-P
__ RED GUNKEL-P
__ RIP HAGERMAN-P
__ ED (BIG ED) KLEPFER-P
__ OTIS LAMBETH-P
__ GROVER (SLIM) LOWDERMILK-P
__ MARTY MCHALE-P (2)
__ WILLIE MITCHELL-P (1)
__ GUY (THE ALABAMA BLOSSOM) MORTON (INJ)-P
__ KEN PENNER-P
__ POP-BOY SMITH-P
__ LEE FOHL-MGR
(*OPENING DAY STARTERS•*)

1917

3RD 88-86 12GB

__ MILO ALLISON-OF
__ JOSH BILLINGS-C
__ RAY CHAPMAN-SS•/INF
__ HANK DEBERRY-C
__ FRED EUNICK-3B
__ JOE (DOC) EVANS-3B
__ JACK GRANEY-OF•
__ LOU GUISTO-1B
__ JOE (MOON) HARRIS-1B•/UTIL
__ IVAN HOWARD-UTIL
__ MARTY KAVANAGH-OF/2B
__ RAY MILLER-1B (1)
__ STEVE O'NEILL-C•
__ BRAGGO ROTH-OF•
__ ELMER SMITH-OF (2)
__ TRIS (THE GREY EAGLE) SPEAKER-OF•
__ TERRY (COTTON TOP) TURNER-3B•/2B
__ BILL WAMBSGANSS-2B•
__ JIM (SARGE) BAGBY-P
__ JOE BOEHLING-P
__ FRITS COUMBE-P
__ STAN COVELESKI-P
__ GEORGE DICKERSON-P
__ AL (PUDGY) GOULD-P
__ ED (BIG ED) KLEPFER-P
__ OTIS LAMBETH-P
__ GUY (THE ALABAMA BLOSSOM) MORTON-P
__ POP-BOY SMITH-P
__ RED TORKELSON-P
__ SMOKEY JOE WOOD (INJ)-P
__ LEE FOHL-MGR
(*OPENING DAY STARTERS•*)

1929

3RD 81-71 24GB

1 JACKIE (RABBIT) TAVENER-SS•
2 CARL (HOOKS) LIND-2B/3B
3 DICK (WIGGLES) (TWITCHES) PORTER-OF/2B
4 JOE SEWELL-3B•
5 EARL (ROCK) AVERILL-OF•
6 LEW FONSECA-1B•
7 CHARLIE (CUCKOO) JAMIESON-OF•
8 LUKE SEWELL-C•
9 GLENN MYATT-C
10 HOWIE (HANK) SHANKS-CH
11 GROVER (SLICK) HARTLEY-C
12 JOE (LEFTY) SHAUTE (INJ)-P
14 JAKE MILLER-P
15 WILLIS (ACE) HUDLIN-P
17 KEN HOLLOWAY-P
18 JOHNNY (JOVO) (BIG SERB) MILJUS, (INJ)-P
21 JIMMY ZINN-P
22 WES FARRELL-P
23 MILT SHOFFNER-P
34 RAY GARDNER-SS
49 MEL (CHIEF) HARDER-P
51 BIBB (JOCKEY) FALK-OF•
57 JOE (UNSER CHOE) HAUSER-1B
61 EDDIE MORGAN-OF
71 JOHNNY HODAPP-2B•
__ CLINT BROWN-P (3G: 9/21-10/6)
__ JOHNNY BURNETT-SS/2B (19G: 4/29-6/28)
__ GEORGE GRANT-P (12G: 4/17-7/7)
__ DAN JESSEE-PR (1G: 8/14)
__ JIM MOORE-P (2G: 4/29-5/6)
__ ROGER (PECK) PECKINPAUGH-MGR

1930

4TH 81-73 21GB

1 DICK (WIGGLES) (TWITCHES) PORTER (INJ) -OF•
2 JOE SEWELL-3B•
3 EARL (ROCK) AVERILL-OF•
4 LEW FONSECA (INJ)-1B/3B
5 BIBB (JOCKEY) FALK-OF
6 JOHNNY HODAPP-2B•
7 CARL (HOOKS) LIND-SS/2B
7 ED MONTAGUE-SS/3B
8 LUKE SEWELL (INJ)-C•
9 GLENN MYATT-C
10 JONAH GOLDMAN-SS•/3B
11 CHARLIE (CUCKOO) JAMIESON-OF•
12 WILLIS (ACE) HUDLIN-P
14 WES FARRELL-P
15 JAKE MILLER-P
16 CLINT BROWN-P
17 MILT SHOFFNER-P
18 MEL (CHIEF) HARDER-P
21 KEN HOLLOWAY-P (1)
21 JOE (MULE) SPRINZ-C
22 BELVE (BILL) BEAN-P
22 JOE (LEFTY) SHAUTE (INJ)-P
23 PETE (JAKE) (AKA JABLONOWSKI) APPLETON-P
24 SAL GLIOTTO-P
39 JOHNNY BURNETT-3B/SS
39 ROXIE LAWSON-P
49 RAY GARDNER-SS
51 EDDIE MORGAN-1B•
56 BOB (SUITCASE BOB) SEEDS-OF
61 GROVER (SLICK) HARTLEY-C
71 HOWIE (HANK) SHANKS-CH
__ LES (BARNEY) BARNHART-P (1G: 9/27)
__ GEORGE DETORE-3B (3G: 9/14-17)
__ ROGER (PECK) PECKINPAUGH-MGR
__ JOE VOSMIK-OF (9G: 9/10-28)
__ RALPH WINEGARNER-3B (5G: 9/20-28)

1931

4TH 78-76 30GB

1 JOHNNY BURNETT-INF/OF
2 DICK (WIGGLES) (TWITCHES) PORTER-OF/2B
3 EARL (ROCK) AVERILL-OF
4 JOHNNY HODAPP-2B
5 LEW FONSECA-1B (1)
5 WILLIE KAMM-3B (2)
6 JOE VOSMIK-OF
7 JONAH GOLDMAN-SS
7 ODELL (BAD NEWS) HALE-INF
8 LUKE SEWELL-C
9 GLENN MYATT-C
10 ROGER (PECK) PECKINPAUGH-MGR
11 JOE (MULE) SPRINZ-C
12 WILLIS (ACE) HUDLIN-P
14 WES FARRELL-P
15 JAKE MILLER (INJ)-P
16 CLINT BROWN-P
17 MILT SHOFFNER-P
18 MEL (CHIEF) HARDER-P
19 MOE BERG-C
20 HOWIE (HANK) SHANKS-CH
21 HOWARD (JUDGE) CRAGHEAD-P
22 BELVE (BILL) BEAN-P
23 PETE (JAKE) (AKA JABLONOWSKI) APPLETON-P
24 ROXIE LAWSON-P
25 FAY (SCOW) THOMAS-P
25 SARGE CONNALLY-P
26 ORAL HILDEBRAND-P
27 MOE BERG-C
28 CHARLIE (CUCKOO) JAMIESON-OF
29 BIBB (JOCKEY) FALK-OF
31 BOB (SUITCASE BOB) SEEDS-OF/1B
32 GEORGE DETORE-INF
33 EDDIE MORGAN-1B
35 BILL (WILD BILL) HUNNEFIELD-SS/2B (1)
35 ED MONTAGUE-SS
35 PETE DONOHUE-P (2)
37 EARL WOLGAMOT-CH
37 BRUCE CONNATSER-1B

1932

4TH 87-65 19GB

1 JOHNNY BURNETT-SS/2B
2 DICK (WIGGLES) (TWITCHES) PORTER-OF
3 EARL (ROCK) AVERILL-OF
4? JOHNNY HODAPP-2B (1) (7G: 4/13-23)
4 BILL CISSELL-2B/SS (2)
5 WILLIE KAMM-3B
6 JOE VOSMIK-OF
7 ED MONTAGUE-SS/3B
8 LUKE SEWELL-C
9 GLENN MYATT-C
10 ROGER (PECK) PECKINPAUGH-MGR
11 FRANKIE PYTLAK-C
12 WILLIS (ACE) HUDLIN-P
14 WES FARRELL-P
15 SARGE CONNALLY-P
16 CLINT BROWN-P
17 PETE (JAKE) (AKA JABLONOWSKI) APPLETON-P (1)
17 JACK RUSSELL-P (2)
18 MEL (CHIEF) HARDER-P
19 ORAL HILDEBRAND-P
20 HOWIE (HANK) SHANKS-CH
21 LEO (LEFTY) MOON-P
21 RALPH WINEGARNER-P
22 BOZE BERGER-SS
22 JOE BOLEY-SS (2)
24 MONTE (HOOT) PEARSON-P
28 CHARLIE (CUCKOO) JAMIESON (INJ)-OF
30 EARL WOLGAMOT-CH
31? BOB (SUITCASE BOB) SEEDS-OF (1)
31 MIKE POWERS-OF
33 EDDIE MORGAN-1B
37 BRUCE CONNATSER-1B

1933

4TH 75-76 23.5GB

1 JOHNNY BURNETT-INF
2 DICK (WIGGLES) (TWITCHES) PORTER-OF
3 EARL (ROCK) AVERILL-OF
4 BILL CISSELL-INF (1)
5 WILLIE KAMM-3B
6 JOE VOSMIK-OF
7 HARLEY (LEFTY) BOSS-1B
8 ROY SPENCER-C
9 GLENN MYATT-C
10 ROGER (PECK) PECKINPAUGH-MGR1
10 WALTER (THE BIG TRAIN) (BARNEY) JOHNSON-MGR2
11 FRANKIE PYTLAK-C
12 WILLIS (ACE) HUDLIN-P
14 WES FARRELL (INJ)-P/OF
15 SARGE CONNALLY-P
16 CLINT BROWN-P
17 BELVE (BILL) BEAN-P
18 MEL (CHIEF) HARDER-P
19 ORAL HILDEBRAND-P
20 BIBB (JOCKEY) FALK-CH
20 PATSY GHARRITY-CH
21 HOWARD (JUDGE) CRAGHEAD-P
21 HAL TROSKY-1B
22 MILT GALATZER-OF/1B
25 ODELL (BAD NEWS) HALE-2B/3B
26 BILL KNICKERBOCKER (INJ) -SS
27 MIKE POWERS-OF
29 JOHNNY OULLIBER-OF
30 EARL WOLGAMOT-CH
30 THORNTON LEE-P
33 EDDIE MORGAN-1B
33 MONTE (HOOT) PEARSON-P

1934

3RD 85-69 16GB

1 JOHNNY BURNETT-INF/OF
2 DICK (WIGGLES) (TWITCHES) PORTER-OF (1)
2 BOB (SUITCASE BOB) SEEDS-OF (2)
3 EARL (ROCK) AVERILL-OF
4 BILL KNICKERBOCKER-SS
5 WILLIE KAMM-3B
6 JOE VOSMIK-OF
7 HAL TROSKY-1B
8 ROY SPENCER-C
8 BILL BRENZEL-C
9 GLENN MYATT (INJ)-C
9 BOB GARBARK-C
10 WALTER (THE BIG TRAIN) (BARNEY) JOHNSON-MGR
11 FRANKIE PYTLAK-C
12 WILLIS (ACE) HUDLIN-P
14 BOB WEILAND-P (2)
15 SARGE CONNALLY-P
16 CLINT BROWN (INJ)-P
17 BELVE (BILL) BEAN-P
18 MEL (CHIEF) HARDER-P
19 ORAL HILDEBRAND-P
20 PATSY GHARRITY-CH
21 LLOYD (GIMPY) BROWN-P
22 THORNTON LEE-P
23 RALPH WINEGARNER-P
24 DENNY GALEHOUSE-P
26 EDDIE MOORE-INF
26 KIT CARSON-OF
29 SAM RICE-OF
30? EARL WOLGAMOT-CH
31 MOE BERG-C (2)
33 MONTE (HOOT) PEARSON-P
34 ODELL (BAD NEWS) HALE-2B/3B
35 DUTCH HOLLAND-OF
35 MILT GALATZER-OF/1B
__ BILL (LEFTY) PERRIN-P (1G: 9/30)

1935

3RD 82-71 12GB

1 MILT GALATZER-OF
2 BOZE BERGER-2B/INF
3 EARL (ROCK) AVERILL-OF
4 BILL KNICKERBOCKER-SS
5 WILLIE KAMM-3B
5 KIT CARSON-OF
6 JOE VOSMIK-OF
7 HAL TROSKY-1B
8 BILL BRENZEL-C
9 GLENN MYATT-C (1)
9 BOB GARBARK-C
10 WALTER (THE BIG TRAIN) (BARNEY) JOHNSON-MGR1
11 FRANKIE PYTLAK-C
12 WILLIS (ACE) HUDLIN-P
14 GREEK GEORGE-C
15 DENNY GALEHOUSE-P
15 EDDIE PHILLIPS-C
16 CLINT BROWN-P
17 BELVE (BILL) BEAN-P (1)
18 MEL (CHIEF) HARDER-P
19 ORAL HILDEBRAND-P
20 PATSY GHARRITY-CH
21 LLOYD (GIMPY) BROWN-P

22 THORNTON LEE-P
23 RALPH WINEGARNER (INJ)-P/UTIL
24 LEFTY STEWART-P (2)
28 THORNTON LEE-P
29 ROY (JEEP) (SAGE) HUGHES-INF
30 MONTE (HOOT) PEARSON-P
30 STEVE O'NEILL-CH/MGR2
31 AB WRIGHT-OF
33 MONTE (HOOT) PEARSON-P
34 ODELL (BAD NEWS) HALE-3B/2B
35 BRUCE (SOUPY) CAMPBELL (ILL)-OF

1936

5TH 80-74 22.5GB

1* MILT GALATZER-OF/1B/P*
2 BOZE BERGER-INF
3 EARL (ROCK) AVERILL-OF
4 BILL KNICKERBOCKER-SS
5 ROY (JEEP) (SAGE) HUGHES-2B
6 JOE VOSMIK-OF
7 HAL TROSKY-1B
8 JOE BECKER (INJ)-C
9* BOB (RAPID ROBERT) FELLER-P*
10 GEORGE (THE BULL) UHLE-P
11 FRANKIE PYTLAK (INJ)-C
12 WILLIS (ACE) HUDLIN-P
14 BILLY SULLIVAN-C/UTIL
15 JOHNNY ALLEN-P
16 GEORGE BLAEHOLDER-P
17 GREEK GEORGE-C
17 PAUL (TEX) KARDOW-P
17 AL (HAPPY) MILNAR-P
18 MEL (CHIEF) HARDER-P
19 ORAL HILDEBRAND-P
20 WALLY SCHANG-CH
21 LLOYD (GIMPY) BROWN (ILL)-P
21 JEFF HEATH-OF
22 THORNTON LEE-P
23 RALPH WINEGARNER-P/UTIL
23 ROY (STORMY) WEATHERLY-OF
24 AL (HAPPY) MILNAR-P
25 DENNY GALEHOUSE-P
30 STEVE O'NEILL-MGR
31 JIM (GEE GEE) GLEESON-OF
31 BILL (GOOBER) ZUBER-P
33 GEORGE BLAEHOLDER-P
34 ODELL (BAD NEWS) HALE-3B/2B
35 BRUCE (SOUPY) CAMPBELL (ILL)-OF
36 DENNY GALEHOUSE-P

1937

4TH 83-71 19GB

1 LYN (BROADWAY) LARY-SS
2 HUGH ALEXANDER-OF
2 ROY (STORMY) WEATHERLY-OF/3B
3 EARL (ROCK) AVERILL-OF
4 ODELL (BAD NEWS) HALE-3B/2B
5 ROY (JEEP) (SAGE) HUGHES-3B/2B
6 MOOSE SOLTERS-OF
7 HAL TROSKY-1B
8 FRANKIE PYTLAK-C
9 BILLY SULLIVAN-UTIL
10 JOE BECKER (INJ)-C
11 EARL WHITEHILL-P
12 WILLIS (ACE) HUDLIN-P
14 BOB (RAPID ROBERT) FELLER-P
15 JOHNNY ALLEN (ILL)-P
16 DENNY GALEHOUSE-P
17 JOE HEVING-P
18 MEL (CHIEF) HARDER-P
19 IVY (POISON) ANDREWS-P (1)
20 WHIT WYATT-P
21 LLOYD (GIMPY) BROWN-P
22 JOHN KRONER-2B/3B
23 BRUCE (SOUPY) CAMPBELL-OF
24 KEN (CURLY) JUNGELS-P
24 BLAS MONACO-2B
24 JEFF HEATH-OF
26 STEVE O'NEILL-MGR
27 WALLY SCHANG-CH
28 GEORGE (THE BULL) UHLE-CH
29 CARL FISCHER-P (1)
29 BILL SODD-PH
35 KEN (BUTCH) KELTNER-3B

1938

3RD 86-66 13GB

1 LYN (BROADWAY) LARY-SS
2 JOHN KRONER-INF
3 EARL (ROCK) AVERILL-OF
4 ODELL (BAD NEWS) HALE-2B
5 SKEETER WEBB-INF
6 MOOSE SOLTERS-OF
7 HAL TROSKY-1B
8 FRANKIE PYTLAK-C
9 ROLLIE HEMSLEY (INJ)-C
10 HANK HELF-C
11 EARL WHITEHILL-P
12 WILLIS (ACE) HUDLIN-P
14 BOB (RAPID ROBERT) FELLER-P
15 JOHNNY ALLEN (INJ)-P
16 DENNY GALEHOUSE-P
17 JOE HEVING-P (1)
18 MEL (CHIEF) HARDER-P
19 KEN (CURLY) JUNGELS-P
19 BILL (GOOBER) ZUBER-P
20 AL (HAPPY) MILNAR-P
21 JOHNNY HUMPHRIES-P
22 ROY (STORMY) WEATHERLY-OF
23 BRUCE (SOUPY) CAMPBELL-OF
24 JEFF HEATH-OF
25 KEN (BUTCH) KELTNER-3B
26 OSSIE VITT-MGR
27 WALLY SCHANG-CH
28 JOHNNY BASSLER-CH
30 CLAY SMITH-P
31 OSCAR GRIMES-2B/1B
32 TOMMY IRWIN-SS
33 CHUCK WORKMAN-OF
34 LOU BOUDREAU-3B
35 LLOYD RUSSELL-PR
36 RAY MACK-2B
__ CHARLEY SUCHE-P (1G: 9/18)

1939

3RD 87-67 20.5GB

1 OSCAR GRIMES-INF
2 BEN CHAPMAN-OF
2 LUKE SEWELL-C/1B/CH
3 EARL (ROCK) AVERILL-OF
4 ODELL (BAD NEWS) HALE-2B/3B
5 SKEETER WEBB-SS
5 LOU BOUDREAU-SS
6 MOOSE SOLTERS-OF (1)
6 RAY MACK-2B/3B
7 HAL TROSKY-1B
8 FRANKIE PYTLAK-C
9 ROLLIE HEMSLEY-C
10 LUKE SEWELL-C/1B/CH
10 FLOYD (ROCK) STROMME-P
10 HARRY EISENSTAT-P (2)
11 JOHNNY BROACA-P
11 LYN (BROADWAY) LARY-SS (1)
11 BEN CHAPMAN-OF
12 WILLIS (ACE) HUDLIN-P
14 BILL (GOOBER) ZUBER-P
15 JOHNNY ALLEN-P
16 JOHNNY BROACA-P
17 JOE (BURRHEAD) DOBSON-P
18 MEL (CHIEF) HARDER-P
19 BOB (RAPID ROBERT) FELLER-P
20 AL (HAPPY) MILNAR-P
21 JOHNNY HUMPHRIES-P
22 ROY (STORMY) WEATHERLY-OF
23 BRUCE (SOUPY) CAMPBELL-OF
24 JEFF HEATH-OF
24 HARRY EISENSTAT-P (2)
25 KEN (BUTCH) KELTNER-3B
26 OSSIE VITT-MGR
27 SKI (SPINACH) MELILLO-CH
28 JOHNNY BASSLER-CH
29 TOM DRAKE (INJ)-P
30 LEFTY SULLIVAN-P
30 MIKE NAYMICK-P
31 BILL LOBE-CH
31 FLOYD (ROCK) STROMME-P
32 JIM SHILLING-2B/SS (1)

1940

2ND 89-65 1GB

1 OSCAR GRIMES (INJ)-1B/3B
3 RUSTY PETERS-INF
4 ODELL (BAD NEWS) HALE-3B
5 LOU BOUDREAU-SS
6 RAY MACK-2B
7 HAL TROSKY-1B
8 FRANKIE PYTLAK (ILL)-C/1B
9 ROLLIE HEMSLEY-C
10 HARRY EISENSTAT-P
11 BEN CHAPMAN-OF
12 WILLIS (ACE) HUDLIN-P (1)
12 NATE ANDREWS-P
14 BILL (GOOBER) ZUBER-P
15 JOHNNY ALLEN-P
16 LUKE SEWELL-CH
17 JOE (BURRHEAD) DOBSON-P
18 MEL (CHIEF) HARDER-P
19 BOB (RAPID ROBERT) FELLER-P
20 AL (HAPPY) MILNAR-P
21 JOHNNY HUMPHRIES-P
22 ROY (STORMY) WEATHERLY-OF
23 BEAU BELL-OF/1B
24 JEFF HEATH-OF
24 CAL (PREACHER) DORSETT-P
25 KEN (BUTCH) KELTNER-3B
26 OSSIE VITT-MGR
27 SKI (SPINACH) MELILLO-CH
28 JOHNNY BASSLER-CH
30 MIKE NAYMICK-P
32 AL SMITH-P
33 KEN (CURLY) JUNGELS-P
33 JEFF HEATH-OF
34 BRUCE (SOUPY) CAMPBELL-OF
35 DIXIE HOWELL-P
40 HANK HELF-C
43 CAL (PREACHER) DORSETT-P
44 BEN CHAPMAN-OF

1941

4TH (TIE) 75-79 26GB

1 OSCAR GRIMES-INF
2 GEE WALKER-OF
3 RUSTY PETERS-INF
4 GENE (RED) DESAUTELS (INJ)-C
5 LOU BOUDREAU-SS
6 RAY MACK-2B
7 HAL TROSKY (INJ)-1B
7 BUCK FRIERSON-OF
8 KEN (BUTCH) KELTNER-3B
9 ROLLIE HEMSLEY-C
10 HARRY EISENSTAT-P
11 JOE HEVING-P
12 NATE ANDREWS-P
12 DUTCH ZWILLING-CH
14 EARL WHITEHILL-CH
14 FABIAN GAFFKE-OF
14 LARRY ROSENTHAL-OF/1B (2)
15 JOE KRAKAUSKAS-P
16 LUKE SEWELL-CH
16 CHUBBY DEAN-P (2)
17 JIM BAGBY, JR.-P
18 MEL (CHIEF) HARDER (INJ)-P
19 BOB (RAPID ROBERT) FELLER-P
20 AL (HAPPY) MILNAR-P
21 CLINT BROWN-P
22 ROY (STORMY) WEATHERLY-OF
22 AL SMITH-P
23 BEAU BELL-OF/1B
23 CAL (PREACHER) DORSETT-P
23 LES (MOE) FLEMING-1B
24 JEFF HEATH-OF
25 KEN (CURLY) JUNGELS-P
25 KEN (BUTCH) KELTNER-3B
26 EARL WHITEHILL-CH
27 ROGER (PECK) PECKINPAUGH-MGR
28 GEORGE (GOOD KID) SUSCE-CH
30 JIM HEGAN-C
32 AL SMITH-P
33 JEFF HEATH-OF
33 CAL (PREACHER) DORSETT-P
33 HANK EDWARDS-OF
34 CLARENCE (SOUP) CAMPBELL-OF
35 RED (PORKY) HOWELL-PH
36 KEN (CURLY) JUNGELS-P
36 STEVE GROMEK-P
38 BOB LEMON-3B
38 CHUCK WORKMAN-PH
40 RED EMBREE-P
43 KEN (CURLY) JUNGELS-P
45 VERN FREIBERGER-1B
45 RED (PORKY) HOWELL-PH
47 JACK CONWAY-SS
__ ORIS (BROWN) HOCKETT-OF (2G: 9/27-28)

1942

4TH 75-79 28GB

1 OSCAR GRIMES-INF
3 RUSTY PETERS-INF
4 GENE (RED) DESAUTELS (INJ)-C
5 LOU BOUDREAU-SS
6 RAY MACK-2B
(7) HAL TROSKY (ILL)-(1B)
7 PETE CENTER-P
8 KEN (BUTCH) KELTNER-3B
9 OTTO (DUTCH) DENNING-C/OF
10 HARRY EISENSTAT-P
11 JOE HEVING-P
12 VERN KENNEDY-P
14 BUSTER (BUS) MILLS-OF
15 JOE KRAKAUSKAS-P
15 TED SEPKOWSKI-2B
16 CHUBBY DEAN-P
17 JIM BAGBY, JR.-P
18 MEL (CHIEF) HARDER-P
20 AL (HAPPY) MILNAR-P
21 CLINT BROWN-P
22 ROY (STORMY) WEATHERLY-OF
23 LES (MOE) FLEMING-1B
24 JEFF HEATH-OF
26 BURT (BARNEY) SHOTTON-CH
27 SKI (SPINACH) MELILLO-CH
28 GEORGE (GOOD KID) SUSCE-CH
31 EDDIE ROBINSON-1B
32 AL SMITH-P
33 HANK EDWARDS-OF
34 ORIS (BROWN) HOCKETT-OF
35 RAY POAT-P
36 STEVE GROMEK-P
38 TOM FERRICK-P
40 JIM HEGAN-C
42 BOB LEMON-3B
45 FABIAN GAFFKE-OF
47 RED EMBREE-P
__ PAUL CALVERT-P (1G: 9/24)
__ ALLIE (SUPERCHIEF) (WAHOO) REYNOLDS-P (2G: 9/17-27)

1943

3RD 82-71 15.5GB

1 ROY CULLENBINE-OF/1B
2 BUDDY ROSAR-C
3 RUSTY PETERS-INF/OF
4 GENE (RED) DESAUTELS-C
5 LOU BOUDREAU-SS/C/MGR
6 RAY MACK-2B
7* PETE CENTER (MIL)-P*
8 KEN (BUTCH) KELTNER-3B
9 OTTO (DUTCH) DENNING-1B
9 MICKEY ROCCO-1B
11 JOE HEVING-P
12 VERN KENNEDY-P
14 EDDIE (SMILEY) TURCHIN-3B/SS
16 CHUBBY DEAN (MIL)-P
17 JIM BAGBY, JR.-P
18 MEL (CHIEF) HARDER (INJ)-P
20 AL (HAPPY) MILNAR-P (1)
21 ALLIE (SUPERCHIEF) (WAHOO) REYNOLDS-P
22 JIM MCDONNELL-C
23 PAT SEEREY-OF
24 JEFF HEATH-OF
25 STEVE GROMEK-P
26 BURT (BARNEY) SHOTTON-CH
27 DEL BAKER-CH
28 GEORGE (GOOD KID) SUSCE (INJ)-C/CH
31 MIKE NAYMICK-P
32 AL SMITH-P
33 HANK EDWARDS (MIL)-OF
34 ORIS (BROWN) HOCKETT-OF
35 RAY POAT-P
36 FRANK (DOLIE) DOLJACK-OF
36 JIMMY GRANT-3B (2)
38 JACK SALVESON-P
39 ED (SPECS) KLIEMAN-P

CLEVELAND INDIANS

46 GENE WOODLING (MIL)-OF
47 PAUL CALVERT-P

1944

5TH (TIE) 72-82 17GB

1 ROY CULLENBINE-OF
2 BUDDY ROSAR (MIL)-C
3 RUSTY PETERS-INF
4 NORM (DUKE) SCHLUETER-C
4 JIM DEVLIN-C
5 LOU BOUDREAU-SS/C/MGR
6* PAUL (LEFTY) O'DEA-UTIL/P*
8 KEN (BUTCH) KELTNER-3B
9 MICKEY ROCCO-1B
11 JOE HEVING-P
12 VERN KENNEDY-P (1)
15 HAL KLEINE-P
16 HAL KLEINE-P
16 HANK RUSZKOWSKI-C
17 JIM BAGBY, JR. (MER)-P
17 MYRIL HOAG-OF (2)
18 MEL (CHIEF) HARDER-P
21 ALLIE (SUPERCHIEF) (WAHOO) REYNOLDS-P
22 JIM BAGBY, JR. (MER)-P
23 PAT SEEREY-OF
24 JEFF HEATH-OF
25 STEVE GROMEK-P
26 BURT (BARNEY) SHOTTON-CH
27 DEL BAKER-CH
28 GEORGE (GOOD KID) SUSCE (INJ)-C/CH
29 JIM MCDONNELL-C
30 RED EMBREE-P
30 BILL (LEFTY) BONNESS-P
31 MIKE NAYMICK-P (1)
32 AL SMITH-P
33 PAUL CALVERT-P
34 ORIS (BROWN) HOCKETT-OF
34 EARL (HOOK) HENRY-P
35 RAY POAT-P
36 JIMMY GRANT-2B/3B (2)
37 STEVE BIRAS-2B
38 RAY MACK-2B
38 RUSS LYON-C
39 ED (SPECS) KLIEMAN-P

1945

5TH 77-72 11GB

1 ROY CULLENBINE-OF/3B (1)
1 DON ROSS-3B (2)
2 AL CIHOCKI-INF
3 BOB ROTHEL-3B
4 JEFF HEATH (INJ)-OF
5 LOU BOUDREAU (INJ)-SS/MGR
6*PAUL (LEFTY) O'DEA-OF/P*
7 ED WHEELER-INF
8 POP (PAPA) WILLIAMS-1B
8 LES (MOE) FLEMING-OF/1B
10 MICKEY ROCCO-1B
11 FRANKIE (BLIMP) HAYES-C (2)
12 RED STEINER-C (1)
14 JIM MCDONNELL-C
15 HAL KLEINE-P
16 HANK RUSZKOWSKI (MIL)-C
17 MYRIL HOAG-OF/P
18 MEL (CHIEF) HARDER-P
19 BOB (RAPID ROBERT) FELLER-P
21 ALLIE (SUPERCHIEF) (WAHOO) REYNOLDS-P
22 JIM BAGBY, JR. (MER)-P
23 PAT SEEREY-OF
24 DUTCH MEYER-2B
25 STEVE GROMEK-P
26 BURT (BARNEY) SHOTTON-CH
27 SKI (SPINACH) MELILLO-CH
28 GEORGE (GOOD KID) SUSCE-CH
30 JACK SALVESON-P
30 RED EMBREE (MIL)-P
32 AL SMITH-P
33 PAUL CALVERT-P
33 STAN BENJAMIN-OF
34 EARL (HOOK) HENRY-P
34 ELMER (DUTCH) WEINGARTNER-SS
35 HAL KLEINE-P
(35) RAY POAT (RET)-(P)
35 JACK SALVESON-P
39 ED (SPECS) KLIEMAN-P
40 PETE CENTER (MIL)-P
41 FELIX MACKIEWICZ-OF
42 PETE CENTER (MIL)-P
42 GENE (RED) DESAUTELS (MIL)-C
42 EDDIE (LEFTY) CARNETT (MIL)-OF/P
50 JACK SALVESON-P

1946

6TH 68-86 36GB

1 DON ROSS-3B/OF
2 RAY MACK-2B
3 DUTCH MEYER-2B
4 JACK CONWAY-INF
5 LOU BOUDREAU-SS/MGR
6*BOB LEMON-P*/OF
7 BLAS MONACO-PH
7 GEORGE CASE-OF
8 LES (MOE) FLEMING-1B/OF
8 HOWIE MOSS-3B (2)
9 KEN (BUTCH) KELTNER-3B
10 MICKEY ROCCO-1B
10 JIMMY WASDELL-1B/OF (2)
11 FRANKIE (BLIMP) HAYES-C (1)
11 MAX PATKIN-CH
12 SHERM LOLLAR-C
12 RUSTY PETERS (MIL)-SS
14 JIM HEGAN-C
15 GEORGE CASE-OF
15 HEINZ (DUTCH) BECKER-1B (2)
16 GENE WOODLING-OF
17 FELIX MACKIEWICZ-OF
18 MEL (CHIEF) HARDER (INJ)-P
19 BOB (RAPID ROBERT) FELLER-P
20 CHARLIE BREWSTER-SS
20 BOB (SARGE) KUZAVA-P
21 ALLIE (SUPERCHIEF) (WAHOO) REYNOLDS-P
22 VIC JOHNSON-P
22 JOE (JITTERY JOE) BERRY-P (2)
23 PAT SEEREY-OF
24 BUSTER (BUS) MILLS-OF/CH
25 STEVE GROMEK-P
26 TOM FERRICK-P (1)
26 TOM JORDAN-C (2)
27 SKI (SPINACH) MELILLO-CH
28 GEORGE (GOOD KID) SUSCE-CH
29 PETE CENTER-P
30 JOE KRAKAUSKAS-P
30 RAY FLANIGAN-P
31 JOHNNY (SPECS) PODGAJNY-P
31 CHARLIE (SHERIFF) GASSAWAY-P
32 HANK EDWARDS-OF
33 ED (SPECS) KLIEMAN-P
33 RALPH (MACK) MCCABE-P
33 LES WEBBER-P (2)
33 RALPH (WIG) WEIGEL-C
34 EDDIE ROBINSON-1B
35 DON BLACK-P
35 JACKIE (JOHNNY) PRICE-SS
36 RED EMBREE (MIL)-P
37 ED (SPECS) KLIEMAN-P
39 TED SEPKOWSKI-3B
39 DALE MITCHELL-OF
40 HOWIE MOSS-3B (2)
42 RALPH (WIG) WEIGEL-C
44 LES WEBBER-P (2)
45 RAY FLANIGAN-P
46 DALE MITCHELL-OF
48 CHARLIE BREWSTER-SS

1947

4TH 80-74 17GB

1 JIMMY WASDELL-PH
2 EDDIE BOCKMAN-INF/OF
3*LYMAN LINDE-P*
3 EDDIE ROBINSON-1B
4 JOE (FLASH) GORDON-2B
5 LOU BOUDREAU-SS/MGR
6 KEN (BUTCH) KELTNER-3B
7 JACK CONWAY-INF
8 LES (MOE) FLEMING-1B
9*CAL (PREACHER) DORSETT-P*
10 JIM HEGAN-C
11 HANK RUSZKOWSKI-C
12 AL LOPEZ-C
14 LARRY DOBY-OF
15 HEINZ (DUTCH) BECKER-PH
15 LES (WIMPY) (LEFTY) WILLIS-P
16 ED (SPECS) KLIEMAN-P
17 AL (FLIP) ROSEN-3B/OF
17 GENE BEARDEN-P
18 MEL (CHIEF) HARDER-P
19 BOB (RAPID ROBERT) FELLER-P
20 ROGER WOLFF-P (1)
20 BOB (SARGE) KUZAVA-P
21 BOB LEMON-P
22 RED EMBREE-P
23 DON BLACK-P
24 AL GETTEL-P
25 STEVE GROMEK-P
26 BOB (SARGE) KUZAVA-P
28 BRYAN STEPHENS-P
29 LES (WIMPY) (LEFTY) WILLIS-P
29 BRYAN STEPHENS-P
29 ERNIE GROTH-P
30 PAT SEEREY-OF
31 GEORGE (CATFISH) METKOVICH-OF/1B
32 HANK EDWARDS (INJ)-OF
33 DALE MITCHELL-OF
34 HAL PECK-OF
35 FELIX MACKIEWICZ-OF (1)
36 TED SEPKOWSKI, OF (1)
36 JOE FRAZIER-OF
39 GENE BEARDEN-P
40 SKI (SPINACH) MELILLO-CH
41 BILL (DEACON) MCKECHNIE-CH
42 GEORGE (GOOD KID) SUSCE-CH
43 TRIS (THE GREY EAGLE) SPEAKER-CH

1948

1ST 97-58 0GB

W WS-BOSN 4-2

2 JOHNNY (BERNIE) BERARDINO-INF
3 EDDIE ROBINSON-1B
4 JOE (FLASH) GORDON-2B/SS
5 LOU BOUDREAU-SS/C/MGR
6 KEN (BUTCH) KELTNER-3B
7*MIKE (THE BIG BEAR) GARCIA-P*
7 AL (FLIP) ROSEN-3B
10 JIM HEGAN-C
12 JOE TIPTON-C
14 LARRY DOBY-OF
15 RAY (DEACON) MURRAY-PH
16 ED (SPECS) KLIEMAN-P
17 BUTCH WENSLOFF-P
18 RUSS CHRISTOPHER-P
19 BOB (RAPID ROBERT) FELLER-P
20 LYMAN LINDE-P
20 SAM (SAD SAM) ZOLDAK-P (2)
21 BOB LEMON-P
22 MIKE (THE BIG BEAR) GARCIA-P
23 DON BLACK (INJ)-P
24 AL GETTEL-P (1)
24 BOB KENNEDY-OF/INF (2)
25 BOB MUNCRIEF-P
26 ERNIE GROTH-P
26 SAM (SAD SAM) ZOLDAK-P (2)
27 STEVE GROMEK-P
28 ERNIE GROTH-P
28 GENE BEARDEN-P
28 RAY (IKE) BOONE-SS
28 LES WEBBER-P
29 BILL (LEFTY) KENNEDY-P (1)
29 RUSS CHRISTOPHER-P
29 SATCHEL PAIGE-P
30 PAT SEEREY-OF(1)
30 SAM (SAD SAM) ZOLDAK-P (2)
30 GENE BEARDEN-P
31 SATCHEL PAIGE,-P
31 ALLIE CLARK-OF/INF
32 HANK EDWARDS (INJ)-OF
34 DALE MITCHELL-OF
35 WALT JUDNICH-OF/1B
36 HAL PECK-OF
38 THURMAN (JOE E.) TUCKER-OF
40 SKI (SPINACH) MELILLO-CH
41 BILL (DEACON) MCKECHNIE-CH
42 MUDDY RUEL-CH
43 MEL (CHIEF) HARDER-CH

1949

3RD 89-65 8GB

1 BOBBY AVILA-2B
2 JOHNNY (BERNIE) BERARDINO-INF
3 MICKEY VERNON-1B
4 JOE (FLASH) GORDON-2B
5 LOU BOUDREAU-SS/INF/MGR
6 KEN (BUTCH) KELTNER-3B
7 AL (FLIP) ROSEN-3B
8 RAY (IKE) BOONE-SS
9 HERM REICH-OF (2)
9 LUKE EASTER-OF
10 JIM HEGAN-C
11 MIKE TRESH-C
14 LARRY DOBY-OF
15 FREDDIE MARSH-PR
17 MILT NIELSEN-OF
18 MINNIE MINOSO-OF
19 BOB (RAPID ROBERT) FELLER-P
20 SAM (SAD SAM) ZOLDAK-P
21 BOB LEMON-P
22 AL BENTON-P
24 EARLY (GUS) WYNN-P
25 MIKE (THE BIG BEAR) GARCIA-P
26 FRANK (PAP) PAPISH-P
27 STEVE GROMEK-P
29 SATCHEL PAIGE-P
30 GENE BEARDEN-P
31 ALLIE CLARK-OF/1B
32 HANK EDWARDS-OF (1)
33 BOB KENNEDY-OF/3B
34 DALE MITCHELL-OF
36 HAL PECK (INJ)-OF
37 LARRY DOBY-OF
38 THURMAN (JOE E.) TUCKER-OF
41 BILL (DEACON) MCKECHNIE-CH
42 MUDDY RUEL-CH
43 MEL (CHIEF) HARDER-CH
44 GEORGE (GOOD KID) SUSCE-CH
45 STEVE O'NEILL-CH

1950

4TH 92-62 6GB

1 BOBBY AVILA-2B/SS
2 JOHNNY (BERNIE) BERARDINO-2B/3B (1)
3 MICKEY VERNON-1B (1)
4 JOE (FLASH) GORDON-2B
5 LOU BOUDREAU-INF/MGR
7 AL (FLIP) ROSEN-3B
8 RAY (IKE) BOONE-SS
9 LUKE EASTER-1B/OF
10 JIM HEGAN-C
11 HERB CONYERS-1B
12 RAY (DEACON) MURRAY-C
14 LARRY DOBY-OF
17 AL (LEFTY) ABER-P
18 MARINO (CHICK) PIERETTI-P
19 BOB (RAPID ROBERT) FELLER-P
20 SAM (SAD SAM) ZOLDAK-P
21 BOB LEMON-P
22 AL BENTON-P
23 JESSE FLORES-P
24 EARLY (GUS) WYNN-P
25 MIKE (THE BIG BEAR) GARCIA-P
26 DICK ROZEK-P
27 STEVE GROMEK-P
28 MARINO (CHICK) PIERETTI-P
28 DICK (LEGS) WEIK-P (2)
30 GENE BEARDEN-P (1)
30 JIM LEMON-OF
31 DICK (LEGS) WEIK-P (2)
31 ALLIE CLARK-OF
33 BOB KENNEDY-OF
34 DALE MITCHELL-OF
35 RAY (DEACON) MURRAY-C
38 THURMAN (JOE E.) TUCKER-OF
41 SKI (SPINACH) MELILLO-CH
42 MUDDY RUEL-CH
43 MEL (CHIEF) HARDER-CH
44 AL (BUCKETFOOT AL) SIMMONS-CH

1951

2ND 93-61 5GB

1 BOBBY AVILA-2B
2 DOUG HANSEN-PR
2 LOU KLEIN-PH
3 DALE MITCHELL-OF
4 JIM HEGAN-C
5 SNUFFY STIRNWEISS-2B/3B
6 MINNIE MINOSO-OF (1)
7 AL (FLIP) ROSEN-3B
8 RAY (IKE) BOONE-SS

CLEVELAND INDIANS

9 LUKE EASTER-1B
10 AL LOPEZ-MGR
11 MERRILL (MERL) COMBS-SS
12 RAY (DEACON) MURRAY-C
12 LOU BRISSIE-P (2)
14 LARRY DOBY-OF
15 BIRDIE TEBBETTS-C
17 GEORGE ZUVERINK-P
18 CHARLIE (BUBBA) HARRIS-P (2)
19 BOB (RAPID ROBERT) FELLER-P
20 CLARENCE MADDERN-OF
21 BOB LEMON-P
22 JOHNNY (THE DUTCH MASTER) (DOUBLE NO-HIT) VANDER MEER-P
22 SAM (TOOTHPICK SAM) JONES-P
23 HAL NARAGON-C
24 EARLY (GUS) WYNN-P
25 MIKE (THE BIG BEAR) GARCIA-P
26 DICK ROZEK-P
27 STEVE GROMEK-P
(28) DICK (LEGS) WEIK (MIL)-(P)
28 JERRY (RED) FAHR-P
29 BOB CHAKALES-P
31 ALLIE CLARK-OF (1)
31 SAM CHAPMAN-OF/1B (2)
32 MILT NIELSEN-PH
32 BARNEY MCCOSKY-OF (3)
33 BOB KENNEDY-OF
35 HARRY (SUITCASE) (GOODY) SIMPSON-OF/1B
36 SAM (TOOTHPICK SAM) JONES-P
37 BOB KENNEDY-OF
38 THURMAN (JOE E.) TUCKER-PH
38 PAUL (PEANUTS) (GULLIVER) LEHNER-OF (4)
40 BILL LOBE-CH
42 JAKE FLOWERS-CH
43 MEL (CHIEF) HARDER-CH
44 RED RUFFING-CH

1952

2ND 93-61 2GB

1 BOBBY AVILA-2B
2 JOHNNY (BERNIE) BERARDINO-INF (1)
2 GEORGE (BO) STRICKLAND-SS/2B (2)
3 DALE MITCHELL-OF
4 JIM HEGAN-C
5 SNUFFY STIRNWEISS-3B
5 HANK (HEENEY) (HEINE) MAJESKI-3B/2B (2)
6 DAVE POPE-OF
6 BILL GLYNN-1B
7 AL (FLIP) ROSEN-3B/INF
8 RAY (IKE) BOONE-SS/INF
9 LUKE EASTER-1B
10 AL LOPEZ-MGR
11 MERRILL (MERL) COMBS-SS/2B
12 LOU BRISSIE-P
14 LARRY DOBY-OF
15 BIRDIE TEBBETTS-C
16 QUINCY TROUPPE-C
17 GEORGE ZUVERINK-P
18 BILL ABERNATHIE-P
18 JOE TIPTON-C (2)
19 BOB (RAPID ROBERT) FELLER-P
20 MICKEY HARRIS-P (2)
21 BOB LEMON-P
22 SAM (TOOTHPICK SAM) JONES-P
23 PETE REISER-OF
24 EARLY (GUS) WYNN-P
25 MIKE (THE BIG BEAR) GARCIA-P
26 DICK ROZEK-P
27 STEVE GROMEK-P
29 BOB CHAKALES-P
29 TED (CORK) WILKS-P
30 BOB CHAKALES-P
31 JIM (BIG JIM) FRIDLEY-OF
31 WALLY WESTLAKE-OF (3)
32 BARNEY MCCOSKY-OF (3)
33 BOB KENNEDY (MIL)-OF/3B
35 HARRY (SUITCASE) (GOODY) SIMPSON-OF/1B
36 TED (CORK) WILKS-P
(37) DICK (LEGS) WEIK (MIL)-(P)
38 PETE (PISTOL PETE) REISER-OF
40 BILL LOBE-CH
42 JAKE FLOWERS-CH
43 MEL (CHIEF) HARDER-CH
44 TONY (COOCH) (CHICK) CUCCINELLO-CH

1953

2ND 92-62 8.5GB

1 BOBBY AVILA-2B
2 GEORGE (BO) STRICKLAND-SS/1B
3 DALE MITCHELL-OF
4 JIM HEGAN-C
5 HANK (HEENEY) (HEINE) MAJESKI-UTIL
6 LARRY DOBY-OF
6 BILL GLYNN-1B/OF
7 AL (FLIP) ROSEN-3B/INF
8 RAY (IKE) BOONE-SS (1)
8 OWEN (RED) FRIEND-INF (2)
9 LUKE EASTER (INJ)-1B
10 AL LOPEZ-MGR
11 ART HOUTTEMAN-P (2)
12 LOU BRISSIE-P
14 BILL GLYNN-1B/OF
14 LARRY DOBY-OF
15 DICK (DANDY) AYLWARD-C
15 JOE GINSBERG-C (2)
16 HANK FOILES-C (2)
17 JIM LEMON-OF/1B
18 JOE TIPTON-C
19 BOB (RAPID ROBERT) FELLER-P
20 BOB CHAKALES-P
21 BOB LEMON-P
22 DAVE HOSKINS-P
24 EARLY (GUS) WYNN-P
25 MIKE (THE BIG BEAR) GARCIA-P
26 BOB HOOPER-P
27 STEVE GROMEK-P (1)
27 BILL (LEFTY) WIGHT-P (2)
28 TED (CORK) WILKS-P
28 DICK (BONES) TOMANEK-P
29 AL (LEFTY) ABER-P (1)
29 ART HOUTTEMAN-P (2)
31 WALLY WESTLAKE-OF
32 BARNEY MCCOSKY-PH
32 AL (FUZZY) SMITH-OF/3B
33 BOB KENNEDY-OF
35 HARRY (SUITCASE) (GOODY) SIMPSON-OF/1B
37 DICK (LEGS) WEIK-PR/(P) (1)
40 BILL LOBE-CH
41 ART HOUTTEMAN-P (2)
42 RED KRESS-CH
43 MEL (CHIEF) HARDER-CH
44 TONY (COOCH) (CHICK) CUCCINELLO-CH
52 DAVE HOSKINS-P

1954

1ST 111-43 0GB

L WS-NYN 4-0

1 BOBBY AVILA-2B/SS
2 GEORGE (BO) STRICKLAND (INJ)-SS
3 DALE MITCHELL-OF/1B
4 JIM HEGAN-C
5 HANK (HEENEY) (HEINE) MAJESKI-2B/3B
6 BILL GLYNN-1B/OF
7 AL (FLIP) ROSEN-3B/INF
8 RUDY REGALADO-3B/2B
9 LUKE EASTER-PH
10 AL LOPEZ-MGR
11 ART HOUTTEMAN-P
12 DON (THE SPHINX) MOSSI-P
14 LARRY DOBY-OF
15 JOE GINSBERG-C
15 MICKEY GRASSO-C
16 HAL (PRINCE HAL) NEWHOUSER-P
17 DAVE PHILLEY-OF
18 HAL NARAGON-C
19 BOB (RAPID ROBERT) FELLER-P
20 RAY NARLESKI-P
21 BOB LEMON-P
22 DAVE HOSKINS-P
23 BOB CHAKALES-P (1)
23 VIC WERTZ-1B/OF (2)
24 EARLY (GUS) WYNN-P
25 MIKE (THE BIG BEAR) GARCIA-P
26 BOB HOOPER-P
28 DICK (BONES) TOMANEK-P
31 WALLY WESTLAKE-OF
32 AL (FUZZY) SMITH-OF/INF
33 BOB KENNEDY-OF (1)
33 JIM DYCK-PH
34 DAVE POPE-OF
36 SAM (BLACKIE) DENTE-SS/2B
37 ROCKY NELSON-1B
38 JOSE (PANTS) SANTIAGO-P
40 BILL LOBE-CH
42 RED KRESS-CH
43 MEL (CHIEF) HARDER-CH
44 TONY (COOCH) (CHICK) CUCCINELLO-CH

1955

2ND 93-61 3GB

1 BOBBY AVILA-2B
2 GEORGE (BO) STRICKLAND-SS
3 DALE MITCHELL-1B/OF
4 JIM HEGAN-C
5 HANK (HEENEY) (HEINE) MAJESKI-3B/2B (1)
5 BOBBY YOUNG-2B/3B (2)
6 JOE ALTOBELLI-1B
7 AL (FLIP) ROSEN-3B/1B
8 RUDY REGALADO-3B/2B
8 KENNY KUHN-SS
9 RALPH KINER-OF
10 AL LOPEZ-MGR
11 ART HOUTTEMAN-P
12 DON (THE SPHINX) MOSSI-P
14 LARRY DOBY-OF
14 TED GRAY-P (2)
15 HANK FOILES-C
16 HAL (PRINCE HAL) NEWHOUSER-P
16 AL (FUZZY) SMITH-OF/INF
17 DAVE PHILLEY-OF (1)
17 RUDY REGALADO-3B/2B
18 HAL NARAGON-C
19 BOB (RAPID ROBERT) FELLER-P
20 RAY NARLESKI-P
21 BOB LEMON-P
23 VIC WERTZ (ILL)-1B/OF
24 EARLY (GUS) WYNN-P
25 MIKE (THE BIG BEAR) GARCIA-P
26 SAL (THE BARBER) MAGLIE-P (2)
27 HERB SCORE-P
28 BUD DALEY-P
30 BILL (LEFTY) WIGHT-P (1)
30 HOOT EVERS-OF (2)
31 WALLY WESTLAKE-OF (1)
31 GENE WOODLING-OF (2)
32 AL (FUZZY) SMITH-OF/INF
32 STU LOCKLIN-OF
33 FERRIS FAIN-1B (2)
34 DAVE POPE-OF (1)
34 JOSE (PANTS) SANTIAGO-P
35 STAN PAWLOSKI-2B
36 SAM (BLACKIE) DENTE-SS/2B
37 HARRY (SUITCASE) (GOODY) SIMPSON-OF
37 BILLY HARRELL-SS
38 ROCKY COLAVITO-OF
40 BILL LOBE-CH
42 RED KRESS-CH
43 MEL (CHIEF) HARDER-CH
44 TONY (COOCH) (CHICK) CUCCINELLO-CH
45 JOE ALTOBELLI-1B
48 HANK AGUIRRE-P
51 JOSE (PANTS) SANTIAGO-P

1956

2ND 88-66 9GB

1 BOBBY AVILA-2B
2 GEORGE (BO) STRICKLAND-INF
3 DALE MITCHELL-OF (1)
4 JIM HEGAN-C
5 BOBBY YOUNG-2B/3B
7 AL (FLIP) ROSEN-3B
8 KENNY KUHN-SS/2B
9 RUDY REGALADO-3B/1B
10 AL LOPEZ-MGR
11 ART HOUTTEMAN-P
12 DON (THE SPHINX) MOSSI-P
14 GENE WOODLING (ILL)-OF
15 HANK FOILES-C (1)
15 EARL AVERILL, JR.-C
16 AL (FUZZY) SMITH-OF/INF
17 RUDY REGALADO-3B/1B
17 CHICO CARRASQUEL-SS/3B
18 HAL NARAGON-C
19 BOB (RAPID ROBERT) FELLER-P
20 RAY NARLESKI (INJ)-P
21 BOB LEMON-P
22 HANK AGUIRRE-P
22 CAL (BUSTER) MCLISH-P
23 VIC WERTZ-1B
24 EARLY (GUS) WYNN-P
25 MIKE (THE BIG BEAR) GARCIA-P
26 SAL (THE BARBER) MAGLIE-P (1)
26 PRESTON WARD-1B/OF (2)
27 HERB SCORE-P
28 BUD DALEY-P
28 HANK AGUIRRE-P
30 HOOT EVERS-PH (1)
31 GENE WOODLING (ILL)-OF
31 JIM BUSBY-OF
32 STU LOCKLIN-OF
33 CAL (BUSTER) MCLISH-P
33 JOE (RABBIT) CAFFIE-OF
34 DAVE POPE-OF (2)
36 SAM MELE,-OF/1B
38 ROCKY COLAVITO-OF
40 BILL LOBE-CH
42 RED KRESS-CH
43 MEL (CHIEF) HARDER-CH
44 TONY (COOCH) (CHICK) CUCCINELLO-CH

1957

6TH 76-77 21.5GB

1 BOBBY AVILA-2B/3B
2 KERBY FARRELL-MGR
3 GEORGE (BO) STRICKLAND-INF
4 JIM HEGAN-C
5 JOE ALTOBELLI-1B/OF
6*JOHNNY GRAY-P*
6 BILLY HARRELL-INF
6 EDDIE ROBINSON-1B (2)
8 KENNY KUHN-INF
9 LARRY RAINES-UTIL
10 BUD DALEY-P
11 ART HOUTTEMAN-P (1)
11 DICK BROWN-C
12 DON (THE SPHINX) MOSSI-P
14 GENE WOODLING-OF
15 RUSS NIXON-C
16 AL (FUZZY) SMITH-3B/OF
17 CHICO CARRASQUEL-SS
18 HAL NARAGON-C
19 *(RET#) BOB FELLER*
20 RAY NARLESKI-P
21 BOB LEMON-P
22 CAL (BUSTER) MCLISH-P
23 VIC WERTZ-1B
24 EARLY (GUS) WYNN-P
25 MIKE (THE BIG BEAR) GARCIA-P
26 PRESTON WARD-1B
26 VITO VALENTINETTI-P (2)
26 HOYT WILHELM-P (2)
27 HERB SCORE (INJ)-P
28 HANK AGUIRRE-P
29 DICK (BONES) TOMANEK-P
30 STAN PITULA (INJ)-P
30 BOB ALEXANDER-P
31 JIM BUSBY-OF (1)
32 ROGER MARIS-OF
33 JOE (RABBIT) CAFFIE-OF
34 JOE (RABBIT) CAFFIE-OF
34 STAN PITULA (INJ)-P
35 BOB USHER-OF (1)
36 DICK WILLIAMS-OF/3B (2)
37 JOHNNY GRAY-P
37 BILLY HARRELL-INF
38 ROCKY COLAVITO-OF
40 BILL LOBE-CH
42 RED KRESS-CH
43 MEL (CHIEF) HARDER-CH
44 EDDIE (THE BRAT) (MUGGSY) STANKY-CH

1958

4TH 77-76 14.5GB

1 BOBBY AVILA-2B/3B
2 BOBBY (NIG) BRAGAN-MGR1
2 EARL AVERILL, JR.-3B
2 RANDY (HANDSOME RANSOM) JACKSON-3B (2)
(3) GEORGE (BO) STRICKLAND (RET)-(SS)
3 WOODIE HELD-UTIL (2)
4 JAY (J.W.) PORTER-C/INF
5 ROGER MARIS-OF (1)
6* ROCKY COLAVITO-OF/1B/P*
7 FRED HATFIELD-3B (1)

CLEVELAND INDIANS

7 BILLY HUNTER-SS/3B (2)
8 MICKEY VERNON-1B
9 MINNIE MINOSO-OF/3B
10 VIC POWER-UTIL (2)
11 DICK BROWN-C
12 DON (THE SPHINX) MOSSI-P
14 LARRY DOBY-OF
15 RUSS NIXON-C
16 BILLY MORAN-2B/SS
17 CHICO CARRASQUEL-2B/3B (1)
18 HAL NARAGON-C
19 *(RET#) BOB FELLER*
20 RAY NARLESKI-P
21 BOB LEMON-P
22 CAL (BUSTER) MCLISH-P
23 VIC WERTZ (INJ)-1B
25 MIKE (THE BIG BEAR) GARCIA (INJ)-P
26 HOYT WILHELM-P (1)
26 DICK BRODOWSKI-P
27 HERB SCORE (INJ)-P
28 HAL WOODESHICK-P
29 DICK (BONES) TOMANEK-P (1)
29 ROD GRABER-OF
30 CARROLL HARDY-OF
31 GARY GEIGER-OF/3B/P
32 CHUCK CHURN-P
32 MORRIE (LEFTY) MARTIN-P (2)
33 JIM (MUDCAT) GRANT-P
34 DON FERRARESE-P
35 STEVE RIDZIK-P
35 JOE (FLASH) GORDON-MGR2
36 PRESTON WARD-3B/1B (1)
37 BOB KELLY-P (2)
37 JIM (SHERIFF) CONSTABLE-P (2)
38 BILLY HARRELL-3B/UTIL
39 GARY BELL-P
40 JO-JO WHITE-CH
42 RED KRESS-CH
43 MEL (CHIEF) HARDER-CH
44 EDDIE (THE BRAT) (MUGGSY) STANKY-CH

1959

2ND 89-65 5GB

1 BILLY MARTIN (INJ)-2B/3B
2 RANDY (HANDSOME RANSOM) JACKSON-3B (1)
3 WOODIE HELD-SS/UTIL
4 GEORGE (BO) STRICKLAND-3B/INF
5 RAY WEBSTER-2B/3B
6 ROCKY COLAVITO-OF
7 GENE LEEK-3B/SS
7 GRANNY HAMNER-INF (2)
8 ED FITZGERALD (INJ)-C (2)
9 MINNIE MINOSO-OF
10 VIC POWER-1B/INF
11 DICK BROWN-C
12 WILLIE (PUDDIN' HEAD) JONES-3B (2)
14 TITO FRANCONA-OF/1B
15 RUSS NIXON-C
17 ELMER VALO-OF
18 HAL NARAGON-C (1)
18 BILLY MORAN-2B/SS
19 *(RET#) BOB FELLER*
20 AL (BOZO) CICOTTE-P
21 BOB LEMON-P
22 CAL (BUSTER) MCLISH-P
23 BOBBY LOCKE-P
23 BUD PODBIELAN-P
23 JAKE STRIKER-P
23 JACK HARSHMAN-P (3)
25 MIKE (THE BIG BEAR) GARCIA-P
26 DICK BRODOWSKI-P
27 HERB SCORE-P
28 RIVERBOAT SMITH-P (2)
29 HUMBERTO ROBINSON-P (1)
29 BOBBY LOCKE-P
30 CARROLL HARDY-OF
31 JIM PERRY-P
32 JOHNNY BRIGGS-P
32 JIM BAXES-2B/3B (2)
33 JIM (MUDCAT) GRANT-P
34 DON FERRARESE-P
35 JOE (FLASH) GORDON-MGR
37 JIMMY PIERSALL-OF/3B
38 DON DILLARD-PH
39 GARY BELL-P
40 JO-JO WHITE-CH
42 RED KRESS-CH
43 MEL (CHIEF) HARDER-CH
43 CHUCK TANNER-OF
45 JIM BOLGER-PH (1)
45 GORDIE COLEMAN-1B

1960

4TH 76-78 21GB

1 MIKE DE LA HOZ-SS/3B
1 JOHNNY TEMPLE-2B/3B
2 KEN ASPROMONTE-2B/3B (2)
3 WOODIE HELD (INJ)-SS
4 GEORGE (BO) STRICKLAND-INF
4 JOE MORGAN-3B/OF (2)
5 BUBBA PHILLIPS-3B/UTIL
5 STEVE DEMETER-3B
6 HARVEY KUENN-OF/3B
6 CHUCK TANNER-OF
7 BUBBA PHILLIPS-3B/UTIL
7 HARVEY KUENN-OF/3B
8 BOB HALE-1B
8 JOHNNY POWERS-OF (2)
8 HANK FOILES-C (2)
8 ROCKY BRIDGES-SS/3B (2)
9 BOB HALE-1B
10 VIC POWER-1B/INF
11 JOHNNY (HONEY) ROMANO-C
12 WALT BOND-OF
14 TITO FRANCONA-OF/1B
15 RUSS NIXON-C (1)
15 JOE KEOUGH-OF (2)
16 JOHNNY BRIGGS-P (1)
16 JOHNNY TEMPLE-2B/3B
17 JOHNNY KLIPPSTEIN-P
18 BARRY LATMAN-P
19 *(RET#) BOB FELLER*
20 MIKE LEE-P
21 BOB LEMON-P
22 DICK STIGMAN-P
23 JACK HARSHMAN-P
24 BARRY LATMAN-P
25 CARL THOMAS-P
25 DON (NEWK) NEWCOMBE-P (2)
26 BOB GRIM-P (1)
26 TY CLINE-OF
27 BARRY LATMAN-P
27 RED WILSON-C (2)
27 PETE WHISENANT-OF (2)
28 BOBBY TIEFENAUER-P
29 BOBBY LOCKE-P
30 CARROLL HARDY-OF (1)
30 CARL (STUBBY) MATHIAS-P
30 TED BOWSFIELD-P (2)
31 JIM PERRY-P
32 CARL (STUBBY) MATHIAS-P
33 JIM (MUDCAT) GRANT-P
34 WYNN (HAWK) HAWKINS-P
34 MIKE DE LA HOZ-SS/3B
35 JOE (FLASH) GORDON-MGR1
35 JIMMY DYKES-MGR3
37 JIMMY PIERSALL-OF
38 DON DILLARD-OF
38 FRANK FUNK-P
39 GARY BELL-P
40 JO-JO WHITE-CH/MGR2
40 LUKE (OLD ACHES & PAINS) APPLING-CH
41 ED FITZGERALD-CH
42 RED KRESS-CH
43 MEL (CHIEF) HARDER-CH
45 TED (CORK) WILKS-CH

1961

5TH 78-83 30.5GB

1 MIKE DE LA HOZ-INF
2 KEN ASPROMONTE-2B (2)
3 WOODIE HELD-SS
4 JOE MORGAN-3B/OF
4 BOB NIEMAN-OF (2)
5 BUBBA PHILLIPS-3B
6 JACK KUBISZYN-INF
7 HAL JONES-1B
7 MIKE DE LA HOZ-INF
8 WILLIE KIRKLAND-OF
9 BOB HALE-PH (1)
9 TY CLINE-OF
10 VIC POWER-1B/2B
11 JOHNNY (HONEY) ROMANO-C
12 WALT BOND-OF
14 TITO FRANCONA-OF/1B
15 VALMY THOMAS-C
16 JOHNNY TEMPLE-2B
17 SAM (SUDDEN SAM) MCDOWELL-P
18 BARRY LATMAN-P
19 *(RET#) BOB FELLER*
20 RUSS HEMAN-P (1)
22 DICK STIGMAN (INJ)-P
23 JOHNNY ANTONELLI-P (1)
23 JOE SCHAFFERNOTH-P (2)
24 BOB ALLEN-P
27 BILL DAILEY-P
27 STEVE HAMILTON-P
29 BOBBY LOCKE-P
30 CHUCK ESSEGIAN-OF (3)
31 JIM PERRY-P
32 AL LUPLOW-OF
33 JIM (MUDCAT) GRANT-P
34 WYNN (HAWK) HAWKINS-P
35 JIMMY DYKES-MGR1
36 DON DILLARD-OF
37 JIMMY PIERSALL-OF
38 FRANK FUNK-P
39 GARY BELL-P
40 LUKE (OLD ACHES & PAINS) APPLING-CH
42 MEL MCGAHA-CH
43 MEL (CHIEF) HARDER-CH/MGR2
45 A. JONES-CH

1962

6TH 80-82 16GB

1 JERRY (SLIM) KINDALL-2B
2 KEN ASPROMONTE-2B/3B (1)
2 MARLAN COUGHTRY-PH
2 JACK KUBISZYN-SS/3B
3 WOODIE HELD-SS/UTIL
4 BOB NIEMAN-PH (1)
4 TOMMIE AGEE-OF
5 BUBBA PHILLIPS-3B/UTIL
6 WILLIE TASBY-OF/3B (2)
7 MIKE DE LA HOZ-2B
7 JIM (MOE) MAHONEY-INF
8 WILLIE KIRKLAND-OF
9 TY CLINE-OF
10 MAX ALVIS-3B
11 JOHNNY (HONEY) ROMANO-C
12 GENE GREEN-OF/1B
14 TITO FRANCONA-1B
15 HAL JONES-1B
16 JIM (MOE) MAHONEY-INF
17 SAM (SUDDEN SAM) MCDOWELL-P
18 BARRY LATMAN-P
19 *(RET#) BOB FELLER*
20 RON TAYLOR-P
20 DICK DONOVAN-P
22 RON TAYLOR-P
23 DICK DONOVAN-P
23 FLOYD WEAVER, P
24 BOB ALLEN-P
25 DOC EDWARD-C
26 DON RUDOLPH-P (1)
26 DAVE TYRIVER-P
26 BOB HARTMAN-P
27 BILL DAILEY-P
28 PEDRO (PETE) RAMOS-P
29 RUBEN GOMEZ-P (1)
29 JACKIE COLLUM-P
30 CHUCK ESSEGIAN-OF
31 JIM PERRY-P
32 AL LUPLOW-OF
33 JIM (MUDCAT) GRANT-P
34 WYNN (HAWK) HAWKINS (MIL)-P
35 WALT BOND-OF
36 DON DILLARD-OF
38 FRANK FUNK-P
39 GARY BELL-P
40 PEDRO (PETE) RAMOS-P
40 RAY KATT-CH
41 SALTY PARKER-CH
42 MEL MCGAHA-MGR
43 MEL (CHIEF) HARDER-CH
45 HANK IZQUIERDO-CH

1963

5TH (TIE) 79-83 25.5GB

1 BIRDIE TEBBETTS-MGR
2 MEL (CHIEF) HARDER-CH
3 GEORGE (BO) STRICKLAND-CH
4 ELMER VALO-CH
5 JIM LAWRENCE-C
5 CAL NEEMAN-C (1)
5 SAMMY TAYLOR-C (3)
6 DOC EDWARDS-C
6 JOE AZCUE-C (2)
7 BOB LIPSKI-C
9 JOHNNY (HONEY) ROMANO (INJ)-C
10 MAX ALVIS-3B
11 JOE ADCOCK-1B
12 WOODIE HELD-2B/UTIL
14 JERRY (SLIM) KINDALL-SS/INF
15 FRED WHITFIELD-1B
16 TONY MARTINEZ-SS
16 LARRY BROWN-SS/2B
17 MIKE DE LA HOZ-UTIL
18 DICK HOWSER-SS (2)
19 *(RET#) BOB FELLER*
21 BOB CHANCE-OF
22 AL LUPLOW-OF
23 GENE GREEN-OF (1)
23 TOMMIE AGEE-OF
24 TITO FRANCONA-OF/1B
25 VIC DAVALILLO (INJ)-OF
27 WILLIE KIRKLAND-OF
28 WILLIE TASBY-OF/2B
29 ELLIS BURTON-OF (1)
30 DICK DONOVAN-P
31 JIM PERRY-P (1)
31 JACK KRALICK-P (2)
32 BARRY LATMAN-P
33 JIM (MUDCAT) GRANT-P
34 SAM (SUDDEN SAM) MCDOWELL-P
35 PEDRO (PETE) RAMOS-P
36 TED ABERNATHY-P
37 TOMMY (T.J.) JOHN-P
38 EARLY (GUS) WYNN-P
39 GARY BELL-P
40 BOB ALLEN-P
42 RON NISCHWITZ-P
43 JACK CURTIS-P
43 GORDON SEYFRIED-P
48 JERRY WALKER-P

1964

6TH (TIE) 79-83 20GB

1 BIRDIE TEBBETTS (ILL)-MGR
2 EARLY (GUS) WYNN-CH
3 GEORGE (BO) STRICKLAND-CH/ACT.MGR
4 ELMER VALO-CH
5 SOLLY HEMUS-CH
6 JOE AZCUE-C
7 JOHNNY (HONEY) ROMANO-C/1B
9 GEORGE BANKS-UTIL
10 MAX ALVIS (ILL)-3B
11 VERN FULLER (INJ)-PH
11 BILLY MORAN-INF (2)
12 WOODIE HELD-UTIL
14 JERRY (SLIM) KINDALL-1B (1)
14 TONY MARTINEZ-2B/SS
15 FRED WHITFIELD-1B
16 LARRY BROWN-2B/SS
17 CHICO SALMON-UTIL
18 DICK HOWSER-SS (2)
19 *(RET#) BOB FELLER*
20 WALLY POST-OF
20 PAUL DICKEN-PH
21 BOB CHANCE-1B/OF
22 AL LUPLOW-OF
24 TITO FRANCONA-OF/1B
25 VIC DAVALILLO-OF
26 CHICO SALMON-UTIL
27 LEON WAGNER-OF
28 AL (FUZZY) SMITH-OF (1)
28 TOMMIE AGEE-OF
30 DICK DONOVAN-P
31 JACK KRALICK-P
32 DUKE SIMS-C
33 JIM (MUDCAT) GRANT-P (1)
33 LUIS TIANT-P
34 JERRY WALKER-P
35 PEDRO (PETE) RAMOS-P (1)
36 TED ABERNATHY-P
37 TOMMY (T.J.) JOHN-P
39 GARY BELL-P
42 SONNY SIEBERT-P
43 GORDON SEYFRIED-P
43 LEE STANGE-P (2)
44 DON MCMAHON-P
45 TOM KELLEY-P
48 JERRY WALKER-P
48 SAM (SUDDEN SAM) MCDOWELL-P

1965

5TH 87-75 15GB

1 BIRDIE TEBBETTS-MGR
2 EARLY (GUS) WYNN-CH
3 GEORGE (BO) STRICKLAND-CH
4 SOLLY HEMUS-CH
6 JOE AZCUE-C
7 CAM CARREON-C
7 PHIL ROOF-C (2)
9 DUKE SIMS-C

10 MAX ALVIS-3B
11 BILLY MORAN-2B/SS
12 RALPH GAGLIANO-PR
12 BILL DAVIS-PH
14 GEORGE BANKS-3B
14 TONY MARTINEZ-PH
15 FRED WHITFIELD-1B
16 LARRY BROWN-SS/2B
17 CHICO SALMON-UTIL
18 DICK HOWSER-SS/2B
19 *(RET#) BOB FELLER*
20 LU CLINTON-OF (3)
21 ROCKY COLAVITO-OF
22 AL LUPLOW-OF
23 CHUCK HINTON-UTIL
24 RICHIE SCHEINBLUM-PH
24 PEDRO GONZALEZ-2B/UTIL (2)
25 VIC DAVALILLO-OF
27 LEON WAGNER-OF
30 DICK DONOVAN-P
31 JACK KRALICK-P
32 RALPH TERRY-P
33 LUIS TIANT-P
34 STEVE HARGAN-P
35 FLOYD WEAVER-P
36 BOBBY TIEFENAUER-P (3)
39 GARY BELL-P
40 STAN WILLIAMS-P
41 MIKE (RED) HEDLUND (INJ)-P
42 SONNY SIEBERT-P
43 LEE STANGE-P
44 DON MCMAHON-P
45 TOM KELLEY-P
48 SAM (SUDDEN SAM) MCDOWELL-P
49 JACK SPRING-P
50 RAY (BUDDY) BARKER-1B (1)

1966

5TH 81-81 17GB

1 BIRDIE TEBBETTS-MGR1
2 EARLY (GUS) WYNN-CH
3 GEORGE (BO) STRICKLAND-CH/MGR2
4 REGGIE OTERO-CH
5 RAY MUELLER-CH
5 BUDDY BOOKER-C
6 JOE AZCUE-C
7 DEL CRANDALL-C
8 BUDDY BOOKER-C
9 DUKE SIMS (INJ)-C
10 MAX ALVIS-3B
11 BILL DAVIS-1B
12 BILL DAVIS-1B
12 JIM (DIAMOND JIM) GENTILE-1B (2)
13 VERN FULLER-2B
14 GEORGE BANKS-PH
15 FRED WHITFIELD-1B
16 LARRY BROWN (INJ)-SS/2B
17 CHICO SALMON-UTIL
18 DICK HOWSER-2B/SS
19 *(RET#) BOB FELLER*
20 PAUL DICKEN-PH
21 ROCKY COLAVITO-OF
21 TONY MARTINEZ-SS/2B
21 JOSE (PAPITO) VIDAL-OF
23 CHUCK HINTON-UTIL
24 PEDRO GONZALEZ-2B/UTIL
25 VIC DAVALILLO-OF
26 JIM LANDIS-OF
27 LEON WAGNER-OF
29 TONY CURRY-PH
31 JACK KRALICK-P
32 JOHN O'DONOGHUE-P
33 LUIS TIANT-P
34 STEVE HARGAN-P
36 BOB ALLEN-P
37 BOB HEFFNER-P
39 GARY BELL-P
40 GEORGE CULVER-P
42 SONNY SIEBERT-P
43 LEE STANGE-P (1)
44 DON MCMAHON-P (1)
45 TOM KELLEY-P
46 DICK (THE MONSTER) RADATZ-P
48 SAM (SUDDEN SAM) MCDOWELL (INJ)-P

1967

8TH 75-87 17GB

2 CLAY BRYANT-CH
3 GEORGE (BO) STRICKLAND-CH
4 PAT MULLIN-CH
5 DEL RICE-CH
6 JOE ADCOCK-MGR
7 JOE AZCUE-C
8 RAY FOSSE-C
9 DUKE SIMS-C
10 MAX ALVIS-3B
11 TONY HORTON-1B (2)
13 VERN FULLER-2B/SS
14 GORDY LUND-SS
15 FRED WHITFIELD-1B
16 LARRY BROWN-SS
17 CHICO SALMON-UTIL
18 GUS GIL-2B/1B
19 *(RET#) BOB FELLER*
20 DON DEMETER-OF/3B (2)
21 ROCKY COLAVITO-OF (1)
21 JIM KING-OF (3)
22 WILLIE SMITH-OF/1B
23 CHUCK HINTON-OF/2B
24 PEDRO GONZALEZ-INF
25 VIC DAVALILLO-OF
26 LEE MAYE-OF/2B
27 LEON WAGNER-OF
28 RICHIE SCHEINBLUM-OF
29 JOSE (PAPITO) VIDAL-OF
31 JACK KRALICK-P
31 ORLANDO PENA-P (2)
32 JOHN O'DONOGHUE-P
33 LUIS TIANT-P
34 STEVE HARGAN-P
35 STAN WILLIAMS-P
36 BOB ALLEN-P
37 STEVE BAILEY-P
39 GARY BELL-P (1)
39 ED CONNOLLY-P
40 GEORGE CULVER-P
41 BOBBY TIEFENAUER-P
42 SONNY SIEBERT-P
45 TOM KELLEY (INJ)-P
46 DICK (THE MONSTER) RADATZ-P (1)
48 SAM (SUDDEN SAM) MCDOWELL-P

1968

3RD 86-75 16.5GB

1 JOSE CARDENAL-OF
2 JACK SANFORD-CH
3 GEORGE (BO) STRICKLAND-CH
4 JOHNNY (SKIDS) LIPON-CH
5 AL (BLACKIE) DARK-MGR
6 JOE AZCUE-C
7 KEN SUAREZ-UTIL
8 RAY FOSSE-C
9 DUKE SIMS-UTIL
10 MAX ALVIS-3B
11 TONY HORTON-1B
13 VERN FULLER-2B/INF
14 DAVE NELSON-2B/SS
15 BILLY HARRIS-INF
16 LARRY BROWN-SS
17 CHICO SALMON-UTIL
19 *(RET#) BOB FELLER*
20 JIMMIE HALL-OF (2)
21 TOMMY HARPER-OF/2B
22 WILLIE SMITH-1B/OF/P (1)
22 LOU (SLICK) JOHNSON-OF
23 LOU (SWEET LOU) PINIELLA-OF
24 EDDIE LEON-SS
24 LOU KLIMCHOCK-INF
25 VIC DAVALILLO-OF (1)
25 RUSS NAGELSON-PH
26 LEE MAYE-OF/1B
27 LEON WAGNER-OF (1)
27 RUSS SNYDER-OF/1B (2)
28 RICHIE SCHEINBLUM-OF
29 JOSE (PAPITO) VIDAL-OF/1B
31 HORACIO PINA-P
32 EDDIE FISHER-P
33 LUIS TIANT-P
34 STEVE HARGAN-P
35 STAN WILLIAMS-P
36 MIKE (RED) HEDLUND-P
37 STEVE BAILEY-P
38 BILLY ROHR-P
38 ROB GARDNER-P
39 MIKE PAUL-P
40 DARRELL SUTHERLAND-P
42 SONNY SIEBERT-P
43 VINCENTE (HUEVO) ROMO-P (2)
44 TOMMY GRAMLY-P
(45) TOM KELLEY (INJ)-(P)
46 HAL (BUD) KURTZ-P
48 SAM (SUDDEN SAM) MCDOWELL-P

1969

6TH E 62-99 46.5GB

1 JOSE CARDENAL-OF/3B
2 JACK SANFORD-CH
3 GEORGE (BO) STRICKLAND-CH
4 JOHNNY (SKIDS) LIPON-CH
5 AL (BLACKIE) DARK-MGR
6 JOE AZCUE-C (1)
7 KEN SUAREZ-C
8 RAY FOSSE-C
9 DUKE SIMS-C/UTIL
10 MAX ALVIS (INJ)-3B/SS
11 TONY HORTON-1B
12 LUKE EASTER-CH
13 VERN FULLER-2B/3B
14 DAVE NELSON (INJ)-2B/OF
16 LARRY BROWN-SS/INF
17 ZOILO (ZORRO) VERSALLES-INF (1)
17 LOU CAMILLI-3B
18 JACK HEIDEMANN-SS
19 *(RET#) BOB FELLER*
20 JIMMIE HALL-OF (1)
20 CAP PETERSON-OF/3B
21 FRANK BAKER-OF
23 CHUCK HINTON-OF/3B
24 EDDIE LEON-SS
25 RUSS NAGELSON-OF/1B
26 LEE MAYE-OF (1)
27 RUSS SNYDER-OF
28 RICHIE SCHEINBLUM-OF
29 LOU KLIMCHOCK-UTIL
31 HORACIO PINA-P
32 JACK HAMILTON-P (1)
33 LUIS TIANT-P
34 STEVE HARGAN-P
35 STAN WILLIAMS-P
36 LARRY BURCHART (INJ)-P
37 GARY KROLL-P
38 PHIL HENNIGAN-P
39 MIKE PAUL-P
40 KEN (HAWK) HARRELSON-OF/1B
41 RON LAW-P
42 SONNY SIEBERT-P (1)
42 DICK ELLSWORTH-P (2)
43 VINCENTE (HUEVO) ROMO-P (1)
43 JUAN PIZARRO-P (2)
48 SAM (SUDDEN SAM) MCDOWELL-P
49 JUAN PIZARRO-P (2)
50 DICK ELLSWORTH-P (2)
54 GARY BOYD-P

1970

5TH E 76-86 32GB

1 AL (BLACKIE) DARK-MGR
2 COT DEAL-CH
3 KERBY FARRELL-CH
4 JOHNNY (SKIDS) LIPON-CH
5 AL (BLACKIE) DARK-MGR
5 *(RET#) LOU BOUDREAU*
8 RAY FOSSE-C
9 DUKE SIMS-UTIL
10 RICH (RED) ROLLINS-3B (2)
11 TONY HORTON (ILL)-1B
12 GRAIG NETTLES-3B/OF
13 VERN FULLER-INF
14 WALT (HOOT) EVERS-CH
16 LARRY BROWN-INF
17 LOU CAMILLI-INF
18 JACK HEIDEMANN-SS
19 *(RET#) BOB FELLER*
22 TED FORD-OF
23 CHUCK HINTON-UTIL
24 EDDIE LEON-2B/INF
25 RUSS NAGELSON-OF/1B (1)
25 BUDDY BRADFORD-OF/3B (2)
26 TED UHLAENDER-OF
27 ROY FOSTER-OF
28 VADA PINSON-OF/1B
29 LOU KLIMCHOCK-1B/2B
29 JOHN LOWENSTEIN-UTIL
31 BARRY MOORE-P (1)
31 STEVE MINGORI-P
32 DEAN CHANCE-P (1)
33 BOB MILLER-P (1)
33 RICK AUSTIN-P
34 STEVE HARGAN (INJ)-P
35 DENNY HIGGINS-P
36 FRED LASHER-P (2)
38 PHIL HENNIGAN-P
39 MIKE PAUL-P
40 KEN (HAWK) HARRELSON (INJ)-1B
42 DICK ELLSWORTH-P (1)
42 JIM RITTWAGE-P
44 VINCE COLBERT-P
45 RICH HAND-P
46 STEVE DUNNING-P
48 SAM (SUDDEN SAM) MCDOWELL-P

1971

6TH E 60-102 43GB

1 AL (BLACKIE) DARK-MGR
2 COT DEAL-CH
3 KERBY FARRELL-CH
4 JOHNNY (SKIDS) LIPON-CH/MGR2
5 *(RET#) LOU BOUDREAU*
6 BOBBY HOFMAN-CH
7 KEN SUAREZ-C
8 RAY FOSSE-C
10 HAROLD (GOMER) HODGE-INF
(11) TONY HORTON (ILL)-(1B)
11 TED UHLAENDER-OF
12 GRAIG NETTLES-3B/OF
14 CHRIS CHAMBLISS-1B
16 LARRY BROWN-SS (1)
16 FRED STANLEY-SS/2B
17 LOU CAMILLI-SS/2B
17 KURT BEVACQUA-UTIL
18 JACK HEIDEMANN (INJ)-SS
19 *(RET#) BOB FELLER*
21 FRANK BAKER-OF
22 TED FORD-OF
23 CHUCK HINTON-UTIL
24 EDDIE LEON-2B/SS
25 BUDDY BRADFORD-OF (1)
25 KURT BEVACQUA-UTIL
26 TED UHLAENDER-OF
27 ROY FOSTER-OF
28 VADA PINSON-OF/1B
29 JOHN LOWENSTEIN (INJ)-UTIL
30 RAY LAMB-P
31 STEVE MINGORI-P
32 ALAN FOSTER-P
33 RICK AUSTIN-P
34 STEVE HARGAN (INJ)-P
35 CAMILO PASCUAL-P
36 CAMILO PASCUAL-P
38 PHIL HENNIGAN-P
39 MIKE PAUL-P
40 KEN (HAWK) HARRELSON (INJ)-1B/OF
40 JIM CLARK-OF/1B
44 VINCE COLBERT-P
45 RICH HAND (INJ)-P
46 STEVE DUNNING-P
47 ED FARMER-P
48 SAM (SUDDEN SAM) MCDOWELL-P
49 MARK BALLINGER-P
50 CHARLES MACHEMEHL-P
51 BOB KAISER-P

1972

5TH E 72-84 14GB

1 DEL UNSER-OF
2 KEN ASPROMONTE-MGR
3 JOE LUTZ-CH
5 *(RET#) LOU BOUDREAU*
6 BOBBY HOFMAN-CH
7 JACK BROHAMER-2B/3B
8 RAY FOSSE-C/1B
9 BUDDY BELL-OF/3B
10 JERRY MOSES-C/1B
11 EDDIE LEON-2B/SS
12 GRAIG NETTLES-3B
14 CHRIS CHAMBLISS (INJ)-1B
15 FRANK DUFFY-SS
16 FRED STANLEY-SS/2B (1)
17 LOU CAMILLI-SS/2B
18 JACK HEIDEMANN-SS
19 *(RET#) BOB FELLER*
20 ALEX JOHNSON-OF
21 WARREN SPAHN-CH
22 TOMMY MCCRAW-OF/1B
23 RON LOLICH-OF
25 KURT BEVACQUA-OF/3B
25 MIKE KILKENNY-P (4)
27 ROY FOSTER-OF
28 ADOLFO PHILLIPS-OF
29 JOHN LOWENSTEIN-OF/1B
30 RAY LAMB-P
31 STEVE MINGORI-P
32 MILT WILCOX-P
33 LOWELL PALMER-P (2)
34 STEVE HARGAN-P
35 GAYLORD PERRY-P
35 TOM HILGENDORF-P
35 BILL BUTLER-P
36 GAYLORD PERRY-P
37 DENNY RIDDLEBERGER-P
38 PHIL HENNIGAN (INJ)-P
40 TOM HILGENDORF-P
41 DICK TIDROW-P
42 MIKE KILKENNY-P (4)
43 MARCELINO LOPEZ-P
44 VINCE COLBERT-P
46 STEVE DUNNING-P

CLEVELAND INDIANS

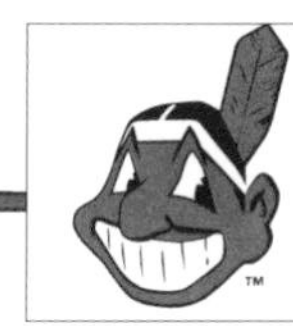

47 ED FARMER-P
52 LARRY JOHNSON-C
61 ROY HATHAWAY-CH
62 LEN JOHNSTON-CH
63 CLAY BRYANT-CH

1973
6TH E 71-91 26GB

2 KEN ASPROMONTE-MGR
3 JOE LUTZ-CH
4 LEO (CHICO) CARDENAS-SS/3B
5 *(RET#) LOU BOUDREAU*
6 ROCKY COLAVITO-CH
7 JOHNNY ELLIS-UTIL
8 ALAN ASHBY-C
9 JERRY KENNEY-2B
10 JACK BROHAMER-2B
11 DAVE DUNCAN (INJ)-C/DH
13 WALT (NO-NECK) WILLIAMS-OF/DH
14 CHRIS CHAMBLISS-1B
15 FRANK DUFFY (INJ)-SS
16 TOM RAGLAND-2B/SS
18 MIKE KEKICH-P (2)
19 *(RET#) BOB FELLER*
20 GEORGE HENDRICK (INJ)-OF
21 WARREN SPAHN-CH
22 RON LOLICH-OF
23 OSCAR GAMBLE-DH/OF
24 CHARLIE SPIKES-OF/DH
25 BUDDY BELL-3B/OF
27 DICK BOSMAN-P (2)
28 RUSTY TORRES-OF
29 JOHN LOWENSTEIN-UTIL
30 RAY LAMB-P
31 STEVE MINGORI-P (1)
31 TOM TIMMERMAN-P (2)
32 JERRY JOHNSON-P
33 KEN (DAFFY) SANDERS-P (2)
33 TED FORD-OF
34 BRENT STROM (INJ)-P
36 GAYLORD PERRY-P
40 TOM HILGENDORF-P
41 DICK TIDROW-P
42 MIKE KILKENNY-P
43 MILT WILCOX (INJ)-P
46 STEVE DUNNING-P (1)
46 MIKE JACKSON-P (2)
46 TOMMY SMITH-OF
47 ED FARMER-P (1)
47 KEN (DAFFY) SANDERS-P (2)
49 DICK BOSMAN,P (2)

1974
4TH E 77-85 14GB

2 KEN ASPROMONTE-MGR
3 CLAY BRYANT-CH
4 ANGEL (REMY) HERMOSO (INJ)-2B
5 *(RET#) LOU BOUDREAU*
6 LARRY DOBY-CH
7 JOHNNY ELLIS (INJ)-1B/UTIL
8 ALAN ASHBY-C
9 LARRY JOHNSON-PR
9 RICO CARTY-DH/1B
10 JACK BROHAMER-2B
11 DAVE DUNCAN-C/UTIL
12 ED CROSBY-INF
13 BRUCE ELLINGSEN-P
14 CHRIS CHAMBLISS-1B (1)
14 DWAIN ANDERSON-2B
14 TOMMY MCCRAW-UTIL (2)
15 FRANK DUFFY-SS
16 OSSIE BLANCO-1B/DH
16 FRITZ PETERSON-P (2)
17 JACK HEIDEMANN-INF (1)
17 LUIS ALVARADO-INF/DH (3)
18 DUANE KUIPER-2B
18 OSSIE BLANCO-1B/DH
19 *(RET#) BOB FELLER*
20 GEORGE HENDRICK-OF/DH
21 TONY PACHECO-CH
22 LERON LEE-OF/DH
23 OSCAR GAMBLE-DH/OF
24 CHARLIE SPIKES-OF
25 BUDDY BELL (INJ)-3B/DH
26 TOMMY SMITH (INJ)-OF/DH
27 DICK BOSMAN-P
28 RUSTY TORRES-OF/DH
29 JOHN LOWENSTEIN-OF/INF
30 FRITZ PETERSON-P (2)
30 JOE LIS-OF (2)
31 TOM TIMMERMAN-P
31 JIM PERRY-P
32 BOB JOHNSON-P
32 BILL GOGOLEWSKI-P
33 FRED BEENE-P (2)
33 FRANK ROBINSON-DH/1B (2)
34 JIM KERN-P
35 CECIL UPSHAW-P (1)
35 TOM BUSKEY-P (2)
36 GAYLORD PERRY-P
38 STEVE KLINE (INJ)-P (2)
39 TOM TIMMERMAN-P
40 TOM HILGENDORF-P
41 DICK TIDROW-P (1)
41 STEVE ARLIN-P (2)
42 JOHNNY JETER-OF
43 MILT WILCOX-P
47 KEN (DAFFY) SANDERS-P (1)
47 BRUCE ELLINGSEN-P
47 FRED BEENE-P (2)

1975
4TH E 79-80 15.5GB

1 KEN BERRY-OF/DH
1 DAVE GARCIA-CH
2 HARVEY (THE KITTEN) HADDIX-CH
3 DAVE GARCIA-CH
3 *(RET#) EARL AVERILL*
(4) ANGEL (REMY) HERMOSO (INJ)-(2B)
4 RICK CERONE-C
4 BILL (SUDS) SUDAKIS-UTIL (2)
5 *(RET#) LOU BOUDREAU*
6 JEFF TORBORG-CH
7 JOHNNY ELLIS-UTIL
8 ALAN ASHBY-C/UTIL
9 RICO CARTY-DH/UTIL
10 JACK BROHAMER (INJ)-2B
11 TOMMY SMITH-OF/DH
12 ED CROSBY-INF
13 BLUE MOON ODOM-P (2)
14 TOMMY MCCRAW-1B/OF/CH
15 FRANK DUFFY-SS
16 FRITZ PETERSON (INJ)-P
17 KEN BERRY-OF/DH
17 DAVE LAROCHE-P
18 DUANE KUIPER-2B/DH
19 *(RET#) BOB FELLER*
20 GEORGE HENDRICK-OF
20 FRANK ROBINSON (INJ)-DH/MGR
21 GEORGE HENDRICK-OF
22 LERON LEE-OF/DH (1)
22 JIM BIBBY-P (2)
23 OSCAR GAMBLE-OF/DH
24 CHARLIE SPIKES-OF/DH
25 BUDDY BELL-3B
26 BOOG POWELL-1B/DH
27 DICK BOSMAN-P (1)
27 RORIC HARRISON-P (2)
28 RICK MANNING-OF/DH
28 JACKIE BROWN-P (2)
29 JOHN LOWENSTEIN-UTIL
30 JOE LIS-1B/DH
30 RICK WAITS-P
31 JIM PERRY-P (1)
31 JACKIE BROWN-P (2)
32 DON HOOD-P
33 ERIC RAICH-P
34 JIM KERN-P
35 TOM BUSKEY (INJ)-P
36 GAYLORD PERRY-P (1)
36 JACKIE BROWN-P (2)
36 RICK WAITS-P
37 DENNIS (ECK) ECKERSLEY-P
(38) STEVE KLINE (INJ)-(P)
39 BOB REYNOLDS-P (3)
40 BOB REYNOLDS-P (3)
42 LARRY ANDERSEN-P
43 DAVE LAROCHE-P
44 JIM STRICKLAND-P
47 FRED BEENE (INJ)-P

1976
4TH E 81-78 16GB

1 DAVE GARCIA-CH
1 GEORGE HENDRICK-OF/DH
2 HARVEY (THE KITTEN) HADDIX-CH
3 *(RET#) EARL AVERILL*
4 RICK CERONE-C
5 *(RET#) LOU BOUDREAU*
6 ROCKY COLAVITO-CH
6 JEFF TORBORG-CH
7 JEFF TORBORG-CH
7 ROCKY COLAVITO-CH
8 ALAN ASHBY-C/UTIL
9 RICO CARTY-DH/UTIL
10 RAY FOSSE-C/DH
11 TOMMY SMITH-OF/DH
12 ED CROSBY-INF
12 ORLANDO GONZALEZ-UTIL
13 RON PRUITT-UTIL
14 LARVELL BLANKS-INF/DH
15 FRANK DUFFY-SS
16 FRITZ PETERSON-P (1)
16 ALFREDO GRIFFIN-SS/DH
17 DAVE LAROCHE-P
18 DUANE KUIPER-2B/UTIL
19 *(RET#) BOB FELLER*
20 FRANK ROBINSON-UTIL/MGR
21 GEORGE HENDRICK-OF/DH
22 JIM BIBBY-P
23 STAN THOMAS-P
24 CHARLIE SPIKES-OF/DH
25 BUDDY BELL-3B/1B
26 BOOG POWELL-1B
27 DOUG HOWARD-UTIL
28 RICK MANNING-OF
29 JOHN LOWENSTEIN-UTIL
30 JOE LIS-OF/DH
31 JACKIE BROWN-P
32 DON HOOD-P
33 ERIC RAICH-P
34 JIM KERN-P
35 TOM BUSKEY (INJ)-P
36 RICK WAITS-P
37 DENNIS (ECK) ECKERSLEY-P
40 HARRY PARKER-P
41 PAT DOBSON-P

1977
5TH E 71-90 28.5GB

00 PAUL DADE-UTIL
1 JOHNNY GRUBB (INJ) OF/DH
2 HARVEY (THE KITTEN) HADDIX-CH
3 *(RET#) EARL AVERILL*
4 JOE NOSSEK-CH
5 *(RET#) LOU BOUDREAU*
6 ROCKY COLAVITO-CH
7 JEFF TORBORG-CH/MGR2
8 ALFREDO GRIFFIN-SS/DH
9 RICO CARTY-DH/1B
10 RAY FOSSE-UTIL (1)
10 JEFF TORBORG-CH/MGR2
11 BILL MELTON-INF/DH
13 RON PRUITT-UTIL
14 LARVELL BLANKS-INF/DH
15 FRANK DUFFY-SS
16 FRED KENDALL-C/DH
17 DAVE LAROCHE-P (1)
17 WAYNE GARLAND-P
18 DUANE KUIPER-2B
19 *(RET#) BOB FELLER*
20 FRANK ROBINSON-MGR1
21 JOHNNY GRUBB (INJ)-OF/DH
22 JIM BIBBY-P
23 WAYNE GARLAND-P
23 BRUCE BOCHTE-OF/UTIL (2)
24 CHARLIE SPIKES-OF/DH
25 BUDDY BELL (INJ)-3B/OF
26 DAVE OLIVER-2B
27 JIM NORRIS-OF/1B
28 RICK MANNING (INJ)-OF
29 ANDRE THORNTON-1B/DH
30 JOHN LOWENSTEIN-UTIL
31 PAUL DADE-UTIL
32 DON HOOD-P
34 JIM KERN-P
35 TOM BUSKEY-P
36 RICK WAITS-P
37 DENNIS (ECK) ECKERSLEY-P
38 BILL LAXTON-P (2)
39 AL FITZMORRIS-P
41 PAT DOBSON-P
42 LARRY ANDERSEN-P
43 SID MONGE-P (2)
44 DON HOOD-P
49 CARDELL CAMPER-P

1978
6TH E 69-90 29GB

00 PAUL DADE-OF/DH
1 JOHNNY GRUBB-OF (1)
2 HARVEY (THE KITTEN) HADDIX-CH
3 *(RET#) EARL AVERILL*
4 DAVE DUNCAN-CH
5 *(RET#) LOU BOUDREAU*
6 ROCKY COLAVITO-CH
7 RON PRUITT-UTIL
7 BERNIE CARBO-DH/OF (2)
8 ALFREDO GRIFFIN-SS
9 RON HASSEY-C
10 JEFF TORBORG-MGR
13 RON PRUITT-UTIL
14 LARVELL BLANKS-INF/DH
14 DAVE FREISLEBEN-P
16 BO DIAZ (INJ)-C
17 WAYNE GARLAND (INJ)-P
18 DUANE KUIPER-2B
19 *(RET#) BOB FELLER*
20 HORACE SPEED (INJ)-OF/DH
21 TOM VERYZER-SS
22 TED COX-UTIL
23 WILLIE HORTON-DH (1)
23 DAN BRIGGS-OF
24 JOE NOSSEK-CH
25 BUDDY BELL-3B/DH
27 JIM NORRIS-UTIL
28 RICK MANNING-OF
29 ANDRE THORNTON-1B
30 LARRY LINTZ-DH
31 WAYNE CAGE-DH/1B
32 DAVID CLYDE-P
34 JIM KERN-P
35 MIKE VAIL-OF/DH (1)
35 GARY ALEXANDER-C/DH (2)
36 RICK WAITS-P
37 DAN SPILLNER-P
38 DAVE FREISLEBEN-P
39 AL FITZMORRIS (INJ)-P (1)
40 RICK WISE-P
(41) PAT DOBSON (INJ)-(P)
41 PAUL REUSCHEL-P (2)
43 SID MONGE-P
44 DON HOOD-P
46 RICK KREUGER-P
48 MIKE PAXTON-P
51 DENNIS KINNEY-P (1)

1979
6TH E 81-80 22GB

00 PAUL DADE-UTIL (1)
1 DAVE GARCIA-CH/MGR2
2 CHUCK (TWIGGY) HARTENSTEIN-CH
3 *(RET#) EARL AVERILL*
4 DAVE DUNCAN-CH
5 *(RET#) LOU BOUDREAU*
9 RON HASSEY-UTIL
10 JEFF TORBORG-MGR1
11 TOBY HARRAH-3B/UTIL
12 DAVE ROSELLO-INF
13 RON PRUITT-UTIL
14 TOM MCCRAW-CH
15 TOM VERYZER-SS
16 BO DIAZ (INJ)-C
17 WAYNE GARLAND (INJ)-P
18 DUANE KUIPER-2B
19 *(RET#) BOB FELLER*
20 HORACE SPEED-OF/DH
21 TOM VERYZER-SS
21 MIKE HARGROVE-OF/UTIL (2)
22 TED COX-UTIL
23 VICTOR CRUZ-P
24 JOE NOSSEK-CH
25 BOBBY BONDS-OF/DH
27 JIM NORRIS-OF/DH
28 RICK MANNING (INJ)-OF
29 ANDRE THORNTON-1B/DH
30 DELL ALSTON-OF/DH
31 WAYNE CAGE-DH/1B
32 DAVID CLYDE(ILL/INJ)-P
33 ERIC WILKINS (INJ)-P
35 GARY ALEXANDER-C/UTIL (2)
36 RICK WAITS-P
37 DAN SPILLNER-P
38 DAVE FREISLEBEN-P
39 LEN BARKER-P
40 RICK WISE-P
41 PAUL REUSCHEL (INJ)-P
42 LARRY ANDERSEN-P
42 SANDY WIHTOL-P
43 SID MONGE-P
44 DON HOOD-P (1)
44 CLIFF JOHNSON-DH/C (2)
47 VICTOR CRUZ-P
48 MIKE PAXTON-P
56 SANDY WIHTOL-P

1980
6TH E 79-81 23GB

1 DAVE GARCIA-MGR
2 DENNY SOMMERS-CH
3 *(RET#) EARL AVERILL*
4 DAVE DUNCAN-CH
5 *(RET#) LOU BOUDREAU*
6 JORGE ORTA-OF/DH
7 ALAN BANNISTER-UTIL (2)
8 JACK BROHAMER-2B/DH (2)
9 RON HASSEY-C/UTIL
10 JERRY DYBZINSKI-INF/DH

CLEVELAND INDIANS

11 TOBY HARRAH-3B/UTIL
12 DAVE ROSELLO-INF/DH
13 RON PRUITT-UTIL (1)
13 DELL ALSTON-OF/DH
14 TOM MCCRAW-CH
15 TOM VERYZER (INJ)-SS
16 BO DIAZ-C
17 WAYNE GARLAND-P
18 DUANE KUIPER (INJ)-2B
19 *(RET#) BOB FELLER*
21 MIKE HARGROVE-1B
23 VICTOR CRUZ-P
24 JOE NOSSEK-CH
26 ANDRES MORA-OF
27 BOB OWCHINKO-P
27 MIGUEL DILONE-OF/DH
28 RICK MANNING-OF
(29) ANDRE THORNTON (INJ)-(1B)
30 DELL ALSTON-OF/DH
34 JOE CHARBONEAU-OF/DH
35 GARY ALEXANDER-UTIL
36 RICK WAITS-P
37 DAN SPILLNER-P
39 LEN BARKER-P
40 JOHN DENNY (INJ)-P
42 BOB OWCHINKO-P
43 SID MONGE-P
44 CLIFF JOHNSON-DH (1)
46 MIKE STANTON-P
47 DON COLLINS-P
48 MIKE PAXTON-P
48 ROSS GRIMSLEY-P (2)
49 GARY GRAY-UTIL
56 SANDY WIHTOL-P

1981

1ST 1/2:6TH E 26-24 5GB
2ND 1/2:5TH E 26-27 5GB
FINAL: 52-51 --GB

1 DAVE GARCIA-MGR
2 DENNY SOMMERS-CH
3 *(RET#) EARL AVERILL*
4 DAVE DUNCAN-CH
5 *(RET#) LOU BOUDREAU*
6 JORGE ORTA-OF
7 ALAN BANNISTER-UTIL
8 VON HAYES-UTIL
9 RON HASSEY-C/UTIL
10 JERRY DYBZINSKI-INF/DH
11 TOBY HARRAH-3B/UTIL
12 DAVE ROSELLO-INF/DH
13 RON PRUITT-UTIL
14 TOM MCCRAW-CH
15 TOM VERYZER-SS
16 BO DIAZ-C/DH
17 WAYNE GARLAND-P
18 DUANE KUIPER-2B
19 *(RET#) BOB FELLER*
20 RICK MANNING-OF
21 MIKE HARGROVE-1B/DH
22 BERT BLYLEVEN-P
22 MIKE FISCHLIN-SS/2B
23 CHRIS BANDO-C/DH
24 JOE NOSSEK-CH
25 PAT KELLY-DH/OF
27 MIGUEL DILONE-OF/DH
28 RICK MANNING-OF
28 BERT BLYLEVEN-P
29 ANDRE THORNTON-DH/1B
30 KARL PAGEL-1B/DH
32 LARRY LITTLETON-OF
34 JOE CHARBONEAU-OF/DH
35 BOB LACEY-P (1)
36 RICK WAITS-P
37 DAN SPILLNER-P
39 LEN BARKER-P
40 JOHN DENNY-P
41 DENNIS LEWALLYN-P
43 SID MONGE-P
44 ED GLYNN-P
45 TOM BRENNAN-P
46 MIKE STANTON-P
(48) ROSS GRIMSLEY (INJ)-(P)

1982

6TH E (TIE) 78-84 17GB

1 DAVE GARCIA-MGR
2 DENNY SOMMERS-CH
3 *(RET#) EARL AVERILL*
4 JOHNNY GORYL-CH
5 *(RET#) LOU BOUDREAU*
6 MEL QUEEN-CH
7 ALAN BANNISTER (INJ)-UTIL
8 VON HAYES-OF/INF
9 RON HASSEY-C/UTIL
10 JERRY DYBZINSKI-SS/3B
11 TOBY HARRAH-3B/INF
14 TOM MCCRAW-CH
15 BILL NAHORODNY-C
16 JACK PERCONTE-2B/DH
17 LARRY MILBOURNE-INF (3)
19 *(RET#) BOB FELLER*
20 RICK MANNING-OF
21 MIKE HARGROVE-1B/DH
22 MIKE FISCHLIN-SS/UTIL
23 CHRIS BANDO (INJ)-C/3B
24 ROD CRAIG-OF/DH
25 SANDY WIHTOL-P
26 BAKE MCBRIDE (INJ)-OF
27 MIGUEL DILONE-OF/DH
28 BERT BLYLEVEN (INJ)-P
29 ANDRE THORNTON-DH/1B
30 KARL PAGEL-1B/DH
31 JOHN BOHNET-P
31 JERRY REED-P (2)
32 ED WHITSON-P
34 JOE CHARBONEAU-OF/DH
(35) SILVIO MARTINEZ (INJ)-(P)
36 RICK WAITS (INJ)-P
37 DAN SPILLNER-P
38 LARY SORENSEN-P
39 LEN BARKER-P
40 JOHN DENNY (INJ)-P (1)
41 DENNIS LEWALLYN-P
41 TOM BRENNAN-P
42 JOHN DENNY (INJ)-P (1)
43 RICK SUTCLIFFE-P
44 RICK SUTCLIFFE-P
44 NEAL HEATON-P
45 TOM BRENNAN-P
48 ED GLYNN-P
50 BUD ANDERSON-P
51 BUD ANDERSON-P
52 CARMEN CASTILLO-OF/DH
54 KEVIN RHOMBERG-UTIL
56 ROD CRAIG-OF/DH

1983

7TH E 70-92 28GB

1 ED NAPOLEON-CH
2 MIKE FERRARO-MGR1
3 *(RET#) EARL AVERILL*
4 JOHNNY GORYL-CH
5 *(RET#) LOU BOUDREAU*
6 DENNY SOMMERS-CH
7 ALAN BANNISTER-UTIL
8 MANNY TRILLO-2B (1)
8 CARMEN CASTILLO-OF/DH
9 RON HASSEY-C/DH
10 PAT TABLER-OF/UTIL
11 TOBY HARRAH (INJ)-3B/UTIL
12 CARMEN CASTILLO-OF/DH
12 KEVIN RHOMBERG-OF/DH
13 JUAN EICHELBERGER-P
14 JULIO FRANCO-SS
15 BRODERICK PERKINS-UTIL
16 JACK PERCONTE-2B
17 JIM ESSIAN-C/3B
18 KEVIN RHOMBERG-OF/DH
18 PAT CORRALES-MGR2
19 *(RET#) BOB FELLER*
20 RICK MANNING-OF (1)
20 GORMAN THOMAS-OF (2)
21 MIKE HARGROVE-1B/DH
22 MIKE FISCHLIN-INF/DH
23 CHRIS BANDO-C
24 GEORGE VUKOVICH-OF
25 WILL CULMER-OF/DH
26 BAKE MCBRIDE (INJ)-OF/DH
27 MIGUEL DILONE-OF (1)
27 RICH BARNES-P
28 BERT BLYLEVEN-P
29 ANDRE THORNTON-DH/1B
30 KARL PAGEL-DH/OF
31? CHUCK ESTRADA-CH
32 OTTO VELEZ-DH
32 RICK BEHENNA-P (2)
35 JERRY REED-P
36 RICK WAITS-P (1)
36 JAMIE EASTERLY-P (2)
37 DAN SPILLNER-P
38 LARY SORENSEN-P
39 LEN BARKER-P (1)
40 ERNIE CAMACHO-P
43 RICK SUTCLIFFE-P
44 NEAL HEATON-P
45 TOM BRENNAN-P
47 DON MCMAHON-CH
48 ED GLYNN-P
51 BUD ANDERSON-P
54 KEVIN RHOMBERG-OF/DH
54 MIKE JEFFCOAT-P

1984

6TH E 75-87 29GB

1 ED NAPOLEON-CH
2 BRETT BUTLER-OF
3 *(RET#) EARL AVERILL*
4 JOHNNY GORYL-CH
4 TONY BERNAZARD-2B/DH
5 *(RET#) LOU BOUDREAU*
6 DENNY SOMMERS-CH
8 CARMEN CASTILLO-OF/DH
9 RON HASSEY-UTIL (1)
9 JAMIE QUIRK-C (2)
10 PAT TABLER-UTIL
11 JEFF MORONKO-3B/DH
12 KEVIN RHOMBERG-UTIL
13 ERNIE CAMACHO-P
14 JULIO FRANCO-SS/DH
15 BRODERICK PERKINS-DH/1B
15 JAMIE EASTERLY (INJ)-P
16 TONY BERNAZARD-2B/DH
16 JERRY WILLARD-C/DH
17 BOBBY BONDS-CH
17 JUNIOR NOBOA-2B/DH
18 PAT CORRALES-MGR
19 *(RET#) BOB FELLER*
20 OTIS NIXON-OF
21 MIKE HARGROVE-1B
22 MIKE FISCHLIN-INF
23 CHRIS BANDO-UTIL
24 GEORGE VUKOVICH-OF
25 GEORGE FRAZIER-P (1)
25 BOBBY BONDS-CH
26 BROOK JACOBY (INJ)-3B/SS
27 RICH BARNES-P
27 MEL HALL-OF/DH (2)
28 BERT BLYLEVEN-P
29 ANDRE THORNTON-DH/1B
30 JOE CARTER-OF/1B
31 STEVE COMER-P
32 RICK BEHENNA (INJ)-P
33 ROY SMITH-P
34 STEVE FARR-P
36 JAMIE EASTERLY (INJ)-P
37 DAN SPILLNER-P (1)
37 DON SCHULZE-P (2)
38 LUIS APONTE-P
40 ERNIE CAMACHO-P
43 RICK SUTCLIFFE-P (1)
43 JERRY UJDUR-P
44 NEAL HEATON-P
45 JOHNNY GORYL-CH
46 TOM WADDELL-P
46 MIKE JEFFCOAT-P
47 DON MCMAHON-CH
49 JEFF BARKLEY-P
50 RAMON ROMERO-P
53 JERRY WILLARD-C/DH
54 MIKE JEFFCOAT-P
54 TOM WADDELL-P
58 STEVE FARR-P
65 JOSE ROMAN-P

1985

7TH E 60-102 39.5GB

1 ED NAPOLEON-CH
1 JACK AKER-CH
2 BRETT BUTLER-OF/DH
3 *(RET#) EARL AVERILL*
4 TONY BERNAZARD-2B/SS
5 *(RET#) LOU BOUDREAU*
6 DENNY SOMMERS-CH
6 DOC EDWARDS-CH
7 PAT CORRALES-MGR
8 CARMEN CASTILLO-OF/DH
9 BUTCH BENTON-C
10 PAT TABLER (INJ)-1B/UTIL
11 JOHNNIE LEMASTER-SS (2)
12 BENNY AYALA-OF/DH
13 ERNIE CAMACHO (INJ)-P
14 JULIO FRANCO-SS/UTIL
16 JERRY WILLARD-C/DH
18 PAT CORRALES-MGR
19 *(RET#) BOB FELLER*
20 OTIS NIXON-OF/DH
21 MIKE HARGROVE-UTIL
22 MIKE FISCHLIN-INF/DH
23 CHRIS BANDO-C
24 GEORGE VUKOVICH-OF
25 BOBBY BONDS-CH
26 BROOK JACOBY-3B/2B
27 MEL HALL (INJ)-OF/DH
28 BERT BLYLEVEN-P (1)
29 ANDRE THORNTON-DH
30 JOE CARTER-OF/UTIL
31 JOSE ROMAN-P
31 CURT WARDLE-P (2)
32 RICK BEHENNA (INJ)-P
33 ROY SMITH (INJ)-P
35 JERRY REED-P
36 JAMIE EASTERLY-P
37 DON SCHULZE-P
38 DAVE VON OHLEN (INJ)-P
39 CURT WARDLE-P (2)
40 KEITH CREEL-P
41 RICH THOMPSON-P
43 BRYAN CLARK-P
44 NEAL HEATON-P
45 JOHNNY GORYL-CH
46 MIKE JEFFCOAT-P (1)
47 DON MCMAHON-CH
47 FRED KOENIG-CH
48 VERN RUHLE-(INJ)-P
49 JEFF BARKLEY-P
50 RAMON ROMERO-P
54 TOM WADDELL-P
55 CURT WARDLE-P (2)
58 JIM WILSON-1B/DH

1986

5TH E 84-78 11.5GB

1 JACK AKER-CH
2 BRETT BUTLER-OF
3 *(RET#) EARL AVERILL*
4 TONY BERNAZARD-2B
5 *(RET#) LOU BOUDREAU*
6 ANDY ALLANSON-C
7 PAT CORRALES-MGR
8 CARMEN CASTILLO-OF/DH
10 PAT TABLER-1B/DH
12 DAVE CLARK-OF/DH
13 ERNIE CAMACHO-P
14 JULIO FRANCO-SS/UTIL
15 DAN ROHN-INF
16 JAY BELL-2B/DH
18 KEN SCHROM-P
19 *(RET#) BOB FELLER*
20 OTIS NIXON-OF/DH
21 GREG SWINDELL-P
22 FRAN MULLINS (INJ)-UTIL
23 CHRIS BANDO-C
24 EDDIE WILLIAMS-OF
25 BOBBY BONDS-CH
26 BROOK JACOBY-3B
27 MEL HALL-OF/DH
28 CORY SNYDER-UTIL
29 ANDRE THORNTON (INJ)-DH
30 JOE CARTER-OF/1B
32 DOC EDWARDS-CH
32 JOHN BUTCHER (INJ)-P (2)
33 BRYAN OELKERS-P
34 JOSE ROMAN-P
35 PHIL NIEKRO-P
36 JAMIE EASTERLY (INJ)-P
37 DON SCHULZE (INJ)-P
38 JOHN BUTCHER (INJ)-P (2)
39 DOUG JONES-P
42 RICH YETT-P
43 SCOTT BAILES-P
44 NEAL HEATON-P (1)
44 FRANK WILLS-P
44 JOHN BUTCHER (INJ)-P (2)
45 JOHNNY GORYL-CH
45 FRANK WILLS-P
46 JIM KERN-P
47 FRED KOENIG-CH
48 DICKIE NOLES (INJ)-P
49 TOM CANDIOTTI-P
53 REGGIE RITTER-P
(54) TOM WADDELL (INJ)-(P)

1987

7TH E 61-101 37GB

1 JACK AKER-CH
1 TOMMY HINZO-2B
2 BRETT BUTLER-OF
3 *(RET#) EARL AVERILL*
4 TONY BERNAZARD-2B (1)
4 BRIAN DORSETT-C
4 DAVE ROBERTS-CH
5 *(RET#) LOU BOUDREAU*
6 ANDY ALLANSON-C
7 PAT CORRALES-MGR1
7 LUIS ISAAC-CH
8 CARMEN CASTILLO-DH/OF
10 PAT TABLER-1B/DH
11 JAMIE EASTERLY (INJ)-P
12 DAVE CLARK-OF/DH
13 ERNIE CAMACHO-P
14 JULIO FRANCO (INJ)-SS/UTIL
15 DAVE GALLAGHER-OF
15 CASEY PARSONS-UTIL
16 JAY BELL-SS
17 JUNIOR NOBOA-INF/DH
18 KEN SCHROM-P
19 *(RET#) BOB FELLER*
20 OTIS NIXON-OF/DH
21 GREG SWINDELL (INJ)-P
22 FRANK WILLS-P
23 CHRIS BANDO-C
24 EDDIE WILLIAMS-3B
24 RICK DEMPSEY (INJ)-C
25 BOBBY BONDS-CH
26 BROOK JACOBY-3B/UTIL
27 MEL HALL-OF/DH
28 CORY SNYDER-OF/SS

CLEVELAND INDIANS

29 ANDRE THORNTON-DH
30 JOE CARTER-1B/UTIL
31 DOUG FROBEL-OF/DH
31 STEVE COMER-CH
32 DOC EDWARDS-CH/MGR2
32 STEVE (LEFTY) CARLTON-P (1)
34 EDDIE WILLIAMS-3B
35 PHIL NIEKRO-P (1)
36 ED VANDE BERG-P
37 MARK HUISMANN-P (2)
39 DON GORDON-P (2)
41 DOC EDWARDS-CH
42 RICH YETT-P
43 SCOTT BAILES-P
44 FRANK WILLS-P
44 ED VANDE BERG-P
44 REGGIE RITTER (INJ)-P
45 JOHNNY GORYL-CH
46 DOUG JONES-P
47 MIKE ARMSTRONG-P
47 DARREL AKERFELDS-P
48 JEFF KAISER (INJ)-P
49 TOM CANDIOTTI-P
52 JOHN FARRELL-P
53 REGGIE RITTER (INJ)-P
53 SAMMY STEWART (INJ)-P
54 TOM WADDELL (INJ)-P

1988

6TH E 78-84 11GB

2 TOM SPENCER-CH
3 *(RET#) EARL AVERILL*
4 DOMINGO RAMOS-3B (1)
4 HOUSTON JIMENEZ-2B/SS
5 *(RET#) LOU BOUDREAU*
6 ANDY ALLANSON-C
7 LUIS ISAAC-CH
8 CARMEN CASTILLO-OF/DH
9 CHARLIE (CHUCK) MANUEL-CH
10 PAT TABLER-DH/1B (1)
10 PAUL ZUVELLA-SS
11 DOUG JONES-P
12 DAVE CLARK-DH/OF
12 PAUL ZUVELLA-SS
14 JULIO FRANCO-2B/DH
15 RON WASHINGTON-INF
16 JAY BELL-SS/DH
17 TOM LAMPKIN-C
17 BILL LASKEY-P
18 RON TINGLEY-C
19 *(RET#) BOB FELLER*
20 WILLIE UPSHAW-1B
21 GREG SWINDELL-P
22 BRAD HAVENS-P (2)
23 CHRIS BANDO-C (1)
24 TERRY FRANCONA-UTIL
25 DAVE CLARK-DH/OF
26 BROOK JACOBY-3B
27 MEL HALL-OF/DH
28 CORY SNYDER-OF/DH
30 JOE CARTER-OF
31 DAN SCHATZEDER-P (1)
31 DAN FIROVA-C
32 DOC EDWARDS-MGR
33 RON KITTLE-DH
34 EDDIE WILLIAMS-3B
35 MARK WILEY-CH
36 REGGIE WILLIAMS-OF
36 RICK RODRIGUEZ-P
37 CHRIS CODIROLI-P
39 DON GORDON-P
40 BUD BLACK (INJ)-P (2)
42 RICH YETT (INJ)-P
43 SCOTT BAILES-P
44 JON PERLMAN (INJ)-P
45 JOHNNY GORYL-CH
46 DOUG JONES-P
47 JEFF KAISER (INJ)-P
49 TOM CANDIOTTI-P
50 JEFF DEDMON-P
52 JOHN FARRELL-P
57 ROD NICHOLS-P
60 ROD ALLEN-DH
68 SCOTT JORDAN-OF
69 LUIS MEDINA-1B
75 MIKE WALKER-P

1989

6TH E 73-89 16GB

1 TOMMY HINZO-INF/DH
2 TOM SPENCER-CH
3 *(RET#) EARL AVERILL*
4 CHARLIE (CHUCK) MANUEL-CH
5 *(RET#) LOU BOUDREAU*
6 ANDY ALLANSON-C
7 LUIS ISAAC-CH
8 MARK SALAS-DH/C
9 PETE O'BRIEN-1B/DH
10 PAUL ZUVELLA-INF/DH
11 DOUG JONES-P
12 JIM DAVENPORT-CH
13 JOEL SKINNER-C
14 JERRY BROWNE-2B/DH
15 DENNY GONZALEZ-DH/3B
15 NEIL ALLEN (INJ)-P
16 FELIX FERMIN-SS/2B
18 RON TINGLEY-C
19 *(RET#) BOB FELLER*
20 ODDIBE MCDOWELL-OF/DH (1)
20 DION JAMES-UTIL (2)
21 GREG SWINDELL (INJ)-P
22 BRAD HAVENS-P (1)
22 KEITH ATHERTON-P
23 LUIS AGUAYO-INF/DH
25 DAVE CLARK-DH/OF
25 NEIL ALLEN (INJ)-P
26 BROOK JACOBY-3B/DH
27 JOE SKALSKI-P
28 CORY SNYDER-OF/UTIL
29 LUIS MEDINA-UTIL
30 JOE CARTER-OF/UTIL
31 PETE DALENA-DH
32 DOC EDWARDS-MGR1
33 PAT KEEDY-UTIL
34 ED WOJNA-P
34 DANNY SHEAFFER-UTIL
35 MARK WILEY-CH
36 TIM STODDARD (INJ)-P
36 ALBERT (JOEY) BELLE-OF/DH
37 STEVE DAVIS-P
38 KEITH ATHERTON-P
38 DAVE HENGEL (INJ)-OF/DH
40 BUD BLACK-P
42 RICH YETT-P
43 SCOTT BAILES-P
44 MIKE YOUNG-DH/OF
45 BRAD KOMMINSK (ILL)-OF
46 JEFF KAISER-P
47 JESSE OROSCO-P
49 TOM CANDIOTTI-P
50 ED WOJNA-P
50 STEVE OLIN-P
52 JOHN FARRELL-P
53 KEVIN WICKANDER-P
54 ROD NICHOLS (INJ)-P
55 BEAU ALLRED-OF/DH
64 RUDY SEANEZ-P
66 BRAD KOMMINSK (ILL)-OF
66 MARK HIGGINS-1B
67 JOE SKALSKI-P
76 TOM MAGRANN-C
__ JOHN HART-MGR2 (19G: 9/12-10/1)

1990

4TH E 77-85 11GB

1 JOHN MCNAMARA-MGR
2 STEVE SPRINGER-3B/DH
2 RAFAEL SANTANA-SS
2 ALEX COLE-OF/DH
3 *(RET#) EARL AVERILL*
4 JOEL SKINNER-C
5 *(RET#) LOU BOUDREAU*
6 MARK MCLEMORE-3B/DH (2)
7 LUIS ISAAC-CH
7 CHRIS JAMES-DH/OF
8 ALBERT (JOEY) BELLE-DH/OF
9 CARLOS BAERGA-INF
10 TOM BROOKENS-INF/DH
11 DOUG JONES-P
12 MIKE HARGROVE-CH
13 LUIS ISAAC-CH
14 JERRY BROWNE-2B
15 SANDY ALOMAR-C
16 FELIX FERMIN-SS/2B
17 KEITH HERNANDEZ (INJ)-1B
18 CHRIS JAMES-DH/OF
18 *(RET#) MEL HARDER*
19 *(RET#) BOB FELLER*
20 DION JAMES-UTIL
21 GREG SWINDELL-P
22 CANDY MALDONADO-OF/DH
23 MITCH WEBSTER-OF/UTIL
24 STAN JEFFERSON-OF/DH (2)
25 RICH DAUER-CH
26 BROOK JACOBY-3B/1B
28 CORY SNYDER-OF/SS
30 SERGIO VALDEZ-P (2)
31 TOM BROOKENS-INF/DH
31 STEVE OLIN-P
32 JOSE MORALES-CH
32 RUDY SEANEZ-P
33 EFRAIN VALDEZ-P
34 JOSE MORALES-CH
35 MARK WILEY-CH
36 MAURO GOZZO-P
37 RAFAEL SANTANA-SS
38 CECILIO GUANTE-P
40 BUD BLACK-P (1)
41 CHARLES NAGY-P
42 AL NIPPER-P
44 JEFF MANTO-1B/3B
44 KEN PHELPS-1B/DH (2)
45 JEFF MANTO-1B/3B
46 JEFF KAISER (INJ)-P
47 JESSE OROSCO-P
48 MIKE WALKER-P
49 TOM CANDIOTTI-P
50 STEVE OLIN-P
50 COLBY WARD-P
51 BILLY WILLIAMS-CH
52 JOHN FARRELL (INJ)-P
53 KEVIN WICKANDER (INJ)-P
54 ROD NICHOLS-P
55 BEAU ALLRED-OF
57 JEFF SHAW-P
59 KEVIN BEARSE-P
68 TURNER WARD-OF/DH

1991

7TH E 57-105 34GB

1 JOHN MCNAMARA-MGR1
2 ALEX COLE-OF/DH
3 *(RET#) EARL AVERILL*
4 JOEL SKINNER-C
5 *(RET#) LOU BOUDREAU*
6 JOSE ESCOBAR-INF
6 EVER MAGALLANES-SS
6 JIM THOME-3B
7 CHRIS JAME (INJ)-DH/UTIL
8 ALBERT (JOEY) BELLE-DH/OF
9 CARLOS BAERGA-3B/INF
10 MARK LEWIS-2B/SS
11 DOUG JONES-P
12 MIKE HARGROVE-CH/MGR2
13 LUIS ISAAC-CH
14 JERRY BROWNE-UTIL
15 SANDY ALOMAR (INJ)-C/DH
16 FELIX FERMIN-SS
(17) KEITH HERNANDEZ (INJ)-(1B)
18 *(RET#) MEL HARDER*
19 *(RET#) BOB FELLER*
20 TURNER WARD-OF/DH (1)
21 GREG SWINDELL-P
22 CARLOS MARTINEZ-DH/1B
22 LUIS LOPEZ-UTIL
23 MITCH WEBSTER-OF (1)
23 LUIS MEDINA-DH
23 MARK WHITEN (INJ)-OF/DH (2)
23 DENIS BOUCHER-P (2)
24 REGGIE JEFFERSON-1B (2)
24 GLENALLEN HILL-OF/DH (2)
25 RICH DAUER-CH
25 JIM THOME-3B
26 BROOK JACOBY-1B/3B (1)
27 DAVE OTTO-P
30 SERGIO VALDEZ-P
31 STEVE OLIN-P
32 RUDY SEANEZ-P
33 EFRAIN VALDEZ-P
34 JOSE MORALES-CH
35 MARK WILEY-CH
36 MAURO GOZZO-P
37 BEAU ALLRED-OF/DH
37 JOSE GONZALEZ-OF (3)
38 SHAWN HILLEGAS-P
39 WILLIE BLAIR-P
40 ERIC KING (INJ)-P
41 CHARLES NAGY-P
42 SHAWN HILLEGAS-P
43 MIKE ALDRETE-UTIL (2)
44 MIKE HUFF-OF/2B (1)
44 TONY PEREZCHICA-INF (2)
45 JEFF MANTO-UTIL
46 BRUCE EGLOFF-P
47 JESSE OROSCO-P
48 MIKE WALKER-P
49 TOM CANDIOTTI-P (1)
49 DENIS BOUCHER-P (2)
50 JEFF MUTIS-P
51 BILLY WILLIAMS-CH
(52) JOHN FARRELL (INJ)-(P)
54 ROD NICHOLS-P
56 EDDIE TAUBANSEE-C
56 MIKE YORK (INJ)-P
57 JEFF SHAW-P
58 GARLAND KISER-P
63 ERIC BELL-P
64 TOM KRAMER-P
66 BRUCE EGLOFF-P
73 WAYNE KIRBY-OF
81 DOM CHITI-CH

1992

4TH E (TIE) 76-86 20GB

0 JUNIOR ORTIZ-C
1 GLENALLEN HILL-OF/DH
2 ALEX COLE-OF/DH (1)
2 JOSE HERNANDEZ-SS
3 *(RET#) EARL AVERILL*
5 *(RET#) LOU BOUDREAU*
6 RON CLARK-CH
7 KENNY LOFTON-OF
8 ALBERT (JOEY) BELLE-DH/OF
9 CARLOS BAERGA-3B/INF
10 MARK LEWIS-2B/SS
11 PAUL SORRENTO-1B/DH
12 CRAIG WORTHINGTON-3B
14 JESSE LEVIS-C/DH
15 SANDY ALOMAR (INJ)-C/DH
16 FELIX FERMIN-UTIL
17 DAVE NELSON-CH
18 *(RET#) MEL HARDER*
19 *(RET#) BOB FELLER*
20 TONY PEREZCHICA-INF/DH
21 MIKE HARGROVE-MGR
22 DAVE ROHDE-3B
23 MARK WHITEN (INJ)-OF/DH
24 RICK ADAIR-CH
25 JIM THOME-3B
26 BROOK JACOBY-3B/1B
27 DAVE OTTO-P
28 DEREK LILLIQUIST-P
30 DOM CHITI-CH
31 STEVE OLIN-P
32 MIKE CHRISTOPHER-P
33 THOMAS HOWARD-OF/DH (2)
34 JOSE MORALES-CH
35 MIKE CHRISTOPHER-P
35 WAYNE KIRBY-OF
36 BRAD ARNSBERG-P
37 DENIS BOUCHER-P
37 DAVE MLICKI-P
38 ERIC PLUNK-P
39 DENNIS COOK-P
41 CHARLES NAGY-P
42 CARLOS MARTINEZ-INF/DH
44 REGGIE JEFFERSON-1B (2)
46 BRUCE EGLOFF-P
47 SCOTT SCUDDER-P
48 TED POWER-P
49 DENIS BOUCHER-P
49 JOSE MESA-P (2)
50 JEFF MUTIS-P
51 KEN BOLEK-CH
52 JOSE MESA-P (2)
53 KEVIN WICKANDER-P
54 ROD NICHOLS-P
55 JEFF NEWMAN-CH
56 ALAN EMBREE-P
57 JEFF SHAW-P
63 ERIC BELL-P
68 JESSE LEVIS-C/DH
77 JACK ARMSTRONG-P

1993

6TH E 76-86 19GB

0 JUNIOR ORTIZ-C
1 SAM HORN-DH
1 GLENALLEN HILL-OF/DH (1)
2 DAN WILLIAMS-CH ASST
3 *(RET#) EARL AVERILL*
5 *(RET#) LOU BOUDREAU*
6 RON CLARK-CH
7 KENNY LOFTON-OF
8 ALBERT (JOEY) BELLE-OF/DH
9 CARLOS BAERGA (INJ)-2B/DH
10 ALVARO ESPINOZA-3B/INF
11 PAUL SORRENTO-1B/UTIL
12 JESSE LEVIS-C/DH
13 LANCE PARRISH (RET)-C
14 DAVE NELSON-CH
15 SANDY ALOMAR (INJ)-C
16 FELIX FERMIN-SS
17 BOB OJEDA (INJ)-P
18 *(RET#) MEL HARDER*
19 *(RET#) BOB FELLER*
20 MARK LEWIS-SS
21 MIKE HARGROVE-MGR
22 GLENALLEN HILL-OF/DH (1)
22 CANDY MALDONADO-OF/DH (2)
23 DAVE MLICKI (INJ)-P
24 RICK ADAIR-CH
24 MANNY RAMIREZ-DH/OF
25 JIM THOME-3B
27 JEFF TREADWAY-INF/DH
28 DEREK LILLIQUIST-P

CLEVELAND INDIANS

29 TOM KRAMER-P
30 DOM CHITI-CH
(31) STEVE OLIN-P (DIED)-(P)
32 MIKE CHRISTOPHER-P
33 THOMAS HOWARD-OF/DH (1)
33 JOSE MESA-P
34 JOSE MORALES-CH
35 WAYNE KIRBY-OF/DH
36 DAVE MLICKI (INJ)-P
36 MIKE BIELECKI-P
36 JEFF MUTIS-P
38 ERIC PLUNK-P
39 DENNIS COOK-P
40 MATT YOUNG-P
40 RANDY MILLIGAN-1B/DH (2)
41 CHARLES NAGY (INJ)-P
42 CARLOS MARTINEZ-INF/DH
43 CLIFF YOUNG (DIED)-P
44 REGGIE JEFFERSON-DH/1B
45 JERRY DIPOTO-P
46 BILL WERTZ-P
47 SCOTT SCUDDER (INJ)-P
48 TED POWER (INJ/REL)-P (1)
48 JASON GRIMSLEY-P
49 JOSE MESA-P
49 BOB MILACKI-P
50 JEFF MUTIS-P
50 JULIAN TAVAREZ-P
51 KEN BOLEK-CH
51 HEATHCLIFF SLOCUMB-P (2)
(52) TIM CREWS (DIED)-(P)
53 KEVIN WICKANDER-P (1)
53 JEREMY HERNANDEZ-P (2)
54 MARK CLARK (INJ)-P
55 JEFF NEWMAN-CH
58 PAUL ABBOTT-P
59 ALBIE LOPEZ-P
64 TOM KRAMER-P

1994

2ND C — 66-47 — 1GB
STRIKE NO POST-SEASON

1 DAVE NELSON-CH
2 MATT MERULLO-C
3 *(RET#) EARL AVERILL*
5 *(RET#) LOU BOUDREAU*
6 LUIS ISAAC-CH
7 KENNY LOFTON-OF
8 ALBERT (JOEY) BELLE-OF/DH
9 CARLOS BAERGA (INJ)-2B/DH
10 ALVARO ESPINOZA-3B/INF
11 PAUL SORRENTO-1B/UTIL
12 JESSE LEVIS-C
13 OMAR VIZQUEL (INJ)-SS
14 DAVE NELSON-CH
14 *(RET#) LARRY DOBY*
15 SANDY ALOMAR (INJ)-C
17 TONY PENA-C
18 *(RET#) MEL HARDER*
19 *(RET#) BOB FELLER*
20 MARK LEWIS-SS/3B
21 MIKE HARGROVE-MGR
22 CANDY MALDONADO-DH
24 MANNY RAMIREZ-DH/OF
25 JIM THOME-3B
26 STEVE FARR (INJ)-P (1)
26 BUDDY BELL-CH
27 PHIL (THE VULTURE) REGAN-CH
28 DEREK LILLIQUIST-P
29 JEFF RUSSELL-P (2)
30 RUBEN AMARO, JR.-OF
32 DENNIS MARTINEZ-P
33 EDDIE MURRAY-DH
34 MATT TURNER (ILL)-P
35WAYNE KIRBY-OF/DH
36 HERBERT PERRY-3B
37 CHAD OGEA-P
38 ERIC PLUNK-P
40 STEVE FARR (INJ)-P (1)
40 JEFF RUSSELL-P (2)
41 CHARLES NAGY-P
42 CHARLIE (CHUCK) MANUEL-CH
43 CHRIS NABHOLZ (INJ)-P (1)
44 RUSS SWAN-P
45 JERRY DIPOTO (INJ)-P
46 BILL WERTZ-P
47 JACK MORRIS (REL)-P
48 JASON GRIMSLEY-P
49 JOSE MESA-P
50 JULIAN TAVAREZ-P
51 LARRY CASIAN-P (2)
52 BRIAN BARNES-P (1)
53 PAUL SHUEY (INJ)-P
54 MARK CLARK (INJ)-P
55 JEFF NEWMAN-CH
59 ALBIE LOPEZ-P
88 RENE GONZALES-3B

1995

1ST C — 100-44 — 0GB
144 GAME SEASON
W ALDS-BOSA 3-0
W ALCS-SEAA 4-2
L WS-ATLN 4-2

1 DAVE NELSON-CH
3 *(RET#) EARL AVERILL*
4 DAVID BELL-3B (1)
5 *(RET#) LOU BOUDREAU*
6 LUIS ISAAC-CH
7 KENNY LOFTON (INJ)-OF
8 ALBERT (JOEY) BELLE-OF
9 CARLOS BAERGA-2B
10 ALVARO ESPINOZA-1B
11 PAUL SORRENTO-1B
12 JESSE LEVIS-C
13 OMAR VIZQUEL-SS
14 *(RET#) LARRY DOBY*
15 SANDY ALOMAR (INJ)-C
16 BILLY RIPKEN-2B/3B
16 SCOOTER TUCKER-C (2)
17 TONY PENA-C
18 *(RET#) MEL HARDER*
19 *(RET#) BOB FELLER*
20 RUBEN AMARO, JR. (INJ)-OF
21 MIKE HARGROVE-MGR
23 JEROMY BERNITZ-OF
24 MANNY RAMIREZ-OF
25 JIM THOME-3B
26 BUDDY BELL-CH
27 DENNIS COOK-P
28 MARK WILEY-CH
29 JEFF NEWMAN-CH
30 GREGG OLSON-P (1)
31 DAVE WINFIELD (INJ)-DH
32 DENNIS MARTINEZ-P
33 EDDIE MURRAY (INJ)-DH
35 WAYNE KIRBY-OF
36 HERBERT PERRY-1B
37 CHAD OGEA-P
38 ERIC PLUNK-P
40 BUD BLACK (REL)-P
41 CHARLES NAGY-P
42 CHARLIE (CHUCK) MANUEL-CH
43 DAN WILLIAMS-CH
44 KEN HILL-P (2)
45 PAUL ASSENMACHER-P
47 JOE ROA-P
48 JASON GRIMSLEY-P
49 JOSE MESA-P
50 JULIAN TAVAREZ-P
52 JOHN FARRELL-P
53 PAUL SHUEY (INJ)-P
54 MARK CLARK-P
55 JEFF NEWMAN-CH
55 OREL (BULLDOG) HERSHISHER (INJ)-P
56 ALAN EMBREE-P
58 BRIAN GILES-OF/DH
59 ALBIE LOPEZ-P
62 JIM POOLE-P

1996

1ST C — 99-62 — 0GB
L ALDS-BALA 3-1

1 DAVE NELSON-CH
2 JEFF KENT-3B (2)
2 EINAR DIAZ-C
3 *(RET#) EARL AVERILL*
4 MARK CARREON (INJ)-OF/1B (2)
5 *(RET#) LOU BOUDREAU*
6 LUIS ISAAC-CH
7 KENNY LOFTON-OF
8 ALBERT (JOEY) BELLE-OF
9 CARLOS BAERGA-2B (1)
9 DAMIAN JACKSON-SS
10 ALVARO ESPINOZA-3B (1)
10 JOSE VIZCAINO-2B (2)
11 TOBY HARRAH-CH
12 GREG SWINDELL-P (2)
12 JEFF KENT-3B (2)
13 OMAR VIZQUEL-SS
14 *(RET#) LARRY DOBY*
15 SANDY ALOMAR, JR.-C
16 JEFF NEWMAN-CH
17 TONY PENA-C
18 *(RET#) MEL HARDER*
19 *(RET#) BOB FELLER*
20 JEROMY BERNITZ-OF (1)
20 KEVIN SEITZER-DH (2)
21 MIKE HARGROVE-MGR
22 BRIAN GILES-OF
23 JULIO FRANCO (INJ)-1B
24 MANNY RAMIREZ-OF
25 JIM THOME-3B
26 CASEY CANDAELE-2B
27 GERONIMO PENA-2B
28 MARK WILEY-CH
29 JACK MCDOWELL (INJ)-P
30 SCOTT LEIUS (INJ)-3B
32 DENNIS MARTINEZ (INJ)-P
33 EDDIE MURRAY-DH (1)
34 BRIAN ANDERSON-P
35 WAYNE KIRBY (WAIV)-OF (1)
35 DANNY GRAVES-P
36 HERBERT PERRY (INJ)-1B
37 CHAD OGEA (INJ)-P
38 ERIC PLUNK-P
39 KENT MERCKER-P (2)
41 CHARLES NAGY-P
42 CHARLIE (CHUCK) MANUEL-CH
43 DAN WILLIAMS-CH
45 PAUL ASSENMACHER-P
46 RYAN THOMPSON-OF
47 JOE ROA-P
48 NIGEL WILSON-DH
49 JOSE MESA-P
50 JULIAN TAVAREZ-P
53 PAUL SHUEY-P
55 OREL (BULLDOG) HERSHISHER-P
56 ALAN EMBREE (INJ)-P
59 ALBIE LOPEZ-P
62 JIM POOLE (INJ)-P (1)

1997

1ST C — 86-75 — 0GB
W ALDS-NYA 3-2
W ALCS-BALA 4-2
L WS-FLAN 4-3

1 TONY FERNANDEZ-2B
2 EINAR DIAZ-C
3 *(RET#) EARL AVERILL*
4 LUIS ISAAC-CH
5 *(RET#) LOU BOUDREAU*
6 BIP ROBERTS-2B/OF (2)
7*JEFF JUDEN-P* (2)
8 DAVE NELSON-CH
9 MATT WILLIAMS-3B
10 PAT BORDERS-C
11 DAMIAN JACKSON-SS (1)
11 JEFF BRANSON-INF (2)
12 CHAD CURTIS (INJ)-OF (1)
12 JEFF JUDEN-P (2)
12 JEFF MANTO-2B (2)
13 OMAR VIZQUEL-SS
14 *(RET#) LARRY DOBY*
15 SANDY ALOMAR, JR.-C/DH
16 JEFF NEWMAN-CH
17 MARQUIS GRISSOM (INJ)-OF
18 *(RET#) MEL HARDER*
19 *(RET#) BOB FELLER*
20 KEVIN SEITZER-1B
21 MIKE HARGROVE-MGR
22 BRIAN GILES-OF
23 JULIO FRANCO-2B/DH (1)
23 DAVID JUSTICE-OF/DH
24 MANNY RAMIREZ-OF
25 JIM THOME-3B
26 CASEY CANDAELE-2B
27 JARET WRIGHT-P
28 MARK WILEY-CH
29 JACK MCDOWELL (INJ)-P
30 TRENIDAD HUBBARD-OF
32 CHARLIE (CHUCK) MANUEL-CH
33 DAVID JUSTICE-OF/DH
34 BRIAN ANDERSON (INJ)-P
35 DANNY GRAVES-P
35 ENRIQUE WILSON-SS/2B
(36) HERBERT PERRY (INJ)-(1B)
36 BRUCE AVEN-OF
37 CHAD OGEA (INJ)-P
38 ERIC PLUNK-P
40 BARTOLO COLON-P
41 CHARLES NAGY-P
42 MIKE JACKSON-P
43 DAN WILLIAMS-CH
44 KEVIN MITCHELL (REL)-DH
44 JEFF MANTO-2B (2)
44 RICHIE SEXSON-PH/1B
45 PAUL ASSENMACHER-P
46 JASON JACOME-P (2)
47 TERRY CLARK (WAIV)-P (1)
48 CHARLIE (CHUCK) MANUEL-CH
49 JOSE MESA-P
50 DAVID WEATHERS-P (2)
51 ALVIN MORMAN (INJ)-P
52 STEVE KLINE-P (1)
52 SEAN CASEY-1B
53 PAUL SHUEY (INJ)-P
54 JOHNNY GORYL-CH
55 OREL (BULLDOG) HERSHISHER (INJ)-P
56 BRUCE AVEN-OF
57 JOHN SMILEY-P (2)
59 ALBIE LOPEZ (INJ)-P

1998

1ST C — 89-73 — 90GB
W ALDS-BOSA 3-1
L ALCS-NYA 4-2

1 AL BUMBRY-CH
2 EINAR DIAZ-C
3 *(RET#) EARL AVERILL*
4 LUIS ISAAC-CH
5 *(RET#) LOU BOUDREAU*
6 JOLBERT CABRERA-SS
6 DAVID BELL-2B (2)
7 KENNY LOFTON-OF
9 SHAWON DUNSTON-2B/UTIL (1)
9 TOREY LOVULLO-2B/3B
10 PAT BORDERS-C
11 JEFF BRANSON (INJ)-2B/INF
12 JEFF MANTO-INF (1)
12 MARK WHITEN-OF/DH
13 OMAR VIZQUEL-SS
14 *(RET#) LARRY DOBY*
15 SANDY ALOMAR, JR.-C/DH
16 DWIGHT (DOC) (DOCTOR K) GOODEN (INJ)-P
17 TRAVIS FRYMAN-3B
18 *(RET#) MEL HARDER*
19 *(RET#) BOB FELLER*
20 STEVE KARSAY-P (2)
21 MIKE HARGROVE-MGR
21 *(RET#) BOB LEMON*
22 BRIAN GILES (INJ)-OF
23 DAVID JUSTICE-OF/DH
24 MANNY RAMIREZ-OF
25 JIM THOME (INJ)-1B/DH
26 JEFF MANTO-INF (3)
27 JARET WRIGHT-P
28 MARK WILEY-CH
28 JOEY CORA-2B (2)
29 GERONIMO BERROA (INJ)-OF/DH (1)
30 RICK KRIVDA-P (1)
30 MIKE HARGROVE-MGR
32 CHARLIE (CHUCK) MANUEL-CH
33 TIM WORRELL-P (2)
33 MATT LUKE-PH (2)
33 CECIL FIELDER (REL)-1B/DH (2)
34 DAVE BURBA-P
35 ENRIQUE WILSON (INJ)-SS/2B
36 TOM MARTIN (INJ)-P
37 CHAD OGEA (INJ)-P
38 ERIC PLUNK-P (1)
39 STEVE REED-P (2)
40 BARTOLO COLON-P
41 CHARLES NAGY-P
42 MIKE JACKSON-P
43 DAN WILLIAMS-CH
43 DOUG JONES-P (2)
44 RICHIE SEXSON-1B/OF/DH
45 PAUL ASSENMACHER-P
46 JASON JACOME-P
47 RON VILLONE (INJ)-P
49 JOSE MESA-P (1)
51 ALVIN MORMAN (INJ)-P (1)
51 JACOB CRUZ-PH
53 PAUL SHUEY (INJ)-P
54 JOHNNY GORYL-CH
55 JEFF NEWMAN-CH
(57) JOHN SMILEY (INJ)-(P)
59 JASON RAKERS-P
60 EDDIE PRIEST-P (2)
61 ALEX RAMIREZ-OF
62 JIM POOLE-P
66 RUSS BRANYAN-3B
RON KARKOVICE (REL)-(C)

1999

1ST C — 97-65 — 0GB
L ALDS-BOSA 3-2

1 WIL CORDERO (INJ)-OF
2 EINAR DIAZ-C
3 *(RET#) EARL AVERILL*
4 LUIS ISAAC-CH
5 *(RET#) LOU BOUDREAU*
6 JOLBERT CABRERA-SS
7 KENNY LOFTON-OF
8 JOHN MCDONALD-INF
9 CLARENCE JONES-CH
9 CHRIS TURNER-C
9 CARLOS BAERGA-3B (2)
10 PAT BORDERS-C (1)
11 BRIAN GRAHAM-CH

CLEVELAND INDIANS

12 ROBERTO ALOMAR-2B
13 OMAR VIZQUEL-SS
14 *(RET#) LARRY DOBY*
15 SANDY ALOMAR, JR. (INJ)-C/DH
16 DWIGHT (DOC) (DOCTOR K) GOODEN (INJ)-P
17 TRAVIS FRYMAN-3B
18 *(RET#) MEL HARDER*
19 *(RET#) BOB FELLER*
20 STEVE KARSAY (INJ)-P
21 *(RET#) BOB LEMON*
22 MARK LANGSTON-P
23 DAVID JUSTICE-OF/DH
24 MANNY RAMIREZ-OF
25 JIM THOME (INJ)-1B/DH
26 JEFF MANTO-INF (1/3)
26 JESSE LEVIS-C
27 JARET WRIGHT (SUS-5D)-P
28 CLARENCE JONES-CH
29 MARK WHITEN (INJ)-OF/DH
29 TYLER HOUSTON-INF (2)
30 MIKE HARGROVE-MGR
32 CHARLIE (CHUCK) MANUEL-CH
33 RUSSELL BRANYAN-3B
33 DAVE STEVENS-P
33 HAROLD BAINES-DH (2)
34 DAVE BURBA-P
35 ENRIQUE WILSON (INJ)-SS/2B
36 TOM MARTIN (INJ)-P
37 PAUL WAGNER-P
38 PHIL (THE VULTURE) REGAN-CH
39 STEVE REED-P
40 BARTOLO COLON-P
41 CHARLES NAGY-P
42 MIKE JACKSON-P
43 DAN WILLIAMS-CH
44 RICHIE SEXSON-1B/OF/DH
45 PAUL ASSENMACHER-P
46 JEFF TAM-P (1)
47 RICH DELUCIA-P
48 JERRY SPRADLIN-P (1)
48 CHRIS HANEY-P
49 TOM CANDIOTTI-P (2)
50 JIM BROWER-P
(51) JACOB CRUZ (INJ)-(OF)
52 DAVE ROBERTS-OF
53 PAUL SHUEY (INJ)-P
54 DAVE RISKE-P
55 JEFF NEWMAN-CH
56 SEAN DEPAULA-P
59 JASON RAKERS-P
61 ALEX RAMIREZ-OF
62 JIM POOLE-P (2)
73 RICKY RINCON (INJ)-P

2000

2ND C 90-72 5GB

1 WIL CORDERO (INJ)-OF (2)
2 EINAR DIAZ-C
3 *(RET#) EARL AVERILL*
4 LUIS ISAAC-CH
5 *(RET#) LOU BOUDREAU*
6 JOLBERT CABRERA-SS
7 KENNY LOFTON-OF
8 JOHN MCDONALD-INF
9 GRADY LITTLE-CH
10 DAVE ROBERTS-OF
11 TED UHLAENDER-CH
12 ROBERTO ALOMAR-2B
13 OMAR VIZQUEL-SS
14 *(RET#) LARRY DOBY*
15 SANDY ALOMAR, JR. (INJ)-C/DH
16 JIM RIGGLEMAN-CH
17 TRAVIS FRYMAN-3B
18 *(RET#) MEL HARDER*
19 *(RET#) BOB FELLER*
20 STEVE KARSAY (INJ)-P
21 *(RET#) BOB LEMON*
22 MIKE MOHLER-P (2)
23 DAVID JUSTICE-OF/DH (1)
23 DAVID SEGUI-DH (2)
23 RICKY LEDEE-OF (2)
24 MANNY RAMIREZ-OF
25 JIM THOME-1B/DH
26 BOB WICKMAN-P (2)
27 JARET WRIGHT (INJ)-P
28 CLARENCE JONES-CH
29 MARK WHITEN-OF/DH
29 STEVE WOODARD-P (2)
30 SCOTT KAMIENIECKI-P (1)
30 WIL CORDERO-OF (2)
31 CHUCK FINLEY-P
32 CHARLIE (CHUCK) MANUEL-MGR
33 RUSSELL BRANYAN-3B
34 DAVE BURBA-P
35 ENRIQUE WILSON (INJ)-SS/2B (1)
36 TOM MARTIN (INJ)-P
37 BOBBY WITT-P
37 JAMIE NAVARRO-P (2)
38 DICK POLE-CH
39 STEVE REED-P
40 BARTOLO COLON-P
41 CHARLES NAGY (INJ)-P
42 *(RET#) JACKIE ROBINSON*
43 DAN WILLIAMS-CH
44 RICHIE SEXSON-1B/OF/DH (1)
45 JUSTIN SPEIER-P
46 PAUL RIGDON-P (1)
46 JASON BERE-P (2)
47 TIM DREW-P
48 CHRIS HANEY-P
50 JIM BROWER-P
51 JACOB CRUZ (INJ)-OF
53 PAUL SHUEY-P
54 DAVE RISKE (INJ)-P
55 JIM DEDRICK-P
56 SEAN DEPAULA (INJ)-P
57 BRIAN WILLIAMS-P (2)
58 JAMIE BREWINGTON-P
59 MARK WATSON-P
59 ALAN NEWMAN-P
60 KANE DAVIS-P (1)
60 BILL SELBY-OF/INF
61 ALEX RAMIREZ-DH (1)
61 CHAN PERRY-OF
62 CAMERON CAIRNCROSS-P
63 ANDREW LORRAINE-P (2)
64 J. D. BRAMMER-P
66 WILLIE J. MARTINEZ-P
67 CHRIS NICHTING-P
73 RICKY RINCON (INJ)-P

2001

1ST C 91-71 0GB
L ALDS-SEAA 3-2

1 MARK LEWIS-3B
2 EINAR DIAZ-C
3 *(RET#) EARL AVERILL*
4 LUIS ISAAC-CH
5 *(RET#) LOU BOUDREAU*
6 JOLBERT CABRERA-OF
7 KENNY LOFTON (INJ)-OF
8 JOHN MCDONALD-INF
9 GRADY LITTLE-CH
10 DAVE ROBERTS (INJ)-OF
11 TED UHLAENDER-CH
12 ROBERTO ALOMAR-2B
13 OMAR VIZQUEL-SS
14 *(RET#) LARRY DOBY*
16 EDDIE TAUBENSEE (INJ)-C
17 TRAVIS FRYMAN (INJ)-3B
18 *(RET#) MEL HARDER*
19 *(RET#) BOB FELLER*
20 STEVE KARSAY (INJ)-P (1)
20 DAVE HOLLINS-DH
21 *(RET#) BOB LEMON*
22 JUAN GONZALEZ-OF
23 ELLIS BURKS-OF/DH
25 JIM THOME-1B/DH
26 BOB WICKMAN-P
27 JARET WRIGHT (INJ)-P
28 CLARENCE JONES-CH
29 STEVE WOODARD (INJ)-P
30 WIL CORDERO (INJ)-OF
31 CHUCK FINLEY (INJ)-P
32 CHARLIE (CHUCK) MANUEL-MGR
33 RUSSELL BRANYAN-3B
34 DAVE BURBA-P
35 JOEL SKINNER-CH
36 SCOTT RADINSKY-P
37 JAKE WESTBROOK-P
38 DICK POLE-CH
39 STEVE REED-P (1)
39 MILTON BRADLEY-OF
40 BARTOLO COLON-P
41 CHARLES NAGY (INJ)-P
42 *(RET#) JACKIE ROBINSON*
43 DAN WILLIAMS-CH
44 RICH RODRIGUEZ-P
45 JUSTIN SPEIER-P (1)
45 TIM LAKER-C
46 MARTY CORDOVA-OF
47 TIM DREW-P
48 ROY SMITH-P
49 JOHN ROCKER-P (2)
50 KARIM GARCIA-OF
51 JACOB CRUZ-OF (1)
51 MIKE BACSIK-P
52 C. C. SABATHIA-P
53 PAUL SHUEY (INJ)-P
54 DAVID RISKE-P
55 DANYS BAEZ-P
57 RYAN DRESE-P
62 CAMERON CAIRNCROSS (INJ)-P
73 RICKY RINCON-P

2002

3RD C 74-88 20.5GB

1 AL BUMBRY-CH
2 EINAR DIAZ (INJ)-C
3 *(RET#) EARL AVERILL*
4 LUIS ISAAC-CH
5 *(RET#) LOU BOUDREAU*
6 ROBBY THOMPSON-CH
8 JOHN MCDONALD-INF
9 BRADY ANDERSON-OF/DH
9 CHAD ALLEN-OF
9 LEE STEVENS-UTIL (2)
10 JOLBERT CABRERA (INJ)-OF/2B/DH
10 CAVELLI (COCO) CRISP-OF
11 MATT LAWTON (INJ)-OF/DH
12 RICKY GUTIERREZ-2B/DH
13 OMAR VIZQUEL-SS
14 *(RET#) LARRY DOBY*
16 EDDIE TAUBENSEE (INJ)-C
16 CHAD PARONTO (INJ)-P
17 TRAVIS FRYMAN-3B
18 *(RET#) MEL HARDER*
19 *(RET#) BOB FELLER*
20 BRUCE AVEN-OF
20 KARIM GARCIA-OF
21 *(RET#) BOB LEMON*
22 EARL SNYDER-1B/3B
23 ELLIS BURKS-DH/OF
24 MILTON BRADLEY-OF/DH
25 JIM THOME-1B/DH
26 BOB WICKMAN (INJ)-P
27 JARET WRIGHT (INJ)-P
28 RUSSELL BRANYAN-UTIL
28 BEN BROUSSARD-OF/1B/DH
29 JEFF DATZ-CH
30 WIL CORDERO (INJ)-OF
30 CHRIS MAGRUDER-OF
31 CHUCK FINLEY (INJ)-P (1)
32 CHARLIE (CHUCK) MANUEL-MGR 1
33 EDDIE MURRAY-CH
34 MARK WOHLERS-P
34 DAVE BURBA-P (2)
35 JOEL SKINNER-CH/MGR2
36 BILL SELBY-UTIL
37 JAKE WESTBROOK (INJ)-P
38 EDDIE PEREZ-C
40 BARTOLO COLON-P (1)
41 CHARLES NAGY (INJ)-P
42 *(RET#) JACKIE ROBINSON*
43 DAN WILLIAMS-BPC
44 JOSH BARD-C
44 TODD DUNWOODY (INJ)-OF
45 MIKE BROWN-CH
45 TERRY MULHOLLAND-P (2)
(46) ALEX ESCOBAR (INJ)-(OF)
46 RICH RODRIGUEZ-P
47 DAVE ELDER-P
48 ROY SMITH-P
49 ALEX HERRERA-P
49 NERIO RODRIGUEZ-P (1)
49 JASON BEVERLIN-P (1)
50 DAVE MAURER-P
51 JERROD RIGGAN-P
52 C. C. SABATHIA-P
53 PAUL SHUEY-P (1)
53 CARL SADLER-P
54 DAVID RISKE-P
55 DANYS BAEZ-P
56 SEAN DEPAULA-P
57 RYAN DRESE-P
58 HEATH MURRAY (INJ)-P
59 JASON C. PHILLIPS (INJ)-P
60 BRIAN TALLET-P
61 BRANDON PHILLIPS-2B
62 GREG LAROCCA-3B/2B
63 VICTOR MARTINEZ-C/DH
64 JASON DAVIS-P
65 CLIFF LEE-P
73 RICKY RINCON-P (1)

2003

4TH C 68-94 22GB

1 CASEY BLAKE-3B/1B
2 ZACH SORENSEN-2B/UTIL
3 *(RET#) EARL AVERILL*
4 LUIS ISAAC-CH
5 *(RET#) LOU BOUDREAU*
6 ALEX ESCOBAR-OF
7 BRANDON PHILLIPS-2B
8 JOHN MCDONALD (INJ)-INF
9 JODY GERUT-OF/DH
10 CAVELLI (COCO) CRISP-OF/DH
11 MATT LAWTON (INJ)-OF/DH
12 RICKY GUTIERREZ (INJ)-INF
13 OMAR VIZQUEL (INJ)-SS
14 *(RET#) LARRY DOBY*
15 TIM LAKER-C
16 CHAD PARONTO-P
18 *(RET#) MEL HARDER*
19 *(RET#) BOB FELLER*
20 KARIM GARCIA (INJ)-OF (1)
20 VICTOR MARTINEZ-C
21 *(RET#) BOB LEMON*
22 ERIC WEDGE-MGR
23 ELLIS BURKS (INJ)-DH
24 MILTON BRADLEY (INJ)-OF/DH
25 BUDDY BELL-CH
(26) BOB WICKMAN (INJ)-(P)
27 JACK CRESSEND-P
28 BEN BROUSSARD-1B
29 JEFF DATZ-CH
30 CHRIS MAGRUDER-OF
30 BRIAN TALLETT-P
31 BRIAN ANDERSON-P (1)
32 TRAVIS HAFNER (INJ)-DH/1B
33 EDDIE MURRAY-CH
34 DAN MICELI-P (2)
34 CLIFF LEE (INJ)-P
35 JOEL SKINNER-CH
36 BILL SELBY-3B
36 NICK BIERBRODT-P (2)
37 JAKE WESTBROOK-P
38 AARON MYETTE (INJ)-P
38 RYAN LUDWICK (INJ)-OF (2)
(39) MARK WOHLERS (INJ) (P)
40 BILLY TRABER (INJ)-P
42 *(RET#) JACKIE ROBINSON*
44 JOSH BARD-C
45 TERRY MULHOLLAND-P
46 JASON BERE (INJ)-P
47 SHANE SPENCER-OF/1B (1)
47 DAVE CORTES-P
47 DAVID LEE-P
48 JOSE SANTIAGO-P
49 DAVE ELDER (INJ)-P
49 CHAD DURBIN-P
50 JASON DAVIS (INJ)-P
51 JERROD RIGGAN-P
52 C. C. SABATHIA-P
53 CARL SADLER-P
54 DAVID RISKE-P
55 DANYS BAEZ-P
56 RICARDO RODRIGUEZ (INJ)-P
56 ANGEL SANTOS-2B/3B
57 CARL WILLIS-CH
57 JASON BOYD (INJ) (SUS:3G-P
59 JASON C. PHILLIPS (INJ)-P
59 ALEX HERRERA-P
60 JHONNY PERALTA-SS/3B
61 BRANDON PHILLIPS-2B
61 JASON STANFORD-P
62 GREG LAROCCA-3B
63 RAFAEL BETANCOURT-P
65 CLIFF LEE (INJ)-P

2004

3RD C 80-82 12GB

00 RICK WHITE-P
1 CASEY BLAKE-3B
2 SANDY MARTINEZ-C (1)
3 *(RET#) EARL AVERILL*
4 LUIS ISAAC-CH
5 *(RET#) LOU BOUDREAU*
6 ALEX ESCOBAR-OF (1)
6 BUDDY BELL-CH
7 BRANDON PHILLIPS-2B
8 JOHN MCDONALD-3B/SS
9 JODY GERUT-OF/DH
10 CAVELLI (COCO) CRISP-OF/DH
11 MATT LAWTON-OF/DH
12 LOU MERLONI-1B
13 OMAR VIZQUEL-SS
14 *(RET#) LARRY DOBY*
15 TIM LAKER-C
16 JHONNY PERALTA-INF
18 *(RET#) MEL HARDER*
19 *(RET#) BOB FELLER*
20 RONNIE BELLIARD-2B
21 *(RET#) BOB LEMON*
22 ERIC WEDGE-MGR
23 BEN BROUSSARD-1B
24 RICK WHITE-P
24 GRADY SIZEMORE-OF
25 BUDDY BELL-CH
26 BOB WICKMAN (INJ)-P
27 JACK CRESSEND-P
29 JEFF DATZ-CH
(30) BRIAN TALLETT (INJ)-(P)
31 JEFF D'AMICO-P
31 MARK LITTLE-P
32 KAZUHITO TADANO (INJ)-P
33 EDDIE MURRAY-CH
34 CLIFF LEE-P
35 JOEL SKINNER-CH
36 JOSE JIMENEZ-P

36 ERNIE YOUNG-OF
37 JAKE WESTBROOK-P
38 RYAN LUDWICK (INJ)-OF
39 SCOTT ELARTON-P (2)
41 VICTOR MARTINEZ-C
42 *(RET#) JACKIE ROBINSON*
44 JOSH BARD (INJ)-C
45 RAUL GONZALEZ-OF
45 JOSH PHELPS-DH (2)
47 DAVID LEE-P
48 TRAVIS HAFNER-1B/DH
49 CHAD DURBIN-P
49 JAKE ROBBINS-P
50 JASON DAVIS-P
52 C. C. SABATHIA-P
53 JEROME ROBERTSON-P (1)
53 JEREMY GUTHRIE-P
54 DAVID RISKE-P
55 SCOTT STEWART-P (1)
55 FRANCISCO CRUCETA-P
56 CLIFF BARTOSH-P
57 CARL WILLIS-CH
57 LOU POTE-P
57 KYLE DENNEY-P
58 JASON ANDERSON (INJ)-P
58 JOE DAWLEY (INJ)-P
59 MATT MILLER-P
61 JASON STANFORD (INJ)-P
62 BOBBY HOWRY-P
63 RAFAEL BETANCOURT (INJ) -P
64 FERNANDO CABRERA-P

2005

2ND C *93-69* *6GB*

1 CASEY BLAKE-OF
2 JHONNY PERALTA-SS
3 *(RET#) EARL AVERILL*
4 LUIS ISAAC-CH
5 *(RET#) LOU BOUDREAU*
6 ROBBY THOMPSON-CH
7 BRANDON PHILLIPS-INF
8 JEFF LIEFER-OF/1B
9 JODY GERUT-OF (1)
9 JASON DUBOIS-OF (2)
10 CAVELLI (COCO) CRISP (INJ) -OF/DH
11 JOSE HERNANDEZ-2B
12 ALEX CORA-2B (1)
14 *(RET#) LARRY DOBY*
15 RAMON VAZQUEZ-2B (2)
16 JUAN GONZALEZ (INJ)-OF
17 AARON BOONE-3B
18 *(RET#) MEL HARDER*
19 *(RET#) BOB FELLER*
20 RONNIE BELLIARD-2B
21 *(RET#) BOB LEMON*
22 ERIC WEDGE-MGR
23 BEN BROUSSARD-1B
24 GRADY SIZEMORE-OF
25 BUDDY BELL-CH (1)
25 RYAN GARKO-C
26 BOB WICKMAN-P
29 JEFF DATZ-CH
30 BRIAN TALLETT-P
31 CLIFF LEE-P
32 KAZUHITO TADANO-P
33 EDDIE MURRAY-CH
34 KEVIN MILLWOOD (INJ)-P
35 JOEL SKINNER-CH
36 JEREMY GUTHRIE-P
37 JAKE WESTBROOK-P
38 RYAN LUDWICK-OF
38 FRANKLIN GUTIERREZ-OF
39 SCOTT ELARTON-P
41 VICTOR MARTINEZ-C
42 *(RET#) JACKIE ROBINSON*
44 JOSH BARD-C
46 BOBBY HOWRY-P
47 SCOTT SAUERBECK-P
48 TRAVIS HAFNER (INJ)-DH
50 JASON DAVIS-P
52 C. C. SABATHIA-P
53 ARTHUR RHODES (INJ) (BRV)-P
54 DAVID RISKE (SUS:3G)-P
56 FERNANDO CABRERA-P
57 CARL WILLIS-CH
59 MATT MILLER (INJ)-P
63 RAFAEL BETANCOURT (INJ) -P
__ DEREK SHELTON-CH

The Indians are loaded with young talented players: Grady Sizemore, Jhonny Peralta, Coco Crisp, Ben Broussard, Victor Martinez—it won't be long before their impact is felt. Crisp (Above) wears #10. He came to the Indians in the Chick Finley trade with the Cardinals in 2002. In his short career with the Tribe he has shown speed and power.

DETROIT TIGERS

1931
DETROIT TIGERS
7TH 61-93 29.5GB

1 HUB WALKER-OF
2 GEE WALKER-OF
3 CHARLIE (MECHANICAL MAN) GEHRINGER (INJ)-2B/1B
4 DALE (MOOSE) ALEXANDER-1B/OF
5 MARTY MCMANUS-3B/INF (1)
5 GENE (RED) DESAUTELS-C
6 FRANK (DOLIE) DOLJACK-OF
7 LOU BROWER-SS/2B
7 BILL (BUMP) AKERS-SS/2B
7 BILLY ROGELL-SS
8 WALLY SCHANG-C
8 MUDDY RUEL-C (2)
9 RAY HAYWORTH-C
11 EARL WHITEHILL-P
12 VIC SORRELL-P
14 WAITE (SCHOOLBOY) HOYT-P (1)
15 GEORGE (THE BULL) UHLE-P
16 TOMMY BRIDGES-P
17 WHIT WYATT (INJ)-P
18 CHIEF HOGSETT-P
19 CHARLIE SULLIVAN-P
22 ROY JOHNSON-OF
24 JOHN (ROCKY) STONE-OF
25 JOE (JUMPIN' JOE) DUGAN-3B
26 IVEY SHIVER-OF
27 MARK KOENIG-INF/P
28 ORLIN COLLIER-P
29 MARV (FRECK) OWEN-INF
29 NOLEN RICHARDSON-3B
34 BUCKY HARRIS-2B/MGR
35 JOHNNY (NIG) GRABOWSKI-C
37 GEORGE QUELLICH-OF
41 ART (RED) (SANDY) HERRING-P
43 JEAN DUBUC-CH
52 ROGER BRESNAHAN-CH

1932
5TH 76-75 29.5GB

1 ROY JOHNSON-OF (1)
2 CHARLIE (MECHANICAL MAN) GEHRINGER (INJ)-2B
3 JOHN (ROCKY) STONE-OF
4 DALE (MOOSE) ALEXANDER-1B (1)
4 EARL WEBB-OF (2)
5 BILLY RHIEL-UTIL
6 BILLY ROGELL-SS/3B
7 BILL LAWRENCE-OF
8 NOLEN RICHARDSON-3B/SS
9 MUDDY RUEL-C
11 VIC SORRELL-P
12 WHIT WYATT-P
14 GEORGE (THE BULL) UHLE-P
15 EARL WHITEHILL, P
16 TOMMY BRIDGES-P
17 CHIEF HOGSETT-P
18 ART (RED) (SANDY) HERRING-P
18 RIP SEWELL-P (2)
21 IZZY GOLDSTEIN-P
22 RIP SEWELL-P (2)
23 RAY HAYWORTH-C
24 GEORGE (GOOD KID) SUSCE-C
25 GENE (RED) DESAUTELS-C
26 HARRY (STINKY) DAVIS-1B
27 GEE WALKER-OF
28 JO-JO WHITE-OF
29 BUCK MARROW-P
31 JEWEL ENS-CH
32 BUCKY HARRIS-MGR
33 HEINIE SCHUBLE-3B/SS
34 HARRY? FRITZ-CH
__ FRANK (DOLIE) DOLJACK-OF (8G: 9/17-25)

1933
5TH 75-79 25GB

1 PETE FOX-OF
2 CHARLIE (MECHANICAL MAN) GEHRINGER-2B
3 JOHN (ROCKY) STONE-OF
4 EARL WEBB-OF (1)
5 BILLY RHIEL-OF
5 JOHNNY PASEK-C
6 BILLY ROGELL-SS
6 GEE WALKER-OF
7 HANK (HAMMERIN' HANK) GREENBERG-1B
8* BOTS NEKOLA-P*
9 FRANK (DOLIE) DOLJACK-OF
9 FRANK (TUBBY) REIBER-C
11 VIC SORRELL-P
12 WHIT WYATT-P (1)
12 VIC FRASIER-P (2)
14 GEORGE (THE BULL) UHLE-P (1)
14 ELDON (SUBMARINE) AUKER-P
15 MARV (FRECK) OWEN-3B
16 TOMMY BRIDGES-P
17 CHIEF HOGSETT-P
18 ART (RED) (SANDY) HERRING-P
19 FIRPO MARBERRY-P
20 LUKE (HOT POTATO) HAMLIN-P
22 CARL FISCHER-P
23 RAY HAYWORTH-C
24 SCHOOLBOY ROWE (INJ)-P
25 GENE (RED) DESAUTELS-C
26 HARRY (STINKY) DAVIS-1B
27 GEE WALKER-OF
28 JO-JO WHITE-OF
31 DEL BAKER-CH/MGR2
32 BUCKY HARRIS-MGR1
33 HEINIE SCHUBLE-INF
__ ROXIE LAWSON-P (4G: 9/6-19)

1934
1ST 101-53 0GB
L WS-STLN 4-3

2 CHARLIE (MECHANICAL MAN) GEHRINGER-2B
3 MICKEY COCHRANE-C/MGR
4 GOOSE GOSLIN-OF
5 HANK (HAMMERIN' HANK) GREENBERG-1B
6 GEE WALKER-OF
7 BILLY ROGELL-SS
8 MARV (FRECK) OWEN-3B
10 TOMMY BRIDGES-P
11 FIRPO MARBERRY-P
12 PETE FOX-OF
13 ELDON (SUBMARINE) AUKER-P
14 SCHOOLBOY ROWE (INJ)-P
15 CARL FISCHER-P
16 VIC FRASIER-P (2)
16 GENERAL CROWDER-P (2)
17 CHIEF HOGSETT-P
18 VIC SORRELL-P
19 STEVE LARKIN-P
19 RED PHILLIPS-P
19 ICEHOUSE WILSON-PH
19 RUDY YORK-C
20 LUKE (HOT POTATO) HAMLIN-P
21 FRANK (TUBBY) REIBER-C
22 HEINIE SCHUBLE-INF
23 RAY HAYWORTH-C
24 FLEA CLIFTON-3B/2B
25 JO-JO WHITE-OF
26 FRANK (DOLIE) DOLJACK-OF/1B
29 LUKE (HOT POTATO) HAMLIN-P
31 CY PERKINS-PH/CH
32 DEL BAKER-CH

1935
1ST 93-58 0GB
W WS-CHIN 4-2

2 CHARLIE (MECHANICAL MAN) GEHRINGER-2B
3 MICKEY COCHRANE-C/MGR
4 GOOSE GOSLIN-OF
5 HANK (HAMMERIN' HANK) GREENBERG-1B
6 GEE WALKER-OF
7 BILLY ROGELL-SS
8 MARV (FRECK) OWEN-3B
9 PETE FOX-OF
10 TOMMY BRIDGES-P
11 FIRPO MARBERRY-P
12 CLYDE HATTER-P
13 ELDON (SUBMARINE) AUKER-P
14 SCHOOLBOY ROWE-P
15 CARL FISCHER-P (1)
15 HUGH SHELLEY-OF
16 GENERAL CROWDER-P
17 CHIEF HOGSETT-P
18 VIC SORRELL-P
19 JOE SULLIVAN-P
21 FRANK (TUBBY) REIBER-C
22 HEINIE SCHUBLE-3B/2B
23 RAY HAYWORTH-C
24 FLEA CLIFTON-INF
25 JO-JO WHITE-OF
26 ROXIE LAWSON-P
27 CHET (CHICK) MORGAN-OF
30 HUB WALKER-OF
31 CY PERKINS-CH
32 DEL BAKER-CH

1936
2ND 83-71 19.5GB

2 CHARLIE (MECHANICAL MAN) GEHRINGER-2B
3 MICKEY COCHRANE (ILL)-C/MGR
4 GOOSE GOSLIN-OF
5 HANK (HAMMERIN' HANK) GREENBERG (INJ)-1B
6 AL (BUCKETFOOT AL) SIMMONS-OF/1B
7 BILLY ROGELL-SS/3B
8 MARV (FRECK) OWEN-3B/1B
9 PETE FOX-OF
10 TOMMY BRIDGES-P
11 GEE WALKER-OF
12 CHAD KIMSEY-P
13 ELDON (SUBMARINE) AUKER-P
14 SCHOOLBOY ROWE-P
15 ROXIE LAWSON-P
16 GENERAL CROWDER-P
16 GLENN MYATT-C
16 BIRDIE TEBBETTS-C
17 CHIEF HOGSETT-P (1)
18 VIC SORRELL-P
19 JOE SULLIVAN-P
21 FRANK (TUBBY) REIBER-C
21 JAKE (WHISTLIN' JAKE) WADE-P
22 JACK (SLUG) BURNS-1B (2)
23 RAY HAYWORTH-C
24 FLEA CLIFTON-INF
24 SALTY PARKER-SS/1B
25 JO-JO WHITE-OF
26 GIL ENGLISH-3B
28 RED PHILLIPS-P
29 JAKE (WHISTLIN' JAKE) WADE-P
29 JACK (SLUG) BURNS-1B (2)
31 CY PERKINS-CH
32 DEL BAKER-CH

1937
2ND 89-65 13GB

2 CHARLIE (MECHANICAL MAN) GEHRINGER-2B
3 MICKEY COCHRANE (INJ)-C/MGR
4 GOOSE GOSLIN-OF/1B
5 HANK (HAMMERIN' HANK) GREENBERG-1B
6 CHET LAABS-OF
7 BILLY ROGELL-SS
8 MARV (FRECK) OWEN-3B
9 PETE FOX-OF
10 TOMMY BRIDGES-P
11 GEE WALKER-OF
12 ELDON (SUBMARINE) AUKER-P
14 SCHOOLBOY ROWE (INJ)-P
15 ROXIE LAWSON-P
16 GEORGE GILL-P
17 BOB (LEFTY) LOGAN-P (1)
17 PAT MCLAUGHLIN-P
18 VIC SORRELL-P
18 CLIFF BOLTON-C
20 RUDY YORK-C/3B
21 CLYDE HATTER-P
21 SLICK COFFMAN-P
22 PAT MCLAUGHLIN-P
23 RAY HAYWORTH-C
24 GIL ENGLISH-2B/3B (1)
24 BOOTS POFFENBERGER-P
25 JO-JO WHITE-OF
26 JACK RUSSELL-P
27 BABE HERMAN-OF
28 BIRDIE TEBBETTS-C
29 JAKE (WHISTLIN' JAKE) WADE-P
30 FLEA CLIFTON-INF
30 CHARLIE GELBERT-SS (2)
31 CY PERKINS-CH
32 DEL BAKER-CH

1938
4TH 84-70 16GB

2 CHARLIE (MECHANICAL MAN) GEHRINGER-2B
3 MICKEY COCHRANE-MGR1
3 CHET LAABS-OF
4 RUDY YORK-C/UTIL
5 HANK (HAMMERIN' HANK) GREENBERG-1B
6 DON ROSS-3B
7 BILLY ROGELL-SS
8 DIXIE (THE PEOPLE'S CHERCE) WALKER-OF
9 PETE FOX-OF
10 TOMMY BRIDGES-P
11 VERN KENNEDY (INJ)-P
12 ELDON (SUBMARINE) AUKER-P
14 SCHOOLBOY ROWE (INJ)-P
14 BOB HARRIS-P
15 ROXIE LAWSON-P
16 GEORGE GILL-P
17 BOOTS POFFENBERGER-P
18 JAKE (WHISTLIN' JAKE) WADE-P
19 ROY CULLENBINE-OF
20 MARK CHRISTMAN-3B/SS
21 SLICK COFFMAN-P
22 JO-JO WHITE-OF
23 RAY HAYWORTH-C (1)
24 BENNY MCCOY-2B/3B
25 CHET LAABS-OF
25 CHET (CHICK) MORGAN-OF
26 HARRY EISENSTAT-P
27 TONY PIET-3B/2B
27 AL BENTON-P
28 BIRDIE TEBBETTS-C
29 AL BENTON-P
31 BING MILLER-CH
32 DEL BAKER-CH/MGR2
34 JOE ROGALSKI-P
35 GEORGE ARCHIE-PH
35 WOODY DAVIS-P
CLYDE HATTER (DIED)-(P)

1939
5TH 81-73 26.5GB

1 BIRDIE TEBBETTS-C
2 CHARLIE (MECHANICAL MAN) GEHRINGER-2B
3 FRANK (DINGLE) CROUCHER-SS/2B
4 RUDY YORK-C/1B
5 HANK (HAMMERIN' HANK) GREENBERG-1B
6 MIKE (PINKY) HIGGINS-3B
7 BILLY ROGELL-INF
8 DIXIE (THE PEOPLE'S CHERCE) WALKER-OF (1)
8 DIXIE PARSONS-C
9 PETE FOX-OF
10 TOMMY BRIDGES-P
11 VERN KENNEDY-P (1)
11 BUD THOMAS-P (3)
12 MARK CHRISTMAN-3B (1)
12 BOBO (BUCK) NEWSOM-P (2)
14 SCHOOLBOY ROWE-P
15 DIZZY TROUT-P
16 GEORGE GILL-P (1)
16 JACHYM-CH
16 HAL (PRINCE HAL) NEWHOUSER-P
17 CHET LAABS-OF (1)
17 GORDIE HINKLE-CH
17 BEAU BELL-OF (2)
18 BOBO (BUCK) NEWSOM-P (2)
18 FRED HUTCHINSON-P
19 ROY CULLENBINE-OF/1B
20 LES (MOE) FLEMING-OF
20 BEAU BELL-OF (2)
21 BARNEY MCCOSKY-OF
22 AL BENTON-P
23 ROXIE LAWSON-P
23 RED KRESS (INJ)-INF
24 HARRY EISENSTAT-P (1)
24 BENNY MCCOY-2B/SS
24 EARL (ROCK) AVERILL-OF (2)
25 SLICK COFFMAN-P
26 BOB HARRIS-P (1)
26 JIM WALKUP-P (2)
26 COTTON PIPPEN-P (2)
27 RED LYNN-P (1)
27 BENNY MCCOY-2B/SS
28 ARCHIE (HAPPY) MCKAIN-P
29 FLOYD GIEBELL-P
30 MERV SHEA-C/CH
31 BING MILLER-CH
32 DEL BAKER-MGR
33 GORDIE HINKLE-CH

1940

1ST 90-64 0GB

L WS-CINN 4-3

1 BIRDIE TEBBETTS-C
2 CHARLIE (MECHANICAL MAN) GEHRINGER-2B
3 FRANK (DINGLE) CROUCHER-INF
4 RUDY YORK-1B
5 HANK (HAMMERIN' HANK) GREENBERG-OF
6 MIKE (PINKY) HIGGINS-3B
7 DICK (ROWDY RICHARD) BARTELL-SS
8 BILLY SULLIVAN-C/3B
9 PETE FOX-OF
10 TOMMY BRIDGES-P
11 BUD THOMAS-P
11 COTTON PIPPEN-P
12 BOBO (BUCK) NEWSOM-P
14 SCHOOLBOY ROWE-P
15 DIZZY TROUT-P
16 HAL (PRINCE HAL) NEWHOUSER-P
17 COTTON PIPPEN-P
17 BUD THOMAS-P
17 PAT MULLIN-OF
18 FRED HUTCHINSON-P
19 AL BENTON-P
20 BRUCE (SOUPY) CAMPBELL-OF
21 BARNEY MCCOSKY-OF
22 DICK CONGER-P
22 FLOYD GIEBELL-P
23 TUCK STAINBACK-OF
24 TOM SEATS-P
25 LYNN (LINE DRIVE) NELSON-P
25 BOB (LEFTY) UHL-P
26 RED KRESS (INJ)-3B/SS/CH
26 JOHNNY GORSICA-P
27 EARL (ROCK) AVERILL-OF
28 ARCHIE (HAPPY) MCKAIN-P
29 CLAY SMITH-P
30 MERV SHEA-CH
31 BING MILLER-CH
32 DEL BAKER-MGR
33 GORDIE? HINKLE-CH
33 DUTCH MEYER-2B
33 SCAT METHA-2B/3B
34 JOHNNY GORSICA-P
__ FRANK SECORY-PH (1G: 4/28)

1941

4TH (TIE) 75-79 26GB

1 BIRDIE TEBBETTS-C
2 CHARLIE (MECHANICAL MAN) GEHRINGER-2B
3 FRANK (DINGLE) CROUCHER-SS
4 RUDY YORK-1B
5 HANK (HAMMERIN' HANK) GREENBERG (MIL)-OF
6 MIKE (PINKY) HIGGINS-3B
7 DICK (ROWDY RICHARD) BARTELL-SS (1)
7 BOYD PERRY-SS/2B
8 BILLY SULLIVAN-C/3B
9 DUTCH MEYER-2B
9 ERIC (BOOB) MCNAIR-3B/SS
10 TOMMY BRIDGES-P
11 DIZZY TROUT-P
12 BOBO (BUCK) NEWSOM-P
14 SCHOOLBOY ROWE-P
15 JOHNNY GORSICA-P
16 HAL (PRINCE HAL) NEWHOUSER-P
17 FLOYD GIEBELL-P
17 HOOT EVERS-OF
17 VIRGIL (FIRE) TRUCKS-P
18 PAT MULLIN-OF
18 RIP RADCLIFF-OF (2)
19 AL BENTON-P
20 BRUCE (SOUPY) CAMPBELL-OF
21 BARNEY MCCOSKY-OF
22 BUD THOMAS-P
17 VIRGIL (FIRE) TRUCKS-P
23 TUCK STAINBACK-OF
24 NED HARRIS-OF
24 DICK WAKEFIELD-OF
24 HAL MANDERS-P
25 EARL COOK-P
25 HAL WHITE-P
26 DICK WAKEFIELD-OF
27 PAT MULLIN-OF
27 LES MUELLER-P
28 ARCHIE (HAPPY) MCKAIN-P (1)
28 MURRAY (MOE) FRANKLIN-SS/3B
29 FRED HUTCHINSON-PH
30 MERV SHEA-CH
31 BING MILLER-CH
32 DEL BAKER-MGR
33 STEVE O'NEILL-CH
34 EARL COOK-P
34 BOB PATRICK-OF

1942

5TH 73-81 30GB

1 BIRDIE TEBBETTS-C
2 CHARLIE (MECHANICAL MAN) GEHRINGER (MIL)-2B/CH
3 JIMMY BLOODWORTH-2B/SS
4 RUDY YORK-1B
5 RIP RADCLIFF-OF/1B
6 MIKE (PINKY) HIGGINS-3B
7 BILLY HITCHCOCK-SS/3B
7 JOHNNY (SKIDS) LIPON-SS
8 DOC (FLIT) CRAMER-OF
9 ERIC (BOOB) MCNAIR-SS (1)
9* JACK (BLACK JACK) WILSON-P* (2)
9 HANK RIEBE-C
10 TOMMY BRIDGES-P
11 DIZZY TROUT-P
12 HAL MANDERS-P
14 SCHOOLBOY ROWE-P (1)
15 JOHNNY GORSICA-P
16 HAL (PRINCE HAL) NEWHOUSER-P
17 CHARLIE FUCHS-P
18 ROY HENSHAW-P
19 AL BENTON-P
20 DON ROSS-OF/3B
21 BARNEY MCCOSKY-OF
22 VIRGIL (FIRE) TRUCKS-P
23 DIXIE PARSONS-C
24 BOB PATRICK (INJ)-OF
24 JACK (BLACK JACK) WILSON-P (2)
25 HAL WHITE-P
26 NED HARRIS-OF
26 DUTCH MEYER-2B
27 MURRAY (MOE) FRANKLIN-SS/2B
28 NED HARRIS-OF
30 MERV SHEA-CH
31 JACK TIGHE-CH
31 AL UNSER-C
32 DEL BAKER-MGR

1943

5TH 78-76 20GB

2 DICK WAKEFIELD-OF
3 JIMMY BLOODWORTH-2B
4 RUDY YORK-1B
5 RIP RADCLIFF-OF/1B
6 MIKE (PINKY) HIGGINS-3B
7 JOE HOOVER-SS
8 DOC (FLIT) CRAMER-OF
9 PAUL RICHARDS-C
10 TOMMY BRIDGES-P
11 DIZZY TROUT-P
12 RUFE GENTRY-P
12 JOE ORRELL-P
14 JOE ORRELL-P
14 PRINCE OANA-P
15 JOHNNY GORSICA-P
16 HAL (PRINCE HAL) NEWHOUSER-P
18 ROY HENSHAW-P
19 STUBBY OVERMIRE-P
20 DON ROSS-OF/INF
21 CHARLIE METRO-OF
22 VIRGIL (FIRE) TRUCKS-P
23 DIXIE PARSONS-C
24 JOE (LITTLE JOE) (J.P.) WOOD-2B/3B
25 HAL WHITE-P
26 NED HARRIS-OF
27 JOHN MCHALE (MIL)-PH
27 JIMMY OUTLAW-OF
30 AL UNSER-C
31 AL VINCENT-CH
32 STEVE O'NEILL-MGR

1944

2ND 88-66 1GB

1 BOB SWIFT-C
2 DICK WAKEFIELD (MIL)-OF
2* CHIEF HOGSETT-P*
3 EDDIE (HOTSHOT) MAYO-2B/SS
4 RUDY YORK-1B
5 DON (JEEP) HEFFNER-2B
5* JAKE MOOTY-P*
6 MIKE (PINKY) HIGGINS-3B
7 RED BOROM-2B/SS
7 JOE HOOVER-SS/2B
8 DOC (FLIT) CRAMER-OF
9 PAUL RICHARDS-C
11 DIZZY TROUT-P
12 RUFE GENTRY-P
14 JOE ORRELL-P
15 JOHNNY GORSICA-P
16 HAL (PRINCE HAL) NEWHOUSER-P
17 BOB (BUNCH) GILLESPIE-P
18 JACK SULLIVAN-2B
19 STUBBY OVERMIRE-P
20 DON ROSS-OF/INF
21 CHARLIE METRO-OF (1)
21 ROY HENSHAW-P
22 HACK MILLER-C
22 JOE ORENGO-INF
23 BOOM-BOOM BECK-P
24 JOE HOOVER-SS/2B
24 JOE ORENGO-INF
25 JOHN MCHALE (MIL)-PH
25 ZEB (RED) EATON-P
25 BUBBA FLOYD-SS
26 CHUCK HOSTETLER-OF
27 JIMMY OUTLAW-OF
28 ART MILLS-CH
30 AL UNSER-2B/C
31 AL VINCENT-CH
31 ART MILLS-CH
32 STEVE O'NEILL-MGR

1945

1ST 88-65 0GB

W WS-CHIN 4-3

1 BOB SWIFT-C
2 ED (BUTCH) (MOUSE) MIERKOWICZ-OF
2 DON ROSS-3B (1)
3 EDDIE (HOTSHOT) MAYO-2B/SS
4 RUDY YORK-1B
5* BILLY PIERCE-P*
5 HANK (HAMMERIN' HANK) GREENBERG (MIL)-OF
6 ROY CULLENBINE-OF (2)
7 JOE HOOVER-SS
8 DOC (FLIT) CRAMER-OF
9 PAUL RICHARDS-C
10 RED BOROM-INF
10 TOMMY BRIDGES (MIL)-P
11 DIZZY TROUT-P
12 RUFE GENTRY (H/O)-P
12 BILLY PIERCE-P
12 JOHN MCHALE-1B
12 JIM (ABBA DABBA) TOBIN-P (2)
14 JOE ORRELL-P
14 JIM (ABBA DABBA) TOBIN-P (2)
15 LES MUELLER-P
16 HAL (PRINCE HAL) NEWHOUSER-P
17 ZEB (RED) EATON-P
18 STUBBY OVERMIRE-P
19 AL BENTON (INJ)-P
20 PAT MCLAUGHLIN-P
20 BILLY PIERCE-P
21 ART HOUTTEMAN-P
22 BOB MAIER-3B/OF
22 JIM (ABBA DABBA) TOBIN-P (2)
23 MILT WELCH-C
23 HACK MILLER-C
24 WALTER WILSON-P
25 JOHN MCHALE-1B
25 PAT MCLAUGHLIN-P
25 GEORGE (UG) CASTER-P (2)
26 PAT MCLAUGHLIN-P
26 CHUCK HOSTETLER-OF
27 GEORGE (UG) CASTER-P (2)
27 JIMMY OUTLAW-OF/3B
28 SKEETER WEBB-SS/2B
29 RUSS KERNS-PH
29 CARL (SKINNY) MCNABB-PH
30 HUB WALKER-OF
30 RED BOROM-INF
31 ART MILLS-CH
31 HACK MILLER-C
32 STEVE O'NEILL-MGR
34 HUB WALKER-OF
35 VIRGIL (FIRE) TRUCKS (MIL)-P
36 PRINCE OANA-P
39 CARL (SKINNY) MCNABB-PH

1946

2ND 92-62 12GB

1 BIRDIE TEBBETTS-C
2 ROY CULLENBINE-OF/1B
3 EDDIE (HOTSHOT) MAYO (INJ)-2B
4 DICK WAKEFIELD-OF
5 HANK (HAMMERIN' HANK) GREENBERG-1B
6 MIKE (PINKY) HIGGINS-3B (1)
6* ART HOUTTEMAN-P*
7 EDDIE (SPARKY) LAKE-SS
8 DOC (FLIT) CRAMER-OF
9 PAUL RICHARDS-C
10 TOMMY BRIDGES-P
11 DIZZY TROUT-P
12 BOB SWIFT-C
14 HOOT EVERS (INJ)-OF
15 HOOT EVERS (INJ)-OF
16 HAL (PRINCE HAL) NEWHOUSER-P
17 HAL WHITE-P
18 STUBBY OVERMIRE-P
19 AL BENTON-P
20 ANSE MOORE-OF
21 BARNEY MCCOSKY-OF (1)
21 GEORGE KELL-3B/1B (2)
22 VIRGIL (FIRE) TRUCKS-P
23 BILLY HITCHCOCK-2B
24 HAL MANDERS-P (1)
24 JOHNNY GROTH-OF
25 GEORGE (UG) CASTER-P
26 JIMMY BLOODWORTH (MIL) -2B
26 NED HARRIS-PH
27 JIMMY OUTLAW-OF/3B
28 SKEETER WEBB- 2B/SS
29 FRED HUTCHINSON-P
30 FRANK SHELLENBACK-CH
31 ART MILLS-CH
32 STEVE O'NEILL-MGR
33 PAT MULLIN-OF
34 RUFE GENTRY-P
34 TED GRAY-P
35 JOHNNY GORSICA (MIL)-P
35 LOU (LENA) KRETLOW-P
37 JOHNNY (SKIDS) LIPON-SS/3B

1947

2ND 85-69 12GB

1 BIRDIE TEBBETTS-C (1)
1 HAL WAGNER-C (2)
2 ROY CULLENBINE-1B
3 EDDIE (HOTSHOT) MAYO-2B
4 DICK WAKEFIELD-OF
6 PAT MULLIN-OF
7 EDDIE (SPARKY) LAKE-SS
8 DOC (FLIT) CRAMER-OF
9 BOB SWIFT-C
11 DIZZY TROUT-P
12 ED (BUTCH) (MOUSE) MIERKOWICZ-OF
14 HOOT EVERS-OF
15 ART HOUTTEMAN-P
16 HAL (PRINCE HAL) NEWHOUSER-P
17 HAL WHITE-P
18 STUBBY OVERMIRE-P
19 AL BENTON-P
20 VIC WERTZ-OF
21 GEORGE KELL-3B
22 VIRGIL (FIRE) TRUCKS-P
23 JOHN MCHALE-1B
24 JOHNNY GORSICA-P
24 JOHNNY GROTH-OF
25 HANK RIEBE-C
26 BEN STEINER-PR
27 JIMMY OUTLAW-OF/3B
28 SKEETER WEBB-2B/SS
29 FRED HUTCHINSON-P
30 FRANK SHELLENBACK-CH
31 ART MILLS-CH
32 STEVE O'NEILL-MGR
33 BILL SWEENEY-CH
34 RUFE GENTRY-P
35 JOHNNY GORSICA-P

1948

5TH 78-76 18.5GB

1 HAL WAGNER-C (1)
1 JOE GINSBERG-C
2 PAUL CAMPBELL-1B
3 EDDIE (HOTSHOT) MAYO-2B/3B
4 DICK WAKEFIELD-OF
5 GEORGE (SAM) VICO-1B
6 PAT MULLIN-OF
7 EDDIE (SPARKY) LAKE (INJ)-2B/3B
8 DOC (FLIT) CRAMER-OF/CH
9 BOB SWIFT-C
10 BILLY PIERCE-P
11 DIZZY TROUT-P
12 ED (BUTCH) (MOUSE) MIERKOWICZ-OF

DETROIT TIGERS

4 HOOT EVERS-OF
5 ART HOUTTEMAN-P
5 GEORGE KELL (INJ)-3B
6 HAL (PRINCE HAL) NEWHOUSER-P
7 HAL WHITE-P
8 STUBBY OVERMIRE-P
9 AL BENTON-P
0 VIC WERTZ-OF
1 GEORGE KELL (INJ)-3B
1 ART HOUTTEMAN-P
2 VIRGIL (FIRE) TRUCKS-P
3 JOHN MCHALE-PH
3 LOU (LENA) KRETLOW-P
4 RUFE GENTRY-P
4 JOHNNY GROTH-OF
5 HANK RIEBE-C
6 JOHNNY (SKIDS) LIPON-SS/INF
7 JIMMY OUTLAW-3B/OF
8 JOHNNY BERO-2B
9 FRED HUTCHINSON-P
0 TED GRAY-P
1 ART MILLS-CH
2 STEVE O'NEILL-MGR
3 BILL SWEENEY-CH
4 TED GRAY-P
6 NEIL BERRY-SS/2B

1949

4TH 87-67 10GB

1 AARON ROBINSON-C
2 JOHNNY (SKIDS) LIPON-SS
3 JOHNNY GROTH-OF
4 DICK WAKEFIELD-OF
5 GEORGE (SAM) VICO-1B
6 PAT MULLIN-OF
7 EDDIE (SPARKY) LAKE-INF
8 NEIL BERRY-2B/SS
9 BOB SWIFT-C
0 RED ROLFE-MGR
1 DIZZY TROUT-P
2 ART HOUTTEMAN (INJ)-P
4 HOOT EVERS-OF
5 ART HOUTTEMAN (INJ)-P
5 PAUL CAMPBELL-1B
6 HAL (PRINCE HAL) NEWHOUSER-P
7 HAL WHITE-P
7 DON (BUTCH) (CAB) KOLLOWAY-INF (2)
8 STUBBY OVERMIRE-P
9 MARV GRISSOM-P
20 VIC WERTZ-OF
21 GEORGE KELL-3B
22 VIRGIL (FIRE) TRUCKS-P
23 SAUL ROGOVIN-P
24 MARLIN STUART-P
25 HANK RIEBE-C
26 HAL WHITE-P
27 JIMMY OUTLAW-PH
28 DICK (ROWDY RICHARD) BARTELL-CH
29 FRED HUTCHINSON-P
30 DON LUND-PH
32 EARL RAPP-PH (1)
32 BOB MAVIS-PR
33 TED LYONS-CH
34 TED GRAY-P
36 LOU (LENA) KRETLOW-P

1950

2ND 95-59 3GB

1 AARON ROBINSON-C
2 JOHNNY (SKIDS) LIPON-SS
3 JOHNNY GROTH-OF
4 JERRY PRIDDY-2B
6 PAT MULLIN-OF
7 EDDIE (SPARKY) LAKE-3B/SS
8 NEIL BERRY-INF
9 BOB SWIFT-C
10 RED ROLFE-MGR
11 DIZZY TROUT-P
12 ART HOUTTEMAN-P
14 HOOT EVERS-OF
15 PAUL CAMPBELL-PH
15 HANK BOROWY-P (3)
16 HAL (PRINCE HAL) NEWHOUSER-P
17 DON (BUTCH) (CAB) KOLLOWAY-1B/2B
19 DICK KRYHOSKI-1B
20 VIC WERTZ-OF
21 GEORGE KELL-3B
22 VIRGIL (FIRE) TRUCKS (INJ)-P
23 SAUL ROGOVIN-P
24 MARLIN STUART-P
24 RAY HERBERT-P
25 HAL WHITE-P
26 MARLIN STUART-P
26 JOE GINSBERG-C
27 CHARLIE (KING KONG) KELLER-OF
28 DICK (ROWDY RICHARD) BARTELL-CH
29 FRED HUTCHINSON-P
30 DICK KRYHOSKI-1B
30BILL (WILD BILL) CONNELLY-P
30 RAY HERBERT-P
31 PAUL CALVERT-P
33 TED LYONS-CH
34 TED GRAY (ILL)-P
35 FRANK (PIG) HOUSE-C
36 RICK FERRELL-CH

1951

5TH 73-81 25GB

1 AARON ROBINSON-C (1)
2 JOHNNY (SKIDS) LIPON-SS
3 JOHNNY GROTH-OF
4 JERRY PRIDDY-2B/SS
5 VIC WERTZ-OF
6 PAT MULLIN-OF
7 GEORGE KELL-3B
8 NEIL BERRY-INF
9 BOB SWIFT (ILL)-C
10 RED ROLFE-MGR
11 DIZZY TROUT-P
12 STEVE (BUD) SOUCHOCK-UTIL
14 HOOT EVERS-OF
15 HANK BOROWY-P
16 HAL (PRINCE HAL) NEWHOUSER (INJ)-P
17 DON (BUTCH) (CAB) KOLLOWAY-1B
18 EARL (LEFTY) JOHNSON-P
18 RUSS SULLIVAN-OF
19 WAYNE (NUBBIN') MCLELAND-P
20 RAY HERBERT (MIL)-P
21 DOC DAUGHERTY-PH
21 BOB (SUGAR) CAIN-P (2)
22 VIRGIL (FIRE) TRUCKS-P
23 SAUL ROGOVIN-P (1)
23 BOB (SUGAR) CAIN-P (2)
24 MARLIN STUART-P
25 HAL WHITE-P
26 JOE GINSBERG-C
27 CHARLIE (KING KONG) KELLER-OF
28 DICK (ROWDY RICHARD) BARTELL-CH
29 FRED HUTCHINSON-P
30 DICK KRYHOSKI-1B
31 PAUL CALVERT-P
31 BOB (SUGAR) CAIN-P (2)
33 TED LYONS-CH
34 TED GRAY (ILL)-P
35 FRANK (PIG) HOUSE-C
36 RICK FERRELL-CH
37 GENE BEARDEN-P (2)
37 DICK MARLOWE-P
46 AL (WHITEY) FEDEROFF-2B

1952

8RD 50-104 45GB

1 JOE GINSBERG-C
1 FRED HATFIELD-3B/SS (2)
2 JOHNNY (SKIDS) LIPON-SS (1)
2 FRED HATFIELD-3B/SS (2)
2 JOE GINSBERG-C
3 JOHNNY GROTH-OF
4 JERRY PRIDDY (INJ)-2B
5 VIC WERTZ-OF (1)
5 CLIFF MAPES-OF
6 PAT MULLIN-OF
7 GEORGE KELL-3B (1)
7 JOHNNY PESKY-INF (2)
8 NEIL BERRY-SS/3B
9 BOB SWIFT-C
10 RED ROLFE-MGR1
10 MATT BATTS (ILL)-C
11 DIZZY TROUT-P (1)
11 WALT (MOOSE) DROPO-1B (2)
12 STEVE (BUD) SOUCHOCK-UTIL
14 HOOT EVERS-PH (1)
14 DON (FOOTSIE) LENHARDT-OF (2)
14 DAVE MADISON-P (2)
15 MATT BATTS (ILL)-C
15 CARL LINHART-PH
16 HAL (PRINCE HAL) NEWHOUSER-P
17 DON (BUTCH) (CAB) KOLLOWAY-1B/2B
18 RUSS SULLIVAN-OF
18 BILL (LEFTY) WIGHT-P (2)
19 BILL (BUD) BLACK-P
19 ALEX GARBOWSKI-PR
19 RUSS SULLIVAN-OF
20 VIC WERTZ-OF (1)
20 BILL TUTTLE-OF
21 ART HOUTTEMAN-P
22 VIRGIL (FIRE) TRUCKS-P
23 WAYNE (NUBBIN') MCLELAND-P
24 MARLIN STUART-P (1)
24 JIM DELSING-OF (2)
25 HAL WHITE-P
26 JOE GINSBERG-C
26 KEN (HOOK) JOHNSON-P
26 HARVEY KUENN-SS
27 MATT BATTS (ILL)-C
28 DICK (ROWDY RICHARD) BARTELL-CH
28 AL (WHITEY) FEDEROFF-2B/SS
29 FRED HUTCHINSON-P/MGR2
30 BENNIE TAYLOR-1B
30 DON LUND-OF
31 WAYNE MCLELAND-P
31 NED GARVER-P (2)
32 GEORGE LERCHEN-OF
32 JOHNNY (HIPPITY) HOPP-OF/1B (2)
33 TED LYONS-CH
34 TED GRAY-P
35 FRANK HOUSE (MIL)-C
36 RICK FERRELL-CH
37 BILL (BUD) BLACK-P
37 DICK MARLOWE-P
38 RUSS SULLIVAN-OF
38 DICK LITTLEFIELD-P
44 BILLY HOEFT-P
(45) RAY HERBERT (MIL)-(P)
46 AL (WHITEY) FEDEROFF-2B/SS

1953

6TH 60-94 40.5GB

1 FRED HATFIELD-INF
2 JOE GINSBERG-C (1)
2* AL (LEFTY) ABER-P* (2)
2 RENO BERTOIA-2B
3 WALT (MOOSE) DROPO-1B
4 JERRY PRIDDY-INF
5 BOB NIEMAN-OF
6 PAT MULLIN-OF
7 JOHNNY PESKY-2B
8 OWEN (RED) FRIEND-2B (1)
8 RAY (IKE) BOONE-3B/SS (2)
9 BOB SWIFT-C/CH
10 MATT BATTS-C
12 STEVE (BUD) SOUCHOCK-OF/1B
14 DAVE MADISON-P
15 GEORGE (BUD) FREESE-PH
16 HAL (PRINCE HAL) NEWHOUSER (INJ)-P
17 BILLY HITCHCOCK-INF
18 BILL (LEFTY) WIGHT-P (1)
18 STEVE GROMEK-P (2)
19 RUSS SULLIVAN-OF
19 RAY SCARBOROUGH-P (2)
20 RAY HERBERT-P
21 ART HOUTTEMAN-P (1)
21 DICK (LEGS) WEIK-P (2)
22 FRANK (WHEELS) (TEX) CARSWELL-OF
22 AL (LEFTY) ABER-P (2)
24 JIM DELSING-OF
25 AL KALINE-OF
26 HARVEY KUENN-SS
27 HAL ERICKSON-P
28 BOB MILLER-P
29 FRED HUTCHINSON-P/MGR
30 DON LUND-OF
31 NED GARVER-P
32 JOHNNY BUCHA-C
33 TED LYONS-CH
34 TED GRAY-P
35 MILT JORDAN-P
35 EARL (IRISH) HARRIST-P (2)
35 RALPH (HAWK) BRANCA-P (2)
36 RICK FERRELL-CH
37 DICK MARLOWE-P
38 JOHN BAUMGARTNER-3B
39 PAUL FOYTACK-P
39 EARL (IRISH) HARRIST-P (2)
44 BILLY HOEFT-P
45 RAY HERBERT-P

1954

5TH 68-86 43GB

1 FRED HATFIELD-2B/3B
2 FRANK (PIG) HOUSE-C
3 WALT (MOOSE) DROPO-1B
4 CHARLIE KRESS-1B/OF (1)
4 WAYNE BELARDI-1B (2)
5 BOB NIEMAN-OF
6 AL KALINE-OF
7 JOHNNY PESKY-PH (1)
7 HARVEY KUENN-SS
8 RAY (IKE) BOONE-3B/SS
9 BOB SWIFT-CH
10 MATT BATTS-C (1)
10 RED WILSON-C (2)
12 STEVE (BUD) SOUCHOCK (INJ)-OF/3B
14 JIM HICKS-P
14 AL LAKEMAN-C
14 HOOT EVERS-OF (3)
15 FRANK BOLLING-2B
16 RENO BERTOIA-INF
17 BILL TUTTLE-OF
18 STEVE GROMEK-P
19 WALT STREULI-C
20 RAY HERBERT-P
21 DICK (LEGS) WEIK-P
21H CHARLIE (CHICK) KING-OF
22 AL (LEFTY) ABER-P
24 JIM DELSING-OF
25 AL KALINE-OF
26 HARVEY KUENN-SS
28 BOB MILLER-P
29 FRED HUTCHINSON-
30 DON LUND-OF
30 DICK (LEGS) WEIK-P
30 FRANK (THE YANKEE KILLER) (MULE) LARY-P
31 NED GARVER-P
33 SCHOOLBOY ROWE-CH
34 TED GRAY (INJ)-P
35 RALPH (HAWK) BRANCA-P (1)
36 JOHNNY (HIPPITY) HOPP-CH
37 DICK MARLOWE-P
38 GEORGE ZUVERINK-P (2)
44 BILLY HOEFT-P
49 DICK DONOVAN-P
50 AL (MOOSE) LAKEMAN-C
50 GEORGE ZUVERINK-P (2)
50 GEORGE (CURLY) BULLARD-SS

1955

5TH 79-75 17GB

1 FRED HATFIELD-2B/INF
2 FRANK (PIG) HOUSE-C
3 FERRIS (BURRHEAD) FAIN-1B (1)
4 WAYNE BELARDI-1B
4 CHARLIE (SMOKEY) MAXWELL-OF/1B (2)
5 BILL TUTTLE-OF
6 AL KALINE-OF
7 HARVEY KUENN-SS
8 RAY (IKE) BOONE-3B
9 JAY (J. W.) PORTER-UTIL
9 EARL (THE EARL OF SNOHOMISH) TORGESON-1B (2)
10 RED WILSON-C
11 BUBBA PHILLIPS-OF/3B
12 STEVE (BUD) SOUCHOCK - PH
12 JOE COLEMAN (INJ)-P (2)
14 BILL (BUD) BLACK-P
14 PETE? FOX-CH
15 GEORGE ZUVERINK-P (1)
15 JIM BUNNING-P
16 RENO BERTOIA-INF
17 FRANK (THE YANKEE KILLER) (MULE) LARY-P
18 STEVE GROMEK-P
19 BOB SCHULTZ-P
19 BABE BIRRER-P
20 JIM SMALL-OF
21 CHARLIE (CHICK) KING-OF
22 AL (LEFTY) ABER-P
24 JIM DELSING-OF
25 HARRY (SWEDE) MALMBERG-2B
26 VAN FLETCHER-P
27 LEO CRISTANTE-P
28 BOB MILLER-P
30 JACK (STRETCH) PHILLIPS-1B/3B
31 NED GARVER-P
32 BUCKY HARRIS-MGR
33 SCHOOLBOY ROWE-CH
34 BILLY HITCHCOCK-CH

35 JACK TIGHE-CH
36 PAUL FOYTACK-P
37 DICK MARLOWE-P
37 RON SAMFORD-SS
38 BILL FROATS-P
40 BEN FLOWERS-P
40 WALT STREULI-C
44 BILLY HOEFT-P
45 BILL FROATS-P
47 DUKE MAAS-P

1956

5TH 82-72 15GB

1 FRED HATFIELD-2B (1)
1 JIM BRIDEWESER-INF (2)
2 FRANK (PIG) HOUSE-C
3 CHARLIE (CHICK) KING-OF
3 BOB KENNEDY-OF/3B (2)
4 CHARLIE (SMOKEY) MAXWELL-OF
5 BILL TUTTLE-OF
6 AL KALINE-OF
7 HARVEY KUENN-SS/OF
8 RAY (IKE) BOONE-3B
9 EARL (THE EARL OF SNOHOMISH) TORGESON-1B
10 RED WILSON-C
11 VIRGIL (FIRE) TRUCKS-P
12 CHARLIE LAU-C
12 BUDDY HICKS-INF
13 BOB MILLER-P
13 BILL TUTTLE-OF
14 BILL (BUD) BLACK-P
14 JIM BUNNING-P
15 JAY (J. W.) PORTER-C/OF
16 RENO BERTOIA-2B/3B
16 WALT MASTERSON-P
17 FRANK (THE YANKEE KILLER) (MULE) LARY-P
18 STEVE GROMEK-P
19 GENE (TWINKLES) (SLICK) HOST-P
20 JIM SMALL-OF
21 PAUL FOYTACK-P
22 AL (LEFTY) ABER-P
23 JAY (J. W.) PORTER-C/OF
23 VIRGIL (FIRE) TRUCKS-P
24 JIM DELSING-OF (1)
24 FRANK BOLLING-2B
25 HAL WOODESHICK-P
26 JIM (DIAMOND JIM) BRADY-P
27 WAYNE BELARDI-1B/OF
28 BOB MILLER-P
29 WALT MASTERSON-P
29 PETE WOJEY-P
30 JACK (STRETCH) PHILLIPS-UTIL
31 NED GARVER (INJ)-P
32 BUCKY HARRIS-MGR
33 GENE (TWINKLES) (SLICK) HOST-P
34 BILLY HITCHCOCK-CH
35 JACK TIGHE-CH
36 JOE (FLASH) GORDON-CH
37 DICK MARLOWE-P (1)
39 WALT STREULI-C
41 JIM BUNNING-P
44 BILLY HOEFT-P
47 DUKE MAAS-P

1957

4TH 78-76 20GB

1 BOBO OSBORNE-OF/1B
1 JACK DITTMER-3B/2B
2 FRANK (PIG) HOUSE-C
3 JOHNNY GROTH-OF (2)
4 CHARLIE (SMOKEY) MAXWELL-OF
5 JIM FINIGAN-3B/2B
6 AL KALINE-OF
7 HARVEY KUENN-SS/INF
8 RAY (IKE) BOONE-1B/3B
9 EARL (THE EARL OF SNOHOMISH) TORGESON-1B (1)
9 DAVE PHILLEY-UTIL (2)
10 RED WILSON-C
11 HARRY BYRD-P
11 EDDIE ROBINSON-1B (1)
12 TOM (KIBBY) YEWCIC-C
12 JOHN TSITOURIS-P
12 MEL CLARK-OF
13 BILL TUTTLE-OF
14 JIM BUNNING-P
15 JAY (J. W.) PORTER-UTIL
16 RENO BERTOIA-3B/INF
17 FRANK (THE YANKEE KILLER) (MULE) LARY-P
18 STEVE GROMEK-P
18 CHUCK DANIEL-P
19 LOU SLEATER-P
19 JACK CRIMIAN-P
20 JIM SMALL-OF
21 PAUL FOYTACK-P
22 AL (LEFTY) ABER-P (2)
23 DUKE MAAS-P
24 FRANK BOLLING-2B
25 BOB SHAW-P
26 STEVE BOROS-3B/SS
27 RON SAMFORD-INF
28 GEORGE THOMAS-3B
29 PETE WOJEY-P
29 BILL TAYLOR-OF
30 JACK (STRETCH) PHILLIPS-PH
30 KARL (OLE) OLSON-OF
31 JIM STUMP-P
32 DON LUND-CH
33 WILLIS (ACE) HUDLIN-CH
34 BILLY HITCHCOCK-CH
35 JACK TIGHE-MGR
41 DON LEE-P
41 JOE (LITTLE JOE) PRESKO-P
44 BILLY HOEFT-P

1958

5TH 77-77 17GB

1 BILLY (THE KID) MARTIN-SS/3B
2 FRANK BOLLING-2B
3 JOHNNY GROTH-OF
4 CHARLIE (SMOKEY) MAXWELL-OF/1B
5 GAIL HARRIS-1B
6 AL KALINE-OF
7 HARVEY KUENN-OF
8 RAY (IKE) BOONE-1B (1)
8 TITO FRANCONA-OF/1B (2)
9 GUS (OZARK IKE) ZERNIAL-OF
10 RED WILSON-C
12 TIM THOMPSON-C
12 CHARLIE LAU-C
14 JIM BUNNING-P
15 JIM HEGAN-C (1)
15 GEORGE THOMAS-OF
16 RENO BERTOIA-3B/UTIL
17 FRANK (THE YANKEE KILLER) (MULE) LARY-P
18 TOM (PLOWBOY) MORGAN-P
19 LOU SLEATER-P
19 JACK FELLER-C
19 BILL FISCHER-P (2)
20 MICKEY (MAURY) MCDERMOTT-P
20 HERM WEHMEIER-P (2)
20 DON LEE-P
20 LOU (THE NERVOUS GREEK) SKIZAS-OF/3B
21 PAUL FOYTACK-P
22 LOU (THE NERVOUS GREEK) SKIZAS-OF/3B
22 OZZIE VIRGIL-3B
23 MILT BOLLING-INF
23 COOT VEAL-SS
24 GEORGE SPENCER-P
24 STEVE BOROS-3B/SS
25 BOB SHAW-P (1)
25 AL (BOZO) CICOTTE-P (2)
26 GEORGE SUSCE-P (2)
27 JOE (LITTLE JOE) PRESKO-P
27 BOB (HURRICANE)-OF (2)
28 VITO VALENTINETTI-P (1)
29 BILL TAYLOR-OF
29 BILL NORMAN-MGR2
30 HANK AGUIRRE-P
31 TOMMY (OLD RELIABLE) (THE CLUTCH) HENRICH-CH
32 DON LUND-CH
33 WILLIS (ACE) HUDLIN-CH
34 BILLY HITCHCOCK-CH
35 JACK TIGHE-MGR1
35 GEORGE ALUSIK-OF
37 HERB MOFORD-P
44 BILLY HOEFT-P
47 BOBO OSBORNE-PH

1959

4TH 76-78 18GB

1 EDDIE (THE WALKING MAN) YOST-3B/2B
2 FRANK BOLLING-2B
3 JOHNNY GROTH-OF
4 CHARLIE (SMOKEY) MAXWELL-OF/1B
5 GAIL HARRIS-1B
6 AL KALINE-OF
7 HARVEY KUENN-OF
8 ROCKY BRIDGES-SS/2B
9 GUS (OZARK IKE) ZERNIAL-1B/OF
10 RED WILSON-C
11 LOU BERBERET-C
11 CHARLIE LAU-C
14 JIM BUNNING-P
15 DON (THE SPHINX) MOSSI-P
16 RAY NARLESKI-P
17 FRANK (THE YANKEE KILLER) (MULE) LARY-P
18 TOM (PLOWBOY) MORGAN-P
19 PETE BURNSIDE-P
20 BARNEY SCHULTZ-P
20 BOB BRUCE-P
20 JIM STUMP-P
21 PAUL FOYTACK-P
22 TED LEPCIO-INF (2)
23 COOT VEAL-SS
24 NEIL CHRISLEY-OF
25 LARRY DOBY-OF (1)
25 RON SHOOP-C
26 GEORGE SUSCE-P
26 JIM STUMP-P
26 BOB SMITH-P (2)
26 STEVE DEMETER-3B
27 JERRY DAVIE-P
28 JIMMY DYKES-MGR2
29 BILL NORMAN-MGR1
30 HANK AGUIRRE-P
30 DAVE SISLER-P (2)
31 TOMMY (OLD RELIABLE) (THE CLUTCH) HENRICH-CH
32 BOBO OSBORNE-1B/OF
33 WILLIS (ACE) HUDLIN-CH
34 BILLY HITCHCOCK-CH
36 OSSIE ALVAREZ-PH
37 JIM PROCTOR-P
41 DAVE SISLER-P (2)
44 BILLY HOEFT-P (1)

1960

6TH 71-83 26GB

1 EDDIE (THE WALKING MAN) YOST-3B
2 FRANK BOLLING-2B
3 JOHNNY GROTH-OF
3 DICK MCAULIFFE-SS
4 CHARLIE (SMOKEY) MAXWELL-OF
5 GAIL HARRIS-1B
5 SANDY AMOROS-OF (2)
5 DICK GERNERT-1B/OF (2)
6 AL KALINE-OF
7 ROCKY COLAVITO-OF
8 ROCKY BRIDGES-3B/SS (1)
8 COOT VEAL-INF
9 CHICO FERNANDEZ-SS
10 RED WILSON-C (1)
10 HANK FOILES-C (3)
11 LOU BERBERET-C
14 JIM BUNNING-P
15 DON (THE SPHINX) MOSSI-P
16 RAY (BABY) SEMPROCH-P
16 PHIL (THE VULTURE) REGAN-P
17 FRANK (THE YANKEE KILLER) (MULE) LARY-P
18 TOM (PLOWBOY) MORGAN-P (1)
18 BILL FISCHER-P (2)
19 PETE BURNSIDE-P
21 PAUL FOYTACK-P
22 CASEY WISE-INF
22 OZZIE VIRGIL-UTIL
23 EM LINDBECK-PH
23 CLEM LABINE-P (2)
24 NEIL CHRISLEY-OF/1B
25 NORM CASH-1B/OF
27 HARRY CHITI-C (2)
28 JIMMY DYKES-MGR1
28 JOE (FLASH) GORDON-MGR3
29 STEVE BILKO-1B
30 DAVE SISLER-P
31 LUKE (OLD ACHES & PAINS) APPLING-CH
31 GEORGE SPENCER-P
32 BOB BRUCE-P
33 TOM FERRICK-CH
34 BILLY HITCHCOCK-CH/MGR2
36 SANDY AMOROS-OF (2)
37 HANK AGUIRRE-P
40 JO-JO WHITE-CH

1961

2ND 101-61 8GB

1 STEVE BOROS (INJ)-3B
2 JAKE WOOD-2B
3 CHUCK COTTIER-SS/2B (1)
3 DICK MCAULIFFE-SS/3B
4 CHARLIE (SMOKEY) MAXWELL-OF
5 DICK GERNERT-PH (1)
5 FRANK (PIG) HOUSE-C
6 AL KALINE-OF/3B
7 ROCKY COLAVITO-OF
8 OZZIE VIRGIL-UTIL
8 RENO BERTOIA-INF (3)
9 CHICO FERNANDEZ-SS/3B
10 DICK BROWN-C
11 HARRY CHITI-C
11 FRED GLADDING-P
11 RON KLINE-P (2)
12 MIKE ROARKE-C
14 JIM BUNNING-P
15 DON (THE SPHINX) MOSSI-P
16 PHIL (THE VULTURE) REGAN-P
17 FRANK (THE YANKEE KILLER) (MULE) LARY-P
18 TERRY FOX-P
19 JIM DONOHUE-P (1)
19 BILL FREEHAN-C
19 JERRY CASALE-P (2)
20 HAL WOODESHICK-P (2)
20 GERRY STALEY-P (3)
21 PAUL FOYTACK-P
22 VIC WERTZ-PH (2)
24 GEORGE THOMAS-OF/SS (1)
24 MANNY MONTEJO-P
25 NORM CASH-1B
26 BILL FISCHER-P (1)
26 GEORGE ALUSIK-OF
27 BOB SCHEFFING-MGR
28 BOBO OSBORNE-1B/3B
31 DON (JEEP) HEFFNER-CH
32 BOB BRUCE (INJ)-P
32 RON NISCHWITZ-P
33 TOM FERRICK-CH
37 HANK AGUIRRE-P
38 GERRY STALEY-P (3)
38 BILL BRUTON-OF
40 BUBBA MORTON-OF
44 PHIL CAVARRETTA-CH
45 HOWIE KOPLITZ-P
46 JOE GRZENDA-P

1962

4TH 85-76 10.5GB

1 STEVE BOROS-3B/2B
2 JAKE WOOD-2B
3 DICK MCAULIFFE-INF
4 CHARLIE (SMOKEY) MAXWELL-OF/1B (1)
5 PURNAL GOLDY-OF
6 AL KALINE (INJ)-OF
7 ROCKY COLAVITO-OF
8 RENO BERTOIA-INF
8 DON BUDDIN-INF (2)
9 CHICO FERNANDEZ-SS/INF
10 DICK BROWN-C
12 MIKE ROARKE-C
14 JIM BUNNING-P
15 DON (THE SPHINX) MOSSI-P
16 PHIL (THE VULTURE) REGAN-P
17 FRANK (THE YANKEE KILLER) (MULE) LARY-P
18 TERRY FOX-P
19 JERRY CASALE-P
19 BILL FAUL-P
20 VIC WERTZ-1B
21 PAUL FOYTACK-P
22 RON KLINE-P
23 SAM (TOOTHPICK SAM) JONES-P
24 FRANK KOSTRO-3B
25 NORM CASH-1B/OF
26 GEORGE ALUSIK-PH (1)
26 BOB FARLEY-1B/OF (2)
27 BOB SCHEFFING-MGR
28 BOBO OSBORNE-UTIL
29 FRED GLADDING-P
29 RON NISCHWITZ-P
31 TOM FLETCHER-P
32 DOUG GALLAGHER-P
33 TOM FERRICK-CH
34 GEORGE (MERCURY) (STUD) (FOGHORN) MYATT-CH
37 HANK AGUIRRE-P
38 BILL BRUTON-OF
40 BUBBA MORTON-OF/1B
44 PHIL CAVARRETTA-CH
45 HOWIE KOPLITZ-P
46 BOB HUMPHREYS-P

1963

5TH 79-83 25.5GB

1 BUBBA PHILLIPS-3B/OF

DETROIT TIGERS

2 JAKE WOOD (INJ)-2B/3B
3 DICK MCAULIFFE-SS/2B
4 WHITEY (THE WHITE RAT) HERZOG-1B/OF
5 PURNAL GOLDY-PH
6 AL KALINE (INJ)-OF
7 ROCKY COLAVITO-OF
8 DON WERT-INF
9 CHICO FERNANDEZ-SS
9 CHUCK DRESSEN-MGR2
10 GUS TRIANDOS-C
11 BILL FREEHAN-C
12 MIKE ROARKE-C
13 BILL FAUL-P
14 JIM BUNNING-P
15 DON (THE SPHINX) MOSSI-P
16 PHIL (THE VULTURE) REGAN-P
17 FRANK (THE YANKEE KILLER) (MULE) LARY-P
18 TERRY FOX-P
20 VIC WERTZ-1B (1)
20 FRED GLADDING-P
20 GATES BROWN-OF
21 PAUL FOYTACK-P (1)
22 TOM (SNAKE) STURDIVANT-P (2)
23 BOB ANDERSON-P
24 FRANK KOSTRO-UTIL (1)
24 GEORGE THOMAS-OF/2B (2)
25 NORM CASH-1B
26 GATES BROWN-OF
27 BOB SCHEFFING-MGR1
28 COOT VEAL-SS
29 MICKEY LOLICH-P
33 TOM FERRICK-CH
33 WILLIE SMITH-P
34 GEORGE (MERCURY) (STUD) (FOGHORN) MYATT-CH
34 DENNY MCLAIN-P
34 PAT MULLIN-CH
35 BOB SWIFT-CH
35 BOB DUSTAL-P
36 JOHN SULLIVAN-C
37 HANK AGUIRRE-P
38 BILL BRUTON-OF
40 BUBBA MORTON-OF (1)
40 WILLIE SMITH-P
40 GEORGE SMITH-2B
41 STUBBY OVERMIRE-CH
41 DICK EGAN-P
42 ALAN KOCH-P
44 PHIL CAVARRETTA-CH
46 LARRY FOSTER-P
48 WILLIE HORTON-OF
51 BOB SWIFT-CH
52 PAT MULLIN-CH
53 STUBBY OVERMIRE-CH
54 WAYNE BLACKBURN-CH

1964
4TH 85-77 14GB

1 BUBBA PHILLIPS-3B/OF
2 JAKE WOOD-UTIL
3 DICK MCAULIFFE-SS
4 DON DEMETER-OF/1B
6 AL KALINE-OF
7 CHUCK DRESSEN-MGR
8 DON WERT-3B/SS
9 JERRY LUMPE-2B
11 BILL FREEHAN-C/1B
12 MIKE ROARKE-C
13 BILL FAUL-P
14 DAVE WICKERSHAM-P
15 LARRY SHERRY (INJ)-P
16 PHIL (THE VULTURE) REGAN-P
17 FRANK (THE YANKEE KILLER) (MULE) LARY-P(1)
18 TERRY FOX-P
19 ED (ROCK) RAKOW-P
20 FRED GLADDING-P
21 HANK AGUIRRE-P
23 WILLIE HORTON-OF
24 GEORGE THOMAS-OF/3B
25 NORM CASH-1B
26 GATES BROWN-OF
29 MICKEY LOLICH-P
33 JULIO (WHIPLASH) NAVARRO-P (2)
34 DENNY MCLAIN-P
36 JOHN SULLIVAN-C
37 BILL ROMAN-1B
37 HANK AGUIRRE-P
38 BILL BRUTON-OF
39 JOHNNIE (DURANGO KID) SEALE-P
40 GEORGE SMITH-2B
41 DICK EGAN-P
42 ALAN KOCH-P (1)
42 JULIO (WHIPLASH) NAVARRO-P (2)
44 FRITZ FISHER-P
45 JIM NORTHRUP-OF
47 JOE SPARMA-P
48 JACK HAMILTON-P
49 MICKEY STANLEY-OF
51 BOB SWIFT-CH
52 PAT MULLIN-CH
53 STUBBY OVERMIRE-CH
54 WAYNE BLACKBURN-CH

1965
4TH 89-73 13GB

1 RAY OYLER-INF
2 JAKE WOOD-INF
3 DICK MCAULIFFE (INJ)-SS
4 DON DEMETER-OF/1B
6 AL KALINE (INJ)-OF/3B
7 CHUCK DRESSEN (ILL)-MGR
8 DON WERT-3B/INF
9 JERRY LUMPE-2B
11 BILL FREEHAN-C
12 MIKE ROARKE-CH
14 DAVE WICKERSHAM-P
15 LARRY SHERRY-P
16 PHIL (THE VULTURE) REGAN-P
17 DENNY MCLAIN-P
18 TERRY FOX-P
19 ED (ROCK) RAKOW-P
19 VERN (WOODY) HOLTGRAVE-P
20 FRED GLADDING-P
21 JOE SPARMA-P
23 WILLIE HORTON-OF/3B
24 GEORGE THOMAS-OF/2B
25 NORM CASH-1B
26 GATES BROWN-OF
27 BILL ROMAN-1B
27 RON NISCHWITZ-P
28 ORLANDO PENA-P (2)
29 MICKEY LOLICH-P
30 JIM NORTHRUP-OF
31 JACK HAMILTON (INJ)-P
32 RON NISCHWITZ-P
32 WAYNE REDMOND-OF
35 JACKIE MOORE-C
36 JOHN SULLIVAN-C
37 HANK AGUIRRE-P
39 JOHNNIE (DURANGO KID) SEALE-P
39 JOHN HILLER-P
40 GEORGE SMITH-INF
42 JULIO (WHIPLASH) NAVARRO-P
46 LEO MARENTETTE-P
49 MICKEY STANLEY-OF
51 BOB SWIFT-CH/ACT MGR
52 PAT MULLIN-CH
53 STUBBY OVERMIRE-CH
55 FRANK SKAFF-CH

1966
3RD 88-74 10GB

1 RAY OYLER-SS
2 JAKE WOOD-INF
3 DICK MCAULIFFE-SS/3B
4 DON DEMETER-OF/1B (1)
6 AL KALINE-OF
7 CHUCK DRESSEN (DIED)-MGR1
8 DON WERT-3B
9 JERRY LUMPE-2B
11 BILL FREEHAN-C/1B
12 MIKE ROARKE-CH
14 DAVE WICKERSHAM-P
15 LARRY SHERRY-P
16 EARL WILSON-P (2)
17 DENNY MCLAIN-P
18 TERRY FOX-P (1)
20 FRED GLADDING-P
21 JOE SPARMA-P
22 JOHNNY PODRES-P (2)
23 WILLIE HORTON-OF
24 MICKEY STANLEY (INJ)-OF
25 NORM CASH-1B
26 GATES BROWN-OF
27 BILL MONBOUQUETTE-P
28 ORLANDO PENA-P
29 MICKEY LOLICH-P
30 JIM NORTHRUP-OF
32 DON PEPPER-1B
34 ORLANDO MCFARLANE-C
35 ARLO BRUNSBERG-C
37 HANK AGUIRRE-P
38 ORLANDO MCFARLANE-C
39 JOHN HILLER-P
42 JULIO (WHIPLASH) NAVARRO-P
44 DICK TRACEWSKI-2B/SS
46 BILL GRAHAM-P
49 GEORGE (MOOSE) KORINCE-P
51 BOB SWIFT (ILL/DIED)-CH/MGR2
52 PAT MULLIN-CH
53 STUBBY OVERMIRE-CH
55 FRANK SKAFF-CH/MGR3

1967
2ND (TIE) 91-71 1GB

1 RAY OYLER-SS
2 JAKE WOOD-INF (1)
3 DICK MCAULIFFE-2B/SS
4 JIM LANDIS-OF
5 JIM NORTHRUP-OF
6 AL KALINE (INJ)-OF
7 EDDIE MATHEWS-3B/1B (2)
8 DON WERT-3B/SS
9 JERRY LUMPE-2B/3B
10 MAYO SMITH-MGR
11 BILL FREEHAN-C/1B
14 DAVE WICKERSHAM-P
15 LARRY SHERRY-P (1)
15 FRED LASHER-P
16 EARL WILSON-P
17 DENNY MCLAIN-P
18 JOHN HILLER-P
19 GEORGE (MOOSE) KORINCE-P
20 FRED GLADDING-P
21 JOE SPARMA-P
22 JOHNNY PODRES-P
23 WILLIE HORTON-OF
24 MICKEY STANLEY-OF/1B
25 NORM CASH-1B
26 GATES BROWN (INJ)-OF
27 BILL MONBOUQUETTE-P (1)
28 ORLANDO PENA-P (1)
28 MIKE MARSHALL-P
29 MICKEY LOLICH-P
30 JOHNNY KLIPPSTEIN-P
30 LENNY GREEN-OF
33 DAVE CAMPBELL-1B
34 JIM PRICE-C
37 HANK AGUIRRE-P
38 BILL HEATH-C (2)
39 WAYNE COMER-OF
40 PAT DOBSON-P
43 TOM MATCHICK-SS
44 DICK TRACEWSKI-INF
50 TONY (COOCH) (CHICK) CUCCINELLO-CH
51 WALLY MOSES-CH
52 HAL NARAGON-CH
53 JOHNNY SAIN-CH
54 BABE BIRRER-CH

1968
1ST 103-59 0GB
W WS-STLN 4-3

1 RAY OYLER-SS
2 TOM MATCHICK-INF
3 DICK MCAULIFFE-2B/SS
5 JIM NORTHRUP-OF
6 AL KALINE-OF/1B
7 EDDIE MATHEWS (INJ)-3B/1B
8 DON WERT-3B
10 MAYO SMITH-MGR
11 BILL FREEHAN-C/UTIL
12 JIM PRICE-C
14 DENNIS RIBANT-P (1)
15 FRED LASHER-P
16 EARL WILSON-P
17 DENNY MCLAIN-P
18 JOHN HILLER-P
21 JOE SPARMA-P
22 PAT DOBSON-P
23 WILLIE HORTON-OF
24 MICKEY STANLEY-OF/INF
25 NORM CASH-1B
26 GATES BROWN-OF/1B
27 WAYNE COMER-OF/C
29 MICKEY LOLICH-P
30 LENNY GREEN-OF
30 ROY FACE-P (2)
33 DAVE CAMPBELL-2B
34 JIM ROOKER-P
37 JOHN WYATT-P (3)
38 LES CAIN-P
39 JON (WARBLER) WARDEN-P
43 DARYL PATTERSON-P
44 DICK TRACEWSKI-INF
46 BOB CHRISTIAN-1B/OF
47 DON MCMAHON-P (2)
50 TONY (COOCH) (CHICK) CUCCINELLO-CH
51 WALLY MOSES-CH
52 HAL NARAGON-CH
53 JOHNNY SAIN-CH

1969
2ND E 90-72 19GB

2 TOM MATCHICK-INF
3 DICK MCAULIFFE (INJ)-2B
4 TOM TRESH-SS/UTIL (2)
5 JIM NORTHRUP-OF
6 AL KALINE-OF/1B
7 CESAR (COCOA) GUTIERREZ-SS (2)
8 DON WERT-3B
9 IKE BROWN-UTIL
10 MAYO SMITH-MGR
11 BILL FREEHAN-C/1B
12 JIM PRICE-C
14 DICK (THE MONSTER) RADATZ-P (1)
15 FRED LASHER-P
16 EARL WILSON-P
17 DENNY MCLAIN-P
18 JOHN HILLER-P
20 BOB REED-P
21 JOE SPARMA-P
22 PAT DOBSON-P
23 WILLIE HORTON-OF
24 MICKEY STANLEY-OF/INF
25 NORM CASH-1B
26 GATES BROWN-OF
27 RON WOODS-OF (1)
28 TOM TIMMERMANN-P
29 MICKEY LOLICH-P
31 WAYNE REDMOND-PH
33 DAVE CAMPBELL-INF
35 MIKE KILKENNY-P
36 NORM MCRAE-P
39 FRED SCHERMAN-P
43 DARYL PATTERSON (MIL)-P
44 DICK TRACEWSKI-INF
47 DON MCMAHON-P (1)
47 GARY TAYLOR-P
50 GROVER RESINGER-CH
51 WALLY MOSES-CH
52 HAL NARAGON-CH
53 JOHNNY SAIN-CH
53 TED KAZANSKI-CH

1970
4TH E 79-83 29GB

2 DALTON JONES-INF
3 DICK MCAULIFFE-2B/INF
4 KEVIN (CASEY) COLLINS-1B
5 JIM NORTHRUP-OF
6 AL KALINE-OF/1B
7 CESAR (COCOA) GUTIERREZ-SS
8 DON WERT-3B/2B
9 IKE BROWN-UTIL
10 MAYO SMITH-MGR
11 BILL FREEHAN (INJ)-C
12 JIM PRICE-C
15 FRED LASHER-P (1)
16 EARL WILSON-P (1)
17 DENNY MCLAIN (INJ)-P
18 JOHN HILLER-P
19 JOE NIEKRO-P
20 BOB REED-P
23 WILLIE HORTON (INJ)-OF
24 MICKEY STANLEY-OF/1B
25 NORM CASH-1B
26 GATES BROWN-OF
27 JERRY ROBERTSON-P
28 TOM TIMMERMANN-P
29 MICKEY LOLICH-P
30 LERRIN LAGROW-P
31 RUSS NAGELSON-OF/1B (2)
33 GENE LAMONT-C
34 TIM HOSLEY-C
35 MIKE KILKENNY-P
36 NORM MCRAE-P
38 LES CAIN-P
39 FRED SCHERMAN-P
41 ELLIOTT MADDOX-UTIL
42 KEN SZOTKIEWICZ (INJ)-SS
43 DARYL PATTERSON-P
46 DENNIS SAUNDERS-P
50 GROVER RESINGER-CH
51 WALLY MOSES-CH
52 LEN OKRIE-CH
53 MIKE ROARKE-CH

1971
2ND E 91-71 12GB

1 BILLY (THE KID) MARTIN-MGR
2 DALTON JONES-UTIL
3 DICK MCAULIFFE-2B/SS
4 AURELIO RODRIGUEZ-3B/SS
5 JIM NORTHRUP-OF/1B
6 AL KALINE-OF/1B
7 CESAR (COCOA) GUTIERREZ-INF

8 ED BRINKMAN-SS
9 IKE BROWN-UTIL
10 TONY TAYLOR-2B/3B (2)
11 BILL FREEHAN-C/OF
12 JIM PRICE (INJ)-C
14 DEAN CHANCE (INJ)-P
15 JOE COLEMAN-P
16 JIM HANNAN-P (1)
16 RON PERRANOSKI-P (2)
(18) JOHN HILLER (ILL)-(P)
19 JOE NIEKRO-P
21 BILL ZEPP-P
23 WILLIE HORTON (INJ)-OF
24 MICKEY STANLEY-OF
25 NORM CASH-1B
26 GATES BROWN-OF
27 BILL DENEHY-P
28 TOM TIMMERMANN-P
29 MICKEY LOLICH-P
32 DAVE BOSWELL-P (1)
32 DEAN CHANCE (INJ)-P
33 GENE LAMONT-C
34 TIM HOSLEY-C/1B
35 MIKE KILKENNY (ILL)-P
36 BILL GILBRETH-P
37 CHUCK SEELBACH-P
38 LES CAIN (INJ)-P
39 FRED SCHERMAN-P
41 JOHN YOUNG-1B
43 DARYL PATTERSON-P (1)
43 JACK WHILLOCK-P
44 KEVIN (CASEY) COLLINS-UTIL
45 JIM FOOR-P
46 MARVIN LANE-OF
50 ART FOWLER-CH
51 JOE (GERMANY) SCHULTZ-CH
52 CHARLIE (SWEDE) SILVERA-CH
53 FRANK SKAFF-CH

1972

1ST E 86-70 0GB
L ALCS-OAKA 3-2

1 BILLY (THE KID) MARTIN-MGR
2 DALTON JONES-PH (1)
3 DICK MCAULIFFE-2B/INF
4 AURELIO RODRIGUEZ-3B/SS
5 JIM NORTHRUP-OF/1B
6 AL KALINE (INJ)-OF/1B
7 JOHN KNOX-2B
8 ED BRINKMAN-SS
9 IKE BROWN-UTIL
10 TONY TAYLOR-INF
11 BILL FREEHAN-C
12 DUKE SIMS-C/OF (2)
14 TOM HALLER-C
15 JOE COLEMAN-P
16 RON PERRANOSKI-P (1)
(18) JOHN HILLER (ILL)-(P)
19 JOE NIEKRO (INJ)-P
20 FRED HOLDSWORTH-P
22 IKE BLESSITT-OF
23 WILLIE HORTON (INJ)-OF
24 MICKEY STANLEY-OF/1B
25 NORM CASH-1B
26 GATES BROWN-OF
28 TOM TIMMERMANN-P
29 MICKEY LOLICH-P
30 LERRIN LAGROW-P
31 PAUL JATA-UTIL
32 GENE LAMONT-C
33 GENE LAMONT-C
33 FRANK (THE CAPITAL PUNISHER) (HONDO) HOWARD-1B/OF (2)
35 MIKE KILKENNY-P (1)
35 CHRIS ZACHARY-P
36 BILL GILBRETH-P
37 CHUCK SEELBACH-P
38 LES CAIN-P
38 WOODIE FRYMAN-P (2)
39 FRED SCHERMAN-P
40 JOHN GAMBLE-SS
42 WAYNE COMER-OF
42 JOE STATON-1B
43 MARVIN LANE-OF
44 BILL SLAYBACK-P
45 JIM FOOR-P
46 BOB STRAMPE-P
47 PHIL MEELER-P
48 DON LESHNOCK-P
50 ART FOWLER-CH
51 JOE (GERMANY) SCHULTZ-CH
52 CHARLIE (SWEDE) SILVERA-CH
53 DICK TRACEWSKI-CH

1973

3RD E 85-77 12GB

1 BILLY (THE KID) MARTIN-MGR1
3 DICK MCAULIFFE-2B/UTIL
4 AURELIO RODRIGUEZ-3B/SS
5 JIM NORTHRUP-OF/1B
6 AL KALINE-OF/1B
7 RICH REESE-1B/OF (1)
7 TOM VERYZER-SS
8 ED BRINKMAN-SS
9 IKE BROWN-UTIL
10 TONY TAYLOR-UTIL
11 BILL FREEHAN-C/UTIL
12 DUKE SIMS-C/OF (1)
14 BILL SLAYBACK-P
15 JOE COLEMAN-P
17 BOB MILLER-P (3)
18 JOHN HILLER-P
20 RICH REESE-1B/OF (1)
20 FRED HOLDSWORTH-P
21 MARVIN LANE-OF
22 RON CASH-OF/3B
23 WILLIE HORTON-OF/DH
24 MICKEY STANLEY-OF
25 NORM CASH-1B/DH
26 GATES BROWN-DH/OF
27 DICK SHARON-OF
28 TOM TIMMERMANN-P (1)
28 ED FARMER-P (2)
29 MICKEY LOLICH-P
30 LERRIN LAGROW (INJ)-P
31 JIM PERRY-P
33 FRANK (THE CAPITAL PUNISHER) (HONDO) HOWARD-DH/1B
34 MIKE STRAHLER-P
35 DAVE LEMANCZYK-P
36 BOB DIDIER-C
37 CHUCK SEELBACH (INJ)-P
38 WOODIE FRYMAN-P
39 FRED SCHERMAN-P
40 JOHN GAMBLE-PR
41 FRED HOLDSWORTH-P
42 JOE STATON-1B
44 JOHN KNOX-2B
45 GARY IGNASIAK-P
50 ART FOWLER-CH
51 JOE (GERMANY) SCHULTZ-CH/MGR2
52 CHARLIE (SWEDE) SILVERA-CH
52 COTTON (COT) DEAL-CH
53 DICK TRACEWSKI-CH

1974

6TH E 72-90 19GB

2 JOHN KNOX-INF/DH
3 GARY SUTHERLAND-2B/INF
4 AURELIO RODRIGUEZ-3B
5 JIM NORTHRUP-OF (1)
6 AL KALINE-DH
7 TOM VERYZER-SS
8 ED BRINKMAN-SS/3B
9 IKE BROWN-3B
10 GENE LAMONT-C
11 BILL FREEHAN-1B/UTIL
12 JERRY MOSES-C
14 BILL SLAYBACK-P
15 JOE COLEMAN-P
17 LUKE WALKER (INJ)-P
18 JOHN HILLER-P
19 DAVE LEMANCZYK-P
20 FRED HOLDSWORTH-P
21 MARVIN LANE-OF/DH
22 BEN OGLIVIE-UTIL
23 WILLIE HORTON (INJ)-OF/DH
24 MICKEY STANLEY (INJ)-OF/INF
25 NORM CASH-1B
26 GATES BROWN-DH
27 DICK SHARON-OF
28 JIM NETTLES-OF
29 MICKEY LOLICH-P
30 LERRIN LAGROW-P
31 VERN RUHLE-P
35 RALPH (MAJOR) HOUK-MGR
36 JIM (STING) RAY-P
37 CHUCK SEELBACH-P
37 DAN MEYER-OF
38 WOODIE FRYMAN-P
39 LEON ROBERTS-OF
40 RON CASH (ILL)-1B/3B
42 RON LEFLORE-OF
43 REGGIE SANDERS-1B/DH
44 LEON ROBERTS-OF
45 JOHN WOCKENFUSS-C
50 JIM HEGAN-CH
51 JOE (GERMANY) SCHULTZ-CH
52 COTTON (COT) DEAL-CH
53 DICK TRACEWSKI-CH

1975

6TH E 57-102 37.5GB

2 JOHN KNOX-INF/DH
3 GARY SUTHERLAND-2B
4 AURELIO RODRIGUEZ-3B
7 TOM VERYZER-SS
8 RON LEFLORE-OF
9 NATE COLBERT-1B/DH (1)
9 CHUCK SCRIVENER-3B/SS
10 GENE LAMONT-C
11 BILL FREEHAN-C/1B
15 JOE COLEMAN-P
16 GENE (STICK) MICHAEL-INF
18 JOHN HILLER (INJ)-P
19 DAVE LEMANCZYK (INJ)-P
21 RAY BARE-P
22 BEN OGLIVIE-OF/UTIL
23 WILLIE HORTON-DH
24 MICKEY STANLEY (INJ)-UTIL
25 DAN MEYER-OF/1B
26 GATES BROWN-PH
27 JACK PIERCE-1B
28 IKE BROOKENS-P
29 MICKEY LOLICH-P
30 LERRIN LAGROW-P
31 VERN RUHLE-P
32 TOM WALKER-P
34 BOB REYNOLDS-P (2)
34 BOB MOLINARO-OF
35 RALPH (MAJOR) HOUK-MGR
36 FERNANDO ARROYO-P
37 TOM MAKOWSKI-P
39 GENE PENTZ-P
40 JERRY MANUEL-2B
42 ART JAMES-OF
43 BILLY BALDWIN-OF/DH
44 LEON ROBERTS-OF/DH
45 JOHN WOCKENFUSS-C
47 TERRY HUMPHREY (INJ)-C
48 ED GLYNN-P
49 STEVE GRILLI-P
50 JIM HEGAN-CH
51 JOE (GERMANY) SCHULTZ-CH
52 STEVE HAMILTON-CH
53 DICK TRACEWSKI-CH

1976

5TH E 74-87 24GB

1 JERRY MANUEL-INF/DH
2 PHIL MANKOWSKI-3B
3 GARY SUTHERLAND-2B (1)
3 PETE GARCIA-2B (2)
4 AURELIO RODRIGUEZ (INJ)-3B
5 MARK WAGNER-SS
7 TOM VERYZER (INJ)-SS
8 RON LEFLORE-OF/DH
9 CHUCK SCRIVENER-INF
10 RUSTY STAUB-OF/DH
11 BILL FREEHAN-C/UTIL
12 MILT MAY (INJ)-C
15 JOE COLEMAN-P (1)
17 DAVE ROBERTS-P
18 JOHN HILLER (INJ)-P
19 DAVE LEMANCZYK (INJ)-P
20 MARK (THE BIRD) FIDRYCH-P
21 RAY BARE-P
22 BEN OGLIVIE-UTIL
23 WILLIE HORTON (INJ)-DH
24 MICKEY STANLEY-UTIL
25 DAN MEYER-UTIL
27 BILL LAXTON-P
28 JIM (CATFISH) CRAWFORD-P
29 FRANK MACCORMACK-P
30 JASON THOMPSON-1B
31 MARV LANE-OF
31 VERN RUHLE-P
33 ALEX JOHNSON-OF/DH
35 RALPH (MAJOR) HOUK-MGR
42 ART JAMES (INJ)-OF
45 JOHN WOCKENFUSS-C
46 BRUCE KIMM-C/DH
48 ED GLYNN-P
49 STEVE GRILLI-P
50 JIM HEGAN-CH
51 JOE (GERMANY) SCHULTZ-CH
52 FRED GLADDING-CH
53 DICK TRACEWSKI-CH
62 MARK (THE BIRD) FIDRYCH-P

1977

4TH E 74-88 26GB

2 PHIL MANKOWSKI-3B/2B
3 TITO FUENTES-2B/DH
4 AURELIO RODRIGUEZ (INJ)-3B/SS
5 MARK WAGNER-SS/2B
7 TOM VERYZER-SS
8 RON LEFLORE-OF
9 CHUCK SCRIVENER-INF
10 RUSTY STAUB-DH
11 BRUCE KIMM-C/DH
12 MILT MAY-C
13 LANCE PARRISH-C
14 JOHN WOCKENFUSS-UTIL
15 LUIS ALVARADO-3B (2)
17 DAVE ROBERTS-P (1)
18 JOHN HILLER-P
19 DAVE ROZEMA-P
20 MARK (THE BIRD) FIDRYCH (INJ)-P
21 RAY BARE-P
22 BEN OGLIVIE-OF/DH
23 WILLIE HORTON-OF (1)
24 MICKEY STANLEY-UTIL
25 TIM CORCORAN-OF/DH
27 BOB SYKES-P
28 JIM (CATFISH) CRAWFORD-P
29 STEVE FOUCAULT-P
30 JASON THOMPSON-1B
31 VERN RUHLE (INJ)-P
32 BRUCE TAYLOR-P
33 STEVE KEMP-OF
34 BOB MOLINARO-PH (1)
35 RALPH (MAJOR) HOUK-MGR
36 FERNANDO ARROYO-P
39 MILT WILCOX-P
40 BOB ADAMS-1B/C
42 ALAN TRAMMELL-SS/C
43 STEVE KEMP-OF
43 LOU WHITAKER-2B
44 TITO FUENTES-2B/DH
47 JACK MORRIS (INJ)-P
48 ED GLYNN-P
49 STEVE GRILLI-P
50 JIM HEGAN-CH
51 FRED HATFIELD-CH
52 FRED GLADDING-CH
53 DICK TRACEWSKI-CH

1978

5TH E 86-76 13.5GB

1 LOU WHITAKER-2B/DH
2 PHIL MANKOWSKI-3B
3 ALAN TRAMMELL-SS
4 AURELIO RODRIGUEZ-3B
5 MARK WAGNER-SS/2B
7 STEVE DILLARD-2B/DH
8 RON LEFLORE-OF
10 RUSTY STAUB-DH
12 MILT MAY-C
13 LANCE PARRISH-C
14 JOHN WOCKENFUSS-OF/DH
18 JOHN HILLER-P
19 DAVE ROZEMA-P
20 MARK (THE BIRD) FIDRYCH (INJ)-P
21 JIM SLATON-P
22 DAVE STEGMAN-OF
24 MICKEY STANLEY-OF/1B
25 TIM CORCORAN-OF/DH
26 GATES BROWN-CH
27 BOB SYKES (INJ)-P
28 JIM (CATFISH) CRAWFORD-P
29 STEVE FOUCAULT-P (1)
30 JASON THOMPSON-1B
31 STEVE BAKER-P
32 BRUCE TAYLOR-P
33 STEVE KEMP-OF
34 CHARLIE SPIKES-OF
35 RALPH (MAJOR) HOUK-MGR
36 FERNANDO ARROYO (INJ)-P
37 KIP YOUNG-P
38 DAVE TOBIK-P
39 MILT WILCOX-P
41 JACK BILLINGHAM-P
42 SHELDON BURNSIDE-P
44 KIP YOUNG-P
47 JACK MORRIS-P
48 ED GLYNN-P
49 STEVE GRILLI-P
50 JIM HEGAN-CH

DETROIT TIGERS

1 FRED HATFIELD-CH
2 FRED GLADDING-CH
3 DICK TRACEWSKI-CH

1979

5TH E 85-76 18GB

1 LOU WHITAKER-2B
2 PHIL MANKOWSKI (INJ)-3B/DH
3 ALAN TRAMMELL-SS
4 AURELIO RODRIGUEZ-3B/1B
5 MARK WAGNER-INF/DH
8 RON LEFLORE-OF/DH
9 DAVE MACHEMER-UTIL
0 RUSTY STAUB (H/O)-DH (1)
1 SPARKY (CAPT. HOOK) ANDERSON-MGR2
2 MILT MAY-C (1)
2 ED PUTNAM-C/1B
3 LANCE PARRISH-C
4 JOHN WOCKENFUSS-UTIL
6 TOM BROOKENS-INF/DH
8 JOHN HILLER (INJ)-P
9 DAVE ROZEMA (INJ)-P
0 MARK (THE BIRD) FIDRYCH (INJ)-P
1 AL GREENE-DH/OF
2 DAVE STEGMAN-OF
3 KIRK GIBSON-OF
4 CHAMP SUMMERS-UTIL (2)
5 TIM CORCORAN-UTIL
6 GATES BROWN-CH
7 JERRY MORALES-OF/DH
8 LES MOSS-MGR1
9 AURELIO LOPEZ-P
0 JASON THOMPSON-1B/DH
1 STEVE BAKER-P
2 BRUCE TAYLOR-P
2 RICKEY PETERS-UTIL
3 STEVE KEMP-OF/DH
4 DAN GONZALES-OF/DH
5 LYNN JONES-OF/DH
6 FERNANDO ARROYO-P
7 KIP YOUNG-P
8 DAVE TOBIK-P
9 MILT WILCOX-P
0 PAT UNDERWOOD-P
1 JACK BILLINGHAM-P
2 SHELDON BURNSIDE-P
3 MIKE CHRIS-P
6 DAN PETRY-P
7 JACK MORRIS-P
8 BRUCE ROBBINS-P
0 BILLY CONSOLO-CH
1 ED BRINKMAN-CH
2 JOHN (GROD) GRODZICKI-CH
3 DICK TRACEWSKI-CH
5 BOOTS DAY-CH

1980

5TH E 84-78 19GB

1 LOU WHITAKER-2B
2 RICHIE HEBNER (INJ)-1B/UTIL
3 ALAN TRAMMELL-SS
5 MARK WAGNER-INF
6 *(RET#) AL KALINE*
9 STAN PAPI-INF (2)
10 AL COWENS-OF/DH (2)
11 SPARKY (CAPT. HOOK) ANDERSON-MGR
13 LANCE PARRISH-C/UTIL
14 JOHN WOCKENFUSS-UTIL
15 DUFFY DYER-C/DH
16 TOM BROOKENS-INF/DH
18 JOHN HILLER (RET)-P
19 DAVE ROZEMA-P
20 MARK (THE BIRD) FIDRYCH-P
22 DAVE STEGMAN-OF/DH
23 KIRK GIBSON (INJ)-OF/DH
24 CHAMP SUMMERS-DH/UTIL
25 TIM CORCORAN-UTIL
26 GATES BROWN-CH
27 JIM LENTINE-OF/DH
28 JERRY UJDUR-P
29 AURELIO LOPEZ-P
30 JASON THOMPSON-1B (1)
32 RICKEY PETERS-OF/DH
33 STEVE KEMP-OF/DH
34 DAN GONZALES-OF/DH
35 LYNN JONES (INJ)-OF/DH
36 DAN SCHATZEDER-P
38 DAVE TOBIK-P
39 MILT WILCOX-P
40 PAT UNDERWOOD-P
41 JACK BILLINGHAM-P (1)
42 SHELDON BURNSIDE-P
44 ROGER WEAVER (INJ)-P
44 BRUCE ROBBINS-P
46 DAN PETRY-P
47 JACK MORRIS-P
48 BRUCE ROBBINS-P
48 ROGER WEAVER (INJ)-P
50 BILLY CONSOLO-CH
51 ALEX GRAMMAS-CH
52 ROGER CRAIG-CH
53 DICK TRACEWSKI-CH

1981

1ST 1/2:4TH E 31-26 3.5GB
2ND 1/2:2ND E (TIE) 29-23 1.5GB
FINAL: 60-49 --GB

1 LOU WHITAKER-2B
2 RICHIE HEBNER-1B/DH
3 ALAN TRAMMELL-SS
6 *(RET#) AL KALINE*
7 RICK LEACH-UTIL
9 STAN PAPI-UTIL
10 AL COWENS-OF
11 SPARKY (CAPT. HOOK) ANDERSON-MGR
12 MARTY CASTILLO-UTIL
13 LANCE PARRISH-C/DH
14 JOHN WOCKENFUSS-UTIL
15 DUFFY DYER-C
15 RON JACKSON-1B (2)
16 TOM BROOKENS-3B
17 BILL FAHEY (INJ)-C
18 MICK KELLEHER-INF
19 DAVE ROZEMA-P
21 DENNIS KINNEY-P
23 KIRK GIBSON-OF/DH
24 CHAMP SUMMERS-DH/OF
26 GATES BROWN-CH
28 JERRY UJDUR-P
29 AURELIO LOPEZ-P
31 KEVIN SAUCIER-P
32 RICKEY PETERS-OF/DH
33 STEVE KEMP-OF/DH
34 DARRELL BROWN-OF/DH
35 LYNN JONES (INJ)-OF/DH
36 DAN SCHATZEDER-P
38 ROGER CRAIG-CH
39 MILT WILCOX-P
41 GEORGE CAPUZZELLO-P
42 LARRY ROTHSCHILD-P
45 DAVE TOBIK-P
46 DAN PETRY-P
47 JACK MORRIS-P
49 DAVE RUCKER-P
50 BILLY CONSOLO-CH
51 ALEX GRAMMAS-CH
53 DICK TRACEWSKI-CH
60 HOWARD BAILEY-P

1982

4TH E 83-79 12GB

1 LOU WHITAKER-2B/DH
2 RICHIE HEBNER-1B/DH (1)
3 ALAN TRAMMELL-SS
4 MIKE LAGA-1B/DH
5 HOWARD JOHNSON-UTIL
6 *(RET#) AL KALINE*
7 RICK LEACH (INJ)-UTIL
11 SPARKY (CAPT. HOOK) ANDERSON-MGR
12 MARTY CASTILLO-C
12 GLENN WILSON-OF/DH
13 LANCE PARRISH-C/OF
14 JOHN WOCKENFUSS-UTIL
15 MIKE IVIE-DH (2)
16 TOM BROOKENS-3B/UTIL
17 BILL FAHEY (INJ)-C
18 MICK KELLEHER-2B/3B (1)
19 DAVE ROZEMA (INJ)-P
20 JERRY TURNER-P
21 ENOS CABELL-1B/UTIL
22 LARRY PASHNICK-P
23 KIRK GIBSON (INJ)-OF/DH
24 BOB JAMES-P (2)
25 MARK DEJOHN-INF
26 GATES BROWN-CH
27 ED MILLER-OF/DH
28 JERRY UJDUR-P
29 AURELIO LOPEZ (INJ)-P
31 KEVIN SAUCIER-P
31 LARRY HERNDON-OF/DH
(32) RICKEY PETERS (INJ)-(OF)
33 KEVIN SAUCIER-P
34 CHET LEMON-OF/DH
35 LYNN JONES-OF/DH
36 ELIAS SOSA-P
38 ROGER CRAIG-CH
39 MILT WILCOX-P
40 PAT UNDERWOOD-P
42 LARRY ROTHSCHILD-P
43 DAVE GUMPERT-P
44 JUAN BERENGUEZ-P
45 DAVE TOBIK-P
46 DAN PETRY-P
47 JACK MORRIS-P
49 DAVE RUCKER-P
50 BILLY CONSOLO-CH
51 ALEX GRAMMAS-CH
53 DICK TRACEWSKI-CH
60 HOWARD BAILEY-P

1983

2ND E 92-70 6GB

1 LOU WHITAKER-2B/DH
2 *(RET#) CHARLIE GEHRINGER*
3 ALAN TRAMMELL-SS
4 MIKE LAGA-DH/1B
5 *(RET#) HANK GREENBERG*
6 *(RET#) AL KALINE*
7 RICK LEACH (INJ)-UTIL
8 MARTY CASTILLO-3B/C
10 JULIO GONZALEZ-INF
11 SPARKY (CAPT. HOOK) ANDERSON-MGR
12 GLENN WILSON-OF
13 LANCE PARRISH-C/DH
14 JOHN WOCKENFUSS-UTIL
15 MIKE IVIE-1B
15 WAYNE KRENCHICKI-INF (2)
16 TOM BROOKENS-3B/UTIL
17 BILL FAHEY (INJ)-C
18 DAVE RUCKER-P (1)
18 BILL NAHORODNY-PH
19 DAVE ROZEMA-P
20 HOWARD JOHNSON-3B/DH
21 ENOS CABELL-1B/UTIL
22 LARRY PASHNICK-P
23 KIRK GIBSON-DH/OF
24 BOB JAMES-P (1)
24 GLENN ABBOTT-P (2)
25 SAL BUTERA-C
26 GATES BROWN-CH
28 JERRY UJDUR-P
29 AURELIO LOPEZ (INJ)-P
30 JOHNNY GRUBB (INJ)-OF/DH
31 LARRY HERNDON-OF/DH
33 JOHN MARTIN-P (2)
34 CHET LEMON-OF
35 LYNN JONES-OF/DH
37 BOB MOLINARO-DH (2)
38 ROGER CRAIG-CH
39 MILT WILCOX (INJ)-P
40 PAT UNDERWOOD-P
40 DOUG BAIR-P (2)
43 DAVE GUMPERT-P
44 JUAN BERENGUEZ-P
46 DAN PETRY-P
47 JACK MORRIS-P
49 DAVE RUCKER-P (1)
50 BILLY CONSOLO-CH
51 ALEX GRAMMAS-CH
53 DICK TRACEWSKI-CH
60 HOWARD BAILEY-P

1984

1ST E 104-58 0GB
W ALCS-KCA 3-0
W WS-SDN 4-1

1 LOU WHITAKER-2B
2 *(RET#) CHARLIE GEHRINGER*
3 ALAN TRAMMELL-SS/DH
4 MIKE LAGA-1B/DH
5 *(RET#) HANK GREENBERG*
6 *(RET#) AL KALINE*
8 MARTY CASTILLO-UTIL
9 DOUG BAKER-INF/DH
11 SPARKY (CAPT. HOOK) ANDERSON-MGR
12 ROD ALLEN-DH/OF
13 LANCE PARRISH-C/DH
14 DAVE BERGMAN-1B/OF
15 RUSTY KUNTZ-OF/DH
16 TOM BROOKENS-INF/DH
17 GLENN ABBOTT-P
17 BILL SCHERRER-P (2)
19 DAVE ROZEMA-P
20 HOWARD JOHNSON-3B/UTIL
21 WILLIE HERNANDEZ-P
23 KIRK GIBSON-OF/DH
24 SCOTT EARL-2B
24 GLENN ABBOTT-P
25 DWIGHT LOWRY-C
26 GATES BROWN-CH
27 BARBERO GARBEY-UTIL
28 CARL WILLIS-P (1)
29 AURELIO LOPEZ (INJ)-P
30 JOHNNY GRUBB-OF/DH
31 LARRY HERNDON-OF/DH
32 RUPPERT JONES-OF/DH
34 CHET LEMON-OF/DH
37 NELSON SIMMONS-OF/DH
38 ROGER CRAIG-CH
39 MILT WILCOX-P
40 DOUG BAIR-P
41 DARRELL EVANS-DH/INF
42 SID MONGE-P (2)
44 JUAN BERENGUEZ-P
46 DAN PETRY-P
47 JACK MORRIS-P
48 ROGER MASON-P
49 RANDY O'NEAL-P
50 BILLY CONSOLO-CH
51 ALEX GRAMMAS-CH
53 DICK TRACEWSKI-CH

1985

3RD E 84-77 15GB

1 LOU WHITAKER-2B
2 *(RET#) CHARLIE GEHRINGER*
3 ALAN TRAMMELL-SS
4 MIKE LAGA-DH/1B
5 *(RET#) HANK GREENBERG*
6 *(RET#) AL KALINE*
8 MARTY CASTILLO-C/3B
9 DOUG BAKER-SS/2B
11 SPARKY (CAPT. HOOK) ANDERSON-MGR
12 CHRIS PITTARO-INF/DH
13 LANCE PARRISH-C/DH
14 DAVE BERGMAN (INJ)-UTIL
15 RUSTY KUNTZ-DH/1B
16 TOM BROOKENS-3B/UTIL
17 BILL SCHERRER-P
18 BOB MELVIN-C
19 SCOTTI MADISON-DH/C
20 JIM WEAVER-DH/OF
20 DOUG FLYNN-INF (2)
21 WILLIE HERNANDEZ-P
23 KIRK GIBSON-OF/DH
26 FRANK TANANA-P (2)
27 BARBERO GARBEY-UTIL
29 AURELIO LOPEZ-P
30 JOHNNY GRUBB-DH/OF
31 LARRY HERNDON-OF
32 ALEX SANCHEZ-OF/DH
34 CHET LEMON-OF
35 WALT TERRELL-P
37 NELSON SIMMONS-OF/DH
39 MILT WILCOX (INJ)-P
40 DOUG BAIR-P (1)
41 DARRELL EVANS-1B/UTIL
42 MICKEY MAHLER-P (2)
43 CHUCK CARY-P
44 JUAN BERENGUEZ-P
46 DAN PETRY-P
47 JACK MORRIS-P
48 BOB STODDARD-P
49 RANDY O'NEAL-P
50 BILLY CONSOLO-CH
51 ALEX GRAMMAS-CH
52 BILLY (MUFF) MUFFETT-CH
53 DICK TRACEWSKI-CH
56 BILLY (MUFF) MUFFETT-CH

1986

3RD E 87-75 8.5GB

1 LOU WHITAKER-2B
2 *(RET#) CHARLIE GEHRINGER*
3 ALAN TRAMMELL-SS/DH
4 MIKE LAGA (INJ)-1B/DH (1)
5 *(RET#) HANK GREENBERG*
6 *(RET#) AL KALINE*
8 MIKE HEATH-C/3B (2)
9 DOUG BAKER-INF/DH
10 DAVE ENGLE (INJ)-UTIL
11 SPARKY (CAPT. HOOK) ANDERSON-MGR
12 DWIGHT LOWRY-UTIL
13 LANCE PARRISH (INJ)-C/DH
14 DAVE BERGMAN-UTIL
15 PAT SHERIDAN-OF/DH
16 TOM BROOKENS-UTIL
17 BILL SCHERRER-P
18 SCOTTI MADISON-3B/DH
19 DARNELL COLES-3B/UTIL
20 JIM SLATON-P (2)
21 WILLIE HERNANDEZ-P
23 KIRK GIBSON (INJ)-OF/DH
25 ERIC KING-P
26 FRANK TANANA-P
27 HARRY SPILMAN-UTIL (1)
27 JOHN PACELLA-P
28 VADA PINSON-CH
29 DAVE COLLINS-OF/DH
30 JOHNNY GRUBB (INJ)-DH/OF
31 LARRY HERNDON-OF/DH
32 BRIAN HARPER-UTIL
33 MATT NOKES-C
34 CHET LEMON-OF

35 WALT TERRELL-P
36 JACK LAZORKO-P
37 BRUCE FIELDS-OF/DH
38 TIM TOLMAN-UTIL
38 MARK THURMOND-P (2)
39 BILL CAMPBELL (INJ)-P
40 DAVE LAPOINT-P (1)
40 JIM SLATON-P (2)
40 MARK THURMOND-P (2)
41 DARRELL EVANS-1B/UTIL
43 CHUCK CARY-P
43 JOHN PACELLA-P
45 BRYAN KELLY-P
46 DAN PETRY (INJ)-P
47 JACK MORRIS-P
49 RANDY O'NEAL-P
50 BILLY CONSOLO-CH
51 ALEX GRAMMAS-CH
53 DICK TRACEWSKI-CH
56 BILLY (MUFF) MUFFETT-CH

1987

1ST E 98-64 0GB
L ALCS-MINA 4-1

1 LOU WHITAKER-2B
2 *(RET#) CHARLIE GEHRINGER*
3 ALAN TRAMMELL-SS
4 BILLY BEAN-OF
5 *(RET#) HANK GREENBERG*
6 *(RET#) AL KALINE*
7 ORLANDO MERCADO-C (1)
7 BILL (MAD DOG) MADLOCK-DH/INF (2)
8 MIKE HEATH-UTIL
9 DOUG BAKER-INF
9 JIM MORRISON-UTIL (2)
11 SPARKY (CAPT. HOOK) ANDERSON-MGR
12 DWIGHT LOWRY-C/1B
14 DAVE BERGMAN-UTIL
15 PAT SHERIDAN-OF
16 TOM BROOKENS-3B/INF
17 TERRY HARPER-DH/OF (1)
17 JIM MORRISON-UTIL (2)
19 DARNELL COLES (INJ)-UTIL (1)
19 DOYLE ALEXANDER-P (2)
21 WILLIE HERNANDEZ (INJ)-P
23 KIRK GIBSON (INJ)-OF/DH
24 ORLANDO MERCADO-C (1)
24 SCOTT LUSADER-OF/DH
25 ERIC KING-P
26 FRANK TANANA-P
27 DICKIE NOLES-P (2)
28 VADA PINSON-CH
30 JOHNNY GRUBB-UTIL
31 LARRY HERNDON-OF/DH
32 JIM WALEWANDER-INF/DH
33 MATT NOKES-C/UTIL
34 CHET LEMON-OF
35 WALT TERRELL-P
36 NATE SNELL-P
38 TIM TOLMAN-OF/DH
39 MIKE HENNEMAN-P
40 MARK THURMOND-P
41 DARRELL EVANS-1B/UTIL
42 MORRIS MADDEN-P
44 JEFF ROBINSON-P
45 BRYAN KELLY-P
46 DAN PETRY-P
47 JACK MORRIS-P
49 NATE SNELL-P
50 BILLY CONSOLO-CH
51 ALEX GRAMMAS-CH
53 DICK TRACEWSKI-CH
56 BILLY (MUFF) MUFFETT-CH

1988

2ND E 88-74 1GB

1 LOU WHITAKER-2B
2 *(RET#) CHARLIE GEHRINGER*
3 ALAN TRAMMELL-SS
4 BILLY BEAN-UTIL
5 *(RET#) HANK GREENBERG*
6 *(RET#) AL KALINE*
7 SCOTT LUSADER-DH/OF
8 MIKE HEATH-C/OF
9 RAY KNIGHT-UTIL
9 FRED LYNN-OF/DH (2)
11 SPARKY (CAPT. HOOK) ANDERSON-MGR
12 LUIS SALAZAR-UTIL
14 DAVE BERGMAN-1B/UTIL
15 PAT SHERIDAN-OF/DH
16 TOM BROOKENS-3B/INF
17 JIM MORRISON-UTIL (1)
17 DON HEINKLE (INJ)-P
19 DOYLE ALEXANDER-P
21 WILLIE HERNANDEZ-P
22 GARY PETTIS-OF/DH
22 RAY KNIGHT-UTIL
23 TOREY LOVULLO-2B/3B
24 SCOTT LUSADER-DH/OF
24 GARY PETTIS-OF/DH
25 ERIC KING-P
26 FRANK TANANA-P
27 MARK HUISMANN-P
28 VADA PINSON-CH
29 BILLY BEANE-OF
30 IVAN DEJESUS-SS
31 LARRY HERNDON-DH/OF
32 JIM WALEWANDER-UTIL
33 MATT NOKES-C/DH
34 CHET LEMON-OF
35 WALT TERRELL-P
36 MIKE TRUJILLO-P
39 MIKE HENNEMAN-P
40 DWAYNE MURPHY-DH
41 DARRELL EVANS-DH/1B
43 TED POWER-P (2)
44 JEFF ROBINSON (INJ)-P
47 JACK MORRIS-P
48 PAUL GIBSON-P
49 STEVE SEARCY-P
50 BILLY CONSOLO-CH
51 ALEX GRAMMAS-CH
53 DICK TRACEWSKI-CH
56 BILLY (MUFF) MUFFETT-CH

1989

7TH E 59-103 30GB

1 LOU WHITAKER-2B/DH
2 *(RET#) CHARLIE GEHRINGER*
3 ALAN TRAMMELL-SS/DH
4 BILLY BEAN-OF/1B (1)
5 *(RET#) HANK GREENBERG*
6 *(RET#) AL KALINE*
7 SCOTT LUSADER (INJ)-OF/DH
8 MIKE HEATH-C/UTIL
9 FRED LYNN-OF/DH
10 ROB RICHIE-OF/DH
11 SPARKY (CAPT. HOOK) ANDERSON-MGR
12 MIKE BRUMELY-UTIL
14 DAVE BERGMAN-1B/UTIL
15 PAT SHERIDAN-OF/DH (1)
15 TRACY JONES-OF/DH (2)
16 DAVID PALMER-P
16 BRIAN DUBOIS-P
17 AL PEDRIQUE-INF
18 RAMON PENA (INJ)-P
19 DOYLE ALEXANDER-P
20 DOUG STRANGE-INF/DH
21 WILLIE HERNANDEZ (INJ)-P
23 TOREY LOVULLO-1B/3B
24 GARY PETTIS (INJ)-OF
25 KENNY WILLIAMS (INJ)-OF/DH
26 FRANK TANANA-P
27 CHARLES HUDSON (INJ)-P
28 VADA PINSON-CH
30 KEITH MORELAND-DH/UTIL (1)
31 KEVIN RITZ-P
32 GARY WARD-UTIL (2)
33 MATT NOKES (INJ)-C/DH
34 CHET LEMON-OF/DH
35 CHRIS BROWN-3B
35 RICK SCHU-3B/UTIL (2)
36 FRANK WILLIAMS (INJ)-P
37 RANDY NOSEK-P
38 SHAWN HOLMAN-P
39 MIKE HENNEMAN-P
41 EDWIN NUNEZ-P
41 RANDY BOCKUS-P
42 DAVE BEARD-P
43 MIKE TRUJILLO-P
43 JEFF DATZ-C/DH
44 JEFF ROBINSON (INJ)-P
46 MIKE SCHWABE-P
47 JACK MORRIS (INJ)-P
48 PAUL GIBSON-P
49 STEVE SEARCY (INJ)-P
50 BILLY CONSOLO-CH
51 ALEX GRAMMAS-CH
52 MATT SINATRO-C
53 DICK TRACEWSKI-CH
55 BRAD HAVENS-P (2)
56 BILLY (MUFF) MUFFETT-CH

1990

3RD E 79-83 9GB

1 LOU WHITAKER-2B/DH
2 *(RET#) CHARLIE GEHRINGER*
3 ALAN TRAMMELL-SS/DH
4 TONY PHILLIPS-3B/UTIL
5 *(RET#) HANK GREENBERG*
6 *(RET#) AL KALINE*
7 SCOTT LUSADER-OF/DH
8 MIKE HEATH-C/UTIL
9 LARRY SHEETS-OF/DH
10 MARK SALAS-UTIL
11 SPARKY (CAPT. HOOK) ANDERSON-MGR
12 RICH ROWLAND-C/DH
12 ED ROMERO-3B/2B
14 DAVE BERGMAN-DH/UTIL
15 TRACY JONES-OF/DH (1)
15 LLOYD MOSEBY-OF/DH
16 BRIAN DUBOIS-P (1)
17 LLOYD MOSEBY-OF/DH
17 CLAY PARKER-P (2)
18 JOHNNY PAREDES-2B (1)
18 LANCE MCCULLERS (INJ)-P (2)
19 JERRY DON GLEATON-P
20 URBANO LUGO-P
21 DARNELL COLES-UTIL (2)
22 MILT CUYLER-OF
23 DAN PETRY (INJ)-P
24 TRAVIS FRYMAN-INF/DH
25 KENNY WILLIAMS-OF/DH (1)
25 JOHN SHELBY-OF/DH (2)
26 FRANK TANANA-P
28 VADA PINSON-CH
30 SCOTT ALDRED-P
31 KEVIN RITZ-P
32 GARY WARD-UTIL
33 MATT NOKES-DH/C (1)
33 JIM LINDEMAN-UTIL
34 CHET LEMON-OF/DH
35 SCOTT ALDRED-P
35 WALT TERRELL-P (2)
37 RANDY NOSEK-P
37 CLAY PARKER-P (2)
39 MIKE HENNEMAN-P
41 EDWIN NUNEZ (INJ)-P
43 STEVE WAPNICK-P
43 MATT KINZER (INJ)-P
44 JEFF ROBINSON (INJ)-P
45 CECIL (BIG DADDY) FIELDER-1B/DH
46 MIKE SCHWABE-P
47 JACK MORRIS-P
48 PAUL GIBSON-P
49 STEVE SEARCY-P
50 BILLY CONSOLO-CH
51 ALEX GRAMMAS-CH
53 DICK TRACEWSKI-CH
56 BILLY (MUFF) MUFFETT-CH

1991

2ND E (TIE) 84-78 7GB

1 LOU WHITAKER-2B/DH
2 *(RET#) CHARLIE GEHRINGER*
3 ALAN TRAMMELL (INJ)-SS/UTIL
4 TONY PHILLIPS-UTIL
5 *(RET#) HANK GREENBERG*
6 *(RET#) AL KALINE*
8 PETE (INKY) INCAVIGLIA-OF/DH
8 JOHN MOSES-OF
9 TONY BERNAZARD-2B/DH
9 SKEETER BARNES-UTIL
10 ANDY ALLANSON-UTIL
11 SPARKY (CAPT. HOOK) ANDERSON-MGR
12 RICH ROWLAND-C/DH
14 DAVE BERGMAN-UTIL
15 LLOYD MOSEBY-OF/DH
16 DAVE HAAS-P
17 LUIS DE LOS SANTOS-UTIL
19 JERRY DON GLEATON (INJ)-P
20 MICKEY TETTLETON-C/UTIL
21 SCOTT LIVINGSTONE-3B
22 MILT CUYLER-OF
23 MARK LEITER-P
24 TRAVIS FRYMAN-3B/SS
25 JOHN SHELBY-OF/DH
25 SHAWN HARE-OF/DH
26 FRANK TANANA-P
27 MARK SALAS-UTIL
28 VADA PINSON-CH
29 ROB DEER-OF/DH
29 PETE (INKY) INCAVIGLIA-OF/DH
29 MARK LEITER-P
30 SCOTT ALDRED-P
31 KEVIN RITZ-P
32 DAN GAKELER-P
34 JOHNNY PAREDES-UTIL
35 WALT TERRELL-P
36 BILL GULLICKSON-P
39 MIKE HENNEMAN (INJ)-P
41 RUSTY MEACHAM-P
42 MIKE DALTON-P
43 MIKE MUNOZ-P
44 ROB DEER-OF/DH
45 CECIL (BIG DADDY) FIELDER-1B/DH
46 DAN PETRY-P (1)
46 JOHN KIELY-P
48 PAUL GIBSON-P
49 STEVE SEARCY-P (1)
49 JEFF KAISER-P
50 BILLY CONSOLO-CH
51 ALEX GRAMMAS-CH
53 DICK TRACEWSKI-CH
55 JOHN CERUTTI-P
56 BILLY (MUFF) MUFFETT-CH
57 JIM DAVENPORT-CH
58 MARK LEITER-P

1992

6TH E 75-87 21GB

1 LOU WHITAKER-2B/DH
2 *(RET#) CHARLIE GEHRINGER*
3 ALAN TRAMMELL (INJ)-SS
4 TONY PHILLIPS-UTIL
5 *(RET#) HANK GREENBERG*
6 *(RET#) AL KALINE*
7 SCOTT LIVINGSTONE-3B
9 SKEETER BARNES-UTIL
10 SHAWN HARE-OF/1B
11 SPARKY (CAPT. HOOK) ANDERSON-MGR
12 RICH ROWLAND-UTIL
13 RICO BROGNA-1B/DH
14 DAVE BERGMAN-UTIL
15 MARK CARREON-OF/DH
16 DAVE HAAS-P
18 GARY PETTIS-OF (2)
19 CHAD KREUTER-C/DH
20 MICKEY TETTLETON-C/UTIL
22 MILT CUYLER-OF
23 MARK LEITER-P
24 TRAVIS FRYMAN-SS/3B
25 ERIC KING-P
25 SHAWN HARE-OF/1B
26 FRANK TANANA-P
27 KURT KNUDSEN-P
28 ROB DEER-OF/DH
30 SCOTT ALDRED-P
31 KEVIN RITZ-P
32 DAN GLADDEN-OF/DH
35 WALT TERRELL-P
36 BILL GULLICKSON-P
39 MIKE HENNEMAN-P
40 PHIL CLARK-OF/DH
42 BUDDY GROOM-P
43 MIKE MUNOZ-P
44 JOHN DOHERTY-P
45 CECIL (BIG DADDY) FIELDER-1B/DH
46 JOHN KIELY-P
48 LES LANCASTER-P
50 BILLY CONSOLO-CH
52 GENE ROOF-CH
53 DICK TRACEWSKI-CH
54 LARRY HERNDON-CH
56 BILLY (MUFF) MUFFETT-CH
59 DAN WHITMER-CH

1993

3RD E (TIE) 85-77 10GB

1 LOU WHITAKER-2B
2 *(RET#) CHARLIE GEHRINGER*
3 ALAN TRAMMELL (INJ)-UTIL
4 TONY PHILLIPS-OF/UTIL
5 *(RET#) HANK GREENBERG*
6 *(RET#) AL KALINE*
7 SCOTT LIVINGSTONE-3B/DH
9 SKEETER BARNES-UTIL
11 SPARKY (CAPT. HOOK) ANDERSON-MGR
12 RICH ROWLAND-C/DH
13 MARK LEITER (INJ)-P
15 GARY THURMAN-OF/DH
16 DAVE HAAS (INJ)-P
16 DAVID WELLS-P
18 DAVE HAAS (INJ)-P
19 CHAD KREUTER-C/UTIL
20 MICKEY TETTLETON-UTIL
21 MIKE MOORE-P
22 MILT CUYLER (INJ)-OF
23 KIRK GIBSON-DH/OF
24 TRAVIS FRYMAN-SS/3B
27 KURT KNUDSEN (INJ)-P
28 ROB DEER-OF/DH (1)
29 DANNY BAUTISTA-OF/DH
30 BILL KRUEGER (INJ)-P
31 LARRY HERNDON-CH
32 DAN GLADDEN (INJ)-OF/DH

DETROIT TIGERS

33 ERIC DAVIS-OF/DH (2)
34 GREG GOHR-P
35 CHRIS GOMEZ-UTIL
36 BILL GULLICKSON (INJ)-P
37 MARK GRATER-P
37 JOE BOEVER-P (2)
38 ROB MACDONALD-P
39 MIKE HENNEMAN-P
40 DAVE JOHNSON (INJ)-P
41 JOHN DESILVA-P (1)
42 BUDDY GROOM-P
43 MIKE MUNOZ-P (1)
43 SEAN BERGMAN-P
44 JOHN DOHERTY-P
45 CECIL (BIG DADDY) FIELDER-1B/DH
46 JOHN KIELY-P
46 MIKE GARDINER-P (2)
48 STORM DAVIS-P (2)
49 TOM BOLTON-P
50 BILLY CONSOLO-CH
52 GENE ROOF-CH
53 DICK TRACEWSKI-CH
56 BILLY (MUFF) MUFFETT-CH
59 DAN WHITMER-CH

1994

5TH E 53-62 18GB

STRIKE NO POST-SEASON

1 LOU WHITAKER-2B
2 *(RET#) CHARLIE GEHRINGER*
3 ALAN TRAMMELL-UTIL
4 TONY PHILLIPS-OF/UTIL
5 *(RET#) HANK GREENBERG*
6 *(RET#) AL KALINE*
7 SCOTT LIVINGSTONE-3B/DH/1B (1)
8 JUAN (SAMMY) SAMUEL-2B
9 SKEETER BARNES-1B
10 PHIL STIDHAM-P
11 SPARKY (CAPT. HOOK) ANDERSON-MGR
12 JOHN FLAHERTY-C
15 GREG CADARET-P
16 DAVID WELLS (INJ)-P
17 RICCARDO INGRAM-OF/PH
19 CHAD KREUTER-C/UTIL
20 MICKEY TETTLETON-C
21 MIKE MOORE-P
22 MILT CUYLER (INJ)-OF
23 KIRK GIBSON-DH/OF
24 TRAVIS FRYMAN-3B
27 KURT KNUDSEN-P
29 DANNY BAUTISTA (INJ)-OF/DH
30 BILL KRUEGER (WAIV)-P
31 LARRY HERNDON-CH
32 JOSE LIMA-P
33 ERIC DAVIS (INJ)-OF/DH
34 GREG GOHR (INJ)-P
35 CHRIS GOMEZ-SS
36 BILL GULLICKSON (INJ)-P
37 JOE BOEVER-P
38 GENE HARRIS (INJ)-P
39 MIKE HENNEMAN (INJ)-P
41 TIM BELCHER-P
42 BUDDY GROOM-P
43 SEAN BERGMAN-P
44 JOHN DOHERTY (INJ)-P
45 CECIL (BIG DADDY) FIELDER-1B/DH
46 MIKE GARDINER-P
48 STORM DAVIS-P
49 JUNIOR FELIX (INJ)-OF
52 GENE ROOF-CH
53 DICK TRACEWSKI-CH
56 BILLY (MUFF) MUFFETT-CH
59 DAN WHITMER-CH

1995

4TH E 60-84 26GB

144 GAME SEASON

1 LOU WHITAKER-2B
2 *(RET#) CHARLIE GEHRINGER*
3 ALAN TRAMMELL (INJ)-SS
4 BOBBY HIGGINSON-OF
5 *(RET#) HANK GREENBERG*
6 *(RET#) AL KALINE*
7 SHANNON PENN-2B
7 STEVE RODRIGUEZ-2B (2)
8 JUAN (SAMMY) SAMUEL-2B (1)
9 CHAD CURTIS-OF
10 SCOTT FLETCHER-INF
11 SPARKY (CAPT. HOOK) ANDERSON-MGR
12 JOHN FLAHERTY-C
13 TODD STEVENSON-OF
15 BRIAN MAXCY-P
16 DAVID WELLS-P
17 TONY CLARK-1B
18 RUDY PEMBERTON-OF/DH
19 FRANKLIN STUBBS-1B
20 DERRICK WHITE-1B
21 MIKE MOORE (WAIV)-P
22 MILT CUYLER (INJ)-OF
23 KIRK GIBSON (RET)-DH/OF
24 TRAVIS FRYMAN-3B
25 RON TINGLEY-C
26 BEN BLOMDAHL-P
27 PAT AHEARNE-P
27 MIKE MYERS-P
28 JOE HALL-OF
29 DANNY BAUTISTA-OF
30 SEAN WHITESIDE-P
31 LARRY HERNDON-CH
32 JOSE LIMA-P
33 MIKE CHRISTOPHER-P
34 GREG GOHR (INJ)-P
35 CHRIS GOMEZ-SS
36 C.J. NITKOWSKI-P
37 JOE BOEVER-P
38 KEVIN WICKANDER (INJ)-P
38 DWAYNE HENRY-P
39 MIKE HENNEMAN-P (1)
40 FELIPE LIRA-P
41 STEVE RODRIGUEZ-2B (2)
42 BUDDY GROOM-P (1)
42 PHIL NEVIN-OF/DH (2)
43 SEAN BERGMAN (INJ)-P
44 JOHN DOHERTY-P
45 CECIL (BIG DADDY) FIELDER-1B/DH
46 MIKE GARDINER (INJ/WAIV)-P
46 CLINT SODOWSKI-P
49 BRIAN BOHANON-P
51 RALPH TREUEL-CH
52 GENE ROOF-CH
53 DICK TRACEWSKI-CH
54 JEFF JONES-CH

1996

5TH E 53-109 39GB

2 *(RET#) CHARLIE GEHRINGER*
3 ALAN TRAMMELL (INJ)-SS
4 BOBBY HIGGINSON (INJ)-OF
5 *(RET#) HANK GREENBERG*
6 *(RET#) AL KALINE*
7 TIM HYERS-PH
7 BRAD AUSMUS-C (2)
8 MARK PARENT-C (1)
8 PHIL HIATT-DH
9 CHAD CURTIS-OF (1)
9 DAMION EASLEY-SS (2)
10 GLENN EZELL-CH
12 JOHN FLAHERTY-C (1)
12 PHIL NEVIN-OF
14 MARK LEWIS-2B
15 BRIAN MAXCY-P
15 DUANE SINGLETON-OF
15 ANDUJAR CEDENO-SS (2)
17 TONY CLARK-1B
18 FRED KENDALL-CH
19 RON OESTER-CH
20 EDDIE WILLIAMS-DH
21 MIKE C. WALKER-P
21 RUBEN SIERRA-OF/DH (2)
22 JUSTIN THOMPSON (INJ)-P
24 TRAVIS FRYMAN-3B
25 BUDDY BELL-MGR
26 BRIAN WILLIAMS-P
27 MIKE MYERS-P
28 OMAR OLIVARES (INJ)-P
29 DANNY BAUTISTA-OF
29 TODD VAN POPPEL-P (2)
30 MELVIN NIEVES (INJ)-OF
31 LARRY HERNDON-CH
32 JOSE LIMA-P
33 MIKE CHRISTOPHER-P
33 RAUL CASANOVAS (INJ)-DH/C
34 GREG GOHR (INJ)-P (1)
34 JOHN CUMMINGS-P (2)
35 CHRIS GOMEZ-SS (1)
36 CURTIS PRIDE (INJ)-DH
37 GREGG OLSON-P (1)
37 TREVOR MILLER-P
38 BOB SCANLAN-P (1)
38 BRIAN MOEHLER-P
39 KIMARA BARTEE-OF
40 FELIPE LIRA-P
41 FAUSTO CRUZ-PH
42 RANDY VERES-P
42 TOM URBANI-P (2)
42 SHANNON PENN-PH
43 RICHIE LEWIS (INJ)-P
43 JEFF MCCURRY-P
43 JOEY EISCHEN-P (2)
45 CECIL (BIG DADDY) FIELDER-1B (1)
46 CLINT SODOWSKI-P
48 C. J. NITKOWSKI-P
49 SCOTT ALDRED (WAIV)-P (1)
49 A.J. SAGER-P
51 RICHIE LEWIS (INJ)-P
52 JOHN FARRELL-P
54 JON MATLACK-CH
55 TERRY FRANCONA-CH
57 GREG KEAGLE-P
59 TODD VAN POPPEL-P (2)

1997

3RD E 79-83 19GB

2 *(RET#) CHARLIE GEHRINGER*
4 BOBBY HIGGINSON (INJ)-OF
5 *(RET#) HANK GREENBERG*
6 *(RET#) AL KALINE*
7 JODY REED-2B
8 MATT WALBECK (INJ)-C
9 DAMION EASLEY-2B
10 BRIAN JOHNSON-C (1)
10 MARCUS JENSEN-C (2)
12 PHIL NEVIN (INJ)-DH
13 PERRY HILL-CH
14 ORLANDO MILLER (INJ)-SS
15 LARRY PARRISH-CH
16 *(RET#) HAL NEWHOUSER*
17 TONY CLARK-1B
18 FRED KENDALL-CH
19 JOHN CUMMINGS-P
20 WILLIE BLAIR (INJ)-P
21 BRIAN HUNTER-OF
22 JUSTIN THOMPSON-P
24 TRAVIS FRYMAN-3B
25 BUDDY BELL-MGR
26 DOUG BROCAIL-P
27 MIKE MYERS-P
28 OMAR OLIVARES (INJ)-P (1)
28 SCOTT SANDERS-P (2)
29 VINCE (VINCENT VAN GO) COLEMAN-OF
29 FRANK CATALANOTTO-2B
30 MELVIN NIEVES (INJ)-OF
31 LARRY HERNDON-CH
32 DAN MICELI-P
33 RAUL CASANOVAS-DH/C
34 JUAN ENCARNACION-OF
35 RICK ADAIR-CH
36 CURTIS PRIDE-OF/DH (1)
37 DEIVI CRUZ-SS
38 BRIAN MOEHLER-P
39 KIMARA BARTEE-OF/DH
40 FELIPE LIRA-P (1)
41 BOB HAMELIN-DH
42 FERNANDO HERNANDEZ-P
43 BUBBA TRAMMELL-OF
43 JOE HALL-OF
44 JOE HALL-OF
44 BUBBA TRAMMELL-OF
46 KEVIN JARVIS-P (3)
48 JERRY WHITE-CH
49 A.J. SAGER-P
50 TIM PUGH (WAIV) P
52 JOSE BAUTISTA (REL)-P (1)
53 JIMMY HURST-OF
54 EDDIE GAILLARD-P
55 ROBERTO DURAN-P
57 GREG KEAGLE-P
58 GLENN DISHMAN-P
59 TODD JONES-P

1998

5TH C 65-97 24GB

2 *(RET#) CHARLIE GEHRINGER*
4 BOBBY HIGGINSON-OF
5 *(RET#) HANK GREENBERG*
6 *(RET#) AL KALINE*
7 JOE OLIVER (REL)-C (1)
8 DEIVI CRUZ (INJ)-SS
9 DAMION EASLEY-2B/SS
10 BIP ROBERTS (INJ)-DH/OF (1)
10 TOBY HARRAH-CH
12 KIMERA BARTEE (INJ)-OF
13 PERRY HILL-CH
14 BILLY RIPKEN (INJ)(WAIV)-INF
14 MATT ANDERSON-P
15 LARRY PARRISH-CH/MGR2
16 *(RET#) HAL NEWHOUSER*
17 TONY CLARK-1B
18 FRED KENDALL-CH
19 JOE RANDA-INF
20 PETE (INKY) INCAVIGLIA (WAIV)-DH (1)
20 JEFF MANTO-1B/OF/DH (2)
20 GABE ALVAREZ-3B/DH
21 BRIAN L. HUNTER-OF
22 JUSTIN THOMPSON-P
25 BUDDY BELL-MGR1
26 DOUG BROCAIL (INJ)-P
27 SCOTT SANDERS-P (1)
27 FRANK CATALANOTTO-2B/INF
28 LUIS GONZALEZ-OF
29 FRANK CATALANOTTO-2B/INF
29 GERONIMO BERROA-DH/OF (2)
30 ANDY TOMBERLIN-DH/OF
30 JOE SIDDALL-C
31 LARRY HERNDON-CH
32 PAUL BAKO-C
33 RAUL CASANOVA (INJ)-DH/C
34 JUAN ENCARNACION (INJ)-OF
35 RICK ADAIR-CH
36 TIM WORRELL-P (1)
36 BRIAN POWELL-P
37 PETE (INKY) INCAVIGILIA (WAIV)-DH (1)
37 TREY BEAMON (INJ)-DH
38 BRIAN MOEHLER-P
39 BRYCE FLORIE (INJ)-P
41 SETH GREISINGER-P
41 DENNY HARRIGER-P
41 ROB FICK-C
42 *(RET#) JACKIE ROBINSON*
43 JASON WOOD-SS/INF (2)
44 SEAN RUNYAN-P
45 DOUG BOCHTLER-P
46 FRANK CASTILLO (INJ)-P
48 JERRY WHITE-CH
49 A.J. SAGER-P
50 SETH GREISINGER-P
51 MATT ANDERSON-P
51 GABE KAPLER-OF
(52) JOHN ROSENGREN (INJ)-(P)
52 MARINO SANTANA-P
54 JEFF JONES-CH
55 ROBERTO DURAN (INJ)-P
56 DEAN CROW-P
57 GREG KEAGLE-P
58 WILL BRUNSON-P (2)
59 TODD JONES-P

1999

3RD C 69-92 27.5GB

2 *(RET#) CHARLIE GEHRINGER*
3 ALAN TRAMMELL-CH
4 BOBBY HIGGINSON (INJ)-OF
5 *(RET#) HANK GREENBERG*
6 *(RET#) AL KALINE*
7 DEAN PALMER-3B
8 DEIVI CRUZ-SS
9 DAMION EASLEY-2B/SS
10 JUAN (SAMMY) SAMUEL-CH
12 BRAD AUSMUS-C
13 LANCE PARRISH-CH
14 MATT ANDERSON-P
15 LARRY PARRISH-MGR
16 *(RET#) HAL NEWHOUSER*
17 TONY CLARK-1B
18 KIMERA BARTEE-OF
19 PERRY HILL-CH
20 WILLIE BLAIR-P
21 BRIAN L. HUNTER-OF (1)
21 GREGG JEFFERIES-OF
22 JUSTIN THOMPSON-P
23 GABE KAPLER-OF
24 KARIM GARCIA-OF
25 GREGG JEFFERIES-OF
25 GABE ALVAREZ-DH
26 DOUG BROCAIL-P
27 FRANK CATALANOTTO-2B/INF
29 KARIM GARCIA-OF
29 LUIS POLONIA-OF
30 DAVE MLICKI-P (2)
31 ROB FICK (INJ)-C
31 DAN WARTHEN-CH
32 JASON WOOD (INJ)-INF
33 RAUL CASANOVAS (INJ)-DH/C
34 JUAN ENCARNACION-OF
35 RICK ADAIR-CH
35 ERIK HILJUS-P
36 JEFF WEAVER-P
37 BILL HASELMAN-C
38 BRIAN MOEHLER (SUS-10D)-P
39 BRYCE FLORIE (INJ)-P (1)

39 ROB FICK (INJ)-C
40 FELIPE LIRA-P
40 NELSON CRUZ-P
41 MASAO KIDA (INJ)-P
42 *(RET#) JACKIE ROBINSON*
43 FRANCISCO CORDERO-P
44 SEAN RUNYAN (INJ)-P
45 DAVE BORKOWSKI-P
46 LUIS GARCIA-INF
46 LUIS POLONIA-OF
48 JOSE MACIAS-2B
49 C. J. NITKOWSKI-P
(50) SETH GREISINGER (INJ)-(P)
51 MEL ROJAS (WAIV)-P (2)
52 BEIKER GRATEROL-P
54 JEFF JONES-CH
55 ERIK HILJUS-P
58 WILL BRUNSON-P
58 WILLIS ROBERTS-P
59 TODD JONES-P

2000

3RD C 79-83 16GB

2 *(RET#) CHARLIE GEHRINGER*
4 BOBBY HIGGINSON-OF
5 *(RET#) HANK GREENBERG*
6 *(RET#) AL KALINE*
7 DEAN PALMER-3B
8 DEIVI CRUZ-SS
9 DAMION EASLEY-2B/SS
10 JUAN (SAMMY) SAMUEL-CH
12 BRAD AUSMUS-C
13 LANCE PARRISH-CH
14 MATT ANDERSON-P
15 BOB MELVIN-CH
16 *(RET#) HAL NEWHOUSER*
17 SHANE HALTER-INF
18 ROB FICK (INJ)-INF
19 JUAN GONZALEZ-OF (2)
20 WILLIE BLAIR-P
21 GREGG JEFFERIES (INJ)-OF
22 LUIS POLONIA-DH (1)
22 DUSTY ALLEN-INF (2)
23 HIDEO NOMO-P
23 *(RET#) WILLIE HORTON*
24 KARIM GARCIA-OF (1)
24 RICH BECKER-OF (2)
25 GABE ALVAREZ-DH (1)
25 HAL MORRIS-1B (2)
26 DOUG BROCAIL-P
27 C. J. NITKOWSKI-P
28 DANNY PATTERSON (INJ)-P
29 WENDELL MAGEE-OF
30 DAVE MLICKI (INJ)-P
31 DAN WARTHEN-CH
32 DOUG MANSOLINO-CH
33 PHIL GARNER-MGR
34 JUAN ENCARNACION-OF
35 ERIC MUNSON-1B
36 JEFF WEAVER-P
37 JIM R. POOLE-P (1)
37 STEVE W. SPARKS-P
38 BRIAN MOEHLER
39 SHANE HALTER-INF
39 JOSE MACIAS-INF
40 NELSON CRUZ-P
41 MASAO KIDA-P
41 ERIK HILJUS-P
42 *(RET#) JACKIE ROBINSON*
43 BILLY MCMILLON-OF
44 TONY CLARK (INJ)-1B
45 DAVE BORKOWSKI-P
46 MARK J. JOHNSON-P
48 BILL MADLOCK-CH
49 ALLEN MCDILL-P
49 ADAM BERNERO-P
49 SEAN RUNYAN-P
(50) SETH GREISINGER (INJ)-(P)
52 KEVIN TOLAR-P
53 JAVIER CARDONA-C
54 RODNEY LINDSEY-OF
55 SEAN RUNYAN-P
56 BRANDON VILLAFUERTE-P
57 ERIC DUBOSE-P
59 TODD JONES-P
66 ANTHONY CHAVEZ-P
67 TILSON BRITO-INF
74 BILLY MCMILLON-OF

2001

3RD C 66-96 25GB

2 *(RET#) CHARLIE GEHRINGER*
4 BOBBY HIGGINSON (INJ)-OF
5 *(RET#) HANK GREENBERG*
6 *(RET#) AL KALINE*
7 DEAN PALMER (INJ)-3B
8 DEIVI CRUZ (INJ)-SS
9 DAMION EASLEY-2B/SS
10 JUAN (SAMMY) SAMUEL-CH
12 BRANDON INGE (INJ)-C
13 LANCE PARRISH-CH
14 MATT ANDERSON-P
15? BOB MELVIN-CH
15 JAVIER CARDONA-C
16 *(RET#) HAL NEWHOUSER*
17 SHANE HALTER-INF
18 ROB FICK-INF
18 HEATH MURRAY, P
19 ROGER CEDENO-OF
20 RYAN JACKSON-1B
(21) MITCH MELUSKEY (INJ)-(C)
22 VICTOR SANTOS-P
23 *(RET#) WILLIE HORTON*
24 JERMAINE CLARK (WAIV)-INF
24 WILLIE BLAIR-P
24 NATE CORNEJO-P
25 ROB FICK (SUS)-INF/C
26 ADAM BERNERO-P
27 C. J. NITKOWSKI-P
28 DANNY PATTERSON
29 WENDELL MAGEE (INJ)-OF
30 DAVE MLICKI (INJ)-P (1)
30 LUIS PINEDA-P
31 DAN WARTHEN-CH
32 DOUG MANSOLINO-CH
33 PHIL GARNER-MGR
34 JUAN ENCARNACION-OF
35 HEATH MURRAY-P
35 RANDALL SIMON-1B
36 JEFF WEAVER-P
37 STEVE W. SPARKS-P
38 BRIAN MOEHLER (INJ)-P
39 JOSE MACIAS-INF
40 MATT PERISHO (INJ)-P
41 CHRIS HOLT-P
42 *(RET#) JACKIE ROBINSON*
42 JOSE LIMA-P (2)
43 BILLY MCMILLON (WAIV)-DH
43 JARROD PATTERSON-3B
43 CHRIS WAKELAND-OF
44 TONY CLARK-1B
45 DAVE BORKOWSKI (INJ)-P
48 BILL MADLOCK-CH
49 PEDRO SANTANA-2B
49 MIKE RIVERA-C
(50) SETH GREISINGER (INJ)-(P)
50 ERIC MUNSON-C
52 KEVIN TOLAR-P
53 JAVIER CARDONA-C
55 MARK REDMAN (INJ)-P (2)
56 ED OTT-CH
57 MATT MILLER-P
57 ADAM PETTYJOHN-P
58 RYAN JACKSON-1B
58 MATT MILLER-P
59 TODD JONES-P (1)

2002

5TH C 55-106 39GB

2 *(RET#) CHARLIE GEHRINGER*
4 BOBBY HIGGINSON (INJ)-OF/DH
5 *(RET#) HANK GREENBERG*
6 *(RET#) AL KALINE*
7 DEAN PALMER (INJ)-DH
8 CRAIG PAQUETTE-UTIL
9 DAMION EASLEY (INJ)-2B
10 JUAN (SAMMY) SAMUEL-CH
12 DAMIAN JACKSON-UTIL
14 MATT ANDERSON (INJ)-P
15 BRANDON INGE-UTIL
16 *(RET#) HAL NEWHOUSER*
17 SHANE HALTER-UTIL
18 FELIPE ALOU-CH
19 MARV RETTENMUND-CH
20 RYAN JACKSON-1B
20 OMAR INFANTE-SS/2B
21 MITCH MELUSKEY (INJ)-C
21 CRAIG MONROE-OF/DH
22 JOSE PANIAGUA-P
22 HIRAM BOCACHICA-OF/UTIL (2)
23 *(RET#) WILLIE HORTON*
24 ADAM BERNERO-P
25 ROB FICK-OF/1B
26 DMITRI YOUNG (INJ)-UTIL
27 ADAM PETTIJOHN-P
27 CHRIS TRUBY-3B (2)
28 DANNY PATTERSON (INJ)-P
29 WENDELL MAGEE-OF/DH
30 KRIS KELLER-P
30 GEORGE LOMBARD-OF/DH (2)
31 DAN WARTHEN-CH
31 JASON BEVERLIN-P (2)
32 JAMIE WALKER-P
33 PHIL GARNER-MGR1
33 ERIC MUNSON-DH/1B
34 NATE CORNEJO-P
35 RANDALL SIMON (INJ)-DH/1B
36 JEFF WEAVER-P (1)
37 STEVE W. SPARKS-P
38 BRIAN MOEHLER (INJ)-P (1)
39 JOSE MACIAS-INF (1)
39 RAMON SANTIAGO (INJ)-SS
40 MATT PERISHO-P
40 OSCAR SALAZAR-INF
40 BRIAN POWELL-P
41 OSCAR HENRIQUEZ (INJ)-P
42 JOSE LIMA-P
43 CARLOS PENA-1B/DH (2)
44 JACOB CRUZ (INJ)-UTIL
44 ANDRES TORRES-OF
45 TERRY PEARSON-P
45 MATT WALBECK-C
46 MIKE MAROTH-P
48 JULIO SANTANA (INJ)-P
49 MIKE RIVERA-C/DH
50 SETH GREISINGER (INJ)-P
50 ANDY VAN HEKKEN-P
52 JEFF FARNSWORTH-P
53 LUIS PUJOLS-MGR2 (2)
54 STEVE MCCATTY-CH
55 MARK REDMAN-P
56 FERNANDO RODNEY-P
57 JUAN ACEVEDO-P
58 MATT MILLER (INJ)-P
58 ERIK SABEL-P
58 SHANE LOUX-P
61 ERIC ECKENSTAHLER-P
62 FRANKLYN GERMAN-P
63 JASON JIMENEZ-P (2)

2003

5TH C 43-119 47GB

2 *(RET#) CHARLIE GEHRINGER*
3 ALAN TRAMMEL-MGR
4 BOBBY HIGGINSON (SUS:2G)-OF/DH
5 *(RET#) HANK GREENBERG*
6 *(RET#) AL KALINE*
7 DEAN PALMER (INJ)-DH
8 MATT WALBECK-C
10 JUAN (SAMMY) SAMUEL-CH
12 CARLOS PENA (INJ)-1B
13 LANCE PARRISH-CH
14 MATT ANDERSON-P
15 BRANDON INGE-C
16 *(RET#) HAL NEWHOUSER*
17 SHANE HALTER-UTIL
18 MICK KELLEHER-CH
19 ALEX SANCHEZ-OF (2)
20 OMAR INFANTE-SS/INF
21 CRAIG PAQUETTE (REL)-1B/OF
21 KEVIN WITT-DH/UTIL
22 KIRK GIBSON-CH
23 *(RET#) WILLIE HORTON*
24 ADAM BERNERO-P (1)
24 WARREN MORRIS-2B
25 DMITRI YOUNG-DH/OF/3B
26 HIRAM BOCACHICA-OF
26 CODY ROSS (INJ)-OF
27 CRAIG MONROE-OF/DH
28 DANNY PATTERSON (INJ)-P
29 BRUCE FIELDS-CH
30 ERNIE YOUNG-DH
30 BEN PETRICK-OF/C (2)
31 ERIC MUNSON (INJ)-3B
32 JAMIE WALKER-P
33 STEVE AVERY-P
34 NATE CORNEJO-P
35 GARY KNOTTS-P
36 ERIC ECKENSTAHLER-P
37 STEVE W. SPARKS-P (1)
38 JEREMY BONDERMAN-P
39 RAMON SANTIAGO-SS/2B
40 A. J. HINCH (INJ)-C
41 WILFREDO LEDEZMA-P
42 *(RET#) JACKIE ROBINSON*
43 EUGENE KINGSALE (INJ)-OF
44 ANDRES TORRES-OF
45 CHRIS MEARS-P
46 MIKE MAROTH-P
48 CHRIS SPURLING-P
49 DANNY KLASSEN-INF
50 RAFAEL LANDESTOY-CH
52 MATT RONEY-P
53 BRIAN SCHMACK-P
54 BOB CLUCK-CH
56 FERNANDO RODNEY-P
58 SHANE LOUX-P
59 NATE ROBERTSON-P
62 FRANKLYN GERMAN-P

2004

4TH C 72-90 20GB

2 *(RET#) CHARLIE GEHRINGER*
3 ALAN TRAMMEL-MGR
4 BOBBY HIGGINSON-OF
5 *(RET#) HANK GREENBERG*
6 *(RET#) AL KALINE*
7 IVAN (PUDGE) RODRIGUEZ-C
8 JUAN (SAMMY) SAMUEL-CH
9 CARLOS GUILLEN-SS
10 JUAN (SAMMY) SAMUEL-CH
10 FERNANDO VINA (INJ)-2B
12 CARLOS PENA-1B
13 LANCE PARRISH-CH
14 MATT ANDERSON-P
15 BRANDON INGE (INJ)-C
16 *(RET#) HAL NEWHOUSER*
17 DANNY PATTERSON-P
18 MICK KELLEHER-CH
19 ALEX SANCHEZ (INJ)-OF
20 OMAR INFANTE-3B
21 JASON JOHNSON-P
22 KIRK GIBSON-CH
23 *(RET#) WILLIE HORTON*
24 RONDELL WHITE-DH/OF
25 DMITRI YOUNG (INJ)-DH/OF
26 MIKE DIFELICE-C (1)
26 GRANDERSON, CURTIS-OF
27 CRAIG MONROE (INJ)-OF/DH
28 GREG NORTON-DH/3B
29 BRUCE FIELDS-CH
30 CHRIS SHELTON-C
31 ERIC MUNSON-3B
32 JAMIE WALKER-P
33 MARCUS THAMES-OF
34 NATE CORNEJO (INJ)-P
35 GARY KNOTTS (INJ)-P
37 NATE ROBERTSON-P
38 JEREMY BONDERMAN-P
40 NOOK LOGAN-OF
41 WILFREDO LEDEZMA-P
42 *(RET#) JACKIE ROBINSON*
43 AL LEVINE-P
44 ANDRES TORRES-OF
44 JASON SMITH-SS
45 LINO URDANETA (INJ)-P
46 MIKE MAROTH-P
(48) CHRIS SPURLING-(P)
49 JOHN ENNIS-P
51 ROBERTO NOVOA-P
51 STEVE COLYER-P
54 BOB CLUCK-CH
55 RYAN RABURN-3B
(56) FERNANDO RODNEY (INJ)-(P)
57 CRAIG DINGMAN-P
59 ESTEBAN YAN-P
62 FRANKLYN GERMAN-P
74 UGUETH URBINA-P

2005

4TH C 71-91 28GB

2 *(RET#) CHARLIE GEHRINGER*
3 ALAN TRAMMEL-MGR
4 BOBBY HIGGINSON-OF
5 *(RET#) HANK GREENBERG*
6 *(RET#) AL KALINE*
7 IVAN (PUDGE) RODRIGUEZ-C
8 JUAN (SAMMY) SAMUEL-CH
9 CARLOS GUILLEN (INJ)-SS
(10) FERNANDO VINA (INJ)-(2B
12 CARLOS PENA-1B
13 LANCE PARRISH-CH
14 RAMON MARTINEZ (INJ)-SS (1)
14 PLACIDO POLANCO (INJ)-2B (2)
15 BRANDON INGE-3B/C
16 *(RET#) HAL NEWHOUSER*
17 JASON SMITH-INF
18 MICK KELLEHER-CH
19 NOOK LOGAN-OF
20 OMAR INFANTE-2B
21 JASON JOHNSON-P
22 KIRK GIBSON-CH
23 *(RET#) WILLIE HORTON*
24 RONDELL WHITE (INJ)-DH/OF
25 DMITRI YOUNG-DH
26 VANCE WILSON-C
27 CRAIG MONROE-OF
28 CURTIS GRANDERSON-OF
29 BRUCE FIELDS-CH
30 MAGGLIO ORDONEZ (INJ)-OF
31 CHRIS SHELTON-1B
32 JAMIE WALKER-P

DETROIT TIGERS

33 MARCUS THAMES-OF
34 MATT GINTER-P
36 JOHN MCDONALD-INF (2)
37 NATE ROBERTSON-P
38 JEREMY BONDERMAN (SUS:5G)-P
39 TONY GIARRATANO-SS
39 JASON KARNUTH-P
40 TROY PERCIVAL (INJ)-P
41 WILFREDO LEDEZMA-P
42 *(RET#) JACKIE ROBINSON*
43 ALEXIS GOMEZ-OF
43 ROMAN COLON-P (2)
44 KYLE FARNSWORTH (SUS:5G)-P (1)
46 MIKE MAROTH-P
48 CHRIS SPURLING-P
49 KEVIN HOOPER-2B
49 JASON GRILLLI-P
50 MARK WOODYARD-P
50 ANDREW GOOD-P
51 VIC DARENSBOURG-P
52 DOUG CREEK-P
53 SEAN DOUGLASS-P
54 BOB CLUCK-CH
56 FERNANDO RODNEY (INJ)-P
57 CRAIG DINGMAN-P
59 JUSTIN VERLANDER-P
62 FRANKLYN GERMAN-P
74 UGUETH URBINA-P (1)

Cecil Fielder gave the Tiger fans something to holler about in the early '90s. Just back from a year in Japan, Big Daddy was hammering the ball. He hit 51 home runs in 1990, and again led the league in '91 with 44. He averaged over 30 per year for the next four seasons. He led the league in RBIs the first three years that he wore a Tiger uniform. He became attached to his number 45 and sought it out when he joined the Yankees and Angels later on.

KANSAS CITY ROYALS

1969
KANSAS CITY ROYALS
4TH W 69-93 28GB

1 JOE FOY-3B/UTIL
2 JO-JO WHITE-CH
3 MEL (CHIEF) HARDER-CH
4 HARRY DUNLOP-CH
5 OWEN (RED) FRIEND-CH
6 JOE (FLASH) GORDON-MGR
7 CHUCK HARRISON-1B
8 ED KIRKPATRICK-UTIL
9 LOU (SWEET LOU) PINIELLA-OF
10 PAUL SCHAAL-INF
11 ELLIE RODRIGUEZ-C
12 JUAN RIOS-INF
13 JIM ROOKER-P
14 JERRY ADAIR-2B/INF
15 BILLY HARRIS-2B
16 JOE KEOUGH-OF/1B
17 DAVE (MOE) MOREHEAD-P
18 PAT KELLY-OF
19 MIKE FIORE-1B/OF
20 JIM CAMPANIS-C
21 BUCK MARTINEZ (SCH)-C/OF
22 JIM ROOKER-P
23 DON O'RILEY-P
24 JACKIE HERNANDEZ-SS
25 MOE DRABOWSKY-P
26 GALEN CISCO-P
27 WALLY BUNKER-P
28 DENNIS PAEPKE-C
29 BILL BUTLER-P
30 GEORGE SPRIGGS-OF
31 HAWK TAYLOR-OF/C
32 MIKE (RED) HEDLUND-P
33 BOB OLIVER-OF/INF
34 TOM (BUGS) BURGMEIER-P
35 ROGER (SPIDER) NELSON-P
36 CHARLIE METRO-CH
37 STEVE JONES-P
38 BILLY HARRIS-2B
38 JERRY CRAM-P
39 LUIS ALCARAZ-INF
40 DAVE WICKERSHAM-P
40 CHRIS ZACHARY-P
41 DICK DRAGO-P
42 CHRIS ZACHARY-P
42 AL FITZMORRIS-P
44 SCOTT NORTHEY-OF
45 FRAN HEALY-C
46 FRED RICO-OF/3B

1970
4TH W (TIE) 65-97 33GB

1 LUIS ALCARAZ-2B
1 COOKIE ROJAS-2B (2)
2 BOB LEMON-CH/MGR2
3 JOE (DODE) SCHULTZ-CH
4 HARRY DUNLOP-CH
5 DANNY CARNEVALE-CH
6 GEORGE SPRIGGS-OF
6 BUCK MARTINEZ (MIL)-C
6 BOBBY FLOYD-SS/3B (2)
7 BILL SORRELL-UTIL
8 ED KIRKPATRICK-C/UTIL
9 LOU (SWEET LOU) PINIELLA-OF/1B
10 PAUL SCHAAL-3B/INF
11 ELLIE RODRIGUEZ-C
12 GEORGE SPRIGGS-OF
13 JIM ROOKER-P
14 JERRY ADAIR-2B
14 GEORGE (BO) STRICKLAND-CH
15 RICH SEVERSON-SS/2B
16 JOE KEOUGH (INJ)-OF/1B
17 DAVE (MOE) MOREHEAD-P
18 PAT KELLY-OF
19 MIKE FIORE-1B (1)
19 TOM MATCHICK-INF (2)
20 JIM CAMPANIS-C/OF
20 JIM YORK-P
21 AURELIO MONTEAGUDO-P
22 TOM (BUGS) BURGMEIER-P
23 AL FITZMORRIS-P
24 JACKIE HERNANDEZ-SS
25 MOE DRABOWSKY-P (1)
26 AMOS OTIS-OF
27 WALLY BUNKER (INJ)-P
28 KEN WRIGHT-P
29 BILL BUTLER-P
30 BOB JOHNSON-P
31 HAWK TAYLOR-C/1B
32 MIKE (RED) HEDLUND (ILL)-P
32 DON O'RILEY-P
33 BOB OLIVER-1B/3B
34 PAUL SPLITTORFF-P
35 ROGER (SPIDER) NELSON (INJ)-P
36 CHARLIE METRO-MGR1
36 TED ABERNATHY-P (3)
41 DICK DRAGO-P
48 KEN WRIGHT-P

1971
2ND W 85-76 16GB

1 COOKIE ROJAS (INJ)-2B/INF
2 FREDDIE PATEK-SS
3 GALEN CISCO-CH
4 HARRY DUNLOP-CH
5 GEORGE (BO) STRICKLAND-CH
5 BOBBY FLOYD-INF
5 TED SAVAGE-OF (2)
5 SANDY VALDESPINO-OF
6 BUCK MARTINEZ-C
7 CHUCK HARRISON-1B
7 TED SAVAGE-OF (2)
8 ED KIRKPATRICK-OF/C
9 LOU (SWEET LOU) PINIELLA (INJ)-OF
10 PAUL SCHAAL-3B
11 GEORGE (BO) STRICKLAND-CH
12 JERRY MAY (INJ)-C
14 JIM ROOKER-P
15 RICH SEVERSON-INF
15 BOBBY FLOYD-INF
16 JOE KEOUGH-OF
17 DENNIS PAEPKE-C/OF
18 GAIL HOPKINS-1B
19 BOBBY KNOOP-2B/3B
20 MONTY MONTGOMERY-P
21 BOB LEMON-MGR
22 TOM (BUGS) BURGMEIER-P
23 AL FITZMORRIS-P
24 CHARLIE LAU-CH
25 LANCE CLEMONS-P
25 MIKE MCCORMICK-P
25 PAUL SPLITTORFF-P
26 AMOS OTIS-OF
27 WALLY BUNKER-P
27 LANCE CLEMONS-P
28 KEN WRIGHT (INJ)-P
29 BILL BUTLER (INJ)-P
32 MIKE (RED) HEDLUND-P
33 BOB OLIVER-UTIL
34 PAUL SPLITTORFF-P
35 ROGER (SPIDER) NELSON-P
36 TED ABERNATHY-P
37 FREDDIE PATEK-SS
40 JIM YORK-P
41 DICK DRAGO-P
43 BRUCE DAL CANTON-P
44 CARL TAYLOR-OF (2)

1972
4TH W 76-78 16.5GB

1 COOKIE ROJAS (INJ)-2B/INF
2 RON HANSEN-INF
3 GALEN CISCO-CH
4 HARRY DUNLOP-CH
5 RICHIE SCHEINBLUM-OF
6 JIM WOHLFORD-2B
7 JOHN MAYBERRY-1B
8 ED KIRKPATRICK-C/1B
9 LOU (SWEET LOU) PINIELLA-OF
10 PAUL SCHAAL-3B/SS
11 GEORGE (BO) STRICKLAND-CH
12 JERRY MAY-C
14 CARL TAYLOR-UTIL
15 BOBBY FLOYD-INF
15 MIKE JACKSON-P
16 JOE KEOUGH-OF
17 DENNIS PAEPKE-C/OF
18 GAIL HOPKINS-1B/3B
19 BOBBY KNOOP-2B/3B
20 MONTY MONTGOMERY-P
21 BOB LEMON-MGR
22 TOM (BUGS) BURGMEIER-P
23 AL FITZMORRIS-P
24 CHARLIE LAU-CH
25 JIM ROOKER-P
25 MIKE JACKSON-P
26 AMOS OTIS-OF
28 KEN WRIGHT-P
29 TOM MURPHY-P (2)
30 STEVE HOVLEY-OF
32 MIKE (RED) HEDLUND-P
33 BOB OLIVER-OF (1)
34 PAUL SPLITTORFF-P
35 ROGER (SPIDER) NELSON (INJ)-P
36 TED ABERNATHY-P
37 FREDDIE PATEK-SS
38 ROGER (SPIDER) NELSON (INJ)-P
39 NORM ANGELINI-P
40 STEVE BUSBY-P
41 DICK DRAGO-P
43 BRUCE DAL CANTON-P

1973
2ND W 88-74 6GB

1 COOKIE ROJAS-2B
2 KURT BEVACQUA-UTIL
3 GALEN CISCO-CH
4 HARRY DUNLOP-CH
5 TOM POQUETTE-OF
6 JIM WOHLFORD-DH/OF
7 JOHN MAYBERRY-1B/DH
8 ED KIRKPATRICK-OF/UTIL
9 LOU (SWEET LOU) PINIELLA-OF/DH
10 PAUL SCHAAL-3B
11 HAL MCRAE-DH/UTIL
12 JERRY MAY-C (1)
12 RICH REICHARDT-DH/OF (2)
14 CARL TAYLOR-UTIL
15 BOBBY FLOYD-2B/SS
16 FRAN HEALY-C/DH
17 FRANK ORTENZIO-OF
18 GAIL HOPKINS-DH/1B
19 FRANK WHITE-SS/2B
20 BARRY RAZIANO-P
22 TOM (BUGS) BURGMEIER-P
22 MARK LITTELL-P
23 AL FITZMORRIS-P
23 STEVE MINGORI-P (2)
24 CHARLIE LAU-CH
25 MIKE JACKSON-P (1)
25 GEORGE BRETT-3B
26 AMOS OTIS-OF/DH
27 MARK LITTELL-P
27 JOE HOERNER-P (2)
28 KEN WRIGHT-P
29 DOUG BIRD-P
30 STEVE HOVLEY-OF/DH
31 JACK MCKEON-MGR
32 GENE GARBER-P
33 STEVE MINGORI-P (2)
34 PAUL SPLITTORFF-P
37 FREDDIE PATEK-SS
39 NORM ANGELINI-P
39 AL FITZMORRIS-P
40 STEVE BUSBY-P
41 DICK DRAGO-P
42 KEITH MARSHALL-OF
42 BUCK MARTINEZ-C
43 BRUCE DAL CANTON-P
44 TOM POQUETTE-OF
45 WAYNE SIMPSON-P

1974
5TH W 77-85 13GB

1 COOKIE ROJAS-2B
2 KURT BEVACQUA-UTIL
3 GALEN CISCO-CH
4 HARRY DUNLOP-CH
5 RICHIE SCHEINBLUM-DH/OF (2)
6 JIM WOHLFORD-OF/DH
7 JOHN MAYBERRY-1B/DH
8 TONY SOLAITA-UTIL
10 PAUL SCHAAL-3B (1)
11 HAL MCRAE-DH/UTIL
13 FERNANDO GONZALEZ-3B/DH (1)
15 BOBBY FLOYD-INF
16 FRAN HEALY-C
17 DENNIS PAEPKE-C/OF
18 AL COWENS-OF/UTIL
19 NELSON (NELLIE) BRILES (INJ)-P
20 FRANK WHITE-INF/DH
21 BUCK MARTINEZ-C
22 DENNIS LEONARD-P
23 STEVE MINGORI-P
24 CHARLIE LAU-CH
25 GEORGE BRETT-3B/SS
26 AMOS OTIS-OF/DH
27 JOE HOERNER-P
28 VADA PINSON-OF/UTIL
29 DOUG BIRD-P
30 RICHIE SCHEINBLUM-DH/OF (2)
30 ORLANDO (BABY BULL) CEPEDA-DH
31 JACK MCKEON-MGR
32 GENE GARBER-P (1)
33 MARTY PATTIN-P
34 PAUL SPLITTORFF-P
37 FREDDIE PATEK-SS
38 AURELIO LOPEZ-P
39 AL FITZMORRIS-P
40 STEVE BUSBY-P
41 LINDY MCDANIEL-P
43 BRUCE DAL CANTON-P
48 RICH REICHARDT-PH

1975
2ND W 91-71 7GB

1 COOKIE ROJAS-2B/DH
2 FREDDIE PATEK-SS/DH
3 HARMON (KILLER) KILLEBREW-DH/1B
4 HARRY DUNLOP-CH
5 GEORGE BRETT-3B/SS
6 JIM WOHLFORD-OF/DH
7 JOHN MAYBERRY-1B/DH
8 TONY SOLAITA-DH/1B
9 GALEN CISCO-CH
9 JAMIE QUIRK-UTIL
10 BOB MCCLURE-P
11 HAL MCRAE-OF/UTIL
12 GARY MARTZ-OF
14 STEVE BOROS-CH
15 BOB STINSON-UTIL
16 FRAN HEALY (INJ)-C/DH
17 MARK LITTELL-P
18 AL COWENS-OF/DH
19 NELSON (NELLIE) BRILES (INJ)-P
20 FRANK WHITE-UTIL
21 BUCK MARTINEZ-C
22 DENNIS LEONARD-P
23 STEVE MINGORI (ILL)-P
24 WHITEY HERZOG-MGR2
25 RODNEY SCOTT-DH/INF
26 AMOS OTIS-OF
27 CHARLIE LAU-CH
28 VADA PINSON-OF/UTIL
29 DOUG BIRD-P
30 JAMIE QUIRK-UTIL
31 JACK MCKEON-MGR1
33 MARTY PATTIN-P
34 PAUL SPLITTORFF-P
35 GEORGE THROOP-P
36 GALEN CISCO-CH
37 FREDDIE PATEK-SS/DH
39 AL FITZMORRIS-P
40 STEVE BUSBY-P
41 LINDY MCDANIEL (ILL)-P
42 GEORGE THROOP-P
43 BRUCE DAL CANTON-P (1)
43 RAY SADECKI-P (3)
44 RODNEY SCOTT-DH/INF

1976
1ST W 90-72 0GB
L ALCS-NYA 3-2

1 COOKIE ROJAS-UTIL
2 FREDDIE PATEK-SS/DH
3 DAVE NELSON-INF/DH
4 CHUCK HILLER-CH
5 GEORGE BRETT-3B/SS
6 JIM WOHLFORD-OF/UTIL
7 JOHN MAYBERRY-1B/DH
8 TONY SOLAITA-DH/1B
9 JAMIE QUIRK-DH/INF
10 TOMMY DAVIS-DH (2)
11 HAL MCRAE-DH/OF
12 JOHN WATHAN (INJ)-C/1B
14 STEVE BOROS-CH
15 BOB STINSON-C
16 FRAN HEALY (INJ)-DH (1)
16 ANDY HASSLER-P (2)
17 MARK LITTELL-P
18 AL COWENS-OF/DH
19 WILLIE WILSON-OF
20 FRANK WHITE-2B/SS
21 BUCK MARTINEZ-C
22 DENNIS LEONARD-P
23 STEVE MINGORI-P
24 WHITEY HERZOG-MGR
25 TOM POQUETTE-OF/DH
26 AMOS OTIS-OF
27 CHARLIE LAU-CH
28 KEN (DAFFY) SANDERS-P (2)
29 DOUG BIRD-P
30 RUPPERT JONES-OF/DH
31 TOM BRUNO-P
32 BOB MCCLURE-P
33 MARTY PATTIN-P
34 PAUL SPLITTORFF (INJ)-P
34 ROGER (SPIDER) NELSON-P
35 TOM BRUNO-P
36 GALEN CISCO-CH
37 RAY SADECKI (REL)-P (1)
37 LARRY GURA-P
39 AL FITZMORRIS-P
40 STEVE BUSBY (INJ)-P

KANSAS CITY ROYALS

42 TOM HALL-P (2)
43 ANDY HASSLER-P (2)
49 JERRY CRAM-P

1977
1st W 102-60 0GB
L ALCS-NYA 3-2

1 COOKIE ROJAS-INF/DH
2 FREDDIE PATEK-SS
3 DAVE NELSON (INJ)-2B/DH
4 CHUCK HILLER-CH
5 GEORGE BRETT-3B/UTIL
6 BOB HEISE-INF
7 JOHN MAYBERRY-1B/DH
8 PETE LACOCK-DH/1B
9 CLINT HURDLE-OF
10 CLINT HURDLE-OF
10 JOE LAHOUD-OF/DH
11 HAL MCRAE-DH/OF
12 JOHN WATHAN-UTIL
14 STEVE BOROS-CH
15 DARRELL PORTER-C/DH
16 ANDY HASSLER (INJ)-P
17 MARK LITTELL-P
18 AL COWENS-OF/DH
19 WILLIE WILSON-OF/DH
19 JOE ZDEB-UTIL
20 FRANK WHITE-2B/SS
21 BUCK MARTINEZ-C
22 DENNIS LEONARD-P
23 STEVE MINGORI-P
24 WHITEY HERZOG-MGR
25 TOM POQUETTE-OF
26 AMOS OTIS-OF
27 CHARLIE LAU-CH
29 DOUG BIRD-P
30 U. L. WASHINGTON-SS
31 RANDY MCGILBERRY-P
32 WILLIE WILSON-OF/DH
33 MARTY PATTIN-P
34 PAUL SPLITTORFF-P
35 JOE LAHOUD-OF/DH
35 GEORGE THROOP-P
36 GALEN CISCO-CH
37 LARRY GURA-P
39 GARY LANCE-P
(40) STEVE BUSBY (INJ)-(P)
42 TOM HALL-P
48 JIM COLBORN-P

1978
1st W 92-70 0GB
L ALCS-NYA 3-1

1 JERRY TERRELL-INF
2 FREDDIE PATEK-SS
3 STEVE BRAUN-OF/3B (2)
4 CHUCK HILLER-CH
5 GEORGE BRETT-3B/SS
6 WILLIE WILSON-OF/DH
7 RANDY BASS-PH
8 PETE LACOCK-1B
9 CLINT HURDLE-OF/UTIL
10 JOE LAHOUD-OF/DH
10 JAMIE QUIRK-3B/SS
11 HAL MCRAE-DH/OF
12 JOHN WATHAN-UTIL
14 STEVE BOROS-CH
15 DARRELL PORTER-C/DH
16 ANDY HASSLER (INJ)-P (1)
16 STEVE FOUCAULT-P (2)
17 RANDY MCGILBERRY-P
17 LUIS SILVERIO-OF/DH
18 AL COWENS (INJ)-OF/UTIL
19 JOE ZDEB-UTIL
20 FRANK WHITE-2B
21 ART KUSNYER-C
22 DENNIS LEONARD-P
23 STEVE MINGORI-P
24 WHITEY HERZOG-MGR
25 TOM POQUETTE-OF/DH
26 AMOS OTIS-OF/DH
27 CHARLIE LAU-CH
28 RANDY MCGILBERRY-P
29 DOUG BIRD-P
30 U. L. WASHINGTON-INF/DH
31 RANDY MCGILBERRY-P
31 DAVE CRIPE-3B
32 LARRY GURA-P
33 MARTY PATTIN-P
34 PAUL SPLITTORFF-P
35 GEORGE THROOP-P
36 GALEN CISCO-CH
37 LARRY GURA-P
37 JIM GAUDET-C
38 RICH GALE-P
39 AL (THE MAD HUNGARIAN) HRABOSKY-P
40 STEVE BUSBY (INJ)-P
40 STEVE FOUCAULT-P (2)
43 BILL PASCHALL-P
48 JIM COLBORN-P (1)

1979
2nd W 85-77 3GB

0 GEORGE SCOTT-UTIL (2)
1 JERRY TERRELL (INJ)-UTIL/P
2 FREDDIE PATEK (INJ)-SS
3 STEVE BRAUN (INJ)-UTIL
4 CHUCK HILLER-CH
5 GEORGE BRETT-3B/UTIL
6 WILLIE WILSON-OF/DH
7 TODD CRUZ-SS/3B
8 PETE LACOCK-1B/DH
9 CLINT HURDLE-UTIL
9 JAMIE QUIRK-UTIL
10 JAMIE QUIRK-UTIL
10 CLINT HURDLE-UTIL
11 HAL MCRAE-DH
12 JOHN WATHAN-UTIL
13 JIM GAUDET-C
14 STEVE BOROS-CH
15 DARRELL PORTER-C/DH
16 JOHN SULLIVAN-CH
18 AL COWENS-OF/DH
19 JOE ZDEB-OF
20 FRANK WHITE (INJ)-2B
21 ED RODRIGUEZ (INJ)-P
22 DENNIS LEONARD (INJ)-P
23 STEVE MINGORI (INJ)-P
24 WHITEY HERZOG-MGR
25 TOM POQUETTE-OF (1)
25 CRAIG CHAMBERLAIN-P
26 AMOS OTIS-OF/DH
27 RENIE MARTIN-P
28 JIM NETTLES-DH/1B
29 DAN (QUIZ) QUISENBERRY-P
30 U. L. WASHINGTON-INF/DH
31 GARY CHRISTENSON-P
32 LARRY GURA-P
33 MARTY PATTIN (INJ)-P
34 PAUL SPLITTORFF-P
35 GEORGE THROOP-P (1)
35 CRAIG EATON-P
36 GALEN CISCO-CH
37 JIM GAUDET-C
38 RICH GALE-P
39 AL (THE MAD HUNGARIAN) HRABOSKY-P
40 STEVE BUSBY-P
42 BILL PASCHALL-P
43 GERMAN BARRANCA-UTIL

1980
1st W 97-65 0GB
W ALCS-NYA 3-0
L WS-PHIN 4-2

1* JERRY TERRELL-UTIL/P*
2 RUSTY TORRES-OF/DH
2 ONIX CONCEPCION-SS
3 STEVE BRAUN-OF/DH (1)
4 BOBBY DETHERAGE-OF
5 GEORGE BRETT (INJ)-3B/1B
6 WILLIE WILSON-OF
7 DAVE CHALK-INF/DH
8 PETE LACOCK-1B/OF
9 JAMIE QUIRK-UTIL
10 CLINT HURDLE-OF
11 HAL MCRAE-DH/OF
12 JOHN WATHAN-UTIL
15 DARRELL PORTER (ILL)-C/DH
18 RANCE MULLINIKS-SS/2B
19 MANNY CASTILLO-SS
19 JOSE CARDENAL-OF (2)
20 FRANK WHITE-2B
21 JEFF TWITTY-P
22 DENNIS LEONARD-P
23 GERMAN BARRANCA-PR
24 WILLIE MAYS AIKENS-1B/DH
25 KEN BRETT-P
25 CRAIG CHAMBERLAIN-P
26 AMOS OTIS-OF
27 RENIE MARTIN-P
28 BILL CONNORS-CH
28 MIKE JONES-P
29 DAN (QUIZ) QUISENBERRY-P
30 U. L. WASHINGTON-SS
31 GARY CHRISTENSON-P
32 LARRY GURA-P
33 MARTY PATTIN-P
34 PAUL SPLITTORFF-P
35 RAWLY EASTWICK-P
36 BILL CONNORS-CH
38 RICH GALE-P
40 STEVE BUSBY-P
41 JIM FREY-MGR
42 JOSE MARTINEZ-CH
43 GORDY MACKENZIE-CH
44 JIMMIE SCHAFFER-CH
50 MIKE JONES-P
52 KEN PHELPS-1B
53 ONIX CONCEPCION-SS
54 JEFF TWITTY-P

1981
1st 1/2:5th W 20-30 12GB
2nd 1/2:2nd E 30-23 0GB
FINAL: 50-53 --GB
L ALDS-OAKA 3-0

2 ONIX CONCEPCION-SS
4 DARRYL MOTLEY-OF
5 GEORGE BRETT-3B
6 WILLIE WILSON-OF
7 DAVE CHALK-INF
9 JAMIE QUIRK-UTIL
10 CLINT HURDLE (INJ)-OF
11 HAL MCRAE-DH/OF
12 JOHN WATHAN-C/UTIL
14 LEE MAY-1B/DH
15 JERRY GROTE-C (1)
16 KEN PHELPS-DH/1B
17 TIM IRELAND-1B
18 RANCE MULLINIKS-INF
20 FRANK WHITE-2B
21 DICK HOWSER-MGR2
22 DENNIS LEONARD-P
23 CESAR GERONIMO-OF
24 WILLIE MAYS AIKENS-1B
25 KEN BRETT-P
26 AMOS OTIS-OF/DH
27 RENIE MARTIN-P
28 BILL PASCHALL-P
29 DAN (QUIZ) QUISENBERRY-P
30 U. L. WASHINGTON-SS
31 JEFF SCHATTINGER-P
32 LARRY GURA-P
33 TIM IRELAND-1B
33 ATLEE HAMMAKER-P
34 PAUL SPLITTORFF-P
35 JIM WRIGHT-P
36 BILL CONNORS-CH
37 JUAN BERENGUER-P (1)
37 PAT SHERIDAN-OF
38 RICH GALE-P
39 GREG KEATLEY-C
40 MIKE JONES-P
41 JIM FREY-MGR1
42 JOSE MARTINEZ-CH
43 GORDY MACKENZIE-CH
44 JIMMIE SCHAFFER-CH
45 DANNY GARCIA-OF/1B
46 RICK RENICK-CH
50 JIM WRIGHT-P
52 KEN PHELPS-DH/1B
53 JUAN BERENGUER-P (1)
53 ONIX CONCEPCION-SS

1982
2nd W 90-72 0GB

2 ONIX CONCEPCION-INF/DH
3 TOM POQUETTE-OF
4 GREG PRYOR-INF
5 GEORGE BRETT-3B/OF
6 WILLIE WILSON (INJ)-OF
7 DON SLAUGHT-C
8 ROCKY COLAVITO-CH
9 JAMIE QUIRK (INJ)-UTIL
10 DICK HOWSER-MGR
11 HAL MCRAE-DH/OF
12 JOHN WATHAN (INJ)-C/1B
14 LEE MAY-1B/DH
15 TIM IRELAND (INJ)-UTIL
16 DENNIS WERTH-1B/C
(17) MIKE JONES (INJ-AUTO)-(P)
20 FRANK WHITE-2B
21 KEITH CREEL-P
22 DENNIS LEONARD (INJ)-P
23 CESAR GERONIMO (INJ)-OF/DH
24 WILLIE MAYS AIKENS-1B
25 JERRY MARTIN-OF/DH
26 AMOS OTIS-OF
27 STEVE HAMMOND-OF/DH
27 BOB TUFTS-P
28 DAVE FROST (INJ)-P
29 DAN (QUIZ) QUISENBERRY-P
30 U. L. WASHINGTON (INJ)-SS/DH
31 MIKE ARMSTRONG-P
32 LARRY GURA-P
33 VIDA BLUE-P
34 PAUL SPLITTORFF-P
35 JIM WRIGHT-P
35 RON JOHNSON-1B
36 GRANT (BUCK) JACKSON-P (1)
36 BOB TUFTS-P
37 DEREK BOTELHO-P
37 BOMBO RIVERA-OF
(38) SCOTT BROWN (INJ)-(P)
39 BILL CASTRO-P
40 BUD BLACK-P
41 JOE NOSSEK-CH
42 JOSE MARTINEZ-CH
43 CLOYD (JUNIOR) BOYER-CH
44 JIMMIE SCHAFFER-CH
45 KELLY HEATH-2B
46 BUDDY BIANCALANA-SS
48 DON HOOD-P
49 DEREK BOTELHO-P
57 MARK RYAL-OF

1983
2nd W 79-83 20GB

1 BUDDY BIANCALANA-SS
2 ONIX CONCEPCION-INF/DH
3 CLIFF PASTORNICKY-3B
4 GREG PRYOR-INF
5 GEORGE BRETT-3B/UTIL
6 WILLIE WILSON (INJ)-OF
7 DON SLAUGHT-C/DH
8 ROCKY COLAVITO-CH
9* JOE SIMPSON-UTIL/P*
10 DICK HOWSER-MGR
11 HAL MCRAE-DH
12 JOHN WATHAN (INJ)-C/UTIL
14 VIDA BLUE-P
14 DARRYL MOTLEY-OF/DH
15 PAT SHERIDAN-OF
16 LEON ROBERTS-OF/DH
(17) MIKE JONES (INJ-AUTO)-(P)
18 STEVE RENKO-P
19 FRANK WILLS-P
20 FRANK WHITE-2B
21 KEITH CREEL-P
22 DENNIS LEONARD (INJ)-P
23 CESAR GERONIMO (INJ)-OF
24 WILLIE MAYS AIKENS-1B/DH
25 JERRY MARTIN (INJ)-OF
26 AMOS OTIS-OF/DH
28 ERIC RASMUSSEN-P (2)
29 DAN (QUIZ) QUISENBERRY-P
30 U. L. WASHINGTON-SS/DH
31 MIKE ARMSTRONG-P
32 LARRY GURA-P
33 VIDA BLUE-P
33 BUTCH DAVIS-OF
34 PAUL SPLITTORFF-P
35 RON JOHNSON-1B/C
36 BOB TUFTS-P
36 GAYLORD PERRY-P (2)
38 MARK HUISMANN-P
39 BILL CASTRO-P
40 BUD BLACK-P
41 JOE NOSSEK-CH
42 JOSE MARTINEZ-CH
43 CLOYD (JUNIOR) BOYER-CH
44 JIMMIE SCHAFFER-CH
45 DANNY JACKSON-P
48 DON HOOD-P

1984
1st W 84-78 0GB

1 BUDDY BIANCALANA-INF/DH
2 ONIX CONCEPCION (INJ)-SS/INF
3 JORGE ORTA-DH/UTIL
4 GREG PRYOR-INF/DH
5 GEORGE BRETT (INJ)-3B
6 WILLIE WILSON (SUB)-OF
7 DON SLAUGHT-C/DH
9 DANE IORG-UTIL (2)
10 DICK HOWSER-MGR
11 HAL MCRAE-DH
12 JOHN WATHAN-UTIL
14 LEE MAY-CH
15 PAT SHERIDAN-OF
16 LEON ROBERTS (INJ)-UTIL/P
17 MIKE JONES-P
18 STEVE BALBONI-1B/DH
19 FRANK WILLS-P
20 FRANK WHITE (INJ)-2B
21 BUCKY DENT-SS/3B
(22) DENNIS LEONARD (INJ)-(P)
23 MARK GUBICZA-P
24 DARRYL MOTLEY-OF
25 DANNY JACKSON-P
27 JOE BECKWITH-P
29 DAN (QUIZ) QUISENBERRY-P

30 U. L. WASHINGTON (INJ)-SS
31 BRET SABERHAGEN-P
32 LARRY GURA-P
33 BUTCH DAVIS-OF/DH
34 PAUL SPLITTORFF-P
35 LYNN JONES (INJ)-OF
37 TUCKER ASHFORD3B
37 CHARLIE LEIBRANDT-P
38 MARK HUISMANN-P
40 BUD BLACK-P
41 MIKE FERRARO-CH
42 JOSE MARTINEZ-CH
43 GARY BLAYLOCK-CH
44 JIMMIE SCHAFFER-CH
45 DANNY JACKSON-P
46 HOWIE BODELL-CH
49 ORLANDO SANCHEZ-C (1)
49 LUIS PUJOLS-C
50 JIM SCRANTON-SS/3B
58 DAVE LEEPER-OF/DH

1985

1st W 91-71 0GB
W ALCS-TORA 4-3
W WS-STLN 4-3

1 BUDDY BIANCALANA-INF/DH
2 ONIX CONCEPCION (INJ)-SS/2B
3 JORGE ORTA-DH
4 GREG PRYOR-INF/DH
5 GEORGE BRETT (INJ)-3B/DH
6 WILLIE WILSON-OF
8 JIM SUNDBERG-C
9 DANE IORG (INJ)-UTIL
10 DICK HOWSER-MGR
11 HAL MCRAE-DH
12 JOHN WATHAN-UTIL
14 LEE MAY-CH
15 PAT SHERIDAN (INJ)-OF/DH
16 JIM SCRANTON-SS/3B
17 MIKE JONES-P
18 JAMIE QUIRK-C/1B
20 FRANK WHITE-2B
21 LONNIE SMITH-OF (2)
22 DENNIS LEONARD (INJ)-P
23 MARK GUBICZA-P
24 DARRYL MOTLEY-OF/DH
25 DANNY JACKSON-P
26 STEVE FARR-P
27 JOE BECKWITH-P
28 OMAR MORENO-OF (2)
29 DAN (QUIZ) QUISENBERRY-P
30 MIKE LACOSS-P
31 BRET SABERHAGEN-P
32 LARRY GURA-P (1)
35 LYNN JONES-OF/DH
36 DAVE LEEPER-DH
37 CHARLIE LEIBRANDT-P
38 MARK HUISMANN-P
40 BUD BLACK-P
41 MIKE FERRARO-CH
42 JOSE MARTINEZ-CH
43 GARY BLAYLOCK-CH
44 JIMMIE SCHAFFER-CH
45 STEVE BALBONI-1B
51 TONY FERREIRA (INJ)-P
61 BOB HEGMAN-2B

1986

3rd W (tie) 75-86 16GB

1 BUDDY BIANCALANA-SS/2B
2 ANGEL SALAZAR (INJ)-SS/2B
3 JORGE ORTA-DH
4 GREG PRYOR-INF
5 GEORGE BRETT-3B/UTIL
6 WILLIE WILSON-OF
7 RUDY LAW-OF/DH
8 JIM SUNDBERG-C
9 JAMIE QUIRK-UTIL
10 DICK HOWSER (ILL)-MGR1
11 HAL MCRAE-DH
12 JOHN WATHAN-CH
13 DAVID CONE-P
14 LEE MAY-CH
15 DWIGHT TAYLOR-DH/OF
16 BO JACKSON-OF/DH
17 MIKE BREWER-OF/DH
18 JAMIE QUIRK-UTIL
20 FRANK WHITE-2B/INF
21 LONNIE SMITH-OF/DH
22 DENNIS LEONARD-P
23 MARK GUBICZA-P
24 DARRYL MOTLEY-OF/DH (1)
25 DANNY JACKSON-P
26 STEVE FARR-P
27 MIKE KINGERY-OF
28 SCOTT BANKHEAD-P
29 DAN (QUIZ) QUISENBERRY-P
31 BRET SABERHAGEN-P
32 BILL PECOTA-3B/SS
33 KEVIN SEITZER-UTIL
34 TERRY BELL-C
35 LYNN JONES-OF/UTIL
36 RONDIN JOHNSON-2B
37 CHARLIE LEIBRANDT-P
38 MARK HUISMANN-P (1)
38 STEVE SHIELDS-P (2)
40 BUD BLACK-P
41 MIKE FERRARO-CH/MGR2
42 JOSE MARTINEZ-CH
43 GARY BLAYLOCK-CH
44 JIMMIE SCHAFFER-CH
45 STEVE BALBONI (INJ)-1B
49 SCOTT BANKHEAD-P
50 ALAN HARGESHEIMER (INJ)-P

1987

2nd W 83-77 2GB

1 BUDDY BIANCALANA-UTIL (1)
2 ANGEL SALAZAR-SS
3 JORGE ORTA-DH
3 ROSS JONES-SS/2B
4 DANNY TARTABULL-OF
5 GEORGE BRETT (INJ)-1B/UTIL
6 WILLIE WILSON-OF/DH
7 ED HEARN (INJ)-C
9 JAMIE QUIRK-C/SS
10 *(RET#) DICK HOWSER*
11 HAL MCRAE-DH/CH
12 JUAN BENIQUEZ-UTIL (1)
12 JOHN WATHAN-MGR2
15 DANNY JACKSON-P
16 BO JACKSON-OF/DH
17 RICK ANDERSON-P
18 BRET SABERHAGEN-P
19 BOB STODDARD-P
20 FRANK WHITE-2B/INF
21 LONNIE SMITH (INJ)-OF/DH
22 JIM EISENREICH-DH
23 MARK GUBICZA-P
24 LARRY OWEN-C
25 DANNY JACKSON-P
25 GARY THURMAN-OF
26 STEVE FARR-P
27 THAD BOSLEY-OF/DH
28 MIKE MACFARLANE-C
28 GENE GARBER-P (2)
29 DAN (QUIZ) QUISENBERRY-P
30 DAVE GUMPERT-P
31 BRET SABERHAGEN-P
31 MELIDO PEREZ-P
31 BOB SHIRLEY-P (2)
32 RICK ANDERSON-P
32 BILL PECOTA-INF/DH
33 KEVIN SEITZER-3B/UTIL
37 CHARLIE LEIBRANDT-P
38 SCOTTI MADISON-1B/C
39 JERRY DON GLEATON-P
40 BUD BLACK-P
41 BILLY (SHOTGUN) GARDNER-MGR1
41 JOE JONES-CH
42 JOSE MARTINEZ-CH
43 GARY BLAYLOCK-CH
44 JIMMIE SCHAFFER-CH
45 STEVE BALBONI-DH/1B
46 ED NAPOLEON-CH
49 JOHN DAVIS-P
53 GARY THURMAN-OF

1988

3rd W 84-77 19.5GB

1 KURT STILLWELL-SS
2 KEVIN SEITZER-3B/UTIL
2 DAVE OWEN-SS
3 BRAD WELLMAN-INF/DH
4 DANNY TARTABULL-OF/DH
5 GEORGE BRETT-1B/UTIL
6 WILLIE WILSON-OF
7 ED HEARN (INJ)-C/DH
8 MIKE MACFARLANE-C
9 JAMIE QUIRK-C/INF
10 *(RET#) DICK HOWSER*
12 JOHN WATHAN-MGR
14 BILL (BILLY BUCK) BUCKNER-DH/1B (2)
16 BO JACKSON (INJ)-OF/DH
17 RICK ANDERSON-P
18 BRET SABERHAGEN-P
19 FLOYD BANNISTER-P
20 FRANK WHITE-2B/DH
21 JEFF MONTGOMERY-P
22 JIM EISENREICH-OF/DH
23 MARK GUBICZA-P
24 LARRY OWEN-C
25 GARY THURMAN-OF/DH
26 STEVE FARR-P
27 THAD BOSLEY-OF/DH (1)
27 LUIS AQUINO-P
28 MIKE LUM-CH
29 DAN (QUIZ) QUISENBERRY-P (1)
29 REY PALACIOS-UTIL
30 PAT TABLER-DH/1B (2)
31 GENE GARBER-P
31 ISRAEL SANCHEZ-P
32 BILL PECOTA-UTIL
33 KEVIN SEITZER-3B/UTIL
34 NICK CAPRA-OF/DH
35 MARK LEE-P
36 TOM (FLASH) GORDON-P
37 CHARLIE LEIBRANDT-P
38 SCOTTI MADISON-UTIL
39 JERRY DON GLEATON-P
40 BUD BLACK-P (1)
41 ADRIAN (PAT) GARRETT-CH
42 BOB SCHAEFER-CH
43 FRANK FUNK-CH
44 JIMMIE SCHAFFER-CH
45 STEVE BALBONI-1B/DH (1)
46 ED NAPOLEON-CH
48 TED POWER-P (1)
51 LUIS DE LOS SANTOS-1B/DH
54 JOSE DEJESUS-P

1989

2nd W 92-70 7GB

1 KURT STILLWELL (INJ)-SS
(2) BUDDY BIANCALANA (INJ)-(SS)
3 BRAD WELLMAN-UTIL
4 DANNY TARTABULL-OF/DH
5 GEORGE BRETT (INJ)-1B/UTIL
6 WILLIE WILSON-OF/DH
7 JOHN MAYBERRY-CH
8 BOB BOONE-C
9 LUIS DE LOS SANTOS-1B
10 *(RET#) DICK HOWSER*
12 JOHN WATHAN-MGR
14 BILL (BILLY BUCK) BUCKNER-1B/DH
15 MIKE MACFARLANE-C/DH
16 BO JACKSON-OF/DH
17 MATT WINTERS-OF/DH
18 BRET SABERHAGEN-P
19 FLOYD BANNISTER (INJ)-P
20 FRANK WHITE-2B
21 JEFF MONTGOMERY-P
22 JIM EISENREICH-OF/DH
23 MARK GUBICZA-P
24 JEFF SCHULZ-OF
25 GARY THURMAN (INJ)-OF/DH
26 STEVE FARR (INJ)-P
27 LUIS AQUINO-P
28 MIKE LUM-CH
29 REY PALACIOS-UTIL
30 PAT TABLER-UTIL
(31) ISRAEL SANCHEZ (INJ)-(P)
32 BILL PECOTA-UTIL
33 KEVIN SEITZER-3B/UTIL
34 STAN CLARKE-P
34 LARRY MCWILLIAMS-P (2)
36 TOM (FLASH) GORDON-P
37 CHARLIE LEIBRANDT-P
38 TERRY LEACH-P (2)
39 JERRY DON GLEATON-P
40 RICK LUECKEN-P
41 ADRIAN (PAT) GARRETT-CH
42 BOB SCHAEFER-CH
43 FRANK FUNK-CH
44 GLENN EZELL-CH
45 BOB BUCHANAN-P
49 STEVE CRAWFORD-P
54 JOSE DEJESUS-P
55 KEVIN APPIER-P

1990

6th W 75-86 27.5GB

1 KURT STILLWELL-SS
2 STEVE JELTZ-UTIL
4 DANNY TARTABULL (INJ)-OF/DH
5 GEORGE BRETT-1B/UTIL
6 WILLIE WILSON-OF/DH
7 JOHN MAYBERRY-CH
8 BOB BOONE (INJ)-C
10 *(RET#) DICK HOWSER*
12 JOHN WATHAN-MGR
14 STORM DAVIS-P
15 MIKE MACFARLANE-C/DH
16 BO JACKSON (INJ)-OF/DH
17 GERALD PERRY-DH/1B
18 BRET SABERHAGEN (INJ)-P
19 JEFF CONINE-1B
20 FRANK WHITE-2B/OF
21 JEFF MONTGOMERY-P
22 JIM EISENREICH-OF/DH
23 MARK GUBICZA (INJ)-P
24 JEFF SCHULZ-OF/DH
25 GARY THURMAN-OF
26 STEVE FARR-P
27 LUIS AQUINO (INJ)-P
28 STEVE CRAWFORD (INJ)-P
29 REY PALACIOS (INJ)-UTIL
30 PAT TABLER-UTIL (1)
31 ISRAEL SANCHEZ-P
32 BILL PECOTA-UTIL
33 KEVIN SEITZER-3B/2B
34 LARRY MCWILLIAMS-P
34 CHRIS CODIROLI-P
35 RICH DOTSON-P
35 PETE FILSON (INJ)-P
36 TOM (FLASH) GORDON-P
37 JAY BALLER-P
38 ANDY MCGAFFIGAN-P (2)
40 DARYL SMITH-P
41 ADRIAN (PAT) GARRETT-CH
42 BOB SCHAEFER-CH
43 FRANK FUNK-CH
44 GLENN EZELL-CH
45 RUSS MORMON-UTIL
47 SEAN BERRY-3B
48 MARK DAVIS (INJ)-P
49 BRENT MAYNE-C
50 TERRY SHUMPERT (INJ)-2B/DH
52 MEL STOTTLEMYRE, JR.-P
54 LUIS ENCARNACION-P
55 KEVIN APPIER-P
56 BRIAN MCRAE-OF
57 JIM CAMPBELL (INJ)-P
58 HECTOR WAGNER-P
59 CARLOS MALDONADO-P

1991

6th W 82-80 13GB

1 KURT STILLWELL-SS
2 NELSON LIRIANO-2B
3 TERRY SHUMPERT-2B
4 DANNY TARTABULL-OF/DH
5 GEORGE BRETT (INJ)-DH/1B
7 TIM SPEHR-C
8 JIM EISENREICH-OF/UTIL
9 BOBBY MOORE-OF
10 *(RET#) DICK HOWSER*
11 HAL MCRAE-MGR3
12 JOHN WATHAN-MGR1
13 CARMELO MARTINEZ-1B/DH (2)
14 STORM DAVIS-P
15 MIKE MACFARLANE (INJ)-C/DH
16 TOM (FLASH) GORDON-P
17 PAUL ZUVELLA-3B
18 BRET SABERHAGEN (INJ)-P
21 JEFF MONTGOMERY-P
23 MARK GUBICZA (INJ)-P
24 WARREN CROMARTIE-UTIL
24 BRENT MAYNE-C/DH
25 GARY THURMAN (INJ)-OF
26 TERRY PUHL-DH/OF
26 DAVE CLARK-OF/DH
26 TODD BENZINGER-1B/DH (2)
27 LUIS AQUINO-P
28 STEVE CRAWFORD (INJ)-P
30 KIRK GIBSON-OF/DH
31 DAVID HOWARD-UTIL
32 BILL PECOTA-3B/UTIL/P
33 KEVIN SEITZER-3B/DH
34 HECTOR WAGNER-P
35 LYNN JONES-CH
36 TOM (FLASH) GORDON-P
37 PAT DOBSON-CH
38 ANDY MCGAFFIGAN-P
38 TODD BENZINGER-1B/DH (2)
39 TOM (BUGS) BURGMEIER-CH
39 STU COLE-2B/DH
39 CARMELO MARTINEZ-1B/DH (2)
39 WES GARDNER-P (2)
41 ADRIAN (PAT) GARRETT-CH
42 BOB SCHAEFER-CH/MGR2
43 DAN SCHATZEDER-P
43 STORM DAVIS-P
44 GLENN EZELL-CH
45 RUSS MORMON-UTIL
47 SEAN BERRY-3B
48 MARK DAVIS (INJ)-P
49 BRENT MAYNE-C
49 WARREN CROMARTIE-UTIL

KANSAS CITY ROYALS

50 ARCHIE CORBIN-P
51 HARVEY PULLIAM-OF
52 MIKE BODDICKER-P
53 JORGE PEDRE-C/1B
55 KEVIN APPIER-P
56 BRIAN MCRAE-OF
57 MIKE MAGNANTE-P
58 JOEL JOHNSTON-P
59 CARLOS MALDONADO-P

1992

6TH W (TIE) 72-90 26GB

2 BOB MELVIN-C/1B
3 TERRY SHUMPERT-2B/SS
5 GEORGE BRETT (INJ)-DH/INF
8 JIM EISENREICH-OF
9 GREGG JEFFERIES-3B/2B
10 *(RET#) DICK HOWSER*
11 HAL MCRAE-MGR
12 WALLY JOYNER-1B
13 DAVID HOWARD-SS/OF
15 MIKE MACFARLANE-C
16 KEITH MILLER-2B/OF
17 JUAN (SAMMY) SAMUEL-OF/2B (2)
19 JEFF CONINE-OF/1B
21 JEFF MONTGOMERY-P
22 KEVIN MCREYNOLDS-OF
23 MARK GUBICZA-P
24 BRENT MAYNE-C/3B
25 GARY THURMAN-OF
26 NEAL HEATON-P (1)
26 RICH SAUVEUR-P
26 CURTIS WILKERSON-INF
27 LUIS AQUINO-P
28 RUSTY MEACHAM-P
29 CHRIS GWYNN (INJ)-OF
30 CURTIS WILKERSON-INF
31 DAVID HOWARD-SS/OF
32 RICO ROSSY-INF
33 CHRIS HANEY-P (2)
35 LYNN JONES-CH
36 TOM (FLASH) GORDON-P
37 JOEL JOHNSTON-P
38 RICK REED-P
40 CURT YOUNG-P (1)
40 KEVIN KOSLOFSKI-OF
41 ADRIAN (PAT) GARRETT-CH
42 BRUCE KISON-CH
43 GUY HANSEN-CH
43 JOE JONES-CH
44 GLENN EZELL-CH
45 LEE MAY-CH
46 NEAL HEATON, P (1)
46 GUY HANSEN-CH
47 DENNIS RASMUSSEN-P (2)
48 MARK DAVIS-P (1)
48 JUAN BERENGUER-P (2)
49 STEVE SHIFFLETT-P
50 BILL SAMPEN-P (2)
51 HARVEY PULLIAM-OF
52 MIKE BODDICKER-P
53 DENNIS MOELLER-P
54 ED PIERCE-P
55 KEVIN APPIER-P
56 BRIAN MCRAE-OF
57 MIKE MAGNANTE-P
58 HIPOLITO PICHARDO-P

1993

3RD W 84-78 10GB

3 TERRY SHUMPERT-2B
4 GARY GAETTI-3B/UTIL (2)
5 GEORGE BRETT-DH
6 DAVID HOWARD (INJ)-UTIL
7 GREG GAGNE-SS
8 CRAIG WILSON-UTIL
10 *(RET#) DICK HOWSER*
11 HAL MCRAE-MGR
12 WALLY JOYNER-1B
13 JOSE (CHICO) LIND-2B
14 CHRIS GWYNN-UTIL
15 MIKE MACFARLANE-C
16 KEITH MILLER (INJ)-UTIL
17 DAVID CONE-P
19 CURTIS WILKERSON (INJ)-2B/SS
21 JEFF MONTGOMERY-P
22 KEVIN MCREYNOLDS-OF/DH
23 MARK GUBICZA-P
24 BRENT MAYNE-C/DH
25 PHIL HIATT-3B/DH
26 HARVEY PULLIAM-OF
27 JEFF GRANGER-P
28 RUSTY MEACHAM (INJ)-P
29 BILLY BREWER-P
30 HUBIE BROOKS-UTIL
31 FRANK DIPINO (INJ)-P
31 GREG CADARET-P (2)
32 RICO ROSSY-INF
33 CHRIS HANEY-P
34 FELIX JOSE-OF/DH
35 HIPOLITO PICHARDO-P
36 TOM (FLASH) GORDON-P
37 MARK GARDNER (INJ)-P
38 RICK REED-P (1)
40 KEVIN KOSLOFSKI-OF/DH
41 JOHN HABYAN-P (2)
42 BRUCE KISON-CH
43 STEVE BOROS-CH
44 GLENN EZELL-CH
45 LEE MAY-CH
46 GUY HANSEN-CH
47 DENNIS RASMUSSEN (INJ)-P
48 BOB (HAMMER) HAMELIN-1B
50 BILL SAMPEN-P
50 STAN BELINDA-P (2)
51 ENRIQUE BURGOS-P
(52) MIKE BODDICKER (INJ) (P) (1)
53 NELSON SANTOVENIA-C
55 KEVIN APPIER-P
56 BRIAN MCRAE-OF
57 MIKE MAGNANTE-P

1994

3RD C 64-51 4GB

STRIKE NO POST-SEASON

3 BOB (HAMMER) HAMELIN-DH
4 TERRY SHUMPERT-2B
5 *(RET#) GEORGE BRETT*
6 DAVID HOWARD-UTIL
7 GREG GAGNE-SS
8 GARY GAETTI (INJ)-3B/UTIL
9 JAMIE QUIRK-CH
10 *(RET#) DICK HOWSER*
11 HAL MCRAE-MGR
12 WALLY JOYNER (INJ)-1B
13 JOSE (CHICO) LIND-2B
15 MIKE MACFARLANE-C
16 KEITH MILLER (INJ)-UTIL
21 JEFF MONTGOMERY-P
22 DAVID CONE-P
23 MARK GUBICZA-P
24 BRENT MAYNE-C/DH
26 NELSON SANTOVENIA-C
27JEFF GRANGER-P
28 RUSTY MEACHAM-P
29 VINCE (VINCENT VAN GO) \ COLEMAN-OF
30 HUBIE BROOKS (REL)-DH/1B
33 CHRIS HANEY-P
34 FELIX JOSE (INJ)-OF/DH
35 HIPOLITO PICHARDO-P
36 TOM (FLASH) GORDON-P
38 BOB MILACKI-P
40 KEVIN KOSLOFSKI-OF/DH
41 BILLY BREWER-P
42 DAVE HENDERSON (INJ)-OF
42? BRUCE KISON-CH
43 STAN BELINDA-P
43? STEVE BOROS-CH
44 GLENN EZELL-CH
45 LEE MAY-CH
47 TOM GOODWIN-OF
52 DWAYNE HOSEY-PH/OF
53 JOSE DEJESUS-P
55 KEVIN APPIER-P
56 BRIAN MCRAE-OF
57 MIKE MAGNANTE (INJ)-P

1995

2ND C 70-74 30GB

144 GAME SEASON

2 BOB BOONE-MGR
3 BOB (HAMMER) HAMELIN-DH
5 *(RET#) GEORGE BRETT*
6 DAVID HOWARD (INJ)-OF
7 GREG GAGNE (INJ)-SS
8 GARY GAETTI-3B/UTIL
9 JAMIE QUIRK-CH
10 *(RET#) DICK HOWSER*
12 WALLY JOYNER-1B
13 JOSE (CHICO) LIND (PERS/WAIV)-2B
14 JEFF GROTEWALD-DH
15 PAT BORDERS-C
15 HENRY MERCEDES-C
16 KEITH MILLER-OF
16 LES NORMAN-OF
17 JEFF COX-CH
18 JOE RANDA-2B
19 GREG (BULL) LUZINSKI-CH
20 *(RET#) FRANK WHITE*
21 JEFF MONTGOMERY-P
22 JON NUNNALLY-OF
23 MARK GUBICZA-P
24 BRENT MAYNE-C/DH
25 PHIL HIATT (INJ)-OF
26 CHRIS JAMES-OF (1)
27 JUAN (SAMMY) SAMUEL-DH (2)
28 RUSTY MEACHAM-P
29 JON NUNNALLY-OFF
29 VINCE (VINCENT VAN GO) COLEMAN-OF (1)
29 MIKE SWEENEY-C
30 GREGG OLSON-P (2)
31 MICHAEL TUCKER-OF
32 TOM BROWNING (INJ)-P
33 CHRIS HANEY (INJ)-P
34 FELIX JOSE (REL)-OF/DH
35 HIPOLITO PICHARDO (INJ)-P
36 TOM (FLASH) GORDON (INJ)-P
37 RUSS MCGINNIS-1B
37 DENNIS RASMUSSEN-P
37 SCOTT ANDERSON-P
37 RICK HUISMAN-P
38 JEFF COX-CH
38 CHRIS STYNES-2B
39 MITCHELL PAGE-CH
40 VINCE (VINCENT VAN GO) COLEMAN-OF (1)
40 JOSE MOTA-2B
41 BILLY BREWER-P
42 BRUCE KISON-CH
42 TOM GOODWIN-OF
43 KEITH LOCKHART-2B/3B
44 JOE VITIELLO-DH
45 JASON JACOME-P
46 EDGAR CACERES-2B
47 DAVE FLEMING-P (2)
48 BRENT COOKSON-DH/OF
49 DOUG LINTON-P
50 MELVIN BUNCH-P
51 JIM PITTSLEY (INJ)-P
51 JOHNNY DAMON-OF
52 DILSON TORRES-P
53 JOSE DEJESUS-P
53 JIM CONVERSE-P
54 BRUCE KISON-CH
55 KEVIN APPIER (INJ)-P
57 MIKE MAGNANTE (INJ)-P

1996

5TH C 75-86 24GB

1 BIP ROBERTS (INJ)-2B
3 BOB (HAMMER) HAMELIN (INJ)-1B
4 KEITH LOCKHART-3B/2B
5 *(RET#) GEORGE BRETT*
6 DAVID HOWARD-UTIL
8 BOB BOONE-MGR
9 JAMIE QUIRK-CH
10 *(RET#) DICK HOWSER*
12 CRAIG PAQUETTE-3B/OF
14 CHRIS STYNES-INF
15 MIKE MACFARLANE-C
16 JOE RANDA (INJ)-3B
17 KEVIN APPIER-P
18 JOHNNY DAMON-OF
19 GREG (BULL) LUZINSKI-CH
20 *(RET#) FRANK WHITE*
21 JEFF MONTGOMERY (INJ)-P
22 JON NUNNALLY-DH
23 MARK GUBICZA (INJ)-P
24 TERRY CLARK-P
24 BOB SCANLAN-P (2)
25 LES NORMAN (INJ)-OF
26 SAL FASANO-C
27 JEFF GRANGER-P
29 MIKE SWEENEY-DH
30 JOSE OFFERMAN-SS
31 MICHAEL TUCKER (INJ)-OF
32 KEVIN YOUNG-1B/3B
33 CHRIS HANEY-P
34 JIM PITTSLEY (INJ)-P
35 HIPOLITO PICHARDO-P
36 HENRY MERCEDES-C
37 RICK HUISMAN-P
38 JIM CONVERSE (INJ)-P
39 MITCHELL PAGE-CH
41 TIM BELCHER-P
42 TOM GOODWIN-OF
43 TOM (BUGS) BURGMEIER-CH
44 JOE VITIELLO-DH
45 JASON JACOME-P
46 PAT LENNON (REL)-OF
46 TIM PUGH (WAIV)-P (2)
46 JAIME BLUMA-P
47 BRIAN BEVIL-P
49 DOUG LINTON-P
50 KEN ROBINSON-P
50 JOSE ROSADO-P
51 JULIO VALERA-P
52 MELVIN BUNCH-P
54 BRUCE KISON-CH
55 GUY HANSEN-CH
56 TIM FOLI-CH
57 MIKE MAGNANTE (INJ) (WAIV)-P
58 ROD MYERS-OF
__ TOM POQUETTE-CH

1997

5TH C 67-94 19GB

1 BIP ROBERTS (INJ)-2B (1)
2 TIM SPEHR-C (1)
2 JED HANSEN-2B
5 *(RET#) GEORGE BRETT*
6 DAVID HOWARD (INJ)-2B
7 JEFF KING-1B
8 BOB BOONE-MGR1
9 JAMIE QUIRK-CH
10 *(RET#) DICK HOWSER*
12 CRAIG PAQUETTE-3B
14 SCOTT COOPER (INJ)-1B/DH
15 MIKE MACFARLANE (INJ)-C
16 SCOTT COOPER (INJ)-1B/DH
16 DEAN PALMER-3B (2)
17 KEVIN APPIER-P
18 JOHNNY DAMON-OF
19 GREG (BULL) LUZINSKI-CH
20 *(RET#) FRANK WHITE*
21 JEFF MONTGOMERY (INJ)-P
22 JON NUNNALLY-OF (1)
22 LARRY SUTTON-1B
24 JERMAINE DYE-OF
(25) JAMIE BLUMA (INJ)-(P)
26 SAL FASANO-C
27 RICKY BONES-P (2)
28 JAY BELL-SS
29 MIKE SWEENEY
30 JOSE OFFERMAN (INJ)-2B
31 ROD MYERS-OF
32 JOE VITIELLO-DH
33 CHRIS HANEY (INJ)-P
34 JIM PITTSLEY-P
35 HIPOLITO PICHARDO (INJ) - P
36 RYAN LONG-OF
36 MATA MARTINEZ,-SS
37 RICH DAUER-CH
38 JIM CONVERSE (INJ)-P
38 RICKY BONES-P (2)
39 MITCHELL PAGE-CH
39 YAMIL BENITEZ-OF
40 RICH DAUER-CH
40 TONY MUSER-MGR2 (2)
41 TIM BELCHER-P
42 TOM GOODWIN-OF (1)
43 SHANE HALTER-2B/OF
44 CHILI DAVIS (INJ)-DH
45 JASON JACOME-P (1)
45 LARRY CASIAN-P (2)
46 MIKE WILLIAMS (REL)-P
46 SCOTT SERVICE-P (2)
47 BRIAN BEVIL-P
48 GREGG OLSON-P (2)
49 MITCH (WILD THING) WILLIAMS (REL)-P
49 JOSE SANTIAGO-P
50 JOSE ROSADO-P
51 JULIO VALERA (INJ)-P
52 MIKE PEREZ-P
52 ROLAND DE LA MAZA-P
53 GLENDON RUSCH (INJ)-P
54 BRUCE KISON-CH
55 GUY HANSEN-CH
56 ALLEN MCDILL-P
56 MATT WHISENANT-P (2)
57 JAMIE WALKER (INJ)-P
58 HECTOR CARRASCO-P (2)
63 ANDY STEWART-C

1998

3RD C 72-89 16.5GB

1 LUIS RIVERA-SS/INF
2 JED HANSEN-2B
3 LUIS RIVERA-SS/INF
4 SHANE HALTER-INF
5 *(RET#) GEORGE BRETT*
6 TERRY PENDLETON (INJ)-3B/DH
7 JEFF KING (INJ)-1B/DH
8 SCOTT LEIUS (INJ)-3B
9 JAMIE QUIRK-CH
10 *(RET#) DICK HOWSER*
12 ERNIE YOUNG (INJ)-OF
12 TIM SPEHR-C (2)
14 FELIX MARTINEZ-SS/2B
15 MIKE MACFARLANE-C (1)
15 CHRIS TURNER-C

15 JEREMY GIAMBI-OF/DH
16 DEAN PALMER-3B
17 KEVIN APPIER (INJ)-P
18 JOHNNY DAMON-OF
19 JEFF CONINE (INJ)-1B
20 FRANK WHITE-CH
21 JEFF MONTGOMERY-P
22 LARRY SUTTON-OF/1B
23 HAL MORRIS (INJ)-1B/OF
24 JERMAINE DYE (INJ)-OF
25 RICH DAUER-CH
26 SAL FASANO (INJ)-C
27 JOE VITIELLO (INJ)-OF
27 DERMAL BROWN-DH/OF
28 PAT RAPP-P
29 MIKE SWEENEY-C
30 JOSE OFFERMAN-2B
31 SHANE MACK (INJ)-OF/DH (2)
32 JOE VITIELLO (INJ)-OF
32 MENDY LOPEZ-SS/3B
33 CHRIS HANEY (INJ)-P
34 JIM PITTSLEY-P
35 HIPOLITO PICHARDO (INJ) -P
36 CARLOS BELTRAN-OF
37 RICH DAUER-CH
37 JEFF SUPPAN-P
38 TOM POQUETTE-CH
40 TONY MUSER-MGR
41 TIM BELCHER-P
42 *(RET#) JACKIE ROBINSON*
(43) ROD MYERS (INJ)-(OF)
43 CARLOS FEBLES-2B
43 TOM (BUGS) BURGMEIER-CH
44 BRIAN BARBER-P
45 BART EVANS (INJ)-P
46 JERMAINE ALLENSWORTH-OF (2)
46 JOSE SANTIAGO-P
47 BRIAN BEVIL (INJ)-P
48 SCOTT SERVICE-P
49 RICKY BONES-P
50 JOSE ROSADO-P
51 DANNY RIOS-P
51 CHRIS HATCHER-OF
52 HECTOR ORTIZ-C
53 GLENDON RUSCH (INJ)-P
54 BRUCE KISON-CH
55 GUY HANSEN-CH
55 TIM BYRDAK-P
55 ALLEN MCDILL-P
56 MATT WHISENANT-P
57 JAMIE WALKER (INJ)-P

1999

4TH C 64-97 32.5GB

1 REY SANCHEZ-SS
2 JED HANSEN-INF
3 CARLOS FEBLES-2B
5 *(RET#) GEORGE BRETT*
6 STEVE SCARSONE-INF
7 JEFF KING-1B/DH
8 SCOTT LEIUS (INJ)-3B
9 JAMIE QUIRK-CH
10 *(RET#) DICK HOWSER*
12 TIM SPEHR-C
13 SAL FASANO-C
14 MENDY LOPEZ-2B
15 JEREMY GIAMBI-OF/DH
16 JOE RANDA-3B
17 KEVIN APPIER (INJ)-P (1)
18 JOHNNY DAMON-OF
19 CHAD KREUTER-C
20 FRANK WHITE-CH
21 JEFF MONTGOMERY-P
22 LARRY SUTTON (INJ-OF/1B
23 LAMAR JOHNSON-CH
24 JERMAINE DYE (INJ)-OF
25 RICH DAUER-CH
26 FELIX MARTINEZ-SS
27 DERMAL BROWN-DH
28 MARK (COYOTE) WILEY-CH
29 MIKE SWEENEY-C
30 BRAD RIGBY-P (2)
31 JOE VITIELLO-INF
32 RAY HOLBERT-INF
33 CHAD DURBIN-P
34 JIM PITTSLEY-P (1)
34 MARC PISCIOTTA-P
34 DEREK WALLACE-P
35 HIPOLITO PICHARDO-P
36 CARLOS BELTRAN-OF
37 JEFF SUPPAN-P
38 SCOTT POSE-OF
39 TERRY MATHEWS (REL)-P
40 TONY MUSER-MGR
41 DON WENGERT-P
41 BLAKE STEIN-P (2)
42 *(RET#) JACKIE ROBINSON*
43 TOM (BUGS) BURGMEIER-CH
44 BRIAN BARBER-P
45 ORBER MORENO-P
46 JOSE SANTIAGO-P
47 JAY WITASICK-P
48 SCOTT SERVICE-P
49 CHRIS FUSSELL-P
50 JOSE ROSADO-P
51 ALVIN MORMAN-P
52 MARK QUINN-OF
53 GLENDON RUSCH (INJ)-P (1)
53 LANCE CARTER-P
54 DAN REICHERT-P
55 MAC SUSUKI-P (2)
56 MATT WHISENANT (REL)-P (1)
57 KEN RAY-P
57 DAN MURRAY-P (2)
58 TIM BYRDAK-P

2000

4TH C 77-85 18GB

1 REY SANCHEZ-SS
2 JORGE FABREGAS (INJ)-C
3 CARLOS FEBLES-2B
4 RAY HOLBERT-INF
5 *(RET#) GEORGE BRETT*
6 TODD DUNWOODY-DH
6 DAVID MCCARTY-INF
7 TODD DUNWOODY-DH
8 LUIS ORDAZ-INF
9 JAMIE QUIRK-CH
10 *(RET#) DICK HOWSER*
12 JEFF REBOULET-INF
14 MARK QUINN-DH
15 CARLOS BELTRAN (INJ)-OF
16 JOE RANDA-3B
17 MAC SUZUKI-P
18 JOHNNY DAMON-OF
19 BRIAN JOHNSON-C
19 WILSON DELGADO-INF (2)
20 FRANK WHITE-CH
22 BRAD RIGBY-P (1)
22 HECTOR ORTIZ-C
23 LAMAR JOHNSON-CH
24 JERMAINE DYE-OF
25 RICH DAUER-CH
27 DERMAL (DEE) BROWN-DH
28 JAY WITASICK-P (1)
28 PAUL SPOLJARIC (INJ)-P
29 MIKE SWEENEY-C
30 BRENT STROM-CH
31 JASON RAKER-P
32 BRETT LAXTON-P
33 CHAD DURBIN-P
34 BLAKE STEIN-P
35 MIGUEL BATISTA-P (2)
36 DAN MURRAY-P
37 JEFF SUPPAN-P
38 SCOTT POSE-OF
39 DOUG BOCHTLER-P
40 TONY MUSER-MGR
41 DAN REICHERT-P
42 *(RET#) JACKIE ROBINSON*
43 TOM (BUGS) BURGMEIER-CH
44 GREGG ZAUN-C
45 ORBER MORENO (INJ)-P
46 JOSE SANTIAGO-P
48 JERRY SPRADLIN-P
49 CHRIS FUSSELL (INJ)-P
50 JOSE ROSADO-P
51 KRIS WILSON-P
52 RICKY BOTTALICO-P
54 ANDY LARKIN-P (2)
56 JEFF D'AMICO-P (1)
57 SCOTT MULLEN-P
58 TIM BYRDAK-P
59 BRIAN MEADOWS-P (2)

2001

5TH C 65-97 26GB

1 REY SANCHEZ-SS (1)
2 BRENT MAYNE-C
3 CARLOS FEBLES (INJ)-2B
4 WILSON DELGADO-3B/2B (1)
4 ANGEL BERROA-SS
5 *(RET#) GEORGE BRETT*
6 DAVID MCCARTY-INF
7 A. J. HINCH-C
8 LUIS ORDAZ-INF
9 JAMIE QUIRK-CH
10 *(RET#) DICK HOWSER*
12 LUIS ALICEA-INF
14 MARK QUINN-OF
15 CARLOS BELTRAN-OF
16 JOE RANDA-3B
17 MAC SUZUKI (INJ)-P (1)
17 NEIFI PEREZ-SS (2)
18 RAUL IBANEZ-OF
19 DOUG HENRY-P
20 FRANK WHITE-CH
22 HECTOR ORTIZ (INJ)-C
23 LAMAR JOHNSON-CH
24 JERMAINE DYE-OF (1)
25 RICH DAUER-CH
26 SAL FASANO-C (2)
26 JEFF AUSTIN-P
27 DERMAL (DEE) BROWN (INJ)-OF
28 TRENIDAD HUBBARD (WAIV)-OF (1)
28 KEN HARVEY-DH/1B
29 MIKE SWEENEY (SUS)-1B/DH
30 BRENT STROM-CH
30 DONNIE SADLER-3B (2)
30 BRANDON BERGER-OF
31 BRIAN MEADOWS (WAIV)-P
33 CHAD DURBIN-P
34 BLAKE STEIN-P
35 AL NIPPER-CH
36 PAUL BYRD-P
37 JEFF SUPPAN-P
38 JASON GRIMSLEY-P
39 ROBERTO HERNANDEZ-P
40 TONY MUSER-MGR
41 DAN REICHERT-P
42 *(RET#) JACKIE ROBINSON*
43 ENDY CHAVEZ-OF
44 GREGG ZAUN (INJ)-C
46 JOSE SANTIAGO-P
46 BRAD VOYLES-P
50 JOSE ROSADO (INJ)-P
51 KRIS WILSON-P
53 CHRIS GEORGE-P
54 MIKE MACDOUGALD-P
55 TONY COGAN-P
57 SCOTT MULLEN (INJ)-P
58 CORY BAILEY-P
__ TOM GAMBOA-CH

2002

4TH C 62-100 32.5GB

1 DONNIE SADLER-UTIL
1 LUIS ORDAZ-INF
2 BRENT MAYNE-C
3 CARLOS FEBLES (INJ)-2B/SS
4 ANGEL BERROA-SS
5 *(RET#) GEORGE BRETT*
6 DAVID MCCARTY- 1B/DH (1)
6 TONY PENA-MGR3 (2)
7 A. J. HINCH-C
8 NEIFI PEREZ-SS/2B
9 ALEXIS GOMEZ-OF
10 *(RET#) DICK HOWSER*
11 CHUCK KNOBLAUCH (INJ)-OF/DH
12 LUIS ALICEA-UTIL
13 JOHN MIZEROCK-MGR2
14 MARK QUINN (INJ)-OF/DH
15 CARLOS BELTRAN-OF/DH
16 JOE RANDA-3B/DH
17 MAC SUZUKI-P
17 DUSTY WATHAN-C
18 RAUL IBANEZ-OF/DH/1B
19 DONZELL MCDONALD-OF
19 KIT PELLOW-3B/1B
20 JOHN HALE (?)-CH
20 *(RET#) FRANK WHITE*
21 TOM GAMBOA-CH
22 JUAN BRITO-C
24 MICHAEL TUCKER-OF/DH
25 RICH DAUER-CH
26 JEFF AUSTIN-P
27 DEE BROWN-OF/DH
29 MIKE SWEENEY (INJ)-1B/DH
30 BRANDON BERGER-OF/DH
31 DARRELL MAY (INJ)-P
32 CHRIS GEORGE (INJ)-P
33 CHAD DURBIN-P
34 BLAKE STEIN (INJ)-P
35 AL NIPPER-CH
35 RYAN BUKVICH-P
36 PAUL BYRD-P
37 JEFF SUPPAN-P
38 JASON GRIMSLEY-P
39 ROBERTO HERNANDEZ (INJ)-P
40? TONY MUSER-MGR1
40 RUNELVYS HERNANDEZ-P
41 DAN REICHERT-P
42 *(RET#) JACKIE ROBINSON*
43 WES OBERMUELLER-P
43 CHAN PERRY-1B
44 BOB SCHAEFER-CH
45 AARON GUIEL-OF/DH
46 BRAD VOYLES-P
47 BRYAN REKAR-P
47 JOHN CUMBERLAND-CH
48 JEREMY AFFELDT (INJ)-P
50 MIKE CARUSO-INF
51 KRIS WILSON (INJ)-P
52 BRIAN SHOUSE-P
52 JEREMY HILL-P
53 MIGUEL ASENCIO-P
54 MIKE MACDOUGALD-P
56 NATE FIELD-P
56 SHAWN SEDLACEK-P
57 SCOTT MULLEN-P
58 CORY BAILEY-P
__ JEFF PENTLAND-CH
__ LUIS SILVERIO-CH

2003

3RD C 83-79 7GB

1 GOOKIE DAWKINS-2B
2 BRENT MAYNE-C
3 CARLOS FEBLES (INJ)-2B
4 ANGEL BERROA-SS
5 *(RET#) GEORGE BRETT*
6 TONY PENA-MGR
7 MENDY LOPEZ-UTIL
8 DEE BROWN (INJ)-OF/DH
9 DAVID DEJESUS-OF
10 *(RET#) DICK HOWSER*
11 TOM PRINCE-C (2)
12 DESI RELAFORD-UTIL
13 JOHN MIZEROCK-CH
14 BRENT ABERNATHY-2B (2)
14 RONDELL WHITE-OF (2)
15 CARLOS BELTRAN (INJ)-OF/DH
16 JOE RANDA-3B
17 LUIS SILVERIO-CH
18 RAUL IBANEZ-OF/1B/DH
19 JARROD PETERSON-3B/DH
19 BRIAN ANDERSON-P (2)
20 *(RET#) FRANK WHITE*
21 TOM GAMBOA-CH
22 JEFF PENTLAND-CH
23 JULIUS MATOS-INF
24 MICHAEL TUCKER (INJ)-OF/DH
25 RONTREZ JOHNSON-OF
25 JOSE LIMA (INJ)-P
26 MIKE DIFELICE (SUS:2G)-C
27 NATE FIELD-P
28 KEN HARVEY-1B/DH
29 MIKE SWEENEY (INJ)-DH/1B
30 BRANDON BERGER-OF/DH
31 ALBIE LOPEZ (INJ)-P
31 PAUL ABBOTT-P
32 CHRIS GEORGE-P
33 MORGAN BURKHART-1B
33 CURTIS LESKANIC-P (2)
34 DARRELL MAY-P
35 RYAN BUKVICH-P
36 KYLE SNYDER (INJ)-P
37 GRAEME LLOYD-P (2)
38 JASON GRIMSLEY-P
39 SEAN LOWE (REL)-P
40 RUNELVYS HERNANDEZ (INJ)-P
41 JIMMY GOBBLE-P
42 *(RET#) JACKIE ROBINSON*
43 AL LEVINE-P (2)
44 BOB SCHAEFER-CH
45 AARON GUIEL-OF
46 BRAD VOYLES-P
47 JOHN CUMBERLAND-CH
48 JEREMY AFFELDT (INJ)-P
49 JAMEY WRIGHT-P
50 JASON GILFILLAN-P
51 KRIS WILSON-P
52 JEREMY HILL-P (1)
53 MIGUEL ASENCIO (INJ)-P
54 MIKE MACDOUGALD-P
55 NATE FIELD-P
55 KEVIN APPIER (INJ)-P (2)
56 LES WALROND-P
57 SCOTT MULLEN-P (1)
58 RICK DEHART-P
59 DANNY (D. J.) CARRASCO-P

2004

5TH C 58-104 34GB

1 ANDRES BLANCO-2B
1 DAMIAN JACKSON-SS (2)
1 WILTON GUERRERO-2B
2 WILTON GUERRERO-2B
2 JOHN BUCK-C
3 MIKE TONIS-C
3 ANDRES BLANCO-2B
3 PAUL PHILLIPS-C
4 ANGEL BERROA (INJ)-SS
5 *(RET#) GEORGE BRETT*
6 TONY PENA-MGR
7 MENDY LOPEZ-1B
8 DEE BROWN (INJ)-OF

ANSAS CITY ROYALS

9 DAVID DEJESUS-OF
0 *(RET#) DICK HOWSER*
1 MATT STAIRS-OF
2 DESI RELAFORD (INJ)-2B
3 JOHN MIZEROCK-CH
4 TONY GRAFFANINO (INJ)-2B
5 CARLOS BELTRAN-OF
6 JOE RANDA-3B
7 LUIS SILVERIO-CH
8 KELLY STINNETT (INJ)-C
9 BRIAN ANDERSON-P
0 *(RET#) FRANK WHITE*
1 DANNY (D. J.) CARRASCO-P
2 JUAN GONZALEZ (INJ)-OF
3 ZACK GREINKE-P
4 RICH THOMPSON-OF
4 BRANDON BERGER-OF
4 RUBEN MATEO-OF (2)
5 BRIAN POLDBERG-CH
6 JEFF PENTLAND-CH
7 DENNY BAUTISTA-P (2)
7 JOSE BAUTISTA-3B (3)
8 KEN HARVEY (INJ)-1B/DH
9 MIKE SWEENEY (INJ)-1B/DH
0 RUBEN GOTAY-2B
1 ADRIAN BROWN-OF
1 BYRON GETTIS-OF
1 DONNIE MURPHY-2B
2 CHRIS GEORGE-P
3 CURTIS LESKANIC-P (1)
4 DARRELL MAY-P
5 RYAN BUKVICH-P
6 CALVIN PICKERING-1B/DH
7 JUSTIN HUISMAN-P
8 JASON GRIMSLEY-P (1)
8 ABRAHAM NUNEZ-OF (2)
9 MIKE MASON-CH
40) RUNELVYS HERNANDEZ (INJ)-(P)
1 JIMMY GOBBLE-P
2 *(RET#) JACKIE ROBINSON*
3 ALEXIS GOMEZ-OF (1)
3 RUDY SEANEZ-P (1)
4 BOB SCHAEFER-CH
5 AARON GUIEL (INJ)-OF/DH
6 MIKE WOOD-P
7 SCOTT SULLIVAN (INJ)-P
8 JEREMY AFFELDT (INJ)-P
9 DENNYS REYES-P
0 JIMMY SERRANO-P
2 JOHN CUMBERLAND-CH
2 MATT KINNEY-P (2)
53) MIGUEL ASENCIO (INJ)-(P)
4 MIKE MACDOUGALD (INJ)-P
5 KEVIN APPIER (INJ)-P
6 JAIME CERDA-P
7 NATE FIELD (INJ)-P
8 SHAWN CAMP-P
9 DANNY (D. J.) CARRASCO-P
9 EDUARDO VILLACIS-P (1)
9 JORGE VASQUEZ-P
1 JAIME CERDA-P
8 SHAWN CAMP-P

2005

5TH C 56-106 43GB

1 DENNY HOCKING-INF
2 JOHN BUCK-C
3 TERRENCE LONG-OF
4 ANGEL BERROA-SS
5 *(RET#) GEORGE BRETT*
6 TONY PENA-MGR1
7 ALBERTO CASTILLO (REL)-C (1)
7 ANDRES BLANCO-INF
8 JOE MCEWING-INF
9 DAVID DEJESUS-OF
0 *(RET#) DICK HOWSER*
1 ELI MARRERO-OF (1)
11 PAUL PHILLIPS-C
12 MATT STAIRS-OF/DH
13 LUIS SILVERIO-CH
13 BILL DORAN-CH
14 TONY GRAFFANINO-2B (1)
15 SHANE COSTA-OF
16 JUSTIN HUBER-1B
17 LUIS SILVERIO-CH
18 JOE JONES-CH
18 CHIP AMBRES-OF
19 BRIAN ANDERSON (INJ)-P
20 *(RET#) FRANK WHITE*
21 DANNY (D. J.) CARRASCO-P
22 JONAH BAYLISS-P
23 ZACK GREINKE-P
24 MARK TEAHEN (INJ)-3B
25 BRIAN POLDBERG-CH
25 BUDDY BELL-MGR2 (2)
26 JEFF PENTLAND-CH
26 ANDRE DAVID-CH
27 DENNY BAUTISTA (INJ)-P
28 KEN HARVEY (INJ)-1B
29 MIKE SWEENEY (INJ)-DH/1B
30 RUBEN GOTAY-3B/2B
31 DONNIE MURPHY (INJ)-2B
33 JOSE LIMA-P
34 MATT DIAZ (INJ)-OF
35 EMIL BROWN-OF
36 CALVIN PICKERING-DH
37 GUY HANSEN-CH
37 STEVE STEMLE (INJ)-P
38 RYAN JENSEN-P
39 KYLE SNYDER-P
40 RUNELVYS HERNANDEZ (SUS:10G)-P
41 JIMMY GOBBLE-P
42 *(RET#) JACKIE ROBINSON*
43 LEO NUNEZ-P
44 BOB SCHAEFER-CH
45 AARON GUIEL-OF
46 MIKE WOOD-P
(47) SCOTT SULLIVAN (INJ)-(P)
48 JEREMY AFFELDT (INJ)-P
49 BRIAN POLDBERG-CH
50 AMBIORIX BURGOS-P
51 ANDY SISCO-P
52 CHRIS DEMARIA-P
53 J. P. HOWELL-P
54 MIKE MACDOUGALD-P
55 GUY HANSEN-CH
56 JAIME CERDA-P
57 NATE FIELD-P
58 SHAWN CAMP (WAIV)-P

Frank White spent his entire career playing for the Royals. His number 20 is one of three retired by the club. He was a superb second baseman, leading the league in fielding three times and selected five times as an All-Star. White was a member of the World Championship team of '85.

1961
LOS ANGELES ANGELS
8TH 70-91 38.5GB

1 JOE KOPPE-INF
2 RED KRESS-CH
3 BOB (MR. TEAM) ELLIOTT-CH
4 GEORGE THOMAS-OF/3B
5 MARV GRISSOM-CH
6 ED SADOWSKI-C
7 BOB (BUCK) RODGERS-C
8 EARL AVERILL, JR.-C/UTIL
9 DEL RICE-C
10 EDDIE YOST (INJ)-3B
11 KEN ASPROMONTE-2B (1)
11 CHUCK TANNER-OF
12 KEN HAMLIN-SS
12 BILLY MORAN-2B/SS
14 GENE LEEK-UTIL
15 TED (BIG KLU) KLUSZEWSKI-1B
16 FRITZIE BRICKELL-SS
17 JIM FREGOSI-SS
18 BILL (THE CRICKET) (SPECS) RIGNEY-MGR
19 JULIO BECQUER-1B (1)
20 STEVE BILKO-1B/OF
21 ROCKY BRIDGES-INF
22 LEO BURKE-PH
22 JOHNNY JAMES-P (2)
24 ART FOWLER-P
26 KEN HUNT-OF/2B
27 LOU (SLICK) JOHNSON-OF
27 LEON (DADDY WAGS) WAGNER-OF
28 ALBIE PEARSON-OF
29 FAYE THRONEBERRY-OF
29 TOM SATRIANO-INF
30 BOB CERV-OF (1)
30 RYNE DUREN-P (2)
31 NED GARVER-P
31 DEAN CHANCE-P
32 TRUMAN (TEX) CLEVENGER-P (1)
32 LEE THOMAS-OF/1B (2)
33 ELI GRBA-P
34 BOB SPROUT-P
35 DANNY ARDELL-1B
35 RAY SEMPROCH-P
37 KEN MCBRIDE-P
39 RON (THE KID) MOELLER-P
40 JERRY CASALE-P (1)
40 JIM DONOHUE-P (2)
41 JACK SPRING-P
41 RON KLINE-P (1)
41 DEAN CHANCE-P
43 TED BOWSFIELD-P
46 RUSS HEMAN-P (2)
47 TOM (PLOWBOY) MORGAN-P
48 JACK PAEPKE-CH

1962
3RD 86-76 10GB

1 JOE KOPPE-SS/INF
2 FRANK LEJA-1B
3 JACK PAEPKE-CH
4 GEORGE THOMAS (MIL)-OF
5 MARV GRISSOM-CH
6 ED SADOWSKI-C
7 BOB (BUCK) RODGERS-C
8 EARL AVERILL, JR.-OF/C
9 DEL RICE-CH
10 EDDIE YOST-3B/1B
10 DICK SIMPSON-OF
11 CHUCK TANNER-OF
11 BILLY CONSOLO-INF (2)
11 JIM FREGOSI-SS
12 BILLY MORAN-2B/SS
14 GENE LEEK (MIL)-UTIL
14 MARLIN COUGHTRY-3B/2B (1)
15 TOM (TIM) BURGESS-1B/OF
16 JIM FREGOSI-SS
16 LEO BURKE-UTIL
17 FRED NEWMAN-P
18 BILL (THE CRICKET) (SPECS) RIGNEY-MGR
19 FELIX TORRES-3B
20 STEVE BILKO (INJ)-1B/OF
21 ROCKY BRIDGES-CH
22 BOB BOTZ-P
23 EDDIE YOST-3B/1B
24 ART FOWLER-P
26 KEN HUNT (INJ) (MIL)-1B
27 LEON (DADDY WAGS) WAGNER-OF
28 ALBIE PEARSON-OF
29 TOM SATRIANO-3B
30 RYNE DUREN-P
31 DEAN CHANCE-P
32 LEE THOMAS-1B/OF
33 ELI GRBA-P
34 BOBBY DARWIN-P
35 GORDIE WINDHORN-OF (2)
35 JULIO (WHIPLASH) NAVARRO-P
36 BO BELINSKY-P
37 KEN MCBRIDE (INJ)-P
38 DICK SIMPSON-OF
39 JOE NUXHALL-P (1)
39 ED KIRKPATRICK-C
40 JIM DONOHUE-P (1)
40 DAN OSINSKI-P (2)
41 JACK SPRING-P
42 FRED NEWMAN-P
43 TED BOWSFIELD-P
47 TOM (PLOWBOY) MORGAN-P
48 GEORGE (RED) WITT-P (1)
48 DON LEE-P (2)
54 BOBBY DARWIN-P

1963
9TH 70-91 34GB

1 JOE KOPPE-UTIL
2 TOM SATRIANO-UTIL
3 JACK PAEPKE-CH
4 GEORGE THOMAS-OF/INF (1)
4 JIMMY PIERSALL-OF (3)
5 MARV GRISSOM-CH
6 ED SADOWSKI-C
7 BOB (BUCK) RODGERS-C
8 ED KIRKPATRICK-C/OF
9 DEL RICE-CH
11 JIM FREGOSI-SS
12 BILLY MORAN-2B
14 FRANK KOSTRO-UTIL (2)
15 BOB (SID) SADOWSKI-OF/INF
16 HANK FOILES-C (2)
17 FRED NEWMAN-P
18 BILL (THE CRICKET) (SPECS) RIGNEY-MGR
19 FELIX TORRES-3B/1B
21 ROCKY BRIDGES-CH
23 CHARLIE DEES-1B
24 ART FOWLER-P
25 BOB PERRY-OF
26 KEN HUNT-OF (1)
27 LEON (DADDY WAGS) WAGNER-OF
28 ALBIE PEARSON-OF
29 TOM SATRIANO-UTIL
30 MIKE LEE-P
31 DEAN CHANCE-P
32 LEE THOMAS-1B/OF
33 ELI GRBA-P
33 AUBREY GATEWOOD-P
35 JULIO (WHIPLASH) NAVARRO-P
36 BO BELINSKY-P
37 KEN MCBRIDE-P
39 BOB (BULLET BOB) TURLEY-P (1)
40 DAN OSINSKI-P
41 JACK SPRING-P
43 MEL NELSON-P
45 RON (THE KID) MOELLER-P (1)
45 BOB DULIBA-P
47 TOM (PLOWBOY) MORGAN-P
48 DON LEE-P
49 PAUL FOYTACK-P (2)

1964
6TH (TIE) 80-82 13GB

1 JOE KOPPE-UTIL
2 TOM SATRIANO-UTIL
3 JACK PAEPKE-CH
4 JIMMY PIERSALL-OF
5 MARV GRISSOM-CH
6 JOE ADCOCK-1B
7 BOB (BUCK) RODGERS-C
8 ED KIRKPATRICK-OF
9 DEL RICE-CH
10 DICK SIMPSON-OF
11 JIM FREGOSI-SS
12 BILLY MORAN-INF (1)
14 VIC POWER-INF (2)
15 LU CLINTON-OF (2)
16 HANK FOILES-PH
16 JACK HIATT-C/1B
17 FRED NEWMAN-P
18 BILL (THE CRICKET) (SPECS) RIGNEY-MGR
19 FELIX TORRES-3B/1B
20 PAUL FOYTACK-P
20 RICK REICHARDT-OF
21 SALTY PARKER-CH
22 BILL KELSO-P
23 CHARLIE DEES-1B
24 ART FOWLER-P/CH
25 BOB PERRY-OF
26 LENNY GREEN-OF (2)
28 ALBIE PEARSON-OF
29 BOBBY KNOOP-2B
31 DEAN CHANCE-P
32 LEE THOMAS-OF/1B (1)
33 AUBREY GATEWOOD-P
33 ED SUKLA-P
34 BARRY LATMAN-P
35 JULIO (WHIPLASH) NAVARRO-P (1)
35 WILLIE SMITH-OF/P
36 BO BELINSKY (SUS)-P
37 KEN MCBRIDE-P
38 GEORGE (LEFTY) BRUNET-P
38 AUBREY GATEWOOD-P
39 BOB (MOOSE) (HORSE) LEE-P
40 DAN OSINSKI-P
41 JACK SPRING-P (1)
41 BOB MEYER-P (2)
42 PAUL SCHAAL-2B/3B
43 GEORGE (LEFTY) BRUNET-P
45 BOB DULIBA-P
47 TOM (PLOWBOY) MORGAN-P INSTR
48 DON LEE-P

1965
CALIFORNIA ANGELS
7TH 75-87 27GB

1 JOE KOPPE-UTIL
2 TOM SATRIANO-UTIL
3 RICK REICHARDT-OF
4 JIMMY PIERSALL-OF
5 MARV GRISSOM-CH
6 JOE ADCOCK-1B
7 BOB (BUCK) RODGERS-C
8 ED KIRKPATRICK-OF
9 DEL RICE-CH
10 DICK SIMPSON-OF
11 JIM FREGOSI-SS
12 COSTEN SHOCKLEY-1B/OF
12 JACKIE HERNANDEZ-SS/3B
14 VIC POWER-INF
15 LU CLINTON-OF (1)
16 PHIL ROOF-C (1)
17 FRED NEWMAN-P
18 BILL (THE CRICKET) (SPECS) RIGNEY-MGR
19 MERRITT RANEW-C
20 JACK PAEPKE-CH
21 SALTY PARKER-CH
23 RON PICHE-P
23 CHARLIE DEES-1B
23 JACK SANFORD-P (2)
23 ED SUKLA-P
24 BOBBY GENE SMITH-OF
24 GINO CIMOLI-OF
25 DICK WANTZ (DIED)-P
26 AL SPANGLER-OF (2)
27 JOSE CARDENAL-OF/INF
28 ALBIE PEARSON-OF
29 BOBBY KNOOP-2B
30 TOM EGAN-C
31 DEAN CHANCE-P
33 MARCELINO LOPEZ-P
34 BARRY LATMAN-P
35 WILLIE SMITH-OF/1B
37 KEN MCBRIDE (INJ)-P
37 JIM COATES-P
38 AUBREY GATEWOOD-P
39 BOB (MOOSE) (HORSE) LEE-P
40 RUDY MAY-P
41 DICK WANTZ (DIED)-P
42 PAUL SCHAAL-3B/2B
43 GEORGE (LEFTY) BRUNET-P
44 JULIO GOTAY-INF
46 JIM COATES-P
48 DON LEE-P (1)
49 JACK SANFORD-P (2)
50 JIM (RED) MCGLOTHLIN-P
51 ED SUKLA-P

1966
6TH 80-82 18GB

1 JOSE CARDENAL-OF
2 TOM SATRIANO-UTIL
3 RICK REICHARDT (ILL)-OF
4 JIMMY PIERSALL-OF
5 MARV GRISSOM-CH
6 JOE ADCOCK-1B
7 BOB (BUCK) RODGERS-C
8 ED KIRKPATRICK-OF/1B
9 DEL RICE-CH
10 BUBBA MORTON-OF
10 WILLIE MONTANEZ-1B
10 JAY JOHNSTONE-OF
11 JIM FREGOSI-SS
12 JACKIE HERNANDEZ-UTIL
14 CHUCK VINSON-1B
15 FRANK MALZONE-3B
16 NORM SIEBERN-1B
17 FRED NEWMAN-P
18 BILL (THE CRICKET) (SPECS) RIGNEY-MGR
19 MINNIE ROJAS-P
20 JACK PAEPKE-CH
21 SALTY PARKER-CH
22 MINNIE ROJAS-P
22 BILL KELSO-P
23 ED SUKLA-P
25 ED BAILEY-PH
25 RAMON LOPEZ-P
25 JIM COATES-P
25 HOWIE (DIZ) REED-P (2)
26 AL SPANGLER-OF
26 JACKIE WARNER-OF
28 ALBIE PEARSON (INJ)-OF
29 BOBBY KNOOP-2B
30 TOM EGAN-C
31 DEAN CHANCE-P
32 LEW BURDETTE-P
33 MARCELINO LOPEZ-P
35 WILLIE SMITH-OF
37 JACKIE WARNER-OF
38 CLYDE WRIGHT-P
39 BOB (MOOSE) (HORSE) LEE-P
40 RUDY MAY (INJ)-P
41 DICK EGAN-P
41 JORGE RUBIO-P
41 BILL KELSO-P
41 HOWIE (DIZ) REED-P (2)
42 PAUL SCHAAL-3B
43 GEORGE (LEFTY) BRUNET-P
45 JIM (RED) MCGLOTHLIN-P
46 JIM COATES-P
46 JORGE RUBIO-P
49 JACK SANFORD-P
50 JIM COATES-P
57 JORGE RUBIO-P

1967
5TH 84-77 7.5GB

1 JOSE CARDENAL-OF
2 TOM SATRIANO-UTIL
3 RICK REICHARDT-OF
4 JIMMY PIERSALL-OF
5 DON MINCHER-1B/OF
6 LEN GABRIELSON-OF (1)
6 ROGER REPOZ-OF (2)
7 BOB (BUCK) RODGERS-C
8 ED KIRKPATRICK-C/OF
9 JIMMIE HALL-OF
10 JAY JOHNSTONE-OF
11 JIM FREGOSI-SS
12 ORLANDO MCFARLANE-C
12 AURELIO RODRIGUEZ-3B
14 BILL (MOOSE) SKOWRON-1B (2)
15 WOODIE HELD-UTIL (2)
16 HAWK TAYLOR-C (2)
17 FRED NEWMAN (INJ)-P
17 MOOSE STUBING-PH
18 BILL (THE CRICKET) (SPECS) RIGNEY-MGR
19 MINNIE ROJAS-P
20 BOB LEMON-CH
21 MIKE ROARKE-CH
22 BILLY HERMAN-CH
23 DON HEFFNER-CH
24 NICK WILLHITE-P (1)
24 JACK HAMILTON-P (2)
25 JOHNNY (PEACHES) WERHAS-UTIL (2)
27 BUBBA MORTON-OF
29 BOBBY KNOOP-2B
30 TOM EGAN (MIL)-C
31 PETE CIMINO-P
32 LEW BURDETTE-P
32 CURT SIMMONS-P (2)
33 MARCELINO LOPEZ-P (1)
34 DON WALLACE-INF
35 JIM (FLUFF) WEAVER-P
37 JORGE RUBIO-P
38 CLYDE WRIGHT (MIL)-P
39 KEN TURNER-P
40 RUDY MAY (INJ)-P
41 BILL KELSO-P
42 PAUL SCHAAL-3B/INF
43 GEORGE (LEFTY) BRUNET-P
44 RICKEY CLARK-P
45 JIM (RED) MCGLOTHLIN-P

A/CALIFORNIA/ANAHEIM/**LOS ANGELES ANGELS**

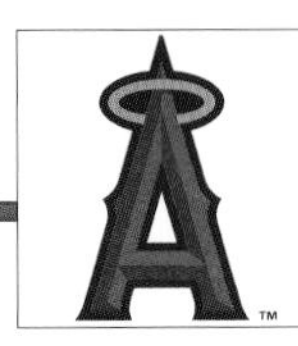

5 JIM COATES-P
5 CURT SIMMONS-P (2)
7 AURELIO RODRIGUEZ-3B
7 BOBBY LOCKE-P
7 JIM (FLUFF) WEAVER-P
7 JIM HIBBS-PH
8 MICKEY MCDERMOTT-CH
9 JACK SANFORD-P (1)
9 CURT SIMMONS-P (2)
0 JIM (FLUFF) WEAVER-P
0 JACK HAMILTON-P (2)
1 JIM HIBBS-PH
1 KEN TURNER-P
2 CLYDE WRIGHT (MIL)-P

1968

8TH (TIE) 67-95 13GB

1 AURELIO RODRIGUEZ (ILL)-3B/2B
2 TOM SATRIANO-UTIL
3 RICK REICHARDT-OF
4 CHUCK COTTIER-3B/2B
5 DON MINCHER-1B/OF
6 ROGER REPOZ-OF
7 BOB (BUCK) RODGERS-C
8 ED KIRKPATRICK-UTIL
9 JIMMIE HALL-OF (1)
9 JIM SPENCER-1B
0 JAY JOHNSTONE-OF
1 JIM FREGOSI-SS
2 ORLANDO MCFARLANE (INJ)-C
2 BOBBY TREVINO-OF
5 WOODIE HELD-UTIL (1)
5 WINSTON LLENAS-3B
5 WAYNE CAUSEY-2B (2)
7 BILL HARRELSON-P
8 BILL (THE CRICKET) (SPECS) RIGNEY-MGR
9 MINNIE ROJAS (INJ)-P
0 BOB LEMON-CH
1 MIKE ROARKE-CH
2 ROCKY BRIDGES-CH
3 DON HEFFNER-CH
4 JACK HAMILTON-P
5 DENNIS BENNETT-P
6 CHUCK HINTON-UTIL
7 BUBBA MORTON-OF/3B
8 VIC DAVALILLO-OF (2)
9 BOBBY KNOOP-2B
0 TOM EGAN-C
1 PETE CIMINO-P
1 LARRY SHERRY-P
1 STEVE KEALEY-P
2 SAMMY ELLIS-P
3 MARTY PATTIN-P
4 BOBBY LOCKE-P
5 JIM (FLUFF) WEAVER-P
5 JARVIS TATUM-OF
7 BOB HEFFNER-P
8 CLYDE WRIGHT-P
9 TOM (BUGS) BURGMEIER-P
1 TOM MURPHY-P
2 PAUL SCHAAL (INJ)-3B
3 GEORGE (LEFTY) BRUNET-P
4 RICKEY CLARK (INJ)-P
5 JIM (RED) MCGLOTHLIN-P
6 TOM MURPHY-P
7 BOBBY LOCKE-P
7 ANDY MESSERSMITH-P
8 MICKEY MCDERMOTT-CH
8 STEVE KEALEY-P
8 BOBBY LOCKE-P
9 TOM MURPHY-P
3 JIMMIE REESE, ? CH

1969

3RD W 71-91 26GB

1 AURELIO RODRIGUEZ (ILL)-3B/2B
2 TOM SATRIANO-UTIL (1)
2 JOE AZCUE-C (3)
3 RICK REICHARDT-OF/1B
4 CHUCK COTTIER-2B
4 SANDY ALOMAR-2B (2)
5 DICK (DR.STRANGEGLOVE) STUART-1B
5 JIM HICKS-OF/1B (2)
6 ROGER REPOZ-OF/1B
7 BOB (BUCK) RODGERS-C
8 JARVIS TATUM-OF
9 JIM SPENCER-1B
10 JAY JOHNSTONE-OF
11 JIM FREGOSI-SS
12 RUBEN AMARO, SR.-INF
14 WINSTON LLENAS-3B
15 WINSTON LLENAS-3B
17 VERN GEISHERT-P
18 BILL (THE CRICKET) (SPECS) RIGNEY-MGR1
19 KEN TATUM-P
20 MARV GRISSOM-CH
21 MIKE ROARKE-CH
22 ROCKY BRIDGES-CH
23 GREG WASHBURN-P
24 EDDIE FISHER-P
26 LOU (SLICK) JOHNSON-OF
27 BUBBA MORTON-OF/1B
28 VIC DAVALILLO-OF/1B (1)
28 RANDY BROWN-C/OF
29 BOBBY KNOOP-2B (1)
30 TOM EGAN (INJ)-C
31 STEVE KEALEY-P
31 PHIL (KEMO) ORTEGA (INJ)-P
32 BILL VOSS-OF/1B
33 PEDRO BORBON-P
34 RUDY MAY-P
35 BILLY COWAN-OF (2)
36 LEFTY PHILLIPS-MGR2
37 BOB CHANCE-1B
38 CLYDE WRIGHT-P
39 HOYT WILHELM-P (1)
39 WALLY WOLF-P
40 LLOYD ALLEN-P
40 BOB PRIDDY-P (2)
41 TOM MURPHY-P
42 MARTY PEREZ-INF
43 GEORGE (LEFTY) BRUNET-P (1)
44 RICKEY CLARK (INJ)-P
45 JIM (RED) MCGLOTHLIN-P
47 ANDY MESSERSMITH-P
48 MICKEY MCDERMOTT-CH
48 VERN GEISHERT-P
49 TOM BRADLEY-P
50 LLOYD ALLEN-P
51 LLOYD ALLEN-P
51 GREG WASHBURN-P
52 RICKEY CLARK (INJ)-P

1970

3RD W 86-76 12GB

1 AURELIO RODRIGUEZ, (ILL)-3B (1)
1 RAY OYLER-SS/3B
2 JOE AZCUE-C
3 RICK REICHARDT-OF/1B (1)
3 MICKEY RIVERS-OF
4 SANDY ALOMAR-2B
5 JIM HICKS-PH
5 TOMMIE REYNOLDS-OF/3B
6 ROGER REPOZ-OF/1B
7 KEN MCMULLEN-3B (2)
8 JARVIS TATUM-OF
9 JIM SPENCER-1B
10 JAY JOHNSTONE-OF
11 JIM FREGOSI-SS
12 CHICO RUIZ-UTIL
14 BILLY COWAN-OF/INF
15 CHICO RUIZ-UTIL
17 ALEX JOHNSON-OF
19 KEN TATUM-P
20 FRED KOENIG-CH
21 NORM SHERRY-CH
22 ROCKY BRIDGES-CH
24 EDDIE FISHER-P
25 TONY GONZALEZ-OF (2)
26 TERRY COX-P
27 PETE (PISTOL PETE) REISER-CH
28 RANDY BROWN-C
29 TOM BRADLEY-P
30 TOM EGAN-C
31 STEVE KEALEY-P
32 BILL VOSS (INJ)-OF
33 DOUG GRIFFIN-2B/3B
34 RUDY MAY-P
36 LEFTY PHILLIPS-MGR
37 DAVE LAROCHE-P
38 CLYDE WRIGHT-P
39 WALLY WOLF-P
39 STEVE KEALEY-P
40 LLOYD ALLEN-P
41 TOM MURPHY-P
42 MARTY PEREZ-INF
42 RAY OYLER-SS/3B
43 GREG GARRETT-P
45 TOMMY SILVERIO-OF/1B
46 MEL QUEEN-P
47 ANDY MESSERSMITH (INJ)-P
48 TERRY COX-P
48 PAUL DOYLE-P (1)
68 HARVEY SHANK-P

1971

4TH W 76-86 25.5GB

1 BRUCE CHRISTENSEN-SS
2 JOE AZCUE (H/O)-C
2 SANDY ALOMAR-2B/SS
3 MICKEY RIVERS (MIL)-OF
3 JEFF TORBORG (INJ)-C
4 SANDY ALOMAR-2B/SS
4 TONY (TONY C) CONIGLIARO (INJ)-OF
5 TOMMIE REYNOLDS-OF/3B
5 MICKEY RIVERS (MIL)-OF
6 ROGER REPOZ-OF/1B
7 KEN MCMULLEN-3B
8 SYD O'BRIEN-UTIL
9 JIM SPENCER-1B
10 TONY (TONY C) CONIGLIARO (INJ)-OF
10 JERRY MOSES-C/OF
11 JIM FREGOSI (INJ)-SS
12 KEN BERRY-OF
14 BILLY COWAN-OF/1B
15 CHICO RUIZ-3B/2B
15 RUDY MEOLI-PH
16 DAVE LAROCHE-P
17 ALEX JOHNSON (SUS)-OF
18 BILLY PARKER-2B
19 JERRY MOSES-C/OF
19 TOMMIE REYNOLDS-OF/3B
20 FRED KOENIG-CH
21 NORM SHERRY-CH
22 ROCKY BRIDGES-CH
24 EDDIE FISHER-P
25 TONY GONZALEZ-OF
27 PETE (PISTOL PETE) REISER-CH
30 FRED LASHER-P
33 TOMMY SILVERIO-2B/3B
34 RUDY MAY (INJ)-P
35 ARCHIE REYNOLDS-P
36 LEFTY PHILLIPS-MGR
37 JOHNNY STEPHENSON-C
38 CLYDE WRIGHT-P
39 ART KUSNYER-C
40 LLOYD ALLEN-P
41 TOM MURPHY-P
42 BRUCE CHRISTENSEN-SS
42 ANDY HASSLER-P
43 JIM MALONEY (INJ)-P
44 RICKEY CLARK-P
45 TOMMY SILVERIO-OF/1B
45 BILLY WYNNE-P
46 MEL QUEEN-P
47 ANDY MESSERSMITH (INJ)-P

1972

5TH W 75-80 18GB

2 SANDY ALOMAR-2B/SS
3 KEN MCMULLEN-3B
4 KEN MCMULLEN-3B
4 DOUG HOWARD-UTIL
5 MICKEY RIVERS-OF
6 ROGER REPOZ-PH
6 CURT MOTTON-OF (2)
7 DEL RICE-MGR
8 SYD O'BRIEN-INF (1)
8 JACK HIATT-C (2)
9 JIM SPENCER-1B/OF
10 JEFF TORBORG (ILL)-C
12 WINSTON LLENAS-UTIL
13 JOHNNY ROSEBORO-CH
14 BILLY COWAN-PH
14 CHRIS COLETTA-OF
15 TOM DUKES (INJ)-P
16 KEN BERRY-OF
17 LEO (CHICO) CARDENAS-SS
18 BILLY PARKER-UTIL
21 BOBBY WINKLES-CH
22 PEANUTS LOWREY-CH
23 JIMMIE REESE-CH
24 EDDIE FISHER-P (1)
27 TOM (PLOWBOY) MORGAN-CH
28 VADA PINSON-OF/1B
29 ANDY KOSCO-OF (1)
29 DOUG HOWARD-UTIL
30 NOLAN RYAN-P
31 JOE AZCUE-C (1)
31 STEVE BARBER-P (2)
32 ALAN FOSTER-P
33 TOMMY SILVERIO-OF
33 BOB OLIVER-1B/OF (2)
34 RUDY MAY-P
35 DICK LANGE-P
36 LEROY (LEE) STANTON-OF
37 JOHNNY STEPHENSON-C
38 CLYDE WRIGHT-P
39 ART KUSNYER-C
40 LLOYD ALLEN-P
41 TOM MURPHY-P (1)
41 DON ROSE-P
44 RICKEY CLARK-P
45 DON ROSE-P
46 MEL QUEEN-P
46 DAVE SELLS-P
47 ANDY MESSERSMITH (INJ)-P
48 PAUL DOYLE-P

1973

4TH W 79-83 15GB

1 BOBBY WINKLES-MGR
2 JOHNNY ROSEBORO-CH
3 RUDY MEOLI-SS/INF
4 DOUG HOWARD-UTIL
5 MICKEY RIVERS-OF
5 MIKE (SUPERJEW) EPSTEIN-1B (2)
6 ALAN GALLAGHER-3B/INF (2)
7 BILLY GRABARKEWITZ-UTIL (1)
7 DAVE CHALK-SS
8 DICK STELMASZEK-C (2)
9 JIM SPENCER-1B/DH (1)
9 RICHIE SCHEINBLUM-OF/DH (2)
10 JEFF TORBORG (INJ)-C
11 JOHNNY STEPHENSON-C
12 WINSTON LLENAS-UTIL
13 BOBBY VALENTINE (INJ)-SS/OF
15 ART KUSNYER-C
16 KEN BERRY-OF
17 BOBBY BROOKS-OF
18 BILLY PARKER-2B/SS
19 JERRY DAVANON-INF
19 CHARLIE SANDS-C
20 FRANK (ROBBY) ROBINSON-DH/OF
21 SALTY PARKER-CH
22 TOMMY MCCRAW-UTIL
23 JIMMIE REESE-CH
24 SANDY ALOMAR-2B/SS
25 RICH HAND-P (2)
27 TOM (PLOWBOY) MORGAN-CH
28 VADA PINSON-OF
29 DAVE SELLS-P
30 NOLAN RYAN-P
31 STEVE BARBER-P
33 BOB OLIVER-UTIL
34 RUDY MAY-P
35 DICK LANGE-P
36 LEROY (LEE) STANTON-OF
38 CLYDE WRIGHT-P
39 ART KUSNYER-C
40 LLOYD ALLEN-P (1)
40 FRANK TANANA-.P
41 AURELIO MONTEAGUDO-P
42 ANDY HASSLER-P
45 RON PERRANOSKI (INJ)-P
46 DAVE SELLS-P
47 RICH HAND-P (2)
47 TERRY WILSHUSEN-P
48 BILL SINGER-P
49 DICK LANGE-P

1974

6TH W 68-94 22GB

1 BOBBY WINKLES-MGR1
1 ORLANDO RAMIREZ-SS
2 JOHNNY ROSEBORO-CH
3 RUDY MEOLI-INF
4 JOE LAHOUD-OF/DH
5 MIKE (SUPERJEW) EPSTEIN-1B
5 JOHN DOHERTY-1B/DH
6 ELLIE RODRIGUEZ-C/DH
7 DAVE CHALK-SS/3B
8 JOHN BALAZ-OF
9 RICHIE SCHEINBLUM-OF/DH (1)
9 PAUL SCHAAL-3B (2)
9 BOB HEISE-INF (2)
10 TOM EGAN-C
12 WINSTON LLENAS (INJ)-UTIL
13 BOBBY VALENTINE (INJ)-UTIL
14 MORRIS NETTLES-OF
14 DOUG HOWARD-UTIL
15 DENNY DOYLE-2B/SS
16 MORRIS NETTLES-OF
17 MICKEY RIVERS (INJ)-OF
19 CHARLIE SANDS (INJ)-C
20 FRANK (ROBBY) ROBINSON-DH/OF (1)
21 SALTY PARKER-CH
22 TOMMY MCCRAW-1B/OF (1)
22 BRUCE BOCHTE-OF/1B
23 WHITEY HERZOG-CH/MGR2/CH
23 DICK WILLIAMS-MGR3
24 SANDY ALOMAR-2B/SS (1)
24 WHITEY HERZOG-CH/MGR2/CH
26 BILL STONEMAN-P

26? BILLY (MUFF) MUFFET-CH
27 TOM (PLOWBOY) MORGAN-CH
29 DAVE SELLS-P
30 NOLAN RYAN-P
31 BARRY RAZIANO-P
32 JOHN DOHERTY-1B/DH
33 BOB OLIVER-UTIL (1)
34 RUDY MAY-P (1)
34 HORACIO PINA-P (2)
35 DICK LANGE-P
36 LEROY (LEE) STANTON (INJ)-OF
37 ED FIGUEROA-P
38 BILL GILBRETH-P
39 KEN SANDERS-P (2)
39 DICK SELMA-P (2)
40 FRANK TANANA-P
41 SKIP LOCKWOOD-P
42 ANDY HASSLER-P
44 DOUG HOWARD-UTIL
44 LUIS QUINTANA-P
45 CHUCK DOBSON-P
47 JOHN CUMBERLAND-P
48 BILL SINGER (INJ)-P
50 JIMMIE REESE-CH
50 CHUCK DOBSON-P
51 ORLANDO PENA-P (2)
52 DON KIRKWOOD-P (2)
66 BILLY MUFFETT-CH

1975

6TH W 72-89 25.5GB

1 ORLANDO RAMIREZ-SS
2 RON JACKSON-UTIL
2 JERRY REMY-2B
3 RUDY MEOLI-UTIL
4 JOE LAHOUD (INJ)-DH/OF
5 JOHN DOHERTY-1B/DH
6 ELLIE RODRIGUEZ (INJ)-C
7 DAVE CHALK-3B
8 JOHN BALAZ-OF/DH
8 ANDY ETCHEBARREN (INJ)-C (2)
9 BILL (SUDS) SUDAKIS-UTIL (1)
9 JOHN BALAZ-OF/DH
10 TOM EGAN-C
10 ADRIAN (PAT) GARRETT-UTIL (2)
11 BOBBY VALENTINE-UTIL (1)
12 WINSTON LLENAS-UTIL
14 BILLY SMITH-INF/DH
15 DENNY DOYLE-2B/3B (1)
15 IKE HAMPTON-UTIL
16 MORRIS NETTLES-OF/DH
17 MICKEY RIVERS-OF/DH
18 BOB ALLIETTA (INJ)-C
19 MICKEY SCOTT-P
20 TOMMY HARPER-DH/UTIL (1)
20 DANNY GOODWIN-DH
21 MIKE MILEY-SS
22 BRUCE BOCHTE (INJ)-1B/DH
23 DICK WILLIAMS-MGR
24 WHITEY HERZOG-CH
25 JERRY ADAIR-CH
26 BILLY (MUFF) MUFFET-CH
27 GROVER RESINGER-CH
28 ORLANDO PENA-P
28 DAVE COLLINS-OF/DH
29 DAVE SELLS-P (1)
29 CHUCK DOBSON-P
29 PAUL DADE-UTIL
30 NOLAN RYAN (INJ)-P
31 TOMMY HARPER-DH/UTIL (1)
32 RON JACKSON-UTIL
33 DON KIRKWOOD-P
34 HORACIO PINA-P
34 JIM BREWER-P (2)
35 DICK LANGE-P
36 LEROY (LEE) STANTON-OF
37 ED FIGUEROA-P
38 DAN BRIGGS-UTIL
39 JOE PACTWA-P
40 FRANK TANANA-P
41 CHARLIE HUDSON-P
42 ANDY HASSLER-P
43 SID MONGE-P
44 LUIS QUINTANA-P
44 JOE PACTWA-P
45 CHUCK DOBSON-P
46 CHUCK HOCKENBERY-P
47 STEVE BLATERIC-P
47 GARY ROSS-P
48 BILL SINGER-P
50 JIMMIE REESE-CH
51 ORLANDO PENA-P
52 DON KIRKWOOD-P

1976

4TH (TIE) W 76-86 14GB

1 ORLANDO RAMIREZ-SS
2 JERRY REMY-2B/DH
3 RUSTY TORRES-OF/UTIL
4 JOE LAHOUD (INJ)-DH/OF (1)
4 DAN BRIGGS-UTIL
7 DAVE CHALK-SS/3B
8 ANDY ETCHEBARREN (INJ)-C
9 TOMMY DAVIS-DH/1B (1)
9 BOB JONES-OF/DH
9 TERRY HUMPHREY-C
10 ADRIAN (PAT) GARRETT-UTIL
10 MIKE EASLER-DH
11 BILLY SMITH-INF/DH
11 MIKE GUERRERO-INF/DH
12 ED HERRMANN-C (1)
12 TOMMY DAVIS-DH/1B (1)
14 BILL MELTON-DH/INF
15 CARLOS LOPEZ-OF/DH
15 IKE HAMPTON-C/SS
16 BILLY SMITH-INF/DH
16 RON JACKSON-3B/UTIL
17 ORLANDO ALVAREZ-OF/DH
18 BOB JONES-OF/DH
19 MICKEY SCOTT (INJ)-P
21 MIKE MILEY-SS
21 JIM BREWER (INJ)-P
22 BRUCE BOCHTE-OF/UTIL
23 DICK WILLIAMS-MGR1
24 VERN HOSCHEIT-CH
25 BOBBY BONDS (INJ)-OF/DH
26 BILLY (MUFF) MUFFET-CH
27 GROVER RESINGER-CH
27 TONY SOLAITA-1B/DH (2)
28 DAVE COLLINS-OF/DH
29 PAUL DADE-UTIL
30 NOLAN RYAN-P
32 RON JACKSON-3B/UTIL
32 CARLOS LOPEZ-OF/DH
33 DON KIRKWOOD-P
34 JIM BREWER (INJ)-P
36 LEROY (LEE) STANTON-OF/DH
37 NORM SHERRY-CH/MGR2
38 DAN BRIGGS-UTIL
38 TIM NORDBROOK-UTIL
39 STEVE DUNNING-P (1)
40 FRANK TANANA-P
41 DICK DRAGO-P
42 ANDY HASSLER-P (1)
42 JOHN VERHOEVEN-P
43 SID MONGE-P
44 MIKE OVERY-P
45 MIKE OVERY-P
45 PAUL HARTZELL-P
47 GARY ROSS-P
48 JOHN VERHOEVEN-P
49? BOB CLEAR-CH
50 JIMMIE REESE-CH
52 GARY WHEELOCK-P
58 PAUL HARTZELL-P

1977

5TH W 74-88 28GB

1 DEL CRANDALL-CH
2 JERRY REMY-2B/3B
3 RUSTY TORRES (INJ)-OF
4 BOBBY GRICH (INJ)-SS
6 DAVE GARCIA-CH/MGR2
7 DAVE CHALK-3B/INF
8 ANDY ETCHEBARREN-C/CH
9 TERRY HUMPHREY-C
10 DAVE KINGMAN-1B/OF (3)
11 MIKE GUERRERO (INJ)-INF/DH
12 DON BAYLOR-OF/UTIL
14 ORLANDO RAMIREZ-UTIL
15 IKE HAMPTON-C/DH
16 RON JACKSON-UTIL
17 ORLANDO RAMIREZ???UTIL
17 DAVE LAROCHE-P (2)
18 BOB JONES-DH
18 RANCE MULLINICKS-SS
19 MICKEY SCOTT-P
19 KEN LANDREAUX-OF
20 DANNY GOODWIN-DH
20 FRANK (ROBBY) ROBINSON-CH
21 DAN BRIGGS-UTIL
22 BRUCE BOCHTE-OF/DH (1)
22 WILLIE AIKENS-UTIL
23 DANNY GOODWIN-DH
24 BILLY (MUFF) MUFFET-CH
24 MARV GRISSOM-CH
25 BOBBY BONDS-OF/DH
26 JOE RUDI (INJ)-OF/DH
27 TONY SOLAITA-1B/DH
28 GIL FLORES-OF/DH
30 NOLAN RYAN-P
31 FRED KUHAULUA-P
32 THAD BOSLEY (INJ)-OF
33 DON KIRKWOOD-P (1)
33 MIKE BARLOW-P
33 KEN BRETT-P (2)
34 KEN BRETT-P (2)
35 MIKE CUELLAR-P
35 BALOR MOORE-P
37 NORM SHERRY-MGR1
38 GARY NOLAN (INJ)-P (2)
39 JOHN CANEIRA-P
40 FRANK TANANA-P
41 DICK DRAGO-P (1)
41 DYAR MILLER-P (2)
42 WAYNE SIMPSON-P
43 SID MONGE-P (1)
43 TOM WALKER-P (2)
44 CARLOS MAY-1B/OF
45 PAUL HARTZELL-P
46 WAYNE SIMPSON-P
47 GARY ROSS (INJ)-P
48 JOHN VERHOEVEN-P (1)
48 GARY NOLAN (INJ)-P (2)
49 BOB CLEAR-CH
50 JOHN CANEIRA-P
50 JIMMIE REESE-CH

1978

2ND (TIE) W 87-75 5GB

1 DAVE GARCIA-MGR1
2 JOHN MCNAMARA-CH
3 RICK MILLER-OF
4 BOBBY GRICH-2B
5 BRIAN DOWNING-C/DH
6 RON FAIRLY-1B/DH
7 DAVE CHALK-SS/UTIL
8 MERV RETTENMUND-OF/DH
9 TERRY HUMPHREY-C/INF
10 LYMAN BOSTOCK (DIED)-OF/DH
11 JIM FREGOSI-MGR2
12 CARNEY LANSFORD-3B/UTIL
14 JIM ANDERSON-SS/2B
15 IKE HAMPTON-UTIL
16 RON JACKSON (INJ)-1B/UTIL
17 DAVE LAROCHE-P
18 RANCE MULLINICKS-SS/DH
19 KEN LANDREAUX-OF/DH
20 DANNY GOODWIN-DH
24 MARV GRISSOM-CH
25 DON BAYLOR-DH/UTIL
26 JOE RUDI (INJ)-OF/UTIL
27 TONY SOLAITA-DH/1B
30 NOLAN RYAN (INJ)-P
33 MIKE BARLOW-P
34 KEN BRETT-P
35 DAVE MACHEMER-INF
36 AL FITZMORRIS-P (2)
37 DAVE FROST-P
38 TOM GRIFFIN-P
39 JOHN CANEIRA-P
40 FRANK TANANA-P
41 DYAR MILLER (INJ)-P
42 CHRIS KNAPP (INJ)-P
45 PAUL HARTZELL-P
46 DON AASE-P
47 AL FITZMORRIS-P (2)
48 BOB SKINNER-CH
49 BOB CLEAR-CH
50 JIMMIE REESE-CH

1979

1ST W 88-74 0GB

L ALCS-BALA 3-1

1 BOBBY KNOOP-CH
2 ORLANDO RAMIREZ-SS/DH
3 RICK MILLER (INJ)-OF/DH
4 BOBBY GRICH (INJ)-2B
5 BRIAN DOWNING-C/DH
6 DERON JOHNSON-CH
(7) DAVE CHALK (INJ)-(SS)
7 BRIAN HARPER-DH
8 MERV RETTENMUND-DH/OF
9 TERRY HUMPHREY (INJ)-C
9 JOHN HARRIS-1B
11 JIM FREGOSI-MGR
12 CARNEY LANSFORD-3B
14 JIM ANDERSON-UTIL
15 DAN FORD-OF
17 DAVE LAROCHE-P
18 RANCE MULLINICKS-SS
19 BERT (CAMPY) CAMPANERIS-SS/DH (2)
20 IKE HAMPTON-UTIL
20 LARRY HARLOW-OF (2)
22 WILLIE AIKENS-1B/DH
23 TOM DONOHUE-C
24 WILLIE DAVIS-OF/DH
25 DON BAYLOR-DH/UTIL
26 JOE RUDI (INJ)-OF/UTIL
27 DERON JOHNSON-CH
28 RALPH (ROADRUNNER) GARR-DH (2)
29 ROD CAREW (INJ)-1B/DH
30 NOLAN RYAN-P
31 DICKIE THON-INF/DH
32 BOBBY CLARK-OF
33 MIKE BARLOW (INJ)-P
33 JIM BARR-P
34 RALPH BOTTING-P
36 MIKE BARLOW (INJ)-P
37 DAVE FROST-P
38 MARK CLEAR-P
39 JOHN MONTAGUE-P (2)
40 FRANK TANANA (INJ)-P
41 DYAR MILLER-P (1)
41 STEVE EDDY-P
41 DAVE SCHULER-P
42 CHRIS KNAPP (INJ)-P
43 RALPH BOTTING-P
45 BOB FERRIS-P
46 DON AASE-P
47 STEVE EDDY-P
48 JIM BARR-P
48 RALPH (ROADRUNNER) GARR-DH (2)
49 BOB CLEAR-CH
50 JIMMIE REESE-CH
51 LARRY SHERRY-CH

1980

6TH W 65-95 31GB

1 BOBBY KNOOP-CH
2 FREDDIE (THE FLEA) PATEK-SS
3 RICK MILLER-OF
4 BOBBY GRICH-2B/1B
5 BRIAN DOWNING (INJ)-C/DH
5 CARNEY LANSFORD-3B
6 DERON JOHNSON-CH
7 MERV RETTENMUND-CH
8 MERV RETTENMUND (RET)-DH
8 DAVE SKAGGS (INJ)-C (2)
9 JOHN HARRIS-1B
9 BRIAN DOWNING (INJ)-C/DH
11 JIM FREGOSI-MGR
12 CARNEY LANSFORD-3B
14 TODD CRUZ-UTIL (1)
14 GIL KUBSKI-OF
15 DAN FORD (INJ)-OF/DH
16 STAN CLIBURN-C
17 DAVE LAROCHE-P
18 AL COWENS-OF/DH (1)
18 JOHN HARRIS-1B
19 BERT (CAMPY) CAMPANERIS-UTIL
20 LARRY HARLOW-OF/UTIL
22 GIL KUBSKI-OF
22 JASON THOMPSON-1B/DH (2)
22 DAVE LEMANCZYK-P (2)
23 TOM DONOHUE-C
24 BRUCE KISON (INJ)-P
25 DON BAYLOR (INJ)-OF/DH
26 JOE RUDI (INJ)-OF/UTIL
27 FREDDIE MARTINEZ-P
28 ED HALICKI-P (2)
29 ROD CAREW-1B/DH
31 DICKIE THON-INF/DH
32 BOBBY CLARK-OF
33 JIM BARR (INJ)-P
34 RALPH BOTTING-P
36 DAN WHITMER-C
37 DAVE FROST (INJ)-P
38 MARK CLEAR-P
39 JOHN MONTAGUE-P
40 FRANK TANANA-P
41 DAVE SCHULER-P
41 ANDY HASSLER-P (2)
42 CHRIS KNAPP-P
43 JIM DORSEY-P
44 BOB FERRIS-P
45 BOB FERRIS-P
45 DAVE LEMANCZYK-P (2)
46 DON AASE-P
47 ANDY HASSLER-P (2)
47 DAVE SCHULER-P
48 RALPH (ROADRUNNER) GARR-DH/OF
48 RALPH BOTTING-P
49 BOB CLEAR-CH
50 JIMMIE REESE-CH
51 LARRY SHERRY-CH

LA/CALIFORNIA/ANAHEIM/**LOS ANGELES ANGELS**

1981
1ST 1/2:4TH W 31-29 6GB
2ND 1/2:7TH W 20-30 8.5GB
FINAL: 51-59 --GB

1 BOBBY KNOOP-CH
2 FREDDIE (THE FLEA) PATEK-INF
3 BRIAN HARPER-OF/DH
3 JUAN BENIQUEZ-OF/DH
3 TOM (BRUNO) BRUNANSKY-OF
3 GENE (SKIP) MAUCH-MGR2
4 BOBBY GRICH-2B
5 BRIAN DOWNING-OF/DH
6* ANGEL MORENO-P*
7 RICK (ROOSTER) BURLESON-SS
8 FRED LYNN-OF
10 BUTCH HOBSON-3B/DH
11 JIM FREGOSI-MGR1
11 JOE FERGUSON-C/OF (2)
12 JUAN BENIQUEZ-OF/DH
12 BRIAN HARPER-OF/DH
13 JOHN HARRIS-1B
14 MERV RETTENMUND-CH
14 ED OTT-C
15 DAN FORD-OF
16 BOB DAVIS-C
17 MERV RETTENMUND-CH
18 PRESTON GOMEZ-CH
19 BERT (CAMPY) CAMPANERIS-INF
20 LARRY HARLOW-OF
21 DARYL SCONIERS-1B/DH
21 ANGEL MORENO-P
22 MICKEY MAHLER-P
23 STEVE LUBRATICH-3B
24 BRUCE KISON (INJ)-P
25 DON BAYLOR-DH/UTIL
26 BILL TRAVERS (INJ)-P
27 FREDDIE MARTINEZ-P
28 JOHN D'ACQUISTO-P
29 ROD CAREW-1B/DH
30 TOM (BRUNO) BRUNANSKY-OF
31 DOUG RAU-(INJ)-P
32 BOBBY CLARK (INJ)-OF
34 JESSE JEFFERSON-P
37 DAVE FROST (INJ)-P
38 GEOFF ZAHN-P
39 MIKE WITT-P
40 LUIS SANCHEZ-P
41 ANDY HASSLER-P
43 KEN FORSCH-P
44 MIKE WITT-P
44 GENE (SKIP) MAUCH-MGR2
45 STEVE RENKO-P
46 DON AASE-P
47 ANGEL MORENO-P
47 TOM (PLOWBOY) MORGAN-CH
48 DOUG RAU (INJ)-P
49 BOB CLEAR-CH
49 MICKEY MAHLER-P
50 JIMMIE REESE-CH

1982
1ST W 93-69 0GB
L ALCS-MILA 3-2

1 BOBBY KNOOP-CH
2 MICK KELLEHER-SS/3B (2)
3 GENE (SKIP) MAUCH-MGR
4 BOBBY GRICH-2B/DH
5 BRIAN DOWNING-OF
6 DARYL SCONIERS-1B/DH
7 RICK (ROOSTER) BURLESON (INJ)-SS
8 BOB BOONE-C
9 ROB WILFONG-UTIL (2)
10 TIM FOLI-SS/INF
11 DOUG DECINCES-3B/SS
12 JUAN BENIQUEZ-OF
13 JOE FERGUSON-C/OF
(14) ED OTT (INJ)-(C)
15 RON JACKSON-1B/3B
16 JOHN (JACK) CURTIS-P (2)
17 MERV RETTENMUND-CH
18 PRESTON GOMEZ-CH
19 FRED LYNN-OF
20 TIM FOLI-SS/INF
20 GARY PETTIS-OF
21 ANGEL MORENO-P
22 MICKEY MAHLER-P
23 LUIS TIANT-P
23 DOUG CORBETT-P (2)
24 BRUCE KISON-P
25 DON BAYLOR-DH
(26) BILL TRAVERS (INJ)-(P)
26 JOHN (JACK) CURTIS-P (2)
26 TOMMY (T.J.) JOHN-P (2)
28 JOHN (JACK) CURTIS-P (2)
29 ROD CAREW-1B
30 GARY PETTIS-OF
30 DAVE GOLTZ (INJ)-P (2)
31 JOSE MORENO-2B/DH
32 BOBBY CLARK-OF
33 LUIS TIANT-P
34 STAN BAHNSEN-P (1)
35 TOMMY (T.J.) JOHN-P (2)
38 GEOFF ZAHN-P
39 MIKE WITT-P
40 LUIS SANCHEZ-P
41 ANDY HASSLER-P
42 RICK STEIRER-P
43 KEN FORSCH-P
44 REGGIE (MR. OCTOBER) JACKSON-OF/DH
45 STEVE RENKO-P
46 DON AASE (INJ)-P
47 TOM (PLOWBOY) MORGAN-CH
47 DAVE GOLTZ (INJ)-P (2)
48 RICK ADAMS-SS
49 BOB CLEAR-CH
50 JIMMIE REESE-CH

1983
5TH (TIE) W 70-92 29GB

1 BOBBY KNOOP-CH
2 JOHN MCNAMARA-MGR
3 RICK ADAMS-INF
3 MIKE O'BERRY-C
4 BOBBY GRICH (INJ)-2B/SS
5 BRIAN DOWNING (INJ)-OF/DH
6 DARYL SCONIERS-UTIL
7 RICK (ROOSTER) BURLESON (INJ)-SS
8 BOB BOONE-C
9 ROB WILFONG-UTIL
10 TIM FOLI (INJ)-SS/3B
11 DOUG DECINCES (INJ)-3B/DH
12 JUAN BENIQUEZ (INJ)-OF/DH
13 JOE FERGUSON-C/OF
14 ED OTT (INJ)-C
15 RON JACKSON-UTIL
16 JOHN (JACK) CURTIS-P
17 ELLIS VALENTINE (INJ)-OF
18 PRESTON GOMEZ-CH
19 FRED LYNN-OF/DH
20 GARY PETTIS-OF
23 DOUG CORBETT-P
24 BRUCE KISON (INJ)-P
25 TOMMY (T.J.) JOHN-P
26 BILL TRAVERS-P
26 *(RET #) GENE AUTRY*
27 BYRON MCLAUGHLIN-P
28 STEVE LUBRATICH-INF
29 ROD CAREW-1B/UTIL
30 DAVE GOLTZ-P
30 DICK SCHOFIELD-SS
31 RICK ADAMS-INF
32 BOBBY CLARK (INJ)-UTIL
33 BOB LACEY-P
34 JERRY NARRON-C/DH
35 TOMMY (T.J.) JOHN-P
35 BILL TRAVERS-P
36 STEVE BROWN-P
37 MIKE BROWN-OF
38 GEOFF ZAHN (INJ)-P
39 MIKE WITT-P
40 LUIS SANCHEZ-P
41 ANDY HASSLER-P
42 RICK STEIRER-P
43 KEN FORSCH-P
44 REGGIE (MR. OCTOBER) JACKSON-DH/OF
(46) DON AASE (INJ)-(P)
47 TOM (PLOWBOY) MORGAN-CH
48 CURT BROWN-P
49 BOB CLEAR-CH
50 JIMMIE REESE-CH

1984
2ND (TIE) W 81-81 3GB

1 BOBBY KNOOP-CH
2 JOHN MCNAMARA-MGR
3 MIKE BROWN-OF/DH
4 BOBBY GRICH-INF
5 BRIAN DOWNING-OF/DH
6 DARYL SCONIERS (INJ)-1B/DH
7 RICK (ROOSTER) BURLESON (INJ)-PH
8 BOB BOONE-C
9 ROB WILFONG-2B/UTIL
10 ROB PICCIOLO-UTIL
11 DOUG DECINCES-3B/DH
12 JUAN BENIQUEZ-OF
15 RON JACKSON-UTIL (1)
15 DERREL THOMAS-UTIL (2)
16 JOHN (JACK) CURTIS (INJ)-P
(17) ELLIS VALENTINE (INJ)-(OF)
18 PRESTON GOMEZ-CH
19 FRED LYNN-OF
20 GARY PETTIS-OF
22 MIKE BROWN-OF/DH
22 DICK SCHOFIELD-SS
23 DOUG CORBETT-P
24 BRUCE KISON (INJ)-P
25 TOMMY (T.J.) JOHN-P
26 *(RET #) GENE AUTRY*
27 FRANK LACORTE (INJ)-P
27 CRAIG SWAN (INJ)-P (2)
29 ROD CAREW-1B/UTIL
30 DICK SCHOFIELD-SS
30 DERREL THOMAS-UTIL (2)
31 FRANK LACORTE (INJ)-P
32 DARRELL MILLER-1B/OF
34 JERRY NARRON-C/1B
35 DAVE (D.W.) SMITH-P
36 STEVE BROWN-P
37 RON ROMANICK-P
38 GEOFF ZAHN-P
39 MIKE WITT-P
40 LUIS SANCHEZ-P
41 JIM SLATON-P
42 RICK STEIRER-P
43 KEN FORSCH (INJ)-P
44 REGGIE (MR. OCTOBER) JACKSON-DH/OF
46 DON AASE (INJ)-P
47 JIM SLATON-P
48 CURT KAUFMAN-P
49 BOB CLEAR-CH
50 JIMMIE REESE-CH
51 MARCEL LACHEMANN-CH
63 STEW CLIBURN-P

1985
2ND W 90-72 1GB

1 BOBBY KNOOP-CH
2 CRAIG GERBER-UTIL
3 GENE (SKIP) MAUCH-MGR
4 BOBBY GRICH-2B/INF
5 BRIAN DOWNING-OF/DH
6 DARYL SCONIERS (INJ) (SUB)-DH/1B
(7) RICK (ROOSTER) BURLESON (INJ)-(SS)
8 BOB BOONE-C
9 ROB WILFONG-2B/DH
10 RON ROMANICK-P
11 DOUG DECINCES-3B/DH
12 JUAN BENIQUEZ-UTIL
13 RUPPERT JONES-OF/DH
15 KIRK MCCASKILL-P
16 JACK HOWELL-3B
17 TONY MACK-P
18 URBANO LUGO-P
19 RUPPERT JONES-OF/DH
19 AL HOLLAND-P (3)
20 GARY PETTIS (INJ)-OF
20 DON SUTTON-P (2)
21 MIKE BROWN-OF/DH (1)
22 DICK SCHOFIELD-SS
23 DOUG CORBETT (INJ)-P
24 RUFINO LINARES-OF
24 GARY PETTIS (INJ)-OF
25 TOMMY (T.J.) JOHN-P (1)
25 GEORGE HENDRICK-OF/DH (2)
26 *(RET #) GENE AUTRY*
27 PAT CLEMENTS-P (1)
27 DON SUTTON-P (2)
29 ROD CAREW-1B/DH
30 DEVON WHITE-OF
(31) FRANK LACORTE (INJ)-(P)
32 DARRELL MILLER (INJ)-UTIL
33 STEW CLIBURN-P
34 JERRY NARRON-UTIL
35 DAVE (D.W.) SMITH-P
36 BOB KIPPER-P (1)
36 PAT KEEDY-3B/OF
37 DONNIE MOORE-P
38 GEOFF ZAHN (INJ)-P
39 MIKE WITT-P
40 LUIS SANCHEZ (INJ)-P
41 JIM SLATON-P
(43) KEN FORSCH (INJ)-(P)
44 REGGIE (MR. OCTOBER) JACKSON-OF/DH
45 JOHN (CANDY MAN) CANDELARIA-P (2)
46 ALAN FOWLKES (INJ)-P
47 MOOSE STUBING-CH
49 BOB CLEAR-CH
50 JIMMIE REESE-CH
51 MARCEL LACHEMANN-CH
56 GUS POLIDOR-SS/OF

1986
1ST W 92-70 0GB
L ALCS-BOSA 4-3

1 BOBBY KNOOP-CH
3 GENE (SKIP) MAUCH-MGR
4 BOBBY GRICH-INF
5 BRIAN DOWNING-OF/DH
6 MARK RYAL-UTIL
7 RICK (ROOSTER) BURLESON-UTIL
8 BOB BOONE-C
9 ROB WILFONG-2B
10 RON ROMANICK-P
11 DOUG DECINCES-3B/UTIL
12 GUS POLIDOR-INF
13 RUPPERT JONES-OF
15 KIRK MCCASKILL-P
16 JACK HOWELL-UTIL
18 URBANO LUGO (INJ)-P
20 GARY PETTIS-OF/DH
20 DON SUTTON-P
21 WALLY JOYNER-1B
22 DICK SCHOFIELD-SS
23 DOUG CORBETT-P
24 GARY PETTIS-OF/DH
25 GEORGE HENDRICK-UTIL
26 *(RET #) GENE AUTRY*
27 DON SUTTON-P
28 MARK MCLEMORE-2B
29 *(RET#) ROD CAREW*
30 DEVON WHITE-OF
31 CHUCK FINLEY-P
32 DARRELL MILLER-UTIL
34 JERRY NARRON-C/DH
36 GARY LUCAS (INJ)-P
37 DONNIE MOORE (INJ)-P
38 TODD FISCHER-P
39 MIKE WITT-P
41 JIM SLATON-P (1)
43 KEN FORSCH-P
43 VERN RUHLE-P
44 REGGIE (MR. OCTOBER) JACKSON-DH/OF
45 JOHN (CANDY MAN) CANDELARIA (INJ)-P
46 MIKE COOK-P
46 WILLIE FRASER-P
47 MOOSE STUBING-CH
47 T. R. BRYDEN-P
48 RAY CHADWICK-P
49 BOB CLEAR-CH
50 JIMMIE REESE-CH
51 MARCEL LACHEMANN-CH
51 TERRY FORSTER (INJ)-P
52 WILLIE FRASER-P
53 MARCEL LACHEMANN-CH
59 CHUCK FINLEY-P
63 T. R. BRYDEN-P

1987
6TH (TIE) W 75-87 10GB

1 BOBBY KNOOP-CH
2 TACK WILSON-OF/DH
3 GENE (SKIP) MAUCH-MGR
3 JOHNNY RAY-2B/DH (2)
4 GENE (SKIP) MAUCH-MGR
5 BRIAN DOWNING-DH/OF
6 MARK RYAL-UTIL
6 BILL (BILLY BUCK) BUCKNER-DH/1B (2)
8 BOB BOONE-C/DH
9 RUPPERT JONES-OF/DH
10 TONY ARMAS-OF
11 DOUG DECINCES-3B/UTIL (1)
12 JIM EPPARD-OF
13 JACK FIMPLE-C
14 GUS POLIDOR-INF
15 KIRK MCCASKILL (INJ)-P
16 JACK HOWELL-OF/INF
17 JACK LAZORKO-P
18 URBANO LUGO-P
19 RICK DOWN-CH
20 DON SUTTON-P
21 WALLY JOYNER-1B
22 DICK SCHOFIELD (INJ)-SS
24 GARY PETTIS-OF
25 GEORGE HENDRICK (INJ)-UTIL
26 *(RET #) GENE AUTRY*
27 WILLIE FRASER-P
28 MARK MCLEMORE-2B/UTIL
29 *(RET#) ROD CAREW*
30 DEVON WHITE-OF
31 CHUCK FINLEY-P
32 DARRELL MILLER (INJ)-UTIL
34 MIGUEL GARCIA-P
34 BRYAN HARVEY-P
35 BUTCH WYNEGAR-C/DH
36 GARY LUCAS-P

37 DONNIE MOORE (INJ)-P
38 GREG MINTON-P (2)
38 BRYAN HARVEY-P
39 MIKE WITT-P
40 JOE COLEMAN-CH
41 DEWAYNE BUICE-P
44 JERRY REUSS-P (3)
45 JOHN (CANDY MAN) CANDELARIA (ALC)-P
46 MIKE COOK-P
47 JACK LAZORKO-P
47 MOOSE STUBING-CH
49 BOB CLEAR-CH
50 JIMMIE REESE-CH
53 MARCEL LACHEMANN-CH
58 JACK FIMPLE-C
61 RICK DOWN-CH

1988

4TH W 75-87 29GB

1 BOBBY KNOOP-CH
2 COOKIE ROJAS-MGR1
3 JOHNNY RAY-2B/UTIL
5 BRIAN DOWNING-DH
6 BILL (BILLY BUCK) BUCKNER-DH/1B (1)
6 DOUG DAVIS-C/3B
6 JOE REDFIELD-3B
6 DOMINGO RAMOS-3B/OF (2)
7 THAD BOSLEY-OF (2)
8 BOB BOONE-C
9 CHICO WALKER-UTIL
9 JUNIOR NOBOA-INF
10 CHICO WALKER-UTIL
11 DANTE BICHETTE-OF
12 JIM EPPARD-UTIL
14 GUS POLIDOR-UTIL
15 KIRK MCCASKILL (INJ)-P
16 JACK HOWELL-3B/OF
17 JACK LAZORKO-P
18 URBANO LUGO-P
19 RICK DOWN-CH
20 TONY ARMAS-OF/DH
21 WALLY JOYNER-1B
22 DICK SCHOFIELD-SS
23 SHERMAN CORBETT-P
23 MIKE BROWN-OF
24 CHILI DAVIS-OF/DH
25 GEORGE HENDRICK-UTIL
26 *(RET #) GENE AUTRY*
27 WILLIE FRASER-P
28 MARK MCLEMORE (INJ)-INF/DH
29 *(RET#) ROD CAREW*
30 DEVON WHITE (INJ)-OF
31 CHUCK FINLEY-P
32 DARRELL MILLER-UTIL
33 STEW CLIBURN-P
34 BRYAN HARVEY-P
35 BUTCH WYNEGAR (INJ)-C
36 MIKE COOK-P
36 SHERMAN CORBETT-P
37 DONNIE MOORE (INJ)-P
38 GREG MINTON (INJ)-P
39 MIKE WITT-P
40 JOE COLEMAN-CH
41 DEWAYNE BUICE (INJ)-P
42 TERRY CLARK-P
43 MIKE COOK-P
43 RAY KRAWCZYK-P
44 RICH MONTELEONE-P
45 VANCE LOVELACE-P
46 DAN PETRY (INJ) P
47 MOOSE STUBING-CH/MGR2
48 FRANK DIMICHELE-P
48 BRIAN DORSETT (INJ)-C
50 JIMMIE REESE-CH
53 MARCEL LACHEMANN-CH
57 RICK RAGASSO-CH
58 JACK FIMPLE-C
59 RAY KRAWCZYK-P

1989

3RD W 91-71 8GB

1 BOBBY KNOOP-CH
2 DERON JOHNSON-CH
3 JOHNNY RAY-2B
4 GARY DISARCINA-SS
5 BRIAN DOWNING-DH
6 BOBBY ROSE-3B/2B
7 CLAUDELL WASHINGTON-OF/DH
7 KENT ANDERSON-UTIL
8 BRIAN BRADY-OF
8 MAX VENABLE-OF
9 GLENN HOFFMAN-INF/DH
10 MARK MCLEMORE-INF/DH
11 JIM EPPARD-1B
12 DOUG (THE RED ROOSTER) (ROJO) RADER-MGR
13 LANCE PARRISH-C/DH
14 BILL SCHROEDER (INJ)-C/1B
14 JOHN ORTON-C
15 KIRK MCCASKILL-P
16 JACK HOWELL-3B/OF
18 CLAUDELL WASHINGTON-OF/DH
19 DANTE BICHETTE-OF/DH
20 TONY ARMAS (INJ)-UTIL
21 WALLY JOYNER-1B
22 DICK SCHOFIELD (INJ)-SS
23 BILL SCHROEDER (INJ)-C/1B
24 CHILI DAVIS-OF/DH
25 JIM ABBOTT-P
26 *(RET #) GENE AUTRY*
27 WILLIE FRASER-P
28 BERT BLYLEVEN-P
29 *(RET#) ROD CAREW*
30 DEVON WHITE-OF/DH
31 CHUCK FINLEY-P
32 RON TINGLEY-C
33 BOB MCCLURE-P
34 BRYAN HARVEY-P
36 SHERMAN CORBETT-P
37 BOB MCCLURE-P
38 GREG MINTON-P
39 MIKE WITT-P
40 JOE COLEMAN-CH
42 TERRY CLARK (INJ)-P
44 RICH MONTELEONE-P
45 VANCE LOVELACE-P
46 DAN PETRY-P
47 MOOSE STUBING-CH
48 MIKE FETTERS-P
50 JIMMIE REESE-CH
53 MARCEL LACHEMANN-CH

1990

4TH W 80-82 23GB

1 BOBBY KNOOP-CH
2 DERON JOHNSON-CH
3 JOHNNY RAY-2B/DH
4 DOUG (THE RED ROOSTER) (ROJO) RADER-MGR
5 BRIAN DOWNING-DH
6 BOBBY ROSE-2B/3B
7 KENT ANDERSON-INF
8 MAX VENABLE-OF/DH
9 LEE STEVENS-1B
10 MARK MCLEMORE (INJ)-2B/3B (1)
10 PETE COACHMAN-INF/DH
11 GARY DISARCINA-SS/2B
12 MARK LANGSTON-P
13 LANCE PARRISH-C/UTIL
14 JOHN ORTON-C
15 KIRK MCCASKILL-P
16 JACK HOWELL-3B/INF
17 DICK SCHOFIELD (INJ)-SS
18 CLAUDELL WASHINGTON-OF (1)
18 LUIS POLONIA-OF/DH (2)
18 DONNIE HILL-UTIL/P
19 DANTE BICHETTE-OF
20 RICK SCHU-UTIL
21 WALLY JOYNER (INJ)-1B
22 DONNIE HILL-UTIL/P
22 LUIS POLONIA-OF/DH (2)
23 BILL SCHROEDER (INJ)-C/1B
24 CHILI DAVIS-DH/OF
25 JIM ABBOTT-P
26 *(RET #) GENE AUTRY*
27 WILLIE FRASER-P
28 BERT BLYLEVEN (INJ)-P
29 *(RET#) ROD CAREW*
30 DEVON WHITE-OF
31 CHUCK FINLEY-P
32 RON TINGLEY (INJ)-C
32 DAVE WINFIELD-OF/DH (2)
33 BOB MCCLURE (INJ)-P
34 BRYAN HARVEY-P
35 CLIFF YOUNG-P
36 SHERMAN CORBETT-P
37 JEFF RICHARDSON-P
38 GREG MINTON (INJ)-P
39 MIKE WITT-P (1)
39 JOE GRAHE-P
40 JOE COLEMAN-CH
41 RON TINGLEY (INJ)-C
43 SCOTT BAILES-P
44 JOE GRAHE-P
45 MARK EICHHORN-P
46 MARK CLEAR-P
46 SCOTT LEWIS-P
47 MOOSE STUBING-CH
48 MIKE FETTERS-P
50 JIMMIE REESE-CH
53 MARCEL LACHEMANN-CH
60 RICK SCHU-UTIL

1991

7TH W 81-81 14GB

1 BOBBY KNOOP-CH
2 DERON JOHNSON-CH
3 GARY GAETTI-3B
4 DOUG (THE RED ROOSTER) (ROJO) RADER-MGR1
6 BOBBY ROSE (INJ)-UTIL
7 BOB (BUCK) RODGERS-MGR2 (2)
8 MAX VENABLE-OF/DH
9 LEE STEVENS-1B/OF
10 LUIS SOJO-2B/UTIL
11 GARY DISARCINA-INF
12 MARK LANGSTON-P
13 LANCE PARRISH-C/UTIL
14 JOHN ORTON-C/DH
15 KIRK MCCASKILL-P
16 JACK HOWELL-UTIL (1)
16 SHAWN ABNER-OF/DH (2)
17 DICK SCHOFIELD-SS
18 DONNIE HILL-UTIL/P
19 BRUCE HINES-CH
20 JOE GRAHE-P
21 WALLY JOYNER-1B
22 LUIS POLONIA-OF/DH
23 FLOYD BANNISTER (INJ)-P
24 RON TINGLEY-C
25 JIM ABBOTT-P
26 *(RET #) GENE AUTRY*
27 DAVE GALLAGHER-OF/DH
(28) BERT BLYLEVEN (INJ)-(P)
29 *(RET#) ROD CAREW*
30 RUBEN AMARO-UTIL
31 CHUCK FINLEY-P
32 DAVE WINFIELD-OF/DH
33 BOB MCCLURE-P
34 BRYAN HARVEY-P
35 CLIFF YOUNG-P
35 CHRIS BEASLEY-P
36 FERNANDO VALENZUELA-P
37 BOB (BUCK) RODGERS-MGR2 (2)
38 BRUCE HINES-CH
38 KEVIN FLORA-2B
39 CHRIS CRON-1B/DH
39 DAVE PARKER-DH (1)
40 MARK DAVIS-OF
41 BARRY LYONS-1B (2)
41 MIKE MARSHALL-1B/DH (2)
43 SCOTT BAILES-P
44 JOE GRAHE-P
44 CHRIS CRON-1B/DH
44 KYLE ABBOTT-P
45 MARK EICHHORN-P
46 SCOTT LEWIS-P
47 JUNIOR FELIX (INJ)-OF
48 MIKE FETTERS-P
49 JEFF ROBINSON-P
50 JIMMIE REESE-CH
51 FRANK (CRANE) REBERGER-CH
53 MARCEL LACHEMANN-CH
57 RICK TURNER-CH
59 KYLE ABBOTT-P

1992

5TH (TIE) W 72-90 24GB

1 BOBBY KNOOP-CH
2 DERON JOHNSON (DIED)-CH
3 GARY GAETTI-3B/1B
5 KEN (OBIE) OBERKFELL-UTIL
6 BOBBY ROSE-2B/1B
7 BOB (BUCK) RODGERS-MGR
8 HUBIE BROOKS-DH/1B
9 VON HAYES (INJ) (REL)-OF/1B
9 LEE STEVENS-1B
10 LUIS SOJO-2B/INF
11 GARY DISARCINA-INF
11 REGGIE WILLIAMS-OF
12 MARK LANGSTON-P
13 LANCE PARRISH-C/UTIL (1)
14 JOHN ORTON-C/DH
15 TIM SALMON-OF
16 ROB DUCEY-OF (2)
17 DICK SCHOFIELD-SS (1)
17 CHAD CURTIS-OF
18 SCOTT LEWIS-P
19 JOE GRAHE-P
20 JOE GRAHE-P
20 MIKE FITZGERALD-C/UTIL
21 ALVIN DAVIS-1B
21 GREG MYERS-C (2)
22 LUIS POLONIA-OF
23 LEE STEVENS-1B
23 MIKE BUTCHER-P
24 RON TINGLEY-C
25 JIM ABBOTT-P
26 *(RET #) GENE AUTRY*
27 DAVE GALLAGHER-OF/DH
28 BERT BLYLEVEN (INJ)-P
29 ROD CAREW-CH
30 CHAD CURTIS-OF
30 *(RET#) NOLAN RYAN*
31 CHUCK FINLEY-P
32 CHUCK CRIM-P
33 JOHN MORRIS (REL.)-OF
33 GARY DISARCINA-INF
34 BRYAN HARVEY-P
37 JOHN (BULL) WATHAN-C
38 JOSE GONZALEZ-OF
39 KEN MACHA-CH
40 DON ROBINSON-P (1)
40 TIM FORTUGNO, P
41 STEVE FREY-P
41 SCOTT BAILES-P
44 JULIO VALERA-P
45 MARK EICHHORN-P
46 DAMION EASLEY-3B/SS
47 JUNIOR FELIX (INJ)-OF
48 MIKE BUTCHER-P
48 HILLY HATHAWAY-P
50 JIMMIE REESE-CH
51 TIM FORTUGNO-P
53 MARCEL LACHEMANN-CH
57 RICK TURNER-CH
73 CHUCK HERNANDEZ-CH
88 RENE GONZALES-INF

1993

5TH (TIE) W 71-91 23GB

1 DAMION EASLEY (INJ)-INF/DH
2 BOBBY KNOOP-CH
3 GARY GAETTI (REL.)-INF/DH (1)
3 JIM WALEWANDER-INF/DH
3 KURT STILLWELL-2B/SS (2)
5 ROD CORREIA-INF/DH
6 J. T. SNOW-1B
7 BOB (BUCK) RODGERS-MGR
9 CHAD CURTIS-OF/DH
10 TOREY LOVULLO-2B/UTIL
11 GREG MYERS-C/DH
12 MARK LANGSTON-P
13 LARRY GONZALES-C/1B
14 JOHN ORTON (INJ)-C
15 TIM SALMON-OF/DH
16 GENE NELSON-P (1)
17 KELLY GRUBER (INJ)-UTIL
18 SCOTT LEWIS-P
19 JOE GRAHE (INJ)-P
20 JEROME WALTON-DH/OF
20 PAUL SWINGLE-P
21 SCOTT SANDERSON-P (1)
21 PHIL LEFTWICH-P
21 EDUARDO PEREZ-3B/DH
22 LUIS POLONIA-OF/DH
23 MIKE BUTCHER (INJ)-P
24 RON TINGLEY-C
25 STAN JAVIER-UTIL
25 JIM EDMONDS-OF
26 *(RET #) GENE AUTRY*
29 ROD CAREW-CH
30 *(RET#) NOLAN RYAN*
31 CHUCK FINLEY-P
32 CHUCK CRIM-P
32 JOE MAGRANE-P (2)
33 GARY DISARCINA (INJ)-SS
34 JULIO VALERA (INJ)-P
35 DOUG LINTON-P (2)
36 JERRY NIELSEN-P
37 JOHN (BULL) WATHAN-CH
38 JOHN FARRELL-P
39 KEN MACHA-CH
40 RUSS SPRINGER (INJ)-P
41 STEVE FREY-P
42 MARK HOLZEMER-P
43 DARRYL SCOTT-P
44 CHILI DAVIS-DH/P
45 EDUARDO PEREZ-3B/DH
45 PHIL LEFTWICH-P
46 TY VAN BURKLEO-1B
47 KEN PATTERSON-P
48 HILLY HATHAWAY-P
50 JIMMIE REESE-CH
53 RICK TURNER-CH
55 CHUCK HERNANDEZ-CH
56 BRIAN ANDERSON-P
57 RICK TURNER-CH
60 RICK WRONA-DH
88 RENE GONZALES-3B/UTIL/P

1994

4TH W 47-68 5.5GB
STRIKE NO POST-SEASON

1 DAMION EASLEY (INJ)-3B
2 BOBBY KNOOP-CH

LA/CALIFORNIA/ANAHEIM/**LOS ANGELES ANGELS**

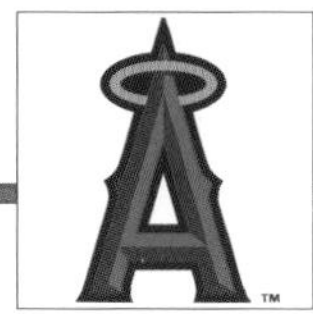

3 HAROLD REYNOLDS-2B
5 ROD CORREIA-2B
6 J. T. SNOW-1B
7 BOB (BUCK) RODGERS-MGR 1
7 MARK DALESANDRO-3B
9 CHAD CURTIS-OF/DH
0 REX HUDLER (INJ)-2B/UTIL
1 GREG MYERS (INJ)-C/DH
2 MARK LANGSTON (INJ)-P
4 JORGE FABREGAS-C
5 TIM SALMON (INJ)-OF/DH
6 GARRET ANDERSON-OF
7 SPIKE OWEN-3B
8 SCOTT LEWIS (INJ)-P
9 JOE GRAHE-P
0 CHRIS TURNER-C
1 CRAIG LEFFERTS (REL)-P
2 BO JACKSON-OF
3 MIKE BUTCHER-P
4 EDUARDO PEREZ-3B/DH/1B
5 JIM EDMONDS-OF/1B
6 *(RET #) GENE AUTRY*
7 MARK LEITER-P
8 BOB PATTERSON-P
9 ROD CAREW-CH
0 *(RET#) NOLAN RYAN*
1 CHUCK FINLEY-P
2 JOE MAGRANE (INJ)-P
3 GARY DISARCINA-SS
5 DWIGHT SMITH-OF (1)
5 ANDREW LORRAINE-P
6 BILL SAMPEN-P
6 JEFF SCHWARZ-P (2)
8 JOHN FARRELL-P
9 KEN MACHA-CH
1 JOHN DOPSON (INJ)-P
3 RUSS SPRINGER-P
4 CHILI DAVIS-DH
5 PHIL LEFTWICH (INJ)-P
7 KEN PATTERSON (INJ)-P
0 JIMMIE REESE (DIED)-CH
3 MARCEL LACHEMANN-MGR 2 (2)
5 CHUCK HERNANDEZ-CH
6 BRIAN ANDERSON (INJ)-P
8 JORGE FABREGAS-C
2 MAX OLIVARES-P

1995

2ND W 78-67 1GB
L P/O-SEAA 1-0

1 DAMION EASLEY-3B
2 BOBBY KNOOP-CH
3 ORLANDO PALMEIRO-OF
5 ROD CORREIA-2B
6 J. T. SNOW-1B
7 MARK DALESANDRO-C
8 KEVIN FLORA-DH (1)
(8) TODD GREENE-(C)
9 CARLOS MARTINEZ (WAIV)-3B
9 DICK SCHOFIELD-SS (2)
0 REX HUDLER (INJ)-OF
1 GREG MYERS (INJ)-C/DH
2 MARK LANGSTON (INJ)-P
3 JOSE LIND (WAIV)-2B (2)
4 JORGE FABREGAS-C
5 TIM SALMON-OF/DH
6 GARRET ANDERSON-OF
7 SPIKE OWEN (INJ)-3B
8 DAVE GALLAGHER (INJ)-OF (2)
9 TONY PHILLIPS-3B/OF
0 CHRIS TURNER-C
1 SCOTT SANDERSON (INJ)-P
2 SHAWN BOSKIE (INJ)-P
3 MIKE BUTCHER-P
4 EDUARDO PEREZ-3B
5 JIM EDMONDS-OF
6 *(RET #) GENE AUTRY*
27 MIKE ALDRETE-1B (2)
28 ANDY ALLENSON (INJ)-C
29 ROD CAREW-CH
30 *(RET#) NOLAN RYAN*
31 CHUCK FINLEY-P
32 JOHN HABYAN-P (2)
33 GARY DISARCINA (INJ)-SS
34 MIKE HARKEY-P (2)
36 MIKE BIELECKI (INJ)-P
37 BOB PATTERSON-P
38 BILL LACHEMANN-CH
39 RICK (ROOSTER) BURLESON-CH
40 TROY PERCIVAL-P
42 MARK HOLZEMER-P
43 RUSS SPRINGER-P (1)
43 RICH MONTELEONE-P
44 CHILI DAVIS (INJ)-DH
46 MIKE JAMES (INJ)-P
47 LEE SMITH-P
48 KEN EDENFIELD-P
50 *(RET#) JIMMIE REESE*
52 JIM ABBOTT-P (2)
53 MARCEL LACHEMANN-MGR
54 ERIK BENNETT-P
55 CHUCK HERNANDEZ-CH
56 BRIAN ANDERSON (INJ)-P
70 JOE MADDON-CH
88 RENE GONZALES-3B
99 MITCH WILLIAMS (REL)-P

1996

4TH W 70-91 19.5GB

1 DAMION EASLEY (INJ)-INF (1)
1? JOHN MCNAMARA (ILL)-MGR2
2 BOBBY KNOOP-CH
3 ORLANDO PALMEIRO-OF
5 GEORGE ARIAS-3B
6 J. T. SNOW-1B
7 PAT BORDERS-C (2)
8 TODD GREENE-C
9 DICK SCHOFIELD (INJ)-SS
10 REX HUDLER-2B
11 DON SLAUGHT (INJ)-C (1)
11 ROBERT EENHOORN-2B (2)
12 MARK LANGSTON (INJ)-P
14 JORGE FABREGAS-C
15 TIM SALMON-OF
16 GARRET ANDERSON-OF
17 BEN VANRYN-P
17 CHUCK MCELROY (INJ)-P (2)
18 RANDY VELARDE-2B
19 JASON DICKSON-P
20 CHRIS TURNER-C
21 SCOTT SANDERSON (INJ) (REL)-P
21 BRAD PENNINGTON (INJ)-P (2)
21 DARRELL MAY-P (2)
22 SHAWN BOSKIE-P
23 TIM WALLACH (REL)-3B (1)
25 JIM EDMONDS (INJ)-OF
26 *(RET #) GENE AUTRY*
27 MIKE ALDRETE-OF (1)
27 DARIN ERSTAD-OF
28 TODD FROHWIRTH-P
28 CHRIS PRITCHETT-1B
29 ROD CAREW-CH
30 *(RET#) NOLAN RYAN*
31 CHUCK FINLEY-P
32 JACK HOWELL (INJ)-3B
33 GARY DISARCINA-SS
(34) BRYAN HARVEY (INJ)-(P)
35 DENNIS SPRINGER-P
36 GREG GOHR-P (2)
37 JEFF SCHMIDT-P
38 BILL LACHEMANN-CH
39 RICK (ROOSTER) BURLESON-CH
40 TROY PERCIVAL-P
42 MARK HOLZEMER (INJ)-P
43 RICH MONTELEONE (INJ)-P
44 CHILI DAVIS-DH
45 PHIL LEFTWICH-P
46 MIKE JAMES-P
47 LEE SMITH (INJ)-P (1)
47 JOE COLEMAN-CH
48 KEN EDENFIELD-P (1)
48 PEP HARRIS-P
50 *(RET#) JIMMIE REESE*
52 JIM ABBOTT-P
53 MARCEL LACHEMANN-MGR1
(54) STEVE ONTIVAEROS (INJ)-(P)
55 CHUCK HERNANDEZ-CH
55 KYLE ABBOTT-P
55 ROBERT ELLIS-P
56 JASON GRIMSLEY-P
57? MICK BILLMEYER-CH
58 MARK EICHHORN (INJ)-P
59 SHAD WILLIAMS-P
60 RYAN HANCOCK-P
65 MIKE HOLTZ-P
70 JOE MADDON-CH/INT MGR3

1997
ANAHEIM ANGELS

2ND W 84-78 6GB

1 TERRY COLLINS-MGR
2 LARRY BOWA-CH
3 ORLANDO PALMEIRO (INJ) OF/DH
4 CRAIG GREBECK-SS/2B
5 LUIS ALICEA-2B
6 CHAD KREUTER-C (2)
7 GEORGE ARIAS-3B (1)
7 ANGEL ENCARNACION-C
8 TODD GREENE (INJ)-C
9 GARY DISARCINA-SS
10 DAVE HOLLINS-3B
11 ROBERT EENHOORN-3B
12 MARK LANGSTON (INJ)-P
13 JIM LEYRITZ-C/1B (1)
14 JORGE FABREGAS-C (1)
15 TIM SALMON-OF
16 GARRET ANDERSON-OF
17 CHUCK MCELROY-P (1)
18 RANDY VELARDE (INJ)-2B
19 JASON DICKSON-P
20 CHRIS TURNER (INJ)-C
21 SHIGETOSHI HASEGAWA-P
22 DARRELL MAY-P
23 MARK GUBICZA (INJ)-P
24 RICKEY HENDERSON-OF (2)
25 JIM EDMONDS (INJ)-OF
26 *(RET #) GENE AUTRY*
27 DARIN ERSTAD-OF
29 ROD CAREW-CH
30 *(RET#) NOLAN RYAN*
31 CHUCK FINLEY (INJ)-P
32 JACK HOWELL (INJ)-1B/DH
33 EDDIE MURRAY (INJ) (REL)-DH (1)
34 ALLEN WATSON-P
35 DENNIS SPRINGER-P
36 GREG CADARET-P
(38) PETER JANICKI-(P)
39 DAVE PARKER-CH
40 TROY PERCIVAL (INJ)-P
41 RICH DE LUCIA (INJ)-P (2)
42 *(RET #) JACKIE ROBINSON*
43 ANTHONY CHAVEZ-P
44 KEVIN GROSS-P
44 KEN HILL-P (2)
46 MIKE JAMES (INJ)-P
47 JOE COLEMAN-CH
48 PEP HARRIS-P
50 *(RET#) JIMMIE REESE*
53 MARCEL LACHEMANN-CH
(55) ROBERT ELLIS-(P)
59 SHAD WILLIAMS-P
61 MIKE BOVEE-P
62 MATT PERISHO-P
65 MIKE HOLTZ-P
70 JOE MADDON-CH
73 TONY PHILLIPS-OF (2)

1998

2ND W 85-77 3GB

1 TERRY COLLINS-MGR
2 LARRY BOWA-CH
3 ORLANDO PALMEIRO (INJ) OF/DH
4 CHAD KREUTER-C (2)
5 CRAIG SHIPLEY (INJ)-3B/UTIL
6 MATT WALBECK-C
7 NORBERTO (PACCO) MARTIN (INJ)-2B
8 TODD GREENE (INJ)-OF/1B
9 GARY DISARCINA-SS
10 DAVE HOLLINS (INJ)-3B
11 ROBERT EENHOORN-3B
11 JUSTIN BAUGHMAN-2B/SS
12 CARLOS GARCIA-2B/UTIL
12 TROY GLAUS-3B
12 CHARLIE O'BRIEN (INJ)-C (2)
12 GREGG JEFFERIES-OF/1B (2)
13 JUSTIN BAUGHMAN-2B/SS
14 TROY GLAUS-3B
15 TIM SALMON (INJ)-DH/OF
16 GARRET ANDERSON-OF
17 TREVOR WILSON-P
18 RANDY VELARDE (INJ)-2B
19 JASON DICKSON-P
20 PHIL NEVIN-C/1B/DH
21 SHIGETOSHI HASEGAWA-P
22 DAMON MASHORE-OF
22 CHARLIE O'BRIEN (INJ)-C (2)
23 RICH ROBERTSON-P
23 STEVE SPARKS-P
24 GEORGE HENDRICK-CH
25 JIM EDMONDS (INJ)-OF
26 *(RET #) GENE AUTRY*
27 DARIN ERSTAD-OF/1B
28 CHRIS PRITCHETT (INJ)-1B
29 ROD CAREW-CH
30 *(RET#) NOLAN RYAN*
31 CHUCK FINLEY-P
32 FRANK BOLICK (REL)-DH/UTIL
32 MIKE FETTERS-P (2)
32 MARK P. JOHNSON-1B/DH
33 JEFF JUDEN-P (2)
34 ALLEN WATSON (INJ)-P
36 GREG CADARET-P (1)
36 MIKE FETTERS-P (2)
38 BEN MOLINA-C
39 OMAR OLIVARES-P
40 TROY PERCIVAL-P
41 RICH DE LUCIA-P
42 *(RET #) JACKIE ROBINSON*
44 KEN HILL (INJ)-P
45 CECIL FIELDER-DH (1)
46 MIKE JAMES (INJ)-P
47 JOE COLEMAN-CH
48 PEP HARRIS (INJ)-P
50 *(RET#) JIMMIE REESE*
53 MARCEL LACHEMANN-CH
55 REGGIE WILLIAMS-OF
56 JARROD WASHBURN-P
59 FRANK BOLICK-INF
65 MIKE HOLTZ-P
(69) ANGEL ENCARNACION (INJ)-(C)
70 JOE MADDON-CH
72 JACK MCDOWELL-P
99 GAR VALLONE (INJ)-P

1999

4TH W 70-92 25GB

1 TERRY COLLINS-MGR
2 LARRY BOWA-CH
3 ORLANDO PALMEIRO (INJ) OF/DH
4 DAVE SILVESTRI-2B
4 BRETT HEMPHILL-C
5 JEFF HUSON-INF
6 MATT WALBECK-C
7 ANDY SHEETS-SS
8 TODD GREENE (SUS-3G)-C
9 GARY DISARCINA (INJ)-SS
10 MIKE COLANGELO (INJ)-OF
11 *(RET#) JIM FREGOSI*
12 REGGIE B. WILLIAMS (INJ)-OF
13 JUSTIN BAUGHMAN (INJ)-2B/SS
14 TROY GLAUS-3B
15 TIM SALMON (INJ)-DH/OF
16 GARRET ANDERSON-OF
17 DARIN ERSTAD-OF/1B
18 RANDY VELARDE-2B (1)
18 JUAN ALVAREZ-P
19 JASON DICKSON (INJ)-P
20 TRENT DURRINGTON-INF
21 SHIGETOSHI HASEGAWA-P
22 CHARLIE O'BRIEN (INJ)-C
23 STEVE SPARKS-P
24 GEORGE HENDRICK-CH
25 JIM EDMONDS (INJ)-OF
26 *(RET #) GENE AUTRY*
27 MIKE FYHRIE-P
28 CHRIS PRITCHETT-1B
29 ROD CAREW-CH
30 *(RET#) NOLAN RYAN*
31 CHUCK FINLEY-P
33 MATT LUKE (INJ)-OF
34 MARK PETKOVSEK-P
36 TIM UNROE-1B
36 RAMON ORTIZ-P
37 STEVE DECKER-C
38 DICK POLE-CH
39 OMAR OLIVARES-P (1)
40 TROY PERCIVAL-P
41 TIM BELCHER (INJ)-P
42 MO VAUGHN (INJ)-1B/DH
43 ALAN LEVINE-P
44 KEN HILL (INJ)-P
45 BRIAN COOPER-P
46 MIKE JAMES (INJ)-P
46 STEVE MINTZ-P
47 JOE COLEMAN-CH
48 PEP HARRIS (INJ)-P
50 *(RET#) JIMMIE REESE*
52 MIKE MAGNANTE-P
55 JEFF DAVANON-OF
56 JARROD WASHBURN-P
57 MICK BILLMEYER-CH
58 LOU POTE-P
60 SCOTT SCHOENEWEIS-P
63 BEN MOLINA-C
65 MIKE HOLTZ-P
70 JOE MADDON-CH
72 JACK MCDOWELL (INJ)-P
__ SAM SUPLIZIO-CH

2000

3RD W 82-80 9.5GB

1 KEITH JOHNSON-1B
1 KEVIN STOCKER-INF (2)
1 BENGIE MOLINA-C
2 ADAM KENNEDY-2B
3 ORLANDO PALMEIRO-OF/DH
4 ALFREDO GRIFFIN-CH

5 BENGIE MOLINA-C
5 RON GANT-OF (2)
6 MATT WALBECK-C
7 MICKEY HATCHER-CH
7 JASON BATES-INF
8 JUSTIN BAUGHMAN-INF
9 GARY DISARCINA (INJ)-SS
10 BENJI GIL-INF
11 *(RET#) JIM FREGOSI*
14 MIKE SCIOSCIA-MGR
15 TIM SALMON-DH/OF
16 GARRET ANDERSON-OF
17 DARIN ERSTAD-OF/1B
18 JUAN ALVAREZ-P
19 JASON DICKSON (INJ)-P
20 TRENT DURRINGTON-2B
21 SHIGETOSHI HASEGAWA-P
22 EDGARD CLEMENTE-OF
23 SCOTT SPIEZIO-DH
24 BUD BLACK-CH
25 TROY GLAUS-3B
26 *(RET #) GENE AUTRY*
27 MIKE FYHRIE-P
28 ERIC WEAVER-P
29 *(RET#) ROD CAREW*
30 *(RET#) NOLAN RYAN*
32 MATT WISE-P
33 SCOTT KARL-P (2)
34 MARK PETKOVSEK-P
35 SETH ETHERTON-P
36 RAMON ORTIZ-P
37 KENT BOTTENFIELD-P (1)
38 KEVIN STOCKER-INF (2)
38 GREG CADARET-P
39 KEITH LUUBA-SS
39 BRYAN WARD-P (2)
40 TROY PERCIVAL-P
41 TIM BELCHER (INJ)-P
42 MO VAUGHN-1B/DH
43 ALAN LEVINE-P
44 KEN HILL-P (1)
45 BRIAN COOPER-P
47 KENT MERCKER (INJ)-P
50 *(RET#) JIMMIE REESE*
53 BRETT HINCHCLIFFE-P
54 DERRICK TURNBOW-P
55 JEFF DAVANON (INJ)-OF
56 JARROD WASHBURN (INJ)-P
57 BEN WEBER-P (2)
58 LOU POTE-P
60 SCOTT SCHOENEWEIS-P
65 MIKE HOLTZ-P
70 JOE MADDON-CH
71 DWAYNE HOSEY-OF
76 SHAWN WOOTEN-C
81 MIKE COLANGELO (INJ)-OF
88 ORLANDO MERCADO-CH

2001

3RD W 75-87 41GB

1 BENGIE MOLINA (INJ)-C
2 ADAM KENNEDY (INJ)-2B
3 ORLANDO PALMEIRO-OF/DH
4 ALFREDO GRIFFIN-CH
5 WALLY JOYNER (RET)-1B
6 JORGE FABREGAS-C
7 MICKEY HATCHER-CH
8 JOSE NIEVES (INJ)-SS
9 GARY DISARCINA (INJ)-SS
10 BENJI GIL-INF
11 *(RET#) JIM FREGOSI*
12 RON ROENICKE-CH
13 BOBBY RAMOS-CH
14 MIKE SCIOSCIA-MGR
15 TIM SALMON (INJ)-DH/OF
16 GARRET ANDERSON-OF
17 DARIN ERSTAD-OF/1B
19 JAMIE BURKE-C
21 SHIGETOSHI HASEGAWA (INJ)-P
22 DAVID ECKSTEIN-INF
23 SCOTT SPIEZIO-DH
24 BUD BLACK-CH
25 TROY GLAUS-3B
26 *(RET #) GENE AUTRY*
28 JOSE MOLINA-C
29 *(RET#) ROD CAREW*
30 *(RET#) NOLAN RYAN*
31 GLENALLEN HILL (INJ) (REL)-OF
32 MATT WISE-P
33 STEVE GREEN-P
34 PAT RAPP-P
36 RAMON ORTIZ-P
37 LARRY BARNES-1B
39 JOSE FERNANDEZ-DH
40 TROY PERCIVAL-P
42 MO VAUGHN (INJ)-1B/DH
43 ALAN LEVINE-P
44 SHAWN WOOTEN-C
45 BRIAN COOPER-P
46 KIMERA BARTEE (INJ)-OF (1)
46 TOBY BORLAND-P
47 MARK LUKASIEWICZ-P
50 *(RET#) JIMMIE REESE*
52 BART MIADICH-P
55 JEFF DAVANON-DH
56 JARROD WASHBURN (INJ)-P
58 LOU POTE-P
59 ISMAEL VALDES (INJ)-P
60 SCOTT SCHOENEWEIS-P
62 SCOT SHIELDS-P
65 MIKE HOLTZ (INJ)-P
70 JOE MADDON-CH
77 BEN WEBER-P
87 RENDY ESPINA (INJ)-P

2002

2ND W (W/C) 99-63 4GB
W ALDS-NYA 3-1
W ALCS-MINA 4-1
W WS-SFN 4-3

1 BENGIE MOLINA-C
2 ADAM KENNEDY-2B
3 ORLANDO PALMEIRO-OF/DH
4 ALFREDO GRIFFIN-CH
5 ALFREDO AMEZANGA-SS
6 JORGE FABREGAS-C (1)
6 CHONE FIGGINS-2B
7 MICKEY HATCHER-CH
8 JOSE NIEVES-SS
9 SAL FASANO-C
10 BENJI GIL (INJ)-INF/DH
11 *(RET#) JIM FREGOSI*
12 RON ROENICKE-CH
13 BOBBY RAMOS-CH
14 MIKE SCIOSCIA-MGR
15 TIM SALMON-OF/DH
16 GARRET ANDERSON-OF/DH
17 DARIN ERSTAD-OF/1B
18 DONNIE WALL-P
18 ALEX OCHOA-OF (2)
20 BRAD FULLMER-DH/1B
21 DENNIS COOK (INJ)-P
22 DAVID ECKSTEIN-SS
23 SCOTT SPIEZIO-1B/UTIL
24 BUD BLACK-CH
25 TROY GLAUS-3B
26 *(RET #) GENE AUTRY*
27 KEVIN APPIER-P
28 JOSE MOLINA-C
29 *(RET#) ROD CAREW*
30 *(RET#) NOLAN RYAN*
32 MATT WISE-P
33 STEVE GREEN-P
33 JEFF DAVANON-OF/DH
34 AARON SELE (INJ)-P
35 CLAY BELLINGER-1B
36 RAMON ORTIZ-P
39 JULIO RAMIREZ (INJ)-OF/DH
40 TROY PERCIVAL-P
41 JOHN LACKEY-P
42 *(RET #) JACKIE ROBINSON*
43 ALAN LEVINE-P
44 SHAWN WOOTEN (INJ)-DH/UTIL
47 MARK LUKASIEWICZ-P
50 *(RET#) JIMMIE REESE*
51 MICKEY CALLAWAY-P
53 BRANDON DONNELLY-P
56 JARROD WASHBURN-P
57 FRANCISCO RODRIGUEZ-P
58 LOU POTE-P
60 SCOTT SCHOENEWEIS-P
62 SCOT SHIELDS-P
70 JOE MADDON-CH
77 BEN WEBER-P

2003

3RD W 77-85 19GB

1 BENGIE MOLINA (INJ)-C
2 ADAM KENNEDY (INJ)-2B
3 TOM GREGORIO-C
4 ALFREDO GRIFFIN-CH
5 ALFREDO AMEZANGA (INJ)-SS
6 CHONE FIGGINS-OF/2B
7 MICKEY HATCHER-CH
8 ERIC OWENS-OF
9 ADAM RIGGS-1B/UTIL
10 BENJI GIL (INJ)-INF
11 *(RET#) JIM FREGOSI*
12 RON ROENICKE-CH
14 MIKE SCIOSCIA-MGR
15 TIM SALMON-OF/DH
16 GARRET ANDERSON-OF/DH
17 DARIN ERSTAD (INJ)-OF
18 RICH RODRIGUEZ-P
20 BRAD FULLMER (INJ)-DH/1B
22 DAVID ECKSTEIN (INJ)-SS
23 SCOTT SPIEZIO-1B/UTIL
24 BUD BLACK-CH
25 TROY GLAUS (INJ)-3B
26 *(RET #) GENE AUTRY*
27 KEVIN APPIER (INJ) (REL)-P (1)
27 TRENT DURRINGTON-2B/3B
28 JOSE MOLINA-C
29 *(RET#) ROD CAREW*
30 *(RET#) NOLAN RYAN*
(32) MATT WISE (INJ)-(P)
34 AARON SELE (INJ)-P
36 RAMON ORTIZ-P
38 GARY GLOVER-P (2)
39 ROBB QUINLAN-1B
40 TROY PERCIVAL (INJ)-P
41 JOHN LACKEY-P
42 *(RET #) JACKIE ROBINSON*
43 JULIO RAMIREZ-OF
44 SHAWN WOOTEN-UTIL
45 BARRY WESSON-OF
45 RAMON ORTIZ-P
46 GARY JOHNSON-OF
47 GARY JOHNSON-OF
47 WILSON DELGADO-2B/SS (2)
50 *(RET#) JIMMIE REESE*
51 MICKEY CALLAWAY (INJ)-P (1)
51 CHRIS BOOTCHECK-P
52 BART MIADICH-P
53 BRENDAN DONNELLY (INJ)-P
54 DERRICK TURNBOW-P
55 JEFF DAVANON-OF
56 JARROD WASHBURN-P
57 FRANCISCO RODRIGUEZ-P
58 GREG JONES-P
60 SCOTT SCHOENEWEIS-P (1)
62 SCOT SHIELDS-P
63 KEVIN GREGG-P
70 JOE MADDON-CH
77 BEN WEBER-P

2004

1ST W 92-70 0GB
L ALDS BOSA 3-0

1 BENGIE MOLINA-C
2 ADAM KENNEDY-2B
4 ALFREDO GRIFFIN-CH
5 ALFREDO AMEZANGA-SS
6 JOSE GUILLEN-OF
7 MICKEY HATCHER-CH
8 JOSH PAUL-C
9 CHONE FIGGINS-3B
10 ADAM RIGGS-UTIL
11 *(RET#) JIM FREGOSI*
12 RON ROENICKE-CH
14 MIKE SCIOSCIA-MGR
15 TIM SALMON (INJ)-OF/DH
16 GARRET ANDERSON-OF/DH
17 DARIN ERSTAD-OF/1B
18 SHANE HALTER-1B
19 CURTIS PRIDE-OF
20 ANDRES GALARRAGA-1B/DH
21 BARTOLO COLON-P
22 DAVID ECKSTEIN-SS
23 DALLAS MCPHERSON-3B
24 BUD BLACK-CH
25 TROY GLAUS (INJ)-3B
26 *(RET #) GENE AUTRY*
27 VLADIMIR GUERRERO-OF
28 JOSE MOLINA-C
29 *(RET#) ROD CAREW*
30 *(RET#) NOLAN RYAN*
34 AARON SELE-P
35 CASEY KOTCHMAN-1B
36 RAMON ORTIZ-P
38 GARY GLOVER-P (2)
39 ROBB QUINLAN (INJ)-1B
40 TROY PERCIVAL (INJ)-P
41 JOHN LACKEY-P
42 *(RET #) JACKIE ROBINSON*
43 RAUL MONDESI (INJ)-OF (2)
45 KELVIM ESCOBAR-P
50 *(RET#) JIMMIE REESE*
52 MATT HENSLEY-P
53 BRENDAN DONNELLY (INJ)-P
54 DERRICK TURNBOW-P
55 JEFF DAVANON (INJ)-OF/DH
56 JARROD WASHBURN-P
57 FRANCISCO RODRIGUEZ-P
(58) GREG JONES-(P)
60 SCOTT DUNN-P
62 SCOT SHIELDS-P
63 KEVIN GREGG-P
65 DUSTY BERGMAN-P
70 JOE MADDON-CH
77 BEN WEBER-P

2005
LOS ANGELES ANGELS

1ST W 95-67 0GB
W ALDS NYA 3-2
L ALCS CHIA 4-1

1 BENGIE MOLINA (INJ)-C
2 ADAM KENNEDY (INJ)-2B
4 ALFREDO GRIFFIN-CH
5 DAVID METRANGA-SS
6 MAICER IZTURIS (INJ)-SS
7 MICKEY HATCHER-CH
8 JOSH PAUL-C
9 CHONE FIGGINS-3B/OF
10 RON ROENICKE-CH
11 *(RET#) JIM FREGOSI*
12 STEVE FINLEY (INJ)-OF
14 MIKE SCIOSCIA-MGR
(15) TIM SALMON (INJ)-(OF)
16 GARRET ANDERSON-OF
17 DARIN ERSTAD-1B
18 ORLANDO CABRERA (INJ)-SS
19 CURTIS PRIDE (INJ)-OF/DH
20 JUAN RIVERA-OF/DH
21 LOU MERLONI (INJ)-INF
23 DALLAS MCPHERSON (INJ 3B
24 BUD BLACK-CH
26 *(RET #) GENE AUTRY*
27 VLADIMIR GUERRERO (INJ OF
28 JOSE MOLINA-C
29 *(RET#) ROD CAREW*
30 *(RET#) NOLAN RYAN*
34 JAKE WOODS-P
35 CASEY KOTCHMAN-1B
36 PAUL BYRD-P
37 GREG JONES-P
38 CHRIS PRIETO-OF
39 ROBB QUINLAN (INJ)-3B
40 BARTOLO COLON-P
41 JOHN LACKEY-P
42 *(RET #) JACKIE ROBINSON*
44 JEFF MATHIS-C
45 KELVIM ESCOBAR (INJ)-P
46 JASON CHRISTIANSEN-P (2
48 ORLANDO MERCADO-CH
49 CHRIS BOOTCHECK-P
50 *(RET#) JIMMIE REESE*
51 ZACH SORENSON-3B/SS
(52) MATT HENSLEY (INJ)-(P)
53 BRENDAN DONNELLY (SUS:10G)-P
54 ERVIN SANTANA-P
55 JEFF DAVANON-OF/DH
56 JARROD WASHBURN (INJ)-P
57 FRANCISCO RODRIGUEZ (INJ)-P
58 JOEL PERALTA-P
59 ESTEBAN YAN-P
62 SCOT SHIELDS-P
63 KEVIN GREGG-P
64 BRET PRINZ (INJ)-P
68 JOE SAUNDERS-P
70 JOE MADDON-CH

WASHINGTON SENATORS/**MINNESOTA TWINS**

The Senators became the second team to wear numbers on their backs on a permanent basis. They began the 1930 season wearing their numbers both home and away.

1930
WASHINGTON SENATORS
2ND 94-60 8GB

1 SAMMY WEST-OF
2 SAM RICE-OF
3 GOOSE GOSLIN-OF (1)
3 HEINIE MANUSH-OF (2)
4 BUDDY MYER-2B
5 JOE JUDGE-1B
6 JOE CRONIN-SS
7 OSSIE BLUEGE-3B/SS
8 JACKIE HAYES-INF
9 JIM MCLEOD-3B/SS
10 RED BARNES-PH (1)
11 JAKE POWELL-OF
11 GEORGE LOEPP-OF
12 MUDDY RUEL-C
13 ART (ART THE GREAT) SHIRES-1B (2)
14 BERNIE TATE-C (1)
15 ROY SPENCER-C
16 PATSY GHARRITY-PH
17 FIRPO MARBERRY-P
18 BUMP HADLEY-P
19 SAD SAM JONES-P
20 GARLAND BRAXTON-P (1)
21 CARL FISCHER-P
21 MYLES THOMAS-P
22 AD LISKA (INJ)-P
23 LLOYD (GIMPY) BROWN-P
24 BOBBY (LEFTY) BURKE-P
25 CARLOS MOORE-P
25 GENERAL CROWDER-P
26 DAVE (SHERIFF) HARRIS-OF
26 BILL (WHISPERING BILL) BARRETT-OF (2)
27 WALTER (THE BIG TRAIN) (BARNEY) JOHNSON-MGR
28 NICK ALTROCK-CH
29 AL (THE CLOWN PRINCE) SCHACHT-CH
32 HARRY CHILD (AKA CHESLEY)-P
38 JOE KUHEL-1B
__ HARLEY (LEFTY) BOSS-PH (3G: 5/22-6/1)
__ PINKY HARGRAVE-C (2) (10G: 9/11-9/28)
__ RAY TREADWAY-3B (6G: 9/17-9/26)

1931
3RD 92-62 16GB

1 BUDDY MYER-2B
2 SAM RICE-OF
3 HEINIE MANUSH-OF
4 JOE CRONIN-SS
5 JOE JUDGE (ILL)-1B
6 SAMMY WEST-OF
7 OSSIE BLUEGE-3B/SS
8 ROY SPENCER-C
9 PINKY HARGRAVE-C
10 CLIFF BOLTON-C
12 FIRPO MARBERRY-P
14 SAD SAM JONES-P
15 GENERAL CROWDER-P
16 BUMP HADLEY-P
17 LLOYD (GIMPY) BROWN-P
18 AD LISKA (INJ)-P
18 WALT MASTERS-P
19 BOBBY (LEFTY) BURKE-P
20 CARL FISCHER-P
21 WALT TAUSCHER-P
22 JACKIE HAYES-INF
23 JOE KUHEL-1B
25 HARRY RICE-OF
26 DAVE (SHERIFF) HARRIS-OF
27 BUCK JORDAN-1B
28 WALTER (THE BIG TRAIN) (BARNEY) JOHNSON-MGR
29 NICK ALTROCK-PH/CH
30 AL (THE CLOWN PRINCE) SCHACHT-CH
31 PATSY GHARRITY-CH
__ BILL (ANDY) ANDRUS-3B (3G: 9/19-9/27)
__ JOHNNY (PATCHEYE) GILL-OF (8G: 9/12-9/27)
__ BABE (BLIMP) PHELPS-PH (3G: 9/17-9/21)
__ MONTE (PROF) WEAVER-P (3G: 9/20-9/26)

1932
3RD 93-61 14GB

1 BUDDY MYER-2B
2 HEINIE MANUSH-OF
3 SAMMY WEST-OF
4 JOE CRONIN-SS
5 CARL REYNOLDS (INJ)-OF
6 JOE JUDGE-1B
7 OSSIE BLUEGE-3B
8 ROY SPENCER-C
9 MOE BERG-C
10 HOWIE (MAPE) MAPLE-C
11 FIRPO MARBERRY-P
12 GENERAL CROWDER-P
14 LLOYD (GIMPY) BROWN-P
15 CARL FISCHER-P
15 DICK COFFMAN-P (2)
16 MONTE (PROF) WEAVER-P
17 BILL MCAFEE-P
17 BOBBY (LEFTY) BURKE-P
17 BUD THOMAS-P
18 FRANK RAGLAND-P
19 BOBBY (LEFTY) BURKE-P
19 WES KINGDON-3B/SS
19 BOB FRIEDRICH-P
20 JIM MCLEOD-SS
20 TOMMY THOMAS-P (2)
21 JOE KUHEL-1B
22 SAM RICE-OF
23 JOHN KERR-INF
24 DAVE (SHERIFF) HARRIS-OF
25 WALTER (THE BIG TRAIN) (BARNEY) JOHNSON-MGR
26 PATSY GHARRITY-CH
27 EDDIE (DORF) AINSMITH-CH
28 NICK ALTROCK-PH/CH
29 AL (THE CLOWN PRINCE) SCHACHT-CH
31 ED (DOC) EDELEN-P
__ DANNY MUSSER-3B (1G:9/18)

1933
1ST 99-53 0GB
L WS-NYN 4-1

1 BUDDY MYER-2B
2 JOE KUHEL-1B
3 HEINIE MANUSH-OF
4 JOE CRONIN-SS/MGR
5 GOOSE GOSLIN-OF
6 FRED (FRITZ) SCHULTE-OF
7 OSSIE BLUEGE-3B
8 LUKE SEWELL-C
9 CLIFF BOLTON-C/OF
10 MOE BERG-C
11 EARL WHITEHILL-P
12 GENERAL CROWDER-P
14 LEFTY STEWART-P
15 TOMMY THOMAS-P
16 MONTE (PROF) WEAVER-P
17 JACK RUSSELL-P
18 BOBBY (LEFTY) BURKE-P
19 BILL MCAFEE-P
19 ED CHAPMAN-P
20 ED (BABE) LINKE-P
21 BUD THOMAS-P
22 SAM RICE-OF
23 JOHN KERR-2B/3B
24 DAVE (SHERIFF) HARRIS-UTIL
25 BOB BOKEN-INF
26 CECIL TRAVIS-3B
26 JOHN CAMPBELL-P
26 ALEX (RED) MCCOLL-P
27 NICK ALTROCK-PH/CH
28 AL (THE CLOWN PRINCE) SCHACHT-CH
30 RAY (POP) PRIM-P
31 CECIL TRAVIS-3B

1934
7TH 66-86 34GB

1 BUDDY MYER-2B
2 JOHN (ROCKY) STONE (INJ)-OF
3 HEINIE MANUSH-OF
4 JOE CRONIN (INJ)-SS/MGR
5 JOE KUHEL (INJ)-1B
6 FRED SINGTON-OF
6 FRED (FRITZ) SCHULTE-OF
7 OSSIE BLUEGE-INF/OF
8 LUKE SEWELL (INJ)-C
9 CLIFF BOLTON-C
9 JAKE POWELL-OF
10 MOE BERG-C (1)
10 ALLEN (BULLET BEN) BENSON-P
11 EARL WHITEHILL-P
12 GENERAL CROWDER-P (1)
12 SYD COHEN-P
14 LEFTY STEWART-P
15 TOMMY THOMAS-P
16 MONTE (PROF) WEAVER-P
17 JACK RUSSELL-P
18 BOBBY (LEFTY) BURKE-P
19 PETE SUSKO-1B
19 JOHNNY (PATCHEYE) GILL-OF
20 CECIL TRAVIS-3B
20 BOB (JUNIOR) KLINE-P (2)
21 ELMER KLUMPP-C
22 GUS DUGAS-OF
22 REESE (DIGGSY) DIGGS-P
22 PETE SUSKO-1B
23 JOHN KERR-3B/2B/CH
24 DAVE (SHERIFF) HARRIS-OF/3B
25 BOB BOKEN-3B/2B (1)
25 RED KRESS-UTIL (2)
26 ALEX (RED) MCCOLL-P
26 MARC FILLEY-P
27 NICK ALTROCK-CH
28 AL (THE CLOWN PRINCE) SCHACHT-CH
29 ED (BABE) LINKE-P
29 ORVILLE ARMBRUST-P
30 RAY (POP) PRIM-P
30 JOHN MILLIGAN-P
32 EDDIE PHILLIPS-C

1935
6TH 67-86 27GB

1 BUDDY MYER-2B
2 JOHN (ROCKY) STONE-OF
2 FRED (FRITZ) SCHULTE-OF
3 HEINIE MANUSH-OF
4 JOHN (ROCKY) STONE-OF
5 JOE KUHEL-1B
5 CECIL TRAVIS-3B/OF
6 JOE KUHEL-1B
7 OSSIE BLUEGE-SS/INF
8 CLIFF BOLTON-C
9 SAMMY HOLBROOK-C
10 JACK (RED) REDMOND-C
10 RED MARION-OF
11 EARL WHITEHILL-P
12 BOBBY (LEFTY) BURKE-P
12 PHIL (SID) HENSIEK-P
12 AL (ELROD) MCLEAN-P
12 DICK LANAHAN-P
14 LEFTY STEWART-P (1)
14 JIM (WHITEY) HAYES-P
14 BUCK (LEFTY) ROGERS-P
15 TOMMY THOMAS-P (1)
15 CHICK STARR-C
16 MONTE (PROF) WEAVER (ILL/INJ)-P
17 JACK RUSSELL-P
18 BOBBY (LEFTY) BURKE-P
18 BUMP HADLEY-P
19 ED (BABE) LINKE-P
20 LEON (LEFTY) PETTIT-P
21 BOBO (BUCK) NEWSOM-P
22 HENRY COPPOLA-P
23 NICK ALTROCK-CH
24 JAKE POWELL-OF/2B
25 FRED SINGTON-OF
26 RED KRESS-UTIL/P
27 NICK ALTROCK-CH
28 LYN (BROADWAY) LARY-SS (1)
28 ALAN (INKY) STRANGE-SS (2)
29 ED (BABE) LINKE-P
29 JOHN KERR-CH
31 BELVE (BILL) BEAN-P
31 DEE MILES-OF
32 BOBBY ESTALELLA-3B
33 BUDDY LEWIS-3B
34 JOHN MIHALIC-SS
35 BUCKY HARRIS-MGR

1936
4TH 82-71 20GB

1 BUDDY MYER (ILL)-2B
2 BUDDY LEWIS-3B
3 JESSE HILL-OF
4 JAKE POWELL-OF (1)
4 BEN CHAPMAN-OF (2)
5 CECIL TRAVIS-SS/UTIL
6 JOHN (ROCKY) STONE-OF
7 JOE KUHEL-1B/3B
8 CARL REYNOLDS-OF
9 CLIFF BOLTON-C
10 WALLY MILLIES-C
11 EARL WHITEHILL-P
12 BOBO (BUCK) NEWSOM-P
14 SYD COHEN-P
14 ED (BABE) LINKE-P
15 JIMMIE DESHONG-P
16 JOE (CROONIN' JOE) CASCARELLA-P (2)
16 JACK RUSSELL-P (1)
17 JACK RUSSELL-P (1)
17 MONTE (PROF) WEAVER-P
18 PETE (JAKE) APPLETON (AKA JABLONOWSKI)-P
19 BILL PHEBUS-P
19 FRED SINGTON-OF
19 HENRY COPPOLA-P
20 KEN (LEFTY) CHASE-P
20 FIRPO MARBERRY-P (2)
20 BILL (BULLFROG) DIETRICH-P (2)
21 JOE BOKINA-P
22 CHICK STARR-C
22 ALEX (GIZ) SABO-C
23 BOBBY ESTALELLA-PH
24 JOHN MIHALIC-2B
24 DEE MILES-OF
25 RED KRESS-INF
27 NICK ALTROCK-CH
27 OSSIE BLUEGE-2B/INF
28 NICK ALTROCK-CH
29 EARL MCNEELY-CH
30 BUCKY HARRIS-MGR
31 SHANTY HOGAN-C
33 ED (BABE) LINKE-P

1937
6TH 73-80 28.5GB

1 BUDDY MYER-2B/OF
2 BUDDY LEWIS-3B
3 AL (BUCKETFOOT AL) SIMMONS-OF
4 BEN CHAPMAN-OF (1)
4 MEL ALMADA-OF (2)
5 CECIL TRAVIS-SS
6 JOHN (ROCKY) STONE-OF
7 JOE KUHEL-1B
8 SHANTY HOGAN-C
9 WALLY MILLIES-C
10 HERB (WORKHORSE) CROMPTON-C
10 RICK FERRELL-C (2)
11 JOE (CROONIN' JOE) CASCARELLA-P (1)
11 BILL PHEBUS-P
12 BOBO (BUCK) NEWSOM-P (1)
12 WES FERRELL-P (2)
14 SYD COHEN-P
15 JIMMIE DESHONG-P
16 JIMMY BLOODWORTH-2B
16 CARL FISCHER-P (2)
17 MONTE (PROF) WEAVER-P
18 PETE (JAKE) APPLETON (AKA JABLONOWSKI)-P
19 ED (BABE) LINKE-P
20 MILT GRAY-C
20 DICK LANAHAN-P
20 BUCKY JACOBS-P
21 BILL PHEBUS-P
21 KEN (LEFTY) CHASE-P
24 JOHN MIHALIC-2B
25 JESSE HILL-OF (1)
25 GEORGE CASE-OF
26 JIMMY WASDELL-1B/OF
26 ALEX (GIZ) SABO-C
27 OSSIE BLUEGE-2B/INF
28 NICK ALTROCK-CH
29 EARL MCNEELY-CH
30 BUCKY HARRIS-MGR
31 FRED SINGTON-OF
32 KEN (LEFTY) CHASE-P
33 DICK LANAHAN-P
34 RED ANDERSON-P
35 JOE (BLACKIE) KOHLMAN-P
36 JOE KRAKAUSKAS-P
38 MIKE (MICKEY) GUERRA-C
40 FRANK TRECHOCK-SS
__ JERRY LYNN-2B (1G: 9/19)
__ JOHNNY (MUTT) RIDDLE-C (1) (8G: 5/4-18)

1938
5TH 75-76 23.5GB

1 BUDDY MYER-2B
2 BUDDY LEWIS-3B
3 ZEKE BONURA-1B
4 MEL ALMADA-OF (1)
4 SAMMY WEST-OF (2)
5 CECIL TRAVIS-SS
6 JOHN (ROCKY) STONE (ILL)-OF
7 AL (BUCKETFOOT AL) SIMMONS-OF
8 RICK FERRELL-C
9 TONY GIULIANI-C
10 WES FERRELL-P (1)
11 KEN (LEFTY) CHASE-P
12 JOE KRAKAUSKAS-P
14 CHIEF HOGSETT-P
15 JIMMIE DESHONG-P

16 DUTCH LEONARD-P
17 MONTE (PROF) WEAVER-P
18 PETE (JAKE) APPLETON (AKA JABLONOWSKI)-P
19 BILL PHEBUS-P
19 JIMMY WASDELL-1B/OF
20 GOOSE GOSLIN-OF
20 JOE (BLACKIE) KOHLMAN-P
21 MICKEY LIVINGSTON-C
22 HARRY KELLEY-P
23 TAFFY WRIGHT-OF
24 JIMMY WASDELL-1B/OF
25 GEORGE CASE-OF
27 OSSIE BLUEGE-INF
28 NICK ALTROCK-CH
29 CLYDE (DEERFOOT) MILAN-CH
30 BUCKY HARRIS-MGR
32 JOE (BLACKIE) KOHLMAN-P
33 JOE (BLACKIE) KOHLMAN-P
__ RENE MONTEAGUDO-P (5G: 9/6-20)

1939

6TH 65-87 41.5GB

1 BUDDY MYER-2B
2 BUDDY LEWIS-3B
3 BOBBY ESTALELLA-OF
4 TAFFY WRIGHT-OF
5 CECIL TRAVIS-SS
6 GEORGE CASE-OF
7 JIMMY WASDELL-1B
7 JIMMY BLOODWORTH-2B/OF
8 RICK FERRELL-C
9 JAKE EARLY-C
10 BUCKY HARRIS-MGR
10 ED LEIP-2B
10 TONY GIULIANI-C
11 KEN (LEFTY) CHASE-P
12 JOE KRAKAUSKAS-P
14 ALEX CARRASQUEL-P
15 JIMMIE DESHONG-P
16 DUTCH LEONARD-P
17 BOBBY LOANE-OF
17 BOB PRICHARD-1B
17 LOU THUMAN-P
18 PETE (JAKE) APPLETON (AKA JABLONOWSKI)-P
19 JOE HAYNES-P
20 BUCKY JACOBS-P
21 CHARLIE GELBERT-INF
22 HARRY KELLEY (INJ)-P
22 ALEX (SPUNK) PITKO-OF
23 SAMMY WEST-OF/1B
24 JOHNNY WELAJ-OF
27 OSSIE BLUEGE-INF
28 NICK ALTROCK-CH
29 CLYDE (DEERFOOT) MILAN-CH
29 HAL (BLONDIE) QUICK-SS
30 BUCKY HARRIS-MGR
31 BUD THOMAS-P (2)
33 WALT MASTERSON-P
34 JOE? FITZGERALD-CH
34 ELMER GEDEON-OF
34 MICKEY VERNON-1B
35 MIKE PALAGYI-P
35 ELMER GEDEON-OF
36 ALEX (SPUNK) PITKO-OF
36 DICK BASS-P
37 ED LEIP-2B
38 BILL (DUTCH) HOLLAND-P
39 HAL (BLONDIE) QUICK-SS
40 MORRIE ADERHOLT-3B
41 LOU THUMAN-P
41 AL EVANS-C
44 EARLY (GUS) WYNN-P

1940

7TH 64-90 26GB

1 BUDDY MYER-2B
2 BUDDY LEWIS-OF/3B
3 ZEKE BONURA-1B (1)
3 JIMMY WASDELL-1B (1)
3* RED ANDERSON-P*
4 GEE WALKER-OF
5 CECIL TRAVIS-3B/SS
6 GEORGE CASE-OF
7 JIMMY POFAHL-SS/2B
8 RICK FERRELL-C
9 JIMMY BLOODWORTH-2B/INF
11 KEN (LEFTY) CHASE-P
12 JOE KRAKAUSKAS-P
14 ALEX CARRASQUEL-P
15 SID HUDSON-P
16 DUTCH LEONARD-P
17 BUCKY JACOBS-P
18 ZEKE BONURA-1B (1)
18 WILLIS (ACE) HUDLIN-P (2)
19 JOE HAYNES-P
20 JAKE EARLY-C
20 DICK HAHN-C
21 CHARLIE GELBERT-INF/P (1)
21 JIM (SUNNY JIM) MALLORY-OF
22 WALT MASTERSON-P
23 SAMMY WEST-1B/OF
24 JOHNNY WELAJ-OF
25 RENE MONTEAGUDO-P
26 BENNY BENGOUGH-CH
27 OSSIE BLUEGE-CH
28 NICK ALTROCK-CH
28 SHERRY ROBERTSON-SS
29 CLYDE (DEERFOOT) MILAN-CH
29 DICK HAHN-C
30 BUCKY HARRIS-MGR
32 AL EVANS-C
34 GIL TORRES-P
34 WILLIS (ACE) HUDLIN-P (2)
34 MICKEY VERNON-1B
35 AL (BOOTS) HOLLINGSWORTH-P
35 JACK SANFORD-1B
__ MORRIE ADERHOLT-2B (1G: 9/8)
__ LOU THUMAN-P (2G: 9/27-29)

1941

6TH (TIE) 70-84 31GB

1 BUDDY MYER-2B
2 DOC (FLIT) CRAMER-OF
3 BUDDY LEWIS-OF/3B
4 BEN CHAPMAN-OF (1)
4 ROBERTO ORTIZ-OF
5 CECIL TRAVIS-SS/3B
6 JIMMY BLOODWORTH-2B/INF
7 GEORGE ARCHIE-3B/1B (1)
8 RICK FERRELL-C (1)
8 JAKE EARLY-C
9 AL EVANS-C
10 GEORGE CASE-OF
11 KEN (LEFTY) CHASE-P
11 JAKE EARLY-C
12 JIMMY POFAHL-SS
13 KEN (LEFTY) CHASE-P
14 ALEX CARRASQUEL-P
14 WALT MASTERSON-P
15 SID HUDSON-P
16 DUTCH LEONARD-P
17 RED ANDERSON-P
17 DANNY (DEACON DANNY) MACFAYDEN-P
17 RONNIE MILLER-P
17 VERN KENNEDY-P (2)
18 RED ANDERSON-P
19 ALEX CARRASQUEL-P
20 JAKE EARLY-C
20 EARLY (GUS) WYNN-P
21 CLIFF BOLTON-C
22 MORRIE ADERHOLT-2B/3B
22 VERN KENNEDY-P (2)
22 SHERRY ROBERTSON-3B
23 SAMMY WEST-OF
24 JOHNNY WELAJ-OF
25 OSSIE BLUEGE-CH
25 HARRY DEAN-P
(26) LOU THUMAN (MIL)-(P)
26 CLYDE (DEERFOOT) MILAN-CH
27 BENNY BENGOUGH-CH
28 BUCKY HARRIS-MGR
29 MICKEY VERNON-1B
30? NICK ALTROCK-CH
31 BILL (GOOBER) ZUBER-P
32 AL EVANS-C
32 STEVE (SMOKEY) SUNDRA-P
33 VERN KENNEDY-P (2)
34 HILLY (TONY) LAYNE-3B
35 JACK SANFORD-1B
36 CHARLIE LETCHAS-2B
__ DICK MULLIGAN-P (1G: 9/24)

1942

7TH 62-89 39.5GB

1 GEORGE CASE-OF
2 STAN SPENCE-OF
3 BRUCE (SOUPY) CAMPBELL (MIL)-OF
4 BOBBY ESTALELLA-3B/OF
5 MICKEY VERNON-1B
6 BOB REPASS-INF
6 RAY HOFFMAN-3B
7 FRANK (DINGLE) CROUCHER (INJ)-2B
8 JAKE EARLY-C
9 AL EVANS-C
10 RAY SCARBOROUGH-P
11 EARLY (GUS) WYNN-P
12 BOBO (BUCK) NEWSOM-P (1)
14 WALT MASTERSON-P
14 MIKE (SHOTGUN) CHARTAK-OF (2)
14 ROY CULLENBINE-OF/3B (2)
15 SID HUDSON-P
16 DUTCH LEONARD (INJ)-P
17 STEVE (SMOKEY) SUNDRA-P (1)
17 BILL TROTTER-P (2)
18 ALEX CARRASQUEL-P
19 JACK (BLACK JACK) WILSON-P (1)
19 LOU BEVIL-P
20 BILL (GOOBER) ZUBER-P
21 PHIL MCCULLOUGH-P
21 BILL KENNEDY-P
22 STAN GALLE (MIL)-3B
23 JIMMY POFAHL-SS
24 ROBERTO ORTIZ-OF
24 JOHN SULLIVAN-SS
24 ELLIS (CAT) CLARY-2B/3B
25 OSSIE BLUEGE-CH
26 CLYDE (DEERFOOT) MILAN-CH
27 BENNY BENGOUGH-CH
28 BUCKY HARRIS-MGR
29 NICK ALTROCK-CH
31 HARDIN (LI'L ABNER) CATHEY-P
32 CHILE GOMEZ-2B/3B
32 ELLIS (CAT) CLARY-2B/3B
32 JOHN SULLIVAN-SS
34 WALT MASTERSON-P
34 AL KVASNAK (MIL)-OF
66 RAY SCARBOROUGH-P
__ DEWEY ADKINS-P (1G: 9/19)
__ GENE (ROWDY) MOORE-OF (1G: 9/22)

1943

2ND 84-69 13.5GB

00 BOBO (BUCK) NEWSOM-P (3)
1 GEORGE CASE-OF
2 STAN SPENCE-OF
3 ELLIS (CAT) CLARY-2B/3B (1)
4 BOB (INDIAN BOB) JOHNSON-OF/INF
5 MICKEY VERNON-1B
6 JERRY PRIDDY-2B/INF
7* DEWEY ADKINS-P*
7 JOHN SULLIVAN-SS
8 JAKE EARLY-C
9 TONY GIULIANI-C
10 RAY SCARBOROUGH (MIL)-P
10 JIM MERTZ-P
10 JOHNNY NIGGELING-P (2)
11 EARLY (GUS) WYNN-P
12 OWEN SCHEETZ-P
12 BILL (LEFTY) LEFEBVRE-P
12 EWALD (LEFTY) PYLE-P
14 JIM MERTZ-P
15 OWEN SCHEETZ-P
15 ALEX KAMPOURIS-UTIL (2)
16 DUTCH LEONARD-P
17 OX MILLER-P (1)
17 RED BARBARY-PH
17 DEWEY ADKINS-P
17 VERN (TURK) CURTIS-P
18 ALEX CARRASQUEL-P
19 MICKEY HAEFNER-P
20 MILO CANDINI-P
21 EWALD (LEFTY) PYLE-P
21 RED ROBERTS-SS/3B
22 RED MARION-OF
22 JAKE POWELL-OF
23 SHERRY ROBERTSON-3B/SS
24 ELLIS (CAT) CLARY-2B/3B (1)
24 GENE (ROWDY) MOORE-OF/1B
25 OSSIE BLUEGE-MGR
26 CLYDE (DEERFOOT) MILAN-CH
27 BENNY BENGOUGH-CH
28 MICKEY HAEFNER-P
28 GEORGE (MERCURY) (STUD) (FOGHORN) MYATT-INF
29 NICK ALTROCK-CH
29 LEW CARPENTER-P
29 RED ROBERTS-SS/3B
29 TOM PADDEN-C (2)
30 BOB (INDIAN BOB) JOHNSON-OF/INF
30 NICK ALTROCK-CH
31 LEFTY (GOOFY) GOMEZ (P/T)-P
31 HARLOND (DARKIE) CLIFT-3B (2)
32 JOHN SULLIVAN-SS
34 RAY SCARBOROUGH (MIL)-P
36 RED MARION-OF
36 ED (BABE) BUTKA-1B
38 RED ROBERTS-SS/3B
40 SHERRY ROBERTSON-3B/SS
43 GEORGE (MERCURY) (STUD) (FOGHORN) MYATT-INF
44 GENE (ROWDY) MOORE-OF/1B
__ ROBERTO ORTIZ-OF (1G: 9/26)

1944

8TH 64-90 25GB

1 GEORGE CASE-OF
2 STAN SPENCE-OF/1B
3 ED BOLAND-OF
3 HARLOND (DARKIE) CLIFT-3B
3 FRED (MUSCLES) VAUGHN-2B/3B
4 ROBERTO ORTIZ-OF
5 JOE KUHEL-1B
6 LUIS SUAREZ-3B
6 JOE VOSMIK-OF
6 EDDIE (THE WALKING MAN YOST-3B/SS
6 GEORGE (BINGO) BINKS-O
7 JOHN SULLIVAN-SS
8 RICK FERRELL-C
9 MIKE (MICKEY) GUERRA-C
10 MICKEY HAEFNER-P
11 EARLY (GUS) WYNN-P
11 JUG THESENGA-P
12 JOHNNY NIGGELING-P (2)
14 MILO CANDINI-P
15 ROGER WOLFF-P
16 DUTCH LEONARD-P
17 BABY ORTIZ-P
17 VERN (TURK) CURTIS (MIL)-P
17 ED BOLAND-OF
17 RENE MONTEAGUDO-OF
18 ALEX CARRASQUEL-P
19 SANDY ULLRICH-P
19 WALT (WALLY) HOLBOROW-P
20 BILL (LEFTY) LEFEBVRE-P
21 PRESTON GOMEZ-2B/SS
22 HILLY (TONY) LAYNE-3B/2B
23 JAKE POWELL-OF/3B
24 GEORGE (MERCURY) (STUD) (FOGHORN) MYATT-2B/UTIL
25 GIL TORRES-3B/INF
26 ED (BABE) BUTKA-1B
27 ROY VALDES-PH
27 AL EVANS (MIL)-C
29 JOE FITZGERALD-CH
30 OSSIE BLUEGE-MGR
31 CLYDE (DEERFOOT) MILAN-CH
32 GEORGE (THE BULL) UHLE-CH
33 NICK ALTROCK-CH
41 BILL ZINSER-P

1945

2ND 87-67 1.5GB

1 GEORGE CASE-OF
2 BUDDY LEWIS (MIL)-OF
3 HARLOND (DARKIE) CLIFT-3B
4 JAKE POWELL-OF/3B (1)
4 DICK KIMBLE-SS
5 JOE KUHEL-1B
6 WALT CHIPPLE-OF
6 HOWIE MCFARLAND-OF
6 MIKE KREEVICH-OF (2)
7 GEORGE (BINGO) BINKS-OF/1B
7 CECIL TRAVIS (MIL)-3B
8 RICK FERRELL-C
9 MIKE (MICKEY) GUERRA-C
10 MICKEY HAEFNER-P
11 DICK KIMBLE-SS
11 AL EVANS-C
12 JOHNNY NIGGELING-P
14 JOE (FIRE) CLEARY-P
15 MARINO (CHICK) PIERETTI-
16 DUTCH LEONARD-P
17 ROGER WOLFF-P
18 ALEX CARRASQUEL-P

WASHINGTON SENATORS/**MINNESOTA TWINS**

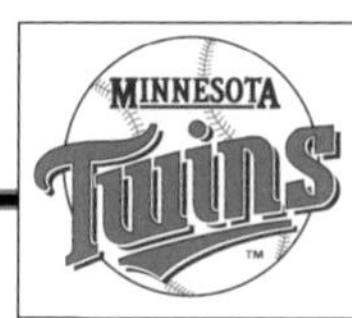

19 WALT (WALLY) HOLBOROW-P
20 FRED (MUSCLES) VAUGHN-2B/SS
21 DICK STONE-P
22 HILLY (TONY) LAYNE-3B
23 CECIL TRAVIS (MIL)-3B
24 GEORGE (MERCURY) (STUD) (FOGHORN) MYATT-2B/UTIL
25 GIL TORRES-SS/3B
27 JOSE (GUINEO) ZARDON-OF
28 SANDY ULLRICH-P
29 JOE FITZGERALD-CH
30 OSSIE BLUEGE-MGR
31 CLYDE (DEERFOOT) MILAN-CH
31 JOE JUDGE-CH
32 ARMANDO ROCHE-P
32 MIKE KREEVICH-OF (2)
32 HOWIE MCFARLAND-OF
33 NICK ALTROCK-CH
34 BERT SHEPARD-P
35 WALT MASTERSON (MIL)-P
35 VINCE VENTURA-OF
38 JOE JUDGE-CH
__ PETE (JAKE) APPLETON (AKA JABLONOWSKI)-P (2) (6G: 9/2-20)

1946

4TH 76-78 28GB

00 BOBO (BUCK) NEWSOM-P (2)
1 SHERRY ROBERTSON-INF/OF
2 BUDDY LEWIS-OF
3 SHERRY ROBERTSON-INF/OF
3 JEFF HEATH-OF (1)
4 MICKEY VERNON-1B
5 STAN SPENCE-OF
6 JERRY PRIDDY-2B
6* JAKE (WHISTLIN' JAKE) WADE-P* (2)
7 CECIL TRAVIS-SS/3B
8 JAKE EARLY-C
8 AL EVANS-C
9 MIKE (MICKEY) GUERRA-C
10 MICKEY HAEFNER-P
11 AL EVANS-C
12 JOHNNY NIGGELING-P (1)
13 SID HUDSON-P
14 SID HUDSON-P
14 RICK FERRELL-CH
15 MARINO (CHICK) PIERETTI-P
16 DUTCH LEONARD-P
16 MICKEY HAEFNER-P
17 ROGER WOLFF-P
18 SID HUDSON-P
19 MAXIE WILSON-P
19 JOE GRACE-OF (2)
20 BILL KENNEDY-P
20 MAXIE WILSON-P
20 MILO CANDINI-P
21 RAY SCARBOROUGH-P
22 GIL COAN-OF
23 WALT MASTERSON-P
23 GEORGE (BINGO) BINKS-OF
24 GEORGE (MERCURY) (STUD) (FOGHORN) MYATT-2B/UTIL
25 GIL TORRES-INF/P
26 JOE KUHEL-1B (1)
26 EARLY (GUS) WYNN (MIL)-P
27 JACK SANFORD-1B
27 BILLY HITCHCOCK-SS/3B (2)
28 EDDIE (THE WALKING MAN) YOST-3B
29 JOE FITZGERALD-CH
30 OSSIE BLUEGE-MGR
31 CLYDE (DEERFOOT) MILAN-CH
32 NICK ALTROCK-CH
33 JOE JUDGE-CH
34 BERT SHEPARD-P
34 SAMMY WEST-CH
34 JAKE (WHISTLIN' JAKE) WADE-P (2)
35 WALT MASTERSON-P
36 VERN (TURK) CURTIS-P
37 RICK FERRELL-CH
38 BILL KENNEDY-P
39 BILLY HITCHCOCK-SS/3B (2)
39 RAY (OX) GOOLSBY-OF
44 AL LAMACCHIA-P (2)

1947

7TH 64-90 33GB

00 BOBO (BUCK) NEWSOM-P (1)
1 GEORGE CASE-OF
1 TOM MCBRIDE-OF/3B
2 BUDDY LEWIS-OF
3 SHERRY ROBERTSON-UTIL
4 MICKEY VERNON-1B
5 STAN SPENCE-OF
6 JERRY PRIDDY-2B
7 CECIL TRAVIS-3B/SS
8 AL EVANS-C
9 FRANK MANCUSO-C
11 JOHN SULLIVAN-SS/2B
12 LUM HARRIS-P
12 MARK CHRISTMAN-SS/2B
13 SID HUDSON (INJ)-P
13 MILO CANDINI-P
14 LOU KNERR-P
15 MARINO (CHICK) PIERETTI-P
16 MICKEY HAEFNER-P
17 TOM FERRICK-P
19 JOE GRACE-OF
19 HAL TOENES-P
20 MILO CANDINI-P
20 SID HUDSON (INJ)-P
21 RAY SCARBOROUGH-P
22 MARK CHRISTMAN-SS/2B
22 BUZZ DOZIER-P
22 GIL COAN-OF
23 SCOTT CARY-P
23 EARL (JUNIOR) WOOTEN-OF
24 GEORGE (MERCURY) (STUD) (FOGHORN) MYATT-2B
25 ED (MOUSE) LYONS-2B
26 EARLY (GUS) WYNN-P
28 EDDIE (THE WALKING MAN) YOST-3B
29 JOE FITZGERALD-CH
30 OSSIE BLUEGE-MGR
31 CLYDE (DEERFOOT) MILAN-CH
32 TOM MCBRIDE-OF/3B
32 EARL (JUNIOR) WOOTEN-OF
33 NICK ALTROCK-CH
34 SAMMY WEST-CH
35 WALT MASTERSON-P
37 RICK FERRELL-C/CH
51 BILL KENNEDY-P
51 FELIX MACKIEWICZ-OF (2)
__ CAL ERMER-2B (1G: 9/26)

1948

7TH 56-97 40GB

1 JOHN SULLIVAN-SS/2B
2 AL KOZAR-2B
3 GIL COAN-OF
4 MICKEY VERNON-1B
5 SHERRY ROBERTSON-OF
6 LEON (LEE) CULBERSON-OF
6 BUD STEWART-OF (2)
7 EDDIE (THE WALKING MAN) YOST-3B
8 AL EVANS-C
9 JAKE EARLY-C
9 LEN OKRIE-C
10 RAY SCARBOROUGH-P
11 JAKE EARLY-C
12 FORREST THOMPSON-P
14 RAMON GARCIA-P
14 LARRY DRAKE-OF
15 MARINO (CHICK) PIERETTI-P (1)
16 MICKEY HAEFNER-P
16 CAL COOPER-P
17 TOM FERRICK-P
18 DICK (LEGS) WEIK-P
18 ANGEL FLEITAS-SS
19 MILO CANDINI-P
20 SID HUDSON-P
21 DICK WELTEROTH-P
22 RAMON GARCIA-P
22 SAMMY MEEKS-SS/2B
22 JIM CLARK-SS/3B
22 ANGEL FLEITAS-SS
23 EARL (JUNIOR) WOOTEN-OF/1B/P
24 MARK CHRISTMAN-SS/INF
25 TOM MCBRIDE-OF
26 EARLY (GUS) WYNN-P
28 JAY DIFANI-PH
28 EARL (IRISH) HARRIST-P (2)
29 JOE FITZGERALD-CH
29 CARDEN GILLENWATER-OF
31 CLYDE (DEERFOOT) MILAN-CH
32 TOM MCBRIDE-OF
32 RICK FERRELL-CH
33 NICK ALTROCK-CH
34 SAMMY WEST-CH
35 WALT MASTERSON-P
36 DICK WELTEROTH-P
36 JOE FITZGERALD-CH
37 RICK FERRELL-CH
40 JOE KUHEL-MGR
77 ANGEL FLEITAS-SS
__ CLYDE VOLLMER-OF (2) (1G: 10/2)

1949

8TH 50-104 47GB

1 AL KOZAR-2B
2 BUDDY LEWIS-OF
3 GIL COAN-OF
4 SAM (BLACKIE) DENTE-SS
5 SHERRY ROBERTSON-UTIL
6 BUD STEWART-OF
7 EDDIE (THE WALKING MAN) YOST-3B
8 AL EVANS-C
9 JAKE EARLY-C
10 RAY SCARBOROUGH-P
11 JAKE EARLY-C
11 RALPH (WIG) WEIGEL-C
11 DIZZY SUTHERLAND-P
12 FORREST THOMPSON-P
12 JAKE EARLY-C
14 EDDIE (SPECS) (BABE) KLEIMAN-P (1)
14 MICKEY HARRIS-P (2)
15 SID HUDSON-P
16 MICKEY HAEFNER-P (1)
16 JULIO GONZALES-P
17 HAL KELLER-PH
18 DICK (LEGS) WEIK-P
19 MILO CANDINI-P
19 JIM PEARCE-P
20 PAUL CALVERT-P
21 DICK WELTEROTH-P
22 CLYDE VOLLMER-OF
23 JOHN SIMMONS-OF
24 MARK CHRISTMAN-INF
25 EDDIE ROBINSON-1B
26 JOE HAYNES-P
27 JAY DIFANI-2B
27 SAM MELE-OF/1B (2)
28 HERM REICH-PH (1)
28 AL GETTEL-P (2)
28 BUZZ DOZIER-P
29 JOE FITZGERALD-CH
31 CLYDE (DEERFOOT) MILAN-CH
32 RICK FERRELL-CH
33 NICK ALTROCK-CH
34 SAMMY WEST-CH
34 MICKEY HARRIS-P (2)
35 WALT MASTERSON-P (1)
35 ROBERTO (MEX) ORTIZ-OF
35 AL GETTEL-P (2)
35 MICKEY HARRIS-P (2)
36 JOE FITZGERALD-CH
36 AL GETTEL-P (2)
37 RICK FERRELL-CH
37 HAL KELLER-PH
37 LLOYD (RED) HITTLE-P
40 JOE KUHEL-MGR

1950

5TH 67-87 31GB

10 AL EVANS-C
11 MIKE (MICKEY) GRASSO-C
12 LEN OKRIE-C
13 CARLOS PASCUAL-P
14 HAL KELLER-C
15 SANDY CONSUEGRA-P
17 MICKEY HARRIS-P
18 JOE HAYNES-P
19 LLOYD (RED) HITTLE-P
19 BOB ROSS-P
19 ROGELIO (LIMONAR) MARTINEZ-P
19 JULIO MORENO-P
20 SID HUDSON-P
21 CONNIE MARRERO-P
22 STEVE NAGY-P
22 AL SIMA-P
22 ELMER (SMOKY) SINGLETON-P
24 JIM PEARCE-P
25 RAY SCARBOROUGH-P
25 BOB (SARGE) KUZAVA-P (2)
26 JOE HAYNES-P
27 DICK (LEGS) WEIK-P (1)
28 DICK WELTEROTH-P
28 ELMER (SMOKY) SINGLETON-P
28 AL SIMA-P
29 GENE BEARDEN-P (2)
30 GIL COAN (INJ)-OF
31 SAM MELE-OF/1B
32 IRV NOREN-OF/1B
33 ROBERTO ORTIZ-OF
33 HAL KELLER-C
33 JULIO MORENO-P
34 BUD STEWART-OF
35 CLYDE VOLLMER-OF (1)
35 TOMMY (OBIE) O'BRIEN-OF (2)
35 JOHNNY OSTROWSKI-OF (2)
40 SAM (BLACKIE) DENTE-SS/2B
41 GEORGE GENOVESE-PH
42 AL KOZAR-2B (1)
42 CASS MICHAELS-2B (2)
43 SHERRY ROBERTSON-UTIL
44 EDDIE ROBINSON-1B (1)
44 MICKEY VERNON-1B (2)
45 EDDIE (THE WALKING MAN) YOST-3B
46 MERL COMBS-SS
46 FRED TAYLOR-1B
50 BUCKY HARRIS-MGR
51 CLYDE (DEERFOOT) MILAN-CH
52 JOE FITZGERALD-CH
53 GEORGE (MERCURY) (STUD) (FOGHORN) MYATT-CH
54 NICK ALTROCK-CH

1951

7TH 62-92 36GB

1 EDDIE (THE WALKING MAN) YOST-3B/OF
2 GIL COAN-OF
3 MICKEY VERNON-1B
4 SAM (BLACKIE) DENTE-INF
5 SHERRY ROBERTSON-OF
6 GENE (SATCHEL) VERBLE-INF
7 CASS MICHAELS-2B
8 IRV NOREN-OF
10 MIKE (MICKEY) GRASSO-C
10 LEN OKRIE-C
10 CLYDE KLUTTZ-C (2)
11 MIKE (MICKEY) GRASSO-C
12 MIKE MCCORMICK-OF
14 SAM MELE-OF/1B
15 MIKE (MICKEY) GRASSO-C
16 WILLIE MIRANDA-2B/1B
17 MICKEY HARRIS-P
18 JOE HAYNES-P
19 GENE BEARDEN-P (1)
19 HANK (HOOKS) WYSE-P (2)
19 BOB PORTERFIELD-P (2)
20 SID HUDSON-P
21 BOB (SARGE) KUZAVA-P (1)
21 FRED SANFORD-P (2)
21 TOM FERRICK-P (2)
22 CONNIE MARRERO-P
23 JULIO MORENO-P
24 ALTON (DEACON) BROWN-P
24 DON JOHNSON-P (2)
25 FRANK SACKA-C
25 FRANK CAMPOS-OF
26 TOM FERRICK-P (2)
26 ROY HAWES-1B
27 DICK STARR-P (2)
27 FRED SANFORD-P (2)
28 AL SIMA-P
29 BOB PORTERFIELD-P (2)
29 BOB ROSS-P
29 DAN PORTER-OF
30 SANDY CONSUEGRA-P
31 DICK STARR-P (2)
32 IRV NOREN-OF
35 PETE RUNNELS-SS
36 FRED TAYLOR-1B
37 DON JOHNSON-P (2)
42 CASS MICHAELS-2B
43 SHERRY ROBERTSON-OF
44 MICKEY VERNON-1B
45 EDDIE (THE WALKING MAN) YOST-3B/OF
46 FRED TAYLOR-1B
50 BUCKY HARRIS-MGR
51 CLYDE (DEERFOOT) MILAN-CH
52 JOE FITZGERALD-CH
53 GEORGE (MERCURY) (STUD) (FOGHORN) MYATT-CH
54 NICK ALTROCK-CH

1952

5TH 78-76 17GB

1 EDDIE (THE WALKING MAN) YOST-3B/OF
2 GIL COAN-OF

3 MICKEY VERNON-1B
4* MIKE FORNIELES-P*
4 TOM (MUSCLES) UPTON-SS
5 SHERRY ROBERTSON-PR (1)
5* RAUL SANCHEZ-P*
6 FLOYD BAKER-2B/INF
7 CASS MICHAELS-2B (1)
7 EARL RAPP-OF (2)
7 FREDDIE MARSH-2B/OF (2)
8 IRV NOREN-OF
8 JACKIE JENSEN-OF (2)
9 HAL KELLER-C
9 GEORGE BRADSHAW-C
10 CLYDE KLUTTZ-C
11 MIKE (MICKEY) GRASSO-C
12 BOBO (BUCK) NEWSOM-P (1)
13 RAUL SANCHEZ-P
14 BUNKY STEWART-P
14 SAM MELE-OF
14 JIM BUSBY-OF (2)
15 HARLEY GROSSMAN-P
15 BUCK VARNER-OF
17 MICKEY HARRIS-P
17 FRANK (THE NAUGATUCK NUGGET) (SPEC) SHEA-P
18 JOE HAYNES-P
19 BOB PORTERFIELD-P
20 SID HUDSON-P (1)
20 WALT MASTERSON-P (2)
21 TOM FERRICK-P
22 CONNIE MARRERO-P
23 JULIO MORENO-P
24 DON JOHNSON-P
25 FRANK CAMPOS-OF
26 ARCHIE WILSON-OF (2)
26 KEN WOOD-OF (2)
27 JERRY SNYDER-2B/SS
28 MEL HODERLEIN-2B
30 SANDY CONSUEGRA-P
31 LOU SLEATER-P (2)
32 FRANK (THE NAUGATUCK NUGGET) (SPEC) SHEA-P
33 RAUL SANCHEZ-P
33 RANDY GUMPERT-P (2)
34 BUNKY STEWART-P
34 FRED TAYLOR-1B
34 LOU SLEATER-P (2)
35 PETE RUNNELS-SS/2B
36 FRED TAYLOR-1B
36 KEN WOOD-OF (2)
37 RAUL SANCHEZ-P
38 GEORGE BRADSHAW-C
50 BUCKY HARRIS-MGR
51 CLYDE (DEERFOOT) MILAN-CH
52 JOE FITZGERALD-CH
53 GEORGE (MERCURY) (STUD) (FOGHORN) MYATT-CH
54 NICK ALTROCK-CH

1953

5TH 76-76 23.5GB

1 EDDIE (THE WALKING MAN) YOST-3B
2 GIL COAN-OF
3 MICKEY VERNON-1B
4 JACKIE JENSEN-OF
6 FLOYD BAKER-3B (1)
6 CARMEN MAURO-OF (2)
6 JERRY SNYDER-SS/2B
7 JIM BUSBY-OF
8 LES (GOOCH) PEDEN-C
8 ED FITZGERALD-C (2)
10 BOB OLDIS-C
10 FRANK SACKA-C
11 MIKE (MICKEY) GRASSO-C
12 WAYNE (TWIG) TERWILLIGER-2B
15 GENE (SATCHEL) VERBLE-SS
15 YO-YO DAVALILLO-SS
16 SONNY DIXON-P
17 FRANK (THE NAUGATUCK NUGGET) (SPEC) SHEA-P
18 CHUCK STOBBS-P
19 BOB PORTERFIELD-P
20 WALT MASTERSON-P
22 CONNIE MARRERO-P
23 JULIO MORENO-P
23 BUNKY STEWART-P
24 CLYDE VOLLMER-OF (2)
25 FRANK CAMPOS-PH
25 JERRY LANE-P
26 KEN WOOD-OF
26 KITE THOMAS-OF/C (2)
27 TOMMY BYRNE-P (2)
28 MEL HODERLEIN-2B/SS
29 TONY ROIG-2B
30 SANDY CONSUEGRA-P (1)
30 BRUCE (SQUEAKY) BARMES-OF
30 TOMMY BYRNE-P (2)
31 DEAN STONE-P
31 JOHNNY (BEAR TRACKS) SCHMITZ-P (2)
32 DEAN STONE-P
35 PETE RUNNELS-SS/2B
36 AL SIMA-P
37 ED FITZGERALD, C (2)
37 JOHNNY (BEAR TRACKS) SCHMITZ-P (2)
38 BUNKY STEWART-P
49 JIM PEARCE-P
50 BUCKY HARRIS-MGR
51 HEINIE MANUSH-CH
52 JOE FITZGERALD-CH
53 GEORGE (MERCURY) (STUD) (FOGHORN) MYATT-CH
54 NICK ALTROCK-CH
55 JOE HAYNES-CH
DAN PORTER (MIL)-(OF)
BOB ROSS (MIL)-(P)

1954

6TH 66-88 45GB

1 EDDIE (THE WALKING MAN) YOST-3B
2 ROY (SQUIRREL) SIEVERS-OF/1B
3 MICKEY VERNON-1B
4 TOMMY UMPHLETT-OF
5 PETE RUNNELS-SS/UTIL
6 JERRY SNYDER-SS/2B
7 JIM BUSBY-OF
8 ED FITZGERALD-C
9 BOB OLDIS-C
10 JOE TIPTON-C
11 JOHNNY PESKY-2B/SS (2)
12 WAYNE (TWIG) TERWILLIGER-2B/INF
14 JIM LEMON-OF
15 CLYDE VOLLMER-OF
16 SONNY DIXON-P (1)
16 GUS KERIAZAKOS-P
17 FRANK (THE NAUGATUCK NUGGET) (SPEC) SHEA-P
18 CHUCK STOBBS-P
19 BOB PORTERFIELD-P
20 JOHNNY (BEAR TRACKS) SCHMITZ-P
21 MICKEY (MAURY) MCDERMOTT-P
22 CONNIE MARRERO-P
23 CARLOS PAULA-OF
24 BUNKY STEWART-P
25 HARMON (KILLER) KILLEBREW-2B
26 DEAN STONE-P
27 CAMILO (LITTLE POTATO) PASCUAL-P
28 MEL HODERLEIN-SS/2B
28 ROY DIETZEL-2B/3B
29 TOM WRIGHT-OF
30 JESSE LEVAN-3B/1B
31 STEVE (HOSS) KORCHECK-C
50 BUCKY HARRIS-MGR
51 HEINIE MANUSH-CH
52 JOE FITZGERALD-CH
53 GEORGE (MERCURY) (STUD) (FOGHORN) MYATT-CH
54 NICK ALTROCK-CH
55 JOE HAYNES-CH

1955

8TH 53-101 43GB

1 EDDIE (THE WALKING MAN) YOST-3B
2 ROY (SQUIRREL) SIEVERS-OF/INF
3 MICKEY VERNON-1B
4 JIM BUSBY-OF (1)
4 JOHNNY GROTH-OF (2)
5 PETE RUNNELS-2B/SS
6 JERRY SNYDER-2B/SS
7 CHUCK DRESSEN-MGR
8 ED FITZGERALD-C
9 BOB OLDIS-C
11 BRUCE (BULL) EDWARDS-C/3B
12 HARMON (KILLER) KILLEBREW-3B/2B
14 JIM LEMON-OF
14 CLINT (SCRAP IRON) COURTNEY-C (2)
15 TED ABERNATHY-P
16 VINCE GONZALES-P
16 BOB (CHICK) CHAKALES-P (2)
17 FRANK (THE NAUGATUCK NUGGET) (SPEC) SHEA-P
18 CHUCK STOBBS-P
19 BOB PORTERFIELD-P
20 JOHNNY (BEAR TRACKS) SCHMITZ-P
21 MICKEY (MAURY) MCDERMOTT-P
22 TOMMY UMPHLETT-OF
24 BUNKY STEWART-P
24 WEBBO CLARKE-P
25 BOBBY KLINE-INF/P
26 DEAN STONE-P
27 CAMILO (LITTLE POTATO) PASCUAL-P
28 PEDRO (PETE) RAMOS-P
29 STEVE (HOSS) KORCHECK-C
29 JERRY SCHOONMAKER-OF
30 BILL CURRIE-P
31 CARLOS PAULA-OF
32 DICK HYDE-P
32 JULIO BECQUER-1B
34 JUAN DELIS-UTIL
35 JESSE LEVAN-PH
35 TOM WRIGHT-OF
36 TONY ROIG-INF
36 JOSE VALDIVIELSO-SS
37 ERNIE ORAVETZ-OF
43 BILL CURRIE-P
51 COOKIE LAVAGETTO-CH
52 JOE FITZGERALD-CH
53 ELLIS (CAT) CLARY-CH
55 JOE HAYNES-CH

1956

7TH 59-95 38GB

1 EDDIE (THE WALKING MAN) YOST-3B/OF
2 ROY (SQUIRREL) SIEVERS-OF/1B
3 KARL (OLE) OLSON-OF
4 TONY ROIG-2B/SS
5 PETE RUNNELS-1B/INF
6 JERRY SNYDER (INJ)-SS/2B
7 CHUCK DRESSEN-MGR
8 ED FITZGERALD-C
9 LOU BERBERET-C
10 LOU BERBERET-C
10 TEX CLEVENGER-P
11 BUD BYERLY-P
11 CLINT (SCRAP IRON) COURTNEY-C
11 TEX CLEVENGER-P
12 HARMON (KILLER) KILLEBREW-3B/2B
14 BUD BYERLY-P
14 TEX CLEVENGER-P
14 CLINT (SCRAP IRON) COURTNEY-C
15 TED ABERNATHY (INJ)-P
16 BOB (CHICK) CHAKALES-P
17 DICK BRODOWSKI-P
18 CHUCK STOBBS-P
21 BOB WIESLER-P
22 JOSE VALDIVIELSO-SS
22 LYLE LUTTRELL-SS
23 JIM LEMON-OF
24 BUNKY STEWART-P
25 HERB PLEWS-2B/INF
26 DEAN STONE-P
27 CAMILO (LITTLE POTATO) PASCUAL-P
28 PEDRO (PETE) RAMOS-P
(29) JERRY SCHOONMAKER (MIL)-(OF)
29 EVELIO HERNANDEZ-P
30 WHITEY (THE WHITE RAT) HERZOG-OF/1B
31 CARLOS PAULA-OF
32 CARLOS PAULA-OF
32 DICK (TUT) TETTELBACH-OF
34 DICK (TUT) TETTELBACH-OF
37 ERNIE ORAVETZ-OF
38 CONNIE GROB-P
39 HAL GRIGGS-P
40 BUD BYERLY-P
41 CONNIE GROB-P
41 TOM WRIGHT-PH
51 COOKIE LAVAGETTO-CH
52 JOE FITZGERALD-CH
53 ELLIS (CAT) CLARY-CH
54 BILLY JURGES-CH
55 JOE HAYNES-CH
STEVE (HOSS) KORCHECK (MIL)-(C)

1957

8TH 55-99 43GB

1 EDDIE (THE WALKING MAN) YOST (INJ)-3B
2 ROY (SQUIRREL) SIEVERS-OF/1B
3 KARL (OLE) OLSON-OF (1)
3 HARMON (KILLER) KILLEBREW-3B/2B
4 DICK (TUT) TETTELBACH-OF
4 FAYE THRONEBERRY-OF (2)
5 PETE RUNNELS-1B/INF
6 JERRY SNYDER-INF
7 CHUCK DRESSEN-MGR1
8 ED FITZGERALD-C
9 LOU BERBERET-C
11 BUD BYERLY-P
12 TEX CLEVENGER-P
14 CLINT (SCRAP IRON) COURTNEY-C
15 TED ABERNATHY-P
16 BOB (CHICK) CHAKALES (1)
16 RUSS (RUSTY) (DUTCH) KEMMERER-P (2)
17 CAMILO (LITTLE POTATO) PASCUAL-P
18 CHUCK STOBBS-P
19 DICK BRODOWSKI-P
19 ART (DUTCH) SCHULT-1B/OF (2)
20 NEIL CHRISLEY-OF
20 MILT BOLLING-INF (2)
21 BOB WIESLER-P
21 BOB USHER-OF (2)
23 JIM LEMON-OF/1B
24 GARLAND (DUCK) SHIFFLETT-P
24 HAL GRIGGS-P
25 HERB PLEWS-2B/INF
26 DEAN STONE-P (1)
26 JOE BLACK-P
28 PEDRO (PETE) RAMOS-P
29 JERRY SCHOONMAKER-OF
30 WHITEY (THE WHITE RAT) HERZOG-OF/1B
31 LYLE LUTTRELL-SS
31 ROCKY BRIDGES-SS/INF (2)
32 DICK (TUT) TETTELBACH-OF
32 DON MINNICK-P
34 NEIL CHRISLEY-OF
34 EVELIO HERNANDEZ-P
34 JIM HEISE-P
35 DICK HYDE-P
36 RALPH LUMENTI-P
39 JULIO BECQUER-1B
51 COOKIE LAVAGETTO-CH/MGR2
53 ELLIS (CAT) CLARY-CH
54 BILLY JURGES-CH
55 BOOM-BOOM BECK-CH

1958

8TH 61-93 31GB

1 EDDIE (THE WALKING MAN) YOST-3B/UTIL
2 ROY (SQUIRREL) SIEVERS-OF/1B
3 HARMON (KILLER) KILLEBREW-3B
4 KEN ASPROMONTE-2B/INF (2)
5 NORM ZAUCHIN-1B
6 ALBIE PEARSON-OF
7 BOBBY MALKMUS-INF
8 ED FITZGERALD-C/1B
9 LOU BERBERET-C (1)
10 STEVE (HOSS) KORCHECK (MIL)-C
11 BUD BYERLY-P (1)
11 JACK SPRING-P
11 VITO VALENTINETTI-P (2)
12 TEX CLEVENGER-P
14 CLINT (SCRAP IRON) COURTNEY-C
15 BOB ALLISON-OF
16 RUSS (RUSTY) (DUTCH) KEMMERER-P
17 CAMILO (LITTLE POTATO) PASCUAL-P
18 CHUCK STOBBS-P (1)
18 BILL FISCHER-P (3)
20 JULIO BECQUER-1B/OF
21 BOB WIESLER-P
21 AL (BOZO) CICOTTE-P (1)
21 JOHN ROMONOSKY-P
22 OSSIE ALVAREZ-INF
22 LYLE LUTTRELL-SS
23 JIM LEMON-OF
24 HAL GRIGGS-P
25 HERB PLEWS-2B/3B
27 RALPH LUMENTI-P
27 JOE ALBANESE-P

28 PEDRO (PETE) RAMOS-P
29 JULIO BECQUER-1B/OF
29 JOHNNY SCHIAVE-2B
30 WHITEY (THE WHITE RAT) HERZOG-OF (1)
30 FAYE THRONEBERRY-OF
31 ROCKY BRIDGES-SS/INF
34 NEIL CHRISLEY-OF/3B
34 JERRY SNYDER-2B/SS
34 JOHN (SHERRIF) CONSTABLE-P (3)
35 DICK HYDE-P
51 COOKIELAVAGETTO-MGR
53 ELLIS (CAT) CLARY-CH
54 BILLY JURGES-CH
55 BOOM-BOOM BECK-CH

1959

8TH 63-91 31GB

1 RENO BERTOIA-2B/INF
2 ROY (SQUIRREL) SIEVERS-1B/OF
3 HARMON (KILLER) KILLEBREW-3B/OF
4 KEN ASPROMONTE-UTIL
5 NORM ZAUCHIN-1B
5 ZOILO (ZORRO) VERSALLES-SS
6 ALBIE PEARSON-OF (1)
6 BILLY CONSOLO-SS/2B (2)
7 BOBBY MALKMUS-PR
7 LENNY GREEN-OF (2)
8 ED FITZGERALD-C/1B (1)
8 HAL NARAGON-C (2)
9 JOHNNY SCHIAVE-2B
9 JAY (J.W.) PORTER-C/1B (1)
10 STEVE (HOSS) KORCHECK-C
11 VITO VALENTINETTI-P
12 TEX CLEVENGER-P
14 CLINT (SCRAP IRON) COURTNEY (ILL)-C
15 RALPH LUMENTI-P
15 VITO VALENTINETTI-P
16 RUSS (RUSTY) (DUTCH) KEMMERER-P
17 CAMILO (LITTLE POTATO) PASCUAL-P
18 BILL FISCHER-P
19 JACK KRALICK-P
19 HAL WOODESHICK-P
21 JIM (KITTY) KAAT-P
22 DAN DOBBEK-OF
23 JIM LEMON-OF
24 HAL GRIGGS-P
25 HERB PLEWS-2B (1)
25 TOM MCAVOY-P
25 BILLY CONSOLO-SS/2B (2)
26 BOB ALLISON-OF
26 MURRAY WALL-P (2)
27 CHUCK STOBBS-P
28 PEDRO (PETE) RAMOS-P
29 JULIO BECQUER-1B
30 FAYE THRONEBERRY-OF
32 RON SAMFORD-SS/2B
34 JOHN ROMONOSKY-P
35 DICK HYDE (INJ)-P
36 JOSIE VALDIVIELSO-SS
37 JACK KRALICK-P
38 JOHN ROMONOSKY-P
39 HAL WOODESHICK-P
45 JACK KRALICK-P
51 COOKIE LAVAGETTO-MGR
53 ELLIS (CAT) CLARY-CH
54 BILLY JURGES-CH
54 SAM MELE-CH
55 BOOM-BOOM BECK-CH

1960

5TH 73-81 24GB

1 RENO BERTOIA-3B/2B
3 HARMON (KILLER) KILLEBREW-1B/3B
4 KEN ASPROMONTE-PH
4 LAMAR (JAKE) JACOBS-PH
5 JOSIE VALDIVIELSO-SS
6 BILLY CONSOLO-INF
7 LENNY GREEN-OF
8 HAL NARAGON-C
9 BILLY (SHOTGUN) GARDNER-2B/SS
10 EARL BATTEY-C
11 TED ABERNATHY-P
11 RUDY HERNANDEZ-P
12 TEX CLEVENGER-P
14 EARL BATTEY-C
14 PEDRO (PETE) RAMOS-P
15 JACK KRALICK-P
16 RUSS (RUSTY) (DUTCH) KEMMERER-P (1)
16 PETE WHISENANT-OF (3)
17 CAMILO (LITTLE POTATO) PASCUAL-P
18 BILL FISCHER-P (1)
18 TOM (PLOWBOY) MORGAN-P
19 HAL WOODESHICK-P
20 DON LEE-P
21 JIM (KITTY) KAAT-P
21 RAY (FARMER) MOORE-P (2)
22 DAN DOBBEK-OF
23 JIM LEMON-OF
25 ZOILO (ZORRO) VERSALLES-SS
26 BOB ALLISON-OF/1B
27 CHUCK STOBBS-P
28 PEDRO (PETE) RAMOS-P
28 DON MINCHER-1B
29 JULIO BECQUER-1B/P
30 FAYE THRONEBERRY-OF
32 DON MINCHER-1B
32 ELMER VALO-OF (2)
34 JIM (KITTY) KAAT-P
35 DICK HYDE-P
35 TED SADOWSKI-P
36 JIM (KITTY) KAAT-P
37 JOHNNY SCHIAVE-2B
38 JACK KRALICK-P
39 HECTOR MAESTRI-P
51 COOKIELAVAGETTO-MGR
52 BOB SWIFT-CH
53 ELLIS (CAT) CLARY-CH
54 SAM MELE-CH
55 CLYDE MCCULLOUGH-CH

1961
MINNESOTA TWINS

7TH 70-90 38GB

1 RENO BERTOIA-3B (1)
1 BILLY (THE KID) MARTIN-2B/SS (2)
2 ZOILO (ZORRO) VERSALLES-SS
3 HARMON (KILLER) KILLEBREW-1B/UTIL
4 BOB ALLISON-OF/1B
5 JOSIE VALDIVIELSO-INF
6 BILLY CONSOLO-INF
6 TED LEPCIO-INF (2)
6 JIM SNYDER-2B
7 LENNY GREEN-OF
8 HAL NARAGON-C
9 BILLY (SHOTGUN) GARDNER-2B/3B (1)
9 RICH (RED) ROLLINS-2B/3B
10 EARL BATTEY-C
11 RON HENRY-C/1B
13 BILL TUTTLE-3B/UTIL (2)
14 PEDRO (PETE) RAMOS-P
14 SAM MELE-CH/MGR2
15 JACK KRALICK-P
16 BERTO CUETO-P
16 TED SADOWSKI-P
17 CAMILO (LITTLE POTATO) PASCUAL-P
18 PAUL GIEL-P (1)
18 LEE STANGE-P
18 DANNY MCDEVITT-P (2)
20 DON LEE-P
21 RAY (FARMER) MOORE-P
22 DAN DOBBEK-OF
23 JIM LEMON-OF
24 PETE WHISENANT-OF
24 DANNY MCDEVITT-P (2)
24 ED PALMQUIST-P (2)
25 LAMAR (JAKE) JACOBS-PH
26 DON MINCHER-1B
27 CHUCK STOBBS-P
28 DON MINCHER-1B
28 JULIO BECQUER-1B/OF/P (2)
28 PEDRO (PETE) RAMOS-P
29 JULIO BECQUER-1B/OF/P (2)
32 ELMER VALO-OF (1)
35 TED SADOWSKI-P
35 GERRY ARRIGO-P
35 JOE ALTOBELLI-OF/1B
36 JIM (KITTY) KAAT-P
38 FRED BRUCKBAUER-P
39 LEE STANGE-P
40 ED PALMQUIST-P (2)
40 BILL (SHORTY) PLEIS-P
41 GARY DOTTER-P
42 GERRY ARRIGO-P
43 AL (BULL) SCHROLL-P
51 COOKIELAVAGETTO-MGR1
52 ED (STEADY EDDIE) LOPAT-CH
53 FLOYD BAKER-CH
54 SAM MELE-CH/MGR2
55 CLYDE MCCULLOUGH-CH

1962

2ND 91-71 5GB

2 ZOILO (ZORRO) VERSALLES-SS
3 HARMON (KILLER) KILLEBREW-OF/1B
4 BOB ALLISON-OF/1B
5 DON MINCHER-1B
6 JIM SNYDER-2B/1B
7 LENNY GREEN-OF
8 HAL NARAGON-C
9 RICH (RED) ROLLINS-3B/SS
10 EARL BATTEY-C
11 GEORGE BANKS-OF/3B
12 BERNIE ALLEN-2B
13 BILL TUTTLE-3B/UTIL
14 SAM MELE-MGR
15 JACK KRALICK-P
16 JOHNNY GORYL-2B/SS
17 CAMILO (LITTLE POTATO) PASCUAL-P
18 DICK STIGMAN-P
19 BILL (SHORTY) PLEIS-P
19 JIM DONOHUE-P (2)
20 DON LEE-P (1)
20 FRANK SULLIVAN-P (2)
21 RAY (FARMER) MOORE-P
22 JERRY ZIMMERMAN-C
23 JIM LEMON (INJ)-OF
27 RUBEN GOMEZ-P (2)
28 VIC POWER-1B/2B
33 JACKIE COLLUM-P (1)
33 JOE BONIKOWSKI-P
33 RUBEN GOMEZ-P (2)
36 JIM (KITTY) KAAT-P
37 TONY OLIVA-OF
38 MARTY MARTINEZ-SS/3B
39 LEE STANGE-P
42 JIM MANNING-P
44 JIM ROLAND-P
45 TED SADOWSKI-P
46 GERRY ARRIGO-P
47 GEORGES MARANDA-P
48 JOE BONIKOWSKI-P
51 GEORGE (BO) STRICKLAND-CH
52 ED FITZGERALD-CH
53 FLOYD BAKER-CH
54 GORDON (MALTZY) MALTZBERGER-CH

1963

5RD 91-70 13GB

1 BERNIE ALLEN-2B
2 ZOILO (ZORRO) VERSALLES-SS
3 HARMON (KILLER) KILLEBREW-OF
4 BOB ALLISON-OF
5 DON MINCHER-1B
6 VIC WERTZ-1B (2)
7 LENNY GREEN-OF
8 JOHNNY GORYL-2B/SS
9 RICH (RED) ROLLINS-3B/2B
10 EARL BATTEY-C
11 GEORGE BANKS-3B
12 BERNIE ALLEN-2B
13 BILL TUTTLE-3B/UTIL
14 SAM MELE-MGR
15 JACK KRALICK-P (1)
15 BILL DAILEY-P
17 CAMILO (LITTLE POTATO) PASCUAL-P
18 DICK STIGMAN-P
19 BILL (SHORTY) PLEIS-P
20 FRANK SULLIVAN-P
20 MIKE FORNIELES-P (2)
20 LEE STANGE-P
21 RAY (FARMER) MOORE-P
22 JERRY ZIMMERMAN-C
23 JIM LEMON (INJ)-OF (1)
24 PAUL RATLIFF-C
26 JAY WARD-3B/OF
27 GARY DOTTER-P
27 MIKE FORNIELES-P (2)
28 VIC POWER,-1B/2B
29 FRED LASHER-P
29 WALLY POST-OF (2)
30 JIMMIE HALL-OF
31 BILL DAILEY-P
31 JIM PERRY-P (2)
32 GARRY ROGGENBURK-P
33 FRED LASHER-P
34 DWIGHT SIEBLER-P
34 JIM ROLAND-P
35 GERRY ARRIGO-P
36 JIM (KITTY) KAAT-P
37 TONY OLIVA-PH
38 MARTY MARTINEZ-SS/3B
39 LEE STANGE-P
40 JULIO BECQUER-PR
43 DON (DINO) WILLIAMS-P
46 GERRY ARRIGO-P
47 GEORGES MARANDA-P
51 HAL NARAGON-CH
52 ED FITZGERALD-CH
53 FLOYD BAKER-CH
54 GORDON (MALTZY) MALTZBERGER-CH

1964

6TH (TIE) 79-83 20GB

1 BERNIE ALLEN (INJ)-2B
2 ZOILO (ZORRO) VERSALLES-SS
3 HARMON (KILLER) KILLEBREW-OF
4 BOB ALLISON-1B/OF
5 DON MINCHER-1B
6 TONY OLIVA-OF
7 LENNY GREEN-OF (1)
7 JIMMIE HALL-OF
8 JOHNNY GORYL-2B/3B
9 RICH (RED) ROLLINS-3B
10 EARL BATTEY-C
11 GEORGE BANKS-PH (1)
11 FRANK KOSTRO-UTIL
12 JOE MCCABE-C
12 RON HENRY-C
14 SAM MELE-MGR
15 BILL DAILEY (INJ)-P
15 AL (RED) WORTHINGTON-P (2)
16 JOE NOSSEK-OF
16 JERRY (SLIM) KINDALL-INF (2)
17 CAMILO (LITTLE POTATO) PASCUAL-P
18 DICK STIGMAN-P
19 BILL (SHORTY) PLEIS-P
20 LEE STANGE-P (1)
20 BILL (SPOT) BETHEA-2B/SS
21 BILL FISCHER-P
21 JIM SNYDER-2B
21 GARY DOTTER-P
21 GARLAND (DUCK) SHIFFLETT-P
22 JERRY ZIMMERMAN-C
23 DAVE BOSWELL-P
24 RICH REESE-1B
25 JIM ROLAND-P
26 JAY WARD-2B/OF
26 CLYDE (BUD) BLOOMFIELD-2B/SS
26 JERRY FOSNOW-P
27 JOHNNY KLIPPSTEIN-P (2)
28 VIC POWER,-1B/2B (1)
29 CHUCK NIESON-P
30 JIMMIE HALL-OF
30 JAY WARD-2B/OF
31 JIM PERRY-P
32 BILL DAILEY (INJ)-P
33 JIM (MUDCAT) GRANT-P (2)
34 DWIGHT SIEBLER-P
35 GERRY ARRIGO-P
36 JIM (KITTY) KAAT-P
37 TONY OLIVA-OF
44 JIM ROLAND-P
48 JOE MCCABE-C
49 CLYDE (BUD) BLOOMFIELD-2B/SS
51 HAL NARAGON-CH
52 ED FITZGERALD-CH
53 FLOYD BAKER-CH
54 GORDON (MALTZY) MALTZBERGER-CH
58 BILL WHITBY-P

1965

1ST 102-60 0GB

L WS-LAN 4-3

1 BILLY (THE KID) MARTIN-CH
2 ZOILO (ZORRO) VERSALLES-SS
3 HARMON (KILLER) KILLEBREW (INJ)-UTIL
4 BOB ALLISON-OF/1B
5 DON MINCHER-1B/OF
6 TONY OLIVA-OF
7 JIMMIE HALL-OF
8 BERNIE ALLEN (INJ)-2B/3B
8 ANDY KOSCO-OF/1B
9 RICH (RED) ROLLINS-3B/2B
10 EARL BATTEY-C
11 FRANK KOSTRO-UTIL
11 FRANK (GUIDO) QUILICI-2B/SS
12 CESAR (PEPITO) TOVAR-UTIL
13 RICH REESE-1B/OF
14 SAM MELE-MGR

15 AL (RED) WORTHINGTON-P
16 JERRY (SLIM) KINDALL-2B/INF
17 CAMILO (LITTLE POTATO) PASCUAL-P
18 DICK STIGMAN-P
19 BILL (SHORTY) PLEIS-P
20 JOHN SEVCIK-C
22 JERRY ZIMMERMAN-C
23 DAVE BOSWELL (ILL)-P
24 JOE NOSSEK-OF/3B
25 JOHN SEVCIK-C
25 DWIGHT SIEBLER-P
26 JERRY FOSNOW-P
26 JIM MERRITT-P
27 JOHNNY KLIPPSTEIN-P
28 SANDY VALDESPINO-OF
29 MEL NELSON-P
30 GARRY ROGGENBURK-P
31 JIM PERRY-P
33JIM (MUDCAT) GRANT-P
34 DWIGHT SIEBLER-P
34 TED UHLAENDER-OF
35 PETE CIMINO-P
36 JIM (KITTY) KAAT-P
41 JOHN SEVCIK-C
44 JIM ROLAND-P
47 SANDY VALDESPINO-OF
51 HAL NARAGON-CH
52 JIM LEMON-CH
53 JOHNNY SAIN-CH

1966

2ND 89-73 9GB

1 BILLY (THE KID) MARTIN-CH
2 ZOILO (ZORRO) VERSALLES-SS
3 HARMON (KILLER) KILLEBREW-3B/UTIL
4 BOB ALLISON-OF
5 DON MINCHER-1B
6 TONY OLIVA-OF
7 JIMMIE HALL-OF
8 ANDY KOSCO-OF/1B
9 RICH (RED) ROLLINS-3B/UTIL
10 EARL BATTEY-C
11 BERNIE ALLEN-2B/3B
12 CESAR (PEPITO) TOVAR-UTIL
13 RICH REESE-PH
14 SAM MELE-MGR
15 AL (RED) WORTHINGTON-P
16 TED UHLAENDER-OF
17 CAMILO (LITTLE POTATO) PASCUAL-P
19 BILL (SHORTY) PLEIS-P
20 RUSS NIXON-C
21 BERNIE ALLEN-2B/3B
22 JERRY ZIMMERMAN-C
23 DAVE BOSWELL-P
24 JOE NOSSEK-OF (1)
24 RON CLARK-3B
25 DWIGHT SIEBLER-P
26 JIM MERRITT-P
27 JOHNNY KLIPPSTEIN-P
28 SANDY VALDESPINO-OF
29 GEORGE MITTERWALD-C
30 GARRY ROGGENBURK-P (1)
30 RON KELLER-P
30 JIM OLLOM-P
31 JIM PERRY-P
32 JIM ROLAND-P
33 JIM (MUDCAT) GRANT-P
34 TED UHLAENDER-OF
34 RON CLARK-3B
35 PETE CIMINO-P
36 JIM (KITTY) KAAT-P
39 JIM ROLAND-P
51 HAL NARAGON-CH
52 JIM LEMON-CH
53 JOHNNY SAIN-CH

1967

2ND (TIE) 91-71 1GB

1 BILLY (THE KID) MARTIN-CH
2 ZOILO (ZORRO) VERSALLES-SS
3 HARMON (KILLER) KILLEBREW-1B/3B
4 BOB ALLISON-OF
5 RICH REESE-1B/OF
5 RUSS NIXON-C
6 TONY OLIVA-OF
7 FRANK (GUIDO) QUILICI-2B/SS
8 RON CLARK (INJ)-3B
9 RICH (RED) ROLLINS-3B
10 EARL BATTEY-C
11 TED UHLAENDER-OF
12 CESAR (PEPITO) TOVAR-UTIL
14 SAM MELE-MGR1
15 AL (RED) WORTHINGTON-P
16 TED UHLAENDER-OF
16 FRANK KOSTRO-OF/3B
17 JIM MERRITT-P
18 JIM OLLOM-P
19 JIM ROLAND-P
20 RUSS NIXON-C
20 RICH REESE-1B/OF
21 WALT (DIED) BOND-OF
21 ROD CAREW-2B
21 HANK IZQUIEDRO-C
22 JERRY ZIMMERMAN-C/CH
23 DAVE BOSWELL-P
24 ANDY KOSCO-OF/1B (1)
24 JACKIE HERNANDEZ-SS/3B
25 DWIGHT SIEBLER-P
25 PAT KELLY (MIL)-PH
26 JIM MERRITT-P
26 MEL NELSON-P
27 RON KLINE-P
28 SANDY VALDESPINO-OF
29 ROD CAREW-2B
30 CARROLL HARDY-OF
31 JIM PERRY-P
32 DEAN CHANCE-P
33 JIM (MUDCAT) GRANT-P
35 GRAIG NETTLES-PH
36 JIM (KITTY) KAAT-P
43 CAL ERMER-MGR2
47 EARLY (GUS) WYNN-CH
52 JIM LEMON-CH
53 EARLY (GUS) WYNN-CH

1968

7TH 79-83 24GB

1 BILLY MARTIN-CH
2 FRANK KOSTRO-OF/1B
3 HARMON (KILLER) KILLEBREW (INJ)-1B/3B
4 BOB ALLISON-OF/1B
5 BOB OLDIS-CH
6 TONY OLIVA-OF
7 FRANK (GUIDO) QUILICI-INF
8 RON CLARK-INF
9 RICH (RED) ROLLINS-3B
10 JOHNNY ROSEBORO-C
10 RICK RENICK-SS
11 TED UHLAENDER-OF
12 CESAR (PEPITO) TOVAR-UTIL/P (ALL POS.)
13 JOHNNY ROSEBORO-C
15 AL (RED) WORTHINGTON-P
16 RON PERRANOSKI-P
17 BUZZ STEPHEN-P
17 JIM MERRITT-P
18 RON KELLER (MIL)-P
19 JIM ROLAND-P
20 RICH REESE-1B/OF
21 TOM HALL-P
21 BOB MILLER-P
22 JERRY ZIMMERMAN-C
23 DAVE BOSWELL-P
24 JACKIE HERNANDEZ-SS/1B
25 BRUCE LOOK-C
26 JIM MERRITT-P
27 DANNY MORRIS-P
28 GRAIG NETTLES-OF/INF
29 ROD CAREW-2B/SS
30 PAT KELLY (MIL)-OF
31 JIM PERRY-P
32 DEAN CHANCE-P
34 GEORGE MITTERWALD-C
36 JIM (KITTY) KAAT (INJ)-P
42 BUZZ STEPHEN-P
43 CAL ERMER-MGR
45 JIM HOLT-OF
46 GEORGE CASE-CH
47 EARLY (GUS) WYNN-CH
48 JOHNNY (GROUCHO) GORYL-CH
49 BOB MILLER-P

1969

1ST W 97-65 0GB
L ALCS-BALA 3-0

1 BILLY (THE KID) MARTIN-MGR
2 FRANK KOSTRO-PH
2 GRAIG NETTLES-OF/3B
3 HARMON (KILLER) KILLEBREW-3B/1B
4 BOB ALLISON-OF/1B
5 LEO (CHICO) CARDENAS-SS
6 TONY OLIVA-OF
7 FRANK (GUIDO) QUILICI-INF
8 RON CLARK-3B (1)
8 RICK DEMPSEY-C
9 CHARLIE (CHUCK) MANUEL-OF
10 RICK RENICK-UTIL
11 TED UHLAENDER-OF
12 CESAR (PEPITO) TOVAR-OF/INF
13 JOHNNY ROSEBORO-C
15 GEORGE MITTERWALD-C/OF
16 RON PERRANOSKI-P
17 JERRY CRIDER-P
17 JOE GRZENDA-P
18 DICK WOODSON-P
18 HERM HILL-OF
19 AL (RED) WORTHINGTON (RET)-P
19 BILL ZEPP-P
20 RICH REESE-1B/OF
21 TOM HALL-P
22 TOM TISCHINSKI-C
23 DAVE BOSWELL-P
24 DANNY MORRIS-P
24 DARRELL (BUCKY) BRANDON-P (2)
25 DAVE BOSWELL-P
25 BILL ZEPP-P
26 JIM HOLT-OF/1B
27 DANNY MORRIS-P
27 CHARLEY WALTERS-P
27 JERRY CRIDER-P
29 ROD CAREW-2B
31 JIM PERRY-P
32 DEAN CHANCE (INJ)-P
33 JOE GRZENDA-P
34 COTTON NASH-1B/OF
35 DICK WOODSON-P
36 JIM (KITTY) KAAT-P
43 ART FOWLER-CH
44 VERN MORGAN-CH
45 JOHNNY (GROUCHO) GORYL-CH
46 CHARLIE (SWEDE) SILVERA-CH
47 EARLY (GUS) WYNN-CH
49 BOB MILLER-P
56 CHARLEY WALTERS-P

1970

1ST W 98-64 0GB
L ALCS-BALA 3-0

2 FRANK (CROW) CROSETTI-CH
3 HARMON (KILLER) KILLEBREW-3B/1B
4 BOB ALLISON-OF/1B
5 LEO (CHICO) CARDENAS-SS
5 DANNY THOMPSON-2B/INF
6 TONY OLIVA-OF
7 FRANK (GUIDO) QUILICI-INF
8 PAUL RATLIFF-C
9 CHARLIE (CHUCK) MANUEL-OF
10 RICK RENICK-UTIL
11 BRANT ALYEA-OF
12 CESAR (PEPITO) TOVAR-OF/INF
15 GEORGE MITTERWALD-C
16 RON PERRANOSKI-P
17 LEO (CHICO) CARDENAS-SS
18 BILL (THE CRICKET) (SPECS) RIGNEY-MGR
19 HERM HILL-OF
20 RICH REESE-1B
21 TOM HALL-P
22 TOM TISCHINSKI-C
23 DAVE BOSWELL (INJ)-P
24 STEVE BARBER-P
24 PETE HAMM-P
25 BILL ZEPP-P
26 JIM HOLT-OF/1B
27 MINNIE MENDOZA-3B/2B
28 BERT BLYLEVEN-P
29 ROD CAREW (INJ)-2B/1B
30 HAL HAYDEL-P
31 JIM PERRY-P
32 DICK WOODSON-P
33 LUIS TIANT-P
34 PETE HAMM-P
34 JIM NETTLES-OF
35 STAN WILLIAMS-P
36 JIM (KITTY) KAAT-P
37 STEVE BRYE-OF
38 RICK DEMPSEY-C
39 JIM NETTLES-OF
40 COTTON NASH-1B
44 VERN MORGAN-CH
45 BOB (BUCK) RODGERS-CH
46 MARV GRISSOM-CH
47 SHERRY ROBERTSON-CH
55 DANNY THOMPSON-2B/INF

1971

5TH W 74-86 26.5GB

2 FRANK (CROW) CROSETTI-CH
3 HARMON (KILLER) KILLEBREW-1B/3B
4 STEVE BRAUN-3B/UTIL
5 DANNY THOMPSON (INJ)-INF
6 TONY OLIVA (INJ)-OF
7 PAUL POWELL-OF
7 JIM NETTLES-OF
8 PAUL RATLIFF-C (1)
8 PHIL ROOF-C (2)
9 CHARLIE (CHUCK) MANUEL-OF
10 RICK RENICK (INJ)-3B/OF
11 BRANT ALYEA-OF
12 CESAR (PEPITO) TOVAR-OF/INF
15 GEORGE MITTERWALD-C
16 RON PERRANOSKI-P (1)
16 BOB GEBHARD-P
17 LEO (CHICO) CARDENAS-SS
18 BILL (THE CRICKET) (SPECS) RIGNEY-MGR
19 SAL CAMPISI-P
19 JIM STRICKLAND-P
20 RICH REESE-1B/OF
21 TOM HALL-P
22 TOM TISCHINSKI-C
23 RAY CORBIN-P
24 STEVE BARBER-P
24 GEORGE THOMAS-UTIL
24 PETE HAMM-P
25 RICK DEMPSEY-C
26 JIM HOLT-OF/1B
27 ERIC SODERHOLM-3B
28 BERT BLYLEVEN-P
29 ROD CAREW-2B/3B
30 HAL HAYDEL-P
31 JIM PERRY-P
32 STEVE LUEBBER-P
33 PETE HAMM-P
34 PETE HAMM-P
35 STAN WILLIAMS-P (1)
36 JIM (KITTY) KAAT-P
37 STEVE BRYE-OF
38 RICK DEMPSEY-C
39 JIM NETTLES-OF
41 RAY CORBIN-P
43 FRANK (GUIDO) QUILICI-CH
44 VERN MORGAN-CH
45 BOB (BUCK) RODGERS-CH
46 MARV GRISSOM-CH
53 JIM STRICKLAND-P

1972

3RD W 77-77 15.5GB

1 ERIC SODERHOLM-3B
2 BOBBY DARWIN-OF
3 HARMON (KILLER) KILLEBREW-1B
4 STEVE BRAUN-UTIL
5 DANNY THOMPSON-SS
6 TONY OLIVA (INJ)-OF
7 JIM NETTLES-OF/1B
8 PHIL ROOF-C
9 CHARLIE (CHUCK) MANUEL-OF
10 RICK RENICK-UTIL
11 STEVE BRYE-OF
12 CESAR (PEPITO) TOVAR-OF
13 DICK WOODSON-P
14 DAN MONZON-INF/OF
15 GEORGE MITTERWALD-C
16 BOB GEBHARD-P
17 DAVE LAROCHE-P
18 BILL (THE CRICKET) (SPECS) RIGNEY-MGR1
19 JIM STRICKLAND-P
20 RICH REESE-1B/OF
21 WAYNE GRANGER-P
22 TOM NORTON (INJ)-P
23 RAY CORBIN-P
24 GLENN BORGMANN-C
25 RICK DEMPSEY-C
25 MIKE ADAMS-OF
26 JIM HOLT-OF/1B
27 BUCKY GUTH-SS
28 BERT BLYLEVEN-P
29 ROD CAREW-2B
30 DAVE GOLTZ-P
31 JIM PERRY-P
32 STEVE LUEBBER-P
36 JIM (KITTY) KAAT (INJ)-P

WASHINGTON SENATORS/**MINNESOTA TWINS**

39 DAVE GOLTZ-P
41 TOM NORTON (INJ)-P
42 RALPH ROWE-CH
43 FRANK (GUIDO) QUILICI-CH/MGR2
44 VERN MORGAN-CH
45 BOB (BUCK) RODGERS-CH
46 AL (RED) WORTHINGTON-CH

1973

3RD W 81-81 13GB

1 ERIC SODERHOLM-3B/SS
1 RICH REESE-1B (2)
2 BOBBY DARWIN-OF/DH
3 HARMON (KILLER) KILLEBREW (INJ)-1B/DH
4 STEVE BRAUN (INJ)-3B/OF
5 DANNY THOMPSON-SS/3B
6 TONY OLIVA-DH
7 JERRY TERRELL-UTIL
8 PHIL ROOF-C
9 LARRY HISLE-OF
10 JOE LIS-1B/DH
11 STEVE BRYE-OF
12 DANNY (MICKEY) WALTON-UTIL
13 DICK WOODSON (INJ)-P
14 DAN MONZON-INF/OF
15 GEORGE MITTERWALD-C/DH
16 DANNY FIFE-P
17 BILL HANDS-P
18 EDDIE BANE-P
19 JIM STRICKLAND-P
20 KEN SANDERS-P (1)
20 VIC ALBURY-P
21 JOE DECKER-P
22 CRAIG KUSICK-UTIL
23 RAY CORBIN-P
24 GLENN BORGMANN-C
24 BILL CAMPBELL-P
25 MIKE ADAMS-OF/DH
26 JIM HOLT-OF/1B
27 GLENN BORGMANN-C
28 BERT BLYLEVEN-P
29 ROD CAREW-2B
30 DAVE GOLTZ-P
35 JERRY TERRELL-UTIL
36 JIM (KITTY) KAAT-P (1)
39 DANNY (MICKEY) WALTON-UTIL
42 RALPH ROWE-CH
43 FRANK (GUIDO) QUILICI-MGR
44 VERN MORGAN-CH
45 BOB (BUCK) RODGERS-CH
46 AL (RED) WORTHINGTON-CH

1974

3RD W 82-80 8GB

1 SERGIO FERRER-SS/2B
2 BOBBY DARWIN-OF
3 HARMON (KILLER) KILLEBREW-DH/1B
4 STEVE BRAUN-OF/3B
5 DANNY THOMPSON (INJ)-SS/UTIL
6 TONY OLIVA-DH
7 JERRY TERRELL-UTIL
8 PHIL ROOF-C
9 LARRY HISLE-OF
10 JOE LIS-UTIL (1)
10 CRAIG KUSICK-1B
10 PAT BOURQUE-1B (2)
11 STEVE BRYE-OF
12 ERIC SODERHOLM-3B/SS
13 DICK WOODSON-P (1)
14 GLENN BORGMANN-C
15 RANDY HUNDLEY (INJ)-C
16 DANNY FIFE-P
17 BILL HANDS-P (1)
17 BILL BUTLER-P
19 TOM BURGMEIER-P
20 VIC ALBURY-P
21 JOE DECKER-P
22 CRAIG KUSICK-1B
23 RAY CORBIN-P
24 BILL CAMPBELL-P
25 LUIS GOMEZ-INF/DH
26 JIM HOLT-1B/OF (1)
28 BERT BLYLEVEN-P
29 ROD CAREW-2B
30 DAVE GOLTZ-P
31 JIM HUGHES-P
32 TOM JOHNSON-P
37 JIM HUGHES-P
42 RALPH ROWE-CH
43 FRANK (GUIDO) QUILICI-MGR
44 VERN MORGAN-CH
45 BOB (BUCK) RODGERS-CH
49 BILL HANDS-P (1)

1975

4TH W 76-83 20.5GB

1 SERGIO FERRER-INF/DH
1 JERRY TERRELL-UTIL
2 BOBBY DARWIN-OF/DH (1)
3 *(RET#) HARMON KILLEBREW*
4 STEVE BRAUN-UTIL
5 DANNY THOMPSON-SS/UTIL
6 TONY OLIVA-DH
7 DANNY (MICKEY) WALTON-UTIL
7 DAVE MCKAY-3B
8 PHIL ROOF (INJ)-C
9 LARRY HISLE (INJ)-OF
10 LYMAN BOSTOCK (INJ)-OF/DH
11 STEVE BRYE (INJ)-OF
12 ERIC SODERHOLM (INJ)-3B/DH
13 TOM LUNDSTEDT-C/DH
14 GLENN BORGMANN-C
15 DAN FORD-OF/DH
16 TOM KELLY-1B/OF
16 EDDIE BANE-P
17 BILL BUTLER-P
18 MIKE PAZIK-P
18 MARK WILEY-P
19 TOM BURGMEIER-P
20 VIC ALBURY-P
21 JOE DECKER (ILL)-P
22 CRAIG KUSICK-1B
22 JOHNNY BRIGGS-1B/UTIL (2)
23 RAY CORBIN (INJ)-P
24 BILL CAMPBELL-P
25 LUIS GOMEZ-INF/DH
26 MIKE POEPPING-OF
27 MARK WILEY-P
28 BERT BLYLEVEN-P
29 ROD CAREW-2B/UTIL
30 DAVE GOLTZ-P
31 JIM HUGHES-P
32 TOM JOHNSON-P
41 MIKE PAZIK-P
42 RALPH ROWE-CH
43 FRANK (GUIDO) QUILICI-MGR
44 VERN MORGAN-CH
45 LEE STANGE-CH
54 MIKE PAZIK-P

1976

3RD W 85-77 5GB

1 JERRY TERRELL-UTIL
2 STEVE BRAUN-UTIL
3 *(RET#) HARMON KILLEBREW*
4 GENE (SKIP) MAUCH-MGR
5 DANNY THOMPSON-SS (1)
5 ROY SMALLEY, JR.-SS (2)
6 TONY OLIVA-DH/CH
7 DAVE MCKAY-INF/DH
8 PHIL ROOF-C (1)
9 LARRY HISLE-OF
10 LYMAN BOSTOCK-OF
11 STEVE BRYE (INJ)-OF/DH
(12) ERIC SODERHOLM (INJ)-(3B)
14 GLENN BORGMANN-C
15 DAN FORD-OF/DH
16 EDDIE BANE-P
16 BUTCH WYNEGAR-C/DH
17 PETE (RED) REDFERN-P
18 EDDIE BANE-P
18 BILL (THE SINGER THROWIN MACHINE) SINGER-P (2)
19 TOM BURGMEIER-P
20 VIC ALBURY (INJ)-P
21 JOE DECKER-P
21 TOM JOHNSON-P
22 CRAIG KUSICK-DH/1B
23 STEVE LUEBBER-P
24 BILL CAMPBELL-P
25 LUIS GOMEZ-UTIL
26 MIKE PAZIK-P
26 MIKE CUBBAGE-SS/UTIL (2)
28 BERT BLYLEVEN-P (1)
29 ROD CAREW-1B/2B
30 DAVE GOLTZ-P
31 JIM HUGHES-P
32 BOB RANDALL-2B
34 STEVE LUEBBER-P
40 MIKE PAZIK-P
40 JOE NOSSEK-CH
41 EDDIE (MOUSE) LYONS-CH
42 DON MCMAHON-CH
43 JERRY ZIMMERMAN-CH
48 BILL (THE SINGER THROWIN MACHINE) SINGER-P (2)

1977

4TH W 84-77 17.5GB

1 JERRY TERRELL-UTIL
2 RANDY BASS-DH
3 *(RET#) HARMON KILLEBREW*
4 GENE (SKIP) MAUCH-MGR
5 ROY SMALLEY, JR.-SS
6 TONY OLIVA-CH
7 ROB WILFONG-2B/DH
8 GLENN ADAMS (INJ)-DH/OF
9 LARRY HISLE-OF/DH
10 LYMAN BOSTOCK-OF
11 TERRY (BUD) BULLING-C/DH
12 RICH CHILES-DH/OF
14 GLENN BORGMANN (INJ)-C
15 DAN FORD-OF/DH
16 BUTCH WYNEGAR-C/3B
17 PETE (RED) REDFERN-P
18 DON (AUTO) CARRITHERS-P
19 TOM BURGMEIER-P
20 GARY SERUM-P
21 TOM JOHNSON-P
22 CRAIG KUSICK-DH/1B
23 PAUL THORMODSGARD-P
24 WILLIE NORWOOD-OF/DH
25 LUIS GOMEZ-UTIL
26 MIKE CUBBAGE-3B/DH
27 DAVE JOHNSON-P
28 JIM SHELLENBACK-P
29 ROD CAREW-1B/UTIL
30 DAVE GOLTZ-P
31 JIM HUGHES-P
32 BOB RANDALL (INJ)-2B/UTIL
32 JEFF HOLLY-P
33 MIKE PAZIK (AUTO)-P
34 RON SCHUELER-P
35 BOB GORINSKI-OF/DH
36 JEFF HOLLY-P
37 BILL BUTLER-P
38 GEOFF ZAHN-P
39 LARRY WOLFE-3B
40 SAM PERLOZZO-2B/3B
41 KARL KUEHL-CH
42 DON MCMAHON-CH
43 JERRY ZIMMERMAN-CH
50 JIM SHELLENBACK-P

1978

4TH W 73-89 19GB

1 LARRY WOLFE-3B/SS
3 *(RET#) HARMON KILLEBREW*
4 GENE (SKIP) MAUCH-MGR
5 ROY SMALLEY, JR.-SS
6 TONY OLIVA-CH
7 ROB WILFONG (INJ)-2B/DH
8 GLENN ADAMS-DH/OF
9 BOMBO RIVERA-OF/DH
10 HOSTEN POWELL-OF/DH
12 RICH CHILES-OF/DH
14 GLENN BORGMANN-C/DH
15 DAN FORD-OF/DH
16 BUTCH WYNEGAR-C/3B
17 PETE (RED) REDFERN-P
18 GREG THAYER-P
19 ROGER ERICKSON-P
20 GARY SERUM-P
21 TOM JOHNSON (INJ)-P
22 CRAIG KUSICK-UTIL
23 PAUL THORMODSGARD-P
24 WILLIE NORWOOD-OF/DH
26 MIKE CUBBAGE-3B/2B
27 DAVE JOHNSON-P
28 MAC SCARCE-P
28 MIKE MARSHALL-P
29 ROD CAREW-1B/UTIL
30 DAVE GOLTZ (INJ)-P
31 DARRELL JACKSON-P
32 BOB RANDALL-2B/UTIL
33 MIKE MARSHALL-P
33 DAVE EDWARDS-OF
34 JOSE MORALES-UTIL
36 JEFF HOLLY-P
37 RORIC HARRISON-P
38 GEOFF ZAHN-P
39 STAN PERZANOWSKI-P
40 JOHN SUTTON-P
40 DARRELL JACKSON-P
41 KARL KUEHL-CH
41 JOHN SUTTON-P
42 CAMILO (LITTLE POTATO) PASCUAL-CH
43 JERRY (ZIM) ZIMMERMAN-CH

1979

4TH W 82-80 6GB

2 JOHN CASTINO-3B/SS
3 *(RET#) HARMON KILLEBREW*
4 GENE (SKIP) MAUCH-MGR
5 ROY SMALLEY, JR.-SS/1B
7 ROB WILFONG-2B/OF
8 GLENN ADAMS-DH/OF
9 BOMBO RIVERA-OF/DH
10 HOSKEN POWELL (INJ)-OF/DH
12 DANNY GOODWIN-DH/1B
12 RICK SOFIELD-OF
14 GLENN BORGMANN-C
15 RON (PAPA JACK) JACKSON-1B/UTIL
16 BUTCH WYNEGAR-C/DH
17 PETE (RED) REDFERN-P
18 PAUL HARTZELL-P
19 ROGER ERICKSON-P
20 GARY SERUM-P
21 JEFF HOLLY-P
21 TERRY FELTON-P
22 CRAIG KUSICK-DH/1B (1)
23 PAUL THORMODSGARD-P
24 WILLIE NORWOOD-OF/DH
25 RICK SOFIELD-OF
25 DANNY GOODWIN-DH/1B
26 MIKE CUBBAGE (INJ)-UTIL
27 JERRY KOOSMAN-P
27 MIKE BACSIK-P
28 MIKE MARSHALL-P
30 DAVE GOLTZ-P
31 KEN BRETT-P (1)
31 DARRELL JACKSON-P
32 BOB RANDALL-UTIL
33 DAVE EDWARDS-OF/DH
34 JOSE MORALES-DH/1B
35 GARY WARD-OF/DH
36 JEFF HOLLY-P
36 JERRY KOOSMAN-P
37 DAN GRAHAM-DH
37 JESUS VEGA-PH
38 GEOFF ZAHN (INJ)-P
40 KEVIN STANFIELD-P
41 KARL KUEHL-CH
42 CAMILO (LITTLE POTATO) PASCUAL-CH
43 JERRY (ZIM) ZIMMERMAN-CH
44 KEN LANDREAUX-OF
45 JOHNNY (GROUCHO) GORYL-CH
48 TERRY FELTON-P

1980

3RD W 77-84 19.5GB

1 JESUS VEGA-DH/1B
2 JOHN CASTINO-3B/SS
3 *(RET#) HARMON KILLEBREW*
4 GENE (SKIP) MAUCH-MGR1
5 ROY SMALLEY, JR.-SS/UTIL
7 ROB WILFONG-2B/OF
8 GLENN ADAMS-DH/OF
9 BOMBO RIVERA (INJ)-OF/DH
10 HOSKEN POWELL-OF
11 SAL BUTERA-C/DH
12 RICK SOFIELD-OF/DH
14 PETE MACKANIN-UTIL
15 RON (PAPA JACK) JACKSON-1B/UTIL
16 BUTCH WYNEGAR-C/DH
17 PETE (RED) REDFERN (INJ)-P
18 GREG JOHNSTON-OF
19 ROGER ERICKSON-P
20 BOB VESELIC-P
21 TERRY FELTON-P
21 LENNY FAEDO-3B/2B
22 JOHN VERHOEVEN-P
23 DOUG CORBETT-P
24 WILLIE NORWOOD-OF/DH
25 DANNY GOODWIN-DH/1B
26 MIKE CUBBAGE-INF/DH
27 MIKE BACSIK-P
27 AL WILLIAMS-P
28 MIKE MARSHALL-P
28 AL WILLIAMS-P
30 FERNANDO ARROYO-P
31 DARRELL JACKSON-P
32 BOB RANDALL-SS
32 MIKE KINNUNEN-P
32 GARY WARD-OF
33 DAVE EDWARDS-OF/DH
34 JOSE MORALES-DH/UTIL
35 MIKE KINNUNEN-P

36 JERRY KOOSMAN-P
37 BOB VESELIC-P
38 GEOFF ZAHN-P
39 BOB VESELIC-P
41 KARL KUEHL-CH
42 CAMILO (LITTLE POTATO) PASCUAL-CH
43 JERRY (ZIM) ZIMMERMAN-CH
44 KEN LANDREAUX-OF/DH
45 JOHNNY (GROUCHO) GORYL-CH/MGR2
50 JOHN VERHOEVEN-P
52 FERNANDO ARROYO-P

1981

1ST 1/2:7TH W 17-39 18GB
2ND 1/2:5TH W 24-29 6.5GB
FINAL: 41-68 --GB

1 TIM CORCORAN-1B/DH
2 JOHN CASTINO-3B/2B
3 *(RET#) HARMON KILLEBREW*
4 MARK FUNDERBURK-OF/DH
5 ROY SMALLEY, JR. (INJ)-SS/UTIL
7 ROB WILFONG-2B
8 GLENN ADAMS-DH
9 MICKEY HATCHER-OF/UTIL
10 HOSKEN POWELL-OF/DH
11 SAL BUTERA-UTIL
12 RICK SOFIELD-OF
14 PETE MACKANIN-UTIL
15 RON (PAPA JACK) JACKSON-1B/UTIL (1)
15 TIM LAUDNER-C/DH
16 BUTCH WYNEGAR (INJ)-C/DH
17 PETE (RED) REDFERN (INJ)-P
18 RAY SMITH (INJ)-C
19 ROGER ERICKSON (INJ)-P
20 BOB VESELIC-P
20 DAVE ENGEL-OF/UTIL
21 GREG JOHNSTON-OF
21 LENNY FAEDO-3B/2B
22 JOHN VERHOEVEN-P
23 DOUG CORBETT-P
24 CHUCK BAKER-INF/DH
25 DANNY GOODWIN-UTIL
26 KENT HRBEK-1B/DH
27 BRAD HAVENS-P
28 AL WILLIAMS-P
30 FERNANDO ARROYO-P
31 DARRELL JACKSON (ILL)-P
32 GARY WARD-OF
33 JACK O'CONNOR-P
34 DON COOPER-P
35 BOB VESELIC-P
36 JERRY KOOSMAN-P (1)
37 TERRY FELTON-P
38 RON WASHINGTON-SS/OF
39 GARY GAETTI-3B/DH
40 JACK HOBBS-P
41 KARL KUEHL-CH
42 BILLY (SHOTGUN) GARDNER-CH/MGR2
43 RICK STELMASZEK-CH
44 MICKEY HATCHER-OF/UTIL
44 JIM LEMON-CH
45 JOHNNY (GROUCHO) GORYL-CH/MGR1
46 JOHNNY PODRES-CH
51 DAVE ENGLE-OF/UTIL

1982

7TH W 60-102 33GB

1 JESUS VEGA-UTIL
2 JOHN CASTINO-2B/UTIL
3 *(RET#) HARMON KILLEBREW*
4 JIM EISENREICH (ILL)-OF
5 ROY SMALLEY, JR. (INJ)-SS (1)
7 ROB WILFONG-2B (1)
7 GREG (BOOMER) WELLS-1B/DH
7 LARRY MILBOURNE-2B (2)
8 GARY GAETTI-3B/UTIL
9 MICKEY HATCHER-UTIL
10 BOBBY MITCHELL-OF
11 SAL BUTERA-C
12 LENNY FAEDO-SS/DH
14 KENT HRBEK-1B/DH
15 TIM LAUDNER-C
16 BUTCH WYNEGAR-C (1)
16 FRANK VIOLA-P
17 PETE (RED) REDFERN (INJ)-P
18 RAY SMITH (INJ)-C
18 TERRY FELTON-P
19 ROGER ERICKSON-P (1)
19 JOHN PACELLA-P (2)
20 DAVE ENGEL-OF/DH
22 BOBBY CASTILLO-P
22 RANDY JOHNSON-DH/OF
23 DOUG CORBETT-P (1)
23 PETE FILSON-P
24 RON WASHINGTON-INF
24 TOM (BRUNO) BRUNANSKY-OF
25 RANDY BUSH-DH/OF
27 BRAD HAVENS-P
28 AL WILLIAMS-P
30 FERNANDO ARROYO-P (1)
30 PAUL BORIS-P
31 DARRELL JACKSON (INJ)-P
32 GARY WARD-OF/DH
33 JACK O'CONNOR-P
34 DON COOPER-P
34 RON DAVIS-P
36 JEFF LITTLE-P
37 TERRY FELTON-P
37 BOBBY CASTILLO-P
38 RON WASHINGTON-INF
39 RON DAVIS-P
40 JACK HOBBS-P
40 PAUL BORIS-P
41 KARL KUEHL-CH
41 FRANK VIOLA-P
42 BILLY (SHOTGUN) GARDNER-MGR
43 RICK STELMASZEK-CH
44 JIM LEMON-CH
45 JEFF LITTLE-P
46 JOHNNY PODRES-CH
48 JACK O'CONNOR-P

1983

5TH W (TIE) 70-92 29GB

1 RAY SMITH-C
1 HOUSTON JIMENEZ-SS
2 JOHN CASTINO-2B/UTIL
3 *(RET#) HARMON KILLEBREW*
4 JIM EISENREICH (ILL)-OF
5 TIM TEUFEL-UTIL
5 RAY SMITH-C
7 SCOTT ULLGER-UTIL
8 GARY GAETTI-3B/UTIL
9 MICKEY HATCHER-UTIL
10 BOBBY MITCHELL-OF
11 TACK WILSON-DH/OF
11 RUSTY KUNTZ-OF (2)
12 LENNY FAEDO (INJ)-SS
12 TACK WILSON-DH/OF
14 KENT HRBEK-1B/DH
15 TIM LAUDNER-C/DH
16 FRANK VIOLA-P
17 BRYAN OELKERS-P
18 KEN SCHROM-P
19 RICK LYSANDER-P
20 DAVE ENGEL-C/UTIL
21 JIM LEWIS-P
22 LEN WHITEHOUSE-P
23 PETE FILSON (INJ)-P
24 TOM (BRUNO) BRUNANSKY-OF/DH
25 RANDY BUSH-DH/1B
26 DARRELL BROWN-OF/DH
27 BRAD HAVENS-P
28 AL WILLIAMS-P
30 MIKE WALTERS-P
31 GREG GAGNE-SS
32 GARY WARD-OF/DH
33 JACK O'CONNOR-P
34 TIM TEUFEL-UTIL
35 GREG GAGNE-SS
35 JAY PETTIBONE-P
37 BOBBY CASTILLO (INJ)-P
38 RON WASHINGTON-SS/UTIL
39 RON DAVIS-P
41 TOM KELLY-CH
42 BILLY (SHOTGUN) GARDNER-MGR
43 RICK STELMASZEK-CH
44 JIM LEMON-CH
45 JIM SHELLENBACK-CH
46 JOHNNY PODRES-CH

1984

2ND W 81-81 3GB

1 HOUSTON JIMENEZ-SS
1 ALVARO ESPINOZA-SS
2 JOHN CASTINO (INJ)-3B
3 *(RET#) HARMON KILLEBREW*
4 JIM EISENREICH (ILL)-DH/OF
4 CHRIS SPEIER-SS (3)
5 HOUSTON JIMENEZ-SS
7 DAVE MEIER-UTIL
8 GARY GAETTI-3B/UTIL
9 MICKEY HATCHER-OF/UTIL
10 JEFF REED-C
11 TIM TEUFEL-2B
12 LENNY FAEDO-SS/DH
14 KENT HRBEK-1B/DH
15 TIM LAUDNER-C/DH
16 FRANK VIOLA-P
17 ED HODGE-P
18 KEN SCHROM (INJ)-P
19 RICK LYSANDER-P
19 LARRY PASHNICK-P
20 DAVE ENGEL-C/DH
21 JEFF REED-C
21 KEITH COMSTOCK-P
21 ANDRE DAVID-OF/DH
22 LEN WHITEHOUSE-P
23 PETE FILSON-P
24 TOM (BRUNO) BRUNANSKY-OF/DH
25 RANDY BUSH-DH/1B
26 DARRELL BROWN-OF/DH
28 AL WILLIAMS (INJ)-P
30 MIKE WALTERS-P
31 MIKE HART-OF
31 GREG GAGNE-PH
32 JOHN BUTCHER-P
33 JACK O'CONNOR-P
34 MIKE SMITHSON-P
34 KIRBY (STUB) PUCKETT-OF
35 PAT PUTNAM-DH (2)
36 CURT WARDLE-P
37 BOBBY CASTILLO (INJ)-P
38 RON WASHINGTON-INF/DH
39 RON DAVIS-P
41 TOM KELLY-CH
42 BILLY (SHOTGUN) GARDNER-MGR
43 RICK STELMASZEK-CH
44 JIM LEMON-CH
46 JOHNNY PODRES-CH
48 MIKE SMITHSON-P
58 LARRY PASHNICK-P

1985

5TH W (TIE) 77-85 14GB

1 ALVARO ESPINOZA-SS
(2) JOHN CASTINO (INJ)-(3B)
3 *(RET#) HARMON KILLEBREW*
5 ROY SMALLEY, JR.-DH/UTIL
6 TONY OLIVA-CH
7 DAVE MEIER-OF/DH
8 GARY GAETTI-3B/UTIL
9 MICKEY HATCHER-OF/UTIL
10 JEFF REED-C
11 TIM TEUFEL-2B/DH
12 MARK SALAS-C/DH
14 KENT HRBEK-1B/DH
15 TIM LAUDNER-C/1B
16 FRANK VIOLA-P
17 DENNIS BURTT-P
18 KEN SCHROM-P
19 RICK LYSANDER-P
20 DAVE ENGEL-UTIL
22 LEN WHITEHOUSE-P
23 PETE FILSON-P
24 TOM (BRUNO) BRUNANSKY-OF
25 RANDY BUSH-UTIL
26 FRANK EUFEMIA-P
27 MARK BROWN-P
28 BERT BLYLEVEN-P (2)
29 STEVE HOWE-P (2)
30 STEVE HOWE-P (2)
31 GREG GAGNE-SS/DH
32 JOHN BUTCHER-P
33 MIKE STENHOUSE-UTIL
34 KIRBY (STUB) PUCKETT-OF
35 TOM KLAWITTER (INJ)-P
36 CURT WARDLE-P (1)
36 MARK PORTUGAL-P
37 RICH YETT-P
38 RON WASHINGTON-INF/DH
39 RON DAVIS-P
40 MARK FUNDERBURK-UTIL
41 TOM KELLY-CH
42 BILLY (SHOTGUN) GARDNER-MGR1
42 DICK SUCH-CH
43 RICK STELMASZEK-CH
44 RAY MILLER-MGR2
45 MARK PORTUGAL-P
46 JOHNNY PODRES-CH
48 MIKE SMITHSON-P
49 STEVE LOMBARDOZZI-2B

1986

6TH W 71-91 21GB

1 ALVARO ESPINOZA-2B/SS
2 CHRIS PITTARO-2B/SS
3 *(RET#) HARMON KILLEBREW*
4 STEVE LOMBARDOZZI-2B
5 ROY SMALLEY, JR.-DH/INF
6 TONY OLIVA-CH
7 MARK DAVIDSON-OF/DH
8 GARY GAETTI-3B/UTIL
9 MICKEY HATCHER-UTIL
10 JEFF REED-C
11 AL WOODS-DH
12 MARK SALAS-C/DH
14 KENT HRBEK-1B/DH
15 TIM LAUDNER-C
16 FRANK VIOLA-P
17 DENNIS BURTT-P
18 ALEX SANCHEZ-DH/OF
19 ROY SMITH-P
20 BILLY BEANE-OF/DH
21 ANDRE DAVID-DH
21 GEORGE FRAZIER-P (2)
22 KEITH ATHERTON-P (2)
23 PETE FILSON-P (1)
23 ROY LEE JACKSON-P
24 TOM (BRUNO) BRUNANSKY-OF/DH
25 RANDY BUSH-OF/UTIL
28 BERT BLYLEVEN-P
30 JUAN AGOSTO-P (2)
31 GREG GAGNE-SS/2B
32 JOHN BUTCHER-P (1)
32 NEAL HEATON-P (2)
33 FRANK PASTORE (INJ)-P
34 KIRBY (STUB) PUCKETT-OF
35 BILL LATHAM-P
36 MARK PORTUGAL-P
37 RAY FONTENOT-P (2)
38 RON WASHINGTON-INF/DH
39 RON DAVIS-P (1)
40 ALLAN ANDERSON-P
41 TOM KELLY-CH/MGR2
42 DICK SUCH-CH
43 RICK STELMASZEK-CH
44 RAY MILLER-MGR1
45 WAYNE (TWIG) TERWILLIGER-CH
48 MIKE SMITHSON-P
49 ALLAN ANDERSON-P
51 ROY SMITH-P

1987

1ST W 86-77 0GB
W ALCS-DETA 4-1
W WS-STLN 4-3

2 CHRIS PITTARO-2B/DH
3 *(RET#) HARMON KILLEBREW*
4 STEVE LOMBARDOZZI-2B
5 ROY SMALLEY, JR.-DH/INF
6 TONY OLIVA-CH
7 GREG GAGNE-SS/UTIL
8 GARY GAETTI-3B/DH
9 GENE LARKIN-DH/1B
10 TOM KELLY-MGR
11 TOM NIETO-C/DH
12 MARK SALAS-C (1)
14 KENT HRBEK-1B/DH
15 TIM LAUDNER-C/UTIL
16 FRANK VIOLA-P
17 LES STRAKER-P
18 DON BAYLOR-DH (2)
19 RANDY NIEMANN-P
20 BILLY BEANE-OF
21 GEORGE FRAZIER-P
22 KEITH ATHERTON-P
23 ROY SMITH-P
24 TOM (BRUNO) BRUNANSKY-OF/DH
25 RANDY BUSH-UTIL
26 AL NEWMAN-UTIL
27 MARK DAVIDSON-OF/DH
28 BERT BLYLEVEN-P
29 *(RET#) ROD CAREW*
30 JEFF BITTIGER-P
31 DAN SCHATSEDER-P (2)
32 DAN GLADDEN-OF/DH
33 SAL BUTERA-C (2)
34 KIRBY (STUB) PUCKETT-OF/DH
36 MARK PORTUGAL-P
36 JOE NIEKRO-P (2)
38 STEVE (LEFTY) CARLTON-P
39 JOE NIEKRO-P (2)
40 JUAN BERENGUER-P
41 JEFF REARDON-P
42 DICK SUCH-CH
43 RICK STELMASZEK-CH
44 RICK RENICK-CH
45 WAYNE (TWIG) TERWILLIGER-CH
46 JOE KLINK-P
48 MIKE SMITHSON-P
49 ALLAN ANDERSON-P

WASHINGTON SENATORS/**MINNESOTA TWINS**

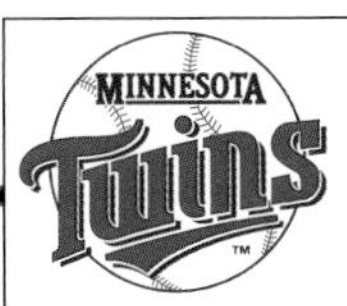

1988

2ND W 91-71 13GB

1 JOHN MOSES-OF/DH
3 *(RET#) HARMON KILLEBREW*
4 STEVE LOMBARDOZZI-INF
5 JIM DWYER-DH/OF (2)
6 TONY OLIVA-CH
7 GREG GAGNE-SS/UTIL
8 GARY GAETTI-3B/UTIL
9 GENE LARKIN-DH/1B
10 TOM KELLY-MGR
11 TOM NIETO-C/DH
12 BRIAN HARPER-C/UTIL
14 KENT HRBEK-1B/DH
15 TIM LAUDNER-C/UTIL
16 FRANK VIOLA-P
17 LES STRAKER (INJ)-P
18 KELVIN TORVE-1B/DH
18 TOMMY HERR (INJ)-2B/UTIL (2)
19 MARK PORTUGAL-P
20 MIKE MASON-P
20 JOHN CHRISTENSEN-OF/DH
21 DOUG BAKER-INF
22 KEITH ATHERTON-P
23 ROY SMITH-P
24 TOM (BRUNO) BRUNANSKY-OF/DH (1)
25 RANDY BUSH-OF/UTIL
26 AL NEWMAN-INF/DH
27 MARK DAVIDSON-UTIL
28 BERT BLYLEVEN-P
29 *(RET#) ROD CAREW*
31 FREDDIE TOLIVER-P
32 DAN GLADDEN-OF/UTIL/P
33 TOMMY HERR (INJ)-2B/UTIL (2)
34 KIRBY (STUB) PUCKETT-OF/DH
36 JOE NIEKRO-P
36 ERIC BULLOCK-OF/DH
37 DAN SCHATZEDER-P (2)
38 STEVE (LEFTY) CARLTON-P
38 KARL BEST-P
39 DWIGHT LOWRY-C
40 JUAN BERENGUER-P
41 JEFF REARDON-P
42 DICK SUCH-CH
43 RICK STELMASZEK-CH
44 RICK RENICK-CH
45 WAYNE (TWIG) TERWILLIGER-CH
46 GERMAN GONZALEZ-P
48 JIM WINN-P
49 ALLAN ANDERSON-P
51 MARK PORTUGAL-P
53 CHARLIE LEA (INJ)-P
57 TIPPY MARTINEZ-P

1989

5TH W 80-82 19GB

1* JOHN MOSES-UTIL/P*
2 WALLY BACKMAN (INJ)-2B/DH
3 *(RET#) HARMON KILLEBREW*
4 ORLANDO MERCADO-C
5 JIM DWYER-DH/OF (1)
6 TONY OLIVA-CH
7 GREG GAGNE-SS/OF
8 GARY GAETTI-3B/UTIL
9 GENE LARKIN-UTIL
10 TOM KELLY-MGR
11 GREG OLSON-C
12 BRIAN HARPER-C/UTIL
14 KENT HRBEK (INJ)-1B/DH
15 TIM LAUDNER-UTIL
16 FRANK VIOLA-P (1)
17 RICK AGUILERA-P (2)
18 SHANE RAWLEY-P
20 VIC RODRIGUEZ-3B/DH
21 DOUG BAKER-INF/DH
22 CARMEN CASTILLO-OF/DH
23 ROY SMITH-P
25 RANDY BUSH-OF/UTIL
26 AL NEWMAN-UTIL
27 LEE TUNNELL-P
29 *(RET#) ROD CAREW*
30 FRANCISCO OLIVERAS-P
31 FREDDIE TOLIVER-P (1)
32 DAN GLADDEN (INJ)-OF/DH/P
33 MIKE COOK-P
34 KIRBY (STUB) PUCKETT-OF/DH
36 STEVE SHIELDS (INJ)-P
36 KEVIN TAPANI-P (2)
38 RANDY ST. CLAIRE-P
39 MIKE DYER-P
40 JUAN BERENGUER-P
41 JEFF REARDON-P
42 DICK SUCH-CH
43 RICK STELMASZEK-CH
44 RICK RENICK-CH
45 WAYNE (TWIG) TERWILLIGER-CH
46 GERMAN GONZALEZ (INJ)-P
47 GARY WAYNE-P
49 ALLAN ANDERSON-P
50 DAVID WEST-P (2)
51 GREG BOOKER-P (2)
52 LENNY WEBSTER-C
53 MARK GUTHRIE-P
54 PAUL SORRENTO-1B/DH
54 TIM DRUMMOND-P
55 PAUL SORRENTO-1B/DH
56 TERRY JORGENSEN-3B
58 CHIP HALE-INF/DH

1990

7TH W 74-88 29GB

0 JUNIOR ORTIZ-C/DH
1* JOHN MOSES-UTIL/P*
2 NELSON LIRIANO-INF/DH (2)
3 *(RET#) HARMON KILLEBREW*
4 CHIP HALE-2B
5 JIM DWYER-DH/OF
5 PEDRO MUNOZ-OF/DH
6 TONY OLIVA-CH
7 GREG GAGNE-SS/UTIL
8 GARY GAETTI-3B/INF
9 GENE LARKIN-DH/UTIL
10 TOM KELLY-MGR
12 BRIAN HARPER-C/UTIL
14 KENT HRBEK (INJ)-1B/UTIL
17 FREDDIE MANRIQUE-2B/DH
19 LARRY CASIAN-P
20 JACK SAVAGE-P
21 DOUG BAKER-2B
22 CARMEN CASTILLO-DH/OF
23 ROY SMITH-P
24 SHANE MACK-OF/DH
25 RANDY BUSH-UTIL
26 AL NEWMAN-2B/UTIL
29 *(RET#) ROD CAREW*
30 TERRY LEACH-P
31 SCOTT LEIUS-SS/3B
32 DAN GLADDEN-OF/DH
34 KIRBY (STUB) PUCKETT-OF/UTIL
35 JOHN (CANDY MAN) CANDELARIA-P (1)
36 KEVIN TAPANI-P
37 PAUL ABBOTT-P
38 RICK AGUILERA-P
40 JUAN BERENGUER-P
41 RICH GARCES-P
41 RICH YETT-P
42 DICK SUCH-CH
43 RICK STELMASZEK-CH
44 RICK RENICK-CH
45 WAYNE (TWIG) TERWILLIGER-CH
45 JOHN (CANDY MAN) CANDELARIA-P (1)
46 SCOTT ERICKSON-P
47 GARY WAYNE-P
49 ALLAN ANDERSON-P
50 DAVID WEST (INJ)-P
52 LENNY WEBSTER-C
53 MARK GUTHRIE-P
54 TIM DRUMMOND-P
55 PAUL SORRENTO-1B/DH
58 CHIP HALE-INF/DH

1991

1ST W 95-67 0GB
W ALCS-TORA 4-1
W WS-ATLN 4-3

0 JUNIOR ORTIZ-C
1 JARVIS BROWN-OF/DH
3 *(RET#) HARMON KILLEBREW*
5 PEDRO MUNOZ-OF/DH
6 TONY OLIVA-CH
6 *(RET#) TONY OLIVA*
7 GREG GAGNE-SS/DH
9 GENE LARKIN-UTIL
10 TOM KELLY-MGR
11 CHUCK KNOBLAUCH-2B/SS
12 BRIAN HARPER-C/UTIL
13 MIKE (PAGS) PAGLIARULO-3B/2B
14 KENT HRBEK (INJ)-1B
15 LENNY WEBSTER-C
17 LARRY CASIAN-P
18 PAUL SORRENTO-1B/DH
19 SCOTT ERICKSON-P
22 CARMEN CASTILLO-OF/DH
23 WILLIE BANKS-P
24 SHANE MACK-OF/DH
25 RANDY BUSH-UTIL
26 AL NEWMAN-INF/DH
29 *(RET#) ROD CAREW*
30 TERRY LEACH-P
31 SCOTT LEIUS-UTIL
32 DAN GLADDEN-OF
34 KIRBY (STUB) PUCKETT-OF
35 STEVE (BED ROCK) BEDROSIAN-P
35 RON GARDENHIRE-CH
36 KEVIN TAPANI-P
37 PAUL ABBOTT-P
38 RICK AGUILERA-P
39 DAVID WEST (INJ)-P
40 STEVE (BED ROCK) BEDROSIAN-P
42 DICK SUCH-CH
43 RICK STELMASZEK-CH
44 CHILI DAVIS-DH/OF
45 WAYNE (TWIG) TERWILLIGER-CH
46 TERRY CROWLEY-CH
47 JACK MORRIS-P
48 GARY WAYNE-P
49 ALLAN ANDERSON-P
50 DAVID WEST (INJ)-P
51 CARL WILLIS-P
53 MARK GUTHRIE-P
55 TERRY CROWLEY-CH
58 DENNY NEAGLE-P
59 TOM EDENS-P
60 WILLIE BANKS-P

1992

2ND W 90-72 6GB

1 JARVIS BROWN-OF/DH
2 DONNIE HILL-UTIL
3 *(RET#) HARMON KILLEBREW*
5 PEDRO MUNOZ-OF/DH
6 *(RET#) TONY OLIVA*
7 GREG GAGNE-SS
9 GENE LARKIN-UTIL
10 TOM KELLY-MGR
11 CHUCK KNOBLAUCH-2B/UTIL
12 BRIAN HARPER-C/DH
13 MIKE (PAGS) PAGLIARULO-3B/2B
14 KENT HRBEK-1B/DH
15 LENNY WEBSTER-C
16 BOB KIPPER-P
16 DEREK PARKS-C
17 LARRY CASIAN-P
17 JEFF REBOULET-UTIL
18 DARREN REED-OF/DH (2)
19 SCOTT ERICKSON-P
20 MIKE TROMBLEY-P
20 PAT MAHOMES-P
21 PAT MAHOMES-P
21 MIKE TROMBLEY-P
22 BILL KRUEGER-P (1)
23 WILLIE BANKS-P
24 SHANE MACK-OF
25 RANDY BUSH-UTIL
26 J. T. BRUETT-OF/DH
27 TERRY JORGENSEN-INF
29 *(RET#) ROD CAREW*
31 SCOTT LEIUS-3B/SS
33 BERNARDO BRITO-OF/DH
34 KIRBY (STUB) PUCKETT-OF/UTIL
35 RON GARDENHIRE-CH
36 KEVIN TAPANI-P
37 PAUL ABBOTT-P
38 RICK AGUILERA-P
39 DAVID WEST (INJ)-P
42 DICK SUCH-CH
43 RICK STELMASZEK-CH
44 CHILI DAVIS-DH/UTIL
45 WAYNE (TWIG) TERWILLIGER-CH
46 TERRY CROWLEY-CH
47 GARY WAYNE-P
47 BILL KRUEGER-P (1)
48 GARY WAYNE-P
48 LARRY CASIAN-P
49 LUIS QUINONES-INF/DH
50 BOB KIPPER-P
51 CARL WILLIS-P
52 MAURO GOZZO-P
53 MARK GUTHRIE-P
57 JOHN SMILEY-P
59 TOM EDENS-P

1993

5TH W (TIE)71-91 23GB

2 PAT MEARES-SS
3 *(RET#) HARMON KILLEBREW*
4 CHIP HALE-INF/DH
5 PEDRO MUNOZ-OF
6 *(RET#) TONY OLIVA*
7 DENNY HOCKING-SS/2B
8 DAVID MCCARTY-UTIL
9 GENE LARKIN (INJ)-UTIL
10 TOM KELLY-MGR
11 CHUCK KNOBLAUCH-2B/UTIL
12 BRIAN HARPER-C/DH
13 MIKE (PAGS) PAGLIARULO-3B (1)
14 KENT HRBEK-1B/DH
15 LENNY WEBSTER-C/DH
16 DEREK PARKS-C
17 JEFF REBOULET-UTIL
18 EDDIE GUARDADO-P (2)
19 SCOTT ERICKSON-P
20 PAT MAHOMES-P
21 MIKE TROMBLEY-P
22 GEORGE TSAMIS-P
23 WILLIE BANKS-P
24 SHANE MACK-OF
25 RANDY BUSH-UTIL
25 RICH BECKER-OF
26 J. T. BRUETT-OF
27 TERRY JORGENSEN-INF
29 *(RET#) ROD CAREW*
31 SCOTT LEIUS (INJ)-SS
32 DAVE WINFIELD-DH/OF
33 BERNARDO BRITO-OF/DH
34 KIRBY (STUB) PUCKETT-OF/DH
35 RON GARDENHIRE-CH
36 KEVIN TAPANI-P
37 SCOTT STAHOVIAK-3B
38 RICK AGUILERA-P
41 RICH GARCES-P
42 DICK SUCH-CH
43 RICK STELMASZEK-CH
44 JIM DESHAIES-P (1)
45 WAYNE (TWIG) TERWILLIGER-CH
46 TERRY CROWLEY-CH
47 BRETT MERRIMAN-P
48 LARRY CASIAN (INJ)-P
49 MIKE HARTLEY-P
51 CARL WILLIS (INJ)-P
52 DEREK LEE-OF
53 MARK GUTHRIE (INJ)-P
57 GREG BRUMMETT-P (2)
59 MIKE MAKSUDIAN (INJ)-1B

1994

4TH C 53-60 14GB
STRIKE NO POST-SEASON

1 ALEX COLE-OF
2 PAT MEARES (INJ)-SS
3 *(RET#) HARMON KILLEBREW*
4 CHIP HALE-3B
5 PEDRO MUNOZ-OF
6 *(RET#) TONY OLIVA*
7 DENNY HOCKING-SS
8 DAVID MCCARTY-1B/UTIL
10 TOM KELLY-MGR
11 CHUCK KNOBLAUCH-2B/UTIL
14 KENT HRBEK (INJ)-1B/DH
16 DEREK PARKS-C
17 JEFF REBOULET-UTIL
18 EDDIE GUARDADO-P
19 SCOTT ERICKSON (INJ)-P
20 PAT MAHOMES (INJ)-P
21 MIKE TROMBLEY-P
22 CARLOS PULIDO-P
23 MATT WALBECK-C
24 SHANE MACK (INJ)-OF
25 RICH BECKER (INJ)-OF
29 *(RET#) ROD CAREW*
31 SCOTT LEIUS-3B
32 DAVE WINFIELD (INJ)-DH/OF
34 KIRBY (STUB) PUCKETT-OF/DH
35 RON GARDENHIRE-CH
36 KEVIN TAPANI-P
38 RICK AGUILERA-P
39 STEVE DUNN-1B
41 DAVE STEVENS-P
42 DICK SUCH-CH
43 RICK STELMASZEK-CH
44 JIM DESHAIES-P
45 WAYNE (TWIG) TERWILLIGER-CH
46 TERRY CROWLEY-CH
47 BRETT MERRIMAN-P
48 LARRY CASIAN-P (1)
51 CARL WILLIS-P
52 KEVIN CAMPBELL-P
53 MARK GUTHRIE-P
54 KEITH GARAGOZZO-P
58 STEVE DUNN-1B
58 ERIK SCHULLSTROM-P

1995

5TH C 56-88 44GB

144 GAME SEASON

1 ALEX COLE-OF
2 PAT MEARES-SS
3 *(RET#) HARMON KILLEBREW*
4 CHIP HALE-3B/1B
5 PEDRO MUNOZ-DH
6 *(RET#) TONY OLIVA*
7 DENNY HOCKING-SS
8 DAVID MCCARTY-1B
9 MATT WALBECK-C
10 TOM KELLY-MGR
11 CHUCK KNOBLAUCH-2B/UTIL
12 MATT MERULLO-C
14 *(RET#) KENT HRBEK*
15 RON COOMER-1B/DH
16 DAN MASTELLER-1B
17 JEFF REBOULET-SS
18 EDDIE GUARDADO-P
19 SCOTT ERICKSON-P (1)
20 PAT MAHOMES-P
21 MIKE TROMBLEY-P
22 BRAD RADKE-P
23 GREG W. HARRIS (REL)-P
24 KEVIN MAAS (INJ)-1B
24 RICCARDO INGRAM-DH
25 RICH BECKER-OF
26 BRIAN RAABE-2B
29 *(RET#) ROD CAREW*
31 SCOTT LEIUS-3B
32 LATROY HAWKINS-P
33 BERNARDO BRITO-DH
33 FRANKIE RODRIGUEZ-P (2)
34 KIRBY (STUB) PUCKETT (INJ)-OF
35 RON GARDENHIRE-CH
36 KEVIN TAPANI-P
37 SCOTT STAHOVIAK-1B
38 RICK AGUILERA-P
39 STEVE DUNN-1B
40 MARTY CORDOVA-OF
41 DAVE STEVENS-P
42 DICK SUCH-CH
43 RICK STELMASZEK-CH
44 JERALD CLARK-OF
45 SCOTT ULLGER-CH
46 TERRY CROWLEY-CH
47 RICH ROBERTSON-P
48 JERRY WHITE-CH
50 MATT LAWTON-OF
51 CARL WILLIS-P
51 SCOTT WATKINS-P
52 KEVIN CAMPBELL-P
52 SCOTT KLINGENBECK-P (2)
53 MARK GUTHRIE-P (1)
54 MO SANFORD-P
55 OSCAR MUNOZ-P
56 JOSE PARRA-P (2)
57 VINCE HORSMAN (WAIV)-P
58 ERIK SCHULLSTROM-P
59 BRAD RADKE-P
99 OSCAR MUNOZ-P

1996

4TH C 78-84 21.5GB

2 PAT MEARES-SS
3 *(RET#) HARMON KILLEBREW*
4 PAUL MOLITOR-DH/1B
5 ROBERTO KELLY (INJ)-OF
6 *(RET#) TONY OLIVA*
7 DENNY HOCKING (INJ)-OF
8 RON COOMER-1B
9 MATT WALBECK-C
10 TOM KELLY-MGR
11 CHUCK KNOBLAUCH-2B
12 CHIP HALE-3B/1B
13 TODD WALKER-3B/2B
14 *(RET#) KENT HRBEK*
15 DAVE HOLLINS-3B (1)
16 DAN SERAFINI-P
17 JEFF REBOULET-2B
18 EDDIE GUARDADO-P
19 GREG HANSELL-P
20 PAT MAHOMES-P (1)
21 MIKE TROMBLEY-P
22 BRAD RADKE-P
23 TOM QUINLAN-3B
24 GREG MYERS (INJ)-C
25 RICH BECKER-OF
26 BRIAN RAABE,-3B
27 MIKE DURANT-C
29 *(RET#) ROD CAREW*
31 DAN NAULTY (INJ)-P
32 LATROY HAWKINS-P
33 FRANKIE RODRIGUEZ-P
(34) KIRBY (STUB) PUCKETT (INJ) (RET)-(OF)
35 RON GARDENHIRE-CH
37 SCOTT STAHOVIAK-1B
38 RICK AGUILERA (INJ)-P
40 MARTY CORDOVA-OF
41 DAVE STEVENS (INJ)-P
42 DICK SUCH-CH
43 RICK STELMASZEK-CH
45 SCOTT ULLGER-CH
46 TERRY CROWLEY-CH
47 RICH ROBERTSON-P
50 MATT LAWTON-OF
51 MIKE MILCHIN (WAIV)-P (1)
51 BRENT BREDE-PH
52 SCOTT KLINGENBECK-P
56 JOSE PARRA-P
57 SCOTT ALDRED-P (2)
57 ERIK BENNETT-P
59 ERIK BENNETT-P
59 TRAVIS MILLER-P

1997

4TH C 68-94 18.5GB

2 PAT MEARES (INJ)-SS
3 *(RET#) HARMON KILLEBREW*
4 PAUL MOLITOR (INJ)-DH
5 ROBERTO KELLY (INJ)-OF (1)
6 *(RET#) TONY OLIVA*
7 DENNY HOCKING-3B/SS
8 RON COOMER-3B/1B
10 TOM KELLY-MGR
11 CHUCK KNOBLAUCH-2B
12 TODD WALKER-3B/2B
14 *(RET#) KENT HRBEK*
15 DARREN JACKSON-OF (1)
16 DAN SERAFINI-P
17 GREG SWINDELL-P
18 EDDIE GUARDADO-P
19 BOB TEWKSBURY-P
20 TRAVIS MILLER-P
21 GREG SWINDELL-P
21 MIKE TROMBLEY-P
22 BRAD RADKE-P
23 TODD RITCHIE-P
24 GREG MYERS (INJ)-C (1)
25 RICH BECKER-OF
26 KEVIN JARVIS (WAIV)-P (2)
26 JAVIER VALENTIN-C
27 DAVID ORTIZ-1B
28 GREG COLBRUNN-1B (1)
29 *(RET#) ROD CAREW*
30 GREGG OLSON-P (1)
31 DAN NAULTY (INJ)-P
32 LATROY HAWKINS-P
33 FRANKIE RODRIGUEZ-P
34 *(RET#) KIRBY PUCKETT*
35 RON GARDENHIRE-CH
36 TERRY STEINBACH-C
37 SCOTT STAHOVIAK (INJ)-1B
38 RICK AGUILERA-P
39 DAMIAN MILLER-C
40 MARTY CORDOVA (INJ)-OF
41 DAVE STEVENS-P (1)
42 DICK SUCH-CH
42 *(RET#) JACKIE ROBINSON*
43 RICK STELMASZEK-CH
44 DICK SUCH-CH
45 SCOTT ULLGER-CH
46 TERRY CROWLEY-CH
47 RICH ROBERTSON-P
48 TORII HUNTER-PR
50 MATT LAWTON-OF
51 BRENT BREDE-1B
52 SHANE BOWERS-P
(56) JOSE PARA (INJ)-(P)
57 SCOTT ALDRED-P
59 CHRIS LATHAM-P

1998

4TH C 70-92 19GB

1 OTIS NIXON (INJ)-OF
2 PAT MEARES-SS
3 *(RET#) HARMON KILLEBREW*
4 PAUL MOLITOR (INJ)-DH
5 BRENT GATES-INF
6 *(RET#) TONY OLIVA*
7 DENNY HOCKING-3B/SS
8 RON COOMER-3B/1B
9 ORLANDO MERCED-1B (1)
9 A. J. PIERZYNSKI-C
10 TOM KELLY-MGR
12 TODD WALKER-3B/2B
14 *(RET#) KENT HRBEK*
15 JON SHAVE-3B/INF
16 DAN SERAFINI-P
17 GREG SWINDELL-P (1)
18 EDDIE GUARDADO-P
20 TRAVIS MILLER-P
21 MIKE TROMBLEY-P
22 BRAD RADKE-P
23 TODD RITCHIE-P
24 HECTOR CARRASCO-P
24 TRAVIS BAPTIST-P
25 ALEX OCHOA-OF
26 JAVIER VALENTIN-C
27 DAVID ORTIZ (INJ)-1B
28 CHRIS LATHAM-OF
29 *(RET#) ROD CAREW*
30 MIKE MORGAN (INJ)-P
31 DAN NAULTY-P
32 LATROY HAWKINS-P
33 FRANKIE RODRIGUEZ-P
34 *(RET#) KIRBY PUCKETT*
35 RON GARDENHIRE-CH
36 TERRY STEINBACH-C
37 SCOTT STAHOVIAK-1B/OF
38 RICK AGUILERA-P
39 BOB TEWKSBURY (INJ)-P
40 MARTY CORDOVA (INJ)-OF
41 ERIC MILTON-P
42 *(RET#) JACKIE ROBINSON*
43 RICK STELMASZEK-CH
44 DICK SUCH-CH
45 SCOTT ULLGER-CH
46 TERRY CROWLEY-CH
47 COREY KOSKIE-3B
48 TORII HUNTER-OF
50 MATT LAWTON-OF
51 DOUG MIENKIEWICZ-1B
53 BENJ SAMPSON-P
58 HECTOR CARRASCO-P

1999

5TH C 63-97 33GB

3 *(RET#) HARMON KILLEBREW*
5 BRENT GATES-INF
6 *(RET#) TONY OLIVA*
7 DENNY HOCKING-3B/SS
8 RON COOMER-3B/1B
9 A. J. PIERZYNSKI-C
10 TOM KELLY-MGR
11 JACQUE JONES-OF
12 TODD WALKER-3B/2B
13 JERRY WHITE-CH
14 *(RET#) KENT HRBEK*
15 CRISTIAN GUZMAN-INF
16 MIDRE CUMMINGS-OF
18 EDDIE GUARDADO (INJ)-P
19 MIKE LINCOLN-P
20 TRAVIS MILLER-P
21 MIKE TROMBLEY-P
22 BRAD RADKE-P
23 BENJ SAMPSON-P
25 DOUG MIENTKIEWICZ-1B
26 JAVIER VALENTIN-C
27 DAVID ORTIZ-INF
28 CHRIS LATHAM-OF
29 *(RET#) ROD CAREW*
31 CHAD ALLEN-OF
32 LATROY HAWKINS-P
33 J. C. ROMERO-P
34 *(RET#) KIRBY PUCKETT*
35 RON GARDENHIRE-CH
36 TERRY STEINBACH (INJ)-C
38 RICK AGUILERA-P (1)
40 MARTY CORDOVA-OF/DH
41 ERIC MILTON-P
42 *(RET#) JACKIE ROBINSON*
43 RICK STELMASZEK-CH
44 DICK SUCH-CH
45 SCOTT ULLGER-CH
46 BOB WELLS-P
47 COREY KOSKIE-3B
48 TORII HUNTER-OF
49 DAN PERKINS-P
50 MATT LAWTON-OF
51 ROB RADLOSKY-P
53 JOE MAYS-P
54 JAY RYAN-P
55 MARK REDMAN-P
56 CLEATUS DAVIDSON-P
57 GARY RATH-P
58 HECTOR CARRASCO-P
66 STEVE LIDDLE-CH
67 RICK KNAPP-CH

2000

5TH C 69-93 26GB

1 JAY CANIZARO-INF
2 LUIS RIVAS-INF
3 *(RET#) HARMON KILLEBREW*
4 PAUL MOLITOR-CH
6 *(RET#) TONY OLIVA*
7 DENNY HOCKING-3B/SS
8 RON COOMER-3B/1B
9 JASON MAXWELL-INF
10 TOM KELLY-MGR
11 JACQUE JONES-OF
12 TODD WALKER-3B/2B (1)
12 DANNY ARDOIN-C
13 JERRY WHITE-CH
14 *(RET#) KENT HRBEK*
15 CRISTIAN GUZMAN-INF
16 MIDRE CUMMINGS-OF (1)
18 EDDIE GUARDADO-P
19 MIKE LINCOLN (INJ)-P
20 TRAVIS MILLER-P
21 ERIC MILTON-P
22 BRAD RADKE (INJ)-P
24 MATTHEW LE CROY-C
25 DOUG MIENTKIEWICZ-1B
26 A. J. PIERZYNSKI-C
27 DAVID ORTIZ-DH
28 MARCUS JENSEN-C
29 *(RET#) ROD CAREW*
30 BRIAN BUCHANAN-OF
31 CHAD ALLEN-OF
32 LATROY HAWKINS-P
33 J. C. ROMERO-P
34 *(RET#) KIRBY PUCKETT*
35 RON GARDENHIRE-CH
38 SEAN BERGMAN-P
38 CASEY BLAKE-INF
39 CHAD MOELLER-C
40 JOHN BARNES-INF
42 BUTCH HUSKEY-OF (1)
42 *(RET#) JACKIE ROBINSON*
43 RICK STELMASZEK-CH
44 DICK SUCH-CH
45 SCOTT ULLGER-CH
46 BOB WELLS-P
47 COREY KOSKIE-3B
48 TORII HUNTER-OF
50 MATT LAWTON-OF
51 MATT KINNEY-P
52 DANNY MOTA-P
53 JOE MAYS-P
54 JAY RYAN-P
55 MARK REDMAN-P
57 JOHAN SANTANA-P
58 HECTOR CARRASCO-P (1)
59 JACK CRESSEND-P
60 RICH BATCHELOR-P
64 BILL SPRINGMAN-CH
68 PHIL ROOF-CH

2001

2ND C 85-77 6GB

(1) JAY CANIZARO (INJ)-(INF
2 LUIS RIVAS-INF
3 *(RET#) HARMON KILLEBREW*
4 PAUL MOLITOR-CH
5 MICHAEL CUDDYER-INF/DH
6 *(RET#) TONY OLIVA*
7 DENNY HOCKING-3B/SS
8 QUENTIN MCCRACKEN-DH
9 JASON MAXWELL-2B
10 TOM KELLY-MGR
11 JACQUE JONES-OF
12 TOM PRINCE-C
13 JERRY WHITE-CH
14 *(RET#) KENT HRBEK*
15 CRISTIAN GUZMAN-SS
16 DOUG MIENTKIEWICZ-1B
17 DUSTAN MOHR-OF
18 EDDIE GUARDADO-P
19 GRANT BALFOUR-P
20 TRAVIS MILLER-P
21 ERIC MILTON-P
22 BRAD RADKE (INJ)-P
23 BOBBY KIELTY-OF
24 MATTHEW LE CROY-C
25 JOE MAYS-P
26 A. J. PIERZYNSKI-C
27 DAVID ORTIZ (INJ)-DH
28 JACK CRESSEND-P
29 *(RET#) ROD CAREW*
30 BRIAN BUCHANAN (INJ)-OF
31 CHAD ALLEN (INJ)-OF
32 LATROY HAWKINS-P
33 J. C. ROMERO-P
34 *(RET#) KIRBY PUCKETT*
35 RON GARDENHIRE-CH
36 RICK REED-P (2)
37 ADAM JOHNSON-P
38 CASEY BLAKE-3B
39 JUAN RINCON-P
40 JOHN BARNES (INJ)-OF
42 *(RET#) JACKIE ROBINSON*
43 RICK STELMASZEK-CH
44 DICK SUCH-CH
45 SCOTT ULLGER-CH
46 BOB WELLS-P
47 COREY KOSKIE-3B
48 TORII HUNTER (INJ)-OF
49 KYLE LOHSE-P
50 MATT LAWTON-OF (1)
52 TONY FIORE-P
53 MIKE DUVALL-P
55 MARK REDMAN (INJ)-P (1)
56 BRAD THOMAS-P
57 JOHAN SANTANA (INJ)-P
58 HECTOR CARRASCO-P
59 JACK CRESSEND-P

WASHINGTON SENATORS/**MINNESOTA TWINS**

59 TODD JONES-P (2)

2002

1st C 94-67 0GB

W ALDS-OAKA 3-2

L ALCS-ANAA 4-1

1 JAY CANIZARO-2B/3B
2 LUIS RIVAS (INJ)-2B
3 *(RET#) HARMON KILLEBREW*
5 MICHAEL CUDDYER-UTIL
6 *(RET#) TONY OLIVA*
7 DENNY HOCKING-UTIL
8 JAVIER VALENTIN-C
9 STEVE LIDDLE-CH
11 JACQUE JONES-OF/DH
12 TOM PRINCE-C
13 JERRY WHITE-CH
14 *(RET#) KENT HRBEK*
15 CRISTIAN GUZMAN-SS
16 DOUG MIENTKIEWICZ-1B
17 DUSTAN MOHR-OF/DH
18 EDDIE GUARDADO-P
19 MIKE TROMBLEY-P
20 TRAVIS MILLER-P
20 JOSE RODRIGUEZ (INJ)-P (2)
21 ERIC MILTON-P
22 BRAD RADKE (INJ)-P
23 BOBBY KIELTY-OF/DH/1B
24 MATTHEW LE CROY-DH/1B/C
25 JOE MAYS (INJ)-P
26 A. J. PIERZYNSKI-C
27 DAVID ORTIZ-DH/1B
28 JACK CRESSEND (INJ)-P
29 *(RET#) ROD CAREW*
30 BRIAN BUCHANAN-OF/DH (1)
31 RICK REED-P
32 LATROY HAWKINS-P
33 J. C. ROMERO-P
34 *(RET#) KIRBY PUCKETT*
35 RON GARDENHIRE-CH
36 WARREN MORRIS-2B
38 CASEY BLAKE-UTIL
39 JUAN RINCON-P
40 RICK ANDERSON-CH
41 MICHAEL RESTOVICH-OF/DH
42 MIKE JACKSON-P
43 RICK STELMASZEK-CH
44 DAVID LAMB-INF
45 SCOTT ULLGER-CH
46 BOB WELLS (INJ)-P
47 COREY KOSKIE-3B
48 TORII HUNTER-OF
49 KYLE LOHSE-P
50 KEVIN FREDERICK-P
51 MATT KINNEY (INJ)-P
52 TONY FIORE-P
54 MIKE RYAN-OF
57 JOHAN SANTANA-P
58 TODD SEARS-1B
62 AL NEWMAN-CH

2003

1st C 90-72 0GB

L ALDS-NYA 3-1

2 LUIS RIVAS (INJ)-2B
3 *(RET#) HARMON KILLEBREW*
5 MICHAEL CUDDYER-UTIL
6 *(RET#) TONY OLIVA*
7 DENNY HOCKING-UTIL
8 CHRIS GOMEZ (INJ)-INF
9 STEVE LIDDLE-CH
11 JACQUE JONES (INJ)-OF/DH
12 TOM PRINCE-C (1)
13 JERRY WHITE-CH
14 *(RET#) KENT HRBEK*
15 CRISTIAN GUZMAN-SS
16 DOUG MIENTKIEWICZ-1B
17 DUSTAN MOHR-OF/DH
18 EDDIE GUARDADO-P
19 GRANT BALFOUR-P
20 LEW FORD (INJ)-OF
21 ERIC MILTON (INJ)-P
22 BRAD RADKE (SUS:5G)-P
23 BOBBY KIELTY-OF/DH/1B (1)
23 SHANNON STEWART-OF/DH (2)
24 MATT LECROY-DH/C/1B
25 JOE MAYS (INJ)-P
26 A. J. PIERZYNSKI-C
27 JUSTIN MORNEAU-DH/1B
29 *(RET#) ROD CAREW*
30 JAMES BALDWIN (F/A)-P
31 RICK REED (INJ)-P
32 LATROY HAWKINS-P
33 J. C. ROMERO-P
34 *(RET#) KIRBY PUCKETT*
35 RON GARDENHIRE-MGR
37 KENNY ROGERS (SUS:5G)-P
38 ADAM JOHNSON-P
39 JUAN RINCON-P
40 RICK ANDERSON-CH
41 MICHAEL RESTOVICH-OF
42 *(RET#) JACKIE ROBINSON*
43 RICK STELMASZEK-CH
44 ROB BOWEN-C
45 SCOTT ULLGER-CH
46 ALEX PRIETO-2B/SS
47 COREY KOSKIE (INJ)-3B
48 TORII HUNTER-OF
49 KYLE LOHSE-P
50 JESSE OROSCO-P (3)
51 CARLOS PULIDO-P
52 TONY FIORE-P
54 MIKE RYAN-OF
55 MIKE FETTERS (INJ)-P
56 BRAD THOMAS-P
57 JOHAN SANTANA-P
57 MIKE NAKAMURA-P
58 TODD SEARS-1B/DH (1)
59 MIKE NAKAMURA-P
62 AL NEWMAN-CH

2004

1st C 92-70 0GB

L ALDS-NYA 3-1

1 JASON KUBEL-OF
2 LUIS RIVAS-2B
3 *(RET#) HARMON KILLEBREW*
4 AUGIE OJEDA-SS
5 MICHAEL CUDDYER-OF/2B
6 *(RET#) TONY OLIVA*
7 JOE MAUER (INJ)-C
8 NICK PINTO (INJ)-2B
9 STEVE LIDDLE-CH
11 JACQUE JONES-OF/DH
12 MICHAEL RYAN-OF
13 JERRY WHITE-CH
14 *(RET#) KENT HRBEK*
15 CRISTIAN GUZMAN-SS
16 DOUG MIENTKIEWICZ-1B (1)
17 ALEX PRIETO-SS
18 JASON BARTLETT-SS
19 GRANT BALFOUR (INJ)-P
20 LEW FORD-OF
21 HENRY BLANCO-C
22 BRAD RADKE-P
23 SHANNON STEWART (INJ)-OF
24 MATT LECROY (INJ)-C
(25) JOE MAYS (INJ)-(P)
26 PAT BORDERS-C (2)
27 JUSTIN MORNEAU-1B
28 JESSE CRAIN-P
29 *(RET#) ROD CAREW*
30 JOSE OFFERMAN-PH
31 J. D. DURBIN-P
32 TERRY TIFFEE-3B/1B
33 J. C. ROMERO-P
34 *(RET#) KIRBY PUCKETT*
35 RON GARDENHIRE-MGR
36 JOE NATHAN-P
38 AARON FULTZ-P
39 JUAN RINCON-P
40 RICK ANDERSON-CH
41 MICHAEL RESTOVICH-OF
42 *(RET#) JACKIE ROBINSON*
43 RICK STELMASZEK-CH
44 ROB BOWEN-C
45 SCOTT ULLGER-CH
45 TERRY MULHOLLAND-P
46 TERRY MULHOLLAND-P
46 SCOTT ULLGER-CH
47 COREY KOSKIE-3B
48 TORII HUNTER (INJ)-OF
49 KYLE LOHSE-P
50 JOE BEIMEL-P
51 CARLOS PULIDO-P
52 CARLOS SILVA-P
54 MATT GUERRIER-P
56 BRAD THOMAS-P
57 JOHAN SANTANA-P
58 SETH GREISINGER-P
62 AL NEWMAN-CH
71 JOE ROA-P

2005

3rd C 83-79 16GB

(1) JASON KUBEL (INJ)-(OF)
2 LUIS RIVAS (INJ)-2B
3 *(RET#) HARMON KILLEBREW*
5 MICHAEL CUDDYER (INJ)-3B/1B
6 *(RET#) TONY OLIVA*
7 JOE MAUER-C
8 NICK PINTO (INJ)-2B/SS
9 STEVE LIDDLE-CH
11 JACQUE JONES-OF
12 MICHAEL RYAN-OF
13 JERRY WHITE-CH
14 *(RET#) KENT HRBEK*
15 BRENT ABERNATHY (INJ)-2B
16 GLENN WILLIAMS (INJ)-2B
17 JUAN CASTRO (INJ)-SS/2B
18 JASON BARTLETT-SS
(19) GRANT BALFOUR (INJ)-(P)
20 LEW FORD-OF/DH
21 JASON TYNER-OF
21 BRET BOONE (REL)-2B (2)
22 BRAD RADKE-P
23 SHANNON STEWART-OF
24 MATT LECROY-C/DH/1B
25 JOE MAYS-P
27 JUSTIN MORNEAU (INJ)-1B
28 JESSE CRAIN-P
29 *(RET#) ROD CAREW*
30 SCOTT BAKER-P
32 TERRY TIFFEE-INF
33 J. C. ROMERO-P
34 *(RET#) KIRBY PUCKETT*
35 RON GARDENHIRE-MGR
36 JOE NATHAN-P
38 LUIS RODRIGUEZ-3B
39 JUAN RINCON (SUS:10G)-P
40 RICK ANDERSON-CH
41 CHRIS HEINTZ-C
42 *(RET#) JACKIE ROBINSON*
43 RICK STELMASZEK-CH
45 TERRY MULHOLLAND-P
46 SCOTT ULLGER-CH
47 FRANCISCO LIRIANO-P
48 TORII HUNTER (INJ)-OF
49 KYLE LOHSE-P
51 CORKY MILLER-C
52 CARLOS SILVA (INJ)-P
54 MATT GUERRIER-P
55 MIKE REDMOND-C
56 TRAVIS BOWYER-P
57 JOHAN SANTANA-P
59 DAVE GASSNER-P
62 AL NEWMAN-CH
71 JOE ROA-P

Gary Gaetti played half of his career with the Twins. In his rookie year he wore #39, but thereafter donned his familiar #8. He was a two-time All-Star and accounted for 56% of his homeruns (201) and 57% of his RBIs (758) while in a Twins uniform. He helped them to their first World Series win in 1987 over St. Louis.

NEW YORK YANKEES

The Yankees were the first team to permanently wear numbers on the backs of their uniforms. The origir numbers selected reflected the postion in the batting order.

1929
NEW YORK YANKEES

2ND 88-66 18GB

NO# MILLER (MIGHTY MITE) (HUG) HUGGINS (DIED)-MGR1
1 EARLE (THE KENTUCKY COLONEL) COMBS-OF
2 MARK KOENIG-INF
3 BABE (BAMBINO) (THE SULTAN OF SWAT) RUTH-OF
4 LOU (THE IRON HORSE) (LARRUPIN' LOU) GEHRIG-1B
5 BOB (LONG BOB) MEUSEL-OF
6 TONY (POOSH 'EM UP TONY) LAZZERI-2B
7 LEO (THE LIP) (LIPPY) DUROCHER-SS/2B
8 JOHNNY (NIG) GRABOWSKI-C
9 BENNY BENGOUGH (INJ)-C
10 BILL DICKEY-C
11 HERB (THE KNIGHT OF KENNETT SQUARE) PENNOCK-P
12 WAITE (SCHOOLBOY) HOYT-P
14 GEORGE PIPGRAS-P
15 HANK JOHNSON (INJ)-P
15 ART JORGENS-C
16 TOM ZACHARY-P
17 FRED (LEFTY) HEIMACH-P
18 WILCY (CY) MOORE-P
19 ED (SATCHELFOOT) WELLS-P
20 MYLES THOMAS-P (1)
20 JULIE WERA-3B
21 GEORGE (TIOGA GEORGE) BURNS-PH (1)
21 GORDON (DUSTY) RHODES-P
22 GENE ROBERTSON-3B (1)
24 LYN (BROADWAY) LARY-INF
25 BEN PASCHAL-OF
26 CEDRIC DURST-OF/1B
27 SAMMY (BABE RUTH'S LEGS) BYRD-OF
28 LIZ FUNK-PR
29 BOB SHAWKEY-CH
30 GORDON (DUSTY) RHODES-P
30 BOTS NEKOLA-P
31 ROY SHERID-P
32 ART JORGENS-C
33 CHARLEY O'LEARY-CH
34 ART FLETCHER-CH/MGR2
_ HARRY MATHEWS-CH

1930
3RD 86-68 16GB

1 EARLE (THE KENTUCKY COLONEL) COMBS-OF
2 MARK KOENIG-SS (1)
2 YATS WUESTLING-SS/3B (2)
3* BABE (BAMBINO) (THE SULTAN OF SWAT) RUTH-OF/P*
4 LOU (THE IRON HORSE) (LARRUPIN' LOU) GEHRIG-1B
5 TONY (POOSH 'EM UP TONY) LAZZERI-2B/UTIL
6 DUSTY COOKE-OF
7 BEN CHAPMAN-3B/2B
8 BILL DICKEY-C
9 BUBBLES HARGRAVE-C
10 BENNY BENGOUGH (INJ)-C
11 WAITE (SCHOOLBOY) HOYT-P (1)
11 OWNIE CARROLL-P (2)
12 GEORGE PIPGRAS-P
14 HANK JOHNSON (INJ)-P
15 ROY SHERID-P
16 HERB (THE KNIGHT OF KENNETT SQUARE) PENNOCK-P
16 TOM ZACHARY-P (1)
17 ED (SATCHELFOOT) WELLS-P
18 TOM ZACHARY-P (1)
18 LOU MCEVOY-P
18 BILL HENDERSON-P
19 GORDON (DUSTY) RHODES-P
19 HARRY RICE-OF/INF (2)
20 BILL WERBER-SS/3B
21 RED RUFFING-P (2)
22 LEFTY (GOOFY) GOMEZ-P
24 LYN (BROADWAY) LARY-SS
25 JIMMIE REESE-2B/3B
26 SAMMY (BABE RUTH'S LEGS) BYRD-OF
27 CEDRIC DURST-OF
28 ART JORGENS-C
29 BOB SHAWKEY-MGR
29 LOU MCEVOY-P
30 ART FLETCHER-CH
30 JIMMY (SUNSET JIMMY) BURKE-CH
31 CHARLEY O'LEARY-CH
32 FRANK (LEFTY) BARNES-P
32 KEN HOLLOWAY-P (2)
32 BILL (HANK) KARLON-OF
33? SAM GIBSON-P (2G:9/16,21)
34 FOSTER (EDDIE) EDWARDS-P

1931
2ND 94-59 13.5GB

1 EARLE (THE KENTUCKY COLONEL) COMBS-OF
2 LYN (BROADWAY) LARY-SS
2 RED ROLFE-SS
3 BABE (BAMBINO) (THE SULTAN OF SWAT) RUTH-OF/1B
4 LOU (THE IRON HORSE) (LARRUPIN' LOU) GEHRIG-1B/OF
5 TONY (POOSH 'EM UP TONY) LAZZERI-2B/3B
6 DUSTY COOKE (INJ)-OF
7 BEN CHAPMAN-OF/2B
8 BILL DICKEY-C
9 CY PERKINS-C
10 ART JORGENS-C
12 GEORGE PIPGRAS-P
14 HANK JOHNSON-P
15 ROY SHERID-P
16 HERB (THE KNIGHT OF KENNETT SQUARE) PENNOCK-P
17 ED (SATCHELFOOT) WELLS-P
18 RED RUFFING-P
19 GORDON (DUSTY) RHODES-P
19 LEFTY WEINERT-P
20 LEFTY (GOOFY) GOMEZ-P
21 GORDON (DUSTY) RHODES-P
22 IVY (POISON) ANDREWS-P
24 JIM (BIG JIM) WEAVER-P
26 JIMMIE REESE-2B
27 JOE SEWELL-3B/2B
28 MYRIL HOAG-OF/3B
29 SAMMY (BABE RUTH'S LEGS) BYRD-OF
30 ART FLETCHER-CH
31 JIMMY (SUNSET JIMMY) BURKE-CH
34 LOU MCEVOY-P
34 IVY (POISON) ANDREWS-P
35 DIXIE (THE PEOPLE'S CHERCE) WALKER-OF

1932
1ST 107-47 0GB

W WS-CHIN 4-0

NO# JOE (MARSE JOE) MCCARTHY-MGR
1 EARLE (THE KENTUCKY COLONEL) COMBS-OF
2 LYN (BROADWAY) LARY-UTIL
3 BABE (BAMBINO) (THE SULTAN OF SWAT) RUTH-OF/1B
4 LOU (THE IRON HORSE) (LARRUPIN' LOU) GEHRIG-1B
5 FRANKIE (CROW) CROSETTI-SS/INF
6 BEN CHAPMAN-OF
7 JACK SALTZGAVER-2B
8 BILL DICKEY (INJ)-C
9 ART JORGENS-C
10 GEORGE PIPGRAS-P
11 LEFTY (GOOFY) GOMEZ-P
12 HERB (THE KNIGHT OF KENNETT SQUARE) PENNOCK-P
14 ED (SATCHELFOOT) WELLS-P
15 RED RUFFING-P
16 GORDON (DUSTY) RHODES-P (1)
16 WILCY (CY) MOORE-P (2)
17 HANK JOHNSON (ILL)-P
17 DANNY (DEACON DANNY) MACFAYDEN-P (2)
18 JOHNNY ALLEN-P
19 JUMBO BROWN-P
20 JOHNNY (FORDHAM JOHNNY) (FIREMAN) (GRANDMA) MURPHY-P
20 CHARLIE DEVENS-P
21 JOE SEWELL-3B
22 DOC FARRELL-INF
23 TONY (POOSH 'EM UP TONY) LAZZERI-2B/3B
24 SAMMY (BABE RUTH'S LEGS) BYRD-OF
26 JOE (GABBY) GLENN-C
27 MYRIL HOAG-OF/1B
28 IVY (POISON) ANDREWS-P (1)
29 ART FLETCHER-CH
30 JIMMY (SUNSET JIMMY) BURKE-CH
31 CY PERKINS-CH
32 DUSTY COOKE (INJ)-OF
32 EDDIE PHILLIPS-C
_ ROY SCHALK-2B (3G:9/17-18)

1933
2ND 91-59 7GB

NO# JOE (MARSE JOE) MCCARTHY-MGR
1 EARLE (THE KENTUCKY COLONEL) COMBS-OF
2 LYN (BROADWAY) LARY-UTIL
3* BABE (BAMBINO) (THE SULTAN OF SWAT) RUTH-OF/1B/P*
4 LOU (THE IRON HORSE) (LARRUPIN' LOU) GEHRIG-1B
5 FRANKIE (CROW) CROSETTI-SS
6 BEN CHAPMAN-OF
7 TONY (POOSH 'EM UP TONY) LAZZERI-2B
8 BILL DICKEY-C
9 ART JORGENS-C
9 JOE (GABBY) GLENN-C
10 GEORGE PIPGRAS-P (1)
10 TONY (PUG) RENSA,-C
11 LEFTY (GOOFY) GOMEZ-P
12 HERB (THE KNIGHT OF KENNETT SQUARE) PENNOCK-P
14 RUSS (SHERIFF) VAN ATTA-P
15 RED RUFFING-P
16 WILCY (CY) MOORE-P
17 DANNY (DEACON DANNY) MACFAYDEN-P
18 JOHNNY ALLEN-P
19 JUMBO BROWN-P
20 DON BRENNAN-P
21 JOE SEWELL-3B
22 DOC FARRELL-SS/2B
24 BILLY WERBER-3B (1)
25 SAMMY (BABE RUTH'S LEGS) BYRD-OF
26 GEORGE (THE BULL) UHLE-P (3)
27 DIXIE (THE PEOPLE'S CHERCE) WALKER-OF
29 ART FLETCHER-CH
30 CY PERKINS-CH
31 JIMMY (SUNSET JIMMY) BURKE-CH
33 PETE (JAKE) APPLETON (AKA JABLONOWSKI)-P
33 CHARLIE DEVENS-P

1934
2ND 94-60 7GB

NO# JOE (MARSE JOE) MCCARTHY-MGR
1 EARLE (THE KENTUCKY COLONEL) COMBS (INJ)-OF
1 GEORGE (TWINKLETOES) SELKIRK-OF
2 LYN (BROADWAY) LARY-1B (1)
2 RED ROLFE-SS/3B
3 BABE (BAMBINO) (THE SULTAN OF SWAT) RUTH-OF
4 LOU (THE IRON HORSE) (LARRUPIN' LOU) GEHRIG-1B/SS
5 FRANKIE (CROW) CROSETTI-SS/INF
6 TONY (POOSH 'EM UP TONY) LAZZERI-2B/3B
7 BEN CHAPMAN-OF
8 BILL DICKEY (INJ)-C
9 ART JORGENS-C
10 DON (JEEP) HEFFNER-2B
11 LEFTY (GOOFY) GOMEZ-P
12 JACK SALTZGAVER-3B/1B
14 RUSS (SHERIFF) VAN ATTA-P
15 RED RUFFING-P
16 JIMMIE DESHONG-P
17 DANNY (DEACON DANNY) MACFAYDEN-P
18 JOHNNY ALLEN (INJ)-P
19 JOHNNY (FORDHAM JOHNNY) (FIREMAN) (GRANDMA) MURPHY-P
20 HARRY SMYTHE-P (1)
20 FLOYD (THREE-FINGER) NEWKIRK-P
20 BURLEIGH (OL' STUBBLEBEARD) GRIMES-P (3)
21 JOHNNY SCHULTE-CH
21 JOHNNY BROACA-P
22 LYN (BROADWAY) LARY-1B (1)
22 VITO TAMULIS-P
23 FLOYD (THREE-FINGER) NEWKIRK-P
24 VITO TAMULIS-P
24 CHARLIE DEVENS-P
25 SAMMY (BABE RUTH'S LEGS) BYRD-OF
26 GEORGE (THE BULL) UHLE-P
26 JOHNNY BROACA-P
27 DIXIE (THE PEOPLE'S CHERCE) WALKER-OF
27 ZACK TAYLOR-C
28 MYRIL HOAG-OF
29 ART FLETCHER-CH
30 JOE SEWELL-CH
33 CHARLIE DEVENS-P

1935
2ND 89-60 3GB

NO# JOE (MARSE JOE) MCCARTHY-MGR
1 EARLE (THE KENTUCKY COLONEL) COMBS (INJ)-OF
2 RED ROLFE-3B/SS
3 GEORGE (TWINKLETOES) SELKIRK-OF
4 LOU (THE IRON HORSE) (LARRUPIN' LOU) GEHRIG-1B
5 FRANKIE (CROW) CROSETTI-SS/INF
5 NOLEN RICHARDSON-SS
6 TONY (POOSH 'EM UP TONY) LAZZERI-2B/SS
7 BEN CHAPMAN-OF
8 BILL DICKEY-C
9 ART JORGENS-C
10 DON (JEEP) HEFFNER-2B
11 LEFTY (GOOFY) GOMEZ-P
12 JACK SALTZGAVER-INF
14 RUSS (SHERIFF) VAN ATTA-P (1)
15 RED RUFFING-P
16 JIMMIE DESHONG-P
17 JUMBO BROWN-P
18 JOHNNY ALLEN (INJ)-P
19 JOHNNY (FORDHAM JOHNNY) (FIREMAN) (GRANDMA) MURPHY-P
20 JOHNNY BROACA-P
21 PAT MALONE-P
22 VITO TAMULIS-P
25 JESSE HILL-OF
26 JOE (GABBY) GLENN-C
27 DIXIE (THE PEOPLE'S CHERCE) WALKER (INJ)-OF
27 BLONDY RYAN-SS (2)
28 MYRIL HOAG-OF
29 ART FLETCHER-CH
30 JOE SEWELL-3B
31 JOHNNY SCHULTE-CH

1936
1ST 102-51 0GB

W WS-NYN 4-2

NO# JOE (MARSE JOE) MCCARTHY-MGR
1 ROY JOHNSON-OF
2 RED ROLFE-3B
3 GEORGE (TWINKLETOES) SELKIRK-OF

NEW YORK YANKEES

4 LOU (THE IRON HORSE) (LARRUPIN' LOU) GEHRIG-1B
5 FRANKIE (CROW) CROSETTI-SS
6 TONY (POOSH 'EM UP TONY) LAZZERI-2B/SS
7 BEN CHAPMAN-OF (1)
7 JAKE POWELL-OF (2)
8 BILL DICKEY-C
9 JOE (JOLTIN' JOE) (THE YANKEE CLIPPER) DIMAGGIO-OF
10 DON (JEEP) HEFFNER-INF
11 LEFTY (GOOFY) GOMEZ-P
12 JACK SALTZGAVER-INF
14 BUMP HADLEY-P
15 RED RUFFING-P
16 MONTE (HOOT) PEARSON-P
17 JUMBO BROWN-P
18 ART JORGENS-C
19 JOHNNY (FORDHAM JOHNNY) (FIREMAN) (GRANDMA) MURPHY-P
20 JOHNNY BROACA-P
21 PAT MALONE-P
22 BOB (SUITCASE BOB) SEEDS-OF/3B
24 STEVE (SMOKEY) SUNDRA-P
25 KEMP WICKER-P
25 TED KLEINHAUS-P
26 JOE (GABBY) GLENN-C
27 DIXIE (THE PEOPLE'S CHERCE) WALKER (INJ)-OF (1)
28 MYRIL HOAG-OF
29 ART FLETCHER-CH
30 EARLE (THE KENTUCKY COLONEL) COMBS-CH
31 JOHNNY SCHULTE-CH
44 BOB (SUITCASE BOB) SEEDS-OF/3B

1937

1ST — 102-52 — 0GB
W WS-NYN 4-1

NO# JOE (MARSE JOE) MCCARTHY-MGR
1 FRANKIE (CROW) CROSETTI-SS
2 RED ROLFE-3B
3 GEORGE (TWINKLETOES) SELKIRK (INJ)-OF
4 LOU (THE IRON HORSE) (LARRUPIN' LOU) GEHRIG-1B
5 JOE (JOLTIN' JOE) (THE YANKEE CLIPPER) DIMAGGIO-OF
6 TONY (POOSH 'EM UP TONY) LAZZERI-2B/SS
7 JAKE POWELL (ILL)-OF
8 BILL DICKEY-C
9 MYRIL HOAG-OF
10 DON (JEEP) HEFFNER-UTIL
11 LEFTY (GOOFY) GOMEZ-P
12 JACK SALTZGAVER-1B
13 SPUD CHANDLER-P
14 BUMP HADLEY-P
15 RED RUFFING-P
16 MONTE (HOOT) PEARSON-P
17 BABE DAHLGREN-PH
18 ART JORGENS-C
19 JOHNNY (FORDHAM JOHNNY) (FIREMAN) (GRANDMA) MURPHY-P
20 JOHNNY BROACA (JMP)-P
20 KEMP WICKER-P
21 PAT MALONE-P
22 ROY JOHNSON-OF (1)
22 TOMMY (OLD RELIABLE) (THE CLUTCH) HENRICH (INJ)-OF
23 FRANK MAKOSKY-P
24 SPUD CHANDLER-P
24 IVY (POISON) ANDREWS-P (2)
25 KEMP WICKER-P
25 JOE (SANDY) VANCE-P
26 JOE (GABBY) GLENN-C
28 BABE DAHLGREN-PH
28 FRANK MAKOSKY-P
29 ART FLETCHER-CH
30 EARLE (THE KENTUCKY COLONEL) COMBS-CH
31 JOHNNY SCHULTE-CH
•34 FRANK MAKOSKY-P
•35 SPUD CHANDLER-P

1938

1ST — 99-53 — 0GB
W WS-CHIN 4-0

NO# JOE (MARSE JOE) MCCARTHY-MGR
1 FRANKIE (CROW) CROSETTI-SS
2 RED ROLFE-3B
3 GEORGE (TWINKLETOES) SELKIRK-OF
4 LOU (THE IRON HORSE) (LARRUPIN' LOU) GEHRIG-1B
5 JOE (JOLTIN' JOE) (THE YANKEE CLIPPER) DIMAGGIO-OF
6 JOE (FLASH) GORDON-2B
7 JAKE POWELL-OF
8 BILL DICKEY-C
9 MYRIL HOAG-OF
10 BILL KNICKERBOCKER-2B/SS
11 LEFTY (GOOFY) GOMEZ-P
12 BABE DAHLGREN-3B/1B
13 LEE STINE-P
14 BUMP HADLEY-P
15 RED RUFFING-P
16 MONTE (HOOT) PEARSON-P
17 TOMMY (OLD RELIABLE) (THE CLUTCH) HENRICH-OF
18 ART JORGENS-C
19 JOHNNY (FORDHAM JOHNNY) (FIREMAN) (GRANDMA) MURPHY-P
20 KEMP WICKER-P
21 SPUD CHANDLER-P
22 JOE (FIREMAN) BEGGS-P
24 IVY (POISON) ANDREWS-P
25 JOE (SANDY) VANCE-P
25 WES FERRELL-P (2)
26 JOE (GABBY) GLENN-C
28 ATLEY (SWAMPY) DONALD-P
29 ART FLETCHER-CH
30 EARLE (THE KENTUCKY COLONEL) COMBS-CH
31 JOHNNY SCHULTE-CH
32 STEVE (SMOKEY) SUNDRA-P
33 LEE STINE-P

1939

1ST — 106-45 — 0GB
W WS-CINN 4-0

NO# JOE (MARSE JOE) MCCARTHY-MGR
1 FRANKIE (CROW) CROSETTI-SS
2 RED ROLFE-3B
3 GEORGE (TWINKLETOES) SELKIRK-OF
4 LOU (THE IRON HORSE) (LARRUPIN' LOU) GEHRIG (ILL)(RET)-1B
4 (RET#) LOU GEHRIG
5 JOE (JOLTIN' JOE) (THE YANKEE CLIPPER) DIMAGGIO-OF
6 JOE (FLASH) GORDON-2B
7 JAKE POWELL-OF
7 TOMMY HENRICH-OF/1B
8 BILL DICKEY-C
9 CHARLIE (KING KONG) KELLER-OF
10 BILL KNICKERBOCKER-2B/SS
11 LEFTY (GOOFY) GOMEZ-P
12 BABE DAHLGREN-1B
14 BUMP HADLEY-P
15 RED RUFFING-P
16 MONTE (HOOT) PEARSON-P
17 TOMMY (OLD RELIABLE) (THE CLUTCH) HENRICH-OF/1B
17 JAKE POWELL-OF
18 ART JORGENS-C
19 JOHNNY (FORDHAM JOHNNY) (FIREMAN) (GRANDMA) MURPHY-P
20 ORAL HILDEBRAND-P
21 SPUD CHANDLER (INJ)-P
22 MARIUS (LEFTY) RUSSO-P
23 STEVE (SMOKEY) SUNDRA-P
24 MARV (BABY FACE) BREUER-P
25 WES FERRELL-P
25 MARIUS (LEFTY) RUSSO-P
26 BUDDY ROSAR-C
27 JOE (MUSCLES) GALLAGHER-OF (1)
27 SPUD CHANDLER (INJ)-P
28 ATLEY (SWAMPY) DONALD-P
29 ART FLETCHER-CH
30 EARLE (THE KENTUCKY COLONEL) COMBS-CH
30 MARIUS (LEFTY) RUSSO-P
31 JOHNNY SCHULTE-CH
32 STEVE (SMOKEY) SUNDRA-P
38 MARIUS (LEFTY) RUSSO-P

1940

3RD — 88-66 — 2GB

NO# JOE (MARSE JOE) MCCARTHY-MGR
1 FRANKIE (CROW) CROSETTI-SS
2 RED ROLFE-3B
3 GEORGE (TWINKLETOES) SELKIRK-OF
4 (RET#) LOU GEHRIG
5 JOE (JOLTIN' JOE) (THE YANKEE CLIPPER) DIMAGGIO-OF
6 JOE (FLASH) GORDON-2B
7 TOMMY (OLD RELIABLE) (THE CLUTCH) HENRICH-OF/1B
8 BILL DICKEY-C
9 CHARLIE (KING KONG) KELLER-OF
10 BILL KNICKERBOCKER-SS/3B
11 LEFTY (GOOFY) GOMEZ (INJ)-P
12 BABE DAHLGREN-1B
14 BUMP HADLEY-P
15 RED RUFFING-P
16 MONTE (HOOT) PEARSON-P
17 JAKE POWELL (INJ)-OF
19 JOHNNY (FORDHAM JOHNNY) (FIREMAN) (GRANDMA) MURPHY-P
20 ORAL HILDEBRAND-P
20 ERNIE (TINY) BONHAM-P
21 SPUD CHANDLER-P
22 MARIUS (LEFTY) RUSSO-P
24 MARV (BABY FACE) BREUER-P
25 STEVE (SMOKEY) SUNDRA-P
26 BUDDY ROSAR-C
27 LEE GRISSOM-P (1)
27 BUSTER (BUS) MILLS-OF
28 ATLEY (SWAMPY) DONALD-P
30 MIKE (SHOTGUN) CHARTAK-OF
31 ART FLETCHER-CH
32 EARLE (THE KENTUCKY COLONEL) COMBS-CH
33 JOHNNY SCHULTE-CH

1941

1ST — 101-53 — 0GB
W WS-BKLN 4-1

NO# JOE (MARSE JOE) MCCARTHY-MGR
1 FRANKIE (CROW) CROSETTI-SS/3B
2 RED ROLFE-3B
3 GEORGE (TWINKLETOES) SELKIRK-OF
4 (RET#) LOU GEHRIG
5 JOE (JOLTIN' JOE) (THE YANKEE CLIPPER) DIMAGGIO-OF
6 JOE (FLASH) GORDON-2B/1B
7 TOMMY (OLD RELIABLE) (THE CLUTCH) HENRICH-OF/1B
8 BILL DICKEY-C
9 CHARLIE (KING KONG) KELLER-OF
10 PHIL (SCOOTER) RIZZUTO-SS
11 LEFTY (GOOFY) GOMEZ-P
12 BUDDY ROSAR-C
14 JERRY PRIDDY-INF
15 RED RUFFING-P
16 JOHNNY LINDELL-PH
17 CHARLEY STANCEU-P
18 STEVE PEEK-P
19 JOHNNY (FORDHAM JOHNNY) (FIREMAN) (GRANDMA) MURPHY-P
20 ERNIE (TINY) BONHAM-P
21 SPUD CHANDLER-P
22 MARIUS (LEFTY) RUSSO-P
24 MARV (BABY FACE) BREUER-P
26 KEN (HAWK) SILVESTRI (ILL)-C
27 FRENCHY BORDAGARAY-OF
28 ATLEY (SWAMPY) DONALD-P
29 GEORGE WASHBURN-P
30 NORM (RED) BRANCH-P
31 ART FLETCHER-CH
32 EARLE (THE KENTUCKY COLONEL) COMBS-CH
33 JOHNNY SCHULTE-CH
34 JOHNNY STURM-1B

1942

1ST — 103-51 — 0GB
L WS-STLN 4-1

NO# JOE (MARSE JOE) MCCARTHY-MGR
1 FRANKIE (CROW) CROSETTI-INF
2 RED ROLFE (ILL)-3B
3 GEORGE (TWINKLETOES) SELKIRK-OF
4 (RET#) LOU GEHRIG
5 JOE (JOLTIN' JOE) (THE YANKEE CLIPPER) DIMAGGIO-OF
6 JOE (FLASH) GORDON-2B
7 TOMMY (OLD RELIABLE) (THE CLUTCH) HENRICH (MIL)-OF/1B
7 ROY CULLENBINE-OF/1B (3)
8 BILL DICKEY (INJ)-C
9 CHARLIE (KING KONG) KELLER-OF
10 PHIL (SCOOTER) RIZZUTO-SS
11 LEFTY (GOOFY) GOMEZ-P
12 BUDDY ROSAR-C
14 JERRY PRIDDY-INF
15 RED RUFFING-P
16 TUCK STAINBACK-OF
17 ED LEVY-1B
18 JOHNNY LINDELL-P
19 JOHNNY (FORDHAM JOHNNY) (FIREMAN) (GRANDMA) MURPHY-P
20 ERNIE (TINY) BONHAM-P
21 SPUD CHANDLER-P
22 MARIUS (LEFTY) RUSSO (INJ)-P
24 MARV (BABY FACE) BREUER-P
25 ED (TRUCK) KEARSE-C
28 ATLEY (SWAMPY) DONALD-P
30 NORM (RED) BRANCH (MIL)-P
(30?) MIKE (SHOTGUN) CHARTAK-PH (1)
30 JIM (MILKMAN JIM) TURNER-P (2)
31 ART FLETCHER-CH
32 EARLE (THE KENTUCKY COLONEL) COMBS-CH
33 JOHNNY SCHULTE-CH
34 BUDDY HASSETT-1B
36 MEL QUEEN-P
38 HANK BOROWY-P
39 MIKE (SHOTGUN) CHARTAK-PH (1)
39 ROLLIE HEMSLEY-C (2)

1943

1ST — 98-56 — 0GB
W WS-STLN 4-1

NO# JOE (MARSE JOE) MCCARTHY-MGR
1 FRANKIE (CROW) CROSETTI (SUS)-INF
2 SNUFFY STIRNWEISS-SS/2B
3 BUD METHENY-OF
4 (RET#) LOU GEHRIG
5 NICK ETTEN-1B
6 JOE (FLASH) GORDON-2B
7 BILLY (THE BULL) JOHNSON-3B
8 BILL DICKEY-C
9 CHARLIE (KING KONG) KELLER-OF
10 ROY (STORMY) WEATHERLY-OF
11 TOMMY BYRNE-P
12 OSCAR GRIMES-SS/1B
14 CHARLEY (BUTCH) WENSLOFF-P
15 HANK BOROWY-P
16 TUCK STAINBACK-OF
17 BILL (GOOBER) ZUBER-P

18 JOHNNY LINDELL-OF
19 JOHNNY (FORDHAM JOHNNY) (FIREMAN) (GRANDMA) MURPHY-P
20 ERNIE (TINY) BONHAM-P
21 SPUD CHANDLER-P
22 MARIUS (LEFTY) RUSSO-P
24 MARV (BABY FACE) BREUER-P
25 AARON ROBINSON (MIL)-PH
26 KEN (ZIGGY) SEARS-C
27 ROLLIE HEMSLEY-C
28 ATLEY (SWAMPY) DONALD-P
29 OSCAR GRIMES-SS/1B
30 JIM (MILKMAN JIM) TURNER-P
31 ART FLETCHER-CH
32 EARLE (THE KENTUCKY COLONEL) COMBS-CH
33 JOHNNY SCHULTE-CH

1944

3RD *83-71* *6GB*

NO# JOE (MARSE JOE) MCCARTHY-MGR
1 TUCK STAINBACK-OF
1 FRANKIE (CROW) CROSETTI (MIL) (RET)-SS
2 SNUFFY STIRNWEISS-2B
3 BUD METHENY-OF
4 *(RET#) LOU GEHRIG*
5 NICK ETTEN-1B
6 DON SAVAGE-3B
7 OSCAR GRIMES-3B/SS
8 JOHNNY LINDELL-OF
9 TUCK STAINBACK-OF
9 HERSH MARTIN-OF
9 ED LEVY-OF
10 MIKE GARBARK-C
11 BOB (RIP) COLLINS-C
12 MIKE (MOLLIE) MILOSEVICH-SS
14 MONK DUBIEL-P
15 HANK BOROWY-P
16 MEL QUEEN-P
16 JOE (FIREMAN) PAGE-P
17 BILL (GOOBER) ZUBER-P
18 JOHNNY (SWEDE) JOHNSON-P
19 HERSH MARTIN-OF
19 AL LYONS (MIL)-P
19 LARRY ROSENTHAL-OF (1)
20 ERNIE (TINY) BONHAM-P
20 BILL (DUTCH) DRESCHER-C
21 SPUD CHANDLER (MIL)-P
21 JOHNNY COONEY-OF (2)
21 BILL BEVENS-P
22 RUSS DERRY-OF
22 BILL (DUTCH) DRESCHER-C
24 AL LYONS (MIL)-P
24 PAUL (BIG POISON) WANER-PH (2)
26 STEVE ROSER-P
27 ROLLIE HEMSLEY (MIL)-C
28 ATLEY (SWAMPY) DONALD-P
29 BILL BEVENS-P
30 JIM (MILKMAN JIM) TURNER-P
31 ART FLETCHER-CH
32 EARLE (THE KENTUCKY COLONEL) COMBS-CH
32 JOHNNY NEUN-CH
33 JOHNNY SCHULTE-CH

1945

4TH *81-71* *6.5GB*

NO# JOE (MARSE JOE) MCCARTHY-MGR
1 SNUFFY STIRNWEISS-2B
2 FRANKIE (CROW) CROSETTI-SS
3 BUD METHENY-OF
4 *(RET#) LOU GEHRIG*
5 NICK ETTEN 1B
6 DON SAVAGE-3B/OF
7 OSCAR GRIMES-3B/1B
8 JOHNNY LINDELL (MIL)-OF
8 AARON ROBINSON (MIL)-C
9 HERSH MARTIN-OF
9 CHARLIE (KING KONG) KELLER-OF
10 MIKE GARBARK-C
11 JOE (FIREMAN) PAGE-P
12 JOE BUZAS-SS
12 CHARLIE (KING KONG) KELLER-OF
14 MONK DUBIEL-P
15 HANK BOROWY-P (1)
15 CHARLIE (KING KONG) KELLER-OF
16 HERB (WORKHORSE) CROMPTON-C
17 BILL (GOOBER) ZUBER-P
18 TUCK STAINBACK-OF
19 KEN HOLCOMBE-P
20 ERNIE (TINY) BONHAM-P
21 BILL BEVENS-P
21 SPUD CHANDLER (MIL)-P
22 PAUL (BIG POISON) WANER (MIL)-PH
22 RED RUFFING-P
24 STEVE ROSER-P
25 AL GETTEL-P
26 MIKE (MOLLIE) MILOSEVICH-SS
27 ROLLIE HEMSLEY (MIL)-C
27 RUSS DERRY-OF
28 ATLEY (SWAMPY) DONALD (INJ)-P
29 BILL (DUTCH) DRESCHER-C
30 JIM (MILKMAN JIM) TURNER-P
31 ART FLETCHER-CH
32 JOHNNY NEUN-CH
33 JOHNNY SCHULTE-CH
35 PAUL (VON) SCHREIBER-P
36 BILL (DUTCH) DRESCHER-C

1946

3RD *87-67* *17GB*

NO# JOE (MARSE JOE) MCCARTHY-MGR1
1 SNUFFY STIRNWEISS-3B/INF
2 FRANKIE (CROW) CROSETTI-SS
3 BUD METHENY-PH
3 ROY (STORMY) WEATHERLY-PH
3 EDDIE BOCKMAN-3B
4 *(RET#) LOU GEHRIG*
5 JOE (JOLTIN' JOE) (THE YANKEE CLIPPER) DIMAGGIO-OF
6 JOE (FLASH) GORDON-2B
7 OSCAR GRIMES-SS/2B (1)
7 BOBBY (DOC) BROWN-SS/3B
7 AARON ROBINSON-C
8 BILL DICKEY-C/MGR2
8 FRANK COLMAN-OF (2)
9 NICK ETTEN-1B
9 AARON ROBINSON-C
10 PHIL (SCOOTER) RIZZUTO-SS
11 JOE (FIREMAN) PAGE-P
12 CHARLIE (KING KONG) KELLER-OF
14 CUDDLES MARSHALL-P
15 TOMMY (OLD RELIABLE) (THE CLUTCH) HENRICH-OF/1B
16 CHARLEY STANCEAU-P (1)
16 BILL BEVENS-P
17 BILL (GOOBER) ZUBER-P (1)
17 MEL QUEEN (MIL)-P
18 KARL DREWS-P
18 RANDY GUMPERT-P
19 JOHNNY (FORDHAM JOHNNY) (FIREMAN) (GRANDMA) MURPHY-P
20 ERNIE (TINY) BONHAM-P
21 SPUD CHANDLER-P
22 RED RUFFING-P
24 GUS NIARHOS-C
24 BILLY (THE BULL) JOHNSON (MIL)-3B
25 AL GETTEL-P
26 STEVE ROSER-P (1)
26 MARIUS (LEFTY) RUSSO-P
26 BILL (DUTCH) DRESCHER-C
26 KARL DREWS-P
27 JOHNNY LINDELL-OF/1B
28 HANK (HEENEY) (HEINE) MAJESKI-3B (1)
28 TOMMY BYRNE-P
29 BILL (DUTCH) DRESCHER-C
29 JOHNNY (FORDHAM JOHNNY) (FIREMAN) (GRANDMA) MURPHY-P
29 CHARLEY STANCEAU-P (1)
29 STEVE (BUD) SOUCHOCK-1B
30 BILL (LEFTY) WIGHT-P
31 RED ROLFE-CH
32 JOHNNY NEUN-CH/MGR3
33 JOHNNY SCHULTE-CH
34 KEN (HAWK) SILVESTRI-C
35 AARON ROBINSON-C
36 JAKE (WHISTLING JAKE) WADE-P (1)
36 AL LYONS-P
37 GUS NIARHOS-C
37 HERB (LEFTY) KARPEL-P
38 MEL QUEEN (MIL)-P
38 FRANK (DUTCH) HILLER-P
38 YOGI BERRA-C
39 TOMMY BYRNE-P
40 HERB (LEFTY) KARPEL-P
40 ROY (STORMY) WEATHERLY-PH
41 STEVE (BUD) SOUCHOCK-1B
42 BILL (DUTCH) DRESCHER-C
42? VIC (THE SPRINGFIELD RIFLE) RASCHI-P (2G:9/23-29)
43 FRANK (DUTCH) HILLER-P

1947

1ST *97-57* *0GB*

W WS-BKLN 4-3

1 SNUFFY STIRNWEISS-2B
2 FRANKIE (CROW) CROSETTI-2B/SS/CH
3 FRANK COLMAN-OF
3 ALLIE CLARK-OF
4 *(RET#) LOU GEHRIG*
5 JOE (JOLTIN' JOE) (THE YANKEE CLIPPER) DIMAGGIO-OF
6 BOBBY (DOC) BROWN-UTIL
7 CHARLIE (CHUCK) DRESSEN-CH
8 AARON ROBINSON-C
9 GEORGE (MAC) MCQUINN-1B
10 PHIL (SCOOTER) RIZZUTO-SS
11 JOE (FIREMAN) PAGE-P
12 CHARLIE (KING KONG) KELLER (INJ)-OF
14 TED SEPKOWSKI-PR
14 RUGGER ARDIZOIA-P
14 LONNY FREY-2B (2)
15 TOMMY (OLD RELIABLE) (THE CLUTCH) HENRICH-OF/1B
16 BILL BEVENS-P
17 MEL QUEEN-P (1)
17 VIC (THE SPRINGFIELD RIFLE) RASCHI-P
18 RANDY GUMPERT-P
19 VIC (THE SPRINGFIELD RIFLE) RASCHI-P
19 KARL DREWS-P
20 FRANK (THE NAUGATUCK NUGGET) (SPEC) SHEA-P
21 SPUD CHANDLER-P
22 ALLIE (SUPERCHIEF) (WAHOO) REYNOLDS-P
24 BILLY (THE BULL) JOHNSON-3B
25 RAY MACK-PR (1)
25 CHARLEY (BUTCH) WENSLOFF-P
26 DON JOHNSON-P
27 JOHNNY LINDELL-OF
28 TOMMY BYRNE-P
28 BILL (LEFTY) WIGHT-P
29 JOHNNY LUCADELLO-2B
29 SHERM LOLLAR-C
30 DICK STARR-P
31 JOHN (RED) CORRIDEN, SR.-CH
32 RALPH (MAJOR) HOUK-C
33 JOHNNY SCHULTE-CH
34 KEN (HAWK) SILVESTRI-C
34 BOBO (BUCK) NEWSOM-P (2)
35 YOGI BERRA-C/OF
36 AL LYONS-P (1)
36 JACK (STRETCH) PHILLIPS-1B
37 BUCKY HARRIS-MGR
38 KARL DREWS-P
42 CHARLEY (BUTCH) WENSLOFF-P
43 VIC (THE SPRINGFIELD RIFLE) RASCHI-P
48 FRANK COLMAN-OF
50 RALPH (MAJOR) HOUK-C
51 GEORGE (MAC) MCQUINN-1B
52 JOHNNY LUCADELLO-2B

1948

3RD *94-60* *2.5GB*

1 SNUFFY STIRNWEISS-2B
2 FRANKIE (CROW) CROSETTI-2B/SS/CH
3 CLIFF MAPES-OF
3 *(RET#) BABE RUTH*
4 *(RET#) LOU GEHRIG*
5 JOE (JOLTIN' JOE) (THE YANKEE CLIPPER) DIMAGGIO-OF
6 BOBBY (DOC) BROWN-UTIL
7 CHARLIE (CHUCK) DRESSEN-CH
8 YOGI BERRA-C/OF
9 GEORGE (MAC) MCQUINN-1B
10 PHIL (SCOOTER) RIZZUTO-SS
11 JOE (FIREMAN) PAGE-P
12 CHARLIE (KING KONG) KELLER (INJ)-OF
13 CLIFF MAPES-OF
14 LONNY FREY-PR (1)
15 TOMMY (OLD RELIABLE) (THE CLUTCH) HENRICH-OF/1B
17 VIC (THE SPRINGFIELD RIFLE) RASCHI-P
18 RANDY GUMPERT-P (1)
18 BOB PORTERFIELD-P
19 KARL DREWS-P (1)
19 DICK STARR-P
20 FRANK (THE NAUGATUCK NUGGET) (SPEC) SHEA-P
21 CUDDLES MARSHALL-P
22 ALLIE (SUPERCHIEF) (WAHOO) REYNOLDS-P
24 BILLY (THE BULL) JOHNSON-3B
25 HANK BAUER-OF
27 JOHNNY LINDELL-OF
28 TOMMY BYRNE-P
29 SHERM LOLLAR-C
30 ED (STEADY EDDIE) LOPAT P
31 JOHN (RED) CORRIDEN, SR. -CH
32 RALPH (MAJOR) HOUK-C
33 JOHNNY SCHULTE-CH
34 JACK (STRETCH) PHILLIPS-1B
35 RED EMBREE-P
36 DICK STARR-P
36 JACK (STRETCH) PHILLIPS-1B
37 BUCKY HARRIS-MGR
38 GUS NIARHOS-C
39 FRANK (DUTCH) HILLER-P
40 CUDDLES MARSHALL-P
40 CHARLIE (SWEDE) SILVERA-C
41 STEVE (BUD) SOUCHOCK-1B
42 BUD STEWART-PH (1)
42 JOE COLLINS-1B
46 CHARLIE (SWEDE) SILVERA-C

1949

1ST *97-57* *0GB*

W WS-BKLN 4-1

1 SNUFFY STIRNWEISS-2B/3B
2 FRANKIE (CROW) CROSETTI-CH
3 *(RET#) BABE RUTH*
4 *(RET#) LOU GEHRIG*
5 JOE (JOLTIN' JOE) (THE YANKEE CLIPPER) DIMAGGIO-OF
6 BOBBY (DOC) BROWN-3B/OF
7 CLIFF MAPES-OF
8 YOGI BERRA (INJ)-C
9 CHARLIE (KING KONG) KELLER-OF
10 PHIL (SCOOTER) RIZZUTO-SS
11 JOE (FIREMAN) PAGE-P
12 RALPH (BUCK) BUXTON-P
14 GENE WOODLING-OF
15 TOMMY (OLD RELIABLE) (THE CLUTCH) HENRICH-OF/1B
17 VIC (THE SPRINGFIELD RIFLE) RASCHI-P
18 BOB PORTERFIELD (INJ)-P
18 FENTON (MUSCLES) MOLE-1B
19 CUDDLES MARSHALL-P
20 FRANK (THE NAUGATUCK NUGGET) (SPEC) SHEA-P
21 FRED SANFORD-P
22 ALLIE (SUPERCHIEF) (WAHOO) REYNOLDS-P
23 DICK KRYHOSKI-1B
23 FENTON (MUSCLES) MOLE-1B
24 BILLY (THE BULL) JOHNSON-INF
25 HANK BAUER-OF
26 HUGH CASEY-P (2)
27 JOHNNY LINDELL-OF
28 TOMMY BYRNE-P
29 CHARLIE (SWEDE) SILVERA-C
30 ED (STEADY EDDIE) LOPAT-P
31 JIM (MILKMAN JIM) TURNER-CH
32 RALPH (MAJOR) HOUK-C
33 BILL DICKEY-CH
35 DUANE PILLETTE-P
35 MICKEY WITEK-PH

NEW YORK YANKEES

36 JACK (STRETCH) PHILLIPS-1B (1)
36 JOHNNY (THE BIG CAT) MIZE-1B (2)
37 CASEY (THE OLD PROFESSOR) STENGEL-MGR
38 GUS NIARHOS-C
39 FRANK (DUTCH) HILLER-P
39 WALLY HOOD-P
41 JOE COLLINS-1B
42 JERRY COLEMAN-2B/SS
52 JIM DELSING-OF

1950

1ST *98-56* *0GB*

W WS-PHIN 4-0

1 SNUFFY STIRNWEISS-2B/3B (1)
2 FRANKIE (CROW) CROSETTI-CH
3 *(RET#) BABE RUTH*
4 *(RET#) LOU GEHRIG*
5 JOE (JOLTIN' JOE) (THE YANKEE CLIPPER) DIMAGGIO-OF
6 BOBBY (DOC) BROWN-3B
7 CLIFF MAPES-OF
8 YOGI BERRA-C
9 DICK WAKEFIELD-OF (1)
9 HANK WORKMAN-1B
10 PHIL (SCOOTER) RIZZUTO-SS
11 JOE (FIREMAN) PAGE-P
12 BILLY (THE KID) MARTIN-2B/3B
14 GENE WOODLING-OF
15 TOMMY (OLD RELIABLE) (THE CLUTCH) HENRICH (INJ)-1B
16 ERNIE NEVEL-P
17 VIC (THE SPRINGFIELD RIFLE) RASCHI-P
18 BOB PORTERFIELD (INJ)-P
18 DAVE MADISON-P
18 WHITEY (CHAIRMAN OF THE BOARD) FORD-P
19 WHITEY (CHAIRMAN OF THE BOARD) FORD-P
20 ERNIE NEVEL-P
21 FRED SANFORD-P
22 ALLIE (SUPERCHIEF) (WAHOO) REYNOLDS-P
23 BOB PORTERFIELD (INJ)-P
24 BILLY (THE BULL) JOHNSON-3B/1B
25 HANK BAUER-OF
26 DON JOHNSON-P (1)
26 TOM FERRICK-P (2)
27 JOHNNY LINDELL-OF (1)
27 LEW BURDETTE-P
28 TOMMY BYRNE-P
29 CHARLIE (SWEDE) SILVERA-C
30 ED (STEADY EDDIE) LOPAT-P
31 JIM (MILKMAN JIM) TURNER-CH
32 RALPH (MAJOR) HOUK-C
33 BILL DICKEY-CH
35 DUANE PILLETTE-P (1)
35 JOE (PROFESSOR) (SPECS) OSTROWSKI-P (2)
36 JOHNNY (THE BIG CAT) MIZE-1B
37 CASEY (THE OLD PROFESSOR) STENGEL-MGR
38 GUS NIARHOS-PR
38 JOHNNY (HIPPITY) HOPP-1B/OF (2)
40 JACKIE JENSEN-OF
41 JOE COLLINS-1B/OF
42 JERRY COLEMAN-2B/SS
54 JIM DELSING-OF (1)

1951

1ST *98-56* *0GB*

W WS-NYN 4-2

1 BILLY (THE KID) MARTIN-UTIL
2 FRANKIE (CROW) CROSETTI-CH
3 *(RET#) BABE RUTH*
4 *(RET#) LOU GEHRIG*
5 JOE (JOLTIN' JOE) (THE YANKEE CLIPPER) DIMAGGIO-OF
6 MICKEY (THE COMMERCE COMET) MANTLE-OF
6 BOBBY (DOC) BROWN-3B
7 CLIFF MAPES-OF (1)
7 BOB CERV-OF
7 MICKEY (THE COMMERCE COMET) MANTLE-OF
8 YOGI BERRA-C
9 BOBBY (DOC) BROWN-3B
9 JIM BRIDEWESER-SS
10 PHIL (SCOOTER) RIZZUTO-SS
11 JOHNNY SAIN-P (2)
12 GIL MCDOUGALD-3B/2B
14 GENE WOODLING-OF
15 TOMMY (OLD RELIABLE) (THE CLUTCH) HENRICH-CH
(16) WHITEY (CHAIRMAN OF THE BOARD) FORD (MIL)-(P)
17 VIC (THE SPRINGFIELD RIFLE) RASCHI-P
18 BOB MUNCRIEF-P
18 JACK KRAMER-P (2)
19 FRANK (THE NAUGATUCK NUGGET) (SPEC) SHEA-P
20 ART SCHALLOCK-P
21 FRED SANFORD-P (1)
21 BOB (SARGE) KUZAVA-P (2)
22 ALLIE (SUPERCHIEF) (WAHOO) REYNOLDS-P
23 BOB PORTERFIELD-P (1)
23 ARCHIE WILSON-OF
24 BILLY (THE BULL) JOHNSON-3B (1)
24 STUBBY OVERMIRE-P (2)
25 HANK BAUER-OF
26 TOM FERRICK-P (1)
26 ART SCHALLOCK-P
26 ERNIE NEVEL-P
27 JACKIE JENSEN-OF
28 TOMMY BYRNE-P (1)
28 TOM (PLOWBOY) MORGAN-P
29 CHARLIE (SWEDE) SILVERA-C
30 ED (STEADY EDDIE) LOPAT-P
31 JIM (MILKMAN JIM) TURNER-CH
32 RALPH (MAJOR) HOUK-C
33 BILL DICKEY-CH
35 JOE (PROFESSOR) (SPECS) OSTROWSKI-P
36 JOHNNY (THE BIG CAT) MIZE-1B
37 CASEY (THE OLD PROFESSOR) STENGEL-MGR
38 JOHNNY (HIPPITY) HOPP-1B
40 JACKIE JENSEN-OF
40 BOB WIESLER (MIL)-P
40 BOBBY HOGUE-P (3)
41 JOE COLLINS-1B/OF
42 JERRY COLEMAN-2B/SS
45 CLINT (SCRAP IRON) COURTNEY-C
52 TOM (PLOWBOY) MORGAN-P

1952

1ST *95-59* *0GB*

W WS-BKLN 4-3

1 BILLY (THE KID) MARTIN (INJ)-2B
2 FRANKIE (CROW) CROSETTI-CH
3 *(RET#) BABE RUTH*
4 *(RET#) LOU GEHRIG*
5 *(RET#) JOE DIMAGGIO*
6 BOBBY (DOC) BROWN (MIL)-3B
6 ANDY CAREY-3B/SS
7 MICKEY (THE COMMERCE COMET) MANTLE-OF/3B
8 YOGI BERRA-C
9 HANK BAUER-OF
10 PHIL (SCOOTER) RIZZUTO-SS
11 JOHNNY SAIN-P
12 GIL MCDOUGALD-3B/2B
14 GENE WOODLING-OF
15 ARCHIE WILSON-PH
(16) WHITEY (CHAIRMAN OF THE BOARD) FORD (MIL)-(P)
17 VIC (THE SPRINGFIELD RIFLE) RASCHI-P
18 JIM (HOT ROD) MCDONALD-P
19 KAL SEGRIST-2B/3B
19 RAY SCARBOROUGH-P (2)
20 ART SCHALLOCK-P
21 BOB (SARGE) KUZAVA-P
22 ALLIE (SUPERCHIEF) (WAHOO) REYNOLDS-P
23 BILL (LEFTY) MILLER-P
24 TOM GORMAN-P
25 JACKIE JENSEN-OF
25 IRV NOREN-OF/1B (2)
27 JIM BRIDEWESER-INF
28 TOM (PLOWBOY) MORGAN (MIL)-P
28 CHARLIE (KING KONG) KELLER-OF
29 CHARLIE (SWEDE) SILVERA-C
30 ED (STEADY EDDIE) LOPAT (INJ)-P
31 JIM (MILKMAN JIM) TURNER-CH
32 RALPH (MAJOR) HOUK-C
33 BILL DICKEY-CH
34 BOB CERV-OF
34 HARRY (LEFTY) SCHAEFFER-P
34 KAL SEGRIST-2B/3B
35 JOE (PROFESSOR) (SPECS) OSTROWSKI-P
36 JOHNNY (THE BIG CAT) MIZE-1B
37 CASEY (THE OLD PROFESSOR) STENGEL-MGR
38 JOHNNY (HIPPITY) HOPP-1B (1)
38 LOREN (BEE BEE) BABE-3B
39 LOREN (BEE BEE) BABE-3B
39 HARRY (LEFTY) SCHAEFFER-P
40 BOBBY HOGUE-P (1)
40 JOHNNY (BEAR TRACKS) SCHMITZ-P (2)
40 EWELL (THE WHIP) BLACKWELL-P (2)
41 JOE COLLINS-1B
42 JERRY COLEMAN (MIL)-2B
54 ANDY CAREY-3B/SS

1953

1ST *99-52* *0GB*

W WS-BKLN 4-2

1 BILLY (THE KID) MARTIN-2B/SS
2 FRANKIE (CROW) CROSETTI-CH
3 *(RET#) BABE RUTH*
4 *(RET#) LOU GEHRIG*
5 *(RET#) JOE DIMAGGIO*
6 ANDY CAREY-INF
7 MICKEY (THE COMMERCE COMET) MANTLE-OF/SS
8 YOGI BERRA-C
9 HANK BAUER-OF
10 PHIL (SCOOTER) RIZZUTO-SS
11 JOHNNY SAIN-P
12 GIL MCDOUGALD-3B/2B
14 GENE WOODLING-OF
15 JOE COLLINS-1B/OF
16 WHITEY (CHAIRMAN OF THE BOARD) FORD-P
17 VIC (THE SPRINGFIELD RIFLE) RASCHI-P
18 JIM (HOT ROD) MCDONALD-P
19 RAY SCARBOROUGH-P (1)
20 ART SCHALLOCK-P
20 WILLIE MIRANDA-SS (2)
21 BOB (SARGE) KUZAVA-P
22 ALLIE (SUPERCHIEF) (WAHOO) REYNOLDS-P
23 BILL (LEFTY) MILLER-P
24 TOM GORMAN-P
25 IRV NOREN-OF
26 GUS TRIANDOS-1B/C
27 JIM BRIDEWESER-INF
28 BILL (BIG BILL) RENNA-OF
29 CHARLIE (SWEDE) SILVERA-C/3B
30 ED (STEADY EDDIE) LOPAT-P
31 JIM (MILKMAN JIM) TURNER-CH
32 RALPH (MAJOR) HOUK-C
33 BILL DICKEY-CH
35 JOHNNY (BEAR TRACKS) SCHMITZ-P (1)
35 STEVE KRALY-P
36 JOHNNY (THE BIG CAT) MIZE-1B
37 CASEY (THE OLD PROFESSOR) STENGEL-MGR
38 LOREN (BEE BEE) BABE-3B (1)
38 WILLIE MIRANDA-SS (2)
38 ART SCHALLOCK-P
40 EWELL (THE WHIP) BLACKWELL (INJ)-P
41 BOB CERV-PH
42 JERRY COLEMAN (MIL)-2B/SS
43 ART (DUTCH) SCHULT-PR
44 FRANK VERDI-SS
45 DON BOLLWEG-1B

1954

2ND *103-51* *8GB*

(1) BILLY (THE KID) MARTIN (MIL)-(2B)
2 FRANKIE (CROW) CROSETTI-CH
3 *(RET#) BABE RUTH*
4 *(RET#) LOU GEHRIG*
5 *(RET#) JOE DIMAGGIO*
6 ANDY CAREY-3B
7 MICKEY (THE COMMERCE COMET) MANTLE-OF/INF
8 YOGI BERRA-C
9 HANK BAUER-OF
10 PHIL (SCOOTER) RIZZUTO-SS
11 JOHNNY SAIN-P
12 GIL MCDOUGALD-2B/3B
14 GENE WOODLING (INJ)-OF
15 JOE COLLINS-1B
16 WHITEY (CHAIRMAN OF THE BOARD) FORD-P
17 ENOS (COUNTRY) SLAUGHTER (INJ)-OF
18 JIM (HOT ROD) MCDONALD (INJ)-P
19 HARRY BYRD-P
19 ART SCHALLOCK-P
20 WILLIE MIRANDA-INF
21 BOB (SARGE) KUZAVA-P (1)
21 JIM KONSTANTY-P (2)
22 ALLIE (SUPERCHIEF) (WAHOO) REYNOLDS-P
23 BILL (LEFTY) MILLER-P
23 TOMMY BYRNE-P
24 TOM GORMAN-P
24 RALPH (HAWK) BRANCA-P (2)
25 IRV NOREN-OF/1B
26 GUS TRIANDOS-1B/C
27 BOBBY (DOC) BROWN (MIL)-3B
27 MARLIN STUART-P (2)
27 WOODIE HELD-SS/3B
28 TOM (PLOWBOY) MORGAN-P
29 CHARLIE (SWEDE) SILVERA-C
30 ED (STEADY EDDIE) LOPAT-P
31 JIM (MILKMAN JIM) TURNER-CH
32 RALPH (MAJOR) HOUK-C/CH
33 BILL DICKEY-CH
36 EDDIE ROBINSON-1B
37 CASEY (THE OLD PROFESSOR) STENGEL-MGR
38 ART SCHALLOCK-P
39 BOB WIESLER-P
41 BOB CERV-OF
42 JERRY COLEMAN-INF
49 LOU BERBERET-C
51 FRANK LEJA-1B
53 BILL (MOOSE) SKOWRON-INF
55 BOB GRIM-P

1955

1ST *96-58* *0GB*

L WS-BKLN 4-3

1 BILLY (THE KID) MARTIN-2B
2 FRANKIE (CROW) CROSETTI-CH
3 *(RET#) BABE RUTH*
4 *(RET#) LOU GEHRIG*
5 *(RET#) JOE DIMAGGIO*
6 ANDY CAREY-3B
7 MICKEY (THE COMMERCE COMET) MANTLE-OF/SS
8 YOGI BERRA-C
9 HANK BAUER-OF/C
10 PHIL (SCOOTER) RIZZUTO-SS/2B
11 JOHNNY SAIN-P (1)
12 GIL MCDOUGALD-2B/3B
14 BILL (MOOSE) SKOWRON-1B/3B
15 JOE COLLINS-1B/OF
16 WHITEY (CHAIRMAN OF THE BOARD) FORD-P
17 ENOS (COUNTRY) SLAUGHTER (INJ)-PH (1)
17 BOBBY RICHARDSON-2B/SS
18 DON LARSEN-P
19 BOB (BULLET BOB) TURLEY-P
20 BILLY HUNTER-SS
21 JIM KONSTANTY-P
22 RIP COLEMAN-P
23 TOMMY BYRNE-P
24 GERRY STALEY-P (2)
25 IRV NOREN-OF
28 TOM (PLOWBOY) MORGAN-P

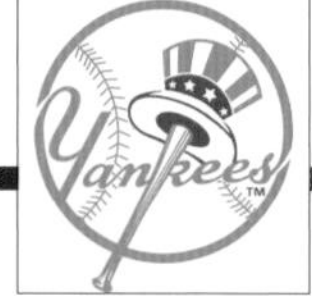

29 CHARLIE (SWEDE) SILVERA-C
30 ED (STEADY EDDIE) LOPAT-P (1)
30 RIP COLEMAN-P
31 JIM (MILKMAN JIM) TURNER-CH
32 ELSTON (ELLIE) HOWARD-OF/C
33 BILL DICKEY-CH
35 LOU BERBERET-C
36 EDDIE ROBINSON-1B
37 CASEY (THE OLD PROFESSOR) STENGEL-MGR
38 ART SCHALLOCK-P (1)
38 JOHNNY BLANCHARD-C
38 TED GRAY-P (3)
39 BOB WIESLER-P
40 TOMMY CARROLL-SS
41 MARV (MARVELOUS MARV) THRONEBERRY-1B
41 BOB CERV-OF
42 JERRY COLEMAN (INJ)-INF
44 DICK (TUT) TETTELBACH-OF
47 TOM (SNAKE) STURDIVANT-P
51 FRANK LEJA-1B
53 JOHNNY KUCKS-P
55 BOB GRIM (INJ)-P

1956

1ST 97-57 0GB
W WS-BKLN 4-3

1 BILLY (THE KID) MARTIN-2B/3B
2 FRANKIE (CROW) CROSETTI-CH
3 *(RET#) BABE RUTH*
4 *(RET#) LOU GEHRIG*
5 *(RET#) JOE DIMAGGIO*
6 ANDY CAREY-3B
7 MICKEY (THE COMMERCE COMET) MANTLE-OF
8 YOGI BERRA-C/OF
9 HANK BAUER-OF
10 PHIL (SCOOTER) RIZZUTO-SS
11 JERRY LUMPE-SS/3B
12 GIL MCDOUGALD-SS/INF
14 BILL (MOOSE) SKOWRON-1B/3B
15 JOE COLLINS-OF/1B
16 WHITEY (CHAIRMAN OF THE BOARD) FORD-P
17 BOBBY RICHARDSON-2B
17 ENOS (COUNTRY) SLAUGHTER (INJ)-OF (2)
18 DON LARSEN-P
19 BOB (BULLET BOB) TURLEY-P
20 BILLY HUNTER (INJ)-SS/3B
21 JIM KONSTANTY-P (1)
21 RALPH TERRY-P
21 SONNY DIXON-P
22 MICKEY (MAURY) MCDERMOTT-P
23 TOMMY BYRNE-P
24 GERRY STALEY-P (1)
25 IRV NOREN (INJ)-OF/1B
28 TOM (PLOWBOY) MORGAN-P
29 CHARLIE (SWEDE) SILVERA-C
30 RIP COLEMAN-P
31 JIM (MILKMAN JIM) TURNER-CH
32 ELSTON (ELLIE) HOWARD-OF/C
33 BILL DICKEY-CH
36 EDDIE ROBINSON-1B (1)
36 NORM SIEBERN (INJ)-OF
37 CASEY (THE OLD PROFESSOR) STENGEL-MGR
39 GEORGE (TEDDY) WILSON-OF (2)
40 TOMMY CARROLL-3B/SS
41 BOB CERV (INJ)-OF
42 JERRY COLEMAN-INF
45 LOU (THE NERVOUS GREEK) SKIZAS-PH (1)
47 TOM (SNAKE) STURDIVANT-P
51 JIM COATES-P
53 JOHNNY KUCKS-P
55 BOB GRIM-P

1957

1ST 98-56 0GB
L WS-MILN 4-3

1 BILLY (THE KID) MARTIN-2B/3B (1)
2 FRANKIE (CROW) CROSETTI-CH
3 *(RET#) BABE RUTH*
4 *(RET#) LOU GEHRIG*
5 *(RET#) JOE DIMAGGIO*
6 ANDY CAREY-3B
7 MICKEY (THE COMMERCE COMET) MANTLE-OF
8 YOGI BERRA-C/OF
9 HANK BAUER-OF
11 JERRY LUMPE-SS/3B
12 GIL MCDOUGALD-SS/INF
14 BILL (MOOSE) SKOWRON-1B
15 JOE COLLINS-1B/OF
16 WHITEY (CHAIRMAN OF THE BOARD) FORD (INJ)-P
17 ENOS (COUNTRY) SLAUGHTER (INJ)-OF
18 DON LARSEN-P
19 BOB (BULLET BOB) TURLEY-P
21 RALPH TERRY-P (1)
21 SAL (THE BARBER) MAGLIE-P (2)
23 TOMMY BYRNE-P
24 AL (BOZO) CICOTTE-P
25 ZEKE BELLA-OF
27 WOODIE HELD-PH (1)
27 BOBBY DEL GRECO-OF (2)
28 ART DITMAR-P
29 BOBBY RICHARDSON-2B
30 BOBBY SHANTZ-P
31 JIM (MILKMAN JIM) TURNER-CH
32 ELSTON (ELLIE) HOWARD-UTIL
33 BILL DICKEY-CH
33 CHARLIE (KING KONG) KELLER-CH
33 RANDY GUMPERT-CH
34 TONY KUBEK-UTIL
36 HARRY (SUITCASE) (GOODY) SIMPSON-OF/1B (2)
37 CASEY (THE OLD PROFESSOR) STENGEL-MGR
39 DARRELL JOHNSON-C
42 JERRY COLEMAN-INF
47 TOM (SNAKE) STURDIVANT-P
53 JOHNNY KUCKS-P
55 BOB GRIM-P

1958

1ST 92-62 0GB
W WS-MILN 4-3

1 BOBBY RICHARDSON-INF
2 FRANKIE (CROW) CROSETTI-CH
3 *(RET#) BABE RUTH*
4 *(RET#) LOU GEHRIG*
5 *(RET#) JOE DIMAGGIO*
6 ANDY CAREY-3B
7 MICKEY (THE COMMERCE COMET) MANTLE-OF
8 YOGI BERRA-C/UTIL
9 HANK BAUER-OF
10 TONY KUBEK-SS/UTIL
11 JERRY LUMPE-3B/SS
12 GIL MCDOUGALD-2B/SS
14 BILL (MOOSE) SKOWRON-1B/3B
16 WHITEY (CHAIRMAN OF THE BOARD) FORD-P
17 ENOS (COUNTRY) SLAUGHTER (INJ)-OF
18 DON LARSEN (INJ)-P
19 BOB (BULLET BOB) TURLEY-P
20 MARV (MARVELOUS MARV) THRONEBERRY-1B/OF
21 SAL (THE BARBER) MAGLIE-P (1)
21 VIRGIL (FIRE) TRUCKS-P (2)
22 DARRELL JOHNSON-C
23 MURRY DICKSON-P (2)
24 DUKE MAAS-P (2)
25 NORM SIEBERN-OF
26 RYNE DUREN-P
27 JOHNNY JAMES-P
27 BOBBY DEL GRECO-OF
28 ART DITMAR-P
29 FRITZIE BRICKELL-2B
30 BOBBY SHANTZ-P
31 JIM (MILKMAN JIM) TURNER-CH
32 ELSTON (ELLIE) HOWARD-UTIL
35 RALPH (MAJOR) HOUK-CH
36 HARRY (SUITCASE) (GOODY) SIMPSON-OF/1B (1)
37 CASEY (THE OLD PROFESSOR) STENGEL-MGR
47 TOM (SNAKE) STURDIVANT (INJ)-P
53 JOHNNY KUCKS-P
55 BOB GRIM-P (1)
55 ZACH MONROE-P

1959

3RD 79-75 15GB

1 BOBBY RICHARDSON-2B/INF
2 FRANKIE (CROW) CROSETTI-CH
3 *(RET#) BABE RUTH*
4 *(RET#) LOU GEHRIG*
5 *(RET#) JOE DIMAGGIO*
6 ANDY CAREY (ILL)3B
7 MICKEY (THE COMMERCE COMET) MANTLE-OF
8 YOGI BERRA-C/OF
9 HANK BAUER-OF
10 TONY KUBEK-SS/UTIL
11 JERRY LUMPE-INF (1)
11 HECTOR LOPEZ-3B/OF (2)
12 GIL MCDOUGALD-INF
14 BILL (MOOSE) SKOWRON (INJ)-1B/3B
15 JIM PISONI-OF (2)
16 WHITEY (CHAIRMAN OF THE BOARD) FORD-P
17 ENOS (COUNTRY) SLAUGHTER (INJ)-OF (1)
18 DON LARSEN-P
19 BOB (BULLET BOB) TURLEY-P
20 MARV (MARVELOUS MARV) THRONEBERRY-1B/OF
21 MARK FREEMAN-P (2)
22 JIM BRONSTAD-P
22 GARY BLAYLOCK-P (2)
23 RALPH TERRY-P (2)
24 DUKE MAAS-P
25 NORM SIEBERN-OF/1B
26 RYNE DUREN-P
28 ART DITMAR-P
29 FRITZIE BRICKELL-SS/2B
30 BOBBY SHANTZ-P
31 JIM (MILKMAN JIM) TURNER-CH
32 ELSTON (ELLIE) HOWARD-UTIL
33 CHARLIE (KING KONG) KELLER-CH
34 CLETE BOYER-SS/3B
35 RALPH (MAJOR) HOUK-CH
37 CASEY (THE OLD PROFESSOR) STENGEL-MGR
38 JOHNNY BLANCHARD-UTIL
39 JIM COATES-P
40 JOHN (GABE) GABLER-P
43 KEN HUNT-OF
44 KEN HUNT-OF
44 GORDON WINDHORN-OF
45 MARK FREEMAN-P (2)
47 TOM (SNAKE) STURDIVANT (INJ)-P (1)
47 ELI GRBA-P
47 CHARLIE (KING KONG) KELLER-CH
49 JIM BRONSTAD-P
51 GORDON WINDHORN-OF
53 JOHNNY KUCKS-P (1)
55 ZACH MONROE-P

1960

1ST 97-57 0GB
L WS-PITN 4-3

1 BOBBY RICHARDSON-2B/3B
2 FRANKIE (CROW) CROSETTI-CH
3 *(RET#) BABE RUTH*
4 *(RET#) LOU GEHRIG*
5 *(RET#) JOE DIMAGGIO*
6 ANDY CAREY-3B/OF
7 MICKEY (THE COMMERCE COMET) MANTLE-OF
8 YOGI BERRA-C/OF
9 ROGER MARIS-OF
10 TONY KUBEK-SS/OF
11 HECTOR LOPEZ-OF/INF
12 GIL MCDOUGALD-3B/2B
14 BILL (MOOSE) SKOWRON-1B
15 JIM PISONI-OF
16 WHITEY (CHAIRMAN OF THE BOARD) FORD-P
17 ELMER VALO-OF (1)
17 BOB CERV-OF/1B (2)
18 FRED KIPP-P
18 ELI GRBA-P
19 BOB (BULLET BOB) TURLEY-P
20 JOE (OATS) DEMAESTRI-2B/SS
22 BILL STAFFORD-P
23 RALPH TERRY-P
24 DUKE MAAS-P
25 KENT HADLEY-1B
25 DALE LONG-1B (2)
25 JESSE GONDER-C
26 RYNE DUREN-P
28 ART DITMAR-P
29 HAL STOWE-P
30 BOBBY SHANTZ-P
32 ELSTON (ELLIE) HOWARD-C/OF
33 BILL DICKEY-CH
34 CLETE BOYER-3B/SS
35 RALPH (MAJOR) HOUK-CH
36 ED (STEADY EDDIE) LOPAT-CH
37 CASEY (THE OLD PROFESSOR) STENGEL-MGR
38 JOHNNY BLANCHARD (ILL)-C
39 JIM COATES-P
40 JOHN (GABE) GABLER-P
43 DERON JOHNSON-3B
44 KEN HUNT-OF
44 JIM HEGAN-CH
46 BILL SHORT-P
47 BILLY SHANTZ-C
47 LUIS ARROYO-P
48 BILL STAFFORD-P
53 JOHNNY JAMES-P

1961

1ST 109-53 0GB
W WS-CINN 4-1

1 BOBBY RICHARDSON-2B
2 FRANKIE (CROW) CROSETTI-CH
3 *(RET#) BABE RUTH*
4 *(RET#) LOU GEHRIG*
5 *(RET#) JOE DIMAGGIO*
6 DERON JOHNSON-3B (1)
6 CLETE BOYER-3B/UTIL
7 MICKEY (THE COMMERCE COMET) MANTLE-OF
8 YOGI BERRA-OF/C
9 ROGER MARIS-OF
10 TONY KUBEK-SS
11 HECTOR LOPEZ-OF
12 BILLY (SHOTGUN) GARDNER-3B/2B (2)
14 BILL (MOOSE) SKOWRON-1B
15 JACK REED-OF
15 TOM TRESH-SS
16 WHITEY (CHAIRMAN OF THE BOARD) FORD-P
17 LEE THOMAS-PH
17 BOB CERV-OF/1B (2)
18 HAL (PORKY) RENIFF-P
19 BOB (BULLET BOB) TURLEY (INJ)-P
20 JOE (OATS) DEMAESTRI-INF
22 BILL STAFFORD-P
23 RALPH TERRY-P
24 DANNY MCDEVITT-P (1)
24 AL DOWNING-P
25 JESSE GONDER-PH
26 RYNE DUREN-P (1)
26 TEX CLEVENGER-P (2)
28 ART DITMAR-P (1)
28 BUD DALEY-P (2)
29 DUKE MAAS-P
29 EARL (THE EARL OF SNOHOMISH) TORGESON-1B (2)
31 JOHNNY SAIN-CH
32 ELSTON (ELLIE) HOWARD-C/1B
34 CLETE BOYER-3B/UTIL
34 BOB HALE-1B (2)
35 RALPH (MAJOR) HOUK-MGR
36 WALLY MOSES-CH
38 JOHNNY BLANCHARD-C/OF
39 JIM COATES-P
44 JIM HEGAN-CH
45 ROLLIE SHELDON-P
47 LUIS ARROYO-P
53 JOHNNY JAMES-P (1)

1962

1ST 96-66 0GB
W WS-SFN 4-3

1 BOBBY RICHARDSON-2B
2 FRANKIE (CROW) CROSETTI-CH
3 *(RET#) BABE RUTH*
4 *(RET#) LOU GEHRIG*
5 *(RET#)* JOE DIMAGGIO
6 CLETE BOYER-3B
7 MICKEY (THE COMMERCE COMET) MANTLE (INJ)-OF
8 YOGI BERRA-C/OF
9 ROGER MARIS-OF
10 TONY KUBEK (MIL)-SS/OF
11 HECTOR LOPEZ-OF/INF
12 BILLY (SHOTGUN) GARDNER-2B/3B (1)
14 BILL (MOOSE) SKOWRON-1B

NEW YORK YANKEES

15 TOM TRESH-SS/OF
16 WHITEY (CHAIRMAN OF THE BOARD) FORD-P
17 BOB CERV-OF/1B (1)
18 HAL (PORKY) RENIFF-P
19 BOB (BULLET BOB) TURLEY-P
21 TEX CLEVENGER-P
22 BILL STAFFORD-P
23 RALPH TERRY-P
24 AL DOWNING-P
25 JOE (PEPI) PEPITONE-OF/1B
26 TEX CLEVENGER-P
26 DALE LONG-1B (2)
27 JACK REED-OF
28 BUD DALEY-P
29 HAL (SKINNY) BROWN-P (2)
30 MARSHALL (SHERIFF) BRIDGES-P
31 JOHNNY SAIN-CH
32 ELSTON (ELLIE) HOWARD-C
34 PHIL LINZ-UTIL
35 RALPH (MAJOR) HOUK-MGR
36 WALLY MOSES-CH
38 JOHNNY BLANCHARD-UTIL
39 JIM COATES-P
40 JACK CULLEN-P
41 JAKE GIBBS-3B
44 JIM HEGAN-CH
45 ROLLIE SHELDON-P
47 LUIS ARROYO (INJ)-P
56 JIM BOUTON-P

1963

1ST 104-57 0GB
L WS-LAN 4-0

1 BOBBY RICHARDSON-2B
2 FRANKIE (CROW) CROSETTI-CH
3 *(RET#) BABE RUTH*
4 *(RET#) LOU GEHRIG*
5 *(RET#) JOE DIMAGGIO*
6 CLETE BOYER-3B/INF
7 MICKEY (THE COMMERCE COMET) MANTLE (INJ)-OF
8 YOGI BERRA-C/CH
9 ROGER MARIS-OF
10 TONY KUBEK-SS/OF
11 HECTOR LOPEZ-OF/2B
14 HARRY BRIGHT-1B/3B (2)
15 TOM TRESH-OF
16 WHITEY (CHAIRMAN OF THE BOARD) FORD-P
18 HAL (PORKY) RENIFF-P
19 STAN WILLIAMS-P
20 BILL KUNKEL-P
22 BILL STAFFORD-P
23 RALPH TERRY-P
24 AL DOWNING-P
25 JOE (PEPI) PEPITONE-1B/OF
26 DALE LONG-1B/CH
27 JACK REED-OF
28 BUD DALEY (INJ)-P
29 TOM METCALF-P
30 MARSHALL (SHERIFF) BRIDGES-P
31 JOHNNY SAIN-CH
32 ELSTON (ELLIE) HOWARD-C
34 PHIL LINZ-UTIL
35 RALPH (MAJOR) HOUK-MGR
38 JOHNNY BLANCHARD-OF
39 STEVE HAMILTON-P (2)
41 JAKE GIBBS-C
42 PEDRO GONZALEZ-2B
44 JIM HEGAN-CH
47 LUIS ARROYO-P
56 JIM BOUTON-P

1964

1ST 99-63 0GB
L WS-STLN 4-3

1 BOBBY RICHARDSON-2B/SS
2 FRANKIE (CROW) CROSETTI-CH
3 *(RET#) BABE RUTH*
4 *(RET#) LOU GEHRIG*
5 *(RET#) JOE DIMAGGIO*
6 DERON JOHNSON-3B (1)
6 CLETE BOYER-3B/SS
7 MICKEY (THE COMMERCE COMET) MANTLE-OF
8 YOGI BERRA-MGR
9 ROGER MARIS-OF
10 TONY KUBEK (INJ)-SS
11 HECTOR LOPEZ-OF/3B
12 MIKE HEGAN-1B
14 HARRY BRIGHT-1B
14 PEDRO (PETE) RAMOS-P (2)
15 TOM TRESH-OF
16 WHITEY (CHAIRMAN OF THE BOARD) FORD-P/CH
18 HAL (PORKY) RENIFF-P
19 STAN WILLIAMS-P
22 BILL STAFFORD-P
23 RALPH TERRY-P
24 AL DOWNING-P
25 JOE (PEPI) PEPITONE-1B/OF
26 ARCHIE MOORE-OF/1B
28 BUD DALEY (INJ)-P
30 MEL STOTTLEMYRE-P
31 JIM (GEE GEE) GLEESON-CH
32 ELSTON (ELLIE) HOWARD-C
34 PHIL LINZ-UTIL
38 JOHNNY BLANCHARD-UTIL
39 STEVE HAMILTON-P
41 JAKE GIBBS-C
42 PEDRO GONZALEZ-UTIL
43 ROGER REPOZ-OF
44 JIM HEGAN-CH
45 ROLLIE SHELDON-P
48 ELVIO JIMENEZ-OF
49 BOB MEYER-P (1)
51 PETE MIKKELSEN-P
56 JIM BOUTON-P

1965

6TH 77-85 25GB

1 BOBBY RICHARDSON-2B
2 FRANKIE (CROW) CROSETTI-CH
3 *(RET#) BABE RUTH*
4 *(RET#) LOU GEHRIG*
5 *(RET#) JOE DIMAGGIO*
6 CLETE BOYER-3B/SS
7 MICKEY (THE COMMERCE COMET) MANTLE (INJ)-OF
9 ROGER MARIS (INJ)-OF
10 TONY KUBEK-SS/UTIL
11 HECTOR LOPEZ-OF//1B
12 PHIL LINZ-UTIL
14 PEDRO (PETE) RAMOS-P
15 TOM TRESH-OF
16 WHITEY (CHAIRMAN OF THE BOARD) FORD-P
17 BOBBY MURCER-SS
18 HAL (PORKY) RENIFF-P
20 HORACE CLARKE-INF
21 JOHNNY KEANE-MGR
22 BILL STAFFORD (INJ)-P
23 JIM BRENNEMAN-P
23 RICH BECK-P
24 AL DOWNING-P
25 JOE (PEPI) PEPITONE-1B/OF
26 ARCHIE MOORE-OF/1B
27 DUKE CARMEL-1B
28 GIL BLANCO-P
29 BOBBY TIEFENAUER-P (2)
29 MIKE JUREWICZ-P
30 MEL STOTTLEMYRE-P
31 COT DEAL-CH
32 ELSTON (ELLIE) HOWARD (INJ)-C/UTIL
35 VERN BENSON-CH
38 JOHNNY BLANCHARD-C (1)
38 DOC EDWARDS-C (2)
39 STEVE HAMILTON-P
41 JAKE GIBBS-C
42 PEDRO GONZALEZ-UTIL (1)
42 RAY (BUDDY) BARKER-1B/3B (2)
43 ROGER REPOZ-OF
44 JIM HEGAN-CH
45 ROLLIE SHELDON-P (1)
45 JACK CULLEN-P
47 BOB SCHMIDT-C
48 ROY WHITE-OF/2B
51 PETE MIKKELSEN-P
53 ROSS MOSCHITTO-OF
56 JIM BOUTON-P
57 ART LOPEZ-OF

1966

10TH 70-89 26.5GB

1 BOBBY RICHARDSON-2B/3B
2 FRANKIE (CROW) CROSETTI-CH
3 *(RET#) BABE RUTH*
4 *(RET#) LOU GEHRIG*
5 *(RET#) JOE DIMAGGIO*
6 CLETE BOYER-3B/SS
7 MICKEY (THE COMMERCE COMET) MANTLE-OF
9 ROGER MARIS-OF
11 HECTOR LOPEZ-OF
12 RUBEN AMARO-SS
14 PEDRO (PETE) RAMOS-P
15 TOM TRESH-OF/3B
16 WHITEY (CHAIRMAN OF THE BOARD) FORD (INJ)-P
17 BOBBY MURCER-SS
18 HAL (PORKY) RENIFF-P
19 BOB (WARRIOR) FRIEND-P (1)
20 HORACE CLARKE-SS/INF
21 JOHNNY KEANE-MGR1
22 FRED (BUBBY) TALBOT-P (2)
23 BILLY BRYAN-C/1B (2)
24 AL DOWNING-P
25 JOE (PEPI) PEPITONE-1B/OF
26? JOHN MILLER-1B/OF
27 DICK (DUCKY) SCHOFIELD-SS (2)
28 STEVE WHITAKER-OF
29 BILL HENRY-P
30 MEL STOTTLEMYRE-P
31 JIM (MILKMAN JIM) TURNER-CH
32 ELSTON (ELLIE) HOWARD-C/1B
33 JOHNNY NEUN-CH
34 MIKE HEGAN-1B
35 VERN BENSON-CH
35 RALPH (MAJOR) HOUK-MGR2
36 WALLY MOSES-CH
39 STEVE HAMILTON-P
40 LU CLINTON-OF
41 JAKE GIBBS (INJ)-C
42 RAY (BUDDY) BARKER-1B
43 ROGER REPOZ-OF (1)
43 MIKE FERRARO-3B
44 JIM HEGAN-CH
45 JACK CULLEN-P
45 STAN BAHNSEN-P
47 JOHN MILLER-1B/OF
48 ROY WHITE-OF/2B
52 FRITZ PETERSON-P
(53) ROSS MOSCHITTO (MIL)-(OF)
56 JIM BOUTON (INJ)-P
58 DOOLEY WOMACK-P
60 STAN BAHNSEN-P
RICH BECK (MIL)-(P)

1967

9TH 72-90 20GB

2 FRANKIE (CROW) CROSETTI-CH
3 *(RET#) BABE RUTH*
4 *(RET#) LOU GEHRIG*
5 *(RET#) JOE DIMAGGIO*
6 CHARLEY SMITH-3B
7 MICKEY (THE COMMERCE COMET) MANTLE-1B
10 DICK HOWSER (INJ)-INF
11 BILL ROBINSON-OF
12 RUBEN AMARO-SS/INF
14 JERRY KENNEY-SS
15 TOM TRESH-OF
16 WHITEY (CHAIRMAN OF THE BOARD) FORD-P
(17) BOBBY MURCER (MIL)-(SS)
17 TOM SHOPAY-OF
18 HAL (PORKY) RENIFF-P (1)
18 STEVE BARBER-P (2)
19 FRITZ PETERSON-P
20 HORACE CLARKE-2B
22 FRED (BUBBY) TALBOT-P
23 BILLY BRYAN-C
23 BOB TILLMAN-C (2)
24 AL DOWNING-P
25 JOE (PEPI) PEPITONE-OF/1B
26 JOHN KENNEDY-INF
27 TOM SHOPAY-OF
28 STEVE WHITAKER-OF
30 MEL STOTTLEMYRE-P
31 JIM (MILKMAN JIM) TURNER-CH
32 ELSTON (ELLIE) HOWARD-C/1B (1)
34 MIKE HEGAN (MIL)-1B/OF
35 RALPH (MAJOR) HOUK-MGR
36 LOREN (BEE BEE) BABE-CH
38 FRANK FERNANDEZ (MIL)-C/OF
39 STEVE HAMILTON-P
40 LU CLINTON-OF
40 BILL (MOMBO) MONBOUQUETTE-P (2)
41 JAKE GIBBS-C
42 RAY (BUDDY) BARKER-1B
43 DALE (MOUNTAIN MAN) ROBERTS-P
44 JIM HEGAN-CH
47 FRANK TEPEDINO-1B
48 ROY WHITE-OF/3B
48 CECIL PERKINS-P
49 CHARLIE SANDS-PH
50 BILLY BRYAN-C
52 JOE VERBANIC-P
53 ROSS MOSCHITTO-OF
54 THAD TILLOTSON-P
56 JIM BOUTON-P
58 DOOLEY WOMACK-P
68 CHARLIE SANDS-PH
70 FRANK TEPEDINO-1B

1968

5TH 83-79 20GB

2 FRANKIE (CROW) CROSETTI-CH
3 *(RET#) BABE RUTH*
4 *(RET#) LOU GEHRIG*
5 *(RET#) JOE DIMAGGIO*
6 CHARLEY SMITH (INJ)-3B
7 MICKEY (THE COMMERCE COMET) MANTLE-1B
9 STEVE WHITAKER-OF
10 DICK HOWSER-INF
11 BILL ROBINSON-OF
12 RUBEN AMARO-SS/INF
14 BOBBY COX-3B
15 TOM TRESH-SS/OF
16 WHITEY (CHAIRMAN OF THE BOARD) FORD-CH
17 GENE (STICK) MICHAEL-SS/P
18 STEVE BARBER-P
19 FRITZ PETERSON-P
20 HORACE CLARKE-2B
21 ROY WHITE-OF/3B
22 FRED (BUBBY) TALBOT-P
23 ELLIE RODRIGUEZ-C
24 AL DOWNING (INJ)-P
25 JOE (PEPI) PEPITONE-OF/1B
26 MIKE FERRARO-3B
28 ANDY KOSCO-OF/1B
29 ROCKY COLAVITO-OF/P (2)
30 MEL STOTTLEMYRE-P
31 JIM (MILKMAN JIM) TURNER-CH
35 RALPH (MAJOR) HOUK-MGR
38 FRANK FERNANDEZ-C/OF
39 STEVE HAMILTON-P
40 BILL (MOMBO) MONBOUQUETTE-P (1)
40 LINDY MCDANIEL-P (2)
41 JAKE GIBBS-C
44 JIM HEGAN-CH
45 STAN BAHNSEN-P
48 ROY WHITE-OF/3B
51 JOHN WYATT-P (2)
51 TONY SOLAITA-1B
52 JOE VERBANIC-P
54 THAD TILLOTSON-P
56 JIM BOUTON-P
56 JOHN CUMBERLAND-P
58 DOOLEY WOMACK-P

1969

5TH E 80-81 28.5GB

1 BOBBY MURCER-OF/3B
2 JERRY KENNEY-3B/UTIL
3 *(RET#) BABE RUTH*
4 *(RET#) LOU GEHRIG*
5 *(RET#) JOE DIMAGGIO*
6 ROY WHITE-OF
7 *(RET#) MICKEY MANTLE*
9 DICK SIMPSON-OF (1)
9 RON WOODS-OF (2)
10 FRANK FERNANDEZ-C/OF
11 BILL ROBINSON-OF/1B
12 BILLY COWAN-OF/1B (1)
12 RON BLOMBERG-OF
14 BOBBY COX-3B/2B
15 TOM TRESH-SS (1)
15 THURMAN MUNSON-C
17 GENE (STICK) MICHAEL-SS
18 MIKE KEKICH-P
19 FRITZ PETERSON-P
20 HORACE CLARKE-2B
21 NATE (PEEWEE) OLIVER-PH (1)
21 JIM LYTTLE-OF
22 FRED (BUBBY) TALBOT-P (1)
22 JACK AKER-P (2)
23 DON NOTTEBART-P (1)
23 JOHNNY ELLIS-C
24 AL DOWNING-P
25 JOE (PEPI) PEPITONE-1B
26 JIMMIE HALL-OF/1B (2)
27 TOM SHOPAY-OF
30 MEL STOTTLEMYRE-P
31 JIM (MILKMAN JIM) TURNER-CH
32 ELSTON (ELLIE) HOWARD-CH
34 DICK HOWSER-CH
35 RALPH (MAJOR) HOUK-MGR
38 LEN BOEHMER-INF
39 STEVE HAMILTON-P
40 LINDY MCDANIEL-P
41 JAKE GIBBS-C
44 JIM HEGAN-CH
45 STAN BAHNSEN-P
46 FRANK TEPEDINO-OF
50 BILL BURBACH-P
51 RON KLIMKOWSKI-P
(52) JOE VERBANIC (INJ)-(P)
54 KEN JOHNSON-P (2)
55 DAVE MCDONALD-1B
56 JOHN CUMBERLAND-P

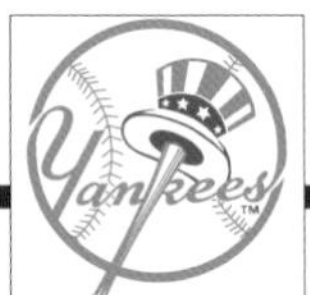

1970

2ND E 93-69 15GB

1 BOBBY MURCER-OF
2 JERRY KENNEY-3B/2B
3 *(RET#) BABE RUTH*
4 *(RET#) LOU GEHRIG*
5 *(RET#) JOE DIMAGGIO*
6 ROY WHITE-OF
7 MICKEY (THE COMMERCE COMET) MANTLE-CH
9 RON WOODS-OF
10 DANNY CATER-1B/UTIL
13 CURT BLEFARY-OF/1B
15 THURMAN MUNSON-C
17 GENE (STICK) MICHAEL-SS/INF
18 MIKE KEKICH (INJ)-P
19 FRITZ PETERSON-P
20 HORACE CLARKE-2B
21 FRANK TEPEDINO-1B/OF
22 JACK AKER-P
23 JOHNNY ELLIS-UTIL
24 RON KLIMKOWSKI-P
25 PETE WARD-1B
26 FRANK BAKER-SS
27 JIM LYTTLE-OF
28 RON HANSEN-INF
29 MIKE MCCORMICK-P (2)
30 MEL STOTTLEMYRE-P
31 JIM (MILKMAN JIM) TURNER -CH
32 ELSTON (ELLIE) HOWARD-CH
34 DICK HOWSER-CH
35 RALPH (MAJOR) HOUK-MGR
37 *(RET#) CASEY STENGEL*
38 STEVE KLINE-P
39 STEVE HAMILTON-P (1)
39 GARY JONES-P
40 LINDY MCDANIEL-P
41 JAKE GIBBS-C
43 ROB GARDNER-P
44 JIM HEGAN-CH
45 STAN BAHNSEN-P
46 BOBBY MITCHELL-OF
49 LOYD COLSON-P
50 BILL BURBACH-P
52 JOE VERBANIC (INJ)-P
54 GARY WASLEWSKI-P (2)
56 JOHN CUMBERLAND-P (1)
56 MIKE MCCORMICK-P (2)

1971

4TH E 82-80 21GB

1 BOBBY MURCER-OF
2 JERRY KENNEY-3B/INF
3 *(RET#) BABE RUTH*
4 *(RET#) LOU GEHRIG*
5 *(RET#) JOE DIMAGGIO*
6 ROY WHITE-OF
7 *(RET#) MICKEY MANTLE*
9 RON WOODS-OF (1)
10 DANNY CATER-1B/3B
11 DANNY (MICKEY) WALTON-OF (2)
12 RON BLOMBERG-OF
13 CURT BLEFARY-OF/1B (1)
14 RON SWOBODA-OF (2)
15 THURMAN MUNSON-C/OF
17 GENE (STICK) MICHAEL-SS
18 MIKE KEKICH-P
19 FRITZ PETERSON-P
20 HORACE CLARKE-2B
21 FRANK TEPEDINO-INF (1)
21 RUSTY TORRES-OF
22 JACK AKER-P
23 JOHNNY ELLIS-1B/C
24 FELIPE ALOU-OF/1B (2)
25 LEN BOEHMER-3B
26 FRANK BAKER-SS
27 JIM LYTTLE-OF
28 RON HANSEN-INF
29 JIM HARDIN (INJ)-P (2)
30 MEL STOTTLEMYRE-P
31 JIM (MILKMAN JIM) TURNER -CH
32 ELSTON (ELLIE) HOWARD-CH
34 DICK HOWSER-CH
35 RALPH (MAJOR) HOUK-MGR
37 *(RET#) CASEY STENGEL*
38 STEVE KLINE-P
39 GARY JONES-P
39 ROB GARDNER-P (2)
40 LINDY MCDANIEL-P
41 JAKE GIBBS-C
43 ROB GARDNER-P (2)
43 TERRY LEY-P
44 JIM HEGAN-CH
45 STAN BAHNSEN-P
46 ROGER HAMBRIGHT-P
50 BILL BURBACH-P
50 ALAN CLOSTER-P
54 GARY WASLEWSKI-P

1972

4TH E 79-76 6.5GB

1 BOBBY MURCER-OF
2 JERRY KENNEY-SS/3B
3 *(RET#) BABE RUTH*
4 *(RET#) LOU GEHRIG*
5 *(RET#) JOE DIMAGGIO*
6 ROY WHITE-OF
7 *(RET#) MICKEY MANTLE*
8 *(RET#) YOGI BERRA*
8 *(RET#) BILL DICKEY*
10 CELERANO SANCHEZ-3B
11 BERNIE ALLEN-3B/2B
12 RON BLOMBERG-OF
14 RON SWOBODA-OF/1B
15 THURMAN MUNSON-C
17 GENE (STICK) MICHAEL-SS
18 MIKE KEKICH-P
19 FRITZ PETERSON-P
20 HORACE CLARKE-2B
21 RUSTY TORRES-OF
22 JACK AKER-P (1)
22 RON KLIMKOWSKI-P
23 JOHNNY ELLIS-C/1B
24 FELIPE ALOU-1B/OF
25 JOHNNY CALLISON-OF
27 RICH MCKINNEY-3B
28 SPARKY LYLE-P
29 WADE BLASINGAME-P (2)
30 MEL STOTTLEMYRE-P
31 JIM (MILKMAN JIM) TURNER -CH
32 ELSTON (ELLIE) HOWARD-CH
32 WADE BLASINGAME-P (2)
33 ROB GARDNER-P
34 DICK HOWSER-CH
35 RALPH (MAJOR) HOUK-MGR
36 HAL LANIER-INF
37 *(RET#) CASEY STENGEL*
38 STEVE KLINE-P
39 CASEY COX-P (2)
40 LINDY MCDANIEL-P
41 FRANK TEPEDINO-PH
42 CHARLIE SPIKES-OF
43 ROB GARDNER-P
44 JIM HEGAN-CH
45 RICH HINTON-P (1)
45 LARRY GOWELL-P
47 FRED BEENE-P
50 ALAN CLOSTER-P
50 DOC MEDICH-P
54 STEVE BLATERIK-P
54 JIM ROLAND-P (2)

1973

4TH E 80-82 17GB

1 BOBBY MURCER-OF
2 MATTY ALOU-OF/UTIL (1)
3 *(RET#) BABE RUTH*
4 *(RET#) LOU GEHRIG*
5 *(RET#) JOE DIMAGGIO*
6 ROY WHITE-OF
7 *(RET#) MICKEY MANTLE*
8 *(RET#) YOGI BERRA*
8 *(RET#) BILL DICKEY*
9 GRAIG NETTLES-3B/DH
10 CELERANO SANCHEZ-UTIL
11 BERNIE ALLEN-2B/DH (1)
11 FRED STANLEY-SS/2B
12 RON BLOMBERG-DH/1B
14 RON SWOBODA-OF/DH
15 THURMAN MUNSON-C/DH
17 GENE (STICK) MICHAEL-SS
18 MIKE KEKICH-P (1)
18 DAVE PAGAN-P
18 MIKE HEGAN-1B (2)
19 FRITZ PETERSON-P
20 HORACE CLARKE-2B
22 HAL LANIER-INF
23 JERRY MOSES-C/DH
24 FELIPE ALOU-1B/OF (1)
24 OTTO VELEZ-OF
25 JOHNNY CALLISON-OF/DH
28 SPARKY LYLE-P
29 CASEY COX-P
29 SAM (SUDDEN SAM) MCDOWELL-P (2)
29 TOM BUSKEY-P
30 MEL STOTTLEMYRE-P
31 JIM (MILKMAN JIM) TURNER -CH
32 ELSTON (ELLIE) HOWARD-CH
34 DICK HOWSER-CH
35 RALPH (MAJOR) HOUK-MGR
36 PAT DOBSON-P (2)
37 *(RET#) CASEY STENGEL*
38 STEVE KLINE (INJ)-P
39 JIM MAGNUSON-P
39 WAYNE GRANGER-P (2)
40 LINDY MCDANIEL-P
42 DOC MEDICH-P
43 JIM RAY HART-DH (2)
44 JIM HEGAN-CH
45 WAYNE GRANGER-P (2)
46 RICK DEMPSEY-C
47 FRED BEENE-P
48 SAM (SUDDEN SAM) MCDOWELL-P (2)
50 DAVE PAGAN-P
50 DUKE SIMS-DH/C (2)

1974

2ND E 89-73 2GB

1 BOBBY MURCER-OF
2 SANDY ALOMAR-2B/DH (2)
3 *(RET#) BABE RUTH*
4 *(RET#) LOU GEHRIG*
5 *(RET#) JOE DIMAGGIO*
6 ROY WHITE-OF/DH
7 *(RET#) MICKEY MANTLE*
8 *(RET#) YOGI BERRA*
8 *(RET#) BILL DICKEY*
9 GRAIG NETTLES-3B/SS
10 CHRIS CHAMBLISS-1B (2)
11 FRED STANLEY-SS/2B
11 SANDY ALOMAR-2B/DH (2)
12 RON BLOMBERG-DH/OF
13 WALT (NO-NECK) WILLIAMS-DH/OF
14 LOU PINIELLA-OF/UTIL
15 THURMAN MUNSON-C/DH
16 WHITEY (CHAIRMAN OF THE
BOARD) FORD-CH
16 *(RET#) WHITEY FORD*
17 GENE (STICK) MICHAEL-INF
18 MIKE HEGAN-1B (1)
18 LARRY MURRAY-OF
19 FRITZ PETERSON-P (1)
19 DICK TIDROW-P (2)
20 HORACE CLARKE-2B/DH (1)
21 BILL VIRDON-MGR
22 JIM MASON-SS
23 ALEX JOHNSON-DH/OF (2)
24 OTTO VELEZ-UTIL
26 FERNANDO GONZALEZ-INF/DH (2)
27 ELLIOTT MADDOX-OF/INF
28 SPARKY LYLE-P
29 TOM BUSKEY-P (1)
29 DICK WOODSON-P
30 MEL STOTTLEMYRE (INJ)-P
31 MEL WRIGHT-CH
32 ELSTON (ELLIE) HOWARD-CH
33 DOC MEDICH-P
34 DICK HOWSER-CH
35 TIPPY MARTINEZ-P
36 PAT DOBSON-P
37 *(RET#) CASEY STENGEL*
38 STEVE KLINE-P (1)
38 CECIL UPSHAW-P (2)
39 LARRY GURA-P
40 TIPPY MARTINEZ-P
40 RICK SAWYER-P
41 DUKE SIMS-C/DH
41 MIKE WALLACE-P (2)
42 LARRY GURA-P
42 KEN WRIGHT-P
43 JIM RAY HART-DH
43 JIM DEIDEL-C
43 RUDY MAY (INJ)-P (2)
44 BILL (SUDS) SUDAKIS-UTIL
46 RICK DEMPSEY-UTIL
47 FRED BEENE-P (1)
48 SAM (SUDDEN SAM) MCDOWELL (INJ)-P
51 TERRY WHITFIELD-OF
53 DAVE PAGAN-P

1975

3RD E 83-77 12GB

1 BILLY (THE KID) MARTIN-MGR2 (2)
2 SANDY ALOMAR-2B
3 *(RET#) BABE RUTH*
4 *(RET#) LOU GEHRIG*
5 *(RET#) JOE DIMAGGIO*
6 ROY WHITE-OF/UTIL
7 *(RET#) MICKEY MANTLE*
8 *(RET#) YOGI BERRA*
8 *(RET#) BILL DICKEY*
9 GRAIG NETTLES-3B
10 CHRIS CHAMBLISS-1B
11 FRED STANLEY-SS/INF
12 RON BLOMBERG-DH/OF
13 WALT (NO-NECK) WILLIAMS-UTIL
14 LOU PINIELLA (ILL)-OF/DH
15 THURMAN MUNSON-C/UTIL
16 WHITEY (CHAIRMAN OF THE BOARD) FORD-CH
18 DAVE BERGMAN-OF
19 DICK TIDROW-P
20 EDDIE LEON-SS
20 EDDIE BRINKMAN-INF (3)
21 BILL VIRDON-MGR1
22 JIM MASON-SS/2B
23 ALEX JOHNSON-DH//OF
24 OTTO VELEZ-1B/DH
24 RICK BLADT-OF
25 BOBBY BONDS-OF/DH
26 RICH COGGINS-OF/DH (2)
27 ELLIOTT MADDOX (INJ)-OF/2B
28 SPARKY LYLE-P
29 JIM (CATFISH) HUNTER-P
31 MEL WRIGHT-CH
32 ELSTON (ELLIE) HOWARD-CH
33 DOC MEDICH-P
34 DICK HOWSER-CH
36 PAT DOBSON-P
37 *(RET#) CASEY STENGEL*
39 LARRY GURA-P
40 TIPPY MARTINEZ-P
41 MIKE WALLACE-P (1)
41 RICK SAWYER-P
42 BOB OLIVER-UTIL
43 RUDY MAY-P
44 TERRY WHITFIELD-OF
45 ED HERRMANN-DH/C
46 RICK DEMPSEY-UTIL
49 KERRY DINEEN-OF
49 RON (LOUISIANA LIGHTNIN') GUIDRY-P
52 LARRY MURRAY-OF
53 DAVE PAGAN-P
54 RON (LOUISIANA LIGHTNIN') GUIDRY-P
62 CLOYD (JUNIOR) BOYER-CH

1976

1ST E 97-62 0GB

W ALCS-KCA 3-2

L WS-CINN 4-0

1 BILLY (THE KID) MARTIN-MGR
2 SANDY ALOMAR-UTIL
3 *(RET#) BABE RUTH*
4 *(RET#) LOU GEHRIG*
5 *(RET#) JOE DIMAGGIO*
6 ROY WHITE-OF
7 *(RET#) MICKEY MANTLE*
8 YOGI BERRA-CH
8 *(RET#) YOGI BERRA*
8 *(RET#) BILL DICKEY*
9 GRAIG NETTLES-3B/SS
10 CHRIS CHAMBLISS-1B/DH
11 FRED STANLEY-SS/2B
12 RON BLOMBERG (INJ)-DH
13 DOYLE ALEXANDER-P (2)
14 LOU PINIELLA-OF/DH
15 THURMAN MUNSON-C/UTIL
16 *(RET#) WHITEY FORD*
17 MICKEY RIVERS-OF
18 TIPPY MARTINEZ-P (1)
18 ELLIE HENDRICKS-C (2)
19 DICK TIDROW-P
20 MICKEY KLUTTS-SS
21 BOB LEMON-CH
22 JIM MASON-SS
23 OSCAR GAMBLE-OF/DH
24 OTTO VELEZ-UTIL
25 WILLIE RANDOLPH-2B
25 GRANT (BUCK) JACKSON-P (2)
26 RICH COGGINS-OF/DH (1)
26 JUAN BERNHARDT-UTIL
26 CESAR (PEPITO) TOVAR-DH/2B (2)
27 ELLIOTT MADDOX (INJ)-OF/DH
28 SPARKY LYLE-P
29 JIM (CATFISH) HUNTER-P
30 WILLIE RANDOLPH-2B
31 ED FIGUEROA-P
32 ELSTON (ELLIE) HOWARD-CH
33 BOB LEMON-CH
34 DICK HOWSER-CH
36 DOCK ELLIS-P
37 *(RET#) CASEY STENGEL*
38 KEN BRETT-P (1)
38 CARLOS MAY-DH/UTIL (2)
39 GENE (STICK) MICHAEL-CH
40 TIPPY MARTINEZ-P (1)
40 FRAN HEALY-C/DH (2)
43 RUDY MAY-P (1)
43 JIM YORK-P
44 TERRY WHITFIELD-OF
46 RICK DEMPSEY-C/OF (1)
46 GENE LOCKLEAR-OF
47 KERRY DINEEN-OF
47 LARRY MURRAY-OF
49 RON (LOUISIANA LIGHTNIN') GUIDRY-P
52 DOYLE ALEXANDER-P (2)

NEW YORK YANKEES

53 DAVE PAGAN-P (1)
53 KEN HOLTZMAN-P (2)

1977

1st E 100-62 0GB
W ALCS-KCA 3-2
W WS-LAN 4-2

1 BILLY (THE KID) MARTIN-MGR
2 PAUL BLAIR-OF/DH
3 *(RET#) BABE RUTH*
4 *(RET#) LOU GEHRIG*
5 *(RET#) JOE DIMAGGIO*
6 ROY WHITE-OF/DH
7 *(RET#) MICKEY MANTLE*
8 YOGI BERRA-CH
8 *(RET#) YOGI BERRA*
8 *(RET#) BILL DICKEY*
9 GRAIG NETTLES-3B/DH
10 CHRIS CHAMBLISS-1B/DH
11 FRED STANLEY-INF
12) RON BLOMBERG (INJ)-(DH)
14 LOU PINIELLA-UTIL
15 THURMAN MUNSON-C/DH
16 *(RET#) WHITEY FORD*
17 MICKEY RIVERS-OF/DH
18 ELLIE HENDRICKS-C
19 DICK TIDROW-P
20 BUCKY DENT-SS
21 CLOYD (JUNIOR) BOYER-CH
22 GIL PATTERSON (INJ)-P
23 STAN THOMAS-P (2)
24 JIM (THE TOY CANON) WYNN-DH/OF (1)
24 MIKE TORREZ-P (2)
25 GEORGE ZEBER-INF/DH
27 MARTY PEREZ-3B (1)
27 DELL ALSTON-UTIL
28 SPARKY LYLE-P
29 JIM (CATFISH) HUNTER (INJ)-P
30 WILLIE RANDOLPH-2B
31 ED FIGUEROA-P
32 ELSTON (ELLIE) HOWARD-CH
33 BOBBY COX-CH
34 DICK HOWSER-CH
35 DON GULLETT (INJ)-P
36 DOCK ELLIS-P (1)
36 MIKE TORREZ-P (2)
36 STAN THOMAS-P (2)
37 *(RET#) CASEY STENGEL*
38 CARLOS MAY-DH/OF (1)
39 MICKEY KLUTTS-(INJ)-3B/SS
40 FRAN HEALY-C
41 CLIFF JOHNSON-UTIL (2)
42 ART FOWLER-CH
44 REGGIE (MR. OCTOBER) JACKSON-OF/DH
46 GENE LOCKLEAR-OF
48 MIKE TORREZ-P (2)
48 DAVE KINGMAN-DH (4)
49 RON (LOUISIANA LIGHTNIN') GUIDRY-P
50 KEN CLAY-P
51 LARRY MCCALL-P
52 STAN THOMAS-P (2)
53 KEN HOLTZMAN-P
54 DAVE BERGMAN-OF/1B
54 GIL PATTERSON (INJ)-P

1978

1st E 100-63 0GB
W ALCS-KCA 3-1
W WS-LAN 4-2

1 BILLY (THE KID) MARTIN-MGR1
2 PAUL BLAIR-OF/INF
3 *(RET#) BABE RUTH*
4 *(RET#) LOU GEHRIG*
5 *(RET#) JOE DIMAGGIO*
6 ROY WHITE-OF/DH
7 *(RET#) MICKEY MANTLE*
8 YOGI BERRA-CH
8 *(RET#) YOGI BERRA*
8 *(RET#) BILL DICKEY*
9 GRAIG NETTLES-3B/SS
10 CHRIS CHAMBLISS-1B/DH
11 FRED STANLEY-INF
12 JIM SPENCER-DH/1B
14 LOU PINIELLA-OF/DH
15 THURMAN MUNSON-C/UTIL
16 *(RET#) WHITEY FORD*
17 MICKEY RIVERS-OF
18 DENNY SHERRILL-DH/3B
19 DICK TIDROW-P
20 BUCKY DENT (INJ)-SS
21 JAY JOHNSTONE-OF/DH (2)
21 BOB LEMON-MGR3
23 DAMASO GARCIA-2B/SS
24 MICKEY KLUTTS (INJ)-3B (1)
24 GARY THOMASSON-OF/DH (2)
25 GEORGE ZEBER-2B
25 BRIAN DOYLE-INF
26 DOMINGO RAMOS-SS
27 DELL ALSTON-PH (1)
27 JAY JOHNSTONE-OF/DH (2)
28 SPARKY LYLE-P
29 JIM (CATFISH) HUNTER (INJ)-P
30 WILLIE RANDOLPH (INJ)-2B
31 ED FIGUEROA-P
32 ELSTON (ELLIE) HOWARD-CH
33 GENE (STICK) MICHAEL-CH
34 DICK HOWSER-CH/MGR2
35 DON GULLETT (INJ)-P
36 RAWLY EASTWICK-P (1)
36 DAVE RAJSICH-P
36 PAUL LINDBLAD-P (2)
37 *(RET#) CASEY STENGEL*
40 FRAN HEALY (INJ)-C
40 BOB KAMMEYER-P
40 LARRY MCCALL-P
40 PAUL LINDBLAD-P (2)
41 CLIFF JOHNSON-DH/UTIL
42 ART FOWLER-CH
43 KEN CLAY (INJ)-P
44 REGGIE (MR. OCTOBER) JACKSON-OF/DH
45 JIM BEATTIE-P
46 MIKE HEATH-C
47 ANDY MESSERSMITH (INJ)-P
48 CLYDE KING-CH
49 RON (LOUISIANA LIGHTNIN') GUIDRY-P
51 LARRY MCCALL-P
52 DAVE RAJSICH-P
53 KEN HOLTZMAN-P (1)
53 LARRY MCCALL-P
53 RON DAVIS-P
54 GOOSE GOSSAGE-P

1979

4th E 89-71 13.5GB

1 BILLY (THE KID) MARTIN-MGR2
2 PAUL BLAIR-OF (1)
2 DARRYL JONES-DH/OF (2)
2 BOBBY MURCER-OF (2)
3 *(RET#) BABE RUTH*
4 *(RET#) LOU GEHRIG*
5 *(RET#) JOE DIMAGGIO*
6 ROY WHITE-DH/OF
7 *(RET#) MICKEY MANTLE*
8 YOGI BERRA-CH
8 *(RET#) YOGI BERRA*
8 *(RET#) BILL DICKEY*
9 GRAIG NETTLES-3B
10 CHRIS CHAMBLISS-1B/DH
11 FRED STANLEY-UTIL
12 JIM SPENCER-DH/1B
14 LOU PINIELLA-OF/DH
15 THURMAN MUNSON (DIED)-C/UTIL
15 *(RET#) THURMAN MUNSON*
16 *(RET#) WHITEY FORD*
17 MICKEY RIVERS-OF (1)
17 OSCAR GAMBLE-OF/DH (2)
18 BRIAN DOYLE-3B/2B
19 DICK TIDROW-P (1)
19 RICK ANDERSON-P
20 BUCKY DENT-SS
21 BOB LEMON-MGR1
22 BOBBY BROWN-OF/DH (2)
23 LUIS TIANT-P
24 DENNIS WERTH-1B
25 TOMMY (T.J.) JOHN-P
26 JUAN BENIQUEZ (INJ)-OF/3B
27 JAY JOHNSTONE-OF/DH (1)
27 DARRYL JONES-DH/OF (2)
27 BRAD GULDEN-C
29 JIM (CATFISH) HUNTER-P
30 WILLIE RANDOLPH-2B
31 ED FIGUEROA (INJ)-P
31 JEFF TORBORG-CH
32 ELSTON (ELLIE) HOWARD-CH
33 MIKE FERRARO-CH
34 LENNY RANDLE-OF/DH
(35) DON GULLETT (INJ)-(P)
36 PAUL MIRABELLA-P
36 JIM (KITTY) KAAT-P (2)
37 *(RET#) CASEY STENGEL*
38 JERRY NARRON-C/DH
39 RON DAVIS-P
40 CHARLIE LAU-CH
41 CLIFF JOHNSON-DH/C (1)
41 GEORGE (BOOMER) SCOTT-DH/1B (3)
42 TOM (PLOWBOY) MORGAN-CH
42 ART FOWLER-CH
43 KEN CLAY-P
44 REGGIE (MR. OCTOBER) JACKSON (INJ)-OF/DH
45 JIM BEATTIE (INJ)-P
46 DON HOOD-P (2)
47 BRUCE ROBINSON-C
47 JIM (KITTY) KAAT-P (2)
47 JEFF TORBORG-CH
48 JIM HEGAN-CH
49 RON (LOUISIANA LIGHTNIN') GUIDRY-P
50 PAUL MIRABELLA-P
50 ROGER SLAGLE-P
52 ROGER SLAGLE-P
52 MIKE GRIFFIN-P
53 RON DAVIS-P
53 RAY BURRIS-P (2)
53 BOB KAMMEYER-P
54 GOOSE GOSSAGE (INJ)-P
55 PAUL MIRABELLA-P
56 DAVE (RAGS) RIGHETTI-P
57 ROY STAIGER-3B
58 BOBBY BROWN-OF/DH (2)
58 BRUCE ROBINSON-C
59 DAMASO GARCIA-SS/3B

1980

1st E 103-59 0GB
L ALCS-KCA 3-0

2 BOBBY MURCER-OF/DH
3 *(RET#) BABE RUTH*
4 *(RET#) LOU GEHRIG*
5 *(RET#) JOE DIMAGGIO*
6 BRAD GULDEN-C
7 *(RET#) MICKEY MANTLE*
8 YOGI BERRA-CH
8 *(RET#) YOGI BERRA*
8 *(RET#) BILL DICKEY*
9 GRAIG NETTLES (ILL)-3B/SS
10 RICK CERONE-C
11 FRED STANLEY-INF
12 JIM SPENCER-1B/DH
13 BOBBY BROWN-OF/DH
14 LOU PINIELLA-OF/DH
15 *(RET#) THURMAN MUNSON*
16 *(RET#) WHITEY FORD*
17 OSCAR GAMBLE-OF/DH
18 BRIAN DOYLE-INF
19 BRAD GULDEN-C
20 BUCKY DENT-SS
21 ERIC SODERHOLM-DH/3B
22 RUPPERT JONES (ILL/INJ0-OF
23 LUIS TIANT (INJ)-P
24 DENNIS WERTH-UTIL
25 TOMMY (T.J.) JOHN-P
26 JOHNNY OATES-C
27 BRAD GULDEN-C
27 PAUL BLAIR-OF
27 AURELIO RODRIGUEZ-3B/2B (2)
28 BOB (BULL) WATSON-1B/DH
30 WILLIE RANDOLPH-2B
31 ED FIGUEROA-P (1)
33 MIKE FERRARO-CH
34 DICK HOWSER-MGR
(35) DON GULLETT (INJ)-(P)
36 JIM (KITTY) KAAT-P (1)
36 GAYLORD PERRY-P (2)
37 *(RET#) CASEY STENGEL*
38 TOM UNDERWOOD-P
39 RON DAVIS-P
40 CHARLIE LAU-CH
41 JEFF TORBORG-CH
42 STAN WILLIAMS-CH
43 DOUG BIRD-P
44 REGGIE (MR. OCTOBER) JACKSON-OF/DH
45 RUDY MAY-P
46 JOE LEFEBVRE-OF
47 BRUCE ROBINSON-C
48 JIM HEGAN-CH
49 RON (LOUISIANA LIGHTNIN') GUIDRY-P
52 MIKE GRIFFIN-P
53 TIM LOLLAR-P
54 GOOSE GOSSAGE-P
55 ROGER HOLT-2B
56 TED WILBORN-OF
57 CLYDE KING-CH
57 DENNY SHERRILL-SS/2B
59 TED WILBORN-OF
61 MARSHALL BRANT-1B/DH

1981

1st 1/2:1st E 34-22 0GB
2nd 1/2:6th E 25-26 5GB
FINAL: 59-48 --GB
W ALDS-MILA 3-2
W ALCS-OAKA 3-0
L WS-LAN 4-2

2 BOBBY MURCER-DH
3 *(RET#) BABE RUTH*
4 *(RET#) LOU GEHRIG*
5 *(RET#) JOE DIMAGGIO*
7 *(RET#) MICKEY MANTLE*
8 YOGI BERRA-CH
8 *(RET#) YOGI BERRA*
8 *(RET#) BILL DICKEY*
9 GRAIG NETTLES-3B/DH
10 RICK CERONE (INJ)-C
11 GENE (STICK) MICHAEL-MGR1
12 JIM SPENCER-1B (1)
12 DAVE REVERING-1B (2)
13 BOBBY BROWN-OF/DH
14 LOU PINIELLA-OF/DH
15 *(RET#) THURMAN MUNSON*
16 *(RET#) WHITEY FORD*
17 OSCAR GAMBLE-OF/DH
18 LARRY MILBOURNE-INF/DH
19 DAVE (RAGS) RIGHETTI-P
20 BUCKY DENT-SS
(21) ERIC SODERHOLM (INJ)-(3B)
21 BOB LEMON-MGR2
22 JERRY MUMPHREY-OF
23 BARRY FOOTE-UTIL (2)
24 DENNIS WERTH (INJ)-UTIL
25 TOMMY (T.J.) JOHN (INJ)-P
26 JOHNNY OATES-C
27 AURELIO RODRIGUEZ-INF/DH
28 BOB (BULL) WATSON (INJ)-1B/DH
30 WILLIE RANDOLPH-2B
31 DAVE WINFIELD-OF/DH
33 MIKE FERRARO-CH
34 DAVE LAROCHE-P
35 BILL CASTRO-P
36 STEVE BALBONI-1B/DH
36 RICK REUSCHEL-P (2)
37 *(RET#) CASEY STENGEL*
38 TOM UNDERWOOD-P (1)
39 RON DAVIS-P
40 CHARLIE LAU-CH
41 JEFF TORBORG-CH
42 STAN WILLIAMS-CH
42 CLYDE KING-CH
43 DOUG BIRD-P (1)
43 GEORGE FRAZIER-P
44 REGGIE (MR. OCTOBER) JACKSON-OF/DH
45 RUDY MAY-P
46 GENE NELSON-P
(47) BRUCE ROBINSON(INJ)-(C)
48 JOE ALTOBELLI-CH
48 RICK REUSCHEL-P (2)
49 RON (LOUISIANA LIGHTNIN') GUIDRY-P
50 CLYDE KING-CH
52 MIKE GRIFFIN-P (1)
53 JERRY WALKER-CH
54 GOOSE GOSSAGE-P
55 ANDRE ROBERTSON-SS/2B
56 BILL CASTRO-P
56 MIKE PATTERSON-OF (2)
57 TUCKER ASHFORD-2B
58 DAVE WEHRMEISTER-P
58 ANDY MCGAFFIGAN-P
66 STEVE BALBONI-1B/DH
67 GENE NELSON-P

1982

5th E 79-83 16GB

2 BOBBY MURCER-DH
3 *(RET#) BABE RUTH*
4 *(RET#) LOU GEHRIG*
5 *(RET#) JOE DIMAGGIO*
6 KEN GRIFFEY, SR.-OF
7 *(RET#) MICKEY MANTLE*
8 YOGI BERRA-CH
8 *(RET#) YOGI BERRA*
8 *(RET#) BILL DICKEY*
9 GRAIG NETTLES-3B/DH
10 RICK CERONE (INJ)-C
11 GENE (STICK) MICHAEL-MGR2
12 DAVE REVERING-1B/DH (1)
12 JOHN MAYBERRY-1B/DH (2)
14 LOU PINIELLA-DH/OF
15 *(RET#) THURMAN MUNSON*
16 *(RET#) WHITEY FORD*
17 OSCAR GAMBLE-DH/OF
18 LARRY MILBOURNE-INF (1)
18 RODNEY SCOTT-SS/2B (2)
18 MIKE PATTERSON-OF/DH
18 ANDRE ROBERTSON-INF
19 DAVE (RAGS) RIGHETTI-P
20 BUCKY DENT-SS (1)
20 EDDIE RODRIGUEZ-2B
21 BOB LEMON-MGR1
22 JERRY MUMPHREY (INJ)-OF
23 BARRY FOOTE (INJ)-C (2)
24 BUTCH HOBSON-DH/1B
24 LEE MAZZILLI-UTIL (2)
25 TOMMY (T.J.) JOHN-P (1)

25 STEFAN WEVER-P
26 SHANE RAWLEY-P
27 BUTCH WYNEGAR (ILL)-C (2)
28 BOB (BULL) WATSON-1B/DH
28 JOHN MAYBERRY-1B/DH (2)
29 DAVE COLLINS-UTIL
30 WILLIE RANDOLPH-2B/DH
31 DAVE WINFIELD-OF/DH
33 MIKE FERRARO-CH
34 ROY SMALLEY, JR.-SS/UTIL (2)
34 DAVE LAROCHE-P
35 BUTCH HOBSON-DH/1B
35 ROGER ERICKSON (INJ)-P (2)
(36) RICK REUSCHEL (INJ)-(P)
36 STEVE BALBONI-1B/DH
37 *(RET#) CASEY STENGEL*
38 DAVE STEGMAN-DH
38 BARRY EVANS-INF
39 ROY SMALLEY, JR.-SS/UTIL (2)
39 MIKE MORGAN-P
40 MICKEY VERNON-CH
41 JEFF TORBORG-CH
42 JERRY WALKER-CH
42 STAN WILLIAMS-CH
42 CLYDE KING-CH/MGR3
43 GEORGE FRAZIER-P
45 RUDY MAY-P
46 JOE (PEPI) PEPITONE-CH
46 SHANE RAWLEY-P
46 DON MATTINGLY-OF/1B
47 CURT KAUFMAN-P
48 JOE ALTOBELLI-CH
49 RON (LOUISIANA LIGHTNIN') GUIDRY-P
50 JOHN PACELLA-P (1)
50 LYNN MCGLOTHEN-P
52 DOYLE ALEXANDER (INJ)-P
53 JAY HOWELL-P
54 GOOSE GOSSAGE (INJ)-P
55 ROY SMALLEY, JR.-SS/UTIL (2)
56 MIKE PATTERSON-OF/DH
56 ANDRE ROBERTSON-INF
57 BOBBY RAMOS-C
58 JUAN ESPINO-C
58 SAMMY ELLIS-CH
61 JIM LEWIS-P
63 MIKE MORGAN-P
66 STEVE BALBONI-1B/DH

1983

3RD E 91-71 7GB

1 BILLY (THE KID) MARTIN-MGR
2 BOBBY MURCER-DH
3 *(RET#) BABE RUTH*
4 *(RET#) LOU GEHRIG*
5 *(RET#) JOE DIMAGGIO*
6 ROY WHITE-CH
7 *(RET#) MICKEY MANTLE*
8 YOGI BERRA-CH
8 *(RET#) YOGI BERRA*
8 *(RET#) BILL DICKEY*
9 GRAIG NETTLES-3B/DH
10 RICK CERONE (INJ)-C/3B
11 JEFF TORBORG-CH
12 ROY SMALLEY, JR.-SS/UTIL
14 LOU PINIELLA-OF/DH
15 *(RET#) THURMAN MUNSON*
16 *(RET#) WHITEY FORD*
17 OSCAR GAMBLE-OF/DH
18 ANDRE ROBERTSON (INJ)-SS/2B
19 DAVE (RAGS) RIGHETTI-P
20 ROWLAND OFFICE-OF
20 BOBBY MEACHAM-SS/3B
21 STEVE KEMP-OF/DH
22 JERRY MUMPHREY-OF (1)
22 OMAR MORENO-OF
23 DON ZIMMER-CH
24 JOHN (COUNT) MONTEFUSCO-P (2)
25 DON BAYLOR-DH/UTIL
26 SHANE RAWLEY-P
27 BUTCH WYNEGAR-C
28 STEVE BALBONI-1B/DH
28 BOB SHIRLEY-P
30 WILLIE RANDOLPH (INJ)-2B
31 DAVE WINFIELD-OF
33 KEN GRIFFEY, SR. (INJ)-1B/UTIL
34 DAVE LAROCHE-P
34 MATT KEOUGH-P (2)
35 ROGER ERICKSON-P
(36) RICK REUSCHEL (INJ)-(P) (1)
37 *(RET#) CASEY STENGEL*
38 CURT KAUFMAN-P
38 DAVE LAROCHE-P
39 OTIS NIXON-OF
39 LARRY MILBOURNE-INF (2)
40 DON ZIMMER-CH
41 JEFF TORBORG-CH
41 SAMMY ELLIS-CH
42 ART FOWLER-CH
43 GEORGE FRAZIER-P
45 RUDY MAY (INJ)-P
46 DON MATTINGLY-UTIL
47? CURT KAUFMAN-P
47 RAY FONTENOT-P
48 DALE MURRAY-P
49 RON (LOUISIANA LIGHTNIN') GUIDRY-P
50 JAY HOWELL (INJ)-P
52 DOYLE ALEXANDER (INJ)-P (1)
52 OTIS NIXON-OF
53 JAY HOWELL (INJ)-P
53 LEE WALLS-CH
54 GOOSE GOSSAGE-P
56 BERT (CAMPY) CAMPANERIS-2B/3B
57 RAY FONTENOT-P
58 JUAN ESPINO-C
62 BRIAN DAYETT-OF
65 JUAN ESPINO-C
66 STEVE BALBONI-1B/DH

1984

3RD E 87-75 17GB

2 TIM FOLI-INF
3 *(RET#) BABE RUTH*
4 *(RET#) LOU GEHRIG*
5 *(RET#) JOE DIMAGGIO*
6 ROY WHITE-CH
7 *(RET#) MICKEY MANTLE*
8 YOGI BERRA-MGR
8 *(RET#) YOGI BERRA*
8 *(RET#) BILL DICKEY*
9 *(RET#) ROGER MARIS*
10 RICK CERONE (INJ)-C
11 TOBY HARRAH-3B/UTIL
12 ROY SMALLEY, JR.-INF/DH (1)
13 KEITH SMITH-SS
14 LOU PINIELLA-OF/DH
15 *(RET#) THURMAN MUNSON*
16 *(RET#) WHITEY FORD*
17 OSCAR GAMBLE (INJ)-DH/OF
18 ANDRE ROBERTSON-SS/2B
19 DAVE (RAGS) RIGHETTI-P
20 BOBBY MEACHAM-SS/2B
21 STEVE KEMP-OF/DH
22 OMAR MORENO-OF/DH
23 DON MATTINGLY-1B/OF
24 JOHN (COUNT) MONTEFUSCO (INJ)-P
25 DON BAYLOR-DH/OF
26 SHANE RAWLEY-P (1)
27 BUTCH WYNEGAR-C
29 BOB SHIRLEY-P
30 WILLIE RANDOLPH-2B
31 DAVE WINFIELD-OF
32 *(RET#) ELSTON HOWARD*
33 KEN GRIFFEY, SR. (INJ)-UTIL
34 SCOTT BRADLEY-OF/C
35 PHIL NIEKRO-P
36 MIKE ARMSTRONG (INJ)-P
37 *(RET#) CASEY STENGEL*
38 JOSE RIJO-P
40 GENE (STICK) MICHAEL-CH
41 SAMMY ELLIS-CH
41 JOE COWLEY-P
42 DOUG HOLMQUIST-CH
43 JERRY MCNERTNEY-CH
44 JEFF TORBORG-CH
45 DENNIS RASMUSSEN-P
46 DON MATTINGLY-1B/OF
46 MIKE (PAGS) PAGLIARULO-3B
47 RAY FONTENOT-P
48 DALE MURRAY (INJ)-P
49 RON (LOUISIANA LIGHTNIN') GUIDRY-P
50 JAY HOWELL (INJ)-P
52 MARK CONNOR-CH
53 MARTY BYSTROM (INJ)-P (2)
55 STAN JAVIER-OF
55 VIC MATA-OF
56 CURT BROWN-P
56 REX HUDLER-2B
58 MIKE O'BERRY-C/3B
62 BRIAN DAYETT-OF/DH
66 JIM DESHAIES-P
67 CLAY CHRISTIANSEN-P

1985

2ND E 97-64 2GB

1 BILLY (THE KID) MARTIN-MGR2
2 DALE BERRA-3B/SS
3 *(RET#) BABE RUTH*
4 *(RET#) LOU GEHRIG*
5 *(RET#) JOE DIMAGGIO*
6 MIKE (PAGS) PAGLIARULO-3B
7 *(RET#) MICKEY MANTLE*
8 YOGI BERRA-MGR1
8 *(RET#) YOGI BERRA*
8 *(RET#) BILL DICKEY*
9 *(RET#) ROGER MARIS*
10 *(RET#) PHIL RIZZUTO*
11 BILLY SAMPLE-OF
12 RON HASSEY-UTIL
13 KEITH SMITH-SS
14 LOU PINIELLA-CH
15 *(RET#) THURMAN MUNSON*
16 *(RET#) WHITEY FORD*
17 VIC MATA-OF
18 ANDRE ROBERTSON (INJ)-INF
19 DAVE (RAGS) RIGHETTI-P
20 BOBBY MEACHAM-SS
21 DAN PASQUA-OF/DH
22 OMAR MORENO-OF/DH (1)
23 DON MATTINGLY-1B
24 RICKEY HENDERSON-OF/DH
25 DON BAYLOR-DH
26 JOHN (COUNT) MONTEFUSCO (INJ)-P
26 NEIL ALLEN-P (2)
26 JOE NIEKRO-P (2)
27 BUTCH WYNEGAR-C
28 BILL (MOMBO) MONBOQUETTE-CH
29 BOB SHIRLEY-P
30 WILLIE RANDOLPH-2B
31 DAVE WINFIELD-OF/DH
32 *(RET#) ELSTON HOWARD*
33 KEN GRIFFEY, SR. (INJ)-OF/UTIL
34 SCOTT BRADLEY (INJ)-DH/C
35 PHIL NIEKRO-P
36 MIKE ARMSTRONG-P
37 *(RET#) CASEY STENGEL*
38 ED WHITSON-P
39 DON COOPER-P
39 NEIL ALLEN-P (2)
40 GENE (STICK) MICHAEL-CH
41 JOE COWLEY-P
42 STUMP MERRILL-CH
42 DOUG HOLMQUIST-CH
43 RICH BORDI-P
44 JEFF TORBORG-CH
45 DENNIS RASMUSSEN-P
46 HENRY COTTO (INJ)-OF
47 ROD SCURRY-P (2)
48 DALE MURRAY-P (1)
48 WILLIE HORTON-CH
49 RON (LOUISIANA LIGHTNIN') GUIDRY-P
50 MARTY BYSTROM (INJ)-P
52 MARK CONNOR-CH
52 JUAN ESPINO-C
53 MARTY BYSTROM (INJ)-P
53 NEIL ALLEN-P (2)
54 BRIAN FISHER-P
55 VIC MATA-OF
55 JUAN BONILLA-2B
56 REX HUDLER-INF
58 JUAN ESPINO-C

1986

2ND E 90-72 5.5GB

1 GENE (STICK) MICHAEL-CH
1 *(RET#) BILLY MARTIN*
2 DALE BERRA-INF/DH
2 WAYNE TOLLESON-SS/INF (2)
3 *(RET#) BABE RUTH*
4 *(RET#) LOU GEHRIG*
5 *(RET#) JOE DIMAGGIO*
6 ROY WHITE-CH
7 *(RET#) MICKEY MANTLE*
8 *(RET#) YOGI BERRA*
8 *(RET#) BILL DICKEY*
9 *(RET#) ROGER MARIS*
10 *(RET#) PHIL RIZZUTO*
11 GARY ROENICKE-UTIL
12 RON HASSEY-C/DH (1)
12 JOEL SKINNER-C (2)
13 MIKE (PAGS) PAGLIARULO-3B
14 LOU PINIELLA-MGR
15 *(RET#) THURMAN MUNSON*
16 *(RET#) WHITEY FORD*
17 MIKE EASLER-DH/OF
18 CLAUDELL WASHINGTON-OF (2)
19 DAVE (RAGS) RIGHETTI-P
20 BOBBY MEACHAM-SS
21 DAN PASQUA-OF/UTIL
22 MIKE FISCHLIN-SS/2B
23 DON MATTINGLY-1B/UTIL
24 RICKEY HENDERSON-OF/DH
25 TOMMY (T.J.) JOHN (INJ)-P
26 JOHN (COUNT) MONTEFUSCO (INJ)-P
26 JOE NIEKRO-P
26 IVAN DEJESUS-SS
26 PAUL ZUVELLA-SS
26 BRYAN (TWIG) LITTLE-2B (2)
27 BUTCH WYNEGAR (ILL)-C
28 ROD SCURRY-P
29 BOB SHIRLEY-P
30 WILLIE RANDOLPH-2B/DH
31 DAVE WINFIELD-OF/UTIL
32 *(RET#) ELSTON HOWARD*
33 KEN GRIFFEY, SR.-OF/DH (1)
33 TIM STODDARD-P (2)
33 RON KITTLE-DH/OF (2)
34 DOUG DRABEK-P
34 RON HASSEY-C/DH (1)
34 MIKE ARMSTONG-P
35 BOB TEWKSBURY-P
36 AL HOLLAND-P
36 MIKE ARMSTONG-P
37 *(RET#) CASEY STENGEL*
38 ED WHITSON-P (1)
38 LEO HERNANDEZ-3B/2B
39 JOE NIEKRO-P
40 GENE (STICK) MICHAEL-CH
40 DON (ZIM) (POPEYE) ZIMMER-CH
41 SAMMY ELLIS-CH
41 SCOTT NIELSON-P
42 STUMP MERRILL-CH
43 TIM STODDARD-P (2)
44 JEFF TORBORG-CH
45 DENNIS RASMUSSEN-P
46 HENRY COTTO-OF/DH
47 ALFONSO PULIDO-P
48 JOE ALTOBELLI-CH
49 RON (LOUISIANA LIGHTNIN') GUIDRY-P
50 PHIL LOMBARDI-OF/C
52 MARK CONNOR-CH
53 AL HOLLAND-P
53 JOHN (COUNT) MONTEFUSCO (INJ)-P
54 BRIAN FISHER-P
56 AL HOLLAND-P
58 JUAN ESPINO-C
62 BRAD ARNSBERG-P
68 BRAD ARNSBERG-P

1987

4TH E 89-73 9GB

1 *(RET#) BILLY MARTIN*
2 WAYNE TOLLESON-SS/3B
3 *(RET#) BABE RUTH*
4 *(RET#) LOU GEHRIG*
5 *(RET#) JOE DIMAGGIO*
6* RICK CERONE-C/1B/P*
7 *(RET#) MICKEY MANTLE*
8 *(RET#) YOGI BERRA*
8 *(RET#) BILL DICKEY*
9 *(RET#) ROGER MARIS*
10 *(RET#) PHIL RIZZUTO*
11 LENN SAKATA (INJ)-3B/2B
12 JOEL SKINNER-C
12 MARK SALAS-UTIL
13 MIKE (PAGS) PAGLIARULO-3B/1B
14 LOU PINIELLA-MGR
15 *(RET#) THURMAN MUNSON*
16 *(RET#) WHITEY FORD*
17 HENRY COTTO-OF
17 PAUL ZUVELLA-INF
17 MIKE EASLER-DH/OF (2)
18 CLAUDELL WASHINGTON-OF/DH
19 DAVE (RAGS) RIGHETTI-P
20 BOBBY MEACHAM-INF/DH
21 DAN PASQUA-UTIL
22 GARY WARD-OF/UTIL
23 DON MATTINGLY-1B/DH
24 RICKEY HENDERSON (INJ)-OF/DH
25 TOMMY (T.J.) JOHN-P
26 PAUL ZUVELLA-INF
26 RICK RHODEN-P
27 KEITH HUGHES-PH (1)
27 MARK SALAS-UTIL
28 RANDY VELARDE-SS
28 HENRY COTTO-OF
29 BOB SHIRLEY-P (1)
29 PAUL ZUVELLA-INF
29 AL HOLLAND-P
29 RANDY VELARDE-SS
30 WILLIE RANDOLPH (INJ)-2B/DH
31 DAVE WINFIELD-OF/DH
32 *(RET#) ELSTON HOWARD*
33 RON KITTLE (INJ)-DH/OF (2)
34 MIKE FERRARO-CH

NEW YORK YANKEES

35 BOB TEWKSBURY-P (1)
35 STEVE TROUT-P
36 JEFF MORONKO-INF/OF
36 BRAD ARNSBERG (INJ)-P
37 *(RET#) CASEY STENGEL*
38 PAT CLEMENTS-P
39 BOBBY MURCER-CH
39 JOE NIEKRO-P (1)
39 BILL GULLICKSON-P (2)
39 ROBERTO KELLY-OF/DH
40 STAN WILLIAMS-CH
41 CHARLES HUDSON-P
42 STUMP MERRILL-CH
43 TIM STODDARD-P
44 JEFF TORBORG-CH
45 DENNIS RASMUSSEN-P (1)
45 BILL GULLICKSON-P (2)
46 HENRY COTTO-OF
46 RICH BORDI-P
46 JERRY ROYSTER-INF/OF (2)
47 JUAN BONILLA-INF/DH
47 PETE FILSON-P
48 NEIL ALLEN-P
49 RON (LOUISIANA LIGHTNIN') GUIDRY-P
50 JAY WARD-CH
51 CECILIO GUANTE (INJ)-P
52 MARK CONNOR-CH
53 KEITH HUGHES-PH (1)
53 ORESTES DESTRADE-1B/DH
54 CECILIO GUANTE (INJ)-P
54 BRAD ARNSBERG (INJ)-P
54 JAY BUHNER-OF
55? MIKE FENNEL-CH
56 AL LEITER-P
57 ROBERTO KELLY-OF/DH
57 JUAN BONILLA-INF/DH
58 JUAN ESPINO-C
58 AL HOLLAND-P
59 ROBERTO KELLY-OF/DH
61 PHIL LOMBARDI-C
61 ORESTES DESTRADE-1B/DH
64 BILL FULTON-P

1988

5TH E | 85-76 | 5GB

1 BILLY (THE KID) MARTIN-MGR1
1 *(RET#) BILLY MARTIN*
2 WAYNE TOLLESON (INJ)-INF
3 *(RET#) BABE RUTH*
4 *(RET#) LOU GEHRIG*
5 *(RET#) JOE DIMAGGIO*
6 CLETE BOYER-CH
6 JACK CLARK-DH/UTIL
7 *(RET#) MICKEY MANTLE*
8 *(RET#) YOGI BERRA*
8 *(RET#) BILL DICKEY*
9 *(RET#) ROGER MARIS*
10 *(RET#) PHIL RIZZUTO*
11 DON SLAUGHT (INJ)-C/DH
12 JOEL SKINNER-C
13 MIKE (PAGS) PAGLIARULO-3B
14 LOU PINIELLA-MGR2
15 *(RET#) THURMAN MUNSON*
16 *(RET#) WHITEY FORD*
17 RAFAEL SANTANA-SS
18 CLAUDELL WASHINGTON-OF/DH
19 DAVE (RAGS) RIGHETTI-P
20 BOBBY MEACHAM (INJ)-INF
21 JOSE CRUZ-DH/OF
21 KEN PHELPS-DH/1B (2)
22 GARY WARD-UTIL
23 DON MATTINGLY-1B/UTIL
24 RICKEY HENDERSON-OF/DH
25 TOMMY (T.J.) JOHN-P
26 RICK RHODEN-P
27 NEIL ALLEN (INJ)-P
28 AL LEITER (INJ)-P
29 RANDY VELARDE-INF
29 LUIS AGUAYO-INF (2)
30 WILLIE RANDOLPH (INJ)-2B
31 DAVE WINFIELD-OF/DH
32 *(RET#) ELSTON HOWARD*
33 JACK CLARK-DH/UTIL
33 STEVE SHIELDS-P
34 MIKE FERRARO-CH
35 LEE GUETTERMAN-P
36 RICH DOTSON-P
37 *(RET#) CASEY STENGEL*
38 PAT CLEMENTS-P
38? HAL MORRIS-OF/DH
39 ROBERTO KELLY-OF/DH
40 CLETE BOYER-CH
40 STEVE SHIELDS-P
40 CLYDE KING-CH
41 CHARLES HUDSON (INJ)-P
42 ART FOWLER-CH
42 STAN WILLIAMS-CH
43 TIM STODDARD-P
44 JEFF TORBORG-CH
45 JOHN (CANDY MAN) CANDELARIA (INJ)-P
46 HIPOLITO PENA-P
46 RANDY VELARDE-INF
47 ALVARO ESPINOZA-2B/SS
47 SCOTT NIELSON-P
48 GEORGE MITTERWALD-CH
48 GENE (STICK) MICHAEL-CH
49 RON (LOUISIANA LIGHTNIN') GUIDRY-P
50 CHRIS CHAMBLISS-PH/CH
51 CECILIO GUANTE (INJ)-P (1)
52 DALE MOHORCIC-P (2)
52 BOB GEREN-C
52 DAVE EILAND-P
54 JAY BUHNER-OF (1)
54 DALE MOHORCIC-P (2)
57 BOB GEREN-C
58 BOB GEREN-C
60 HIPOLITO PENA-P
62 HAL MORRIS-OF/DH

1989

5TH E | 74-87 | 14.5GB

1 *(RET#) BILLY MARTIN*
2 WAYNE TOLLESON-INF/DH
3 *(RET#) BABE RUTH*
4 *(RET#) LOU GEHRIG*
5 *(RET#) JOE DIMAGGIO*
6 STEVE SAX-2B
7 *(RET#) MICKEY MANTLE*
8 *(RET#) YOGI BERRA*
8 *(RET#) BILL DICKEY*
9 *(RET#) ROGER MARIS*
10 *(RET#) PHIL RIZZUTO*
11 DON SLAUGHT-C/DH
12 TOM BROOKENS (INJ)-UTIL
13 MIKE (PAGS) PAGLIARULO-3B/DH (1)
13 MIKE BLOWERS-3B
15 *(RET#) THURMAN MUNSON*
16 *(RET#) WHITEY FORD*
(17) RAFAEL SANTANA (INJ)-(SS)
18 RANDY VELARDE-3B/SS
19 DAVE (RAGS) RIGHETTI-P
20 ALVARO ESPINOZA-SS
21 KEN PHELPS-DH/1B (1)
21 HAL MORRIS-UTIL
22 GARY WARD-OF/DH (1)
22 HAL MORRIS-UTIL
22 LUIS POLONIA-OF/DH (2)
23 DON MATTINGLY-1B/UTIL
24 RICKEY HENDERSON-OF (1)
24 DEION (NEON DEION) SANDERS (FB)-OF
24 MARCUS LAWTON-OF/DH
25 TOMMY (T.J.) JOHN-P
25 GREG CADARET-P (2)
26 STAN JEFFERSON-OF/DH (1)
26 JIMMY JONES-P
26 STEVE KIEFER (INJ)-3B
27 JAMIE QUIRK-UTIL (1)
27 MEL HALL (INJ)-OF/DH
28 AL LEITER-P (1)
28 JESSE BARFIELD-OF (2)
28 DAVE EILAND-P
28 DALE MOHORCIC-P
29 DAVE LAPOINT (INJ)-P
29 JESSE BARFIELD-OF (2)
30 BUCKY DENT-MGR2
(31) DAVE WINFIELD (INJ)-(OF)
32 *(RET#) ELSTON HOWARD*
33 BOB BROWER-OF
33 SCOTT NIELSON-P
33 ERIC PLUNK-P (2)
34 RICH DOTSON-P (1)
34 DON SCHULTZE-P (1)
34 BOBBY DAVIDSON-P
34 WALT TERRELL-P (2)
35 LEE GUETTERMAN-P
36 RICH DOTSON-P (1)
36 BILLY CONNORS-CH
37 *(RET#) CASEY STENGEL*
38 CLAY PARKER-P
39 ROBERTO KELLY-OF
40 ANDY HAWKINS-P
41 LANCE MCCULLERS-P
42 BILLY CONNORS-CH
42 DAVE LAPOINT (INJ)-P
43 LEE ELIA-CH
43 GENE (STICK) MICHAEL-CH
44 JOHN STEARNS-CH
45 JOHN (CANDY MAN) CANDELARIA (INJ)-P (1)
45 KEVIN MMAHAT-P
46 DALLAS GREEN-MGR1
47 PAT CORRALES-CH
47 CHAMP SUMMERS-CH
48 FRANK (THE CAPITAL PUNISHER) (HONDO) HOWARD-CH
50 STEVE BALBONI-DH/1B
51 DON SCHULTZE-P (1)
51 CHUCK CARY (INJ)-P
52 CHARLIE (IRISH) FOX-CH
52 MIKE FERRARO-CH
53 BOB GEREN-C/DH
54 DALE MOHORCIC-P
54 DON SCHULTZE-P (1)
54 GOOSE GOSSAGE-P (2)
55 SCOTT NIELSON-P
55? MIKE FENNEL-CH
56 BRIAN DORSETT-C
57 HENSLEY (BAM-BAM) MEULENS-3B

1990

7TH E | 67-95 | 21GB

1 *(RET#) BILLY MARTIN*
2 WAYNE TOLLESON-INF/DH
3 *(RET#) BABE RUTH*
4 *(RET#) LOU GEHRIG*
5 *(RET#) JOE DIMAGGIO*
6 STEVE SAX-2B
7 *(RET#) MICKEY MANTLE*
8 *(RET#) YOGI BERRA*
8 *(RET#) BILL DICKEY*
9 *(RET#) ROGER MARIS*
10 *(RET#) PHIL RIZZUTO*
11 RICK CERONE (INJ)-UTIL
12 ALVARO ESPINOZA-SS
12 JIM LEYRITZ-3B/UTIL
13 ALVARO ESPINOZA-SS
15 *(RET#) THURMAN MUNSON*
16 *(RET#) WHITEY FORD*
17 CLAUDELL WASHINGTON-(INJ)-OF/DH (2)
18 RANDY VELARDE-UTIL
19 DAVE (RAGS) RIGHETTI-P
20 BUCKY DENT-MGR1
20 ALVARO ESPINOZA-SS
21 DEION (NEON DEION) SANDERS (FB)-OF/DH
21 KEVIN MAAS-1B/DH
21 MIKE BLOWERS-3B
22 LUIS POLONIA-DH (1)
22 MIKE WITT (INJ)-P (2)
23 DON MATTINGLY (INJ)-1B/UTIL
24 MIKE BLOWERS-3B
24 KEVIN MAAS-1B/DH
25 GREG CADARET-P
26 JIMMY JONES-P
27 MEL HALL-DH/OF
28 TIM LEARY-P
28 ALAN MILLS-P
28 BRIAN DORSETT-C
29 JESSE BARFIELD-OF
30 BUCKY DENT-MGR1
31 DAVE WINFIELD (INJ)-OF/DH (1)
31 BRIAN DORSETT-C
31 HENSLEY (BAM-BAM) MEULENS-3B
32 *(RET#) ELSTON HOWARD*
33 ERIC PLUNK-P
34 PASCUAL PEREZ (INJ)-P
35 LEE GUETTERMAN-P
36 BILLY CONNORS-CH
37 *(RET#) CASEY STENGEL*
38 CLAY PARKER-P (1)
38 MATT NOKES-UTIL (2)
39 ROBERTO KELLY-OF/DH
40 ANDY HAWKINS-P
41 LANCE MCCULLERS-P (1)
41 STUMP MERRILL-MGR2
41 DARRELL EVANS-CH
42 DAVE LAPOINT (INJ)-P
43 JEFF ROBINSON-P
44 MIKE FERRARO-CH
45 STEVE BALBONI-DH/1B
46 JOE SPARKS-CH
46 STUMP MERRILL-MGR2
47 CHAMP SUMMERS-CH
47 MARC HILL-CH
48 BUCK SHOWALTER-CH
50 JOHN HABYAN-P
50 OSCAR AZOCAR-OF/DH
51 CHUCK CARY (INJ)-P
52 MARK CONNOR-CH
53 BOB GEREN-C/DH
54 TIM LEARY-P
55 RICH MONTELEONE-P
56 MARK LEITER-P
58 DAVE EILAND-P
59 DAVE EILAND-P
59 STEVE ADKINS-P
60 JOHN HABYAN-P
61 JOHN HABYAN-P
62 STEVE ADKINS-P
63 JIM WALEWANDER-INF/DH
64 ALAN MILLS-P
69 ALAN MILLS-P

1991

5TH E | 71-91 | 20GB

1 *(RET#) BILLY MARTIN*
2 GRAIG NETTLES-CH
3 *(RET#) BABE RUTH*
4 *(RET#) LOU GEHRIG*
5 *(RET#) JOE DIMAGGIO*
6 STEVE SAX-2B/3B
7 *(RET#) MICKEY MANTLE*
8 *(RET#) YOGI BERRA*
8 *(RET#) BILL DICKEY*
9 *(RET#) ROGER MARIS*
10 *(RET#) PHIL RIZZUTO*
11 BUCK SHOWALTER-CH
12 JIM LEYRITZ-UTIL
12 TOREY LOVULLO-3B
12 CARLOS RODRIGUEZ-SS/2B
13 TOREY LOVULLO-3B
14 MIKE BLOWERS-3B
14 PAT KELLY-3B/2B
15 *(RET#) THURMAN MUNSON*
16 *(RET#) WHITEY FORD*
17 SCOTT LUSADER (INJ)-OF/DH
17 PAT SHERIDAN-OF/DH
18 RANDY VELARDE-UTIL
20 ALVARO ESPINOZA-SS/3B/P
21 SCOTT SANDERSON-P
22 STUMP MERRILL-MGR
23 DON MATTINGLY-1B/DH
24 KEVIN MAAS-DH/1B
25 GREG CADARET-P
26 STEVE FARR-P
27 MEL HALL-OF/DH
28 DAVE EILAND-P
29 JESSE BARFIELD (INJ)-OF
31 HENSLEY (BAM-BAM) MEULENS-UTIL
32 *(RET#) ELSTON HOWARD*
33 ERIC PLUNK-P
34 PASCUAL PEREZ (INJ)-P
35 LEE GUETTERMAN-P
36 MIKE WITT (INJ)-P
36 MIKE HUMPHREYS-UTIL
37 *(RET#) CASEY STENGEL*
38 MATT NOKES-C/DH
39 ROBERTO KELLY (INJ)-OF
40 ANDY HAWKINS-P (1)
40 SCOTT KAMIENIECKI (INJ)-P
41 WADE TAYLOR-P
42 JOHN HABYAN-P
43 TOREY LOVULLO-3B
43 JEFF JOHNSON-P
44 MIKE FERRARO-CH
45 RICH MONTELEONE-P
46 FRANK (THE CAPITAL PUNISHER) (HONDO) HOWARD-CH
47 MARC HILL-CH
48 BUCK SHOWALTER-CH
48 JOHN RAMOS-C/DH
50 ALAN MILLS-P
51 CHUCK CARY (INJ)-P
51 BERNIE WILLIAMS-OF
52 MARK CONNOR-CH
53 BOB GEREN-C
54 TIM LEARY-P
55 RICH MONTELEONE-P
57 JOHN HABYAN-P
57 STEVE HOWE (INJ)-P
60 DARRIN CHAPIN-P

1992

4TH E (TIE) | 76-86 | 20GB

1 *(RET#) BILLY MARTIN*
2 MIKE GALLEGO-2B/SS
3 *(RET#) BABE RUTH*
4 *(RET#) LOU GEHRIG*
5 *(RET#) JOE DIMAGGIO*
6 CLETE BOYER-CH
7 *(RET#) MICKEY MANTLE*
8 *(RET#) YOGI BERRA*
8 *(RET#) BILL DICKEY*
9 *(RET#) ROGER MARIS*
10 *(RET#) PHIL RIZZUTO*
11 BUCK SHOWALTER-MGR
12 JIM LEYRITZ-UTIL
13 GERALD WILLIAMS-OF
14 PAT KELLY-2B
15 *(RET#) THURMAN MUNSON*
16 *(RET#) WHITEY FORD*
17 ANDY (STANKY) STANKIEWICZ-SS/2B
18 RANDY VELARDE-UTIL
19 DION JAMES-OF/DH
20 MIKE STANLEY-UTIL
21 SCOTT SANDERSON-P
22 SCOTT KAMIENIECKI (INJ)-P
23 DON MATTINGLY-1B/DH
24 KEVIN MAAS-DH/1B
25 GREG CADARET-P
26 STEVE FARR-P
27 MEL HALL-OF/DH
28 CHARLIE HAYES-3B/1B

29 JESSE BARFIELD (INJ)-OF
31 MIKE HUMPHREYS-OF/DH
31 BOB WICKMAN-P
32 *(RET#) ELSTON HOWARD*
33 MELIDO PEREZ-P
34 MIKE HUMPHREYS-OF/DH
34 JERRY NIELSEN-P
35 LEE GUETTERMAN-P
35 CURT YOUNG-P (2)
36 SHAWN HILLEGAS-P
36 RUSS SPRINGER-P
37 *(RET#) CASEY STENGEL*
38 MATT NOKES-C
39 ROBERTO KELLY (INJ)-OF
40 TONY CLONINGER-CH
41 RUSS SPRINGER-P
41 TIM BURKE-P
42 JOHN HABYAN-P
43 JEFF JOHNSON-P
43 SAM MILITELLO-P
45 DANNY TARTABULL-OF/DH
46 FRANK (THE CAPITAL PUNISHER) (HONDO) HOWARD-CH
48 RUSS (MONK) MEYER-CH
49 JEFF JOHNSON-P
50 ED NAPOLEON-CH
51 BERNIE WILLIAMS-OF
52 MARK CONNOR-CH
53 GLENN SHERLOCK-CH??
54 TIM LEARY-P
54 STERLING HITCHCOCK-P
55 RICH MONTELEONE-P
56 DAVE SILVESTRI-SS
57 STEVE HOWE (INJ)-P
59 HENSLEY (BAM-BAM) MEULENS-3B
60 J. T. SNOW-1B/DH

1993

2ND E 88-74 7GB

1 *(RET#) BILLY MARTIN*
2 MIKE GALLEGO-INF/DH
3 *(RET#) BABE RUTH*
4 *(RET#) LOU GEHRIG*
5 *(RET#) JOE DIMAGGIO*
6 CLETE BOYER-CH
7 *(RET#) MICKEY MANTLE*
8 *(RET#) YOGI BERRA*
8 *(RET#) BILL DICKEY*
9 *(RET#) ROGER MARIS*
10 *(RET#) PHIL RIZZUTO*
11 BUCK SHOWALTER-MGR
12 WADE BOGGS-3B/DH
13 JIM LEYRITZ-UTIL
14 PAT KELLY-2B
15 *(RET#) THURMAN MUNSON*
16 *(RET#) WHITEY FORD*
17 SPIKE OWEN-SS/DH
18 RANDY VELARDE (INJ)-UTIL
19 DION JAMES-OF/UTIL
20 MIKE STANLEY-C/DH
21 PAUL O'NEILL (INJ)-OF/DH
22 JIMMY KEY-P
23 DON MATTINGLY (INJ)-1B/DH
24 KEVIN MAAS-DH/1B
25 JIM ABBOTT-P
26 STEVE FARR-P
27 BOB WICKMAN-P
28 SCOTT KAMIENIECKI-P
28 ANDY (STANKY) STANKIEWICZ-INF/DH
29 MIKE HUMPHREYS-OF/DH
31 HENSLEY (BAM-BAM) MEULENS-UTIL
31 FRANK TANANA-P (2)
32 *(RET#) ELSTON HOWARD*
33 MELIDO PEREZ (INJ)-P
34 SAM MILITELLO-P
34 ANDY COOK-P
34 STERLING HITCHCOCK-P
35 ANDY (STANKY) STANKIEWICZ-INF/DH
35 PAUL GIBSON-P (2)
36 GERALD WILLIAMS-OF/DH
37 *(RET#) CASEY STENGEL*
38 MATT NOKES-C/DH
39 MIKE WITT (INJ)-P
40 TONY CLONINGER-CH
41 JAKE GIBBS-CH
42 JOHN HABYAN-P (1)
42 DOMINGO JEAN-P
43 JEFF JOHNSON-P
43 PAUL ASSENMACHER-P (2)
44 *(RET#) REGGIE JACKSON*
45 DANNY TARTABULL-DH/OF
46 FRANK (THE CAPITAL PUNISHER) (HONDO) HOWARD-CH
47 DAVE SILVESTRI-SS/3B
47 LEE SMITH-P (2)
48 RICK DOWN-CH
50 ED NAPOLEON-CH
51 BERNIE WILLIAMS-OF
52 MARK CONNOR-CH
53 NEAL HEATON-P
53 MARK HUTTON-P
54 BOBBY MUNOZ-P
55 RICH MONTELEONE-P
57 STEVE HOWE (INJ)-P

1994

1ST E 70-43 0GB
STRIKE NO POST-SEASON

1 *(RET#) BILLY MARTIN*
2 MIKE GALLEGO (INJ)-INF/DH
3 *(RET#) BABE RUTH*
4 *(RET#) LOU GEHRIG*
5 *(RET#) JOE DIMAGGIO*
6 CLETE BOYER-CH
7 *(RET#) MICKEY MANTLE*
8 *(RET#) YOGI BERRA*
8 *(RET#) BILL DICKEY*
9 *(RET#) ROGER MARIS*
10 *(RET#) PHIL RIZZUTO*
11 BUCK SHOWALTER-MGR
12 WADE BOGGS-3B/DH
13 JIM LEYRITZ-DH
14 PAT KELLY (INJ)-2B
15 *(RET#) THURMAN MUNSON*
16 *(RET#) WHITEY FORD*
17 LUIS POLONIA-OF
18 RANDY VELARDE (INJ)-UTIL
19 BOB OJEDA (REL)-P
19 KEVIN ELSTER (INJ)-SS
20 MIKE STANLEY (INJ)-C/DH
21 PAUL O'NEILL-OF/DH
22 JIMMY KEY-P
23 DON MATTINGLY (INJ)-1B/DH
24 RUSS DAVIS-3B
25 JIM ABBOTT-P
26 DARYL BOSTON-OF
27 BOB WICKMAN-P
28 SCOTT KAMIENIECKI-P
29 GERALD WILLIAMS-OF/DH
30 WILLIE RANDOLPH-CH
31 XAVIER HERNANDEZ (INJ)-P
32 *(RET#) ELSTON HOWARD*
33 MELIDO PEREZ (INJ)-P
34 GREG A. HARRIS (REL)-P (2)
34 ROB MURPHY-P (2)
35 PAUL GIBSON (INJ)-P
36 BILLY CONNORS-CH
37 *(RET#) CASEY STENGEL*
38 MATT NOKES (INJ)-C/DH
39 DONN PALL (REL)-P (1)
40 TONY CLONINGER-CH
41 STERLING HITCHCOCK-P
43 BOB MELVIN (INJ)-1B (1)
44 *(RET#) REGGIE JACKSON*
45 DANNY TARTABULL-DH/OF
46 TERRY MULHOLLAND-P
47 DAVE SILVESTRI-INF
48 RICK DOWN-CH
50 ROBERT EENBOOM-SS
51 BERNIE WILLIAMS-OF
52 MARK HUTTON-P
54 JEFF REARDON (REL)-P
54 JOE AUSANIO-P
55 BRIAN BUTTERFIELD-CH
57 STEVE HOWE (INJ)-P

1995

2ND E (W/C) 79-65 7GB
144 GAME SEASON
L ALDS-SEAA 3-2

1 *(RET#) BILLY MARTIN*
2 DEREK JETER-SS
3 *(RET#) BABE RUTH*
4 *(RET#) LOU GEHRIG*
5 *(RET#) JOE DIMAGGIO*
6 TONY FERNANDEZ-SS
7 *(RET#) MICKEY MANTLE*
8 *(RET#) YOGI BERRA*
8 *(RET#) BILL DICKEY*
9 *(RET#) ROGER MARIS*
10 *(RET#) PHIL RIZZUTO*
11 BUCK SHOWALTER-MGR
12 WADE BOGGS-3B/DH
13 JIM LEYRITZ-DH
14 PAT KELLY (INJ)-2B
15 *(RET#) THURMAN MUNSON*
16 *(RET#) WHITEY FORD*
17 LUIS POLONIA (WAIV)-OF
17 RUBEN RIVERA-OF
18 RANDY VELARDE-UTIL
19 JACK MCDOWELL-P
20 MIKE STANLEY-C
21 PAUL O'NEILL (INJ)-OF
22 JIMMY KEY (INJ)-P
23 DON MATTINGLY (INJ)-1B/DH
24 RUSS DAVIS-3B
25 SCOTT BANKHEAD-P
25 RUBEN SIERRA-DH/OF (2)
26 KEVIN ELSTER-SS (1)
26 DARRYL STRAWBERRY (SUB)-DH/OF
27 BOB WICKMAN-P
28 SCOTT KAMIENIECKI (INJ)-P
29 GERALD WILLIAMS-OF
30 WILLIE RANDOLPH-CH
31 BRIAN BOEHRINGER-P
32 *(RET#) ELSTON HOWARD*
33 MELIDO PEREZ (INJ)-P
34 BOB MACDONALD-P
35 JOHN WETTELAND-P (2)
36 BILLY CONNORS-CH
36 DAVID CONE-P (2)
37 *(RET#) CASEY STENGEL*
38 JEFF PATTERSON-P
38 JOSIAS MANZANILLO (INJ)-P
39 DION JAMES-OF
40 TONY CLONINGER-CH
41 STERLING HITCHCOCK-P
42 MARIANO RIVERA-P
43 DAVE SILVESTRI-SS/DH (1)
43 NARDI CONTRARAS-CH
44 *(RET#) REGGIE JACKSON*
45 DANNY TARTABULL-DH/OF (1)
46 ANDY PETTITE-P
47 DAVE EILAND-P
47 RICK HONEYCUTT-P (2)
48 RICK DOWN-CH
50 ROBERT EENBOOM-SS/2B
51 BERNIE WILLIAMS-OF
54 JOE AUSANIO-P
55 BRIAN BUTTERFIELD-CH
56 DAVE PAVLAS-P
57 STEVE HOWE-P
62 JORGE POSADA-C

1996

1ST E 92-70 0GB
W ALDS-TEXA 3-1
W ALCS-BALA 4-1
W WS-ATLN 4-2

1 *(RET#) BILLY MARTIN*
2 DEREK JETER-SS
3 *(RET#) BABE RUTH*
4 *(RET#) LOU GEHRIG*
5 *(RET#) JOE DIMAGGIO*
6 JOE TORRE-MGR
7 *(RET#) MICKEY MANTLE*
8 *(RET#) YOGI BERRA*
8 *(RET#) BILL DICKEY*
9 *(RET#) ROGER MARIS*
10 *(RET#) PHIL RIZZUTO*
11 DWIGHT (DOC) GOODEN-P
12 WADE BOGGS-3B
13 JIM LEYRITZ-C/DH
14 PAT KELLY (INJ)-2B
15 *(RET#) THURMAN MUNSON*
16 *(RET#) WHITEY FORD*
17 KENNY ROGERS-P
18 MARIANO DUNCAN (INJ)-2B
19 LUIS SOJO-3B (2)
20 ROBERT EENHOORN (WAIV)-SS/2B (1)
20 MIKE ALDRETE-DH/P (2)
21 PAUL O'NEILL (INJ)-OF
22 JIMMY KEY (INJ)-P
24 TINO MARTINEZ-1B
25 RUBEN SIERRA-DH/OF (1)
25 CECIL (BIG DADDY) FIELDER-DH (2)
25 JOE GIRARDI-C
26 ANDY FOX-3B
27 BOB WICKMAN-P (1)
27 GRAEME LLOYD-P (2)
28 SCOTT KAMIENIECKI (INJ)-P
28 RUBEN RIVERA-OF
28 DAVID WEATHERS-P
29 GERALD WILLIAMS-OF (1)
29 RICKY BONES-P (2)
30 WILLIE RANDOLPH-CH
31 TIM (ROCK) RAINES (INJ)-OF
32 *(RET#) ELSTON HOWARD*
(33) MELIDO PEREZ (INJ)-(P)
33 CHARLIE HAYES-3B (2)
34 MEL STOTTLEMYRE-CH
35 JOHN WETTELAND (INJ)-P
36 DAVID CONE (INJ)-P
37 *(RET#) CASEY STENGEL*
38 MATT HOWARD-2B
38 DAVE EILAND-P
39 DION JAMES (REL)-OF
39 MATT LUKE-OF
39 PAUL GIBSON-P
39 BRIAN BOEHRINGER-P
39 DARRYL (STRAW) STRAWBERRY-DH
40 TONY CLONINGER-CH
41 JORGE POSADA-C
41 BRIAN BOEHRINGER-P
42 MARIANO RIVERA-P
43 JEFF NELSON-P
44 *(RET#) REGGIE JACKSON*
45 JOE GIRARDI-C
45 CECIL (BIG DADDY) FIELDER-DH (2)
46 ANDY PETTITE-P
47 RUBEN RIVERA-OF
47 BILLY BREWER-P
47 DAVE PAVLAS-P
48 DON (POPEYE) (ZIM) ZIMMER-CH
50 CHRIS CHAMBLISS-CH
51 BERNIE WILLIAMS (INJ)-OF
52 MARK HUTTON (INJ)-P (1)
52 DAVID WEATHERS-P (2)
53 JOSE CARDENAL-CH
54 JIM MECIR-P
55 RAMIRO MENDOZA-P
55 WALLY WHITEHURST-P
55 JORGE POSADA-C
56 DALE POLLEY-P
57 STEVE HOWE (REL)-P
57 RAMIRO MENDOZA-P
60 TIM MCINTOSH-C/1B
TONY FERNANDEZ (INJ)-(INF)

1997

2ND E (W/C) 96-66 2GB
L ALDS-CLEA 3-2

1 *(RET#) BILLY MARTIN*
2 DEREK JETER-SS
3 *(RET#) BABE RUTH*
4 *(RET#) LOU GEHRIG*
5 *(RET#) JOE DIMAGGIO*
6 JOE TORRE-MGR
7 *(RET#) MICKEY MANTLE*
8 *(RET#) YOGI BERRA*
8 *(RET#) BILL DICKEY*
9 *(RET#) ROGER MARIS*
10 *(RET#) PHIL RIZZUTO*
11 DWIGHT (DOC) GOODEN (INJ)-P
12 WADE BOGGS-3B
13 CHARLIE HAYES-3B
14 PAT KELLY (INJ)-2B
15 *(RET#) THURMAN MUNSON*
16 *(RET#) WHITEY FORD*
17 KENNY ROGERS-P
18 MARIANO DUNCAN-2B (1)
18 MIKE STANLEY-C/DH (2)
18 ANDY FOX-INF
19 LUIS SOJO-2B (2)
20 JORGE POSADA-C
20 MIKE STANLEY-C/DH (2)
21 PAUL O'NEILL-OF
22 MARK WHITEN-OF
22 JORGE POSADA-C
23 *(RET#) DON MATTINGLY*
24 TINO MARTINEZ-1B
25 JOE GIRARDI-C
26 SCOTT POSE-OF
26 ANDY FOX-3B
26 REY SANCHEZ-2B (2)
27 GRAEME LLOYD-P
28 CHAD CURTIS-OF (2)
29 MIKE STANTON-P
30 WILLIE RANDOLPH-CH
31 TIM (ROCK) RAINES (INJ)-OF
32 *(RET#) ELSTON HOWARD*
33 DAVID WELLS-P
34 MEL STOTTLEMYRE-CH
35 HIDEKI IRABU-P
36 DAVID CONE (INJ)-P
37 *(RET#) CASEY STENGEL*
38 SCOTT POSE-OF
38 HOMER BUSH-2B
39 DARRYL (STRAW) STRAWBERRY-DH
40 TONY CLONINGER-CH
41 BRIAN BOEHRINGER-P
42 MARIANO RIVERA-P
43 JEFF NELSON-P
44 *(RET#) REGGIE JACKSON*
45 CECIL (BIG DADDY) FIELDER (INJ)-DH (2)
46 ANDY PETTITE-P
47 IVAN CRUZ-DH/1B
48 DON (POPEYE) (ZIM) ZIMMER-CH
50 CHRIS CHAMBLISS-CH
51 BERNIE WILLIAMS (INJ)-OF
52 DAVID WEATHERS-P (1)
52 DANNY RIOS-P
52 PETE (INKY) INCAVIGLIA-DH (2)
52 JOE BOROWSKI-P (2)
53 JOSE CARDENAL-CH
54 JIM MECIR-P
55 RAMIRO MENDOZA-P
63 DANNY RIOS-P
63 MICHAEL FIGGA-C

NEW YORK YANKEES

1998

1ST E 114-48 0GB
W ALDS-TEXA 3-0
W ALCS-CLEA 4-2
W WS-SDN 4-0

1 *(RET#) BILLY MARTIN*
2 DEREK JETER (INJ)-SS
3 *(RET#) BABE RUTH*
4 *(RET#) LOU GEHRIG*
5 *(RET#) JOE DIMAGGIO*
6 JOE TORRE-MGR
7 *(RET#) MICKEY MANTLE*
8 *(RET#) YOGI BERRA*
8 *(RET#) BILL DICKEY*
9 *(RET#) ROGER MARIS*
0 *(RET#) PHIL RIZZUTO*
1 CHUCK KNOBLAUCH-2B
3 WILLIE BANKS-P (1)
3 MIKE FIGGA-C
3 HIDEKI IRABU-P
5 *(RET#) THURMAN MUNSON*
6 *(RET#) WHITEY FORD*
7 DALE SVEUM (REL)-INF/DH
8 SCOTT BROSIUS-3B
9 LUIS SOJO (INJ)-2B
20 JORGE POSADA-C
21 PAUL O'NEILL-OF
22 HOMER BUSH-2B/INF/DH
23 *(RET#) DON MATTINGLY*
24 TINO MARTINEZ-1B
25 JOE GIRARDI-C
26 SHANE SPENCER-OF
26 ORLANDO (EL DUQUE) HERNANDEZ-P
27 GRAEME LLOYD (INJ)-P
28 CHAD CURTIS-OF
29 MIKE STANTON-P
30 WILLIE RANDOLPH-CH
31 TIM (ROCK) RAINES-OF
32 *(RET#) ELSTON HOWARD*
33 DAVID WELLS-P
34 MEL STOTTLEMYRE-CH
36 DAVID CONE-P
37 *(RET#) CASEY STENGEL*
38 RICKY LEDEE-OF
39 DARRYL (STRAW) STRAWBERRY-DH
40 TONY CLONINGER-CH
40 DARREN HOLMES (INJ)-P
41 DARREN HOLMES (INJ)-P
41 TONY CLONINGER-CH
42 MARIANO RIVERA (INJ)-P
43 JEFF NELSON (INJ)-P
44 *(RET#) REGGIE JACKSON*
45 CHILI DAVIS (INJ)-DH
46 ANDY PETTITE-P
47 SHANE SPENCER-OF/1B
48 CHRIS CHAMBLISS-CH
50 DON (POPEYE) (ZIM) ZIMMER-CH
51 BERNIE WILLIAMS (INJ)-OF
52 MIKE BUDDIE-P
53 JOSE CARDENAL-CH
54 TODD ERDOS-P
55 RAMIRO MENDOZA-P
57 JOE BOROWSKI (INJ)-P (2)
58 MIKE JERZEMBECK-P
59 RYAN BRADLEY-P
60 MIKE LOWELL-3B/DH
61 JIM BRUSKE-P (3)
62 JAY TESSMER-P
69 HOMER BUSH-2B

1999

1ST E 98-64 0GB
W ALDS-TEXA 3-0
W ALCS-BOSA 4-1
W WS-ATLN 4-0

1 *(RET#) BILLY MARTIN*
2 DEREK JETER-SS
3 *(RET#) BABE RUTH*
4 *(RET#) LOU GEHRIG*
5 *(RET#) JOE DIMAGGIO*
6 JOE TORRE-MGR
7 *(RET#) MICKEY MANTLE*
8 *(RET#) YOGI BERRA*
8 *(RET#) BILL DICKEY*
9 *(RET#) ROGER MARIS*
10 *(RET#) PHIL RIZZUTO*
11 CHUCK KNOBLAUCH-2B
12 ROGER (ROCKET) CLEMENS (INJ)-P
13 MIKE FIGGA-C (1)
13 JEFF MANTO-1B (2)
13 JIM LEYRITZ-C (2)
14 HIDEKI IRABU-P
15 *(RET#) THURMAN MUNSON*
16 *(RET#) WHITEY FORD*
17 RICKY LEDEE-OF
18 SCOTT BROSIUS-3B
19 LUIS SOJO (INJ)-2B
20 JORGE POSADA-C
21 PAUL O'NEILL-OF
22 TONY TARASCO-OF
22 ROGER (ROCKET) CLEMENS (INJ)-P
23 *(RET#) DON MATTINGLY*
24 TINO MARTINEZ-1B
25 JOE GIRARDI-C
26 ORLANDO (EL DUQUE) HERNANDEZ-P
27 TONY FOSSAS-P
27 ALLEN WATSON-P (3)
28 CHAD CURTIS-OF
29 MIKE STANTON-P
30 WILLIE RANDOLPH-CH
31 DAN NAULTY-P
32 *(RET#) ELSTON HOWARD*
34 MEL STOTTLEMYRE-CH
35 CLAY BELLINGER-INF
36 DAVID CONE-P
37 *(RET#) CASEY STENGEL*
38 JASON GRIMSLEY-P
39 DARRYL (STRAW) STRAWBERRY (SUS)-DH
40 TONY CLONINGER-CH
41 TONY CLONINGER-CH
41 MIKE BUDDIE-P
42 MARIANO RIVERA-P
43 JEFF NELSON (INJ)-P
44 *(RET#) REGGIE JACKSON*
45 CHILI DAVIS
46 ANDY PETTITE-P
47 SHANE SPENCER (INJ)-OF/1B
48 CHRIS CHAMBLISS-CH
50 DON (POPEYE) (ZIM) ZIMMER-CH
51 BERNIE WILLIAMS (INJ)-OF
52 ED YARNELL-P
53 JOSE CARDENAL-CH
54 TODD ERDOS-P
55 RAMIRO MENDOZA-P
57 JAY TESSMER-P
57 JEFF JUDEN-P
(58) MIKE JERZEMBECK-(P)
58 ALFONSO SORIANO-DH/SS
59 D'ANGELO JIMENEZ-INF
(63) MIKE JERZEMBECK-(P)
(67) DARRELL EINERTSON (INJ)-(P)

2000

1ST E 87-74 0GB
W ALDS-OAKA 3-2
W ALCS-SEAA 4-2
W WS-NYN 4-1

1 *(RET#) BILLY MARTIN*
2 DEREK JETER-SS
3 *(RET#) BABE RUTH*
4 *(RET#) LOU GEHRIG*
5 *(RET#) JOE DIMAGGIO*
6 JOE TORRE-MGR
7 *(RET#) MICKEY MANTLE*
8 *(RET#) YOGI BERRA*
8 *(RET#) BILL DICKEY*
9 *(RET#) ROGER MARIS*
10 *(RET#) PHIL RIZZUTO*
11 CHUCK KNOBLAUCH-2B
12 DENNY NEAGLE-P (2)
13 JIM LEYRITZ-C (1)
13 JOSE VIZCAINO-INF (2)
14 WILSON DELGADO-INF (1)
14 LUIS SOJO-INF (2)
15 *(RET#) THURMAN MUNSON*
16 *(RET#) WHITEY FORD*
17 RICKY LEDEE-OF (1)
17 DWIGHT (DOC) GOODEN-P (3)
18 SCOTT BROSIUS-3B
19 ROBERTO KELLY (INJ)-OF
19 LUIS POLONIA-DH (2)
20 JORGE POSADA-C
21 PAUL O'NEILL-OF
22 ROGER (ROCKET) CLEMENS (INJ)-P
23 *(RET#) DON MATTINGLY*
24 TINO MARTINEZ-1B
25 CHRIS TURNER-C
26 ORLANDO (EL DUQUE) HERNANDEZ (INJ)-P
27 ALLEN WATSON (INJ)-P
28 DAVID JUSTICE-OF (2)
29 MIKE STANTON-P
30 TIM (ROCK) RAINES-OF
30 WILLIE RANDOLPH-CH
31 LANCE JOHNSON-OF
31 BEN FORD-P
31 GLENALLEN HILL-OF/DH (2)
32 *(RET#) ELSTON HOWARD*
33 RYAN THOMPSON-OF
33 JOSE CANSECO-DH (2)
34 MEL STOTTLEMYRE-CH
35 CLAY BELLINGER-INF
36 DAVID CONE-P
37 *(RET#) CASEY STENGEL*
38 JASON GRIMSLEY-P
40 TONY CLONINGER-CH
41 ED YARNELL-P
41 TONY CLONINGER-CH
42 MARIANO RIVERA-P
43 JEFF NELSON-P
44 *(RET#) REGGIE JACKSON*
45 FELIX JOSE-OF
45 RYAN THOMPSON-OF
46 ANDY PETTITE-P
47 SHANE SPENCER (INJ)-OF
48 CHRIS CHAMBLISS-CH
50 TODD ERDOS-P (1)
50 DON (POPEYE) (ZIM) ZIMMER-CH
51 BERNIE WILLIAMS-OF
53 ALFONSO SORIANO-INF
54 LEE MAZZILLI-CH
55 RAMIRO MENDOZA (INJ)-P
56 DARRELL EINERTSON-P
56 TED LILLY-P
57 JAKE WESTBROOK-P
58 RANDY CHOATE-P
60 CRAIG DINGMAN-P
62 WILSON DELGADO-INF (1)
62 JAY TESSMER-P
63 RANDY KEISLER-P
88 RYAN THOMPSON-OF

2001

1ST E 95-65 0GB
W ALDS-OAKA 3-2
W ALCS-SEAA 4-1
L WS-ARIN 4-3

1 *(RET#) BILLY MARTIN*
2 DEREK JETER (INJ)-SS
3 *(RET#) BABE RUTH*
4 *(RET#) LOU GEHRIG*
5 *(RET#) JOE DIMAGGIO*
6 JOE TORRE-MGR
7 *(RET#) MICKEY MANTLE*
8 *(RET#) YOGI BERRA*
8 *(RET#) BILL DICKEY*
9 *(RET#) ROGER MARIS*
10 *(RET#) PHIL RIZZUTO*
11 CHUCK KNOBLAUCH-2B
12 CLAY BALLINGER-INF
13 MICHAEL COLEMAN-OF
14 JOE OLIVER-C
14 WILSON DELGADO-I (2)
15 *(RET#) THURMAN MUNSON*
16 *(RET#) WHITEY FORD*
17 DARREN BRAGG-OF (2)
17 GERALD WILLIAMS-OF (2)
18 SCOTT BROSIUS (INJ)-3B
19 LUIS SOJO-INF
20 JORGE POSADA (SUS)-C
21 PAUL O'NEILL-OF
22 ROGER (ROCKET) CLEMENS (INJ)-P
23 *(RET#) DON MATTINGLY*
24 TINO MARTINEZ-1B
25 RANDY VELARDE-2B (2)
26 ORLANDO (EL DUQUE) HERNANDEZ (INJ)-P
27 ALLEN WATSON (INJ)-P
28 DAVID JUSTICE (INJ)-OF/DH
29 MIKE STANTON-P
30 WILLIE RANDOLPH-CH
32 *(RET#) ELSTON HOWARD*
33 ALFONSO SORIANO-INF
34 MEL STOTTLEMYRE-CH
35 MIKE (MOOSE) MUSSINA-P
36 BOBBY ESTALELLA-C
37 *(RET#) CASEY STENGEL*
38 RANDY CHOATE-P
39 MARK WOHLERS-P (2)
40 TONY CLONINGER-CH
41 BRIAN BOEHRINGER-P
41 STERLING HITCHCOCK-P (2)
42 MARIANO RIVERA-P
43 TODD GREENE-C
44 *(RET#) REGGIE JACKSON*
45 HENRY RODRIGUEZ (INJ)-OF
45 JAY WITASICK-P (2)
46 ANDY PETTITE (INJ)-P
47 SHANE SPENCER (INJ)-OF
48 SCOTT SEABOL-OF
48 ROBERT PEREZ-OF
51 BERNIE WILLIAMS-OF
52 DON (POPEYE) (ZIM) ZIMMER-CH
53 TOM DENBO-CH
54 LEE MAZZILLI-CH
55 RAMIRO MENDOZA (INJ)-P
56 TODD WILLIAMS (INJ)-P
56 JUAN RIVERA-OF
57 CARLOS ALMANZAR-P
57 MARK WOHLERS-P (2)
57 ERICK ALMONTE-SS
58 RANDY CHOATE-P
58 RANDY KEISLER-P
59 DONZELL MCDONALD-OF
60 DARRELL EINERTSON (INJ)-P
60 NICK JOHNSON-1B
61 TED LILLY-P
62 BRETT JODIE-P
62 BRANDON KNIGHT-P
65 ADRIAN HERNANDEZ-P
71 CHRISTIAN PARKER (INJ)-P

2002

1ST E 103-58 0GB
L ALDS-ANAA 3-1

1 *(RET#) BILLY MARTIN*
2 DEREK JETER-SS
3 *(RET#) BABE RUTH*
4 *(RET#) LOU GEHRIG*
5 *(RET#) JOE DIMAGGIO*
6 JOE TORRE-MGR
7 *(RET#) MICKEY MANTLE*
8 *(RET#) BILL DICKEY*
8 *(RET#) YOGI BERRA*
9 *(RET#) ROGER MARIS*
10 *(RET#) PHIL RIZZUTO*
11 CHRIS WIDGER-C
12 ALFONSO SORIANO-2B
13 LEE MAZZILLI-CH
14 ENRIQUE WILSON-UTIL
15 *(RET#) THURMAN MUNSON*
16 *(RET#) WHITEY FORD*
17 GERALD WILLIAMS-OF
17 ALEX ARIAS-3B/SS
18 MARCUS THAMES,-OF
18 JEFF WEAVER-P (2)
19 ROBIN VENTURA-3B/1B
20 JORGE POSADA-C/DH
22 ROGER (ROCKET) CLEMENS-P
23 *(RET#) DON MATTINGLY*
25 JASON GIAMBI-1B/DH
26 ORLANDO (EL DUQUE) HERNANDEZ (INJ)-P
27 RONDELL WHITE-OF/DH
28 JOHN VANDER WAL-OF/DH/1B
29 MIKE STANTON-P
30 WILLIE RANDOLPH-CH
31 STEVE KARSAY-P
32 *(RET#) ELSTON HOWARD*
33 DAVID WELLS-P
34 MEL STOTTLEMYRE-CH
35 MIKE (MOOSE) MUSSINA-P
36 NICK JOHNSON-1B/DH
37 *(RET#) CASEY STENGEL*
38 RANDY CHOATE-P
39 RON COOMER-3B/DH/1B
41 STERLING HITCHCOCK (INJ)-P
42 MARIANO RIVERA (INJ)-P
43 TED LILLY-P (1)
43 RAUL MONDESI-OF (2)
44 *(RET#) REGGIE JACKSON*
45 ALBERTO CASTILLO-C
46 ANDY PETTITTE (INJ)-P
47 SHANE SPENCER-OF
48 JAY TESSMER-P
48 BRANDON KNIGHT-P
51 BERNIE WILLIAMS-OF/DH
52 RICH MONTELEONE-CH
53 DON (POPEYE) (ZIM) ZIMMER-CH
53 MIKE THURMAN-P
54 DON (POPEYE) (ZIM) ZIMMER-CH
55 RAMIRO MENDOZA-P
56 RICK DOWN-CH
57 KARIM GARCIA-OF (1)
57 DREW HENSON-DH
59 JUAN RIVERA (INJ)-OF
61 TED LILLY-P (1)
65 ADRIAN HERNANDEZ-P

2003

1ST E 101-61 0GB
W ALDS-MINA 3-1
W ALCS-BOSA 4-3
L WS-FLAN 4-2

1 *(RET#) BILLY MARTIN*
2 DEREK JETER (INJ)-SS
3 *(RET#) BABE RUTH*
4 *(RET#) LOU GEHRIG*
5 *(RET#) JOE DIMAGGIO*
6 JOE TORRE-MGR
7 *(RET#) MICKEY MANTLE*
8 *(RET#) BILL DICKEY*
8 *(RET#) YOGI BERRA*
9 *(RET#) ROGER MARIS*
10 *(RET#) PHIL RIZZUTO*
11 ERICK ALMONTE-SS
11 CURTIS PRIDE-OF
11 DAVID DELLUCCI (INJ)-OF (2)
12 ALFONSO SORIANO-2B
13 ANTONIO OSUNA (INJ)-P
14 ENRIQUE WILSON-INF
15 *(RET#) THURMAN MUNSON*
16 *(RET#) WHITEY FORD*
17 JOHN FLAHERTY-C
18 JEFF WEAVER-P
19 ROBIN VENTURA-3B (1)
19 AARON BOONE-3B (2)
20 JORGE POSADA-C

22 ROGER (ROCKET) CLEMENS-P
23 *(RET#) DON MATTINGLY*
24 RUBEN SIERRA-DH/OF (2)
25 JASON GIAMBI-1B/DH
(26) JON LIEBER (INJ)-(P)
27 TODD ZEILE-3B/1B/DH (1)
27 LUIS SOTO-INF
28 CHRIS LATHAM-OF
28 CHARLES GIPSON-OF
28 KARIM GARCIA-OF (2)
29 BUBBA TRAMMELL (INJ) (RET)-DH/OF
30 WILLIE RANDOLPH-CH
(31) STEVE KARSAY (INJ)-(P)
32 *(RET#) ELSTON HOWARD*
33 DAVID WELLS (BRV)-P
34 MEL STOTTLEMYRE-CH
35 MIKE (MOOSE) MUSSINA-P
36 NICK JOHNSON (INJ)-1B/DH
37 *(RET#) CASEY STENGEL*
38 RANDY CHOATE-P
38 BRET PRINZ-P (2)
38 DREW HENSON-3B
39 CHRIS HAMMOND-P
40 DAN MICELI-P (3)
40 GABE WHITE (INJ)-P (2)
41 STERLING HITCHCOCK-P (1)
41 JORGE DE PAULA-P
42 MARIANO RIVERA (INJ)-P
43 RAUL MONDESI-OF (1)
43 JEFF NELSON-P (2)
44 *(RET#) REGGIE JACKSON*
45 JASON ANDERSON-P (1)
45 ARMANDO BENITEZ-P (2)
45 FELIX HEREDIA (INJ)-P (2)
46 ANDY PETTITTE (INJ)-P
47 AL REYES-P
47 JESSE OROSCO-P (2)
47 ERICK ALMONTE-SS
48 FERNANDO SEGUIGNOL-1B
51 BERNIE WILLIAMS (INJ)-OF
52 RICH MONTELEONE-CH
52 JOSE CONTRERAS (INJ)-P
53 LEE MAZZILLI-CH
54 DON (POPEYE) (ZIM) ZIMMER-CH
55 HIDEKI MATSUI-OF
56 RICK DOWN-CH
57 JUAN ACEVEDO (REL)-P (1)
57 MICHEL HERNANDEZ-C
59 JUAN RIVERA-OF
60 BRANDON CLAUSSEN-P
60 ERICK ALMONTE-SS

2004

1ST E — 101-61 — 0GB
W ALDS-MINA 3-1
L ALCS-BOSA 4-3

1 *(RET#) BILLY MARTIN*
2 DEREK JETER-SS
3 *(RET#) BABE RUTH*
4 *(RET#) LOU GEHRIG*
5 *(RET#) JOE DIMAGGIO*
6 JOE TORRE-MGR
7 *(RET#) MICKEY MANTLE*
8 *(RET#) BILL DICKEY*
8 *(RET#) YOGI BERRA*
9 *(RET#) ROGER MARIS*
10 *(RET#) PHIL RIZZUTO*
11 GARY SHEFFIELD-OF
12 KENNY LOFTON (INJ)-OF
13 ALEX RODRIGUEZ-3B
14 ENRIQUE WILSON-2B
15 *(RET#) THURMAN MUNSON*
16 *(RET#) WHITEY FORD*
17 JOHN FLAHERTY-C
18 HOMER BUSH-INF
18 JOHN OLERUD-1B (2)
19 BUBBA CROSBY-OF
20 JORGE POSADA-C
22 JON LIEBER (INJ)-P
23 *(RET#) DON MATTINGLY*
23 DON MATTINGLY-CH
24 RUBEN SIERRA-DH
25 JASON GIAMBI (INJ)-1B/DH
26 ORLANDO (EL DUQUE) HERNANDEZ (INJ)-P
27 KEVIN BROWN (INJ)-P
28 ESTEBAN LOAIZA-P (2)
29 TONY CLARK-1B
30 WILLIE RANDOLPH-CH
31 STEVE KARSAY (INJ)-P
32 *(RET#) ELSTON HOWARD*
33 JAVIER VAZQUEZ-P
34 MEL STOTTLEMYRE-CH
35 MIKE (MOOSE) MUSSINA-P
36 TOM (FLASH) GORDON-P
37 *(RET#) CASEY STENGEL*
38 TRAVIS LEE (INJ)-1B
39 ANDY PHILLIPS-INF
40 GABE WHITE-P (1)
40 C. J. NITKOWSKI-P (2)
41 MIGUEL CAIRO-2B
42 MARIANO RIVERA-P
43 JORGE DE PAULA (INJ)-P
44 *(RET#) REGGIE JACKSON*
45 FELIX HEREDIA-P
46 DONOVAN OSBORNE-P
47 BRET PRINZ-P
48 PAUL QUANTRILL-P
51 BERNIE WILLIAMS (INJ)-OF
52 RICH MONTELEONE-CH
52 JOSE CONTRERAS-P (1)
53 LUIS SOJO-CH
54 ROY WHITE-CH
55 HIDEKI MATSUI-OF
56 SCOTT PROCTOR-P
56 TANYAN STURTZE-P
57 ALEX GRAMAN-P
57 SCOTT PROCTOR-P
57 BRAD HALSEY-P
60 SAM MARSONEK (INJ)-P
60 FELIX ESCALONA-SS
61 JUAN PADILLA-P (1)
61 BRAD HALSEY-P

2005

1ST E — 95-67 — 0GB
L ALDS-LAA 3-2

1 *(RET#) BILLY MARTIN*
2 DEREK JETER-SS
3 *(RET#) BABE RUTH*
4 *(RET#) LOU GEHRIG*
5 *(RET#) JOE DIMAGGIO*
6 JOE TORRE-MGR
7 *(RET#) MICKEY MANTLE*
8 *(RET#) BILL DICKEY*
8 *(RET#) YOGI BERRA*
9 *(RET#) ROGER MARIS*
10 *(RET#) PHIL RIZZUTO*
11 GARY SHEFFIELD-OF
12 TONY WOMACK-2B/OF
13 ALEX RODRIGUEZ-3B
14 ROBINSON CANO-2B
14 RUSS JOHNSON-UTIL
14 ANDY PHILLIPS-UTIL
15 *(RET#) THURMAN MUNSON*
16 *(RET#) WHITEY FORD*
17 JOHN FLAHERTY-C
18 ANDY PHILLIPS-UTIL
18 BUBBA CROSBY-OF
19 BUBBA CROSBY-OF
19 AL LEITER-P (2)
20 JORGE POSADA-C
22 ROBINSON CANO-2B
23 *(RET#) DON MATTINGLY*
23 DON MATTINGLY-CH
24 TINO MARTINEZ-1B
25 JASON GIAMBI-1B/DH
26 REY SANCHEZ (INJ)-INF
26 MARK BELLHORN-INF (2)
27 KEVIN BROWN (INJ)-P
28 RUBEN SIERRA (INJ)-DH
29 MIKE STANTON (REL)-P (1)
29 TIM REDDING-P (2)
29 FELIX ESCALONA-INF
31 STEVE KARSAY (REL)-P
31 JASON ANDERSON-P
31 AARON SMALL-P
32 *(RET#) ELSTON HOWARD*
33 JARET WRIGHT (INJ)-P
34 MEL STOTTLEMYRE-CH
35 MIKE (MOOSE) MUSSINA-P
36 TOM (FLASH) GORDON-P
37 *(RET#) CASEY STENGEL*
38 BUDDY GROOM-P (1)
38 RAMIRO MENDOZA-P
39 KEVIN REESE-OF
39 MELKY CABRERA-OF
39 SHAWN CHACON-P (2)
40 CHIEN-MING WANG (INJ)-P
41 RANDY JOHNSON-P
42 MARIANO RIVERA-P
43 SCOTT PROCTOR-P
44 *(RET#) REGGIE JACKSON*
45 CARL PAVANO (INJ)-P
46 DARRELL MAY-P (2)
46 ALAN EMBREE-P (2)
47 FELIX RODRIGUEZ (INJ)-P
48 PAUL QUANTRILL (SUS:3G) -P (1)
48 WAYNE FRANKLIN-P
49 *(RET#) RON GUIDRY*
50 MATT LAWTON-OF (3)
51 BERNIE WILLIAMS-OF/DH
52 JOE GIRARDI-CH
53 LUIS SOJO-CH
54 ROY WHITE-CH
55 HIDEKI MATSUI-OF
56 SCOTT PROCTOR-P
56 TANYAN STURTZE (INJ)-P
57 NEIL ALLEN-CH
58 COLTER BEAN-P
58 SEAN HENN-P
58 ALEX GRAMAN-P
60 WIL NIEVES-C
61 JORGE DE PAULA-P

Louisiana Lightnin' Ron Guidry (Above, top) had one of the greatest Yankee seasons of all time in 1978. He was 25-3 for an incredible .893 with 9 shutouts. Donnie Ballgame Don Mattingly (Above, bottom) started his career on fire—an AL All-Star six years in a row. He won the batting title in 1984 with .343. He was also one of the slickest fielding first basemen to ever play the game winning nine Gold Gloves. Back problems hurt his career truncated four seasons and forced him to retire early.

PHILADELPHIA/KANSAS CITY/ OAKLAND ATHLETICS

Connie Mack's Athletics, seeking to cut expenses, only wore numbers on their away uniforms after the League's dictum that every team should use numbers to identify players. Mack did not wish to jeopardize the sale of scorecards at home. This practice lasted from 1931 through 1936.

1931-1936: (Games: HOME, *AWAY*) Unnumbered and unidentified players.

1931
PHILADELPHIA ATHLETICS
1ST 107-45 0GB
L WS-STLN 4-3

NO# CONNIE (THE TALL TACTICIAN) MACK-MGR
2 MICKEY COCHRANE-C
3 JIMMIE (DOUBLE X) (BEAST) FOXX-1B/UTIL
4 MAX (CAMERA EYE) (TILLY) BISHOP-2B
5 JIMMY DYKES-3B/SS
6 JOE BOLEY-SS/2B
7 AL (BUCKETFOOT AL) SIMMONS-OF
8 MULE HAAS (INJ)-OF
9 BING MILLER-OF
10 LEFTY GROVE-P
11 GEORGE (MOOSE) EARNSHAW-P
12 RUBE WALBERG-P
13 BILL SHORES-P
14 EDDIE ROMMEL-P
15 ROY (POPEYE) MAHAFFEY-P
16 HANK MCDONALD-P
17 JIM PETERSON-P
18 LEW KRAUSSE, SR.-P
19 SOL (BUCK) CARTER-P
20 JOHNNIE HEVING-C
21 JOE PALMISANO-C/2B
22 ERIC (BOOB) MCNAIR-INF
23 DIB WILLIAMS-SS/UTIL
24 PHIL (HOOK) TODT-1B
25 JIMMY MOORE-OF
26 DOC CRAMER (INJ)-OF
28 WAITE (SCHOOLBOY) HOYT-P (2)
30 KID GLEASON-CH
31 EDDIE (COCKY) COLLINS-CH
32 EARLE MACK-CH
NO# LOU FINNEY-OF (9G:9/12,14,14,15,16,18, 19,21,22@HOME)

1932
2ND 94-60 13GB

NO# CONNIE (THE TALL TACTICIAN) MACK-MGR
2 MICKEY COCHRANE-C/OF
3 JIMMIE (DOUBLE X) (BEAST) FOXX-1B/3B
4 MAX (CAMERA EYE) (TILLY) BISHOP-2B
5 JIMMY DYKES-3B/INF
6 JOE BOLEY-SS (1)
6 DIB WILLIAMS-SS/UTIL
7 AL (BUCKETFOOT AL) SIMMONS-OF
8 MULE HAAS-OF
9 BING MILLER-OF
10 LEFTY GROVE-P
11 GEORGE (MOOSE) EARNSHAW-P
12 RUBE WALBERG-P
14 EDDIE ROMMEL-P
15 ROY (POPEYE) MAHAFFEY-P
16 SUGAR CAIN-P
17 JOE BOWMAN-P
17 IRV STEIN-P
18 LEW KRAUSSE, SR.-P
19 JIMMIE DESHONG-P
19 TONY FREITAS-P
20 JOHNNIE HEVING-C
21 ED MADJESKI-C
22 ERIC (BOOB) MCNAIR-SS
23 DIB WILLIAMS-SS/UTIL
23 OSCAR (OKKIE) ROETTGER-1B
23 JOHN (SKINS) JONES-OF
24 JOE BOLEY-SS (1)
24 AL REISS-SS
24 JIM (TIM) MCKEITHAN-P
25 ED COLEMAN (INJ)-OF
26 DOC CRAMER (INJ)-OF
30 KID GLEASON-CH
31 EDDIE (COCKY) COLLINS-CH
32 EARLE MACK-CH
42 ED (CY) CIHOCKI-PH

1933
3RD 79-72 19.5GB

NO# CONNIE (THE TALL TACTICIAN) MACK-MGR
2 MICKEY COCHRANE-C
3 JIMMIE (DOUBLE X) (BEAST) FOXX-1B/SS
4 MAX (CAMERA EYE) (TILLY) BISHOP-2B
5 MIKE (PINKY) HIGGINS-3B
6 DIB WILLIAMS-SS/INF
6 ERIC (BOOB) MCNAIR-SS/2B
7 LOU FINNEY-OF
8 DOC CRAMER-OF
9 BING MILLER-OF/1B
10 LEFTY GROVE-P
11 GEORGE (MOOSE) EARNSHAW-P
12 RUBE WALBERG-P
14 GOWELL (LEFTY) CLASET-P
15 ROY (POPEYE) MAHAFFEY-P
16 SUGAR CAIN-P
17 JIM (TIM) MCKEITHAN-P
18 BOBBY COOMBS-P
19 TONY FREITAS-P
20 DICK (KEWPIE DICK) BARRETT-P
20 BILL (BULLFROG) DIETRICH-P
21 ED MADJESKI-C
21 HANK MCDONALD-P (1)
22 ERIC (BOOB) MCNAIR-SS/2B
22 ED MADJESKI-C
23 DIB WILLIAMS-SS/INF
24 JIM (TIM) MCKEITHAN-P
24 ED (CY) CIHOCKI-INF
25 ED COLEMAN-OF
26 DOC CRAMER-OF
26 BOB (INDIAN BOB) JOHNSON-OF
27 JIM PETERSON-P
31 EDDIE ROMMEL-CH
32 EARLE MACK-CH
33 RUSS (LENA) (SLATS) BLACKBURNE-CH
46 JOHNNY (FOOTSIE) MARCUM-P
NO# FRANKIE (BLIMP) HAYES-C (3G:9/21,28,30@HOME)
NO# EMIL ROY-P (1G:9/30@HOME)
NO# HANK WINSTON-P (1G:9/30@HOME)
NO# JOE ZAPUSTAS-OF (2G:9/28,30@HOME)

1934
5TH 68-82 31GB

NO# CONNIE (THE TALL TACTICIAN) MACK-MGR
2 CHARLIE BERRY-C
3 JIMMIE (DOUBLE X) (BEAST) FOXX-1B/3B
4 DIB WILLIAMS-2B/SS
5 MIKE (PINKY) HIGGINS-3B
6 DIB WILLIAMS-2B/SS
6 ERIC (BOOB) MCNAIR-SS
7 BOB (INDIAN BOB) JOHNSON-OF
8 DOC CRAMER-OF
9 BING MILLER-OF
9 ED COLEMAN-OF
10 JERRY MCQUAIG-OF
10 CHARLIE MOSS-C
11 SUGAR CAIN-P
12 JOHNNY (FOOTSIE) MARCUM-P
14 BILL (BULLFROG) DIETRICH-P
15 ROY (POPEYE) MAHAFFEY-P
15 MORT (DUTCH) FLOHR-P
16 BOB (JUNIOR) KLINE-P (1)
16 SUGAR CAIN-P
16 ROY VAUGHN-P
17 ROY (POPEYE) MAHAFFEY-P
19 ED LAGGER-P
19 HARRY (MATTY) MATUZAK-P
20 JOE (CROONING JOE) CASCARELLA-P
21 ED MADJESKI-C (1)
21 AL BENTON-P
22 ERIC (BOOB) MCNAIR-SS
22 RABBIT WARSTLER-2B/SS
23 LOU FINNEY-OF/1B
24 JIM (TIM) MCKEITHAN-P
25 ED COLEMAN-OF
26 DOC CRAMER-OF
26 WHITEY WILSHERE-P
27 BING MILLER-OF
28 FRANKIE (BLIMP) HAYES-C
30 EARLE MACK-CH
31 RUSS (LENA) (SLATS) BLACKBURNE-CH
32 EARLE MACK-CH
32 EDDIE ROMMEL-CH
__ GEORGE (UG) CASTER-P (5G:*9/10,14,19*,AWAY, 24,26@HOME)
__ JACK (BLACK JACK) WILSON-P (2G: *9/9,14*,AWAY)

1935
8TH 58-91 34GB

NO# CONNIE (THE TALL TACTICIAN) MACK-MGR
2 JIMMIE (DOUBLE X) (BEAST) FOXX-1B/UTIL
3 JIMMIE (DOUBLE X) (BEAST) FOXX-1B/UTIL
3 ALEX HOOKS-1B
4 DIB WILLIAMS-2B (1)
5 MIKE (PINKY) HIGGINS-3B
6 DIB WILLIAMS-2B (1)
6 ERIC (BOOB) MCNAIR-SS/INF
7 BOB (INDIAN BOB) JOHNSON-OF
8 DOC CRAMER-OF
9 ED COLEMAN-OF (1)
9* WOODY UPCHURCH-P*
10 CHARLIE BERRY-C
11 SUGAR CAIN-P (1)
11 GEORGE BLAEHOLDER-P (2)
12 JOHNNY (FOOTSIE) MARCUM-P
14 BILL (BULLFROG) DIETRICH-P
15 ROY (POPEYE) MAHAFFEY-P
15 CARL DOYLE-P
15 GEORGE (UG) CASTER-P
16 SUGAR CAIN-P (1)
16 DUTCH LIEBER-P
17 ROY (POPEYE) MAHAFFEY-P
18 GEORGE TURBEVILLE-P
19 WALLY MOSES (INJ)-OF
20 JOE (CROONING JOE) CASCARELLA-P (1)
20 GEORGE TURBEVILLE-P
20 WEDO (SOUTHERN) MARTINI-P
20 VALLIE (CHIEF) EAVES-P
21 AL BENTON-P
22 ERIC (BOOB) MCNAIR-SS/INF
22 RABBIT WARSTLER-2B/3B
23 LOU FINNEY-OF/1B
24 WHITEY WILSHERE-P
24 EARL HUCKLEBERRY-P
25 ED COLEMAN-OF (1)
26 DOC CRAMER-OF
26 CONNIE MACK, JR.-CH
27 CHARLIE MOSS-C
27 PAUL RICHARDS-C (2)
28 SKEETER NEWSOME-INF/OF
30 EARLE MACK-CH
31 RUSS (LENA) (SLATS) BLACKBURNE-CH
32 EARLE MACK-CH
41 GEORGE BLAEHOLDER-P (2)
67 BILL PATTON-C (9G:6/29,30,*7/6*,20,21,22, 9/7,28,28)
68 HERMAN FINK-P (5G:9/16,18,*22,24,25*)
70 BERNIE SNYDER-2B/SS (10G:9/15,15,18,*21,22,24, 25*,28,28,29)
__ BILL CONROY-C§ (1G:*9/21*-1st G of DH)
__ JACK OWENS-C§ (1G:*9/21*-2nd G of DH)
__ AL VEACH-P (2G:*9/22*,28)
NO# BILL FERRAZZI-P (3G:9/7,9,15@HOME)
NO# JACK PEERSON-SS (10G:9/7,7,8,9,15,17,18, 28,28,29@HOME)

§ Probably wore same shirt

1936
8TH 53-100 49GB

NO# CONNIE (THE TALL TACTICIAN) MACK-MGR
2 FRANKIE (BLIMP) HAYES-C
3 FRED (LEFTY) ARCHER-P
3 JIM OGLESBY-1B
4 RABBIT WARSTLER-2B (1)
5 MIKE (PINKY) HIGGINS-3B
6 SKEETER NEWSOME-SS/UTIL
7 BOB (INDIAN BOB) JOHNSON-OF/INF
8 GEORGE (POOCH) (COUNT) PUCCINELLI-OF
9 WALLY MOSES-OF
10 CHARLIE BERRY-C/CH
11 GORDON (DUSTY) RHODES-P
12 CHARLIE MOSS-C
12 HANK JOHNSON-P
14 BILL (BULLFROG) DIETRICH-P (1)
14 RANDY GUMPERT-P
15 PETE NAKTENIS-P
16 RED BULLOCK-P
16 DUTCH LIEBER-P
17 BUCK ROSS-P
18 CARL DOYLE-P
19 HARRY KELLEY-P
20 GEORGE TURBEVILLE-P
20 RANDY GUMPERT-P
21 WOODY UPCHURCH-P
21 BILL (SWISH) NICHOLSON-OF
22 HERMAN FINK-P
23 LOU FINNEY-1B/OF
24 WHITEY WILSHERE (INJ)-P
25 BILL CONROY-C
26 DOC CRAMER-OF
26 EMIL (LEFTY) MAILHO-OF
27 AL NIEMIEC-2B/SS
27 HUGH (HAL) LUBY-2B
28 CHUBBY DEAN-1B
29 RUSTY PETERS-UTIL
29 HOD LISENBEE-P
30 EARLE MACK-CH
31 RUSS (LENA) (SLATS) BLACKBURNE-CH
32 ? MCFARLAND-CH
37 HARRY (MATTY) MATUZAK-P
45 DICK CULLER-2B/SS
45 JACK PEERSON-SS
46 STU FLYTHE-P
NO# EDDIE SMITH-P (2G:9/20,25@HOME)

1937
7TH 54-97 46.5GB

NO# CONNIE (THE TALL TACTICIAN) MACK-MGR
1 FRANKIE (BLIMP) HAYES-C
2 EARLE BRUCKER (INJ)-C
3* CHUBBY DEAN-1B/P*
4 BILL CISSELL-2B
4 WAYNE AMBLER-2B
5 BILL WERBER-3B/OF
6 SKEETER NEWSOME-SS
7 BOB (INDIAN BOB) JOHNSON-OF/2B
8 LOU FINNEY-UTIL
8 EDDIE YOUNT-OF
9 WALLY MOSES-OF
10 BILL CONROY-C/1B
10 WARREN HUSTON-INF
10 DOYT MORRIS-OF
11 LYNN (LINE DRIVE) NELSON-P
12 RUSTY PETERS-2B/INF
14 RANDY GUMPERT-P
15 JESSE HILL-OF (2)
16 HARRY KELLEY-P
16 BABE BARNA-OF/1B
17 BUCK ROSS-P
18 HERMAN FINK-P
19 AL WILLIAMS-P
19 ACE PARKER-UTIL
19 RANDY GUMPERT-P
20 GEORGE (UG) CASTER-P
21 BUD THOMAS-P
22 EDDIE SMITH-P
23 JACK ROTHROCK-OF/2B
24 GEORGE TURBEVILLE-P
25 AL WILLIAMS-P
25 BILL CONROY-C/1B
26 DOC CRAMER-OF
26 ACE PARKER-UTIL
27 EARLE MACK-CH
28 RUSS (LENA) (SLATS) BLACKBURNE-CH
29 CHARLIE BERRY-CH
31 ACE PARKER-UTIL
32 EARLE MACK-CH
35 GENE HASSON-1B
41 FRED (LEFTY) ARCHER-P
61 BILL (LEFTY) KALFASS-P
__ HAL WAGNER-C (1G:10/3)

1938
8TH 53-99 46GB

NO# CONNIE (THE TALL TACTICIAN) MACK-MGR

1 WALLY MOSES-OF
2 SKEETER NEWSOME (INJ)-SS
3 BILLY WERBER-3B
4 BOB (INDIAN BOB) JOHNSON-OF/INF
5 GENE HASSON-1B
6 LOU FINNEY-1B/OF
7 DARIO LODIGIANI-2B
7 STAN SPERRY-2B
8 FRANKIE (BLIMP) HAYES-C
9 EARLE BRUCKER-C/1B
10 PAUL EASTERLING-OF
10 DICK SIEBERT (INJ)-1B (2)
11 DAVE SMITH-P
11 RUSTY PETERS-SS
12 WAYNE AMBLER-SS/2B
14 BABE BARNA-OF
14 SAM CHAPMAN-OF
15 HARRY KELLEY-P (1)
16 GEORGE (UG) CASTER-P
17 BUCK ROSS-P
18 EDDIE SMITH-P
19 HAL WAGNER-C
19 CHUBBY DEAN-P
20 BUD THOMAS-P
21 AL WILLIAMS-P
22 LYNN (LINE DRIVE) NELSON-P
23 NICK ETTEN-1B
24 NELSON (NELS) (NELLIE) POTTER-P
24 IRV BARTLING-SS/3B
25 ACE PARKER-UTIL
25 RALPH (BUCK) BUXTON-P
26 RANDY GUMPERT-P
26 HAL WAGNER-C
27 EARLE MACK-CH
28 RUSS (LENA) (SLATS) BLACKBURNE-CH
29 CHARLIE BERRY-C/CH
30 MULE HAAS-OF/1B
30 JIM RENINGER-P
31 RANDY GUMPERT-P

1939

7TH 55-97 51.5GB

NO# CONNIE (THE TALL TACTICIAN) MACK-MGR
1 WALLY MOSES-OF
2 SKEETER NEWSOME-SS/2B
3 BOB MCNAMARA-INF
3 BILL LILLARD-SS
4 BOB (INDIAN BOB) JOHNSON-OF/2B
5 DICK SIEBERT-1B
6 LOU FINNEY-OF (1)
6 AL (BRONK) BRANCATO-3B/SS
7 DARIO LODIGIANI-3B/2B
8 FRANKIE (BLIMP) HAYES-C
9 EARLE BRUCKER- C
10 SAM CHAPMAN-OF/1B
11 DEE MILES-OF
12 SEP GANTENBEIN-2B/INF
13 BILL BECKMANN-P
14 WAYNE AMBLER-SS/2B
15 BOB JOYCE-P
16 GEORGE (UG) CASTER (ILL)-P
17 BUCK ROSS-P
18 EDDIE SMITH-P (1)
18 ERIC (BLUE DEVIL) (DUKIE) TIPTON-OF
19 CHUBBY DEAN-P
20 BUD THOMAS-P (1)
20 SAM PAGE-P
20 WALT MASTERS-P
21 ROY (TARZAN) PARMELEE-P
21 JIM RENINGER-P
21 JIM SCHELLE-P
22 LYNN (LINE DRIVE) NELSON-P
23 BOB MCNAMARA-INF
23 DAVE SMITH-P
24 NELSON (NELS) (NELLIE) POTTER-P
25 COTTON PIPPEN-P (1)
25 FRED (CHAPPIE) CHAPMAN-SS
26 HAL WAGNER-C
26 EDDIE COLLINS, JR.-OF/2B
27 EARLE MACK-CH
28 RUSS (LENA) (SLATS) BLACKBURNE-CH
29 CHARLIE BERRY-CH
30 JIM RENINGER-P
30 HARRY O'NEILL-C
31 DAVE SMITH-P
31 LES (BUSTER) MCCRABB-P
32 DAVE KEEFE-CH
34 BILL NAGEL-INF/P
35 BILL BECKMANN-P
36 HARRY O'NEILL-C
36 NICK ETTEN-1B

1940

8TH 54-100 36GB

NO# CONNIE (THE TALL TACTICIAN) MACK-MGR
1 WALLY MOSES-OF
2 BENNY MCCOY-2B/3B
3 BILL LILLARD-SS/2B
4 BOB (INDIAN BOB) JOHNSON-OF
5 DICK SIEBERT-1B
6 AL (BUCKETFOOT AL) SIMMONS-OF/CH
7 CRASH DAVIS-2B/SS
8 FRANKIE (BLIMP) HAYES-C
9 EARLE BRUCKER- C
10 SAM CHAPMAN-OF
11 DEE MILES-OF
12 SEP GANTENBEIN-UTIL
14 CARL MILES-P
16 GEORGE (UG) CASTER-P
17 BUCK ROSS-P
18 AL (BRONK) BRANCATO-3B/SS
19 CHUBBY DEAN-P
20 HERMAN BESSE-P
21 ED (THE WILD ELK OF THE WASATCH) HEUSSER-P
22 BUDDY HANCKEN-C
22 PORTER (LEFTY) VAUGHAN-P
23 PHIL (BABE) MARCHILDON-P
24 NELSON (NELS) (NELLIE) POTTER-P
25 FRED (CHAPPIE) CHAPMAN-SS
25 JACK WALLAESA-SS
26 HAL WAGNER (INJ)-C
27 EARLE MACK-CH
28 RUSS (LENA) (SLATS) BLACKBURNE-CH
29 CHARLIE BERRY-CH
30 JOHNNY BABICH-P
31 LES (BUSTER) MCCRABB-P
32 DAVE KEEFE-CH
33 PAT MCLAUGHLIN-P
34 AL RUBELING-3B/2B
35 BILL BECKMANN-P
37 DARIO LODIGIANI-PH
38 ELMER VALO-OF
39 BUDDY HANCKEN-C
40 ERIC (BLUE DEVIL) (DUKIE) TIPTON-OF
41 JACK WALLAESA-SS

1941

8TH 64-90 37GB

NO# CONNIE (THE TALL TACTICIAN) MACK-MGR
1 WALLY MOSES-OF
2 BENNY MCCOY-2B
3 PETE (PECKY) SUDER-3B/SS
4 BOB (INDIAN BOB) JOHNSON-OF/1B
5 DICK SIEBERT-1B
6 SAM CHAPMAN-OF
7 DEE MILES-OF
8 FRANKIE (BLIMP) HAYES-C
9 HAL WAGNER-C
10 AL (BRONK) BRANCATO-3B/SS
11 FRED (CHAPPIE) CHAPMAN-SS
12 CRASH DAVIS-2B/1B
14 EDDIE COLLINS, JR.-OF
15 RANKIN JOHNSON, JR.-P
15 ELMER VALO-OF
16 JACK KNOTT-P
16 ROGER WOLFF-P
17 BUCK ROSS-P (1)
17 TEX SHIRLEY-P
17 BUMP HADLEY-P (2)
18 LUM HARRIS-P
19 CHUBBY DEAN-P (1)
20 HERMAN BESSE-P
21 PHIL (BABE) MARCHILDON-P
22 PORTER (LEFTY) VAUGHAN-P
23 FRED CALIGIURI-P
24 NELSON (NELS) (NELLIE) POTTER-P (1)
24 PAT TOBIN-P
25 BILL BECKMANN-P
26 EARLE BRUCKER-CH
27 EARLE MACK-CH
28 AL (BUCKETFOOT AL) SIMMONS-OF/CH
28 TOM FERRICK-P
29 LES (BUSTER) MCCRABB-P
30 JOHNNY BABICH-P
31 DAVE KEEFE-CH
32 FELIX (MAC) MACKIEWICZ-OF
32 BUMP HADLEY-P (2)
33 JOHN LEOVICH-C
34 TOM FERRICK-P
35 DON RICHMOND-3B
35 RAY POOLE-PH
38 ERIC (BLUE DEVIL) (DUKIE) TIPTON-OF
39 AL RUBELING-3B/2B
42 DICK FOWLER-P
55 DON RICHMOND-3B

1942

8TH 55-99 48GB

NO# CONNIE (THE TALL TACTICIAN) MACK-MGR
1 MIKE KREEVICH-OF
2 BILL KNICKERBOCKER (INJ)-2B/SS
2 KEN RICHARDSON-UTIL
3 PETE (PECKY) SUDER-SS/INF
4 BOB (INDIAN BOB) JOHNSON-OF
5 DICK SIEBERT-1B
6 BUDDY BLAIR-3B
7 DEE MILES-OF
8 FRANKIE (BLIMP) HAYES-C (1)
8 BOB SWIFT-C (2)
9 HAL WAGNER-C
10 JACK WALLAESA-SS
10 PHIL (BABE) MARCHILDON-P
11 KEN RICHARDSON-UTIL
11 GEORGE YANKOWSKI-C
11 BRUCE KONOPKA-1B
12 CRASH DAVIS-INF
14 EDDIE COLLINS, JR. (MIL)-OF
14 LARRY ESCHEN-SS/2B
14 ERIC (BOOB) MCNAIR-SS/2B (2)
15 ELMER VALO-OF
16 LARRY ESCHEN-SS/2B
16 JACK KNOTT (MIL)-P
17 TEX SHIRLEY-P
18 LUM HARRIS-P
19 FELIX (MAC) MACKIEWICZ-OF
19 ROGER WOLFF-P
20 HERMAN BESSE-P
21 PHIL (BABE) MARCHILDON-P
22 DICK FOWLER-P
23 FRED CALIGIURI-P
24 RUSS CHRISTOPHER-P
25 BILL BECKMANN-P (1)
25 BOB HARRIS-P (2)
26 EARLE BRUCKER-CH
27 EARLE MACK-CH
28 AL (BUCKETFOOT AL) SIMMONS-CH
29 LES (BUSTER) MCCRABB-P
29 BOB SAVAGE-P
30 ROGER WOLFF-P
31 DAVE KEEFE-CH
32 DICK FOWLER-P
33 RUSS (LENA) (SLATS) BLACKBURNE-CH
34 JIM CASTIGLIA (MIL)-C
35 JIM CASTIGLIA (MIL)-C
35 JACK KNOTT (MIL)-P
35 ELMER VALO-OF
37 TAL (TED) ABERNATHY-P
45 JACK KNOTT (MIL)-P
_ DICK ADKINS-SS (3G: 9/19-27)
_ JOE COLEMAN-P (1G: 9/19)
_ SAM LOWRY-P (1G: 9/19)

1943

2ND 49-105 49GB

NO# CONNIE (THE TALL TACTICIAN) MACK-MGR
1 JO-JO WHITE-OF
2 EDDIE (HOTSHOT) MAYO-3B
2? ED BUSCH-SS (4G:9/30-10/3)
3 PETE (PECKY) SUDER-2B/INF
4 BOBBY ESTALELLA-OF
5 DICK SIEBERT-1B
6 IRV HALL-SS/INF
7 LOU CIOLA-P
7 FELIX (MAC) MACKIEWICZ-OF
7? GEORGE KELL-3B (1G:9/28)
8 BOB SWIFT-C
9 HAL WAGNER-C
10 FRANK SKAFF-INF
10? TONY PARISSE-C (6G:9/22-10/3)
11 BRUCE KONOPKA (MIL)-PH
11 JOHNNY WELAJ (MIL)-OF
11? BILL BURGO-OF (17G:9/22-10/3)
12 JIMMY RIPPLE-OF
12 JIM TYACK-OF
12? JOE RULLO-2B (16G:9/22-10/3)
14 BERT KUCYZNSKI-P
14 CARL SCHEIB-P
14? LEW (NOISY) FLICK-OF (1G:9/28)
14 BRUCE KONOPKA (MIL)-PH
14 VERN BENSON (MIL)-PH
15 ELMER VALO (MIL)-OF
16 ROGER WOLFF-P
17 RUSS CHRISTOPHER-P
18 LUM HARRIS-P
19 FELIX (MAC) MACKIEWICZ-OF
19 JESSE FLORES-P
20 HERMAN BESSE-P
21 DON BLACK-P
22 SAM LOWRY-P
22 DON (JEEP) HEFFNER-2B/1B (2)
23 ORIE ARNTZEN-P
24 EVERETT FAGAN (MIL)-P
25 TOM CLYDE-P
25 BUD MAINS-P
26 EARLE BRUCKER-PH/CH
27 EARLE MACK-CH
28 AL (BUCKETFOOT AL) SIMMONS-CH
28 RUSS (LENA) (SLATS) BLACKBURNE-CH
29 DAVE KEEFE-CH
30 ROGER WOLFF-P
30? WOODY WHEATON-OF (7G:9/28-10/3)
31 DAVE KEEFE-CH
31 JOHN BURROWS-P (1)
32 DAVE KEEFE-CH
33 RUSS (LENA) (SLATS) BLACKBURNE-CH
37 TAL (TED) ABERNATHY-P
_ CHARLIE BOWLES (MIL)-P (2G:9/25,25)
_ NORM BROWN-P (1G:10/3)
_ GEORGE STALLER-OF (21G:9/14-10/3)

1944

5TH (TIE) 72-82 17GB

NO# CONNIE (THE TALL TACTICIAN) MACK-MGR
1 JO-JO WHITE-OF/SS (1)
2 ED BUSCH-SS/INF
3* JOHN MCGILLEN-P*
3 HAL EPPS-OF (2)
4 BOBBY ESTALELLA-OF/1B
5 DICK SIEBERT-1B/OF
6 IRV HALL-2B/INF
7 GEORGE KELL-3B
8 FRANKIE (BLIMP) HAYES-C
9 HAL WAGNER-C (1)
9 FORD (ROCKY) (SNAPPER) GARRISON-OF (2)
10 TONY PARISSE-C
11 BILL BURGO-OF
11 BILL (FIBBER) MCGHEE-1B
12 JOE RULLO-2B/1B
12 LARRY ROSENTHAL-OF (2)
14? LEW (NOISY) FLICK-OF (19G:)
14 CHARLIE METRO-UTIL (2)
15 BOB GARBARK-C
16 BOBO (BUCK) NEWSOM-P
17 RUSS CHRISTOPHER-P
18 LUM HARRIS-P
19 JESSE FLORES-P
20 JOE (JITTERY JOE) BERRY-P
21 DON BLACK-P
22 BILL MILLS-C
22 JOE BURNS-3B/2B
23 BOBBY WILKINS-SS
23 BILL MILLS-C
24 CARL SCHEIB-P
25 TAL (TED) ABERNATHY-P
26 EARLE BRUCKER-PH/CH
27 EARLE MACK-CH
28 RUSS (LENA) (SLATS) BLACKBURNE-CH
29 DAVE KEEFE-CH
30 WOODY WHEATON-P/OF
31 LUKE (HOT POTATO) HAMLIN-P
32 AL (BUCKETFOOT AL) SIMMONS-OF/CH
32 JOHN MCGILLEN-P
_ HAL PECK-OF (2G:9/29,29)

PHILADELPHIA/KANSAS CITY/ OAKLAND ATHLETICS

__ JIM PRUETT-C (3G:9/26-10/1)

1945
8TH 52-98 34.5GB

NO# CONNIE (THE TALL TACTICIAN) MACK-MGR
1 HAL PECK-OF
2 ED BUSCH-SS/INF
3*CHARLIE (SHERIFF) GASSAWAY-P*
3 FORD (ROCKY) (SNAPPER) GARRISON (MIL)-OF
4 BOBBY ESTALELLA-OF
5 DICK SIEBERT-1B
6 IRV HALL-2B
7 GEORGE KELL-3B
8 FRANKIE (BLIMP) HAYES-C (1)
8 GREEK GEORGE (SUS)-C
9 JIM PRUETT-C
9 BUDDY ROSAR (RET)-C
10 SAM CHAPMAN (MIL)-OF
10 MAYO SMITH-OF
10 JOE (DODE) CICERO-OF
11 BUDDY ROSAR (RET)-C
11 CHARLIE BOWLES (MIL)-P
12 LARRY ROSENTHAL-OF
12 GREEK GEORGE (SUS)-C
12 ERNIE KISH-OF
13 JOE BURNS-3B/2B
14 JOE ASTROTH-C
14 BILL (FIBBER) MCGHEE-OF/1B
15 CHARLIE METRO-OF
15 JOE ASTROTH-C
16 BOBO (BUCK) NEWSOM-P
17 RUSS CHRISTOPHER-P
18 STEVE (SPLINTER) GERKIN-P
18 AL (BRONK) BRANCATO-SS
19 JESSE FLORES-P
20 JOE (JITTERY JOE) BERRY-P
21 DON BLACK (SUS)-P
22 JOE BURNS-3B/2B
22 BOBBY WILKINS-SS
23 WOODY CROWSON-P
23 PHIL (BABE) MARCHILDON (MIL)-P
24 CARL SCHEIB (MIL)-P
24 BILL (WILD BILL) CONNELLY -P
25 DICK FOWLER (MIL)-P
25 JOE (DODE) CICERO-OF
26 EARLE BRUCKER-CH
27 EARLE MACK-CH
29 DAVE KEEFE-CH
30 LOU KNERR-P
31 LARRY DRAKE-OF
32 AL (BUCKETFOOT AL) SIMMONS-OF/CH
35 CHARLIE BOWLES (MIL)-P
36 PHIL (BABE) MARCHILDON (MIL)-P

1946
8TH 49-105 55GB

NO# CONNIE (THE TALL TACTICIAN) MACK-MGR
1 FORD (ROCKY) (SNAPPER) GARRISON-OF
1 TUCK STAINBACK-OF
2 RUSS DERRY-OF
3 HAL PECK-OF
3 HANK (HEENEY) (HEINE) MAJESKI-3B (2)
4 SAM CHAPMAN-OF
5 GEORGE (MAC) MCQUINN-1B
6 IRV HALL-2B/SS
7 GEORGE KELL-3B (1)
7 BARNEY MCCOSKY-OF (2)
8 BUDDY ROSAR-C
9 GENE (RED) DESAUTELS-C
10 JACK WALLAESA-SS
(11) FRED CALIGIURI (MIL)-(P)
12 PETE (PECKY) SUDER-SS/UTIL
14 JAKE CAULFIELD-SS/3B
14 JOE ASTROTH-C
15 GENE HANDLEY-2B/INF
16 BOBO (BUCK) NEWSOM-P (1)
17 RUSS CHRISTOPHER-P
18 LUM HARRIS-P
19 JESSE FLORES-P
20 JOE (JITTERY JOE) BERRY-P (1)
21 ELMER VALO-OF
22 OSCAR GRIMES-INF (2)
23 PHIL (BABE) MARCHILDON-P
(24) CARL SCHEIB (MIL)-(P)
24 HERMAN BESSE-P
25 DICK FOWLER-P
26 EARLE BRUCKER-CH
27 EARLE MACK-CH
28 PAT COOPER-P
28 PORTER (LEFTY) VAUGHAN-P
29 DAVE KEEFE-CH
30 LOU KNERR-P
31 LEE GRIFFITH-P
31 NORM BROWN-P
32 AL (BUCKETFOOT AL) SIMMONS-CH
33 GEORGE (DODO) ARMSTRONG-C
35 JACK KNOTT-P
36 BRUCE KONOPKA-CH
36 HANK (HEENEY) (HEINE) MAJESKI-3B (2)
36 JOE COLEMAN-P
37 BOB SAVAG-P
38 VERN BENSON-OF
38 EVERETT FAGAN (MIL)-P
40 BILL MCCAHAN-P
41 DON RICHMOND-3B

1947
5TH 78-76 19GB

NO# CONNIE (THE TALL TACTICIAN) MACK-MGR
1 EDDIE JOOST-SS
2 GENE HANDLEY (INJ)-INF
3 HANK (HEENEY) (HEINE) MAJESKI-3B/INF
4 SAM CHAPMAN-OF
5 FERRIS FAIN-1B
6 DICK ADAMS-1B/OF
7 BARNEY MCCOSKY-OF
8 BUDDY ROSAR-C
9 MIKE (MICKEY) GUERRA-C
10 ELMER VALO-OF
11 GEORGE (BINGO) BINKS-OF/1B
12 PETE (PECKY) SUDER-2B/INF
14 DON RICHMOND-3B/2B
14 HERMAN FRANKS-C
15 PAT COOPER-1B
15 AUSTIN KNICKERBOCKER-OF
16 BOB SAVAGE-P
17 RUSS CHRISTOPHER-P
17 LOU BRISSIE-P
18 BILL (BULLFROG) DIETRICH-P
19 JOE COLEMAN-P
19 JESSE FLORES-P
20 JOE COLEMAN-P
21 PHIL (BABE) MARCHILDON-P
23 BILL MCCAHAN-P
24 CARL SCHEIB-P
25 DICK FOWLER-P
26 EARLE BRUCKER-CH
27 EARLE MACK-CH
28 CHET LAABS-OF
28 NELLIE FOX-2B
29 DAVE KEEFE-CH
30 AUSTIN KNICKERBOCKER-OF
30 TOM KIRK-PH
31 RAY POOLE-PH
31 MICKEY RUTNER-3B
32 AL (BUCKETFOOT AL) SIMMONS-CH

1948
4TH 84-70 12.5GB

NO# CONNIE (THE TALL TACTICIAN) MACK-MGR
1 EDDIE JOOST-SS
2 SKEETER WEBB-2B/SS
3 HANK (HEENEY) (HEINE) MAJESKI-3B/SS
4 SAM CHAPMAN-OF
5 FERRIS FAIN-1B
6 RUDY YORK-1B
7 BARNEY MCCOSKY-OF
8 BUDDY ROSAR-C
9 MIKE (MICKEY) GUERRA-C
10 ELMER VALO-OF
11 GEORGE (BINGO) BINKS-OF (1)
11 RAY COLEMAN-OF (2)
12 PETE (PECKY) SUDER-2B
14 HERMAN FRANKS-C
15 DON WHITE-OF/3B
16 BOB SAVAGE-P
17 CHARLIE (BUBBA) HARRIS-P
18 BILL (BULLFROG) DIETRICH-P
18 WALT HOLBOROW-P
19 LOU BRISSIE-P
20 JOE COLEMAN-P
21 PHIL (BABE) MARCHILDON-P
22 NELSON (NELS) (NELLIE) POTTER-P (2)
22 ALEX KELLNER-P
23 BILL MCCAHAN (INJ)-P
24 CARL SCHEIB-P/OF
25 DICK FOWLER (INJ)-P
26 EARLE BRUCKER, SR.-CH
26 EARLE BRUCKER, JR.-C
27 EARLE MACK-CH
29 DAVE KEEFE-CH
30 BILLY (KID) DEMARS-INF
32 AL (BUCKETFOOT AL) SIMMONS-CH
41 NELLIE FOX-2B
56 BOB WELLMAN-1B/OF

1949
5TH 81-73 16GB

NO# CONNIE (THE TALL TACTICIAN) MACK-MGR
1 EDDIE JOOST-SS
2 WALLY MOSES-OF
3 HANK (HEENEY) (HEINE) MAJESKI-3B
4 SAM CHAPMAN-OF
5 FERRIS FAIN-1B
6 TAFFY WRIGHT-OF
(7) BARNEY MCCOSKY (INJ)-(OF)
8 BUDDY ROSAR-C
9 JOE ASTROTH-C
10 ELMER VALO-OF
11 HANK BIASATTI-1B
12 PETE (PECKY) SUDER-2B/INF
15 DON WHITE-OF/3B
16 TOD DAVIS-INF
17 CHARLIE (BUBBA) HARRIS-P
18 NELLIE FOX-2B
19 LOU BRISSIE-P
20 JOE COLEMAN-P
21 PHIL (BABE) MARCHILDON (INJ)-P
22 ALEX KELLNER-P
23 BILL MCCAHAN-P
24 CARL SCHEIB-P/OF
25 DICK FOWLER-P
26 EARLE BRUCKER, SR.-CH
27 EARLE MACK-CH
28 JIM WILSON-P
29 DAVE KEEFE-CH
30 BOBBY SHANTZ-P
31 LES (BUSTER) MCCRABB-CH
32 AL (BUCKETFOOT AL) SIMMONS-CH
33 BOBBY ESTALELLA (MEX)-OF
34 CLEM HAUSMANN-P
34 AUGIE GALAN-OF (2)
35 JIMMY DYKES-CH
37 MIKE (MICKEY) GUERRA-C

1950
8TH 52-102 46GB

NO# CONNIE (THE TALL TACTICIAN) MACK-MGR
1 EDDIE JOOST-SS
2 WALLY MOSES-OF
3 BEN GUINTINI-OF
4 SAM CHAPMAN-OF
5 PAUL (PEANUTS) (GULLIVER) LEHNER-OF
6 BOB (DUKE) DILLINGER-3B
7 BARNEY MCCOSKY-OF
8 FERRIS FAIN-1B
9 JOE ASTROTH-C
10 ELMER VALO-OF
11 BILLY HITCHCOCK-2B/SS
12 PETE (PECKY) SUDER-INF
14 GENE (MOUSEY) MARKLAND-2B
15 JOE TIPTON-C
17 JOHNNY KUCAB-P
18 KERMIT WAHL-INF
19 LOU BRISSIE-P
20 JOE COLEMAN-P
21 JOE MURRAY-P
22 ALEX KELLNER-P
23 BOB HOOPER-P
24 CARL SCHEIB-P/OF
25 DICK FOWLER (INJ)-P
26 MOE BURTSCHY (INJ)-P
27 EARLE MACK-CH
28 EDDIE (SPECS) (BABE) KLIEMAN-P
28 ROBERTO ORTIZ-OF (2)
29 DAVE KEEFE-CH
30 BOBBY SHANTZ-P
31 LES (BUSTER) MCCRABB-P/CH
32 MICKEY COCHRANE-CH
33 BING MILLER-CH
35 JIMMY DYKES-CH/ASST MGR
36 HANK (HOOKS) WYSE-P
36 HARRY BYRD-P
37 MIKE (MICKEY) GUERRA-C
38 BOB WELLMAN-OF
38 MOE BURTSCHY (INJ)-P
38 BOB RINKER-C
39 HARRY BYRD-P

1951
6TH 70-84 28GB

1 EDDIE JOOST-SS
2 WALLY MOSES-OF
3 LOU LIMMER-1B
4 SAM CHAPMAN-OF (1)
5 PAUL (PEANUTS) (GULLIVER) LEHNER-OF (1)
5 DAVE PHILLEY-OF/3B (2)
5 HANK (HEENEY) (HEINE) MAJESKI-3B (2)
6 EDDIE SAMCOF-2B
6 GUS (OZARK IKE) (ZEKE) ZERNIAL-OF (2)
6 LOU KLEIN-2B (2)
7 BARNEY MCCOSKY-OF (1)
7 ALLIE CLARK-OF/3B (2)
8 FERRIS FAIN (INJ)-1B/OF
9 JOE ASTROTH-C
10 ELMER VALO-OF
11 BILLY HITCHCOCK-INF
12 PETE (PECKY) SUDER-2B/INF
14 RAY (DEACON) MURRAY-C (2)
15 JOE TIPTON-C
16 TOD DAVIS-2B/3B
17 CHARLIE (BUBBA) HARRIS-P (1)
17 DAVE PHILLEY-OF/3B (2)
18 KERMIT WAHL-3B (1)
19 LOU BRISSIE-P
19 GUS (OZARK IKE) (ZEKE) ZERNIAL-OF (2)
20 JOE COLEMAN-P
21 SAM (SAD SAM) ZOLDAK-P
22 ALEX KELLNER-P
23 BOB HOOPER-P
24 CARL SCHEIB-P/OF
25 DICK FOWLER-P
26 MORRIE (LEFTY) MARTIN-P
29 TOM (REBEL) OLIVER-CH
30 BOBBY SHANTZ-P
31 LES (BUSTER) MCCRABB-CH
32 CHIEF BENDER-CH
33 BING MILLER-CH
35 JIMMY DYKES-MGR
36 HANK (HOOKS) WYSE-P (1)
37 JOHNNY KUCAB-P
38 BOB WELLMAN-OF
38 MOE BURTSCHY (INJ)-P
39 HARRY BYRD-P
42 MORRIE (LEFTY) MARTIN-P

1952
4TH 79-75 16GB

1 EDDIE JOOST-SS
2 SKEETER KELL-2B
3 HAL BEVAN-3B (2)
4 TOM (HAM) HAMILTON-1B
5 HANK (HEENEY) (HEINE) MAJESKI-3B (1)
5 CASS MICHAELS-2B (3)
6 KITE THOMAS-OF
7 ALLIE CLARK (INJ)-OF/1B
8 FERRIS FAIN-1B
9 JOE ASTROTH-C
10 ELMER VALO-OF
11 BILLY HITCHCOCK-3B/1B
12 PETE (PECKY) SUDER-INF
14 RAY (DEACON) MURRAY-C
15 JOE TIPTON-C (1)
16 JACK LITTRELL-SS/3B
16 SHERRY ROBERTSON-UTIL (2)
17 DAVE PHILLEY-OF/3B
18 TEX HOYLE-P
19 GUS (OZARK IKE) (ZEKE) ZERNIAL-OF
20 BOBO (BUCK) NEWSOM-P (2)
21 SAM (SAD SAM) ZOLDAK-P
21 WALT KELLNER-P
22 ALEX KELLNER-P
23 BOB HOOPER-P
24 CARL SCHEIB-P/OF
25 DICK FOWLER-P
26 MORRIE (LEFTY) MARTIN (INJ)-P
28 WALLY MOSES-CH
29 TOM (REBEL) OLIVER-CH
30 BOBBY SHANTZ-P
31 LES (BUSTER) MCCRABB-CH
32 CHIEF BENDER-CH
33 BING MILLER-CH
34 ED WRIGHT-P
35 JIMMY DYKES-MGR
36 LEN MATARAZZO-P
37 JOHNNY KUCAB-P

37 MARION FRICANO-P
38 CHARLIE BISHOP-P
39 HARRY BYRD-P

1953

7TH 59-95 41.5GB

1 EDDIE JOOST-SS
2 JOE (OATS) DEMAESTRI-SS
3 LOREN (BEE BEE) BABE-3B/SS (2)
4 TOM (HAM) HAMILTON-1B/OF
5 CASS MICHAELS-2B
6 KITE THOMAS-OF (1)
6 CARMEN MAURO-OF/3B (3)
7 ALLIE CLARK-OF (1)
7 TOMMY (T-BONE) GIORDANO-2B
7 SPIDER WILHELM-SS
8 EDDIE ROBINSON-1B
9 JOE ASTROTH-C
10 ELMER VALO (INJ)-OF
11 NEAL WATLINGTON-C
11 DON (BUTCH) (CAB) KOLLOWAY-3B
12 PETE (PECKY) SUDER-INF
14 RAY (DEACON) MURRAY-C
15 FRANK (LEFTY) FANOVICH-P
16 ED MCGHEE-OF
17 DAVE PHILLEY-OF/3B
18 BILL HARRINGTON (MIL)-P
19 GUS (OZARK IKE) (ZEKE) ZERNIAL-OF
20 BOBO (BUCK) NEWSOM-P
21 WALT KELLNER-P
22 ALEX KELLNER-P
23 DICK ROZEK-P
23 BOB TRICE-P
24 CARL SCHEIB-P/OF
25 JOE COLEMAN (ILL)-P
26 MORRIE (LEFTY) MARTIN-P
28 WALLY MOSES-CH
29 TOM (REBEL) OLIVER-CH
29 BOBO (BUCK) NEWSOM-P
30 BOBBY SHANTZ (INJ)-P
31 LES (BUSTER) MCCRABB-CH
32 CHIEF BENDER-CH
33 BING MILLER-CH
34 RINTY MONAHAN-P
35 JIMMY DYKES-MGR
36 JOHNNY MACKINSON-P
36 TOMMY (T-BONE) GIORDANO-2B
37 MARION FRICANO-P
38 CHARLIE BISHOP-P
39 HARRY BYRD-P
40 JOHNNY MACKINSON-P
41 BILL HARRINGTON (MIL)-P
41 JOHNNY MACKINSON-P
45 NEAL WATLINGTON-C

1954

8TH 51-103 60GB

1 EDDIE JOOST-INF/MGR
2 JOE (OATS) DEMAESTRI-SS/INF
3 JACK LITTRELL-SS
4 DON BOLLWEG-1B
5 VIC POWER-OF/INF
6 SPOOK JACOBS-2B
8 BILL RENNA-OF
9 JOE ASTROTH-C
10 ELMER VALO-OF
11 BILLY SHANTZ-C
12 PETE (PECKY) SUDER-INF
14 LOU LIMMER-1B
15 JIM FINIGAN-3B
16 ED MCGHEE-OF (1)
17 BILL UPTON-P
17 BILL OSTER-P
18 JIM ROBERTSON-C
19 GUS (OZARK IKE) (ZEKE) ZERNIAL (INJ)-OF/1B
20 ART DITMAR-P
20 JOE TAYLOR-OF
22 ALEX KELLNER-P
23 BOB TRICE-P
23 DICK ROZEK-P
24 CARL SCHEIB-P (1)
24 SONNY DIXON-P (2)
25 ARNIE PORTOCARRERO-P
26 MORRIE (LEFTY) MARTIN-P (1)
26 AL SIMA-P (2)
28 WALLY MOSES-CH
29 AUGIE GALAN-CH
30 BOBBY SHANTZ (INJ)-P
31 LES (BUSTER) MCCRABB-CH
32 JOHNNY GRAY-P
33 MOE BURTSCHY-P
34 JOHNNY GRAY-P
35 ROLLIE HEMSLEY-CH
36 HAL (BUD) RAETHER-P
37 MARION FRICANO-P
38 CHARLIE BISHOP-P
40 LEE WHEAT-P
40 BILL WILSON-OF (2)
42 OZZIE VAN BRABANT-P
48 LOU LIMMER-1B
49 DICK ROZEK-P
49 DUTCH ROMBERGER-P

1955

KANSAS CITY ATHLETICS

6TH 63-91 33GB

1 HAL BEVAN-3B
1 HECTOR LOPEZ-3B/2B
2 JOE (OATS) DEMAESTRI-SS
2 ALEX GEORGE-SS
3 DON BOLLWEG-1B
3 TOM SAFFELL-OF
4 JIM FINIGAN-2B/3B
5 LOU BOUDREAU-MGR
6 DON PLARSKI-OF
6 SPOOK JACOBS-2B
6 JERRY SCHYPINSKI-SS/2B
7 VIC POWER-1B
8 DICK KRYHOSKI-1B
8 GLENN COX-P
9 JACK LITTRELL (INJ)-INF
10 ERIC MACKENZIE-C
10 HECTOR LOPEZ-3B/2B
11 JOE ASTROTH-C
12 PETE (PECKY) SUDER-2B
12 CLETE BOYER-INF
14 JOHNNY GRAY-P
14 JOHNNY SAIN-P (2)
15 OZZIE VAN BRABANT-P
15 WALT CRADDOCK-P
16 LEE WHEAT-P
16 VIC RASCHI-P (2)
17 MARION FRICANO-P
17 RAY HERBERT-P
18 CLOYD (JUNIOR) BOYER-P
19 ART (CHIC) CECCARELLI-P
20 ALEX KELLNER-P
21 BOBBY SHANTZ-P
22 BILLY SHANTZ-C
23 BOB TRICE-P
24 SONNY DIXON-P
25 ARNIE PORTOCARRERO (INJ)-P
26 CHARLIE BISHOP-P
26 BILL HARRINGTON (MIL)-P
27 MOE BURTSCHY-P
27 GUS KERIAZAKOS-P
28 ART DITMAR-P
29 BOB SPICER-P
29 MARION FRICANO-P
29 MIKE KUME-P
30 GUS (OZARK IKE) (ZEKE) ZERNIAL-OF
31 LOU SLEATER-P
31 BILL STEWART-OF
32 BILL WILSON-OF/P
33 JIM ROBERTSON-C
33 ENOS (COUNTRY) SLAUGHTER-OF (2)
34 BILL RENNA-OF
35 ELMER VALO-OF
36 EWELL (THE WHIP) BLACKWELL-P
37 TOM GORMAN-P
38 BILL STEWART-OF
38 HARRY (SUITCASE) (GOODY) SIMPSON-OF/1B (2)
40 GEORGE SUSCE-CH
41 HARRY (WILDFIRE) CRAFT-CH
42 SKI (SPINACH) MELILLO-CH
43 BURLEIGH (OL' STUBBLEBEARD) GRIMES-CH

1956

8TH 52-102 45GB

1 MIKE BAXES-SS/2B
2 JOE (OATS) DEMAESTRI-SS/2B
4 JIM FINIGAN-2B/3B
5 LOU BOUDREAU-MGR
6 SPOOK JACOBS-2B (1)
6 AL PILARCIK-OF
7 VIC POWER-1B/UTIL
8 RANCE PLESS-1B/3B
9 JOE GINSBERG-C (1)
9 GEORGE (LEFTY) BRUNET-P
9 HAL SMITH-C (2)
10 HECTOR LOPEZ-3B/UTIL
11 JOE ASTROTH-C
11 TIM THOMPSON-C
12 CLETE BOYER-2B/3B
14 BILL BRADFORD-P
14 BILL HARRINGTON (MIL)-P
14 JACK MCMAHAN-P (2)
15 WALT CRADDOCK-P
16 GLENN COX-P
17 TROY (DUTCH) HERRIAGE-P
18 LOU (LENA) KRETLOW-P
19 ART (CHIC) CECCARELLI-P
20 ALEX KELLNER-P
21 BOBBY SHANTZ (INJ)-P
22 TIM THOMPSON-C
23 LOU (LENA) KRETLOW-P
23 TOM LASORDA-P
23 WALLY BURNETTE-P
24 JACK CRIMIAN-P
25 ARNIE PORTOCARRERO-P
25 EDDIE ROBINSON-1B (2)
26 BILL HARRINGTON (MIL)-P
26 JOSE (PANTS) SANTIAGO-P
27 LOU (LENA) KRETLOW-P
28 ART DITMAR-P
29 BOB SPICER-P
30 GUS (OZARK IKE) (ZEKE) ZERNIAL-OF
31 DAVE MELTON-OF
32 JOSE (PANTS) SANTIAGO-P
33 ENOS (COUNTRY) SLAUGHTER-OF (1)
33 LOU (LENA) KRETLOW-P
34 BILL RENNA-OF
35 ELMER VALO-OF (1)
35 LOU (THE NERVOUS GREEK) SKIZES-OF (2)
36 MOE BURTSCHY-P
36 JIM PISONI-OF
37 TOM GORMAN-P
38 HARRY (SUITCASE) (GOODY) SIMPSON-OF/1B
39 JOHNNY GROTH-OF
39 CARL DUSER-P
40 GEORGE SUSCE-CH
41 HARRY (WILDFIRE) CRAFT-CH
42 SKI (SPINACH) MELILLO-CH
53 GEORGE (LEFTY) BRUNET-P

1957

7TH 59-94 38.5GB

1 BILLY HUNTER-2B/INF
2 JOE (OATS) DEMAESTRI-SS
4 MILT GRAFF-2B
4 BILLY (THE KID) MARTIN-INF (2)
5 LOU BOUDREAU-MGR1
7 VIC POWER-1B/UTIL
9 HAL SMITH-C
10 HECTOR LOPEZ-3B/UTIL
11 IRV NOREN-1B/OF (1)
11 MILT GRAFF-2B
12 CLETE BOYER-2B/3B
12 DAVE HILL-P
15 RIP COLEMAN-P
15 HARRY TAYLOR-P
16 AL (LEFTY) ABER-P (2)
17 TOM (PLOWBOY) MORGAN-P
19 MICKEY MCDERMOTT-P
20 ALEX KELLNER-P
21 JACK URBAN-P
21 ED BLAKE-P
22 TIM THOMPSON-C
23 VIRGIL (FIRE) TRUCKS-P
23 WALLY BURNETTE-P
24 WALLY BURNETTE-P
25 ARNIE PORTOCARRERO-P
26 RALPH TERRY-P (2)
26 RYNE DUREN-P
28 GLENN COX-P
28 GENE (TWINKLES) (SLICK) HOST-P
28 WALLY BURNETTE-P
30 GUS (OZARK IKE) (ZEKE) ZERNIAL-OF/1B
31 NED GARVER-P
32 JIM PISONI-OF
32 BOB MARTYN-OF
33 BOB CERV-OF
34 HAL (BUD) RAETHER-P
35 LOU (THE NERVOUS GREEK) SKIZES-OF/3B
36 JIM (GEE GEE) GLEESON-CH
37 TOM GORMAN-P
38 HARRY (SUITCASE) (GOODY) SIMPSON-1B/OF (1)
38 WOODIE HELD-OF
39 JOHNNY GROTH-OF (1)
40 SPUD CHANDLER-CH
41 HARRY (WILDFIRE) CRAFT-CH/MGR2
42 BOB SWIFT-CH
46 JIM (GEE GEE) GLEESON-CH

1958

7TH 73-81 19GB

1 BILLY HUNTER-INF (1)
1 CHICO CARRASQUEL-3B/SS (2)
2 JOE (OATS) DEMAESTRI-SS
3 DAVE MELTON-OF
4 MILT GRAFF-2B
4 LOU KLIMCHOCK-2B
5 WOODIE HELD-UTIL (1)
5 HARRY (SUITCASE) (GOODY) SIMPSON-1B/OF (2)
6* WALT CRADDOCK-P*
7 VIC POWER-1B/2B (1)
7 PRESTON WARD-UTIL (2)
8 HARRY CHITI-C
9 HAL SMITH-3B/UTIL
10 HECTOR LOPEZ-2B/UTIL
11 MIKE BAXES-2B/SS
12 FRANK (PIG) HOUSE-C
13 BILL TUTTLE-OF
14 CARL DUSER-P
15 CARL DUSER-P
15 DICK (BONES) TOMANEK-P (2)
16 GLENN COX-P
17 HARRY CHITI-C
18 KENT HADLEY-1B
20 ALEX KELLNER-P (1)
20 JOHN TSITOURIS-P
21 JACK URBAN-P
22 BUD DALEY-P
22 WHITEY HERZOG-OF/1B (2)
23 VIRGIL (FIRE) TRUCKS-P (1
24 WALLY BURNETTE-P
24 BOB DAVIS-P
26 RALPH TERRY-P
27 KEN JOHNSON-P
28 BUD DALEY-P
29 MURRY DICKSON-P (1)
30 WALT CRADDOCK-P
31 NED GARVER-P
32 BOB MARTYN-OF
33 BOB CERV-OF
34 DUKE MAAS-P (1)
34 BOB GRIM-P (2)
35 DAVE MELTON-OF
35 JIM SMALL-OF
35 ROGER MARIS-OF (2)
36 FRANK (PIG) HOUSE-C
37 TOM GORMAN-P
38 RAY HERBERT-P
39 DON (JEEP) HEFFNER-CH
39 DICK (BONES) TOMANEK-P (2)
39 HOWIE (DIZ) REED-P
40 SPUD CHANDLER-CH
40 BOB GRIM-P (2)
41 HARRY (WILDFIRE) CRAFT-MGR
42 BOB SWIFT-CH
47 MURRY DICKSON-P (1)

1959

7TH 66-88 28GB

1 WAYNE (TWIG) TERWILLIGER-2B/INF
2 JOE (OATS) DEMAESTRI-SS
3 ROGER MARIS (ILL)-OF
5 HARRY (SUITCASE) (GOODY) SIMPSON-1B/OF (1)
5 LOU KLIMCHOCK-2B
7 PRESTON WARD-1B/OF
7* AL (STRETCH) GRUNWALD-P*
8 HARRY CHITI-C
9 HAL SMITH-3B/C
10 HECTOR LOPEZ-2B(1)
10 JOE MORGAN-3B (2)
11 JOHN TSITOURIS-P
11 JERRY LUMPE-INF (2)
12 FRANK (PIG) HOUSE-C
13 BILL TUTTLE-OF
14 RUSS SNYDER-OF
14 TOMMY CARROLL-SS/3B
15 DICK (BONES) TOMANEK-P
16 HOWIE (DIZ) REED-P
17 ZEKE BELLA-OF/1B
18 KENT HADLEY-1B
20 RUSS (THE MAD MONK) (ROWDY) MEYER-P
20 HOWIE (DIZ) REED-P
20 JOHN TSITOURIS-P
21 MURRY DICKSON-P
22 WHITEY HERZOG (ILL)-OF/1B
23 DICK WILLIAMS-3B/UTIL
26 RALPH TERRY-P (1)
26 JOHNNY KUCKS-P (2)
28 BUD DALEY-P
30 GEORGE (LEFTY) BRUNET-P
30 RAY (IKE) BOONE-1B/3B (2)
30 RAY (JABBO) JABLONSKI-3B (2)
31 NED GARVER-P
32 BOB MARTYN-PR
32 TOM (SNAKE) STURDIVANT-P (2)
33 BOB CERV-OF
34 BOB GRIM-P
35 KEN JOHNSON-P
35 MARK FREEMAN-P (2)
36 RIP COLEMAN-P (1)
36 MARTY KUTYNA-P
36 EVANS KILLEEN-P

'HILADELPHIA/KANSAS CITY/
)AKLAND ATHLETICS

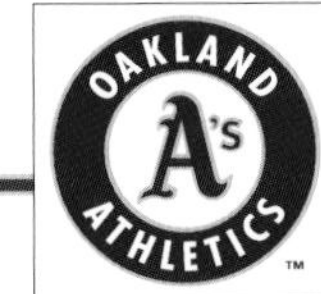

7 TOM GORMAN-P
8 RAY HERBERT-P
9 DON (JEEP) HEFFNER-CH
0 JOHNNY SAIN-CH
1 HARRY (WILDFIRE) CRAFT-MGR
2 BOB SWIFT-CH
7 TOM (SNAKE) STURDIVANT-P (2)
3 JOHNNY KUCKS-P (2)

1960

8TH 58-96 39GB

1 WAYNE (TWIG) TERWILLIGER-2B
1 ANDY CAREY-3B (2)
2 KEN HAMLIN-SS
3 MARV (MARVELOUS MARV) THRONEBERRY-1B
4 RAY (JABBO) JABLONSKI-3B
4 LOU KLIMCHOCK-2B
5 BOB JOHNSON-INF
6 JIM DELSING-OF
6 WHITEY HERZOG (ILL)-OF/1B
7 NORM SIEBERN-OF/1B
8 HARRY CHITI-C (1)
9 HANK BAUER-OF
0 PETE DALEY-C/OF
1 JERRY LUMPE-2B/SS
2 HANK FOILES-C (1)
2 DANNY (DUSTY) (BEAK) KRAVITZ-C (2)
3 BILL TUTTLE-OF
4 RUSS SNYDER-OF
5 BOB DAVIS-P
6 HOWIE (DIZ) REED-P
7 KEN JOHNSON-P
8 DON LARSEN-P
0 JOHN TSITOURIS (INJ)-P
2 PETE DALEY-C/OF
3 DICK WILLIAMS-UTIL
4 DICK HALL-P
6 JOHNNY KUCKS-P
7 GEORGE (LEFTY) BRUNET-P (1)
7 RAY BLEMKER-P
7 BOB GIGGIE-P (2)
7 JOHNNY BRIGGS-P (2)
8 BUD DALEY-P
0 BOB (MR. TEAM) ELLIOTT-MGR
1 NED GARVER-P
2 LEO (KIKI) KIELY-P
3 BOB CERV-OF (1)
4 LEO (KIKI) KIELY-P
6 MARTY KUTYNA-P
7 LEO POSADA-OF
7 BOB TROWBRIDGE-P
8 RAY HERBERT-P
9 DON (JEEP) HEFFNER-CH
0 WALKER (WALK) COOPER-CH
2 FRED (FAT FREDDIE) FITZSIMMONS-CH
5 DAVE WICKERSHAM-P
7 CHET BOAK-2B
8 JIM MCMANUS-1B

1961

9TH (TIE) 61-100 47.5GB

1 DICK HOWSER-SS
2 WAYNE CAUSEY-3B/INF
3 MARV (MARVELOUS MARV) THRONEBERRY-1B/OF
3 GENE STEPHENS-OF (2)
4 LOU KLIMCHOCK-UTIL
4 OZZIE VIRGIL, SR.-2B
5 BILLY BRYAN-C
6 ANDY CAREY-3B (1)
6 DERON JOHNSON-OF/INF (2)
7 NORM SIEBERN-1B/OF
8 HAYWOOD SULLIVAN-C/UTIL
9 HANK BAUER-OF/MGR2
10 BOB (THE ROPE) BOYD-1B (1)
10 JIM (JUNGLE JIM) RIVERA-OF (2)
11 JERRY LUMPE-2B
12 JOE PIGNATANO-C/3B
13 BILL TUTTLE-OF (1)
14 AL PILARCIK-OF (1)
14 BOBBY DEL GRECO-OF (2)
14 WES COVINGTON-OF (3)
16 OZZIE VIRGIL, SR.-2B
16 GORDON MACKENZIE-C
16 RENO BERTOIA-3B/2B (2)
16 CHUCK ESSIGIAN-OF
17 KEN JOHNSON-P (1)
18 DON LARSEN-P (1)
18 BILLY BRYAN-C
19 LEO POSADA-OF
20 JIM ARCHER-P
21 JAY HANKINS-OF
22 CLINT (SCRAP IRON) COURTNEY-C
22 BOBBY PRESCOTT-OF
22 STAN JOHNSON-OF
23 JERRY WALKER-P
24 LEW KRAUSSE, JR.-P
25 FRANK CIPRIANI-OF
26 BOB SHAW-P (2)
27 DAVE WICKERSHAM (INJ)-P
27 JOHN WYATT-P
27 MICKEY MCDERMOTT-P (2)
27 PAUL GIEL-P (2)
28 BUD DALEY-P (1)
28 ART DITMAR-P (2)
29 BILL KIRK-P
30 NORM BASS-P
31 BILL FISCHER-P (2)
32 BILL KUNKEL-P
33 JOE NUXHALL-P
35 ED (ROCK) RAKOW-P
36 ED KEEGAN-P
37 TED (CORK) WILKS-CH
38 RAY HERBERT-P (1)
38 BILL FISCHER-P (2)
38 GERRY STALEY-P (2)
39 JOE (FLASH) GORDON-MGR1
39 JOHNNY (THE BIG CAT) MIZE-CH
40 DARIO LODIGIANI-CH
41 JO-JO WHITE-CH
42 ED FITZGERALD-CH
43 DAN PFISTER-P
44 JOHNNY (THE BIG CAT) MIZE-CH
45 CHARLIE SHOEMAKER-2B

1962

9TH 72-90 24GB

1 DICK HOWSER (INJ)-SS
2 WAYNE CAUSEY-INF
3 GENE STEPHENS-OF
3 GEORGE ALUSIK-OF/1B (2)
4 GINO CIMOLI-OF
5 BOBBY DEL GRECO-OF
6 DERON JOHNSON (MIL)-OF/INF
6 BILLY CONSOLO-SS (3)
7 NORM SIEBERN-1B
8 HAYWOOD SULLIVAN-C/1B
9 HANK BAUER-MGR
10 JOE AZCUE (INJ)-C
11 JERRY LUMPE-2B/SS
12 MANNY JIMENEZ-OF
15 JOSE TARTABULL-OF
16 ED CHARLES-3B/2B
17 JOHN WOJCIK-OF
17 CHARLIE SHOEMAKER-2B
17 HECTOR MARTINEZ-PH
18 BILLY BRYAN-C
19 LEO POSADA-OF
19 ORLANDO PENA-P
20 JIM ARCHER-P
21 ED (ROCK) RAKOW-P
22 NORM BASS-P
22 BOB GIGGIE-P
22 DON WILLIAMS-P
23 JERRY WALKER-P
24 DIEGO SEGUI-P
25 BILL KUNKEL-P
26 DAVE WICKERSHAM-P
27 DAN PFISTER-P
28 ART DITMAR-P
28 BILL FISCHER-P
29 BILL FISCHER-P
29 DANNY MCDEVITT-P
30 MARLAN COUGHTRY-3B (2)
31 DAN OSINSKI-P (1)
31 RUPE TOPPIN-P
33 JOHN WYATT-P
34 BOB GRIM-P
34 GORDON JONES-P
34 MOE DRABOWSKY-P (2)
35 GORDIE WINDHORN-OF
36 FRED NORMAN-P
36 GRANNY HAMNER-P
37 ED (STEADY EDDIE) LOPAT-CH
38 BILL KERN-OF
40 DARIO LODIGIANI-CH
41 JO-JO WHITE-CH
42 GUS NIARHOS-CH
47 DANNY MCDEVITT-P

1963

8TH 73-89 31.5GB

1 DICK HOWSER-SS (1)
1 SAMMY ESPOSITO-INF (2)
2 WAYNE CAUSEY-SS/3B
3 GEORGE ALUSIK (INJ)-OF
4 GINO CIMOLI-OF
5 BOBBY DEL GRECO-OF/3B
6 CHUCK ESSIGIAN-OF
7 NORM SIEBERN-1B/OF
8 HAYWOOD SULLIVAN-C/1B
8 DICK GREEN-SS/2B
8 CHARLIE LAU-C (2)
9 JAY HANKINS-OF
9 TOMMIE REYNOLDS-OF
9 HECTOR MARTINEZ-OF
10 JOE AZCUE-C (1)
10 DOC EDWARDS-C (2)
11 JERRY LUMPE-2B
12 MANNY JIMENEZ-OF
12 KEN (HAWK) HARRELSON-1B/OF
14 CHARLIE LAU-C (2)
15 JOSE TARTABULL-OF
16 ED CHARLES-3B
17 JOHN WOJCIK-OF
18 BILLY BRYAN-C
18 TOM (SNAKE) STURDIVANT-P (3)
19 ORLANDO PENA-P
20 MANNY JIMENEZ-OF
20 DALE WILLIS-P
20 TOM (SNAKE) STURDIVANT-P (3)
21 ED (ROCK) RAKOW-P
22 NORM BASS-P
22 JOSE SANTIAGO-P
23 DIEGO SEGUI-P
24 DALE WILLIS-P
25 MOE DRABOWSKY-P
25 DAVE THIES-P
26 DAVE WICKERSHAM-P
27 FRED NORMAN-P
27 DAN PFISTER (INJ)-P
28 BILL FISCHER-P
29 TONY LARUSSA-SS/2B
30 ED (STEADY EDDIE) LOPAT-MGR
31 AURELIO MONTEAGUDO-P
32 PETE LOVRICH-P
33 JOHN WYATT-P
34 BILL LANDIS-P
35 JOHN O'DONOGHUE-P
37 ED (STEADY EDDIE) LOPAT-MGR
40 JIMMY DYKES-CH
41 MEL MCGAHA-CH
42 GUS NIARHOS-CH
43 TED BOWSFIELD-P

1964

10TH 57-105 42GB

1 DICK GREEN-2B
2 WAYNE CAUSEY-SS/INF
3 GEORGE ALUSIK-OF/1B
4 GINO CIMOLI-OF (1)
4 KEN (HAWK) HARRELSON-OF/1B
4 JOHN WOJCIK-OF
5 NELSON MATHEWS-OF
6 JIM (DIAMOND JIM) GENTILE-1B
7 ROCKY COLAVITO-OF
8 GEORGE WILLIAMS-UTIL
9 BILLY BRYAN-C
10 DOC EDWARDS-C/1B
11 DAVE DUNCAN-C
12 KEN (HAWK) HARRELSON-OF/1B
12 MANNY JIMENEZ-OF
13 BLUE MOON ODOM-P
14 CHARLIE LAU-C (1)
14 CHARLIE SHOEMAKER-2B
14 DAN PFISTER-P
14 LARRY STAHL-OF
15 JOSE TARTABULL-OF
16 ED CHARLES-3B
17 JOHN WOJCIK-OF
17 DIEGO SEGUI-P
18 TOM (SNAKE) STURDIVANT-P (1)
18 WES STOCK-P (2)
19 VERN HANDRAHAN-P
19 BERT (CAMPY) CAMPANERIS-UTIL
20 MANNY JIMENEZ-OF
21 JACK AKER-P
21 LEW KRAUSSE, JR.-P
21 JOSE SANTIAGO-P
22 JOSE SANTIAGO-P
22 ORLANDO PENA-P
23 RICK JOSEPH-1B/3B
24 ORLANDO PENA-P
25 MOE DRABOWSKY-P
26 JOHN O'DONOGHUE-P
27 DAN PFISTER-P
27 KEN (DAFFY) SANDERS-P
30 ED (STEADY EDDIE) LOPAT-MGR1
30 BOB MEYER-P (3)
31 AURELIO MONTEAGUDO-P
31 LEW KRAUSSE, JR.-P
33 JOHN WYATT-P
35 TOMMIE REYNOLDS-OF
36 JOE GRZENDA-P
40 JIMMY DYKES-CH
41 MEL MCGAHA-CH/MGR2
42 GUS NIARHOS-CH
43 TED BOWSFIELD-P
44 LUKE APPLING-CH
48 BABE DAHLGREN-CH
49 TOM FERRICK-CH

1965

10TH 59-103 43GB

1 DICK GREEN-2B
2 WAYNE CAUSEY-INF
3 MIKE HERSHBERGER-OF
4 JIM (DIAMOND JIM) GENTILE-1B (1)
5 NELSON MATHEWS-OF
5 LU CLINTON-OF
6 KEN (HAWK) HARRELSON-1B/OF
7 JIM LANDIS-OF
8 SKIP LOCKWOOD-3B
9 BILLY BRYAN-C
10 DOC EDWARDS-C/1B (1)
10 JOSE TARTABULL-OF
11 JESSE HICKMAN-P
11 RENE LACHEMANN-C
12 TOMMIE REYNOLDS-OF
13 BLUE MOON ODOM-P
14 AURELIO MONTEAGUDO-P
14 JOHNNY BLANCHARD-C/OF (2)
15 JOHN SANDERS-PR
15 ROLLIE SHELDON-P (2)
16 ED CHARLES-3B/INF
17 DIEGO SEGUI-P
18 WES STOCK-P
19 BERT (CAMPY) CAMPANERIS-SS/ALL/P
20 DON BUSCHHORN (INJ)-P
21 LEW KRAUSSE, JR.-P
21 SANTIAGO ROSARIO-1B/OF
22 JIM DICKSON-P
23 TOM HARRISON-P
23 JACK AKER-P
24 ORLANDO PENA-P (1)
24 LARRY STAHL, OF
25 MOE DRABOWSKY-P
25 LEW KRAUSSE, JR.-P
26 JOHN O'DONOGHUE-P
27 JIM (CATFISH) HUNTER-P
28 FRED (BUBBY) TALBOT-P
29 JOSE SANTIAGO-P
29 SATCHEL PAIGE, P
29 AURELIO MONTEAGUDO-P
30 ED (STEADY EDDIE) LOPAT-CH
32 PAUL LINDBLAD-P
33 JOHN WYATT-P
34 DICK JOYCE-P
35 TOM HARRISON-P
38 RANDY SCHWARTZ-1B
40 WHITEY HERZOG-CH
41 MEL MCGAHA-MGR1
41 HAYWOOD SULLIVAN-MGR2
42 GUS NIARHOS-CH
43 DON (THE SPHINX) MOSSI-P
44 LUKE APPLING-CH
46 RON (STRETCH)-P
48 GABBY HARTNETT-CH
49 TOM FERRICK-CH

1966

7TH 74-86 23GB

1 DICK GREEN-2B/3B
2 WAYNE CAUSEY-3B/SS (1)
2 DANNY CATER-UTIL (2)
3 MIKE HERSHBERGER-OF
4 PHIL ROOF-C
4 KEN (HAWK) HARRELSON-1B/OF (1)
5 AL (BLACKIE) DARK-MGR
6 KEN (HAWK) HARRELSON-1B/OF (1)
6 PHIL ROOF-C
6 SAL BANDO-3B (2)
7 ERNIE FAZIO-2B/SS
8 KEN SUAREZ-C
8 DON BLASINGAME-2B (2)
9 BILLY BRYAN-C/1B (1)
9 ROGER REPOZ-OF/1B (2)
10 JOSE TARTABULL-OF (1)
11 JESSE HICKMAN-P
11 RON STONE-OF/1B
11 TIM TALTON-C/1B
12 OSSIE CHAVARRIA-UTIL
13 BLUE MOON ODOM-P
14 LARRY STAHL-OF
15 ROLLIE SHELDON-P (1)
15 WES STOCK-P
15 GUIDO GRILLI-P (2)
16 ED CHARLES-3B/UTIL
17 JIM DUCKWORTH (INJ)-P (2)
17 JOE GRZENDA-P
18 WES STOCK-P
18 RENE LACHEMANN-C
19 BERT (CAMPY) CAMPANERIS-SS
20 LEW KRAUSSE, JR.-P
21 MANNY JIMENEZ-OF
21 JIM GOSGER-OF (2)
22 JESSE HICKMAN-P

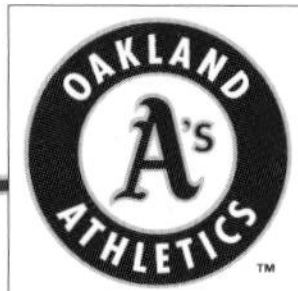

22 JIM DICKSON-P
22 JOHN DONALDSON-2B
23 JACK AKER-P
24 GUIDO GRILLI-P (2)
24 JOE NOSSEK-OF/3B (2)
25 PAUL LINDBLAD-P
26 RALPH TERRY-P (1)
26 VERN HANDRAHAN-P
27 JIM (CATFISH) HUNTER (ILL) -P
28 FRED (BUBBY) TALBOT-P (1)
28 JIM DICKSON-P
28 RICK MONDAY-OF
28 BILL STAFFORD-P
29 LEW KRAUSSE, JR.-P
29 JESSE HICKMAN-P
29 CHUCK DOBSON (INJ)-P
30 GIL BLANCO-P
31 JESSE HICKMAN-P
31 RANDY SCHWARTZ-1B
31 JIM DUCKWORTH (INJ)-P (2)
32 BILL EDGERTON-P
33 JOHN WYATT-P (1)
33 JIM NASH-P
34 AURELIO MONTEAGUDO-P (1)
34 KEN (DAFFY) SANDERS-P (2)
35 JOE GRZENDA-P
35 KEN SUAREZ-C
36 GIL BLANCO-P
37 VERN HANDRAHAN-P
40 BOBBY HOFMAN-CH
41 AL VINCENT-CH
42 COT DEAL-CH
44 LUKE APPLING-CH
46 PAUL LINDBLAD-P
47 CHUCK DOBSON (INJ)-P
51 RON STONE-OF/1B
59 OSSIE CHAVARRIA-UTIL

1967
10TH 62-99 29.5GB

1 DICK GREEN-3B/INF
2 DANNY CATER-UTIL
3 MIKE HERSHBERGER-OF
4 PHIL ROOF-C
4 BOBBY HOFMAN-CH
5 AL (BLACKIE) DARK-MGR1
6 SAL BANDO-3B
6 KEN (HAWK) HARRELSON-1B (2)
7 RICK MONDAY-OF
8 KEN SUAREZ-C
9 ROGER REPOZ-OF/1B (1)
10 ALLAN (THE PANAMANIAN EXPRESS) LEWIS-PH
10 JOHN DONALDSON-2B/SS
10 OSSIE CHAVARRIA, -UTIL
10 HOSS BOWLIN-3B
11 TIM TALTON-C/1B
12 OSSIE CHAVARRIA-UTIL
12 JOHN DONALDSON-2B/SS
13 BLUE MOON ODOM-P
14 TED KUBIAK-INF
15 JOE RUDI-1B/OF
16 ALLAN (THE PANAMANIAN EXPRESS) LEWIS-PH
16 ED CHARLES-3B (1)
16 ROBERTO RODRIGUEZ-P
17 KEN SUAREZ, C
17 ROBERTO RODRIGUEZ-P
18 WES STOCK-P/CH
19 BERT (CAMPY) CAMPANERIS-SS
20 LEW KRAUSSE, JR.-P
21 JIM GOSGER-OF
22 BILL STAFFORD-P
22 BILL EDGERTON-P
23 JACK AKER-P
24 JOE NOSSEK-OF
24 PAUL LINDBLAD-P
25 PAUL LINDBLAD-P
26 DIEGO SEGUI-P
27 JIM (CATFISH) HUNTER-P
28 RICK MONDAY-OF
29 CHUCK DOBSON-P
30 JIM NASH-P
31 REGGIE (MR. OCTOBER) JACKSON-OF
31 BOB DULIBA-P
32 BILL EDGERTON-P
32 TONY PIERCE-P
33 GIL BLANCO-P
33 LUKE APPLING-CH/MGR2
33 JACK SANFORD-P (2)
34 RAMON (RAY) WEBSTER-1B/OF
35 DAVE DUNCAN-C
40 BOBBY HOFMAN-CH
41 AL VINCENT-CH
42 COT DEAL-CH
42 GEORGE LAUZERIQUE-P
44 LUKE APPLING-CH/MGR2
45 JOE RUDI-1B/OF

1968
OAKLAND ATHLETICS
6TH 82-80 21GB

1 DICK GREEN-UTIL
2 DANNY CATER-1B/UTIL
3 MIKE HERSHBERGER-OF
4 PHIL ROOF (INJ)-C
5 JOE (YANKEE CLIPPER) (JOLTIN JOE) DIMAGGIO-CH
6 SAL BANDO-3B/OF
7 RICK MONDAY-OF
8 JOE RUDI-OF
9 REGGIE (MR. OCTOBER) JACKSON-OF
10 TONY LARUSSA-PH
10 DAVE DUNCAN-C
11 WARREN BOGLE-P
12 JOHN DONALDSON-2B/INF
13 BLUE MOON ODOM-P
14 TED KUBIAK (MIL) 2B/SS
15 FLOYD ROBINSON-OF (1)
15 ALLAN (THE PANAMANIAN EXPRESS) LEWIS-OF
16 JOE KEOUGH-OF/1B
17 ED SPRAGUE-P
17 JIM (PAG) PAGLIARONI (INJ) -C
18 RENE LACHEMANN-C
19 BERT (CAMPY) CAMPANERIS-SS/OF
20 LEW KRAUSSE, JR.-P
21 JIM GOSGER-OF
22 ED SPRAGUE-P
23 JACK AKER-P
24 DIEGO SEGUI-P
25 PAUL LINDBLAD-P
26 DIEGO SEGUI-P
27 JIM (CATFISH) HUNTER-P
28 GEORGE LAUZERIQUE-P
29 CHUCK DOBSON-P
30 JIM NASH-P
31 RAMON (RAY) WEBSTER-1B
32 TONY PIERCE-P
32 ROLLIE FINGERS-P
32 KEN (DAFFY) SANDERS-P
33 BOB KENNEDY-MGR
38 ROLLIE FINGERS-P
40 BILL (BARNACLE BILL) (SAILOR BILL) POSEDEL-CH
41 JOHN MCNAMARA-CH
42 SHERMAN LOLLAR-CH

1969
4TH W 69-93 28GB

1 DICK GREEN-2B
2 DANNY CATER-1B/UTIL
3 MIKE HERSHBERGER (INJ)-OF
4 PHIL ROOF (INJ)-C
5 JOE (YANKEE CLIPPER) (JOLTIN JOE) DIMAGGIO-CH
6 SAL BANDO-3B
7 RICK MONDAY (INJ)-OF
8 ALLAN (THE PANAMANIAN EXPRESS) LEWIS-OF
9 REGGIE (MR. OCTOBER) JACKSON-OF
10 DAVE DUNCAN-C
11 TONY LARUSSA-PH
11 JOHN WYATT-P
11 JUAN PIZARRO-P (3)
12 JOHN DONALDSON (INJ)-2B/INF (1)
12 LARRY HANEY-C (2)
13 BLUE MOON ODOM (INJ)-P
14 TED KUBIAK-2B/SS
15 BOBBY BROOKS-OF
16 MARCEL LACHEMANN-P
17 JIM (PAG) PAGLIARONI-C (1)
17 FRED (BUBBY) TALBOT-P (3)
19 BERT (CAMPY) CAMPANERIS-SS/OF
20 LEW KRAUSSE, JR.-P
21 VIDA BLUE-P
22 ED SPRAGUE-P
23 RAMON (RAY) WEBSTER-1B
24 JOE NOSSEK-OF (1)
24 MARCEL LACHEMANN-P
24 GENE TENACE-C
25 PAUL LINDBLAD-P
26 JOE RUDI-OF/1B
27 JIM (CATFISH) HUNTER-P
28 GEORGE LAUZERIQUE-P
28 VIDA BLUE-P
29 CHUCK DOBSON-P
30 JIM NASH (INJ)-P
31 JOSE TARTABULL-OF
32 BOB JOHNSON-1B/2B (2)
33 JIM ROLAND-P
34 ROLLIE FINGERS-P
35 TOMMIE REYNOLDS (INJ)-OF
35 JOHN WYATT-P
36 TITO FRANCONA-1B/OF (2)
37 BILL MCNULTY-OF
40 BILL (BARNACLE BILL) (SAILOR BILL) POSEDEL-CH
41 JOHN MCNAMARA-CH/MGR2
42 HANK BAUER-MGR1
42 JUAN PIZARRO-P (3)
43 BOBBY HOFMAN-CH
44 VERN HOSCHIET-CH

1970
4TH W 65-97 33GB

1 DICK GREEN-2B/UTIL
2 JOHN DONALDSON-INF
3* DOOLEY WOMACK-P*
5 DON MINCHER-1B
6 SAL BANDO-3B
7 RICK MONDAY-OF
8 FELIPE ALOU-OF/1B
9 REGGIE (MR. OCTOBER) JACKSON-OF
10 DAVE DUNCAN-C
11 JOHN MCNAMARA-MGR
12 LARRY HANEY-C
12 TOMMY DAVIS-OF/1B (3)
13 BLUE MOON ODOM (INJ)-P
14 ROBERTO (BABY) PENA-SS/3B (1)
14 MARCEL LACHEMANN-P
15 BOBBY BROOKS-OF
16 MARCEL LACHEMANN-P
16 DOOLEY WOMACK-P
17 ROBERTO (BABY) PENA-SS/3B (1)
17 FRED (BUBBY) TALBOT-P
17 VIDA BLUE-P
19 BERT (CAMPY) CAMPANERIS-SS
21 JIM DRISCOLL-2B/SS
22 TONY LARUSSA-2B
23 ROBERTO RODRIQUEZ-P (1)
23 STEVE HOVLEY-1B (2)
24 DIEGO SEGUI-P
25 PAUL LINDBLAD-P
26 JOE RUDI-OF/1B
27 JIM (CATFISH) HUNTER-P
28 JIM (MUDCAT) GRANT-P (1)
29 CHUCK DOBSON-P
30 DON MINCHER-1B
31 JOSE TARTABULL-OF
32 BOB JOHNSON-3B/1B
32 ALLAN (THE PANAMANIAN EXPRESS) LEWIS-OF
33 JIM ROLAND (INJ)-P
34 ROLLIE FINGERS-P
35 DARRELL OSTEEN (MIL)-P
35 VIDA BLUE-P
36 TITO FRANCONA-1B/OF (1)
36 BOB LOCKER-P (2)
37 DARRELL OSTEEN (MIL)-P
38 AL DOWNING-P (1)
38 GENE TENACE-C
39 FRANK FERNANDEZ-C/OF
40 BILL (BARNACLE BILL) (SAILOR BILL) POSEDEL-CH
41 CHARLIE LAU-CH
43 BOBBY HOFMAN-CH
44 VERN HOSCHIET-CH
45 ROBERTO RODRIQUEZ-P (1)
46 FRED (BUBBY) TALBOT-P
50 BOB LOCKER-P (2)

1971
2ND W 85-76 16GB

1 DICK GREEN-2B/SS
2 ANGEL MANGUAL-OF
3 RON CLARK-PH
5 DON MINCHER-1B (1)
5 MIKE EPSTEIN-1B (2)
6 SAL BANDO-3B
7 RICK MONDAY-OF
8 FELIPE ALOU-OF (1)
8 LARRY BROWN-INF (2)
9 REGGIE (MR. OCTOBER) JACKSON-OF
10 DAVE DUNCAN-C
11 DWAIN ANDERSON-INF
12 TOMMY DAVIS-UTIL
13 BLUE MOON ODOM-P
14 MARCEL LACHEMANN-P
16 MARCEL LACHEMANN-P
16 JIM (MUDCAT) GRANT-P (2)
17 RON KLIMKOWSKI-P
19 BERT (CAMPY) CAMPANERIS-SS
20 JIM PANTHER-P
20 MIKE HEGAN-1B/OF (2)
22 DAROLD KNOWLES-P (2)
22 JIM (MUDCAT) GRANT-P (2)
23 DICK WILLIAMS-MGR
24 DIEGO SEGUI-P
25 PAUL LINDBLAD-P (1)
25 GEORGE HENDRICK-OF
26 JOE RUDI-OF/1B
27 JIM (CATFISH) HUNTER-P/PH
28 STEVE HOVLEY-OF
29 CHUCK DOBSON (INJ)-P
31 GEORGE HENDRICK-OF
32 DAROLD KNOWLES-P (2)
33 JIM ROLAND-P
34 ROLLIE FINGERS-P
35 VIDA BLUE-P
36 BOB LOCKER-P
38 GENE TENACE-C/OF
39 FRANK FERNANDEZ-C
39 CURT BLEFARY-UTIL (2)
40 BILL (BARNACLE BILL) (SAILOR BILL) POSEDEL-CH
41 JERRY LUMPE-CH
42 TONY LARUSSA-INF (1)
43 IRV NOREN-CH
44 VERN HOSCHIET-CH
52 RAMON (RAY) WEBSTER-1B (2)
56 ROB GARDNER-P (1)
58 PAT GARRETT-OF
58 DARYL PATTERSON-P (2)

1972
1ST W 93-62 0GB
W ALCS-DETA 3-2
W WS-CINN 4-3

1 DICK GREEN (INJ)-2B/SS
2 ANGEL MANGUAL-OF
3 LARRY HANEY-C/2B
3 PAT GARRETT-OF
3 WES STOCK-CH (2)
4 TIM CULLEN-2B/INF
4 RON CLARK-2B/3B (1)
4 DON MINCHER-1B (2)
5 MIKE EPSTEIN-1B
6 SAL BANDO-3B/2B
7 BRANT ALYEA-OF (1)
7 ART SHAMSKY-PH (2)
8 LARRY BROWN (INJ)-2B/3B
9 REGGIE (MR. OCTOBER) JACKSON-OF
10 DAVE DUNCAN-C
11 DWAIN ANDERSON-SS/3B (1)
11 MARTY MARTINEZ-INF (2)
11 TED KUBIAK-2B/3B (2)
12 ORLANDO (THE BABY BULL) (CHA CHA) CEPEDA-PH (2)
12 GONZALO MARQUEZ-1B
13 BLUE MOON ODOM (INJ)-P
14 DON SHAW-P (2)
14 MATTY ALOU-OF/1B (2)
15 BOBBY BROOKS-OF
15 (DOWNTOWN) OLLIE BROWN-OF (2)
16 TIM CULLEN-2B/INF
17 DENNY MCLAIN-P (1)
17 GARY WASLEWSKI-P
18 BILL MCNULTY-3B
19 BERT (CAMPY) CAMPANERIS-SS
20 MIKE HEGAN-1B/OF
21 DAL MAXVILL-2B/SS (2)
22 JOE HORLEN-P
23 DICK WILLIAMS-MGR
24 DIEGO SEGUI-P (1)
24 BILL VOSS-OF (2)
24 ALLAN (THE PANAMANIAN EXPRESS) LEWIS-OF
25 GEORGE HENDRICK-OF
26 JOE RUDI-OF/3B
27 JIM (CATFISH) HUNTER-P
(29) CHUCK DOBSON (INJ)-(P
30 KEN HOLTZMAN-P
32 DAROLD KNOWLES-P
33 JIM ROLAND-P (1)
33 DAVE HAMILTON-P
33 MIKE KILKENNY-P (2)
34 ROLLIE FINGERS-P
35 VIDA BLUE-P
36 BOB LOCKER-P
38 GENE TENACE-UTIL
39 CURT BLEFARY-UTIL (1)
40 BILL (BARNACLE BILL) (SAILOR BILL) POSEDEL-CH
41 JERRY ADAIR-CH
43 IRV NOREN-CH
44 VERN HOSCHIET-CH

1973
1ST W 94-68 0GB
W ALCS-BALA 3-2
W WS-NYN 4-3

1 DICK GREEN-2B/INF
2 ANGEL MANGUAL-UTIL
3 WES STOCK-CH
3 JAY JOHNSTONE-UTIL
3 PHIL GARNER-3B
4 BILLY NORTH-OF/DH
5 RICH MCKINNEY-UTIL
6 SAL BANDO-3B/DH
7* HORACIO PINA-P*

PHILADELPHIA/KANSAS CITY/ OAKLAND ATHLETICS

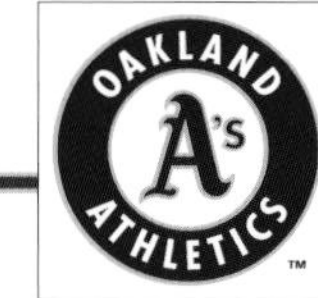

7 DERON JOHNSON-DH/1B (2)
8 MANNY TRILLO-2B
9 REGGIE (MR. OCTOBER) JACKSON-OF/DH
0 RAY FOSSE-C/DH
1 TED KUBIAK-INF
2 GONZALO MARQUEZ-UTIL (1)
2 RICO CARTY-DH (3)
3 BLUE MOON ODOM (INJ)-P
4 VIDA BLUE-P
5 LARRY HANEY-C (1)
5 TIM HOSLEY-C
6 BILLY CONIGLIARO (INJ)-OF/2B
7 MIKE ANDREWS-2B/DH (2)
8 GENE TENACE-1B/UTIL
9 BERT (CAMPY) CAMPANERIS-SS
0 MIKE HEGAN-UTIL (1)
1 DAL MAXVILL-INF (1)
2 ROB GARDNER-P (1)
2 JESUS ALOU-OF/DH (2)
3 DICK WILLIAMS-MGR
4 PAUL LINDBLAD-P
4 ALLAN (THE PANAMANIAN EXPRESS) LEWIS-DH/OF
5 PAUL LINDBLAD-P
6 JOE RUDI-OF/UTIL
7 JIM (CATFISH) HUNTER-(INJ)-P
8 HORACIO PINA-P
9 CHUCK DOBSON-P
0 KEN HOLTZMAN-P
2 DAROLD KNOWLES-P
3 DAVE HAMILTON-P
4 ROLLIE FINGERS-P
5 JOSE MORALES-DH (1)
5 VIDA BLUE-P
5 GLENN ABBOTT-P
6 GLENN ABBOTT-P
7 VIC DAVALILLO-1B/DH (2)
8 PAT BOURQUE-DH/1B
0 WES STOCK-CH
1 JERRY ADAIR-CH
2 WES STOCK-CH
3 IRV NOREN-CH
4 VERN HOSCHIET-CH

1974

1ST W 90-72 0GB
W ALCS-BALA 3-1
W WS-LAN 4-1

1 DICK GREEN-2B
2 ANGEL MANGUAL-UTIL
2 HERB WASHINGTON-PR
3 HERB WASHINGTON-PR
3 PHIL GARNER-INF/DH
4 BILLY NORTH-OF/DH
5 AL (BLACKIE) DARK-MGR
6 SAL BANDO-3B/DH
7 DERON JOHNSON-DH (1)
8 MANNY TRILLO (INJ)-2B
9 REGGIE (MR. OCTOBER) JACKSON-OF/DH
0 RAY FOSSE (INJ) C/DH
1 TED KUBIAK-INF/DH
2 LARRY HANEY-C/INF
3 BLUE MOON ODOM (INJ)-P
4 VIDA BLUE-P
5 CLAUDELL WASHINGTON-DH/OF
6 DAL MAXVILL-INF (2)
8 GENE TENACE-1B/UTIL
9 BERT (CAMPY) CAMPANERIS-SS/DH
0 LEON HOOTEN-P
1 RICH MCKINNEY-UTIL
2 JESUS ALOU-DH/OF
3 GAYLEN PITTS-INF
3 BILL PARSONS-P
3 TIM HOSLEY-C
4 JOHN DONALDSON-2B/3B
5 PAUL LINDBLAD-P
6 JOE RUDI-OF/UTIL
27 JIM (CATFISH) HUNTER-P
28 CHAMP SUMMERS-OF/DH
29 PHIL GARNER-INF/DH
30 KEN HOLTZMAN-P
32 DAROLD KNOWLES-P
33 DAVE HAMILTON-P
34 ROLLIE FINGERS-P
(36) BOB LOCKER (INJ)-(P)
36 GLENN ABBOTT-P
37 VIC DAVALILLO-OF/DH
37 GLENN ABBOTT-P
38 PAT BOURQUE-1B (1)
38 JIM HOLT-1B/DH (2)
36 GLENN ABBOTT-P
(39) BOB LOCKER (INJ)-(P)
39 BILL PARSONS-P
40 WES STOCK-CH
41 JERRY ADAIR-CH
42 WES STOCK-CH
43 IRV NOREN-CH
43 BOBBY WINKLES-CH
43 BOB HOFMAN-CH
44 VERN HOSCHIET-CH
44 BOB HOFMAN-CH
44 BOBBY WINKLES-CH
45 BOB HOFMAN-CH
50 BILL PARSONS-P

1975

1ST W 98-64 0GB
L ALCS-BOSA 3-0

1 DON HOPKINS-DH/OF
2 ANGEL MANGUAL-OF/DH
3 HERB WASHINGTON-PR
3 CESAR (PEPITO) TOVAR-INF/DH (2)
4 BILLY NORTH-OF/DH
5 AL (BLACKIE) DARK-MGR
6 SAL BANDO-3B
7 CHARLIE SANDS-DH
7 BILLY WILLIAMS-DH/1B
7 DENNY WALLING-OF
8 BILLY GRABARKEWITZ-2B/DH
9 REGGIE (MR. OCTOBER) JACKSON-OF/DH
10 RAY FOSSE -UTIL
11 TED KUBIAK-INF (1)
11 RICH MCKINNEY-1B/DH
12 LARRY HANEY-C/3B
13 BLUE MOON ODOM-P (1)
13 TOMMY SANDT-2B
14 VIDA BLUE-P
15 CLAUDELL WASHINGTON-OF
16 MIKE NORRIS (INJ)-P
17 DICK BOSMAN-P (2)
18 GENE TENACE-C/UTIL
19 BERT (CAMPY) CAMPANERIS-SS
20 CRAIG MITCHELL-P
21 TOMMY HARPER-UTIL (2)
22 JIM TODD-P
23 GAYLEN PITTS-INF
24 CHARLIE CHANT-OF/DH
25 PAUL LINDBLAD-P
26 JOE RUDI (INJ)-1B/UTIL
28 BILLY WILLIAMS-DH/1B
29 PHIL GARNER-2B/SS
30 KEN HOLTZMAN-P
31 MATT ALEXANDER (INJ)-UTIL
32 TED MARTINEZ-INF (2)
33 DAVE HAMILTON-P
34 ROLLIE FINGERS-P
35 SONNY SIEBERT (INJ)-P
36 JIM PERRY-P (2)
37 GLENN ABBOTT-P
38 JIM HOLT-UTIL
39 JIM TODD-P
39 STAN BAHNSEN-P (2)
41 DAL MAXVILL-CH
42 WES STOCK-CH
43 BOB HOFMAN-CH
44 BOBBY WINKLES-CH
45 DAL MAXVILL-SS/2B
50 JIM TODD-P

1976

2ND W 87-74 2.5GB

1 DON HOPKINS-PR
2 ANGEL MANGUAL-OF/DH
2 PHIL GARNER-2B
2 CESAR (PEPITO) TOVAR (INJ)-OF/DH (1)
3 CESAR (PEPITO) TOVAR (INJ)-OF/DH (1)
3 PHIL GARNER-2B
4 BILLY NORTH-OF/DH
5 DENNY WALLING-OF
5 JEFF NEWMAN-C (2)
6 SAL BANDO-3B/UTIL
7 CHUCK TANNER-MGR
10 WAYNE GROSS-UTIL
11 RON FAIRLY-1B (2)
12 LARRY HANEY-C
13 TOMMY SANDT-INF
14 VIDA BLUE-P
15 CLAUDELL WASHINGTON-OF/DH
16 MIKE NORRIS-P
17 DICK BOSMAN-P
18 GENE TENACE (INJ)-1B/UTIL
19 BERT (CAMPY) CAMPANERIS-SS
20 CRAIG MITCHELL-P
20 DON BAYLOR-UTIL
21 LARRY LINTZ-UTIL
22 JIM TODD-P
23 NATE COLBERT-DH
24 MIKE TORREZ-P
25 PAUL LINDBLAD-P
26 JOE RUDI-OF/UTIL
27 CHRIS BATTON-P
28 BILLY WILLIAMS-DH/OF
29 PHIL GARNER-2B
30 TIM HOSLEY-C (2)
31 MATT ALEXANDER-OF/DH
(32) TED MARTINEZ (REL)-(INF)
34 ROLLIE FINGERS-P
35 KEN MCMULLEN-INF/DH
36 PAUL MITCHELL-P
37 GLENN ABBOTT-P
38 JIM HOLT-DH
39 STAN BAHNSEN-P
41 JOE LONNETT-CH
42 WES STOCK-CH
43 AL MONCHAK-CH
44 JOE LONNETT-CH
44 WILLIE (STRETCH) MCCOVEY-DH (2)
45 LARRY LINTZ-UTIL
45 STAN BAHNSEN-P
46 GARY WOODS-OF/DH

1977

7TH W 63-98 38.5GB

1 JACK MCKEON-MGR1
1 BOBBY WINKLES-MGR2
2 MATT ALEXANDER-UTIL
3 RODNEY SCOTT-UTIL
4 BILLY NORTH (INJ)-OF/DH
5 JEFF NEWMAN-C
6 MITCHELL PAGE-OF/DH
7 MARTY PEREZ-2B/INF (2)
8 ROB PICCIOLO-SS
9 RICH MCKINNEY-UTIL
10 WAYNE GROSS-3B/1B
11 TONY ARMAS-OF/SS
12 JERRY TABB-1B/DH
14 VIDA BLUE-P
15 JOE COLEMAN-P
16 MIKE NORRIS-P
17 DOUG BAIR-P
18 MIKE JORGENSEN-UTIL (2)
19 SHELDON MALLORY (INJ)-UTIL
20 LARRY MURRAY-UTIL
21 LARRY LINTZ-INF/DH
22 RICK LANGFORD-P
23 JIM UMBARGER-P (1)
24 MIKE TORREZ-P
24 PAUL MITCHELL-P (1)
24 STEVE DUNNING-P
25 TIM HOSLEY-UTIL
26 JIM TYRONE-OF/UTIL
26 DOUG BAIR-P
27 MARK WILLIAMS-OF
27 MATT KEOUGH-P
28 PABLO TORREALBA-P
29 CRAIG MITCHELL-P
30 JIM UMBARGER-P (1)
30 JOE COLEMAN-P
31 DAVE GIUSTI-P (1)
32 EARL WILLIAMS (INJ) DH/UTIL
33 DOC MEDICH (INJ)-P (1)
34 BOB LACEY-P
35 MANNY SANGUILLEN-C/UTIL
36 PAUL MITCHELL-P (1)
36 DOCK ELLIS-P (2)
37 STEVE MCCATTY-P
41 CAL ERMER-CH
42 LEE STANGE-CH
43 RED SCHOENDIENST-CH
45 STAN BAHNSEN-P (1)
46 BOB LACEY-P
52 DAVE GIUSTI-P (1)
53 DOC MEDICH (INJ)-P (1)
60 DICK ALLEN (SUS/RET)-1B/DH
99 WILLIE CRAWFORD-OF/DH (2)

1978

6TH W 69-93 23GB

1 BOBBY WINKLES-MGR1
1 JACK MCKEON-MGR2
2 RED SCHOENDIENST-CH
3 MIKE GUERRERO-SS
3* CRAIG MINETTO-P*
4 BILLY NORTH-OF (1)
4 GLENN BURKE (INJ)-UTIL (2)
5 JEFF NEWMAN-UTIL
6 MITCHELL PAGE-OF/DH
7 MIKE EDWARDS-2B/UTIL
8 ROB PICCIOLO-INF
9 MIKE ADAMS-INF/DH
9 JOE WALLIS-OF/DH (2)
10 WAYNE GROSS-3B/1B
11 TONY ARMAS (INJ)-OF/DH
12 GARY THOMASSON-OF/1B (1)
13 DELL ALSTON-UTIL (2)
14 JERRY TABB-1B/DH
15 JOE COLEMAN-P (1)
15 M IKE MORGAN-P
16 MIKE NORRIS-P
16 TAYLOR DUNCAN-INF/DH
17 MARTY PEREZ-INF
17 MARK BUDASKA-OF
17 MIKE NORRIS-P
18 JIM ESSIAN-C/UTIL
19 MIGUEL DILONE-UTIL
20 LARRY MURRAY-OF
20 RICO CARTY-DH (2)
22 RICK LANGFORD-P
23 WILLIE HORTON-DH/OF (2)
24 DAVE REVERING-1B/DH
26 SCOTT MEYER-C
27 MATT KEOUGH-P
28 STEVE RENKO-P
30 TIM HOSLEY-C/DH
30 ALAN WIRTH-P
31 STEVE STAGGS-INF/DH
32 CRAIG MINETTO-P
33 ELIAS SOSA-P
33 DAVE HEAVERLO-P
34 BOB LACEY-P
36 DWAYNE MURPHY-OF/DH
37 TIM CONROY-P
37 GARY ALEXANDER-UTIL (1)
38 JOHN HENRY JOHNSON-P
40 PETE BROBERG-P
41 LEE STANGE-CH
42 JACK MCKEON-MGR2
43 BOBBY HOFMAN-CH
44 TITO FUENTES-2B
44 DARRELL WOODARD-INF/DH
46 BOB LACEY-P
48 BRUCE ROBINSON-C
52 ALAN WIRTH-P
54 STEVE MCCATTY-P
60 DAVE HEAVERLO-P

1979

7TH W 54-108 34GB

1 JIM MARSHALL-MGR
3 MIKE GUERRERO-SS
5 JEFF NEWMAN-C/UTIL
6 MITCHELL PAGE-DH/OF
7 MIKE EDWARDS-2B/UTIL
8 ROB PICCIOLO-SS/UTIL
9 JOE WALLIS (INJ)-OF
10 WAYNE GROSS-3B/UTIL
11 TONY ARMAS (INJ)-OF
12 MICKEY KLUTTS-INF/DH (2)
14 GLENN BURKE (RET)-OF
15 M IKE MORGAN-P
16 DAVE CHALK-INF (3)
17 MIKE NORRIS (INJ)-P
18 JIM ESSIAN-UTIL
19 MIGUEL DILONE-OF (1)
20 LARRY MURRAY-OF/2B
21 DWAYNE MURPHY-OF/DH
22 RICK LANGFORD-P
23 DEREK BRYANT (INJ)-OF/DH
24 DAVE REVERING-1B/DH
25 JIM MARSHALL-MGR
27 MATT KEOUGH-P
28 JIM TODD-P
30 ALAN WIRTH-P
31 MILT RAMIREZ-INF
32 CRAIG MINETTO-P
33 DAVE HAMILTON-P
34 BOB LACEY (INJ)-P
35 RICKEY HENDERSON-OF
36 DWAYNE MURPHY-OF/DH
38 JOHN HENRY JOHNSON-P (1)
41 LEE STANGE-CH
42 JIM SAUL-CH
43 LEE WALLS-CH
44 GEORGE MITTERWALD-CH
48 MIKE HEATH-UTIL
50 BRIAN KINGMAN-P
54 STEVE MCCATTY-P
60 DAVE HEAVERLO-P

1980

2ND W 83-79 14GB

1 BILLY (THE KID) MARTIN-MGR
3 MIKE GUERRERO-SS
4 RANDY ELLIOTT-DH
4 ORLANDO GONZALEZ-UTIL
5 JEFF NEWMAN-UTIL
6 MITCHELL PAGE-DH
7 MIKE EDWARDS-UTIL
8 ROB PICCIOLO-UTIL
10 WAYNE GROSS-3B/UTIL
11 TONY ARMAS-OF
12 MICKEY KLUTTS (INJ)-INF/DH
13 DAVE REVERING-1B/DH
(14) GLENN BURKE (INJ)-(OF)
16 MIKE DAVIS-UTIL
17 MIKE NORRIS (INJ)-P
18 JIM ESSIAN-C/UTIL
19 JEFF COX-2B
21 DWAYNE MURPHY-OF/DH
22 RICK LANGFORD-P
24 JEFF COX-2B
25 DAVE HAMILTON-P
27 MATT KEOUGH-P
28 RICH BORDI-P
29 RICK LYSANDER-P
30 ALAN WIRTH-P
32 CRAIG MINETTO-P

33 DAVE HAMILTON-P
34 BOB LACEY-P
35 RICKEY HENDERSON-OF/DH
38 JEFF JONES-P
39 DAVE MCKAY-2B/INF
40 ERNIE CAMACHO-P
41 CLETE BOYER-CH
42 ART FOWLER-CH
43 LEE WALLS-CH
44 GEORGE MITTERWALD-CH
45 RAY COSEY-PH
45 ALAN WIRTH-P
48 MIKE HEATH-UTIL
50 BRIAN KINGMAN-P
53 ERNIE CAMACHO-P
54 STEVE MCCATTY-P
58 MARK SOUZA-P
59 DAVE BEARD-P

1981

1ST 1/2:1ST W 37-23 0GB
2ND 1/2:2ND W 27-22 1GB
FINAL: 64-45 --GB
W ALDS-KCA 3-0
L ALCS-NYA 3-0

1 BILLY (THE KID) MARTIN-MGR
2 MIKE HEATH-C/OF
3 SHOOTY BABITT-2B
5 JEFF NEWMAN-C/1B
6 MITCHELL PAGE-DH
7 RICK BOSETTI-OF/DH (2)
8 ROB PICCIOLO-SS
9 MICKEY KLUTTS (INJ)-3B
10 WAYNE GROSS-3B/UTIL
11 FRED STANLEY-SS/2B
12 MICKEY KLUTTS (INJ)-3B
12 JIM SPENCER-1B (2)
13 DAVE REVERING-1B/DH (1)
14 MIKE PATTERSON-OF/DH (1)
14 KEITH DRUMRIGHT-2B/DH
15 MARK BUDASKA-DH
15 JIMMY SEXTON-3B/DH
16 MIKE DAVIS-UTIL
17 MIKE NORRIS-P
18 BRIAN DOYLE-2B
19 JEFF COX-2B
20 TONY ARMAS-OF
21 DWAYNE MURPHY-OF/DH
22 RICK LANGFORD-P
24 KELVIN MOORE-1B
25 TIM HOSLEY (RET)-DH/1B
27 MATT KEOUGH-P
28 RICH BORDI-P
29 JIM NETTLES-OF
31 TOM UNDERWOOD-P (2)
32 CRAIG MINETTO-P
32 ED FIGUEROA-P
33 DAVE BEARD-P
34 BO MCLAUGHLIN (INJ)-P
35 RICKEY HENDERSON-OF
37 BOB KEARNEY-C
38 JEFF JONES-P
39 DAVE MCKAY-INF
40 GEORGE MITTERWALD-CH
41 CLETE BOYER-CH
42 ART FOWLER-CH
43 LEE WALLS-CH
44 CLIFF JOHNSON-DH/1B
45 JACKIE MOORE-CH
47 MIKE PATTERSON-OF/DH (1)
48 MIKE HEATH-C/OF
50 BRIAN KINGMAN-P
51 BOB OWCHINKO-P
53 BOB OWCHINKO-P
54 STEVE MCCATTY-P
55 DAVE BEARD-P
56 ED FIGUEROA-P
59 DAVE BEARD-P
60 DAVE HEAVERLO-P

1982

5TH W 68-94 25GB

1 BILLY (THE KID) MARTIN-MGR
2 MIKE HEATH-C/UTIL
3 JEFF BURROUGHS-DH/OF
4 DAN MEYER-1B/UTIL
5 JEFF NEWMAN-UTIL
6 MITCHELL PAGE-DH
7 RICK BOSETTI-OF
8 ROB PICCIOLO-SS (1)
8 KEVIN BELL-3B/DH
9 MICKEY KLUTTS-3B
10 WAYNE GROSS-3B/UTIL
10 DANNY GOODWIN-DH
11 FRED STANLEY-SS/2B
12 JIM SPENCER-1B
13 DARRELL BROWN-OF/DH
15 DAVEY LOPES-2B/OF
16 MIKE DAVIS-OF/1B
17 MIKE NORRIS-P
18 TONY PHILLIPS-SS
19 JIMMY SEXTON-3B/DH
20 TONY ARMAS-OF/DH
21 DWAYNE MURPHY-OF/UTIL
22 RICK LANGFORD-P
23 CHRIS CODIROLI-P
25 KELVIN MOORE-1B
26 JOE RUDI-UTIL
27 MATT KEOUGH-P
28 DANNY GOODWIN-DH
29 BRIAN KINGMAN-P
30 BOB KEARNEY-C
31 TOM UNDERWOOD-P
32 JOHN (COUNT) (COUNT OF MONTE CRISTO) D'ACQUISTO-P
32 FERNANDO ARROYO-P (2)
33 DAVE BEARD-P
34 BO MCLAUGHLIN-P
35 RICKEY HENDERSON-OF/DH
36 STEVE BAKER-P
37 TIM CONROY-P
38 JEFF JONES (INJ)-P
39 DAVE MCKAY-INF
40 GEORGE MITTERWALD-CH
41 CLETE BOYER-CH
42 ART FOWLER-CH
44 CLIFF JOHNSON (INJ)-DH/1B
45 JACKIE MOORE-CH
46 CHARLIE METRO-CH
47 DENNIS KINNEY-P
50 BRIAN KINGMAN-P
51 BOB OWCHINKO-P
54 STEVE MCCATTY-P
56 DENNIS KINNEY-P

1983

4TH W 74-88 25GB

2 MIKE HEATH (INJ)-C/UTIL
3 JEFF BURROUGHS-DH
4 DAN MEYER (INJ)-UTIL
4 CARNEY LANSFORD (INJ)-3B/SS
5 CARNEY LANSFORD (INJ)-3B/SS
6 MITCHELL PAGE-DH/OF
7 DAN MEYER (INJ)-UTIL
8 RICKEY PETERS-OF/DH
9 GARRY HANCOCK-UTIL
9 DARRYL CIAS-C
10 WAYNE GROSS-1B/UTIL/P
11 GARRY HANCOCK-UTIL
11 LUIS QUINONES-INF/DH
13 GORMAN HEIMUELLER-P
14 STEVE BOROS-MGR
15 DAVEY LOPES-2B/UTIL
16 MIKE DAVIS (INJ)-OF/DH
17 MIKE NORRIS (INJ)-P
18 TONY PHILLIPS-SS/UTIL
19 MARSHALL BRANT-1B/DH
21 DWAYNE MURPHY-OF/DH
22 RICK LANGFORD (INJ)-P
23 CHRIS CODIROLI-P
24 TIM CONROY-P
25 KELVIN MOORE-1B
25 DONNIE HILL-SS
(26) JOE RUDI (INJ)-(UTIL)
27 MATT KEOUGH-P (1)
28 BILLY WILLIAMS-CH
29 CURT YOUNG-P
30 BOB KEARNEY-C/DH
31 TOM UNDERWOOD-P
32 BILL KRUEGER (INJ)-P
33 DAVE BEARD-P
34 BILL ALMON-UTIL
35 RICKEY HENDERSON-OF/DH
36 STEVE BAKER-P (1)
37 TIM CONROY-P
37 RON SCHUELER-CH
38 JEFF JONES (INJ)-P
39 TOM BURGMEIER (INJ)-P
40 ED FARMER-P (2)
41 CLETE BOYER-CH
42 JACKIE MOORE-CH
43 RON SCHUELER-CH
43 MIKE WARREN-P
44 ED NOTTLE-CH
45 RICH WORTHAM-P
46 MIKE WARREN-P
47 RUSTY MCNEALY-DH/OF
48 BEN CALLAHAN-P
49 MARK SMITH-P
51 RON SCHUELER-CH
51 DAVE HUDGENS-1B/DH
52 LUIS QUINONES-INF/DH
53 BERT BRADLEY-P
54 STEVE MCCATTY-P
55 KEITH ATHERTON-P
64 BILL KRUEGER (INJ)-P

1984

4TH W 77-85 7GB

2 MIKE HEATH-C/UTIL
3 JEFF BURROUGHS-DH/OF
4 CARNEY LANSFORD-3B
6 MICKEY TETTLETON-C
7 DAN MEYER-1B/DH
8 JOE MORGAN-2B/DH
9* MARK WAGNER-UTIL/P*
9 GARRY HANCOCK-UTIL
10 DAVE KINGMAN-DH/1B
11 GARRY HANCOCK-UTIL
13 GORMAN HEIMUELLER-P
14 STEVE BOROS-MGR1
15 DAVEY LOPES (INJ)-UTIL (1)
16 MIKE DAVIS-OF/DH
(17) MIKE NORRIS (INJ)-(P)
18 TONY PHILLIPS-UTIL
18 DAVE DUNCAN-CH
19 JIM ESSIAN (INJ)-UTIL
20 BRUCE BOCHTE-1B/DH
21 DWAYNE MURPHY-OF
22 RICK LANGFORD (INJ)-P
23 CHRIS CODIROLI-P
24 TIM CONROY-P
25 DONNIE HILL (ILL)-INF/DH
26 BILLY WILLIAMS-CH
27 LARY SORENSEN-P
28 STEVE KIEFER-UTIL
29 CURT YOUNG-P
30 CHUCK RAINEY-P (2)
32 BILL KRUEGER-P
33 MIKE TORREZ-P (2)
34 BILL ALMON-UTIL
35 RICKEY HENDERSON-OF
36 BILL CAUDILL-P
37 RON SCHUELER-CH
38 JEFF JONES (INJ)-P
38 LARY SORENSEN-P
39 TOM BURGMEIER (INJ)-P
40 LARY SORENSEN-P
41 CLETE BOYER-CH
42 JACKIE MOORE-CH/MGR2
43 MIKE WARREN-P
44 WES STOCK-CH
45 BOB DIDIER-CH
46 DAVE MCKAY-CH
48 RAY BURRIS-P
52 JEFF BETTENDORF-P
52 DAVE LEIPER-P
54 STEVE MCCATTY-P
55 KEITH ATHERTON-P

1985

4TH W (TIE) 77-85 14GB

2 MIKE HEATH-C/UTIL
3 ALFREDO GRIFFIN-SS
4 CARNEY LANSFORD (INJ)-3B
5 STEVE HENDERSON-OF/DH
6 MICKEY TETTLETON-C/DH
7 CHARLIE O'BRIEN-C
8 ROB PICCIOLO (ILL)-UTIL
9 DAN MEYER-UTIL
9 MIKE GALLEGO-INF
10 DAVE KINGMAN-DH/1B
11 DAVE COLLINS-OF
12 DUSTY BAKER-UTIL
15 DONNIE HILL (INJ)-2B
16 MIKE DAVIS-OF
(17) MIKE NORRIS (INJ/SUB)-(P)
18 TONY PHILLIPS (INJ)-3B/2B
20 BRUCE BOCHTE-1B
20 DON SUTTON-P (1)
21 DWAYNE MURPHY-OF
22 RICK LANGFORD (INJ)-P
23 CHRIS CODIROLI-P
24 TIM CONROY-P
25 DONNIE HILL (INJ)-2B
25 TOMMY (T.J.) JOHN-P (2)
26 BILLY WILLIAMS-CH
27 DON SUTTON-P (1)
28 STEVE KIEFER-3B/DH
29 CURT YOUNG (INJ)-P
32 BILL KRUEGER-P
33 JOSE CANSECO-OF
34 TOM TELLMAN (INJ)-P
36 STEVE MURA-P
38 JOSE RIJO-P
39 DAVE MCKAY-CH
40 JEFF KAISER-P
41 CLETE BOYER-CH
42 JACKIE MOORE-MGR
43 MIKE WARREN-P
44 WES STOCK-CH
45 BOB DIDIER-CH
46 DAVE MCKAY-CH
48 TOM BIRTSAS-P
49 TOM BIRTSAS-P
50 JAY HOWELL-P
53 STEVE ONTIVEROS-P
54 STEVE MCCATTY-P
55 KEITH ATHERTON-P

1986

3RD (TIE) W 76-86 16GB

2 TONY PHILLIPS (INJ)-2B/UTIL
3 ALFREDO GRIFFIN-SS
4 CARNEY LANSFORD-3B/UTIL
5 STEVE HENDERSON-OF/DH
6 MICKEY TETTLETON (INJ)-C
7 JERRY WILLARD-C/DH
8 BILL BATHE-P
9 MIKE GALLEGO-INF
10 DAVE KINGMAN-DH/1B
10 TONY LARUSSA-MGR3
11 WAYNE GROSS-3B
12 DUSTY BAKER-UTIL
14 BRUCE BOCHTE-1B/DH
15 DONNIE HILL-INF/DH
16 MIKE DAVIS-OF
17 LENN SAKATA-2B/DH
18 TONY PHILLIPS (INJ)-2B/UTIL
18 DAVE DUNCAN-CH
20 BRUCE BOCHTE-1B/DH
21 DWAYNE MURPHY (INJ)-OF/DH
22 RICK LANGFORD-P
23 CHRIS CODIROLI (INJ)-P
24 RUSTY TILLMAN-OF
25 DONNIE HILL-INF/DH
25 MARK MCGWIRE-3B
26 DAVE KINGMAN-DH/1B
27 RICK RODRIGUEZ-P
29 CURT YOUNG-P
30 MOOSE HAAS-P
30 STAN JAVIER-OF/DH
31 RICKEY PETERS (INJ)-UTIL
32 BILL KRUEGER (INJ)-P
33 JOSE CANSECO-OF/DH
34 DAVE STEWART-P (2)
35 BILL MOONEYHAM-P
36 TERRY STEINBACH-C
38 JOSE RIJO-P
39 DAVE MCKAY-CH
40 DOUG BAIR-P
42 JACKIE MOORE-MGR1
43 RON PLAZA-CH
44 WES STOCK-CH
45 BOB DIDIER-CH
46 JEFF NEWMAN-CH/MGR2
46 JOE RUDI-CH
47 JOAQUIN ANDUJAR (INJ)-P
48 TOM BIRTSAS-P
49 ROB NELSON-1B/DH
50 JAY HOWELL (INJ)-P
51 ERIC PLUNK-P
52 DOUG BAIR-P
52 DAVE LEIPER-P
53 STEVE ONTIVEROS (INJ)-P
54 JERRY WILLARD-C/DH
54 FERNANDO ARROYO-P
55 KEITH ATHERTON-P (1)
57 DAVE VON OHLEN-P
58 DARREL AKERFELDS-P
59 TOM DOZIER-P

1987

3RD W 81-81 4GB

2 TONY PHILLIPS (INJ)-2B/UTIL
3 ALFREDO GRIFFIN-SS/2B
4 CARNEY LANSFORD-3B/UTIL
5 JIM (FRENCHY) LEFEBVRE-CH
6 MICKEY TETTLETON-UTIL
7 JERRY WILLARD (INJ)-UTIL
9 MIKE GALLEGO (INJ)-INF
10 TONY LARUSSA-MGR
11 RON CEY-UTIL
11 JOHNNIE LEMASTER-INF/DH
11 MATT SINATRO-C
12 RICK RODRIGUEZ-P
14 TONY BERNAZARD-2B/DH (2)
15 RENE LACHEMANN-CH
16 MIKE DAVIS-OF/DH
17 WALT WEISS-SS/DH
18 DAVE DUNCAN-CH
19 GENE NELSON-P
21 DWAYNE MURPHY (INJ)-UTIL
22 LUIS POLONIA-OF/DH
23 CHRIS CODIROLI-P
24 ALEX SANCHEZ-OF/DH
24 STEVE HENDERSON-OF/DH
25 MARK MCGWIRE-1B/UTIL
26 JOE RUDI-CH
27 RICK RODRIGUEZ-P
27 JOSE RIJO-P
28 STAN JAVIER (INJ)-OF/DH
29 CURT YOUNG-P
30 MOOSE HAAS (INJ)-P
31 BRIAN HARPER-DH/OF
32 BILL KRUEGER-P (1)
32 GREG CADARET-P
33 JOSE CANSECO-OF/DH
34 DAVE STEWART-P
36 TERRY STEINBACH-C/UTIL
37 BILL CAUDILL (INJ)-P
38 JOSE RIJO-P
38 DAVE OTTO-DH/OF
39 DAVE MCKAY-CH
40 ROB NELSON-1B (1)
40 RICK HONEYCUTT-P
41 STORM DAVIS-P (2)
43 RENE LACHEMANN-CH
43 DENNIS ECKERSLEY-P
44 REGGIE (MR. OCTOBER) JACKSON-DH/OF
45 MIKE PAUL-CH
46 JOE RUDI-CH

PHILADELPHIA/KANSAS CITY/ OAKLAND ATHLETICS

46 GARY LAVELLE-P (2)
47 JOAQUIN ANDUJAR (INJ)-P
49 ROB NELSON-1B (1)
49 DENNIS LAMP-P
50 JAY HOWELL (INJ)-P
51 ERIC PLUNK-P
52 DAVE LEIPER-P (1)
53 STEVE ONTIVEROS-P
55 BOB (BULL) WATSON-CH
57 DAVE VON OHLEN-P

1988

1ST W 104-58 0GB

W ALCS-BOSA 4-0

L WS-LAN 4-1

00 DON BAYLOR-DH
2 TONY PHILLIPS (INJ)-UTIL
3 ORLANDO MERCADO-C
4 CARNEY LANSFORD-3B/UTIL
5 JIM (FRENCHY) LEFEBVRE-CH
6 FELIX JOSE-OF
7 WALT WEISS-SS
9 MIKE GALLEGO-INF
10 TONY LARUSSA-MGR
11 MATT SINATRO-C
12 DON BAYLOR-DH
14 STORM DAVIS-P
15 RENE LACHEMANN-CH
17 GLENN HUBBARD-2B/DH
18 DAVE DUNCAN-CH
19 GENE NELSON-P
(20) MATT YOUNG (INJ)-(P)
21 DOUG JENNINGS (INJ)-UTIL
22 LUIS POLONIA-OF/DH
24 RON HASSEY-C/DH
25 MARK MCGWIRE-1B/OF
27 ED JURAK-3B
28 STAN JAVIER-UTIL
29 CURT YOUNG-P
30 LANCE BLANKENSHIP-2B/DH
31 DAVE MCKAY-CH
32 GREG CADARET-P
33 JOSE CANSECO-OF/DH
34 DAVE STEWART-P
35 BOB WELCH-P
36 TERRY STEINBACH (INJ)-C/UTIL
37 RICH BORDI-P
38 DAVE OTTO-P
39 DAVE PARKER (INJ)-UTIL
40 RICK HONEYCUTT-P
41 STORM DAVIS-P
41 JIM CORSI-P
42 DAVE HENDERSON-OF
43 DENNIS ECKERSLEY-P
44 DAVE MCKAY-CH
45 MIKE PAUL-CH
46 JOE RUDI-CH
46 RICH BORDI-P
48 DOUG JENNINGS (INJ)-UTIL
51 ERIC PLUNK-P
52 JEFF SHAVER-P
53 STEVE ONTIVEROS (INJ)-P
54 TODD BURNS-P
55 BOB (BULL) WATSON-CH

1989

1ST W 99-63 0GB

W ALCS-TORA 4-1

W WS-SFN 4-0

2 TONY PHILLIPS-2B/UTIL
3 DICK SCOTT-SS
3 JAMIE QUIRK-UTIL (2)
4 CARNEY LANSFORD-3B/UTIL
5 ART KUSNYER-CH
6 FELIX JOSE-OF
7 WALT WEISS (INJ)-SS
8 DAVE MCKAY-CH
9 MIKE GALLEGO-SS/UTIL
10 TONY LARUSSA-MGR
11 BILLY BEANE-UTIL
12 LANCE BLANKENSHIP-UTIL
14 STORM DAVIS-P
15 RENE LACHEMANN-CH
17 GLENN HUBBARD-2B/DH
18 DAVE DUNCAN-CH
19 GENE NELSON-P
20 MATT YOUNG (INJ)-P
21 DOUG JENNINGS-OF
21 MIKE MOORE-P
22 LUIS POLONIA-OF (1)
23 MIKE MOORE-P
23 CHRIS BANDO-C
24 RON HASSEY-UTIL
24 RICKEY HENDERSON-OF/DH (2)
25 MARK MCGWIRE-1B/DH
27 BILLY BEANE-UTIL
27 RON HASSEY-UTIL
28 STAN JAVIER-OF/INF
29 CURT YOUNG-P
30 CHRIS BANDO-C
30 LARRY ARNDT-1B/3B
31 DAVE MCKAY-CH
31 SCOTT HEMOND-3B
32 GREG CADARET-P (1)
33 JOSE CANSECO (INJ)-OF/DH
34 DAVE STEWART-P
35 BOB WELCH-P
36 TERRY STEINBACH-C/UTIL
38 DAVE OTTO-P
39 DAVE PARKER-DH/OF
40 RICK HONEYCUTT-P
41 JIM CORSI-P
42 DAVE HENDERSON-OF/DH
43 DENNIS ECKERSLEY (INJ)-P
44 KEN PHELPS-1B/DH (2)
45 MERV RETTENMUND-CH
46 TOMMIE REYNOLDS-CH
46 BILL DAWLEY-P
47 TOMMIE REYNOLDS-CH
51 ERIC PLUNK-P (1)
51 DANN HOWITT-OF/1B
53 BRIAN SNYDER-P
54 TODD BURNS-P

1990

1ST W 103-59 0GB

W ALCS-BOSA 4-0

L WS-CINN 4-0

2 DOUG JENNINGS-UTIL
3 JAMIE QUIRK-UTIL
3 HAROLD BAINES-DH (2)
4 CARNEY LANSFORD-3B/UTIL
5 ART KUSNYER-CH
6 FELIX JOSE-OF/DH (1)
6 JAMIE QUIRK-UTIL
7 WALT WEISS-SS
8 DAVE MCKAY-CH
9 MIKE GALLEGO-UTIL
10 TONY LARUSSA-MGR
12 LANCE BLANKENSHIP-UTIL
15 RENE LACHEMANN-CH
16 DARREN LEWIS-OF/DH
17 MIKE NORRIS-P
18 DAVE DUNCAN-CH
19 GENE NELSON-P
21 MIKE MOORE-P
22 SCOTT SANDERSON-P
24 RICKEY HENDERSON-OF/DH
25 MARK MCGWIRE-1B/DH
27 RON HASSEY-UTIL
27 *(RET#) CATFISH HUNTER*
28 STAN JAVIER-OF/DH (1)
29 CURT YOUNG-P
30 WILLIE RANDOLPH-2B/DH (2)
31 SCOTT HEMOND-3B/2B
33 JOSE CANSECO-OF/DH
34 DAVE STEWART-P
35 BOB WELCH-P
36 TERRY STEINBACH-C/UTIL
38 DAVE OTTO (INJ)-P
40 RICK HONEYCUTT-P
(41) JIM CORSI (INJ)-(P)
42 DAVE HENDERSON (INJ)-OF/DH
43 DENNIS ECKERSLEY-P
44 KEN PHELPS-DH/1B (1)
45 MERV RETTENMUND-CH
46 MIKE BORDICK-INF
47 TOMMIE REYNOLDS-CH
48 STEVE HOWARD-OF/DH
49 STEVE CHITREN-P
51 DANN HOWITT-UTIL
51 WILLIE MCGEE-OF/DH (2)
52 TROY AFENIR-C/DH
54 TODD BURNS-P
55 OZZIE CANSECO-DH/OF
57 REGGIE HARRIS (ILL)-P
58 JOE KLINK-P
59 JOE BITKER-P (1)

1991

4TH W 84-78 11GB

2* VANCE LAW-UTIL/P*
3 HAROLD BAINES-DH/OF
4 CARNEY LANSFORD (INJ)-3B/DH
5 ART KUSNYER-CH
6 JAMIE QUIRK-UTIL
7 WALT WEISS (INJ)-SS
8 DAVE MCKAY-CH
9 MIKE GALLEGO-2B/SS
10 TONY LARUSSA-MGR
11 ERNEST RILES-3B/INF
12 LANCE BLANKENSHIP-UTIL
13 DOUG JENNINGS-UTIL
14 FRED MANRIQUE-SS/2B
15 RENE LACHEMANN-CH
15 RON DARLING-P (3)
16 WILLIE WILSON-OF/DH
17 KIRK DRESSENDORFER (ILL)-P
17 RON DARLING-P (3)
18 DAVE DUNCAN-CH
19 GENE NELSON (INJ)-P
20 RICK (ROOSTER) BURLESON-CH
21 MIKE MOORE-P
22 KIRK DRESSENDORFER (ILL)-P
23 DANN HOWITT-OF/1B
24 RICKEY HENDERSON-OF/DH
25 MARK MCGWIRE-1B
26 BROOK JACOBY-3B/1B (2)
27 *(RET#) CATFISH HUNTER*
29 CURT YOUNG-P
30 ERIC SHOW-P
31 SCOTT HEMOND-UTIL
32 REGGIE HARRIS-P
33 JOSE CANSECO-OF/DH
34 DAVE STEWART-P
35 BOB WELCH-P
36 TERRY STEINBACH-C/UTIL
37 JOE SLUSARSKI-P
38 DANA ALLISON-P
40 RICK HONEYCUTT (INJ)-P
41 ANDY HAWKINS-P (2)
42 DAVE HENDERSON (INJ)-OF/UTIL
43 DENNIS ECKERSLEY-P
44 REGGIE (MR. OCTOBER) JACKSON-CH
45 JOHNNY GUZMAN-P
45 SCOTT BROSIUS-2B
46 MIKE BORDICK-INF
47 TOMMIE REYNOLDS-CH
48 BRAD KOMMINSK-OF
49 STEVE CHITREN-P
50 BRUCE WALTON-P
52 TROY AFENIR-C/DH
53 JOHN BRISCOE-P
54 TODD BURNS (INJ)-P
55 JOHN BRISCOE-P
55 KEVIN CAMPBELL-P
56 ANDY HAWKINS-P (2)
57 RON WITMEYER-1B
58 JOE KLINK (INJ)-P
59 TODD VAN POPPLE-P

1992

1ST W 96-66 0GB

L ALCS-TORA 4-2

2 RANDY READY-UTIL
2 SCOTT BROSIUS-UTIL
3 HAROLD BAINES-DH/OF
4 CARNEY LANSFORD (INJ)-3B/INF
5 ART KUSNYER-CH
6 WILLIE WILSON-OF/DH
7 MIKE KINGERY-OF
8 DAVE MCKAY-CH
9 JAMIE QUIRK-UTIL
10 TONY LARUSSA-MGR
11 DOUG (THE RED ROOSTER) (ROJO) RADER-CH
12 LANCE BLANKENSHIP-UTIL
14 MIKE BORDICK-2B/SS
15 RENE LACHEMANN-CH
16 SCOTT HEMOND-UTIL
17 RON DARLING-P
18 DAVE DUNCAN-CH
19 GENE NELSON-P
20 RANDY READY-UTIL
21 MIKE MOORE-P
22 WALT WEISS (INJ)-SS
23 DANN HOWITT-OF/1B
23 JEFF RUSSELL-P (2)
24 RICKEY HENDERSON-OF/DH
25 MARK MCGWIRE-1B
26 VINCE HORSMAN-P
27 *(RET#) CATFISH HUNTER*
28 ERIC FOX-OF
29 TROY NEEL-UTIL
29 RUBEN SIERRA-OF/DH (2)
30 JERRY BROWNE-UTIL
31 SCOTT HEMOND-UTIL
31 KELLY DOWNS-P
32 BOBBY WITT-P (2)
33 JOSE CANSECO-OF/DH (1)
34 DAVE STEWART-P
35 BOB WELCH-P
36 TERRY STEINBACH-C/1B
37 JOE SLUSARSKI-P
38 JEFF PARRETT-P
39 HENRY MERCEDES-C
40 RICK HONEYCUTT (INJ)-P
41 JOHNNY GUZMAN-P
42 DAVE HENDERSON (INJ)-OF
43 DENNIS ECKERSLEY-P
44 REGGIE (MR. OCTOBER) JACKSON-CH
46 MIKE BORDICK-2B/SS
47 TOMMIE REYNOLDS-CH
48 JIM CORSI-P
50 BRUCE WALTON-P
52 MIKE RACZKA-P
53 JOHN BRISCOE-P
54 GOOSE GOSSAGE-P
55 KEVIN CAMPBELL-P
56 TODD REVENIG-P
57 SHAWN HILLEGAS-P (2)

1993

7TH W 71-91 26GB

2 SCOTT HEMOND-UTIL
3 CRAIG PAQUETTE-3B/UTIL
5 ART KUSNYER-CH
6 DALE SVEUM-UTIL
7 SCOTT BROSIUS-UTIL
8 DAVE MCKAY-CH
10 TONY LARUSSA-MGR
11 KURT ABBOTT-UTIL
12 LANCE BLANKENSHIP-UTIL
13 BRENT GATES-2B
14 MIKE BORDICK-SS/2B
15 STORM DAVIS-P (1)
16 TROY NEEL-DH/1B
17 RON DARLING-P
18 DAVE DUNCAN-CH
20 KEVIN SEITZER-UTIL/P (1)
21 RUBEN SIERRA-OF/DH
23 MIKE ALDRETE-UTIL
24 RICKEY HENDERSON-OF/DH (1)
25 MARK MCGWIRE (INJ)-1B
26 VINCE HORSMAN-P
27 *(RET#) CATFISH HUNTER*
28 ERIC FOX-OF/DH
29 CURT YOUNG (INJ)-P
30 JERRY BROWNE (INJ)-OF/INF
31 KELLY DOWNS-P
32 BOBBY WITT-P
34 *(RET#) ROLLIE FINGERS*
35 BOB WELCH-P
36 TERRY STEINBACH (INJ)-C/UTIL
37 JOE SLUSARSKI-P
38 MARCOS ARMAS-UTIL
39 HENRY MERCEDES-C/DH
40 RICK HONEYCUTT (INJ)-P
42 DAVE HENDERSON-OF/DH
43 DENNIS ECKERSLEY-P
46 JOE BOEVER-P (1)
47 TOMMIE REYNOLDS-CH
47 MIGUEL JIMENEZ-P
48 ERIC HELFAND-C
49 SCOTT LYDY-OF/DH
50 BOB ALEJO-CH
50 STEVE KARSAY-P
51 ROGER SMITHBERG-P
52 EDWIN NUNEZ-P
53 JOHN BRISCOE-P
54 GOOSE GOSSAGE-P
55 KEVIN CAMPBELL-P
(56) TODD REVENIG (INJ)-(P)
57 SHAWN HILLEGAS-P
58 MIKE MOHLER-P
59 TODD VAN POPPEL-P

1994

2ND W 51-63 1GB

STRIKE NO POST-SEASON

2 SCOTT HEMOND-UTIL/C
3 CRAIG PAQUETTE-3B
4 CARNEY LANSFORD-CH
5 ART KUSNYER-CH
6 JIM (FRENCHY) LEFEBVRE-CH
6 STEVE SAX (INJ)-2B
7 SCOTT BROSIUS (INJ)-3B
8 DAVE MCKAY-CH
9 JUNIOR NOBOA-2B (1)
9 ERNIE YOUNG-OF
10 TONY LARUSSA-MGR
11 JIM (FRENCHY) LEFEBVRE-CH
12 LANCE BLANKENSHIP (INJ)-UTIL
13 BRENT GATES (INJ)-2B
14 MIKE BORDICK-SS
15 TOMMIE REYNOLDS-CH
16 TROY NEEL (INJ)-DH/1B
17 RON DARLING-P
18 DAVE DUNCAN-CH
19 DAVE (RAGS) RIGHETTI (REL)-P (1)
19 JIM BOWIE-1B
20 STEVE KARSAY (INJ)-P
21 RUBEN SIERRA-OF/DH
22 BILL TAYLOR (INJ)-P
23 MIKE ALDRETE-OF
24 RICKEY HENDERSON (INJ)-OF/DH
25 MARK MCGWIRE (INJ)-1B
26 VINCE HORSMAN-P
27 *(RET#) CATFISH HUNTER*
28 STAN JAVIER-OF
29 GERONIMO BERROA (INJ)-OF/DH
31 MIKE BRUMLEY-2B
31 ERIC FOX-OF
32 BOBBY WITT-P
34 *(RET#) ROLLIE FINGERS*
35 BOB WELCH-P
36 TERRY STEINBACH-C/UTIL
37 FRANCISCO MATOS-2B
38 STEVE PHOENIX-P
40 CARLOS REYES (INJ)-P
41 FAUSTO CRUZ-3B/SS

42 JEFF SCHAEFER-2B/3B
43 DENNIS ECKERSLEY-P
47 TOMMIE REYNOLDS-CH
47 MIGUEL JIMENEZ-P
48 ERIC HELFAND-C
50 STEVE ONTIVEROS-P
51 ROGER SMITHBERG-P
52 EDWIN NUNEZ (REL)-P
52 DAVE LEIPER-P
53 JOHN BRISCOE (INJ)-P
55 MARK ACRE-P
57 ED VOSBERG-P
58 MIKE MOHLER-P
59 TODD VAN POPPEL-P

1995

4TH W 67-77 11.5GB
144 GAME SEASON

2 MIKE GALLEGO-2B
3 CRAIG PAQUETTE-3B
4 CARNEY LANSFORD-CH
5 ART KUSNYER-CH
6 ERIC HELFAND-C
7 SCOTT BROSIUS-3B
8 DAVE MCKAY-CH
9 ERNIE YOUNG-OF
10 TONY LARUSSA-MGR
11 JIM (FRENCHY) LEFEBVRE-CH
12 BRIAN HARPER (RET)-C
13 BRENT GATES-2B
14 MIKE BORDICK (INJ)-SS
15 TOMMIE REYNOLDS-CH
16 JASON GIAMBI-INF/DH
17 RON DARLING (REL)-P
18 DAVE DUNCAN-CH
19 MIKE HARKEY (WAIV)-P (1)
19 GEORGE WILLIAMS-C
21 RUBEN SIERRA (INJ)-OF/DH (1)
23 MIKE ALDRETE-OF/1B (1)
24 RICKEY HENDERSON-OF
25 MARK MCGWIRE (INJ)-1B
26 CHRIS EDDY-P
27 *(RET#) CATFISH HUNTER*
28 STAN JAVIER-OF
29 GERONIMO BERROA-DH
30 TODD STOTTLEMYRE-P
31 JOHN WASDIN-P
33 ANDY TOMBERLIN-OF
34 *(RET#) ROLLIE FINGERS*
35 DAVE STEWART (RET)-P
36 TERRY STEINBACH (INJ)-C
37 CARLOS REYES-P
38 SCOTT BAKER-P
38 STEVE PHOENIX-P
39 STEVE WOJCIECHOWSKI-P
40 RICK HONEYCUTT-P (1)
41 JIM CORSI (INJ)-P
42 GEORGE WILLIAMS-C
43 DENNIS ECKERSLEY-P
44 JOSE HERRERA-OF
45 DANNY TARTABULL (INJ)-DH (2)
48 FAUSTO CRUZ-SS
48 ARIETO PRIETO (INJ)-P
50 STEVE ONTIVEROS (INJ)-P
51 DOUG JOHNS-P
52 DAVE LEIPER-P (1)
52 RAMON FERMIN-P
53 JOHN BRISCOE (INJ)-P
55 MARK ACRE (INJ)-P
56 DON WENGERT (INJ)-P
58 MIKE MOHLER-P
59 TODD VAN POPPEL-P

1996

3RD W 78-84 12GB

2 ALLEN BATTLE-OF
3 BOB CLUCK-CH
5 PEDRO MUNOZ (INJ)-OF
6 TOREY LOVULLO-3B
7 SCOTT BROSIUS (INJ)-3B
8 BRENT GATES (INJ)-2B
9 DUFFY DYER-CH
11 ERNIE YOUNG-OF
12 MATT STAIRS-OF
13 SCOTT SPIEZIO-3B
14 MIKE BORDICK-SS
15 DENNY WALLING-CH
16 JASON GIAMBI-1B/OF
17 CARLOS REYES-P
18 ART HOWE-MGR
19 GEORGE WILLIAMS-C
21 IZZY MOLINA-C
22 BILL TAYLOR (INJ)-P
23 PHIL PLANTIER-OF
24 BRIAN LESHER-OF
25 MARK MCGWIRE (INJ)-DH/1B
26 RAFAEL BOURNIGAL-SS
27 *(RET#) CATFISH HUNTER*
28 TONY BASTISTA-3B/2B
29 GERONIMO BERROA-DH
30 AARON SMALL-P
30 JAY WITASICK-P
31 JOHN WASDIN-P
32 MIKE MOHLER-P
33 DAMON MASHORE (INJ)-OF
34 *(RET#) ROLLIE FINGERS*
35 BRAD FISCHER-CH
36 TERRY STEINBACH-C
37 STEVE MONTGOMERY-P
38 RON WASHINGTON-CH
39 STEVE WOJCIECHOWSKI-P
40 RAFAEL BOURNIGAL-SS
40 WILLIE ADAMS-P
41 JIM CORSI (INJ)-P
42 BUDDY GROOM-P
44 JOSE HERRERA-DH
45 KERWIN MOORE-OF
48 ARIETO PRIETO (INJ)-P
49 WILLIE ADAMS-P
49 WEBSTER GARRISON-2B/1B
50 DAVE TELGHEDER-P
51 DOUG JOHNS-P
52 JAY WITASICK-P
53 JOHN BRISCOE-P
54 BOBBY CHOUINARD-P
55 MARK ACRE-P
56 DON WENGERT-P
58 PAUL FLETCHER-P
59 TODD VAN POPPEL (WAIV)-P (1)

1997

4TH W 65-97 25GB

2 JASON MCDONALD-OF
3 BOB CLUCK-CH
4 MIGUEL TEJADA-SS
5 BRIAN LESHER-OF
6 BRENT MAYNE-C
7 SCOTT BROSIUS (INJ)-3B
8 SCOTT SHELDON-SS
8 TILSON BRITO-SS (2)
9 DUFFY DYER-CH
11 ERNIE YOUNG-OF
12 MATT STAIRS-OF
13 IZZY MOLINA-C
14 BEN GRIEVE-OF
15 DENNY WALLING-CH
16 JASON GIAMBI-OF
17 DAVE MAGADAN-3B/1B/DH
18 ART HOWE-MGR
19 GEORGE WILLIAMS (INJ)-C
20 STEVE KARSAY (INJ)-P
21 SCOTT SPIEZIO (INJ)-2B
22 BILL TAYLOR (INJ)-P
23 PATRICK LENNON (INJ)-OF
24 BUDDY GROOM-P
25 MARK MCGWIRE-DH/1B (1)
26 RAFAEL BOURNIGAL (INJ)-INF/SS
27 *(RET#) CATFISH HUNTER*
28 TONY BASTISTA (INJ)-SS
29 GERONIMO BERROA-DH (1)
29 T. J. MATHEWS-P (2)
30 AARON SMALL-P
31 DAMON MASHORE (INJ)-OF
32 MIKE MOHLER-P
33 JOSE CANSECO (INJ)-OF
34 *(RET#) ROLLIE FINGERS*
35 BRAD FISCHER-CH
37 CARLOS REYES (INJ)-P
38 RON WASHINGTON-CH
39 STEVE WOJCIECHOWSKI (INJ)-P
40 WILLIE ADAMS-P
41 ERIC LUDWICK-P (2)
42 BUDDY GROOM-P
44 RICHIE LEWIS-P (1)
45 MIKE OQUIST (INJ)-P
46 BOB ALEJO-CH
47 BILLY BREWER (INJ)-P (1)
47 MARK BELLHORN-2B
48 ARIETO PRIETO (INJ)-P
49 GARY HAUGHT-P
49 ANDREW LORRAINE-P
50 DAVE TELGHEDER (INJ)-P
51 RICHIE LEWIS-P (1)
51 SCOTT SHELDON-SS
51 JIMMY HAYNES-P
52 JAY WITASICK-P
53 STEVE MONTGOMERY-P
53 JOHN JOHNSTONE-P (2)
55 MARK ACRE-P
56 DON WENGERT-P
57 BRAD RIGBY (INJ)-P
58 TIM KUBINSKI (INJ)-P
59 DANE JOHNSON-P

1998

4TH W 74-88 14GB

2 JASON MCDONALD (INJ)-OF
3 BIP ROBERTS-2B/UTIL (2)
4 MIGUEL TEJADA (INJ)-SS
5 SHANE MACK-OF (1)
5 MIKE MACFARLANE-C
6 MIKE BLOWERS-3B/1B
7 KURT ABBOTT (INJ)-SS/UTIL
7 KEVIN MITCHELL (INJ) (REL)-DH/OF/1B
8 ED SPRAGUE, JR.-3B/1B (2)
9 DUFFY DYER-CH
10 MARK BELLHORN-DH
11 GARY JONES-CH
12 MATT STAIRS-OF
13 IZZY MOLINA-C
14 BEN GRIEVE-OF
15 DENNY WALLING-CH
15 SHANE MACK-OF (1)
16 JASON GIAMBI-OF
17 DAVE MAGADAN (INJ)-3B/1B/DH
18 ART HOWE-MGR
(19) GEORGE WILLIAMS (INJ)-(C)
20 BRIAN LESHER (INJ)-OF
21 SCOTT SPIEZIO (INJ)-2B
22 BILL TAYLOR-P
23 A. J. HINCH-C
24 RICKEY HENDERSON-OF
26 RAFAEL BOURNIGAL-INF/SS
27 *(RET#) CATFISH HUNTER*
28 JACK VOIGT-1B/UTIL
28 MARK HOLZEMER-P
29 BUDDY GROOM-P
30 AARON SMALL-P
30 TIM WORRELL-P (3)
30 ERIC CHAVEZ-3B
31 KEVIN MITCHELL (INJ) (REL)-DH/OF/1B
31 GIL HEREDIA-P
32 MIKE MOHLER-P
33 T. J. MATHEWS-P
34 *(RET#) ROLLIE FINGERS*
35 BRAD FISCHER-CH
36 MIKE FETTERS (INJ)-P (1)
37 KENNY ROGERS-P
38 RON WASHINGTON-CH
39 JASON WOOD-SS (1)
(40) WILLIE ADAMS (INJ)-(P)
41 JIM DOUGHERTY-P
42 *(RET#) JACKIE ROBINSON*
44 MIKE OQUIST-P
45 JORGE VELANDIA-SS/2B
46 BOB ALEJO-CH
47 RICK PETERSON-CH
48 ARIETO PRIETO-P
49 TOM CANDIOTTI-P
50 DAVE TELGHEDER (INJ)-P
51 JIMMY HAYNES-P
52 JAY WITASICK-P
53 RYAN CHRISTENSON-OF
54 MIKE NEILL (INJ)-OF
55 JASON WOOD-INF
56 STEVE CONNELLY-P
(57) BRAD RIGBY-(P)
59 BLAKE STEIN-P

1999

2ND W 87-76 8GB

2 JASON MCDONALD (INJ)-OF
3 ERIC CHAVEZ-3B
4 MIGUEL TEJADA (INJ)-SS
5 JOHN JAHA-INF
6 TONY PHILLIPS (INJ)-OF
7 FRANK MENECHINO-INF
8 OLMEDO SAENZ (INJ)-INF
8 RANDY VELARDE-INF (2)
9 OLMEDO SAENZ (INJ)-INF
(10) MARK BELLHORN-(DH)
12 MATT STAIRS-OF
13 JORGE VELANDIA (INJ)-INF
14 BEN GRIEVE-OF
15 MIKE MACFARLANE-C
16 JASON GIAMBI-OF
17 RON MAHAY-P
18 ART HOWE-MGR
19 KEVIN APPIER-P (2)
20 KEVIN JARVIS (INJ)-P
21 SCOTT SPIEZIO (INJ)-2B
22 BILL TAYLOR-P (1)
22 RICH BECKER-OF (2)
23 A. J. HINCH-C
24 DOUG JONES-P
(26) ERIC STUCKENSCHNEIDE (INJ)-(OF)
27 *(RET#) CATFISH HUNTER*
28 RYAN CHRISTENSON-OF
29 BUDDY GROOM-P
30 TIM (ROCK) RAINES (INJ)-OF/DH
31 GIL HEREDIA-P
33 T. J. MATHEWS (INJ)-P
34 *(RET#) ROLLIE FINGERS*
35 BRAD FISCHER-CH
36 TIM WORRELL (INJ)-P
37 KENNY ROGERS-P (1)
38 RON WASHINGTON-CH
40 OMAR OLIVARES-P (2)
41 THAD BOSLEY-CH
42 *(RET#) JACKIE ROBINSON*
44 MIKE OQUIST-P
45 DAVE HUDGENS-CH
47 RICK PETERSON-CH
(48) ARIETO PRIETO (INJ)-(P)
48 JASON (IZZY) ISRINGHAUSEN-P (2)
49 TOM CANDIOTTI-P (1)
49 GREG MCMICHAEL-P (2)
51 JIMMY HAYNES-P
52 TIM HUDSON-P
55 RAMON HERNANDEZ-C
56 CHAD HARVILL-P
57 BRAD RIGBY-P (1)
58 BRETT LAXTON-P
58 TED KUBINSKI-P
59 BLAKE STEIN-P (1)
61 LUIS VIZCAINO-P

2000

1ST W 91-70 0GB
L ALDS-NYA 3-2

2 JOSE ORTIZ-INF
3 ERIC CHAVEZ-3B
4 MIGUEL TEJADA-SS
5 JOHN JAHA (INJ)-INF
6 SAL FASANO-C
7 JEREMY GIAMBI-OF
8 RANDY VELARDE-INF
9 OLMEDO SAENZ-INF
10 MIKE STANLEY-1B (2)
11 FRANK MENECHINO-INF
12 MATT STAIRS-OF
13 JORGE VELANDIA (INJ)-INF (1)
14 BEN GRIEVE-OF
15 TIM HUDSON-P
16 JASON GIAMBI-INF
17 RON MAHAY-P (1)
18 ART HOWE-MGR
19 KEVIN APPIER-P
20 MARK MULDER-P
21 BO PORTER-OF
22 RICH BECKER-OF (1)
22 MARCUS JONES-P
22 ERIC BYRNES-OF
23 A. J. HINCH-C
24 DOUG JONES-P
26 SCOTT SERVICE-P
27 *(RET#) CATFISH HUNTER*
28 RYAN CHRISTENSON-OF
29 JEFF TAM-P
30 ARIETO PRIETO-P
31 GIL HEREDIA-P
33 T. J. MATHEWS-P
34 *(RET#) ROLLIE FINGERS*
35 BRAD FISCHER-CH
36 ADAM PIATT-P
37 TERRENCE LONG-OF
38 RON WASHINGTON-CH
39 KEN MACHA-CH
40 OMAR OLIVARES (INJ)-P
41 THAD BOSLEY-CH
42 *(RET#) JACKIE ROBINSON*
44 JASON (IZZY) ISRINGHAUSEN-P
45 MIKE QUADE-CH
45 JIM MECIR-P (2)
47 RICK PETERSON-CH
48 JIM MECIR-P (2)
49 MARK BELLHORN-INF
50 MARIO VALDEZ-INF
52 MIKE MAGNANTE-P
53 BARRY ZITO-P
55 RAMON HERNANDEZ-C
56 RICH SAUVEUR-P
56 TERRY BURROWS-P
59 TODD BELITZ-P
61 LUIS VIZCAINO-P
68 STEVE GAJKOWSKI-P

2001

2ND W (W/C) 102-60 14GB
L ALDS-NYA 3-2

2 JOSE ORTIZ (INJ)-INF (1)
2 F. P. SANTAGELO-2B
3 ERIC CHAVEZ-3B
4 MIGUEL TEJADA-SS
5 JOHN JAHA (INJ) (RET)-INF/DH
5 RON GANT-OF/DH (2)
6 ADAM PIATT (INJ)-OF
7 JEREMY GIAMBI-OF/DH
8 JOHNNY DAMON-OF
9 OLMEDO SAENZ-INF/DH
11 FRANK MENECHINO-INF
12 TERRENCE LONG-OF
13 SAL FASANO-C
13 BILLY MCMILLON (INJ)-OF (2)
14 MARK BELLHORN-3B
15 TIM HUDSON-P
16 JASON GIAMBI-INF
17 TOM WILSON-C
18 ART HOWE-MGR
19 MARK GUTHRIE-P
20 MARK MULDER-P
21 CORY LIDLE-P
22 ERIC BYRNES-DH
23 MARIO VALDEZ (INJ)-INF
24 GREG MYERS-DH
24 JERMAINE DYE-OF (2)
26 JERMAINE DYE-OF (2)
26 ROB RYAN-DH
27 *(RET#) CATFISH HUNTER*
28 RYAN CHRISTENSON-OF (1)
28 GREG MYERS-DH

PHILADELPHIA/KANSAS CITY/
OAKLAND ATHLETICS

29 JEFF TAM-P
30 ROBIN JENNINGS-OF (1)
30 ANDY ABAD-1B
31 GIL HEREDIA-P
32 CHAD HARVILLE (INJ)-P
33 T. J. MATHEWS-P
34 *(RET#) ROLLIE FINGERS*
35 BRAD FISCHER-CH
37 ERIK HILJUS-P
38 RON WASHINGTON-CH
39 KEN MACHA-CH
41 THAD BOSLEY-CH
42 *(RET#) JACKIE ROBINSON*
44 JASON (IZZY) ISRINGHAUSEN-P
45 JIM MECIR (INJ)-P
47 RICK PETERSON-CH
48 MIKE QUADE-CH
49 BILLY MCMILLON-OF (2)
49 MARK FYHRIE-P (2)
51 LUIS VIZCAINO-P
52 MIKE MAGNANTE-P
53 CHAD BRADFORD-P
55 RAMON HERNANDEZ-C
75 BARRY ZITO-P

2002

1ST W 94-67 0GB
L ALDS-MINA 3-2

2 CARLOS PENA-1B (1)
2 JASON GRABOWSKI-OF
3 ERIC CHAVEZ-3B/*DH*
4 MIGUEL TEJADA-SS
5 RAY DURHAM-DH/2B (2)
6 ADAM PIATT-*OF/1B*
7 JEREMY GIAMBI-OF/DH *(1)*
7 JOHN MABRY-OF/1B (2)
8 RANDY VELARDE (INJ)-INF/DH
9 OLMEDO SAENZ-INF/DH
10 SCOTT HATTEBERG-1B/DH
11 FRANK MENECHINO-INF
12 TERRENCE LONG-OF
14 MARK ELLIS-2B/INF
15 TIM HUDSON-P
(17) MARIO VALDEZ (INJ)-(OF)
18 ART HOWE-MGR
19 LARRY SUTTON-1B/OF
20 MARK MULDER-P
21 CORY LIDLE-P
22 ERIC BYRNES-OF/DH
23 DAVID JUSTICE-OF/DH
24 JERMAINE DYE-OF/DH
26 CODY MCKAY-C
27 *(RET#) CATFISH HUNTER*
28 GREG MYERS-C
29 JEFF TAM-P
30 MIKE COLANGELO-OF
30 JOSE FLORES-UTIL
31 MIKE HOLTZ-P (1)
31 TED LILLY (INJ)-P (2)
34 *(RET#) ROLLIE FINGERS*
35 BRAD FISCHER-CH
37 ERIK HILJUS-P
38 RON WASHINGTON-CH
39 KEN MACHA-CH
40 ESTEBAN GERMAN-2B
41 THAD BOSLEY-CH
42 *(RET#) JACKIE ROBINSON*
44 BILLY KOCH-P
45 JIM MECIR-P
46 MIKE VENAFRO-P
47 RICK PETERSON-CH
47 JOHN MABRY-OF/1B (2)
48 MIKE QUADE-CH
49 MIKE FYHRIE-P (2)
52 MIKE MAGNANTE-P
53 CHAD BRADFORD-P
55 RAMON HERNANDEZ-C
56 AARON HARANG-P
57 MICAH BOWIE-P
73 RICARDO RINCON-P (2)
75 BARRY ZITO-P

2003

1ST W 96-66 0GB
L ALDS-BOSA 3-2

2 CHRIS SINGLETON-OF
3 ERIC CHAVEZ-3B
4 MIGUEL TEJADA-SS
5 RON GANT-OF/DH
6 JOSE GUILLEN-OF (2)
7 MARK JOHNSON-C
8 ADAM PIATT (WAIV)-OF (1)
8 BOBBY CROSBY-SS
10 SCOTT HATTEBERG-1B/DH
11 FRANK MENECHINO-INF
12 TERRENCE LONG (SUS:2G)-OF
13 BILLY MCMILLON-OF/DH
14 MARK ELLIS-2B
15 TIM HUDSON-P
16 RICH HARDEN-P
17 ADAM MELHUSE-C/INF
18 DAVID MCCARTY (WAIV)-OF/1B (1)
18 GRAHAM KOONCE-1B
20 MARK MULDER (INJ)-P
21 MIKE EDWARDS-OF
22 ERIC BYRNES-OF
23 JASON GRABOWSKI-OF/3B
24 JERMAINE DYE (INJ)-OF
27 *(RET#) CATFISH HUNTER*
29 KEITH FOULKE-P
31 TED LILLY-P
32 CHAD HARVILLE-P
33 JEREMY FIKAC-P
34 *(RET#) ROLLIE FINGERS*
35 BRAD FISCHER-CH
37 STEVE W. SPARKS-P (2)
38 RON WASHINGTON-CH
39 KEN MACHA-MGR
40 ESTEBAN GERMAN-2B
41 THAD BOSLEY-CH
42 *(RET#) JACKIE ROBINSON*
44 ERUBIEL DURAZO-DH/1B
45 JIM MECIR (INJ)-P
46 RICK PETERSON-CH
47 TERRY FRANCONA-CH
48 DAVE HUDGENS-CH
49 MIKE NEU-P
51 MIKE WOOD-P
52 BOB GEREN-CH
53 CHAD BRADFORD-P
54 JOHN HALAMA-P
55 RAMON HERNANDEZ-C
56 AARON HARANG-P (1)
57 MICAH BOWIE (INJ)-P
58 JUSTIN DUCHSCHERER-P
73 RICARDO RINCON-P
75 BARRY ZITO-P

2004

2ND W 91-71 1GB

2 MARK MCLEMORE (INJ)-2B/3B
3 ERIC CHAVEZ (INJ)-3B
6 MIKE ROSE-C
7 BOBBY CROSBY-SS
10 SCOTT HATTEBERG-1B
11 FRANK MENECHINO-INF (1)
12 ESTEBAN GERMAN-2B
13 BILLY MCMILLON-OF/DH
(14) MARK ELLIS-(2B)
15 TIM HUDSON (INJ)-P
17 ADAM MELHUSE-C
18 ERIC KARROS-1B
18 MARK REDMAN-P
20 MARK MULDER-P
21 MARK KOTSAY-OF
22 ERIC BYRNES-OF
23 BOBBY KIELTY-OF
24 JERMAINE DYE-OF/DH
26 DAMIAN MILLER-C
27 *(RET#) CATFISH HUNTER*
28 OCTAVIO DOTEL-P (2)
29 CHRIS HAMMOND-P
31 CHAD HARVILLE-P
31 KIRK SAARLOOS (INJ)-P
32 CHAD HARVILLE-P
32 ERIC KARROS-1B
33 NICK SWISHER-OF
34 *(RET#) ROLLIE FINGERS*
35 BRAD FISCHER-CH
38 RON WASHINGTON-CH
39 KEN MACHA-MGR
40 RICH HARDEN-P
41 CURT YOUNG-CH
42 *(RET#) JACKIE ROBINSON*
44 ERUBIEL DURAZO-DH
45 JIM MECIR-P
46 CHRIS SPEIER-CH
46 JAIRO GARCIA-P
47 RAMON CASTRO-2B
48 DAVE HUDGENS-CH
49 MARCO SCUTARO-INF
52 BOB GEREN-CH
53 ARTHUR RHODES-P
54 CHAD BRADFORD-P
55 MARK REDMAN-P
57 JUSTIN LEHR-P
58 JUSTIN DUCHSCHERER-P
64 JOE BLANTON-P
73 RICARDO RINCON-P
75 BARRY ZITO-P

2005

2ND W 88-74 7GB

3 ERIC CHAVEZ-3B
4 JERMAINE CLARK-OF/2B
6 KEITH GINTER-2B
7 BOBBY CROSBY (INJ)-SS
10 SCOTT HATTEBERG-1B/DH
11 DAN JOHNSON-1B
12 MATT WATSON-OF
13 KEIICHI YABU-P
14 MARK ELLIS-2B
15 RENE LACHEMANN-CH
16 JAY PAYTON-OF (2)
17 ADAM MELHUSE-C
18 JASON KENDALL-C
19 MARCO SCUTARO-2B/SS
20 HUSTON STREET-P
21 MARK KOTSAY-OF
22 ERIC BYRNES-OF (1)
22 ALBERTO CASTILLO-C (2)
23 BOBBY KIELTY-OF
24 DANNY HAREN-P
26 CHARLES THOMAS-OF
27 *(RET#) CATFISH HUNTER*
28 HIRAM BOCACHICA-OF
29 OCTAVIO DOTEL (INJ)-P
30 SETH ETHERTON-P
31 KIRK SAARLOOS-P
33 NICK SWISHER (INJ)(BRV)-OF
34 *(RET#) ROLLIE FINGERS*
35 BRAD FISCHER-CH
37 JOE KENNEDY-P
38 RON WASHINGTON-CH
39 KEN MACHA-MGR
40 RICH HARDEN (INJ)-P
41 CURT YOUNG-CH
42 *(RET#) JACKIE ROBINSON*
43 *(RET#) DENNIS ECKERSLEY*
44 ERUBIEL DURAZO-DH
45 JAY WITASICK-P (2)
46 JAIRO GARCIA-P
47 RON FLORES-P
48 DAVE HUDGENS-CH
49 TIM HARIKKALA-P
49 FREDDIE BYNUM-INF
50 KIKO CALERO (INJ)-P
51 JUAN CRUZ-P
52 BOB GEREN-CH
(53) CHAD BRADFORD (INJ)-(P) (1)
55 JOE BLANTON-P
56 RYAN GLYNN-P
57 BRITT REAMES-P
58 JUSTIN DUCHSCHERER-P
73 RICARDO RINCON-P
75 BARRY ZITO-P

Big Mac. Mark McGwire broke in with a smash. He set the single season homerun record for rookies with 49 in 1987. He also had a slugging percentage of .618. He was a 7-time All-Star with the A's, but his exhilarating race with Sammy Sosa to the record 70 HRs in 1998 stands out as his greatest achievement.

SEATTLE MARINERS

1977
SEATTLE MARINERS
6TH W 64-98 38GB

1 BILL STEIN-3B/UTIL
2 JULIO CRUZ-2B/DH
3 SKIP JUTZE-C
4 STEVE BRAUN-OF/UTIL
5 DAVE COLLINS-OF/DH
6 LARRY COX-C
7 DAN MEYER-1B
8 CARLOS LOPEZ (INJ)-OF/DH
9 RUPPERT JONES-OF/DH
10 LARRY MILBOURNE-INF/DH
11 TOMMY SMITH-OF
12 CRAIG REYNOLDS-SS
14 JOSE BAEZ-2B/UTIL
15 BOB STINSON-C/DH
16 GARY WHEELOCK (INJ)-P
17 GLENN ABBOTT-P
18 JOE LIS-1B/C
18 KEVIN PASLEY-C (2)
19 BOB GALASSO-P
20 TOMMY MOORE-P
20 JIMMY SEXTON-SS
21 TOM MCMILLAN-SS
22 DARRELL JOHNSON-MGR
23 STAN THOMAS (INJ)-P (1)
23 LUIS (PUCHY) DELGADO-OF
24 FRANK MACCORMACK-P
25 JOHN MONTAGUE-P
26 JUAN BERNHARDT (INJ)-DH
27 DIEGO SEGUI-P
28 VADA PINSON-CH
29 TOM HOUSE (INJ)-P (2)
30 DAVE PAGAN-P (1)
30 BYRON MCLAUGHLIN-P
31 DON BRYANT-CH
32 WES STOCK-CH
33 JIM BUSBY-CH
34 PAUL MITCHELL-P (2)
35 GREG ERARDI-P
36 LEE STANTON-OF/DH
37 MIKE KEKICH (INJ)-P
38 BILL LAXTON (INJ)-P (1)
38 RAY FOSSE-C/DH (2)
39 STEVE BURKE-P
40 RICK HONEYCUTT-P
41 MIKE KEKICH (INJ)-P
41 DOC MEDICH-P (2)
43 ENRIQUE ROMO-P
45 DICK POLE (INJ)-P
46 RICK JONES (INJ)-P

1978
7TH W 56-104 35GB

1 BILL STEIN-3B/DH
2 JULIO CRUZ-2B/UTIL
3 BILL PLUMMER-C
4 STEVE BRAUN-DH/OF (1)
6 BOB ROBERTSON (INJ)-DH/1B
7 DAN MEYER (INJ)-1B/UTIL
8 LEON ROBERTS-OF/DH
9 RUPPERT JONES (ILL)-OF
10 LARRY MILBOURNE-INF/DH
11 CHARLIE BEAMON-DH/1B
12 CRAIG REYNOLDS-SS
13 DICK POLE-P
14 JOSE BAEZ-UTIL
14 TOM PACIOREK-UTIL (2)
15 BOB STINSON-C/DH
17 GLENN ABBOTT-P
18 KEVIN PASLEY-C
20 MIKE PARROTT (INJ)-P
22 DARRELL JOHNSON-MGR
23 BRUCE BOCHTE-OF/UTIL
25 JOHN MONTAGUE (INJ)-P
26 JUAN BERNHARDT-UTIL
27 JIM TODD-P
28 VADA PINSON-CH
29 TOM HOUSE-P
30 BYRON MCLAUGHLIN-P
31 DON BRYANT-CH
32 WES STOCK-CH
33 JIM BUSBY-CH
34 PAUL MITCHELL-P
(35) SANTO ALCALA-(P)
36 LEE STANTON-DH/OF
38 JIM COLBURN-P (2)
39 STEVE BURKE (INJ)-P
40 RICK HONEYCUTT (INJ)-P
41 SHANE RAWLEY-P
42 SHANE RAWLEY-P
42 TOM BROWN-P
43 ENRIQUE ROMO-P
43 JOHN HALE-OF/DH
44 ENRIQUE ROMO-P
45 DICK POLE-P
46 RICK JONES-P
48 JIM COLBORN-P (2)
51 BILL (MAZ) MAZEROSKI-CH

1979
6TH W 67-95 21GB

1 BILL STEIN (INJ)-INF
2 BOBBY VALENTINE-UTIL
5 LARRY COX-C
6 JULIO CRUZ (INJ) 2B
7 DAN MEYER-3B/UTIL
8 LEON ROBERTS-OF/DH
9 RUPPERT JONES-OF
10 LARRY MILBOURNE-INF
11 MARIO MENDOZA-SS
12 CHARLIE BEAMON-UTIL
14 TOM PACIOREK-OF/1B
15 BOB STINSON-C
17 GLENN ABBOTT (INJ)-P
18 JOE SIMPSON-OF/DH
19 RODNEY CRAIG-OF
20 MIKE PARROTT-P
21 RAFAEL VASQUEZ-P
22 DARRELL JOHNSON-MGR
23 BRUCE BOCHTE-1B
24 ROB DRESSLER-P
25 JOHN MONTAGUE-P (1)
26 JUAN BERNHARDT-PH
26 JIM LEWIS-P
27 BYRON MCLAUGHLIN-P
28 VADA PINSON-CH
29 ROY BRANCH-P
30 BILL (MAZ) MAZEROSKI-CH
31 DON BRYANT-CH
32 WES STOCK-CH
33 RANDY STEIN-P
34 PAUL MITCHELL-P (1)
35 JOE DECKER-P
35 WAYNE TWITCHELL-P (2)
36 ODELL JONES-P
37 RICH HINTON-P (2)
38 FLOYD BANNISTER-P
40 RICK HONEYCUTT-P
41 SHANE RAWLEY (INJ)-P
43 JOHN HALE-OF/DH
53 WILLIE HORTON-DH

1980
7TH W 59-103 38GB

1 BILL STEIN (INJ)-UTIL
2 LARRY MILBOURNE-UTIL
3 JERRY NARRON-C/DH
4 JIM ANDERSON-UTIL
5 LARRY COX-C
6 JULIO CRUZ-2B/DH
7 DAN MEYER-OF/UTIL
8 LEON ROBERTS-OF/DH
9 BILL (MAZ) MAZEROSKI-CH
10 TED COX-3B
11 MARIO MENDOZA-SS
12 JUAN BENIQUEZ (INJ)-OF/DH
14 TOM PACIOREK-UTIL
15 BOB STINSON-C
15 DAVE EDLER-3B
16 GARY WHEELOCK (INJ)-P
17 GLENN ABBOTT-P
18 JOE SIMPSON-OF/1B
19 RODNEY CRAIG-OF
20 MIKE PARROTT (INJ)-P
21 MARC HILL-C (2)
22 DARRELL JOHNSON-MGR1
22 KIM ALLEN-UTIL
23 BRUCE BOCHTE-1B/DH
24 ROB DRESSLER-P
25 RICK ANDERSON-P
26 REGGIE WALTON-OF/DH
27 BYRON MCLAUGHLIN-P
28 VADA PINSON-CH
30 MAURY WILLS-MGR2
31 DON BRYANT-CH
32 WES STOCK-CH
35 FRANK FUNK-CH
38 FLOYD BANNISTER-P
40 RICK HONEYCUTT-P
41 SHANE RAWLEY-P
44 MANNY SARMIENTO-P
45 JIM BEATTIE-P
49 DAVE ROBERTS-P (2)
50 DAVE HEAVERLO-P
53 WILLIE HORTON (INJ)-DH
54 BYRON MCLAUGHIN-P
60 DAVE HEAVERLO-P

1981
1ST 1/2: 6TH W 21-36 14.5GB
2ND 1/2:5TH W 23-29 6.5GB
FINAL: 6TH W 44-65 --GB

1 LENNY RANDLE-3B/UTIL
2 KIM ALLEN-UTIL
3 JERRY NARRON-C
4 JIM ANDERSON-SS/3B
5 JEFF BURROUGHS-OF/DH
6 JULIO CRUZ-2B/SS
7 DAN MEYER-UTIL
8 VANCE MCHENRY-SS/DH
9 TERRY (BUD) BULLING-C
10 CANANEA REYES-CH
11 JIM MALER-1B/DH
12 TOMMY DAVIS-CH
14 TOM PACIOREK-OF
15 RENE LACHEMANN-MGR2
16 RICK AUERBACH (INJ)-SS
17 GLENN ABBOTT-P
18 JOE SIMPSON-OF/1B
19 FLOYD BANNISTER-P
20 MIKE PARROTT-P
21 KEN CLAY-P
22 RICHIE ZISK-DH
23 BRUCE BOCHTE-1B/UTIL
24 DAVE EDLER-3B/SS
26 RANDY STEIN-P
27 CASEY PARSONS-OF/1B
27 BRAD GULDEN-C
28 JERRY DON GLEATON-P
29 GARY GRAY-UTIL
30 MAURY WILLS-MGR1
31 BRIAN ALLARD (INJ)-P
32 WES STOCK-CH
32 BUD BLACK-P
33 REGGIE WALTON (INJ)-OF/DH
34 BOB STODDARD-P
35 FRANK FUNK-CH
36 BUD BLACK-P
38 FLOYD BANNISTER-P
38 PAUL SERNA-SS/2B
39 LARRY ANDERSEN-P
40 DICK DRAGO-P
41 SHANE RAWLEY-P
42 DAVE HENDERSON-OF
43 BOB GALASSO (INJ)-P
44 DAN FIROVA-C
45 JIM BEATTIE-P
48 BRYAN CLARK-P
49 KEN CLAY-P
__ VITO LUCARELLI-CH?
__ LEW TEMPLE-CH?

1982
4TH W 76-86 17GB

1 LENNY RANDLE-UTIL
1 DAVE EDLER-UTIL
2 DOMINGO RAMOS-SS
2 ORLANDO MERCADO-C/DH
3 PAUL SERNA-UTIL
4 RENE LACHEMANN-MGR
5 DAVE REVERING-1B (3)
6 JULIO CRUZ-2B/UTIL
7 JIM ESSIAN (INJ)-C
8 RICK SWEET-C (2)
9 BILL PLUMMER-CH
10 DAVE DUNCAN-CH
11 TERRY (BUD) BULLING-C
12 MANNY CASTILLO-3B/2B
14 STEVE STROUGHTER-DH/OF
15 CHUCK COTTIER-CH
16 AL COWENS-OF/DH
(17) GLENN ABBOTT (INJ)-(P)
18 JOE SIMPSON-OF
19 FLOYD BANNISTER-P
20 THAD BOSLEY-OF
20 RICH BORDI-P
21 GENE NELSON-P
21 TODD CRUZ-SS
22 RICHIE ZISK-DH
23 BRUCE BOCHTE-OF/UTIL
24 GENE NELSON-P
25 RICH BORDI-P
25 MIKE MOORE-P
26 VANCE MCHENRY-SS/DH
26 JOHN MOSES-OF
27 JERRY DON GLEATON-P
28 VADA PINSON-CH
29 GARY GRAY-1B/DH
30 ED NUNEZ (INJ)-P
(31) BRIAN ALLARD (INJ)-(P)
32 ED VANDE BERG-P
33 JIM MALER-1B/DH
34 BOB STODDARD-P
35 RON MUSSELMAN-P
36 GAYLORD PERRY-P
37 BILL CAUDILL-P
39 LARRY ANDERSEN-P
41 BILL CAUDILL-P
42 DAVE HENDERSON-OF
43 GENE NELSON-P
44 DAN FIROVA-C
44 BOBBY BROWN-OF/DH
45 JIM BEATTIE-P
46 MIKE STANTON-P
48 BRYAN CLARK-P

1983
7TH W 60-102 39GB

1 DAVE EDLER-UTIL
1 DEL CRANDALL-MGR2
2 ORLANDO MERCADO-C
3 DOMINGO RAMOS-INF/DH
4 RENE LACHEMANN-MGR1
5 STEVE HENDERSON-OF/DH
6 JULIO CRUZ-2B/DH (1)
6 JAMIE NELSON-C
7 SPIKE OWEN-SS
8 RICK SWEET-C
9 BILL PLUMMER-CH
9 PHIL ROOF-CH
10 RICKY NELSON-OF/DH
11 TERRY (BUD) BULLING-C
11 DARNELL COLES-3B
12 MANNY CASTILLO-UTIL/P
14 TONY BERNAZARD-2B (2)
15 CHUCK COTTIER-CH
16 AL COWENS (INJ)-OF/DH
17 GLENN ABBOTT (INJ)-P (1)
18 ROD ALLEN-DH/OF
18 HAROLD REYNOLDS-2B
20 JAMIE ALLEN-3B/DH
21 TODD CRUZ-SS (1)
21 RON ROENICKE-UTIL (2)
22 RICHIE ZISK-DH
23 PAT PUTNAM-1B/DH
24 GENE NELSON-P
25 MIKE MOORE-P
26 JOHN MOSES-OF/DH
28 VADA PINSON-CH
29 PHIL BRADLEY-OF/DH
30 ED NUNEZ-P
32 ED VANDE BERG-P
33 JIM MALER-1B/DH
34 BOB STODDARD-P
35 FRANK FUNK-CH
36 GAYLORD PERRY-P (1)
37 BILL CAUDILL-P
39 KARL BEST-P
40 MATT YOUNG-P
42 DAVE HENDERSON-OF/DH
44 KEN PHELPS-1B/DH
45 JIM BEATTIE (INJ)-P
46 MIKE STANTON-P
47 AL CHAMBERS-DH/OF
48 BRYAN CLARK-P
49 ROY THOMAS-P

1984
5TH W 74-88 10GB

1 DEL CRANDALL-MGR1
2 ORLANDO MERCADO-C
3 DOMINGO RAMOS-INF
4 PHIL ROOF-CH
5 STEVE HENDERSON-OF/DH
6 BILL NAHORODNY-C/1B
7 SPIKE OWEN-SS
8 LARRY MILBOURNE-UTIL
9 BARRY BONNELL-OF/UTIL
10 RICKY NELSON-DH/OF
11 BOB KEARNEY-C
12 MARK LANGSTON-P
13 IVAN CALDERON (INJ)-OF
14 JACK PERCONTE-2B
15 CHUCK COTTIER-CH/MGR2
16 AL COWENS-OF/DH
17 JIM PRESLEY-3B/DH
18 RICK SWEET-BP P ???
19 DARNELL COLES-UTIL
20 GORMAN THOMAS (INJ)-OF/DH
21 ALVIN DAVIS-1B/DH
22 RICHIE ZISK (INJ)-(DH)
23 PAT PUTNAM-UTIL (1)
24 HAROLD REYNOLDS-2B
25 MIKE MOORE-P
26 JOHN MOSES-OF/DH
27 PHIL (THE VULTURE) REGAN-CH
29 PHIL BRADLEY-OF/DH
30 ED NUNEZ-P
31 SALOME BAROJAS-P (2)
32 ED VANDE BERG-P
33 DAVE BEARD (INJ)-P
34 BOB STODDARD-P
35 FRANK FUNK-CH
36 BEN HINES-CH
36 LEE GUETTERMAN-P
37 DAVE GEISEL-P
38 DANNY TARTABULL-SS/2B
39 KARL BEST-P
40 MATT YOUNG-P
41 DAVE VALLE-C

SEATTLE MARINERS

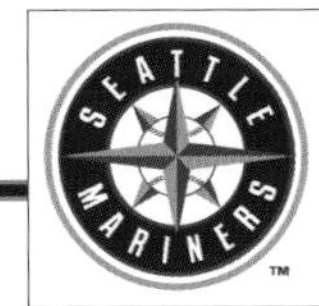

42 DAVE HENDERSON-OF/DH
43 MARTY MARTINEZ-CH
44 KEN PHELPS-DH/1B
45 JIM BEATTIE-P
46 MIKE STANTON-P
47 AL CHAMBERS-OF/DH
49 ROY THOMAS-P
52 PAUL MIRABELLA-P

1985

5TH W 74-88 17GB

1 DONNIE SCOTT-C
3 DOMINGO RAMOS-INF
4 PHIL ROOF-CH
5 DAVE VALLE (INJ)-C
6 JIM (MOE) MAHONEY-CH
7 SPIKE OWEN-SS
8 DERON JOHNSON-CH
9 BARRY BONNELL (INJ)-UTIL
10 MARTY MARTINEZ-CH
11 BOB KEARNEY (INJ)-C
12 MARK LANGSTON (INJ)-P
13 IVAN CALDERON (INJ)-OF/UTIL
14 JACK PERCONTE-2B
15 CHUCK COTTIER-MGR
16 AL COWENS-OF/DH
17 JIM PRESLEY-3B
18 BILL SWIFT-P
19 DARNELL COLES-UTIL
20 GORMAN THOMAS (INJ)-DH
21 ALVIN DAVIS-1B
22 IVAN CALDERON (INJ)-OF/UTIL
23 AL CHAMBERS-PH
24 HAROLD REYNOLDS-2B
25 MIKE MOORE-P
26 JOHN MOSES-OF
27 PHIL (THE VULTURE) REGAN-CH
28 RICKY NELSON-OF
29 PHIL BRADLEY-OF
30 ED NUNEZ-P
31 SALOME BAROJAS-P
32 ED VANDE BERG-P
33 BRIAN SNYDER-P
34 JIM LEWIS-P
35 MIKE MORGAN (INJ)-P
37 DAVE GEISEL-P
38 DANNY TARTABULL-SS/3B
39 KARL BEST (INJ)-P
40 MATT YOUNG-P
41 DAVE TOBIK-P
42 DAVE HENDERSON-OF
43 FRANK WILLS-P
44 KEN PHELPS-DH/1B
45 JIM BEATTIE (INJ)-P
46 MIKE STANTON-P (1)
46 JACK LAZORKO-P
49 ROY THOMAS-P
50 BOB LONG-P
51 BILL WILKINSON-P
52 PAUL MIRABELLA-P
LARRY MILBOURNE (INJ)-(UTIL)

1986

7TH W 67-95 25GB

1 STEVE YEAGER-C
1 SPIKE OWEN-SS (1)
2 ROSS JONES-INF/DH
3 DOMINGO RAMOS-INF/DH
4 DANNY TARTABULL-OF/UTIL
5 DAVE VALLE (INJ)-C/1B
6 JIM (MOE) MAHONEY-CH
7 SPIKE OWEN-SS (1)
7 STEVE YEAGER-C
8 DERON JOHNSON-CH
9 BARRY BONNELL-UTIL
10 MARTY MARTINEZ-CH/MGR2
11 BOB KEARNEY (INJ)-C
12 MARK LANGSTON-P
14 MICKEY BRANTLEY-OF
15 CHUCK COTTIER-MGR1
16 AL COWENS-OF/DH
16 RICKY NELSON-DH/OF
17 JIM PRESLEY-3B
18 BILL SWIFT-P
19 HAROLD REYNOLDS-2B
20 GORMAN THOMAS-DH/1B (1)
21 ALVIN DAVIS-1B/DH
22 IVAN CALDERON-OF (1)
22 SCOTT BRADLEY-C/DH (2)
23 DICK WILLIAMS-MGR3
24 HAROLD REYNOLDS-2B
24 PHIL ROOF-CH
25 MIKE MOORE-P
26 JOHN MOSES-OF/UTIL
27 PHIL (THE VULTURE) REGAN-CH
28 OZZIE VIRGIL, SR.-CH
28 MARK HUISMANN-P (2)
29 PHIL BRADLEY-OF
30 ED NUNEZ (INJ)-P
31 JERRY REED (INJ)-P
32 OZZIE VIRGIL, SR.-CH
34 MILT WILCOX-P
35 MIKE MORGAN-P
36 LEE GUETTERMAN-P
37 MIKE BROWN-P (2)
38 DANNY TARTABULL-OF/UTIL
38 DAVE HENGEL-DH/OF (2)
39 KARL BEST-P
40 MATT YOUNG-P
42 DAVE HENDERSON-OF/DH (1)
43 MIKE TRUJILLO-P (2)
44 KEN PHELPS-1B/DH
45 JIM BEATTIE (INJ)-P
46 PETE LADD-P
47 STEVE FIREOVID-P
(49) ROY THOMAS (INJ)-(P)
51 REY QUINONES-SS (2)
52 PAUL MIRABELLA-P

1987

4TH W 78-84 7GB

1 RICH RENTERIA-UTIL
3 DOMINGO RAMOS-INF/DH
4 HAROLD REYNOLDS-2B
5 MARIO DIAZ-SS
6 DONELL NIXON-OF/DH
7 MIKE KINGERY-OF/DH
9 SCOTT BRADLEY-C/UTIL
10 DAVE VALLE-C/UTIL
11 BOB KEARNEY-C
11 EDGAR MARTINEZ-3B/DH
12 MARK LANGSTON-P
13 BILL WILKINSON-P
14 MICKEY BRANTLEY (INJ)-OF/DH
15 SCOTT BANKHEAD-P
16 MIKE MORGAN-P
17 JIM PRESLEY-3B/UTIL
19 RICH MONTELEONE-P
20 DAVE HENGEL-OF/DH
21 ALVIN DAVIS-1B
22 BILLY CONNORS-CH
23 DICK WILLIAMS-MGR
24 PHIL ROOF-CH
25 MIKE MOORE-P
26 JOHN MOSES-OF/UTIL
27 MARK HUISMANN-P (1)
27 CLAY PARKER-P
28 BOBBY TOLAN-CH
29 PHIL BRADLEY-OF
30 ED NUNEZ-P
31 JERRY REED-P
32 OZZIE VIRGIL, SR.-CH
33 FRANK (THE CAPITAL PUNISHER) (HONDO) HOWARD-CH
34 LEE GUETTERMAN-P
35 BRICK SMITH-1B/DH
36 GARY (SARGE) MATTHEWS-DH (2)
37 STAN CLARKE-P
38 JERRY NARRON-C
40 STEVE SHIELDS (INJ)-P
42 JOHN CHRISTENSEN (INJ)-OF/DH
43 MIKE TRUJILLO-P
44 KEN PHELPS-DH/1B
46 JIM WEAVER-OF
47 MIKE BROWN-P
48 DENNIS POWELL-P
49 ROY THOMAS-P
51 REY QUINONES-SS
54 MIKE CAMPBELL-P

1988

7TH W 68-93 35.5GB

1 RICH RENTERIA-UTIL
2 DARNELL COLES-OF/UTIL
3 BILL PLUMMER-CH
4 HAROLD REYNOLDS-2B
5 MARIO DIAZ-INF
6 JIM SNYDER-MGR2
7 MIKE KINGERY-OF/1B
8 JIM SNYDER-CH
8 GREG (PEEWEE) BRILEY-OF
9 SCOTT BRADLEY-UTIL
10 DAVE VALLE (INJ)-C/UTIL
11 EDGAR MARTINEZ-3B
12 MARK LANGSTON-P
13 BILL WILKINSON (INJ)-P
14 MICKEY BRANTLEY (INJ)-OF/DH
15 SCOTT BANKHEAD (INJ)-P
16 DAVE HENGEL-OF/DH
17 JIM PRESLEY-3B/DH
18 BILL SWIFT-P
19 ROD SCURRY-P
20 HOWIE BEDELL-CH
21 ALVIN DAVIS-1B/DH
22 GLENN WILSON-OF/DH (1)
23 DICK WILLIAMS-MGR1
24 PHIL ROOF-CH
25 MIKE MOORE-P
27 MIKE CAMPBELL-P
28 HENRY COTTO-OF/DH
29 BRUCE FIELDS-OF/DH
30 ED NUNEZ-P (1)
30 JOHN RABB-UTIL
31 JERRY REED-P
32 OZZIE VIRGIL, SR.-CH
32 GENE WALTER-P (2)
33 FRANK (THE CAPITAL PUNISHER) (HONDO) HOWARD-CH
34STEVE TROUT (INJ)-P
35 BRICK SMITH-1B
35 BILL MCGUIRE-C
36 BILLY CONNORS-CH
37 JULIO SOLANO-P
38 MIKE JACKSON-P
39 ERIK HANSON-P
40 MIKE SCHOOLER-P
41 ROD SCURRY-P
43 JAY BUHNER-OF/1B (2)
44 KEN PHELPS-DH/1B (1)
44 TERRY TAYLOR-P
45 STEVE BALBONI-DH/1B (2)
48 DENNIS POWELL-P
50TERRY TAYLOR-P
51 REY QUINONES-SS/DH

1989

6TH W 73-89 26GB

00 JEFFREY LEONARD-DH/OF
2 DARNELL COLES-OF/UTIL
3 BILL PLUMMER-CH
4 HAROLD REYNOLDS-2B/DH
5 JIM LEFEBVRE-MGR
6 BOB DIDIER-CH
7 MIKE KINGERY-OF
8 GREG (PEEWEE) BRILEY-OF/UTIL
9 SCOTT BRADLEY-UTIL
10 DAVE VALLE (INJ)-C
11 EDGAR MARTINEZ-3B
12 MARK LANGSTON-P (1)
13 OMAR VIZQUEL-SS
14 MICKEY BRANTLEY-OF/DH
15 SCOTT BANKHEAD-P
17 JIM PRESLEY-3B/UTIL
18 BILL SWIFT-P
19 JAY BUHNER (INJ)-OF/1B
20 MIKE PAUL-CH
21 ALVIN DAVIS-1B/DH
22 RUSTY KUNTZ-CH
23 MARIO DIAZ-INF
24 KEN GRIFFEY, JR. (INJ)-OF
25 MIKE DUNNE-P (2)
27 MIKE CAMPBELL-P
28 HENRY COTTO-OF/DH
29 BRUCE FIELDS-OF
30 GENE CLINES-CH
31 JERRY REED-P
(32) GENE WALTER (INJ)-(P)
34 STEVE TROUT-P
34 KEITH COMSTOCK-P
35 BILL MCGUIRE-C (1)
36 BRIAN HOLMAN-P (2)
37 JULIO SOLANO-P
38 MIKE JACKSON-P
39 ERIK HANSON (INJ)-P
40 MIKE SCHOOLER-P
41 MIKE DUNNE-P (2)
41 GENE HARRIS-P (2)
41 CLINT ZAVARAS-P
43 DAVE COCHRANE-UTIL
47 GENE HARRIS-P (2)
48 DENNIS POWELL-P
49 TOM NIEDENFUER (INJ)-P
51 REY QUINONES-SS (1)
51 RANDY JOHNSON-P (2)
52 LUIS DELEON-P
54 JIM WILSON-DH

1990

5TH W 77-85 26GB

00 JEFFREY LEONARD-DH/OF
1 MATT YOUNG-P*
2 JEFF SCHAEFER-INF
3 BILL PLUMMER-CH
4 HAROLD REYNOLDS-2B
5 JIM LEFEBVRE-MGR
6 BOB DIDIER-CH
7 MIKE BRUMLEY (INJ)-UTIL
8 GREG (PEEWEE) BRILEY-OF/DH
9 SCOTT BRADLEY-UTIL
10 DAVE VALLE (INJ)-C/1B
11 EDGAR MARTINEZ-3B/DH
12 PETE O'BRIEN (INJ)-1B/UTIL
13 OMAR VIZQUEL (INJ)-SS
14 TINO MARTINEZ-1B
15 SCOTT BANKHEAD (INJ)-P
16 GENE CLINES-CH
17 MATT SINATRO-C
18 BILL SWIFT-P
19 JAY BUHNER (INJ)-OF/1B
20 MIKE PAUL-CH
21 ALVIN DAVIS-DH/1B
22 RUSTY KUNTZ-CH
23 MIKE GARDINER-P
24 KEN GRIFFEY, JR. (INJ)-OF/DH
25 TRACY JONES (INJ)-OF/DH (2)
27 BRENT KNACKERT-P
28 HENRY COTTO-OF/DH
29 BRIAN GILES-INF/DH
30 MATT YOUNG-P
30 KEN GRIFFEY, SR.-OF (2)
31 JERRY REED-P (1)
32 KEITH COMSTOCK-P
33 DARNELL COLES-OF/UTIL (1)
34 DAVE BURBA-P
36 BRIAN HOLMAN (INJ)-P
37 GARY EAVE-P
37 RUSS SWAN (INJ)-P (2)
38 MIKE JACKSON-P
39 ERIK HANSON-P
40 MIKE SCHOOLER (INJ)-P
(41) CLINT ZAVARAS (INJ)-(P)
42 VANCE LOVELACE-P
43 DAVE COCHRANE-UTIL
45 BRYAN CLARK-P
47 GENE HARRIS (INJ)-P
48 DENNIS POWELL-P (1)
48 BRYAN CLARK-P
51 RANDY JOHNSON-P
53 SCOTT MEDVIN-P
54 JOSE MELENDEZ-P
55 RICH DELUCIA-P
65 GARY EAVE-P

1991

5TH W 83-79 12GB

1 GREG (PEEWEE) BRILEY-OF/UTIL
2 JEFF SCHAEFER-INF/DH
3 BILL PLUMMER-CH
4 HAROLD REYNOLDS-2B/DH
5 JIM LEFEBVRE-MGR
6 RON CLARK-CH
7 ALONZO POWELL-OF/UTIL
8 RICH AMARAL (INJ)-INF/DH
9 SCOTT BRADLEY-UTIL
10 DAVE VALLE-C/1B
11 EDGAR MARTINEZ-3B/DH
12 PETE O'BRIEN-1B/UTIL
13 OMAR VIZQUEL-SS/2B
14 TINO MARTINEZ-1B/DH
15 SCOTT BANKHEAD (INJ)-P
16 GENE CLINES-CH
17 MATT SINATRO-C
18 BILL SWIFT-P
19 JAY BUHNER-OF
20 MIKE PAUL-CH
21 ALVIN DAVIS-DH/1B
22 RUSTY KUNTZ-CH
23 PAT RICE-P
24 KEN GRIFFEY, JR.-OF/DH
25 TRACY JONES (INJ)-DH/OF
26 PAT LENNON-DH/OF
28 HENRY COTTO (INJ)-OF/DH
30 KEN GRIFFEY, SR. (INJ)-OF/DH
32 KEITH COMSTOCK-P
34 DAVE BURBA-P
36 BRIAN HOLMAN-P
37 RUSS SWAN-P
38 MIKE JACKSON-P
39 ERIK HANSON (INJ)-P
40 MIKE SCHOOLER (INJ)-P
43 DAVE COCHRANE-UTIL
44 BILL KRUEGER-P
45 CHRIS HOWARD-C
46 ROB MURPHY (INJ)-P
47 GENE HARRIS-P
49 DAN WARTHEN-CH
51 RANDY JOHNSON-P
52 CALVIN JONES-P
55 RICH DELUCIA-P
56 DAVE FLEMING-P

1992

7TH W 64-98 32GB

1 GREG (PEEWEE) BRILEY-OF/UTIL

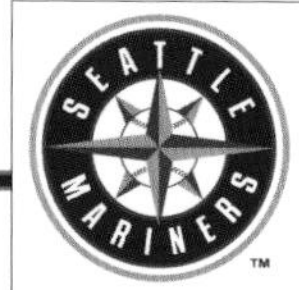

SEATTLE MARINERS

2 JEFF SCHAEFER-INF/DH
3 LANCE PARRISH-DH (2)
4 HAROLD REYNOLDS-2B/DH
5 RUSS NIXON-CH
6 SCOTT BRADLEY-UTIL
6 BERT HEFFERNAN-C
6 JOHN MOSES-OF
7 KEVIN MITCHELL (INJ)-OF/DH
8 RICH AMARAL-UTIL
9 BILL PLUMMER-MGR
10 DAVE VALLE-C
11 EDGAR MARTINEZ-3B/DH
12 PETE O'BRIEN-1B/DH
13 OMAR VIZQUEL-SS
14 MARTY MARTINEZ-CH
15 KEVIN BROWN-P
15 DAVE SCHMIDT-P
15 BILL HASELMAN-C
16 GENE CLINES-CH
16 KEVIN BROWN-P
17 MATT SINATRO-C
19 JAY BUHNER-OF
20 SHANE TURNER-3B
22 RUSTY KUNTZ-CH
23 TINO MARTINEZ-1B/DH?
23 DANN HOWITT-OF
24 KEN GRIFFEY, JR.-OF/DH
25 ROGER HANSEN-CH
28 HENRY COTTO-OF/DH
29 MIKE SCHOOLER (INJ)-P
31 ERIC GUNDERSON-P
32 CLAY PARKER-P
33 PAT LENNON-OF
34 JIM ACKER-P
34 BRET BOONE-2B
35 DAVE FLEMING-P
(36) BRIAN HOLMAN-(P)
37 RUSS SWAN-P
38 MIKE BLOWERS-3B
39 ERIK HANSON (INJ)-P
40 JEFF NELSON-P
42 KERRY WOODSON-P
43 DAVE COCHRANE-UTIL
44 DANN HOWITT-OF
45 CHRIS HOWARD-C
46 BRIAN FISHER-P
47 GENE HARRIS-P
47 JUAN AGOSTO-P
47 MIKE WALKER-P
48 DENNIS POWELL-P
49 DAN WARTHEN-CH
49 JUAN AGOSTO-P (2)
50 MARK GRANT-P
51 RANDY JOHNSON-P
52 CALVIN JONES-P
53 SHAWN BARTON-P
54 RANDY KRAMER-P
54 TIM LEARY-P
55 RICH DELUCIA-P
59 CLAY PARKER-P

1993

4TH W 82-80 12GB

1 BRIAN TURANG-UTIL
2 SAM PERLOZZO-CH
3 LEE ELIA-CH
4 MACKEY SASSER (INJ)-UTIL
5 BRET BOONE-2B/DH
6 FERNANDO VINA-INF/DH
7 JOHN MCLAREN-CH
8 RICH AMARAL-2B/UTIL
9 PETE O'BRIEN-UTIL
10 DAVE VALLE-C
11 EDGAR MARTINEZ (INJ)-DH/3B
13 OMAR VIZQUEL-SS/DH
14 LOU (SWEET LOU) PINIELLA-MGR
15 GREG LITTON-UTIL
16 MIKE BLOWERS-3B/UTIL
17 RUSS SWAN-P
18 DAVE MAGADAN-INF/DH (2)
19 JAY BUHNER-OF/DH
20 GREG PIRKL-1B/DH
22 WALLY BACKMAN-3B/2B
22 DWAYNE HENRY (INJ)-P (2)
23 TINO MARTINEZ (INJ)-1B/DH
24 KEN GRIFFEY, JR.-OF/UTIL
25 MIKE FELDER-OF/UTIL
26 DAVE WAINHOUSE-P
27 LEE TINSLEY-OF/DH
28 HENRY COTTO-OF/DH (1)
28 MARC NEWFIELD-DH/OF
29 CHRIS BOSIO (INJ)-P
30 KEN GRIFFEY, SR.-CH
32 SAMMY ELLIS-CH
32 ERIK PLANTENBERG-P
33 BILL HASELMAN-UTIL
34 ERIK PLANTENBERG-P
34 RANDY (THE BIG UNIT) JOHNSON
35 DAVE FLEMING (INJ)-P
37 NORM CHARLTON (INJ)-P
38 BRAD HOLMAN-P
39 ERIK HANSON-P
40 JEFF NELSON-P
40 ZAK SHINALL-P
40 LARRY SHEETS-DH/OF
41 JIM CONVERSE-P
(42) KERRY WOODSON (INJ)-(P)
42 TED POWER-P (2)
42 ROGER SALKELD-P
43 JEFF NELSON-P
44 DANN HOWITT-OF/DH
45 CHRIS HOWARD-C
46 MIKE HAMPTON-P
47 JOHN CUMMINGS-P
48 DENNIS POWELL-P
48 DWAYNE HENRY-P (2)
48 TED POWER-P (2)
49 SAM MEJIAS-CH
50 BOB AYRAULT-P (2)
50 KEVIN KING-P
51 RANDY (THE BIG UNIT) JOHNSON
52 STEVE ONTIVEROS-P
54 TIM LEARY-P
55 RICH DELUCIA-P
BRIAN HOLMAN (INJ)-(P)

1994

3RD W 49-63 2GB
STRIKE NO POST-SEASON

1 BRIAN TURANG (INJ)-UTIL
2 SAM PERLOZZO-CH
3 ALEX RODRIGUEZ-SS
4 LEE ELIA-CH
5 ERIC ANTHONY (INJ)-OF
6 DAN WILSON-C
7 JOHN MCLAREN-CH
8 RICH AMARAL-2B/UTIL
9 LUIS SOJO-2B
10 FELIX FERMIN-SS
11 EDGAR MARTINEZ (INJ)-DH/3B
12 ERIK PLANTENBERG-P
13 BOBBY AYALA-P
14 LOU (SWEET LOU) PINIELLA-MGR
15 MACKEY SASSER (INJ/REL)-UTIL
16 MIKE BLOWERS-3B/UTIL
17 KEITH MITCHELL (INJ)-DH
18 REGGIE JEFFERSON (INJ)-DH/1B
19 JAY BUHNER-OF/DH
20 GREG PIRKL-DH
22 ROGER SALKELD-P
23 TINO MARTINEZ-1B/DH
24 KEN GRIFFEY, JR.-OF/UTIL
25 JIM CONVERSE-P
26 GEORGE GLINATSIS-P
27 TOREY LOVULLO-2B
28 MARC NEWFIELD-OF
29 CHRIS BOSIO (INJ)-P
31 BOBBY THIGPEN-P
31 JERRY WILLARD-1B
32 SAMMY ELLIS-CH
33 BILL HASELMAN-C
34 GREG HIBBARD (INJ)-P
34 QUINN MACK-OF
34 SHAWN BOSKIE (INJ)-P (3)
35 DAVE FLEMING (INJ)-P
36 DALE SVEUM-3B
37 GREG HIBBARD (INJ)-P
40 DARREN BRAGG-DH/C
41 MILT HILL-P (2)
42 JEFF DARWIN-P
43 JEFF NELSON-P
44 JOHN CUMMINGS (INJ)-P
45 JOHN CUMMINGS (INJ)-P
45 CHRIS H. HOWARD-C
46 BOB WELLS-P
47 TIM DAVIS-P
(48) TED POWER (INJ)-(P)
49 SAM MEJIAS-CH
50 KEVIN KING-P
51 RANDY (THE BIG UNIT) JOHNSON
54 GOOSE GOSSAGE-P
55 BILL RISLEY-P

1995

1ST W 79-66 0GB
W P/O-CALA 1-0
W ALDS-NYA 3-2
L ALCS-CLEA 4-2

1 ALEX DIAZ-OF
2 SAM PERLOZZO-CH
3 ALEX RODRIGUEZ-SS
4 LEE ELIA-CH
5 BOBBY CUELLAR-CH
6 DAN WILSON-C
7 JOHN MCLAREN-CH
8 RICH AMARAL-OF
9 LUIS SOJO (INJ)-2B
10 FELIX FERMIN (INJ)-SS
11 EDGAR MARTINEZ-DH
12 DOUG STRANGE-3B
13 BOBBY AYALA-P
14 LOU (SWEET LOU) PINIELLA-MGR
15 MATT SINATRO-CH
16 MIKE BLOWERS-3B
17 MATT SINATRO-CH
18 CHAD KREUTER (INJ)-C
19 JAY BUHNER (INJ)-OF
20 GREG PIRKL (INJ)-1B
22 RAFAEL CARMONA-P
23 TINO MARTINEZ-1B
24 KEN GRIFFEY, JR. (INJ)-OF
25 CHRIS BOSIO-P
26 WARREN NEWSON-OF (2)
27 MARC NEWFIELD-OF (1)
28 JOEY CORA-2B
29 CHRIS BOSIO (INJ)-P
29 WARREN NEWSON-OF (2)
29 VINCE (VINCENT VAN GO) COLEMAN-OF (2)
31 TIM BELCHER-P
32 JIM CONVERSE-P (1)
32 RAFAEL CARMONA-P
32 GARY THURMAN-OF
33 RON VILLONE-P (1)
33 BOB WOLCOTT-P
34 DARREN BRAGG-OF
35 DAVE FLEMING-P (1)
35 SCOTT DAVISON-P
36 CHRIS WIDGER-C
37 NORM CHARLTON-P (2)
38 SALOMON TORRES-P (2)
39 TIM HARIKKALA-P
40 DARREN BRAGG-OF (2)
40 ANDY BENES-P (2)
41 STEVE FREY (INJ/WAIV)-P
41 ARQUIMEDEZ POZO-2B
42 JIM MECIR-P
43 JEFF NELSON-P
44 JOHN CUMMINGS (INJ)-P
44 BILL KRUEGER-P (2)
45 CHRIS H. HOWARD-C
46 BOB WELLS-P
47 TIM DAVIS-P
48 LEE GUETTERMAN-P
49 SAM MEJIAS-CH
50 KEVIN KING-P
51 RANDY (THE BIG UNIT) JOHNSON
55 BILL RISLEY-P
ERIC GUNDERSON (INJ)-(P) (2)
GREG HIBBARD (INJ)-(P)

1996

2ND W 85-76 4.5GB

1 ALEX DIAZ (INJ)-OF
2 STEVE SMITH-CH
3 ALEX RODRIGUEZ (INJ)-SS
4 LEE ELIA-CH
5 BOBBY CUELLAR-CH
6 DAN WILSON-C
7 JOHN MCLAREN-CH
8 RICH AMARAL-OF
9 LUIS SOJO (WAIV)-2B (1)
10 JEFF MANTO (WAIV)-2B (2)
10 DAVE HOLLINS-3B (2)
11 EDGAR MARTINEZ (INJ)-DH
12 DOUG STRANGE-1B
13 BOBBY AYALA (INJ)-P
14 LOU (SWEET LOU) PINIELLA-MGR
15 MATT SINATRO-CH
16 PAUL MENHART (INJ)-P
17 JOHN MARZANO-C
18 RUSS DAVIS (INJ)-3B
19 JAY BUHNER-OF
20 GREG PIRKL (REL)-1B (2)
20 MARK WHITEN-OF (3)
22 RAFAEL CARMONA-P
23 BLAS MINOR-P (2)
24 KEN GRIFFEY, JR. (INJ)-OF
25 CHRIS BOSIO (INJ)-P
26 RAUL IBANEZ-DH
(27) GREG HIBBARD (INJ)-(P)
28 JOEY CORA-2B
29 RICKY JORDAN (INJ) (REL)-1B
30 ANDY SHEETS-SS
32 EDWIN HURTADO (INJ)-P
33 BOB WOLCOTT-P
34 BRIAN R. HUNTER-1B/OF
35 SCOTT DAVISON-P
36 CHRIS WIDGER-C
37 NORM CHARLTON-P
38 SALOMON TORRES-P
39 TIM HARIKKALA-P
40 JOE KLINK-P
40 SAM MEJIAS-CH
40 MANNY MARTINEZ (WAIV)-OF (1)
40 GREG MCCARTHY-P
41 STERLING HITCHCOCK-P
42 MIKE JACKSON-P
43 RUSTY MEECHAM-P
44 PAUL SORRENTO-1B
45 TERRY MULHOLLAND-P (2)
46 BOB WELLS-P
47 TIM DAVIS (INJ)-P
48 LEE GUETTERMAN-P
49 SAM MEJIAS-CH
50 JAMIE MOYER-P (2)
51 RANDY (THE BIG UNIT) JOHNSON (INJ)-P
52 MATT WAGNER-P
53 BOB MILACKI-P
56 DARREN BRAGG-OF (1)
96 MAKATO (MAC) SUSUKI-P

1997

1ST W 90-72 0GB
L ALDS-CLEA 4-2

2 STEVE SMITH-CH
3 ALEX RODRIGUEZ (INJ)-SS
4 LEE ELIA-CH
5 LEE TINSLEY (INJ)-OF
6 DAN WILSON-C
7 JOHN MCLAREN-CH
8 RICH AMARAL-OF
9 BRENT GATES-2B/3B
10 ROBERTO KELLY-OF (2)
11 EDGAR MARTINEZ-DH
12 ANDY SHEETS-INF
13 JEFF FASSERO-P
14 LOU (SWEET LOU) PINIELLA-MGR
15 MATT SINATRO-CH
16 MIKE BLOWERS-1B
17 JOHN MARZANO-C
18 RUSS DAVIS (INJ)-3B
19 JAY BUHNER-OF
20 MIKE MADDUX (INJ) (REL)-P
22 RAFAEL CARMONA-P
23 JOSE CRUZ, JR.-OF (1)
23 PAUL SPOLJARIC-P (2)
24 KEN GRIFFEY, JR.-OF
25 JOHN MOSES-CH
26 ALVARO ESPINOZA (INJ) (REL)-2B
26 OMAR OLIVARES-P (2)
27 SCOTT SANDERS-P (1)
27 OMAR OLIVARES-P (2)
27 KEN CLOUDE-P
28 JOEY CORA-2B
29 ROB DUCEY (INJ)-OF
30 RAUL IBANEZ-OF/DH
30 BRIAN RAABE-2B (1)
31 BOBBY AYALA-P
32 DENNIS MARTINEZ-P
33 BOB WOLCOTT-P
34 GIOMAR GUEVARA-DH
35 DAN ROHRMEIER-DH
36 DEREK LOWE-P (1)
37 NORM CHARLTON-P
38 SALOMON TORRES (WAIV)-P (1)
39 EDWIN HURTADO-P
39 GREG MCCARTHY-P
40 GREG MCCARTHY-P
40 MIKE TIMLIN-P (2)
41 JOSIAS MANZANILLO (INJ)-P
41 FELIPE LIRA-P (2)
42 *(RET#) JACKIE ROBINSON*
43 RICK WILKINS (INJ)-C (2)
44 PAUL SORRENTO-1B
46 BOB WELLS-P
47 TIM DAVIS (INJ)-P
49 SAM MEJIAS-CH
50 JAMIE MOYER (INJ)-P
51 RANDY (THE BIG UNIT) JOHNSON-P
52 HEATHCLIFF SLOCUMB-P (2)
54 NARDI CONTRERAS-CH
59 MARK HOLZEMER-P

1998

3RD W 76-85 11.5GB

1 GLENALLEN HILL (WAIV)-OF (1)
2 RICK WILKINS-C (1)
2 DAVID BELL-2B (3)

SEATTLE MARINERS

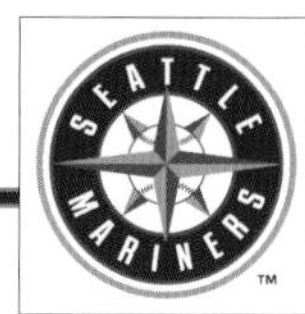

3 ALEX RODRIGUEZ-SS
4 GUIOMAR GUIVARA (INJ)-2B
5 CARLOS GUILLEN-2B
6 DAN WILSON-C
7 JOHN MCLAREN-CH
8 RICH AMARAL (INJ)-OF
9 JEFF HUSON-UTIL
9 JOE OLIVER-C (2)
10 STEVE SMITH-CH
11 EDGAR MARTINEZ-DH
12 SHANE MONAHAN-OF
13 JEFF FASSERO (INJ)-P
14 LOU (SWEET LOU) PINIELLA-MGR
15 MATT SINATRO-CH
16 CHARLES GIPSON-INF
17 JOHN MARZANO-C
18 RUSS DAVIS-3B
19 JAY BUHNER-OF
20 ROB DUCEY (INJ)-OF
21 DAVID SEGUI-1B
(22) RAFAEL CARMONA (INJ)-(P)
23 PAUL SPOLJARIC-P
23 DAVID MCCARTY-OF/1B
24 KEN GRIFFEY, JR.-OF
25 JOHN MOSES-CH
26 BILL (C.) SWIFT-P
27 KEN CLOUDE-P
28 JOEY CORA-2B (1)
29 JESSE BARFIELD-CH
30 ROBERT PEREZ-OF (1)
30 JOSE PANIAGUA-P
31 BOBBY AYALA-P
33 RYAN RADMANOVICH-OF
(34) GIOMAR GUEVARA (INJ)-(DH)
34 PAUL SPOLJARIC-P
35 STAN WILLIAMS-CH
38 RAUL IBANEZ (INJ)-OF
39 GREG MCCARTHY-P
40 MIKE TIMLIN-P
41 FELIPE LIRA-P
41 MAC SUSUKI-P
42 *(RET#) JACKIE ROBINSON*
44 JIM BULLINGER-P
44 RICO ROSSY-3B/INF
46 BOB WELLS (INJ)-P
(47) TIM DAVIS (INJ)-(P)
48 TONY FOSSAS-P (1)
48 RICKY CRADLE-OF
48 PAUL ABBOTT-P
49 SAM MEJIAS-CH
50 JAMIE MOYER-P
51 RANDY (THE BIG UNIT) JOHNSON-P (1)
52 HEATHCLIFF SLOCUMB-P
54 NARDI CONTRERAS-CH (1)
54 STEVE GAJKOWSKI-P
59 GIOMAR GUEVARA (INJ)-2B
59 DAVID HOLDRIDGE-P
(62) RANDY VERES (INJ)-(P)
62 RAUL CHAVEZ-C
62 ANDREW LORRAINE-P

1999

3RD W 79-83 16GB

1 CHARLES GIPSON (INJ)-OF
2 RAFAEL BOURNIGAL-INF
3 ALEX RODRIGUEZ (INJ)-SS
4 GIOMAR GUEVARA-INF
4 MIKE BLOWERS-3B (2)
5 RAUL IBANEZ-OF
6 DAN WILSON-C
7 JOHN MCLAREN-CH
8 CARLOS GUILLEN (INJ)-INF
10 STEVE SMITH-CH
11 EDGAR MARTINEZ-DH
12 SHANE MONAHAN-OF
13 JEFF FASSERO (INJ)-P (1)
14 LOU (SWEET LOU) PINIELLA-MGR
15 MATT SINATRO-CH
16 SAM MEJIAS-CH
17 TOM LAMPKIN-C
18 RUSS DAVIS-3B
19 JAY BUHNER-OF
20 MATT MIESKE-OF (1)
21 DAVID SEGUI-1B (1)
22 BRIAN L. HUNTER-OF (2)
23 MARK LEITER (INJ)-P
23 ROBERT RAMSAY-P
24 KEN GRIFFEY, JR.-OF
25 DAVID BELL-2B
26 DOMINGO CEDENO-SS (1)
26 RAFAEL CARMONA-P
27 BUTCH HENRY (INJ)-P
28 KEN CLOUDE-P
29 JESSE BARFIELD-CH
30 JOSE PANIAGUA-P
31 MELVIN BUNCH-P
31 TODD WILLIAMS-P
32 BRETT HINCHLIFFE-P
33 FRANKIE RODRIGUEZ-P
34 FREDDY GARCIA-P
35 STAN WILLIAMS-CH
37 DAMASO MARTE-P
37 RYAN JACKSON-INF
40 OZZIE TIMMONS-OF
41 MAC SUSUKI-P (1)
41 ALLEN WATSON (REL)-P (2)
41 STEVE SINCLAIR-P (2)
42 BUTCH HUSKEY-OF (1)
43 TOM DAVEY-P (2)
45 RYAN FRANKLIN-P
45 PAUL ABBOTT-P
46 JORDAN ZIMMERMAN (INJ)-P
47 JOHN MABRY (INJ)-OF
48 SEAN SPENCER-P
48 PAUL ABBOTT-P
49 JOSE MESA-P
50 JAMIE MOYER-P
52 ERIC WEAVER (INJ)-P
54 JOHN HALAMA-P
55 GIL MECHE-P
56 DENNIS STARK-P

2000

2ND W (W/C) 91-71 .5GB
W ADLS 3-0
L ACLS-NYA 4-2

1 CHARLES GIPSON-OF
3 ALEX RODRIGUEZ (INJ)-SS
4 MARK MCLEMORE-INF
5 JOHN OLERUD-1B
6 DAN WILSON-C
7 JOHN MCLAREN-CH
8 CARLOS GUILLEN-INF
9 MIKE CAMERON-OF
9 JOE OLIVER-C
10 LARRY BOWA-CH
11 EDGAR MARTINEZ-DH
12 JOHN MOSES-CH
13 ANTHONY SANDERS-OF
14 LOU (SWEET LOU) PINIELLA-MGR
15 MATT SINATRO-CH
16 STAN JAVIER-OF
16 CHRIS WIDGER-C (2)
17 TOM LAMPKIN (INJ)-C
18 JOE OLIVER-C
18 AL MARTIN-OF (2)
19 JAY BUHNER-OF
20 CARLOS E. HERNANDEZ-3B
22 KAZUHIRO SASAKI-P
23 RAUL IBANEZ-OF
25 DAVID BELL-2B
27 PAT AHEARNE-P
28 STAN JAVIER-OF
29 GERALD PERRY-CH
30 AARON SELE-P
31 BRIAN LESHER-OF/INF
33 FRANKIE RODRIGUEZ (INJ)-P
34 FREDDY GARCIA-P
35 BRYAN PRICE-CH
35 RICKEY HENDERSON-OF (2)
36 JOSE PANIAGUA-P
37 ROBERT RAMSAY-P
38 JOEL PINEIRO-P
39 ROBERT MACHADO-C
40 BRETT TOMKO-P
42 *(RET#) JACKIE ROBINSON*
44 MIKE CAMERON-OF
47 JOHN MABRY-OF (1)
48 PAUL ABBOTT-P
49 JOSE MESA-P
50 JAMIE MOYER-P
53 ARTHUR RHODES-P
54 JOHN HALAMA-P
55 GIL MECHE (INJ)-P
58 KEVIN HODGES-P
65 BRIAN LESHER-OF/INF

2001

1ST W 116-46 0GB
W ADLS-CLEA 3-2
L ACLS-NYA 4-1

1 CHARLES GIPSON-OF
2 LEE ELIA-CH
4 MARK MCLEMORE-INF
5 JOHN OLERUD-1B
6 DAN WILSON-C
7 JOHN MCLAREN-CH
8 CARLOS GUILLEN-INF
10 ANTHONY SANDERS-OF
10 ED SPRAGUE (INJ)-1B/DH
11 EDGAR MARTINEZ (INJ)-DH
12 JOHN MOSES-CH
13 RAMON VAZQUEZ-SS
14 LOU (SWEET LOU) PINIELLA-MGR
15 MATT SINATRO-CH
16 CHRIS WIDGER (INJ)-C
17 TOM LAMPKIN-C
18 PAT BORDERS-C
19 JAY BUHNER (INJ)-OF
20 SCOTT PODSEDNIK-OF
22 KAZUHIRO SASAKI-P
23 AL MARTIN-OF
25 DAVID BELL-2B
27 GERALD PERRY-CH
28 STAN JAVIER (INJ)-OF
29 BRET BOONE-2B
30 AARON SELE-P
31 DAVE MYERS-CH
32 BRYAN PRICE-CH
34 FREDDY GARCIA-P
36 JOSE PANIAGUA (SUS3)-P
37 NORM CHARLTON (INJ)-P
38 JOEL PINEIRO-P
40 BRETT TOMKO-P
42 *(RET#) JACKIE ROBINSON*
43 JEFF NELSON-P
44 MIKE CAMERON-OF
45 RYAN FRANKLIN-P
48 PAUL ABBOTT (INJ)-P
50 JAMIE MOYER-P
51 ICHIRO SUZUKI-OF
53 ARTHUR RHODES-P
54 JOHN HALAMA-P
55 GIL MECHE (INJ)-P
61 BRIAN FUENTES-P
67 DENNIS STARK-P

2002

3RD W 93-69 10GB

1 CHARLES GIPSON-OF/UTIL
2 LEE ELIA-CH
4 MARK MCLEMORE-OF/UTIL
5 JOHN OLERUD-1B/DH
6 DAN WILSON-C/1B
7 JOHN MCLAREN-CH
8 CARLOS GUILLEN-SS/DH
9 JEFF CIRILLO-3B/1B
10 PAT BORDERS-DH/C
11 EDGAR MARTINEZ (INJ)-DH
12 JOHN MOSES-CH
13 BEN DAVIS-C/1B
14 LOU (SWEET LOU) PINIELLA-MGR
15 MATT SINATRO-CH
16 WILLIE BLOOMQUIST-UTIL
17 SHIGETOSHI HASEGAWA-P
18 EUGENE KINGSALE-OF (1)
20 SCOTT PODSEDNIK-OF/DH
21 RUBEN SIERRA-OF/DH
22 KAZUHIRO SASAKI-P
23 LUIS UGUETO-DH/INF
25 DESI RELAFORD-UTIL
26 MARK WATSON-P
26 RON WRIGHT-DH
27 GERALD PERRY-CH
29 BRET BOONE-2B
30 JOSE OFFERMAN-UTIL (2)
31 DAVE MYERS-CH
32 BRYAN PRICE-CH
33 JAMES BALDWIN-P
34 FREDDY GARCIA-P
36 JUSTIN KAYE-P
36 DOUG CREEK-P (2)
38 JOEL PINEIRO-P
39 RAFAEL SORIANO (INJ)-P
39 BRIAN FITZGERALD-P
39 CHRIS SNELLING (INJ)-OF
40 JULIO MATEO-P
42 *(RET#) JACKIE ROBINSON*
43 JEFF NELSON (INJ)-P
44 MIKE CAMERON-OF
45 RYAN FRANKLIN-P
47 ISMAEL VALDES-P (2)
48 PAUL ABBOTT (INJ)-P
50 JAMIE MOYER-P
51 ICHIRO SUZUKI-OF/DH
52 AARON TAYLOR-P
53 ARTHUR RHODES-P
54 JOHN HALAMA-P

2003

2ND W 93-69 3GB

1 REY SANCHEZ-SS (2)
2 RANDY WINN-OF
3 BOB MELVIN-MGR
4 MARK MCLEMORE-UTIL
5 JOHN OLERUD-1B
6 DAN WILSON (INJ)-C
7 JEFF CIRILLO (INJ)-3B
8 CARLOS GUILLEN (INJ)-SS/3B
9 RENE LACHEMANN-CH
10 PAT BORDERS-C/3B
11 EDGAR MARTINEZ-DH
12 JOHN MOSES-CH
13 BEN DAVIS-C
16 WILLIE BLOOMQUIST-UTIL
17 SHIGETOSHI HASEGAWA-P
20 J. J. PUTZ-P
22 KAZUHIRO SASAKI (INJ)-P
23 LUIS UGUETO-INF
(28) GREG COLBRUNN (INJ)-(1B)
29 BRET BOONE-2B
30 CHAD MEYERS-DH/OF
31 DAVE MYERS-CH
32 GIOVANNI CARRARA-P
33 LAMAR JOHNSON-CH
34 FREDDY GARCIA-P
35 BRYAN PRICE-CH
36 JAMAL STRONG-DH/OF
38 JOEL PINEIRO-P
39 RAFAEL SORIANO-P
40 JULIO MATEO-P
42 *(RET#) JACKIE ROBINSON*
43 JEFF NELSON-P (1)
44 MIKE CAMERON-OF
45 RYAN FRANKLIN-P
46 AARON LOOPER-P
47 JOHN MABRY (INJ)-OF/DH
49 ORLANDO GOMEZ-CH
49 ARMANDO BENITEZ-P (3)
50 JAMIE MOYER-P
51 ICHIRO SUZUKI-OF
53 ARTHUR RHODES-P
54 AARON TAYLOR-P
55 GIL MECHE-P
59 MATT J. WHITE-P (2)
59 BRIAN SWEENEY-P

2004

4TH W 63-99 29GB

1 RAMON SANTIAGO-SS
2 RANDY WINN-OF
3 BOB MELVIN-MGR
4 PAUL MOLITOR-CH
5 JOHN OLERUD (REL)-1B (1)
6 DAN WILSON-C
7 MIGUEL OLIVO (INJ)-C (2)
8 MIKE ALDRETE-CH
8 MIGUEL OLIVO (INJ)-C (2)
9 QUINTON MCCRACKEN-OF/DH (1)
10 PAT BORDERS-C (1)
11 EDGAR MARTINEZ-DH
12 JOLBERT CABRERA-UTIL
13 BEN DAVIS-C (1)
15 RENE LACHEMANN-CH
16 WILLIE BLOOMQUIST-UTIL
17 SHIGETOSHI HASEGAWA-P
18 EDDIE GUARDADO (INJ)-P
20 J. J. PUTZ-P
22 JOSE LOPEZ-SS
23 SCOTT SPIEZIO-3B/1B
25 DAVE HANSEN-INF/DH (1)
25 MIKE ALDRETE-CH
26 JUSTIN LEONE (INJ)-3B
28 RAUL IBANEZ (INJ)-OF/1B
29 BRET BOONE-2B
30 MICKEY LOPEZ-2B/DH
31 DAVE MYERS-CH
32 KEVIN JARVIS-P (1)
32 CHA SEUNG BAEK-P
33 BUCKY JACOBSON-1B/DH
34 FREDDY GARCIA-P (1)
35 RICH AURILIA-SS (1)
35 BRYAN PRICE-CH
35 MASAO KIDA-P (2)
36 JAMAL STRONG-DH/OF
38 JOEL PINEIRO-P
39 RAFAEL SORIANO-P
40 JULIO MATEO-P
41 RANDALL WILLIAMS-P
42 *(RET#) JACKIE ROBINSON*
43 MATT THORNTON-P
44 HIRAM BOCACHICA-OF
45 RYAN FRANKLIN-P
47 RON VILLONE-P
48 TRAVIS BLACKLEY-P
49 ORLANDO GOMEZ-CH
50 JAMIE MOYER-P
51 ICHIRO SUZUKI-OF/DH
52 GEORGE SHERRILL-P
53 MIKE MYERS-P (1)
53 GREG DOBBS-3B
54 AARON TAYLOR (INJ)-P
55 GIL MECHE-P
56 BOBBY MADRITSCH-P
57 SCOTT ATCHISON-P
58 JEREMY REED-OF
59 RENE RIVERA-C

2005

4TH W 69-93 26GB

1 RAMON SANTIAGO-INF

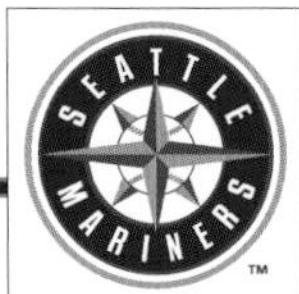

SEATTLE MARINERS

2 RANDY WINN-OF (1)
2 MIGUEL OJEDA-C (2)
(3) POKEY REESE (INJ)-(SS)
4 JOSE LOPEZ-2B
5 ADRIAN BELTRE-3B
6 DAN WILSON (INJ)-C
7 JEREMY REED-OF
8 MIGUEL OLIVO-C (1)
8 YORVIT TORREALBA-C (2)
9 RON HASSEY-CH
10 DAVE HANSEN (INJ)-INF
12 WILSON VALDEZ-SS (1)
12 MIKE MORSE (SUS:10G)-SS
13 CARLOS GARCIA-CH
15 JEFF NEWMAN-CH
16 WILLIE BLOOMQUIST (INJ)-3B
17 SHIGETOSHI HASEGAWA-P
18 EDDIE GUARDADO-P
20 J. J. PUTZ-P
21 MIKE HARGROVE-MGR
22 JOSE LOPEZ-2B
22 GREG DOBBS-1B/DH
23 SCOTT SPIEZIO (INJ)(REL)-1B
25 DON BAYLOR-CH
(26) JUSTIN LEONE (INJ)-(3B)
27 SCOTT ATCHISON (INJ)-P
28 RAUL IBANEZ-OF/DH
29 BRET BOONE (REL)-2B (1)
30 AARON SELE (REL)-P
30 RENE RIVERA-C
31 WIKI GONZALEZ-C
32 CHRIS SNELLING (INJ)-OF
34 BRYAN PRICE-CH
35 MASAO KIDA-P
36 JAMAL STRONG (SUS:10G)-OF
37 PAT BORDERS (REL)-C
37 CLINT NAGEOTTE-P
38 JOEL PINEIRO (INJ)-P
39 RAFAEL SORIANO (INJ)-P
40 JULIO MATEO-P (1)
41 JIM SLATON-CH
42 *(RET#) JACKIE ROBINSON*
43 JEFF NELSON (BRV)-P
44 RICHIE SEXSON-1B
45 RYAN FRANKLIN (SUS:10G)-P
46 YUNIESKY BETANCOURT-SS
47 RON VILLONE-P (1)
49 JORGE CAMPILLO (INJ)-P
50 JAMIE MOYER-P
51 ICHIRO SUZUKI-OF
52 GEORGE SHERRILL-P
53 MATT THORNTON-P
54 MATT THORNTON-P
54 SHIN-SOO CHOO-P
55 GIL MECHE-P
56 BOBBY MADRITSCH (INJ)-P
58 JEFF HARRIS-P
59 RENE RIVERA-C
59 FELIX HERNANDEZ-P
62 JAIME BUBELA-OF

Ichiro Suzuki burst upon the Seattle scene in 2001. He slashed hits to all fields with his unorthodox swing. He has averaged 226 hits per year. That's averaged. In 2004, he had 262 hits that beat out George Sisler's 64-year-old record by five. But that's only part of the story. Imagine this, as an outfielder Suzuki has been involved in nearly as many DPs (10) as he has made errors (11) in the five years since leaving Japan. Because of his unusual number (#51), he is outside the parameters of the Dream Teams in Chapter 8.

TAMPA BAY DEVIL RAYS

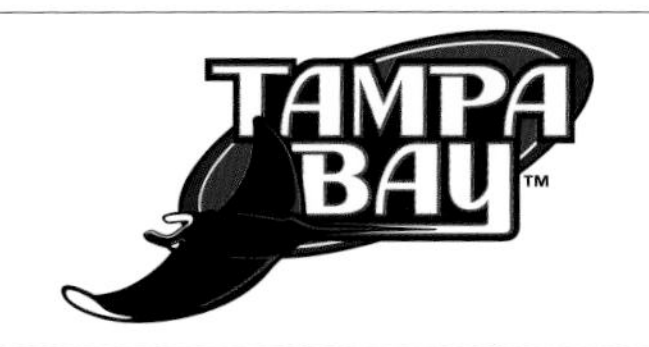

1998
TAMPA BAY DEVIL RAYS
5TH E 63-99 51GB

2 RANDY WINN-OF/DH
3 QUENTON MCCRACKEN-OF/DH
4 AARON LEDESMA-SS
5 STEVE HENDERSON-CH
6 ORLANDO GOMEZ-CH
6 JOHN FLAHERTY (INJ)-C
7 GREG RIDDOCH-CH
8 MIKE DIFELICE-C
9 BOBBY SMITH (INJ)-3B/INF
10 RICH BUTLER (INJ)-OF
11 LARRY ROTHSCHILD-MGR
12 WADE BOGGS (INJ)-3B/DH
13 MIGUEL CAIRO-2B/DH
14 DAVE MARTINEZ (INJ)-OF
15 KERRY ROBINSON-OF
16 TIM LAKER-C (1)
17 DAVE SILVESTRI-UTIL
19 KEVIN STOCKER (INJ)-SS
20 MIGUEL CAIRO-INF
20 SCOTT MCCLAIN-1B/3B
21 BUBBA TRAMMELL-OF
22 BILLY HATCHER-CH
23 JOHN FLAHERTY (INJ)-C
24 MIKE KELLY (INJ)-OF
(25) VAUGHN ESHELMANN (INJ)-(P)
26 TIM LAKER-C (1)
27 JEROME WALTON (INJ) (REL)-OF
27 RICK WHITE-P
28 EDDIE GAILLARD-P
29 FRED (CRIME DOG) MCGRIFF-1B
30 ROLANDO ARROJO (INJ)-P
31 TONY SAUNDERS-P
32 ALBIE LOPEZ (INJ)-P
33 FRANK (THE CAPITOL PUNISHER) (HONDO) HOWARD-CH
(34)HERBERT PERRY (INJ)-(1B)
35 DENNIS SPRINGER-P
36 MATT RUEBEL-P
36 TERRELL WADE (INJ)-P
37 SCOTT ALDRED-P
38 RICK WILLIAMS-CH
39 ROBERTO HERNANDEZ-P
40 WILSON ALVAREZ (INJ)-P
41 JASON JOHNSON (INJ)-P
42 *(RET#) JACKIE ROBINSON*
43 ESTEBAN YAN-P
44 PAUL SORRENTO-1B/DH
45 JIM MECIR-P
46 DAN CARLSON-P
47 MIKE DUVALL-P
48 DAVE EILAND-P
51 RICK WHITE-P
52 RAMON TATIS (INJ)-P
53 MATT RUEBEL-P
55 RICK GORECKI (INJ)-P
56 BRYAN REKAR (INJ)-P
57 BRAD PENNINGTON-P
60 JULIO SANTANA-P (2)

1999
5TH E 69-93 29GB

2 RANDY WINN-OF/DH
3 QUENTON MCCRACKEN (INJ)-OF/DH
4 AARON LEDESMA (INJ)-SS
5 LEON ROBERTS-CH
6 JOHN FLAHERTY (INJ)-C
7 GREG RIDDOCH-CH
8 MIKE DIFELICE-C
9 BOBBY SMITH (INJ)-3B/INF
10 RICH BUTLER (INJ)-(OF)
11 LARRY ROTHSCHILD-MGR
12 WADE BOGGS (INJ)-3B/DH
13 MIGUEL CAIRO-2B/DH
14 DAVE MARTINEZ (INJ)-OF
15 DAVID LAMB-INF
17 ROLANDO ARROJO-P
18 JULIO FRANCO-INF
19 KEVIN STOCKER (INJ)-SS
21 BUBBA TRAMMELL-OF
22 BILLY HATCHER-CH
23 ORLANDO GOMEZ-CH
24 RYAN RUPE-P
25 FRANK (THE CAPITOL PUNISHER) (HONDO) HOWARD-CH
26 TONY GRAFFANINO-INF
27 CORY LIDLE (INJ)-P
28 EDDIE GAILLARD-P
29 FRED (CRIME DOG) MCGRIFF-1B
30 SCOTT ALDRED-P (1)
30 JOSE GUILLEN-OF (2)
31 TONY SAUNDERS (INJ)-P
32 ALBIE LOPEZ (INJ)-P
33 JOSE CANSECO (INJ)-DH
34 DAN WHEELER-P
35 HERBERT PERRY (INJ)-3B
37 SCOTT ALDRED-P (1)
37 NORM CHARLTON (THE GENIUS)-P
38 RICK WILLIAMS-CH
39 ROBERTO HERNANDEZ-P
40 WILSON ALVAREZ (INJ)-P
41 DANNY CLYBURN-OF
42 *(RET#) JACKIE ROBINSON*
43 ESTEBAN YAN-P
44 PAUL SORRENTO (INJ)-1B/DH
45 JIM MECIR (INJ)-P
46 ALAN NEWMAN-P
47 MIKE DUVALL-P
48 DAVE EILAND-P
50 TERRELL LOWERY-OF
51 RICK WHITE-P
53 BOBBY WITT-P
(55) RICK GORECKI (INJ)-(P)
56 BRYAN REKAR (INJ)-P
60 JULIO SANTANA (INJ)-P (1)
61 MICKEY CALLAWAY-P
62 JEFF SPARKS-P
63 JIM MORRIS-P
71 STEVE COX-INF

2000
5TH E 69-92 18GB

1 MIGUEL CAIRO-2B/DH
2 RANDY WINN-OF/DH
3 QUENTON MCCRACKEN (INJ)-OF/DH
4 GERALD WILLIAMS-OF
5 LEON ROBERTS-CH
6 JOHN FLAHERTY (INJ)-C
7 JOSE CARDENAL-CH
8 MIKE DIFELICE-C
9 BOBBY SMITH (INJ)-3B/INF
9 VINNY CASTILLA-3B
10 RUSS JOHNSON-INF (2)
11 LARRY ROTHSCHILD-MGR
12 *(RET#) WADE BOGGS*
13 MIGUEL CAIRO-2B/DH
13 OZZIE GUILLEN-INF (2)
14 DAVE MARTINEZ-OF (1)
14 JASON TYNER-OF (2)
15 KENNY KELLY-OF
16 DWIGHT (DOC) GOODEN, (REL)-P (2)
16 FELIX MARTINEZ-INF
18 BILL RUSSELL-CH
19 KEVIN STOCKER-SS (1)
20 VINNY CASTILLA-3B
20 BOBBY SMITH (INJ)-3B/INF
21 BUBBA TRAMMELL-OF (1)
21 AUBREY HUFF-INF
22 BILLY HATCHER-CH
23 GREG VAUGHN-OF
24 RYAN RUPE-P
25 ORLANDO GOMEZ-CH
26 TONY GRAFFANINO-INF(1)
27 CORY LIDLE (INJ)-P
28 STEVE COX-OF
29 FRED (CRIME DOG) MCGRIFF-1B
30 JOSE GUILLEN-OF
31 TONY SAUNDERS (INJ) (RET)-P
32 ALBIE LOPEZ-P
33 JOSE CANSECO-DH (1)
34 DAN WHEELER-P
35 HERBERT PERRY (INJ)-3B (1)
35 BRYAN REKAR-P
36 MARK GUTHRIE-P (2)
36 TONY FIORIE-P
37 BILLY TAYLOR-P (2)
38 RICK WILLIAMS-CH
38 DOUG CREEK-P
39 ROBERTO HERNANDEZ-P
40 WILSON ALVAREZ (INJ)-P
41 PAUL WILSON-P
42 *(RET#) JACKIE ROBINSON*
43 ESTEBAN YAN-P
44 OZZIE TIMMONS-OF
45 JIM MECIR (INJ)-P (1)
45 TREVOR ENDERS-P
46 STEVE TRACHSEL-P (1)
47 MIKE DUVALL-P
48 DAVE EILAND (INJ)-P
49 TANYON STURTZE-P (2)
51 RICK WHITE-P (1)
54? BILL FISCHER-CH
55 TOBY HALL-C
56 BRYAN REKAR-P
57 JUAN GUZMAN (INJ)-P
58 TRAVIS HARPER-P
62 JEFF SPARKS-P
63 JIM MORRIS-P
66 JACE BREWER-INF
71 DAMIAN ROLLS (INJ)-INF
73 ALLEN BATTLE-OF
76 CHRIS MICHALAK-P

2001
5TH E 62-100 34GB
W ADLS-CLEA 3-2
L ACLS-NYA 4-1

2 RANDY WINN-OF/DH
3 BRENT ABERNATHY-2B
4 GERALD WILLIAMS (REL)-OF (1)
5 TERRY COLLINS-CH
6 JOHN FLAHERTY-C
7 JOSE CARDENAL-CH
7 LEE MAY-CH
8 MIKE DIFELICE-C
9 VINNY CASTILLA (REL)-3B
9 CHRIS GOMEZ-SS
10 JARED SANDBERG-3B
11 LARRY ROTHSCHILD-MGR1
12 WADE BOGGS-CH
14 JASON TYNER-OF
15 PAUL HOOVER-C
16 FELIX MARTINEZ (INJ)-INF
18 BEN GRIEVE-OF
19 AUBREY HUFF-3B
20 BOBBY SMITH (WAIV)-3B/INF
22 BILLY HATCHER-CH
23 GREG VAUGHN-OF
24 RYAN RUPE-P
25 DARREN (DUTCH) DAULTON-CH
25 RUSS JOHNSON (INJ)-SS/2B
26 ANDY SHEETS-SS
27 BOBBY SEAY-P
28 STEVE COX (INJ)-OF/1B
29 FRED (CRIME DOG) MCGRIFF-1B (1)
30 JOSE GUILLEN (INJ)-OF
32 ALBIE LOPEZ-P (1)
32 NICK BIERBRODT-P (2)
33 DAMIAN ROLLS-INF
34 DAN WHEELER-P
35 BRYAN REKAR (INJ)-P
36 TONY FIORIE-P
37 RUSTY MEACHAM-P
38 DOUG CREEK-P
40 WILSON ALVAREZ (INJ)-P
41 PAUL WILSON-P
42 *(RET#) JACKIE ROBINSON*
43 ESTEBAN YAN (INJ)-P
44 KEN HILL (REL)-P
44 TOBY HALL-C
45 DEWON BRAZELTON-P
46 JESUS COLOME-P
48 ARIEL PRIETO (INJ)-P
49 TANYON STURTZE-P
50 MIKE JUDD (INJ)-P
50 JOE KENNEDY-P
51 JEFF WALLACE (INJ)-P
52 BRIAN ROSE-P
53 JASON STANDRIDGE-P
54 BILL FISCHER-CH
55 GLENN EZELL-CH
55 TOBY HALL-C
56 HAL MCRAE-CH/MGR 2
(57) JUAN GUZMAN (INJ)-(P)
58 TRAVIS HARPER-P
59 MICKEY CALLAWAY-P
60 VICTOR ZAMBRANO-P
61 TRAVIS PHELPS-P

2002
5TH E 55-106 48GB

2 RANDY WINN-OF/DH
3 BRENT ABERNATHY-2B
4 JASON CONTI-OF
5 FELIX ESCALONA-INF
6 JOHN FLAHERTY-C
8 CARL CRAWFORD-OF
9 CHRIS GOMEZ-SS
10 JARED SANDBERG-3B/UTIL
11 HAL MCRAE-MGR
12 *(RET#) WADE BOGGS*
14 JASON TYNER-OF
15 TOM FOLEY-CH
15 PAUL HOOVER-C
17 JOE KENNEDY-P
18 BEN GRIEVE-OF/DH
19 AUBREY HUFF-DH/1B/3B
20 BOBBY SMITH-INF
20 DAVE MCCARTY-OF (2)
22 BILLY HATCHER-CH
23 GREG VAUGHN (INJ)-DH/OF
24 RYAN RUPE (INJ)-P
25 RUSS JOHNSON (PERS)-3B/INF
26 ANDY SHEETS-INF
28 STEVE COX-1B/DH
29 JASON SMITH-UTIL
33 DAMIAN ROLLS-OF
(34) DAN REICHERT (P)-(2)
35 LEE MAY-CH
36 LUIS DE LOS SANTOS-P
37 BRANDON BACKE-P
38 DOUG CREEK-P (1)
38 LANCE CARTER-P
39 LEE GARDNER-P
40 WILSON ALVAREZ (INJ)-P
41 PAUL WILSON-P
42 *(RET#) JACKIE ROBINSON*
43 ESTEBAN YAN-P
44 TOBY HALL-C
45 DEWON BRAZELTON-P
46 JESUS COLOME-P
47 LEE MAY-CH
48 DELVIN JAMES-P
49 TANYON STURTZE-P
50 JACKIE BROWN-CH
51 STEVE KENT-P
52 TOM MARTIN (INJ)-P
53 JASON STANDRIDGE-P
54 JASON JIMENEZ-P (1)
55 GLENN EZELL-CH
58 TRAVIS HARPER-P
59 JORGE SOSA (INJ)-P
60 VICTOR ZAMBRANO-P
61 TRAVIS PHELPS-P

2003
5TH E 63-99 38GB

1 ANTONIO PEREZ-2B/INF
2 BILLY HATCHER-CH
3 BRENT ABERNATHY (WAIV)-2B (1)
3 FELIX ESCALONA-SS/INF
3 JASON SMITH-3B
3 JEFF LEIFER (WAIV)-3B (2)
3 ADAM PIATT-OF (2)
4 LEE ELIA-CH
5 ROCCO BALDELLI-OF
7 JOHN MCLAREN-CH
8 MARLON ANDERSON-2B/OF
9 AL MARTIN-DH/OF
10 REY ORDONEZ (INJ)-SS
11 JASON TYNER-OF
12 *(RET#) WADE BOGGS*
13 CARL CRAWFORD-OF
14 LOU (SWEET LOU) PINIELLA-MGR
15 TOM FOLEY-CH
15 MATT SINATRO-CH
16 TRAVIS LEE (INJ)-1B
16 TOM FOLEY-CH
17 JOE KENNEDY (INJ)-P
18 BEN GRIEVE (INJ)-DH/OF
19 AUBREY HUFF-OF/UTIL
20 JAVIER VALENTIN-C/DH
22 BILLY HATCHER-CH
22 TERRY SHUMPERT (INJ)-UTIL
23 JULIO LUGO-SS (2)
24 GEORGE LOMBARD-OF
25 DAMIAN EASLEY (REL)-INF
25 MATT DIAZ-OF
26 JARED SANDBERG-3B
27 BOBBY SEAY (INJ)-P
28 JIM PARQUE (INJ) (REL)-P
29 CHRIS BOSIO-CH
30 BRANDON BACKE-P
32 NICK BIERBRODT-P (1)
32 ADAM PIATT-OF/DH (2)
33 DAMIAN ROLLS (INJ)-3B/OF
35 MILT MAY-CH
35 CHRIS TRUBY-3B
37 BRANDON BACKE-P
37 SETH MCCLUNG (INJ)-P
37 BRANDON BACKE-P
38 LANCE CARTER-P
39 STEVE PARRIS (INJ) (REL)-P
39 PETE LAFOREST-DH/C
40 AL LEVINE-P (1)
40 DOUG WAECHTER-P
41 ROB BELL-P
42 *(RET#) JACKIE ROBINSON*
43 MIKE VENAFRO (REL)-P
43 JON SWITZER-P
44 TOBY HALL-C
45 DEWON BRAZELTON-P
46 MARK MALASKA-P
47 LEE MAY-CH

47 VICTOR ZAMBRANO-P
48 JOHN ROCKER-P
49 JESUS COLOME (INJ)-P
50 JACKIE BROWN-CH
50 CHAD GAUDIN-P
51 JEREMI GONZALEZ-P
53 JASON STANDRIDGE-P
54 JEREMI GONZALEZ-P
55 GLENN EZELL-CH
57 CARLOS REYES-P
58 TRAVIS HARPER-P
59 JORGE SOSA-P
60 JONNY GOMES-DH

2004

4TH E 70-91 30.5GB

1 REY SANCHEZ-2B
2 BILLY HATCHER-CH
4 LEE ELIA-CH
5 ROCCO BALDELLI (INJ)-OF
6 TOM FOLEY-CH
7 JOHN MCLAREN-CH
8 JASON ROMANO-PR (1)
9 ROBERT FICK-1B (1)
9 B. J. UPTON-SS
10 DAMIAN ROLLS-UTIL
11 GEOFF BLUM-3B/2B
12 *(RET#) WADE BOGGS*
13 CARL CRAWFORD-OF
14 LOU (SWEET LOU) PINIELLA-MGR
15 MATT SINATRO-CH
17 CHARLES GIPSON-UTIL
19 AUBREY HUFF-3B/1B/DH
20 MIDRE CUMMINGS-OF
22 JOSE CRUZ-OF
23 JULIO LUGO-SS/2B
24 TINO MARTINEZ-1B/DH
25 MATT DIAZ-DH/OF
26 BROOK FORDYCE-C
27 GEOFF BLUM-3B/2B
28 DANYS BAEZ-P
29 FRED MCGRIFF (REL)-DH/1B
30 MARK HENDRICKSON-P
31 TODD RITCHIE-P
32 DAMIAN ROSS-P
33 EDUARDO PEREZ (INJ)-1B/DH
34 PAUL ABBOTT-P (1)
35 B. J. UPTON-SS/DH/3B
35 RANDALL SIMON-DH/1B (2)
36 JORGE SOSA-P
38 LANCE CARTER-P
40 DOUG WAECHTER (INJ)-P
41 ROB BELL-P
42 *(RET#) JACKIE ROBINSON*
43 JOEY GATHRIGHT-OF
43 DICKY GONZALEZ-P
44 TOBY HALL-C
45 DEWON BRAZELTON-P
46 BOBBY SEAY-P
47 VICTOR ZAMBRANO-P (1)
47 FRANKLIN NUNEZ-P
49 JESUS COLOME (INJ)-P
50 CHAD GAUDIN-P
51 TREVER MILLER-P
52 JOHN HALAMA-P
53 JASON STANDRIDGE (INJ)-P
53 JOHN WEBB-P
54 JEREMI GONZALEZ-P
55 CHUCK HERNANDEZ-CH
57 BARTOLOME FORTUNATO-P (1)
57 SCOTT KAZMIR-P
58 TRAVIS HARPER-P
59 JORGE BAUTISTA-3B (2)
59 JORGE CANTU-2B
60 JONNY GOMES-DH

2005

5TH E 67-95 28GB

1 JOEY GATHRIGHT-OF
2 ALEX SANCHEZ (SUS:3G)-OF (1)
2 FERNANDO CORTEZ-3B
3 JORGE CANTU-2B
4 LEE ELIA-CH
(5) ROCCO BALDELLI (INJ)-(OF)
6 TOM FOLEY-CH
7 JOHN MCLAREN (SUS:3G)-CH
8 ALEX GONZALEZ (INJ)-3B
10 CHRIS SINGLETON-OF
11 HIDEO NOMO (REL)-P (1)
12 *(RET#) WADE BOGGS*
13 CARL CRAWFORD-OF
14 LOU (SWEET LOU) PINIELLA-MGR
15 CASEY FOSSUM-P
16 TRAVIS LEE (INJ)-1B
17 KEVIN CASH-C
18 NICK GREEN-2B
19 AUBREY HUFF-OF/DH/1B
20 BILLY HATCHER-CH
21 JOSH PHELPS-DH
22 MATT SINATRO-CH
23 JULIO LUGO-SS
24 CHARLES JOHNSON-C
24 ERIC MUNSON-1B/DH
26 SCOTT KAZMIR-P
27 DAMON HOLLINS-OF
28 DANYS BAEZ-P
29 REGGIE TAYLOR-OF
30 MARK HENDRICKSON (INJ)-P
31 JONNY GOMES-OF/DH
33 EDUARDO PEREZ-1B
36 TIM LAKER-C
37 SETH MCCLUNG-P
38 LANCE CARTER (SUS:3G)-P
39 PETE LAFOREST-C
40 DOUG WAECHTER (INJ)-P
41 ROB BELL (INJ)-P
42 *(RET#) JACKIE ROBINSON*
44 TOBY HALL-C
45 DEWON BRAZELTON (SUS:5G)-P
47 FRANKLIN NUNEZ-P
48 JON SWITZER-P
48 JOE BOROWSKI-P (2)
49 JESUS COLOME (INJ)-P
51 TREVER MILLER-P
52 LEE GARDNER-P
53 JOHN WEBB-P
54 CHAD ORVELLA-P
55 CHUCK HERNANDEZ-CH
56 TIM CORCORAN-P
58 TRAVIS HARPER-P
97 JOE BEIMEL-P

Two of the promising young stars in Tampa Bay, Scott Kazmir (Above, right) arrived via the Victor Zambrano trade in July 2004 and Rocco Baldelli (Right) who missed the entire 2005 season recovering from surgery. Both players create an air of excitement wherever they go.

1961
WASHINGTON SENATORS
9TH (TIE) 61-100 47.5GB

1 WILLIE TASBY-OF
2 R.C. STEVENS-1B
2 EDDIE BRINKMAN-3B
3 MICKEY VERNON-MGR
4 DANNY O'CONNELL-3B/2B
5 COOT VEAL-SS
6 BILLY KLAUS-UTIL
7 CHUCK COTTIER-2B (2)
8 PETE DALEY-C
9 MARTY KEOUGH-OF
10 HARRY BRIGHT-UTIL
11 BUD ZIPFEL-1B
11 DUTCH DOTTERER-C
12 GENE GREEN-C/OF
14 GENE WOODLING-OF
15 DAVE SISLER-P
16 PETE BURNSIDE-P
17 JOHNNY KLIPPSTEIN-P
18 ED HOBAUGH-P
19 MIKE (THE BIG BEAR) GARCIA-P
19 HAL WOODESHICK-P (1)
19 KEN RETZER-C
20 DICK DONOVAN-P
21 BENNY DANIELS-P
22 MARTY KUTYNA-P
23 TOM CHENEY (INJ)-P (2)
23 RUDY HERNANDEZ-P
24 CARL (STUBBY) MATHIAS-P
24 HECTOR MAESTRI-P
25 DALE LONG-1B
26 JOHN (GABE) GABLER-P
27 JOE MCCLAIN-P
28 CHET BOAK-2B
29 BOB JOHNSON-INF
29 JIM (MOE) MAHONEY-SS/2B
29 RON STILLWELL-SS
30 JIM KING-OF/C
32 CHUCK HINTON-OF
32 JOE HICKS-OF
34 CARL BOULDIN-P
34 CLAUDE OSTEEN-P (2)
35 TOM (SNAKE) STURDIVANT-P (1)
40 SID HUDSON-CH
41 GEORGE CASE-CH
42 ROLLIE HEMSLEY-CH
43 GEORGE (GOOD KID) SUSCE-CH
47 TOM (SNAKE) STURDIVANT-P (1)
47 ROY HEISER-P

1962
10TH 60-101 35.5GB

1 WILLIE TASBY-OF (1)
1* JACK JENKINS-P*
3 MICKEY VERNON-MGR
4 DANNY O'CONNELL-3B/2B
5 KEN HAMLIN-SS/2B
6 JOHNNY SCHIAVE-3B/2B
7 CHUCK COTTIER-2B
8 RON STILLWELL-2B/SS
9 KEN RETZER-C
10 HARRY BRIGHT-1B/UTIL
11 BUD ZIPFEL-1B/OF
12 BOB SCHMIDT-C
14 GENE WOODLING-OF (1)
15 DAVE STENHOUSE-P
16 PETE BURNSIDE-P
17 BOB BAIRD-P
17 FREDDIE GREEN-P
18 ED HOBAUGH-P
19 JIM HANNAN-P
20 RAY RIPPLEMEYER-P
21 BENNY DANIELS-P
22 MARTY KUTYNA-P
23 TOM CHENEY-P
24 CLAUDE OSTEEN-P
25 DALE LONG-1B (1)
25 DON LOCK-OF
26 DON RUDOLPH-P (2)
27 JOE MCCLAIN-P
27 CARL BOULDIN-P
28 STEVE HAMILTON-P
29 BOB JOHNSON-3B/UTIL
30 JIM KING-OF
31 JOE HICKS-OF
32 CHUCK HINTON-OF/INF
33 DON RUDOLPH-P (2)
34 JOHN KENNEDY-SS/3B
34 CLAUDE OSTEEN-P
37 JIMMY PIERSALL-OF
38 EDDIE BRINKMAN-SS/3B
38 CARL BOULDIN-P
40 SID HUDSON-CH
41 GEORGE CASE-CH
42 ROLLIE HEMSLEY-CH
43 GEORGE (GOOD KID) SUSCE-CH

1963
10TH 56-106 48.5GB

1 MARV BREEDING-INF (1)
1 TOM BROWN-1B/OF
2 BARRY SHETRONE-PH
2 JOHN KENNEDY-3B/SS
3 MICKEY VERNON-MGR1
3 CAL NEEMAN-C
4 DON LOCK-OF
5 HOBIE LANDRITH-C (2)
6 JOHNNY SCHIAVE-3B/2B
6 KEN RETZER-C
7 CHUCK COTTIER-2B/INF
8* BOB BAIRD-P*
9 MINNIE MINOSO-OF/3B
10 DON LEPPERT-C
11 EDDIE BRINKMAN-SS
12 TOM BROWN-1B/OF
12 BOB SCHMIDT-C
12 DON BLASINGAME-2B (2)
14 GIL HODGES-MGR2
15 DAVE STENHOUSE (INJ)-P
16 RON (THE KID) MOELLER-P (2)
17 JIM DUCKWORTH-P
18 PETE BURNSIDE-P (2)
20 KEN HUNT-OF (2)
21 BENNY DANIELS-P
22 JACK JENKINS-P
22 ED ROEBUCK-P (2)
22 ART QUIRK-P
23 TOM CHENEY-P
24 CLAUDE OSTEEN-P
25 BOBO OSBORNE-1B/3B
26 JIM HANNAN-P
27 RON KLINE-P
28 STEVE HAMILTON-P (1)
28 JIM COATES-P (1)
28 STEVE RIDZIK-P
29 DICK PHILLIPS-INF
30 JIM KING-OF
32 CHUCK HINTON-OF/INF
33 DON RUDOLPH-P
34 LOU KLIMCHOCK-2B (1)
34 DON (POPEYE) ZIMMER-3B/2B (2)
36 JOHN KENNEDY-3B/SS
36 ED HOBAUGH-P
37 JIMMY PIERSALL-OF (1)
37 ED ROEBUCK-P (2)
39 JIM BRONSTAD-P
34 CARL BOULDIN-P
40 SID HUDSON-CH
41 GEORGE CASE-CH
41 DANNY O'CONNELL-CH
42 EDDIE (THE WALKING MAN) YOST-CH
43 GEORGE (GOOD KID) SUSCE-CH

1964
9TH 62-100 42GB

1 DON BLASINGAME-2B
2 JOHN KENNEDY-3B/INF
3 BILL (MOOSE) SKOWRON-1B (1)
3 JOE CUNNINGHAM-1B (2)
4 DON LOCK-OF
5 FRED (SQUEAKY) VALENTINE-OF
6 KEN HUNT-OF
6 WILLIE KIRKLAND-OF (2)
7 CHUCK COTTIER-INF
8 MIKE BRUMLEY-C
9 ROY (SQUIRREL) SIEVERS-1B (2)
10 DON LEPPERT-C
11 EDDIE BRINKMAN-SS
12 ROY (SQUIRREL) SIEVERS-1B (2)
12 KEN HUNT-OF
14 GIL HODGES-MGR
15 DAVE STENHOUSE (INJ)-P
16 DON LOUN-P
16 HOWIE KOPLITZ-P
17 JIM DUCKWORTH (INJ)-P
18 FRANK KREUTZER-P (2)
18 CARL BOULDIN-P
19 JIM HANNAN-P
20 KEN RETZER-C
20 TOM CHENEY (INJ)-P
21 BENNY DANIELS-P
23 TOM CHENEY (INJ)-P
23 DON (POPEYE) ZIMMER-UTIL
24 CLAUDE OSTEEN-P
25 PETE CRAIG-P
25 MARSHALL (SHERIFF) BRIDGES-P
26 ALAN KOCH-P (2)
27 RON KLINE-P
28 STEVE RIDZIK-P
29 DICK PHILLIPS-1B/3B
30 JIM KING-OF
31 WILLIE KIRKLAND-OF (2)
32 CHUCK HINTON-OF/3B
33 DON RUDOLPH-P
34 BUSTER NARUM-P
35 BUSTER NARUM-P
35 PETE CRAIG-P
37 ED ROEBUCK-P (1)
37 JIM BRONSTAD-P
40 SID HUDSON-CH
41 DANNY O'CONNELL-CH
42 EDDIE (THE WALKING MAN) YOST-CH
43 GEORGE (GOOD KID) SUSCE-CH
44 HOBIE LANDRITH-CH

1965
8TH 70-92 32GB

1 DON BLASINGAME-2B
2 KEN MCMULLEN-3B/UTIL
3 JOE CUNNINGHAM-1B
4 DON LOCK-OF
5 DICK NEN-1B
6 WILLIE KIRKLAND-OF
7 CHUCK COTTIER-PH
7 KEN HAMLIN-INF
8 MIKE BRUMLEY-C
9 FRANK (THE CAPITAL PUNISHER) (HONDO) HOWARD-OF
10 BOB CHANCE-1B/OF
11 EDDIE BRINKMAN-SS
12 WOODY HELD-OF/INF
14 GIL HODGES-MGR
16 MIKE MCCORMICK-P
17 BARRY MOORE-P
17 JIM DUCKWORTH-P
17 RYNE DUREN-P (2)
18 FRANK KREUTZER-P
19 JIM HANNAN-P
20 BUSTER NARUM-P
21 BENNY DANIELS-P
22 NICK WILLHITE-P (1)
22 MARSHALL (SHERIFF) BRIDGES-P
23 DON (POPEYE) ZIMMER-UTIL
24 PETE RICHERT-P
25 ROY (SQUIRREL) SIEVERS-1B
25 BRANT ALYEA-1B/OF
26 PHIL (KEMO) ORTEGA-P
27 RON KLINE-P
28 STEVE RIDZIK-P
29 DOUG CAMILLI-C
30 JIM KING-OF
31 HOWIE KOPLITZ-P
31 JOE MCCABE-C
32 PAUL CASANOVA-C
34 FRED (SQUEAKY) VALENTINE-OF
35 PETE CRAIG-P
35 DALLAS GREEN-P
36 JOE COLEMAN-P
37 JIM FRENCH-C
40 SID HUDSON-CH
41 RUBE WALKER-CH
42 EDDIE (THE WALKING MAN) YOST-CH
43 GEORGE (GOOD KID) SUSCE-CH
44 GEORGE (GOOD KID) SUSCE-CH
45 GEORGE CASE-CH

1966
8TH 71-88 25.5GB

1 DON BLASINGAME-2B/SS (1)
1 TIM CULLEN-3B/2B
2 KEN MCMULLEN-3B/UTIL
3 JOE CUNNINGHAM-1B
3 KEN (HAWK) HARRELSON-1B (2)
4 DON LOCK-OF
5 DICK NEN-1B
6 WILLIE KIRKLAND-OF
7 KEN HAMLIN-2B/3B
8 MIKE BRUMLEY-C
9 FRANK (THE CAPITAL PUNISHER) (HONDO) HOWARD-OF
10 BOB CHANCE-1B
11 EDDIE BRINKMAN-SS
12 JOHN ORSINO (INJ)-PH
14 GIL HODGES-MGR
15 BOB (RABBIT) SAVERINE-2B/UTIL
16 MIKE MCCORMICK-P
17 JIM DUCKWORTH-P (1)
17 HANK ALLEN-OF
18 FRANK KREUTZER-P
18 BOB HUMPHREYS-P
18 DICK LINES-P
18 FRANK KREUTZER-P
19 JIM HANNAN-P
20 BUSTER NARUM-P
20 PAUL CASANOVA-C
21 DOUG CAMILLI (INJ)-C
22 DICK PHILLIPS-1B
22 PAUL CASANOVA-C
22 TOM CHENEY-P
23 BOB HUMPHREYS-P
24 PETE RICHERT-P
25 BARRY MOORE-P
25 ALAN CLOSTER-P
25 DICK BOSMAN-P
26 PHIL (KEMO) ORTEGA-P
27 RON KLINE-P
28 JIM FRENCH-C
29 CASEY COX-P
30 JIM KING-OF
30 FRANK KREUTZER-P
31 HOWIE KOPLITZ (INJ)-P
31 DAVE BALDWIN-P
32 FRANK KREUTZER-P
32 DIEGO SEGUI-P
34 FRED (SQUEAKY) VALENTINE-OF/1B
35 PETE CRAIG-P
36 JOE COLEMAN-P
37 JOE COLEMAN-P
38 DICK BOSMAN-P
41 RUBE WALKER-CH
42 EDDIE (THE WALKING MAN) YOST-CH
43 GEORGE (GOOD KID) SUSCE-CH
44 JOE PIGNATANO-CH

1967
6TH (TIE) 76-85 15.5GB

1 TIM CULLEN-UTIL
2 KEN MCMULLEN-3B
3 KEN (HAWK) HARRELSON-1B (1)
3 JOHN ORSINO-1B/C
4 CAP PETERSON-OF
5 DICK NEN-1B/OF
6 HANK ALLEN-OF
7 BERNIE ALLEN-2B
8 PAUL CASANOVA-C
9 FRANK (THE CAPITAL PUNISHER) (HONDO) HOWARD-OF/1B
10 JIM FRENCH-C
11 EDDIE BRINKMAN-SS
12 MIKE (SUPERJEW) EPSTEIN-1B (2)
14 GIL HODGES-MGR
15 BOB (RABBIT) SAVERINE-UTIL
16 BOB PRIDDY-P
17 CAMILO (LITTLE POTATO) PASCUAL-P
18 DICK LINES-P
19 JIM HANNAN-P
20 JOE COLEMAN-P
21 DOUG CAMILLI-C
22 DICK NOLD-P
23 BOB HUMPHREYS-P
24 PETE RICHERT-P (1)
24 FRANK BERTAINA-P (2)
25 BARRY MOORE-P
26 PHIL (KEMO) ORTEGA-P
27 DICK BOSMAN-P
28 BUSTER NARUM-P
29 CASEY COX-P
30 JIM KING-OF/C (1)
30 FRANK COGGINS-2B
31 BOB CHANCE-1B
31 DAVE BALDWIN-P
32 DAROLD KNOWLES-P
34 FRED (SQUEAKY) VALENTINE-OF
36 ED STROUD-OF (2)
37 DAVE BALDWIN-P
38 DICK NOLD-P
38 BUSTER NARUM-P
38 CASEY COX-P
41 RUBE WALKER-CH
42 EDDIE (THE WALKING MAN) YOST-CH

43 GEORGE (GOOD KID) SUSCE-CH
44 JOE PIGNATANO-CH

1968

10TH 65-96 37.5GB

1 FRANK COGGINS-2B
2 KEN MCMULLEN-3B/SS
3 BRANT ALYEA-OF
4 CAP PETERSON-OF
5 HANK ALLEN-UTIL
5 GARY HOLMAN-1B/OF
6 RON HANSEN-SS/3B (1)
6 DICK BILLINGS-OF/3B
6 TIM CULLEN-INF (2)
7 BERNIE ALLEN-2B/3B
8 PAUL CASANOVA-C
9 FRANK (THE CAPITAL PUNISHER) (HONDO) HOWARD-OF/1B
10 JIM FRENCH-C
11 EDDIE BRINKMAN-UTIL
12 MIKE (SUPERJEW) EPSTEIN-1B
14 BILLY BRYAN-C
16 JIM HANNAN-P
17 CAMILO (LITTLE POTATO) PASCUAL-P
18 CAMILO (LITTLE POTATO) PASCUAL-P
19 GERRY SCHOEN-P
20 JOE COLEMAN-P
21 BILL HAYWOOD-P
22 BILL DENEHY-P
22 GENE MARTIN-OF
23 BOB HUMPHREYS-P
24 FRANK BERTAINA-P
25 BARRY MOORE-P
26 PHIL (KEMO) ORTEGA-P
27 DICK BOSMAN-P
28 DENNY HIGGINS-P
29 CASEY COX-P
30 DEL UNSER-OF/1B
31 JIM MILES-P
32 DAROLD KNOWLES (MIL)-P
34 FRED (SQUEAKY) VALENTINE-OF (1)
34 STEVE JONES-P
35 HANK ALLEN-UTIL
35 SAM BOWENS-OF
36 ED STROUD-OF
37 DAVE BALDWIN-P
40 JIM LEMON-MGR
41 SID HUDSON-CH
42 NELLIE FOX-CH
43 BOBBY HOFMAN-CH
44 DOUG CAMILLI-(C)/CH

1969

4TH E 86-76 23GB

1 TIM CULLEN-INF
2 KEN MCMULLEN-3B
3 BRANT ALYEA-OF/1B
5 GARY HOLMAN-1B/OF
5 LEE MAYE-OF (2)
6 MIKE (SUPERJEW) EPSTEIN-1B
7 BERNIE ALLEN-2B/3B
8 PAUL CASANOVA-C
9 TED (SPLENDID SPLINTER) (THUMPER) (TEDDY BALLGAME) WILLIAMS-MGR
10 JIM FRENCH-C
11 EDDIE BRINKMAN-UTIL
12 DOUG CAMILLI-CH
14 DICK SMITH-OF
15 ZOILO (ZORRO) VERSALLES-INF
16 JIM HANNAN-P
17 CAMILO (LITTLE POTATO) PASCUAL-P (1)
17 TOBY HARRAH-SS
20 JOE COLEMAN-P
21 JIM MILES-P
21 JIM SHELLENBACK-P (2)
22 JAN DUKES-P
22 FRANK KREUTZER-P
23 BOB HUMPHREYS-P
24 FRANK BERTAINA-P (1)
24 JIM MILES-P
25 BARRY MOORE-P
26 DICK BILLINGS-OF/3B
27 DICK BOSMAN-P
28 DENNY HIGGINS-P
29 CASEY COX-P
30 DEL UNSER-OF/1B
31 SAM BOWENS-OF
31 CISCO CARLOS-P (2)
32 DAROLD KNOWLES (MIL)-P
33 FRANK (THE CAPITAL PUNISHER) (HONDO) HOWARD-OF/1B
35 HANK ALLEN-OF/INF
36 ED STROUD-OF
37 DAVE BALDWIN-P
40 JOE CAMACHO-CH
41 SID HUDSON-CH
42 NELLIE FOX-CH
43 GEORGE (GOOD KID) SUSCE-CH
44 WAYNE (TWIG) TERWILLIGER-CH

1970

6TH E 70-92 38GB

1 TIM CULLEN-2B/SS
2 KEN MCMULLEN-3B (1)
2 AURELIO RODRIGUEZ-3B/SS (2)
3 RICK REICHARDT-OF/3B (2)
4 DICK NEN-1B
4 TOMMY GRIEVE-OF
4 LARRY BIITTNER-PH
5 LEE MAYE-OF/3B (1)
6 MIKE (SUPERJEW) EPSTEIN-1B
7 BERNIE ALLEN-2B/3B
8 PAUL CASANOVA-C
9 TED (SPLENDID SPLINTER) (THUMPER) (TEDDY BALLGAME) WILLIAMS-MGR
10 JIM FRENCH-C/OF
11 EDDIE BRINKMAN-SS
12 WAYNE COMER-OF/3B (2)
13 JOHNNY ROSEBORO-C/CH
14 DAVE NELSON-2B
16 JIM HANNAN-P
17 PEDRO (PETE) RAMOS-P
18 DICK SUCH-P
18 BILL GOGOLEWSKI-P
19 JOE GRZENDA-P
19 CISCO CARLOS-P
20 JOE COLEMAN-P
20 JEFF BURROUGHS-OF
21 JIM SHELLENBACK-P
22 JAN DUKES-P
23 BOB HUMPHREYS-P (1)
23 JACKIE BROWN-P
23 DICK BOSMAN-P
24 GREG GOOSSEN-1B/OF (2)
27 DICK BOSMAN-P
28 HORACIO PINA-P
29 CASEY COX-P
30 DEL UNSER-OF
31 JOE GRZENDA-P
32 DAROLD KNOWLES-P
33 FRANK (THE CAPITAL PUNISHER) (HONDO) HOWARD-OF/1B
34 GEORGE (LEFTY) BRUNET-P (1)
34 DENNY RIDDLEBERGER-P
35 HANK ALLEN-OF (1)
35 DICK BILLINGS-C
36 ED STROUD-OF
40 JOE CAMACHO-CH
41 SID HUDSON-CH
42 NELLIE FOX-CH
43 GEORGE (GOOD KID) SUSCE-CH
44 WAYNE (TWIG) TERWILLIGER-CH
45 DEL (BABE) WILBER-CH

1971

5TH E 63-96 38.5GB

1 TIM CULLEN-2B/SS
2 DON WERT-INF
2 LENNY RANDLE-2B
3 TOMMY MCCRAW-OF/1B
4 LARRY BIITTNER-OF/1B
5 PAUL CASANOVA-C
6 MIKE (SUPERJEW) EPSTEIN-1B (1)
6 DON MINCHER-1B (2)
7 BERNIE ALLEN-2B/3B
8 DICK BILLINGS-UTIL
9 TED (SPLENDID SPLINTER) (THUMPER) (TEDDY BALLGAME) WILLIAMS-MGR
10 JIM FRENCH-C/OF
10 BILL FAHEY-C
11 TOBY HARRAH-SS/3B
13 BILL GOGOLEWSKI-P
14 JOE FOY-INF
14 DAVE NELSON-3B/2B
14 JIM MASON-SS
15 TOM RAGLAND-2B
15 DAVE NELSON-3B/2B
16 JIM SHELLENBACK-P
17 DENNY MCLAIN-P
18 PETE BROBERG-P
19 DENNY RIDDLEBERGER-P
20 JEFF BURROUGHS-OF
21 CURT FLOOD-OF
21 TOM RAGLAND-2B
23 JACKIE BROWN-P
24 MIKE THOMPSON-P
25 FRANK FERNANDEZ-OF/C
26 JERRY JANESKI-P
27 DICK BOSMAN-P
28 HORACIO PINA-P
29 CASEY COX-P
30 DEL UNSER-OF
31 JOE GRZENDA-P
32 DAROLD KNOWLES-P (1)
32 PAUL LINDBLAD-P (2)
33 FRANK (THE CAPITAL PUNISHER) (HONDO) HOWARD-OF/1B
34 RICK STELMASZEK-C
35 RICHIE SCHEINBLUM-OF
37 ELLIOTT MADDOX-OF/3B
39 RICHIE SCHEINBLUM-OF
40 JOE CAMACHO-CH
41 SID HUDSON-CH
42 NELLIE FOX-CH
43 GEORGE (GOOD KID) SUSCE-CH
44 WAYNE (TWIG) TERWILLIGER-CH
45 AL (ZEKE) ZARILLA-CH

1972
TEXAS RANGERS

6TH W 54-100 38.5GB

1 DAVE NELSON-3B/OF
2 LENNY RANDLE-2B/UTIL
2 JIM MASON-SS/3B
3 TED FORD-OF
4 LARRY BIITTNER-1B/OF
5 DON MINCHER-1B (1)
6 DON MINCHER-1B (1)
6 TOMMY GRIEVE-OF
7 TED KUBIAK-INF (1)
7 VIC HARRIS-2B/SS
8 DICK BILLINGS-C/UTIL
9 TED (SPLENDID SPLINTER) (THUMPER) (TEDDY BALLGAME) WILLIAMS-MGR
10 MARTY MARTINEZ-INF (3)
11 TOBY HARRAH (ILL)-SS
12 KEN SUAREZ-C
12 BILL FAHEY-C
13 BILL GOGOLEWSKI-P
14 JIM MASON-SS/3B
14 DALTON JONES-UTIL (2)
15 HAL KING-C
15 RICH HINTON-P (2)
16 JIM SHELLENBACK-P
16 JAN DUKES-P
17 DON STANHOUSE (INJ)-P
18 PETE BROBERG-P
19 JERRY JANESKI-P
20 JEFF BURROUGHS (INJ)-OF/1B
21 TOM RAGLAND-INF
22 JIM DRISCOLL-2B/3B
23 ELLIOTT MADDOX-OF
24 STEVE LAWSON-P
25 RICH HAND-P
27 DICK BOSMAN-P
28 HORACIO PINA-P
29 CASEY COX-P (1)
30 MIKE PAUL-P
31 JIM PANTHER-P
32 PAUL LINDBLAD-P
33 FRANK (THE CAPITAL PUNISHER) (HONDO) HOWARD-1B/OF (1)
34 JIM ROLAND-P (3)
35 JOE LOVITTO-OF
35 RICH HINTON-P (2)
39 RICHIE SCHEINBLUM-OF
40 JOE CAMACHO-CH
41 SID HUDSON-CH
42 NELLIE FOX-CH
43 GEORGE (GOOD KID) SUSCE-CH
44 WAYNE (TWIG) TERWILLIGER-CH
46 RICH HINTON-P (2)
50 JAN DUKES-P

1973

6TH W 57-105 37GB

1 DAVE NELSON-2B
1 BILLY (THE KID) MARTIN-MGR3
2 JIM MASON-SS/INF
3 JIM SPENCER-1B/DH (2)
4 LARRY BIITTNER-UTIL
5 RICO CARTY-OF/DH (1)
5* JIM KREMMEL-P*
6 TOMMY GRIEVE-OF/DH
7 VIC HARRIS-OF/INF
8 DICK BILLINGS (INJ)-UTIL
10 KEN SUAREZ-C
11 TOBY HARRAH (INJ)-SS/3B
13 BILL GOGOLEWSKI-P
14 CHARLES HUDSON (INJ)-P
15 ALEX JOHNSON-DH/OF
16 JIM SHELLENBACK-P
16 JIM MERRITT-P
17 DON STANHOUSE-P
17 JACKIE BROWN-P
17 JIM FREGOSI-INF (2)
18 PETE BROBERG-P
19 SONNY SIEBERT (INJ)-P (2)
20 JEFF BURROUGHS-OF/UTIL
21 LENNY RANDLE-2B/UTIL
21 BILL (SUDS) SUDAKIS-UTIL
22 RICK HENNINGER-P
22 JIM BIBBY-P (2)
23 ELLIOTT MADDOX (INJ)-OF/UTIL
24 PETE MACKANIN-SS/3B
25 RICH HAND-P (1)
25 RICO CARTY-OF/DH (1)
26 MIKE (SUPERJEW) EPSTEIN-1B (1)
26 LLOYD ALLEN-P (2)
27 DICK BOSMAN-P (1)
27 STEVE DUNNING-P (2)
28 BILL GOGOLEWSKI-P
29 STEVE FOUCAULT (INJ)-P
30 MIKE PAUL-P (1)
31 JACKIE BROWN-P
32 DICK STELMASZEK-C (1)
32 DAVID CLYDE-P
33 DON DURHAM-P
34 DON DURHAM-P
35 JOE LOVITTO-3B/OF
35 RICK HENNINGER-P
37 DON CASTLE-DH
38 BILL (MAD DOG) MADLOCK-3B
39 RICK WAITS-P
40 WHITEY HERZOG-MGR1
41 CHUCK HILLER-CH
42 JACKIE MOORE-CH
43 CHUCK ESTRADA-CH
46 STEVE DUNNING-P (2)
49 CHARLES HUDSON (INJ)-P
__ DEL (BABE) WILBER-MGR2 (1G: 9/1)

1974

2ND W 84-76 5GB

1 BILLY (THE KID) MARTIN-MGR
2 DUKE SIMS-UTIL (2)
3 JIM SPENCER-1B/DH
4 MIKE CUBBAGE-3B/2B
5 DAVE NELSON (INJ)-2B/DH
6 TOMMY GRIEVE-UTIL
7 CESAR (PEPITO) TOVAR-OF/DH
7 LENNY RANDLE-3B/UTIL
8 DICK BILLINGS-UTIL (1)
8 BOBBY JONES-OF
9 JOE LOVITTO-OF/1B
10 JIM SUNDBERG-C
11 TOBY HARRAH-SS/3B
12 CESAR (PEPITO) TOVAR-OF/DH
15 ALEX JOHNSON-OF/DH (1)
16 JIM MERRITT (INJ)-P
17 JIM FREGOSI-1B/3B
18 PETE BROBERG-P
18 LARRY BROWN-INF
19 FERGUSON (FERGIE) JENKINS-P
19 LEO (CHICO) CARDENAS-UTIL
20 JEFF BURROUGHS-OF/UTIL
21 MIKE HARGROVE-1B/UTIL
22 JIM BIBBY-P
23 STAN THOMAS-P
24 PETE MACKANIN-SS
25 JIM SHELLENBACK-P
26 STEVE HARGAN-P
27 STEVE DUNNING-P
27 DON STANHOUSE-P
27 ROY HOWELL-3B
28 JACKIE BROWN-P
29 STEVE FOUCAULT-P
30 LLOYD ALLEN-P (1)
30 DAVE MOATES-PR
31 FERGUSON (FERGIE) JENKINS-P
32 DAVID CLYDE-P

WASHINGTON SENATORS/**TEXAS RANGERS**

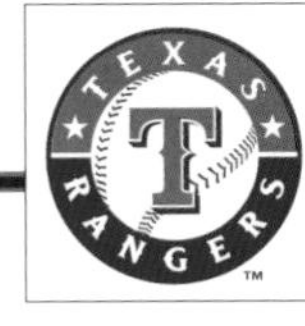

33 LENNY RANDLE-3B/UTIL
34 BILL HANDS-P (2)
35 JOE LOVITTO-OF/1B
36 DON STANHOUSE-P
37 BILL FAHEY-C
38 TOM ROBSON-1B/DH
40 ART FOWLER-CH
40 PETE BROBERG-P
41 ART FOWLER-CH
42 JACKIE MOORE-CH
43 CHARLIE (SWEDE) SILVERA-CH
44 FRANK LUCCHESI-CH
45 MERRILL (MERL) COMBS-CH
46 JEFF TERPKO-P
47 CHARLIE (SWEDE) SILVERA-CH
49 FRANK LUCCHESI-CH
49 BILL HANDS-P (2)
50 DON STANHOUSE-P
53 MERRILL (MERL) COMBS-CH

1975

3RD W — 79-83 — 19GB

1 BILLY (THE KID) MARTIN-MGR1 (1)
2 JOE LOVITTO (INJ)-UTIL
3 JIM SPENCER-1B/DH
3 WILLIE DAVIS-OF (1)
3 EDDIE BRINKMAN-3B (2)
4 MIKE CUBBAGE-INF/DH
5 DAVE NELSON (INJ)-2B/DH
6 TOMMY GRIEVE-OF/DH
7 LENNY RANDLE-3B/UTIL
8 BOBBY JONES-OF/DH
9 JOE LOVITTO (INJ)-UTIL
9 JIM SPENCER-1B/DH
10 JIM SUNDBERG-C
11 TOBY HARRAH-SS/INF
12 CESAR (PEPITO) TOVAR-OF/DH (1)
13 ROY HOWELL-3B/DH
14 BILL FAHEY (INJ)-C
15 WILLIE DAVIS-OF (1)
15 ROY SMALLEY-UTIL
16 JIM MERRITT (INJ)-P
17 JIM FREGOSI-UTIL
18 MIKE KEKICH-P
18 STAN PERZANOWSKI-P
19 LEO (CHICO) CARDENAS-INF
20 JEFF BURROUGHS-OF/DH
21 MIKE HARGROVE-OF/UTIL
22 JIM BIBBY-P (1)
23 STAN THOMAS-P
24 MIKE KEKICH-P
25 CLYDE WRIGHT-P
26 STEVE HARGAN-P
27 ROY HOWELL-3B/DH
27 TOMMY MOORE-P (2)
28 JACKIE BROWN-P (1)
28 TOMMY MOORE-P (2)
29 STEVE FOUCAULT-P
30 DAVE MOATES-OF/DH
31 FERGUSON (FERGIE) JENKINS-P
32 DAVID CLYDE-P
33 LENNY RANDLE-3B/UTIL
33 JIM GIDEON-P
34 BILL HANDS (INJ)-P
34 MIKE BACSIK-P
35 RON PRUITT-C/OF
36 GAYLORD PERRY-P (2)
38 TOM ROBSON-1B/DH
38 CLYDE WRIGHT-P
39 JIM GIDEON-P
40 JIM UMBARGER-P
41 ART FOWLER-CH
42 JACKIE MOORE-CH
43 CHARLIE (SWEDE) SILVERA-CH
44 FRANK LUCCHESI-CH/MGR2
45 MERRILL (MERL) COMBS-CH
46 JEFF TERPKO-P
47? BILL GERNERT-CH
49 BILL HANDS (INJ)-P

1976

4TH (TIE) W — 76-86 — 14GB

3 JOE LAHOUD-DH/OF (2)
4 MIKE CUBBAGE-INF/DH (1)
4 DANNY THOMPSON-INF (2)
5 KEN PAPE-INF/DH
6 TOMMY GRIEVE-DH/OF
7 LENNY RANDLE-2B/UTIL
9 JOHNNY ELLIS (INJ)-C/DH
10 JIM SUNDBERG-C
11 TOBY HARRAH-SS/UTIL
12 JUAN BENIQUEZ-OF/2B
13 ROY HOWELL-3B/DH
14 BILL FAHEY-C
15 ROY SMALLEY-2B/SS (1)
15 GREG PRYOR-INF
16 GENE CLINES-OF/DH
17 JIM FREGOSI-UTIL
18 STAN PERZANOWSKI-P
19 FRITZ PETERSON (INJ)-P (2)
20 JEFF BURROUGHS-OF/DH
21 MIKE HARGROVE-1B/DH
22 DOUG AULT-1B/DH
23 NELSON (NELLIE) BRILES-P
25 MIKE BACSIK-P
25 LEN BARKER-P
26 STEVE HARGAN-P
28 BURT BLYLEVEN-P (2)
29 STEVE FOUCAULT-P
30 DAVE MOATES-OF/DH
33 CRAIG SKOK-P
34 MIKE BACSIK-P
34 NELSON (NELLIE) BRILES-P
35 STEVE BARR-P
36 GAYLORD PERRY-P
38 TOMMY BOGGS-P
40 JIM UMBARGER-P
42 JACKIE MOORE-CH
43 JOE HOERNER-P
44 FRANK LUCCHESI-MGR
45 PAT CORRALES-CH
46 JEFF TERPKO-P
47 BILL GERNERT-CH
47 TOMMY BOGGS-P
48 BILL (SINGER THROWING MACHINE) SINGER-P (1)
54 SID HUDSON-CH

1977

2ND W — 94-68 — 8GB

1 BUMP WILLS-2B/UTIL
2 SANDY ALOMAR-UTIL
3 JIM MASON-INF/DH (2)
5 BILLY HUNTER-MGR4
6 TOMMY GRIEVE (INJ)-OF/DH
7 LEW BEASLEY-UTIL
8 CONNIE RYAN-CH
9 JOHNNY ELLIS-UTIL
10 JIM SUNDBERG-C
11 TOBY HARRAH-3B/SS
12 JUAN BENIQUEZ-OF
12? EDDIE (THE BRAT) (MUGGSY) STANKY-MGR2 (1G: 6/18)
13 ROY HOWELL-UTIL (1)
13 KURT BEVACQUA-UTIL
14 BILL FAHEY-C
15 CLAUDELL WASHINGTON-OF/DH
16 CLAUDELL WASHINGTON-OF/DH
16 DAVE MAY-OF/DH
17 JIM FREGOSI (INJ)-3B/DH (1)
17 DOCK ELLIS-P (3)
18 PAT PUTNAM-1B/DH
18 ED KIRKPATRICK-UTIL (2)
19 BERT (CAMPY) CAMPANERIS-SS
20 KEN HENDERSON (INJ)-OF/DH
21 MIKE HARGROVE-1B
22 TOMMY BOGGS-P
23 WILLIE HORTON-DH/OF (2)
24 GARY GRAY-OF
24 PAUL LINDBLAD-P
24 MIKE WALLACE-P
24 BOBBY CUELLAR-P
25 PAUL LINDBLAD-P
26 STEVE HARGAN-P (1)
26 KEITH SMITH-OF
27 JOHN POLONI-P
27 MIKE WALLACE-P
28 BURT BLYLEVEN-P
29 ROGER MORET (INJ)-P
30 EDDIE MILLER-DH/OF
31 MIKE MARSHALL (INJ)-P (2)
32 DAROLD KNOWLES-P
33 DOYLE ALEXANDER-P
34 NELSON (NELLIE) BRILES-P (1)
35 ADRIAN DEVINE-P
36 GAYLORD PERRY-P
37 MIKE BACSIK-P
38 TOMMY BOGGS-P
39 LEN BARKER-P
40 JIM UMBARGER-P
41 CONNIE RYAN-CH/MGR3
42 ROGER MORET (INJ)-P
44 FRANK LUCCHESI-MGR1
45 PAT CORRALES-CH
47 FRED KOENIG-CH
48 MIKE BACSIK-P
53 BOBBY CUELLAR-P
54 SID HUDSON-CH

1978

2ND (TIE) W — 87-75 — 5GB

0 AL OLIVER (INJ)-OF/DH
1 BUMP WILLS-2B
2 SANDY ALOMAR-INF/DH
3 JIM MASON-INF/DH
4 NELSON NORMAN-SS/3B
5 BILLY HUNTER-MGR1
6 JOHNNY GRUBB-OF/DH (2)
7 BILLY SAMPLE-DH/OF
8 CONNIE RYAN-CH
9 JOHNNY ELLIS-C/DH
10 JIM SUNDBERG-C/DH
11 TOBY HARRAH-3B/SS
12 JUAN BENIQUEZ (INJ)-OF
13 KURT BEVACQUA-INF/DH
15 CLAUDELL WASHINGTON (INJ)-OF/DH (1)
15? LA RUE WASHINGTON-2B/DH (3G: 9/7-10/1)
16 PAUL MIRABELLA-P
17 DOCK ELLIS-P
18 PAT PUTNAM-DH/1B
19 BERT (CAMPY) CAMPANERIS-SS/DH
20 BOBBY THOMPSON-OF/DH
21 MIKE HARGROVE-1B/DH
22 RICHIE ZISK-OF/DH
23 GARY GRAY-OF
24 BOBBY BONDS-OF/DH (2)
25 PAUL LINDBLAD-P (1)
26 REGGIE CLEVELAND-P (2)
27 DOC MEDICH-P
28 STEVE COMER-P
29 ROGER MORET (ILL)-P
31 FERGUSON (FERGIE) JENKINS-P
32 JON MATLACK-P
33 DOYLE ALEXANDER-P
34 JOHN LOWENSTEIN-UTIL
35 MIKE JORGENSEN-UTIL
35 GARY GRAY-OF
39 LEN BARKER-P
40 JIM UMBARGER-P
41 RAY MILLER-CH
42 JIMMIE SCHAFFER-CH
42 DOC MEDICH-P
43 GREG MAHLBERG-C
44 DANNY DARWIN-P
45 PAT CORRALES-CH/MGR2
46 JIMMIE SCHAFFER-CH
47 FRED KOENIG-CH
48 BOBBY THOMPSON-OF/DH
52 STEVE COMER-P
54 SID HUDSON-CH

1979

3RD W — 83-79 — 5GB

0 AL OLIVER (INJ)-OF/DH
1 BUMP WILLS-2B
3 LARVELL BLANKS (INJ)-INF/DH
4 NELSON NORMAN-SS/2B
5 BILLY SAMPLE-OF/DH
6 JOHNNY GRUBB (INJ)-OF/DH
7 OSCAR GAMBLE (INJ)-DH/OF (1)
8 CONNIE RYAN-CH
9 JOHNNY ELLIS-DH/UTIL
10 JIM SUNDBERG-C
11 STEVE COMER-P
12 OSCAR GAMBLE (INJ)-DH/OF (1)
12 DAVE CHALK-UTIL (2)
12 ERIC SODERHOLM-UTIL (2)
14 DAVE ROBERTS (INJ)-UTIL
15 LA RUE WASHINGTON-UTIL
17 DOCK ELLIS-P (1)
17 BOB BABCOCK-P
17 MICKEY RIVERS-OF/DH (2)
18 PAT PUTNAM-1B/DH
19 BERT (CAMPY) CAMPANERIS-SS (1)
20 BOB BABCOCK-P
22 RICHIE ZISK-OF/DH
23 GARY GRAY-OF
23 BRIAN ALLARD-P
24 BRIAN ALLARD-P
24 WILLIE MONTANEZ-1B/DH (2)
25 BUDDY BELL-3B/SS
26 DAVE RAJSICH-P
27 JERRY DON GLEATON-P
28 SPARKY LYLE-P
30 ED FARMER-P (1)
30 GREG MAHLBERG-C
31 FERGUSON (FERGIE) JENKINS-P
32 JON MATLACK (INJ)-P
33 DOYLE ALEXANDER (INJ)-P
34 JIM KERN-P
35 MIKE JORGENSEN (INJ)-UTIL
37 LARRY MCCALL-P
38 JOHN HENRY JOHNSON-P (2)
39 GARY HOLLE-1B
41 JACKIE BROWN-CH
42 DOC MEDICH-P
44 DANNY DARWIN-P
45 PAT CORRALES-MGR
47 FRED KOENIG-CH
48 FRANK LUCCHESI-CH

1980

4TH W — 76-85 — 20.5GB

0 AL OLIVER (INJ)-OF/UTIL
1 BUMP WILLS-2B
2 MIKE RICHARDT-2B/DH
3 PEPE FRIAS-SS/INF (1)
4 NELSON NORMAN-SS
5 BILLY SAMPLE-OF/DH
6 JOHNNY GRUBB-OF/DH
7 BUD HARRELSON (INJ)-SS/2B
8 DANNY (MICKEY) WALTON-DH
9 JOHNNY ELLIS-UTIL
10 JIM SUNDBERG-C
11 STEVE COMER (INJ)-P
12 ODIE DAVIS-SS/3B
12 BRIAN ALLARD-P
14 DAVE ROBERTS-UTIL
15 JERRY DON GLEATON-P
16 KEN CLAY-P
17 MICKEY RIVERS-OF/DH
18 PAT PUTNAM-1B/UTIL
19 JIM NORRIS-UTIL
20 BOB BABCOCK-P
20 RUSTY STAUB-DH/1B
22 RICHIE ZISK-DH/OF
23 BRIAN ALLARD-P
24 ED FIGUEROA-P (2)
25 BUDDY BELL-3B/SS
26 DAVE RAJSICH-P
27 JERRY DON GLEATON-P
28 SPARKY LYLE-P (1)
28 DENNIS LEWALLYN-P
29 TUCKER ASHFORD-3B/SS
29 JOHN BUTCHER-P
30 MIKE HART-OF
31 FERGUSON (FERGIE) JENKINS (SUB)-P
32 JON MATLACK-P
33 DON KAINER-P
33 DOC MEDICH-P
34 JIM KERN (INJ)-P
35 ADRIAN DEVINE (INJ)-P
36 GAYLORD PERRY-P (1)
37 RICH DONNELLY-CH
38 JOHN HENRY JOHNSON-P
41 JACKIE BROWN-CH
42 DOC MEDICH-P
42 JACKIE MOORE-CH
43 JACKIE MOORE-CH
43 DON KAINER-P
44 DANNY DARWIN-P
45 PAT CORRALES-MGR
46 BOB BABCOCK-P
47 BOB BABCOCK-P
47 FRED KOENIG-CH
48 FRANK LUCCHESI-CH
49 CHARLIE HOUGH-P (2)

1981

1ST 1/2:2ND W — 31-29 — 1.5GB
2ND 1/2:3RD W — 20-30 — 4.5GB
FINAL: — 57-48 — --GB

0 AL OLIVER-DH/1B
1 BUMP WILLS-2B/DH
3 WAYNE TOLLESON-3B/SS
4 NELSON NORMAN-SS
5 BILLY SAMPLE (INJ)-OF
6 JOHNNY GRUBB-OF
7 LEON ROBERTS-OF
8 BOBBY JOHNSON-C/1B
9 JOHNNY ELLIS-1B/DH
10 JIM SUNDBERG-C/OF
11 STEVE COMER-P
12 LEN WHITEHOUSE-P
13 BILL STEIN-UTIL
14 MARIO MENDOZA-SS
15 LEN WHITEHOUSE-P
16 LEON ROBERTS-OF
16 TOM POQUETTE-OF (2)
17 MICKEY RIVERS-OF
18 PAT PUTNAM-1B/OF
19 TOMMY HELMS-CH

20 LARRY COX-C
20 DON WERNER-DH
21 DAN DURAN-OF/1B
22 DARRELL JOHNSON-CH
23 DON (POPEYE) ZIMMER-MGR
24 RICK LISI-OF
24 DAVE SCHMIDT-P
25 BUDDY BELL-3B/SS
27 BOBBY JONES-OF
29 JOHN BUTCHER-P
30 MARK WAGNER-OF
31 FERGUSON (FERGIE) JENKINS-P
32 RICK HONEYCUTT-P
32 JON MATLACK-P
33 DOC MEDICH-P
34 JIM KERN (INJ)-P
35 BOB LACEY-P (2)
37 TOMMY HELMS-CH
38 JOHN HENRY JOHNSON-P
39 BOB BABCOCK-P
40 DARRELL JOHNSON-CH
40 RICK HONEYCUTT-P
41 JACKIE BROWN-CH
42 WAYNE (TWIG) TERWILLIGER-CH
44 DANNY DARWIN-P
46 BOB BABCOCK-P
47 FRED KOENIG-CH
49 CHARLIE HOUGH-P
53 MARK MERCER-P

1982

6TH W 64-98 29GB

1 BILL STEIN-UTIL
2 MIKE RICHARDT-2B/UTIL
3 WAYNE TOLLESON-INF
4 NICK CAPRA-OF
5 BILLY SAMPLE-OF/DH
6 JOHNNY GRUBB-OF/DH
6 LAMAR JOHNSON-DH/1B
7 LEON ROBERTS-OF/DH (1)
7 BUCKY DENT-SS (2)
8 BOBBY JOHNSON-C/1B
9 BOBBY JOHNSON-C/1B
9 LARRY PARRISH-OF/UTIL
10 JIM SUNDBERG-C/OF
11 STEVE COMER (INJ)-P
12 DAVE HOSTETLER-1B/DH
14 MARIO MENDOZA-SS
15 LARRY PARRISH-OF/UTIL
16 LEE MAZZILLI (INJ)-OF/DH (1)
16 MIKE MASON-P
17 MICKEY RIVERS (INJ)-DH
18 PAT PUTNAM-UTIL
19 TOMMY HELMS-CH
20 DON WERNER-DH
21 DOUG FLYNN-2B/SS (1)
22 DARRELL JOHNSON-CH/MGR2
23 DON (POPEYE) ZIMMER-MGR1
23 PETE O'BRIEN-UTIL
24 DAVE SCHMIDT-P
25 BUDDY BELL-3B/SS
26 GEORGE WRIGHT-OF
27 LAMAR JOHNSON-DH/1B
28 FRANK TANANA-P
29 JOHN BUTCHER-P
30 MARK WAGNER (ILL)-SS
32 JON MATLACK-P
33 DOC MEDICH-P (1)
33 JIM FARR-P
34 PAUL MIRABELLA-P
35 JIM FARR-P
35 TOM HENKE-P
35 RANDY BASS-DH/1B (2)
38 TERRY BOGENER-OF/DH
40 RICK HONEYCUTT-P
41 JACKIE BROWN-CH
42 WAYNE (TWIG) TERWILLIGER-CH
44 DANNY DARWIN-P
47 FRED KOENIG-CH
48 MIKE SMITHSON-P
49 CHARLIE HOUGH-P
50 JOHN BUTCHER-P
54 DANNY BOITANO-P

1983

3RD W 77-85 22GB

1 BILL STEIN-INF/DH
2 MIKE RICHARDT (INJ)-2B
3 WAYNE TOLLESON-2B/UTIL
4 NICK CAPRA-OF
5 BILLY SAMPLE-OF
6 BOBBY JONES-UTIL
7 BUCKY DENT-SS/DH
8 BOBBY JOHNSON-C/1B
9 PETE O'BRIEN-1B/DH
10 JIM SUNDBERG-C
11 DOUG (THE RED ROOSTER) (ROJO) RADER-MGR
12 DAVE HOSTETLER-DH/1B
13 TOMMY DUNBAR-OF/DH
14 LARRY BIITTNER-UTIL
15 LARRY PARRISH-OF/DH
16 MIKE MASON-P
17 MICKEY RIVERS-DH/OF
18 GLENN EZELL-CH
19 CURTIS WILKERSON-INF
21 ODELL JONES (INJ)-P
22 MERV RETTENMUND-CH
23 GLENN EZELL-CH
23 VICTOR CRUZ-P
24 DAVE SCHMIDT (INJ)-P
25 BUDDY BELL-3B
26 GEORGE WRIGHT-OF
28 FRANK TANANA-P
29 JOHN BUTCHER-P
30 MARK WAGNER-SS
31 DAVE STEWART-P (2)
32 JON MATLACK-P
35 TOM HENKE-P
37 RICH DONNELLY-CH
38 RICKY WRIGHT-P (2)
40 RICK HONEYCUTT-P (1)
41 DAVE TOBIK-P
42 WAYNE (TWIG) TERWILLIGER-CH
43 DONNIE SCOTT-C
44 DANNY DARWIN-P
46 JIM ANDERSON-UTIL
48 MIKE SMITHSON-P
49 CHARLIE HOUGH-P
51 AL LACHOWICZ-P
52 DICK SUCH-CH

1984

7TH W 69-92 14.5GB

1 BILL STEIN (INJ)-UTIL
2 MIKE RICHARDT-2B (1)
2 ALAN BANNISTER (INJ)-UTIL (2)
3 WAYNE TOLLESON-2B/UTIL
5 BILLY SAMPLE-OF/DH
6 BOBBY JONES-UTIL
9 PETE O'BRIEN-1B/OF
10 NED YOST-C
11 DOUG (THE RED ROOSTER) (ROJO) RADER-MGR
12 DAVE HOSTETLER-1B/DH
13 TOMMY DUNBAR-OF/DH
14 JIM ANDERSON-INF
15 LARRY PARRISH-DH/UTIL
16 MIKE MASON-P
17 MICKEY RIVERS-DH/OF
18 GLENN EZELL-CH
19 CURTIS WILKERSON-SS/2B
20 KEVIN BUCKLEY-DH
20 JEFF KUNKEL-SS/DH
21 ODELL JONES-P
22 MERV RETTENMUND-CH
22 JIM BIBBY-P
24 DAVE SCHMIDT-P
25 BUDDY BELL-3B
26 GEORGE WRIGHT (INJ)-OF/DH
28 FRANK TANANA-P
29 MERV RETTENMUND-CH
30 MARV FOLEY-UTIL
31 DAVE STEWART-P
32 GARY WARD-OF/DH
35 TOM HENKE-P
36 DWAYNE HENRY-P
36 DICKIE NOLES-P (2)
37 RICH DONNELLY-CH
38 RICKY WRIGHT-P
41 DAVE TOBIK-P
42 WAYNE (TWIG) TERWILLIGER-CH
43 DONNIE SCOTT-C
44 DANNY DARWIN-P
45 DWAYNE HENRY-P
49 CHARLIE HOUGH-P
52 DICK SUCH-CH
53 JOEY MCLAUGHLIN-P (2)

1985

7TH W 62-99 28.5GB

0 ODDIBE MCDOWELL-OF/DH
1 BILL STEIN-UTIL
2 ALAN BANNISTER-UTIL
2 BOBBY VALENTINE-MGR2
3 WAYNE TOLLESON-INF/DH
4 DON SLAUGHT (INJ)-C
5 DOUG (THE RED ROOSTER) (ROJO) RADER-MGR1
5 ALAN BANNISTER-UTIL
6 BOBBY JONES-UTIL
7 GLENN BRUMMER-C/UTIL
8 LUIS PUJOLS (INJ)-C
9 PETE O'BRIEN-1B
10 ART HOWE-CH
11 DOUG (THE RED ROOSTER) (ROJO) RADER-MGR1
11 TOBY HARRAH-2B/UTIL
12 GENO PETRALLI-C
13 TOMMY DUNBAR-DH/OF
15 LARRY PARRISH (INJ)-OF/UTIL
16 MIKE MASON-P
17 ELLIS VALENTINE-OF/DH
18 GLENN EZELL-CH
19 CURTIS WILKERSON-SS/UTIL
20 JEFF KUNKEL-SS
21 GLENN EZELL-CH
21 DUANE WALKER-OF/DH (2)
22 MERV RETTENMUND-CH
22 STEVE BUECHELE-3B/2B
23 JOSE GUZMAN-P
24 DAVE SCHMIDT-P
25 BUDDY BELL-3B (1)
26 GEORGE WRIGHT-OF/DH
27 GREG A. HARRIS-P
28 FRANK TANANA-P (1)
28 BOB SEBRA-P (2)
29 JOSE GUZMAN-P
29 MATT WILLIAMS-P
30 DAVE ROZEMA (INJ)-P
31 DALE MURRAY-P (2)
32 GARY WARD-OF/DH
33 GLEN COOK-P
35 TOM HOUSE-CH
36 DICKIE NOLES (INJ)-P
37 RICH DONNELLY-CH
38 RICKY WRIGHT-P
39 NICK CAPRA-OF
40 TOMMY BOGGS-P
40 JEFF RUSSELL-P
41 CHRIS WELSH-P
42 WAYNE (TWIG) TERWILLIGER-CH
43 DAVE STEWART-P (1)
44 CLIFF JOHNSON (INJ)-DH (1)
44 RICK SURHOFF-P (2)
45 DWAYNE HENRY-P
46 BURT HOOTON-P
48 DAVE STEWART-P (1)
49 CHARLIE HOUGH-P
52 DICK SUCH-CH
59 DUANE WALKER-OF/DH (2)

1986

2ND W 87-75 5GB

0 ODDIBE MCDOWELL-OF/DH
1 SCOTT FLETCHER-SS/UTIL
2 BOBBY VALENTINE-MGR
3 JERRY BROWNE-2B
3 RUBEN SIERRA-OF/DH
4 DON SLAUGHT-C/DH
5 PETE (INKY) INCAVIGLIA-OF/DH
5 MIKE STANLEY-UTIL
6 BOBBY JONES-OF/1B
7 ORLANDO MERCADO-C
9 PETE O'BRIEN-1B
10 ART HOWE-CH
11 TOBY HARRAH-2B
12 GENO PETRALLI-UTIL
13 JOE FERGUSON-CH
14 TIM FOLI-CH
15 LARRY PARRISH-DH/3B
16 MIKE MASON-P
17 DARRELL PORTER-C/DH
18 ED CORREA-P
19 CURTIS WILKERSON-INF/DH
20 JEFF KUNKEL-SS/DH
22 STEVE BUECHELE-3B/UTIL
23 JOSE GUZMAN-P
24 RICKY WRIGHT (INJ)-P
25 DARRELL PORTER-C/DH
26 GEORGE WRIGHT-OF/DH
27 GREG A. HARRIS-P
28 MITCH (WILD THING) WILLIAMS-P
29 PETE (INKY) INCAVIGLIA-OF/DH
30 DAVE ROZEMA-P
31 TOM ROBSON-CH
32 GARY WARD (ILL)-OF/DH
34 TOM PACIOREK-UTIL
34 DALE MOHORCIC-P
35 TOM HOUSE-CH
38 RICKY WRIGHT (INJ)-P
38 RON MERIDITH-P
40 JEFF RUSSELL-P
41 JOE FERGUSON-CH
42 MICKEY MAHLER-P (1)
43 BOB BROWER-OF/DH
43 KEVIN BROWN-P
44 TOM PACIOREK-UTIL
45 DWAYNE HENRY (INJ)-P
46 MIKE LOYND-P
47 RUBEN SIERRA-OF/DH
48 BOBBY WITT-P
49 CHARLIE HOUGH (INJ)-P
50 MICKEY MAHLER-P (1)
50 MIKE LOYND-P

1987

6TH (TIE) W 75-87 10GB

0 ODDIBE MCDOWELL-OF
1 SCOTT FLETCHER-SS
2 BOBBY VALENTINE-MGR
3 GREG TABOR-2B/DH
3 RUBEN SIERRA-OF
4 DON SLAUGHT-C/DH
5 MIKE STANLEY-UTIL
8 JERRY BROWNE-2B/DH
9 PETE O'BRIEN-1B/UTIL
10 ART HOWE-CH
12 GENO PETRALLI-UTIL
13 JOE FERGUSON-CH
14 TIM FOLI-CH
15 LARRY PARRISH-DH/UTIL
16 MIKE MASON-P (1)
16 BOB MALLOY-P
17 DARRELL PORTER-UTIL
18 CECIL ESPY-OF
18 ED CORREA (INJ)-P
19 CURTIS WILKERSON-INF/DH
20 JEFF KUNKEL (INJ)-UTIL
21 ED CORREA (INJ)-P
21 RUBEN SIERRA-OF
22 STEVE BUECHELE-3B/UTIL
23 JOSE GUZMAN-P
26 DAVE OLIVER-CH
27 GREG A. HARRIS-P
28 MITCH (WILD THING) WILLIAMS-P
29 PETE (INKY) INCAVIGLIA-OF/DH
30 MIKE JEFFCOAT-P
31 TOM ROBSON-CH
33 BOB BROWER-OF/DH
34 DALE MOHORCIC-P
35 TOM HOUSE-CH
36 BOBBY WITT (INJ)-P
38 RON MERIDITH-P
39 PAUL KILGUS-P
40 JEFF RUSSELL (INJ)-P
41 TOM O'MALLEY-3B/2B
42 KEITH CREEL-P
44 TOM PACIOREK (INJ)-UTIL
45 DWAYNE HENRY-P
46 MIKE LOYND-P
48 SCOTT ANDERSON-P
49 CHARLIE HOUGH-P
50 GARY MIELKE-P
51 DAVE MEIER-OF
53 ED CORREA (INJ)-P
57 STEVE HOWE (SUS)-P

1988

6TH W 70-91 33.5GB

0 ODDIBE MCDOWELL-OF/DH
1 SCOTT FLETCHER-SS
2 BOBBY VALENTINE-MGR
5 MIKE STANLEY-UTIL
6 CECIL ESPY-UTIL
7 CHAD KREUTER-C
8 JERRY BROWNE-2B
9 PETE O'BRIEN-1B/DH
10 ART HOWE-CH
10 JIM SUNBERG-C (2)
12 GENO PETRALLI-C/UTIL
13 LARRY SEE-UTIL
14 DAVEY LOPES-CH
15 LARRY PARRISH-DH (1)
15 DAVEY LOPES-CH
16 ART HOWE-CH
17 BARBARO GARBEY (INJ)-UTIL
(18) ED CORREA (INJ)-(P)
18 CECIL ESPY-UTIL
19 CURTIS WILKERSON-2B/UTIL
20 JEFF KUNKEL-UTIL/P
21 RUBEN SIERRA-OF/DH
22 STEVE BUECHELE-3B/2B
23 JOSE GUZMAN-P
24 STEVE KEMP-UTIL
(25) BRAD ARNSBERG (INJ)-(P)
26 DAVE OLIVER-CH
27 JIM STEELS-UTIL
28 MITCH (WILD THING) WILLIAMS-P

WASHINGTON SENATORS/**TEXAS RANGERS**

9 PETE (INKY) INCAVIGLIA (INJ)-OF/DH
0 MIKE JEFFCOAT-P
1 TOM ROBSON-CH
2 RAY HAYWARD (INJ)-P
3 BOB BROWER-OF/DH
4 DALE MOHORCIC-P (1)
4 STEVE WILSON-P
5 TOM HOUSE-CH
6 BOBBY WITT-P
7 JOSE CECENA (INJ)-P
8 CRAIG MCMURTRY-P
9 PAUL KILGUS-P
0 JEFF RUSSELL-P
1 KEVIN BROWN-P
2 GUY HOFFMAN-P
3 ED VANDE BERG-P
3 GUY HOFFMAN-P
5 DWAYNE HENRY-P
6 TONY FOSSAS-P
7 KEVIN REIMER-DH
8 SCOTT MAY-P
9 CHARLIE HOUGH-P
1 CECELIO GUANTE-P (2)
2 DICK EGAN-CH
3) ED CO9RREA (INJ)-(P)
4 DEWAYNE VAUGHN-P

1989

4TH W 83-79 16GB

1 SCOTT FLETCHER-SS/DH (1)
2 BOBBY VALENTINE-MGR
3 RAFAEL PALMEIRO-1B/DH
3 HAROLD BAINES-DH/OF (2)
5 MIKE STANLEY-UTIL
6 CECIL ESPY-UTIL
7 CHAD KREUTER-C
8 JACK DAUGHERTY-UTIL
9 RICK LEACH-UTIL
0 JIM SUNBERG-C/DH
0 TOBY HARRAH-CH
2 GENO PETRALLI-C/DH
3 HAROLD BAINES-DH/OF (2)
3 JUAN GONZALEZ-OF
4 JULIO FRANCO-2B/DH
5 DAVEY LOPES-CH
6 DEAN PALMER-UTIL
7 SAMMY SOSA-OF/DH (1)
7 FRED MANRIQUE-INF (2)
9 THAD BOSLEY-OF/DH
9 JEFF STONE-DH/OF (1)
9 JUAN GONZALEZ-OF
0 JEFF KUNKEL-UTIL/P
1 RUBEN SIERRA-OF
2 STEVE BUECHELE-3B/UTIL
23) JOSE GUZMAN (INJ)-(P)
4 DARREL AKERFELDS-P
5 BUDDY BELL-DH/INF
5 RAFAEL PALMEIRO-1B/DH
6 DAVE OLIVER-CH
7 JOHN BARFIELD-P
8 BRAD ARNSBERG-P
9 PETE (INKY) INCAVIGLIA-OF/DH
0 MIKE JEFFCOAT-P
1 TOM ROBSON-CH
2 THAD BOSLEY-OF/DH
4 NOLAN RYAN-P
5 TOM HOUSE-CH
6 BOBBY WITT-P
7 KENNY ROGERS-P
8 CRAIG MCMURTRY (INJ)-P
9 JAMIE MOYER (INJ)-P
0 JEFF RUSSELL-P
1 KEVIN BROWN-P
2 SCOTT COOLBAUGH-3B/DH
3 WILSON ALVAREZ-P
4 DREW HALL-P
7 KEVIN REIMER-DH
9 CHARLIE HOUGH-P
0 GARY MIELKE-P
51 CECELIO GUANTE-P
52 DICK EGAN-CH
54 PAUL WILMET-P

1990

3RD W 83-79 23GB

2 BOBBY VALENTINE-MGR
3 HAROLD BAINES-DH/OF (1)
4 CECIL ESPY-UTIL
5 MIKE STANLEY-UTIL
6 CECIL ESPY-UTIL
7 CHAD KREUTER-C/DH
8 JACK DAUGHERTY-UTIL
9 JEFF HUSON-SS/INF
11 TOBY HARRAH-CH
12 GENO PETRALLI-C/INF
14 JULIO FRANCO-2B/DH
15 DAVEY LOPES-CH
17 JOHN RUSSELL-UTIL
18 KEVIN BELCHER-OF
19 JUAN GONZALEZ-OF/DH
20 JEFF KUNKEL (INJ)-UTIL
21 RUBEN SIERRA-OF/DH
22 STEVE BUECHELE (INJ)-3B/2B
(23) JOSE GUZMAN (INJ)-(P)
24 GARY PETTIS-OF/DH
25 RAFAEL PALMEIRO-1B/DH
26 DAVE OLIVER-CH
27 JOHN BARFIELD-P
28 BRAD ARNSBERG-P
29 PETE (INKY) INCAVIGLIA-OF/DH
30 MIKE JEFFCOAT (INJ)-P
31 TOM ROBSON-CH
32 THAD BOSLEY-OF/DH
33 BILL HASELMAN-DH/C
34 NOLAN RYAN-P
35 TOM HOUSE-CH
36 BOBBY WITT-P
37 KENNY ROGERS-P
38 CRAIG MCMURTRY-P
39 JAMIE MOYER-P
40 JEFF RUSSELL (INJ)-P
41 KEVIN BROWN (INJ)-P
42 SCOTT COOLBAUGH-3B
43 SCOTT CHIAMPARINO-P
44 JOHN HOOVER-P
44 JOE BITKER-P (2)
45 BRIAN BOHANON-P
47 KEVIN REIMER-DH
48 GERALD ALEXANDER-P
49 CHARLIE HOUGH-P
50 GARY MIELKE (INJ)-P
51 RAMON MANON-P
57 GARY GREEN-SS

1991

3RD W 85-77 10GB

1 GARY GREEN (INJ)-SS
2 BOBBY VALENTINE-MGR
3 JOSE HERNANDEZ-SS/3B
3 DENNY WALLING-3B/OF
4 MONTY FARISS-UTIL
5 MIKE STANLEY-UTIL
6 MARIO DIAZ-INF/DH
7 CHAD KREUTER-C
7 IVAN (PUDGE) RODRIGUEZ-C
8 JACK DAUGHERTY (INJ)-UTIL
9 JEFF HUSON-SS/INF
10 NICK CAPRA-OF
10 MARK PARENT (INJ)-C
11 TOBY HARRAH-CH
12 GENO PETRALLI (INJ)-UTIL
13 ORLANDO GOMEZ-CH
14 JULIO FRANCO-2B
15 DAVEY LOPES-CH
16 DEAN PALMER-UTIL
17 JOHN RUSSELL (INJ)-UTIL
18 TONY SCRUGGS-OF
19 JUAN GONZALEZ-OF/DH
(20) JEFF KUNKEL (INJ)-(UTIL)
21 RUBEN SIERRA-OF
22 STEVE BUECHELE-3B/INF (1)
23 JOSE GUZMAN-P
24 GARY PETTIS-OF/DH
25 RAFAEL PALMEIRO-1B/DH
26 DAVE OLIVER-CH
27 JOHN BARFIELD-P
28 BRAD ARNSBERG (INJ)-P
29 OIL CAN BOYD-P (2)
30 MIKE JEFFCOAT-P
31 TOM ROBSON-CH
32 HECTOR FAJARDO-P (2)
32 TERRY MATHEWS-P
32 CALVIN SCHIRALDI-P
33 DONALD HARRIS-OF/DH
34 NOLAN RYAN-P
35 TOM HOUSE-CH
36 BOBBY WITT (INJ)-P
37 KENNY ROGERS-P
38 CALVIN SCHIRALDI-P
38 TERRY MATHEWS-P
39 ROB MAURER-1B/DH
40 JEFF RUSSELL-P
41 KEVIN BROWN-P
42 ERIC NOLTE-P (2)
43 SCOTT CHIAMPARINO (INJ)-P
44 BARRY MANUEL-P
44 JOE BITKER-P
45 BRIAN BOHANON (INJ)-P
47 KEVIN REIMER-OF/DH
48 GERALD ALEXANDER-P
52 JIM POOLE-P (1)
52 WAYNE ROSENTHAL-P
54 GOOSE GOOSAGE-P
55 BRIAN DOWNING-DH
56 MARK PETKOVSEK-P

1992

4TH W 77-85 19GB

1 JEFF FRYE-2B
2 BOBBY VALENTINE-MGR1
3 JEFF RUSSELL (INJ)-C/OF
4 MONTY FARISS-UTIL
5 BRIAN DOWNING-DH
6 PERRY HILL-CH
7 IVAN (PUDGE) RODRIGUEZ-C
8 AL NEWMAN-2B/UTIL
8 JACK DAUGHERTY-1B/OF
9 JEFF HUSON-UTIL
10 DICKIE THON-SS
11 TOBY HARRAH-CH/MGR2
12 GENO PETRALLI-UTIL
13 ORLANDO GOMEZ-CH
14 JULIO FRANCO (INJ)-UTIL
15 JOHN CANGELOSI-OF
15 DAVID HULSE-OF
16 DEAN PALMER-3B
17 FLOYD BANNISTER-P
18 DON CARMAN-P
18 DONALD HARRIS-OF/DH
19 JUAN GONZALEZ-OF/DH
20 JEFF ROBINSON-P (1)
20 MARIO DIAZ-INF
21 RUBEN SIERRA-OF/DH (1)
22 JACK DAUGHERTY-1B/OF
22 FLOYD BANNISTER-P
23 JOSE GUZMAN-P
24 MIKE CAMPBELL-P
24 RAY STEPHENS-C
25 RAFAEL PALMEIRO-1B/DH
26 DAVE OLIVER-CH
28 TODD BURNS-P
29 EDWIN NUNEZ-P (2)
29 STEVE FIREOVID-P
30 MIKE JEFFCOAT-P
31 TOM ROBSON-CH
33 DONALD HARRIS-OF/DH
33 JOSE CANSECO-OF/DH (2)
34 NOLAN RYAN (INJ)-P
35 TOM HOUSE-CH
36 BOBBY WITT (INJ)-P
37 KENNY ROGERS-P
38 TERRY MATHEWS-P
39 ROB MAURER-1B/DH
40 JEFF RUSSELL-P (1)
41 KEVIN BROWN-P
42 DAN SMITH-P
43 SCOTT CHIAMPARINO-P
44 BARRY MANUEL-P
45 BRIAN BOHANON (INJ)-P
46 LANCE MCCULLERS-P
46 MATT WHITESIDE-P
47 KEVIN REIMER-OF/DH
48 GERALD ALEXANDER-P
49 DANNY LEON-P
50 RAY BURRIS-CH
52 WAYNE ROSENTHAL-P
53 DAN PELTIER-OF
54 CHRIS COLON-SS
57 RUSS MCGINNIS-UTIL
59 ROGER PAVLIK-P
66 DOUG (CRASH) DAVIS-C

1993

2ND W 86-76 8GB

(1) JEFF FRYE (INJ)-(INF)
2 MANNY LEE (INJ)-SS/DH
3 BILLY RIPKEN (INJ)-INF
4 CHRIS JAMES-OF (2)
5 GARY REDUS-UTIL
6 MARIO DIAZ-INF
7 IVAN (PUDGE) RODRIGUEZ-C/DH
8 JOHN RUSSELL (INJ)-UTIL
9 JEFF HUSON (INJ)-INF/DH
10 JON SHAVE-SS/2B
11 CRAIG LEFFERTS-P
12 GENO PETRALLI (INJ)-UTIL
13 BUTCH DAVIS-OF/DH
14 JULIO FRANCO-DH
15 DAVID HULSE-OF/DH
16 DEAN PALMER (INJ)-3B/SS
17 DAN PELTIER-OF/1B
18 DONALD HARRIS-OF/DH
19 JUAN GONZALEZ-OF/DH
20 DOUG STRANGE-2B/INF
22 BENJI GIL-SS
23 MIKE SCHOOLER-P
23 GENE NELSON-P (2)
24 STEVE DREYER-P
25 RAFAEL PALMEIRO-1B
26 DAVE OLIVER-CH
27 MATT WHITESIDE-P
28 TODD BURNS-P (1)
28 DARREN OLIVER-P
29 DOUG DASCENZO-OF/DH
31 ROBB NEN (INJ)-P (1)
31 CRIS CARPENTER-P (2)
32 CHARLIE LEIBRANDT (INJ)-P
33 JOSE CANSECO (INJ)-OF/DH/P
34 NOLAN RYAN (INJ)-P
36 STEVE BALBONI-DH
37 KENNY ROGERS-P
38 BOB PATTERSON-P
39 RICK REED-P (2)
40 ROB DUCEY-OF
41 KEVIN BROWN-P
42 JACKIE MOORE-CH
43 MICKEY HATCHER-CH
44 KEVIN KENNEDY-MGR
45 BRIAN BOHANON-P
46 WILLIE UPSHAW-CH
47 PERRY HILL-CH
48 CLAUDE OSTEEN-CH
50 TOM HENKE-P
51 JEFF BRONKEY-P
59 ROGER PAVLIK-P

1994

1ST W 52-62 0GB

STRIKE NO POST-SEASON

0 JUNIOR ORTIZ-C
1 JEFF FRYE (INJ)-2B
2 MANNY LEE (INJ)-SS
3 BILLY RIPKEN (INJ)-2B/3B
4 CHRIS JAMES (INJ)-OF
5 GARY REDUS (INJ)-UTIL
6 ESTEBAN BELTRE-SS
7 IVAN (PUDGE) RODRIGUEZ-C/DH
8 ODDIBE MCDOWELL (INJ)-OF
(9) JEFF HUSON (INJ)-(INF)
(10) JON SHAVE (INJ)-(INF)
11 CHUCK JACKSON-2B
12 ROB DUCEY-OF
13 BUTCH DAVIS-OF/DH
15 DAVID HULSE-OF/DH
16 DEAN PALMER (INJ)-3B/SS
19 JUAN GONZALEZ-OF/DH
20 DOUG STRANGE (INJ)-2B/INF
21 JOHN DETTMER-P
22 WILL (THE THRILL) CLARK-1B
24 STEVE DREYER-P
25 JAMES HURST-P
26 DAVE OLIVER-CH
27 MATT WHITESIDE-P
28 DARREN OLIVER-P
29 RUSTY GREER-OF
30 HECTOR FAJARDO-P
31 CRIS CARPENTER-P
32 RICKY HELLING-P
33 JOSE CANSECO-OF/DH
35 DAN SMITH (INJ)-P
36 TIM LEARY (INJ)-P
37 KENNY ROGERS-P
38 TERRY BURROWS-P
39 RICK REED-P
39 DUFF BRUMLEY-P
40 RICK HONEYCUTT (INJ)-P
41 KEVIN BROWN-P
42 JACKIE MOORE-CH
43 MICKEY HATCHER-CH
44 KEVIN KENNEDY-MGR
45 BRIAN BOHANON-P
46 WILLIE UPSHAW-CH
47 PERRY HILL-CH
47 BRUCE HURST (RET)-P
48 CLAUDE OSTEEN-CH
49 PERRY HILL-CH
50 TOM HENKE (INJ)-P
52 JAY HOWELL-P
59 ROGER PAVLIK (INJ)-P
61 JAMES HURST-P
77 JACK ARMSTRONG (INJ)-P

1995

3RD W 74-70 4.5GB

144 GAME SEASON

1 JEFF FRYE (INJ)-2B
2 OTIS NIXON-OF
3 MARK MCLEMORE-OF
4 LOU FRAZIER-OF (2)
5 BUCKY DENT-CH
5 JERRY NARRON-CH
6 ESTEBAN BELTRE-SS
7 IVAN (PUDGE) RODRIGUEZ-C
8 RUDY JARAMILLO-CH
9 LUIS ORTIZ-3B
10 DAVE VALLE-C
11 JERRY NARRON-CH
12 ED NAPOLEON-CH

13 MIKE PAGLIARULO-1B
14 BILLY HATCHER-OF
14 JOHN MARZANO-C
15 MICKEY TETTLETON-DH
16 DEAN PALMER (INJ)-3B
17 DICK BOSMAN-CH
18 ERIC FOX-OF
(19) JUAN GONZALEZ (INJ)-(OF)
20 BUCKY DENT-CH
21 JOHN DETTMER-P
21 JACK VOIGT-UTIL (2)
21 CANDY MALDONADO-OF (2)
22 WILL (THE THRILL) CLARK-1B
23 BENJI GIL-SS
24 STEVE BUCHELE (REL)-3B (2)
24 CRAIG WORTHINGTON-3B (2)
25 LARRY HARDY-CH
26 JOHNNY OATES-MGR
27 MATT WHITESIDE (INJ)-P
28 DARREN OLIVER (INJ)-P
29 RUSTY GREER-OF
30 HECTOR FAJARDO-P (1)
30 SAM HORN-DH
31 ROGER MCDOWELL-P
32 RICKY HELLING-P
36 BOBBY WITT-P
37 KENNY ROGERS-P
38 TERRY BURROWS-P
39 BOB TEWKSBURY (INJ)-P
40 JEFF RUSSELL (INJ)-P
40 DANNY DARWIN-P (2)
41 CHRIS H. HOWARD-DH (2)
42 DENNIS COOK-P (2)
44 DANNY DARWIN-P (2)
45 SHAWN HARE-DH
46 KEVIN GROSS-P
48 JOSE ALBERRO-P
51 MARK BRANDENBERG-P
52 ED VOSBERG-P
53 TERRY BURROWS-P
54 CHRIS NICHTING-P
55 WILSON HEREDIA-P (1)
57 SCOTT TAYLOR-P
59 ROGER PAVLIK-P
61 PERRY HILL-CH

1996

1ST W 90-72 0GB
L ALDS-NYA 3-1

1 KURT STILLWELL (INJ)-2B
2 DAMON BUFORD-OF
3 MARK MCLEMORE-OF
4 DARRYL HAMILTON-OF
5 JERRY NARRON-CH
6 KEVIN L. BROWN-C
7 IVAN (PUDGE) RODRIGUEZ-C
8 RUDY JARAMILLO-CH
9 LUIS ORTIZ-3B
10 DAVE VALLE-C
11 LEE STEVENS (INJ)-1B
12 ED NAPOLEON-CH
14 LOU FRAZIER-DH
15 MICKEY TETTLETON-DH
16 DEAN PALMER-3B
17 DICK BOSMAN-CH
18 KEVIN ELSTER-SS
19 JUAN GONZALEZ (INJ)-OF
20 BUCKY DENT-CH
21 WARREN NEWSON-OF
22 WILL (THE THRILL) CLARK-1B
23 BENJI GIL (INJ)-SS
24 CRAIG WORTHINGTON (REL)-3B
24 JACK VOIGT-OF/3B
25 LARRY HARDY-CH
26 JOHNNY OATES-MGR
27 MATT WHITESIDE-P
28 DARREN OLIVER-P
29 RUSTY GREER-OF
30 RIKKERT FANEYTE-2B/OF
32 RICKY HELLING-P (1)
32 MIKE STANTON-P (2)
33 JOHN BURKETT-P
34 *(RET#) NOLAN RYAN*
36 BOBBY WITT-P
37 GIL HEREDIA-P
39 MIKE HENNEMAN-P
40 JEFF RUSSELL-P
(41) CHRIS H. HOWARD-(INJ)-(P)
42 DENNIS COOK-P
44 KEN HILL-P
46 KEVIN GROSS (INJ)-P
48 JOSE ALBERRO-P
51 MARK BRANDENBERG-P (1)
52 ED VOSBERG-P
(54) CHRIS NICHTING (INJ)-(P)
56 DANNY PATTERSON (INJ)-P
59 ROGER PAVLIK-P
88 RENE GONZALES-1B

1997

3RD W 77-85 13GB

1 DOMINGO CEDENO (INJ)-SS/2B
2 DAMON BUFORD-OF
3 MARK MCLEMORE (INJ)-2B
4 FERNANDO TATIS-3B
5 JERRY NARRON-CH
6 KEVIN L. BROWN-C
7 IVAN (PUDGE) RODRIGUEZ-C
8 RUDY JARAMILLO-CH
9 BILLY RIPKEN (INJ)-SS/2B
10 HENRY MERCEDES-C
11 LEE STEVENS (INJ)-1B/OF
12 ED NAPOLEON-CH
13 JIM LEYRITZ-C/1B (2)
14 DAVE SILVESTRI (INJ)-SS
14 ALEX DIAZ-PH
15 MICKEY TETTLETON (INJ) (RET)-DH
16 DEAN PALMER-3B (1)
17 DICK BOSMAN-CH
18 MIKE SIMMS (INJ)-OF
19 JUAN GONZALEZ (INJ)-OF
20 BUCKY DENT-CH
21 WARREN NEWSON (INJ)-OF
22 WILL (THE THRILL) CLARK-1B
23 BENJI GIL-SS
24 MIKE DEVEREAUX (REL)-OF
24 TOM GOODWIN-OF (2)
25 LARRY HARDY-CH
26 JOHNNY OATES-MGR
27 MATT WHITESIDE-P
28 DARREN OLIVER-P
29 RUSTY GREER-OF
30 HANLEY FRIAS-SS
31 XAVIER HERNANDEZ (INJ)-P
32 RICKY HELLING-P (2)
33 JOHN BURKETT (INJ)-P
34 *(RET#) NOLAN RYAN*
35 JOHN WETTELAND-P
36 BOBBY WITT-P
37 MARC SAGMOEN-OF
42 *(RET#) JACKIE ROBINSON*
44 KEN HILL (INJ)-P (1)
45 ERIC MOODY-P
46 TERRY CLARK-P (2)
47 TANYON STURTZE-P
48 JOSE ALBERRO (WAIV)-P (1)
48 WILSON HEREDIA-P
52 ED VOSBERG-P (1)
52 BRYAN EVERSGERD-P
53 ERIC GUNDERSON (INJ)-P
56 DANNY PATTERSON (INJ)-P
58 CORY BAILEY-P (1)
58 SCOTT BAILES-P
59 ROGER PAVLIK (INJ)-P
60 JULIO SANTANA-P

1998

1ST W 88-74 0GB
L ALDS-NYA 3-0

1 DOMINGO CEDENO-INF
3 MARK MCLEMORE (INJ)-2B
4 FERNANDO TATIS-3B (1)
4 MILT CUYLER-OF/DH
5 JERRY NARRON-CH
7 IVAN (PUDGE) RODRIGUEZ-C
8 RUDY JARAMILLO-CH
(9) RICK WRONA-(C)
9 LEE STEVENS (INJ)-1B/OF
10 LUIS ALICEA-2B/3B/DH
11 LEE STEVENS (INJ)-1B/OF
11 ROYCE CLAYTON-SS (2)
12 ED NAPOLEON-CH
14 ALEX DIAZ-PH
14 SCOTT SHELDON-UTIL
14 ROB SASSER-PH
16 MIKE SIMMS-OF/DH
17 DICK BOSMAN-CH
18 KEVIN ELSTER (INJ) (WAIV)-SS
18 CHRIS TREMIE-DH
19 JUAN GONZALEZ-OF
20 BUCKY DENT-CH
21 WARREN NEWSON-OF/DH (2)
22 WILL (THE THRILL) CLARK (INJ)-1B
23 TIM CRABTREE-P
24 TOM GOODWIN-OF
25 LARRY HARDY-CH
25 ESTEBAN LOAIZA-P (2)
26 JOHNNY OATES-MGR
27 TODD ZEILE-3B (3)
28 DARREN OLIVER (INJ)-P (1)
29 RUSTY GREER-OF
30 AARON SELE-P
31 XAVIER HERNANDEZ (INJ)-P
32 RICKY HELLING-P
33 JOHN BURKETT-P
34 *(RET#) NOLAN RYAN*
35 JOHN WETTELAND-P
36 BOBBY WITT-P (1)
36 GREG CADARET-P (2)
37 BILL HASELMAN-C
39 ROBERTO KELLY (INJ)-OF
40 MATT PERISHO-P
42 *(RET#) JACKIE ROBINSON*
43 AL LEVINE-P
44 TODD STOTTLEMYRE-P (2)
45 JONATHAN JOHNSON-P
48 LARRY HARDY-CH
49 TONY FOSSAS-P (2)
(50) MARK BRANDENBURG (INJ)-(P)
51 TODD VAN POPPEL-P (1)
53 ERIC GUNDERSON-P
54 ESTEBAN LOAIZA-P (2)
56 DANNY PATTERSON (INJ)-P
58 SCOTT BAILES (INJ)-P
59 ROGER PAVLIK (INJ)-P
60 JULIO SANTANA-P (1)

1999

1ST W 95-67 0GB
L ALDS-NYA 3-0

3 MARK MCLEMORE (INJ)-2B
4 SCOTT SHELDON-INF
5 JERRY NARRON-CH
6 GREGG ZAUN-C
7 IVAN (PUDGE) RODRIGUEZ-C
8 RUDY JARAMILLO-CH
9 LEE STEVENS (INJ)-1B/OF
10 LUIS ALICEA-2B/3B/DH
11 ROYCE CLAYTON (INJ)-SS
12 ED NAPOLEON-CH
13 JEFF FASSERO-P (2)
15 JON SHAVE-INF
15 MIKE SIMMS (INJ)-OF/DH
17 DICK BOSMAN-CH
19 JUAN GONZALEZ-OF
20 BUCKY DENT-CH
21 RUBEN MATEO (INJ)-OF
23 TIM CRABTREE-P
24 TOM GOODWIN-OF
25 RAFAEL PALMEIRO-1B
26 JOHNNY OATES-MGR
27 TODD ZEILE-3B
28 ESTEBAN LOAIZA (INJ)-P
29 RUSTY GREER-OF
30 AARON SELE-P
32 RICKY HELLING-P
33 JOHN BURKETT (INJ)-P
34 *(RET#) NOLAN RYAN*
35 JOHN WETTELAND-P
36 MIKE MORGAN-P
37 COREY LEE-P
38 RUBEN MATEO (INJ)-OF
38 RYAN GLYNN-P
39 ROBERTO KELLY (INJ)-OF
40 RYAN GLYNN-P
40 MATT PERISHO-P
41 SCARBOROUGH GREEN-OF
42 *(RET#) JACKIE ROBINSON*
43 MICHAEL VENAFRO-P
44 KELLY DRANSFELDT-SS
46 DOUG DAVIS-P
48 LARRY HARDY-CH
50 JONATHAN JOHNSON-P
51 MIKE MUNOZ-P
52 DANNY KOLB-P
53 ERIC GUNDERSON-P
54 MARK CLARK-P
56 DANNY PATTERSON-P
59 JEFF ZIMMERMAN-P

2000

4TH W 71-91 20.5GB

1 DAVE MARTINEZ-OF (3)
2 JASON MCDONALD-OF
2 MIKE YOUNG-2B
3 CHAD CURTIS-OF
4 SCOTT SHELDON-INF
5 JERRY NARRON-CH
6 TOM EVANS (INJ)-INF
7 IVAN (PUDGE) RODRIGUEZ (INJ)-C
8 RUDY JARAMILLO-CH
9 PEDRO VALDES-OF
10 LUIS ALICEA-2B/3B/DH
11 ROYCE CLAYTON-SS
12 ED NAPOLEON-CH
12 RICKY LEDEE-OF (3)
13 MIKE LAMB-INF
14 DARREN OLIVER-P
15 RUBEN SIERRA-OF/DH
17 DICK BOSMAN-CH
18 GABE KAPLER-OF
19 JUAN GONZALEZ-OF (1)
20 BUCKY DENT-CH
21 RUBEN MATEO (INJ)-OF
(22) JUSTIN THOMPSON (INJ)-(P)
23 TIM CRABTREE-P
24 DAVID SEGUI-1B (1)
25 RAFAEL PALMEIRO-1B
26 JOHNNY OATES-MGR
27 FRANK CATALANOTTO-INF
28 ESTEBAN LOAIZA-P (1)
28 RUBEN SIERRA-OF/DH
29 RUSTY GREER-OF
30 FRANCISCO CORDERO-P
32 RICKY HELLING-P
33 BILL HASELMAN-C
34 *(RET#) NOLAN RYAN*
35 JOHN WETTELAND-P
37 KENNY ROGERS-P
38 RYAN GLYNN-P
39 B. J. WASZGIS-C
40 MATT PERISHO-P
41 SCARBOROUGH GREEN-OF
42 *(RET#) JACKIE ROBINSON*
43 MICHAEL VENAFRO-P
44 KELLY DRANSFELDT-SS
45 DARWIN CUBILLAN-P (2)
46 DOUG DAVIS-P
48 LARRY HARDY-CH
49 BRIAN SIKORSKI-P
50 JONATHAN JOHNSON-P
51 MIKE MUNOZ (INJ)-P
52 DANNY KOLB (INJ)-P
54 MARK CLARK-P
55 RANDY KNORR-C
59 JEFF ZIMMERMAN-P

2001

4TH W 73-89 43GB

2 MICHAEL YOUNG-2B
3 ALEX RODRIGUEZ-SS
4 SCOTT SHELDON-3B
5 JERRY NARRON-CH/MGR2
6 DOUG MIRABELLI-C (1)
6* ROB BELL-P*
7 IVAN (PUDGE) RODRIGUEZ (INJ)-C
8 RUDY JARAMILLO-CH
9 CHAD CURTIS (INJ)-OF
11 KEN CAMINITI (INJ) (REL)-3B (1)
11 CHRIS MAGRUDER-OF
12 RICKY LEDEE (INJ)-OF
13 MIKE LAMB-3B
14 ANDRES GALARRAGA-DH (1)
15 CARLOS PENA-1B
16 BO PORTER-OF
17 DOUG DAVIS-P
18 RANDY VELARDE (INJ)-INF (1)
19 GABE KAPLER (INJ)-OF
20 BUCKY DENT-CH
21 RUBEN MATEO-OF
21 CRAIG MONROE-OF
(22) JUSTIN THOMPSON (INJ)-(P)
23 PAT MAHOMES-P
24 RUBEN SIERRA-OF/DH
25 RAFAEL PALMEIRO-1B
26 JOHNNY OATES-MGR1
27 FRANK CATALANOTTO-2B
28 DARREN OLIVER (INJ)-P
29 RUSTY GREER (INJ)-OF
30 FRANCISCO CORDERO (INJ)-P
31 BOBBY JONES-CH
32 RICKY HELLING-P
33 BILL HASELMAN (INJ)-C
34 *(RET#) NOLAN RYAN*
35 TIM CRABTREE (INJ)-P
36 MIKE HUBBARD (INJ)-C
37 KENNY ROGERS-P
38 RYAN GLYNN-P
39 AARON MYETTE-P
41 JUAN MORENO (INJ)-P
42 *(RET#) JACKIE ROBINSON*
43 MICHAEL VENAFRO-P
44 J. D. SMART (INJ)-P
44 KELLY DRANSFELDT-SS
45 JEFF BRANTLEY (REL)-P
45 JUSTIN DUCHSCHERER-P
46 MARK PETKOVSEK-P

WASHINGTON SENATORS/**TEXAS RANGERS**

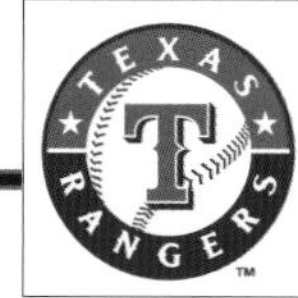

47 REID NICHOLS-CH
48 LARRY HARDY-CH
50 JONATHAN JOHNSON-P
50 BRANDON VILLAFUERTE-P
51 R. A. DICKEY-P
52 DANNY KOLB (INJ)-P
52 JUAN MORENO (INJ)-P
52 DANNY KOLB (INJ)-P
53 JOAQUIN BENOIT-P
55 CHRIS MICHALAK-P
56 KEVIN FOSTER-P
57 CLIFF BRUMBAUGH-OF
57 MARCUS JENSEN-C
58 MIKE JUDD-P (2)
59 JEFF ZIMMERMAN-P
__ BOBBY CUELLAR-CH

2002

4TH W 72-90 31GB

1 STEVE SMITH-CH
2 CARL EVERETT (INJ)-OF/DH
3 ALEX (A-ROD) RODRIGUEZ-SS
4 JASON ROMANO-OF/UTIL (1)
4 DONNIE SADLER-UTIL (2)
5 JERRY NARRON-MGR
6* ROB BELL-P*
6 TRAVIS HAFNER-DH/1B
7 IVAN (PUDGE) RODRIGUEZ (INJ)-C/DH
8 RUDY JARAMILLO-CH
9 JAMIE QUIRK-CH
10 MIKE YOUNG-2B/INF
11 TERRY FRANCONA-CH
12 HANK BLALOCK-3B
13 MIKE LAMB-UTIL
14 ISMAEL VALDES-P (1)
15 RYAN LUDWICK-OF
16 DAVE BURBA (REL)-P (1)
16 JASON HART-OF/1B
17 DOUG DAVIS-P
18 GABE KAPLER-OF (1)
19 JUAN GONZALEZ (INJ)-OF/DH
20 DEMARLO HALE-CH
21 REYNALDO GARCIA-P
21 TODD HOLLANDSWORTH-OF (2)
21 CALVIN MURRAY-OF/DH (2)
22 HECTOR ORTIZ-C
23 TODD GREENE-C/1B
24 RUBEN RIVERA-OF/DH
25 RAFAEL PALMEIRO-1B/DH
27 FRANK CATALANOTTO (INJ)-UTIL
28 KEVIN MENCH-OF/DH
29 RUSTY GREER (INJ)-OF/DH
30 ROB BELL-P
31 FRANCISCO CORDERO (INJ)-P
32 DAN MICELI-P
32 ANTHONY TELFORD-P
33 BILL HASELMAN-C/DH
34 *(RET#) NOLAN RYAN*
35 HERBERT PERRY-3B/UTIL
37 KENNY ROGERS-P
38 AARON MYETTE-P
39 JAY POWELL (INJ)-P
40 RUDY SEANEZ (INJ)-P
42 *(RET #) JACKIE ROBINSON*
43 STEVE WOODWARD-P
44 RICH RODRIGUES (INJ)-P
45 HIDEKI IRABU (INJ) (ILL)-P
46 DENNYS REYES-P (2)
47 TODD VAN POPPEL-P
48 COLBY LEWIS-P
49 JOHN ROCKER (INJ)-P
49 DANILO (DANNY) LEON-P
50 RANDY FLORES-P (1)
50 C. J. NITKOWSKI-P
51 JUAN ALVAREZ-P
52 DANNY KOLB (INJ)-P
53 JOAQUIN BENOIT-P
54 CHRIS MICHALAK-P
55 OREL HERSHISER-CH
56 BEN KOZLOWSKI-P
(59) JEFF ZIMMERMAN (INJ)-(P)
61 CHAN HO PARK (INJ)-P
__ OSCAR ACOSTA-CH

2003

4TH W 71-91 25GB

1 STEVE SMITH-CH
2 CARL EVERETT-OF (1)
2 RAMON NIVAR-OF
3 ALEX (A-ROD) RODRIGUEZ-SS
4 DONNIE SADLER-UTIL
5 EINAR DIAZ-C
6 DOUG GLANVILLE (INJ)-OF (1)
8 RUDY JARAMILLO-CH
9 HANK BLALOCK-3B/2B
10 MIKE YOUNG-2B/SS
11 BUCK SHOWALTER-MGR
12 CHAD KREUTER (REL)-C
13 MIKE LAMB-UTIL
14 ISMAEL VALDES (INJ)-P
15 RYAN LUDWICK-OF (1)
16 RYAN CHRISTENSON-OF
17 DOUG DAVIS-P (1)
17 LAYNCE NIX-OF
18 DON WAKAMATSU-CH
19 JUAN GONZALEZ (INJ)-OF/DH
20 DEMARLO HALE-CH
21 RUBEN SIERRA-DH/OF (1)
21 JASON JONES-OF/DH
22 TODD GREENE (INJ)-C/1B
23 MARK TEIXEIRA-1B/UTIL
24 JERMAINE CLARK (WAIV)-UTIL (1)(3)
25 RAFAEL PALMEIRO-DH/1B
27 TODD GREENE (INJ)-C/1B
27 MARCUS THAMES-OF
28 KEVIN MENCH (INJ)-OF
(29) RUSTY GREER (INJ)-(OF)
31 FRANCISCO CORDERO-P
32 RON MAHAY-P
34 *(RET#) NOLAN RYAN*
35 HERBERT PERRY (INJ)-1B/3B
36 MICKEY CALLAWAY-P (2)
37 RYAN DRESE-P
38 AARON FULTZ (INJ)-P
39 JAY POWELL (INJ)-P
40 MARIO RAMOS-P
41 UGUETH URBINA-P (1)
41 JUAN DOMINGUEZ-P
42 *(RET #) JACKIE ROBINSON*
43 ESTEBAN YAN-P (1)
43 TONY MOUNCE-P
44 ALAN BENES-P (2)
45 R. A. DICKEY-P
46 JOHN THOMSON-P
47 TODD VAN POPPEL (INJ) (REL)-P (1)
47 TONY MOUNCE-P
47 SHANE SPENCER-OF/1B/DH (2)
48 COLBY LEWIS-P
49 VICTOR SANTOS-P
50 C. J. NITKOWSKI-P
50 ROBERT ELLIS-P
51 GERALD LAIRD-C
52? MARK CONNOR-CH
53 JOAQUIN BENOIT (INJ)-P
54 ERASMO RAMIREZ-P
55 OREL HERSHISER-CH
56 ROSMAN GARCIA-P
57 REYNALDO GARCIA-P
58 BRIAN SHOUSE-P
(59) JEFF ZIMMERMAN (INJ)-(P)
61 CHAN HO PARK (INJ)-P

2004

3RD W 89-73 3GB

1 STEVE SMITH-CH
2 RAMON NIVAR-OF
4 MANNY ALEXANDER-SS
5 DANNY ARDOIN-C
5 ANDY FOX-2B (2)
6 GERALD LAIRD (INJ)-C
7 ERIC YOUNG-UTIL
8 RUDY JARAMILLO-CH
9 HANK BLALOCK-3B
10 MIKE YOUNG-2B/SS
11 BUCK SHOWALTER-MGR
12 ALFONSO SORIANO-2B
13 CHAD ALLEN-OF/DH
14 GARY MATTHEWS, JR.-OF
15 KEN HUCKABY-C (3)
16 DEMARLO HALE-CH
17 LAYNCE NIX-OF
18 DON WAKAMATSU-CH
19 JASON CONTI-OF
19 SCOTT ERICKSON-P (2)
20 BRAD FULLMER (INJ)-DH/1B
22 DAVE DELLUCCI-OF
23 MARK TEIXEIRA (INJ)-1B/DH
24 ADRIAN GONZALEZ-1B
27 ROD BARAJAS-C
28 KEVIN MENCH-OF
(29) RUSTY GREER (INJ)-(OF)
30 RICARDO RODRIGUEZ (INJ)-P
31 FRANCISCO CORDERO-P
32 RON MAHAY-P
33 BRIAN JORDAN (INJ)-OF/DH
34 *(RET#) NOLAN RYAN*
35 HERBERT PERRY (INJ)-DH/1B/3B
36 MICKEY CALLAWAY (INJ)-P
37 KENNY ROGERS-P
38 RYAN DRESE-P
39 JAY POWELL (INJ)-P
40 CARLOS ALMANZAR-P
41 JUAN DOMINGUEZ-P
42 *(RET #) JACKIE ROBINSON*
43 JEFF NELSON (INJ)-P
44 KAMERON LOE-P
45 R. A. DICKEY (INJ)-P
46 DOUG BROCAIL-P
47 JOHN WASDIN-P
48 COLBY LEWIS (INJ)-P
49 SAM NARRON-P (1)
50 FRANK FRANCISCO-P
51 NICK BIERBRODT-P
51 NICK BACSIK, JR.-P
52 MARK CONNOR-CH
53 JOAQUIN BENOIT-P
54 ERASMO RAMIREZ-P
55 OREL HERSHISER-CH
56 ROSMAN GARCIA-P
56 MICHAEL TEJERA-P (2)
57 NICK REGILIO-P
57 TRAVIS HUGHES-P
58 BRIAN SHOUSE (INJ)-P
(59) JEFF ZIMMERMAN (INJ)-(P)
61 CHAN HO PARK-P

2005

3RD W 79-83 16GB

1 STEVE SMITH-CH
2 ANDRES TORRES-OF
4 ESTEBAN GERMAN-2B
6 GERALD LAIRD (INJ)-C
7 MARK DEROSA-OF/SS
8 RUDY JARAMILLO-CH
9 HANK BLALOCK-3B
10 MIKE YOUNG-SS
11 BUCK SHOWALTER-MGR
12 ALFONSO SORIANO-2B
13 CHAD ALLEN-OF/DH
14 GARY MATTHEWS, JR. (INJ)-OF
15 SANDY ALOMAR, JR.-C
16 DEMARLO HALE-CH
17 LAYNCE NIX (INJ)-OF
18 DON WAKAMATSU-CH
(20) GREG COLBRUNN (INJ)-(DH)
21 STEVE KARSAY-P (2)
22 DAVE DELLUCCI-OF/DH
23 MARK TEIXEIRA-1B
24 ADRIAN GONZALEZ-1B/DH
25 MARSHALL MCDOUGALL-INF
25 PHIL NEVIN-1B/DH (2)
27 ROD BARAJAS-C
28 KEVIN MENCH-OF
30 RICARDO RODRIGUEZ (INJ)-P
31 FRANCISCO CORDERO-P
32 RON MAHAY (INJ)-P
34 *(RET#) NOLAN RYAN*
35 RYAN BUKVICH (INJ)-P
36 C. J. WILSON-P
37 KENNY ROGERS-P
38 RYAN DRESE-P (1)
38 JUSTIN THOMPSON-P
39 PEDRO ASTACIO (INJ)-P (1)
39 JAMES BALDWIN-P (2)
39 SCOTT FELDMAN-P
40 CARLOS ALMANZAR (INJ) (BRV)-P
40 EDISON VOLQUEZ-P
41 JUAN DOMINGUEZ-P
42 *(RET #) JACKIE ROBINSON*
43 KAMERON LOE-P
44 JASON STANDRIDGE-P (1)
44 JASON BOTTS-OF/DH
45 R. A. DICKEY (INJ)-P
46 DOUG BROCAIL-P
47 JOHN WASDIN-P
48 MATT RILEY-P
48 KEVIN GRYBOSKI (SUS:3G)-P (2)
49 CHRIS YOUNG-P
50 FRANK FRANCISCO (INJ)-P
51 RICHARD HIDALGO (INJ)-OF
52 MARK CONNOR-CH
53 JOAQUIN BENOIT (INJ)-P
54 ERASMO RAMIREZ (INJ)-P
55 OREL HERSHISER-CH
56 MICHAEL TEJERA-P
57 NICK REGILIO (INJ)-P
58 BRIAN SHOUSE-P
59 JOSH RUPE-P
61 CHAN HO PARK-P (1)

Ruben Sierra wore a Texas Rangers uniform in ten of his years in the Bigs. He preferred #21, but has worn numbers 47, 3, 16, 28, and 24 while on the Rangers. He has hit the majority (180) of his HRs while with the club. A four-time All-Star, he led the AL in triples (14) and RBI (119) and slugging (.543) in 1989—his best year.

TORONTO BLUE JAYS

1977
TORONTO BLUE JAYS
7TH E 54-107 45.5GB

1 BOB BAILOR (INJ)-UTIL
2 STEVE STAGGS-2B
3 STEVE BOWLING-OF
4 PHIL ROOF (INJ)-C
5 SAM EWING-UTIL
6 RON FAIRLY-DH/UTIL
7 ROY HARTSFIELD-MGR
8 ALAN ASHBY-C
9 RICK CERONE (INJ)-C
10 JIM MASON-SS (1)
10 DOUG (THE RED ROOSTER) (ROJO) RADER-UTIL (2)
11 JOHN SCOTT-OF/DH
12 ERNIE WHITT-C
13 ROY HOWELL (INJ)-3B/DH (2)
15 BOB MILLER-CH
16 TIM NORDBROOK-SS (2)
18 JIM CLANCY-P
19 OTTO VELEZ-OF/DH
20 AL WOODS-OF/DH
21 TOM BRUNO-P
22 DENNIS DEBARR-P
23 DAVE LEMANCZYK-P
24 CHUCK (TWIGGY) HARTENSTEIN (INJ)-P
25 DOUG AULT-1B/DH
26 STEVE HARGAN-P (1)
27 JEFF BYRD-P
28 MIKE DARR-P
29 HECTOR TORRES-SS/INF
30 PETE VUCKOVICH-P
31 BOBBY DOERR-CH
33 MIKE WILLIS-P
34 JESSE JEFFERSON-P
35 GARY WOODS-OF
36 JERRY GARVIN-P
38 PETE GARCIA-2B/DH
39 DAVE MCKAY-INF/DH
41 HARRY WARNER-CH
42 JACKIE MOORE-CH
43 DON LEPPERT-CH
44 JERRY JOHNSON-P
45 TOM MURPHY-P (2)
48 BILL (SINGER THROWING MACHINE) SINGER (INJ)-P

1978
7TH E 59-102 40GB

1 BOB BAILOR (INJ)-OF/INF
3 BRIAN MILNER-C
5 SAM EWING-DH/OF
7 ROY HARTSFIELD-MGR
8 ALAN ASHBY-C
9 RICK CERONE-C/DH
10 JOHN MAYBERRY-1B/DH
11 LUIS GOMEZ-SS
12 ERNIE WHITT-C
13 ROY HOWELL-3B/UTIL
14 TOMMY HUTTON-OF/1B (1)
14 BUTCH ALBERTS-DH
15 BOB MILLER-CH
16 TIM NORDBROOK-SS (1)
16 JOE COLEMAN-P (2)
17 TIM JOHNSON-SS/2B (2)
18 JIM CLANCY-P
19 OTTO VELEZ-OF/UTIL
20 AL WOODS-OF
21 RICO CARTY-DH (1)
21 MARK WILEY-P (2)
22 RICK BOSETTI-OF
23 DAVE LEMANCZYK-P
24 TOM UNDERWOOD-P
25 DOUG AULT-UTIL
26 WILLIE UPSHAW-UTIL
27 VICTOR CRUZ-P
29 GARTH IORG-2B
31 BOBBY DOERR-CH
32 DON KIRKWOOD (INJ)-P
33 MIKE WILLIS-P
34 JESSE JEFFERSON-P
35 GARY WOODS-OF
36 JERRY GARVIN-P
38 BALOR MOORE-P
39 DAVE MCKAY-2B/UTIL
40 JOE COLEMAN-P (2)
41 HARRY WARNER-CH
42 JACKIE MOORE-CH
43 DON LEPPERT-CH
44 TOM BUSKEY-P
45 TOM MURPHY-P
46 DAVE WALLACE-P
47 VICTOR CRUZ-P
(48) BILL (SINGER THROWING MACHINE) SINGER (INJ)-(P)
48 WILLIE HORTON-DH (3)

1979
7TH E 53-109 50.5GB

1 BOB BAILOR-OF/UTIL
2 DANNY AINGE (SCH)-2B/DH
4 ALFREDO GRIFFIN-SS
5 BOBBY BROWN-OF (1)
5 BOB ROBERTSON-1B/DH
5 CRAIG KUSICK-UTIL/P (2)
7 ROY HARTSFIELD-MGR
8 BOB DAVIS-C
9 RICK CERONE-C
10 JOHN MAYBERRY-1B
11 LUIS GOMEZ-INF
13 ROY HOWELL-3B/DH
15 BOB MILLER-CH
16 BUTCH EDGE-P
17 TIM JOHNSON-INF
18 JIM CLANCY (INJ)-P
19 OTTO VELEZ-UTIL
20 AL WOODS-OF/DH
21 RICO CARTY-DH
22 RICK BOSETTI-OF
23 DAVE LEMANCZYK (INJ)-P
24 TOM UNDERWOOD-P
25 STEVE LUEBBER-P
25 DAVE FREISLEBEN-P
27 TONY SOLAITA-DH/1B (2)
29 PEDRO HERNANDEZ-PR
30 JOE CANNON-OF/DH
31 BOBBY DOERR-CH
32 JACKSON TODD-P
33 MIKE WILLIS-P
34 JESSE JEFFERSON-P
36 JERRY GARVIN (INJ)-P
37 TED WILBORN-OF/DH
37 DAVE STIEB-P
38 BALOR MOORE-P
39 DAVE MCKAY-2B/3B
40 MARK LEMONGELLO-P
41 HARRY WARNER-CH
42 JACKIE MOORE-CH
43 DON LEPPERT-CH
44 TOM BUSKEY (INJ)-P
45 TOM MURPHY-P
45 STEVE GRILLI-P
46 DYAR MILLER-P (2)
46 STEVE LUEBBER-P
47 PHIL HUFFMAN-P

1980
7TH E 67-95 36GB

1 BOB BAILOR-UTIL/P
2 DANNY AINGE (SCH)-UTIL
3 BOBBY MATTICK-MGR
4 ALFREDO GRIFFIN-SS
6 PAT KELLY-C
7 DAMASO GARCIA-2B/DH
8 BOB DAVIS-C
9 BARRY BONNELL-OF/DH
10 JOHN MAYBERRY-1B/DH
11 MIKE MACHA-3B/C
11 STEVE BRAUN-DH/3B (2)
12 ERNIE WHITT-C
13 ROY HOWELL-3B/DH
14 DENIS MENKE-CH
15 LLOYD MOSEBY-OF/DH
16 GARTH IORG-UTIL
17 DOMINGO RAMOS-INF/DH
18 JIM CLANCY-P
19 OTTO VELEZ (INJ)-DH/1B
20 AL WOODS-OF/DH
21 KEN SCHROM-P
22 RICK BOSETTI (INJ)-OF
23 DAVE LEMANCZYK-P (1)
23 MIKE WILLIS-P
24 JIMY WILLIAMS-CH
25 DOUG AULT-UTIL
26 WILLIE UPSHAW-UTIL
28 JOHN FELSKE-CH
30 JOE CANNON-OF/DH
31 BOBBY DOERR-CH
32 JACK KUCEK-P
33 MIKE WILLIS-P
34 JESSE JEFFERSON-P (1)
36 JERRY GARVIN-P
37 DAVE STIEB-P
38 BALOR MOORE-P
40 JACKSON TODD-P
41 AL WIDMAR-CH
42 PAUL MIRABELLA-P
44 TOM BUSKEY-P
46 JOEY MCLAUGHLIN-P
46 MIKE BARLOW-P
48 LUIS LEAL-P
49 PAUL HODGSON-OF/DH
50 JOEY MCLAUGHLIN-P

1981
1ST 1/2: 7TH E 16-42 19GB
2ND 1/2: 7TH E 21-27 7.5GB
FINAL: E 37-69 -- GB

2 DANNY AINGE-UTIL
2 FRED MANRIQUE-INF/DH
3 BOBBY MATTICK-MGR
4 ALFREDO GRIFFIN-SS/INF
6 DAN WHITMER-C
7 DAMASO GARCIA-2B/DH
8 KEN MACHA-UTIL
9 BARRY BONNELL-OF
10 JOHN MAYBERRY-1B/DH
11 GEORGE BELL-OF/DH
12 ERNIE WHITT-C
13 BUCK MARTINEZ-C
14 DENIS MENKE-CH
15 LLOYD MOSEBY-OF
16 GARTH IORG-INF/DH
17 MARK BOMBACK-P
18 JIM CLANCY-P
19 OTTO VELEZ-DH/1B
20 AL WOODS-OF/DH
22 RICK BOSETTI-OF/DH (1)
23 MIKE WILLIS-P
24 JIMY WILLIAMS-CH
24 BOB PATE-OF
25 ROY LEE JACKSON-P
26 WILLIE UPSHAW-UTIL
28 JOHN FELSKE-CH
29 JESSE BARFIELD-OF
30 JUAN BERENGUER-P (2)
31 BOBBY DOERR-CH
32 CHARLIE BEAMON-DH/1B
33 DALE MURRAY-P
34 TED COX-INF/DH
36 JERRY GARVIN-P
37 DAVE STIEB-P
38 NINO ESPINOSA-P (2)
40 JACKSON TODD-P
41 AL WIDMAR-CH
42 PAUL MIRABELLA-P
43 GREG WELLS-1B/DH
45 MARK BOMBACK-P
46 MIKE BARLOW-P
48 LUIS LEAL-P
50 JOEY MCLAUGHLIN-P
51 PAUL MIRABELLA-P
51 NINO ESPINOSA-P (2)
52 JUAN BERENGUER-P (2)

1982
6TH E (TIE) 78-84 17GB

3 WAYNE NORDHAGEN (INJ)-DH/OF (1) (3)
3 LEON ROBERTS-DH/OF (2)
3 WAYNE NORDHAGEN (INJ)-DH/OF (1) (3)
4 ALFREDO GRIFFIN-SS
5 RANCE MULLINIKS-3B/SS
6 BOBBY COX-MGR
7 DAMASO GARCIA-2B/DH
8 JOHN SULLIVAN-CH
9 BARRY BONNELL-OF/UTIL
10 JOHN MAYBERRY-DH/1B (1)
10 DAVE REVERING-DH/1B (2)
12 ERNIE WHITT-C/DH
13 BUCK MARTINEZ-C
14 GENO PETRALLI-C/3B
15 LLOYD MOSEBY-OF
16 GARTH IORG-INF/DH
17 MARK BOMBACK-P
18 JIM CLANCY-P
19 OTTO VELEZ-DH
20 AL WOODS-OF/DH
21 KEN SCHROM-P
22 HOSKEN POWELL-OF/DH
24 JIMY WILLIAMS-CH
25 ROY LEE JACKSON-P
26 WILLIE UPSHAW-1B/DH
28 MARK EICHHORN-P
29 JESSE BARFIELD-OF/DH
30 WAYNE NORDHAGEN (INJ)-DH/OF (1) (3)
31 DAVE BAKER-3B
33 DALE MURRAY-P
34 STEVE SENTENEY-P
35 DAVE GEISEL-P
35 DICK DAVIS-OF/DH (2)
36 JERRY GARVIN-P
37 DAVE STIEB-P
38 JIM GOTT-P
39 PEDRO HERNANDEZ-UTIL
41 AL WIDMAR-CH
42 PAUL MIRABELLA-P
43 CITO GASTON-CH
45 TONY JOHNSON-OF/DH
48 LUIS LEAL-P
50 JOEY MCLAUGHLIN (INJ)-P
51 DAVE GEISEL-P
55 GLENN ADAMS-DH

1983
4TH E 89-73 9GB

1 TONY FERNANDEZ-SS/DH
4 ALFREDO GRIFFIN-SS/UTIL
5 RANCE MULLINIKS-3B/INF
6 BOBBY COX-MGR
7 DAMASO GARCIA-2B
8 JOHN SULLIVAN-CH
9 BARRY BONNELL-OF/UTIL
10 DAVE COLLINS-OF/UTIL
11 GEORGE BELL-OF/DH
12 ERNIE WHITT-C
13 BUCK MARTINEZ-C
14 GENO PETRALLI-C/DH
15 LLOYD MOSEBY-OF
16 GARTH IORG-DH/OF
17 RANDY MOFFITT-P
18 JIM CLANCY-P
22 HOSKEN POWELL-OF/UTIL
23 MITCH WEBSTER-OF/DH
24 JIMY WILLIAMS-CH
25 ROY LEE JACKSON-P
26 WILLIE UPSHAW-1B/DH
27 MICKEY KLUTTS-3B/DH
29 JESSE BARFIELD-OF/DH
30 MIKE MORGAN (INJ)-P
31 JIM ACKER-P
33 JORGE ORTA-DH/OF
34 STAN CLARKE-P
35 DAVE GEISEL-P
36 DON COOPER-P
37 DAVE STIEB-P
38 JIM GOTT-P
41 AL WIDMAR-CH
43 CITO GASTON-CH
44 CLIFF JOHNSON-DH/1B
45 MATT WILLIAMS-P
47 DOYLE ALEXANDER-P (2)
48 LUIS LEAL-P
50 JOEY MCLAUGHLIN-P

1984
2ND E 89-73 15GB

1 TONY FERNANDEZ (INJ)-UTIL
1 TOBY HERNANDEZ-C
2 FRED MANRIQUE-2B/DH
3 JIMY WILLIAMS-CH
4 ALFREDO GRIFFIN-SS/UTIL
5 RANCE MULLINIKS-3B/INF
6 BOBBY COX-MGR
7 DAMASO GARCIA-2B/DH
8 JOHN SULLIVAN-CH
9 RICK LEACH-UTIL/P
10 DAVE COLLINS-OF/UTIL
11 GEORGE BELL-OF/UTIL
12 ERNIE WHITT-C
13 BUCK MARTINEZ-C/DH
14 GENO PETRALLI-C/DH
15 LLOYD MOSEBY-OF
16 GARTH IORG-UTIL
17 KELLY GRUBER-UTIL
18 JIM CLANCY-P
20 RON SHEPHERD-OF/DH
22 JIMMY KEY-P
23 MITCH WEBSTER-UTIL
24 WILLIE AIKENS (SUB)-DH/1B
25 ROY LEE JACKSON-P
26 WILLIE UPSHAW-1B/DH
27 JIMMY KEY-P
29 JESSE BARFIELD-OF/DH
30 RON MUSSELMAN-P
31 JIM ACKER-P
33 DOYLE ALEXANDER-P
35 BRYAN CLARK-P
37 DAVE STIEB-P
38 JIM GOTT-P
41 AL WIDMAR-CH
42 BILLY SMITH-CH
43 CITO GASTON-CH
44 CLIFF JOHNSON-DH/1B
48 LUIS LEAL-P
50 JOEY MCLAUGHLIN-P (1)
53 DENNIS LAMP-P

1985
1ST E 99-62 0GB
L ALCS-KCA 4-3

0 AL OLIVER-DH/1B (2)
00 CLIFF JOHNSON-DH/1B (2)
1 TONY FERNANDEZ-SS
3 JIMY WILLIAMS-CH
4 MANNY LEE-INF
5 RANCE MULLINIKS-3B
6 BOBBY COX-MGR
7 DAMASO GARCIA-2B
8 JOHN SULLIVAN-CH
9 RICK LEACH-1B/OF
11 GEORGE BELL-OF/3B

TORONTO BLUE JAYS

12 ERNIE WHITT-C
13 BUCK MARTINEZ (INJ)-C
15 LLOYD MOSEBY-OF
16 GARTH IORG-3B/2B
17 KELLY GRUBER-3B/2B
18 JIM CLANCY (INJ)-P
21 RON SHEPHERD-OF/DH
22 JIMMY KEY-P
23 MITCH WEBSTER-OF/DH (1)
23 CECIL FIELDER-1B
24 WILLIE AIKENS-DH
25 LEN MATUSZEK-DH/1B (1)
25 STEVE DAVIS-P
26 WILLIE UPSHAW-1B/DH
28 LOU THORNTON-OF/DH
29 JESSE BARFIELD-OF
30 RON MUSSELMAN-P
31 JIM ACKER-P
33 DOYLE ALEXANDER-P
34 STAN CLARKE-P
36 BILL CAUDILL-P
37 DAVE STIEB-P
38 STEVE NICOSIA-C
39 GARY ALLENSON-C
41 AL WIDMAR-CH
42 BILLY SMITH-CH
43 CITO GASTON-CH
44 JEFF BURROUGHS-DH
46 GARY LAVELLE-P
48 LUIS LEAL-P
49 TOM FILER-P
50 TOM HENKE-P
53 DENNIS LAMP-P
54 JEFF HEARRON-C
55 JOHN CERUTTI-P

1986

4TH E 86-76 9.5GB

00 CLIFF JOHNSON-DH/1B
1 TONY FERNANDEZ-SS
3 JIMY WILLIAMS-MGR
4 MANNY LEE-INF
5 RANCE MULLINIKS-3B/UTIL
7 DAMASO GARCIA-2B/UTIL
8 JOHN SULLIVAN-CH
9 RICK LEACH-UTIL
11 GEORGE BELL-OF/UTIL
12 ERNIE WHITT-C
13 BUCK MARTINEZ-C/DH
15 LLOYD MOSEBY-OF/DH
16 GARTH IORG-INF
17 KELLY GRUBER-UTIL
18 JIM CLANCY-P
19 FRED (CRIME DOG) MCGRIFF-DH/1B
21 RON SHEPHERD-OF/DH
22 JIMMY KEY-P
23 CECIL FIELDER-UTIL
24 JOHN MCLAREN-CH
25 STEVE DAVIS-P
26 WILLIE UPSHAW-1B/DH
29 JESSE BARFIELD-OF
31 JIM ACKER-P (1)
31 DUANE WARD-P (2)
32 LUIS AQUINO-P
33 DOYLE ALEXANDER-P (1)
33 JOE JOHNSON-P (2)
34 STAN CLARKE-P
35 JEFF MUSSELMAN-P
36 BILL CAUDILL-P
37 DAVE STIEB-P
38 MARK EICHHORN-P
39 DON GORDON-P
40 MICKEY MAHLER-P (2)
41 AL WIDMAR-CH
42 BILLY SMITH-CH
43 CITO GASTON-CH
44 CLIFF JOHNSON-DH/1B
(46) GARY LAVELLE (INJ)-(P)
(49) TOM FILER (INJ)-(P)
50 TOM HENKE-P
53 DENNIS LAMP-P
54 JEFF HEARRON-C
55 JOHN CERUTTI-P

1987

2ND E 96-66 2GB

1 TONY FERNANDEZ-SS
2 NELSON LIRIANO-2B
3 JIMY WILLIAMS-MGR
4 MANNY LEE-INF/DH
5 RANCE MULLINIKS-INF/DH
7 JUAN BENIQUEZ-UTIL (2)
8 JOHN SULLIVAN-CH
9 RICK LEACH-UTIL
10 MIKE SHARPERSON-2B (1)
11 GEORGE BELL-OF/UTIL
12 ERNIE WHITT-C
13 JEFF MUSSELMAN-P
14 ALEXIS INFANTE-PR
15 LLOYD MOSEBY-OF/DH
16 GARTH IORG-2B/UTIL
17 KELLY GRUBER-3B/UTIL
18 JIM CLANCY-P
19 FRED (CRIME DOG) MCGRIFF-DH/1B
21 CHARLIE MOORE-C/OF
22 JIMMY KEY-P
23 CECIL FIELDER-DH/INF
24 JOHN MCLAREN-CH
26 WILLIE UPSHAW-1B
27 JEFF DEWILLIS-C
28 LOU THORNTON-DH/OF
29 JESSE BARFIELD-OF
31 DUANE WARD-P
33 JOE JOHNSON-P
35 JEFF MUSSELMAN-P
35 PHIL NIEKRO-P (2)
36 DAVID WELLS-P
37 DAVE STIEB-P
38 MARK EICHHORN-P
39 DON GORDON-P (1)
40 ROB DUCEY-OF/DH
41 AL WIDMAR-CH
42 BILLY SMITH-CH
43 CITO GASTON-CH
45 JOSE NUNEZ-P
46 GARY LAVELLE (INJ)-P (1)
46 MIKE FLANAGAN-P (2)
47 MATT STARK (INJ)-C
50 TOM HENKE-P
52 GREG MYERS-C
55 JOHN CERUTTI-P

1988

3RD E (TIE) 87-75 2GB

1 TONY FERNANDEZ-SS
2 NELSON LIRIANO-INF/DH
3 JIMY WILLIAMS-MGR
4 MANNY LEE-2B/UTIL
5 RANCE MULLINIKS-DH/3B
6 SIL CAMPUSANO (INJ)-OF/DH
7 JUAN BENIQUEZ-DH/OF
7 JOHN MCLAREN-CH
8 JOHN SULLIVAN-CH
9 RICK LEACH-UTIL
10 PAT BORDERS (INJ)-C/UTIL
11 GEORGE BELL-OF/UTIL
12 ERNIE WHITT-C
13 JEFF MUSSELMAN (INJ)-P
14 ALEXIS INFANTE-UTIL
15 LLOYD MOSEBY-OF/DH
16 TODD STOTTLEMYRE-P
17 KELLY GRUBER-3B/UTIL
18 JIM CLANCY-P
19 FRED (CRIME DOG) MCGRIFF-1B
20 ROB DUCEY-OF
21 MARK ROSS-P
22 JIMMY KEY (INJ)-P
23 CECIL FIELDER-UTIL
24 JOHN MCLAREN-CH
27 TONY CASTILLO-P
28 LOU THORNTON-OF/DH
29 JESSE BARFIELD-OF/DH
31 DUANE WARD-P
33 SAL BUTERA-C
36 DAVID WELLS-P
37 DAVE STIEB-P
38 MARK EICHHORN-P
40 ROB DUCEY-OF
40 DOUG BAIR-P
41 AL WIDMAR-CH
42 BILLY SMITH-CH
43 CITO GASTON-CH
44 FRANK WILLS-P
45 JOSE NUNEZ-P
46 MIKE FLANAGAN-P
(47) MATT STARK (INJ)-(C)
50 TOM HENKE-P
54 GALEN CISCO-CH
55 JOHN CERUTTI-P
57 WINSTON LLENAS-CH

1989

1ST E 89-73 0GB
L ALCS-OAKA 4-1

1 TONY FERNANDEZ-SS
2 NELSON LIRIANO-2B/DH
3 JIMY WILLIAMS-MGR1
3 MOOKIE WILSON-OF (2)
4 MANNY LEE (INJ)-UTIL
5 RANCE MULLINIKS-DH/3B
7 JOHN MCLAREN-CH
8 JOHN SULLIVAN-CH
9 BOB BRENLY-UTIL (1)
9 JOHN OLERUD-1B/DH
10 PAT BORDERS (INJ)-C/DH
11 GEORGE BELL-OF/DH
12 ERNIE WHITT-C/DH
13 JEFF MUSSELMAN (SUB)-P
13 LEE MAZZILLI-UTIL (2)
14 ALEXIS INFANTE-UTIL
15 LLOYD MOSEBY-OF/DH
16 GREG MYERS (INJ)-C/DH
17 KELLY GRUBER-3B/UTIL
18 TOM LAWLESS-UTIL
19 FRED (CRIME DOG) MCGRIFF-1B/DH
20 ROB DUCEY (INJ) OF
21 FRANCISCO CABRERRA-DH (1)
21 OZZIE VIRGIL-DH/C
22 JIMMY KEY-P
24 JIM ACKER-P (2)
25 MIKE SQUIRES-CH
27 TONY CASTILLO-P (1)
28 AL LEITER (INJ)-P (2)
29 JESSE BARFIELD-OF (1)
29 GLENALLEN HILL-OF/DH
30 TODD STOTTLEMYRE-P
31 DUANE WARD-P
32 STEVE CUMMINGS-P
33 ALEX SANCHEZ-P
34 KEVIN BASTISTE-OF
36 DAVID WELLS-P
37 DAVE STIEB-P
38 DEWAYNE BUICE-P
41 AL WIDMAR-CH
42 XAVIER HERNANDEZ-P
43 CITO GASTON-CH/MGR2
44 FRANK WILLS-P
45 JOSE NUNEZ-P
46 MIKE FLANAGAN-P
47 MAURO GOZZO-P
50 TOM HENKE-P
54 JUNIOR FELIX-OF/DH
55 JOHN CERUTTI-P
56 MARTY PATTIN-CH

1990

2ND E 86-76 2GB

1 TONY FERNANDEZ-SS
2 NELSON LIRIANO-2B (1)
3 MOOKIE WILSON-OF/DH
4 MANNY LEE-2B/SS
5 RANCE MULLINIKS-UTIL
6 LUIS SOJO-UTIL
7 JOHN MCLAREN-CH
8 JOHN SULLIVAN-CH
9 JOHN OLERUD-DH/1B
10 PAT BORDERS-C/DH
11 GEORGE BELL-OF/DH
12 KENNY WILLIAMS-OF/DH (2)
15 GENE TENACE-CH
16 TODD STOTTLEMYRE-P
16 TOM QUINLAN-3B
17 KELLY GRUBER-3B/UTIL
18 TOM LAWLESS-UTIL
19 FRED (CRIME DOG) MCGRIFF-1B/DH
20 ROB DUCEY-OF
21 GREG MYERS-C
22 JIMMY KEY (INJ)-P
24 GLENALLEN HILL-OF/DH
25 MIKE SQUIRES-CH
26 OZZIE VIRGIL-C/DH
26 JIM EPPARD-PH
27 WILLIE BLAIR-P
28 AL LEITER (INJ)-P
30 TODD STOTTLEMYRE-P
31 DUANE WARD-P
32 STEVE CUMMINGS-P
34 JIM ACKER-P
35 BUD BLACK-P (2)
36 DAVID WELLS-P
37 DAVE STIEB-P
38 RICK LUECKEN-P (2)
39 PAUL KILGUS-P
40 MARK WHITEN-OF/DH
40 BUD BLACK-P (2)
41 FRANK WILLS-P
42 GALEN CISCO-CH
43 CITO GASTON-MGR
44 FRANK WILLS-P
45 ROB MACDONALD-P
46 MIKE FLANAGAN-P
46 TOM GILLES-P
47 JUNIOR FELIX-OF/DH
48 JOHN (CANDY MAN) CANDELARIA-P (2)
50 TOM HENKE-P
55 JOHN CERUTTI-P
59 CARLOS DIAZ-C

1991

1ST E 91-71 0GB
L ALCS-MINA 4-1

1 EDDIE ZOSKY-SS
2 ROBERTO ALOMAR-2B
3 MOOKIE WILSON-OF/DH
4 MANNY LEE-SS
5 RANCE MULLINIKS (INJ)-DH/3B
6 MIKE SQUIRES-CH
7 RICH HACKER-CH
8 JOHN SULLIVAN-CH
9 JOHN OLERUD-1B/DH
10 PAT BORDERS-C
12 KENNY WILLIAMS-OF/DH (1)
12 ROBERTO ALOMAR-2B
13 KENNY WILLIAMS-OF/DH (1)
14 DEREK BELL-OF
15 GENE TENACE-CH
15 PAT TABLER-DH/UTIL
17 KELLY GRUBER (INJ)-3B/DH
18 GENE TENACE-CH
19 DEVON WHITE-OF
19 RAY GIANNELLI-3B
20 ROB DUCEY-OF/DH
21 GREG MYERS-C
22 JIMMY KEY-P
23 MARK WHITEN-OF (1)
23 CANDY MALDONADO-OF (2)
24 GLENALLEN HILL-DH/OF (1)
24 TURNER WARD-OF (2)
25 MIKE SQUIRES-CH
25 DEVON WHITE-OF
26 VINCE HORSMAN-P
26 MICKEY WESTON-P
27 WILLIE FRASER-P (1)
27 CORY SNYDER-UTIL
28 AL LEITER (INJ)-P
29 JOE CARTER-OF/DH
30 TODD STOTTLEMYRE-P
31 DUANE WARD-P
33 ED SPRAGUE-UTIL
34 JIM ACKER-P
35 DENIS BOUCHER-P (1)
36 DAVID WELLS-P
37 DAVE STIEB (INJ)-P
39 DAVE PARKER-DH (2)
40 MIKE TIMLIN-P
41 PAT HENTGEN-P
42 GALEN CISCO-CH
43 CITO GASTON-MGR
44 FRANK WILLS-P
45 ROB MACDONALD-P
46 KEN DAYLEY (ILL)-P
49 RANDY KNORR-C
49 TOM CANDIOTTI-P (2)
50 TOM HENKE (INJ)-P
53 DAVID WEATHERS-P
54 RANDY KNORR-C
56 HECTOR TORRES-CH
66 JUAN GUZMAN-P
88 RENE GONZALES-INF

1992

1ST E 96-66 0GB
W ALCS-OAKA 4-2
W WS-ATLN 4-2

1 EDDIE ZOSKY-SS
2 MANNY LEE-SS
3 BOB BAILOR-CH
4 ALFREDO GRIFFIN-SS/2B
5 RANCE MULLINIKS-PH
7 RICH HACKER-CH
8 JOHN SULLIVAN-CH
9 JOHN OLERUD-1B/DH
10 PAT BORDERS-C
11 JEFF KENT-INF (1)
11 DAVID CONE-P (2)
12 ROBERTO ALOMAR-2B/DH
14 DEREK BELL-OF/DH
15 PAT TABLER-UTIL
16 TOM QUINLAN-3B
17 KELLY GRUBER-3B
18 GENE TENACE-CH
19 DOMINGO MARTINEZ-1B
20 ROB DUCEY-OF/DH
21 GREG MYERS-C/DH
21 MIKE MAKSUDIAN-1B
22 JIMMY KEY-P
23 CANDY MALDONADO-OF/DH
24 TURNER WARD-OF
25 DEVON WHITE-OF/DH
26 DOUG LINTON-P
27 RANDY KNORR-C
28 AL LEITER (INJ)-P
29 JOE CARTER-OF/UTIL
30 TODD STOTTLEMYRE-P
31 DUANE WARD-P
32 DAVE WINFIELD-DH/OF
33 ED SPRAGUE-UTIL
34 MARK EICHHORN-P (2)
35 RICKY TRLICEK-P
36 DAVID WELLS-P
37 DAVE STIEB (INJ)-P
39 LARRY HISLE-CH
40 MIKE TIMLIN-P
41 PAT HENTGEN-P

42 GALEN CISCO-CH
43 CITO GASTON-MGR
45 ROB MACDONALD-P
(46) KEN DAYLEY (INJ)-(P)
47 JACK MORRIS-P
48 MARK EICHHORN-P (2)
50 TOM HENKE (INJ)-P
53 DAVID WEATHERS-P
66 JUAN GUZMAN-P

1993

1ST E 95-67 0GB
W ALCS-CHIA 4-2
W WS-PHIN 4-2

(1) EDDIE ZOSKY (INJ)-(INF)
1 TONY FERNANDEZ-SS (2)
2 LUIS SOJO-INF
2 ROB BUTLER (INJ)-OF
3 BOB BAILOR-CH
4 ALFREDO GRIFFIN (INJ)-INF
5 DOMINGO MARTINEZ-1B/3B
6 CARLOS DELGADO-C/DH
7 RICH HACKER-CH
8 JOHN SULLIVAN-CH
9 JOHN OLERUD-1B/DH
10 PAT BORDERS-C
11 DARNELL COLES-UTIL
12 ROBERTO ALOMAR-2B
14 DARRIN JACKSON-OF (1)
14 RICKEY HENDERSON-OF (2)
16 TURNER WARD (INJ)-OF/1B
18 GENE TENACE-CH
19 PAUL MOLITOR-DH/1B
21 WILLIAM CANATE (ILL)-OF/1B
22 DICK (DUCKY) SCHOFIELD (INJ)-SS
24 TURNER WARD-OF
24 RICKEY HENDERSON-OF (2)
25 DEVON WHITE-OF
26 DOUG LINTON-P (1)
27 RANDY KNORR-C
28 AL LEITER-P
29 JOE CARTER-OF/DH
30 TODD STOTTLEMYRE-P
31 DUANE WARD-P
32 HUCK FLENER-P
33 ED SPRAGUE-3B
34 DAVE STEWART (INJ)-P
39 LARRY HISLE-CH
40 MIKE TIMLIN-P
41 PAT HENTGEN-P
42 GALEN CISCO-CH
43 CITO GASTON-MGR
44 SCOTT BROW-P
45 NICK LEYVA-CH
46 KEN DAYLEY-P
47 JACK MORRIS (INJ)-P
48 MARK EICHHORN-P
49 TONY CASTILLO-P
50 DANNY COX-P
54 WOODY WILLIAMS-P
56 SHAWN GREEN-OF/DH
66 JUAN GUZMAN-P
70 DOMINGO CEDENO-SS/2B

1994

3RD E 55-60 16GB
STRIKE NO POST-SEASON

2 ROB BUTLER-OF
3 BOB BAILOR-CH
4 DICK (DUCKY) SCHOFIELD-INF
6 CARLOS DELGADO-OF
8 ALEX GONZALEZ (INJ)-SS
9 JOHN OLERUD-1B/DH
10 PAT BORDERS-C
11 DARNELL COLES-DH
12 ROBERTO ALOMAR-2B
15 SHAWN GREEN-OF
16 NICK LEYVA-CH
17 ROBERT PEREZ-OF
18 GENE TENACE-CH
19 PAUL MOLITOR-DH
20 DOMINGO CEDENO-2B
24 GREG CADARET (REL)-P
24 DAVE RIGHETTI-P (2)
25 DEVON WHITE-OF
26 MIKE HUFF (INJ)-OF
27 RANDY KNORR-C
28 AL LEITER (INJ)-P
29 JOE CARTER-OF/DH
30 TODD STOTTLEMYRE-P
31 DUANE WARD (INJ)-P
33 ED SPRAGUE-3B
34 DAVE STEWART (INJ)-P
36 DARREN HALL-P
37 RANDY ST. CLAIRE-P
38 AARON SMALL-P
39 LARRY HISLE-CH
40 MIKE TIMLIN (INJ)-P
41 PAT HENTGEN-P
42 GALEN CISCO-CH
43 CITO GASTON-MGR
44 SCOTT BROW-P
45 PAUL SPOLJARIC-P
46 DENNIS HOLMBERG-CH
49 TONY CASTILLO-P
50 DANNY COX (INJ)-P
53 BRAD CORNETT-P
54 WOODY WILLIAMS-P
58 BRAD CORNETT-P
66 JUAN GUZMAN-P

1995

5TH E 56-88 30GB

0 CANDY MALDONADO-OF (1)
1 TOMAS PEREZ-SS
3 BOB BAILOR-CH
6 CARLOS DELGADO (INJ)-OF
7 SHANNON STEWART-OF
8 ALEX GONZALEZ-SS
9 JOHN OLERUD-1B
11 DAVID CONE-P (1)
12 ROBERTO ALOMAR-2B
13 LANCE PARRISH-C
14 HOWARD BATTLE-3B
15 SHAWN GREEN-OF
16 NICK LEYVA-CH
17 ROBERT PEREZ-OF
18 GENE TENACE-CH
19 PAUL MOLITOR-DH
20 DOMINGO CEDENO-2B
22 BRAD CORNETT (INJ)-P
23 CANDY MALDONADO-OF (1)
25 DEVON WHITE (INJ)-OF
26 MIKE HUFF (INJ)-OF
27 RANDY KNORR (INJ)-C
28 AL LEITER-P
29 JOE CARTER-OF
31 DUANE WARD (INJ)-P
32 EDWIN HURTADO-P
33 ED SPRAGUE-3B
36 DARREN HALL (INJ)-P
37 TIM CRABTREE-P
38 GIOVANNI CARRERA-P
39 LARRY HISLE-CH
40 MIKE TIMLIN (INJ)-P
41 PAT HENTGEN-P
42 GALEN CISCO-CH
43 CITO GASTON-MGR
44 DANNY DARWIN (REL)-P (1)
44 KEN ROBINSON-P
46 DENNIS HOLMBERG-CH
47 JIMMY ROGERS-P
48 RICARDO JORDAN-P
49 TONY CASTILLO-P
50 DANNY COX (INJ)-P
52 JEFF WARE-P
53 ANGEL (SANDY) MARTINEZ-C
54 WOODY WILLIAMS (INJ)-P
55 PAUL MENHART-P
66 JUAN GUZMAN (INJ)-P

1996

4TH E 74-88 18GB

1 TOMAS PEREZ-2B
2 OTIS NIXON (INJ)-OF
3 MIGUEL CAIRO-2B
4 ALFREDO GRIFFIN-CH
5 JACOB BRUMFIELD-OF (2)
6 FELIPE CRESPO (INJ)-3B
7 SHANNON STEWART-OF
8 ALEX GONZALEZ-SS
9 JOHN OLERUD-DH
11 JUAN (SAMMY) SAMUEL (INJ)-2B
14 TILSON BRITO-2B
15 SHAWN GREEN-OF
16 NICK LEYVA-CH
17 ROBERT PEREZ-OF
18 GENE TENACE-CH
19 FRANK VIOLA (REL)-P
20 DOMINGO CEDENO-2B (1)
21 CARLOS DELGADO-1B
22 CHARLIE O'BRIEN-C
24 PAUL SPOLJARIC (INJ)-P
27 SCOTT BROW (WAIV)-P
28 WILLIE UPSHAW-CH
29 JOE CARTER-OF
32 BRIAN BOHANON-P
33 ED SPRAGUE-3B
34 MEL QUEEN-CH
35 ANGEL (SANDY) MARTINEZ (INJ)-C
36 MARTY JANZEN-P
37 TIM CRABTREE-P
38 GIOVANNI CARRERA-P (1)
38 HUCK FLENER-P
39 ERIK HANSON-P
40 MIKE TIMLIN-P
41 PAT HENTGEN-P
43 CITO GASTON-MGR
45 JOSE SILVA-P
46 JULIO MOSQUERA-C
48 PAUL QUANTRILL-P
49 TONY CASTILLO-P (1)
49 LUIS ANDUJAR-P (2)
50 DANE JOHNSON (WAIV)-P
52 JEFF WARE-P
53 ANGEL (SANDY) MARTINEZ-C
54 WOODY WILLIAMS (INJ)-P
55 BILL RISLEY (INJ)-P
57 JUAN GUZMAN (INJ)-P

1997

5TH E 76-86 22GB

1 TOMAS PEREZ (INJ)-2B/OF
2 OTIS NIXON (INJ)-OF (1)
3 FELIPE CRESPO-3B
4 ALFREDO GRIFFIN-CH
5 JACOB BRUMFIELD (INJ)-OF
6 CARLOS DELGADO (INJ)-OF
7 SHANNON STEWART-OF
8 ALEX GONZALEZ (INJ)-2B/SS
10 JIM LETT-CH
11 JUAN (SAMMY) SAMUEL-DH/2B
12 TILSON BRITO-(WAIV)-2B (1)
12 RICH BUTLER-OF
13 CARLOS GARCIA-2B/SS
14 GENE TENACE-CH
14 RUBEN SIERRA (REL)-OF (2)
15 SHAWN GREEN-OF
16 NICK LEYVA-CH
17 ROBERT PEREZ-OF
18 BENITO SANTIAGO (INJ)-C
19 DAN PLESAC-P
20 WOODY WILLIAMS-P
21 ROGER (ROCKET) CLEMENS-P
22 CHARLIE O'BRIEN-C
23 JOSE CRUZ, JR.-OF (2)
24 PAUL SPOLJARIC (INJ)-P (1)
24 MARIANO DUNCAN-2B (2)
25 CARLOS DELGADO-DH
26 WILLIE UPSHAW-CH
28 TOM EVANS-3B
29 JOE CARTER-OF/1B
30 WOODY WILLIAMS-P
31 ROBERT PERSON (INJ)-P
33 ED SPRAGUE, JR. (INJ)-3B
34 MEL QUEEN, JR.-CH
35 ANGEL (SANDY) MARTINEZ-C
36 MARTY JANZEN-P
37 TIM CRABTREE (INJ)-P
38 HUCK FLENER-P
39 ERIK HANSON (INJ)-P
40 MIKE TIMLIN-P (1)
40 CARLOS ALMANZAR-P
41 PAT HENTGEN-P
42 *(RET#) JACKIE ROBINSON*
43 CITO GASTON-MGR1
43 JOE CARTER-OF/1B
45 KELVIN ESCOBAR-P
46 JULIO MOSQUERA-C
48 PAUL QUANTRILL-P
49 LUIS ANDUJAR-P
50 CRIS CARPENTER-P
52 KEN ROBINSON-P
54 WOODY WILLIAMS (INJ)-P
54 OMAR DAAL-P (2)
55 BILL RISLEY (INJ)-P
57 JUAN GUZMAN (INJ)-P

1998

3RD E 88-74 26GB

00 JOSE CANSECO-DH/OF
1 TONY FERNANDEZ-SS
2 CRAIG GREBECK-2B/INF
2 TOM EVANS-3B
3 FELIPE CRESPO-3B
4 CRAIG GREBECK-2B/INF
5 MARK DALESANDRO-C
6 KEVIN WITT-1B
7 EDDIE RODRIGUEZ-CH
8 ALEX GONZALEZ-2B/SS
9 DARRIN FLETCHER (INJ)-C
10 JIM LETT-CH
11 JUAN (SAMMY) SAMUEL-DH/2B
12 TONY PHILLIPS-OF (1)
13 TOMAS PEREZ-SS/2B
14 KEVIN L. BROWN (INJ)-C
15 SHAWN GREEN-OF
17 TIM JOHNSON-MGR
18 BENITO SANTIAGO (INJ)-C
19 DAN PLESAC-P
20 MIKE STANLEY-DH/1B (1)
20 PATRICK LENNON-OF
21 ROGER (ROCKET) CLEMENS-P
22 SAL BUTERA-CH
23 JOSE CRUZ, JR.-OF
24 SHANNON STEWART-OF
25 CARLOS DELGADO (INJ)-1B/DH
26 CHRIS CARPENTER-P
28 RANDY MYERS-P (1)
30 WOODY WILLIAMS-P
31 ROBERT PERSON-P
33 ED SPRAGUE, JR.-3B (1)
33 JOSE CANSECO-DH/OF
34 MEL QUEEN, JR.-CH
36 GARY (SARGE) MATTHEWS-CH
37 DAVE STIEB-P
39 ERIK HANSON (INJ)-P
39 NERIO RODRIGUEZ-P (2)
40 CARLOS ALMANZAR-P
41 PAT HENTGEN (INJ)-P
42 *(RET#) JACKIE ROBINSON*
44 JOSE CANSECO-DH/OF
45 KELVIM ESCOBAR (INJ)-P
48 PAUL QUANTRILL-P
49 LUIS ANDUJAR-P
50 CRIS CARPENTER-P
50 BEN VANRYN (WAIV)-P (3)
52 ROY HALLADAY-P
53 STEVE SINCLAIR-P
55 BILL RISLEY-P
57 JUAN GUZMAN-P (1)
58 SHANNON WITHEM-P
59 MARK DALESANDRO-INF
__ JACK HUBBARD-CH

1999

3RD E 84-78 14GB

1 TONY FERNANDEZ-SS
2 JACOB BRUMFIELD-DH (2)
3 NORBERTO (PACO) MARTIN-2B
3 VERNON WELLS-OF
4 CRAIG GREBECK (INJ)-2B/INF
5 MARK DALESANDRO-C
6 KEVIN WITT-1B
7 PAT KELLY-2B
7 TONY BATISTA-SS (2)
8 ALEX GONZALEZ (INJ)-2B/SS
9 DARRIN FLETCHER-C
10 JIM LETT-CH
11 JIM FREGOSI-MGR
12 WILLIE GREENE-INF
13 PETER MUNRO-P
14 KEVIN L. BROWN (INJ)-C
15 SHAWN GREEN-OF
16 LLOYD (SHAKER) MOSEBY-CH
17 DAVE HOLLINS-3B/DH
17 CURTIS GOODWIN-OF (2)
18 HOMER BUSH (INJ)-INF
19 DAN PLESAC-P (1)
19 DAVID SEGUI (INJ)-1B (2)
20 PATRICK LENNON-OF
20 ROB BUTLER-OF
21 WILLIS OTANEZ (INJ)-INF (2)
22 MIKE MATHENY (INJ)-C
23 JOSE CRUZ, JR. (INJ)-OF
24 SHANNON STEWART-OF
25 CARLOS DELGADO (INJ)-1B/DH
26 CHRIS CARPENTER-P
27 ANTHONY SANDERS-OF
28 CASEY BLAKE-INF
29 GERONIMO BERROA (INJ)-OF
29 PAT BORDERS-C (2)
30 MARTY PEVEY-CH
31 ROBERT PERSON-P (1)
31 CHRIS WOODWARD-SS
32 ROY HALLADAY-P
33 DAVID WELLS-P
34 MEL QUEEN, JR.-CH
35 TERRY BEVINGTON-CH
36 GARY (SARGE) MATTHEWS-CH
37 GRAEME LLOYD-P
39 NERIO RODRIGUEZ-P
40 ERIC LUDWICK (WAIV)-P

TORONTO BLUE JAYS

40 PAUL SPOLJARIC-P (2)
41 PAT HENTGEN-P
42 *(RET#) JACKIE ROBINSON*
43 TOM DAVEY-P (1)
43 JOHN HUDEK-P (3)
44 BILLY KOCH-P
45 JOHN BALE-P
46 STEVE SINCLAIR-P (1)
46 MIKE ROMANO-P
47 KELVIM ESCOBAR-P
48 PAUL QUANTRILL-P
50 JOEY HAMILTON (INJ)-P
51 GARY GLOVER-P
52 JOHN FRASCATORE-P (2)
(55) BILL RISLEY (INJ)-(P)
56 BRIAN MCRAE-OF (3)
69 PETER MUNRO-P

2000

3RD E 83-79 4.5GB

1 MICKEY MORANDINI-2B (2)
3 LEE ELIA-CH
4 CRAIG GREBECK-2B/INF
7 TONY BATISTA-INF
8 ALEX GONZALEZ (INJ)-2B/SS
9 DARRIN FLETCHER-C
10 VERNON WELLS-OF
11 JIM FREGOSI-MGR
13 PETER MUNRO (INJ)-P
14 DAVE MARTINEZ-OF (4)
15 CHAD MOTTOLA-OF
15 MARTY CORDOVA-OF
16 ANDY THOMPSON-OF
18 HOMER BUSH-INF
19 JOSH PHELPS-P
20 BRAD FULLMER-DH
21 CHARLIE GREENE-C
21 ESTEBAN LOAIZA-P (2)
22 RICK LANGFORD-CH
22 ROB DUCEY-OF (2)
22 CHAD MOTTOLA-OF
23 JOSE CRUZ, JR.-OF
24 SHANNON STEWART-OF
25 CARLOS DELGADO (INJ)-1B/DH
26 CHRIS CARPENTER-P
27 TODD GREENE-DH
28 LANCE PAINTER-P
29 BOBBY KNOOP-CH
30 ALBERTO CASTILLO-C
31 CHRIS WOODWARD-SS
32 ROY HALLADAY-P
33 DAVID WELLS-P
34 DARWIN CUBILLAN-P (1)
35 TERRY BEVINGTON-CH
36 CLAYTON ANDREWS-P
36 PEDRO BORBON-P
37 FRANK CASTILLO-P
38 MARK GUTHRIE-P (3)
39 ERIC GUNDERSON-P
40 MATT DEWITT (INJ)-P
41 CITO GASTON-CH
42 *(RET#) JACKIE ROBINSON*
43 RAUL MONDESI (INJ)-OF
44 BILLY KOCH-P
46 STEVE TRACHSEL-P (2)
47 KELVIM ESCOBAR-P
48 PAUL QUANTRILL-P
49 JOHN BALE-P
50 LEO ESTRELLA-P
50 JOEY HAMILTON (INJ)-P
51 PEDRO BORBON-P
52 JOHN FRASCATORE-P
54 PASQUAL COCO-P
55 ROBERT ELLIS-P
55 DEWAYNE WISE (INJ)-OF
56 ROLY DE ARMAS-OF

2001

3RD E 80-82 16GB

1 COOKIE ROJAS-CH
1 TONY FERNANDEZ-3B (2)
2 CESAR IZTURIS-SS
3 JEFF FRYE (INJ)-2B
4 COOKIE ROJAS-CH
5 CHRIS WOODWARD (INJ)-2B
7 TONY BATISTA (WAIV)-3B
7 FELIPE LOPEZ-3B
8 ALEX GONZALEZ-2B/SS
9 DARRIN FLETCHER-C
10 VERNON WELLS-OF
11 RYAN FREEL-2B
12 LUIS LOPEZ-1B
13 BUCK MARTINEZ-MGR
(15) ANDY THOMPSON (INJ)-(OF)
16 GARTH IORG-CH
17 CHRIS MICHALAK (WAIV)-P
17 JOSH PHELPS-C
18 HOMER BUSH (INJ)-INF
19 DAN PLESAC-P
20 BRAD FULLMER-DH
21 ESTEBAN LOAIZA-P
22 BRIAN SIMMONS-OF
23 JOSE CRUZ, JR. (INJ)-OF
24 SHANNON STEWART-OF
25 CARLOS DELGADO-1B/DH
26 CHRIS CARPENTER-P
27 CHRIS LATHAM-OF
28 LANCE PAINTER-P
28 BRANDON LYON-P
29 SCOTT EYRE-P
30 ALBERTO CASTILLO-C
32 ROY HALLADAY-P
(33) MIKE SIROTKA (INJ)-(P)
35 TERRY BEVINGTON-CH
36 BOB FILE-P
36 SCOTT EYRE-P
36 BOB FILE-P
37 BRIAN BOWLES-P
38 PASQUAL COCO-P
39 STEVE PARRIS (INJ)-P
40 KEVIN BEIRNE-P
41 CITO GASTON-CH
42 *(RET#) JACKIE ROBINSON*
43 RAUL MONDESI-OF
44 BILLY KOCH-P
45 KELVIM ESCOBAR-P
47 GIL PATTERSON-CH
48 PAUL QUANTRILL-P
49 MATT DEWITT-P
50 JOEY HAMILTON (REL)-P
51 PEDRO BORBON-P
52 JOHN FRASCATORE-P
53 MARK CONNOR-CH

2002

3RD E 78-84 25.5GB

2 DAVE BERG-UTIL
3 ORLANDO HUDSON-2B
4 COOKIE ROJAS-CH
5 CHRIS WOODWARD-SS/INF
6 JOE LAWRENCE-2B
7 FELIPE LOPEZ-SS/2B
8 PEDRO SWANN-DH/OF
9 DARRIN FLETCHER (RET)-C/DH
10 VERNON WELLS-OF
11 ERIC HINSKE-3B
13 BUCK MARTINEZ-MGR1
14 CARLOS TOSCA-CH/MGR2
15 TOM WILSON-C/DH/1B
16 GARTH IORG-CH
16 DEWAYNE WISE-OF/DH
17 JOSH PHELPS-DH/C
18 HOMER BUSH-2B (1)
19 DAN PLESAC-P (1)
19 CLIFF POLLITTE-P (2)
20 KEN HUCKABY-C
21 ESTEBAN LOAIZA (INJ)-P
23 JOSE CRUZ, JR. (INJ)-OF/DH
24 SHANNON STEWART-OF/DH
25 CARLOS DELGADO-1B/DH
26 CHRIS CARPENTER (INJ)-P
28 BRANDON LYON-P
29 SCOTT EYRE-P (1)
29 KEVIN CASH-C
30 BRIAN LESHER-1B/OF
32 ROY HALLADAY-P
(33) MIKE SIROTKA (INJ)-(P)
34 JUSTIN MILLER-P
35 COREY THURMAN-CH
36 BOB FILE-P
37 BRIAN BOWLES-P
38 PASQUAL COCO-P
39 STEVE PARRIS (INJ)-P
40 SCOTT CASSIDY-P
41 PETE WALKER-P (2)
42 *(RET#) JACKIE ROBINSON*
43 RAUL MONDESI-OF/DH (1)
43 SCOTT CASSIDY-P
43 MARK HENDRICKSON-P
44 LUKE PROKOPEC (INJ)-P
45 KELVIM ESCOBAR-P
46 JASON KERSCHNER-P (2)
47 GIL PATTERSON-CH
49 FELIX HEREDIA-P
50 BRIAN COOPER-P
51 PEDRO BORBON-P (1)
52 BRUCE WALTON-CH
53 MARK CONNOR-CH
53 MIKE SMITH-P
54 JAYSON WERTH-OF
55 GUTTIEREZ-CH??
55 BRIAN BUTTERFIELD-CH
57 SCOTT WIGGINS-P
58 JOHN GIBBONS-CH

2003

3RD E 86-76 15GB

2 DAVE BERG (INJ)-UTIL
3 ORLANDO HUDSON-2B
5 CHRIS WOODWARD-SS
6 HOWIE CLARK-UTIL
7* JOSH TOWERS-P*
9 TOM WILSON-C/1B
10 VERNON WELLS-OF
11 ERIC HINSKE (INJ)-3B
13 JAYSON WERTH (INJ)-OF
14 CARLOS TOSCA-MGR
16 MIKE BORDICK-INF
17 JOSH PHELPS (INJ)-DH/1B
19 CLIFF POLLITTE (INJ)-P
20 KEN HUCKABY-C
21 CORY LIDLE (INJ)-P
23 SHANNON STEWART-OF (1)
24 BOBBY KIELTY-OF/1B (2)
25 CARLOS DELGADO-1B/DH
26 BRUCE BOWLES-P
27 FRANK CATALANOTTO-OF/DH/1B
28 GREG MYERS-C/DH
29 KEVIN CASH-C
30 DOUG LINTON-P
31 TANYON STURTZE-P
32 ROY HALLADAY-P
33 JEFF TAM-P
(34) JUSTIN MILLER (INJ)-(P)
35 COREY THURMAN-P
(36) BOB FILE (INJ)-(P)
37 REED JOHNSON-OF
38 JOHN WASDIN-P
39 DOUG CREEK (INJ)-P
41 PETE WALKER (INJ)-P
42 *(RET#) JACKIE ROBINSON*
43 MARK HENDRICKSON-P
44 AQUILINO LOPEZ-P
45 KELVIM ESCOBAR-P
46 JASON KERSCHNER-P
47 GIL PATTERSON-CH
48 DOUG DAVIS-P (2)
50 VINNY CHULK-P
51 TREVER MILLER-P
52 BRUCE WALTON-CH
53 SCOTT SERVICE-P (2)
54 DAN REICHERT-P
55 BRIAN BUTTERFIELD-CH
56 MIKE BARNETT-CH
57 JUAN ACEVEDO (BRV)-P (2)
58 JOHN GIBBONS-CH

2004

5TH E 67-94 33.5GB

1 ORLANDO HUDSON-2B
2 DAVE BERG-DH/OF
3 CHRIS GOMEZ-SS
4 FRANK MENECHINO-INF/DH
5 CHRIS WOODWARD (INJ)-SS
6 HOWIE CLARK-3B
7* JOSH TOWERS-P*
8 RUSS ADAMS-SS
9 GREGG ZAUN-C
10 VERNON WELLS-OF
11 ERIC HINSKE-3B
12 JOE BREEDEN-CH
14 CARLOS TOSCA-MGR1
15 ALEXIS RIOS-OF
16 GUILLERMO QUIROZ-C
17 JOSH PHELPS-DH/1B (1)
18 SIMON POND-OF/DH
20 BOBBY ESTALELLA-C (2)
21 GABE GROSS-OF
23 JASON KERSHNER-P
24 SEAN DOUGLASS-P
25 CARLOS DELGADO-1B/DH
26 VALERIO DE LOS SANTOS (INJ)-P
27 FRANK CATALANOTTO (INJ)-OF/DH
28 GREG MYERS (INJ)-C
29 KEVIN CASH-C
30 JUSTIN SPEIER (INJ)-P
31 TED LILLY-P
32 ROY HALLADAY-P
33 CHAD HERMANSON-OF
34 JUSTIN MILLER-P
35 BRANDON LEAGUE-P
36 BOB FILE (INJ)-P
37 REED JOHNSON-OF
39 GUSTAVO CHACIN-P
41 PAT HENTGEN (RET)-P
42 *(RET#) JACKIE ROBINSON*
43 MIGUEL BATISTA-P
44 AQUILINO LOPEZ-P
46 KERRY LIGTENBERG (INJ)-P
47 GIL PATTERSON-CH
48 KEVIN FREDERICK-P
49 DAVE BUSH-P
50 VINNY CHULK-P
51 TERRY ADAMS-P (1)
51 DAVE MAURER-P
51 RYAN GLYNN-P
52 BRUCE WALTON-CH
53 MIKE NAKAMURA-P
54 JASON FRASOR-P
55 BRIAN BUTTERFIELD-CH
56 MIKE BARNETT-CH
58 JOHN GIBBONS-CH/MGR2
59 ADAM PETERSON-P

2005

3RD E 80-82 15GB

1 ORLANDO HUDSON-2B
2 AARON HILL-INF/DH
3 REED JOHNSON-OF
4 FRANK MENECHINO-2B/DH
5 JOHN GIBBONS-MGR
6 JOHN MCDONALD-SS (1)
7* JOSH TOWERS-P*
8 RUSS ADAMS-SS
9 GREGG ZAUN (INJ)-C
10 VERNON WELLS-OF
11 ERIC HINSKE-3B/1B
12 ERNIE WHITT-CH
14 MICKEY BRANTLEY-CH
15 ALEXIS RIOS-OF
16 GUILLERMO QUIROZ-C
18 GABE GROSS-OF
20 KEN HUCKABY-C
22 BRANDON LEAGUE-OF
24 JOHN-FORD GRIFFIN-OF
27 FRANK CATALANOTTO (BRV)-OF
28 GREG MYERS-C
28 SHAUN MARCUM-P
29 SHEA HILLENBRAND-UTIL
30 JUSTIN SPEIER-P
31 TED LILLY (INJ)-P
32 ROY HALLADAY (INJ)-P
34 JUSTIN MILLER-P
35 CHAD GAUDIN-P
37 SCOTT DOWNS-P
38 BRAD ARNSBERG-P
39 GUSTAVO CHACIN-P
40 DUSTIN MCGOWAN-P
41 PETE WALKER-P
42 *(RET#) JACKIE ROBINSON*
43 MIGUEL BATISTA-P
47 COREY KOSKIE (INJ)-3B
48 MATT WHITESIDE
49 DAVE BUSH-P
50 VINNY CHULK-P
52 BRUCE WALTON-CH
54 JASON FRASOR-P
55 BRIAN BUTTERFIELD-CH
56 MIKE BARNETT-CH
58 ANDY DOMINIQUE-C
60 SCOTT SCHOENEWEIS-P

Jim Clancy reached his high in wins—16 in '82.

ARIZONA DIAMONDBACKS

1998
ARIZONA DIAMONDBACKS
5TH W 55-97 33GB

2 HANLEY FRIAS (INJ)-INF
5 ANDY STANKIEWICZ-INF
6 ANDY FOX-OF/3B
7 DANNY KLASSEN-SS
9 MATT WILLIAMS (INJ)-3B
10 TONY BATISTA-INF
11 BUCK SHOWALTER-MGR
12 JORGE FABREGAS (INJ)-C (1)
14 BRENT BREDE-OF
14 CARLOS TOSCA-CH
15 BRENT BREDE-OF
16 TRAVIS LEE (INJ)-1B
17 JIM PRESLEY-CH
18 CHRIS C. JONES-OF (1)
19 WILLIE BLAIR-P (1)
20 JEFF SUPPAN-P (1)
21 DWAYNE MURPHY-CH
22 DEVON WHITE-OF
23 BERNARD GILKEY-OF (2)
24 KAREM GARCIA-OF
25 DAVID DELLUCCI-OF
26 DAMIAN MILLER-C
(27) CORY LIDLE (INJ)-(P)
29 HENSLEY MEULENS-OF
29 BOB WOLCOTT-P
30 GREGG OLSON-P
31 RUSS SPRINGER-P (1)
31 AARON SMALL-P (2)
32 ALAN EMBREE-P (2)
33 JAY BELL-SS
34 BRIAN ANDERSON-P
35 KELLY STINNETT-C
36 CLINT SADOWSKY-P
37 OMAR DAAL (INJ)-P
38 JOEL ADAMSON (INJ)-P
39 BARRY MANUEL-P
40 ANDY BENES-P
41 EDDIE DIAZ-2B
42 *(RET #) JACKIE ROBINSON*
43 YAMIL BENITEZ-OF
(44) KEN ROBINSON (INJ)-(P)
44 AMAURY TELEMACO-P (2)
46 SCOTT BROW-P (1)
46 WILLIE BANKS-P (2)
47 FELIX RODRIGUEZ (INJ)-P
48 CHRIS MICHALAK-P
49 BRYAN COREY-P
50 BEN FORD-P
51 MIKE ROBERTSON (WAIV) INF/OF
52 MARK CONNOR-CH
53 GLENN SHERLOCK-CH
55 BRIAN BUTTERFIELD-CH
57 RICKY PICKETT-P
57 BOBBY CHOUINARD-P (2)
58 EFRAIN VALDEZ-P
60 HANLEY FRIAS (INJ)-INF
66 NEIL WEBER-P
67 VLADIMIR NUNEZ-P

1999
1ST W 100-62 0 GB
L NLDS-NYN 3-1

2 HANLEY FRIAS-INF
4 DANTE POWELL-OF
5 TONY WOMACK-2B/OF
6 ANDY FOX-OF/3B
7 DANNY KLASSEN-SS
9 MATT WILLIAMS-3B
10 TONY BATISTA-INF (1)
11 BUCK SHOWALTER-MGR
10 TURNER WARD-OF (2)
12 STEVE FINLEY-OF
14 CARLOS TOSCA-CH
15 ROB RYAN-OF
16 TRAVIS LEE (INJ)-1B
17 JIM PRESLEY-CH
18 EDDIE DIAZ-2B
19 DAN PLESAC-P (2)
20 LUIS GONZALEZ-OF
21 DWAYNE MURPHY-CH
22 GREG SWINDELL (INJ)-P
23 BERNARD GILKEY-OF
25 DAVID DELLUCCI (INJ)-OF
26 DAMIAN MILLER-C
27 ARMANDO REYNOSO-P
28 GREG COLBRUNN-1B
29 LENNY HARRIS-INF (2)
30 GREGG OLSON-P
31 MATT MANTEI-P (2)
32 TODD STOTTLEMYRE (INJ)-P
33 JAY BELL-SS
34 BRIAN ANDERSON-P
35 KELLY STINNETT-C
36 ERIK SABEL-P
37 OMAR DAAL-P
40 ANDY BENES-P
41 BOBBY CHOUINARD-P
42 *(RET #) JACKIE ROBINSON*
43 DAN CARLSON-P
44 AMAURY TELEMACO (INJ)-P (1)
44 ERUBIEL DURAZO-INF
45 VICENTE PADILLA-P
46 DARREN HOLMES-P
47 ERNIE YOUNG-P
48 VLADIMIR NUNEZ-P (1)
48 ROD BARAJAS-C
49 BYUNG HYUN KIM-P
50 JOHN FRISCATORE-P (1)
50 ED VOSBERG-P (2)
51 RANDY JOHNSON-P
52 MARK CONNOR-CH
53 GLENN SHERLOCK-CH
55 BRIAN BUTTERFIELD-CH
BRIAN SHOUSE (INJ)-(P)

2000
3RD W 85-77 12GB

2 HANLEY FRIAS-INF
3 DANNY KLASSEN-INF
4 CRAIG COUNSELL-INF
5 TONY WOMACK-INF
6 ANDY FOX-OF/3B (1)
9 MATT WILLIAMS-3B
10 TURNER WARD-OF
11 BUCK SHOWALTER-MGR
12 STEVE FINLEY-OF
13 JASON CONTI-OF
14 CARLOS TOSCA-CH
15 ROB RYAN-OF
16 TRAVIS LEE (INJ)-1B (1)
17 JIM PRESLEY-CH
19 DAN PLESAC-P
20 LUIS GONZALEZ-OF
21 DWAYNE MURPHY-CH
22 GREG SWINDELL-P
23 BERNARD GILKEY-OF (1)
23 MATT MIESKE-OF (2)
25 DAVID DELLUCCI (INJ)-OF
26 DAMIAN MILLER-C
27 ARMANDO REYNOSO-P
28 GREG COLBRUNN-1B
29 LENNY HARRIS-INF (1)
29 DANNY BAUTISTA-OF (2)
30 TODD STOTTLEMYRE (INJ)-P
31 MATT MANTEI-P
33 JAY BELL-SS
34 BRIAN ANDERSON-P
35 KELLY STINNETT-C
36 MIKE MORGAN-P
37 OMAR DAAL-P (1)
38 CURT SCHILLING-P (2)
39 ALEX CABRERA-INF
40 DARREN HOLMES-P (1)(4)
42 *(RET #) JACKIE ROBINSON*
44 ERUBIEL DURASO-INF
45 VICENTE PADILLA-P (1)
46 RUSS SPRINGER-P
47 JOHNNY RUFFIN-P
48 ROD BARAJAS-C
49 BYUNG HYUN KIM-P
50 GERALDO GUZMAN-P
51 RANDY JOHNSON-P
52 MARK CONNOR-CH
55 BRIAN BUTTERFIELD-CH
56 NELSON FIGUEROA-P
56 JOHNNY RUFFIN-P
__ TODD REVENIG-CH
__ KERRY WOODSON-CH

2001
1ST W 92-70 0 GB
W NLDS-STL 3-2
W NLCS-ATL 4-1
W WS NYA 4-3

2 JUAN SOSA-3B
3 BOB MELVIN-CH
4 CRAIG COUNSELL-INF
5 TONY WOMACK (INJ)-INF
6 JASON CONTI-OF (1)
6 RYAN CHRISTENSON-OF (2)
8 ROB RYAN-OF (1)
8 RYAN CHRISTENSON-OF (2)
8 MIKE DIFELICE (SUS-2G)-C
9 MATT WILLIAMS (INJ)-3B
10 ALEX CLINTON-SS
12 STEVE FINLEY-OF
13 MIDRE CUMMINGS-OF
14 EDDIE RODRIGUEZ-CH
15 BOB BRENLY-MGR
16 REGGIE SANDERS (INJ)-OF
17 MARK GRACE-1B
19 JACK CUST-OF
20 LUIS GONZALEZ-OF
21 DWAYNE MURPHY-CH
22 GREG SWINDELL-P
25 DAVID DELLUCCI (INJ)-OF
26 DAMIAN MILLER-C
27 ARMANDO REYNOSO (INJ)-P
28 GREG COLBRUNN (INJ)-1B
29 DANNY BAUTISTA-OF
(30) TODD STOTTLEMYRE (INJ)-(P)
31 MATT MANTEI (INJ)-P
32 BOB WELCH-CH
32 ALBIE LOPEZ-P (2)
33 JAY BELL-2B
34 BRIAN ANDERSON (INJ)-P
35 CHRIS SPEIER-CH
36 MIKE MORGAN (INJ)-P
37 JUNIOR SPIVEY-2B
38 CURT SCHILLING-P
39 CHAD MOELLER-C
40 BOBBY WITT (INJ)-P
41 BRET PRINZ-P
42 *(RET #) JACKIE ROBINSON*
43 MIGUEL BATISTA-P
44 ERUBIEL DURASO (INJ)-1B
45 KEN HUCKABY-C
46 RUSS SPRINGER (INJ)-P
47 NICK BIERBRODT-P (1)
48 ROD BARAJAS-C
49 BYUNG HYUN KIM-P
50 GERALDO GUZMAN-P
51 RANDY JOHNSON-P
52 MIKE MOHLER-P
53 GLENN SHERLOCK-CH
54 ROY BROHAWN-P
55 ROBERT ELLIS-P
56 ERIK SABEL-P
57 ERIC KNOTT-P
58 MIKE KOPLOVE-P
61 LYLE OVERBAY-INF

2002
1ST W 98-64 0 GB
L NLDS-STL 3-0

3 BOB MELVIN-CH
4 CRAIG COUNSELL (INJ)-INF
5 TONY WOMACK (INJ)-SS/OF
6 QUINTON MCCRACKEN-OF
7 DANNY KLASSEN-3B/SS
8 FELIX JOSE-OF
9 MATT WILLIAMS (INJ)-3B
10 ALEX CLINTON-INF
11 JOSE GUILLEN-OF (1)
11 MARK LITTLE-OF (3)
12 STEVE FINLEY-OF
14 EDDIE RODRIGUEZ-CH
15 BOB BRENLY-MGR
16 CHAD MOELLER-C
17 MARK GRACE-1B/P
18 CHRIS DONNELS (INJ)-3B/1B
19 ROBIN YOUNT-CH
20 LUIS GONZALEZ-OF
21 DWAYNE MURPHY-CH
22 GREG SWINDELL (INJ)-P
23 LYLE OVERBAY-1B
24 JOHN PATTERSON-P
25 DAVID DELLUCCI-OF
26 DAMIAN MILLER-C
27 ARMANDO REYNOSO (INJ)-P
28 GREG COLBRUNN (INJ)-1B/3B
29 DANNY BAUTISTA (INJ)-OF
30 TODD STOTTLEMYRE (INJ)-P
31 MATT MANTEI (INJ)-P
32 RICH HELLING-P
33 JAY BELL (INJ)-INF
34 BRIAN ANDERSON-P
35 MIKE MYERS-P
36 MIKE MORGAN (INJ)-P
37 JUNIOR SPIVEY-2B
38 CURT SCHILLING-P
39 MIKE FETTERS-P
40 BOBBY WITT (INJ)-P
41 BRET PRINZ-P
42 *(RET#) JACKIE ROBINSON*
43 MIGUEL BATISTA-P
44 ERUBIEL DURASO-1B/OF
47 EDDIE OROPESA-P
48 ROD BARAJAS-C/1B
49 BYUNG HYUN KIM-P
50 CHUCK KNIFFIN-CH
51 RANDY JOHNSON-P
52 DUANER SANCHEZ-P (1)
52 JOSE PARRA-P
53 GLENN SHERLOCK-CH
58 MIKE KOPLOVE-P

2003
3RD W 84-78 16.5GB

3 CARLOS BAERGA-INF
4 CRAIG COUNSELL (INJ)-INF
5 TONY WOMACK (INJ)-SS (1)
6 QUINTON MCCRACKEN-OF
7 ROBBY HAMMOCK-C/UTIL
8 FELIX JOSE-OF/PH
9 MATT WILLIAMS (REL)-3B
10 ALEX CLINTON-SS/INF
11 MATT KATA-2B/INF
12 STEVE FINLEY-OF
14 EDDIE RODRIGUEZ-CH
15 BOB BRENLY-MGR
16 CHAD MOELLER-C
17 MARK GRACE (INJ) (RET)-1B
19 ROBIN YOUNT-CH
20 LUIS GONZALEZ-OF
21 DWAYNE MURPHY-CH
23 LYLE OVERBAY-PH
24 JOHN PATTERSON-P
25 DAVID DELLUCCI (INJ)-OF (1)
25 MIGUEL BATISTA (SUS:10G)-P
26 RICKY BOTTALICO-P
27 LUIS TERRERO-OF
28 SHEA HILLENBRAND (INJ)-1B/3B (2)
29 DANNY BAUTISTA (INJ)-OF
31 MATT MANTEI (INJ)-P
34 STEPHEN RANDOLPH (INJ)-P
35 MIKE MYERS-P
36 SCOTT SERVICE-P (1)
36 BRADY RAGGIO-P
37 JUNIOR SPIVEY (INJ)-2B
38 CURT SCHILLING (INJ)-P
40 EDDIE OROPESA-P
40 DENNYS REYES-P (2)
41 BRET PRINZ (INJ)-P (1)
42 *(RET#) JACKIE ROBINSON*
43 MIGUEL BATISTA (SUS:10G)-P
43 RAUL MONDESI-OF (2)
45 ELMER DESSENS-P
47 JOSE VALVERDE-P
48 ROD BARAJAS (INJ)-C
49 BYUNG HYUN KIM (INJ)-P (1)
49 EDGAR GONZALEZ-P
50 CHUCK KNIFFIN-CH
51 RANDY JOHNSON (INJ)-P
52 ANDREW GOOD-P
53 GLENN SHERLOCK-CH
54 STEPHEN RANDOLPH (INJ)-P
54 EDDIE OROPESA-P
55 BRANDON WEBB (INJ)-P
56 OSCAR VILLARREAL-P
57 CHRIS CAPUANO-P
58 MIKE KOPLOVE (INJ)-P

2004
5TH W 51-111 42GB

1 ANDY GREEN-2B
2 ROBERTO ALOMAR-2B (1)
2 JERRY GIL-2B
3 CARLOS BAERGA (INJ)-1B
4 DONNIE SADLER-SS
4 QUINTON MCCRACKEN-OF (2)
5 SCOTT HAIRSTON-2B
6 BRENT MAYNE-C (1)
7 ROBBY HAMMOCK (INJ)-C
8 MATT KATA (INJ)-2B
9 RICH SCHU-CH
10 ALEX CLINTON-INF
11 RICHIE SEXSON (INJ)-1B
12 STEVE FINLEY-OF (1)
14 EDDIE RODRIGUEZ-CH
13 JEFF FASSERO-P (2)
15 BOB BRENLY-MGR1
15 KOYIE HILL (INJ)-C
16 CASEY FOSSUM (INJ)-P
17 BOBBY ESTALELLA-C (1)
17 TOMMY JONES-CH
18 CHAD TRACY-3B
19 ROBIN YOUNT-CH
20 LUIS GONZALEZ-OF
22 MIKE KOPLOVE-P
23 STEVE SPARKS-P
25 ALAN ZINTER-1B
26 DOUG DEVORE-OF
27 LUIS TERRERO-OF
28 SHEA HILLENBRAND-3B/1B
29 DANNY BAUTISTA-OF
31 MATT MANTEI-P
32 LANCE CORMIER-P
33 RANDY CHOATE-P

ARIZONA DIAMONDBACKS

34 STEPHEN RANDOLPH-P
35 GREG COLBRUNN (INJ)-1B
36 SCOTT SERVICE (INJ)-P
37 SHANE REYNOLDS (INJ)-P
39 BRIAN BRUNDY-P
39 MIKE FETTERS-P
40 SHANE NANCE (INJ)-P
41 GREG AQUINO-P
42 *(RET#) JACKIE ROBINSON*
43 JOSH KROEGER-OF
43 BRANDON VILLAFUERTE-P
44 MIKE GOSLING-P
45 ELMER DESSENS-P (1)
45 CHAD DURBIN-P (2)
47 JOSE VALVERDE-P
48 JUAN BRITO-C
49 EDGAR GONZALEZ-P
50 CHUCK KNIFFIN-CH
51 RANDY JOHNSON-P
52 ANDREW GOOD-P
53 GLENN SHERLOCK-CH
54 CASEY DAIGLE-P
55 BRANDON WEBB-P
56 OSCAR VILLARREAL-P
__ AL PEDRIQUE-CH/MGR2
__ LORENZO BUNDY-CH
__ DENNIS LEWALLYN-CH

2005

2TH W *77-85* *5GB*

1 ANDY GREEN-2B
(2) JERRY GIL (INJ)-(2B)
2 BRETT BUTLER-CH
3 BOB MELVIN-MGR
4 CRAIG COUNSELL-SS/2B
5 KOYIE HILL (INJ)-C
6 QUINTON MCCRACKEN-OF
8 MIKE ALDRETE-CH
9 SCOTT HAIRSTON-INF
10 ROYCE CLAYTON-SS
11 MATT KATA-2B (1)
12 ALEX CLINTON-SS
13 MARK DAVIS-CH
14 CARLOS TOSCA-CH
15 SHAWN GREEN-OF/1B
16 CONOR JACKSON-1B/OF
17 BRANDON WEBB-P
18 CHAD TRACY-3B
19 CHRIS SNYDER-C
20 LUIS (GONZO) GONZALEZ (BRV)-OF
21 RANDY CHOATE-P
22 JOSE CRUZ, JR. (INJ)-OF (1)
23 JAVIER VAZQUEZ-P
25 TROY GLAUS-3B
27 LUIS TERRERO (INJ)-OF
28 BUDDY GROOM-P (2)
29 CLAUDIO VARGAS-P (2)
30 BRIAN BRUNEY-P
31 MATT HERGES-P (2)
32 LANCE CORMIER-P
33 JAY BELL-CH
34 TONY CLARK-1B
35 KELLY STINNETT-C
36 KERRY LIGTENBERG-P
37 BRAD HALSEY-P
38 BRANDON LYON (INJ)-P
39 JAVIER LOPEZ-P (2)
41 GREG AQUINO (INJ)-P
42 *(RET#) JACKIE ROBINSON*
44 MIKE GOSLING-P
45 CLAUDIO VARGAS-P (2)
45 TIM WORRELL-P (2)
47 JOSE VALVERDE (INJ)-P
48 RUSS ORTIZ (INJ)-P
49 EDGAR GONZALEZ-P
50 JASON BULGER
52 BRANDON, MEDDERS-P
53 GLENN SHERLOCK-CH
55 SHAWN ESTES (INJ)-P
56 OSCAR VILLARREAL (INJ)-P
57 ARMANDO ALMANZA-P
57 DUSTIN NIPPERT-P
76 MIKE KOPLOVE-P

Veteran outfielder, Luis Gonzalez has been an All-Star four times. He led the National League in hits with 206 in 1999. Gonzo got the game winning hit in the seventh game of the World Series defeating the powerful Yankees.

1932
BOSTON BRAVES
5TH 77-77 13GB

1 RABBIT MARANVILLE-2B
2 RED WORTHINGTON (INJ)-OF
3 WALLY BERGER-OF/1B
4 WES SCHULMERICH-OF
5 ART (ART THE GREAT) SHIRES (INJ)-1B
5 BUCK JORDAN-1B
6 BILL (BUMP) AKERS-INF
7 FRITZ KNOTHE-3B
8 AL SPOHRER-C
9 PINKY HARGRAVE (INJ)-C
9 BUCKY WALTERS-3B
10 BILLY URBANSKI-SS
11 ED (BIG ED) BRANDT-P
12 SOCKS SEIBOLD-P
14 TOM ZACHARY-P
15 BEN CANTWELL-P
16 FRED FRANKHOUSE-P
17 BRUCE CUNNINGHAM-P
18 BOB BROWN-P
19 HUCK BETTS-P
20 RANDY MOORE-UTIL
21 OX ECKHARDT-PH
21 HUB (SHUCKS PRUETT (INJ)-P
22 FREDDY LEACH-OF
23 JOHNNY SCHULTE-C (2)
24 BILL (WEE WILLIE) SHERDEL-P (1)
24 HOD FORD-INF (2)
27 LEO (BLACKIE) MANGUM-P
28 DUTCH HOLLAND-OF
30 EARL CLARK-OF
32 HANK GOWDY-CH
33 DUFFY LEWIS-CH
34 BILL (DEACON) MCKECHNIE-MGR

1933
4TH 83-71 9GB

1 RABBIT MARANVILLE-2B
2 RED WORTHINGTON (INJ)-OF
3 WALLY BERGER-OF
4 RANDY MOORE-OF/1B
5 BUCK JORDAN-1B
6 BILLY URBANSKI-SS
7 FRITZ KNOTHE-3B/SS (1)
7 PINKY WHITNEY-3B/2B (2)
8 SHANTY HOGAN-C
9 AL SPOHRER-C
10 DUTCH HOLLAND-OF
10 JOE MOWRY-OF
11 WES SCHULMERICH-OF (1)
11 ED (BIG ED) BRANDT-P
12 HOD FORD-INF
12 BOB SMITH-P (2)
14 ED (BIG ED) BRANDT-P
14 WES SCHULMERICH-OF (1)
14 HAL (SHERIFF) LEE-OF (2)
15 TOM ZACHARY-P
16 BEN CANTWELL-P
17 BOB BROWN-P
18 HUCK BETTS-P
19 SOCKS SEIBOLD-P
20 FRED FRANKHOUSE-P
21 LEO (BLACKIE) MANGUM-P
22 EARL CLARK-OF
22 TOMMY THOMPSON-OF
23 PINKY HARGRAVE-C
24 ED (JACK) FALLENSTEIN-P
26 AL (A-1) WRIGHT-2B
26 RAY (IRON MAN) STARR-P (2)
27 DICK GYSELMAN-INF
31 HANK GOWDY-CH
32 DUFFY LEWIS-CH
33 BILL (DEACON) MCKECHNIE-MGR

1934
4TH 78-73 16GB

(1) RABBIT MARANVILLE (INJ) -(2B)
2 BILLY URBANSKI-SS
3 WALLY BERGER-OF
4 RANDY MOORE-OF/1B
5 BUCK JORDAN-1B
6 PINKY WHITNEY-3B/INF
7 RED WORTHINGTON-OF (1)
8 SHANTY HOGAN-C
9 AL SPOHRER-C
10 HAL (SHERIFF) LEE-OF/2B
11 ED (BIG ED) BRANDT-P
12 BEN CANTWELL-P
14 FRED FRANKHOUSE-P
15 HUCK BETTS-P
16 TOM ZACHARY-P
16 DICK (KEWPIE DICK) OLIVER (BARRETT)-P (1)
16 ELBIE FLETCHER-1B
16 BEN CANTWELL-P
17 BOB SMITH-P
18 JIM (JUMBO JIM) ELLIOTT-P (2)
20 BOB BROWN-P
21 LEO (BLACKIE) MANGUM-P
23 JOE MOWRY-OF/2B
23 DAN MCGEE-SS
23 JOHNNIE (TY TY) (KATZ) TYLER-OF
24 DICK GYSELMAN-3B/2B
25 TOMMY THOMPSON-OF
26 CLARENCE PICKREL-P
28 MARTY MCMANUS-2B/3B
29 FLINT (SHAD) RHEM-P (2)
30 LES MALLON-2B
31 HANK GOWDY-CH
32 DUFFY LEWIS-CH
33 BILL (DEACON) MCKECHNIE-MGR
34 HOWIE EVIS-CH

1935
8TH 38-115 61.5GB

1 RABBIT MARANVILLE-2B
2 BILLY URBANSKI-SS
3 BABE (BAMBINO) (THE SULTAN OF SWAT) RUTH-OF
4 WALLY BERGER-OF
5 BUCK JORDAN-1B/UTIL
6 PINKY WHITNEY-3B/2B
7 RANDY MOORE-OF/1B
8 SHANTY HOGAN-C
9 AL SPOHRER-C
10 HAL (SHERIFF) LEE-OF
10 JOE MOWRY-OF
11 ED (BIG ED) BRANDT-P
12 BOB BROWN-P
13 FLINT (SHAD) RHEM-P
14 FRED FRANKHOUSE-P
15 HUCK BETTS-P
16 BEN CANTWELL-P
17 BOB SMITH-P
18 TOMMY THOMPSON-OF
19 JOE MOWRY-OF
20 LES MALLON-2B/UTIL
21 LEO (BLACKIE) MANGUM-P
21 DANNY (DEACON DANNY) MACFAYDEN-P (2)
22 BILL (BUDDY) LEWIS-C
22 RAY (IRON MAN) MUELLER-C
23 ELBIE FLETCHER-1B
24 JOHNNIE (TY TY) (KATZ) TYLER-OF
26 JOE COSCARART-INF
27 AL BLANCHE-P
28 LARRY BENTON-P
30 ART (MOOSE) DOLL-C
31 HANK GOWDY-CH
32 DUFFY LEWIS-CH
33 BILL (DEACON) MCKECHNIE-MGR
__ ED MORIARTY-2B (8G: 6/21-7/5)

1936
6TH 71-83 21GB

1 GENE (ROWDY) MOORE-OF
2 BILLY URBANSKI-SS/3B
3 TONY (COOCH) (CHICK) CUCCINELLO-2B
4 WALLY BERGER-OF
5 BUCK JORDAN-1B
6 PINKY WHITNEY-3B (1)
6 MICKEY HASLIN-3B/2B (2)
7 AL LOPEZ-C/1B
8 BILL (BUDDY) LEWIS-C
9* ROY WEIR-P*
10 HAL (SHERIFF) LEE-OF
12 BOB BROWN-P
13 TOMMY THOMPSON-OF/1B
14 DANNY (DEACON DANNY) MACFAYDEN-P
15 TINY CHAPLIN-P
16 BEN CANTWELL-P
17 JOHNNY (TOBACCO CHEWIN' JOHNNY) LANNING-P
18 RAY BENGE-P (1)
19 ANDY PILNEY-PH
20 WAYNE (OSSIE)(FISH HOOK) OSBORNE-P
20 RAY (IRON MAN) MUELLER-C
20 SWEDE LARSEN-2B
21 JOHNNY BABICH-P
22 JOE COSCARART-3B/INF
24 BOBBY REIS-P
25 GENE FORD-P
25 GUY (MISSISSIPPI MUDCAT) BUSH-P (2)
26 AMBY MURRAY-P
27 JIM (IRISH) MCCLOSKY-P
28 HAL (AL) WEAFER-P
29 ART (MOOSE) DOLL-P
30 ED MORIARTY-PH
30 RABBIT WARSTLER-SS (2)
31 HANK GOWDY-CH
32 BOB SMITH-P
33 BILL (DEACON) MCKECHNIE-MGR
36 AL BLANCHE-P
40 JIM (IRISH) MCCLOSKY-P
__ FABIAN KOWALIK-P (3) (1G: 8/5)

1937
5TH 79-73 16GB

1 GENE (ROWDY) MOORE-OF
2 BILLY URBANSKI (INJ)-PH
2 GIL ENGLISH-3B (2)
3 TONY (COOCH) (CHICK) CUCCINELLO-2B
4 WALLY BERGER-OF (1)
4 JOHNNY (MUTT) RIDDLE-C (2)
5 ELBIE FLETCHER-1B (2)
6 VINCE DIMAGGIO-OF
7 AL LOPEZ-C
8 RABBIT WARSTLER-SS
9 DEBS (TEX) GARMS-OF/3B
10 RAY (IRON MAN) MUELLER-C
11 ROY WEIR (INJ)-P
12 BUCK JORDAN-PH (1)
12 ROY JOHNSON-OF/3B (2)
14 DANNY (DEACON DANNY) MACFAYDEN-P
16 VIC FRASIER-P
16 LOU FETTE-P
17 JOHNNY (TOBACCO CHEWIN' JOHNNY) LANNING-P
18 GUY (MISSISSIPPI MUDCAT) BUSH-P
19 BEAUTY MCGOWAN-OF
19 FRANK (THE GREAT GABBO) GABLER-P (2)
20 IRA HUTCHINSON-P
22 LINK WASEM-C
22 FRANK (THE GREAT GABBO) GABLER-P (2)
22 MILT SHOFFNER-P
23 JIM (MILKMAN JIM) TURNER -P
24 BOBBY REIS-OF/1B/P
25 BOB SMITH-P
29 EDDIE (HOTSHOT) MAYO-3B
30 BILL (DEACON) MCKECHNIE-MGR
31 HANK GOWDY-CH
32 TOMMY THEVENOW-INF

1938
5TH 77-75 12GB

1 GENE (ROWDY) MOORE (INJ)-OF
2 GIL ENGLISH-UTIL
3 TONY (COOCH) (CHICK) CUCCINELLO-2B
4 MAX WEST-OF/1B
5 ELBIE FLETCHER-1B
6 VINCE DIMAGGIO-OF/2B
7 AL LOPEZ (INJ)-C
8 RABBIT WARSTLER-SS/2B
9 DEBS (TEX) GARMS-UTIL
10 RAY (IRON MAN) MUELLER (INJ)-C
11 ROY WEIR-P
11 ART KENNEY-P
11 JOE (JERSEY JOE) STRIPP-3B (2)
12 ROY JOHNSON-OF
12 RALPH MCLEOD-OF
14 DANNY (DEACON DANNY) MACFAYDEN (INJ)-P
15 MILT SHOFFNER (ILL)-P
16 LOU FETTE-P
17 JOHNNY (TOBACCO CHEWIN' JOHNNY) LANNING-P
18 DICK (LIEF) ERRICKSON-P
19 JOHNNY (MUTT) RIDDLE-C
20 IRA HUTCHINSON-P
21 HARL MAGGERT-OF/3B
22 BOB KAHLE-PH
23 JIM (MILKMAN JIM) TURNER -P
24 BOBBY REIS-P/UTIL
25 BUTCH SUTCLIFFE-C
25 JOHNNY NIGGERLING-P
25 TOMMY REIS-P (2)
26 HIKER MORAN-P
26 MIKE BALAS-P
27 FRANK (THE GREAT GABBO) GABLER-P (1)
27 TOM EARLEY-P
29 EDDIE (HOTSHOT) MAYO-3B/2B
29 TOM (SUGAR) KANE-2B
29 JIM HITCHCOCK-SS/2B
29 JOE (TWEET) WALSH-SS
30 ART (MOOSE) DOLL-P
31 CASEY (THE OLE PROFESSOR) STENGEL-MGR
32 GEORGE (HIGHPOCKETS) KELLY-CH
33 MIKE KELLY-CH
34 JOHNNY COONEY-OF/1B

1939
7TH 63-88 32.5GB

1 BAMA ROWELL-OF
1 EDDIE (EPPIE) MILLER (INJ)-SS
2 HANK (HEENEY) (HEINE) MAJESKI-3B
2 OTTO HUBER-2B/3B
3 TONY (COOCH) (CHICK) CUCCINELLO (INJ)-2B
4 MAX WEST-OF
5 ELBIE FLETCHER-1B (1)
5 SIBBY SISTI-INF
6 BUDDY HASSETT-1B/OF
7 AL LOPEZ-C
8 RABBIT WARSTLER-INF
9 DEBS (TEX) GARMS-OF/3B
10 PHIL MASI-C
11 TOM EARLEY-P
12 FRED FRANKHOUSE-P
14 DANNY (DEACON DANNY) MACFAYDEN-P
15 MILT SHOFFNER-P (1)
15 WHITEY WIETELMANN-SS/2B
16 LOU FETTE-P
17 JOHNNY (TOBACCO CHEWIN' JOHNNY) LANNING-P
18 DICK (LIEF) ERRICKSON-P
19 JOE SULLIVAN-P
20 AL (BUCKETFOOT AL) SIMMONS-OF (1)
20 GEORGE (BARNEY) BARNICLE-P
21 BILL (BARNICLE BILL) (SAILOR BILL) POSEDEL-P
22 JIMMY OUTLAW-OF/3B
23 JIM (MILKMAN JIM) TURNER (INJ)-P
24 JOHNNY COONEY-OF/1B
25 OTTO HUBER-2B/3B
25 RALPH HODGIN-OF
25 SIBBY SISTI-INF
26 HIKER MORAN-P
27 AL VEIGEL-P
28 OLIVER HILL-PH
29 STAN (POLO) ANDREWS-C
31 CASEY (THE OLE PROFESSOR) STENGEL-MGR
32 GEORGE (HIGHPOCKETS) KELLY-CH
33 MIKE KELLY-CH
34 JOE CALLAHAN-P
36 BILL (BROADWAY BILL) SCHUSTER-SS/3B
37 RED BARKELY-SS/3B
38 CHET ROSS-OF
40 ROY WEIR-P
41 CHET CLEMENS-OF

1940
7TH 65-87 34.5GB

1 SIBBY SISTI-3B/2B
2 BUDDY HASSETT-1B/OF
3 LES SCARSELLA-1B
3 AL GLOSSOP-INF (2)
4 MAX WEST-OF/1B
3 TONY (COOCH) (CHICK) CUCCINELLO-3B (1)

BOSTON/MILWAUKEE/ ATLANTA BRAVES

5* ACE WILLIAMS-P*
6 CHET ROSS-OF
7 EDDIE (EPPIE) MILLER (INJ)-SS
8 AL LOPEZ-C (1)
8 GENE (ROWDY) MOORE-OF (2)
8 RAY BERRES-C (2)
9 JOHNNY COONEY-OF/1B
10 PHIL MASI-C
11 STAN (POLO) ANDREWS-C
12 RABBIT WARSTLER-INF (1)
12 ART (LEFTY) JOHNSON-P
14 MEL (PRIMO) PREIBISCH-OF
14 HANK (HEENEY) (HEINE) MAJESKI-PH
15 WHITEY WIETELMANN-INF
16 BAMA ROWELL-2B/OF
17 DON MANNO-OF
17 BOBBY LOANE-OF
18 LOU FETTE-P (1)
18 SIGGIE (CHOPS) BROSKIE-C
19 DICK (LIEF) ERRICKSON-P
20 BILL (BARNICLE BILL) (SAILOR BILL) POSEDEL-P
21 JOE SULLIVAN-P
22 JIM (ABBA DABBA) TOBIN (INJ)-P
23 BILL SWIFT-P
23 MANNY (GYP) SALVO-P
24 DICK COFFMAN-P
25 NICK (JUMBO) STRINCEVICH-P
26 TOM EARLEY-P
27 GEORGE (BARNEY) BARNICLE-P
28 AL (PIE) PIECHOTA-P
29 RAY BERRES-C (2)
30 JOE CALLAHAN-P
30 BUDDY GREMP-1B
31 MANNY (GYP) SALVO-P
31 CLAUDE WILBORN-OF
31 FRANK (HANK) LAMANNA-P
32 CASEY (THE OLE PROFESSOR) STENGEL-MGR
33 GEORGE (HIGHPOCKETS) KELLY-CH
34 AL (BEARTRACKS) JAVERY-P

1941

7TH 62-92 38GB

1 SIBBY SISTI-3B/INF
2 BUDDY HASSETT-1B
3 EARL (ROCK) AVERILL-OF
3 SKIPPY ROBERGE-INF
4 MAX WEST-OF
5 BABE DAHLGREN-1B/3B (1)
5* JOHNNY HUTCHINGS-P*(2)
6 CHET ROSS (INJ)-OF
7 EDDIE (EPPIE) MILLER-SS
8 GENE (ROWDY) MOORE-OF
9 JOHNNY COONEY-OF/1B
10 PHIL MASI-C
11 RAY BERRESOC
14 HANK (HEENEY) (HEINE) MAJESKI-3B
15 WHITEY WIETELMANN-INF
15 JOHN DUDRA-INF
16 BAMA ROWELL-2B/UTIL
17 BILL (BARNICLE BILL) (SAILOR BILL) POSEDEL-P
18 AL (BEARTRACKS) JAVERY-P
19 DICK (LIEF) ERRICKSON-P
20 EDDIE (LEFTY) CARNETT-P
20 FRANK DEMAREE-OF (2)
21 JOE SULLIVAN-P (1)
22 JIM (ABBA DABBA) TOBIN-P
23 MANNY (GYP) SALVO-P
24 FRANK (HANK) LAMANNA-P
25 NICK (JUMBO) STRINCEVICH-P (1)
26 TOM EARLEY-P
27 GEORGE (BARNEY) BARNICLE-P
27 AL MONTGOMERY-C
28 AL (PIE) PIECHOTA-P
29 ART (LEFTY) JOHNSON-P
30 WES FERRELL-P
31 PAUL (BIG POISON) WANER -OF/1B (2)
32 CASEY (THE OLE PROFESSOR) STENGEL-MGR
33 GEORGE (HIGHPOCKETS) KELLY-CH
33 BUDDY GREMP-UTIL
35 DON MANNO-UTIL
36 MEL (PRIMO) PREIBISCH-OF
37 BUSTER BRAY-OF
37 LLOYD (LITTLE POISON) WANER-OF (2)

1942

7TH 59-89 44GB

1 TOMMY (KELLY) HOLMES-OF
2 SIBBY SISTI-2B/OF
3 NANNY FERNANDEZ-3B/OF
4 MAX WEST-1B/OF
5 ERNIE (SCHNOZZ) (BOCCI) LOMBARDI-C
6 CHET ROSS-OF
7 EDDIE (EPPIE) MILLER-SS
8 PAUL (BIG POISON) WANER -OF
9 JOHNNY COONEY-OF/1B
10 PHIL MASI-C/OF
11 CLYDE KLUTTZ-C
12 FRANK DEMAREE-OF
14 SKIPPY ROBERGE-INF
15 TONY (COOCH) (CHICK) CUCCINELLO-3B/2B
16 LEFTY WALLACE-P
16 WARREN SPAHN-P
17 JOHNNY HUTCHINGS-P
18 AL (BEARTRACKS) JAVERY-P
19 DICK (LIEF) ERRICKSON-P (1)
19 MIKE SANDLOCK-SS
20 GEORGE DIEHL-P
20 FRANK MCELYEA-OF
21 BILL DONOVAN-P
22 JIM (ABBA DABBA) TOBIN-P
23 MANNY (GYP) SALVO-P
24 FRANK (HANK) LAMANNA-P
24 JIM (SID) HICKEY-P
25 WHITEY WIETELMANN-INF
26 TOM EARLEY-P
(27) AL MONTGOMERY (DIED)-(C)
27 LOU TOST-P
28 JOHNNY SAIN-P
29 ART (LEFTY) JOHNSON (MIL)-P
30 BUDDY GREMP (MIL)-1B/3B
31 DUCKY DETWEILER-3B
32 CASEY (THE OLE PROFESSOR) STENGEL-MGR
33 GEORGE (HIGHPOCKETS) KELLY-CH

1943

6TH 68-85 36.5GB

1 TOMMY (KELLY) HOLMES-OF
2 EDDIE JOOST-3B/INF
3 JOHNNY MCCARTHY (INJ/MIL)-1B
4 CHUCK WORKMAN-OF/INF
6 CHET ROSS-OF
7 WHITEY WIETELMANN-SS
8 BEN GERAGHTY-INF
8 HEINIE HELTZEL-3B
9* KERBY FARRELL-1B/P*
10 PHIL MASI-C
11 BILL BRUBAKER-3B/1B
12 CLYDE KLUTTZ-C
14 JOE BURNS-3B/OF
15 TONY (COOCH) (CHICK) CUCCINELLO-INF (1)
16 HUGH POLAND-C (2)
17 CONNIE CREEDEN-PH
18 AL (BEARTRACKS) JAVERY-P
19 RED BARRETT-P
20 GEORGE DIEHL-P
21 BILL DONOVAN (MIL)-P
21? CARL LINDQUIST-P (2G: 9/27-10/3)
22 JIM (ABBA DABBA) TOBIN-P
24 MANNY (GYP) SALVO-P (1)(3)
25 NATE ANDREWS-P
26 GEORGE JEFFCOAT-P
26 BEN (BIG BEN) CARDONI-P
27 LOU TOST-P
28 ROY TALCOTT-P
29 BUTCH NIEMAN-OF
30 CONNIE RYAN-2B/3B
31 BOB COLEMAN-CH
32 CASEY (THE OLE PROFESSOR) STENGEL-MGR
33 GEORGE (HIGHPOCKETS) KELLY-CH
34 DAVE (BLIMP) (PORKY) ODOM-P
35 SAM GENTILE-PH
35 RAY MARTIN (MIL)-P
36 ALLYN (FISH HOOK) STOUT -P
36 DANNY (DEACON DANNY) MACFAYDEN-P
42? JOHN DAGENHARD-P (2G: 9/28-10/3)
__ BUCK ETCHISON-1B (10G: 9/22-10/3)

1944

6TH 65-89 40GB

1 TOMMY (KELLY) HOLMES-OF
2 DAMON (DEE) PHILLIPS-3B/SS
2 BEN GERAGHTY-2B/3B
2 FRANK DREWS-2B
3 BUCK ETCHISON-1B
4 CHUCK WORKMAN-OF/3B
5 DAMON (DEE) PHILLIPS-3B/SS
5 AB WRIGHT-OF
6 CHET ROSS-OF
6 MIKE SANDLOCK-3B/SS
7 WHITEY WIETELMANN-SS/INF
8 CONNIE RYAN (MIL)-2B/3B
8 BEN GERAGHTY-2B/3B
8 DICK CULLER-SS
9* MAX MACON-1B/OF/P*
10 PHIL MASI-C/INF
11 CLYDE KLUTTZ-C
12 GENE PATTON-PR
14 HUGH POLAND-C
14 STEVE SHEMO-2B/3B
15 CHET CLEMENS (MIL)-OF
15 WARREN HUSTON-INF
16 BUTCH NIEMAN-OF
17 JIM (SID) HICKEY (MIL)-P
17 JOHNNY HUTCHINGS-P
18 AL (BEARTRACKS) JAVERY-P
19 RED BARRETT-P
20 BEN (BIG BEN) CARDONI-P
21 CARL LINDQUIST-P
21 PAT CAPRI-2B
22 JIM (ABBA DABBA) TOBIN-P
25 NATE ANDREWS-P
26 HARRY MACPHERSON-P
27 ROLAND GLADU-3B/OF
28 CHET ROSS-OF
28 WOODY RICH-P
29 STEW HOFFERTH-C
30 IRA HUTCHINSON-P
31 BOB COLEMAN-MGR
32 BENNY BENGOUGH-CH
33 TOM SHEEHAN-CH
34 FRANK DREWS-2B
34 ROLAND GLADU-3B/OF
34 STAN (BETZ) KLOPP-P
35 GEORGE WOODEND-P
43 IRA HUTCHINSON-P
EDDIE JOOST (RET)-(INF)

1945

6TH 67-85 30GB

1 TOMMY (KELLY) HOLMES-OF
2 FRANK DREWS (INJ)-2B
3 JOE MACK-1B
3 JOE (DUCKY) (MUSCLES) MEDWICK-OF/1B (2)
4 STAN WENTZEL-OF
4 CARDEN GILLENWATER-OF
5 TOMMY NELSON-3B/2B
5 JOE (DUCKY) (MUSCLES) MEDWICK-OF/1B (2)
5 VINCE SHUPE-1B
6 CHUCK WORKMAN-3B/OF
7* WHITEY WIETELMANN (INJ)-2B/INF/P*
8 DICK CULLER-SS/3B
9* LEFTY WALLACE-P*
9 EDDIE JOOST (INJ)-2B/3B
9 STEW HOFFERTH-C
10 PHIL MASI-C/1B
11 CLYDE KLUTTZ-C (1)
11 TOMMY NELSON-3B/2B
11 IRA HUTCHINSON-P
12 JOE HEVING-P
12 NORM WALLEN-3B
13 MORT COOPER (INJ)-P
14 ED WRIGHT-P
14 BILL (SQUARE JAW) RAMSEY-OF
15 LEFTY WALLACE-P
15 BOB WHITCHER0P
15 EWALD (LEFTY) PYLE-P (2)
16 BUTCH NIEMAN-OF
17 JOHNNY HUTCHINGS-P
18 AL (BEARTRACKS) JAVERY (INJ)-P
19 IRA HUTCHINSON-P
19 RED BARRETT-P (1)
20 BEN (BIG BEN) CARDONI-P
20 BOB LOGAN, (LEFTY)-P
21 STEW HOFFERTH-C
21 CHARLIE COZART-P
22 JIM (ABBA DABBA) TOBIN-P (1)
22 ELMER (SMOKY) SINGLETON-P
23 LOU FETTE-P
24 DON HENDRICKSON-P
24 TOM EARLEY-P
25 NATE ANDREWS-P
25 BEN (BIG BEN) CARDONI-P
26 HAL SCHACKER-P
26 BILL (BIG BILL) LEE-P (2)
27 EDDIE JOOST (INJ)-2B/3B
28 STEVE SHEMO-INF
28 MORRIE ADERHOLT-OF/2B (2)
29 BILL (SQUARE JAW) RAMSEY-OF
29 MIKE (SLUGS) ULISNEY-C
31 BOB COLEMAN-MGR1
32 BENNY BENGOUGH-CH
33 DEL BISSONETTE-CH/MGR2

1946

4TH 81-72 15.5GB

1 TOMMY (KELLY) HOLMES-OF
2 JOHNNY (JACK) BARRETT (INJ)-OF
2 SIBBY SISTI-3B
3 TOMMY NEILL-OF
3 JOHNNY MCCARTHY-1B
4 MAX WEST-1B (1)
4 BAMA ROWELL-OF
4 RAY SANDERS (INJ)-1B
5 RAY SANDERS (INJ)-1B
5 BAMA ROWELL-OF
6 CHUCK WORKMAN-OF (1)
6 DON PADGETT-C (2)
7* WHITEY WIETELMANN-INF/P*
8 CONNIE RYAN-2B/3B
9 BOB KEELY-CH
9 HUGH POLAND-C
10 PHIL MASI-C
11 NANNY FERNANDEZ-3B/UTIL
12 JOHNNY (HIPPITY) HOPP-1B/OF
13 MORT COOPER-P
14 DICK CULLER-SS
15 ELMER (SMOKY) SINGLETON-P
15 BOB BRADY-C
16 ED WRIGHT-P
17 JOHNNY HUTCHINGS-P
17 STEVE ROSER-P (2)
18 HUGH POLAND-C
18 ACE WILLIAMS-P
18 ERNIE WHITE-P
19 LEFTY WALLACE-P
19 FRANK (RED) BARRETT-P
20 SKIPPY ROBERGE-3B
20 BILLY HERMAN-INF (2)
21 AL (BEARTRACKS) JAVERY (INJ)-P
21 WARREN SPAHN (MIL)-P
22 EARL REID-P
22 DANNY LITWHILER-OF/3B (2)
23 ACE WILLIAMS-P
23 EARL REID-P
23 ALVIN (AL) (BLACKIE) DARK -SS/OF
24 CARDEN GILLENWATER-OF
25 BILL (BARNICLE BILL) (SAILOR BILL) POSEDEL-P
26 BILL (BIG BILL) LEE-P
27 STEW HOFFERTH-C
27 KEN O'DEA-C
28 JOHNNY COONEY-CH
29 JAKE FLOWERS-CH
30 BILLY SOUTHWORTH-MGR
31 DICK MULLIGAN-P
31 MIKE MCCORMICK-OF (2)
32 DUCKY DETWEILER-PH
32 JOHNNY NIGGELING-P
33 JOHNNY SAIN-P
34 DON HENDRICKSON-P
34 LEFTY WALLACE-P

34 SI JOHNSON-P (2)
35 DON HENDRICKSON-P
36 SI JOHNSON-P (2)
38 JIM KONSTANTY-P
MAX MACON (MIL)-(P)
RAY MARTIN (MIL)-(P)
__ DAMON (DEE) PHILLIPS-PH (2G: 9/22-29)

1947

3RD 86-68 8GB

1 TOMMY (KELLY) HOLMES-OF
2 TOMMY NEILL-OF
3 BOB (MR. TEAM) ELLIOTT-3B
4 DANNY LITWHILER-OF
5 BAMA ROWELL-OF/INF
6 FRANK (BUCK) MCCORMICK-1B (2)
7 SIBBY SISTI-SS/2B
8 CONNIE RYAN-2B/SS
9 EARL (THE EARL OF SNOHOMISH) TORGESON-1B
10 PHIL MASI-C
11 NANNY FERNANDEZ-UTIL
11 RAY MARTIN-P
12 JOHNNY (HIPPITY) HOPP-OF
13 MORT COOPER-P (1)
14 DICK CULLER-SS
15 DANNY MURTAUGH-2B/3B
16 ED WRIGHT-P
18 ANDY KARL-P
20 MAX MACON-P
21 WARREN SPAHN-P
22 HANK CAMELLI-C
23 BOB BRADY-PH
24 ANDY KARL-P
24 JOHNNY (TOBACCO CHEWIN' JOHNNY) LANNING-P
25 RED BARRETT-P
26 CLYDE (HARDROCK) SHOUN-P (2)
27 JOHNNY (NIG) BEAZLEY (INJ)-P
28 JOHNNY COONEY-CH
29 ERNIE WHITE (INJ)-P
30 BILLY SOUTHWORTH-MGR
31 MIKE MCCORMICK-OF
32 DICK MULLIGAN-P
33 JOHNNY SAIN-P
34 WALT LANFRANCONI-P
35 BOB KEELY-CH
36 SI JOHNSON-P
37 GLENN (LEFTY) ELLIOTT-P
96 BILL (BIG BILL)(NINETY-SIX) VOISELLE-P (2)
RAY SANDERS (INJ)-(1B)

1948

1ST 91-62 0GB

L WS-CLEA 4-2

1 TOMMY (KELLY) HOLMES-OF
2 ALVIN (AL) (BLACKIE) DARK-SS
3 BOB (MR. TEAM) ELLIOTT-3B
4 DANNY LITWHILER-OF (1)
4 JEFF HEATH (INJ)-OF
4 MARV (TWITCH) RICKERT-OF (2)
5 JIM RUSSELL (ILL)-OF
5 RAY SANDERS-PH
6 FRANK (BUCK) MCCORMICK-1B
7 SIBBY SISTI-SS/2B
8 CONNIE RYAN-2B/3B
9 EARL (THE EARL OF SNOHOMISH) TORGESON-1B
10 PHIL MASI-C
11 PAUL BURRIS-C
11 RAY MARTIN-P
12 EDDIE (THE BRAT) (MUGGSY) STANKY (INJ)-2B
13 RED BARRETT-P
14 BOBBY STURGEON-INF
15 BILL SALKELD-C
16 ED WRIGHT-P
16 GLENN (LEFTY) ELLIOTT-P
17 JOHNNY (NIG) BEAZLEY (INJ)-P
18 GLENN (LEFTY) ELLIOTT-P
19 CLINT (CONNIE) CONATSER-OF
20 MARV (TWITCH) RICKERT-OF (2)
21 WARREN SPAHN-P
22 NELSON (NELS) (NELLIE) POTTER-P (3)
24 VERN BICKFORD-P
25 AL LYONS-P/OF
26 CLYDE (HARDROCK) SHOUN-P
27 FREDDIE FITZSIMMONS-CH
28 JOHNNY COONEY-CH
29 ERNIE WHITE-P
30 BILLY SOUTHWORTH-MGR
31 MIKE MCCORMICK-OF
33 JOHNNY SAIN-P
34 JOHNNY ANTONELLI-P
35 BOB KEELY-CH
36 SI JOHNSON-CH
37 BOBBY HOGUE-P
38 JIM PRENDERGAST-P
96 BILL (BIG BILL)(NINETY-SIX) VOISELLE-P

1949

4TH 75-79 22GB

1 TOMMY (KELLY) HOLMES-OF
2 ALVIN (AL) (BLACKIE) DARK-SS/3B
3 BOB (MR. TEAM) ELLIOTT-3B
4 JEFF HEATH (INJ)-OF
5 JIM RUSSELL-OF
6 RAY SANDERS (INJ)-1B
7 SIBBY SISTI-UTIL
8 CONNIE RYAN-INF
9 EARL (THE EARL OF SNOHOMISH) TORGESON (INJ)-1B
10 PHIL MASI-C (1)
10 MICKEY LIVINGSTON (INJ)-C (2)
11 PETE (PISTOL PETE) REISER-OF/3B
12 EDDIE (THE BRAT) (MUGGSY) STANKY (INJ)-2B
13 RED BARRETT-P
14 AL (MOOSE) LAKEMAN-1B
14 ED (HORN) SAUER-OF/3B
15 BILL SALKELD-C
16 STEVE KUCZEK-PH
17 JOHNNY (NIG) BEAZLEY-P
17 ELBIE FLETCHER-1B
18 GLENN (LEFTY) ELLIOTT-P
19 CLINT (CONNIE) CONATSER-OF
21 WARREN SPAHN-P
22 NELSON (NELS) (NELLIE) POTTER-P
23 DON THOMPSON-OF
23 DEL CRANDALL-C
24 VERN BICKFORD-P
25 BOB HALL-P
26 CLYDE (HARDROCK) SHOUN-P (1)
26 MICKEY LIVINGSTON (INJ)-C (2)
28 JOHNNY COONEY-CH/MGR2
29 JIMMY BROWN-CH
30 BILLY SOUTHWORTH-MGR1
31 MARV (TWITCH) RICKERT-OF/1B
33 JOHNNY SAIN-P
34 JOHNNY ANTONELLI-P
35 BOB KEELY-CH
36 SI JOHNSON-CH
37 BOBBY HOGUE-P
38 RAY MARTIN-P
96 BILL (BIG BILL)(NINETY-SIX) VOISELLE-P

1950

4TH 83-71 8GB

1 TOMMY (KELLY) HOLMES-OF
2 GENE (SKIP) MAUCH-INF
3 BOB (MR. TEAM) ELLIOTT-3B
4 SID GORDON-OF/3B
5 SAM (JET) JETHROE-OF
6* MURRAY WALL-P*
6 BOB ADDIS-OF
7 SIBBY SISTI-UTIL
8 CONNIE RYAN-2B (1)
9 EARL (THE EARL OF SNOHOMISH) TORGESON-1B
10 BUDDY KERR-SS
11 PETE (PISTOL PETE) REISER-OF/3B
12 ROY (SPEC) HARTSFIELD-2B
14 PAUL BURRIS-C
15 LUIS OLMO-OF/3B
16 DAVE COLE-P
17 BOB (MR. CHIPS) CHIPMAN-P
18 EMIL (ANTELOPE) (DUTCH) VERBAN-2B (2)
19 ERNIE JOHNSON-P
20 DICK DONOVAN-P
21 WARREN SPAHN-P
22 WALT LINDEN-C
22 MICKEY HAEFNER-P (2)
23 DEL CRANDALL-C/1B
24 VERN BICKFORD-P
25 BOB HALL-P
26 NORMIE (JUMBO) ROY-P
27 WILLARD MARSHALL-OF
28 JOHNNY COONEY-CH
29 JIMMY BROWN-CH
30 BILLY SOUTHWORTH-MGR
31 BUCKY WALTERS-P/CH
33 JOHNNY SAIN-P
34 JOHNNY ANTONELLI-P
35 BOB KEELY-CH
36 DICK DONOVAN-P
36 MAX SURKONT-P
37 BOBBY HOGUE-P
39 DICK MANVILLE-P
39 WALKER (WALK) COOPER-C (2)

1951

4TH 76-78 20.5GB

1 TOMMY (KELLY) HOLMES-OF/MGR2
1 RAY (IRON MAN) MUELLER (INJ)-C
2 GENE (SKIP) MAUCH-INF
3 BOB (MR. TEAM) ELLIOTT-3B
4 SID GORDON-OF/3B
5 SAM (JET) JETHROE-OF
6 BOB ADDIS-OF
7 SIBBY SISTI-UTIL
7 EBBA ST. CLAIRE (INJ)-C
8 RAY (IRON MAN) MUELLER (INJ)-C
8 BOB THORPE-PH
9 EARL (THE EARL OF SNOHOMISH) TORGESON-1B
10 BUDDY KERR-SS/2B
11 BLIX DONNELLY-P
11 PHIL (FLIP) PAINE-P
11 SID SCHACHT-P (2)
12 ROY (SPEC) HARTSFIELD-2B
13 SIBBY SISTI-UTIL
14 BOB (MR. CHIPS) CHIPMAN-P
15 LUIS OLMO-OF/3B
16 DAVE COLE-P
17 CHET NICHOLS, JR.-P
18 LUIS (CANENA) MARQUEZ-OF
19 JIM WILSON-P
20 DICK DONOVAN-P
21 WARREN SPAHN-P
22 GEORGE ESTOCK-P
(23) DEL CRANDALL (MIL)-(C)
23 JOHNNY (YATCHA) LOGAN-SS
24 VERN BICKFORD (INJ)-P
26 DAVE COLE-P
27 WILLARD MARSHALL-OF
28 JOHNNY COONEY-CH
29 JIMMY BROWN-CH
30 BILLY SOUTHWORTH-MGR1
31 BUCKY WALTERS-CH
33 JOHNNY SAIN-P (1)
33 LEW BURDETTE-P
(34) JOHNNY ANTONELLI (MIL)-(P)
35 BOB KEELY-CH
36 MAX SURKONT-P
37 BOBBY HOGUE-P (1)
37 SID SCHACHT-P (2)
39 WALKER (WALK) COOPER-C
44 BOB (MR. CHIPS) CHIPMAN-P

1952

7TH 64-89 32GB

1 TOMMY (KELLY) HOLMES-MGR1
2 BILLY KLAUS-SS
4 SID GORDON-OF/3B
5 SAM (JET) JETHROE-OF
6 BILL REED-2B
6 JACK DITTMER-2B
7 JACK (SOUR MASH JACK) DANIELS-OF
8 PETE WHISENANT-OF
9 EARL (THE EARL OF SNOHOMISH) TORGESON-1B/OF
10 JACK CUSICK-SS/3B
11 SHELDON (AVAILABLE) JONES-P
12 ROY (SPEC) HARTSFIELD-2B
13 SIBBY SISTI-UTIL
14 PAUL BURRIS-C
16 BOB (MR. CHIPS) CHIPMAN-P
18 BOB THORPE-OF
19 JIM WILSON-P
20 DICK DONOVAN-P
21 WARREN SPAHN-P
22 BERT THIEL-P
22 VIRGIL JESTER-P
23 JOHNNY (YATCHA) LOGAN-SS
24 VERN BICKFORD (INJ)-P
27 WILLARD MARSHALL-OF (1)
28 JOHNNY COONEY-CH
29 DAVE COLE-P
30 DICK HOOVER-P
30 DAVE COLE-P
31 BUCKY WALTERS-CH
32 ERNIE JOHNSON-P
33 LEW BURDETTE-P
(34) JOHNNY ANTONELLI (MIL)-(P)
35 BOB KEELY-CH
36 MAX SURKONT-P
37 GEORGE CROWE-1B
39 WALKER (WALK) COOPER-C
40 BUS (BUZZY) CLARKSON-SS/3B
40 VIRGIL JESTER-P
40 CHARLIE (JOLLY CHOLLY) GRIMM-MGR2
41 EDDIE MATHEWS-3B
42 EBBA ST. CLAIRE-C
44 BUS (BUZZY) CLARKSON-SS/3B
56 GENE CONLEY-P
DEL CRANDALL (MIL)-(C)
CHET NICHOLS, JR.(MIL)-(P)
PHIL (FLIP) PAINE (MIL)-(P)

1953

MILWAUKEE BRAVES

2ND 92-62 13GB

1 DEL CRANDALL-C
2 BILLY KLAUS-PH
2 HARRY HANEBRINK-2B/3B
3 JIM PENDLETON-OF/SS
4 SID GORDON-OF
6 JACK DITTMER-2B
9 JOE ADCOCK-1B
10 BOB BUHL-P
13 SIBBY SISTI-UTIL
14 PAUL BURRIS-C
15 DON LIDDLE-P
16 DAVE (GABBY) JOLLY-P
18 BOB THORPE-OF
19 JIM WILSON-P
21 WARREN SPAHN-P
22 VIRGIL JESTER-P
23 JOHNNY (YATCHA) LOGAN-SS
24 VERN BICKFORD-P
26 MEL ROACH-2B
28 JOHNNY COONEY-CH
29 MEL ROACH-2B
30 DAVE COLE-P
31 BUCKY WALTERS-CH
32 ERNIE JOHNSON-P
33 LEW BURDETTE-P
34 JOHNNY ANTONELLI-P
35 BOB KEELY-CH
36 MAX SURKONT-P
37 GEORGE CROWE-1B
38 BILLY BRUTON-OF
39 WALKER (WALK) COOPER-C
40 CHARLIE (JOLLY CHOLLY) GRIMM-MGR
41 EDDIE MATHEWS-3B
42 EBBA ST. CLAIRE-C
43 DON LIDDLE-P
47 JOEY JAY-P
48 ANDY (HANDY ANDY) (PRUSCHKA) PAFKO-OF
CHET NICHOLS, JR.(MIL)-(P)
PHIL (FLIP) PAINE (MIL)-(P)

BOSTON/MILWAUKEE/ ATLANTA BRAVES

1954

3RD 89-65 8GB

1 DEL CRANDALL-C
3 JIM PENDLETON-OF
4 DANNY O'CONNELL-2B/INF
5 HANK (HAMMERIN' HANK) AARON (INJ)-OF
6 JACK DITTMER-2B
7 BILLY (DOC) QUEEN-OF
8 SAM CALDERONE-C
9 JOE ADCOCK-1B
10 BOB BUHL-P
11 PHIL (FLIP) PAINE-P
12 RAY CRONE-P
13 SIBBY SISTI-PR
14 MEL ROACH-1B
15 CHARLIE GORIN-P
16 CHET NICHOLS, JR.-P
16 DAVE (GABBY) JOLLY-P
17 DAVE (GABBY) JOLLY-P
17 CHET NICHOLS, JR.-P
19 JIM WILSON-P
20 RAY CRONE-P
20 DAVE KOSLO-P (2)
21 WARREN SPAHN-P
22 GENE CONLEY-P
23 JOHNNY (YATCHA) LOGAN-SS
24 CHARLIE WHITE-C
27 GEORGE (CATFISH) METKOVICH-1B/OF
28 JOHNNY COONEY-CH
30 ROY SMALLEY, SR.-INF
31 BUCKY WALTERS-CH
32 ERNIE JOHNSON-P
33 LEW BURDETTE-P
34 BOBBY (THE FLYING SCOT) THOMSON (INJ)-OF
35 BOB KEELY-CH
38 BILLY BRUTON-OF
40 CHARLIE (JOLLY CHOLLY) GRIMM-MGR
41 EDDIE MATHEWS-3B/OF
42 SAM CALDERONE-C
47 JOEY JAY-P
48 ANDY (HANDY ANDY) (PRUSCHKA) PAFKO-OF

1955

2ND 85-69 13.5GB

1 DEL CRANDALL-C
2 MEL WRIGHT-CH
3 JIM PENDLETON-UTIL
4 DANNY O'CONNELL-2B/INF
6 JACK DITTMER-2B
7 DEL RICE-C (2)
9 JOE ADCOCK (INJ)-1B
10 BOB BUHL-P
11 PHIL (FLIP) PAINE-P
12 RAY CRONE-P
14 MEL ROACH (MIL)-(INF)
15 CHARLIE GORIN-P
16 DAVE (GABBY) JOLLY-P
17 CHET NICHOLS, JR.-P
18 CHUCK TANNER-OF
19 BENNIE TAYLOR-1B
20 DAVE KOSLO-P
20 RAY CRONE-P
21 WARREN SPAHN-P
22 GENE CONLEY-P
23 JOHNNY (YATCHA) LOGAN-SS
24 CHARLIE WHITE-C
24 BOB ROSELLI-C
27 DANNY O'CONNELL-2B/INF
28 JOHNNY COONEY-CH
29 ROBERTO VARGAS-P
30 JOHN EDELMAN-P
31 BUCKY WALTERS-CH
32 ERNIE JOHNSON-P
33 LEW BURDETTE-P
34 BOBBY (THE FLYING SCOT) THOMSON (INJ)-OF
35 BOB KEELY-CH
38 BILLY BRUTON-OF
39 GEORGE CROWE-1B
40 CHARLIE (JOLLY CHOLLY) GRIMM-MGR
41 EDDIE MATHEWS-3B
44 HANK (HAMMERIN' HANK) AARON (INJ)-OF/2B
47 JOEY JAY-P
48 ANDY (HANDY ANDY) (PRUSCHKA) PAFKO-OF/3B
49 HUMBERTO ROBINSON-P

1956

2ND 92-62 1GB

1 DEL CRANDALL-C
2 FRED (PUDGE) HANEY-MGR2
3 JIM PENDLETON-INF
3 JOHNNY (MUTT) RIDDLE-CH
4 DANNY O'CONNELL-2B/INF
5 FELIX MANTILLA-SS/3B
6 JACK DITTMER-2B
7 DEL RICE-C
8 JOHNNY (MUTT) RIDDLE-CH
9 JOE ADCOCK-1B
10 BOB BUHL-P
11 PHIL (FLIP) PAINE-P
11 JIM PENDLETON-INF
14 FRANK TORRE-1B
16 DAVE (GABBY) JOLLY-P
17 CHET NICHOLS, JR.-P
17 TAYLOR (TAY) PHILLIPS-P
18 CHUCK TANNER-OF
19 RED MURFF (INJ)-P
20 RAY CRONE-P
21 WARREN SPAHN-P
22 GENE CONLEY-P
23 JOHNNY (YATCHA) LOGAN-SS
24 BOB ROSELLI-C
25 BOBBY (THE FLYING SCOT) THOMSON (INJ)-OF/3B
28 EARL HERSCH-OF
30 BOB TROWBRIDGE-P
31 CHARLIE (CHINSKI) ROOT-CH
32 ERNIE JOHNSON-P
33 LEW BURDETTE-P
35 BOB KEELY-CH
36 LOU SLEATER-P
38 BILLY BRUTON-OF
39 TOBY ATWELL-C (2)
40 CHARLIE (JOLLY CHOLLY) GRIMM-MGR1
41 EDDIE MATHEWS-3B
41 WES COVINGTON-OF
44 HANK (HAMMERIN' HANK) AARON (INJ)-OF/2B
48 ANDY (HANDY ANDY) (PRUSCHKA) PAFKO-OF
49 HUMBERTO ROBINSON-P
MEL ROACH (MIL)-(INF)

1957

1ST 95-59 0GB
W WS-NYA 4-3

1 DEL CRANDALL-C/UTIL
2 FRED (PUDGE) HANEY-MGR
3 JOHNNY (MUTT) RIDDLE-CH
4 DANNY O'CONNELL-2B (1)
4 RED SCHOENDIENST-2B/OF(2)
5 FELIX MANTILLA-UTIL
6 HARRY HANEBRINK-3B
7 DEL RICE (INJ)-C
8 CONNIE RYAN-CH
9 JOE ADCOCK (INJ)-1B
10 BOB BUHL-P
12 BOB (HURRICANE) HAZLE-OF
12 DICK COLE-INF
14 FRANK TORRE-1B
15 CARL (SWATS) SAWATSKI-C
16 DAVE (GABBY) JOLLY-P
17 TAYLOR (TAY) PHILLIPS-P
18 CHUCK TANNER-OF (1)
18 JOHN (THUMPER) DEMERIT-OF (2)
19 RED MURFF (INJ)-P
19 HAWK TAYLOR-C
20 RAY CRONE-P (1)
20 DON MCMAHON-P
21 WARREN SPAHN-P
22 GENE CONLEY-P
23 JOHNNY (YATCHA) LOGAN-SS
24 PHIL (FLIP) PAINE-P
25 BOBBY (THE FLYING SCOT) THOMSON (INJ)-OF (1)
25 NIPPY JONES-1B/OF
29 MEL ROACH-2B
29 BOB MALKMUS-2B
30 BOB TROWBRIDGE-P
31 CHARLIE (CHINSKI) ROOT-CH
32 ERNIE JOHNSON-P
33 LEW BURDETTE-P
34 JUAN PIZARRO-P
35 BOB KEELY-CH
38 BILLY BRUTON (INJ)-OF
41 EDDIE MATHEWS-3B
43 WES COVINGTON-OF
44 HANK (HAMMERIN' HANK) AARON (INJ)-OF/2B
47 JOEY JAY-P
48 ANDY (HANDY ANDY) (PRUSCHKA) PAFKO-OF
56 RAY SHEARER-OF

1958

1ST 92-62 0GB
L WS-NYA 4-3

1 DEL CRANDALL-C
2 FRED (PUDGE) HANEY-MGR
3 JOHN FITZPATRICK-CH
4 RED SCHOENDIENST (ILL)-2B
5 FELIX MANTILLA-UTIL
6 HARRY HANEBRINK-OF/3B
7 DEL RICE-C
8 BILLY HERMAN-CH
9 JOE ADCOCK-1B/OF
10 BOB BUHL (INJ)-P
11 EDDIE HAAS-OF
11 JOE KOPPE-SS
12 BOB (HURRICANE) HAZLE-OF (1)
12 MEL ROACH (INJ)-UTIL
14 FRANK TORRE-1B
15 CARL (SWATS) SAWATSKI-C (1)
15 HAWK TAYLOR-OF
16 CARL WILLEY-P
17 BOB RUSH-P
18 JOHN (THUMPER) DEMERIT-OF
19 HAWK TAYLOR-OF
20 DON MCMAHON-P
21 WARREN SPAHN-P
22 GENE CONLEY (INJ) -P
23 JOHNNY (YATCHA) LOGAN-SS
24 BOB ROSELLI-PH
25 DICK LITTLEFIELD-P
25 BOB ROSELLI-PH
26 HARRY HANEBRINK-OF/3B
27 CASEY WISE-INF
29 MEL ROACH (INJ)-UTIL
29 JOHN (THUMPER) DEMERIT-OF
30 BOB TROWBRIDGE-P
31 WHIT WYATT-CH
32 ERNIE JOHNSON-P
33 LEW BURDETTE-P
34 JUAN PIZARRO-P
34 GEORGE (GOOD KID) SUSCE-CH
38 BILLY BRUTON (INJ)-OF
40 EDDIE HAAS-OF
41 EDDIE MATHEWS-3B
43 WES COVINGTON-OF
44 HANK (HAMMERIN' HANK) AARON (INJ)-OF/2B
47 JOEY JAY-P
48 ANDY (HANDY ANDY) (PRUSCHKA) PAFKO-OF
49 HUMBERTO ROBINSON-P

1959

1ST (TIE) 86-68 0GB
L P/O-LAN 2-0

1 DEL CRANDALL-C
2 FRED (PUDGE) HANEY-MGR
3 JOHN FITZPATRICK-CH
4 RED SCHOENDIENST (ILL)-2B
5 WHIT WYATT-CH
6 STAN (STASH) LOPATA-C/1B
7 DEL RICE (INJ)-C
8 BILLY HERMAN-CH
9 JOE ADCOCK-1B/OF
10 BOB BUHL (INJ)-P
11 JOHNNY O'BRIEN-2B
11 BOBBY AVILA-2B (3)
12 MEL ROACH (INJ)-UTIL
13 CHUCK COTTIER-2B
14 FRANK TORRE-1B
15 MICKEY VERNON-1B/OF
16 CARL WILLEY-P
17 BOB RUSH-P
18 FELIX MANTILLA-2B/UTIL
19 JOE MORGAN-2B (1)
19 CASEY WISE-2B/SS
19 RAY (IKE) BOONE-1B (3)
20 DON MCMAHON-P
21 WARREN SPAHN-P
23 JOHNNY (YATCHA) LOGAN-SS
24 JIM PISONI-OF (1)
24 LEE MAYE-OF
25 ENOS (COUNTRY) SLAUGHTER-OF (2)
28 AL SPANGLER-OF
29 JOHN (THUMPER) DEMERIT-OF
30 BOB TROWBRIDGE-P
31 BOB HARTMAN-P
32 BOB GIGGIE-P
33 LEW BURDETTE-P
34 JUAN PIZARRO-P
36 GEORGE (GOOD KID) SUSCE-CH
38 BILLY BRUTON-OF
41 EDDIE MATHEWS-3B
43 WES COVINGTON (INJ)-OF
44 HANK (HAMMERIN' HANK) AARON (INJ)-OF/3B
47 JOEY JAY-P
48 ANDY (HANDY ANDY) (PRUSCHKA) PAFKO (INJ)-OF

1960

2ND 88-66 7GB

1 DEL CRANDALL-C
3 BOB SCHEFFING-CH
4 RED SCHOENDIENST-2B
5 WHIT WYATT-CH
6 CHARLIE LAU-C
7 CHUCK DRESSEN-MGR
8 GEORGE (MERCURY) (STUD) (FOGHORN) MYATT-CH
9 JOE ADCOCK-1B
10 BOB BUHL-P
11 EDDIE HAAS-OF
12 MEL ROACH-UTIL
13 CHUCK COTTIER-2B
14 FRANK TORRE-1B
15 STAN (STASH) LOPATA-C
15 JOE TORRE-PH
16 CARL WILLEY-P
17 BOB RUSH-P (1)
18 FELIX MANTILLA-UTIL
19 RAY (IKE) BOONE-1B (1)
19 ALVIN (AL) (BLACKIE) DARK-UTIL (2)
20 DON MCMAHON-P
21 WARREN SPAHN-P
23 JOHNNY (YATCHA) LOGAN-SS
24 LEE MAYE-OF
25 AL SPANGLER-OF
30 GEORGE (LEFTY) BRUNET-P (2)
31 GEORGE (LEFTY) BRUNET-P (2)
32 BOB GIGGIE-P (1)
32 DON NOTTEBART-P
33 LEW BURDETTE-P
34 JUAN PIZARRO-P
35 RON PICHE-P
36 KEN MACKENZIE-P
36 TERRY FOX-P
38 BILLY BRUTON-OF
41 EDDIE MATHEWS-3B
42 MIKE KRSNICH-OF
42 LEN GABRIELSON-OF
43 WES COVINGTON-OF
44 HANK (HAMMERIN' HANK) AARON (INJ)-OF/2B
47 JOEY JAY-P
48 ANDY (HANDY ANDY) (PRUSCHKA) PAFKO-CH

1961

4TH 83-71 10GB

1 DEL CRANDALL (INJ)-C
2 FRANK BOLLING-2B
3 BILLY MARTIN-PH (1)
3 BOB BOYD-1B (2)
5 WHIT WYATT-CH
6 CHARLIE LAU-C (1)
6 BIRDIE TEBBETTS-MGR2
7 CHUCK DRESSEN-MGR1
8 GEORGE (MERCURY) (STUD) (FOGHORN) MYATT-CH
9 JOE ADCOCK-1B
10 BOB BUHL-P
11 ROY MCMILLAN-SS
12 MEL ROACH-OF/1B (1)
12 FRANK THOMAS-OF/1B (2)
15 JOE TORRE-C
16 CARL WILLEY-P
17 MOE DRABOWSKI-P
18 FELIX MANTILLA-UTIL
19 SETH (MOE) MOREHEAD-P
19 GINO CIMOLI-OF (2)
20 DON MCMAHON-P
21 WARREN SPAHN-P
22 SAMMY WHITE-C

23 JOHNNY (YATCHA) LOGAN-SS (1)
24 LEE MAYE-OF
25 AL SPANGLER-OF
26 HAWK TAYLOR-OF/C
29 JOHN (THUMPER) DEMERIT-OF
30 GEORGE (LEFTY) BRUNET (ILL)-P
30 NEIL CHRISLEY-PH
30 MACK (MACK THE KNIFE) JONES-OF
32 DON NOTTEBART-P
33 LEW BURDETTE-P
35 RON PICHE-P
35 CLAUDE (FRENCHY) RAYMOND-P
36 KEN MACKENZIE-P
36 BOB HENDLEY-P
40 PHIL ROOF-C/PR
40 TONY CLONINGER-P
40 CHI CHI OLIVO-P
41 EDDIE MATHEWS-3B
43 WES COVINGTON-OF (1)
43 JOHNNY ANTONELLI-P (2)
44 HANK (HAMMERIN' HANK) AARON (INJ)-OF/3B
48 ANDY (HANDY ANDY) (PRUSCHKA) PAFKO-CH

1962

5TH 86-76 15.5GB

1 DEL CRANDALL-C/1B
2 FRANK BOLLING-2B
3 BILL ADAIR-CH
4 JIMMY DYKES-CH
5 WHIT WYATT-CH
6 BIRDIE TEBBETTS-MGR
8 BOB UECKER-C
9 JOE ADCOCK-1B
10 BOB BUHL-P (1)
10 JACK CURTIS-P (2)
11 ROY MCMILLAN-SS
12 HANK (BULLDOG) FISCHER-P
15 JOE TORRE-C
16 CARL WILLEY-P
18 LOU KLIMCHOCK-PH
18 LOU (SLICK) JOHNSON-OF
19 DENIS MENKE-UTIL
20 DON MCMAHON-P (1)
20 GUS BELL-OF (2)
21 WARREN SPAHN-P
22 CECIL (SLEWFOOT) BUTLER-P
23 DENNY LEMASTER-P
24 LEE MAYE (ILL)-OF
25 HOWIE BEDELL-OF
25 KEN ASPROMONTE-2B/3B (2)
26 BOB SHAW-P
27 AMADO SAMUEL-INF
28 TOMMIE AARON-UTIL
29 DENIS MENKE-UTIL
29 HAWK TAYLOR (MIL)-OF
30 MACK (MACK THE KNIFE) JONES-OF
30 JIM (SHERIFF) CONSTABLE-P
32 DON NOTTEBART-P
33 LEW BURDETTE-P
35 CLAUDE (FRENCHY) RAYMOND-P
36 BOB HENDLEY-P
39 MIKE KRSNICH-UTIL
40 TONY CLONINGER-P
41 EDDIE MATHEWS-3B/1B
44 HANK (HAMMERIN' HANK) AARON (INJ)-OF/3B
45 ETHAN BLACKABY-OF
45 HANK (BULLDOG) FISCHER-P
48 ANDY (HANDY ANDY) (PRUSCHKA) PAFKO-CH

1963

6TH 84-78 15GB

1 DEL CRANDALL-C/1B
2 FRANK BOLLING-2B
3 KEN (HAWK) SILVESTRI-CH
4 JO-JO WHITE-CH
5 WHIT WYATT-CH
6 DIXIE (THE PEOPLE'S CHERCE) WALKER-CH
8 BOB UECKER-C
9 NORM LARKER-1B (1)
10 BOBBY(NIG) BRAGAN-MGR
11 ROY MCMILLAN-SS
12 GENE OLIVER-1B/UTIL (2)
14 WOODY-WOODWARD-SS
15 JOE TORRE-C/UTIL
16 LOU KLIMCHOCK-1B (2)
17 GENE OLIVER-1B/UTIL (2)
18 BOBBY TIEFENAUER-P
19 DENIS MENKE-UTIL
20 GUS BELL-PH
21 WARREN SPAHN-P
22 WADE BLASINGAME-P
23 DENNY LEMASTER-P
24 LEE MAY-OF
25 DAN SCHNEIDER-P
26 BOB SHAW-P
27 AMADO SAMUEL-SS/2B
28 TOMMIE AARON-UTIL
29 HAWK TAYLOR (INJ)-OF
30 MACK (MACK THE KNIFE) JONES-OF
31 TY CLINE-OF
31 BUBBA MORTON-OF (2)
32 FRANK FUNK-P
33 LEW BURDETTE-P (1)
34 HANK (BULLDOG) FISCHER-P
35 CLAUDE (FRENCHY) RAYMOND-P
36 BOB HENDLEY-P
37 BOB SADOWSKI-P
38 RON PICHE-P
39 LEN GABRIELSON-UTIL
40 TONY CLONINGER-P
41 EDDIE MATHEWS-3B/OF
42 DON DILLARD-OF
44 HANK (HAMMERIN' HANK) AARON (INJ)-OF
77 RICO CARTY-PH

1964

5TH 88-74 5GB

2 FRANK BOLLING-2B
3 KEN (HAWK) SILVESTRI-CH
4 JO-JO WHITE-CH
5 WHIT WYATT-CH
6 DIXIE (THE PEOPLE'S CHERCE) WALKER-CH
7 MIKE DE LA HOZ-INF
8 MERRITT RANEW-C (2)
9 ED BAILEY-C
10 BOBBY(NIG) BRAGAN-MGR
11 ROY MCMILLAN-SS (1)
11 LOU KLIMCHOCK-3B/2B
12 GENE OLIVER-1B/C
14 WOODY WOODWARD-INF
15 JOE TORRE-C/1B
16 SANDY ALOMAR, SR.-SS
17 PHIL ROOF-C
17 FRANK (THE YANKEE KILLER) (MULE) LARY-P (3)
18 BOBBY TIEFENAUER-P
19 DENIS MENKE-SS/INF
20 GUS BELL-PH
20 CLAY (HAWK) CARROLL-P
21 WARREN SPAHN-P
22 DICK KELLEY (INJ)-P
23 DENNY LEMASTER-P
24 LEE MAY-OF/3B
25 DAN SCHNEIDER (INJ)-P
26 BILLY HOEFT-P
27 GARY KOLB-UTIL
29 FELIPE ALOU (INJ)-OF/1B
30 CHI-CHI OLIVO-P
31 TY CLINE-OF/1B
32 CECIL (SLEWFOOT) BUTLER-P
34 HANK (BULLDOG) FISCHER-P
35 PHIL NIEKRO-P
36 WADE BLASINGAME-P
37 BOB SADOWSKI-P
38 JOHN BRAUN-P
39 LEN GABRIELSON-1B/OF (1)
39 DAVE EILERS-P
40 TONY CLONINGER-P
41 EDDIE MATHEWS-3B/1B
42 ETHAN BLACKABY-OF
43 RICO CARTY-OF
44 HANK (HAMMERIN' HANK) AARON (INJ)-OF/2B
45 JACK SMITH-P
46 ARNIE UMBACH-P
47 BILL SOUTHWORTH-3B
53 JACK SMITH-P

1965

5TH 86-76 11GB

2 FRANK BOLLING-2B
3 KEN (HAWK) SILVESTRI-CH
4 JO-JO WHITE-CH
5 WHIT WYATT-CH
6 DIXIE (THE PEOPLE'S CHERCE) WALKER-CH
7 MIKE DE LA HOZ-INF
10 BOBBY(NIG) BRAGAN-MGR
11 LOU KLIMCHOCK-1B
12 GENE OLIVER-1B/UTIL
14 WOODY WOODWARD-SS/2B
15 JOE TORRE-C/1B
16 SANDY ALOMAR, SR.-SS/2B
18 BOBBY TIEFENAUER-P (1)
18 JOHNNY BLANCHARD-OF (3)
19 DENIS MENKE (INJ)-INF
20 CLAY (HAWK) CARROLL-P
20 DICK KELLEY (INJ)-P
22 DICK KELLEY (INJ)-P
23 DENNY LEMASTER (INJ)-P
24 LEE MAY-OF/3B (1)
26 DAN OSINSKI-P
27 GARY KOLB-OF (1)
27 BILLY COWAN-OF (2)
28 TOMMIE AARON-1B
28 JESSE GONDER-C (2)
29 FELIPE ALOU-OF/INF
30 CHI-CHI OLIVO-P
30 KEN JOHNSON-P (2)
31 TY CLINE-OF/1B
32 JIM BEAUCHAMP-1B (2)
33 BILLY O'DELL-P
34 HANK (BULLDOG) FISCHER-P
35 PHIL NIEKRO-P
36 WADE BLASINGAME-P
37 BOB SADOWSKI-P
38 CHI-CHI OLIVO-P
39 DAVE EILERS-P (1)
39 FRANK THOMAS-1B/OF (3)
40 TONY CLONINGER-P
41 EDDIE MATHEWS-3B
42 DON DILLARD-OF
43 RICO CARTY-OF
44 HANK (HAMMERIN' HANK) AARON (INJ)-OF
48 MACK (MACK THE KNIFE) JONES-OF

1966

ATLANTA BRAVES

5TH 85-77 10GB

2 FRANK BOLLING-2B
3 KEN (HAWK) SILVESTRI-CH
4 JO-JO WHITE-CH
5 WHIT WYATT-CH
6 GROVER RESINGER-CH
7 MIKE DE LA HOZ-INF
8 BILLY HITCHCOCK-CH/MGR2
9 LEE THOMAS-1B (1)
9 GEORGE (SONNY)KOPACZ-1B
10 BOBBY(NIG) BRAGAN-MGR1
11 MARTY KEOUGH-1B/OF
11 LEE BALES-2B/3B
11 FELIX MILLAN-INF
12 GENE OLIVER (INJ)-UTIL
14 WOODY WOODWARD-2B/SS
15 JOE TORRE-C/1B
16 SANDY ALOMAR, SR.-2B/SS
18 ADRIAN (PAT) GARRETT-OF
18 FELIX MILLAN-INF
19 DENIS MENKE-SS/INF
20 CLAY (HAWK) CARROLL-P
22 DICK KELLEY-P
23 DENNY LEMASTER-P
24 HERB HIPPAUF-P
24 BILL ROBINSON-OF
25 DAN SCHNEIDER-P
26 JAY RITCHIE-P
26 JOHN HERRNSTEIN-OF (3)
27 TY CLINE-OF/1B (2)
28 RON REED-P
29 FELIPE ALOU-1B/UTIL
30 KEN JOHNSON-P
31 GARY GEIGER-OF
32 ARNIE UMBACH-P
33 BILLY O'DELL-P (1)
33 DON SCHWALL-P (2)
33 PAT JARVIS-P
34 HANK (BULLDOG) FISCHER-P (1)
34 CHARLIE VAUGHAN-P
34 JOEY JAY-P (2)
35 PHIL NIEKRO-P
36 WADE BLASINGAME (INJ)-P
37 TED ABERNATHY-P (2)
37 DON SCHWALL-P (2)
38 CHI-CHI OLIVO-P
39 TED ABERNATHY-P (2)
40 TONY CLONINGER-P
41 EDDIE MATHEWS-3B
42 JOEY JAY-P (2)
43 RICO CARTY-OF/UTIL
44 HANK (HAMMERIN' HANK) AARON (INJ)-OF/2B
45 EDDIE SADOWSKI-C
48 MACK (MACK THE KNIFE) JONES-OF/1B
52 CECIL UPSHAW-P

1967

7TH 77-85 24.5GB

2 MARTY MARTINEZ-UTIL
3 KEN (HAWK) SILVESTRI-CH/MGR2
4 BOB KENNEDY-CH
5 WHIT WYATT-CH
6 CLETE BOYER-3B/SS
7 MIKE DE LA HOZ-INF
8 BILLY HITCHCOCK-MGR1
9 BILL ADAIR-CH
10 CHARLIE LAU-PH (2)
11 FELIX MILLAN-2B
11 TITO FRANCONA-1B/OF (2)
12 GENE OLIVER-C (1)
12 BOB UECKER-C (2)
14 WOODY WOODWARD-2B/SS
15 JOE TORRE-C/1B
16 ANGEL (REMY) HERMOSO-SS/2B
17 FELIX MILLAN-2B
18 DAVE NICHOLSON-OF
19 DENIS MENKE-SS/3B
20 CLAY (HAWK) CARROLL-P
22 DICK KELLEY-P
23 DENNY LEMASTER-P
24 RAMON HERNANDEZ-P
25 CITO GASTON-OF
26 JAY RITCHIE-P
27 TY CLINE (INJ)-OF (1)
27 ED (ROCK) RAKOW-P
28 JIM BEAUCHAMP-PH
28 MIKE LUM-OF
29 FELIPE ALOU-1B/OF
30 KEN JOHNSON-P
31 GARY GEIGER-OF
32 GEORGE STONE-P
32 GLEN CLARK-PH
33 PAT JARVIS-P
34 CECIL UPSHAW-P
35 PHIL NIEKRO-P
36 WADE BLASINGAME-P (1)
36 CLAUDE (FRENCHY) RAYMOND-P (2)
37 DON SCHWALL-P
38 RON REED-P
40 TONY CLONINGER (ILL)-P
41 JIM BRITTON-P
42 BOB BRUCE-P
42 JIM BRITTON-P
43 RICO CARTY-OF/1B
44 HANK (HAMMERIN' HANK) AARON (INJ)-OF/2B
47 RAMON HERNANDEZ-P
48 MACK (MACK THE KNIFE) JONES-OF

1968

5TH 81-81 16GB

2 MARTY MARTINEZ-UTIL
3 KEN (HAWK) SILVESTRI-CH
4 JIM FANNING-CH
5 HARRY DORISH-CH
6 CLETE BOYER (INJ)-3B
7 GIL GARRIDO-SS
8 JIM BUSBY-CH
9 BILLY GOODMAN-CH
10 BOB TILLMAN-C
11 DERON JOHNSON (INJ)-1B/3B
12 DUSTY BAKER-OF
14 WOODY WOODWARD-INF (1)
14 BOB JOHNSON-3B/2B (2)
15 JOE TORRE (INJ)-C/1B
16 SONNY JACKSON (INJ)-SS
17 FELIX MILLAN-2B
18 TOMMIE AARON-UTIL
19 TITO FRANCONA-OF/1B
20 CLAY (HAWK) CARROLL-P (1)
22 DICK KELLEY-P
23 STU MILLER-P
23 MILT (GIMPY) PAPPAS-P (2)
23 TED DAVIDSON-P (2)
23 WAYNE CAUSEY-INF (3)
24 AL SANTORINI-P
26 LUM HARRIS-MGR
28 MIKE LUM-OF
29 FELIPE ALOU-OF
30 KEN JOHNSON-P
32 GEORGE STONE-P

3OSTON/MILWAUKEE/ ATLANTA BRAVES

2 TED DAVIDSON-P (2)
2 MILT (GIMPY) PAPPAS-P (2)
3 PAT JARVIS-P
4 CECIL UPSHAW-P
5 PHIL NIEKRO-P
6 CLAUDE (FRENCHY) RAYMOND-P
7 SKIP GUINN-P
7 RICK KESTER-P
8 RON REED-P
9 WALT HRINIAK-C
0 TONY CLONINGER-P (1)
0 GEORGE STONE-P
2 JIM BRITTON-P
43) RICO CARTY (ILL)-(OF)
3 MIKE PAGE-OF
3 AL SANTORINI-P
4 HANK (HAMMERIN' HANK) AARON (INJ)-OF/1B
7 STU MILLER-P
8 SANDY VALDESPINO-OF
8 RALPH (ROAD RUNNER) GARR-PH
5 SATCHEL PAIGE-CH

1969

1ST W 93-69 0GB

L NLCS-NYN 3-0

2 DARRELL EVANS-3B
2 JIM BREAZEALE-1B
3 KEN (HAWK) SILVESTRI-CH
4 BOB DIDIER-C
5 HARRY DORISH-CH
6 CLETE BOYER-3B
7 GIL GARRIDO-SS
8 JIM BUSBY-CH
9 BILLY GOODMAN-CH
0 BOB TILLMAN-C
1 BOB ASPROMONTE-UTIL
1 RALPH (ROAD RUNNER) GARR-OF
1 DARRELL EVANS-3B
2 DUSTY BAKER-OF
4 BOB ASPROMONTE-UTIL
6 SONNY JACKSON (INJ)-SS
7 FELIX MILLAN-2B
8 TOMMIE AARON-1B/OF
9 TITO FRANCONA-OF/1B (1)
20 ORLANDO (BABY BULL) (CHA CHA) CEPEDA-1B
22 GARRY HILL-P
22 MIKE MCQUEEN-P
23 LARRY MAXIE-P
25 RICO CARTY-OF
26 LUM HARRIS-MGR
28 MIKE LUM-OF
29 FELIPE ALOU-OF
30 KEN JOHNSON-P (1)
30 ORLANDO (BABY BULL) (CHA CHA) CEPEDA-1B
31 GARY NEIBAUER-P
32 MILT (GIMPY) PAPPAS-P
33 PAT JARVIS-P
34 CECIL UPSHAW-P
35 PHIL NIEKRO-P
36 CLAUDE (FRENCHY) RAYMOND-P (1)
36 OSCAR BROWN-OF
37 RICK KESTER-P
37 BOB PRIDDY-P (3)
38 RON REED-P
39 WALT HRINIAK (INJ)-C (1)
39 HOYT WILHELM-P (2)
40 GEORGE STONE-P
42 JIM BRITTON-P
43 CHARLIE VAUGHAN-P
43 TONY GONZALEZ-OF (2)
44 HANK (HAMMERIN' HANK) AARON (INJ)-OF/1B
45 PAUL DOYLE-P
46 BOB PRIDDY-P (3)
47 HOYT WILHELM-P (2)
48 RALPH (ROAD RUNNER) GARR-OF
65 SATCHEL PAIGE-CH

1970

5TH W 76-86 26GB

3 KEN (HAWK) SILVESTRI-CH
4 BOB DIDIER-C
5 HARRY DORISH-CH
6 CLETE BOYER-3B/SS
7 GIL GARRIDO-SS/2B
8 JIM BUSBY-CH
9 BILLY GOODMAN-CH
10 BOB TILLMAN-C
11 DARRELL EVANS-3B
12 DUSTY BAKER-OF
14 BOB ASPROMONTE-UTIL
15 HAL KING-C
16 SONNY JACKSON-SS
17 FELIX MILLAN-2B
18 TOMMIE AARON-1B/OF
19 JIMMIE HALL-OF (2)
22 MIKE MCQUEEN-P
23 JIM NASH-P
23 JIMMIE HALL-OF (2)
24 JIM NASH-P
24 STEVE BARBER-P (2)
25 RICO CARTY-OF
26 LUM HARRIS-MGR
27 RON KLINE-P
27 RICK KESTER-P
28 MIKE LUM-OF
29 LARRY JASTER-P
29 AUBREY GATEWOOD-P
29 DON CARDWELL-P (2)
30 ORLANDO (BABY BULL) (CHA CHA) CEPEDA-1B
31 GARY NEIBAUER-P
32 MILT (GIMPY) PAPPAS-P (1)
32 EARL WILLIAMS-1B/3B
33 PAT JARVIS-P
(34) CECIL UPSHAW (INJ)-(P)
35 PHIL NIEKRO-P
36 JULIO (WHIPLASH) NAVARRO-P
37 BOB PRIDDY-P
38 RON REED (INJ)-P
39 HOYT WILHELM-P (1)
40 GEORGE STONE-P
(42) JIM BRITTON (INJ)-(P)
43 TONY GONZALEZ-OF (1)
44 HANK (HAMMERIN' HANK) AARON (INJ)-OF/1B
45 OSCAR BROWN-OF
48 RALPH (ROAD RUNNER) GARR-OF
50 AUBREY GATEWOOD-P
(51) JIM BRITTON (INJ)-(P)
53 RICK KESTER-P

1971

3RD W 82-80 8GB

2 JIM BREAZEALE-1B
3 KEN (HAWK) SILVESTRI-CH
4 BOB DIDIER-C
5 HARRY DORISH-CH
6 CLETE BOYER-3B/SS
6 TONY LARUSSA-INF (2)
7 GIL GARRIDO-INF
8 JIM BUSBY-CH
9 MARTY PEREZ-SS/2B
10 CONNIE RYAN-CH
11 DARRELL EVANS-3B/OF
12 DUSTY BAKER-OF
14 MARV STAEHLE-2B/3B
14 LEO FOSTER-INF
15 HAL KING-C
16 SONNY JACKSON-OF
17 FELIX MILLAN-2B
18 TOMMIE AARON-1B/3B
18 ZOILO (ZORRO) VERSALLES-INF
19 TOMMIE AARON-1B/3B
22 MIKE MCQUEEN (INJ)-P
23 JIM NASH-P
24 STEVE BARBER-P
(25) RICO CARTY (INJ)-(OF)
26 LUM HARRIS-MGR
28 MIKE LUM-OF/1B
29 RON HERBEL-P
30 ORLANDO (BABY BULL) (CHA CHA) CEPEDA (INJ) -1B
31 GARY NEIBAUER-P
31 LEO FOSTER-INF
32 EARL WILLIAMS-C/INF
33 PAT JARVIS-P
34 CECIL UPSHAW-P
35 PHIL NIEKRO-P
36 TOM KELLEY-P
37 BOB PRIDDY-P
38 RON REED-P
39 HOYT WILHELM-P (1)
39 TOM HOUSE-P
40 GEORGE STONE-P
41 EDDIE MATHEWS-CH
44 HANK (HAMMERIN' HANK) AARON-1B/OF
45 OSCAR BROWN-OF
47 TOM KELLEY-P
48 RALPH (ROAD RUNNER) GARR-OF

1972

4TH W 70-84 25GB

2 JIM BREAZEALE-1B/3B
3 KEN (HAWK) SILVESTRI-CH
4 BOB DIDIER-C
4 LARVELL BLANKS-INF
5 LEW BURDETTE-CH
6 BOB DIDIER-C
7 GIL GARRIDO-INF
8 JIM BUSBY-CH
9 MARTY PEREZ-SS
11 DARRELL EVANS-3B
12 DUSTY BAKER-OF
15 PAUL CASANOVA-C
16 SONNY JACKSON (INJ)-UTIL
17 FELIX MILLAN-2B
18 ROWLAND OFFICE-OF
19 ROD GILBREATH-2B/3B
22 MIKE MCQUEEN (INJ)-P
23 JIM NASH-P (1)
23 LARRY JASTER-P
24 STEVE BARBER-P (1)
24 JIMMY FREEMAN-P
25 RICO CARTY (INJ)-OF
26 LUM HARRIS-MGR1
27 JIM HARDIN-P
28 MIKE LUM-OF/1B
30 ORLANDO (BABY BULL) (CHA CHA) CEPEDA (INJ) -1B (1)
30 DENNY MCLAIN-P (2)
31 GARY NEIBAUER-P (1)
32 EARL WILLIAMS-C/INF
33 PAT JARVIS-P
34 CECIL UPSHAW-P
35 PHIL NIEKRO-P
36 TOM KELLEY-P
37 RON SCHUELER-P
38 RON REED-P
39 TOM HOUSE-P
39 JOE HOERNER-P (2)
40 GEORGE STONE-P
41 EDDIE MATHEWS-CH/MGR2
43 JOE HOERNER-P (2)
44 HANK (HAMMERIN' HANK) AARON-1B/OF
45 OSCAR BROWN-OF
48 RALPH (ROAD RUNNER) GARR-OF

1973

5TH W 76-85 22.5GB

1 CONNIE RYAN-CH
3 KEN (HAWK) SILVESTRI-CH
4 LARVELL BLANKS-INF
5 PAUL CASANOVA-C
6 DAVEY JOHNSON-2B
7 ROY (SPEC) HARTSFIELD-CH
7 JOE (PEPI) PEPITONE-1B (2)
7 FRANK TEPEDINO-1B
8 JIM BUSBY-CH
9 MARTY PEREZ-SS
11 DARRELL EVANS-3B/1B
12 DUSTY BAKER-OF
14 DICK DIETZ-1B/C
15 JOHNNY OATES (INJ)-C
16 SONNY JACKSON-OF/SS
17 LEO FOSTER-SS
18 JACK PIERCE-1B
18 FREDDIE VELAZQUEZ-C
19 ROD GILBREATH-3B
20 OSCAR BROWN (INJ)-OF
(22) MIKE MCQUEEN (INJ)-(P)
22 JIM PANTHER-P
24 RORIC HARRISON-P
24 LARRY HOWARD-C
25 DANNY (BEAR) FRISELLA (INJ)-P
25 LARRY HOWARD-C
26 TOM HOUSE-P
27 PAT DOBSON-P (1)
27 ADRIAN DEVINE-P
28 MIKE LUM-1B/OF
29 CHUCK GOGGIN-UTIL (2)
30 DAVE CHEADLE-P
31 GARY NEIBAUER-P
32 MAX LEON-P
33 LEW BURDETTE-CH
34 CECIL UPSHAW-P (1)
34 DANNY (BEAR) FRISELLA (INJ)-P
35 PHIL NIEKRO-P
36 TOM KELLEY-P
36 JOE NIEKRO-P
37 RON SCHUELER-P
38 RON REED (INJ)-P
39 GARY GENTRY (INJ)-P
40 JIMMY FREEMAN-P
40 JOE NIEKRO-P
41 EDDIE MATHEWS-MGR
42 NORM MILLER (INJ)-OF
43 JOE HOERNER (INJ)-P (1)
43 AL CLOSTER-P
44 HANK (HAMMERIN' HANK) AARON-OF
45 WENTY FORD-P
48 RALPH (ROAD RUNNER) GARR-OF
49 CARL MORTON-P

1974

3RD W 88-74 14GB

1 CONNIE RYAN-CH
3 KEN (HAWK) SILVESTRI-CH
4 LARVELL BLANKS-SS
5 PAUL CASANOVA-C
6 DAVEY JOHNSON-1B/2B
7 FRANK TEPEDINO-1B
8 JIM BUSBY-CH
9 MARTY PEREZ-2B/INF
10 CRAIG ROBINSON-SS
11 DARRELL EVANS-3B
12 DUSTY BAKER-OF
14 CLYDE KING-MGR2
15 JOHNNY OATES-C
16 SONNY JACKSON-OF
17 LEO FOSTER-UTIL
18 JACK PIERCE-1B
18 IVAN MURRELL-OF/1B
19 ROD GILBREATH-2B
22 ROWLAND OFFICE-OF
23 HERM STARRETTE-CH
24 RORIC HARRISON (INJ)-P
25 GARY GENTRY (INJ)-P
26 TOM HOUSE-P
27 M IKE BEARD-P
28 MIKE LUM (INJ)-1B/OF
29 VIC CORRELL-C
31 MAX LEON-P
32 JOE NIEKRO-P
33 JACK AKER-P (1)
34 DANNY (BEAR) FRISELLA-P
35 PHIL NIEKRO-P
36 JOE NIEKRO-P
36 LEW KRAUSSE, JR.-P
38 RON REED (INJ)-P
39 JOHN FULLER-OF
41 EDDIE MATHEWS-MGR1
41 MIKE THOMPSON-P (2)
42 NORM MILLER-OF
44 HANK (HAMMERIN' HANK) AARON-OF
45 JAMIE EASTERLY-P
47 BUZZ CAPRA-P
48 RALPH (ROAD RUNNER) GARR-OF
49 CARL MORTON-P
50 MAX LEON-P

1975

5TH W 67-94 40.5GB

1 EDDIE HAAS-CH
3 KEN (HAWK) SILVESTRI-CH
4 LARVELL BLANKS-SS/2B
6 DAVEY JOHNSON-PH
6 CONNIE RYAN-MGR2
7 FRANK TEPEDINO-1B
8 JIM BUSBY-CH
9 MARTY PEREZ (INJ)-2B/SS
10 CRAIG ROBINSON-SS (1)
10 ROB BELLOIR-SS/2B
11 DARRELL EVANS-3B/1B
12 DUSTY BAKER-OF
13 BOB BEALL-1B
13 BLUE MOON ODOM-P (3)
14 CLYDE KING-MGR1
15 JOHNNY OATES-C (1)
15 ED GOODSON-1B/3B (2)
16 BOB BEALL-1B
18 EARL WILLIAMS-1B/C
18 LUKE APPLING-CH
19 ROD GILBREATH-INF
20 JOE NOLAN-C
22 ROWLAND OFFICE-OF
23 HERM STARRETTE-CH
24 RORIC HARRISON-P (1)
25 GARY GENTRY-P
25 FRANK LACORTE-P
26 TOM HOUSE-P
27 DAVE MAY-OF
28 MIKE LUM-1B/OF
29 VIC CORRELL-C
30 BRUCE DAL CANTON-P (2)
31 MAX LEON-P
32 EARL WILLIAMS-1B/C
33 MIKE THOMPSON-P
34 RAY SADECKI-P (2)
35 PHIL NIEKRO-P
36 PABLO TORREALBA-P
36 ADRIAN DEVINE-P
37 M IKE BEARD-P
38 RON REED-P (1)

38 ELIAS SOSA-P
39 PABLO TORREALBA-P
39 RORIC HARRISON-P (1)
40 FRANK LACORTE-P
41 ADRIAN DEVINE-P
42 BIFF POCOROBA-C
43 CITO GASTON-OF/1B
43 BRUCE DAL CANTON-P (2)
45 JAMIE EASTERLY-P
47 BUZZ CAPRA (INJ)-P
48 RALPH (ROAD RUNNER) GARR-OF
49 CARL MORTON-P
DICK ALLEN (REF)-(1B) (1)

1976

6TH W 70-92 32GB

1 DAVE BRISTOL-MGR
3 DALE MURPHY-C
4 JERRY ROYSTER-3B/SS
5 EDDIE HAAS-CH
6 CHRIS CANNIZZARO-CH
7 CHRIS CANNIZZARO-CH
7 KEN HENDERSON-OF
8 VERN BENSON-CH
9 MARTY PEREZ-INF (1)
9 MIKE EDEN-2B
10 ROB BELLOIR-INF
11 DARRELL EVANS-1B/3B (1)
12 TOM PACIOREK-UTIL
14 ROGER MORET (INJ)-P
15 DARREL CHANEY-SS/INF
16 CRAIG ROBINSON-INF (2)
17 ANDY MESSERSMITH (INJ)-P
18 BRIAN ASSELSTINE-OF
18 TERRY CROWLEY (REL)-PH (1)
19 ROD GILBREATH-2B/3B
20 MIKE MARSHALL (INJ)-P (2)
22 ROWLAND OFFICE (INJ)-OF
23 HERM STARRETTE-CH
24 JIM (THE TOY CANNON) WYNN-OF
25 FRANK LACORTE-P
25 WILLIE MONTANEZ-1B (2)
26 FRANK LACORTE-P
27 DAVE MAY-OF
28 KEN HENDERSON-OF
28 PABLO TORREALBA-P
29 VIC CORRELL-C
30 BRUCE DAL CANTON-P
31 MAX LEON-P
32 EARL WILLIAMS-C/1B (1)
32 PETE VARNEY-C (2)
33 RICK CAMP-P
34 LEE LACY-UTIL (1)
34 PRESTON HANNA-P
34 PAT ROCKETT-SS
35 PHIL NIEKRO-P
36 ADRIAN DEVINE (INJ)-P
37 MIKE BEARD-P
38 ELIAS SOSA-P (1)
38 AL AUTRY-P
40 DICK RUTHVEN-P
42 BIFF POCOROBA (INJ)-C
43 CITO GASTON-OF/1B
45 JAMIE EASTERLY-P
46 ROGER MORET (INJ)-P
47 BUZZ CAPRA (INJ)-P
48 JUNIOR MOORE-UTIL
49 CARL MORTON-P
50 MIKE MARSHALL (INJ)-P (2)

1977

6TH W 61-101 37GB

1 DAVE BRISTOL-MGR1/4
2 BARRY BONNELL-OF/3B
3 DALE MURPHY-C
4 BIFF POCOROBA-C
5 EDDIE HAAS-CH
6 CHRIS CANNIZZARO-CH
7 JEFF BURROUGHS-OF
8 VERN BENSON-CH/MGR3
9 PAT ROCKETT (INJ)-SS
10 ROB BELLOIR-INF
11 JOE NOLAN-C
12 TOM PACIOREK-UTIL
13 JERRY ROYSTER-UTIL
14 JUNIOR MOORE-3B/2B
15 DARREL CHANEY (INJ-SS/2B
16 CRAIG ROBINSON-SS
17 ANDY MESSERSMITH (INJ)-P
18 BRIAN ASSELSTINE-OF
19 ROD GILBREATH-2B/3B
20 MIKE MARSHALL-P (1)
20 DAVE CAMPBELL-P
20 LARRY WHISENTON-PH
22 ROWLAND OFFICE-OF/1B
23 JOHNNY SAIN-CH
24 MICKEY MAHLER-P
25 WILLIE MONTANEZ (INJ)-1B
26 FRANK LACORTE-P
27 ANDY MESSERSMITH (INJ)-P
29 VIC CORRELL-C
31 MAX LEON (SUS)-P
32 DAVE CAMPBELL-P
33 RICK CAMP (INJ)-P
34 DUANE THEISS-P
34 EDDIE (BUDDY) SOLOMON-P
35 PHIL NIEKRO-P
36 GARY (SARGE) MATTHEWS-OF
37 MIKE BEARD-P
37 EDDIE (BUDDY) SOLOMON-P
37 JOEY MCLAUGHLIN-P
38 STEVE KLINE-P
39 MIKE DAVEY-P
40 DICK RUTHVEN (INJ)-P
42 DON COLLINS-P
43 CITO GASTON-OF/1B
44 *(RET#) HANK AARON*
45 JAMIE EASTERLY (INJ)-P
47 BUZZ CAPRA-P
48 LARRY BRADFORD-P
48 JOEY MCLAUGHLIN-P
49 PRESTON HANNA-P
50 BOB JOHNSON-P
50 STEVE HARGAN-P (3)
52 DUANE THEISS-P
52 DON COLLINS-P
54 MIKE DAVEY-P
58 JOE NOLAN-C
TED TURNER-MGR2 (1G:5/11)

1978

6TH W 69-93 26GB

1 JERRY ROYSTER-SS/INF
2 BARRY BONNELL-OF/3B
3 DALE MURPHY-1B/C
4 BIFF POCOROBA (INJ)-C
5 BOB HORNER-3B
6 BOBBY COX-MGR
7 JEFF BURROUGHS-OF
8 CHRIS CANNIZZARO-CH
9 PAT ROCKETT-SS
10 ROB BELLOIR-SS/3B
11 JOE NOLAN-C
12 TOM PACIOREK-1B (1)
12 JERRY MADDOX-3B
12 HANK SMALL-1B
14 TOM (TIM) BURGESS-CH
15 DARREL CHANEY-INF
16 CHICO RUIZ-2B/3B
17 EDDIE MILLER-OF
17 GLENN HUBBARD (INJ)-2B
18 BRIAN ASSELSTINE (INJ)-OF
18 LARRY WHISENTON-OF
19 ROD GILBREATH-3B/2B
20 LARRY WHISENTON-OF
20 BRUCE BENEDICT-C
22 ROWLAND OFFICE-OF/1B
24 MICKEY MAHLER-P
25 BOB BEALL-1B/OF
26 FRANK LACORTE-P
26 GENE GARBER-P (2)
27 LARRY MCWILLIAMS-P
28 ADRIAN DEVINE (INJ)-P
30 BRIAN ASSELSTINE (INJ)-OF
31 MAX LEON-P
32 DAVE CAMPBELL-P
33 RICK CAMP-P
34 DUANE THEISS-P
35 PHIL NIEKRO-P
36 GARY (SARGE) MATTHEWS (INJ)-OF
37 EDDIE (BUDDY) SOLOMON (INJ)-P
39 MIKE DAVEY-P
40 DICK RUTHVEN-P (1)
40 CRAIG SKOK-P
42 FRANK LACORTE-P
43 CITO GASTON-OF/1B (1)
44 *(RET#) HANK AARON*
45 JAMIE EASTERLY-P
48 CLOYD (JUNIOR) BOYER-CH
49 PRESTON HANNA-P
50 TOMMY BOGGS-P
56 JIM BOUTON-P

1979

6TH W 66-94 23.5GB

1 JERRY ROYSTER-2B/3B
2 BARRY BONNELL-OF/3B
3 DALE MURPHY (INJ)-1B/C
4 BIFF POCOROBA (INJ)-C
5 BOB HORNER (INJ)-3B
6 BOBBY COX-MGR
7 JEFF BURROUGHS-OF
8 ALEX GRAMMAS-CH
9 PEPE FRIAS-SS
10 BOBBY DEWS-CH
11 JOE NOLAN-C
14 EDDIE MILLER-OF
15 DARREL CHANEY-UTIL
16 LARRY BRADFORD-P
16 JIM WESSINGER-2B
17 GLENN HUBBARD-2B
18 LARRY WHISENTON-OF
20 BRUCE BENEDICT-C
22 ROWLAND OFFICE-OF/1B
23 TOMMIE AARON-CH
24 MICKEY MAHLER-P
25 BOB BEALL-1B
26 GENE GARBER-P
27 LARRY MCWILLIAMS (INJ)-P
28 ADRIAN DEVINE-P
28 MIKE LUM-1B/OF
29 RICK MATULA-P
30 BRIAN ASSELSTINE (INJ)-OF
31 MIKE MACHA-3B
32 BO MCLAUGHLIN-P (2)
34 LARRY BRADFORD-P
35 PHIL NIEKRO-P
36 GARY (SARGE) MATTHEWS-OF
37 EDDIE (BUDDY) SOLOMON-P
38 LARRY BRADFORD-P
38 ADRIAN DEVINE-P
39 RICK MAHLER-P
40 CRAIG SKOK-P
40 LARRY BRADFORD-P
42 FRANK LACORTE-P (1)
43 TONY BRIZZOLARA-P
44 *(RET#) HANK AARON*
45 JAMIE EASTERLY-P
46 JOEY MCLAUGHLIN-P
46 CHARLIE SPIKES-OF
48 CLOYD (JUNIOR) BOYER-CH
49 PRESTON HANNA (INJ)-P
50 TOMMY BOGGS-P
50 JOEY MCLAUGHLIN-P
51 TOMMY BOGGS-P
54 RICK MATULA-P

1980

4TH W 81-80 11GB

1 JERRY ROYSTER-UTIL
2 BOBBY DEWS-CH
3 DALE MURPHY-OF/1B
4 BIFF POCOROBA (INJ)-C
5 BOB HORNER-3B/1B
6 BOBBY COX-MGR
7 JEFF BURROUGHS-OF
8 JOHN SULLIVAN-CH
9 LUIS GOMEZ-SS
10 CHRIS CHAMBLISS-1B
11 JOE NOLAN-C (1)
14 CHICO RUIZ-INF
14 EDDIE MILLER-OF
15 BILL NAHORODNY-C/1B
16 LARVELL BLANKS-INF
17 GLENN HUBBARD-2B
19 TERRY HARPER-OF
20 BRUCE BENEDICT-C
22 GARY COOPER-OF
23 TOMMIE AARON-CH
26 GENE GARBER-P
27 LARRY MCWILLIAMS-P
28 MIKE LUM-OF/1B
29 RICK MATULA-P
30 BRIAN ASSELSTINE (INJ)-OF
33 DOYLE ALEXANDER-P
34 LARRY BRADFORD-P
35 PHIL NIEKRO-P
36 GARY (SARGE) MATTHEWS-OF
37 RICK CAMP-P
39 AL (THE MAD HUNGARIAN) HRABOSKY-P
40 TOMMY BOGGS-P
42 RICK MAHLER-P
44 *(RET#) HANK AARON*
46 CHARLIE SPIKES-OF
47 RAFAEL RAMIREZ-SS
48 CLOYD (JUNIOR) BOYER-CH
49 PRESTON HANNA-P

1981

1ST 1/2:4TH W 25-29 9.5GB
2ND 1/2:5TH W 25-27 7.5GB
FINAL: 50-56 --GB

1 JERRY ROYSTER-3B/2B
2 BOBBY DEWS-CH
3 DALE MURPHY-OF/1B
4 BIFF POCOROBA-3B/C
5 BOB HORNER (INJ)-3B
6 BOBBY COX-MGR
8 JOHN SULLIVAN-CH
9* LUIS GOMEZ-INF/P*
10 CHRIS CHAMBLISS-1B
11 KEN SMITH-1B
12 LARRY OWEN-C
14 MATT SINATRO-C
15 BILL NAHORODNY-C/1B
15 PAUL RUNGE-SS
16 RAFAEL RAMIREZ-SS
17 GLENN HUBBARD-2B
18 CLAUDELL WASHINGTON-OF
19 TERRY HARPER-OF
20 BRUCE BENEDICT-C
22 BOB PORTER-PH
22 BRETT BUTLER-OF
23 TOMMIE AARON-CH
24 JOHN (COUNT) MONTEFUSCO-P
25 RUFINO LINARES-OF
26 GENE GARBER (INJ)-P
27 LARRY MCWILLIAMS-P
28 MIKE LUM-OF (1)
28 LARRY WHISENTON-OF
29 RICK MATULA-P
30 BRIAN ASSELSTINE (INJ)-OF
31 ALBERT HALL-OF
32 STEVE (BEDROCK) BEDROSIAN-P
34 LARRY BRADFORD-P
35 PHIL NIEKRO-P
36 GAYLORD PERRY-P
37 RICK CAMP-P
39 AL (THE MAD HUNGARIAN) HRABOSKY (INJ)-P
40 TOMMY BOGGS-P
41 BOB WALK-P
42 RICK MAHLER-P
43 BOB WALK-P
44 *(RET#) HANK AARON*
45 EDDIE MILLER-OF
46 GAYLORD PERRY-P
47 BROOK JACOBY-3B
48 CLOYD (JUNIOR) BOYER-CH
49 PRESTON HANNA-P
50 BOB WALK (INJ)-P
50 JOSE ALVAREZ-P

1982

1ST W 89-73 0GB
L NLCS-STLN 3-0

1 JERRY ROYSTER-UTIL
2 ALBERT HALL-PR
3 DALE MURPHY-OF
4 BIFF POCOROBA-C/3B
5 BOB HORNER-3B
6 RANDY JOHNSON-2B/3B
7 BOB PORTER-OF/1B
8 BOB WATSON-1B/OF
9 JOE TORRE-MGR
10 CHRIS CHAMBLISS-1B
11 KEN SMITH-1B/OF
14 MATT SINATRO-C
15 BOB WALK-P
15 PAUL RUNGE-PH
15 CLAUDELL WASHINGTON-OF
16 RAFAEL RAMIREZ-SS
17 GLENN HUBBARD-2B
18 CLAUDELL WASHINGTON-OF
18 PAUL ZUVELLA-SS
19 TERRY HARPER (INJ)-OF
20 BRUCE BENEDICT-C
22 BRETT BUTLER-OF
23 TOMMIE AARON-CH
24 LARRY OWEN-C
25 RUFINO LINARES-OF
26 GENE GARBER (INJ)-P
27 LARRY MCWILLIAMS-P (1)
27 PASCUAL PEREZ-P
28 LARRY WHISENTON-OF
30 KEN DAYLEY-P
31 ALBERT HALL-PR
31 DONNIE MOORE-P
32 STEVE (BEDROCK) BEDROSIAN-P
33 DONNIE MOORE-P
34 TOM HAUSMAN-P
35 PHIL NIEKRO-P
36 CARLOS DIAZ-P (1)

BOSTON/MILWAUKEE/ ATLANTA BRAVES

6 SONNY JACKSON-CH
7 RICK CAMP-P
8 JOE COWLEY (INJ)-P
9 AL (THE MAD HUNGARIAN) HRABOSKY-P
0 TOMMY BOGGS (INJ)-P
2 RICK MAHLER-P
3 BOB WALK-P
4 *(RET#) HANK AARON*
5 BOB (HOOT) (GIBBY) GIBSON-CH
8 CARLOS DIAZ-P (1)
9 PRESTON HANNA-P (1)
0 BOB WALK (INJ)-P
0 JOSE ALVAREZ-P
2 JOE PIGNATANO-CH
3 DAL MAXVILL-CH
4 RUBE WALKER-CH

1983

2ND W 88-74 3GB

1 JERRY ROYSTER-UTIL
2 ALBERT HALL-OF
3 DALE MURPHY-OF
4 BIFF POCOROBA-C
5 BOB HORNER (INJ)-3B/1B
6 RANDY JOHNSON-3B/2B
7 BRAD KOMMINSK-OF
8 BOB WATSON-1B
9 JOE TORRE-MGR
0 CHRIS CHAMBLISS-1B
1 KEN SMITH-1B
1 MIKE JORGENSEN-1B/OF (2)
2 PAUL RUNGE-2B
4 MATT SINATRO-C
5 CLAUDELL WASHINGTON-OF
6 RAFAEL RAMIREZ-SS
7 GLENN HUBBARD-2B
8 PAUL ZUVELLA-SS
9 TERRY HARPER-OF
0 BRUCE BENEDICT-C
2 BRETT BUTLER-OF
3 TOMMIE AARON-CH
4 LARRY OWEN-C
6 GENE GARBER (INJ)-P
7 PASCUAL PEREZ-P
8 GERALD PERRY-1B/OF
9 CRAIG MCMURTRY-P
0 KEN DAYLEY-P
1 DONNIE MOORE-P
2 STEVE (BEDROCK) BEDROSIAN-P
3 PETE FALCONE-P
5 PHIL NIEKRO-P
6 GERALD PERRY-1B/OF
6 SONNY JACKSON-CH
7 RICK CAMP (INJ)-P
9 LEN BARKER-P (2)
0 TOMMY BOGGS (INJ)-P
2 RICK MAHLER-P
3 BOB WALK-P
4 *(RET#) HANK AARON*
5 BOB (HOOT) (GIBBY) GIBSON-CH
7 BROOK JACOBY-3B
8 TONY BRIZZOLARA-P
9 RICK BEHENNA-P (1)
9 JEFF DEDMON-P
1 TERRY FORSTER-P
2 JOE PIGNATANO-CH
3 DAL MAXVILL-CH
4 RUBE WALKER-CH
7 SONNY JACKSON-CH

1984

2ND W 80-82 12GB

1 JERRY ROYSTER-UTIL
2 ALBERT HALL-OF
3 DALE MURPHY-OF
4 BIFF POCOROBA-PH
5 BOB HORNER (INJ)-3B/
6 RANDY JOHNSON-3B
7 BRAD KOMMINSK-OF
8 BOB WATSON-1B
9 JOE TORRE-MGR
10 CHRIS CHAMBLISS-1B
11 MIKE JORGENSEN-1B/OF (1)
11 RUFINO LINARES-OF
12 PAUL RUNGE-INF
14 MATT SINATRO-C
15 CLAUDELL WASHINGTON-OF
16 RAFAEL RAMIREZ-SS
17 GLENN HUBBARD-2B
18 PAUL ZUVELLA-2B/SS
19 TERRY HARPER-OF
20 BRUCE BENEDICT-C
23 TOMMIE AARON-CH
24 KEN (OBIE) OBERKFELL (INJ)-3B/2B (2)
25 ALEX TREVINO-C (2)
26 GENE GARBER-P
27 PASCUAL PEREZ (SUS)-P
28 GERALD PERRY-1B/OF
29 CRAIG MCMURTRY-P
30 KEN DAYLEY-P (1)
30 MILT THOMPSON-OF
31 DONNIE MOORE (INJ)-P
32 STEVE (BEDROCK) BEDROSIAN (INJ)-P
33 PETE FALCONE-P
34 ZANE SMITH-P
36 EDDIE HAAS-CH
37 RICK CAMP-P
39 LEN BARKER (INJ)-P
42 RICK MAHLER-P
44 *(RET#) HANK AARON*
45 BOB (HOOT) (GIBBY) GIBSON-CH
47 MIKE PAYNE-P
48 TONY BRIZZOLARA-P
49 JEFF DEDMON-P
51 TERRY FORSTER (INJ)-P
52 JOE PIGNATANO-CH
53 DAL MAXVILL-CH
54 RUBE WALKER-CH
55 LUKE (OLE ACHES & PAINS) APPLING-CH

1985

5TH W 66-96 29GB

2 ALBERT HALL-OF
3 DALE MURPHY-OF
5 RICK CERONE-C
7 BOBBY WINE, SR.-CH/MGR2
8 LARRY OWEN-C
10 CHRIS CHAMBLISS-1B
11 BOB HORNER-1B/3B
12 PAUL RUNGE-INF
14 ANDRES THOMAS-SS
15 CLAUDELL WASHINGTON-OF
16 RAFAEL RAMIREZ-SS
17 GLENN HUBBARD-2B
18 PAUL ZUVELLA-2B/SS
19 TERRY HARPER-OF
20 BRUCE BENEDICT-C
22 EDDIE HAAS-MGR1
23 DAVE SCHULER-P
24 KEN (OBIE) OBERKFELL (INJ)-3B/2B
26 GENE GARBER-P
27 PASCUAL PEREZ (INJ)-P
28 GERALD PERRY-1B/OF
29 CRAIG MCMURTRY-P
30 MILT THOMPSON-OF
31 JOHN RABB-OF
32 STEVE (BEDROCK) BEDROSIAN-P
33 JOHNNY SAIN-CH
34 ZANE SMITH (INJ)-P
36 BRAD KOMMINSK-OF
37 RICK CAMP-P
38 JOE JOHNSON-P
39 LEN BARKER (INJ)-P
40 BRUCE SUTTER-P
42 RICK MAHLER-P
43 STEVE SHIELDS-P
44 *(RET#) HANK AARON*
49 JEFF DEDMON-P
50 BRIAN SNITKER-CH
51 TERRY FORSTER-P
52 LEO MAZZONE-CH
53 DAL MAXVILL-CH
53 BOBBY DEWS-CH
55 JOE JOHNSON-P
57 STEVE SHIELDS-P
61 DAVE SCHULER-P

1986

6TH W 72-89 23.5GB

1 ALBERT HALL-OF
2 ALBERT HALL-OF
2 RUSS NIXON-CH
3 DALE MURPHY-OF
4 BOB SKINNER-CH
5 BILLY SAMPLE-OF/2B
6 BILLY SAMPLE-OF/2B
6 DARRYL MOTLEY-OF (2)
7 CHUCK TANNER-MGR
8 WILLIE STARGELL-CH
9 OZZIE VIRGIL, JR.-C
10 CHRIS CHAMBLISS-1B
11 BOB HORNER-1B
12 PAUL RUNGE-2B
14 ANDRES THOMAS-SS
15 CLAUDELL WASHINGTON (INJ)-OF (1)
16 RAFAEL RAMIREZ-UTIL
17 GLENN HUBBARD-2B
18 OMAR MORENO-OF
19 TERRY HARPER-OF
20 BRUCE BENEDICT-C
22 KEN GRIFFEY, SR.-OF/1B (2)
23 TED (SIMBA) SIMMONS-UTIL
24 KEN (OBIE) OBERKFELL-3B/2B
26 GENE GARBER-P
28 GERALD PERRY-OF/1B
29 CRAIG MCMURTRY (INJ)-P
30 PAUL ASSENMACHER-P
31 ED OLWINE-P
33 JOHNNY SAIN-CH
34 ZANE SMITH (INJ)-P
36 BRAD KOMMINSK-3B/OF
37 DOYLE ALEXANDER-P (2)
38 JOE JOHNSON-P (1)
38 JIM ACKER-P (2)
39 CLIFF SPECK-P
39 CRAIG MCMURTRY (INJ)-P
40 BRUCE SUTTER (INJ)-P
42 RICK MAHLER-P
43 STEVE SHIELDS-P
44 *(RET#) HANK AARON*
45 CHARLIE PULEO-P
46 DAVID PALMER-P
48 DUANE WARD-P (1)
49 JEFF DEDMON-P
50 TONY BARTIROME-CH
52 AL MONCHAK-CH
53 RUSS NIXON-CH
55 RICH MORALES-CH
56 DUANE WARD-P (1)
57 CHARLIE PULEO-P
59 PAUL ASSENMACHER-P

1987

5TH W 69-92 20.5GB

1 ALBERT HALL-OF
2 RUSS NIXON-CH
3 DALE MURPHY-OF
4 BOB SKINNER-CH
5 RON GANT-2B
6 DARRYL MOTLEY-OF
7 CHUCK TANNER-MGR
8 WILLIE STARGELL-CH
9 OZZIE VIRGIL, JR.-C
10 DION JAMES-OF
11 TERRY BELL-PH
12 PAUL RUNGE-INF
14 ANDRES THOMAS (INJ)-SS
15 GARY ROENICKE-OF/1B
16 RAFAEL RAMIREZ (INJ)-SS/3B
17 GLENN HUBBARD-2B
18 TRENCH DAVIS-PH
19 GRAIG NETTLES-3B/1B
20 BRUCE BENEDICT-C
22 KEN GRIFFEY, SR.-OF/1B
23 TED (SIMBA) SIMMONS-UTIL
24 KEN (OBIE) OBERKFELL-3B/2B
25 PETE SMITH-P
25 LARRY MCWILLIAMS-P
26 GENE GARBER-P (1)
27 MIKE FISCHLIN-PR
28 GERALD PERRY-1B/OF
29 STEVE ZIEM-P
30 PAUL ASSENMACHER-P
31 ED OLWINE-P
32 JEFF BLAUSER-SS
33 JOHNNY SAIN-CH
33 DOYLE ALEXANDER (INJ)-P (1)
34 ZANE SMITH-P
35 PHIL NIEKRO-P (3)
36 CHUCK CARY-P
37 RANDY O'NEAL-P (1)
37 JOE BOEVER-P
38 JIM ACKER-P
39 BRUCE DAL CANTON-CH
(40) BRUCE SUTTER (INJ)-(P)
42 RICK MAHLER-P
43 KEVIN COFFMAN-P
44 *(RET#) HANK AARON*
45 CHARLIE PULEO-P
46 DAVID PALMER (INJ)-P
47 TOM GLAVINE-P
48 MARTY CLARY-P
49 JEFF DEDMON-P
50 TONY BARTIROME-CH
52 AL MONCHAK-CH
55 RICH MORALES-CH
59 STEVE ZIEM-P
DAMASO GARCIA (INJ)-(2B)

1988

6TH W 54-106 39.5GB

1 ALBERT HALL (INJ)-OF
2 RUSS NIXON-MGR2
3 DALE MURPHY-OF
4 BOB SKINNER-CH
4 JERRY ROYSTER-UTIL
5 RON GANT-2B/3B
6 LONNIE (SKATES) SMITH-OF
7 CHUCK TANNER-MGR1
7 BOBBY WINE-CH
8 WILLIE STARGELL-CH
8 JODY DAVIS-C (2)
9 OZZIE VIRGIL, JR.-C
10 DION JAMES-OF
11 ROY MAJTYKA-CH
12 PAUL RUNGE-INF
13 JUAN EICHELBERGER-P
14 ANDRES THOMAS-SS
15 GARY ROENICKE-OF/1B
16 TOMMY GREGG-OF (2)
17 MARK LEMKE-2B
18 DAMASO GARCIA-2B
19 TERRY BLOCKER-OF
20 BRUCE BENEDICT-C
22 KEN GRIFFEY, SR.-OF/1B (1)
23 TED (SIMBA) SIMMONS-1B/C
24 KEN (OBIE) OBERKFELL-3B/2B (1)
25 PETE SMITH-P
26 RICK MAHLER-P
27 JIM MORRISON-3B/OF/P (2)
28 GERALD PERRY-1B
29 TERRY BLOCKER-OF
29 JOHN SMOLTZ-P
30 PAUL ASSENMACHER-P
31 ED OLWINE (INJ)-P
32 JEFF BLAUSER-SS/2B
34 ZANE SMITH (INJ)-P
36 CHUCK CARY (INJ)-P
37 JOE BOEVER-P
38 JIM ACKER (INJ)-P
39 BRUCE DAL CANTON-CH
40 BRUCE SUTTER-P
40 JOSE ALVAREZ-P
42 RICK MAHLER-P
42 BRUCE SUTTER-P
43 KEVIN COFFMAN-P
44 *(RET#) HANK AARON*
45 CHARLIE PULEO-P
47 TOM GLAVINE-P
48 GARY EAVE-P
49 JUAN EICHELBERGER-P
49 GERMAN JIMENEZ-P
50 KEVIN BLANKENSHIP-P (1)
50 TONY BARTIROME-CH
52 AL MONCHAK-CH
54 CLARENCE JONES-CH
55 BRIAN SNITKER-CH
57 JOHN SMOLTZ-P

1989

6TH W 63-97 28GB

1 ODDIBE MCDOWELL-OF (2)
2 RUSS NIXON-MGR
3 DALE MURPHY-OF
4 JEFF BLAUSER-3B/UTIL
5 RON GANT-3B/OF
6* JOHN RUSSELL-UTIL/P*
7 BOBBY WINE-CH
7 JODY DAVIS-C/1B
8 JODY DAVIS-C/1B
8 JOHN MIZEROCK-C
9 DREW DENSON-1B
9 BOBBY WINE-CH
10 DION JAMES-OF/1B (1)
10 ED WHITED-3B/1B
11 ROY MAJTYKA-CH
11 DARRELL EVANS-1B/3B
12 JEFF WETHERBY-OF
14 ANDRES THOMAS-SS
15 ED WHITED-3B/1B
15 JEFF TREADWAY-2B/3B
16 TOMMY GREGG (INJ)-OF/1B
17 MARK LEMKE-2B
18 GERONIMO BERROA-OF
18 CLARENCE JONES-CH
19 TERRY BLOCKER-OF/P
19 ED ROMERO-INF (2)
19 FRANCISCO CABRERA-1B/C (2)
20 BRUCE BENEDICT-C
22 GERONIMO BERROA-OF
23 DAVID JUSTICE-OF
24 DEREK LILLIQUIST-P
25 PETE SMITH-P
26 ROY MAJTYKA-CH
27 LONNIE (SKATES) SMITH-OF
28 GERALD PERRY (INJ)-1B
29 JOHN SMOLTZ-P
30 PAUL ASSENMACHER-P (1)
30 MIKE STANTON-P

33 TOMMY GREENE-P
34 ZANE SMITH-P (1)
34 SERGIO VALDEZ-P
36 TONY CASTILLO-P
37 JOE BOEVER-P
38 JIM ACKER-P (1)
38 KELLY MANN-C
39 BRUCE DAL CANTON-CH
40 JOSE ALVAREZ (INJ-P
(42) BRUCE SUTTER (INJ)-(P)
43 JAY ALDRICH-P (2)
44 *(RET#) HANK AARON*
45 CHARLIE PULEO-P
46 DWAYNE HENRY-P
47 TOM GLAVINE-P
48 GARY EAVE-P
48 MARTY CLARY-P
49 MARK EICHHORN-P
50 KENT MERCKER-P
52 RUSTY RICHARDS-P
54 CLARENCE JONES-CH
55 BRIAN SNITKER-CH

1990
6TH W 65-97 26GB
1 ODDIBE MCDOWELL-OF
2 RUSS NIXON-MGR1
3 DALE MURPHY-OF (1)
4 JEFF BLAUSER-SS/UTIL
5 RON GANT-OF
6 ALEX INFANTE-INF
6 BOBBY COX-MGR2
7 JODY DAVIS-1B/C
8 ALEX INFANTE-INF
8 VICTOR ROSARIO-SS/2B
9 BOBBY WINE-CH
10 GREG OLSON-C/3B
11 MIKE BELL-1B
12 ERNIE WHITT (INJ)-C
14 ANDRES THOMAS-SS/3B
15 JEFF TREADWAY-2B
16 TOMMY GREGG-1B/OF
17 NICK ESASKY (ILL)-1B
17 JIMMY KREMERS-C
18 JIM PRESLEY-3B/1B
19 FRANCISCO CABRERA-1B/C
20 MARK LEMKE (INJ)-INF
21 *(RET#) WARREN SPAHN*
22 JIMY WILLIAMS-CH
23 DAVID JUSTICE-1B/OF
24 DEREK LILLIQUIST-P (1)
24 JIM VATCHER-OF (2)
25 PETE SMITH (INJ)-P
26 ROY MAJTYKA-CH
27 LONNIE (SKATES) SMITH-OF
28 CLARENCE JONES-CH
28 JOE HESKETH-P (2)
29 JOHN SMOLTZ-P
30 MIKE STANTON (INJ)-P
31 JIM VATCHER-OF (2)
32 CHARLIE LEIBRANDT (INJ)-P
33 TOMMY GREENE-P (1)
33 JEFF PARRETT-P (2)
34 SERGIO VALDEZ-P (1)
34 PAUL MARAK-P
35 PHIL NIEKRO-CH
36 TONY CASTILLO-P
37 JOE BOEVER-P (1)
37 GERONIMO BERROA-OF
38 KELLY MANN-C
38 JOE HESKETH-P (2)
39 BRUCE DAL CANTON-CH
39 PAT CORRALES-CH
40 MARVIN FREEMAN-P (2)
40 CHARLIE KERFELD-P (2)
41 *(RET#) EDDIE MATHEWS*
42 STEVE AVERY-P
43 DOUG SISK (INJ)-P
44 *(RET#) HANK AARON*
45 CHARLIE LEIBRANDT (INJ)-P
46 DWAYNE HENRY-P
47 TOM GLAVINE-P
48 MARTY CLARY-P
49 RICK LUECKEN-P (1)
50 KENT MERCKER-P
52 RUSTY RICHARDS-P
54 LEO-MAZZONE-CH
55 BRIAN SNITKER-CH
55 MARK GRANT-P (2)

1991
1ST W 94-68 0GB
W NLCS-PITN 4-3
L WS-MINA 4-3
1 OTIS NIXON-OF
2 RAFAEL BELLIARD-SS
4 JEFF BLAUSER-INF
5 RON GANT-OF
6 BOBBY COX-MGR
(7) NICK ESASKY (ILL)-(1B)
8 MIKE HEATH (INJ)-C
9 TERRY PENDLETON-3B
10 GREG OLSON-C
11 MIKE BELL-1B
12 SID BREAM (INJ)-1B
14 BRIAN HUNTER-1B/OF
15 JEFF TREADWAY-2B
16 TOMMY GREGG (INJ)-OF/1B
17 KEITH MITCHELL-OF
17 DANNY HEEP-OF/1B
18 JIM CLANCY-P (2)
19 FRANCISCO CABRERA-C/1B
20 MARK LEMKE-2B/3B
21 *(RET#) WARREN SPAHN*
22 JIMY WILLIAMS-CH
23 DAVID JUSTICE (INJ)-OF
24 DEION (NEON) SANDERS (FBL)-OF
25 PETE SMITH (INJ)-P
26 JIM BEAUCHAMP-CH
26 ALEJANDRO PENA-P (2)
27 LONNIE (SKATES) SMITH-OF
28 CLARENCE JONES-CH
29 JOHN SMOLTZ-P
30 MIKE STANTON-P
31 JERRY WILLARD-C
32 CHARLIE LEIBRANDT-P
33 STEVE AVERY-P
34 RICO ROSSY-SS
35 *(RET#) PHIL NIEKRO*
36 TONY CASTILLO-P (1)
36 MIKE BIELECKI-P (2)
37 JIM BEAUCHAMP-CH
38 CLARENCE JONES-CH
39 PAT CORRALES-CH
40 MARVIN FREEMAN (INJ)-P
41 *(RET#) EDDIE MATHEWS*
42 STEVE AVERY-P
42 ARMANDO REYNOSO-P
42 RICK MAHLER-P (2)
43 DOUG SISK (INJ)-P
43 MARK WOHLERS-P
44 *(RET#) HANK AARON*
45 VINNY CASTILLA-SS
46 RANDY ST. CLAIRE-P
46 DAN PETRY-P (2)
47 TOM GLAVINE-P
48 JUAN BERENGUER (INJ)-P
49 JEFF PARRETT-P
49 DAMON BERRYHILL-C (2)
50 KENT MERCKER-P
52 NED YOST-CH
54 LEO-MAZZONE-CH
(55) MARK GRANT (INJ)-(P)

1992
1ST W 98-64 0GB
W NLCS-PITN 4-3
L WS-TORA 4-2
1 OTIS NIXON-OF
2 RAFAEL BELLIARD-SS/2B
4 JEFF BLAUSER-INF
5 RON GANT-OF
6 BOBBY COX-MGR
7 MELVIN NIEVES-OF
8 JAVY LOPEZ-C
9 TERRY PENDLETON-3B
10 GREG OLSON-C
11 DAMON BERRYHILL-C
12 SID BREAM-1B
14 BRIAN HUNTER-1B/OF
15 JEFF TREADWAY-2B/3B
16 TOMMY GREGG-OF
18 STEVE LYONS-OF/2B (1)
18 RYAN KLESKO-1B
19 FRANCISCO CABRERA-C
20 MARK LEMKE-2B/3B
21 *(RET#) WARREN SPAHN*
22 JIMY WILLIAMS-CH
23 DAVID JUSTICE (INJ)-OF/1B
24 DEION (NEON) SANDERS (FBL)-OF
25 PETE SMITH (INJ)-P
26 ALEJANDRO PENA-P
27 LONNIE (SKATES) SMITH-OF
28 CLARENCE JONES-CH
29 JOHN SMOLTZ-P
30 MIKE STANTON-P
31 JERRY WILLARD-C (1)
31 JEFF REARDON-P (2)
32 CHARLIE LEIBRANDT-P
33 STEVE AVERY-P
35 *(RET#) PHIL NIEKRO*
36 MIKE BIELECKI-P
37 JIM BEAUCHAMP-CH
38 DAVID NIED-P
39 PAT CORRALES-CH
40 MARVIN FREEMAN (INJ)-P
41 *(RET#) EDDIE MATHEWS*
42 ARMANDO REYNOSO-P
43 MARK WOHLERS-P
44 *(RET#) HANK AARON*
45 VINNY CASTILLA-3B/SS
46 RANDY ST. CLAIRE-P
47 TOM GLAVINE-P
48 JUAN BERENGUER (INJ)-P (1)
48 MARK DAVIS-P (2)
50 KENT MERCKER-P
51 BEN RIVERA-P (1)
51 PEDRO BORBON-P
52 NED YOST-CH
54 LEO-MAZZONE-CH

1993
1ST W 104-58 0GB
L NLCS-PHIN 4-2
1 OTIS NIXON-OF
2 RAFAEL BELLIARD-SS/2B
4 JEFF BLAUSER-SS
5 RON GANT-OF
6 BOBBY COX-MGR
8 JAVY LOPEZ-C
9 TERRY PENDLETON-3B
10 GREG OLSON (INJ)-C
11 DAMON BERRYHILL-C
12 SID BREAM-1B
14 BRIAN HUNTER (INJ)-1B/OF
15 RAMON CARABALLO-2B
16 CHIPPER JONES-SS
18 RYAN KLESKO-1B/OF
19 FRANCISCO CABRERA-1B/C
20 MARK LEMKE-2B
21 *(RET#) WARREN SPAHN*
22 JIMY WILLIAMS-CH
23 DAVID JUSTICE-OF
24 DEION (NEON) SANDERS (SUS?)-OF
25 PETE SMITH (INJ)-P
26 TONY TARASCO-OF
27 FRED (CRIME DOG) MCGRIFF-1B (2)
28 CLARENCE JONES-CH
29 JOHN SMOLTZ-P
30 MIKE STANTON-P
31 GREG MADDUX-P
32 BILL PECOTA-UTIL
33 STEVE AVERY-P
35 *(RET#) PHIL NIEKRO*
36 STEVE (BEDROCK) BEDROSIAN-P
37 JIM BEAUCHAMP-CH
38 GREG MCMICHAEL-P
39 PAT CORRALES-CH
40 MARVIN FREEMAN (INJ)-P
41 *(RET#) EDDIE MATHEWS*
42 NED YOST-CH
43 MARK WOHLERS-P
44 *(RET#) HANK AARON*
47 TOM GLAVINE-P
50 KENT MERCKER-P
51 PEDRO BORBON, JR.-P
52 JAY HOWELL-P
54 LEO MAZZONE-CH

1994
2ND E 68-46 6GB
STRIKE NO POST-SEASON
2 RAFAEL BELLIARD-SS/2B
4 JEFF BLAUSER (INJ)-SS
6 BOBBY COX-MGR
8 JAVY LOPEZ-C
9 TERRY PENDLETON (INJ)-3B
10 GREGG OLSON (INJ)-P
11 CHARLIE O'BRIEN-C
12 DAVE GALLAGHER-OF
14 ROBERTO KELLY-OF (2)
(16) CHIPPER JONES (INJ)-SS
17 JARVIS BROWN-OF
18 RYAN KLESKO-1B/OF
19 MIKE MORDECAI-SS
20 MARK LEMKE-2B
21 *(RET#) WARREN SPAHN*
22 JIMY WILLIAMS-CH
23 DAVID JUSTICE-OF
24 DEION (NEON) SANDERS-OF (1)
25 MIKE KELLY-OF
26 TONY TARASCO-OF
27 FRED (CRIME DOG) MCGRIFF-1B
28 CLARENCE JONES-CH
29 JOHN SMOLTZ-P
30 MIKE STANTON-P
31 GREG MADDUX-P
32 BILL PECOTA-UTIL
33 STEVE AVERY-P
34 MIKE BIELECKI-P
35 *(RET#) PHIL NIEKRO*
36 STEVE (BEDROCK) BEDROSIAN-P
37 JIM BEAUCHAMP-CH
38 GREG MCMICHAEL-P
39 PAT CORRALES-CH
40 GREGG OLSON (INJ)-P
41 *(RET#) EDDIE MATHEWS*
42 NED YOST-CH
43 MARK WOHLERS-P
44 *(RET#) HANK AARON*
45 JOSE OLIVA-3B
47 TOM GLAVINE-P
49 MILT HILL-P (1)
49 BRAD WOODALL-P
50 KENT MERCKER-P
54 LEO MAZZONE-CH

1995
1ST E 90-54 0GB
144 GAME SEASON
W NLDS-COLN 3-1
W NLCS-CINN 4-0
W WS-CLEA 4-2
2 RAFAEL BELLIARD-SS
3 *(RET#) DALE MURPHY*
4 JEFF BLAUSER-SS
6 BOBBY COX-MGR
7 DWIGHT SMITH-OF
8 JAVY LOPEZ-C
9 MARQUIS GRISSOM-OF
10 CHIPPER JONES-3B
11 CHARLIE O'BRIEN-C
12 EDDIE PEREZ-C
15 BRIAN KOWITZ-OF
16 MIKE MORDECAI-SS
17 LUIS POLONIA-OF (2)
18 RYAN KLESKO-OF
20 MARK LEMKE-2B
21 *(RET#) WARREN SPAHN*
22 JIMY WILLIAMS-CH
23 DAVID JUSTICE-OF
24 MIKE DEVEREAUX-OF (2)
25 MIKE KELLY-OF
26 MIKE SHARPERSON-3B
26 ALEJANDRO PENA-P
27 FRED (CRIME DOG) MCGRIFF-1B
28 CLARENCE JONES-CH
29 JOHN SMOLTZ-P
30 MIKE STANTON-P (1)
30 ED GIOVANOLA-INF
31 GREG MADDUX-P
32 BILL PECOTA-UTIL
33 STEVE AVERY-P
34 MATT MURRAY-P (1)
34 DARRELL MAY-P
35 *(RET#) PHIL NIEKRO*
36 STEVE (BEDROCK) BEDROSIAN-P
36 TERRILL WADE-P
37 JIM BEAUCHAMP-CH
38 GREG MCMICHAEL-P
39 PAT CORRALES-CH
40 ROD NICHOLS-P
41 *(RET#) EDDIE MATHEWS*
42 NED YOST-CH
43 MARK WOHLERS-P
44 *(RET#) HANK AARON*
45 JOSE OLIVA-3B (1)
46 JASON SCHMIDT-P
47 TOM GLAVINE-P
48 BRAD WOODALL-P
49 TERRY CLARK-P
49 TOM THOBE-P
49 BRAD WOODALL-P
50 KENT MERCKER-P
51 PEDRO BORBON, JR.-P
52 BRAD CLONTZ-P
54 LEO MAZZONE-CH

1996
1ST E 96-66 0GB
W NLDS-LAN 3-0
W NLCS-STLN 4-3
L WS-NYA 4-2
1 LUIS POLONIA-OF (2)
2 RAFAEL BELLIARD-SS
3 *(RET#) DALE MURPHY*
4 JEFF BLAUSER (INJ)-SS
5 TYLER HOUSTON-1B (1)
5 PABLO MARTINEZ-PH
5 TERRY PENDLETON-3B (2)
6 BOBBY COX-MGR
7 DWIGHT SMITH-OF
8 JAVY LOPEZ-C

BOSTON/MILWAUKEE/ ATLANTA BRAVES

9 MARQUIS GRISSOM-OF
10 CHIPPER JONES-3B
11 ED GIOVANOLA-2B
12 EDDIE PEREZ-C
14 TONY GRAFFANINO-2B
14 DANNY BAUTISTA (INJ)-OF
15 DANNY BAUTISTA (INJ)-OF
15 DENNY NEAGLE-P (2)
16 MIKE MORDECAI (INJ)-SS
17 ED GIOVANOLA-2B
17 LUIS POLONIA-OF (2)
18 RYAN KLESKO-OF
19 JEROME WALTON (INJ)-OF
20 MARK LEMKE (INJ)-2B
21 *(RET#) WARREN SPAHN*
22 JIMY WILLIAMS-CH
23 DAVID JUSTICE(INJ)-OF
24 JERMAINE DYE-OF
25 MARK WHITEN-OF (2)
25 ANDRUW JONES-OF
26 MIKE BIELECKI-P
27 FRED (CRIME DOG) MCGRIFF-1B
28 CLARENCE JONES-CH
29 JOHN SMOLTZ-P
30 JOE AYRAULT-C
31 GREG MADDUX-P
32 KEVIN LOMON- P
33 STEVE AVERY (INJ)-P
34 DEAN HARTGRAVES-P (2)
35 *(RET#) PHIL NIEKRO*
36 TERRILL WADE-P
37 JIM BEAUCHAMP-CH
38 GREG MCMICHAEL-P
39 PAT CORRALES-CH
41 *(RET#) EDDIE MATHEWS*
42 NED YOST-CH
43 MARK WOHLERS-P
44 *(RET#) HANK AARON*
46 JASON SCHMIDT (INJ)-P (1)
47 TOM GLAVINE-P
48 BRAD WOODALL-P
49 TOM THOBE-P
49 CARL SCHUTZ-P
50 JOE BOROWSKI-P
51 PEDRO BORBON, JR. (INJ)-P
52 BRAD CLONTZ-P
54 LEO MAZZONE-CH

1997

1ST E 101-61 0GB
W NLDS-HOUN 3-0
L NLCS-FLAN 4-2

1 KEITH LOCKHARDT-2B
2 RAFAEL BELLIARD-SS
3 *(RET#) DALE MURPHY*
4 JEFF BLAUSER-SS
5 ? WEST-CH
6 BOBBY COX-MGR
7 KENNY LOFTON (INJ)-OF
8 JAVY LOPEZ-C
9 TIM SPEHR-C (2)
10 CHIPPER JONES-3B
11 ED GIOVANOLA-SS
12 EDDIE PEREZ-C
14 TONY GRAFFANINO-2B
15 DENNY NEAGLE-P
16 MIKE MORDECAI (INJ)-SS
17 DANNY BAUTISTA (INJ)-OF
18 RYAN KLESKO-OF
19 TOMMY GREGG-OF
20 MARK LEMKE (INJ)-2B
21 *(RET#) WARREN SPAHN*
22 BOBBY DEWS-CH
23 GREG COLBRUNN-PH (2)
24 MICHAEL TUCKER-OF
25 ANDRUW JONES-OF
26 MIKE BIELECK (INJ)-P
27 FRED (CRIME DOG) MCGRIFF-1B
28 CLARENCE JONES-CH
29 JOHN SMOLTZ-P
30 BRAD CLONTZ-P
31 GREG MADDUX-P
32 ALAN EMBREE-P
33 RANDALL SIMON-1B
(34) DEAN HARTGRAVES (INJ)-(P)
(34) BRYAN HARVEY (INJ)-(P)
34 KEVIN MILLWOOD-P
35 *(RET#) PHIL NIEKRO*
36 TERRILL WADE (INJ)-P
37 JIM BEAUCHAMP-CH
38 MIKE CATHER-P
39 PAT CORRALES-CH
40 CHAD FOX-P
41 *(RET#) EDDIE MATHEWS*
42 NED YOST-CH
43 MARK WOHLERS-P
44 *(RET#) HANK AARON*
45 PAUL BYRD-P
(46) YORKIS PEREZ (REL)-(P)
46 KERRY LIGTHENBERG-P
47 TOM GLAVINE-P
48 GREG MYERS-C (2)
49 CHRIS BROCK-P
50 JOE BOROWSKI-P (1)
50 JOHN LEROY-P
(51) PEDRO BORBON, JR. (INJ)-(P)
54 LEO MAZZONE-CH
(56) SCOTT BROW-(P)
(57) JAMIE WALKER-(P)

1998

1ST E 106-56 0GB
W NLDS-CHIN 3-0
L NLCS-SDN 4-2

1 KEITH LOCKHARDT-2B
2 RAFAEL BELLIARD (INJ)-SS
3 *(RET#) DALE MURPHY*
6 BOBBY COX-MGR
7 MARK DEROSA-INF
8 JAVY LOPEZ-C
9 WES HELMS-3B
10 CHIPPER JONES-3B
11 TONY GRAFFANINO-2B
12 EDDIE PEREZ-C
13 OZZIE GUILLEN-SS (2)
14 ANDRES (THE BIG CAT) GALARRAGA-1B
15 DENNY NEAGLE-P
16 DAMON HOLLINS-OF
17 DANNY BAUTISTA (INJ)-OF
18 RYAN KLESKO-OF
19 CURTIS PRIDE (INJ)-OF
20 MARTY MALLOY-INF
21 *(RET#) WARREN SPAHN*
22 WALT WEISS-SS
23 GREG COLBRUNN-1B (2)
24 MICHAEL TUCKER-OF
25 ANDRUW JONES-OF
26 GEORGE LOMBARD-OF
27 GERALD (ICE) WILLIAMS-OF
28 CLARENCE JONES-CH
29 JOHN SMOLTZ (INJ)-P
30 RAY HOLBERT-INF (1)
30 NORM (THE GENIUS) CHARLTON-P (2)
31 GREG MADDUX-P
32 DENNIS (EL PRESIDENTE) MARTINEZ-P
33 RANDALL SIMON-1B
34 KEVIN MILLWOOD-P
35 *(RET#) PHIL NIEKRO*
36 ALAN EMBREE-P (1)
36 RUSS SPRINGER-P (2)
37 JIM BEAUCHAMP-CH
38 MIKE CATHER-P
39 PAT CORRALES-CH
40 RUDY SEANEZ-P
41 *(RET#) EDDIE MATHEWS*
42 NED YOST-CH
43 MARK WOHLERS-P
44 *(RET#) HANK AARON*
45 PAUL BYRD (WAIV)-P (1)
45 ODALIS PEREZ-P
46 KERRY LIGTHENBERG-P
47 TOM GLAVINE-P
48 BRIAN EDMONDSON-(WAIV)-P (1)
48 BRUCE CHEN-P
49 JOHN ROCKER-P
50 ADAM BUTLER-P
(51) PEDRO BORBON, JR. (INJ)-(P)
52 BOBBY DEWS-CH
54 LEO MAZZONE-CH
59 FRANK FULTZ-CH
(60) DAMIAN MOSS (INJ)-(P)

1999

1ST E 103-59 0GB
W NLDS-HOUN 3-1
W NLCS-NYN 4-2
L WS-NYA 4-0

1 OTIS NIXON (INJ)-OF
2 MARK DEROSA-INF
3 *(RET#) DALE MURPHY*
4 JORGE FABREGAS-C (2)
5 NED YOST-CH
6 BOBBY COX-MGR
7 KEITH LOCKHARDT-2B
8 JAVY LOPEZ (INJ)-C
(9) WES HELMS (INJ)-(3B)
9 HOWARD BATTLE-INF
10 CHIPPER JONES-3B
11 PASQUAL MATOS-C
12 EDDIE PEREZ-C
13 OZZIE GUILLEN-SS
(14) ANDRES (THE BIG CAT) GALARRAGA (ILL)-1B
15 RANDALL SIMON-1B
16 JOSE HERNANDEZ-INF (2)
17 GLENN HUBBARD-CH
18 RYAN KLESKO-OF/1B
19 BRIAN R. HUNTER-OF/1B
20 FREDDY GARCIA-OF (2)
21 *(RET#) WARREN SPAHN*
22 WALT WEISS-SS
23 DON BAYLOR-CH
24 BRETT BOONE-2B
25 ANDRUW JONES-OF
26 GEORGE LOMBARD-OF
27 GERALD (ICE) WILLIAMS-OF
28 JOHN HUDEK (INJ)-P (2)
28 GREG MYERS (INJ)-C (2)
29 JOHN SMOLTZ (INJ)-P
30 KEVIN MCGLINCHY-P
31 GREG MADDUX-P
32 JUSTIN SPEIER-P
33 BRIAN JORDAN-OF
34 KEVIN MILLWOOD-P
35 *(RET#) PHIL NIEKRO*
36 RUSS SPRINGER-P
37 MIKE REMLINGER-P
38 MIKE CATHER-P
38 SEAN BERGMAN-P (2)
39 PAT CORRALES-CH
40 RUDY SEANEZ (INJ)-P
41 *(RET#) EDDIE MATHEWS*
42 *(RET#) JACKIE ROBINSON*
43 MARK WOHLERS (INJ)-P (1)
43 MICAH BOWIE-P (1)
43 TERRY MULHOLLAND-P (2)
43 ODALIS PEREZ (INJ)-P
44 *(RET#) HANK AARON*
45 ODALIS PEREZ (INJ)-P
45 TERRY MULHOLLAND-P (2)
46 KERRY LIGTHENBERG (INJ-P
47 TOM GLAVINE-P
48 BRUCE CHEN-P
49 JOHN ROCKER-P
50 DERRIN EBERT-P
51 JOE WINKELSAS-P
51 HOWARD BATTLE-INF
51 DAVID CORTES-P
52 BOBBY DEWS-CH
54 LEO MAZZONE-CH
56 EVERETT STULL-P
59 FRANK FULTZ-CH
(60) DAMIAN MOSS (INJ)-(P)

2000

1ST E 95-67 0GB
L NLDS-STLN 3-0

1 RAFAEL FURCAL-SS/2B
2 MARK DEROSA-INF
3 *(RET#) DALE MURPHY*
4 QUILVIO VERAS (INJ)-2B
5 NED YOST-CH
6 BOBBY COX-MGR
7 KEITH LOCKHARDT-2B
8 JAVY LOPEZ (INJ)-C
9 PAUL BAKO-C (3)
10 CHIPPER JONES-3B
11 STEVE SISCO-OF
12 EDDIE PEREZ (INJ)-C
14 ANDRES (THE BIG CAT) GALARRAGA-1B
15 B. J. SURHOFF-OF (2)
16 REGGIE SANDERS (INJ)-OF
17 GLENN HUBBARD-CH
18 WES HELMS-INF
19 BRIAN R. HUNTER-OF/1B (1)
19 JOHN BURKETT-P
20 FERNANDO LUNAR-C (1)
20 TIM UNROE-INF
21 *(RET#) WARREN SPAHN*
22 WALT WEISS-SS
23 BOBBY (BOBBY BO) BONILLA-OF
24 WALLY JOYNER-1B
25 ANDRUW JONES-OF
26 GEORGE LOMBARD-OF
27 TRENIDAD HUBBARD-OF (1)
27 MIKE HUBBARD-C (1)
28 MERV RETTENMUND-CH
29 JOHN SMOLTZ (INJ)-P
30 KEVIN MCGLINCHY (INJ)-P
31 GREG MADDUX-P
32 STEVE AVERY (INJ)-P
33 BRIAN JORDAN-OF
34 KEVIN MILLWOOD-P
35 *(RET#) PHIL NIEKRO*
36 LUIS RIVERA-P (1)
36 STAN BELINDA-P (2)
37 MIKE REMLINGER-P
38 GREG MCMICHAEL (INJ)-P
39 PAT CORRALES-CH
40 RUDY SEANEZ (INJ)-P
41 *(RET#) EDDIE MATHEWS*
42 *(RET#) JACKIE ROBINSON*
43 ODALIS PEREZ (INJ)-P
44 *(RET#) HANK AARON*
45 TERRY MULHOLLAND-P
46 KERRY LIGTHENBERG (INJ-P
47 TOM GLAVINE-P
48 BRUCE CHEN-P (1)
48 ANDY ASHBY-P (2)
49 JOHN ROCKER-P
50 DON WENGERT-P
50 SCOTT KAMIENIECKI-P (2)
51 DAVID CORTES-P
51 JASON MARQUIS-P
52 BOBBY DEWS-CH
54 LEO MAZZONE-CH
56 GABE MOLINA-P (2)
56 DAVE STEVENS-P
57 PEDRO SWANN-OF
58 CHRIS SEELBACH-P
59 FRANK FULTZ-CH
70 ISRAEL VILLEGAS-P

2001

1ST E 88-74 0GB
W NLDS-HOUN 3-0
L NLCS-ARIN 4-1

1 RAFAEL FURCAL (INJ)-SS/2B
2 RICO BROGNA-1B
2 REY SANCHEZ-SS (2)
3 *(RET#) DALE MURPHY*
4 QUILVIO VERAS (INJ)-2B
4 JULIO FRANCO-1B
5 NED YOST-CH
6 BOBBY COX-MGR
7 KEITH LOCKHARDT-2B
8 JAVY LOPEZ-C
9 PAUL BAKO-C
10 CHIPPER JONES-3B
11 KURT ABBOTT (INJ)-SS
11 KEN CAMINITI-3B (2)
12 EDDIE PEREZ (INJ)-C
14 DAVE MARTINEZ-1B
15 B. J. SURHOFF-OF
16 MARK DEROSA-INF
17 GLENN HUBBARD-CH
18 WES HELMS-INF
19 JOHN BURKETT-P
20 MARCUS GILES-3B
20 STEVE KARSAY-P (2)
21 *(RET#) WARREN SPAHN*
22 JESSE GARCIA-SS
23 BERNARD GILKEY (INJ)-OF
24 MARCUS GILES-3B
25 ANDRUW JONES-OF
(26) GEORGE LOMBARD (INJ)-(OF)
27 DAMIAN MOSS (INJ)-P
28 MERV RETTENMUND-CH
29 JOHN SMOLTZ (INJ)-P
30 KEVIN MCGLINCHY (INJ)-P
30 WILSON BETEMIT-SS
31 GREG MADDUX (INJ)-P
32 JOSE CABRERA-P
33 BRIAN JORDAN-OF
34 KEVIN MILLWOOD (INJ)-P
35 *(RET#) PHIL NIEKRO*
36 JOE SLUSARSKI (INJ)-P
36 STEVE KARSAY-P (2)
36 STEVE REED-P (2)
37 MIKE REMLINGER-P
38 JASON MARQUIS-P
39 PAT CORRALES-CH
40 JOE NELSON-P
40 CORY ALDRIDGE-P
41 *(RET#) EDDIE MATHEWS*
42 *(RET#) JACKIE ROBINSON*
43 MARC VALDES-P
43 TIM SPOONEYBARGER-P
44 *(RET#) HANK AARON*
45 ODALIS PEREZ-P
46 KERRY LIGTHENBERG-P
47 TOM GLAVINE-P
48 MATT WHITESIDE (REL)-P
48 RUDY SEANEZ-P (2)
49 JOHN ROCKER-P (1)
49 SCOTT SOBKOWIAK (INJ)-P
50 STEVE REED-P (2)
50 TREY MOORE-P
51 CHRIS SEELBACH-P
52 BOBBY DEWS-CH
54 LEO MAZZONE-CH
59 FRANK FULTZ-CH
61 DAMIAN MOSS (INJ)-P
64 SCOTT SOBKOWIAK (INJ)-P

2002

1ST E 101-59 0GB
L NLDS-SFN 3-2

1 RAFAEL FURCAL-SS/2B
2 JESSE GARCIA-1B

3 *(RET#) DALE MURPHY*
4 JULIO FRANCO-1B
4 MATT FRANCO-1B/OF
5 NED YOST-CH
6 BOBBY COX-MGR
7 KEITH LOCKHARDT-2B/3B
8 JAVY LOPEZ-C
9 TERRY PENDLETON-CH
10 CHIPPER JONES-OF
11 GARY SHEFFIELD-OF
(14) DAVE MARTINEZ (INJ)-(OF)
15 B. J. SURHOFF (INJ)-1B/OF
16 MARK DEROSA (INJ)-2B/UTIL
17 GLENN HUBBARD-CH
18 WES HELMS (INJ)-1B/3B
19 VINNY CASTILLA-3B
20 HENRY BLANCO-C
21 *(RET#) WARREN SPAHN*
22 MARCUS GILES (INJ)-2B/3B
23 JULIO FRANCO-1B
24 MARCUS GILES-3B
25 ANDRUW JONES-OF
(26) GEORGE LOMBARD (INJ)-(OF)
26 ANDY PRATT-P
27 DAMIAN MOSS-P
28 RYAN LANGERHANS-OF
28 DARREN BRAGG-OF
29 JOHN SMOLTZ-P
30 AARON SMALL-P
30 JUNG BONG-P
31 GREG MADDUX-P
32 ALBIE LOPEZ-P
33 JOEY DAWLEY-P
34 KEVIN MILLWOOD-P
35 *(RET#) PHIL NIEKRO*
36 CHRIS HAMMOND-P
37 MIKE REMLINGER-P
38 JASON MARQUIS-P
39 PAT CORRALES-CH
40 DARREN HOLMES-P
41 *(RET#) EDDIE MATHEWS*
42 *(RET#) JACKIE ROBINSON*
43 TIM SPOONEYBARGER-P
44 *(RET#) HANK AARON*
45 JOHN ENNIS-P
45 TREY HODGES-P
46 KERRY LIGTHENBERG-P
47 TOM GLAVINE-P
48 JOHN FOSTER (INJ) (ILL)-P
49 KEVIN GRYBOSKI-P
50 STEVE TORREALBA-C
52 BOBBY DEWS-CH
54 LEO MAZZONE-CH
59 FRANK FULTZ-CH

2003

1ST E 101-61 0GB
L NLDS-CHIN 3-2

1 RAFAEL FURCAL-SS
2 JESSE GARCIA-INF
3 *(RET#) DALE MURPHY*
4 MATT FRANCO-1B/OF
5 ROBERT FICK (INJ)-1B
6 BOBBY COX-MGR
8 JAVY LOPEZ-C
9 TERRY PENDLETON-CH
10 CHIPPER JONES-OF
11 GARY SHEFFIELD (BRV)-OF
12 MIKE HESSMAN-UTIL
14 JULIO FRANCO (INJ)-1B
16 MARK DEROSA-2B/UTIL
17 GLENN HUBBARD-CH
18 RYAN LANGERHANS-OF
19 VINNY CASTILLA-3B
20 HENRY BLANCO-C
21 *(RET#) WARREN SPAHN*
22 MARCUS GILES-2B
23 JOHNNY ESTRADA-C
25 ANDRUW JONES-OF
26 WILL CUNNANE-P
27 JARET WRIGHT-P (2)
28 DARREN BRAGG-OF
29 JOHN SMOLTZ (INJ)-P
30 HORACIO RAMIREZ-P
31 GREG MADDUX-P
32 MIKE HAMPTON (INJ)-P
33 FREDDI GONZALEZ-CH
34 ROBERTO HERNANDEZ (INJ-P
35 *(RET#) PHIL NIEKRO*
(36) PAUL BYRD (INJ)-(P)
37 SHANE REYNOLDS-P
38 JASON MARQUIS-P
39 PAT CORRALES-CH
40 DARREN HOLMES (INJ)-P
41 *(RET#) EDDIE MATHEWS*
42 *(RET#) JACKIE ROBINSON*
43 JOEY DAWLEY-P
44 *(RET#) HANK AARON*
45 TREY HODGES-P
46 RAY KING-P
48 RUSS ORTIZ-P
49 KEVIN GRYBOSKI (INJ)-P
50 WILL CUNNANE-P
50 KENT MERCKER-P (2)
51 JUNG BONG-P
52 BOBBY DEWS-CH
54 LEO MAZZONE-CH
56 BRIAN SNITKER-INT CH
59 FRANK FULTZ-CH
__ OTIS NIXON-CH

2004

1ST E 96-66 0GB
L NLDS-HOUN 3-2

1 RAFAEL FURCAL-SS
2 JESSE GARCIA-INF
3 *(RET#) DALE MURPHY*
6 BOBBY COX-MGR
7 J. D. DREW-OF
8 ELI MARRERO (INJ)-OF
9 TERRY PENDLETON-CH
10 CHIPPER JONES-OF
11 DEWAYNE WISE (INJ)-OF
12 EDDIE PEREZ-C
14 JULIO FRANCO-1B
15 MIKE HESSMAN-3B
16 MARK DEROSA-3B
17 GLENN HUBBARD-CH
19 ADAM LAROCHE (INJ)-1B
20 DARRON HOLLINS-OF
20 NICK GREEN-2B
21 *(RET#) WARREN SPAHN*
22 MARCUS GILES-2B
23 JOHNNY ESTRADA-C
24 WILSON BETEMIT-SS/3B
25 ANDRUW JONES-OF
26 WILL CUNNANE-P
26 CHARLES THOMAS-OF
27 JARET WRIGHT-P
28 SAM MCCONNELL-P
29 JOHN SMOLTZ-P
30 HORACIO RAMIREZ (INJ)-P
32 MIKE HAMPTON-P
33 FREDDI GONZALEZ-CH
34 ARMANDO ALMANZA (INJ)-P
34 JOSE CAPELLAN-P
35 *(RET#) PHIL NIEKRO*
36 PAUL BYRD (INJ)-P
37 CHRIS REITSMA-P
38 TOM MARTIN-P (2)
39 PAT CORRALES-CH
40 C. J. NITKOWSKI-P
40 ROMAN COLON-P
41 *(RET#) EDDIE MATHEWS*
42 *(RET#) JACKIE ROBINSON*
43 TRAVIS SMITH-P
44 *(RET#) HANK AARON*
45 DAN MEYER-P
46 TIM DREW (INJ)-P
48 RUSS ORTIZ-P
49 KEVIN GRYBOSKI-P
50 KENT MERCKER-P
51 JUAN CRUZ-P
52 JOHN THOMSON-P
53 BOBBY DEWS-CH
54 LEO MAZZONE-CH
57 ANTONIO ALFONSECA-P
59 FRANK FULTZ-CH

2005

1ST E 90-72 0GB
L NLDS-HOUN 3-1

1 RAFAEL FURCAL-SS
3 *(RET#) DALE MURPHY*
4 PETE ORR-UTIL
6 BOBBY COX-MGR
7 JEFF FRANCOEUR-OF
8 BRAYAN PENA-C
9 TERRY PENDLETON-CH
10 CHIPPER JONES (INJ)-OF
11 ANDY MARTE-INF
12 EDDIE PEREZ (INJ)-C
14 JULIO FRANCO-1B
15 TIM HUDSON (INJ)-P
16 BRIAN MCCANN-C
17 GLENN HUBBARD-CH
18 RYAN LANGERHANS-OF
19 ADAM LAROCHE-1B
20 TODD HOLLANDSWORTH-OF (2)
21 *(RET#) WARREN SPAHN*
22 MARCUS GILES-2B
23 JOHNNY ESTRADA-C
24 WILSON BETEMIT-3B/SS
25 ANDRUW JONES-OF
26 KYLE DAVIES-P
27 FRANK BROOKS-P
27 KELLY JOHNSON-OF
28 JOEY DEVINE-P
29 JOHN SMOLTZ-P
30 HORACIO RAMIREZ-P
32 MIKE HAMPTON (INJ)-P
33 BRIAN JORDAN (INJ)-OF
34 JORGE SOSA-P
35 *(RET#) PHIL NIEKRO*
36 JORGE VAZQUEZ-P
36 CHUCK JAMES-P
37 CHRIS REITSMA-P
38 TOM MARTIN (REL)-P
38 JIM BROWER-P (2)
39 PAT CORRALES-CH
40 ROMAN COLON-P (1)
40 KYLE FARNSWORTH-P (2)
41 *(RET#) EDDIE MATHEWS*
42 *(RET#) JACKIE ROBINSON*
43 RAUL MONDESI-OF
43 J. POWELL (INJ)-P
44 *(RET#) HANK AARON*
45 FREDI GONZALEZ-CH
46 JOHN FOSTER (INJ)-P
48 SETH GREISINGER-P
48 BLAINE BOYER-P
49 KEVIN GRYBOSKI-P (1)
49 MACAY MCBRIDE-P
50 ADAM BERNERO-P
50 ANTHONY LEREW-P
51 DAN KOLB-P
52 JOHN THOMSON (INJ)-P
53 BOBBY DEWS-CH
54 LEO MAZZONE-CH
57 MATT CHILDERS-P
59 FRANK FULTZ-CH

Looking as disgruntled as he does unfamiliar, Dale Murphy looks back on a career that was predominently in a Braves uniform. He was an All-Star seven times with Atlanta. Dale won back-to-back MVPs in 1982-83. He led the NL in HRs twice, RBIs twice and slugging twice. He fell short by two of reaching the coveted 400-home run plateau. The Braves retired his #3 in 1994, the year after he retired from the game.

CHICAGO CUBS

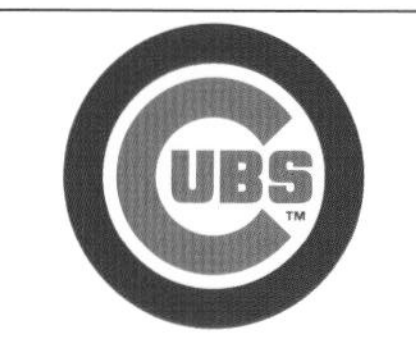

1932
CHICAGO CUBS
1ST 90-64 0GB
L WS-NYA 4-0

1 WOODY ENGLISH-3B/SS
2 BILLY HERMAN-2B
3 KIKI CUYLER (INJ)-OF
4 RIGGS (OLD HOSS) STEPHENSON-OF
5 JOHNNY MOORE-OF
6 CHARLIE (JOLLY CHOLLY) GRIMM-1B/MGR2
7 GABBY HARTNETT-C/1B
8 ROLLIE HEMSLEY-C/OF
9 ROGERS (RAJAH) HORNSBY-OF/3B/MGR1
9 MARK KOENING-SS
11 BILLY JURGES (INJ)-SS/3B
12 CHARLIE (CHINSKI) ROOT-P
14 GUY (MISSISSIPPI MUDCAT) BUSH-P
15 PAT MALONE-P
16 BURLEIGH (OL' STUBBLE-BEARD) GRIMES-P
17 LON (THE ARKANSAS HUMMINGBIRD) WARNEKE-P
18 BOB SMITH-P
19 JAKIE MAY-P
21 BUD TINNING-P
22 MARV GUDAT-OF/1B/P
23 LEROY HERRMANN-P
24 MARV GUDAT-OF/1B/P
31 STAN (SMILIN' STAN) HACK -3B
34 ZACK TAYLOR-C
41 JOHN (RED) CORRIDEN, SR.-CH
42 CHARLEY O'LEARY-CH
49 VINCE BARTON-OF
49 CARROLL (LEFTY) YERKES-P
51 FRANK DEMAREE-OF
56 LANCE RICHBOURG-OF
NO# ED BAECHT-P (1G: 4/20)
NO# BOBO (BUCK) NEWSOM-P (1G:6/4)
NO# DANNY TAYLOR-OF (1) (TO BKLN:5/7)
NO# HARRY TAYLOR-1B (10G: 4/14-5/28)

1933
3RD 86-68 6GB

1 WOODY ENGLISH-3B/SS
2 BILLY HERMAN-2B
3 KIKI CUYLER (INJ)-OF
4 BABE HERMAN-OF
5 RIGGS (OLD HOSS) STEPHENSON-OF
6 FRANK DEMAREE-OF
7 CHARLIE (JOLLY CHOLLY) GRIMM-1B/MGR
8 HARVEY (GINK) HENDRICK-UTIL
9 GABBY HARTNETT-C
11 BILLY JURGES-SS
12 MARK KOENING-INF
14 ZACK TAYLOR-C
15 GILLY CAMPBELL-C
16 LON (THE ARKANSAS HUMMINGBIRD) WARNEKE-P
17 GUY (MISSISSIPPI MUDCAT) BUSH-P
18 PAT MALONE-P
19 CHARLIE (CHINSKI) ROOT-P
21 BURLEIGH (OL' STUBBLE-BEARD) GRIMES-P
21 LEROY HERRMANN-P
22 BUD TINNING-P
23 LYNN (LINE DRIVE) NELSON -P
31 JIM MOSOLF-OF
31 TAYLOR DOUTHIT-OF (2)
34 ROY HENSHAW-P
41 CARROLL (LEFTY) YERKES-P
41 DOLPH CAMILLI-1B
42 CHARLEY O'LEARY-CH
42 BERYL RICHMOND-P
49 STAN (SMILIN' STAN) HACK -3B
51 JOHN (RED) CORRIDEN, SR.-CH
56 JOHNNY SCHULTE-CH
61 BABE (BLIMP) PHELPS-C

1934
3RD 86-65 8GB

1 WOODY ENGLISH-INF
2 BILLY HERMAN-2B
3 KIKI CUYLER-OF
4 BABE HERMAN-OF/1B
5 RIGGS (OLD HOSS) STEPHENSON-OF
6 CHUCK KLEIN-OF
7 CHARLIE (JOLLY CHOLLY) GRIMM-1B/MGR
8 BILLY JURGES-SS
9 GABBY HARTNETT-C
11 BENNIE TATE-C
11 CHICK WIEDEMEYER-P
12 JIM (BIG JIM) WEAVER-P (2)
12 BOB O'FARRELL-C (2)
14 CHARLIE (CHINSKI) ROOT-P
15 DICK WARD-P
15 JIM (BIG JIM) WEAVER-P (2)
16 LON (THE ARKANSAS HUMMINGBIRD) WARNEKE-P
17 GUY (MISSISSIPPI MUDCAT) BUSH-P
18 PAT MALONE-P
19 BILL (BIG BILL) LEE-P
21 ROY (POP) JOINER-P
22 BUD TINNING-P
23 LYNN (LINE DRIVE) NELSON -P
31 AUGIE GALAN-INF
34 STAN (SMILIN' STAN) HACK -3B
41 DOLPH CAMILLI-1B (1)
41 DON HURST-1B (2)
42 TUCK STAINBACK-OF/3B
43 PHIL CAVARRETTA-1B
51 JOHN (RED) CORRIDEN, SR.-CH
56 MIKE KELLY-CH
61 BABE (BLIMP) PHELPS-C

1935
1ST 100-54 0GB
L WS-DETA 4-2

1 WOODY ENGLISH-3B/SS
2 BILLY HERMAN-2B
3 KIKI CUYLER-OF (1)
4 CHUCK KLEIN-OF
5 TUCK STAINBACK-OF
6 FRANK DEMAREE-OF
7 FRED LINDSTROM-OF/3B
8 CHARLIE (JOLLY CHOLLY) GRIMM-1B/MGR
9 GABBY HARTNETT-C
11 BILLY JURGES-SS
12 LON (THE ARKANSAS HUMMINGBIRD) WARNEKE-P
14 LARRY FRENCH-P
15 BILL (BIG BILL) LEE-P
16 TEX CARLETON-P
17 CHARLIE (CHINSKI) ROOT-P
18 CLAY BRYANT-P
18 JOHNNY (PATCHEYE) GILL-PH
21 HUGH CASEY-P
22 ROY HENSHAW-P
23 ROY (POP) JOINER-P
23 CLYDE (HARDROCK) SHOUN-P
24 FABIAN KOWALIK-P
39 STAN (SMILIN' STAN) HACK -3B/1B
41 KEN O'DEA-C
42 WALTER (TARZAN) STEPHENSON-C
43 PHIL CAVARRETTA-1B
51 AUGIE GALAN-OF
56 JOHN (RED) CORRIDEN, SR.-CH
61 ROY (HARDROCK) JOHNSON-CH

1936
2ND (TIE) 87-67 5GB

1 WOODY ENGLISH-INF
2 BILLY HERMAN-2B
3 GENE LILLARD-SS/3B
4 CHUCK KLEIN-OF (1)
4 ETHAN ALLEN-OF (2)
5 TUCK STAINBACK-OF
6 FRANK DEMAREE-OF
7 CHARLIE (JOLLY CHOLLY) GRIMM-1B/MGR
8 JOHNNY (PATCHEYE) GILL-OF
9 GABBY HARTNETT-C
11 BILLY JURGES-SS
12 LON (THE ARKANSAS HUMMINGBIRD) WARNEKE-P
14 LARRY FRENCH-P
15 BILL (BIG BILL) LEE-P
16 TEX CARLETON-P
17 CHARLIE (CHINSKI) ROOT-P
18 CLAY BRYANT-P
22 ROY HENSHAW-P
23 CLYDE (HARDROCK) SHOUN-P
24 FABIAN KOWALIK-P (1)
24 CURT (COONSKIN) DAVIS-P (2)
39 STAN (SMILIN' STAN) HACK -3B/1B
41 KEN O'DEA-C
42 WALTER (TARZAN) STEPHENSON-C
43 PHIL CAVARRETTA-1B
51 AUGIE GALAN-OF
56 JOHN (RED) CORRIDEN, SR.-CH
61 ROY (HARDROCK) JOHNSON-CH

1937
2ND 93-61 3GB

1 CHARLIE (JOLLY CHOLLY) GRIMM-MGR
2 GABBY HARTNETT-C
3 RIPPER COLLINS (INJ)-1B
4 BILLY HERMAN-2B
5 BILLY JURGES-SS
6 STAN (SMILIN' STAN) HACK -3B/1B
7 AUGIE GALAN-OF/INF
8 JOE MARTY-OF
9 FRANK DEMAREE-OF
11 BILL (BIG BILL) LEE-P
12 KEN O'DEA-C
14 LARRY FRENCH-P
15 LONNY (JUNIOR) FREY-UTIL
16 TEX CARLETON-P
17 CHARLIE (CHINSKI) ROOT-P
18 CLAY BRYANT-P
19 JOHN (RED) CORRIDEN, SR.-CH
20 ROY (HARDROCK) JOHNSON-CH
21 CLYDE (HARDROCK) SHOUN-P
22 CURT (COONSKIN) DAVIS (ILL)-P
23 PHIL CAVARRETTA-OF/1B
24 ROY (TARZAN) PARMELEE-P
39 BOB GARBARK-PH
39 BOB (LEFTY) LOGAN-P (2)
41 JOHN BOTTARINI-C/OF
42 TUCK STAINBACK-OF
43 DUTCH MEYER-PR
43 NEWT KIMBALL-P
43 CARL REYNOLDS-OF
49 KIRBY HIGBE-P
56 JOHN (RED) CORRIDEN, SR.-CH
61 ROY (HARDROCK) JOHNSON-CH

1938
1ST 89-63 0GB
L WS-NYA 4-0

1 CHARLIE (JOLLY CHOLLY) GRIMM-MGR1
2 GABBY HARTNETT-C/MGR2
3 RIPPER COLLINS-1B
4 BILLY HERMAN-2B
5 BILLY JURGES-SS
6 STAN (SMILIN' STAN) HACK -3B
7 AUGIE GALAN-OF
8 JOE MARTY-OF
9 FRANK DEMAREE-OF
11 BILL (BIG BILL) LEE-P
12 KEN O'DEA-C
14 LARRY FRENCH-P
15 TONY (POOSH 'EM UP) LAZZERI-UTIL/CH
16 TEX CARLETON-P
17 CHARLIE (CHINSKI) ROOT-P
18 CLAY BRYANT-P
19 JOHN (RED) CORRIDEN, SR.-CH
20 ROY (HARDROCK) JOHNSON-CH
21 STEVE MESNER-SS
22 DIZZY DEAN (INJ)-P
23 PHIL CAVARRETTA-OF/1B
25 KIRBY HIGBE-P
26 NEWT KIMBALL-P
28 STEVE MESNER-SS
28 JACK RUSSELL-P
29 BOBBY MATTICK-SS
29 KIRBY HIGBE-P
30 JIM (BIG TRAIN) ASBELL-OF
32 COAKER TRIPLETT-OF
32 NEWT KIMBALL-P
39 BOB GARBARK-C/1B
41 BOB (LEFTY) LOGAN-P
41 VANCE PAGE-P
43 CARL REYNOLDS-OF
56 AL (TUB) (PARD) EPPERLY-P

1939
4TH 84-70 13GB

2 GABBY HARTNETT-C/MGR
3 PHIL CAVARRETTA (INJ)-1B/OF
4 BILLY HERMAN-2B
5 DICK (ROWDY RICHARD) BARTELL-SS/3B
6 STAN (SMILIN' STAN) HACK -3B
7 AUGIE GALAN-OF
8 JOE MARTY-OF (1)
8 BILL (SWISH) NICHOLSON-OF
9 HANK LEIBER-OF
11 BILL (BIG BILL) LEE-P
12 GUS (BLACKIE) MANCUSO-C
13 CLAUDE PASSEAU-P (2)
14 LARRY FRENCH-P
15 STEVE MESNER-INF
15 BOBBY MATTICK-SS
16 RAY (COWBOY) HARRELL-P (1)
17 CHARLIE (CHINSKI) ROOT-P
18 CLAY BRYAN (INJ)-P
19 JOHN (RED) CORRIDEN, SR.-CH
20 ROY (HARDROCK) JOHNSON-CH
22 DIZZY DEAN-P
23 VERN OLSEN-P
24 JIM (GEE GEE) GLEESON-OF
25 KIRBY HIGBE-P (1)
27 GENE LILLARD-P
28 JACK RUSSELL-P
31 EARL WHITEHILL (INJ)-P
32 RIP RUSSELL-1B
39 BOB GARBARK-C
41 VANCE PAGE-P
43 CARL REYNOLDS-OF

1940
5TH 75-79 25.5GB

2 GABBY HARTNETT-C/1B/MGR
3 PHIL CAVARRETTA (INJ)-1B
4 BILLY HERMAN-2B
5 BILLY ROGELL-INF
6 STAN (SMILIN' STAN) HACK -3B
7 AUGIE GALAN (INJ)-OF/2B
8 BILL (SWISH) NICHOLSON-OF
9 HANK LEIBER-OF/1B
10 AL TODD-C
11 BILL (BIG BILL) LEE-P
12 RIP RUSSELL-1B/3B
13 CLAUDE PASSEAU-P
14 LARRY FRENCH-P
15 BOBBY MATTICK-SS/3B
16 KEN RAFFENSBERGER-P
17 CHARLIE (CHINSKI) ROOT-P
18 CLAY BRYAN (INJ)-P
18 ZEKE BONURA-1B (2)
19 JOHN (RED) CORRIDEN, SR.-CH
20 GEORGE (THE BULL) UHLE-CH
21 CLYDE MCCULLOUGH-C
22 DIZZY DEAN (INJ)-P
23 VERN OLSEN-P
24 JIM (GEE GEE) GLEESON-OF
25 JAKE MOOTY-P
28 BOBBY STURGEON-SS
31 DOM (DIM DOM) DALLESSANDRO-OF
39 BOB (RIP) COLLINS-C
41 VANCE PAGE-P
43 JULIO BONETTI-P
43 RABBIT WARSTLER-SS/2B (2)

1941
6TH 70-84 30GB

1 JIMMIE (ACE) WILSON-MGR
2 AL TODD-PH
4 BILLY HERMAN-2B (1)

4 CHARLIE GILBERT-OF
5 BILLY MYERS-SS/2B
5 CLYDE MCCULLOUGH-C
6 STAN (SMILIN' STAN) HACK -3B/1B
7 AUGIE GALAN-OF (1)
7* JOHNNY (BEAR TRACKS) SCHMITZ-P*
8 BILL (SWISH) NICHOLSON-OF
9 HANK LEIBER (INJ)-OF/1B
10 BILLY MYERS-SS/2B
11 BILL (BIG BILL) LEE-P
12 RIP RUSSELL-1B
12 JOHNNY (MR. CHIPS) HUDSON-INF
13 CLAUDE PASSEAU-P
14 LARRY FRENCH-P (1)
14 KEN RAFFENSBERGER-P
15 LOU STRINGER-2B/SS
16 KEN RAFFENSBERGER-P
16 WIMPY QUINN-P
16 BABE DAHLGREN-1B (2)
17 CHARLIE (CHINSKI) ROOT-P
18 WIMPY QUINN-P
19 LOU (THE MAD RUSSIAN) NOVIKOFF-OF
19 BARNEY OLSEN-OF
20 EMIL KUSH-P
20 HANK GORNICKI-P (2)
21 CLYDE MCCULLOUGH-C
21 FRANK (JELLY) JELINCICH-OF
22 DIZZY DEAN (INJ)-P
23 VERN OLSEN-P
24 GREEK GEORGE-C
25 JAKE MOOTY-P
26 LOU (THE MAD RUSSIAN) NOVIKOFF-OF
27 EDDIE WAITKUS-1B
27 RUSS (BABE) MEERS-P
27 LENNY MERULLO-SS
28 BOBBY STURGEON-SS/INF
29 BARNEY OLSEN-OF
31 DOM (DIM DOM) DALLESSANDRO-OF
31 JOHNNY (BEAR TRACKS) SCHMITZ-P
32 PAUL (LI'L ABNER) ERICKSON-P
33 BOB SCHEFFING-C
35 LENNY MERULLO-SS
37 DICK SPALDING-CH
38 CHARLIE (JOLLY CHOLLY) GRIMM-CH
38 KIKI CUYLER-CH
40 TOT PRESSNELL-P
41 VANCE PAGE-P
41 VALLIE (CHIEF) EAVES-P
44 PHIL CAVARRETTA-OF/1B

1942

6TH 70-84 30GB

1 JIMMIE (ACE) WILSON-MGR
2 MARV (COONIE) FELDERMAN-C
2 PAUL GILLESPIE-C
4 CHARLIE GILBERT-OF
5 CLYDE MCCULLOUGH-C
6 STAN (SMILIN' STAN) HACK -3B
7 DOM (DIM DOM) DALLESSANDRO-OF
8 BILL (SWISH) NICHOLSON-OF
9 CHICO HERNANDEZ-C
11 BILL (BIG BILL) LEE (INJ)-P
12 RIP RUSSELL-UTIL
13 CLAUDE PASSEAU-P
14 LOU (THE MAD RUSSIAN) NOVIKOFF-OF
14 VALLIE (CHIEF) EAVES-P
15 LOU STRINGER-2B/3B
16 BABE DAHLGREN-1B (1)
16 JIMMIE (DOUBLE X) (BEAST) FOXX (INJ)-1B/C (2)
17 HI BITHORN-P
19 LOU (THE MAD RUSSIAN) NOVIKOFF-OF
19 LON (THE ARKANSAS HUMMINGBIRD) WARNEKE-P (2)
21 BOB BOWMAN-P
21 DICK (LIEF) ERRICKSON-P (2)
22 EMIL KUSH-P
23 VERN OLSEN-P
25 JAKE MOOTY-P
28 BOBBY STURGEON (INJ)-INF
30 BILL FLEMING-P
30 JESSE FLORES-P
31 JOHNNY (BEAR TRACKS) SCHMITZ-P
31 JOE (JITTERY JOE) BERRY-P
32 CY BLOCK-3B/2B
32 PAUL (LI'L ABNER) ERICKSON-P
33 BOB SCHEFFING-C
35 LENNY MERULLO-SS
37 DICK SPALDING-CH
38 KIKI CUYLER-CH
40 TOT PRESSNELL-P
43 PEANUTS LOWREY-OF
44 PHIL CAVARRETTA-1B/OF
45 ED HANYZEWSKI-P
45 HANK (HOOKS) WYSE-P
46 BILL FLEMING-P
46 MARV (TWITCH) RICKERT-OF
48 WHITEY PLATT-OF

1943

5TH 74-79 30.5GB

8 PETE (PICCOLO PETE) ELKO-3B
10 CLYDE MCCULLOUGH (INJ) -C
11 AL TODD-C
11 MICKEY KREITNER-C
12 CHICO HERNANDEZ-C
13 CLAUDE PASSEAU-P
14 LOU (THE MAD RUSSIAN) NOVIKOFF (H/O)-OF
20 STAN (SMILIN' STAN) HACK -3B
20 DON (PEP) JOHNSON-2B
21 LENNY MERULLO-SS/INF
21 BILL (BROADWAY BILL) SCHUSTER-SS
22 STU MARTIN-INF
22 CHARLIE GILBERT-OF
24 HEINZ (DUTCH) BECKER-1B
24 ED (HORN) SAUER-OF/3B
25 EDDIE (THE BRAT) (MUGGSY) STANKY-2B/INF
30 PAUL (DUKE) DERRINGER-P
31 BILL (BIG BILL) LEE (INJ)-P
31 DALE ALDERSON-P
32 LON (THE ARKANSAS HUMMINGBIRD) WARNEKE-P
33 ANDY (HANDY ANDY) (PRUSCHKA) PAFKO-OF
33 JAKE MOOTY-P
33 HANK (HOOKS) WYSE-P
34 ED HANYZEWSKI-P
35 HI BITHORN-P
36 BILL FLEMING-P
36 JOHN BURROWS-P (2)
37 JOHN BURROWS-P (2)
37 PAUL (LI'L ABNER) ERICKSON-P
38 DICK (KEWPIE DICK) BARRETT-P (1)
38 JOHN BURROWS-P (2)
38 MICKEY LIVINGSTON-C/1B (2)
39 RAY (POP) PRIM-P
40 JIMMIE (ACE) WILSON-MGR
41 DICK SPALDING-CH
42 KIKI CUYLER-CH
43 BILL (SWISH) NICHOLSON-OF
44 PHIL CAVARRETTA-1B/OF
45 HANK (HOOKS) WYSE-P
45 LOU (THE MAD RUSSIAN) NOVIKOFF (H/O)-OF
46 DOM (DIM DOM) DALLESSANDRO-OF
47 PEANUTS LOWREY-OF/INF
47 JOHNNY OSTROWSKI-OF/3B
48 WHITEY PLATT-OF
50 WALTER SIGNER-P
51 IVAL (GOODIE) GOODMAN-OF

1944

4TH 79-79 30GB

10 BILLY HOLM-C
11 MICKEY KREITNER-C
12 ROY EASTERWOOD-C
12 DEWEY (DEE) WILLIAMS-C
13 CLAUDE PASSEAU-P
20 DON (PEP) JOHNSON-2B
21 LENNY MERULLO-SS/1B
22 BILL (BROADWAY BILL) SCHUSTER-SS/2B
23 ROY (JEEP) (SAGE) HUGHES-3B/SS
24 PAUL GILLESPIE-C
24 TONY YORK-SS/3B
25 EDDIE (THE BRAT) (MUGGSY) STANKY-INF (1)
25 STAN (SMILIN' STAN) HACK -3B
26 JIMMIE (DOUBLE X) (BEAST) FOXX-3B/C
26 CHARLIE BREWSTER-SS
30 PAUL (DUKE) DERRINGER-P
31 DALE ALDERSON (MIL)-P
31 BOB (MR. CHIPS) CHIPMAN -P (2)
32 BILL FLEMING-P
33 HANK (HOOKS) WYSE-P
34 ED HANYZEWSKI (INJ)-P
35 HY VANDENBERG-P
36 JOHN BURROWS-P
37 PAUL (LI'L ABNER) ERICKSON-P
38 BEN (RED) MANN-PR
38 MACK STEWART-P
39 HANK MIKLOS-P
39 RED LYNN-P
40 JIMMIE (ACE) WILSON-MGR1
40 CHARLIE (JOLLY CHOLLY) GRIMM-MGR3
41 MILT STOCK-CH
42 ROY (HARDROCK) JOHNSON-CH/MGR2
43 BILL (SWISH) NICHOLSON-OF
44 PHIL CAVARRETTA-1B/OF
45 LOU (THE MAD RUSSIAN) NOVIKOFF-OF
45 BEN (RED) MANN-PR
46 DOM (DIM DOM) DALLESSANDRO-OF
47 DALE ALDERSON (MIL)-P
48 ANDY (HANDY ANDY) (PRUSCHKA) PAFKO-OF
49 ED (HORN) SAUER-OF/3B
49 FRANK SECORY-OF
50 JOE STEPHENSON (MIL)-C
50 JOHNNY OSTROWSKI-OF
51 IVAL (GOODIE) GOODMAN-OF
52 PETE (PICCOLO PETE) ELKO-3B
_ CHARLIE (SHERIFF) GASSAWAY-P (2G: 9/25-10/1)

1945

1ST 96-56 0GB

L WS-DETA 4-3

5 JOHNNY MOORE-PH
6 STAN (SMILIN' STAN) HACK -3B/1B
7 HEINZ (DUTCH) BECKER-1B
8 LEN RICE (INJ)-C
9 CLYDE MCCULLOUGH (MIL)-PH§
10 PAUL GILLESPIE-C/OF
11 MICKEY LIVINGSTON-C/1B
12 DEWEY (DEE) WILLIAMS-C
13 CLAUDE PASSEAU-P
20 DON (PEP) JOHNSON-2B
21 LENNY MERULLO-SS
22 BILL (BROADWAY BILL) SCHUSTER-INF
23 ROY (JEEP) (SAGE) HUGHES (INJ)-INF
26 RAY (IRON MAN) STARR-P (2)
26 HANK BOROWY-P (2)
27 WALTER SIGNER-P
27 GEORGE (THREE STAR) HENNESSEY-P
30 PAUL (DUKE) DERRINGER-P
31 BOB (MR. CHIPS) CHIPMAN -P (2)
32 RAY (IRON MAN) STARR-P (2)
32 LOYD CHRISTOPHER-OF (2)
33 HANK (HOOKS) WYSE-P
34 ED HANYZEWSKI-P
35 HY VANDENBERG-P
36 JORGE (PANCHO) COMELLAS-P
36 LON (THE ARKANSAS HUMMINGBIRD) WARNEKE-P
37 PAUL (LI'L ABNER) ERICKSON-P
38 MACK STEWART-P
38 JOHNNY MOORE-PH
38 RAY (IRON MAN) STARR-P (2)
39 RAY (POP) PRIM-P
40 CHARLIE (JOLLY CHOLLY) GRIMM-MGR
41 MILT STOCK-CH
42 ROY (HARDROCK) JOHNSON-CH
43 BILL (SWISH) NICHOLSON-OF
44 PHIL CAVARRETTA-1B/OF
45 ED (HORN) SAUER-OF
47 PEANUTS LOWREY-OF/SS
48 ANDY (HANDY ANDY) (PRUSCHKA) PAFKO-OF
49 FRANK SECORY-OF
50 JOHNNY OSTROWSKI-3B
51 REGGIE OTERO-1B
52 RED SMITH-CH
53 CY BLOCK (MIL)-2B/3B

§ PLAYED IN WORLD SERIES ONLY

1946

3RD 82-71 14.5GB

6 STAN (SMILIN' STAN) HACK (INJ)-3B
6 DEWEY (DEE) WILLIAMS-C
7 HEINZ (DUTCH) BECKER-PH (1)
7 BOBBY STURGEON-SS/2B
9 CLYDE MCCULLOUGH-C
10 BOB SCHEFFING-C
11 MICKEY LIVINGSTON (INJ)-C/1B
12 LOU STRINGER-INF
13 CLAUDE PASSEAU-P
13 HAL MANDERS-P (2)
15 RED ADAMS-P
17 RUSS (BABE) MEERS-P
17 HANK SCHENZ-3B
18 RUSS BAUERS-P
18 RED ADAMS-P
19 EMMETT (PINKY) O'NEILL-P (1)
19 DOYLE (PORKY) LADE-P
20 DON (PEP) JOHNSON (INJ)-2B
21 LENNY MERULLO-SS
22 CHARLIE GILBERT-OF (1)
22 RABBIT GARRIOTT-PH
23 VERN OLSEN-P
25 HI BITHORN-P
26 HANK BOROWY-P
27 AL GLOSSOP-2B/SS
27 JOHNNY OSTROWSKI-3B/2B
29 EMIL KUSH-P
31 BOB (MR. CHIPS) CHIPMAN -P
32 BILL FLEMING-P
32 TED (PORKY) PAWELEK-C
33 HANK (HOOKS) WYSE-P
34 ED HANYZEWSKI-P
34 CY BLOCK-3B
35 MARV (TWITCH) RICKERT-OF
36 EDDIE WAITKUS-1B
37 PAUL (LI'L ABNER) ERICKSON-P
38 BOBBY STURGEON-SS/2B
38 RUSS (THE MAD MONK) (MONK) (ROWDY) MEYER-P
39 RAY (POP) PRIM (INJ)-P
40 CHARLIE (JOLLY CHOLLY) GRIMM-MGR
41 MILT STOCK-CH
42 ROY (HARDROCK) JOHNSON-CH
43 BILL (SWISH) NICHOLSON-OF
44 PHIL CAVARRETTA-OF/1B
45 BILLY JURGES-SS/INF
46 DOM (DIM DOM) DALLESSANDRO-OF
47 PEANUTS LOWREY-OF/3B
48 ANDY (HANDY ANDY) (PRUSCHKA) PAFKO-OF
49 FRANK SECORY-OF
50 JOHNNY OSTROWSKI-3B/2B
52 RED SMITH-CH
53 JOHNNY (BEAR TRACKS) SCHMITZ-P
54 CLARENCE MADDERN-OF

1947

6TH 69-85 25GB

5 HANK SCHENZ-3B
6 STAN (SMILIN' STAN) HACK (INJ)-3B
7 BOBBY STURGEON-INF
9 CLYDE MCCULLOUGH-C

CHICAGO CUBS

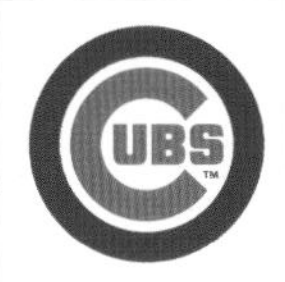

0 BOB SCHEFFING-C
1 MICKEY LIVINGSTON-C (1)
1 CLIFF (KIF) ABERSON-OF
2 DEWEY (DEE) WILLIAMS-C
3 CLAUDE PASSEAU-P
7 RUSS (BABE) MEERS-P
0 DON (PEP) JOHNSON-2B/3B
1 LENNY MERULLO-SS
1 SAL MADRID-SS
2 LONNY (JUNIOR) FREY-2B (1)
2 RALPH (BRUZ) HAMNER-P
3 DOYLE (PORKY) LADE-P
4 BILL (BIG BILL) LEE-P
4 OX MILLER-P
6 HANK BOROWY-P
8 RUSS (THE MAD MONK) (MONK) (ROWDY) MEYER (INJ)-P
9 EMIL KUSH-P
1 BOB (MR. CHIPS) CHIPMAN -P
2 BOB CARPENTER-P (2)
3 HANK (HOOKS) WYSE-P
4 FREDDY SCHMIDT-P (3)
5 MARV (TWITCH) RICKERT-OF/1B
5 RALPH (BRUZ) HAMNER-P
6 EDDIE WAITKUS-1B
7 PAUL (LI'L ABNER) ERICKSON-P
0 CHARLIE (JOLLY CHOLLY) GRIMM-MGR
1 MILT STOCK-CH
2 ROY (HARDROCK) JOHNSON-CH
3 BILL (SWISH) NICHOLSON-OF
4 PHIL CAVARRETTA-OF/1B
5 BILLY JURGES-SS/CH
6 DOM (DIM DOM) DALLESSANDRO-OF
7 PEANUTS LOWREY-3B/UTIL
8 ANDY (HANDY ANDY) (PRUSCHKA) PAFKO-OF
9 RAY MACK-2B (2)
2 RED SMITH-CH
3 JOHNNY (BEAR TRACKS) SCHMITZ-P

1948

8TH 64-90 27.5GB

2* TONY JACOBS-P*
5 HANK SCHENZ-2B/3B
6 JEFF CROSS-SS/2B (2)
7 DICK CULLER-SS/2B
7 EMIL (THE ANTELOPE) (DUTCH) VERBAN-2B (2)
8 RUBE WALKER-C
9 CLYDE MCCULLOUGH-C
0 BOB SCHEFFING-C
1 CLIFF (KIF) ABERSON-OF
1 MERV SHEA-CH
6 DON CARLSEN-P
7 WARREN HACKER-P
7 JESS DOBERNIC-P
8 CARL (SWATS) SAWATSKI-PH
8 JEFF CROSS-SS/2B (2)
8 WARREN HACKER-P
9 HAL JEFFCOAT-OF
0 DON (PEP) JOHNSON-2B/3B
0 DUMMY LYNCH-2B
2 CLARENCE MADDERN-OF
3 DOYLE (PORKY) LADE-P
4 BEN WADE-P
6 HANK BOROWY-P
7 DUTCH MCCALL-P
8 RUSS (THE MAD MONK) (MONK) (ROWDY) MEYER-P
29 EMIL KUSH-P
30 BOB RUSH-P
31 BOB (MR. CHIPS) CHIPMAN -P
32 CLIFF (LEFTY) CHAMBERS-P
(33) HANK (HOOKS) WYSE (INJ)-(P)
33 GENE (SKIP) MAUCH-2B/SS (2)
35 RALPH (BRUZ) HAMNER-P
36 EDDIE WAITKUS-1B/OF
37 PAUL (LI'L ABNER) ERICKSON-P (1)
39 ROY SMALLEY, SR.-SS
40 CHARLIE (JOLLY CHOLLY) GRIMM-MGR
41 MILT STOCK-CH
41 CARMEN MAURO-OF
42 ROY (HARDROCK) JOHNSON-CH
43 BILL (SWISH) NICHOLSON-OF
44 PHIL CAVARRETTA-1B/OF
45 BILLY JURGES-SS/CH
47 PEANUTS LOWREY-OF/INF
48 ANDY (HANDY ANDY) (PRUSCHKA) PAFKO-3B
52 RED SMITH-CH
53 JOHNNY (BEAR TRACKS) SCHMITZ-P

1949

8TH 61-93 36GB

3 FRANKIE (THE FORDHAM FLASH) FRISCH-MGR2
4 SMOKY BURGESS-C
4 HAL JEFFCOAT-OF
5 HANK SCHENZ-3B
5 BOB RAMAZZOTTI-INF (2)
6 FRANKIE GUSTINE-3B/2B
6 WAYNE (TWIG) TERWILLIGER-2B
6 BILL SERENA-3B
7 EMIL (THE ANTELOPE) (DUTCH) VERBAN-2B
8 RUBE WALKER-C
8 SMOKY BURGESS-C
9 MICKEY OWEN (MEX)-C
9 RUBE NOVOTNEY-C
10 BOB SCHEFFING (ILL)-C
11 CLIFF (KIF) ABERSON-OF
11 BOB MUNCRIEF-P (2)
12 CAL (BUSTER) MCLISH-P
16 MICKEY OWEN (MEX)-C
16 HANK EDWARDS (INJ)-OF (2)
17 JESS DOBERNIC-P (1)
17 BOB RUSH-P
18 WARREN HACKER-P
19 HAL JEFFCOAT-OF
20 DUTCH LEONARD-P
20 DWAIN (LEFTY) SLOAT-P
22 CLARENCE MADDERN-1B
22 HERM REICH-1B/OF (3)
23 DOYLE (PORKY) LADE-P
26 MONK DUBIEL-P
27 BILL SERENA-3B
29 EMIL KUSH-P
30 BOB RUSH-P
31 BOB (MR. CHIPS) CHIPMAN -P
32 DUTCH LEONARD-P
33 GENE (SKIP) MAUCH-INF
34 MORT COOPER-P
35 RALPH (BRUZ) HAMNER-P
36 JIM KIRBY-PH
37 DEWEY ADKINS-P
39 ROY SMALLEY, SR.-SS
40 CHARLIE (JOLLY CHOLLY) GRIMM-MGR1
42 ROY (HARDROCK) JOHNSON-CH
43 HARRY (THE HAT) WALKER-OF (1)
43 HANK SAUER-OF (2)
44 PHIL CAVARRETTA-1B/OF
45 MERV SHEA-CH
47 PEANUTS LOWREY-OF/3B (1)
47 FRANKIE BAUMHOLTZ-OF (2)
48 ANDY (HANDY ANDY) (PRUSCHKA) PAFKO-OF/3B
53 JOHNNY (BEAR TRACKS) SCHMITZ-P

1950

7TH 64-89 26.5GB

2 RANDY (HANDSOME RANSOM) JACKSON-3B
3 FRANKIE (THE FORDHAM FLASH) FRISCH-MGR
4 HAL JEFFCOAT (INJ)-OF
5 BOB RAMAZZOTTI-INF
6 BILL SERENA-3B
7 EMIL (THE ANTELOPE) (DUTCH) VERBAN-UTIL (1)
8 RUBE WALKER-C
9 HANK SAUER-OF/1B
10 BOB SCHEFFING-C (1)
10 RON (ROLLO) NORTHEY-OF (2)
11 CARL (SWATS) SAWATSKI-C
12 MICKEY OWEN-C
16 HANK EDWARDS-OF
16 HARRY CHITI-C
17 BOB RUSH-P
18 WARREN HACKER-P
20 DUTCH LEONARD-P
21 WAYNE (TWIG) TERWILLIGER-2B/UTIL
22 BOB BORKOWSKI-OF/1B
23 DOYLE (PORKY) LADE-P
24 PAUL (LEFTY) MINNER-P
26 MONK DUBIEL-P
29 PRESTON WARD (INJ)-1B
30 FRANK (DUTCH) HILLER-P
32 HARRY CHITI-C
33 ANDY VARGA-P
34 JOHNNY (THE DUTCH MASTER) (DOUBLE NO-HIT) VANDER MEER-P
38 JOHNNY KLIPPSTEIN-P
39 ROY SMALLEY, SR.-SS
41 CARMEN MAURO-OF
42 ROY (HARDROCK) JOHNSON-CH
44 PHIL CAVARRETTA (INJ)-1B/OF
45 FRANK (DUTCH) HILLER-P
47 SPUD DAVIS-CH
48 ANDY (HANDY ANDY) (PRUSCHKA) PAFKO-OF
49 BILL BAKER-CH
53 JOHNNY (BEAR TRACKS) SCHMITZ-P
96 BILL (NINETY-SIX) (BIG BILL) VOISELLE-P

1951

8TH 62-92 34.5GB

2 RANDY (HANDSOME RANSOM) JACKSON-3B
3 FRANKIE (THE FORDHAM FLASH) FRISCH-MGR1
4 HAL JEFFCOAT-OF
5 BOB RAMAZZOTTI-INF
6 BILL SERENA (INJ)-3B
6 FRED (FUZZY) RICHARDS-1B
7 FRANKIE BAUMHOLTZ-OF
8 RUBE WALKER-C (1)
8 BRUCE (BULL) EDWARDS-C/1B (2)
9 HANK SAUER-OF/1B
11 SMOKY BURGESS-C
12 MICKEY OWEN-C
17 BOB RUSH-P
18 WARREN HACKER-P
18 BOB KELLY-P
20 DUTCH LEONARD-P
21 WAYNE (TWIG) TERWILLIGER-2B (1)
21 EDDIE MIKSIS-2B (2)
22 BOB BORKOWSKI-OF
23 ANDY VARGA-P
24 PAUL (LEFTY) MINNER-P
26 MONK DUBIEL-P
27 CAL (BUSTER) MCLISH-P
(29) PRESTON WARD (MIL)-(1B)
30 FRANK (DUTCH) HILLER-P
32 BOB SCHULTZ-P
32 HARRY CHITI-C
33 BOB KELLY-P
35 TURK LOWN-P
36 JOHNNY KLIPPSTEIN-P
37 JACK CUSICK-SS
39 ROY SMALLEY, SR. (INJ)-SS
40 DEE FONDY-1B
40 CHUCK CONNORS-1B
41 CARMEN MAURO-OF
42 ROY (HARDROCK) JOHNSON-CH
44 PHIL CAVARRETTA-1B/MGR2
47 SPUD DAVIS-CH
48 ANDY (HANDY ANDY) (PRUSCHKA) PAFKO-OF (1)
48 GENE HERMANSKI-OF (2)
49 CHARLIE (CHINSKI) ROOT-CH
53 JOHNNY (BEAR TRACKS) SCHMITZ-P (1)
53 JOE HATTEN-P (2)

1952

5TH 77-77 19.5GB

2 RANDY (HANDSOME RANSOM) JACKSON-3B/OF
4 HAL JEFFCOAT-OF
5 BOB RAMAZZOTTI (INJ)-INF
6 BILL SERENA-3B/2B
7 FRANKIE BAUMHOLTZ-OF
8 BRUCE (BULL) EDWARDS-C/2B
9 HANK SAUER-OF
10 BOB SCHULTZ-P
10 RON (ROLLO) NORTHEY-PH
11 TOBY ATWELL-C
12 BOB USHER-PH
12 TOMMY (BUCKSHOT) BROWN-INF (2)
16 BOB ADDIS-OF
17 BOB RUSH-P
18 WARREN HACKER-P
19 JOE HATTEN-P
19 DICK MANVILLE-P
20 DUTCH LEONARD-P
21 EDDIE MIKSIS-2B/SS
22 BOB BORKOWSKI-OF
22 GENE HERMANSKI-OF
24 PAUL (LEFTY) MINNER-P
25 JOHNNY PRAMESA-C
26 MONK DUBIEL-P
(29) PRESTON WARD (MIL)-(1B)
30 WILLIE (THE KNUCK) RAMSDELL-P
30 VERN FEAR-P
32 HARRY CHITI-C
33 BOB KELLY-P
34 BOB SCHULTZ-P
35 TURK LOWN-P
36 JOHNNY KLIPPSTEIN-P
37 VERN FEAR-P
39 ROY SMALLEY, SR.-SS
40 DEE FONDY-1B
41 BUD HARDIN-SS/2B
42 ROY (HARDROCK) JOHNSON-CH
43 LEON BRINKOPF-SS
43 CAL HOWE-P
44 PHIL CAVARRETTA-1B/MGR
47 SPUD DAVIS-CH
49 CHARLIE (CHINSKI) ROOT-CH
53 CAL HOWE-P

1953

7TH 65-89 40GB

2 RANDY (HANDSOME RANSOM) JACKSON-3B
3 RAY BLADES-CH
3 HAL JEFFCOAT-OF
4 HAL JEFFCOAT-OF
4 RALPH KINER-OF (2)
5 BOB RAMAZZOTTI (INJ)-2B
6 BILL SERENA-3B/2B
7 FRANKIE BAUMHOLTZ-OF
8 CLYDE MCCULLOUGH-C
9 HANK SAUER (INJ)-OF
10 DALE (BOB) TALBOT-OF
11 TOBY ATWELL-C (1)
11 JOE GARAGIOLA-C (2)
12 TOMMY (BUCKSHOT) BROWN-SS/OF
14 PAUL SCHRAMKA-OF
14 ERNIE BANKS-SS
15 CARL (SWATS) SAWATSKI-C
16 BOB ADDIS-OF (1)
16 HOWIE POLLET-P (2)
17 BOB RUSH-P
18 WARREN HACKER-P
20 DUTCH LEONARD-P
21 EDDIE MIKSIS-2B/SS
22 GENE HERMANSKI-OF (1)
22 GEORGE (CATFISH) METKOVICH-OF/1B (2)
24 PAUL (LEFTY) MINNER-P
26 SHELDON (AVAILABLE) JONES-P
26 BILL MOISAN-P
28 JIM WILLIS-P
29 PRESTON WARD-OF/1B (1)
29 RAY BLADES-CH
30 DUKE SIMPSON-P
31 FRED (LEFTY) BACZEWSKI-P (1)
33 BOB KELLY-P (1)
33 BUBBA CHURCH-P (2)
34 BOB SCHULTZ-P (1)
35 TURK LOWN-P
36 JOHNNY KLIPPSTEIN-P
36 DON ELSTON-P
37 GENE BAKER-2B
39 ROY SMALLEY, SR.-SS
40 DEE FONDY-1B
42 ROY (HARDROCK) JOHNSON-CH
44 PHIL CAVARRETTA-PH/MGR
47 SPUD DAVIS-CH
49 CHARLIE (CHINSKI) ROOT-CH

1954

7TH 64-90 33GB

1 BILL SERENA-3B/2B
2 RANDY (HANDSOME RANSOM) JACKSON-3B

4 RALPH KINER-OF
5 BRUCE (BULL) EDWARDS-PH
6 STAN (SMILIN' STAN) HACK-MGR
7 FRANKIE BAUMHOLTZ-OF
8 CLYDE MCCULLOUGH (INJ)-C/3B
8 BRUCE (BULL) EDWARDS-PH
9 HANK SAUER-OF
10 DALE (BOB) TALBOT-OF
11 JOE GARAGIOLA-C (1)
12 CHRIS KITSOS-SS
14 ERNIE BANKS-SS
16 HOWIE POLLET-P
17 BOB RUSH-P
18 WARREN HACKER-P
19 HAL JEFFCOATL, SR.-P
20 DUTCH LEONARD-P
21 EDDIE MIKSIS-UTIL
22 JIM DAVIS-P
23 DAVE COLE (INJ)-P
23 BUBBA CHURCH-P
24 PAUL (LEFTY) MINNER-P
25 WALKER (WALK) COOPER-C (2)
27 JIM BROSNAN-P
28 JIM WILLIS-P
28 HAL (HOOT) RICE-OF (2)
30 VERN MORGAN-3B
31 AL LARY-P
33 BILL (MUMBLES) TREMEL-P
34 JOHN PYECHA-P
35 TURK LOWN-P
36 JOHNNY KLIPPSTEIN-P
37 GENE BAKER-2B
38 BOB ZICK-P
39 DAVE COLE (INJ)-P
40 DEE FONDY-1B
41 RAY BLADES-CH
46 BOB SCHEFFING-CH
48 JIM FANNING-C
48 LUIS (CANENA) MARQUEZ-OF (1)
49 STEVE BILKO-1B (2)
52 DON ROBERTSON-OF
55 EL TAPPE-C

1955

6TH 72-81 26GB

1 JIM FANNING-C
2 RANDY (HANDSOME RANSOM) JACKSON-3B
3 GALE WADE-OF
3 OWEN (RED) FRIEND-3B/SS (2)
4 TED TAPPE-OF
5 VERN MORGAN-3B
6 STAN (SMILIN' STAN) HACK-MGR
7 FRANKIE BAUMHOLTZ-OF
8 CLYDE MCCULLOUGH-C
9 HANK SAUER-OF
11 BOB (SPOOK) SPEAKE-OF/1B
14 ERNIE BANKS-SS
16 HOWIE POLLET-P
17 BOB RUSH-P
18 WARREN HACKER-P
19 HAL JEFFCOATL, SR.-P
20 DUTCH LEONARD-P
21 EDDIE MIKSIS-OF/3B
22 JIM DAVIS-P
23 BUBBA CHURCH-P
24 PAUL (LEFTY) MINNER-P
25 WALKER (WALK) COOPER-C
26 BOB THORPE-P
27 SAM (TOOTHPICK SAM) JONES-P
28 LLOYD (CITATION) MERRIMAN-OF (2)
29 JOHN ANDRE-P
30 JIM (DUTCH) BOLGER-OF
31 AL LARY-PR
32 HARRY CHITI-C
33 BILL (MUMBLES) TREMEL-P
35 VICENTE AMOR-P
37 GENE BAKER-2B
40 DEE FONDY-1B
41 RAY BLADES-CH
42 HY COHEN-P
43 HARRY PERKOWSKI-P
45 DON (TIGER) KAISER-P
46 BOB SCHEFFING-CH
46 RAY HAYWORTH-CH
48 JIM KING-OF
53 DAVE HILLMAN-P
55 EL TAPPE-C

1956

8TH 60-94 33GB

1 JIM FANNING-C
2 GALE WADE-OF
3 OWEN (RED) FRIEND-PH
5 FRANK KELLERT-1B
6 STAN (SMILIN' STAN) HACK-MGR
7 DON (TIGER) HOAK-3B
8 CLYDE MCCULLOUGH-C
10 RICHIE MYERS-PH
12 ED WINCENIAK-3B/2B
14 ERNIE BANKS-SS
15 HOBIE LANDRITH-C
15 JOHNNY BRIGGS-P
16 JOHNNY BRIGGS-P
17 BOB RUSH-P
18 WARREN HACKER-P
19 PEPPER (THE WILD HORSE OF THE OSAGE) MARTIN-CH
20 DUTCH LEONARD-CH
21 EDDIE MIKSIS-UTIL
22 JIM DAVIS-P
23 JERRY (SLIM) KINDALL-SS
24 PAUL (LEFTY) MINNER-P
25 JIM HUGHES-P (2)
26 MOE DRABOWSKI-P
27 SAM (TOOTHPICK SAM) JONES-P
30 PETE WHISENANT-OF
31 TURK LOWN-P
32 HARRY CHITI-C
33 BILL (MUMBLES) TREMEL-P
34 RUSS (THE MAD MONK) (MONK) (ROWDY) MEYER (INJ)-P (1)
37 GENE BAKER-2B
39 MONTE IRVIN-OF
40 DEE FONDY-1B
41 RAY BLADES-CH
42 JIM BROSNAN-P
43 WALT (MOOSE) MORYN-OF
45 DON (TIGER) KAISER-P
47 SOLLY DRAKE-OF
48 JIM KING-OF
50 GEORGE PIKTUZIS-P
50 JIM HUGHES-P (2)
53 DAVE HILLMAN-P
55 EL TAPPE-C
57 VITO VALENTINETTI-P

1957

7TH (TIE) 62-92 33GB

1 JIM FANNING-C
2 LEE WALLS-OF/3B (2)
3 JIM (DUTCH) BOLGER-OF/3B
4 JOHNNY GORYL-3B
5 BOBBY DEL GRECO-OF (1)
5 FRANK ERNAGA-OF
6 JACK LITTRELL-INF
7 CASEY WISE-2B/SS
7 BOBBY ADAMS-3B/2B
8 CHARLIE (SWEDE) SILVERA-C
9 BOB (ARCH) LENNON-OF
9 GORDON (MOOSE) (DUKE) MASSA-C
11 BOB (SPOOK) SPEAKE-OF/1B
12 ED WINCENIAK-INF
12 BOBBY MORGAN-2B/3B (2)
14 ERNIE BANKS-SS/3B
15 JACKIE COLLUM-P (1)
15 JIM (WOODY) WOODS-PR
16 BOB (BUTCH) WILL-OF
16 JOHNNY BRIGGS-P
17 BOB RUSH-P
18 DICK (HUMMER) DROTT-P
20 ELMER (SMOKY) SINGLETON (INJ)-P
22 RAY (IRON MAN) MUELLER-CH
23 JERRY (SLIM) KINDALL-INF
25 BOB SCHEFFING-MGR
26 MOE DRABOWSKI-P
27 BOB ANDERSON-P
27 DALE LONG-1B (2)
28 GLEN HOBBIE-P
29 TOM POHOLSKY-P
30 CAL NEEMAN-C
31 TURK LOWN-P
32 BOB ANDERSON-P
33 FREDDIE (FAT FREDDIE) FITZSIMMONS-CH
34 DICK LITTLEFIELD-P
36 DON ELSTON-P (2)
37 GENE BAKER-2B (1)
37 EDDIE HAAS-OF
39 JACK LITTRELL-INF
39 CHUCK TANNER-OF (2)
40 DEE FONDY-1B (1)
40 ED MAYER-P
42 JIM BROSNAN-P
43 WALT (MOOSE) MORYN-OF
45 DON (TIGER) KAISER-P
46 ED MICKELSON-1B
52 GEORGE (MERCURY) (FOGHORN) (STUD) MYATT-CH
53 DAVE HILLMAN-P
57 VITO VALENTINETTI-P (1)

1958

5TH (TIE) 72-82 20GB

2 LEE WALLS-OF
3 JIM (DUTCH) BOLGER-OF
4 JOHNNY GORYL-3B/2B
5 TONY TAYLOR-2B/3B
6 CHUCK TANNER-OF
7 WALT (MOOSE) MORYN-OF
8 DALE LONG-1B/C
9 BOBBY (THE FLYING SCOT) THOMSON-OF/3B
10 EL TAPPE-C
11 CAL NEEMAN-C
12 BOBBY MORGAN- PH
12 DICK (FOOTER) (TREADS) JOHNSON-PH
14 ERNIE BANKS-SS
15 SAMMY TAYLOR-C
16 BOBBY ADAMS-3B/2B
16 BOB (BUTCH) WILL-OF
16 BOBBY ADAMS-INF
17 FRANK ERNAGA-PH
17 AL (BLACKIE) DARK-3B (2)
18 DICK (HUMMER) DROTT-P
19 MOE THACKER-C
19 BILL HENRY-P
19 PAUL SMITH-1B (2)
20 ELMER (SMOKY) SINGLETON (INJ)-P
20 ED MAYER-P
20 MARCELINO SOLIS-P
20 CHARLIE (CHICK) KING-OF
21 DAVE HILLMAN-P
22 GORDON (MOOSE) (DUKE) MASSA-PH
22 FREDDY RODRIGUEZ-P
22 LOU JACKSON-OF
23 JIM BROSNAN-P (1)
23 MOE THACKER-C
23 JOHN BUZHARDT-P
23 JERRY (SLIM) KINDALL-2B
24 GENE (SUDS) FODGE-P
24 BILL (GABE) GABLER-PH
25 BOB SCHEFFING-MGR
26 MOE DRABOWSKI-P
27 DOLAN (NICK) NICHOLS-P
27 JIM MARSHALL-1B/OF (2)
28 GLEN HOBBIE-P
29 TAYLOR (TAY) PHILLIPS-P
30 JOHNNY BRIGGS-P
31 TURK LOWN-P (1)
31 DICK ELLSWORTH-P
32 BOB ANDERSON-P
32 HERSH (BUSTER) FREEMAN-P (2)
33 FREDDIE (FAT FREDDIE) FITZSIMMONS-CH
34 GEORGE (MERCURY) (FOGHORN) (STUD) MYATT-CH
35 ROGERS (RAJAH) HORNSBY-CH
36 DON ELSTON-P
42 ELMER (SMOKY) SINGLETON (INJ)-P
52 GEORGE (MERCURY) (FOGHORN) (STUD) MYATT-CH
53 DAVE HILLMAN-P
57 ROGERS (RAJAH) HORNSBY-CH

1959

5TH (TIE) 74-80 13GB

2 LEE WALLS-OF
4 JOHNNY GORYL-2B/3B
4 BILLY WILLIAMS-OF
5 TONY TAYLOR-2B/SS
6 EARL AVERILL-UTIL
7 WALT (MOOSE) MORYN-OF
8 DALE LONG-1B/
9 BOBBY (THE FLYING SCOT) THOMSON-OF/3B
10 EL TAPPE-CH
11 CAL NEEMAN-C
12 JIM MARSHALL-1B/OF
14 ERNIE BANKS-SS
15 SAMMY TAYLOR-C
16 BOBBY ADAMS-1B
16 RANDY (HANDSOME RANSOM) JACKSON-3B/OF (2)
17 AL (BLACKIE) DARK-3B/INF
18 DON EADDY-3B
20 CHARLIE (CHICK) KING-OF (1)
20 IRV NOREN-OF/1B (2)
21 GEORGE ALTMAN-OF
22 ED DONNELLY-P
25 BOB SCHEFFING-MGR
30 DICK (HUMMER) DROTT-P
31 DAVE HILLMAN-P
32 BOB ANDERSON-P
33 FREDDIE (FAT FREDDIE) FITZSIMMONS-CH
34 GEORGE (MERCURY) (FOGHORN) (STUD) MYATT-CH
35 ROGERS (RAJAH) HORNSBY-CH
36 DON ELSTON-P
37 BILL HENRY-P
38 JOHN BUZHARDT-P
39 MOE DRABOWSKI-P
40 GLEN HOBBIE-P
41 TAYLOR (TAY) PHILLIPS-P (1)
41 ART (CHIC) CECCARELLI-P
41 SETH (MOE) MOREHEAD-P (2)
42 ELMER (SMOKY) SINGLETON-P
42 LOU JACKSON-OF
43 ART (DUTCH) SCHULT-1B/OF
43 BOB (RIVERBOAT) SMITH-P
43 BOB PORTERFIELD-P (2)
45 MORRIE (LEFTY) MARTIN-P
45 BEN JOHNSON-P
46 JOE SCHAFFERNOTH (INJ) P

1960

7TH 60-94 35GB

1 RICHIE (WHITEY) ASHBURN-OF
2 EL TAPPE-C/CH
3 LOU KLEIN-CH
3 HARRY (WILDFIRE) CRAFT-CH
4 CHARLIE (CHINSKI) ROOT-CH
4 VEDIE HIMSL-CH
5 TONY TAYLOR-2B/SS (1)
5 LOU BOUDREAU-MGR2
6 EARL AVERILL-UTIL (1)
6 JIM MCKNIGHT-2B/OF
7 WALT (MOOSE) MORYN-OF (1)
9 DEL RICE-C (1)
9 JIM HEGAN-C
9 DICK BERTELL-C
10 RON SANTO-3B
11 CAL NEEMAN-C (1)
11 ED BOUCHEE-1B (2)
12 DICK GERNERT-1B/OF (1)
12 NELSON MATHEWS-OF
14 ERNIE BANKS-SS
15 SAMMY TAYLOR (INJ)-C
15 RON SANTO-3B
16 JERRY (SLIM) KINDALL-2B/SS
17 DON (POPEYE) ZIMMER-UTIL
18 AL HEIST-OF
19 SAMMY DRAKE-3B/2B
20 IRV NOREN-1B/OF (1)
20 DANNY MURPHY-OF
20 GRADY HATTON-2B
21 GEORGE ALTMAN-OF/1B
22 MOE THACKER-C
23 ART (DUTCH) SCHULT OF/1B
24 LOU (SLICK) JOHNSON-OF
25 FRANK THOMAS UTIL
28 BOB (BUTCH) WILL-OF
30 DICK (HUMMER) DROTT-P
31 JOHN GOETZ-P
31 MARK FREEMAN-P
32 BOB ANDERSON-P
34 DICK BURWELL-P
36 DON ELSTON-P
37 DICK ELLSWORTH-P
38 SETH (MOE) MOREHEAD-P
39 MOE DRABOWSKI-P
40 GLEN HOBBIE-P
41 ART (CHIC) CECCARELLI-P
41 JIM HEGAN-C
41 BILLY WILLIAMS-OF

CHICAGO CUBS

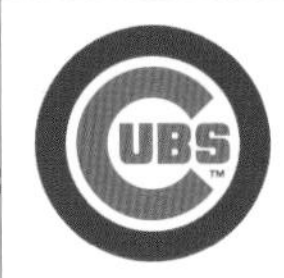

42 LOU BOUDREAU-MGR2
43 ART (DUTCH) SCHULT-OF/1B
43 AL (BULL) SCHROLL-P
43 DON CARDWELL-P (2)
45 BEN JOHNSON-P
45 JIM BREWER-P
45 MEL WRIGHT-P
46 JOE SCHAFFERNOTH-P
50 CHARLIE (JOLLY CHOLLY) GRIMM-MGR1

1961

7TH *64-90* *29GB*

1 RICHIE (WHITEY) ASHBURN-OF
6 DICK BERTELL-C
7 SAMMY TAYLOR-C
8 MOE THACKER-C
8 GEORGE (BUD) FREESE-PH
9 CUNO BARRAGAN (INJ)-C
10 RON SANTO-3B
11 ED BOUCHEE-1B
12 MEL ROACH-1B/2B (2)
14 ERNIE BANKS-SS/UTIL
16 JERRY (SLIM) KINDALL-2B/SS
17 DON (POPEYE) ZIMMER-2B/UTIL
18 ANDRE (ANDY) RODGERS-UTIL
19 SAMMY DRAKE-OF
20 JIM MCANANY-OF
21 GEORGE ALTMAN-OF/1B
22 AL HEIST-OF
23 NELSON MATHEWS-OF
24 LOU BROCK-OF
25 FRANK THOMAS-OF/1B (1)
25 MOE THACKER-C
25 MOE MORHARDT-1B
26 BILLY WILLIAMS-OF
27 DANNY MURPHY-OF
28 BOB (BUTCH) WILL-OF/1B
30 DICK (HUMMER) DROTT-P
32 BOB ANDERSON-P
33 KEN HUBBS-2B
34 DICK BURWELL (MIL)-P
36 DON ELSTON-P
37 DICK ELLSWORTH-P
40 GLEN HOBBIE-P
41 BARNEY SCHULTZ-P
42 JACK CURTIS-P
43 DON CARDWELL-P
45 MEL WRIGHT-P
46 JOE SCHAFFERNOTH-P (1)
48 JIM BREWER-P
50 CHARLIE (JOLLY CHOLLY) GRIMM-CH
51 BOBBY ADAMS-CH
52 EL TAPPE-CH/MGR3
53 HARRY (WILDFIRE) CRAFT-CH/MGR2
54 VEDIE HIMSL-MGR1
55 RIPPER COLLINS-CH
56 RUBE WALKER-CH
57 GOLDIE HOLT-CH
58 FRED MARTIN-CH
59 DICK COLE-CH
60 LOU KLEIN-CH/MGR4

1962

9TH *59-103* *42.5GB*

6 DICK BERTELL-C
7 SAMMY TAYLOR-C (1)
8 MOE THACKER-C
9 CUNO BARRAGAN-C
10 RON SANTO-3B/SS
11 MOE MORHARDT-PH
11 ALEX GRAMMAS-INF (2)
14 ERNIE BANKS-1B/3B
15 JIM MCKNIGHT-UTIL
16 KEN HUBBS-2B
18 ANDRE (ANDY) RODGERS-SS/1B
19 ELDER WHITE-SS/2B
19 DARYL ROBERTSON-SS/3B
20 JIM MCANANY-PH
20 BILLY OTT-OF
21 GEORGE ALTMAN-OF/1B
22 BILLY OTT-OF
22 JIM MCANANY-PH
23 NELSON MATHEWS-OF
23 BOBBY GENE SMITH-OF (2)
24 LOU BROCK-OF
26 BILLY WILLIAMS-OF
27 DANNY MURPHY-OF
27 DON LANDRUM-OF (2)
28 BOB (BUTCH) WILL-OF/1B
30 GEORGE GERBERMAN-P
31 DAVE (JUG) GERARD-P
31 BOB BUHL-P (2)
32 BOB ANDERSON-P
32 JACK WARNER-P
34 CAL KOONCE-P
35 MORRIE STEEVENS--P
36 DON ELSTON-P
37 DICK ELLSWORTH-P
38 JACK WARNER-P
38 JIM BREWER-P
39 TONY BALSAMO-P
39 PAUL TOTH-P (2)
40 GLEN HOBBIE-P
41 BARNEY SCHULTZ-P
42 JACK CURTIS-P (1)
42 FREDDIE BURDETTE-P
43 DON CARDWELL-P
45 DAVE (JUG) GERARD-P
46 AL LARY-P
47 DON PRINCE-P
50 CHARLIE (JOLLY CHOLLY) GRIMM-CH
51 BOBBY ADAMS-CH
52 EL TAPPE-C/CH/MGR1
53 BUCK O'NEIL-CH
54 VEDIE HIMSL-CH
55 RIPPER COLLINS-CH
56 RUBE WALKER-CH
57 GOLDIE HOLT-CH
58 FRED MARTIN-CH
60 LOU KLEIN-CH/MGR2
63 CHARLIE METRO-CH/MGR3

1963

7TH *82-80* *17GB*

5 JIMMIE SCHAFFER-C
6 DICK BERTELL-C
7 MERRITT RANEW-C/1B
9 CUNO BARRAGAN-C
10 RON SANTO-3B
11 ALEX GRAMMAS-SS
12 KEN ASPROMONTE-2B/1B
14 ERNIE BANKS-1B
15 KEN ASPROMONTE-2B/1B
15 LEO BURKE-2B/1B (2)
16 KEN HUBBS-2B
17 STEVE BOROS-1B/OF
18 ANDRE (ANDY) RODGERS-SS
19 ELLIS BURTON-OF (2)
19 JIMMY STEWART-SS/2B
20 BILLY COWAN-OF
21 ELLIS BURTON-OF (2)
23 NELSON MATHEWS-OF
24 LOU BROCK-OF
26 BILLY WILLIAMS-OF
27 DON LANDRUM-OF
28 BOB (BUTCH) WILL-1B
29 JOHN BOCCABELLA-1B
30 DICK LEMAY-P
30 JACK WARNER-P
31 BOB BUHL-P
32 JACK WARNER-P
33 PAUL MUDROCK-P
33 JACK WARNER-P
34 CAL KOONCE-P
36 DON ELSTON-P
37 DICK ELLSWORTH-P
38 JIM BREWER-P
39 PAUL TOTH-P
40 GLEN HOBBIE-P
41 BARNEY SCHULTZ-P (1)
41 TOM BAKER-P
42 FREDDIE BURDETTE-P
43 LINDY MCDANIEL-P
46 LARRY JACKSON-P
50 CHARLIE (JOLLY CHOLLY) GRIMM-CH
51 BOBBY ADAMS-CH
54 VEDIE HIMSL-CH
55 RIPPER COLLINS-CH
56 RUBE WALKER-CH
57 GOLDIE HOLT-CH
58 FRED MARTIN-CH
59 MEL WRIGHT-CH
61 BOB KENNEDY-MGR

1964

8TH *76-86* *17GB*

5 JIMMIE SCHAFFER (INJ)-C
6 DICK BERTELL-C
7 MERRITT RANEW-C (1)
7 RON CAMPBELL-2B
8 VIC ROZNOVSKY-C
10 RON SANTO-3B
11 PAUL POPOVICH-PH
11 DON KESSINGER-SS
12 LEN GABRIELSON-OF/1B (2)
14 ERNIE BANKS-1B
15 LEO BURKE-UTIL
(16) KEN HUBBS (DIED)-(2B)
17 JOEY AMALFITANO-2B/INF
18 ANDRE (ANDY) RODGERS-SS
19 JIMMY STEWART-UTIL
20 BILLY COWAN-OF
21 ELLIS BURTON-OF
22 JOHN BOCCABELLA-1B/OF
24 LOU BROCK-OF (1)
26 BILLY WILLIAMS-OF
27 DON LANDRUM-OF
27 DOUG CLEMENS-OF (2)
28 LEE GREGORY-P
28 BILLY OTT-OF
30 WAYNE SCHURR-P
31 BOB BUHL-P
32 ERNIE BROGLIO-P (2)
33 JACK SPRING-P
33 LEW BURDETTE-P (2)
34 CAL KOONCE-P
34 JACK WARNER-P
36 DON ELSTON-P
37 DICK ELLSWORTH-P
38 JOHN FLAVIN-P
38 DICK SCOTT-P
39 PAUL TOTH-P
39 PAUL (JAKE) JAECKEL-P
40 GLEN HOBBIE-P (1)
40 JACK WARNER-P
40 ERNIE BROGLIO-P (2)
41 STERLING SLAUGHTER-P
42 FREDDIE BURDETTE-P
43 LINDY MCDANIEL-P
45 FRED NORMAN-P
45 BOBBY SHANTZ-P (2)
46 LARRY JACKSON-P
51 BOBBY ADAMS-CH
52 EL TAPPE-CH
53 BUCK O'NEIL-CH
54 VEDIE HIMSL-CH
55 ALEX GRAMMAS-CH
56 RUBE WALKER-CH
57 GOLDIE HOLT-CH
58 FRED MARTIN-CH
59 MEL WRIGHT-CH
60 LOU KLEIN-CH
61 BOB KENNEDY-MGR
62 WALT DIXON-CH
63 GEORGE (BUD) FREESE-CH
64 JOE MACKO-CH

1965

8TH *72-90* *25GB*

6 DICK BERTELL-C (1)
6 ED BAILEY-C/1B (2)
7 ROBERTO (BABY) PENA-SS
7 HARVEY KUENN-OF/1B (2)
8 VIC ROZNOVSKY-C
10 RON SANTO-3B
11 DON KESSINGER-SS
12 LEN GABRIELSON-OF/1B (1)
13 BILL FAUL-P
14 ERNIE BANKS-1B
15 RON CAMPBELL-PH
15 LEO BURKE-C/OF
15 HARVEY KUENN-OF/1B (2)
17 JOEY AMALFITANO-2B/SS
18 GLENN BECKERT-2B
19 JIMMY STEWART-OF/SS
20 DON LANDRUM-OF
21 GEORGE ALTMAN-OF/1B
22 JOHN BOCCABELLA-1B/OF
23 DON YOUNG-OF
24 ELLIS BURTON-OF
25 CHRIS KRUG-C
26 BILLY WILLIAMS-OF
27 DOUG CLEMENS-OF
29 HARRY BRIGHT-PH
29 BYRON BROWNE, OF
30 KEN HOLTZMAN-P
31 BOB BUHL-P
32 ERNIE BROGLIO-P
33 LEW BURDETTE-P (1)
33 BOB HENDLEY-P (2)
34 CAL KOONCE-P
36 BOB HUMPHREYS-P
37 DICK ELLSWORTH-P
39 TED ABERNATHY-P
40 JACK WARNER-P
40 BILLY HOEFT-P
42 CHUCK (TWIGGY) HARTENSTEIN-PR
43 LINDY MCDANIEL-P
46 LARRY JACKSON-P
48 FRANK (THE BEAU) BAUMANN-P
50 WHITEY LOCKMAN-CH
51 BOBBY ADAMS-CH
52 EL TAPPE-CH
53 BUCK O'NEIL-CH
54 STAN (SMILIN' STAN) HACK-CH
55 AL (BLACKIE) DARK-CH
56 RUBE WALKER-CH
57 GOLDIE HOLT-CH
58 FRED MARTIN-CH
59 MEL (CHIEF) HARDER-CH
60 LOU KLEIN-CH/MGR2
61 BOB KENNEDY-MGR1
62 WALT DIXON-CH
63 GEORGE (BUD) FREESE-CH
64 LES PEDEN-CH

1966

10TH *59-103* *36GB*

2 LEO (THE LIP) (LIPPY) DUROCHER-MGR
3 FREDDIE (FAT FREDDIE) FITZSIMMONS-CH
4 RUBE WALKER-CH
5 WHITEY LOCKMAN-CH
7 HARVEY KUENN-OF (1)
7 PETE (PISTOL PETE) REISER-CH
7 JOHN HERRNSTEIN-OF (2)
8 LEE THOMAS-1B/OF (2)
9 RANDY HUNDLEY-C
10 RON SANTO-3B
11 DON KESSINGER-SS
12 JOHN BOCCABELLA (INJ)-UTIL
13 BILL FAUL-P
14 ERNIE BANKS-1B/3B
17 JOEY AMALFITANO-INF
18 GLENN BECKERT-2B/SS
19 JIMMY STEWART-UTIL
20 TY CLINE-OF (1)
20 ADOLFO PHILLIPS-OF (2)
21 GEORGE ALTMAN-OF/1B
22 PAUL POPOVICH-2B
23 RON CAMPBELL-SS/3B
23 CARL WARWICK-OF
25 DON BRYANT-C
25 CHRIS KRUG-C
26 BILLY WILLIAMS-OF
27 BILL HANDS-P
27 BOB (SHORTY) RAUDMAN-OF
28 ROBERTO (BABY) PENA-SS
28 MARTY KEOUGH-OF (2)
29 BYRON BROWNE-OF
30 KEN HOLTZMAN-P
31 BOB BUHL-P (1)
31 FERGUSON (FERGIE) JENKINS-P (2)
32 ERNIE BROGLIO-P
32 RICH NYE-P
33 BOB HENDLEY-P
34 FRANK THOMAS-PH
34 CAL KOONCE-P
36 ROBIN ROBERTS-P (2)
37 DICK ELLSWORTH-P
39 TED ABERNATHY-P (1)
39 CURT SIMMONS-P (2)
40 BILLY HOEFT-P (1)
41 ADOLFO PHILLIPS-OF (2)
41 FRED NORMAN-P
42 CHUCK (TWIGGY) HARTENSTEIN-P
43 DON LEE (INJ)-P
43 WES COVINGTON-OF (1)
45 LEN CHURCH-P
45 BILLY CONNORS-P
45 DAVE DOWLING-P
46 LARRY JACKSON-P (1)
46 DAVE DOWLING-P
47 ARNIE EARLEY-P
47 CHUCK ESTRADA-P
49 BILL HANDS-P
50 ARNIE EARLEY-P
67 BILLY CONNORS-P

1967

3RD *87-74* *14GB*

2 LEO (THE LIP) (LIPPY) DUROCHER-MGR
3 JOE BECKER-CH
4 RUBE WALKER-CH
5 JOEY AMALFITANO-PH/CH
6 JOHNNY STEPHENSON-C
6 DICK BERTELL-C
7 PETE (PISTOL PETE) REISER-CH
8 LEE THOMAS-OF/1B
9 RANDY HUNDLEY-C
10 RON SANTO-3B
11 DON KESSINGER-SS
12 JOHN BOCCABELLA-UTIL
14 ERNIE BANKS-1B
15 NORM GIGON-UTIL
18 GLENN BECKERT-2B
19 JIMMY STEWART-PH (1)
20 ADOLFO PHILLIPS-OF
21 GEORGE ALTMAN-OF/1B
21 AL SPANGLER-OF

21 CLARENCE JONES-OF/1B
22 PAUL POPOVICH-INF
25 JOE CAMPBELL-OF
25 TED SAVAGE-OF/3B (2)
26 BILLY WILLIAMS-OF
27 BOB (SHORTY) RAUDMAN-OF
27 CLARENCE JONES-OF/1B
29 BYRON BROWNE-OF
30 KEN HOLTZMAN (MIL)-P
31 FERGUSON (FERGIE) JENKINS-P
32 RICH NYE-P
33 BOB HENDLEY-P (1)
33 ROB GARDNER-P
33 BOB SHAW-P (2)
34 CAL KOONCE-P (1)
34 JIM ELLIS-P
35 DICK CALMUS-P
36 BILL STONEMAN-P
37 RAY CULP-P
38 RICK JAMES-P
39 CURT SIMMONS-P (1)
40 DON LARSEN-P
40 PETE MIKKELSON-P (2)
41 FRED NORMAN-P
41 ROB GARDNER,-P
42 CHUCK (TWIGGY) HARTENSTEIN-P
43 DICK (THE MONSTER) RADATZ-P (2)
45 DICK CALMUS-P
45 JOHN UPHAM-P
46 DICK (THE MONSTER) RADATZ-P (2)
47 BOB SHAW-P (2)
48 RICK JAMES-P
48 JOE NIEKRO-P
49 BILL HANDS-P
50 BILL STONEMAN-P
51 PETE MIKKELSON-P (2)
52 JIM ELLIS-P

1968

3RD 84-78 13GB

2 LEO (THE LIP) (LIPPY) DUROCHER-MGR
3 JOE BECKER-CH
4 RUBE WALKER-CH
5 JOEY AMALFITANO-CH
6 JOHNNY STEPHENSON-PH
6 RANDY BOBB-C
7 PETE (PISTOL PETE) REISER-CH
8 BILL PLUMMER-C
9 RANDY HUNDLEY-C
10 RON SANTO-3B
11 DON KESSINGER-SS
12 JOHN BOCCABELLA-C/OF
12 GENE OLIVER-UTIL (2)
14 ERNIE BANKS-1B
15 DICK NEN-1B
17 JOSE ARCIA-UTIL
18 GLENN BECKERT-2B
19 LEE ELIA-INF
20 ADOLFO PHILLIPS-OF
21 AL SPANGLER-OF
22 VIC LAROSE-2B/SS
22 BOBBY TIEFENAUER-P
24 JOHN FELSKE-C
24 JIMMY MCMATH-OF
25 TED SAVAGE-OF (1)
25 WILLIE SMITH-OF/1B/P (2)
26 BILLY WILLIAMS-OF
27 PHIL (THE VULTURE) REGAN-P (2)
28 JIM HICKMAN-OF
29 CLARENCE JONES-1B
30 KEN HOLTZMAN-P
31 FERGUSON (FERGIE) JENKINS-P
32 RICH NYE-P
33 GARY ROSS-P
33 RAMON HERNANDEZ-P
34 JOPHERY BROWN-P
36 BILL STONEMAN-P
37 JOHN UPHAM-P/OF
37 FRANK (CRANE) REBERGER-P
38 DARCY FAST-P
38 BOBBY TIEFENAUER-P
39 ARCHIE REYNOLDS-P
40 PETE MIKKELSON-P (1)
40 JACK LAMABE-P
41 LOU (SLICK) JOHNSON-OF (1)
42 CHUCK (TWIGGY) HARTENSTEIN-P
47 JOPHERY BROWN-P
48 JOE NIEKRO-P
49 BILL HANDS-P
54 FRANK (CRANE) REBERGER-P

1969

2ND E 92-70 8GB

2 LEO (THE LIP) (LIPPY) DUROCHER-MGR
3 JOE BECKER-CH
4 RUBE WALKER-CH
5 JOEY AMALFITANO-CH
8 KEN RUDOLPH-C/OF
9 RANDY HUNDLEY-C
10 RON SANTO-3B
11 DON KESSINGER-SS
12 GENE OLIVER-UTIL/CH
14 ERNIE BANKS-1B
15 NATE (PEEWEE) OLIVER-2B (2)
18 GLENN BECKERT (INJ)-2B
19 BILL HEATH-C
19 CHARLEY SMITH-PH
20 ADOLFO PHILLIPS-OF (1)
20 RICK BLADT-OF
20 OSCAR GAMBLE-OF
21 AL SPANGLER-OF
22 PAUL POPOVICH-UTIL (2)
23 MANNY JIMENEZ-OF
23 JIMMIE HALL-OF (3)
25 WILLIE SMITH-OF/1B
26 BILLY WILLIAMS-OF
27 PHIL (THE VULTURE) REGAN-P
28 JIM HICKMAN-OF
29 DON YOUNG-OF
30 KEN HOLTZMAN-P
31 FERGUSON (FERGIE) JENKINS-P
32 RICH NYE-P
33 GARY ROSS-P (1)
34 HANK AGUIRRE-P
36 JOE DECKER-P
37 TED ABERNATHY-P
38 JIM COLBORN-P
38 DON NOTTEBART-P (2)
39 ARCHIE REYNOLDS-P
39 DICK SELMA-P (2)
42 JIM QUALLS (INJ)-OF/2B
43 JOHNNY HAIRSTON-C/OF
45 ALEC DISTASO-P
46 ARCHIE REYNOLDS-P
46 KEN JOHNSON-P (3)
48 JOE NIEKRO-P (1)
48 DON NOTTEBART-P (2)
48 DAVE LEMONDS-P
48 JIM COLBORN-P
49 BILL HANDS-P
50 DICK SELMA-P (2)
50 KEN JOHNSON-P (3)
50 KEN RUDOLPH-C/OF

1970

2ND E 84-75 5GB

2 LEO (THE LIP) (LIPPY) DUROCHER-MGR
3 JOE BECKER-CH
4 RUBE WALKER-CH
5 JOEY AMALFITANO-CH
6 JOHNNY CALLISON-OF
7 PEANUTS LOWREY-CH
8 KEN RUDOLPH-C
8 JOE (PEPI) PEPITONE-OF/1B (2)
9 RANDY HUNDLEY (INJ)-C
10 RON SANTO-3B/OF
11 DON KESSINGER-SS
12 J. C. MARTIN-C/1B
14 ERNIE BANKS (INJ)-1B
15 KEN RUDOLPH-C
16 ROGER METZGER-SS
17 TERRY HUGHES-3B/OF
18 GLENN BECKERT-2B/OF
19 PHIL GAGLIANO-INF (2)
20 BOOTS DAY-OF (1)
20 AL SPANGLER-OF/CH
21 JACK HIATT-C/1B (2)
22 PAUL POPOVICH-INF
23 JIMMIE HALL-OF (1)
23 ADRIAN (PAT) GARRETT-PH
24 CLEO JAMES-OF
25 WILLIE SMITH-1B/OF
26 BILLY WILLIAMS-OF
27 PHIL (THE VULTURE) REGAN-P
28 JIM HICKMAN-OF/1B
29 JOE (PEPI) PEPITONE-OF/1B (2)
29 BROCK DAVIS-OF
29 TOMMY DAVIS-OF (3)
30 KEN HOLTZMAN-P
31 FERGUSON (FERGIE) JENKINS-P
32 JIM COSMAN-P
32 JIMMY DUNEGAN-P
32 MILT (GIMPY) PAPPAS-P (2)
34 HANK AGUIRRE-P
34 JIMMY DUNEGAN-P
35 HOYT WILHELM-P (2)
36 JOE DECKER-P
37 TED ABERNATHY-P (1)
37 HERMAN FRANKS-CH
38 ROE SKIDMORE-PH
39 ARCHIE REYNOLDS-P
39 HOYT WILHELM-P (2)
40 LARRY GURA-P
41 CLEO JAMES-OF
42 JUAN PIZARRO-P
43 ROBERTO RODRIQUEZ-P (3)
45 BOB MILLER-P (3)
46 JUAN PIZARRO-P
46 STEVE BARBER-P (1)
48 JIM COLBORN-P
49 BILL HANDS-P
50 JUAN PIZARRO-P
50 ROBERTO RODRIQUEZ-P (3)

1971

3RD E (TIE) 83-79 14GB

1 MEL WRIGHT-CH
2 LEO (THE LIP) (LIPPY) DUROCHER-MGR
3 AL SPANGLER-PH/CH
4 RUBE WALKER-CH
5 JOEY AMALFITANO-CH
6 JOHNNY CALLISON-OF
7 PEANUTS LOWREY-CH
8 JOE (PEPI) PEPITONE (INJ)-1B/OF
9 RANDY HUNDLEY (INJ)-C
10 RON SANTO-3B/OF
11 DON KESSINGER-SS
12 J. C. MARTIN-C/OF
14 ERNIE BANKS (INJ)-1B
15 KEN RUDOLPH-C
16 GARRY JESTADT-INF3B (1)
16 GENE HISER-OF
18 GLENN BECKERT (INJ)-2B
19 DANNY BREEDEN-C
19 PAT BOURQUE-1B
20 JOSE ORTIZ-OF
21 HECTOR TORRES-SS/2B
22 PAUL POPOVICH-INF
23 RAMON (RAY) WEBSTER-1B
23 CARMEN FANZONE-UTIL
24 CLEO JAMES-OF/3B
25 HAL BREEDEN-OF
25 BILLY NORTH-OF
26 BILLY WILLIAMS-OF
27 PHIL (THE VULTURE) REGAN-P
28 JIM HICKMAN-OF/1B
29 BROCK DAVIS-OF
30 KEN HOLTZMAN-P
31 FERGUSON (FERGIE) JENKINS-P
32 MILT (GIMPY) PAPPAS-P
33 BILL BONHAM-P
36 JOE DECKER-P
37 EARL STEPHENSON-P
38 RON TOMPKINS-P
40 LARRY GURA-P
43 CHRIS CANNIZZARO-C (2)
44 BURT HOOTON-P
45 BOB MILLER-P (1)
45 RAY NEWMAN-P
46 JUAN PIZARRO-P
47 FRANK FERNANDEZ-C (4)
48 JIM COLBORN-P
49 BILL HANDS-P
54 RAY NEWMAN-P

1972

2ND E 85-70 11GB

1 JOSE CARDENAL-OF
2 LEO (THE LIP) (LIPPY) DUROCHER-MGR 1
3 LARRY JANSEN-CH
4 HANK AGUIRRE-CH
5 Q. V. LOWE-CH
6 PETE (PISTOL PETE) REISER-CH
7 RICK MONDAY-OF
8 JOE (PEPI) PEPITONE (RET)-1B
9 RANDY HUNDLEY-C
10 RON SANTO (INJ)-3B/UTIL
11 DON KESSINGER-SS
12 J. C. MARTIN (INJ)-C
14 ERNIE BANKS-CH
15 KEN RUDOLPH-C
16 GENE HISER-OF
16 WHITEY LOCKMAN-MGR2
17 DAVE ROSELLO-SS
17 FRANK COGGINS-PH
18 GLENN BECKERT-2B
19 PAT BOURQUE-1B
20 CHRIS WARD-PH
21 GENE HISER-OF
22 PAUL POPOVICH (ILL)-INF
23 CARMEN FANZONE-UTIL
24 ART SHAMSKY-1B
24 TOMMY DAVIS-1B/OF (1)
24 PETE LACOCK-OF
25 BILLY NORTH-OF
26 BILLY WILLIAMS-OF
27 PHIL (THE VULTURE) REGAN-P (1)
27 JIM TYRONE-OF
28 JIM HICKMAN-1B/OF
29 AL MONTREUIL-2B
30 DAN MCGINN-P
31 FERGUSON (FERGIE) JENKINS-P
32 MILT (GIMPY) PAPPAS-P
33 BILL BONHAM-P
34 CLINT COMPTON-P
36 JOE DECKER-P
36 TOM PHOEBUS-P (2)
37 STEVE HAMILTON-P
37 JOE DECKER-P
38 JACK AKER-P (2)
39 RICK REUSCHEL-P
39 ELLIE HENDRICKS-C (2)
40 LARRY GURA-P
43 RICK REUSCHEL-P
44 BURT HOOTON-P
46 JUAN PIZARRO-P
47 FRANK FERNANDEZ-C
48 RICK REUSCHEL-P
49 BILL HANDS-P

1973

5TH E 77-84 5GB

1 JOSE CARDENAL-OF
2 BOBBY ADAMS-CH
3 LARRY JANSEN-CH
4 HANK AGUIRRE-CH
5 ADRIAN (PAT) GARRETT-OF/C
6 PETE (PISTOL PETE) REISER-CH
7 RICK MONDAY-OF
8 JOE (PEPI) PEPITONE-1B (1)
8 TOM LUNDSTEDT-C
9 RANDY HUNDLEY-C
10 RON SANTO-3B
11 DON KESSINGER-SS
12 ANDRE (ANDY) THORNTON-1B
14 ERNIE BANKS-CH
15 KEN RUDOLPH-C
16 WHITEY LOCKMAN-MGR
17 DAVE ROSELLO-2B/SS
17 DAVE LAROCHE-P
18 GLENN BECKERT (INJ)-2B
19 PAT BOURQUE-1B (1)
19 GONZALO MARQUEZ-1B (2)
21 GENE HISER-OF
22 PAUL POPOVICH-INF
23 CARMEN FANZONE-UTIL
24 CLEO JAMES-OF
25 ADRIAN (PAT) GARRET-OF/C
25 PETE LACOCK-OF
26 BILLY WILLIAMS-OF/1B
27 PETE (PISTOL PETE) REISER-CH
28 JIM HICKMAN-1B/OF
29 CLEO JAMES-OF
29 DAVE ROSELLO-2B/SS
29 MATT ALEXANDER-OF
31 FERGUSON (FERGIE) JENKINS-P
32 MILT (GIMPY) PAPPAS-P
33 BILL BONHAM-P
34 RAY BURRIS-P
35 MIKE PAUL-P (2)
36 BOB LOCKER-P
37 DAVE LAROCHE-P
38 JACK AKER-P
40 LARRY GURA-P
42 MATT ALEXANDER-OF
42 TONY LARUSSA-PR
43 RICO CARTY-OF (2)
44 BURT HOOTON-P
46 JUAN PIZARRO-P (1)
48 RICK REUSCHEL-P

1974

6TH E 66-96 22GB

1 JOSE CARDENAL-OF
2 JIM MARSHALL-CH
3 AL SPANGLER-CH

CHICAGO CUBS

4 VIC HARRIS (INJ)-2B
5 ADRIAN (PAT) GARRETT-UTIL
6 J. C. MARTIN-CH
7 RICK MONDAY-OF
8 DICK STELMASZEK-C
8 TOM LUNDSTEDT-C
9 STEVE SWISHER-C
10 BILLY GRABARKEWITZ-INF (2)
11 DON KESSINGER-SS
12 ANDRE (ANDY) THORNTON-1B/3B
15 GEORGE MITTERWALD-C
16 WHITEY LOCKMAN-MGR1
16 ROB SPERRING-2B/SS
17 DAVE LAROCHE-P
18 BILL (MAD DOG) MADLOCK (INJ)-3B
19 GONZALO MARQUEZ-1B
20 CHRIS WARD-OF/1B
21 GENE HISER-OF
23 CARMEN FANZONE-UTIL
24 JERRY MORALES-OF
25 PETE LACOCK-OF/1B
25 JIM MARSHALL-MGR2
26 BILLY WILLIAMS (INJ)-1B/OF
27 JIM TYRONE-OF/3B
28 RON DUNN-2B/3B
29 DAVE ROSELLO-2B/SS
30 STEVE STONE-P
32 TOM DETTORE-P
33 BILL BONHAM-P
34 RAY BURRIS-P
35 MIKE PAUL-P
36 HORACIO PINA-P (1)
37 HANK AGUIRRE-CH
39 JIM TODD-P
40 HERB HUTSON (INJ)-P
42 MATT ALEXANDER-UTIL
44 BURT HOOTON-P
45 OSCAR ZAMORA-P
46 PETE (PISTOL PETE) REISER-CH
47 KEN FRAILING-P
48 RICK REUSCHEL-P
49 JIM KREMMEL-P

1975

5TH E (TIE) 75-87 17.5GB

1 JOSE CARDENAL-OF
2 JIM SAUL-CH
3 JACK BLOOMFIELD-CH
4 VIC HARRIS-UTIL
5 IRV NOREN-CH
6 TIM HOSLEY-C
7 RICK MONDAY-OF
9 STEVE SWISHER-C
11 DON KESSINGER-SS/3B
12 ANDRE (ANDY) THORNTON (INJ)-1B/3B
15 GEORGE MITTERWALD-C/1B
16 ROB SPERRING-UTIL
17 DAVE ROSELLO-SS
18 BILL (MAD DOG) MADLOCK (INJ)-3B
19 MANNY TRILLO-2B/SS
21 GENE HISER-OF
22 RON DUNN-UTIL
23 PETE LACOCK-1B/OF
24 JERRY MORALES-OF
25 JIM MARSHALL-MGR
27 JIM TYRONE-OF
27 CHAMP SUMMERS-OF
28 ADRIAN (PAT) GARRETT-1B (1)
28 JOE WALLIS-OF
29 DAVE ROSELLO-SS
29 JIM TYRONE-OF
30 STEVE STONE-P
31 DAROLD KNOWLES-P
31 TOM DETTORE-P
32 TOM DETTORE-P
32 DAROLD KNOWLES-P
33 BILL BONHAM-P
34 RAY BURRIS-P
35 GEOFF ZAHN (INJ)-P (2)
35 BUDDY SCHULTZ-P
36 BOB LOCKER-P
37 WILLIE PRALL-P
38 WILLIE PRALL-P
38 GEOFF ZAHN (INJ)-P (2)
39 EDDIE WATT-P
39 TOM DETTORE-P
39 KEN CROSBY-P
40 EDDIE (BUDDY) SOLOMON-P
42 MILT WILCOX-P
43 PAUL REUSCHEL-P
44 BURT HOOTON-P (1)
45 OSCAR ZAMORA (INJ)-P
46 MARV GRISSOM-CH
47 KEN FRAILING-P
48 RICK REUSCHEL-P
49 EDDIE WATT-P
49 DONNIE MOORE-P
50 EDDIE (BUDDY) SOLOMON-P

1976

4TH E 75-87 26GB

1 JOSE CARDENAL-OF
2 JIM SAUL-CH
3 JACK BLOOMFIELD-CH
4 HARRY DUNLOP-CH
5 RANDY HUNDLEY-C
6 TIM HOSLEY-C (1)
7 RICK MONDAY-OF/1B
8 ED PUTNAM-C/1B
9 STEVE SWISHER-C
12 ANDRE (ANDY) THORNTON-1B (1)
12 JERRY TABB-1B
15 GEORGE MITTERWALD-C/1B
16 ROB SPERRING-UTIL
16 MARV GRISSOM-CH
17 DAVE ROSELLO-SS
18 BILL (MAD DOG) MADLOCK (INJ)-3B
19 MANNY TRILLO-2B/SS
20 MICK KELLEHER-SS/INF
21 MIKE ADAMS-UTIL
22 WAYNE TYRONE-UTIL
23 PETE LACOCK-1B/OF
24 JERRY MORALES-OF
25 JIM MARSHALL-MGR
26 LARRY BIITTNER-1B/OF
27 CHAMP SUMMERS-UTIL
28 JOE WALLIS-OF
30 STEVE STONE (INJ)-P
31 TOM DETTORE (REL)-P
31 JOE COLEMAN-P (2)
32 DAROLD KNOWLES-P
33 BILL BONHAM-P
34 RAY BURRIS-P
35 BUDDY SCHULTZ-P
36 RAMON HERNANDEZ-P (2)
38 GEOFF ZAHN-P
39 KEN CROSBY-P
40 MIKE KRUKOW-P
42 BRUCE SUTTER-P
43 PAUL REUSCHEL-P
44 MIKE GARMAN-P
45 OSCAR ZAMORA-P
46 MARV GRISSOM-CH
47 KEN FRAILING-P
48 RICK REUSCHEL-P
50 STEVE RENKO-P (2)
51 JOE COLEMAN-P (2)

1977

4TH E 81-81 20GB

1 JOSE CARDENAL (INJ) OF/INF
2 PEANUTS LOWREY-CH
3 HERMAN FRANKS-MGR
4 RANDY HUNDLEY (RET)-C/CH
5 AL (BLACKIE) DARK-CH (1)
6 BARNEY SCHULTZ-CH
7 BOBBY MURCER-OF/INF
9 STEVE SWISHER-C
10 MIKE SEMBER-2B
11 IVAN DEJESUS-SS
12 BOBBY DARWIN-OF (2)
15 GEORGE MITTERWALD-C/1B
16 STEVE ONTIVEROS-3B
17 DAVE ROSELLO-INF
17 DAVE ROBERTS-P (2)
18 GENE CLINES-OF
19 MANNY TRILLO-2B
20 MICK KELLEHER (INJ)-INF
21 GREG GROSS-OF
22 BILL (BILLY BUCK) BUCKNER (INJ)-1B
23 MIKE GORDON-C
24 JERRY MORALES-OF
26 LARRY BIITTNER-1B/OF/P
27 JOE WALLIS (INJ)-OF
30 MIKE ADAMS-UTIL
31 JIM TODD-P
33 BILL BONHAM-P
34 RAY BURRIS-P
36 RAMON HERNANDEZ-P (1)
38 WILLLIE HERNANDEZ-P
39 MIKE KRUKOW-P
40 PETE BROBERG-P
41 DAVE ROBERTS-P (2)
42 BRUCE SUTTER (INJ)-P
43 PAUL REUSCHEL-P
44 DAVE GIUSTI-P (2)
45 DENNIS LAMP-P
45 JACK BLOOMFIELD-CH
(47) KEN FRAILING (INJ)-(P)
47 DENNIS LAMP-P
48 RICK REUSCHEL-P
49 DONNIE MOORE-P
50 STEVE RENKO (ILL)-P (1)

1978

3RD E 79-83 11GB

1 COOKIE ROJAS-CH
2 PEANUTS LOWREY-CH
3 HERMAN FRANKS-MGR
4 MIKE ROARKE-CH
5 JOEY AMALFITANO-CH
6 LARRY COX (INJ)-C
7 BOBBY MURCER-OF
9 DAVE RADER-C
9 TIM BLACKWELL-C
10 DAVE KINGMAN (INJ)-OF/1B
11 IVAN DEJESUS-SS
12 RUDY MEOLI-2B/3B
15 MIKE SEMBER-3B/SS
16 STEVE ONTIVEROS (INJ)-3B/1B
17 ED PUTNAM-UTIL
18 GENE CLINES-OF
19 MANNY TRILLO-2B
20 MICK KELLEHER-INF
21 GREG GROSS-OF
22 BILL (BILLY BUCK) BUCKNER-1B
23 MIKE GORDON-C
24 HEITY CRUZ-OF/3B (1)
25 SCOT THOMPSON-OF/1B
26 LARRY BIITTNER-1B/OF
27 JOE WALLIS-OF (1)
27 MIKE VAIL-OF/3B (2)
30 KEN HOLTZMAN-P (2)
31 DAVEY JOHNSON-3B (2)
32 RODNEY SCOTT-UTIL
32 JERRY WHITE-OF (2)
34 RAY BURRIS-P
35 WOODIE FRYMAN-P (1)
37 MANNY SEOANE-P
38 WILLLIE HERNANDEZ-P
39 MIKE KRUKOW-P
40 LYNN MCGLOTHEN-P (2)
41 DAVE ROBERTS-P
42 BRUCE SUTTER-P
43 PAUL REUSCHEL (INJ)-P (1)
45 JACK BLOOMFIELD-CH
45 KARL PAGEL-PH
46 DAVE GEISEL-P
47 DENNIS LAMP-P
48 RICK REUSCHEL-P
49 DONNIE MOORE-P

1979

5TH E 80-82 18GB

1 COOKIE ROJAS-CH
2 PEANUTS LOWREY-CH
3 HERMAN FRANKS-MGR1
4 MIKE ROARKE-CH
5 JOEY AMALFITANO-CH/MGR2
6 TED SIZEMORE-2B (1)
7 BOBBY MURCER-OF (1)
7 BRUCE KIMM-C
8 BARRY FOOTE-C
9 TIM BLACKWELL-C
10 DAVE KINGMAN-OF
11 IVAN DEJESUS-SS
12 STEVE MACKO-2B/3B
15 STEVE DILLARD-2B/3B
16 STEVE ONTIVEROS-3B/1B
17 KURT SEIBERT-2B
18 GENE CLINES (RET)-PH/CH
20 MICK KELLEHER-INF
22 BILL (BILLY BUCK) BUCKNER-1B
24 KEN HENDERSON-OF (2)
25 SCOT THOMPSON-OF
26 LARRY BIITTNER-OF/1B
27 MIKE VAIL-OF/3B
28 JERRY MARTIN-OF
29 STEVE DAVIS-2B/3B
30 KEN HOLTZMAN (INJ)-P
32 SAMMY MEJIAS-OF (1)
32 MIGUEL DILONE-OF (2)
33 GEORGE RILEY-P
34 RAY BURRIS-P (1)
35 DOUG CAPILLA-P (2)
36 BILL CAUDILL-P
38 WILLLIE HERNANDEZ-P
39 MIKE KRUKOW-P
40 LYNN MCGLOTHEN-P
41 DICK TIDROW-P (2)
42 BRUCE SUTTER-P
45 KARL PAGEL-PH
46 DAVE GEISEL-P
47 DENNIS LAMP-P
48 RICK REUSCHEL-P
49 DONNIE MOORE-P

1980

6TH E 64-98 27GB

1 COOKIE ROJAS-CH
2 MIKE TYSON-2B
3 GENE CLINES-CH
4 MIKE ROARKE-CH
5 JOEY AMALFITANO-CH/MGR2
6 MIKE O'BERRY-C
7 CLIFF JOHNSON-UTIL (2)
8 BARRY FOOTE (INJ)-C
9 TIM BLACKWELL-C
10 DAVE KINGMAN (INJ)-OF/1B
11 IVAN DEJESUS-SS
12 STEVE MACKO (INJ)-INF
15 STEVE DILLARD-INF
16 STEVE ONTIVEROS (INJ)-3B
16 BILL HAYES-C
17 JESUS FIGUEROA-OF
18 PRESTON GOMEZ-MGR1
20 MICK KELLEHER-INF
21 LENNY RANDLE-3B/UTIL
22 BILL (BILLY BUCK) BUCKNER-1B/OF
23 JIM TRACY-OF/1B
24 KEN HENDERSON (INJ)-OF
25 SCOT THOMPSON (INJ)-OF/1B
26 BILLY WILLIAMS-CH
27 MIKE VAIL-OF
28 JERRY MARTIN-OF
30 CARLOS LEZCANO-OF
33 LARRY BIITTNER-1B/OF
33 LEE SMITH-P
34 RANDY MARTZ-P
35 DOUG CAPILLA-P
36 BILL CAUDILL-P
37 GEORGE RILEY-P
38 WILLLIE HERNANDEZ-P
39 MIKE KRUKOW-P
40 LYNN MCGLOTHEN-P
41 DICK TIDROW-P
42 BRUCE SUTTER-P
45 KARL PAGEL-PH
46 LEE SMITH-P
47 DENNIS LAMP-P
48 RICK REUSCHEL-P

1981

1ST 1/2:6TH E 15-37 17.5GB
2ND 1/2:5TH E 23-28 6GB
FINAL: 38-65 --GB

1 COOKIE ROJAS-CH
2 PEANUTS LOWREY-CH
3 GENE CLINES-CH
4 JACK HIATT-CH
5 JOEY AMALFITANO-MGR
6 LES MOSS-CH
7 JODY DAVIS-C
8 BARRY FOOTE-C (1)
9 TIM BLACKWELL-C
10 LEON (BULL) DURHAM-OF/1B
11 IVAN DEJESUS-SS
(12) STEVE MACKO (ILL)-(INF)
15 STEVE DILLARD-INF
16 BILL HAYES-C
18 MIKE TYSON-2B
19 PAT TABLER-2B
20 JOE STRAIN-2B
20 SCOTT FLETCHER-INF
21 TY WALLER-UTIL
22 BILL (BILLY BUCK) BUCKNER-1B
23 JIM TRACY-OF
24 JERRY MORALES-OF
25 SCOT THOMPSON-OF/1B
25 BOBBY BONDS-OF
26 BILLY WILLIAMS-CH
27 HEITY CRUZ-2B/SS
28 STEVE HENDERSON-OF
29 SCOT THOMPSON-OF/1B
30 CARLOS LEZCANO-OF
32 MEL HALL-OF
33 MIKE LUM-OF/1B (2)
34 RANDY MARTZ-P
35 DOUG CAPILLA-P
36 BILL CAUDILL-P
37 KEN KRAVEC-P
38 WILLLIE HERNANDEZ-P
39 MIKE KRUKOW-P
40 LYNN MCGLOTHEN-P (1)
40 DAVE GEISEL-P
41 DICK TIDROW-P

44 KEN REITZ-3B
45 JAY HOWELL-P
46 LEE SMITH-P
47 GARY (GENE) KRUG-PH
47 DOUG BIRD-P (2)
48 RICK REUSCHEL-P (1)
49 RAWLY EASTWICK (INJ)-P
50 DOUG BIRD-P (2)
50 MIKE GRIFFIN-P (2)

1982

5TH E 73-89 19GB

1 LARRY BOWA-SS
2 JOHN VUKOVICH-CH
3 BILLY CONNORS-CH
4 LEE ELIA-MGR
5 GORDY MACKENZIE-CH
6 KEITH MORELAND-OF/INF
7 JODY DAVIS-C
8 TOM HARMON-CH
9 LARRY COX-C
9 BUTCH BENTON-C
10 LEON (BULL) DURHAM-OF/1B
11 DAN BRIGGS (INJ) OF/1B
15 JUNIOR KENNEDY-INF
17 BUMP WILLS-2B
18 SCOT THOMPSON (INJ)-OF/1B
19 PAT TABLER-3B
20 SCOTT FLETCHER-SS
21 TY WALLER-OF/3B
21 JAY JOHNSTONE-OF (2)
22 BILL (BILLY BUCK) BUCKNER-1B
23 RYNE (RYNO) SANDBERG-3B/2B
23 JIM TRACY-OF
24 JERRY MORALES (INJ)-OF
25 GARY WOODS-OF
26 BILLY WILLIAMS-CH
27 MEL HALL-OF
28 STEVE HENDERSON-OF
29 BOBBY MOLINARO-OF (1)
29 TY WALLER-OF/3B
30 HEITY CRUZ-OF
31 FERGIE JENKINS-P
32 MEL HALL-OF
32 DAN LARSON-P
33 ALLEN RIPLEY-P
34 RANDY MARTZ (INJ)-P
36 MIKE PROLY-P
37 KEN KRAVEC-P
38 WILLLIE HERNANDEZ-P
39 BILL CAMPBELL-P
41 DICK TIDROW-P
43 HERMAN SEGELKE-P
43 RANDY STEIN-P
46 LEE SMITH-P
47 DOUG BIRD-P
48 DICKIE NOLES-P
50 RANDY STEIN-P
50 TOM FILER-P

1983

5TH E 71-91 19GB

1 LARRY BOWA-SS
2 JOHN VUKOVICH-CH
3 BILLY CONNORS-CH
4 LEE ELIA-MGR1
4 CHARLIE FOX-MGR2
5 RUBEN AMARO, SR.-CH
6 KEITH MORELAND-OF/C
7 JODY DAVIS-C
8 DUFFY DYER-CH
9 FRED KOENIG-CH
10 LEON (BULL) DURHAM (INJ)-OF/1B
11 RON CEY-3B
12 CARMELO MARTINEZ-UTIL
15 JUNIOR KENNEDY-INF
15 MIKE DIAZ-C
16 STEVE LAKE-C
17 JAY LOVIGLIO-PH
17 DAN ROHN-2B/SS
18 SCOT THOMPSON-OF/1B
19 DAVE OWEN-SS/3B
20 WAYNE NORDHAGEN-OF
20 THAD BOSLEY-OF
21 JAY JOHNSTONE-OF
22 BILL (BILLY BUCK) BUCKNER-1B/OF
23 RYNE (RYNO) SANDBERG-2B/SS
24 JERRY MORALES-OF
25 GARY WOODS-OF/2B
26 FRITZ (FRITZIE) CONNALLY-3B
27 MEL HALL (INJ)-OF
29 TOM VERYZER-SS/3B
30 CHUCK RAINEY-P
31 FERGIE JENKINS-P
32 CRAIG LEFFERTS-P
33 JOE CARTER-OF
34 STEVE TROUT-P
36 MIKE PROLY-P
37 PAUL MOSKAU-P
37 BILL JOHNSON-P
38 WILLLIE HERNANDEZ-P (1)
38 TOM GRANT-OF
39 BILL CAMPBELL-P
41 WARREN BRUSSTAR-P
42 RICH BORDI-P
43 DON SCHULZE-P
44 DICK RUTHVEN-P (2)
46 LEE SMITH-P
47 RICK REUSCHEL-P (2)
48 DICKIE NOLES (SUB)-P
50 ALAN HARGESHEIMER-P
52 REGGIE PATTERSON-P
60 CRAIG LEFFERTS-P

1984

1ST E 96-65 0GB

L NLCS-SDN 3-2

1 LARRY BOWA-SS
2 JOHN VUKOVICH-CH
3 BILLY CONNORS-CH
4 DON (POPEYE) ZIMMER-CH
5 RUBEN AMARO, SR.-CH
6 KEITH MORELAND-OF/UTIL
7 JODY DAVIS-C
8 JIM FREY-MGR
9 JOHNNY OATES-CH
10 LEON (BULL) DURHAM-1B
11 RON CEY-3B
12 DAVEY LOPES-OF/2B (2)
15 RON HASSEY (INJ)-C/1B (2)
16 STEVE LAKE (ILL)-C
17 DAN ROHN-2B/SS
18 RICHIE HEBNER (INJ)-UTIL
19 DAVE OWEN-INF
20 BOB DERNIER-OF
21 JAY JOHNSTONE-OF
22 BILL (BILLY BUCK) BUCKNER-1B/OF (1)
22 BILLY HATCHER-OF
23 RYNE (RYNO) SANDBERG-2B
24 BILLY HATCHER-OF
24 SCOTT SANDERSON (INJ)-P
25 GARY WOODS-OF/2B
27 MEL HALL-OF (1)
27 THAD BOSLEY-OF
28 HENRY COTTO-OF
29 TOM VERYZER (INJ)-INF
30 CHUCK RAINEY-P (1)
33 PORFI ALTAMIRANO-P
34 STEVE TROUT-P
36 GARY (SARGE) MATTHEWS-OF
37 BILL JOHNSON-P
38 RON MERIDITH-P
39 GEORGE FRAZIER-P (2)
40 DENNIS ECKERSLEY-P (2)
40 RICK SUTCLIFFE-P (2)
41 WARREN BRUSSTAR-P
42 RICH BORDI-P
43 DON SCHULZE-P (1)
43 DENNIS ECKERSLEY-P (2)
44 DICK RUTHVEN (INJ)-P
46 LEE SMITH-P
47 RICK REUSCHEL (INJ)-P
48 DICKIE NOLES-P (1)
48 RICK REUSCHEL (INJ)-P
49 TIM STODDARD-P
52 REGGIE PATTERSON-P

1985

4TH E 77-84 23.5GB

1 LARRY BOWA-SS (1)
2 JOHN VUKOVICH-CH
3 BILLY CONNORS-CH
4 DON (POPEYE) ZIMMER-CH
5 RUBEN AMARO, SR.-CH
6 KEITH MORELAND-OF/UTIL
7 JODY DAVIS-C
8 JIM FREY-MGR
9 JOHNNY OATES-CH
10 LEON (BULL) DURHAM-1B
11 RON CEY-3B
12 SHAWON DUNSTON-SS
12 DAVEY LOPES-UTIL
16 STEVE LAKE-C
18 RICHIE HEBNER-UTIL
19 DAVE OWEN-INF
20 BOB DERNIER (INJ)-OF
21 SCOTT SANDERSON (INJ)-P
22 BILLY HATCHER-OF
23 RYNE (RYNO) SANDBERG-2B/SS
24 BRIAN DAYETT (INJ)-OF
25 GARY WOODS-OF/2B
27 THAD BOSLEY-OF
28 CHRIS SPEIER-INF
30 DARRIN JACKSON-OF
30 CHICO WALKER-OF/2B
31 RAY FONTENOT-P
32 JOHNNY ABREGO-P
32 LARRY GURA-P (2)
34 STEVE TROUT (INJ)-P
35 JON PERLMAN-P
36 GARY (SARGE) MATTHEWS (INJ)-OF
38 RON MERIDITH-P
39 GEORGE FRAZIER-P
40 RICK SUTCLIFFE (INJ)-P
41 WARREN BRUSSTAR-P
42 LARY SORENSEN-P
43 DENNIS ECKERSLEY (INJ)-P
44 DICK RUTHVEN (INJ)-P
45 DAVE GUMPERT (INJ)-P
46 LEE SMITH-P
47 DEREK BOTELHO-P
48 JAY BALLER-P
49 STEVE ENGEL-P
50 DAVE BEARD-P
52 REGGIE PATTERSON-P

1986

5TH E 70-90 37GB

1 DAVE MARTINEZ-OF
2 JOHN VUKOVICH-CH/MGR2
3 BILLY CONNORS-CH
4 DON (POPEYE) ZIMMER-CH
4 GENE (STICK) MICHAEL-MGR3
5 RUBEN AMARO, SR.-CH
6 KEITH MORELAND-OF/UTIL
7 JODY DAVIS-C/1B
8 JIM FREY-MGR1
9 JOHNNY OATES-CH
10 LEON (BULL) DURHAM-1B
11 RON CEY-3B
12 SHAWON DUNSTON-SS
12 DAVEY LOPES-3B/OF (1)
16 STEVE LAKE-C (1)
16 TERRY FRANCONA-OF/1B
18 STEVE CHRISTMAS (INJ)-C/1B
19 MANNY TRILLO-INF
20 BOB DERNIER (INJ)-OF
21 SCOTT SANDERSON-P
22 JERRY MUMPHREY-OF
22 JOHN VUKOVICH-CH
23 RYNE (RYNO) SANDBERG-2B
24 BRIAN DAYETT-OF
25 RAFAEL PALMEIRO-OF
26 BILLY WILLIAMS-CH
27 THAD BOSLEY-OF
28 CHRIS SPEIER-INF
29 CHICO WALKER-OF
31 RAY FONTENOT-P (1)
31 GREG MADDUX-P
33 MATT KEOUGH-P (1)
33 FRANK DIPINO-P
34 STEVE TROUT-P
36 GARY (SARGE) MATTHEWS-OF
37 ED LYNCH-P (2)
39 GEORGE FRAZIER-P (1)
39 RON DAVIS-P (2)
40 RICK SUTCLIFFE-P
41 MIKE MARTIN-C
43 DENNIS ECKERSLEY-P
44 DICK RUTHVEN-P
44 DREW HALL-P
45 DAVE GUMPERT-P
46 LEE SMITH-P
48 JAY BALLER-P
49 JAMIE MOYER-P
50 GUY HOFFMAN-P

1987

6TH E 76-85 18.5GB

1 DAVE MARTINEZ-OF
2 JOHN VUKOVICH-CH
3 HERM STARRETTE-CH
4 GENE (STICK) MICHAEL-MGR1
5 JIM SNYDER-CH
6 KEITH MORELAND-3B/1B
7 JODY DAVIS-C
8 ANDRE DAWSON-OF
9 JOHNNY OATES-CH
10 LEON (BULL) DURHAM-1B
11 JIM SUNDBERG-C
12 SHAWON DUNSTON (INJ)-SS
16 PAUL NOCE-INF
17 MIKE BRUMLEY-SS/2B
18 WADE ROWDON-3B
19 MANNY TRILLO-INF
20 BOB DERNIER-OF
21 SCOTT SANDERSON-P
22 JERRY MUMPHREY-OF
23 RYNE (RYNO) SANDBERG-2B
24 BRIAN DAYETT-OF
25 RAFAEL PALMEIRO-OF/1B
26 BILLY WILLIAMS-CH
28 LUIS QUINONES-INF
29 CHICO WALKER-OF
30 DARRIN JACKSON-OF
31 GREG MADDUX-P
33 FRANK DIPINO-P
34 STEVE TROUT (INJ)-P (1)
34 DAMON BERRYHILL-C
36 GARY (SARGE) MATTHEWS-OF (1)
37 ED LYNCH-P
39 RON DAVIS-P (1)
40 RICK SUTCLIFFE-P
41 MIKE MASON-P (2)
42 BOB TEWKSBURY (INJ)-P (2)
44 DREW HALL-P
46 LEE SMITH-P
47 DICKIE NOLES (INJ)-P (1)
48 JAY BALLER-P
49 JAMIE MOYER-P
50 LES LANCASTER-P
52 FRANK LUCCHESI-MGR2

1988

4TH E 77-85 24GB

1 DAVE MARTINEZ-OF
1 RICK WRONA-C
2 JOE ALTOBELLI-CH
2 VANCE LAW-3B/OF
3 JOSE MARTINEZ-CH
4 DON (POPEYE) ZIMMER-MGR
5 CHUCK COTTIER-CH
6 JOE ALTOBELLI-CH
7 JODY DAVIS-C (1)
8 ANDRE DAWSON-OF
9 DAMON BERRYHILL-C
10 LEON (BULL) DURHAM-1B (1)
11 JIM SUNDBERG-C (1)
12 SHAWON DUNSTON-SS
17 MARK GRACE-1B
18 ANGEL SALAZAR-INF
19 MANNY TRILLO-INF
20 DAVE MEIER-3B
21 SCOTT SANDERSON (INJ)-P
22 JERRY MUMPHREY-OF
23 RYNE (RYNO) SANDBERG-2B
24 GARY VARSHO-OF
25 RAFAEL PALMEIRO-OF/1B
27 ROLANDO ROOMES-OF
28 MARK GRACE-1B
28 MITCH WEBSTER-OF (2)
29 DOUG DASCENZO-OF
30 DARRIN JACKSON-OF
31 GREG MADDUX-P
32 CALVIN SCHIRALDI-P
33 FRANK DIPINO-P
34 DICK POLE-CH
35 LARRY COX-CH
36 MIKE BIELECKI-P
37 PAT PERRY-P (2)
38 MIKE CAPEL,-P
40 RICK SUTCLIFFE-P
41 JEFF PICO-P
42 BOB TEWKSBURY-P
44 DREW HALL-P
45 AL NIPPER (INJ)-P
47 BILL LANDRUM-P
48 MIKE HARKEY-P
49 JAMIE MOYER-P
50 LES LANCASTER (INJ)-P
51 JEFF PICO-P
51 KEVIN BLANKENSHIP-P (2)
54 GOOSE GOSSAGE (INJ)-P

1989

1ST E 93-69 0GB

L NLCS-SFN 4-1

1 RICK WRONA-C
2 VANCE LAW-3B/OF
3 JOSE MARTINEZ-CH
4 DON (POPEYE) ZIMMER-MGR
5 CHUCK COTTIER-CH
6 JOE ALTOBELLI-CH
7 JOE GIRARDI-C
8 ANDRE DAWSON (INJ)-OF
9 DAMON BERRYHILL (INJ)-C
10 LLOYD MCCLENDON-UTIL
11 PHIL STEPHENSON-OF (1)
11 LUIS SALAZAR-3B/OF (2)

CHICAGO CUBS

12 SHAWON DUNSTON-SS
15 DOMINGO RAMOS-SS/3B
16 GREG SMITH-2B/OF
17 MARK GRACE-1B
18 DWIGHT SMITH-OF
19 CURTIS WILKERSON-UTIL
20 JEROME WALTON (INJ)-OF
21 SCOTT SANDERSON-P
23 RYNE (RYNO) SANDBERG-2B
24 GARY VARSHO-OF
25 MARVELL WYNNE-OF (2)
28 MITCH (WILD THING) WILLIAMS-P
29 DOUG DASCENZO-OF
30 DARRIN JACKSON-OF (1)
30 PAUL ASSENMACHER-P (2)
31 GREG MADDUX-P
32 CALVIN SCHIRALDI-P (1)
33 MITCH WEBSTER-OF
34 DICK POLE-CH
35 LARRY COX-CH
36 MIKE BIELECKI-P
37 PAT PERRY (INJ)-P
38 DEAN WILKINS-P
39 PAUL KILGUS-P
40 RICK SUTCLIFFE-P
41 JEFF PICO-P
43 JOE KRAEMER-P
44 STEVE WILSON-P
45 PAUL ASSENMACHER-P (2)
50 LES LANCASTER-P
51 KEVIN BLANKENSHIP-P

1990

4TH E (TIE) 77-85 18GB

1 RICK WRONA-PH
3 JOSE MARTINEZ-CH
4 DON (POPEYE) ZIMMER-MGR
5 CHUCK COTTIER-CH
6 JOE ALTOBELLI-CH
7 JOE GIRARDI-C
8 ANDRE DAWSON-OF
9 DAMON BERRYHILL (INJ)-C
10 LLOYD MCCLENDON-UTIL (1)
11LUIS SALAZAR-3B/OF
12 SHAWON DUNSTON-SS
15 DOMINGO RAMOS-INF
16 GREG SMITH-SS/2B
17 MARK GRACE-1B
18 DWIGHT SMITH-OF
19 CURTIS WILKERSON-UTIL
20 JEROME WALTON (INJ)-OF
22 MIKE HARKEY (INJ)-P
23 RYNE (RYNO) SANDBERG-2B
24 GARY VARSHO-OF
25 MARVELL WYNNE-OF
27 DERRICK MAY-OF
28 MITCH (WILD THING) WILLIAMS (INJ)-P
29 DOUG DASCENZO-OF/P
30 DAVE CLARK-OF
31 GREG MADDUX-P
32 HECTOR VILLANUEVA-C/1B
33 LANCE DICKSON=P
34 DICK POLE-CH
36 MIKE BIELECKI-P
37 BILL LONG-P (2)
38 DEAN WILKINS-P
38 RANDY KRAMER-P (2)
39 JOSE NUNEZ-P
40 RICK SUTCLIFFE (INJ)-P
41 JEFF PICO-P
42 KEVIN COFFMAN-P
43 LANCE DICKSON-P
43 JOE KRAEMER-P
44 STEVE WILSON-P
45 PAUL ASSENMACHER-P
46 DAVE PAVLAS-P
47 SHAWN BOSKIE (INJ)-P
48 PHIL ROOF-CH
50 LES LANCASTER-P
51 KEVIN BLANKENSHIP-P

1991

4TH E 77-83 20GB

1 ERIK PAPPAS-C
1 DOUG STRANGE-3B
2 RICK WILKINS-C
3 JOSE MARTINEZ-CH
4 DON (POPEYE) ZIMMER-MGR1
5 CHUCK COTTIER-CH
6 JOE ALTOBELLI-CH
7 JOE GIRARDI (INJ)-C
8 ANDRE DAWSON-OF
9 DAMON BERRYHILL-C (1)
10 LUIS SALAZAR-3B/UTIL
11 GEORGE BELL-OF
12 SHAWON DUNSTON-SS
15 REY SANCHEZ-SS/2B
16 JOSE VIZCAINO-INF
17 MARK GRACE-1B
18 DWIGHT SMITH-OF
19 HECTOR VILLANUEVA-C/1B
20 JEROME WALTON-OF
22 MIKE HARKEY (INJ)-P
23 RYNE (RYNO) SANDBERG-
24 CHICO WALKER-UTIL
25 GARY SCOTT-3B
27 DERRICK MAY-OF
28 CED LANDRUM-OF
29 DOUG DASCENZO-OF/P
30 BOB SCANLAN-P
31 GREG MADDUX-P
32 DANNY JACKSON (INJ)-P
33 YORKIS PEREZ-P
34 DICK POLE-CH
35 CHUCK MCELROY-P
36 MIKE BIELECKI-P (1)
37 ERIK PAPPAS-C
38 BILLY CONNORS-CH
39 LADDIE RENFROE-P
39 SCOTT MAY-P
40 RICK SUTCLIFFE (INJ)-P
41 JIM ESSIAN-MGR3
42 DAVE SMITH (INJ)-P
44 STEVE WILSON-P (1)
45 PAUL ASSENMACHER-P
46 DAVE PAVLAS-P
47 SHAWN BOSKIE-P
48 PHIL ROOF-CH
49 FRANK CASTILLO-P
50 LES LANCASTER-P
51 HEATHCLIFF (HEATH) SLOCUMB-P

1992

4TH E 78-84 18GB

1 DOUG STRANGE-3B/2B
2 RICK WILKINS-C
3 JOSE MARTINEZ-CH
4 BILLY CONNORS-CH
5 JIM LEFEBVRE-MGR
6 REY SANCHEZ-SS/2B
7 JOE GIRARDI (INJ)-C
8 ANDRE DAWSON-OF
10 LUIS SALAZAR-UTIL
11 JEFF KUNKEL-UTIL
12 SHAWON DUNSTON (INJ)-SS
15 CHUCK COTTIER-CH
16 JOSE VIZCAINO-INF
17 MARK GRACE-1B
18 DWIGHT SMITH-OF
19 HECTOR VILLANUEVA-C/1B
20 JEROME WALTON-OF
21 ALEX ARIAS-SS
21 SAMMY SOSA-OF
22 MIKE HARKEY (INJ)-P
23 RYNE (RYNO) SANDBERG-2B
24 CHICO WALKER-UTIL (1)
24 STEVE BUECHELE-3B/2B (2)
25 GARY SCOTT-3B/SS
26 BILLY WILLIAMS-CH
27 DERRICK MAY-OF
28 KAL DANIELS-OF (2)
29 DOUG DASCENZO-OF
30 BOB SCANLAN-P
31 GREG MADDUX-P
32 DANNY JACKSON (INJ)-P
32 JESSIE HOLLINS-P
34 KEN PATTERSON-P
35 CHUCK MCELROY-P
36 MIKE MORGAN-P
38 JEFF ROBINSON-P
39 FERNANDO RAMSEY-OF
41 TOM TREBELHORN-CH
42 DAVE SMITH (INJ)-P
44 JEFF HARTSOCK-P
45 PAUL ASSENMACHER-P
46 SAMMY ELLIS-CH
47 SHAWN BOSKIE-P
48 DENNIS RASMUSSEN-P (1)
49 FRANK CASTILLO-
50 ALEX ARIAS-SS
51 HEATHCLIFF (HEATH) SLOCUMB-P
52 JIM BULLINGER-P
53 GEORGE PEDRE-C

1993

4TH E 84-78 13GB

1 TOMMY SHIELDS-UTIL
2 RICK WILKINS-C
3 JOSE MARTINEZ-CH
4 BILLY CONNORS-CH
5 JIM LEFEBVRE-MGR1
6 WILLIE WILSON-OF
9 MATT WALBECK-C
10 STEVE LAKE-C
11 REY SANCHEZ-SS
12 SHAWON DUNSTON (INJ)-SS
13 TURK WENDELL-P
15 CHUCK COTTIER-CH
16 JOSE VIZCAINO-INF
17 MARK GRACE-1B
18 DWIGHT SMITH (INJ)-OF
19 KEVIN ROBERSON-OF
20 ERIC YELDING-UTIL
21 SAMMY SOSA-OF
22 MIKE HARKEY (INJ)-P
23 RYNE (RYNO) SANDBERG-2B
24 STEVE BUECHELE-3B/1B
25 CANDY MALDONATO-OF (1)
25 KARL (TUFFY) RHODES-OF (2)
26 BILLY WILLIAMS-CH
27 DERRICK MAY-OF
28 RANDY MYERS-P
29 JOSE GUZMAN-P
30 BOB SCANLAN-P
32 DAN PLESAC-P
34 GLENALLEN HILL-OF (2)
35 CHUCK MCELROY-P
36 MIKE MORGAN-P
37 GREG HIBBARD-P
38 JOSE BAUTISTA-P
39 EDDIE ZAMBRANO-OF/1B
40 TONY MUSER-CH
41 TOM TREBELHORN-CH
42 GLENALLEN HILL-OF (2)
44 BILL BRENNAN-P
45 PAUL ASSENMACHER-P (1)
46 STEVE TRACHSEL-P
47 SHAWN BOSKIE-P
49 FRANK CASTILLO-P
51 HEATHCLIFF (HEATH) SLOCUMB-P (1)
52 JIM BULLINGER-P
53 DOUG JENNINGS-1B
JESSIE HOLLINS (INJ)-(P)

1994

5TH C 49-64 16.5GB
STRIKE NO POST-SEASON

2 RICK WILKINS-C
3 JOSE MARTINEZ-CH
4 GLENALLEN HILL-OF
5 CHUCK COTTIER-CH
6 WILLIE WILSON (INJ/REL)-OF
7 MIKE MAKSUDIAN-1B
8 MARK PARENT-C
11 REY SANCHEZ-SS
12 SHAWON DUNSTON-SS
13 TURK WENDELL-P
16 ANTHONY YOUNG (INJ)-P
17 MARK GRACE-1B
18 JOSE HERNANDEZ-3B
19 KEVIN ROBERSON (INJ)-OF
20 TODD HANEY-2B
21 SAMMY SOSA-OF
22 EDDIE ZAMBRANO-1B
23 RYNE (RYNO) SANDBERG-2B
24 STEVE BUECHELE-3B/1B
25 KARL (TUFFY) RHODES-OF
26 BILLY WILLIAMS-CH
27 DERRICK MAY-OF
28 RANDY MYERS-P
29 JOSE GUZMAN (INJ)-P
31 KEVIN FOSTER-P
32 CHUCK CRIM-P
35 WILLIE BANKS-P
36 MIKE MORGAN (INJ)-P
37 DAN PLESAC-P
38 JOSE BAUTISTA (INJ)-P
40 TONY MUSER-CH
41 TOM TREBELHORN-MGR
42 MOE DRABOWSKI-CH
43 MARV FOLEY-CH
45 RANDY VERES-P
46 STEVE TRACHSEL (INJ)-P
47 SHAWN BOSKIE-P (1)
47 DONN PALL-P (2)
(49) FRANK CASTILLO (INJ)-(P)
51 BLAISE ILSLEY (INJ)-P
52 JIM BULLINGER-P
53 DAVE OTTO-P

1995

3RD C 73-71 12GB
144 GAME SEASON

2 RICK WILKINS-C
3 MAX OLIVERAS-CH
5 JIM RIGGLEMAN-MGR
6 MIKE HUBBARD-C
7 JOE KMAK-C
8 TODD PRATT-C
8 MARK PARENT-C (2)
9 SCOTT SERVAIS-C (2)
10 SCOTT BULLETT-OF
11 REY SANCHEZ-2B
12 SHAWON DUNSTON-SS
13 TURK WENDELL-P
15 MATT FRANCO-INF
16 ANTHONY YOUNG-P
17 MARK GRACE-1B
18 JOSE HERNANDEZ-3B
19 KEVIN ROBERSON (INJ)-OF
20 HOWARD (HOJO JOHNSON-3B
21 SAMMY SOSA-OF
23 RYNE (RYNO) SANDBERG (RET)-2B
24 STEVE BUECHELE-3B (1)
24 TODD HANEY-2B/3B
25 KARL (TUFFY) RHODES-OF (1)
25 LUIS (GONZO) GONZALES-OF (2)
26 BILLY WILLIAMS-CH
27 WILLIE BANKS-P (1)
27 TODD ZEILE-1B/3B (2)
28 RANDY MYERS-P
(29) JOSE GUZMAN (INJ)-(P)
30 OZZIE TIMMONS-OF
31 FERGIE JENKINS-CH
32 KEVIN FOSTER-P
33 TOM EDENS-P
34 TANYON STURTZE-P
36 MIKE MORGAN-P (1)
36 DAVID SWARTZBAUGH-P
38 JAIME NAVARRO-P
39 MIKE C. WALKER-P
40 TONY MUSER-CH
41 BRYAN HICKERSON-P (1)
41 ROBERTO RIVERA-P
42 DAN RADISON-CH
43 DAVE BIALAS-CH
46 STEVE TRACHSEL-P
47 MIKE PEREZ-P
49 FRANK CASTILLO-P
51 TERRY ADAMS-P
52 JIM BULLINGER-P
53 CHRIS NABHOLZ (INJ)-P
55 LARRY CASIAN-P
56 BRIAN MCRAE-OF
57 RICH GARCES-P (1)

1996

4TH C 76-86 12GB

1 DOUG GLANVILLE-OF
2 FELIX FERMIN (REL)-2B
3 MAX OLIVERAS-CH
4 BRIAN DORSETT-C
5 JIM RIGGLEMAN-MGR
6 MIKE HUBBARD-C
7 TYLER HOUSTON-1B (2)
9 SCOTT SERVAIS-C
10 SCOTT BULLETT (INJ)-OF
11 REY SANCHEZ (INJ)-SS
12 LEO GOMEZ-3B
13 TURK WENDELL-P
15 TERRY SHUMPERT (INJ)-3B
16 DAVE MAGADAN (INJ)-INF
17 MARK GRACE (INJ)-1B
18 JOSE HERNANDEZ-3B
19 BROOKS KIESCHNICK-OF
20 BRET BARBERIE-2B
21 SAMMY SOSA (INJ)-OF
23 RYNE (RYNO) SANDBERG -2B
24 TODD HANEY-2B
25 LUIS (GONZO) GONZALES-OF
26 BILLY WILLIAMS-CH
27 DOUG JONES (WAIV)-P (1)
28 PEDRO VALDES-OF
29 JOSE GUZMAN (INJ)(WAIV)-P (1)
30 OZZIE TIMMONS-OF
31 FERGIE JENKINS-CH
32 KEVIN FOSTER-P
33 MIKE CAMPBELL (INJ)-P
34 TANYON STURTZE-P
35 BOB PATTERSON-P
36 DAVID SWARTZBAUGH-P
37 BRANT BROWN-1B
38 JAIME NAVARRO-P
39 ROBIN JENNINGS-PH
40 TONY MUSER-CH
42 DAN RADISON-CH
43 DAVE BIALAS-CH
44 AMAURY TELEMACO (INJ)-P
45 KENT BOTTENFIELD-P
46 STEVE TRACHSEL (INJ)-P

47 MIKE PEREZ-P
49 FRANK CASTILLO-P
51 TERRY ADAMS-P
52 JIM BULLINGER-P
55 LARRY CASIAN-P
56 BRIAN MCRAE-OF
59 RODNEY MYERS-P

1997
5TH C 68-94 16GB
1 DOUG GLANVILLE-OF
1 LANCE JOHNSON-OF (2)
2 MAKO OLIVERAS-CH
3 DAN RADISON-CH
5 JIM RIGGLEMAN-MGR
6 MIKE HUBBARD-C
7 TYLER HOUSTON (INJ)-C
8 DOUG GLANVILLE-OF
9 SCOTT SERVAIS-C
10 TERRELL LOWERY-PH
11 REY SANCHEZ (INJ)-SS/2B (1)
12 SHAWON DUNSTON (INJ)-SS (1)
13 TURK WENDELL-P (1)
15 KEVIN ORIE (INJ)-3B
17 MARK GRACE (INJ)-1B
18 JOSE HERNANDEZ-2B/SS/OF
19 BROOKS KIESCHNICK-OF
20 MIGUEL CAIRO-2B/SS
21 SAMMY SOSA-OF
22 DAVE CLARK-OF
23 RYNE (RYNO) SANDBERG-2B
24 MANNY ALEXANDER-SS (2)
25 DAVE HANSEN-3B
26 BILLY WILLIAMS-CH
27 PHIL (THE VULTURE) REGAN-CH
29 ROBIN JENNINGS-OF
31 KEVIN FOSTER (INJ)-P
33 TERRY ADAMS-P
33 RAMON MOREL-P (2)
34 KENT BOTTENFIELD-P
35 BOB PATTERSON-P
36 KEVIN TAPANI (INJ)-P
37 BRANT BROWN-OF/1B
38 DAVID SWARTZBAUGH-P
40 TONY MUSER-CH (1)
40 DAVE STEVENS-P (2)
41 MARC PISCIOTTA-P
42 DAN RADISON-CH
42 *(RET#) JACKIE ROBINSON*
43 DAVE BIALAS-CH
44 AMAURY TELEMACO-P
45 TERRY MULHOLLAND-P (1)
45 KENT BOTTENFIELD-P
46 STEVE TRACHSEL (INJ)-P
47 MIGUEL BATISTA-P
48 MARK CLARK-P (2)
49 FRANK CASTILLO-P (1)
51 MEL ROJAS-P (1)
51 TERRY ADAMS-P
52 RAMON TATIS-P
54 JEREMI GONZALEZ-P
55 LARRY CASIAN (INJ)-P (1)
56 BRIAN MCRAE-OF (1)
59 RODNEY L. MYERS-P

1998
2ND C (WC) 90-73 12.5GB
1 LANCE JOHNSON (INJ)-OF
2 JEFF PENTLAND-CH
3 DAN RADISON-CH
4 JEFF BLAUSER (INJ)-SS
5 JIM RIGGLEMAN-MGR
6 GLENALLEN HILL-OF (2)
7 TYLER HOUSTON (INJ)-C
8 SANDY MARTINEZ-C
8 GARY GAETTI-3B (2)
9 SCOTT SERVAIS-C
10 TERRELL LOWERY-OF
11 JOSE NIEVES-SS
12 MICKEY MORANDINI-2B
15 KEVIN ORIE-3B (1)
15 SANDY MARTINEZ-C
17 MARK GRACE-1B
19 JASON HARDTKE-INF
20 MATT MIESKE-OF
21 SAMMY SOSA-OF
22 DAVE CLARK-OF
24 MANNY ALEXANDER-SS
25 DERRICK WHITE (WAIV)-OF (1)
25 ORLANDO MERCED-1B (3)
26 BILLY WILLIAMS-CH
27 PHIL (THE VULTURE) REGAN-CH
28 PEDRO VALDEZ (INJ)-OF
(29) ROBIN JENNINGS (INJ)-(OF)
30 JEREMI GONZALEZ (INJ)-P
31 KEVIN FOSTER (INJ)-P
33 DON WENGERT-P (2)
34 KERRY WOOD-P
35 BOB PATTERSON (INJ) (WAIV)-P
35 FELIX HEREDIA-P (2)
36 KEVIN TAPANI-P
37 BRANT BROWN (INJ)-OF/1B
38 MIKE MORGAN-P (2)
39 TOM GAMBOA-CH
40 HENRY RODRIGUEZ (INJ)-OF
41 MARC PISCIOTTA-P
42 *(RET#) JACKIE ROBINSON*
43 DAVE BIALAS-CH
44 AMAURY TELEMACO (WAIV)-P (1)
44 TONY FOSSAS (WAIV)-P (2)
44 CHRIS HANEY-P (2)
45 TERRY MULHOLLAND-P
46 STEVE TRACHSEL-P
47 ROD (THE SHOOTER) BECK-P
48 DAVE STEVENS-P
49 KENNIE STEENSTRA-P
49 FELIX HEREDIA-P (2)
50 JASON MAXWELL-INF
51 TERRY ADAMS-P
52 MATT KARCHNER-P (2)
53 KURT MILLER-P
54 MARK CLARK-P
56 JUSTIN SPEIER-P (1)
58 BEN VANRYN-P (1)
59 RODNEY L. MYERS-P

1999
6TH C 67-95 30GB
1 LANCE JOHNSON (INJ)-OF
2 JEFF PENTLAND-CH
3 DAN RADISON-CH
4 JEFF BLAUSER (INJ)-SS
5 JIM RIGGLEMAN-MGR
6 GLENALLEN HILL-OF
7 TYLER HOUSTON-C (1)
7 SHANE ANDREWS-3B (2)
8 GARY GAETTI-3B
9 BENITO SANTIAGO-C
11 JOSE NIEVES-INF
12 MICKEY MORANDINI-2B
15 SANDY MARTINEZ-C
16 JEFF REED-C (2)
17 MARK GRACE-1B
18 JOSE HERNANDEZ-3B/SS (1)
18 COLE LINIAK-INF
19 CURTIS GOODWIN-OF (1)
19 JOSE MOLINA-C
20 CHAD MEYERS-OF
21 SAMMY SOSA-OF
24 MANNY ALEXANDER-SS
26 BILLY WILLIAMS-CH
27 SCOTT SANDERS-P
28 ROOSEVELT BROWN-OF
29 ROBIN JENNINGS (INJ)-OF
30 MARK GUTHRIE-P (2)
31 BRAD WOODALL-P (1)
31 BOBBY AYALA-P (2)
32 JON LIEBER-P
33 DAN SERAFINI-P
33 BRIAN MCNICHOL-P
(34) KERRY WOOD (INJ)-(P)
35 BO PORTER-OF
36 KEVIN TAPANI (INJ)-P
37 DOUG CREEK-P
38 MARTY DEMERRITT-CH
38 RICK AGUILERA (INJ)P (2)
39 TOM GAMBOA-CH
40 HENRY RODRIGUEZ-OF
41 STEVE RAIN-P
42 *(RET#) JACKIE ROBINSON*
43 DAVE BIALAS-CH
44 KYLE FARNSWORTH-P
45 TERRY MULHOLLAND-P (1)
46 STEVE TRACHSEL-P
47 ROD (THE SHOOTER) BECK (INJ)-P (1)
48 MARTY DEMERRITT-CH
49 FELIX HEREDIA-P
51 TERRY ADAMS (INJ)-P
52 MATT KARCHNER (INJ)-P
53 KURT MILLER (INJ)-P
53 MICAH BOWIE-P (2)
54 JEREMI GONZALEZ-P
55 ANDREW LORRAINE-P
56 RAY KING-P
58 RICHIE BARKER-P
59 RODNEY L. MYERS-P

2000
6TH C 65-97 30GB
1 DAVE MARTINEZ-1B (2)
2 JEFF PENTLAND-CH
2 SANDY ALOMAR, SR.-CH
3 GENE GLYNN-CH
4 SANDY ALOMAR, SR.-CH
4 JEFF PENTLAND-CH
5 RENE LACHEMANN-CH
6 GLENALLEN HILL (INJ)-OF (1)
6 ROSS GLOAD-OF
7 ERIC YOUNG-2B
8 JOE GIRARDI-C
9 DAMON BUFORD-OF
11 JOSE NIEVES-INF
12 RICKY GUTIERREZ-INF
14 *(RET#) ERNIE BANKS*
15 JULIO ZULETA-INF
16 JEFF REED-C
17 MARK GRACE-1B
18 COLE LINIAK-INF
19 JOSE MOLINA-C
20 CHAD MEYERS-OF
21 SAMMY SOSA-OF
22 TARRIK BROCK-OF
22 RONDELL WHITE (INJ)-OF
23 *(RET#) RYNE SANDBERG*
24 SHANE ANDREWS (INJ)-INF
25 DON (GROOVE) BAYLOR-MGR
26 BILLY WILLIAMS-CH
27 COREY PATTERSON-OF
28 ROOSEVELT BROWN-OF
29 JEFF HUSON-INF
30 MARK GUTHRIE-P (1)
30 RAUL GONZALEZ-OF
32 JON LIEBER-P
34 KERRY WOOD (INJ)-P
35 DANNY YOUNG-P
35 BRANT BROWN-OF (2)
35 SCOTT DOWNS-P (1)
35 WILL OHMAN-P
36 KEVIN TAPANI-P
37 SCOTT DOWNS-P (1)
37 BRANT BROWN-OF (2)
37 JERRY SPRADLIN-P (2)
38 RICK AGUILERA-P
39 WILLIE GREENE-INF
40 HENRY RODRIGUEZ-OF (1)
40 OSWALDO MAIRENA-P
41 STEVE RAIN-P
42 *(RET#) JACKIE ROBINSON*
44 KYLE FARNSWORTH-P
45 TIM WORRELL-P (2)
46 OSCAR ACOSTA-CH
47 TODD VAN POPPEL-P
48 OSCAR ACOSTA-CH
48 RUBEN QUEVEDO-P
49 FELIX HEREDIA-P
50 PHIL NORTON-P
51 BRIAN WILLIAMS-P (1)
51 GARY MATTHEWS, JR.-OF
52 MATT KARCHNER-P
52 JOEY NATION-P
54 JEREMI GONZALEZ (INJ)-P
55 ANDREW LORRAINE-P (1)
55 JAMIE ARNOLD-P (2)
57 AUGIE OJEDA,INF
58 MIKE MAHONEY, C
59 ISMAEL VALDES (INJ)-P (1)
76 DANIEL GARIBAY-P

2001
3RD C 88-74 5GB
1 AUGIE OJEDA-2B
2 SANDY ALOMAR, SR.-CH
3 GENE GLYNN-CH
4 JEFF PENTLAND-CH
5 RENE LACHEMANN-CH
6 RON COOMER (INJ)-1B
7 ERIC YOUNG-2B
8 OSCAR ACOSTA-CH
9 DAMON BUFORD (WAIV)-OF
9 TODD HUNDLEY (INJ)-C
11 TODD DUNWOODY-OF
11 MICHAEL TUCKER-OF (2)
12 RICKY GUTIERREZ-INF
13 JEFF FASSERO-P
14 *(RET#) ERNIE BANKS*
15 JULIO ZULETA-1B
16 DELINO DESHIELDS-OF (2)
19 GARY MATTHEWS, JR.-OF (1)
20 COREY PATTERSON-OF
21 SAMMY SOSA-OF
22 RONDELL WHITE (INJ)-OF
23 *(RET#) RYNE SANDBERG*
24 MATT STAIRS-1B
24 MICHAEL TUCKER-OF (2)
25 DON (GROOVE) BAYLOR-MGR
26 BILLY WILLIAMS-CH
27 JOE GIRARDI-C
28 ROOSEVELT BROWN-OF
29 ROBERT MACHADO-C
29 FRED MCGRIFF-1B (2)
30 MATT STAIRS-1B
31 MIKE FYHRIE (INJ)-P (1)
32 JON LIEBER-P
33 BILL MUELLER-3B
34 KERRY WOOD-P
35 WILL OHMAN-P
36 KEVIN TAPANI-P
37 SCOTT CHIASSON-P
38 MANNY AYBAR-P
38 CARLOS ZAMBRANO-P
40 MANNY AYBAR-P
40 MIGUEL CAIRO-2B (1)
40 CHAD MEYERS-OF
41 DAVID WEATHERS-P (2)
42 *(RET#) JACKIE ROBINSON*
44 KYLE FARNSWORTH-P
45 TOM (FLASH) GORDON (INJ)-P
46 JASON BERE-P
47 TODD VAN POPPEL-P
48 JOE BOROWSKI-P
49 DAVID WEATHERS-P (2)
50 JULIAN TAVAREZ-P
51 JUAN CRUZ-P
54 RON MAHAY-P
55 COURTNEY DUNCAN (INJ)-P
56 JASON SMITH-SS (1)
72 ROBERT MACHADO-C
94 FELIX HEREDIA-P
99 TODD HUNDLEY-C

2002
5TH C 67-95 30GB
1 AUGIE OJEDA-INF
2 SANDY ALOMAR, SR.-CH
3 GENE GLYNN-CH
3 CHAD HERMANSON-OF (2)
4 JEFF PENTLAND-CH (1)
5 RENE LACHEMANN-CH/MGR2
6 DARREN LEWIS-OF
8 ALEX GONZALEZ-SS
9 TODD HUNDLEY-C
10 BRUCE KIMM-MGR3
11 CHRIS STYNES-2B/3B
12 ANGEL ECHEVARRIA-OF/1B
13 JEFF FASSERO-P (1)
14 *(RET#) ERNIE BANKS*
15 MARIO ENCARNACION-OF
15 KEVIN ORIE-3B
16 DELINO DESHIELDS-2B
17 BOBBY HILL-2B
18 MOISES ALOU-OF
19 HEE SEOP CHOI-1B
20 COREY PATTERSON-OF
21 SAMMY SOSA-OF
22 MARK PRIOR (INJ)-P
23 *(RET#) RYNE SANDBERG*
24 ROOSEVELT BROWN-OF
25 DON (GROOVE) BAYLOR-MGR1
26 *(RET#) BILLY WILLIAMS*
27 JOE GIRARDI-C
28 MARK BELLHORN-2B/INF
29 FRED MCGRIFF-1B
30 MATT CLEMENT-P
31 DONOVAN OSBORNE (INJ)-P
32 JON LIEBER (INJ)-P
33 BILL MUELLER (INJ)-3B (1)
34 KERRY WOOD-P
35 ALAN BENES-P
36 RICK KRANITZ-CH
37 SCOTT CHIASSON-P
38 CARLOS ZAMBRANO (INJ)-P
39 STEVE SMYTH-P
41 JESUS SANCHEZ-P
42 *(RET#) JACKIE ROBINSON*
43 DAVE BIALAS-CH
44 KYLE FARNSWORTH (INJ)-P
45 TOM (FLASH) GORDON (INJ)-P (1)
46 JASON BERE (INJ)-P
47 LARRY ROTHSCHILD-CH
48 JOE BOROWSKI-P
49 WILL CUNNANE-P
51 JUAN CRUZ-P
52 PAT MAHOMES-P
53 FRANCIS BELTRAN-P
54 RON MAHAY-P
55 COURTNEY DUNCAN-P
57 ANTONIO ALFONSECA-P
58 MARK MAHONEY-C
72 ROBERT MACHADO-C/1B (1)

CHICAGO CUBS

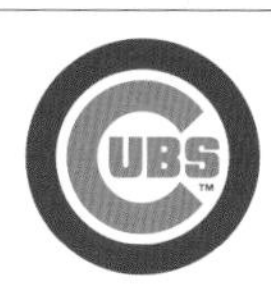

2003

1ST C 88-74 0GB
W NLDS-ATLN 3-2
L NLCS-FLAN 4-3

1 AUGIE OJEDA-SS
1 KENNY LOFTON-OF (2)
2 GENE CLINES-CH
3 WENDELL KIM-CH (2)
4 DOUG GLANVILLE-OF (2)
5 TOM GOODWIN (INJ)-OF
5 TONY WOMACK-2B (3)
6 RAMON MARTINEZ-INF
7 RAMON MARTINEZ-INF
7 KENNY LOFTON-OF (2)
8 ALEX GONZALEZ-SS
9 PAUL BAKO-C
10 *(RET#) RON SANTO*
11 MARK GRUDZIELANEK (INJ) -2B
12 DUSTY BAKER-MGR
(13) WILL OHMAN (INJ)-(P)
14 *(RET#) ERNIE BANKS*
15 JOSE HERNANDEZ-INF (2)
16 ARAMIS RAMIREZ-3B (2)
17 BOBBY HILL-2B (1)
18 MOISES ALOU-OF
19 HEE SEOP CHOI (INJ)-1B
20 COREY PATTERSON (INJ)-OF
21 SAMMY SOSA (INJ) (SUS:5G)-OF
22 MARK PRIOR (INJ)-P
23 *(RET#) RYNE SANDBERG*
24 DAVE KELTON-OF
24 TOM GOODWIN (INJ)-OF
25 TROY O'LEARY-OF
26 *(RET#) BILLY WILLIAMS*
27 DAMIAN MILLER-C
28 MARK BELLHORN-2B/INF (1)
28 DAVE KELTON-OF
29 LENNY HARRIS (WAIV) (REL)-PH/2B (1)
29 JOSH PAUL-C (2)
30 MATT CLEMENT-P
31 MARK GUTHRIE (INJ)-P
32 ERIC KARROS-1B
34 KERRY WOOD-P
35 ALAN BENES-P (1)
35 RANDALL SIMON-1B (2)
36 GARY (SARGE) MATTHEWS-CH
37 MIKE REMLINGER-P
38 CARLOS ZAMBRANO-P
40 TODD WELLEMEYER-P
42 *(RET#) JACKIE ROBINSON*
43 DAVE VERES (INJ)-P
44 KYLE FARNSWORTH (SUS:3G)-P
45 TRENIDAD HUBBARD-OF
46 DICK POLE-CH (2)
47 LARRY ROTHSCHILD-CH
48 JOE BOROWSKI-P
50 PHIL NORTON-P (1)
51 JUAN CRUZ-P
52 SERGIO MITRE-P
55 SHAWN ESTES-P
57 ANTONIO ALFONSECA, (INJ) (SUS:7G)-P
59 JUAN LOPEZ-CH
62 FELIX SANCHEZ-P
(89) SCOTT CHIASSON (INJ)-(P)

2004

3RD C 89-73 16GB

1 JOSE MACIAS (INJ)-UTIL
2 GENE CLINES-CH
3 WENDELL KIM-CH
4 JASON DUBOIS-OF
5 MICHAEL BARRETT-C
5 NOMAR GARCIAPARRA-SS (2)
6 RAMON E. MARTINEZ (INJ)-SS/INF
7 TODD WALKER-2B
8 ALEX GONZALEZ (INJ)-SS (1)
8 NOMAR GARCIAPARRA-SS (2)
8 MICHAEL BARRETT-C
9 PAUL BAKO-C
10 *(RET#) RON SANTO*
11 MARK GRUDZIELANEK (INJ)-2B
12 DUSTY BAKER-MGR
13 REY ORDONEZ-SS
13 NEIFI PEREZ-SS (2)
14 *(RET#) ERNIE BANKS*
16 ARAMIS RAMIREZ-3B
17 CALVIN MURRAY-OF
18 MOISES ALOU-OF
19 DAMIAN JACKSON-SS (1)
19 BRENDAN HARRIS-2B (1)
19 MIKE DIFELICE-C (2)
20 COREY PATTERSON-OF
21 SAMMY SOSA-OF
22 MARK PRIOR (INJ)-P
23 *(RET#) RYNE SANDBERG*
24 TOM GOODWIN-OF
25 DEREK LEE-1B
26 *(RET#) BILLY WILLIAMS*
27 DAVID KELTON-OF
28 TODD HOLLANDSWORTH (INJ)-1B
29 ANDY PRATT-P (1)
29 REY ORDONEZ-SS
29 BEN GRIEVE-OF (2)
30 MATT CLEMENT-P
31 GREG MADDUX-P
32 LA TROY HAWKINS-P
33 RYAN DEMPSTER (INJ)-P
33 GLENDON RUSCH-P
34 KERRY WOOD-P
36 GARY (SARGE) MATTHEWS-CH
37 MIKE REMLINGER (INJ)-P
38 CARLOS ZAMBRANO-P
40 TODD WELLEMEYER-P
41 LARRY ROTHSCHILD-CH
42 *(RET#) JACKIE ROBINSON*
43 MICHAEL WUERTZ-P
44 KYLE FARNSWORTH-P
46 DICK POLE-CH
48 JOE BOROWSKI (INJ)-P
49 JEREMY ANDERSON-P (1)
50 KENT MERCKER-P (1)
51 JON LEICESTER-P
52 SERGIO MITRE-P
53 FRANCIS BELTRAN-P (1)
59 JUAN LOPEZ-CH

2005

4TH C 79-83 21GB

1 JOSE MACIAS-3B/2B
2 GENE CLINES-CH
3 JEROMY BURNITZ-OF
4 JASON DUBOIS-OF (1)
4 BEN GRIEVE-OF
5 MICHAEL BARRETT-C
5 NOMAR GARCIAPARRA (INJ)-SS/3B
7 TODD WALKER (INJ)-2B
8 MICHAEL BARRETT-C
9 HENRY BLANCO-C
9 JODY GERUT-OF (2)
9 SCOTT MCCLAIN-1B/3B
10 *(RET#) RON SANTO*
11 RONNY CEDENO-SS
12 DUSTY BAKER-MGR
13 NEIFI PEREZ-SS
14 *(RET#) ERNIE BANKS*
15 JERRY HAIRSTON (INJ)-UTIL
16 ARAMIS RAMIREZ (INJ)-3B
17 ADAM GREENBERG (INJ)-OF
19 ENRIQUE WILSON-INF
19 MATT MURTON-OF
20 COREY PATTERSON-OF
22 MARK PRIOR (INJ)-P
23 *(RET#) RYNE SANDBERG*
24 HENRY BLANCO-C
25 DEREK LEE-1B
26 *(RET#) BILLY WILLIAMS*
28 TODD HOLLANDSWORTH -OF (1)
29 MIKE FONTENOT-2B
31 GREG MADDUX-P
32 LA TROY HAWKINS-P (1)
32 JEROME WILLIAMS-P (2)
33 GLENDON RUSCH-P
34 KERRY WOOD (INJ)-P
35 CHRIS SPEIER-CH
36 GARY (SARGE) MATTHEWS-CH
37 MIKE REMLINGER (INJ)-P (1)
37 JERMAINE VAN BUREN-P
38 CARLOS ZAMBRANO-P
39 DICK POLE-CH
40 TODD WELLEMEYER-P
41 LARRY ROTHSCHILD-CH
42 *(RET#) JACKIE ROBINSON*
43 MICHAEL WUERTZ-P
44 ROBERTO NOVOA-P
45 BEN GRIEVE-OF
45 WILL OHMAN-P
46 RYAN DEMPSTER-P
47 CHAD FOX (INJ)-P
48 JOE BOROWSKI (INJ)-P (1)
48 SCOTT WILLIAMSON (INJ)-P
49 JOHN KORONKA-P
50 WILL OHMAN-P
50 MATT LAWTON-OF (2)
51 JON LEICESTER-P
52 SERGIO MITRE-P
53 RICH HILL-P
55 RYAN THERIOT-2B
56 CLIFF BARTOSH-P
58 GEOVANY SOTO-C
59 JUAN LOPEZ-CH

Ryne Sandberg broke in with the Phillies in 1981, but only batted .167 in 13 games. They dealt him to the Cubs where he became their franchise player of the '80s and '90s. The Cubs lost both playoff appearances (1984 vs. Padres and 1989 vs. Giants) through no fault of Ryno's who batted .368 and .400 respectively. The 10-time All-Star led the NL in runs three times, HRs once and in 1984 he hit 19 HRs and a league-high 19 triples. He led all second basemen in fielding 4 times. He retired in 1994 and returned to play two more seasons where he tacked on 37 HR, 139 R, 253 H, 54 2B, 156 RBI, and 210 BB.

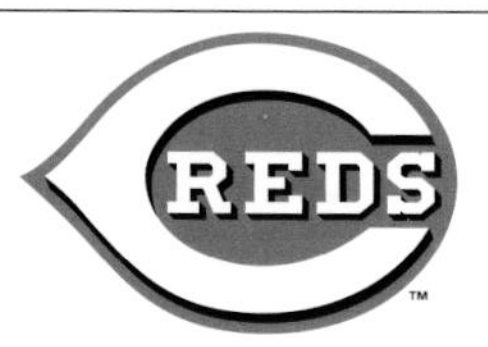

CINCINNATI REDS

It was reported in several sources that the Reds wore numbers on their sleeves as far back as 1883 and again in 1888. If it were the case, they would have been the first professional baseball team to wear numbers.

1932
CINCINNATI REDS
8TH 60-94 30GB

1 GEORGE (BOOTS) GRANTHAM-2B/1B
2 WALLY GILBERT-3B
3 ESTEL (CRABBY) CRABTREE-OF
4 HARVEY (GINK) HENDRICK-1B (2)
5 BABE HERMAN-OF
6 CHICK HAFEY (ILL)-OF
7 ERNIE (SCHNOZZ) (BOCCI) LOMBARDI-C
8 WALLY ROETTGER-OF
9 TAYLOR DOUTHIT-OF
10 LEO (THE LIP) (LIPPY) DUROCHER-SS
11 CLYDE (PETE) MANION-C
12 RED (THE NASHVILLE NARCISSUS) LUCAS-P
14 SI JOHNSON-P
15 RAY (JOCKEY) KOLP-P
16 BENNY FREY-P (2)
17 OWNIE CARROLL-P
18 EPPA (JEPTHA) RIXEY-P
19 LARRY BENTON-P
20 JACK OGDEN-P
21 WHITEY HILCHER-P
22 CASPER ASBJORNSON-C ASBY (NAME CHANGE)-C
23 ANDY (HANDY ANDY) HIGH-3B/2B
24 JO-JO MORRISSEY-UTIL
30 MICKEY (DOC) DOOLAN-CH
31 DAN (HOWLING DAN) (DAPPER DAN) HOWLEY-MGR
33 BOBBY WALLACE-CH
NO# OTTO (SQUEAKY) BLUEGE-PR (1G:4/22)
NO# MICKEY HEATH (ILL)-1B (39G: 4/12-6/5)
NO# CLIFF HEATHCOTE-PH (1) (8G: 4/21-6/6)
NO# HARRY (SLUG) HEILMANN (ILL)-1B (15G: 4/15-5/31)
NO# JIMMY SHEVLIN-1B (7G: 4/27-5/4)
NO# BIFF WYSONG-P (7G: 4/13-5/7)

1933
8TH 58-94 33GB

1 GEORGE (BOOTS) GRANTHAM (INJ)-2B/1B
2 JO-JO MORRISSEY-2B/INF
3 JIM (SUNNY JIM) BOTTOMLEY-1B
4 CHICK HAFEY-OF
5 JOHNNY MOORE-OF
6 ROLLIE HEMSLEY-C (1)
6 JACK CROUCH-C (2)
7 ERNIE (SCHNOZZ) (BOCCI) LOMBARDI-C
8 WALLY ROETTGER-OF
9 HARRY RICE-OF/3B
10 LEO (THE LIP) (LIPPY) DUROCHER-SS (1)
10 SPARKY ADAMS-3B/SS (2)
11 TAYLOR DOUTHIT-PR (1)
11 ALLYN (FISH HOOK) STOUT-P (2)
12 RED (THE NASHVILLE NARCISSUS) LUCAS-P
14 SI JOHNSON-P
15 RAY (JOCKEY) KOLP-P
16 BENNY FREY-P
18 EPPA (JEPTHA) RIXEY-P
19 LARRY BENTON-P
21 PAUL (DUKE) DERRINGER-P (2)
23 ANDY (HANDY ANDY) HIGH-3B/2B
24 CLYDE (PETE) MANION-C
27 BOB SMITH-P (1)
27 TOMMY (TONY) ROBELLO-2B/3B
29 JACK QUINN-P
31 OTTO (SQUEAKY) BLUEGE-SS/INF
34 JEWEL ENS-CH
35 DONIE BUSH-MGR
__ EDDIE HUNTER-3B (1G: 8/5)

1934
8TH 52-99 42GB

1 JIM (SUNNY JIM) BOTTOMLEY-1B
2 TONY PIET-2B/3B
2 TED PETOSKEY-OF
3 MARK KOENIG-3B/INF
4 SPARKY ADAMS-3B/SS
5 JAKE FLOWERS-PH
6 GORDON (OSKIE) SLADE-SS/2B
7 WES SCHULMERICH-OF (2)
8 ADAM COMOROSKY-OF
9 CHICK HAFEY-OF
10 JOHNNY MOORE-OF (1)
10 HARLIN (SAMSON) POOL-OF
10 FRANK (BUCK) MCCORMICK-1B
11 IVEY (CHICK) SHIVER-OF
12 LINC BLAKELY-OF
12 JIMMY SHEVLIN-1B
14 PAUL (DUKE) DERRINGER-P
15 SI JOHNSON-P
16 LARRY BENTON-P
17 DAZZY VANCE-P (1)
18 ALLYN (FISH HOOK) STOUT-P
19 DON BRENNAN-P
19 WHITEY WISTERT-P
20 SYL JOHNSON-P (1)
20 TED KLEINHANS-P (2)
21 RAY (JOCKEY) KOLP-P
22 JOE (LEFTY) SHAUTE-P
22 HARRY (HANK) MCCURDY-1B
23 TOMMY (TONY) ROBELLO-2B/3B
23 TONY FREITAS-P
23 TOMMY (TONY) ROBELLO-2B/3B
24 JIM LINDSEY-P (1)
24 LEE GRISSOM-P
25 CLYDE (PETE) MANION-C
26 BOB O'FARRELL-C/MGR1 (1)
26 CHUCK DRESSEN-MGR3
27 ERNIE (SCHNOZZ) (BOCCI) LOMBARDI-C
28 BENNY FREY-P
29 BURT (BARNEY) SHOTTON-CH/MGR2
30 VAL PICINICH-CH
30 ALEX KAMPOURIS-2B
31 BILL MARSHALL-2B
32 LEE GRISSOM-P
__ JUNIE (LEFTY) BARNES-P (2G: 9/12-30)
__ SHERMAN EDWARDS-P (1G: 9/21)
__ BERYL RICHMOND-P (6G: 9/12-29)

1935
6TH 68-85 31.5GB

1 JIM (SUNNY JIM) BOTTOMLEY-1B
3 ALEX KAMPOURIS-2B/SS
4 BILLY SULLIVAN-INF
5 BILLY MYERS-SS
6 GORDON (OSKIE) SLADE-UTIL
7 CHUCK DRESSEN-MGR
8 TONY PIET-OF (1)
8 KIKI CUYLER-OF (2)
9 LEW RIGGS-3B
10 IVAL (GOODIE) GOODMAN-OF (1)
11 CHICK HAFEY (INJ)-OF
11 TED PETOSKEY-OF
11 BABE HERMAN-OF/1B (2)
12 SAMMY (BABE RUTH'S LEGS) BYRD-OF
14 ADAM COMOROSKY-OF
15 HARLIN (SAMSON) POOL-OF
17 ERNIE (SCHNOZZ) (BOCCI) LOMBARDI-C
18 HANK (POPEYE) ERICKSON-C
18 CALVIN CHAPMAN-SS/2B
19 GILLY CAMPBELL-UTIL
20 LEROY HERRMANN-P
21 SI JOHNSON-P
22 BENNY FREY-P
23 TONY FREITAS-P
24 DANNY (DEACON DANNY) MACFAYDEN-P (1)
24 LES SCARSELLA-1B
25 PAUL (DUKE) DERRINGER-P
25 LEE GAMBLE-OF
26 AL (BOOTS) HOLLINGSWORTH-P
27 GENE SCHOTT-P
28 DON BRENNAN-P
29 BILLY SULLIVAN-INF
29 EMMETT (RAMROD) NELSON-P
30 WHITEY HILCHER-P
31 TOM SHEEHAN-CH
32 LEE GRISSOM-P
33 GEORGE (HIGHPOCKETS) KELLY-CH

1936
5TH 74-80 18GB

1 GILLY CAMPBELL-C/1B
2 ERNIE (SCHNOZZ) (BOCCI) LOMBARDI-C
3 ALEX KAMPOURIS-2B/OF
4 KIKI CUYLER-OF
5 BILLY MYERS-SS
6 BABE HERMAN-OF/1B
7 CHUCK DRESSEN-MGR
8 SAMMY (BABE RUTH'S LEGS) BYRD-OF
9 LEW RIGGS-3B
10 IVAL (GOODIE) GOODMAN-OF
11 LES SCARSELLA-1B
11 GEORGE MCQUINN-OF
12 IVEY WINGO-CH
13 EDDIE (EPPIE) MILLER-SS/2B
14 CALVIN CHAPMAN-UTIL
15 LEE HANDLEY-2B/3B
16 HUB WALKER-OF/UTIL
17 TOMMY THEVENOW-INF
17 EDDIE JOOST-SS/2B
19 AL (BOOTS) HOLLINGSWORTH-P
20 GENE SCHOTT-P
21 LEE STINE-P
22 BENNY FREY-P
24 SI JOHNSON-P (1)
24 WILD BILL HALLAHAN-P (2)
25 PAUL (DUKE) DERRINGER-P
26 TONY FREITAS-P
27 EMMETT (RAMROD) NELSON-P
27 DEE MOORE-P
28 DON BRENNAN-P
29 TOM SHEEHAN-CH
30 GEORGE (HIGHPOCKETS) KELLY-CH
31 EMMETT (RAMROD) NELSON-P
31 WHITEY HILCHER-P
32 LEE GRISSOM-P
32 PEACHES DAVIS-P
35 WHITEY MOORE-P
39 JAKE MOOTY-P

1937
8TH 56-98 40GB

1* DEE MOORE-P*/C
1 GILLY CAMPBELL-C/1B
1 GUS BRITTAIN-C/CH
2 ERNIE (SCHNOZZ) (BOCCI) LOMBARDI-C
3 ALEX KAMPOURIS-2B
4 KIKI CUYLER-OF
5 BILLY MYERS-SS/2B
6 JIMMY OUTLAW-3B
7 CHUCK DRESSEN-MGR1
7 HARRY CHOZEN-C
8 CHARLIE GELBERT-INF (1)
8 KIDDO DAVIS-OF (2)
9 LEW RIGGS-3B/INF
10 IVAL (GOODIE) GOODMAN-OF
11 LES SCARSELLA-1B/OF
12? IVEY WINGO-CH
12 RED BARRETT-P
12 FRANK (BUCK) MCCORMICK-UTIL
14 CHICK HAFEY-OF
15 PHIL (MICKEY) WEINTRAUB-OF (1)
15 HARRY (WILDFIRE) CRAFT-OF
16 HUB WALKER-OF/2B
17 JUMBO BROWN-P (1)
17 DOUBLE JOE DWYER-PH
17 JOE (CROONING JOE) CASCARELLA-P (2)
18 PEACHES DAVIS-P
19 AL (BOOTS) HOLLINGSWORTH-P
20 GENE SCHOTT-P
21 WILD BILL HALLAHAN-P
22 EDDIE JOOST-2B
23 TED KLEINHANS-P
23 WHITEY MOORE-P
24 SPUD DAVIS-C
25 PAUL (DUKE) DERRINGER-P
26 JAKE MOOTY-P
26 ARNIE MOSER-PH
27 JOHNNY (DOUBLE NO-HIT) (DUTCH MASTER) VANDER MEER-P
28 DON BRENNAN-P (1)
28 PAUL (DUTCH) GEHRMAN-P
29 TOM SHEEHAN-CH
29 PINKY JORGENSEN-OF
30 GEORGE (HIGHPOCKETS) KELLY-CH
30 FRANK (BUCK) MCCORMICK-UTIL
31 CHARLIE ENGLISH-3B/2B
31 JOHNNY (DOUBLE NO-HIT) (DUTCH MASTER) VANDER MEER-P
32 LEE GRISSOM-P
33 EDDIE (EPPIE) MILLER-SS/3B
34 BUCK JORDAN-1B (2)
35 GILLY CAMPBELL-C/1B
36 WHITEY MOORE-P
37 DUTCH MELE-OF
38 GUS BRITTAIN-C
39 ? HUGHES-CH
__ BOBBY WALLACE-MGR2 (25G: 9/9-10/3)

1938
4TH 82-68 6GB

35 ERNIE (SCHNOZZ) (BOCCI) LOMBARDI-C
36 SPUD DAVIS-C (1)
37 FRANK (BUCK) MCCORMICK-1B
38 ALEX KAMPOURIS-2B (1)
39 BILLY MYERS-SS/2B
40 LEW RIGGS-3B
41 IVAL (GOODIE) GOODMAN-OF
42 DUSTY COOKE-OF
43 LEE GAMBLE-OF
44 HARRY (WILDFIRE) CRAFT-OF
45 BUCK JORDAN-PH (1)
45 NOLEN RICHARDSON-SS
45 JUSTIN (OTT) STEIN-SS/2B (2)
46 RAY BENGE-P
46 DON LANG-INF
47 LONNY (JUNIOR) FREY-2B/SS
48 KIDDO DAVIS-OF
49 NINO BONGIOVANNI-OF
50 WILLARD (BILL) HERSHBERGER-C/2B
51 JIMMY OUTLAW-PH
51 DON LANG-INF
52 PAUL (DUKE) DERRINGER-P
53 LEE GRISSOM (INJ)-P
54 GENE SCHOTT-P
55 PEACHES DAVIS-P
56 AL (BOOTS) HOLLINGSWORTH-P (1)
56 BUCKY WALTERS-P (2)
57 JOHNNY (DOUBLE NO-HIT) (DUTCH MASTER) VANDER MEER-P
58 JOE (CROONING JOE) CASCARELLA-P
59 TED KLEINHANS-P
59 DICK WEST-PH
60 WHITEY MOORE-P
61 RED BARRETT-P
62 WALLY BERGER-OF (2)
63 JIM (BIG JIM) WEAVER-P (2)
65 BILL (DEACON) MCKECHNIE-MGR
66 HANK GOWDY-CH
67 EDD ROUSH-CH

1939
1ST 97-57 0GB
L WS-NYA 4-0

1 BILL (DEACON) MCKECHNIE-MGR
2 HANK GOWDY-CH
3 JIMMIE (ACE) WILSON-C/CH
4 ERNIE (SCHNOZZ) (BOCCI) LOMBARDI-C
5 WILLARD (BILL) HERSHBERGER-C/2B
10 FRANK (BUCK) MCCORMICK-1B
11 LONNY (JUNIOR) FREY-2B

CINCINNATI REDS

2 BILLY MYERS-SS
4 NOLEN RICHARDSON-SS
4 HANK JOHNSON-P
4 ART JACOBS (INJ)-P
5 LEW RIGGS-3B
6 LES SCARSELLA (INJ)-PH
7 EDDIE JOOST-2B/SS
8 BILL WERBER-3B
9 MILT GALATZER-1B
2 WALLY BERGER-OF
3 HARRY (WILDFIRE) CRAFT-OF
4 IVAL (GOODIE) GOODMAN-OF
5 LEE GAMBLE-OF
6 FRENCHY BORDAGARAY-OF/2B
7 NINO BONGIOVANNI-OF
8 VINCE DIMAGGIO-OF
0 PAUL (DUKE) DERRINGER-P
1 BUCKY WALTERS-P
2 LEE GRISSOM-P
3 JOHNNY (DOUBLE NO-HIT) (DUTCH MASTER) VANDER MEER-P
4 JIM (BIG JIM) WEAVER-P
5 WHITEY MOORE-P
6 BUD HAFEY-OF (1)
6 WES LIVENGOOD-P
6 JOHNNY NIGGELING-P
7 PEACHES DAVIS-P
7 MILT SHOFFNER-P (2)
8 RED BARRETT-P
8 PETE NAKTENIS-P
8 AL (BUCKETFOOT AL) SIMMONS-OF (2)
8 DICK WEST-OF/C
9 JUNIOR THOMPSON-P
1 ELMER RIDDLE-P

1940

1ST 100-53 0GB
W WS-DETA 4-3

1 BILL (DEACON) MCKECHNIE-MGR
2 HANK GOWDY-CH
3 JIMMIE (ACE) WILSON-C/CH
4 ERNIE (SCHNOZZ) (BOCCI) LOMBARDI-C
5 WILLARD (BILL) HERSHBERGER (DIED)-C/2B
5 DICK WEST-C
6 BILL BAKER-C
0 FRANK (BUCK) MCCORMICK-1B
1 LONNY (JUNIOR) FREY-2B
2 BILLY MYERS-SS
5 LEW RIGGS-3B
7 EDDIE JOOST-INF
8 BILL WERBER-3B
0 MIKE MCCORMICK-OF
1 VINCE DIMAGGIO-OF (1)
1 JOHNNY RIZZO-OF (2)
1 MORRIE (MOE) (SNOOKER) ARNOVICH-OF (2)
2 WALLY BERGER-OF (1)
2 MIKE DEJAN-OF
2 JIMMY RIPPLE-OF (2)
3 HARRY (WILDFIRE) CRAFT-OF/1B
4 IVAL (GOODIE) GOODMAN-OF
5 LEE GAMBLE-OF
5 WITT (LEFTY) GUISE-P
0 PAUL (DUKE) DERRINGER-P
1 BUCKY WALTERS-P
3 JOHNNY (DOUBLE NO-HIT) (DUTCH MASTER) VANDER MEER-P
4 JIM (MILKMAN JIM) TURNER-P
35 WHITEY MOORE-P
37 MILT SHOFFNER-P
39 JUNIOR THOMPSON-P
40 JOHNNY HUTCHINGS-P
41 ELMER RIDDLE-P
42 RED BARRETT-P
43 JOE (FIREMAN) BEGGS-P

1941

3RD 88-66 12GB

1 BILL (DEACON) MCKECHNIE-MGR
2 HANK GOWDY-CH
3 JEWEL ENS-CH
4 ERNIE (SCHNOZZ) (BOCCI) LOMBARDI-C
5 DICK WEST-C
6 BILL BAKER-C
7 JOHNNY (MUTT) RIDDLE-C
9 RAY LAMANNO-C
10 FRANK (BUCK) MCCORMICK-1B
11 LONNY (JUNIOR) FREY-2B
12 BENNY ZIENTARA-2B
15 BOBBY MATTICK-INF
16 BENNY ZIENTARA-2B
16 CHUCK ALENO-3B/1B
17 PEP YOUNG-3B (1)
17 EDDIE JOOST-SS/INF
18 BILL WERBER-3B
19 EDDIE SHOKES-PH
19 RAY LAMANNO-C
20 MIKE MCCORMICK-OF
21 JIM (GEE GEE) GLEESON-OF
22 JIMMY RIPPLE-OF
23 HARRY (WILDFIRE) CRAFT-OF/1B
24 IVAL (GOODIE) GOODMAN (ILL)-OF
25 ERNIE (CHIEF) KOY-OF (2)
25 HANK SAUER-OF
26 EDDIE (MONGOOSE) LUKON-OF
27 EDDIE (MONGOOSE) LUKON-OF
27 LLOYD (LITTLE POISON) WANER-OF (3)
29 HANK SAUER-OF
30 PAUL (DUKE) DERRINGER-P
31 BUCKY WALTERS-P
32 MONTE (HOOT) PEARSON-P
33 JOHNNY (DOUBLE NO-HIT) (DUTCH MASTER) VANDER MEER-P
34 JIM (MILKMAN JIM) TURNER (INJ)-P
35 WHITEY MOORE-P
37 RAY (IRON MAN) STARR-P
38 JOHNNY HUTCHINGS-P (1)
39 JUNIOR THOMPSON-P
40 BOB (LEFTY) LOGAN-P
41 ELMER RIDDLE-P
43 JOE (FIREMAN) BEGGS-P

1942

4TH 76-76 29GB

1 BILL (DEACON) MCKECHNIE-MGR
2 HANK GOWDY-CH
3 RAY BLADES-CH
4 AL (MOOSE) LAKEMAN-OF
5 DICK WEST-C/OF
7 ROLLIE HEMSLEY-C (1)
9 RAY LAMANNO-C
10 FRANK (BUCK) MCCORMICK-1B
11 LONNY (JUNIOR) FREY-2B
12 JOE ABREU-3B/2B
15 BOBBY MATTICK-SS
16 CHUCK ALENO-3B/2B
16 DAMON (DEE) PHILLIPS-SS
17 EDDIE JOOST-SS/2B
18 BERT HAAS-3B/UTIL
20 MIKE MCCORMICK (INJ)-OF
21 JIM (GEE GEE) GLEESON-OF
21 MAX MARSHALL-OF
23 HARRY (WILDFIRE) CRAFT-OF
23 ERIC (BLUE DEVIL)(DUKIE) TIPTON-OF
24 IVAL (GOODIE) GOODMAN-OF
25 ERNIE (CHIEF) KOY-PH (1)
27 GEE WALKER-OF
28 FRANKIE KELLEHER-OF
28 HANK SAUER-1B
29 HANK SAUER-1B
29 FRANK SECORY-OF
29 CLYDE VOLLMER-OF
30 PAUL (DUKE) DERRINGER-P
31 BUCKY WALTERS-P
33 JOHNNY (DOUBLE NO-HIT) (DUTCH MASTER) VANDER MEER-P
34 JIM (MILKMAN JIM) TURNER -P (1)
35 WHITEY MOORE-P (1)
35 CLYDE (HARDROCK) SHOUN-P (2)
37 RAY (IRON MAN) STARR-P
39 JUNIOR THOMPSON-P
41 ELMER RIDDLE-P
43 JOE (FIREMAN) BEGGS-P
44 EWELL (THE WHIP) BLACKWELL-P
47 EWELL (THE WHIP) BLACKWELL-P

1943

2ND 87-67 18GB

1 BILL (DEACON) MCKECHNIE-MGR
2 HANS LOBERT-CH
3 ESTEL (CRABBY) CRABTREE-OF
4 AL (MOOSE) LAKEMAN-OF
5 DICK WEST-C/OF
6 TONY DEPHILLIPS-C
7 RAY (IRON MAN) MUELLER-C
10 FRANK (BUCK) MCCORMICK-1B
11 LONNY (JUNIOR) FREY-2B
15 EDDIE (EPPIE) MILLER-SS
16 STEVE MESNER-3B
17 WOODIE WILLIAMS-INF
18 BERT HAAS-UTIL
19 CHARLIE BREWSTER-2B (1)
(20) MIKE MCCORMICK (MIL)-(OF)
20 DAIN (DING-A-LING) (SNIFFY) CLAY-OF
21 MAX MARSHALL-OF
22 FRANKIE KELLEHER-OF
22 LONNIE GOLDSTEIN-1B
23 ERIC (BLUE DEVIL)(DUKIE) TIPTON-OF
27 GEE WALKER-OF
28 CHUCK ALENO-OF
29 JACK NIEMES-P
31 BUCKY WALTERS-P
33 JOHNNY (DOUBLE NO-HIT) (DUTCH MASTER) VANDER MEER-P
34 ED (THE WILD ELK OF THE WASATCH) HEUSSER-P
35 CLYDE (HARDROCK) SHOUN-P
37 RAY (IRON MAN) STARR-P
38 BOB MALLOY-P
39 ROCKY STONE-P
41 ELMER RIDDLE-P
43 JOE (FIREMAN) BEGGS-P

1944

3RD 89-65 16GB

1 BILL (DEACON) MCKECHNIE-MGR
2 HANS LOBERT-CH
3 ESTEL (CRABBY) CRABTREE-OF/1B/CH
4 AL (MOOSE) LAKEMAN-PH
5 JOE JUST-C
6 LEN RICE-C
6 JOHNNY (MUTT) RIDDLE-C
7 RAY (IRON MAN) MUELLER-C
8 JIMMIE (ACE) WILSON-CH
10 FRANK (BUCK) MCCORMICK-1B
11 EDDIE (EPPIE) MILLER-SS
12 KERMIT WAHL-3B
14 CHUCK ALENO-INF
16 STEVE MESNER-3B
17 WOODIE WILLIAMS-INF
18 BUCK FAUSETT-3B/P
20 DAIN (DING-A-LING) (SNIFFY) CLAY-OF
21 MAX MARSHALL (MIL)-OF
21 JO-JO WHITE-OF (2)
22 TONY CRISCOLA-OF
23 ERIC (BLUE DEVIL) (DUKIE) TIPTON-OF
24 CHUCHO RAMOS-OF
26 MIKE KOSMAN-PR
27 GEE WALKER-OF
28 JAKE EISENHARDT-P
29 CLYDE (HARDROCK) SHOUN-P
30 KENT (PETE) PETERSON-P
31 BUCKY WALTERS-P
33 ARNOLD (HOOK) (LEFTY) CARTER-P
34 ED (THE WILD ELK OF THE WASATCH) HEUSSER-P
35 BOB KATZ-P
35 JIM KONSTANTY-P
36 CLYDE (HARDROCK) SHOUN-P
37 HARRY (GUNBOAT) GUMBERT-P (2)
38 BOB MALLOY (MIL)-P
39 BOB FERGUSON (MIL)-P
39 KENT (PETE) PETERSON-P
41 ELMER RIDDLE (INJ)-P
41 HARRY (GUNBOAT) GUMBERT-P (2)
42 TOMMY DE LA CRUZ-P
43 JOE (FIREMAN) BEGGS (MIL)-P
43 HOWIE FOX-P
43 JOE NUXHALL-P
43 BILL LOHRMAN-P (2)
__ JODIE BEELER-2B/3B (3G:9/21-10/1)

1945

7TH 61-93 37GB

1 BILL (DEACON) MCKECHNIE-MGR
2 JIMMIE (ACE) WILSON-CH
3 HANK GOWDY-CH
4 AL (MOOSE) LAKEMAN-C
5 JOE JUST-C
5 AL UNSER-C
6 JOHNNY (MUTT) RIDDLE-C
10 FRANK (BUCK) MCCORMICK-1B
11 EDDIE (EPPIE) MILLER (INJ) -SS
12 KERMIT WAHL-INF
15 EDDIE (MONGOOSE) LUKON (MIL)-OF
15 WALLY FLAGER-SS (1)
16 STEVE MESNER-3B/2B
17 WOODIE WILLIAMS-2B
18 EARL (IRISH) HARRIST-P
18 RAY (PEP) MEDEIROS-PR
19 HERM WEHMEIER-P
20 DAIN (DING-A-LING) (SNIFFY) CLAY-OF
21 DICK SIPEK-OF
22 AL LIBKE-OF/P/1B
23 ERIC (BLUE DEVIL) (DUKIE) TIPTON-OF
27 GEE WALKER-OF/3B
28 HANK SAUER (MIL)-OF/1B
31 BUCKY WALTERS (INJ)-P
33 ARNOLD (HOOK) (LEFTY) CARTER-P
34 ED (THE WILD ELK OF THE WASATCH) HEUSSER-P
35 MIKE MODAK-P
35 MEL BOSSER-P
36 GUY (MISSISSIPPI MUDCAT) BUSH-P
36 VERN KENNEDY-P (2)
37 HOWIE FOX-P
38 ELMER RIDDLE (SUS)-P
39 JOE BOWMAN-P (2)
41 BOOM-BOOM BECK-P (1)
42 HOD LISENBEE-P
42 JOHNNY HETKI-P
43 FRANK DASSO-P

1946

6TH 67-87 30GB

1 BILL (DEACON) MCKECHNIE-MGR
2 JIMMIE (ACE) WILSON-CH
3 HANK GOWDY-CH
4 AL (MOOSE) LAKEMAN-C
5 RAY LAMANNO-C
6 GEE WALKER-CH
7 RAY (IRON MAN) MUELLER-C
11 LONNY (JUNIOR) FREY-2B/OF
12 BOBBY ADAMS-2B/UTIL
13 EDDIE (EPPIE) MILLER-SS
14 CLAUDE CORBITT-SS
15 GRADY HATTON-3B/OF
16 BENNY ZIENTARA-2B/3B
17 EDDIE SHOKES-1B
18 BERT HAAS-1B/3B
19 BOB USHER-OF/3B
20 DAIN (DING-A-LING) (SNIFFY) CLAY-OF
21 HOWIE MOSS-OF (1)
22 AL LIBKE-OF/P
23 LONNIE GOLDSTEIN-PH
23 MIKE MCCORMICK-OF (1)
24 MAX WEST-OF (2)
27 EDDIE (MONGOOSE) LUKON-OF
28 GARLAND (KNOBBY) LAWING-OF (1)
28 CLYDE VOLLMER-OF
31 BUCKY WALTERS-P
32 CLAY LAMBERT-P
33 JOHNNY (DOUBLE NO-HIT) (DUTCH MASTER) VANDER MEER-P
34 ED (THE WILD ELK OF THE WASATCH) HEUSSER-P
35 NATE ANDREWS-P (1)
36 CLYDE (HARDROCK) SHOUN-P
37 HOWIE FOX-P
38 BOB MALLOY (MIL)-P
38 FRANK DASSO-P

40 JOHNNY HETKI-P
41 HARRY (GUNBOAT) GUMBERT-P
42 GEORGE BURPO-P
43 JOE (FIREMAN) BEGGS-P
44 BOB MALLOY (MIL)-P
46 CLYDE VOLLMER-OF
47 EWELL (THE WHIP) BLACKWELL-P

1947

5TH 73-81 21GB

1 JOHNNY NEUN-MGR
2 GEORGE (HIGHPOCKETS) KELLY-CH
3 PHIL PAGE-CH
4 AL (MOOSE) LAKEMAN-PH (1)
5 RAY LAMANNO-C
6 HUGH POLAND-C (2)
7 RAY (IRON MAN) MUELLER-C
10 VIRGIL (RED) STALLCUP-SS
12 BOBBY ADAMS-2B
13 EDDIE (EPPIE) MILLER-SS
14 EDDIE (EPPIE) MILLER-SS
15 GRADY HATTON-3B
16 BENNY ZIENTARA-2B/3B
17 CHARLIE (CHUCK) KRESS-1B
17 BABE YOUNG-1B (2)
18 BERT HAAS-OF/1B
19 KERMIT WAHL-INF
20 TED (BIG KLU) KLUSZEWSKI-1B
21 FRANKIE BAUMHOLTZ-OF
23 AUGIE GALAN-OF
24 BOB USHER-OF/3B
24 TOMMY TATUM-OF/2B (2)
25 CLYDE VOLLMER-OF
27 EDDIE (MONGOOSE) LUKON-OF
31 BUCKY WALTERS-P
32 CLAY LAMBERT-P
33 JOHNNY (DOUBLE NO-HIT) (DUTCH MASTER) VANDER MEER-P
34 EDDIE ERAUTT-P
35 MIKE SCHULTZ-P
35 HARRY PERKOWSKI-P
36 CLYDE (HARDROCK) SHOUN-P (1)
36 KEN RAFFENSBERGER-P (2)
37 BUD (RED) LIVELY-P
38 KENT (PETE) PETERSON-P
40 JOHNNY HETKI-P
41 HARRY (GUNBOAT) GUMBERT-P
42 KEN (SOUP) POLIVKA-P
43 JOE (FIREMAN) BEGGS-P (1)
44 BOB MALLOY-P
45 HERM WEHMEIER-P
47 EWELL (THE WHIP) BLACKWELL-P
(48) ELMER RIDDLE-(P)

1948

7TH 64-89 27GB

1 JOHNNY NEUN-MGR1
2 GEORGE (HIGHPOCKETS) KELLY-CH
3 PHIL PAGE-CH
5 RAY LAMANNO-C
6 HUGH POLAND-PH
7 RAY (IRON MAN) MUELLER (INJ)-C
8 DEWEY (DEE) WILLIAMS-C
10 VIRGIL (RED) STALLCUP-SS
12 BOBBY ADAMS-2B/3B
14 CLAUDE CORBITT-INF
15 GRADY HATTON-3B/UTIL
16 BENNY ZIENTARA-INF
17 BABE YOUNG-1B/OF (1)
18 TED (BIG KLU) KLUSZEWSKI-1B
19 HOWIE (STRETCH) (STEEPLE) SCHULTZ-1B (2)
21 FRANKIE BAUMHOLTZ-OF
22 JOHNNY WYROSTEK-OF
23 AUGIE GALAN-OF
25 CLYDE VOLLMER-OF (1)
28 MARV (TWITCH) RICKERT-PH (1)
28 DANNY LITWHILER-OF/3B (2)
29 HANK SAUER-OF/1B
31 BUCKY WALTERS-P/MGR2
32 WALKER (FOOTS) CRESS-P
33 JOHNNY (DOUBLE NO-HIT) (DUTCH MASTER) VANDER MEER-P
34 EDDIE ERAUTT-P
36 KEN RAFFENSBERGER-P
37 BUD (RED) LIVELY-P
37 STEVE (FLIP) FILIPOWICZ-OF
38 KENT (PETE) PETERSON-P
40 JOHNNY HETKI-P
41 HARRY (GUNBOAT) GUMBERT-P
43 HOWIE FOX-P
44 TOMMY HUGHES-P
44 JIM (BONES) BLACKBURN-P
45 HERM WEHMEIER-P
47 EWELL (THE WHIP) BLACKWELL (INJ)-P
48 KEN HOLCOMBE-P
48 KEN BURKHART-P (2)

1949

7TH 62-92 35GB

1 BUCKY WALTERS-MGR1
2 LUKE SEWELL-CH/MGR2
3 TONY CUCCINELLO-CH
4 PHIL PAGE-CH
6 DIXIE HOWELL-C
7 RAY (IRON MAN) MUELLER-C (1)
7 WALKER (WALK) COOPER-C (2)
9 JOHNNY PRAMESA-C
10 VIRGIL (RED) STALLCUP-SS
11 JIMMY BLOODWORTH-2B/INF
12 BOBBY ADAMS-2B/3B
14 CLAUDE CORBITT-INF
14 SAMMY MEEKS-2B/SS
15 GRADY HATTON-3B
17 CHARLIE (CHUCK) KRESS-1B (1)
17 JESS DOBERNIC-P (2)
18 TED (BIG KLU) KLUSZEWSKI-1B
20 LLOYD (CITATION) MERRIMAN-OF
21 FRANKIE BAUMHOLTZ-OF (1)
21 PEANUTS LOWREY-OF (2)
22 JOHNNY WYROSTEK-OF
28 DANNY LITWHILER-OF/3B
29 HANK SAUER-OF/1B (1)
29 WALLY POST-OF
29 HARRY (THE HAT) WALKER-OF/1B (2)
30 KENT (PETE) PETERSON-P
31 BUCKY WALTERS-MGR1
31 HERM WEHMEIER-P
32 WALKER (FOOTS) CRESS-P
33 JOHNNY (DOUBLE NO-HIT) (DUTCH MASTER) VANDER MEER-P
34 EDDIE ERAUTT-P
35 HARRY PERKOWSKI-P
36 KEN RAFFENSBERGER-P
37 BUD (RED) LIVELY-P
39 JESS DOBERNIC-P (2)
39 DIXIE HOWELL-P
40 FRANK (LEFTY) FANOVICH-P
41 HARRY (GUNBOAT) GUMBERT-P
43 HOWIE FOX-P
45 HERM WEHMEIER-P
47 EWELL (THE WHIP) BLACKWELL (INJ)-P
48 KEN BURKHART-P
49 FRANK FANOVICH-P
50 LUKE SEWELL-CH/MGR2
53 PHIL PAGE-CH

1950

6TH 66-87 24.5GB

2 TED TAPPE-PH
5 HOBIE LANDRITH-C
6 DIXIE HOWELL-C
7 WALKER (WALK) COOPER-C
7 BOB SCHEFFING-C (2)
8 HOBIE LANDRITH-C
9 JOHNNY PRAMESA-C
10 VIRGIL (RED) STALLCUP-SS
11 JIMMY BLOODWORTH-2B (1)
12 BOBBY ADAMS-2B/3B
14 SAMMY MEEKS-SS/2B
15 GRADY HATTON-3B/INF
16 CONNIE RYAN-2B (2)
17 JOE ADCOCK-OF/1B
18 TED (BIG KLU) KLUSZEWSKI-1B
20 LLOYD (CITATION) MERRIMAN-OF
21 PEANUTS LOWREY-OF/2B (1)
22 JOHNNY WYROSTEK-OF/1B
23 RON NORTHEY-OF (1)
23 JIM (DUTCH) BOLGER-OF
24 BOB USHER-OF
25 MARV RACKLEY-PH
28 DANNY LITWHILER-OF
30 KENT (PETE) PETERSON-P
31 HERM WEHMEIER-P
32 FRANK SMITH-P
33 JOHNNY HETKI-P
34 EDDIE ERAUTT-P
35 HARRY PERKOWSKI-P
36 KEN RAFFENSBERGER-P
38 BUD BYERLY-P
38 JIM (JAY) AVREA-P
40 WILLIE (THE KNUCK) RAMSDELL-P (2)
43 HOWIE FOX-P
47 EWELL (THE WHIP) BLACKWELL-P
50 LUKE SEWELL-MGR
51 TONY (COOCH) (CHICK) CUCCINELLO-CH
52 GUS (BLACKIE) MANCUSO-CH
53 PHIL PAGE-CH

1951

6TH 68-86 28.5GB

5 HOBIE LANDRITH-C
6 DIXIE HOWELL-C
7 BOB SCHEFFING-C (1)
9 JOHNNY PRAMESA-C
10 VIRGIL (RED) STALLCUP-SS
11 ROY MCMILLAN-INF
12 BOBBY ADAMS-UTIL
14 SAMMY MEEKS-SS/2B
15 GRADY HATTON-3B/OF
16 CONNIE RYAN-2B/UTIL
18 TED (BIG KLU) KLUSZEWSKI-1B
20 LLOYD (CITATION) MERRIMAN-OF
21 JOE ADCOCK-OF
22 JOHNNY WYROSTEK-OF/1B
24 BOB USHER-OF
25 WALLY POST-OF
25 HANK EDWARDS (INJ)-OF (2)
26 TED TAPPE-PH
26 BARNEY MCCOSKY-OF (2)
28 DANNY LITWHILER-OF
30 KENT (PETE) PETERSON-P
30 JIM (DUTCH) BOLGER-OF
31 HERM WEHMEIER-P
32 FRANK SMITH-P
33 JIM (BONES) BLACKBURN-P
34 EDDIE ERAUTT-P
35 HARRY PERKOWSKI-P
36 KEN RAFFENSBERGER-P
38 BUD BYERLY-P
40 WILLIE (THE KNUCK) RAMSDELL-P
43 HOWIE FOX-P
45 ED BLAKE-P
47 EWELL (THE WHIP) BLACKWELL-P
50 LUKE SEWELL-MGR
51 TONY (COOCH) (CHICK) CUCCINELLO-CH
52 DANNY LITWHILER-CH
53 PHIL PAGE-CH

1952

6TH 69-85 27.5GB

5 HOBIE LANDRITH-C
6 DIXIE HOWELL-C
7 ANDY SEMINICK-C
9 JOE ROSSI-C
10 VIRGIL (RED) STALLCUP-SS
10 EDDIE KAZAK-3B/1B (2)
11 ROY MCMILLAN-SS
12 BOBBY ADAMS-3B
13 EDDIE PELLAGRINI-INF
15 GRADY HATTON-2B
16 JOHNNY TEMPLE-2B
18 TED (BIG KLU) KLUSZEWSKI-1B
(20) LLOYD (CITATION) MERRIMAN (MIL)-(OF)
22 JOHNNY WYROSTEK-OF/1B (1)
22 WILLARD MARSHALL-OF (2)
23 DICK SISLER-OF (1)
23 JIM GREENGRASS-OF
23 WALLY WESTLAKE-OF (2)
24 BOB BORKOWSKI-OF/1B
25 HANK EDWARDS-OF (1)
25 NILES JORDAN-P
26 JOE ADCOCK-OF/1B
28 WALLY POST (ILL)-OF
28 CAL ABRAMS-OF (2)
31 HERM WEHMEIER-P
32 FRANK SMITH-P
35 HARRY PERKOWSKI-P
36 KEN RAFFENSBERGER-P
38 BUD BYERLY-P
38 BUD PODBIELAN-P (2)
39 JOE NUXHALL-P
40 NILES JORDAN-P
40 BUBBA CHURCH-P (2)
41 FRANK HILLER-P
45 ED BLAKE-P
45 PHIL HAUGSTAD-P
45 JOHNNY (BEAR TRACKS) SCHMITZ-P (3)
47 EWELL (THE WHIP) BLACKWELL-P (1)
50 LUKE SEWELL-MGR1
50 ROGERS HORNSBY-MGR3
51 EARLE BRUCKER-CH/MGR
52 BEN CHAPMAN-CH
53 PHIL PAGE-CH

1953

6TH 68-87 37GB

3 HOBIE LANDRITH-C
5 HOBIE LANDRITH-C
5 FRANK BALDWIN-C
6 HANK FOILES-OF (1)
6 ED BAILEY-C
7 ANDY SEMINICK-C
8 FRANK BALDWIN-C
11 ROY MCMILLAN-SS
12 BOBBY ADAMS-3B
14 ROCKY BRIDGES-2B/INF
15 GRADY HATTON-INF
16 JOHNNY TEMPLE-2B
18 TED (BIG KLU) KLUSZEWSKI-1B
(20) LLOYD (CITATION) MERRIMAN (MIL)-(OF)
20 GEORGE LERCHEN-OF
20 BOB MARQUIS-OF
22 WILLARD MARSHALL-OF
23 JIM GREENGRASS-OF
24 BOB BORKOWSKI-OF/1B
25 GUS BELL-OF
27 JOE SZEKELY-OF
28 WALLY POST-OF
31 HERM WEHMEIER-P
32 FRANK SMITH-P
33 BOB KELLY-P (2)
34 EDDIE ERAUTT-P (1)
34 JACKIE COLLUM-P (2)
35 HARRY PERKOWSKI-P
36 KEN RAFFENSBERGER-P
37 CLYDE KING-P
38 BUD PODBIELAN-P
39 JOE NUXHALL-P
41 BUBBA CHURCH-P (1)
45 ED BLAKE-P
46 ERNIE NEVEL-P
46 FRED (LEFTY) BACZEWSKI-P (2)
47 HOWIE JUDSON-P
48 BARNEY MARTIN-P
50 ROGERS HORNSBY-MGR1
51 FORD (ROCKY) GARRISON-CH
52 BUSTER MILLS-CH/MGR2

1954

5TH 74-80 23GB

1 BIRDIE TEBBETTS-MGR
2 DICK (ROWDY RICHARD) BARTELL-CH
3 TOM FERRICK-CH
5 HOBIE LANDRITH-C
6 ED BAILEY-C
7 ANDY SEMINICK-C
10 CHUCK HARMON-3B/1B
11 ROY MCMILLAN-SS
12 BOBBY ADAMS-3B/2B
14 ROCKY BRIDGES-INF
15 GRADY HATTON-PH (1)
15 JIM (DUTCH) BOLGER-OF
15 JOHNNY (SKIDS) LIPON-PH
16 JOHNNY TEMPLE-2B
18 TED (BIG KLU) KLUSZEWSKI-1B
19 DICK MURPHY-PH
19 CONNIE RYAN-PH
20 LLOYD (CITATION) MERRIMAN-OF

CINCINNATI REDS

21 NINO ESCALERA-UTIL
23 JIM GREENGRASS-OF
24 BOB BORKOWSKI-OF/1B
25 GUS BELL-OF
28 WALLY POST-OF
31 HERM WEHMEIER-P (1)
31 KARL DREWS-P (2)
31 CLIFF ROSS-P
32 FRANK SMITH-P
34 JACKIE COLLUM-P
35 HARRY PERKOWSKI-P
36 KEN RAFFENSBERGER-P
36 KARL DREWS-P (2)
36 JERRY LANE-P
36 MARIO (BABE) PICONE-P (2)
38 BUD PODBIELAN-P
39 JOE NUXHALL-P
42 MOE SAVRANSKY-P
46 FRED (LEFTY) BACZEWSKI-P
47 HOWIE JUDSON-P
49 CORKY VALENTINE-P
51 ART FOWLER-P
53 GEORGE ZUVERINK-P
53 KARL DREWS-P (2)
54 JIM PEARCE-P

1955

5TH 75-79 23.5GB

1 BIRDIE TEBBETTS-MGR
2 DICK (ROWDY RICHARD) BARTELL-CH
3 TOM FERRICK-CH
4 JIMMY DYKES-CH
5 HOBIE LANDRITH (INJ)-C
6 ED BAILEY-C
6 MATT BATTS-C
7 ANDY SEMINICK-C (1)
7 SMOKY BURGESS-C (2)
10 CHUCK HARMON-UTIL
11 ROY MCMILLAN-SS
12 BOBBY ADAMS-3B/2B (1)
12 RAY (JABBO) JABLONSKI-3B/OF
12 MILT SMITH-3B/2B
14 ROCKY BRIDGES-3B/INF
15 RAY (JABBO) JABLONSKI-3B/OF
16 JOHNNY TEMPLE-2B
18 TED (BIG KLU) KLUSZEWSKI-1B
19 DICK MURPHY-PH
21 NINO ESCALERA-UTIL
22 BOB THURMAN-OF
23 JIM GREENGRASS-OF (1)
23 STAN PALYS-OF/1B (2)
24 BOB BORKOWSKI-OF/1B (1)
24 SAM MELE-OF/1B (2)
25 GUS BELL-OF
26 JOE (OX) BROVIA-PH
26 BOB (HURRICANE) HAZLE-OF
27 GLEN GORBOUS-OF (1)
27 AL SILVERA-OF
28 WALLY POST-OF
30 HERSH (BUSTER) FREEMAN-P (2)
31 JERRY LANE-P
31 DON GROSS-P
32 JIM PEARCE-P
33 STEVE RIDZIK-P (2)
34 JACKIE COLLUM-P
35 JOHNNY KLIPPSTEIN-P
36 RUDY (BUSTER) MINARCIN-P
37 BOB HOOPER-P
38 BUD PODBIELAN (INJ)-P
39 JOE NUXHALL-P
42 GERRY STALEY-P (1)
43 MAURY FISHER-P
46 FRED (LEFTY) BACZEWSKI-P
49 CORKY VALENTINE-P
49 JOE BLACK-P (2)
51 ART FOWLER-P
54 RUDY (BUSTER) MINARCIN-P

1956

3RD 91-63 2GB

1 BIRDIE TEBBETTS-MGR
2 FRANK (BUCK) MCCORMICK-CH
3 TOM FERRICK-CH
4 JIMMY DYKES-CH
6 ED BAILEY-C
7 SMOKY BURGESS-C
9 BRUCE (BULL) EDWARDS-C/INF
9 MATT BATTS-C
9 JOE FRAZIER-OF (2)
10 CHUCK HARMON-OF/1B (1)
10 ALEX GRAMMAS-INF (2)
11 ROY MCMILLAN-SS
12 RAY (JABBO) JABLONSKI-3B/2B
14 ROCKY BRIDGES-UTIL
15 GEORGE (BIG GEORGE) CROWE-1B
16 JOHNNY TEMPLE-2B/OF
18 TED (BIG KLU) KLUSZEWSKI-1B
20 FRANK ROBINSON-OF
22 BOB THURMAN-OF
23 STAN PALYS-OF
24 BOBBY BALCENA-OF
24 JOE FRAZIER-OF (2)
25 GUS BELL-OF
26 JIM DYCK-3B/1B (2)
26 RUSS (THE MAD MONK) (MONK) (ROWDY) MEYER-P (2)
27 AL SILVERA-OF
27 CURT FLOOD-PH
28 WALLY POST-OF
30 HERSH (BUSTER) FREEMAN-P
31 DON GROSS-P
32 FRANK SMITH-P
34 JACKIE COLLUM-P
35 JOHNNY KLIPPSTEIN-P
36 JOHN OLDHAM-PR
36 PAUL (LEFTY) LAPALME-P (2)
37 ART (DUTCH) SCHULT-OF
39 JOE NUXHALL-P
40 TOM ACKER-P
42 HAL JEFFCOAT-P
43 BILL (LEFTY) KENNEDY-P
43 LARRY JANSEN-P
46 BROOKS (BULL) LAWRENCE-P
48 PAT SCANTLEBURY-P
49 JOE BLACK-P
51 ART FOWLER-P

1957

4TH 80-74 15GB

1 BIRDIE TEBBETTS-MGR
2 FRANK (BUCK) MCCORMICK-CH
3 TOM FERRICK-CH
4 JIMMY DYKES-CH
6 ED BAILEY-C
7 SMOKY BURGESS-C
8 DON PAVLETICH (MIL)-PH
9 DON PAVLETICH (MIL)-PH
9 DUTCH DOTTERER-C
10 ALEX GRAMMAS-INF
11 ROY MCMILLAN-SS
12 DON (TIGER) HOAK-3B/2B
14 ROCKY BRIDGES-INF (1)
14 CURT FLOOD-PH
15 GEORGE (BIG GEORGE) CROWE-1B
16 JOHNNY TEMPLE-2B/OF
17 BOBBY HENRICH-UTIL
18 TED (BIG KLU) KLUSZEWSKI (INJ)-1B
19 BILL (LEFTY) KENNEDY-P
19 BOBBY (SCROGGY) DURNBAUGH-SS
20 FRANK ROBINSON-OF/1B
22 BOB THURMAN-OF
24 JERRY LYNCH-OF/C
25 GUS BELL-OF
27 ART (DUTCH) SCHULT-OF
27 JOE TAYLOR-OF
28 WALLY POST-OF
29 PETE WHISENANT-OF
30 HERSH (BUSTER) FREEMAN-P
31 DON GROSS-P
32 RAUL SANCHEZ-P
34 CLAUDE OSTEEN-P
34 CHARLIE RABE-P
35 JOHNNY KLIPPSTEIN-P
36 WARREN HACKER-P (1)
36 VICENTE AMOR-P
38 BUD PODBIELAN-P
39 JOE NUXHALL-P
40 TOM ACKER-P
42 HAL JEFFCOAT-P
45 DAVE SKAUGSTAD-P
46 BROOKS (BULL) LAWRENCE-P
47 JAY HOOK-P
51 ART FOWLER-P

1958

4TH 76-78 16GB

1 BIRDIE TEBBETTS-MGR1
2 JOHNNY RIDDLE-CH
3 TOM FERRICK-CH
4 JIMMY DYKES-CH/MGR2
6 ED BAILEY-C
7 SMOKY BURGESS-C
9 DUTCH DOTTERER-C
10 ALEX GRAMMAS-INF
11 ROY MCMILLAN-SS
12 DON (TIGER) HOAK-3B/SS
15 GEORGE (BIG GEORGE) CROWE-1B
16 JOHNNY TEMPLE-2B/1B
17 BOBBY HENRICH-UTIL
18 STEVE BILKO-1B (1)
18 WALT (MOOSE) DROPO-1B (2)
19 DEE FONDY-1B/OF
20 FRANK ROBINSON-OF/3B
22 BOB THURMAN-OF
23 CHUCK COLES-OF
24 JERRY LYNCH-OF
25 GUS BELL-OF
26 JIM (BIG JIM) FRIDLEY-OF
28 EDDIE MIKSIS-UTIL (2)
28 VADA PINSON-OF
29 PETE WHISENANT-OF/2B
30 HERSH (BUSTER) FREEMAN-P (1)
30 DON (NEWK) NEWCOMBE-P (2)
31 CHARLIE RABE-P
31 JIM O'TOOLE-P
31 GENE (LEFTY) HAYDEN-P
32 HARVEY (THE KITTEN) HADDIX-P
33 FRED HATFIELD-2B/3B
33 TED WIEAND-P
35 JOHNNY KLIPPSTEIN-P (1)
35 TED WIEAND-P
36 DON (NEWK) NEWCOMBE-P (2)
37 BOB PURKEY-P
39 JOE NUXHALL-P
40 TOM ACKER-P
41 ALEX KELLNER-P (2)
42 HAL JEFFCOAT-P
43 WILLARD SCHMIDT-P
43 ORLANDO PENA-P
44 WILLARD SCHMIDT-P
45 BOB KELLY-P
45 TURK LOWN-P (2)
45 DAN MOREJON-OF
46 BROOKS (BULL) LAWRENCE-P
47 BILL (LEFTY) WIGHT-P
47 JAY HOOK-P
48 TURK LOWN-P (2)

1959

5TH (TIE) 74-80 13GB

1 MAYO SMITH-MGR1
1 FRED HUTCHINSON-MGR2
2 CLYDE KING-CH
2 COTTON DEAL-CH
3 WALLY MOSES-CH
4 REGGIE OTERO-CH
6 ED BAILEY-C
8 DON PAVLETICH-PR
9 DUTCH DOTTERER-C
10 EDDIE KASKO-SS/INF
10 WILLARD SCHMIDT, -P
11 ROY MCMILLAN (INJ)-SS
12 JIM PENDLETON-OF/INF
14 WILLIE (PUDDIN' HEAD) JONES-3B (3)
15 FRANK THOMAS-UTIL
16 JOHNNY TEMPLE-2B/1B
17 BOBBY HENRICH- SS/3B
18 WALT (MOOSE) DROPO-1B (1)
18 CLIFF COOK-3B
19 WHITEY LOCKMAN-UTIL (2)
20 FRANK ROBINSON-1B/OF
22 BOB THURMAN-PH
22 BUDDY GILBERT-OF
23 DEL ENNIS-OF (1)
23 WILLIE (PUDDIN' HEAD) JONES-3B (3
24 JERRY LYNCH-OF
25 GUS BELL-OF
27 JOHNNY POWERS-OF
28 VADA PINSON-OF
29 PETE WHISENANT-OF
31 JIM O'TOOLE-P
32 MIKE CUELLAR-P
32 CLAUDE OSTEEN-P
35 BOB MABE-P
36 DON (NEWK) NEWCOMBE-P
37 BOB PURKEY-P
39 JOE NUXHALL-P
40 TOM ACKER-P
41 JIM BAILEY-P
42 HAL JEFFCOAT-P (1)
42 JIM BROSNAN-P (2)
43 ORLANDO PENA-P
44 WILLARD SCHMIDT-P
46 BROOKS (BULL) LAWRENCE-P
47 LUIS ARROYO-P (1)
47 DON RUDOLPH-P (2)
47 JAY HOOK-P

1960

6TH 67-87 28GB

1 FRED HUTCHINSON-MGR
2 COTTON DEAL-CH
3 WALLY MOSES-CH
4 REGGIE OTERO-CH
6 ED BAILEY-C
8 FRANK (PIG) HOUSE-C
9 DUTCH DOTTERER-C
9 JOE AZCUE-C
10 EDDIE KASKO-3B/INF
11 ROY MCMILLAN-SS/2B
12 BILLY (THE KID) MARTIN-2B
14 WILLIE (PUDDIN' HEAD) JONES-3B/2B
17 ELIO CHACON-2B/OF
17 LEO (CHICO) CARDENAS-SS
18 GORDY COLEMAN-1B
19 WHITEY LOCKMAN-1B
19 CLIFF COOK-3B/OF
20 FRANK ROBINSON-1B/UTIL
21 ROGELIO ALVAREZ-1B
22 JOE GAINES-OF
22 TONY GONZALEZ-OF (1)
24 JERRY LYNCH-OF
25 GUS BELL-OF
27 LEE WALLS-OF/1B
27 HARRY ANDERSON-1B/OF (2)
28 VADA PINSON-OF
29 PETE WHISENANT-PH (1)
29 WALLY POST-OF (2)
31 JIM O'TOOLE-P
32 CLAUDE OSTEEN-P
34 TED WIEAND-P
34 MARSHALL (SHERRIF) BRIDGES-P (2)
35 RAUL SANCHEZ-P
36 DON (NEWK) NEWCOMBE-P (1)
37 BOB PURKEY-P
39 JOE NUXHALL-P
40 CAL (BUSTER) MCLISH-P
42 JIM BROSNAN-P
43 ORLANDO PENA-P
44 BILL HENRY-P
45 DUANE RICHARDS-P
46 BROOKS (BULL) LAWRENCE-P
46 BOB GRIM-P (2)
46 JIM MALONEY-P
47 JAY HOOK-P

1961

1ST 93-61 0GB

L WS-NYA 4-1

1 FRED HUTCHINSON-MGR
2 DICK SISLER-CH
3 JIM (MILKMAN JIM) TURNER-CH
4 REGGIE OTERO-CH
6 ED BAILEY-C (1)
6 JOHNNY EDWARDS-C
6 BOB SCHMIDT-C (2)
8 JERRY (PIG) ZIMMERMAN-C
9 HAL BEVAN-PH
9 DARRELL JOHNSON-C (2)
10 EDDIE KASKO-SS/INF
11 CLIFF COOK-3B/OF
11 JIM BAUMER-C
12 GENE (AUGIE) FREESE-3B/2B
14 WILLIE (PUDDIN' HEAD) JONES-3B
15 DICK GERNERT-3B (2)
16 LEO (CHICO) CARDENAS-SS
17 ELIO CHACON-2B/OF
18 GORDY COLEMAN-1B
19 DON BLASINGAME-2B (2)
20 FRANK ROBINSON-OF/3B
21 JOE GAINES-OF
24 JERRY LYNCH-OF
25 GUS BELL-OF
27 HARRY ANDERSON-1B/OF
27 PETE WHISENANT-UTIL/CH (2)
28 VADA PINSON-OF
29 WALLY POST-OF
30 JOEY JAY-P

31 JIM O'TOOLE-P
32 CLAUDE OSTEEN-P (1)
34 MARSHALL (SHERRIF) BRIDGES-P
34 SHERMAN (ROADBLOCK) JONES-P
37 BOB PURKEY-P
38 HOWIE NUNN (INJ)-P
40 KEN JOHNSON-P (2)
41 KEN HUNT-P
42 JIM BROSNAN-P
44 BILL HENRY-P
46 JIM MALONEY-P
47 JAY HOOK-P

1962

3RD 98-64 3.5GB

1 FRED HUTCHINSON-MGR
2 DICK SISLER-CH
3 JIM (MILKMAN JIM) TURNER -CH
4 REGGIE OTERO-CH
5 DARRELL JOHNSON-C (1)
6 JOHNNY EDWARDS-C
7 JESSE GONDER-PH
8 DON PAVLETICH-1B/C
9 HANK FOILES-C
10 EDDIE KASKO-3B/SS
11 ROGELIO ALVAREZ-1B
12 GENE (AUGIE) FREESE (INJ) -3B
14 TOMMY HARPER-3B
14 DON (POPEYE) ZIMMER-INF (2)
15 CLIFF COOK-3B (1)
16 LEO (CHICO) CARDENAS-SS
17 COOKIE ROJAS-2B/3B
18 GORDY COLEMAN-1B
19 DON BLASINGAME-2B
20 FRANK ROBINSON-OF
21 JOE GAINES-OF
23 OTIS DOUGLAS-CH
24 JERRY LYNCH-OF
25 MARTY KEOUGH-OF/1B
27 PETE WHISENANT-CH
28 VADA PINSON-OF
29 WALLY POST-OF
30 JOEY JAY-P
31 JIM O'TOOLE-P
32 SAMMY ELLIS-P
34 MOE DRABOWSKY-P (1)
37 BOB PURKEY-P
38 DAVE HILLMAN-P (1)
38 HOWIE NUNN-P
38 JOHN TSITOURIS-P
39 BOB MILLER-P (1)
39 TED WILLS-P (2)
40 DAVE SISLER-P
41 JOE NUXHALL-P (2)
42 JIM BROSNAN-P
43 HOWIE NUNN-P
44 BILL HENRY-P
46 JIM MALONEY-P
47 JOHNNY KLIPPSTEIN-P

1963

5TH 86-76 13GB

1 FRED HUTCHINSON-MGR
2 DICK SISLER-CH
3 JIM (MILKMAN JIM) TURNER -CH
4 REGGIE OTERO-CH
6 JOHNNY EDWARDS-C
7 JESSE GONDER-C (1)
7 SAMMY TAYLOR-C (2)
8 DON PAVLETICH-1B/C
9 HANK FOILES-C (1)
9 GENE GREEN-C
9 DARYL (BIG DEE) SPENCER-3B (2)
10 EDDIE KASKO-INF
11 HARRY BRIGHT-1B (1)
12 GENE (AUGIE) FREESE-3B/OF
14 PETE (CHARLIE HUSTLE) ROSE-2B/OF
16 LEO (CHICO) CARDENAS-SS
17 TOMMY HARPER-OF/3B
18 GORDY COLEMAN-1B
19 DON BLASINGAME-2B/3B (1)
19 CHARLIE NEAL-INF (2)
20 FRANK ROBINSON-OF/1B
21 KEN WALTERS-OF/1B
24 JERRY LYNCH-OF (1)
24 BOB SKINNER-OF (2)
25 MARTY KEOUGH-1B/OF
28 VADA PINSON-OF
29 WALLY POST-OF (1)
30 JOEY JAY-P
31 JIM O'TOOLE-P
33 AL (RED) WORTHINGTON-P
36 RAY SHORE-CH
37 BOB PURKEY-P
38 JOHN TSITOURIS-P
41 JOE NUXHALL-P
42 JIM BROSNAN-P (1)
43 DOM ZANNI-P (2)
44 BILL HENRY-P
46 JIM MALONEY-P
47 JIM COATES-P (2)
48 JIM (BEAR) OWENS-P

1964

2ND 92-70 1GB

1 FRED HUTCHINSON (ILL)-MGR1
2 DICK SISLER-CH/MGR2
3 JIM (MILKMAN JIM) TURNER -CH
4 REGGIE OTERO-CH
5 JOHNNY TEMPLE-PH/CH
6 JOHNNY EDWARDS-C
7 JIMMIE COKER-C
8 DON PAVLETICH-C/1B
9 HAL SMITH-C
10 STEVE BOROS-3B
11 DERON JOHNSON-1B/UTIL
12 BOBBY KLAUS-INF (1)
14 PETE (CHARLIE HUSTLE) ROSE-2B
15 CHICO RUIZ-3B/2B
16 LEO (CHICO) CARDENAS-SS
17 TOMMY HARPER-OF/3B
18 GORDY COLEMAN-1B
19 TOMMY HELMS-PH
20 FRANK ROBINSON-OF
22 MEL QUEEN-OF
24 BOB SKINNER-OF (1)
24 TONY PEREZ-1B
25 MARTY KEOUGH-OF/1B
28 VADA PINSON-OF
30 JOEY JAY-P
31 JIM O'TOOLE-P
32 SAMMY ELLIS-P
33 AL (RED) WORTHINGTON-P (1)
33 RYNE DUREN-P (2)
34 CHET NICHOLS-P
36 RAY SHORE-CH
37 BOB PURKEY-P
38 JOHN TSITOURIS-P
41 JOE NUXHALL-P
42 BILLY MCCOOL-P
44 BILL HENRY-P
46 JIM MALONEY-P
50 TOMMY HELMS-PH
53 JIM DICKSON-P

1965

4TH 89-73 8GB

(1) FRED HUTCHINSON (DIED)-(MGR)
2 DICK SISLER-MGR
3 JIM (MILKMAN JIM) TURNER -CH
4 REGGIE OTERO-CH
5 FRANK (FEZ) OCEAK-CH
6 JOHNNY EDWARDS-C
7 JIMMIE COKER-C
8 DON PAVLETICH-C/1B
10 STEVE BOROS-3B
11 DERON JOHNSON-3B
12 ART SHAMSKY-OF/1B
14 PETE (CHARLIE HUSTLE) ROSE-2B
15 CHICO RUIZ (INJ)-3B/SS
16 LEO (CHICO) CARDENAS-SS
17 TOMMY HARPER-OF/INF
18 GORDY COLEMAN-1B
19 TOMMY HELMS-INF
20 FRANK ROBINSON-OF
22 MEL QUEEN-OF
23 LEE MAY, PH
24 TONY PEREZ-1B
25 MARTY KEOUGH-1B/OF
26 CHARLIE JAMES-OF
28 VADA PINSON-OF
30 JOEY JAY-P
31 JIM O'TOOLE-P
32 SAMMY ELLIS-P
33 DOM ZANNI-P
35 GERRY ARRIGO-P
36 RAY SHORE-CH
37 ROGER CRAIG-P
38 JOHN TSITOURIS-P
39 BOBBY LOCKE-P
41 JOE NUXHALL-P
42 BILLY MCCOOL-P
44 BILL HENRY-P (1)
44 JIM DUFFALO-P (2)
46 JIM MALONEY-P
47 GERRY ARRIGO-P
54 DARRELL OSTEEN-P
56 TED DAVIDSON-P

1966

7TH 76-84 18GB

1 *(RET#)FRED HUTCHINSON*
2 ROY SIEVERS-CH
3 MEL (CHIEF) HARDER-CH
4 DAVE BRISTOL-CH/MGR2
6 JOHNNY EDWARDS-C
7 JIMMIE COKER-C/OF
8 DON PAVLETICH-C/1B
9 WHITEY WIETELMANN-CH
10 DON (JEEP) HEFFNER-MGR1
10 VERN BENSON-CH
11 DERON JOHNSON-OF/INF
12 ART SHAMSKY-OF
13 RAY SHORE-CH
14 PETE (CHARLIE HUSTLE) ROSE-2B/3B
15 CHICO RUIZ-UTIL
16 LEO (CHICO) CARDENAS-SS
17 TOMMY HARPER-OF
18 GORDY COLEMAN-1B
19 TOMMY HELMS-3B/2B
20 DICK SIMPSON-OF
22 MEL QUEEN-OF/P
23 LEE MAY-1B
24 TONY PEREZ-1B
27 JACK BALDSCHUN-P
28 VADA PINSON-OF
30 HANK (BULLDOG) FISCHER-P (2)
31 JIM O'TOOLE-P
32 SAMMY ELLIS-P
33 DOM ZANNI-P
34 MILT (GIMPY) PAPPAS-P
35 GERRY ARRIGO-P (1)
36 RAY SHORE-CH
36 TED DAVIDSON-P
38 JOHN TSITOURIS-P
38 HANK (BULLDOG) FISCHER-P (2)
41 JOE NUXHALL (INJ)-P
42 BILLY MCCOOL-P
43 DON NOTTEBART-P
46 JIM MALONEY-P
47 JACK BALDSCHUN-P
54 DARRELL OSTEEN-P
56 TED DAVIDSON-P
68 WHITEY WIETELMANN-CH

1967

4TH 87-75 14.5GB

1 *(RET#)FRED HUTCHINSON*
2 JIMMY BRAGAN-CH
3 MEL (CHIEF) HARDER-CH
4 DAVE BRISTOL-MGR
5 JOHNNY BENCH-C
6 JOHNNY EDWARDS-C
7 JIMMIE COKER-C
8 DON PAVLETICH-C/INF
9 WHITEY WIETELMANN-CH
10 VERN BENSON-CH
11 DERON JOHNSON-1B/3B
12 ART SHAMSKY-OF
13 RAY SHORE-CH
14 PETE (CHARLIE HUSTLE) ROSE-OF/2B
15 CHICO RUIZ-UTIL
16 LEO (CHICO) CARDENAS (INJ)-SS
17 TOMMY HARPER (INJ)-OF
18 GORDY COLEMAN-1B
19 TOMMY HELMS-2B/SS
20 DICK SIMPSON-OF
22 MEL QUEEN-P
23 LEE MAY-1B/OF
24 TONY PEREZ-3B/INF
25 FLOYD ROBINSON-OF
27 JACK BALDSCHUN-P
28 VADA PINSON-OF
32 SAMMY ELLIS-P
33 TED ABERNATHY-P
34 MILT (GIMPY) PAPPAS-P
35 GERRY ARRIGO-P
36 BOB (MOOSE) (HORSE) LEE-P (2)
36 TED DAVIDSON (INJ)-P
38 JOHN TSITOURIS-P
38 GARY NOLAN-P
39 JACK BALDSCHUN-P
39 BOB (MOOSE) (HORSE) LEE-P (2)
39 DARRELL OSTEEN-P
40 LEN BOEHMER-2B
42 BILLY MCCOOL-P
43 DON NOTTEBART-P
45 JAKE WOOD-OF (2)
46 JIM MALONEY-P
48 BOB (MOOSE) (HORSE) LEE-P (2)
54 DARRELL OSTEEN-P
57 TED ABERNATHY-P

1968

4TH 83-79 14GB

1 *(RET#)FRED HUTCHINSON*
2 JIMMY BRAGAN-CH
3 MEL (CHIEF) HARDER-CH
4 DAVE BRISTOL-MGR
5 JOHNNY BENCH-C
6 BOB JOHNSON-SS/1B (1)
6 WOODY WOODWARD-INF (2)
7 PAT CORRALES-C
8 DON PAVLETICH (INJ)-1B/C
9 HAL (CORA) SMITH-CH
10 VERN BENSON-CH
11 HAL MCRAE-2B
12 MACK (MACK THE KNIFE) JONES-OF
14 PETE (CHARLIE HUSTLE) ROSE-OF/INF
15 CHICO RUIZ-INF
16 LEO (CHICO) CARDENAS -SS
17 FRED WHITFIELD-1B
19 TOMMY HELMS-2B/INF
22 MEL QUEEN (INJ)-P
23 LEE MAY-1B/OF
24 TONY PEREZ-3B
25 JIMMIE SCHAFFER-C
26 BILL KELSO-P
27 MR. RED LOGO
28 VADA PINSON-OF
29 ALEX JOHNSON-OF
30 JAY RITCHIE-P
31 DAN MCGINN-P
32 MILT (GIMPY) PAPPAS-P (1)
32 TONY CLONINGER-P (2)
33 TED ABERNATHY-P
35 GERRY ARRIGO-P
36 TED DAVIDSON-P (1)
36 CLAY (HAWK) CARROLL-P (2)
37 JOHN TSITOURIS-P
38 GARY NOLAN-P
39 GEORGE CULVER-P
40 TONY CLONINGER-P (2)
41 BILL KELSO-P
42 BILLY MCCOOL (INJ)-P
45 JAKE WOOD-OF
46 JIM MALONEY-P
48 BOB (MOOSE) (HORSE) LEE-P
55 JIM BEAUCHAMP-OF/1B

1969

3RD W 89-73 4GB

1 *(RET#)FRED HUTCHINSON*
2 JIMMY BRAGAN-CH
4 DAVE BRISTOL-MGR
5 JOHNNY BENCH-C
6 WOODY WOODWARD-SS/2B
7 PAT CORRALES-C
8 DANNY BREEDEN-C
9 HAL (CORA) SMITH-CH
10 VERN BENSON-CH
(11) HAL MCRAE (INJ)-(2B)
12 DARREL CHANEY-SS
14 PETE (CHARLIE HUSTLE) ROSE-OF/2B
15 CHICO RUIZ-UTIL
16 JIMMY STEWART-UTIL
17 FRED WHITFIELD-1B
18 MIKE DE LA HOZ-PH
19 TOMMY HELMS-2B/SS
20 TED SAVAGE-OF/2B
21 CLYDE MASHORE-PH
22 MEL QUEEN-P
23 LEE MAY-1B/OF
24 TONY PEREZ-3B
25 BERNIE CARBO-PH
27 MR. RED LOGO
28 BOBBY TOLAN-OF
29 ALEX JOHNSON-OF
30 JIM MERRITT-P
31 HARVEY (THE KITTEN) HADDIX-CH
33 CAMILO (LITTLE POTATO) PASCUAL-P (2)
34 JOSE PENA-P
34 PEDRO RAMOS-P (2)
35 GERRY ARRIGO-P
36 CLAY (HAWK) CARROLL-P

CINCINNATI REDS

37 WAYNE GRANGER-P
38 GARY NOLAN (INJ)-P
39 GEORGE CULVER-P
40 TONY CLONINGER-P
42 BILL SHORT-P
42 DENNIS RIBANT,-P (2)
43 JACK (FAT JACK) FISHER-P
44 JOHN NORIEGA-P
44 AL JACKSON-P (2)
46 JIM MALONEY (INJ)-P
55 JIM BEAUCHAMP-OF/1B

1970

1ST W 102-60 0GB
W NLCS-PITN 3-0
L WS-BALA 4-1

1 *(RET#)FRED HUTCHINSON*
2 ALEX GRAMMAS-CH
3 GEORGE SCHERGER-CH
4 LARRY SHEPARD-CH
5 JOHNNY BENCH-C/UTIL
6 WOODY WOODWARD-INF
7 PAT CORRALES-C
9 BILL PLUMMER-C
10 SPARKY ANDERSON-MGR
11 HAL MCRAE-OF/INF
12 DARREL CHANEY-INF
13 DAVE CONCEPCION-SS/2B
14 PETE (CHARLIE HUSTLE) ROSE-OF
15 FRANK DUFFY-SS
16 JIMMY STEWART-UTIL
17 JAY WARD-INF
17 TY CLINE (ILL)-OF/1B (2)
18 TED (BIG KLU) KLUSZEWSKI-CH
19 TOMMY HELMS-2B/SS
22 ANGEL BRAVO-OF
23 LEE MAY-1B
24 TONY PEREZ-3B/1B
25 BERNIE CARBO-OF
27 MR. RED LOGO
28 BOBBY TOLAN-OF
30 JIM MERRITT (INJ)-P
31 JIM (RED) MCGLOTHLIN-P
33 MEL BEHNEY (MIL)-P
34 PEDRO BORBON-P
34 BO BELINSKY-P
35 DON GULLETT-P
36 CLAY (HAWK) CARROLL-P
37 WAYNE GRANGER-P
38 GARY NOLAN-P
39 RAY WASHBURN-P
40 TONY CLONINGER-P
42 JOHN NORIEGA-P
43 MILT WILCOX-P
45 WAYNE SIMPSON (INJ)-P
46 JIM MALONEY (INJ)-P
50 DAVE CONCEPCION-SS/2B
56 DON GULLETT-P

1971

4TH W (TIE) 79-83 11GB

1 *(RET#)FRED HUTCHINSON*
2 ALEX GRAMMAS-CH
3 GEORGE SCHERGER-CH
4 LARRY SHEPARD-CH
5 JOHNNY BENCH-C/UTIL
6 WOODY WOODWARD-INF
7 PAT CORRALES-C
9 BILL PLUMMER-C
10 SPARKY ANDERSON-MGR
11 HAL MCRAE-OF
12 DARREL CHANEY-INF
13 DAVE CONCEPCION-SS/UTIL
14 PETE (CHARLIE HUSTLE) ROSE-OF
15 FRANK DUFFY-SS (1)
15 GEORGE FOSTER-OF (2)
16 JIMMY STEWART-UTIL
17 TY CLINE-OF/1B
18 TED (BIG KLU) KLUSZEWSKI-CH
19 TOMMY HELMS-2B
20 WILLIE SMITH-1B
22 ANGEL BRAVO-PH
22 AL (THE BULL) FERRARA-OF
23 LEE MAY-1B
24 TONY PEREZ-3B/1B
25 BERNIE CARBO-OF
27 MR. RED LOGO
(28) BOBBY TOLAN (INJ)-(OF)
29 BUDDY BRADFORD-OF (2)
30 JIM MERRITT-P
31 JIM (RED) MCGLOTHLIN-P
34 PEDRO BORBON-P
35 DON GULLETT-P
36 CLAY (HAWK) CARROLL-P
37 WAYNE GRANGER-P
38 GARY NOLAN-P
39 JOE GIBBON-P
40 TONY CLONINGER-P
42 STEVE BLATERIC-P
43 MILT WILCOX-P
44 ED SPRAGUE-P
45 WAYNE SIMPSON-P
47 GREG GARRETT-P
48 ROSS GRIMSLEY-P

1972

1ST W 95-59 0GB
W NLCS-PITN 3-2
L WS-OAKA 4-3

1 *(RET#)FRED HUTCHINSON*
2 ALEX GRAMMAS-CH
3 GEORGE SCHERGER-CH
4 LARRY SHEPARD-CH
5 JOHNNY BENCH-C/UTIL
6 WOODY WOODWARD-INF
7 PAT CORRALES-C (1)
7 SONNY RUBERTO-C
8 JOE MORGAN-2B
9 BILL PLUMMER (INJ)-C/INF
10 SPARKY ANDERSON-MGR
11 HAL MCRAE-OF/3B
12 DARREL CHANEY-INF
13 DAVE CONCEPCION-SS/INF
14 PETE (CHARLIE HUSTLE) ROSE-OF
15 GEORGE FOSTER-OF
16 DENIS MENKE-3B/1B
17 JULIAN JAVIER-INF
18 TED (BIG KLU) KLUSZEWSKI-CH
20 CESAR GERONIMO-OF
21 TOM HALL-P
22 TED UHLAENDER-OF
24 TONY PEREZ-1B
25 BERNIE CARBO-OF (1)
25 JOE HAGUE-1B/OF (2)
27 MR. RED LOGO
28 BOBBY TOLAN-OF
30 JIM MERRITT-P
31 JIM (RED) MCGLOTHLIN-P
34 PEDRO BORBON-P
35 DON GULLETT-P
36 CLAY (HAWK) CARROLL-P
38 GARY NOLAN-P
39 JOE GIBBON-P (1)
43 JACK BILLINGHAM-P
44 ED SPRAGUE-P
45 WAYNE SIMPSON-P
48 ROSS GRIMSLEY-P
49 DAVE TOMLIN-P

1973

1ST W 99-63 0GB
L NLCS-NYN 3-2

1 *(RET#)FRED HUTCHINSON*
2 ALEX GRAMMAS-CH
3 GEORGE SCHERGER-CH
4 LARRY SHEPARD-CH
5 JOHNNY BENCH-C/UTIL
6 BOB BARTON-C
6 HAL KING-C
8 JOE MORGAN-2B
9 BILL PLUMMER-C/3B
10 SPARKY ANDERSON-MGR
11 DENIS MENKE-3B/INF
12 DARREL CHANEY-INF
13 DAVE CONCEPCION (INJ)-SS/OF
14 PETE (CHARLIE HUSTLE) ROSE-OF
15 GEORGE FOSTER-OF
16 PHIL GAGLIANO-UTIL
17 ED CROSBY-SS/2B (2)
18 TED (BIG KLU) KLUSZEWSKI-CH
20 CESAR GERONIMO-OF
21 TOM HALL-P
22 DAN DRIESSEN-UTIL
23 ANDY KOSCO-OF/1B
24 TONY PEREZ-1B
25 JOE HAGUE-OF/1B
26 RICHIE SCHEINBLUM-OF (1)
27 MR. RED LOGO
27 GENE LOCKLEAR-OF (1)
27 MR. RED LOGO
28 BOBBY TOLAN-OF
29 LARRY STAHL-OF/1B
30 KEN GRIFFEY-OF
31 JIM (RED) MCGLOTHLIN-P (1)
32 FRED NORMAN-P (2)
33 ED ARMBRISTER-OF
34 PEDRO BORBON-P
35 DON GULLETT-P
36 CLAY (HAWK) CARROLL-P
38 GARY NOLAN (INJ)-P
41 TOM HALL-P
43 JACK BILLINGHAM-P
44 ED SPRAGUE-P (1)
44 DICK BANEY-P
45 ROGER (SPIDER) NELSON (INJ)-P
48 ROSS GRIMSLEY-P
49 DAVE TOMLIN-P
50 DICK BANEY-P

1974

2ND W 98-64 4GB

1 *(RET#)FRED HUTCHINSON*
2 ALEX GRAMMAS-CH
3 GEORGE SCHERGER-CH
4 LARRY SHEPARD-CH
5 JOHNNY BENCH-C/INF
6 HAL KING-C
8 JOE MORGAN-2B
9 BILL PLUMMER-C/3B
10 SPARKY ANDERSON-MGR
11 JUNIOR KENNEDY-2B/3B
12 DARREL CHANEY-INF
13 DAVE CONCEPCION-SS
14 PETE (CHARLIE HUSTLE) ROSE-OF
15 GEORGE FOSTER-OF
16 PHIL GAGLIANO-INF
17 TERRY CROWLEY-OF/1B
18 TED (BIG KLU) KLUSZEWSKI-CH
20 CESAR GERONIMO-OF
21 TOM HALL-P
22 DAN DRIESSEN-3B/UTIL
23 ANDY KOSCO (INJ)-3B/OF
24 TONY PEREZ-1B
25 RAY KNIGHT-3B
26 MERV RETTENMUND-OF
27 MR. RED LOGO
28 ROGER FREED-1B
30 KEN GRIFFEY-OF
31 CLAY KIRBY-P
32 FRED NORMAN-P
33 ED ARMBRISTER-OF
34 PEDRO BORBON-P
35 DON GULLETT-P
36 CLAY (HAWK) CARROLL-P
37 WILL MCENANEY-P
(38) GARY NOLAN (INJ)-(P)
39 RAWLY EASTWICK-P
43 JACK BILLINGHAM-P
44 PAT DARCY-P
44 DICK BANEY-P
45 ROGER (SPIDER) NELSON (INJ)-P
46 PAT OSBURN-P
47 MIKE MCQUEEN-P
48 ROSS GRIMSLEY-P
49 RAWLY EASTWICK-P
51 TOM CARROLL-P
58 PAT DARCY-P

1975

1ST W 108-54 0GB
W NLCS-PITN 3-0
W WS-BOSA 4-3

1 *(RET#)FRED HUTCHINSON*
2 ALEX GRAMMAS-CH
3 GEORGE SCHERGER-CH
4 LARRY SHEPARD-CH
5 JOHNNY BENCH-C/UTIL
7 DON WERNER-C
8 JOE MORGAN-2B
9 BILL PLUMMER-C
10 SPARKY ANDERSON-MGR
12 DARREL CHANEY-INF
13 DAVE CONCEPCION-SS/3B
14 PETE (CHARLIE HUSTLE) ROSE-3B/OF
15 GEORGE FOSTER-OF/1B
16 JOHN VUCKOVICH-3B
17 TERRY CROWLEY-OF/1B
18 TED (BIG KLU) KLUSZEWSKI-CH
20 CESAR GERONIMO-OF
21 TOM HALL-P (1)
22 DAN DRIESSEN-1B/OF
23 DOUG FLYNN-INF
24 TONY PEREZ-1B
26 MERV RETTENMUND-OF/3B
27 MR. RED LOGO
30 KEN GRIFFEY-OF
31 CLAY KIRBY-P
32 FRED NORMAN-P
33 ED ARMBRISTER-OF
34 PEDRO BORBON-P
35 DON GULLETT (INJ)-P
36 CLAY (HAWK) CARROLL-P
37 WILL MCENANEY-P
(38) GARY NOLAN (INJ)-(P)
43 JACK BILLINGHAM-P
44 PAT DARCY-P
49 RAWLY EASTWICK-P
51 TOM CARROLL-P

1976

1ST W 102-60 0GB
W NLCS-PHIN 3-0

1 *(RET#)FRED HUTCHINSON*
2 RUSS NIXON-CH
3 GEORGE SCHERGER-CH
4 LARRY SHEPARD-CH
5 JOHNNY BENCH-C/UTIL
7 DON WERNER-C
8 JOE MORGAN-2B
9 BILL PLUMMER-C
10 SPARKY ANDERSON-MGR
11 BOB BAILEY-OF/3B
13 DAVE CONCEPCION-SS/3B
14 PETE (CHARLIE HUSTLE) ROSE-3B/OF
15 GEORGE FOSTER-OF/1B
18 TED (BIG KLU) KLUSZEWSKI-CH
19 JOEL YOUNGBLOOD-UTIL
20 CESAR GERONIMO-OF
21 MIKE LUM-OF
22 DAN DRIESSEN-1B/OF
23 DOUG FLYNN-INF
24 TONY PEREZ-1B
27 MR. RED LOGO
30 KEN GRIFFEY-OF
32 FRED NORMAN-P
33 ED ARMBRISTER-OF
34 PEDRO BORBON-P
35 DON GULLETT (INJ)-P
36 RICH HINTON-P
37 WILL MCENANEY-P
38 GARY NOLAN-P
40 PAT ZACHRY-P
42 SANTO ALCALA-P
43 JACK BILLINGHAM-P
44 PAT DARCY-P
45 MANNY SARMIENTO-P
49 RAWLY EASTWICK-P
53 JOE HENDERSON-P

1977

2ND W 88-74 10GB

1 *(RET#)FRED HUTCHINSON*
2 RUSS NIXON-CH
3 GEORGE SCHERGER-CH
4 LARRY SHEPARD-CH
5 JOHNNY BENCH-C/UTIL
7 DON WERNER-C
8 JOE MORGAN-2B
9 BILL PLUMMER-C
10 SPARKY ANDERSON-MGR
11 BOB BAILEY-1B/OF (1)
13 DAVE CONCEPCION-SS
14 PETE (CHARLIE HUSTLE) ROSE-3B
15 GEORGE FOSTER-OF/1B
18 TED (BIG KLU) KLUSZEWSKI-CH
20 CESAR GERONIMO-OF
21 MIKE LUM-1B/OF
22 DAN DRIESSEN-1B
23 DOUG FLYNN-INF (1)
23 RICK AUERBACH-2B/SS
25 RAY KNIGHT-UTIL
27 MR. RED LOGO
28 CHAMP SUMMERS-OF/3B
30 KEN GRIFFEY-OF
30 MARIO SOTO-P
31 PAUL MOSKAU-P
32 FRED NORMAN-P
33 ED ARMBRISTER-OF
34 PEDRO BORBON-P
35 WOODIE FRYMAN (RET)-P
36 MARIO SOTO-P
36 ANGEL TORRES-P
37 DALE MURRAY-P
38 GARY NOLAN (JAP)-P (1)
40 PAT ZACHRY-P (1)
40 JOE HOERNER-P
41 TOM (TOM TERRIFIC) SEAVER-P (2)
42 SANTO ALCALA-P (1)
42 JOE HOERNER-P
43 JACK BILLINGHAM-P
44 MIKE CALDWELL-P (1)
44 DOUG CAPILLA-P (2)
45 MANNY SARMIENTO-P
46 ANGEL TORRES-P
47 TOM HUME-P
49 RAWLY EASTWICK-P (1)
50 DAN DUMOULIN,P
50 JOE HENDERSON-P
53 JOE HENDERSON-P
53 DAN DUMOULIN-P

1978

2ND W 92-69 2.5GB

- **1** *(RET#)FRED HUTCHINSON*
- **2** RUSS NIXON-CH
- **3** GEORGE SCHERGER-CH
- **4** LARRY SHEPARD-CH
- **5** JOHNNY BENCH (INJ)-C/UTIL
- **5** ALEX GRAMMAS-CH
- **7** DON WERNER-C
- **8** JOE MORGAN-2B
- **9** VIC CORRELL-C
- **10** SPARKY ANDERSON-MGR
- **11** RON PLAZA-CH
- **13** DAVE CONCEPCION-SS
- **14** PETE (CHARLIE HUSTLE) ROSE-3B/UTIL
- **15** GEORGE FOSTER-OF/1B
- **16** RON OESTER-SS
- **17** MIKE GRACE-3B
- **18** TED (BIG KLU) KLUSZEWSKI-CH
- **19** KEN HENDERSON-OF (2)
- **20** CESAR GERONIMO-OF
- **21** MIKE LUM-OF/1B
- **22** DAN DRIESSEN-1B
- **23** RICK AUERBACH- INF
- **25** RAY KNIGHT-UTIL
- **26** JUNIOR KENNEDY-2B/3B
- **27** MR. RED LOGO
- **28** CHAMP SUMMERS-OF/3B
- **29** DAVE COLLINS-OF
- **30** KEN GRIFFEY-OF
- **31** PAUL MOSKAU-P
- **32** FRED NORMAN-P
- **34** PEDRO BORBON-P
- **36** MARIO SOTO-P
- **37** DALE MURRAY-P (1)
- **37** DAVE TOMLIN-P
- **40** DOUG BAIR-P
- **41** TOM (TOM TERRIFIC) SEAVER-P
- **42** BILL BONHAM,-P
- **43** DAVE TOMLIN-P
- **44** DOUG CAPILLA-P
- **45** MANNY SARMIENTO-P
- **47** TOM HUME-P
- **50** DAN DUMOULIN,P
- **51** MIKE LACOSS-P
- **56** HARRY SPILMAN-PH
- **58** ARTURO DEFREITAS-1B

1979

1ST W 90-71 0GB
L NLCS-PITN 3-0

- **1** *(RET#)FRED HUTCHINSON*
- **2** RUSS NIXON-CH
- **3** JOHN MCNAMARA-MGR
- **4** HARRY DUNLOP-CH
- **5** JOHNNY BENCH-C/1B
- **6** BILL FISCHER-CH
- **7** HEITY CRUZ-OF
- **8** JOE MORGAN-2B
- **9** VIC CORRELL-C
- **11** RON PLAZA-CH
- **12** HARRY SPILMAN-1B/3B
- **13** DAVE CONCEPCION-SS
- **15** GEORGE FOSTER (INJ)-OF
- **16** RON OESTER-SS
- **19** KEN HENDERSON- (INJ)-OF (1)
- **20** CESAR GERONIMO-OF
- **21** ARTURO DEFREITAS-1B/OF
- **21** RAFAEL SANTO DOMINGO-PH
- **22** DAN DRIESSEN-1B
- **23** RICK AUERBACH- INF
- **25** RAY KNIGHT-3B
- **26** JUNIOR KENNEDY-INF
- **27** MR. RED LOGO
- **28** CHAMP SUMMERS-OF/1B (1)
- **28** SAMMY MEJIAS-OF (2)
- **29** DAVE COLLINS-OF/1B
- **30** KEN GRIFFEY (INJ)-OF
- **31** PAUL MOSKAU-P
- **32** FRED NORMAN-P
- **33** PAUL BLAIR-OF (2)
- **34** PEDRO BORBON-P (1)
- **35** FRANK PASTORE-P
- **36** MARIO SOTO (INJ)-P
- **37** DAVE TOMLIN-P
- **40** DOUG BAIR-P
- **41** TOM (TOM TERRIFIC) SEAVER-P
- **42** BILL BONHAM (INJ)-P
- **44** DOUG CAPILLA-P (1)
- **44** CHARLIE LEIBRANDT-P
- **45** MANNY SARMIENTO-P
- **47** TOM HUME-P
- **51** MIKE LACOSS-P
- **53** FRANK PASTORE-P

1980

3RD W 89-73 3.5GB

- **1** *(RET#)FRED HUTCHINSON*
- **2** RUSS NIXON-CH
- **3** JOHN MCNAMARA-MGR
- **4** HARRY DUNLOP-CH
- **5** JOHNNY BENCH-C
- **6** BILL FISCHER-CH
- **7** HEITY CRUZ-OF
- **9** VIC CORRELL (INJ)-C
- **11** RON PLAZA-CH
- **12** HARRY SPILMAN-UTIL
- **13** DAVE CONCEPCION-SS/2B
- **15** GEORGE FOSTER (INJ)-OF
- **16** RON OESTER-INF
- **17** JOE NOLAN-C (2)
- **19** DON WERNER-C
- **20** CESAR GERONIMO-OF
- **22** DAN DRIESSEN-1B
- **23** RICK AUERBACH- INF (1)
- **25** RAY KNIGHT-3B
- **26** JUNIOR KENNEDY-2B
- **27** MR. RED LOGO
- **28** SAMMY MEJIAS-OF
- **29** DAVE COLLINS-OF
- **30** KEN GRIFFEY-OF
- **31** PAUL MOSKAU-P
- **34** SHELDON BURNSIDE-P
- **35** FRANK PASTORE (INJ)-P
- **36** MARIO SOTO-P
- **37** DAVE TOMLIN-P
- **38** BRUCE BERENYI-P
- **40** DOUG BAIR-P
- **41** TOM (TOM TERRIFIC) SEAVER (INJ)-P
- **42** BILL BONHAM (INJ)-P
- **43** JAY HOWELL-P
- **44** CHARLIE LEIBRANDT-P
- **47** TOM HUME-P
- **48** GEOFF COMBE-P
- **49** JOE PRICE-P
- **51** MIKE LACOSS-P
- **56** PAUL HOUSEHOLDER-OF
- **57** EDDIE MILNER-PH

1981

1ST 1/2:2ND W 35-21 .5GB
2ND 1/2:2ND W 31-21 1.5GB
FINAL: 66-42 --GB

- **1** *(RET#)FRED HUTCHINSON*
- **2** RUSS NIXON-CH
- **3** JOHN MCNAMARA-MGR
- **4** HARRY DUNLOP-CH
- **5** JOHNNY BENCH (INJ)-1B/C
- **6** BILL FISCHER-CH
- **7** RAFAEL LANDESTOY-2B (2)
- **9** MIKE O'BERRY-C
- **11** RON PLAZA-CH
- **12** HARRY SPILMAN-UTIL (1)
- **12** GERMAN BARRANCA-PH
- **13** DAVE CONCEPCION-SS
- **15** GEORGE FOSTER-OF
- **16** RON OESTER-2B/SS
- **17** JOE NOLAN-C
- **19** NEIL FIALA-PH (2)
- **20** EDDIE MILNER-PH
- **21** PAUL HOUSEHOLDER-OF
- **22** DAN DRIESSEN-1B
- **23** MIKE VAIL-OF
- **25** RAY KNIGHT-3B
- **26** JUNIOR KENNEDY-2B/3B
- **27** MR. RED LOGO
- **28** SAMMY MEJIAS-OF
- **29** DAVE COLLINS-OF
- **30** KEN GRIFFEY-OF
- **31** PAUL MOSKAU-P
- **33** LARRY BIITTNER-1B/OF
- **35** FRANK PASTORE-P
- **36** MARIO SOTO-P
- **37** GEOFF COMBE-P
- **38** BRUCE BERENYI-P
- **40** DOUG BAIR-P (1)
- **40** JOE EDELEN-P (2)
- **41** TOM (TOM TERRIFIC) SEAVER-P
- **(42)** BILL BONHAM (INJ)-(P)
- **43** SCOTT BROWN-P
- **44** CHARLIE LEIBRANDT-P
- **47** TOM HUME-P
- **49** JOE PRICE-P
- **51** MIKE LACOSS-P
- **53** SCOTT BROWN-P

1982

6TH W 62-101 28GB

- **1** *(RET#)FRED HUTCHINSON*
- **2** RUSS NIXON-CH/MGR2
- **3** JOHN MCNAMARA-MGR1
- **3** GEORGE SCHERGER-CH
- **4** HARRY DUNLOP-CH
- **5** JOHNNY BENCH (INJ)-3B/UTIL
- **6** BILL FISCHER-CH
- **7** RAFAEL LANDESTOY-UTIL
- **8** JOE AMALFITANO-CH
- **9** MIKE O'BERRY-C
- **11** RON PLAZA-CH
- **12** GERMAN BARRANCA-PH
- **13** DAVE CONCEPCION-SS/INF
- **16** RON OESTER-2B/INF
- **17** TOM LAWLESS-2B
- **19** WAYNE KRENCHICKI-3B/2B
- **20** EDDIE MILNER (INJ)-OF
- **21** PAUL HOUSEHOLDER-OF
- **22** DAN DRIESSEN-1B
- **23** MIKE VAIL-OF
- **24** DAVE VAN GORDER-C
- **26** DUANE WALKER-OF
- **27** MR. RED LOGO
- **28** CESAR CEDENO-OF/1B
- **29** ALEX TREVINO-C/3B
- **30** CLINT HURDLE-OF
- **32** BOB SHIRLEY-P
- **33** LARRY BIITTNER-OF/1B
- **34** JIM KERN-P (1)
- **34** BILL SCHERRER-P
- **35** FRANK PASTORE-P
- **36** MARIO SOTO-P
- **37** GREG HARRIS-P
- **38** BRUCE BERENYI-P
- **40** JOE EDELEN-P
- **41** TOM (TOM TERRIFIC) SEAVER (INJ)-P
- **44** CHARLIE LEIBRANDT-P
- **45** BEN HAYES-P
- **47** TOM HUME (INJ)-P
- **49** JOE PRICE-P
- **50** BEN HAYES-P
- **50** BRAD LESLEY-P

1983

6TH W 74-88 17GB

- **1** *(RET#)FRED HUTCHINSON*
- **2** GARY REDUS-OF
- **3** GEORGE SCHERGER-CH
- **4** STEVE CHRISTMAS-C
- **4** ALAN KNICELY-C/UTIL
- **5** JOHNNY BENCH (INJ)-UTIL
- **6** BILL FISCHER-CH
- **7** RUSS NIXON-MGR
- **8** RAFAEL LANDESTOY-UTIL (1)
- **8** STEVE CHRISTMAS-C
- **9** DANN BILARDELLO-C
- **10** TOM FOLEY-SS/2B
- **11** RON PLAZA-CH
- **11** ALAN KNICELY-C/UTIL
- **12** WAYNE KRENCHICKI-3B/2B (1)
- **12** NICK ESASKY-3B
- **13** DAVE CONCEPCION-SS/INF
- **15** NICK ESASKY-3B
- **15** WAYNE KRENCHICKI-3B/2B (1)
- **15** SKEETER BARNES-1B/3B
- **16** RON OESTER-2B
- **17** KELLY PARIS-INF
- **19** TOMMY HELMS-CH
- **20** EDDIE MILNER-OF
- **21** PAUL HOUSEHOLDER-OF
- **22** DAN DRIESSEN (INJ)-1B
- **23** JEFF JONES-OF/1B
- **24** DAVE VAN GORDER-C
- **25** CHARLIE PULEO (INJ)-P
- **26** DUANE WALKER-OF
- **27** MR. RED LOGO
- **28** CESAR CEDENO-OF/1B
- **29** ALEX TREVINO-C/3B
- **30** DALLAS WILLIAMS-OF
- **32** RICH GALE-P
- **33** GREG HARRIS-P
- **34** BILL SCHERRER-P
- **35** FRANK PASTORE-P
- **36** MARIO SOTO-P
- **37** GREG HARRIS-P
- **38** BRUCE BERENYI-P
- **42** KEEFE CATO-P
- **45** BEN HAYES-P
- **46** JEFF RUSSELL-P
- **47** TOM HUME (INJ)-P
- **48** TED POWER-P
- **49** JOE PRICE (INJ)-P
- **50** BRAD LESLEY-P

1984

5TH W 70-92 22GB

- **1** *(RET#)FRED HUTCHINSON*
- **2** GARY REDUS-OF
- **3** GEORGE SCHERGER-CH
- **4** BRAD GULDEN-C
- **6** BRUCE KIMM-CH
- **7** PAUL HOUSEHOLDER-OF (1)
- **8** JOE SPARKS-CH
- **9** VERN RAPP-MGR1
- **10** TOM FOLEY-INF
- **11** DANN BILARDELLO-C
- **12** NICK ESASKY-3B/1B
- **13** DAVE CONCEPCION-SS/INF
- **14** PETE (CHARLIE HUSTLE) ROSE-1B/MGR2 (2)
- **15** WAYNE KRENCHICKI-INF
- **16** RON OESTER-2B/SS
- **17** TOM LAWLESS-2B/3B (1)
- **19** TOMMY HELMS-CH
- **20** EDDIE MILNER (ILL)-OF
- **21** SKEETER BARNES-3B/OF
- **22** DAN DRIESSEN-1B (1)
- **23** DAVE VAN GORDER-C/1B
- **24** TONY PEREZ-1B
- **25** CHARLIE PULEO-P
- **26** DUANE WALKER (INJ)-OF
- **27** MR. RED LOGO
- **28** CESAR CEDENO-OF/1B
- **29** ALEX TREVINO-C (1)
- **31** JOHN FRANCO-P
- **32** BOB OWCHINKO-P
- **33** RON ROBINSON-P
- **34** BILL SCHERRER-P (1)
- **34** ALAN KNICELY-1B/C
- **35** FRANK PASTORE-P
- **36** MARIO SOTO-P
- **37** MIKE SMITH-P
- **37** ANDY MCGAFFIGAN-P (2)
- **38** BRUCE BERENYI-P (1)
- **38** JAY TIBBS-P
- **39** DAVE PARKER-OF
- **40** STAN WILLIAMS-CH
- **40** CARL WILLIS-P (2)
- **42** KEEFE CATO-P
- **44** ERIC DAVIS-OF
- **(45)** BEN HAYES (INJ)-(P)
- **45** JIM (KITTY) KAAT-CH
- **46** JEFF RUSSELL-P
- **47** TOM HUME-P
- **48** TED POWER-P
- **49** JOE PRICE-P
- **50** BRAD LESLEY-P
- **53** MIKE SMITH-P
- **54** TOM BROWNING-P
- **56** WADE ROWDON-SS/3B
- **58** RON ROBINSON-P
- **59** FRED TOLIVER-P

1985

2ND W 89-72 5.5GB

- **1** *(RET#)FRED HUTCHINSON*
- **2** GARY REDUS-OF
- **3** GEORGE SCHERGER-CH
- **6** BRUCE KIMM-CH
- **7** BILLY (KID) DEMARS-CH
- **8** BO DIAZ-C (2)
- **9** MAX VENABLE-OF
- **10** TOM FOLEY-INF (1)
- **10** TOM RUNNELS-SS/2B
- **11** DANN BILARDELLO-C
- **12** NICK ESASKY-UTIL
- **13** DAVE CONCEPCION-SS/3B
- **14** PETE (CHARLIE HUSTLE) ROSE-1B/MGR
- **15** WAYNE KRENCHICKI-3B/2B
- **16** RON OESTER-2B
- **17** WADE ROWDON-3B
- **19** TOMMY HELMS-CH
- **20** EDDIE MILNER-OF
- **21** PAUL O'NEILL-OF
- **23** DAVE VAN GORDER-C
- **24** TONY PEREZ-1B
- **25** BUDDY BELL-3B (2)
- **26** DUANE WALKER-OF (1)
- **27** MR. RED LOGO
- **28** CESAR CEDENO-OF/1B (1)
- **31** JOHN FRANCO-P
- **32** TOM BROWNING-P
- **33** RON ROBINSON-P
- **34** ALAN KNICELY-C (1)
- **34** MIKE SMITH-P
- **35** FRANK PASTORE (INJ)-P
- **36** MARIO SOTO-P
- **37** ANDY MCGAFFIGAN-P
- **38** JAY TIBBS-P
- **39** DAVE PARKER-OF
- **40** CARL WILLIS-P
- **42** JOHN STUPER-P
- **44** ERIC DAVIS-OF
- **45** JIM (KITTY) KAAT-CH
- **46** ROB MURPHY-P
- **47** TOM HUME-P
- **48** TED POWER-P
- **49** JOE PRICE (INJ)-P
- **51** BOB BUCHANAN (INJ)-P
- **53** MIKE SMITH-P

CINCINNATI REDS

54 ROB MURPHY-P
56 WADE ROWDON-3B

1986

2ND W 86-76 10GB

1 *(RET#)FRED HUTCHINSON*
2 SCOTT BREEDEN-CH
3 GEORGE SCHERGER-CH
4 BRUCE KIMM-CH
6 BO DIAZ-C
7 BILLY (KID) DEMARS-CH
9 MAX VENABLE-OF
10 TOM RUNNELS-2B/3B
11 KURT STILLWELL-SS
12 NICK ESASKY (INJ)-1B/UTIL
13 DAVE CONCEPCION (INJ)-INF
14 PETE (CHARLIE HUSTLE) ROSE-1B/MGR
15 BARRY LARKIN-SS/2B
16 RON OESTER-2B
17 WADE ROWDON-UTIL
19 TOMMY HELMS-CH
20 EDDIE MILNER-OF
21 PAUL O'NEILL-PH
22 SAL BUTERA-C/P
23 DAVE VAN GORDER (INJ)-C
24 TONY PEREZ-1B
25 BUDDY BELL-3B/2B
27 MR. RED LOGO
28 KAL DANIELS-OF
29 TRACY JONES (INJ)-OF/1B
31 JOHN FRANCO-P
32 TOM BROWNING-P
33 RON ROBINSON-P
34 BILL GULLICKSON-P
36 MARIO SOTO (INJ)-P
37 MIKE SMITH-P
38 SCOTT TERRY-P
39 DAVE PARKER-OF
40 CARL WILLIS-P
40 JOHN DENNY-P
42 CARL WILLIS-P
43 BILL LANDRUM-P
44 ERIC DAVIS-OF
45 CHRIS WELSH-P
46 ROB MURPHY-P
48 TED POWER-P
49 JOE PRICE (INJ)-P
59 SCOTT TERRY-P
79 JOE LETT-CH

1987

2ND W 84-78 6GB

1 *(RET#)FRED HUTCHINSON*
2 SCOTT BREEDEN-CH
3 JOE LETT-CH
4 BRUCE KIMM-CH
6 BO DIAZ-C
7 BILLY (KID) DEMARS-CH
8 TERRY MCGRIFF-C
9 MAX VENABLE-OF
10 TERRY FRANCONA-1B/OF
11 KURT STILLWELL-INF
12 NICK ESASKY (INJ)-1B/UTIL
13 DAVE CONCEPCION-INF
14 PETE (CHARLIE HUSTLE) ROSE-MGR
15 BARRY LARKIN-SS
16 RON OESTER (INJ)-2B
19 TOMMY HELMS-CH
21 PAUL O'NEILL-OF/1B/P
22 SAL BUTERA-C (1)
22 DAVE COLLINS-OF
23 LLOYD MCCLENDON-UTIL
24 TONY PEREZ-CH
25 BUDDY BELL-3B
26 LEO GARCIA-OF
27 MR. RED LOGO
28 KAL DANIELS-OF
29 TRACY JONES-OF
30 GUY HOFFMAN-P
31 JOHN FRANCO-P
32 TOM BROWNING-P
33 RON ROBINSON-P
34 BILL GULLICKSON-P (1)
35 PAT PACILLO-P
36 MARIO SOTO (INJ)-P
37 BILL SCHERRER-P
38 PAT PERRY-P (2)
39 DAVE PARKER-OF/1B
40 JEFF MONTGOMERY-P
41 JERRY REUSS-P (2)
41 TOM HUME-P (2)
43 BILL LANDRUM-P
44 ERIC DAVIS-OF
45 DENNIS RASMUSSEN-P (2)
46 ROB MURPHY-P
47 FRANK WILLIAMS-P
48 TED POWER-P
50 GUY HOFFMAN-P
58 JEFF TREADWAY-2B

1988

2ND W 87-74 7GB

1 *(RET#)FRED HUTCHINSON*
2 SCOTT BREEDEN-CH
3 JOE LETT-CH
4 BRUCE KIMM-CH
4 DAVE BRISTOL-CH
6 BO DIAZ (INJ)-C
7 LENNY HARRIS-3B/2B
8 TERRY MCGRIFF-C
9 EDDIE MILNER (SUB)-OF
9 LUIS QUINONES-INF
10 LEON (BULL) DURHAM (SUB)-1B (2)
11 BARRY LARKIN-SS
12 NICK ESASKY-1B
13 DAVE CONCEPCION-INF/P
14 PETE (CHARLIE HUSTLE) ROSE-MGR
15 JEFF TREADWAY (INJ)-2B
16 RON OESTER (INJ)-2B/SS
17 CHRIS SABO-3B/SS
19 TOMMY HELMS-CH
20 DANNY JACKSON-P
21 PAUL O'NEILL-OF/1B
22 DAVE COLLINS-OF/1B
23 LEE MAY-CH
24 TONY PEREZ-CH
25 BUDDY BELL (INJ)3B/1B (1)
25 KEN GRIFFEY, SR.-1B (2)
26 LEO GARCIA-OF
26 VAN SNIDER-OF
27 JOSE RIJO-P
28 KAL DANIELS-OF
29 TRACY JONES-OF (1)
29 HERM WINNINGHAM-OF (2)
30 GUY HOFFMAN-P
30 LLOYD MCCLENDON-UTIL
30 KEN GRIFFEY, SR.-1B (2)
31 JOHN FRANCO-P
32 TOM BROWNING-P
33 RON ROBINSON (INJ)-P
34 JEFF REED-C (2)
35 PAT PACILLO-P
35 RANDY ST. CLAIRE-P (2)
36 MARIO SOTO-P (1)
37 NORM (GENIOUS) CHARLTON-P
38 PAT PERRY-P (1)
38 KEITH BROWN-P
39 RON ROENICKE-OF
40 JACK ARMSTRONG-P
42 TIM BIRTSAS-P
43 BILL LANDRUM-P
43 JEFF GRAY-P
44 ERIC DAVIS-OF
45 DENNIS RASMUSSEN-P (1)
45 CANDY SIERRA-P (2)
46 ROB MURPHY-P
47 NORM (GENIOUS) CHARLTON-P
47 FRANK WILLIAMS-P
48 TED POWER-P
48 TIM BIRTSAS-P
49 ROB DIBBLE-P
51 MARTY BROWN-3B
51 RANDY ST. CLAIRE-P (2)
56 LENNY HARRIS-3B/2B
57 VAN SNIDER-OF

1989

5TH W 75-87 17GB

1 *(RET#)FRED HUTCHINSON*
2 SCOTT BREEDEN-CH
3 JOE LETT-CH
4 DAVE BRISTOL-CH
6 BO DIAZ (INJ)-C
7 LENNY HARRIS-3B/2B (1)
7 MARIANO DUNCAN-UTIL (2)
8 TERRY MCGRIFF-C
9 LUIS QUINONES-INF
9 JOE OLIVER-C
10 MANNY TRILLO-INF
10 LUIS QUINONES-INF
11 BARRY LARKIN (INJ)-SS
12 JOEL YOUNGBLOOD-OF
14 PETE (CHARLIE HUSTLE) ROSE-MGR1
15 SKEETER BARNES-PH
15 JEFF RICHARDSON-SS/3B
16 RON OESTER (INJ)-2B/SS
17 CHRIS SABO (INJ)-3B
19 TOMMY HELMS-CH/MGR2
20 DANNY JACKSON (INJ)-P
21 PAUL O'NEILL (INJ)-OF
22 DAVE COLLINS-OF
23 LEE MAY-CH
24 TONY PEREZ-CH
25 TODD BENZINGER-1B
26 VAN SNIDER-OF
27 JOSE RIJO (INJ)-P
28 KAL DANIELS (INJ)-OF (1)
28 SCOTT MADISON-3B
29 HERM WINNINGHAM-OF
30 KEN GRIFFEY, SR.-OF/1B
31 JOHN FRANCO-P
32 TOM BROWNING-P
33 RON ROBINSON (INJ)-P
34 JEFF REED-C
35 MIKE GRIFFIN-P
36 ROLANDO ROOMES-OF
37 NORM (GENIOUS) CHARLTON-P
(39) JEFF SELLERS (INJ)-(P)
40 JACK ARMSTRONG-P
42 RICK MAHLER-P
43 KENT TEKULVE-P
44 ERIC DAVIS-OF
45 BOB SEBRA-P (2)
47 SCOTT SCUDDER-P
48 TIM BIRTSAS-P
49 ROB DIBBLE-P
51 MARTY BROWN-3B
54 TIM LEARY-P (2)
55 MIKE ROESLER-P
56 SCOTT SCUDDER-P
56 ROSARIO RODRIGUEZ-P

1990

1ST W 91-71 0GB
W NLCS-PITN 4-2
W WS-OAKA 4-0

1 *(RET#)FRED HUTCHINSON*
2 SAM PERLOZZO-CH
3 LARRY ROTHSCHILD-CH
4 JACKIE MOORE-CH
7 MARIANO DUNCAN-UTIL
8 TERRY MCGRIFF-C (1)
8 ALEX TREVINO-C (3)
9 JOE OLIVER-C
9 TERRY MCGRIFF-C (1)
10 LUIS QUINONES-INF
11 BARRY LARKIN-SS
12 BILLY BATES-2B (2)
12 PAUL NOCE-PH
15 GLENN BRAGGS-OF (2)
16 RON OESTER-2B/3B
17 CHRIS SABO-3B
19 BILL DORAN-2B/3B (2)
20 DANNY JACKSON (INJ)-P
21 PAUL O'NEILL-OF
22 BILLY HATCHER-OF
23 HAL MORRIS-1B/OF
24 TONY PEREZ-CH
25 TODD BENZINGER-1B/OF
26 TERRY LEE-1B
27 JOSE RIJO-P
28 RANDY MYERS-P
29 HERM WINNINGHAM-OF
30 KEN GRIFFEY, SR.-1B/OF (1)
32 TOM BROWNING-P
33 RON ROBINSON-P (1)
33 GINO MINUTELLI-P
34 JEFF REED-C
35 STAN WILLIAMS-CH
36 ROLANDO ROOMES-OF (1)
37 NORM (GENIOUS) CHARLTON-P
38 KEITH BROWN-P
40 JACK ARMSTRONG-P
41 LOU (SWEET LOU) PINIELLA-MGR
42 RICK MAHLER-P
43 TIM LAYANA-P
44 ERIC DAVIS-OF
45 CHRIS HAMMOND-P
47 SCOTT SCUDDER-P
48 TIM BIRTSAS-P
49 ROB DIBBLE-P
52 CHRIS HAMMOND-P
55 GLENN SUTKO-C
56 ROSARIO RODRIGUEZ-P
59 KIP GROSS-P

1991

5TH W 74-88 20GB

1 *(RET#)FRED HUTCHINSON*
2 SAM PERLOZZO-CH
3 LARRY ROTHSCHILD-CH
4 JACKIE MOORE-CH
6 DONNIE SCOTT-C
7 MARIANO DUNCAN-UTIL
9 JOE OLIVER-C
10 LUIS QUINONES-INF
11 BARRY LARKIN-SS
15 GLENN BRAGGS (INJ)-OF
17 CHRIS SABO-3B
19 BILL DORAN-2B/UTIL
20 CHRIS JONES-OF
21 PAUL O'NEILL-OF
22 BILLY HATCHER-OF
23 HAL MORRIS-1B/OF
24 TONY PEREZ-CH
25 TODD BENZINGER-1B/OF (1)
25 CARMELO MARTINEZ-1B/OF (3)
26 TERRY LEE-1B
27 JOSE RIJO (INJ)-P
28 RANDY MYERS-P
29 HERM WINNINGHAM-OF
32 TOM BROWNING-P
33 GINO MINUTELLI-P
34 JEFF REED-C
35 STAN WILLIAMS-CH
36 DON CARMAN-P
36 KIP GROSS-P
37 NORM (GENIOUS) CHARLTON (INJ)-P
38 KEITH BROWN-P
39 MILT HILL-P
40 JACK ARMSTRONG-P
41 LOU (SWEET LOU) PINIELLA-MGR
42 REGGIE JEFFERSON-1B (1)
42 STAN JEFFERSON-OF
43 TIM LAYANA-P
44 ERIC DAVIS (ILL)-OF
45 CHRIS HAMMOND (INJ)-P
47 SCOTT SCUDDER (INJ)-P
48 TED POWER-P
49 ROB DIBBLE-P
52 MO SANFORD-P
53 REGGIE SANDERS (INJ)-OF
54 STEVE FOSTER-P
55 GLENN SUTKO-C
57 FREDDIE BENAVIDES-SS/2B
59 KIP GROSS-P

1992

2ND W 90-72 8GB

1 *(RET#)FRED HUTCHINSON*
2 SAM PERLOZZO-CH
3 LARRY ROTHSCHILD-CH
4 JACKIE MOORE-CH
6 DAN WILSON-C
7 RICK WRONA-C/1B
8 JOHN MCLAREN-CH
9 JOE OLIVER-C/1B
10 BIP ROBERTS (INJ)-UTIL
11 BARRY LARKIN (INJ)-SS
12 FREDDIE BENAVIDES-INF
15 GLENN BRAGGS-OF
16 REGGIE SANDERS (INJ)-OF
17 CHRIS SABO (INJ)-3B
19 BILL DORAN-2B/1B
20 JEFF BRANSON-INF
21 PAUL O'NEILL-OF
22 BILLY HATCHER-OF (1)
23 HAL MORRIS (INJ)-1B
24 TONY PEREZ-CH
25 SCOTT BANKHEAD-P
26 DARNELL COLES-UTIL
27 JOSE RIJO-P
28 SCOTT RUSKIN-P
29 GREG SWINDELL-P
30 DAVE MARTINEZ-OF/1B
31 TIM BELCHER-P
32 TOM BROWNING (INJ)-P
34 JEFF REED-C
35 GERONIMO BERROA-OF
37 NORM (GENIOUS) CHARLTON (INJ)-P
38 TROY AFENIR-C
39 MILT HILL-P
40 GARY GREEN-SS/3B
41 LOU (SWEET LOU) PINIELLA-MGR
45 CHRIS HAMMOND (INJ)-P
46 JACOB BRUMFIELD-OF
47 SCOTT BRADLEY-C (2)
48 DWAYNE HENRY-P
49 ROB DIBBLE-P
50 SCOTT BANKHEAD-P
50 TOM BOLTON-P (2)
52 TONY MENENDEZ-P
54 STEVE FOSTER-P
55 TIM PUGH-P
56 WILLIE GREENE-3B
57 TIM COSTO-1B
58 CESAR HERNANDEZ-OF
59 KEITH BROWN-P
59 BOBBY AYALA-P

1993

5TH W 73-89 31GB

00 JOSE CARDENAL-CH
1 *(RET#)FRED HUTCHINSON*
2 DAVE MILEY-CH
3 RON OESTER-CH
3 BOBBY VALENTINE-CH

4 DAVE BRISTOL-CH
4 RAY KNIGHT-CH
5 *(RET#)JOHNNY BENCH*
6 DAN WILSON-C
7 KEVIN MITCHELL (INJ)-OF
8 JUAN (SAMMY) SAMUEL-INF/OF
9 JOE OLIVER-C/UTIL
10 BIP ROBERTS (INJ)-UTIL
11 BARRY LARKIN (INJ)-SS
12 WILLIE GREENE (INJ)-SS/3B
15 DAVEY JOHNSON-MGR2
16 REGGIE SANDERS-OF
17 CHRIS SABO-3B
18 TIM COSTO-UTIL
19 RANDY MILLIGAN-1B/OF (1)
20 JEFF BRANSON-INF
21 JACK DAUGHERTY-OF/1B (2)
22 CECIL ESPY-OF
22 THOMAS HOWARD-OF (2)
23 HAL MORRIS (INJ)-1B
24 TONY PEREZ-MGR1
25 GREG CADARET-P (1)
26 TOMMY GREGG-OF (2)
27 JOSE RIJO-P
28 SCOTT RUSKIN-P
30 ROBERTO (BOBBY) KELLY (INJ)-OF
31 TIM BELCHER-P (1)
32 TOM BROWNING (INJ)-P
33 BRIAN DORSETT-C/1B
34 SCOTT SERVICE-P (2)
35 DON GULLETT-CH
39 MILT HILL-P
40 TIM PUGH-P
41 JEFF REARDON-P
42 GARY VARSHO-OF
43 BILL LANDRUM (INJ)-P
44 JOHN ROPER-P
45 KEVIN WICKANDER-P (2)
45 KEITH HUGHES-OF
46 JACOB BRUMFIELD-OF/2B
48 DWAYNE HENRY-P (1)
48 JERRY SPRADLIN-P
49 ROB DIBBLE (INJ)-P
50 KEITH GORDON-OF
51 GREG TUBBS-OF
52 LARRY LUEBBERS-P
53 KEVIN WICKANDER-P (2)
54 STEVE FOSTER (INJ)-P
55 TIM PUGH-P
55 ROSS POWELL-P
56 JEFF KAISER-P (1)
56 MIKE ANDERSON-P
57 JOHN SMILEY (INJ)-P
58 CESAR HERNANDEZ-OF
58 JOHNNY RUFFIN-P
59 BOBBY AYALA-P
60 BRIAN KOELLING-2B/SS
61 CHRIS BUSHING-P
62 KEITH KESSINGER-SS

1994

1ST C 66-48 0GB
STRIKE NO POST-SEASON

1 *(RET#)FRED HUTCHINSON*
2 JOEL YOUNGBLOOD-CH
3 GRANT (BUCK) JACKSON-CH
4 JACOB BRUMFIELD-OF
5 *(RET#)JOHNNY BENCH*
(6) RON GANT (INJ)-(OF)
7 KEVIN MITCHELL-OF
8 BOB BOONE-CH
9 JOE OLIVER (INJ)-C
10 EDDIE TAUBENSEE-C (2)
11 BARRY LARKIN-SS
12 WILLIE GREENE-3B
12 DEION SANDERS-OF (2)
16 REGGIE SANDERS-OF
18 DAVEY JOHNSON-MGR
19 JEROME WALTON (INJ)-PH
20 JEFF BRANSON-INF
21 TONY FERNANDEZ-3B
22 THOMAS HOWARD-OF
23 HAL MORRIS (INJ)-1B
25 RAY KNIGHT-CH
26 STEVE PEGUES-OF (1)
27 JOSE RIJO-P
28 LENNY HARRIS-INF
29 BRET BOONE-2B
30 ROBERTO (BOBBY) KELLY-OF (1)
30 BRIAN R. HUNTER-1B
31 CHUCK MCELROY-P
32 TOM BROWNING (INJ)-P
33 BRIAN DORSETT-C
34 SCOTT SERVICE-P
35 DON GULLETT-CH
39 ERIK HANSON (INJ)-P
40 TIM PUGH-P
41 JOHN ROPER-P
42 KEVIN JARVIS-P
44 JOHN ROPER-P
45 JEFF BRANTLEY-P
46 PETE SCHOUREK-P
47 JOHNNY RUFFIN-P
48 JERRY SPRADLIN (WAIV)-P (1)
(49) ROB DIBBLE (INJ)-(P)
53 RICH DELUCIA-P
(54) STEVE FOSTER (INJ)-(P)
55 TIM FORTUGNO-P
56 HECTOR CARRASCO (INJ)-P
57 JOHN SMILEY-P
58 HECTOR CARRASCO (INJ)-P

1995

1ST C 85-59 0GB
W NLDS-LAN 3-0
L NLCS-ATLN 4-0
144 GAME SEASON

1 *(RET#)FRED HUTCHINSON*
2 JOEL YOUNGBLOOD-CH
3 GRANT (BUCK) JACKSON-CH
4 HAL MCRAE-CH
5 *(RET#)JOHNNY BENCH*
6 RON GANT-OF
7 DARREN LEWIS-OF (2)
8 DAMON BERRYHILL-C
9 ERIC ANTHONY-OF
10 EDDIE TAUBENSEE-C
11 BARRY LARKIN-SS
12 WILLIE GREENE-3B
15 DAVEY JOHNSON-MGR
16 REGGIE SANDERS-OF
17 MARK LEWIS-3B
18 BENITO SANTIAGO (INJ)-C
19 JEROME WALTON-OF
20 JEFF BRANSON-1B
21 DEION (NEON DEION) SANDERS-OF (1)
21 MARK PORTUGAL-P (2)
22 THOMAS HOWARD-OF
23 HAL MORRIS-1B
25 RAY KNIGHT-CH
26 JOHNNY RUFFIN-P
27 JOSE RIJO (INJ)-P
28 LENNY HARRIS-1B
29 BRET BOONE-2B
30 BRIAN R. HUNTER-OF
31 CHUCK MCELROY-P
32 KEVIN JARVIS-P
34 PETE SMITH-P
34 DAVE BURBA-P (2)
35 DON GULLETT-CH
36 DAVID (BOOMER) WELLS-P (2)
37 XAVIER HERNANDEZ-P
38 MIKE REMLINGER-P (2)
39 CRAIG WORTHINGTON-3B
40 TIM PUGH-P
41 BRAD PENNINGTON-P (2)
42 KEVIN JARVIS-P
42 MIKE JACKSON-P
44 JOHN ROPER-P (1)
44 FRANK VIOLA-P
45 JEFF BRANTLEY-P
46 PETE SCHOUREK-P
47 SCOTT SULLIVAN-P
48 RICK REED-P
49 C. J. NITKOWSKI-P
49 NIGEL WILSON-OF
51 ERIC OWENS-3B
53 RICH DELUCIA-P
(57) STEVE FOSTER (INJ)-(P)
55 TIM FORTUGNO-P
57 JOHN SMILEY-P
58 HECTOR CARRASCO (INJ)-P
61 STEVE GIBRALTER-OF
62 JOHN COURTRIGHT-P
65 MATT GROTT-P
77 MARIANO DUNCAN-UTIL (2)

1996

3RD C 81-81 7GB

00 CURTIS GOODWIN-OF
1 *(RET#)FRED HUTCHINSON*
2 JOEL YOUNGBLOOD-CH
4 HAL MCRAE-CH
5 *(RET#)JOHNNY BENCH*
7 CURTIS GOODWIN-OF
7 KEVIN MITCHELL (SUS)-OF (2)
9 JOE OLIVER-C
10 EDDIE TAUBENSEE-C
11 BARRY LARKIN-SS
12 WILLIE GREENE (INJ)-3B
15 MIKE KELLY-OF
16 REGGIE SANDERS (INJ)-OF
17 CHRIS SABO (SUS)(INJ)-3B
18 ERIC OWENS-3B
19 ERIC ANTHONY (INJ)-OF (1)
20 JEFF BRANSON-1B
21 MARK PORTUGAL (INJ)-P
22 THOMAS HOWARD (INJ)-OF
23 HAL MORRIS (INJ)-1B
25 RAY KNIGHT-MGR
26 JOHNNY RUFFIN-P
(27) JOSE RIJO (INJ)-(P)
28 LENNY HARRIS-2B
29 BRET BOONE (INJ)-2B
30 VINCE (VINCENT VAN GO) COLEMAN (WAIV)-OF
30 EDUARDO PEREZ-1B
31 CHUCK MCELROY (INJ)-P (1)
31 LEE SMITH-P (2)
31 MIKE MORGAN-P (2)
32 KEVIN JARVIS-P
33 STEVE GIBRALTER-OF
34 DAVE BURBA-P
35 DON GULLETT-CH
36 SCOTT SERVICE-P
37 XAVIER HERNANDEZ-P (1)
37 DEREK LILLIQUIST (REL)-P
39 TIM BELK-1B
39 PEDRO A. MARTINEZ-P (2)
40 TIM PUGH (WAIV)-P (1)
40 GIOVANNI CARRARA-P (2)
40 TIM PUGH (WAIV)-P (3)
41 JEFF SHAW-P
42 ROGER SALKELD-P
43 MIKE REMLINGER-P
44 ERIC DAVIS (INJ)-OF
45 JEFF BRANTLEY (INJ)-P
46 PETE SCHOUREK (INJ)-P
47 TOM HUME-CH
47 LEE SMITH-P (2)
48 JERRY SPRADLIN-P
49 TOM HUME-CH
50 MARC BOMBARD-CH
51 BROOK FORDYCE-C
52 KEITH MITCHELL-OF
53 MARCUS MOORE-P
53 TIM PUGH (WAIV)-P (1) (3)
(54) STEVE FOSTER (INJ)-(P)
54 CHAD MOTTOLA-OF
55 JIM LETT-CH
56 SCOTT SULLIVAN-P
57 JOHN SMILEY-P
58 HECTOR CARRASCO-P
59 CURT LYONS-P

1997

3RD C 76-86 8GB

0 RON (O) OESTER-CH
00 CURTIS GOODWIN-OF
1 *(RET#)FRED HUTCHINSON*
2 JOEL YOUNGBLOOD-CH
3 POKEY REESE-SS/3B
4 DAMIAN JACKSON-SS/2B (2)
5 *(RET#)JOHNNY BENCH*
6 BROOK FORDYCE-C
7 JOE OLIVER-C
9 TERRY PENDLETON (INJ) (REL)-3B
10 EDDIE TAUBENSEE-C
11 BARRY LARKIN (INJ)-SS
12 WILLIE GREENE-3B
14 PETE ROSE, JR.-3B
15 MIKE KELLY-OF
16 REGGIE SANDERS (INJ)-OF
17 AARON BOONE-3B
18 ERIC OWENS-3B
19 DENIS MENKE-CH
20 JEFF BRANSON-SS (1)
20 CHRIS STYNES-2B (2)
21 DEION (NEON DEION) SANDERS-OF
22 RUBEN SIERRA-OF (1)
22 JON NUNNALLY-OF (2)
23 HAL MORRIS (INJ)-1B
25 RAY KNIGHT-MGR1
(27) JOSE RIJO (INJ)-(P)
28 LENNY HARRIS-OF
29 BRET BOONE (INJ)-2B
30 KEN GRIFFEY, SR.-CH
31 OZZIE TIMMONS-OF
31 JACK MCKEON-MGR2
32 KEVIN JARVIS (INJ)-P (1)
32 DANNY GRAVES-P (2)
(33) STEVE GIBRALTER (INJ)-(OF)
34 DAVE BURBA (INJ)-P
35 DON GULLETT-CH
36 MIKE MORGAN (INJ)-P
37 STAN BELINDA-P
38 KENT MERCKER (INJ)-P
39 EDUARDO PEREZ-1B/OF/3B
40 RICKY BONES-P (1)
40 BRETT TOMKO-P
41 JEFF SHAW-P
42 *(RET#)JACKIE ROBINSON*
43 MIKE REMLINGER-P
44 PAT WATKINS-3B/OF
45 JEFF BRANTLEY (INJ)-P
46 PETE SCHOUREK (INJ)-P
47 TOM HUME-CH
48 GABE WHITE-P
49 JOEY EISCHEN (INJ)-P
50 SCOTT SERVICE-P (1)
50 JAMES CROWELL-P
51 JEFF TABAKA-P
52 SCOTT WINCHESTER-P
53 PEDRO A. MARTINEZ-P
56 SCOTT SULLIVAN-P
57 JOHN SMILEY (INJ)-P (1)
58 HECTOR CARRASCO-P (1)
58 RICHIE LEWIS-P (2)
61 GIOVANNI CARRARA-P
67 FELIX RODRIGUEZ-P

1998

4TH C 77-85 25GB

0 RON (O) OESTER-CH
0 STEVE LARKIN-1B
1 *(RET#)FRED HUTCHINSON*
2 HARRY DUNLOP-CH
3 POKEY REESE (INJ)-SS/3B
4 DAMIAN JACKSON-SS/2B
4 JEFFREY HAMMONDS-OF (2)
5 *(RET#)JOHNNY BENCH*
6 BROOK FORDYCE (INJ)-C
7 RON (O) OESTER-CH
8 *(RET#)JOE MORGAN*
9 PAT WATKINS-OF
10 EDDIE TAUBENSEE-C
11 BARRY LARKIN (INJ)-SS
12 WILLIE GREENE-3B (1)
12 DAMIAN JACKSON-SS/2B
15 JACK MCKEON-MGR
16 REGGIE SANDERS-OF
17 AARON BOONE-3B
18 *(RET#)TED KLUSZEWSKI*
19 DENIS MENKE-CH
20 *(RET#)FRANK ROBINSON*
21 SEAN CASEY (INJ)-1B
22 JON NUNNALLY-OF
23 CHRIS STYNES-3B/1B
25 DMITRI YOUNG-1B/OF
26 STEVE COOKE (INJ)-P
(27) JOSE RIJO (INJ)-(P)
28 LENNY HARRIS-OF (1)
28 PAUL KONERKO-1B/OF
29 BRET BOONE-2B
30 KEN GRIFFEY, SR.-CH
31 SCOTT SULLIVAN-P
32 DANNY GRAVES-P
33 MARC KROON (INJ)-P (2)
33 JOHN HUDEK-P (2)
34 MIKE FRANK (INJ)-OF
35 DON GULLETT-CH
36 GABE WHITE-P
37 STAN BELINDA (INJ)-P
38 PETE HARNISCH-P
39 EDUARDO PEREZ-1B/OF/3B
40 BRETT TOMKO-P
41 JEFF SHAW-P (1)
42 *(RET#)JACKIE ROBINSON*
43 MIKE REMLINGER-P
44 SCOTT WINCHESTER-P
45 MARK HUTTON (INJ)-P
45 TONY TARASCO-OF
46 MELVIN NIEVES (INJ)-OF
48 RICARDO JORDAN-P
48 RICK KRIVDA-P (2)
49 DAVID WEATHERS (WAIV)P
49 DENNIS REYES-P (2)
51 EDDIE PRIEST-P (1)
51 JASON BERE-P (2)
53 TODD WILLIAMS,-P
54 KEITH GLAUBER (INJ)-P
56 SCOTT KLINGENBECK (WAIV)-P
57 ROBERTO PETAGINE-1B
58 STEVE PARRIS-P
62 GUILLERMO GARCIA-INF

1999

2ND C 96-67 1.5GB

00 KERRY ROBINSON-OF
1 *(RET#)FRED HUTCHINSON*
2 HARRY DUNLOP-CH
3 POKEY REESE (INJ)-SS/3B
4 DAMIAN JACKSON-OF
5 *(RET#)JOHNNY BENCH*

CINCINNATI REDS

6 TRAVIS DAWKINS-INF
7 MARK SWEENEY-OF
8 *(RET#)JOE MORGAN*
9 HAL MORRIS (INJ)-1B
10 EDDIE TAUBENSEE-C
11 BARRY LARKIN (INJ)-SS
12 CHRIS STYNES-2B
15 DANNY NEAGLE (INJ)-P
16 RON (O) OESTER-CH
17 AARON BOONE-3B
18 *(RET#)TED KLUSZEWSKI*
19 DENIS MENKE-CH
20 *(RET#)FRANK ROBINSON*
21 SEAN CASEY (INJ)-1B
22 DAVE COLLINS-CH
23 GREG VAUGHN-OF
25 DMITRI YOUNG-1B/OF
26 JOHN HUDEK-P (1)
26 JASON LARUE-C
28 MARK LEWIS-3B
29 BRIAN JOHNSON-C
30 KEN GRIFFEY, SR.-CH
31 JACK MCKEON-MGR
32 DANNY GRAVES-P
33 STEVE AVERY-P
34 MICHAEL TUCKER-OF
35 DON GULLETT-CH
36 GABE WHITE-P
37 STAN BELINDA (INJ)-P
38 PETE HARNISCH-P
39 MARK WOHLERS (INJ)-P (2)
39 RALPH MILLIARD-2B
40 BRETT TOMKO-P
41 RON VILLONE-P
42 *(RET#)JACKIE ROBINSON*
43 B. J. RYAN-P (1)
43 RALPH MILLIARD-2B
43 MARK WOHLERS (INJ)-P (2)
44 MIKE CAMERON-OF
46 JASON BERE (INJ)-P (1)
47 TOM HUME-CH
48 SCOTT WILLIAMSON-P
49 DENNIS REYES-P
(51) SCOTT WINCHESTER (INJ)-(P)
56 SCOTT SULLIVAN-P
57 RICK GREENE-P
57 JUAN GUZMAN-P (2)
58 STEVE PARRIS-P

2000

2ND C 85-77 10GB

1 *(RET#)FRED HUTCHINSON*
2 JASON LARUE-C
3 POKEY REESE (INJ)-SS/3B
4 CHRIS STYNES-3B
5 *(RET#)JOHNNY BENCH*
6 BENITO SANTIAGO-C
7 ALEX OCHOA-OF
8 *(RET#)JOE MORGAN*
9 DANTE BICHETTE-OF (1)
10 EDDIE TAUBENSEE-C
11 BARRY LARKIN (INJ)-SS
12 D. T. CROMER-INF
12 JUAN CASTRO-INF
15 DANNY NEAGLE-P (1)
16 RON (O) OESTER-CH
17 AARON BOONE (INJ)-3B
18 *(RET#)TED KLUSZEWSKI*
19 DENIS MENKE-CH
20 *(RET#)FRANK ROBINSON*
21 SEAN CASEY (INJ)-1B
22 DAVE COLLINS-CH
23 HAL MORRIS-1B (1)
23 KIMERA BARTEE-OF
24 *(RET#)TONY PEREZ*
25 DMITRI YOUNG-1B/OF
26 TRAVIS (GOOKIE) DAWKINS -SS
26 CHRIS SEXTON-INF
28 MARK LEWIS-3B (1)
28 MIKE BELL-INF
29 ROB BELL-P
30 KEN GRIFFEY, JR.-OF
31 JACK MCKEON-MGR
32 DANNY GRAVES-P
33 KEN GRIFFEY, SR.-CH
34 MICHAEL TUCKER-OF
35 DON GULLETT-CH
36 GABE WHITE-P (1)
36 MANNY AYBAR-P (2)
36 D. T. CROMER-INF
37 NORM (GENIOUS) CHARLTON-P
38 PETE HARNISCH-P
39 D. T. CROMER-INF
39 HECTOR MERCADO-P
41 RON VILLONE-P
42 *(RET#)JACKIE ROBINSON*
43 OSVALDO FERNANDEZ (INJ)-P
44 BRIAN L. HUNTER-OF (2)
45 ELMER DESSENS-P
46 BROOKS KIESCHNICK-INF
47 TOM HUME-CH
48 SCOTT WILLIAMSON-P
49 DENNIS REYES-P
51 MARK WOHLERS (INJ)-P
52 ANDY LARKIN-P (1)
52 JOHN RIEDLING-P
53 LARRY LUEBBERS-P
54 BRADY CLARK-OF
55 MARK BERRY-CH
56 SCOTT SULLIVAN-P
58 STEVE PARRIS-P
59 KEITH GLAUBER-P
71 MIKE HUBBARD-C (2)
__ SCOTT WINCHESTER-P (5G:)

2001

5TH C 66-96 27GB

1 *(RET#)FRED HUTCHINSON*
2 DEION (NEON DEION) SANDERS (REL)-OF
2 TODD WALKER-2B (2)
3 POKEY REESE-SS/3B
4 BRANDON LARSON-OF
5 *(RET#)JOHNNY BENCH*
6 WILTON GUERRERO-2B
7 ALEX OCHOA-OF (1)
8 *(RET#)JOE MORGAN*
9 BOB BOONE-MGR
10 TIM FOLI-CH
11 BARRY LARKIN (INJ)-SS
12 JUAN CASTRO-INF
15 DONNIE SADLER-2B
16 RON (O) OESTER-CH
17 AARON BOONE (INJ)-3B
18 *(RET#)TED KLUSZEWSKI*
19 BILL DORAN-CH
20 *(RET#)FRANK ROBINSON*
21 SEAN CASEY-1B
22 BRADY CLARK-OF
23 JASON LARUE-C
24 *(RET#)TONY PEREZ*
25 DMITRI YOUNG-1B/OF
26 ROBIN JENNINGS-OF (3)
27 JOSE RIJO-P
28 RUBEN RIVERA-OF
29 ROB BELL-P (1)
29 JUAN ACEVADO-P
30 KEN GRIFFEY, JR. (INJ)-OF
31 KELLY STINNETT-C
32 DANNY GRAVES-P
33 KEN GRIFFEY, SR.-CH
34 MICHAEL TUCKER-OF (1)
34 CALVIN PICKERING-1B
35 DON GULLETT-CH
36 D. T. CROMER-1B
37 SCOTT WINCHESTER (INJ)-P
37 CORKY MILLER-C
38 PETE HARNISCH (INJ)-P
39 JUSTIN ATCHLEY-P
39 RAUL GONZALEZ-OF
40 SETH ETHERTON (INJ)-P
41 CHRISTOPHER REITSMA-P
42 *(RET#)JACKIE ROBINSON*
43 OSVALDO FERNANDEZ-P
44 ADAM DUNN-OF
45 ELMER DESSENS-P
46 JOHN RIEDLING (INJ)-P
47 TOM HUME-CH
48 SCOTT WILLIAMSON (INJ)-P
49 DENNIS REYES-P
50 BRIAN REITH-P
50 JOEY HAMILTON-P
51 MARK WOHLERS-P (1)
51 SCOTT MACRAE-P
52 HECTOR MERCADO-P
53 JIM BROWER-P
54 BILL SELBY-3B
54 JARED FERNANDEZ-P
55 MARK BERRY-CH
56 SCOTT SULLIVAN-P
57 CHRIS NICHTING-P (1)
58 FRANKIE RODRIGUEZ-P
59 LANCE DAVIS-P
60 CHRIS PIERSOLL-P

2002

3RD C 78-84 19GB

1 *(RET#)FRED HUTCHINSON*
3 GOOKIE DAWKINS-2B/3B
4 JIM LEFEBVRE-CH
5 *(RET#)JOHNNY BENCH*
6 WILTON GUERRERO-2B (1)
6 JOSE GUILLEN-OF (2)
7 JUAN CASTRO (INJ)-INF
8 *(RET#)JOE MORGAN*
9 BOB BOONE-MGR
10 TIM FOLI-CH
11 BARRY LARKIN-SS
12 TODD WALKER-2B
15 RUBEN MATEO-OF
16 BRANDON LARSON (INJ)-UTIL
17 AARON BOONE-3B/SS
18 *(RET#)TED KLUSZEWSKI*
19 REGGIE TAYLOR-OF
20 *(RET#)FRANK ROBINSON*
21 SEAN CASEY (INJ)-1B
22 BRADY CLARK-OF (1)
23 JASON LARUE (INJ)-C
24 *(RET#)TONY PEREZ*
25 RAY KNIGHT-CH
26 WILY MO PENA-OF
27 JOSE RIJO (INJ) P
28 AUSTIN KEARNS (INJ)-OF
29 JUAN ACEVADO-P
29 RAUL GONZALEZ-OF (1)
30 KEN GRIFFEY, JR. (INJ)-OF
31 KELLY STINNETT (INJ)-C
32 DANNY GRAVES-P
33 JOSE CARDENAL-CH
33 RUSSELL BRANYAN-OF/INF (2)
34 JUAN ENCARNACION-OF (1)
34 RYAN DEMPSTER-P (2)
35 DON GULLETT-CH
36 GABE WHITE (INJ)-P
37 CORKY MILLER-C
38 BRIAN MOEHLER-P (2)
39 JOSE SILVA (INJ)-P
41 CHRIS REITSMA-P
42 *(RET#)JACKIE ROBINSON*
43 JIMMY HAYNES-P
44 ADAM DUNN-OF/1B
45 ELMER DESSENS-P
46 JOHN RIEDLING (INJ)-P
47 TOM HUME-CH
48 SCOTT WILLIAMSON-P
49 LUIS PINEDA (INJ)-P
50 JOEY HAMILTON-P
52 BRUCE CHEN-P (3)
53 JIM BROWER-P (1)
53 JARED FERNANDEZ-P
54 LUKE HUDSON-P
55 MARK BERRY-CH?BPC
55 SHAWN ESTES-P (2)
56 SCOTT SULLIVAN-P
59 CARLOS ALMANZAR (INJ)-P

2003

5TH C 69-93 19GB

1 *(RET#)FRED HUTCHINSON*
2 JOSE CARDENAL-CH
3 RYAN FREEL (INJ)-OF/2B
3 D'ANGELO JIMENEZ-2B (2)
4 RAINIER OLMEDO (SUS:3G) -SS/2B
5 *(RET#)JOHNNY BENCH*
6 JOSE GUILLEN(SUS:3G)-OF (1)
6 RYAN FREEL (INJ)-OF/2B
7 JUAN CASTRO (INJ)-INF
8 *(RET#)JOE MORGAN*
9 BOB BOONE-MGR 1
10 TIM FOLI-CH
10 FREDDIE BENAVIDES-CH
11 BARRY LARKIN (INJ)-SS
12 FELIPE LOPEZ-SS/INF
12 DAVE MILEY-MGR 2
15 RUBEN MATEO-OF
16 BRANDON LARSON (INJ)-3B/OF
17 AARON BOONE-3B/INF (1)
18 *(RET#)TED KLUSZEWSKI*
19 REGGIE TAYLOR (INJ)-OF
20 *(RET#)FRANK ROBINSON*
21 SEAN CASEY (INJ) (SUS:3G) -1B
22 CORKY MILLER-C
23 JASON LARUE-C
24 *(RET#)TONY PEREZ*
25 RAY KNIGHT-CH
26 WILY MO PENA (INJ)-OF
28 AUSTIN KEARNS (INJ)-OF
29 JUAN ACEVADO (INJ)-P
30 KEN GRIFFEY, JR. (INJ)-OF
31 KELLY STINNETT (INJ)-C (1)
32 DANNY GRAVES (INJ)-P
33 RUSSELL BRANYAN (INJ)-UTIL
34 RYAN DEMPSTER (INJ)-P
35 DON GULLETT-CH
36 GABE WHITE (INJ)-P (1)
37 STEPHEN SMITHERMAN-OF
38 RYAN WAGNER-P
39 JOSIAS MANZANILLO-P
39 AARON HARANG-P (2)
40 PAUL WILSON (SUS: G) (INJ)-P
41 CHRIS REITSMA-P
42 *(RET#)JACKIE ROBINSON*
43 JIMMY HAYNES (INJ)-P
44 ADAM DUNN (SUS:3G) (INJ) -OF/1B
45 JIMMY ANDERSON-P
45 TODD VAN POPPEL-P (2)
46 JOHN RIEDLING (INJ)-P
47 TOM HUME-CH
48 SCOTT WILLIAMSON-P (1)
48 JOE VALENTINE-P
49 FELIX HEREDIA (WAIV)-P (1)
50 KENT MERCKER-P (1)
50 DAN SERAFINI-P
51 JEFF AUSTIN-P
52 BRIAN REITH-P
53 MIKE BUDZINSKI-OF
54 JOEY HAMILTON-P
(55) LUKE PROKOPEC (INJ)-(P)
56 SCOTT SULLIVAN (INJ)-P (1)
57 TOM ROBSON-CH
57 JOHN BALE (INJ)-P
58 JOSH HALL-P
59 MARK BERRY-CH
60 TIM HUMMEL-3B
61 MARK WATSON (INJ)-P
62 SETH ETHERTON-P
63 DERNELL STENSON (DD)-OF
64 JIM CHAMBLEE-3B
65 SCOTT RANDALL-P
66 PHIL NORTON-P (2)
67 DANE SARDINHA-C
68 ERIC VALENT-OF
70 MATT BELISLE-P
71 JUAN CERROS-P

2004

4TH C 76-86 29GB

1 *(RET#)FRED HUTCHINSON*
2 FELIPE LOPEZ-SS
3 D'ANGELO JIMENEZ-2B
4 RAINIER OLMEDO -SS
5 *(RET#)JOHNNY BENCH*
6 RYAN FREEL-3B
7 JUAN CASTRO (INJ)-3B
8 *(RET#)JOE MORGAN*
9 JACOB CRUZ-OF
10 JASON ROMANO (INJ)-2B
11 BARRY LARKIN-SS
12 DAVE MILEY-MGR
15 COREY LIDLE-P (1)
16 BRANDON LARSON (INJ)-UTIL
17 JAVIER VALENTIN-C
18 *(RET#)TED KLUSZEWSKI*
19 ANDERSON MACHADO-SS
20 *(RET#)FRANK ROBINSON*
21 SEAN CASEY-1B
22 CORKY MILLER-C
23 JASON LARUE (INJ)-C
24 *(RET#)TONY PEREZ*
25 JOHN VANDER WAL-OF
26 WILY MO PENA-OF
28 AUSTIN KEARNS (INJ)-OF
29 JUAN ACEVADO-P
30 KEN GRIFFEY, JR. (INJ)-OF
31 JUNG BONG-P
32 DANNY GRAVES (INJ)-P
33 MIKE MATHEWS (INJ)-P
34 BRANDON CLAUSSEN-P
35 DON GULLETT-CH
36 GABE WHITE-P (2)
38 RYAN WAGNER-P
39 AARON HARANG-P
40 PAUL WILSON (INJ)-P
41 JESUS SANCHEZ-P
41 MATT BELISLE-P
42 *(RET#)JACKIE ROBINSON*
43 JIMMY HAYNES (REL)-P
43 ANDERSON MACHADO-SS
43 JOSH HANCOCK-P (2)
44 ADAM DUNN-OF/1B
45 TODD VAN POPPEL-P
46 JOHN RIEDLING (BRV)-P
47 TOM HUME-CH
48 JOE VALENTINE-P
49 CHRIS CHAMBLISS-CH
50 JERRY NARRON-CH
51 PHIL NORTON-P
52 BRIAN REITH-P
53 RANDY WHISLER-CH
54 LUKE HUDSON-P
55 MARK BERRY-CH
56 AARON MYETTE-P
57 JERMAINE CLARK-2B
(58) JOSH HALL (INJ)-(P)
59 TODD JONES-P (1)
60 TIM HUMMEL-3B
60 JUAN PADILLA-P (2)

2005

5TH C 73-89 27GB

1 *(RET#)FRED HUTCHINSON*
2 FELIPE LOPEZ-SS
3 D'ANGELO JIMENEZ-2B
4 RAINIER OLMEDO (INJ)-SS
5 *(RET#)JOHNNY BENCH*
6 RYAN FREEL (INJ)-3B/UTIL
7 JASON ROMANO-OF
7 AARON HOLBERT-INF
8 *(RET#) JOE MORGAN*
9 JACOB CRUZ-OF
10 *(RET#) SPARKY ANDERSON*
12 DAVE MILEY-MGR1
12 EDWIN ENCARNACION-3B
15 LUIS LOPEZ (INJ)-3B/2B
16 JOE RANDA-3B (1)
17 JAVIER VALENTIN-C
18 *(RET#)TED KLUSZEWSKI*
19 ANDERSON MACHADO (INJ)(WAIV)-SS (1)
19 CHRIS DENORFIA-OF
20 *(RET#)FRANK ROBINSON*
21 SEAN CASEY-1B
22 ERIC MILTON-P
23 JASON LARUE (BRV)-C
24 *(RET#)TONY PEREZ*
25 DAVID WEATHERS-P
26 WILY MO PENA (INJ)-OF
27 WILLIAM BERGOLIA-INF
28 AUSTIN KEARNS-OF
29 KENNY KELLY (INJ)-OF (1)
29 MIGUEL PEREZ-C
30 KEN GRIFFEY, JR.-OF
31 MATT BELISLE-P
32 DANNY GRAVES (REL) (WAIV)-P (1)
32 JOHN MOSES-CH
33 RICH AURILIA (INJ)-2B/INF
34 BRANDON CLAUSSEN-P
35 DON GULLETT-CH
35 JASON STANDRIDGE-P (2)
36 RAMON ORTIZ (INJ)-P
37 BRIAN SHACKLEFORD-P
38 RYAN WAGNER (INJ)-P
39 AARON HARANG-P
40 PAUL WILSON (INJ)-P
41 JERRY NARRON-CH/MGR2
42 *(RET#)JACKIE ROBINSON*
43 JOSH HANCOCK (INJ)-P
44 ADAM DUNN-OF
46 ALLAN SIMPSON-P (2)
47 TOM HUME-CH
48 JOE VALENTINE-P
49 CHRIS CHAMBLISS-CH
50 KENT MERCKER-P
51 JUNG BONG (INJ)-P
52 RICKY STONE-P
52 CHRIS BOOKER-P
53 RANDY WHISLER-CH
54 LUKE HUDSON (INJ)-P
55 MARK BERRY-CH
56 TODD COFFEY-P
57 RANDY KEISLER (INJ)-P
58 VERN RUHLE-CH
59 DANE SARDINHA-C
67 ELIZARDO RAMIREZ-P
77 BEN WEBER (INJ)-P

Barry Larkin was a 9-time All-Star shortstop for the Reds. He played 19 years and 2180 games for them from 1986-2004. As a Red, he batted .295, scored 1329 runs, knocked in another 960 with 441 doubles, 76 triples and 198 HRs. He also walked 999 times and stole 379 bases. With Larkin as captain and shortstop, the Reds won the 1990 WS vs. Oakland where he batted .353. In his only other appearance in post-season play (1995), he batted .385 in the NLDS defeating the Dodgers and .389 in the NLCS vs. the Braves in a losing cause.

COLORADO ROCKIES

1993
COLORADO ROCKIES
6TH W 67-95 37GB
1 JERRY ROYSTER-CH
2 GERALD YOUNG-OF
3 DALE MURPHY (RET)-OF
3 JERRY ROYSTER-CH
4 NELSON LIRIANO-INF
5 ALEX COLE-OF
6 DARYL BOSTON-OF
7 JOE GIRARDI (INJ) -C
8 ROBERTO MEJIA-2B
9 VINNY CASTILLA-SS
10 DANTE BICHETTE-OF
12 FREDDIE BENAVIDES (INJ)-INF
13 CHARLIE HAYES-3B/SS
14 ANDRES GALARRAGA (INJ)-1B
15 PEDRO CASTELLANO-INF
16 DANNY SHEAFFER-UTIL
17 DAVID NIED (INJ)-P
18 BRUCE RUFFIN-P
19 WILLIE BLAIR-P
20 JIM TATUM-UTIL
21 ERIC YOUNG-2B/OF
22 ERIC WEDGE (INJ)-C
23 DON (POPEYE) ZIMMER-CH
24 JERALD CLARK-OF/1B
25 DON BAYLOR-MGR
26 AMOS OTIS-CH
27 BUTCH HENRY-P (1)
27 GREG W. HARRIS -P (2)
28 BRYN SMITH (INJ)-P
28 LANCE PAINTER-P
29 RON HASSEY-CH
30 KEITH SHEPHERD -P
32 SCOTT ALDRED-P
32 JAYHAWK OWENS-C
33 CHRIS JONES-OF
34 SCOTT SERVICE-P (1)
34 MO SANFORD-P
36 LARRY BEARNARTH-CH
37 JAY GAINER-1B
38 JEFF PARRETT (INJ)-P
39 STEVE REED-P
40 DARREN HOLMES-P
41 MARK KNUDSON-P
42 ARMANDO REYNOSO-P
43 ANDY ASHBY-P (1)
43 MIKE MUNOZ-P (2)
45 CURT LESKANIC-P
46 KENT BOTTENFIELD-P (2)
47 LANCE PAINTER-P
47 BRUCE HURST (INJ)-P (2)
49 SCOTT FREDRICKSON-P
53 GARY WAYNE-P
54 MARCUS MOORE-P
55 MARK GRANT-P (2)
KEVIN RITZ (INJ)-(P)

1994
3RD W 53-64 6.5GB
STRIKE NO POST SEASON
1 TRENIDAD HUBBARD-OF
2 GENE GLYNN-CH
4 NELSON LIRIANO-INF
7 JOE GIRARDI (INJ)-C
8 ROBERTO MEJIA-2B
9 VINNY CASTILLA-SS
10 DANTE BICHETTE-OF
12 MIKE KINGERY-OF
13 CHARLIE HAYES-3B
14 ANDRES GALARRAGA (INJ) 1B
16 DANNY SHEAFFER-UTIL/C
17 DAVID NIED (INJ)-P
18 BRUCE RUFFIN-P
19 WILLIE BLAIR-P
20 HOWARD (HOJO) JOHNSON-OF
21 ERIC YOUNG-OF
22 WALT WEISS-SS
23 DON (POPEYE) ZIMMER-CH
24 DWIGHT (DEWEY) EVANS-CH
25 DON BAYLOR-MGR
26 ELLIS BURKS (INJ)-OF
27 MIKE HARKEY-P
27 TY VAN BURKLEO-1B
28 LANCE PAINTER-P
29 RON HASSEY-CH
30 KEVIN RITZ-P
31 GREG W. HARRIS-P
32 MIKE HARKEY-P
33 CHRIS C. JONES-OF
34 JAYHAWK OWENS-C
35 JOHN VANDER WAL-1B
36 LARRY BEARNARTH-CH
38 JIM CZAJKOWSKI-P
39 STEVE REED-P
40 DARREN HOLMES (INJ)-P
41 BILL PLUMMER-CH
42 ARMANDO REYNOSO (INJ) P
43 MIKE MUNOZ-P
44 MARVIN FREEMAN-P
45 CURT LESKANIC-P
46 KENT BOTTENFIELD (INJ)-P (1)
46 GREG W. HARRIS-P
47 MARK THOMPSON-P
53 BRUCE WALTON-P
54 MARCUS MOORE-P
SCOTT FREDRICKSON (INJ) (P)

1995
2ND W (WC) 77-67 1GB
L NLDS-ATLN 3-1
1 TRENIDAD HUBBARD-OF
2 GENE GLYNN-CH
3 QUINTON MCCRACKEN-OF
4 CRAIG COUNSELL-SS
6 JASON BATES-2B
7 JOE GIRARDI-C
8 ROBERTO MEJIA-2B
9 VINNY CASTILLA-3B
10 DANTE BICHETTE-OF
11 MATT NOKES-C (2)
12 MIKE KINGERY-OF
14 ANDRES GALARRAGA-1B
15 PEDRO CASTELLANO-3B
16 CURT LESKANIC-P
17 DAVID NIED-P
18 BRUCE RUFFIN-P
19 JIM TATUM-1B
20 BILL SWIFT-P
21 ERIC YOUNG-OF
22 WALT WEISS-SS
23 DON (POPEYE) ZIMMER (RET)-CH
24 HARVEY PULLIAM-OF
25 DON BAYLOR-MGR
26 ELLIS BURKS-OF
27 JORGE BRITO-C
28 LANCE PAINTER-P
29 RON HASSEY-CH
30 KEVIN RITZ-P
31 ROGER BAILEY-P
31 BRET SABERHAGEN-P (2)
32 MARK THOMPSON-P
33 LARRY WALKER-OF
34 JAYHAWK OWENS-C
35 JOHN VANDER WAL-OF
36 LARRY BEARNARTH-CH
37 RICK MATHEWS-CH
38 BRIAN REKAR-P
38 BRET SABERHAGEN-P (2)
38 ROGER BAILEY-P
39 STEVE REED-P
40 DARREN HOLMES-P
41 ART HOWE-CH
42 ARMANDO REYNOSO-P
43 MIKE MUNOZ-P
44 MARVIN FREEMAN-P
47 OMAR OLIVARES-P (1)
47 BRYAN HICKERSON-P (2)
48 A. J. SAGER-P
49 JUAN ACEVEDO-P
53 JOE GRAHE-P
55 JOE GRAHE-P
56 BRIAN REKAR-P

1996
3RD W 83-79 8GB
1 TERRY JONES-C
2 GENE GLYNN-CH
3 QUINTON MCCRACKEN-OF
5 NEIFI PEREZ-2B
6 JASON BATES-2B
7 TRENIDAD HUBBARD-OF (1)
9 VINNY CASTILLA-3B
10 DANTE BICHETTE-OF
11 ANGEL ECHEVARRIA-OF
12 PEDRO CASTELLANO (WAIV)-2B
13 RYAN HAWBLITZEL-P
14 ANDRES GALARRAGA-1B
15 JEFF REED-C
16 CURT LESKANIC (INJ)-P
17 DAVID NIED-P
18 BRUCE RUFFIN-P
19 JAMEY WRIGHT-P
20 BILL SWIFT (INJ)-P
21 ERIC YOUNG (INJ)-2B
22 WALT WEISS-SS
23 BRYAN REKAR-P
24 KEN GRIFFEY, SR.-CH
25 DON BAYLOR-MGR
26 ELLIS BURKS-OF
27 JORGE BRITO-C
27 MILT THOMPSON-OF (2)
27 STEVE DECKER-C (2)
28 LANCE PAINTER (INJ)-P
29 HARVEY PULLIAM-OF
29 ERIC ANTHONY-OF
30 KEVIN RITZ-P
(31) BRET SABERHAGEN (INJ)-(P)
32 MARK THOMPSON-P
33 LARRY WALKER (INJ)-OF
34 JAYHAWK OWENS (INJ)-C
35 JOHN VANDER WAL-OF
36 MIKE FARMER-P
37 JOHN BURKE-P
38 ROGER BAILEY (INJ)-P
39 STEVE REED-P
40 DARREN HOLMES-P
41 ROBBIE BECKETT-P
42 ARMANDO REYNOSO-P
43 MIKE MUNOZ (INJ)-P
44 MARVIN FREEMAN (REL)-P (1)
44 ALAN COCKRELL-OF
45 FRANK FUNK-CH
46 PAUL ZUVELLA-CH
47 JACKIE MOORE-CH
48 JOHN HABYAN (REL)-P
50 GARVIN ALSTON-P

1997
3RD W 83-79 7GB
2 GENE GLYNN-CH
3 QUINTON MCCRACKEN-OF
5 NEIFI PEREZ-SS/2B
6 JASON BATES-2B
7 CRAIG COUNSELL-PR (1)
8 KIRT MANWARING-C
9 VINNY CASTILLA-3B
10 DANTE BICHETTE-OF
11 ANGEL ECHEVARRIA (INJ)-OF
12 BRIAN RAABE-3B (2)
13 CLINT HURDLE-CH
14 ANDRES GALARRAGA-1B
15 JEFF REED-C
16 CURT LESKANIC (INJ)-P
17 TODD HELTON-OF/1B
18 BRUCE RUFFIN (INJ)-P
19 JAMEY WRIGHT (INJ)-P
20 BILL SWIFT (INJ)(REL)-P
21 ERIC YOUNG-2B (1)
22 WALT WEISS (INJ)-SS
23 BRYAN REKAR-P
24 HARVEY PULLIAM-OF
25 DON BAYLOR-MGR
26 ELLIS BURKS (INJ)-OF
28 DARNELL COLES (JAP)-OF
28 RENE GONZALEZ-PH
30 KEVIN RITZ (INJ)-P
31 ROGER BAILEY (INJ)-P
32 MARK THOMPSON-P
33 LARRY WALKER-OF
34 PEDRO ASTACIO-P
35 JOHN VANDER WAL-OF
36 BOBBY JONES-P
37 JOHN BURKE-P
38 JEFF MCCURRY-P
39 STEVE REED-P
40 DARREN HOLMES-P
41 ROBBIE BECKETT-P
42 *(RET#) JACKIE ROBINSON*
43 MIKE MUNOZ-P
44 MIKE DE JEAN (INJ)-P
45 JERRY DIPOTO-P
46 P. J. CAREY-CH
47 JACKIE MOORE-CH
47 NATE MINCHEY-P
48 FRANK CASTILLO-P (2)
49 FRANK FUNK-CH
(50) GARVIN ALSTON (INJ)-(P)
51 PEDRO ASTACIO-P (2)
52 JOHN THOMSON (INJ)-P
53 MARK HUTTON-P (2)
54 TIM SCOTT-P (2)

1998
4TH W 77-85 21GB
1 CURTIS GOODWIN-OF
2 GENE GLYNN-CH
3 MIKE LANSING-2B
4 JACKIE MOORE-CH
5 NEIFI PEREZ-SS
6 JASON BATES (INJ)-2B
7 KURT ABBOTT-INF (2)
8 KIRT MANWARING-C
9 VINNY CASTILLA-3B
10 DANTE BICHETTE-OF
11 ANGEL ECHEVARRIA-OF
12 DARRYL HAMILTON-OF
13 CLINT HURDLE-CH
15 JEFF REED-C
16 CURT LESKANIC (INJ)-P
17 TODD HELTON-OF/1B
19 DERRICK WHITE-OF (2)
19 EDGARD CLEMENTE-OF
20 MIKE SAIPE-P
21 JAMEY WRIGHT-P
22 NELSON LIRIANO-INF
22 MARK STRITTMATTER-C
23 CHUCK MCELROY-P
24 JEFF BARRY-OF
24 DERRICK GIBSON-OF
25 DON BAYLOR-MGR
26 ELLIS BURKS-OF (1)
27 DARRYL HAMILTON-OF (2)
28 GREG COLBRUNN-1B (1)
28 TERRY SHUMPERT-INF
29 MARK THOMPSON (INJ)-P
30 KEVIN RITZ (INJ)-P
(31) ROGER BAILEY (INJ)-(P)
32 MARK THOMPSON-P
32 MARK BROWNSON-P
33 LARRY WALKER (INJ)-OF
34 PEDRO ASTACIO-P
35 JOHN VANDER WAL-OF (1)
36 BOBBY M. JONES-P
(37) JOHN BURKE (INJ)-(P)
38 LARIEL GONZALEZ-P
39 GREG COLBRUNN-1B/OF
39 JIM STOOPS-P
41 DAVID WAINHOUSE-P
42 *(RET) JACKIE ROBINSON*
43 MIKE MUNOZ-P
44 MIKE DE JEAN-P
45 JERRY DIPOTO-P
47 DAVE VERES-P
49 FRANK FUNK-CH
50 BILL HAYES-CH
52 JOHN THOMSON (INJ)-P
53 FRED RATH-P
57 DARRYL KILE-P

1999
5TH W 72-90 28GB
2 CHRIS PETERSEN-SS
2 JUAN SOSA-OF
3 MIKE LANSING-2B
4 CHRIS SEXTON-OF
5 NEIFI PEREZ-SS
6 BRUCE KIMM-CH
7 KURT ABBOTT-INF
8 KIRT MANWARING-C
9 VINNY CASTILLA-3B
10 DANTE BICHETTE-OF
11 JIM LEYLAND-MGR
12 DARRYL HAMILTON-OF (1)
12 EDGARD CLEMENTE-OF
13 CLINT HURDLE-CH
15 JEFF REED-C (1)
15 BEN PETRICK-C
16 CURT LESKANIC-P
17 TODD HELTON-OF/1B
19 EDGARD CLEMENTE-OF
20 LORENZO BUNDY-CH
21 JAMEY WRIGHT-P
22 PAT WATKINS-OF
22 TERRY SHUMPERT-INF
23 CHUCK MCELROY-P (1)
23 JOHN CANGELOSI-OF
24 DERRICK GIBSON-OF
26 RICH DONNELLY-CH
27 MIKE KELLY-OF
27 JEFF BARRY-OF
28 LENNY HARRIS-INF (1)
29 MILT MAY-CH
(30) KEVIN RITZ (INJ)-(P)
31 J. R. PHILLIPS-OF
32 MARK BROWNSON-P
33 LARRY WALKER (INJ)-OF
34 PEDRO ASTACIO-P
35 HENRY BLANCO-C
36 BOBBY (M.) JONES-P
37 TOMMY SANDT-CH
39 ANGEL ECHEVARRIA-OF (1)
41 BRIAN BOHANON-P
42 *(RET#) JACKIE ROBINSON*
43 DAVID WAINHOUSE-P
43 DAVID LEE-P
44 MIKE DE JEAN-P
45 JERRY DIPOTO-P
47 DAVE VERES-P
48 RIGO BELTRAN-P
49 ROBERTO RAMIREZ-P
51 LUTHER HACKMAN-P
52 JOHN THOMSON (INJ)-P
53 MIKE PORZIO-P
54 DAVID LEE-P
56 BRIAN MCRAE-OF (2)
57 DARRYL KILE-P

2000

4TH W 82-80 15GB

1 DAVE GARCIA-CH
2 AARON LEDESMA-SS
2 JEFF FRYE-INF (2)
3 MIKE LANSING-2B (1)
4 JEFFREY HAMMONDS-OF
5 NEIFI PEREZ-SS
6 JEFF FRYE-INF (2)
6 JUAN PIERRE-OF
7 JEFF CIRILLO-3B
8 BRENT MAYNE-C
11 TOBY HARRAH-CH
12 BRIAN L. HUNTER-OF (1)
13 CLINT HURDLE-CH
14 TODD WALKER-INF (2)
15 BEN PETRICK-C
16 FRED KENDALL-CH
17 TODD HELTON-OF/1B
18 MIKE DEJEAN (INJ)-P
19 SCOTT KARL (INJ)-P
20 DALLAS WILLIAMS-CH
21 MASATO YOSHII-P
22 TERRY SHUMPERT-INF
23 JEFF MANTO-INF
23 BUBBA CARPENTER-C
23 ELVIS PENA-INF
24 TOM GOODMAN-OF (1)
25 BUDDY BELL-MGR
26 RICH DONNELLY-CH
27 TODD HOLLANDSWORTH -OF (2)
28 MIKE MYERS-P
29 SCOTT SERVAIS (INJ)-C (1)
29 CARLOS MENDOZA-OF
30 ROLANDO ARROJO-P (1)
30 ADAM MELHUSE-INF (2)
31 DARREN BRAGG-OF
31 DAVID MORAGA-P (2)
32 KEVIN JARVIS (INJ)-P
33 LARRY WALKER (INJ)-OF
34 PEDRO ASTACIO-P
35 BUTCH HUSKEY-OF (2)
36 GABE WHITE-P (2)
37 STAN BELINDA-P (1)
38 MANNY AYBAR-P (1)
39 ANGEL ECHEVARRIA-OF
40 BRIAN ROSE-P (2)
41 BRIAN BOHANON-P
42 *(RET#) JACKIE ROBINSON*
43 BOBBY CHOUINARD-P
44 MIKE DEJEAN (INJ)-P
44 ROLANDO ARROJO-P (1)
45 JERRY DIPOTO (INJ)-P
46 JOHN WASDIN-P (2)
47 GIOVANNI CARRARA-P
48 CRAIG HOUSE-P
49 JOSE JIMENEZ-P
50 JULIAN TAVAREZ-P
51 DAVID LEE-P
53 MARCEL LACHEMANN-CH
54 RICK CROUSHORE-P
54 PETE WALKER-P
71 PETE WALKER-P
WALT MCKEEL (INJ)-(C)

2001

5TH W 73-89 19 GB

1 DAVE GARCIA-CH
2 BRENT BUTLER-2B
3 RON GANT-OF (1)
3 ALEX OCHOA-OF (2)
4 JUAN URIBE-SS
5 NEIFI PEREZ (INJ)-SS (1)
6 BEN PETRICK-C
7 JEFF CIRILLO (INJ)-3B
8 BRENT MAYNE-C (1)
9 JUAN PIERRE-OF
10 MIKE HAMPTON-P
11 TOBY HARRAH-CH
12 TODD WALKER-2B (1)
12 JOSE ORTIZ-2B (2)
13 CLINT HURDLE-CH
14 GREG NORTON-1B
15 DENNY NEAGLE (INJ)-P
16 FRED KENDALL-CH
16 KEVIN SEFCIK-SS
16 MAC SUSUKI (WAIV)-P (2)
16 KIMERA BARTEE-OF (2)
17 TODD HELTON-OF/1B
19 MARK LITTLE (INJ)-OF
20 DALLAS WILLIAMS-CH
21 ADAM MELHUSE-C
22 TERRY SHUMPERT-INF
23 JOE DAVENPORT-P
23 JACOB CRUZ (INJ)-OF (2)
25 BUDDY BELL-MGR
26 RICH DONNELLY-CH
27 TODD HOLLANDSWORTH (INJ)-OF
28 MIKE MYERS-P
29 RON VILLONE-P (1)
29 GARY BENNETT-C (3)
30 JUSTIN SPEIER-P (2)
31 ROBIN JENNINGS-OF (2)
31 SAL FASANO-C (3)
32 DAN MICELI-P (2)
33 LARRY WALKER-OF
34 PEDRO ASTACIO-P (1)
35 CLIFF BRUMBAUGH-OF (2)
36 GABE WHITE-P
37 KANE DAVIS (INJ)-P (2)
39 JAY POWELL-P (2)
40 SCOTT ELARTON (INJ)-P (2)
41 BRIAN BOHANON (INJ)-P
42 *(RET#) JACKIE ROBINSON*
43 BOBBY CHOUINARD-P
44 MIKE DEJEAN-P (1)
44 MARIO ENCARNACION-OF
46 JOHN WASDIN-P (1)
46 TODD BELITZ-P
47 HORACIO ESTRADA-P
48 CHRIS NICHTING-P (2)
49 JOSE JIMENEZ (INJ)-P
50 JUAN ACEVADO (INJ)-P (1)
51 CRAIG DINGMAN (INJ)-P
52 JOHN THOMSON (INJ)-P
53 MARCEL LACHEMANN-CH
54 TIM CHRISTMAN-P
55 BROOKS KIESCHNICK (INJ) OF
56 SHAWN CHACON-P
57 JASON JENNINGS-P

2002

4TH W 73-89 25 GB

1 DAVE GARCIA-CH
2 JOSE ORTIZ-2B/3B
2 MIKE GALLEGO-CH
3 JASON ROMANO-UTIL (2)
4 JUAN URIBE-SS
5 BRENT BUTLER-2B/INF
6 BEN PETRICK-OF/C
7* TODD ZEILE-3B/P*
8 BOBBY ESTALELLA (INJ)-C
9 JUAN PIERRE-OF
10 MIKE HAMPTON-P
11 TOBY HARRAH-CH
12 JOSE ORTIZ-2B/3B
13 CLINT HURDLE-CH/MGR2
14 GREG NORTON-3B/UTIL
15 DENNY NEAGLE-P
16 FRED KENDALL-CH
16 JOSE JIMENEZ-P
17 TODD HELTON-1B/OF
18 FRED KENDALL-CH
19 MARK LITTLE (INJ)-OF (1)
19 GABE KAPLER-OF (2)
20 DALLAS WILLIAMS-CH
21 JACK CUST-OF
22 TERRY SHUMPERT-UTIL
23 RUSS GLOAD-1B/OF
25 BUDDY BELL-MGR1
25 SANDY ALOMAR, JR.-C (2)
26 RICH DONNELLY-CH
26 WALT MCKEEL-C
27 TODD HOLLANDSWORTH-OF (1)
27 JAY PAYTON-OF (2)
29 GARY BENNETT-C
30 JUSTIN SPEIER (INJ)-P
32 JASON JENNINGS-P
33 LARRY WALKER-OF
34 SHAWN CHACON (INJ)-P
35 AARON COOK-P
38 PETE HARNISCH (INJ)-(P)
39 BRIAN FUENTES-P
(40) SCOTT ELARTON (INJ)-(P)
41 DENNY STARK-P
42 *(RET#) JACKIE ROBINSON*
44 ALAN COCKRELL-CH
45 VICTOR SANTOS-P
46 MARK COREY-P (2)
47 CHRIS NICHTING-P
48 MIKE JAMES-P
49 DENNYS REYES-P (1)
50 BENNY AGBAYANI-OF (1)
51 RICK WHITE-P (1)
51 RANDY FLORES-P (2)
52 JOHN THOMSON-P (1)
52 SEAN LOWE-P (2)
53 COREY VANCE-P
54 KENT MERCKER (INJ)-P
55 JIM WRIGHT-CH
59 TODD JONES-P

2003

4TH W 74-88 26.5 GB

1 PABLO OZUNA (INJ)-UTIL
2 SANDY ALOMAR, SR.-CH
3 RENE REYES-OF
4 JUAN URIBE (INJ)-SS/2B
5 BRENT BUTLER-INF
5 TONY WOMACK-SS/2B (2)
6 BEN PETRICK-OF/C (1)
6 MANDY ROMERO-C
7 CHRIS STYNES-3B/2B
8 BOBBY ESTALELLA (INJ)-C
9 JAMIE QUIRK-CH
10 RONNIE BELLIARD (INJ)-2B
11 LUKE ALLEN-PH
12 CLINT BARMES-SS
13 CLINT HURDLE-MGR
14 GREG NORTON-UTIL
15 DENNY NEAGLE (INJ)-P
16 JOSE JIMENEZ-P
17 TODD HELTON-1B
18 JOSE HERNANDEZ-SS (1)
19 GABE KAPLER-OF (1)
19 KIT PELLOW-C
20 GREG VAUGHN-OF
21 CHRIS RICHARD (INJ)-OF/1B
23 CHARLES JOHNSON-C
24 JAY PAYTON-OF
25 MARK SWEENEY-OF/1B
26 MARK BELLHORN (INJ)-UTIL (2)
27 VIC DARENSBOURG-P (1)
27 GARRETT ATKINS-3B
28 AARON COOK-P
29 DAVE COLLINS-CH
30 JUSTIN SPEIER-P
31 GREGG ZAUN-C (2)
32 JASON JENNINGS-P
33 LARRY WALKER-OF
34 SHAWN CHACON (INJ)-P
35 NELSON CRUZ (INJ) (REL)-P
36 BOB APODACA-CH
37 DARREN OLIVER-P
39 STEVE REED-P
40 SCOTT ELARTON (INJ)-P
40 BRIAN FUENTES-P
41 DENNY STARK (INJ)-P
42 *(RET#) JACKIE ROBINSON*
43 DAN MICELI-P (1)
43 ADAM BERNERO-P (2)
44 PRESTON WILSON-OF
45 JAVIER LOPEZ-P
46 MATT MILLER-P
47 CORY VANCE-P
49 JASON YOUNG-P
50 SCOTT ELARTON (INJ)-P
51 JOE ROA (F/A)(WAIV)-P (2)
52 DUANE ESPY-CH
53 RICK MATHEWS-CH
55 JESUS SANCHEZ-P
59 TODD JONES-P (1)
71 CHIN-HUI TSAO (INJ)-P

2004

4TH W 68-94 25 GB

2 SANDY ALOMAR, SR.-CH
3 JORGE PIEDRA-OF
4 LUIS GONZALEZ-2B
5 MATT HOLLIDAY-3B/OF
6 AARON MILES-2B
7 RENE REYES-OF
8 JAMIE QUIRK-CH
9 VINNIE CASTILLA-3B
10 ROYCE CLAYTON-SS
11 BRAD HAWPE-OF
12 CLINT BARMES-SS
13 JEFF FASSERO-P (1)
13 CLINT HURDLE-MGR
14 CLINT HURDLE-MGR
(15) DENNY NEAGLE (INJ)-(P)
16 DENNY HOCKING-OF
16 JAMEY WRIGHT-P
17 TODD HELTON-1B
18 ANDY TRACY-1B
19 KIT PELLOW-OF
20 TODD GREENE-C
21 CHOO FREEMAN-OF
23 CHARLES JOHNSON-C
24 VLADIMIR NUNEZ-P
25 MARK SWEENEY-OF
26 JEFF FRANCIS-P
27 GARRETT ATKINS-3B
28 AARON COOK (INJ)-P
29 DAVE COLLINS-CH
30 J. D. CLOSSER-C
32 JASON JENNINGS-P
33 LARRY WALKER-OF (1)
34 SHAWN CHACON-P
35 JEREMY BURNITZ-OF
36 BOB APODACA-CH
37 JOE KENNEDY-P
38 KEVIN JARVIS-P (1)
39 STEVE REED-P
40 BRIAN FUENTES-P
41 DENNY STARK (INJ)-P
42 *(RET#) JACKIE ROBINSON*
43 ADAM BERNERO (INJ)-P
44 PRESTON WILSON-OF
45 JAVIER LOPEZ-P
46 TIM HARIKKALA-P
47 SCOTT DOHMANN-P
49 JASON YOUNG (INJ)-P
50 SCOTT ELARTON-P (1)
50 TRAVIS DRISKILL-P
51 ALLAN SIMPSON-P
52 DUANE ESPY-CH
53 RICK MATHEWS-CH
55 SHAWN ESTES-P
50 SCOTT ELART
71 CHIN-HUI TSAO (INJ)-P
99 TURK WENDELL (INJ)-P

2005

5TH W 67-95 15 GB

1 ANDERSON MACHADO (WAIV)-INF (2)
2 MIKE GALLEGO-CH
3 JORGE PIEDRA (SUS:10G)-OF
4 LUIS GONZALEZ-2B/UTIL
5 MATT HOLLIDAY (INJ)-OF
6 AARON MILES (INJ)-2B
7 J. D. CLOSSER-C
8 DESI RELAFORD (INJ)(REL) INF
8 OMAR QUINTANILLA-SS/2B
9 JAMIE QUIRK-CH
10 JEFF BAKER-3B
11 BRAD HAWPE (INJ)-OF
12 CLINT BARMES (INJ)-SS
13 CLINT HURDLE-MGR
14 MATT ANDERSON-P
15 ALFREDO AMEZAGA (WAIV -3B (1)
16 JAMEY WRIGHT-P
17 TODD HELTON (INJ)-1B
18 MIKE DEJEAN-P (2)
19 RYAN SPILBORGHS-OF
20 TODD GREENE (INJ)-C
21 CHOO FREEMAN-OF
22 DUSTAN MOHR-OF
23 RYAN SPEIER-P
25 MICHAEL RESTOVICH-OF (
25 EDDY GARABITO-2B
26 JEFF FRANCIS-P
27 GARRETT ATKINS (INJ)-3B
28 AARON COOK (INJ)-P
29 DAVE COLLINS-CH
30 JOSE ACEVEDO-P
31 CORY SULLIVAN-OF
32 JASON JENNINGS (INJ)-P
34 SHAWN CHACON-P (1)
34 LARRY BIGBIE-OF (2)
35 ERIC BYRNES-OF (2)
35 MIKE ESPOSITO-P
36 BOB APODACA-CH
37 JOE KENNEDY-P (1)
38 RYAN SHEALY-1B
39 BLAINE NEAL-P (2)
40 BRIAN FUENTES-P
41 JAY WITASICK-P (1)
42 *(RET#) JACKIE ROBINSON*
44 PRESTON WILSON-OF (1)
45 JAVIER LOPEZ (WAIV)-P (1)
45 ZACH DAY-P (2)
46 BOBBY SEAY-P
47 SCOTT DOHMANN-P
48 TIM OLSON-SS
49 BYUNG-HYUN KIM-P
50 DAVID CORTES-P
51 ALLAN SIMPSON-P (1)
51 SUN WOO (SUNNY) KIM (INJ)-P (2)
51 AQUILINO LOPEZ-P (1)
52 DUANE ESPY-CH
53 RICK MATHEWS-CH
54 RANDY WILLIAMS (WAIV)-P (2)
55 DANNY ARDOIN-C
58 DAN MICELI (INJ)-P
60 MATTHEW MERRICKS (INJ)-P
71 CHIN-HUI TSAO (INJ)-P

FLORIDA MARLINS

1993

FLORIDA MARLINS

6TH E 64-98 33GB

1 COOKIE ROJAS-CH
2 SCOTT POSE-OF
3 CARL EVERETT-OF
4 MONTY FARISS-OF
6 RICH RENTERIA-UTIL
8 BRET BARBERIE (INJ)-2B
09 BENITO SANTIAGO-C/OF
10 BOB MCCLURE-P
10 GARY SHEFFIELD-3B (2)
11 CHRIS HAMMOND-P
12 DOUG (THE RED ROOSTER) (ROJO) RADER-CH
13 ROB NATAL-C
14 GUS POLIDOR-2B/3B
15 RENE LACHEMANN-MGR
16 GERONIMO BERROA-OF
17 DARRELL WHITMORE-OF
18 DAVE MAGADAN-3B/1B (1)
19 JEFF CONINE-OF/1B
20 GREG BRILEY-OF
21 CHUCK CARR-OF
22 WALT WEISS-SS
24 ALEX ARIAS-INF
24 RICHIE LEWIS-P
25 MATIAS CARRILLO-OF
26 RICHIE LEWIS-P
26 ALEX ARIAS-INF
27 LUIS AQUINO (INJ)-P
28 VADA PINSON-CH
29 HENRY COTTO-OF (2)
30 NIGEL WILSON-OF
31 ROBB NEN-P (2)
33 FRANK (CRANE) REBERGER-CH
34 BRYAN HARVEY-P
35 DAVID WEATHERS-P
36 CHRIS HAMMOND-P
39 ORESTES DESTRADE-1B
40 JOHN JOHNSTONE-P
41 JIM CORSI-P
42 RICH RODRIGUEZ-P (2)
(43) SCOTT CHIAMPARINO (INJ)-(P)
44 CRIS CARPENTER-P (1)
46 RYAN BOWEN (INJ)-P
47 JUNIOR FELIX-OF
48 PAT RAPP-P
49 CHARLIE HOUGH-P
50 TERRY MCGRIFF-C
51 TREVOR HOFFMAN-P (1)
52 MITCH LYDEN-C
53 MARCEL LACHEMANN-CH
54 MATT TURNER-P
55 STEVE DECKER (INJ)-C
58 JOE KLINK-P
77 JACK ARMSTRONG-P

1994

5TH E 51-64 23.5 GB

BB STRIKE

1 COOKIE ROJAS-CH
3 CARL EVERETT (INJ)-OF
4 GREG COLBRUNN (INJ)-1B
6 RICH RENTERIA (INJ)-UTIL
7 KURT ABBOTT-SS
8 BRET BARBERIE-2B
09 BENITO SANTIAGO-C/OF
10 GARY SHEFFIELD (INJ)-3B
11 CHRIS HAMMOND (INJ)-P
12 DOUG (THE RED ROOSTER) (ROJO) RADER-CH
13 BOB NATAL-C
14 JERRY BROWNE-3B/OF
15 RENE LACHEMANN-MGR
16 GREG O'HALLORAN-1B
17 DARRELL WHITMORE-OF
18 DAVE MAGADAN (INJ)-3B
19 JEFF CONINE-OF/1B
20 JESUS TAVAREZ-OF
21 CHUCK CARR-OF
22 RON TINGLEY (F/A)-C (1)
23 CHARLES JOHNSON-C
24 RICHIE LEWIS-P
25 MATIAS CARRILLO-OF
26 ALEX ARIAS-INF
27 LUIS AQUINO (INJ)-P
28 VADA PINSON-CH
29 MARIO DIAZ-INF
31 ROBB NEN-P
33 FRANK (CRANE) REBERGER-CH
34 BRYAN HARVEY (INJ)-P
35 DAVID WEATHERS-P
37 MIKE JEFFCOAT-P
37 RICH SCHEID-P
38 MARK GARDNER (INJ)-P
39 ORESTES DESTRADE-1B
40 JOHN JOHNSTONE-P
42 JEREMY HERNANDEZ (INJ)-P
43 RON TINGLEY (FREE)-C (1)
43 RUSS MORMAN-1B
44 WILLIE FRASER-P
46 RYAN BOWEN (INJ)-P
47 JEFF MUTIS-P
48 PAT RAPP-P
49 CHARLIE HOUGH (RET)-P
50 BRIAN DRAHMAN-P
51 TERRY MATHEWS-P
53 MARCEL LACHEMANN (1) -CH
53 KURT MILLER-P
58 YORKIS PEREZ (INJ)-P
MICHAEL MYERS (INJ)-(P)

1995

4TH E 67-76 22.5 GB

(144 GAMES)

1 COOKIE ROJAS-CH
3 QUILVIO VERAS-2B
4 GREG COLBRUNN-1B
6 TOMMY GREGG-1B
7 KURT ABBOTT-SS
8 ANDRE DAWSON-OF
9 TERRY PENDLETON-3B
10 GARY SHEFFIELD (INJ)-OF
12 JOE BREEDEN-CH
13 BOB NATAL-C
14 JERRY BROWNE-2B
15 RENE LACHEMANN-MGR
16 EDDIE ZOSKY-SS
17 DARRELL WHITMORE-OF
18 MATT MANTEI-P
19 JEFF CONINE-OF/1B
20 JESUS TAVAREZ-OF
21 CHUCK CARR-OF
22 RUSTY KUNTZ-CH
23 CHARLES JOHNSON-C
24 RICHIE LEWIS-P
25 STEVE DECKER-C
26 ALEX ARIAS-INF
27 MATT DUNBAR-P
27 RICH GARCES-P
28 MARK GARDNER-P
29 MARIO DIAZ-SS
30 WILLIE BANKS-P (3)
31 ROBB NEN-P
32 MIKE MYERS-P (1)
32 ALEJANDRO PENA-P (2)
33 RICK WILLIAMS-CH
33 JOHN BURKETT-P
34 BRYAN HARVEY (INJ)-P
35 DAVID WEATHERS-P
36 BOBBY WITT-P (1)
37 RICH SCHEID-P
37 AARON SMALL-P
38 MARK GARDNER-P
39 ORESTES DESTRADE (JAP)-1B
40 JOHN JOHNSTONE-P
42 JEREMY HERNANDEZ-P
43 JOSE MORALES-CH
44 ALEJANDRO PENA-P (2)
44 ROB MURPHY-P (2)
44 MARC VALDES-P
45 RUSS NORMAN-OF/1B
46 RYAN BOWEN-P
47 LARRY ROTHSCHILD-CH
48 PAT RAPP-P
50 BUDDY GROOM-P
51 TERRY MATHEWS-P
52 RANDY VERES-P
58 YORKIS PEREZ-P
59 JAY POWELL-P

1996

3RD E 80-82 16 GB

1 COOKIE ROJAS-CH/MGR2
2 DEVON WHITE-OF
3 QUILVIO VERAS (INJ)-2B
4 GREG COLBRUNN (INJ)-1B
6 JOE ORSULAK-OF
7 KURT ABBOTT (INJ)-SS
8 ANDRE DAWSON (INJ)-OF
9 TERRY PENDLETON-3B (1)
9 GREGG ZAUN-C (2)
10 GARY SHEFFIELD (INJ)-OF
11 CHRIS HAMMOND (INJ) (WAIV)-P
12 JOE BREEDEN-CH
13 BOB NATAL-C
14 CRAIG GREBECK (INJ)-2B
15 RENE LACHEMANN-MGR1
16 EDGAR RENTERIA (INJ)-SS
18 MATT MANTEI (INJ)-P
19 JEFF CONINE-OF/1B
20 JESUS TAVAREZ-OF
21 JOHN BOLES-MGR3
22 RUSTY KUNTZ-CH
23 CHARLES JOHNSON (INJ)-C
(24) WILSON HEREDIA (INJ)(P)
24 FELIX HEREDIA-P
25 AL LEITER-P
26 ALEX ARIAS-SS
27 KEVIN BROWN (INJ)-P
29 JOE SIDDALL-C
29 JOSH BOOTY-3B
31 ROBB NEN-P
32 ALEJANDRO PENA (INJ)-P
33 JOHN BURKETT-P (1)
33 RICK HELLING-P (2)
34 JOSE MORALES-CH
34 LUIS CASTILLO-2B
35 DAVID WEATHERS-P (1)
35 JERRY BROOKS-C/1B
36 ANDY LARKIN-P
37 RALPH MILLIARD-2B
38 RICK WILLIAMS-CH
39 JAY POWELL (INJ)-P
40 BILLY MCMILLON-OF
43 MIGUEL BATISTA-P
44 MARC VALDES-P
45 RUSS MORMAN-1B
46 DONN PALL-P
47 LARRY ROTHSCHILD-CH
48 PAT RAPP-P
50 BILL HURST-P
51 TERRY MATHEWS (INJ)-P(1)
52 MARK HUTTON-P (2)
53 KURT MILLER-P
56 JOEL ADAMSON-P
58 YORKIS PEREZ-P
59 JAY POWELL-P
61 LIVAN HERNANDEZ-P

1997

2ND E (WC) 92-70 9 GB

W NLDS-SFN 3-0

W NLCS-ATLN 4-2

W WS-CLEA 4-3

1 LUIS CASTILLO (INJ)-2B
2 JOSH BOOTY-3B
3 EDGAR RENTERIA-SS
4 MARK KOTSAY-OF
6 JERRY MANUEL-CH
7 KURT ABBOTT-2B/SS
8 JIM EISENREICH-OF
9 GREGG ZAUN-C
10 GARY SHEFFIELD (INJ)-OF
11 JIM LEYLAND-MGR
12 BRUCE KIMM-CH
13 BOB NATAL-C
14 JOHN WEHNER (INJ)-OF
15 CLIFF FLOYD (INJ)-OF/1B
16 EDGAR RENTERIA-SS
17 JERRY MANUEL-CH
17 TODD DUNWOODY-OF
18 MOISES ALOU-OF
19 JEFF CONINE-1B
20 DARREN (DUTCH) DAULTON-1B
21 RALPH MILLIARD-2B
22 DEVON WHITE-OF
23 CHARLES JOHNSON-C
24 BOBBY (BOBBY BO) BONILLA-3B
25 AL LEITER (INJ)-P
26 ALEX ARIAS (INJ)-SS
27 KEVIN BROWN-P
28 JOHN CANGELOSI-OF/P
29 MILT MAY-CH
30 MATT WHISENANT (INJ)-P (1)
30 CRAIG COUNSELL-2B (2)
31 ROBB NEN-P
32 ALEX FERNANDEZ-P
33 RICK HELLING-P (1)
33 KIRT OJALA-P
35 KURT MILLER (INJ)-P
37 TOMMY SANDT-CH
38 ROB STANIFER-P
39 JAY POWELL-P
40 BILLY MCMILLON-OF (1)
41 TONY SAUNDERS (INJ)-P
42 DENNIS COOK-P
43 RUSS MORMAN-1B
44 DONN PALL-P
45 RICH DONNELLY-CH
47 LARRY ROTHSCHILD-CH
48 PAT RAPP-P (1)
49 FELIX HEREDIA-P
52 MARK HUTTON-P (1)
52 ED VOSBERG (2)-P
57 ANTONIO ALFONSECA-P
61 LIVAN HERNANDEZ-P

1998

5TH E 54-108 52 GB

1 LUIS CASTILLO-2B
2 JOSH BOOTY-3B
3 RYAN JACKSON-OF/1B
4 MARK KOTSAY-OF
4 RANDY KNORR-C
7 MARK KOTSAY-OF
8 JIM EISENREICH-OF (1)
8 PRESTON WILSON-1B (2)
9 GREGG ZAUN-C
10 GARY SHEFFIELD-OF (1)
11 JIM LEYLAND-MGR
12 BRUCE KIMM-CH
13 DAVE BERG-3B/SS
14 JOHN WEHNER-UTIL
15 CLIFF FLOYD-OF/1B
16 EDGAR RENTERIA (INJ)-SS
17 TODD DUNWOODY-OF
18 KEVIN MILLAR (INJ)-1B
19 JOHN ROSKOS-INF
20 VICTOR DARENSBOURG-P
20 BRIAN EDMONDSON-P (2)
21 JESUS SANCHEZ-P
22 ALEX GONZALEZ-INF
23 CHARLES JOHNSON-C (1)
24 KIRT OJALA-P
25 BOBBY (BOBBY BO) BONILLA-3B (1)
25 TODD ZEILE-3B (2)
25 DERRICK LEE-INF
27 DERRICK LEE-INF
27 TODD ZEILE-3B (2)
27 KEVIN ORIE-3B (2)
28 JOHN CANGELOSI-OF
29 MILT MAY-CH
30 CRAIG COUNSELL (INJ)-2B
31 RICH DUBEE-CH
31 MIKE PIAZZA-C (2)
(32) ALEX FERNANDEZ (INJ)-(P)
33 MATT MANTEI (INJ)-P
34 BRIAN MEADOWS (INJ)-P
36 ANDY LARKIN-P
37 TOMMY SANDT-CH
38 ROB STANIFER-P
39 JAY POWELL-P (1)
39 BRIAN DAUBACH-INF
40 VICTOR DARENSBOURG-P
40 CHRIS HAMMOND-P
41 OSCAR HENRIQUEZ-P
42 *(RET) JACKIE ROBINSON*
40 ERIC LUDWICK (INJ)-P
44 DONN PALL-P
45 RICH DONNELLY-CH
46 GABE GONZALEZ-P
47 RAFAEL MEDINA (INJ)-P
48 MANUEL BARRIOS-P (1)
49 FELIX HEREDIA-P (1)
50 RYAN DEMPSTER-P
51 JUSTIN SPEIER-P (2)
52 MIKE REDMOND (INJ)-C
54 JOE FONTONOT (INJ)-P
57 ANTONIO ALFONSECA (INJ) -P
58 DAVE BERG-P
61 LIVAN HERNANDEZ-P

1999

5TH E 64-98 39GB

1 LUIS CASTILLO-2B
6 RAMON CASTRO-C
7 MARK KOTSAY-OF
8 TONY TAYLOR-CH
8 ALEX GONZALEZ-INF
9 GUILLERMO GARCIA-C
10 DAVE BERG-INF
11 ALEX GONZALEZ-INF
12 JOE BREEDEN-CH
13 JOHN BOLES-MGR
14 JORGE FABREGAS-C (1)
15 CLIFF FLOYD (INJ)-OF/1B
16 JOE MALOOF-CH
17 TODD DUNWOODY-OF
18 KEVIN MILLAR-1B
19 JOHN ROSKOS-INF
20 BRIAN EDMONDSON-P
21 JESUS SANCHEZ-P
22 RUSTY KUNTZ-CH
23 DANNY BAUTISTA-OF
24 KIRT OJALA-P
25 DERRICK LEE-INF
26 TIM HYERS-1B
27 KEVIN ORIE (INJ)-3B
28 MIKE LOWELL-3B
29 BRUCE AVEN-OF
30 CRAIG COUNSELL (INJ)-2B (1)
30 CHRIS CLAPINSKI-INF
31 RICH DUBEE-CH
32 ALEX FERNANDEZ (INJ)-P
33 MATT MANTEI-P (1)
34 BRIAN MEADOWS-P
36 VLADIMIR NUNEZ-P (2)
37 LUIS GONZALEZ-CH/INT MGR

37 JULIO RAMIREZ-OF
38 REID CORNELIUS-P
30 VLADIMIR NUNEZ-P (2)
40 VICTOR DARENSBOURG-P
41 BRADEN LOOPER-P
42 *(RET) JACKIE ROBINSON*
43 ARCHIE CORBIN-P
43 A. J. BURNETT-P
44 PRESTON WILSON-1B
45 AMAURY GARCIA-INF
46 RYAN DEMPSTER-P
47 RAFAEL MEDINA-P
48 BRENT BILLINGSLY-P
49 DENNIS SPRINGER,P
50 ARCHIE CORBIN-P
52 MIKE REDMOND-C
55 ARMANDO ALMANZA-P
57 ANTONIO ALFONSECA-P
58 MICHAEL TEJERA-P
59 HECTOR ALMONTE-P
61 LIVAN HERNANDEZ-P (1)

2000

3RD E 79-82 15.5GB

1 LUIS CASTILLO-2B
2 CHRIS CLAPINSKI-INF
3 PABLO OZUNA-INF
6 ANDY FOX-UTIL (2)
7 MARK KOTSAY-OF
8 TONY TAYLOR-CH
9 MENDY LOPEZ-INF
10 DAVE BERG-INF
11 ALEX GONZALEZ (INJ)-INF
12 JOE BREEDEN-CH
13 JOHN BOLES-MGR
14 SANDY MARTINEZ-C
15 KEVIN MILLAR-INF
16 JOEMALOOF-CH
17 RAMON CASTRO-C
18 MARK SMITH-OF
19 MIKE LOWELL-3B
20 BRIAN EDMONDSON (INJ)-P
21 JESUS SANCHEZ-P
22 RUSTY KUNTZ-CH
22 VIC DARENSBOURG-P
23 DANNY BAUTISTA-OF (1)
23 CHUCK SMITH-P
25 DERRICK LEE-INF
26 PAUL BAKO-C (2)
26 MANNY AYBAR-P (3)
26 NATHAN ROLISON-INF
27 MANNY AYBAR-P (3)
28 BRAD PENNY (INJ)-P
29 RICKY BONES-P
30 CLIFF FLOYD (INJ)-OF
31 RICH DUBEE-CH
32 ALEX FERNANDEZ (INJ)-P
33 FREDI GONZALEZ-CH
34 DAN MICELI-P
35 JASON GRILLI-P
36 VLADIMIR NUNEZ-P
37 BRANT BROWN-OF (1)
38 REID CORNELIUS-P
40 VIC DARENSBOURG-P
40 HENRY RODRIGUEZ-OF(2)
41 BRADEN LOOPER-P
42 *(RET#) JACKIE ROBINSON*
43 A. J. BURNETT-P
44 PRESTON WILSON-1B
45 CHUCK SMITH-P
46 RYAN DEMPSTER-P
47 RON MAHAY-P (2)
50 JOE STRONG-P
52 MIKE REDMOND-C
55 ARMANDO ALMANZA-P
57 ANTONIO ALFONSECA-P
(58) MICHAEL TEJERA (INJ)-(P)
MIKE GULAN-(INF)

2001

4TH E 76-86 12 GB

1 LUIS CASTILLO-2B
3 PABLO OZUNA-INF
4 LYLE MOUTON-OF
4 ERIC OWENS (INJ)-OF
6 ANDY FOX (INJ)-UTIL
7 ERIC OWENS-OF
8 TONY TAYLOR-CH
9 RYAN MCGUIRE-OF
10 DAVE BERG-INF
11 ALEX GONZALEZ-INF
12 JOE BREEDEN-CH
13 JOHN BOLES-MGR 1
14 RYAN THOMPSON-OF
15 KEVIN MILLAR-INF
16 JOE MALOOF-CH
17 RAMON CASTRO (WAIV)-C
18 JEFF ABBOTT (INJ)-OF
19 MIKE LOWELL-3B
21 JESUS SANCHEZ-P
22 VIC DARENSBOURG (INJ)-P
23 CHARLES JOHNSON-C
24 TONY PEREZ-MGR 2
25 DERRICK LEE-1B
27 CHAD MATTOLA-OF
27 MIKE GULAN-3B
28 BRAD PENNY-P
28 RICH DUBEE-CH
29 RICKY BONES-P
30 CLIFF FLOYD-OF
31 RICH DUBEE-CH
31 BRAD PENNY-P
32 ALEX FERNANDEZ (INJ)-P
33 FREDI GONZALEZ-CH
34 DAN MICELI-P (1)
35 LYNN JONES-CH
36 VLADIMIR NUNEZ (INJ)-P
37 JASON GRILLI-P
41 BRADEN LOOPER-P
42 *(RET#) JACKIE ROBINSON*
43 A. J. BURNETT (INJ)-P
44 PRESTON WILSON (INJ)-1B
45 CHUCK SMITH (INJ)-P
46 RYAN DEMPSTER-P
47 JOHN MABRY (INJ)-1B (2)
48 JOHNNY RUFFIN-P
49 BENITO BAEZ-P
50 JOE STRONG-P
51 MATT CLEMENT-P
52 MIKE REDMOND-C
53 JUAN ACEVADO-P (2)
54 BLAINE NEAL-P
55 ARMANDO ALMANZA-P
56 GARY KNOTTS-P
56 KEVIN OLSEN-P
57 ANTONIO ALFONSECA-P
61 JOSH BECKETT-P

2002

4TH E 79-83 23GB

1 LUIS CASTILLO-2B
2 MARTY MALLOY-2B/3B
3 PABLO OZUNA (INJ)-UTIL
4 BRIAN BANKS-OF/INF
5 *(RET#) CARL BARGER*
6 ANDY FOX-SS/UTIL
7 PERRY HILL-CH
8 HOMER BUSH-2B/SS (2)
10 JEFF TORBORG-MGR
11 ALEX GONZALEZ (INJ)-SS
12 MIKE MORDECAI-SS/INF (2)
13 OZZIE GUILLEN-CH
15 KEVIN MILLAR-OF/INF
16 ERIC OWENS-OF
17 RAMON CASTRO-C
19 MIKE LOWELL-3B
22 VIC DARENSBOURG-P
23 CHARLES JOHNSON-C
25 DERRICK LEE-1B
27 ABRAHAM NUNEZ-OF
28 BILL ROBINSON-CH
30 CLIFF FLOYD-OF (1)
30 TIM (ROCK) RAINES, SR.-OF
31 BRAD PENNY (INJ)-P
32 TIM (ROCK) RAINES, SR.-OF
32 NATE ROBERTSON-P
33 TOBY BORLAND-P
34 A. J. BURNETT (INJ)-P
35 GARY KNOTTS-P
36 VLADIMIR NUNEZ-P
38 BRAD ARNSBERG-CH
40 RICK RENICK-CH
41 BRADEN LOOPER-P
42 (RET) *JACKIE ROBINSON*
43 A. J. BURNETT-P
43 JUAN ENCARNACION-OF (2)
44 PRESTON WILSON-OF
45 OSWALDO MAIRENA-P
45 CARL PAVANO-P (2)
46 RYAN DEMPSTER-P (1)
46 CARL PAVANO-P (2)
46 OSWALDO MAIRENA-P
46 JUAN ENCARNACION-OF (2)
47 GRAEME LLOYD-P (2)
48 JUSTIN WAYNE-P
50 JULIAN TAVAREZ-P
52 MIKE REDMOND-C
53 NATE TEUT-P
54 BLAINE NEAL-P
55 ARMANDO ALMANZA (INJ)-P
56 KEVIN OLSEN-P
58 MICHAEL TEJERA-P
61 JOSH BECKETT (INJ)-P
62 HANSEL IZQUIERDO-P
__ JEFF COX-CH

2003

2ND E W/C 91-71 10GB
W NLDS-SFN 3-1
W NLCS-CHIN 4-3
W WS-NYA 4-2

1 LUIS CASTILLO-2B
4 GERALD WILLIAMS-OF
5 *(RET#) CARL BARGER*
6 ANDY FOX-UTIL
7 IVAN (PUDGE) RODRIGUEZ-C
9 JUAN PIERRE-OF
10 JEFF TORBORG-MGR1
10 LENNY HARRIS-PH/OF (2)
11 ALEX GONZALEZ-SS
12 MIKE MORDECAI-INF
13 OZZIE GUILLEN-CH
14 TODD HOLLANDSWORTH (INJ)-OF
15 JACK MCKEON-MGR2
16 PERRY HILL-CH
17 RAMON CASTRO-C
18 LENNY HARRIS-PH/OF (2)
18 JEFF CONINE-OF (2)
19 MIKE LOWELL (INJ)-3B
20 MIGUEL CABRERA-OF/3B
21 CHAD ALLEN-OF
21 JOSH BECKETT (INJ)-P
22 BRIAN BANKS-OF/1B
23 DOUG DAVIS-CH
25 DERRICK LEE-1B
26 WAYNE ROSENTHAL-CH
(27) ABRAHAM NUNEZ (INJ)-(OF)
28 BILL ROBINSON-CH
29 ARMANDO ALMANZA (INJ)-P
31 BRAD PENNY-P
32 JUAN ALVAREZ-P
33 TOBY BORLAND (ILL)-P
34 A. J. BURNETT (INJ)-P
35 DONTRELL WILLIS-P
36 VLADIMIR NUNEZ-P
38 BRAD ARNSBERG-CH
38 RICK HELLING-P (2)
39 BLAINE NEAL-P
40 NATE BUMP-P
41 BRADEN LOOPER-P
42 (RET) *JACKIE ROBINSON*
43 JUAN ENCARNACION-OF
44 ALLEN LEVRAULT-P
45 CARL PAVANO-P
47 JEFF COX-CH
48 JUSTIN WAYNE (INJ)-P
49 CHAD FOX-P (2)
52 MIKE REDMOND-C
55 MARK REDMAN (INJ)-P
56 KEVIN OLSEN (INJ)-P
57 TOMMY PHELPS (INJ)-P
58 MICHAEL TEJERA-P
61 JOSH BECKETT (INJ)-P
67 PIERRE ARSENAULT-CH
74 URGUETH URBINA-P (2)
91 TIM SPOONEYBARGER (INJ)-(P)

2004

3RD E 83-79 13GB

1 LUIS CASTILLO-2B
2 DAMIAN EASLEY-2B
3 CHRIS AGUILA-3B
5 *(RET#) CARL BARGER*
6 MATT TREANOR-C
7 PERRY HILL-CH
8 TONY TAYLOR-CH
9 JUAN PIERRE-OF
10 LENNY HARRIS-3B
11 ALEX GONZALEZ-SS
12 MIKE MORDECAI-SS
14 JOSH WILLINGHAM-OF
14 PAUL LO DUCA-C/1B (2)
15 JACK MCKEON-MGR
16 WIL CORDERO-1B
17 RAMON CASTRO (INJ)-C
18 JEFF CONINE-OF
19 MIKE LOWELL-3B
20 MIKE NEU-P
21 JOSH BECKETT (INJ)-P
23 DOUG DAVIS-CH
24 MIGUEL CABRERA-OF/3B
25 HEE SEOP CHOI-1B (1)
25 DAVID WEATHERS-P (3)
26 WAYNE ROSENTHAL-CH
27 ABRAHAM NUNEZ-OF (1)
28 BILL ROBINSON-CH
29 LARRY SUTTON-OF
31 BRAD PENNY-P (1)
31 ISMAEL VALDEZ-P (2)
33 TOBY BORLAND-P
34 A. J. BURNETT (INJ)-P
35 DONTRELL WILLIS-P
37 DARREN OLIVER-P (1)
37 RUDY SEANEZ-P (2)
38 JOSIAS MANZANILLO-P
39 BEN HOWARD-P
40 NATE BUMP-P
41 FRANKLYN GRACESQUI-P
42 (RET) *JACKIE ROBINSON*
43 JUAN ENCARNACION-OF (2)
44 CHAD FOX (INJ)-P
45 CARL PAVANO-P
46 MATT PERISHO-P
47 JEFF COX-CH
48 JUSTIN WAYNE-P
49 ARMANDO BENITEZ (INJ)-P
50 AARON SMALL-P
52 MIKE REDMOND-C
54 LOGAN KENSING-P
57 TOMMY PHELPS-P
58 MICHAEL TEJERA-P (1)
67 PIERRE ARSENAULT-CH
88 BILLY KOCH-P (2)
(91) TIM SPOONEYBARGER (INJ)-P

2005

3RD E (TIED) 83-79 7G

1 LUIS CASTILLO-2B
2 DAMIAN EASLEY-2B
3 CHRIS AGUILA-OF
4 ROBERT ANDINO-INF/SS
5 *(RET#) CARL BARGER*
6 MATT TREANOR-C
7 PERRY HILL-CH
9 JUAN PIERRE-OF
10 LENNY HARRIS-UTIL
11 ALEX GONZALEZ-SS
12 JOE DILLON-UTIL
12 MIKE MORDECAI-INF
14 JOSH WILLINGHAM (INJ)-C
15 JACK MCKEON-MGR
16 PAUL LO DUCA-C
18 JEFF CONINE-OF/1B
19 MIKE LOWELL-3B
20 JOSH WILSON-SS/2B
21 JOSH BECKETT (INJ)-P
22 AL LEITER (REL)-P (1)
22 RYAN JORGENSEN-C
22 JOE DILLON-UTIL
23 RANDY MESSENGER-P
24 MIGUEL CABRERA-OF
25 CARLOS DELGADO (INJ)-1
26 VALERIO DE LOS SANTOS-
27 CHAD BENTZ-P
27 JEREMY HERMIDA-OF
28 BILL ROBINSON-CH
30 LUIS DORANTE-CH
31 ISMAEL VALDEZ (INJ)-P
32 TRAVIS SMITH-P
33 HARRY DUNLOP-CH
34 A. J. BURNETT-P
35 DONTRELL WILLIS-P
36 BRIAN MOEHLER-P
37 FRANK CASTILLO-P
38 MARK WILEY-CH
40 NATE BUMP (INJ)-P
41 JOHN RIEDLING (INJ)-P
42 (RET) *JACKIE ROBINSON*
43 JUAN ENCARNACION-OF
45 JIM MECIR (INJ)-P
46 MATT PERISHO-P (1)
47 JEFF COX-CH
48 SCOTT OLSEN-P
48 PAUL QUANTRILL-P (3)
49 YORMAN BAZARDO (INJ)-P
49 RON VILLONE-P (2)
50 TODD JONES-P
51 CHRIS RESOP-P
52 JIM CROWELL-P
54 LOGAN KENSING (INJ)-P
55 JOSH JOHNSON-P
56 JASON VARGAS-P
57 ANTONIO ALFONSECA (IN -P
59 GUILLERMO MOTA (INJ)-P
67 PIERRE ARSENAULT-CH
(91) TIM SPOONEYBARGER (INJ)-(P)

1962

HOUSTON COLT 45's

8TH 64-96 36.5GB

1 HARRY (WILDFIRE) CRAFT-MGR
2 JIM (CHOPPY) ADAIR-CH
3 BOBBY (NIG) BRAGAN-CH
4 JIM BUSBY-OF/C/CH
5 COT DEAL-CH
6 LUM HARRIS-CH
7 MERRITT RANEW-C
8 HAL SMITH-C/INF
9 JIM CAMPBELL-C
10 NORM LARKER-1B/OF
11 JOEY AMALFITANO-2B/3B
14 BOB ASPROMONTE-3B/INF
15 BOB LILLIS-SS/INF
16 BILLY GOODMAN-INF
16 CARL WARWICK-OF (2)
17 DICK GERNERT-1B
17 BOB CERV-OF (2)
17 PIDGE BROWNE-1B
18 DON BUDDIN-SS/3B (1)
18 J C HARTMAN-SS
19 ERNIE FAZIO-SS
19 GEORGE WILLIAMS-2B
20 DON TAUSSIG-OF
20 CARL WARWICK-OF (2)
21 AL SPANGLER-OF
22 AL HEIST-OF
23 JIM PENDLETON-UTIL
24 JOHNNY WEEKLY-OF
24 DAVE ROBERTS-OF/1B
25 ROMAN MEJIAS-OF
26 JOHNNY TEMPLE-2B/3B (2)
27 PIDGE BROWNE-1B
27 BOB CERV-OF (2)
27 RON DAVIS-OF
30 BOB BRUCE-P
31 AL (BOZO) CICOTTE-P
31 DON MCMAHON-P (2)
32 JIM UMBRICHT-P
33 DEAN STONE-P (1)
33 GEORGE (LEFTY) BRUNET-P
34 DAVE GIUSTI-P
35 JIM GOLDEN-P
36 KEN JOHNSON-P
36 GEORGE (RED) WITT-P (2)
36 DICK (HUMMER) DROTT (INJ)-P
39 RUSS (RUSTY)(DUTCH) KEMMERER-P (2)
39 JOHN ANDERSON-P (2)
40 KEN JOHNSON-P
42 BOBBY SHANTZ-P (1)
43 DICK (TURK) FARRELL-P
44 BOBBY TIEFENAUER-P
46 JIM UMBRICHT-P
46 HAL WOODESHICK-P

1963

9TH 66-96 33GB

1 HARRY (WILDFIRE) CRAFT-MGR
2 JIM (CHOPPY) ADAIR-CH
3 PETE RUNNELS-INF
4 JIM BUSBY-OF/C/CH
4 GLENN (SPARKY) VAUGHAN-SS/3B
5 COT DEAL-CH
6 LUM HARRIS-CH
6 JERRY GROTE-C
7 JOHN BATEMAN-C
8 HAL SMITH-C
8 DAVE ADLESH-C
9 JIM CAMPBELL-C
9 HAL SMITH-C
10 RUSTY STAUB-1B/OF
11 ERNIE FAZIO-2B/INF
12 JOE MORGAN-2B
13 DICK (TURK) FARRELL-P
14 BOB ASPROMONTE-3B/1B
15 BOB LILLIS-SS/INF
16 JOHNNY TEMPLE-2B/3B
16 MIKE WHITE-2B
17 AARON (HAWK) POINTER-OF
18 J C HARTMAN-SS
18 JIMMY (THE TOY CANNON) WYNN-UTIL
19 SONNY JACKSON-SS
20 CARL WARWICK-OF/1B
21 AL SPANGLER-OF
22 JOHN PACIOREK-OF
23 IVAN MURRELL-OF
24 DAVE ADLESH-C
26 JOHNNY WEEKLY (INJ)-OF
26 CARROLL HARDY-OF
27 HOWIE GOSS-OF
29 BROCK DAVIS-OF
30 BOB BRUCE-P
31 DON MCMAHON-P
32 JIM UMBRICHT-P
33 GEORGE (LEFTY) BRUNET-P (1)
34 RANDY CARDINAL-P
34 JIM DICKSON-P
35 JIM GOLDEN-P
36 DICK (HUMMER) DROTT-P
38 HAL (SKINNY) BROWN-P
39 RUSS (RUSTY)(DUTCH) KEMMERER-P
40 KEN JOHNSON-P
41 DANNY COOMBS-P
42 JAY DAHL-P
43 DON NOTTEBART-P
44 JIM DICKSON-P
44 CHRIS ZACHARY-P
44 JOE HOERNER-P
46 HAL WOODESHICK-P
47 LARRY YELLEN-P

1964

9TH 66-96 27GB

1 HARRY (WILDFIRE) CRAFT-MGR1
2 NELLIE FOX-2B
3 PETE RUNNELS-1B
4 JIM BUSBY-OF/C/CH
5 COT DEAL-CH
6 LUM HARRIS-CH/MGR2
7 JOHN BATEMAN-C
8 JERRY GROTE-C
8 DAVE ADLESH-C
9 JOHN (PORK CHOP) HOFFMAN-C
10 RUSTY STAUB-1B/OF
11 EDDIE KASKO-SS/3B
13 DICK (TURK) FARRELL-P
14 BOB ASPROMONTE-3B
15 BOB LILLIS-INF
16 MIKE WHITE-OF/INF
17 STEVE HERTZ-3B
20 JIM BEAUCHAMP-OF/1B
20 CARROLL HARDY-OF
21 AL SPANGLER-OF
22 JOE GAINES-OF (2)
22 JIM BEAUCHAMP-OF/1B
23 WALT BOND-1B/OF
24 JIMMY (THE TOY CANNON) WYNN-OF
25 IVAN MURRELL-OF
26 JOHNNY WEEKLY (INJ)-OF
26 DAVE ROBERTS-OF/1B
27 JOE GAINES-OF (2)
28 WALT (NO-NECK) WILLIAMS-OF
29 BROCK DAVIS-OF
29 SONNY JACKSON-SS
30 BOB BRUCE-P
31 DON LARSEN-P (2)
(32) JIM UMBRICHT (DIED)-(P)
33 JIM (BEAR) OWENS-P
34 DAVE GIUSTI-P
34 GORDON JONES-P
35 JOE MORGAN-2B
36 CLAUDE (FRENCHY) RAYMOND-P
37 LARRY YELLEN-P
37 CHRIS ZACHARY-P
38 HAL (SKINNY) BROWN-P
39 DAVE GIUSTI-P
40 KEN JOHNSON-P
42 JIM (CHOPPY) ADAIR-CH
43 DON NOTTEBART-P
44 JOE HOERNER-P
44 DANNY COOMBS (MIL)-P
45 DON BRADEY-P
46 HAL WOODESHICK-P
47 LARRY YELLEN-P
49 LARRY DIERKER-P

1965

HOUSTON ASTROS

9TH 65-97 32GB

2 NELLIE FOX-INF/CH
3 JIM (CHOPPY) ADAIR-CH
4 JIM BUSBY-CH
4 JIM (DIAMOND JIM) GENTILE-1B (2)
5 HOWIE POLLET-CH
6 CLINT (SCRAP IRON) COURTNEY-CH
7 JOHN BATEMAN-C
7 GUS TRIANDOS-C (2)
8 DAVE ADLESH-C
8 RON BRAND-C/UTIL
10 RUSTY STAUB-OF/1B
11 EDDIE KASKO (INJ)-SS/3B
13 DICK (TURK) FARRELL-P
14 BOB ASPROMONTE-3B/INF
15 BOB LILLIS-SS/INF
16 MIKE WHITE-3B
17 CHUCK HARRISON-1B
18 JOE MORGAN-2B
19 SONNY JACKSON-SS/3B
20 JIM BEAUCHAMP-OF/1B (1)
20 LEE MAYE-OF (2)
21 AL SPANGLER-OF (1)
21 JIM (STING) RAY-P
22 CHUCK HARRISON-1B
23 WALT BOND-1B/OF
24 JIMMY (THE TOY CANNON) WYNN-OF
25 JIM (MOE) MAHONEY-SS
26 LUM HARRIS-MGR
27 GENE RATLIFF-PH
28 JOE GAINES-OF
30 BOB BRUCE-P
31 DON LARSEN-P (1)
31 JACK LAMABE-P (2)
31 FRANK THOMAS-UTIL (2)
32 *(RET#) JIM UMBRICHT*
33 JIM (BEAR) OWENS-P
34 KEN MACKENZIE-P
34 NORM MILLER-OF
35 JIM (STING) RAY-P
35 CHUCK HARRISON-1B
35 MIKE CUELLAR-P
36 CLAUDE (FRENCHY) RAYMOND-P
37 CHRIS ZACHARY-P
38 ROBIN ROBERTS-P (2)
39 DAVE GIUSTI-P
40 KEN JOHNSON-P (1)
40 RON TAYLOR-P (2)
40 DON LEE-P (2)
41 JIM BUSBY-CH
41 CARROLL SEMBERA-P
42 BRUCE VON HOFF-P
43 DON NOTTEBART-P
44 DANNY COOMBS (MIL)-P
46 HAL WOODESHICK-P (1)
46 GORDON JONES-P
46 DON ARLICH-P
46 RON TAYLOR-P (2)
48 DON LEE-P (2)
49 LARRY DIERKER-P
52 JIM (DIAMOND JIM) GENTILE-1B (2)
54 NORM MILLER-OF
57 JOHN (PORK CHOP) HOFFMAN-C

1966

8TH 72-90 23GB

1 GRADY HATTON-MGR
2 NELLIE FOX-CH
3 GORDON JONES-CH
3 JIM BUSBY-CH
4 JIM (DIAMOND JIM) GENTILE-1B (1)
5 JIM BUSBY-CH
5 GORDON JONES-CH
6 AL HEIST-CH
7 JOHN BATEMAN-C
8 BILL HEATH-C
9 RON BRAND-UTIL
10 RUSTY STAUB-OF/1B
11 JULIO GOTAY-3B
11 GENE (AUGIE) FREESE-UTIL (2)
12 NATE COLBERT-PH
13 DICK (TURK) FARRELL-P
14 BOB ASPROMONTE-3B/INF
15 BOB LILLIS-INF
16 SONNY JACKSON-SS
17 CHUCK HARRISON-1B
18 JOE MORGAN (INJ)-2B
20 LEE MAYE-OF
21 DAVE NICHOLSON-OF
22 GREG SIMS-OF
22 RON DAVIS-OF
23 DON WILSON-P
24 JIMMY (THE TOY CANNON) WYNN (INJ)-OF
25 FELIX MANTILLA-UTIL
27 DAVE ADLESH-C
28 AARON (HAWK) POINTER-OF
29 BROCK DAVIS-OF
30 BOB BRUCE-P
31 GARY KROLL-P
32 *(RET#) JIM UMBRICHT*
33 JIM (BEAR) OWENS-P
34 NORM MILLER-OF/3B
34 AURELIO MONTEAGUDO-P (2)
35 MIKE CUELLAR-P
36 CLAUDE (FRENCHY) RAYMOND-P
37 CHRIS ZACHARY-P
37 AURELIO MONTEAGUDO-P (2)
38 ROBIN ROBERTS-P/CH (1)
38 JIM (STING) RAY-P
38 BOB (BULL) WATSON-PH
39 DAVE GIUSTI-P
40 RON TAYLOR (INJ)-P
41 CARROLL SEMBERA-P
42 FRANK CARPIN-P
43 JIM (STING) RAY-P
43 DON LEE-P (1)
44 DANNY COOMBS-P
46 BARRY LATMAN-P
46 DON ARLICH-P
46 JOE GAINES-OF
48 BARRY LATMAN-P
49 LARRY DIERKER-P
50 CHRIS ZACHARY-P

1967

9TH 69-93 32.5GB

1 GRADY HATTON-MGR
2 NELLIE FOX-CH
3 JIM BUSBY-CH
4 DAVE ADLESH-C
5 GORDON JONES-CH
5 HAL KING-C
6 AL HEIST-CH
7 JOHN BATEMAN-C
8 BILL HEATH-C (1)
8 JACKIE BRANDT-UTIL (2)
9 RON BRAND-UTIL
10 RUSTY STAUB-OF
11 EDDIE MATHEWS-1B/3B (1)
11 BOB (BULL) WATSON-1B
12 LEE BALES-2B/SS
12 DOUG (THE RED ROOSTER) (ROJO) RADER-1B/3B
13 DICK (TURK) FARRELL-P (1)
14 BOB ASPROMONTE-3B
15 BOB LILLIS-INF
16 SONNY JACKSON-SS
17 CHUCK HARRISON-1B
18 JOE MORGAN-2B/OF
19 HOWIE (DIZ) REED-P
20 JIM LANDIS-OF (3)
20 IVAN MURRELL-OF
21 NORM MILLER (MIL)-OF
21 LEE BALES-2B/SS
22 RON DAVIS-OF
23 DON WILSON-P
23 AARON (HAWK) POINTER-OF
24 JIMMY (THE TOY CANNON) WYNN-OF
25 BO BELINSKY-P
26 JOHN BUZHARDT-P (3)
27 DAVE ADLESH-C
27 CHRIS ZACHARY-P
28 AARON (HAWK) POINTER-OF
28 JULIO GOTAY-INF
29 ALONZO (CANDY) HARRIS-PH
30 BO BELINSKY-P
31 DANNY COOMBS-P
31 DICK (TURK) FARRELL-P (1)
31 LARRY SHERRY-P (2)
31 BRUCE VON HOFF-P
32 *(RET#) JIM UMBRICHT*
33 JIM (BEAR) OWENS-P/CH
34 JOE (LOCO) HERRARA-PH
35 MIKE CUELLAR-P
36 CLAUDE (FRENCHY) RAYMOND-P (1)
36 DAVE EILERS-P
37 CHRIS ZACHARY-P
37 LARRY SHERRY-P (2)
38 BRUCE VON HOFF-P
39 DAVE GIUSTI-P
40 DON WILSON-P
41 CARROLL SEMBERA-P
42 LEE BALES-2B/SS
42 PAT HOUSE-P
44 DANNY COOMBS-P
44 ARNIE EARLEY-P
44 TOM DUKES-P
45 BRUCE VON HOFF-P
46 DAN SCHNEIDER-P
47 WADE BLASINGAME-P
48 BARRY LATMAN-P
48 TOM DUKES-P
49 LARRY DIERKER (MIL)-P

1968

10TH 72-90 25GB

00 JOHN MAYBERRY-1B

1 GRADY HATTON-MGR1
2 SALTY PARKER-CH
3 MEL MCGAHA-CH
4 BUDDY HANCKEN-CH
5 JIM (BEAR) OWENS-CH
6 DAVE ADLESH-C
7 JOHN BATEMAN-C
8 HAL KING-C
9 RON BRAND-UTIL
10 RUSTY STAUB-1B/OF
11 DENIS MENKE-2B/INF
12 DOUG (THE RED ROOSTER) (ROJO) RADER-3B/1B
14 BOB ASPROMONTE-UTIL
15 HECTOR TORRES-SS/2B
17 JULIO GOTAY-2B/3B
18 JOE MORGAN (INJ)-2B/OF
20 IVAN MURRELL-OF
20 LEON MCFADDEN-SS
21 NORM MILLER-OF
22 RON DAVIS-OF (1)
22 NATE COLBERT-OF/1B
22 JOE (LOCO) HERRARA-OF/2B
23 DENNY LEMASTER-P
24 JIMMY (THE TOY CANNON) WYNN-OF
25 HARRY (THE HAT) WALKER-MGR2
26 BOB (BULL) WATSON-OF
26 NATE COLBERT-OF/1B
27 BOB (BULL) WATSON-OF
28 LEE THOMAS-OF/1B
30 JOHN BUZHARDT-P
31 DANNY COOMBS-P
32 *(RET#) JIM UMBRICHT*
33 HAL GILSON-P (2)
33 JOHN BUZHARDT-P
35 MIKE CUELLAR-P
36 WADE BLASINGAME (INJ)-P
37 BYRON BROWNE-OF
37 DICK SIMPSON-OF (2)
39 DAVE GIUSTI-P
40 DON WILSON-P
(41) CARROLL SEMBERA (INJ)-(P)
42 STEVE SHEA-P
43 PAT HOUSE-P
44 DANNY COOMBS-P
44 TOM DUKES-P
45 JIM (STING) RAY-P
47 WADE BLASINGAME (INJ)-P
48 FRED GLADDING (INJ)-P
49 LARRY DIERKER-P
50 PAT HOUSE-P
50 DANNY (MICKEY) WALTON-PH
51 STEVE SHEA-P
52 HAL GILSON-P (2)

1969

5TH W 81-81 12GB

2 SALTY PARKER-CH
3 MEL MCGAHA-CH
4 BUDDY HANCKEN-CH
5 JIM (BEAR) OWENS-CH
6 DON BRYANT-C
7 JOHNNY EDWARDS-C
10 TOMMY DAVIS-OF (2)
11 DENIS MENKE-SS/INF
12 DOUG (THE RED ROOSTER) (ROJO) RADER-3B/1B
13 CURT BLEFARY-1B/OF
14 MARTY MARTINEZ-UTIL/P
15 HECTOR TORRES (INJ)-SS
17 JULIO GOTAY-2B/3B
18 JOE MORGAN-2B/OF
19 GARY GEIGER-OF
20 LEON MCFADDEN-OF/SS
21 NORM MILLER-OF
22 JESUS ALOU (INJ)-OF
23 DENNY LEMASTER-P
24 JIMMY (THE TOY CANNON) WYNN-OF
25 HARRY (THE HAT) WALKER-MGR
26 KEITH LAMPARD-OF
27 BOB (BULL) WATSON-UTIL
28 SANDY VALDESPINO-OF (1)
31 DANNY COOMBS-P
32 *(RET#) JIM UMBRICHT*
33 JOHN MAYBERRY-PH
34 CESAR GERONIMO-OF
35 SKIP GUINN-P
36 WADE BLASINGAME-P
37 DOOLEY WOMACK-P (1)
37 SCIPIO SPINKS-P
38 TOM GRIFFIN-P
40 DON WILSON-P
41 DANNY COOMBS-P
41 DAN SCHNEIDER-P
41 BILL HENRY-P
42 JACK BILLINGHAM-P
43 RON WILLIS-P (2)
44 JIM BOUTON-P (2)
45 JIM (STING) RAY-P
47 BOB WATKINS-P
48 FRED GLADDING-P
49 LARRY DIERKER-P
50 RON WILLIS-P (2)
56 JIM BOUTON-P (2)
58 DAN SCHNEIDER-P

1970

4TH W 79-83 23GB

2 SALTY PARKER-CH
3 MEL MCGAHA-CH
4 BUDDY HANCKEN-CH
5 JIM (BEAR) OWENS-CH
6 DON BRYANT-C
7 JOHNNY EDWARDS-C
9 JOE (PEPI) PEPITONE-1B/OF (1)
10 TOMMY DAVIS-OF (1)
10 LARRY HOWARD-UTIL
11 DENIS MENKE-SS/UTIL
12 DOUG (THE RED ROOSTER) (ROJO) RADER-3B/1B
14 MARTY MARTINEZ-UTIL
15 HECTOR TORRES-SS/2B
18 JOE MORGAN-2B
19 GARY GEIGER-OF
20 LEON MCFADDEN-PR
20 CESAR GERONIMO-OF
21 NORM MILLER-OF/C
22 JESUS ALOU (INJ)-OF
23 DENNY LEMASTER-P
24 JIMMY (THE TOY CANNON) WYNN-OF
25 HARRY (THE HAT) WALKER-MGR
26 KEITH LAMPARD-OF/1B
27 BOB (BULL) WATSON-1B/UTIL
28 CESAR CEDENO-OF
31 JACK DILAURO-P
32 *(RET#) JIM UMBRICHT*
33 JOHN MAYBERRY-1B
36 WADE BLASINGAME-P
37 SCIPIO SPINKS-P
38 TOM GRIFFIN-P
39 DAN OSINSKI-P
39 GEORGE CULVER-P (2)
40 DON WILSON-P
41 RON COOK-P
42 JACK BILLINGHAM-P
43 DAN OSINSKI-P
43 KEN FORSCH-P
44 JIM BEAUCHAMP-OF (1)
45 JIM (STING) RAY-P
46 BUDDY HARRIS-P
48 FRED GLADDING-P
49 LARRY DIERKER-P
53 MIKE MARSHALL-P (1)
56 JIM BOUTON-P

1971

4TH W (TIE) 79-83 11GB

2 SALTY PARKER-CH
3 HUB KITTLE-CH
4 BUDDY HANCKEN-CH
5 JIM (BEAR) OWENS-CH
7 JOHNNY EDWARDS (INJ)-C
8 JACK HIATT (INJ)-C/1B
10 LARRY HOWARD-C
11 DENIS MENKE-1B/INF
12 DOUG (THE RED ROOSTER) (ROJO) RADER-3B
14 MARTY MARTINEZ-INF
15 ROGER METZGER-SS
16 RAY BUSSE-SS/3B
17 JAY SCHLUETER-OF
18 JOE MORGAN-2B
19 DERREL THOMAS-2B
20 CESAR GERONIMO-OF
21 NORM MILLER (INJ)-OF/C
22 JESUS ALOU-OF
23 DENNY LEMASTER-P
24 JIMMY (THE TOY CANNON) WYNN-OF
25 HARRY (THE HAT) WALKER-MGR
27 BOB (BULL) WATSON-OF/1B
28 CESAR CEDENO-OF/1B
29 RICH CHILES-OF
30 WADE BLASINGAME-P
31 LARRY YOUNT-P
32 *(RET#) JIM UMBRICHT*
33 GEORGE CULVER-P
33 JOHN MAYBERRY-1B
35 SKIP GUINN-P
36 WADE BLASINGAME-P
37 SCIPIO SPINKS-P
38 TOM GRIFFIN-P
39 GEORGE CULVER-P
40 DON WILSON-P
41 RON COOK (INJ)-P
42 JACK BILLINGHAM-P
43 KEN FORSCH-P
44 BILL GREIF-P
45 JIM (STING) RAY-P
46 BUDDY HARRIS-P
48 FRED GLADDING-P
49 LARRY DIERKER (INJ)-P
50 J. R. RICHARD-P
52 BILL GREIF-P

1972

2ND W 84-69 10.5GB

1 SALTY PARKER-CH
2 SALTY PARKER-CH/MGR2
2 LEO (THE LIP)(LIPPY) DUROCHER-MGR3 (2)
3 HUB KITTLE-CH
4 BUDDY HANCKEN-CH
5 JIM (BEAR) OWENS-CH
6 CLIFF JOHNSON-C
7 JOHNNY EDWARDS-C
8 JACK HIATT-C (1)
8 GARY SUTHERLAND-2B/3B
9 BOB STINSON-C/OF
10 LARRY HOWARD-C/OF
11 JIMMY STEWART-UTIL
12 DOUG (THE RED ROOSTER) (ROJO) RADER-3B
14 ROGER METZGER-SS
15 DAVE ROBERTS-P
18 BOBBY FENWICK-INF
19 TOMMY HELMS-2B
21 NORM MILLER-OF
22 JESUS ALOU-OF
23 LEE MAY-1B
24 JIMMY (THE TOY CANNON) WYNN-OF
25 HARRY (THE HAT) WALKER-MGR1
27 BOB (BULL) WATSON-OF/1B
28 CESAR CEDENO-OF
29 RICH CHILES-OF
32 *(RET#) JIM UMBRICHT*
36 WADE BLASINGAME-P (1)
37 JOE GIBBON-P (2)
37 MIKE COSGROVE-P
38 TOM GRIFFIN-P
39 GEORGE CULVER-P
40 DON WILSON-P
42 JIM YORK-P
43 KEN FORSCH-P
45 JIM (STING) RAY-P
47 JERRY REUSS-P
48 FRED GLADDING-P
49 LARRY DIERKER-P
50 J. R. RICHARD-P

1973

4TH W 82-80 17GB

1 GRADY HATTON-CH
2 LEO (THE LIP)(LIPPY) DUROCHER-MGR
3 HUB KITTLE-CH
4 PRESTON GOMEZ-CH
5 BOB LILLIS-CH
6 CLIFF JOHNSON-1B
7 JOHNNY EDWARDS (ILL)-C
8 GARY SUTHERLAND-2B/3B
9 OTIS THORNTON-C
10 LARRY HOWARD-C (1)
10 RAFAEL BATISTA-1B
11 JIMMY STEWART-UTIL
12 DOUG (THE RED ROOSTER) (ROJO) RADER-3B
14 ROGER METZGER-SS
15 DAVE ROBERTS-P
16 BOB LILLIS-CH
16 RAY BUSSE-SS/3B (2)
17 GARY SUTHERLAND-2B/3B
17 HECTOR TORRES-SS/2B
19 TOMMY HELMS-2B
20 TOMMIE AGEE-OF (1)
20 DAVE CAMPBELL-UTIL (3)
21 NORM MILLER (INJ)-OF
21 GREG GROSS-OF
22 JESUS ALOU-OF (1)
22 MIKE EASLER-OF
23 LEE MAY-1B
24 JIMMY (THE TOY CANNON) WYNN-OF
25 BOB GALLAGHER-OF/1B
26 SKIP JUTZE-C
27 BOB (BULL) WATSON-OF/UTIL
28 CESAR CEDENO-OF
30 JIM (CATFISH) CRAWFORD-P
32 *(RET#) JIM UMBRICHT*
34 CECIL UPSHAW-P(2)
37 MIKE COSGROVE-P
38 TOM GRIFFIN (INJ)-P
39 JUAN PIZARRO-P (2)
40 DON WILSON-P
42 JIM YORK-P
43 KEN FORSCH-P
45 JIM (STING) RAY-P
46 DOUG KONIECZNY-P
47 JERRY REUSS-P
48 FRED GLADDING-P
49 LARRY DIERKER (INJ)-P
50 J. R. RICHARD-P
51 JUAN PIZARRO-P (2)

1974

4TH W 81-81 21GB

1 GRADY HATTON-CH
2 ROGER CRAIG-CH
3 HUB KITTLE-CH
4 PRESTON GOMEZ-MGR
4 BOB LILLIS-CH
5 BOB LILLIS-CH
6 CLIFF JOHNSON-C/1B
7 JOHNNY EDWARDS-C
8 MILT MAY-C
9 MICK KELLEHER-SS
10 LARRY MILBOURNE-UTIL
11 DENIS MENKE-INF
12 DOUG (THE RED ROOSTER) (ROJO) RADER-3B
14 ROGER METZGER-SS
15 DAVE ROBERTS-P
16 RAY BUSSE-3B
18 PRESTON GOMEZ-MGR
19 TOMMY HELMS-2B
20 DAVE CAMPBELL (INJ)-UTIL
21 GREG GROSS-OF
22 MIKE EASLER-PH
23 LEE MAY-1B
24 CLAUDE OSTEEN-P (1)
24 RAMON DE LOS SANTOS-P
25 BOB GALLAGHER-OF/1B
26 SKIP JUTZE -C
26 WILBUR HOWARD-OF
27 BOB (BULL) WATSON-OF/1B
28 CESAR CEDENO-OF
31 (DOWNTOWN) OLLIE BROWN-OF (1)
31 MIKE NAGY-P
31 PAUL SIEBERT-P
32 *(RET#) JIM UMBRICHT*
37 MIKE COSGROVE-P
38 TOM GRIFFIN-P
40 DON WILSON-P
42 JIM YORK-P
43 KEN FORSCH-P
44 FRED SCHERMAN-P
45 MIKE NAGY-P
46 DOUG KONIECZNY-P
47 JERRY JOHNSON-P
49 LARRY DIERKER-P
50 J. R. RICHARD-P

1975

6TH W 64-97 43.5GB

2 ROGER CRAIG-CH
3 HUB KITTLE-CH
4 JIM WILLIAMS-CH
5 BOB LILLIS-CH
6 CLIFF JOHNSON-UTIL
7 BILLVIRDON-MGR2
8 MILT MAY-C
9 SKIP JUTZE-C
10 LARRY MILBOURNE-2B/SS
11 ROB ANDREWS-2B/SS
12 DOUG (THE RED ROOSTER) (ROJO) RADER-3B/SS
14 ROGER METZGER-SS
15 DAVE ROBERTS-P
16 JERRY DAVANON-INF
17 KEN BOSWELL-2B/3B
18 PRESTON GOMEZ-MGR1
19 TOMMY HELMS-INF
20 RAFAEL BATISTA-PH
21 GREG GROSS-OF
22 MIKE EASLER-PH
23 ENOS CABELL-UTIL
24 ART GARDNER-OF
25 JOSE (CHEO) CRUZ-OF
26 WILBUR HOWARD-OF
27 BOB (BULL) WATSON-1B/OF
28 CESAR CEDENO (INJ)-OF
29 JESUS DE LA ROSA-PH
30 JIM (CATFISH) CRAWFORD-P
31 PAUL SIEBERT-P

OUSTON COLT 45's/**ASTROS**

2 *(RET#) JIM UMBRICHT*
5 WAYNE GRANGER-P
6 JOE NIEKRO-P
7 MIKE COSGROVE-P
8 TOM GRIFFIN (INJ)-P
2 JIM YORK-P
3 KEN FORSCH (INJ)-P
4 FRED SCHERMAN-P (1)
4 JOSE SOSA-P
6 DOUG KONIECZNY-P
8 MIKE STANTON-P
9 LARRY DIERKER-P
0 J. R. RICHARD-P

1976

3RD W 80-82 22GB

2 MEL WRIGHT-CH
3 TONY PACHECO-CH
4 DEACON JONES-CH
5 BOB LILLIS-CH
6 CLIFF JOHNSON-UTIL
7 BILLVIRDON-MGR
8 ED HERRMANN-C (2)
9 SKIP JUTZE-C
0 LARRY MILBOURNE-2B
1 ROB ANDREWS-2B/SS
4 ROGER METZGER-SS/2B
5 ALEX TAVERAS-SS/2B
6 JERRY DAVANON-INF
7 KEN BOSWELL-UTIL
8 ART HOWE-3B/2B
0 RICH CHILES-OF
1 GREG GROSS-OF
2 LEON ROBERTS-OF
3 ENOS CABELL-3B/1B
5 JOSE (CHEO) CRUZ-OF
6 WILBUR HOWARD-OF/2B
7 BOB (BULL) WATSON-1B
8 CESAR CEDENO-OF
9 AL JAVIER-OF
0 GENE PENTZ (INJ)-P
1 PAUL SIEBERT-P
2 *(RET#) JIM UMBRICHT*
33) JOE MCINTOSH (INJ)-(P)
4 DAN LARSON-P
5 JOE SAMBITO-P
6 JOE NIEKRO-P
7 MIKE COSGROVE-P
8 TOM GRIFFIN-P (1)
9 MIKE BARLOW-P
9 BO MCLAUGHLIN-P
2 LARRY HARDY-P
3 KEN FORSCH-P
4 JOSE SOSA-P
5 GIL RONDON-P
7 JOAQUIN (JACK) ANDUJAR-P
9 LARRY DIERKER-P
0 J. R. RICHARD-P
1 MARK LEMONGELLO-P
2 JOAQUIN (JACK) ANDUJAR-P
3 LARRY HARDY-P

1977

3RD W 81-81 17GB

2 MEL WRIGHT-CH
3 TONY PACHECO-CH
4 DEACON JONES-CH
5 BOB LILLIS-CH
6 CLIFF JOHNSON-OF/1B (1)
6 CRAIG CACEK-1B
7 BILLVIRDON-MGR
8 ED HERRMANN-C
9 CLIFF JOHNSON-OF/1B (1)
9 JULIO GONZALEZ-SS/2B
0 MIKE FISCHLIN-SS
1 ROB SPERRING-INF
3 JOE FERGUSON-C/1B
4 ROGER METZGER (INJ)-SS/2B
16 JIM FULLER-OF/1B
17 KEN BOSWELL-2B/3B
18 ART HOWE (INJ)-2B/INF
20 JOE CANNON-OF
21 WILLIE CRAWFORD-OF (1)
21 TERRY PUHL-OF
22 LEON ROBERTS, OF
23 ENOS CABELL-3B/INF
24 ART GARDNER-OF
25 JOSE (CHEO) CRUZ-OF
26 WILBUR HOWARD-OF/2B
27 BOB (BULL) WATSON-1B
28 CESAR CEDENO-OF
29 DENNY WALLING-OF
30 GENE PENTZ-P
31 DANNY (MICKEY) WALTON-1B
32 *(RET#) JIM UMBRICHT*
33 TOM DIXON-P
34 DAN LARSON-P
35 JOE SAMBITO-P
36 JOE NIEKRO-P
37 TOM DIXON-P
38 FLOYD BANNISTER (INJ)-P
39 BO MCLAUGHLIN-P
42 MARK LEMONGELLO-P
43 KEN FORSCH-P
45 ROY THOMAS-P
46 DOUG KONIECZNY (INJ)-P
47 JOAQUIN (JACK) ANDUJAR (INJ)-P
50 J. R. RICHARD-P
52 JULIO GONZALEZ-SS/2B
53 LUIS PUJOLS-C
60 ??? ALFONSO-CH

1978

5TH W 74-88 21GB

2 MEL WRIGHT-CH
3 TONY PACHECO-CH
4 DEACON JONES-CH
5 BOB LILLIS-CH
6 REGGIE BALDWIN-C
7 BILLVIRDON-MGR
8 ED HERRMANN-C (1)
8 LUIS PUJOLS-C/1B
9 JULIO GONZALEZ-INF
10 MIKE FISCHLIN-SS
13 JOE FERGUSON-C (1)
13 BRUCE BOCHY-C
14 ROGER METZGER-SS/2B (1)
15 KEITH DRUMRIGHT-2B
16 DAVE BERGMAN-1B/OF
17 RAFAEL LANDESTOY-SS/UTIL
18 ART HOWE (INJ)-2B/INF
19 JIM OBRADOVICH-1B
20 JOE CANNON-OF
21 TERRY PUHL-OF
22 JESUS ALOU-OF
23 ENOS CABELL-3B/INF
24 JIMMY SEXTON-INF
25 JOSE (CHEO) CRUZ-OF/1B
26 WILBUR HOWARD-UTIL
27 BOB (BULL) WATSON-1B
28 CESAR CEDENO (INJ)-OF
29 DENNY WALLING-OF
30 GENE PENTZ (INJ)-P
31 DAN WARTHEN-P
32 *(RET#) JIM UMBRICHT*
34 RICK WILLIAMS-P
35 JOE SAMBITO-P
36 JOE NIEKRO-P
37 TOM DIXON-P
38 FLOYD BANNISTER-P
39 BO MCLAUGHLIN-P
42 MARK LEMONGELLO-P
43 KEN FORSCH-P
44 OSCAR ZAMORA-P
45 FRANK RICCELLI-P
46 JEFFREY LEONARD-OF
47 JOAQUIN (JACK) ANDUJAR (INJ)-P
48 VERN RUHLE-P
50 J. R. RICHARD-P
51 OSCAR ZAMORA-P

1979

2ND W 89-73 1.5GB

2 MEL WRIGHT-CH
3 TONY PACHECO-CH
4 DEACON JONES-CH
5 BOB LILLIS-CH
6 REGGIE BALDWIN-C/1B
7 BILLVIRDON-MGR
8 LUIS PUJOLS-C
9 JULIO GONZALEZ-INF
11 ALAN KNICELY-C/3B
12 CRAIG REYNOLDS-SS
13 BRUCE BOCHY-C
14 ALAN ASHBY (INJ)-C
16 DAVE BERGMAN-1B
17 RAFAEL LANDESTOY-2B/SS
18 ART HOWE (INJ)-2B/INF
20 DANNY HEEP-OF
21 TERRY PUHL-OF
22 JESUS ALOU-OF/1B/CH
23 ENOS CABELL-3B/1B
24 JIMMY SEXTON-INF
25 JOSE (CHEO) CRUZ-OF
27 BOB (BULL) WATSON-1B (1)
28 CESAR CEDENO-1B/OF
29 DENNY WALLING-OF
30 JEFFREY LEONARD-OF
31 FRANK LACORTE-P (2)
32 *(RET#) JIM UMBRICHT*
33 TOM WIEDENBAUER-OF
33 GEORGE THROOP-P (2)
34 GORDY PLADSON-P
35 JOE SAMBITO-P
36 JOE NIEKRO-P
37 TOM DIXON (INJ)-P
38 RICK WILLIAMS-P
39 BO MCLAUGHLIN-P (1)
39 PETE LADD-P
41 GARY WILSON-P
41 BOBBY SPROWL-P
42 PETE LADD-P
42 BERT ROBERGE (INJ)-P
43 KEN FORSCH (INJ)-P
45 FRANK RICCELLI (INJ)-P
46 RANDY NIEMANN-P
47 JOAQUIN (JACK) ANDUJAR (INJ)-P
48 VERN RUHLE (INJ)-P
50 J. R. RICHARD-P
54 MIKE MENDOZA-P
65 RICK WILLIAMS-P

1980

1ST W 93-70 0GB
W 1G P/O -LAN
L NLCS-PHIN 3-2

2 MEL WRIGHT-CH
3 DON LEPPERT-CH
4 DEACON JONES-CH
5 BOB LILLIS-C/3B
6 LUIS PUJOLS-C/3B
7 BILLVIRDON-MGR
8 JOE MORGAN-2B
9 JULIO GONZALEZ-SS/3B
10 MIKE FISCHLIN-SS
11 ALAN KNICELY-PH
12 CRAIG REYNOLDS-SS
13 BRUCE BOCHY-C/1B
14 ALAN ASHBY-C
15 GARY WOODS-OF
16 DAVE BERGMAN-1B/OF
17 RAFAEL LANDESTOY-INF
18 ART HOWE (INJ)-1B/INF
20 DANNY HEEP-1B
21 TERRY PUHL-OF
22 SCOTT LOUCKS-OF
23 ENOS CABELL-3B/1B
25 JOSE (CHEO) CRUZ-OF
26 GORDY PLADSON-P
28 CESAR CEDENO-1B/OF
29 DENNY WALLING-1B/OF
30 JEFFREY LEONARD-OF/1B
31 FRANK LACORTE-P
32 *(RET#) JIM UMBRICHT*
33 GORDY PLADSON-P
34 NOLAN RYAN-P
35 JOE SAMBITO-P
36 JOE NIEKRO-P
38 RICK WILLIAMS-P
40 BOBBY SPROWL-P
41 BOBBY SPROWL-P
42 BERT ROBERGE-P
43 KEN FORSCH-P
45 DAVE SMITH-P
46 RANDY NIEMANN-P
47 JOAQUIN (JACK) ANDUJAR (INJ)-P
48 VERN RUHLE-P
50 J. R. RICHARD (ILL)-P

1981

1ST 1/2:3RD W 28-29 8GB
2ND 1/2:1ST W 33-20 0GB
FINAL: P/O W 61-49 --GB
L: WDS- LAN 3-2

1 BERT PENA-SS
2 MEL WRIGHT-CH
3 DON LEPPERT-CH
3 PHIL GARNER-2B (2)
4 DEACON JONES-CH
5 BOB LILLIS-CH
6 LUIS PUJOLS-C
7 BILLVIRDON-MGR
8 DAVE ROBERTS-UTIL
9 JOE PITTMAN-2B/3B
10 DICKIE THON-INF
11 ALAN KNICELY-C/OF
12 CRAIG REYNOLDS-SS
14 ALAN ASHBY-C
15 MIKE IVIE (ILL)-1B (2)
16 DAVE BERGMAN-1B (1)
16 HARRY SPILMAN-1B (2)
17 RAFAEL LANDESTOY-2B (1)
18 ART HOWE-3B/1B
20 DON SUTTON-P
21 TERRY PUHL-OF
22 SCOTT LOUCKS-OF
22 GARY WOODS-OF
23 KIKO GARCIA-INF
24 DANNY HEEP-1B/OF
25 JOSE (CHEO) CRUZ-OF
26 GORDY PLADSON-P
27 BILLY SMITH-P
28 CESAR CEDENO-1B/OF
29 DENNY WALLING-1B/OF
30 JEFFREY LEONARD-1B/OF (1)
30 TONY SCOTT-OF (2)
31 FRANK LACORTE-P
32 *(RET#) JIM UMBRICHT*
34 NOLAN RYAN-P
35 JOE SAMBITO-P
36 JOE NIEKRO-P
38 TIM TOLMAN-OF
39 BOB KNEPPER-P
41 BOBBY SPROWL-P
43 DON LEPPERT-CH
44 GORDY PLADSON-P
45 DAVE SMITH-P
(46) RANDY NIEMANN (INJ)-(P)
47 JOAQUIN (JACK) ANDUJAR (INJ)-P (1)
48 VERN RUHLE-P
(50) J. R. RICHARD (ILL)-(P)

1982

5TH W 77-85 12GB

2 MEL WRIGHT-CH
3 PHIL GARNER-2B/3B
4 DEACON JONES-CH
5 BOB LILLIS-CH/MGR2
6 LUIS PUJOLS-C
7 BILLVIRDON-MGR1
8 KEVIN BASS-OF (2)
9 JOE PITTMAN-3B/OF (1)
10 DICKIE THON-SS/INF
11 ALAN KNICELY-UTIL
12 CRAIG REYNOLDS-SS/3B
14 ALAN ASHBY-C
15 MIKE IVIE-PH (1)
16 HARRY SPILMAN-1B
17 RANDY MOFFITT-P
18 ART HOWE (INJ)-3B/1B
19 BILL DORAN-2B
20 DON SUTTON-P (1)
21 TERRY PUHL-OF
22 RAY KNIGHT-1B/3B
23 KIKO GARCIA (INJ)-INF
24 DANNY HEEP-OF/1B
25 JOSE (CHEO) CRUZ-OF
26 SCOTT LOUCKS-OF
27 FRANK LACORTE-P
29 DENNY WALLING-OF/1B
30 TONY SCOTT-CH
31 FRANK LACORTE-P
31 DAN BOONE-P (2)
32 *(RET#) JIM UMBRICHT*
34 NOLAN RYAN-P
35 JOE SAMBITO (INJ)-P
36 JOE NIEKRO-P
37 LARRY RAY-OF
38 TIM TOLMAN-OF/1B
39 BOB KNEPPER-P
42 BERT ROBERGE-P
43 DON LEPPERT-CH
44 GORDY PLADSON-P
45 DAVE SMITH (INJ)-P
46 FRANK DIPINO-P
47 MARK ROSS-P
48 VERN RUHLE-P
(50) J. R. RICHARD (ILL)-(P)
51 MIKE LACOSS-P
52 GEORGE CAPPUZZELLO-P
55 LES MOSS-CH
56? TONY PACHECO-CH

1983

3RD W 85-77 6GB

1 BERT PENA-SS
2 MEL WRIGHT-CH
3 PHIL GARNER-3B
4 JOHN MIZEROCK (INJ)-C
5 BOB LILLIS-MGR
6 LUIS PUJOLS-C
8 KEVIN BASS-OF
10 DICKIE THON-SS
11 FRANK DIPINO-P
12 CRAIG REYNOLDS-UTIL
14 ALAN ASHBY (ILL)-C
15 DENIS MENKE-CH
16 HARRY SPILMAN-1B/C
(18) ART HOWE (INJ)-(INF)
19 BILL DORAN-2B
20 GEORGE BJORKMAN-C
21 TERRY PUHL-OF
22 RAY KNIGHT-1B
24 OMAR MORENO-OF (1)
25 JOSE (CHEO) CRUZ-OF
26 SCOTT LOUCKS-OF
27 FRANK LACORTE (INJ)-P
28 JERRY MUMPHREY-OF (2)
29 DENNY WALLING-UTIL
30 TONY SCOTT-OF
31 JEFF HEATHCOCK-P
32 *(RET#) JIM UMBRICHT*
33 MIKE SCOTT (INJ)-P

34 NOLAN RYAN (INJ)-P
(35) JOE SAMBITO (INJ)-(P)
36 JOE NIEKRO-P
38 TIM TOLMAN-1B/OF
39 BOB KNEPPER-P
43 DON LEPPERT-CH
45 DAVE SMITH-P
46 BILL DAWLEY-P
46 FRANK DIPINO-P
48 VERN RUHLE-P
(50) J. R. RICHARD (ILL)-(P)
51 MIKE LACOSS (INJ)-P
52 JULIO SOLANO-P
53 MIKE MADDEN (INJ)-P
54 JERRY WALKER-CH
55 LES MOSS-CH

1984

2ND W (TIE) 80-82 12GB

1 BERT PENA-SS
2 COT DEAL-CH
3 PHIL GARNER-3B/2B
(4) JOHN MIZEROCK (INJ)-(C)
5 BOB LILLIS-MGR
6 MARK BAILEY-C
7 ALAN BANNISTER-SS/OF (1)
10 DICKIE THON (INJ)-SS
11 FRANK DIPINO-P
12 CRAIG REYNOLDS-SS/3B
13 TOM WIEGHAUS-C
14 ALAN ASHBY (INJ)-C
15 DENIS MENKE-CH
16 HARRY SPILMAN-1B/C
17 KEVIN BASS-OF
19 BILL DORAN-2B/SS
20 JIM PANKOVITS-UTIL
21 TERRY PUHL (INJ)-OF
22 RAY KNIGHT-3B/1B (1)
23 ENOS CABELL-1B
25 JOSE (CHEO) CRUZ-OF
(26) SCOTT LOUCKS (INJ)-(OF)
27 GLENN DAVIS-1B
28 JERRY MUMPHREY-OF
29 DENNY WALLING-UTIL
30 TONY SCOTT-OF (1)
30 MIKE RICHARDT-PH (2)
32 *(RET#) JIM UMBRICHT*
33 MIKE SCOTT-P
34 NOLAN RYAN-P
35 JOE SAMBITO (INJ)-P
36 JOE NIEKRO-P
38 TIM TOLMAN-OF/1B
39 BOB KNEPPER-P
43 DON LEPPERT-CH
45 DAVE SMITH-P
46 BILL DAWLEY-P
47 MARK ROSS-P
48 VERN RUHLE-P
49 JEFF CALHOUN-P
51 MIKE LACOSS-P
52 JULIO SOLANO-P
53 MIKE MADDEN-P
54 JERRY WALKER-CH
55 LES MOSS-CH

1985

3RD W (TIE) 83-79 12GB

1 BERT PENA (INJ)-INF
2 COT DEAL-CH
3 PHIL GARNER-3B/2B
4 JOHN MIZEROCK-C
5 BOB LILLIS-MGR
6 MARK BAILEY-C/1B
9 ERIC BULLOCK-OF
10 DICKIE THON (INJ)-SS
11 FRANK DIPINO-P
12 CRAIG REYNOLDS-SS/2B
14 ALAN ASHBY (INJ)-C
15 DENIS MENKE-CH
16 HARRY SPILMAN-1B/C
17 KEVIN BASS-OF
18 TIM TOLMAN-OF/1B
19 BILL DORAN-2B
20 JIM PANKOVITS (INJ)-UTIL
21 TERRY PUHL (INJ)-OF
22 CHRIS JONES-OF
23 ENOS CABELL-1B (1)
23 GERMAN RIVERA-3B
24 TY GAINEY-OF
25 JOSE (CHEO) CRUZ-OF
27 GLENN DAVIS-1B/OF
28 JERRY MUMPHREY-OF
29 DENNY WALLING-UTIL
31 JEFF HEATHCOCK-P
32 *(RET#) JIM UMBRICHT*
33 MIKE SCOTT-P
34 NOLAN RYAN-P
36 JOE NIEKRO-P (1)
37 CHARLEY KERFELD-P
39 BOB KNEPPER-P
41 MARK KNUDSON-P
42 RON MATHIS-P
43 DON LEPPERT-CH
43 JIM DESHAIES-P
45 DAVE SMITH-P
46 BILL DAWLEY-P
47 MARK ROSS-P
48 MATT GALANTE-CH
49 JEFF CALHOUN-P
52 JULIO SOLANO-P
53 MIKE MADDEN (INJ)-P
54 JERRY WALKER-CH
55 LES MOSS-CH

1986

1ST W 96-66 0GB
L NLCS-NYN 4-2

1 BERT PENA-INF
3 PHIL GARNER-3B/2B
4 JOHN MIZEROCK-C
6 MARK BAILEY-C/1B
7 ROBBIE WINE-C
8 YOGI BERRA-CH
9 ERIC BULLOCK-OF
10 DICKIE THON-SS
11 FRANK DIPINO-P (1)
11 DAVEY LOPES-OF/3B (2)
12 CRAIG REYNOLDS-UTIL/P
14 ALAN ASHBY-C
15 DENIS MENKE-CH
17 KEVIN BASS-OF
18 GENE TENACE-CH
19 BILL DORAN-2B
20 JIM PANKOVITS-UTIL
21 TERRY PUHL-OF
22 HAL LANIER-MGR
23 DAN DRIESSEN-1B (2)
24 TY GAINEY-OF
25 JOSE (CHEO) CRUZ-OF
26 LOUIE MEADOWS-OF
27 GLENN DAVIS-1B
28 BILLY HATCHER-OF
29 DENNY WALLING-3B/UTIL
30 TONY WALKER-OF
32 *(RET#) JIM UMBRICHT*
33 MIKE SCOTT-P
34 NOLAN RYAN (INJ)-P
35 AURELIO LOPEZ-P
37 CHARLEY KERFELD-P
38 MANNY HERNANDEZ-P
39 BOB KNEPPER-P
41 MARK KNUDSON-P (1)
42 TOM FUNK-P
43 JIM DESHAIES-P
44 DANNY DARWIN-P (2)
45 DAVE SMITH-P
46 MATT KEOUGH-P (2)
47 LARRY ANDERSEN-P (2)
48 MATT GALANTE-CH
48 MATT KEOUGH-P (2)
49 JEFF CALHOUN-P
51 RAFAEL MONTALVO-P
52 JULIO SOLANO-P
53 MIKE MADDEN-P
55 LES MOSS-CH

1987

3RD W 76-86 14GB

1 BERT PENA-SS/3B
2 GERALD YOUNG-OF
3 PHIL GARNER-3B/2B (1)
3 BUDDY BIANCALANA-SS/2B (2)
4 DALE BERRA-SS/2B
6 MARK BAILEY-C
7 ROBBIE WINE (ILL)-C
8 YOGI BERRA-CH
9 TROY AFENIR-C
10 DICKIE THON (INJ)-SS
11 DAVEY LOPES (INJ)-OF
11 DENIS MENKE-CH
11 KEN CAMINITI-3B
12 CRAIG REYNOLDS-SS/3B
13 RON MATHIS-P
14 ALAN ASHBY-C
15 DENIS MENKE-CH
15 DAVEY LOPES (INJ)-OF
16 DENIS MENKE-CH
17 KEVIN BASS-OF
18 GENE TENACE-CH
19 BILL DORAN-2B/SS
20 JIM PANKOVITS-UTIL
21 TERRY PUHL-OF
22 HAL LANIER-MGR
23 CHUCK JACKSON-UTIL
24 TY GAINEY-OF
25 JOSE (CHEO) CRUZ-OF
26 PAUL HOUSEHOLDER-OF
27 GLENN DAVIS-1B
28 BILLY HATCHER-OF
29 DENNY WALLING-3B/UTIL
30 TONY WALKER-OF
30 RONN REYNOLDS-C
30 TY WALLER-OF
31 JEFF HEATHCOCK-P
32 *(RET#) JIM UMBRICHT*
33 MIKE SCOTT-P
34 NOLAN RYAN-P
35 AURELIO LOPEZ-P
37 CHARLEY KERFELD (INJ)-P
38 MANNY HERNANDEZ-P
39 BOB KNEPPER-P
43 JIM DESHAIES-P
44 DANNY DARWIN-P
45 DAVE SMITH-P
47 LARRY ANDERSEN-P
48 MATT GALANTE-CH
49 JUAN AGOSTO-P
50 ROCKY CHILDRESS-P
52 JULIO SOLANO-P
53 DAVE MEADS-P
55 LES MOSS-CH
56 ROB MALLICOAT-P

1988

5TH W 82-80 12.5GB

1 CASEY CANDAELE-2B (2)
2 GERALD YOUNG-OF
3 CAMERON DREW-OF
4 CRAIG BIGGIO-C
5 STEVE HENDERSON-OF/1B
6 MARK BAILEY-C
6 HARRY SPILMAN-1B (2)
8 YOGI BERRA-CH
9 ALEX TREVINO-C/OF
10 GENE CLINES-CH
11 KEN CAMINITI-3B
12 CRAIG REYNOLDS-INF
13 ERNIE CAMACHO-P
14 ALAN ASHBY (INJ)-C
15 DENIS MENKE-CH
16 RAFAEL RAMIREZ-SS
17 KEVIN BASS-OF
18 JOHN FISHEL-OF
19 BILL DORAN-2B/SS
20 JIM PANKOVITS-INF
21 TERRY PUHL-OF
22 HAL LANIER-MGR
23 CHUCK JACKSON-UTIL
(24) TY GAINEY (INJ)-(OF)
25 BUDDY BELL-3B/2B (2)
26 LOUIE MEADOWS-OF
27 GLENN DAVIS-1B
28 BILLY HATCHER-OF
29 DENNY WALLING (INJ)-UTIL (1)
29 CRAIG SMAJSTRLA-2B
31 JEFF HEATHCOCK-P
31 BOB FORSCH-P (2)
32 *(RET#) JIM UMBRICHT*
33 MIKE SCOTT-P
34 NOLAN RYAN-P
35 BRIAN MEYER-P
(37) CHARLEY KERFELD (INJ)-(P)
39 BOB KNEPPER-P
41 JEFF HEATHCOCK-P
42 LARRY ANDERSEN-P
43 JIM DESHAIES-P
44 DANNY DARWIN-P
45 DAVE SMITH-P
47 JOAQUIN (JACK) ANDUJAR (INJ)-P
48 MATT GALANTE-CH
49 JUAN AGOSTO-P
50 ROCKY CHILDRESS-P
53 DAVE MEADS-P
54 MARC HILL-CH
55 LES MOSS-CH

1989

3RD W 86-76 6GB

2 GERALD YOUNG-OF
3 PHIL GARNER-CH
4 CRAIG BIGGIO-C/OF
4 STEVE LOMBARDOZZI-2B/3B
5 ED NAPOLEON-CH
6* GREG GROSS-UTIL/P*
7 CRAIG BIGGIO-C/OF
8 YOGI BERRA-CH
9 ALEX TREVINO-UTIL
10 HARRY SPILMAN-1B/C
11 KEN CAMINITI-3B
12 CRAIG REYNOLDS-UTIL/P
13 GLENN WILSON-OF (2)
14 ALAN ASHBY-C
15 RON WASHINGTON-2B/3B
15 ERIC YELDING-UTIL
16 RAFAEL RAMIREZ-SS
17 KEVIN BASS (INJ)-OF
18 ART HOWE-MGR
19 BILL DORAN-2B
20 DAN SCHATZEDER (INJ)-P
21 TERRY PUHL-OF/1B
22 ROGER MASON-P
23 ERIC ANTHONY-OF
24 ED OTT-CH
26 LOUIE MEADOWS-OF/1B
27 GLENN DAVIS-1B
28 BILLY HATCHER-OF (1)
28 CARL NICHOLS-C
31 BOB FORSCH-P
32 *(RET#) JIM UMBRICHT*
33 MIKE SCOTT-P
35 BRIAN MEYER-P
36 RICK RHODEN (INJ)-P
38 JIM CLANCY-P
39 BOB KNEPPER-P (1)
42 MARK DAVIDSON-OF
43 JIM DESHAIES-P
44 DANNY DARWIN-P
45 DAVE SMITH-P
47 LARRY ANDERSEN-P
48 MATT GALANTE-CH
49 JUAN AGOSTO-P
51 MARK PORTUGAL-P
52 JOSE CANO-P
(53) DAVE MEADS (INJ)-(P)
55 LES MOSS-CH
67 ROGER MASON-P

1990

4TH W (TIE) 75-87 16GB

1 CASEY CANDAELE-UTIL
2 GERALD YOUNG-OF
2 RICH GEDMAN-C (2)
3 PHIL GARNER-CH
4 STEVE LOMBARDOZZI (IN
-INF
4 KARL (TUFFY) RHODES-O
5 ED NAPOLEON-CH
6 DAVE ROHDE-INF
7 CRAIG BIGGIO-C/OF
9 ALEX TREVINO-C/1B (1)
9 TERRY MCGRIFF-C (2)
10 KEN OBERKFELL-INF
11 KEN CAMINITI-3B
12 GLENN WILSON-OF/1B
13 GLENN WILSON-OF/1B
14 ED OTT-CH
15 ERIC YELDING-OF/INF
16 RAFAEL RAMIREZ-SS
17 JEFF BALDWIN-OF
17 ANDUJAR CEDENO-SS
18 ART HOWE-MGR
19 BILL DORAN-2B (1)
20 DAN SCHATZEDER-P (1)
21 TERRY PUHL (INJ)-OF/1B
22 FRANKLIN STUBBS-1B/OF
22 MARK DAVIDSON (INJ)-OF
23 ERIC ANTHONY-OF
24 MARK DAVIDSON (INJ)-OF
24 FRANKLIN STUBBS-1B/OF
26 LOUIE MEADOWS-OF (1)
26 LUIS (GONZO) GONZALEZ 3B/1B
27 GLENN DAVIS (INJ)-1B
28 CARL NICHOLS-UTIL
29 JAVIER ORTIZ (INJ)-OF
30 MIKE SIMMS-1B
31 XAVIER HERNANDEZ-P
32 *(RET#) JIM UMBRICHT*
33 MIKE SCOTT-P
35 BRIAN MEYER-P
36 BILL GULLICKSON-P
37 CHARLEY KERFELD-P (1)
38 JIM CLANCY-P
42 RUDY JARAMILLO-CH
43 JIM DESHAIES-P
44 DANNY DARWIN-P
45 DAVE SMITH-P
47 LARRY ANDERSEN-P (1)
48 MATT GALANTE-CH
49 JUAN AGOSTO-P
51 MARK PORTUGAL-P
52 AL OSUNA-P
53 TERRY CLARK-P
54 BOB CLUCK-CH
54 BRIAN FISHER-P
54 RANDY HENNIS-P
55 BRIAN FISHER-P
55 BOB CLUCK-CH

1991

6TH W 65-97 29GB

1 CASEY CANDAELE-2B/UTIL
2 GERALD YOUNG-OF
3 PHIL GARNER-CH
4 KARL (TUFFY) RHODES-OF
5 JEFF BAGWELL-1B
6 DAVE ROHDE-INF
7 CRAIG BIGGIO-C/UTIL
9 SCOTT SERVAIS (INJ)-C
10 KEN OBERKFELL-1B/3B

HOUSTON COLT 45's/ASTROS

0 TONY EUSEBIO-C
1 KEN CAMINITI-3B
2 STEVE FINLEY-OF
4 ED OTT-CH
5 ERIC YELDING-SS/OF
6 RAFAEL RAMIREZ-INF
7 ANDUJAR CEDENO-SS
8 ART HOWE-MGR
9 CURT SCHILLING-P
0 MARK MCLEMORE (INJ)-2B
0 JOSE TOLENTINO-1B/OF
1 ERIC ANTHONY-OF
2 MARK DAVIDSON-OF
3 ANDY MOTA-2B
6 LUIS (GONZO) GONZALEZ-OF
7 PETE HARNISCH-P
8 CARL NICHOLS-C
8 KENNY LOFTON-OF
9 JAVIER ORTIZ-OF
0 MIKE SIMMS-OF
1 XAVIER HERNANDEZ (INJ)-P
2 *(RET#) JIM UMBRICHT*
3 MIKE SCOTT (INJ)-P
5 MIKE CAPEL-P
6 DEAN WILKINS-P
6 GARY COOPER-3B
7 JIMMY JONES (INJ)-P
8 JIM CLANCY-P (1)
9 CHRIS GARDNER-P
1 JIM CORSI-P
2 RUDY JARAMILLO-CH
3 JIM DESHAIES-P
4 JEFF JUDEN-P
6 RYAN BOWEN-P
7 DWAYNE HENRY-P
8 MATT GALANTE-CH
9 JUAN AGOSTO-P
1 MARK PORTUGAL-P
3 BRIAN WILLIAMS-P
4 BOB CLUCK-CH
5 BOB CLUCK-CH
6 ROB MALLICOAT-P
7 DARRYL KILE-P
3 MARK MCLEMORE (INJ)-2B

1992

4TH W 81-81 17GB

1 CASEY CANDAELE-UTIL
2 GERALD YOUNG-OF
4 KARL (TUFFY) RHODES-OF
5 JEFF BAGWELL-1B
6 EDDIE TAUBENSEE-C
7 CRAIG BIGGIO-2B
9 SCOTT SERVAIS-C
0 ERNEST RILES-INF
1 KEN CAMINITI-3B
2 STEVE FINLEY-OF/C
3 ERNEST RILES-INF
4 ED OTT-CH
5 ERIC YELDING-SS/OF
6 RAFAEL RAMIREZ-SS/3B
7 ANDUJAR CEDENO-SS
8 ART HOWE-MGR
9 JUAN GUERRERO-UTIL
0 EDDIE (SCOOTER) TUCKER-C
1 ERIC ANTHONY-OF
2 MIKE SIMMS-OF/1B
3 DOUG JONES-P
4 CHRIS JONES-OF
5 DENNY WALLING-PH
5 *(RET#) JOSE CRUZ*
6 LUIS (GONZO) GONZALEZ-OF
7 PETE HARNISCH-P
8 PETE (INKY) INCAVIGLIA-OF
9 AL OSUNA-P
0 SHANE REYNOLDS-P
0 BENNY DISTEFANO-OF/1B
1 XAVIER HERNANDEZ-P
32 *(RET#) JIM UMBRICHT*
37 JIMMY JONES (INJ)-P
38 SHANE REYNOLDS-P
41 WILLIE BLAIR-P
41 RYAN BOWEN-P
42 RUDY JARAMILLO-CH
46 RYAN BOWEN-P
47 ROB MURPHY-P
48 MATT GALANTE-CH
49 RICH SCHEID-P
50 BUTCH HENRY-P
51 MARK PORTUGAL-P
52 TOM SPENCER-CH
52 AL OSUNA-P
53 BRIAN WILLIAMS-P
54 JOE BOEVER-P
55 BOB CLUCK-CH
56 ROB MALLICOAT-P
57 DARRYL KILE-P
68 BENNY DISTEFANO-OF/1B

1993

3RD W 85-77 19GB

1 CASEY CANDAELE-UTIL
3 CHRIS DONNELS-INF
4 KARL (TUFFY) RHODES-OF (1)
4 A. MIKE BRUMLEY-UTIL
5 JEFF BAGWELL-1B
6 EDDIE TAUBENSEE-C
7 CRAIG BIGGIO-2B
9 SCOTT SERVAIS-C
10 ANDUJAR CEDENO-SS/3B
11 KEN CAMINITI-3B
12 STEVE FINLEY-OF
14 ED OTT-CH
15 DOUG DRABEK-P
16 CHRIS JAMES-OF (1)
17 ANDUJAR CEDENO-SS/3B
17 KEVIN BASS-OF
18 ART HOWE-MGR
19 JIM LINDEMAN-1B
20 KEVIN BASS-OF
21 GREG SWINDELL-P
22 JACK DAUGHERTY-1B/OF (1)
23 DOUG JONES-P
24 ERIC ANTHONY-OF
25 *(RET#) JOSE CRUZ*
26 LUIS (GONZO) GONZALEZ-OF
27 PETE HARNISCH-P
28 JOSE URIBE-SS
29 AL OSUNA-P
30 RICK PARKER-UTIL
31 XAVIER HERNANDEZ-P
32 *(RET#) JIM UMBRICHT*
35 JACK DAUGHERTY-1B/OF (1)
36 EDDIE (SCOOTER) TUCKER-C
37 SHANE REYNOLDS-P
42 RUDY JARAMILLO-CH
44 JEFF JUDEN-P
46 TOM EDENS (INJ)-P
47 MARK GRANT-P (1)
48 MATT GALANTE-CH
49 JUAN AGOSTO-P
51 MARK PORTUGAL-P
52 TOM SPENCER-CH
53 BRIAN WILLIAMS-P
54 ERIC BELL-P
55 BOB CLUCK-CH
(56) ROB MALLICOAT (INJ)-(P)
57 DARRYL KILE-P
59 TODD JONES-P

1994

2ND C 66-49 0.5GB
STRIKE NO POST-SEASON

1 JULIO LINARES-CH
2 TERRY COLLINS-MGR
3 CHRIS DONNELS-3B
4 ANDY STANKIEWICZ (INJ)-2B
5 JEFF BAGWELL-1B
6 EDDIE TAUBENSEE-C (1)
7 CRAIG BIGGIO-2B
9 SCOTT SERVAIS-C
10 ANDUJAR CEDENO-SS
11 KEN CAMINITI-3B
12 STEVE FINLEY (INJ)-OF
15 DOUG DRABEK-P
(16) BRAULIO CASTILLO (INJ)-(OF)
17 KEVIN BASS-OF
18 JAMES MOUTON-OF
19 BRIAN L. HUNTER-OF
20 TONY EUSEBIO-C
21 GREG SWINDELL-P
22 MIKE SIMMS-OF
24 ORLANDO MILLER-SS
25 *(RET#) JOSE CRUZ*
26 LUIS (GONZO) GONZALEZ-OF
27 PETE HARNISCH (INJ)-P
28 MIKE FELDER-OF
28 MILT THOMPSON-OF
29 ROBERTO PETAGINE-1B
30 MEL STOTTLEMYRE-CH
31 SID BREAM (INJ)-1B
32 *(RET#) JIM UMBRICHT*
35 JOHN HUDEK-P
37 SHANE REYNOLDS-P
38 MIKE HAMPTON-P
39 BEN HINES-CH
43 DAVE VERES-P
46 TOM EDENS-P (1)
48 MATT GALANTE-CH
51 MIKE FELDER-OF
52 ROSS POWELL-P
53 BRIAN WILLIAMS (INJ)-P
55 STEVE HENDERSON-CH
56 BEN HINES-CH
57 DARRYL KILE-P
59 TODD JONES-P
99 MITCH (WILD THING) WILLIAMS (REL)-P

1995

2ND C 76-49 9GB
144 GAME SEASON

1 JULIO LINARES-CH
2 TERRY COLLINS-MGR
3 CHRIS DONNELS-3B (1)
3 RICK WILKINS-C (2)
4 ANDY STANKIEWICZ-2B
5 JEFF BAGWELL-1B
6 JAMES MOUTON-OF
7 CRAIG BIGGIO-2B
9 SCOTT SERVAIS-C (1)
9 JERRY GOFF-C
10 MIKE HAMPTON-P
12 RICKY GUTIERREZ-SS
14 DEREK BELL-OF
15 DOUG DRABEK-P
16 CRAIG SHIPLEY-3B
16 DERRICK MAY-OF (2)
17 PHIL PLANTIER-OF (1)
17 PAT BORDERS-C (2)
18 JAMES MOUTON-OF
18 DAVE MAGADAN-3B
18 CRAIG SHIPLEY-3B
19 BRIAN L. HUNTER-OF
20 TONY EUSEBIO-C
21 GREG SWINDELL-P
21 PHIL NEVIN-3B (1)
21 DAVE HAJEK-PH
22 MIKE SIMMS-OF
22 DAVE MAGADAN-3B
23 MIKE SIMMS-OF
24 ORLANDO MILLER-SS
25 *(RET#) JOSE CRUZ*
26 LUIS (GONZO) GONZALEZ-OF (1)
27 JOHN CANGELOSI-OF
28 MILT THOMPSON-OF
29 JESSE BARFIELD-CH
30 MEL STOTTLEMYRE-CH
31 EDDIE (SCOOTER) TUCKER-C
32 *(RET#) JIM UMBRICHT*
35 JOHN HUDEK-P
36 EDDIE (SCOOTER) TUCKER-C
36 A. MIKE BRUMLEY-OF/1B
37 SHANE REYNOLDS-P
38 CRAIG MCMURTRY-P
39 MIKE HENNEMAN-P (2)
41 PEDRO A. MARTINEZ-P
41 GREG SWINDELL-P
42 PEDRO A. MARTINEZ-P
43 DAVE VERES-P
46 DOUG BROCAIL-P
48 MATT GALANTE-CH
49 JIM DOUGHERTY-P
52 ROSS POWELL-P (1)
55 STEVE HENDERSON-CH
56 BEN HINES-CH
57 DARRYL KILE-P
58 DEAN HARTGRAVES-P
59 TODD JONES-P

1996

2ND C 82-80 6GB

1 JULIO LINARES-CH
2 TERRY COLLINS-MGR
3 RICK WILKINS-C (1)
3 KIRT MANWARING-C (2)
4 DAVE HAJEK-2B
5 JEFF BAGWELL-1B
6 JAMES MOUTON-OF
7 CRAIG BIGGIO-2B
9 JERRY GOFF-C
9 RANDY KNORR-C
10 MIKE HAMPTON-P
12 RICKY GUTIERREZ-SS
13 BILLY WAGNER (INJ)-P
14 DEREK BELL-OF
15 DOUG DRABEK (INJ)-P
16 DERRICK MAY (INJ)-OF (2)
17 SEAN BERRY-3B
18 RICK SWEET-CH
19 BRIAN L. HUNTER (INJ)-OF
20 TONY EUSEBIO (INJ)-C
21 GREG SWINDELL (INJ) (WAIV)-P
21 RAY MONTGOMERY-PH
22 ANTHONY YOUNG-P
22 ANDUJAR CEDENO (INJ)-SS (3)
23 MIKE SIMMS-OF
24 ORLANDO MILLER-SS
25 *(RET#) JOSE CRUZ*
27 JOHN CANGELOSI-OF
28 BILL SPIERS-3B
29 BOB ABREU-2B
30 DAVE HAJEK-PH
31 XAVIER HERNANDEZ-P
32 *(RET#) JIM UMBRICHT*
34 *(RET#) NOLAN RYAN*
35 JOHN HUDEK (INJ)-P
36 MARK SMALL-P
37 SHANE REYNOLDS-P
39 JOHN JOHNSTONE-P
41 XAVIER HERNANDEZ-P
41 JEFF TABAKA-P
42 BRENT STROM-CH
44 DANNY DARWIN-P (2)
45 CHRIS HOLT-P
46 DOUG BROCAIL (INJ)-P
48 MATT GALANTE-CH
49 JIM DOUGHERTY-P
51 ALVIN MORMAN-P
52 TERRY CLARK (INJ)-P
55 STEVE HENDERSON-CH
56 DONNE WALL-P
57 DARRYL KILE-P
58 DEAN HARTGRAVES (WAIV)-P (1)
59 TODD JONES (INJ)-P

1997

1ST C 84-78 0GB
L NLDS-ATLN 3-0

2 LUIS RIVERA-INF
4 PAT LISTACH (REL)-SS
4 TONY PENA-C (2)
5 JEFF BAGWELL-1B
6 JAMES MOUTON-OF
7 CRAIG BIGGIO-2B
8 ALAN ASHBY-CH
9 RANDY KNORR-C
10 MIKE HAMPTON-P
11 BRAD AUSMUS-C
12 RICKY GUTIERREZ (INJ)-INF
13 BILLY WAGNER-P
14 DEREK BELL (INJ)-OF
15 RICHARD HIDALGO-OF
16 TOM MCCRAW-CH
17 SEAN BERRY (INJ)-3B
18 BILL VIRDON-CH
19 RUSS JOHNSON-3B
20 TONY EUSEBIO-C
21 CHUCK CARR-OF (2)
22 THOMAS HOWARD-OF
24 MIKE CUBBAGE-CH
25 JOSE (CHEO) CRUZ, SR.-CH
25 *(RET#) JOSE CRUZ*
26 LUIS (GONZO) GONZALEZ-OF
27 TIM BOGAR-SS
28 BILL SPIERS-3B
29 KEN RAMOS-OF
29 J. R. PHILLIPS-PH
31 RUSS SPRINGER (INJ)-P
32 *(RET#) JIM UMBRICHT*
34 *(RET#) NOLAN RYAN*
35 JOHN HUDEK-P
(36) MARK SMALL (INJ)-(P)
37 SHANE REYNOLDS (INJ)-P
39 RAY MONTGOMERY (INJ)-OF
41 TOM MARTIN (INJ)-P
42 JOSE LIMA-P
43 BLAS MINOR-P
45 CHRIS HOLT-P
48 VERN RUHLE-CH
49 LARRY DIERKER-MGR
50 SID (EL SID) FERNANDEZ (INJ)(RET)-P
51 JOSE CABRERA-P
52 MIKE MAGNANTE-P
53 BOBBY ABREU-OF
54 TOMMY GREENE-P
54 OSCAR HENRIQUEZ-P
55 MANUEL BARRIOS-P
56 DONNE WALL-P
57 DARRYL KILE-P
59 RAMON GARCIA-P

1998

1ST C 102-60 0GB
L NLDS-SDN 3-1

3 CARL EVERETT-OF
4 DAVE ENGLE-CH
4 MITCH MELUSKEY-C
5 JEFF BAGWELL (INJ)-1B
7 CRAIG BIGGIO-2B
8 MATT GALANTE-CH
9 RUSS JOHNSON-INF
10 MIKE HAMPTON (INJ)-P
11 BRAD AUSMUS-C
12 RICKY GUTIERREZ-INF

13 BILLY WAGNER (INJ)-P
14 DEREK BELL-OF
15 RICHARD HIDALGO (INJ)-OF
16 RICHARD HIDALGO-OF
16 TOM MCCRAW-CH
17 SEAN BERRY-3B
18 BILL VIRDON-CH
18 MOISES ALOU-OF
19 DOUG HENRY-P
20 TONY EUSEBIO-C
22 PETE (INKY) INCAVIGLIA (INJ)-PH (2)
23 MIKE GRZANICH-P
24 MIKE CUBBAGE-CH
25 JOSE (CHEO) CRUZ, SR.-CH
25 *(RET#) JOSE CRUZ*
27 TIM BOGAR-SS
28 BILL SPIERS-3B/1B
29 J. R. PHILLIPS-UTIL
31 DARYLE WARD-INF
32 *(RET#) JIM UMBRICHT*
34 *(RET#) NOLAN RYAN*
35 DAVE CLARK-OF
36 JACK HOWELL (INJ)-1B/3B
37 SHANE REYNOLDS-P
38 SEAN BERGMAN-P
39 RAY MONTGOMERY (INJ)-OF
39 JAY POWELL-P (2)
41 PETE SCHOUREK (INJ)-P (1)
42 JOSE LIMA-P
43 DOUG HENRY-P
43 BOB SCANLAN-P
44 REGGIE HARRIS-P
(45) CHRIS HOLT (INJ)-(P)
46 TREVER MILLER-P
47 C. J. NITKOWSKI-P
48 VERN RUHLE-CH
49 LARRY DIERKER-MGR
50 SCOTT ELARTON-P
51 JOSE CABRERA (INJ)-P
51 RANDY (THE BIG UNIT) JOHNSON-P (2)
52 MIKE MAGNANTE (INJ)-P
54 JOHN HALAMA-P
55 BRIAN SIKORSKY-P
(59) RAMON GARCIA (INJ)-(P)

1999

1ST C 97-65 0GB

L NLDS-ATLN 3-1

1 ALEX DIAZ (INJ)-OF
2 HARRY SPILMAN-CH
3 CARL EVERETT-OF
4 CARLOS HERNANDEZ-SS
5 JEFF BAGWELL-1B
6 PAUL BAKO-C
7 CRAIG BIGGIO-2B
8 MATT GALANTE-CH
9 RUSS JOHNSON-SS
10 MIKE HAMPTON (INJ)-P
11 KEN CAMINITI (INJ)-3B
12 RICKY GUTIERREZ (INJ)-INF
13 BILLY WAGNER (INJ)-P
14 DEREK BELL-OF
15 RICHARD HIDALGO (INJ)-OF
16 TOM MCCRAW-CH
17 RANDY KNORR-C
18 MOISES ALOU (INJ)-OF
19 DOUG HENRY (INJ)-P
20 TONY EUSEBIO-C
21 MITCH MELUSKEY (INJ)-C
22 LANCE BERKMAN-OF
23 MATT MIESKE-OF (2)
24 MIKE CUBBAGE-CH
25 JOSE (CHEO) CRUZ, SR.-CH
25 *(RET#) JOSE CRUZ*
27 TIM BOGAR-SS
28 BILL SPIERS-3B/1B
29 GLEN BARKER-OF
30 JOHN TAMARGO-CH
31 DARYLE WARD-1B
32 *(RET#) JIM UMBRICHT*
34 *(RET#) NOLAN RYAN*
35 RYAN THOMPSON-OF
36 JACK HOWELL (INJ)-1B/3B
37 SHANE REYNOLDS-P
38 SEAN BERGMAN (INJ)-P (1)
38 STAN JAVIER-OF (2)
39 JAY POWELL-P
42 JOSE LIMA-P
44 CHRIS HOLT-P
45 CHRIS HOLT-P
46 TREVER MILLER-P
47 JEFF MCCURRY-P
48 VERN RUHLE-CH
49 LARRY DIERKER-MGR
50 SCOTT ELARTON-P
51 JOSE CABRERA-P
52 WADE MILLER-P
53 BRIAN WILLIAMS-P
56 DEAN CROW-P
58 JOE SLUSARSKI-P

2000

4TH C 72-90 23GB

1 KEITH GINTER-INF
2 MORGAN ENGSBERG-INF
4 JULIO LUGO-INF
5 JEFF BAGWELL-1B
6 PAUL BAKO-C (1)
6 CHRIS TRUBY-INF
7 CRAIG BIGGIO (INJ)-2B
8 MATT GALANTE-CH
9 RUSS JOHNSON-SS (1)
10 TRIPP CROMER (INJ)-INF
11 KEN CAMINITI (INJ)-3B
13 BILLY WAGNER (INJ)-P
14 ROGER CEDENO (INJ)-OF
15 RICHARD HIDALGO-OF
16 DWIGHT GOODEN (REL)-P (1)
16 MARC VALDES-P
17 LANCE BERKMAN-OF
18 MOISES ALOU (INJ)-OF
19 DOUG HENRY-P (1)
20 TONY EUSEBIO-C
21 MITCH MELUSKEY (INJ)-C
22 TOM MCCRAW-CH
23 MATT MIESKE-OF (1)
23 EDDIE ZOSKY-INF
24 MIKE CUBBAGE-CH
25 JOSE (CHEO) CRUZ, SR.-CH
25 *(RET#) JOSE CRUZ*
27 TIM BOGAR-SS
28 BILL SPIERS-3B/1B
29 GLEN BARKER-OF
30 JOHN TAMARGO-CH
31 DARYLE WARD-OF
32 *(RET#) JIM UMBRICHT*
34 *(RET#) NOLAN RYAN*
36 MIKE MADDUX-P
36 SCOTT LINEBRINK-P (2)
37 SHANE REYNOLDS-P
38 RUSTY MEACHAM-P
39 JAY POWELL (INJ)-P
41 SCOTT LINEBRINK-P (2)
41 OCTAVIO DOTEL-P
42 JOSE LIMA-P
44 CHRIS HOLT-P
45 BRIAN POWELL-P
46 YORKIS PEREZ-P
46 RAUL CHAVEZ-C
48 VERN RUHLE-CH
49 LARRY DIERKER-MGR
50 SCOTT ELARTON-P
51 JOSE CABRERA-P
52 WADE MILLER-P
53 WAYNE FRANKLIN-P
54 JASON GREEN-P
56 KIP GROSS-P
56 FRANK CHARLES-C
58 JOE SLUSARSKI-P
59 TONY MCKNIGHT-P
72 RAUL CHAVEZ-C

2001

1ST C 93-69 0GB

L NLDS-ATLN 3-0

1 KEITH GINTER-2B
3 ADAM EVERETT-SS
4 JULIO LUGO-INF
5 JEFF BAGWELL-1B
6 CHRIS TRUBY-INF
7 CRAIG BIGGIO-2B
8 MATT GALANTE-CH
9 MIKE CUBBAGE-CH
10 JOSE VIZCAINO-SS
11 BRAD AUSMUS-C
12 HARRY SPILMAN-CH
13 BILLY WAGNER (INJ)-P
14 CHARLIE HAYES (INJ)(REL)-3B
15 RICHARD HIDALGO-OF
16 ORLANDO MERCED (INJ)-OF
17 LANCE BERKMAN-OF
18 MOISES ALOU (INJ)-OF
19 VINNY CASTILLA-3B (2)
20 TONY EUSEBIO-C
21 SCOTT SERVAIS (INJ)-C
22 MENDY LOPEZ (WAIV)-SS (1)
23 DAVE MLICKI-P (2)
24 GLEN BARKER-OF
25 JOSE (CHEO) CRUZ, SR.-CH
25 *(RET#) JOSE CRUZ*
26 DOUG BROCAIL (INJ)-P
27 PEDRO ASTACIO (INJ)-P (2)
28 BILL SPIERS (INJ)-3B/1B
29 OCTAVIO DOTEL-P
30 JOHN TAMARGO-CH
31 DARYLE WARD-OF
32 *(RET#) JIM UMBRICHT*
34 *(RET#) NOLAN RYAN*
35 RICKY STONE-P
36 SCOTT LINEBRINK-P
37 SHANE REYNOLDS (INJ)-P
38 MIKE JACKSON-P
39 JAY POWELL-P (1)
39 RON VILLONE-P (2)
41 NELSON CRUZ-P
42 JOSE LIMA (SUS 5G)-P (1)
43 DAVE MLICKI-P (2)
43 MIKE WILLIAMS-P (2)
44 RAY OSWALT-P
45 BRIAN POWELL-P
45 WILFREDO RODRIGUEZ-P
47 KENT BOTTENFIELD (INJ)-P
48 BURT HOOTEN-CH
49 LARRY DIERKER-MGR
50 SCOTT ELARTON (INJ)-P (1)
51 JOSE CABRERA-P
51 TIM REDDING-P
52 WADE MILLER-P
53 WAYNE FRANKLIN-P
55 CARLOS E. HERNANDEZ-P
58 JOE SLUSARSKI (WAIV)-P (2)
58 JIM MANN-P
59 TONY MCKNIGHT-P (1)

2002

2ND C 84-78 13GB

1 KEITH GINTER-INF (1)
2 GREGG ZAUN-C
4 JULIO LUGO (INJ)-SS
5 JEFF BAGWELL-1B
6 TONY PENA-CH (1)
7 CRAIG BIGGIO-2B/OF
8 GREGG ZAUN-C
8 MARK LORETTA-INF (2)
10 JOSE VIZCAINO-INF
11 BRAD AUSMUS-C
12 HARRY SPILMAN-CH
13 BILLY WAGNER-P
14 MORGAN ENSBERG-3B
15 RICHARD HIDALGO-OF
16 ORLANDO MERCED-OF/INF
17 LANCE BERKMAN-OF
20 RICKY STONE-P
21 BRIAN L. HUNTER (ILL)-OF
22 JIMY WILLIAMS-MGR
23 DAVE MLICKI (INJ)-P
24 JASON LANE-OF
25 JOSE (CHEO) CRUZ, SR.-CH
25 *(RET#) JOSE CRUZ*
(26) DOUG BROCAIL (INJ)-(P)
27 GEOFF BLUM-3B/UTIL
28 ADAM EVERETT-SS
29 OCTAVIO DOTEL-P
30 JOHN TAMARGO-CH
31 DARYLE WARD-OF
32 *(RET#) JIM UMBRICHT*
34 *(RET#) NOLAN RYAN*
35 HIPOLITO PICHARDO (INJ) (RET)-P
35 RICKY STONE-P
35 PEDRO BORBON-P (2)
36 SCOTT LINEBRINK-P
37 SHANE REYNOLDS (INJ)-P
38 GENE LAMONT-CH
39 T. J. MATHEWS (INJ)-P
41 NELSON CRUZ-P
42 *(RET#) JACKIE ROBINSON*
43 ALAN ZINTER-1B/C
44 RAY OSWALT-P
45 BARRY WESSON-OF
45 TOM (FLASH) GORDON-P (2)
46 RAUL CHAVEZ-C
48 BURT HOOTEN-CH
49 *(RET#) LARRY DIERKER*
50 KIRK SAARLOOS-P
51 TIM REDDING-P
52 WADE MILLER (INJ)-P
53 PETER MUNRO-P
54 BRAD LIDGE-P
55 CARLOS E. HERNANDEZ (INJ)-P
58 JIM MANN-P
59 BRANDON PUFFER-P
60 JERIOME ROBERTSON-P

2003

2ND C 87-75 1GB

1 COLIN PORTER-OF
1 DAVID MATRANGA-2B
2 GREGG ZAUN-C (1)
2 MITCH MELUSKEY-PH
3 TRIPP CROMER-2B
4 JULIO LUGO-SS (1)
4 ERIC BRUNTLETT-INF
5 JEFF BAGWELL-1B
6 MARK BAILEY-CH
7 CRAIG BIGGIO-OF
8 HARRY SPILMAN-CH
9 COLIN PORTER-OF
10 JOSE VIZCAINO (INJ)-INF
11 BRAD AUSMUS-C
12 JEFF KENT (INJ) (SUS:2G)-2B
13 BILLY WAGNER-P
14 MORGAN ENSBERG-3B
15 RICHARD HIDALGO (INJ)-OF
16 ORLANDO MERCED-OF/1B
17 LANCE BERKMAN-OF
20 RICKY STONE-P
21 BRIAN L. HUNTER-OF
22 JIMY WILLIAMS-MGR
23 KIRK SAARLOOS-P
24 JASON LANE-OF
25 JOSE (CHEO) CRUZ, SR.-C
25 *(RET#) JOSE CRUZ*
27 GEOFF BLUM-3B/INF
28 ADAM EVERETT-SS
29 OCTAVIO DOTEL-P
30 JOHN TAMARGO-CH
31 BRUCE CHEN (WAIV)-P (1)
31 RON VILLONE-P
32 *(RET#) JIM UMBRICHT*
34 *(RET#) NOLAN RYAN*
35 NATE BLAND-P
36 SCOTT LINEBRINK-P (1)
(37) SHANE REYNOLDS (INJ)-(P)
38 GENE LAMONT-CH
39 BRIAN MOEHLER (INJ)-P
40 DAN MICELI-P (4)
41 JONATHAN JOHNSON-P
41 JARED FERNANDEZ-P
42 *(RET#) JACKIE ROBINSON*
44 RAY OSWALT (INJ)-P
45 MIKE GALLO-P
46 RAUL CHAVEZ-C
48 BURT HOOTEN-CH
49 *(RET#) LARRY DIERKER*
50 RICK WHITE (WAIV)-P (2)
51 TIM REDDING-P
52 WADE MILLER-P
53 PETER MUNRO-P
54 BRAD LIDGE-P
(55) CARLOS E. HERNANDEZ (INJ)-(P)
56 JARED FERNANDEZ-P
56 KIRK BULLINGER-P
58 DAN MICELI-P (4)
59 BRANDON PUFFER-P
60 JERIOME ROBERTSON-P
60 RODRIGO ROSARIO (INJ)-P
62 JERIOME ROBERTSON-P

2004

2ND C W/C 92-70 3GB

W NLDS-ATLN 3-2

L NLCS-STLN 4-3

1 WILLY TAVERAS-OF
2 CHRIS BURKE-2B
3 JIMY WILLIAMS-MGR1
3 PHIL GARNER-MGR2
4 ERIC BRUNTLETT-2B
5 JEFF BAGWELL-1B
6 MARK BAILEY-CH
7 CRAIG BIGGIO-OF
8 HARRY SPILMAN-CH
8 GARY GAETTI-CH
10 JOSE VIZCAINO-INF/SS
11 BRAD AUSMUS-C
12 JEFF KENT-2B
14 MORGAN ENSBERG-3B
15 RICHARD HIDALGO (INJ)-OF (1)
15 CARLOS BELTRAN-OF (2)
17 LANCE BERKMAN-OF
19 ORLANDO PALMEIRO-OF
20 RICKY STONE-P (1)
21 ANDY PETTITTE (INJ)-P
22 ROGER (ROCKET) CLEMENS-P
24 JASON LANE-OF
25 JOSE (CHEO) CRUZ, SR.-CH
25 *(RET#) JOSE CRUZ*
26 MIKE LAMB-3B
27 CARLOS HERNANDEZ-P
28 ADAM EVERETT (INJ)-SS
29 OCTAVIO DOTEL-P (1)
30 JOHN TAMARGO-CH
31 BRANDON DUCKWORTH-P
32 *(RET#) JIM UMBRICHT*
34 *(RET#) NOLAN RYAN*
35 DAVID WEATHERS-P (2)
35 DAN WHEELER-P (2)

36 RUSS SPRINGER-P
37 BRANDON BACKE-P
37 DARREN OLIVER-P (2)
38 GENE LAMONT-CH
41 JARED FERNANDEZ-P
41 BRANDON BACKE-P
42 *(RET#) JACKIE ROBINSON*
43 CHAD HARVILLE-P (2)
44 RAY OSWALT (INJ)-P
45 MIKE GALLO-P
46 RAUL CHAVEZ-C
47 JEREMI GRIFFITHS-P
48 BURT HOOTEN-CH
48 JIM HICKEY-CH

2005

2ND C W/C 89-73 11GB
W NLDS-ATLN 3-1
W NLCS-STLN 4-2
L WS-CHIA 4-0

1 WILLY TAVERAS-OF
2 CHRIS BURKE-UTIL
3 PHIL GARNER-MGR
4 ERIC BRUNTLETT-UTIL
5 JEFF BAGWELL (INJ)-1B
6 MARK BAILEY-CH
7 CRAIG BIGGIO-2B/OF
8 GARY GAETTI-CH
9 HUMBERTO QUINTERO (INJ)-C
10 JOSE VIZCAINO-INF
11 BRAD AUSMUS-C
14 MORGAN ENSBERG-3B
15 CECIL COOPER-CH
16 JASON LANE-OF
17 LANCE BERKMAN (INJ)-1B/OF
19 ORLANDO PALMEIRO-OF
21 ANDY PETTITTE-P
22 ROGER (ROCKET) CLEMENS-P
24 JASON LANE-OF
25 JOSE (CHEO) CRUZ, SR.-CH
25 *(RET#) JOSE CRUZ*
26 MIKE LAMB-1B/3B
28 ADAM EVERETT-SS
29 DOUG MANSOLINO-CH
30 LUKE SCOTT-OF
31 JOHN FRANCO (REL)-P
31 CHARLES GIPSON-OF
32 *(RET#) JIM UMBRICHT*
34 *(RET#) NOLAN RYAN*
35 DAN WHEELER-P
36 RUSS SPRINGER-P
37 TODD SELF-OF
38 EZEQUIEL ASTACIO-P
41 BRANDON BACKE (INJ)-P
42 *(RET#) JACKIE ROBINSON*
43 CHAD HARVILLE (WAIV)-P (1)
43 SCOTT STRICKLAND-P
44 RAY OSWALT-P
45 MIKE GALLO-P
46 RAUL CHAVEZ-C
48 JIM HICKEY-CH
49 *(RET#) LARRY DIERKER*
50 CHAD QUALLS-P
51 WANDY RODRIGUEZ-P
52 CHARLTON JIMERSON-OF
53 MIKE BURNS-P
54 BRAD LIDGE-P
56 BRANDON DUCKWORTH-P
58 TRAVIS DRISKILL-P

Two of the original "Killer Bees", Craig Biggio (left) and Jeff Bagwell (right), finally had their dream come true in 2005 only to have it burst before they knew what happened. They played their entire careers with Houston and finally made it to the World Series, but the White Sox brought that dream to an abrupt end by sweeping the Astros in four. Put their awsome careers together: 3,214 runs, 5,109 hits, 1,092 2B, 84 3B, 709 HR, 2,592 RBI, 8,496 TB, 2,498 BB, 609 SB and batted a combined .290 in the process. They were hit by pitches 401 times to add to their collective On Base Average.

1932

BROOKLYN DODGERS

3RD 81-73 9GB

1 JOHNNY FREDERICK-OF
2 MICKEY FINN-2B
3 JOE (JERSEY JOE)STRIPP-3B/1B
4 HACK WILSON-OF
5 TONY (COOCH) (CHICK) CUCCINELLO-2B
6 LEFTY O'DOUL-OF
7 GLENN (BUCKSHOT) WRIGHT-SS
8 GORDON (OSKIE) SLADE-SS
9 DANNY TAYLOR-OF (2)
10 AL LOPEZ-C
11 CLYDE (SUKEY) SUKEFORTH-C
12 VAL PICINICH-C
14 BUD CLANCY-1B
14 GEORGE (HIGHPOCKETS) KELLY-1B
15 DAZZY VANCE-P
16 VAN LINGLE MUNGO-P
17 WATTY (LEFTY) CLARK-P
18 FRED (LEFTY) HEIMACH-P
19 RAY PHELPS-P
20 SLOPPY THURSTON-P
21 JOE (LEFTY) SHAUTE-P
22 JACK QUINN-P
24 CY MOORE-P
24 ED PIPGRAS-P
25 MAX ROSENFELD-OF
26 FAY (SCOW) THOMAS-P
31 CASEY (THE OLD PROFESSOR) STENGEL-CH
32 OTTO (MOONIE) MILLER-CH
33 MAX (SCOOPS) CAREY-MGR
38 DICK SIEBERT-1B
DEL BISSONETTE (INJ)- (1B)
NO# IKE BOONE-OF (13G: 4/12-5/9)
NO# BRUCE CALDWELL-1B (7G: 5/29-6/6)
NO# ALTA COHEN-OF (9G: 4/12-5/11)
NO# WAITE (SCHOOLBOY) HOYT-P (1) (8G: 4/12-6/4)
NO# ART JONES-P (1G: 4/23)
NO# BOBBY REIS-3B (1G: 4/30)
NO# PAUL RICHARDS-C (3G: 4/17-5/11)
NO# FRESCO (TOMMY) THOMPSON-INF (3G: 4/12-5/14)

1933

6TH 65-88 26.5GB

1 JOHNNY FREDERICK-OF
2 JOE JUDGE-1B (1)
3 JOE (JERSEY JOE)STRIPP-3B/1B
4 HACK WILSON-OF
5 TONY (COOCH) (CHICK) CUCCINELLO-2B
6 LEFTY O'DOUL-OF (1)
6 SAM (SAMBO) LESLIE-1B (2)
7 GLENN (BUCKSHOT) WRIGHT (INJ)-SS
8 JAKE FLOWERS-UTIL
9 DANNY TAYLOR-OF
10 AL LOPEZ-C
11 CLYDE (SUKEY) SUKEFORTH-C
11 LONNY (JUNIOR) FREY-SS
12 VAL PICINICH-C (1)
14 DEL BISSONETTE-1B
14 JOE (SLUG) (POODLES) HUTCHESON-OF
15 OWNIE CARROLL-P
16 VAN LINGLE MUNGO-P
17 WATTY (LEFTY) CLARK (INJ)-P (1)
17 BUZZ BOYLE-OF
18 FRED (LEFTY) HEIMACH (INJ)-P
18 BERT DELMAS-2B
19 CHINK OUTEN-C
20 SLOPPY THURSTON-P
21 JOE (LEFTY) SHAUTE-P
22 ROSY RYAN-P
24 JIMMY (LORD) JORDAN-INF
25 MAX ROSENFELD-OF
26 LU BLUE-1B
27 DUTCH LEONARD-P
28 RAY BENGE-P
30 BOOM-BOOM BECK-P
31 CASEY (THE OLD PROFESSOR) STENGEL-CH
32 OTTO (MOONIE) MILLER-CH
33 MAX (SCOOPS) CAREY-MGR
35 ROSY RYAN-P
39 RAY (LUKE) LUCAS-P

1934

6TH 71-81 23.5GB

1 JOHNNY FREDERICK-OF
2 JIM BUCHER (INJ)-INF
3 JOE (JERSEY JOE)STRIPP (INJ)-3B/1B
4 HACK WILSON-OF (1)
5 TONY (COOCH) (CHICK) CUCCINELLO-2B
6 SAM (SAMBO) LESLIE-1B
7 JOHNNY MCCARTHY-SS
8 LONNY (JUNIOR) FREY-SS
9 DANNY TAYLOR-OF
10 AL LOPEZ-C
11 CLYDE (SUKEY) SUKEFORTH-C
11 NICK TREMARK-OF
12 JIMMY (LORD) JORDAN-INF
14 WALLY MILLIES-C
15 OWNIE CARROLL-P
16 VAN LINGLE MUNGO-P
17 BUZZ BOYLE-OF
18 LEN KOENECKE-OF
20 GLENN (PETE) CHAPMAN-OF/2B
21 PHIL PAGE-P
21 HARRY SMYTHE-P (2)
22 RAY BERRES-C
23 CHARLIE (LEFTY) PERKINS-P
24 WATTY (LEFTY) CLARK-P (2)
25 LES (BIG ED) (NEMO) MUNNS-P
26 RAY (LUKE) LUCAS-P
26 JOHNNY BABICH-P
27 DUTCH LEONARD-P
28 RAY BENGE-P
29 ART (RED) (SANDY) HERRING-P
30 BOOM-BOOM BECK-P
31 CASEY (THE OLD PROFESSOR) STENGEL-CH
32 OTTO (MOONIE) MILLER-CH
33 CHICK (?) FRASER-CH
34 TOMMY ZACHARY-P (2)
__ BERT (SONNY) HOGG-3B (2G: 6/1-2)

1935

5TH 70-83 29.5GB

1 BUZZ BOYLE-OF
2 JIM BUCHER-UTIL
3 JOE (JERSEY JOE)STRIPP-3B/1B
4 FRENCHY BORDAGARAY-OF
5 TONY (COOCH) (CHICK) CUCCINELLO-2B
5 JOHNNY COONEY-OF
6 SAM (SAMBO) LESLIE-1B
6 RAOUL (ROD) DEDEAUX-SS
7 GEORGE (MOOSE) EARNSHAW-P (2)
8 LONNY (JUNIOR) FREY-SS
9 DANNY TAYLOR-OF
10 AL LOPEZ-C
11 NICK TREMARK-OF
12 JIMMY (LORD) JORDAN-INF
14 FRANK (LEFTY) LAMANSKE-P
14 FRANK SKAFF-3B
15 BOB (LEFTY) LOGAN-P
15 TOM (RATTLESNAKE) BAKER-P
16 VAN LINGLE MUNGO-P
17 WATTY (LEFTY) CLARK-P
18 LEN KOENECKE (DIED)-OF
19 BABE (BLIMP) PHELPS-C
20 HARRY EISENSTAT-P
20 ZACK TAYLOR-C
21 DAZZY VANCE-P
21 BUSTER (BUS) MILLS-OF
22 CURLY ONIS-C
22 VINCE (BALDY) SHERLOCK-2B
23 JOHNNY MCCARTHY-SS
24 BOBBY REIS-UTIL/P
25 LES (BIG ED) (NEMO) MUNNS-P
26 JOHNNY BABICH-P
27 DUTCH LEONARD-P
28 RAY BENGE-P
28 HARVEY (BUCK) GREEN-P
30 BOB BARR-P
31 CASEY (THE OLD PROFESSOR) STENGEL-CH
32 OTTO (MOONIE) MILLER-CH
33 CHICK (?) FRASER-CH
34 TOMMY ZACHARY-P
__ WHITEY OCK-C (1G: 9/29)

1936

7TH 67-87 25GB

1 FRED LINDSTROM (INJ)-OF
2 JIM BUCHER-UTIL
3 JOE (JERSEY JOE)STRIPP-3B/1B
4 FRENCHY BORDAGARAY-OF
5 JACK RADTKE-INF
5 BEN GERAGHTY-INF
6 BUDDY HASSETT-1B
7 GEORGE (MOOSE) EARNSHAW-P (1)
7? JOHNNY (MR. CHIPS) HUDSON-INF (6G: 6/20-7/1)
8 LONNY (JUNIOR) FREY-SS
9 DANNY TAYLOR-OF
9 TOM (LONG TOM) WINSETT-OF
10 RAY BERRES-C
11 GEORGE WATKINS-OF (2)
12 JIMMY (LORD) JORDAN-INF
14 OX ECKHARDT-OF
14 HARRY EISENSTAT-P
15 JOHNNY COONEY-OF
16 VAN LINGLE MUNGO-P
17 WATTY (LEFTY) CLARK-P
18 DICK SIEBERT-OF
19 BABE (BLIMP) PHELPS-C
20 ZACK TAYLOR-C
21 SID (PUDGE) GAUTREAUX-C
22 TOM (RATTLESNAKE) BAKER-P
23 GEORGE JEFFCOAT-P
24 RANDY MOORE-OF
25 ED (BIG ED) BRANDT-P
26 FRED FRANKHOUSE-P
27 DUTCH LEONARD (INJ)-P
28 NICK TREMARK-OF
29 HARRY EISENSTAT-P
30 MAX BUTCHER-P
31 CASEY (THE OLD PROFESSOR) STENGEL-CH
31 EDDIE WILSON (INJ)-OF
32 OTTO (MOONIE) MILLER-CH
33 CHICK (?) FRASER-CH
34 TOMMY ZACHARY-P (1)
34 HANK WINSTON-P
36 CASEY (THE OLD PROFESSOR) STENGEL-CH

1937

6TH 62-91 33.5GB

1 WOODY ENGLISH-SS/2B
2 JIM BUCHER-UTIL
3 JOE (JERSEY JOE)STRIPP-INF
4 TONY MALINOSKY-INF
4 BERT HAAS-OF/1B
5 COOKIE LAVAGETTO-2B/3B
6 BUDDY HASSETT-1B
7 LINDSAY (RED) BROWN-SS
7 JOHNNY (MR. CHIPS) HUDSON-INF
8 SID (PUDGE) GAUTREAUX-C
8 PAUL CHERVINKO-C
9 BABE (BLIMP) PHELPS-C
10 RANDY MOORE-OF (1)
10 FRED (FAT FREDDIE) FITZSIMMONS (INJ)-P (2)
11 FRED FRANKHOUSE-P
12 LUKE (HOT POTATO) HAMLIN-P
14 ROY SPENCER-C
15 MAX BUTCHER (INJ)-P
16 VAN LINGLE MUNGO (INJ)-P
17 WATTY (LEFTY) CLARK-P/CH
18 HARRY EISENSTAT-P
18 GEORGE (FLASH) FALLON-2B
19 JIM LINDSEY-P
19 RALPH (LEFTY) BIRKHOFER-P
20 GEORGE CISAR-OF
21 NICK POLLY-3B
22 TOM (RATTLESNAKE) BAKER-P (1)
22 ROY HENSHAW-P
23 GEORGE JEFFCOAT (ILL)-P
23 EDDIE WILSON-OF
24 JAKE DANIEL-1B
24 JIM PETERSON-P
24 BUCK MARROW-P
25 JOHNNY COONEY-OF
26 HEINIE MANUSH-OF
27 EDDIE (PEPPER) MORGAN-1B/OF
27 BEN CANTWELL-P (2)
28 EDDIE WILSON-OF
28 ART PARKS-OF
29 TOM (LONG TOM) WINSETT-OF
30 GIB BRACK-OF
31 ANDY (HANDY ANDY) HIGH-CH
32 OTTO (MOONIE) MILLER-CH
32 GOODY ROSEN-OF
33 BURLEIGH (OL' STUBBLEBEARD) GRIMES-MGR
34 ELMER KLUMPP-C
34 WAITE (SCHOOLBOY) HOYT-P (2)

1938

7TH 69-81 17.5GB

1 WOODY ENGLISH-INF
1 PACKY ROGERS-UTIL
2 LEO (THE LIP) (LIPPY) DUROCHER-SS
3 PETE COSCARART-2B
4 DOLPH CAMILLI-1B
5 COOKIE LAVAGETTO-3B/2B
6 JOHNNY (MR. CHIPS) HUDSON-2B/SS
7 RAY THOMAS-C
7 PACKY ROGERS-UTIL
7 WOODY WILLIAMS-SS/3B
8 PAUL CHERVINKO-C
8 GILLY CAMPBELL-C
9 BABE (BLIMP) PHELPS-C
10 ROY SPENCER-C
11 FRED FRANKHOUSE-P
12 LUKE (HOT POTATO) HAMLIN-P
13 BURLEIGH (OL' STUBBLEBEARD) GRIMES-MGR
14 FRED (FAT FREDDIE) FITZSIMMONS (INJ)-P
15 WAITE (SCHOOLBOY) HOYT-P
15 VITO TAMULIS-P (2)
16 VAN LINGLE MUNGO-P
17 MAX BUTCHER-P (1)
17 ORIS (BROWN) HOCKETT-OF
18 TOT PRESSNELL-P
20 ERNIE (CHIEF) KOY-OF
21 BILL (SAILOR BILL) (BARNACLE BILL) POSEDEL-P
22 BUDDY HASSETT-OF/1B
(23) GEORGE JEFFCOAT (ILL)-(P)
23 WAYNE LAMASTER-P (2)
24 BUCK MARROW-P
24 LEE (BUCK) ROGERS-P (2)
25 KIKI CUYLER-OF
26 HEINIE MANUSH-OF (1)
26 MERV SHEA-C
27 GOODY ROSEN-OF
28 MERV SHEA-C
28 BERT HAAS-OF/1B
29 TOM (LONG TOM) WINSETT-OF
29 TOM SHEEHAN-CH
30 GIB BRACK-OF
30 TUCK STAINBACK-OF (3)
31 ANDY (HANDY ANDY) HIGH-CH
31 EDDIE (PEPPER) MORGAN-1B/OF
32 JESSE (POP) HAINES-CH
33 ERNIE (CHIEF) KOY-OF
35 BABE (BAMBINO) (SULTAN OF SWAT) RUTH-CH
36 DYKES POTTER-P
37 OTTO (MOONIE) MILLER-CH
37 FRED SINGTON-OF

BROOKLYN/**LOS ANGELES DODGERS**

_ JOHN (SHERIFF) GADDY-P (2G: 9/27,10/2)
_ GREEK GEORGE-C (7G: 9/22-10/2)
_ RAY HAYWORTH-C (2) (5G: 9/16-10/2)
_ SAM (SUBWAY SAM) NAHEM -P (1G: 10/2)
_ JIM (COWBOY) WINFORD-P (2G: 9/16,22)

1939

3RD 84-69 12.5GB

1 GENE (ROWDY) MOORE-OF
2 LEO (THE LIP) (LIPPY) DUROCHER-SS/MGR
3 PETE COSCARART-2B/INF
4 DOLPH CAMILLI-1B
5 COOKIE LAVAGETTO-3B
6 JOHNNY (MR. CHIPS) HUDSON-2B/SS
7 CHUCK DRESSEN-CH
8 ART PARKS-OF
9 BABE (BLIMP) PHELPS-C
10 RAY HAYWORTH-C (1)
10 CARL DOYLE-P
11 TONY (POOSH'EM UP) LAZZERI-2B/3B (1)
11 DIXIE (THE PEOPLE'S CHERCE) WALKER (INJ)-OF (2)
12 LUKE (HOT POTATO) HAMLIN-P
14 FRED (FAT FREDDIE) FITZSIMMONS (INJ)-P
15 VITO TAMULIS-P
16 VAN LINGLE MUNGO-P
17 JIMMY RIPPLE-OF (2)
17 WHIT WYATT-P
18 TOT PRESSNELL-P
19 IRA HUTCHINSON-P
20 ERNIE (CHIEF) KOY-OF
21 AL TODD-C
22 RED EVANS-P
22 LINDSEY DEAL-OF
23 CHRIS HARTJE-C
24 BILL CROUCH-P
24 AL (BOOTS) HOLLINGSWORTH-P (2)
25 HUGH CASEY-P
26 BILL CROUCH-P
26 LYN (BROADWAY) LARY-SS/3B (2)
27 GOODY ROSEN-OF
28 FRED SINGTON-OF
28 BERT HAAS-OF/1B
29 ORIS (BROWN) HOCKETT-OF
29 MEL ALMADA-OF (2)
30 TUCK STAINBACK-OF
31 BILL KILLIFER-CH
32 ART PARKS-OF
32 BOOTS POFFENBERGER (INJ)-P
34 GENE SCHOTT-P
42 GEORGE JEFFCOAT-P

1940

2ND 88-65 12GB

1 CHARLIE GILBERT-OF
1 PEE WEE REESE (INJ)-SS
2 LEO (THE LIP) (LIPPY) DUROCHER-SS/MGR
3 PETE COSCARART-2B/INF
4 DOLPH CAMILLI-1B
5 COOKIE LAVAGETTO (ILL)-3B
6 JOHNNY (MR. CHIPS) HUDSON-INF
7 CHUCK DRESSEN-CH
7 JOE (DUCKY) (MUSCLES) MEDWICK-OF (2)
8 JOE VOSMIK-OF
9 BABE (BLIMP) PHELPS-C
10 GUS (BLACKIE) MANCUSO-C
11 DIXIE (THE PEOPLE'S CHERCE) WALKER (INJ)-OF
12 LUKE (HOT POTATO) HAMLIN-P
14 FRED (FAT FREDDIE) FITZSIMMONS-P
15 VITO TAMULIS-P
16 VAN LINGLE MUNGO (INJ)-P/CH
17 WHIT WYATT-P
18 TOT PRESSNELL-P
18 STEVE (THE MAD RUSSIAN) RACHUNOK-P
19 HERMAN FRANKS-C
20 ERNIE (CHIEF) KOY-OF (1)
20 WES FLOWERS-P
21 WES FERRELL-P
21 LOU FETTE-P (2)
21 LEE GRISSOM-P (2)
22 BEN TINCUP-CH
23 ED HEAD-P
24 JOE (MUSCLES) GALLAGHER-OF (2)
25 HUGH CASEY-P
26 CARL DOYLE-P (1)
26 CURT (COONSKIN) DAVIS-P (2)
27 TONY GIULIANI-C
28 TEX CARLETON-P
29 JIMMY WASDELL-OF/1B (2)
30 ROY CULLENBINE-OF (1)
31 GENE (ROWDY) MOORE-OF (1)
32 JIMMY RIPPLE-OF (1)
32 LEE GRISSOM-P (2)
33 NEWT KIMBALL-P (1)
33 DON ROSS-3B
34 CHARLIE GILBERT-OF
34 PETE (PISTOL PETE) REISER-UTIL
36 MAX MACON-P
77 JOE (DUCKY) (MUSCLES) MEDWICK-OF (2)
77 CHUCK DRESSEN-CH

1941

1ST 100-54 0GB

L WS-NYA 4-1

1 PEE WEE REESE-SS
2 LEO (THE LIP) (LIPPY) DUROCHER-SS/MGR
3 PETE COSCARART-2B/SS
4 DOLPH CAMILLI-1B
5 COOKIE LAVAGETTO-3B
6 TONY GIULIANI-C
6 JOE (DUCKY) (MUSCLES) MEDWICK-OF
7 CHUCK DRESSEN-CH
8 JOE VOSMIK-OF
8 JIMMY WASDELL-OF/1B
9 BABE (BLIMP) PHELPS (JMP)-C
10 MICKEY OWEN-C
11 DIXIE (THE PEOPLE'S CHERCE) WALKER (INJ)-OF
12 LUKE (HOT POTATO) HAMLIN-P
14 FRED (FAT FREDDIE) FITZSIMMONS-P
15 VITO TAMULIS-P (2)
15 TOM DRAKE-P
16 VAN LINGLE MUNGO-P/CH
16 BILLY HERMAN-2B (2)
17 WHIT WYATT-P
18 LEW RIGGS-INF
19 HERMAN FRANKS-C
20 KEMP WICKER-P
20 LARRY FRENCH-P (2)
21 NEWT KIMBALL-P
22 BILL SWIFT-P
22 JOHNNY ALLEN-P (2)
23 ED HEAD-P
24 PAUL (BIG POISIN) WANER-OF (1)
24 TOMMY TATUM-OF
24 AUGIE GALAN-OF (2)
25 HUGH CASEY-P
26 CARL DOYLE-P
26 CURT (COONSKIN) DAVIS-P
27 PETE (PISTOL PETE) REISER-UTIL
28 MACE BROWN-P (2)
29 JIMMY WASDELL-OF/1B
29 ED (RUBE) ALBOSTA-P
30 RED CORRIDEN-CH
31 AL KAMPOURIS (INJ-2B
32 LEE GRISSOM-P (1)
32 BOB (MR. CHIPS) CHIPMAN-P
33 MACE BROWN-P (2)
38 TONY GIULIANI-C
47 GEORGE PFISTER-C
77 JOE (DUCKY) (MUSCLES) MEDWICK-OF

1942

2ND 104-50 2GB

1 PEE WEE REESE-SS
2 LEO (THE LIP) (LIPPY) DUROCHER-MGR
3 AL KAMPOURIS-2B
3 STAN ROJEK-PR
4 DOLPH CAMILLI-1B
5 ARKY VAUGHAN-3B/INF
6 JOE (DUCKY) (MUSCLES) MEDWICK-OF
7 CHUCK DRESSEN-CH
8* SCHOOLBOY ROWE-P* (2)
8* BOBO NEWSOM-P* (2)
9 BILLY SULLIVAN-C
10 MICKEY OWEN-C
11 DIXIE (THE PEOPLE'S CHERCE) WALKER (INJ)-OF
12 BOB (MR. CHIPS) CHIPMAN-P
12 BABE DAHLGREN-1B (3)
13 KIRBY HIGBE-P
14 FRED (FAT FREDDIE) FITZSIMMONS-P
16 BILLY HERMAN-2B/1B
17 WHIT WYATT-P
18 LEW RIGGS-INF
19 CLIFF DAPPER-C
20 LARRY FRENCH-P
21 NEWT KIMBALL-P
22 JOHNNY ALLEN-P (2)
23 ED HEAD-P
24 AUGIE GALAN-OF
25 HUGH CASEY-P
26 CURT (COONSKIN) DAVIS-P
27 PETE (PISTOL PETE) REISER (INJ)-UTIL
28 MAX MACON-P
30 RED CORRIDEN-CH
31 LES WEBBER-P
32 JOHNNY RIZZO-OF
33 CHET KEHN-P
37 FRENCHY BORDAGARAY-OF

1943

3RD 81-72 23.5GB

1 PAUL (BIG POISIN) WANER-OF
2 LEO (THE LIP) (LIPPY) DUROCHER-SS/MGR
3 AL KAMPOURIS-2B (1)
3 RED BARKLEY-SS
3 BOYD BARTLEY-SS
3 AL CAMPANIS-2B
4 DOLPH CAMILLI (RET)-1B
4 GIL HODGES-3B
4 JOE ORENGO-3B (2)
5 ARKY VAUGHAN-3B/INF
6 CHUCK DRESSEN-CH
6 HAL PECK-PH
6 CARDEN GILLENWATER-OF
7 JOE (DUCKY) (MUSCLES) MEDWICK-OF (1)
7 CHUCK DRESSEN-CH
8* BOBO NEWSOM-P* (1)
8 HOWIE (STRETCH) (STEEPLE) SCHULTZ-1B
9 BILL HART-INF
10 MICKEY OWEN-C
11 DIXIE (THE PEOPLE'S CHERCE) WALKER-OF
12 RUBE MELTON-P
12 REX BARNEY-1B
13 KIRBY HIGBE-P
14 FRED (FAT FREDDIE) FITZSIMMONS-P
14 CHRIS (BUD) HAUGHEY-P
14 GENE HERMANSKI (MIL)-OF
15 BOBBY (NIG) BRAGAN-C/INF
16 BILLY HERMAN-2B/1B
17 WHIT WYATT (INJ)-P
18 JOHNNY COONEY-1B/OF
18 CARDEN GILLENWATER-OF
19 FRENCHY BORDAGARAY-OF
20 AL GLOSSOP-UTIL
21 NEWT KIMBALL-P (1)
21 LUIS OLMO-OF
22 JOHNNY ALLEN (INJ)-P (1)
22 BOB (MR. CHIPS) CHIPMAN-P
22 BILL SAYLES-P (2)
23 ED HEAD-P
24 AUGIE GALAN-OF
26 CURT (COONSKIN) DAVIS-P
27 DEE MOORE-C (1)
27 FRITZ OSTERMUELLER-P (2)
28 MAX MACON-P/1B
28 HAL (SKEETS) GREGG-P
30 RED CORRIDEN-CH
31 LES WEBBER-P
32 RUBE MELTON-P
32 BILL LOHRMAN-P (2)
33 PAT ANKENMAN (MIL)-SS
35 CLYDE (SUKEY) SUKEFORTH-CH
36 FRENCHY BORDAGARAY-OF

1944

7TH 63-91 42GB

1 PAUL (BIG POISIN) WANER-OF (1)
2 LEO (THE LIP) (LIPPY) DUROCHER-MGR
3 EDDIE (BAZOOKA) (FIDDLER) BASINSKI-2B/SS
3 GENE (SKIP) MAUCH-SS
3 ART (RED)(SANDY) HERRING-P
4 GIL ENGLISH-INF
5 CLANCY SMYRES-PH
5* BEN CHAPMAN-P*
6 JACK BOLLING (MIL)-1B
6 BILL HART-3B/SS
7 CHUCK DRESSEN-CH
8 HOWIE (STRETCH) (STEEPLE) SCHULTZ-1B
9 LLOYD (LITTLE POISIN) WANER-OF (1)
9 TOMMY (BUCKSHOT) BROWN-SS
10 MICKEY OWEN-C
11 DIXIE (THE PEOPLE'S CHERCE) WALKER-OF
12 BOB (MR. CHIPS) CHIPMAN-P (1)
12 EDDIE (THE BRAT) (MUGGSY) STANKY-INF (2)
13 TOMMY WARREN-P
13 RALPH (HAWK) BRANCA-P
14 RUBE MELTON-P
15 BOBBY (NIG) BRAGAN-C/INF
15 STAN (POLO) ANDREWS-C
16 PAT ANKENMAN-2B/SS
16 BARNEY KOCH-2B/SS
16 EDDIE MIKSIS-3B/SS
17 WHIT WYATT (INJ)-P
18 JOHNNY COONEY-1B/OF
18 CLYDE KING-P
18 LOU ROCHELLI (MIL)-2B
19 ED HEAD (MIL)-P
19 CHARLIE FUCHS-P
19 TOM (LEFTY) SUNKEL-P
19 MORRIE ADERHOLT-OF
20 TOMMY WARREN-P
20 CHARLIE OSGOOD-P
21 LUIS OLMO-OF/UTIL
22 BILL LOHRMAN-P (1)
22 FRANK WURM-P
22 JACK FRANKLIN-P
24 AUGIE GALAN-OF
25 WES FLOWERS-P
26 CURT (COONSKIN) DAVIS-P
27 FRITZ OSTERMUELLER-P (1)
27 CLAUDE CROCKER-P
28 HAL (SKEETS) GREGG-P
30 RED CORRIDEN-CH
31 LES WEBBER-P
32 FATS DANTONIO-C
32 RAY HAYWORTH-C
33 FRENCHY BORDAGARAY-OF
34 ROY JARVIS (MIL)-C
34 CAL (BUSTER) MCLISH-P
35 CLYDE (SUKEY) SUKEFORTH-CH
35 GOODY ROSEN-OF
38 CHINK ZACHARY-P
_ RED DURRETT-OF (11G: 9/14-10/1)
_ JOHN WELLS-P (4G: 9/14-10/1)

1945

3RD 87-67 11GB

1 MIKE SANDLOCK-UTIL
2 LEO (THE LIP) (LIPPY) DUROCHER-2B/MGR
3 FATS DANTONIO-C
3 BABE HERMAN-OF
3 RED DURRETT-OF
4 BABE HERMAN-OF
5* BEN CHAPMAN-P* (1)
5 JOHNNY PEACOCK-C (2)
6 BILL HART-3B/SS
7 CHUCK DRESSEN-CH
8 HOWIE (STRETCH) (STEEPLE) SCHULTZ-1B
8 ED (BIG ED) STEVENS-1B
8 CLAUDE CORBITT-3B
9 BARNEY WHITE-INF
9 TOMMY (BUCKSHOT) BROWN-SS
10 MICKEY OWEN (MIL)-C
10 ERNIE RUDOLPH-P

11 DIXIE (THE PEOPLE'S CHERCE) WALKER-OF
12 EDDIE (THE BRAT) (MUGGSY) STANKY-2B
13 RALPH (HAWK) BRANCA-P
13 JOHN DOUGLAS-1B
14 LEE PFUND-P
15 STAN (POLO) ANDREWS-C (1)
16 ART (RED)(SANDY) HERRING-P
17 TOM SEATS-P
18 VIC LOMBARDI-P
19 MORRIE ADERHOLT-OF (1)
19 CY BUKER-P
21 LUIS OLMO-OF/UTIL
22 RAY HATHAWAY-P
23 CY BUKER-P
24 AUGIE GALAN-1B/OF/3B
25 OTHO (NICK) NITCHOLAS-P
25 DON LUND-PH
26 CURT (COONSKIN) DAVIS-P
27 EDDIE (BAZOOKA) (FIDDLER) BASINSKI-2B/SS
27? CLAUDE CROCKER-P (1G: 9/30)
28 HAL (SKEETS) GREGG-P
29 CLYDE KING-P
30 RED CORRIDEN-CH
31 LES WEBBER-P
31 EDDIE (BAZOOKA) (FIDDLER) BASINSKI-2B/SS
32 RAY HAYWORTH-C/CH
32 BABE HERMAN-OF
32 LES WEBBER-P
33 FRENCHY BORDAGARAY-OF
34 FATS DANTONIO-C
34 CLYDE (SUKEY) SUKEFORTH-CH
35 GOODY ROSEN-OF
38 CHINK ZACHARY-P

1946

2ND 96-60 2GB

L PLAYOFF-STLN 2-0

1 PEE WEE REESE-SS
2 LEO (THE LIP) (LIPPY) DUROCHER-MGR
3 STAN ROJEK-INF
4 MIKE SANDLOCK-C/3B
5 CARL (SKOONJ) (THE READING RIFLE) FURILLO-OF
5 COOKIE LAVAGETTO-3B
6 CARL (SKOONJ) (THE READING RIFLE) FURILLO-OF
7 CHUCK DRESSEN-CH
8 HOWIE (STRETCH) (STEEPLE) SCHULTZ-1B
9 JACK GRAHAM-1B
10 EARL NAYLOR-PH
10 LEW RIGGS-3B
10 BRUCE (BULL) EDWARDS-C
11 DIXIE (THE PEOPLE'S CHERCE) WALKER-OF
12 EDDIE (THE BRAT) (MUGGSY) STANKY-2B
13 KIRBY HIGBE-P
14 FERRELL (ANDY) ANDERSON-C
15 LEW RIGGS-3B
15 DICK WHITMAN-OF
16 BILLY HERMAN-3B/2B (1)
16 JOE (DUCKY) (MUSCLES) MEDWICK-OF/1B
17 BOB RAMAZZOTTI-3B/2B
18 VIC LOMBARDI-P
19 JOE HATTEN-P
20 RALPH (HAWK) BRANCA-P
21 ART (RED)(SANDY) HERRING-P
22 GENE HERMANSKI-OF
23 ED HEAD (INJ) P
24 AUGIE GALAN-1B/OF/3B
25 HUGH CASEY-P
26 CURT (COONSKIN) DAVIS-P
26 REX BARNEY-P
27 PETE (PISTOL PETE) REISER -OF/3B
28 HAL (SKEETS) GREGG-P
29 CARL (SKOONJ) (THE READING RIFLE) FURILLO-OF
29 HANK BEHRMAN-P
30 RED CORRIDEN-CH
31 DICK WHITMAN-OF
31 HANK BEHRMAN-P
31 OTIS (SCAT) DAVIS-PR
32 LES WEBBER-P (1)
32 JOE TEPSIC-OF
33 DON PADGETT-C (1)
34 HANK BEHRMAN-P
34 JEAN PIERRE ROY-P
34 EDDIE MIKSIS (MIL)-SS/2B
35 GOODY ROSEN-OF (1)
35 CAL (BUSTER) MCLISH (MIL)-P
36 ED (BIG ED) STEVENS-1B
37 RUBE MELTON (MIL)-P
38 BOB RAMAZZOTTI-3B/2B
38 PAUL (LEFTY) MINNER (INJ) -P
39 JOHN CORRIDEN, JR.-C
40 HARRY TAYLOR-P
49 JOHN CORRIDEN, JR.-C
__ GLEN MOULDER-P (1G: 4/26)
__ CLYDE (SUKEY) SUKEFORTH -CH
LUIS OLMO (MEX)-(OF)
MICKEY OWEN (MEX)-(C)

1947

1ST 94-60 0GB

L WS-NYA 4-3

BURT (BARNEY) SHOTTON-MGR2
1 PEE WEE REESE-SS
(2) LEO (THE LIP) (LIPPY) DUROCHER (SUS)-(MGR)
3 STAN ROJEK-INF
4 DUKE (THE SILVER FOX) SNIDER-OF
5 COOKIE LAVAGETTO-3B
6 CARL (SKOONJ) (THE READING RIFLE) FURILLO-OF
7 PETE (PISTOL PETE) REISER (INJ)-OF/3B
8 HOWIE (STRETCH) (STEEPLE) SCHULTZ-1B
8 HAL (SKEETS) GREGG-P*
9 ARKY VAUGHAN-OF/3B
10 BRUCE (BULL) EDWARDS-C
11 DIXIE (THE PEOPLE'S CHERCE) WALKER-OF
11 JACK BANTA-P
12 EDDIE (THE BRAT) (MUGGSY) STANKY-2B
13 KIRBY HIGBE-P (1)
13 RALPH (HAWK) BRANCA-P
14 DICK WHITMAN-OF
14 GIL HODGES-C
15 CLYDE (SUKEY) SUKEFORTH-MGR1/CH
16 RAY BLADES-CH
16 CLYDE KING-P
17 TOMMY TATUM-OF (1)
17 DON LUND-OF
18 VIC LOMBARDI-P
19 JOE HATTEN-P
20 RALPH (HAWK) BRANCA-P
20 PHIL HAUGSTAD-P
21 CLYDE KING-P
21 SPIDER JORGENSEN-3B
22 GENE HERMANSKI-OF
23 GEORGE (LEFTY) DOCKINS-P
23 DAN BANKHEAD-P
24 BOBBY (NIG) BRAGAN-C
25 HUGH CASEY-P
26 REX BARNEY-P
27 RAY BLADES-CH
28 HAL (SKEETS) GREGG-P
29 HANK BEHRMAN-P (1)(3)
30 AL GIONFRIDDO-OF (2)
31 JAKE PITLER-CH
32 WILLIE (THE KNUCK) RAMSDELL-P
33 TOMMY (BUCKSHOT) BROWN (MIL)-UTIL
34 EDDIE MIKSIS-UTIL
35 MARV RACKLEY-OF
36 ED (BIG ED) STEVENS-1B
37 RUBE MELTON-P
39 ED CHANDLER-P
40 CLYDE (SUKEY) SUKEFORTH-MGR1/CH
40 DON LUND-OF
40 ERV PALICA-P
41 HARRY TAYLOR-P
42 JACKIE ROBINSON-1B
43 JOHNNY VAN CUYK-P
LUIS OLMO (MEX)-(OF)
MICKEY OWEN (MEX)-(C)

1948

3RD 84-70 7.5GB

BURT (BARNEY) SHOTTON-MGR3
1 PEE WEE REESE-SS
2 LEO (THE LIP) (LIPPY) DUROCHER-MGR1
3 BILLY COX-INF
4 DUKE (THE SILVER FOX) SNIDER-OF
5 TOMMY (BUCKSHOT) BROWN-3B/1B
6 CARL (SKOONJ) (THE READING RIFLE) FURILLO-OF
7 PETE (PISTOL PETE) REISER (INJ)-OF/3B
8 DON LUND-OF (1)
8 GEORGE (SHOTGUN) SHUBA-OF
9 ARKY VAUGHAN-OF/3B
10 BRUCE (BULL) EDWARDS (INJ)-C/UTIL
11 JACK BANTA-P
12 ERV PALICA-P
13 RALPH (HAWK) BRANCA-P
14 GIL HODGES-1B/C
15 CLYDE (SUKEY) SUKEFORTH-CH
16 CLYDE KING-P
17 BOB RAMAZZOTTI-INF
17 CARL (OISK) ERSKINE-P
18 DICK WHITMAN-OF
19 JOE HATTEN-P
20 PHIL HAUGSTAD-P
20 ELMER SEXAUER-P
20 HANK BEHRMAN-P
21 SPIDER JORGENSEN (INJ)-3B
22 GENE HERMANSKI-OF
23 JOHNNY HALL-P
24 BOBBY (NIG) BRAGAN-C
25 HUGH CASEY (INJ)-P
26 REX BARNEY-P
27 RAY BLADES-CH/MGR2
28 PREACHER ROE-P
29 GENE (SKIP) MAUCH-INF (1)
29 HANK BEHRMAN-P
30 DWAIN (LEFTY) SLOAT-P
31 JAKE PITLER-CH
32 WILLIE (THE KNUCK) RAMSDELL-P
33 TOMMY (BUCKSHOT) BROWN-3B/1B
33 ROY (CAMPY) CAMPANELLA-C
33 WILLIE (THE KNUCK) RAMSDELL-P
34 EDDIE MIKSIS-INF
35 MARV RACKLEY-OF
36 PRESTON WARD-1B
37 JOHNNY VAN CUYK-P
38 PAUL (LEFTY) MINNER-P
39 ROY (CAMPY) CAMPANELLA-C
40 ERV PALICA-P
41 HARRY TAYLOR (ILL)-P
42 JACKIE ROBINSON-2B/INF
44 GENE (SKIP) MAUCH-INF (1)
45 JOHNNY HALL-P
52 PRESTON WARD-1B
56 ROY (CAMPY) CAMPANELLA-C
LUIS OLMO (MEX)-(OF)
MICKEY OWEN (MEX)-(C)

1949

1ST 97-57 0GB

L WS-NYA 4-1

BURT (BARNEY) SHOTTON-MGR
1 PEE WEE REESE-SS
3 BILLY COX-INF
4 DUKE (THE SILVER FOX) SNIDER-OF
5 TOMMY (BUCKSHOT) BROWN-OF
6 CARL (SKOONJ) (THE READING RIFLE) FURILLO-OF
7 MIKE MCCORMICK-OF
8 GEORGE (SHOTGUN) SHUBA-OF
9 BOB RAMAZZOTTI-INF (1)
10 BRUCE (BULL) EDWARDS-C/UTIL
11 JACK BANTA-P
12 ERV PALICA-P
13 RALPH (HAWK) BRANCA-P
14 GIL HODGES-1B
15 CLYDE (SUKEY) SUKEFORTH-CH
16 MORRIE (LEFTY) MARTIN-P
17 CARL (OISK) ERSKINE-P
18 DICK WHITMAN-OF
19 JOE HATTEN-P
21 SPIDER JORGENSEN-3B
22 GENE HERMANSKI-OF
23 PAT MCGLOTHIN-P
26 REX BARNEY-P
27 MILT STOCK-CH
28 PREACHER ROE-P
31 JAKE PITLER-CH
32 CAL ABRAMS-OF
34 EDDIE MIKSIS-INF
35 MARV RACKLEY-OF (1)(3)
35 JOHNNY (HIPPITY) HOPP-OF/1B
35 MARV RACKLEY-OF (1)(3)
36 CHUCK CONNORS-PH
36 DON (NEWK) NEWCOMBE-P
37 JOHNNY VAN CUYK-P
37 LUIS OLMO (MEX)-OF
38 PAUL (LEFTY) MINNER-P
39 ROY (CAMPY) CAMPANELLA-C
40 BUD PODBIELAN-P
(41) HARRY TAYLOR (ILL)-(P)
42 JACKIE ROBINSON-2B

1950

2ND 89-65 2GB

BURT (BARNEY) SHOTTON-MGR
1 PEE WEE REESE-SS/3B
2 BOBBY MORGAN-3B/SS
3 BILLY COX-INF
4 DUKE (THE SILVER FOX) SNIDER-OF
5 TOMMY (BUCKSHOT) BROWN-OF
6 CARL (SKOONJ) (THE READING RIFLE) FURILLO-OF
7 STEVE LEMBO-C
8 GEORGE (SHOTGUN) SHUBA-OF
8 CAL ABRAMS-OF
10 BRUCE (BULL) EDWARDS-C/1B
11 JACK BANTA (INJ)-P
11 CARL (OISK) ERSKINE-P
11 AL (TUB)(PARD) EPPERLY-P
11 JOE LANDRUM-P
12 ERV PALICA-P
13 RALPH (HAWK) BRANCA-P
14 GIL HODGES-1B
15 CLYDE (SUKEY) SUKEFORTH-CH
17 CARL (OISK) ERSKINE-P
18 WAYNE BELARDI-1B
19 JOE HATTEN-P
21 SPIDER JORGENSEN-3B (1)
22 GENE HERMANSKI-OF
23 PAT MCGLOTHIN-P
25 CHRIS VAN CUYK-P
26 REX BARNEY-P
27 MILT STOCK-CH
28 PREACHER ROE-P
31 JAKE PITLER-CH
32 CAL ABRAMS-OF
33 WILLIE (THE KNUCK) RAMSDELL-P (1)
33 JIM ROMANO-P
34 EDDIE MIKSIS-INF
35 MAL MALLETTE-P
36 DON (NEWK) NEWCOMBE-P
37 JIM RUSSELL-OF
38 BILLY LOES-P
39 ROY (CAMPY) CAMPANELLA-C
40 BUD PODBIELAN-P
41 CLEM LABINE-P
42 JACKIE ROBINSON-2B
43 DAN BANKHEAD-P

1951

2ND 97-60 1GB

L PLAYOFF-NYN 2-1

1 PEE WEE REESE-SS
3 BILLY COX-INF
4 DUKE (THE SILVER FOX) SNIDER-OF
5 TOMMY (BUCKSHOT) BROWN-OF (1)
6 CARL (SKOONJ) (THE READING RIFLE) FURILLO-OF
7 CHUCK DRESSEN-MGR
9 ROCKY BRIDGES-INF
10 BRUCE (BULL) EDWARDS-C/1B (1)
10 RUBE WALKER-C (2)
11 MICKEY LIVINGSTON-C
12 ERV PALICA-P

BROOKLYN/**LOS ANGELES DODGERS**

13 RALPH (HAWK) BRANCA-P
14 GIL HODGES-1B
15 CLYDE (SUKEY) SUKEFORTH-CH
16 EARL MOSSOR-P
17 CARL (OISK) ERSKINE-P
18 WAYNE BELARDI-1B
19 JOE HATTEN-P (1)
19 JOHNNY (BEAR TRACKS) SCHMITZ-P (2)
20 PHIL HAUGSTAD-P
22 GENE HERMANSKI-OF (1)
22 ANDY (HANDY ANDY) (PRUSCHKA) PAFKO-OF (2)
23 CLYDE KING-P
24 HANK EDWARDS-PH (1)
25 CHRIS VAN CUYK-P
27 COOKIE LAVAGETTO-CH
28 PREACHER ROE-P
29 DON THOMPSON-OF
31 JAKE PITLER-CH
32 CAL ABRAMS-OF
34 EDDIE MIKSIS-INF (1)
34 WAYNE (TWIG) TERWILLIGER-2B/3B (2)
36 DON (NEWK) NEWCOMBE-P
37 JIM RUSSELL-OF
38 DICK WILLIAMS-OF
39 ROY (CAMPY) CAMPANELLA-C
40 BUD PODBIELAN-P
41 CLEM LABINE-P
42 JACKIE ROBINSON-2B
43 DAN BANKHEAD-P

1952

1ST 96-57 0GB
L WS-NYA 4-3

1 PEE WEE REESE-SS
2 BOBBY MORGAN-INF
3 BILLY COX (INJ)-3B/INF
4 DUKE (THE SILVER FOX) SNIDER-OF
5 SANDY AMOROS-OF
6 CARL (SKOONJ) (THE READING RIFLE) FURILLO-OF
7 CHUCK DRESSEN-MGR
8 GEORGE (SHOTGUN) SHUBA-OF
9 ROCKY BRIDGES-INF
10 RUBE WALKER-C
12 RALPH (HAWK) BRANCA-P
14 GIL HODGES-1B
15 JOHNNY (DOC) RUTHERFORD-P
16 KEN LEHMAN-P
17 CARL (OISK) ERSKINE-P
18 STEVE LEMBO-C
18 JIM HUGHES-P
19 JOHNNY (BEAR TRACKS) SCHMITZ-P (1)
19 JOE LANDRUM-P
22 BILLY HERMAN-CH
23 CLYDE KING-P
25 CHRIS VAN CUYK-P
27 COOKIE LAVAGETTO-CH
28 PREACHER ROE-P
29 TOMMY (KELLY) HOLMES-OF (2)
30 BILLY LOES-P
31 JAKE PITLER-CH
32 CAL ABRAMS-OF (1)
32 ROCKY NELSON-1B
34 RON NEGRAY-P
(36) DON (NEWK) NEWCOMBE (MIL)-(P)
38 DICK WILLIAMS-OF/UTIL
39 ROY (CAMPY) CAMPANELLA-C
40 BUD PODBIELAN-P (1)
41 CLEM LABINE-P
42 JACKIE ROBINSON-2B
45 RAY (FARMER) MOORE-P
46 BEN WADE-P
47 GEORGE PFISTER-CH
48 ANDY (HANDY ANDY) (PRUSCHKA) PAFKO-OF
49 JOE BLACK-P
ERV PALICA (MIL)-(P)

1953

1ST 105-49 0GB
L WS-NYA 4-2

1 PEE WEE REESE-SS
2 BOBBY MORGAN-SS/3B
3 BILLY COX (INJ)-3B/INF
4 DUKE (THE SILVER FOX) SNIDER-OF
5 WAYNE BELARDI (INJ)-1B
6 CARL (SKOONJ) (THE READING RIFLE) FURILLO-OF
7 CHUCK DRESSEN-MGR
8 GEORGE (SHOTGUN) SHUBA-OF
9 DIXIE HOWELL-PH
9 DICK TEED-PH
10 RUBE WALKER-C
11 WAYNE BELARDI (INJ)-1B
13 RALPH (HAWK) BRANCA-P (1)
14 GIL HODGES-1B
17 CARL (OISK) ERSKINE-P
18 JIM HUGHES-P
19 JIM (JUNIOR) GILLIAM-2B
20 CARMEN MAURO-OF (1)
22 BILLY HERMAN-CH
23 ERV PALICA (MIL)-P
25 BOB MILLIKEN-P
27 COOKIE LAVAGETTO-CH
28 PREACHER ROE-P
29 DON THOMPSON-OF
30 BILLY LOES-P
31 JAKE PITLER-CH
32 BILL ANTONELLO-OF
34 RUSS (MONK) (THE MAD MONK) (ROWDY) MEYER-P
(36) DON (NEWK) NEWCOMBE (MIL)-(P)
38 DICK WILLIAMS-OF
39 ROY (CAMPY) CAMPANELLA-C
41 CLEM LABINE-P
42 JACKIE ROBINSON-OF/INF
45 JOHNNY PODRES-P
46 BEN WADE-P
46 GLENN MICKENS-P
48 RUSS (MONK) (THE MAD MONK) (ROWDY) MEYER-P
48 RAY (FARMER) MOORE-P
48 CARMEN MAURO-OF (1)
49 JOE BLACK-P
53 BOB MILLIKEN-P

1954

2ND 92-62 5GB

1 PEE WEE REESE-SS
3 BILLY COX (INJ)-3B/INF
4 DUKE (THE SILVER FOX) SNIDER-OF
5 WAYNE BELARDI-PH (1)
5 CHUCK KRESS-1B (2)
6 CARL (SKOONJ) (THE READING RIFLE) FURILLO-OF
8 GEORGE (SHOTGUN) SHUBA-OF
10 RUBE WALKER-C
12 ERV PALICA-P
14 GIL HODGES-1B
15 SANDY AMOROS-OF
17 CARL (OISK) ERSKINE-P
18 JIM HUGHES-P
19 JIM (JUNIOR) GILLIAM-2B
21 TIM THOMPSON-C/OF
22 BILLY HERMAN-CH
23 DON (POPEYE) ZIMMER-SS
24 WALTER (SMOKEY) ALSTON -MGR
25 BOB (BOBO) MILLIKEN-P
27 PETE WOJEY-P
27 TOM LASORDA-P
28 PREACHER ROE-P
29 DON THOMPSON-OF
29 TOM LASORDA-P
30 BILLY LOES-P
31 JAKE PITLER-CH
33 TED LYONS-CH
34 RUSS (MONK) (THE MAD MONK) (ROWDY) MEYER-P
35 PETE WOJEY-P
36 DON (NEWK) NEWCOMBE-P
38 DICK WILLIAMS-OF
38 BOB DARNELL-P
39 ROY (CAMPY) CAMPANELLA (INJ)-C
40 WALT (MOOSE) MORYN-OF
41 CLEM LABINE-P
42 JACKIE ROBINSON-OF/INF
43 DON (TIGER) HOAK-3B
45 JOHNNY PODRES (ILL)-P
46 BEN WADE-P (1)
48 KARL SPOONER-P
49 JOE BLACK (INJ)-P

1955

1ST 98-55 0GB
W WS-NYA 4-3

1 PEE WEE REESE-SS
4 DUKE (THE SILVER FOX) SNIDER-OF
6 CARL (SKOONJ) (THE READING RIFLE) FURILLO-OF
8 GEORGE (SHOTGUN) SHUBA-OF
10 RUBE WALKER-C
12 FRANK KELLERT-1B
13 JIM HUGHES-P
14 GIL HODGES-1B/OF
15 SANDY AMOROS-OF
17 CARL (OISK) ERSKINE-P
18 JIM HUGHES-P
18 CHUCK TEMPLETON-P
19 JIM (JUNIOR) GILLIAM-2B
22 BILLY HERMAN-CH
23 DON (POPEYE) ZIMMER-INF
24 WALTER (SMOKEY) ALSTON -MGR
27 TOM LASORDA-P
27 BOB BORKOWSKI-OF (2)
28 CHUCK TEMPLETON-P
30 BILLY LOES-P
31 JAKE PITLER-CH
32 SANDY KOUFAX (INJ)-P
33 JOE BECKER-CH
34 RUSS (MONK) (THE MAD MONK) MEYER (INJ)-P
36 DON (NEWK) NEWCOMBE-P
37 ED ROEBUCK-P
39 ROY (CAMPY) CAMPANELLA (INJ)-C
40 WALT (MOOSE) MORYN-OF
40 ROGER CRAIG-P
41 CLEM LABINE-P
42 JACKIE ROBINSON-3B/UTIL
43 DON (TIGER) HOAK-3B
45 JOHNNY PODRES-P
46 DON BESSENT-P
48 KARL SPOONER (INJ)-P
49 JOE BLACK-P (1)
49 WALT (MOOSE) MORYN-OF
51 BERT HAMRIC-PH
54 DIXIE HOWELL-C

1956

1ST 93-61 0GB
L WS-NYA 4-3

1 PEE WEE REESE-SS/3B
2 RANDY (HANDSOME RANSOM) JACKSON-3B
3 CHICO FERNANDEZ-SS
4 DUKE (THE SILVER FOX) SNIDER-OF
6 CARL (SKOONJ) (THE READING RIFLE) FURILLO-OF
8 ROCKY NELSON-1B (1)
8 DALE MITCHELL-OF/PH (2)
9 GINO CIMOLI-OF
10 RUBE WALKER-C
14 GIL HODGES-1B/OF
15 SANDY AMOROS-OF
16 KEN LEHMAN-P
17 CARL (OISK) ERSKINE-P
18 JIM HUGHES-P (1)
19 JIM (JUNIOR) GILLIAM-2B/OF
21 ROCKY NELSON-1B (1)
22 BILLY HERMAN-CH
23 DON (POPEYE) ZIMMER (INJ)-INF
24 WALTER (SMOKEY) ALSTON -MGR
27 DON DEMETER-OF
28 CHUCK TEMPLETON-P
28 RALPH (HAWK) BRANCA-P
30 BILLY LOES-P (1)
31 JAKE PITLER-CH
32 SANDY KOUFAX-P
33 JOE BECKER-CH
34 BOB DARNELL-P
34 BOB ASPROMONTE-PH
35 SAL (THE BARBER) MAGLIE -P (2)
36 DON (NEWK) NEWCOMBE-P
37 ED ROEBUCK-P
38 DICK WILLIAMS-PH (1)
39 ROY (CAMPY) CAMPANELLA-C
40 ROGER CRAIG-P
41 CLEM LABINE-P
42 JACKIE ROBINSON-3B/UTIL
43 CHARLIE NEAL-2B/SS
44 BOB ASPROMONTE-PH
45 JOHNNY PODRES (MIL)-P
46 DON BESSENT-P
49 CHUCK TEMPLETON-P
50 CHICO FERNANDEZ-SS
53 DON DRYSDALE-P
54 DIXIE HOWELL-C

1957

3RD 84-70 11GB

1 PEE WEE REESE-3B/SS
2 RANDY (HANDSOME RANSOM) JACKSON (INJ) -3B
3 ELMER VALO-OF
4 DUKE (THE SILVER FOX) SNIDER-OF
6 CARL (SKOONJ) (THE READING RIFLE) FURILLO-OF
8 JOHNNY ROSEBORO-C/1B
9 GINO CIMOLI-OF
10 RUBE WALKER-C
12 JIM (DIAMOND JIM) GENTILE-1B
14 GIL HODGES-1B/OF
15 SANDY AMOROS-OF
16 KEN LEHMAN-P (1)
16 DANNY MCDEVITT-P
17 CARL (OISK) ERSKINE (INJ)-P
19 JIM (JUNIOR) GILLIAM-2B/OF
21 BILL HARRIS-P
22 BILLY HERMAN-CH
23 DON (POPEYE) ZIMMER-INF
24 WALTER (SMOKEY) ALSTON -MGR
26 FRED KIPP-P
31 JAKE PITLER-CH
32 SANDY KOUFAX-P
33 JOE BECKER-CH
35 SAL (THE BARBER) MAGLIE -P (1)
36 DON (NEWK) NEWCOMBE-P
37 ED ROEBUCK-P
39 ROY (CAMPY) CAMPANELLA-C
40 ROGER CRAIG-P
41 CLEM LABINE-P
43 CHARLIE NEAL-2B/SS
45 JOHNNY PODRES-P
46 DON BESSENT-P
49 RENE VALDEZ-P
49 BOB KENNEDY-OF/3B (2)
50 DON ELSTON-P (1)
50 ROD MILLER-PH
51 GREG (MOE) MULLEAVY-CH
53 DON DRYSDALE-P
55 JACKIE COLLUM-P (2)
58 JOE PIGNATANO-C

1958

LOS ANGELES DODGERS

7TH 71-83 21GB

1 PEE WEE REESE-SS/3B
2 RANDY (HANDSOME RANSOM) JACKSON-3B (1)
2 DON DEMETER-OF
3 ELMER VALO-OF
4 DUKE (THE SILVER FOX) SNIDER-OF
5 NORM LARKER-OF/1B
6 CARL (SKOONJ) (THE READING RIFLE) FURILLO-OF
7 CHUCK DRESSEN-CH
8 JOHNNY ROSEBORO-C/1B
9 GINO CIMOLI-OF
10 RUBE WALKER-C/CH
11 DICK GRAY-3B
11 BOB LILLIS-SS
12 BABE BIRRER-P
14 GIL HODGES-1B/UTIL
16 DANNY MCDEVITT-P
16 BOB WILSON-OF
16 BOB GIALLOMBARDO-P
17 CARL (OISK) ERSKINE-P
19 JIM (JUNIOR) GILLIAM-2B/OF
22 JOHNNY PODRES-P
23 DON (POPEYE) ZIMMER-SS/INF
24 WALTER (SMOKEY) ALSTON -MGR
25 FRANK (HONDO) (CAPITAL PUNISHER) HOWARD-OF
26 FRED KIPP-P
27 DON DEMETER-OF
27 JIM (DIAMOND JIM) GENTILE-1B
29 RALPH (TAMI) MAURIELLO-P
30 BOB LILLIS-SS
31 GREG (MOE) MULLEAVY-CH

32 SANDY KOUFAX-P
33 JOE BECKER-CH
33 STEVE BILKO-1B (2)
35 LARRY SHERRY-P
35 JOHNNY KLIPPSTEIN-P (2)
36 DON (NEWK) NEWCOMBE-P (1)
36 STEVE BILKO-1B
37 ED ROEBUCK-P
37 BABE BIRRER-P
38 RON NEGRAY-P
(39) ROY (CAMPY) CAMPANELLA (INJ) (C)
40 ROGER CRAIG-P
40 STAN WILLIAMS-P
41 CLEM LABINE-P
43 CHARLIE NEAL-2B/SS
45 DON MILES-OF
46 DON BESSENT (INJ)-P
51 LARRY SHERRY-P
53 DON DRYSDALE-P
55 JACKIE COLLUM-P
55 RON FAIRLY-OF
58 JOE PIGNATANO-C
61 EARL ROBINSON-3B

1959

1ST 88-68 0GB
W WS-CHIA 4-2

1 PEE WEE REESE-CH
2 DON DEMETER-OF
4 DUKE (THE SILVER FOX) SNIDER-OF
5 NORM LARKER-1B/OF
6 CARL (SKOONJ) (THE READING RIFLE) FURILLO-OF
7 CHUCK DRESSEN-CH
8 RON FAIRLY-OF
9 WALLY MOON-OF
11 DICK GRAY-3B (1)
11 BOB LILLIS-SS
12 TOMMY DAVIS-PH
14 GIL HODGES-1B/3B
16 DANNY MCDEVITT-P
17 CARL (OISK) ERSKINE-P
18 SOLLY DRAKE-OF (1)
18 SANDY AMOROS-OF
19 JIM (JUNIOR) GILLIAM-3B/UTIL
20 RIP REPULSKI-OF
21 BILL HARRIS-P
22 JOHNNY PODRES-P
23 DON (POPEYE) ZIMMER-SS/INF
24 WALTER (SMOKEY) ALSTON-MGR
25 FRANK (HONDO) (CAPITAL PUNISHER) HOWARD-OF
26 FRED KIPP-P
29 JIM BAXES-3B (1)
29 CHUCK ESSEGIAN-OF (2)
30 BOB LILLIS-SS
30 MAURY WILLS-SS
31 GREG (MOE) MULLEAVY-CH
32 SANDY KOUFAX-P
33 JOE BECKER-CH
34 NORM SHERRY-C
35 JOHNNY KLIPPSTEIN-P
37 GENE SNYDER-P
38 ROGER CRAIG-P
40 STAN WILLIAMS-P
41 CLEM LABINE-P
43 CHARLIE NEAL-2B/SS
44 JOHNNY ROSEBORO-C/1B
45 ART FOWLER-P
45 CHUCK CHURN-P
51 LARRY SHERRY-P
53 DON DRYSDALE-P
58 JOE PIGNATANO-C

1960

4TH 82-72 13GB

2 DON DEMETER-OF
4 DUKE (THE SILVER FOX) SNIDER-OF
5 NORM LARKER-1B/OF
6 CARL (SKOONJ) (THE READING RIFLE) FURILLO-PH
8 JOHNNY ROSEBORO-C/1B
9 WALLY MOON-OF
10 BOBBY (NIG) BRAGAN-CH
11 BOB LILLIS-INF
12 TOMMY DAVIS-PH
14 GIL HODGES-1B/3B
15 IRV NOREN-PH (2)
15 ED (ROCK) RAKOW-P
16 DANNY MCDEVITT-P
17 PHIL (KEMO) ORTEGA-P
18 SANDY AMOROS-OF (1)
18 CHARLEY SMITH-3B
19 JIM (JUNIOR) GILLIAM-3B/UTIL
20 RIP REPULSKI-OF (1)
21 ED (ROCK) RAKOW-P
22 JOHNNY PODRES-P
23 ED PALMQUIST-P
24 WALTER (SMOKEY) ALSTON-MGR
25 FRANK (HONDO) (CAPITAL PUNISHER) HOWARD-OF
26 WILLIE DAVIS-OF
27 PETE (PISTOL PETE) REISER-CH
28 BOB ASPROMONTE-SS/3B
29 CHUCK ESSEGIAN-OF
30 MAURY WILLS-SS
31 GREG (MOE) MULLEAVY-CH
32 SANDY KOUFAX-P
33 JOE BECKER-CH
34 NORM SHERRY-C
35 DOUG CAMILLI-C
37 ED ROEBUCK-P
38 ROGER CRAIG (INJ)-P
40 STAN WILLIAMS-P
41 CLEM LABINE-P (1)
41 JIM GOLDEN-P
43 CHARLIE NEAL-2B/SS
44 JOHNNY ROSEBORO-C/1B
44 RON FAIRLY-OF
51 LARRY SHERRY-P
53 DON DRYSDALE-P
58 JOE PIGNATANO-C

1961

2ND 89-65 4GB

2 LEO (THE LIP) (LIPPY) DUROCHER-CH
3 WILLIE DAVIS-OF
4 DUKE (THE SILVER FOX) SNIDER (INJ)-OF
5 NORM LARKER-1B/OF
6 RON FAIRLY-OF/1B
7 DON DEMETER-OF (1)
7 DARYL (BIG DEE) SPENCER-3B/SS (2)
8 JOHNNY ROSEBORO-C/1B
9 WALLY MOON-OF
10 CLAY BRYANT-CH
11 BOB LILLIS-INF (1)
12 TOMMY DAVIS-OF/3B
14 GIL HODGES-1B
15 TIM HARKNESS-1B
16 RON PERRANOSKI-P
17 PHIL (KEMO) ORTEGA-P
18 CHARLEY SMITH-3B/SS (1)
19 JIM (JUNIOR) GILLIAM-3B/UTIL
20 DICK (TURK) FARRELL-P (2)
22 JOHNNY PODRES-P
23 ED PALMQUIST-P (1)
23 GORDIE WINDHORN-OF
24 WALTER (SMOKEY) ALSTON-MGR
25 FRANK (HONDO) (CAPITAL PUNISHER) HOWARD-OF
27 PETE (PISTOL PETE) REISER-CH
28 BOB ASPROMONTE-INF
30 MAURY WILLS-SS
32 SANDY KOUFAX-P
33 JOE BECKER-CH
34 NORM SHERRY-C
35 DOUG CAMILLI-C
37 ED ROEBUCK (INJ)-P
38 ROGER CRAIG-P
40 STAN WILLIAMS-P
41 JIM GOLDEN-P
43 CHARLIE NEAL-2B/SS
51 LARRY SHERRY-P
53 DON DRYSDALE-P
54 CARL WARWICK-OF (1)

1962

2ND 102-63 1GB
L PLAYOFF-SFN 2-1

2 LEO (THE LIP) (LIPPY) DUROCHER-CH
3 WILLIE DAVIS-OF
4 DUKE (THE SILVER FOX) SNIDER (INJ)-OF
6 RON FAIRLY-1B/OF
7 LEE WALLS-UTIL
8 JOHNNY ROSEBORO-C/1B
9 WALLY MOON-OF
11 LARRY (POSSUM) BURRIGHT-2B/SS
12 TOMMY DAVIS-OF/3B
14 KEN MCMULLEN-OF
15 TIM HARKNESS-1B
16 RON PERRANOSKI-P
17 PHIL (KEMO) ORTEGA-P
19 JIM (JUNIOR) GILLIAM-2B/UTIL
20 DARYL (BIG DEE) SPENCER-3B/SS
21 ANDY CAREY-3B
22 JOHNNY PODRES-P
23 WILLARD HUNTER-P (1)
24 WALTER (SMOKEY) ALSTON-MGR
25 FRANK (HONDO) (CAPITAL PUNISHER) HOWARD-OF
27 PETE (PISTOL PETE) REISER-CH
30 MAURY WILLS-SS
31 GREG (MOE) MULLEAVY-CH
32 SANDY KOUFAX (INJ)-P
33 JOE BECKER-CH
34 NORM SHERRY-C
35 DOUG CAMILLI-C
37 ED ROEBUCK-P
38 JOE MOELLER-P
40 STAN WILLIAMS-P
41 JACK SMITH-P
44 DICK TRACEWSKI-SS
45 PETE RICHERT-P
51 LARRY SHERRY-P
53 DON DRYSDALE-P

1963

1ST 99-63 0GB
W WS-NYA 4-0

2 LEO (THE LIP) (LIPPY) DUROCHER-CH
3 WILLIE DAVIS-OF
5 DICK NEN-1B
6 RON FAIRLY-1B/OF
7 LEE WALLS-UTIL
8 JOHNNY ROSEBORO-C/1B
9 WALLY MOON-OF
11 LARRY (POSSUM) BURRIGHT-3B/UTIL
12 TOMMY DAVIS-OF/3B
14 BILL (MOOSE) SKOWRON-1B/3B
15 BOB MILLER-P
16 RON PERRANOSKI-P
17 PHIL (KEMO) ORTEGA-P
19 JIM (JUNIOR) GILLIAM-2B/UTIL
20 DARYL (BIG DEE) SPENCER-3B/SS (1)
20 DICK SCOTT-P
20 AL (THE BULL) FERRARA-OF
22 JOHNNY PODRES-P
23 DON (POPEYE) ZIMMER-INF (1)
23 MARV BREEDING-INF (2)
24 WALTER (SMOKEY) ALSTON-MGR
25 FRANK (HONDO) (CAPITAL PUNISHER) HOWARD-OF
26 DERRILL GRIFFITH-2B
27 PETE (PISTOL PETE) REISER-CH
28 NICK WILLHITE-P
29 NATE (PEEWEE) OLIVER-2B/SS
30 MAURY WILLS-SS
31 GREG (MOE) MULLEAVY-CH
32 SANDY KOUFAX (INJ)-P
33 JOE BECKER-CH
34 DICK CALMUS-P
35 DOUG CAMILLI-C
36 ROY GLEASON-PH
37 ED ROEBUCK-P (1)
39 KEN ROWE-P
41 JACK SMITH-P
44 DICK TRACEWSKI-SS/2B
45 PETE RICHERT-P
51 LARRY SHERRY-P
53 DON DRYSDALE-P

1964

6TH (TIE) 80-82 13GB

2 LEO (THE LIP) (LIPPY) DUROCHER-CH
3 WILLIE DAVIS-OF
6 RON FAIRLY-1B
7 LEE WALLS-OF/C
8 JOHNNY ROSEBORO-C
9 WALLY MOON-OF
10 JEFF TORBORG-C
11 KEN MCMULLEN-UTIL
12 TOMMY DAVIS-OF
14 JOHNNY (PEACHES) WERHAS-3B
15 BOB MILLER-P
16 RON PERRANOSKI-P
17 PHIL (KEMO) ORTEGA-P
19 JIM (JUNIOR) GILLIAM-2B/UTIL
20 LARRY MILLER-P
21 JIM BREWER-P
22 JOHNNY PODRES (INJ)-P
23 BART SHIRLEY-3B/SS
24 WALTER (SMOKEY) ALSTON-MGR
25 FRANK (HONDO) (CAPITAL PUNISHER) HOWARD-OF
26 DERRILL GRIFFITH-2B
27 PETE (PISTOL PETE) REISER-CH
28 WES PARKER-OF/1B
29 NATE (PEEWEE) OLIVER-2B/SS
30 MAURY WILLS-SS
31 GREG (MOE) MULLEAVY-CH
32 SANDY KOUFAX-P
33 JOE BECKER-CH
35 DOUG CAMILLI-C
37 NICK WILLHITE-P
38 JOE MOELLER-P
39 HOWIE (DIZ) REED-P
40 BILL (THE SINGER THROWING MACHINE) SINGER-P
41 LARRY MILLER-P
43 WILLIE CRAWFORD-OF
44 DICK TRACEWSKI-SS/2B
45 PETE RICHERT-P
47 JOHN PURDIN-P
53 DON DRYSDALE-P

1965

1ST 97-65 0GB
W WS-MINA 4-3

3 WILLIE DAVIS-OF
5 JIM LEFEBVRE-2B
6 RON FAIRLY-OF/1B
8 JOHNNY ROSEBORO-C/3B
9 WALLY MOON-OF
10 JEFF TORBORG-C
11 JOHN KENNEDY-3B/SS
12 TOMMY DAVIS (INJ)-OF
14 JOHNNY (PEACHES) WERHAS-3B
15 BOB MILLER-P
16 RON PERRANOSKI-P
17 HECTOR (HEC) VALLE-C
18 PRESTON GOMEZ-CH
19 JIM (JUNIOR) GILLIAM-2B/UTIL/CH
20 AL (THE BULL) FERRARA-OF
21 JIM BREWER (INJ)-P
22 JOHNNY PODRES-P
23 CLAUDE OSTEEN-P
24 WALTER (SMOKEY) ALSTON-MGR
25 DICK SMITH-OF
26 DERRILL GRIFFITH-2B
28 WES PARKER-OF/1B
29 NATE (PEEWEE) OLIVER-2B/SS
30 MAURY WILLS-SS
31 DON LEJOHN-3B
31 PRESTON GOMEZ-CH
32 SANDY KOUFAX-P
33 DANNY OZARK-CH
35 JOHN PURDIN-P
36 LEFTY PHILLIPS-CH
37 MIKE KEKICH-P
39 HOWIE (DIZ) REED-P
40 BILL (THE SINGER THROWING MACHINE) SINGER-P
41 LOU (SLICK) JOHNSON-OF
43 WILLIE CRAWFORD-OF
44 DICK TRACEWSKI-INF
45 NICK WILLHITE-P (2)
53 DON DRYSDALE-P

1966

1ST 95-67 0GB
L WS-BALA 4-0

2 *BART SHIRLEY-SS*
2 *DICK (DUCKY) SCHOFIELD-3B/SS (3)*
3 WILLIE DAVIS-OF
4 *TOMMY HUTTON-1B*
5 JIM LEFEBVRE-*2B/3B*
6 RON FAIRLY-*OF/1B*
7 *DICK (DR STRANGEGLOVE) STUART-1B (2)*
8 JOHNNY ROSEBORO-C/3B
9 AL (THE BULL) FERRARA-OF
10 JEFF TORBORG-C
11 JOHN KENNEDY-*INF*
12 TOMMY DAVIS-*OF/3B*
15 BOB MILLER-P
16 RON PERRANOSKI-P
17 *JIM BARBIERI-OF*
18 PRESTON GOMEZ-CH
19 JIM (JUNIOR) GILLIAM-2B/UTIL/CH

BROOKLYN/**LOS ANGELES DODGERS**

0 *DON SUTTON-P*
1 JIM BREWER (INJ)-P
2 JOHNNY PODRES-P *(1)*
3 CLAUDE OSTEEN-P
4 WALTER (SMOKEY) ALSTON -MGR
5 *WES COVINGTON-OF (2)*
6 DERRILL GRIFFITH-2B
7 *PHIL(THE VULTURE) REGAN -P*
8 WES PARKER-OF/1B
9 NATE (PEEWEE) OLIVER-*INF*
0 MAURY WILLS-SS/*3B*
1 *JIM CAMPANIS-C*
2 SANDY KOUFAX-P
3 DANNY OZARK-CH
6 LEFTY PHILLIPS-CH
8 *JOE MOELLER-P*
9 HOWIE (DIZ) REED-P (1)
0 BILL (THE SINGER THROWING MACHINE) SINGER-P
1 LOU (SLICK) JOHNSON-OF
3 WILLIE CRAWFORD-OF
5 NICK WILLHITE-P
3 DON DRYSDALE-P

1967

8TH 73-89 28.5GB

2 *DICK (DUCKY) SCHOFIELD-3B/SS*
3 WILLIE DAVIS-OF
5 JIM LEFEBVRE-3B/INF
6 RON FAIRLY-*OF/1B*
8 JOHNNY ROSEBORO-C/3B
9 AL (THE BULL) FERRARA-OF
0 JEFF TORBORG-C
1 TOMMY DEAN-SS
2 BOB BAILEY-INF
4 JOHNNY (PEACHES) WERHAS-PH
4 LEN GABRIELSON-OF (2)
5 BOB MILLER-P
6 RON PERRANOSKI-P
7 NATE (PEEWEE) OLIVER-UTIL
8 PRESTON GOMEZ-CH
9 JIM (JUNIOR) GILLIAM-CH
20 *DON SUTTON-P*
21 JIM BREWER-P
22 DANNY OZARK-CH
23 CLAUDE OSTEEN-P
24 WALTER (SMOKEY) ALSTON -MGR
25 JIM CAMPANIS-C
26 GENE (STICK) MICHAEL-SS
27 *PHIL(THE VULTURE) REGAN -P*
28 WES PARKER-OF/1B
33 RON HUNT-2B/3B
34 LUIS ALCARAZ-2B
35 JIM HICKMAN-UTIL/P
36 LEFTY PHILLIPS-CH
37 DICK EGAN-P
38 *JOE MOELLER-P*
39 BOB (MOOSE)(HORSE) LEE-P (1)
40 BILL (THE SINGER THROWING MACHINE) SINGER-P
41 JIM HICKMAN-UTIL/P
41 LOU (SLICK) JOHNSON (INJ)-OF
43 WILLIE CRAWFORD-OF
44 ALAN FOSTER-P
46 BRUCE BRUBAKER-P
52 CARROLL BERINGER-CH
53 DON DRYSDALE-P
54 JOHN DUFFIE-P

1968

7TH (TIE) 76-86 21GB

2 ZOILO (ZORRO) VERSALLES-SS
3 WILLIE DAVIS-OF
5 JIM LEFEBVRE (INJ)-UTIL
6 RON FAIRLY-*OF/1B*
7 BOB BAILEY-3B/UTIL
8 DANNY OZARK-CH
9 AL (THE BULL) FERRARA (INJ)-OF
10 JEFF TORBORG-C
11 *BART* SHIRLEY-SS
12 JIM FAIREY-OF
14 LEN GABRIELSON-OF
15 TOM HALLER-C
16 ROCKY COLAVITO-OF (1)
16 BILL (SUDS) SUDAKIS-3B
17 HANK AGUIRRE-P
18 PRESTON GOMEZ-CH
19 JIM (JUNIOR) GILLIAM-CH
20 DON SUTTON-P
21 JIM BREWER-P
22 JIM (MUDCAT) GRANT-P
23 CLAUDE OSTEEN-P
24 WALTER (SMOKEY) ALSTON -MGR
25 JIM CAMPANIS-C
26 PAUL POPOVICH-2B/INF
27 PHIL(THE VULTURE) REGAN -P (1)
27 JOE MOELLER-P
28 WES PARKER-1B/OF
30 CLEO JAMES-OF
31 TED SAVAGE-OF (2)
34 LUIS ALCARAZ-2B
35 JOHN PURDIN-P
36 LEFTY PHILLIPS-CH
37 MIKE KEKICH-P
38 JACK BILLINGHAM-P
40 BILL (THE SINGER THROWING MACHINE) SINGER-P
43 WILLIE CRAWFORD-OF
44 ALAN FOSTER (INJ)-P
45 KEN BOYER-3B/1B (2)
47 VICENTE (HUEVO) ROMO-P (1)
47 WILLIE CRAWFORD-OF
52 CARROLL BERINGER-CH
53 DON DRYSDALE-P

1969

4TH W 85-77 8GB

1 BILLY GRABARKEWITZ-INF
2 BOBBY VALENTINE-PR
3 WILLIE DAVIS-OF
4 TOMMY HUTTON-1B
5 JIM LEFEBVRE-INF
6 RON FAIRLY (INJ)-1B/OF (1)
6 STEVE GARVEY-PH
7 ROY (SPEC) HARTSFIELD-CH
8 BOB STINSON-C
9 ANDY KOSCO-OF/1B
10 JEFF TORBORG-C
11 MANNY MOTA-OF (2)
12 VON JOSHUA-OF
14 LEN GABRIELSON-OF
15 TOM HALLER-C
16 BILL (SUDS) SUDAKIS-3B
17 JIM BUNNING-P (2)
18 BILL RUSSELL-OF
19 JIM (JUNIOR) GILLIAM-CH
20 DON SUTTON-P
21 JIM BREWER-P
22 PAUL POPOVICH-2B/INF (1)
23 CLAUDE OSTEEN-P
24 WALTER (SMOKEY) ALSTON -MGR
25 JOE MOELLER-P
26 RED ADAMS-CH
27 WILLIE CRAWFORD-OF
28 WES PARKER (ILL)-1B/OF
29 JACK JENKINS-P
30 MAURY WILLS-SS (2)
31 AL MCBEAN-P (2)
33 DANNY OZARK-CH
34 BOBBY DARWIN-P
35 JOHN PURDIN-P
38 BILL BUCKNER-PH
38 JIM BUNNING-P (2)
40 BILL (THE SINGER THROWING MACHINE) SINGER-P
41 TED SIZEMORE-2B/UTIL
42 RAY LAMB-P
43 JOHN MILLER-UTIL
44 ALAN FOSTER-P
45 KEN BOYER-1B
46 PETE MIKKELSEN-P
52 CARROLL BERINGER-CH
53 DON DRYSDALE (INJ)-P
54 AL MCBEAN-P (2)

1970

2ND W 87-74 14.5GB

1 BILLY GRABARKEWITZ-INF
3 WILLIE DAVIS-OF
5 JIM LEFEBVRE-INF
6 STEVE GARVEY-3B/2B
7 ROY (SPEC) HARTSFIELD-CH
8 BOB STINSON-C
9 ANDY KOSCO-OF/1B
10 JEFF TORBORG-C
11 MANNY MOTA-OF
12 VON JOSHUA-OF
13 JOE FERGUSON-C
14 LEN GABRIELSON-OF
15 TOM HALLER-C
16 BILL (SUDS) SUDAKIS-UTIL
17 CAMILO (LITTLE POTATO) PASCUAL-P
17 TOM PACIOREK-OF
18 BILL RUSSELL-OF
19 JIM (JUNIOR) GILLIAM-CH
20 DON SUTTON-P
21 JIM BREWER-P
22 BILL (BILLY BUCK) BUCKNER-OF/1B
23 CLAUDE OSTEEN-P
24 WALTER (SMOKEY) ALSTON -MGR
25 JOE MOELLER-P
26 RED ADAMS-CH
27 WILLIE CRAWFORD-OF
28 WES PARKER-1B/OF
30 MAURY WILLS-SS
31 AL MCBEAN-P (1)
31 CHARLIE HOUGH-P
31 GARY MOORE-OF/1B
33 DANNY OZARK-CH
34 RAY LAMB-P
35 FRED NORMAN-P (1)
37 MIKE STRAHLER-P
38 SANDY VANCE-P
40 BILL (THE SINGER THROWING MACHINE) SINGER (ILL)-P
41 TED SIZEMORE (INJ)-2B/UTIL
44 ALAN FOSTER-P
45 JERRY STEPHENSON-P
46 PETE MIKKELSEN (ILL)-P
49 JOSE PENA-P
49 CHARLIE HOUGH-P
52 CARROLL BERINGER-CH

1971

2ND W 89-73 1GB

1 BILLY GRABARKEWITZ (INJ) -INF
2 BOBBY VALENTINE-UTIL
3 WILLIE DAVIS-OF
5 JIM LEFEBVRE-2B/3B
6 STEVE GARVEY-3B
7 ROY (SPEC) HARTSFIELD-CH
8 DUKE SIMS-C
10 RON (PENGUIN) CEY-PH
11 MANNY MOTA-OF
12 VON JOSHUA-OF
13 JOE FERGUSON-C
14 TOM HALLER-C
15 DICK ALLEN-3B/UTIL
16 BILL (SUDS) SUDAKIS (INJ) -UTIL
17 TOM PACIOREK-OF
18 BILL RUSSELL-UTIL
19 JIM (JUNIOR) GILLIAM-CH
20 DON SUTTON-P
21 JIM BREWER-P
22 BILL (BILLY BUCK) BUCKNER-OF/1B
23 CLAUDE OSTEEN-P
24 WALTER (SMOKEY) ALSTON -MGR
25 JOE MOELLER-P
26 RED ADAMS-CH
27 WILLIE CRAWFORD-OF
28 WES PARKER-1B/OF
29 JOSE PENA-P
30 MAURY WILLS-SS
31 HOYT WILHELM-P (2)
33 DANNY OZARK-CH
35 BOBBY DARWIN-OF
37 MIKE STRAHLER-P
38 SANDY VANCE-P
40 BILL (THE SINGER THROWING MACHINE) SINGER (ILL)-P
44 AL DOWNING-P
46 PETE MIKKELSEN-P
48 DOYLE ALEXANDER-P
49 CHARLIE HOUGH-P
50 BOB O'BRIEN-P
52 CARROLL BERINGER-CH

1972

3RD W 85-70 10.5GB

1 BILLY GRABARKEWITZ (INJ) -INF
2 BOBBY VALENTINE-UTIL
3 WILLIE DAVIS-OF
5 JIM LEFEBVRE-2B/3B
6 STEVE GARVEY-3B/1B
7 ROY (SPEC) HARTSFIELD-CH
8 DUKE SIMS-C (1)
8 DICK DIETZ (INJ)-C
9 TERRY MCDERMOTT-1B
10 RON (PENGUIN) CEY-3B
11 MANNY MOTA-OF
13 JOE FERGUSON-C/OF
14 CHRIS CANNIZZERO-C
15 DAVEY LOPES-2B
16 DICK DIETZ (INJ)-C
16 RON PERRANOSKI-P (2)
17 TOM PACIOREK-1B/OF
18 BILL RUSSELL-SS/OF
19 JIM (JUNIOR) GILLIAM-CH
20 DON SUTTON-P
21 JIM BREWER-P
22 BILL (BILLY BUCK) BUCKNER-OF/1B
23 CLAUDE OSTEEN-P
24 WALTER (SMOKEY) ALSTON -MGR
25 TOMMY (T.J.) JOHN-P
26 RED ADAMS-CH
27 WILLIE CRAWFORD-OF
28 WES PARKER-1B/OF
29 JOSE PENA-P
30 MAURY WILLS-SS/3B
31 HOYT WILHELM-P
31 DOUG RAU-P
32 *(RET#) SANDY KOUFAX*
33 DANNY OZARK-CH
34 LEE LACY (INJ)-2B
36 FRANK ROBINSON-OF
37 MIKE STRAHLER-P
39 *(RET#) ROY CAMPANELLA*
40 BILL (THE SINGER THROWING MACHINE) SINGER-P
41 STEVE YEAGER-C
42 *(RET#) JACKIE ROBINSON*
44 AL DOWNING-P
45 PETE RICHERT-P
46 PETE MIKKELSEN-P
49 CHARLIE HOUGH-P
52 CARROLL BERINGER-CH

1973

2ND W 95-66 3.5GB

2 PAUL POWELL-OF
2 ORLANDO ALVARAZ-PH
3 WILLIE DAVIS-OF
5 KEN MCMULLEN (INJ)-3B
6 STEVE GARVEY-1B/OF
7 STEVE YEAGER-C
8 JERRY ROYSTER-3B/2B
10 RON (PENGUIN) CEY-3B
11 MANNY MOTA-OF
12 VON JOSHUA (INJ)-OF
13 JOE FERGUSON-C/OF
14 CHRIS CANNIZZERO-C
15 DAVEY LOPES-2B/UTIL
17 TOM PACIOREK-OF/1B
18 BILL RUSSELL-SS
19 JIM (JUNIOR) GILLIAM-CH
20 DON SUTTON-P
21 JIM BREWER-P
22 BILL (BILLY BUCK) BUCKNER-1B/OF
23 CLAUDE OSTEEN-P
24 WALTER (SMOKEY) ALSTON -MGR
25 TOMMY (T.J.) JOHN-P
26 RED ADAMS-CH
27 WILLIE CRAWFORD-OF
28 JIM FAIREY-PH
29 GREG HEYDEMAN-P
31 DOUG RAU-P
32 *(RET#) SANDY KOUFAX*
34 LEE LACY-2B
38 GEOFF ZAHN-P
39 *(RET#) ROY CAMPANELLA*
40 GEORGE CULVER-P (1)
41 GREG SHANAHAN-P
42 *(RET#) JACKIE ROBINSON*
44 AL DOWNING-P
45 PETE RICHERT-P
47 ANDY MESSERSMITH-P
49 CHARLIE HOUGH-P
50 EDDIE SOLOMON-P
52 TOM LASORDA-CH
54 MONTY BASGALL-CH

1974

1ST W 102-60 0GB
W NLCS-PITN 3-1
L WS-OAKA 4-1

1 RICK AUERBACH-INF
2 ORLANDO ALVARAZ-OF
4 KEVIN PASLEY-C
5 KEN MCMULLEN (RET)-3B/2B
6 STEVE GARVEY-1B
7 STEVE YEAGER-C
8 JERRY ROYSTER-UTIL
10 RON (PENGUIN) CEY-3B
11 MANNY MOTA-PH/OF
12 VON JOSHUA-OF

13 JOE FERGUSON-C/OF
14 IVAN DEJESUS-SS
15 DAVEY LOPES-2B
16 GAIL HOPKINS-C/1B
17 TOM PACIOREK-OF/1B
18 BILL RUSSELL-SS
19 JIM (JUNIOR) GILLIAM-CH
20 DON SUTTON-P
21 JIM BREWER (INJ)-P
22 BILL (BILLY BUCK) BUCKNER-OF/1B
23 JIMMY (THE TOY CANNON) WYNN-OF
24 WALTER (SMOKEY) ALSTON -MGR
25 TOMMY (T.J.) JOHN (INJ)-P
26 RED ADAMS-CH
27 WILLIE CRAWFORD-OF
28 MIKE (IRON MIKE) MARSHALL-P
31 DOUG RAU-P
32 *(RET#) SANDY KOUFAX*
34 LEE LACY-2B/3B
36 RICK RHODEN-P
38 GEOFF ZAHN-P
39 *(RET#) ROY CAMPANELLA*
40 REX HUDSON-P
41 GREG SHANAHAN-P
42 *(RET#) JACKIE ROBINSON*
43 JOHN HALE-OF
44 AL DOWNING-P
46 CHUCK MANUEL-PH
47 ANDY MESSERSMITH-P
49 CHARLIE HOUGH-P
50 EDDIE SOLOMON-P
52 TOM LASORDA-CH
54 MONTY BASGALL-CH

1975

2ND W 88-74 20GB

1 RICK AUERBACH (INJ)-INF
2 ORLANDO ALVARAZ-PH
5 KEN MCMULLEN-3B/1B
6 STEVE GARVEY-1B
7 STEVE YEAGER-C
8 JERRY ROYSTER- UTIL
9 LERON LEE-OF (2)
10 RON (PENGUIN) CEY-3B
11 MANNY MOTA-PH/OF
12 PAUL POWELL-C/OF
13 JOE FERGUSON (INJ)-C/OF
14 IVAN DEJESUS-SS
15 DAVEY LOPES-2B/UTIL
16 CHUCK MANUEL-PH
17 TOM PACIOREK-OF
17 JOE SIMPSON-OF
18 BILL RUSSELL (INJ)-SS
19 JIM (JUNIOR) GILLIAM-CH
20 DON SUTTON-P
21 JIM BREWER-P (1)
22 BILL (BILLY BUCK) BUCKNER (INJ)-OF/1B
23 JIMMY (THE TOY CANNON) WYNN-OF
24 WALTER (SMOKEY) ALSTON -MGR
(25) TOMMY (T.J.) JOHN (INJ)-(P)
26 RED ADAMS-CH
27 WILLIE CRAWFORD-OF
28 MIKE (IRON MIKE) MARSHALL (INJ)-P
31 DOUG RAU-P
32 *(RET#) SANDY KOUFAX*
34 LEE LACY-UTIL
35 DENNIS LEWALLYN-P
36 RICK RHODEN-P
37 HENRY CRUZ-OF
38 GEOFF ZAHN-P (1)
39 *(RET#) ROY CAMPANELLA*
40 REX HUDSON-P
41 DAVE SELLS-P (2)
42 *(RET#) JACKIE ROBINSON*
43 JOHN HALE-OF
44 AL DOWNING-P
45 STAN WALL-P
46 JUAN (MANITO) MARICHAL-P
46 BURT HOOTON-P (2)
47 ANDY MESSERSMITH-P
49 CHARLIE HOUGH-P
50 EDDIE SOLOMON-P
52 TOM LASORDA-CH
54 MONTY BASGALL-CH
71 PAUL POWELL-C/OF

1976

2ND W 92-70 10GB

1 RICK AUERBACH-INF
2 ELLIE RODRIGUEZ-C
3 GLENN BURKE-OF
4 KEVIN PASLEY-C
5 TED SIZEMORE-2B/C
6 STEVE GARVEY-1B
7 STEVE YEAGER-C
8 REGGIE SMITH-OF (2)
9 LERON LEE-OF
10 RON (PENGUIN) CEY-3B
11 MANNY MOTA-PH/OF
12 DUSTY BAKER-OF
13 JOE FERGUSON-OF/C (1)
14 IVAN DEJESUS-SS/3B
15 DAVEY LOPES-2B/OF
17 JOE SIMPSON-OF
18 BILL RUSSELL-SS
19 JIM (JUNIOR) GILLIAM-CH
20 DON SUTTON-P
21 ED GOODSON-UTIL
22 BILL (BILLY BUCK) BUCKNER (INJ)-OF/1B
24 WALTER (SMOKEY) ALSTON -MGR
25 TOMMY (T.J.) JOHN-P
26 RED ADAMS-CH
27 ELIAS SOSA-P (2)
28 MIKE (IRON MIKE) MARSHALL-P (1)
31 DOUG RAU-P
32 *(RET#) SANDY KOUFAX*
34 LEE LACY-UTIL
35 DENNIS LEWALLYN-P
36 RICK RHODEN-P
37 HENRY CRUZ-OF
38 ELIAS SOSA-P (2)
39 *(RET#) ROY CAMPANELLA*
41 JIM LYTTLE-OF (2)
42 *(RET#) JACKIE ROBINSON*
43 JOHN HALE-OF
44 AL DOWNING-P
45 STAN WALL-P
46 BURT HOOTON-P
48 RICK SUTCLIFFE-P
48 DANNY (MICKEY) WALTON-PH
49 CHARLIE HOUGH-P
52 TOM LASORDA-CH
54 MONTY BASGALL-CH
55 SERGIO ROBLES-C

1977

1ST W 98-64 0GB
W NLCS-PHIN 3-1
L WS-NYA 4-2

2 TOM LASORDA-MGR
3 GLENN BURKE-OF
4 KEVIN PASLEY-C (1)
5 JOHNNY OATES-C
6 STEVE GARVEY-1B
7 STEVE YEAGER-C
8 REGGIE SMITH-OF
9 JERRY GROTE-C/3B (2)
10 RON (PENGUIN) CEY-3B
11 MANNY MOTA-PH/OF
12 DUSTY BAKER-OF
15 DAVEY LOPES-2B
16 RICK MONDAY-OF/1B
17 JOE SIMPSON-OF/1B
18 BILL RUSSELL-SS
19 JIM (JUNIOR) GILLIAM-CH
20 DON SUTTON-P
21 ED GOODSON-1B/3B
22 BOOG POWELL-PH/1B
23 TED MARTINEZ (INJ)-INF
24 *(RET#) WALTER ALSTON*
25 TOMMY (T.J.) JOHN-P
26 RED ADAMS-CH
27 ELIAS SOSA-P
28 PRESTON GOMEZ-CH
29 MIKE GARMAN-P
31 DOUG RAU-P
32 *(RET#) SANDY KOUFAX*
33 VIC DAVALILLO-OF
34 LEE LACY (INJ)-UTIL
35 DENNIS LEWALLYN-P
36 RICK RHODEN-P
37 HANK WEBB-P
38 LANCE RAUTZHAN-P
39 *(RET#) ROY CAMPANELLA*
41 BOBBY CASTILLO-P
42 *(RET#) JACKIE ROBINSON*
43 JOHN HALE-OF
44 HANK WEBB-P
44 AL DOWNING (INJ)-P
44 RON WASHINGTON-SS
45 STAN WALL-P
46 BURT HOOTON-P
48 RICK SUTCLIFFE-P
49 CHARLIE HOUGH-P
51 JEFF LEONARD-OF
54 MONTY BASGALL-CH
56 RAFAEL LANDESTOY-2B/SS
60 LANCE RAUTZHAN-P

1978

1ST W 95-67 0GB
W NLCS-PHIN 3-1
L WS-NYA 4-2

2 TOM LASORDA-MGR
3 GLENN BURKE-OF (1)
3 ENZO HERNANDEZ-SS
3 RUDY LAW-OF
4 BILLY NORTH-OF (2)
5 JOHNNY OATES-C
6 STEVE GARVEY-1B
7 STEVE YEAGER (INJ)-C
8 REGGIE SMITH-OF
9 JERRY GROTE (INJ)-C/3B
10 RON (PENGUIN) CEY-3B
11 MANNY MOTA-PH
12 DUSTY BAKER-OF
13 JOE FERGUSON-C/OF (2)
15 DAVEY LOPES-2B/OF
16 RICK MONDAY-OF/1B
17 JOE SIMPSON-OF
18 BILL RUSSELL-SS
19 JIM (JUNIOR) GILLIAM (DIED)-CH
19 *(RET#) JUNIOR GILLIAM*
20 DON SUTTON-P
21 DENNIS LEWALLYN-P
23 TED MARTINEZ (INJ)-INF
24 *(RET#) WALTER ALSTON*
25 TOMMY (T.J.) JOHN-P
26 RED ADAMS-CH
28 PRESTON GOMEZ-CH
29 MIKE GARMAN-P (1)
29 GERRY HANNAHS-P
31 DOUG RAU-P
32 *(RET#) SANDY KOUFAX*
33 VIC DAVALILLO-OF/1B
34 LEE LACY-UTIL
35 DENNIS LEWALLYN-P
35 BOB WELCH-P
36 RICK RHODEN-P
38 LANCE RAUTZHAN-P
39 *(RET#) ROY CAMPANELLA*
40 BRAD GULDEN-C
41 BOBBY CASTILLO-P
43 RICK SUTCLIFFE-P
45 JIM LEFEBVRE-CH
46 BURT HOOTON-P
48 DAVE STEWART-P
49 CHARLIE HOUGH-P
51 TERRY FORSTER-P
52 MYRON WHITE-OF
54 MONTY BASGALL-CH
57 PEDRO GUERRERO-1B
58 MARK CRESSE-CH

1979

3RD W 79-83 11.5GB

1 DERRELL THOMAS-OF/UTIL
2 TOM LASORDA-MGR
5 JOHNNY OATES-C
6 STEVE GARVEY-1B
7 STEVE YEAGER-C
8 REGGIE SMITH (INJ)-OF
9 GARY THOMASSON-OF/1B
10 RON (PENGUIN) CEY-3B
11 MANNY MOTA-PH/OF
12 DUSTY BAKER-OF
13 JOE FERGUSON-C/OF
14 VON JOSHUA-OF
15 DAVEY LOPES-2B
16 RICK MONDAY (INJ)-OF
18 BILL RUSSELL-SS
19 *(RET#) JUNIOR GILLIAM*
20 DON SUTTON-P
21 DENNIS LEWALLYN-P
21 JERRY REUSS-P
23 TED MARTINEZ-INF
24 *(RET#) WALTER ALSTON*
25 JERRY REUSS-P
26 RED ADAMS-CH
27 JOE BECKWITH-P
28 PRESTON GOMEZ-CH
29 GERRY HANNAHS-P
31 DOUG RAU (INJ)-P
32 *(RET#) SANDY KOUFAX*
33 VIC DAVALILLO-OF/PH
34 DERRELL THOMAS-OF/UTIL
34 KEN BRETT-P (2)
35 BOB WELCH (INJ)-P
36 LERRIN LAGROW (INJ)-P (2)
37 LERRIN LAGROW (INJ)-P (2)
37 BOBBY CASTILLO-P
38 LANCE RAUTZHAN-P (1)
39 *(RET#) ROY CAMPANELLA*
41 BOBBY CASTILLO-P
41 JERRY REUSS-P
42 *(RET#) JACKIE ROBINSON*
43 RICK SUTCLIFFE-P
44 MICKEY HATCHER-OF/3B
45 JIM LEFEBVRE-CH
46 BURT HOOTON-P
47 ANDY MESSERSMITH-P
49 CHARLIE HOUGH-P
50 LERRIN LAGROW (INJ)-P (2)
51 TERRY FORSTER (INJ)-P
54 MONTY BASGALL-CH
56 DAVE PATTERSON-P
57 PEDRO GUERRERO-1B
58 MARK CRESSE-CH

1980

2ND W 92-71 1GB

1 GARY WEISS-PR
2 TOM LASORDA-MGR
3 RUDY LAW-OF
4 *(RET#) DUKE SNIDER*
6 STEVE GARVEY-1B
7 STEVE YEAGER-C
8 REGGIE SMITH (INJ)-OF
9 GARY THOMASSON-OF/1B
10 RON (PENGUIN) CEY-3B
11 MANNY MOTA-PH/CH
12 DUSTY BAKER-OF
13 JOE FERGUSON (INJ)-C/OF
14 MIKE SCOSCIA-C
15 DAVEY LOPES-2B
16 RICK MONDAY-OF
17 BOBBY MITCHELL-OF
18 BILL RUSSELL (INJ)-SS
19 *(RET#) JUNIOR GILLIAM*
20 DON SUTTON-P
21 JAY JOHNSTONE-OF
22 DON STANHOUSE (INJ)-P
23 VIC DAVALILLO-PH/1B
24 *(RET#) WALTER ALSTON*
26 RED ADAMS-CH
27 JOE BECKWITH-P
28 PEDRO (PETE) GUERRERO (INJ)-UTIL
29 DON STANHOUSE (INJ)-P
30 DERRELL THOMAS-OF/UTIL
(31) DOUG RAU (INJ)-(P)
32 *(RET#) SANDY KOUFAX*
33 VIC DAVALILLO-PH/1B
33 DANNY OZARK-CH
34 FERNANDO VALENZUELA-P
35 BOB WELCH (INJ)-P
36 PEPE FRIAS-SS (2)
37 BOBBY CASTILLO-P
38 DAVE GOLTZ-P
39 *(RET#) ROY CAMPANELLA*
41 JERRY REUSS-P
42 *(RET#) JACKIE ROBINSON*
43 RICK SUTCLIFFE-P
44 MICKEY HATCHER-OF/3B
47 JACK PERCONTE-2B
46 BURT HOOTON-P
49 CHARLIE HOUGH-P (1)
51 TERRY FORSTER (INJ)-P
54 MONTY BASGALL-CH
57 STEVE HOWE-P
58 MARK CRESSE-CH

1981

1ST 1/2:1ST W 36-21 0GB
2ND 1/2:4TH W 27-26 6GB
FINAL: 63-47 --GB
W NLDS-HOUN 3-2
W NLCS-MONN 3-2
W WS-NYA 4-2

1 GARY WEISS-SS
2 TOM LASORDA-MGR
4 *(RET#) DUKE SNIDER*
5 MIKE MARSHALL-UTIL
6 STEVE GARVEY-1B
7 STEVE YEAGER-C
8 REGGIE SMITH (INJ)-1B
9 JERRY GROTE-C
10 RON (PENGUIN) CEY-3B
11 MANNY MOTA-CH
12 DUSTY BAKER-OF
13 JOE FERGUSON-OF (1)
14 MIKE SCOSCIA-C
15 DAVEY LOPES (INJ)-2B
16 RICK MONDAY-OF
17 BOBBY MITCHELL-OF
18 BILL RUSSELL-SS
19 *(RET#) JUNIOR GILLIAM*
21 JAY JOHNSTONE-OF/1B
22 MARK BRADLEY-OF
24 *(RET#) WALTER ALSTON*
25 TED POWER-P
26 ALEJANDRO PENA-P
27 JOE BECKWITH (ILL)-P
28 PEDRO (PETE) GUERRERO-OF/INF
29 RON PERRANOSKI-CH
30 DERRELL THOMAS-UTIL
32 *(RET#) SANDY KOUFAX*
33 DANNY OZARK-CH
34 FERNANDO VALENZUELA-P

BROOKLYN/LOS ANGELES DODGERS

5 BOB WELCH-P
6 PEPE FRIAS-INF
7 BOBBY CASTILLO-P
8 DAVE GOLTZ-P
9 *(RET#) ROY CAMPANELLA*
0 ALEJANDRO PENA-P
1 JERRY REUSS-P
2 *(RET#) JACKIE ROBINSON*
3 RICK SUTCLIFFE-P
4 KEN LANDREAUX-OF
5 JACK PERCONTE-2B
6 BURT HOOTON-P
7 TOM NIEDENFUER-P
7 CANDY MALDONADO-OF
8 DAVE STEWART-P
9 TOM NIEDENFUER-P
0 RON ROENICKE-OF
1 TERRY FORSTER-P
2 STEVE SAX-2B
4 MONTY BASGALL-CH
7 STEVE HOWE-P
8 MARK CRESSE-CH

1982

2ND W 88-74 1GB

2 TOM LASORDA-MGR
3 STEVE SAX-2B
4 *(RET#) DUKE SNIDER*
5 MIKE MARSHALL-OF/1B
6 STEVE GARVEY-1B
7 STEVE YEAGER (INJ)-C
8 MARK BELANGER-SS/2B
9 DON CROW-C
0 RON (PENGUIN) CEY-3B
1 MANNY MOTA-PH/CH
2 DUSTY BAKER-OF
4 MIKE SCOSCIA-C
6 RICK MONDAY-OF/1B
8 BILL RUSSELL-SS
9 *(RET#) JUNIOR GILLIAM*
0 CANDY MALDONADO-OF
1 JAY JOHNSTONE-PH (1)
1 RICKY WRIGHT-P
2 MARK BRADLEY-OF
3 DAVE SAX-OF
4 *(RET#) WALTER ALSTON*
5 TED POWER-P
6 ALEJANDRO PENA-P
7 JOE BECKWITH-P
8 PEDRO (PETE) GUERRERO-OF/3B
9 RON PERRANOSKI-CH
0 DERRELL THOMAS (INJ)-UTIL
1 JORGE ORTA-OF
2 *(RET#) SANDY KOUFAX*
3 DANNY OZARK-CH
4 FERNANDO VALENZUELA-P
5 BOB WELCH-P
6 STEVE SHIRLEY-P
7 RICKY WRIGHT-P
7 ALEX TAVERAS-INF
8 DAVE GOLTZ-P (1)
9 *(RET#) ROY CAMPANELLA*
0 RON ROENICKE-OF
1 JERRY REUSS-P
2 *(RET#) JACKIE ROBINSON*
3 JOSE MORALES-PH (2)
4 KEN LANDREAUX-OF
5 VICENTE (HUEVO) ROMO (INJ)-P
6 BURT HOOTON (INJ)-P
7 GREG BROCK-1B
8 DAVE STEWART-P
9 TOM NIEDENFUER-P
0 VICENTE (HUEVO) ROMO (INJ)-P
1 TERRY FORSTER-P
4 MONTY BASGALL-CH
7 STEVE HOWE-P
8 MARK CRESSE-CH

1983

1ST W 91-71 0GB

L NLCS-PHIN 3-1

2 TOM LASORDA-MGR
3 STEVE SAX-2B
4 *(RET#) DUKE SNIDER*
5 MIKE MARSHALL-OF/1B
7 STEVE YEAGER-C
8 JOEY AMALFITANO-CH
9 GREG BROCK-1B
10 DAVE ANDERSON-SS/3B
11 MANNY MOTA-PH/CH
12 DUSTY BAKER-OF
14 MIKE SCOSCIA (INJ)-C
15 GIL REYES-C
16 RICK MONDAY-OF/1B
17 GREG BROCK-1B
17 RAFAEL LANDESTOY-UTIL (2)
18 BILL RUSSELL-SS
19 *(RET#) JUNIOR GILLIAM*
20 CANDY MALDONADO-OF
21 RICKY WRIGHT-P (1)
22 DAVE SAX-C
23 DAVE SAX-C
23 R. J. REYNOLDS-OF
23 RICK HONEYCUTT-P (2)
24 *(RET#) WALTER ALSTON*
25 GERMAN RIVERA-3B
26 ALEJANDRO PENA-P
27 JOE BECKWITH-P
28 PEDRO (PETE) GUERRERO-3B/1B
29 RON PERRANOSKI-CH
30 DERRELL THOMAS (INJ)-OF/UTIL
31 JACK FIMPLE-C
32 *(RET#) SANDY KOUFAX*
33 SID BREAM-1B
34 FERNANDO VALENZUELA-P
35 BOB WELCH-P
37 ALEX TAVERAS-INF
38 PAT ZACHRY-P
39 *(RET#) ROY CAMPANELLA*
40 RON ROENICKE-OF (1)
40 RICK HONEYCUTT-P (2)
41 JERRY REUSS-P
42 *(RET#) JACKIE ROBINSON*
43 JOSE MORALES-1B
44 KEN LANDREAUX-OF
46 BURT HOOTON-P
47 LARRY WHITE-P
48 DAVE STEWART-P (1)
49 TOM NIEDENFUER-P
50 SID FERNANDEZ-P
52 CECIL ESPY-OF
54 MONTY BASGALL-CH
55 OREL HERSHISER-P
56 RICH RODAS-P
57 STEVE HOWE (SUB)-P
58 MARK CRESSE-CH

1984

4TH W 79-83 13GB

1 *(RET#) PEE WEE REESE*
2 TOM LASORDA-MGR
3 STEVE SAX-2B
4 *(RET#) DUKE SNIDER*
5 MIKE MARSHALL-OF/1B
7 STEVE YEAGER-C
8 JOEY AMALFITANO-CH
9 GREG BROCK (INJ)-1B
10 DAVE ANDERSON-SS/3B
11 MANNY MOTA-CH
14 MIKE SCOSCIA-C
15 GIL REYES-C
16 RICK MONDAY-1B/OF
17 RAFAEL LANDESTOY-UTIL
17 ED AMELUNG-OF
18 BILL RUSSELL-SS/UTIL
19 *(RET#) JUNIOR GILLIAM*
20 CANDY MALDONADO-OF/3B
21 BOB BAILOR (INJ)-INF
22 FRANKLIN STUBBS-1B/OF
23 R. J. REYNOLDS-OF
24 *(RET#) WALTER ALSTON*
25 GERMAN RIVERA-3B
26 ALEJANDRO PENA-P
27 CARLOS DIAZ-P
28 PEDRO (PETE) GUERRERO-OF/INF
29 RON PERRANOSKI-CH
31 JACK FIMPLE-C
32 *(RET#) SANDY KOUFAX*
33 SID BREAM-1B
34 FERNANDO VALENZUELA-P
35 BOB WELCH-P
37 MIKE VAIL-OF
38 PAT ZACHRY-P
39 *(RET#) ROY CAMPANELLA*
40 RICK HONEYCUTT-P
41 JERRY REUSS (INJ)-P
42 *(RET#) JACKIE ROBINSON*
43 JOSE MORALES-PH
43 KEN HOWELL-P
44 KEN LANDREAUX-OF
45 TERRY WHITFIELD (INJ)-OF
46 BURT HOOTON-P
47 LARRY WHITE-P
49 TOM NIEDENFUER (INJ)-P
50 TONY BREWER-OF
51 LEMMIE MILLER-OF
54 MONTY BASGALL-CH
55 OREL HERSHISER-P
56 RICH RODAS (INJ)-P
(57) STEVE HOWE (SUB)-(P)
58 MARK CRESSE-CH

1985

1ST W 95-67 0GB

L NLCS-STLN 4-2

0 AL OLIVER-OF
1 *(RET#) PEE WEE REESE*
2 TOM LASORDA-MGR
3 STEVE SAX-2B/3B
4 *(RET#) DUKE SNIDER*
5 MIKE MARSHALL (ILL)-OF/1B
7 STEVE YEAGER-C
8 JOEY AMALFITANO-CH
9 GREG BROCK-1B
10 DAVE ANDERSON (INJ)-3B/INF
11 MANNY MOTA-CH
12 MARIANO DUNCAN-SS/2B
12 JAY JOHNSTONE (INJ)-PH
14 MIKE SCOSCIA-C
15 GIL REYES-C
16 RON PERRANOSKI-CH
17 LEN MATUSZEK-UTIL (2)
18 BILL RUSSELL (INJ)-UTIL
19 *(RET#) JUNIOR GILLIAM*
20 CANDY MALDONADO-OF/3B
21 BOB BAILOR (INJ)-UTIL
22 FRANKLIN STUBBS-1B
23 R. J. REYNOLDS-OF (1)
23 ENOS CABELL-UTIL (2)
24 *(RET#) WALTER ALSTON*
25 MARIANO DUNCAN-SS/2B
26 ALEJANDRO PENA (INJ)-P
27 CARLOS DIAZ-P
28 PEDRO (PETE) GUERRERO-OF/INF
29 RALPH BRYANT-OF
32 *(RET#) SANDY KOUFAX*
33 SID BREAM-1B (1)
34 FERNANDO VALENZUELA-P
35 BOB WELCH (INJ)-P
36 JOSE GONZALEZ-OF
37 MIKE RAMSEY-SS/2B
37 BOBBY CASTILLO-P
39 *(RET#) ROY CAMPANELLA*
40 RICK HONEYCUTT-P
41 JERRY REUSS-P
42 *(RET#) JACKIE ROBINSON*
43 KEN HOWELL-P
44 KEN LANDREAUX-OF
45 TERRY WHITFIELD-OF
46 TOM BRENNAN-P
48 DENNIS POWELL-P
48 MIKE RAMSEY-SS/2B
49 TOM NIEDENFUER-P
50 TONY BREWER-OF
50 BRIAN HOLTON-P
51 REGGIE WILLIAMS-OF
52 BILL (MAD DOG) MADLOCK-3B (2)
53 *(RET#) DON DRYSDALE*
54 MONTY BASGALL-CH
55 OREL HERSHISER-P
56 RICH RODAS (INJ)-P
57 STEVE HOWE-P (1)
57 STU PEDERSON-OF
58 MARK CRESSE-CH

1986

5TH W 73-89 23GB

1 *(RET#) PEE WEE REESE*
2 TOM LASORDA-MGR
3 STEVE SAX-2B
4 *(RET#) DUKE SNIDER*
5 MIKE MARSHALL-OF
7 CESAR CEDENO-OF
8 JOEY AMALFITANO-CH
9 GREG BROCK (INJ)-1B
10 DAVE ANDERSON (INJ)-INF
11 MANNY MOTA-CH
12 BILL (MAD DOG) MADLOCK-3B/1B
13 DON MCMAHON-CH
14 MIKE SCOSCIA (INJ)-C
16 RON PERRANOSKI-CH
17 LEN MATUSZEK (INJ)-UTIL
18 BILL RUSSELL-UTIL
19 *(RET#) JUNIOR GILLIAM*
20 ED AMELUNG-OF
20 LARRY SEE-1B
21 REGGIE WILLIAMS-OF
22 FRANKLIN STUBBS-OF/1B
23 ENOS CABELL-1B/UTIL
24 *(RET#) WALTER ALSTON*
25 MARIANO DUNCAN (INJ)-SS
26 ALEJANDRO PENA (INJ)-P
27 CARLOS DIAZ-P
28 PEDRO (PETE) GUERRERO (INJ)-OF/1B
29 ALEX TREVINO-C/1B
31 ED VANDE BERG-P
33 JEFF HAMILTON-3B/SS
34 FERNANDO VALENZUELA-P
35 BOB WELCH-P
36 BEN HINES-CH
37 JACK FIMPLE-C/INF
38 CRAIG SHIPLEY-INF
39 *(RET#) ROY CAMPANELLA*
40 RICK HONEYCUTT-P
41 JERRY REUSS (INJ)-P
42 *(RET#) JACKIE ROBINSON*
43 KEN HOWELL-P
44 KEN LANDREAUX (INJ)-OF
45 TERRY WHITFIELD-OF
45 JOE BECKWITH-P
46 RALPH BRYANT-OF
47 JOSE GONZALEZ-OF
48 DENNIS POWELL (INJ)-P
49 TOM NIEDENFUER-P
51 REGGIE WILLIAMS-OF
51 BRIAN HOLTON-P
52 BALVINO GALVEZ-P
53 *(RET#) DON DRYSDALE*
54 MONTY BASGALL-CH
55 OREL HERSHISER-P
57 STU PEDERSON-OF
58 MARK CRESSE-CH

1987

4TH W 73-89 17GB

1 *(RET#) PEE WEE REESE*
2 TOM LASORDA-MGR
3 STEVE SAX-2B/UTIL
4 *(RET#) DUKE SNIDER*
5 MIKE MARSHALL-OF
7 TRACY WOODSON (INJ)-3B/1B
8 JOEY AMALFITANO-CH
9 MICKEY HATCHER-3B/UTIL
10 DAVE ANDERSON-INF
11 MANNY MOTA-CH
12 BILL (MAD DOG) MADLOCK-3B/1B (1)
12 DANNY HEEP-OF/1B
14 MIKE SCOSCIA-C
15 GIL REYES-C
16 RON PERRANOSKI-CH
17 LEN MATUSZEK (INJ)-1B
18 BILL RUSSELL-CH
19 *(RET#) JUNIOR GILLIAM*
20 PHIL GARNER-INF (2)
21 REGGIE WILLIAMS-OF
22 FRANKLIN STUBBS-OF/1B
23 TIM LEARY-P
24 *(RET#) WALTER ALSTON*
25 MARIANO DUNCAN (INJ)-SS/UTIL
26 ALEJANDRO PENA-P
27 TITO LANDRUM-OF (2)
28 PEDRO (PETE) GUERRERO-OF/1B
29 ALEX TREVINO-C/UTIL
31 JOHN (T-BONE) SHELBY-OF (2)
32 *(RET#) SANDY KOUFAX*
33 JEFF HAMILTON (INJ)-3B/SS
34 FERNANDO VALENZUELA-P
35 BOB WELCH-P
36 MATT YOUNG-P
37 MIKE RAMSEY-OF
37 GLENN HOFFMAN-SS (2)
38 CRAIG SHIPLEY-SS/3B
39 *(RET#) ROY CAMPANELLA*
40 RICK HONEYCUTT-P (1)
40 MIKE DEVEREAUX-OF
41 JERRY REUSS-P (1)
41 BRAD HAVENS (INJ)-P
42 *(RET#) JACKIE ROBINSON*
43 KEN HOWELL-P
44 KEN LANDREAUX-OF
45 CHRIS GWYNN-OF
46 RALPH BRYANT-OF
47 JOSE GONZALEZ-OF
48 ORLANDO MERCADO-C (2)
49 TOM NIEDENFUER-P (1)
49 TIM BELCHER-P
50 JACK SAVAGE-P
51 BRIAN HOLTON-P
52 TIM CREWS-P
53 *(RET#) DON DRYSDALE*
54 RON DAVIS-P (2)
55 OREL HERSHISER-P
56 BRAD WELLMAN (INJ)-INF
56 MIKE RAMSEY-OF
57 SHAWN HILLEGAS-P
58 MARK CRESSE-CH
59 BILL KRUEGER-P (2)
60 MIKE SHARPERSON-3B/2B (2)
88 MIKE RAMSEY-OF

1988

1ST W 94-67 0GB

W NLCS-NYN 4-3

W WS-OAKA 4-1

1 *(RET#) PEE WEE REESE*

2 TOM LASORDA-MGR
3 STEVE SAX-2B
4 *(RET#) DUKE SNIDER*
5 MIKE MARSHALL-OF/!B
7 ALFREDO GRIFFIN (INJ)-SS
8 JOEY AMALFITANO-CH
9 MICKEY HATCHER-OF/INF
10 DAVE ANDERSON-INF
11 MANNY MOTA-CH
12 DANNY HEEP-OF/1B/P
13 JOE FERGUSON-CH
14 MIKE SCOSCIA-C
15 GIL REYES-C
16 RON PERRANOSKI-CH
17 RICK DEMPSEY-C
18 BILL RUSSELL-CH
19 *(RET#) JUNIOR GILLIAM*
20 DON SUTTON (INJ)-P
21 TRACY WOODSON-3B/1B
22 FRANKLIN STUBBS-OF/1B
23 KIRK GIBSON-OF
24 *(RET#) WALTER ALSTON*
26 ALEJANDRO PENA-P
27 MIKE SHARPERSON-INF
28 PEDRO (PETE) GUERRERO-3B/UTIL (1)
29 RICKY HORTON-P (2)
30 JOHN TUDOR-P (2)
31 JOHN (T-BONE) SHELBY-OF
32 *(RET#) SANDY KOUFAX*
33 JEFF HAMILTON (INJ)-3B/INF
34 FERNANDO VALENZUELA-P
35 BILL BRENNAN-P
36 JOSE GONZALEZ-OF
36 BEN HINES-CH
37 MIKE DAVIS-OF
38 JOSE GONZALEZ-OF
39 *(RET#) ROY CAMPANELLA*
40 MIKE DEVEREAUX-OF
41 BRAD HAVENS-P (1)
41 BILL KRUEGER-P
42 *(RET#) JACKIE ROBINSON*
43 KEN HOWELL (INJ)-P
45 CHRIS GWYNN (INJ)-OF
47 JESSE OROSCO-P
48 RAMON MARTINEZ-P
49 TIM BELCHER-P
50 JAY HOWELL-P
51 BRIAN HOLTON-P
52 TIM CREWS-P
54 TIM LEARY-P
53 *(RET#) DON DRYSDALE*
55 OREL HERSHISER-P
56 RICKY HORTON-P (2)
57 SHAWN HILLEGAS-P (1)
58 MARK CRESSE-CH

1989

4TH W 77-83 14GB

1 *(RET#) PEE WEE REESE*
2 TOM LASORDA-MGR
3* JEFF HAMILTON-3B/INF/P*
4 *(RET#) DUKE SNIDER*
5 MIKE MARSHALL (INJ)-OF/!B
7 ALFREDO GRIFFIN-SS
8 JOEY AMALFITANO-CH
9* MICKEY HATCHER-OF/INF/P*
10 DAVE ANDERSON-INF
11 MANNY MOTA-CH
12 WILLIE RANDOLPH-2B
13 JOE FERGUSON-CH
14 MIKE SCOSCIA-C
15 CHRIS GWYNN (INJ)-OF
16 RON PERRANOSKI-CH
17 RICK DEMPSEY-C
18 BILL RUSSELL-CH
19 *(RET#) JUNIOR GILLIAM*
20 WILLIE RANDOLPH-2B
20 MIKE DAVIS (INJ)-OF
21 TRACY WOODSON-3B
22 FRANKLIN STUBBS (INJ)-OF/1B
23 KIRK GIBSON (INJ)-OF
24 *(RET#) WALTER ALSTON*
25 MARIANO DUNCAN-UTIL (1)
25 DARRIN FLETCHER-C
26 ALEJANDRO PENA-P
27 MIKE SHARPERSON-INF
28 KAL DANIELS (INJ)-OF (2)
29 RICKY HORTON-P (1)
29 LENNY HARRIS-UTIL (2)
30 JOHN TUDOR (INJ)-P
31 JOHN (T-BONE) SHELBY-OF
32 *(RET#) SANDY KOUFAX*
33 EDDIE MURRAY-1B/3B
34 FERNANDO VALENZUELA-P
35 BEN HINES-CH
36 MIKE MORGAN-P
37 MIKE DAVIS (INJ)-OF
38 JOSE GONZALEZ-OF
39 *(RET#) ROY CAMPANELLA*
40 BILLY BEAN-OF (2)
42 *(RET#) JACKIE ROBINSON*
43 MIKE HARTLEY-P
44 JOSE VISCAINO-SS
45 CHRIS GWYNN (INJ)-OF
45 MIKE HUFF-OF
48 RAMON MARTINEZ-P
49 TIM BELCHER-P
50 JAY HOWELL-P
51 JEFF FISCHER-P
52 TIM CREWS-P
53 *(RET#) DON DRYSDALE*
54 TIM LEARY-P (1)
55 OREL HERSHISER-P
56 MIKE MUNOZ-P
57 JOHN WETTELAND-P
58 MARK CRESSE-CH
59 RAY SEARAGE-P

1990

2ND W 86-76 5GB

1 *(RET#) PEE WEE REESE*
2 TOM LASORDA-MGR
3 JEFF HAMILTON (INJ)-3B
4 *(RET#) DUKE SNIDER*
5 STAN JAVIER-OF (2)
7 ALFREDO GRIFFIN-SS
8 JOEY AMALFITANO-CH
9 MICKEY HATCHER-UTIL
10 JUAN (SAMMY) SAMUEL-2B/OF
12 WILLIE RANDOLPH-2B (1)
12 LUIS LOPEZ-1B
14 MIKE SCOSCIA-C
15 CHRIS GWYNN-OF
16 RON PERRANOSKI-CH
17 RICK DEMPSEY-C
18 BILL RUSSELL-CH
19 *(RET#) JUNIOR GILLIAM*
20 BRIAN TRAXLER-1B
20 DARREN HOLMES-P
21 HUBIE BROOKS-OF
22 DON AASE (INJ)-P
23 KIRK GIBSON (INJ)-OF
24 *(RET#) WALTER ALSTON*
25 DARRIN FLETCHER-C (1)
25 DENNIS COOK-P (2)
26 PAT PERRY (INJ)-P
27 MIKE SHARPERSON-3B/INF
28 KAL DANIELS-OF
29 LENNY HARRIS-3B/UTIL
30 JOSE OFFERMANN-SS
31 JOHN (T-BONE) SHELBY-OF (1)
31 JIM NEIDLINGER-P
31 JIM POOLE-P
32 *(RET#) SANDY KOUFAX*
33 EDDIE MURRAY-1B
34 FERNANDO VALENZUELA-P
35 JIM GOTT (INJ)-P
36 MIKE MORGAN-P
37 BEN HINES-CH
38 JOSE GONZALEZ-OF
39 *(RET#) ROY CAMPANELLA*
40 BARRY LYONS-C (2)
40 TERRY WELLS-P
40 JOHN WETTELAND-P
41 CARLOS HERNANDEZC
42 *(RET#) JACKIE ROBINSON*
43 DAVE HANSEN-3B
44 JOSE VISCAINO-SS/2B
46 MIKE HARTLEY-P
48 RAMON MARTINEZ-P
49 TIM BELCHER (INJ)-P
50 JAY HOWELL (INJ)-P
51 DAVE WALSH-P
51 TERRY WELLS-P
52 TIM CREWS-P
53 *(RET#) DON DRYSDALE*
54 MIKE MADDUX-P
54 JIM POOLE-P
55 OREL HERSHISER (INJ)-P
56 MIKE MUNOZ-P
57 JOHN WETTELAND-P
58 MARK CRESSE-CH
59 RAY SEARAGE (INJ)-P

1991

2ND W 93-69 1GB

1 *(RET#) PEE WEE REESE*
2 TOM LASORDA-MGR
3 JEFF HAMILTON-3B/SS
4 *(RET#) DUKE SNIDER*
5 STAN JAVIER-OF/1B
7 ALFREDO GRIFFIN-SS
8 GARY (KID) CARTER-C/1B
10 JUAN (SAMMY) SAMUEL-2B
12? JOEY AMALFITANO-CH
12 GREG SMITH-2B
13 ROGER (BUBBLES) MCDOWELL (INJ)-P (2)
14 MIKE SCOSCIA-C
15 CHRIS GWYNN-OF
16 RON PERRANOSKI-CH
17 BOB OJEDA-P
18 BILL RUSSELL-CH
19 *(RET#) JIM GILLIAM*
20 MITCH WEBSTER-OF/1B (2)
22 BRETT BUTLER-OF
23 ERIC KARROS-1B
24 *(RET#) WALTER ALSTON*
25 DENNIS COOK-P
27 MIKE SHARPERSON-INF
28 KAL DANIELS-OF
29 LENNY HARRIS-3B/UTIL
30 JOSE OFFERMANN-SS
31 JIM NEIDLINGER-P
32 *(RET#) SANDY KOUFAX*
33 EDDIE MURRAY-1B/3B
35 JIM GOTT-P
36 MIKE MORGAN-P
37 BEN HINES-CH
38 JOSE GONZALEZ-OF (1)
38 STEVE WILSON-P (2)
39 *(RET#) ROY CAMPANELLA*
40 BARRY LYONS-C (1)
40 BUTCH DAVIS-PH
41 CARLOS HERNANDEZ-C
42 *(RET#) JACKIE ROBINSON*
43 DAVE HANSEN-3B
44 STEVE WILSON-P (2)
44 DARRYL STRAWBERRY-OF
45 KEVIN GROSS-P
46 MIKE HARTLEY-P (1)
47 TOM GOODWIN-OF
48 RAMON MARTINEZ-P
49 TIM BELCHER-P
50 JAY HOWELL (INJ)-P
52 TIM CREWS-P
53 *(RET#) DON DRYSDALE*
54 JOHN (CANDY MAN) CANDELARIA-P
55 OREL HERSHISER-P
56 MIKE CHRISTOPHER-P
57 JOHN WETTELAND-P
58 MARK CRESSE-CH

1992

6TH W 63-99 35GB

1 *(RET#) PEE WEE REESE*
2 TOM LASORDA-MGR
4 *(RET#) DUKE SNIDER*
5 STAN JAVIER-OF/1B (1)
7 BILLY ASHLEY-OF
8 JOEY AMALFITANO-CH
10 JUAN (SAMMY) SAMUEL-2B (1)
11 MANNY MOTA-CH
12 DAVE ANDERSON-INF
13 JOE FERGUSON-CH
14 MIKE SCOSCIA-C
15 DAVE HANSEN-3B
16 RON PERRANOSKI-CH
17 BOB OJEDA-P
19 *(RET#) JIM GILLIAM*
20 MITCH WEBSTER-OF/1B
21 ERIC YOUNG,INF
22 BRETT BUTLER-OF
23 ERIC KARROS-1B
24 *(RET#) WALTER ALSTON*
25 MIKE PIAZZA-C
26 HENRY RODRIGUEZ-OF
27 MIKE SHARPERSON-INF
28 KAL DANIELS-OF
28 RAFAEL BOURNIGAL-SS
29 LENNY HARRIS-3B/UTIL
30 JOSE OFFERMANN-SS
31 ROGER (BUBBLES) MCDOWELL (INJ)-P
32 *(RET#) SANDY KOUFAX*
33 ERIC DAVIS-OF
35 JIM GOTT-P
36 TODD BENZINGER-1B/OF
37 BEN HINES-CH
38 STEVE WILSON-P
39 *(RET#) ROY CAMPANELLA*
(40) RUDY SEANEZ (INJ) (P)
41 CARLOS HERNANDEZ-C
42 *(RET#) JACKIE ROBINSON*
44 DARRYL STRAWBERRY-OF
45 PEDRO MARTINEZ-P
46 KEVIN GROSS-P
47 TOM GOODWIN-OF
48 RAMON MARTINEZ-P
49 TOM CANDIOTTI-P
50 JAY HOWELL (INJ)-P
52 TIM CREWS-P
53 *(RET#) DON DRYSDALE*
54 JOHN (CANDY MAN) CANDELARIA-P
55 OREL HERSHISER-P
56 PEDRO ASTACIO-P
57 KIP GROSS-P
58 MARK CRESSE-CH
59 PEDRO ASTACIO-P

1993

4TH W 81-81 23GB

1 *(RET#) PEE WEE REESE*
2 TOM LASORDA-MGR
3 JODY REED (INJ)-2B
4 *(RET#) DUKE SNIDER*
7 BILLY ASHLEY-OF
8 JOEY AMALFITANO-CH
11 MANNY MOTA-CH
13 JOE FERGUSON-CH
15 DAVE HANSEN-3B
16 RON PERRANOSKI-CH
17 ROGER (BUBBLES) MCDOWELL-P
19 *(RET#) JIM GILLIAM*
20 MITCH WEBSTER-OF
21 RAFAEL BOURNIGAL-SS/2
22 BRETT BUTLER-OF
23 ERIC KARROS-1B
24 *(RET#) WALTER ALSTON*
25 TIM WALLACH-3B/1B
26 HENRY RODRIGUEZ-OF/1B
27 MIKE SHARPERSON-INF/O
28 CORY SNYDER-OF/INF
29 LENNY HARRIS-INF/OF
30 JOSE OFFERMANN-SS
31 MIKE PIAZZA-C/1B
32 *(RET#) SANDY KOUFAX*
33 ERIC DAVIS-OF (1)
35 JIM GOTT-P
36 RICK TRLICEK-P
37 BEN HINES-CH
38 TODD WORRELL (INJ)-P
39 *(RET#) ROY CAMPANELLA*
41 CARLOS HERNANDEZ-C
42 *(RET#) JACKIE ROBINSON*
43 RAUL MONDESI-OF
44 DARRYL STRAWBERRY (INJ)-OF
45 PEDRO J. MARTINEZ-P
46 KEVIN GROSS-P
47 TOM GOODWIN-OF
48 RAMON MARTINEZ-P
49 TOM CANDIOTTI-P
50 STEVE WILSON-P
53 *(RET#) DON DRYSDALE*
54 OMAR DAAL-P
55 OREL HERSHISER-P
56 PEDRO ASTACIO-P
57 ROD NICHOLS-P
57 KIP GROSS-P
58 MARK CRESSE-CH
60 JOHN DESILVA-P (2)
64 JERRY BROOKS-OF

1994

1ST W 58-56 0GB

STRIKE NO POST-SEASON

1 *(RET#) PEE WEE REESE*
2 TOM LASORDA-MGR
4 *(RET#) DUKE SNIDER*
5 DAVE HANSEN (INJ)-3B
7 BILLY ASHLEY-OF
8 JOEY AMALFITANO-CH
9 REGGIE SMITH-CH
10 CHRIS GWYNN-OF
12 JEFF TREADWAY (INJ)-3B
14 DELINO DESHIELDS (INJ)-2B
15 DAVE HANSEN (INJ)-3B
15 TOM PRINCE-C
16 RON PERRANOSKI-CH
17 ROGER (BUBBLES) MCDOWELL-P
18 BILL RUSSELL-CH
19 *(RET#) JIM GILLIAM*
20 MITCH WEBSTER-OF
21 RAFAEL BOURNIGAL-SS
22 BRETT BUTLER-OF
23 ERIC KARROS-1B
24 *(RET#) WALTER ALSTON*
26 CARLOS HERNANDEZ (INJ)-C
28 CORY SNYDER (INJ)-OF/INF
29 TIM WALLACH-3B/1B
30 JOSE OFFERMANN-SS
31 MIKE PIAZZA-C
32 *(RET#) SANDY KOUFAX*
33 GAREY INGRAM-2B
35 JIM GOTT (INJ)-P
37 DARREN DREIFORT-P
38 TODD WORRELL (INJ)-P
39 *(RET#) ROY CAMPANELLA*
40 HENRY RODRIGUEZ-OF/1B
42 *(RET#) JACKIE ROBINSON*

43 RAUL MONDESI-OF
44 DARRYL STRAWBERRY (INJ/WAIV)-OF (1)
45 AL OSUNA-P
46 KEVIN GROSS-P
47 GARY WAYNE-P
48 RAMON MARTINEZ-P
49 TOM CANDIOTTI-P
52 BRIAN BARNES-P (2)
53 *(RET#) DON DRYSDALE*
54 OMAR DAAL-P
55 OREL HERSHISER-P
56 PEDRO ASTACIO-P
57 RUDY SEANEZ-P
58 MARK CRESSE-CH
59 ISMAEL VALDEZ-P
60 EDDIE PYE-SS
61 CHAN HO PARK-P
94 DON YI-INTREPRETOR

1995

1st W 78-66 0GB
L NLDS-CINN 3-0
144 GAME SEASON

1 *(RET#) PEE WEE REESE*
2 TOM LASORDA-MGR
3 EDDIE PYE-2B
4 *(RET#) DUKE SNIDER*
5 DAVE HANSEN-3B
7 BILLY ASHLEY-OF
8 JOEY AMALFITANO-CH
9 REGGIE SMITH-CH
10 CHRIS GWYNN-OF
12 JEFF TREADWAY-3B (1)
12 KARIM GARCIA-OF
13 ANTONIO OSUNA-P
14 DELINO DESHIELDS-2B
15 TOM PRINCE (INJ)-C
16 HIDEO NOMO-P
17 DAVE WALLACE-CH
18 BILL RUSSELL-CH
19 *(RET#) JIM GILLIAM*
20 MITCH WEBSTER-OF
21 ROBERTO KELLY-OF
22 DICK SCHOFIELD-3B
22 CHAD FONVILLE-SS (2)
22 BRETT BUTLER-OF
23 ERIC KARROS-1B
24 *(RET#) WALTER ALSTON*
25 MIKE BUSCH-1B/3B
26 CARLOS HERNANDEZ-C
27 ROGER CEDENO-OF
28 TODD HOLLANDSWORTH (INJ)-OF
29 TIM WALLACH (INJ)-3B/1B
30 JOSE OFFERMANN-SS
31 MIKE PIAZZA (INJ)-C
32 *(RET#) SANDY KOUFAX*
33 GAREY INGRAM-2B
36 NOE MUNOZ-C
36 TODD WILLIAMS-P
38 TODD WORRELL-P
39 *(RET#) ROY CAMPANELLA*
40 HENRY RODRIGUEZ-OF/1B (1)
40 WILLIE BANKS-P
41 REGGIE WILLIAMS-OF
41 JOHN CUMMINGS-P
42 *(RET#) JACKIE ROBINSON*
43 RAUL MONDESI-OF
45 NOE MUNOZ-C
45 JOSE PARRA-P
45 JIM BRUSKE-P
46 ROB MURPHY-P
46 RICK PARKER-OF
46 KEVIN TAPANI-P
48 RAMON MARTINEZ-P
49 TOM CANDIOTTI-P
50 ANTONIO OSUNA-P
50 FELIX RODRIGUEZ-P
51 JOEY EISCHEN-P
52 GREG HANSELL-P
52 MARK GUTHRIE-P (2)
53 *(RET#) DON DRYSDALE*
54 OMAR DAAL-P
56 PEDRO ASTACIO-P
57 RUDY SEANEZ-P
58 MARK CRESSE-CH
59 ISMAEL VALDEZ-P
60 JUAN CASTRO-3B/SS
61 CHAN HO PARK-P
65 JOSE PARRA-P
66 TODD WILLIAMS-P

1996

2nd W 90-72 1GB
WC L NLDS-ATLN 3-0

1 *(RET#) PEE WEE REESE*
2 TOM LASORDA (ILL) (RET)-MGR1
3 CHAD FONVILLE-UTIL
4 *(RET#) DUKE SNIDER*
5 DAVE HANSEN-3B
7 GREG GAGNE (INJ)-SS
8 JOEY AMALFITANO-CH
9 REGGIE SMITH-CH
10 CHAD CURTIS-OF (2)
11 MANNY MOTA-CH
12 KARIM GARCIA-PH
13 ANTONIO OSUNA-P
14 DELINO DESHIELDS-2B
15 TOM PRINCE-C
16 HIDEO NOMO-P
17 DAVE WALLACE-CH
18 BILL RUSSELL-CH/MGR2
19 *(RET#) JIM GILLIAM*
20 MIKE BLOWERS (INJ)-3B
21 BILLY ASHLEY (INJ)-OF
22 BRETT BUTLER (ILL)-OF
23 ERIC KARROS-1B
24 *(RET#) WALTER ALSTON*
25 MIKE BUSCH (INJ)-OF
26 CARLOS HERNANDEZ (INJ)-C
27 ROGER CEDENO-OF
28 TODD HOLLANDSWORTH-OF
29 MILT THOMPSON (WAIV)-OF/PH (1)
29 TIM WALLACH (RET)-PH (2)
30 WILTON GUERRERO-INF
31 MIKE PIAZZA-C
32 *(RET#) SANDY KOUFAX*
(35) RICK GORECKI (INJ)-(P)
35 DAVE CLARK-OF (2)
36 SCOTT RADINSKY (INJ)-P
37 DARREN DREIFORT (INJ-P
38 TODD WORRELL-P
39 *(RET#) ROY CAMPANELLA*
40 RICK PARKER-PH/OF
41 JOHN CUMMINGS-P (1)
42 *(RET#) JACKIE ROBINSON*
43 RAUL MONDESI-OF
44 MARK GUTHRIE-P
45 JIM BRUSKE-P
48 RAMON MARTINEZ (INJ)-P
49 TOM CANDIOTTI (INJ)-P
50 FELIX RODRIGUEZ-P
51 JOEY EISCHEN-P (1)
52 DARREN HALL (INJ)-P
53 *(RET#) DON DRYSDALE*
55 WAYNE KIRBY-OF (2)
56 PEDRO ASTACIO-P
58 MARK CRESSE-CH
59 ISMAEL VALDEZ-P
60 JUAN CASTRO-SS
61 CHAN HO PARK-P
62 ORESTE MARRERO-PH

1997

2nd W 88-74 2GB

1 *(RET#) PEE WEE REESE*
2 *(RET#) TOM LASORDA*
3 CHAD FONVILLE-2B (1)
4 *(RET#) DUKE SNIDER*
5 CHIP HALE-3B
7 GREG GAGNE-SS
8 JOEY AMALFITANO-CH
9 REGGIE SMITH-CH
10 OTIS NIXON-OF (2)
11 MANNY MOTA-CH
12 KARIM GARCIA-OF
13 ANTONIO OSUNA-P
14 MIKE SCIOSCIA-CH
15 TOM PRINCE-C
16 HIDEO NOMO-P
17 DAVE WALLACE-CH
18 BILL RUSSELL-MGR
19 *(RET#) JIM GILLIAM*
20 DARREN LEWIS-OF (2)
21 BILLY ASHLEY-OF
22 BRETT BUTLER (INJ)-OF
23 ERIC KARROS-1B
24 *(RET#) WALTER ALSTON*
25 JUAN CASTRO (INJ)-2B/SS
26 EDDIE WILLIAMS-OF (1)
26 ERIC YOUNG-2B (2)
27 TODD ZEILE-3B
28 TODD HOLLANDSWORTH (INJ)-OF
29 ERIC ANTHONY-OF
30 WILTON GUERRERO-2B
31 MIKE PIAZZA-C
32 *(RET#) SANDY KOUFAX*
33 EDDIE MURRAY-1B (2)
35 WAYNE KIRBY-OF
36 SCOTT RADINSKY-P
37 DARREN DREIFORT (INJ-P
38 TODD WORRELL-P
39 *(RET#) ROY CAMPANELLA*
41 TRIPP CROMER (INJ)-SS/2B
42 *(RET#) JACKIE ROBINSON*
43 RAUL MONDESI-OF
44 MARK GUTHRIE-P
45 ROGER CEDENO (INJ) SS/OF
46 NELSON LIRIANO (INJ)-PH
48 RAMON MARTINEZ (INJ)-P
49 TOM CANDIOTTI-P
50 MIKE HARKEY-P
51 ADAM RIGGS-2B
52 DARREN HALL-P
53 *(RET#) DON DRYSDALE*
54 HENRY BLANCO-3B
55 RICK GORECKI (INJ)-P
56 PEDRO ASTACIO-P (1)
56 GAREY INGRAM-OF
57 DENNIS REYES-P
58 MARK CRESSE-CH
59 ISMAEL VALDEZ-P
60 MICHAEL JUDD-P
61 CHAN HO PARK-P
66 PAUL KONERKO-INF

1998

3rd 83-79 15GB

1 *(RET#) PEE WEE REESE*
2 *(RET#) TOM LASORDA*
3 ALEX CORA-2B
4 *(RET#) DUKE SNIDER*
5 GARY SHEFFIELD-OF (2)
5 JOSE VIZCAINO-INF (2)
7 PAUL KONERKO-1B (1)
7 TRIPP CROMER (INJ)-SS/2B
8 JOEY AMALFITANO-CH
9 REGGIE SMITH-CH
9 MICKEY HATCHER-CH
10 JOSE VIZCAINO-INF (2)
10 GARY SHEFFIELD-OF (2)
11 MANNY MOTA-CH
12 MIKE DEVEREAUX-OF
12 JIM EISENREICH-OF (2)
13 ANTONIO OSUNA-P
14 MIKE SCIOSCIA-CH
15 TOM PRINCE-C
16 HIDEO NOMO-P (1)
16 MARK GRUDZIELANEK-SS (2)
17 DAVE WALLACE-CH
17 JUAN CASTRO-2B/SS
18 BILL RUSSELL-MGR 1
19 *(RET#) JIM GILLIAM*
20 *(RET#) DON SUTTON*
21 ERIC YOUNG (INJ)-2B
22 THOMAS HOWARD-OF
22 GLENN HOFFMAN-MGR 2
23 ERIC KARROS (INJ)-1B
24 *(RET#) WALTER ALSTON*
25 JUAN CASTRO-2B/SS
25 BOBBY (BOBBY BO) BONILLA-3B (2)
26 CHARLES JOHNSON-C (2)
27 TODD ZEILE-3B (1)
27 MANUEL BARRIOS-P
28 TODD HOLLANDSWORTH (INJ)-OF
29 ADRIAN BELTRE-3B
30 WILTON GUERRERO-2B (1)
30 MARK GRUDZIELANEK-SS \ (2)
31 MIKE PIAZZA-C (1)
31 JOHN (T-BONE) SHELBY-CH
32 *(RET#) SANDY KOUFAX*
33 GREG GREGSON-CH
33 CARLOS PEREZ-P (2)
35 GREG MCMICHAEL-P (2)
36 SCOTT RADINSKY-P
37 DARREN DREIFORT-P
38 DAVE MLICKI-P (2)
39 *(RET#) ROY CAMPANELLA*
40 MATT LUKE (WAIV)-1B (1)(3)
41 TRIPP CROMER (INJ)-SS/2B
41 JEFF SHAW-P (2)
42 *(RET#) JACKIE ROBINSON*
43 RAUL MONDESI-OF
44 MARK GUTHRIE-P
45 ROGER CEDENO (INJ) SS/OF
46 JIM BRUSKE-P (1)
47 TRENIDAD HUBBARD (INJ)-OF
48 RAMON MARTINEZ (INJ)-P
49 FRANK LANKFORD-P
49 GARY RATH-P
49 CHARLIE HOUGH-CH
50 BRAD CLONTZ-P (1)
50 WILL BRUNSON-P (1)
52 DARREN HALL (INJ)-P
53 *(RET#) DON DRYSDALE*
(54) HENRY BLANCO (INJ)-(3B)
56 ERIC WEAVER-P
57 DENNIS REYES-P
57 BRIAN BOHANON-P (2)
58 MARK CRESSE-CH
58 SHAWN MALONEY-P
59 ISMAEL VALDEZ (INJ)-P
60 MICHAEL JUDD-P
61 CHAN HO PARK-P
62 MIKE METCALFE-INF
63 ANGEL PENA-C
64 PAUL LO DUCA-INF
67 JEFF KUBENKO-P
70 DAMON HOLLINS-OF

1999

3rd W 77-85 23GB

1 *(RET#) PEE WEE REESE*
2 *(RET#) TOM LASORDA*
3 ALEX CORA (INJ)-2B
4 *(RET#) DUKE SNIDER*
5 JOSE VIZCAINO-INF
7 TRIPP CROMER (INJ)-SS/2B
8 MARK GRUDZIELANEK (INJ)-SS
9 TODD HUNDLEY-C
10 GARY SHEFFIELD-OF
11 MANNY MOTA-CH
12 JIM TRACY-CH
13 ANTONIO OSUNA (INJ)-P
15 DAVEY JOHNSON-MGR
16 PAUL LO DUCA-C
17 JUAN CASTRO-INF
19 *(RET#) JIM GILLIAM*
20 *(RET#) DON SUTTON*
21 ERIC YOUNG-2B
22 DEVON WHITE-OF
23 ERIC KARROS-1B
24 *(RET#) WALTER ALSTON*
25 DAVE HANSEN-1B
26 RICK DEMPSEY-CH
27 KEVIN BROWN-P
28 TODD HOLLANDSWORTH (INJ)-OF
29 ADRIAN BELTRE-3B
30 BRENT COOKSON-OF
30 CRAIG COUNSELL-INF (2)
31 JOHN (T-BONE) SHELBY-CH
32 *(RET#) SANDY KOUFAX*
33 CARLOS PEREZ-P
35 GLENN HOFFMAN-CH
36 ANGEL PENA-C
37 DARREN DREIFORT-P
38 DAVE MLICKI-P (1)
38 CLAUDE OSTEEN-CH
39 *(RET#) ROY CAMPANELLA*
41 JEFF SHAW-P
42 *(RET#) JACKIE ROBINSON*
43 RAUL MONDESI-OF
44 RICK DOWN-CH
45 JEFF KUBENKA-P
46 RICK WILKINS-C
46 DOUG BOCHTLER-P
47 TRENIDAD HUBBARD (INJ)-OF
48 JACOB BRUMFIELD-OF (1)
48 ERIC GAGNE-P
49 CHARLIE HOUGH-CH
49 MATT HERGES-P
50 PEDRO BORBON-P
51 MEL ROJAS-P (1)
51 MIKE MADDUX-P (2)
52 JAIME ARNOLD-P
53 *(RET#) DON DRYSDALE*
54 CHANCE SANFORD-INF
54 JEFF WILLIAMS-P
55 ONAN MASAOKA-P
56 ROBINSON CHECO-P
59 ISMAEL VALDEZ (INJ)-P
60 MICHAEL JUDD-P
61 CHAN HO PARK-P
70 ONAN MASAOKA-P
75 ALAN MILLS-P

2000

2nd W 86-76 11GB

1 *(RET#) PEE WEE REESE*
2 *(RET#) TOM LASORDA*
3 ALEX CORA-2B
4 *(RET#) DUKE SNIDER*
5 DAVEY JOHNSON-MGR
7 JOSE VIZCAINO-INF (1)
8 MARK GRUDZIELANEK (INJ)-SS
9 TODD HUNDLEY-C
10 GARY SHEFFIELD-OF
11 MANNY MOTA-CH
12 JIM TRACY-CH
13 ANTONIO OSUNA-P
14 F. P. SANTANGELO (INJ)-OF
15 SHAWN GREEN-OF
16 PAUL LODUCA-C
17 GERONIMO BERROA (INJ)-OF
18 JIM LEYRITZ-UTIL (2)

19 *(RET#) JIM GILLIAM*
20 *(RET#) DON SUTTON*
21 CHAD KREUTER-C
22 DEVON WHITE-OF
23 ERIC KARROS-1B
24 *(RET#) WALTER ALSTON*
25 DAVE HANSEN-1B
26 RICK DEMPSEY-CH
27 KEVIN BROWN-P
28 TODD HOLLANDSWORTH-OF (1)
28 TOM GOODWIN-OF (2)
29 ADRIAN BELTRE-3B
30 GREGG OLSON-P
31 JOHN (T-BONE) SHELBY-CH
32 *(RET#) SANDY KOUFAX*
33 CARLOS PEREZ-P
35 GLENN HOFFMAN-CH
37 DARREN DREIFORT-P
38 CLAUDE OSTEEN-CH
39 *(RET#) ROY CAMPANELLA*
40 ONAN MASAOKA-P
41 JEFF SHAW-P
42 *(RET#) JACKIE ROBINSON*
43 KEVIN ELSTER-INF
44 RICK DOWN-CH
45 MIKE METCALFE-OF
45 ADAM MELHUSE-1B (1)
45 JEFF BRANSON-P
46 TREVER MILLER-P (1)
46 HIRAM BOCACHICA-INF
47 SHAWN GILBERT-OF
47 BRUCE AVEN-OF (2)
48 ERIC GAGNE-P
49 MATT HERGES-P
50 CHRIS DONNELS (INJ)-INF
51 TERRY ADAMS-P
52 JAIME ARNOLD-P (1)
52 AL REYES-P (2)
53 *(RET#) DON DRYSDALE*
54 JEFF WILLIAMS-P
55 OREL HERSHISER-P
56 MIKE FETTERS-P
57 LUKE PROKOPEC-P
59 ISMAEL VALDEZ (INJ)-P (2)
60 MICHAEL JUDD-P
61 CHAN HO PARK-P
67 KRIS FOSTER (INJ)-P
75 ALAN MILLS-P (1)

2001

3RD W 86-76 6GB

1 *(RET#) PEE WEE REESE*
2 *(RET#) TOM LASORDA*
3 ALEX CORA-2B
4 *(RET#) DUKE SNIDER*
5 JIM RIGGLEMAN-CH
7 JEFF BRANSON-2B
8 MARK GRUDZIELANEK (INJ)-2B
9 MARQUIS GRISSOM (SUS)-OF
10 GARY SHEFFIELD-OF
11 MANNY MOTA-CH
12 JIM TRACY-MGR
14 JEFF REBOULET-SS
15 SHAWN GREEN-OF
16 PAUL LO DUCA-C
17 JIM LETT-CH
18 TIM BOGAR (INJ)-INF
19 *(RET#) JIM GILLIAM*
20 *(RET#) DON SUTTON*
21 CHAD KREUTER-C
23 ERIC KARROS (INJ)-1B
24 *(RET#) WALTER ALSTON*
25 DAVE HANSEN (INJ)-1B
26 BRIAN JOHNSON-C
27 KEVIN BROWN (INJ)-P
28 TOM GOODWIN (INJ)-OF
29 ADRIAN BELTRE (INJ)-3B
30 GREGG OLSON-P
30 JAMES BALDWIN-P (2)
31 JOHN (T-BONE) SHELBY-CH
32 *(RET#) SANDY KOUFAX*
(33) CARLOS PEREZ (INJ)-(P)
33 HIRAM BOCACHICA-INF
35 GLENN HOFFMAN-CH
36 ANGEL PENA-C
37 DARREN DREIFORT (INJ)-P
38 ERIC GAGNE-P
39 *(RET#) ROY CAMPANELLA*
40 MIKE TROMBLEY-P
41 JEFF SHAW-P
42 *(RET#) JACKIE ROBINSON*
43 ANDY ASHBY (INJ)-P
44 JACK CLARK-CH
44 PHIL HIATT-3B
45 JIM COLBORN-CH
45 JOSE NUNEZ-P
45 DENNIS SPRINGER-P
45 TERRY MULHOLLAND-P (2)
46 HIRAM BOCACHICA-INF
46 BRUCE AVEN-P
47 JESSE OROSCO (INJ)-P
49 MATT HERGES-P
50 CHRIS DONNELS-INF
51 TERRY ADAMS-P
52 AL REYES-P
53 *(RET#) DON DRYSDALE*
54 JEFF WILLIAMS-P
55 GIOVANNI CARRARA-P
56 MIKE FETTERS (INJ)-P (1)
56 DENNIS SPRINGER-P
57 LUKE PROKOPEC (INJ)-P
59 MCKAY CHRISTENSEN-OF
61 CHAN HO PARK-P
62 JOSE NUNEZ-P (1)

2002

3RD W 92-70 6GB

1 *(RET#) PEE WEE REESE*
2 *(RET#) TOM LASORDA*
3 CESAR IZTURIS-SS
4 *(RET#) DUKE SNIDER*
5 JIM RIGGLEMAN-CH
5 TYLER HOUSTON-INF (2)
7 MIKE KINKADE-1B/OF
8 MARK GRUDZIELANEK-2B
9 MARQUIS GRISSOM-OF
10 HIDEO NOMO-P
11 MANNY MOTA-CH
12 JIM (TRACE) TRACY-MGR
13 ALEX CORA-SS/2B
14 JEFF REBOULET (INJ)-INF
15 SHAWN GREEN-OF
16 PAUL LO DUCA-C/1B/OF
17 KAZUHISA ISHII-P
18 JIM LETT-CH
19 *(RET#) JIM GILLIAM*
20 *(RET#) DON SUTTON*
21 CHAD KREUTER-C
22 JACK CLARK-CH
23 ERIC KARROS-1B
24 *(RET#) WALTER ALSTON*
25 DAVE HANSEN-1B/3B
26 HIRAM BOCACHICA-INF
26 WILKIN RUAN-OF
27 KEVIN BROWN (INJ)-P
28 JIM RIGGLEMAN-CH
29 ADRIAN BELTRE-3B
30 DAVE ROBERTS-OF
31 JOHN (T-BONE) SHELBY-CH
32 *(RET#) SANDY KOUFAX*
33 BRIAN JORDAN-OF
35 GLENN HOFFMAN-CH
36 OMAR DAAL-P
37 DARREN DREIFORT-P
38 ERIC GAGNE-P
39 *(RET#) ROY CAMPANELLA*
40 DAVE ROSS-C
41 ODALIS PEREZ-P
41 JOE THURSTON-2B
42 *(RET#) JACKIE ROBINSON*
43 ANDY ASHBY-P
44 PAUL SHUEY-P (2)
45 TERRY MULHOLLAND-P (1)
45 ODALIS PEREZ-P
46 PAUL QUANTRILL-P
47 JESSE OROSCO-P
48 JIM COLBORN-CH
49 LUKE ALLEN-OF
49 BRIAN COREY-P
50 JOLBERT CABRERA-UTIL (2)
51 ROBERT ELLIS-P
52 CHIN-FENG CHEN-OF
53 *(RET#) DON DRYSDALE*
54 JEFF WILLIAMS-P
55 GIOVANNI CARRARA-P
56 DENNIS SPRINGER-P
57 VICTOR ALVAREZ-P
58 KEVIN BIERNE-P
59 GUILLERMO MOTA-P

2003

2ND W 85-77 15.5GB

1 *(RET#) PEE WEE REESE*
2 *(RET#) TOM LASORDA*
3 CESAR IZTURIS-SS
4 *(RET#) DUKE SNIDER*
5 JASON ROMANO-OF
6 JOLBERT CABRERA-UTIL
7 MIKE KINKADE-UTIL
8 RON COOMER (INJ)-1B/3B
9 TODD HUNDLEY (INJ)-C
10 HIDEO NOMO-P
11 MANNY MOTA-CH
12 JIM (TRACE) TRACY-MGR
13 ALEX CORA-2B/SS
14 LARRY BARNES-1B/OF
15 SHAWN GREEN-OF
16 PAUL LO DUCA-C/1B
17 KAZUHISA ISHII (INJ)-P
18 JIM LETT-CH
19 *(RET#) JIM GILLIAM*
20 *(RET#) DON SUTTON*
21 JEROMY BURNITZ-OF (2)
22 JACK CLARK-CH
22 GEORGE HENDRICK-CH
23 ROBIN VENTURA-1B/3B (2)
24 *(RET#) WALTER ALSTON*
25 JIM RIGGLEMAN-CH
25 RICKEY HENDERSON-OF
26 WILKIN RUAN-OF
27 KEVIN BROWN (INJ)-P
28 FRED MCGRIFF (INJ)-1B
29 ADRIAN BELTRE-3B
30 DAVE ROBERTS (INJ)-OF
31 JOHN (T-BONE) SHELBY-CH
32 *(RET#) SANDY KOUFAX*
33 BRIAN JORDAN (INJ)-OF
35 GLENN HOFFMAN-CH
36 DARYLE WARD (INJ)-1B/OF
36 EDWIN JACKSON-P
37 DARREN DREIFORT (INJ)-P
38 ERIC GAGNE-P
39 *(RET#) ROY CAMPANELLA*
40 DAVE ROSS-C
41 CHAD HERMANSON (INJ)-OF
42 *(RET#) JACKIE ROBINSON*
43 ANDY ASHBY (INJ)-P
44 PAUL SHUEY (INJ)-P
45 ODALIS PEREZ-P
46 PAUL QUANTRILL-P
47 WILSON ALVAREZ-P
48 JIM COLBORN-CH
49 JOE THURSTON-2B
49 BUBBA CROSBY-OF (1)
49 SCOTT MULLEN-P (2)
50 STEVE COLYER-P
51 TOM MARTIN-P
52 CHIN-FENG CHEN-PH
53 *(RET#) DON DRYSDALE*
54 TROY BROHAWN (INJ)-P
55 KOYIE HILL-PH
(56) DEREK THOMPSON (INJ)-(P)
57 VICTOR ALVAREZ-P
58 RODNEY MYERS-P
59 GUILLERMO MOTA-P
60 MASAO KIDA-P

2004

1ST W 93-69 0GB
L NLDS-STLN 3-1

1 *(RET#) PEE WEE REESE*
2 *(RET#) TOM LASORDA*
3 CESAR IZTURIS-SS
4 *(RET#) DUKE SNIDER*
5 HEE SEOP CHOI-1B (2)
6 BRENT MAYNE-C
7 TOM WILSON-C (2)
8 OLMEDA SAENZ-3B/1B
(9) TODD HUNDLEY (INJ)-(C)
10 HIDEO NOMO (INJ)-P
11 MANNY MOTA-CH
12 JIM (TRACE) TRACY-MGR
12 STEVE FINLEY-OF (2)
13 ALEX CORA-2B
15 SHAWN GREEN-1B/OF
16 PAUL LO DUCA-C/1B (1)
16 STEVE FINLEY-OF (2)
16 JIM (TRACE) TRACY-MGR
17 KAZUHISA ISHII (INJ)-P
18 JIM LETT-CH
18 JOSE HERNANDEZ-2B
19 *(RET#) JIM GILLIAM*
20 *(RET#) DON SUTTON*
21 MILTON BRADLEY-OF
22 EDWIN JACKSON-P
23 ROBIN VENTURA-3B/1B
24 *(RET#) WALTER ALSTON*
25 TIM WALLACH-CH
26 ANTONIO PEREZ-SS
27 JOSE LIMA-P
28 JASON WERTH-OF
29 ADRIAN BELTRE-3B
30 DAVE ROBERTS (INJ)-OF (1)
31 JOHN (T-BONE) SHELBY-CH
32 *(RET#) SANDY KOUFAX*
33 JASON GRABOWSKI-3B
35 GLENN HOFFMAN-CH
36 JEFF WEAVER-P
37 DARREN DREIFORT (INJ)-P
38 ERIC GAGNE-P
39 *(RET#) ROY CAMPANELLA*
40 DAVE ROSS-C
41 MIKE VENAFRO-P
42 *(RET#) JACKIE ROBINSON*
43 JUAN ENCARNACION-OF (1)
43 YHENCY BRAZOBAN-P
(44) PAUL SHUEY (INJ)-(P)
45 ODALIS PEREZ-P
46 RODNEY MYERS-P
46 ELMER DESSENS-P (2)
47 WILSON ALVAREZ-P
48 JIM COLBORN-CH
49 JOE THURSTON-2B
49 BUBBA CROSBY-OF (1)
50 DUANER SANCHEZ-P
51 TOM MARTIN-P (1)
52 CHIN-FENG CHEN-OF
53 *(RET#) DON DRYSDALE*
54 JOSE FLORES-SS
55 GIOVANNI CARRARA-P
56 JIM RIGGLEMAN-CH
57 SCOTT STEWART-P (2)
58 BRIAN FALKENBORG (INJ)-P
59 GUILLERMO MOTA-P (1)
60 MASAO KIDA-P (1)

2005

4TH W 71-91 11G

1 *(RET#) PEE WEE REESE*
2 *(RET#) TOM LASORDA*
3 CESAR IZTURIS (INJ)-SS
4 *(RET#) DUKE SNIDER*
5 HEE SEOP CHOI-1B
6 JASON GRABOWSKI (INJ)-
7 J. D. DREW (INJ)-OF
8 OLMEDA SAENZ-1B/3B
9 JASON PHILLIPS-C
10 JOSE VALENTIN (INJ)-3B
11 MANNY MOTA-CH
12 JEFF KENT-2B
13 OSCAR ROBLES-SS/3B
15 SCOTT ERICKSON-P
16 JIM (TRACE) TRACY-MGR
17 JASON REPKO-OF
18 PAUL BAKO (INJ)-C
18 JIM LETT-CH
19 *(RET#) JIM GILLIAM*
20 *(RET#) DON SUTTON*
21 MILTON BRADLEY (INJ)-OF
22 JOSE CRUZ, JR.-OF (3)
23 DEREK LOWE-P
24 *(RET#) WALTER ALSTON*
25 TIM WALLACH-CH
25 MIKE EDWARDS-3B/OF
26 ANTONIO PEREZ (INJ)-SS
27 D. J. HOULTON-P
28 JASON WERTH (INJ)-OF
30 JOHN (T-BONE) SHELBY-CH
31 BRAD PENNY (INJ)-P
32 *(RET#) SANDY KOUFAX*
33 RICKY LEDEE (INJ)-OF
35 GLENN HOFFMAN-CH
36 JEFF WEAVER-P
(37) DARREN DREIFORT (INJ)-
38 ERIC GAGNE (INJ)-P
39 *(RET#) ROY CAMPANELLA*
40 STEVE SCHMOLL-P
41 DIONER NAVARRO-C
42 *(RET#) JACKIE ROBINSON*
43 JUAN ENCARNACION-OF (1)
43 YHENCY BRAZOBAN-P
44 JON DEBUS-CH
45 ODALIS PEREZ (INJ)-P
46 ELMER DESSENS (INJ)-P
47 WILSON ALVAREZ (INJ)-P
48 JIM COLBORN-CH
49 CODY ROSS-OF
49 WILLY AYBAR-INF
50 DUANER SANCHEZ-P
51 JONATHAN BROXTON-P
52 CHIN-FENG CHEN-OF
52 BRIAN MYROW-1B
53 *(RET#) DON DRYSDALE*
54 MIKE ROSE-C
55 GIOVANNI CARRARA-P
56 DEREK THOMPSON-P
56 HONG-CHIH KUO-P
57 FRANQUELIS OSORIO-P
58 BUDDY CARLYLE-P
58 EDWIN JACKSON-P
59 KELLY WUNSCH (INJ)-P
66 NORIHIRO NAKAMURA-INF

SEATTLE PILOTS/ MILWAUKEE BREWERS

The 1969 expansion Seattle Pilots were an American League club in the Western Division. The franchise moved to Milwaukee the following year and were renamed the Brewers, still residing in the AL West. In 1972, they moved to the AL East. They then moved to the newly created AL Central in 1994. Their last move was in 1998 when they jumped to the NL Central to help balance the schedules.

1969
SEATTLE PILOTS

6TH AL-W 64-98 33GB

1 RAY OYLER-SS
2 FRANKIE (CROW) CROSETTI-CH
3 JOE (DODE) SCHULTZ-MGR
4 SAL (THE BARBER) MAGLIE -CH
5 DON MINCHER-1B
6 EDDIE O'BRIEN-CH
7 RON PLAZA-CH
8 MIKE HEGAN-OF/1B
8 MIKE FERRARO-PH
9 RICH (RED) ROLLINS (INJ)-3B/SS
10 LARRY HANEY-C (1)
10 JOHN DONALDSON-2B/INF (2)
11 JOHN KENNEDY (INJ)-SS/3B
12 TOMMY DAVIS-OF/1B (1)
12 DANNY (MICKEY) WALTON-OF
13 STEVE BARBER (INJ)-P
14 JIM GOSGER-OF (1)
14 MICKEY FUENTES-P
14 GORDY LUND--INF
15 JERRY MCNERTNEY-C
16 DICK SIMPSON-OF (2)
17 JIM (PAG) PAGLIARONI (INJ)-UTIL (2)
18 GUS GIL-INF
19 STEVE WHITAKER-OF
20 WAYNE COMER-OF/UTIL
21 TOMMY HARPER-3B/UTIL
22 FRED (CHICKEN) STANLEY-SS/2B
23 JACK AKER-P
23 FRED (BUBBY) TALBOT-P (2)
24 DIEGO SEGUI-P
25 JOHN GELNAR-P
26 MERRITT RANEW-UTIL
27 DARRELL (BUCKY) BRANDON-P (1)
27 BOB LOCKER-P (2)
28 MIKE MARSHALL-P
28 SANDY VALDESPINO-OF (2)
30 FREDDIE VELAZQUEZ-C
30 RON CLARK-INF (2)
31 JOSE (PAPITO) VIDAL-OF
31 SIBBY SISTI-CH
32 DICK BANEY-P
32 GENE BRABENDER-P
33 MARTY PATTIN-P
34 GREG GOOSSEN-1B/OF
35 JOHN MORRIS-P
36 STEVE HOVLEY-OF
38 BOB MEYER-P
39 GEORGE (LEFTY) BRUNET-P
39 GARY BELL-P (1)
39 GARY ROGGENBURK-P (2)
40 BILL EDGERTON-P
40 JERRY STEPHENSON-P
41 JERRY STEPHENSON-P
41 DOOLEY WOMACK-P (2)
42 SKIP LOCKWOOD-P
43 JOHN O-DONOGHUE-P
44 GARY ROGGENBURK-P (2)
45 GARY TIMBERLAKE (MIL)-C
45 DICK BANEY-P
46 GARY ROGGENBURK-P (2)
46 DICK BATES-P
51 BILLY WILLIAMS-OF
56 JIM BOUTON-P (1)
57 DARRELL (BUCKY) BRANDON-P (1)
57 GEORGE (LEFTY) BRUNET-P

1970
MILWAUKEE BREWERS

4TH AL-W (TIE) 65-97 33GB

1 TED KUBIAK-2B/SS
2 TED SAVAGE-OF/1B
4 DAVE BRISTOL-MGR
5 PHIL ROOF-C/1B
6 MIKE HERSHBERGER (INJ)-OF
7 RUSS SNYDER-OF
8 MIKE HEGAN-1B/OF
9 RICH (RED) ROLLINS-3B (1)
9 TITO FRANCONA-1B (2)
10 MAX ALVIS-3B
11 JOHN KENNEDY (INJ)-SS/3B (1)
11 DAVE MAY-OF (2)
12 DANNY (MICKEY) WALTON-OF
15 JERRY MCNERTNEY-C/1B
16 GUS GIL-2B/3B
17 PETE KOEGEL-OF
18 WES STOCK-CH
19 BOB BURDA-OF/1B (2)
20 WAYNE COMER-OF/UTIL (1)
20 KEN SANDERS-P
21 TOMMY HARPER-3B/UTIL
22 BERNIE SMITH-OF
23 CAL ERMER-CH
23 BOB LOCKER-P (1)
24 JACKIE MOORE-CH
24 LEW KRAUSSE-P
25 JOHN GELNAR-P
26 ROY MCMILLAN-CH
27 BOB LOCKER-P (1)
27 CAL ERMER-CH
28 SANDY VALDESPINO-OF (1)
28 ROBERTO (BABY) PENA-SS/INF (2)
30 LEW KRAUSSE-P
30 JACKIE MOORE-CH
31 BRUCE BRUBAKER-P
32 GENE BRABENDER-P
33 MARTY PATTIN-P
34 GREG GOOSSEN-1B (1)
35 JOHN MORRIS (ILL)-P
36 STEVE HOVLEY-OF (1)
36 AL DOWNING-P (2)
38 BOB MEYER-P
39 BOB BOLIN-P (1)
40 FLOYD WICKER-OF
41 RAY PETERS-P
42 SKIP LOCKWOOD-P
43 JOHN O-DONOGHUE-P (1)
44 HANK ALLEN-OF/INF (2)
45 FRED (CHICKEN) STANLEY-SS/2B
46 DAVE BALDWIN-P
47 BOB HUMPHREYS-P (2)
48 WAYNE TWITCHELL-P
49 GEORGE LAUZERIQUE-P
49 DICK ELLSWORTH-P (2)
50 BOB HUMPHREYS-P (2)
MICKEY FUENTES (DIED)-(P)

1971

6TH AL-W 69-92 32GB

1 TED KUBIAK-2B/SS (1)
1 JOSE CARDENAL-OF (2)
2 TED SAVAGE-OF (1)
2 BOB HEISE-UTIL (2)
4 DAVE BRISTOL-MGR
5 PHIL ROOF-C (1)
5 PAUL RATLIFF-C (2)
6 ELLIE RODRIGUEZ-C
7 DANNY (MICKEY) WALTON-OF/3B (1)
7 FRANK TEPEDINO-INF (2)
8 MIKE HEGAN-1B (1)
8 ROB ELLIS-OF/3B
9 AL YATES-OF
9 DICK (DUCKY) SCHOFIELD-SS (2)
10 ANDY KOSKO-UTIL
11 DAVE MAY-OF
12 JOHNNY BRIGGS-1B/OF (2)
15 DARRELL PORTER-C
16 RON THEOBALD-2B/INF
17 PETE KOEGEL-OF (1)
18 WES STOCK-CH
19 TOM MATCHICK-3B/2B
19 RICK AUERBACH-SS
20 KEN SANDERS-P
21 TOMMY HARPER-3B/UTIL
22 BERNIE SMITH-OF
22 GUS GIL-INF
23 BOB MITCHELL-OF
24 LEW KRAUSSE-P
25 JOHN GELNAR-P
25 BOB REYNOLDS-P (2)
26 ROY MCMILLAN-CH
27 CAL ERMER-CH
28 ROBERTO (BABY) PENA-INF
29 LARRY BEARNARTH-P
30 JACKIE MOORE-CH
31 HARVEY KUENN-CH
32 BILL VOSS-OF
33 MARTY PATTIN-P
34 JIM HANNAN-P (2)
35 JOHN MORRIS (INJ)-P
38 MARCELINO LOPEZ-P
40 FLOYD WICKER-OF (1)
40 JERRY BELL-P
41 JIM SLATON-P
42 SKIP LOCKWOOD-P
49 DICK ELLSWORTH-P
49 FLOYD WEAVER-P
50 BOB REYNOLDS-P (2)
51 JERRY BELL-P
52 BILL PARSONS-P

1972

6TH AL-E 65-91 21GB

1 DEL CRANDALL-MGR3
2 BOB HEISE-INF
3 JOE LAHOUD-OF
4 DAVE BRISTOL-MGR1
5 GEORGE (BOOMER) SCOTT -1B/3B
6 ELLIE RODRIGUEZ-C
7 SYD O'BRIEN-3B/2B
7 RON CLARK-2B/3B
9 BILLY CONIGLIARO (RET)-OF
10 TOMMIE REYNOLDS-UTIL
11 DAVE MAY-OF
12 JOHNNY BRIGGS-0F/1B
14 (DOWNTOWN) OLLIE BROWN-OF/3B (3)
15 DARRELL PORTER-C
16 RON THEOBALD-2B
17 PAUL RATLIFF-C
17 JOE AZCUE-C (2)
18 WES STOCK-CH
19 RICK AUERBACH-SS
20 KEN SANDERS-P
21 CURT MOTTON-OF (1)
22 BROCK DAVIS-OF
24 KEN BRETT (INJ)-P
25 FRANK LINZY-P
26 ROY MCMILLAN-CH/MGR2
27 JIM LONBORG-P
29 JIM LONBORG-P
30 JACKIE MOORE-CH
30 CHUCK TAYLOR-P (2)
31 HARVEY KUENN-CH
32 BILL VOSS-OF (1)
33 MIKE FERRARO-3B/SS
35 EARL STEPHENSON-P
38 EARL STEPHENSON-P
39 JOHN FELSKE-C/1B
40 JERRY BELL (INJ)-P
41 JIM SLATON-P
42 SKIP LOCKWOOD-P
43 GARY RYERSON-P
43 RAY NEWMAN-P
48 JIM COLBORN-P
49 RAY NEWMAN-P
49 ARCHIE REYNOLDS-P
52 BILL PARSONS-P

1973

5TH AL-E 74-88 23GB

1 DEL CRANDALL-MGR
2 BOB HEISE-UTIL
3 JOE LAHOUD-DH/OF
4 TIM JOHNSON-SS
5 GEORGE (BOOMER) SCOTT -1B/DH
6 ELLIE RODRIGUEZ-C
7 DON (BROOKS) MONEY-3B/SS
9 PETE GARCIA-2B
10 BOB SHAW-CH
11 DAVE MAY-OF/DH
12 JOHNNY BRIGGS-0F/DH
14 (DOWNTOWN) OLLIE BROWN-DH/OF
15 DARRELL PORTER-C/DH
17 BOBBY MITCHELL-OF/DH
18 BOB SHAW-CH
18 AL WIDMAR-CH
19 RICK AUERBACH-SS
21 CHRIS SHORT-P
21 JOHN VUKOVICH-INF
22 CHARLIE MOORE-C
22 ROB GARDNER-P (2)
23 EDUARDO RODRIGUEZ-P
24 JOE NOSSEK-CH
25 FRANK LINZY-P
26 BOB COLUCCIO-OF/DH
27 CHRIS SHORT-P
29 ED SPRAGUE-P (3)
30 JIM WALTON-CH
31 HARVEY KUENN-CH
32 JOE NOSSEK-CH
32 WILBUR HOWARD-OF/DH
33 CARLOS VELAZQUEZ-P
33 ROB GARDNER-P (2)
34 KEVIN KOBEL-P
38 BILL CHAMPION-P
39 JOHN FELSKE-C/1B
40 JERRY BELL-P
41 JIM SLATON-P
42 SKIP LOCKWOOD-P
43 GARY RYERSON-P
44 GORMAN THOMAS-UTIL
46 KEN REYNOLDS-P
48 JIM COLBORN-P
49 RAY NEWMAN-P
52 BILL PARSONS-P

1974

5TH AL-E 76-86 15GB

1 DEL CRANDALL-MGR
2 BOBBY SHELDON-2B/DH
2 JACK LIND-SS/2B
3 DERON JOHNSON-1B/DH
4 TIM JOHNSON-UTIL
5 GEORGE (BOOMER) SCOTT -1B/DH
6 MIKE HEGAN-UTIL
7 DON (BROOKS) MONEY-3B/UTIL
8 ROB ELLIS-UTIL
9 PETE GARCIA-2B
11 DAVE MAY-OF/DH
12 JOHNNY BRIGGS-OF/DH
14 FELIPE ALOU-OF
14 BOB HANSEN-DH/1B
15 DARRELL PORTER-C/DH
16 KEN BERRY-OF/DH
17 BOBBY MITCHELL-DH/OF
18 AL WIDMAR-CH
19 ROBIN YOUNT-SS
20 BILL CASTRO-P
21 JOHN VUKOVICH-INF
22 CHARLIE MOORE-C/DH
23 EDUARDO RODRIGUEZ-P
24 JOE NOSSEK-CH
25 ED SPRAGUE (INJ)-P
25 BILL TRAVERS-P
26 BOB COLUCCIO-OF/DH
27 BILL CASTRO-P
27 ROGER MILLER-P
29 JIM SLATON-P
29 ED SPRAGUE (INJ)-P
30 JIM WALTON-CH
31 HARVEY KUENN-CH
32 JOE NOSSEK-CH
32 HARVEY KUENN-CH
34 KEVIN KOBEL-P
35 BILL CASTRO-P
35 DICK SELMA-P (2)
37 SIXTO LEZCANO-OF
38 CLYDE WRIGHT-P
39 BILL CHAMPION-P
40 JERRY BELL-P
41 EDUARDO RODRIGUEZ-P
41 JIM SLATON-P
42 TOM MURPHY-P
43 LARRY ANDERSON-P
44 GORMAN THOMAS-OF/DH
46 BILL TRAVERS-P
48 JIM COLBORN (INJ)-P
50 DICK SELMA-P (2)

1975

5TH AL-E 68-94 28GB

1 DEL CRANDALL-MGR1
2 BOBBY SHELDON-2B/DH
2 KURT BEVACQUA-INF/DH
3 GORMAN THOMAS-OF/DH
4 TIM JOHNSON (INJ)-UTIL
5 GEORGE (BOOMER) SCOTT -1B/DH
6 MIKE HEGAN-UTIL
7 DON (BROOKS) MONEY (INJ)-3B/SS
8 ROB ELLIS-UTIL
8 JACK LIND-SS/2B
9 PETE GARCIA (INJ)-2B/DH
11 KURT BEVACQUA-INF/DH
12 JOHNNY BRIGGS (INJ)-OF (1)
12 BOBBY DARWIN (INJ)-OF/DH (2)
15 DARRELL PORTER-C/DH
16 SIXTO LEZCANO-OF/DH
17 BOBBY MITCHELL-OF/DH
18 TOM HAUSMAN (INJ)-P
19 ROBIN YOUNT-SS
20 LAFAYETTE CURRENCE -P
20 BILL CASTRO (INJ)-P
22 CHARLIE MOORE-UTIL
23 EDUARDO RODRIGUEZ (INJ)-P
24 JOE NOSSEK-CH
25 BILL TRAVERS-P
25 TOM HAUSMAN (INJ)-P
26 BOB COLUCCIO-OF (1)
26 BILL SHARP-OF (2)
29 ED SPRAGUE (INJ)-P
30 JIM WALTON-CH
32 HARVEY KUENN-MGR2
33 TOMMY BIANCO-UTIL
35 BILL CASTRO (INJ)-P
36 RICK AUSTIN-P

37 KEN MCBRIDE-CH
38 TOM HAUSMAN (INJ)-P
39 BILL CHAMPION (INJ)-P
40 PETE BROBERG-P
41 JIM SLATON-P
42 TOM MURPHY (INJ)-P
43 LARRY ANDERSON-P
43 RICK AUSTIN-P
44 HANK (HAMMERIN' HANK) AARON-DH/OF
45 LARRY ANDERSON-P
46 JERRY AUGUSTINE-P
46 BILL TRAVERS-P
48 JIM COLBORN-P
49 PAT OSBORN-P

1976

5TH AL-E 66-95 32GB

2 ALEX GRAMMAS-MGR
3 GORMAN THOMAS (INJ)-UTIL
4 TIM JOHNSON (INJ)-UTIL
5 GEORGE (BOOMER) SCOTT-DH
6 MIKE HEGAN-UTIL
7 DON (BROOKS) MONEY-3B/UTIL
8 JACK HEIDEMANN-INF/DH (2)
9 PETE GARCIA (INJ)-2B/DH (1)
9 GARY SUTHERLAND-UTIL (2)
10 ART KUSNYER-C
11 KURT BEVACQUA-INF/DH
11 JIMMY ROSARIO-OF/DH
11 JIM GANTNER-3B/DH
12 BOBBY DARWIN-OF/DH (1)
12 BERNIE CARBO-OF/DH (2)
14 VON JOSHUA-OF/DH (2)
15 DARRELL PORTER-C/DH
16 SIXTO LEZCANO-OF/DH
17 BOB HANSEN-DH/1B
17 STEVE BOWLING-OF/DH
18 TOM HAUSMAN-P
19 ROBIN YOUNT-SS/OF
22 CHARLIE MOORE-UTIL
23 EDUARDO RODRIGUEZ-P
24 JIMMY BRAGAN-CH
25 BILL TRAVERS-P
26 BILL SHARP-OF/DH
27 RAY SADECKI-P (2)
28 VON JOSHUA-OF/DH (2)
29 ED SPRAGUE (INJ)-P
30 MOOSE HAAS-P
31 GARY BEARE-P
31 DANNY (BEAR) FRISELLA-P (2)
32 HARVEY KUENN-CH
34 KEVIN KOBEL-P
34 RAY SADECKI-P (2)
34 DANNY (BEAR) FRISELLA-P (2)
35 BILL CASTRO-P
37 HAL (CURA) SMITH-CH
38 CAL (BUSTER) MCLISH-CH
39 BILL CHAMPION-P
39 DANNY THOMAS-OF
40 PETE BROBERG-P
41 JIM SLATON-P
42 TOM MURPHY-P (1)
42 DANNY (BEAR) FRISELLA-P (2)
43 RICK AUSTIN
44 HANK (HAMMERIN' HANK) AARON-DH/OF
44 *(RET#) HANK AARON*
46 JERRY AUGUSTINE-P
48 JIM COLBORN-P
49 DANNY (BEAR) FRISELLA-P (2)

1977

6TH AL-E 67-95 33GB

1 TIM JOHNSON (INJ)-UTIL
2 ALEX GRAMMAS-MGR
3 ED KIRKPATRICK-UTIL (3)
4 MIKE HEGAN-UTIL
5 JAMIE QUIRK-DH/UTIL
6 SAL BANDO-3B/UTIL
7 DON (BROOKS) MONEY-2B/UTIL
8 JACK HEIDEMANN-DH-2B
8 JIM (THE TOY CANNON) WYNN-OFDH (2)
10 BOB MCCLURE-P
11 STEVE BRYE-OF/DH
12 LARRY HANEY-C
14 JIM WOHLFORD-OF/UTIL
15 CECIL COOPER-1B/DH
16 SIXTO LEZCANO (INJ)-OF
17 KEN MCMULLEN-UTIL
18 BARRY CORT (INJ)-P
19 ROBIN YOUNT-SS
20 DANNY THOMAS-OF/DH
21 LENN SAKATA-2B
21 BOBBY SHELDON-DH/2B
22 CHARLIE MOORE-C
23 EDUARDO RODRIGUEZ-P
24 JIMMY BRAGAN-CH
25 BILL TRAVERS (INJ)-P
26 DICK DAVIS-OF/DH
28 VON JOSHUA-OF
29 GARY BEARE-P
30 MOOSE HAAS-P
31 ED ROMERO-SS
31 JIM GANTNER-3B/DH
32 HARVEY KUENN-CH
33 FRANK (THE CAPITAL PUNISHER)(HONDO) HOWARD-CH
35 BILL CASTRO-P
37 HAL (CURA) SMITH-CH
38 CAL (BUSTER) MCLISH-CH
39 DANNY THOMAS-OF/DH
39 LARY SORENSEN-P
40 SAM HINDS-P
41 JIM SLATON-P
44 *(RET#) HANK AARON*
45 RICH FOLKERS-P
46 JERRY AUGUSTINE-P
48 BOB MCCLURE-P
48 MIKE CLADWELL-P (2)
49 LARY SORENSEN-P
56 DICK DAVIS-OF/DH

1978

3RD AL-E 93-69 6.5GB

1 TIM JOHNSON-SS (1)
1 TIM NORDBROOK (INJ)-SS (2)
2 LENN SAKATA-2B
4 PAUL MOLITOR-2B/UTIL
5 TONY MUSER-1B
6 SAL BANDO-3B/UTIL
7 DON (BROOKS) MONEY-UTIL
8 ANDY ETCHEBARREN (INJ)-C
9 LARRY HISLE-OF/DH
10 BOB MCCLURE-P
11 JEFF YURAK-OF
11 DAVE MAY-OF/DH (1)
11 JIM GANTNER-INF
12 LARRY HANEY-C/CH
(13) RAY FOSSE (INJ)-(C)
14 JIM WOHLFORD-OF/DH
15 CECIL COOPER (INJ)-1B/DH
16 SIXTO LEZCANO (INJ)-OF/DH
17 JIM GANTNER-INF
19 ROBIN YOUNT (INJ)-SS
20 GORMAN THOMAS-OF
21 BUCK MARTINEZ-C
22 CHARLIE MOORE-C
23 EDUARDO RODRIGUEZ-P
24 BEN OGLIVIE-OF/UTIL
25 BILL TRAVERS (INJ)-P
26 DICK DAVIS-OF/DH
27 ANDY REPLOGLE-P
30 MOOSE HAAS (INJ)-P
31 GEORGE BAMBERGER-MGR
32 HARVEY KUENN-CH
33 FRANK (THE CAPITAL PUNISHER)(HONDO) HOWARD-CH
35 BILL CASTRO-P
36 MARK BOMBACK-P
37 BUCK RODGERS-CH
38 CAL (BUSTER) MCLISH-CH
39 LARY SORENSEN-P
40 WILLIE MUELLER-P
40 RANDY STEIN-P
43 RANDY STEIN-P
44 *(RET#) HANK AARON*
46 JERRY AUGUSTINE-P
47 ED FARMER-P
48 MIKE CLADWELL-P
49 ANDY REPLOGLE-P
49 WILLIE MUELLER-P

1979

2ND AL-E 95-66 8GB

1 TIM NORDBROOK-SS
2 LENN SAKATA-2B
4 PAUL MOLITOR-2B/UTIL
6* SAL BANDO-3B/UTIL/P*
7 DON (BROOKS) MONEY (INJ)-DH/INF
9 LARRY HISLE (INJ)-DH/OF
10 BOB MCCLURE-P
12 LARRY HANEY-CH
13 RAY FOSSE-UTIL
13 BOB GALASSO-P
14 JIM WOHLFORD-OF/DH
15 CECIL COOPER-1B/DH
16 SIXTO LEZCANO-OF/DH
17 JIM GANTNER-INF/P
18 BOB GALASSO-P
19 ROBIN YOUNT-SS
20 GORMAN THOMAS-OF/DH
21 BUCK MARTINEZ-C/P
22 CHARLIE MOORE-C
23 REGGIE CLEVELAND-P
24 BEN OGLIVIE-OF/UTIL
25 BILL TRAVERS-P
26 DICK DAVIS-DH/OF
27 ANDY REPLOGLE-P
29 LANCE RAUTZHAN-P (2)
30 MOOSE HAAS-P
31 GEORGE BAMBERGER-MGR
32 HARVEY KUENN-CH
33 FRANK (THE CAPITAL PUNISHER)(HONDO) HOWARD-CH
34 DANNY BOITANO-P
35 BILL CASTRO-P
36 BOB GALASSO-P
37 BUCK RODGERS-CH
38 CAL (BUSTER) MCLISH-CH
39 LARY SORENSEN-P
41 JIM SLATON-P
42 FRANK LACORTE-P (1)
43 PAUL MITCHELL-P (2)
44 *(RET#) HANK AARON*
45 BOB GALASSO-P
46 JERRY AUGUSTINE-P
47 REGGIE CLEVELAND-P
48 MIKE CLADWELL-P
50 ANDY REPLOGLE-P

1980

3RD AL-E 86-76 17GB

4 PAUL MOLITOR (INJ)-2B/UTIL
6 SAL BANDO-UTIL
7 DON (BROOKS) MONEY (INJ)-3B/UTIL
8 JOHN POFF-UTIL
9 LARRY HISLE (INJ)-DH
10 BOB MCCLURE-P
12 LARRY HANEY-CH
15 CECIL COOPER-1B/DH
16 SIXTO LEZCANO (INJ)-OF/DH
17 JIM GANTNER-INF
18 RON HANSEN-CH
19 ROBIN YOUNT-SS/DH
20 GORMAN THOMAS-OF/DH
21 BUCK MARTINEZ-C
22 CHARLIE MOORE-C
23 REGGIE CLEVELAND-P
24 BEN OGLIVIE-OF/DH
25 BILL TRAVERS-P
26 DICK DAVIS-DH/OF
28 VIC HARRIS-UTIL
29 MARK BROUHARD-UTIL
30 MOOSE HAAS-P
31 GEORGE BAMBERGER (ILL)-MGR2
32 HARVEY KUENN-CH
33 FRANK (THE CAPITAL PUNISHER)(HONDO) HOWARD-CH
34 DANNY BOITANO-P
34 ED ROMERO-INF
35 BILL CASTRO-P
37 BUCK RODGERS-MGR1/CH/MGR3
38 CAL (BUSTER) MCLISH-CH
39 LARY SORENSEN-P
40 JOHN FLINN-P
41 JIM SLATON-P
42 DAVE LAPOINT-P
43 PAUL MITCHELL-P
44 *(RET#) HANK AARON*
45 DANNY BOITANO-P
45 BUSTER (RICKEY) KEETON-P
46 JERRY AUGUSTINE-P
47 FRED HOLDSWORTH-P
48 MIKE CLADWELL-P
50 BUSTER (RICKEY) KEETON-P
56 NED YOST-C
62 DAVE LAPOINT-P

1981

1ST 1/2:3RD E 31-25 3GB
2ND 1/2:1ST E 31-22 0GB
FINAL: 62-47 --GB
L ALDS-NYA 3-2

4 PAUL MOLITOR (INJ)-2B/UTIL
5 NED YOST-C
6 SAL BANDO-UTIL
7 DON (BROOKS) MONEY (INJ)-3B/UTIL
9 LARRY HISLE (INJ)-DH
10 BOB MCCLURE (INJ)-P
11 ED ROMERO-INF
12 LARRY HANEY-CH
13 ROY HOWELL-UTIL
15 CECIL COOPER-1B/DH
16 MARSHALL EDWARDS-OF/DH
17 JIM GANTNER-2B
18 RON HANSEN-CH
19 ROBIN YOUNT-SS/DH
20 GORMAN THOMAS-OF/DH
22 CHARLIE MOORE-C
23 REGGIE CLEVELAND-P
23 TED (SIMBA) SIMMONS-C/UTIL
24 BEN OGLIVIE-OF/DH
25 REGGIE CLEVELAND-P
26 DONNIE MOORE-P
27 THAD BOSLEY-OF/DH
27 DONNIE MOORE-P
28 JAMIE EASTERLY-P
29 MARK BROUHARD-
30 MOOSE HAAS-P
32 HARVEY KUENN-CH
34 ROLLIE FINGERS-P
35 RANDY LERCH-P
36 HARRY WARNER-CH
37 BUCK RODGERS-MGR
38 CAL (BUSTER) MCLISH-CH
41 JIM SLATON-P
42 WILLIE MUELLER-P
43 CHUCK PORTER-P
44 *(RET#) HANK AARON*
45 BUSTER (RICKEY) KEETON-P
46 JERRY AUGUSTINE-P
47 DWIGHT BERNARD-P
48 MIKE CLADWELL-P
49 FRANK DIPINO-P
50 PETE VUCKOVICH-P
51 WILLIE MUELLER-P
56 JAMIE EASTERLY-P

1982

1ST E 95-67 0GB
W ALCS-CALA 3-2
L WS-STLN 4-3

4 PAUL MOLITOR (INJ)-3B/UTIL
5 NED YOST-C/DH
7 DON (BROOKS) MONEY-UTIL
8 ROB PICCIOLO-INF/DH (2)
9 LARRY HISLE (INJ)-DH
10 BOB MCCLURE-P
11 ED ROMERO-UTIL
12 LARRY HANEY-CH
13 ROY HOWELL-DH/UTIL
15 CECIL COOPER-1B/DH
16 MARSHALL EDWARDS-OF/DH
17 JIM GANTNER (INJ)-2B
18 RON HANSEN-CH
19 ROBIN YOUNT-SS/DH
20 GORMAN THOMAS-OF
21 DON SUTTON-P (2)
22 CHARLIE MOORE-OF/UTIL
23 TED (SIMBA) SIMMONS-C/D
24 BEN OGLIVIE-OF/DH
26 KEVIN BASS-OF/DH (1)
26 BOB SKUBE-OF/DH
27 PETE LADD-P
28 JAMIE EASTERLY-P
29 MARK BROUHARD-OF/DH
30 MOOSE HAAS-P
32 HARVEY KUENN-CH/MGR2
33 DOC MEDICH-P (2)
34 ROLLIE FINGERS (INJ)-P
35 RANDY LERCH-P
36 HARRY WARNER-CH
37 BUCK RODGERS-MGR1
38 CAL (BUSTER) MCLISH-CH
41 JIM SLATON-P
43 CHUCK PORTER-P
44 *(RET#) HANK AARON*
45 PAT DOBSON-CH
45 DOUG JONES-P
46 JERRY AUGUSTINE-P
47 DWIGHT BERNARD-P
48 MIKE CLADWELL-P
50 PETE VUCKOVICH-P
54 DOUG JONES-P

SEATTLE PILOTS/ MILWAUKEE BREWERS

1983
5TH AL-E 87-75 11GB
1 DAVE GARCIA-CH
2 RANDY READY-DH/3B
4 PAUL MOLITOR-3B/DH
5 NED YOST (INJ)-C
7 DON (BROOKS) MONEY (INJ)-UTIL
8 ROB PICCIOLO-INF/DH
9 JOE TORRE-MGR
10 BOB MCCLURE-P
11 ED ROMERO-UTIL
12 LARRY HANEY-CH
13 ROY HOWELL-DH
14 DION JAMES-OF/DH
15 CECIL COOPER-1B/DH
16 MARSHALL EDWARDS-OF/DH
17 JIM GANTNER-2B
18 RON HANSEN-CH
19 ROBIN YOUNT-SS/DH
20 GORMAN THOMAS-OF (1)
20 DON SUTTON-P
21 DON SUTTON-P
22 CHARLIE MOORE-OF/UTIL
23 TED (SIMBA) SIMMONS-C/DH
24 BEN OGLIVIE-OF/DH
26 BOB SKUBE-UTIL
26 ANDY BEENE-P
27 PETE LADD-P
28 JAMIE EASTERLY-P (1)
28 RICK MANNING-OF (2)
29 MARK BROUHARD (INJ)-OF/DH
30 MOOSE HAAS-P
32 HARVEY KUENN-MGR
(34) ROLLIE FINGERS (INJ)-(P)
36 RICK WAITS (INJ)-P (2)
39 BILL SCHROEDER-C
40 BOB GIBSON-P
41 JIM SLATON-P
42 TOM TELLMAN-P
43 CHUCK PORTER-P
44 *(RET#) HANK AARON*
45 PAT DOBSON-CH
46 JERRY AUGUSTINE (INJ)-P
47 JAIME COCANOWER-P
48 MIKE CLADWELL-P
49 TOM CANDIOTTI-P
50 PETE VUCKOVICH (INJ)-P
54 ANDY BEENE-P

1984
7TH AL-E 67-94 36.5GB
1 DAVE GARCIA-CH
2 RANDY READY-3B
4 PAUL MOLITOR (INJ)-3B/DH
5 DOUG LOMAN-OF
8 JIM SUNDBERG (INJ)-C
9 RENE LACHEMANN-MGR
10 BOB MCCLURE-P
11 ED ROMERO-UTIL
12 LARRY HANEY-CH
13 ROY HOWELL-UTIL
14 DION JAMES-OF
15 CECIL COOPER-1B/DH
17 JIM GANTNER-2B
19 ROBIN YOUNT-SS/DH
20 DON SUTTON-P
21 BILL SCHROEDER-UTIL
21 JIM KERN-P (2)
22 CHARLIE MOORE-OF/C
23 TED (SIMBA) SIMMONS-DH/INF
24 BEN OGLIVIE-OF/DH
25 BOBBY CLARK (INJ)-OF
26 ANDY BEENE-P
26 WILLIE LOZADO-INF/DH
27 PETE LADD-P
28 RICK MANNING-OF/DH
29 MARK BROUHARD-OF/DH
30 MOOSE HAAS-P
31 JIM KERN-P (2)
33 JACK LAZORKO-P
34 ROLLIE FINGERS (INJ)-P
35 TOM TREBELHORN-CH
36 RICK WAITS-P
39 PAUL HARTZELL-P
40 BOB GIBSON-P
41 JACK LAZORKO-P
41 RAY SEARAGE-P
42 TOM TELLMAN-P
43 CHUCK PORTER (INJ)-P
44 *(RET#) HANK AARON*
45 PAT DOBSON-CH
46 JERRY AUGUSTINE-P
46 ANDY BEENE-P
47 JAIME COCANOWER-P
48 MIKE CLADWELL(INJ)-P
49 TOM CANDIOTTI (INJ)-P
(50) PETE VUCKOVICH (INJ)-(P)

1985
6TH AL-E 71-90 28GB
1 ERNEST RILES-SS/DH
2 RANDY READY (INJ)-UTIL
4 PAUL MOLITOR-3B/DH
5 DOUG LOMAN-OF
7 PAUL HOUSEHOLDER-OF/DH
8 ANDY ETCHEBARREN-CH
9 BILLY JO ROBIDOUX-UTIL
10 BOB MCCLURE-P
11 ED ROMERO-UTIL
12 LARRY HANEY-CH
14 DION JAMES (INJ)-OF/DH
15 CECIL COOPER-1B/DH
16 MIKE FELDER-OF
17 JIM GANTNER-2B/INF
18 DANNY DARWIN-P
19 ROBIN YOUNT-OF/UTIL
20 RAY BURRIS-P
20 RICK WAITS-P
21 BILL SCHROEDER (INJ)-UTIL
22 CHARLIE MOORE-C/OF
23 TED (SIMBA) SIMMONS-DH/UTIL
24 BEN OGLIVIE-OF/DH
25 BOBBY CLARK-OF
26 BRIAN GILES-INF/DH
27 PETE LADD-P
28 RICK MANNING-OF/DH
29 MARK BROUHARD-OF/DH
30 MOOSE HAAS-P
31 GEORGE BAMBERGER-MGR
33 FRANK (THE CAPITAL PUNISHER)(HONDO) HOWARD-CH
34 ROLLIE FINGERS (INJ)-P
35 TONY MUSER-CH
36 RICK WAITS-P
36 CARLOS PONCE-UTIL
37 JIM KERN-P
37 BRAD LESLEY-P
38 HERMAN STARRETTE-CH
39 TIM LEARY-P
40 BOB GIBSON-P
41 RAY SEARAGE-P
42 JIM KERN-P
42 DAVE HUPPERT-C
43 CHUCK PORTER (INJ)-P
44 *(RET#) HANK AARON*
45 ANDY ETCHEBARREN-CH
46 BILL WEGMAN-P
47 JAIME COCANOWER-P
48 RAY BURRIS-P
49 TEDDY HIGUERA-P
50 PETE VUCKOVICH (INJ)-P
55 TEDDY HIGUERA-P
58 ERNEST RILES-SS/DH

1986
6TH AL-E 91-71 7GB
1 ERNEST RILES-SS
2 RANDY READY-UTIL (1)
2 EDDIE DIAZ-SS
3 JUAN CASTILLO-UTIL
4 PAUL MOLITOR (INJ)-3B/UTIL
5 RICK CERONE-C
7 PAUL HOUSEHOLDER-OF/DH
8 ANDY ETCHEBARREN-CH
9 JIM ADDUCI-1B
10 BOB MCCLURE-P (1)
10 JUAN NIEVES-P
11 RICK CERONE-C
12 LARRY HANEY-CH
13 BILLY JO ROBIDOUX (INJ)-1B/DH
15 CECIL COOPER-1B/DH
16 MIKE FELDER (INJ)-OF/DH
17 JIM GANTNER-2B/UTIL
18 DANNY DARWIN-P (1)
19 ROBIN YOUNT-OF/UTIL
20 JUAN NIEVES-P
20 GORMAN THOMAS-DH/1B (2)
21 BILL SCHROEDER-UTIL
22 CHARLIE MOORE-C/UTIL
24 BEN OGLIVIE-OF/DH
25 MARK CLEAR-P
26 GLENN BRAGGS-OF/DH
27 DALE SVEUM-INF
28 RICK MANNING-OF/DH
29 CHRIS BOSIO-P
30 STEVE KIEFER-SS
31 GEORGE BAMBERGER-MGR1
32 TOM TREBELHORN-CH/MGR2
33 FRANK (THE CAPITAL PUNISHER)(HONDO) HOWARD-CH
34 JOHN HENRY JOHNSON-P
35 TONY MUSER-CH
36 GLENN BRAGGS-OF/DH
37 DAN PLESAC-P
38 HERMAN STARRETTE-CH
39 TIM LEARY-P
40 BOB GIBSON-P
41 RAY SEARAGE-P (1)
41 MIKE BIRKBECK-P
41 MARK KNUDSON-P (2)
42 TOM TREBELHORN-MGR2
44 *(RET#) HANK AARON*
45 ROB DEER-OF/1B
46 BILL WEGMAN-P
47 JAIME COCANOWER-P
48 BRYAN CLUTTERBUCK-P
49 TEDDY HIGUERA-P
50 PETE VUCKOVICH (RET)-P

1987
3RD AL-E 91-71 7GB
1 ERNEST RILES (INJ)-3B/SS
3 JUAN CASTILLO-2B/INF
4 PAUL MOLITOR (INJ)-DH/INF
5 B. J. SURHOFF-C/UTIL
7 DALE SVEUM-SS/2B
8 ANDY ETCHEBARREN-CH
9 GREG BROCK-1B
10 DAVE HILTON-CH
11 CHARLIE O'BRIEN-C
12 LARRY HANEY-CH
13 BILLY JO ROBIDOUX-1B/DH
14 JIM PACIOREK-UTIL
15 CECIL COOPER-DH
16 MIKE FELDER-UTIL
17 JIM GANTNER (INJ)-INF/DH
19 ROBIN YOUNT-OF/DH
20 JUAN NIEVES-P
21 BILL SCHROEDER-UTIL
22 STEVE STANICEK-DH
24 CHUCK (TWIGGY) HARTENSTEIN-CH
25 MARK CLEAR-P
26 GLENN BRAGGS-OF/DH
27 PAUL MIRABELLA-P
28 RICK MANNING-OF/DH
29 CHRIS BOSIO-P
30 STEVE KIEFER-3B/2B
31 ALEX MADRID-P
32 CHUCK CRIM-P
34 MARK CIARDI-P
35 TONY MUSER-CH
36 BRAD KOMMINSK-OF/DH
37 DAN PLESAC-P
38 JOHN HENRY JOHNSON-P
39 LEN BARKER
40 MIKE BIRKBECK (INJ)-P
41 MARK KNUDSON-P
42 TOM TREBELHORN-MGR
43 DAVE STAPLETON-P
44 *(RET#) HANK AARON*
45 ROB DEER-OF/UTIL
46 BILL WEGMAN-P
48 RAY BURRIS (RET)-P
48 JAY ALDRICH-P
49 TEDDY HIGUERA-P
61 ALEX MADRID-P
63 JAY ALDRICH-P

1988
3RD AL-E (TIE) 87-75 2GB
00 JEFFREY LEONARD-OF/DH (2)
1 ERNEST RILES-INF/DH (1)
1 GARY SHEFFIELD-SS
2 MIKE YOUNG-DH/OF
3 JUAN CASTILLO (INJ)-INF/DH
4 PAUL MOLITOR-3B/UTIL
5 B. J. SURHOFF-C/UTIL
7 DALE SVEUM (INJ)-SS/UTIL
8 ANDY ETCHEBARREN-CH
9 GREG BROCK (INJ)-1B/DH
10 DAVE HILTON-CH
11 CHARLIE O'BRIEN-C
12 LARRY HANEY-CH
13 BILLY JO ROBIDOUX-1B/DH
14 JIM ADDUCI-UTIL
16 MIKE FELDER (INJ)-UTIL
17 JIM GANTNER-2B/3B
18 DARRYL HAMILTON-OF/DH
19 ROBIN YOUNT-OF/DH
20 JUAN NIEVES (INJ)-P
21 BILL SCHROEDER (INJ)-UTIL
(22) STEVE STANICEK (INJ)-(DH)
22 CHARLIE O'BRIEN-C
23 JOEY MEYER-DH/1B
24 CHUCK (TWIGGY) HARTENSTEIN-CH
25 MARK CLEAR (INJ)-P
26 GLENN BRAGGS (INJ)-OF/DH
27 PAUL MIRABELLA-P
28 ODELL JONES-P
29 CHRIS BOSIO-P
30 STEVE KIEFER-2B/3B
32 CHUCK CRIM-P
35 TONY MUSER-CH
37 DAN PLESAC-P
38 DON AUGUST-P
39 TOM FILER (INJ)-P
40 MIKE BIRKBECK-P
41 MARK KNUDSON-P
42 TOM TREBELHORN-MGR
43 DAVE STAPLETON (INJ)-P
44 *(RET#) HANK AARON*
45 ROB DEER-OF/DH
46 BILL WEGMAN-P
49 TEDDY HIGUERA-P

1989
4TH AL-E 81-81 8GB
1 GARY SHEFFIELD-SS
3 JUAN CASTILLO-2B
4 PAUL MOLITOR-3B/UTIL
5 B. J. SURHOFF-C/UTIL
6 BILL SPIERS-SS/UTIL
(7) DALE SVEUM (INJ)-(SS)
8 ANDY ETCHEBARREN-CH
9 GREG BROCK (INJ)-1B/DH
10 GUS POLIDOR-INF/DH
10 DUFFY DYER-CH
11 LAVEL FREEMAN-DH
11 GREG VAUGHN-OF/DH
12 LARRY HANEY-CH
14 GUS POLIDOR-INF/DH
15 ED ROMERO-INF (3)
16 MIKE FELDER-UTIL
17 JIM GANTNER (INJ)-2B/DH
19 ROBIN YOUNT-OF/DH
(20) JUAN NIEVES (INJ)-(P)
21 JERRY REUSS-P (2)
22 CHARLIE O'BRIEN-C
23 JOEY MEYER-DH/1B
24 CHUCK (TWIGGY) HARTENSTEIN-CH
25 DAVE ENGLE-UTIL
26 GLENN BRAGGS-OF/DH
27 PAUL MIRABELLA-P
28 JEFF PETEREK-P
29 CHRIS BOSIO-P
30 TERRY FRANCONA-UTIL/P
31 DUFFY DYER-CH
31 JAIME NAVARRO-P
32 CHUCK CRIM-P
33 JAY ALDRICH-P (1)
33 GEORGE CANALE-1B
34 BILLY BATES (INJ)-2B
35 TONY MUSER-CH
36 TONY FOSSAS-P
36 RAY KRAWCZYK-P
37 DAN PLESAC-P
38 DON AUGUST-P
39 TOM FILER (INJ)-P
40 MIKE BIRKBECK (INJ-P
41 MARK KNUDSON-P
42 TOM TREBELHORN-MGR
43 RANDY VERES-P
44 *(RET#) HANK AARON*
45 ROB DEER-OF/DH
46 BILL WEGMAN (INJ)-P
47 BILL KRUEGER-P
48 BRYAN CLUTTERBUCK (INJ)-P
49 TEDDY HIGUERA (INJ)-P
51 JAIME NAVARRO-P

1990
6TH AL-E 74-88 14GB
2 EDDIE (KIKI) DIAZ-INF/DH
4 PAUL MOLITOR (INJ)-INF/DH
5 B. J. SURHOFF-C/3B
6 BILL SPIERS (INJ)-SS
7 DALE SVEUM-INF
8 ANDY ETCHEBARREN-CH
9 GREG BROCK-1B
10 DUFFY DYER-CH
11 GARY SHEFFIELD-3B
12 LARRY HANEY-CH
14 GUS POLIDOR-INF
14 JULIO MACHADO-P (2)
16 MIKE FELDER-UTIL
17 JIM GANTNER (INJ)-2B/3B
18 DARRYL HAMILTON-OF/DH
19 ROBIN YOUNT-OF/DH

(20) JUAN NIEVES (INJ)-(P)
21 KEVIN BROWN-P (2)
22 CHARLIE O'BRIEN-C (1)
22 GEORGE CANALE-1B/DH
23 GREG VAUGHN-OF/DH
24 CHUCK (TWIGGY) HARTENSTEIN-CH
24 DARRYL HAMILTON-OF/DH
25 DON BAYLOR-CH
26 GLENN BRAGGS-OF/DH (1)
26 TIM MCINTOSH-C
27 PAUL MIRABELLA-P
28 TOM FILER (INJ)-P
29 CHRIS BOSIO (INJ)-P
30 TERRY FRANCONA-1B/DH
30 TOM EDENS-P
30 KEVIN BROWN-P (2)
30 BOB SEBRA-P
31 JAIME NAVARRO-P
32 CHUCK CRIM-P
33 GEORGE CANALE-1B/DH
33 RON ROBINSON-P (2)
34 BILLY BATES-2B (1)
34 MARK LEE-P
34 DENNIS POWELL-P (2)
35 NARCISO ELVIRA-P
35 MIKE CAPEL-P
36 TONY FOSSAS-P
37 DAN PLESAC-P
38 DON AUGUST-P
38 RON ROBINSON-P (2)
39 DAVE PARKER-DH/1B
41 MARK KNUDSON-P
42 TOM TREBELHORN-MGR
43 RANDY VERES-P
44 *(RET#) HANK AARON*
45 ROB DEER-OF/UTIL
46 BILL WEGMAN (INJ)-P
47 BILL KRUEGER-P
48 TOM EDENS-P
49 TEDDY HIGUERA-P
50 MARK LEE-P
50 KEVIN BROWN-P (2)
50 RAY BURRIS-CH
53 NARCISO ELVIRA-P

1991

4TH AL-E 83-79 8GB

3 DANTE BICHETTE-OF/3B
4 PAUL MOLITOR-DH/1B
5 B. J. SURHOFF-C/UTIL
6 BILL SPIERS-SS/UTIL
7 DALE SVEUM-INF/DH
8 ANDY ETCHEBARREN-CH
9 GREG BROCK-1B
10 DUFFY DYER-CH
11 GARY SHEFFIELD (INJ)-3B/DH
12 LARRY HANEY-CH
13 FRED (CHICKEN) STANLEY-CH
14 RICK DEMPSEY-C/1B/P
17 JIM GANTNER-3B/2B
18 JIM OLANDER-OF/DH
18 JULIO MACHADO-P
19 ROBIN YOUNT-OF/DH
20 KEVIN BROWN-P
21 CAL ELDRED-P
22 CANDY MALDONADO (INJ)-OF/DH (1)
22 GEORGE CANALE-1B
23 GREG VAUGHN-OF/DH
24 DARRYL HAMILTON-OF
25 DON BAYLOR-CH
26 TIM MCINTOSH-UTIL
28 DOUG HENRY-P
29 CHRIS BOSIO (INJ)-P
30 KEVIN BROWN-P
30 WILLIE RANDOLPH-2B/DH
31 JAIME NAVARRO-P
32 CHUCK CRIM-P
33 RON ROBINSON (INJ)-P
34 MARK LEE-P
37 DAN PLESAC-P
38 DON AUGUST-P
39 MATIAS CARILLO
40 DARREN HOLMES-P
41 MARK KNUDSON (INJ)-P
42 TOM TREBELHORN-MGR
43 JIM HUNTER-P
44 *(RET#) HANK AARON*
45 EDWIN NUNEZ (INJ)-P
46 BILL WEGMAN-P
47 JIM AUSTIN (INJ)-P
48 JULIO MACHADO-P
49 TEDDY HIGUERA (INJ)-P
50 RAY BURRIS-CH
53 MIKE IGNASIAK (INJ)-P
59 CHRIS GEORGE-P

1992

2ND AL-E 92-70 4GB

0 FRANKLIN STUBBS-1B/OF
2 WILLIAM SUERO-2B/SS
3 PHIL GARNER-MGR
4 PAUL MOLITOR-DH/1B
5 B. J. SURHOFF-C/UTIL
6 ANDY ALLANSON-C
7 DALE SVEUM-INF/DH
8 DANTE BICHETTE-OF
9 BILL SPIERS-INF
10 DUFFY DYER-CH
11 DAVE NILSSON-C/1B
12 SCOTT FLETCHER-2B/INF
13 DAVE NILSSON-C/1B
14 TIM FOLI-CH
16 PAT LISTACH-SS/UTIL
17 JIM GANTNER-INF
18 ALEX DIAZ-OF
19 ROBIN YOUNT-OF/DH
20 KEVIN SEITZER-3B/INF
21 CAL ELDRED-P
22 MIKE EASLER-CH
23 GREG VAUGHN-OF/DH
24 DARRYL HAMILTON-OF
25 RICKY BONES-P
26 TIM MCINTOSH-UTIL
27 NEAL HEATON-P
28 DOUG HENRY-P
29 CHRIS BOSIO-P
30 BRUCE RUFFIN-P
31 JAIME NAVARRO-P
32 JOHN JAHA-1B/DH
33 RON ROBINSON-P
35 BILL CASTRO-CH
36 MIKE FETTERS-P
37 DAN PLESAC-P
39 JIM TATUM-3B
40 DARREN HOLMES-P
41 EDWIN NUNEZ-P
42 JIM AUSTIN-P
44 *(RET#) HANK AARON*
45 DON ROWE-CH
45 EDWIN NUNEZ-P
46 BILL WEGMAN-P
47 JESSE OROSCO-P
54 JOSE VALENTIN-2B/3B

1993

7TH AL-E 69-93 26GB

1 ALEX DIAZ (INJ)-OF/DH
2 WILLIAM SUERO-2B/3B
2 JOSE VALENTIN-SS
3 PHIL GARNER-MGR
5 B. J. SURHOFF-3B/UTIL
8 DICKIE THON-INF/DH
9 BILL SPIERS-2B/UTIL
10 DUFFY DYER-CH
11 DAVE NILSSON (INJ)-C/UTIL
12 GENE CLINES-CH
13 BILL DORAN (INJ)-2B/1B
14 TIM FOLI-CH
16 PAT LISTACH (INJ)-SS/OF
18 TOM (BRUNO) BRUNANSKY (INJ)-OF/DH
19 ROBIN YOUNT-OF/UTIL
20 KEVIN SEITZER-UTIL (2)
21 CAL ELDRED-P
22 TOM LAMPKIN-UTIL
23 GREG VAUGHN-OF/DH
24 DARRYL HAMILTON-OF/DH
25 RICKY BONES-P
26 TIM MCINTOSH-C (1)
26 JUAN BELL-UTIL (2)
27 JOE KMAK-C
28 DOUG HENRY-P
29 KEVIN REIMER-DH/OF
30 MATT MIESKE-OF
31 JAIME NAVARRO-P
32 JOHN JAHA-1B/INF
33 TROY O'LEARY-OF
35 BILL CASTRO-CH
36 MIKE FETTERS-P
37 GRAEME LLOYD-P
38 ANGEL MIRANDA (INJ)-P
39 RAFAEL NOVOA-P
40 MIKE IGNASIAK-P
42 JIM AUSTIN-P
43 MARK KIEFER-P
44 *(RET#) HANK AARON*
45 DON ROWE-CH
46 BILL WEGMAN (INJ)-P
47 JESSE OROSCO-P
48 CARLOS MALDONADO-P
49 TEDDY HIGUERA (INJ)-P
50 MATT MAYSEY-P
51 JOSIAS MANZANILLO-P (1)
52 CARLOS MALDONADO-P
52 MIKE BODDICKER (INJ)-P (2)

1994

5TH AL-C 53-62 15GB
STRIKE NO POST-SEASON

1 ALEX DIAZ (INJ)-OF/DH
2 JOSE VALENTIN-SS
3 PHIL GARNER-MGR
5 B. J. SURHOFF (INJ)-UTIL
8 JODY REED-2B
9 BILL SPIERS-3B
10 DUFFY DYER-CH
11 DAVE NILSSON-C/UTIL
12 BRIAN HARPER (INJ)-C/DH
14 TIM FOLI-CH
15 GENE CLINES-CH
15 MIKE MATHENY-C
16 PAT LISTACH (INJ)-SS
18 TOM (BRUNO) BRUNANSKY (INJ)-OF/DH (1)
18 DAVE VALLE (INJ)-C (2)
18 DUANE SINGLETON-OF
19 *(RET#) ROBIN YOUNT*
20 KEVIN SEITZER (INJ)-UTIL
21 CAL ELDRED-P
22 MIKE MATHENY-C
23 GREG VAUGHN (INJ)-DH/OF
24 DARRYL HAMILTON (INJ)-OF/DH
25 RICKY BONES-P
26 JEFF CIRILLO-3B
27 TURNER WARD-OF
28 DOUG HENRY (INJ)-P
29 JEFF BRONKEY (INJ)-P
30 MATT MIESKE-OF
31 JAIME NAVARRO-P
32 JOHN JAHA-1B/INF
33 TROY O'LEARY-OF
34 *(RET#) ROLLIE FINGERS*
35 BILL CASTRO-CH
36 MIKE FETTERS-P
37 GRAEME LLOYD-P
38 ANGEL MIRANDA (INJ)-P
39 BOB SCANLON-P
40 MIKE IGNASIAK (INJ)-P
41 JOSE MERCEDES (INJ)-P
42 RICK WRONA-C
43 MARK KIEFER-P
44 *(RET#) HANK AARON*
45 DON ROWE-CH
46 BILL WEGMAN (INJ)-P
47 JESSE OROSCO-P
49 TEDDY HIGUERA-P

1995

4TH AL-C 65-79 35GB
144 GAME SEASON

1 FERNANDO VINA-2B
2 JOSE VALENTIN-SS
3 PHIL GARNER-MGR
5 B. J. SURHOFF-1B
8 TIM UNROE-1B
8 MARK LORETTA-SS
9 JOE OLIVER (INJ)-C
10 DUFFY DYER-CH
11 DAVE NILSSON-OF
12 DERRICK MAY-OF (1)
13 BRIAN GIVENS-P
14 TIM FOLI-CH
15 DAVID HULSE-OF
16 PAT LISTACH-2B
18 DUANE SINGLETON-OF
19 *(RET#) ROBIN YOUNT*
20 KEVIN SEITZER-UTIL
21 CAL ELDRED (INJ)-P
22 MIKE MATHENY-C
23 GREG VAUGHN-DH
24 DARRYL HAMILTON-OF
25 RICKY BONES-P
26 JEFF CIRILLO-3B
27 TURNER WARD (INJ)-OF
28 LAMAR JOHNSON-CH
29 JEFF BRONKEY (INJ)-P
30 MATT MIESKE-OF
31 JAMIE MCANDREW (INJ)-P
32 JOHN JAHA-1B
33 RON RIGHTNOWAR-P
34 *(RET#) ROLLIE FINGERS*
35 BILL CASTRO-CH
36 MIKE FETTERS (INJ)-P
37 GRAEME LLOYD (INJ)-P
38 ANGEL MIRANDA (INJ)-P
39 BOB SCANLON (INJ)-P
40 MIKE IGNASIAK (INJ)-P
41 JOSE MERCEDES (INJ)-P
42 SCOTT KARL-P
43 MARK KIEFER-P
44 *(RET#) HANK AARON*
45 DON ROWE-CH
46 BILL WEGMAN-P
47 AL REYES (INJ)-P
48 JOE SLUSARSKI-P
49 JAMIE MCANDREW (INJ)-P
49 RON DIBBLE-P (2)
49 BRAD WOODALL-P
50 STEVE SPARKS-P
51 SID ROBERSON-P
52 KEVIN WICKANDER-P (2)
53 MIKE THOMAS (INJ)-P

1996

3RD AL-C 80-82 19.5GB

1 FERNANDO VINA-2B
2 JOSE VALENTIN-SS
3 PHIL GARNER-MGR
4 PAT LISTACH (INJ)-2B
7 DANNY PEREZ-PH
7 BRIAN BANKS-OF
8 MARK LORETTA-SS
9 TIM UNROE-1B
10 MARC NEWFIELD-OF (2)
11 KELLY STINNETT-C
12 CHRIS BANDO-CH
13 BRIAN GIVENS-P
14 DAVE NILSSON (INJ)-1B
15 DAVID HULSE (INJ)-OF
16 JESSE LEVIS-C
17 JIM GANTNER-CH
18 KEVIN KOSLOSKI-OF
18 TODD DUNN-OF
19 *(RET#) ROBIN YOUNT*
20 KEVIN SEITZER-1B (1)
20 JEROMY BURNITZ-OF (2)
21 CAL ELDRED (INJ)-P
22 MIKE MATHENY-C
23 GREG VAUGHN-DH (1)
24 CHUCK CARR (INJ)-OF
25 RICKY BONES-P (1)
26 JEFF CIRILLO-3B
27 TURNER WARD (INJ)-OF
28 LAMAR JOHNSON-CH
29 GERALD WILLIAMS-OF (2)
30 MATT MIESKE-OF
(31) JAMIE MCANDREW (INJ)-(P)
31 TIM VANEGMOND-P
32 JOHN JAHA-1B
33 JEFF D'AMICO-P
34 *(RET#) ROLLIE FINGERS*
35 BILL CASTRO-CH
36 MIKE FETTERS-P
37 GRAEME LLOYD-P (1)
37 BOB WICKMAN-P (2)
38 ANGEL MIRANDA-P
39 TERRY BURROWS-P
39 BRYCE FLORIE-P (2)
40 BEN MCDONALD-P
41 JOSE MERCEDES-P
42 SCOTT KARL-P
43 MARK KIEFER-P
43 DOUG JONES-P (2)
44 *(RET#) HANK AARON*
45 DON ROWE-CH
46 CRIS CARPENTER-P
47 AL REYES-P
48 MARSHALL BOZE-P
49 MIKE POTTS-P
49 RON VILLONE-P (2)
50 STEVE SPARKS-P
51 RAMON GARCIA-P
52 KEVIN WICKANDER (INJ) (REL)-P

1997

3RD AL-C 78-83 8GB

1 FERNANDO VINA (INJ)-2B
2 JOSE VALENTIN (INJ)-SS
3 PHIL GARNER-MGR
5 KELLY STINNETT (INJ)-C
7 BRIAN BANKS-1B
7 CHUCK TANNER-CH
8 MARK LORETTA-SS
9 TIM UNROE-1B
10 MARC NEWFIELD (INJ)-OF
11 ANTONE WILLIAMSON-1B
12 CHRIS BANDO-CH
13 JEFF D'AMICO (INJ)-P
14 DAVE NILSSON-DH
15 JEFF HUSON-2B
16 JESSE LEVIS-C
17 JIM GANTNER-CH
18 TODD DUNN-OF
19 *(RET#) ROBIN YOUNT*
20 JEROMY BURNITZ-OF
21 CAL ELDRED-P
22 MIKE MATHENY-C
24 CHUCK CARR (REL)-OF (1)
24 DARRIN JACKSON-OF (2)
25 ANGEL MIRANDA (INJ)(REL)-P
25 JULIO FRANCO-DH (2)
26 JEFF CIRILLO-3B
27 BOB WICKMAN-P
28 LAMAR JOHNSON-CH
28 JACK VOIGT-OF/1B

SEATTLE PILOTS/
MILWAUKEE BREWERS

29 GERALD WILLIAMS-OF
30 MATT MIESKE (INJ)-OF
31 PETE HARNISCH-P (2)
32 JOHN JAHA (INJ)-1B
33 JAMIE MCANDREW-P
34 *(RET#) ROLLIE FINGERS*
35 BILL CASTRO-CH
36 MIKE FETTERS (INJ)-P
37 MARK DAVIS-P
37 STEVE WOODARD (INJ)-P
38 JOEL ADAMSON-P
39 BRYCE FLORIE (INJ)-P
40 BEN MCDONALD (INJ)-P
41 JOSE MERCEDES-P
42 SCOTT KARL-P
43 DOUG JONES-P
44 *(RET#) HANK AARON*
45 DON ROWE-CH
46 SEAN MALONEY-P
46 PAUL WAGNER-P (2)
47 AL REYES-P
48 STEVE WOODARD (INJ)-P
48 MARK DAVIS-P
49 RON VILLONE-P
(50) STEVE SPARKS (INJ)-(P)
51 EDDY DIAZ-2B
52 MIKE MISURACA-P
53 GREG HANSELL-P

1998

5TH NL-C 74-88 28GB

1 FERNANDO VINA-2B
2 JOSE VALENTIN-SS
3 PHIL GARNER-MGR
5 GEOFF JENKINS-OF
7 DAVE NILSSON (INJ)-OF
8 MARK LORETTA-SS
9 MARQUIS GRISSOM-OF
10 MARC NEWFIELD-OF
11 RONNIE BELLIARD-INF
12 CHRIS BANDO-CH
(13) JEFF D'AMICO (INJ)-(P)
14 JEFF JUDEN (WAIV)-P (1)
16 JESSE LEVIS (INJ)-C
(18) TODD DUNN (INJ)-(OF)
19 *(RET#) ROBIN YOUNT*
20 JEROMY BURNITZ-OF
21 CAL ELDRED (INJ)-P
22 MIKE MATHENY (INJ)-C
23 LAMAR JOHNSON-CH
23 MARCUS JENSEN-C
24 DARREN JACKSON (INJ)-OF
25 BRIAN BANKS-OF/C/3B
26 JEFF CIRILLO-3B
27 BOB WICKMAN-P
28 MIKE MYERS-P
29 JIM LEFEBVRE-CH
30 MIKE (HAMMER) HAMLIN-1B
31 BRONSON PATRICK-P
32 JOHN JAHA (INJ)-1B
33 BOBBY HUGHES-C
34 *(RET#) ROLLIE FINGERS*
35 BILL CASTRO-CH
36 JOEL YOUNGBLOOD-CH
37 STEVE WOODARD-P
38 DOUG MANSOLINO-CH
39 ERIC OWENS-OF
39 ERIC PLUNK-P (2)
40 CHAD FOX (INJ)-P
41 JOSE MERCEDES
42 SCOTT KARL-P
43 DOUG JONES-P (1)
43 JOE HUDSON-P
44 *(RET#) HANK AARON*
45 DON ROWE-CH
46 PAUL WAGNER (INJ)(REL)-P
46 BILL PULSIPHER-P
47 AL REYES (INJ)-P
48 BRAD WOODALL-P
49 DAVID WEATHERS-P (2)
50 GREG MARTINEZ-OF
52 BOBBY CHOUINARD (WAIV)-P (1)
52 TRAVIS SMITH
52 RAFAEL ROQUE-P
53 ROD HENDERSON-P
57 GREGORY MULLINS-P
58 VALERIO DE LOS SANTOS-P
63 BRAD WOODALL-P

1999

5TH NL-C 74-87 22.5GB

1 FERNANDO VINA (INJ)-2B
2 JOSE VALENTIN (INJ)-SS
3 PHIL GARNER-MGR1
4 *(RET#) PAUL MOLITOR*
5 GEOFF JENKINS-OF
7 SEAN BERRY-3B
8 MARK LORETTA-SS
9 MARQUIS GRISSOM-OF
10 RONNIE BELLIARD-INF
11 HIDEO NOMO-P
12 BOB MELVIN-CH
13 JEFF D'AMICO (INJ)-P
14 DAVE NILSSON (INJ)-OF
16 LOU COLLIER-SS
18 CHARLIE GREEN-C
19 *(RET#) ROBIN YOUNT*
20 JEROMY BURNITZ-OF
21 CAL ELDRED (INJ)-P
22 RICH BECKER-OF (1)
23 BRIAN BANKS-OF/C/3B
24 ALEX OCHOA-OF
25 JIM ABBOTT-P
26 JEFF CIRILLO-3B
27 BOB WICKMAN-P
28 MIKE MYERS-P
29 JIM LEFEBVRE-CH/MGR2
30 RON JACKSON-CH
31 BOBBY HUGHES (INJ)-C
32 ROCKY COPPINGER-P (2)
33 LYLE MOUTON-OF
34 *(RET#) ROLLIE FINGERS*
35 BILL CASTRO-CH
36 DOUG MANSOLINO-CH
37 STEVE WOODARD-P
38 ERIC PLUNK-P
39 BILL CAMPBELL-CH
40 CHAD FOX (INJ)-P
41 KYLE PETERSON-P
42 SCOTT KARL-P
43 JIM PITTSLEY-P (2)
44 *(RET#) HANK AARON*
45 REGGIE HARRIS-P
45 EDDIE ZOSKY-2B
46 BILL PULSIPHER (INJ)-P
47 AL REYES-P (1)
47 EDDIE ZOSKY-2B
47 JASON BERE-P (2)
48 STEVE FALTEISEK-P
49 DAVID WEATHERS-P
50 ROBINSON CANCEL-C
51 HORACIO ESTRADA-P
51 CARL DALE-P
52 RAFAEL ROQUE-P
53 ROD HENDERSON-P
54 HECTOR RAMIREZ-P
58 VALERIO DE LOS SANTOS-P

2000

3RD NL-C 73-89 22GB

00 CURTIS LESKANIC-P
1 LUIS M. LOPEZ-INF
2 TYLER HOUSTON-INF
3 JERRY ROYSTER-CH
4 *(RET#) PAUL MOLITOR*
5 GEOFF JENKINS-OF
7 SEAN BERRY-3B (1)
8 MARK LORETTA-SS
9 MARQUIS GRISSOM-OF
10 RONNIE BELLIARD-INF
11 RICHIE SEXSON-OF (2)
12 HENRY BLANCO-C
13 JEFF D'AMICO (INJ)-P
14 CHARLIE HAYES-INF
15 B. J. SURHOFF-OF (2)
16 LOU COLLIER-SS
18 JOSE HERNANDEZ-INF
19 *(RET#) ROBIN YOUNT*
20 JEROMY BURNITZ-OF
21 JAMEY WRIGHT-P
22 KEVIN BARKER-1B
23 MARK SWEENEY (INJ)-OF
24 JAMES MOUTON-OF
25 RAUL CASANOVA-C
(26) KYLE PETERSON (INJ)-(P)
27 BOB WICKMAN-P (1)
27 KEVIN L. BROWN-C
28 VALERIO DE LOS SANTOS-P
29 ROD CARREW-CH
30 DAVEY LOPES-MGR
31 PAUL RIGDON-P (2)
(32) ROCKY COPPINGER (INJ)-(P)
33 LYLE MOUTON (INJ)-OF
34 *(RET#) ROLLIE FINGERS*
35 BILL CASTRO-CH
36 BOB APODACA-CH
37 STEVE WOODARD-P (1)
37 KANE DAVIS-P (2)
38 JAIME NAVARRO-P (1)
38 ANGEL ETCHEVARRIA-INF (2)
38 SANTIAGO PEREZ-INF
39 CHRIS C. JONES-OF
39 CURTIS LESKANIC-P
(40) CHAD FOX (INJ)-(P)
41 MATT T. WILLIAMS-P
41 EVERETT STULL-P
41 MIKE BUDDIE-P
42 *(RET#) JACKIE ROBINSON*
43 CHRIS SPEIER-CH
44 *(RET#) HANK AARON*
45 GARY (MUGS)(HARDROCK) ALLENSON-CH
46 RAY KING-P
47 JASON BERE-P (1)
48 HORACIO ESTRADA-P
49 DAVID WEATHERS-P
(50) ROBINSON CANCEL (INJ)-(C)
50 BOB SCANLAN-P
51 JIMMY HAYNES-P
52 RAFAEL ROQUE-P
53 JUAN ACEVEDO-P
55 ALLEN LEVRAULT-P
58 HECTOR RAMIREZ-P
59 JOHN SNYDER (INJ)-P
79 DWIGHT BERNARD-CH
88 JIM BRUSKE (INJ)-P
GLENN DISHMAN-(P)
ANTONE WILLIAMSON-(INF)

2001

4TH NL-C 68-94 25GB

00 CURTIS LESKANIC-P
1 LUIS M. LOPEZ-INF
2 TYLER HOUSTON (INJ)-INF
3 JERRY ROYSTER-CH
4 *(RET#) PAUL MOLITOR*
5 GEOFF JENKINS (INJ)-OF
7 TONY FERNANDEZ (WAIV)-3B (1)
7 ALEX SANCHEZ-OF
8 MARK LORETTA (INJ)-SS
9 ROBERT PEREZ-OF (2)
9 ELVIS PENA-2B
10 RONNIE BELLIARD-INF
11 RICHIE SEXSON-OF
12 HENRY BLANCO-C
13 JEFF D'AMICO (INJ)-P
14 MIKE COOLBAUGH-SS
15 BEN SHEETS (INJ)-P
16 LOU COLLIER-SS
18 JOSE HERNANDEZ-INF
19 *(RET#) ROBIN YOUNT*
20 JEROMY BURNITZ-OF
21 JAMEY WRIGHT (INJ)-P
22 DEVON WHITE-OF
23 MARK LEITER (INJ)-P
24 JAMES MOUTON (INJ)-OF
25 RAUL CASANOVA (INJ)-C
26 KYLE PETERSON-P
27 LANCE PAINTER (INJ)-P (2)
28 VALERIO DE LOS SANTOS (INJ)-P
29 ROD CARREW-CH
30 DAVEY LOPES-MGR
31 PAUL RIGDON (INJ)-P
32 NICK NEUGEBAUER (INJ)-P
33 WILL CUNNANE (WAIV)-P
33 MARK SWEENEY-OF
34 *(RET#) ROLLIE FINGERS*
35 BILL CASTRO-CH
36 BOB APODACA-CH
37 RUBEN QUEVEDO-P
38 BRANDON KOLB-P
39 ANGEL ECHEVARRIA-UTIL
40 CHAD FOX-P
41 JEFFREY HAMMONDS (INJ)-OF
42 *(RET#) JACKIE ROBINSON*
43 LUIS SALAZAR-CH
44 *(RET#) HANK AARON*
45 GARY (MUGS)(HARDROCK) ALLENSON-CH
46 RAY KING-P
47 MIKE BUDDIE-P
48 MIKE DEJEAN-P
49 DAVID WEATHERS-P (1)
49 KEVIN L. BROWN-C
(50) EVERETT STULL (INJ)-(P)
50 JESSE LEVIS-C
51 JIMMY HAYNES (INJ)-P
52 MAC SUZUKI-P (3)
53 GUS GANDARILLAS-P
55 ALLEN LEVRAULT-P
56 ROCKY COPPINGER-P

2002

6TH C 56-106 41GB

(00) CURTIS LESKANIC (INJ)-(P)
1 LUIS M. LOPEZ (INJ)-SS (1)
1 KEITH GINTER-3B (2)
2 TYLER HOUSTON-3B (1)
2 BILL HALL-SS/3B
3 JERRY ROYSTER-CH/MGR2
4 *(RET#) PAUL MOLITOR*
5 GEOFF JENKINS (INJ)-OF
6 JORGE FABREGAS-C (2)
7 ERIC YOUNG-2B
8 MARK LORETTA-INF (1)
9 PAUL BAKO-C
10 RON BELLIARD-2B/3B
11 RICHIE SEXSON-1B
12 MATT STAIRS-OF
13 DAVE PEMBER-P
14 CECIL COOPER-CH
15 BEN SHEETS-P
16 LENNY HARRIS-OF/INF
18 JOSE HERNANDEZ-SS
19 *(RET#) ROBIN YOUNT*
21 JAMEY WRIGHT (INJ)-P (1)
22 ALEX SANCHEZ (INJ)-OF
23 ALEX OCHOA-OF (1)
23 ANDREW LORRAINE-P
25 RAUL CASANOVA (INJ)-C (1)
26 MARCUS JENSEN-C
26 WAYNE FRANKLIN-P
27 RYAN CHRISTENSON-OF
28 VALERIO DE LOS SANTOS-P
29 DAVE COLLINS-CH
30 DAVEY LOPES-MGR1
30 JIMMY OSTING (INJ)-P
30 MIKE MATTHEWS-P (2)
(31) PAUL RIGDON (INJ)-(P)
32 NICK NEUGEBAUER (INJ)-P
33 JIM RUSHFORD-OF
35 BILL CASTRO-CH
36 GARY MATTHEWS-CH
36 WAYNE FRANKLIN-P
37 RUBEN QUEVEDO-P
38 RYAN THOMPSON-OF
39 GLENDON RUSCH-P
40 CHAD FOX (INJ)-P
41 JEFFREY HAMMONDS-OF
42 *(RET#) JACKIE ROBINSON*
43 DAVE STEWART (RES)-CH
43 MATT CHILDERS-P
44 *(RET#) HANK AARON*
45 GARY (MUGS) (HARDROCK) ALLENSON-CH
46 RAY KING-P
47 MIKE BUDDIE-P
47 SHANE NANCE (INJ)-P
48 MIKE DEJEAN-P
49 JOSE CABRERA-P
50 EVERETT STULL-P
51 LUIS VIZCAINO-P
52 NELSON FIGUEROA-P
53 BEN DIGGINS-P
55 IZZY ALCANTARA-OF/1B
56 JASON DUROCHER-P
59 BRIAN MALLETTE-P
72 ROBERT MERCHADO-C/1B (2)
81 BEN DIGGINS-P
95 TAKAHITO NOMURA-P

2003

6TH C 56-106 41GB

2 BILL HALL-SS/2B
3 NED YOST-MGR
4 *(RET#) PAUL MOLITOR*
5 GEOFF JENKINS (INJ)-OF
6 KEITH GINTER-INF
7 ERIC YOUNG-2B (1)
9 ENRIQUE CRUZ-INF
10 ROYCE CLAYTON-SS
11 RICHIE SEXSON-1B
12 EDDIE PEREZ-C
(13) DAVE PEMBER (INJ)-(P)
14 DAVE NELSON-CH
15 BEN SHEETS-P
16 BUTCH WYNEGAR-CH
18 WES HELMS (INJ)-3B
19 *(RET#) ROBIN YOUNT*
20 SCOTT PODSEDNIK-OF
21 KEITH OSIK-C
22 ALEX SANCHEZ-OF (1)
22 JASON CONTI-OF
23 RICKIE WEEKS-2B
24 JOHN VANDER WAL-OF
25 RICH DAUER-CH
26 WAYNE FRANKLIN-P
27 BRADY CLARK (INJ)-OF
28 VALERIO DE LOS SANTOS (INJ)-P (1)
29 JASON CONTI-OF
29 MARK SMITH-OF
30 WES OBERMUELLER-P
31 LUIS MARTINEZ-P
(32) NICK NEUGEBAUER (INJ)-(P)
33 CURTIS LESKANIC-P (1)
33 DAVID MANNING-P
35 BILL CASTRO-CH
36 MIKE MADDUX-CH
37 RUBEN QUEVEDO (INJ)-P
39 GLENDON RUSCH (INJ)-P

40 JOHN FOSTER-P
41 JEFFREY HAMMONDS (INJ) (REL)-OF (1)
41 DANNY KOLB-P
42 *(RET#) JACKIE ROBINSON*
43 DAVE BURBA-P
43 MIKE CRUDALE-P (2)
44 *(RET#) HANK AARON*
45 RICH DONNELLY-CH
46 TODD RITCHIE (INJ)-P
47 SHANE NANCE-P
48 MIKE DEJEAN-P (1)
48 MIKE CRUDALE-P (2)
49 DOUG DAVIS-P (3)
50 MATT KINNEY-P
51 LUIS VIZCAINO-P
52 MATT FORD (INJ)-P
53 LEO ESTRELLA-P
55 BROOKS KIESCHNICK-P
56 JAYSON DUROCHER (INJ)-P
57 PETE ZOCCOLILLO-OF

2004

6TH C *67-94* *37.5GB*

1 COREY HART-OF
2 BILL HALL-SS
3 NED YOST-MGR
4 *(RET#) PAUL MOLITOR*
5 GEOFF JENKINS-OF
6 KEITH GINTER-2B
8 MATT ERICKSON-3B
8 MARK L. JOHNSON-C
9 JEFF LIEFER-OF
10 DAVE KRYNZEL-OF
11 LYLE OVERBAY-1B
12 BEN GRIEVE-OF (1)
14 DAVE NELSON-CH
15 BEN SHEETS-P
16 BUTCH WYNEGAR-CH
18 WES HELMS (INJ)-3B
19 *(RET#) ROBIN YOUNT*
20 SCOTT PODSEDNIK-OF
21 CHAD MOELLER-C
22 TRENT DURRINGTON-3B
24 CHRIS MAGRUDER-OF
25 RICH DAUER-CH
26 MATT WISE-P
27 BRADY CLARK-OF
29 GARY BENNETT-C
30 CRAIG COUNSELL-SS
31 RUSSELL BRANYAN-3B
31 ADRIAN HERNANDEZ-P
33 WES OBERMUELLER-P
35 BILL CASTRO-CH
36 MIKE MADDUX-CH
37 JUNIOR SPIVEY (INJ)-2B
38 CHRIS SAENZ-P
38 BEN FORD-P
39 CHRIS CAPUANO (INJ)-P
40 BEN HENDRICKSON-P
41 DANNY KOLB-P
42 *(RET#) JACKIE ROBINSON*
43 DAVE BURBA-P (1)
44 *(RET#) HANK AARON*
45 RICH DONNELLY-CH
46 MIKE ADAMS-P
47 JORGE DE LA ROSA-P
48 BEN FORD-P
48 PEDRO LIRIANO-P
49 DOUG DAVIS-P
50 MATT KINNEY-P (1)
50 TRAVIS PHELPS-P
51 LUIS VIZCAINO-P
53 VICTOR SANTOS-P
55 BROOKS KIESCHNICK-P
57 JEFF BENNETT-P
58 GARY GLOVER-P

2005

3RD C *81-81* *19GB*

1 COREY HART-OF
2 BILL HALL-SS/INF
3 NED YOST-MGR
4 *(RET#) PAUL MOLITOR*
5 GEOFF JENKINS-OF
6 JEFF CIRILLO (INJ)-3B
7 J. J. HARDY-SS
8 NELSON CRUZ-OF
10 DAVE KRYNZEL-OF
11 LYLE OVERBAY-1B
14 DAVE NELSON-CH
15 BEN SHEETS (INJ)-P
16 BUTCH WYNEGAR-CH
18 WES HELMS-3B/1B
19 *(RET#) ROBIN YOUNT*
21 CHAD MOELLER-C
22 TRENT DURRINGTON-3B
23 RICKIE WEEKS-2B
24 CHRIS MAGRUDER-OF
25 RICH DAUER-CH
26 DAMIAN MILLER-C
27 BRADY CLARK (INJ)-OF
28 PRINCE FIELDER-1B
29 JULIO MOSQUERA-C
30 RICK HELLING-P
31 RUSSELL BRANYAN (INJ)-3B
32 RICH DONNELLY-CH
33 WES OBERMUELLER-P
35 BILL CASTRO-CH
36 MIKE MADDUX-CH
37 JUNIOR SPIVEY-2B (1)
37 DANA EVELAND-P
38 MATT WISE (INJ)-P
39 CHRIS CAPUANO-P
41 TOMMY PHELPS-P
42 *(RET#) JACKIE ROBINSON*
43 JUSTIN LEHR-P
44 *(RET#) HANK AARON*
45 CARLOS LEE-OF
46 MIKE ADAMS-P
47 JORGE DE LA ROSA-P
48 JULIO SANTANA (INJ)-P
49 DOUG DAVIS-P
51 KANE DAVIS-P
52 RICKY BOTTALICO-P
52 JOSE CAPELLAN-P
53 VICTOR SANTOS-P
55 TOMO OHKA-P (2)
58 GARY GLOVER-P
59 DERRICK TURNBOW-P
(70) MIKE JONES (INJ) -(P)

Both were members of Harvey's Wallbangers' 1982 American League pennant-winning club. They flew into the World Series versus the Cardinals firing on all cylinders and won the first game 10-0. However, St. Louis regrouped and went on to win in seven. Robin Yount (Above) had twelve hits and Paul Molitor (Below) collected eleven. They're both in the Hall of Fame.

NEW YORK METS

1962
NEW YORK METS
10TH 40-120 60.5GB

1 RICHIE (WHITEY) ASHBURN -OF/2B
2 ELIO CHACON-SS/INF
2 MARV (MARVELOUS MARV) THRONEBERRY-1B (2)
3 GUS BELL-OF (1)
3 ED BOUCHEE-1B
4 CHARLIE NEAL-2B/INF
5 HOBIE LANDRITH-C (1)
5 JOE PIGNATANO-C (2)
6 JIM MARSHALL-1B/OF (1)
6 CLIFF COOK-3B/OF (2)
6 RICK HERRSCHER-UTIL
7 SAMMY DRAKE-2B/3B
7 ELIO CHACON-SS/INF
8 CHRIS CANNIZZARO-C/OF
9 JIM HICKMAN-OF
10 ROD (HOT ROD) KANEHL-UTIL
11 ED BOUCHEE-1B
11 GENE WOODLING-OF (2)
12 SAMMY DRAKE-2B/3B
12 CHOO CHOO COLEMAN-C
14 GIL HODGES-1B
15 AL JACKSON-P
16 BOBBY GENE SMITH-OF (1)
16 SAMMY TAYLOR (INJ)-C (2)
17 DON (POPEYE) ZIMMER-3B (1)
17 CHOO CHOO COLEMAN-C
18 FELIX MANTILLA-3B/INF
19 KEN MACKENZIE-P
20 CRAIG ANDERSON-P
21 ED KRANEPOOL-1B
22 BOB MOORHEAD-P
23 JOE CHRISTOPHER-OF
24 BOB L. MILLER-P
25 FRANK THOMAS-OF/INF
26 HERB MOFORD-P
26 VINEGAR BEND MIZELL-P (2)
26 GALEN CISCO-P (2)
27 DAVE HILLMAN-P (2)
27 LARRY FOSS-P
28 CLEM LABINE-P
28 SHERMAN (ROADBLOCK) JONES-P
29 JOHN (THUMPER) DEMERIT -OF
29 WILLARD HUNTER-P (2)
34 DAVE HILLMAN-P (2)
35 RAY DAVIAULT-P
36 SHERMAN (ROADBLOCK) JONES-P
36 BOB G. MILLER-P
37 CASEY (THE OLD PRO-FESSOR) STENGEL-MGR
38 ROGER CRAIG-P
43 JOE GINSBERG-C
44 HARRY CHITI-C
47 JAY HOOK-P
48 RED KRESS-CH
51 COOKIE LAVAGETTO-CH
52 SOLLY HEMUS-CH
53 ROGERS (RAJAH) HORNSBY-CH
54 RED RUFFING-CH

1963
10TH 51-111 48GB

1 CLIFF COOK-UTIL
1 DUKE CARMEL-OF/1B (2)
2 MARV (MARVELOUS MARV) THRONEBERRY-1B
3 TIM HARKNESS-1B
4 CHARLIE NEAL-3B/SS (1)
4 DUKE SNIDER-OF
5 NORM SHERRY-C
6 LARRY (POSSUM) BURRIGHT-INF
7 CHICO FERNANDEZ-INF (2)
8 CHRIS CANNIZZARO-C
9 JIM HICKMAN-OF/3B
10 ROD (HOT ROD) KANEHL-UTIL
11 DUKE SNIDER-OF
12 JESSE GONDER-C (2)
13 ROGER CRAIG-P
14 GIL HODGES-1B (1)
15 AL JACKSON-P
16 SAMMY TAYLOR-C (1)
16 DICK SMITH-OF/1B
17 CHOO CHOO COLEMAN-C/OF
18 PUMPSIE GREEN-3B
19 KEN MACKENZIE-P (1)
19 ED BAUTA-P (2)
20 CRAIG ANDERSON-P
21 ED KRANEPOOL-OF/1B
22 JOE HICKS-OF
23 JOE CHRISTOPHER-OF
25 FRANK THOMAS-OF/INF
26 GALEN CISCO-P
28 CARL WILLEY-P
29 DON ROWE-P
31 LARRY BEARNARTH-P
33 RON HUNT-2B/3B
34 JIMMY PIERSALL-OF (2)
34 CLEON JONES-OF
36 TRACY STALLARD-P
37 CASEY (THE OLD PRO-FESSOR) STENGEL-MGR
38 ROGER CRAIG-P
39 STEVE DILLON-P
40 AL MORAN-SS/3B
41 GROVER POWELL-P
43 TED SCHREIBER-INF
47 JAY HOOK-P
51 COOKIE LAVAGETTO-CH
52 SOLLY HEMUS-CH
53 ERNIE WHITE-CH
54 CLYDE MCCULLOUGH-CH

1964
10TH 53-109 40GB

1 CHARLEY SMITH-3B/UTIL
2 GEORGE ALTMAN-OF
3 TIM HARKNESS (INJ)-1B
4 WAYNE GRAHAM-3B
6 LARRY (POSSUM) BURRIGHT-2B
6 BOBBY KLAUS-INF
7 AMADO SAMUEL-INF
8 CHRIS CANNIZZARO-C
9 JIM HICKMAN-OF/3B
10 ROD (HOT ROD) KANEHL-UTIL
11 ROY MCMILLAN-SS (2)
12 JESSE GONDER-C
15 AL JACKSON-P
16 DICK SMITH-1B/OF
17 DENNIS RIBANT-P
17 FRANK (THE YANKEE KILLER)(MULE) LARY-P (2)
19 HAWK TAYLOR-C/OF
20 CRAIG ANDERSON-P
21 ED KRANEPOOL-1B/OF
22 JACK (FAT JACK) FISHER-P
23 JOE CHRISTOPHER-OF
24 JERRY HINSLEY-P
25 FRANK THOMAS-UTIL (1)
25 GARY KROLL-P (2)
26 GALEN CISCO-P
27 TOM PARSONS-P
28 CARL WILLEY (INJ)-P
31 LARRY BEARNARTH-P
33 RON HUNT-2B/3B
36 TRACY STALLARD-P
37 CASEY (THE OLD PRO-FESSOR) STENGEL-MGR
38 ED BAUTA-P
38 WILLARD HUNTER-P
39 STEVE DILLON-P
40 AL MORAN-SS/3B
42 LARRY ELLIOTT-OF
43 BILL WAKEFIELD-P
45 RON LOCKE-P
47 JAY HOOK-P
47 TOM PARSONS-P
47 DARRELL SUTHERLAND-P
47 TOM (SNAKE) STURDIVANT-P (2)
49 JOHNN STEPHENSON-3B/OF
51 WES WESTRUM-CH
52 MICKEY (JEEP) HEFFNER-CH
53 MEL (CHIEF) HARDER-CH
54 SHERIFF ROBINSON-CH

1965
10TH 50-112 47GB

1 CHARLEY SMITH-3B/INF
2 CHUCK HILLER-2B/UTIL (2)
3 BILLY COWAN-UTIL (1)
3 BUD HARRELSON-SS
5 CHRIS CANNIZZARO-C
6 BOBBY KLAUS-INF
7 ED KRANEPOOL-1B
8 YOGI BERRA-C/CH
9 JIM HICKMAN-OF/INF
10 KEVIN (CASEY) COLLINS (INJ)-3B/SS
11 ROY MCMILLAN-SS
12 JESSE GONDER-C (1)
14 RON SWOBODA-OF
15 AL JACKSON-P
16 LARRY MILLER-P
16 DANNY NAPOLEON-OF/3B
17 FRANK (THE YANKEE KILLER)(MULE) LARY-P (1)
17 JIMMIE SCHAFFER-C (2)
18 DENNIS RIBANT-P
18 GARY KOLB-UTIL (2)
19 HAWK TAYLOR-C/1B
19 JOHNNY STEPHENSON-C/OF
20 JIM BETHKE-P
20 GREG GOOSSEN-C
21 WARREN SPAHN-P/CH (1)
21 BOB MOORHEAD-P
22 JACK (FAT JACK) FISHER-P
23 JOE CHRISTOPHER-OF
24 JOHNNY LEWIS-OF
25 GARY KROLL-P
26 GALEN CISCO-P
27 TOM PARSONS-P
28 CARL WILLEY-P
28 JIM BETHKE-P
29 ROB GARDNER-P
30 DENNIS RIBANT-P
31 LARRY BEARNARTH-P
33 RON HUNT (INJ)-2B/3B
34 CLEON JONES-OF
34 DENNIS MUSGRAVES (INJ)-P
35 LARRY MILLER-P
36 DENNIS MUSGRAVES (INJ)-P
36 JIM BETHKE-P
37 CASEY (THE OLD PRO-FESSOR) STENGEL-MGR1
38 DAVE EILERS-P (2)
39 DICK SELMA-P
41 JIM BETHKE-P
41 DENNIS MUSGRAVES (INJ)-P
41 GORDIE RICHARDSON-P
43 DARRELL SUTHERLAND-P
45 TUG MCGRAW-P
49 JOHNNY STEPHENSON-3B/OF
51 WES WESTRUM-CH/MGR2
52 MICKEY (JEEP) HEFFNER-CH
53 SHERIFF ROBINSON-CH

1966
9TH 65-95 28.5 GB

1 ED BRESSOUD-SS/INF
2 CHUCK HILLER-UTIL
3 BUD HARRELSON-SS
4 RON SWOBODA-OF
5 SHAUN FITZMAURICE-OF
6 LOU KLIMCHOCK-PH
6 JIM HICKMAN (INJ)-OF/1B
7 ED KRANEPOOL-1B/OF
8 YOGI BERRA-CH
9 WES WESTRUM-MGR
10 GREG GOOSSEN-C
11 ROY MCMILLAN-SS
12 JOHNNY STEPHENSON-C/OF
14 KEN BOYER-3B/1B
15 JERRY GROTE-C/3B
16 DANNY NAPOLEON-OF
17 DICK (DR. STRANGEGLOVE) STUART-1B (1)
17 BOB (WARRIOR) FRIEND-P (2)
17 LARRY ELLIOTT-OF
18 AL LUPLOW-OF
19 HAWK TAYLOR-C/1B
20 CHOO CHOO COLEMAN-C
20 BOB (WARRIOR) FRIEND-P (2)
21 CLEON JONES-OF
22 JACK (FAT JACK) FISHER-P
23 BILLY MURPHY-OF
24 JOHNNY LEWIS-OF
25 DALLAS GREEN-P
25 RALPH TERRY P (2)
26 JERRY ARRIGO (INJ)-P (2)
26 BOB SHAW-P (2)
27 JIM HICKMAN (INJ)-OF/1B
27 DALLAS GREEN-P
28 BILL HEPLER-P
29 ROB GARDNER-P
30 DENNIS RIBANT-P
31 LARRY BEARNARTH-P
32 JACK HAMILTON-P
33 RON HUNT-2B/INF
34 NOLAN RYAN-P
34 DICK SELMA-P
34 JERRY ARRIGO (INJ)-P (2)
35 LARRY MILLER-P
37 *(RET#) CASEY STENGEL*
38 DAVE EILERS-P
38 RALPH TERRY-P (2)
39 DICK SELMA-P
40 GORDIE RICHARDSON-P
40 DICK RUSTECK (INJ)-P
41 GORDIE RICHARDSON-P
43 DICK RUSTECK (INJ)-P
43 DARRELL SUTHERLAND-P
45 DARRELL SUTHERLAND-P
45 TUG MCGRAW (INJ)-P
46 RALPH TERRY-P (2)
46 BILL HEPLER-P
49 DICK RUSTECK (INJ)-P
51 WES WESTRUM-MGR
52 HARVEY (THE KITTEN) HADDIX-CH
53 SHERIFF ROBINSON-CH
54 WHITEY-HERZOG-CH

1967
10TH 61-101 40.5GB

1 JERRY BUCHEK-2B/INF
2 CHUCK HILLER (INJ)-2B (1)
2 PHIL LINZ-UTIL (2)
3 BUD HARRELSON-SS
4 RON SWOBODA-OF/1B
5 SANDY ALOMAR-INF (1)
5 ED CHARLES-3B (2)
6 BART SHIRLEY-2B
6 BOB JOHNSON-INF (2)
7 ED KRANEPOOL-1B
8 YOGI BERRA-CH
9 WES WESTRUM-MGR1
10 GREG GOOSSEN-C
12 TOMMY DAVIS-OF/1B
14 KEN BOYER-3B/1B (1)
15 JERRY GROTE-C
16 TOMMIE REYNOLDS-UTIL
17 HAWK TAYLOR-C (1)
17 DON BOSCH-OF
18 AL LUPLOW-OF (1)
18 JOE MOOCK-3B
18 AL LUPLOW-OF (1)
19 KEVIN (CASEY) COLLINS-2B
20 JOHN SULLIVAN-C
21 CLEON JONES-OF
22 JACK (FAT JACK) FISHER-P
23 BOB HEISE-INF
24 JOHNNY LEWIS-OF
24 KEN BOSWELL-2B/3B
25 AMOS OTIS-OF/3B
25 BOB JOHNSON-INF (2)
25 LARRY STAHL-OF
26 BOB SHAW-P (1)
26 BILL GRAHAM-P
27 DON CARDWELL (INJ)-P
28 DENNIS BENNETT-P (2)
29 DANNY (BEAR) FRISELLA-P
29 RALPH TERRY-P
29 NICK WILLHITE-P (2)
30 DICK SELMA-P
30 BILL CONNORS-P
31 LES ROHR-P
32 JACK HAMILTON-P (1)
32 NICK WILLHITE-P (2)
32 HAL (PORKY) RENIFF-P (2)
33 CHUCK ESTRADA-P
33 BOB HENDLEY-P (2)
34 JACK LAMABE-P (2)
34 CAL KOONCE-P (2)
35 DON SHAW (MIL)-P
35 BILLY WYNNE-P
36 JERRY KOOSMAN-P
37 *(RET#) CASEY STENGEL*
38 RALPH TERRY-P
38 DENNIS BENNETT-P (2)
38 CAL KOONCE-P (2)
38 BILL CONNORS-P
38 BILLY WYNNE-P
39 DICK SELMA-P
40 JERRY HINSLEY-P
40 JOE GRZENDA-P
41 TOM (TOM TERRIFIC) SEAVER-P
42 LES ROHR-P
42 RON TAYLOR-P
43 JERRY HINSLEY-P
43 JOE GRZENDA-P
44 BILL DENEHY-P
44 AL SCHMELZ-P
45 JACK LAMABE-P (2)
45 TUG MCGRAW-P
46 DON SHAW (MIL)-P
47 JERRY KOOSMAN-P
48 JOE GRZENDA-P
52 HARVEY (THE KITTEN) HADDIX-CH

53 SHERIFF ROBINSON-CH
54 SALTY PARKER-CH/MGR2

1968

9TH 73-89 24GB

1 JERRY BUCHEK-UTIL
2 PHIL LINZ-2B
3 BUD HARRELSON-SS
4 RON SWOBODA-OF/1B
5 ED CHARLES-3B/1B
6 AL WEIS-INF
7 ED KRANEPOOL-1B/OF
8 YOGI BERRA-CH
9 J. C. MARTIN-C/1B
10 GREG GOOSSEN-1B/C
10 DUFFY DYER-C
10 MIKE JORGENSEN-1B
11 BOB HEISE-SS/2B
12 KEN BOSWELL (INJ)-2B
14 GIL HODGES-MGR
15 JERRY GROTE-C
16 KEVIN (CASEY) COLLINS-INF
17 DON BOSCH-OF
18 DUFFY DYER-C
19 KEVIN (CASEY) COLLINS-INF
20 TOMMIE AGEE-OF
21 CLEON JONES-OF
22 GREG GOOSSEN-1B/C
23 BOB HEISE-SS/2B
24 ART SHAMSKY-OF/1B
25 LARRY STAHL-OF/1B
27 DON CARDWELL-P
29 DANNY (BEAR) FRISELLA-P
30 NOLAN RYAN (INJ)-P
31 LES ROHR-P
34 CAL KOONCE-P
35 DON SHAW-P
36 JERRY KOOSMAN-P
37 *(RET#) CASEY STENGEL*
38 AL JACKSON-P
39 DICK SELMA-P
40 BILL SHORT-P
41 TOM (TOM TERRIFIC) SEAVER-P
42 RON TAYLOR-P
43 JIM MCANDREW-P
45 BILL CONNORS-P
46 DON SHAW-P
52 JOE PIGNATANO-CH
53 EDDIE (THE WALKING MAN) YOST-CH
54 RUBE WALKER-CH

1969

1ST E 100-62 0GB
W NLCS-ATLN 3-0
W WS-BALA 4-1

1 KEVIN (CASEY) COLLINS-3B (1)
1 BOBBY PFEIL-UTIL
3 BUD HARRELSON-SS
4 RON SWOBODA-OF
5 ED CHARLES-3B
6 AL WEIS-INF
7 ED KRANEPOOL-1B/OF
8 YOGI BERRA-CH
9 J. C. MARTIN-C/1B
10 DUFFY DYER-C
11 WAYNE (RED) GARRETT-3B/INF
12 KEN BOSWELL-2B
14 GIL HODGES-MGR
15 JERRY GROTE-C
17 ROD GASPAR-OF
18 JIM GOSGER-OF
20 TOMMIE AGEE-OF
21 CLEON JONES-OF/1B
22 DONN CLENDENON-1B/OF (2)
24 ART SHAMSKY (INJ)-OF/1B
25 AMOS OTIS-OF/3B
27 DON CARDWELL-P
28 BOB HEISE-SS
29 DANNY (BEAR) FRISELLA-P
29 BOB JOHNSON-P
30 NOLAN RYAN (INJ)-P
31 JACK DILAURO-P
33 LES ROHR-P
34 CAL KOONCE-P
36 JERRY KOOSMAN-P
37 *(RET#) CASEY STENGEL*
38 AL JACKSON-P (1)
38 JESSE HUDSON-P
39 GARY GENTRY-P
41 TOM (TOM TERRIFIC) SEAVER-P
42 RON TAYLOR-P
43 JIM MCANDREW-P
45 TUG MCGRAW-P
52 JOE PIGNATANO-CH
53 EDDIE (THE WALKING MAN) YOST-CH
54 RUBE WALKER-CH

1970

3RD E 83-79 6GB

3 BUD HARRELSON-SS
4 RON SWOBODA-OF
5 JOE FOY-3B
6 AL WEIS-2B/SS
7 ED KRANEPOOL-1B
8 YOGI BERRA-CH
10 DUFFY DYER-C
11 WAYNE (RED) GARRETT-INF
12 KEN BOSWELL-2B
14 GIL HODGES-MGR
15 JERRY GROTE-C
16 MIKE JORGENSEN-1B/OF
17 ROD GASPAR-OF
17 TED MARTINEZ-2B/SS
18 DAVEMARSHALL-OF
19 TIM FOLI-SS/3B
20 TOMMIE AGEE-OF
21 CLEON JONES-OF/1B
22 DONN CLENDENON-1B/OF
24 ART SHAMSKY-OF/1B
27 DON CARDWELL-P (1)
29 KEN SINGLETON-OF
30 NOLAN RYAN-P
31 RON HERBEL-P (2)
32 DEAN CHANCE-P (2)
33 RAY SADECKI-P
34 CAL KOONCE-P (1)
34 DANNY (BEAR) FRISELLA-P
36 JERRY KOOSMAN (INJ)-P
37 *(RET#) CASEY STENGEL*
38 RICH FOLKERS-P
39 GARY GENTRY-P
41 TOM (TOM TERRIFIC) SEAVER-P
42 RON TAYLOR-P
43 JIM MCANDREW-P
44 LEROY STANTON-OF
45 TUG MCGRAW-P
52 JOE PIGNATANO-CH
53 EDDIE (THE WALKING MAN) YOST-CH
54 RUBE WALKER-CH

1971

3RD E (TIE) 83-79 14GB

2 BOB ASPROMONTE-3B
3 BUD HARRELSON-SS
5 FRANK ESTRADA-C
6 AL WEIS-2B/3B
7 ED KRANEPOOL-1B/OF
8 YOGI BERRA-CH
10 DUFFY DYER-C
11 WAYNE (RED) GARRETT (MIL)-INF
12 KEN BOSWELL-2B
14 GIL HODGES-MGR
15 JERRY GROTE-C
16 MIKE JORGENSEN-OF/1B
17 TED MARTINEZ-UTIL
18 DAVE MARSHALL-OF
19 TIM FOLI-SS/3B
20 TOMMIE AGEE-OF
21 CLEON JONES-OF
22 DONN CLENDENON-1B
23 LEROY STANTON-OF
24 ART SHAMSKY (INJ)-OF/1B
25 DON HAHN-OF
28 JOHN (THE HAMMER) MILNER-OF
29 KEN SINGLETON-OF
30 NOLAN RYAN-P
31 DON ROSE-P
32 JON MATLACK-P
33 RAY SADECKI-P
34 DANNY (BEAR) FRISELLA-P
35 JON MATLACK-P
35 CHARLIE WILLIAMS-P
36 JERRY KOOSMAN (INJ)-P
37 *(RET#) CASEY STENGEL*
38 BUZZ CAPRA-P
39 GARY GENTRY-P
41 TOM (TOM TERRIFIC) SEAVER-P
42 RON TAYLOR-P
43 JIM MCANDREW-P
45 TUG MCGRAW-P
47 CHARLIE WILLIAMS-P
52 JOE PIGNATANO-CH
53 EDDIE (THE WALKING MAN) YOST-CH
54 RUBE WALKER-CH

1972

3RD E 83-73 13.5GB

1 LUTE BARNES-2B/SS
2 JIM FREGOSI-3B/INF
3 BUD HARRELSON (INJ)-SS
4 RUSTY STAUB (INJ)-OF
5 JIM BEAUCHAMP-1B/OF
7 ED KRANEPOOL-1B/OF
8 YOGI BERRA-MGR
9 BILL SUDAKIS (INJ)-1B/C
10 DUFFY DYER-C/OF
11 WAYNE (RED) GARRETT-3B/2B
12 KEN BOSWELL-2B
(14) GIL HODGES (DIED)-(MGR)
14 *(RET#) GIL HODGES*
15 JERRY GROTE (INJ)-UTIL
17 TED MARTINEZ-UTIL
18 DAVEMARSHALL-OF
19 TOMMY MOORE-P
20 TOMMIE AGEE-OF
21 CLEON JONES-OF/1B
23 DAVE SCHNECK-OF
24 JIM BEAUCHAMP-1B/OF
24 WILLIE (SAY HEY) MAYS-OF/1B (2)
25 DON HAHN-OF
28 JOHN (THE HAMMER) MILNER-OF/1B
32 JON MATLACK-P
33 RAY SADECKI-P
34 DANNY (BEAR) FRISELLA-P
35 JOE NOLAN-C
36 JERRY KOOSMAN-P
37 *(RET#) CASEY STENGEL*
38 BUZZ CAPRA-P
39 GARY GENTRY-P
40 TOMMY MOORE-P
40 BRENT STROM-P
41 TOM (TOM TERRIFIC) SEAVER-P
42 CHUCK TAYLOR-P (1)
42 HANK WEBB-P
43 JIM MCANDREW-P
44 BOB RAUCH-P
45 TUG MCGRAW-P
48 JOE NOLAN-C
52 JOE PIGNATANO-CH
53 EDDIE (THE WALKING MAN) YOST-CH
54 RUBE WALKER-CH
55 SHERIFF ROBINSON-CH

1973

1ST E 82-79 0GB
W NLCS-CINN 3-2
L WS-OAKA 4-3

1 LUTE BARNES-PH
2 JIM FREGOSI-UTIL (1)
3 BUD HARRELSON (INJ)-SS
4 RUSTY (LE GRAND ORANGE) STAUB-OF
5 JIM BEAUCHAMP-1B
6 GREG HARTS-PH
7 ED KRANEPOOL-1B/OF
8 YOGI BERRA-MGR
9 GEORGE THEODORE (INJ)-OF/1B
10 DUFFY DYER-C
11 WAYNE (RED) GARRETT-3B/INF
12 KEN BOSWELL-3B/2B
14 *(RET#) GIL HODGES*
15 JERRY GROTE (INJ)-C/3B
16 FELIX MILLAN-2B
17 TED MARTINEZ-UTIL
18 GEORGE THEODORE (INJ)-OF/1B
19 BRIAN OSTROSSER-SS
19 JIM GOSGER-OF
20 JERRY MAY-C (2)
21 CLEON JONES (INJ)-OF/1B
23 DAVE SCHNECK-OF
24 WILLIE (SAY HEY) MAYS-OF/1B
25 DON HAHN-OF
27 CRAIG SWAN-P
28 JOHN (THE HAMMER) MILNER-1B/OF
29 RICH CHILES-OF
30 HANK WEBB-P
30 JERRY MAY-C (2)
30 JOHN STROHMAYER-P (2)
30 BOB MILLER-P (2)
31 HARRY PARKER-P
32 JON MATLACK-P
33 RAY SADECKI-P
34 PHIL HENNIGAN-P
34 JOHN STROHMAYER-P (2)
34 BOB APODACA-P
36 JERRY KOOSMAN-P
37 *(RET#) CASEY STENGEL*
38 BUZZ CAPRA-P
39 TOMMY MOORE-P
39 JOHN STROHMAYER-P (2)
40 GEORGE STONE-P
41 TOM (TOM TERRIFIC) SEAVER-P
42 RON HODGES-C
43 JIM MCANDREW-P
45 TUG MCGRAW-P
46 CRAIG SWAN-P
51 ROY MCMILLAN-CH
52 JOE PIGNATANO-CH
53 EDDIE (THE WALKING MAN) YOST-CH
54 RUBE WALKER-CH
55 JOE FITZGERALD-CH

1974

5TH E 71-91 17GB

2 BROCK PEMBERTON-1B
3 BUD HARRELSON (INJ)-SS
4 RUSTY (LE GRAND ORANGE) STAUB-OF
5 JIM GOSGER-OF
6 RICH PUIG-2B/3B
7 ED KRANEPOOL-OF/1B
8 YOGI BERRA-MGR
9 GEORGE THEODORE-1B/OF
10 DUFFY DYER-C
11 WAYNE (RED) GARRETT-3B/SS
12 KEN BOSWELL-UTIL
14 *(RET#) GIL HODGES*
15 JERRY GROTE (INJ)-C
16 DAVE SCHNECK-OF
17 FELIX MILLAN-2B
18 BENNY AYALA-OF
20 IKE HAMPTON-C
21 CLEON JONES (INJ)-OF
22 HANK WEBB-P
22 JACK AKER, (INJ)-P (2)
23 TED MARTINEZ-UTIL
24 WILLIE (SAY HEY) MAYS-CH
25 DON HAHN-OF
26 BRUCE BOISCLAIR-OF
27 JERRY CRAM-P
27 CRAIG SWAN (INJ)-P
28 JOHN (THE HAMMER) MILNER-1B
29 HANK WEBB-P
30 BOB MILLER-P
31 HARRY PARKER-P
32 JON MATLACK-P
33 RAY SADECKI-P
34 BOB APODACA-P
35 RANDY STERLING-P
36 JERRY KOOSMAN-P
37 *(RET#) CASEY STENGEL*
38 JERRY CRAM-P
39 JOHN STROHMAYER-P
40 GEORGE STONE (INJ)-P
41 TOM (TOM TERRIFIC) SEAVER-P
42 RON HODGES-C
45 TUG MCGRAW (INJ)-P
48 NINO ESPINOSA-P
51 ROY MCMILLAN-CH
52 JOE PIGNATANO-CH
53 EDDIE (THE WALKING MAN) YOST-CH
54 RUBE WALKER-CH

1975

3RD E (TIE) 82-80 10.5GB

1 GENE CLINES-OF
2 BROCK PEMBERTON-PH
3 BUD HARRELSON (INJ)-SS
5 MIKE PHILLIPS-SS/2B (2)
7 ED KRANEPOOL-1B/OF
8 YOGI BERRA-MGR1
9 JOE TORRE-3B/1B
10 RUSTY (LE GRAND ORANGE) STAUB-OF
11 WAYNE (RED) GARRETT-3B/SS
12 JACK HEIDEMANN-INF
14 *(RET#) GIL HODGES*
15 JERRY GROTE-C
16 JOHN STEARNS-C
17 FELIX MILLAN-2B
19 TOM HALL-P (2)
21 CLEON JONES (INJ)-OF
22 BOB GALLAGHER-OF
23 JESUS ALOU-OF
24 WILLIE (SAY HEY) MAYS-CH
25 DEL UNSER-OF
26 DAVE KINGMAN-OF/INF
27 CRAIG SWAN-P
28 JOHN (THE HAMMER) MILNER-OF/1B
29 HANK WEBB-P
31 HARRY PARKER (INJ)-P (1)

NEW YORK METS

31 MIKE VAIL-OF
32 JON MATLACK-P
33 KEN (DAFFY) SANDERS-P
34 BOB APODACA (INJ)-P
35 ROY STAIGER-3B
36 JERRY KOOSMAN-P
37 *(RET#) CASEY STENGEL*
38 JERRY CRAM-P
38 SKIP LOCKWOOD-P
39 NINO ESPINOSA-P
40 GEORGE STONE (INJ)-P
41 TOM (TOM TERRIFIC) SEAVER-P
42 RON HODGES-C
42 TOM HALL-P (2)
44 MAC SCARCE-P
45 RICK BALDWIN-P
48 RANDY TATE-P
50 PHIL CAVARRETTA-CH
51 ROY MCMILLAN-CH/MGR2
52 JOE PIGNATANO-CH
53 EDDIE (THE WALKING MAN) YOST-CH
54 RUBE WALKER-CH

1976

3RD E 86-76 15GB

1 LEO FOSTER-INF
2 ROY STAIGER-3B/SS
3 BUD HARRELSON-SS
4 BRUCE BOISCLAIR-OF
5 MIKE PHILLIPS-INF
6 MIKE VAIL-OF
7 ED KRANEPOOL-1B/OF
9 JOE TORRE-1B/3B
11 WAYNE (RED) GARRETT-INF (1)
11 PEPE MANGUAL-OF (2)
12 JACK HEIDEMANN-SS/2B (1)
12 LEE MAZZILLI-OF
12 JOHN STEARNS-C
14 *(RET#) GIL HODGES*
15 JERRY GROTE-C/OF
16 JOHN STEARNS-C
16 LEE MAZZILLI-OF
17 FELIX MILLAN-2B
18 BENNY AYALA-OF
19 TOM HALL-P (1)
21 BILLY BALDWIN-OF
22 JAY KLEVEN-C
23 LEON BROWN-OF
24 WILLIE (SAY HEY) MAYS-CH
25 DEL UNSER-OF (1)
25 JIM DWYER-OF (2)
26 DAVE KINGMAN-OF/1B
27 CRAIG SWAN-P
28 JOHN (THE HAMMER) MILNER-OF/1B
29 MICKEY LOLICH-P
30 HANK WEBB-P
32 JON MATLACK-P
33 KEN (DAFFY) SANDERS-P (1)
34 BOB APODACA (INJ)-P
36 JERRY KOOSMAN-P
37 *(RET#) CASEY STENGEL*
38 SKIP LOCKWOOD-P
39 NINO ESPINOSA-P
41 TOM (TOM TERRIFIC) SEAVER-P
42 RON HODGES-C
44 BOB MYRICK-P
45 RICK BALDWIN-P
50 PHIL CAVARRETTA-CH
51 ROY MCMILLAN-CH
52 JOE PIGNATANO-CH
53 EDDIE (THE WALKING MAN) YOST-CH
54 RUBE WALKER-CH
55 JOE FRAZIER-MGR

1977

6TH E 64-98 37GB

1 LEO FOSTER-INF
1 BOBBY VALENTINE (INJ)-INF (2)
2 ROY STAIGER-3B/SS
3 BUD HARRELSON (INJ)-SS
4 BRUCE BOISCLAIR-OF/1B
5 MIKE PHILLIPS-INF (1)
5 STEVE HENDERSON-OF
6 MIKE VAIL-OF
7 ED KRANEPOOL-OF/1B
9 JOE TORRE-1B/3B/MGR2
11 PEPE MANGUAL-OF
11 LENNY RANDLE-3B/UTIL (2)
12 JOHN STEARNS-C/1B
14 *(RET#) GIL HODGES*
15 JERRY GROTE-C/3B (1)
16 LEE MAZZILLI-OF
17 FELIX MILLAN (INJ)-2B
18 JOEL YOUNGBLOOD-UTIL (2)
19 LUIS ALVARADO-2B (1)
20 JOHNNY PACELLA-P
22 DOC MEDICH-P (3)
23 DOUG FLYNN-INF (2)
24 WILLIE (SAY HEY) MAYS-CH
26 DAVE KINGMAN-OF/1B (1)
27 CRAIG SWAN-P
28 JOHN (THE HAMMER) MILNER-1B/OF
30 JACKSON TODD-P
31 ROY LEE JACKSON-P
32 JON MATLACK (INJ)-P
33 RAY SADECKI-P
33 DAN NORMAN-OF
34 BOB APODACA-P
35 LUIS ROSADO-1B/C
36 JERRY KOOSMAN-P
37 *(RET#) CASEY STENGEL*
38 SKIP LOCKWOOD-P
39 NINO ESPINOSA-P
40 PAT ZACHRY-P (2)
41 TOM (TOM TERRIFIC) SEAVER-P
42 RON HODGES-C
43 PAUL SIEBERT-P (2)
44 BOB MYRICK-P
45 RICK BALDWIN-P
46 PAUL SIEBERT-P (2)
51 DENNY SOMMERS-CH
52 JOE PIGNATANO-CH
53 TOM BURGESS-CH
54 RUBE WALKER-CH
55 JOE FRAZIER-MGR1

1978

6TH E 66-96 24GB

3 SERGIO FERRER-INF
4 BRUCE BOISCLAIR-OF/1B
5 STEVE HENDERSON-OF
7 ED KRANEPOOL-OF/1B
9 JOE TORRE-MGR
10 KEN HENDERSON (INJ)-OF (1)
11 LENNY RANDLE-3B/2B
12 JOHN STEARNS-C/3B
14 *(RET#) GIL HODGES*
15 BUTCH BENTON-C
16 LEE MAZZILLI-OF
17 GIL FLORES-OF
18 JOEL YOUNGBLOOD-UTIL
19 TIM FOLI (INJ)-SS
20 KEN HENDERSON (INJ)-OF (1)
21 ELLIOTT MADDOX-OF/INF
22 DALE MURRAY-P (2)
23 DOUG FLYNN-2B/SS
24 WILLIE (SAY HEY) MAYS-CH
25 WILLIE MONTANEZ-1B
26 MIKE BRUHERT-P
27 CRAIG SWAN-P
28 DWIGHT BERNARD-P
29 ALEX TREVINO-C/3B
29 ROY LEE JACKSON-P
29 KEVIN KOBEL-P
30 MARDIE CORNEJO-P
31 DWIGHT BERNARD-P
31 ROY LEE JACKSON-P
32 TOM HAUSMAN-P
33 DAN NORMAN-OF
(34) BOB APODACA (INJ)-(P)
36 JERRY KOOSMAN-P
37 *(RET#) CASEY STENGEL*
38 SKIP LOCKWOOD-P
39 NINO ESPINOSA-P
40 PAT ZACHRY (INJ)-P
42 RON HODGES-C
43 PAUL SIEBERT-P
44 BOB MYRICK-P
45 BUTCH METZGER-P
47 MARDIE CORNEJO-P
48 JUAN BERENGUER-P
49 KEVIN KOBEL-P
50 PHIL CAVARRETTA-CH
51 DENNY SOMMERS-CH
52 JOE PIGNATANO-CH
53 DAL (MAXIE) MAXVILL-CH
54 RUBE WALKER-CH

1979

6TH E 63-99 35GB

1 SERGIO FERRER-INF
3 RICHIE HEBNER-3B/1B
4 BRUCE BOISCLAIR (INJ)-OF/1B
5 STEVE HENDERSON (INJ)-OF
6 JOSE CARDENAL (INJ)-OF/1B
7 ED KRANEPOOL-1B/OF
8 DAN NORMAN-OF
9 JOE TORRE-MGR
10 KELVIN CHAPMAN-2B/3B
11 FRANK TAVERAS-SS (2)
12 JOHN STEARNS-C/UTIL
14 *(RET#) GIL HODGES*
16 LEE MAZZILLI-OF/1B
17 GIL FLORES-OF
18 JOEL YOUNGBLOOD-OF/INF
19 TIM FOLI-SS (1)
20 JOHNNY PACELLA-P
21 ELLIOTT MADDOX (INJ)-OF/3B
22 DALE MURRAY-P (1)
23 DOUG FLYNN-2B/SS
24 WILLIE (SAY HEY) MAYS-CH
25 WILLIE MONTANEZ-1B (1)
26 RAY BURRIS (INJ)-P (3)
27 CRAIG SWAN-P
28 DWIGHT BERNARD-P
29 ALEX TREVINO-UTIL
30 MIKE SCOTT-P
30 DOCK ELLIS-P (2)
31 ROY LEE JACKSON-P
32 TOM HAUSMAN (INJ)-P
33 PETE FALCONE-P
(34) BOB APODACA (INJ)-(P)
35 DOCK ELLIS-P (2)
36 WAYNE TWITCHELL-P (1)
36 RAY BURRIS (INJ)-P (3)
37 *(RET#) CASEY STENGEL*
38 SKIP LOCKWOOD (INJ)-P
40 PAT ZACHRY (INJ)-P
42 RON HODGES-C
43 JUAN BERENGUER-P
(44) BOB MYRICK (INJ)-(P)
44 ANDY HASSLER-P (2)
45 JEFF REARDON-P
46 NEIL ALLEN (INJ)-P
47 JESSE OROSCO-P
48 JUAN BERENGUER-P
48 ED GLYNN-P
49 KEVIN KOBEL (INJ)-P
50 ANDY HASSLER-P (2)
51 DICK SISLER-CH
52 JOE PIGNATANO-CH
53 CHUCK COTTIER-CH
54 RUBE WALKER-CH
61 JESSE OROSCO-P

1980

5TH E 67-85 24GB

1 MOOKIE WILSON-OF
2 PHIL MANKOWSKI (INJ/ILL)-3B
3 MARIO RAMIREZ-INF
4 JOSE MORENO-2B/3B
5 STEVE HENDERSON-OF
6 JOSE CARDENAL-OF/1B (1)
8 DAN NORMAN-OF
9 JOE TORRE-MGR
11 FRANK TAVERAS-SS
12 JOHN STEARNS (INJ)-C/INF
13 NEIL ALLEN-P
14 *(RET#) GIL HODGES*
15 BUTCH BENTON-C
15 CLAUDELL WASHINGTON-OF (2)
16 LEE MAZZILLI-1B/OF
17 JERRY MORALES-OF
18 JOEL YOUNGBLOOD-OF/INF
19 PHIL MANKOWSKI (INJ/ILL)-3B
20 JOHNNY PACELLA-P
21 ELLIOTT MADDOX-3B/UTIL
22 JOSE MORENO-2B/3B
22 MIKE JORGENSEN-1B/OF
23 DOUG FLYNN (INJ)-2B/SS
25 JERRY MORALES-OF
25 BILL ALMON-INF (2)
26 RAY BURRIS (INJ)-P
27 CRAIG SWAN (INJ)-P
28 MARK BOMBACK-P
28 WALLY BACKMAN-2B/SS
29 ALEX TREVINO-UTIL
30 MIKE SCOTT-P
31 ROY LEE JACKSON-P
32 TOM HAUSMAN-P
33 PETE FALCONE-P
34 RAY BURRIS (INJ)-P
35 ED LYNCH-P
36 MARK BOMBACK-P
37 *(RET#) CASEY STENGEL*
39 WALLY BACKMAN-2B/SS
39 HUBIE BROOKS-3B
40 PAT ZACHRY (INJ)-P
42 RON HODGES (INJ)-C
43 JUAN BERENGUER-P
45 JEFF REARDON-P
46 NEIL ALLEN-P
46 SCOTT HOLMAN-P
47 ROY LEE JACKSON-P
48 ED GLYNN-P
49 KEVIN KOBEL-P
49 DYAR MILLER-P
50 ED LYNCH-P
51 DICK SISLER-CH
52 JOE PIGNATANO-CH
53 CHUCK COTTIER-CH
54 RUBE WALKER-CH
56 DYAR MILLER-P
58 LUIS ROSADO-1B
60 AL OSMUNDSON-CH

1981

1ST 1/2:5TH E 17-34 15GB
2ND 1/2:4TH E 24-28 5.5GB
FINAL: 41-62 --GB

1 MOOKIE WILSON-OF
3 MIKE CUBBAGE-3B
4 BOB BAILOR-UTIL
5 MIKE HOWARD-OF
6 WALLY BACKMAN-2B/3B
7 HUBIE BROOKS-3B/UTIL
9 JOE TORRE-MGR
10 RUSTY (LE GRAND ORANGE) STAUB-1B
11 FRANK TAVERAS-SS
12 JOHN STEARNS-C/INF
13 NEIL ALLEN-P
14 *(RET#) GIL HODGES*
15 DAVE ROBERTS-P
15 MIKE HOWARD-OF
16 LEE MAZZILLI-OF
17 BRIAN GILES-2B/SS
17 ELLIS VALENTINE-OF (2)
18 JOEL YOUNGBLOOD (INJ)-OF
19 RON GARDENHIRE-INF
20 GREG A. HARRIS-P
22 MIKE JORGENSEN-1B/OF
23 DOUG FLYNN-2B/SS
25 RANDY JONES (INJ)-P
25 CHARLIE PULEO-P
26 DAVE (KONG) KINGMAN-1B/OF
27 CRAIG SWAN (INJ)-P
28 MIKE MARSHALL-P
29 ALEX TREVINO-UTIL
30 MIKE SCOTT-P
31 ED LYNCH-P
32 TOM HAUSMAN (INJ)-P
33 PETE FALCONE-P
34 ED LYNCH-P
34 DAVE ROBERTS-P
35 ED LYNCH-P
35 RANDY JONES (INJ)-P
36 DANNY BOITANO-P
37 *(RET#) CASEY STENGEL*
38 TIM LEARY (INJ)-P
40 PAT ZACHRY-P
42 RON HODGES-C
43 TERRY LEACH-P
44 JEFF REARDON-P (1)
44 RAY SEARAGE-P
45 BOB (HOOT) GIBSON-CH
47 JESSE OROSCO-P
48 ED GLYNN-P
49 DYAR MILLER-P
51 DERON JOHNSON-CH
52 JOE PIGNATANO-CH
53 CHUCK COTTIER-CH
54 RUBE WALKER-CH

1982

6TH E 65-97 27GB

1 MOOKIE WILSON-OF
3 BUD HARRELSON-CH
4 BOB BAILOR-UTIL
5 MIKE HOWARD-OF/2B
6 WALLY BACKMAN (INJ)-2B/INF
7 HUBIE BROOKS-3B
8 RICK SWEET-PH (1)
8 RONN REYNOLDS-C
8 PHIL MANKOWSKI-3B
9 BRUCE BOCHY-C/1B
10 RUSTY (LE GRAND ORANGE) STAUB-OF/1B/CH
11 TOM VERYZER (INJ)-2B/SS
12 JOHN STEARNS (INJ)-C/1B
13 NEIL ALLEN (INJ)-P
14 *(RET#) GIL HODGES*
15 GEORGE FOSTER-OF
17 ELLIS VALENTINE-OF
18 JOEL YOUNGBLOOD-OF/2B (1)
19 RON GARDENHIRE-SS/INF
20 RICK OWNBEY-P
21 GARY RAJSICH-OF/1B

22 MIKE JORGENSEN-1B/OF
23 BRIAN GILES-2B/SS
25 CHARLIE PULEO-P
26 DAVE (KONG) KINGMAN-1B
27 CRAIG SWAN-P
28 SCOTT HOLMAN-P
29 TOM GORMAN-P (2)
30 MIKE SCOTT-P
31 GEORGE BAMBERGER-MGR
32 TOM HAUSMAN (INJ)-P (1)
32 CARLOS DIAZ-P (2)
33 PETE FALCONE-P
34 RUSTY TILLMAN-OF
35 RANDY JONES-P
36 ED LYNCH-P
37 *(RET#) CASEY STENGEL*
39 DOUG SISK-P
40 PAT ZACHRY-P
42 RON HODGES-C
43 TERRY LEACH-P
45 BRENT GAFF-P
47 JESSE OROSCO-P
48 CARLOS DIAZ-P (2)
49 WALT TERRELL-P
51 JIM FREY-CH
53 BUD HARRELSON-CH
55 FRANK (THE CAPITAL PUNISHER)(HONDO) HOWARD-CH
56 BILL MONBOUQUETTE-CH

1983

6TH E 68-94 22GB

1 MOOKIE WILSON-OF
2 JOSE OQUENDO-SS
4 BOB BAILOR-UTIL
5 MIKE HOWARD-OF
6 WALLY BACKMAN-2B/3B
7 HUBIE BROOKS-3B/2B
8 RONN REYNOLDS-C
9 MARK BRADLEY-OF
10 RUSTY (LE GRAND ORANGE) STAUB-1B/OF
11 TUCKER ASHFORD-UTIL
12 JOHN STEARNS (INJ)-PR
13 NEIL ALLEN-P (1)
14 *(RET#) GIL HODGES*
15 GEORGE FOSTER-OF
17 KEITH (MEX) HERNANDEZ-1B (2)
18 DARRYL STRAWBERRY-OF
19 RON GARDENHIRE-SS
20 RICK OWNBEY-P
20 MIKE FITZGERALD-C
21 GARY RAJSICH-1B
22 MIKE JORGENSEN-1B (1)
23 BRIAN GILES-2B/SS
25 DANNY HEEP-OF/1B
26 DAVE (KONG) KINGMAN-1B/OF
27 CRAIG SWAN-P
28 SCOTT HOLMAN-P
29 TOM GORMAN-P
30 MIKE TORREZ-P
31 GEORGE BAMBERGER-MGR1
32 CARLOS DIAZ-P
33 CLINT HURDLE-3B/OF
34 JUNIOR ORTIZ-C (2)
36 ED LYNCH-P
37 *(RET#) CASEY STENGEL*
38 TIM LEARY-P
39 DOUG SISK-P
41 TOM (TOM TERRIFIC) SEAVER-P
42 RON HODGES-C
43 TERRY LEACH-P
44 RON DARLING-P
45 BRENT GAFF-P
47 JESSE OROSCO-P
48 MIKE BISHOP-C
48 CARLOS DIAZ-P
49 WALT TERRELL-P
51 JIM FREY-CH
53 BOBBY VALENTINE-CH
54 BILL MONBOUQUETTE-CH
55 FRANK (THE CAPITAL PUNISHER)(HONDO) HOWARD-CH/MGR2
56 GENE DUSAN-CH

1984

2ND E 90-72 6.5GB

1 MOOKIE WILSON-OF
2 JOSE OQUENDO-SS
3 RAFAEL SANTANA-SS
5 DAVEY JOHNSON-MGR
6 WALLY BACKMAN-2B/SS
7 HUBIE BROOKS-3B/SS
8 JOHN GIBBONS (INJ)-C
9 JERRY MARTIN (SUS)-OF/1B
10 RUSTY (LE GRAND ORANGE) STAUB-1B
11 KELVIN CHAPMAN-2B/3B
12 JOHN STEARNS (INJ)-C/1B
14 *(RET#) GIL HODGES*
15 GEORGE FOSTER-OF
16 DWIGHT (DOC) GOODEN-P
17 KEITH (MEX) HERNANDEZ-1B
18 DARRYL STRAWBERRY-OF
19 RON GARDENHIRE-SS/INF
20 MIKE FITZGERALD-C
21 ROSS JONES-SS/3B
21 HERM WINNINGHAM-OF
22 BOBBY VALENTINE-CH
22 RAY KNIGHT-3B/1B (2)
25 DANNY HEEP-OF/1B
26 BILL ROBINSON-CH
27 CRAIG SWAN-P (1)
27 WES GARDNER-P
28 BOBBY VALENTINE-CH
29 TOM GORMAN-P
30 MIKE TORREZ-P (1)
31 BRUCE BERENYI-P (2)
32 DICK TIDROW-P
32 KEVIN MITCHELL-3B
34 JUNIOR ORTIZ-C
35 BILLY BEANE-OF
35 JOHN CHRISTENSEN-OF
36 ED LYNCH-P
37 *(RET#) CASEY STENGEL*
38 TIM LEARY-P
39 DOUG SISK-P
40 CALVIN SCHIRALDI-P
42 RON HODGES-C
44 RON DARLING-P
45 BRENT GAFF-P
47 JESSE OROSCO-P
48 MEL STOTTLEMYRE, SR.-CH
49 WALT TERRELL-P
50 SID (EL SID) FERNANDEZ-P
51 VERN HOSCHEIT-CH
55 FRANK (THE CAPITAL PUNISHER)(HONDO) HOWARD-CH

1985

2ND E 98-64 3GB

1 MOOKIE WILSON (INJ)-OF
2 BOBBY VALENTINE-CH (1)
2 LARRY BOWA-SS/2B (2)
3 RAFAEL SANTANA-SS
4 LENNY DYKSTRA-OF
5 DAVEY JOHNSON-MGR
6 WALLY BACKMAN-2B/SS
7 JOHN CHRISTENSEN-OF
8 GARY (KID) CARTER-C/UTIL
9 RONN REYNOLDS-C
10 RUSTY (LE GRAND ORANGE) STAUB-OF
11 KELVIN CHAPMAN-2B/3B
12 RON DARLING-P
13 CLINT HURDLE-C/OF
14 *(RET#) GIL HODGES*
15 GEORGE FOSTER-OF
16 DWIGHT (DOC) GOODEN-P
17 KEITH (MEX) HERNANDEZ-1B
18 DARRYL STRAWBERRY (INJ)-OF
19 RON GARDENHIRE (INJ)-INF
20 HOWARD (HOJO) JOHNSON-3B/UTIL
21 TERRY BLOCKER-OF
22 RAY KNIGHT-INF
23 BUD HARRELSON-CH
25 DANNY HEEP-OF/1B
26 BOBBY VALENTINE-CH (1)
26 TERRY LEACH-P
27 WES GARDNER-P
28 BILL ROBINSON-CH
29 TOM GORMAN-P
30 MEL STOTTLEMYRE, SR.-CH
31 BRUCE BERENYI (INJ)-P
33 BILL LATHAM-P
35 JOHN CHRISTENSEN-OF
35 BILLY BEANE-OF
35 JOE SAMBITO-P
36 ED LYNCH-P
37 *(RET#) CASEY STENGEL*
38 RICK AGUILERA-P
39 DOUG SISK-P
40 CALVIN SCHIRALDI-P
42 ROGER MCDOWELL-P
44 BILL LATHAM-P
44 TOM PACIOREK-OF/1B (2)
(45) BRENT GAFF (INJ)-(P)
45 RANDY NIEMANN-P
47 JESSE OROSCO-P
48 RANDY MYERS-P
50 SID (EL SID) FERNANDEZ-P
51 VERN HOSCHEIT-CH
52 GREG PAVLICK-CH
64 BILL LATHAM-P

1986

1ST E 108-54 0GB

W NLCS-HOUN 4-2

W WS-BOSA 4-3

1 MOOKIE WILSON (INJ)-OF
2 KEVIN ELSTER-SS
3 RAFAEL SANTANA-SS/2B
4 LENNY DYKSTRA-OF
5 DAVEY JOHNSON-MGR
6 WALLY BACKMAN-2B
7 JOHN GIBBONS-C
7 KEVIN MITCHELL-UTIL
8 GARY (KID) CARTER-C/UTIL
11 TIM TEUFEL-INF
12 RON DARLING-P
13 LEE MAZZILLI-OF/1B (2)
14 *(RET#) GIL HODGES*
15 GEORGE FOSTER-OF (1)
16 DWIGHT (DOC) GOODEN-P
17 KEITH (MEX) HERNANDEZ-1B
18 DARRYL STRAWBERRY (INJ)-OF
19 BOB (BOBBY O) OJEDA-P
20 HOWARD (HOJO) JOHNSON-3B/UTIL
22 RAY KNIGHT-3B/1B
23 BUD HARRELSON-CH
25 DANNY HEEP-OF
26 TERRY LEACH-P
27 TIM CORCORAN-1B
27 STAN JEFFERSON-OF
28 BILL ROBINSON-CH
29 DAVE MAGADAN-1B
29 TIM CORCORAN-1B
30 MEL STOTTLEMYRE, SR.-CH
31 BRUCE BERENYI-P
32 STAN JEFFERSON-OF
32 RICK ANDERSON-P
33 BARRY LYONS-C
35 KEVIN MITCHELL-UTIL
35 JOHN GIBBONS-C
36 ED LYNCH (INJ)-P (1)
37 *(RET#) CASEY STENGEL*
38 RICK AGUILERA-P
39 DOUG SISK-P
40 RANDY NIEMANN-P
42 ROGER MCDOWELL-P
43 BOB (BOBBY O) OJEDA-P
43 JOHN MITCHELL-P
47 JESSE OROSCO-P
48 RANDY MYERS-P
49 ED HEARN-C
50 SID (EL SID) FERNANDEZ-P
51 VERN HOSCHEIT-CH
52 GREG PAVLICK-CH
66 JOHN MITCHELL-P

1987

2ND E 92-70 3GB

1 MOOKIE WILSON-OF
2 BILL ALMON-UTIL (2)
3 RAFAEL SANTANA-SS
4 LENNY DYKSTRA-OF
5 DAVEY JOHNSON-MGR
6 WALLY BACKMAN-2B
7 CLINT HURDLE-1B
8 GARY (KID) CARTER-C/UTIL
9 GREGG JEFFERIES-PH
10 SID (EL SID) FERNANDEZ-P
11 TIM TEUFEL-2B/1B
12 RON DARLING-P
13 LEE MAZZILLI-OF/1B
14 *(RET#) GIL HODGES*
15 RICK AGUILERA (INJ)-P
16 DWIGHT (DOC) GOODEN (SUB)-P
17 KEITH (MEX) HERNANDEZ-1B
18 DARRYL STRAWBERRY-OF
19 BOB (BOBBY O) OJEDA (INJ)-P
20 HOWARD (HOJO) JOHNSON-3B/UTIL
21 KEVIN ELSTER-SS
22 KEVIN MCREYNOLDS-OF
23 BUD HARRELSON-CH
25 AL PEDRIQUE-SS/2B (1)
25 KEITH MILLER (INJ)-2B
26 TERRY LEACH-P
27 RANDY MILLIGAN-PH
28 BILL ROBINSON-CH
29 DAVE MAGADAN-3B/1B
30 MEL STOTTLEMYRE, SR.-CH
31 GENE WALTER-P
32 MARK CARREON-OF
32 TOM EDENS-P
33 BARRY LYONS-C
34 SAM PERLOZZO-CH
37 *(RET#) CASEY STENGEL*
38 RICK AGUILERA (INJ)-P
38 BOB GIBSON-P
39 DOUG SISK-P
40 JEFF INNIS-P
42 ROGER MCDOWELL (INJ)-P
43 JOHN MITCHELL-P
44 DAVID CONE (INJ)-P
45 JOHN (CANDY MAN) CANDELARIA-P
47 JESSE OROSCO-P
48 RANDY MYERS-P
49 DON SCHULZE-P
50 SID (EL SID) FERNANDEZ-P
51 VERN HOSCHEIT-CH

1988

1ST E 100-60 0GB

L NLCS-LAN 4-3

1 MOOKIE WILSON-OF
2 MACKEY SASSER-UTIL
3 BUD HARRELSON-CH
4 LENNY DYKSTRA-OF
5 DAVEY JOHNSON-MGR
6 WALLY BACKMAN-2B
7 BOB MCCLURE-P (2)
8 GARY (KID) CARTER-C/INF
9 GREGG JEFFERIES-3B/2B
11 TIM TEUFEL-2B/1B
12 RON DARLING-P
13 LEE MAZZILLI-OF/1B
14 *(RET#) GIL HODGES*
15 RICK AGUILERA (INJ)-P
16 DWIGHT (DOC) GOODEN-P
17 KEITH (MEX) HERNANDEZ (INJ)-1B
18 DARRYL STRAWBERRY-OF
19 BOB (BOBBY O) OJEDA-P
20 HOWARD (HOJO) JOHNSON-3B/SS
21 KEVIN ELSTER-SS
22 KEVIN MCREYNOLDS-OF
23 BUD HARRELSON-CH
25 KEITH MILLER (INJ)-UTIL
26 TERRY LEACH-P
27 BOB MCCLURE-P (2)
28 BILL ROBINSON-CH
29 DAVE MAGADAN-3B/1B
30 MEL STOTTLEMYRE, SR.-CH
31 GENE WALTER-P (1)
32 MARK CARREON-OF
33 BARRY LYONS-C/1B
34 SAM PERLOZZO-CH
37 *(RET#) CASEY STENGEL*
40 JEFF INNIS-P
41 *(RET#) TOM SEAVER*
42 ROGER MCDOWELL-P
43 JOHN MITCHELL-P
44 DAVID CONE-P
45 EDWIN NUNEZ-P (2)
46 DAVID WEST-P
48 RANDY MYERS-P
50 SID (EL SID) FERNANDEZ-P
52 GREG PAVLICK-CH

1989

2ND E 87-75 6GB

1 MOOKIE WILSON-OF (1)
2 MACKEY SASSER-C/3B
3 BUD HARRELSON-CH
4 LENNY DYKSTRA-OF (1)
4 LOU THORNTON-OF
5 DAVEY JOHNSON-MGR
7 JUAN (SAMMY) SAMUEL-OF (2)
8 GARY (KID) CARTER (INJ)-C/1B
9 GREGG JEFFERIES-2B/3B
10 DAVE MAGADAN-1B/3B
11 TIM TEUFEL-2B/1B
12 RON DARLING-P
13 LEE MAZZILLI-OF/1B (1)
13 JEFF MUSSELMAN-P (2)
14 *(RET#) GIL HODGES*
15 RICK AGUILERA (INJ)-P (1)
15 JEFF MCKNIGHT-INF
15 RON DARLING-P
16 DWIGHT (DOC) GOODEN (INJ)-P
17 KEITH (MEX) HERNANDEZ (INJ)-1B
18 DARRYL STRAWBERRY-OF
19 BOB (BOBBY O) OJEDA-P
20 HOWARD (HOJO) JOHNSON-3B/SS

NEW YORK METS

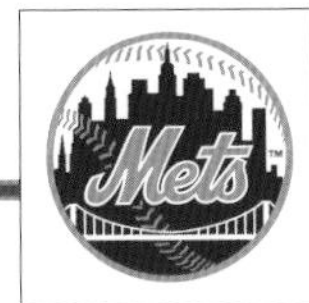

1 KEVIN ELSTER-SS
2 KEVIN MCREYNOLDS-OF
5 KEITH MILLER-UTIL
6 TERRY LEACH-P (1)
6 KEVIN TAPANI-P (1)
7 TOM O'MALLEY-3B
8 BILL ROBINSON-CH
9 DAVE MAGADAN-1B/3B
9 FRANK VIOLA-P (2)
0 MEL STOTTLEMYRE, SR.-CH
1 JULIO MACHADO-P
2 MARK CARREON-OF
3 BARRY LYONS-C
4 SAM PERLOZZO-CH
5 CRAIG SHIPLEY-SS/3B
6 MANNY HERNANDEZ-P
7 *(RET#) CASEY STENGEL*
8 BLAINE BEATTY-P
8 RICK AGUILERA (INJ)-P (1)
9 PHIL LOMBARDI-C/1B
0 JEFF INNIS-P
1 *(RET#) TOM SEAVER*
2 ROGER MCDOWELL-P (1)
3 JOHN MITCHELL-P
4 DAVID CONE-P
6 DAVID WEST-P (1)
7 WALLY WHITEHURST-P
8 RANDY MYERS-P
9 DON AASE-P
0 SID (EL SID) FERNANDEZ-P
2 GREG PAVLICK-CH
5 MIKE CUBBAGE-CH

1990
2ND E 91-71 4GB
1 LOU THORNTON-OF
1 CHUCK CARR-OF
2 MACKEY SASSER-C/1B
3 BUD HARRELSON-CH/MGR2
4 MIKE CUBBAGE-CH
5 DAVEY JOHNSON-MGR1
6 MIKE MARSHALL-1B/OF (1)
6 DARREN REED-OF
6 ALEX TREVINO-C (2)
7 DARYL BOSTON-OF (2)
9 GREGG JEFFERIES-2B/3B
0 DAVE MAGADAN-1B/3B
1 TIM TEUFEL-INF
2 KEITH HUGHES-OF
3 JEFF MUSSELMAN-P
4 *(RET#) GIL HODGES*
5 RON DARLING-P
6 DWIGHT (DOC) GOODEN-P
8 DARRYL STRAWBERRY-OF
9 BOB (BOBBY O) OJEDA-P
20 HOWARD (HOJO) JOHNSON-3B/SS
21 KEVIN ELSTER (INJ)-SS
22 KEVIN MCREYNOLDS-OF
23 KEVIN BROWN-P (1)
23 CHUCK HILLER-CH
25 KEITH MILLER-UTIL
26 ALEJANDRO PENA-P
27 TOM O'MALLEY-3B/1B
28 TOMMY HERR-2B (2)
29 FRANK VIOLA-P
30 MEL STOTTLEMYRE, SR.-CH
31 JOHN FRANCO-P
32 DOC EDWARDS-CH
33 BARRY LYONS (INJ)-C (1)
33 CHARLIE O'BRIEN-C (2)
34 JULIO VALERA-P
34 MARIO DIAZ-SS/2B
35 ORLANDO MERCADO-C (1)
35 PAT TABLER-OF (2)
36 DAVE LIDDELL-C
36 KEVIN BAEZ-SS
37 *(RET#) CASEY STENGEL*
(38) BLAINE BEATTY (INJ)-(P)
39 KELVIN TORVE-1B/OF
40 JEFF INNIS-P
43 KEVIN BROWN-P (1)
43 DAN SCHATZEDER-P (2)
44 DAVID CONE-P
45 MARK CARREON (INJ)-OF
46 CHRIS JELIC-OF
47 WALLY WHITEHURST-P
48 JULIO MACHADO-P (1)
49 TODD HUNDLEY-C
50 SID (EL SID) FERNANDEZ-P
52 GREG PAVLICK-CH

1991
5TH E 77-84 20.5GB
0 TERRY MCDANIEL-OF
1 VINCE (VINCENT VAN GO) COLEMAN (INJ)-OF
2 MACKEY SASSER-UTIL
3 BUD HARRELSON-MGR1
4 MIKE CUBBAGE-CH/MGR2
5 CHARLIE O'BRIEN-C
6 DARYL BOSTON-OF
7 HUBIE BROOKS (INJ)-OF
9 GREGG JEFFERIES-2B/3B
10 DAVE MAGADAN (INJ)-1B
11 TIM TEUFEL-INF (1)
11 GARRY TEMPLETON-UTIL (2)
13 RICK CERONE-C
14 *(RET#) GIL HODGES*
15 RON DARLING-P (1)
16 DWIGHT (DOC) GOODEN (INJ)-P
17 DAVID CONE-P
19 JEFF GARDNER-SS/2B
20 HOWARD (HOJO) JOHNSON-3B/UTIL
21 KEVIN ELSTER-SS
22 KEVIN MCREYNOLDS-OF
23 CHRIS DONNELS-1B/3B
25 KEITH MILLER-UTIL
26 ALEJANDRO PENA-P (1)
27 CHUCK CARR (INJ)-OF
28 TOMMY HERR-2B/OF (1)
29 FRANK VIOLA-P
30 MEL STOTTLEMYRE, SR.-CH
31 JOHN FRANCO-P
32 DOC EDWARDS-CH
33 ANTHONY YOUNG-P
34 JULIO VALERA-P
36 TONY CASTILLO-P (2)
37 *(RET#) CASEY STENGEL*
38 BLAINE BEATTY-P
39 KELVIN TORVE-1B
39 RICH SAUVEUR-P
40 JEFF INNIS-P
41 *(RET#) TOM SEAVER*
43 DOUG SIMONS-P
44 DAVID CONE-P
44 TIM BURKE-P (2)
45 MARK CARREON-OF
46 TERRY BROSS-P
47 WALLY WHITEHURST-P
48 PETE SCHOUREK-P
49 TODD HUNDLEY-C
50 SID (EL SID) FERNANDEZ (INJ)-P
51 TOM SPENCER-CH
52 GREG PAVLICK-CH
65 DOUG SIMONS-P

1992
5TH E 72-90 24GB
1 VINCE (VINCENT VAN GO) COLEMAN (INJ)-OF
2 MACKEY SASSER-UTIL
3 JUNIOR NOBOA-INF
4 MIKE CUBBAGE-CH
5 JEFF MCKNIGHT-UTIL (2)
6 DARYL BOSTON-OF
7 D. J. DOZIER-OF
8 DAVE GALLAGHER (INJ)-OF
9 TODD HUNDLEY-C
10 JEFF TORBORG-MGR
11 DICK SCHOFIELD-SS (2)
12 WILLIE RANDOLPH (INJ)-2B
13 RODNEY MCCRAY-OF
13 STEVE SPRINGER-2B/3B
14 *(RET#) GIL HODGES*
15 KEVIN ELSTER (INJ)-SS
15 JEFF MCKNIGHT-UTIL (2)
16 DWIGHT (DOC) GOODEN-P
17 DAVID CONE-P (1)
18 BRET SABERHAGEN-P
19 ANTHONY YOUNG-P
20 HOWARD (HOJO) JOHNSON (INJ)-OF
21 KEVIN BASS-OF (2)
22 CHARLIE O'BRIEN-C
23 CHRIS DONNELS- 3B/2B
25 BOBBY (BOBBY BO) BONILLA-OF/1B
26 BARRY FOOTE-CH
27 TOM MCCRAW-CH
28 DAVE LAROCHE-CH
29 DAVE MAGADAN, (INJ)-3B/1B
30 MEL STOTTLEMYRE, SR.-CH
31 JOHN FRANCO (INJ)-P
32 BILL PECOTA-INF
33 EDDIE MURRAY-1B
34 CHICO WALKER-UTIL (2)
35 LEE GUETTERMAN-P (2)
36 KEVIN BAEZ (INJ)-SS
37 *(RET#) CASEY STENGEL*
38 PAT HOWELL-OF
39 JEFF KENT-INF
40 JEFF INNIS-P
41 *(RET#) TOM SEAVER*
43 MARK DEWEY-P
44 TIM BURKE-P (1)
44 TOM FILER-P
44 RYAN THOMPSON-OF
45 PAUL GIBSON-P
46 BARRY JONES-P (2)
47 WALLY WHITEHURST-P
48 PETE SCHOUREK-P
49 JOE VITKO-P
49 MIKE BIRKBECK-P
50 SID (EL SID) FERNANDEZ (INJ)-P
53 ERIC HILLMAN-P

1993
7TH E 59-103 38GB
1 TONY FERNANDEZ-SS (1)
1 KEVIN BAEZ-SS
2 WAYNE HOUSIE-OF
2 DOUG SAUNDERS-INF
3 DARRIN JACKSON (ILL)-OF (2)
4 MIKE CUBBAGE-CH
5 JEROMY BURNITZ-OF
6 JOE ORSULAK-OF/1B
7 JEFF MCKNIGHT-UTIL
7 BOBBY WINE, SR.-CH
8 DAVE GALLAGHER-OF/1B
9 TODD HUNDLEY-C
10 JEFF TORBORG-MGR1
10 BUTCH HUSKEY-3B
11 VINCE (VINCENT VAN GO) COLEMAN (INJ) (SUS)-OF
12 JEFF KENT-2B/INF
14 *(RET#) GIL HODGES*
15 DARRELL JOHNSON-CH
16 DWIGHT (DOC) GOODEN (INJ)-P
17 JEFF MCKNIGHT-UTIL
18 BRET SABERHAGEN (INJ)-P
19 ANTHONY YOUNG-P
20 HOWARD (HOJO) JOHNSON (INJ)-3B
22 CHARLIE O'BRIEN-C
23 TIM BOGAR (INJ)-SS/INF
25 BOBBY (BOBBY BO) BONILLA (INJ)-OF/INF
26 BARRY FOOTE-CH
26 CED LANDRUM-OF
27 TOM MCCRAW-CH
28 DAVE LAROCHE-CH
28 BOBBY JONES-P
29 FRANK TANANA (INJ)-P (1)
30 MEL STOTTLEMYRE, SR.-CH
31 JOHN FRANCO (INJ)-P
33 EDDIE MURRAY-1B
34 CHICO WALKER-UTIL
35 KENNY GREER-P
36 KEVIN BAEZ-SS
36 TITO NAVARRO-SS
37 *(RET#) CASEY STENGEL*
38 DAVE TELGHEDER-P
39 JOSIAS MANZANILLO-P (2)
40 JEFF INNIS-P
41 *(RET#) TOM SIEVER*
43 MICKEY WESTON-P
44 RYAN THOMPSON-OF
45 PAUL GIBSON-P (1)
45 MAURO (GOOSE) GOZZO-P
46 DALLAS GREEN-MGR2
47 MIKE DRAPER (INJ)-P
48 PETE SCHOUREK-P
(49) JOE VITKO (INJ)-(P)
50 SID (EL SID) FERNANDEZ (INJ)-P
51 MIKE MADDUX-P
53 ERIC HILLMAN-P
56 JEFF KAISER-P

1994
3RD E 55-58 18.5GB
STRIKE NO POST-SEASON
1 FERNANDO VINA (INJ)-INF
3 LUIS RIVERA-SS
4 MIKE CUBBAGE-CH
5 JEROMY BURNITZ-OF
6 JOE ORSULAK-OF/1B
7 BOBBY WINE, SR.-CH
8 STEVE SWISHER-CH
9 TODD HUNDLEY-C
10 DAVID SEGUI-1B
11 RICK PARKER (INJ)-OF
12 JEFF KENT-2B/INF
13 JONATHAN HURST-P
14 *(RET#) GIL HODGES*
15 JOSE VIZCAINO-SS
16 DWIGHT (DOC) GOODEN (INJ/SUB)-P
17 BRET SABERHAGEN (INJ)-P
18 JEFF MCKNIGHT (INJ)-2B
19 SHAWN HARE-OF
20 RYAN THOMPSON-OF
21 DAVID SEGUI-1B
22 KEVIN MCREYNOLDS (INJ)-OF
23 TIM BOGAR (INJ)-SS/INF
25 BOBBY (BOBBY BO) BONILLA-OF/INF
26 RICO BROGNA-1B
27 TOM MCCRAW-CH
28 BOBBY J. JONES-P
29 JIM LINDEMAN-1B
30 DOUG LINTON-P
31 JOHN FRANCO-P
32 PETE SMITH (INJ)-P
33 KELLY STINNETT-C
34 FRANK SEMINARA-P
37 *(RET#) CASEY STENGEL*
38 DAVE TELGHEDER-P
39 JOSIAS MANZANILLO (INJ)-P
40 ERIC GUNDERSON-P
41 *(RET#) TOM SIEVER*
43 MIKE REMLINGER-P
44 JOHN CANGELOSI (REL)-OF
45 MAURO (GOOSE) GOZZO-P
46 DALLAS GREEN-MGR
47 JASON JACOME-P
48 ROGER MASON-P (2)
50 JUAN CASTILLO-P
51 MIKE MADDUX (INJ)-P
52 GREG PAVLICK-CH
53 ERIC HILLMAN-P
55 FRANK (THE CAPITAL PUNISHER)(HONDO) HOWARD-CH

1995
2ND E (TIE) 69-75 21GB
144 GAME SEASON
1 RICKY OTERO-OF
2 DAMON BUFORD-OF (2)
3 CARL EVERETT-OF
4 MIKE CUBBAGE-CH
5 BROOK FORDYCE-C
5 CHRIS JONES-OF
6 JOE ORSULAK-OF/1B
7 BOBBY WINE, SR.-CH
9 TODD HUNDLEY-C
10 TOM MCCRAW-CH
11 AARON LEDESMA-INF
12 JEFF KENT-2B
13 EDGARDO ALFONZO-2B
14 *(RET#) GIL HODGES*
15 JOSE VIZCAINO-SS
16 DWIGHT (DOC) GOODEN (SUS)-P
17 BRET SABERHAGEN-P (1)
18 JEFF BARRY-OF
19 BILL SPIERS-1B
20 RYAN THOMPSON-OF
21 DAVID SEGUI-1B (1)
21 BILL PULSIPHER-P
22 BRETT BUTLER-OF (1)
22 ALEX OCHOA-OF
23 TIM BOGAR-SS/INF
25 BOBBY (BOBBY BO) BONILLA-3B (1)
26 RICO BROGNA-1B
27 PETE HARNISCH (INJ)-P
28 BOBBY J. JONES-P
29 ROBERT PERSON-P
30 ALBERTO CASTILLO-C
31 JOHN FRANCO-P
33 KELLY STINNETT-C
34 BLAS MINOR (INJ)-P
35 DOUG HENRY-P
36 MIKE BIRKBECK-P
36 DON FLORENCE-P
37 *(RET#) CASEY STENGEL*
38 DAVE MLICKI-P
39 JOSIAS MANZANILLO-P (1)
40 ERIC GUNDERSON-P (1)
40 DAVE TELGHEDER-P
41 *(RET#) TOM SIEVER*
42 BUTCH HUSKEY-3B/OF
43 MIKE REMLINGER-P (1)
43 PAUL BYRD-P
44 KEVIN LOMON-P
44 JASON (IZZY) ISRINGHAUSEN-P
45 JERRY DIPOTO-P
46 DALLAS GREEN-MGR
47 JASON JACOME-P (1)
47 REID CORNELIUS-P (2)
49 PETE WALKER-P
52 GREG PAVLICK-CH
55 FRANK (THE CAPITAL PUNISHER)(HONDO) HOWARD-CH
55 BLAS MINOR (INJ)-P

1996
4TH E 71-91 25GB
0 REY ORDONEZ-SS
1 LANCE JOHNSON-OF

2 BOBBY VALENTINE-MGR2
3 CARL EVERETT (INJ)-OF
4 MIKE CUBBAGE-CH
5 CHRIS JONES-OF
6 CARLOS BAERGA-3B (2)
7 BOBBY WINE, SR.-CH
7 CHARLIE GREENE-C
8 STEVE SWISHER-CH
9 TODD HUNDLEY-C
10 TOM MCCRAW-CH
11 TIM BOGAR-1B
12 JEFF KENT-2B (1)
12 ALVARO ESPINOZA-INF (2)
13 EDGARDO ALFONZO-2B
14 *(RET#) GIL HODGES*
15 JOSE VIZCAINO-SS (1)
15 MATT FRANCO-3B
17 BRENT MAYNE-C
18 KEVIN ROBERSON-OF
19 JASON HARDTKE-2B
20 ROBERTO PETAGINE-1B
(21) BILL PULSIPHER (INJ)-(P)
22 ALEX OCHOA-OF
23 BERNARD GILKEY-OF
26 RICO BROGNA (INJ)-1B
27 PETE HARNISCH (INJ)-P
28 BOBBY J. JONES-P
29 ROBERT PERSON-P
30 ALBERTO CASTILLO-C
31 JOHN FRANCO-P
32 PAUL WILSON (INJ)-P
33 ANDY TOMBERLIN-OF
34 BLAS MINOR-P (1)
34 RICK TRLICEK-P
35 DOUG HENRY-P
37 *(RET#) CASEY STENGEL*
38 DAVE MLICKI-P
(39) JUAN ACEVADO (INJ)-(P)
40 MIKE FYHRIE-P
41 *(RET#) TOM SIEVER*
42 BUTCH HUSKEY (INJ)-3B
43 PAUL BYRD (INJ)-P
44 JASON (IZZY) ISRINGHAUSEN (INJ)-P
45 JERRY DIPOTO-P
46 DALLAS GREEN-MGR1
47 DEREK WALLACE-P
48 PEDRO MARTINEZ, A.-P (1)
49 BOB MACDONALD (WAIV)-P
52 GREG PAVLICK-CH
53 RAFAEL LANDESTOY-CH
54 MARK CLARK-P
55 FRANK (THE CAPITAL PUNISHER)(HONDO) HOWARD-CH
56 BOB APODACA-CH

1997

3RD E 88-74 13GB

0 REY ORDONEZ-SS
1 LANCE JOHNSON (INJ)-OF (1)
1 MOOKIE WILSON-CH
2 BOBBY VALENTINE-MGR
3 CARL EVERETT-OF
4 COOKIE ROJAS-CH
5 JOHN OLERUD-1B
6 MANNY ALEXANDER (INJ)-2B/SS (1)
6 CARLOS MENDOZA-OF
8 CARLOS BAERGA-2B
9 TODD HUNDLEY (INJ)-C
10 GARY THURMAN-OF
10 KEVIN MORGAN-3B
10 ROBERTO PETAGINE-1B
11 CORY LIDLE-P
12 SHAWN GILBERT (INJ)-SS
13 EDGARDO ALFONZO-3B
14 *(RET#) GIL HODGES*
15 MATT FRANCO-1B
17 LUIS LOPEZ-1B
18 TAKASHI KASHIWADA-P
19 JASON HARDTKE-2B
20 BRUCE BENEDICT-CH
(21) BILL PULSIPHER (INJ)-(P)
22 ALEX OCHOA-OF
23 BERNARD GILKEY-OF
25 YORKIS PEREZ (INJ)-P
26 BARRY MANUEL-P
27 PETE HARNISCH (INJ)-P (1)
28 BOBBY J. JONES-P
29 STEVE BIESER-OF
30 ALBERTO CASTILLO-C
31 JOHN FRANCO-P
(32) PAUL WILSON (INJ)-(P)
33 ANDY TOMBERLIN (INJ)-OF
34 BOB APODACA-CH
35 RICK REED-P
36 GREG MCMICHAEL-P
37 *(RET#) CASEY STENGEL*
38 DAVE MLICKI-P
39 JUAN ACEVADO-P
40 ARMANDO REYNOSO-P
41 *(RET#) TOM SIEVER*
42 BUTCH HUSKEY-3B
43 TOBY BORLAND-P (1)
43 TODD PRATT-C
44 JASON (IZZY) ISRINGHAUSEN (INJ)-P
45 RANDY NIEMANN-CH
46 BRIAN BOHANON-P
(47) DEREK WALLACE (INJ)-(P)
48 RICARDO JORDAN-P
49 JOE CRAWFORD-P
50 RICK TRLICEK (INJ)-P (2)
51 MOOKIE WILSON-CH
51 MEL ROJAS-P (2)
53 TOM ROBSON-CH
54 MARK CLARK-P (1)
56 BRIAN MCRAE-OF (2)
66 JOE CRAWFORD-P
99 TURK WENDELL-P (2)

1998

2ND E 88-74 18GB

1 MOOKIE WILSON-CH
2 BOBBY VALENTINE-MGR
3 VANCE WILSON (INJ)-C
4 COOKIE ROJAS-CH
5 JOHN OLERUD-1B
6 RICH BECKER-OF (1)
6 TONY PHILLIPS-OF (3)
7 TODD PRATT (INJ)-C
8 CARLOS BAERGA-2B
9 TODD HUNDLEY (INJ)-C/OF
10 REY ORDONEZ-SS
11 PRESTON WILSON-OF (1)
11 WAYNE KIRBY-OF
12 SHAWN GILBERT-INF
12 JORGE FABREGAS-C (2)
13 EDGARDO ALFONZO (INJ)-3B
14 *(RET#) GIL HODGES*
15 MATT FRANCO (INJ)-UTIL/PH
16 HIDEO NOMO-P (2)
17 LUIS LOPEZ-INF/UTIL
18 CRAIG PAQUETTE (INJ)-3B
18 TODD HANEY-2B/OF
19 JIM TATUM-INF/C
19 LENNY HARRIS-OF (2)
20 BRUCE BENEDICT-CH
21 BILL PULSIPHER (INJ)-P (1)
21 MASATO YOSHII-P
22 AL LEITER (INJ)-P
23 BERNARD GILKEY (INJ)-OF (1)
23 JERMAINE ALLENSWORTH, -OF (3)
25 JAY PAYTON-OF
26 RALPH MILLIARD-INF
27 DENNIS COOK-P
28 BOBBY J. JONES-P
29 MASATO YOSHII-P
29 OCTAVIO DOTEL-P
30 ALBERTO CASTILLO (WAIV) -C
31 JOHN FRANCO-P
31 MIKE PIAZZA-C (3)
(32) PAUL WILSON (INJ)-(P)
33 TIM SPEHR, (INJ)-C (1)
33 MIKE KINKADE-INF
34 BOB APODACA-CH
35 RICK REED-P
36 GREG MCMICHAEL-P (1)(3)
36 JEFF TAM-P
37 *(RET#) CASEY STENGEL*
38 DAVE MLICKI-P (1)
38 JEFF TAM-P
39 RICK WILKINS-C (2)
39 BENNY AGBAYANI-OF
39 JOSIAS MANZANILLO-P
40 ARMANDO REYNOSO (INJ)-P
41 *(RET#) TOM SIEVER*
42 BUTCH HUSKEY (INJ)-OF
43 JOHN HUDEK-P (1)
43 RIGO BELTRAN-P
(44) JASON (IZZY) ISRINGHAUSEN (INJ)-(P)
45 RANDY NIEMANN-CH
45 JOHN FRANCO-P
46 BRIAN BOHANON-P (1)
46 WILLIE BLAIR-P (2)
48 RANDY NIEMANN-CH
49 BRAD CLONTZ (INJ)-P (2)
(50) HECTOR MERCADO (INJ)-(P)
51 MEL ROJAS-P
53 TOM ROBSON-CH
56 BRIAN MCRAE-OF
99 TURK WENDELL-P

1999

2ND E (W/C) 97-66 6.5GB
W NLDS-ARIN 3-1
L NLCS-ATLN 4-2

1 MOOKIE WILSON-CH
2 BOBBY VALENTINE-MGR
3 VANCE WILSON (INJ)-C
4 ROBIN VENTURA-3B
5 JOHN OLERUD-1B
6 MELVIN MORA-3B
7 TODD PRATT-C
8 COOKIE ROJAS-CH
10 REY ORDONEZ-SS
(11) JAY PAYTON (INJ)-(OF)
11 SHANE HALTER-INF
12 SHAWON DUNSTON-UTIL (2)
13 EDGARDO ALFONZO (INJ)-3B
14 *(RET#) GIL HODGES*
15 MATT FRANCO (INJ)-UTIL/PH
17 LUIS LOPEZ-INF/UTI
18 DARRYL HAMILTON-OF (2)
19 ROGER CEDENO-OF
20 BRUCE BENEDICT-CH
21 MASATO YOSHII-P
22 AL LEITER (INJ)-P
23 PAT MAHOMES-P
24 RICKEY HENDERSON-OF
25 BOBBY (BOBBY BO) BONILLA (INJ)-OF
26 TERRANCE LONG-OF
26 BILL TAYLOR-P (2)
27 DENNIS COOK-P
28 BOBBY J. JONES (INJ)-P
29 OCTAVIO DOTEL-P
30 ALLEN WATSON-P (1)
30 JORGE TOCA-INF
31 MIKE PIAZZA-C
33 MIKE KINKADE-INF
34 BOB APODACA-CH
34 CHUCK MCELROY-P (2)
35 RICK REED (INJ)-P
36 GREG MCMICHAEL (INJ)-P (1)
37 *(RET#) CASEY STENGEL*
38 JEFF TAM (INJ)-P (2)
39 JOSIAS MANZANILLO-P
41 *(RET#) TOM SIEVER*
42 *(RET#) JACKIE ROBINSON*
43 RIGO BELTRAN-P (1)
44 JASON (IZZY) ISRINGHAUSEN P (1)
(44) JAY PAYTON (INJ)-(OF)
45 JOHN FRANCO (INJ)-P
46 JERMAINE ALLENSWORTH-OF
48 RANDY NIEMANN-CH
48 DAN MURRAY-P (1)
48 GLENSON RUSCH-P (2)
49 ARMANDO BENITEZ-P
50 BENNY AGBAYANI-OF
52 DAVE WALLACE-CH
53 TOM ROBSON-CH
53 MICKEY BRANTLEY-CH
54 AL JACKSON-CH
55 OREL HERSHISHER-P
56 BRIAN MCRAE-OF (1)
73 KENNY ROGERS-P (2)
99 TURK WENDELL-P

2000

2ND E (W/C) 94-68 1GB
W NLDS-SFN 3-1
W NLCS-STLN 4-1
L WS-NYA 4-1

1 MOOKIE WILSON-CH
2 BOBBY VALENTINE-MGR
3 VANCE WILSON (INJ)-C
4 ROBIN VENTURA-3B
5 MARK JOHNSON-OF
5 ORLANDO MILLER-INF
6 MELVIN MORA-3B (1)
6 TIMO PEREZ-OF
7 TODD PRATT-C
8 COOKIE ROJAS-CH
9 TODD ZEILE-1B
10 REY ORDONEZ (INJ)-SS
11 JASON TYNER-OF (1)
11 JORGE VELANDIA-INF (2)
12 JOHN STEARNS-CH
13 EDGARDO ALFONZO-3B
14 *(RET#) GIL HODGES*
15 MATT FRANCO (INJ)-UTIL/PH
16 DEREK BELL-OF
17 MIKE BORDICK-SS (2)
18 DARRYL HAMILTON (INJ)-OF
19 LENNY HARRIS-INF (2)
20 KURT ABBOTT-INF
21 BOBBY M. JONES-P
22 AL LEITER-P
23 PAT MAHOMES-P
24 RICKEY HENDERSON-OF (1)
25 BILL PULSIPHER-P (1)
26 JON NUNNALLY (JAP)-OF (1)
26 DAVID LAMB-INF
27 DENNIS COOK-P
28 BOBBY J. JONES (INJ)-P
29 ERIC CAMMACK-P
30 JORGE TOCA-INF
31 MIKE PIAZZA-C
32 MIKE HAMPTON-P
33 MIKE KINKADE-INF (1)
33 BUBBA TRAMMELL-OF (2)
34 JERROD RIGGAN-P
35 RICK REED-P
36 GRANT ROBERTS-P
37 *(RET#) CASEY STENGEL*
39 JIM MANN-P
40 RYAN MCGUIRE-OF
41 *(RET#) TOM SIEVER*
42 *(RET#) JACKIE ROBINSON*
44 JAY PAYTON-OF
45 JOHN FRANCO-P
46 RICH RODRIGUEZ-P
47 JOE MCEWING-UTIL
48 GLENSON RUSCH-P
49 ARMANDO BENITEZ-P
50 BENNY AGBAYANI-OF
51 RICK WHITE-P (2)
52 DAVE WALLACE-CH
53 TOM ROBSON-CH
54 AL JACKSON-CH
99 TURK WENDELL-P

2001

3RD E 82-80 6GB

1 MOOKIE WILSON-CH
2 BOBBY VALENTINE-MGR
3 VANCE WILSON-C
4 ROBIN VENTURA-3B
5 TSUYOSHI SHINJO (INJ)-OI
6 TIMO PEREZ (INJ)-OF
7 TODD PRATT-C (1)
7 GARY BENNETT-C (2)
8 DESI RELAFORD-SS
9 TODD ZEILE-1B
10 REY ORDONEZ (INJ)-SS
11 JORGE VELANDIA (INJ)-SS
12 JOHN STEARNS-CH
13 EDGARDO ALFONZO (INJ)-3B
14 *(RET#) GIL HODGES*
17 KEVIN APPIER-P
18 DARRYL HAMILTON (REL)-OF
19 LENNY HARRIS-INF
20 MARK P. JOHNSON-OF
(21) BOBBY M. JONES (INJ)-(F
22 AL LEITER (INJ)-P
23 BRIAN ROSE (WAIV)-P (1)
23 MATT LAWTON-OF (2)
25 ALEX ESCOBAR-OF
26 JASON PHILIPS-C
27 DENNIS COOK-P (1)
27 MARK COREY-P
28 ERIC CAMMACK (INJ)-P
29 STEVE TRACHSEL-P
30 JORGE TOCA-1B
31 MIKE PIAZZA-C
32 BRETT HINCHLIFFE-P
32 BRUCE CHEN-P (2)
33 DONNE WALL (INJ)-P
34 TOM MARTIN-P
35 RICK REED-P (1)
36 GRANT ROBERTS-P
37 *(RET#) CASEY STENGEL*
38 JERROD RIGGAN-P
39 DICKY GONZALEZ-P
40 RICK CROUSHORE (INJ)-P
40 C. J. NITKOWSKI-P (2)
41 *(RET#) TOM SIEVER*
42 *(RET#) JACKIE ROBINSON*
43 PETE WALKER-P
44 JAY PAYTON (INJ)-OF
45 JOHN FRANCO-P
47 JOE MCEWING-UTIL
48 GLENSON RUSCH-P
49 ARMANDO BENITEZ-P
50 BENNY AGBAYANI (INJ)-OF
51 RICK WHITE (INJ)-P
52 RANDY NIEMANN-CH
53 DAVE ENGLE-CH
54CHARLIE HOUGH-CH
55 BOBBY FLOYD-CH
56 DARREN BRAGG-OF (1)
99 TURK WENDELL-P (1)

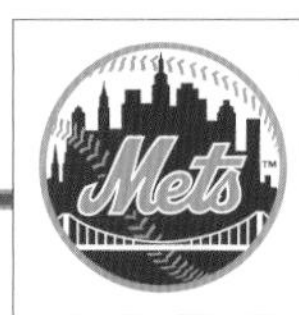

2002

5TH E 75-86 26.5GB

1 MOOKIE WILSON-CH
2 BOBBY VALENTINE-MGR
3 VANCE WILSON-C/1B
4 JOHN VALENTIN-INF
5 MARK JOHNSON-1B/OF
6 TIMO PEREZ-OF
7 JASON PHILLIPS-C
8 MATT GALANTE-CH
9 TY WIGGINGTON-UTIL
0 REY ORDONEZ-SS
2 ROBERTO ALOMAR-2B
3 EDGARDO ALFONZO-3B
4 *(RET#) GIL HODGES*
5 BRADY CLARK-OF (2)
7 SATORU KOMIYAMA-P
8 JEFF D'AMICO-P
9 ROGER CEDENO-OF
0 JEROMY BURNITZ-OF
1 BOBBY M. JONES-P (1)
1 MARK LITTLE-OF (2)
1 RAUL GONZALEZ-OF (2)
2 AL LEITER-P
3 MCKAY CHRISTENSEN-OF
3 ESIX SNEAD-OF
5 GARY MATTHEWS, JR.-PH (1)
5 SCOTT STRICKLAND-P (2)
6 MARCOS SCUTARO-UTIL
7 MARK COREY-P
7 JASON MIDDLEBROOK-P (2)
9 STEVE TRACHSEL-P
30) JORGE TOCA (INJ)-(1B)
1 MIKE PIAZZA-C
2 BRUCE CHEN-P (1)
3 MIKE BACSIK-P
4 PEDRO ASTACIO-P
5 DAVID WEATHERS-P
6 GRANT ROBERTS-P
7 *(RET#) CASEY STENGEL*
8 JAE SEO-P
8 PAT STRANGE-P
9 STEVE REED-P (2)
0 TONY TARASCO-OF/1B
1 *(RET#) TOM SIEVER*
2 MO VAUGHN-1B
3 PETE WALKER-P (1)
3 JAIME CERDA-P
4 JAY PAYTON-OF (1)
45) JOHN FRANCO (INJ)-(P)
6 TYLER WALKER-P
7 JOE MCEWING-UTIL
8 KANE DAVIS (INJ)-P
9 ARMANDO BENITEZ-P
0 JOHN THOMSON-P (2)
1 TOM ROBSON-CH
1 CHRIS CHAMBLISS-CH
2 RANDY NIEMANN-CH
3 DAVE ENGLE-CH
3 MARK GUTHRIE-P
4CHARLIE HOUGH-CH
5 SHAWN ESTES-P (1)
5 PEDRO FELICIANO-P

2003

5TH E 66-95 34.5GB

0 TONY CLARK-1B
2 GARY PETTIS-CH
3 VANCE WILSON-C
4 MATT GALANTE-CH
5 TSUYOSHI SHINJO-OF
6 TIMO PEREZ (INJ)-OF
7 JOSE REYES (INJ)-SS
9 TY WIGGINGTON-3B
0 REY SANCHEZ (INJ)-SS/2B (1)
0 JOE DIPASTINO-C
1 JOE (LITTLE MAC) MCEWING-UTIL
12 ROBERTO ALOMAR-2B (1)
12 DANNY GARCIA-2B
13 JORGE VELANDIA-SS
14 *(RET#) GIL HODGES*
15 DENNY WALLING-CH
16 DAVID CONE (INJ) (RET)-P
17 GRAEME LLOYD-P (1)
17 JASON ANDERSON-P (2)
18 ART HOWE-MGR
19 ROGER CEDENO-OF
20 JEROMY BURNITZ (INJ)-OF (1)
20 PRENTICE REDMAN-OF
21 RAUL GONZALEZ-OF
22 AL LEITER (INJ)-P
23 JASON PHILLIPS-1B/C
25 DON BAYLOR (ILL)-CH
26 MARCOS SCUTARO-2B
27 JASON MIDDLEBROOK-P
27 MIKE GLAVINE-1B
28 SCOTT STRICKLAND (INJ)-P
29 STEVE TRACHSEL-P
30 CLIFF FLOYD (INJ)-OF
31 MIKE PIAZZA (INJ) (SUS:4G)-C
32 MIKE STANTON (INJ)-P
33 MIKE BACSIK-P
34 PEDRO ASTACIO (INJ)-P
35 DAVID WEATHERS-P
36 GRANT ROBERTS (INJ)-P
37 *(RET#) CASEY STENGEL*
38 PAT STRANGE-P
39 DAN WHEELER-P
40 JAE SEO-P
41 *(RET#) TOM SIEVER*
42 MO VAUGHN (INJ)1B
43 JAIME CERDA-P
44 JAY BELL (INJ)-INF
45 JOHN FRANCO (INJ)-P
46 JEREMY GRIFFITHS-P
47 TOM GLAVINE-P
48 AARON HEILMAN-P
49 ARMANDO BENITEZ-P (1)
49 ORBER MORENO-P
50 MATT WATSON-OF
52 RICK WAITS-CH
52 TONY CLARK-1B
53 VERN RUHLE-CH
55 PEDRO FELICIANO-P
56 EDWIN ALMONTE-P (2)
57 JASON ROACH-P
61 JEFF DUNCAN-OF

2004

5TH E 71-91 25GB

1 ESIX SNEAD-OF
2 GARY PETTIS-CH
3 VANCE WILSON (INJ)-C
4 MATT GALANTE-CH
5 DAVID WRIGHT-3B
6 RICKY GUTIERREZ-2B (1)
6 TOM WILSON-C (1)
6 JAY KEPPINGER-2B/SS
7 JOSE REYES (INJ)-2B/SS
9 TY WIGGINGTON-3B/INF (1)
9 CRAIG BRAZELL-1B
10 JEFF DUNCAN-OF
10 BRIAN BUCHANAN-OF (2)
10 JOE HIETPAS-C
11 JOE (LITTLE MAC) MCEWING-UTIL
12 DANNY GARCIA-2B
13 MATT GINTER (INJ)-P
14 *(RET#) GIL HODGES*
15 DENNY WALLING-CH
15 RICHARD HIDALGO-OF (2)
17 WILSON DELGARDO-SS
18 ART HOWE-MGR
19 SCOTT ERICKSON-P
19 HEATH BELL-P
20 KARIM GARCIA-OF (1)
20 RICKY BOTTALICO-P
21 GERALD WILLIAMS-OF
22 AL LEITER-P
23 JASON PHILLIPS-C/1B
25 KAZUO MATSUI-SS
26 JAE WEONG SEO-P
27 TODD ZEILE-1B/3B/C
(28) SCOTT STRICKLAND (INJ)-(P)
29 STEVE TRACHSEL-P
30 CLIFF FLOYD-OF
31 MIKE PIAZZA-1B/C
32 MIKE STANTON-P
33 TYLER YATES-P
34 RICKY BOTTALICO-P
34 KRIS BENSON-P (2)
35 DAVID WEATHERS-P (1)
35 MIKE DEJEAN-P (2)
36 GRANT ROBERTS (INJ)-P
37 *(RET#) CASEY STENGEL*
38 JAMES BALDWIN-P
38 VICTOR ZAMBRANO (INJ)-P (2)
39 DAN WHEELER-P (1)
40 BRADEN LOOPER-P
41 *(RET#) TOM SIEVER*
(42) MO VAUGHN (INJ)-(1B)
43 SHANE SPENCER (INJ) (REL)-OF
43 BARTOLOME FORTUNATO-P
44 MIKE CAMERON-OF
45 JOHN FRANCO-P
46 JOSE PARRA-P
47 TOM GLAVINE-P
48 AARON HEILMAN-P
49 ORBER MORENO-P
50 VICTOR DIAZ-OF/2B
51 RICK PETERSON-CH
52 DON BAYLOR-CH
53 RICK WAITS-CH
53 BOBBY FLOYD-CH
55 PEDRO FELICIANO-P
57 ERIC VALENT-OF/1B

2005

3RD E (TIED) 83-79 7GB

1 ANDERSON HERNANDEZ-2B/SS
2 SANDY ALOMAR, SR.-CH
3 MIGUEL CAIRO (INJ)-2B
4 CHRIS WOODWARD-UTIL
5 DAVID WRIGHT-3B
7 JOSE REYES-SS
10 SHINGO TAKATSU-P (2)
11 RAMON CASTRO (INJ)-C
12 WILLIE RANDOLPH-MGR
13 BRIAN DAUBACH-1B
14 *(RET#) GIL HODGES*
15 CARLOS BELTRAN-OF
16 DOUG MIENTKIEWICZ-1B
17 DAE-SUNG KOO (INJ)-P
18 MARLON ANDERSON-UTIL
19 HEATH BELL-P
20 VICTOR DIAZ-OF
21 GERALD WILLIAMS-OF
22 ROYCE RING-P
23 KAZUHISA ISHII (INJ)-P
25 KAZUO MATSUI (INJ)-2B
26 JAE WEONG SEO-P
27 MIKE MATTHEWS-P
27 MIKE JACOBS-1B
28 JUAN PADILLA-P
29 STEVE TRACHSEL (INJ)-P
30 CLIFF FLOYD-OF
31 MIKE PIAZZA (INJ)-C
32 DANNY GRAVES-P (2)
33 MIKE DIFELICE-C
33 JOSE SANTIAGO-P
34 KRIS BENSON (INJ)-P
35 MIKE DEJEAN-P (1)
35 JOSE OFFERMAN-1B (2)
36 MANNY AYBAR-P
37 *(RET#) CASEY STENGEL*
38 VICTOR ZAMBRANO-P
39 ROBERTO HERNANDEZ-P
40 BRADEN LOOPER-P
41 *(RET#) TOM SIEVER*
42 *(RET#) JACKIE ROBINSON*
(43) BARTOLOME FORTUNATO (INJ)-(P)
44 MIKE CAMERON (INJ)-OF
46 FELIX HEREDIA (INJ)-P
46 TIM HAMULACK-P
47 TOM GLAVINE-P
48 AARON HEILMAN-P
50 MANNY ACTA-CH
51 RICK PETERSON-CH
53 JERRY MANUEL-CH
54 RICK DOWN-CH
56 GUY CONTI-CH
57 ERIC VALENT-OF

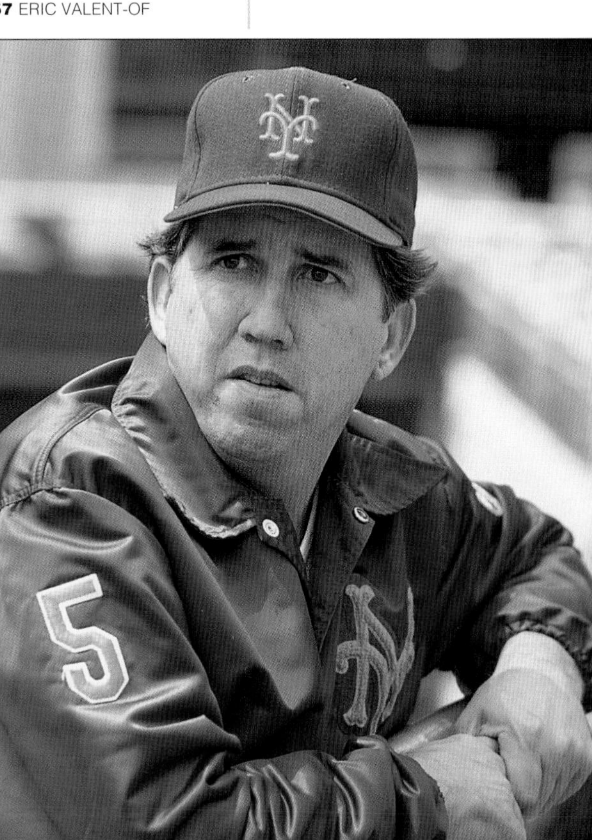

Davey Johnson (#5) managed the Mets to their last World Championship in 1986. They won 108 games that year. They went on to beat Houston in the NLCS. Everyone remembers Mookie Wilson's knubber down the first base line that opened the gates to victory over the Red Sox in seven games. Johnson finished first in 1988 also, but lost to the Dodgers in the NLCS 4-2. Of his 14 years managing, he finished first in his division five times. He ended his career with 1148 wins and 888 losses. That's a percentage of .564. Tommy Lasorda had .526 and the Ole Professor Casey Stengel had .508, believe it or not.

1932
PHILADELPHIA PHILLIES
4TH 78-76 12GB

1 KIDDO DAVIS-OF
2 DICK (ROWDY RICHARD) BARTELL-SS
3 CHUCK KLEIN-OF
4 DON HURST-1B
5 PINKY WHITNEY-3B/2B
6 HAL (SHERIFF) LEE-OF
7 SPUD DAVIS-C
8 HARRY (HANK) MCCURDY-C
9 AL TODD-C
10 EDDIE DELKER-2B (2)
11 BERNIE FRIBERG-2B
12 LES MALLON-2B/3B
14 FRED BRICKELL-OF
15 CLIFF HEATHCOTE-1B (2)
16 RAY BENGE-P
17 JACK BERLY-P
18 PHIL (FIDGETY PHIL) COLLINS-P
19 CLISE DUDLEY-P
20 HAL ELLIOTT-P
21 JUMBO JIM ELLIOTT-P
22 SNIPE HANSEN-P
23 GEORGE KNOTHE-2B
24 ED HOLLEY-P
25 FLINT (SHAD) RHEM-P (2)
26 BURT (BARNEY) SHOTTON MGR
27 JACK ONSLOW-CH
28 REGGIE GRABOWSKI-P
29 BOB ADAMS-P
30 AD LISKA-P
NO# STEW BOLEN-P (5G: 4/20-5/16)
NO# RUBE BRESSLER-OF (1) (27G: 4/15-6/14)
NO# CHET (NICK) NICHOLS-P (11G: 4/18-5/29)
NO# RUSS SCARRITT-OF (11G: 4/16-5/25)
NO# DOUG (POCO) TAITT-PH (4G: 4/18-5/4)
NO# HUGH WILLINGHAM-PH (4G: 4/20-30)

1933
7TH 69-92 31GB

1 CHICK FULLIS-OF/3B
2 DICK (ROWDY RICHARD) BARTELL-SS
3 CHUCK KLEIN-OF
4 GUS DUGAS-1B/OF
4 FRANK RAGLAND-P
5 PINKY WHITNEY-3B/2B (1)
5 FRITZ KNOTHE-3B/2B (2)
5 MICKEY HASLIN-2B
6 HAL (SHERIFF) LEE-OF (1)
6 WES SCHULMERICH-OF (2)
7 MICKEY FINN (DIED)-2B
7 JIM MCLEOD-3B/SS
8 SPUD DAVIS-C
9 HARRY (HANK) MCCURDY-C
10 AL TODD-C/OF
11 EDDIE DELKER-2B/3B
12 JACK WARNER-2B/INF
14 FRED BRICKELL-OF
14 ALTA (SCHOOLBOY) COHEN-OF
15 DON HURST-1B
16 PHIL (FIDGETY PHIL) COLLINS-P
17 JUMBO JIM ELLIOTT-P
18 CLARENCE PICKREL-P
18 REGGIE GRABOWSKI-P
18 MICKEY HASLIN-2B
19 SNIPE HANSEN-P
20 JACK BERLY-P
21 ED HOLLEY-P
22 AD LISKA-P
23 CY MOORE-P
24 FLINT (SHAD) RHEM-P
25 FRANK PEARCE-P
26 NEWT HUNTER-CH
26 BURT (BARNEY) SHOTTON MGR
27 BURT (BARNEY) SHOTTON MGR
27 NEWT HUNTER-CH
28 JOHN JACKSON-P
31 HUGH WILLINGHAM-PH
__ CHARLIE BUTLER-P (1G: 5/1)

1934
7TH 56-93 37GB

10 JOE (SOCKS) HOLDEN-C
11 AL TODD-C
12 JIMMIE (ACE) WILSON-C/INF/MGR
20 DICK (ROWDY RICHARD) BARTELL-SS
21 LOU CHIOZZA-2B/UTIL
22 MICKEY HASLIN-INF
23 MARTY HOPKINS-3B (1)
23 ANDY (HANDY ANDY) HIGH-3B/2B
23 BUD CLANCY-1B
24 DON HURST-1B (1)
24 DOLPH CAMILLI-1B (2)
25 IRV JEFFRIES-2B/3B
30 ETHAN ALLEN-OF
31 CHICK FULLIS-OF (1)
31 KIDDO DAVIS-OF (2)
32 HARVEY (GINK) HENDRICK OF/INF
33 PRINCE OANA-OF
33 JOHNNY MOORE-OF (2)
34 FREDDIE FRINK-OF
34 ART (SPEEDY) RUBLE-OF
34 HACK WILSON-OF (2)
35 WES SCHULMERICH-OF (1)
35 BUCKY WALTERS-3B/2B/P (2)
40 PHIL (FIDGETY PHIL) COLLINS-P
41 GEORGE DARROW-P
42 CURT DAVIS-P
43 JUMBO JIM ELLIOTT-P (1)
43 EUEL (CHIEF) MOORE-P
44 REGGIE GRABOWSKI-P
45 SNIPE HANSEN-P
46 ED HOLLEY-P (1)
47 TED KLEINHANS-P (1)
47 SYL JOHNSON-P (2)
48 CY MOORE-P
49 CY MALIS-P
49 BILL LOHRMAN-P
49 FRANK PEARCE-P
50 HANS LOBERT-CH
51 DICK SPALDING-CH
__ ED BOLAND-OF (8G: 9/11-24)

1935
7TH 64-89 35.5GB

10 BUBBER JONNARD-C
10 JOE (SOCKS) HOLDEN-C
11 AL TODD-C
11 HAL KELLEHER-P
12 JIMMIE (ACE) WILSON-C/2B/MGR
20 BUCKY WALTERS-3B/2B/P
21 LOU CHIOZZA-2B/3B
22 BLONDY RYAN-INF (1)
22 DINO (DYNAMO) CHIOZZA-SS
22 CHILE GOMEZ-SS/2B
23 JOHNNY VERGEZ-3B/SS
24 DOLPH CAMILLI-1B
25 ART BRAMHALL-SS/3B
25 MICKEY HASLIN (ILL)-SS/INF
30 ETHAN ALLEN-OF
31 GEORGE WATKINS-OF
32 ORVILLE JORGENS-P
33 JOHNNY MOORE-OF
34 ED BOLAND-OF
34 FRED (FRITZ) LUCAS-OF
40 PHIL (FIDGETY PHIL) COLLINS-P (1)
40 HUGH (LOSING PITCHER) MULCAHY-P
41 PRETZEL PEZZULLO-P
42 MICKEY HASLIN (ILL)-SS/INF
42 CURT DAVIS-P
43 EUEL (CHIEF) MOORE-P (1)
44 ORVILLE JORGENS-P
45 SNIPE HANSEN-P (1)
45 RAY (POP) PRIM-P
46 JOE BOWMAN-P
47 SYL JOHNSON-P
48 JIM BIVIN-P
49 FRANK PEARCE-P
50 HANS LOBERT-CH
51 DICK SPALDING-CH
__ TOMMY THOMAS-P (2) (4G: 5/21-30)

1936
8TH 54-100 38GB

10 EARL GRACE-C
11 BILL ATWOOD-C
12 JIMMIE (ACE) WILSON-C/1B/MGR
20 CHARLIE SHEERIN-INF
20 RAY BENGE-P (2)
20 STAN SPERRY-2B
21 LEO NORRIS-SS/2B
22 CHILE GOMEZ-2B/SS
23 JOHNNY VERGEZ-3B (1)
23 STAN SPERRY-2B
23 RAY BENGE-P (2)
24 DOLPH CAMILLI-1B
25 MICKEY HASLIN-2B/3B (1)
25 PINKY WHITNEY-3B/2B (2)
30 ETHAN ALLEN-OF (1)
30 WALT BASHORE-OF/3B
32 CHUCK KLEIN-OF (2)
32 ERNIE (DAVE) SULIK-OF
32 GENE CORBETT-1B
33 JOHNNY MOORE-OF
34 LOU CHIOZZA-OF/INF
34 MORRIS (SNOOKER) (MOE) ARNOVICH-OF
36 CHUCK KLEIN-OF
37 GEORGE WATKINS-OF (1)
37 ERNIE (DAVE) SULIK-OF
40 BUCKY WALTERS-P/2B/3B
41 PRETZEL PEZZULLO-P
41 PETE SIVESS-P
41 TOM ZACHARY-P (2)
42 CURT DAVIS-P (1)
42 FABIAN KOWALIK-P (2)
42 HUGH (LOSING PITCHER) MULCAHY-P
43 HERB (HUB) (LEFTY) HARRIS-P
43 HAL KELLEHER-P
44 ORVILLE JORGENS-P
45 EUEL (CHIEF) MOORE-P
46 JOE BOWMAN-P
47 SYL JOHNSON-P
48 CLAUDE PASSEAU-P
50 HANS LOBERT-CH
51 DICK SPALDING-CH
__ LEFTY BERTRAND-P (1G: 4/15)
__ ELMER (SWEDE) BURKART-P (2G: 9/14-27)
__ JOE (SOCKS) HOLDEN-PH (1G: 4/21)

1937
7TH 61-92 34.5GB

10 EARL GRACE-C
11 BILL ATWOOD-C
12 JIMMIE (ACE) WILSON-C/1B/MGR
20 GEORGE (TOM) SCHAREIN-SS
21 LEO NORRIS-INF
22 GENE CORBETT-3B/2B
22 WALTER (TARZAN) STEPHENSON-C
23 DEL YOUNG-2B
24 EARL (SNITZ) BROWN-OF/1B
25 PINKY WHITNEY-3B
26 BILL (ANDY) ANDRUS-3B
26 ELMER (SWEDE) BURKART-P
27 DOLPH CAMILLI-1B
30 HERSH MARTIN-OF
33 JOHNNY MOORE-OF
34 MORRIS (SNOOKER) (MOE) ARNOVICH-OF
36 CHUCK KLEIN-OF
37 FRED TAUBY-OF
37 HOWIE (LEFTY) GORMAN-OF
40 BUCKY WALTERS-P/3B
41 LARRY CRAWFORD-P
41 PETE SIVESS-P
41 BOB (THIN MAN) ALLEN-P
42 HUGH (LOSING PITCHER) MULCAHY-P
43 HAL KELLEHER-P
44 ORVILLE JORGENS-P
45 BOBBY (LEFTY) BURKE-P
45 WAYNE LAMASTER-P
46 BUCKY WALTERS-P/3B
47 SYL JOHNSON-P
47 WALTER (TARZAN) STEPHENSON-C
48 CLAUDE PASSEAU-P
49 WALT MASTERS-P
50 HANS LOBERT-CH
– LEON (LEFTY) PETTIT-P (3G: 5/29-6/8)

1938
8TH 45-105 43GB

1 CHUCK KLEIN-OF
2 HERSH MARTIN-OF
3 MORRIS (SNOOKER) (MOE) ARNOVICH-OF
4 RAY STOVIAK-OF
4 ART REBEL-OF
5 PINKY WHITNEY-3B/INF
6 GEORGE (TOM) SCHAREIN-INF
7 DEL YOUNG-SS/2B
8 EARL (SNITZ) BROWN-1B/OF
8 JUSTIN (OTT) STEIN-3B/2B
8 BUCK JORDAN-3B/1B (2)
9 EMMETT (HEINIE) MUELLER -2B/3B
10 CAP CLARK-C
11 BILL ATWOOD-C
12 JIMMIE (ACE) WILSON-C/MGR1
13 CLAUDE PASSEAU-P
14 PHIL (MICKEY) WEINTRAUB-1B
15 HUGH (LOSING PITCHER) MULCAHY-P
16 TOM REIS-P (1)
16 TUCK STAINBACK-OF (2)
16 GIB (GIBBY) BRACK-OF (2
17 BUCKY WALTERS-P/3B (1
17 AL (BOOTS) HOLLINGSWORTH-P (2)
18 AL SMITH-P
19 WILD BILL HALLAHAN-P
20 PETE SIVESS-P
21 ED HEUSSER-P
21 WAYNE LAMASTER-P (1)
22 SYL JOHNSON-P
23 GENE CORBETT, 1B
23 HOWIE (LEFTY) GORMAN-PH
24 HAL KELLEHER-P
24 MAX BUTCHER-P (2)
25 HANS LOBERT-CH/MGR2
28 SPUD DAVIS-C (2)
__ ELMER (SWEDE) BURKART-P (2G: 9/26-10/2)
__ EDDIE (ITZY) FEINBERG-SS/OF (10G: 9/11-10/2)
__ TOM LANNING-P (3G: 9/14-10/2)
__ ALEX PITKO-OF (7G: 9/11-10/2)

1939
8TH 45-106 50.5GB

1 DOC PROTHRO-MGR
2 HANS LOBERT-CH
3* SYL JOHNSON-P*
4 SPUD DAVIS-C
5* IKE PEARSON-P*
5 BILL ATWOOD-C
5 JOHNNY (LEFTY) WATWOOD-1B
6 GUS SUHR-1B (2)
7 JOE KRACHER-C
7* AL (BOOTS) HOLLINGSWORTH-P* (1
7* BUD HAFEY-OF/P* (2)
8* MAX BUTCHER-P* (1)
8 WALLY MILLIES-C
9* HUGH (LOSING PITCHER) MULCAHY-P*
10 CHARLIE LETCHAS-C
10 DAVE COBLE-C
11 JENNINGS (JINX) POINDEXTER-P
11 BILL KERSIECK-P
12 JIM HENRY-P
12 RAY HARRELL-P (2)
13 CLAUDE PASSEAU-P (1)
14 ELMER (SWEDE) BURKART-P
14 AL SMITH-P
14 KIRBY HIGBE-P (2)
15 BOOM-BOOM BECK-P
16 MAX BUTCHER-P (1)
16 STAN BENJAMIN-OF/3B
16 LES POWERS-1B
16 ROY (JEEP) (SAGE) HUGHES-2B (2)
17 AL (BOOTS) HOLLINGSWORTH-P (1)
17 DEL YOUNG-SS/2B
18 GEORGE (TOM) SCHAREIN-SS
18 AL SMITH-P
19 PINKY MAY-3B
20 PINKY WHITNEY-INF
20 JIM SHILLING-OF
21 EMMETT (HEINIE) MUELLER-UTIL
22 JACK BOLLING-1B
23 WALLY MILLIES-C
23 BUD BATES-OF
23 JENNINGS (JINX)

PHILADELPHIA PHILLIES

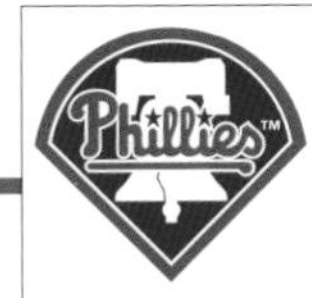

POINDEXTER-P
4 MORRIS (SNOOKER) (MOE) ARNOVICH-OF
5 HERSH MARTIN-OF
6 CHUCK KLEIN-OF (1)
6 BENNIE WARREN-C
7 GIB (GIBBY) BRACK-OF/1B
8 LE GRANT SCOTT-OF
8 BILL HOFFMAN-P
8 ROY (JEEP) (SAGE) HUGHES-2B (2)
3 ROY BRUNER-P
4 GENE SCHOTT-P (1)
4 BILL ATWOOD-C
4 LEN GABRIELSON (INJ)-1B
5 ELMER (SWEDE) BURKART-P
5 JOE MARTY-OF/P (2)
_ EDDIE (ITZY) FEINBERG-2B/SS (6G: 5/8-23)

1940

8TH 50-103 50GB

1 DOC PROTHRO-MGR
2 HANS LOBERT-CH
3* SYL JOHNSON-P*
4* ART MAHAN-1B/P*
4 DANNY LITWHILER-OF
5 BILL ATWOOD-C
6 GUS SUHR-1B
6* CY BLANTON-P*
6 SAM FILE-SS/3B
7 STAN BENJAMIN-OF
7 GEORGE JUMONVILLE-SS/3B
7* CY BLANTON-P*
7 WALLY BERGER-OF/1B (2)
8 MEL MAZZERA-OF/1B
8 ED LEVY-PH
8* FRANK (LEFTY) HOERST-P*
9* HUGH (LOSING PITCHER) MULCAHY-P*
0 HAM SCHULTE-2B/SS
2 IKE PEARSON-P
4 KIRBY HIGBE-P
5 BOOM-BOOM BECK-P
6 LEFTY SMOLL-P
7 DEL YOUNG-SS/2B
7 CHARLIE FRYE-P
8 GEORGE (TOM) SCHAREIN-SS
8 HAL MARNIE-2B
9 PINKY MAY-3B/SS
20 BOBBY BRAGAN-SS/3B
21 EMMETT (HEINIE) MUELLER-UTIL
22 JOHNNY PODGAJNY-P
23 WALLY MILLIES-C
4 MORRIS (SNOOKER) (MOE) ARNOVICH-OF (1)
24 MAXIE WILSON-P
25 HERSH MARTIN-OF
25 AL MONCHAK-SS/2B
25 NEB STEWART-OF
26 BENNIE WARREN-C/1B
27 PAUL (LEFTY) MASTERSON-P
28 DANNY LITWHILER-OF
28 LLOYD BROWN-P
28 ROY (JEEP) (SAGE) HUGHES-2B
29 CHUCK KLEIN-OF
31 EMMETT (HEINIE) MUELLER-UTIL
33 ROY BRUNER-P
33 JOHNNY RIZZO-OF/3B (3)
34 SI JOHNSON-P
35 JOE MARTY-OF

1941

8TH 43-111 57GB

1 PROTHRO, DOC MGR
2 HANS LOBERT-CH
3 MICKEY LIVINGSTON-C/1B
4 DANNY LITWHILER-OF
5 JOHNNY RIZZO-OF/3B
6* BILL CROUCH-P* (1)
6 PAUL BUSBY-OF
7 STAN BENJAMIN-OF/INF
8* RUBE MELTON-P*
9* GENE LAMBERT-P*
9 BILL NAGEL-UTIL
9 HAL MARNIE-2B
10 VITO TAMULIS-P (1)
10 LEE GRISSOM-P (2)
11 FRANK (LEFTY) HOERST-P
12 IKE PEARSON-P
14 CY BLANTON-P
15 BOOM-BOOM BECK-P
16 GEORGE JUMONVILLE-SS/3B
16 DANNY MURTAUGH-2B/SS
17 JOHNNY PODGAJNY-P
19 PINKY MAY-3B/SS
20 BOBBY BRAGAN-SS/INF
21 EMMETT (HEINIE) MUELLER (INJ)-UTIL
23 WALLY MILLIES-C
23 PAUL (LEFTY) MASTERSON-P
23 JIM CARLIN-OF/3B
24 HAL MARNIE-2B
24 BILL NAGEL-UTIL
25 NICK ETTEN-1B
26 BENNIE WARREN-C
28 ROY (JEEP) (SAGE) HUGHES-2B
29 CHUCK KLEIN-OF
30 BILL HARMAN-C/P
31 EMMETT (HEINIE) MUELLER (INJ)-UTIL
33 DALE JONES-P
34 SI JOHNSON-P
35 JOE MARTY-OF
ROY BRUNER (MIL)-(P)
HUGH MULCAHY (LOSING PITCHER) (MIL)-(P)

1942

8TH 42-109 62.5GB

1 HANS LOBERT-MGR
2 HANS LOBERT-MGR
2 BILL KILLIFER-CH
3 CHUCK KLEIN-PH/CH
5 BILL BURICH-SS/3B
5 BENNIE WARREN-C/1B
6 MICKEY LIVINGSTON-C/1B
7 DANNY LITWHILER-OF
7 HAL MARNIE-INF
7* BOOM-BOOM BECK-P*
8* SI JOHNSON-P*
8* HILLY FLITCRAFT-P*
8* PAUL (LEFTY) MASTERSON-P*
9* GENE LAMBERT-P*
10 BOOM-BOOM BECK-P
10 ANDY LAPIHUSKA-P
11 DANNY LITWHILER-OF
11 CY BLANTON-P
11 BOOM-BOOM BECK-P
12 BILL PETERMAN-C
12 ERNIE KOY-OF (2)
14 ED MURPHY-1B
14 FRANK (LEFTY) HOERST-P
15 TOMMY HUGHES-P
15 BOOM-BOOM BECK-P
15 HAL MARNIE-INF
16 HILLY FLITCRAFT-P
16 SI JOHNSON-P
17 RUBE MELTON-P
18 SAM NAHEM-P
19 IKE PEARSON-P
20 JOHNNY PODGAJNY-P
20 BOBBY BRAGAN-SS/UTIL
22 NICK ETTEN-1B
24 BENNIE WARREN-C/1B
24 AL GLOSSIP-2B/3B
25 BENNIE CULP-C
25 BERT HODGE-3B
26 PINKY MAY-3B
27 DANNY MURTAUGH-INF
28 BILL BURICH-SS/3B
28 TOMMY HUGHES-P
30 STAN BENJAMIN-OF/1B
30 ED FREED-OF
31 DANNY LITWHILER-OF
31 GEORGE HENNESSEY-P
32 EARL NAYLOR-OF/1B/P
33 RON (ROLLO) NORTHEY-OF
34 LLOYD (LITTLE POISON) WANER-OF

1943

7TH 64-90 41GB

1 DANNY MURTAUGH (MIL)-2B
2 PINKY MAY-3B
3 BABE DAHLGREN-UTIL
4 DANNY LITWHILER-OF (1)
4 COAKER TRIPLETT-OF (2)
5 EARL NAYLOR-OF
5 BUSTER ADAMS-OF (2)
6* AL (LEFTY) GERHEAUSER-P*
6* ANDY KARL-P* (2)
7 MICKEY LIVINGSTON-C/1B (1)
8 CHUCK KLEIN-OF
9 PAUL BUSBY-OF
10 SI JOHNSON (MIL)-P
10 DEE MOORE-UTIL (2)
11 AL (LEFTY) GERHEAUSER-P
12 CHARLIE FUCHS-P (1)
12 DALE MATTHEWSON-P
14 RON (ROLLO) NORTHEY-OF
15 BOOM-BOOM BECK-P
15 BOB FINLEY-C
15 ANDY SEMINICK-C/OF
15 KEN RAFFENSBERGER-P
16 JACK KRAUS-P
17 JOHNNY PODGAJNY-P (1)
17 ROGERS MCKEE-P
17 DUTCH DIETZ-P (2)
18 TOM PADDEN-C (1)
18 GEORGE EYRICH (MIL)-P
19 GLEN STEWART-SS/UTIL
20 BILL WEBB-P
20 RAY HAMRICK-2B/SS
20 CHARLIE BREWSTER-SS (2)
21 ANDY LAPIHUSKA-P
21 DICK CONGER-P
22 SCHOOLBOY ROWE-P
23 EARL WHITEHILL-P
24 BUCKY HARRIS-MGR1
25 GARTON DEL SAVIO-SS
25 DALE MATTHEWSON-P
25 BILL LEE-P (2)
26 DICK BARRETT-P
27 NEWT KIMBALL-P (2)
28 JIMMY WASDELL-1B/OF (2)
29 BENNY CULP-C
33 FREDDIE FITZSIMMONS-MGR2
38 BILL LEE-P (2)
__ DEACON DONAHUE-P (2G: 9/16-22)
__ MANNY SALVO-P (2) (1G: 5/13)

1944

8TH 61-92 43.5GB

1 CHARLIE LETCHAS-INF
2 MOON MULLEN-2B/UTIL
2 BUSTER ADAMS-OF
2 BENNY CULP-C
3* ROGERS MCKEE-P*
3 JIMMY WASDELL-OF/1B
3* ANDY KARL-P*
4 COAKER TRIPLETT-OF
4 RON (ROLLO) NORTHEY-OF
5 BUSTER ADAMS-OF
5 COAKER TRIPLETT-OF
6 CHARLIE LETCHAS-INF
7* KEN RAFFENSBERGER-P*
7 TED CIESLAK-3B/OF
8 GLEN STEWART-3B/INF
9 MERV SHEA-C/CH
9 BOB FINLEY-C
10 HARRY SHUMAN-P
10 CHET COVINGTON-P
10 CHARLIE RIPPLE-P
11 AL (LEFTY) GERHEAUSER-P
11 VERN KENNEDY-P (2)
12 DEACON DONAHUE-P
12 DICK BARRETT-P
14 RON (ROLLO) NORTHEY-OF
14 FREDDIE FITZSIMMONS-MGR
15 ANDY SEMINICK-C/OF
15 KEN RAFFENSBERGER-P
16 CHARLEY SCHANZ-P
17 MOON MULLEN-2B/UTIL
17 BILL LEE-P
18 AL VERDEL-P
19 GLEN STEWART-3B/INF
19 DEACON DONAHUE-P
19 JOHNNY PEACOCK-C/2B (2)
20 BENNY CULP-C
20 RAY HAMRICK (MIL)-SS
20 DALE MATTHEWSON-P
20 RALPH (PUTSY) CABALLERO-3B
21 NICK GOULISH-PH
21 HEINIE HELTZEL-SS
21 GRANNY HAMNER-SS
22 TURKEY TYSON-PH
22 CHARLEY SCHANZ-P
22 CHET COVINGTON-P
23 BENNY CULP-C
23 JOHN FICK-P
23 LEE RILEY-OF
23 TED CIESLAK-3B/OF
24 AL (LEFTY) GERHEAUSER-P
24 ANDY SEMINICK-C/OF
25 MERV SHEA-C/CH
26 DICK BARRETT-P
26 CHUCK KLEIN-OF
27 BARNEY MUSSILL-P
28 ANDY KARL-P
28 NICK GOULISH-PH
28 JIMMY WASDELL-OF/1B
29 BARNEY MUSSILL-P
29 TONY LUPIEN-1B
30 AL VERDEL-P
30 JOE ANTOLICK-C
31 BOB FINLEY-C
31 BENNY CULP-C
33 FREDDIE FITZSIMMONS-MGR
36? LOU LUCIER-P (2) (1G: 10/1)

1945

8TH 46-108 52GB

1 BITSY MOTT-SS/INF
2 BUSTER ADAMS-OF (1)
2 JOHN ANTONELLI-3B/INF (2)
3 JIMMY WASDELL-OF/1B
4* JIMMIE FOXX-INF/P*
5 VANCE DINGES-OF/1B
6 FRED DANIELS-2B/3B
6 GRANNY HAMNER (MIL)-SS
7 NICK PICCIUTO-3B/2B
7 VINCE DIMAGGIO-OF
8 GARVIN HAMNER-INF
8 ED WALCZAK-2B/SS
8 WALLY FLAGER-SS/2B (2)
9 GUS MANCUSO-C
10 JOHNNY PEACOCK-C (1)
10 HAL SPINDEL-C
10 WHIT WYATT-P
11 WHIT WYATT-P
11 ANDY KARL-P
12 DICK BARRETT-P
14 FREDDIE FITZSIMMONS-MGR1
15 KEN RAFFENSBERGER-P
15 DICK MAUNEY-P
16 CHARLEY SCHANZ (ILL)-P
17 BILL LEE-P (1)
17 HUGH (LOSING PITCHER) MULCAHY (MIL)-P
18 CHARLIE SPROULL-P
19 VERN KENNEDY-P (1)
19 JACK KRAUS-P
20 DICK COFFMAN-P
21 DON HASENMAYER (MIL)-2B/3B
22 RENE MONTEAGUDO-OF/P
23 ANDY KARL-P
24 ANDY SEMINICK-C/OF
25 MERV SHEA-CH
26 CHUCK KLEIN-CH
27 COAKER TRIPLETT-OF
28 RALPH (PUTSY) CABALLERO-3B
28 GLENN CRAWFORD-OF/INF (2)
29 OSCAR JUDD-P (2)
31 IZZY LEON-P
32 STAN ANDREWS-C (2)
33 ANDY KARL-P
33 WALLY FLAGER-SS/2B (2)
34 MITCH CHETKOVICH-P
34 BEN CHAPMAN-UTIL/P/MGR2 (2)
35 CHARLIE RIPPLE-P
36 LOU LUCIER-P
36 LEFTY SCOTT-P
36 JAKE POWELL-OF (2)
37 NICK GOULISH-OF
37 DON GRATE-P

1946

5TH 69-85 28GB

1 JOHNNY WYROSTEK-OF
2 KEN RICHARDSON-2B
2 ROLLIE HEMSLEY (INJ)-C
3 JIMMY WASDELL-OF/1B (1)
3* ELI HODKEY-P*
4 RON (ROLLO) NORTHEY-OF
5 JIM (RAWHIDE) TABOR-3B
6 ROY (JEEP) (SAGE) HUGHES-INF
7 BEN CHAPMAN-P/MGR
8* CHARLIE RIPPLE-P*
9 EMIL (ANTELOPE) (DUTCH) VERBAN-2B (2)
10 DICK MULLIGAN-P (1)
11 BENNY BENGOUGH-CH
12 ELI HODKEY-P
14 DEL ENNIS-OF
15 DICK MAUNEY-P
16 KEN RAFFENSBERGER-P
17 OSCAR JUDD-P
18 CHARLEY SCHANZ-P
19 SCHOOLBOY ROWE-P
20 SI JOHNSON-P (1)
21 IKE PEARSON-P
21 CHARLIE GILBERT-OF (2)

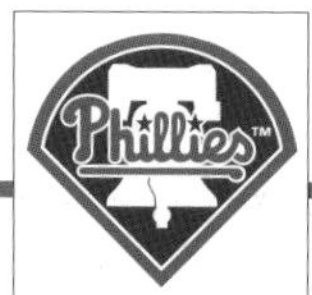

22 FRANK (LEFTY) HOERST-P
23 HAL SPINDEL-C
23 CHARLIE LETCHAS (MIL)-2B
24 ANDY SEMINICK-C
25 BENNY CULP-C
26 FRANK (BUCK) MCCORMICK-1B
27 JOHN O'NEIL-SS
28 TOMMY HUGHES-P
29 SKEETER NEWSOME-SS/INF
30 RON (ROLLO) NORTHEY-OF
30 BLIX DONNELLY-P (2)
31 CY PERKINS-CH
32 ART LOPATKA-P
33 ANDY KARL-P
34 VINCE DIMAGGIO-OF (1)
(37) RAY HAMRICK (MIL)-(INF)
37 GRANNY HAMNER-SS
38 AL JURISICH-P
39 LOU (THE MAD RUSSIAN) NOVIKOFF-OF
39 AL (HAPPY) MILNAR-P (2)
39 LOU POSSEHL-P
40 JOHNNY HUMPHRIES-P
40 DON HASENMAYER-3B
41 VANCE DINGES-1B/OF
42 CHARLEY STANCEAU-P (2)
43 GLENN CRAWFORD-PH
43 DON GRATE-P
44 ANDY KARL-P
46 DEE MOORE-C/1B
47 ROLLIE HEMSLEY (INJ)-C
47 VANCE DINGES-1B/OF
48 HUGH (LOSING PITCHER) MULCAHY-P
50 EMIL (ANTELOPE) (DUTCH) VERBAN-2B (2)
__ BILL BURICH (MIL)-3B (2G: 6/8-12)
__ DICK KOECHER-P (1G: 9/29)
GEORGE EYRICH (MIL)-(P)
ROGERS MCKEE (MIL)-(P)
MOON MULLEN (MIL)-(INF)

1947

7TH (TIE) 62-92 32GB

1 JOHNNY WYROSTEK-OF
2 BUSTER ADAMS-OF
3 CHARLIE GILBERT-OF
4 RON (ROLLO) NORTHEY-OF (1)
4 HARRY (THE HAT) WALKER-OF/1B (2)
5 JIM (RAWHIDE) TABOR-3B
6 SKEETER NEWSOME-SS/INF
7 BEN CHAPMAN-MGR
8 DON PADGETT-C
9 EMIL (ANTELOPE) (DUTCH) VERBAN-2B
10 FRANK (BUCK) MCCORMICK-1B (1)
10 HOWIE (STRETCH) (STEEPLE) SCHULTZ-1B (2)
11 BENNY BENGOUGH-CH
12 LOU FINNEY-PH
12 WILLIE (PUDDIN' HEAD) JONES-3B
14 DEL ENNIS-OF
15 DICK MAUNEY-P
16 KEN RAFFENSBERGER-P (1)
17 OSCAR (OSSIE) JUDD-P
18 CHARLEY SCHANZ-P
19 SCHOOLBOY ROWE-P
20 DUTCH LEONARD-P
21 AL JURISICH-P
22 JACK ALBRIGHT (INJ)-SS
22 RALPH LAPOINTE-SS
23 RALPH LAPOINTE-SS
24 ANDY SEMINICK-C
25 BENNY CULP-CH
26 HOWIE (STRETCH) (STEEPLE) SCHULTZ-1B (2)
26 AL (MOOSE) LAKEMAN-1B/C (2)
26 DICK (HIGHPOCKETS) KOECHER-P
27 FREDDY SCHMIDT-P (2)
27 KEN HEINTZELMAN-P (2)
27 RALPH (PUTSY) CABALLERO-3B
28 TOMMY HUGHES-P
29 LOU POSSEHL-P
30 BLIX DONNELLY-P
31 CY PERKINS-CH
32 ROLLIE HEMSLEY (INJ)-C
32 CURT SIMMONS-P
33 FREDDY SCHMIDT-P (2)
34 HUGH POLAND-C (1)
34 FRANK (LEFTY) HOERST-P
34 FREDDY SCHMIDT-P (2)
35 LEE (JEEP) HANDLEY-3B/INF
35 GRANNY HAMNER-SS
36 NICK ETTEN-1B
36 AL (MOOSE) LAKEMAN-1B/C (2)
37 HOMER SPRAGINS-P
__ JESSE LEVAN-OF (2G: 9/27-28)

1948

6TH 66-88 25.5GB

1 GRANNY HAMNER-2B/INF
1 RICHIE (WHITEY) ASHBURN (INJ)-OF
2 RALPH (PUTSY) CABALLERO-3B/2B
3 BERT HAAS (INJ)-3B/1B
4 HARRY (THE HAT) WALKER-OF/INF
5 EDDIE (EPPIE) MILLER-SS
6 DICK SISLER-1B
7 BEN CHAPMAN-MGR1
7 EDDIE SAWYER-MGR3
8 DON PADGETT-C
9 EMIL (ANTELOPE) (DUTCH) VERBAN-2B (1)
9* JOCKO THOMPSON-P*
11 BENNY BENGOUGH-CH
12 HOWIE (STRETCH) (STEEPLE) SCHULTZ-1B (1)
12 LOU POSSEHL-P
14 DEL ENNIS-OF
15 BAMA ROWELL-UTIL
16 JOHNNY BLATNIK-OF
17 GRANNY HAMNER-2B/INF
17 OSCAR (OSSIE) JUDD-P
17 HAL WAGNER-C (2)
18 SAM (SUBWAY SAM) NAHEM-P
18 JACKIE MAYO-OF
19 SCHOOLBOY ROWE-P
20 DUTCH LEONARD-P
21 ED (THE WILD ELK OF THE WASATCH) HEUSSER-P
22 DON PADGETT-C
24 ANDY SEMINICK-C
25 AL (MOOSE) LAKEMAN-C/P
26 DICK (HIGHPOCKETS) KOECHER-P
26 JIM KONSTANTY-P
27 KEN HEINTZELMAN-P
28 CURT SIMMONS-P
30 BLIX DONNELLY-P
31 CY PERKINS-CH
32 DUSTY COOKE-CH/MGR2
33 GRANNY HAMNER-2B/INF
34 MONK DUBIEL-P
35 CHARLIE (BUD) BICKNELL-P
36 AL (LEFTY) PORTO-P
36 NICK (JUMBO) STRINCEVICH-P (2)
36 ROBIN ROBERTS-P
37 LOU GRASMICK-P
37 LOU POSSEHL-P
37 WILLIE (PUDDIN' HEAD) JONES-3B
41 STAN (STASH) LOPATA-C
41 PAUL (LI'L ABNER) ERICKSON-P (2)

1949

3RD 81-73 16GB

1 RICHIE (WHITEY) ASHBURN (INJ)-OF
2 GRANNY HAMNER-SS
3 BERT HAAS-PH (1)
3 BILL GLYNN-1B
3 EDDIE (EPPIE) MILLER-2B/SS
4 EDDIE WAITKUS (INJ)-1B
5 EDDIE (EPPIE) MILLER-2B/SS
6 WILLIE (PUDDIN' HEAD) JONES-3B
7 BUDDY BLATTNER-INF
8 DICK SISLER-1B
9 RALPH (PUTSY) CABALLERO-2B/SS
9 MIKE GOLIAT-2B/1B
11 BENNY BENGOUGH-CH
12 BILL (SWISH) NICHOLSON-OF
14 DEL ENNIS-OF
15 JACKIE MAYO-OF
16 JOHNNY BLATNIK-OF
17 STAN (HONDO) HOLLMIG-OF
19 SCHOOLBOY ROWE-P
20 HANK BOROWY-P
21 ANDY SEMINICK-C
22 KEN TRINKLE-P
24 EDDIE SAWYER-MGR
25 KEN (HAWK) SILVESTRI-C
26 HAL WAGNER-C
27 KEN HEINTZELMAN-P
28 CURT SIMMONS-P
29 STAN (STASH) LOPATA-C
30 BLIX DONNELLY-P
31 CY PERKINS-CH
32 DUSTY COOKE-CH
33 ED (BUTCH) SANICKI-OF
34 RUSS (MONK) (THE MAD MONK) (ROWDY) MEYER-P
35 JIM KONSTANTY-P
36 ROBIN ROBERTS-P
37 JOCKO THOMPSON-P
38 GEORGE (MOOSE) EARNSHAW-CH
39 CHARLIE (BUD) BICKNELL-P
40 ROBERT (MAJE) MCDONNELL-CH
41 BOB MILLER-P

1950

1ST 91-63 0GB

L WS-NYA 4-0

1 RICHIE (WHITEY) ASHBURN (INJ)-OF
2 GRANNY HAMNER-SS
3 RALPH (PUTSY) CABALLERO-INF
4 EDDIE WAITKUS-1B
5 JIMMY BLOODWORTH-INF (2)
6 WILLIE (PUDDIN' HEAD) JONES-3B
8 DICK SISLER-1B
9 MIKE GOLIAT-2B/1B
11 BENNY BENGOUGH-CH
12 BILL (SWISH) NICHOLSON-OF
14 DEL ENNIS-OF
15 JACKIE MAYO-OF
16 JOHNNY BLATNIK-OF (1)
16 KEN (HOOK) JOHNSON-P (2)
17 STAN (HONDO) HOLLMIG-OF
18 MILO CANDINI-P
19 BOB MILLER-P
20 HANK BOROWY-P (1)
20 STEVE RIDZIK-P
21 ANDY SEMINICK-C
23 BUBBA CHURCH-P
24 EDDIE SAWYER-MGR
25 KEN (HAWK) SILVESTRI-C
27 KEN HEINTZELMAN-P
28 CURT SIMMONS-P
29 STAN (STASH) LOPATA-C
30 BLIX DONNELLY-P
31 CY PERKINS-CH
32 DUSTY COOKE-CH
33 JOCKO THOMPSON-P
34 RUSS (MONK) (THE MAD MONK) (ROWDY) MEYER-P
35 JIM KONSTANTY-P
36 ROBIN ROBERTS-P
37 DICK WHITMAN-OF
38 GEORGE (MOOSE) EARNSHAW-CH
39 PAUL (STU) STUFFEL-P
40 ROBERT (MAJE) MCDONNELL-CH
41 JACK BRITTIN-P

1951

5TH 73-81 23.5GB

1 RICHIE (WHITEY) ASHBURN-OF
2 GRANNY HAMNER-SS
3 RALPH (PUTSY) CABALLERO-2B/INF
4 EDDIE WAITKUS-1B
5 JIMMY BLOODWORTH-2B/1B
5 TOMMY (BUCKSHOT) BROWN-UTIL (2)
6 WILLIE (PUDDIN' HEAD) JONES-3B
8 DICK SISLER-OF
9 MIKE GOLIAT-2B/3B (1)
9 DICK YOUNG-2B
10 DEL (BABE) WILBER-C
11 BENNY BENGOUGH-CH
12 BILL (SWISH) NICHOLSON-OF
13 EDDIE PELLIGRINI-INF
14 DEL ENNIS-OF
15 ED (BUTCH) SANICKI-OF
15 JACKIE MAYO-OF
16 LOU POSSEHL-P
17 STAN (HONDO) HOLLMIG-OF
18 MILO CANDINI-P
19 BOB MILLER (INJ)-P
20 ANDY (SWEDE) HANSEN-P
21 ANDY SEMINICK-C
22 KARL DREWS-P
23 BUBBA CHURCH-P
24 EDDIE SAWYER-MGR
25 KEN (HAWK) SILVESTRI-C/2B
27 KEN HEINTZELMAN-P
(28) CURT SIMMONS (MIL)-(P)
29 STAN (STASH) LOPATA-C
31 CY PERKINS-CH
32 DUSTY COOKE-CH
33 JOCKO THOMPSON-P
34 RUSS (MONK) (THE MAD MONK) (ROWDY) MEYER P
35 JIM KONSTANTY-P
36 ROBIN ROBERTS-P
37 DICK WHITMAN-OF
37 TOMMY (BUCKSHOT) BROWN-UTIL (2)
37 JIMMY BLOODWORTH-2B/1B
37 MEL CLARK-OF
38 LEO CRISTANTE-P
39 KEN (HOOK) JOHNSON-P
40 ROBERT (MAJE) MCDONNELL-CH
41 JACK BRITTIN-P
41 NILES JORDAN-P

1952

4TH 87-67 9.5GB

1 RICHIE (WHITEY) ASHBURN -OF
2 GRANNY HAMNER-SS
3 RALPH (PUTSY) CABALLERO-INF
4 EDDIE WAITKUS-1B
5 TOMMY (BUCKSHOT) BROWN-OF/1B (1)
5 DICK YOUNG-2B
6 WILLIE (PUDDIN' HEAD) JONES-3B
7 JACK (LUCKY) LOHRKE-INF
8 CONNIE RYAN-2B
9 NIPPY JONES-1B
10 DEL (BABE) WILBER-PH (1)
11 BENNY BENGOUGH-CH
12 BILL (SWISH) NICHOLSON-OF
14 DEL ENNIS-OF
15 JACKIE MAYO-OF
16 MEL CLARK-OF
17 JOHNNY WYROSTEK-OF (2)
18 HOWIE FOX-P
19 BOB MILLER-P
20 ANDY (SWEDE) HANSEN-P
21 SMOKY BURGESS-C
22 KARL DREWS-P
23 BUBBA CHURCH-P (1)
24 EDDIE SAWYER-MGR1
24 STEVE O'NEILL-MGR2
27 KEN HEINTZELMAN-P
28 CURT SIMMONS-P
29 STAN (STASH) LOPATA-C
31 CY PERKINS-CH
32 DUSTY COOKE-CH
32 EDDIE (HOTSHOT) MAYO-CH
33 KENT (PETE) PETERSON-P
34 RUSS (MONK) (THE MAD MONK) (ROWDY) MEYER-P
35 JIM KONSTANTY-P
36 ROBIN ROBERTS-P
37 STEVE RIDZIK-P
40 ROBERT (MAJE) MCDONNELL-CH
41 LOU POSSEHL-P
41 PAUL (STU) STUFFEL-P

1953

3RD (TIE) 83-71 22GB

1 RICHIE (WHITEY) ASHBURN -OF
2 GRANNY HAMNER-2B/SS
3 TOMMY (RABBIT) GLAVIANO-INF
4 EDDIE WAITKUS-1B
6 WILLIE (PUDDIN' HEAD) JONES-3B

PHILADELPHIA PHILLIES

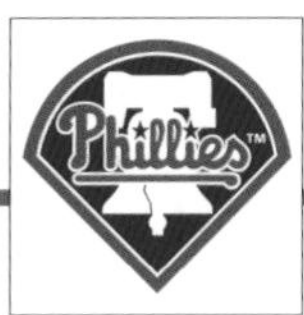

7 JACK (LUCKY) LOHRKE-INF
7 TED KAZANSKI-SS
8 CONNIE RYAN-2B/1B (1)
9 EARL (THE EARL OF SNOHOMISH) TORGESON-1B
1 BENNY BENGOUGH-CH
2 BILL (SWISH) NICHOLSON-OF
4 DEL ENNIS-OF
5 JACKIE (BUTCH) MAYO-OF
6 MEL CLARK (INJ)-OF
7 JOHNNY WYROSTEK-OF
8 JOHNNY LINDELL-P/OF (2)
9 BOB MILLER-P
0 ANDY (SWEDE) HANSEN-P
1 SMOKY BURGESS-C
2 KARL DREWS-P
3 STAN PALYS-OF
4 STEVE O'NEILL-MGR
7 KENT (PETE) PETERSON-P
8 CURT SIMMONS (INJ)-P
9 STAN (STASH) LOPATA-C
1 CY PERKINS-CH
2 EDDIE (HOTSHOT) MAYO-CH
3 TOM (MONEYBAGS) QUALTERS-P
4 PAUL (STU) STUFFEL-P
4 THORNTON KIPPER-P
5 JIM KONSTANTY-P
6 ROBIN ROBERTS-P
7 STEVE RIDZIK-P
0 ROBERT (MAJE) MCDONNELL-CH

1954

4TH 75-79 22GB

1 RICHIE (WHITEY) ASHBURN-OF
2 GRANNY HAMNER-2B/SS
4 BOBBY MORGAN-SS/INF
5 MICKEY MICELOTTA-SS
5 JIM (IGOR) COMMAND-3B
6 WILLIE (PUDDIN' HEAD) JONES-3B
7 TED KAZANSKI-SS
8 TERRY MOORE-MGR2
9 EARL (THE EARL OF SNOHOMISH) TORGESON-1B
0 DANNY SCHELL-OF
1 BENNY BENGOUGH-CH
2 STAN (TUCKER) JOK-PH (1)
4 DEL ENNIS-OF/1B
5 STAN PALYS-OF
6 MEL CLARK-OF
7 JOHNNY WYROSTEK-OF/1B
8 JOHNNY LINDELL-PH
9 BOB MILLER-P
0 MURRY DICKSON-P
1 SMOKY BURGESS-C
2 KARL DREWS-P (1)
2 HERM WEHMEIER-P (2)
4 STEVE O'NEILL-MGR1
5 GUS NIARHOS-C
6 BOB (GREENIE) GREENWOOD (INJ)-P
7 RON MROZINSKI-P
8 CURT SIMMONS-P
9 STAN (STASH) LOPATA-C/1B
1 EARLE (THE KENTUCKY COLONEL) COMBS-CH
2 EDDIE (HOTSHOT) MAYO-CH
3 TOM (MONEYBAGS) QUALTERS-P
4 THORNTON KIPPER-P
5 JIM KONSTANTY-P (1)
6 ROBIN ROBERTS-P
37 STEVE RIDZIK-P
38 FLOYD BAKER-3B/2B (2)
40 ROBERT (MAJE) MCDONNELL-CH
44 PAUL PENSON-P

1955

4TH 77-77 21.5GB

1 RICHIE (WHITEY) ASHBURN-OF
2 GRANNY HAMNER-2B/SS
3 PEANUTS LOWREY-OF/INF
4 BOBBY MORGAN-2B/INF
5 MICKEY MICELOTTA-SS
6 WILLIE (PUDDIN' HEAD) JONES-3B
7 TED KAZANSKI-SS/3B
8 BOB BOWMAN-OF
9 EARL (THE EARL OF SNOHOMISH) TORGESON-1B (1)
9* SAUL ROGOVIN-P* (2)
9 JOHN (GOOSE) EASTON-PR
10 DANNY SCHELL-PH
10 JIM GREENGRASS-OF/3B (2)
11 BENNY BENGOUGH-CH
12 BOB (SARGE) KUZAVA-P (2)
14 DEL ENNIS-OF/1B
15 STAN PALYS-OF (1)
16 MEL CLARK-OF
17 ROY SMALLEY-SS/INF
18 JIM (BEAR) OWENS-P
18 JIM (IGOR) COMMAND-PH
19 BOB MILLER-P
20 MURRY DICKSON-P
21 SMOKY BURGESS-C (1)
21 ANDY SEMINICK-C (2)
22 HERM WEHMEIER-P
24 MAYO SMITH-MGR
25 GUS NIARHOS-C
26 BOB (GREENIE) GREENWOOD-P
27 RON MROZINSKI-P
28 CURT SIMMONS-P
29 STAN (STASH) LOPATA-C/1B
31 WHIT WYATT-CH
32 WALLY MOSES-CH
34 THORNTON KIPPER-P
36 ROBIN ROBERTS-P
37 STEVE RIDZIK-P (1)
37 GLEN GORBOUS-OF (2)
38 FLOYD BAKER-3B/2B
38 RON NEGRAY-P
40 ROBERT (MAJE) MCDONNELL-CH
42 JACK MEYER-P
43 LYNN LOVENGUTH-P
44 DAVE COLE-P
44 EDDIE WAITKUS-1B (2)
45 JACK SPRING-P
45 FRED VAN DUSEN-PH
47 MARV BLAYLOCK-1B/OF
48 JIM WESTLAKE-PH

1956

5TH 71-83 22GB

1 RICHIE (WHITEY) ASHBURN-OF
2* GRANNY HAMNER-SS/2B/P*
4 BOBBY MORGAN-3B/2B (1)
4 SOLLY HEMUS-2B/3B (2)
6 WILLIE (PUDDIN' HEAD) JONES-3B
7 TED KAZANSKI-2B/SS
8 BOB BOWMAN-OF
9 GLEN GORBOUS-OF
11 BENNY BENGOUGH-CH
12 MARV BLAYLOCK-1B/OF
14 DEL ENNIS-OF
15 WALLY WESTLAKE-PH
15 ELMER VALO-OF (2)
16 FRANK BAUMHOLTZ-OF
17 ROY SMALLEY-SS
19 BOB MILLER-P
20 MURRY DICKSON-P (1)
20 HARVEY (THE KITTEN) HADDIX-P (2)
21 ANDY SEMINICK-C
22 HERM WEHMEIER-P (1)
22 BEN FLOWERS-P (2)
23 JIM GREENGRASS-OF/3B
24 MAYO SMITH-MGR
25 STU MILLER-P (2)
26 SAUL ROGOVIN-P
28 CURT SIMMONS-P
29 STAN (STASH) LOPATA-C/1B
30 BOB ROSS-P
31 WHIT WYATT-CH
32 WALLY MOSES-CH
33 DUANE (DEE) PILLETTE-P
34 MACK BURK-C
35 JOE LONNETT-C
36 ROBIN ROBERTS-P
38 RON NEGRAY-P
39 JIM (BEAR) OWENS-P
39 ED BOUCHEE-1B
40 ROBERT (MAJE) MCDONNELL-CH
42 JACK MEYER-P
44 DICK (TURK) FARRELL-P
45 ANGELO LIPETRI-P
48 JACK SANFORD-P

1957

5TH 77-77 18GB

1 RICHIE (WHITEY) ASHBURN-OF
2* GRANNY HAMNER-SS/2B/P*
3 BOBBY MORGAN-2B (1)
3 DON LANDRUM-OF
4 SOLLY HEMUS-2B
5 ED BOUCHEE-1B
6 WILLIE (PUDDIN' HEAD) JONES-3B
7 TED KAZANSKI-INF
8 JOHN KENNEDY-3B
9 HARRY ANDERSON-OF
10 BOB BOWMAN-OF
11 BENNY BENGOUGH-CH
12 MARV BLAYLOCK-1B/OF
14 RIP REPULSKI-OF
16 FRANK BAUMHOLTZ-PH
16 WARREN HACKER-P (2)
17 ROY SMALLEY-SS
19 BOB MILLER-P
20 HARVEY (THE KITTEN) HADDIX-P
21 ANDY SEMINICK-C/CH
22 JIM HEARN-P
24 MAYO SMITH-MGR
26 SAUL ROGOVIN-P
26 RON (ROLLO) NORTHEY-PH (2)
28 CURT SIMMONS-P
29 STAN (STASH) LOPATA-C/1B
31 WHIT WYATT-CH
32 WALLY MOSES-CH
33 TOM (MONEYBAGS) QUALTERS-P
35 JOE LONNETT-C
36 ROBIN ROBERTS-P
39 JACK SANFORD-P
40 ROBERT (MAJE) MCDONNELL-CH
42 JACK MEYER-P
43 DICK (TURK) FARRELL-P
44 SETH (MOE) MOREHEAD-P
45 CHICO FERNANDEZ-SS
46 DON CARDWELL-P
49 WARREN HACKER-P (2)
50 GLEN GORBOUS-OF
50 CHUCK HARMON-OF/INF (2)
JIM (BEAR) OWENS (MIL)-(P)

1958

8TH 69-85 23GB

1 RICHIE (WHITEY) ASHBURN-OF
2 GRANNY HAMNER (INJ)-INF
4 SOLLY HEMUS-2B/3B
5 ED BOUCHEE (ILL)-1B
6 WILLIE (PUDDIN' HEAD) JONES-3B/1B
7 TED KAZANSKI-INF
8 JOE LONNETT-C
9 HARRY ANDERSON-OF/1B
10 BOB BOWMAN-OF
11 BENNY BENGOUGH-CH
12 DAVE PHILLEY-OF/1B
14 WALLY POST-OF
15 RIP REPULSKI-OF
16 CHICO FERNANDEZ-SS
17 ROY SMALLEY-SS
17 CHICO FERNANDEZ-SS
18 PANCHO HERRERA-3B/1B
19 BOB MILLER-P
21 ANDY SEMINICK-CH
22 JIM HEARN-P
24 MAYO SMITH-MGR1
24 EDDIE SAWYER-MGR2
25 DON ERICKSON-P
27 JIMMIE COKER-C
28 CURT SIMMONS-P
29 STAN (STASH) LOPATA-C/1B
31 BILL (BARNACLE BILL) (SAILOR BILL) POSEDEL-CH
32 WALLY MOSES-CH
33 TOM (MONEYBAGS) QUALTERS-P (1)
33 JOHN ANDERSON-P
34 MACK BURK (MIL)-PH
36 ROBIN ROBERTS-P
37 CHUCK ESSEGIAN-OF
37 BOBBY YOUNG-2B
38 JOHNNY GRAY-P
38 JIM HEGAN-C (2)
39 JACK SANFORD-P
41 BOB CONLEY-P
42 JACK MEYER-P
43 DICK (TURK) FARRELL-P
44 SETH (MOE) MOREHEAD-P
46 DON CARDWELL-P
47 CARL (SWATS) SAWATSKI-C
48 RAY (BABY) SEMPROCH-P
49 WARREN HACKER-P
50 ANGELO LIPETRI-P
50 CHUCK HARMON-OF/INF
__ HANK MASON-P (1G: 9/12)
JIM (BEAR) OWENS (MIL)-(P)

1959

8TH 64-90 23GB

1 RICHIE (WHITEY) ASHBURN-OF
2 GRANNY HAMNER-SS/3B (1)
2 SPARKY ANDERSON-2B
4 GENE (AUGIE) FREESE-3B/2B
5 ED BOUCHEE-1B
6 WILLIE (PUDDIN' HEAD) JONES-3B/1B (1)
6 JIM (DUTCH) BOLGER-OF (2)
7 JOE LONNETT-C
7 JOHN (GOOSE) EASTON-PH
8 VALMY THOMAS-C/3B
9 HARRY ANDERSON-OF
10 BOB BOWMAN-OF/P
11 BENNY BENGOUGH-CH
12 DAVE PHILLEY-OF/1B
14 WALLY POST-OF
15 JOE KOPPE-SS/2B
16 JOHN (GOOSE) EASTON-PH
17 CHICO FERNANDEZ-SS/2B
18 CHRIS SHORT-P
20 HARRY HANEBRINK-UTIL
21 DICK CARTER-CH
22 JIM HEARN-P
22 RUBEN GOMEZ-P
24 EDDIE SAWYER-MGR
28 CURT SIMMONS (INJ)-P
29 GENE CONLEY (INJ)-P
31 KEN (HAWK) SILVESTRI-CH
33 AL SCHROLL-P (1)
34 HUMBERTO ROBINSON-P (2)
35 SOLLY DRAKE-OF (2)
36 ROBIN ROBERTS-P
38 JIM HEGAN-C (1)
39 JOHNNY (MUTT) RIDDLE-CH
40 RUBEN GOMEZ-P
41 FREDDY RODRIGUEZ-P
42 JACK MEYER-P
43 DICK (TURK) FARRELL-P
44 SETH (MOE) MOREHEAD-P (1)
44 TAYLOR (TAY) PHILLIPS-P (2)
45 SPARKY ANDERSON-2B
46 DON CARDWELL-P
47 CARL (SWATS) SAWATSKI-C
48 RAY (BABY) SEMPROCH-P
49 JIM (BEAR) OWENS-P
50 ED KEEGAN-P
51 TOM FERRICK-CH

1960

8TH 59-95 36GB

1 AL (BLACKIE) DARK-3B/1B (1)
1 JOE MORGAN-3B
1 BOBBY WINE-SS
2 BOBBY MALKMUS-INF
3 BOBBY DEL GRECO-OF
4 TED LEPCIO-INF
5 ED BOUCHEE-1B (1)
5 CAL NEEMAN-C (2)
6 JOHNNY CALLISON (INJ)-OF (1)
7 TONY CURRY-OF
8 TONY TAYLOR-2B/3B (2)
9 HARRY ANDERSON-OF/1B (1)
9 LEE WALLS-UTIL (2)
10 JIMMIE COKER-C
11 CLAY DALRYMPLE-C
12 DAVE PHILLEY-OF/1B (1)
14 WALLY POST-OF (1)
15 JOE KOPPE (INJ)-SS/3B
16 BOBBY GENE SMITH-OF/3B
17 KEN WALTERS-OF
18 PANCHO HERRERA-1B/2B
20 RUBEN AMARO-SS
21 DICK CARTER-CH
21 PEANUTS LOWREY-CH
22 RUBEN GOMEZ-P
22 TONY GONZALEZ-OF (2)
23 JOHN BUZHARDT-P
24 EDDIE SAWYER-MGR1
28 CURT SIMMONS-P (1)
28 ART MAHAFFEY-P
29 GENE CONLEY-P
30 JIM (WOODY) WOODS-3B
31 KEN (HAWK) SILVESTRI-CH

32 GENE (SKIP) MAUCH-MGR3
34 HUMBERTO ROBINSON-P
36 ROBIN ROBERTS-P
37 HANK MASON-P
39 ANDY COHEN-CH/MGR2/CH
41 CHRIS SHORT-P
42 JACK MEYER (INJ)-P
43 DICK (TURK) FARRELL-P
44 TAYLOR (TAY) PHILLIPS-P
44 AL NEIGER-P
46 DON CARDWELL-P (1)
46 DALLAS GREEN-P
49 JIM (BEAR) OWENS-P

1961

8TH 47-107 46GB

1 AL VINCENT-CH
2 BOB LEMON-CH
3 PEANUTS LOWREY-CH
4 GENE (SKIP) MAUCH-MGR
5 BOB (SID) SADOWSKI-3B
5 GEORGE WILLIAMS-2B
6 JOHNNY CALLISON-OF
7 TONY CURRY-OF
7 PANCHO HERRERA-1B
8 TONY TAYLOR (INJ)-2B/3B
9 LEE WALLS-UTIL
10 CAL NEEMAN-C
10 DARRELL JOHNSON-C (1)
10 JIMMIE COKER-C
10 AL KENDERS-C
11 CLAY DALRYMPLE-C
12 CHOO CHOO COLEMAN-C
14 DON FERRARESE-P
15 JOE KOPPE-SS (1)
15 CHARLEY SMITH-3B/SS (2)
16 BOBBY GENE SMITH-OF
17 KEN WALTERS-OF/INF
18 PANCHO HERRERA-1B
18 ELMER VALO-OF (2)
19 BOBBY MALKMUS-INF
20 RUBEN AMARO-SS/INF
22 TONY GONZALEZ-OF
23 JOHN BUZHARDT-P
24 DON DEMETER-OF/1B (2)
25 KEN LEHMAN-P
26 PAUL BROWN-P
26 BOBBY DEL GRECO-OF (1)
27 JACK BALDSCHUN-P
28 ART MAHAFFEY-P
29 FRANK SULLIVAN-P
30 JIM (WOODY) WOODS-3B
36 ROBIN ROBERTS (INJ)-P
39 PAUL BROWN-P
41 CHRIS SHORT-P
42 JACK MEYER-P
43 DICK (TURK) FARRELL-P (1)
43 WES COVINGTON-OF (4)
46 DALLAS GREEN-P
49 JIM (BEAR) OWENS-P

1962

7TH 81-80 20GB

1 AL VINCENT-CH
2 AL WIDMAR-CH
3 PEANUTS LOWREY-CH
4 GENE (SKIP) MAUCH-MGR
5 ROY (SQUIRREL) SIEVERS-1B/OF
6 JOHNNY CALLISON-OF
7 TED SAVAGE-OF
8 TONY TAYLOR-2B/SS
9 SAMMY WHITE-C
10 BOB OLDIS-C
11 CLAY DALRYMPLE-C
12 TONY GONZALEZ (INJ)-OF
14 DON FERRARESE-P (1)
14 BOBBY LOCKE-P (2)
14 TED SAVAGE-OF
15 BILLY CONSOLO-3B (1)
16 FRANK TORRE-1B
17 JIMMIE COKER(MIL)-C
17 JACK DAVIS-OF
18 FRANK SULLIVAN-P (1)
19 BOBBY MALKMUS-INF
20 RUBEN AMARO (MIL)-SS/1B
21 JOHN HERRNSTEIN-OF
23 PAUL BROWN (ILL)-P
23 DENNIS BENNETT-P
24 DON DEMETER-3B/UTIL
25 TONY GONZALEZ (INJ)-OF
26 CAL (BUSTER) MCLISH-P
27 JACK BALDSCHUN-P
28 ART MAHAFFEY-P
29 JOHN BOOZER-P
31 MEL ROACH-UTIL
32 BILLY KLAUS-INF
36 *(RET#) ROBIN ROBERTS*
39 PAUL BROWN (ILL)-P
41 CHRIS SHORT-P
42 BOBBY WINE-SS/3B
43 WES COVINGTON-OF
46 DALLAS GREEN-P
47 BILL SMITH-P
48 JACK HAMILTON-P
49 JIM (BEAR) OWENS-P
50 ED KEEGAN-P

1963

4TH 87-75 12GB

1 AL VINCENT-CH
2 AL WIDMAR-CH
3 PEANUTS LOWREY-CH
4 GENE (SKIP) MAUCH-MGR
5 ROY (SQUIRREL) SIEVERS-1B
6 JOHNNY CALLISON-OF
7 BOBBY WINE-SS/3B
8 TONY TAYLOR-2B/3B
9 MICKEY HARRINGTON-PR
9 CAL EMERY-1B
10 BOB OLDIS-C
11 CLAY DALRYMPLE-C
12 DON (TIGER) HOAK-3B
14 FRANK TORRE-1B
16 COOKIE ROJAS-2B/OF
17 EARL AVERILL JR.-UTIL
18 RYNE DUREN-P
20 RUBEN AMARO-INF
21 JIM LEMON-OF (2)
23 DENNIS BENNETT (INJ)-P
24 DON DEMETER-OF/INF
25 TONY GONZALEZ-OF
26 CAL (BUSTER) MCLISH-P
27 JACK BALDSCHUN-P
28 ART MAHAFFEY-P
29 JOHN BOOZER-P
32 BILLY KLAUS-INF
32 DICK ALLEN-OF/3B
34 BOBBY LOCKE-P
34 WAYNE GRAHAM-OF
36 *(RET#) ROBIN ROBERTS*
37 RAY CULP-P
39 PAUL BROWN-P
41 CHRIS SHORT-P
43 WES COVINGTON-OF
44 JOHN HERRNSTEIN-OF/1B
45 JOHNNY KLIPPSTEIN-P
46 DALLAS GREEN-P
48 JACK HAMILTON-P

1964

2ND (TIE) 92-70 1GB

1 GEORGE (MERCURY) (STUD) (FOGHORN) MYATT-CH
2 AL WIDMAR-CH
3 PEANUTS LOWREY-CH
4 GENE (SKIP) MAUCH-MGR
5 ROY (SQUIRREL) SIEVERS-1B (1)
5 BOB OLDIS-CH
6 JOHNNY CALLISON-OF
7 BOBBY WINE-SS/3B
8 TONY TAYLOR-2B
9 GUS TRIANDOS-C/1B
10 DANNY CATER (INJ)-OF/INF
11 CLAY DALRYMPLE-C
12 DON (TIGER) HOAK-PH
12 JOHNNY BRIGGS-OF/1B
14 JIM BUNNING-P
15 DICK ALLEN-3B
16 COOKIE ROJAS-UTIL
17 COSTEN SHOCKLEY-1B
17 ED ROEBUCK-P (2)
18 RYNE DUREN-P (1)
18 RICK WISE-P
19 JOHN BOOZER-P
20 RUBEN AMARO-UTIL
22 JOHN HERRNSTEIN-OF/1B
23 DENNIS BENNETT-P
25 TONY GONZALEZ-OF
26 CAL (BUSTER) MCLISH (INJ)-P
26 ALEX JOHNSON-OF
27 JACK BALDSCHUN-P
28 ART MAHAFFEY-P
29 JOHN BOOZER-P
29 PAT CORRALES-PH
31 COSTEN SHOCKLEY-1B
32 DICK ALLEN-3B
34 BOBBY LOCKE-P
34 BOB OLDIS-CH
34 COSTEN SHOCKLEY-1B
34 PAT CORRALES-PH
35 BOBBY SHANTZ-P (3)
36 *(RET#) ROBIN ROBERTS*
37 RAY CULP (INJ)-P
41 CHRIS SHORT-P
43 WES COVINGTON-OF
45 JOHNNY KLIPPSTEIN-P (1)
45 FRANK THOMAS-1B (2)
46 DALLAS GREEN-P
53 BOBBY SHANTZ-P (3)
54 ADOLFO PHILLIPS-OF
54 ED ROEBUCK-P (2)
55 GARY KROLL-P (1)
58 MORRIE STEEVENS-P
58 JOHNNY BRIGGS-OF/1B
59 DAVE BENNETT-P
60 ALEX JOHNSON-OF
62 RICK WISE-P
62 VIC POWER-1B (3)

1965

6TH 85-76 11.5GB

1 GEORGE (MERCURY) (STUD) (FOGHORN) MYATT-CH
2 CAL (BUSTER) MCLISH-CH
3 PEANUTS LOWREY-CH
4 GENE (SKIP) MAUCH-MGR
5 BOB OLDIS-CH
6 JOHNNY CALLISON-OF
7 DICK (DR. STRANGEGLOVE) STUART-1B/3B
8 TONY TAYLOR-2B/3B
9 GUS TRIANDOS-C
10 PAT CORRALES-C
11 CLAY DALRYMPLE-C
12 JOHNNY BRIGGS-OF
13 BOBBY WINE-SS/1B
14 JIM BUNNING-P
15 DICK ALLEN-3B/SS
16 COOKIE ROJAS-UTIL
17 ED ROEBUCK-P
20 RUBEN AMARO-INF
21 RAY HERBERT-P
22 JOHN HERRNSTEIN-1B/OF
23 MORRIE STEEVENS-P
23 ADOLFO PHILLIPS-OF
24 FRANK THOMAS-1B
24 BILL SORRELL-3B
25 TONY GONZALEZ-OF
26 ALEX JOHNSON-OF
27 JACK BALDSCHUN-P
28 ART MAHAFFEY-P
29 BOBBY DEL GRECO-OF
29 GRANT (BUCK) JACKSON-P
30 RYNE DUREN-P (1)
30 LEW BURDETTE-P (2)
31 GARY WAGNER-P
33 BO BELINSKY-P
36 *(RET#) ROBIN ROBERTS*
37 RAY CULP-P
41 CHRIS SHORT-P
43 WES COVINGTON-OF
46 FERGUSON (FERGIE) JENKINS-P
47 MORRIE STEEVENS-P
64 GARY WAGNER-P

1966

4TH 87-75 8GB

1 GEORGE (MERCURY) (STUD) (FOGHORN) MYATT-CH
2 CAL (BUSTER) MCLISH-CH
3 PEANUTS LOWREY-CH
4 GENE (SKIP) MAUCH-MGR
5 BOB OLDIS-CH
6 JOHNNY CALLISON-OF
7 BOBBY WINE-SS/OF
8 TONY TAYLOR-2B/3B
9 BOB UECKER-C
10 BILL WHITE-1B
11 CLAY DALRYMPLE-C
12 JOHNNY BRIGGS (INJ)-OF
14 JIM BUNNING-P
15 DICK ALLEN-3B/OF
16 COOKIE ROJAS-2B/UTIL
17 DOUG CLEMENS-OF/1B
18 PHIL LINZ-INF
19 JOHN BOOZER-P
19 TERRY FOX-P (2)
20 JACKIE BRANDT-OF
21 RAY HERBERT-P
22 JOHN HERRNSTEIN-OF (1)
22 HARVEY KUENN-OF/INF (2)
23 ADOLFO PHILLIPS-OF (1)
24 DICK GROAT-SS/INF
25 TONY GONZALEZ-OF
26 JOE VERBANIC-P
27 ED ROEBUCK-P
27 STEVE RIDZIK-P
27 JOHN MORRIS-P
28 RICK WISE-P
28 ROGER CRAIG-P
29 GRANT (BUCK) JACKSON-P
30 FERGUSON (FERGIE) JENKINS-P (1)
30 BOB BUHL-P (2)
31 GARY WAGNER-P
32 GARY SUTHERLAND-SS
32 DAROLD KNOWLES-P
33 BO BELINSKY-P
34 TERRY FOX-P (2)
34 JIMMIE SCHAFFER-C
35 ROGER CRAIG-P
36 *(RET#) ROBIN ROBERTS*
37 RAY CULP-P
38 RICK WISE-P
41 CHRIS SHORT-P
42 STEVE RIDZIK-P
43 ROGER CRAIG-P
46 LARRY JACKSON-P (2)

1967

5TH 82-80 19.5GB

1 GEORGE (MERCURY) (STUD) (FOGHORN) MYATT-CH
2 ANDY SEMINICK-CH
3 DON (TIGER) HOAK-CH
4 GENE (SKIP) MAUCH-MGR
5 LARRY SHEPARD-CH
6 JOHNNY CALLISON-OF
7 BOBBY WINE-SS/OF
8 TONY TAYLOR-2B/3B
9 BOB UECKER-C (1)
9 GENE OLIVER-C/1B (2)
10 BILL WHITE (INJ)-1B
11 CLAY DALRYMPLE-C
12 JOHNNY BRIGGS-OF
14 JIM BUNNING-P
15 DICK ALLEN (INJ)-3B/OF
16 COOKIE ROJAS-2B/UTIL
17 DOUG CLEMENS-OF
18 PHIL LINZ-SS/3B
18 CHUCK HILLER-2B (2)
20 JACKIE BRANDT-OF (1)
20 RICK JOSEPH-1B
21 PEDRO (PETE) RAMOS-P
21 JIMMIE SCHAFFER-C
22 RUBEN GOMEZ-P
23 DON LOCK-OF
24 DICK GROAT-SS (1)
24 BILLY COWAN-OF
25 TONY GONZALEZ-OF
26 DALLAS GREEN-P
27 DICK HALL-P
28 JOHN BOOZER-P
28 PEDRO (PETE) RAMOS-P
29 GRANT (BUCK) JACKSON-
30 BOB BUHL-P
30 LARRY LOUGHLIN-P
31 GARY WAGNER-P
32 RUBEN GOMEZ-P
32 DICK (TURK) FARRELL-P (2
34 TERRY HARMON-PR
35 DICK HALL-P
35 GARY SUTHERLAND-SS/OF
36 *(RET#) ROBIN ROBERTS*
37 DICK ELLSWORTH-P
38 RICK WISE-P
39 DICK (TURK) FARRELL-P (2
41 CHRIS SHORT (INJ)-P
43 DICK THOENEN-P
46 LARRY JACKSON-P
47 LARRY LOUGHLIN-P
47 DALLAS GREEN-P

1968

7TH (TIE) 76-86 21GB

1 GEORGE (MERCURY) (STUD) (FOGHORN) MYATT-CH/MGR2/CH
2 ANDY SEMINICK-CH
3 AL WIDMAR-CH
4 GENE (SKIP) MAUCH-MGR1
5 DON (BROOKS) MONEY-SS
6 JOHNNY CALLISON-OF
7 BOBBY WINE (INJ)-SS/3B
8 TONY TAYLOR-3B/INF
9 MIKE RYAN-C
10 BILL WHITE-1B
11 CLAY DALRYMPLE-C
12 JOHNNY BRIGGS-OF/1B
14 WOODIE FRYMAN-P
15 DICK ALLEN-OF/3B
16 COOKIE ROJAS-2B/C
17 DOUG CLEMENS-OF
18 GARY SUTHERLAND-UTIL
19 BOB SKINNER-MGR3
20 RICK JOSEPH-UTIL
21 LARRY COLTON-P
22 WOODIE FRYMAN-P
23 DON LOCK-OF
24 LARRY HISLE-OF
25 TONY GONZALEZ-OF
27 DICK HALL-P
28 JOHN BOOZER-P
29 GRANT (BUCK) JACKSON-F
30 JEFF (JESSE) JAMES-P
31 GARY WAGNER-P

PHILADELPHIA PHILLIES

32 DICK (TURK) FARRELL-P
33 PAUL BROWN-P
33 JERRY JOHNSON-P
34 ROBERTO (BABY) PENA-SS
36 *(RET#) ROBIN ROBERTS*
37 HOWIE BEDELL-PH
37 JOHN SULLIVAN-C
38 RICK WISE-P
41 CHRIS SHORT-P
46 LARRY JACKSON-P
48 JERRY JOHNSON-P

1969

5TH E 63-99 37GB

1 BOB SKINNER-MGR1
2 DAVE WATKINS-UTIL
3 RON STONE-OF
4 LARRY HISLE (INJ)-OF
5 DON (BROOKS) MONEY-SS
6 JOHNNY CALLISON-OF
7 VIC ROZNOVSKY-C
8 TONY TAYLOR-INF
9 MIKE RYAN-C
10 GENE STONE-1B
11 DERON JOHNSON-OF/INF
12 JOHNNY BRIGGS-OF/1B
15 DICK ALLEN (SUS)-1B
16 COOKIE ROJAS-2B/OF
18 RICK JOSEPH-INF
19 TERRY HARMON-INF
21 JOHN BOOZER-P
22 WOODIE FRYMAN-P
23 DON LOCK-OF/1B (1)
23 RICH BARRY-OF
23 LEROY REAMS-PH
24 BILLY WILSON (INJ)-P
25 AL RAFFO-P
25 SCOTT REID-OF
26 LOWELL PALMER-P
28 JOHN BOOZER-P
28 LOU PERAZA-P
29 GRANT (BUCK) JACKSON-P
30 JEFF (JESSE) JAMES-P
31 GARY WAGNER-P (1)
31 BILLY CHAMPION-P
32 DICK (TURK) FARRELL-P
33 JERRY JOHNSON-P
34 BARRY LERSCH-P
36 *(RET#) ROBIN ROBERTS*
38 LOU PERAZA-P
38 RICK WISE-P
41 CHRIS SHORT (INJ)-P
42 JOHN BOOZER-P
46 LARRY JACKSON-P
46 BILLY (KID) DEMARS-CH
47 GEORGE (MERCURY) (STUD) (FOGHORN) MYATT-CH/MGR2/CH
48 ANDY SEMINICK-CH
49 AL WIDMAR-CH

1970

5TH E 73-88 15.5GB

1 FRANK LUCCHESI-MGR
2 GEORGE (MERCURY) (STUD) (FOGHORN) MYATT-CH
3 BILLY (KID) DEMARS-CH
4 RAY RIPPLEMEYER-CH
5 DOC EDWARDS-C/CH
6 TIM MCCARVER (INJ)-C
7 MIKE COMPTON-C
8 TONY TAYLOR-UTIL
9 MIKE RYAN (INJ)-C
10 LARRY BOWA-SS/2B
11 DERON JOHNSON-1B/3B
12 JOHNNY BRIGGS (INJ)-OF/1B
14 JIM BUNNING-P
15 DENNY DOYLE-2B
16 DON (BROOKS) MONEY (INJ)-SS
17 TERRY HARMON-INF
18 RICK JOSEPH-OF/INF
19 DEL BATES-C
20 JIM HUTTO-UTIL
21 RON STONE-OF/1B
22 WOODIE FRYMAN (INJ)-P
22 LARRY HISLE-OF
23 OSCAR GAMBLE-OF
24 BILLY WILSON-P
24 BYRON BROWNE-OF
25 SCOTT REID-OF
26 LOWELL PALMER-P
27 SAM PARRILLA-OF
27 DICK SELMA-P
29 GRANT (BUCK) JACKSON-P
30 JOHN VUKOVICH-SS/3B
31 BILLY CHAMPION-P
32 FRED (FIREBALL) WENZ-P
33 WILLIE MONTANEZ-OF/1B
33 MIKE JACKSON-P
34 BARRY LERSCH-P
35 WOODIE FRYMAN (INJ)-P
37 BILLY WILSON-P
38 RICK WISE-P
39 DICK SELMA-P
40 LOWELL PALMER-P
41 CHRIS SHORT-P
42 GREG LUZINSKI-1B
43 JOE HOERNER-P
45 BILL LAXTON-P
46 JOE LIS-OF
47 KEN REYNOLDS-P
CURT FLOOD (H/O)-(OF)

1971

6TH E 67-95 30GB

1 FRANK LUCCHESI-MGR
2 GEORGE (MERCURY) (STUD) (FOGHORN) MYATT-CH
3 BILLY (KID) DEMARS-CH
4 RAY RIPPLEMEYER-CH
5 DOC EDWARDS-CH
6 TIM MCCARVER (INJ)-C
8 TONY TAYLOR-INF (1)
9 MIKE RYAN-C
10 LARRY BOWA-SS
11 DERON JOHNSON-1B/3B
12 JOHNNY BRIGGS-OF (1)
12 PETE KOEGEL-C/OF (2)
14 JIM BUNNING-P
15 DENNY DOYLE (INJ)-2B
16 DON (BROOKS) MONEY-UTIL
17 TERRY HARMON-INF
18 BOBBY PFEIL-UTIL
19 GREG LUZINSKI-1B
20 ROGER FREED-OF/C
21 RON STONE-OF/1B
22 LARRY HISLE-OF
23 OSCAR GAMBLE-OF
24 BYRON BROWNE (INJ)-OF
25 JOE LIS-OF
26 JOHN VUKOVICH-3B
27 WILLIE MONTANEZ-OF/1B
28 BOBBY PFEIL-UTIL
29 MANNY MUNIZ-P
30 JOHN VUKOVICH-3B
31 BILLY CHAMPION-P
32 DARRELL (BUCKY) BRANDON-P
33 WAYNE TWITCHELL-P
34 BARRY LERSCH-P
35 WOODIE FRYMAN-P
36 *(RET#) ROBIN ROBERTS*
37 BILLY WILSON-P
38 RICK WISE-P
39 DICK SELMA (INJ)-P
40 LOWELL PALMER-P
40 MIKE ANDERSON-OF
41 CHRIS SHORT-P
42 KEN REYNOLDS-P
42 GREG LUZINSKI-1B
43 JOE HOERNER-P
46 JOE LIS-OF
47 KEN REYNOLDS-P

1972

6TH E 59-97 37.5GB

1 FRANK LUCCHESI-MGR1
1 BOBBY WINE-CH
2 GEORGE (MERCURY) (STUD) (FOGHORN) MYATT-CH
2 BRANDY DAVIS-CH
3 BILLY (KID) DEMARS-CH
4 RAY RIPPLEMEYER-CH
5 DOC EDWARDS-CH
6 TIM MCCARVER (INJ)-C (1)
6 JOHN BATEMAN-C (2)
7 BOBBY WINE-CH
8 PAUL OWENS-MGR2
9 MIKE RYAN-C
10 LARRY BOWA-SS
11 DERON JOHNSON (INJ)-1B
12 PETE KOEGEL-UTIL
14 TOMMY HUTTON-1B/OF
15 DENNY DOYLE-2B
16 DON (BROOKS) MONEY-3B/SS
17 TERRY HARMON-INF
18 CRAIG ROBINSON-SS
19 GREG LUZINSKI-OF/1B
20 ROGER FREED-OF
21 RON STONE-OF
21 BILL ROBINSON-OF
22 MIKE ANDERSON-OF
22 MIKE SCHMIDT-3B/2B
23 OSCAR GAMBLE-OF/1B
23 JIM NASH (INJ)-P (2)
24 BYRON BROWNE-OF
24 BILL ROBINSON-OF
25 JOE LIS-OF
27 WILLIE MONTANEZ-OF/1B
30 DARRELL (BUCKY) BRANDON-P
31 BILLY CHAMPION-P
32 STEVE (LEFTY) CARLTON-P
33 WAYNE TWITCHELL-P
34 BARRY LERSCH (ILL)-P
35 WOODIE FRYMAN-P (1)
35 DAVE DOWNS-P
36 *(RET#) ROBIN ROBERTS*
37 BILLY WILSON (INJ)-P
38 BOB TERLECKI-P
39 DICK SELMA-P
40 BOB BOONE-C (2)
41 CHRIS SHORT (INJ)-P
42 JIM NASH (INJ)-P (2)
43 JOE HOERNER-P (1)
43 GARY NEIBAUER-P (2)
44 MAC SCARCE-P
47 KEN REYNOLDS-P

1973

6TH E 71-91 11.5GB

1 CARROLL BERINGER-CH
2 BILLY (KID) DEMARS-CH
3 DANNY OZARK-MGR
4 RAY RIPPLEMEYER-CH
5 LARRY COX-C
5 BILLY GRABARKEWITZ-UTIL (2)
6 JIM ESSIAN-C
7 BOBBY WINE-CH
8 BOB BOONE-C
9 MIKE RYAN-C
10 LARRY BOWA (INJ)-SS
11 DERON JOHNSON-1B (1)
12 CESAR (PEPITO) TOVAR (INJ)-UTIL
14 TOMMY HUTTON-1B
15 DENNY DOYLE-2B
16 JOSE PAGAN-UTIL
17 TERRY HARMON-INF
18 CRAIG ROBINSON-SS/2B
19 GREG LUZINSKI-OF
20 MIKE SCHMIDT-3B/INF
21 RON DIORIO-P
22 MIKE ANDERSON (INJ)-OF
24 BILL ROBINSON-OF/3B
25 DEL UNSER-OF
27 WILLIE MONTANEZ-1B/OF
28 MIKE ROGODZINZKI-OF
29 MIKE ROGODZINZKI-OF
30 DARRELL (BUCKY) BRANDON-P
31 KEN BRETT-P
32 STEVE (LEFTY) CARLTON-P
33 WAYNE TWITCHELL-P
34 BARRY LERSCH-P
35 GEORGE CULVER-P (2)
36 *(RET#) ROBIN ROBERTS*
37 BILLY WILSON-P
38 LARRY CHRISTENSON-P
39 DICK SELMA-P
39 DAVE WALLACE-P
40 DICK RUTHVEN (ILL)-P
41 JIM LONBORG-P
44 MAC SCARCE-P
49 MIKE WALLACE-P
50 JIM ESSIAN-C
DAVE DOWNS (INJ)-(P)

1974

3RD E 80-82 8GB

1 CARROLL BERINGER-CH
2 BILLY (KID) DEMARS-CH
3 DANNY OZARK-MGR
4 RAY RIPPLEMEYER-CH
5 LARRY COX-C
6 JIM ESSIAN-C/INF
7 BOBBY WINE-CH
8 BOB BOONE-C
9 JOHN STEARNS-C
10 LARRY BOWA-SS
11 JERRY MARTIN-OF
12 TONY TAYLOR-INF
14 TOMMY HUTTON-1B/OF
15 ALAN BANNISTER-OF/SS
17 TERRY HARMON-SS/2B
18 BILLY GRABARKEWITZ-OF/3B (1)
19 GREG LUZINSKI (INJ)-OF
20 MIKE SCHMIDT-3B
21 RON DIORIO-P
21 JAY JOHNSTONE-OF
22 MIKE ANDERSON-OF/1B
23 (DOWNTOWN) OLLIE BROWN-OF
24 BILL ROBINSON-OF
25 DEL UNSER-OF
26 GENE GARBER-P (2)
27 WILLIE MONTANEZ-1B/OF
28 MIKE ROGODZINZKI-OF
30 DAVE CASH-2B
31 FRANK LINZY-P
32 STEVE (LEFTY) CARLTON-P
33 WAYNE TWITCHELL (INJ)-P
34 TOM UNDERWOOD-P
35 GEORGE CULVER-P
36 *(RET#) ROBIN ROBERTS*
37 RON SCHUELER-P
38 LARRY CHRISTENSON-P
39 EDDIE WATT-P
40 DICK RUTHVEN-P
41 JIM LONBORG-P
43 ED FARMER-P
44 MAC SCARCE-P
45 RON DIORIO-P
45 PETE RICHERT (INJ)-P (2)
47 JESUS HERNAIZ-P
48 ERSKINE THOMASON-P
49 MIKE WALLACE-P (1)
49 DAVE WALLACE-P
DAVE DOWNS (INJ)-(P)

1975

2ND E 86-76 6.5GB

1 CARROLL BERINGER-CH
2 BILLY (KID) DEMARS-CH
3 DANNY OZARK-MGR
4 RAY RIPPLEMEYER-CH
5 LARRY COX-C
5 RON CLARK-PH
6 JIM ESSIAN-C
6 JOHNNY OATES-C (2)
7 BOBBY WINE-CH
8 BOB BOONE-C/3B
10 LARRY BOWA (INJ)-SS
11 JERRY MARTIN-OF
11 TIM MCCARVER-C/1B (2)
12 TONY TAYLOR-INF
14 TOMMY HUTTON-1B/OF
15 ALAN BANNISTER-OF/INF
15 DICK ALLEN-1B (2)
16 ALAN BANNISTER-OF/INF
17 TERRY HARMON-INF
19 GREG LUZINSKI-OF
20 MIKE SCHMIDT-3B/SS
21 JAY JOHNSTONE-OF
22 MIKE ANDERSON-OF/1B
23 (DOWNTOWN) OLLIE BROWN-OF
24 JOHN MONTAGUE-P (2)
25 DON HAHN-OF
25 JERRY MARTIN-OF
25 JOHN MONTAGUE-P (2)
26 GENE GARBER-P
27 WILLIE MONTANEZ-1B (1)
28 MIKE ROGODZINZKI-OF
29 GARRY MADDOX (INJ)-OF (2)
29 CY ACOSTA-P
30 DAVE CASH-2B
31 CY ACOSTA-P
31 GARRY MADDOX (INJ)-OF (2)
32 STEVE (LEFTY) CARLTON-P
33 WAYNE TWITCHELL-P
34 TOM UNDERWOOD-P
35 TOM HILGENDORF-P
36 *(RET#) ROBIN ROBERTS*
37 RON SCHUELER-P
38 LARRY CHRISTENSON-P
40 DICK RUTHVEN-P
41 JIM LONBORG (INJ)-P
43 JOE HOERNER (INJ)-P
44 WAYNE SIMPSON-P
44 LARRY FRITZ-PH
45 TUG MCGRAW-P
46 JOHN MONTAGUE-P (2)
47 RANDY LERCH-P
DAVE DOWNS (INJ)-(P)

1976

1ST E 101-61 0GB

L NLCS-CINN 3-0

1 CARROLL BERINGER-CH
2 BILLY (KID) DEMARS-CH
3 DANNY OZARK-MGR
4 RAY RIPPLEMEYER-CH
5 FRED ANDREWS-2B
5 TIM BLACKWELL-C
6 JOHNNY OATES (INJ)-C
7 BOBBY WINE-CH
8 BOB BOONE-C/1B
9 BILL NAHORODNY-C
10 LARRY BOWA-SS
11 TIM MCCARVER-C/1B
12 TONY TAYLOR (INJ)-2B/3B
14 TOMMY HUTTON-1B/OF
15 DICK ALLEN (INJ)-1B
16 FRED ANDREWS-2B

17 TERRY HARMON-INF
19 GREG LUZINSKI-OF
20 MIKE SCHMIDT-3B
21 JAY JOHNSTONE-OF/1B
22 JOHN VUKOVICH-3B/1B
23 (DOWNTOWN) OLLIE BROWN-OF
25 JERRY MARTIN-OF/1B
26 GENE GARBER-P
26 FRED ANDREWS-2B
28 RICK BOSETTI-OF
28 BOBBY TOLAN-OF
29 RICK BOSETTI-OF
30 DAVE CASH-2B
31 GARRY MADDOX-OF
32 STEVE (LEFTY) CARLTON-P
33 WAYNE TWITCHELL-P
34 TOM UNDERWOOD-P
36 *(RET#) ROBIN ROBERTS*
37 RON SCHUELER-P
38 LARRY CHRISTENSON-P
39 JIM (KITTY) KAAT-P
41 JIM LONBORG-P
42 RON REED-P
45 TUG MCGRAW-P
47 RANDY LERCH-P

1977

1ST E 101-61 0GB
L NLCS-LAN 3-1

1 CARROLL BERINGER-CH
2 BILLY (KID) DEMARS-CH
3 DANNY OZARK-MGR
4 RAY RIPPLEMEYER-CH
5 TIM BLACKWELL-C
6 TED SIZEMORE-2B
7 BOBBY WINE-CH
8 BOB BOONE-C/3B
9 BARRY FOOTE-C (2)
10 LARRY BOWA-SS
11 TIM MCCARVER-C/1B
12 TONY TAYLOR-CH
14 TOMMY HUTTON-1B/OF
15 JIM MORRISON-3B
15 DAVEY JOHNSON-INF
16 FRED ANDREWS-2B
17 TERRY HARMON-INF
18 RICHIE HEBNER-1B/INF
19 GREG LUZINSKI-OF
20 MIKE SCHMIDT-3B/INF
21 JAY JOHNSTONE-OF/1B
22 DANE IORG-1B (1)
22 BAKE MCBRIDE-OF (2)
23 (DOWNTOWN) OLLIE BROWN-OF
25 JERRY MARTIN-OF/1B
26 GENE GARBER-P
28 BOBBY TOLAN-1B (1)
28 JOHN VUKOVICH-PH
30 MIKE BUSKEY-SS
30 JIM MORRISON-3B
31 GARRY MADDOX-OF
32 STEVE (LEFTY) CARLTON-P
33 WAYNE TWITCHELL-P (1)
33 DAN WARTHEN-P (2)
34 TOM UNDERWOOD-P (1)
35 MANNY SEOANE-P
36 *(RET#) ROBIN ROBERTS*
38 LARRY CHRISTENSON-P
39 JIM (KITTY) KAAT-P
40 WARREN BRUSSTAR-P
41 JIM LONBORG (INJ)-P
42 RON REED-P
43 MIKE BUSKEY-SS
45 TUG MCGRAW (INJ)-P
47 RANDY LERCH-P

1978

1ST E 90-72 0GB
L NLCS-LAN 3-1

1 JOSE CARDENAL-1B/OF
2 BILLY (KID) DEMARS-CH
3 DANNY OZARK-MGR
4 RAY RIPPLEMEYER-CH
5 CARROLL BERINGER-CH
6 TED SIZEMORE (INJ)-2B
7 BOBBY WINE-CH
8 BOB BOONE-C/UTIL
9 BARRY FOOTE-C
10 LARRY BOWA-SS
11 TIM MCCARVER-C/1B
12 TONY TAYLOR-CH
14 BUD HARRELSON-2B/SS
15 DAVEY JOHNSON-INF (1)
15 JIM MORRISON-UTIL
16 JIM MORRISON-UTIL
16 TODD CRUZ-SS
17 ORLANDO GONZALEZ-OF/1B
18 RICHIE HEBNER-1B/INF
19 GREG LUZINSKI-OF
20 MIKE SCHMIDT-3B/SS
21 JAY JOHNSTONE-1B/OF (1)
21 BAKE MCBRIDE-OF
22 BAKE MCBRIDE-OF
24 PETE MACKANIN-3B/1B
25 JERRY MARTIN-OF/1B
26 GENE GARBER-P (1)
26 KERRY DINEEN-OF
27 LONNIE SMITH-OF
30 JIM MORRISON-UTIL
31 GARRY MADDOX-OF
32 STEVE (LEFTY) CARLTON-P
33 KEVIN SAUCIER-P
34 KEITH MORELAND-C
35 HORACIO PINA-P
36 *(RET#) ROBIN ROBERTS*
38 LARRY CHRISTENSON-P
39 JIM (KITTY) KAAT-P
40 WARREN BRUSSTAR-P
41 JIM LONBORG-P
42 RON REED-P
44 DICK RUTHVEN-P (2)
45 TUG MCGRAW-P
46 DANNY BOITANO-P
47 RANDY LERCH-P
48 DAN LARSON-P
48 TODD CRUZ-SS
49 RAWLY EASTWICK-P (2)

1979

4TH E 84-78 14GB

1 JOSE CARDENAL-OF/1B (1)
1 *(RET#) RICHIE ASHBURN*
2 BILLY (KID) DEMARS-CH
3 DANNY OZARK-MGR1
4 HERM STARRETTE-CH
5 BOB TIEFENAUER-CH
6 DAVE RADER-C
7 BOBBY WINE-CH
8 BOB BOONE (INJ)-C/3B
9 MANNY TRILLO (INJ)-2B
10 LARRY BOWA-SS
11 TIM MCCARVER-C/OF
12 TONY TAYLOR-CH
14 PETE (CHARLIE HUSTLE) ROSE-1B/INF
15 BUD HARRELSON (RET)-2B/SS
15 RAMON AVILES-2B
17 PETE MACKANIN (INJ)-INF
18 RUDY MEOLI-INF
18 JOHN VUKOVICH-3B/2B
19 GREG LUZINSKI-OF
20 MIKE SCHMIDT-3B/SS
21 BAKE MCBRIDE-OF
22 MIKE ANDERSON-OF/P
23 GREG GROSS-OF
24 PETE MACKANIN (INJ)-INF
24 KEITH MORELAND-C
25 DEL UNSER-OF/1B
26 JOHN POFF-OF/1B
27 LONNIE SMITH-OF
31 GARRY MADDOX-OF
32 STEVE (LEFTY) CARLTON-P
33 KEVIN SAUCIER-P
34 KEITH MORELAND-C
34 JACK KUCEK-P (2)
35 NINO ESPINOSA-P
36 *(RET#) ROBIN ROBERTS*
38 LARRY CHRISTENSON (INJ)-P
39 JIM (KITTY) KAAT-P (1)
40 WARREN BRUSSTAR (INJ)-P
41 JIM LONBORG-P
42 RON REED-P
43 DOUG BIRD-P
44 DICK RUTHVEN (INJ)-P
45 TUG MCGRAW-P
46 DALLAS GREEN-MGR2
47 RANDY LERCH-P
48 DAN LARSON-P
48 DICKIE NOLES-P
49 RAWLY EASTWICK-P
50 DAN LARSON-P

1980

1ST E 91-71 0GB
W NLCS-HOUN 3-2
W WS-KCA 4-2

1 *(RET#) RICHIE ASHBURN*
2 BILLY (KID) DEMARS-CH
3 LEE ELIA-CH
4 HERM STARRETTE-CH
5 MIKE RYAN-CH
6 KEITH MORELAND-UTIL
7 BOBBY WINE-CH
8 BOB BOONE-C
9 MANNY TRILLO-2B
10 LARRY BOWA-SS
11 TIM MCCARVER-1B
11 OZZIE VIRGIL-C
12 RUBEN AMARO-CH
14 PETE (CHARLIE HUSTLE) ROSE-1B
15 RAMON AVILES-SS/2B
16 LUIS AGUAYO-2B/SS
17 DON MCCORMACK-C
18 JOHN VUKOVICH-INF
19 GREG LUZINSKI (INJ)-OF
20 MIKE SCHMIDT-3B
21 BAKE MCBRIDE-OF
22 JAY LOVIGLIO-2B
23 GREG GROSS-OF/1B
24 KEITH MORELAND-UTIL
24 OZZIE VIRGIL-C
25 DEL UNSER-1B/OF
27 LONNIE SMITH-OF
28 ORLANDO ISALES-OF
29 ORLANDO ISALES-OF
29 GEORGE VUKOVICH-OF
30 BOB DERNIER-OF
31 GARRY MADDOX-OF
32 STEVE (LEFTY) CARLTON-P
33 KEVIN SAUCIER (INJ)-P
34 SCOTT MUNNINGHOFF-P
35 NINO ESPINOSA (INJ)-P
36 *(RET#) ROBIN ROBERTS*
38 LARRY CHRISTENSON (INJ)-P
39 MARTY BYSTROM-P
39 SPARKY LYLE-P (2)
39 LERRIN LAGROW-P
40 WARREN BRUSSTAR (INJ)-P
41 BOB WALK-P
42 RON REED-P
43 MARK DAVIS-P
44 DICK RUTHVEN (INJ)-P
45 TUG MCGRAW-P
46 DALLAS GREEN-MGR
47 RANDY LERCH-P
48 DICKIE NOLES-P
49 DAN LARSON-P
50 MARTY BYSTROM-P

1981

1ST 1/2: 1ST E 34-21 0GB
2ND 1/2: 3RD E 25-27 4.5GB
FINAL: 59-48 --GB
L NLDS-MONN 3-2

1 *(RET#) RICHIE ASHBURN*
2 BILLY (KID) DEMARS-CH
3 LEE ELIA-CH
4 HERM STARRETTE-CH
5 MIKE RYAN-CH
6 KEITH MORELAND-UTIL
7 BOBBY WINE-CH
8 BOB BOONE-C
9 MANNY TRILLO-2B
10 LARRY BOWA-SS
11 OZZIE VIRGIL-C
12 RUBEN AMARO-CH
14 PETE (CHARLIE HUSTLE) ROSE-1B
15 RAMON AVILES-INF
16 LUIS AGUAYO-INF
17 DON MCCORMACK-C
18 JOHN VUKOVICH-INF
20 MIKE SCHMIDT-3B
21 BAKE MCBRIDE-OF
23 GREG GROSS-OF
24 RYNE SANDBERG-SS/2B
25 DEL UNSER-1B/OF
26 LEN MATUSZEK-1B/3B
26 DICK DAVIS-OF
27 LONNIE SMITH-OF
28 SPARKY LYLE-P
29 GEORGE VUKOVICH-OF
30 MIKE PROLY-P
30 BOB DERNIER-OF
31 GARRY MADDOX-OF
32 STEVE (LEFTY) CARLTON-P
34 GARY (SARGE) MATTHEWS-OF
35 NINO ESPINOSA-P (1)
35 JERRY REED-P
36 *(RET#) ROBIN ROBERTS*
38 LARRY CHRISTENSON (INJ)-P
39 SPARKY LYLE-P
40 WARREN BRUSSTAR-P
42 RON REED-P
43 MARK DAVIS-P
44 DICK RUTHVEN-P
45 TUG MCGRAW-P
46 DALLAS GREEN-MGR
47 RANDY LERCH-P
48 DICKIE NOLES-P
49 DAN LARSON-P
50 MARTY BYSTROM-P

1982

2ND E 89-73 3GB

1 *(RET#) RICHIE ASHBURN*
2 DERON JOHNSON-CH
3 CLAUDE OSTEEN-CH
4 DAVE BRISTOL-CH
5 MIKE RYAN-CH
6 BO DIAZ-C
7 BOBBY WINE-CH
8 PAT CORRALES-MGR
9 MANNY TRILLO-2B
10 DAVE ROBERTS-UTIL
11 OZZIE VIRGIL-C
11 IVAN DEJESUS-SS/3B
12 LEN MATUSZEK-3B/1B
14 PETE (CHARLIE HUSTLE) ROSE-1B
15 JULIO FRANCO-SS/3B
16 LUIS AGUAYO-INF
17 OZZIE VIRGIL-C
18 IVAN DEJESUS-SS/3B
18 BOB MOLINARO-PH (2)
19 DAVE ROBERTS-UTIL
20 MIKE SCHMIDT-3B
21 SID MONGE-P
21 GREG GROSS-OF
21 ED FARMER-P
22 BOB DERNIER-OF
22 ED FARMER-P
23 GREG GROSS-OF
24 LEN MATUSZEK-3B/1B
24 BOB DERNIER-OF
25 DEL UNSER-1B/OF
25 WILLIE MONTANEZ-1B (2)
26 DICK DAVIS-OF (1)
26 BILL ROBINSON-OF/1B (2)
27 ALEX SANCHEZ-OF
28 SPARKY LYLE-P (1)
29 GEORGE VUKOVICH-OF
30 PORFI ALTAMIRANO-P
31 GARRY MADDOX-OF
32 STEVE (LEFTY) CARLTON-P
34 GARY (SARGE) MATTHEWS-OF
35 JERRY REED-P (1)
36 *(RET#) ROBIN ROBERTS*
37 STAN BAHNSEN-P (2)
38 LARRY CHRISTENSON-P
39 MIKE KRUKOW-P
40 WARREN BRUSSTAR-P (1)
40 JOHN DENNY-P (2)
41 JAY BALLER-P
42 RON REED-P
44 DICK RUTHVEN-P
45 TUG MCGRAW (INJ)-P
46 ED FARMER-P
49 SID MONGE-P
50 MARTY BYSTROM (INJ)-P
57 PORFI ALTAMIRANO-P

1983

1ST E 90-72 0GB
W NLCS-LAN 3-1
L WS-BALA 4-1

1 *(RET#) RICHIE ASHBURN*
2 DERON JOHNSON-CH
3 CLAUDE OSTEEN-CH
4 DAVE BRISTOL-CH
5 MIKE RYAN-CH
5 PAT CORRALES-MGR1
5 PAUL OWENS-MGR2
6 BO DIAZ-C
7 BOBBY WINE-CH
8 JOE MORGAN-2B
9 JUAN (SAMMY) SAMUEL-2B
9 VON HAYES-OF
(10) DAVE ROBERTS (INJ)-(C)
11 IVAN DEJESUS-SS
12 LEN MATUSZEK-1B
14 PETE (CHARLIE HUSTLE) ROSE-1B/OF
15 LARRY MILBOURNE-INF (1)
15 STEVE JELTZ-INF
16 LUIS AGUAYO (INJ)-INF
16 JUAN SAMUEL-2B
17 OZZIE VIRGIL-C
18 PAT CORRALES-MGR1
18 KIKO GARCIA-INF
19 AL HOLLAND-P
20 MIKE SCHMIDT-3B/SS
21 GREG GROSS-OF/1B
22 ED FARMER (INJ)-P (1)
23 JEFF STONE-OF
23 JOE LEFEBVRE-UTIL (2)
24 BOB DERNIER-OF
24 TONY PEREZ-1B
25 BOB MOLINARO-PH (1)
25 MIKE RYAN-CH
26 VON HAYES-OF
26 BOB MOLINARO-PH (1)
27 ALEX SANCHEZ-OF
28 BILL ROBINSON-UTIL
28 SEXTO LEZCANO-OF (2)
28 TIM CORCORAN-1B
29 BOB DERNIER-OF
29 DARREN (DUTCH) DAULTON-C

PHILADELPHIA PHILLIES

30 PORFI ALTAMIRANO-P
31 GARRY MADDOX-OF
32 STEVE (LEFTY) CARLTON-P
34 GARY (SARGE) MATTHEWS-OF
35 TONY GHELFI-P
36 *(RET#) ROBIN ROBERTS*
37 TONY PEREZ-1B
38 LARRY CHRISTENSON (INJ)-P
39 DON CARMAN-P
40 JOHN DENNY-P
42 RON REED-P
43 CHARLIE HUDSON-P
43 WILLIE HERNANDEZ-P (2)
43 SEXTO LEZCANOOF (2)
44 DICK RUTHVEN-P (1)
44 STEVE COMER-P
45 TUG MCGRAW (INJ)-P
46 KEVIN GROSS-P
47 TONY GHELFI-P
47 LARRY ANDERSEN-P
48 KEVIN GROSS-P
48 WILLIE HERNANDEZ-P (2)
49 SID MONGE-P (1)
49 CHARLIE HUDSON-P
50 MARTY BYSTROM (INJ)-P

1984

4TH E 81-81 15.5GB

0 AL OLIVER-1B/OF (2)
1 *(RET#) RICHIE ASHBURN*
2 DERON JOHNSON-CH
3 CLAUDE OSTEEN-CH
4 DAVE BRISTOL-CH
5 PAUL OWENS-MGR
6 BO DIAZ (INJ)-C
7 JOHN FELSKE-CH
8 JUAN (SAMMY) SAMUEL-2B
9 VON HAYES-OF
10 MIKE (SPANKY) LAVALLIERE-C
11 IVAN DEJESUS-SS
12 LEN MATUSZEK (INJ)-1B/OF
15 JOHN WOCKENFUSS-1B/3B
15 STEVE JELTZ-SS/3B
16 LUIS AGUAYO-INF
17 OZZIE VIRGIL-C
18 KIKO GARCIA-INF
19 AL HOLLAND-P
20 MIKE SCHMIDT-3B/INF
21 GREG GROSS-OF/1B
22 TIM CORCORAN-1B/OF
23 JOE LEFEBVRE (INJ)-OF/3B
24 JERRY KOOSMAN-P
25 MIKE RYAN-CH
26 JEFF STONE-OF
27 GLENN WILSON-OF/3B
28 SEXTO LEZCANO-OF
29 BILL CAMPBELL-P
29 JOHN RUSSELL-OF/C
30 STEVE JELTZ-SS/3B
31 GARRY MADDOX (INJ)-OF
32 STEVE (LEFTY) CARLTON-P
33 TIM CORCORAN-1B/OF
33 DAVE WEHRMEISTER-P
(35) TONY GHELFI (INJ)-(P)
36 *(RET#) ROBIN ROBERTS*
37 JOHN RUSSELL-OF/C
37 JIM KERN-P (1)
37 RENIE MARTIN-P (2)
37 JERRY KOOSMAN-P
(38) LARRY CHRISTENSON (INJ)-(P)
39 DON CARMAN-P
39 BILL CAMPBELL-P
40 JOHN DENNY (INJ)-P
41 STEVE FIREOVID-P
42 DON CARMAN-P
44 STEVE FIREOVID-P
45 TUG MCGRAW (INJ)-P
46 KEVIN GROSS-P
47 LARRY ANDERSEN-P
48 SHANE RAWLEY-P (2)
49 CHARLIE HUDSON-P
50 MARTY BYSTROM-P (1)
52 FRANCISCO MELENDEZ-1B
53 RICK SCHU-3B
56 DAVE WEHRMEISTER-P

1985

5TH E 75-87 26GB

1 *(RET#) RICHIE ASHBURN*
2 LEE ELIA-CH
3 CLAUDE OSTEEN-CH
4 DAVE BRISTOL-CH
5 MIKE RYAN-CH
6 BO DIAZ (INJ)-C (1)
6 ALAN KNICELY-1B (2)
7 JOHN FELSKE-MGR
8 JUAN (SAMMY) SAMUEL-2B
9 VON HAYES-OF
10 DARREN (DUTCH) DAULTON (INJ)-C
11 TOM FOLEY-SS (2)
12 GLENN WILSON-OF
14 JOHN WOCKENFUSS-1B/C
15 RICK SCHU-3B
16 LUIS AGUAYO-INF
17 OZZIE VIRGIL-C
18 KIKO GARCIA-SS/3B
18 DERREL THOMAS-UTIL
19 AL HOLLAND-P (1)
20 MIKE SCHMIDT-1B/INF
21 GREG GROSS (INJ)-OF/1B
22 TIM CORCORAN-1B/OF
(23) JOE LEFEBVRE (INJ)-(OF)
24 JERRY KOOSMAN (INJ)-P
25 DEL UNSER-CH
26 JEFF STONE-OF
27 KENT TEKULVE-P (2)
29 JOHN RUSSELL-OF/1B
30 STEVE JELTZ-SS
31 GARRY MADDOX-OF
32 STEVE (LEFTY) CARLTON (INJ)-P
33 DAVE SHIPANOFF-P
36 *(RET#) ROBIN ROBERTS*
38 PAT ZACHRY-P
38 DAVE STEWART-P (2)
39 DAVE RUCKER-P
40 JOHN DENNY-P
42 DON CARMAN-P
43 FREDDIE TOLIVER-P
46 KEVIN GROSS-P
47 LARRY ANDERSEN-P
48 SHANE RAWLEY-P
49 CHARLIE HUDSON-P
50 ROCKY CHILDRESS-P
56 RICK SURHOFF-P (1)

1986

2ND E 86-75 21.5GB

1 *(RET#) RICHIE ASHBURN*
2 JIM DAVENPORT-CH
3 CLAUDE OSTEEN-CH
4 LEE ELIA-CH
5 MIKE RYAN-CH
6 JOHN RUSSELL-C
7 JOHN FELSKE-MGR
8 JUAN (SAMMY) SAMUEL-2B
9 VON HAYES-1B/OF
10 DARREN (DUTCH) DAULTON (INJ)-C
11 TOM FOLEY-INF (1)
11 GREG LEGG-2B/SS
12 GLENN WILSON-OF
14 JEFF STONE-OF
15 RICK SCHU-3B
16 LUIS AGUAYO-INF
17 RON ROENICKE-OF
18 FRANCISCO MELENDEZ-1B
20 MIKE SCHMIDT-3B/1B
21 GREG GROSS-OF/1B
22 GARY REDUS (INJ)-OF
23 JOE LEFEBVRE-OF
24 MILT THOMPSON-OF
25 DEL UNSER-CH
26 JEFF STONE-OF
26 CHRIS JAMES (INJ)-OF
27 KENT TEKULVE-P
28 MILT THOMPSON-OF
28 SHANE RAWLEY (INJ)-P
29 RONN REYNOLDS-C
29 WILLIE HERNANDEZ-P (2)
30 STEVE JELTZ-SS
31 GARRY MADDOX (INJ)-OF
32 STEVE (LEFTY) CARLTON (INJ)-P (1)
33 TOM GORMAN-P
33 MIKE JACKSON-P
34 CHRIS JAMES (INJ)-OF
34 JEFF BITTIGER-P
35 DAN SCHATZEDER-P (2)
35 RANDY LERCH-P
36 *(RET#) ROBIN ROBERTS*
37 TOM HUME (INJ)-P
38 DAVE STEWART-P (1)
39 DAVE RUCKER-P
40 STEVE (BEDROCK) BEDROSIAN-P
41 TOM HUME (INJ)-P
42 DON CARMAN-P
43 FREDDIE TOLIVER (INJ)-P
44 MIKE MADDUX-P
46 KEVIN GROSS-P
47 LARRY ANDERSEN-P (1)
47 BRUCE RUFFIN-P
48 SHANE RAWLEY (INJ)-P
48 MARVIN FREEMAN-P
49 CHARLIE HUDSON-P
50 ROCKY CHILDRESS-P

1987

4TH E (TIE) 80-82 15GB

1 *(RET#) RICHIE ASHBURN*
2 JIM DAVENPORT-CH
3 CLAUDE OSTEEN-CH
4 LEE ELIA-CH/MGR2
5 MIKE RYAN-CH
6 JOHN RUSSELL-OF/C
7 JOHN FELSKE-MGR1
7 KEN DOWELL-SS
7 KEN JACKSON-SS
8 JUAN (SAMMY) SAMUEL-2B
9 VON HAYES-1B/OF
10 DARREN (DUTCH) DAULTON (INJ)-C/1B
11 GREG LEGG-INF
12 GLENN WILSON-OF/P
13 LANCE PARRISH-C
14 JEFF STONE (INJ)-OF
15 RICK SCHU-3B/1B
16 LUIS AGUAYO-INF
17 RON ROENICKE-OF
18 CHRIS JAMES-OF
19 KEITH HUGHES-OF (2)
20 MIKE SCHMIDT-3B/INF
21 GREG GROSS-OF/1B
24 MILT THOMPSON-OF
25 DEL UNSER-CH
26 CHRIS JAMES-OF
27 KENT TEKULVE-P
28 SHANE RAWLEY-P
30 STEVE JELTZ-SS/OF
31 JEFF CALHOUN (INJ)-P
33 MIKE JACKSON-P
34 MIKE EASLER-OF (1)
34 DOUG BAIR-P
35 DAN SCHATZEDER-P (1)
36 *(RET#) ROBIN ROBERTS*
38 WALLY RITCHIE-P
39 JOE COWLEY-P
40 STEVE (BEDROCK) BEDROSIAN-P
41 TOM HUME-P (1)
42 DON CARMAN-P
43 DAN SCHATZEDER-P (1)
43 FREDDIE TOLIVER (INJ)-P
44 MIKE MADDUX-P
45 GREG JELKS-UTIL
46 KEVIN GROSS-P
47 BRUCE RUFFIN-P
50 TOM NEWELL-P
52 TODD FROHWIRTH-P

1988

6TH E 65-96 35.5GB

1 *(RET#) RICHIE ASHBURN*
2 DAVE BRISTOL-CH
3 CLAUDE OSTEEN-CH
4 LEE ELIA-MGR1
5 MIKE RYAN-CH
6 JOHN RUSSELL-C
7 JOHN VUKOVICH-CH/MGR2
8 JUAN (SAMMY) SAMUEL-2B /UTIL
9 VON HAYES (INJ) 1B/UTIL
10 DARREN (DUTCH) DAULTON (INJ)-C/1B
11 GREG LEGG-INF
11 KEITH MILLER-UTIL
12 TONY TAYLOR-CH
13 LANCE PARRISH-C/1B
14 TOMMY BARRETT-2B
15 JACKIE GUTIERREZ-SS/3B
15 BILL ALMON-INF
16 LUIS AGUAYO-INF (1)
17 RICKY JORDAN-1B
18 CHRIS JAMES-OF/3B
19 MIKE YOUNG-OF (1)
20 MIKE SCHMIDT (INJ) 3B/1B
21 GREG GROSS-OF/1B
22 BOB DERNIER-OF
24 MILT THOMPSON-OF
25 DEL UNSER-CH
25 SHANE TURNER-3B/SS
26 CHRIS JAMES-OF/3B
26 RON JONES-OF
27 KENT TEKULVE-P
28 SHANE RAWLEY-P
29 PHIL BRADLEY-OF
30 STEVE JELTZ-SS
31 JEFF CALHOUN (INJ)-P
31 SALOME BAROJAS-P
33 GREG HARRIS-P
34 ALEX MADRID-P
34 BILL SCHERRER-P (2)
35 DANNY CLAY-P
35 AL PARDO-C
36 *(RET#) ROBIN ROBERTS*
37 BOB SEBRA-P
37 BRAD MOORE-P
38 WALLY RITCHIE-P
39 SCOTT SERVICE-P
40 STEVE (BEDROCK) BEDROSIAN (ILL)-P
42 DON CARMAN-P
43 BILL DAWLEY (INJ)-P
44 MIKE MADDUX-P
45 DAVID PALMER (INJ)-P
46 KEVIN GROSS-P
47 BRUCE RUFFIN-P
48 MARVIN FREEMAN-P
52 TODD FROHWIRTH-P

1989

6TH E 67-95 26GB

1 *(RET#) RICHIE ASHBURN*
2 LARRY BOWA-CH
3 DAROLD KNOWLES-CH
4 DENIS MENKE-CH
4 LENNY (NAILS) DYKSTRA-OF (2)
5 MIKE RYAN-CH
6 DWAYNE MURPHY-OF
7 JOHN VUKOVICH-CH
8 JUAN (SAMMY) SAMUEL-OF (1)
8 CHARLIE HAYES-3B (2)
9 VON HAYES-OF/INF
10 DARREN (DUTCH) DAULTON-C
11 JOHN KRUK-OF/1B (2)
12 TONY TAYLOR-CH
13 ROGER MCDOWELL-P
14 TOMMY BARRETT-2B
14 DENIS MENKE-CH
15 FLOYD YOUMANS (INJ)-P
16 NICK LEYVA-MGR
17 RICKY JORDAN-1B
18 CHRIS JAMES-OF/3B (1)
18 JIM ADDUCI-1B/OF
19 TOM NIETO (INJ)-C
20 MIKE SCHMIDT-3B
21 DICKIE THON-SS
22 BOB DERNIER-OF
23 ERIC BULLOCK-OF
23 RANDY READY-UTIL (2)
24 CURT FORD-OF/INF
25 STEVE LAKE (INJ)-C
26 RON JONES (INJ)-OF
27 RANDY O'NEAL-P
28 TOMMY HERR-2B
29 TOMMY BARRETT-2B
30 STEVE JELTZ-UTIL
30 DENNIS COOK-P (2)
31 MARK RYAL-OF/1B
31 AL PARDO-C
32 *(RET #) STEVE CARLTON*
33 GREG HARRIS-P (1)
33 STEVE STANICEK-PH
34 ALEX MADRID-P
36 *(RET#) ROBIN ROBERTS*
37 BOB SEBRA-P (1)
37 KEITH MILLER-UTIL
38 PAT COMBS-P
39 DENNIS COOK-P (2)
40 STEVE (BEDROCK) BEDROSIAN-P (1)
40 TERRY MULHOLLAND-P (2)
41 STEVE ONTIVEROS (INJ)-P
42 DON CARMAN-P
43 KEN HOWELL-P
44 MIKE MADDUX-P
45 TERRY MULHOLLAND-P (2)
46 LARRY MCWILLIAMS-P (1)
47 BRUCE RUFFIN-P
48 MARVIN FREEMAN (INJ)-P
49 JEFF PARRETT-P
50 GORDON DILLARD-P
51 CHUCK MCELROY-P
52 TODD FROHWIRTH-P
54 JASON GRIMSLEY-P

1990

4TH E (TIE) 77-85 18GB

1 *(RET#) RICHIE ASHBURN*
2 LARRY BOWA-CH
3 DAROLD KNOWLES-CH
3 DALE MURPHY-OF (2)
4 LENNY (NAILS) DYKSTRA-OF
6 SIL CAMPUSANO-OF
8 CHARLIE HAYES-3B/INF
9 VON HAYES-OF
10 DARREN (DUTCH) DAULTON-C
11 JOHN KRUK-OF/1B
11 TOM NIETO-C
12 MICKEY MORANDINI-2B
13 ROGER MCDOWELL-P
14 DENIS MENKE-CH
15 DAVE HOLLINS-3B/1B
16 NICK LEYVA-MGR

17 RICKY JORDAN-1B
18 JOHN VUKOVICH-CH
19 TOM NIETO-C
19 JOHN KRUK-OF/1B
20 RON JONES (INJ)-OF
20 *(RET#) MIKE SCHMIDT*
21 DICKIE THON-SS
22 HAL LANIER-CH
23 RANDY READY-OF/2B
24 CARMELO MARTINEZ-1B/OF (1)
24 DARRIN FLETCHER-C (2)
25 STEVE LAKE (INJ)-C
26 RON JONES (INJ)-OF
27 CURT FORD-OF
28 TOMMY HERR-2B (1)
28 JOHN KRUK-OF/1B
(29) TOMMY BARRETT (INJ)-(2B)
29 LOUIE MEADOWS-OF (2)
30 JOE BOEVER-P (2)
31 JIM VATCHER-OF (1)
31 WES CHAMBERLAIN-OF
32 *(RET #)STEVE CARLTON*
(33) FLOYD YOUMANS (INJ)-(P)
33 DAROLD KNOWLES-CH
34 DICKIE NOLES (INJ)-P
35 DARREL AKERFELDS-P
36 *(RET#) ROBIN ROBERTS*
37 ROD BOOKER-INF
38 PAT COMBS-P
39 DENNIS COOK-P (1)
41 STEVE ONTIVEROS (INJ)-P
42 DON CARMAN-P
43 KEN HOWELL-P
45 TERRY MULHOLLAND-P
46 BRAD MOORE-P
47 BRUCE RUFFIN-P
48 MARVIN FREEMAN-P (1)
48 BRAD MOORE-P
48 JASON GRIMSLEY-P
49 JEFF PARRETT-P (1)
49 TOMMY GREENE-P (2)
51 CHUCK MCELROY-P
52 TODD FROHWIRTH-P
53 CHUCK MALONE-P
54 JASON GRIMSLEY-P
54 JOSE DEJESUS-P
60 DICKIE NOLES (INJ)-P

1991

3RD E 78-84 20GB

1 *(RET#) RICHIE ASHBURN*
2 LARRY BOWA-CH
3 DALE MURPHY-OF
4 LENNY (NAILS) DYKSTRA (INJ)-OF
6 WALLY BACKMAN-2B/3B
7 KIM BATISTE-SS
8 CHARLIE HAYES-3B/SS
9 VON HAYES (INJ)-OF
10 DARREN (DUTCH) DAULTON (INJ)-C
11 SIL CAMPUSANO-OF
11 JIM FREGOSI-MGR2
12 MICKEY MORANDINI-2B
13 ROGER MCDOWELL-P (1)
14 DENIS MENKE-CH
15 DAVE HOLLINS-3B/1B
16 NICK LEYVA-MGR1
16 BRAULIO CASTILLO-OF
17 RICKY JORDAN-1B
18 JOHN VUKOVICH-CH
19 JIM LINDEMAN-OF/1B
20 *(RET#) MIKE SCHMIDT*
21 DICKIE THON-SS
22 HAL LANIER-CH
23 RANDY READY (INJ)-2B
24 DARRIN FLETCHER-C
25 STEVE LAKE-C
26 RON JONES (INJ)-OF
27 RICK SCHU-3B/1B
28 MITCH WILLIAMS-P
29 JOHN KRUK-1B/OF
30 JOE BOEVER-P
31 WES CHAMBERLAIN-OF
32 *(RET #)STEVE CARLTON*
33 JOHN MORRIS-OF
34 DANNY COX-P
35 DARREL AKERFELDS-P
35 DOUG LINDSEY-C
36 *(RET#) ROBIN ROBERTS*
37 ROD BOOKER-SS/3B
38 PAT COMBS-P
39 WALLY RITCHIE-P
40 ANDY ASHBY-P
(41) STEVE ONTIVEROS (INJ)-(P)
42 DAVE LAPOINT-P
42 MIKE HARTLEY-P (2)
(43) KEN HOWELL (INJ)-(P)
44 AMALIO CARRENO-P
45 TERRY MULHOLLAND-P
46 JOHNNY PODRES-CH
47 BRUCE RUFFIN-P
48 JASON GRIMSLEY-P
49 TOMMY GREENE-P
50 STEVE SEARCY-P (2)
51 CLIFF BRANTLEY-P
52 TIM MAUSER-P
54 JOSE DEJESUS-P

1992

6TH E 70-92 26GB

1 *(RET#) RICHIE ASHBURN*
2 LARRY BOWA-CH
3 DALE MURPHY (INJ)-OF
4 LENNY (NAILS) DYKSTRA-(INJ) OF
5 KIM BATISTE-SS
6 WALLY BACKMAN (INJ)-2B/3B
7 MARIANO DUNCAN-UTIL
8 DALE SVEUM-INF (1)
9 DALE SVEUM-INF (1)
9 TOM MARSH (INJ)-OF
10 DARREN (DUTCH) DAULTON (INJ)-C
11 JIM FREGOSI-MGR
12 MICKEY MORANDINI-2B
14 DENIS MENKE-CH
15 DAVE HOLLINS-3B/1B
16 BRAULIO CASTILLO-OF
17 RICKY JORDAN-1B
18 JOHN VUKOVICH-CH
19 JIM LINDEMAN-OF/1B
20 *(RET#) MIKE SCHMIDT*
21 PAT COMBS-P
22 STAN JAVIER-OF (2)
23 BRAD BRINK-P
23 TODD PRATT-C
24 STEVE SEARCY-P
24 JUAN BELL-SS
25 MIKE RYAN-CH
26 MEL ROBERTS-CH
27 JOE MILLETTE-INF
28 MITCH WILLIAMS-P
29 JOHN KRUK-1B/OF
30 STEVE LAKE-C
31 STEVE SCARSONE-2B (1)
31 BRAD BRINK-P
32 *(RET #)STEVE CARLTON*
33 RUBEN AMARO, JR.-OF
34 DANNY COX-P
34 BEN RIVERA-P (2)
35 DON ROBINSON-P (2)
36 *(RET#) ROBIN ROBERTS*
37 JULIO PEGUERO-OF
38 CURT SCHILLING-P
39 WALLY RITCHIE-P
40 DON ROBINSON-P (2)
40 ANDY ASHBY-P
41 DARRIN CHAPIN-P
41 MIKE WILLIAMS-P
42 MIKE HARTLEY-P
(43) KEN HOWELL (INJ)-(P)
44 WES CHAMBERLAIN-OF
45 TERRY MULHOLLAND-P
46 JOHNNY PODRES-CH
47 KYLE ABBOTT-P
48 JEFF GROTEWOLD-UTIL
48 JOSE DELEON-P (2)
49 TOMMY GREENE-P
50 BARRY JONES-P (1)
50 JOSE DELEON-P (2)
51 CLIFF BRANTLEY-P
52 KEITH SHEPHERD-P
52 MICKEY WESTON-P
53 GREG MATHEWS-P
(54) JOSE DEJESUS (INJ)-(P)
55 BOB AYRAULT-P
56 JAY BALLER-P

1993

1ST E 97-65 0GB
W NLCS-ATLN 4-2
L WS-TORA 4-2

1 *(RET#) RICHIE ASHBURN*
2 LARRY BOWA-CH
4 LENNY (NAILS) DYKSTRA-OF
5 KIM BATISTE-3B/SS
7 MARIANO DUNCAN-2B/SS
8 JIM EISENREICH-OF/1B
9 MIKE RYAN-CH
10 DARREN (DUTCH) DAULTON-C
11 JIM FREGOSI-MGR
12 MICKEY MORANDINI-2B
14 DENIS MENKE-CH
15 DAVE HOLLINS-3B
16 TONY LONGMIRE-OF
17 RICKY JORDAN-1B
18 JOHN VUKOVICH-CH
19 KEVIN STOCKER-SS
20 *(RET#) MIKE SCHMIDT*
22 PETE (INKY) INCAVIGLIA-OF
23 TODD PRATT (INJ)-C
24 JUAN BELL-SS (1)
24 JOE MILLETTE-SS/3B
25 MILT THOMPSON-OF
26 MEL ROBERTS-CH
27 DANNY JACKSON-P
28 TYLER GREEN-P
29 JOHN KRUK-1B
30 JEFF MANTO-3B/SS
31 BRAD BRINK-P
32 *(RET #)STEVE CARLTON*
33 RUBEN AMARO, JR.-OF
34 BEN RIVERA-P
35 DOUG LINDSEY-C (1)
36 *(RET#) ROBIN ROBERTS*
37 BOBBY THIGPEN-P (2)
38 CURT SCHILLING-P
39 DONN PALL-P (2)
40 DAVID WEST-P
41 MIKE WILLIAMS-P
44 WES CHAMBERLAIN-OF
45 TERRY MULHOLLAND (INJ)-P
46 JOHNNY PODRES-CH
47 LARRY ANDERSEN-P
48 MARK DAVIS-P (1)
48 ROGER MASON-P (2)
49 TOMMY GREENE-P
50 JOSE DELEON-P (1)
52 TIM MAUSER-P (1)
(54) JOSE DEJESUS (INJ)-(P)
55 BOB AYRAULT-P (1)
57 KEVIN FOSTER-P
58 PAUL FLETCHER-P
99 MITCH WILLIAMS-P

1994

4TH E 54-61 20.5GB
STRIKE NO POST-SEASON

1 *(RET#) RICHIE ASHBURN*
2 LARRY BOWA-CH
3 TODD PRATT-C
3 BILLY HATCHER-OF (2)
4 LENNY (NAILS) DYKSTRA (INJ)-OF
5 KIM BATISTE-3B/SS
6 TODD PRATT-C
7 MARIANO DUNCAN (INJ)-2B
8 JIM EISENREICH-OF/1B
9 MIKE RYAN-CH
10 DARREN (DUTCH) DAULTON (INJ)-C
11 JIM FREGOSI-MGR
12 MICKEY MORANDINI-2B
14 DENIS MENKE-CH
15 DAVE HOLLINS (INJ)-3B
16 TONY LONGMIRE-OF
17 RICKY JORDAN-1B
18 JOHN VUKOVICH-CH
19 KEVIN STOCKER-SS
20 *(RET#) MIKE SCHMIDT*
21 TOM MARSH-OF
22 PETE (INKY) INCAVIGLIA-OF
23 DOUG JONES-P
24 MIKE LIEBERTHAL-C
25 MILT THOMPSON-OF (1)
26 MEL ROBERTS-CH
27 DANNY JACKSON-P
29 JOHN KRUK (INJ)-1B
30 TOM QUINLAN-3B
31 RANDY READY-INF
32 *(RET #)STEVE CARLTON*
33 FERNANDO VALENZUELA-P
34 BEN RIVERA (INJ)-P
35 BOBBY MUNOZ-P
36 *(RET#) ROBIN ROBERTS*
37 JEFF JUDEN-P
38 CURT SCHILLING (INJ)-P
40 DAVID WEST-P
41 MIKE WILLIAMS-P
42 TOBY BORLAND-P
43 JEFF JUDEN-P
44 WES CHAMBERLAIN (INJ)-OF (1)
45 SHAWN BOSKIE-P (2)
45 TOM EDENS-P (2)
46 JOHNNY PODRES-CH
47 LARRY ANDERSEN (INJ)-P
48 ROGER MASON-P (1)
48 PAUL QUANTRILL-P (2)
49 TOMMY GREENE (INJ)-P
50 ANDY CARTER-P
51 HEATHCLIFF SLOCUMB-P
52 RICKY BOTTALICO-P
56 BOB WELLS-P
NORM (THE GENIUS) CHARLTON (INJ)-(P)

1995

2ND E (TIE) 69-75 21GB
144 GAME SEASON

00 OMAR OLIVARES-P
1 *(RET#) RICHIE ASHBURN*
2 LARRY BOWA-CH
3 KEVIN ELSTER-INF (2)
4 LENNY (NAILS) DYKSTRA (INJ)-OF
5 GARY VARSHO-OF
6 GENE SCHALL-1B
7 MARIANO DUNCAN-2B (1)
8 JIM EISENREICH-OF
9 MIKE RYAN-CH
10 DARREN (DUTCH) DAULTON-C
11 JIM FREGOSI-MGR
12 MICKEY MORANDINI-2B
13 CHARLIE HAYES-3B
14 DENIS MENKE-CH
15 DAVE HOLLINS-3B (1)
15 GARY BENNETT-PH
16 TONY LONGMIRE-OF
17 DAVE GALLAGHER-OF (1)
18 JOHN VUKOVICH-CH
18 ANDY VAN SLYKE (INJ)-OF (2)
19 KEVIN STOCKER-SS
20 *(RET#) MIKE SCHMIDT*
21 TOM MARSH-OF
22 MARK WHITEN-OF (2)
23 RANDY READY-INF
23 KEVIN JORDAN-INF
24 MIKE LIEBERTHAL-C
25 GREGG JEFFERIES-OF
26 MEL ROBERTS-CH
27 LENNY WEBSTER-C
28 TYLER GREEN-P
29 STEVE FREY-P (3)
30 KEVIN FLORA-OF (2)
31 RANDY READY-INF
31 KEVIN SEFCIK-PH
32 *(RET #)STEVE CARLTON*
33 GENE HARRIS-P
33 RUSS SPRINGER-P (2)
34 ANDY VAN SLYKE (INJ)-OF (2)
35 BOBBY MUNOZ (INJ)-P
36 *(RET#) ROBIN ROBERTS*
37 NORM (THE GENIUS) CHARLTON-P (1)
37 CHUCK RICCI-P
38 CURT SCHILLING (INJ)-P
39 KYLE ABBOTT-P
40 DAVID WEST (INJ)-P
41 MIKE WILLIAMS-P
42 TOBY BORLAND (INJ)-P
43 JEFF JUDEN-P
44 JIM DESHAIES-P
44 MIKE GRACE-P
45 MICHAEL MIMBS-P
46 JOHNNY PODRES-CH
47 DENNIS SPRINGER-P
48 PAUL QUANTRILL-P
49 TOMMY GREENE (INJ)-P
50 ANDY CARTER-P
50 SID FERNANDEZ-P (2)
51 HEATHCLIFF SLOCUMB-P
52 RICKY BOTTALICO-P
52 RYAN KARP-P
58 PAUL FLETCHER-P

1996

5TH E 67-95 29GB

1 *(RET#) RICHIE ASHBURN*
2 LARRY BOWA-CH
3 JOHN VUKOVICH-CH
4 LENNY (NAILS) DYKSTRA (INJ)-OF
5 MIKE BENJAMIN (INJ)-2B
5 GENE SCHALL-1B
6 GENE SCHALL-1B
6 SCOTT ROLEN (INJ)-3B
7 GLENN MURRAY (INJ) (WAIV)-OF
8 JIM EISENREICH (INJ)-OF
9 PETE (INKY) INCAVIGLIA-OF (1)
10 DARREN (DUTCH) DAULTON (INJ) (RET)-C
11 JIM FREGOSI-MGR
12 MICKEY MORANDINI (INJ)-2B
14 DENIS MENKE-CH
15 RICKY OTERO-OF
(16) TONY LONGMIRE (INJ)-(OF)
17 J. R. PHILLIPS-1B (2)
17 DESI RELAFORD-OF

PHILADELPHIA PHILLIES

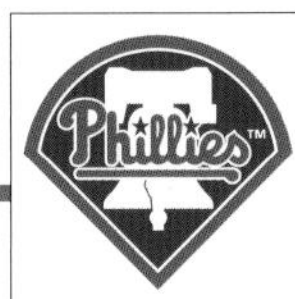

8 BENITO SANTIAGO-C
9 KEVIN STOCKER-SS
0 *(RET#) MIKE SCHMIDT*
1 JON ZUBER-1B
1 RON BLAZIER-P
2 MARK WHITEN (REL)-OF (1)
2 GARY BENNETT-C (2)
3 KEVIN JORDAN (INJ)-1B
4 MIKE LIEBERTHAL (INJ)-C
5 GREGG JEFFERIES (INJ)-OF
6 LEE TINSLEY (INJ)-OF (1)
6 DAVID DOSTER-2B
7 TODD ZEILE-3B (1)
7 BOBBY ESTALELLA-C
28) TYLER GREEN (INJ)-(P)
9 STEVE FREY-P
9 WENDELL MAGEE, JR.-OF
0 DAVE CASH-CH (2)
1 KEVIN SEFCIK-3B
2 *(RET #) STEVE CARLTON*
3 RUSS SPRINGER-P
4 HOWARD BATTLE-3B
4 MANNY MARTINEZ-OF (2)
4 GLENN DISHMAN-P (2)
5 BOBBY MUNOZ (INJ)-P
6 *(RET#) ROBIN ROBERTS*
7 RUBEN AMARO, JR.-OF
8 CURT SCHILLING (INJ)-P
9 RICH HUNTER-P
0 DAVID WEST (INJ)-P
1 MIKE WILLIAMS-P
2 TOBY BORLAND-P
3 DAVE LEIPER (REL)-P (1)
3 RAFAEL QUILRICO-P
3 BRONSON HEFLIN-P
3 JON ZUBER-1B
4 MIKE GRACE (INJ)-P
5 TERRY MULHOLLAND-P (1)
6 JOHNNY PODRES-CH
7 MICHAEL MIMBS (INJ)-P
8 RICARDO JORDAN-P
49) TOMMY GREENE (INJ)-(P)
9 JEFF PARRETT-P (2)
0 SID (EL SID) FERNANDEZ (INJ)-P
1 KEN RYAN-P
2 RICKY BOTTALICO-P
4 CARLOS CRAWFORD-P
5 MATT BEECH-P
6 CALVIN MADURO-P
7 LARRY MITCHELL-P
8 JIM WRIGHT-CH
9 JOE RIGOLI-CH

1997
5TH E 68-94 33GB

1 *(RET#) RICHIE ASHBURN*
2 RICO BROGNA-1B
3 CHUCK COTTIER-CH
(4) LENNY (NAILS) DYKSTRA (INJ)-(OF)
5 ROB BUTLER (INJ)-OF
7 TERRY FRANCONA-MGR
8 MARK PARENT-C
9 BRAD MILLS-CH
0 DARREN (DUTCH) DAULTON-C (1)
1 KEVIN SEFCIK-2B
2 MICKEY MORANDINI-2B
4 REX HUDLER (INJ)-OF
5 RICKY OTERO-OF
6 MIDRE CUMMINGS-OF (2)
7 SCOTT ROLEN-3B
8 JOHN VUKOVICH-CH
9 KEVIN STOCKER-SS
20 *(RET#) MIKE SCHMIDT*
21 MARK PORTUGAL (INJ)-P
22 RON BLAZIER-P
23 KEVIN JORDAN (INJ)-INF
24 MIKE LIEBERTHAL-C
25 GREGG JEFFERIES (INJ)-OF
27 BOBBY ESTALELLA-C
28 TYLER GREEN (INJ)-P
29 WENDELL MAGEE, JR.-OF
30 DESI RELAFORD-SS
31 MARK LEITER-P
32 *(RET #) STEVE CARLTON*
33 SCOTT RUFFCORN-P
34 DERRICK MAY-OF
34 MIKE ROBERTSON (INJ)-1B
35 BOBBY MUNOZ-P
35 RYAN NYE-P
36 *(RET#) ROBIN ROBERTS*
37 RUBEN AMARO, JR.-OF
38 CURT SCHILLING-P
40 REGGIE HARRIS-P
41 ERIK PLANTENBERG-P
41 BILLY MCMILLON-OF (2)
42 GALEN CISCO-CH
44 MIKE GRACE (INJ)-P
45 DANNY TARTABULL (INJ)-OF
47 MICHAEL MIMBS-P
48 JERRY SPRADLIN-P
49 EDGAR RAMOS-P
49 BILLY BREWER (INJ)-P (2)
50 CALVIN MADURO-P
51 KEN RYAN (INJ)-P
52 RICKY BOTTALICO-P
53 TONY BARRON-OF
54 GARRETT STEPHENSON (INJ)-P
55 MATT BEECH-P
56 HAL MCRAE-CH
57 RYAN KARP-P
58 DARRIN WINSTON-P
59 JOE RIGOLI-CH
61 WAYNE GOMES-P

1998
3RD E 75-87 31GB

1 *(RET#) RICHIE ASHBURN*
2 RICO BROGNA-1B
3 CHUCK COTTIER-CH
(4) LENNY (NAILS) DYKSTRA (INJ) (RET)-(OF)
5 MARK LEWIS-2B
6 DOUG GLANVILLE-OF
7 TERRY FRANCONA-MGR
8 MARK PARENT-C
9 BRAD MILLS-CH
11 KEVIN SEFCIK-2B
14 REX HUDLER (WAIV)-OF
14 GARY BENNETT-C
16 MARLON ANDERSON-2B
17 SCOTT ROLEN-3B
18 JOHN VUKOVICH-CH
20 *(RET#) MIKE SCHMIDT*
21 MARK PORTUGAL (INJ)-P
(22) RON BLAZIER (INJ)-(P)
23 KEVIN JORDAN-INF
24 MIKE LIEBERTHAL-C
25 GREGG JEFFERIES-OF (1)
26 ALEX ARIAS-INF
27 BOBBY ESTALELLA-C
28 TYLER GREEN (INJ)-P
29 WENDELL MAGEE, JR.-OF
30 DESI RELAFORD-SS
31 MARK LEITER-P
32 *(RET #) STEVE CARLTON*
33 RUBEN AMARO, JR.-OF
34 PAUL BYRD-P (2)
36 *(RET #) ROBIN ROBERTS*
37 MATT WHITESIDE-P
38 CURT SCHILLING-P
39 RYAN NYE-P
39 TOBY BORLAND-P
40 JON ZUBER-PH
42 *(RET #) JACKIE ROBINSON*
43 GALEN CISCO-CH
44 MIKE GRACE-P
45 YORKIS PEREZ (INJ)-P
46 CARLTON LOEWER-P
47 MIKE WELCH-P
48 JERRY SPRADLIN-P
49 BILLY BREWER (INJ)-P
51 KEN RYAN (INJ)-P
52 RICKY BOTTALICO (INJ)-P
53 BOBBY ABREU-OF
54 GARRETT STEPHENSON-P
55 MATT BEECH (INJ)-P
56 HAL MCRAE-CH
57 ROBERT DODD-P
58 DARRIN WINSTON-P
59 JOE RIGOLI-CH
61 WAYNE GOMES-P

1999
3RD E 77-85 26GB

1 *(RET#) RICHIE ASHBURN*
2 RICO BROGNA-1B
3 CHUCK COTTIER-CH
4 TOREY LOVULLO-INF
5 RON GANT-OF
6 DOUG GLANVILLE-OF
7 TERRY FRANCONA-MGR
8 DESI RELAFORD (INJ)-SS
9 BRAD MILLS-CH
11 KEVIN SEFCIK-2B
12 TOM PRINCE (INJ)-C
14 GARY BENNETT-C
15 DAVE DOSTER-2B
16 MARLON ANDERSON-2B
17 SCOTT ROLEN-3B
18 JOHN VUKOVICH-CH
19 DOMINGO CEDENO-INF (2)
20 *(RET#) MIKE SCHMIDT*
23 KEVIN JORDAN-1B
24 MIKE LIEBERTHAL-C
25 ROB DUCEY-OF
26 ALEX ARIAS-INF
27 BOBBY ESTALELLA-C
(28) TYLER GREEN (INJ)-(P)
29 WENDELL MAGEE, JR.-OF
30 SCOTT ALDRED-P (2)
31 ROBERT PERSON-P (2)
32 *(RET #) STEVE CARLTON*
33 CHAD OGEA-P
34 PAUL BYRD-P
35 CLIFF POLITTE-P
36 *(RET #) ROBIN ROBERTS*
37 JOEL BENNETT-P
37 ANTHONY SHUMAKER-P
38 CURT SCHILLING-P
42 JIM POOLE-P (1)
42 *(RET #) JACKIE ROBINSON*
43 GALEN CISCO-CH
44 MIKE GRACE-P
45 JEFF BRANTLEY (INJ)-P
46 CARLTON LOEWER-P
47 AMAURY TELEMACO-P (2)
48 YORKIS PEREZ-P
49 BILLY BREWER-P
50 PAUL SPOLJARIC-P (1)
50 JOE GRAHE-P
51 KEN RYAN (INJ)-P
52 STEVE SCHRENK-P
53 BOBBY ABREU-OF
54 RANDY WOLF-P
55 MATT BEECH-P
56 HAL MCRAE-CH
57 STEVE MONTGOMERY-(INJ)-P
59 RAMON HENDERSON-CH
61 WAYNE GOMES (INJ)-P

2000
5TH E 65-97 30GB

1 *(RET#) RICHIE ASHBURN*
2 RICO BROGNA-1B (1)
3 CHUCK COTTIER-CH
5 RON GANT-OF (1)
6 DOUG GLANVILLE-OF
7 TERRY FRANCONA-MGR
8 DESI RELAFORD (INJ)-SS (1)
9 BRAD MILLS-CH
10 TRAVIS LEE-OF (2)
11 KEVIN SEFCIK-UTIL
12 MICKEY MORANDINI-2B (1)
13 TOMAS PEREZ-INF
14 GARY BENNETT-C
15 CLEMENTE ALVAREZ-C
16 MARLON ANDERSON-2B
17 SCOTT ROLEN-3B
18 JOHN VUKOVICH-CH
19 BRIAN R. HUNTER-INF (2)
20 *(RET#) MIKE SCHMIDT*
21 KENT BOTTENFIELD-P (2)
22 TOM PRINCE-C
23 KEVIN JORDAN-1B
24 MIKE LIEBERTHAL-C
25 ROB DUCEY-OF (1)(3)
26 ALEX ARIAS-INF
27 DAVID NEWHAN-OF (2)
28 CHRIS PRITCHETT-1B
28 REGGIE TAYLOR-OF
29 JIMMY ROLLINS-INF
30 SCOTT ALDRED (INJ)-P
31 ROBERT PERSON-P
32 *(RET #) STEVE CARLTON*
33 KIRK BULLINGER-P
33 PAT BURRELL-1B
34 PAUL BYRD (INJ)-P
35 CLIFF POLITTE-P
36 *(RET #) ROBIN ROBERTS*
37 BRYAN WARD-P (1)
37 OMAR DAAL-P (2)
38 CURT SCHILLING-P (1)
39 BRUCE CHEN-P (2)
40 GALEN CISCO-CH
41 JASON BOYD (INJ)-P
42 MIKE JACKSON (INJ)-P
43 ANDY ASHBY-P (1)
43 THOMAS JACQUEZ-P
44 CARLOS REYES (INJ) P (1)
44 VICENTE PADILLA-P (2)
45 JEFF BRANTLEY-P
46 TREVER MILLER-P (2)
46 MARK HOLZEMER-P
47 AMAURY TELEMACO-P
48 DAVID COGGIN-P
50 ED VOSBERG-P
51 DOUG NICKLE-P
52 STEVE SCHRENK-P
53 BOBBY ABREU-OF
54 RANDY WOLF-P
55 CHRIS BROCK-P
56 HAL MCRAE-CH
59 RAMON HENDERSON-CH
60 JASON BOYD (INJ)-P
61 WAYNE GOMES (INJ)-P

2001
2ND E 86-76 2GB

P *(RET#) PETE ALEXANDER*
P *(RET#) CHUCK KLEIN*
1 *(RET#) RICHIE ASHBURN*
2 ROB DUCEY (INJ)-OF
3 TODD PRATT-C (2)
4 GARY BENNETT-C (1)
4 MATT WALBECK-C
5 PAT BURRELL-OF
6 DOUG GLANVILLE-OF
7 RICHIE HEBNER-CH
8 MARLON ANDERSON-2B
9 DAVID NEWHAN (INJ)-2B
9 TOMAS PEREZ-INF
10 LARRY BOWA-MGR
11 JIMMY ROLLINS-SS
12 BRIAN L. HUNTER (INJ)-OF
13 TOMAS PEREZ-INF
13 TURK WENDELL-P (2)
14 *(RET#) JIM BUNNING*
15 ERIC VALENT-OF
16 TRAVIS LEE-1B
17 SCOTT ROLEN-3B
18 JOHN VUKOVICH-CH
19 JOHNNY ESTRADA-C
20 *(RET#) MIKE SCHMIDT*
21 GREG GROSS-CH
22 JASON MICHAELS-OF
23 KEVIN JORDAN-1B
24 MIKE LIEBERTHAL (INJ)-C
25 TURNER WARD-OF
26 MARK BOMBARD-INT CH
27 RICKY BOTTALICO (INJ)-P
28 REGGIE TAYLOR-OF
29 P. J. FORBES-UTIL
30 TONY SCOTT-CH
31 ROBERT PERSON (SUS)-P
32 *(RET #) STEVE CARLTON*
33 RHEAL CORMIER (INJ)-P
34 PAUL BYRD-P
34 NICK PUNTO-SS
35 CLIFF POLITTE (INJ)-P
36 *(RET #) ROBIN ROBERTS*
37 OMAR DAAL-P
39 BRUCE CHEN-P (1)
39 DENNIS COOK (INJ)-P (2)
40 JOSE SANTIAGO-P
42 *(RET #) JACKIE ROBINSON*
43 RANDY WOLF (INJ)-P
44 VICENTE PADILLA (INJ)-P
45 CHRIS BROCK-P
46 VERN RUHLE-CH
47 AMAURY TELEMACO-P
48 DAVID COGGIN-P
49 JOSE MESA-P
50 ED VOSBERG-P
51 DOUG NICKLE-P
52 FELIPE CRESPO-1B (2)
53 BOBBY ABREU-OF
54 EDDIE OROPESA (INJ)-P
56 BRANDON DUCKWORTH-P
57 NELSON FIGUEROA-P
59 RAMON HENDERSON-CH
61 WAYNE GOMES (INJ)-P (1)
65 EDDIE OROPESA-P
99 TURK WENDELL-P (2)

2002
3RD E 80-81 21.5GB

P *(RET#) PETE ALEXANDER*
P *(RET#) CHUCK KLEIN*
1 *(RET#) RICHIE ASHBURN*
3 TODD PRATT-C/1B
5 PAT BURRELL-OF
6 DOUG GLANVILLE-OF
7 JOHN MABRY-1B/OF (1)
7 JASON GIAMBI-1B/OF (2)
8 MARLON ANDERSON-2B
9* TOMAS PEREZ-INF/P*
10 LARRY BOWA-MGR
11 JIMMY ROLLINS-SS
12 ERIC VALENT-OF/1B
(13) TURK WENDELL (INJ)-(P)
14 *(RET#) JIM BUNNING*
15 DAVE HOLLINS (ILL)-1B
16 TRAVIS LEE-1B
17 SCOTT ROLEN-3B (1)
18 JOHN VUKOVICH-CH
19 DAN PLESAC-P (2)
20 *(RET#) MIKE SCHMIDT*
21 GREG GROSS-CH
22 JASON MICHAELS-OF/3B
23 PLACIDO POLANCO-3B (2)
24 MIKE LIEBERTHAL-C
25 GARY VARSHO-CH
27 RICKY BOTTALICO (INJ)-P
28 ERIC JUNGE-P
29 MARLON BYRD-OF
30 TONY SCOTT-CH
31 ROBERT PERSON (INJ)-P
32 *(RET#) STEVE CARLTON*
33 RICKY LEDEE-OF

34 NICK PUNTO-INF
35 CLIFF POLITTE-P (1)
35 JOE ROA-P
36 *(RET#) ROBIN ROBERTS*
37 RHEAL CORMIER-P
39 JOHNNY ESTRADA-C
40 JOSE SANTIAGO-P
41 BRETT MYERS-P
42 *(RET #)JACKIE ROBINSON*
43 RANDY WOLF-P
44 VICENTE PADILLA -P
46 VERN RUHLE-CH
48 DAVID COGGIN (INJ)-P
49 JOSE MESA-P
50 MIKE TIMLIN-P (2)
51 DOUG NICKLE-P (1)
51 TERRY ADAMS-P
52 CARLOS SILVA-P
53 BOBBY ABREU-OF
54 HECTOR MERCADO-P
56 BRANDON DUCKWORTH-P
59 RAMON HENDERSON-CH

2003

3RD E 86-76 15GB

P *(RET#) PETE ALEXANDER*
𝔓 *(RET#) CHUCK KLEIN*
1 *(RET#) RICHIE ASHBURN*
2 TYLER HOUSTON (INJ)-3B
3 TODD PRATT-C/1B
4 DAVID BELL (INJ)-3B/2B
5 PAT BURRELL-OF
6 JIMMY ROLLINS-SS
7 GARY VARSHO-CH
8 NICK PUNTO-INF
9 TOMAS PEREZ-INF
10 LARRY BOWA-MGR
12 ANDERSON MACHADO-3B
13 TURK WENDELL (INJ)-P
14 *(RET#) JIM BUNNING*
16 JOE KERRIGAN-CH
18 JOHN VUKOVICH-CH
19 DAN PLESAC-P
20 *(RET#) MIKE SCHMIDT*
21 GREG GROSS-CH
22 JASON MICHAELS (INJ)-OF
23 TRAVIS CHAPMAN-3B
24 MIKE LIEBERTHAL-C
25 JIM THOME-1B
26 CHASE UTLEY-2B
27 PLACIDO POLANCO (INJ)-2B/3B
28 ERIC JUNGE-P
28 VALERIO DE LOS SANTOS-P (2)
29 MARLON BYRD (INJ)-OF
30 TONY SCOTT-CH
31 BRANDON DUCKWORTH (INJ)-P
32 *(RET#) STEVE CARLTON*
33 RICKY LEDEE-OF
34 KEVIN MILLWOOD-P
35 JOE ROA (WAIV) (F/A)-P (1)
35 KELLY STINNETT-C (2)
36 *(RET#) ROBIN ROBERTS*
37 RHEAL CORMIER-P
39 BRETT MYERS-P
41 MIKE WILLIAMS (BRV)-P (2)
42 *(RET #)JACKIE ROBINSON*
43 RANDY WOLF-P
44 VICENTE PADILLA-P
47 AMAURY TELEMACO-P
(48) DAVID COGGIN (INJ)-(P)
49 JOSE MESA-P
50 JOSH HANCOCK-P
51 TERRY ADAMS (INJ)-P
52 CARLOS SILVA (SUS:6G)-P
53 BOBBY ABREU-OF
54 HECTOR MERCADO (INJ)-P
56 GEOFF GEARY-P
57 RYAN MADSON-P
59 RAMON HENDERSON-CH

2004

2ND E 86-76 10GB

P *(RET#) PETE ALEXANDER*
𝔓 *(RET#) CHUCK KLEIN*
1 *(RET#) RICHIE ASHBURN*
2 A. J. HINCH-C
3 TODD PRATT-C
4 DAVID BELL-3B
5 PAT BURRELL (INJ)-OF
6 DOUG GLANVILLE-OF
7 GARY VARSHO-CH
8 GREG GROSS-CH
9 TOMAS PEREZ-3B
10 LARRY BOWA-MGR
11 JIMMY ROLLINS-SS
12 RYAN HOWARD-1B
13 BILLY WAGNER-P
14 *(RET#) JIM BUNNING*
15 MILT THOMPSON-CH
16 JOE KERRIGAN-CH
18 JOHN VUKOVICH-CH
20 *(RET#) MIKE SCHMIDT*
21 ERIC MILTON-P
22 JASON MICHAELS-OF
23 SHAWN WOOTEN-3B
24 MIKE LIEBERTHAL-C
25 JIM THOME-1B
26 CHASE UTLEY-2B
27 PLACIDO POLANCO (INJ)-2B
(28) ERIC JUNGE (INJ)-(P)
29 MARLON BYRD-OF
30 CORY LIDLE-P (2)
31 RAMON HENDERSON-CH
32 *(RET#) STEVE CARLTON*
33 RICKY LEDEE (INJ)-OF (1)
34 KEVIN MILLWOOD (INJ)-P
35 ROBERTO HERNANDEZ (INJ)-P
36 *(RET#) ROBIN ROBERTS*
37 RHEAL CORMIER-P
38 TIM WORRELL-P
39 BRETT MYERS-P
40 PAUL ABBOTT-P (2)
41 FLOYD GAVIN-P
42 *(RET #)JACKIE ROBINSON*
43 RANDY WOLF (INJ)-P
44 VICENTE PADILLA (INJ)-P
46 ELIZARDO RAMIREZ-P (1)
47 AMAURY TELEMACO (INJ)-P
47 FELIX RODRIGUEZ-P (2)
49 FELIX RODRIGUEZ-P (2)
50 JOSH HANCOCK-P (1)
51 BRIAN POWELL (INJ)-P
53 BOBBY ABREU-OF
56 GEOFF GEARY-P
57 AMAURY TELEMACO (INJ)-P
58 LOU COLLIER-3B
59 RAMON HENDERSON-CH
59 TODD JONES-P (2)
63 RYAN MADSON-P
75 JIM CROWELL-P

2005

2ND E 88-74 2GB

P *(RET#) PETE ALEXANDER*
𝔓 *(RET#) CHUCK KLEIN*
1 *(RET#) RICHIE ASHBURN*
3 TODD PRATT-C
4 DAVID BELL-3B
5 PAT BURRELL-OF
6 RYAN HOWARD-1B
7 KENNY LOFTON (INJ)-OF
8 SHANE VICTORINO-OF
9 TOMAS PEREZ-INF
11 JIMMY ROLLINS-SS
12 RAMON MARTINEZ-INF (2)
13 BILLY WAGNER-P
14 *(RET#) JIM BUNNING*
15 MILT THOMPSON-CH
16 BILL DANCY-CH
19 GARY VARSHO-CH
20 *(RET#) MIKE SCHMIDT*
21 JON LIEBER-P
22 JASON MICHAELS-OF
23 MARK BOMBARD-CH
24 MIKE LIEBERTHAL-C
25 JIM THOME (INJ)-1B
26 CHASE UTLEY-2B
27 PLACIDO POLANCO-2B (1)
27 MARK KATA-INF (2)
28 RICH DUBEE-CH
29 MARLON BYRD (INJ)-OF (1)
29 DANNY SANDOVAL-SS
29 MICHAEL TUCKER-OF (2)
30 CORY LIDLE (INJ)-P
31 RAMON HENDERSON-CH
32 *(RET#) STEVE CARLTON*
33 JOSE OFFERMAN-INF (1)
33 AQUILINO LOPEZ-P (2)
34 GAVIN FLOYD-P
36 *(RET#) ROBIN ROBERTS*
37 RHEAL CORMIER-P
38 TIM WORRELL (INJ)-P (1)
39 BRETT MYERS-P
41 CHARLIE MANUEL-MGR
42 *(RET #)JACKIE ROBINSON*
43 RANDY WOLF (INJ)-P
44 VICENTE PADILLA (INJ)-P
46 AARON FULTZ-P
47 ENDY CHAVEZ-OF (2)
48 PEDRO LIRIANO-P
50 ROB TEJEDA-P
51 TERRY ADAMS-P
53 BOBBY ABREU-OF
56 GEOFF GEARY (INJ)-P
57 AMAURY TELEMACO-P
58 EUDE BRITO-P
63 RYAN MADSON-P
74 UGUETH URBINA-P (2)

They called him "Nails." Lenny Dykstra wore the #4 for his entire career. It usually was a number reserved for sluggers, but the feisty little outfielder held his own. He led the National League in hits (192) and batted .325 in 1990. Lenny had a super year in '93 where he led the league in runs scored (143), hits (194) and walks (129). He also batted .305, his on-base percentage was .423 and he slugged .482. He helped the Phils get to the World Series that year only to have Toronto's Joe Carter end their season abruptly with his walk-off HR in Game 6.

PITTSBURGH PIRATES

1932
PITTSBURGH PIRATES
2ND 86-68 4GB

10 LLOYD (LITTLE POISON) WANER-OF
11 PAUL (BIG POISON) WANER-OF
12 ADAM COMOROSKY-OF
14 DAVE BARBEE-OF
15 GUS DUGAS-OF
20 PIE TRAYNOR-3B
21 ARKY VAUGHAN-SS
22 TONY PIET-2B
24 GUS SUHR-1B
25 TOMMY THEVENOW (INJ)-SS/3B
25 BILL BRUBAKER-3B
26 HOWDIE GROSKLOSS-SS
30 EARL GRACE-C
31 TOM PADDEN-C
32 HAL FINNEY (INJ)-C
33 GEORGE (MOON) GIBSON-MGR
34 DOC CRANDALL-CH
35 GROVER (SLICK) HARTLEY-CH
40 RAY (WIZ) KREMER-P
41 HEINIE (THE COUNT OF LUXEMBURG) MEINE-P
42 LARRY FRENCH-P
43 STEVE SWETONIC-P
44 BILL HARRIS-P
45 BILL SWIFT-P
46 LEON (SHAG) CHAGNON-P
47 GLENN SPENCER-P
47 HAL SMITH-P
48 ERV BRAME-P
NO# BILL BRENZEL-C (9G: 4/13-5/9)
NO# WOODY JENSEN-OF (7G: 4/16-5/19)

1933
2ND 87-67 5GB

10 LLOYD (LITTLE POISON) WANER-OF
11 PAUL (BIG POISON) WANER-OF
12 FREDDY LINDSTROM-OF
14 ADAM COMOROSKY-OF
15 BILL BRUBAKER-3B
16 WOODY JENSEN-OF
20 PIE TRAYNOR-3B
21 ARKY VAUGHAN-SS
22 TONY PIET-2B
23 BILL BRUBAKER-3B
23 VAL PICINICH-C (2)
24 GUS SUHR-1B
25 TOMMY THEVENOW (INJ)-INF
26 PEP YOUNG-2B/SS
30 EARL GRACE-C
31 TOM PADDEN-C
32 HAL FINNEY-C
33 GEORGE (MOON) GIBSON-MGR
34 DOC CRANDALL-CH
35 GROVER (SLICK) HARTLEY-CH
36 HONUS (THE FLYING DUTCHMAN) WAGNER-CH
40 RAY (WIZ) KREMER-P
40 RED NONNENKAMP-PH
41 HEINIE (THE COUNT OF LUXEMBURG) MEINE-P
42 LARRY FRENCH-P
43 STEVE SWETONIC-P
44 BILL HARRIS-P
45 BILL SWIFT-P
46 LEON (SHAG) CHAGNON-P
47 HAL SMITH-P
48 WAITE (SCHOOLBOY) HOYT-P
49 RALPH (LEFTY) BIRKOFER-P
50 CLISE DUDLEY-P

1934
5TH 74-76 19.5GB

10 LLOYD (LITTLE POISON) WANER-OF
11 PAUL (BIG POISON) WANER-OF
12 FREDDY LINDSTROM-OF
14 WALLY ROETTGER-OF
16 WOODY JENSEN-OF
20 PIE TRAYNOR-3B/MGR2
21 ARKY VAUGHAN-SS
22 COOKIE LAVAGETTO-2B
23 BILL BRUBAKER-3B
23 BURLEIGH (OL' STUBBLEBEARD) GRIMES-P (2)
24 GUS SUHR-1B
25 TOMMY THEVENOW (INJ)-INF
26 PEP YOUNG-2B/SS
30 EARL GRACE-C
31 TOM PADDEN-C
32 HAL FINNEY-C
33 GEORGE (MOON) GIBSON-MGR1
34 DOC CRANDALL-CH
35 PAT VELTMAN-C
36 HONUS (THE FLYING DUTCHMAN) WAGNER-CH
37 BURLEIGH (OL' STUBBLEBEARD) GRIMES-P (2)
40 RED (THE NASHVILLE NARCISSUS) LUCAS-P
41 HEINIE (THE COUNT OF LUXEMBURG) MEINE-P
42 LARRY FRENCH-P
43 CY BLANTON-P
44 BILL HARRIS-P
44 ED HOLLEY-P (2)
45 BILL SWIFT-P
46 LEON (SHAG) CHAGNON-P
47 HAL SMITH (ILL)-P
48 WAITE (SCHOOLBOY) HOYT-P
49 RALPH (LEFTY) BIRKOFER-P
50 LLOYD (EPPA) JOHNSON-P
_ STEAMBOAT STRUSS-P (1G: 9/30)

1935
4TH 86-67 13.5GB

10 LLOYD (LITTLE POISON) WANER-OF
11 PAUL (BIG POISON) WANER-OF
12 CLAUDE PASSEAU-P
14 BABE HERMAN-OF/1B (1)
15 STEVE SWETONIC-PR
16 WOODY JENSEN-OF
20 PIE TRAYNOR (INJ)-3B/1B/MGR
21 ARKY VAUGHAN-SS
22 COOKIE LAVAGETTO-2B/3B
22 EARL (SNITZ) BROWNE-1B
24 GUS SUHR-1B/OF
25 TOMMY THEVENOW-INF
26 PEP YOUNG-2B/UTIL
27 BILL BRUBAKER-3B
30 EARL GRACE-C
31 TOM PADDEN-C
33 JEWEL ENS-CH
36 HONUS (THE FLYING DUTCHMAN) WAGNER-CH
37 AUBREY EPPS-C
40 RED (THE NASHVILLE NARCISSUS) LUCAS-P
41 GUY (THE MISSISSIPPI MUDCAT) BUSH-P
43 JIM (BIG JIM) WEAVER-P
44 JACK SALVESON-P (1)
45 BILL SWIFT-P
46 CY BLANTON-P
47 HAL SMITH-P
47 BUD HAFEY-OF (2)
48 WAITE (SCHOOLBOY) HOYT-P
49 RALPH (LEFTY) BIRKOFER-P
50 MACE BROWN-P
52 WAYNE (OSSIE) (FISH HOOK) OSBORNE-P

1936
4TH 84-70 8GB

10 LLOYD (LITTLE POISON) WANER-OF
11 PAUL (BIG POISON) WANER-OF
12 BUD HAFEY-OF
14 FRED (FRITZ) SCHULTE-OF
15 JOHNNY (UGLY) DICKSHOT-OF
16 WOODY JENSEN-OF
20 PIE TRAYNOR-MGR
21 ARKY VAUGHAN-SS
22 COOKIE LAVAGETTO-INF
24 GUS SUHR-1B/OF
25 BILL BRUBAKER-3B
26 PEP YOUNG-2B
30 AL TODD (INJ)-C
31 TOM PADDEN-C
32 HAL FINNEY-C
33 JEWEL ENS-CH
36 HONUS (THE FLYING DUTCHMAN) WAGNER-CH
40 RED (THE NASHVILLE NARCISSUS) LUCAS-P
41 GUY (THE MISSISSIPPI MUDCAT) BUSH-P (1)
43 JIM (BIG JIM) WEAVER-P
44 JACK TISING-P
45 BILL SWIFT-P
46 CY BLANTON-P
47 MACE BROWN-P
48 WAITE (SCHOOLBOY) HOYT (ILL)-P
49 RALPH (LEFTY) BIRKOFER-P
51 RUSS BAUERS-P
51 JOHNNY WELCH-P (2)
_ EARL (SNITZ) BROWNE-OF/1B (8G: 9/14-9/27)

1937
3RD 86-68 10GB

10 LLOYD (LITTLE POISON) WANER-OF
11 PAUL (BIG POISON) WANER-OF
14 FRED (FRITZ) SCHULTE-OF
15 JOHNNY (UGLY) DICKSHOT-OF
16 WOODY JENSEN-OF
20 PIE TRAYNOR-3B/MGR
21 ARKY VAUGHAN-SS/OF
22 LEE (JEEP) HANDLEY-2B/3B
24 GUS SUHR-1B
25 BILL BRUBAKER-3B/INF
26 PEP YOUNG-INF
27 JOE BOWMAN-P
30 AL TODD-C
31 TOM PADDEN-C
32 BILL (BROADWAY BILL) SCHUSTER-SS
33 JEWEL ENS-CH
34 JOHNNY GOOCH-CH
36 HONUS (THE FLYING DUTCHMAN) WAGNER-CH
40 RED (THE NASHVILLE NARCISSUS) LUCAS-P
43 JIM (BIG JIM) WEAVER-P
44 KEN HEINTZELMAN-P
45 BILL SWIFT-P
46 CY BLANTON-P
47 MACE BROWN-P
48 WAITE (SCHOOLBOY) HOYT-P (1)
48 RAY BERRES-C
49 ED (BIG ED) BRANDT-P
50 JIM (ABBA DABBA)TOBIN-P
51 RUSS BAUERS-P

1938
2ND 86-64 2GB

10 LLOYD (LITTLE POISON) WANER-OF
11 PAUL (BIG POISON) WANER-OF
12 JOHNNY RIZZO-OF
16 WOODY JENSEN-OF
17 JOHNNY (UGLY) DICKSHOT-OF
20 LEE (JEEP) HANDLEY-3B
21 ARKY VAUGHAN-SS/OF
22 TOMMY THEVENOW-INF
24 GUS SUHR-1B
25 BILL BRUBAKER-UTIL
26 PEP YOUNG-2B
30 AL TODD-C
32 RAY BERRES-C
33 JEWEL ENS-CH
34 JOHNNY GOOCH-CH
34 PIE TRAYNOR-MGR
35 PIE TRAYNOR-MGR
35 HONUS (THE FLYING DUTCHMAN) WAGNER-CH
36 HONUS (THE FLYING DUTCHMAN) WAGNER-CH
36 JEWEL ENS-CH
36 HEINIE MANUSH-PH (2)
37 JOHNNY GOOCH-CH
40 RED (THE NASHVILLE NARCISSUS) LUCAS-P
41 BOB KLINGER-P
44 RIP SEWELL-P
45 BILL SWIFT-P
46 CY BLANTON-P
47 MACE BROWN-P
48 JOE BOWMAN (INJ)-P
49 ED (BIG ED) BRANDT-P
50 JIM (ABBA DABBA)TOBIN-P
51 RUSS BAUERS-P
52 TOMMY THEVENOW-INF
53 KEN HEINTZELMAN-P

1939
6TH 68-85 28.5GB

5* OAD SWIGART-P*
7 EDDIE YOUNT-PH
10 LLOYD (LITTLE POISON) WANER-OF/3B
11 PAUL (BIG POISON) WANER-OF
12 JOHNNY RIZZO-OF
14 HEINIE MANUSH-OF
14 CHUCK KLEIN-OF (2)
16 WOODY JENSEN-OF
16 ELBIE FLETCHER-1B (2)
17 FERN (DANNY) BELL-OF/3B
18 MAURICE (BOMBER) VAN ROBAYS-OF/3B
20 LEE (JEEP) HANDLEY-3B
21 ARKY VAUGHAN-SS
22 JACK (RED) JUELICH-2B/3B
22 FRANKIE GUSTINE-3B
23 PEP RAMBERT-P
24 GUS SUHR-1B (1)
24 BOB (MR. TEAM) ELLIOTT-OF
25 BILL BRUBAKER-INF
26 PEP YOUNG-2B
30 RAY (IRON MAN) MUELLER-C
31 GEORGE (GOOD BOY) SUSCE-C
32 RAY BERRES-C
33 JEWEL ENS-CH
34 JOHNNY GOOCH-CH
35 PIE TRAYNOR-MGR
36 HONUS (THE FLYING DUTCHMAN) WAGNER-CH
38 JOE (DODE) SCHULTZ-C
40 BILL CLEMENSEN-P
40 MAX BUTCHER-P (2)
41 BOB KLINGER-P
42 JOHNNY (WHIZ) GEE-P
44 RIP SEWELL-P
45 BILL SWIFT-P
46 CY BLANTON (INJ)-P
47 MACE BROWN-P
48 JOE BOWMAN-P
49 BILL CLEMENSEN-P
50 JIM (ABBA DABBA)TOBIN-P
51 RUSS BAUERS (INJ)-P
53 KEN HEINTZELMAN-P

1940
4TH 78-76 28.5GB

2 ED LEIP-2B
3 ARKY VAUGHAN-SS/3B
3 ELBIE FLETCHER-1B
4 LEE (JEEP) HANDLEY-3B/2B
4 PEP YOUNG-INF
5 ELBIE FLETCHER-1B
5 ARKY VAUGHAN-SS/3B
6 PEP YOUNG-INF
6 LEE (JEEP) HANDLEY-3B/2B
7 JOHNNY RIZZO-OF (1)
8 VINCE DIMAGGIO-OF (2)
8 BOB (MR. TEAM) ELLIOTT-OF
9 PAUL (BIG POISON) WANER-OF
9 VINCE DIMAGGIO-OF (2)
10 LLOYD (LITTLE POISON) WANER-OF/3B
11 SPUD DAVIS-C
12 RAY BERRES-C (1)
12 AL LOPEZ-C (2)
14 RAY (IRON MAN) MUELLER-C
15 BILL BRUBAKER-INF
16 FRANKIE GUSTINE-2B
17 DICK LANAHAN-P
17 MAURICE (BOMBER) VAN ROBAYS-OF/1B
18 DEBS (TEX) GARMS-3B/OF
19 MAX BUTCHER-P
20 BOB KLINGER-P
21 JOE BOWMAN-P
22 DUTCH DIETZ-P
22 DANNY (DEACON DANNY) MACFAYDEN-P
23 PEP RAMBERT-P
23 FRANK (FATS) KALIN-OF
(24) JOHNNY (WHIZ) GEE (INJ)-(P)

25 MACE BROWN-P
26 OAD SWIGART-P
27 RAY (COWBOY) HARRELL-P
28 MAURICE (BOMBER) VAN ROBAYS- OF/1B
28 DICK LANAHAN-P
29 JOHNNY (TOBACCO CHEWIN' JOHNNY) LANNING-P
30 RIP SEWELL-P
31 RUSS BAUERS-P
32 KEN HEINTZELMAN-P
33 HONUS (THE FLYING DUTCHMAN) WAGNER-CH
34 JAKE FLOWERS-CH
35 FRANKIE (THE FORDHAM FLASH) FRISCH-MGR
35 DUTCH DIETZ-P
36 MIKE KELLY-CH
37 BOB (MR. TEAM) ELLIOTT-OF
37 VINCE DIMAGGIO-OF (2)
37 FERN (DANNY) BELL-PH
38 ED FERNANDES-C
38 JOE (DODE) SCHULTZ-C

1941

4TH 81-73 19GB

1 BILL BAKER-C (2)
2 RIPPER COLLINS-1B/OF
3 ELBIE FLETCHER-1B
4 STU MARTIN-INF
5 ARKY VAUGHAN-SS/3B
6 LEE (JEEP) HANDLEY-3B
8 BOB (MR. TEAM) ELLIOTT-OF
9 VINCE DIMAGGIO-OF
10 LLOYD (LITTLE POISON) WANER-OF (1)
10 ED LEIP-2B
11 SPUD DAVIS-C
12 AL LOPEZ-C
14 BUD STEWART-OF
15 ALF ANDERSON-SS
16 FRANKIE GUSTINE-2B/3B
17 MAURICE (BOMBER) VAN ROBAYS-OF
17 CULLEY RIKARD-OF
18 DEBS (TEX) GARMS-3B/OF
19 MAX BUTCHER-P
20 BOB KLINGER-P
21 JOE BOWMAN-P
21 BILL CLEMENSEN-P
22 DUTCH DIETZ-P
24 JOHNNY (WHIZ) GEE-P
24 BILL BRANDT-P
25 MACE BROWN-P (1)
25 NICK (JUMBO) STRINCEVICH-P (2)
(26) OAD SWIGART (MIL)-(P)
26 JOE SULLIVAN-P (2)
28 DICK LANAHAN-P
28 VINNIE SMITH-C
29 JOHNNY (TOBACCO CHEWIN' JOHNNY) LANNING-P
30 RIP SEWELL-P
31 RUSS BAUERS-P
32 KEN HEINTZELMAN-P
33 HONUS (THE FLYING DUTCHMAN) WAGNER-CH
34 JAKE FLOWERS-CH
35 FRANKIE (THE FORDHAM FLASH) FRISCH-MGR
36 MIKE KELLY-CH
37 BILL CLEMENSEN-P
37 DICK CONGER-P
38 JOE (DODE) SCHULTZ-C
38 BILLY COX-SS
39 LEFTY WILKIE-P
40 CULLEY RIKARD-OF

1942

5TH 68-81 38.5GB

1 BILL BAKER (INJ)-C
3 ELBIE FLETCHER-1B
4 HUCK GEARY (ILL)-SS
4 STU MARTIN (MMAR)-INF
5 PETE COSCARART-SS/2B
(6) LEE (JEEP) HANDLEY (INJ) -(3B)
6 ED LEIP (MIL)-PR
8 BOB (MR. TEAM) ELLIOTT-3B/OF
9 VINCE DIMAGGIO-OF
10 ED LEIP (MIL)-PR
10 BABE (BLIMP) PHELPS-C
11 JIMMY WASDELL-OF/1B
12 AL LOPEZ-C
13 LUKE (HOT POTATO) HAMLIN-P
14 BUD STEWART-UTIL
14 JOHNNY WYROSTEK-OF
15 ALF ANDERSON-SS
16 FRANKIE GUSTINE-2B/UTIL
17 MAURICE (BOMBER) VAN ROBAYS-OF
18 JOHNNY (JACK) BARRETT-OF
19 MAX BUTCHER (INJ)-P
20 BOB KLINGER-P
22 DUTCH DIETZ-P
23 JOHNNY WYROSTEK-OF
23 FRANK COLMAN-OF
(24) JOHNNY (WHIZ) GEE (INJ) -(P)
24 BILL BRANDT-P
24 KEN (CURLY) JUNGELS-P
25 NICK (JUMBO) STRINCEVICH-P
25 HARRY SHUMAN-P
27 HANK GORNICKI-P
29 JOHNNY (TOBACCO CHEWIN' JOHNNY) LANNING-P
30 RIP SEWELL-P
32 KEN HEINTZELMAN (INJ)-P
32 JIM RUSSELL-OF
33 HONUS (THE FLYING DUTCHMAN) WAGNER-CH
34 JAKE FLOWERS-CH
35 FRANKIE (THE FORDHAM FLASH) FRISCH-MGR
36 SPUD DAVIS-CH
37 DICK CONGER-P
39 LEFTY WILKIE-P
40 CULLEY RIKARD (INJ)-OF
40 JACK HALLETT-P

1943

4TH 80-74 25GB

1 BILL BAKER-C
2 TONY (MOSQUITO) ORDENANA-C
3 ELBIE FLETCHER-1B
4 HUCK GEARY-SS
4 AL RUBELING-2B/3B
5 PETE COSCARART-2B/INF
8 BOB (MR. TEAM) ELLIOTT-3B/INF
9 VINCE DIMAGGIO-OF/SS
11 JIMMY WASDELL-PH (1)
11 TOMMY (OBIE) O'BRIEN-OF/3B
12 AL LOPEZ-C/3B
(14) BUD STEWART (RET)-(OF)
14 JOHNNY WYROSTEK-UTIL
16 FRANKIE GUSTINE-SS/INF
17 MAURICE (BOMBER) VAN ROBAYS-OF
18 JOHNNY (JACK) BARRETT-OF
19 MAX BUTCHER (INJ)-P
20 BOB KLINGER-P
21 WALLY (PREACHER) HEBERT-P
22 DUTCH DIETZ-P (1)
22 HANK CAMELLI-C
23 FRANK COLMAN-OF
23 COOKIE CUCCURULLO-P
24 BILL BRANDT-P
25 HARRY SHUMAN-P
26 TOMMY (OBIE) O'BRIEN-OF/3B
26 JOHNNY (WHIZ) GEE-P
27 HANK GORNICKI-P
29 JOHNNY (TOBACCO CHEWIN' JOHNNY) LANNING (MIL)-P
30 RIP SEWELL-P
32 JIM RUSSELL-OF/1B
33 HONUS (THE FLYING DUTCHMAN) WAGNER-CH
34 JAKE FLOWERS-CH
35 FRANKIE (THE FORDHAM FLASH) FRISCH-MGR
36 SPUD DAVIS-CH
39 JOHNNY (SPECS) PODGAJNY-P (2)
40 JACK HALLETT (MIL)-P
41 XAVIER (MR. X) RESCIGNO-P

1944

2ND 90-63 14.5GB

3 BILL RODGERS-OF
3? AL GIONFRIDDO-OF (4G: 9/23-10/1)
4 AL RUBELING-UTIL
5 PETE COSCARART-2B/UTIL
6 LEE (JEEP) HANDLEY-INF
7 BABE DAHLGREN-1B
8 BOB (MR. TEAM) ELLIOTT-3B/SS
9 VINCE DIMAGGIO-OF/3B
10 HANK CAMELLI-C
11 TOMMY (OBIE) O'BRIEN-OF/3B
12 AL LOPEZ-C
(14) BUD STEWART (RET) (MIL) -(UTIL)
14 FRANKIE ZAK-SS
15 ROY WISE-P
15 LLOYD (LITTLE POISON) WANER-OF (2)
16 FRANKIE GUSTINE-SS/INF
17 LEN (MEOW) GILMORE-P
17 VIC BARNHART-SS
18 JOHNNY (JACK) BARRETT-OF
19 MAX BUTCHER-P
20 RAY (IRON MAN) STARR-P
21 FRITZ OSTERMUELLER-P (2)
22 NICK (JUMBO) STRINCEVICH-P
23 FRANK COLMAN-OF/1B
25 JOE VITELLI-P
26 JOHNNY (WHIZ) GEE-P (1)
27 COOKIE CUCCURULLO-P
29 PREACHER ROE-P
30 RIP SEWELL-P
32 JIM RUSSELL-OF
33 HONUS (THE FLYING DUTCHMAN) WAGNER-CH
34 JAKE FLOWERS-CH
35 FRANKIE (THE FORDHAM FLASH) FRISCH-MGR
36 SPUD DAVIS-C/CH
41 XAVIER (MR. X) RESCIGNO-P
_ HANK SWEENEY-1B (1G: 10/1)

1945

4TH 82-72 16GB

1 BILL SALKELD-C
3 BILL RODGERS (MIL)-PH
3 AL GIONFRIDDO-OF
4 JACK SALTZGAVER-2B/3B
5 PETE COSCARART-2B/SS
6 LEE (JEEP) HANDLEY-3B
7 BABE DAHLGREN-1B
8 BOB (MR. TEAM) ELLIOTT-3B/OF
10 HANK CAMELLI-C
11 TOMMY (OBIE) O'BRIEN (ILL)-OF
12 AL LOPEZ-C
14 FRANKIE ZAK-SS/2B
15 LLOYD (LITTLE POISON) WANER-OF
16 FRANKIE GUSTINE-SS/UTIL
17 VIC BARNHART-SS/3B
18 JOHNNY (JACK) BARRETT-OF
19 MAX BUTCHER-P
20 RAY (IRON MAN) STARR-P (1)
20 BOOM-BOOM BECK-P (2)
21 FRITZ OSTERMUELLER (MIL)-P
22 NICK (JUMBO) STRINCEVICH-P
23 FRANK COLMAN-1B/OF
25 JOE VITELLI-PR
25 JOHNNY (TOBACCO CHEWIN' JOHNNY) LANNING (MIL)-P
27 COOKIE CUCCURULLO-P
29 PREACHER ROE-P
30 RIP SEWELL-P
32 JIM RUSSELL-OF
33 HONUS (THE FLYING DUTCHMAN) WAGNER-CH
34 JAKE FLOWERS-CH
35 FRANKIE (THE FORDHAM FLASH) FRISCH-MGR
36 SPUD DAVIS-C/CH
40 AL GERHEAUSER-P
41 XAVIER (MR. X) RESCIGNO-P
45 KEN (CORAL) GABLES-P

1946

7TH 63-91 34GB

1 BILL SALKELD-C
2 JIMMY BROWN-INF
3 AL GIONFRIDDO (ILL)-OF
4 BILLY COX-SS
5 PETE COSCARART-SS
6 LEE (JEEP) HANDLEY-3B/2B
7 MAURICE (BOMBER) VAN ROBAYS-OF/1B
8 BOB (MR. TEAM) ELLIOTT-OF/3B
9 BURGESS (WHITEY) WHITEHEAD-INF
10 HANK CAMELLI-C
11 LEE HOWARD-P
11 AL TATE-P
11 CHUCK WORKMAN-OF/3B (2)
12 AL LOPEZ (INJ)-C
14 FRANKIE ZAK-SS
15 ELBIE FLETCHER-1B
16 FRANKIE GUSTINE-2B/INF
17 VIC BARNHART-PH
18 JOHNNY (JACK) BARRETT-OF (1)
19 MAURICE (BOMBER) VAN ROBAYS-OF/1B
20 KEN HEINTZELMAN-P
21 FRITZ OSTERMUELLER (MIL)-P
22 NICK (JUMBO) STRINCEVICH-P
23 FRANK COLMAN-OF/1B (1
24 ED (RUBE) ALBOSTA-P
25 JOHNNY (TOBACCO CHEWIN' JOHNNY) LANNING-P
26 HANK GORNICKI-P
27 JUNIOR WALSH-P
28 VINNIE SMITH (INJ)-C
28 HANK GORNICKI-P
29 PREACHER ROE-P
30 RIP SEWELL-P
31 LEFTY WILKIE-P
31 ROY JARVIS (MIL)-C
32 JIM RUSSELL-OF/1B
33 HONUS (THE FLYING DUTCHMAN) WAGNER-CH
34 DEL BISSONETTE-CH
35 FRANKIE (THE FORDHAM FLASH) FRISCH-MGR1
36 SPUD DAVIS-CH/MGR2
37 ALF ANDERSON-PH
39 JACK HALLETT-P
40 AL GERHEAUSER-P
41 CHUCK WORKMAN-OF/3B (2
42 JIM HOPPER-P
43 RALPH KINER-OF
44 BILL BAKER-C/1B
45 KEN (CORAL) GABLES-P
46 ED BAHR-P
47 BILL CLEMENSEN-P
49 BEN GUINTINI-OF
BILLY SULLIVAN (MIL)-(C)

1947

7TH (TIE) 62-92 32GB

1 BILL SALKELD-C
1 DIXIE HOWELL-C
2 JIMMY BLOODWORTH-2B
2* AL LYONS-P* (2)
3 ELBIE FLETCHER-1B
4 RALPH KINER-OF
5 HANK (HAMMERIN' HANK) GREENBERG-1B
6 BILLY COX-SS
7 WHITEY WIETELMANN-INF
8 EDDIE (BAZOOKA) (FIDDLER) BASINSKI-2B
10 CLYDE KLUTTZ-C
11 BILLY HERMAN-INF/MGR1
12 CULLEY RIKARD-OF
13 KIRBY HIGBE-P (2)
14 GENE WOODLING-OF
14 BILLY SULLIVAN-C
15 WALLY WESTLAKE-OF
16 FRANKIE GUSTINE-3B
16 PETE CASTIGLIONE-SS
17 JIM RUSSELL-OF/1B
18 AL GIONFRIDDO-OF (1)
18 HANK BEHRMAN-P (2)
19 HUGH (LOSING PITCHER) MULCAHY-P
20 KEN HEINTZELMAN-P (1)
21 FRITZ OSTERMUELLER-P
22 NICK (JUMBO) STRINCEVICH-P
23 LOU TOST-P
23 MEL QUEEN-P (2)
24 ED BAHR-P
25 KEN (CORAL) GABLES-P
26 ELMER (SMOKY) SINGLETON-P

PITTSBURGH PIRATES

7 ART (RED) (SANDY) HERRING-P
8 STEVE NAGY-P
9 PREACHER ROE-P
0 RIP SEWELL-P
1 ROY JARVIS-C
2 JIM RUSSELL-OF/1B
2 ROGER WOLFF-P (2)
3 HONUS (THE FLYING DUTCHMAN) WAGNER-CH
5 ERNIE (TINY) BONHAM-P
6 JIM BAGBY, JR.-P
7 J. R. MCKEE-CH
8 ZACK TAYLOR-CH
9 BILL BURWELL-CH/MGR2
0 CAL (BUSTER) MCLISH-P
2 BILLY SULLIVAN-C
2 GENE (SKIP) MAUCH-2B/SS
_ LEE HOWARD-P (2G: 9/23-25)

1948

4TH 83-71 8.5GB

1 BILLY MEYER-MGR
2 BILL BURWELL-CH
3 JOHNNY (MUTT) RIDDLE-C/CH
4 RALPH KINER-OF
5 ED (BIG ED) STEVENS-1B
6 STAN ROJEK-SS
7 DANNY MURTAUGH-2B
8 MONTY BASGALL-2B
9 ED FITZGERALD-C
0 CLYDE KLUTTZ-C
1 DIXIE (THE PEOPLE'S CHERCE) WALKER-OF
2 JOHNNY (HIPPITY) HOPP-OF/1B
3 KIRBY HIGBE-P
4 MAX WEST-1B/OF
5 WALLY WESTLAKE-OF
6 FRANKIE GUSTINE-3B
7 GRADY WILSON-SS
7 TED BEARD-OF
8 EDDIE BOCKMAN-3B/2B
9 GOLDIE HOLT-CH
1 FRITZ OSTERMUELLER-P
2 NICK (JUMBO) STRINCEVICH-P (1)
3 MEL QUEEN-P
4 BOB CHESNES-P
5 CAL (BUSTER) MCLISH-P
6 ELMER (SMOKY) SINGLETON-P
7 LENNY LEVY-CH
8 VIC LOMBARDI-P
9 DON GUTTERIDGE-PH
9 PETE CASTIGLIONE-SS
0 RIP SEWELL-P
1 EARL TURNER-C
2 HAL (SKEETS) GREGG-P
3 HONUS (THE FLYING DUTCHMAN) WAGNER-CH
4 JUNIOR WALSH-P
5 ERNIE (TINY) BONHAM-P
6 WOODY MAIN-P
7 ELMER RIDDLE-P

1949

6TH 71-83 26GB

1 BILLY MEYER-MGR
2 LES (MOE) FLEMING-1B
3 EDDIE BOCKMAN-3B/2B
3 JOHNNY (MUTT) RIDDLE-CH
4 RALPH KINER-OF
5 ED (BIG ED) STEVENS-1B
5 JACK (STRETCH) PHILLIPS-1B/3B (2)
6 STAN ROJEK-SS
7 DANNY MURTAUGH-2B
8 MONTY BASGALL-2B/3B
8 CLYDE MCCULLOUGH-C
9 ED FITZGERALD-C
10 MONTY BASGALL-2B/3B
11 DIXIE (THE PEOPLE'S CHERCE) WALKER-OF/1B
12 JOHNNY (HIPPITY) HOPP-1B/OF (1) (3)
13 KIRBY HIGBE-P (1)
14 WALT JUDNICH-OF
14 DINO (DINGO) RESTELLI-OF/1B
15 WALLY WESTLAKE-OF
16 PETE CASTIGLIONE-3B/UTIL
17 TED BEARD-OF
17 PHIL MASI-C/1B (2)
17 MARV RACKLEY-OF (2)
17 BOBBY (ROCKY) RHAWN-3B (2)
18 TOM SAFFELL-OF
19 JACK (GABBY) (SCAT) CASSINI-PR
19 BILL (BUGS) WERLE-P
20 BILL (BUGS) WERLE-P
20 ERNIE (TINY) BONHAM (DIED)-P
21 ELMER RIDDLE-P
22 MURRY DICKSON-P
23 CLIFF (LEFTY) CHAMBERS-P
24 BOB CHESNES-P
25 HUGH CASEY-P (1)
27 RAY POAT-P (2)
28 VIC LOMBARDI-P
29 BILL (BUGS) WERLE-P
29 JUNIOR WALSH-P
30 RIP SEWELL-P
31 GOLDIE HOLT-CH
32 HAL (SKEETS) GREGG-P
32 BILL (SAILOR BILL) (BARNACLE BILL) POSEDEL-CH
33 HONUS (THE FLYING DUTCHMAN) WAGNER-CH
34 JOHNNY (MUTT) RIDDLE-CH
35 ERNIE (TINY) BONHAM (DIED)-P
35 LENNY LEVY-CH
37 HAL (SKEETS) GREGG-P
37 ELMER RIDDLE-P
37 HARRY (GUNBOAT) GUMBERT-P (2)
40 BOB MUNCRIEF-P (1)

1950

8TH 57-96 33.5GB

1 BILLY MEYER-MGR
2 HANK SCHENZ-INF
3 JOHNNY (MUTT) RIDDLE-CH
3 DALE COOGAN-1B
3 BOB (DUKE) DILLINGER-3B
4 RALPH KINER-OF
5 JACK (STRETCH) PHILLIPS-1B/3B/P
6 STAN ROJEK-SS/2B
7 DANNY MURTAUGH-2B
8 CLYDE MCCULLOUGH (INJ)-C
9 ED FITZGERALD-C
9 RAY (IRON MAN) MUELLER-C
10 EARL TURNER-C
10 JOHNNY (BERNIE) BERARDINO-2B/3B (2)
11 NANNY FERNANDEZ-3B
11 DANNY O'CONNELL-SS/3B
12 JOHNNY (HIPPITY) HOPP-1B/OF (1) (3)
13 MARV (TWITCH) RICKERT-OF (1)
13 BILL (WILD BILL) PIERRO-P
14 GEORGE (BO) STRICKLAND-2B/3B
15 WALLY WESTLAKE-OF
16 PETE CASTIGLIONE-INF
17 TED BEARD (INJ)-OF
18 TOM SAFFELL-OF
18 GUS BELL-OF
19 BILL (BUGS) WERLE-P
20 VERN (DEACON) LAW-P
20 HAL (SKEETS) GREGG-P
21 BILL (WILD BILL) PIERRO-P
21 GUS BELL-OF
21 TOM SAFFELL-OF
22 MURRY DICKSON-P
23 CLIFF (LEFTY) CHAMBERS-P
24 BOB CHESNES-P
24 HANK BOROWY-P (2)
25 BILL MACDONALD-P
27 MEL QUEEN-P
28 VIC LOMBARDI-P
29 JUNIOR WALSH-P
30 WOODY MAIN-P
30 FRANK (PAP) PAPISH-P
31 GOLDIE HOLT-CH
33 HONUS (THE FLYING DUTCHMAN) WAGNER-CH
34 JOHNNY (MUTT) RIDDLE-CH
35 LENNY LEVY-CH
37 ED (BIG ED) STEVENS-1B
37 HARRY (GUNBOAT) GUMBERT-P
38 FRANK (RED) BARRETT-P
39 WOODY MAIN-P
40 WINDY MCCALL-P

1951

7TH 64-90 32.5GB

1 BILLY MEYER-MGR
2 DALE LONG-1B
2 JOE GARAGIOLA-C (2)
3 BOB (DUKE) DILLINGER-3B (1)
3 CLYDE MCCULLOUGH-C
4 RALPH KINER-OF/1B
5 JACK (STRETCH) PHILLIPS-1B/3B
6 STAN ROJEK-SS (1)
6 ROCKY NELSON-1B/OF
7 DANNY MURTAUGH-2B/3B
7 DICK SMITH-3B
8 CLYDE MCCULLOUGH-C
8 BILL (HOPALONG) HOWERTON-OF/3B (2)
9 ED FITZGERALD-C
10 HANK SCHENZ-2B/3B (1)
10 MONTY BASGALL-2B
10 JACK MERSON-2B
11 GEORGE (CATFISH) METKOVICH-OF/1B
12 JACK MAGUIRE-2B/3B
12 MONTY BASGALL-2B
12 DICK COLE-2B/SS (2)
13 TED BEARD-OF
14 GEORGE (BO) STRICKLAND-SS/2B
15 WALLY WESTLAKE-3B/OF (1)
15 ERV (FOUR-SACK) DUSAK-UTIL/P (2)
16 PETE CASTIGLIONE-3B/SS
17 TOM SAFFELL-OF
18 GUS BELL-OF
19 BILL (BUGS) WERLE-P
20 VERN (DEACON) LAW-P
21 DINO (DINGO) RESTELLI-OF
22 MURRY DICKSON-P
23 CLIFF (LEFTY) CHAMBERS-P (1)
23 PAUL (LEFTY) PETTIT-P
24 PAUL (LEFTY) LAPALME-P
24 DON CARLSEN-P
25 BOB (WARRIOR) FRIEND-P
26 BILL (T-BONE) KOSKI-P
27 PETE (PISTOL PETE) REISER-OF/3B
27 FRANK THOMAS-OF
28 JOE MUIR-P
28 TED (CORK) WILKS-P (2)
29 JUNIOR WALSH-P
30 CON DEMPSEY-P
30 HOWIE POLLET-P (2)
•**31** JOE MUIR-P
33 HONUS (THE FLYING DUTCHMAN) WAGNER-CH
34 JUNIOR WALSH-P
35 HARRY FISHER-PH
36 MEL QUEEN-P
37 PAUL (LEFTY) PETTIT-P
38 LEN YOCHIM-P
39 HARRY FISHER-PH
40 MILT STOCK-CH
41 BABE HERMAN-CH
42 BILL (SAILOR BILL) (BARNACLE BILL) POSEDEL-CH
43 SAM NARRON-CH
BILL MACDONALD (MIL)-(P)
DANNY O'CONNELL (MIL)-(INF)

1952

8TH 42-112 54.5GB

1 BILLY MEYER-MGR
2 JOE GARAGIOLA-C
3 CLYDE MCCULLOUGH-C/1B
4 RALPH KINER-OF
5 JACK (STRETCH) PHILLIPS-1B
5 TONY BARTIROME-1B
6 LEE WALLS-OF
6 DICK SMITH-INF
7 GUS BELL-OF
7 DICK HALL-OF/3B
8 BILL (HOPALONG) HOWERTON-OF/3B (1)
8 BOBBY DEL GRECO-OF
9 ED FITZGERALD-C/3B
10 JACK MERSON-2B/3B
11 HOWIE POLLET-P
12 BOBBY DEL GRECO-OF
12 JOHNNY (BERNIE) BERARDINO-2B (2)
14 GEORGE (BO) STRICKLAND-INF (1)
14 SONNY SENERCHIA-3B
15 ERV (FOUR-SACK) DUSAK-OF
16 PETE CASTIGLIONE-3B/UTIL
17 BRANDY DAVIS-OF
18 GUS BELL-OF
19 BILL (BUGS) WERLE-P
19 HARRY FISHER-P
19 GEORGE (RED) MUNGER-P (2)
20 JIM (BILL) DUNN-P
20 RON KLINE-P
21 RON NECCIAI-P
21 TED BEARD-OF
22 MURRY DICKSON-P
23 JIM WAUGH-P
24 DON CARLSEN-P
24 DICK GROAT-SS
25 BOB (WARRIOR) FRIEND-P
26 CLEM (SCOOTER) KOSHOREK-INF
27 JIM SUCHECKI-P
28 TED (CORK) WILKS-P (1)
28 FRANK THOMAS-OF
29 JIM MANGAN-C
30 JOE MUIR-P
30 BILL (DING DONG)BELL-P
31 DICK SMITH-INF
32 PAUL (LEFTY) LAPALME-P
32 DICK SMITH-INF
34 ED WOLFE-P
35 WOODY MAIN-P
36 CAL HOGUE-P
36 MEL QUEEN-P
40 MILT STOCK-CH
41 CLYDE (SUKEY) SUKEFORTH-CH
42 BILL (SAILOR BILL) (BARNACLE BILL) POSEDEL-CH
43 SAM NARRON-CH
44 GEORGE (CATFISH) METKOVICH-1B/OF
BILL (T-BONE) KOSKI (MIL)-(P)
VERN (DEACON) LAW (MIL)-(P)
BILL MACDONALD (MIL)-(P)
DANNY O'CONNELL (MIL)-(INF)

1953

8TH 50-104 55GB

2 FRED (PUDGE) HANEY-MGR
3 JOE GARAGIOLA-C (1)
4 RALPH KINER-OF (1)
5 DICK HALL-2B
5 PRESTON WARD-1B (2)
6 MIKE SANDLOCK-C
7 DICK SMITH-SS
7 GENE HERMANSKI-OF (2)
9 ED FITZGERALD-C (1)
9 BOB SCHULTZ-P* (2)
9 NICK KOBACK-C
10 DANNY O'CONNELL, 3B/2B
10 JACK SHEPARD-C
11 HOWIE POLLET-P (1)
11 TOBY ATWELL-C (2)
12 DICK COLE-INF
13 EDDIE PELLAGRINI-INF
14 FELIPE (MONTY) MONTEMAYOR-OF
15 FRANK THOMAS-OF
16 PETE CASTIGLIONE-3B (1)
17 CARLOS BERNIER-OF
17 BRANDY DAVIS-OF
18 CAL ABRAMS-OF
19 BOB (WARRIOR) FRIEND-P
20 PAUL (LEFTY) PETTIT-P
21 DICK SMITH-1B/OF
22 MURRY DICKSON-P
23 JIM WAUGH-P
24 PAUL (LEFTY) LAPALME-P
25 BILL MACDONALD-P
26 ELROY (ROY) FACE-P
27 EDDIE O'BRIEN-SS
28 JOHNNY LINDELL-P/1B (1)
29 JOHNNY HETKI-P
30 JOHNNY O'BRIEN-2B/SS
31 VIC JANOWICZ-C
32 CAL HOGUE-P
32 ROGER BOWMAN-P
35 WOODY MAIN-P
36 BOB HALL-P
37 CLEM (SCOOTER) KOSHOREK-IPH
(38) RON NECCIAI (MIL)-(P)
39 BOB ADDIS-PH (2)
40 JOHN FITZPATRICK-CH

41 CLYDE (SUKEY) SUKEFORTH-CH
42 BILL (SAILOR BILL) (BARNACLE BILL) POSEDEL-CH
43 SAM NARRON-CH
44 GEORGE (CATFISH) METKOVICH-1B/OF (1)
44 HAL RICE-OF (2)
57 PETE NATON (MIL)-C
TONY BARTIROME (MIL)-(1B)
BILL (DING DONG) BELL (MIL)-(P)
DICK GROAT (MIL)-(SS)
RON KLINE (MIL)-(P)
BILL (T-BONE) KOSKI (MIL)-(P)
VERN (DEACON) LAW (MIL)-(P)
JIM MANGAN (MIL)-(C)

1954

8TH 53-101 44GB

00 JOE (FIREMAN) PAGE-P
1 *(RET#) BILLY MEYER*
2 FRED (PUDGE) HANEY-MGR
3 BOB SKINNER-1B/OF
4 SID GORDON-OF/3B
5 PRESTON WARD-UTIL
6 DICK SMITH-3B
7 CURT ROBERTS-2B
8 GAIR ALLIE-SS/3B
9 NICK KOBACK-C
10 JACK SHEPARD-C
11 TOBY ATWELL-C
12 DICK COLE-SS/INF
13 EDDIE PELLAGRINI-INF
14 JERRY LYNCH-OF
15 FRANK THOMAS-OF
17 DICK HALL-OF
18 CAL ABRAMS-OF (1)
18 LAURIN PEPPER-P
19 BOB (WARRIOR) FRIEND-P
20 SAM (JET) JETHROE-OF
20 JIM MANGAN (MIL)-C
23 GEORGE O'DONNELL-P
24 PAUL (LEFTY) LAPALME-P
25 CAL HOGUE-P
26 GAIL HENLEY-OF
27 DICK LITTLEFIELD-P (2)
28 WALKER (WALK) COOPER-C (1)
29 JOHNNY HETKI-P
30 NELLIE KING-P
31 VIC JANOWICZ-3B/OF
32 VERN (DEACON) LAW-P
34 BOB PURKEY-P
35 MAX SURKONT-P
38 LEN YOCHIM-P
39 JAKE THIES-P
40 JOHN FITZPATRICK-CH
41 CLYDE (SUKEY) SUKEFORTH-CH
43 SAM NARRON-CH
44 HAL RICE-OF (1)
44 LUIS (CANENA) MARQUEZ-OF (2)
46 BILL HALL-C
TONY BARTIROME (MIL)-(1B)
BILL (DING DONG) BELL (MIL)-(P)
DICK GROAT (MIL)-(SS)
RON KLINE (MIL)-(P)
BILL (T-BONE) KOSKI (MIL)-(P)
PETE NATON (MIL)-(C)
EDDIE O'BRIEN (MIL)-(SS)
JOHNNY O'BRIEN (MIL)-(INF)

1955

8TH 60-94 38.5GB

1 *(RET#) BILLY MEYER*
2 FRED (PUDGE) HANEY-MGR
3 GEORGE (BUD) FREESE-3B
4 SID GORDON-3B/OF (1)
5 PRESTON WARD-1B/OF
6 DICK SMITH-SS
6 JOHNNY O'BRIEN (MIL/INJ)-2B
7 CURT ROBERTS-2B
7 EDDIE O'BRIEN (MIL)-OF/INF
8 GENE (AUGIE) FREESE-3B/2B
9 NICK KOBACK-C
10 JACK SHEPARD-C
11 TOBY ATWELL-C
12 DICK COLE-INF
13 ROBERTO CLEMENTE-OF
14 FELIPE (MONTY) MONTEMAYOR-OF
14 JOHNNY POWERS-OF
15 FRANK THOMAS-OF
16 TOM SAFFELL-OF (1)
17 HARDY PETERSON-C
18 JERRY LYNCH-OF/C
19 BOB (WARRIOR) FRIEND-P
20 RED SWANSON-P
20 BILL (DING DONG) BELL-P
21 EARL SMITH-OF
21 ROBERTO CLEMENTE-OF
22 RON KLINE-P
23 LAURIN PEPPER-P
24 DICK GROAT-SS
25 ROMAN MEJIAS-OF
26 ELROY (ROY) FACE-P
27 DICK LITTLEFIELD-P
28 BEN WADE-P
28 PAUL MARTIN-P
29 DALE LONG-1B
30 NELLIE KING-P
30 DICK HALL-P
31 ROGER BOWMAN-P
31 LINO DONOSO-P
32 VERN (DEACON) LAW-P
•34 FRED WATERS-P
34 BOB PURKEY-P
35 MAX SURKONT-P
36 FRED WATERS-P
37 AL (STRETCH) GRUNWALD-P
38 DICK HALL-P
39 JAKE THIES-P
40 JOHN FITZPATRICK-CH
41 CLYDE (SUKEY) SUKEFORTH-CH
43 SAM NARRON-CH
PAUL SMITH (MIL)-(1B)

1956

7TH 66-88 27GB

1 *(RET#) BILLY MEYER*
2 BOBBY (NIG) BRAGAN-MGR
3 DALE LONG-1B
4 BOB SKINNER-OF/INF
5 PRESTON WARD-OF/3B (1)
6* JOHNNY O'BRIEN-INF/P*
7* EDDIE O'BRIEN-UTIL/P*
8 GENE (AUGIE) FREESE-3B/2B
9 CURT ROBERTS-2B
9 BILL (MAZ) MAZEROSKI-2B
10 JACK SHEPARD-C/1B
11 TOBY ATWELL-C (1)
11 HOWIE POLLET-P (2)
12 DICK COLE-INF
13 RED SWANSON-P
14 JERRY LYNCH (ILL)-OF
14 JOHNNY POWERS-OF
15 FRANK THOMAS-3B/UTIL
16 LEE WALLS-OF/3B
17 RED SWANSON-P
17 DANNY (DUSTY) (BEAK) KRAVITZ-C/3B
18 BOBBY DEL GRECO-OF/3B (1)
18 BILL VIRDON-OF (2)
19 BOB (WARRIOR) FRIEND-P
20 GEORGE (RED) MUNGER-P
21 ROBERTO CLEMENTE-OF/INF
22 RON KLINE-P
23 LAURIN PEPPER-P
24 DICK GROAT-SS/3B
25 JACK MCMAHAN-P (1)
26 ELROY (ROY) FACE-P
27 DICK LITTLEFIELD-P (1)
27 CHOLLY NARANJO-P
27 SPOOK JACOBS-2B
29 NELLIE KING-P
30 DICK HALL (INJ)-P
31 BILL HALL-C
32 VERN (DEACON) LAW-P
33 *(RET#) HONUS WAGNER*
34 BOB PURKEY-P
35 MAX SURKONT-P (1)
35 LUIS ARROYO-P
35 FRED WATERS-P
37 BOB GARBER-P
38 HANK FOILES-C (2)
40 JOHN FITZPATRICK-CH
40 DANNY MURTAUGH-CH
41 CLYDE (SUKEY) SUKEFORTH-CH
43 SAM NARRON-CH
45 LINO DONOSO-P
PAUL SMITH (MIL)-(1B)

1957

7TH 62-92 33GB

1 *(RET#) BILLY MEYER*
2 BOBBY (NIG) BRAGAN-MGR1
3 DALE LONG-1B (1)
3 DEE FONDY-1B (2)
4 BOB SKINNER-OF/INF
5 BUDDY PRITCHARD-SS/2B
6* JOHNNY O'BRIEN-P*/INF
8 GENE (AUGIE) FREESE-3B/UTIL
9 BILL (MAZ) MAZEROSKI-2B
10 DICK RAND-C
11 PAUL SMITH-OF/1B
12 JIM PENDLETON-UTIL
14 JOHNNY POWERS-OF/2B
15 FRANK THOMAS-UTIL
16 LEE WALLS-OF (1)
16 JOE TRIMBLE-P
16 EDDIE O'BRIEN-P
17 DANNY (DUSTY) (BEAK) KRAVITZ-C
17 HARDY PETERSON-C
18 BILL VIRDON-OF
19 BOB (WARRIOR) FRIEND-P
20 HANK FOILES-C
21 ROBERTO CLEMENTE-OF
22 RON KLINE-P
23 GENE BAKER-INF (2)
24 DICK GROAT-SS/3B
25 ROMAN MEJIAS (INJ)-OF
26 ELROY (ROY) FACE-P
28 CHUCK CHURN-P
29 NELLIE KING-P
30 DICK HALL (INJ)-P
30 BENNIE DANIELS-P
31 LAURIN PEPPER-P
31 KEN HAMLIN-SS
31 WHAMMY DOUGLAS-P
32 VERN (DEACON) LAW-P
33 *(RET#) HONUS WAGNER*
34 BOB PURKEY-P
35 RED SWANSON-P
36 JOE TRIMBLE-P
37 BOB (SARGE) KUZAVA-P (1)
37 BOB SMITH (INJ)-P (2)
•38 GEORGE (RED) WITT-P
39 LUIS ARROYO-P
40 DANNY MURTAUGH-CH/MGR2
41 CLYDE (SUKEY) SUKEFORTH-CH
42 LENNY LEVY-CH
43 SAM NARRON-CH
52 GEORGE (RED) WITT-P

1958

2ND 84-70 8GB

1 *(RET#) BILLY MEYER*
3 TED (BIG KLU) KLUSZEWSKI-1B
4 BOB SKINNER-OF
6 JOHNNY O'BRIEN-PH (1)
6 DICK (DUCKY) SCHOFIELD-SS/3B (2)
7 R C STEVENS-1B
7 DICK (DR. STRANGEGLOVE) STUART-1B
8 GENE (AUGIE) FREESE-3B (1)
8 HARRY BRIGHT-3B
9 BILL (MAZ) MAZEROSKI-2B
11 PAUL SMITH-PH (1)
11 BILL HALL-C
12 JIM PENDLETON-PH
14 JOHNNY POWERS-OF
15 FRANK THOMAS-3B/UTIL
16 EDDIE O'BRIEN-P
16 BOB PORTERFIELD-P (2)
17 HARDY PETERSON-C
18 BILL VIRDON-OF
19 BOB (WARRIOR) FRIEND-P
20 HANK FOILES-C
21 ROBERTO CLEMENTE-OF
22 RON KLINE-P
23 GENE BAKER (INJ)-3B/2B
23 HARRY BRIGHT-3B
24 DICK GROAT-SS
25 ROMAN MEJIAS-OF
26 ELROY (ROY) FACE-P
28 DANNY (DUSTY) (BEAK) KRAVITZ-C
29 GEORGE (RED) WITT-P
30 BENNIE DANIELS-P
30 GEORGE (RED) WITT-P
32 VERN (DEACON) LAW-P
33 *(RET#) HONUS WAGNER*
34 CURT RAYDON-P
35 DON WILLIAMS-P
37 BOB SMITH-P
38 DON GROSS-P
40 DANNY MURTAUGH-MGR
41 BILL BURWELL-CH
42 LENNY LEVY-CH
43 SAM NARRON-CH
44 FRANK (FEZ) OCEAK-CH
47 GEORGE PEREZ-P
48 RON BLACKBURN-P
DICK HALL (RET)-(P)

1959

4TH 78-76 9GB

1 *(RET#) BILLY MEYER*
3 TED (BIG KLU) KLUSZEWSKI-1B (1)
4 BOB SKINNER-OF/1B
6 SMOKY BURGESS-C
7 DICK (DR. STRANGEGLOVE) STUART-1B/OF
8 HARRY BRIGHT-UTIL
9 BILL (MAZ) MAZEROSKI-2B
10 DANNY (DUSTY) (BEAK) KRAVITZ-C
11 DICK (DUCKY) SCHOFIELD-SS/3B
12 DON (TIGER) HOAK-3B
14 ROCKY NELSON-1B/OF
15 ROMAN MEJIAS-OF
16 BOB PORTERFIELD-P (1)(3
18 BILL VIRDON-OF
19 BOB (WARRIOR) FRIEND-P
20 HANK FOILES (INJ)-C
20 HARDY PETERSON-C
21 ROBERTO CLEMENTE (INJ)-OF
22 RON KLINE-P
23 JOE CHRISTOPHER-OF
23 HARRY (SUITCASE) (GOODY) SIMPSON-OF (3)
24 DICK GROAT-SS
25 ROMAN MEJIAS-OF
26 ELROY (ROY) FACE-P
28 R C STEVENS-1B
30 DICK HALL-P
30 GEORGE (RED) WITT (INJ)-P
31 HARVEY (THE KITTEN) HADDIX-P
32 VERN (DEACON) LAW-P
33 *(RET#) HONUS WAGNER*
34 PAUL GIEL-P
34 DON WILLIAMS-P
35 DON WILLIAMS-P
35 FRED GREEN-P
36 RON BLACKBURN (MIL)-P
37 BOB SMITH-P (1)
37 DON GROSS-P
37 JIM UMBRICHT-P
38 DON GROSS-P
38 AL JACKSON-P
39 BENNIE DANIELS-P
40 DANNY MURTAUGH-MGR
41 BILL BURWELL-CH
42 JIMMY DYKES-CH
42 GEORGE DETORE-CH
43 SAM NARRON-CH
44 FRANK (FEZ) OCEAK-CH
45 LENNY LEVY-CH
48 KEN HAMLIN-SS
GENE BAKER (INJ)-(3B)

1960

1ST 95-59 0GB

W WS-NYA 4-3

1 *(RET#) BILLY MEYER*
2 BOB OLDIS-C
4 BOB SKINNER-OF
5 HAL SMITH-C
6 SMOKY BURGESS-C
7 DICK (DR. STRANGEGLOVE) STUART-1B
7 R C STEVENS-1B
8 HARRY BRIGHT-PH
9 BILL (MAZ) MAZEROSKI-2B
10 DANNY (DUSTY) (BEAK) KRAVITZ-C (1)
11 DICK (DUCKY) SCHOFIELD-INF
12 DON (TIGER) HOAK-3B
14 ROCKY NELSON-1B
15 ROMAN MEJIAS-PH
16 GENE BAKER-3B/2B
18 BILL VIRDON-OF
19 BOB (WARRIOR) FRIEND-P
20 GINO CIMOLI-OF
21 ROBERTO CLEMENTE-OF
22 JOE GIBBON-P
23 JOE CHRISTOPHER-OF
24 DICK GROAT-SS
26 ELROY (ROY) FACE-P
28 PAUL GIEL-P
29 BENNIE DANIELS-P
29 EARL FRANCIS-P
29 CLEM LABINE-P (3)

ITTSBURGH PIRATES

0 GEORGE (RED) WITT-P
0 VINEGAR BEND MIZELL-P (2)
1 HARVEY (THE KITTEN) HADDIX-P
2 VERN (DEACON) LAW-P
3 *(RET#) HONUS WAGNER*
5 FRED GREEN-P
7 JIM UMBRICHT-P
7 TOM CHENEY-P
8 DON GROSS-P
8 DIOMEDES OLIVO-P
9 GEORGE (RED) WITT-P
0 DANNY MURTAUGH-MGR
1 BILL BURWELL-CH
2 MICKEY VERNON-PH/CH
3 SAM NARRON-CH
4 FRANK (FEZ) OCEAK-CH
5 LENNY LEVY-CH
8 DICK BARONE-SS

1961

6TH 75-79 18GB

1 *(RET#) BILLY MEYER*
2 BOB OLDIS-C
2 DON LEPPERT-C
4 BOB SKINNER-OF
5 HAL SMITH-C
6 SMOKY BURGESS-C
7 DICK (DR. STRANGEGLOVE) STUART-1B/OF
9 BILL (MAZ) MAZEROSKI-2B
1 DICK (DUCKY) SCHOFIELD-UTIL
2 DON (TIGER) HOAK-3B
4 ROCKY NELSON-1B
5 ROMAN MEJIAS- OF
5 TOM (SNAKE) STURDIVANT-P (2)
6 GENE BAKER-3B/2B
6 JOHNNY (YATCHA) LOGAN-3B/SS (2)
7 DONN CLENDENON-OF
8 BILL VIRDON-OF
9 BOB (WARRIOR) FRIEND-P
0 GINO CIMOLI-OF (1)
0 WALT MORYN-OF (2)
1 ROBERTO CLEMENTE-OF
2 JOE GIBBON-P
3 JOE CHRISTOPHER-OF
4 DICK GROAT-SS/3B
5 AL JACKSON-P
6 ELROY (ROY) FACE-P
7 EARL FRANCIS-P
8 BOBBY SHANTZ-P
9 CLEM LABINE-P
0 VINEGAR BEND MIZELL-P
1 HARVEY (THE KITTEN) HADDIX-P
2 VERN (DEACON) LAW (INJ)-P
3 *(RET#) HONUS WAGNER*
4 TOM CHENEY-P (1)
4 AL MCBEAN-P
5 FRED GREEN-P
7 JIM UMBRICHT-P
7 LARRY FOSS-P
9 GEORGE (RED) WITT (INJ)-P
0 DANNY MURTAUGH-MGR
1 BILL BURWELL-CH
2 RON (ROLLO) NORTHEY-CH
3 SAM NARRON-CH
4 FRANK (FEZ) OCEAK-CH
5 LENNY LEVY-CH

1962

4TH 93-68 8GB

1 *(RET#) BILLY MEYER*
2 DON LEPPERT-C
3 ELMO PLASKETT-C
3 ORLANDO MCFARLAND-C
3 BOB BAILEY-3B
4 BOB SKINNER-OF
5 HOWIE GOSS-OF
6 SMOKY BURGESS-C
7 DICK (DR. STRANGEGLOVE) STUART-1B/OF
8* BOB PRIDDY-P*
8 WILLIE STARGELL-OF
9 BILL (MAZ) MAZEROSKI-2B
11 DICK (DUCKY) SCHOFIELD-INF
12 DON (TIGER) HOAK-3B
14 LARRY ELLIOT-OF
14 JIM MARSHALL-1B (2)
15 TOM (SNAKE) STURDIVANT-P
16 JOHNNY (YATCHA) LOGAN-3B
17 DONN CLENDENON-1B/OF
18 BILL VIRDON-OF
19 BOB (WARRIOR) FRIEND-P
21 ROBERTO CLEMENTE-OF
22 JOE GIBBON-P
23 CAL NEEMAN-C
24 DICK GROAT-SS
25 COOT VEAL-PH
26 ELROY (ROY) FACE-P
27 EARL FRANCIS-P
29 TOMMIE SISK-P
30 VINEGAR BEND MIZELL-P (1)
30 TOM BUTTERS-P
31 HARVEY (THE KITTEN) HADDIX-P
32 VERN (DEACON) LAW-P
33 *(RET#) HONUS WAGNER*
34 AL MCBEAN-P
36 JACK LAMABE-P
37 TOMMIE SISK-P
38 DIOMEDES OLIVO-P
39 BOB VEALE-P
40 DANNY MURTAUGH-MGR
41 BILL BURWELL-CH
42 RON (ROLLO) NORTHEY-CH
43 SAM NARRON-CH
44 FRANK (FEZ) OCEAK-CH
45 LENNY LEVY-CH

1963

8TH 74-88 25GB

1 *(RET#) BILLY MEYER*
2 TED SAVAGE (INJ)-OF
2 ELMO PLASKETT-C/3B
3 JIM (PAG) PAGLIARONI-C
4 BOB SKINNER-OF (1)
5 LARRY ELLIOT-PH
6 SMOKY BURGESS-C
7 BOB BAILEY-3B/SS
8 WILLIE STARGELL-OF/1B
9 BILL (MAZ) MAZEROSKI-2B
10 VIRGIL (FIRE) TRUCKS-CH
11 DICK (DUCKY) SCHOFIELD-SS/INF
12 GENE ALLEY-INF
14 TED SAVAGE (INJ)-OF
14 LARRY ELLIOT-PH
15 TOM (SNAKE) STURDIVANT-P (1)
15 MANNY MOTA-OF/2B
16 RON BRAND-UTIL
16 JULIO GOTAY-2B
16 TOM PARSONS-P
17 DONN CLENDENON-1B
18 BILL VIRDON-OF
19 BOB (WARRIOR) FRIEND-P
21 ROBERTO CLEMENTE-OF
22 JOE GIBBON-P
23 JOHNNY (YATCHA) LOGAN-SS/3B
24 JERRY LYNCH-OF
25 TOMMIE SISK-P
26 ELROY (ROY) FACE-P
27 EARL FRANCIS-P
29 DON SCHWALL-P
30 DON CARDWELL-P
31 HARVEY (THE KITTEN) HADDIX-P
32 VERN (DEACON) LAW (RET)-P
33 *(RET#) HONUS WAGNER*
34 AL MCBEAN-P
36 TOM BUTTERS-P
39 BOB VEALE-P
40 DANNY MURTAUGH-MGR
41 DON OSBORN-CH
42 RON (ROLLO) NORTHEY-CH
43 SAM NARRON-CH
44 FRANK (FEZ) OCEAK-CH
45 LENNY LEVY-CH
47 GENE BAKER-CH

1964

6TH (TIE) 80-82 13GB

1 *(RET#) BILLY MEYER*
2 DAVE WISSMAN-OF
3 JIM (PAG) PAGLIARONI-C
4 REX JOHNSTON-OF
4 JERRY MAY-C
5 JERRY MAY-C
5 ORLANDO MCFARLANE-C/OF
6 SMOKY BURGESS-C (1)
7 BOB BAILEY-3B/UTIL
8 WILLIE STARGELL-OF/1B
9 BILL (MAZ) MAZEROSKI-2B
11 DICK (DUCKY) SCHOFIELD-SS
12 GENE (AUGIE) FREESE-3B
14 GENE ALLEY-INF
15 MANNY MOTA-OF/UTIL
16 WILBUR WOOD-P (2)
17 DONN CLENDENON-1B
18 BILL VIRDON-OF
19 BOB (WARRIOR) FRIEND-P
20 JOHN GELNAR-P
21 ROBERTO CLEMENTE-OF
22 JOE GIBBON-P
23 JULIO GOTAY-PH
23 STEVE BLASS-P
24 JERRY LYNCH-OF
25 TOMMIE SISK-P
26 ELROY (ROY) FACE-P
27 EARL FRANCIS-P
29 DON SCHWALL-P
29 FRED GREEN-P
30 DON CARDWELL (INJ)-P
31 TOM BUTTERS-P
31 BOB PRIDDY-P
32 VERN (DEACON) LAW-P
33 *(RET#) HONUS WAGNER*
34 AL MCBEAN-P
35 FRANK BORK-P
36 TOM BUTTERS-P
36 FRANK BORK-P
37 BOB PRIDDY-P
38 JOHN GELNAR-P
39 BOB VEALE-P
40 DANNY MURTAUGH-MGR
41 DON OSBORN-CH
42 MICKEY VERNON-CH
43 SAM NARRON-CH
44 FRANK (FEZ) OCEAK-CH
45 LENNY LEVY-CH
47 ORLANDO MCFARLANE-C/OF
57 FRANK BORK-P
61 DAVE WISSMAN-OF

1965

3RD 90-72 7GB

1 *(RET#) BILLY MEYER*
2 HAL SMITH-C/CH
3 HARRY (THE HAT) WALKER-MGR
4 JOHNNY PESKY-CH
5 ALEX GRAMMAS-CH
6 CLYDE KING-CH
7 BOB BAILEY-3B/OF
8 WILLIE STARGELL-OF/1B
9 BILL (MAZ) MAZEROSKI-2B
10 JIM (PAG) PAGLIARONI-C
11 DICK (DUCKY) SCHOFIELD-SS (1)
11 JOSE PAGAN-3B/SS (2)
12 GENE (AUGIE) FREESE-3B (1)
12 JERRY MAY-C
14 GENE ALLEY-SS/INF
15 MANNY MOTA-OF
16 DEL CRANDALL-C
17 DONN CLENDENON-1B/3B
18 BILL VIRDON-OF
19 BOB (WARRIOR) FRIEND-P
20 FRANK CARPIN-P
21 ROBERTO CLEMENTE-OF
22 JOE GIBBON-P
23 GEORGE SPRIGGS-OF
24 JERRY LYNCH-OF
25 TOMMIE SISK-P
26 ELROY (ROY) FACE (INJ)-P
27 BOB OLIVER-OF
28 OZZIE VIRGIL, SR.-UTIL
29 DON SCHWALL-P
30 ANDRE (ANDY) RODGERS-INF
31 TOM BUTTERS-P
31 LUKE WALKER-P
32 VERN (DEACON) LAW-P
33 *(RET#) HONUS WAGNER*
34 AL MCBEAN-P
35 WILBUR WOOD-P
39 BOB VEALE-P
43 DON CARDWELL-P

1966

3RD 92-70 3GB

1 *(RET#) BILLY MEYER*
2 HAL SMITH-CH
3 HARRY (THE HAT) WALKER-MGR
4 JOHNNY PESKY-CH
5 ALEX GRAMMAS-CH
6 CLYDE KING-CH
7 BOB BAILEY-3B/OF
8 WILLIE STARGELL-OF/1B
9 BILL (MAZ) MAZEROSKI-2B
10 JIM (PAG) PAGLIARONI-C
11 JOSE PAGAN-UTIL
12 JERRY MAY-C
14 GENE ALLEY-SS
15 MANNY MOTA-OF/3B
16 ANDRE (ANDY) RODGERS (INJ)-INF
17 DONN CLENDENON-1B
18 MATTY ALOU-OF
19 PETE MIKKELSEN-P
20 JESSE GONDER-C
21 ROBERTO CLEMENTE-OF
22 WOODIE FRYMAN-P
23 GEORGE SPRIGGS-PH
23 DON BOSCH-OF
24 JERRY LYNCH-OF
25 TOMMIE SISK-P
26 ELROY (ROY) FACE-P
27 LUKE WALKER-P
28 STEVE BLASS-P
29 DON SCHWALL-P (1)
29 BILLY O'DELL-P (2)
31 LUKE WALKER-P
31 BILLY O'DELL-P (2)
32 VERN (DEACON) LAW (INJ)-P
33 *(RET#) HONUS WAGNER*
34 AL MCBEAN-P
37 BOB PURKEY-P
38 JIM SHELLENBACK-P
39 BOB VEALE-P
43 DON CARDWELL-P
45 DAVE ROBERTS 1B
45 GENE (STICK) MICHAEL-INF

1967

6TH 81-81 20.5GB

1 *(RET#) BILLY MEYER*
2 HAL SMITH-CH
3 HARRY (THE HAT) WALKER-MGR1
3 BOB ROBERTSON-1B
4 JOHNNY PESKY-CH
5 ALEX GRAMMAS-CH
6 CLYDE KING-CH
7 ANDRE (ANDY) RODGERS (INJ)-INF
8 WILLIE STARGELL-OF/1B
9 BILL (MAZ) MAZEROSKI-2B
10 JIM (PAG) PAGLIARONI (INJ)-C
11 JOSE PAGAN-UTIL
12 JERRY MAY-C
14 GENE ALLEY-SS
15 MANNY MOTA-OF/3B
16 ANDRE (ANDY) RODGERS (INJ)-INF
17 DONN CLENDENON-1B
18 MATTY ALOU-OF/1B
19 PETE MIKKELSEN-P (1)
19 BRUCE DALCANTON-P
20 JESSE GONDER-C
20 AL LUPLOW-OF (2)
21 ROBERTO CLEMENTE-OF
22 WOODIE FRYMAN-P
23 GEORGE SPRIGGS-OF
24 MANNY JIMENEZ-OF
25 TOMMIE SISK-P
26 ELROY (ROY) FACE-P
28 STEVE BLASS-P
29 JUAN PIZARRO-P
30 MAURY WILLS-3B/SS
31 BILLY O'DELL-P
32 VERN (DEACON) LAW (INJ)-P
33 *(RET#) HONUS WAGNER*
34 AL MCBEAN-P
35 JOHN GELNAR-P
35 MANNY SANGUILLEN-C
36 DENNIS RIBANT-P
37 BILL SHORT-P
37 JOHN GELNAR-P
38 JIM SHELLENBACK-P
38 BOB MOOSE-P
39 BOB VEALE-P
40 DANNY MURTAUGH-MGR2

1968

6TH 80-82 17GB

1 *(RET#) BILLY MEYER*
2 CHUCK HILLER-2B
2 FREDDIE (THE FLEA) PATEK (INJ)-UTIL
(3) BOB ROBERTSON (ILL)-(1B)
4 BILL VIRDON-OF/CH
4 LARRY SHEPARD-MGR
5 ALEX GRAMMAS-CH
6 DON LEPPERT-CH
7 LARRY SHEPARD-MGR
7 BILL VIRDON-OF/CH
8 WILLIE STARGELL-OF/1B
9 BILL (MAZ) MAZEROSKI-2B
10 GARY KOLB-UTIL
11 JOSE PAGAN-UTIL
12 JERRY MAY-C
14 JIM BUNNING-P
15 MANNY MOTA-UTIL

16 CHRIS CANNIZZARO-C
17 DONN CLENDENON-1B
18 MATTY ALOU-OF
20 RICHIE HEBNER-PH
21 ROBERTO CLEMENTE-OF
22 GENE ALLEY-SS/2B
23 LUKE WALKER (ILL)-P
24 MANNY JIMENEZ-OF
25 TOMMIE SISK-P
26 ELROY (ROY) FACE-P (1)
27 RON KLINE-P
28 STEVE BLASS-P
29 JUAN PIZARRO-P (1)
29 AL OLIVER-OF
30 MAURY WILLS-3B/SS
31 BILL HENRY-P (2)
32 VERN (DEACON) LAW-CH
33 *(RET#) HONUS WAGNER*
34 AL MCBEAN-P
36 CARL TAYLOR-C/OF
37 DOCK ELLIS-P
38 BOB MOOSE-P
39 BOB VEALE-P
40 DAVE WICKERSHAM-P
40 DOCK ELLIS-P
43 BRUCE DALCANTON-P

1969

3RD E 88-74 12GB

1 *(RET#) BILLY MEYER*
2 FREDDIE (THE FLEA) PATEK -SS
3 RON DAVIS-OF
4 LARRY SHEPARD-MGR1
5 ALEX GRAMMAS-CH/MGR2
6 DON LEPPERT-CH
7 BILL VIRDON-CH
8 WILLIE STARGELL-OF/1B
9 BILL (MAZ) MAZEROSKI (INJ)-2B
10 GARY KOLB-C
11 JOSE PAGAN-UTIL
12 JERRY MAY (INJ)-C
14 JIM BUNNING-P (1)
14 JOHNNY JETER-OF
15 JOSE MARTINEZ-UTIL
16 AL OLIVER-1B/OF
18 MATTY ALOU-OF
19 JIM SHELLENBACK-P (1)
19 JOE GIBBON-P (2)
20 RICHIE HEBNER-3B/1B
21 ROBERTO CLEMENTE-OF
22 GENE ALLEY (INJ) INF
23 LUKE WALKER-P
24 GENE GARBER-P
25 BOB ROBERTSON-1B
25 BO BELINSKY-P
27 RON KLINE-P (1)
28 STEVE BLASS-P
29 PEDRO (PETE) RAMOS-P (1)
29 AL OLIVER-1B/OF
29 LOU MARONE-P
30 DAVE CASH-2B
31 GENE GARBER-P
31 ANGEL MANGUAL-OF
32 VERN (DEACON) LAW-CH
33 *(RET#) HONUS WAGNER*
35 MANNY SANGUILLEN-C
36 CARL TAYLOR-OF/1B
38 BOB MOOSE-P
39 BOB VEALE-P
40 DOCK ELLIS-P
42 CHUCK (TWIGGY) HARTENSTEIN-P
43 BRUCE DALCANTON-P
44 CARL TAYLOR-OF/1B
45 FRANK BROSSEAU-P

1970

1ST E 89-73 0GB
L NLCS-CINN 3-0

1 *(RET#) BILLY MEYER*
2 FREDDIE (THE FLEA) PATEK-SS
3 RON DAVIS-OF
5 DAVE RICKETTS-C/CH
6 BOB ROBERTSON-1B/UTIL
6 GEORGE KOPACZ-1B
7 BOB ROBERTSON-1B/UTIL
8 WILLIE STARGELL-OF/1B
9 BILL (MAZ) MAZEROSKI-2B
10 DAVE CASH-2B
10 GEORGE KOPACZ-1B
11 JOSE PAGAN-UTIL
12 JERRY MAY-C
13 ED ACOSTA-P
14 GENE ALLEY-SS/INF
15 JOSE MARTINEZ-INF
15 GENE CLINES-OF
16 AL OLIVER-OF/1B
17 DOCK ELLIS-P
18 MATTY ALOU-OF
19 JOE GIBBON-P
20 RICHIE HEBNER-3B
21 ROBERTO CLEMENTE-OF
22 CHUCK (TWIGGY) HARTENSTEIN-P (1)
22 ORLANDO PENA-P
22 GEORGE (LEFTY) BRUNET-P (2)
23 LUKE WALKER-P
24 JOHN LAMB-P
24 JIM NELSON-P
25 JOHNNY JETER-OF
27 BRUCE DALCANTON-P
28 STEVE BLASS (INJ)-P
29 LOU MARONE-P
29 MILT MAY-PH
30 DAVE CASH-2B
31 DAVE GIUSTI-P
33 *(RET#) HONUS WAGNER*
35 MANNY SANGUILLEN-C
36 ORLANDO PENA-P
36 GENE GARBER-P
36 AL MCBEAN-P (2)
36 DICK COLPAERT-P
36 FRED CAMBRIA-P
38 BOB MOOSE (INJ)-P
39 BOB VEALE-P
40 DANNY MURTAUGH-MGR
41 BILL VIRDON-CH
42 DON OSBORN-CH
43 DON LEPPERT-CH
44 FRANK (FEZ) OCEAK-CH
46 ED ACOSTA-P
46 ORLANDO PENA-P
47 JIM (MUDCAT) GRANT-P (2)
50 FRED CAMBRIA-P

1971

1ST E 97-65 0GB
W NLCS-SFN 3-1
W WS-BALA 4-3

1 *(RET#) BILLY MEYER*
2 JACKIE HERNANDEZ-SS/3B
3 LORENZO (RIMP) LANIER-OF
4 CHARLIE SANDS-C
5 DAVE RICKETTS-CH
6 RENNIE STENNETT-2B
7 BOB ROBERTSON-1B
8 WILLIE STARGELL-OF
9 BILL (MAZ) MAZEROSKI-2B/3B
10 RICHIE ZISK-OF
11 JOSE PAGAN-UTIL
14 GENE ALLEY-SS/3B
15 GENE CLINES-OF
16 AL OLIVER-OF/1B
17 DOCK ELLIS-P
18 VIC DAVALILLO-OF/1B
19 JIM (MUDCAT) GRANT-P (1)
20 RICHIE HEBNER-3B
21 ROBERTO CLEMENTE-OF
22 NELSON BRILES-P
22 JIM (MUDCAT) GRANT-P (1)
22 RICHIE ZISK-OF
23 LUKE WALKER-P
24 JOHN LAMB-P
25 BRUCE KISON-P
27 BOB JOHNSON-P
28 STEVE BLASS (INJ)-P
29 MILT MAY-C
30 DAVE CASH-2B/INF
31 DAVE GIUSTI-P
32 JIM NELSON-P
32 BOB MILLER-P (3)
33 *(RET#) HONUS WAGNER*
34 NELSON (NELLIE) BRILES-P
35 MANNY SANGUILLEN-C
36 RAMON HERNANDEZ-P
37 BRUCE KISON-P
37 FRANK TAVERAS-PR
38 BOB MOOSE-P
39 BOB VEALE-P
40 DANNY MURTAUGH-MGR
41 BILL VIRDON-CH
42 DON OSBORN-CH
43 DON LEPPERT-CH
44 FRANK (FEZ) OCEAK-CH
45 CARL TAYLOR-OF (1)
45 FRANK BROSSEAU-P
48 LORENZO (RIMP) LANIER-OF
50 FRANK TAVERAS-PR
51 RAMON HERNANDEZ-P

1972

1ST E 96-59 0GB
L NLCS-CINN 3-2

1 *(RET#) BILLY MEYER*
2 JACKIE HERNANDEZ-SS/3B
3 RICHIE HEBNER-3B
4 CHARLIE SANDS-C
5 DAVE RICKETTS-CH
6 RENNIE STENNETT-UTIL
7 BOB ROBERTSON-UTIL
8 WILLIE STARGELL-1B/OF
9 BILL (MAZ) MAZEROSKI-2B/3B
10 FRANK TAVERAS-SS
11 JOSE PAGAN-3B/OF
12 CHUCK GOGGIN-2B
12 GENE GARBER-P
14 GENE ALLEY-SS/3B
15 GENE CLINES-OF
16 AL OLIVER-OF/1B
17 DOCK ELLIS-P
18 VIC DAVALILLO-OF/1B
20 *(RET#) PIE TRAYNOR*
21 ROBERTO CLEMENTE (INJ) -OF
22 RICHIE ZISK-OF
23 LUKE WALKER (INJ)-P
25 BRUCE KISON-P
27 BOB JOHNSON-P
28 STEVE BLASS-P
29 MILT MAY-C
30 DAVE CASH-2B
31 DAVE GIUSTI-P
32 BOB MILLER-P
33 *(RET#) HONUS WAGNER*
34 NELSON (NELLIE) BRILES-P
35 MANNY SANGUILLEN-C/OF
36 RAMON HERNANDEZ-P
37 FERNANDO GONZALEZ-3B
38 BOB MOOSE-P
39 BOB VEALE-P (1)
39 JIM MCKEE-P
41 BILL VIRDON-MGR
42 DON OSBORN-CH
43 DON LEPPERT-CH
44 FRANK (FEZ) OCEAK-CH
45 JOE MORGAN-CH
49 JIM MCKEE-P

1973

3RD E 80-82 2.5GB

1 *(RET#) BILLY MEYER*
2 JACKIE HERNANDEZ-SS
3 RICHIE HEBNER-3B
4 JIM CAMPANIS-PH
5 DAVE RICKETTS-CH
6 RENNIE STENNETT-UTIL
7 BOB ROBERTSON-1B
8 WILLIE STARGELL-OF
9 BILL (MAZ) MAZEROSKI-CH
11 JERRY MCNERTNEY-C
11 DAL MAXVILL-SS (2)
12 CHUCK GOGGIN-C (1)
12 JOHN MORLAN-P
14 GENE ALLEY-SS/3B
15 GENE CLINES (INJ)-OF
16 AL OLIVER-OF/1B
17 DOCK ELLIS (INJ)-P
18 VIC DAVALILLO-OF/1B (1)
19 JIM ROOKER-P
20 *(RET#) PIE TRAYNOR*
21 *(RET#) ROBERTO CLEMENTE (DIED)*
22 RICHIE ZISK-OF
23 LUKE WALKER-P
25 BRUCE KISON (INJ)-P
27 BOB JOHNSON-P
28 STEVE BLASS-P
29 MILT MAY-C
30 DAVE CASH-2B/3B
31 DAVE GIUSTI-P
32 JOHN MORLAN-P
32 TOM DETTORE-P
33 *(RET#) HONUS WAGNER*
34 NELSON (NELLIE) BRILES-P
35 MANNY SANGUILLEN-C/OF
36 RAMON HERNANDEZ-P
37 FERNANDO GONZALEZ-3B
38 BOB MOOSE-P
39 JIM MCKEE-P
39 DAVE (THE COBRA) PARKER-OF
40 DANNY MURTAUGH-MGR2
41 BILL VIRDON-MGR1
42 MEL WRIGHT-CH
43 DON LEPPERT-CH
44 JOHN LAMB-P
45 DAVE AUGUSTINE-OF
46 JIM MCKEE-P
48 JOHN LAMB-P
49 CHRIS ZACHARY-P
58 JIM FOOR-P

1974

1ST E 88-74 0GB
L NLCS-LAN 3-1

1 *(RET#) BILLY MEYER*
2 JOSE PAGAN-CH
3 RICHIE HEBNER-3B
4 BOB SKINNER-CH
5 MIKE RYAN-C
6 RENNIE STENNETT-2B/OF
7 BOB ROBERTSON-1B
8 WILLIE STARGELL-OF/1B
10 FRANK TAVERAS-SS
11 DAL MAXVILL-SS (1)
11 MARIO MENDOZA-SS
12 JOHN MORLAN-P
14 KURT BEVACQUA-3B/OF (1)
14 ART HOWE-3B/SS
15 GENE CLINES-OF
16 AL OLIVER-OF/1B
17 DOCK ELLIS (INJ)-P
19 JIM ROOKER-P
20 *(RET#) PIE TRAYNOR*
21 *(RET#) ROBERTO CLEMENTE*
22 RICHIE ZISK-OF
23 ED KIRKPATRICK-UTIL
24 PAUL POPOVICH-2B/SS
25 BRUCE KISON-P
26 ED OTT-OF
27 ED OTT-OF
27 DAVE AUGUSTINE-OF
28 STEVE BLASS-P
30 KEN BRETT (INJ)-P
31 DAVE GIUSTI-P
32 JIM SADOWSKI-P
32 DARYL PATTERSON-P
32 KENT TEKULVE-P
33 *(RET#) HONUS WAGNER*
34 KEN MACHA-C
35 MANNY SANGUILLEN-C/OF
36 RAMON HERNANDEZ-P
37 MIGUEL DILONE-OF
38 BOB MOOSE (ILL)-P
39 DAVE (THE COBRA) PARKER (INJ)-OF/1B
40 DANNY MURTAUGH-MGR
41 JERRY REUSS-P
42 DON OSBORN-CH
43 DON LEPPERT-CH
44 LARRY DEMERY-P
45 DARYL PATTERSON-P
45 CHUCK BRINKMAN-C (2)
46 JIM MINSHALL-P
49 JUAN PIZARRO-P
56 JUAN JIMENEZ-P

1975

1ST E 92-69 0GB
L NLCS-CINN 3-0

1 *(RET#) BILLY MEYER*
2 JOSE PAGAN-CH
3 RICHIE HEBNER-3B
4 BOB SKINNER-CH
5 DUFFY DYER-C
6 RENNIE STENNETT-2B
7 BOB ROBERTSON-1B
8 WILLIE STARGELL-1B
10 FRANK TAVERAS-SS
11 MARIO MENDOZA-SS/3B
12 WILLIE RANDOLPH-2B/3B
12 CRAIG REYNOLDS-SS
14 ART HOWE-3B/SS
15 MIGUEL DILONE-OF
16 AL OLIVER-OF/1B
17 DOCK ELLIS-P
18 CRAIG REYNOLDS-SS
18 WILLIE RANDOLPH-2B/3B
19 JIM ROOKER-P
20 *(RET#) PIE TRAYNOR*
21 *(RET#) ROBERTO CLEMENTE*
22 RICHIE ZISK-OF
23 ED KIRKPATRICK-1B/OF
24 PAUL POPOVICH-2B/SS
24 OMAR MORENO-OF
25 BRUCE KISON-P
26 ED OTT-C
27 KENT TEKULVE-P
28 BILL ROBINSON-OF
29 JIM MINSHALL-P
30 KEN BRETT (INJ)-P
31 DAVE GIUSTI-P
33 *(RET#) HONUS WAGNER*
35 MANNY SANGUILLEN-C
36 RAMON HERNANDEZ-P
38 BOB MOOSE (INJ)-P
39 DAVE (THE COBRA) PARKER-OF
40 DANNY MURTAUGH-MGR
41 JERRY REUSS-P
42 DON OSBORN-CH
43 DON LEPPERT-CH
44 LARRY DEMERY-P
45 JOHN (CANDY MAN) CANDELARIA-P
46 JIM MINSHALL-P

ITTSBURGH PIRATES

8 SAM (SUDDEN SAM) MCDOWELL-P
0 JOHN (CANDY MAN) CANDELARIA-P
0 ODELL JONES-P

1976
2ND E 92-70 5GB
1 *(RET#) BILLY MEYER*
2 JOSE PAGAN-CH
3 RICHIE HEBNER-3B
4 BOB SKINNER-CH
5 DUFFY DYER-C
6 RENNIE STENNETT-2B/SS
7 BOB ROBERTSON-1B
8 WILLIE STARGELL-1B
0 FRANK TAVERAS-SS
1 MARIO MENDOZA-INF
2 CRAIG REYNOLDS-SS/2B
4 ED OTT (INJ)-C
5 TOMMY HELMS-INF
6 AL OLIVER-OF/1B
7 DOUG BAIR-P
8 OMAR MORENO-OF
9 JIM ROOKER-P
0 *(RET#) PIE TRAYNOR*
1 *(RET#) ROBERTO CLEMENTE*
2 RICHIE ZISK-OF
3 ED KIRKPATRICK- OF/3B
5 BRUCE KISON-P
7 KENT TEKULVE-P
8 BILL ROBINSON-UTIL
0 RICK LANGFORD-P
1 DAVE GIUSTI (INJ)-P
2 DOC MEDICH-P
3 *(RET#) HONUS WAGNER*
4 DOC MEDICH-P
5 MANNY SANGUILLEN-C
6 RAMON HERNANDEZ-P (1)
7 MIGUEL DILONE-OF
8 BOB MOOSE (DIED)-P
9 DAVE (THE COBRA) PARKER-OF
0 DANNY MURTAUGH (DIED)-MGR
1 JERRY REUSS-P
2 DON OSBORN-CH
3 DON LEPPERT-CH
4 LARRY DEMERY-P
5 JOHN (CANDY MAN) CANDELARIA-P
6 TONY ARMAS-OF
50 RICK LANGFORD-P

1977
2ND E 96-66 5GB
1 *(RET#) BILLY MEYER*
2 JOSE PAGAN-CH
3 JOE LONNETT-CH
3 PHIL GARNER-3B/INF
4 CHUCK TANNER-MGR
4 DALE BERRA-3B
5 DUFFY DYER-C
6 RENNIE STENNETT (INJ)-2B
7 BOB ROBERTSON (INJ)-(1B)
7 CHUCK TANNER-MGR
8 WILLIE STARGELL (INJ)-1B
10 FRANK TAVERAS-SS
1 MARIO MENDOZA-INF/P
2 FERNANDO GONZALEZ-UTIL
3 FERNANDO GONZALEZ-UTIL
4 ED OTT-C
5 TOMMY HELMS-PH (1)
5 MIKE EASLER-OF
6 AL OLIVER-OF
7 PHIL GARNER-3B/INF
8 OMAR MORENO-OF
9 JIM ROOKER-P
20 *(RET#) PIE TRAYNOR*
21 *(RET#) ROBERTO CLEMENTE*
22 JERRY HAIRSTON-OF/2B (2)
23 ED KIRKPATRICK- UTIL (1)
23 GRANT (BUCK) JACKSON-P
24 TOMMY HELMS-PH (1)
24 BOBBY TOLAN-1B/OF (2)
25 BRUCE KISON-P
26 MIKE EDWARDS-2B
27 KENT TEKULVE-P
28 BILL ROBINSON-UTIL
29 KEN MACHA-UTIL
29 JIM FREGOSI-1B/3B (2)
30 KEN MACHA-UTIL
31 AL HOLLAND-P
31 TIM JONES-P
33 *(RET#) HONUS WAGNER*
34 DAVE PAGAN-P (2)
35 GRANT (BUCK) JACKSON-P
35 JOE LONNETT-CH
36 ODELL JONES-P
37 MIGUEL DILONE (INJ)-OF
38 JIM ROOKER-P
39 DAVE PARKER-OF/2B
40 *(RET#) DANNY MURTAUGH*
41 JERRY REUSS-P
42 AL MONCHAK-CH
43 LARRY SHERRY-CH
44 LARRY DEMERY-P
45 JOHN (CANDY MAN) CANDELARIA-P
46 AL HOLLAND-P
47 ED WHITSON-P
48 TIM JONES-P
51 TERRY FORSTER-P
54 GOOSE GOSSAGE-P
55 DAVE PAGAN-P (2)

1978
2ND E 88-73 1.5GB
1 *(RET#) BILLY MEYER*
2 JOSE PAGAN-CH
3 PHIL GARNER-3B/INF
4 DALE BERRA-3B/SS
5 DUFFY DYER-C
6 RENNIE STENNETT (INJ)-2B/3B
7 CHUCK TANNER-MGR
8 WILLIE STARGELL (INJ)-1B
10 FRANK TAVERAS-SS
11 MARIO MENDOZA-INF
12 MATT ALEXANDER-PR
13 FERNANDO GONZALEZ-2B/3B (1)
14 ED OTT-C/OF
15 DOE BOYLAND-1B
16 JOHN (THE HAMMER) MILNER-OF/1B
16 STEVE NICOSIA-C
16 WILL MCENANEY-P
18 OMAR MORENO-OF
19 JIM ROOKER-P
20 *(RET#) PIE TRAYNOR*
21 *(RET#) ROBERTO CLEMENTE*
22 BERT BLYLEVEN-P
23 GRANT (BUCK) JACKSON-P
24 WILL MCENANEY-P
25 BRUCE KISON (INJ)-P
26 JIM BIBBY-P
27 KENT TEKULVE-P
28 BILL ROBINSON-OF/INF
29 JIM FREGOSI (RET)-3B/1B (1)
29 KEN MACHA-3B
30 KEN MACHA-3B
30 DAVE HAMILTON-P (2)
31 JOE LONNETT-CH
31 ED WHITSON-P
32 JOE LONNETT-CH
33 *(RET#) HONUS WAGNER*
34 JOHN (THE HAMMER) MILNER-OF/1B
35 MANNY SANGUILLEN-1B/C
36 ODELL JONES-P
37 ALBERTO LOIS-OF
38 JIM BIBBY-P
39 DAVE PARKER-OF/2B
40 *(RET#) DANNY MURTAUGH*
41 JERRY REUSS-P
42 AL MONCHAK-CH
43 DON ROBINSON-P
44 LARRY DEMERY (INJ)(P)
44 WILL MCENANEY-P
44 CITO GASTON-OF (2)
45 JOHN (CANDY MAN) CANDELARIA-P
46 STEVE BRYE-OF
48 CLAY (HAWK) CARROLL-P
49 DAVE MAY-PH (3)
51 LARRY SHERRY-CH
54 DAVE MAY-PH (3)

1979
1ST E 98-64 0GB
W NLCS-CINN 3-0
W WS-BALA 4-3
1 *(RET#) BILLY MEYER*
2 GARY HARGIS-PR
3 PHIL GARNER-INF
4 DALE BERRA-SS/3B
5 DOE BOYLAND-PH
5 BILL (MAD DOG) MADLOCK-3B (2)
6 RENNIE STENNETT-2B
7 CHUCK TANNER-MGR
8 WILLIE STARGELL-1B
10 FRANK TAVERAS-SS (1)
10 TIM FOLI-SS (2)
11 ALBERTO LOIS-PR
12 DOCK ELLIS-P (3)
14 ED OTT-C
15 ENRIQUE ROMO-P
16 STEVE NICOSIA-C
17 LEE LACY-OF/2B
18 OMAR MORENO-OF
19 JIM ROOKER-P
20 *(RET#) PIE TRAYNOR*
21 *(RET#) ROBERTO CLEMENTE*
22 BERT BLYLEVEN-P
23 GRANT (BUCK) JACKSON-P
24 MIKE EASLER-OF
25 BRUCE KISON-P
26 JIM BIBBY-P
27 KENT TEKULVE-P
28 BILL ROBINSON-OF/INF
31 ED WHITSON-P (1)
32 JOE LONNETT-CH
33 *(RET#) HONUS WAGNER*
34 JOHN (THE HAMMER) MILNER-OF/1B
35 MANNY SANGUILLEN-C/1B
36 MATT ALEXANDER-OF/SS
39 DAVE PARKER-OF
40 *(RET#) DANNY MURTAUGH*
41 RICK RHODEN (INJ)-P
41 JOE COLEMAN-P (2)
42 AL MONCHAK-CH
43 DON ROBINSON-P
44 RICK RHODEN (INJ)-P
45 JOHN (CANDY MAN) CANDELARIA-P
48 BOB SKINNER-CH
49 DAVE ROBERTS-P (2)
51 DON OSBORN-CH
57 HARVEY (THE KITTEN) HADDIX-CH

1980
3RD E 83-79 8GB
1 *(RET#) BILLY MEYER*
2 BERNIE CARBO-PH (2)
3 PHIL GARNER-2B/SS
4 DALE BERRA-INF
5 BILL (MAD DOG) MADLOCK-3B
6 TONY PENA-C
7 CHUCK TANNER-MGR
8 WILLIE STARGELL (INJ)-1B
10 TIM FOLI-SS
11 TONY PENA-C
11 KURT BEVACQUA-UTIL (2)
12 BOB BEALL-PH
14 ED OTT-C/OF
15 ENRIQUE ROMO-P
16 STEVE NICOSIA-C
17 LEE LACY-OF/3B
18 OMAR MORENO-OF
19 JIM ROOKER (INJ)-P
20 *(RET#) PIE TRAYNOR*
21 *(RET#) ROBERTO CLEMENTE*
22 BERT BLYLEVEN-P
23 GRANT (BUCK) JACKSON-P
24 MIKE EASLER-OF
25 PASCUAL PEREZ-P
26 JIM BIBBY-P
27 KENT TEKULVE-P
28 BILL ROBINSON-1B/OF
29 RICK RHODEN-P
30 MICKEY MAHLER-P
31 ROD SCURRY-P
31 HARVEY (THE KITTEN) HADDIX-CH
32 JOE LONNETT-CH
33 *(RET#) HONUS WAGNER*
34 JOHN (THE HAMMER) MILNER-1B/OF
35 MANNY SANGUILLEN-1B
36 MATT ALEXANDER-OF/2B
39 DAVE PARKER-OF
40 *(RET#) DANNY MURTAUGH*
41 ANDY HASSLER-P (1)
42 AL MONCHAK-CH
43 DON ROBINSON-P
44 EDDIE (BUDDY) SOLOMON-P
45 JOHN (CANDY MAN) CANDELARIA-P
46 MARK LEE-P
48 BOB SKINNER-CH
49 DAVE ROBERTS-P (1)
49 VANCE LAW-INF
51 JESSE JEFFERSON-P (2)
57 HARVEY (THE KITTEN) HADDIX-CH
57 ROD SCURRY-P

1981
1ST 1/2:4TH E 25-23 5.5GB
2ND 1/2:6TH E 21-3 9.5GB
FINAL: 46-58 --GB
1 *(RET#) BILLY MEYER*
2 VANCE LAW-INF
3 PHIL GARNER-2B (1)
3 JOHNNY RAY-2B
4 DALE BERRA-INF
5 BILL (MAD DOG) MADLOCK-3B
6 TONY PENA-C
7 CHUCK TANNER-MGR
8 WILLIE STARGELL-1B
10 TIM FOLI-SS
11 KURT BEVACQUA-1B
12 DOE BOYLAND-PH
14 WILLIE MONTANEZ-1B
15 ENRIQUE ROMO-P
16 STEVE NICOSIA-C
17 LEE LACY-OF/3B
18 OMAR MORENO-OF
19 ROD SCURRY-P
20 *(RET#) PIE TRAYNOR*
21 *(RET#) ROBERTO CLEMENTE*
22 ODELL JONES-P
23 GRANT (BUCK) JACKSON-P (1)
24 MIKE EASLER-OF
25 PASCUAL PEREZ-P
26 JIM BIBBY-P
27 KENT TEKULVE-P
28 BILL ROBINSON (INJ)-UTIL
29 RICK RHODEN-P
30 JASON THOMPSON-1B
31 HARVEY (THE KITTEN) HADDIX-CH
32 JOE LONNETT-CH
33 *(RET#) HONUS WAGNER*
34 JOHN (THE HAMMER) MILNER-1B (1)
34 BOB LONG-P
35 GARY ALEXANDER-1B/OF
36 MATT ALEXANDER-OF
39 LUIS TIANT-P
39 DAVE PARKER-OF
40 *(RET#) DANNY MURTAUGH*
42 AL MONCHAK-CH
43 DON ROBINSON (INJ)-P
44 EDDIE (BUDDY) SOLOMON-P
45 JOHN (CANDY MAN) CANDELARIA (INJ)-P
46 MARK LEE-P
47 ERNIE CAMACHO-P
48 BOB SKINNER-CH
49 VICTOR CRUZ-P
50 PASCUAL PEREZ-P
57 BOB LONG-P

1982
4TH E 84-78 8GB
1 *(RET#) BILLY MEYER*
2 JIM MORRISON-UTIL (2)
3 JOHNNY RAY-2B
4 DALE BERRA-SS/3B
5 BILL (MAD DOG) MADLOCK-3B/1B
6 TONY PENA-C
7 CHUCK TANNER-MGR
8 WILLIE STARGELL-1B
8 *(RET#) WILLIE STARGELL*
10 KEN REITZ-3B
10 RICHIE HEBNER-UTIL (2)
11 JIM SMITH-INF
12 BRIAN HARPER-OF
14 WILLIE MONTANEZ-1B/OF (1)
14 JOHN (THE HAMMER) MILNER-1B (2)
15 ENRIQUE ROMO-P
16 STEVE NICOSIA-C/OF
17 LEE LACY-OF/3B
18 OMAR MORENO-OF
19 ROD SCURRY-P
20 *(RET#) PIE TRAYNOR*
21 *(RET#) ROBERTO CLEMENTE*
22 LEE TUNNELL-P
23 TOM GRIFFIN-P
23 RANDY NIEMANN-P
23 GRANT (BUCK) JACKSON-P (2)
24 MIKE EASLER-OF
25 NELSON NORMAN-2B/SS
(26) JIM BIBBY (INJ)-(P)
27 KENT TEKULVE-P
28 BILL ROBINSON-OF (1)
28 WAYNE NORDHAGEN-OF (2)
28 DICK DAVIS-OF (3)
29 RICK RHODEN-P
30 JASON THOMPSON-1B
31 HARVEY (THE KITTEN) HADDIX-CH

32 JOE LONNETT-CH
33 *(RET#) HONUS WAGNER*
34 ROSS BAUMGARTEN (INJ)-P
35 GRANT (BUCK) JACKSON-P (2)
36 JUNIOR ORTIZ-C
37 RAFAEL BELLIARD-SS
38 MANNY SARMIENTO-P
39 DAVE PARKER (INJ)-OF
40 *(RET#) DANNY MURTAUGH*
41 PAUL MOSKAU (INJ)-P
42 AL MONCHAK-CH
43 DON ROBINSON-P
44 EDDIE (BUDDY) SOLOMON-P (1)
45 JOHN (CANDY MAN) CANDELARIA-P
46 PAUL MOSKAU (INJ)-P
46 REGGIE WALTON-OF
47 CECILIO GUANTE-P
48 BOB SKINNER-CH
49 LARRY MCWILLIAMS-P (2)
50 HEDI (EDDIE) VARGAS-1B
51 DOUG FROBEL-OF
54 RANDY NIEMANN-P

1983

2ND E 84-78 6GB

1 *(RET#) BILLY MEYER*
2 JIM MORRISON-INF
3 JOHNNY RAY-2B
4 DALE BERRA-SS
5 BILL (MAD DOG) MADLOCK-3B
6 TONY PENA-C
7 CHUCK TANNER-MGR
8 *(RET#) WILLIE STARGELL*
10 RICHIE HEBNER-UTIL
11 LEE MAZZILLI-OF/1B
12 BRIAN HARPER-OF/1B
14 MILT MAY-C (2)
15 RON WOTUS-SS/2B
16 STEVE NICOSIA (INJ)-C (1)
16 JOE ORSULAK-OF
17 LEE LACY-OF
18 GENE TENACE-UTIL
19 ROD SCURRY-P
20 *(RET#) PIE TRAYNOR*
21 *(RET#) ROBERTO CLEMENTE*
22 LEE TUNNELL-P
23 RANDY NIEMANN-P
24 MIKE EASLER-OF
25 JOSE DELEON-P
26 JIM BIBBY-P
27 KENT TEKULVE-P
28 BOB OWCHINKO-P
29 RICK RHODEN-P
30 JASON THOMPSON-1B
31 HARVEY (THE KITTEN) HADDIX-CH
32 JOE LONNETT-CH
33 *(RET#) HONUS WAGNER*
34 DAVE TOMLIN-P
36 JUNIOR ORTIZ-C (1)
36 MARVELL WYNNE-OF
37 RAFAEL BELLIARD-SS
38 MANNY SARMIENTO-P
39 DAVE PARKER-OF
40 *(RET#) DANNY MURTAUGH*
41 JOSE DELEON-P
41 JIM WINN-P
42 AL MONCHAK-CH
43 DON ROBINSON (INJ)-P
44 JIM WINN-P
45 JOHN (CANDY MAN) CANDELARIA-P
46 RANDY NIEMANN-P
46 MIGUEL DILONE-PR (3)
47 CECILIO GUANTE-P
48 BOB SKINNER-CH
49 LARRY MCWILLIAMS-P
51 DOUG FROBEL-OF
58 ALFONSO PULIDO-P

1984

6TH E 75-87 21.5GB

1 *(RET#) BILLY MEYER*
2 JIM MORRISON-INF
3 JOHNNY RAY-2B
4 DALE BERRA-SS/3B
5 BILL (MAD DOG) MADLOCK (INJ)-3B/1B
6 TONY PENA-C
7 CHUCK TANNER-MGR
8 *(RET#) WILLIE STARGELL*
10 BENNY DISTEFANO-OF/1B
11 JOE ORSULAK-OF
11 LEE MAZZILLI-OF/1B
12 BRIAN HARPER (INJ)-OF/C
14 MILT MAY-C
15 RON WOTUS-SS/2B
16 JOE ORSULAK-OF
16 LEE MAZZILLI-OF/1B
17 LEE LACY-OF/2B
18 BOB WALK (INJ)-P
19 ROD SCURRY (SUB)-P
20 *(RET#) PIE TRAYNOR*
21 *(RET#) ROBERTO CLEMENTE*
22 LEE TUNNELL-P
23 GRANT (BUCK) JACKSON-CH
24 JOHN TUDOR-P
25 JOSE DELEON-P
26 AMOS OTIS (INJ)-OF
26 ALFONSO PULIDO-P
27 KENT TEKULVE-P
28 DENNY GONZALEZ-UTIL
29 RICK RHODEN-P
30 JASON THOMPSON-1B
31 HARVEY (THE KITTEN) HADDIX-CH
32 JOE LONNETT-CH
33 *(RET#) HONUS WAGNER*
34 MIKE BIELECKI-P
35 CHRIS GREEN-P
36 MARVELL WYNNE-OF
37 RAFAEL BELLIARD (INJ)-SS/2B
39 MITCHELL PAGE-PH
40 *(RET#) DANNY MURTAUGH*
41 JIM WINN-P
42 AL MONCHAK-CH
43 DON ROBINSON (INJ)-P
45 JOHN (CANDY MAN) CANDELARIA-P
47 CECILIO GUANTE-P
48 BOB SKINNER-CH
49 LARRY MCWILLIAMS-P
50 HEDI (EDDIE) VARGAS-1B
51 DOUG FROBEL-OF
53 JEFF ZASKE-P
55 RICH PETERSON-CH
58 ALFONSO PULIDO-P
61 RAY KRAWCZYK-P
62 CHRIS GREEN-P

1985

6TH E 57-104 43.5GB

1 *(RET#) BILLY MEYER*
2 JIM MORRISON-UTIL
3 JOHNNY RAY-2B
4 BOB SKINNER-CH
5 BILL (MAD DOG) MADLOCK 3B/1B (1)
5 SID BREAM-1B (2)
6 TONY PENA-C/1B
7 CHUCK TANNER-MGR
8 WILLIE STARGELL-CH
10 TIM FOLI-SS
10 JOHNNIE LEMASTER (INJ)-SS (3)
11 JOE ORSULAK-OF
12 TRENCH DAVIS-OF
12 BILL ALMON-UTIL
13 STEVE KEMP-OF
15 GEORGE HENDRICK-OF (1)
15 PAT CLEMENTS-P (2)
16 LEE MAZZILLI-1B/OF
17 SCOTT LOUCKS-OF
17 JERRY DYBZINSKI-SS
17 MIKE BROWN-OF (2)
18 BOB WALK-P
19 ROD SCURRY (SUB)-P (1)
20 *(RET#) PIE TRAYNOR*
21 *(RET#) ROBERTO CLEMENTE*
22 LEE TUNNELL-P
23 GRANT (BUCK) JACKSON-CH
24 DENNY GONZALEZ-UTIL
25 JOSE DELEON-P
26 JUNIOR ORTIZ-C
27 KENT TEKULVE-P (1)
27 JOHNNIE LEMASTER (INJ)-SS (3)
27 SAMMY KHALIFA-SS
28 SIXTO LEZCANO-OF
29 RICK RHODEN-P
30 JASON THOMPSON-1B
31 MILT GRAFF-CH
32 STEVE DEMETER-CH
33 *(RET#) HONUS WAGNER*
34 MIKE BIELECKI-P
35 AL HOLLAND-P (2)
35 DAVE TOMLIN-P
36 MARVELL WYNNE-OF
37 RAFAEL BELLIARD-SS
39 MITCHELL PAGE-PH
39 R. J. REYNOLDS-OF (2)
40 *(RET#) DANNY MURTAUGH*
41 JIM WINN-P
43 DON ROBINSON-P
44 JEFF ZASKE-P
45 JOHN (CANDY MAN) CANDELARIA-P (1)
46 RAY KRAWCZYK-P
47 CECILIO GUANTE-P
48 RICK REUSCHEL-P
49 LARRY MCWILLIAMS (INJ)-P
51 DOUG FROBEL-OF (1)
51 BOB KIPPER-P (2)
55 RICK PETERSON-CH
58 ALFONSO PULIDO-P
RON WOTUS (INJ)-(INF)

1986

6TH E 64-98 44GB

0 U L WASHINGTON-SS/2B
1 *(RET#) BILLY MEYER*
2 JIM MORRISON-3B/INF
3 JOHNNY RAY-2B
4 MIKE BROWN-OF
5 SID BREAM-1B/OF
6 TONY PENA-C/1B
7 BARRY BONDS-OF
8 *(RET#) WILLIE STARGELL*
10 MIKE DIAZ-UTIL
11 JOE ORSULAK-OF
12 BILL ALMON-UTIL
13 TRENCH DAVIS-OF
13 RICH RENTERIA-2B
14 JIM LEYLAND-MGR
14 BENNY DISTEFANO-OF/1B
14 MIKE DIAZ-UTIL
15 PAT CLEMENTS-P
16 LEE MAZZILLI-OF/1B (1)
16 HIPOLITO PENA-P
17 BOB WALK-P
18 BILL VIRDON-CH
19 MICK KELLEHER-CH
20 *(RET#) PIE TRAYNOR*
21 *(RET#) ROBERTO CLEMENTE*
23 STEVE KEMP-OF
23 R. J. REYNOLDS-OF
24 BARRY BONDS-OF
25 JOSE DELEON-P (1)
25 BOBBY (BOBBY BO) BONILLA-UTIL (2)
26 JUNIOR ORTIZ-C
27 SAMMY KHALIFA-SS/2B
28 U L WASHINGTON-SS/2B
29 RICK RHODEN-P
30 BOB PATTERSON-P
31 BENNY DISTEFANO-OF/1B
31 JIM LEYLAND-MGR
32 GENE LAMONT-CH
33 *(RET#) HONUS WAGNER*
34 MIKE BIELECKI-P
36 RICH SAUVEUR-P
37 RAFAEL BELLIARD-SS/2B
37 RON SCHUELER-CH
38 RAFAEL BELLIARD-SS/2B
39 R. J. REYNOLDS-OF
40 *(RET#) DANNY MURTAUGH*
41 JIM WINN-P
43 DON ROBINSON (INJ)-P
45 RON SCHUELER-CH
45 RICH DONNELLY-CH
46 RAY KRAWCZYK (INJ)-P
47 CECILIO GUANTE (INJ)-P
48 RICK REUSCHEL-P
49 LARRY MCWILLIAMS-P
50 BARRY JONES-P
51 BOB KIPPER (INJ)-P
52 RICH DONNELLY-CH
54 STAN FANSLER-P
56 RICH RENTERIA-2B
57 JOHN SMILEY-P

1987

4TH E (TIE) 80-82 15GB

1 *(RET#) BILLY MEYER*
2 JIM MORRISON-INF (1)
2 MACKEY SASSER-C (2)
3 JOHNNY RAY-2B (1)
3 U L WASHINGTON-SS/3B
4 MIKE (SPANKY) LAVALLIERE-C
4 *(RET#) RALPH KINER*
5 SID BREAM-1B
6 RAFAEL BELLIARD (INJ)-SS/2B
7 ANDY(SLICK) VAN SLYKE-OF/1B
7 DARNELL COLES-UTIL (2)
8 *(RET#) WILLIE STARGELL*
9 *(RET#) BILL MAZEROSKI*
10 JIM LEYLAND-MGR
12 BILL ALMON-UTIL (1)
12 MIKE (SPANKY) LAVALLIERE-C
13 JOSE (CHICO) LIND-2B
14 MIKE DIAZ-UTIL
15 DOUG DRABEK (INJ)-P
16 HIPOLITO PENA-P
16 BOB KIPPER-P
17 BOB WALK-P
18 ANDY (SLICK) VAN SLYKE-OF/1B
19 HOUSTON JIMENEZ-SS/2B
19 TERRY HARPER-OF (2)
20 *(RET#) PIE TRAYNOR*
21 *(RET#) ROBERTO CLEMENTE*
22 JOHN CANGELOSI-OF
22 AL PEDRIQUE-SS/INF (2)
23 R. J. REYNOLDS-OF
24 BARRY BONDS-OF
25 BOBBY (BOBBY BO) BONILLA-3B/UTIL
26 JUNIOR ORTIZ-C
27 SAMMY KHALIFA-SS
28 DENNY GONZALEZ-SS
28 MIGUEL GARCIA-P (2)
29 ONIX CONCEPCION (INJ)-PH
29 FELIX FERMIN (INJ)-SS
30 BOB PATTERSON-P
31 RAY MILLER-CH
32 GENE LAMONT-CH
33 *(RET#) HONUS WAGNER*
34 MIKE BIELECKI-P
35 JIM GOTT-P (2)
36 BRIAN FISHER-P
37 TOMMY SANDT-CH
38 VICENTE PALACIOS-P
39 MILT MAY-CH
40 *(RET#) DANNY MURTAUGH*
41 MIKE DUNNE-P
42 LOGAN EASLEY-P
43 DON ROBINSON-P (1)
43 JEFF ROBINSON-P (2)
44 TOM PRINCE-C
44 JOHN CANGELOSI-OF
45 RICH DONNELLY-CH
46 TOM PRINCE-C
47 TOMMY GREGG-OF
48 RICK REUSCHEL-P (1)
49 HIPOLITO PENA-P
49 DON ROBINSON-P (1)
50 BARRY JONES-P
51 BOB KIPPER-P
52 DORN TAYLOR-P
52 DON ROBINSON-P (1)
53 MARK ROSS-P
54 BRIAN FISHER-P
55 TIM DRUMMOND-P
56 TIM DRUMMOND-P
56 DAVE JOHNSON-P
57 JOHN SMILEY-P
58 BUTCH DAVIS-OF
58 BRETT GIDEON-P
64 HOUSTON JIMENEZ-SS/2B

1988

2ND E 85-75 15GB

1 *(RET#) BILLY MEYER*
2 ORESTES DESTRADE-1B
3 DENNY GONZALEZ-INF
3 RUBEN RODRIGUEZ-C
4 *(RET#) RALPH KINER*
5 SID BREAM-1B
6 RAFAEL BELLIARD-SS/2B
7 DARNELL COLES-UTIL (1)
7 RUBEN RODRIGUEZ-C
8 *(RET#) WILLIE STARGELL*
9 *(RET#) BILL MAZEROSKI*
10 JIM LEYLAND-MGR
11 GLENN WILSON-OF (2)
12 MIKE (SPANKY) LAVALLIERE-C
13 JOSE (CHICO) LIND-2B
14 MIKE DIAZ (INJ)-UTIL (1)
14 KEN OBERKFELL-2B/3B (2)
15 DOUG DRABEK-P
16 BOB KIPPER-P
17 BOB WALK-P
18 ANDY (SLICK) VAN SLYKE-OF
19 GARY REDUS-OF (2)
20 *(RET#) PIE TRAYNOR*
21 *(RET#) ROBERTO CLEMENTE*
22 AL PEDRIQUE-SS/3B
23 R. J. REYNOLDS-OF
24 BARRY BONDS-OF
25 BOBBY (BOBBY BO) BONILLA-3B
26 JUNIOR ORTIZ (INJ)-C
27 MIGUEL GARCIA-P
29 FELIX FERMIN-SS

PITTSBURGH PIRATES

0 BENNY DISTEFANO-1B/OF

1 RAY MILLER-CH

2 GENE LAMONT-CH

3 *(RET#) HONUS WAGNER*

4 RICK REED-P

5 JIM GOTT-P

6 DAVE RUCKER-P

7 TOMMY SANDT-CH

8 VICENTE PALACIOS-P

9 MILT MAY-CH

0 *(RET#) DANNY MURTAUGH*

1 MIKE DUNNE-P

3 JEFF ROBINSON-P

4 JOHN CANGELOSI-OF/P

5 RICH DONNELLY-CH

6 TOM PRINCE-C

7 TOMMY GREGG-OF (1)

7 RANDY MILLIGAN-1B/OF

9 JEFF ROBINSON-P

0 BARRY JONES-P (1)

0 DAVE LAPOINT-P (2)

4 BRIAN FISHER-P

5 DAVE HOSTETLER-1B/C

5 SCOTT MEDVIN-P

7 JOHN SMILEY-P

9 MORRIS MADDEN-P

0 RANDY KRAMER-P

1989

5TH E 74-88 19GB

0 ORTIZ, JUNIOR C

1 *(RET#) BILLY MEYER*

2 GARY REDUS-1B/OF

3 JAY BELL-SS

4 *(RET#) RALPH KINER*

5 SID BREAM (INJ)-1B

6 RAFAEL BELLIARD-SS/2B

7 JEFF KING-INF

8 *(RET#) WILLIE STARGELL*

9 *(RET#) BILL MAZEROSKI*

10 JIM LEYLAND-MGR

11 GLENN WILSON-OF/1B

12 MIKE (SPANKY) LAVALLIERE (INJ)-C

13 JOSE (CHICO) LIND-2B

14 KEN OBERKFELL-1B/2B (1)

15 DOUG DRABEK-P

16 BOB KIPPER (INJ)-P

17 BOB WALK-P

18 ANDY (SLICK) VAN SLYKE (INJ)-OF

19 ALBERT HALL-OF

20 *(RET#) PIE TRAYNOR*

21 *(RET#) ROBERTO CLEMENTE* (OF)

22 LOGAN EASLEY-P

22 DANN BILARDELLO-C

23 R. J. REYNOLDS-OF

24 BARRY BONDS-OF

25 BOBBY (BOBBY BO) BONILLA-3B/UTIL

26 JUNIOR ORTIZ-C

26 NEAL HEATON-P

27 MIGUEL GARCIA-P

28 RANDY KRAMER-P

29 BILLY HATCHER-OF

30 BENNY DISTEFANO-UTIL

31 RAY MILLER-CH

32 GENE LAMONT-CH

33 *(RET#) HONUS WAGNER*

34 RICK REED-P

35 JIM GOTT (INJ)-P

36 BRUCE KIMM-CH

37 TOMMY SANDT-CH

38 SCOTT LITTLE-OF

38 BOB PATTERSON-P

39 MILT MAY-CH

40 *(RET#) DANNY MURTAUGH*

41 MIKE DUNNE-P (1)

41 SCOTT LITTLE-OF

41 MIKE SMITH-P

42 STEVE CARTER-OF

43 BILL LANDRUM-P

44 JOHN CANGELOSI-OF

45 RICH DONNELLY-CH

46 TOM PRINCE-C

46 DOUG BAIR-P

49 JEFF ROBINSON-P

51 REY QUINONES-SS (2)

52 DORN TAYLOR-P

54 BRIAN FISHER (INJ)-P

55 SCOTT MEDVIN-P

57 JOHN SMILEY-P

58 ROGER SAMUELS-P

59 MORRIS MADDEN-P

60 RANDY KRAMER-P

60 STAN BELINDA-P

1990

1ST E 95-67 0GB

L NLCS-CINN 4-2

1 *(RET#) BILLY MEYER*

2 GARY REDUS-1B/OF

3 JAY BELL-SS

4 *(RET#) RALPH KINER*

5 SID BREAM-1B

6 RAFAEL BELLIARD-INF

7 JEFF KING-3B/1B

8 *(RET#) WILLIE STARGELL*

9 *(RET#) BILL MAZEROSKI*

10 JIM LEYLAND-MGR

11 DON SLAUGHT-C

12 MIKE (SPANKY) LAVALLIERE-C

13 JOSE (CHICO) LIND-2B

14 TOM PRINCE-C

15 DOUG DRABEK-P

16 BOB KIPPER (INJ)-P

17 BOB WALK-P

18 ANDY (SLICK) VAN SLYKE-OF

19 ORLANDO MERCED-OF/C

19 WALLY BACKMAN-3B/2B

20 *(RET#) PIE TRAYNOR*

21 *(RET#) ROBERTO CLEMENTE*

22 DANN BILARDELLO-C

23 R. J. REYNOLDS-OF

24 BARRY BONDS-OF

25 BOBBY (BOBBY BO) BONILLA-OF/INF

26 NEAL HEATON-P

27 MARK RYAL-OF

28 RANDY KRAMER-P (1)

29 MARK ROSS-P

29 RANDY TOMLIN-P

30 MARK ROSS-P

30 JAY TIBBS-P (2)

30 LLOYD MCCLENDON-OF (2)

31 RAY MILLER-CH

32 GENE LAMONT-CH

33 *(RET#) HONUS WAGNER*

34 RICK REED-P

35 WALT TERRELL-P (1)

35 CARMELO MARTINEZ-1B/OF (2)

36 BRUCE KIMM-CH

37 TOMMY SANDT-CH

38 BOB PATTERSON-P

39 MILT MAY-CH

40 *(RET#) DANNY MURTAUGH*

41 ZANE SMITH-P (2)

41 MARK HUISMANN-P

42 STEVE CARTER-OF

43 BILL LANDRUM-P

44 JOHN CANGELOSI-OF

45 RICH DONNELLY-CH

46 TOM PRINCE-C

46 DOUG BAIR-P

47 JERRY REUSS-P

48 TED POWER (INJ)-P

50 STAN BELINDA-P

51 CARLOS GARCIA-SS

52 MOISES ALOU-OF (1)

53 MIKE YORK-P

54 ORLANDO MERCED-OF

56 SCOTT RUSKIN-P (1)

57 JOHN SMILEY (INJ)-P

58 MIKE ROESLER-P

58 VICENTE PALACIOS-P

60 STAN BELINDA-P

1991

1ST E 98-64 0GB

L NLCS-ATLN 4-3

1 *(RET#) BILLY MEYER*

2 GARY REDUS-1B/OF

3 JAY BELL-SS

4 *(RET#) RALPH KINER*

5 JOSE GONZALEZ-OF (2)

6 ORLANDO MERCED-1B/C

7 JEFF KING (INJ)-3B

8 *(RET#) WILLIE STARGELL*

9 *(RET#) BILL MAZEROSKI*

10 JIM LEYLAND-MGR

11 DON SLAUGHT-C

12 MIKE (SPANKY) LAVALLIERE-C

13 JOSE (CHICO) LIND-2B

14 TOM PRINCE-C/1B

15 DOUG DRABEK-P

16 BOB KIPPER-P

17 BOB WALK (INJ)-P

18 ANDY (SLICK) VAN SLYKE-OF

19 CURTIS WILKERSON-INF

20 *(RET#) PIE TRAYNOR*

21 *(RET#) ROBERTO CLEMENTE*

22 LLOYD MCCLENDON-UTIL

22 STEVE BUECHELE-3B (2)

23 BOBBY (BOBBY BO) BONILLA-OF/INF

24 BARRY BONDS-OF

26 NEAL HEATON-P

27 STEVE BUECHELE-3B (2)

27 MARK HUISMANN-P

28 CARMELO MARTINEZ-1B (1)

28 JEFF BANISTER-PH

29 RANDY TOMLIN-P

30 ROSARIO RODRIGUEZ-P

31 RAY MILLER-CH

32 GENE LAMONT-CH

33 *(RET#) HONUS WAGNER*

34 RICK REED-P

36 JOE REDFIELD-3B

36 JEFF RICHARDSON-3B/SS

37 TOMMY SANDT-CH

38 BOB PATTERSON-P

39 MILT MAY-CH

40 *(RET#) DANNY MURTAUGH*

41 ZANE SMITH-P

42 GARY VARSHO-OF

43 BILL LANDRUM-P

45 RICH DONNELLY-CH

46 HECTOR FAJARDO-P (1)

47 SCOTT BULLETT-OF

47 JEFF SCHULZ-PH

48 ROGER MASON-P

50 STAN BELINDA-P

51 CARLOS GARCIA-INF

52 JOHN WEHNER (INJ)-3B

53 MITCH WEBSTER-OF (2)

56 CECIL ESPY-OF

57 JOHN SMILEY-P

58 VICENTE PALACIOS (INJ)-P

64 PAUL MILLER-P

69 JEFF SCHULZ-PH

1992

1ST E 96-66 0GB

L NLCS-ATLN 4-3

1 *(RET#) BILLY MEYER*

2 GARY REDUS-1B/OF

3 JAY BELL-SS

4 *(RET#) RALPH KINER*

5 ALEX COLE-OF (2)

6 ORLANDO MERCED-1B/OF

7 JEFF KING (INJ)-UTIL

8 *(RET#) WILLIE STARGELL*

9 *(RET#) BILL MAZEROSKI*

10 JIM LEYLAND-MGR

11 DON SLAUGHT-C

12 MIKE (SPANKY) LAVALLIERE-C

13 JOSE (CHICO) LIND-2B

14 TOM PRINCE-C/3B

15 DOUG DRABEK-P

17 BOB WALK (INJ)-P

18 ANDY (SLICK) VAN SLYKE-OF

20 *(RET#) PIE TRAYNOR*

21 *(RET#) ROBERTO CLEMENTE*

22 STEVE BUECHELE-3B (1)

22 JOHN WEHNER (INJ)-3B

23 LLOYD MCCLENDON-OF/1B

24 BARRY BONDS-OFC

25 KIRK GIBSON-OF

25 WILL PENNYFEATHER-OF

26 DENNIS LAMP-P

26 JEFF ROBINSON-P (2)

26 STEVE COOKE-P

28 ALBERT (AL) MARTIN-OF

29 RANDY TOMLIN-P

31 RAY MILLER-CH

32 DENNY NEAGLE-P

33 *(RET#) HONUS WAGNER*

34 DANNY JACKSON-P (2)

35 DAVE CLARK-OF

36 ALEX COLE-OF (2)

36 KEVIN YOUNG-3B/1B

37 TOMMY SANDT-CH

38 BOB PATTERSON-P

39 MILT MAY-CH

40 *(RET#) DANNY MURTAUGH*

41 ZANE SMITH-P

42 GARY VARSHO-OF

43 PAUL WAGNER-P

44 TERRY COLLINS-CH

45 RICH DONNELLY-CH

48 ROGER MASON-P

49 JERRY DON GLEATON-P

49 TIM WAKEFIELD-P

50 STAN BELINDA-P

51 CARLOS GARCIA-2B/SS

52 JOHN WEHNER (INJ)-3B

53 MIGUEL BATISTA-P

56 CECIL ESPY-OF

57 DANNY COX-P (2)

58 VICENTE PALACIOS-P

61 VICTOR COLE-P

64 PAUL MILLER-P

66 BLAS MINOR-P

1993

5TH E 75-87 22GB

1 *(RET#) BILLY MEYER*

3 JAY BELL-SS

4 *(RET#) RALPH KINER*

6 ORLANDO MERCED-OF/1B

7 JEFF KING-3B/INF

8 *(RET#) WILLIE STARGELL*

9 *(RET#) BILL MAZEROSKI*

10 JIM LEYLAND-MGR

11 DON SLAUGHT-C

12 MIKE (SPANKY) LAVALLIER (REL)-C (1)

13 CARLOS GARCIA-2B/SS

14 TOM PRINCE-C

15 DENNY NEAGLE-P

16 TOM FOLEY-INF

17 BOB WALK-P

18 ANDY (SLICK) VAN SLYKE (INJ)-OF

19 BILL VIRDON-CH

20 *(RET#) PIE TRAYNOR*

21 *(RET#) ROBERTO CLEMENTE*

22 JOHN WEHNER-UTIL

23 LLOYD MCCLENDON-OF/1B

24 DENNIS MOELLER-P

25 WILL PENNYFEATHER-OF

26 STEVE COOKE-P

27 LONNIE (SKATES) SMITH-OF (1)

28 ALBERT (AL) MARTIN-OF

29 RANDY TOMLIN (INJ)-P

30 MIDRE CUMMINGS-OF

31 RAY MILLER-CH

32 DENNY NEAGLE-P

32 DANNY MICELI-P

33 *(RET#) HONUS WAGNER*

35 DAVE CLARK-OF

36 KEVIN YOUNG-1B/3B

37 TOMMY SANDT-CH

39 MILT MAY-CH

40 *(RET#) DANNY MURTAUGH*

41 ZANE SMITH (INJ)-P

42 BRIAN SHOUSE-P

43 PAUL WAGNER-P

44 TERRY COLLINS-CH

44 BEN SHELTON-OF/1B

45 JOHN (CANDY MAN) CANDELARIA (REL)-P

46 RICH DONNELLY-CH

47 SCOTT BULLETT-OF

48 DAVE OTTO-P

48 RICH AUDE-1B/OF

49 TIM WAKEFIELD-P

50 STAN BELINDA-P (1)

50 MARK DEWEY-P

51 TONY WOMACK-SS

53 GLENN WILSON-OF

53 PAUL MILLER-P

55 BLAS MINOR-P

56 JOHN HOPE-P

57 JERRY GOFF-C

58 RICH ROBERTSON-P

59 ANDY TOMBERLIN-OF

61 FREDDIE TOLIVER-P

64 JOEL JOHNSTON-P

65 MARK PETKOVSEK-P

66 BLAS MINOR-P

66 BEN SHELTON-OF

66 JEFF BALLARD-P

67 TONY MENENDEZ-P

ALEJANDRO PENA (INJ)-(P)

1994

3RD C (TIE) 53-61 13GB

STRIKE NO POST-SEASON

1 *(RET#) BILLY MEYER*

3 JAY BELL-SS

4 *(RET#) RALPH KINER*

5 JERRY GOFF-C

5 LANCE PARRISH-C

6 ORLANDO MERCED-OF/1B

7 JEFF KING (INJ)-3B/INF

8 *(RET#) WILLIE STARGELL*

9 *(RET#) BILL MAZEROSKI*

10 JIM LEYLAND-MGR

11 DON SLAUGHT-C

12 JOHN WEHNER (INJ)-OF

13 CARLOS GARCIA-2B

14 BRIAN R. HUNTER-1B (1)

15 DENNY NEAGLE-P

16 TOM FOLEY (INJ)-INF

18 ANDY (SLICK) VAN SLYKE (INJ)-OF

19 BILL VIRDON-CH

20 *(RET#) PIE TRAYNOR*

21 *(RET#) ROBERTO CLEMENTE*

22 GARY VARSHO-1B/OF

23 LLOYD MCCLENDON-OF/1B

25 WILL PENNYFEATHER-OF
25 STEVE PEGUES-OF (2)
26 STEVE COOKE-P
28 ALBERT (AL) MARTIN (INJ)-OF
29 RANDY TOMLIN (INJ)-P
30 MIDRE CUMMINGS-OF
31 RAY MILLER-CH
32 DANNY MICELI-P
33 *(RET#) HONUS WAGNER*
34 ALEJANDRO PENA (INJ) (WAIV)-P
35 DAVE CLARK-OF
36 KEVIN YOUNG-1B
37 TOMMY SANDT-CH
39 MILT MAY-CH
40 *(RET#) DANNY MURTAUGH*
41 ZANE SMITH (INJ)-P
43 PAUL WAGNER-P
44 RICK WHITE-P
45 RICH DONNELLY-CH
46 JUNIOR NOBOA-SS (2)
47 JON LIEBER-P
50 MARK DEWEY (INJ)-P
54 SPIN WILLIAMS-CH
55 BLAS MINOR-P
56 JOHN HOPE-P
57 JERRY GOFF-C
59 RAVELO (RAVIOLI) MANZANILLO-P
62 MIKE DYER-P
63 JEFF TABAKA-P (1)
63 RICH W. ROBERTSON-P
64 JOEL JOHNSTON-P
66 JEFF BALLARD-P

1995

5TH C 58-86 27GB
144 GAME SEASON

1 *(RET#) BILLY MEYER*
2 ANGELO ENCARNACION-C
3 JAY BELL-SS
4 *(RET#) RALPH KINER*
5 JACOB BRUMFIELD-OF
6 ORLANDO MERCED-OF
7 JEFF KING (INJ)-3B
8 *(RET#) WILLIE STARGELL*
9 *(RET#) BILL MAZEROSKI*
10 JIM LEYLAND-MGR
11 DON SLAUGHT-C
12 JOHN WEHNER-OF
13 CARLOS GARCIA-2B
14 MARK PARENT-C
15 DENNY NEAGLE-P
16 NELSON LIRIANO-2B
17 MACKEY SASSER-C
18 BILL VIRDON-CH
19 DAN PLESAC-P
20 *(RET#) PIE TRAYNOR*
21 *(RET#) ROBERTO CLEMENT*
22 FREDDY GARCIA-OF/3B
25 STEVE PEGUES-OF
28 ALBERT (AL) MARTIN-OF
29 KEVIN YOUNG-3B
30 MIDRE CUMMINGS-OF
31 RAY MILLER-CH
32 DANNY MICELI-P
33 *(RET#) HONUS WAGNER*
34 ESTEBAN LOAIZA-P
35 DAVE CLARK-OF
36 MARK JOHNSON-1B
37 TOMMY SANDT-CH
38 JIM GOTT-P
39 MILT MAY-CH
40 *(RET#) DANNY MURTAUGH*
41 JASON CHRISTIANSEN-P
42 LEE HANCOCK-P
43 PAUL WAGNER-P
44 RICK WHITE-P
45 RICH DONNELLY-CH
46 GARY WILSON-P
47 JON LIEBER-P
48 RICH AUDE-1B
49 ROSS POWELL-P (2)
50 DENNIS KONUSZEWSKI-P
53 JEFF MCCURRY-P
54 SPIN WILLIAMS-CH
55 STEVE PARRIS-P
55 RAMON MOREL-P
56 JIM GOTT-P
56 JOHN HOPE-P
57 JOHN ERICKS-P
59 RAVELO (RAVIOLI) MANZANILLO-P
60 STEVE PARRIS-P
60 MIKE MADDUX-P
62 MIKE DYER-P

1996

5TH C 73-89 15GB

1 *(RET#) BILLY MEYER*
2 ANGELO ENCARNACION-C
3 JAY BELL-SS
4 *(RET#) RALPH KINER*
5 JACOB BRUMFIELD-OF (1)
6 ORLANDO MERCED (INJ)-OF
7 JEFF KING-3B
8 *(RET#) WILLIE STARGELL*
9 *(RET#) BILL MAZEROSKI*
10 JIM LEYLAND-MGR
11 MIKE KINGERY (INJ)-OF
12 JOHN WEHNER-OF/3B
13 CARLOS GARCIA (INJ)-2B
15 DENNY NEAGLE-P (1)
16 NELSON LIRIANO-2B
17 CHARLIE HAYES-3B (1)
17 DALE SVEUM-INF
18 JASON KENDALL-C
19 DAN PLESAC-P
20 *(RET#) PIE TRAYNOR*
21 *(RET#) ROBERTO CLEMENT*
23 GENE LAMONT-CH
24 ZANE SMITH (INJ)-P
25 TREY BEAMON-OF
26 STEVE COOKE-P
27 JOE BOEVER-P
27 STEVE PARRIS (INJ)-P
28 ALBERT (AL) MARTIN-OF
29 JOHN HOPE-P
30 MIDRE CUMMINGS-OF
31 RAY MILLER-CH
32 DANNY MICELI-P
33 *(RET#) HONUS WAGNER*
34 ESTEBAN LOAIZA-P
35 DAVE CLARK-OF (1)
36 MARK JOHNSON-1B
37 TOMMY SANDT-CH
38 CHRIS PETERS-P
39 MILT MAY-CH
40 *(RET#) DANNY MURTAUGH*
41 JASON CHRISTIANSEN-P
42 LEE HANCOCK-P
42 JASON SCHMIDT-P (2)
43 PAUL WAGNER (INJ)-P
44 DANNY DARWIN-P (1)
44 JOE BOEVER-P (2)
45 RICH DONNELLY-CH
46 JERMAINE ALLENSWORTH-OF
47 JON LIEBER-P
48 RICH AUDE-1B
49 MATT RUEBEL-P
51 TONY WOMACK-2B
53 DAVE WAINHOUSE-P
54 SPIN WILLIAMS-CH
55 RAMON MOREL-P
57 JOHN ERICKS-P
61 DARRELL MAY (WAIV)-P (1)
62 MARC WILKINS-P
63 KEITH OSIK-C
67 FRANCISCO CORDOVA-P
71 ELMER DESSENS-P
75 RICH LOISELLE-P

1997

2ND C 79-83 5GB

1 *(RET#) BILLY MEYER*
2 KEVIN POLCOVICH-SS
3 SHAWON DUNSTON-SS (2)
4 *(RET#) RALPH KINER*
5 TONY WOMACK-2B
6 LOU COLLIER-INF
8 *(RET#) WILLIE STARGELL*
9 *(RET#) BILL MAZEROSKI*
10 KEVIN ELSTER (INJ)-SS
11 JOSE GUILLEN-OF
12 TURNER WARD-OF
13 ADRIAN BROWN-OF
15 KEITH OSIK-C/2B
16 JOE RANDA (INJ)-3B
17 DALE SVEUM-3B
18 JASON KENDALL-C
19 EMIL BROWN-OF
20 *(RET#) PIE TRAYNOR*
21 *(RET#) ROBERTO CLEMENT*
22 FREDDY GARCIA-3B
23 LLOYD MCCLENDON-CH
25 MARK SMITH-OF
26 STEVE COOKE-P
28 ALBERT (AL) MARTIN (INJ)-OF
29 KEVIN YOUNG (INJ)-1B/OF
30 MIDRE CUMMINGS-OF (1)
30 EDDIE WILLIAMS-1B (2)
32 GENE LAMONT-MGR
33 *(RET#) HONUS WAGNER*
34 ESTEBAN LOAIZA-P
35 MARC WILKINS-P
36 MARK JOHNSON-1B
36 JASON JOHNSON-P
37 JOE JONES-CH
38 CHRIS PETERS-P
39 JEFF GRANGER-P
39 JEFF WALLACE-P
40 *(RET#) DANNY MURTAUGH*
41 JASON CHRISTIANSEN-P
42 JASON SCHMIDT-P
43 PAUL WAGNER (INJ)-P (1)
44 RICK RENICK-CH
45 JACK JONES-CH
45 JACK LIND-CH
46 JERMAINE ALLENSWORTH (INJ)-OF
47 JON LIEBER-P
48 ABRAHAM NUNEZ-SS
49 MATT RUEBEL (INJ)-P
50 PETE VUCKOVICH-CH
51 RICH LOISELLE-P
53 DAVE WAINHOUSE-P
54 SPIN WILLIAMS-CH
55 RAMON MOREL (WAIV)-P (1)
56 JOSE SILVA-P
57 JOHN ERICKS (INJ)-P
63 CLINT SODOWSKI (INJ)-P
67 FRANCISCO CORDOVA-P
71 ELMER DESSENS-P
73 RICARDO RINCON-P

1998

6TH C 69-93 33GB

1 *(RET#) BILLY MEYER*
2 KEVIN POLCOVICH-SS
4 *(RET#) RALPH KINER*
5 TONY WOMACK-2B
6 LOU COLLIER (INJ)-SS
8 *(RET#) WILLIE STARGELL*
9 *(RET#) BILL MAZEROSKI*
10 ABRAHAM NUNEZ-INF
11 JOSE GUILLEN-OF
12 TURNER WARD-OF
13 ADRIAN BROWN-OF
14 FREDDY GARCIA-INF
15 KEITH OSIK-C
16 ARAMIS RAMIREZ-3B
17 DOUG STRANGE (INJ)-3B
18 JASON KENDALL-C
19 EMIL BROWN-OF
20 *(RET#) PIE TRAYNOR*
21 *(RET#) ROBERTO CLEMENT*
22 JASON SCHMIDT-P
23 LLOYD MCCLENDON-CH
25 MARK SMITH (INJ)-OF
27 TIM LAKER-C/1B (2)
28 ALBERT (AL) MARTIN-OF
29 KEVIN YOUNG-1B/OF
30 MANNY MARTINEZ-OF
31 CHANCE SANFORD-INF
32 GENE LAMONT-MGR
33 *(RET#) HONUS WAGNER*
34 ESTEBAN LOAIZA-P (1)
35 MARC WILKINS (INJ)-P
36 JAVIER MARTINEZ-P
37 JOE JONES-CH
38 CHRIS PETERS-P
(39) JEFF WALLACE (INJ)-(P)
40 *(RET#) DANNY MURTAUGH*
41 JASON CHRISTIANSEN-P
42 *(RET#) JACKIE ROBINSON*
44 RICK RENICK-CH
45 JACK LIND-CH
46 JERMAINE ALLENSWORTH (INJ)-OF (1)
47 JON LIEBER-P
48 SEAN LAWRENCE-P
49 JEFF TABAKA (INJ)-P
50 PETE VUCKOVICH-CH
51 RICH LOISELLE (INJ)-P (1)
53 JEFF MCCURRY-P
54 SPIN WILLIAMS-CH
56 JOSE SILVA (INJ)-P
57 TODD VAN POPPEL-P (3)
(60) KANE DAVIS (INJ)-(P)
62 STEVE BIESER-OF
64 MIKE WILLIAMS-P
67 FRANCISCO CORDOVA-P
70 CHANCE SANFORD-INF
71 ELMER DESSENS (INJ)-P
73 RICARDO RINCON (INJ)-P
TONY RUNION-(P)

1999

3RD C 78-83 18.5GB

1 *(RET#) BILLY MEYER*
2 PAT MEARES (INJ)-SS
3 CHAD HERMANSEN-OF
4 *(RET#) RALPH KINER*
5 ED SPRAGUE, JR.-3B
6 MIKE BENJAMIN (INJ)-SS
7 JOHN WEHNER-UTIL
8 *(RET#) WILLIE STARGELL*
9 *(RET#) BILL MAZEROSKI*
10 ABRAHAM NUNEZ-INF
11 JOSE GUILLEN-OF (1)
11 DALE SVEUM-3B/INF
12 TURNER WARD-OF (1)
13 ADRIAN BROWN-OF
14 FREDDY GARCIA-INF (1)
15 KEITH OSIK-C
16 ARAMIS RAMIREZ-3B
17 DOUG STRANGE (INJ)-3B
17 JOE OLIVER-C
18 JASON KENDALL (INJ)-C
19 EMIL BROWN-OF
20 *(RET#) PIE TRAYNOR*
21 *(RET#) ROBERTO CLEMENT*
22 JASON SCHMIDT-P
23 LLOYD MCCLENDON-CH
24 BRIAN GILES-OF
25 IVAN CRUZ (INJ)-1B
26 JASON PHILLIPS-P
27 JOE JONES-CH
28 ALBERT (AL) MARTIN-OF
29 KEVIN YOUNG-1B/OF
30 WARREN MORRIS-2B
31 YAMID HAAD-C
32 GENE LAMONT-MGR
33 *(RET#) HONUS WAGNER*
34 KRIS BENSON-P
35 MARC WILKINS (INJ)-P
(36) JAVIER MARTINEZ (INJ)-(P)
37 BRANT BROWN-OF
38 CHRIS PETERS (INJ)-P
39 JEFF WALLACE-P
40 *(RET#) DANNY MURTAUGH*
41 JASON CHRISTIANSEN-P
42 *(RET#) JACKIE ROBINSON*
43 MIKE WILLIAMS (INJ)-P
44 RICK RENICK-CH
45 JACK LIND-CH
46 PETE SCHOUREK (INJ)-P
47 SCOTT SAUERBECK-P
48 TODD RITCHIE-P
(49) JEFF TABAKA (INJ)-(P)
50 PETE VUCKOVICH-CH
51 RICH LOISELLE (INJ)-P
54 SPIN WILLIAMS-CH
55 JIMMY ANDERSON-P
56 JOSE SILVA (INJ)-P
57 GREG HANSELL-P
59 BRAD CLONTZ-P
60 JASON BOYD-P
63 TIM LAKER-C
64 MIKE GARCIA-P
66 CHRIS TREMIE-C
67 FRANCISCO CORDOVA-P
68 JIM DOUGHERTY-P

2000

5TH C 69-93 26GB

1 *(RET#) BILLY MEYER*
2 PAT MEARES-SS
3 CHAD HERMANSEN-OF
4 *(RET#) RALPH KINER*
5 TIKE REDMAN-OF
6 MIKE BENJAMIN-SS
8 *(RET#) WILLIE STARGELL*
9 *(RET#) BILL MAZEROSKI*
10 ABRAHAM NUNEZ-INF
12 WIL CORDERO-OF (1)
12 JOHN WEHNER-UTIL
13 ADRIAN BROWN (INJ)-OF
14 EMIL BROWN-OF
15 KEITH OSIK-C
16 ARAMIS RAMIREZ-3B
18 JASON KENDALL (INJ)-C
19 LUIS SOJO-INF (1)
19 ALEX HERNANDEZ-INF
20 *(RET#) PIE TRAYNOR*
21 *(RET#) ROBERTO CLEMENT*
22 JASON SCHMIDT (INJ)-P
23 LLOYD MCCLENDON-CH
24 BRIAN GILES-OF
25 IVAN CRUZ-1B
25 ENRIQUE WILSON (INJ)-INF(2)
26 TRENT JEWETT-CH
26 BRIAN SMITH-P
27 JOE JONES-CH
27 ADAM HYZDU-OF
28 JOHN VANDER WAL-OF
29 KEVIN YOUNG-1B/OF
30 WARREN MORRIS-2B
31 CHRIS PETERS-P
32 GENE LAMONT-MGR
33 *(RET#) HONUS WAGNER*
34 KRIS BENSON-P

ITTSBURGH PIRATES

5 MARC WILKINS-P
7 BRUCE AVEN-OF (1)
9 JEFF WALLACE-P
0 *(RET#) DANNY MURTAUGH*
1 JASON CHRISTIANSEN-P (1)
2 *(RET#) JACKIE ROBINSON*
3 MIKE WILLIAMS-P
4 RICK RENICK-CH
5 JACK LIND-CH
5 DAN SERAFINI-P (2)
6 TOMMY SANDT-CH
7 SCOTT SAUERBECK-P
8 TODD RITCHIE (INJ)-P
9 JOSIAS MANZANILLO-P
0 PETE VUCKOVICH-CH
1 RICH LOISELLE (INJ)-P
2 BRAD CLONTZ-P
4 SPIN WILLIAMS-CH
5 JIMMY ANDERSON-P
6 JOSE SILVA-P
7 STEVE SPARKS-P
8 BRIAN O'CONNOR-P
9 TRAVIS BAPTIST-P
0 JOSE PARRA-P
1 ALEX RAMIREZ-OF (2)
2 CORY BAILEY-P
4 MIKE GARCIA-P
4 MATT SKRMETTA-P (2)
7 FRANCISCO CORDOVA-P
9 BRONSON ARROYO-P

2001

6TH C 62-100 31GB

1 *(RET#) BILLY MEYER*
2 PAT MEARES-SS
3 CHAD HERMANSEN-OF
4 *(RET#) RALPH KINER*
5 TIKE REDMAN-OF
6 MIKE BENJAMIN (INJ)-SS
7 JOHN WEHNER-3B
8 *(RET#) WILLIE STARGELL*
9 *(RET#) BILL MAZEROSKI*
0 ABRAHAM NUNEZ-INF
1 HUMBERTO COTA-C
2 JACK WILSON-SS
3 ADRIAN BROWN (INJ)-OF
4 DEREK BELL (INJ)-OF
5 KEITH OSIK (INJ)-C
6 ARAMIS RAMIREZ-3B
7 EMIL BROWN-OF (1)
7 ARMANDO RIOS (INJ)-OF (2)
8 JASON KENDALL (SUS)-C
9 BILL VIRDON-CH
0 *(RET#) PIE TRAYNOR*
1 *(RET#) ROBERTO CLEMENT*
2 JASON SCHMIDT (INJ)-P (1)
2 GARY MATTHEWS, JR.-OF (2)
3 LLOYD MCCLENDON-MGR
4 BRIAN GILES-OF
5 ENRIQUE WILSON (INJ)-INF (1)
5 LUIS FIGUEROA-2B
5 MENDY LOPEZ-2B (2)
7 ALEX HERNANDEZ (INJ)-INF
8 JOHN VANDER WAL-OF (1)
8 RYAN VOGELSONG-P (2)
9 KEVIN YOUNG (SUS)-1B/OF
0 WARREN MORRIS (INJ)-2B
1 OMAR OLIVARES-P
2 FRANCISCO CORDOVA (INJ)-P
3 *(RET#) HONUS WAGNER*
4 KRIS BENSON (INJ)-P
5 DAVE CLARK-CH
6 BILLY TAYLOR-P
6 CRAIG WILSON-C/1B
7 TOMMY SANDT-CH
8 RAMON MARTINEZ (RET)-P
38 DON WENGERT-P
38 ADAM HYZDU-OF
39 MIKE FETTERS-P (2)
40 *(RET#) DANNY MURTAUGH*
42 *(RET#) JACKIE ROBINSON*
43 MIKE WILLIAMS-P (1)
44 TRENT JEWITT-CH
45 TERRY MULHOLLAND (I NJ) -P (1)
45 TONY MCKNIGHT-P (2)
46 DAMASO MARTE-P
47 SCOTT SAUERBECK-P
48 TODD RITCHIE-P
49 JOSIAS MANZANILLO-P
50 MARC WILKINS-P
50 ANDY BARKETT-OF
50 MARC WILKINS-P
51 RICH LOISELLE (INJ)-P
52 BRUCE TANNER-CH
53 JOE BEIMEL-P
54 SPIN WILLIAMS-CH
55 JIMMY ANDERSON-P
56 JOSE SILVA-P
57 MIKE LINCOLN-P
58 DAVE WILLIAMS-P
59 ROB MACKOWIAK (INJ)-2B
69 BRONSON ARROYO-P

2002

4TH C 72-89 24.5GB

1 *(RET#) BILLY MEYER*
(2) PAT MEARES (INJ)-(2B)
3 POKEY REESE-2B
4 *(RET#) RALPH KINER*
6 MIKE BENJAMIN-INF
7 ARMANDO RIOS (INJ)-OF
8 *(RET#) WILLIE STARGELL*
9 *(RET#) BILL MAZEROSKI*
10 ABRAHAM NUNEZ-2B/SS
11 HUMBERTO COTA-C
12 JACK WILSON-SS
13 ADRIAN BROWN-OF
15 KEITH OSIK-C/UTIL
16 ARAMIS RAMIREZ-3B
17 MENDY LOPEZ-PH
18 JASON KENDALL-C
19 BILL VIRDON-CH
20 *(RET#) PIE TRAYNOR*
21 *(RET#) ROBERTO CLEMENTE*
(22) RYAN VOGELSONG (INJ)-(P)
23 LLOYD MCCLENDON-MGR
24 BRIAN GILES-OF
26 J. J. DAVIS-OF
27 JOSH FOGG-P
28 RON VILLONE-P
29 KEVIN YOUNG-1B
31 CHAD HERMANSEN-OF (1)
31 SALOMON TORRES-P
32 KIP WELLS-P
33 *(RET#) HONUS WAGNER*
34 KRIS BENSON (INJ)-P
35 DAVE CLARK-CH
36 CRAIG WILSON-OF/1B/C
37 TOMMY SANDT-CH
38 ADAM HYZDU-OF/1B
39 MIKE FETTERS-P (1)
39 AL REYES-P
40 *(RET#) DANNY MURTAUGH*
42 *(RET #)JACKIE ROBINSON*
43 MIKE WILLIAMS-P
44 TRENT JEWITT-CH
45 DUANER SANCHEZ-P (2)
46 BRIAN MEADOWS-P
47 SCOTT SAUERBECK-P
48 SEAN LOWE-P (1)
49 JOSIAS MANZANILLO (INJ)-P
52 BRUCE TANNER-CH
53 JOE BEIMEL-P
54 SPIN WILLIAMS-CH
55 JIMMY ANDERSON-P
56 TONY ALVAREZ-OF
57 MIKE LINCOLN-P
58 DAVE WILLIAMS (INJ)-P
59 ROB MACKOWIAK-OF/INF
69 BRONSON ARROYO-P
71 BRIAN BOEHRINGER-P

2003

4TH C 75-87 13GB

1 *(RET#) BILLY MEYER*
2 JACK WILSON-SS
3 POKEY REESE (INJ)-2B
4 *(RET#) RALPH KINER*
5 TIKE REDMAN-OF
6 ABRAHAM O. NUNEZ-2B/SS
7 KENNY LOFTON-OF (1)
8 *(RET#) WILLIE STARGELL*
9 *(RET#) BILL MAZEROSKI*
10 ALVARO ESPINOZA-CH
11 HUMBERTO COTA-C
12 MATT STAIRS (INJ)-OF/1B
13 JOHN RUSSELL-CH
16 ARAMIS RAMIREZ-3B (1)
16 JOSE HERNANDEZ-SS (3)
17 BOBBY HILL (INJ)-2B (2)
18 JASON KENDALL (SUS:3G)-C
19 REGGIE SANDERS-OF
20 *(RET#) PIE TRAYNOR*
21 *(RET#) ROBERTO CLEMENTE*
22 RYAN VOGELSONG-P
23 LLOYD MCCLENDON-MGR
24 BRIAN GILES-OF (1)
25 PETE MACKANIN-CH
26 J. J. DAVIS-OF
27 JOSH FOGG (INJ)-P
28 GERALD PERRY-CH
29 KEVIN YOUNG (REL)-1B
30 J. R. HOUSE-PH
31 SALOMON TORRES (INJ)-P
32 KIP WELLS-P
33 *(RET#) HONUS WAGNER56*
34 KRIS BENSON (INJ)-P
35 RANDALL SIMON (INJ) (SUS:3G)-1B (1)
36 CRAIG WILSON-OF/1B/C
37 JEFF SUPPAN-P (1)
37 NELSON FIGUEROA-P
38 ADAM HYZDU-OF
38 JASON BAY (INJ)-OF (2)
39 PAT MAHOMES-P
39 JOHN GRABOW-P
40 *(RET#) DANNY MURTAUGH (1977)*
41 JEFF D'AMICO-P
42 *(RET #)JACKIE ROBINSON*
43 MIKE WILLIAMS-P (1)
44 DENNYS REYES-P (1)
44 MARK COREY-P
45 DUANER SANCHEZ-P
46 BRIAN MEADOWS-P
47 SCOTT SAUERBECK-P (1)
48 RUSTY KUNTZ-CH
48 JIM MANN-P
48 OLIVER PEREZ-P (2)
49 JEFF REBOULET-2B/3B
50 JULIAN TAVAREZ (SUS:3G)-P
51 MIKE GONZALEZ-P
52 BRUCE TANNER-CH
53 JOE BEIMEL-P
54 SPIN WILLIAMS-CH
55 CARLOS RIVERA-1B
57 MIKE LINCOLN (INJ)-P
(58) DAVE WILLIAMS (INJ)-(P)
59 ROB MACKOWIAK-OF/INF
71 BRIAN BOEHRINGER-P
PAT MEARES (INJ)(INF)

2004

5TH C 72-89 32.5GB

1 *(RET#) BILLY MEYER*
2 JACK WILSON-SS
3 CHRIS STYNES-3B
4 *(RET#) RALPH KINER*
5 TIKE REDMAN-OF
7 ABRAHAM O. NUNEZ-INF
8 *(RET#) WILLIE STARGELL*
9 *(RET#) BILL MAZEROSKI*
10 ALVARO ESPINOZA-CH
11 HUMBERTO COTA-C
12 FREDDY SANCHEZ (INJ)-3B
13 JOHN RUSSELL-CH
14 JOSE CASTILLO-2B
15 RUSTY KUNTZ-CH
16 SALOMON TORRES-P
17 BOBBY HILL-2B
18 JASON KENDALL-C
19 TY WIGGINGTON-3B (2)
20 *(RET#) PIE TRAYNOR*
21 *(RET#) ROBERTO CLEMENTE*
22 RYAN VOGELSONG-P
23 LLOYD MCCLENDON-MGR
24 RUBEN MATEO-OF (1)
25 PETE MACKANIN-CH
26 J. J. DAVIS (INJ)-OF
27 JOSH FOGG-P
28 GERALD PERRY-CH
30 J. R. HOUSE-C
31 DARYLE WARD-OF/1B
32 KIP WELLS-P
33 *(RET#) HONUS WAGNER*
34 KRIS BENSON (INJ)-P (1)
35 RANDALL SIMON-1B (1)
36 CRAIG WILSON-OF/1B
37 MIKE JOHNSTON (INJ)-P
38 JASON BAY (INJ)-OF
39 JOHN GRABOW-P
40 *(RET#) DANNY MURTAUGH*
41 BRIAN BOEHRINGER (INJ)-P
42 *(RET #)JACKIE ROBINSON*
43 RAUL MONDESI-OF (1)
43 WILLIS ROBERTS-P
44 MARK COREY-P
46 BRIAN MEADOWS-P
47 JOHN VAN BENSCHOTEN-P
48 OLIVER PEREZ-P
49 JOSE MESA-P
50 JASON BOYD-P
50 JOSE BATISTA-3B (4)
51 MIKE GONZALEZ-P
52 BRUCE TANNER-CH
53 IAN SNELL-P
54 SPIN WILLIAMS-CH
55 CARLOS RIVERA-1B
56 TONY ALVAREZ-3B
57 FRANK BROOKS-P
58 DAVE WILLIAMS (INJ)-P
59 ROB MACKOWIAK-OF/3B
61 SEAN BURNETT (INJ)-P

2005

6TH C 67-95 33GB

00 RICK WHITE-P
1 *(RET#) BILLY MEYER*
2 JACK WILSON-SS
3 ROB MACKOWIAK-UTIL
4 *(RET#) RALPH KINER*
5 TIKE REDMAN-OF
6 ALFREDO AMEZAGA (WAIV) -INF (2)
7 JOSE BAUTISTA-3B
8 *(RET#) WILLIE STARGELL*
9 *(RET#) BILL MAZEROSKI*
10 ALVARO ESPINOZA-CH
11 HUMBERTO COTA (INJ)-C
12 FREDDY SANCHEZ-3B/2B
13 JOHN RUSSELL-CH
14 JOSE CASTILLO (INJ)-2B
15 RUSTY KUNTZ-CH
16 SALOMON TORRES-P
17 BOBBY HILL-3B
19 TY WIGGINGTON-3B
20 *(RET#) PIE TRAYNOR*
21 *(RET#) ROBERTO CLEMENTE*
22 RYAN VOGELSONG-P
23 LLOYD MCCLENDON (SUS:1G)-MGR1
25 PETE MACKANIN-CH/MGR2
26 CHRIS DUFFY (INJ)-OF
27 JOSH FOGG-P
28 GERALD PERRY (SUS:8G)-CH
29 DAVID ROSS-C (1)
29 JODY GERUT-OF (3)
30 PAUL MAHOLM-P
31 DARYLE WARD-1B
32 KIP WELLS-P
33 *(RET#) HONUS WAGNER*
34 BENITO SANTIAGO (INJ) (REL)-C
34 MICHAEL RESTOVICH-OF (2)
35 BRAD ELDRED-1B
36 CRAIG WILSON (INJ)-1B/OF
37 MIKE JOHNSTON-P
38 JASON BAY-OF
39 JOHN GRABOW-P
40 *(RET#) DANNY MURTAUGH*
41 RYAN DOUMIT-C
42 *(RET #)JACKIE ROBINSON*
43 RAY SADLER-OF
46 BRIAN MEADOWS-P
(47) JOHN VAN BENSCHOTEN (INJ)-(P)
48 OLIVER PEREZ (INJ)-P
49 JOSE MESA-P
50 MATT LAWTON-OF (1)
51 MIKE GONZALEZ (INJ)-P
52 BRUCE TANNER-CH
53 IAN SNELL-P
54 SPIN WILLIAMS-CH
55 MARK REDMAN-P
56 RONNY PAULINO-C
57 ZACH DUKE (INJ)-P
58 DAVE WILLIAMS-P
59 NATE MCLOUTH-OF
60 BRYAN BULLINGTON-P
61 TOM GORZELANNY-P
62 MATT CAPPS-P
66 J. J. FURMANIAK-INF (2)
88 RICK WHITE-P

ST. LOUIS CARDINAL

The Cardinals wore numbers on their sleeves during 1923 and 1924. Evidence indicates that it wa probably only at their home games. The practice was then discontinued. The unknown numbers a shown with games played, *HOME games are in italic* and AWAY games in roman. Numbers were introduced permanently on June 25, 1932 following the dictum from the League office.

1923
ST. LOUIS CARDINALS
[WORE #'S ON SLEEVES]
5TH 79-74 16GB

NO# BRANCH (MAHATMA) RICKEY-MGR
1 MAX FLACK-OF
2 JACK SMITH-OF
3 RAY BLADES-OF/3B
4 ROGERS (RAJAH) HORNSBY (ILL)-2B
5 JIM (SUNNY JIM) BOTTOMLEY-1B
6 MILT STOCK-3B
7 HY MYERS-OF
8 DOC LAVAN-INF
9 HEINIE MUELLER-OF
10 JIMMY HUDGENS-1B/2B
11 SPECS TOPORCER-UTIL
11 LES BELL-SS
12 LES (MAJOR) MANN-OF (1)
12 TIGE STONE-OF/P
14 EDDIE (DORF) AINSMITH-C (1)
14 CHARLIE (NIG) NIEBERGALL-C
15 VERNE (STINGER) (TUBBY) CLEMONS-C
16 HARRY (HANK) MCCURDY-C
17 BILL (SPITTIN' BILL) DOAK-P
18 JEFF PFEFFER-P
19 JOHNNY (STUD) STUART-P
20 EDDIE DYER-OF/P
21 CLYDE (FOOTS) BARFOOT-P
22 JAKE FLOWERS-INF
23 BILL (WEE WILLIE) SHERDEL-P
24 BURT (BARNEY) SHOTTON-PR
25 JOE SUGDEN-CH
26 SPECS TOPORCER-UTIL
31 JESSE (POP) HAINES-P
49 FRED TONEY-P
51 LOU NORTH-P
61 HOWARD (TY) FREIGAU-SS/UTIL
71 TAYLOR DOUTHIT-OF
NO# BILL PERTICA-P (1G: 4/20)
NO# JOE (GERMANY) SCHULTZ-PH (2G: 4/18,21)
__ GEORGE KOPSHAW-PH (2G: *8/4,5*)
__ EPP SELL-P (5G: 4/17,5/9,20,27,*29*)
__ SPEED WALKER-PH (2G:*9/15,15*)
__ FRED WIGINGTON-P (4G:4/20,22,5/7,*9/24*)

1924
[WORE #'S ON SLEEVES]
6TH 65-89 28.5GB

NO# BRANCH (MAHATMA) RICKEY-MGR
1 JACK SMITH-OF
2 RAY BLADES-OF/INF
3 MAX FLACK-OF
4 JIM (SUNNY JIM) BOTTOMLEY-1B
6 ROGERS (RAJAH) HORNSBY-2B
7 HEINIE MUELLER-OF/1B
8 JIMMY (SCOOPS) COONEY-SS/INF
9 HY MYERS-UTIL
11 SPECS TOPORCER-INF
12 HOWARD (TY) FREIGAU-3B/SS
16 HI BELL-P
17 CHARLIE (NIG) NIEBERGALL-C
18 JESSE (POP) HAINES-P
19 LEO DICKERMAN-P (2)
20 ERNIE VICK-C
23 BILL (WEE WILLIE) SHERDEL-P
26 MIKE GONZALEZ-C
41 JOHNNY (STUD) STUART-P
49 JEFF PFEFFER-P (1)
51 ALLAN SOTHORON-P
61 EDDIE DYER-P
71 WATTIE HOLM-OF/UTIL
NO# ED CLOUGH-OF (7G: 8/28-9/6)
NO# DOC LAVAN-2B/SS (4G: 4/23-5/4)
NO# RAY SHEPHERDSON-C (3G: 9/19,20,24)
NO# VINCE SHIELDS-P (2G: 9/20,25)
NO# BOB VINES-P (2G: 9/3,27)
__ LES BELL-SS (17G: *4/15-22*, 4/23-5/4)
__ JACK BERLY-P (4G: *4/22*, 9/6-27)
__ JOE (GOOBERS) BRATCHER-OF (4G: *8/26*, 8/28-29)
__ VERNE (STINGER) (TUBBY) CLEMONS-C (25G: *4/21-22*,27,7/29, 8/10, *20-24*, 28-31,9/1, 6, *7-8*,13-27,*28*)
__ PEA RIDGE DAY-P (3G: 9/19-23, *28*)
__ ART (SWEDE) DELANEY-P (8G: *4/16,5/15*,30-6/18)
__ BILL (SPITTIN' BILL) DOAK-P (1) (11G: *4/15-20,27, 5/10-28*, 6/6)
__ TAYLOR DOUTHIT-OF (53G: *4/16*-7/2,9/7-*28*)
__ JESSE (PETE) FOWLER-P (13G: 8/8-10,*20-26*,28-9/27)
__ CHICK HAFEY-OF (24G: 8/28-9/6,*7-10*,12-20)
__ LOU NORTH-P (1) (6G: *4/15-18*,23,6/6-7)
__ FLINT (SHAD) RHEM-P (6G: 9/6-24,*28*)
__ JOE (GERMANY) SCHULTZ-OF (1) (12G: *4/15-21*,27,5/1-3,*15, 18*,30-31)
__ TOMMY THEVENOW-SS (23G: 9/4-*28*)
__ TERRY (COTTON TOP) (TANK) TURNER-CH

1932
ST. LOUIS CARDINALS
[WORE #'S ON BACKS]
6TH (TIE) 72-82 18GB

1 SKEETER WEBB-SS
1 SPARKY ADAMS-3B
2 PEPPER (THE WILD HOSS OF THE OSAGE) MARTIN-OF/3B
3 FRANKIE (THE FORDHAM FLASH) FRISCH-2B
4 JIM (SUNNY JIM) BOTTOMLEY-1B
5 ERNIE ORSATTI-OF
6 GEORGE (WATTY) WATKINS-OF
7 RAY BLADES-OF
8 RIPPER COLLINS-1B/OF
9 JIMMY REESE-2B
10 JAKE FLOWERS-3B
11 CHARLIE GELBERT-SS
12 JIMMIE (ACE) WILSON-C
14 GUS (BLACKIE) MANCUSO-C
15 MIKE GONZALEZ-C
16 JESSE (POP) HAINES-P
17 DIZZY DEAN-P
18 TEX CARLETON-P
19 JIM LINDSEY-P
20 PAUL (DUKE) ('OOM PAUL) DERRINGER-P
21 ALLYN (FISH HOOK) STOUT-P
22 BILL (WILD BILL) HALLAHAN-P
23 SYL JOHNSON-P
24 WATTIE HOLM-OF
24 RUBE BRESSLER-OF (2)
24 CHARLIE (SWAMP BABY) WILSON-SS
25 GABBY STREET-MGR
26 BUZZY WARES-CH
28 JOE (DUCKY) (MUSCLES) MEDWICK-OF
30 GEORGE (COUNT) (POOCH) PUCCINELLI-OF
31 DICK TERWILLIGER-P
__ BILL DELANCEY-C (8G: 9/11-9/26)
__ RAY (IRON MAN) STARR-P (3G: 9/11-9/26)
__ JIM (COWBOY) WINFORD-P (4G: 9/10-9/24)
NO# RAY CUNNINGHAM-INF (11G: 5/13-6/18)
NO# EDDIE DELKER-INF (1) (20G: TR TO PHIN 6/7)
NO# HOD FORD-SS (1) (1G: 4/18) (REL: 5/8)
NO# BENNY FREY-P (1) (2G: 4/21-4/28)
NO# HARVEY (GINK) HENDRICK-3B (1) (28G: 4/15-6/5)
NO# JOEL HUNT-OF (12G: 4/13-5/20)
NO# RAY PEPPER-OF (21G: 4/15-5/27)
NO# FLINT (SHAD) RHEM-P (1) (6G: 4/12-5/9)
NO# BILL (WEE WILLIE) SHERDEL-P (2) (3G: 5/22-6/11)
NO# BUD TEACHOUT-P (1G: 4/15)

1933
5TH 82-71 9.5GB

1 SPARKY ADAMS-SS (1)
2 CHARLIE (SWAMP BABY) WILSON-SS
2 LEO (THE LIP) (LIPPY) DUROCHER-SS (2)
3 FRANKIE (THE FORDHAM FLASH) FRISCH-2B/MGR
4 ROGERS (RAJAH) HORNSBY-2B (1)
5 GEORGE (WATTY) WATKINS-OF
6 ERNIE ORSATTI-OF
7 JOE (DUCKY) (MUSCLES) MEDWICK-OF
8 BOB O'FARRELL-C
9 JIMMIE (ACE) WILSON-C
10 BILL WALKER-P
11 PAT CRAWFORD-3B
12 RIPPER COLLINS-1B
14 GORDON (OSKIE) SLADE-INF
14 BURGESS (WHITEY) WHITEHEAD-INF
15 TEX CARLETON-P
16 JESSE (POP) HAINES-P
17 DIZZY DEAN-P
18 DAZZY VANCE-P
19 PAUL (DUKE) ('OOM PAUL) DERRINGER-P (1)
20 JIM LINDSEY-P
20 PAUL (DUKE) ('OOM PAUL) DERRINGER-P (1)
20 BURLEIGH GRIMES-P (2)
21 JIM MOONEY-P
21 ALLYN (FISH HOOK) STOUT-P (1)
21 GENE (ROWDY) MOORE-OF
22 BILL (WILD BILL) HALLAHAN-P
23 ALLYN (FISH HOOK) STOUT-P (1)
24 ETHAN ALLEN-OF
25 GABBY STREET-MGR1
25 MIKE GONZALEZ-CH
26 BUZZY WARES-CH
27 ESTEL (CRABBY) CRABTREE-OF
28 PEPPER (THE WILD HOSS OF THE OSAGE) MARTIN-3B
29 RAY PEPPER-OF
30 SYL JOHNSON-P
31 BILL (BUDDY) LEWIS-C
31 JOE (MULE) SPRINZ-C

1934
1ST 95-58 0GB
W WS-DETA 4-3

1* PEPPER (THE WILD HOSS OF THE OSAGE) MARTIN-3B/P*
2 LEO (THE LIP) (LIPPY) DUROCHER-SS
3 FRANKIE (THE FORDHAM FLASH) FRISCH-2B/MGR
4 KIDDO DAVIS-OF (1)
4 CHICK FULLIS-OF (2)
5 ERNIE ORSATTI-OF
6 JACK ROTHROCK-OF
7 JOE (DUCKY) (MUSCLES) MEDWICK-OF
8 SPUD DAVIS-C
9 BILL DELANCEY-C
10 BUSTER MILLS-OF
11 PAT CRAWFORD-3B
12 RIPPER COLLINS-1B
14 BURGESS (WHITEY) WHITEHEAD-INF
15 TEX CARLETON-P
16 JESSE (POP) HAINES-P
17 DIZZY DEAN-P
18 BILL WALKER-P
19 JIM (COWBOY) WINFORD-P
19 DAZZY VANCE-P (2)
20 BURLEIGH ('OL STUBBLEBEARD) GRIMES-P (1)
21 PAUL (DAFFY) DEAN-P
22 BILL (WILD BILL) HALLAHAN-P
24 GENE (ROWDY) MOORE-OF
25 MIKE GONZALEZ-CH
26 BUZZY WARES-CH
27 FRANCIS HEALY-UTIL
27 CLARENCE (LEFTY) HEISE-P
28 JIM MOONEY-P
29 LEW RIGGS-PH
31 FLINT (SHAD) RHEM-P (1
31 JIM LINDSEY-P (2)
31 RED WORTHINGTON-PH (2)

1935
2ND 96-58 4GB

1 PEPPER (THE WILD HOSS OF THE OSAGE) MARTI OF/3B
2 LEO (THE LIP) (LIPPY) DUROCHER-SS
3 FRANKIE (THE FORDHAM FLASH) FRISCH-2B/MG
4 CHARLIE GELBERT-INF
5 ERNIE ORSATTI-OF
6 JACK ROTHROCK-OF
7 JOE (DUCKY) (MUSCLES) MEDWICK-OF
8 SPUD DAVIS-C
9 BILL DELANCEY-C
10 DICK WARD-P
10 LYLE (PUNCH) JUDY-2B
10 GENE (ROWDY) MOORE-C
11 TERRY MOORE-OF
12 RIPPER COLLINS-1B
14 BURGESS (WHITEY) WHITEHEAD-INF
15 MAYS COPELAND-P
16 JESSE (POP) HAINES-P
17 DIZZY DEAN-P
18 BILL WALKER-P
19 BILL (FIDDLER BILL) MCGEE-P
19 BUD TINNING-P
19 MIKE RYBA-P
20 AL (OBBIE) ECKERT-P
20 TONY KAUFMANN-P
20 RAY (COWBOY) HARRELL
21 PAUL (DAFFY) DEAN-P
22 BILL (WILD BILL) HALLAHAN-P
24 LYNN (DIG) KING-OF
24 NUBS KLEINKE-P
25 MIKE GONZALEZ-CH
26 BUZZY WARES-CH
27 DICK WARD-P
27 JIM (COWBOY) WINFORD-
28 PHIL (FIDGETY PHIL) COLLINS-P (2)
29 BOB O'FARRELL-C
32 ED (THE WILD ELK OF THE WASATCH) HEUSSER-P
33 CHARLIE (SWAMP BABY) WILSON-3B
33 SAM NARRON-C
35 TOM (LONG TOM) WINSET OF

1936
2ND (TIE) 87-67 5GB

1 PEPPER (THE WILD HOSS OF THE OSAGE) MARTII 3B
2 LEO (THE LIP) (LIPPY) DUROCHER-SS
3 FRANKIE (THE FORDHAM FLASH) FRISCH-INF/MGR
4 CHARLIE GELBERT-INF
5 LYNN (DIG) KING-OF
6 STU MARTIN-INF
7 JOE (DUCKY) (MUSCLES) MEDWICK-OF
8 SPUD DAVIS-C
9 BRUCE (BRUSIE) OGRODOWSKI-C
10 JOHNNY (BIG CAT) (BIG JOHN) MIZE-1B

ST. LOUIS CARDINALS

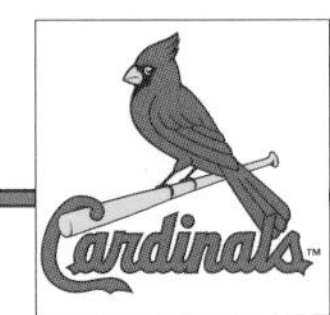

1 TERRY MOORE-OF
2 RIPPER COLLINS-1B
4 ED (THE WILD ELK OF THE WASATCH) HEUSSER-P
5 ROY (TARZAN) PARMELEE-P
6 JESSE (POP) HAINES-P
7 DIZZY DEAN-P
8 SI JOHNSON-P (2)
9 MIKE RYBA-P
9 FLINT (SHAD) RHEM-P
0 NELSON POTTER-P
0 COTTON PIPPEN-P
1 PAUL (DAFFY) DEAN-P
1 WALTER (SMOKEY) ALSTON-1B
1 BILL WALKER-P
2 BILL (WILD BILL) HALLAHAN-P (1)
2 BILL COX-P
2 DON (FIRPO) GUTTERIDGE-3B
3 BUZZY WARES-CH
3 GEORGE (MOOSE) EARNSHAW-P (2)
4 LES (NEMO) (BIG ED) MUNNS-P
4 BILL (FIDDLER BILL) MCGEE-P
5 MIKE GONZALEZ-CH
6 BUZZY WARES-CH
7 JIM (COWBOY) WINFORD-P
9 PAT ANKENMANN-SS
0 EDDIE (PEPPER) MORGAN-OF
0 ART GARIBALDI-3B
0 HEINIE SCHUBEL-3B
0 JOHNNY VERGEZ-3B (2)
LOU (WEASER) SCOFFIC-OF
1 CHICK FULLIS-OF
3 GEORGE (MOOSE) EARNSHAW-P (2)

1937

4TH 81-73 15GB

1 PEPPER (THE WILD HOSS OF THE OSAGE) MARTIN-OF/3B
2 LEO (THE LIP) (LIPPY) DUROCHER-SS
3 FRANKIE (THE FORDHAM FLASH) FRISCH-2B/MGR
4 DON PADGETT-OF
5 DON (FIRPO) GUTTERIDGE-INF
6 STU MARTIN-2B
7 JOE (DUCKY) (MUSCLES) MEDWICK-OF
8 MICKEY OWEN-C
9 BRUCE (BRUSIE) OGRODOWSKI-C
0 JOHNNY (BIG CAT) (BIG JOHN) MIZE-1B
1 HERB BREMER-C
1 TERRY MOORE-OF
2 SI JOHNSON-P
4 FRENCHY BORDAGARAY-3B/OF
5 JIMMY BROWN-INF
6 JESSE (POP) HAINES-P
7 DIZZY DEAN-P
8 LON (THE ARKANSAS HUMMINGBIRD) WARNEKE-P
9 MIKE RYBA-P
0 BOB (LEFTY) WEILAND-P
1 TOM (LEFTY) SUNKEL-P
1 PAUL (DAFFY) DEAN-P
2 DICK SIEBERT-1B
2 ABE WHITE-P
2 RANDY MOORE-OF (2)
2 HOWIE (SPUD) KRIST-P
24 NUBS KLEINKE-P
24 BILL (FIDDLER BILL) MCGEE-P
25 MIKE GONZALEZ-CH
26 BUZZY WARES-CH
27 JIM (COWBOY) WINFORD-P
27 SHERIFF BLAKE-P (2)
28 RAY (COWBOY) HARRELL-P
29 NATE ANDREWS-P
30 HERB BREMER-C
31 JOHNNIE CHAMBERS-P

1938

6TH 71-80 17.5GB

1 PEPPER (THE WILD HOSS OF THE OSAGE) MARTIN-OF/3B
2 TERRY MOORE-OF
3 FRANKIE (THE FORDHAM FLASH) FRISCH-MGR1
4 DON PADGETT-OF/C
5 DON (FIRPO) GUTTERIDGE-INF
6 STU MARTIN-2B
7 JOE (DUCKY) (MUSCLES) MEDWICK-OF
8 MICKEY OWEN-C
9 ENOS (COUNTRY) SLAUGHTER-OF
10 JOHNNY (BIG CAT) (BIG JOHN) MIZE-1B
11 HERB BREMER-C
12 SI JOHNSON-P
14 FRENCHY BORDAGARAY-OF/3B
15 JIMMY BROWN-INF
16 MAX MACON-P
17 JOE (JERSEY JOE) STRIPP-3B (1)
17 GUY (THE MISSISSIPPI MUDCAT) BUSH-P
17 HAL EPPS-OF
18 LON (THE ARKANSAS HUMMINGBIRD) WARNEKE-P
19 MIKE RYBA-P
19 PREACHER ROE-P
19 PAUL (DAFFY) DEAN-P
20 BOB (LEFTY) WEILAND-P
22 LYNN MYERS-SS
22 DICK SIEBERT-1B (1)
24 CREEPY CRESPI-SS
25 MIKE GONZALEZ-CH/MGR2
26 BUZZY WARES-CH
27 CURT (COONSKIN) DAVIS-P
28 RAY (COWBOY) HARRELL-P
29 BILL (FIDDLER BILL) MCGEE-P
30 JIM BUCHER-2B
30 MORT COOPER-P
31 ROY (KID) HENSHAW-P
32 MAX LANIER-P
33 HOWIE (SPUD) KRIST-P
36 CLYDE (HARDROCK) SHOUN-P

1939

2ND 92-61 4.5GB

1 LYNN MYERS-INF
2 LYN (BROADWAY) LARY-INF (3)
3 JIMMY BROWN-INF
4 JOE ORENGO-SS
◊**4** JOHNNY ECHOLS-PR
◊**4** EDDIE (SPARKY) LAKE-SS
5 DON (FIRPO) GUTTERIDGE-3B
6 STU MARTIN-2B
7 JOE (DUCKY) (MUSCLES) MEDWICK-OF
8* TERRY MOORE-OF/P*
9 ENOS (COUNTRY) SLAUGHTER-OF
10 JOHNNY (BIG CAT) (BIG JOHN) MIZE-1B
11 PEPPER (THE WILD HOSS OF THE OSAGE) MARTIN-3B
12 HERMAN FRANKS-C
12 BUSTER ADAMS-PH
13 HERB BREMER-C
13 HERMAN FRANKS-C
14 MICKEY OWEN-C
15 HERMAN FRANKS-C
16 DON PADGETT-C/1B
17 LYNN (DIG) KING-OF
18 FRANK (RED) BARRETT-P
19 CREEPY CRESPI-2B
19 JOHNNY (HIPPITY) HOPP-1B
20 BOB (LEFTY) WEILAND-P
21 LON (THE ARKANSAS HUMMINGBIRD) WARNEKE-P
22 NATE ANDREWS-P
22 PAUL (DAFFY) DEAN-P
23 KEN RAFFENSBERGER-P
23 BOB REPASS-2B
24 CLYDE (HARDROCK) SHOUN-P
25 MORT COOPER-P
26 BOB BOWMAN-P
27 CURT (COONSKIN) DAVIS-P/PH
28 TOM (LEFTY) SUNKEL-P
29 BILL (FIDDLER BILL) MCGEE-P
30 MAX LANIER-P
32 MURRY DICKSON-P
35 MIKE GONZALEZ-CH
36 BUZZY WARES-CH
37 RAY BLADES-MGR

1940

3RD 84-69 16GB

1 EDDIE (SPARKY) LAKE-INF
2* ERNIE WHITE-P*
◊**2** CREEPY CRESPI-INF
3 JIMMY BROWN-INF
4 MARTY (SLATS) (OCTOPUS) (MR. SHORTSTOP) MARION-SS
5 DON (FIRPO) GUTTERIDGE-3B
6 STU MARTIN-2B
7 JOE (DUCKY) (MUSCLES) MEDWICK-OF (1)
◊**7*** NEWT KIMBALL-P* (2)
8 TERRY MOORE-OF
9 ENOS (COUNTRY) SLAUGHTER-OF
10 JOHNNY (BIG CAT) (BIG JOHN) MIZE-1B
11 PEPPER (THE WILD HOSS OF THE OSAGE) MARTIN-OF/3B
12 JOHNNY (HIPPITY) HOPP-OF/1B
14 MICKEY OWEN-C
15 BILL DELANCEY (ILL)-C
16 DON PADGETT-OF/C
17 HAL EPPS-OF
17 IRA HUTCHINSON-P
17 WALKER (WALK) COOPER-C
18 JOE ORENGO-INF
19 RED JONES-OF
19 ERNIE (CHIEF) KOY-OF (2)
20 BOB (LEFTY) WEILAND-P
21 LON (THE ARKANSAS HUMMINGBIRD) WARNEKE-P
22 MURRY DICKSON-P
23 MAX LANIER-P
24 CLYDE (HARDROCK) SHOUN-P
25 MORT COOPER-P
26 BOB BOWMAN-P
27 CURT (COONSKIN) DAVIS-P (1)
27 CARL DOYLE-P (2)
28 JACK RUSSELL-P
28 CARDEN GILLENWATER-OF
29 BILL (FIDDLER BILL) MCGEE-P
30 MAX LANIER-P
30 IRA HUTCHINSON-P
30 ERNIE WHITE-P
31 CARL DOYLE-P (2)
31 HARRY (THE CAT) BRECHEEN-P
31 GENE LILLARD-P
34 RAY BLADES-MGR1
35 MIKE GONZALEZ-CH/MGR2
36 BILLY SOUTHWORTH-MGR3
36 BUZZY WARES-CH
37 RAY BLADES-CH
40 BILLY SOUTHWORTH-MGR3
42 HARRY (THE HAT) WALKER-OF

1941

2ND 97-56 2.5GB

1 EDDIE (SPARKY) LAKE-INF
3 JIMMY BROWN-3B
4 MARTY (SLATS) (OCTOPUS) (MR. SHORTSTOP) MARION-SS
5 STEVE MESNER-3B
5 WHITEY KUROWSKI-3B
6 PEP YOUNG-INF (2)
6 HARRY (THE HAT) WALKER-OF
6 STAN (THE MAN) (STOSH) MUSIAL-OF
7 CREEPY CRESPI-2B
8 TERRY MOORE-OF
9 ENOS (COUNTRY) SLAUGHTER-OF
10 JOHNNY (BIG CAT) (BIG JOHN) MIZE-1B
11 ESTEL (CRABBY) CRABTREE-OF
12 JOHNNY (HIPPITY) HOPP-OF/1B
13 MORT COOPER-P
14 GUS (BLACKIE) MANCUSO-C
15 WALKER (WALK) COOPER-C
16 DON PADGETT-OF/C/1B
18 LON (THE ARKANSAS HUMMINGBIRD) WARNEKE-P
19 ERNIE (CHIEF) KOY-OF (1)
19 ERV (FOUR SACK) DUSAK-OF
20 COAKER TRIPLETT-OF
21 LON (THE ARKANSAS HUMMINGBIRD) WARNEKE-P
21 JOHNNY BEAZLEY-P
23 MAX LANIER-P
24 CLYDE (HARDROCK) SHOUN-P
26 HOWIE (SPUD) KRIST-P
28 ERNIE WHITE-P
29 BILL (FIDDLER BILL) MCGEE-P (1)
29 WALTER SESSI-C
30 IRA HUTCHINSON-P
33 HANK GORNICKI-P (1)
33 CHARLIE MARSHALL-C
34 JOHNNY GRODZICKI-P
34 BILL CROUCH-P (2)
35 MIKE GONZALEZ-CH
36 BUZZY WARES-CH
37 SAM NAHEM-P
37 HOWIE POLLET-P
38 JOHNNY BEAZLEY-P
40 BILLY SOUTHWORTH-MGR
42 HERSH LYONS-P
42 HARRY (GUNBOAT) GUMBERT-P (2)

1942

1ST 106-48 0GB

W WS-NYA 4-1

1 WHITEY KUROWSKI-3B
2 JEFF CROSS-SS
2 BUDDY BLATTNER-INF
3 JIMMY BROWN-INF
4 MARTY (SLATS) (OCTOPUS) (MR. SHORTSTOP) MARION-SS
5 RAY SANDERS-1B
6 STAN (THE MAN) (STOSH) MUSIAL-OF
7 CREEPY CRESPI-2B
8 TERRY MOORE-OF
9 ENOS (COUNTRY) SLAUGHTER-OF
10 HARRY (THE HAT) WALKER-OF
11 ESTEL (CRABBY) CRABTREE-OF
11 HOWIE POLLET-P
12 JOHNNY (HIPPITY) HOPP-1B
13 MORT COOPER-P
14 GUS (BLACKIE) MANCUSO-C (1)
14 MORT COOPER-P
15 WALKER (WALK) COOPER-C
16 KEN O'DEA-C
17 ERV (FOUR SACK) DUSAK-OF/3B
18 LON (THE ARKANSAS HUMMINGBIRD) WARNEKE-P (1)
19 ERV (FOUR SACK) DUSAK-OF/3B
19 HARRY (GUNBOAT) GUMBERT-P
20 COAKER TRIPLETT-OF
21 JOHNNY BEAZLEY-P
22 MURRY DICKSON-P
23 MAX LANIER-P
24 CLYDE (HARDROCK) SHOUN-P (1)
24 MORT COOPER-P
25 MIKE GONZALEZ-CH
26 HOWIE (SPUD) KRIST-P
26 BUZZY WARES-CH
27 HOWIE POLLET-P
27 BILL BECKMANN-P (2)
28 ERNIE WHITE-P
29 HOWIE (SPUD) KRIST-P
30 BILLY SOUTHWORTH-MGR
32 SAM NARRON-C
33 JOHNNY BEAZLEY-P
34 BILL LOHRMAN-P (1)
35 MIKE GONZALEZ-CH
35 WHITEY MOORE-P (2)
36 BUZZY WARES-CH
37 HOWIE POLLET-P
42 HARRY (GUNBOAT) GUMBERT-P

1943

1ST 105-49 0GB

L WS-NYA 4-1

1 WHITEY KUROWSKI-3B

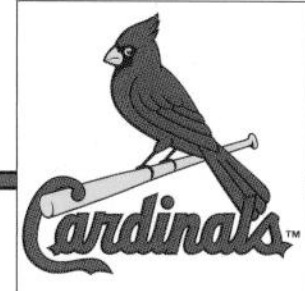

ST. LOUIS CARDINAL

2 LOU KLEIN-2B/SS
3 JIMMY BROWN-INF
4 MARTY (SLATS) (OCTOPUS) (MR. SHORTSTOP) MARION-SS
5 RAY SANDERS-1B
6 STAN (THE MAN) (STOSH) MUSIAL-OF
7 GEORGE (FLASH) FALLON-2B
8 BUSTER ADAMS-OF (1)
8 DANNY LITWHILER-OF (2)
9 DEBS (TEX) GARMS-OF/3B
10 HARRY (THE HAT) WALKER-OF
11 HOWIE POLLET-P
11 AL BRAZLE-P
12 JOHNNY (HIPPITY) HOPP-OF/1B
13 MORT COOPER-P
14 BUSTER ADAMS-OF (1)
15 WALKER (WALK) COOPER-C
16 KEN O'DEA-C
17 FRANK DEMAREE-OF
18 GEORGE (RED) MUNGER-P
19 HARRY (GUNBOAT) GUMBERT-P
20 COAKER TRIPLETT-OF (1)
21 MAX LANIER-P
22 MURRY DICKSON-P
23 MAX LANIER-P
25 MIKE GONZALEZ-CH
26 BUZZY WARES-CH
27 BUD BYERLY-P
28 ERNIE WHITE-P
29 HOWIE (SPUD) KRIST-P
30 BILLY SOUTHWORTH-MGR
31 HARRY (THE CAT) BRECHEEN-P
32 SAM NARRON-C
35 HOWIE (SPUD) KRIST-P

1944
1ST 105-49 0GB
W WS-STLA 4-2

1 WHITEY KUROWSKI-3B
2 BOB KEELY-C
3 EMIL (ANTELOPE) (DUTCH) VERBAN-2B
4 MARTY (SLATS) (OCTOPUS) (MR. SHORTSTOP) MARION-SS
5 RAY SANDERS-1B
6 STAN (THE MAN) (STOSH) MUSIAL-OF
7 GEORGE (FLASH) FALLON-INF
8 AUGIE BERGAMO-OF
8 DANNY LITWHILER-OF
9 DEBS (TEX) GARMS-OF/3B
10 PEPPER (THE WILD HOSS OF THE OSAGE) MARTIN-OF
11 FREDDY SCHMIDT-P
12 JOHNNY (HIPPITY) HOPP-OF
13 MORT COOPER-P
14 BILL TROTTER-P
15 WALKER (WALK) COOPER-C
16 KEN O'DEA-C
17 AUGIE BERGAMO-OF
18 GEORGE (RED) MUNGER-P
18 JOHN ANTONELLI-INF
19 HARRY (GUNBOAT) GUMBERT-P (1)
20 BLIX DONNELLY-P
21 MAX LANIER-P
25 MIKE GONZALEZ-CH
26 BUZZY WARES-CH
27 BUD BYERLY-P
28 TED (CORK) WILKS-P
29 AL JURISICH-P
30 BILLY SOUTHWORTH-MGR
31 HARRY (THE CAT) BRECHEEN-P
32 MIKE NAYMICK-P (2)

1945
2ND 95-59 3GB

1 WHITEY KUROWSKI-3B
2 BOB KEELY-C
2 LOU KLEIN-INF
3 EMIL (ANTELOPE) (DUTCH) VERBAN-2B
4 MARTY (SLATS) (OCTOPUS) (MR. SHORTSTOP) MARION-SS
5 RAY SANDERS-1B
6 RED SCHOENDIENST-OF
7 GEORGE (FLASH) FALLON-INF
7 PEP YOUNG-INF
8 ART REBEL-OF
8 DAVE BARTOSCH-OF
9 DEBS (TEX) GARMS-3B/OF
10 KEN BURKHART-P
11 DEL RICE-C
12 JOHNNY (HIPPITY) HOPP-OF/1B
13 MORT COOPER-P (1)
13 RED BARRETT-P (2)
14 BUSTER ADAMS-OF (2)
15 GLENN GARDNER-P
15 WALKER (WALK) COOPER-C
16 KEN O'DEA-C
17 AUGIE BERGAMO-OF
18 JIM (SUNNY JIM) MALLORY-OF (1)
18 BOB KEELY-C
19 JACK (TEX) CREEL-P
20 BLIX DONNELLY-P
21 MAX LANIER-P
22 JOHN ANTONELLI-3B (1)
22 BILL CROUCH-P
23 GEORGE (LEFTY) DOCKINS-P
24 ART LOPATKA-P
25 MIKE GONZALEZ-CH
26 BUZZY WARES-CH
27 BUD BYERLY-P
28 TED (CORK) WILKS-P
29 AL JURISICH-P
30 BILLY SOUTHWORTH-MGR
31 HARRY (THE CAT) BRECHEEN-P
32 STAN (PARTY) PARTENHEIMER-P
34 GLENN (SHORTY) CRAWFORD-OF (1)
35 GLENN (SHORTY) CRAWFORD-OF (1)
35 GENE CRUMLING-C

1946
1ST 98-58 0GB
W NLP/O-BKLN 2-0
W WS-BOSA 4-3

1 WHITEY KUROWSKI-3B
2 RED SCHOENDIENST-2B
3 EMIL (ANTELOPE) (DUTCH) VERBAN-2B
4 MARTY (SLATS) (OCTOPUS) (MR. SHORTSTOP) MARION-SS
5 HARRY (THE HAT) WALKER-OF
6 STAN (THE MAN) (STOSH) MUSIAL-1B/OF
7 LOU KLEIN (MEX)-2B
7 NIPPY JONES-2B
8 TERRY MOORE-OF
9 CLYDE KLUTTZ-C (2)
9 ENOS (COUNTRY) SLAUGHTER-OF
10 KEN BURKHART-P
11 HOWIE POLLET-P
13 RED BARRETT-P
14 BUSTER ADAMS-OF
15 DICK SISLER-1B
16 KEN O'DEA-C (1)
16 AL BRAZLE-P
17 JOE GARAGIOLA-C
18 DEL RICE-C
19 ERV (FOUR SACK) DUSAK-UTIL
20 BLIX DONNELLY-P (1)
20 GEORGE (RED) MUNGER-P
21 MAX LANIER (MEX)-P
21 JOHNNY BEAZLEY-P
22 MURRY DICKSON-P
23 DEL (BABE) WILBER-C
24 BILL ENDICOTT-OF
25 MIKE GONZALEZ-CH
26 BUZZY WARES-CH
27 JOHNNY BEAZLEY-P
27 AL BRAZLE-P
28 TED (CORK) WILKS-P
29 HOWIE (SPUD) KRIST-P
30 EDDIE DYER-MGR
31 HARRY (THE CAT) BRECHEEN-P
33 JOHNNY GRODZICKI (INJ)-P
34 FRED MARTI (MEX)-P
35 JEFF CROSS-INF
36 AL BRAZLE-P
37 FREDDY SCHMIDT-P
38 WALTER (WATSIE) SESSI-C
39 RED MUNGER-P
39 CLYDE KLUTTZ-C (2)
42 KEN BURKHART-P
42 DANNY LITWHILER-OF (1)

1947
2ND 89-65 5GB

1 WHITEY KUROWSKI-3B
2 RED SCHOENDIENST-2B
3 JEFF CROSS-INF
4 MARTY (SLATS) (OCTOPUS) (MR. SHORTSTOP) MARION-SS
5 HARRY (THE HAT) WALKER-OF (1)
5 RON (ROUND MAN) (ROLLO) NORTHEY-OF (2)
6 STAN (THE MAN) (STOSH) MUSIAL-1B
7 ERV (FOUR SACK) DUSAK-OF
7 NIPPY JONES-1B
8 TERRY MOORE-OF
9 ENOS (COUNTRY) SLAUGHTER-OF
10 HARRY (THE HAT) WALKER-OF (1)
10 KEN BURKHART-P
11 HOWIE POLLET-P
14 GERRY STALEY-P
15 DICK SISLER-1B
16 BERNIE CREGER-SS
17 JOE GARAGIOLA-C
18 DEL RICE-C
19 NIPPY JONES-1B
19 ERV (FOUR SACK) DUSAK-OF
20 GEORGE (RED) MUNGER-P
21 JOE (DUCKY) (MUSCLES) MEDWICK-OF
22 MURRY DICKSON-P
23 DEL (BABE) WILBER-C
25 TONY KAUFMANN-CH
26 BUZZY WARES-CH
27 AL BRAZLE-P
28 TED (CORK) WILKS-P
29 FREDDY SCHMIDT-P (1)
30 EDDIE DYER-MGR
31 HARRY (THE CAT) BRECHEEN-P
32 CHUCK DIERING-OF
33 JOHNNY GRODZICKI-P
34 JIM HEARN-P
35 KEN (HOOKS) JOHNSON-P
39 GEORGE (RED) MUNGER-P
40 DEL (BABE) WILBER-C

1948
2ND 85-69 6.5GB

1 WHITEY KUROWSKI-3B
2 RED SCHOENDIENST-2B
3 JEFF CROSS-INF (1)
3 BOBBY YOUNG-2B
3 NIPPY JONES-1B
4 MARTY (SLATS) (OCTOPUS) (MR. SHORTSTOP) MARION-SS
5 RON (ROUND MAN) (ROLLO) NORTHEY-OF
6 STAN (THE MAN) (STOSH) MUSIAL-OF
7 ERV (FOUR SACK) DUSAK-OF
8 TERRY MOORE-OF
9 ENOS (COUNTRY) SLAUGHTER-OF
10 KEN BURKHART-P (1)
10 BABE YOUNG-1B (2)
11 HOWIE POLLET-P
12 EDDIE KAZAK-3B
14 GERRY STALEY-P
15 BILL BAKER-C
16 RALPH LAPOINTE-INF
17 JOE GARAGIOLA-C
18 DEL RICE-C
19 NIPPY JONES-1B
20 GEORGE (RED) MUNGER-P
21 JOE (DUCKY) (MUSCLES) MEDWICK-OF
21 HAL (HOOT) RICE-OF
22 MURRY DICKSON-P/PH
23 DEL (BABE) WILBER-C
24 JOHNNY BUCHA-C
25 TONY KAUFMANN-CH
26 BUZZY WARES-CH
27 AL BRAZLE-P
28 TED (CORK) WILKS-P
29 DON LANG-3B
30 EDDIE DYER-MGR
31 HARRY (THE CAT) BRECHEEN-P
32 CHUCK DIERING-OF
34 JIM HEARN-P
35 KEN (HOOKS) JOHNSON-P
36 AL PAPAI-P
37 CLARENCE BEERS-P
39 RAY YOCHIM-P
41 LARRY (IRISH) MIGGINS-OF

1949
2ND 96-58 1GB

1 WHITEY KUROWSKI-3B
2 RED SCHOENDIENST-2B
3 NIPPY JONES-1B
4 MARTY (SLATS) (OCTOPUS) (MR. SHORTSTOP) MARION-SS
5 RON (ROUND MAN) (ROLLO) NORTHEY-OF
6 STAN (THE MAN) (STOSH) MUSIAL-1B
7 ERV (FOUR SACK) DUSAK-OF
8 TERRY MOORE-CH
9 ENOS (COUNTRY) SLAUGHTER-OF
10 ED SAUER-OF (1)
10 DEL (BABE) WILBER-C
11 HOWIE POLLET-P
12 TOMMY (RABBIT) GLAVIANO-3B
14 GERRY STALEY-P
15 BILL BAKER-INF
16 HAL (HOOT) RICE-OF
17 JOE GARAGIOLA-C
18 DEL RICE-C
19 ROCKY NELSON-1B
20 GEORGE (RED) MUNGER-P
21 EDDIE KAZAK-INF
22 SOLLY HEMUS-2B
23 MAX LANIER (MEX)-P
23 CLOYD (JUNIOR) BOYER-P
24 KURT (DUTCH) KRIEGER-P
25 TONY KAUFMANN-CH
26 BUZZY WARES-CH
27 AL BRAZLE-P
28 TED (CORK) WILKS-P
29 LOU KLEIN (MEX)-INF
30 EDDIE DYER-MGR
31 HARRY (THE CAT) BRECHEEN-P
32 CHUCK DIERING-OF
33 BILL REEDER-P
34 JIM HEARN-P
34 STEVE BILKO-1B
35 KEN (HOOKS) JOHNSON-P
36 FRED MARTIN (MEX)-P
36 BILL (HOPALONG) HOWERTON-OF
39 GEORGE (RED) MUNGER-P
39 RAY YOCHIM-P
39 FRED MARTIN (MEX)-P
40 BILL REEDER-P
40 DEL (BABE) WILBER-C
41 RUSS DERRY-PH

1950
5TH 78-75 12.5GB

1 HARRY (THE HAT) WALKER-OF
1 HAL (HOOT) RICE-OF
2 RED SCHOENDIENST-2B
3 NIPPY JONES-1B
4 MARTY (SLATS) (OCTOPUS) (MR. SHORTSTOP) MARION-SS
5 STEVE BILKO-1B
5 JOHNNY LINDELL-OF (2)
6 STAN (THE MAN) (STOSH) MUSIAL-1B
7* ERV (FOUR SACK) DUSAK-P*/OF
8 TERRY MOORE-CH
9 ENOS (COUNTRY) SLAUGHTER-OF
10 TOM POHOLSKY-P
11 HOWIE POLLET-P
12 TOMMY (RABBIT) GLAVIANO-3B
14 GERRY STALEY-P
15 JOHNNY BUCHA-C
17 JOE GARAGIOLA-C
18 DEL RICE-C
19 ROCKY NELSON-1B
20 GEORGE (RED) MUNGER-P
21 EDDIE KAZAK-3B
22 SOLLY HEMUS-3B
23 MAX LANIER-P
24 CLOYD (JUNIOR) BOYER-P
25 TONY KAUFMANN-CH
26 BUZZY WARES-CH
27 AL BRAZLE-P
28 TED (CORK) WILKS-P
29 DANNY GARDELLA-PH

ST. LOUIS CARDINALS

30 EDDIE DYER-MGR
31 HARRY (THE CAT) BRECHEEN-P
32 CHUCK DIERING-OF
33 EDDIE (EPPIE) MILLER-INF
34 JIM HEARN-P (1)
34 ED MICKELSON-1B
35 KEN (HOOKS) JOHNSON-P (1)
35 JOHNNY (CHIEF) BLATNIK-OF (2)
36 BILL (HOPALONG) HOWERTON-OF
37 PEANUTS LOWREY-2B (2)
38 COTTON (COT) DEAL-P
39 FRED MARTIN-P
40 ED (BUTCH) MIERKOWICZ-PH
40 DON BOLLWEG-1B
41 AL PAPAI-P (2)

1951

3RD 81-73 15.5GB

1 EDDIE KAZAK-3B
1 BILLY (THE BULL) JOHNSON-3B (2)
2 RED SCHOENDIENST-2B
3 NIPPY JONES-1B
4 MARTY (SLATS) (OCTOPUS) (MR. SHORTSTOP) MARION-SS
5 STEVE BILKO-1B
6 STAN (THE MAN) (STOSH) MUSIAL-OF
7 SOLLY HEMUS-INF
8 TERRY MOORE-CH
9 ENOS (COUNTRY) SLAUGHTER-OF
11 HOWIE POLLET-P (1)
12 TOMMY (RABBIT) GLAVIANO-3B
14 GERRY STALEY-P
15 DICK COLE-2B (1)
16 BILL SARNI-C
17 JOE GARAGIOLA-C (1)
17 WALLY WESTLAKE-OF (2)
18 DEL RICE-C
19 ROCKY NELSON-1B/OF (1)
19 STAN ROJEK-SS (2)
20 GEORGE (RED) MUNGER-P
21 JOE (LITTLE JOE) PRESKO-P
21 JACKIE COLLUM-P
22 BOB (HOBBY) HABENICHT-P
23 MAX LANIER-P
24 CLOYD (JUNIOR) BOYER-P
25 ERV (FOUR SACK) DUSAK-P (1)
25 JACK CRIMIAN-P
25 DICK BOKELMANN-P
26 BUZZY WARES-CH
27 AL BRAZLE-P
28 TED (CORK) WILKS-P (1)
28 CLIFF (LEFTY) CHAMBERS-P (2)
29 TOM POHOLSKY-P
30 KURT (DUTCH) KRIEGER-P
30 BOB SCHEFFING-C (2)
31 HARRY (THE CAT) BRECHEEN-P
32 CHUCK DIERING-OF
33 RAY BLADES-CH
34 LARRY (SYMPHONY) CIAFFONE-OF
34 DAN LEWANDOWSKI-P
35 MIKE RYBA-CH
36 BILL (HOPALONG) HOWERTON-OF (1)
36 JAY VAN NOY-OF
36 VERN BENSON-3B/OF
37 PEANUTS LOWREY-OF
38 DON RICHMOND-3B
38 HARRY (THE HAT) WALKER-OF
39 HAL (HOOT) RICE-OF
40 DON BOLLWEG-1B
42 KURT (DUTCH) KRIEGER-P

1952

3RD 88-66 8.5GB

1 EDDIE KAZAK-3B (1)
1 BILLY (THE BULL) JOHNSON-3B
2 RED SCHOENDIENST-2B
3 EDDIE KAZAK-3B (1)
3 VIRGIL (RED) STALLCUP-SS (2)
5 STEVE BILKO-1B
6 STAN (THE MAN) (STOSH) MUSIAL-OF/P
7 SOLLY HEMUS-INF
8 TERRY MOORE-CH
9 ENOS (COUNTRY) SLAUGHTER-OF
11 TOMMY (RABBIT) GLAVIANO-3B
12 EDDIE (THE BRAT) (MUGGSY) STANKY-MGR/2B
14 GERRY STALEY-P
15 WALLY WESTLAKE-OF (1)
15 DICK SISLER-1B (2)
16 BILL SARNI-C
17 LES FUSSELMAN-C
18 DEL RICE-C
20 GEORGE (RED) MUNGER-P (1)
20 BILL (BUGS) WERLE-P (2)
21 JOE (LITTLE JOE) PRESKO-P
22 BILL (BUGS) WERLE-P (2)
22 MIKE CLARK-P
23 LARRY (IRISH) MIGGINS-OF
24 CLOYD (JUNIOR) BOYER-P
25 JACK CRIMIAN-P
25 DICK BOKELMANN-P
25 VERN BENSON-3B
26 BUZZY WARES-CH
27 AL BRAZLE-P
28 CLIFF (LEFTY) CHAMBERS-P
29 JOHNNY (MUTT) RIDDLE-CH
31 HARRY (THE CAT) BRECHEEN-P
32 JACKIE COLLUM-P
33 VINEGAR BEND MIZELL-P
35 MIKE RYBA-CH
36 GENE (SKIP) MAUCH-SS
36 STU MILLER-P
37 PEANUTS LOWREY-OF
38 HERB GORMAN-PH
39 HAL (HOOT) RICE-OF
40 NEAL HERTWECK-1B
41 FRED HAHN-P
42 HARVEY (THE KITTEN) HADDIX-P
43 EDDIE YUHAS-P
44 WILLARD SCHMIDT-P
44 BOBBY TIEFENAUER-P
46 VERN BENSON-3B
TOM POHOLSKY (MIL)-(P)

1953

3RD (TIE) 83-71 22GB

1 BILLY (THE BULL) JOHNSON-3B
1 PETE CASTIGLIONE-3B (2)
2 RED SCHOENDIENST-2B
3 VIRGIL (RED) STALLCUP-PH
5 STEVE BILKO-1B
6 STAN (THE MAN) (STOSH) MUSIAL-OF
7 SOLLY HEMUS-INF
8 RIP REPULSKI-OF
10 GRANT (SNAP) DUNLAP-OF
10 HARRY ELLIOTT-OF
11 RAY (JABBO) JABLONSKI-3B
12 EDDIE (THE BRAT) (MUGGSY) STANKY-MGR/2B
14 GERRY STALEY-P
15 DICK SISLER-1B
15 FRED (FRITZ) MAROLEWSKI-1B
16 DICK RAND-C
17 LES FUSSELMAN-C
17 SAL YVARS-C (2)
18 DEL RICE-C
19 VERN BENSON-PH
19 DICK (DUCKY) SCHOFIELD-SS
20 EDDIE PHILLIPS-PR
21 JOE (LITTLE JOE) PRESKO-P
22 MIKE CLARK-P
25 DICK BOKELMANN-P
25 EDDIE ERAUTT-P (2)
26 HAL WHITE-P (2)
27 AL BRAZLE-P
28 CLIFF (LEFTY) CHAMBERS-P
29 JOHNNY (MUTT) RIDDLE-CH
30 DIXIE (THE PEOPLE'S CHERCE) WALKER-CH
32 JACKIE COLLUM-P (1)
32 EDDIE ERAUTT-P (2)
32 JOE (LITTLE JOE) PRESKO-P
33 VINEGAR BEND MIZELL-P
35 MIKE RYBA-CH
36 STU MILLER-P
37 PEANUTS LOWREY-UTIL
38 FERRELL ANDERSON-C
39 HAL (HOOT) RICE-OF (1)
39 JOHN ROMONOSKY-P
41 JACK (PREACHER) FASZHOLZ-P
42 HARVEY (THE KITTEN) HADDIX-P
43 EDDIE YUHAS-P
47 WILLARD SCHMIDT-P
TOM POHOLSKY (MIL)-(P)

1954

6TH 72-82 25GB

1 PETE CASTIGLIONE-3B
2 RED SCHOENDIENST-2B
4 ALEX GRAMMAS-INF
5 STEVE BILKO-1B (1)
6 STAN (THE MAN) (STOSH) MUSIAL-OF
7 SOLLY HEMUS-INF
8 RIP REPULSKI-OF
10 TOM ALSTON-1B
10 BEN WADE-P (2)
11 RAY (JABBO) JABLONSKI-3B/1B
12 EDDIE (THE BRAT) (MUGGSY) STANKY-MGR
14 GERRY STALEY-P
15 BILL SARNI-C
17 VIC (SPRINGFIELD RIFLE) RASCHI-P
18 DEL RICE-C
19 DICK (DUCKY) SCHOFIELD-SS
20 WALLY MOON-OF
21 SAL YVARS-C
22 COT DEAL-P
23 TOM POHOLSKY-P
24 JOE (COBRA JOE) FRAZIER-OF/1B
25 ROYCE LINT-P
26 HAL WHITE-P
27 AL BRAZLE-P
28 TOM BURGESS-OF
28 JOE CUNNINGHAM-1B
29 JOHNNY (MUTT) RIDDLE-CH
31 BROOKS (BULL) LAWRENCE-P
31 CARL SCHEIB-P (2)
32 JOE (LITTLE JOE) PRESKO-P
33 BILL (BARNACLE BILL) POSEDEL-CH
34 BILL GREASON-P
35 MIKE RYBA-CH
36 STU MILLER-P
37 PEANUTS LOWREY-OF
39 RALPH BEARD-P
39 MEL WRIGHT-P
40 MEMO LUNA-P
42 HARVEY (THE KITTEN) HADDIX-P
45 GORDON JONES-P

1955

7TH 68-86 30.5GB

1* TONY JACOBS-P*
2 RED SCHOENDIENST-2B
3 DON BLASINGAME-INF
4 ALEX GRAMMAS-SS
5 HARRY (THE HAT) WALKER-OF/MGR2
6 STAN (THE MAN) (STOSH) MUSIAL-1B
7 SOLLY HEMUS-INF
8 RIP REPULSKI-OF
9 BILL VIRDON-OF
10 PETE WHISENANT-OF
10 TOM ALSTON-1B
11 HARRY ELLIOTT-OF
12 EDDIE (THE BRAT) (MUGGSY) STANKY-MGR1
14 KEN BOYER-3B
15 BILL SARNI-C
16 DICK RAND-C
17 VIC (SPRINGFIELD RIFLE) RASCHI-P (1)
17 MEL WRIGHT-P
18 DEL RICE-C (1)
18 NELS BURBRINK-C
19 DICK (DUCKY) SCHOFIELD-SS
20 WALLY MOON-OF/1B
21 BOB STEPHENSON-INF
23 TOM POHOLSKY-P
24 JOE (COBRA JOE) FRAZIER-OF
25 FRANK SMITH-P
27 LOU KAHN-CH
28 JOHN MACKINSON-P
29 JOHNNY (MUTT) RIDDLE-CH
30 DIXIE (THE PEOPLE'S CHERCE) WALKER-CH
31 BROOKS (BULL) LAWRENCE-P
31 AL GETTEL-P
33 BILL (BARNACLE BILL) POSEDEL-CH
34 BOBBY TIEFENAUER-P
35 PAUL LAPALME-P
37 FLOYD WOOLDRIDGE-P
37 BEN FLOWERS-P (2)
38 LUIS (YO-YO) ARROYO-P
39 LARRY JACKSON-P
40 HERB MOFORD-P
41 FLOYD WOOLDRIDGE-P
41 LINDY MCDANIEL-P
42 HARVEY (THE KITTEN) HADDIX-P
43 BARNEY SCHULTZ-P
44 WILLARD SCHMIDT-P
44 GORDON JONES-P

1956

4TH 76-78 17GB

2 RED SCHOENDIENST-2B (1)
2 WHITEY LOCKMAN-OF/1B (2)
3 DON (BLAZER) BLASINGAME-INF
4 ALEX GRAMMAS-SS (1)
6 STAN (THE MAN) (STOSH) MUSIAL-1B
7 SOLLY HEMUS-INF (1)
7 ROCKY NELSON-1B/OF (2)
8 RIP REPULSKI-OF
9 BILL VIRDON-OF (1)
9 BOBBY DEL GRECO-OF (2)
10 HANK SAUER-OF
11 AL (BLACKIE) DARK-SS (2)
14 KEN BOYER-3B
15 BILL SARNI-C (1)
15 RAY KATT-C (2)
16 ELLIS (OLD FOLKS) KINDER-P (1)
17 VINEGAR BEND MIZELL-P
18 HAL (CURA) SMITH-C
19 DICK (DUCKY) SCHOFIELD-SS
20 WALLY MOON-OF/1B
21 JACKIE (FLAKEY) BRANDT-OF (1)
21 DON LIDDLE-P (2)
22 TOM ALSTON-1B
23 TOM POHOLSKY-P
24 JOE (COBRA JOE) FRAZIER-OF (1)
24 BOB BLAYLOCK-P
24 CHUCK HARMON-UTIL (2)
25 MAX SURKONT-P (2)
25 JIM KONSTANTY-P (2)
28 JOE CUNNINGHAM-1B
28 GRADY HATTON-INF (2)
29 FRED HUTCHINSON-MGR
30 WALKER (WALK) COOPER-C
32 JACKIE COLLUM-P
33 BILL (BARNACLE BILL) POSEDEL-CH
34 TERRY MOORE-CH
35 PAUL LAPALME-P (1)
36 STU MILLER-P (1)
36 MURRY DICKSON-P (2)
37 BEN FLOWERS-P (1)
37 HERM WEHMEIER-P (2)
38 CHARLIE (MULE) PEETE-OF
39 LARRY JACKSON-P
40 JOHNNY (HIPPITY) HOPP-CH
41 LINDY MCDANIEL-P
42 HARVEY (THE KITTEN) HADDIX-P (1)
42 BOBBY MORGAN-INF (2)
44 WILLARD SCHMIDT-P
45 GORDON JONES-P
45 DICK LITTLEFIELD-P

1957

2ND 87-67 8GB

3 DON (BLAZER) BLASINGAME-2B
4 EDDIE MIKSIS-OF (1)
6 STAN (THE MAN) (STOSH) MUSIAL-1B
7 DEL ENNIS-OF
8 IRV NOREN-OF (2)
9 JIM KING-OF
10 EDDIE KASKO-INF
11 AL (BLACKIE) DARK-SS/3B
14 KEN BOYER-OF/3B
15 BOBBY GENE SMITH-OF
16 HOBIE LANDRITH-C
17 VINEGAR BEND MIZELL-P
18 HAL (CURA) SMITH-C
19 DICK (DUCKY) SCHOFIELD-SS

20 WALLY MOON-OF
22 TOM ALSTON-1B
23 SAM (TOOTHPICK SAM) JONES-P
24 GENE GREEN-OF
25 HOYT WILHELM-P (1)
25 MORRIE MARTIN-P (2)
26 JIM DAVIS-P (1)
26 BOB MILLER-P
27 CHUCK HARMON-OF (1)
27 FRANK BARNES-P
28 JOE CUNNINGHAM-1B/OF
29 FRED HUTCHINSON-MGR
30 WALKER (WALK) COOPER-C
33 BILL (BARNACLE BILL) POSEDEL-CH
33 AL (BOOTS) HOLLINGSWORTH-CH
34 TERRY MOORE-CH
35 STAN (SMILING STAN) HACK-CH
36 MURRY DICKSON-P
37 HERM WEHMEIER-P
38 BILLY (MUFF) MUFFETT-P
39 LARRY JACKSON-P
40 LYNN LOVENGUTH-P
41 LINDY MCDANIEL-P
42 TOM CHENEY-P
43 LLOYD MERRITT-P
44 WILLARD SCHMIDT-P
45 VON MCDANIEL-P
45 BOB SMITH-P (1)
46 DON LASSETTER-OF
46 BOB KUZAVA-P (2)

1958

5TH (TIE) 72-82 20GB

3 DON (BLAZER) BLASINGAME-2B
6 STAN (THE MAN) (STOSH) MUSIAL-1B
7 DEL ENNIS-OF
8 IRV NOREN-OF
10 EDDIE KASKO-INF
11 AL (BLACKIE) DARK-INF (1)
12 GENE GREEN-OF/C
14 KEN BOYER-3B
15 BOBBY GENE SMITH-OF
16 HOBIE LANDRITH-C
17 VINEGAR BEND MIZELL-P
18 HAL (CURA) SMITH-C
19 DICK (DUCKY) SCHOFIELD-SS (1)
19 RUBEN AMARO-INF
19 JOHNNY O'BRIEN-INF/P (2)
20 WALLY MOON-OF
21 JOE (CASH) TAYLOR-OF (1)
21 RAY KATT-C
21 CURT FLOOD-OF
22 PHIL CLARK-P
22 BILLY (MUFF) MUFFETT-P
22 JOE (CASH) TAYLOR-OF (1)
23 SAM (TOOTHPICK SAM) JONES-P
24 BENNY (PAPELERO) VALENZUELA-3B
24 GENE (AUGIE) FREESE-INF (2)
25 MORRIE MARTIN-P (1)
27 FRANK BARNES-P
27 NELSON CHITTUM-P
28 JOE CUNNINGHAM-1B/OF
29 FRED HUTCHINSON-MGR1
30 BILL SMITH-P
32 BOB MABE-P
32 ELLIS BURTON-OF
33 AL (BOOTS) HOLLINGSWORTH-CH
34 TERRY MOORE-CH
35 STAN (SMILING STAN) HACK-CH/MGR2
36 LEE (SKEETER) TATE-SS
37 HERM WEHMEIER-P (1)
37 JIM (PROFESSOR) BROSNAN-P (2)
38 BILLY (MUFF) MUFFETT-P
38 CHUCK STOBBS-P (2)
39 LARRY JACKSON-P
41 LINDY MCDANIEL-P
42 CURT FLOOD-OF/3B
43 SAL (THE BARBER) MAGLIE-P (2)
44 TOM FLANAGAN-P
44 PHIL (FLIP) PAINE P
45 VON MCDANIEL-P
45 BILL (LEFTY) WIGHT-P (2)
TOM CHENEY-(MIL)-(P)

1959

7TH 71-83 15GB

1 GENE GREEN-OF/C
2 HAL (CURA) SMITH-C
3 HARRY (THE HAT) WALKER-CH
4 HOWIE POLLET-CH
5 JOHNNY KEANE-CH
6 STAN (THE MAN) (STOSH) MUSIAL-1B
7 SOLLY HEMUS-INF/MGR
8 IRV NOREN-OF/1B (1)
9 RAY KATT-C/CH
10 ALEX GRAMMAS-SS
11 DON (BLAZER) BLASINGAME-2B
12 GENE GREEN-OF/C
12 BILL WHITE-OF/1B
14 KEN BOYER-3B
15 JOE CUNNINGHAM-OF/1B
16 RAY (JABBO) JABLONSKI-INF (1)
16 BOB BLAYLOCK-P
18 GEORGE CROWE-1B
19 LEE (SKEETER) TATE-INF
20 JOE (POP) DURHAM-OF
20 DUKE CARMEL-OF
21 CURT FLOOD-OF
22 GINO CIMOLI-OF
24 BOB BLAYLOCK,-P
24 JACK URBAN-P
24 BOB DULIBA-P
24 BOBBY GENE SMITH-OF
25 WALLY SHANNON-INF
25 IRV NOREN-OF/1B (1)
25 CHARLIE (CHICK) KING-OF (2)
25 CHARLIE O'ROURKE, PH
26 BILL WHITE-OF/1B
27 DICK GRAY-UTIL (2)
29 CHUCK ESSEGIAN-OF (1)
29 GENE OLIVER-UTIL
30 MARSHALL (SHERIFF) BRIDGES-P
30 BILL SMITH-P
32 ERNIE BROGLIO-P
33 VINEGAR BEND MIZELL-P
34 ALEX KELLNER-P
36 PHIL CLARK-P
36 HAL JEFFCOAT-P (2)
37 JIM (PROFESSOR) BROSNAN-P (1)
38 TOM CHENEY-P
38 TOM HUGHES-P
39 LARRY JACKSON-P
41 LINDY MCDANIEL-P
42 MARV GRISSOM-P
44 GARY BLAYLOCK-P (1)
44 J.W. PORTER-C/1B (2)
45 DEAN STONE-P
47 DICK RICKETTS-P
49 BOB MILLER-P
51 TIM MCCARVER-C
57 HOWIE NUNN, P
58 BOB (HOOT) (GIBBY) GIBSON-P

1960

3RD 86-68 9GB

1 CARL (SWATS) SAWATSKI-C
2 HAL (CURA) SMITH-C
3 HARRY (THE HAT) WALKER-CH
4 BOB NIEMAN-OF
5 JOHNNY KEANE-CH
6 STAN (THE MAN) (STOSH) MUSIAL-1B
7 SOLLY HEMUS-MGR
8 DARRELL JOHNSON-C/CH
9 RAY KATT-CH
9 TIM MCCARVER-C
10 ALEX GRAMMAS-INF
11 ELLIS BURTON-OF
12 BILL WHITE-1B/OF
14 KEN BOYER-3B
15 JOE CUNNINGHAM-OF/1B
17 ED OLIVARES-2B
18 GEORGE CROWE-1B
19 BOB (SID) SADOWSKI-2B
20 DARYL (BIG DEE) SPENCER-INF
21 CURT FLOOD-OF/2B
22 LEON (DADDY WAGS) WAGNER-OF
22 JOHN GLENN-OF
22 GARY KOLB-OF
23 CAL BROWNING-P
23 CHARLIE JAMES-OF
24 BOB DULIBA-P
24 DON LANDRUM-OF
25 WALLY SHANNON-INF
25 JULIAN (HOOLIE) (PHANTOM) JAVIER-2B
26 HOWIE POLLET-CH
27 DICK GRAY-INF
27 FRANK BARNES-P
27 JULIO GOTAY-INF
28 WALT (MOOSE) MORYN-OF (2)
29 DEL RICE-C (2)
30 MARSHALL (SHERIFF) BRIDGES-P (1)
30 ROCKY BRIDGES 2B (3)
31 BOB (HOOT) (GIBBY) GIBSON-P
31 CURT SIMMONS-P (2)
32 ERNIE BROGLIO-P
33 VINEGAR BEND MIZELL-P (1)
33 ED BAUTA-P
34 CHRIS CANNIZZARO-C
35 BOB MILLER-P
35 MEL NELSON-P
36 FRANK BARNES-P
36 BOB MILLER-P
37 RAY SADECKI-P
38 DOUG CLEMENS-OF
39 LARRY JACKSON-P
41 LINDY MCDANIEL-P
42 WALT (MOOSE) MORYN-OF (2)
43 DUKE CARMEL-OF
44 RON KLINE-P
45 BOB (HOOT) (GIBBY) GIBSON-P
46 BOB GRIM-P (3)

1961

5TH 80-74 13GB

1 CARL (SWATS) SAWATSKI-C/OF
2 RED SCHOENDIENST-2B
3 HARRY (THE HAT) WALKER-CH
4 BOB NIEMAN-OF (1)
4 JIMMIE SCHAFFER-C
5 JOHNNY KEANE-CH/MGR2
6 STAN (THE MAN) (STOSH) MUSIAL-OF
7 SOLLY HEMUS-MGR1
8 DARRELL JOHNSON-CH
8 VERN BENSON-CH
9 HAL (CURA) SMITH-C
10 ALEX GRAMMAS-INF
12 BILL WHITE-1B
14 KEN BOYER-3B
15 JOE CUNNINGHAM-OF/1B
17 JERRY BUCHEK-SS
18 GEORGE CROWE-PH
18 CRAIG ANDERSON-P
19 JULIO GOTAY-SS
20 DARYL (BIG DEE) SPENCER-SS (1)
20 TIM MCCARVER-C
21 CURT FLOOD-OF
23 CHARLIE JAMES-OF
24 DON LANDRUM-OF/2B
24 CARL WARWICK-OF (2)
24 ED OLIVARES-OF
25 JULIAN (HOOLIE) (PHANTOM) JAVIER-2B
26 HOWIE POLLET-CH
27 DON TAUSSIG-OF
28 WALT (MOOSE) MORYN-OF (1)
29 GENE OLIVER-C/OF
31 CURT SIMMONS-P
32 ERNIE BROGLIO-P
33 AL (BOZO) CICOTTE-P
34 CHRIS CANNIZZARO-C
35 BOB (FLEA) LILLIS-INF (2)
36 BOB MILLER-P
37 RAY SADECKI-P
38 MICKEY MCDERMOTT-P (1)
38 ED BAUTA-P
39 LARRY JACKSON-P
40 DOUG CLEMENS-OF
41 LINDY MCDANIEL-P
43 BOBBY TIEFENAUER-P
44 RAY WASHBURN-P
45 BOB (HOOT) (GIBBY) GIBSON-P

1962

6TH 84-78 17.5GB

1 CARL (SWATS) SAWATSKI-C
2 RED SCHOENDIENST-INF/CH
3 HARRY (THE HAT) WALKER-CH
4 JIMMIE SCHAFFER-C
5 JOHNNY KEANE-MGR
6 STAN (THE MAN) (STOSH) MUSIAL-OF
8 VERN BENSON-CH
9 MINNIE MINOSO-OF
10 ALEX GRAMMAS-INF (1)
12 BILL WHITE-1B/OF
14 KEN BOYER-3B
17 FRED WHITFIELD-1B
18 HAL SMITH (ILL)-CH
19 JULIO GOTAY-INF
20 GARY KOLB-OF
21 CURT FLOOD-OF
22 DOUG CLEMENS-OF
22 GARY KOLB-OF
23 CHARLIE JAMES-OF
24 DON LANDRUM-OF (1)
24 BOB BURDA-OF
25 JULIAN (HOOLIE) (PHANTOM) JAVIER-2B
26 HOWIE POLLET-CH
27 CARL WARWICK-OF (1)
27 DAL (MAXIE) MAXVILL-SS
28 MIKE (MOONMAN) SHANNON-OF
29 GENE OLIVER-UTIL
31 CURT SIMMONS-P
32 ERNIE BROGLIO-P
33 BOB DULIBA-P
34 BOB DULIBA-P
34 BOBBY SHANTZ-P (2)
35 JOHN ANDERSON-P (1)
35 BOBBY GENE SMITH-OF (3)
36 BOBBY LOCKE-P (1)
36 DON FERRARESE-P (2)
37 RAY SADECKI-P
38 ED BAUTA-P
39 LARRY JACKSON-P
40 HARVEY BRANCH-P
41 LINDY MCDANIEL-P
42 PAUL TOTH-P (1)
44 RAY WASHBURN-P
45 BOB (HOOT) (GIBBY) GIBSON-P

1963

2ND 93-69 6GB

1 CARL (SWATS) SAWATSKI-C
2 RED SCHOENDIENST-PH/CH
3 JOE (GERMANY) SCHULTZ-CH
4 HOWIE POLLET-CH
5 JOHNNY KEANE-MGR
6 STAN (THE MAN) (STOSH) MUSIAL-OF
8 VERN BENSON-CH
(9) HAL SMITH (ILL)-(CH)
10 JEOFF LONG-PH
11 JERRY BUCHEK-SS
12 BILL WHITE-1B
14 KEN BOYER-3B
15 TIM MCCARVER-C
16 PHIL GAGLIANO-INF
17 JIM BEAUCHAMP-OF
18 LEO BURKE-OF/3B (1)
18 MIKE (MOONMAN) SHANNON-OF
19 JACK DAMASKA-UTIL
19 BUD BLOOMFIELD-3B
20 GARY KOLB-INF/OF
21 CURT FLOOD-OF
22 DOUG CLEMENS-OF
23 CHARLIE JAMES-OF
24 DICK GROAT-SS
25 JULIAN (HOOLIE) (PHANTOM) JAVIER-2B
26 GEORGE ALTMAN-OF
27 DAL (MAXIE) MAXVILL-INF
28 DUKE CARMEL-OF/1B (1)
28 KEN MACKENZIE-P (2)
29 GENE OLIVER-C (1)
29 MOE THACKER-C
29 CORKY WITHROW-OF
30 HARRY (THE FLAME THROWER) FANOK-P
31 CURT SIMMONS-P
32 ERNIE BROGLIO-P
33 LEW BURDETTE-P (2)
34 BOBBY SHANTZ-P
35 SAM (TOOTHPICK SAM) JONES-P
36 BARNEY SCHULTZ-P (2)
37 RAY SADECKI-P
38 ED BAUTA-P (1)
38 DAVE RICKETTS-C
39 RON TAYLOR-P
41 DIOMEDES OLIVO-P
44 RAY WASHBURN-P
45 BOB (HOOT) (GIBBY) GIBSON-P
47 BOB HUMPHREYS-P

1964

1ST 93-69 0GB

W WS-NYA 4-3

2 RED SCHOENDIENST-CH

ST. LOUIS CARDINALS

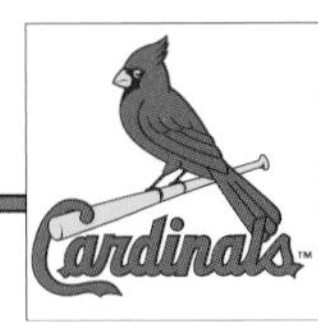

3 JOE (GERMANY) SCHULTZ-CH
4 HOWIE POLLET-CH
5 JOHNNY KEANE-MGR
6 *(RET#) STAN MUSIAL*
8 VERN BENSON-CH
9 BOB (UKE) UECKER-C
0 JEOFF LONG-OF/1B (1)
0 JOE MORGAN-PH
1 JERRY BUCHEK-INF
2 BILL WHITE-1B
4 KEN BOYER-3B
5 TIM MCCARVER-C
6 PHIL GAGLIANO-UTIL
7 CARL WARWICK-PH/OF
8 MIKE (MOONMAN) SHANNON-OF
9 BOB SKINNER-OF (2)
0 LOU BROCK-OF (2)
1 CURT FLOOD-OF
2 DOUG CLEMENS-OF (1)
2 GORDIE RICHARDSON-P
2 JACK SPRING-P (3)
3 CHARLIE JAMES-OF
4 DICK GROAT-SS
5 JULIAN (HOOLIE) (PHANTOM) JAVIER-2B
6 ED SPIEZIO-3B
7 DAL (MAXIE) MAXVILL-UTIL
8 JOHNNY LEWIS-OF
9 DAVE DOWLING-P
0 HARRY (THE FLAME THROWER) FANOK-P
1 CURT SIMMONS-P
2 ERNIE BROGLIO-P (1)
3 LEW BURDETTE-P (1)
3 BARNEY SCHULTZ-P
4 BOBBY SHANTZ-P (1)
5 MIKE CUELLAR-P
6 BARNEY SCHULTZ-P
7 RAY SADECKI-P
9 RON TAYLOR-P
0 GLEN HOBBIE-P (2)
1 ROGER CRAIG-P
1 DAVE BAKENHASTER-P
4 RAY WASHBURN-P
5 BOB (HOOT) (GIBBY) GIBSON-P
7 BOB HUMPHREYS-P

1965

7TH 80-81 16.5GB

2 RED SCHOENDIENST-MGR
3 JOE (DODE) SCHULTZ-CH
4 JOE BECKER,-CH
6 *(RET#) STAN MUSIAL*
7 MICKEY VERNON-CH
8 BOB (BOBO) MILLIKEN-CH
9 BOB (UKE) UECKER-C
10 DAVE RICKETTS-C
11 JERRY BUCHEK-INF
12 BILL WHITE-1B
14 KEN BOYER-3B
15 TIM MCCARVER-C
16 PHIL GAGLIANO- INF
17 CARL WARWICK-OF (1)
17 BOBBY TOLAN-OF
18 MIKE (MOONMAN) SHANNON-OF
19 BOB SKINNER-OF
20 LOU BROCK-OF
21 CURT FLOOD-OF
22 TED SAVAGE-OF
23 TITO FRANCONA-OF/1B
24 DICK GROAT-SS
25 JULIAN (HOOLIE) (PHANTOM) JAVIER-2B
26 ED SPIEZIO-3B
27 DAL (MAXIE) MAXVILL-SS
28 BOB PURKEY-P
29 DON DENNIS-P
30 GEORGE KERNEK-1B
31 CURT SIMMONS-P
32 STEVE (LEFTY) CARLTON-P
33 BARNEY SCHULTZ-P
34 NELSON (NELLIE) BRILES-P
35 DENNIS AUST-P
36 EARL FRANCIS-P
37 RAY SADECKI-P
39 RON TAYLOR-P (1)
39 LARRY JASTER-P
40 TRACY STALLARD-P
44 RAY WASHBURN-P
45 BOB (HOOT) (GIBBY) GIBSON-P
46 HAL WOODESHICK-P (2)

1966

6TH 83-79 12GB

1 CHARLEY SMITH-INF
2 RED SCHOENDIENST-MGR
3 JOE (DODE) SCHULTZ-CH
4 JOE BECKER-CH
5 DICK SISLER-CH
6 *(RET#) STAN MUSIAL*
7 PAT CORRALES-C
8 BOB (BOBO) MILLIKEN-CH
11 JERRY BUCHEK-INF
12 ALEX JOHNSON-OF
14 GEORGE KERNEK-1B
15 TIM MCCARVER-C
16 PHIL GAGLIANO-INF
17 BOBBY TOLAN-OF/1B
18 MIKE (MOONMAN) SHANNON-OF
19 BOB SKINNER-OF
20 LOU BROCK-OF
21 CURT FLOOD-OF
22 TED SAVAGE-OF
23 TITO FRANCONA-1B/OF
24 JIMY WILLIAMS (MIL)-INF
25 JULIAN (HOOLIE) (PHANTOM) JAVIER-2B
26 ED SPIEZIO-3B
27 DAL (MAXIE) MAXVILL-SS
28 ORLANDO (BABY BULL) (CHA CHA) CEPEDA-1B (2)
29 DON DENNIS-P
30 ART MAHAFFEY-P
31 CURT SIMMONS-P (1)
31 DICK HUGHES-P
32 STEVE (LEFTY) CARLTON-P
34 NELSON (NELLIE) BRILES-P
35 DENNIS AUST-P
36 RON WILLIS-P
37 RAY SADECKI-P (1)
37 RON PICHE-P
38 AL (LITTLE AL) JACKSON-P
39 LARRY JASTER-P
40 TRACY STALLARD-P
42 JIM COSMAN-P
43 JOE HOERNER-P
44 RAY WASHBURN-P
45 BOB (HOOT) (GIBBY) GIBSON-P
46 HAL WOODESHICK-P

1967

1ST 101-60 0GB

W WS-BOSA 4-3

1 JOHNNY (HONEY) ROMANO-C
2 RED SCHOENDIENST-MGR
3 JOE (DODE) SCHULTZ-CH
4 BILLY (MUFF) MUFFETT-CH
5 DICK SISLER-CH
6 *(RET#) STAN MUSIAL*
8 BOB (BOBO) MILLIKEN-CH
9 ROGER MARIS-OF
10 DAVE RICKETTS-C
11 EDDIE BRESSOUD-INF
12 ALEX JOHNSON-OF
14 STEVE HUNTZ-2B
15 TIM MCCARVER-C
16 PHIL GAGLIANO-INF
17 BOBBY TOLAN-OF
18 MIKE (MOONMAN) SHANNON-3B
20 LOU BROCK-OF
21 CURT FLOOD-OF
22 TED SAVAGE-PH (1)
23 JACK LAMABE-P (3)
24 JIMY WILLIAMS-SS
25 JULIAN (HOOLIE) (PHANTOM) JAVIER-2B
26 ED SPIEZIO-3B/OF
27 DAL (MAXIE) MAXVILL-SS
28 JACK LAMABE-P (3)
30 ORLANDO (BABY BULL) (CHA CHA) CEPEDA-1B
31 DICK HUGHES-P
32 STEVE (LEFTY) CARLTON-P
34 NELSON (NELLIE) BRILES-P
36 RON WILLIS-P
38 AL (LITTLE AL) JACKSON-P
39 LARRY JASTER-P
42 JIM COSMAN-P
43 JOE HOERNER-P
44 RAY WASHBURN-P
45 BOB (HOOT) (GIBBY) GIBSON-P
46 HAL WOODESHICK-P
47 JACK LAMABE-P (3)
48 MIKE TORREZ-P

1968

1ST 97-65 0GB

L WS-DETA 4-3

2 RED SCHOENDIENST-MGR
3 JOE (DODE) SCHULTZ-CH
4 BILLY (MUFF) MUFFETT-CH
5 DICK SISLER-CH
6 *(RET#) STAN MUSIAL*
7 JOHNNY EDWARDS-C
8 BOB (BOBO) MILLIKEN-CH
9 ROGER MARIS-OF
10 DAVE RICKETTS-C
11 DICK (DUCKY) SCHOFIELD-SS
12 DICK SIMPSON, OF (1)
14 RON DAVIS-OF (2)
14 JOE HAGUE-OF
15 TIM MCCARVER-C
16 PHIL GAGLIANO-INF
17 BOBBY TOLAN-OF/1B
18 MIKE (MOONMAN) SHANNON-3B
20 LOU BROCK-OF
21 CURT FLOOD-OF
23 TED (SIMBA) SIMMONS-C
25 JULIAN (HOOLIE) (PHANTOM) JAVIER-2B
26 ED SPIEZIO-OF/3B
27 DAL (MAXIE) MAXVILL-SS
29 WAYNE GRANGER-P
30 ORLANDO (BABY BULL) (CHA CHA) CEPEDA-1B
31 DICK HUGHES-P
32 STEVE (LEFTY) CARLTON-P
34 NELSON (NELLIE) BRILES-P
35 FLOYD WICKER-OF
36 RON WILLIS-P
39 LARRY JASTER-P
43 JOE HOERNER-P
44 RAY WASHBURN-P
45 BOB (HOOT) (GIBBY) GIBSON-P
46 PETE MIKKELSEN-P (2)
47 HAL (LEFTY) GILSON-P
47 MEL NELSON-P
48 MIKE TORREZ-P

1969

4TH E 87-75 13GB

2 RED SCHOENDIENST-MGR
3 GEORGE KISSELL-CH
4 BILLY (MUFF) MUFFETT-CH
5 DICK SISLER-CH
6 *(RET#) STAN MUSIAL*
7 BILL WHITE-1B
8 BOB (BOBO) MILLIKEN-CH
9 JOE TORRE-1B
10 DAVE RICKETTS-C
11 BOOTS DAY-OF
12 JOE HAGUE-OF
14 STEVE HUNTZ-INF
15 TIM MCCARVER-C
16 PHIL GAGLIANO-INF
17 VIC DAVALILLO-OF/P (2)
18 MIKE (MOONMAN) SHANNON-3B
19 GARY WASLEWSKI-P (1)
19 TOM HILGENDORF-P
20 LOU BROCK-OF
21 CURT FLOOD-OF
22 JIM (MUDCAT) GRANT-P (2)
23 TED (SIMBA) SIMMONS-C
24 JIM HICKS-OF (1)
24 JOE NOSSEK-OF (2)
25 JULIAN (HOOLIE) (PHANTOM) JAVIER-2B
26 JERRY DAVANON-SS (2)
27 DAL (MAXIE) MAXVILL-SS
28 VADA PINSON-OF
29 BYRON BROWNE-OF
29 BOB JOHNSON-INF (1)
30 SAL CAMPISI-P
32 STEVE (LEFTY) CARLTON-P
33 REGGIE CLEVELAND-P
33 JIM ELLIS-P
34 NELSON (NELLIE) BRILES-P
35 DENNIS RIBANT-P (1)
35 MEL NELSON-P
35 CHIP COULTER-2B
36 RON WILLIS-P (1)
37 LERON LEE-OF
38 JERRY DAVANON-SS (2)
39 DAVE GIUSTI-P
42 CHUCK TAYLOR-P
43 JOE HOERNER-P
44 RAY WASHBURN-P
45 BOB (HOOT) (GIBBY) GIBSON-P
46 SANTIAGO GUZMAN-P
47 MEL NELSON-P
48 MIKE TORREZ-P
49 JERRY REUSS-P
50 SANTIAGO GUZMAN-P

1970

4TH E 76-86 13GB

1 JOSE CARDENAL-OF
2 RED SCHOENDIENST-MGR
3 GEORGE KISSELL-CH
4 BILLY (MUFF) MUFFETT-CH
4 ED CROSBY-SS
5 DICK SISLER-CH
6 *(RET#) STAN MUSIAL*
7 VERN BENSON-CH
8 BOB (BOBO) MILLIKEN-CH
9 JOE TORRE-C/3B
10 JIM CAMPBELL-PH
11 COOKIE ROJAS-UTIL (1)
11 JOE NOSSEK-OF
12 JOE HAGUE-OF/1B
14 ED CROSBY-SS
15 DICK ALLEN-1B
16 PHIL GAGLIANO-INF (1)
16 JIM BEAUCHAMP-OF/1B (2)
17 VIC DAVALILLO-OF
18 MIKE (MOONMAN) SHANNON (ILL)-3B
19 TOM HILGENDORF-P
20 LOU BROCK-OF
21 JERRY JOHNSON-P (1)
21 FRANK BERTAINA-P
22 RICH NYE-P (1)
22 REGGIE CLEVELAND-P
22 CHUCK (TWIGGY) HARTENSTEIN-P (2)
22 JERRY DAVANON-INF
23 TED (SIMBA) SIMMONS-C
24 JIM KENNEDY-INF
24 JORGE ROQUE-OF
25 JULIAN (HOOLIE) (PHANTOM) JAVIER-2B
26 LUIS MELENDEZ-OF
26 CHUCK (TWIGGY) HARTENSTEIN-P (2)
27 DAL (MAXIE) MAXVILL-SS
29 BART ZELLER-C/CH
30 SAL CAMPISI-P
31 HARRY PARKER-P
32 STEVE (LEFTY) CARLTON-P
33 REGGIE CLEVELAND-P
34 NELSON (NELLIE) BRILES-P
35 FRANK LINZY-P (2)
36 SANTIAGO GUZMAN-P
36 TED ABERNATHY-P (2)
37 LERON LEE-OF
38 JOSE (CHEO) CRUZ-OF
39 GEORGE CULVER-P (1)
39 AL (THE MAD HUNGARIAN) HRABOSKY-P
40 BOB CHLUPSA-P
40 TED ABERNATHY-P (2)
41 MILT RAMIREZ-INF
42 CHUCK TAYLOR-P
43 BILLYMCCOOL, P
44 CARL TAYLOR-UTIL
45 BOB (HOOT) (GIBBY) GIBSON-P
46 JERRY DAVANON-INF
47 FRED NORMAN-P (2)
48 MIKE TORREZ-P
49 JERRY REUSS-P
50 SANTIAGO GUZMAN-P
50 CHUCK (TWIGGY) HARTENSTEIN-P (2)

1971

2ND E 90-72 7GB

1 JOSE CARDENAL-OF (1)
1 TED KUBIAK-SS/2B (2)
2 RED SCHOENDIENST-MGR
3 GEORGE KISSELL-CH
6 *(RET#) STAN MUSIAL*
7 VERN BENSON-CH
8 VERN BENSON-CH
9 JOE TORRE-3B
10 BOB BURDA-1B/OF
11 DICK (DUCKY) SCHOFIELD-INF (1)
12 JOE HAGUE-1B/OF
14 KEN BOYER-CH
15 JERRY MCNERTNEY-C
16 JIM BEAUCHAMP-1B/OF
17 MATTY ALOU-OF/1B
19 BOB STINSON-C
20 LOU BROCK-OF
21 JORGE ROQUE-OF
21 STAN WILLIAMS-P (2)
22 REGGIE CLEVELAND-P
23 TED (SIMBA) SIMMONS-C
25 JULIAN (HOOLIE) (PHANTOM) JAVIER-2B/3B
26 LUIS MELENDEZ-OF
27 DAL (MAXIE) MAXVILL-SS
28 MOE DRABOWSKI-P
29 TED SIZEMORE-2B/UTIL
31 HARRY PARKER-P
32 STEVE (LEFTY) CARLTON-P
33 BARNEY SCHULTZ-CH

34 GEORGE BRUNETP
34 AL SANTORINI-P (2)
35 FRANK LINZY-P
36 SANTIAGO GUZMAN-P
36 CHRIS ZACHARY-P
37 LERON LEE-OF (1)
37 BOB REYNOLDS-P (1)
37 DENNIS (DENNY) HIGGINS-P
38 JOSE (CHEO) CRUZ-OF
39 AL (THE MAD HUNGARIAN) HRABOSKY-P
40 BOB CHLUPSA-P
41 MILT RAMIREZ-INF
41 TED SIZEMORE-2B/UTIL
42 CHUCK TAYLOR-P
43 RUDY ARROYO-P
44 DON SHAW-P
45 BOB (HOOT) (GIBBY) GIBSON-P
46 MIKE JACKSON-P
47 FRED NORMAN-P (1)
48 MIKE TORREZ-P (1)
48 DARYL PATTERSON-P (3)
49 JERRY REUSS-P
50 LEE THOMAS-CH

1972

4TH E 75-81 21.5GB

1 BERNIE CARBO-OF
2 RED SCHOENDIENST-MGR
3 GEORGE KISSELL-CH
4 ED CROSBY-INF
6 *(RET#) STAN MUSIAL*
8 VERN BENSON-CH
9 JOE TORRE-3B
10 MIKE FIORE-1B (1)
10 MIKE TYSON-2B
11 MARTY MARTINEZ-INF (1)
12 JOE HAGUE-1B (1)
12 BERNIE CARBO-OF (2)
14 KEN BOYER-CH
15 JERRY MCNERTNEY-C
16 DONN CLENDENON-1B
16 RON ALLEN-1B
17 MATTY ALOU-OF (1)
17 BILL VOSS-OF (3)
19 SKIP JUTZE-C
19 DWAIN ANDERSON-INF (2)
20 LOU BROCK-OF
21 BRANT ALYEA-OF (2)
21 JORGE ROQUE-OF
22 REGGIE CLEVELAND-P
23 TED (SIMBA) SIMMONS-C
24 JORGE ROQUE-OF
24 SCIPIO SPINKS-P
25 MICK KELLEHER-INF
25 TONY CLONINGER-P
26 LUIS MELENDEZ-OF
27 DAL (MAXIE) MAXVILL-SS (1)
28 MOE DRABOWSKI-P (1)
28 RICH FOLKERS-P
30 CHARLIE HUDSON-P
31 JOE GRZENDA-P
32 BILL STEIN-3B/OF
33 BARNEY SCHULTZ-CH
34 AL SANTORINI-P
35 DIEGO SEGUI-P (2)
36 SANTIAGO GUZMAN-P
36 JOHN CUMBERLAND-P (2)
37 DENNIS (DENNY) HIGGINS-P
38 JOSE (CHEO) CRUZ-OF
39 AL (THE MAD HUNGARIAN) HRABOSKY-P
40 RICK WISE-P
41 TED SIZEMORE-2B
42 RAY BARE-P
44 DON SHAW-P (1)
44 LOWELL PALMER-P (1)
45 BOB (HOOT) (GIBBY) GIBSON-P
46 DON DURHAM-P
47 KEN REITZ-3B
47 LANCE CLEMONS-P
48 JIM BIBBY-P
50 DON DURHAM-P
50 LEE THOMAS-CH
◊**56** TIM PLODINEC-P

1973

2ND E 81-81 1.5GB

1 BERNIE CARBO-OF
2 RED SCHOENDIENST-MGR
3 GEORGE KISSELL-CH
4 ED CROSBY-INF (1)
4 MATTY ALOU-OF (2)
5 RAY BUSSE-SS (1)
5 TOM HEINTZELMAN-2B
6 *(RET#) STAN MUSIAL*
7 LARRY HANEY-C (2)
8 VERN BENSON-CH
9 JOE TORRE-1B/3B
10 MIKE TYSON-2B
10 DAVE CAMPBELL-2B (2)
11 HECTOR (HEITY) CRUZ-OF
12 LARRY HANEY-C (2)
14 TERRY HUGHES-3B
15 TIM MCCARVER-1B/C
16 MARC HILL-C
17 CIRILIO (TOMMY) CRUZ-OF
18 BOB FENWICK-INF
18 DAVE CAMPBELL-2B (2)
19 DWAIN ANDERSON-INF (1)
19 JIM DWYER-OF
20 LOU BROCK-OF
21 BAKE MCBRIDE-OF
22 REGGIE CLEVELAND-P
23 TED (SIMBA) SIMMONS-C
24 SCIPIO SPINKS-P
25 MICK KELLEHER-INF
25 JIM DWYER-OF
26 LUIS MELENDEZ-OF
27 ALAN FOSTER-P
28 RICH FOLKERS-P
29 WAYNE GRANGER-P (1)
29 LEW KRAUSSE-P
30 JOHNNY LEWIS-CH
31 JOHN ANDREWS-P
32 BILL STEIN-OF
33 BARNEY SCHULTZ-CH
34 AL SANTORINI-P
34 TOM MURPHY-P
34 ORLANDO PENA-P (2)
35 DIEGO SEGUI-P
36 ORLANDO PENA-P (2)
36 TOM MURPHY-P
37 JOHN ANDREWS-P
38 JOSE (CHEO) CRUZ-OF
39 AL (THE MAD HUNGARIAN) HRABOSKY-P
40 RICK WISE-P
41 TED SIZEMORE-2B
44 KEN REITZ-3B
45 BOB (HOOT) (GIBBY) GIBSON-P
46 MIKE THOMPSON-P
47 TOMMIE AGEE-OF (2)
48 JIM BIBBY-P (1)
48 EDDIE FISHER-P (2)
48 ED SPRAGUE-P (2)
49 MIKE NAGY-P
50 TONY AUFERIO-CH
51 EDDIE FISHER-P (2)

1974

2ND E 86-75 1.5GB

1 LUIS (FRITO BANDITO) (PIMBA) ALVARADO-SS
2 RED SCHOENDIENST-MGR
3 GEORGE KISSELL-CH
5 TOM HEINTZELMAN-2B
6 *(RET#) STAN MUSIAL*
7 REGGIE SMITH-OF
8 VERN BENSON-CH
9 JOE TORRE-1B/3B
10 MIKE TYSON-2B
11 JACK HEIDEMANN-SS (2)
12 RICH BILLINGS-C (2)
14 DAVE RICKETTS-CH
15 TIM MCCARVER-C/1B (1)
15 BARRY LERSCH-P
16 MARC HILL-C
17 *(RET#) DIZZY DEAN*
18 KEITH (MEX) HERNANDEZ-1B
19 RICHIE SCHEINBLUM-OF (3)
20 LOU BROCK-OF
21 BAKE MCBRIDE-OF
22 JOHN CURTIS-P
23 TED (SIMBA) SIMMONS-C
24 DANNY GODBY-OF
24 JIM HICKMAN-1B
25 JIM DWYER-OF
26 LUIS MELENDEZ-OF
27 ALAN FOSTER-P
28 RICH FOLKERS-P
29 JERRY DAVANON-INF
29 STAN PAPI-INF
29 BOB HEISE-2B (1)
29 JERRY MUMPHREY-OF
30 JOHNNY LEWIS-CH
31 BOB FORSCH-P
32 RON HUNT-INF (2)
33 BARNEY SCHULTZ-CH
34 PETE RICHERT-P (1)
34 CLAUDE OSTEEN-P (2)
36 ORLANDO PENA-P (1)
36 JOHN DENNY-P
37 BOB FORSCH-P
38 JOSE (CHEO) CRUZ-OF
39 AL (THE MAD HUNGARIAN) HRABOSKY-P
40 SONNY SIEBERT-P
40 RAY BARE-P
41 TED SIZEMORE-2B
42 JOHN DENNY-P
42 SONNY SIEBERT-P
43 MIKE GARMAN-P
44 KEN REITZ-3B
45 BOB (HOOT) (GIBBY) GIBSON-P
46 MIKE THOMPSON-P (1)
46 LARRY HERNDON-OF
47 LYNN MCGLOTHEN-P
48 JERRY MUMPHREY-OF
49 LARRY HERNDON-OF
50 CLAUDE OSTEEN-P (2)

1975

3RD E (TIE) 82-80 10.5GB

2 RED SCHOENDIENST-MGR
3 GEORGE KISSELL-CH
5 EDDIE BRINKMAN-SS (1)
5 WILLIE DAVIS-OF (2)
6 *(RET#) STAN MUSIAL*
7 REGGIE SMITH-OF/1B
8 VERN BENSON-CH
9 KEN RUDOLPH-C
10 MIKE TYSON-2B
11 HECTOR (HEITY) CRUZ-OF
12 RICH BILLINGS-C
12 BUDDY BRADFORD-OF (2)
14 DAVE RICKETTS-CH
15 RON FAIRLY-1B/OF
16 RICH BILLINGS-C
17 *(RET#) DIZZY DEAN*
18 KEITH (MEX) HERNANDEZ-1B
19 TEDDY MARTINEZ-INF (1)
19 MARIO GUERRERO-SS
20 LOU BROCK-OF
21 BAKE MCBRIDE-OF
22 JOHN CURTIS-P
23 TED (SIMBA) SIMMONS-C
24 KEN REYNOLDS-P
24 DANNY CATER-1B
24 MIKE BARLOW-P
25 JIM DWYER-OF (1)
25 LARRY LINTZ-2B (2)
26 LUIS MELENDEZ-OF
27 TOMMY MOORE-P (1)
27 MIKE BARLOW-P
28 MICK KELLEHER-INF
29 JERRY MUMPHREY-OF
29 DON HAHN-OF (2)
30 JOHNNY LEWIS-CH
31 BOB FORSCH-P
32 RON BRYANT-P (2)
32 MIKE WALLACE-P (2)
33 BARNEY SCHULTZ-CH
34 HARRY PARKER-P (2)
35 GREG TERLECKY-P
36 JOHN DENNY-P
37 RAY SADECKI-P (1)
37 DOUG HOWARD-1B
38 ELIAS SOSA-P (1)
38 RON REED-P (2)
39 AL (THE MAD HUNGARIAN) HRABOSKY-P
40 RYAN KUROSAKI-P
41 TED SIZEMORE-2B
42 HARRY (ERIC) RASMUSSEN-P
42 RON REED-P (2)
43 MIKE GARMAN-P
44 KEN REITZ-3B
45 BOB (HOOT) (GIBBY) GIBSON-P
47 LYNN MCGLOTHEN-P

1976

5TH E 72-90 29GB

2 RED SCHOENDIENST-MGR
3 LEE RICHARD-INF
4 VIC HARRIS-2B/OF
5 WILLIE CRAWFORD-OF
6 *(RET#) STAN MUSIAL*
7 REGGIE SMITH-UTIL (1)
7 SAM MEJIAS-OF
8 FRED KOENIG-CH
9 KEN RUDOLPH-C
10 MIKE TYSON-2B
11 DON KESSINGER-SS
12 JOHN TAMARGO-C
13 JOE FERGUSON-C (2)
14 LUIS ALVARADO-2B
15 RON FAIRLY-1B/OF (1)
16 DOUG CLAREY-2B
17 *(RET#) DIZZY DEAN*
18 PRESTON GOMEZ-CH
19 GARRY TEMPLETON-SS
20 LOU BROCK-OF
21 BAKE MCBRIDE-OF
22 JOHN CURTIS-P
23 TED (SIMBA) SIMMONS-C
24 EDDIE (BUDDY) SOLOMON-P
25 HECTOR (HEITY) CRUZ-3B
26 LUIS MELENDEZ-OF (1)
26 DOUG CAPILLA-P
27 MIKE ANDERSON-OF
28 CHARLIE CHANT-OF
29 JERRY MUMPHREY-OF
30 JOHNNY LEWIS-CH
31 BOB FORSCH-P
32 MIKE WALLACE-P
33 BOB (BOBO) MILLIKEN-CH
34 DANNY (BEAR) FRISELLA-P (1)
34 TOM WALKER-P
34 EDDIE (BUDDY) SOLOMON-P
36 JOHN DENNY-P
37 KEITH (MEX) HERNANDEZ-1B
38 BILL GREIF-P (2)
39 AL (THE MAD HUNGARIAN HRABOSKY-P
40 MIKE POTTER-OF
41 PETE FALCONE-P
42 HARRY (ERIC) RASMUSSEN-P
44 LERRIN LAGROW-P
45 *(RET#) BOB GIBSON*
46 MIKE PROLY-P
47 LYNN MCGLOTHEN-P
48 STEVE WATERBURY-P
48 EDDIE (BUDDY) SOLOMON-P
48 BILL GREIF-P (2)
49 EDDIE (BUDDY) SOLOMON-P
50 TOM ZIMMER-CH

1977

3RD E 83-79 18GB

1 GARRY TEMPLETON-SS
2 *(RET#) RED SCHOENDIENST*
3 SONNY RUBERTO-CH
4 MO MOZZALI-CH
5 MIKE PHILLIPS-INF (2)
6 *(RET#) STAN MUSIAL*
7 ROGER FREED,1B/OF
8 JACK KROL-CH
9 VERN RAPP-MGR
10 MIKE TYSON-2B
11 DON KESSINGER-SS (1)
11 JIM DWYER-OF
12 JOHN TAMARGO-C
14 DAVE RADER-C
15 BENNY AYALA-OF
16 JERRY DAVANON-2B
16 TAYLOR DUNCAN-3B
17 *(RET#) DIZZY DEAN*
18 CLAUDE OSTEEN-CH
19 JOEL YOUNGBLOOD-OF/3B (1)
19 DANE IORG-OF (2)
20 LOU BROCK-OF
21 BAKE MCBRIDE-OF (1)
21 RICK BOSETTI-OF
22 BUDDY SCHULTZ-P
23 TED (SIMBA) SIMMONS-C
24 KEN (OBIE) OBERKFELL-2B
25 HECTOR (HEITY) CRUZ-OF
26 DOUG CAPILLA-P (1)
26 RAWLY EASTWICK-P (2)
27 MIKE ANDERSON-OF
29 JERRY MUMPHREY-OF
30 TONY SCOTT-OF
31 BOB FORSCH-P
33 KEN REITZ-3B
33 CLAY (HAWK) CARROLL-P (1)
34 JOHN (D) D'ACQUISTO-P (1
34 BUTCH METZGER-P (2)
35 IKE (JOHNNY) SUTTON-P
36 JOHN DENNY-P
37 KEITH (MEX) HERNANDEZ-1B
38 JOHN URREA-P
39 AL (THE MAD HUNGARIAN) HRABOSKY-P
40 MIKE POTTER-OF
40 TOM UNDERWOOD-P (2)
41 PETE FALCONE-P
42 ERIC RASMUSSEN-P
43 JOHN (D) D'ACQUISTO-P (1
43 MIKE POTTER-OF
44 KEN REITZ-3B
45 *(RET#) BOB GIBSON*
49 LARRY DIERKER-P

ST. LOUIS CARDINALS

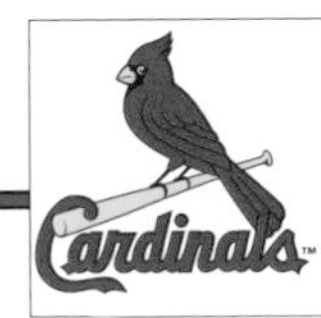

1978

5TH E 69-93 21GB

1 GARRY TEMPLETON-SS
2 *(RET#) RED SCHOENDIENST*
2 STEVE SWISHER-C
3 SONNY RUBERTO-CH
4 MO MOZZALI-CH
5 MIKE PHILLIPS-INF
6 *(RET#) STAN MUSIAL*
7 ROGER FREED-1B/OF
8 JACK KROL-CH/MGR
9 VERN RAPP-MGR1
10 MIKE TYSON-2B
11 JIM DWYER-OF (1)
11 WAYNE GARRETT-3B (2)
12 JOHN TAMARGO-C (1)
14 DAVE RICKETTS-CH
14 KEN BOYER-MGR2
15 DAVE RICKETTS-CH
16 TERRY KENNEDY-C
17 *(RET#) DIZZY DEAN*
18 CLAUDE OSTEEN-CH
19 DANE IORG-OF
20 LOU BROCK-OF
21 JIM LENTINE-OF
21 GARY SUTHERLAND-2B
21 BOB COLUCCIO-OF
22 BUDDY SCHULTZ-P
23 TED (SIMBA) SIMMONS-C
24 KEN (OBIE) OBERKFELL-2B
25 JERRY MORALES-OF
25 GEORGE HENDRICK-OF (2)
26 DAVE HAMILTON-P (1)
26 ROB DRESSLER-P
27 GEORGE HENDRICK-OF (2)
29 JERRY MUMPHREY-OF
30 TONY SCOTT-OF
31 BOB FORSCH-P
32 MARK LITTELL-P
34 DAN O'BRIEN-P
35 SILVIO MARTINEZ-P
36 JOHN DENNY-P
37 KEITH (MEX) HERNANDEZ-1B
38 JOHN URREA-P
39 AURELIO LOPEZ-P
41 PETE FALCONE-P
42 ERIC RASMUSSEN-P (1)
42 ROY THOMAS-P
43 GEORGE FRAZIER-P
44 KEN REITZ-3B
45 *(RET#) BOB GIBSON*
46 PETE VUCKOVICH-P
49 TOM BRUNO-P
50 MIKE RAMSEY-SS

1979

3RD E 86-76 12GB

1 GARRY TEMPLETON-SS
2 RED SCHOENDIENST-CH
3 TOM GRIEVE-OF
3 KEITH SMITH-OF
4 MIKE TYSON-2B
5 MIKE PHILLIPS-INF
6 *(RET#) STAN MUSIAL*
7 ROGER FREED-1B/OF
8 JACK KROL-CH
9 STEVE SWISHER-C
11 BERNIE CARBO-OF
14 KEN BOYER-MGR
15 DAVE RICKETTS-CH
16 TERRY KENNEDY-C
17 *(RET#) DIZZY DEAN*
18 CLAUDE OSTEEN-CH
19 DANE IORG-OF
20 LOU BROCK-OF
21 JIM LENTINE-OF
21 MIKE DIMMEL-OF
22 BUDDY SCHULTZ-P
23 TED (SIMBA) SIMMONS-C
24 KEN (OBIE) OBERKFELL-2B
25 GEORGE HENDRICK-OF
26 DAN O'BRIEN-P
27 DAL (MAXIE) MAXVILL-CH
28 TOM HERR-2B
29 JERRY MUMPHREY-OF
30 TONY SCOTT-OF
31 BOB FORSCH-P
32 MARK LITTELL-P
34 DAN O'BRIEN-P
34 DAROLD KNOWLES-P
35 SILVIO MARTINEZ-P
36 JOHN DENNY-P
37 KEITH (MEX) HERNANDEZ-1B
38 JOHN URREA-P
39 GEORGE FRAZIER-P
41 JOHN FULGHAM-P
42 BOB SYKES-P
43 GEORGE FRAZIER-P
43 ROY THOMAS-P
44 KEN REITZ-3B
45 *(RET#) BOB GIBSON*
46 PETE VUCKOVICH-P
47 WILL MCENANEY-P
48 KIM SEAMAN-P
49 TOM BRUNO-P
51 DAROLD KNOWLES-P

1980

4TH E 74-88 17GB

00 BOBBY BONDS-OF
1 GARRY TEMPLETON-SS
2 RED SCHOENDIENST-CH/MGR
3 KEITH SMITH-OF
3 WHITEY (THE WHITE RAT) HERZOG-MGR
4 JOE DESA-1B/OF
4 MIKE (SUPER SUB) RAMSEY-INF
5 MIKE PHILLIPS-INF
6 *(RET#) STAN MUSIAL*
8 JACK KROL-CH/MGR
9 STEVE SWISHER-C
10 LEON (BULL) DURHAM-OF
11 BERNIE CARBO-OF (1)
11 KEITH SMITH-OF
14 KEN BOYER-MGR
15 DAVE RICKETTS-CH
16 TERRY KENNEDY-C
17 *(RET#) DIZZY DEAN*
18 CLAUDE OSTEEN-CH
19 DANE IORG-OF
20 *(RET#) LOU BROCK*
21 JIM LENTINE-OF (1)
21 TERRY (TITO) LANDRUM-OF
22 BUDDY SCHULTZ-P
23 TED (SIMBA) SIMMONS-C
24 KEN (OBIE) OBERKFELL-2B
25 GEORGE HENDRICK-OF
26 BOBBY BONDS-OF
26 DON HOOD-P
27 DAL (MAXIE) MAXVILL-CH
28 TOM HERR-2B
30 TONY SCOTT-OF
31 BOB FORSCH-P
32 MARK LITTELL-P
33 DONNIE MOORE-P
34 DAROLD KNOWLES-P
34 JIM OTTEN-P
34 PEDRO BORBON-P
35 SILVIO MARTINEZ-P
36 JIM (KITTY) KAAT-P (2)
37 KEITH (MEX) HERNANDEZ-1B
38 JOHN URREA-P
39 GEORGE FRAZIER-P
40 TY WALLER-3B
40 JIM OTTEN-P
40 JOHN MARTIN-P
40 PETE VUCKOVICH-P
41 JOHN FULGHAM-P
42 BOB SYKES-P
43 ROY THOMAS-P
43 JEFF LITTLE-P
44 KEN REITZ-3B
45 *(RET#) BOB GIBSON*
46 PETE VUCKOVICH-P
46 ANDY RINCON-P
47 AL OLMSTED-P
48 KIM SEAMAN-P
48 JOHN LITTLEFIELD-P
49 PEDRO BORBON-P
50 JOHN LITTLEFIELD-P
50 KIM SEAMAN-P

1981

1ST 1/2:2ND E 30-20 1.5GB
2ND 1/2:2ND E 29-23 4.5GB
FINAL: 59-43 --GB

1 GARRY TEMPLETON-SS
2 RED SCHOENDIENST-CH
3 DAVE RICKETTS-CH
4 CHUCK HILLER-CH
5 MIKE (SUPER SUB) RAMSEY-INF
6 *(RET#) STAN MUSIAL*
8 HAL LANIER-CH
9 HUB KITTLE-CH
10 KEN (OBIE) OBERKFELL-3B
11 GLENN BRUMMER-C
14 JULIO GONZALEZ-2B
15 DARRELL PORTER-C
16 SIXTO LEZCANO-OF
17 *(RET#) DIZZY DEAN*
18 GENE TENACE-C
19 DANE IORG-OF
20 *(RET#) LOU BROCK*
21 TERRY (TITO) LANDRUM-OF
22 DAVID GREEN-OF
23 ORLANDO SANCHEZ-C
24 KEN (OBIE) OBERKFELL-3B
24 WHITEY (THE WHITE RAT) HERZOG-MGR
25 GEORGE HENDRICK-OF
26 STEVE BRAUN-OF
27 WHITEY (THE WHITE RAT) HERZOG-MGR
28 TOM HERR-2B
29 GENE ROOF-OF
30 TONY SCOTT-OF (1)
30 JOAQUIN ANDUJAR-P (2)
31 BOB FORSCH-P
32 BOB SHIRLEY-P
33 JOHN MARTIN-P
34 MARK LITTELL-P
35 SILVIO MARTINEZ-P
36 JIM (KITTY) KAAT-P
37 KEITH (MEX) HERNANDEZ-1B
38 JOHN URREA-P
39 LARY SORENSEN-P
40 JIM OTTEN-P
40 DOUG BAIR-P (2)
41 JOHN FULGHAM (INJ)-P
42 BRUCE SUTTER-P
43 DOUG BAIR-P (2)
44 JOE EDELEN-P (1)
45 *(RET#) BOB GIBSON*
46 ANDY RINCON-P
47 DAVE LAPOINT-P
47 JOAQUIN ANDUJAR-P (2)
49 LUIS DELEON-P
50 NEIL FIALA-PH (1)
50 JULIO GONZALEZ-2B

1982

1ST E 92-70 0GB
W NLCS-ATLN 3-0
W WS-MILA 4-3

1 OZZIE (THE WIZARD) SMITH-SS
2 RED SCHOENDIENST-CH
3 DAVE RICKETTS-CH
4 CHUCK HILLER-CH
5 MIKE (SUPER SUB) RAMSEY-INF
6 *(RET#) STAN MUSIAL*
8 HAL LANIER-CH
9 HUB KITTLE-CH
10 KEN (OBIE) OBERKFELL-3B
11 GLENN BRUMMER-C
14 JULIO GONZALEZ-3B
15 DARRELL PORTER-C
17 *(RET#) DIZZY DEAN*
18 GENE TENACE-C
19 DANE IORG-OF
20 *(RET#) LOU BROCK*
21 TERRY (TITO) LANDRUM-OF
22 DAVID GREEN-OF
23 ORLANDO SANCHEZ-C
24 WHITEY (THE WHITE RAT) HERZOG-MGR
25 GEORGE HENDRICK-OF
26 STEVE BRAUN-OF
27 LONNIE SMITH-OF
28 TOM HERR-2B
29 GENE ROOF-OF
31 BOB FORSCH-P
32 JEFF LAHTI-P
33 JOHN MARTIN-P
34 MARK LITTELL-P
34 ERIC RASMUSSEN-P
35 KELLY PARIS-INF
36 JIM (KITTY) KAAT-P
37 KEITH (MEX) HERNANDEZ-1B
38 STEVE MURA-P
39 DAVE LAPOINT-P
40 DOUG BAIR-P
42 BRUCE SUTTER-P
44 JEFF KEENER-P
45 *(RET#) BOB GIBSON*
46 ANDY RINCON-P
47 JOAQUIN ANDUJAR-P
48 JOHN STUPER-P
50 JEFF LAHTI-P
51 WILLIE MCGEE-OF

1983

4TH E 79-83 11GB

1 OZZIE (THE WIZARD) SMITH-SS
2 RED SCHOENDIENST-CH
3 DAVE RICKETTS-CH
4 CHUCK HILLER-CH
5 MIKE (SUPER SUB) RAMSEY-INF
6 *(RET#) STAN MUSIAL*
7 JEFF DOYLE-2B
8 HAL LANIER-CH
9 HUB KITTLE-CH
10 KEN (OBIE) OBERKFELL-3B
11 GLENN BRUMMER-C
12 FLOYD RAYFORD-3B
13 NEIL ALLEN-P (2)
14 RAFAEL SANTANA-INF
14 JIM ADDUCI-1B
15 DARRELL PORTER-C
16 JAMIE QUIRK-C
17 *(RET#) DIZZY DEAN*
18 ANDY (SLICK) VAN SLYKE-OF
19 DANE IORG-OF
20 *(RET#) LOU BROCK*
21 TERRY (TITO) LANDRUM-OF (1)
21 JIMMY SEXTON-SS
22 DAVID GREEN-OF
23 ORLANDO SANCHEZ-C
23 DAROLD KNOWLES-CH
24 WHITEY (THE WHITE RAT) HERZOG-MGR
25 GEORGE HENDRICK-OF
26 STEVE BRAUN-OF
27 LONNIE SMITH-OF
28 TOM HERR-2B
29 GENE ROOF-OF (1)
30 BILLY LYONS-INF
31 BOB FORSCH-P
32 JEFF LAHTI-P
33 JOHN MARTIN-P (1)
34 ERIC RASMUSSEN-P (1)
34 DANNY COX-P
35 KEVIN HAGEN-P
35 DAVE RUCKER-P (2)
36 JIM (KITTY) KAAT-P
36 DAVE RUCKER-P (2)
37 KEITH (MEX) HERNANDEZ-1B (1)
38 DAVE VON OHLEN-P
39 DAVE LAPOINT-P
40 DOUG BAIR-P (1)
41 STEVE BAKER-P (2)
42 BRUCE SUTTER-P
43 RALPH CITARELLA-P
44 JEFF KEENER-P
45 *(RET#) BOB GIBSON*
47 JOAQUIN ANDUJAR-P
48 JOHN STUPER-P
51 WILLIE MCGEE-OF

1984

6TH E 75-87 21.5GB

1 OZZIE (THE WIZARD) SMITH-SS
2 RED SCHOENDIENST-CH
3 DAVE RICKETTS-CH
4 MIKE ROARKE-CH
5 MIKE (SUPER SUB) RAMSEY-INF (1)
5 JOSE (URIBE) GONZALEZ-INF
5 CHRIS SPEIER-SS (2)
6 *(RET#) STAN MUSIAL*
7 ART HOWE-INF
7 JOSE (URIBE) GONZALEZ-INF
8 HAL LANIER-CH
9 JAMIE QUIRK-CH (1)
9 TERRY PENDLETON-3B
10 KEN (OBIE) OBERKFELL-3B (1)
11 GLENN BRUMMER-C
13 NEIL ALLEN-P
14 *(RET#) KEN BOYER*
15 DARRELL PORTER-C
16 NICK LEYVA-CH
17 *(RET#) DIZZY DEAN*
18 ANDY (SLICK) VAN SLYKE-OF
19 DANE IORG-OF (1)
19 MIKE JORGENSEN-1B (2)
20 *(RET#) LOU BROCK*
21 TERRY (TITO) LANDRUM-OF
22 DAVID GREEN-OF
23 TOM NIETO-C
24 WHITEY (THE WHITE RAT) HERZOG-MGR
25 GEORGE HENDRICK-OF
26 STEVE BRAUN-OF
27 LONNIE SMITH-OF
28 TOM HERR-2B
30 BILLY LYONS-INF
31 BOB FORSCH-P
32 JEFF LAHTI-P
33 GARY RAJSICH-1B
34 DANNY COX-P
35 KEVIN HAGEN-P
35 DAVE RUCKER-P
37 PAUL HOUSEHOLDER-OF (2)
38 DAVE VON OHLEN-P
39 DAVE LAPOINT-P

40 RICK OWNBEY-P
42 BRUCE SUTTER-P
43 RALPH CITARELLA-P
44 ANDY HASSLER-P
45 *(RET#) BOB GIBSON*
46 KEN DAYLEY-P (2)
47 JOAQUIN ANDUJAR-P
48 JOHN STUPER-P
48 JOHNNY LEWIS-CH
49 RICKY HORTON-P
50 KURT KEPSHIRE-P
51 WILLIE MCGEE-OF
55 MARK SALAS-OF/C
85 *(RET#) AUGIE BUSCH, SR.*

1985

1ST E 101-61 0GB
W NLCS-LAN 4-2
L WS-KCA 4-3

1 OZZIE (THE WIZARD) SMITH-SS
2 RED SCHOENDIENST-CH
3 DAVE RICKETTS-CH
4 MIKE ROARKE-CH
6 *(RET#) STAN MUSIAL*
7 ART HOWE-INF
7 CESAR CEDENO-1B (2)
8 HAL LANIER-CH
9 TERRY PENDLETON-3B
10 RANDY HUNT-C
10 MIKE (SPANKY) LAVALLIERE-C
11 IVAN DEJESUS-INF
12 CURT FORD-OF
12 TOM LAWLESS-INF
13 NEIL ALLEN-P (1)
14 *(RET#) KEN BOYER*
15 DARRELL PORTER-C
16 NICK LEYVA-CH
17 *(RET#) DIZZY DEAN*
18 ANDY (SLICK) VAN SLYKE-OF
19 MIKE JORGENSEN-1B
20 *(RET#) LOU BROCK*
21 TERRY (TITO) LANDRUM-OF
22 JACK CLARK-1B
23 TOM NIETO-C
24 WHITEY (THE WHITE RAT) HERZOG-MGR
25 BRIAN HARPER-UTIL
26 STEVE BRAUN-OF
27 LONNIE SMITH-OF (1)
27 CURT FORD-OF
28 TOM HERR-2B
29 VINCE (VINCENT VAN GO) COLEMAN-OF
30 JOHN TUDOR-P
31 BOB FORSCH-P
32 JEFF LAHTI-P
33 MATT KEOUGH-P
34 DANNY COX-P
36 JOE BOEVER-P
37 PAT PERRY-P
38 JOE BOEVER-P
38 TODD WORRELL-P
39 BILL CAMPBELL-P
40 DOUG BAIR-P (2)
41 ANDY HASSLER-P
44 ANDY HASSLER-P
45 *(RET#) BOB GIBSON*
46 KEN DAYLEY-P
47 JOAQUIN ANDUJAR-P
48 JOHN TUDOR-P
48 JOHNNY LEWIS-CH
49 RICKY HORTON-P
50 KURT KEPSHIRE-P
51 WILLIE MCGEE-OF
85 *(RET#) AUGIE BUSCH, SR.*

1986

3RD E 79-82 28.5GB

1 OZZIE (THE WIZARD) SMITH-SS
2 RED SCHOENDIENST-CH
3 DAVE RICKETTS-CH
4 MIKE ROARKE-CH
5 MIKE HEATH-C (1)
5 JOSE OQUENDO-INF
5 FREDDIE MANRIQUE-INF
6 *(RET#) STAN MUSIAL*
7 RICH HACKER-CH
8 JOHNNY LEWIS-CH
9 TERRY PENDLETON-3B
10 MIKE (SPANKY) LAVALLIERE-C
11 MIKE (SPANKY) LAVALLIERE-C
11 JOSE OQUENDO-INF
12 TOM LAWLESS-INF
13 CLINT HURDLE-UTIL
14 *(RET#) KEN BOYER*
15 JIM LINDEMAN-OF
16 NICK LEYVA-CH
17 *(RET#) DIZZY DEAN*
18 ANDY (SLICK) VAN SLYKE-OF
20 *(RET#) LOU BROCK*
21 TERRY (TITO) LANDRUM-OF
22 JACK CLARK-1B
23 TOM NIETO-C
23 ALAN KNICELEY-1B
24 WHITEY (THE WHITE RAT) HERZOG-MGR
25 STEVE LAKE-C (2)
25 JERRY WHITE-OF
27 CURT FORD-OF
28 TOM HERR-2B
29 VINCE (VINCENT VAN GO) COLEMAN-OF
30 JOHN TUDOR-P
31 BOB FORSCH-P
32 JEFF LAHTI (INJ)-P
33 JOHN MORRIS-OF
34 DANNY COX-P
35 MIKE LAGA-1B (2)
35 RAY BURRIS-P
36 JOE BOEVER-P
37 PAT PERRY-P
38 TODD WORRELL-P
39 TIM CONROY-P
40 RICK OWNBEY-P
41 BILL EARLEY-P
43 GREG BARGAR-P
45 *(RET#) BOB GIBSON*
46 KEN DAYLEY-P
47 RAY SOFF-P
49 RICKY HORTON-P
50 KURT KEPSHIRE-P
51 WILLIE MCGEE-OF
53 GREG MATHEWS-P
85 *(RET#) AUGIE BUSCH, SR.*

1987

1ST E 95-67 0GB
W NLCS-SFN 4-3
L WS-MINA 4-3

1 OZZIE (THE WIZARD) SMITH-SS
2 RED SCHOENDIENST-CH
3 DAVE RICKETTS-CH
4 MIKE ROARKE-CH
5 ROD BOOKER-INF
6 *(RET#) STAN MUSIAL*
7 RICH HACKER-CH
8 JOHNNY LEWIS-CH
9 TERRY PENDLETON-3B
10 ROD BOOKER-INF
10 DOUG DECINCES-3B (2)
11 JOSE OQUENDO-UTIL
12 TOM LAWLESS-INF
14 *(RET#) KEN BOYER*
15 JIM LINDEMAN-OF
16 NICK LEYVA-CH
17 *(RET#) DIZZY DEAN*
18 DAVID GREEN-OF
19 TOM PAGNOZZI-C
20 *(RET#) LOU BROCK*
21 TERRY (TITO) LANDRUM-OF (1)
21 LANCE JOHNSON-OF
22 JACK CLARK-1B
23 DAN DRIESSEN-1B
24 WHITEY (THE WHITE RAT) HERZOG-MGR
25 STEVE LAKE-C
26 ROD BOOKER-INF
26 TONY PENA-C
27 CURT FORD-OF
28 TOM HERR-2B
29 VINCE (VINCENT VAN GO) COLEMAN-OF
30 JOHN TUDOR-P
31 BOB FORSCH-P
(32) JEFF LAHTI (INJ)-(P)
33 JOHN MORRIS-OF
34 DANNY COX-P
35 MIKE LAGA-1B
36 STEVE PETERS-P
37 PAT PERRY-P (1)
37 SCOTT TERRY-P
38 TODD WORRELL-P
39 DAVE LAPOINT-P (1)
39 RANDY O'NEAL-P (2)
40 TIM CONROY-P
41 JOE MAGRANE-P
42 LEE TUNNELL-P
45 *(RET#) BOB GIBSON*
46 KEN DAYLEY-P
47 RAY SOFF-P
48 BILL DAWLEY-P
49 RICKY HORTON-P
51 WILLIE MCGEE-OF
53 GREG MATHEWS-P
53? SKEETER BARNES-3B
85 *(RET#) AUGIE BUSCH, SR.*

1988

5TH E 76-86 25GB

1 OZZIE (THE WIZARD) SMITH-SS
2 RED SCHOENDIENST-CH
3 DAVE RICKETTS-CH
4 MIKE ROARKE-CH
5 BOB HORNER-1B
6 *(RET#) STAN MUSIAL*
7 RICH HACKER-CH
8 JOHNNY LEWIS-CH
9 TERRY PENDLETON-3B
10 ROD BOOKER-INF
11 JOSE OQUENDO-UTIL
12 TOM LAWLESS-INF
14 *(RET#) KEN BOYER*
15 JIM LINDEMAN-OF
16 NICK LEYVA-CH
17 *(RET#) DIZZY DEAN*
18 LUIS ALICEA-2B
19 TOM PAGNOZZI-C
20 *(RET#) LOU BROCK*
21 DENNY WALLING-INF (2)
21 DUANE WALKER-P
22 TIM JONES-INF
23 TOM (BRUNO) BRUNANSKY-OF (2)
24 WHITEY (THE WHITE RAT) HERZOG-MGR
25 STEVE LAKE-C
26 TONY PENA-C
27 CURT FORD-OF
28 TOM HERR-2B (1)
28 DAN (QUIZ) QUISENBERRY-P (2)
28 PEDRO (PETE) GUERRERO-1B (2)
29 VINCE (VINCENT VAN GO) COLEMAN-OF
30 JOHN TUDOR-P (1)
31 BOB FORSCH-P (1)
32 JOE MAGRANE-P
33 JOHN MORRIS-OF
34 DANNY COX-P
35 MIKE LAGA-1B
36 STEVE PETERS-P
37 SCOTT TERRY-P
38 TODD WORRELL-P
39 RANDY O'NEAL-P
40 DAN (QUIZ) QUISENBERRY-P (2)
41 JOE MAGRANE-P
41 SCOTT ARNOLD-P
43 KEN HILL-P
44 CHRIS CARPENTER-P
45 *(RET#) BOB GIBSON*
46 KEN DAYLEY-P
47 GIBSON ALBA-P
48 JOSE DELEON-P
49 LARRY MCWILLIAMS-P
50 JOHN COSTELLO-P
51 WILLIE MCGEE-OF
53 GREG MATHEWS-P
56 KEN HILL-P
57 MIKE FITZGERALD-1B
58 SCOTT ARNOLD-P
85 *(RET#) AUGIE BUSCH, SR.*

1989

3RD E 87-75 7GB

1 OZZIE (THE WIZARD) SMITH-SS
2 RED SCHOENDIENST-CH
3 DAVE RICKETTS-CH
4 MIKE ROARKE-CH
5 JIM RIGGLEMAN-CH
6 *(RET#) STAN MUSIAL*
7 RICH HACKER-CH
8 JOHNNY LEWIS-CH
9 TERRY PENDLETON-3B
10 ROD BOOKER-INF
11 JOSE OQUENDO-UTIL
12 CRAIG WILSON-3B
14 *(RET#) KEN BOYER*
15 JIM LINDEMAN-OF
16 JIM RIGGLEMAN-CH
16 LEON DURHAM-1B
17 *(RET#) DIZZY DEAN*
19 TOM PAGNOZZI-C
20 *(RET#) LOU BROCK*
21 DENNY WALLING-INF
22 TIM JONES-UTIL
23 TOM (BRUNO) BRUNANSKY-OF
24 WHITEY (THE WHITE RAT) HERZOG-MGR
25 MILT THOMPSON-OF
26 TONY PENA-C
27 TODD ZEILE-C
28 PEDRO (PETE) GUERRERO-1B
29 VINCE (VINCENT VAN GO) COLEMAN-OF
30 DON HEINKEL-P
32 JOE MAGRANE-P
33 JOHN MORRIS-OF
34 DANNY COX (INJ)-P
35 FRANK DIPINO-P
37 SCOTT TERRY-P
38 TODD WORRELL-P
39 BOB TEWKSBURY-P
40 DAN (QUIZ) QUISENBERRY-P
42 TED POWER-P
43 KEN HILL-P
44 CHRIS CARPENTER-P
45 *(RET#) BOB GIBSON*
46 KEN DAYLEY-P
48 JOSE DELEON-P
49 RICKY HORTON-P (2)
50 JOHN COSTELLO-P
51 WILLIE MCGEE-OF
53 GREG MATHEWS (INJ)-P
58 TODD ZEILE-C
59 MATT KINZER-P
85 *(RET#) AUGIE BUSCH, SR.*

1990

6TH E 70-92 25GB

1 OZZIE (THE WIZARD) SMITH-SS
2 RED SCHOENDIENST-CH/MGR2
3 DAVE RICKETTS-CH
4 MIKE ROARKE-CH
5 JIM RIGGLEMAN-CH
5 FELIX JOSE-OF (2)
6 *(RET#) STAN MUSIAL*
7 RICH HACKER-CH
8 TIM JONES-UTIL
9 TERRY PENDLETON-3B
10 REX HUDLER-OF/INF (2)
11 JOSE OQUENDO-2B
12 CRAIG WILSON-3B
14 *(RET#) KEN BOYER*
15 DAVE COLLINS-1B/OF
16 RAY LANKFORD-OF
17 *(RET#) DIZZY DEAN*
19 TOM PAGNOZZI-C
20 *(RET#) LOU BROCK*
21 DENNY WALLING-INF
22 JOE TORRE-MGR3
23 TOM (BRUNO) BRUNANSKY-OF (1)
23 BERNARD GILKEY-OF
24 WHITEY (THE WHITE RAT) HERZOG-MGR1
25 MILT THOMPSON-OF
26 STEVE BRAUN-CH
26 OMAR OLIVARES-P
27 TODD ZEILE-C/3B
28 PEDRO (PETE) GUERRERO-1B
29 VINCE (VINCENT VAN GO) COLEMAN-OF
30 JOHN TUDOR-P
32 JOE MAGRANE-P
33 JOHN MORRIS-OF
34 DANNY COX (INJ)-P
35 FRANK DIPINO-P
36 BRYN SMITH-P
37 SCOTT TERRY-P
38 TODD WORRELL (INJ)-P
39 BOB TEWKSBURY-P
41 TOM NIEDENFUER-P
42 MIKE PEREZ-P
43 KEN HILL-P
44 CHRIS CARPENTER-P
45 *(RET#) BOB GIBSON*
46 KEN DAYLEY-P
47 LEE SMITH-P (2)
48 JOSE DELEON-P
49 RICKY HORTON-P
50 JOHN COSTELLO-P (1)
51 WILLIE MCGEE-OF (1)
53 GREG MATHEWS (INJ)-P
54 RAY STEPHENS-C
55 OMAR OLIVARES-P
56 TIM SHERRILL-P
58 ROD BREWER-1B
60 GERONIMO PENA-2B
61 STAN CLARKE-P
62 HOWARD HILTON-P
62 ERNIE CAMACHO-P (2)
63 MIKE PEREZ-P
85 *(RET#) AUGIE BUSCH, SR.*

1991

2ND E 84-78 14GB

1 OZZIE (THE WIZARD) SMITH-SS

ST. LOUIS CARDINALS

2 RED SCHOENDIENST-CH
3 DAVE RICKETTS-CH
4 GAYLEN PITTS-CH
5 FELIX JOSE-OF
6 *(RET#) STAN MUSIAL*
7 GERONIMO PENA-2B
8 TIM JONES-UTIL
9 JOE TORRE-MGR
10 REX HUDLER-OF/INF
11 JOSE OQUENDO-2B
12 CRAIG WILSON-3B
14 *(RET#) KEN BOYER*
15 DAVE COLLINS-CH
16 RAY LANKFORD-OF
17 *(RET#) DIZZY DEAN*
18 LUIS ALICEA-2B
19 TOM PAGNOZZI-C
20 *(RET#) LOU BROCK*
21 GERALD PERRY-1B
22 BOB MCCLURE-P (2)
23 BERNARD GILKEY-OF
25 MILT THOMPSON-OF
26 OMAR OLIVARES-P
27 TODD ZEILE-C/3B
28 PEDRO (PETE) GUERRERO-1B
29 RICH GEDMAN-C
30 BUCKY DENT-CH
(32) JOE MAGRANE (INJ)-(P)
34 FELIX JOSE-OF
(35) FRANK DIPINO (INJ)-(P)
36 BRYN SMITH-P
37 SCOTT TERRY-P
(38) TODD WORRELL (INJ)-(P)
39 BOB TEWKSBURY-P
40 JOE COLEMAN-CH
41 JAMIE MOYER-P
42 MIKE PEREZ-P
43 KEN HILL-P
44 CHRIS CARPENTER-P
45 *(RET#) BOB GIBSON*
46 WILLIE FRASER-P (2)
47 LEE SMITH-P
48 JOSE DELEON-P
49 JUAN AGOSTO-P
50 MARK GRATER-P
52 RHEAL CORMIER-P
54 RAY STEPHENS-C
55 STAN ROYER-OF
56 TIM SHERRILL-P
58 ROD BREWER-1B
63 MARK CLARK-P
85 *(RET#) AUGIE BUSCH, SR.*

1992

3RD E 83-79 13GB

1 OZZIE (THE WIZARD) SMITH-SS
2 RED SCHOENDIENST-CH
3 BRIAN JORDAN (INJ)-OF
4 GAYLEN PITTS-CH
5 STAN ROYER-3B/1B
6 *(RET#) STAN MUSIAL*
7 GERONIMO PENA (INJ)-2B
8 TIM JONES (INJ)-UTIL
9 JOE TORRE-MGR
10 REX HUDLER (INJ)-UTIL
11 JOSE OQUENDO (INJ)-2B/SS
12 CRAIG WILSON-UTIL
14 *(RET#) KEN BOYER*
15 DAVE COLLINS-CH
16 RAY LANKFORD-OF
17 *(RET#) DIZZY DEAN*
18 LUIS ALICEA (INJ)-2B/SS
19 TOM PAGNOZZI-C
20 *(RET#) LOU BROCK*
21 GERALD PERRY-1B
22 BOB MCCLURE-P
23 BERNARD GILKEY-OF
24 DON BAYLOR-CH
25 MILT THOMPSON-OF
26 OMAR OLIVARES-P
27 TODD ZEILE-3B
28 PEDRO (PETE) GUERRERO (INJ)-1B/OF
29 RICH GEDMAN-C
30 BUCKY DENT-CH
31 DONOVAN OSBORNE-P
32 JOE MAGRANE (INJ)-P
33 ROD BREWER-1B/OF
34 FELIX JOSE-OF
35 FRANK DIPINO (INJ)-P
36 BRYN SMITH (INJ)-P
(37) SCOTT TERRY (INJ)-(P)
38 TODD WORRELL (INJ)-P
39 BOB TEWKSBURY-P
40 JOE COLEMAN-CH
41 ANDRES (THE BIG CAT) GALARRAGA (INJ)-1B
42 MIKE PEREZ-P
43 CHUCK CARR-OF
44 CHRIS CARPENTER-P
45 *(RET#) BOB GIBSON*
46 OZZIE CANSECO-OF
47 LEE SMITH-P
48 JOSE DELEON-P (1)
49 JUAN AGOSTO-P (1)
50 BRIAN JORDAN-OF
50 BIEN FIGUEROA-SS/2B
52 RHEAL CORMIER-P
54 TRACY WOODSON-3B/1B
55 MARK CLARK-P
85 *(RET#) AUGIE BUSCH, SR.*

1993

3RD E 87-75 10GB

00 OMAR OLIVARES-P
1 OZZIE (THE WIZARD) SMITH-SS
2 RED SCHOENDIENST-CH
3 BRIAN JORDAN (INJ)-OF
4 GAYLEN PITTS-CH
5 STAN ROYER-3B/1B
6 *(RET#) STAN MUSIAL*
7 JACK HIBBARD-CH
8 TIM JONES-SS/2B
9 JOE TORRE-MGR
10 CHRIS CHAMBLISS-CH
11 JOSE OQUENDO (INJ)-SS/2B
12 ERIK PAPPAS-UTIL
14 *(RET#) KEN BOYER*
15 DAVE COLLINS-CH
16 RAY LANKFORD (INJ)-OF
17 *(RET#) DIZZY DEAN*
18 LUIS ALICEA-2B/UTIL
19 TOM PAGNOZZI (INJ)-C
20 *(RET#) LOU BROCK*
21 GERONIMO PENA (INJ)-2B
22 MARK WHITEN-OF
23 BERNARD GILKEY-OF/1B
25 GREGG JEFFERIES-1B/2B
26 LES LANCASTER (INJ)-P
27 TODD ZEILE-3B
28 GERALD PERRY-1B/OF
29 HECTOR VILLANUEVA-C
29 MARC RONAN-C
30 BUCKY DENT-CH
31 DONOVAN OSBORNE (INJ)-P
32 JOE MAGRANE-P (1)
33 ROD BREWER-OF/1B/P
34 TOM URBANI-P
35 STEVE DIXON-P
36 PAUL KILGUS (INJ)-P
38 ALLEN WATSON-P
39 BOB TEWKSBURY-P
40 JOE COLEMAN-CH
41 TOM URBANI-P
41 TODD BURNS-P (2)
42 MIKE PEREZ (INJ)-P
43 RENE AROCHA (INJ)-P
44 TRIPP CROMER-SS
45 *(RET#) BOB GIBSON*
46 ROB MURPHY-P
47 LEE SMITH-P (1)
47 RICH BATCHELOR-P
48 OZZIE CANSECO-OF
50 LES LANCASTER (INJ)-P
51 LEE GUETTERMAN-P
52 RHEAL CORMIER-P
54 TRACY WOODSON-3B/1B
55 LONNIE MACLIN-OF
85 *(RET#) AUGIE BUSCH, SR.*

1994

3RD C (TIE) 53-61 13GB

STRIKE NO POST-SEASON

1 OZZIE (THE WIZARD) SMITH-SS
2 RED SCHOENDIENST-CH
3 BRIAN JORDAN (INJ)-OF
4 GAYLEN PITTS-CH
5 STAN ROYER (REL)-3B (1)
6 *(RET#) STAN MUSIAL*
7 TERRY MCGRIFF-C
8 JOSE CARDENAL-CH
9 JOE TORRE-MGR
10 CHRIS CHAMBLISS-CH
11 JOSE OQUENDO (INJ) SS/2B
12 ERIK PAPPAS-UTIL
14 *(RET#) KEN BOYER*
15 GERALD YOUNG-OF
16 RAY LANKFORD-OF
17 *(RET#) DIZZY DEAN*
18 LUIS ALICEA-2B/UTIL
(19) TOM PAGNOZZI (INJ)-(C)
20 *(RET#) LOU BROCK*
21 GERONIMO PENA (INJ)-2B
22 MARK WHITEN (INJ)-OF
23 BERNARD GILKEY-OF/1B
24 BRYAN EVERSGERD-P
25 GREGG JEFFERIES-1B/2B
26 OMAR OLIVARES-P
27 TODD ZEILE-3B
28 GERALD PERRY-1B/OF
30 BUCKY DENT-CH
(31) DONOVAN OSBORNE (INJ)-(P)
32 JOHN HABYAN (INJ)-P
33 RICH RODRIGUEZ-P
34 TOM URBANI-P
35 JOE COLEMAN-CH
(36) PAUL KILGUS (INJ)-(P)
37 RHEAL CORMIER (INJ)-P
38 ALLEN WATSON-P
39 BOB TEWKSBURY-P
40 RICK SUTCLIFFE (INJ)-P
41 STEVE DIXON-P
42 MIKE PEREZ (INJ)-P
43 RENE AROCHA-P
44 TRIPP CROMER-SS
45 *(RET#) BOB GIBSON*
46 ROB MURPHY (WAIV)-P (1)
47 JOHN MABRY-OF
50 JOHN FRASCATORE-P
52 RHEAL CORMIER (INJ)-P
53 SCOT COOLBAUGH-1B
54 TERRY MCGRIFF-C
54 FRANK CIMORELLI-P
57 WILLIE SMITH-P
58 VICENTE PALACIOS-P
59 GARY BUCKLES-P
85 *(RET#) AUGIE BUSCH, SR.*

1995

4TH C 62-81 22.5GB

144 GAME SEASON

1 OZZIE (THE WIZARD) SMITH (INJ)-SS
2 RED SCHOENDIENST-CH
3 BRIAN JORDAN-OF
4 GAYLEN PITTS-CH
5 DANNY SHEAFFER-C
6 *(RET#) STAN MUSIAL*
7 TRIPP CROMER-SS
8 JOSE CARDENAL-CH
9 JOE TORRE-MGR1
10 CHRIS CHAMBLISS-CH
11 JOSE OQUENDO-2B
12 MARK RIGGINS-CH
14 *(RET#) KEN BOYER*
15 DARNELL COLES-1B
16 RAY LANKFORD-OF
17 *(RET#) DIZZY DEAN*
18 MANNY LEE (INJ)-2B
18 CHRIS (SPUDS) SABO-1B
19 TOM PAGNOZZI (INJ)-C
20 *(RET#) LOU BROCK*
21 GERONIMO PENA (INJ)-2B
22 MIKE JORGENSEN-MGR2
23 BERNARD GILKEY-OF
24 TOM URBANI-P
25 TIM HULETT-2B/SS
25 RAMON CARABALLO-2B
25 DAVID BELL-2B/3B
26 SCOTT HEMOND-C/2B
27 TODD ZEILE-1B (1)
28 GERALD PERRY-1B
29 DANNY JACKSON (INJ)-P
30 MARK SWEENEY-1B/OF
31 DONOVAN OSBORNE-P
32 JOHN HABYAN-P
33 RICH RODRIGUEZ (INJ)-P
34 TOM URBANI-P
34 SCOTT COOPER-3B
35 ALLEN BATTLE-OF
36 MIKE MORGAN-P (2)
37 DOUG CREEK-P
38 ALLEN WATSON-P
39 CORY BAILEY-P
41 RICH DELUCIA-P
42 JOSE OLIVA-3B (2)
43 RENE AROCHA-P
44 KEN HILL-P
45 *(RET#) BOB GIBSON*
46 SCOTT COOPER-3B
46 MARK PETKOVSEK-P
47 JOHN MABRY-OF
48 TONY FOSSAS-P
49 JEFF PARRETT-P
50 TOM HENKE-P
51 T. J. MATHEWS-P
52 BRIAN BARBER-P
54 RAY GIANNELLI-1B/OF
55 TERRY BRADSHAW-PH/OF
58 VICENTE PALACIOS-P
60 JOHN FRASCATORE-P
85 *(RET#) AUGIE BUSCH, SR.*

1996

1ST C 88-74 0GB

W NLDS-SDN 3-0

L NLCS-ATLN 4-3

1 OZZIE (THE WIZARD) SMITH (INJ)-SS
2 *(RET#) RED SCHOENDIENST*
3 BRIAN JORDAN (INJ)-OF
4 DANNY SHEAFFER-C
5 RON GANT (INJ)-OF
6 *(RET#) STAN MUSIAL*
8 GARY GAETTI (INJ)-3B
9 MARK DEJOHN-CH
9 *(RET#) ENOS SLAUGHTER*
10 TONY LA RUSSA-MGR
11 ROYCE CLAYTON-SS
12 LUIS ALICEA-2B
13 AARON HOLBERT-2B
14 *(RET#) KEN BOYER*
15 TOMMIE REYNOLDS-CH
16 RAY LANKFORD-OF
17 *(RET#) DIZZY DEAN*
18 DAVE DUNCAN-CH
19 TOM PAGNOZZI (INJ)-C
20 *(RET#) LOU BROCK*
21 CORY BAILEY-P
22 MIKE GALLEGO (INJ)-2B
23 MARK SWEENEY-1B
24 TOM URBANI-P (1)
24 DMITRI YOUNG-1B
25 GEORGE HENDRICK-CH
27 DAVID BELL-2B
28 RON HASSEY-CH
29 DANNY JACKSON (INJ/ILL)-P
30 TODD STOTTLEMYRE-P
31 DONOVAN OSBORNE (INJ)-P
32 RICK HONEYCUTT-P
33 T. J. MATHEWS-P
34 MARK DEJOHN-CH
35 MIGUEL MEJIA (INJ)-OF
36 MIKE MORGAN (INJ) (REL)-P (1)
38 PAT BORDERS-C (1)
39 DAVE MCKAY-CH
40 ANDY BENES-P
41 ALAN BENES-P
43 DENNIS ECKERSLEY (INJ)-P
44 RICH BATCHELOR-P
45 *(RET#) BOB GIBSON*
46 MARK PETKOVSEK (INJ)-P
47 JOHN MABRY-OF
48 TONY FOSSAS-P
49 JEFF PARRETT (REL)-P (1)
49 MIKE DIFELICE-C
50 JOHN FRASCATORE-P
51 WILLIE MCGEE-OF/1B
52 BRIAN BARBER-P
55 TERRY BRADSHAW-PH/OF
57 MIKE BUSBY-P
57 ERIC LUDWICK-P
85 *(RET#) AUGIE BUSCH, SR.*

1997

4TH C 73-89 11GB

1 *(RET#) OZZIE SMITH*
2 *(RET#) RED SCHOENDIENST*
3 BRIAN JORDAN (INJ)-OF
4 CARNEY LANSFORD-CH
5 RON GANT (INJ)-OF
6 *(RET#) STAN MUSIAL*
7 DELINO DESHIELDS-2B
8 GARY GAETTI (INJ)-3B
9 *(RET#) ENOS SLAUGHTER*
10 TONY LA RUSSA-MGR
11 ROYCE CLAYTON-SS
12 DANNY SHEAFFER-C
14 *(RET#) KEN BOYER*
15 RENE LACHEMANN-CH
16 RAY LANKFORD (INJ)-OF
17 *(RET#) DIZZY DEAN*
18 DAVE DUNCAN-CH
19 TOM PAGNOZZI (INJ)-C
20 *(RET#) LOU BROCK*
21 MIKE GULAN-PH
22 MIKE GALLEGO (INJ) (WAIV)-2B
22 SCARBOROUGH GREEN-OF
23 MARK SWEENEY-OF/1B (1)
23 PHIL PLANTIER-OF (2)
24 DMITRI YOUNG (INJ)-1B
25 GEORGE HENDRICK-CH
25 MARK (BIG MAC) MCGWIRE-1B (2)
26 ELI MARRERO-C
27 DAVID BELL (INJ)-INF
28 LANCE PAINTER (INJ)-P
29 DANNY JACKSON (INJ/ILL)-P (1)
29 SCOTT LIVINGSTONE-UTIL (2)

30 TODD STOTTLEMYRE-P
31 DONOVAN OSBORNE (INJ)-P
32 RICK HONEYCUTT (INJ) (RET)-P
33 T. J. MATHEWS-P (1)
33 JOSE BAUTISTA-P (2)
34 MARK DEJOHN-CH
34 FERNANDO VALENZUELA (REL)-P (2)
34 SEAN LOWE-P
35 MATT MORRIS-P
37 MIKE DIFELICE-C
38 STEVE SCARSONE-2B
38 ROBERTO MIJIAS-2B
38 BRADY RAGGIO-P
38 MANNY AYBAR-P
39 DAVE MCKAY-CH
40 ANDY BENES (INJ)-P
41 ALAN BENES (INJ)-P
42 *(RET#) JACKIE ROBINSON*
43 DENNIS ECKERSLEY-P
44 RICH BATCHELOR-P (1)
45 *(RET#) BOB GIBSON*
46 MARK PETKOVSEK (INJ)-P
47 JOHN MABRY (INJ)-1B
48 TONY FOSSAS-P
49 TOM LAMPKIN-C (1)
50 JOHN FRASCATORE-P
51 WILLIE MCGEE-OF
52 LUIS ORDAZ-SS
53 RIGO BELTRAN-P
54 MIKE BUSBY-P
56 MICAH FRANKLIN-OF
56 JEFF BERBLINGER-INF
57 ERIC LUDWICK-P (1)
57 CURTIS KING-P
61 TOM MCGRAW-P
64 BRADY RAGGIO-P
67 ROBERTO MEJIA-2B
85 *(RET#) AUGIE BUSCH, SR.*

1998

3RD C 83-79 19GB

1 *(RET#) OZZIE SMITH*
2 *(RET#) RED SCHOENDIENST*
3 BRIAN JORDAN-OF
4 CARNEY LANSFORD-CH
5 RON GANT (INJ)-OF
6 *(RET#) STAN MUSIAL*
7 DELINO DESHIELDS (INJ)-2B
8 GARY GAETTI (REL)-3B
8 J. D. DREW-OF
9 *(RET#) ENOS SLAUGHTER*
10 TONY LA RUSSA-MGR
11 ROYCE CLAYTON-SS (1)
11 FERNANDO TATIS-3B (2)
11 LUIS ORDAZ-SS
12 SHAWN GILBERT-INF (2)
12 PAT KELLY-2B
13 DAVID HOWARD (INJ)-INF
14 *(RET#) KEN BOYER*
15 RENE LACHEMANN-CH
16 RAY LANKFORD-OF
17 *(RET#) DIZZY DEAN*
18 DAVE DUNCAN-CH
19 TOM PAGNOZZI (INJ) (REL)-C
20 *(RET#) LOU BROCK*
21 BRIAN R. HUNTER (REL)-OF
21 BRYAN EVERSGERD-P
23 LUIS ORDAZ-SS
23 FERNANDO TATIS-3B (2)
24 RICK CROUSHORE-P
25 MARK (BIG MAC) MCGWIRE-1B
26 ELI MARRERO (INJ)-C
27 DAVID BELL-INF (1)
27 PLACIDO POLANCO-INF
28 LANCE PAINTER-P
29 DAVID HOWARD (INJ)-INF
30 TODD STOTTLEMYRE-P (1)
31 DONOVAN OSBORNE (INJ)-P
32 DARREN OLIVER-P (2)
33 DAVE MCKAY-CH
34 MARK DEJOHN-CH
35 MATT MORRIS (INJ)-P
36 BOBBY WITT-P (2)
37 KENT BOTTENFIELD-P
38 MANNY AYBAR-P
39 DAVE (THE COBRA) PARKER-CH
40 CLIFF POLITTE-P
(41) ALAN BENES (INJ)-(P)
42 *(RET#) JACKIE ROBINSON*
43 KENT MERCKER-P
44 JEFF BRANTLEY (INJ)-P
45 *(RET#) BOB GIBSON*
46 MARK PETKOVSEK-P
47 JOHN MABRY-1B
48 SEAN LOWE-P
48 JOE (LITTLE MAC) MCEWING-INF
49 TOM LAMPKIN-C
50 JOHN FRASCATORE-P
51 WILLIE MCGEE-OF
52 LUIS ORDAZ-SS
52 JOSE JIMENEZ-P
53 JUAN ACEVEDO-P
54 MIKE BUSBY-P
55 BRADEN LOOPER-P
57 CURTIS KING-P
58 BRADY RAGGIO-P
58 MARK LITTLE-OF
67 PLACIDO POLANCO-INF
85 *(RET#) AUGIE BUSCH, SR.*

1999

4TH C 75-86 21.5GB

1 *(RET#) OZZIE SMITH*
2 *(RET#) RED SCHOENDIENST*
3 EDGAR RENTERIA-SS
4 MIKE EASLER-CH
5 THOMAS HOWARD-OF
6 *(RET#) STAN MUSIAL*
7 J. D. DREW (INJ)-OF
8 ADAM KENNEDY-2B
9 *(RET#) ENOS SLAUGHTER*
10 TONY LA RUSSA-MGR
11 JOSE OQUENDO-CH
13 LUIS ORDAZ-SS
14 *(RET#) KEN BOYER*
15 RENE LACHEMANN-CH
16 RAY LANKFORD-OF
17 *(RET#) DIZZY DEAN*
18 DAVE DUNCAN-CH
20 *(RET#) LOU BROCK*
21 SHAWON DUNSTON-UTIL (1)
21 CRAIG PAQUETTE-UTIL
22 DARREN BRAGG (INJ)-OF
23 FERNANDO TATIS-3B
24 ERIC DAVIS (INJ)-OF
25 MARK (BIG MAC) MCGWIRE-1B
26 ELI MARRERO (INJ)-C
27 PLACIDO POLANCO-INF
28 LANCE PAINTER-P
29 DAVID HOWARD (INJ)-INF
30 ALBERTO CASTILLO-C
31 DONOVAN OSBORNE (INJ)-P
32 MIKE MOHLER-P
33 DARREN OLIVER-P
34 MARK DEJOHN-CH
(35) MATT MORRIS (INJ)-(P)
36 SCOTT RADINSKY (INJ)-P
37 KENT BOTTENFIELD-P
38 MANNY AYBAR-P
39 DAVE MCKAY-CH
(41) ALAN BENES (INJ)-(P)
42 *(RET#) JACKIE ROBINSON*
43 KENT MERCKER-P (1)
43 MARK THOMPSON-P
44 RICK CROUSHORE-P
45 *(RET#) BOB GIBSON*
47 JOE (LITTLE MAC) MCEWING-2B
48 RICK HEISERMAN-INF
48 EDUARDO PEREZ-1B
49 JOSE JIMENEZ-P
50 CLINT SODOWSKY-P
51 WILLIE MCGEE-OF
52 RICKY BOTTALICO-P
53 JUAN ACEVEDO-P
54 MIKE BUSBY-P
55 GARRETT STEPHENSON-P
57 CURTIS KING (INJ)-P
58 HEATHCLIFF SLOCUMB (INJ)-P (2)
59 MARCUS JENSEN-C
62 RICK HEISERMAN-INF
63 LARRY LUEBBERS-P
66 RICH ANKIEL-P
85 *(RET#) AUGIE BUSCH, SR.*

2000

1ST C 95-67 0GB
W NLDS-ATLN 3-0
L NLCS-NYN 4-1

1 *(RET#) OZZIE SMITH*
2 *(RET#) RED SCHOENDIENST*
3 EDGAR RENTERIA-SS
4 FERNANDO VINA-2B
5 THOMAS HOWARD-OF
6 *(RET#) STAN MUSIAL*
7 J. D. DREW (INJ)-OF
8 CHRIS RICHARD-1B (1)
8 CARLOS A. HERNANDEZ-C (2)
9 *(RET#) ENOS SLAUGHTER*
10 TONY LA RUSSA-MGR
11 JOSE OQUENDO-CH
12 SHAWON DUNSTON-UTIL
13 CASEY CANDAELE-INF
13 LUIS SATURRIA-OF
14 *(RET#) KEN BOYER*
15 JIM EDMONDS-OF
16 RAY LANKFORD-OF
17 *(RET#) DIZZY DEAN*
18 DAVE DUNCAN-CH
19 MIKE EASLER-CH
20 *(RET#) LOU BROCK*
21 CRAIG PAQUETTE-UTIL
22 MIKE MATHENY-C
22 WILL (THE THRILL) CLARK-1B (2)
23 FERNANDO TATIS-3B
24 ERIC DAVIS (INJ)-OF
25 MARK (BIG MAC) MCGWIRE (INJ)-1B
26 ELI MARRERO (INJ)-C
27 PLACIDO POLANCO-INF
28 LARRY SUTTON-INF
29 RICK WILKINS-C
31 ALAN BENES (INJ)-P
32 MIKE MOHLER-P (1)
32 KEITH MCDONALD-C
33 EDUARDO PEREZ-1B
34 MARK DEJOHN-CH
35 MATT MORRIS (INJ)-P
36 SCOTT RADINSKY (INJ)-P
37 DARREN HOLMES-P (2)
38 MARTY MASON-CH
39 DAVE MCKAY-CH
40 ANDY BENES-P
41 PAT HENTGEN-P
42 *(RET#) JACKIE ROBINSON*
43 DAVE VERES-P
44 DAVID WAINHOUSE (INJ)-P
44 MIKE MATHENY-C
45 *(RET#) BOB GIBSON*
46 MARK THOMPSON (INJ)-P
47 JESS OROSCO (INJ)-P
48 JASON CHRISTIANSEN-P (2)
49 MIKE JAMES-P
50 MIKE MATTHEWS (INJ)-P
50 MIKE TIMLIN-P (2)
(51) WILLIE MCGEE (RET)-(OF)
52 JOSE RODRIGUEZ-P
55 GARRETT STEPHENSON-P
56 JUSTIN BRUNETTE-P
57 DARRYL KILE-P
58 HEATHCLIFF SLOCUMB (INJ)-P (1)
60 STEVE BIESER-OF
63 LUTHER HACKMAN-P
66 RICH ANKIEL-P
67 GENE STECHSCHULTE-P
68 BRITT REAMES-P
88 DAVID WAINHOUSE (INJ)-P
85 *(RET#) AUGIE BUSCH, SR.*

2001

1ST C TIE (W/C) 93-69 0GB
L NLDS-ARIN 3-2

1 *(RET#) OZZIE SMITH*
2 *(RET#) RED SCHOENDIENST*
3 EDGAR RENTERIA-SS
4 FERNANDO VINA-2B
5 ALBERT PUJOLS-3B/1B/OF
6 *(RET#) STAN MUSIAL*
7 J. D. DREW (INJ)-OF
8 CARLOS A. HERNANDEZ-C
9 *(RET#) ENOS SLAUGHTER*
10 TONY LA RUSSA-MGR
11 JOSE OQUENDO-CH
12 MITCHELL PAGE-CH
13 KERRY ROBINSON-OF
14 *(RET#) KEN BOYER*
15 JIM EDMONDS-OF
16 RAY LANKFORD-OF (1)
17 *(RET#) DIZZY DEAN*
18 DAVE DUNCAN-CH
19 MIKE EASLER-CH
19 WOODY WILLIAMS-P (2)
20 *(RET#) LOU BROCK*
21 CRAIG PAQUETTE-UTIL
22 MIKE MATHENY-C
23 LUIS SATURRIA-OF
24 BOBBY (BOBBY BO) BONILLA (INJ) (SUS)-UTIL
25 MARK (BIG MAC) MCGWIRE (INJ)-1B
26 ELI MARRERO (INJ)-C
27 PLACIDO POLANCO-INF
28 LARRY SUTTON (WAIV)-INF (1)
28 BILL ORTEGA-OF
29 STUBBY CLAPP-2B
30 DUSTIN HERMANSON-P
31 ALAN BENES-P
32 KEITH MCDONALD-C
34 MARK DEJOHN-CH
35 MATT MORRIS (INJ)-P
36 GENE STECHSCHULTE-P
37 T. J. MATHEWS-P
38 MARTY MASON-CH
39 DAVE MCKAY-CH
40 ANDY BENES-P
41 JASON KARMUTH-P
41 MIGUEL CAIRO-3B
42 *(RET#) JACKIE ROBINSON*
43 DAVE VERES-P
44 STEVE KLINE-P
45 *(RET#) BOB GIBSON*
46 JEFF TABAKA (INJ)-P
47 JOHN MABRY-1B/OF (1)
48 JASON CHRISTIANSEN (INJ)-P (1)
49 MIKE JAMES (INJ)-P
50 MIKE TIMLIN (INJ)-P
51 BUD SMITH-P
52 BUD SMITH-P
55 GARRETT STEPHENSON (INJ)-P
57 DARRYL KILE-P
60 MIKE MATTHEWS-P
63 LUTHER HACKMAN (INJ)-P
65 CHAD HUTCHINSON-P
66 RICH ANKIEL-P
67 GENE STECHSCHULTE-P
85 *(RET#) AUGIE BUSCH, SR.*

2002

1ST C 97-65 0GB
W NLDS-ARIN 3-0
L NLCS-SFN 4-1

0 KERRY ROBINSON-OF
1 *(RET#) OZZIE SMITH*
2 *(RET#) RED SCHOENDIENST*
3 EDGAR RENTERIA-SS
4 FERNANDO VINA-2B
5 ALBERT PUJOLS-OF/INF
6 *(RET#) STAN MUSIAL*
7 J. D. DREW-OF
8 MIKE DIFELICE-C
9 *(RET#) ENOS SLAUGHTER*
10 TONY LA RUSSA-MGR
11 JOSE OQUENDO-CH
12 MITCHELL PAGE-CH
13 KERRY ROBINSON-OF
13 JEFF FASSERO-P (2)
14 *(RET#) KEN BOYER*
15 JIM EDMONDS-OF
16 SCOTT ROLEN-3B (2)
16 IVAN CRUZ-1B
17 *(RET#) DIZZY DEAN*
18 DAVE DUNCAN-CH
19 WOODY WILLIAMS (INJ)-P
20 *(RET#) LOU BROCK*
21 TINO MARTINEZ-1B
22 MIKE MATHENY-C/1B
23 JAMEY WRIGHT-P (2)
24 JOE PETTINI-CH
26 ELI MARRERO-OF/C/1B
27 PLACIDO POLANCO-3B/INF (1)
27 SCOTT ROLEN-3B (2)
28 MIKE COOLBAUGH-3B
30 WILSON DELGADO-SS
31 CHUCK FINLEY-P (2)
33 EDUARDO PEREZ-OF/INF
34 MARK DEJOHN-CH
35 MATT MORRIS-P
36 GENE STECHSCHULTE-P
38 MARTY MASON-CH
39 DAVE MCKAY-CH
40 ANDY BENES (INJ)-P
41 MIGUEL CAIRO-UTIL
42 *(RET #)JACKIE ROBINSON*
43 DAVE VERES-P
44 JASON (IZZY) ISRINGHAUSEN-P
45 *(RET#) BOB GIBSON*
46 JASON SIMONTACCHI-P
47 LUTHER HACKMAN-1B
48 MIKE MATTHEWS-P (1)
49 STEVE KLINE (INJ)-P
50 MIKE TIMLIN-P (1)
50 RICK WHITE-P (2)
51 *(RET#) WILLIE MCGEE*
52 BUD SMITH-P
52 MATT DUFF-P
52 NERIO RODRIGUEZ-P (2)
53 TRAVIS SMITH-P
54 MIKE CRUDALE-P

ST. LOUIS CARDINALS

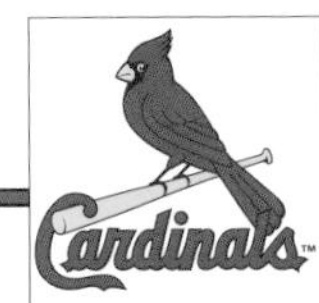

55 GARRETT STEPHENSON (INJ)-P
56 GABE MOLINA-P
57 DARRYL KILE (DD)-P
58 KEVIN JOSEPH-P
58 JOSE RODRIGUEZ-P (1)
60 JOSH PEARCE-P
63 LUTHER HACKMAN-P
(66) RICK ANKIEL (INJ)-(P)
85 *(RET#) AUGIE BUSCH, SR.*
99 SO TAGUCHI-OF

2003

3RD C 85-77 3GB

0 KERRY ROBINSON-OF
1 *(RET#) OZZIE SMITH*
2 *(RET#) RED SCHOENDIENST*
3 EDGAR RENTERIA-SS
4 FERNANDO VINA (INJ)-2B
5 ALBERT PUJOLS (SUS:2G)-OF/1B
6 *(RET#) STAN MUSIAL*
7 J. D. DREW (INJ)-OF
8 JOE GIRARDI (INJ)-C
9 *(RET#) ENOS SLAUGHTER*
10 TONY LA RUSSA-MGR
11 JOSE OQUENDO-CH
12 MITCHELL PAGE-CH
12 MIGUEL CAIRO-UTIL
13 JEFF FASSERO-P
14 *(RET#) KEN BOYER*
15 JIM EDMONDS-OF
16 ORLANDO PALMEIRO-OF
17 *(RET#) DIZZY DEAN*
18 DAVE DUNCAN-CH
19 WOODY WILLIAMS-P
20 *(RET#) LOU BROCK*
21 TINO MARTINEZ-1B
22 MIKE MATHENY (SUS:3G)-C/1B
23 CAL ELDRED-P
24 JOE PETTINI-CH
26 ELI MARRERO (INJ)-OF/C
27 SCOTT ROLEN-3B
28 LANCE PAINTER (INJ)-P
(29) CHRIS CARPENTER (INJ)-(P)
30 BRETT TOMKO-P
31 BO HART-2B
32 DUSTIN HERMANSON-P (1)
32 CHRIS WIDGER (INJ)-C
33 EDUARDO PEREZ (INJ)-OF/INF
35 MATT MORRIS (INJ)-P
(36) GENE STECHSCHULTE (INJ)-(P)
37 MIKE DEJEAN-P (2)
38 MARTY MASON-CH
39 DAVE MCKAY-CH
40 KIKO CALERO (INJ)-P
41 MIGUEL CAIRO-UTIL
41 STERLING HITCHCOCK-P (2)
42 *(RET #)JACKIE ROBINSON*
43 KEVIN OHME-P
43 ESTEBAN YAN (REL)-P (2)
44 JASON (IZZY) ISRINGHAUSEN (INJ)-P
45 *(RET#) BOB GIBSON*
46 JASON SIMONTACCHI-P
47 WILSON DELGADO-INF (1)
47 MIKE DEJEAN-P (2)
48 RUSS SPRINGER (INJ)-P
49 STEVE KLINE-P
50 CHRIS WIDGER (INJ)-C
50 DAN HAREN-P
52 PEDRO BORBON, JR.-P
53 JASON PEARSON-P
54 MIKE CRUDALE-P (1)
55 GARRETT STEPHENSON (INJ)-P
56 GABE MOLINA-P
60 JOSH PEARCE-P
(66) RICK ANKIEL (INJ)-(P)
77 JIMMY JOURNELL (INJ)-P
85 *(RET#) AUGIE BUSCH, SR.*
99 SO TAGUCHI-OF

2004

1ST C 105-57 0GB
W NLDS-LAN 3-1
W NLCS-HOUN 4-3
L WS-BOSA 4-0

1 *(RET#) OZZIE SMITH*
2 *(RET#) RED SCHOENDIENST*
3 EDGAR RENTERIA-SS
4 TONY WOMACK-2B
5 ALBERT PUJOLS-1B
6 *(RET#) STAN MUSIAL*
7 HECTOR LUNA-SS/2B
8 MARLON ANDERSON-2B
9 *(RET#) ENOS SLAUGHTER*
10 TONY LA RUSSA-MGR
11 JOSE OQUENDO-CH
12 MITCHELL PAGE-CH
12 RAY LANKFORD (INJ)-OF
14 *(RET#) KEN BOYER*
15 JIM EDMONDS-OF
16 REGGIE SANDERS-OF
17 *(RET#) DIZZY DEAN*
18 DAVE DUNCAN-CH
19 WOODY WILLIAMS-P
20 *(RET#) LOU BROCK*
21 JASON MARQUIS-P
22 MIKE MATHENY (INJ)-C
23 CAL ELDRED-P
24 JOE PETTINI-CH
26 CODY MCKAY-C/P/3B
27 SCOTT ROLEN-3B
28 ROGER CEDENO (INJ)-OF
28 COLIN PORTER-OF
29 CHRIS CARPENTER (INJ)-P
31 BO HART-2B
32 ROGER CEDENO (INJ)-OF
33 MIKE LINCOLN (INJ)-P
33 LARRY WALKER-OF (2)
34 STEVE KLEIN (INJ)-P
35 MATT MORRIS-P
36 MIKE LINCOLN (INJ)-P
37 JEFF SUPPAN-P
38 MARTY MASON-CH
39 DAVE MCKAY-CH
40 KIKO CALERO (INJ)-P
41 YADIER MOLINA-C
42 *(RET #)JACKIE ROBINSON*
44 JASON (IZZY) ISRINGHAUSEN-P
45 *(RET#) BOB GIBSON*
46 JASON SIMONTACCHI-P
47 JOHN MABRY-OF/1B
49 RICK ANKIEL (INJ)-P
50 JULIAN TAVAREZ-P
52 AL REYES-P
54 JOSH PEARCE-P
55 DANNY HAREN-P
56 RAY KING-P
60 JOSH PEARCE-P
61 RANDY FLORES-P
68 CARMEN CALI-P
85 *(RET#) AUGIE BUSCH, SR.*
99 SO TAGUCHI-OF

2005

1ST C 100-62 0GB
W NLDS-SDN 3-0
L NLCS-HOUN 4-2

1 *(RET#) OZZIE SMITH*
2 *(RET#) RED SCHOENDIENST*
3 ABRAHAM NUNEZ-3B
4 EINAR DIAZ-C
5 ALBERT PUJOLS-1B
6 *(RET#) STAN MUSIAL*
7 HECTOR LUNA-SS/OF
8 HAL MACRAE-CH
9 *(RET#) ENOS SLAUGHTER*
10 TONY LA RUSSA-MGR
11 JOSE OQUENDO-CH
12 MARK GRUDZIELANEK-2B
14 *(RET#) KEN BOYER*
15 JIM EDMONDS-OF
16 REGGIE SANDERS (INJ)-OF
17 *(RET#) DIZZY DEAN*
18 DAVE DUNCAN (SUS:4G)-CH
19 ROGER CEDENO (INJ)-OF
20 *(RET#) LOU BROCK*
21 JASON MARQUIS-P
22 DAVID ECKSTEIN-SS
23 CAL ELDRED (INJ)-P
24 JOE PETTINI-CH
26 ANTHONY REYES-P
27 SCOTT ROLEN (INJ)-3B
28 SCOTT SEABOL-3B/UTIL
29 CHRIS CARPENTER-P
30 MARK MULDER-P
32 KEVIN JARVIS-P
33 LARRY WALKER (INJ)-OF
34 RANDY FLORES (INJ)-P
35 MATT MORRIS (INJ)-P
(36) MIKE LINCOLN (INJ)-(P)
37 JEFF SUPPAN-P
38 MARTY MASON-CH
39 DAVE MCKAY-CH
40 BILL PULSIPHER (INJ)-P
41 YADIER MOLINA (INJ)-C
42 *(RET #)JACKIE ROBINSON*
43 JOHN GALL-OF
44 JASON (IZZY) ISRINGHAUSEN (INJ)-P
45 *(RET#) BOB GIBSON*
46 MIKE MAHONEY-C
47 JOHN MABRY-OF/1B/3B
48 BRAD THOMPSON-P
50 JULIAN TAVAREZ-P
52 AL REYES-P
53 GABE WHITE-P
53 JON RODRIGUEZ-OF
54 CARMEN CALI-P
55 SKIP SCHUMAKER-OF
56 RAY KING-P
60 ADAM WAINWRIGHT-P
61 TYLER JOHNSON-P
62 CHRIS DUNCAN-1B
77 JIMMY JOURNELL-P
85 *(RET#) AUGIE BUSCH, SR.*
99 SO TAGUCHI-OF

The franchise player of the St. Louis Cardinals—Stan Musial. The fans in Brooklyn nicknamed him "The Man" because of the way he tore up Ebbetts Field on every visit. He ended his 22-year career with 1949 runs, 3630 hits, 725 doubles, 177 triples, 475 HRs, 1951 RBIs, 1599 walks, and a lifetime average of .331. He was a 7-time batting champ, appeared in 24 All-Star Games, won three MVPs, hit 5 home runs in a doubleheader, had 4 HRs in consecutive ABs (not the same game), is in the Hall of Fame and the Cardinals retired his number "6" when he retired in 1963.

1969
SAN DIEGO PADRES

6TH W 52-110 41GB

1 (DOWNTOWN) OLLIE BROWN-OF
1 SPARKY ANDERSON-CH
2 JOHN SIPIN (INJ)-2B
3 TOMMY DEAN-SS/2B
4 DUKE SNIDER-CH
5 JOSE ARCIA-2B/UTIL
6 WALLY MOON-CH
7 ED SPIEZIO-3B/OF
8 CHRIS CANNIZZARO-C
9 AL (THE BULL) FERRARA-OF
10 SPARKY ANDERSON-CH
10 SONNY RUBERTO-C
11 ROBERTO (BABY) PENA-INF
12 BILL DAVIS-1B
12 RON SLOCUM-INF
14 LARRY STAHL-OF/1B
15 FRED KENDALL-C
15 DAVE ROBERTS-P
16 TOMMIE SISK-P
16 VAN KELLY-3B/2B
17 NATE COLBERT-1B
18 PRESTON GOMEZ -MGR
19 WHITEY WIETELMANN-CH
20 IVAN MURRELL-OF/1B
21 CITO GASTON-OF
22 DICK KELLEY-P
23 AL SANTORINI-P
24 WALT HRINIAK-C (2)
24 CHRIS KRUG-C
25 TOMMIE SISK-P
25 TONY GONZALES-OF (1)
26 CHRIS KRUG-C
26 (DOWNTOWN) OLLIE BROWN-OF
27 JACK BALDSCHUN-P
27 STEVE ARLIN-P
29 JACK BALDSCHUN-P
29 FRANKIE LIBRAN-SS
30 MIKE CORKINS-P
31 DAVE ROBERTS-P
31 FRANKIE LIBRAN-SS
31 LEON EVERITT-P
31 RAFAEL ROBLES-SS
32 JERRY MORALES-OF
33 GARY ROSS-P (2)
34 AL MCBEAN-P (1)
34 JOHNNY PODRES-P
34 WALT HRINIAK-C (2)
35 RAFAEL ROBLES-SS
36 JERRY DAVANON-2B/SS (1)
36 FRED KENDALL-C
36 VAN KELLY-3B/2B
37 JOHN SIPIN (INJ)-2B
37 JOE NIEKRO-P (2)
38 ROGER CRAIG-CH
39 DICK SELMA-P (1)
39 JIM WILLIAMS-OF
42 BILLY MCCOOL-P
43 CLAY KIRBY-P
44 TOM DUKES-P
44 STEVE ARLIN-P
45 RON SLOCUM-INF
45 JOHNNY PODRES-P
46 FRANK (CRANE) REBERGER-P
47 JOE NIEKRO-P (2)
48 GARY ROSS-P (2)
50 LEON EVERITT-P

1970

6TH W 63-99 39GB

1 BOB BARTON-C
2 DAVE GARCIA-CH
3 TOMMY DEAN (INJ)-SS
4 BOB SKINNER-CH
5 JOSE ARCIA-UTIL
6 RAFAEL ROBLES-SS
7 ED SPIEZIO-3B
8 CHRIS CANNIZZARO-C
9 AL (THE BULL) FERRARA-OF
10 DAVE CAMPBELL-2B
11 RAMON WEBSTER-1B/OF
12 RON SLOCUM-C/INF
14 LARRY STAHL-OF
15 DAVE ROBERTS-P
16 VAN KELLY-3B/2B
16 FRED KENDALL-C
17 NATE COLBERT-1B/3B
18 PRESTON GOMEZ-MGR
19 WHITEY WIETELMANN-CH
20 IVAN MURRELL-OF/1B
21 CITO GASTON-OF
22 RON WILLIS-P
23 AL SANTORINI-P
24 JERRY NYMAN-P
25 STEVE HUNTZ-SS/3B
26 (DOWNTOWN) OLLIE BROWN-OF
27 JACK BALDSCHUN-P
30 MIKE CORKINS-P
31 JERRY NYMAN-P
31 PAUL DOYLE-P (2)
31 ROBERTO RODRIGUEZ-P (2)
32 JERRY MORALES-OF
33 GARY ROSS-P
34 RON HERBEL-P (1)
34 DAVE ROBINSON-OF
37 PAT DOBSON-P
38 ROGER CRAIG-CH
39 JIM WILLIAMS-OF
41 STEVE ARLIN-P
42 EARL WILSON-P (2)
43 CLAY KIRBY-P
44 TOM DUKES (INJ)-P
46 DANNY COOMBS-P
49 RAFAEL ROBLES-SS
50 PAUL DOYLE-P (2)
DICK KELLEY (INJ)-(P)

1971

6TH W 61-100 28.5GB

1 BOB BARTON-C
2 DAVE GARCIA-CH
3 TOMMY DEAN-INF
4 BOB SKINNER-CH
6 DON MASON-2B/3B
7 ED SPIEZIO (INJ)-3B/OF
8 CHRIS CANNIZZARO-C (1)
8 JOHNNIE JETER-OF
8 ANGEL BRAVO-OF (2)
9 AL (THE BULL) FERRARA-OF (1)
10 DAVE CAMPBELL (INJ)-UTIL
11 ENZOHERNANDEZ-SS
12 RON SLOCUM-C
12 GARRY JESTADT-INF (2)
13 RAMON (RAY) WEBSTER-PH (1)
14 LARRY STAHL-OF/1B
15 DAVE ROBERTS-P
16 FRED KENDALL-C/INF
17 NATE COLBERT-1B
18 PRESTON GOMEZ-MGR
19 WHITEY WIETELMANN-CH
20 IVAN MURRELL-OF
21 CITO GASTON-OF
22 STEVE ARLIN-P
23 AL SANTORINI-P (1)
23 MIKE CALDWELL-P
24 LERON LEE-OF (2)
25 ROD GASPAR-OF
26 (DOWNTOWN) OLLIE BROWN-OF
28 MIKE IVIE-C
29 RAMON (RAY) WEBSTER-PH (1)
29 JAY FRANKLIN-P
30 MIKE CORKINS-P
32 JERRY MORALES-OF
33 GARY ROSS-P
34 DAVE ROBINSON-OF
35 FRED NORMAN-P (2)
36 TOM PHOEBUS-P
37 ED ACOSTA-P
37 BOB MILLER-P (2)
38 ROGER CRAIG-CH
39 JAY FRANKLIN-P
41 STEVE ARLIN-P
41 BILL LAXTON-P
42 DICK KELLEY-P
43 CLAY KIRBY-P
44 AL SEVERINSEN-P
46 DANNY COOMBS-P
48 BILL LAXTON-P

1972

6TH W 58-95 36.5GB

1 BOB BARTON-C
1 JOHNNY GRUBB-OF
1 MIKE FIORE-PH (2)
2 DAVE GARCIA-CH
3 CURT BLEFARY-UTIL (2)
4 BOB SKINNER-CH
6 DON MASON-2B/3B
6 FRED STANLEY-INF (2)
7 ED SPIEZIO-3B (1)
7 JOE GODDARD-C
8 JETER, JOHNNIE- OF
9 DON (POPEYE) ZIMMER-CH/MGR2
10 DAVE CAMPBELL-3B/2B
10 RANDY ELLIOTT-OF
11 ENZO HERNANDEZ-SS/OF
12 GARRY JESTADT-INF
14 LARRY STAHL-OF/1B
15 RALPH GARCIA-P
16 FRED KENDALL-C/1B
17 NATE COLBERT-1B
18 PRESTON GOMEZ-MGR1
18 DAVE HILTON-3B
19 WHITEY WIETELMANN-CH
20 IVAN MURRELL-OF
20 DAVE ROBERTS-3B/UTIL
21 CITO GASTON (INJ)-OF
22 STEVE ARLIN-P
23 MIKE CALDWELL-P
24 LERON LEE (INJ)-OF
25 MIKE KILKENNY-P (3)
26 (DOWNTOWN) OLLIE BROWN-OF (1)
27 BILL GREIF-P
28 PAT CORRALES-C (2)
30 DERRELL THOMAS-2B/UTIL
31 RAFAEL ROBLESL-SS/3B
32 JERRY MORALES-OF/3B
33 GARY ROSS-P
34 RANDY ELLIOTT-OF
35 FRED NORMAN-P
36 TOM PHOEBUS-P (1)
36 STEVE SIMPSON-P
37 ED ACOSTA-P
38 ROGER CRAIG-CH
39 MIKE CORKINS-P
40 MIKE CORKINS-P
42 RON TAYLOR-P
42 AL SEVERINSEN-P
43 CLAY KIRBY-P
44 AL SEVERINSEN-P
44 SCHAEFFER, MARK-P
46 SCHAEFFER, MARK-P
47 GARCIA, RALPH-P

1973

6TH W 60-102 39GB

1 JOHNNY GRUBB-OF
2 DAVE GARCIA-CH
4 BOB SKINNER-CH
5 GENE LOCKLEAR-OF (2)
6 BOB DAVIS-C
6 DON MASON-2B/3B
6 RICH MORALES-2B/SS (2)
8 DAVE MARSHALL-OF
9 DON (POPEYE) ZIMMER-MGR
10 DAVE CAMPBELL-INF (1)
10 DWAIN ANDERSON-SS/3B (2)
11 ENZO HERNANDEZ (INJ)-SS
14 IVAN MURRELL-OF/1B
16 FRED KENDALL-C
17 NATE COLBERT-1B
18 DAVE HILTON-3B/2B
19 WHITEY WIETELMANN-CH
20 DAVE ROBERTS-3B/2B
21 CITO GASTON-OF
22 STEVE ARLIN-P
23 MIKE CALDWELL-P
24 LERON LEE-OF
27 BILL GREIF-P
28 PAT CORRALES-C
29 PAT CORRALES-C
30 DERRELL THOMAS-SS/2B
31 DAVE WINFIELD-OF/1B
32 JERRY MORALES-OF
33 GARY ROSS-P
35 FRED NORMAN-P (1)
35 RANDY JONES-P
37 BOB MILLER-P (1)
40 MIKE CORKINS-P
42 BOB MILLER-P (1)
42 FRANK SNOOK-P
43 CLAY KIRBY (INJ)-P
44 VICENTE (HUEVO) ROMO-P
45 JOHNNY PODRES-CH
47 RICH TROEDSON-P

1974

6TH W 60-102 42GB

1 JOHNNY GRUBB-OF/3B
1 JOHN MCNAMARA-MGR
2 JOHN MCNAMARA-MGR
2 JOHNNY GRUBB-OF/3B
3 RANDY ELLIOTT-OF/1B
4 JACK BLOOMFIELD-CH
5 GENE LOCKLEAR-OF
5 BILL ALMON-SS
6 RICH MORALES-2B/SS
7 HORACE CLARKE-2B (2)
8 DAVE HILTON-3B/2B
8 CHRIS CANNIZZARO-C
9 BILL (BARNACLE BILL) POSEDEL-CH
10 CHRIS CANNIZZARO-C
10 DAVE HILTON-3B/2B
11 ENZO HERNANDEZ-SS
12 JOHN SCOTT-OF
12 JIM DAVENPORT-CH
15 MIKE IVIE-1B
16 FRED KENDALL-C
17 NATE COLBERT-1B
18 GLENN BECKERT (INJ)-2B/3B
19 WHITEY WIETELMANN-CH
20 DAVE ROBERTS-3B/UTIL
21 CITO GASTON-OF
22 STEVE ARLIN-P (1)
22 MIKE JOHNSON-P
23 BERNIE WILLIAMS-OF
23 ROD GASPAR-OF/1B
24 JOE MCINTOSH-P
25 LARRY HARDY-P
25 ROD GASPAR-OF/1B
26 BOB BARTON-C
27 BILL GREIF-P
28 BOBBY TOLAN (INJ)-OF
29 LOWELL PALMER-P
30 DERRELL THOMAS-2B/UTIL
31 DAVE WINFIELD-OF/1B
32 MATTY ALOU-OF/1B
32 GENE LOCKLEAR-OF
33 GARY ROSS-P
34 JIM DAVENPORT-CH
34 JOHN SCOTT-OF
35 RANDY JONES-P
36 JIM MCANDREW-P
36 BILL LAXTON-P
37 DAVE TOMLIN-P
38 MIKE JOHNSON-P
38 RUSTY GERHARDT-P
40 MIKE CORKINS (INJ)-P
41 BILL LAXTON-P
42 JERRY TURNER-OF
43 DAVE FREISLEBEN-P
44 WILLIE (STRETCH) MCCOVEY-1B
45 VICENTE (HUEVO) ROMO-P
46 RALPH GARCIA-P
47 RICH TROEDSON-P
48 DAN SPILLNER-P
50 RUSTY GERHARDT-P

1975

4TH W 71-91 37GB

1 JOHN MCNAMARA-MGR
2 JOHNNY GRUBB-OF/3B
3 BILL (THE CRICKET)(SPECS) RIGNEY-CH
4 RANDY HUNDLEY-C
5 BILL ALMON-SS
6 JOHN SCOTT-OF
6 DON HAHN-OF (3)
7 BOB DAVIS-C
8 TED KUBIAK-3B/INF (2)
9 DICK SISLER-CH
10 DAVE HILTON (ILL)-3B/2B
11 ENZO HERNANDEZ-SS
12 JIM DAVENPORT-CH
13 DICK SHARON-OF
14 DAVE FREISLEBEN-P
15 MIKE IVIE-UTIL
16 FRED KENDALL-C
17 JERRY MOSES-C (1)
18 GLENN BECKERT (INJ)-2B/3B
18 STEVE HUNTZ-3B/2B
19 WHITEY WIETELMANN-CH
20 DAVE ROBERTS-3B/2B
21 ALAN FOSTER (INJ)-P
22 BRENT STROM (INJ)-P
23 TITO FUENTES-2B
24 JOE MCINTOSH-P
25 LARRY HARDY-P
26 RICH FOLKERS-P
27 BILL GREIF-P
28 BOBBY TOLAN-OF/1B
29 TOM (PLOWBOY) MORGAN-CH
30 HECTOR TORRES-INF
31 DAVE WINFIELD-OF
32 GENE LOCKLEAR-OF
33 BOBBY VALENTINE-OF (2)
34 DANNY (BEAR) FRISELLA-P
35 RANDY JONES-P
36 BUTCH METZGER-P
37 DAVE TOMLIN-P
38 RUSTY GERHARDT-P
40 SONNY SIEBERT-P (1)
40 JERRY JOHNSON-P
42 JERRY TURNER-OF
43 DAVE FREISLEBEN-P
44 WILLIE (STRETCH) MCCOVEY-1B

AN DIEGO PADRES

3 DAN SPILLNER-P

1976

5TH W 73-89 29GB

1 JOHN MCNAMARA-MGR
2 JOHNNY GRUBB (INJ)-OF/INF
3 WILLIE DAVIS-OF
5 JOE AMALFITANO-CH
6 BILL ALMON-SS
7 BOB DAVIS-C
8 TED KUBIAK-INF
9 DICK SISLER-CH
1 ENZO HERNANDEZ-SS
2 TUCKER ASHFORD-3B
2 DOUG (THE RED ROOSTER) (ROJO) RADER-3B
4 DAVE FREISLEBEN-P
5 MIKE IVIE-1B/UTIL
6 FRED KENDALL-C
7 DOUG (THE RED ROOSTER) (ROJO) RADER-3B
7 MERV RETTENMUND-OF
8 MIKE CHAMPION-2B
9 WHITEY WIETELMANN-CH
1 ALAN FOSTER-P
2 BRENT STROM-P
3 TITO FUENTES-2B
4 DAVE WEHRMEISTER-P
4 KEN REYNOLDS-P
5 LUIS MELENDEZ-OF (2)
6 RICH FOLKERS-P
7 BILL GREIF-P (1)
7 RICK SAWYER-P
0 HECTOR TORRES-INF
1 DAVE WINFIELD-OF
2 GENE LOCKLEAR-OF (1)
3 BOBBY VALENTINE-OF/1B
3 TOM GRIFFIN-P (2)
4 KEN REYNOLDS-P
5 RANDY JONES-P
6 BUTCH METZGER-P
7 DAVE TOMLIN-P
8 ROGER CRAIG-CH
0 JERRY JOHNSON-P
2 JERRY TURNER-OF
3 MIKE DUPREE-P
4 WILLIE (STRETCH) MCCOVEY-1B
4 BOB OWCHINKO-P
6 TUCKER ASHFORD-3B
8 DAN SPILLNER (INJ)-P

1977

5TH W 69-93 29GB

1 JOHN MCNAMARA-MGR1
1 AL (BLACKIE) DARK-MGR3
2 JERRY TURNER-OF
2 LUIS MELENDEZ-OF
3 DAVE ROBERTS-C/INF
4 BOB SKINNER-CH/MGR2
5 JOE AMALFITANO-CH
5 AL (BLACKIE) DARK-MGR3
6 BILL ALMON-SS
7 BOB DAVIS-C
8 PAT SCANLON-UTIL
0 MIKE CHAMPION-2B
1 ENZO HERNANDEZ (INJ)-SS
2 DOUG (THE RED ROOSTER) (ROJO) RADER-3B (1)
3 BOBBY VALENTINE-OF/1B (1)
4 DAVE FREISLEBEN-P
5 MIKE IVIE-1B/3B
6 JOHN D'ACQUISTO-P (2)
7 MERV RETTENMUND-OF/3B
8 GENE TENACE-C/INF
9 WHITEY WIETELMANN-CH
0 JERRY TURNER-OF
20 GEORGE HENDRICK-OF
21 GARY SUTHERLAND-INF
22 BRENT STROM (INJ)-P
23 TITO FUENTES-2B
24 DAVE WEHRMEISTER-P
25 LUIS MELENDEZ-OF
25 GEORGE HENDRICK-OF
26 RICH FOLKERS-P
26 DAVE (KONG) KINGMAN-OF /INF (2)
27 RICK SAWYER-P
28 DON WILLIAMS-CH
29 GENE RICHARDS-OF/1B
31 DAVE WINFIELD-OF
33 TOM GRIFFIN-P
34 ROLLIE FINGERS-P
35 RANDY JONES (INJ)-P
36 BUTCH METZGER-P (1)
37 DAVE TOMLIN-P
37 BRIAN GREER-PH
38 ROGER CRAIG-CH
39 VIC BERNAL-P
40 PAUL SIEBERT-P
44 BOB OWCHINKO-P
46 TUCKER ASHFORD-3B/INF
46 PAUL SIEBERT-P
47 BOB SHIRLEY-P
48 DAN SPILLNER-P

1978

4TH W 84-78 11GB

1 OZZIE SMITH-SS
2 RICK SWEET-C
3 DAVE ROBERTS-UTIL
4 DOUG (THE RED ROOSTER) (ROJO) RADER- CH
4 PHIL ROOF-CH
6 BILL ALMON-3B/INF
7 BOB DAVIS-C
8 BARRY EVANS-3B
9 GENE RICHARDS-OF/1B
9 WHITEY WIETELMANN-CH
10 MIKE CHAMPION-2B/3B
12 TUCKER ASHFORD-INF
14 FERNANDO GONZALEZ-2B (2)
14 DAVE FREISLEBEN-P (1)
14 JIM BESWICK-OF
15 BRODERICK PERKINS-1B
16 JOHN D'ACQUISTO-P
17 OSCAR GAMBLE-OF
18 GENE TENACE-1B/UTIL
19 WHITEY WIETELMANN-CH
19 GENE RICHARDS-OF/1B
20 JERRY TURNER-OF
21 CHUCK BAKER-2B/SS
22 BILLY HERMAN-CH
23 CHUCK ESTRADA-CH
24 DAVE WEHRMEISTER-P
25 GEORGE HENDRICK-OF (1)
25 JIM WILHELM-OF
26 DON REYNOLDS-OF
27 MARK WILEY-P (1)
27 TONY CASTILLO-C
28 DON WILLIAMS-CH
29 MICKEY LOLICH (INJ)-P
30 DERREL THOMAS-UTIL
31 DAVE WINFIELD-OF/1B
32 OZZIE SMITH-SS
32 BOB SHIRLEY-P
33 JUAN EICHELBERGER-P
34 ROLLIE FINGERS-P
35 RANDY JONES-P
36 GAYLORD PERRY-P
38 ROGER CRAIG-MGR
40 PHIL ROOF-CH
41 ERIC RASMUSSEN-P (2)
42 MARK LEE-P
44 BOB OWCHINKO-P
45 RICK SWEET-C
47 BOB SHIRLEY-P
48 DAN SPILLNER-P (1)
48 DENNIS KINNEY-P (2)
59 STEVE MURA-P

1979

5TH W 68-93 22GB

1 OZZIE SMITH-SS
3 BILL FAHEY-C
4 JAY JOHNSTONE-OF/1B (2)
4 PAUL DADE-3B/OF (2)
5 FRED KENDALL-C/1B
6 BILL ALMON-UTIL
7 KURT BEVACQUA-UTIL
8 BARRY EVANS-UTIL
9 BRIAN GREER-OF
12 DOUG (THE RED ROOSTER) (ROJO) RADER- CH
13 FERNANDO GONZALEZ-2B
13 BOBBY TOLAN-1B/OF
15 BRODERICK PERKINS-1B
16 JOHN D'ACQUISTO-P
17 GENE RICHARDS-OF
18 GENE TENACE-1B/C
19 WHITEY WIETELMANN-CH
20 JERRY TURNER-OF
21 MIKE HARGROVE-1B (1)
21 JAY JOHNSTONE-OF/1B (2)
21 PAUL DADE-3B/OF (2)
22 BILLY HERMAN-CH
23 CHUCK ESTRADA-CH
24 DAN BRIGGS-1B/OF
25 JIM WILHELM-OF
26 DON REYNOLDS-OF
27 STEVE MURA (INJ)-P
28 DON WILLIAMS-CH
29 MICKEY LOLICH-P
30 TIM FLANNERY-2B
31 DAVE WINFIELD-OF
32 BOB SHIRLEY-P
33 JUAN EICHELBERGER-P
34 ROLLIE FINGERS (INJ)-P
35 RANDY JONES-P
36 GAYLORD PERRY (INJ)-P
37 JAY JOHNSTONE-OF/1B (2)
38 ROGER CRAIG-MGR
40 SAM PERLOZZO-2B
41 ERIC RASMUSSEN-P
42 MARK LEE-P
44 BOB OWCHINKO-P
48 DENNIS KINNEY-P
49 TOM TELLMANN-P
50 STEVE MURA (INJ)-P
59 STEVE MURA (INJ)-P

1980

6TH W 73-89 19.5GB

1 OZZIE SMITH-SS
2 JERRY COLEMAN-MGR
3 BILL FAHEY-C
4 PAUL DADE-UTIL
4 AURELIO RODRIGUEZ-3B/SS (1)
4 LUIS SALAZAR-3B/OF
5 FRED KENDALL-C/1B
5 RANDY BASS-1B
6 TIM FLANNERY-2B/3B
7 KURT BEVACQUA-3B/1B (1)
7 CRAIG STIMAC-C/3B
8 BARRY EVANS-INF
11 CHUCK BAKER-SS
13 BOBBY TOLAN-CH
15 BRODERICK PERKINS-1B /OF
16 JOHN D'ACQUISTO-P (1)
17 GENE RICHARDS-OF
18 GENE TENACE-C/1B
19 AL HEIST-CH
20 JERRY TURNER (INJ)-OF
21 PAUL DADE-UTIL
22 VON JOSHUA-OF/1B
23 CHUCK ESTRADA-CH
25 WILLIE MONTANEZ-1B (1)
27 STEVE MURA-P
28 JERRY MUMPHREY-OF
29 DON WILLIAMS-CH
30 DAVE CASH-2B
31 DAVE WINFIELD-OF
32 BOB SHIRLEY-P
33 JUAN EICHELBERGER (INJ) -P
34 ROLLIE FINGERS-P
35 RANDY JONES (INJ)-P
36 MIKE ARMSTRONG-P
37 DICK PHILLIPS-CH
40 RICK WISE (INJ)-P
41 ERIC RASMUSSEN-P
42 GEORGE STABLEIN-P
43 GARY LUCAS-P
47 DENNIS BLAIR-P
48 DENNIS KINNEY-P
49 TOM TELLMANN-P
51 JACK CURTIS-P
56 DICK PHILLIPS-CH

1981

1ST 1/2:6TH W 23-33 12.5GB
2ND 1/2:6TH W 18-36 15.5GB
FINAL: 6TH W 41-69 --GB

1 OZZIE SMITH-SS
2 ALAN WIGGINS-OF
3 JUAN BONILLA-2B
4 LUIS SALAZAR-3B/OF
5 RANDY BASS-1B
6 TIM FLANNERY-3B/2B
7 CRAIG STIMAC-PH
8 BARRY EVANS-INF
9 STEVE SWISHER-C
10 MIKE PHILLIPS-2B/SS (1)
10 DOUG GWOSDZ-C
12 MARIO RAMIREZ-SS/3B
13 JUAN EICHELBERGER -P
14 JOSE MORENO-OF/2B
15 BRODERICK PERKINS-1B/ OF
16 TERRY KENNEDY-C
17 GENE RICHARDS-OF
18 JOE LEFEBVRE-OF
20 JERRY TURNER-OF (1)
22 BOBBY TOLAN-CH
22 RUPPERT JONES-OF
23 CHUCK ESTRADA-CH
24 DAVE EDWARDS-OF
25 GARY LUCAS-P
26 CHRIS WELSH-P
27 STEVE MURA-P
28 RUPPERT JONES-OF
28 BOBBY TOLAN-CH
30 DAN BOONE-P
33 FRANK (CAPITAL PUNISHER)(HONDO) HOWARD-MGR
34 JACK KROL-CH
36 MIKE ARMSTRONG-P
37 ED BRINKMAN-CH
38 JOHN URREA-P
39 ED (BIG ED) STEVENS-CH
40 RICK WISE (INJ)-P
41 FRED KUHAULUA-P
43 GARY LUCAS-P
44 ERIC SHOW-P
48 TIM LOLLAR-P
50 JOHN LITTLEFIELD-P
51 FRED KUHAULUA-P
51 JACK CURTIS-P
62 STEVE FIREOVID-P

1982

4TH W 81-81 8GB

1 GARRY TEMPLETON-SS
2 ALAN WIGGINS (SUB)-OF/2B
3 JUAN BONILLA (INJ)-2B
4 LUIS SALAZAR-3B/UTIL
5 RANDY BASS-1B (1)
5 RON TINGLEY-C
6 TIM FLANNERY-2B/INF
7 KURT BEVACQUA-UTIL
8 JOE PITTMAN-2B/SS (2)
9 STEVE SWISHER (INJ)-C
10 DOUG GWOSDZ-C
11 JERRY MANUEL-INF
11 GEORGE HINSHAW-OF
12 MARIO RAMIREZ-INF
13 JUAN EICHELBERGER -P
14 SIXTO LEZCANO-OF
15 BRODERICK PERKINS-1B/OF
16 TERRY KENNEDY-C/1B
17 GENE RICHARDS (INJ)-OF/1B
18 JOE LEFEBVRE-UTIL
19 TONY GWYNN-OF
20 RICK LANCELLOTTI-1B/OF
21 JODY LANSFORD-1B
22 RUPPERT JONES-OF
23 DICK WILLIAMS-MGR
24 DAVE EDWARDS-OF/1B
25 GARY LUCAS-P
26 CHRIS WELSH-P
27 JOHN (COUNT) MONTEFUSCO-P
28 BOBBY TOLAN-CH
29 DAN BOONE-P (1)
30 DAN BOONE-P (1)
30 ERIC SHOW-P
32 OZZIE VIRGIL-CH
34 JACK KROL-CH
35 LUIS DELEON-P
39 FLOYD CHIFFER-P
40 RICK WISE-P
40 ANDY HAWKINS-P
43 DAVE DRAVECKY-P
44 ERIC SHOW-P
45 MIKE GRIFFIN-P
46 NORM SHERRY-CH
48 TIM LOLLAR-P
51 JACK CURTIS-P (1)
54 JOHN (COUNT) MONTEFUSCO-P
55 LUIS DELEON-P
63 ANDY HAWKINS-P

1983

4TH W 81-81 10GB

1 GARRY TEMPLETON-SS
2 ALAN WIGGINS-OF/1B
3 JUAN BONILLA-2B
4 LUIS SALAZAR-3B/SS
6 STEVE GARVEY (INJ)-1B
7 KURT BEVACQUA-UTIL
9 RUPPERT JONES-OF
10 DOUG GWOSDZ-C
11 TIM FLANNERY-INF
12 MARIO RAMIREZ-INF
14 SIXTO LEZCANO-OF (1)
15 BRUCE BOCHY-C
16 TERRY KENNEDY-C/1B
17 GENE RICHARDS-OF/1B
18 JOE LEFEBVRE-UTIL (1)
18 KEVIN MCREYNOLDS-OF
19 TONY GWYNN (INJ)-OF
20 JERRY TURNER-OF
20 BOBBY BROWN-OF
21 JODY LANSFORD-1B
22 GEORGE HINSHAW-OF
23 DICK WILLIAMS-MGR
25 GARY LUCAS-P
26 CHRIS WELSH-P (1)
27 JOHN (COUNT) MONTEFUSCO-P (1)
27 DENNIS RASMUSSEN-P
28 BOBBY TOLAN-CH
29 ELIAS SOSA-P
30 ERIC SHOW-P
31 ED WHITSON (INJ)-P

32 OZZIE VIRGIL-CH
33 HARRY DUNLOP-CH
34 JACK KROL-CH
35 LUIS DELEON-P
36 EDDIE RODRIGUEZ-INF
38 MARK THURMOND-P
39 FLOYD CHIFFER-P
39 ELIAS SOSA-P
40 ANDY HAWKINS-P
42 SID MONGE-P (2)
43 DAVE DRAVECKY-P
44 MARTY DECKER-P
46 NORM SHERRY-CH
47 DENNIS RASMUSSEN-P
48 TIM LOLLAR-P
49 MIKE COUCHEE (INJ)-P
49 SID MONGE-P (2)
50 GERRY DAVIS-OF
51 GREG BOOKER-P
58 MARK THURMOND-P
62 STEVE FIREOVID-P

1984

1ST W 92-70 0GB
W NLCS-CHIN 3-2
L WS-DETA 4-1

1 GARRY TEMPLETON-SS
2 ALAN WIGGINS-2B
4 LUIS SALAZAR-UTIL
6 STEVE GARVEY-1B
7 KURT BEVACQUA-UTIL
9 GRAIG NETTLES-3B
10 DOUG GWOSDZ-C
11 TIM FLANNERY-INF
12 MARIO RAMIREZ-INF
14 CARMELO MARTINEZ-OF/1B
15 BRUCE BOCHY-C
16 TERRY KENNEDY-C
18 KEVIN MCREYNOLDS-OF
19 TONY GWYNN -OF
20 BOBBY BROWN-OF
23 DICK WILLIAMS-MGR
24 CHAMP SUMMERS-1B
25 FLOYD CHIFFER-P
29 DEACON JONES-CH
30 ERIC SHOW-P
31 ED WHITSON-P
32 OZZIE VIRGIL-CH
33 HARRY DUNLOP-CH
34 JACK KROL-CH
35 LUIS DELEON (INJ)-P
37 CRAIG LEFFERTS-P
38 MARK THURMOND-P
39 EDDIE MILLER-OF
40 ANDY HAWKINS-P
41 RON ROENICKE-OF
42 SID MONGE-P (1)
42 GREG HARRIS-P (2)
43 DAVE DRAVECKY-P
46 NORM SHERRY-CH
48 TIM LOLLAR-P
51 GREG BOOKER-P
54 GOOSE GOSSAGE-P

1985

3RD W (TIE) 83-79 12GB

1 GARRY TEMPLETON-SS
2 ALAN WIGGINS (SUB)-2B (1)
3 JERRY ROYSTER-UTIL
4 AL BUMBRY-OF
6 STEVE GARVEY-1B
7 KURT BEVACQUA-UTIL
9 GRAIG NETTLES-3B
10 EDDIE RODRIGUEZ-PH
11 TIM FLANNERY-2B/3B
12 MARIO RAMIREZ-INF
14 CARMELO MARTINEZ-OF/1B
15 BRUCE BOCHY-C
16 TERRY KENNEDY-C/1B
17 MIGUEL DILONE-OF (2)
18 KEVIN MCREYNOLDS-OF
19 TONY GWYNN -OF
20 BOBBY BROWN-OF
23 DICK WILLIAMS-MGR
26 ED WOJNA-P
26 GERRY DAVIS-OF
29 DEACON JONES-CH
30 ERIC SHOW-P
31 LAMARR HOYT-P
32 OZZIE VIRGIL-CH
33 HARRY DUNLOP-CH
34 JACK KROL-CH
35 LUIS DELEON-P
36 GALEN CISCO-CH
37 CRAIG LEFFERTS-P
38 MARK THURMOND-P
39 ROY LEE JACKSON-P
40 ANDY HAWKINS-P
43 DAVE DRAVECKY-P
46 BOB PATTERSON-P
48 GENE WALTER-P
49 TIM STODDARD-P
50 LANCE MCCULLERS-P
51 GREG BOOKER-P
54 GOOSE GOSSAGE (INJ)-P

1986

4TH W 74-88 22GB

1 GARRY TEMPLETON-SS
2 BIP ROBERTS-2B
3 JERRY ROYSTER-UTIL
4 SANDY ALOMAR-CH
5 RANDY READY-3B (2)
6 STEVE GARVEY-1B
7 MARVELL WYNNE-OF
8* DANE IORG-UTIL/P*
8 JOHN KRUK-OF/1B
9 GRAIG NETTLES-3B
10 BENITO SANTIAGO-C
11 TIM FLANNERY-2B/INF
12 RANDY ASADOOR-3B/2B
12 MARK WASINGER-3B/2B
14 CARMELO MARTINEZ-UTIL
15 BRUCE BOCHY-C
16 TERRY KENNEDY-C/1B
17 TIM PYZNARSKI-1B
18 KEVIN MCREYNOLDS-OF
19 TONY GWYNN-OF
20 GARY GREEN-SS
22 STEVE BOROS-MGR
24 DAVE LAPOINTE-P (2)
26 ED WOJNA-P
27 MARK PARENT-C
29 DEACON JONES-CH
30 ERIC SHOW (INJ)-P
31 LAMARR HOYT-P
32 ED WHITSON-P (2)
33 HARRY DUNLOP-CH
34 JACK KROL-CH
36 GALEN CISCO-CH
37 CRAIG LEFFERTS-P
38 THURMOND MARK-P (1)
38 ED WHITSON-P (2)
40 ANDY HAWKINS-P
41 LANCE MCCULLERS-P
43 DAVE DRAVECKY (INJ)-P
45 JIMMY JONES-P
47 BOB STODDARD-P
48 GENE WALTER-P
49 TIM STODDARD-P (1)
49 DAVE LAPOINTE-P (2)
50 ED VOSBERG-P
51 GREG BOOKER-P
54 GOOSE GOSSAGE-P
58 RAY HAYWOOD-P

1987

6TH W 65-97 25GB

1 GARRY TEMPLETON-SS
2 SANDY ALOMAR-CH
4 JOEY CORA-2B/SS
5 RANDY READY-3B/UTIL
6 STEVE GARVEY (INJ)-1B
7 KEVIN MITCHELL-3B/OF (1)
7 ROB NELSON-1B (2)
8 JOHN KRUK-1B/OF
9 BENITO SANTIAGO-C
10 LARRY BOWA-MGR
11 TIM FLANNERY-2B/INF
13 MARK DAVIS-P (2)
14 CARMELO MARTINEZ-OF/1B
15 BRUCE BOCHY-C
16 MARVELL WYNNE-OF
19 TONY GWYNN-OF
21 JIM STEELS-OF
22 STAN JEFFERSON-OF
23 SHANE (MACK THE KNIFE) MACK-OF
24 LUIS SALAZAR-UTIL/P
25 RAY HAYWOOD-P
26 ED WOJNA-P
27 MARK PARENT-C
28 SHAWN ABNER-OF
29 DEACON JONES-CH
30 ERIC SHOW-P
31 ED WHITSON-P
32 ED WHITSON-P
32 KEITH COMSTOCK-P
33 HARRY DUNLOP-CH
34 STORM DAVIS (INJ)-P (1)
35 CHRIS BROWN-3B (2)
36 GALEN CISCO-CH
37 CRAIG LEFFERTS-P (1)
37 ERIC NOLTE-P
38 GREG RIDDOCH-CH
39 TOM GORMAN (INJ)-P
40 ANDY HAWKINS (INJ)-P
41 LANCE MCCULLERS-P
43 DAVE DRAVECKY-P (1)
43 DAVE LEIPER-P (2)
45 JIMMY JONES-P
47 RANDY BYERS-OF
48 MARK DAVIS-P (2)
51 GREG BOOKER-P
52 JIM STEELS-OF
52 MARK GRANT-P (2)
54 GOOSE GOSSAGE (INJ)-P
55 MARK GRANT-P (2)

1988

3RD W 83-78 11GB

1 GARRY TEMPLETON-SS/3B
2 SANDY ALOMAR-CH
3 GREG RIDDOCH-CH
4 SANDY ALOMAR, JR.-PH
5 RANDY READY-UTIL
6 KEITH MORELAND-1B/UTIL
6 *(RET#) STEVE GARVEY*
7 ROB NELSON-1B
7 KEITH MORELAND-1B/UTIL
8 JOHN KRUK-1B/OF
9 BENITO SANTIAGO-C
10 LARRY BOWA-MGR1
10 BIP ROBERTS-INF
11 TIM FLANNERY-INF
12 ROBERTO ALOMAR-2B
14 CARMELO MARTINEZ-OF/1B
15 JACK MCKEON-MGR2
16 MARVELL WYNNE-OF
19 TONY GWYNN-OF
21 DICKIE THON-INF
22 STAN JEFFERSON-OF
23 SHANE (MACK THE KNIFE) MACK-OF
24 JERALD CLARK-OF
26 AMOS OTIS-CH
27 MARK PARENT-C
28 SHAWN ABNER-OF
30 ERIC SHOW-P
31 ED WHITSON-P
32 KEITH COMSTOCK-P
34 DENNIS SOMMERS-CH
35 CHRIS BROWN-3B
36 PAT DOBSON-CH
37 ERIC NOLTE-P
40 ANDY HAWKINS-P
41 LANCE MCCULLERS-P
43 DAVE LEIPER-P
43 DENNIS RASMUSSEN-P (2)
45 JIMMY JONES-P
46 GREG W. HARRIS-P
47 RANDY BYERS-OF
48 MARK DAVIS-P
51 GREG BOOKER-P
52 DAVE LEIPER-P
53 CANDY SIERRA-P (1)
54 GOOSE GOSSAGE (INJ)-P
55 MARK GRANT-P

1989

2ND W 89-73 3GB

1 GARRY TEMPLETON-SS/3B
2 SANDY ALOMAR-CH
3 GREG RIDDOCH-CH
4 LUIS SALAZAR-3B/UTIL (1)
4 JOEY CORA-INF
5 RANDY READY-UTIL (1)
6 *(RET#) STEVE GARVEY*
7 ROB NELSON-1B
8 JOHN KRUK-OF (1)
9 BENITO SANTIAGO-C
10 BIP ROBERTS-UTIL
11 TIM FLANNERY-3B/2B
12 ROBERTO ALOMAR-2B
13 MIKE (PAGS) PAGLIARULO-3B (2)
14 CARMELO MARTINEZ-OF/1B
15 JACK MCKEON-MGR2
16 MARVELL WYNNE-OF (1)
17 SANDY ALOMAR, JR.-C
18 CHRIS JAMES-OF/3B (2)
19 TONY GWYNN-OF
20 GARY GREEN-SS/3B
21 PHIL STEPHENSON-1B (2)
22 DARRIN (D. J.) JACKSON-OF (2)
24 JERALD CLARK-OF
25 JACK CLARK-1B/OF
26 AMOS OTIS-CH
27 MARK PARENT-C
28 SHAWN ABNER-OF
30 ERIC SHOW (INJ)-P
31 ED WHITSON-P
32 CALVIN SCHIRALDI-P (2)
34 DENNY SOMMERS-CH
35 WALT TERRELL-P (1)
36 PAT DOBSON-CH
37 ERIC NOLTE-P
38 PAT CLEMENTS-P
39 DAN MURPHY-P
40 ANDY BENES-P
41 FREDDIE TOLIVER-P (2)
43 DENNIS RASMUSSEN-P
46 GREG W. HARRIS-P
47 BRUCE (LEFTY) HURST-P
48 MARK DAVIS-P
51 GREG BOOKER-P (1)
51 DON SCHULZE-P (2)
52 DAVE LEIPER (INJ)-P
55 MARK GRANT-P

1990

4TH W (TIE) 75-87 16GB

1 GARRY TEMPLETON-SS/3B
2 SANDY ALOMAR-CH
3 GREG RIDDOCH-CH/MGR2
4 DARRIN (D. J.) JACKSON-OF
5 JOEY CORA-UTIL
6 *(RET#) STEVE GARVEY*
7 ROB NELSON-PH
8 FRED LYNN-OF
9 BENITO SANTIAGO (INJ)-C
10 BIP ROBERTS-OF/INF
11 CRAIG LEFFERTS-P
12 ROBERTO ALOMAR-2B/SS
13 MIKE (PAGS) PAGLIARULO-3B
14 ATLEE (HAM)(CHIEF) HAMMAKER-P (2)
15 JACK MCKEON-MGR1
16 MERV RETTENMUND-CH
16? JACK MALOOF-CH
17 JOE CARTER-OF/1B
19 TONY GWYNN-OF
21 PHIL STEPHENSON-1B
22 EDDIE WILLIAMS-3B
23 ROB PICCIOLO-CH
24 JERALD CLARK-1B/OF
25 JACK CLARK (INJ)-1B
25 TOM LAMPKIN-C
26 AMOS OTIS-CH
26 DEREK (THE GEORGIA BULLDOG) LILLIQUIST-P (2)
27 MARK PARENT-C
28 SHAWN ABNER-OF
29 JIM SNYDER-CH
30 ERIC SHOW-P
31 ED WHITSON-P
32 CALVIN SCHIRALDI-P
33 TOM HOWARD-OF
34 DENNY SOMMERS-CH
34 BRUCE KIMM-CH
35 RAFAEL VALDEZ-P
36 PAT DOBSON-CH
36 MIKE ROURKE-CH
38 PAT CLEMENTS-P
40 ANDY BENES-P
41 MIKE DUNNE (INJ)-P
42 RICH RODRIGUEZ-P
43 DENNIS RASMUSSEN-P
44 JOHN DAVIS-P
46 GREG W. HARRIS-P
47 BRUCE (LEFTY) HURST-P
51 GREG BOOKER-P (1)
53 PAUL FARIES-INF
54 RONN REYNOLDS-C
55 MARK GRANT-P (1)

1991

3RD W 84-78 10GB

1 GARRY TEMPLETON-3B/SS (1)
2 TONY FERNANDEZ-SS
2 JIM VATCHER-OF
3 GREG RIDDOCH-MGR
4* DARRIN (D. J.) JACKSON-OF/P*
5 ROB PICCIOLO-CH
6 *(RET#) STEVE GARVEY*
7 MARTY (BUBBLE) BARRETT (INJ)-2B/3B
7 DANN BILARDELLO-C
8 BRIAN DORSETT-1B
8 TONY FERNANDEZ-SS
09 BENITO SANTIAGO (INJ)-C
10 BIP ROBERTS-2B/OF
11 CRAIG LEFFERTS-P
12 SCOTT COOLBAUGH-3B
14 ATLEE (HAM)(CHIEF) HAMMAKER (INJ)-P
15 MIKE ALDRETE-OF (1)
15 JOSE MOTA-2B/SS
16 MERV RETTENMUND-CH
17 JIM SNYDER-CH
18 JIM PRESLEY-3B
18 CRAIG SHIPLEY-SS/2B
19 TONY GWYNN (INJ)-OF
20 TIM TEUFEL-2B/3B (2)
21 PHIL STEPHENSON (INJ)-PH
22 OSCAR AZOCAR-OF

SAN DIEGO PADRES

3 PAUL FARIES-INF
4 JERALD CLARK-OF/1B
5 TOM LAMPKIN-C
6 DEREK (THE GEORGIA BULLDOG) LILLIQUIST-P (2)
7 LARRY ANDERSEN-P
8 SHAWN ABNER-OF (1)
8 JACK HOWELL-3B (2)
9 FRED MCGRIFF-1B
0 KEVIN WARD-OF
1 ED WHITSON (INJ)-P
2 ADAM PETERSON-P
3 TOM HOWARD-OF
4 BRUCE KIMM-CH
6 MIKE ROURKE-CH
7 ERIC NOLTE-P (1)
8 PAT CLEMENTS (INJ)-P
9 WES GARDNER-P (1)
9 JIM LEWIS-P
0 ANDY BENES-P
1 STEVE ROSENBERG-P
2 RICH RODRIGUEZ-P
3 DENNIS RASMUSSEN (INJ)-P
5 JOHN (ELVIS) COSTELLO-P
6 GREG W. HARRIS (INJ)-P
7 BRUCE (LEFTY) HURST-P
8 JOSE MELENDEZ-P
0 JEREMY HERNANDEZ-P
1 MIKE MADDUX-P
4 TIM SCOTT-P
6 RICKY BONES, -P

1992

3RD W 82-80 16GB

1 TONY FERNANDEZ-SS
2 JIM VATCHER-OF
3 GREG RIDDOCH-MGR1
4 DARRIN (D. J.) JACKSON-OF
5 ROB PICCIOLO-CH
6 *(RET#) STEVE GARVEY*
7 DANN BILARDELLO (INJ)-C
8 GARY PETTIS-OF (1)
8 JIM RIGGLEMAN-MGR2
9 BENITO SANTIAGO (INJ)-C
10 GARY SHEFFIELD-3B
11 CRAIG LEFFERTS-P (1)
15 KURT STILLWELL (INJ)-INF
16 MERV RETTENMUND-CH
17 JIM SNYDER-CH
18 CRAIG SHIPLEY-SS/2B
19 TONY GWYNN (INJ)-OF
20 TIM TEUFEL-2B/3B
21 PHIL STEPHENSON-PH
22 OSCAR AZOCAR-OF
23 PAUL FARIES-INF
24 JERALD CLARK-OF/1B
25 TOM LAMPKIN-C
27 LARRY ANDERSEN (INJ)-P
28 RANDY MYERS-P
29 FRED MCGRIFF-1B
30 KEVIN WARD-OF
(31) ED WHITSON (INJ)-(P)
33 TOM HOWARD-OF
33 GENE HARRIS-P
34 BRUCE KIMM-CH
36 MIKE ROURKE-CH
37 LARRY ANDERSEN (INJ)-P
38 PAT CLEMENTS (INJ)-P
38 JIM DESHAIES-P
40 ANDY BENES-P
41 JEFF GARDNER-2B
42 RICH RODRIGUEZ-P
43 GUILLERMO VELASQUEZ-1B
44 FRANK SEMINARA-P
45 DAVE EILAND (INJ)-P
46 GREG W. HARRIS (INJ)-P
47 BRUCE (LEFTY) HURST (INJ)-P
48 JOSE MELENDEZ-P
49 DOUG BROCAIL-P
50 JEREMY HERNANDEZ-P
51 MIKE MADDUX (INJ)-P
54 TIM SCOTT-P
58 DAN WALTERS-C

1993

7TH W 61-101 43GB

1 LUIS LOPEZ-2B
3 DARRELL SHERMAN-OF
4 DEREK BELL-OF/3B
5 ROB PICCIOLO-CH
6 *(RET#) STEVE GARVEY*
7 RICKY GUTIERREZ-SS/UTIL
8 JIM RIGGLEMAN-MGR
10 GARY SHEFFIELD-3B (1)
10 MELVIN NIEVES-OF
11 DAN WALTERS-C
11 BRAD AUSMUS-C
12 JEFF GARDNER-2B/INF
13 BRUCE BOCHY-CH
15 KURT STILLWELL (INJ)-SS/3B (1)
16 MERV RETTENMUND-CH
17 BOB GEREN-C/INF
17 JARVIS BROWN-OF
18 CRAIG SHIPLEY-INF/OF
19 TONY GWYNN (INJ)-OF
20 TIM TEUFEL-INF
21 BILLY BEAN-OF/1B
22 DAN RADISON-CH
23 GUILLERMO VELASQUEZ-1B/OF
24 PHIL PLANTIER-OF
25 KEVIN HIGGINS-C/UTIL
26 ARCHI CIANFROCCO-3B/1B (2)
27 SCOTT SANDERS-P
28 DAVE STATON-1B
29 FRED MCGRIFF-1B (1)
30 PHIL CLARK-UTIL
33 GENE HARRIS-P
34 TREVOR HOFFMAN-P (2)
36 MIKE ROURKE-CH
37 KERRY TAYLOR-P
39 PAT GOMEZ (INJ)-P
40 ANDY BENES-P
41 WALLY WHITEHURST (INJ)-P
42 RICH RODRIGUEZ-P (1)
42 PEDRO A. MARTINEZ-P
43 ANDY ASHBY-P (2)
44 FRANK SEMINARA-P
45 DAVE EILAND-P
45 MARK DAVIS-P (2)
46 GREG W. HARRIS-P (1)
47 BRUCE (LEFTY) HURST (INJ)-P (1)
48 ROGER MASON-P (1)
49 DOUG BROCAIL-P
50 JEREMY HERNANDEZ-P (1)
50 MARK ETTLES-P
52 TIM MAUSER-P (2)
54 TIM SCOTT-P (1)
54 RUDY SEANEZ-P
58 TIM WORRELL-P

1994

4TH W 47-70 12.5GB
STRIKE NO POST-SEASON

1 LUIS LOPEZ-2B
2 KEITH LOCKHART-3B
3 MELVIN NIEVES-OF
4 DEREK BELL (SUS)-OF
5 ROB PICCIOLO-CH
6 *(RET#) STEVE GARVEY*
7 RICKY GUTIERREZ-SS
8 JIM RIGGLEMAN-MGR
9 SCOTT LIVINGSTON-3B (2)
10 BIP ROBERTS-2B
11 BRAD AUSMUS-C
12 RAY HOLBERT-SS
15 BRUCE BOCHY-CH
16 MERV RETTENMUND-CH
17 TIM HYERS (INJ)-OF/1B
18 CRAIG SHIPLEY (INJ)-INF
19 TONY GWYNN (INJ)-OF
20 RAY MCDAVID-OF
21 BILLY BEAN-OF/1B
22 DAN RADISON-CH
23 EDDIE WILLIAMS-1B
24 PHIL PLANTIER-OF
26 ARCHI CIANFROCCO-3B
27 SCOTT SANDERS (INJ)-P
28 BRIAN JOHNSON-C
30 PHIL CLARK-OF/1B
31 DAVE STATON-1B
32 DAVE BIALAS-CH
33 GENE HARRIS-P (1)
33 BILL KRUEGER-P
34 SONNY SIEBERT-CH
36 TIM WORRELL (INJ)-P
37 KERRY TAYLOR-P
38 DONNIE ELLIOTT (INJ)-P
39 BRYCE FLORIE (INJ)-P
40 ANDY BENES-P
41 WALLY WHITEHURST (INJ)-P
42 PEDRO A. MARTINEZ-P
43 ANDY ASHBY-P
44 A. J. SAGER-P
46 JEFF TABAKA-P (2)
47 JOSE MARTINEZ-P
48 MARK DAVIS (REL)-P
48 MIKE CAMPBELL-P
49 DOUG BROCAIL (INJ)-P
50 JOEY HAMILTON-P
51 TREVOR HOFFMAN-P
52 TIM MAUSER (INJ)-P

1995

3RD W 70-74 8GB
144 GAME SEASON

(1) LUIS LOPEZ (INJ)-(SS)
2 JODY REED-2B
3 MELVIN NIEVES-OF
4 ANDUJAR CEDENO-SS
5 ROB PICCIOLO-CH
6 *(RET#) STEVE GARVEY*
7 PHIL PLANTIER-OF (2)
8 GRAIG NETTLES-CH
8 SCOTT LIVINGSTON-3B
9 SCOTT LIVINGSTON-3B
9 GRAIG NETTLES-CH
10 BIP ROBERTS-2B
11 BRAD AUSMUS-C
12 STEVE FINLEY-OF
14 DAVEY LOPES-CH
14 MARC NEWFIELD-OF (2)
15 BRUCE BOCHY-MGR
16 MERV RETTENMUND-CH
17 TIM HYERS-OF
18 RAY HOLBERT-2B
19 TONY GWYNN-OF
21 KEN CAMINITI-3B
23 EDDIE WILLIAMS-1B
24 ROBERTO PETAGINE-1B
25 BRIAN JOHNSON-C
26 BRIAN WILLIAMS-P
27 SCOTT SANDERS-P
29 ARCHI CIANFROCCO-UTIL
30 PHIL CLARK-OF
31 BILLY BEAN-OF
33 BILL KRUEGER-P
33 GLENN DISHMAN-P
34 FERNANDO VALENZUELA-P
36 TIM WORRELL-P
38 DONNIE ELLIOTT-P
39 BRYCE FLORIE-P
40 ANDY BENES-P
42 DAVEY LOPES-CH
43 ANDY ASHBY-P
44 SONNY SIEBERT-CH
45 DOUG BOCHTLER-P
46 JEFF TABAKA-P
47 WILLIE BLAIR-P
48 BILL KRUEGER-P
48 DUSTIN HERMANSON-P
49 RON VILLONE-P
50 JOEY HAMILTON-P
51 TREVOR HOFFMAN-P
52 TIM MAUSER-P
54 MARC KROON-P
55 ANDRES BERUMEN-P

1996

1ST W 91-71 0GB
L NLDS-STLN 3-0

1 LUIS LOPEZ (INJ)-SS
2 JIM TATUM-3B (2)
3 JODY REED-2B
4 TIM FLANNERY-CH
5 ROB PICCIOLO-CH
6 *(RET#) STEVE GARVEY*
7 GREG VAUGHN-OF (2)
8 SCOTT LIVINGSTONE (INJ)-PH
9 CHRIS GWYNN (INJ)-OF
10 ANDUJAR CEDENO-SS (1)
10 CHRIS GOMEZ-SS (2)
11 BRAD AUSMUS-C (1)
12 STEVE FINLEY-OF
13 TODD STEVERSON-PH
14 MARC NEWFIELD-OF (1)
15 BRUCE BOCHY-MGR
16 MERV RETTENMUND-CH
17 DOUG DASCENZO-OF
18 CRAIG SHIPLEY (INJ)-SS/OF
19 TONY GWYNN (INJ)-OF
20 GRADY LITTLE-CH
21 KEN CAMINITI-3B
22 WALLY JOYNER (INJ)-1B
23 JOHN FLAHERTY-C (2)
24 RICKEY HENDERSON-OF
25 BRIAN JOHNSON-C
27 SCOTT SANDERS-P
28 ROB DEER, ROB-PH
29 ARCHI CIANFROCCO (INJ)-3B/1B
31 BOB TEWKSBURY-P
33 GLENN DISHMAN (WAIV)-P (1)
34 FERNANDO VALENZUELA-P
35 JASON THOMPSON-1B
35 AL OSUNA-P (2)
36 TIM WORRELL-P
37 DAN WARTHEN-CH
39 BRYCE FLORIE-P (1)
39 PETE WALKER-P
40 MIKE OQUIST-P
42 DAVEY LOPES-CH
43 ANDY ASHBY (INJ)-P
44 SEAN BERGMAN-P
45 DOUG BOCHTLER-P
47 WILLIE BLAIR-P
48 DUSTIN HERMANSON-P
49 RON VILLONE-P (1)
50 JOEY HAMILTON-P
51 TREVOR HOFFMAN-P
53 DARIO VERAS-P
55 ANDRES BERUMEN-P
59 SEAN MULLIGAN-C

1997

4TH W 76-86 14GB

3 MANDY ROMERO-C
4 QUILVIO VERAS-2B
5 ROB PICCIOLO-CH
6 *(RET#) STEVE GARVEY*
7 PHIL PLANTIER (INJ)-OF (1)
8 SCOTT LIVINGSTONE (INJ) 3B (1)
8 MARK SWEENEY-OF (2)
9 CARLOS HERNANDEZ (INJ)-C
10 CHRIS GOMEZ-SS
11 TIM FLANNERY-CH
12 STEVE FINLEY (INJ)-OF
13 JORGE VELANDIA-2B/SS
14 DON SLAUGHT-C
14 GEORGE ARIAS-3B (2)
15 BRUCE BOCHY-MGR
16 MERV RETTENMUND-CH
18 CRAIG SHIPLEY (INJ)-INF
19 TONY GWYNN-OF
20 CHRIS JONES-OF
21 KEN CAMINITI (INJ)-3B
22 WALLY JOYNER (INJ)-1B
23 JOHN FLAHERTY-C
24 RICKEY HENDERSON (INJ)-OF (1)
25 GREG VAUGHN-OF
26 JERRY SHUMPERT (INJ)-INF
27 DERRICK LEE-1B
28 RUBEN RIVERA-OF
29 ARCHI CIANFROCCO (INJ) -3B/1B
31 TREY BEAMON-PH
32 TIM SCOTT (REL)-P (1)
32 MARC KROON-P
33 TERRY BURROWS-P
34 FERNANDO VALENZUELA-P (1)
34 DANNY JACKSON (RET)-P (2)
35 *(RET#) RANDY JONES*
36 TIM WORRELL-P
37 DAN WARTHEN-CH
38 GREG BOOKER-CH
39 WILL CUNNANE-P
40 SEAN BERGMAN-P
41 STERLING HITCHCOCK (INJ)-P
42 DAVEY LOPES-CH
43 ANDY ASHBY-P
44 TODD ERDOS-P
45 DOUG BOCHTLER (INJ)-P
46 RICH BATCHELER-P (2)
47 PETE SMITH-P
48 HEATH MURRAY (INJ)-P
50 JOEY HAMILTON (INJ)-P
51 TREVOR HOFFMAN-P
52 JOEY LONG-P
53 DARIO VERAS-P
54 PAUL MENHART-P
55 JIM BRUSKE (INJ)-P
65 CARLOS HERNANDEZ (INJ)-C

1998

1ST W 98-64 0GB
W NLDS-HOU 3-1
W NLCS-ATL 4-2
L WS-NYA 4-0

2 ANDY SHEETS-INF
3 MANDY ROMERO-C (1)
3 ANDY SHEETS-INF
4 QUILVIO VERAS-2B
5 ROB PICCIOLO-CH
6 *(RET#) STEVE GARVEY*
7 JAMES MOUTON (INJ)-OF
8 MARK SWEENEY-OF
9 CARLOS HERNANDEZ-C
10 CHRIS GOMEZ-SS
11 TIM FLANNERY-CH
12 STEVE FINLEY-OF
13 JIM LEYRITZ-C (2)
14 GEORGE ARIAS-3B
15 BRUCE BOCHY-MGR
16 MERV RETTENMUND-CH
17 ED GIOVANOLA-INF
18 RANDY MYERS-P (2)
19 TONY GWYNN-OF

20 GREG MYERS (INJ)-C
21 KEN CAMINITI (INJ)-3B
22 WALLY JOYNER-1B
23 GREG VAUGHN-OF
24 MARK LANGSTON (INJ)-P
25 EDDIE WILLIAMS-1B
25 BEN DAVIS-C
26 DON WENGERT-P (1)
26 SCOTT SANDERS-P (2)
27 KEVIN BROWN-P
28 RUBEN RIVERA-OF
29 ARCHI CIANFROCCO (INJ) -3B/1B
30 DAVEY LOPES-CH
31 MATT CLEMENT-P
32 MARC KROON-P (1)
32 ROBERTO RAMIREZ-P
33 DAN MICELI-P
34 DAVE STEWART-CH
35 *(RET#) RANDY JONES*
36 DONNE WALL-P
37 BRIAN BOEHRINGER-P
38 GREG BOOKER-CH
39 WILL CUNNANE (INJ)-P
41 STERLING HITCHCOCK-P
42 DAVEY LOPES-CH
42 *(RET#) JACKIE ROBINSON*
43 ANDY ASHBY-P
44 JOHN VANDER WAL-1B (2)
47 PETE J. SMITH-P (1)
49 BEN VANRYN-P (2)
50 JOEY HAMILTON-P
51 TREVOR HOFFMAN-P
(52) ED VOSBERG (INJ)-(P)
55 JIM BRUSKE-P (2)
56 CARLOS REYES-P (1)
58 STAN SPENCER-P

1999

4TH W 74-88 26GB

1 CARLOS GARCIA-3B
1 CARLOS BAERGA-2B (1)
2 DAMIAN JACKSON-SS
3 ERIC OWENS-OF
4 QUILVIO VERAS-2B
5 ROB PICCIOLO-CH
6 *(RET#) STEVE GARVEY*
7 WIKLENMAN (WIKI) GONZALEZ- C
8 MERV RETTENMUND-CH
(9) CARLOS HERNANDEZ (INJ)-(C)
10 CHRIS GOMEZ (INJ)-SS
11 TIM FLANNERY-CH
12 DAVE MAGADAN-3B
13 JIM LEYRITZ (INJ) C (1)
14 GEORGE ARIAS (INJ)-3B
15 BRUCE BOCHY-MGR
16 REGGIE SANDERS (INJ)-OF
17 ED GIOVANOLA-INF
18 WOODY WILLIAMS-P
19 TONY GWYNN (INJ)-OF
20 GREG MYERS (INJ)-C (1)
21 GARY MATTHEWS, JR.-OF
22 WALLY JOYNER (INJ)-1B
23 PHIL NEVIN-OF/C
24 DAVID NEWHAN-INF
25 BEN DAVIS-C
26 MIKE DARR-OF
27 HEATH MURRAY-P
28 RUBEN RIVERA-OF
29 JOHN VANDER WAL-OF
30 DAVEY LOPES-CH
31 MATT CLEMENT-P
32 ROBERTO RIVERA-P
33 DAN MICELI-P
34 STAN SPENCER-P
35 *(RET#) RANDY JONES*
36 DONNE WALL-P
37 BRIAN BOEHRINGER (INJ)-P
38 GREG BOOKER-CH
39 WILL CUNNANE (INJ)-P
40 CARLOS ALMANZAR (INJ)-P
41 STERLING HITCHCOCK-P
42 *(RET#) JACKIE ROBINSON*
43 ANDY ASHBY-P
44 CARLOS REYES-P
45 DAVE SMITH-CH
46 DOMINGO GUZMAN-P
48 RANDY MYERS (INJ)-P
49 MATT WHITESIDE-P
50 MATT WHISENANT-P (2)
51 TREVOR HOFFMAN-P
52 ED VOSBERG (INJ)-P (1)
58 BUDDY CARLYLE-P

2000

5TH W 76-86 21GB

2 DAMIAN JACKSON-SS
3 ALAN TRAMMELL-CH
4 ED SPRAGUE-3B (1)(3)
5 ROB PICCIOLO-CH
6 *(RET#) STEVE GARVEY*
7 WIKLENMAN (WIKI) GONZALEZ-C
8 ERIC OWENS-OF
9 CARLOS HERNANDEZ-C (1)
9 GABE ALVAREZ-INF (2)
10 CHRIS GOMEZ (INJ)-SS
11 TIM FLANNERY-CH
12 DAVE MAGADAN-3B
13 BEN DAVIS-C
14 DAVID NEWHAN-INF (1)
14 DESI RELAFORD-SS (2)
15 BRUCE BOCHY-MGR
16 KEVIN NICHOLSON-INF
17 JOHN MABRY-OF (2)
18 WOODY WILLIAMS-P
19 TONY GWYNN (INJ)-OF
20 AL MARTIN-OF (1)
20 GREG LAROCCA-INF
21 DUSTY ALLEN-OF (1)
21 MATT CLEMENT-P
22 XAVIER NADY-3B
22 JOHN ROSKOS-OF
23 PHIL NEVIN-OF/C
24 BEN OGLIVIE-CH
24 JOE VITIELLO-INF
25 KORY DEHAAN (INJ)-OF
26 MIKE DARR-OF
27 STEVE MONTGOMERY (INJ)-P
28 RUBEN RIVERA-OF
29 BRET BOONE-2B
30 RYAN KLESKO-1B
31 MATT CLEMENT-P
32 STAN SPENCER (INJ)-P
33 WILL CUNNANE-P
34 BRIAN MEADOWS-P (1)
34 JAY WITASICK-P(2)
35 *(RET#) RANDY JONES*
36 DONNE WALL (INJ)-P
37 BRIAN BOEHRINGER (INJ)-P
38 GREG BOOKER-CH
39 CARLOS REYES-P (2)
39 GEORGE WILLIAMS-C
40 CARLOS ALMANZAR-P
41 STERLING HITCHCOCK (INJ)-P
42 *(RET#) JACKIE ROBINSON*
43 TOM DAVEY-P
43 DOMINGO GUZMAN-P
44 RODRIGO LOPEZ-P
44 TOM DAVEY-P
45 DAVE SMITH-CH
(46) CARLTON LOEWER (INJ)-(P)
47 BRANDON KOLB-P
48 RANDY MYERS (INJ)-P
49 MATT WHITESIDE-P
50 MATT WHISENANT (WAIV)-P
51 TREVOR HOFFMAN-P
52 DUANE ESPY-CH
53 ADAM EATON-P
54 DAVE MAURER-P
55 DANSERAFINI-P (1)
55 BRIAN TOLLBERG-P
56 KEVIN WALKER-P
57 TODD ERDOS-P (2)
58 BUDDY CARLYLE-P
58 HEATHCLIFF SLOCUM-P (2)
66 RODNEY L. MYERS (INJ)-P
77 GEORGE WILLIAMS-C

2001

4TH W 79-83 13GB

1 SANTIAGO PEREZ-2B
2 DAMIAN JACKSON-SS
3 ALAN TRAMMELL-CH
4 D'ANGELO JIMENEZ-3B
5 ROB PICCIOLO-CH
6 *(RET#) STEVE GARVEY*
7 WIKLENMAN (WIKI) GONZALEZ (INJ)-C
8 CESAR CRESPO-2B
9 ALEX ARIAS (INJ)-1B
10 CHRIS GOMEZ (WAIV)-SS (1)
10 EMIL BROWN-OF (2)
11 TIM FLANNERY-CH
12 DAVE MAGADAN-3B/1B
13 BEN DAVIS-C
14 MARK KOTSAY (INJ)-OF
15 BRUCE BOCHY-MGR
16 ADAM RIGGS-3B
16 RAY LANKFORD-OF (2)
17 DONALDO MENDEZ (INJ)-SS
18 WOODY WILLIAMS-P (1)
18 KEVIN WITT-3B
19 TONY GWYNN (INJ)-OF
20 RICK WILKINS-C
21 MIKE COLANGELO-OF
23 PHIL NEVIN-3B
24 RICKEY HENDERSON-OF
26 MIKE DARR (INJ)-OF
27 BUBBA TRAMMELL-OF
28 BOBBY J. JONES-P
29 RODNEY L. MYERS (INJ)-P
30 RYAN KLESKO-1B
31 *(RET#) DAVE WINFIELD*
32 KEVIN JARVIS-P
34 JAY WITASICK-P (1)
35 *(RET#) RANDY JONES*
36 DAVID LEE (INJ)-P
37 JOSE NUNEZ-P (2)
38 GREG BOOKER-CH
39 WESCAR SERRANO-P
40 JIMMY OSTING-P
41 STERLING HITCHCOCK (INJ)-P
42 *(RET#) JACKIE ROBINSON*
43 CHUCK MCELROY-P (2)
44 TOM DAVEY (INJ)-P
45 DAVE SMITH-CH
46 CARLTON LOEWER (INJ)-P
47 RUDY SEANEZ-P (1)
48 DARRELL AKERFELDS-CH
49 DAVID LUNDQUIST-P
50 BRIAN LAWRENCE-P
51 TREVOR HOFFMAN-P
52 DUANE ESPY-CH
53 ADAM EATON (INJ-P
54 DAVE MAURER-P
54 JASON MIDDLEBROOK-P
55 BRIAN TOLLBERG (INJ)-P
56 KEVIN WALKER (INJ)-P
57 JEREMY FIKAC-P
58 BRETT JODIE-P (2)
59 JUNIOR HERNDON-P (2)
66 RODNEY L. MYERS (INJ)-P

2002

5TH W 66-96 32GB

1 RAMON VAZQUEZ-2B/INF
2 CESAR CRESPO-UTIL
3 ALAN TRAMMELL-CH
4* D'ANGELO JIMENEZ-INF/P*
5 ROB PICCIOLO-CH
6 *(RET#) STEVE GARVEY*
7 WIKLENMAN (WIKI) GONZALEZ (INJ)-C
8 CESAR CRESPO-UTIL
8 DEIVI CRUZ-SS
9 RON GANT-OF
10 DEIVI CRUZ-SS
10 JULIUS MATOS-UTIL
11 TIM FLANNERY-CH
12 TRENIDAD HUBBARD-OF/INF
14 MARK KOTSAY-OF
15 BRUCE BOCHY-MGR
16 RAY LANKFORD (INJ)-OF
17 JONATHAN JOHNSON-P
18 KORY DEHAAN-OF
18 EUGENE KINGSALE-OF (2)
19 *(RET#) TONY GWYNN*
20 BRETT TOMKO-P
21 SEAN BURROUGHS (INJ)-3B/2B
23 PHIL NEVIN (INJ)-3B/1B
24 KEVIN BARKER-1B
24 ALEX PELAEX-INF
25 TOM LAMPKIN-C
27 BUBBA TRAMMELL-OF
28 BOBBY J. JONES-P
29 JAVIER CARDONA-C
29 KORY DEHAAN-OF
30 RYAN KLESKO-1B/OF
31 *(RET#) DAVE WINFIELD*
32 KEVIN JARVIS (INJ)-P
33 MARK SWEENEY-1B/OF
33 WIL NIEVES-C
34 BRIAN BUCHANAN-1B/OF (2)
35 *(RET#) RANDY JONES*
36 BEN HOWARD-P
37 JOSE NUNEZ (INJ)-P
38 GREG BOOKER-CH
39 STEVE REED-P (1)
39 BOBBY M. JONES-P (2)
40 MATT DEWITT (INJ)-P
41 ALAN EMBREE-P (1)
41 TOM DAVEY (INJ)-P
41 CLAY CONDREY-P
42 *(RET#) JACKIE ROBINSON*
43 JUAN MORENO-P
43 KEVIN PICKFORD-P
43 DOUG NICKLE-P (2)
44 TOM DAVEY (INJ)-P
44 JAKE PEAVY-P
45 DENNIS TANKERSLEY-P
46 JASON SHIELL-P
46 RODNEY L. MYERS-P
46 JASON KERSHNER-P (1)
47 WIL NIEVES-C
47 BRANDON VILLAFUERTE-P
47 DAVID LUNDQUIST (INJ)-P
48 DARRELL AKERFELDS-CH
49 ERIC CYR (INJ)-P
50 BRIAN LAWRENCE-P
51 TREVOR HOFFMAN-P
52 DUANE ESPY-CH
53 ADAM EATON (INJ)-P
54 JASON MIDDLEBROOK (INJ)-P (1)
54 MIKE BYNUM-P
55 BRIAN TOLLBERG (INJ)-P
56 KEVIN WALKER (INJ)-P
57 JEREMY FIKAC-P
58 JASON BOYD-P
58 MIKE HOLTZ (INJ)-P (2)
58 J. J. TRUJILLO-P
59 OLIVER PEREZ-P
59 JASON PEARSON-P
ROBERT RAMSAY (INJ)-(P)

2003

5TH W 64-98 36.5GB

1 RAMON VAZQUEZ (INJ)-SS/INF
2 JASON BAY (INJ)-OF (1)
3 SHANE VICTORINO-OF
3 KAHLIL GREENE-SS
5 ROB PICCIOLO-CH
6 *(RET#) STEVE GARVEY*
7 WIKLENMAN (WIKI) GONZALEZ-C
8 MARK LORETTA-2B
9 TODD SEARS-1B (2)
10 MIKE RIVERA-C
11 HUMBERTO QUINTERO-C
12 DAVE MAGADAN-CH
13 GARY MATTHEWS, JR.-OF (2)
14 MARK KOTSAY-OF
15 BRUCE BOCHY-MGR
16 LUTHER HACKMAN-P
17 JERMAINE CLARK-OF (2)
17 DONALDO MENDEZ-SS
18 KEITH LOCKHARDT (INJ) (REL)-2B
19 *(RET#) TONY GWYNN*
20 MIGUEL OJEDA-C/1B
21 JARET WRIGHT (WAIV)-P (1)
22 XAVIER NADY-OF
23 PHIL NEVIN (INJ)-1B/OF
24 DAVEY LOPES-CH
24 BRIAN GILES-OF (2)
25 DAVE HANSEN-INF
27 RONDELL WHITE-OF (1)
28 LOU MERLONI (INJ)-UTIL (1)
29 GARY BENNETT (INJ) (SUS:1G)-C
30 RYAN KLESKO (INJ)-1B
31 *(RET#) DAVE WINFIELD*
32 KEVIN JARVIS (INJ)-P
33 SEAN BURROUGHS-3B
34 BRIAN BUCHANAN-OF/1B
35 *(RET#) RANDY JONES*
37 CARLTON LOEWER-P
37 JOE ROA-P (3)
38 GREG BOOKER-CH
38 SCOTT LINEBRINK-P (2)
39 CHARLES NAGY-P
39 BEN HOWARD-P
40 TONY MUSER-CH
41 CLAY CONDREY (INJ)-P
42 *(RET#) JACKIE ROBINSON*
43 BRANDON VILLAFUERTE-P
44 JAKE PEAVY-P
45 DENNIS TANKERSLEY-P
45 ROD BECK-P
46 JAY WITASICK (INJ)-P
47 JESSE OROSCO-P (1)
48 DARRELL AKERFELDS-CH
49 MIKE MATTHEWS-P
50 BRIAN LAWRENCE-P
51 TREVOR HOFFMAN (INJ)-P
52 MATT HERGES-P (1)
53 ADAM EATON (INJ)-P
54 MIKE BYNUM-P
55 BRIAN TOLLBERG-P
56 KEVIN WALKER (INJ)-P
57 RANDY KEISLER-P
58 LUTHER HACKMAN-P
58 ROGER DEAGO-P
59 OLIVER PEREZ-P (1)
__ DARREN BALSLEY-CH

2004

3RD W 87-75 6GB

1 RAMON VAZQUEZ (INJ)-INF

SAN DIEGO PADRES

2 KERRY ROBINSON-OF
3 KAHLIL GREENE-SS
5 ROB PICCIOLO-CH
6 *(RET#) STEVE GARVEY*
7 FREDDY GUZMAN-OF
8 MARK LORETTA-2B
9 ALEX GONZALEZ-SS (3)
10 JON KNOTT-1B
11 HUMBERTO QUINTERO-C
12 DAVE MAGADAN-CH
13 ANTONIO OSUNA (INJ)-P
14 TERRANCE LONG-OF
15 BRUCE BOCHY-MGR
16 AKINORI OTSUKA-P
17 JAY PAYTON-OF
18 DARREN BRAGG-OF (1)
19 *(RET#) TONY GWYNN*
20 MIGUEL OJEDA-C
21 RICH AURILIA-SS/3B (2)
22 XAVIER NADY-OF
23 PHIL NEVIN-1B
24 BRIAN GILES-OF
25 DAVEY LOPES-CH
27 DAVE HANSEN-3B (2)
29 ROBERT FICK-OF (2)
30 RYAN KLESKO (INJ)-OF/1B
31 *(RET#) DAVE WINFIELD*
32 SEAN BURROUGHS-3B
33 DAVID WELLS-P
34 BRIAN BUCHANAN-OF (1)
35 *(RET#) RANDY JONES*
36 DARREN BALSLEY-CH
37 BRIAN SWEENEY-P
38 SCOTT LINEBRINK-P
39 BLAINE NEAL-P
40 TONY MUSER-CH
41 STERLING HITCHCOCK (INJ)-P
42 *(RET#) JACKIE ROBINSON*
43 EDDIE OROPESA-P
43 ANDY ASHBY-P
44 JAKE PEAVY-P
45 ROD BECK-P
46 JAY WITASICK-P
47 JUSTIN GERMANO-P
48 DARRELL AKERFELDS-CH
49 DENNIS TANKERSLEY-P
50 BRIAN LAWRENCE-P
51 TREVOR HOFFMAN-P
52 RICKY STONE-P (2)
53 ADAM EATON-P
54 MARTY MCLEARY-P
54 MIKE BYNUM-P
55 RAMON HERNANDEZ-C
58 JASON SZUMINSKI-P
58 BRANDON PUFFER-P (1)
58 STEVE WATKINS-P
59 ISMAEL VALDEZ-P (1)

2005

1ST W — 82-80 — 0GB

L NLDS-STLN 3-0

2 DAMIAN JACKSON-UTIL
3 KAHLIL GREENE (INJ)-SS
4 BEN JOHNSON-OF
5 ROB PICCIOLO-CH
6 *(RET#) STEVE GARVEY*
(7) FREDDY GUZMAN (INJ)-(OF)
7 ERIC YOUNG (INJ)-2B/OF
8 MARK LORETTA (INJ)-2B
9 JESSE GARCIA-SS
9 DAVID ROSS-C (2)
10 DAVE ROBERTS (INJ)-OF
11 MARK SWEENEY-OF/1B
12 DAVE MAGADAN-CH
13 ROBERT FICK-C/1B
14 ADAM HYZDU-OF (1)
14 MIGUEL OLIVO-C (2)
15 BRUCE BOCHY-MGR
16 AKINORI OTSUKA-P
17 WOODY WILLIAMS (INJ)-P
18 PAUL MCANULTY-INF
19 *(RET#) TONY GWYNN*
20 MIGUEL OJEDA-C (1)
20 MANNY ALEXANDER-INF
22 XAVIER NADY-OF/1B
23 PHIL NEVIN-1B (1)
24 BRIAN GILES-OF
25 DAVEY LOPES-CH
27 GEOFF BLUM (INJ)-3B (1)
28 JOE RANDA-3B (2)
29 CHRIS HAMMOND (INJ)-P
30 RYAN KLESKO-OF/1B
31 *(RET#) DAVE WINFIELD*
33 SEAN BURROUGHS-3B
34 DARRELL MAY-P (1)
34 PEDRO ASTACIO-P (2)
35 *(RET#) RANDY JONES*
36 DARREN BALSLEY-CH
37 RUDY SEANEZ (INJ)-P
38 SCOTT LINEBRINK-P
39 TIM REDDING (INJ)-P (1)
39 WILSON VALDEZ-SS (2)
40 TONY MUSER-CH
41 BRIAN FALKENBERG-P
42 *(RET#) JACKIE ROBINSON*
44 JAKE PEAVY-P
46 PAUL QUANTRILL-P (2)
47 TIM STAUFFER-P
48 DARRELL AKERFELDS-CH
49 DENNYS REYES (REL)-P
49 CRAIG BRESLOW-P
50 BRIAN LAWRENCE-P
51 TREVOR HOFFMAN-P
52 CLAY HENSLEY-P
53 ADAM EATON (INJ)-P
55 RAMON HERNANDEZ (INJ)-C
56 SCOTT CASSIDY-P (2)
57 RANDY WILLIAMS-P (1)
58 CHRIS OXSPRING-P
61 CHAN HO PARK-P (2)

Kahlil Greene, the Padres young shortstop, performing one of his acrobatic displays. He can handle the bat as well. He's had 15 home runs each of the last two seasons.

1932
NEW YORK GIANTS
6TH (TIE) 72-82 18GB

NO# JOHN (LITTLE NAPOLEON) (MUGGSY) MCGRAW-MGR1
1 HUGHIE CRITZ-2B
2 JO-JO (THE GAUSE GHOST) MOORE-OF
2 LEN KOENECKE-OF
3 FRED LINDSTROM-OF/3B
3 EDDIE MOORE-INF
4 BILL (MEMPHIS BILL) TERRY-1B/MGR2
5 MEL (MASTER MELVIN) OTT -OF
6 TRAVIS (STONEWALL) JACKSON (INJ)-SS
7 SHANTY HOGAN-C
8 JOHNNY VERGEZ-3B/SS
9 BOB O'FARRELL-C
10 CARL (THE MEALTICKET) (KING CARL) HUBBELL-P
11 FREDDIE (FAT FREDDIE) FITZSIMMONS-P
12 BILL WALKER-P
14 JIM MOONEY-P
15 HI BELL-P
16 DOLF (THE PRIDE OF HAVANA) LUQUE-P
17 SAM GIBSON-P
18 HAL (PRINCE HAL) SCHUMACHER-P
19 WAITE (SCHOOLBOY) HOYT-P (2)
20 SAM (SAMBO) LESLIE-1B
21 CHICK FULLIS-OF/2B
22 ETHAN ALLEN-OF
23 GIL ENGLISH-3B/SS
24 ED MARSHALL-SS
24 FRANCIS HEALY-C
25 CLARENCE MITCHELL-P/CH
26 IVAN (IVY) OLSON-CH
27 TOMMY CLARKE-CH
28 ART MCLARNEY-SS
29 PAT VELTMAN-PH
30 JOHNNY (TIP) TOBIN-PH
35 ROY (TARZAN) PARMELEE-P

1933
1ST 91-61 0GB
W WS-WASA 4-1

1 JO-JO (THE GAUSE GHOST) MOORE-OF
2 KIDDO DAVIS-OF
3 BILL (MEMPHIS BILL) TERRY (INJ)-1B/MGR
4 MEL (MASTER MELVIN) OTT-OF
5 TRAVIS (STONEWALL) JACKSON-SS/3B
6 HUGHIE CRITZ-2B
7 JOHNNY VERGEZ (ILL)-3B
7 CHUCK DRESSEN-3B
8 GUS (BLACKIE) MANCUSO-C
9 PAUL RICHARDS-C
10 WATTY (LEFTY) CLARK-P (2)
11 CARL (THE MEALTICKET) (KING CARL) HUBBELL-P
12 FREDDIE (FAT FREDDIE) FITZSIMMONS-P
14 PHIL (MICKEY) WEINTRAUB-OF
14 BILL SHORES-P
15 HI BELL-P
16 RAY (IRON MAN) STARR-P (1)
16 LEFTY O'DOUL-OF (2)
17 HAL (PRINCE HAL) SCHUMACHER-P
18 ROY (TARZAN) PARMELEE-P
19 GLENN SPENCER-P
20 DOLF (THE PRIDE OF HAVANA) LUQUE-P
21 AL SMITH-P/CH
22 SAM (SAMBO) LESLIE-1B (1)
22 BILL SHORES-P
23 BLONDY RYAN-SS
24 BERNIE JAMES-INF
25 JACK SALVESON-P
26 HOMER PEEL-OF
27 JOE MALAY-1B
27 HANK LEIBER-OF
28 HARRY (THE HORSE) DANNING-C
28 GEORGE (THE BULL) UHLE-P (2)
31 TOMMY CLARKE-CH
32 FRANK (PANCHO) SNYDER-CH
44 JOHNNY VERGEZ (ILL)-3B

1934
2ND 93-60 2GB

1 JO-JO (THE GAUSE GHOST) MOORE-OF
2 GEORGE WATKINS-OF
3 BILL (MEMPHIS BILL) TERRY (INJ)-1B/MGR
4 MEL (MASTER MELVIN) OTT-OF
5 TRAVIS (STONEWALL) JACKSON-SS/3B
6 HUGHIE CRITZ-2B
7 JOHNNY VERGEZ-3B
8 GUS (BLACKIE) MANCUSO-C
9 PAUL RICHARDS-C
10 HARRY (THE HORSE) DANNING-C
11 CARL (THE MEALTICKET) (KING CARL) HUBBELL-P
12 FREDDIE (FAT FREDDIE) FITZSIMMONS-P
14 SLICK CASTLEMAN-P
14 PHIL (MICKEY) WEINTRAUB-OF
15 HI BELL-P
16 LEFTY O'DOUL-OF
17 HAL (PRINCE HAL) SCHUMACHER-P
18 ROY (TARZAN) PARMELEE (ILL)-P
19 JOE BOWMAN-P
20 DOLF (THE PRIDE OF HAVANA) LUQUE-P
21 AL SMITH-P
22 GEORGE (BOOTS) GRANTHAM-1B/3B
22 PHIL (MICKEY) WEINTRAUB-OF
23 BLONDY RYAN-INF
24 FRESCO (TOMMY) THOMPSON-PH
25 JACK SALVESON-P
26 HOMER PEEL-OF
27 HANK LEIBER-OF
28 WATTY (LEFTY) CLARK-P (1)
28 JACK SALVESON-P
31 TOMMY CLARKE-CH
32 FRANK (PANCHO) SNYDER-CH

1935
3RD 91-62 8.5GB

1 JO-JO (THE GAUSE GHOST) MOORE-OF
2 DICK (ROWDY RICHARD) BARTELL-SS
3 BILL (MEMPHIS BILL) TERRY (INJ)-1B/MGR
4 MEL (MASTER MELVIN) OTT-OF/3B
5 TRAVIS (STONEWALL) JACKSON-3B
6 HUGHIE CRITZ-2B
7 KIDDO DAVIS-OF
8 GUS (BLACKIE) MANCUSO-C
9 PAUL RICHARDS-C (1)
9 GLENN MYATT-C (2)
10 HARRY (THE HORSE) DANNING-C
11 CARL (THE MEALTICKET) (KING CARL) HUBBELL-P
12 FREDDIE (FAT FREDDIE) FITZSIMMONS (INJ)-P
14 ALLYN (FISH HOOK) STOUT-P
15 LEON (SHAG) CHAGNON-P
15 HARRY (GUNBOAT) GUMBERT-P
15 EUEL (CHIEF) MOORE-P (2)
16 HANK LEIBER-OF
17 HAL (PRINCE HAL) SCHUMACHER-P
18 ROY (TARZAN) PARMELEE -P
20 DOLF (THE PRIDE OF HAVANA) LUQUE-P/CH
21 AL SMITH-P
22 AL CUCCINELLO-2B/3B
22 JOE MALAY-PH
23 MARK KOENIG-2B/INF
24 AL CUCCINELLO-2B/3B
25 FRANK (THE GREAT GABBO) GABLER-P
27 PHIL (MICKEY) WEINTRAUB-1B/OF
31 TOMMY CLARKE-CH
32 FRANK (PANCHO) SNYDER-CH
33 SLICK CASTLEMAN-P

1936
1ST 92-62 0GB
L WS-NYA 4-2

1 JO-JO (THE GAUSE GHOST) MOORE-OF
2 DICK (ROWDY RICHARD) BARTELL-SS
3 BILL (MEMPHIS BILL) TERRY (INJ)-1B/MGR
4 MEL (MASTER MELVIN) OTT-OF
5 HANK LEIBER-OF/1B
6 TRAVIS (STONEWALL) JACKSON-3B/SS
7 BURGESS (WHITEY) WHITEHEAD-2B
8 GUS (BLACKIE) MANCUSO-C
9 HARRY (THE HORSE) DANNING-C
10 HARRY (GUNBOAT) GUMBERT-P
11 CARL (THE MEALTICKET) (KING CARL) HUBBELL-P
12 FREDDIE (FAT FREDDIE) FITZSIMMONS (INJ)-P
14 SLICK CASTLEMAN-P
15 DICK COFFMAN-P
16 FIRPO MARBERRY-P
17 HAL (PRINCE HAL) SCHUMACHER-P
18 AL SMITH-P
19 FRANK (THE GREAT GABBO) GABLER-P
20 EDDIE (HOTSHOT) MAYO-3B
20 JOE (SMOKEY JOE) MARTIN -3B
21 ROY SPENCER-C
21 CHARLIE ENGLISH-2B
22 MARK KOENIG-INF
23 JIMMY RIPPLE-OF
24 KIDDO DAVIS-OF
25 TOMMY CLARKE-CH
25 JOHNNY MCCARTHY-1B
26 SAM (SAMBO) LESLIE-1B
30 DOLF (THE PRIDE OF HAVANA) LUQUE-P
32 FRANK (PANCHO) SNYDER-CH
__ JIM (BIG JIM) SHEEHAN-C (1G: 9/26)
__ BABE YOUNG-PH (1G: 9/26)

1937
1ST 95-57 0GB
W WS-NYA 4-1

1 JO-JO (THE GAUSE GHOST) MOORE-OF
1 LOU CHIOZZA-3B/UTIL
2 DICK (ROWDY RICHARD) BARTELL-SS
3 MEL (MASTER MELVIN) OTT-OF/3B
3 HANK LEIBER (INJ)-OF
3 WALLY BERGER-OF (2)
4 HANK LEIBER (INJ)-OF
4 MEL (MASTER MELVIN) OTT-OF/3B
5 JO-JO (THE GAUSE GHOST) MOORE-OF
6 JOHNNY MCCARTHY-1B
7 BURGESS (WHITEY) WHITEHEAD-2B
8 GUS (BLACKIE) MANCUSO-C
9 HARRY (THE HORSE) DANNING-C
10 HARRY (GUNBOAT) GUMBERT-P
11 CARL (THE MEALTICKET) (KING CARL) HUBBELL-P
12 FREDDIE (FAT FREDDIE) FITZSIMMONS (INJ)-P (1)
12 TOM (RATTLESNAKE) BAKER-P (2)
14 DICK COFFMAN-P
15 SLICK CASTLEMAN (INJ)-P
15 PHIL (MICKEY) WEINTRAUB- (2)
16 CLIFF (MICKEY MOUSE) (MOUNTAIN MUSIC) MELTON-P
17 HAL (PRINCE HAL) SCHUMACHER-P
18 AL SMITH-P
19 FRANK (THE GREAT GABBO) GABLER-P (1)
19 BEN CANTWELL-P (1)
19 DON BRENNAN-P (2)
20 SAM (SAMBO) LESLIE-1B
21 MICKEY HASLIN-INF
22 BLONDY RYAN-INF
23 JIMMY RIPPLE-OF
24 KIDDO DAVIS-OF (1)
24 BILL LOHRMAN-P
25 ED MADJESKI-C
26 HANK LEIBER (INJ)-OF
27 HY VANDENBERG-P
28 JUMBO BROWN-P (2)
30 BILL (MEMPHIS BILL) TERRY -MGR
31 DOLF (THE PRIDE OF HAVANA) LUQUE-P
32 FRANK (PANCHO) SNYDER-CH

1938
3RD 83-67 5GB

1 JO-JO (THE GAUSE GHOST) MOORE-OF
2 DICK (ROWDY RICHARD) BARTELL-SS
3 JIMMY RIPPLE-OF
4 MEL (MASTER MELVIN) OTT-3B/OF
5 HANK LEIBER-OF
6 JOHNNY MCCARTHY-1B
(7) BURGESS (WHITEY) WHITEHEAD (ILL)-(2B)
7 GEORGE (MERCURY) (FOGFHORN) (STUD) MYATT-SS/3B
7 MICKEY HASLIN-3B/2B
7 ALEX KAMPOURIS-2B (2)
8 GUS (BLACKIE) MANCUSO-C
9 HARRY (THE HORSE) DANNING-C
10 HARRY (GUNBOAT) GUMBERT-P
11 CARL (THE MEALTICKET) (KING CARL) HUBBELL-P
12 BILL LOHRMAN-P
14 DICK COFFMAN-P
15 SLICK CASTLEMAN-P
16 CLIFF (MICKEY MOUSE) (MOUNTAIN MUSIC) MELTON-P
17 HAL (PRINCE HAL) SCHUMACHER-P
18 HY VANDENBERG-P
18 OSCAR GEORGY-P
19 MICKEY HASLIN-3B/2B
19 BOB (SUITCASE BOB) SEEDS-OF
20 SAM (SAMBO) LESLIE-1B
21 WALLY BERGER-OF (1)
21 HAL (?) KRAUSE-CH
22 BLONDY RYAN-INF
22 BILL CISSELL-2B/3B
23 JOHNNIE (HANS) WITTIG-P
24 JUMBO BROWN-P
25 TOM (RATTLESNAKE) BAKER-P
26 LOU CHIOZZA (INJ)-UTIL
26 ALEX KAMPOURIS-2B (2)
27 MICKEY HASLIN-3B/2B
28 LES POWERS-PH
29 TOM (RATTLESNAKE) BAKER-P
30 BILL (MEMPHIS BILL) TERRY -MGR
31 TOMMY CLARKE-CH
31 TRAVIS (STONEWALL) JACKSON (INJ)-CH
32 FRANK (PANCHO) SNYDER-CH
33? DOLF (THE PRIDE OF HAVANA) LUQUE-CH

1939
5TH 77-74 18.5GB

1 SKEETER SCALZI-SS/3B
1 GEORGE (MERCURY) (FOGFHORN) (STUD) MYATT (INJ)-3B
2 BURGESS (WHITEY) WHITEHEAD-2B/INF
2 AL GLOSSOP-2B
3 JO-JO (THE GAUSE GHOST) MOORE-OF
4 MEL (MASTER MELVIN) OTT-OF/3B

5 ZEKE BONURA-1B
6 FRANK DEMAREE-OF
7 BILLY JURGES-SS
8 HARRY (THE HORSE) DANNING-C
9 KEN O'DEA-C
0 HARRY (GUNBOAT) GUMBERT-P
1 CARL (THE MEALTICKET) (KING CARL) HUBBELL-P
2 BILL LOHRMAN-P
4 DICK COFFMAN-P
4 RAY HAYWORTH-C (2)
5 SLICK CASTLEMAN-P
5 TOM (BIG TOM) GORMAN-P
6 CLIFF (MICKEY MOUSE) (MOUNTAIN MUSIC) MELTON-P
7 HAL (PRINCE HAL) SCHUMACHER-P
8 MANNY (GYP) SALVO-P
9 GEORGE (MERCURY) (FOGFHORN) (STUD) MYATT (INJ)-3B
9 JOHNNIE (HANS) WITTIG-P
9 RED LYNN-P (2)
9 TOM (HEAVE-O) (THE ARM) HAFEY-3B
9 TONY (POOSH 'EM UP) LAZZERI-3B (2)
0 JUMBO BROWN-P
1 LOU CHIOZZA (INJ)-3B/SS
1 BABE YOUNG-1B
21 AL GLOSSOP-2B
22 ALEX KAMPOURIS-2B
23 JOHNNY MCCARTHY-1B/OF/P
24 JIMMY RIPPLE-OF (1)
25 BOB (SUITCASE BOB) SEEDS-OF
26 RED LYNN-P (2)
27 HY VANDENBERG-P
28 JOHNNY (UGLY) DICKSHOT-OF
29 JOHNNIE (HANS) WITTIG-P
30 BILL (MEMPHIS BILL) TERRY-MGR
31 TRAVIS (STONEWALL) JACKSON-CH
32 FRANK (PANCHO) SNYDER-CH

1940

6TH *72-80* *27.5GB*

1 JO-JO (THE GAUSE GHOST) MOORE-OF
2 BILLY JURGES (INJ)-SS
2 RED TRAMBACK-OF
3 FRANK DEMAREE-OF
4 MEL (MASTER MELVIN) OTT-OF/3B
5 BABE YOUNG-1B
6 MICKEY WITEK-SS/2B
7 BURGESS (WHITEY) WHITEHEAD-3B/INF
8 HARRY (THE HORSE) DANNING-C
9 KEN O'DEA (INJ)-C
10 HARRY (GUNBOAT) GUMBERT-P
11 CARL (THE MEALTICKET) (KING CARL) HUBBELL-P
12 BILL LOHRMAN-P
14 RED LYNN-P
15 CLIFF (MICKEY MOUSE) (MOUNTAIN MUSIC) MELTON-P
17 HAL (PRINCE HAL) SCHUMACHER-P
18 JOHNNY MCCARTHY-1B/OF/P
19 ROY (POP) JOINER-P
20 JUMBO BROWN-P
21 PAUL (DAFFY) DEAN-P
22 HY VANDENBERG-P
22 WILLIS (ACE) HUDLIN-P (4)
22 BOB CARPENTER-P
23 GLEN (GABBY) STEWART-3B/SS
24 BUSTER MAYNARD-OF
24 BURGESS (WHITEY) WHITEHEAD-3B/INF
25 GLEN (GABBY) STEWART-3B/SS
26 JOHNNY RUCKER-OF
27 AL GLOSSOP-2B (1)
27 TONY (COOCH) (CHICK) CUCCINELLO-2B/3B (2)
29 BOB (SUITCASE BOB) SEEDS-OF
30 BILL (MEMPHIS BILL) TERRY-MGR
31 TRAVIS (STONEWALL) JACKSON-CH
32 FRANK (PANCHO) SNYDER-CH
33 RAY HAYWORTH-C (2)

1941

5TH *74-79* *25.5GB*

1 JOHNNY RUCKER-OF
2 BILLY JURGES-SS
3 HARRY (THE HORSE) DANNING-C/1B
4 MEL (MASTER MELVIN) OTT-OF
5 BABE YOUNG-1B
6 JOE ORENGO-INF
7 BURGESS (WHITEY) WHITEHEAD-32B/3B
8 KEN O'DEA-C
9 GABBY HARTNETT-C
10 HARRY (GUNBOAT) GUMBERT-P (1)
10 RUBE FISCHER-P
11 CARL (THE MEALTICKET) (KING CARL) HUBBELL-P
12 BILL LOHRMAN-P
14 DICK (ROWDY RICHARD) BARTELL-3B/SS (2)
15 CLIFF (MICKEY MOUSE) (MOUNTAIN MUSIC) MELTON-P
16 BOB BOWMAN-P
17 HAL (PRINCE HAL) SCHUMACHER-P
18 BUMP HADLEY-P (1)
18 HARRY FELDMAN-P
19 JOHNNIE (HANS) WITTIG-P
20 JUMBO BROWN-P
20 BABE BARNA-OF
21 PAUL (DAFFY) DEAN-P
21 BILL (FIDDLER BILL) MCGEE-P (2)
22 MORRIE (SNOOKER) (MOE) ARNOVICH-OF
23 JO-JO (THE GAUSE GHOST) MOORE-OF
24 FRANK DEMAREE-OF (1)
24 SID GORDON-OF
25 MICKEY WITEK-SS/2B
26 JOHNNY RUCKER-OF
26 ODELL (BAD NEWS) HALE-2B (2)
26 TOM (LEFTY) SUNKEL-P
27 ACE ADAMS-P
28 BOB CARPENTER-P
29 JOHN (RED) DAVIS-3B
30 BILL (MEMPHIS BILL) TERRY-MGR
31 DOLF (THE PRIDE OF HAVANA) LUQUE-CH
32 FRANK (PANCHO) SNYDER-CH
33 JACK ARAGON-PR
33 DAVE KOSLO-P
34 JOHNNY MCCARTHY-1B/OF
35 RAE BLAEMIRE-C
36 HUGH EAST-P

1942

3RD *85-67* *20GB*

1 BILLY WERBER-3B
1 SID GORDON-3B
2 WILLARD MARSHALL-OF
3 JOHNNY (THE BIG CAT) (BIG JAWN) MIZE-1B
4 MEL (MASTER MELVIN) OTT-OF/MGR
5* HANK LEIBER-OF/P*
6 CONNIE RYAN-2B
7 BILLY JURGES-SS
8 HARRY (THE HORSE) DANNING-C
9 RAY BERRES-C
10 BILL (FIDDLER BILL) MCGEE-P
11 CARL (THE MEALTICKET) (KING CARL) HUBBELL-P
12 BOB CARPENTER-P
14 DICK (ROWDY RICHARD) BARTELL-3B/SS
15 CLIFF (MICKEY MOUSE) (MOUNTAIN MUSIC) MELTON (INJ)-P
16 TOM (LEFTY) SUNKEL-P
17 HAL (PRINCE HAL) SCHUMACHER-P
18 HARRY FELDMAN-P
19 HOWIE MOSS-OF
19 BILL (NINETY-SIX) (BIG BILL) VOISELLE-P
20 VAN LINGLE MUNGO-P
20 HUGH EAST-P
21 DAVE KOSLO-P
21 CHARLIE (IRISH) FOX-C
22 BILL LOHRMAN-P (2)
23 BABE BARNA-OF
24 GUS (BLACKIE) MANCUSO-C (2)
25 MICKEY WITEK-2B
26 BUSTER MAYNARD-UTIL
27 ACE ADAMS-P
28 BABE YOUNG-OF/1B
30 BUBBER JONNARD-CH
31 DOLF (THE PRIDE OF HAVANA) LUQUE-CH

1943

8TH *55-98* *49.5GB*

1 SID GORDON-UTIL
2 MICKEY WITEK-2B
3 JOHNNY RUCKER-OF
4 MEL (MASTER MELVIN) OTT-OF/3B/MGR
5 BABE BARNA-OF (1)
5* BILL (NINETY-SIX) (BIG BILL) VOISELLE-P*
6 BUSTER MAYNARD-OF/3B
7 BILLY JURGES-SS/3B
8 GUS (BLACKIE) MANCUSO-C
9 HUGH POLAND-C (1)
9 ERNIE (SCHNOZZ) (BOCCI) LOMBARDI-C
10 RAY BERRES-C
11 CARL (THE MEALTICKET) (KING CARL) HUBBELL (INJ)-P
12 JOHNNIE (HANS) WITTIG-P
14 DICK (ROWDY RICHARD) BARTELL-3B/SS
15 CLIFF (MICKEY MOUSE) (MOUNTAIN MUSIC) MELTON (INJ)-P
16 TOM (LEFTY) SUNKEL-P
16 KEN (LEFTY) CHASE-P (2)
17 VAN LINGLE MUNGO-P
18 HARRY FELDMAN-P
18 BUDDY KERR-SS
19 KEN TRINKLE-P
19 JOE (DUCKY) (MUSCLES) MEDWICK-OF/1B (2)
20 BILL SAYLES-P (1)
20 JOHNNY ALLEN-P (2)
21 NAP REYES-1B/3B
21 JOHNNY ALLEN-P (2)
22 BILL LOHRMAN-P (1)
22 CHARLIE MEAD-OF
24 BOBBY COOMBS-P
25 JOE STEPHENSON-C
26 JOE ORENGO-1B (1)
27 ACE ADAMS-P
28 JOE ORENGO-1B (1)
28 FRANK SEWARD-P
29 RUBE FISCHER-P
29 VIC BRADFORD-OF
30 BUBBER JONNARD-CH
31 DOLF (THE PRIDE OF HAVANA) LUQUE-CH
32 HUGH EAST (MIL)-P

1944

5TH *67-87* *38GB*

1 JOHNNY RUCKER-OF
1 BILLY JURGES-INF
2 HUGH (HAL) LUBY-3B/INF
3 JOE (DUCKY) (MUSCLES) MEDWICK-OF
4 MEL (MASTER MELVIN) OTT-OF/3B/MGR
5 PHIL (MICKEY) WEINTRAUB-1B
6 NAP REYES-UTIL
7 BILLY JURGES-INF
7 JOHNNY RUCKER-OF
8 ERNIE (SCHNOZZ) (BOCCI) LOMBARDI-C
9 GUS (BLACKIE) MANCUSO-C
10 BUDDY KERR-SS
11 *(RET#) CARL HUBBELL*
12 GEORGE HAUSMANN-2B
14 HARRY FELDMAN-P
15 RUBE FISCHER-P
16 CLIFF (MICKEY MOUSE) (MOUNTAIN MUSIC) MELTON (INJ)-P
17 BILL (NINETY-SIX) (BIG BILL) VOISELLE-P
18 EWALD PYLE-P
19 FRANK SEWARD-P
20 WALTER (FOOTIE) OCKEY-P
20 JOHNNY (WHIZ) GEE-P (2)
21 KEN (WHITEY) MILLER-P
21 BOB BARTHELSON-P
22 JOHNNY ALLEN-P
23 KEN BRONDELL-P
24 CHARLIE MEAD-OF
24 ANDY (SWEDE) HANSEN-P
25 BRUCE (FATSO) SLOAN-OF
26 LOU (CRIP) POLLI-P
26 RED TREADWAY-OF
27 ACE ADAMS-P
28 CHARLIE MEAD-OF
29 RAY BERRES-C
30 BUBBER JONNARD-CH
31 DOLF (THE PRIDE OF HAVANA) LUQUE-CH
32 ROY NICHOLS-2B/3B
32 JACK (BUDDY) BREWER-P
33 DANNY GARDELLA-OF
34 STEVE (FLIP) FILIPOWICZ-OF/C
35 WALTER (FOOTIE) OCKEY-P
36 FRANK ROSSO-P
37 KEN (WHITEY) MILLER-P
38 ROY NICHOLS 2B/3B

1945

5TH *78-74* *19GB*

1 JOHNNY RUCKER-OF
2 RED TREADWAY-OF
3 JOE (DUCKY) (MUSCLES) MEDWICK-OF (1)
3 CHARLIE MEAD-OF
3 JIM (SUNNY JIM) MALLORY-OF (2)
4 MEL (MASTER MELVIN) OTT-OF/MGR
5 ROY ZIMMERMAN-1B/OF
5 PHIL (MICKEY) WEINTRAUB-1B
6 NAP REYES-3B/1B
7 BILLY JURGES-3B/SS
7 JOHNNY (MR. CHIPS) HUDSON-3B/2B
8 ERNIE (SCHNOZZ) (BOCCI) LOMBARDI-C
9 RAY BERRES-C
10 BUDDY KERR-SS
11 *(RET#) CARL HUBBELL*
12 GEORGE HAUSMANN-2B
14 HARRY FELDMAN-P
15 RUBE FISCHER-P
(16) CLIFF (MICKEY MOUSE) (MOUNTAIN MUSIC) MELTON (SUS)-(P)
16 VAN LINGLE MUNGO-P
17 BILL (NINETY-SIX) (BIG BILL) VOISELLE-P
18 EWALD PYLE-P (1)
18 RAY (COWBOY) HARRELL-P
18 DON FISHER-P
19 LOREN BAIN-P
19 SAL (THE BARBER) MAGLIE-P
20 JOHNNY (WHIZ) GEE (RET)-P
21 JACK (BUDDY) BREWER-P
22 ROY LEE-P
22 WHITEY LOCKMAN (MIL)-OF
23 RAY (COWBOY) HARRELL-P
23 CLYDE KLUTTZ-C (2)
24 SLIM EMMERICH-P
26 BILLY JURGES-3B/SS
27 ACE ADAMS-P
28 ANDY (SWEDE) HANSEN (MIL)-P
28 ADRIAN ZABALA-P
29 RAY BERRES-C
29 AL GARDELLA-OF/1B
30 BUBBER JONNARD-CH
31 DOLF (THE PRIDE OF HAVANA) LUQUE-CH
33 DANNY GARDELLA-OF/1B
34 STEVE (FLIP) FILIPOWICZ-OF
35 MIKE (LEFTY) SCHEMER-1B
37 BILL DEKONING-C
— JACK PHILLIPS-P (2G: 7/13-18)

1946

8TH *61-93* *36GB*

1 BILL (THE CRICKET) (SPECS) RIGNEY-3B/SS
2 MICKEY WITEK (INJ)-2B/3B
3 JOHNNY (THE BIG CAT) (BIG JAWN) MIZE-1B
4 MEL (MASTER MELVIN) OTT-OF/MGR
5 BABE YOUNG-1B/OF
6 SID GORDON-OF/3B
7 WALKER (WALK) COOPER (INJ)-C

8 ERNIE (SCHNOZZ) (BOCCI) LOMBARDI-C
9 CLYDE KLUTTZ-C (1)
9* HAL (PRINCE HAL) SCHUMACHER-P*
9 VINCE DIMAGGIO-OF (2)
10 BUDDY KERR-SS/3B
11 *(RET#) CARL HUBBELL*
12 JOHNNY (WHIZ) GEE-P
13 HAL (PRINCE HAL) SCHUMACHER-P
14 HARRY FELDMAN (MEX)-P
14 TEX (TEXAS JACK) KRAUS-P
15 BUDDY BLATTNER-2B/1B
16 VINCE DIMAGGIO-OF (2)
16 JOHN CARDEN-P
16 MARV GRISSOM-P
17 BILL (NINETY-SIX) (BIG BILL) VOISELLE-P
18 DON FISHER-P
18 JACK GRAHAM-OF/1B
19 JIM GLADD-C
20 BOB CARPENTER (INJ)-P
21 JACK (BUDDY) BREWER-P
21 JACK GRAHAM-OF/1B
21 DICK LAJESKIE-2B
22 DAVE KOSLO-P
23 MONTE KENNEDY-P
23 BOBBY (THE FLYING SCOT) (THE STATEN ISLAND SCOT) THOMSON-3B
24 BOB JOYCE-P
24 WOODY ABERNATHY-P
25 MIKE BUDNICK-P
26 KEN TRINKLE-P
27 ACE ADAMS (MEX)-P
27 GOODY ROSEN-OF (2)
28 JACK GRAHAM-OF/1B
28 SHELDON (AVAILABLE) JONES-P
28 NATE ANDREWS-P (2)
29 SLIM EMMERICH-P
29 MICKEY GRASSO-C
29 GARLAND (KNOBBY) LAWING-OF (2)
30 BUBBER JONNARD-CH
31 RED KRESS-P/CH
32 DICK (ROWDY RICHARD) BARTELL-3B/2B
33 GROVER (SLICK) HARTLEY-CH
34 GROVER (SLICK) HARTLEY-CH
35 WILLARD MARSHALL-OF
36 MONTE KENNEDY-P
36 BENNIE WARREN-C
37 JOHNNY RUCKER-OF
38 MIKE (LEFTY) SCHEMER-PH
39 JESS PIKE-OF
40 MORRIE (SNOOKER) (MOE) ARNOVICH-OF
41 JACK GRAHAM-OF/1B
41 BUSTER MAYNARD-OF
42 JUNIOR THOMPSON-P
VIC BRADFORD (MIL)-(OF)

1947

4TH 81-73 13GB

1 TRAVIS (STONEWALL) JACKSON-CH
2 RED KRESS-CH
3 HANK GOWDY-CH
4 MEL (MASTER MELVIN) OTT-PH/MGR
5 WALKER (WALK) COOPER-C
6 ERNIE (SCHNOZZ) (BOCCI) LOMBARDI-C
7 SAL YVARS-C
8 MICKEY LIVINGSTON-C (2)
9 BENNIE WARREN-C
10 BUDDY KERR-SS
11 *(RET#) CARL HUBBELL*
12 BUDDY BLATTNER-2B/3B
13 MORT COOPER-P (2)
14 BABE YOUNG-PH (1)
14 BOBBY (ROCKY) RHAWN-2B/3B
15 JOHNNY (THE BIG CAT) (BIG JAWN) MIZE-1B
16 JACK (LUCKY) LOHRKE-3B
17 MICKEY WITEK-2B/3B
18 BILL (THE CRICKET) (SPECS) RIGNEY-2B/INF
19 BOBBY (THE FLYING SCOT) (THE STATEN ISLAND SCOT) THOMSON-OF/2B
20 SID GORDON-OF/3B
21 LLOYD (GARY) GEARHART-OF
23 CLINT (THE HONDO HURRICANE) (FLOPPY) HARTUNG-P/OF
24 WOODY ABERNATHY-P
24 JOE LAFATA-OF/1B
25 WHITEY LOCKMAN (INJ)-PH
27 WILLARD MARSHALL-OF
28 WHITEY LOCKMAN (INJ)-PH
28 FUZZ WHITE-OF
30 BILL (NINETY-SIX) (BIG BILL) VOISELLE-P
30 CLARENCE (HOOKS) IOTT-P (2)
30 RAY POAT-P
31 DAVE KOSLO-P
32 MONTE KENNEDY-P
33 BOB CARPENTER (INJ)-P (1)
33 JOE (FIREMAN) BEGGS-P (2)
34 KEN TRINKLE-P
35 JUNIOR THOMPSON-P
35 CLARENCE (HOOKS) IOTT-P (2)
37 MARIO (BABE) PICONE-P
38 HUB ANDREWS-P
39 BILL AYERS-P
39 SHELDON (AVAILABLE) JONES-P
40 MIKE BUDNICK-P
40 WES WESTRUM-C
44 ANDY (SWEDE) HANSEN-P
46 LARRY JANSEN-P

1948

5TH 78-76 13.5GB

1 TRAVIS (STONEWALL) JACKSON-CH
2 RED KRESS-CH
2 LEO (THE LIP) (LIPPY) DUROCHER-MGR2
3 HANK GOWDY-CH
4 MEL (MASTER MELVIN) OTT-MGR1
4 LEO (THE LIP) (LIPPY) DUROCHER-MGR2
5 WALKER (WALK) COOPER-(INJ)-C
6 WES WESTRUM-C
7 RED KRESS-CH
8 MICKEY LIVINGSTON-C
8 JACK HARSHMAN-1B
10 BUDDY KERR-SS
11 *(RET#) CARL HUBBELL*
12 BOBBY (ROCKY) RHAWN-SS/3B
14 JOHNNY MCCARTHY-1B
15 JOHNNY (THE BIG CAT) (BIG JAWN) MIZE-1B
16 JACK (LUCKY) LOHRKE-3B/2B
17 BUDDY BLATTNER-2B/3B
18 BILL (THE CRICKET) (SPECS) RIGNEY-2B/SS
19 BOBBY (THE FLYING SCOT) (THE STATEN ISLAND SCOT) THOMSON-OF
20 SID GORDON-3B/OF
21 LES LAYTON-OF
22 BOBBY (ROCKY) RHAWN-SS/3B
22 DON (MANDRAKE THE MAGICIAN) MUELLER-OF
23 CLINT (THE HONDO HURRICANE) (FLOPPY) HARTUNG-P/OF
25 WHITEY LOCKMAN-OF
26 JOE LAFATA-PH
27 WILLARD MARSHALL-OF
28 JACK CONWAY-INF
28 LONNY (JUNIOR) FREY-2B (2)
29 RED WEBB-P
30 RAY POAT-P
31 DAVE KOSLO-P
32 MONTE KENNEDY-P
33 JOE (FIREMAN) BEGGS-P
33 CLEM (STEAMBOAT) DREISEWERD-P (2)
33 HAL (DUTCH) BAMBERGER-OF
34 KEN TRINKLE-P
35 LOU LOMBARDO-P
36 MICKEY MCGOWAN-P
36 ALEX (WHITEY) KONIKOWSKI-P
37 SHELDON (AVAILABLE) JONES-P
38 HUB ANDREWS-P
39 PETE MILNE-OF
40 JACK HALLETT-P
44 ANDY (SWEDE) HANSEN-P
45 SAL YVARS-C
46 LARRY JANSEN-P
48 BOBO (BUCK) NEWSOM-P
49 THORNTON (LEFTY) LEE-P
49 PAUL (LI'L ABNER) ERICKSON-P (3)

1949

5TH 73-81 24GB

1 FRANKIE (THE FORDHAM FLASH) FRISCH-CH (1)
2 LEO (THE LIP) (LIPPY) DUROCHER-MGR
3 HERMAN FRANKS-PH/CH
4 *(RET#) MEL OTT*
5 WALKER (WALK) COOPER-C (1)
5 RED KRESS-CH
6 FREDDIE (FAT FREDDIE) FITZSIMMONS-CH
7 RED KRESS-CH
7 WALKER (WALK) COOPER-C (1)
7 MONTE IRVIN-UTIL
8 MICKEY LIVINGSTON-C (1)
8 RAY (IRON MAN) MUELLER-C (2)
9 PETE MILNE-OF
9 WES WESTRUM-C
10 BUDDY KERR-SS
11 *(RET#) CARL HUBBELL*
12 BOBBY (ROCKY) RHAWN-SS/3B (1)
12 GEORGE HAUSMANN (MEX)-2B
14 FRANK SHELLENBACK-CH
15 JOHNNY (THE BIG CAT) (BIG JAWN) MIZE-1B (1)
16 PETE MILNE-OF
16 HANK THOMPSON-2B/3B
17 ROGER BOWMAN-P
17 JACK (LUCKY) LOHRKE-3B/2B
18 BILL (THE CRICKET) (SPECS) RIGNEY-INF
20 SID GORDON-3B/UTIL
21 HANK BEHRMAN-P
22 DON (MANDRAKE THE MAGICIAN) MUELLER-OF
23 BOBBY (THE FLYING SCOT) (THE STATEN ISLAND SCOT) THOMSON-OF
24 JOE LAFATA (ILL)-1B
25 WHITEY LOCKMAN-OF
26 BOBBY HOFMAN-2B
26 DAVEY WILLIAMS-2B
27 WILLARD MARSHALL-OF
28 RUDY RUFER-SS
29 AUGIE GALAN-1B/OF (1)
29 ADRIAN ZABALA (MEX)-P
30 RAY POAT-P (1)
30 KIRBY HIGBE-P (2)
31 DAVE KOSLO-P
32 MONTE KENNEDY-P
(35) SAL (THE BARBER) MAGLIE (MEX)-(P)
36 CLINT (THE HONDO HURRICANE) (FLOPPY) HARTUNG-P/OF
37 SHELDON (AVAILABLE) JONES-P
38 RED WEBB-P
39 BERT HAAS-1B/3B (2)
44 ANDY (SWEDE) HANSEN-P
46 LARRY JANSEN-P
47 DICK CULLER-SS
48 ANDY TOMASIC-P
48 SAL YVARS-C
ACE ADAMS (MEX)-(P)
HARRY FELDMAN (MEX)-(P)
DANNY GARDELLA (MEX)-(OF)
NAP REYES (MEX)-(INF)

1950

3RD 86-68 5GB

1 FRANK SHELLENBACK-CH
2 LEO (THE LIP) (LIPPY) DUROCHER-MGR
3 HERMAN FRANKS-CH
4 *(RET#) MEL OTT*
5 FREDDIE (FAT FREDDIE) FITZSIMMONS-CH
6 SAM CALDERONE-C
7 RAY (IRON MAN) MUELLER-C (1)
7 SAL YVARS-C
9 WES WESTRUM-C
10 MARV BLAYLOCK-PH
10 SPIDER JORGENSEN-3B (2)
11 *(RET#) CARL HUBBELL*
12 EDDIE (THE BRAT) (MUGGSY) STANKY-2B
14 RUDY RUFER-SS
15 JACK HARSHMAN-1B
15 TOOKIE GILBERT-1B
16 HANK THOMPSON-3B/OF
17 JACK (LUCKY) LOHRKE-3B/2B
18 BILL (THE CRICKET) (SPECS) RIGNEY-2B/3B
19 ALVIN (BLACKIE) DARK-SS
20 NAP REYES-1B
20 MONTE IRVIN-UTIL
21 MIKE MCCORMICK-PH (1)
21 JIM HEARN-P (2)
22 DON (MANDRAKE THE MAGICIAN) MUELLER-OF
23 BOBBY (THE FLYING SCOT) (THE STATEN ISLAND SCOT) THOMSON-OF
24 JACK MAGUIRE-OF/1B
25 WHITEY LOCKMAN-OF
26 PETE MILNE-PH
30 KIRBY HIGBE-P
30 GEORGE SPENCER-P
31 DAVE KOSLO-P
32 MONTE KENNEDY-P
33 JACK KRAMER-P
34 JIM HEARN-P (2)
35 SAL (THE BARBER) MAGLIE-P
36 CLINT (THE HONDO HURRICANE) (FLOPPY) HARTUNG-P/OF
37 SHELDON (AVAILABLE) JONES-P
39 ROY (STORMY) WEATHERLY-OF
44 ANDY (SWEDE) HANSEN-P
46 LARRY JANSEN-P

1951

1ST 98-59 0GB
W NL/PO-BKLN 2-1
L WS-NYA 4-2

1 FRANK SHELLENBACK-CH
2 LEO (THE LIP) (LIPPY) DUROCHER-MGR
3 HERMAN FRANKS-CH
4 *(RET#) MEL OTT*
5 FREDDIE (FAT FREDDIE) FITZSIMMONS-CH
5 RAY NOBLE-C
6 RAY NOBLE-C
6 FREDDIE (FAT FREDDIE) FITZSIMMONS-CH
7 SAL YVARS-C
9 WES WESTRUM-C
10 HANK SCHENZ-PR (2)
11 *(RET#) CARL HUBBELL*
12 EDDIE (THE BRAT) (MUGGSY) STANKY-2B
14 DAVEY WILLIAMS-2B
15 ARTIE WILSON-INF
16 HANK THOMPSON-3B
17 JACK (LUCKY) LOHRKE-3B/SS
18 BILL (THE CRICKET) (SPECS) RIGNEY-2B/3B
19 ALVIN (BLACKIE) DARK-SS
20 MONTE IRVIN-OF/1B
21 JIM HEARN-P
22 DON (MANDRAKE THE MAGICIAN) MUELLER-OF
23 BOBBY (THE FLYING SCOT (THE STATEN ISLAND SCOT) THOMSON-OF/3B
24 JACK MAGUIRE-OF (1)
24 WILLIE (SAY HEY) MAYS-OF
25 WHITEY LOCKMAN-1B/OF
26 CLINT (THE HONDO HURRICANE) (FLOPPY) HARTUNG-OF
27 SPIDER JORGENSEN-OF/3B
27 EARL RAPP-PH (1)
30 GEORGE SPENCER-P
31 DAVE KOSLO-P
32 MONTE KENNEDY-P
33 JACK KRAMER-P (1)
35 SAL (THE BARBER) MAGLIE-P
37 SHELDON (AVAILABLE) JONES-P
38 ROGER BOWMAN-P
38 RED HARDY-P
38 ALEX (WHITEY) KONIKOWSKI-P
39 GEORGE BAMBERGER-P
38 AL CORWIN-P
44 AL GETTEL-P
46 LARRY JANSEN-P

NEW YORK/**SAN FRANCISCO GIANTS**

1952

2ND 92-62 4.5GB

1 FRANK SHELLENBACK-CH
2 LEO (THE LIP) (LIPPY) DUROCHER-MGR
3 HERMAN FRANKS-CH
4 *(RET#) MEL OTT*
5 RAY NOBLE-C
6 FREDDIE (FAT FREDDIE) FITZSIMMONS-CH
7 SAL YVARS-C
8 RAY KATT-C
8 BILL (HOPALONG) HOWERTON-OF (2)
9 WES WESTRUM-C
10 DAVEY WILLIAMS-2B
11 *(RET#) CARL HUBBELL*
12 BOB (MR. TEAM) ELLIOTT-OF/3B
14 BOBBY HOFMAN-INF
16 HANK THOMPSON-OF/INF
17 AL CORWIN-P
17 GEORGE BAMBERGER-P
18 BILL (THE CRICKET) (SPECS) RIGNEY-INF
19 ALVIN (BLACKIE) DARK-SS
20 MONTE IRVIN (INJ)-OF
21 JIM HEARN-P
22 DON (MANDRAKE THE MAGICIAN) MUELLER-OF
23 BOBBY (THE FLYING SCOT) (THE STATEN ISLAND SCOT) THOMSON-3B/OF
24 WILLIE (SAY HEY) MAYS (MIL)-OF
24 MARIO (BABE) PICONE-P
25 WHITEY LOCKMAN-1B
26 BILL (WILD BILL) CONNELLY-P
26 DICK WAKEFIELD-PH
26 HAL (SKEETS) GREGG-P
28 CHUCK DIERING-OF
29 JACK HARSHMAN-P
30 GEORGE SPENCER-P
30 DARYL SPENCER-SS/3B
31 DAVE KOSLO-P
32 MONTE KENNEDY-P
33 CLINT (THE HONDO HURRICANE) (FLOPPY) HARTUNG-OF
35 SAL (THE BARBER) MAGLIE-P
37 BOB (MR. TEAM) ELLIOTT-OF/3B
37 MAX LANIER-P
38 ROGER BOWMAN-P
38 DUSTY RHODES-OF
39 JACK HARSHMAN-P
40 AL CORWIN-P
40 GEORGE (TEDDY) WILSON-OF/1B (2)
42 MAX LANIER-P
46 LARRY JANSEN (INJ)-P
49 HOYT WILHELM-P
ALEX (WHITEY) KONIKOWSKI (MIL)-(P)

1953

5TH 70-84 35GB

1 FRANK SHELLENBACK-CH
2 LEO (THE LIP) (LIPPY) DUROCHER-MGR
3 HERMAN FRANKS-CH
4 *(RET#) MEL OTT*
5 SAM CALDERONE-C
6 FREDDIE (FAT FREDDIE) FITZSIMMONS-CH
7 SAL YVARS-C (1)
8 RAY NOBLE-C
8 RAY KATT-C
9 WES WESTRUM-C
10 DAVEY WILLIAMS-2B
11 *(RET#) CARL HUBBELL*
12 DARYL SPENCER-INF
14 BOBBY HOFMAN-3B/2B
16 HANK THOMPSON-3B/UTIL
17 TOOKIE GILBERT-1B
18 BILL (THE CRICKET) (SPECS) RIGNEY-3B/2B
19 ALVIN (BLACKIE) DARK-SS/UTIL/P
20 MONTE IRVIN-OF
21 JIM HEARN-P
22 DON (MANDRAKE THE MAGICIAN) MUELLER-OF
23 BOBBY (THE FLYING SCOT) (THE STATEN ISLAND SCOT) THOMSON-OF
(24) WILLIE (SAY HEY) MAYS (MIL)-(OF)
25 WHITEY LOCKMAN-1B/OF
26 BILL (WILD BILL) CONNELLY-P
26 AL (RED) WORTHINGTON-P
27 AL CORWIN-P
28 RUBEN GOMEZ-P
30 GEORGE SPENCER-P
31 DAVE KOSLO-P
32 MONTE KENNEDY-P
35 SAL (THE BARBER) MAGLIE-P
36 SAM CALDERONE-C
37 MAX LANIER-P (1)
38 DUSTY RHODES-OF
40 GEORGE (TEDDY) WILSON-PH
42 FRANK (DUTCH) HILLER-P
42 MARV GRISSOM-P (2)
46 LARRY JANSEN-P
49 HOYT WILHELM-P

1954

1ST 97-57 0GB

W WS-CLEA 4-0

1 FRANK SHELLENBACK-CH
2 LEO (THE LIP) (LIPPY) DUROCHER-MGR
3 HERMAN FRANKS-CH
4 *(RET#) MEL OTT*
5 ERIC RODIN-OF
6 FREDDIE (FAT FREDDIE) FITZSIMMONS-CH
7 EBBA ST. CLAIRE-C
8 RAY KATT-C
9 WES WESTRUM-C
10 DAVEY WILLIAMS-2B
11 *(RET#) CARL HUBBELL*
12 JOEY AMALFITANO-3B/2B
14 BOBBY HOFMAN-INF
15 BILLY (SHOTGUN) GARDNER-INF
16 HANK THOMPSON-3B/UTIL
17 RON SAMFORD-2B
18 FOSTER CASTLEMAN-3B
19 ALVIN (BLACKIE) DARK-SS
20 MONTE IRVIN-OF/INF
21 JIM HEARN-P
22 DON (MANDRAKE THE MAGICIAN) MUELLER-OF
23 BOB (ARCH) LENNON-PH
23 HOOT EVERS-OF (2)
24 WILLIE (SAY HEY) MAYS -OF
25 WHITEY LOCKMAN-1B/OF
26 DUSTY RHODES-OF
27 BILL TAYLOR-OF
28 RUBEN GOMEZ-P
30 GEORGE SPENCER-P
31 PAUL GIEL-P
32 AL CORWIN-P
33 AL (RED) WORTHINGTON-P
34 ALEX (WHITEY) KONIKOWSKI-P
34 AL CORWIN-P
34 RAY MONZANT-P
35 SAL (THE BARBER) MAGLIE-P
36 MARIO (BABE) PICONE-P (1)
36 JOE GARAGIOLA-C (2)
37 DON LIDDLE-P
38 ALEX (WHITEY) KONIKOWSKI-P
40 WINDY MCCALL-P
41 AL CORWIN-P
41 HARVEY GENTRY-PH
42 MARV GRISSOM-P
43 JOHNNY ANTONELLI-P
46 LARRY JANSEN-P
49 HOYT WILHELM-P

1955

3RD 80-74 18.5GB

1 FRANK SHELLENBACK-CH
2 LEO (THE LIP) (LIPPY) DUROCHER-MGR
3 HERMAN FRANKS-CH
4 *(RET#) MEL OTT*
6 FREDDIE (FAT FREDDIE) FITZSIMMONS-CH
7 MICKEY GRASSO-C
8 RAY KATT-C
9 WES WESTRUM-C
10 DAVEY WILLIAMS (INJ)-2B
10 GIL COAN-OF (3)
11 *(RET#) CARL HUBBELL*
12 JOEY AMALFITANO-SS/3B
14 BOBBY HOFMAN-INF/C
15 BILLY (SHOTGUN) GARDNER-INF
15 GAIL HARRIS-1B
16 HANK THOMPSON-3B/INF
17 BILLY (SHOTGUN) GARDNER-INF
18 FOSTER CASTLEMAN-3B
19 ALVIN (BLACKIE) DARK-SS
20 MONTE IRVIN-OF
21 JIM HEARN-P
22 DON (MANDRAKE THE MAGICIAN) MUELLER-OF
24 WILLIE (SAY HEY) MAYS -OF
25 WHITEY LOCKMAN-OF/1B
26 DUSTY RHODES-OF
27 BILL TAYLOR-OF
28 RUBEN GOMEZ-P
30 GEORGE SPENCER-P
30 SID GORDON-3B/OF (2)
31 PAUL GIEL-P
34 AL CORWIN-P
34 WAYNE (TWIG) TERWILLIGER-2B/INF
35 SAL (THE BARBER) MAGLIE-P (1)
37 DON LIDDLE-P
39 PETE BURNSIDE-P
40 WINDY MCCALL-P
41 RAY MONZANT-P
42 MARV GRISSOM-P
43 JOHNNY ANTONELLI-P
46 LARRY JANSEN-P
49 HOYT WILHELM-P

1956

6TH 67-87 26GB

1 DAVEY WILLIAMS-CH
2 RAY (IRON MAN) MUELLER-CH
3 BUCKY WALTERS-CH
4 *(RET#) MEL OTT*
8 RAY KATT-C (1)
8 BILL SARNI (ILL)-C (2)
9 WES WESTRUM-C
10 WAYNE (TWIG) TERWILLIGER-2B
10 RED SCHOENDIENST-2B (2)
11 *(RET#) CARL HUBBELL*
12 FOSTER CASTLEMAN-3B/INF
14 BOBBY HOFMAN-INF/C
15 GAIL HARRIS-1B
15 BILL SARNI (ILL)-C (2)
16 HANK THOMPSON-UTIL
17 OZZIE VIRGIL, SR.-C
18 BILL (THE CRICKET) (SPECS) RIGNEY-MGR
19 ALVIN (BLACKIE) DARK (INJ)-SS (1)
20 DARYL SPENCER- SS/INF
21 JIM HEARN-P
22 DON (MANDRAKE THE MAGICIAN) MUELLER-OF
24 WILLIE (SAY HEY) MAYS -OF
25 WHITEY LOCKMAN-OF/1B (1)
25 JACKIE BRANDT-OF (2)
26 DUSTY RHODES-OF
27 BILL TAYLOR-OF
28 GIL COAN-OF
28 RUBEN GOMEZ-P
29 GEORGE (TEDDY) WILSON-OF (1)
29 MIKE MCCORMICK-P
30 BOB (ARCH) LENNON-OF
30 DICK LITTLEFIELD-P (2)
31 RUBEN GOMEZ-P
31 ROY WRIGHT-P
32 AL (RED) WORTHINGTON (INJ)-P
33 JIM MANGAN-C
34 ED BRESSOUD-SS
36 BOB (ARCH) LENNON-OF
36 MAX SURKONT-P (3)
37 DON LIDDLE-P (1)
38 JOE MARGONERI-P
39 JIM (SHERIFF) CONSTABLE-P
40 WINDY MCCALL-P
41 RAY MONZANT-P
42 MARV GRISSOM-P
43 JOHNNY ANTONELLI-P
44 STEVE RIDZIK-P
45 BILL WHITE-1B/OF
49 HOYT WILHELM-P

1957

6TH 69-85 26GB

1 DAVEY WILLIAMS-CH
2 TOMMY (OLD RELIABLE) (THE CLUTCH) HENRICH-CH
2 DANNY O'CONNELL-2B/3B (2)
3 BUCKY WALTERS-CH
4 *(RET#) MEL OTT*
5 RAY KATT-C
6 HANK SAUER-OF
7 RED SCHOENDIENST-2B (1)
7 TOMMY (OLD RELIABLE) (THE CLUTCH) HENRICH-CH
8? BILL SARNI-CH
9 WES WESTRUM-C
10 RAY (JABBO) JABLONSKI-3B/UTIL
11 *(RET#) CARL HUBBELL*
12 FOSTER CASTLEMAN-INF
14 GAIL HARRIS-1B
15 ANDRE (ANDY) RODGERS-SS/3B
16 VALMY THOMAS-C
17 OZZIE VIRGIL, SR.-UTIL
18 BILL (THE CRICKET) (SPECS) RIGNEY-MGR
20 DARYL SPENCER- SS/INF
21 BILL TAYLOR-PH (1)
21 BOBBY (THE FLYING SCOT) (THE STATEN ISLAND SCOT) THOMSON-OF/3B (2)
22 DON (MANDRAKE THE MAGICIAN) MUELLER-OF
23 BOBBY HOFMAN-PH
23 STU MILLER-P
24 WILLIE (SAY HEY) MAYS -OF
25 WHITEY LOCKMAN-1B/OF
26 DUSTY RHODES-OF
28 RUBEN GOMEZ-P
29 MIKE MCCORMICK-P
32 AL (RED) WORTHINGTON-P
35 PETE BURNSIDE-P
36 MAX SURKONT-P
38 JOE MARGONERI-P
38 JIM DAVIS-P (2)
39 CURT BARCLAY-P
40 WINDY MCCALL-P
41 RAY MONZANT-P
42 MARV GRISSOM-P
43 JOHNNY ANTONELLI-P
44 STEVE RIDZIK-P
44 RAY CRONE-P (2)
46 RAY (JABBO) JABLONSKI-3B/UTIL
46 JIM (SHERIFF) CONSTABLE-P
47 GORDON JONES-P
48 ED BRESSOUD-SS/3B
49 SANDY CONSUEGRA-P (2)

1958
SAN FRANCISCO GIANTS

3RD 80-74 12GB

2 SALTY PARKER-CH
3 HERMAN FRANKS-CH
4 *(RET#) MEL OTT*
6 HANK SAUER-OF
7 VALMY THOMAS-C
9 WES WESTRUM-C
10 RAY (JABBO) JABLONSKI-3B
11 *(RET#) CARL HUBBELL*
12 JIM DAVENPORT-3B/SS
14 DON TAUSSIG-OF
15 ANDRE (ANDY) RODGERS-SS
16 ED BRESSOUD-INF
17 JIM FINIGAN-2B/3B
17 BILL WHITE (MIL)-1B/OF
18 BILL (THE CRICKET) (SPECS) RIGNEY-MGR
19 DANNY O'CONNELL-2B/3B
20 DARYL SPENCER- SS/2B
22 JIM KING-OF
22 JACKIE BRANDT (MIL)-OF
22 DANNY O'CONNELL-2B/3B
23 BOB (SPOOK) SPEAKE-OF
24 WILLIE (SAY HEY) MAYS -OF
25 WHITEY LOCKMAN-UTIL
26 BOB (SPOOK) SPEAKE-OF
27 BOB SCHMIDT-C
28 RUBEN GOMEZ-P
29 WILLIE KIRKLAND-OF
30 ORLANDO (THE BABY BULL) (CHA-CHA) CEPEDA-1B
31 PAUL GIEL-P
32 AL (RED) WORTHINGTON-P

35 PETE BURNSIDE-P
35 JOHN FITZGERALD-P
37 STU MILLER-P
38 GORDON JONES-P
38 JOE (MOSES) SHIPLEY-P
39 CURT BARCLAY-P
39 LEON (DADDY WAGS) WAGNER-OF
40 MIKE MCCORMICK-P
41 RAY MONZANT-P
42 MARV GRISSOM-P
43 JOHNNY ANTONELLI-P
44 RAY CRONE-P
44 DON JOHNSON-P
45 NICK TESTA-C/CH
47 NICK TESTA (RET)-C
48 JIM (SHERIFF) CONSTABLE-P
49 FELIPE ALOU-OF
51 DOM ZANNI-P

1959

3RD 83-71 4GB

1 BILL (BARNACLE BILL) (SAILOR BILL) POSEDEL-CH
2 SALTY PARKER-CH
3 WES WESTRUM-C
4 *(RET#) MEL OTT*
5 HOBIE LANDRITH-C
6 HANK SAUER-OF
8 ROGER MCCARDELL-C
9 BOB SCHMIDT-C
10 JOSE PAGAN-INF
11 *(RET#) CARL HUBBELL*
12 JIM DAVENPORT-3B/SS
15 ANDRE (ANDY) RODGERS-SS
16 ED BRESSOUD-SS/INF
17 ANDRE (ANDY) RODGERS-SS
18 BILL (THE CRICKET) (SPECS) RIGNEY-MGR
19 SAM (TOOTHPICK SAM) JONES-P
20 DARYL SPENCER- 2B/SS
21 LEON (DADDY WAGS) WAGNER-OF
22 DANNY O'CONNELL-2B/3B
23 FELIPE ALOU-OF
24 WILLIE (SAY HEY) MAYS -OF
25 JACKIE BRANDT-OF/INF
26 BOB (SPOOK) SPEAKE-PH
26 DUSTY RHODES-PH
27 JIM HEGAN-C (2)
28 MARSHALL RENFROE-P
29 WILLIE KIRKLAND-OF
30 ORLANDO (THE BABY BULL) (CHA-CHA) CEPEDA-1B/UTIL
32 AL (RED) WORTHINGTON-P
33 JACK SANFORD-P
34 DOM ZANNI-P
36 BILLY (MUFF) MUFFETT-P
36 BUD BYERLY-P
37 STU MILLER-P
38 GORDON JONES-P
39 CURT BARCLAY-P
39 EDDIE FISHER-P
40 MIKE MCCORMICK-P
41 RAY MONZANT (RET)-P
42 JOE (MOSES) SHIPLEY-P
43 JOHNNY ANTONELLI-P
44 WILLIE (STRETCH) MCCOVEY-1B

1960

5TH 79-75 16GB

1 BILL (BARNACLE BILL) (SAILOR BILL) POSEDEL-CH
2 SALTY PARKER-CH
3 WES WESTRUM-C
4 *(RET#) MEL OTT*
5 HOBIE LANDRITH-C
6 NEIL WILSON-C
6 TOM SHEEHAN-MGR2
7 DALE LONG-1B (1)
9 BOB SCHMIDT-C
10 DON BLASINGAME-2B
11 *(RET#) CARL HUBBELL*
12 JIM DAVENPORT-3B/SS
14 JOEY AMALFITANO-UTIL
15 JOSE PAGAN-SS/3B
16 ED BRESSOUD-SS
17 ANDRE (ANDY) RODGERS-UTIL
18 BILL (THE CRICKET) (SPECS) RIGNEY-MGR1
19 SAM (TOOTHPICK SAM) JONES-P
20 DALE LONG-1B (1)
22 DON CHOATE-P
23 FELIPE ALOU-OF
24 WILLIE (SAY HEY) MAYS -OF
25 JIM MARSHALL-1B/OF
26 MATTY ALOU-OF
27 JUAN (MANITO) MARICHAL-P
28 BILLY LOES-P
29 WILLIE KIRKLAND-OF
30 ORLANDO (THE BABY BULL) (CHA-CHA) CEPEDA-OF/1B
31 BILLY O'DELL-P
32 AL (RED) WORTHINGTON-P
32 DAVE PHILLEY-OF/3B (2)
33 JACK SANFORD-P
35 GEORGES MARANDA-P
36 BUD BYERLY-P
36 SHERMAN (ROADBLOCK) JONES-P
37 STU MILLER-P
39 EDDIE FISHER-P
40 MIKE MCCORMICK-P
41 RAY MONZANT-P
42 JOE (MOSES) SHIPLEY-P
43 JOHNNY ANTONELLI-P
44 WILLIE (STRETCH) MCCOVEY-1B

1961

3RD 85-69 8GB

1 ALVIN (BLACKIE) DARK-MGR
2 SALTY PARKER-CH
3 WES WESTRUM-C
3 WHITEY LOCKMAN-CH
4 *(RET#) MEL OTT*
5 HOBIE LANDRITH-C
6 WHITEY LOCKMAN-CH
6 ED BAILEY-C/OF (2)
7 HARVEY KUENN-OF/INF
9 BOB SCHMIDT-C (1)
9 WES WESTRUM-CH
10 DON BLASINGAME-PH (1)
11 *(RET#) CARL HUBBELL*
12 JIM DAVENPORT-3B
14 JOEY AMALFITANO-2B/3B
15 JOSE PAGAN-SS/3B
16 ED BRESSOUD-SS
18 BOB FARLEY-OF/1B
19 SAM (TOOTHPICK SAM) JONES-P
21 ERNIE BOWMAN-INF
23 FELIPE ALOU-OF
24 WILLIE (SAY HEY) MAYS -OF
25 JIM MARSHALL-1B/OF
26 CHUCK HILLER-2B
27 JUAN (MANITO) MARICHAL-P
28 BILLY LOES-P
30 ORLANDO (THE BABY BULL) (CHA-CHA) CEPEDA-OF/1B
31 BILLY O'DELL-P
33 JACK SANFORD-P
34 JOHN (HORSE) ORSINO-C
36 DOM ZANNI-P
37 STU MILLER-P
39 EDDIE FISHER-P
39 DICK LEMAY-P
40 MIKE MCCORMICK-P
41 MATTY ALOU-OF
42 BOB BOLIN-P
44 WILLIE (STRETCH) MCCOVEY-1B
45 JIM DUFFALO-P
46 LARRY JANSEN-CH
51 TOM HALLER-C

1962

1ST 103-62 0GB

L WS-NYA 4-3

1 ALVIN (BLACKIE) DARK-MGR
2 JOE PIGNATANO-C (1)
3 WHITEY LOCKMAN-CH
4 *(RET#) MEL OTT*
5 TOM HALLER-C
6 ED BAILEY-C
7 HARVEY KUENN-OF/3B
9 WES WESTRUM-CH
11 *(RET#) CARL HUBBELL*
12 JIM DAVENPORT-3B
14 DICK PHILLIPS-1B
14 CARL BOLES-OF
15 JOSE PAGAN-SS
17 CAP PETERSON-SS
18 DON LARSEN-P
19 BILLY PIERCE-P
20 BOB NIEMAN-OF (2)
21 ERNIE BOWMAN-INF
22 GAYLORD PERRY-P
23 FELIPE ALOU-OF
24 WILLIE (SAY HEY) MAYS -OF
26 CHUCK HILLER-2B
27 JUAN (MANITO) MARICHAL-P
28 GAYLORD PERRY-P
28 BOB GARIBALDI-P
30 ORLANDO (THE BABY BULL) (CHA-CHA) CEPEDA-1B/OF
31 BILLY O'DELL-P
33 JACK SANFORD-P
34 JOHN (HORSE) ORSINO-C
37 STU MILLER-P
38 MANNY MOTA-UTIL
39 DICK LEMAY-P
40 MIKE MCCORMICK (INJ)-P
41 MATTY ALOU-OF
42 BOB BOLIN-P
44 WILLIE (STRETCH) MCCOVEY-OF/1B
45 JIM DUFFALO-P
46 LARRY JANSEN-CH

1963

3RD 88-74 11GB

1 ALVIN (BLACKIE) DARK-MGR
2 JIMMIE COKER-C
3 WHITEY LOCKMAN-CH
4 *(RET#) MEL OTT*
5 TOM HALLER-C/OF
6 ED BAILEY-C
7 HARVEY KUENN-OF/3B
9 WES WESTRUM-CH
10 JOSE CARDENAL-OF
11 *(RET#) CARL HUBBELL*
12 JIM DAVENPORT-3B/INF
14 JESUS ALOU-OF
14 JOEY AMALFITANO-2B/3B
15 JOSE PAGAN-SS/UTIL
16 NORM LARKER-1B (2)
16 JIM RAY HART-3B
17 CAP PETERSON-UTIL
18 DON LARSEN-P
19 BILLY PIERCE-P
20 BILLY HOEFT (INJ)-P
21 ERNIE BOWMAN-INF
22 JACK (FAT JACK) FISHER-P
23 FELIPE ALOU-OF
24 WILLIE (SAY HEY) MAYS -OF/SS
26 CHUCK HILLER-2B
27 JUAN (MANITO) MARICHAL-P
28 BOB GARIBALDI-P
30 ORLANDO (THE BABY BULL) (CHA-CHA) CEPEDA-1B/OF
31 BILLY O'DELL-P
33 JACK SANFORD-P
34 RON HERBEL-P
34 JIM (SHERIFF) CONSTABLE P
35 GAYLORD PERRY-P
36 FRANK LINZY-P
36 GAYLORD PERRY-P
40 JOHN PREGENZER-P
41 MATTY ALOU-OF
42 BOB BOLIN-P
44 WILLIE (STRETCH) MCCOVEY-OF/1B
45 JIM DUFFALO (INJ)-P
46 LARRY JANSEN-CH
48 AL (LEFTY) STANEK-P

1964

4TH 90-72 3GB

1 ALVIN (BLACKIE) DARK-MGR
3 WHITEY LOCKMAN-CH
4 *(RET#) MEL OTT*
5 TOM HALLER-C/OF
6 HERMAN FRANKS-CH
7 HARVEY KUENN- UTIL
8 COOKIE LAVAGETTO-CH
9 DEL CRANDALL-C
10 JOSE CARDENAL-OF
10 GIL GARRIDO-SS
10 MASANORI MURAKAMI-P
11 *(RET#) CARL HUBBELL*
12 JIM DAVENPORT-INF
14 JESUS ALOU (INJ)-OF
15 JOSE PAGAN-SS/OF
16 JIM RAY HART-3B/OF
17 CAP PETERSON-UTIL
18 DON LARSEN-P (1)
18 JOHN PREGENZER-P
19 BILLY PIERCE-P
21 GIL GARRIDO-SS
21 JOSE CARDENAL-OF
22 HAL LANIER-2B/SS
24 WILLIE (SAY HEY) MAYS -OF/INF
25 DICK ESTELLE-P
26 CHUCK HILLER-2B/3B
27 JUAN (MANITO) MARICHAL-P
28 DUKE (THE SILVER FOX) SNIDER-OF
29 BOB SHAW-P
30 ORLANDO (THE BABY BULL) (CHA-CHA) CEPEDA-1B/OF
31 BILLY O'DELL-P
33 JACK SANFORD (INJ)-P
34 RON HERBEL-P
36 GAYLORD PERRY-P
37 KEN MACKENZIE-P
38 BOB HENDLEY-P
39 RANDY HUNDLEY-C
41 MATTY ALOU (INJ)-OF
42 BOB BOLIN-P
44 WILLIE (STRETCH) MCCOVEY-OF/1B
45 JIM DUFFALO (INJ)-P
46 LARRY JANSEN-CH

1965

2ND 95-67 2GB

1 BOB BARTON-C
1 RANDY HUNDLEY-C
2 JACK HIATT-C/1B
3 HERMAN FRANKS-MGR
4 *(RET#) MEL OTT*
5 TOM HALLER-C
6 ED BAILEY-C/1B (1)
6 DICK BERTELL-C (2)
7 HARVEY KUENN-OF/1B (1)
7 LEN GABRIELSON-OF/1B (2)
8 COOKIE LAVAGETTO-CH
9 CHARLIE (IRISH) FOX-CH
10 BOB SCHRODER-2B/3B
11 *(RET#) CARL HUBBELL*
12 JIM DAVENPORT-INF
14 JESUS ALOU-OF
15 JOSE PAGAN-SS (1)
15 DICK (DUCKY) SCHOFIELD-SS (2)
16 JIM RAY HART-3B/OF
17 CAP PETERSON-OF
21 LEN GABRIELSON-OF/1B (2
21 WARREN SPAHN-P (2)
22 HAL LANIER-2B/SS
23 KEN HENDERSON-OF
24 WILLIE (SAY HEY) MAYS -OF
25 DICK ESTELLE-P
25 BOB BURDA-1B/OF
25 (DOWNTOWN) OLLIE BROWN-OF
26 CHUCK HILLER-2B (1)
26 TITO FUENTES-INF
27 JUAN (MANITO) MARICHAL-P
28 DICK ESTELLE-P
29 BOB SHAW-P
30 ORLANDO (THE BABY BULL) (CHA-CHA) CEPEDA (INJ)-1B/OF
31 BOB BURDA-1B/OF
32 BILL HANDS-P
33 JACK SANFORD-P (1)
34 RON HERBEL-P
35 FRANK LINZY-P
36 GAYLORD PERRY-P
37 MASANORI MURAKAMI-P
38 BOB HENDLEY-P (1)
38 BOB PRIDDY-P
41 MATTY ALOU-OF/P
42 BOB BOLIN-P
43 BOB BARTON-C
44 WILLIE (STRETCH) MCCOVEY-1B
45 JIM DUFFALO-P (1)
45 BILL HENRY-P (2)
46 LARRY JANSEN-CH
47 BOB PRIDDY-P
48 (DOWNTOWN) OLLIE BROWN-OF

1966

2ND 93-68 1.5GB

1 BOB BARTON-C

2 JACK HIATT-1B
2 DICK DIETZ-C
3 HERMAN FRANKS-MGR
4 *(RET#) MEL OTT*
5 TOM HALLER-C/1B
5) DICK BERTELL (INJ)-(C)
7 LEN GABRIELSON-OF/1B
8 COOKIE LAVAGETTO-CH
9 CHARLIE (IRISH) FOX-CH
0 BOB SCHRODER-SS
1 *(RET#) CARL HUBBELL*
2 JIM DAVENPORT-INF
4 JESUS ALOU-OF
5 DICK (DUCKY) SCHOFIELD-SS (1)
5 BOB SCHRODER-SS
6 JIM RAY HART-3B/OF
7 CAP PETERSON-OF/1B
1 BOB GARIBALDI-P
2 HAL LANIER-2B/SS
3 TITO FUENTES-SS/2B
4 WILLIE (SAY HEY) MAYS-OF
5 (DOWNTOWN) OLLIE BROWN-OF
6 TITO FUENTES-SS/2B
7 JUAN (MANITO) MARICHAL-P
8 JOE GIBBON-P
9 BOB SHAW-P (1)
9 JACK HIATT-1B
0 ORLANDO (THE BABY BULL) (CHA-CHA) CEPEDA-OF/1B (1)
0 BILLY HOEFT-P (2)
1 BOB BURDA-1B/OF
4 RON HERBEL-P
5 FRANK LINZY-P
6 GAYLORD PERRY-P
7) MASANORI MURAKAMI (INJ)-(P)
7 RAY SADECKI-P (2)
8 BOB PRIDDY-P
9 LINDY MCDANIEL-P
0 OZZIE VIRGIL,SR.-UTIL
1 DON MASON-2B
2 BOB BOLIN-P
3 DON LANDRUM-OF
3 KEN HENDERSON-OF
4 WILLIE (STRETCH) MCCOVEY-1B
5 BILL HENRY-P
6 LARRY JANSEN-CH
6 BILL (BUGS) WERLE-CH
7 FRANK JOHNSON-OF
8 (DOWNTOWN) OLLIE BROWN-OF
9 RICH ROBERTSON-P

1967

2ND — 91-71 — 10.5GB

1 BOB BARTON-C
2 DICK DIETZ-C
3 HERMAN FRANKS-MGR
4 *(RET#) MEL OTT*
5 TOM HALLER-C/OF
6 PEANUTS LOWREY-CH
7 JACK HIATT-UTIL
8 COOKIE LAVAGETTO-CH
9 CHARLIE (IRISH) FOX-CH
0 BOB SCHRODER-2B/3B
1 *(RET#) CARL HUBBELL*
2 JIM DAVENPORT-INF
4 JESUS ALOU-OF
5 KEN HENDERSON-OF
6 JIM RAY HART-3B/OF
7 CESAR GUTIERREZ-SS/2B
7 BOBBY (LUKE) ETHERIDGE-3B
8 BILL SORRELL-OF
8 DAVE MARSHALL-PR
19 FRANK JOHNSON-OF
19 TY CLINE-OF (2)
20 DICK GROAT-SS/2B (2)
22 HAL LANIER-SS/2B
23 TITO FUENTES-2B/SS
24 WILLIE (SAY HEY) MAYS-OF
25 (DOWNTOWN) OLLIE BROWN-OF
27 JUAN (MANITO) MARICHAL (INJ)-P
28 JOE GIBBON-P
29 NORM SIEBERN-1B/OF (1)
32 NESTOR CHAVEZ-P
34 RON HERBEL-P
35 FRANK LINZY-P
36 GAYLORD PERRY-P
37 RAY SADECKI-P
39 LINDY MCDANIEL-P
40 MIKE MCCORMICK-P
41 DON MASON-2B
41 NESTOR CHAVEZ-P
42 BOB BOLIN-P
43 RICH ROBERTSON-P
44 WILLIE (STRETCH) MCCOVEY-1B
45 BILL HENRY-P
45 RON BRYANT-P
46 LARRY JANSEN-CH
46 BILL HENRY-P
49 RON BRYANT-P
50 NESTOR CHAVEZ-P

1968

2ND — 88-74 — 9GB

1 BOB BARTON-C
2 DICK DIETZ-C
3 HERMAN FRANKS-MGR
4 *(RET#) MEL OTT*
5 WES WESTRUM-CH
6 PEANUTS LOWREY-CH
7 JACK HIATT-C/1B
8* BILL MONBOUQUETTE-P* (2)
9 CHARLIE (IRISH) FOX-CH
10 BOB SCHRODER-INF
11 *(RET#) CARL HUBBELL*
12 JIM DAVENPORT-3B/INF
14 JESUS ALOU-OF
15 KEN HENDERSON-OF
16 JIM RAY HART-3B/OF
18 DAVE MARSHALL-OF
19 TY CLINE-OF/1B
20 FRANK JOHNSON-UTIL
21 DON MASON-INF
22 HAL LANIER-SS
24 WILLIE (SAY HEY) MAYS-OF/1B
25 (DOWNTOWN) OLLIE BROWN-OF
25 BOBBY BONDS-OF
27 JUAN (MANITO) MARICHAL-P
28 JOE GIBBON-P
29 NATE (PEEWEE) OLIVER (ILL)-INF
33 RON HUNT-2B
34 RON HERBEL-P
35 FRANK LINZY-P
36 GAYLORD PERRY-P
37 RAY SADECKI-P
38 WES WESTRUM-CH
39 LINDY MCDANIEL-P (1)
39 BILL MONBOUQUETTE-P (2)
40 MIKE MCCORMICK-P
42 BOB BOLIN-P
43 RICH ROBERTSON-P
44 WILLIE (STRETCH) MCCOVEY-1B
45 BILL HENRY-P (1)
46 LARRY JANSEN-CH

1969

2ND W — 90-72 — 3GB

1 BOB BARTON-C
2 DICK DIETZ-C
3 OZZIE VIRGIL, SR.-C/CH
4 *(RET#) MEL OTT*
5 WES WESTRUM-CH
7 JACK HIATT (INJ)-C/1B
9 JOHN HARRELL-C
9 WES WESTRUM-CH
10 JOHNNY STEPHENSON-C/3B
11 *(RET#) CARL HUBBELL*
12 JIM DAVENPORT-3B/UTIL
14 GEORGE FOSTER-OF
15 KEN HENDERSON (INJ)-OF
16 JIM RAY HART-OF/3B
17 BOBBY (LUKE) ETHERIDGE-3B/SS
18 DAVE MARSHALL-OF
19 BOB BURDA-1B/OF
20 FRANK JOHNSON-OF
21 DON MASON-INF
22 HAL LANIER-SS
23 CLYDE KING-MGR
24 WILLIE (SAY HEY) MAYS-OF/1B
25 BOBBY BONDS-OF
26 RON BRYANT-P
27 JUAN (MANITO) MARICHAL-P
28 JOE GIBBON-P (1)
28 RON KLINE-P (2)
29 TITO FUENTES (INJ)-3B/SS
31 CESAR (COCA) GUTIERREZ-3B/SS (1)
33 RON HUNT-2B/3B
34 RON HERBEL-P
35 FRANK LINZY-P
36 GAYLORD PERRY-P
37 RAY SADECKI-P
38 LEON (DADDY WAGS) WAGNER-OF
39 BOB GARIBALDI-P
40 MIKE MCCORMICK-P
41 MIKE DAVISON-P
42 BOB BOLIN-P
44 WILLIE (STRETCH) MCCOVEY-1B
45 RICH ROBERTSON-P
46 LARRY JANSEN-CH
47 DON MCMAHON-P (2)

1970

3RD W — 86-76 — 16GB

2 DICK DIETZ-C
3 OZZIE VIRGIL, SR.-C/CH
4 *(RET#) MEL OTT*
5 JOHNNY STEPHENSON-C/OF
7 CHARLIE (IRISH) FOX-MGR2
9 WES WESTRUM-CH
10 AL GALLAGHER-3B
11 *(RET#) CARL HUBBELL*
12 JIM DAVENPORT-3B/CH
14 GEORGE FOSTER-OF
15 KEN HENDERSON-OF
16 JIM RAY HART-3B/OF
17 BOB HEISE-INF
18 RUSS GIBSON-C
19 BOB BURDA-1B/OF (1)
20 BERNIE WILLIAMS-OF
21 DON MASON-2B
22 HAL LANIER-SS/INF
23 CLYDE KING-MGR1
23 TITO FUENTES (INJ)-INF
24 WILLIE (SAY HEY) MAYS-OF/1B
25 BOBBY BONDS-OF
26 RON BRYANT-P
27 JUAN (MANITO) MARICHAL (ILL)-P
29 TITO FUENTES (INJ)-INF
29 ED GOODSON-1B
30 JIM JOHNSON-P
30 DON CARRITHERS-P
31 BOB TAYLOR-OF/C
32 RON BRYANT-P
33 RON HUNT-2B/3B
34 RON BRYANT-P
35 FRANK LINZY-P (1)
35 JERRY JOHNSON-P (2)
36 GAYLORD PERRY-P
37 FRANK JOHNSON-OF/1B
37 STEVE WHITAKER-OF
38 SKIP PITLOCK-P
38 BILL FAUL-P
39 FRANK (CRANE) REBERGER-P
40 MIKE MCCORMICK-P (1)
40 JOHN CUMBERLAND-P (2)
41 MIKE DAVISON-P
41 MIGUEL PUENTE-P
44 WILLIE (STRETCH) MCCOVEY-1B
45 RICH ROBERTSON-P
46 LARRY JANSEN-CH
47 DON MCMAHON-P
49 JIM JOHNSON-P

1971

1ST W — 90-72 — 0GB
L NLCS-PITN 3-1

1 JOHN MCNAMARA-CH
2 DICK DIETZ-C
3 OZZIE VIRGIL, SR.-CH
4 *(RET#) MEL OTT*
5 FRAN HEALY-C
6 DAVE RADER-C
7 CHARLIE (IRISH) FOX-MGR
8 DAVE RADER-C
9 WES WESTRUM-CH
10 AL GALLAGHER-3B
11 *(RET#) CARL HUBBELL*
14 GEORGE FOSTER-OF (1)
14 FRANK DUFFY-INF (2)
15 KEN HENDERSON-OF/1B
16 JIM RAY HART-3B/OF
17 BOB HEISE-INF (1)
18 RUSS GIBSON-C
19 JIM WILLOUGHBY-P
19 FLOYD WICKER-OF (2)
20 BERNIE WILLIAMS-OF
22 HAL LANIER-INF
23 TITO FUENTES (INJ)-INF
24 WILLIE (SAY HEY) MAYS-OF/1B
25 BOBBY BONDS-OF
27 JUAN (MANITO) MARICHAL-P
28 JERRY JOHNSON-P
30 DON CARRITHERS-P
31 CHRIS ARNOLD-2B
32 RON BRYANT (INJ)-P
33 STEVE STONE-P
33 JIM BARR-P
34 ED GOODSON-1B
35 JERRY JOHNSON-P
35 STEVE STONE-P
35 CHRIS SPEIER-SS
36 GAYLORD PERRY-P
37 FRANK JOHNSON-1B/OF
37 JIM HOWARTH-OF
38 STEVE HAMILTON-P
39 FRANK (CRANE) REBERGER (INJ)-P
40 JOHN CUMBERLAND-P
43 JIMMY ROSARIO-OF
44 WILLIE (STRETCH) MCCOVEY (INJ)-1B
45 RICH ROBERTSON-P
45 DAVE KINGMAN-1B/OF
46 LARRY JANSEN-CH
47 DON MCMAHON-P
50 JIM WILLOUGHBY-P

1972

5TH W — 69-86 — 26.5GB

1 JOHN MCNAMARA-CH
3 OZZIE VIRGIL, SR.-CH
4 *(RET#) MEL OTT*
5 FRAN HEALY-C
5 JOEY AMALFITANO-CH
6? JOEY AMALFITANO-CH
6 FRAN HEALY-C
7 CHARLIE (IRISH) FOX-MGR
8 ANDY GILBERT-CH
10 AL GALLAGHER-3B
11 *(RET#) CARL HUBBELL*
12 GARY THOMASSON-1B/OF
14 DAVE RADER-C
15 KEN HENDERSON-OF
16 JIM RAY HART-3B
17 CHRIS ARNOLD-INF
18 RUSS GIBSON-C
19 JIM WILLOUGHBY-P
19 JIM HOWARTH-OF/1B
20 BERNIE WILLIAMS-OF
21 ED GOODSON (INJ)-1B
22 DAMIE BLANCO-INF
22 JIMMY ROSARIO-OF
23 TITO FUENTES-2B
24 WILLIE (SAY HEY) MAYS-OF (1)
24 *(RET#) WILLIE MAYS*
25 BOBBY BONDS-OF
26 RANDY MOFFITT-P
26 DAVE KINGMAN-UTIL
27 JUAN (MANITO) MARICHAL-P
28 JERRY JOHNSON-P
29 STEVE STONE-P
30 DON CARRITHERS-P
31 CHRIS ARNOLD-INF
31 GARRY MADDOX-OF
32 RON BRYANT-P
33 JIM BARR-P
34 ED GOODSON (INJ)-1B
35 CHRIS SPEIER-SS
36 SAM (SUDDEN SAM) MCDOWELL (INJ)-P
36 GARY (SARGE) MATTHEWS-OF
38 JOHN MORRIS-P
38 ELIAS SOSA-P
39 RANDY MOFFITT-P
41 JOHN CUMBERLAND-P (1)
41 FRANK (CRANE) REBERGER-P
42 JOHN MORRIS-P
42 JIM WILLOUGHBY-P
43 JIMMY ROSARIO-OF
44 WILLIE (STRETCH) MCCOVEY (INJ)-1B
45 DAVE KINGMAN-UTIL
46 ANDY GILBERT-CH
47 DON MCMAHON-P
48 SAM (SUDDEN SAM) MCDOWELL (INJ)-P
49 CHARLIE WILLIAMS-P

1973

3RD W — 88-74 — 11GB

1 JOHN MCNAMARA-CH
3 MIKE SADEK-C
4 *(RET#) MEL OTT*
5 JOEY AMALFITANO-CH
7 CHARLIE (IRISH) FOX-MGR
8 ANDY GILBERT-CH
10 AL GALLAGHER-3B (1)
10 MIKE PHILLIPS-INF
11 *(RET#) CARL HUBBELL*
12 GARY THOMASSON-1B/OF
14 DAVE RADER-C

16 JIM RAY HART-3B (1)
16 STEVE ONTIVEROS-1B/OF
17 CHRIS ARNOLD-C/INF
18 DAMIE BLANCO-INF
19 JIM HOWARTH-OF/1B
21 ED GOODSON-3B
23 TITO FUENTES-2B/3B
24 *(RET#) WILLIE MAYS*
25 BOBBY BONDS-OF
26 DAVE KINGMAN-INF/P
27 JUAN (MANITO) MARICHAL-P
29 BRUCE MILLER-INF
30 DON CARRITHERS-P
31 GARRY MADDOX-OF
32 RON BRYANT-P
33 JIM BARR-P
34 JOHN D'ACQUISTO-P
35 CHRIS SPEIER-SS/2B
36 GARY (SARGE) MATTHEWS-OF
38 ELIAS SOSA-P
39 RANDY MOFFITT-P
40 TOM BRADLEY-P
42 JIM WILLOUGHBY-P
43 JOHN MORRIS (INJ)-P
44 WILLIE (STRETCH) MCCOVEY-1B
47 DON MCMAHON (RET)-P/CH
48 SAM (SUDDEN SAM) MCDOWELL-P (1)
49 CHARLIE WILLIAMS-P

1974
5TH W 72-90 30GB
1 OZZIE VIRGIL, SR.-CH
2 KEN RUDOLPH-C
4 *(RET#) MEL OTT*
5 JOEY AMALFITANO-CH
7 CHARLIE (IRISH) FOX-MGR1
8 ANDY GILBERT-CH
9 WES WESTRUM-MGR2
10 MIKE PHILLIPS-INF
11 *(RET#) CARL HUBBELL*
12 GARY THOMASSON-OF/1B
14 DAVE RADER-C
16 STEVE ONTIVEROS-3B/UTIL
17 CHRIS ARNOLD-INF
18 DAMIE BLANCO-PH
19 JIM HOWARTH-OF
20 GLENN REDMON-2B
21 ED GOODSON-1B/3B
23 TITO FUENTES-2B
24 *(RET#) WILLIE MAYS*
25 BOBBY BONDS-OF
26 DAVE KINGMAN-1B/UTIL
28 ED HALICKI-P
29 BRUCE MILLER-INF
30 JOHN BOCCABELLA-C
31 GARRY MADDOX-OF
32 RON BRYANT (INJ)-P
33 JIM BARR-P
34 JOHN D'ACQUISTO-P
35 CHRIS SPEIER-SS/2B
36 GARY (SARGE) MATTHEWS-OF
37 MIKE CALDWELL-P
38 ELIAS SOSA-P
39 RANDY MOFFITT-P
40 TOM BRADLEY-P
41 DON ROSE-P
42 JIM WILLOUGHBY-P
43 JOHN MORRIS-P
43 STEVE BARBER-P
46 GARY LAVELLE-P
47 DON MCMAHON (RET)-P/CH
48 BUTCH METZGER-P
49 CHARLIE WILLIAMS-P
50 JOHN (COUNT) MONTEFUSCO-P

1975
3RD W 80-81 27.5GB
1 OZZIE VIRGIL, SR.-CH
2 MARC HILL-C/3B
3 MIKE SADEK-C
4 *(RET#) MEL OTT*
5 JOEY AMALFITANO-CH
8 ANDY GILBERT-CH
9 WES WESTRUM-MGR2
10 MIKE PHILLIPS-2B/3B (1)
10 JOHNNIE LEMASTER-SS
11 *(RET#) CARL HUBBELL*
12 GARY THOMASSON-OF/1B
14 DAVE RADER-C
15 CHRIS ARNOLD-2B/OF
15 JACK CLARK-OF/3B
16 STEVE ONTIVEROS-3B/UTIL
17 RANDY MOFFITT-P
18 CRAIG ROBINSON-SS/2B (2)
19 VON JOSHUA-OF
20 BOBBY MURCER-OF
21 ED GOODSON-1B/3B (1)
22 WILLIE MONTANEZ-1B (2)
24 *(RET#) WILLIE MAYS*
25 ROB DRESSLER-P
26 JOHN (COUNT) MONTEFUSCO-P
27 *(RET#) JUAN MARICHAL*
28 ED HALICKI-P
29 BRUCE MILLER-INF
30 DERREL THOMAS-2B/OF
31 GARRY MADDOX-OF (1)
32 RON BRYANT (RET)-P (1)
32 JAKE BROWN-OF
33 JIM BARR-P
34 JOHN D'ACQUISTO (INJ)-P
35 CHRIS SPEIER-SS/3B
36 GARY (SARGE) MATTHEWS (INJ)-OF
37 MIKE CALDWELL-P
38 HORACE SPEED-OF
39 RANDY MOFFITT-P
40 TOM BRADLEY-P
40 TOMMY TOMS-P
41 GREG MINTON-P
43 GLENN ADAMS-OF
44 *(RET#) WILLIE MCCOVEY*
46 GARY LAVELLE-P
47 DON MCMAHON-CH
49 CHARLIE WILLIAMS-P
50 JOHN (COUNT) MONTEFUSCO-P
56 PETE FALCONE-P
58 GARY ALEXANDER-C
60 DAVE HEAVERLO-P

1976
4TH W 74-88 28GB
1 CRAIG ROBINSON-INF (1)
1 MARTY PEREZ-2B/SS (2)
2 MARC HILL-C/1B
3 MIKE SADEK-C
4 *(RET#) MEL OTT*
5 BOBBY WINKLES-CH
8 BOB RODGERS-CH
9 JIM DAVENPORT-CH
10 JOHNNIE LEMASTER-SS
11 *(RET#) CARL HUBBELL*
12 GARY THOMASSON (INJ)-OF/1B
14 DAVE RADER-C
15 CHRIS ARNOLD-INF
15 JACK CLARK-OF/3B
16 STEVE ONTIVEROS-UTIL
17 RANDY MOFFITT-P
18 BILL (THE CRICKET) (SPECS) RIGNEY-MGR
19 VON JOSHUA-OF (1)
20 BOBBY MURCER-OF
21 KEN REITZ-3B/SS
22 WILLIE MONTANEZ-1B (1)
24 *(RET#) WILLIE MAYS*
25 ROB DRESSLER-P
26 JOHN (COUNT) MONTEFUSCO-P
27 *(RET#) JUAN MARICHAL*
28 ED HALICKI-P
29 BRUCE MILLER-2B/3B
30 DERREL THOMAS (INJ)-UTIL
31 LARRY HERNDON-OF
33 JIM BARR-P
34 JOHN D'ACQUISTO-P
35 CHRIS SPEIER-SS/INF
36 GARY (SARGE) MATTHEWS-OF
37 MIKE CALDWELL-P
39 BOB KNEPPER-P
41 GREG MINTON-P
41 DARRELL EVANS-1B/3B (2)
43 GLENN ADAMS-OF
44 *(RET#) WILLIE MCCOVEY*
45 FRANK RICCELLI-P
46 GARY LAVELLE-P
47 CHARLIE WILLIAMS-P
49 CHARLIE WILLIAMS-P
51 TOMMY TOMS-P
55 FRANK FUNK-CH
56 FRANK FUNK-CH
58 GARY ALEXANDER-C
60 DAVE HEAVERLO-P

1977
4TH W 75-87 23GB
2 MARC HILL-C
3 MIKE SADEK-C
4 *(RET#) MEL OTT*
5 BOBBY WINKLES-CH
6 JOE ALTOBELLI-MGR
8 TOM HALLER-CH
9 JIM DAVENPORT-CH
10 JOHNNIE LEMASTER-SS/3B
11 *(RET#) CARL HUBBELL*
12 GARY THOMASSON-OF/1B
14 KEN RUDOLPH-C (1)
16 RANDY ELLIOTT-OF
17 RANDY MOFFITT-P
18 BILL (MAD DOG) MADLOCK-3B/2B
19 TIM FOLI (INJ)-SS/UTIL (2)
20 VIC HARRIS-UTIL
21 ROB ANDREWS-2B
22 JACK CLARK-OF
23 HERM STARRETTE-CH
24 *(RET#) WILLIE MAYS*
26 JOHN (COUNT) MONTEFUSCO (INJ)-P
27 *(RET#) JUAN MARICHAL*
28 ED HALICKI-P
30 DERREL THOMAS-OF/UTIL
31 LARRY HERNDON (INJ)-OF
32 TOM HEINTZELMAN-PH
33 JIM BARR-P
34 TERRY CORNUTT-P
35 CHRIS SPEIER-SS (1)
36 SKIP JAMES-1B
36 TIM FOLI (INJ)-SS/UTIL (2)
39 BOB KNEPPER-P
40 JOHN (JACK) CURTIS-P
41 DARRELL EVANS-UTIL
42 GREG MINTON-P
42 GARY ALEXANDER-C/OF
44 WILLIE (STRETCH) MCCOVEY-1B
45 TERRY WHITFIELD-OF
46 GARY LAVELLE-P
47 LYNN MCGLOTHEN (INJ)-P
49 CHARLIE WILLIAMS-P
51 TOMMY TOMS-P
60 DAVE HEAVERLO-P

1978
3RD W 89-73 6GB
1 DAVE BRISTOL-CH
2 MARC HILL-C/1B
3 MIKE SADEK (INJ)-C
4 *(RET#) MEL OTT*
5 BOBBY WINKLES-CH
5 TOM HALLER-CH
6 JOE ALTOBELLI-MGR
8 TOM HALLER-CH
9 JIM DAVENPORT-CH
9 HEITY CRUZ-OF/3B (2)
10 JOHNNIE LEMASTER-SS/2B
11 *(RET#) CARL HUBBELL*
12 JIM DAVENPORT-CH
14 VIDA BLUE-P
15 MIKE IVIE-1B/OF
16 ROGER METZGER-SS (2)
17 RANDY MOFFITT-P
18 BILL (MAD DOG) MADLOCK-2B/1B
20 VIC HARRIS-UTIL
21 ROB ANDREWS-2B/SS
22 JACK CLARK-OF
23 HERM STARRETTE-CH
24 *(RET#) WILLIE MAYS*
25 PHIL NATSU-P
26 JOHN (COUNT) MONTEFUSCO-P
27 *(RET#) JUAN MARICHAL*
28 ED HALICKI (INJ)-P
30 JOHN TAMARGO-C (2)
31 LARRY HERNDON-OF
32 TOM HEINTZELMAN-INF
33 JIM BARR-P
34 TERRY CORNUTT-P
34 TOM HEINTZELMAN-INF
35 DENNIS LITTLEJOHN-C
35 ART GARDNER-PH
36 SKIP JAMES-1B
36 JIM DWYER-OF/1B (2)
37 ED PLANK-P
38 GREG MINTON-P
39 BOB KNEPPER-P
40 JOHN (JACK) CURTIS-P
41 DARRELL EVANS-3B
42 TERRY CORNUTT-P
44 WILLIE (STRETCH) MCCOVEY-1B
45 TERRY WHITFIELD-OF
46 GARY LAVELLE-P
47 LYNN MCGLOTHEN-P (1)
49 CHARLIE WILLIAMS-P

1979
4TH W 71-91 19.5GB
1 DAVE BRISTOL-CH/MGR2
2 MARC HILL (INJ)-C/1B
3 MIKE SADEK-C/OF
4 *(RET#) MEL OTT*
5 TOM HALLER-CH
6 JOE ALTOBELLI-MGR1
8 LARRY SHEPARD-CH
9 HEITY CRUZ-OF/3B (1)
10 JOHNNIE LEMASTER-SS/2B
11 *(RET#) CARL HUBBELL*
12 JIM DAVENPORT-CH
14 VIDA BLUE-P
15 MIKE IVIE-UTIL
16 ROGER METZGER-INF
17 RANDY MOFFITT (INJ)-P
18 BILL (MAD DOG) MADLOCK-2B/1B (1)
19 AL HOLLAND-P
20 JOE STRAIN-2B/3B
21 ROB ANDREWS-2B/3B
22 JACK CLARK-OF/3B
23 GREG JOHNSTON-OF
23 PHIL NATSU-P
24 *(RET#) WILLIE MAYS*
25 PHIL NATSU-P
25 DAVE ROBERTS-P (1)
26 JOHN (COUNT) MONTEFUSCO (INJ)-P
27 *(RET#) JUAN MARICHAL*
28 ED HALICKI (ILL)-P
29 JOE COLEMAN-P (1)
29 ED WHITSON-P (2)
30 JOHN TAMARGO-C (1)
30 BOB KEARNEY-C
31 LARRY HERNDON-OF
32 PHIL NATSU-P
32 ED WHITSON-P (2)
34 PEDRO BORBON-P (2)
36 BILLY NORTH-OF
37 ED PLANK-P
38 GREG MINTON (INJ)-P
39 BOB KNEPPER-P
40 JOHN (JACK) CURTIS-P
41 DARRELL EVANS-3B
43 TOM GRIFFIN-P
44 WILLIE (STRETCH) MCCOVEY-1B
45 TERRY WHITFIELD-OF
46 GARY LAVELLE-P
47 DENNIS LITTLEJOHN-C
48 DAVE ROBERTS-P (1)
49 MAX VENABLE-OF

1980
5TH W 75-86 17GB
1 DAVE BRISTOL-MGR
2 MARC HILL-C (1)
2 JOE PETTINI-INF
3 MIKE SADEK-C
4 *(RET#) MEL OTT*
5 JIM LEFEBVRE-CH
6 RENNIE STENNETT-2B
7 MILT MAY-C
8 VERN BENSON-CH
9 JIM WOHLFORD-OF
10 JOHNNIE LEMASTER-SS
11 *(RET#) CARL HUBBELL*
12 JIM DAVENPORT-CH
14 VIDA BLUE (INJ)-P
15 MIKE IVIE (ILL) (RET)-1B
16 ROGER METZGER-SS/2B
17 RANDY MOFFITT (ILL)-P
18 CHRIS BOURJOS-OF
19 AL HOLLAND-P
20 JOE STRAIN (INJ)-INF
21 GUY SULARZ-2B/3B
22 JACK CLARK (INJ)-OF
23 PHIL NATSU-P
24 *(RET#) WILLIE MAYS*
26 JOHN (COUNT) MONTEFUSCO (INJ)-P
27 *(RET#) JUAN MARICHAL*
28 ED HALICKI-P (1)
28 MIKE ROWLAND-P
29 RICH MURRAY (INJ)-1B
31 LARRY HERNDON-OF
32 ED WHITSON-P
33 ALLEN RIPLEY-P
34 PHIL NATSU-P
34 BILL BORDLEY-P
35 DENNIS LITTLEJOHN-C
35 MIKE ROWLAND-P
36 BILLY NORTH-OF
38 GREG MINTON-P
39 BOB KNEPPER-P
40 ALAN HARGESHEIMER-P
41 DARRELL EVANS-3B/1B
42 MILT MAY-C
42 JOHN VAN ORNUM-CH
43 TOM GRIFFIN-P
44 WILLIE (STRETCH) MCCOVEY (RET)-1B
45 TERRY WHITFIELD-OF
46 GARY LAVELLE-P
47 BILL BORDLEY-P
47 DON MCMAHON-CH

FRED BREINING-P
MAX VENABLE-OF
JEFF STEMBER-P

1981

1/2:5TH W 27-32 10GB
1/2:2ND E 29-23 3.5GB
AL: 56-55 --GB

JIM WOHLFORD-OF
JOE PETTINI-INF
MIKE SADEK-C
(RET#) MEL OTT
JIM LEFEBVRE-CH
RENNIE STENNETT-2B
MILT MAY-C
JOE MORGAN-2B
DON BUFORD-CH
JOHNNIE LEMASTER-SS
(RET#) CARL HUBBELL
JIM DAVENPORT-CH
VIDA BLUE-P
MIKE IVIE-1B (1)
BOB BRENLY-UTIL
JEFF RANSOM-C
DAVE BERGMAN-1B/OF (2)
RANDY MOFFITT (ILL)-P
BOB TUFTS-P
AL HOLLAND-P
FRANK ROBINSON-MGR
GUY SULARZ-2B/3B
BILLY SMITH-INF
JACK CLARK-OF
ENOS CABELL-1B/3B
(RET#) WILLIE MAYS
JERRY MARTIN-OF
DOYLE ALEXANDER-P
JEFF LEONARD-OF/1B (2)
(RET#) JUAN MARICHAL
MIKE ROWLAND-P
CHILI DAVIS-OF
LARRY HERNDON-OF
ED WHITSON-P
ALLEN RIPLEY-P
DOYLE ALEXANDER-P
BILL BORDLEY (INJ)-P
BILLY NORTH-OF
GREG MINTON-P
ALAN HARGESHEIMER-P
DARRELL EVANS-3B/1B
JOHN VAN ORNUM-CH
TOM GRIFFIN-P
(RET#) WILLIE MCCOVEY
ALLEN RIPLEY-P
GARY LAVELLE-P
DON MCMAHON-CH
FRED BREINING-P
MAX VENABLE-OF
BOB TUFTS-P
VERN BENSON-CH

1982

3RD W 87-75 2GB

JIM WOHLFORD-OF
JOE PETTINI-SS/3B
JEFF RANSOM-C
JOHN RABB-OF
(RET#) MEL OTT
JIM LEFEBVRE-CH
CHAMP SUMMERS-OF/1B
MILT MAY-C
JOE MORGAN-2B/3B
DON BUFORD-CH
JOHNNIE LEMASTER-SS
(RET#) CARL HUBBELL
JIM DAVENPORT-CH
REGGIE SMITH-1B
BOB BRENLY (INJ)-C/3B
DAVE BERGMAN-1B/OF
ATLEE HAMMAKER-P
DUANE KUIPER-2B
AL HOLLAND-P
20 FRANK ROBINSON-MGR
21 GUY SULARZ-INF
22 JACK CLARK-OF
23 JOSE BARRIOS-1B
24 *(RET#) WILLIE MAYS*
25 RON PRUITT-C/OF
26 JEFF LEONARD (INJ)-OF/1B
27 *(RET#) JUAN MARICHAL*
28 ANDY MCGAFFIGAN-P
29 JIM BARR-P
29 ALAN FOWLKES-P
30 CHILI DAVIS-OF
31 MIKE CHRIS-P
32 RICH GALE-P
33 JIM BARR-P
(34) BILL BORDLEY (INJ)-(P)
34 MIKE CHRIS-P
35 TOM O'MALLEY-INF
36 DAN SCHATZEDER-P (1)
36 BRAD WELLMAN-2B
38 GREG MINTON-P
39 RENIE MARTIN-P
40 MARK DEMPSEY-P
41 DARRELL EVANS-3B/INF
42 JOHN VAN ORNUM-CH
43 SCOTT GARRELTS-P
44 *(RET#) WILLIE MCCOVEY*
45 BILL LASKEY-P
46 GARY LAVELLE-P
47 DON MCMAHON-CH
48 FRED BREINING-P
49 MAX VENABLE (ILL)-OF
52 SCOTT GARRELTS-P
53 ALAN FOWLKES-P
54 SCOTT GARRELTS-P
55 MARK DEMPSEY-P

1983

5TH W 79-83 12GB

1 DANNY OZARK-CH
2 JOE PETTINI-SS/3B
3 DANNY OZARK-CH
4 *(RET#) MEL OTT*
5 JOHN RABB-OF
5 WALLACE JOHNSON-2B (2)
6 CHAMP SUMMERS (INJOF
7 MILT MAY-C (1)
7 STEVE NICOSIA-C (2)
8 BRAD WELLMAN-2B/SS
8 JOEL YOUNGBLOOD-UTIL
9 DON BUFORD-CH
10 JOHNNIE LEMASTER-SS
11 *(RET#) CARL HUBBELL*
12 JIM DAVENPORT-CH
12 TOM MCCRAW-CH
13 MARK DAVIS-P
14 RON PRUITT-PH
14 ATLEE HAMMAKER (INJ)-P
15 BOB BRENLY-C/UTIL
16 DAVE BERGMAN-1B/OF
17 ATLEE HAMMAKER (INJ)-P
17 RENIE MARTIN-P
18 DUANE KUIPER (INJ)-2B
19 BILL LASKEY (INJ)-P
20 FRANK ROBINSON-MGR
21 GUY SULARZ-SS/3B
22 JACK CLARK-OF/1B
23 HERM STARRETTE-CH
24 *(RET#) WILLIE MAYS*
25 DAN GLADDEN-OF
25 MARK CALVERT-P
25 PAT LARKIN-P
25 BRIAN KINGMAN-P
25 RICH MURRAY-1B
26 JEFF LEONARD-OF
27 *(RET#) JUAN MARICHAL*
28 ANDY MCGAFFIGAN-P
29 RANDY LERCH-P (2)
30 CHILI DAVIS-OF
31 MIKE CHRIS-P
31 CHRIS SMITH-UTIL
32 MIKE VAIL-1B/OF (1)
32 CHRIS SMITH-UTIL
32 MARK CALVERT-P
33 JIM BARR-P
34 MIKE KRUKOW (INJ)-P
35 TOM O'MALLEY-3B
36 TOM MCCRAW-CH
37 JEFF RANSOM-C
38 GREG MINTON-P
39 RENIE MARTIN-P
39 MIKE KRUKOW (INJ)-P
40 MARK DEMPSEY-P
41 DARRELL EVANS-1B/INF
42 JOHN VAN ORNUM-CH
43 SCOTT GARRELTS-P
44 *(RET#) WILLIE MCCOVEY*
45 BILL LASKEY (INJ)-P
46 GARY LAVELLE-P
48 FRED BREINING-P
49 MAX VENABLE-OF
50 MARK CALVERT-P
54 SCOTT GARRELTS-P

1984

6TH W 66-96 26GB

0 AL OLIVER-1B (1)
1 DANNY OZARK-CH/MGR2
2 JOE PITTMAN-INF
2 JIM DAVENPORT-CH
4 *(RET#) MEL OTT*
5 JOHN RABB-UTIL
6 DON BUFORD-CH
7 STEVE NICOSIA (INJ)-C
8 JOEL YOUNGBLOOD-3B/UTIL
9 MANNY TRILLO (INJ)-2B/3B
10 JOHNNIE LEMASTER-SS
11 *(RET#) CARL HUBBELL*
12 TOM MCCRAW-CH
12 DUSTY BAKER-OF
13 MARK DAVIS-P
14 ATLEE HAMMAKER (INJ)-P
15 BOB BRENLY-C/UTIL
16 FRAN MULLINS (INJ)-INF
17 RENIE MARTIN-P (1)
17 BOB LACEY-P
18 DUANE KUIPER-2B/1B
19 BILL LASKEY-P
20 FRANK ROBINSON-MGR1
21 TOM MCCRAW-CH
22 JACK CLARK (INJ)-OF/1B
23 HERM STARRETTE-CH
24 *(RET#) WILLIE MAYS*
25 DAN GLADDEN-OF
25 GENE RICHARDS-OF
26 JEFF LEONARD -OF
27 *(RET#) JUAN MARICHAL*
29 RANDY LERCH (INJ)-P
30 CHILI DAVIS-OF
31 SCOTT GARRELTS-P
31 JEFF CORNELL-P
32 MARK CALVERT-P
32 DAN GLADDEN-OF
33 ALEX SANCHEZ-OF
34 MARK GRANT-P
35 TOM O'MALLEY-3B (1)
35 CHRIS BROWN-3B
36 BRAD WELLMAN-INF
37 RANDY GOMEZ-C
38 GREG MINTON-P
39 MIKE KRUKOW-P
41 SCOT THOMPSON-1B/OF
42 JOHN VAN ORNUM-CH
44 *(RET#) WILLIE MCCOVEY*
45 ROB DEER-OF
46 GARY LAVELLE-P
47 MARK GRANT-P
47 FRANK WILLIAMS-P
49 JEFF ROBINSON-P
50 SCOTT GARRELTS-P
51 GEORGE RILEY-P

1985

6TH W 62-100 33GB

1 JIM DAVENPORT-MGR1
1 RICK ADAMS-INF
2 CHUCK HILLER-CH
3 *(RET#) BILL TERRY*
4 *(RET#) MEL OTT*
6 ROCKY BRIDGES-CH
7* ATLEE HAMMAKER-P*
8 JOEL YOUNGBLOOD-OF/3B
9 MANNY TRILLO-2B/3B
10 JOHNNIE LEMASTER-SS (1)
10 RON ROENICKE-OF
11 *(RET#) CARL HUBBELL*
12 JIM DAVENPORT-MGR1
13 MARK DAVIS-P
14 VIDA BLUE-P
15 BOB BRENLY-C/INF
18 DUANE KUIPER (INJ)-PH
19 BILL LASKEY-P (1)
19 ROGER MASON-P
20 JEFF LEONARD-OF
21 TOM MCCRAW-CH
22 DAVID GREEN-1B/OF
23 JOSE URIBE-SS/2B
24 *(RET#) WILLIE MAYS*
25 DAN DRIESSEN-1B (2)
26 GARY RAJSICH-1B
26 MATT NOKES-C
27 *(RET#) JUAN MARICHAL*
28 ROB DEER-OF/1B
29 ALEX TREVINO-C/3B
30 CHILI DAVIS-OF
32 DAN GLADDEN-OF
33 MIKE JEFFCOAT-P (2)
33 ROGER CRAIG-MGR2
34 BOBBY MOORE-P
35 CHRIS BROWN-3B
36 BRAD WELLMAN (INJ)-INF
38 GREG MINTON-P
39 MIKE KRUKOW (INJ)-P
40 DAVE LAPOINT-P
41 SCOT THOMPSON-1B/OF (1)
41 MIKE WOODARD-2B
42 JACK MULL-CH
43 COLIN WARD-P
44 *(RET#) WILLIE MCCOVEY*
46 MIKE JEFFCOAT-P (2)
47 FRANK WILLIAMS-P
48 BOB MILLER-CH
49 JEFF ROBINSON-P
50 SCOTT GARRELTS-P
51 JIM GOTT-P

1986

3RD W 83-79 13GB

1 MIKE ALDRETE-1B/OF
2 LUIS QUINONES-INF
3 *(RET#) BILL TERRY*
4 *(RET#) MEL OTT*
5 BOB LILLIS-CH
6 ROBBY THOMPSON-2B/SS
(7) ATLEE HAMMAKER (INJ)-(P)
7 BOB MELVIN-C/3B
8 JOEL YOUNGBLOOD-UTIL
8 GORDON MACKENZIE-CH
9 RANDY KUTCHER-UTIL
9 RICK LANCELLOTTI-1B/OF
10 BRAD GULDEN-C
11 *(RET#) CARL HUBBELL*
12 PHIL OUELLETTE-C
12 CHRIS JONES-PH
13 MARK DAVIS-P
14 VIDA BLUE (INJ) P
(14) ATLEE HAMMAKER (INJ)-(P)
15 BOB BRENLY-C/INF
16 HARRY SPILMAN-UTIL (2)
18 BOB MELVIN-C/3B
19 ROGER MASON (INJ)-P
19 BILL LASKEY-P
20 JEFF LEONARD (INJ)-OF
21 CANDY MALDONADO-OF/3B
22 WILL (THE THRILL) CLARK (INJ)-1B
23 JOSE URIBE-SS
24 *(RET#) WILLIE MAYS*
25 DAN DRIESSEN-1B (1)
26 CHUCK HENSLEY-P
26 RANDY BOCKUS-P
27 *(RET#) JUAN MARICHAL*
28 JOSE MORALES-CH
29 CANDY MALDONADO-OF/3B
29 MIKE LACOSS-P
30 CHILI DAVIS-OF
31 RICK LANCELLOTTI-1B/OF
32 DAN GLADDEN (INJ)-OF
32 STEVE CARLTON-P (2)
33 ROGER CRAIG-MGR
34 NORM SHERRY-CH
35 CHRIS BROWN (INJ)-3B/SS
36 BRAD WELLMAN-INF
37 KELLY DOWNS-P
38 GREG MINTON (INJ)-P
39 MIKE KRUKOW-P
40 JUAN BERENGUER-P
41 MIKE WOODARD-INF
42 MIKE LACOSS-P
42 BILL FAHEY-CH
43 GORDON MACKENZIE-CH
44 *(RET#) WILLIE MCCOVEY*
45 BILL LASKEY-P
45 ROGER MASON (INJ)-P
45 TERRY MULHOLLAND-P
46 MARK GRANT-P
47 FRANK WILLIAMS-P
48 ROGER MASON (INJ)-P
49 JEFF ROBINSON-P
50 SCOTT GARRELTS-P
51 JIM GOTT-P
52 TERRY MULHOLLAND-P
52 MARK GRANT-P

1987

1ST W 90-72 0GB
L NLCS-STLN 4-3

00 JEFF LEONARD (INJ)-OF
1 DON (POPEYE) ZIMMER-CH
2 CHRIS SPEIER-INF
3 *(RET#) BILL TERRY*
4 *(RET#) MEL OTT*
5 BOB LILLIS-CH
6 ROBBY THOMPSON-2B
7 BOB MELVIN-C/1B
8 JOEL YOUNGBLOOD-OF/3B
9 RANDY KUTCHER-UTIL
9 IVAN DEJESUS-SS
9 ROB WILFONG-2B
9 KEVIN MITCHELL-3B/UTIL (2)
10 MACKEY SASSER-C (1)
10 MATT WILLIAMS-SS/3B
11 *(RET#) CARL HUBBELL*
12 MARK WASINGER-INF
13 MARK DAVIS-P (1)
14 ATLEE HAMMAKER (INJ)-P
15 BOB BRENLY-C/INF
16 HARRY SPILMAN-UTIL
17 KIRT MANWARING-C
17 MACKEY SASSER-C (1)
18 FRANCISCO MELENDEZ-1B
19 RANDY KUTCHER-UTIL
20 EDDIE MILNER (SUB)-OF
21 CANDY MALDONADO (INJ) -OF
22 WILL (THE THRILL) CLARK-1B
23 JOSE URIBE (INJ)-SS

24 *(RET#) WILLIE MAYS*
25 MIKE ALDRETE-OF/1B
26 RANDY BOCKUS-P
26 JESSIE REID-OF
27 *(RET#) JUAN MARICHAL*
28 JOSE MORALES-CH
29 MIKE LACOSS-P
30 CHILI DAVIS-OF
32 MARK DAVIS-P (1)
32 CRAIG LEFFERTS-P (2)
33 ROGER CRAIG-MGR
33 CHILI DAVIS-OF
34 NORM SHERRY-CH
35 CHRIS BROWN (INJ)-3B/SS (1)
36 KEITH COMSTOCK-P (1)
37 KELLY DOWNS-P
38 GREG MINTON-P (1)
38 ROGER CRAIG-MGR
39 MIKE KRUKOW-P
40 JOHN BURKETT-P
40 DON ROBINSON-P (2)
41 MIKE WOODARD-INF
41 DAVE HENDERSON-OF (2)
42 BILL FAHEY-CH
43 GORDON MACKENZIE-CH
43 DAVE DRAVECKY-P (2)
44 *(RET#) WILLIE MCCOVEY*
46 JON PERLMAN-P
46 MARK GRANT-P (1)
47 JOE PRICE-P
48 ROGER MASON-P
48 DON ROBINSON-P (2)
48 RICK REUSCHEL-P (2)
49 JEFF ROBINSON-P (1)
49 RANDY BOCKUS-P
50 SCOTT GARRELTS-P
51 JIM GOTT-P (1)
51 JOHN BURKETT-P
52 MARK GRANT-P (1)
55 KEITH COMSTOCK-P (1)
55 MARK GRANT-P (1)
55 GORDIE MACKENZIE-CH
60 MATT WILLIAMS-SS/3B

1988

4TH W 83-79 11.5GB

00 JEFF LEONARD (INJ)-OF (1)
1 TONY PEREZCHICA-2B
1 ERNEST RILES-INF (2)
2 BRETT BUTLER-OF
3 *(RET#) BILL TERRY*
4 *(RET#) MEL OTT*
5 BOB LILLIS-CH
6 ROBBY THOMPSON-2B
7 BOB MELVIN-C/1B
7 KEVIN MITCHELL-3B/OF
8 JOEL YOUNGBLOOD-OF
9 KEVIN MITCHELL-3B/OF
9 BOB MELVIN-C/1B
10 MATT WILLIAMS-SS/3B
11 *(RET#) CARL HUBBELL*
12 DUSTY BAKER-CH
14 ATLEE HAMMAKER-P
15 BOB BRENLY-C/INF
16 HARRY SPILMAN-1B (1)
17 KIRT MANWARING-C
18 FRANCISCO MELENDEZ (INJ)-1B/OF
19 ROGER MASON-P
19 LARY SORENSEN-P
20 PHIL GARNER (INJ)-3B
21 CANDY MALDONADO-OF
22 WILL (THE THRILL) CLARK-1B
23 JOSE URIBE (INJ)-SS
24 *(RET#) WILLIE MAYS*
25 MIKE ALDRETE-OF/1B
26 JESSIE REID-PH
26 CHARLIE HAYES-OF/3B
27 *(RET#) JUAN MARICHAL*
28 JOSE MORALES-CH
29 MIKE LACOSS (INJ)-P
30 RUSTY TILLMAN-OF
30 DONELL NIXON-OF
31 RANDY BOCKUS-P
32 CRAIG LEFFERTS-P
33 RANDY KUTCHER-UTIL
33 RON DAVIS-P
33 MARK WASINGER-3B
34 NORM SHERRY-CH
35 CHRIS SPEIER-INF
36 DENNIS COOK-P
37 KELLY DOWNS (INJ)-P
38 ROGER CRAIG-MGR
39 MIKE KRUKOW (INJ)-P
40 DON ROBINSON-P
41 TREVOR WILSON-P
42 BILL FAHEY-CH
43 DAVE DRAVECKY (INJ) (ILL) -P
44 *(RET#) WILLIE MCCOVEY*
45 TERRY MULHOLLAND (INJ)-P
47 JOE PRICE (INJ)-P
48 RICK REUSCHEL-P
49 JEFF BRANTLEY-P
50 SCOTT GARRELTS-P
51 JOHN BURKETT-P
54 ANGEL ESCOBAR-SS/3B
55 GORDIE MACKENZIE-CH
58 ROGER SAMUELS-P

1989

1ST W 92-70 0GB
W NLCS-CHIN 4-1
L WS-OAKA 4-0

1 ERNEST RILES-UTIL
2 BRETT BUTLER-OF
3 *(RET#) BILL TERRY*
4 *(RET#) MEL OTT*
5 BOB LILLIS-CH
6 ROBBY THOMPSON-2B
7 KEVIN MITCHELL-OF/3B
8 ED JURAK-UTIL
8 MIKE LAGA-1B
9 MATT WILLIAMS-3B/SS
10 KEN (OBIE) OBERKFELL-INF (2)
11 *(RET#) CARL HUBBELL*
12 DUSTY BAKER-CH
13 ERNIE CAMACHO-P
14 ATLEE HAMMAKER (INJ)-P
15 GREG LITTON-UTIL
16 TERRY KENNEDY-C/1B
17 KIRT MANWARING-C
18 BILL BATHE-C
19 JAMES STEELS-1B/OF
19 BOB BRENLY-C/INF (2)
20 WENDELL KIM-CH
21 CANDY MALDONADO-OF
22 WILL (THE THRILL) CLARK-1B
23 JOSE URIBE (INJ)-SS
24 *(RET#) WILLIE MAYS*
25 TRACY JONES-OF (1)
25 PAT SHERIDAN-OF (2)
26 CHARLIE HAYES-3B (1)
26 MIKE BENJAMIN-SS
27 *(RET#) JUAN MARICHAL*
28 BOB KNEPPER-P (2)
29 MIKE LACOSS (INJ)-P
30 DONELL NIXON-OF
31 DENNIS COOK-P (1)
31 DON ROBINSON-P
32 CRAIG LEFFERTS-P
(33) KARL BEST (INJ)-(P)
33 RUSS SWAN-P
34 NORM SHERRY-CH
35 CHRIS SPEIER (INJ)-INF
36 RANDY MCCAMENT-P
37 KELLY DOWNS (INJ)-P
38 ROGER CRAIG-MGR
39 MIKE KRUKOW (INJ)-P
40 DON ROBINSON-P
40 STEVE (BEDROCK) BEDROSIAN-P (2)
41 TREVOR WILSON-P
42 BILL FAHEY-CH
43 DAVE DRAVECKY (ILL) (INJ) -P
44 *(RET#) WILLIE MCCOVEY*
45 JIM WEAVER-OF
45 STEVE (BEDROCK) BEDROSIAN-P (2)
45 TERRY MULHOLLAND (INJ)-P
47 JOE PRICE (INJ)-P (1)
48 RICK REUSCHEL-P
49 JEFF BRANTLEY-P
50 SCOTT GARRELTS-P
51 JOHN BURKETT-P
52 RUSS SWAN-P
53 STU TATE-P
54 GOOSE GOSSAGE-P (1)

1990

3RD W 85-77 6GB

1 ERNEST RILES-INF
2 BRETT BUTLER-OF
3 *(RET#) BILL TERRY*
4 *(RET#) MEL OTT*
5 BOB LILLIS-CH
6 ROBBY THOMPSON-2B
7 KEVIN MITCHELL-OF
8 GARY (THE KID) CARTER-C/1B
9 MATT WILLIAMS-3B
10 DAVE ANDERSON-INF
11 *(RET#) CARL HUBBELL*
12 DUSTY BAKER-CH
13 ERNIE CAMACHO-P (1)
14 ATLEE HAMMAKER (INJ)-P (1)
14 MARK DEWEY-P
15 GREG LITTON-UTIL
16 TERRY KENNEDY-C/1B
17 KIRT MANWARING-C
17 KEVIN BASS (INJ)-OF
18 BILL BATHE (INJ)-C
19 KEVIN BASS (INJ)-OF
19 KIRT MANWARING-C
20 WENDELL KIM-CH
21 MIKE LAGA-1B
21 MARK LEONARD-OF
22 WILL (THE THRILL) CLARK-1B
23 JOSE URIBE-SS
24 *(RET#) WILLIE MAYS*
25 RICK LEACH (SUB)-OF/1B
26 ANDY MCGAFFIGAN-P (1)
26 MIKE BENJAMIN-SS
26 MIKE KINGERY-OF
27 *(RET#) JUAN MARICHAL*
28 ED VOSBERG-P
28 PAUL MCCLELLAN-P
28 TONY PEREZCHICA-2B/SS
29 MIKE LACOSS (INJ)-P
30 MARK THURMOND (INJ)-P
31 DON ROBINSON (INJ)-P
32 BRAD KOMMINSK-OF (1)
32 JOHN BURKETT-P
32 RICK PARKER-UTIL
(33) JOSE ALVAREZ (INJ)-(P)
33 JOHN BURKETT-P
34 NORM SHERRY-CH
35 ANDRES SANTANA-SS
36 RANDY MCCAMENT-P
36 RAFAEL NOVOA-P
37 KELLY DOWNS (INJ)-P
38 ROGER CRAIG-MGR
39 BOB KNEPPER-P
39 MIKE LAGA-1B
40 STEVE (BEDROCK) BEDROSIAN-P
41 TREVOR WILSON-P
42 BILL FAHEY-CH
44 *(RET#) WILLIE MCCOVEY*
45 BRAD KOMMINSK-OF (1)
45 MARK BAILEY-C
45 FRANCISCO OLIVERAS-P
46 TREVOR WILSON-P
47 DAN (QUIZ) QUISENBERRY-P
47 STEVE DECKER-C
48 RICK REUSCHEL (INJ)-P
49 JEFF BRANTLEY-P
50 SCOTT GARRELTS-P
51 MIKE BENJAMIN-SS
51 GREG BOOKER-P
52 PAUL MCCLELLAN-P
53 ERIC GUNDERSON-P
54 ???
55 RANDY O'NEAL-P
59 RUSS SWAN-P (1)
59 RICK RODRIGUEZ-P

1991

4TH W 75-87 19GB

1 MARK LEONARD-OF
2 DARREN LEWIS-OF
3 *(RET#) BILL TERRY*
4 *(RET#) MEL OTT*
5 BOB LILLIS-CH
6 ROBBY THOMPSON-2B
7 KEVIN MITCHELL-OF/1B
8 KIRT MANWARING-C
9 MATT WILLIAMS-3B/SS
10 DAVE ANDERSON-INF
11 *(RET#) CARL HUBBELL*
12 DUSTY BAKER-CH
14 MIKE REMLINGER-P
15 GREG LITTON-*ALL POS.*
16 TERRY KENNEDY-C/1B
17 KEVIN BASS (INJ)-OF
18 MIKE BENJAMIN-SS/3B
19 DAVE RIGHETTI-P
20 WENDELL KIM-CH
21 TONY PEREZCHICA-SS/2B (1)
21 DARNELL COLES-OF/1B
21 ROYCE CLAYTON-SS
22 WILL (THE THRILL) CLARK-1B
23 JOSE URIBE (INJ)-SS
24 *(RET#) WILLIE MAYS*
25 MIKE FELDER-UTIL
26 MIKE KINGERY-OF
27 *(RET#) JUAN MARICHAL*
28 TOMMY HERR-2B/3B
29 MIKE LACOSS-P
31 DON ROBINSON-P
32 RICK PARKER (INJ)-OF
32 TREVOR WILSON-P
33 JOHN BURKETT-P
34 NORM SHERRY-CH
35 STEVE DECKER-C
36 GIL HEREDIA-P
37 KELLY DOWNS-P
38 ROGER CRAIG-MGR
39 TONY PEREZCHICA-SS/2B (1)
39 TED WOOD-OF
40 BUD BLACK-P
41 TREVOR WILSON-P
41 BRYAN HICKERSON-P
42 BILL FAHEY-CH
44 *(RET#) WILLIE MCCOVEY*
45 FRANCISCO OLIVERAS-P
46 JOSE SEGURA-P
47 ROD BECK-P
48 RICK REUSCHEL (INJ)-P
48 PAUL MCCLELLAN-P
49 JEFF BRANTLEY-P
50 SCOTT GARRELTS (INJ)-P
51 WILLIE MCGEE (INJ)-OF
52 PAUL MCCLELLAN-P
53 ERIC GUNDERSON-P

1992

5TH W 72-90 26GE

1 MARK LEONARD-OF
2 DARREN LEWIS-OF
3 *(RET#) BILL TERRY*
4 *(RET#) MEL OTT*
5 BOB LILLIS-CH
6 ROBBY THOMPSON-2B
7 JOHN PATTERSON-2B/OF
8 KIRT MANWARING-C/3B
9 MATT WILLIAMS-3B/C
10 ROYCE CLAYTON-SS/3B
11 *(RET#) CARL HUBBELL*
12 DUSTY BAKER-CH
14 CHRIS JAMES-OF
14 BOB BRENLY-CH
15 GREG LITTON-UTIL
15 BOB BRENLY-CH
16 CARLOS ALFONSO-CH
17 KEVIN BASS-OF (1)
17 GREG LITTON-UTIL
18 MIKE BENJAMIN-SS/3B
19 DAVE RIGHETTI-P
20 WENDELL KIM-CH
21 KEVIN ROGERS-P
22 WILL (THE THRILL) CLARK-1B
23 JOSE URIBE-SS
24 *(RET#) WILLIE MAYS*
25 MIKE FELDER-OF/2B
26 BILL SWIFT-P
27 *(RET#) JUAN MARICHAL*
28 CORY SNYDER-UTIL
29 GREG LITTON-UTIL
29 STEVE HOSEY-OF
30 JIM MCNAMARA-C
30 CHRIS JAMES-OF
31 JIM PENA-P
32 TREVOR WILSON-P
33 JOHN BURKETT-P
34 DAVE BURBA-P
35 STEVE DECKER-C
36 GIL HEREDIA-P
36 STEVE REED-P
37 KELLY DOWNS-P (1)
37 MARK BAILEY-C
38 ROGER CRAIG-MGR
39 TED WOOD-OF
40 BUD BLACK-P
41 BRYAN HICKERSON-P
42 MIKE JACKSON-P
44 *(RET#) WILLIE MCCOVEY*
45 FRANCISCO OLIVERAS-P
46 CRAIG COLBERT-C/INF
47 ROD BECK-P
48 PAT RAPP-P
49 JEFF BRANTLEY-P
51 WILLIE MCGEE-OF
52 LARRY CARTER-P
58 KEVIN ROGERS-P

1993

2ND W 103-59 1GB

(RET#) CHRISTY MATHEWSO
(RET#) JOHN MCGRAW
1 DAVE MARTINEZ (INJ)-OF
2 DARREN LEWIS-OF
3 *(RET#) BILL TERRY*
4 *(RET#) MEL OTT*
5 BOB LILLIS-CH
6 ROBBY THOMPSON-2B
7 JOHN PATTERSON (INJ)-2E
8 KIRT MANWARING-C
9 MATT WILLIAMS-3B
10 ROYCE CLAYTON-SS
11 *(RET#) CARL HUBBELL*

NEW YORK/**SAN FRANCISCO GIANTS**

2 DUSTY BAKER-MGR
4 TODD BENZINGER (INJ)-UTIL
5 BOB BRENLY-CH
6 BOBBY BONDS-CH
7 DAVE MARTINEZ (INJ)-OF
7 LUIS MERCEDES-OF (2)
8 MIKE BENJAMIN (INJ)-INF
9 DAVE RIGHETTI-P
0 WENDELL KIM-CH
1 PAUL FAIRIES-INF
2 WILL (THE THRILL) CLARK-1B
3 STEVE SCARSONE (INJ)-INF
4 *(RET#) WILLIE MAYS*
5 BARRY BONDS-OF
6 BILL SWIFT-P
7 *(RET#) JUAN MARICHAL*
8 KEVIN ROGERS-P
9 SCOTT SANDERSON-P (2)
9 STEVE HOSEY-OF
0 JIM MCNAMARA-C
0 JIM DESHAIES-P (2)
1 J. R. PHILLIPS-1B
2 TREVOR WILSON (INJ)-P
3 JOHN BURKETT-P
4 DAVE BURBA-P
5 SALOMON TORRES-P
6 GINO MINUTELLI-P
6 ERIK JOHNSON-INF
6 TIM LAYANA-P
7 ANDY ALLANSON-C/1B
7 TERRY BROSS-P
8 STEVE SCARSONE (INJ)-INF
8 RIKKERT FANEYTE-OF
0 BUD BLACK (INJ)-P
1 BRYAN HICKERSON-P
2 MIKE JACKSON-P
4 *(RET#) WILLIE MCCOVEY*
5 MARK CARREON-OF
6 CRAIG COLBERT (INJ)-C/INF
7 ROD BECK-P
8 DICK POLE-CH
9 JEFF BRANTLEY-P
0 GREG BRUMMETT-P (1)
1 WILLIE MCGEE-OF
2 JEFF REED (INJ)-C

1994

2ND W 53-61 3.5GB
STRIKE NO POST-SEASON
(RET#) CHRISTY MATHEWSON
(RET#) JOHN MCGRAW
1 DAVE MARTINEZ (INJ)-OF
2 DARREN LEWIS-OF
3 *(RET#) BILL TERRY*
4 *(RET#) MEL OTT*
5 BOB LILLIS-CH
6 ROBBY THOMPSON (INJ)-2B
7 JOHN PATTERSON-2B
8 KIRT MANWARING-C
9 MATT WILLIAMS-3B
0 ROYCE CLAYTON-SS
1 *(RET#) CARL HUBBELL*
2 DUSTY BAKER-MGR
3 J. R. PHILLIPS-1B
4 TODD BENZINGER (INJ)-UTIL
5 BOB BRENLY-CH
6 BOBBY BONDS-CH
7 DARRYL (STRAW) STRAWBERRY (SUB)-OF (2)
8 MIKE BENJAMIN (INJ)-INF/SS
9 MARK PORTUGAL (INJ)-P
0 WENDELL KIM-CH
1 MARK LEONARD-OF
2 RIKKERT FANEYTE-OF
23 STEVE SCARSONE-3B
24 *(RET#) WILLIE MAYS*
25 BARRY BONDS-OF
26 BILL SWIFT (INJ)-P
27 *(RET#) JUAN MARICHAL*
28 KEVIN ROGERS (INJ)-P
31 STEVE FREY-P
31 ERIK JOHNSON-2B
(32) TREVOR WILSON (INJ)-(P)
33 JOHN BURKETT-P
34 DAVE BURBA-P
35 SALOMON TORRES-P
36 TONY MENEDEZ-P
38 PAT GOMEZ-P
40 BUD BLACK (INJ)-P
41 BRYAN HICKERSON-P
42 MIKE JACKSON (INJ)-P
43 KENT BOTTENFIELD-P (2)
44 *(RET#) WILLIE MCCOVEY*
45 MARK CARREON (INJ)-OF
46 STEVE FREY-P
47 ROD BECK (INJ)-P
48 DICK POLE-CH
49 BRAD BRINK-P
50 BILL VAN LANDINGHAM (INJ)-P
51 WILLIE MCGEE (INJ)-OF
52 JEFF REED-C
55 RICH MONTELEONE (INJ)-P
58 DENNY SOMMERS-CH

1995

4TH W 67-77 11GB
144 GAME SEASON
(RET#) CHRISTY MATHEWSON
(RET#) JOHN MCGRAW
1 GLENALLEN HILL-OF
2 DARREN LEWIS-OF
2 MARK LEONARD-OF
3 *(RET#) BILL TERRY*
4 *(RET#) MEL OTT*
5 BOB LILLIS-CH
6 ROBBY THOMPSON (INJ)-2B
7 JOHN PATTERSON-2B
8 KIRT MANWARING-C
9 MATT WILLIAMS (INJ)-3B
10 ROYCE CLAYTON-SS
11 *(RET#) CARL HUBBELL*
12 DUSTY BAKER-MGR
13 J. R. PHILLIPS-1B
14 TODD BENZINGER (INJ)-UTIL
14 SHAWN BARTON-P
15 BOB BRENLY-CH
16 BOBBY BONDS-CH
18 MIKE BENJAMIN-2B
19 MARK PORTUGAL-P (1)
20 WENDELL KIM-CH
21 DEION SANDERS-OF (2)
22 DAVID MCCARTY-OF (2)
23 STEVE SCARSONE-2B
24 *(RET#) WILLIE MAYS*
25 BARRY BONDS-OF
26 STEVE MINTZ-P
27 *(RET#) JUAN MARICHAL*
29 PAT GOMEZ-P
30 JAMIE BREWINGTON-P
31 MARK LEITER-P
32 TREVOR WILSON (INJ)-P
33 JOSE BAUTISTA-P
34 DAVE BURBA-P (1)
34 SCOTT SERVICE-P
35 SALOMON TORRES-P (1)
35 CARLOS VALDEZ-P
36 KENNY GREER-P
36 SHAWN ESTES-P
37 CHRIS HOOK-P
38 PAT GOMEZ-P
38 JOSE BAUTISTA-P
39 RIKKERT FANEYTE-OF
40 MARK DEWEY-P
41 STEVE FREY-P (1)
41 JOEL CHIMELIS-INF
41 SERGIO VALDEZ-P
42 JOHN ROPER-P (2)
44 *(RET#) WILLIE MCCOVEY*
45 MARK CARREON-1B/OF
45 TERRY MULHOLLAND (INJ)-P
46 TERRY MULHOLLAND-P
46 MARK CARREON-1B/OF
47 ROD BECK-P
48 DICK POLE-CH
49 TOM LAMPLIN-C
50 BILL VAN LANDINGHAM-P
51 ENRIQUE BURGOS-P
52 JEFF REED-C
53 JOE ROSSELLI-P
56 MARVIN BERNARD-OF
57 RICH AURILIA-SS
61 CHRIS HOOK-P
72 LUIS AQUINO-P (2)

1996

4TH W 68-94 23GB
(RET#) CHRISTY MATHEWSON
(RET#) JOHN MCGRAW
1 GLENALLEN HILL (INJ)-OF
2 MEL HALL (WAIV)-OF
2 RICK WILKINS-C (2)
3 *(RET#) BILL TERRY*
4 *(RET#) MEL OTT*
5 BOB LILLIS-CH
6 ROBBY THOMPSON (INJ)-2B
7 MARVIN BENARD-OF
8 KIRT MANWARING (INJ)-C (1)
8 DESI WILSON-1B
9 MATT WILLIAMS (INJ)-3B
10 DAVID MCCARTY (INJ)-OF
11 *(RET#) CARL HUBBELL*
12 DUSTY BAKER-MGR
14 JEFF JUDEN-P (1)
14 TRENIDAD HUBBARD-OF (2)
15 JIM DAVENPORT-CH
16 BOBBY BONDS-CH
17 J. R. PHILLIPS-1B (1)
18 KIM BASTISTE (INJ) (REL)-SS
19 JIM POOLE-P (2)
20 WENDELL KIM-CH
21 SHAWON DUNSTON (INJ)-SS
22 OSVALDO FERNANDEZ-P
23 STEVE SCARSONE (WAIV)-2B
24 *(RET#) WILLIE MAYS*
25 BARRY BONDS-OF
26 MARK GARDNER (ILL)-P
27 *(RET#) JUAN MARICHAL*
28 STAN JAVIER (INJ)-OF
29 STEVE DECKER-C (1)
29 DAN CARLSON-P
30 MARCUS JENSEN-C
30 DAN PELTIER-OF
31 MARK LEITER-P (1)
32 BILL MUELLER-3B
33 STEVE BOURGEOIS-P
34 ALLEN WATSON (INJ)-P
35 RICH AURILIA (INJ)-SS
36 SHAWN ESTES-P
36 JAY CANIZARO-2B
37 CHRIS HOOK (REL)-P
38 JOSE BAUTISTA (WAIV)-P
40 MARK DEWEY-P
41 RICH DELUCIA (INJ)-P
42 SHAWN BARTON (REL)-P
42 KEITH WILLIAMS-OF
42 KIRK RUETER-P (2)
44 *(RET#) WILLIE MCCOVEY*
45 MARK CARREON-OF (1)
47 ROD BECK-P
48 DICK POLE-CH
49 TOM LAMPLIN (INJ)-C
50 BILL VAN LANDINGHAM-P
51 DOUG CREEK-P
52 DAX JONES-OF
54 TIM SCOTT-P (2)
55 SHAWN ESTES-P
60 WILSON DELGADO-SS
62 JACOB CRUZ-OF
65 STEVE SODERSTROM-P
66 DOUG MIRABELLI-C

1997

2ST W 90-72 0GB
L NLDS-FLAN 3-0
(RET#) CHRISTY MATHEWSON
(RET#) JOHN MCGRAW
2 RICK WILKINS (REL)-C (1)
2 DOUG MIRABELLI-C
3 *(RET#) BILL TERRY*
4 *(RET#) MEL OTT*
5 DARRYL HAMILTON (INJ)-OF
6 J. T. SNOW-1B
7 MARVIN BENARD-OF
8 DAMON BERRYHILL-C
10 JOSE VIZCAINO-SS
11 *(RET#) CARL HUBBELL*
12 DUSTY BAKER-MGR
14 MARK LEWIS (INJ)-3B/2B
15 SONNY JACKSON-CH
16 RON PERRANOSKI-CH
17 CARLOS ALFONSO-CH
18 BRIAN JOHNSON-C (2)
19 JIM POOLE-P
20 GENE (ROAD RUNNER) CLINES-CH
21 JEFF KENT-2B/1B
22 OSVALDO FERNANDEZ (INJ)-P
23 DANTE POWELL-OF
24 *(RET#) WILLIE MAYS*
25 BARRY BONDS-OF
26 MARK GARDNER-P
27 *(RET#) JUAN MARICHAL*
28 STAN JAVIER-OF
29 DAN CARLSON (INJ)-P
30 MARCUS JENSEN-C (1)
30 JACOB CRUZ-OF
32 BILL MUELLER (INJ)-3B
33 RICH RODRIGUEZ-P
34 GLENALLEN HILL-OF
35 RICH AURILIA-SS
36 WILSON DELGADO-SS
37 JOE ROA-P
37 JOHN JOHNSTONE (WAIV)-P (1)
38 WILSON DELGADO-SS
38 JACOB CRUZ-OF
38 KEITH FOULKE-P (1)
39 ROBERTO HERNANDEZ-P (2)
40 DANNY DARWIN-P (2)
40 WILSON ALVAREZ-P (2)
41 RICH DELUCIA-P (1)
41 JOHN JOHNSTONE-P (1)
41 CORY BAILEY-P (2)
42 KIRK RUETER-P
42 *(RET#) JACKIE ROBINSON*
43 RENE AROCHA-P
43 DANNY DARWIN-P (2)
44 *(RET#) WILLIE MCCOVEY*
45 KIRK RUETER-P
45 TERRY MULHOLLAND-P (2)
46 KIRK RUETER-P
47 ROD BECK-P
48 DICK POLE-CH
49 RENE AROCHA-P
49 PAT RAPP (INJ)-P (2)
50 BILL VAN LANDINGHAM-P
51 DOUG CREEK-P
52 JULIAN TAVAREZ-P
55 SHAWN ESTES (INJ)-P
57 DOUG HENRY-P

1998

2ND W 89-74 9.5GB
(RET#) CHRISTY MATHEWSON
(RET#) JOHN MCGRAW
1 ALEX DIAZ (WAIV)-OF
1 DOUG MIRABELLI-C
1 ARMANDO RIOS-OF
2 CHRIS (C.) JONES-OF (2)
3 *(RET#) BILL TERRY*
4 *(RET#) MEL OTT*
5 DARRYL HAMILTON-OF (1)
6 J. T. SNOW-1B
7 MARVIN BENARD-OF
8 WILSON DELGADO-SS
8 SHAWON DUNSTON-INF (2)
9 BRENT MAYNE-C
10 JOSE VIZCAINO-SS (1)
10 RON WOTUS-CH
11 *(RET#) CARL HUBBELL*
12 DUSTY BAKER-MGR
13 CHARLIE HAYES-3B
14 REY SANCHEZ-SS
15 SONNY JACKSON-CH
16 RON PERRANOSKI-CH
17 CARLOS ALFONSO-CH
18 BRIAN JOHNSON (INJ)-C
19 JIM POOLE-P (1)
19 DOUG MIRABELLI-C
20 GENE (ROAD RUNNER) CLINES-CH
21 JEFF KENT (INJ)-2B
(22) OSVALDO FERNANDEZ (INJ)-(P)
23 ELLIS BURKS-OF (2)
24 *(RET#) WILLIE MAYS*
25 BARRY BONDS-OF
26 MARK GARDNER-P
27 *(RET#) JUAN MARICHAL*
28 STAN JAVIER-OF
29 DOUG MIRABELLI-C
29 JOE CARTER-OF (2)
30 JACOB CRUZ-OF (1)
30 DANTE POWELL-OF
31 ROBB NEN-P
32 BILL MUELLER-3B
33 RICH RODRIGUEZ-P
34 RAMON (E.) MARTINEZ-2B
35 RICH AURILIA (INJ)-SS
35 JEFF BALL-1B
39 STEVE REED-P (1)
39 STEVE SODERSTROM-P
40 WILSON ALVAREZ-P
41 CORY BAILEY-P
42 *(RET#) JACKIE ROBINSON*
43 DANNY DARWIN-P
44 *(RET#) WILLIE MCCOVEY*
45 DEAN HARTGRAVES-P
46 KIRK RUETER-P
47 JOSE MESA-P (2)
48 RUSSELL ORTIZ-P
49 JOHN JOHNSTONE-P
50 JULIAN TAVAREZ (INJ)-P
51 CHRIS BROCK-P
52 ALVIN MORMAN (INJ)-P (2)
53 OREL (BULLDOG) HERSHISER-P
55 SHAWN ESTES (INJ)-P
59 JUAN LOPEZ-CH
62 WILSON DELGADO-INF

1999

2ND W 86-76 14GB
(RET#) CHRISTY MATHEWSON

(RET#) JOHN MCGRAW
1 ARMANDO RIOS (INJ)-OF
2 EDWARDS GUZMAN-3B
3 *(RET#) BILL TERRY*
4 *(RET#) MEL OTT*
6 J. T. SNOW-1B
7 MARVIN BENARD-OF
8 CALVIN MURRAY-OF
9 BRENT MAYNE-C
10 RON WOTUS-CH
11 *(RET#) CARL HUBBELL*
12 DUSTY BAKER-MGR
13 CHARLIE HAYES-3B
14 F. P. SANTANGELO-OF
15 SONNY JACKSON-CH
16 RON PERRANOSKI-CH
17 CARLOS ALFONSO-CH
18 JAY CANIZARO-2B
19 DOUG MIRABELLI-C
20 GENE (ROAD RUNNER) CLINES-CH
21 JEFF KENT-2B
23 ELLIS BURKS-OF
24 *(RET#) WILLIE MAYS*
25 BARRY BONDS-OF
26 MARK GARDNER-P
27 *(RET#) JUAN MARICHAL*
28 STAN JAVIER-OF (1)
29 SCOTT SERVAIS (INJ)-C
30 *(RET#) ORLANDO CEPEDA*
31 ROBB NEN-P
32 BILL MUELLER-3B
33 RICH RODRIGUEZ-P
34 RAMON (E.) MARTINEZ-2B
35 RICH AURILIA (INJ)-SS
36 JOE NATHAN-P
37 MIGUEL DEL TORO-P
39 BRONSWELL PATRICK-P
42 *(RET#) JACKIE ROBINSON*
43 JERRY SPRADLIN-P (2)
44 *(RET#) WILLIE MCCOVEY*
45 CHRIS BROCK (INJ)-P
46 KIRK RUETER-P
47 FELIX RODRIGUEZ-P
48 RUSSELL ORTIZ-P
49 JOHN JOHNSTONE-P
50 JULIAN TAVAREZ (INJ)-P
55 SHAWN ESTES (INJ)-P
56 ALAN EMBREE-P
59 JUAN LOPEZ-CH
61 LIVAN HERNANDEZ-P (2)
62 WILSON DELGADO-INF

2000

1ST W 97-65 0GB
L NLDS-NYN 3-1

(RET#) CHRISTY MATHEWSON
(RET#) JOHN MCGRAW
1 ARMANDO RIOS-OF
3 *(RET#) BILL TERRY*
4 *(RET#) MEL OTT*
5 ROBBY THOMPSON-CH
6 J. T. SNOW-1B
7 MARVIN BENARD-OF
8 CALVIN MURRAY-OF
9 SCOTT SERVAIS-C (2)
10 RON WOTUS-CH
11 *(RET#) CARL HUBBELL*
12 DUSTY BAKER-MGR
14 TERRELL LOWERY-OF
15 DOUG MIRABELLI-C
15 GUISEPPE CHIARAMONTE-C
16 SONNY JACKSON-CH
18 RUSS DAVIS-INF
19 DAVE RIGHETTI-CH
20 GENE (ROAD RUNNER) CLINES-CH
21 JEFF KENT-2B
22 DAMON MINOR-INF
23 ELLIS BURKS-OF
24 *(RET#) WILLIE MAYS*
25 BARRY BONDS-OF
26 MARK GARDNER-P
27 *(RET#) JUAN MARICHAL*
28 JUAN MELO-INF
29 BOBBY ESTALELLA-C
30 *(RET#) ORLANDO CEPEDA*
31 ROBB NEN-P
32 BILL MUELLER-3B
34 RAMON (E.) MARTINEZ-2B
35 RICH AURILIA (INJ)-SS
36 JOE NATHAN (INJ)-P
37 MIGUEL DEL TORO-P
38 AARON FULTZ-P
39 PEDRO FELIZ-INF
41 SCOTT LINEBRINK-P (1)
41 CHAD ZERBE-P
42 *(RET#) JACKIE ROBINSON*
44 *(RET#) WILLIE MCCOVEY*
46 KIRK RUETER-P
47 FELIX RODRIGUEZ-P
48 RUSS ORTIZ-P
49 JOHN JOHNSTONE (INJ)-P
51 RYAN VOGELSONG-P
52 FELIPE CRESPO-OF
55 SHAWN ESTES-P
56 ALAN EMBREE-P
57 BEN WEBER-P (1)
57 DOUG HENRY-P (2)
59 JUAN LOPEZ-CH
61 LIVAN HERNANDEZ-P

2001

2ND W 90-72 2GB

(RET#) CHRISTY MATHEWSON
(RET#) JOHN MCGRAW
1 ARMANDO RIOS-OF (1)
1 CODY RANSOM-SS
2* WAYNE GOMES (INJ)-P* (2)
3 *(RET#) BILL TERRY*
4 *(RET#) MEL OTT*
5 ROBBY THOMPSON-CH
6 J. T. SNOW (INJ)-1B
7 MARVIN BENARD-OF
8 CALVIN MURRAY-OF
9 EDWARDS GUZMAN-3B
9 YORVIT TORREALBA-C
10 RON WOTUS-CH
11 *(RET#) CARL HUBBELL*
12 DUSTY BAKER-MGR
13 EDWARDS GUZMAN-3B
14 RYAN VOGELSONG-P (1)
14 ANDRES GALARRAGA-1B (2)
15 SONNY JACKSON-CH
15 RYAN JENSEN-P
16 SONNY JACKSON-CH
17 CARLOS ALFONSO-CH
18 RUSS DAVIS (REL)-INF
18 JAY LEACH-OF
19 DAVE RIGHETTI-CH
20 GENE (ROAD RUNNER) CLINES-CH
21 JEFF KENT-2B
22 ERIC DAVIS (INJ)-OF
23 SHAWON DUNSTON (INJ)-OF
24 *(RET#) WILLIE MAYS*
25 BARRY BONDS-OF
26 MARK GARDNER-P
27 *(RET#) JUAN MARICHAL*
28 JOHN VANDER WAL-OF (2)
29 BOBBY ESTALELLA-C
29 JASON SCHMIDT-P (2)
30 *(RET#) ORLANDO CEPEDA*
31 ROBB NEN-P
32 RYAN VOGELSONG-P (1)
32 KURT AINSWORTH-P
33 BENITO SANTIAGO-C
34 RAMON (E.) MARTINEZ-2B
35 RICH AURILIA-SS
37 DAMON MINOR (INJ)-INF
38 AARON FULTZ-P
39 PEDRO FELIZ-INF
40 JASON CHRISTIANSEN-P (2)
41 CHAD ZERBE-P
42 *(RET#) JACKIE ROBINSON*
43 RYAN JENSEN-P
43 BRIAN BOEHRINGER-P
44 *(RET#) WILLIE MCCOVEY*
45 TIM WORRELL (INJ)-P
46 KIRK RUETER-P
47 FELIX RODRIGUEZ-P
48 RUSS ORTIZ-P
(49) JOHN JOHNSTONE (INJ)-(P)
52 FELIPE CRESPO (INJ)-OF (1)
55 SHAWN ESTES (INJ)-P
56 ALAN EMBREE (INJ)-P (1)
56 DANTE POWELL-OF
59 JUAN LOPEZ-CH
61 LIVAN HERNANDEZ-P

2002

2ND W (W/C) 95-66 2.5GB
W NLDS-ATLN 3-2
W NLCS-STLN 4-1
L WS-ANAA 4-3

(RET#) CHRISTY MATHEWSON
(RET#) JOHN MCGRAW
1 KENNY LOFTON-OF (2)
2 CODY RANSOM-SS
3 *(RET#) BILL TERRY*
4 *(RET#) MEL OTT*
5 TSUYOSHI SHINJO-OF
6 J. T. SNOW-1B
7 MARVIN BENARD (INJ)-OF
8 CALVIN MURRAY-OF (1)
8 TOM GOODWIN-OF
9 YORVIT TORREALBA-C
10 RON WOTUS-CH
11 *(RET#) CARL HUBBELL*
12 DUSTY BAKER-MGR
14 TONY TORCATO-OF
15 RYAN JENSEN-P
15 SONNY JACKSON-CH
16 SONNY JACKSON-CH
16 REGGIE SANDERS-OF
17 CARLOS ALFONSO-CH
18 JOE LEFEBVRE-CH
19 DAVE RIGHETTI-CH
20 GENE (ROAD RUNNER) CLINES-CH
21 JEFF KENT-2B
22 JASON SCHMIDT-P
22 MANNY AYBAR-P
22 KURT AINSWORTH-P
23 SHAWON DUNSTON (INJ)-OF/INF
24 *(RET#) WILLIE MAYS*
25 BARRY BONDS-OF
26 JAY WITASICK-P
27 *(RET#) JUAN MARICHAL*
28 DAVID BELL-3B/INF
29 JASON SCHMIDT-P
30 *(RET#) ORLANDO CEPEDA*
31 ROBB NEN-P
32 KURT AINSWORTH-P
32 BILL MUELLER-3B (2)
33 BENITO SANTIAGO-C
34 RAMON (E.) MARTINEZ-UTIL
35 RICH AURILIA-SS
36 JOE NATHAN-P
37 DAMON MINOR-1B
38 AARON FULTZ-P
39 PEDRO FELIZ-UTIL
40 JASON CHRISTIANSEN (INJ)-P (2)
41 CHAD ZERBE-P
42 *(RET #)JACKIE ROBINSON*
43 RYAN JENSEN-P
44 *(RET#) WILLIE MCCOVEY*
45 TIM WORRELL-P
46 KIRK RUETER-P
47 FELIX RODRIGUEZ-P
48 RUSS ORTIZ-P
49 SCOTT EYRE-P (2)
50 MANNY AYBAR-P
51 TROY BROHAWN-P
52 TREY LUNSFORD-C
59 JUAN LOPEZ-CH
61 LIVAN HERNANDEZ-P

2003

1ST W 100-61 0GB
L NLDS-FLAN 3-1

(RET#) CHRISTY MATHEWSON
(RET#) JOHN MCGRAW
1 NEIFI PEREZ-INF
2 CODY RANSOM-SS
3 *(RET#) BILL TERRY*
4 *(RET#) MEL OTT*
5 RAY DURHAM (INJ)-2B
6 J. T. SNOW (INJ)-1B
7 MARVIN BENARD (INJ)-OF
8 YORVIT TORREALBA (BRV)-C
9 MARQUIS GRISSOM-OF
10 RON WOTUS-CH
11 *(RET#) CARL HUBBELL*
13 EDGARDO ALFONZO-3B/2B
14 ANDRES GALARRAGA-1B
15 GENE GLYNN-CH
16 MANNY AYBAR-P
16 JEFFREY HAMMONDS-OF (2)
17 CARLOS ALFONSO-CH
18 JOE LEFEBVRE-CH
19 DAVE RIGHETTI-CH
20 TONY TORCATO-OF
21 RUBEN RIVERA (WAIV)-OF
21 CARLOS VALDERRAMA-OF
21 ERIC YOUNG-2B (2)
22 JOSE CRUZ, JR.-OF
23 FELIPE ALOU-MGR
24 *(RET#) WILLIE MAYS*
25 BARRY BONDS (BRV)-OF
26 MARK GARDNER-CH
27 *(RET#) JUAN MARICHAL*
28 DAMIAN MOSS-P (1)
28 LANCE NIEKRO-1B
29 JASON SCHMIDT (BRV)-P
30 *(RET#) ORLANDO CEPEDA*
(31) ROBB NEN (INJ)-(P)
32 KURT AINSWORTH (INJ)-P (1)
32 DUSTIN HERMANSON (INJ)-P (2)
33 BENITO SANTIAGO (INJ)-C
34 JESSE FOPPERT (INJ)-P
35 RICH AURILIA (INJ)-SS
36 JOE NATHAN-P
37 ALBERTO CASTILLO (INJ)-C
38 JIM BROWER-P
39 PEDRO FELIZ-UTIL
40 JASON CHRISTIANSEN (INJ)-P
41 CHAD ZERBE (INJ)-P
42 *(RET #)JACKIE ROBINSON*
43 RYAN JENSEN (INJ)-P
43 SIDNEY PONSON-P (2)
44 *(RET#) WILLIE MCCOVEY*
45 TIM WORRELL-P
46 KIRK RUETER (INJ)-P
47 FELIX RODRIGUEZ (INJ)-P
48 MATT HERGES-P (2)
49 SCOTT EYRE-P
50 KEVIN CORREIA-P
50 ALBERTO CASTILLO (INJ)-C
50 TODD LINDEN-OF
51 JEFFREY HAMMONDS-OF (2)
51 BRIAN POWELL-P
51 TONY TORCATO-OF
52 TREY LUNSFORD-C
53 KEVIN CORREIA-P
55 LUIS PUJOLS-CH
56 JASON ELLISON-OF
59 JEROME WILLIAMS-P
60 FRANCISCO SANTOS-OF/1
60 NOAH LOWRY-P

2004

2ND W 91-71 2GB

(RET#) CHRISTY MATHEWSO
(RET#) JOHN MCGRAW
1 DAMON MINOR-1B
2 CODY RANSOM-SS
3 *(RET#) BILL TERRY*
4 *(RET#) MEL OTT*
5 RAY DURHAM (INJ)-2B
6 J. T. SNOW-1B
7 PEDRO FELIZ-3B
8 YORVIT TORREALBA-C
9 MARQUIS GRISSOM-OF
10 NEIFI PEREZ-SS (1)
10 RON WOTUS-CH
11 *(RET#) CARL HUBBELL*
13 EDGARDO ALFONZO-3B
14 BRIAN DALLIMORE-SS
15 GENE GLYNN-CH
17 CARLOS ALFONSO-CH
18 JOE LEFEBVRE-CH
19 DAVE RIGHETTI-CH
20 MICHAEL TUCKER-OF
21 TONY TORCATO-OF
22 DUSTIN MOHR-OF
23 FELIPE ALOU-MGR
24 *(RET#) WILLIE MAYS*
25 BARRY BONDS-OF
26 MARK GARDNER-CH
27 *(RET#) JUAN MARICHAL*
28 WAYNE FRANKLIN (INJ)-P
29 JASON SCHMIDT (INJ)-P
30 *(RET#) ORLANDO CEPEDA*
(31) ROBB NEN (INJ)-(P)
32 DUSTIN HERMANSON-P
33 DAVID AARDSMA-P
33 RICKY LEDEE-OF (2)
34 JESSE FOPPERT (INJ)-P
35 DEIVI CRUZ-SS
36 A. J. PIERZYNSKI-C
37 MERKIN VALDEZ-P
37 BRIAN COOPER-P
38 JIM BROWER-P
40 JASON CHRISTIANSEN-P
41 BRAD HENNESSEY-P
42 *(RET #)JACKIE ROBINSON*
43 DAVE BURBA-P (2)
44 *(RET#) WILLIE MCCOVEY*
45 TYLER WALKER-P
46 KIRK RUETER-P
47 FELIX RODRIGUEZ-P (1)
48 MATT HERGES-P
49 SCOTT EYRE (INJ)-P
50 BRET TOMKO (INJ)-P
51 NOAH LOWRY-P
52 JUSTIN KNOEDLER-C
53 LEO ESTRELLA-P
54 KEVIN WALKER-P
55 LUIS PUJOLS-CH
56 JASON ELLISON-OF
57 JEROME WILLIAMS (INJ)-P

2005

3RD W 75-87 7GB

(RET#) CHRISTY MATHEWSO
(RET#) JOHN MCGRAW
1 ADAM SHABALA-OF
1 ANGEL CHAVEZ-2B/SS
2 BRIAN DALLIMORE-2B
2 RANDY WINN-OF (2)
3 *(RET#) BILL TERRY*
4 *(RET#) MEL OTT*
5 RAY DURHAM-2B

NEW YORK/**SAN FRANCISCO GIANTS**

6 J. T. SNOW-1B
7 PEDRO FELIZ-1B/OF
8 YORVIT TORREALBA-C (1)
8 YAMID HAAD-C
9 MARQUIS GRISSOM (INJ) (REL)-OF
0 RON WOTUS-CH
1 *(RET#) CARL HUBBELL*
2 EDGARDO ALFONZO (INJ)-3B
3 OMAR VIZQUEL-SS
4 JEFF FASSERO-P
5 GENE GLYNN-CH
6 JOE LEFEBVRE-CH
7 CARLOS ALFONSO-CH
8 MOISES ALOU (INJ)-OF
9 DAVE RIGHETTI-CH
0 MICHAEL TUCKER-OF (1)
1 TONY TORCATO-OF
1 ALEX SANCHEZ (INJ)-OF
1 JASON ELLISON-OF
2 MIKE MATHENY (BRV)-C
3 FELIPE ALOU-MGR
4 *(RET#) WILLIE MAYS*
5 BARRY BONDS (INJ)-OF
6 MARK GARDNER-CH
7 *(RET#) JUAN MARICHAL*
8 LANCE NIEKRO-1B
9 JASON SCHMIDT (INJ)-P
0 *(RET#) ORLANDO CEPEDA*
2 BRIAN DALLIMORE-2B
2 LATROY HAWKINS (INJ)-P (2)
3 AL LEVINE-P
3 JUSTIN KNOEDLER-C
4 JESSE FOPPERT (INJ)-P (1)
4 DANIEL ORTMEIER-OF
5 DEIVI CRUZ-SS (1)
5 BRET TOMKO-P
7 JACK TASCHNER-P
8 JIM BROWER (REL)-P (1)
8 BRANDON PUFFER-P
8 MATT KINNEY-P
9 TODD LINDEN-OF
0 JASON CHRISTIANSEN-P (1)
0 DOUG CLARK-OF
1 BRAD HENNESSEY-P
2 *(RET #)JACKIE ROBINSON*
3 MATT CAIN-P
4 *(RET#) WILLIE MCCOVEY*
5 TYLER WALKER (INJ)-P
6 KIRK RUETER (INJ)-P
7 SCOTT EYRE-P
8 MATT HERGES-P (1)
9 ARMANDO BENITEZ (INJ)-P
0 BRET TOMKO-P
1 NOAH LOWRY-P
2 BRIAN COOPER-P
3 KEVIN CORREIA-P
4 SCOTT MUNTER-P
5 LUIS PUJOLS-CH
6 JASON ELLISON-OF
7 JEROME WILLIAMS-P (1)
7 JULIO RAMIREZ-OF
9 JEREMY ACCARDO-P

Will "The Thrill" Clark had his best years with the Giants. He led the NL in RBIs and walks in 1988, scored the most runs a year later when the Giants faced the A's in the "Earthquake" Series. His versatility stood out when he led the league in slugging percentage and won a Gold Glove at first base in 1991. The six-time All-Star played in the post season twice with San Francisco, twice with Texas and one last time with the Cardinals in 2000. He liked the double deuces, #22.

1969

MONTREAL EXPOS

6TH E 52-110 48GB

1 GARY SUTHERLAND-2B/UTIL
2 JOHN BATEMAN (INJ)-C
3 BOB BAILEY (INJ)-1B/UTIL
4 GENE (SKIP) MAUCH-MGR
5 TY CLINE-OF/1B
6 RON FAIRLY (INJ)-1B/OF (2)
7 BOBBY WINE-SS/INF
8 KEVIN COLLINS-2B/3B (2)
9 MACK (MACK THE KNIFE) JONES-OF
10 RUSTY (LE GRAND ORANGE) STAUB-OF
11 RON BRAND-C/OF
12 JOHN BOCCABELLA-C
14 ELROY FACE-P
14 MARV STAEHLE-2B
15 MANNY MOTA-OF (1)
16 CLAUDE (FRENCHY) RAYMOND-P (2)
17 DONN CLENDENON-1B/OF (1)
17 KEVIN COLLINS-2B/3B (2)
17 DICK (THE MONSTER) RADATZ-P (2)
18 STEVE RENKO-P
19 DON BOSCH (INJ)-OF
20 STEVE SHEA-P
20 ADOLFO PHILLIPS (ILL)-OF (2)
21 LARRY JASTER-P
22 MUDCAT GRANT-P
22 LEO MARENTETTE-P
22 STEVE RENKO-P
22 DICK (THE MONSTER) RADATZ-P (2)
23 DON SHAW-P
24 MIKE WEGENER-P
25 DAN MCGINN-P
26 BILL STONEMAN-P
27 JERRY ROBERTSON-P
28 CARROLL SEMBERA-P
29 HOWIE (DIZ) REED-P
30 MAURY WILLS-SS/2B (1)
31 JERRY ZIMMERMAN-CH
32 CAL (BUSTER) MCLISH-CH
33 HARRY (PEANUTS) LOWREY-CH
34 BOB OLDIS-CH
35 JIM FAIREY-OF
36 FLOYD WICKER-OF
37 ANGEL (REMY) HERMOSO-2B/SS
37 JOSE (LOCO) HERRERA-UTIL
38 JOSE (LOCO) HERRERA-UTIL
39 COCO LABOY-3B
41 GERRY JESTADT-SS
42 BOB REYNOLDS-P
43 DON HAHN-OF
44 CARL MORTON-P
46 STEVE SHEA-P
47 GARY WASLEWSKI-P (2)

1970

6TH E 73-89 16GB

1 GARY SUTHERLAND-2B/INF
2 JOHN BATEMAN-C
3 BOB BAILEY-UTIL
4 GENE (SKIP) MAUCH-MGR
5 TY CLINE (ILL)-PH (1)
5 CLYDE MASHORE-OF
6 RON FAIRLY (INJ)-1B/OF
7 BOBBY WINE-SS
8 JIM QUALLS-2B/OF
9 MACK (MACK THE KNIFE) JONES-OF
10 RUSTY (LE GRAND ORANGE) STAUB-OF
11 RON BRAND-UTIL
12 JOHN BOCCABELLA-UTIL
14 MARV STAEHLE-2B/SS
15 BALOR MOORE-P
16 CLAUDE (FRENCHY) RAYMOND-P
17 BILL DILLMAN-P
18 STEVE RENKO-P
20 ADOLFO PHILLIPS-OF
21 JOE SPARMA-P
22 JACK HIATT-C/1B (1)
22 RICH NYE-P (2)
23 FRED WHITFIELD-1B
23 JOHN O'DONOGHUE-P
24 MIKE WEGENER (INJ)-P
25 DAN MCGINN-P
26 BILL STONEMAN-P
28 CARROLL SEMBERA-P
28 BOOTS DAY-OF (2)
28 MIKE MARSHALL-P (2)
29 HOWIE (DIZ) REED-P
30 KEN JOHNSON-P
31 JERRY ZIMMERMAN-CH
32 CAL (BUSTER) MCLISH-CH
33 DICK WILLIAMS-CH
34 JIMMY BRAGAN-CH
35 JIM FAIREY-OF
36 JOHN STROHMEYER-P
37 ANGEL (REMY) HERMOSO-2B/3B
37 BOOTS DAY-OF (2)
38 JOSE (LOCO) HERRERA-PH
39 COCO LABOY-3B/2B
42 JIM GOSGER-OF/1B
43 DON HAHN-OF
44 CARL MORTON-P
47 GARY WASLEWSKI-P (1)

1971

5TH E 71-90 25.5GB

1 GARY SUTHERLAND-2B/UTL
2 JOHN BATEMAN-C
3 BOB BAILEY-3B/UTIL
4 GENE (SKIP) MAUCH-MGR
5 CLYDE MASHORE-OF/3B
6 RON FAIRLY-1B/OF
7 BOBBY WINE (INJ)-SS
8 BOOTS DAY-OF
9 MACK (MACK THE KNIFE) JONES-OF
10 RUSTY (LE GRAND ORANGE) STAUB-OF
11 RON BRAND-UTIL
12 JOHN BOCCABELLA-UTIL
14 RON SWOBODA (ROCKY)-OF (1)
14 LARRY DOBY-CH
16 CLAUDE (FRENCHY) RAYMOND-P
17 LARRY DOBY-CH
17 DAVE MCDONALD-1B/OF
18 STEVE RENKO-P
20 RICH HACKER-SS
21 ERNIE MCANALLY-P
22 TERRY HUMPHREY-C
23 JOHN O'DONOGHUE-P
24 MIKE TORREZ-P (2)
25 DAN MCGINN-P
26 BILL STONEMAN-P
27 JIM BRITTON (INJ)-P
28 MIKE MARSHALL-P
29 HOWIE (DIZ) REED-P
30 DON (POPEYE) ZIMMER-CH
31 JERRY ZIMMERMAN-CH
32 CAL (BUSTER) MCLISH-CH
33 RON HUNT-2B/3B
34 JIMMY BRAGAN-CH
35 JIM FAIREY-OF
36 JOHN STROHMEYER-P
37 STAN SWANSON-OF
39 COCO LABOY-3B/2B
42 JIM GOSGER-OF/1B
43 RON WOODS-OF (2)
44 CARL MORTON-P
49 ERNIE MCANALLY-P
50 STAN SWANSON-OF

1972

5TH E 70-86 26.5GB

2 JOHN BATEMAN-C (1)
2 MCCARVER, TIM-UTIL (2)
3 BOB BAILEY-3B/UTIL
4 GENE (SKIP) MAUCH-MGR
5 CLYDE MASHORE-OF
6 RON FAIRLY-OF/1B
7 BOBBY WINE-INF
8 BOOTS DAY-OF
11 PEPE MANGUAL-OF
12 JOHN BOCCABELLA-UTIL
14 LARRY DOBY-CH
15 BALOR MOORE-P
16 MIKE JORGENSEN-1B/OF
18 STEVE RENKO-P
19 TIM FOLI-SS/2B
20 TOM WALKER-P
21 ERNIE MCANALLY-P
22 TERRY HUMPHREY (INJ)-C
23 DENNY LEMASTER-P
23 HAL BREEDEN-1B/OF
24 MIKE TORREZ-P
25 HECTOR TORRES-UTIL/P
26 BILL STONEMAN-P
28 MIKE MARSHALL-P
29 KEN SINGLETON-OF
30 DON (POPEYE) ZIMMER-CH
31 JERRY ZIMMERMAN-CH
32 CAL (BUSTER) MCLISH-CH
33 RON HUNT-2B/3B
34 JIMMY BRAGAN-CH
35 JIM FAIREY-OF
36 JOHN STROHMEYER-P
39 COCO LABOY (INJ)-INF
42 JOE GILBERT-P
43 RON WOODS-OF
44 CARL MORTON-P

1973

4TH E 79-83 3.5GB

1 DAVE BRISTOL-CH
2 JIM LYTTLE-OF
3 BOB BAILEY-3B/OF
4 GENE (SKIP) MAUCH-MGR
5 CLYDE MASHORE (ILL)-OF/2B
6 RON FAIRLY-OF/1B
7 BOB STINSON-C/3B
8 DAY BOOTS-OF
9 BERNIE ALLEN-2B/3B (2)
11 PEPE MANGUAL-OF
12 JOHN BOCCABELLA-C/1B
14 LARRY DOBY-CH
15 BALOR MOORE-P
16 MIKE JORGENSEN-1B/OF
17 JORGE ROQUE-OF
17 CURT BROWN-OF
18 STEVE RENKO-P
19 TIM FOLI (INJ)-SS/UTIL
20 TOM WALKER-P
21 ERNIE MCANALLY-P
22 TERRY HUMPHREY-C
23 HAL BREEDEN-1B
24 MIKE TORREZ-P
25 MICKEY SCOTT-P (2)
26 BILL STONEMAN (INJ-P
28 MIKE MARSHALL-P
29 KEN SINGLETON-OF
30 DON (POPEYE) ZIMMER-CH
31 JERRY ZIMMERMAN-CH
32 CAL (BUSTER) MCLISH-CH
33 RON HUNT (INJ)-2B/3B
34 PAT JARVIS (INJ)-P
35 CRAIG CASKEY-P
36 JOHN STROHMEYER-P (1)
36 CHUCK TAYLOR-P
38 PEPE FRIAS-UTIL
39 COCO LABOY-3B/2B
42 JOE GILBERT-P
43 RON WOODS-OF
45 STEVE ROGERS-P
48 FELIPE ALOU-OF/1B (2)
50 MICKEY SCOTT-P (2)
51 LARRY LINTZ-2B/SS
52 TONY SCOTT-OF
53 JOHN MONTAGUE-P
54 BARRY FOOTE-PH
56 JIM COX-2B
58 JOSE MORALES-PH (2)

1974

4TH E 79-83 8.5GB

1 WILLIE DAVIS-OF
2 JIM LYTTLE-OF
2 JIM NORTHRUP-OF (2)
3 BOB BAILEY-OF/3B
4 GENE (SKIP) MAUCH-MGR
5 DAVE BRISTOL-CH
6 RON FAIRLY-1B/OF
7 BOB STINSON (INJ)-C
8 DAY BOOTS-OF
9 BARRY FOOTE-C
10 JIM COX (INJ)-2B
11 PEPE MANGUAL-OF
12 LARRY LINTZ-INF
15 BALOR MOORE-P
16 MIKE JORGENSEN-1B/OF
17 LARRY BIITTNER-OF
18 STEVE RENKO-P
19 TIM FOLI-SS/3B
20 TOM WALKER-P
21 ERNIE MCANALLY-P
22 TERRY HUMPHREY-C
23 HAL BREEDEN-1B
24 MIKE TORREZ-P
25 DON DEMOLA-P
27 DALE MURRAY-P
28 DENNIS BLAIR-P
29 KEN SINGLETON-OF
31 JERRY ZIMMERMAN-CH
32 CAL (BUSTER) MCLISH-CH
33 RON HUNT-3B/INF (1)
34 JOSE MORALES-C
36 CHUCK TAYLOR-P
37 JERRY WHITE-OF
38 PEPE FRIAS-UTIL
40 DON CARRITHERS-P
42 PAT SCANLON-3B
43 RON WOODS-OF
45 STEVE ROGERS-P
46 WALT HRINIAK-CH
48 BOB GEBHARD-P
49 WARREN CROMARTIE-OF
50 DON DEMOLA-P
50 LARRY PARRISH-3B
52 TONY SCOTT-OF
53 JOHN MONTAGUE-P
54 BARRY FOOTE-C
55 TERRY ENYART-P
57 GARY (THE KID) CARTER-C/OF
58 JOSE MORALES-C

1975

5TH E (TIE) 75-87 17.5GB

1 DAVE BRISTOL-CH
2 RICH COGGINS (ILL)-OF (1)
3 BOB BAILEY (INJ)-OF/3B
4 GENE (SKIP) MAUCH-MGR
5 PETE MACKANIN-2B/INF
8 GARY (THE KID) CARTER-C/OF
9 BARRY FOOTE-C
10 JIM COX-2B
11 PEPE MANGUAL-OF
12 LARRY LINTZ-2B/SS (1)
15 LARRY PARRISH-3B/INF
16 MIKE JORGENSEN-1B/OF
17 LARRY BIITTNER-OF
18 STEVE RENKO-P
19 TIM FOLI-SS/2B
20 DAVE MCNALLY (RET)-P
20 JIM LYTTLE-OF
21 FRED SCHERMAN-P (2)
23 HAL BREEDEN-1B
24 NATE COLBERT-1B (2)
25 DON DEMOLA-P
26 DAVE MCNALLY (RET)-P
26 DON STANHOUSE-P
27 DALE MURRAY (ILL)-P
28 DENNIS BLAIR-P
30 TONY SCOTT-OF
31 JERRY ZIMMERMAN-CH
32 CAL (BUSTER) MCLISH-CH
33 CHIP LANG-P
34 JOSE MORALES-UTIL
35 WOODIE FRYMAN-P
36 CHUCK TAYLOR-P
37 JERRY WHITE-OF
38 PEPE FRIAS (INJ)-INF
39 DAN WARTHEN-P
40 DON CARRITHERS (INJ)-P
42 PAT SCANLON-3B/1B
43 JIM DWYER-OF (2)
44 BOMBO RIVERA-OF
44 FRED SCHERMAN-P (2)
45 STEVE ROGERS-P
46 WALT HRINIAK, -CH
50 LARRY PARRISH-3B/INF
52 TONY SCOTT-OF
53 JOHN MONTAGUE-P (1)
53 LARRY JOHNSON-C
54 DON CARRITHERS (INJ)-P
54 ELLIS VALENTINE-OF
55 FRED SCHERMAN-P (2)

1976

6TH E 55-107 46GB

1 OZZIE VIRGIL-CH
3 CHARLIE (IRISH) FOX-MGR2
5 PETE MACKANIN-2B/UTIL
6 KARL KUEHL-MGR1
8 GARY (THE KID) CARTER-C/OF
9 BARRY FOOTE-C/INF
10 JIM COX-2B
11 PEPE MANGUAL-OF (1)
11 WAYNE (RED) GARRETT-2B/3B (2)
12 RODNEY SCOTT-2B/SS
12 GERRY HANNAHS-P
14 LARRY DOBY-CH
15 LARRY PARRISH-3B
16 MIKE JORGENSEN-1B/OF
17 LARRY BIITTNER-OF (1)
17 ANDRE (ANDY) THORNTON-1B/OF (2)
18 STEVE RENKO-P (1)
18 JOE KERRIGAN-P
19 TIM FOLI-SS/3B
20 JIM LYTTLE-OF (1)
21 FRED SCHERMAN-P
21 CHUCK TAYLOR-P
22 ELLIS VALENTINE-OF
23 ROGER FREED-1B/OF
24 NATE COLBERT-OF/1B (1)
24 ANDRE (HAWK) DAWSON-OF

MONTREAL EXPOS/**WASHINGTON NATIONALS**

25 DON DEMOLA (INJ)-P
25 DEL UNSER-OF (2)
26 DON STANHOUSE-P
27 DALE MURRAY-P
28 DENNIS BLAIR-P
29 GARY ROENICKE-OF
30 RODNEY SCOTT-2B/SS
31 CLAY KIRBY-P
32 EARL WILLIAMS-1B (2)
33 CHIP LANG-P
34 JOSE MORALES-1B/C
35 WOODIE FRYMAN-P
36 CHUCK TAYLOR-P
36 STEVE DUNNING-P (2)
37 JERRY WHITE-OF
38 PEPE FRIAS-UTIL
39 DAN WARTHEN-P
40 DON CARRITHERS-P
41 RON PICHE-CH
42 PAT SCANLON-3B/1B
43 JIM DWYER-OF (1)
44 BOMBO RIVERA-OF
45 STEVE ROGERS (INJ)-P
46 BILL ADAIR-CH
47 WAYNE GRANGER-P
47 LARRY DOBY JOHNSON-C
48 LARRY BEARNARTH-CH
49 WARREN CROMARTIE-OF
52 BILL ATKINSON-P
56 JOE KEENER-P
57 LARRY LANDRETH-P

1977

5TH E 75-87 26GB

1 OZZIE VIRGIL-CH
2 JIM BREWER-CH
3 MICKEY VERNON-CH
4 CHRIS SPEIER-SS (2)
5 PETE MACKANIN-UTIL
6 BILLY (SHOTGUN) GARDNER-CH
8 GARY (THE KID) CARTER-C/OF
9 BARRY FOOTE-C (1)
10 ANDRE (HAWK) DAWSON-OF
11 WAYNE (RED) GARRETT-3B/2B
12 STAN PAPI-INF
14 SAM MEJIAS-OF
15 LARRY PARRISH-3B
16 MIKE JORGENSEN-1B (1)
16 TOM WALKER-P (1)
16 FRED HOLDSWORTH-P
17 ELLIS VALENTINE (INJ)-OF
18 JOE KERRIGAN-P
19 TIM FOLI-SS (1)
20 WILL MCENANEY-P
21 LARRY LANDRETH-P
22 STAN BAHNSEN-P (2)
23 DICK WILLIAMS-MGR
24 TONY PEREZ-1B
25 DEL UNSER-OF/1B
26 DON STANHOUSE-P
28 HAL DUES-P
30 DAVE CASH-2B
31 JACKIE BROWN-P
32 SANTO ALCALA-P (2)
33 SANTO ALCALA-P (2)
33 WAYNE TWITCHELL-P (2)
34 JOSE MORALES-C/1B
35 GERRY HANNAHS-P
37 JERRY WHITE-OF
38 PEPE FRIAS-INF
39 DAN WARTHEN-P (1)
42 BILL ATKINSON-P
43 DAN SCHATZEDER-P
44 TIM BLACKWELL-C (2)
45 STEVE ROGERS-P
48 JEFF TERPKO-P
49 WARREN CROMARTIE-OF

1978

4TH E 76-86 14GB

1 OZZIE VIRGIL-CH
2 JIM BREWER-CH
3 MICKEY VERNON-CH
4 CHRIS SPEIER-SS
6 BILLY (SHOTGUN) GARDNER-CH
8 GARY (THE KID) CARTER-C/1B
9 BOB REECE-C
10 ANDRE (HAWK) DAWSON-OF
11 WAYNE (RED) GARRETT-3B (1)
12 STAN PAPI-INF
14 SAM MEJIAS-OF/P
15 LARRY PARRISH-3B
16 FRED HOLDSWORTH (INJ)-P
17 ELLIS VALENTINE-OF
18 GERRY PIRTLE-P
20 BOB JAMES-P
21 SCOTT SANDERSON-P
22 STAN BAHNSEN (INJ)-P
23 DICK WILLIAMS-MGR
24 TONY PEREZ-1B
25 DEL UNSER-1B/OF
28 HAL DUES-P
29 MIKE GARMAN-P (2)
30 DAVE CASH-2B
32 DAROLD KNOWLES-P
33 WAYNE TWITCHELL-P
34 ED HERRMANN-C
35 GERRY HANNAHS-P
35 WOODIE FRYMAN-P (2)
36 RUDY MAY (INJ)-P
36 DAN SCHATZEDER-P
37 JERRY WHITE-OF (1)
37 TOM HUTTON-1B/OF (2)
38 PEPE FRIAS-2B/SS
39 JERRY FRY-C
40 SCOTT SANDERSON-P
40 NORM SHERRY-CH
42 BILL ATKINSON-P
43 DAN SCHATZEDER-P
43 RUDY MAY (INJ)-P
44 BOBBY RAMOS-C
45 STEVE ROGERS (INJ)-P
46 DAVID PALMER-P
47 RANDY MILLER-P
48 ROSS GRIMSLEY II-P
49 WARREN CROMARTIE-OF

1979

2ND E 95-65 2GB

1 OZZIE VIRGIL-CH
2 JIM BREWER-CH
3 VERN RAPP-CH
3 RODNEY SCOTT-2B/SS
4 CHRIS SPEIER-SS
5 DUFFY DYER-C
6 RUSTY STAUB-1B/OF (2)
7 TONY BERNAZARD-2B
8 GARY (THE KID) CARTER-C/1B
9 VERN RAPP-CH
10 ANDRE (HAWK) DAWSON-OF
12 JIM MASON-SS/3B
14 TOM HUTTON-1B/OF
15 LARRY PARRISH-3B
16 FELIPE ALOU-CH
17 ELLIS VALENTINE-OF
18 JERRY WHITE-OF
19 RODNEY SCOTT-2B/SS
20 BOB JAMES-P
21 SCOTT SANDERSON-P
22 STAN BAHNSEN-P
23 DICK WILLIAMS-MGR
24 TONY PEREZ-1B
25 TONY SOLAITA-C (1)
27 ELIAS SOSA-P
29 DALE MURRAY-P (2)
30 DAVE CASH-2B
31 KEN MACHA-UTIL
32 JERRY WHITE-OF
32 TIM (ROCK) RAINES-PR
34 BILL GULLICKSON-P
35 WOODIE FRYMAN-P
36 DAN SCHATZEDER-P
37 BILL (SPACEMAN) LEE-P
40 NORM SHERRY-CH
42 BILL ATKINSON-P
43 RUDY MAY-P
45 STEVE ROGERS (INJ)-P
46 DAVID PALMER-P
47 JOHN TAMARGO-C (2)
48 ROSS GRIMSLEY II-P
49 WARREN CROMARTIE-OF
57 RANDY BASS-1B
58 PAT MULLIN-CH

1980

2ND E 90-72 1GB

1 OZZIE VIRGIL-CH
2 TONY BERNAZARD-2B/SS
3 RODNEY SCOTT-2B/SS
4 CHRIS SPEIER-SS/3B
5 WILLIE MONTANEZ-1B (2)
7 RON LEFLORE-OF
8 GARY (THE KID) CARTER-C
9 VERN RAPP-CH
10 ANDRE (HAWK) DAWSON-OF
12 JOHN (THE COUNT) D'ACQUISTO-P (2)
14 TOM HUTTON-UTIL/P
15 LARRY PARRISH (INJ)-3B
16 FELIPE ALOU-CH
17 ELLIS VALENTINE (INJ)-OF
18 JERRY WHITE-OF
19 BILL ALMON-SS/2B (1)
21 SCOTT SANDERSON-P
22 STAN BAHNSEN-P
23 DICK WILLIAMS-MGR
24 BOB PATE-OF
25 ROWLAND OFFICE-OF
26 JOHN TAMARGO-C
27 ELIAS SOSA-P
28 HAL DUES-P
29 DALE MURRAY-P
30 TIM (ROCK) RAINES-2B/OF
31 KEN MACHA-UTIL
32 FRED NORMAN-P
34 BILL GULLICKSON-P
35 WOODIE FRYMAN-P
36 GALEN CISCO-CH
37 BILL (SPACEMAN) LEE-P
39 PAT MULLIN-CH
40 NORM SHERRY-CH
43 JERRY MANUEL-SS
44 BOBBY RAMOS-C
45 STEVE ROGERS -P
46 DAVID PALMER (INJ)-P
47 CHARLIE LEA-P
47 STEVE RATZER-P
48 ROSS GRIMSLEY II-P (1)
49 WARREN CROMARTIE-1B/OF
53 CHARLIE LEA-P
54 BRAD MILLS-3B
58 TIM WALLACH-OF/1B

1981

1ST 1/2:3RD E 30-25 4GB
2ND 1/2:1ST E 30-23 0GB
FINAL: 1ST E 60-48 0GB
W NLDS PHIN 3-2
L NLCS LAN 3-2

1 OZZIE VIRGIL-CH
2 BRAD MILLS-3B/2B
3 RODNEY SCOTT-2B
4 CHRIS SPEIER-SS
5 WILLIE MONTANEZ-1B (1)
5 JOHN (THE HAMMER) MILNER-1B (2)
6 CHRIS SMITH-2B
6 JIM FANNING-MGR2
8 GARY (THE KID) CARTER-C/1B
9 VERN RAPP-CH
10 ANDRE (HAWK) DAWSON-OF
12 MIKE PHILLIPS-SS/2B (2)
14 TOM HUTTON-1B/OF
15 LARRY PARRISH-3B
16 FELIPE ALOU-CH
16 TERRY FRANCONA-OF/1B
17 ELLIS VALENTINE-OF (1)
18 JERRY WHITE-OF
19 MIKE GATES-2B
19 GRANT (BUCK) JACKSON-P (2)
21 SCOTT SANDERSON-P
22 STAN BAHNSEN-P
23 DICK WILLIAMS-MGR1
24 BOB PATE-OF
25 ROWLAND OFFICE (INJ)-OF
27 ELIAS SOSA-P
29 TIM WALLACH-OF/UTIL
30 TIM (ROCK) RAINES-OF/2B
31 JEFF REARDON-P (2)
32 TOM GORMAN-P
33 DAN BRIGGS-1B/OF
34 BILL GULLICKSON-P
35 WOODIE FRYMAN-P
36 GALEN CISCO-CH
37 BILL (SPACEMAN) LEE-P
39 PAT MULLIN-CH
40 NORM SHERRY-CH
41 STEVE BOROS-CH
42 TONY JOHNSON-OF
43 JERRY MANUEL (INJ)-2B/SS
44 BOBBY RAMOS-C
45 STEVE ROGERS-P
(46) DAVID PALMER (INJ)-(P)
47 STEVE RATZER-P
48 RAY BURRIS-P
49 WARREN CROMARTIE-1B/OF
50 TOM WIEGHAUS-C
51 RICK ENGLE-P
53 LEA CHARLIE-P
54 CHRIS SMITH-2B
55 DAVE HOSTETLER-1B
56 PAT ROONEY-OF
62-WALLACE JOHNSON-2B
66 BRYN SMITH-P

1982

3RD E 82-80 8GB

0 AL OLIVER-1B
1 WALLACE JOHNSON-2B
2 BILLY (KID) DEMARS-CH
3 RODNEY SCOTT-2B (1)
3 BRYAN (TWIG) LITTLE-2B/SS (2)
4 CHRIS SPEIER-SS
5 JOHN (THE HAMMER) MILNER-1B (1)
6 CHRIS SMITH-PH
6 JIM FANNING-MGR
7 BRAD MILLS-3B
8 GARY (THE KID) CARTER-C
9 VERN RAPP-CH
10 ANDRE (HAWK) DAWSON-OF
11 FRANK TAVERAS-SS/2B
12 MIKE PHILLIPS-2B/SS
14 STEVE BOROS-CH
16 TERRY FRANCONA (INJ) OF/1B
17 TIM BLACKWELL-C
18 JERRY WHITE-OF
19 MIKE GATES-2B2B
20 BOB JAMES-P (1)
21 SCOTT SANDERSON-P
23 DOUG FLYNN-2B (2)
24 BRAD MILLS-3B
25 ROWLAND OFFICE-OF
25 JOEL YOUNGBLOOD-OF (2)
27 ROY JOHNSON-OF
29 TIM WALLACH-3B/UTIL
30 TIM (ROCK) RAINES-OF/2B
32 TOM GORMAN-P (1)
32 MIKE STENHOUSE-PH
33 BRAD GULDEN-C
34 BILL GULLICKSON-P
35 WOODIE FRYMAN-P
36 GALEN CISCO-CH
37 BILL (SPACEMAN) LEE-P
37 DAVE TIMLIN-P
38 BRYN SMITH-P
40 BOB GEBHARD-CH
41 JEFF REARDON-P
42 KEN PHELPS-PH
43 DAN SCHATZEDER-P (2)
49 DAN NORMAN-OF
45 STEVE ROGERS-P
46 DAVID PALMER (INJ)-P
47 RANDY LERCH-P (2)
48 RAY BURRIS-P
49 WARREN CROMARTIE-OF/1B
53 CHARLIE LEA-P

1983

3RD E 86-76 6GB

0 AL OLIVER-1B/OF
1 WALLACE JOHNSON-PH (1)
2 BILLY (KID) DEMARS-CH
3 BRYAN (TWIG) LITTLE-SS/2B
4 CHRIS SPEIER-SS
5 JIM WOHLFORD-OF
6 ANGEL SALAZAR-SS
7 BILL VIRDON-MGR
8 GARY (THE KID) CARTER-C/1B
9 VERN RAPP-CH
10 ANDRE (HAWK) DAWSON-OF
11 TOM WIEGHAUS-C
12 MIKE PHILLIPS-SS/2B
15 TERRY CROWLEY-1B
16 TERRY FRANCONA-OF/1B
17 TIM BLACKWELL-C
17 MANNY TRILLO-2B (2)
18 JERRY WHITE-OF
21 SCOTT SANDERSON (INJ)-P
22 MEL WRIGHT-CH
23 DOUG FLYNN-2B/SS
24 BRAD MILLS-3B/1B
25 MIKE FUENTES-PH
26 CHRIS WELSH-P (2)
28 BRYN SMITH-P
29 TIM WALLACH-3B
30 TIM (ROCK) RAINES-OF/2B
31 RAZOR (RAY) SHINES-OF
32 MIKE STENHOUSE-OF/1B
33 MIKE VAIL-UTIL (2)
34 BILL GULLICKSON-P
35 WOODIE FRYMAN (INJ)-P
36 GALEN CISCO-CH
37 TOM DIXON-P
39 GREG BARGAR-P
40 JOE KERRIGAN-CH
41 JEFF REARDON-P
42 BOB JAMES-P (2)
43 DAN SCHATZEDER-P
44 BOBBY RAMOS-C

45 STEVE ROGERS-P
(46) DAVID PALMER (INJ)-(P)
47 RANDY LERCH-P (1)
47 GENE ROOF-OF (2)
48 RAY BURRIS-P
49 WARREN CROMARTIE-OF/1B
50 DICK GRAPENTHIN-P
51 ANGEL SALAZAR-SS
53 CHARLIE LEA-P

1984

5TH E 78-83 18GB

1 TONY SCOTT-OF (2)
2 BILLY (KID) DEMARS-CH
3 BRYAN (TWIG) LITTLE-2B/SS
4 CHRIS SPEIER-SS/3B (1)
4 MIKE RAMSEY-SS/2B (2)
5 JIM WOHLFORD-OF
6 ANGEL SALAZAR-SS
6 JIM FANNING-MGR2
7 BILL VIRDON-MGR1
8 GARY (THE KID) CARTER-C/1B
10 ANDRE (HAWK) DAWSON-OF
11 ANGEL SALAZAR- SS
12 RUSS NIXON-CH
13 DERREL THOMAS-UTIL (1)
14 PETE (CHARLIE HUSTLE) ROSE-1B/OF (1)
15 MIKE FUENTES-OF
16 TERRY FRANCONA (INJ) 1B/OF
17 FELIPE ALOU-CH
18 MIGUEL DILONE-OF
19 FRED BREINING (INJ)-P
19 RENE GONZALES-SS
20 GREG HARRIS-P (1)
20 TOM LAWLESS-2B (2)
23 DOUG FLYNN-2B/SS
24 DAN DRIESSEN-1B (2)
25 GARY LUCAS-P
27 ROY JOHNSON-OF
28 BRYN SMITH-P
29 TIM WALLACH-3B/SS
30 TIM (ROCK) RAINES-OF/2B
31 RAZOR (RAY) SHINES-1B/3B
32 MIKE STENHOUSE-OF/1B
33 SAL BUTERA-C
34 BILL GULLICKSON-P
35 RON JOHNSON-1B/OF
36 GALEN CISCO-CH
37 ANDY MCGAFFIGAN-P (1)
37 WALLACE JOHNSON-1B
38 JOE HESKETH-P
39 GREG BARGAR-P
40 JOE KERRIGAN-CH
41 JEFF REARDON-P
42 BOB JAMES-P
43 DAN SCHATZEDER-P
44 BOBBY RAMOS-C
45 STEVE ROGERS-P
46 DAVID PALMER (INJ)-P
48 FRED BREINING (INJ)-P
49 MAX VENABLE-OF
50 DICK GRAPENTHIN-P
51 RANDY ST. CLAIRE-P
53 CHARLIE LEA-P

1985

3RD E 84-77 16.5GB

1 U L WASHINGTON (INJ)-INF
2 VANCE LAW-2B/UTIL
3 HERM WINNINGHAM-OF
4 AL NEWMAN-2B/SS
5 JIM WOHLFORD-OF
6 STEVE NICOSIA (INJ)-C/1B (1)
6 FRED MANRIQUE-INF
7 HUBIE BROOKS-SS
9 RUSS NIXON-CH
10 ANDRE (HAWK) DAWSON-OF
11 SAL BUTERA-C
12 ANDRES GALARRAGA-1B
14 NED YOST-C
16 TERRY FRANCONA-UTIL
17 SKEETER BARNES-UTIL
18 MIGUEL DILONE-OF (1)
18 MIKE O'BERRY-C
19 BILL LASKEY-P (2)
20 MIKE FITZGERALD-C
21 MIKE FITZGERALD-C
22 DAN DRIESSEN-1B (1)
22 DOUG FROBEL-OF (2)
23 DOUG FLYNN-2B/SS (1)
23 MITCH WEBSTER-OF (2)
24 MICKEY MAHLER-P (1)
24 SCOT THOMPSON-OF/1B (2)
25 GARY LUCAS (INJ)-P
26 RON HANSEN-CH
27 ROY JOHNSON-OF
28 BRYN SMITH-P
29 TIM WALLACH-3B
30 TIM (ROCK) RAINES-OF
31 RAZOR (RAY) SHINES-1B
32 JACK O'CONNOR-P
33 FLOYD YOUMANS-P
34 BILL GULLICKSON-P
35 RICK RENICK-CH
36 LARRY BEARNARTH-CH
37 BUCK RODGERS-MGR
38 JOE HESKETH (INJ)-P
40 JOE KERRIGAN-CH
41 JEFF REARDON-P
42 BERT ROBERGE (INJ)-P
43 DAN SCHATZEDER (INJ)-P
44 TIM BURKE-P
45 STEVE ROGERS-P
46 DAVID PALMER (INJ)-P
47 DICK GRAPENTHIN-P
48 MICKEY MAHLER-P (1)
49 ED GLYNN-P
51 RANDY ST. CLAIRE-P
(53) CHARLIE LEA (INJ)-(P)
54 TIM BURKE-P
54 JOHN DOPSON-P
55 JOHN DOPSON-P

1986

4TH E 78-83 29.5GB

1 BOBBY WINKLES-CH
2* VANCE LAW (ILL-F)-2B/UTIL/P*
3 HERM WINNINGHAM-OF/SS
4 AL NEWMAN-2B/SS
5 JIM WOHLFORD-OF/3B
6 WALLACE JOHNSON-1B
7 HUBIE BROOKS (INJ)-SS
9 CASEY CANDAELE-2B/3B
10 ANDRE (HAWK) DAWSON-OF
11 DANN BILARDELLO-C
12 ANDRES GALARRAGA (INJ)-1B
14 BILLY MOORE-1B/OF
15 WAYNE KRENCHICKI-UTIL
16 TOM FOLEY-INF
17 RIVERA, LUIS-SS
18 JOE KERRIGAN-CH
19 RENE GONZALES-SS/3B
20 MIKE FITZGERALD (INJ)-C
22 BOB MCCLURE-P (2)
23 MITCH WEBSTER-OF
24 JASON THOMPSON-1B
24 DAVE TOMLIN (INJ)-P
25 GEORGE WRIGHT-OF (2)
26 RON HANSEN-CH
27 ANDY MCGAFFIGAN-P
28 BRYN SMITH (INJ)-P
29 TIM WALLACH-3B
30 TIM (ROCK) RAINES-OF
31 KEN MACHA-CH
32 DENNIS MARTINEZ-P (2)
33 FLOYD YOUMANS-P
34 TOM NIETO-C
35 RICK RENICK-CH
36 LARRY BEARNARTH-CH
37 BUCK RODGERS-MGR
38 JOE HESKETH (INJ)-P
39 JAY TIBBS-P
40 BERT ROBERGE-P
40 BOB MCCLURE-P (2)
41 JEFF REARDON-P
42 BERT ROBERGE-P
43 DAN SCHATZEDER-P (1)
43 BOB OWCHINKO-P
44 TIM BURKE-P
46 GEORGE RILEY-P
47 RANDY HUNT-C
48 BOB SEBRA-P
49 JEFF PARRETT-P
50 SERGIO VALDEZ-P
51 RANDY ST. CLAIRE-P
52 CURT BROWN-P
(53) CHARLIE LEA (INJ)-(P)
55 WIL TEJADA-C

1987

3RD E 91-71 4GB

1 BOBBY WINKLES-CH
2* VANCE LAW-2B/UTIL/P*
3 HERM WINNINGHAM-OF
4 DAVE ENGLE-UTIL
5 REID NICHOLS-OF/3B
6 WALLACE JOHNSON-1B
7 HUBIE BROOKS (INJ)-SS
9 CASEY CANDAELE-UTIL
12 LUIS RIVERA-SS
14 ANDRES GALARRAGA-1B
16 TOM FOLEY-INF
17 FLOYD YOUMANS (INJ)-P
18 RON HANSEN-CH
19 JOHN STEFERO-C
20 MIKE FITZGERALD-C/INF
21 ALONZO POWELL-OF
22 BOB MCCLURE-P
23 MITCH WEBSTER-OF
24 JEFF REED (INJ)-C
26 RON HANSEN-CH
26 NEAL HEATON-P
27 ANDY MCGAFFIGAN-P
28 BRYN SMITH-P
29 TIM WALLACH-3B
30 TIM (ROCK) RAINES-OF
31 KEN MACHA-CH
32 BILL CAMPBELL-P
32 DENNIS MARTINEZ-P
33 JACK DAUGHERTY-1B
33 NELSON NORMAN-SS
34 PASQUEL PEREZ (SUB)-P
35 UBALDO HEREDIA-P
36 LARRY BEARNARTH-CH
37 BUCK RODGERS-MGR
38 JOE HESKETH (INJ)-P
39 JEFF FISCHER-P
39 BILL CAMPBELL-P
40 LARY SORENSEN-P
41 NEAL HEATON-P
41 TOM ROMANO-OF
42 LARY SORENSEN-P
42 JACKIE MOORE-CH
44 TIM BURKE-P
47 NELSON SANTOVENIA-C
47 RAZOR SHINES-1B
48 BOB SEBRA-P
49 JEFF PARRETT-P
50 JAY TIBBS-P
51 RANDY ST. CLAIRE-P
52 CURT BROWN-P
53 CHARLIE LEA (INJ)-P

1988

3TH E 81-81 19GB

1 BOBBY WINKLES-CH
3 HERM WINNINGHAM-OF (1)
3 DAVE MARTINEZ-OF (2)
4 DAVE ENGLE-UTIL
5 CASEY CANDAELE-2B (1)
5 JOHNNY PAREDES-2B/OF
6 WALLACE JOHNSON-1B
7 HUBIE BROOKS-OF
9 CASEY CANDAELE-2B (1)
9 GRAIG NETTLES-3B/1B
11 WIL TEJADA-C
12 LUIS RIVERA-SS
14 ANDRES GALARRAGA-1B
15 JEFF HUSON-UTIL
16 TOM FOLEY-2B/INF
17 FLOYD YOUMANS (SUB)-P
18 RON HANSEN-CH
19 LEONEL CARRION-CH
20 MIKE FITZGERALD-C/OF
22 BOB MCCLURE-P (1)
23 MITCH WEBSTER-OF (1)
23 TOM O'MALLEY-3B
24 JEFF REED-C (1)
24 TRACY JONES-OF (2)
25 REX HUDLER-UTIL
26 NEAL HEATON-P
27 ANDY MCGAFFIGAN-P
28 BRYN SMITH-P
29 TIM WALLACH-3B/2B
30 TIM (ROCK) RAINES-OF
31 KEN MACHA-CH
32 DENNIS MARTINEZ-P
34 PASQUEL PEREZ (INJ)-P
35 OTIS NIXON-OF
36 LARRY BEARNARTH-CH
37 BUCK RODGERS-MGR
38 JOE HESKETH-P
39 RICH SAUVEUR-P
43 MIKE SMITH-P
44 TIM BURKE-P
47 NELSON SANTOVENIA-C
49 JEFF PARRETT (INJ)-P
50 TIM BARRETT-P
51 RANDY ST. CLAIRE-P (1)
51 RANDY JOHNSON-P
52 JOE SPARKS-CH
54 JOHN DOPSON-P
57 RANDY JOHNSON-P
59 BRIAN HOLMAN-P

1989

4TH E 81-81 12GB

1 DAVE MARTINEZ-OF
2 GIL REYES-C
3 JUNIOR NOBOA-INF
4 DAMASO GARCIA-2B/3B
(5) JOHNNY PAREDES (INJ)-(2B)
5 JIM DWYER-PH (2)
6 WALLACE JOHNSON-1B
7 HUBIE BROOKS-OF
9 MARQUIS GRISSOM-OF
11 SPIKE OWEN-SS
12 MARK LANGSTON-P (2)
14 ANDRES GALARRAGA-1B
15 JEFF HUSON-UTIL
16 TOM FOLEY-2B/INF
17 RAFAEL LANDESTOY-CH
18 RON HANSEN-CH
19 JOE SPARKS-CH
20 MIKE FITZGERALD-UTIL
22 NELSON SANTOVENIA (INJ)-C
23 ZANE SMITH-P (2)
24 MIKE ALDRETE-OF/1B
25 REX HUDLER-UTIL
26 BRETT GIDEON-P
27 ANDY MCGAFFIGAN-P
28 BRYN SMITH-P
29 TIM WALLACH-3B/P
30 TIM (ROCK) RAINES-OF
31 KEN MACHA-CH
32 DENNIS MARTINEZ-P
33 LARRY WALKER-OF
34 PASQUEL PEREZ-P
35 OTIS NIXON-OF
36 LARRY BEARNARTH-CH
37 BUCK RODGERS-MGR
38 JOE HESKETH-P
41 STEVE FREY-P
42 JACKIE MOORE-CH
43 GENE HARRIS-P (1)
43 URBANO LUGO-P
44 TIM BURKE-P
45 JOHN (CANDY MAN) CANDELARIA-P (2)
46 KEVIN GROSS-P
48 RICH THOMPSON-P
49 MARTY PEVEY-C/OF
51 RANDY ST. CLAIRE-P (1)
56 MARK GARDNER-P
59 BRIAN HOLMAN-P (1)
59 URBANO LUGO-P
61 GENE HARRIS-P (1)

1990

3RD E 85-77 10GB

1* DAVE MARTINEZ-OF/P*
3* JUNIOR NOBOA-UTIL/P*
4 DELINO DESHIELDS-2B
5 JOHNNY PAREDES-2B (2)
6 WALLACE JOHNSON-1B
9 MARQUIS GRISSOM (INJ)-OF
10 TOM RUNNELLS-CH
11 SPIKE OWEN-SS
12 HAL MCRAE-CH
14 ANDRES GALARRAGA-1B
15 ORLANDO MERCADO-C (2)
16 TOM FOLEY-INF
17 HAL MCRAE-CH
18 MOISES ALOU-OF (2)
19 TOM RUNNELLS-CH
19 JERRY GOFF-UTIL
20 MIKE FITZGERALD-C/OF
21 TOMMY HARPER-CH
22 NELSON SANTOVENIA (INJ)-C
23 OIL CAN BOYD-P
24 MIKE ALDRETE-OF/1B
24 DAVE SCHMIDT (INJ)-P
25 REX HUDLER-PH (1)
25 MIKE ALDRETE-OF/1B
26 BRETT GIDEON (INJ)-P
27 ROLANDO ROOMES-OF (2)
28 DAVE SCHMIDT (INJ)-P
29 TIM WALLACH-3B
30 TIM (ROCK) RAINES-OF
31 KEN MACHA-CH
32 DENNIS MARTINEZ-P
33 LARRY WALKER-OF
34 ZANE SMITH-P (1)
34 SCOTT RUSKIN-P (2)
35 OTIS NIXON-OF/SS
36 LARRY BEARNARTH-CH
37 BUCK RODGERS-MGR
38 JOE HESKETH-P (1)
38 ERIC BULLOCK-PH
40 MARK GARDNER-P
41 STEVE FREY-P
42 BOB MALLOY-P
43 CHRIS NABHOLZ-P
44 TIM BURKE (INJ)-P
45 DREW HALL (INJ)-P
46 KEVIN GROSS-P
47 BRIAN BARNES-P
48 RICH THOMPSON-P
49 HOWARD FARMER-P

0 HOWARD FARMER-P
0 JOHN COSTELLO (INJ)-P (2)
1 MEL ROJAS-P
2 SCOTT ANDERSON-P
4 DALE MOHORCIC-P
5 BILL SAMPEN-P
6 MARK GARDNER-P

1991

6TH E 71-90 26.5GB

1 DAVE MARTINEZ-OF
2 GIL REYES-C
3 JUNIOR NOBOA-UTIL
4 DELINO DESHIELDS-2B
(5) DARREN REED (INJ)-(OF)
6 NIKCO RIESGO-OF
6 JERRY MANUEL-CH
9 MARQUIS GRISSOM-OF
0 TOM RUNNELLS-CH/MRG2
1 SPIKE OWEN-SS
2 HAL MCRAE-CH (1)
2 KENNY WILLIAMS-OF (2)
4 ANDRES GALARRAGA (INJ)-1B
5 RON DARLING-P (2)
6 TOM FOLEY-INF
7 RAFAEL LANDESTOY-CH
18) MOISES ALOU (INJ)-(OF)
20 MIKE FITZGERALD (INJ)-UTIL
21 TOMMY HARPER-CH
22 NELSON SANTOVENIA (INJ)-C
22 IVAN CALDERONE-OF/1B
23 OIL CAN BOYD-P (1)
23 JOHN VANDER WAL-OF
24 RON HASSEY (INJ)-C
25 BRET BARBERIE-INF
26 DAVE SCHMIDT-P
26 NELSON SANTOVENIA (INJ)-C/1B
27 IVAN CALDERONE-OF/1B
28 MARK GARDNER-P
29 TIM WALLACH-3B
31 KEN MACHA-CH
32 DENNIS MARTINEZ-P
33 LARRY WALKER-OF/1B
34 SCOTT RUSKIN-P
35 JAY WARD-CH
36 LARRY BEARNARTH-CH
37 BUCK RODGERS-MGR1 (1)
38 ERIC BULLOCK-OF/1B
39 JEFF FASSERO-P
40 DAVE WAINHOUSE-P
41 STEVE FREY-P
42 RICK MAHLER-P (1)
42 CHRIS HANEY-P
43 CHRIS NABHOLZ (INJ)-P
44 TIM BURKE-P (1)
44 KENNY WILLIAMS-OF (2)
47 BRIAN BARNES-P
48 DOUG PIATT-P
48 BILL LONG-P
50 BARRY JONES-P
51 MEL ROJAS-P
55 BILL SAMPEN-P
58 DOUG PIATT-P

1992

2ND E 87-75 9GB

1 TODD HANEY-2B
2 JERRY WILLARD-1B (2)
3 MATT STAIRS-OF
4 DELINO DESHIELDS-2B
5 DARREN REED (INJ)-OF (1)
5 SEAN BERRY-3B
6 JERRY MANUEL-CH
8 GARY (THE KID) CARTER-C/1B
9 MARQUIS GRISSOM-OF
10 TOM RUNNELLS-MGR1
11 SPIKE OWEN-SS
12 WIL CORDERO-SS/2B
13 ROB NATAL-C
13 RICK CERONE-C
14 ARCHI CIANFROCCO-UTIL
15 GREG COLBRUNN-1B
16 TOM FOLEY-UTIL
17 FELIPE ALOU-CH/MGR2
18 MOISES ALOU-OF
18 STEVE LYONS-OF/1B (2)
19 JERRY GOFF-PH
20 PETE YOUNG-P
21 TOMMY HARPER-CH
22 IVAN CALDERONE (INJ)-OF
23 JOHN VANDER WAL-OF/1B
24 DARRIN FLETCHER (ILL)-C
25 BRET BARBERIE-INF
26 SERGIO VALDEZ-P
27 ERIC BULLOCK-PH
28 MARK GARDNER-P
29 TIM WALLACH-3B/1B
32 DENNIS MARTINEZ-P
33 LARRY WALKER-OF
34 BILL LANDRUM (INJ)-P
35 JAY WARD-CH
36 SCOTT SERVICE-P
36 MATT MAYSEY-P
37 JONATHAN HURST-P
39 JEFF FASSERO-P
40 BILL LANDRUM (INJ)-P
41 DOUG SIMONS-P
42 CHRIS HANEY-P (1)
42 BILL KRUEGER-P (2)
43 CHRIS NABHOLZ-P
44 KEN HILL-P
45 JOE KERRIGAN-CH
45 DOUG SIMONS-P
46 KENT BOTTENFIELD-P
47 BRIAN BARNES-P
50 BILL RISLEY-P
51 MEL ROJAS-P
52 GIL HEREDIA-P (2)
53 TIM LAKER-C
55 BILL SAMPEN-P (1)
57 JOHN WETTELAND-P
59 MATT STAIRS-OF

1993

2ND E 94-68 3GB

1 TIM JOHNSON-CH
2 TIM SPEHR-C
3 MIKE LANSING-INF
4 DELINO DESHIELDS (INJ)-2B
5 SEAN BERRY-3B
6 JERRY MANUEL-CH
7 LOU FRAZIER-UTIL
8 *(RET#) GARY CARTER*
9 MARQUIS GRISSOM-OF
10 *(RET#) RUSTY STAUB*
11 TED WOOD-OF
12 WIL CORDERO-SS/3B
13 JEFF FASSERO-P
14 ARCHI CIANFROCCO-1B (1)
14 KENT BOTTENFIELD-P (1)
14 DERRICK WHITE-1B
15 GREG COLBRUNN (INJ)-1B
16 MIKE GARDINER-P (1)
16 CURTIS PRIDE-OF
17 FELIPE ALOU-MGR
18 MOISES ALOU-OF
19 TIM LAKER-C
20 PETE YOUNG-P
21 TOMMY HARPER-CH
22 SCOTT ALDRED (INJ)-P (2)
23 JOHN VANDER WAL-1B/OF
24 DARRIN FLETCHER-C
25 MATT STAIRS-OF
25 CHARLIE MONTOYO-2B
26 SERGIO VALDEZ-P
26 JOE SIDDALL-UTIL
27 MEL ROJAS-P
27 BUTCH HENRY-P (2)
28 FRANK BOLICK-1B/3B
30 CLIFF FLOYD-1B
31 LUIS PUJOLS-CH
31 JEFF SHAW-P
32 DENNIS MARTINEZ-P
33 LARRY WALKER-OF/1B
34 GIL HEREDIA-P
35 TIM MCINTOSH-OF/C (2)
37 RONDELL WHITE-OF
38 JIMMY JONES (INJ)-P
38 DENIS BOUCHER-P
39 JEFF FASSERO-P
39 RANDY READY-INF
41 BRIAN BARNES-P
42 JEFF SHAW-P
42 KIRK RUETER-P
43 CHRIS NABHOLZ (INJ)-P
44 KEN HILL-P
45 JOE KERRIGAN-CH
46 KENT BOTTENFIELD-P (1)
46 ORESTE MARRERO-1B
47 BRIAN BARNES-P
50 BILL RISLEY-P
51 MEL ROJAS-P
53 BRUCE WALTON-P
53 BRIAN LOONEY-P
54 TIM SCOTT-P (2)
55 FRANK BOLICK-1B/3B
57 JOHN WETTELAND-P
59 MIKE LANSING-INF
67 PIERRE ARSENAULT-CH

1994

1ST E 74-40 0GB
STRIKE NO POST-SEASON

1 TIM JOHNSON-CH
2 TIM SPEHR-C
3 MIKE LANSING-2B
4 JEFF GARDNER-2B/3B
5 SEAN BERRY-3B
6 JERRY MANUEL-CH
7 LOU FRAZIER-OF
8 *(RET#) GARY CARTER*
9 MARQUIS GRISSOM-OF
10 *(RET#) RUSTY STAUB*
12 WIL CORDERO-SS
13 JEFF FASSERO (INJ)-P
15 FREDDIE BENAVIDES-2B
17 FELIPE ALOU-MGR
18 MOISES ALOU-OF
20 ROD HENDERSON-P
21 TOMMY HARPER-CH
22 RONDELL WHITE-OF
23 JUAN BELL-SS
24 DARRIN FLETCHER-C
25 LENNY WEBSTER-C
27 BUTCH HENRY-P
30 CLIFF FLOYD-1B
31 JEFF SHAW-P
33 LARRY WALKER-OF
34 GIL HEREDIA-P
35 BRIAN LOONEY-P
37 PEDRO J. MARTINEZ-P
38 DENIS BOUCHER-P
39 RANDY MILLIGAN-1B
41 HEATH HAYNES-P
42 KIRK RUETER-P
44 KEN HILL-P
45 JOE KERRIGAN-CH
45 PEDRO J. MARTINEZ-P
47 GABE WHITE-P
48 JOEY EISCHEN-P
51 MEL ROJAS-P
54 TIM SCOTT (INJ)-P
55 LUIS PUJOLS-CH
57 JOHN WETTELAND (INJ)-P
67 PIERRE ARSENAULT-CH

1995

5TH E 66-78 24GB
144-GAME SEASON

1 YAMIL BENITEZ-OF
2 TIM SPEHR-C
3 MIKE LANSING-2B
4 MARK GRUDZIELANEK-2B
5 SEAN BERRY-3B
6 JERRY MANUEL-CH
7 LOU FRAZIER-OF (1)
7 F. P. SANTANGELO-OF
8 *(RET#) GARY CARTER*
9 DAVE SILVESTRI-SS (2)
10 *(RET#) RUSTY STAUB*
11 SHANE ANDREWS-3B/1B
12 WIL CORDERO-SS
13 JEFF FASSERO-P
14 JEFF TREADWAY-2B (2)
15 CHAD FONVILLE-SS (1)
15 CURTIS PRIDE-OF
16 TOM FOLEY-2B
17 FELIPE ALOU-MGR
18 MOISES ALOU-OF
19 TIM LAKER-C
21 TOMMY HARPER-CH
22 RONDELL WHITE-OF
23 JIM TRACY-CH
24 DARRIN FLETCHER-C
25 DAVID SEGUI-OF (2)
26 BRYAN EVERSGERD-P
27 BUTCH HENRY-P
28 ROBERTO KELLY-OF (1)
28 JOE SIDDELL-C
29 GREG A. HARRIS-P
30 CLIFF FLOYD-1B
31 JEFF SHAW-P
32 JOE KERRIGAN-CH
33 CARLOS PEREZ-P
34 GIL HEREDIA-P
37 PEDRO J. MARTINEZ-P
39 J. J. THOBE-P
40 HENRY RODRIGUEZ (INJ)-1B (2)
41 UGUETH URBINA-P
42 KIRK RUETER-P
43 CURT SCHMIDT-P
44 TONY TARASCO-OF
45 PEDRO J. MARTINEZ-P
46 JOSE DELEON-P (2)
47 GABE WHITE-P
48 TAVO ALVAREZ-P
49 REID CORNELIUS-P (1)
49 WILLIE FRASER-P
51 MEL ROJAS-P
52 DAVE LEIPER-P (2)
54 TIM SCOTT-P
55 LUIS PUJOLS-CH
55 ??? FRANKS-CH
57 JOHN WETTELAND (INJ)-P
59 UGUETH URBINA-P
63 CURT SCHMIDT-P
67 PIERRE ARSENAULT-CH
72 LUIS AQUINO-P (1)

1996

2ND E 88-74 8GB

1 TOMMY HARPER-CH
2 TIM SPEHR (INJ)-C
3 MIKE LANSING-2B
4 MARK GRUDZIELANEK-2B
5 ANDY STANKIEWICZ (INJ)-2B
6 JERRY MANUEL-CH
7 F. P. SANTANGELO-OF/3B
8 *(RET#) GARY CARTER*
9 DAVE SILVESTRI-3B
10 *(RET#) RUSTY STAUB*
11 SHANE ANDREWS-3B
12 RAUL CHAVEZ-C
13 JEFF FASSERO-P
14 JEFF JUDEN-P (2)
15 YAMIL BENITEZ-OF
16 RICK SCHU-3B
16 ROB LUKACHYK-PH
17 FELIPE ALOU-MGR
18 MOISES ALOU (INJ)(SUS)-OF
(19) TIM LAKER (INJ)-(C)
21 DAVID SEGUI (INJ)-OF
22 RONDELL WHITE (INJ)-OF
23 JIM TRACY-CH
24 DARRIN FLETCHER-C
25 LENNY WEBSTER-C
26 ALEX PACHECO-P
27 VLADIMIR GUERRERO-OF
29 SHERMAN OBANDO (INJ)-OF
30 CLIFF FLOYD-1B/OF
31 MARK LEITER-P (2)
32 JOE KERRIGAN-CH
(33) CARLOS PEREZ (INJ)-(P)
36 JOSE PANIAGUA (INJ)-P
37 RHEAL CORMIER (INJ)-P
39 MIKE DYER-P
40 HENRY RODRIGUEZ-OF/1B
41 UGUETH URBINA-P
42 KIRK RUETER (INJ)-P (1)
43 DAVE VERES-P
44 BARRY MANUEL-P
45 PEDRO J. MARTINEZ-P
46 TONY BARRON-PH
47 OMAR DAAL-P
48 TAVO ALVAREZ (INJ)-P
51 MEL ROJAS-P
52 DAVE LEIPER-P (2)
54 TIM SCOTT-P (1)
55 LUIS PUJOLS-CH
59 ALEX PACHECO-P
66 DEREK AUCOIN-P
67 PIERRE ARSENAULT-CH

1997

4TH E 78-84 23GB

1 TOMMY HARPER-CH
2 ORLANDO CABRERA-SS
3 MIKE LANSING-2B
4 MARK GRUDZIELANEK-SS
5 ANDY STANKIEWICZ (INJ)-SS
7 F. P. SANTANGELO (INJ)-OF
8 *(RET#) GARY CARTER*
9 RYAN MCGUIRE-1B/OF
10 *(RET#) RUSTY STAUB*
10 *(RET#) ANDRE DAWSON*
11 SHANE ANDREWS (INJ)-3B
12 RAUL CHAVEZ-C
13 RHEAL CORMIER-P
14 JEFF JUDEN-P (1)
14 BRAD FULLMER-1B
15 DOUG STRANGE (INJ)-3B
16 CHRIS WIDGER-C
17 FELIPE ALOU-MGR
18 MARC VALDES-P
19 JOE ORSULAK-OF
21 DAVID SEGUI (INJ)-1B
22 RONDELL WHITE (INJ)-OF
23 JIM TRACY-CH
24 DARRIN FLETCHER-C
25 PETE MACKANIN-CH
26 BOBBY CUELLAR-CH
27 VLADIMIR GUERRERO (INJ)-OF
29 SHERMAN OBANDO (INJ)-OF
30 DUSTIN HERMANSON-P
31 HENSLEY MEULENS-1B/OF
32 ANTHONY TELFORD-P
33 CARLOS PEREZ-P
34 RICK DEHART-P
36 JOSE PANIAGUA-P
37 JOSE VIDRO-PH
38 EVERETT STULL-P

40 HENRY RODRIGUEZ-OF
41 UGUETH URBINA-P
42 *(RET#) JACKIE ROBINSON*
43 DAVE VERES (INJ)-P
44 SALOMON TORRES-P (2)
44 STEVE KLINE-P (2)
45 PEDRO J. MARTINEZ-P
47 OMAR DAAL (WAIV)-P (1)
47 MIKE JOHNSON-P (2)
49 LEE SMITH (RET)-P
51 MIKE THURMAN-P
52 JIM BULLINGER-P
53 STEVE FALTEISEK-P
54 SHAYNE BENNETT-P
55 LUIS PUJOLS-CH
67 PIERRE ARSENAULT-CH

1998

4TH E 65-97 41GB

1 TOMMY HARPER-CH
2 ORLANDO CABRERA-2B
3 MIKE HUBBARD-C
4 MARK GRUDZIELANEK-SS (1)
4 WILTON GUERRERO-2B (2)
5 MIKE BARRETT-3B
6 RYAN MCGUIRE-1B/OF
7 F. P. SANTANGELO-OF
8 *(RET#) GARY CARTER*
9 RYAN MCGUIRE-1B/OF
9 TERRY JONES-OF
10 *(RET#) RUSTY STAUB*
10 *(RET#) ANDRE DAWSON*
11 SHANE ANDREWS-3B
12 ROBERT PEREZ (INJ)-OF (2)
13 BOB HENLEY-C
14 DERRICK MAY-OF
15 MIKE MORDECAI (INJ)-INF
16 CHRIS WIDGER-C
17 FELIPE ALOU-MGR
18 MARC VALDES (INJ)-P
20 BRAD FULLMER-1B
21 SHAYNE BENNETT-P
22 RONDELL WHITE (INJ)-OF
23 JIM (TRACE) TRACY-CH
24 SCOTT LIVINGSTONE-3B/1B
25 PETE MACKANIN-CH
26 BOBBY CUELLAR-CH
27 VLADIMIR GUERRERO-OF
28 JAVIER VAZQUEZ-P
29 TREY MOORE (INJ)-P
30 DUSTIN HERMANSON (INJ)-P
31 SHAWN BOSKIE-P
32 ANTHONY TELFORD-P
33 CARLOS PEREZ-P (1)
33 FERNANDO SEGUIGNOL-OF
34 RICK DEHART-P
35 MIKE THURMAN-P
36 RAY HOLBERT-SS (2)
37 JOSE VIDRO-PH
38 KIRK BULLINGER-P
41 UGUETH URBINA-P
42 *(RET#) JACKIE ROBINSON*
43 TIM YOUNG-P
44 STEVE KLINE-P
45 CARL PAVANO-P
47 MIKE JOHNSON-P
48 MIGUEL BATISTA-P
49 JEREMY POWELL-P
50 DAROND STOVALL-OF
51 MIKE MADDUX (INJ)-P
54 BOB HENLEY (INJ)-C
55 LUIS PUJOLS-CH
67 PIERRE ARSENAULT-CH

1999

4TH E 68-94 35GB

1 TOMMY HARPER-CH
2 GENE GLYNN-CH
3 JOSE VIDRO-2B
4 WILTON GUERRERO-2B
5 MIKE BARRETT (INJ)-3B
6 RYAN MCGUIRE-1B/OF
7 ORLANDO MERCED-OF
8 *(RET#) GARY CARTER*
9 TERRY JONES-OF
10 *(RET#) RUSTY STAUB*
10 *(RET#) ANDRE DAWSON*
11 SHANE ANDREWS (INJ)-3B (1)
12 MIKE MORDECAI-OF
13 BOB HENLEY (INJ)-C
14 JOSE FERNANDEZ-INF
16 CHRIS WIDGER-C
17 FELIPE ALOU-MGR
18 ORLANDO CABRERA-2B
19 FERNANDO SEGUIGNOL-INF
20 BRAD FULLMER-1B
21 SHAYNE BENNETT-P
22 RONDELL WHITE (INJ)-OF
23 JAVIER VAZQUEZ-P
24 JAMES MOUTON-OF
25 PETE MACKANIN-CH
26 BOBBY CUELLAR-CH
27 VLADIMIR GUERRERO-OF
28 TED LILLY-P
29 TREY MOORE (INJ)-P
30 DUSTIN HERMANSON-P
31 MANNY MARTINEZ-OF
32 ANTHONY TELFORD-P
33 PETER BERGERON-OF
34 RICK DEHART-P
34 CHRIS STOWERS-OF
35 MIKE THURMAN-P
36 BOBBY AYALA-P (1)
37 DARRON COX (INJ)-C
38 ROBERT MACHADO-C
40 GUILLERMO MOTA-P
41 UGUETH URBINA-P
42 *(RET#) JACKIE ROBINSON*
43 DAN C. SMITH-P
44 STEVE KLINE-P
45 CARL PAVANO-P
47 MIKE JOHNSON-P
48 MIGUEL BATISTA-P
49 JEREMY POWELL-P
50 GEOFF BLUM-INF
51 MIKE MADDUX (INJ)-P (1)
51 MEL ROJAS (REL)-P (3)
51 TONY ARMAS, JR.-P
52 SCOTT STRICKLAND-P
53 TRACE COQUILLETTE-INF
55 LUIS PUJOLS-CH
55 ROBERT MACHADO-C
56 J. D. SMART-P
67 PIERRE ARSENAULT-CH

2000

4TH E 67-95 28GB

1 TERRY JONES (INJ)-OF
2 TOMAS DE LA ROSA-INF
3 JOSE VIDRO-2B
4 WILTON GUERRERO-2B
5 MIKE BARRETT (INJ)-3B
6 PAT ROESSLER-CH
7 PERRY HILL-CH
8 *(RET#) GARY CARTER*
9 LEE STEVENS-INF
10 *(RET#) RUSTY STAUB*
10 *(RET#) ANDRE DAWSON*
11 GEOFF BLUM-3B
12 MIKE MORDECAI-OF
14 HIDEKI IRABU (INJ)-P
15 LENNY WEBSTER-C
16 CHRIS WIDGER-C (1)
17 FELIPE ALOU-MGR
18 ORLANDO CABRERA-2B
19 FERNANDO SEGUIGNOL-INF
20 SCOTT STRICKLAND-P
21 CHARLIE O'BRIEN-C
22 RONDELL WHITE (INJ)-OF (1)
23 JAVIER VAZQUEZ-P
24 MILTON BRADLEY-OF
25 PETE MACKANIN-CH
26 BOBBY CUELLAR-CH
27 VLADIMIR GUERRERO-OF
28 TRACE COQUILLETTE-INF
29 TREY MOORE-P
30 DUSTIN HERMANSON-P
31 BRAD RIGBY-P (2)
32 ANTHONY TELFORD-P
33 PETER BERGERON-OF
35 MIKE THURMAN-P
36 TONY ARMAS (INJ)-P
(37) GRAEME LLOYD (INJ)-(P)
38 BRAD ARNSBERG-CH
39 BRIAN SCHNEIDER-C
40 GUILLERMO MOTA-P
41 UGUETH URBINA (INJ)-P
42 *(RET#) JACKIE ROBINSON*
43 FELIPE LIRA-P
44 STEVE KLINE-P
45 CARL PAVANO (INJ)-P
46 ANDY TRACY-INF
47 MIKE JOHNSON-P
48 MIGUEL BATISTA-P (1)
48 JIM POOLE-P (2)
48 DAVID MORAGA-P (1)
48 SCOTT DOWNS (INJ)-P (2)
49 JEREMY POWELL-P
50 MATT BLANK (INJ)-P
51 SCOTT FORSTER-P
52 T. J. TUCKER (INJ)-P
53 MATT SKRMETTA-P (1)
53 SEAN SPENCER-P
54 JULIO SANTANA-P
55 LUIS PUJOLS-CH
56 TALMADGE NUNNARI-INF
57 YOVANNY LARA (INJ)-P
58 TONY ARMAS, JR. (INJ)-P
58 YOHANNY VALERA-C
67 PIERRE ARSENAULT-CH

2001

5TH E 68-94 20GB

1 JEFF TORBORG-MGR 2
2 TOMAS DE LA ROSA-SS
3 JOSE VIDRO (INJ)-2B
4 RYAN MINOR-3B
5 MIKE BARRETT-C
6 PAT ROESSLER-CH
7 PERRY HILL-CH
8 *(RET#) GARY CARTER*
9 LEE STEVENS-INF
10 *(RET#) RUSTY STAUB*
10 *(RET#) ANDRE DAWSON*
11 GEOFF BLUM-3B
12 MIKE MORDECAI-UTIL
13 OZZIE GUILLEN-ASST. CH
14 HIDEKI IRABU (INJ)(REL)-P
15 RANDY KNORR-C
16 SANDY MARTINEZ (INJ)-C
16 TERRY JONES (INJ)-OF
17 FELIPE ALOU-MGR1
18 ORLANDO CABRERA-2B
19 FERNANDO SEGUIGNOL-INF
20 SCOTT STRICKLAND-P
21 FERNANDO TATIS (INJ)-3B
22 ANDY TRACY-3B/1B
23 JAVIER VAZQUEZ-P
24 MILTON BRADLEY-OF (1)
24 TOMO OHKA-P (2)
25 MARK SMITH-OF
26 JEFF COX-CH
26 BOB SCANLAN-P
27 VLADIMIR GUERRERO-OF
28 CURTIS PRIDE (INJ)-OF
29 ROB DUCEY (INJ)-OF
30 TIM RAINES (INJ)-OF (1)
31 MIKE JOHNSON-P
31 DARWIN CUBILLAN-P
32 ANTHONY TELFORD (INJ)-P
33 PETER BERGERON-OF
34 BRITT REAMES-P
35 MIKE THURMAN (INJ)-P
36 TONY ARMAS, JR.-P
37 SCOTT DOWNS (INJ)-P
38 BRAD ARNSBERG-CH
39 BRIAN SCHNEIDER-C
40 GUILLERMO MOTA (INJ)-P
41 UGUETH URBINA-P
42 *(RET#) JACKIE ROBINSON*
43 FELIPE LIRA-P
44 RICK RENICK-CH
45 CARL PAVANO (INJ)-P
46 BOBBY MUNOZ-P
47 GRAEME LLOYD-P
48 CHRIS PETERS-P
48 JOEY EISCHEN-P
48 BRAD WILKERSON-OF
50 MATT BLANK-P
51 SCOTT STEWART (INJ)-P
55 MASATO YOSHII-P
56 TROY MATTES-P
58 JOEY EISCHEN-P
59 HENRY MATEO-2B
67 PIERRE ARSENAULT-CH

2002

2ND E 83-79 19GB

1 JOSE MACIAS-OF/INF (2)
2 JOSE MACIAS-OF/INF (2)
2 JAMEY CARROLL-INF
3 JOSE VIDRO-2B
4 WILTON GUERRERO-UTIL (2)
5 MIKE BARRETT-C/1B
6 BRAD WILKERSON-OF/1B
7 WENDELL KIM-CH
8 *(RET#) GARY CARTER*
9 LEE STEVENS-1B (1)
10 *(RET#) RUSTY STAUB*
10 *(RET#) ANDRE DAWSON*
11 PETER BERGERON-OF
12 MIKE MORDECAI-UTIL (1)
13 BOB NATAL-CH
14 ANDRES (BIG CAT) GALARRAGA-1B
17 TOM MCCRAW-CH
18 ORLANDO CABRERA-SS
19 ENDY CHAVEZ-OF
20 FRANK ROBINSON-MGR
21 FERNANDO TATIS-3B
22 LOU COLLIER-UTIL
22 MATT CEPICKY-OF
23 JAVIER VAZQUEZ-P
24 TOMO OHKA-P
25 SCOTT STRICKLAND-P (1)
25 TROY O'LEARY-OF
26 CHRIS TRUBY-UTIL (1)
26 WIL CORDERO-OF/1B (2)
27 VLADIMIR GUERRERO-OF
28 JERRY MORALES-CH
29 HENRY MATEO-INF
29 MATT CEPICKY-OF
30 CLIFF FLOYD-OF (2)
31 SUN WOO KIM-P (2)
32 BRUCE CHEN-P (2)
32 JIM BROWER-P (2)
33 DICK POLE-CH
34 BRITT REAMES-P
36 TONY ARMAS, JR.-P
(37) SCOTT DOWNS (INJ)-(P)
38 ED VOSBERG-P
39 BRIAN SCHNEIDER-C/OF
40 HENRY RODRIGUEZ-OF
40 BARTOLO COLON-P (2)
41 MANNY ACTA-CH
42 *(RET#) JACKIE ROBINSON*
43 DAN SMITH-P
45 CARL PAVANO-P (1)
47 GRAEME LLOYD-P (1)
47 TIM DREW-P
49 DICK POLE-CH
49 MATT HERGES-P
51 SCOTT STEWART-P
52 T. J. TUCKER-P
54 ZACH DAY-P
55 MASATO YOSHII-P
58 JOEY EISCHEN-P

2003

4TH E 83-79 18GB

1 JOSE MACIAS-OF/3B
2 JAMEY CARROLL-INF
3 JOSE VIDRO-2B
4 HENRY MATEO-2B/UTIL
5 MIKE BARRETT (INJ)-C
6 BRAD WILKERSON-OF/1B
7 WENDELL KIM-CH (1)
7 BRAD MILLS-CH
7 TODD ZEILE-3B (2)
8 *(RET#) GARY CARTER*
10 *(RET#) RUSTY STAUB*
10 *(RET#) ANDRE DAWSON*
12 WIL CORDERO-1B
13 BOB NATAL-CH
14 MANNY ACTA-CH
15 JEFF LIEFER (WAIV)-OF (1)
16 CLAUDE RAYMOND-CH
17 TOM MCCRAW-CH
18 ORLANDO CABRERA-SS
19 ENDY CHAVEZ-OF
20 FRANK ROBINSON-MGR
21 FERNANDO TATIS (INJ)-3B
22 RON CALLOWAY-OF
23 JAVIER VAZQUEZ-P
24 TOMO OHKA-P
(26) ORLANDO (EL DUQUE) HERNANDEZ-(P)
27 VLADIMIR GUERRERO (INJ)-OF
28 JERRY MORALES-CH
29 MATT CEPICKY-OF
31 SUN WOO KIM-P
32 ANTHONY FERRARI-P
32 JOE VITIELLO-OF/1B
33 CLAUDIO VARGAS (INJ)-P
34 BRITT REAMES-P
35 EDWARDS GUZMAN-UTIL
36 TONY ARMAS, JR. (INJ)-P
37 SCOTT DOWNS-P
39 BRIAN SCHNEIDER-C
41 ERIC KNOTT-P
42 *(RET#) JACKIE ROBINSON*
43 DAN SMITH (INJ)-P
44 JULIO MANON-P
45 JEFF LIEFER (WAIV)-OF (1)
45 VIC DARENSBOURG-P (2)
47 TIM DREW-P
49 DICK POLE-CH (1)
49 RANDY ST. CLAIRE-CH
50 JOSE MERCEDES-P
51 SCOTT STEWART (INJ)-P
52 T. J. TUCKER-P
53 RON CALLOWAY-OF
53 ROY CORCORAN-P
54 ZACH DAY (INJ)-P
56 LUIS AYALA (INJ)-P
58 JOEY EISCHEN (INJ)-P
59 BRYAN HEBSON-P
59 HECTOR ALMONTE-P (2)
60 ROCKY BIDDLE-P
61 LIVAN HERNANDEZ-P
62 CHAD CORDERO- P

2004

5TH E 67-95 29GB

1 JOSH LABANDEIRA-SS
2 CARL EVERETT (INJ)-OF (1)
2 MAICER IZTURIS-2B
3 JOSE VIDRO (INJ)-2B
4 HENRY MATEO-2B
5 JAMEY CARROLL-3B
6 BRAD WILKERSON-OF/1B
7 BRAD MILLS-CH
7 TONY BATISTA-3B
8 *(RET#) GARY CARTER*

MONTREAL EXPOS/**WASHINGTON NATIONALS**

9 EINAR DIAZ-C
10 *(RET#) RUSTY STAUB*
10 *(RET#) ANDRE DAWSON*
11 PETER BERGERON-OF
11 ALEX GONZALEZ-SS (2)
12 ANDY FOX-2B (1)
12 BRENDAN HARRIS-2B (2)
13 BOB NATAL-CH
14 MANNY ACTA-CH
16 CLAUDE RAYMOND-CH
17 TOM MCCRAW-CH
18 ORLANDO CABRERA-SS (1)
19 ENDY CHAVEZ-OF
20 FRANK ROBINSON-MGR
21 JOHN PATTERSON (INJ)-P
22 RON CALLOWAY-OF
23 BRIAN SCHNEIDER-C
24 NICK JOHNSON (INJ)-1B
28 JERRY MORALES-CH
29 MATT CEPICKY-OF
30 TIM (ROCK) RAINES-CH
31 SUN WOO KIM-P
32 CHAD CORDERO-P
33 CLAUDIO VARGAS-P
34 TOMO OHKA (INJ)-P
35 VAL PASCUCCI-OF
36 TONY ARMAS, JR. (INJ)-P
37 LUIS LOPEZ-1B
37 SCOTT DOWNS-P
38 RYAN CHURCH-OF
39 FRANCIS, BELTRAN (INJ)-P (2)
40 JEREMY FICAK-P
42 *(RET#) JACKIE ROBINSON*
(43) DAN SMITH (INJ)-(P)
45 EDDIE RODRIGUEZ-CH
47 ROY CORCORAN-P
49 RANDY ST. CLAIRE-CH
49 SHAWN HILL-P
50 RIGO BELTRAN-P
50 GARY MAJEWSKI-P
51 JON RAUCH (INJ)-P (2)
52 T. J. TUCKER-P
53 JUAN RIVERA-OF
54 ZACH DAY (INJ)-P
56 LUIS AYALA-P
57 CHAD BENTZ-P
58 JOEY EISCHEN (INJ)-P
59 JOE HORGAN-P
60 ROCKY BIDDLE-P
61 LIVAN HERNANDEZ-P

2005
WASHINGTON NATIONALS

5TH E *81-81* *9GB*

00 BRANDON WATSON-OF
1 TYRELL GOODWIN-OF
2 JAMEY CARROLL-2B
3 JOSE VIDRO (INJ)-2B
4 HENRY MATEO (INJ)-2B
4 DEIVI CRUZ-INF (2)
5 CARLOS BAERGA-INF
6 JOSE GUILLEN (SUS:1G)-OF
7 BRAD WILKERSON-OF/1B
8 *(RET#) GARY CARTER*
9 VINNY CASTILLA-3B
10 *(RET#) RUSTY STAUB*
10 *(RET#) ANDRE DAWSON*
11 JEFFREY HAMMONDS (INJ) (RET)-OF
11 JUNIOR SPIVEY-2B (2)
12 DON BUFORD-CH
13 ANTONIO OSUNA (INJ) (REL)-P
14 EDDIE RODRIGUEZ-CH
15 CRISTIAN GUZMAN-SS
16 BOB NATAL-CH
17 TOM MCCRAW-CH
18 TERRMEL SLEDGE (INJ)-OF
19 RYAN CHURCH-OF
20 FRANK ROBINSON-MGR
21 ESTEBAN LOAIZA-P
22 JOHN PATTERSON (INJ)-P
23 BRIAN SCHNEIDER-C
24 NICK JOHNSON (INJ)-1B
25 WIL CORDERO (INJ)(REL)-1B
25 RYAN ZIMMERMAN-3B
26 J. J. DAVIS-OF
26 MARLON BYRD-UTIL (2)
28 TONY BLANCO (INJ)-OF
29 GARY BENNETT-C
30 *(RET#) TIM RAINES*
31 SUN WOO (SUNNY) KIM-P (1)
31 DARRELL RASNER-P
32 CHAD CORDERO-P
34 TOMO OHKA (INJ)-P (1)
34 TRAVIS HUGHES-P
35 RICK SHORT-2B
36 TONY ARMAS, JR. (INJ)-P
37 DAVE HUPPERT-CH
38 GARY MAJEWSKI-P
39 KENNY KELLY-OF (2)
40 ZACH DAY (INJ)-P (1)
42 *(RET#) JACKIE ROBINSON*
44 PRESTON WILSON-OF (2)
45 CLAUDIO VARGAS (INJ)-P (1)
45 RYAN DRESE-P (2)
46 RANDY ST. CLAIRE-CH
47 ENDY CHAVEZ-OF (1)
47 C. J. NITKOWSKI-P
47 MATT CEPICKY-P
47 MATT WHITE-P
48 HECTOR CARRASCO-P
51 JON RAUCH (INJ)-P
52 T. J. TUCKER (INJ)-P
54 BRENDAN HARRIS-3B
54 JOHN HALAMA (REL)-P (2)
55 KEITH OSIK-C
56 LUIS AYALA-P
57 JASON BERGMANN-P
58 JOEY EISCHEN (INJ)-P
61 LIVAN HERNANDEZ-P

Tim Raines played for the Expos for 13 seasons. He was one of the most exciting players to watch. He was always a threat to get on base and then to steal another. He finished with a .294 BA, had 113 triples and stole 808 bases with one of the highest percentages in the history of the game. Rock led the league in steals 4 times, and was once the batting champ in 1986 with .334. A seven-time All-Star with Montreal looks on as Tim Raines, Jr. tries to follow in his footsteps, very tough shoes to fill. With the Montreal franchise moving to Washington for the 2005 season, many of the great Montreal teams (especially 1994 when they might have gone to the World Series if there were one) and much of the fantastic talent that was developed there may soon be forgotten.

The Best: Number by Number

Imagine a team where Hall of Famers Goose Goslin, Jim Bottomley, Al Simmons, Bill Terry and Heinie Manush couldn't even make it!

All of these players wore #3 during their careers, but so did Jimmie Foxx, Ducky Medwick, Earl Averill, Chuck Klein and Babe Ruth.

What an exciting thing it would be if we could ignore the sands of time and create the best possible teams, "Dream Teams," of all the players who wore the same number. Just imagine the fun it would be to watch all the number 4's running around the field. Of course, no names would be worn on the shirts either. And the P. A. announcer would inform the crowd, "Pinch-hitting for number 4, is number 4..."

Such Dream Teams have been selected for the numbers 1--50. Each team consists of eight position players, a pinch-hitter/DH, a utility player, a right-handed and left-handed pitcher, a reliever plus a manager and two coaches.

An effective cross-section of the players eligible was needed to determine the teams. Inequities appear to exist in every ranking method used today. New formulae were created to show a position player in an average yearly performance offensively and defensively, and against the competition of his day.

What was wanted was the player at the peak of his abilities averaged across his career. League leading statistics were viewed as evidence of his level against his contemporaries.

Pitchers were inspected by average yearly numbers, the quality of the inning pitched and how they fared versus their competitors.

Relief pitchers were measured against other relievers. Giving the save as much credence as a win made it easier to select the better fireman. If all pitchers were to be evaluated on an equal basis, the save would be worth 33% of a win at best. However, it was unnecessary to do that here.

More complete statistical listings can be found in "Ground Rules" on page 521.

Here are the formulae that were used:

POSITION PLAYER FORMULA

1. RUNS/YR + HITS/YR + HR/YR + RBI/YR + SB/YR = GROSS # (GRO)
2. B AV + OB AV + SLG AV + DEF TITLES*/YR + OFF TITLES**/YR ÷ 5 = TOTAL AVERAGES (TOT AV)
3. (TOT AV x 1000) + GROSS = PLAYER #

PITCHER FORMULA

1. WINS/YR + SHUTOUTS/YR + SAVES/YR = GROSS # (GRO)
2. H/IP + HR/IP + BB/IP - K/IP =QUALITY INNING (QI)
3. GROSS - ERA = CUMULATIVE # (CUM)
4. W/L% + P TITLES§/YR - QI ÷ 3 = AVERAGING (AVG)
5. (CUM x 100) + (AVG x 1000) = PITCHER #

**Defensive Titles included are fielding percentage and/ or Gold Glove. (One or the other, no duplication.)*

***Offensive Titles included are: runs, hits, 2B, 3B, HR, RBI, BB, B AV, OB AV, SLG AV and SB.*

§Pitching Titles included are: wins, shutouts, saves, innings, complete games, W/L %, strikeouts, ERA, OPP B AV, and OPP OnBase AV.

If a player had worn that Dream Team's particular number, his entire career was considered as an entity and qualified him for that team. However, only the position(s) that the player actually played while wearing that number were permitted.

A player may have worn a certain number in the twilight of his career, but here we considered the player's entire career as a unit and therefore the player at his peak was the player on any given team in any number.

Some teams were exceptionally tough to choose. Many favorites had to be overlooked to be true to the numbers. Offensive, defensive and pitching titles have swung the tide in favor of many players, while some outstanding players without any titles may have finished second. I have tried to be fair in those cases. Andre Dawson won few titles, but was one of the perennial stars of his era, so he did make Teams 8 and 10. Richie Ashburn won many titles that soared him above many star players. He still made Team 1 though.

A point system was established to help in the selection of the managers. In the case where no manager had worn a number (#48), coaches who had managed during their careers were evaluated. Interim managers weren't used.

A manager got one point for winning a divisional title, three points for winning the pennant, five points for a World Series win and three points for the highest won/lost % in that particular group competing. If a tie, the manager with a World Series title won. If neither of them had a Series win, then the best won/lost percentage as a manager earned the job.

Coaches were selected by years of service, the theory being that they must have been doing something right. In case of a tie, the nod went to anyone with managerial experience. If neither had any, the one with the higher "Player Number" was chosen.

Each team's official stats are listed while an additional line is added showing the formulated stats. The team as a whole is enumerated as well.

On the pages following immediately are Dream Teams 1-9, 11, 14, 16, 19, 21, 24, 26, 29 and 32 in detail. Following that are the remaining teams through 50.

HOW TO READ THE TEAM CHART

Let's follow Jim Bottomley's line as an example of a position player. The top line is his career stats: 1,177 runs scored, 2,313 hits, 219 homeruns, 1,422 runs batted in, 58 stolen bases, .310 batting average, .369 on-base average, .500 slug-ging percentage and he fielded .988. The second line shows calculations based on his 16 years of playing: he scored 73.5 runs a year, had 144.5 hits per year, 13.6 homeruns a year, 88.8 runs knocked in a year and 3.6 steals. He never lead the league in fielding, but lead in 7 offensive categories. The **Total Averages** column averages 5 percentages: (.323) batting, on base, slugging, defensive titles and offensive titles per career. (These two columns are seen in "Ground Rules"). The **Gross** (324.0) adds up the first 5 calculations. The **Player #** (647.0) adds Total Averages (remove the decimal) and Gross Number.

Use Matt Young as an example for pitching. The top row of numbers are career stats: he won 55 games, had 5 shutouts, saved 25 more, gave up 1,207 hits, 99 homeruns, 565 walks and struck out 857. His won/lost % was .367 and his ERA 4.40. The bottom row shows that in his 10-year career he averaged 5.5 wins a year, .5 shutouts, and 2.5 saves. He pitched 1,190 innings. He gave up 1.014 hits, .083 homeruns, .474 walks and struck out .720 batters each inning. Adding the hits, homers and walks, then subtracting the strikeouts gives a **Quality Inning (QI)** of .851. If a pitcher yields less and strikes out more, his QI is reduced, the lower the better. He won no pitching titles **(PIT)** and adding the averages of W, SH, and SV gives him a **GROSS (GRO)** of 8.5. His **Cumulative # (CUM)** of 4.10 subtracts the ERA from the GRO. **Averaging (AVG)** -0.161 is the result of adding the W/L% and the pitching titles per career (See "Ground Rules") and subtracting the QI then dividing by three. The **Pitcher #** (249) adds or subtracts the AVG from the CUM. (For pitchers, the decimals are removed to arrive at the number.)

TEAM 1		R	H	HR	RBI	SB	B AV	OB AV	SG AV	FA		TOT		PLAY
MGR BILL McKECHNIE	YRS	R/YR	H/YR	HR/Y	RBI/Y	SB/Y				DEF	OFF	AV	GRO	#
1B JIM BOTTOMLEY		1177	2313	219	1422	58	.310	.369	.500	.988				
	16	73.5	144.5	13.6	88.8	3.6				0	7	.323	324.0	647.0
2B BOBBY DOERR		1094	2042	223	1247	54	.288	.362	.461	.980				
	14	78.1	145.8	15.9	89.0	3.8				4	2	.307	332.6	639.6
SS OZZIE SMITH		1257	2460	28	793	580	.262	.339	.328	.978				
	19	66.2	129.5	1.5	41.7	30.5				14	0	.333	269.6	602.6
3B GEORGE KELL		881	2054	78	870	51	.306	.368	.414	.969				
	15	58.7	136.9	5.2	58.0	3.4				7	5	.377	262.2	639.2
LF KENNY LOFTON		1363	2142	120	702	567	.299	.373	.425	.984				
	15	90.9	123.2	10.4	46.8	37.8				4	7	.366	326.5	692.5
CF RICHIE ASHBURN		1322	2574	29	586	234	.308	.397	.382	.983				
	15	88.1	171.6	1.9	39.0	15.8				0	16	.430	316.4	746.4
RF CHUCK KLEIN		1168	2076	300	1201	79	.320	.379	.543	.962				
	17	68.7	122.1	17.6	70.6	4.6				0	19	.471	283.6	754.6
C DEL CRANDALL		585	1276	179	657	26	.254	.315	.404	.989				
	16	36.5	79.7	11.1	41.0	1.6				4	0	.244	169.9	413.9
PH/DH EARLE COMBS		1186	1866	58	632	96	.325	.397	.462	.974				
	12	98.8	155.5	4.8	52.6	8.0				0	4	.303	319.8	622.8
UTIL PEEWEE REESE		1338	2170	126	885	232	.269	.366	.377	.962				
	16	83.6	135.6	7.8	55.3	14.5				1	3	.252	296.8	548.8

CH CROSETTI, KNOOP		W	SH	SV		H	HR	BB	K		WL%			ERA			PITCH
PITCHERS	YRS	W/Y	SH/Y	SV/Y	IP	H/IP	HR/IP	BB/IP	K/IP	QI		PIT	GRO		CUM	AVG	#
RHP LEW FONSECA		0	0	0		0	0	0	0		.000			0.00			
	1	0.0	0.0	0.0	1	.000	.000	.000	.000	.000		0	0.0		0.00	0	0
LHP MATT YOUNG		55	5	25		1207	99	565	857		.367			4.40			
	10	5.5	0.5	2.5	1190	1.014	.083	.474	.720	.851		0	8.5		4.10	-161	249
RFP DEE MOORE		0	0	0		3	0	2	3		.000			0.00			
	1	0.0	0.0	0.0	7	.428	.000	.285	.428	.285		0	0.0		0.00	-95	-95

PLAYER TOTAL **6307.4** *PITCHER TOTAL* **154** *TEAM TOTAL* **6461.4**

TEAM 1

The pitching is non-existent, but the rest of the team boasts 8 out of 10 Hall of Famers. The infield alone has won the fielding crown at their respective positions 29 times, including catcher. Offensively, they have won 63 titles. Fifty-eight times they have been chosen to All-Star teams.

Lew Fonseca pitched one game for the White Sox capping a 12-year career where he won a batting title and finished at .316 lifetime. He later capitalized on his familiarity of the game by turning to motion pictures. Most of the movie footage done professionally of Major League Baseball following WWII was done by Lew. He shot many a pennant race and World Series.

At least this team would have looked good and been well documented.

TEAM 2

Four Hall of Fame second basemen: Gehringer, Herman, Schoendienst and Fox, vied for this club. Three HOF catchers, too: Cochrane, Hartnett and the Schnozz, Lombardi. The only other position player Hall of Famer on the club is Heinie Manush in left field. Derek Jeter makes it at short.

Colorful Leo "The Lip" Durocher is beaten out by equally colorful Tommy Lasorda for manager. Everyone in the ballpark could tell Leo or Tommy without a scorecard.

Pitching leaves a lot to be desired. Bobby Reeves (-701), an infielder, is the best right-handed pitcher. Chief Hogsett (67) leads the lefties and Al Aber (18) is the best out of the bullpen. This fact drops the team to dead last.

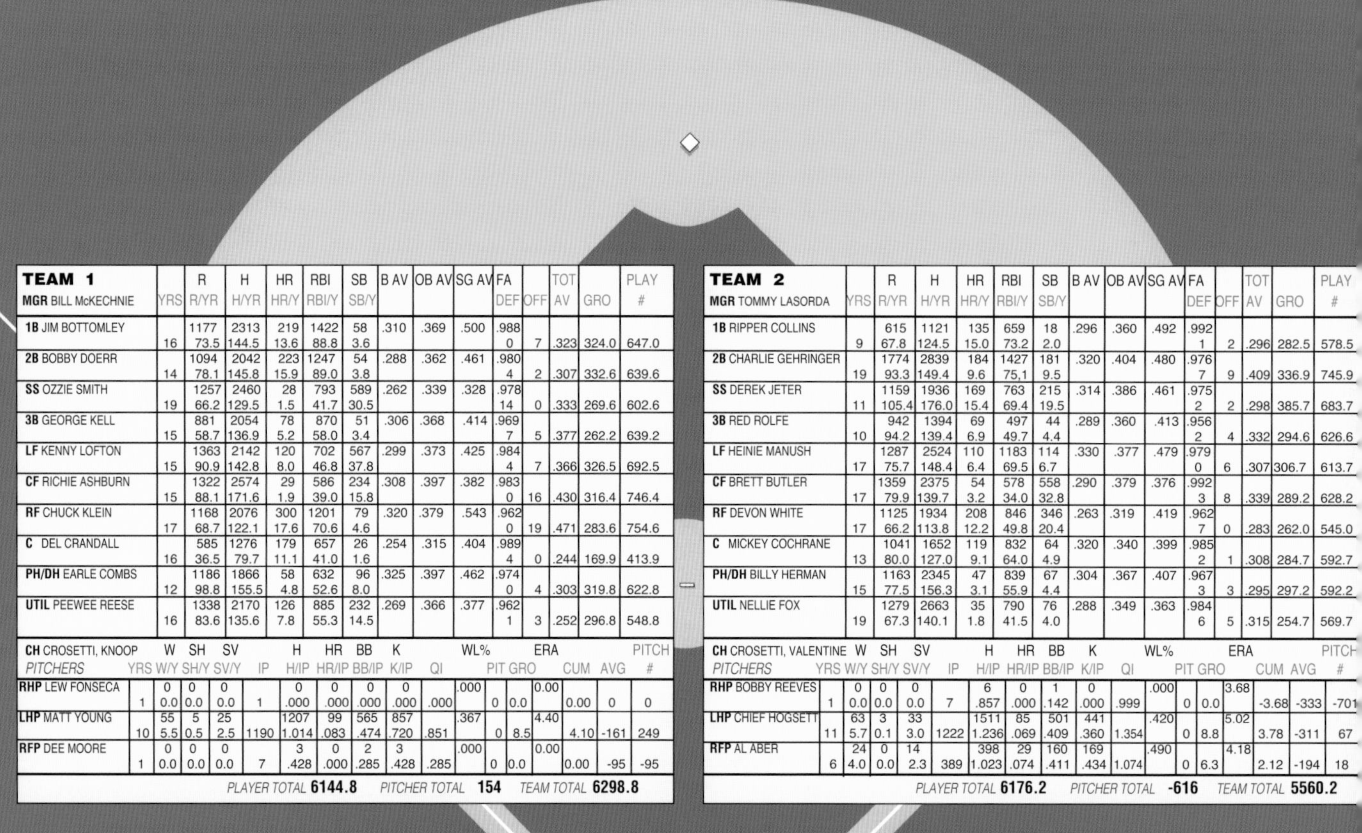

TEAM 1 — **MGR** BILL McKECHNIE

Player	YRS	R	R/YR	H	H/YR	HR	HR/Y	RBI	RBI/Y	SB	SB/Y	B AV	OB AV	SG AV	FA	DEF	OFF	TOT AV	GRO	PLAY #
1B JIM BOTTOMLEY	16	1177	73.5	2313	144.5	219	13.6	1422	88.8	58	3.6	.310	.369	.500	.988	0	7	.323	324.0	647.0
2B BOBBY DOERR	14	1094	78.1	2042	145.8	223	15.9	1247	89.0	54	3.8	.288	.362	.461	.980	4	2	.307	332.6	639.6
SS OZZIE SMITH	19	1257	66.2	2460	129.5	28	1.5	793	41.7	589	30.5	.262	.339	.328	.978	14	0	.333	269.6	602.6
3B GEORGE KELL	15	881	58.7	2054	136.9	78	5.2	870	58.0	51	3.4	.306	.368	.414	.969	7	5	.377	262.2	639.2
LF KENNY LOFTON	15	1363	90.9	2142	142.8	120	8.0	702	46.8	567	37.8	.299	.373	.425	.984	4	7	.366	326.5	692.5
CF RICHIE ASHBURN	15	1322	88.1	2574	171.6	29	1.9	586	39.0	234	15.8	.308	.397	.382	.983	0	16	.430	316.4	746.4
RF CHUCK KLEIN	17	1168	68.7	2076	122.1	300	17.6	1201	70.6	79	4.6	.320	.379	.543	.962	0	19	.471	283.6	754.6
C DEL CRANDALL	16	585	36.5	1276	79.7	179	11.1	657	41.0	26	1.6	.254	.315	.404	.989	4	0	.244	169.9	413.9
PH/DH EARLE COMBS	12	1186	98.8	1866	155.5	58	4.8	632	52.6	96	8.0	.325	.397	.462	.974	0	4	.303	319.8	622.8
UTIL PEEWEE REESE	16	1338	83.6	2170	135.6	126	7.8	885	55.3	232	14.5	.269	.366	.377	.962	1	3	.252	296.8	548.8

CH CROSETTI, KNOOP

PITCHERS	YRS	W	W/Y	SH	SH/Y	SV	SV/Y	IP	H	H/IP	HR	HR/IP	BB	BB/IP	K	K/IP	QI	WL%	PIT	GRO	ERA	CUM	AVG	PITCH #
RHP LEW FONSECA	1	0	0.0	0	0.0	0	0.0	1	0	.000	0	.000	0	.000	0	.000	.000	.000	0	0.0	0.00	0.00	0	0
LHP MATT YOUNG	10	55	5.5	5	0.5	25	2.5	1190	1207	1.014	99	.083	565	.474	857	.720	.851	.367	0	8.5	4.40	4.10	-161	249
RFP DEE MOORE	1	0	0.0	0	0.0	0	0.0	7	3	.428	0	.000	2	.285	3	.428	.285	.000	0	0.0	0.00	0.00	-95	-95

PLAYER TOTAL **6144.8** *PITCHER TOTAL* **154** *TEAM TOTAL* **6298.8**

TEAM 2 — **MGR** TOMMY LASORDA

Player	YRS	R	R/YR	H	H/YR	HR	HR/Y	RBI	RBI/Y	SB	SB/Y	B AV	OB AV	SG AV	FA	DEF	OFF	TOT AV	GRO	PLAY #
1B RIPPER COLLINS	9	615	67.8	1121	124.5	135	15.0	659	73.2	18	2.0	.296	.360	.492	.992	1	2	.296	282.5	578.5
2B CHARLIE GEHRINGER	19	1774	93.3	2839	149.4	184	9.6	1427	75,1	181	9.5	.320	.404	.480	.976	7	9	.409	336.9	745.9
SS DEREK JETER	11	1159	105.4	1936	176.0	169	15.4	763	69.4	215	19.5	.314	.386	.461	.975	2	2	.298	385.7	683.7
3B RED ROLFE	10	942	94.2	1394	139.4	69	6.9	497	49.7	44	4.4	.289	.360	.413	.956	2	4	.332	294.6	626.6
LF HEINIE MANUSH	17	1287	75.7	2524	148.4	110	6.4	1183	69.5	114	6.7	.330	.377	.479	.979	0	6	.307	306.7	613.7
CF BRETT BUTLER	17	1359	79.9	2375	139.7	54	3.2	578	34.0	558	32.8	.290	.379	.376	.992	3	8	.339	289.2	628.2
RF DEVON WHITE	17	1125	66.2	1934	113.8	208	12.2	846	49.8	346	20.4	.263	.319	.419	.962	7	0	.283	262.0	545.0
C MICKEY COCHRANE	13	1041	80.0	1652	127.0	119	9.1	832	64.0	64	4.9	.320	.340	.399	.985	2	1	.308	284.7	592.7
PH/DH BILLY HERMAN	15	1163	77.5	2345	156.3	47	3.1	839	55.9	67	4.4	.304	.367	.407	.967	3	3	.295	297.2	592.2
UTIL NELLIE FOX	19	1279	67.3	2663	140.1	35	1.8	790	41.5	76	4.0	.288	.349	.363	.984	6	5	.315	254.7	569.7

CH CROSETTI, VALENTINE

PITCHERS	YRS	W	W/Y	SH	SH/Y	SV	SV/Y	IP	H	H/IP	HR	HR/IP	BB	BB/IP	K	K/IP	QI	WL%	PIT	GRO	ERA	CUM	AVG	PITCH #
RHP BOBBY REEVES	1	0	0.0	0	0.0	0	0.0	7	6	.857	0	.000	1	.142	0	.000	.999	.000	0	0.0	3.68	-3.68	-333	-701
LHP CHIEF HOGSETT	11	63	5.7	3	0.1	33	3.0	1222	1511	1.236	85	.069	501	.409	441	.360	1.354	.420	0	8.8	5.02	3.78	-311	67
RFP AL ABER	6	24	4.0	0	0.0	14	2.3	389	398	1.023	29	.074	160	.411	169	.434	1.074	.490	0	6.3	4.18	2.12	-194	18

PLAYER TOTAL **6176.2** *PITCHER TOTAL* **-616** *TEAM TOTAL* **5560.2**

TEAM 3

The only positions with non-Hall of Famers are infielders Alex Rodriguez and Eric Chavez. This awesome crew had over 140 offensive titles, although Babe Ruth had 60 of them by himself. The Babe also pitched two games and had complete game victories in 1930 and 1933 while wearing #3, but how could you possibly take his bat away? David Wells, a Ruth freak, wore #3 in Boston briefly.

This crew was fifth in RBIs (12,699) and twelfth in homeruns with 2,956 even with Ruth in the lineup. Team 25 walked away with the HR title with 1,109 more than this club!

TEAM 4

The only player not in the Hall of Fame is shortstop Miguel Tejada. This powerhouse is near the top in offense, but fields awful pitching. Charlie Root is the only bonafide pitcher, the others are position players that filled in.

This group will need all the runs it can get to offset the pitching. But take a look at this murderer's row. They've won over 125 offensive titles with great hitting and great power. They have combined for over 3,300 HRs, gotten more than 22,000 hits, scored more than 13,000 runs, and knocked in another 12,000+ runs. Seven of ten bat over .300; four slug over .500 while two are over .600. Awesome!

Only Molitor shows some speed though.

TEAM 3 **MGR** BILL TERRY	YRS	R R/YR	H H/YR	HR HR/Y	RBI RBI/Y	SB SB/Y	B AV	OB AV	SG AV	FA DEF	OFF	TOT AV	GRO	PLAY #
1B JIMMIE FOXX	20	1751 87.5	2646 132.3	534 26.7	1922 96.1	87 4.3	.325	.428	.609	.992 3	21	.512	346.9	858.9
2B FRANKIE FRISCH	19	1532 80.6	2880 151.5	105 5.5	1244 65.4	419 22.0	.316	.369	.432	.974 3	5	.307	325.0	632.0
SS ALEX RODRIGUEZ	12	1245 103.8	1901 158.4	429 35.8	1226 102.2	226 18.8	.307	.385	.577	.978 2	14	.520	419.6	939.6
3B ERIC CHAVEZ	8	593 85.6	1026 149.2	190 27.1	644 93.1	40 5.8	.275	.350	.496	.965 3	1	.320	360.4	680.4
LF DUCKY MEDWICK	17	1198 70.4	2471 145.3	205 12.0	1383 81.3	42 2.4	.324	.362	.505	.980 1	13	.402	311.4	713.4
CF EARL AVERILL	13	1224 94.1	2019 155.3	238 18.3	1164 89.5	70 5.3	.318	.395	.534	.970 0	2	.280	362.5	642.5
RF BABE RUTH	22	2174 98.8	2873 130.5	714 32.4	2213 100.5	123 5.5	.342	.474	.690	.968 1	60	.855	367.7	1222.7
C MICKEY COCHRANE	13	1041 80.0	1652 127.0	119 9.1	832 64.0	64 4.9	.320	.340	.399	.985 2	1	.308	284.7	592.7
PH/DH CHUCK KLEIN	17	1168 68.7	2076 122.1	300 17.6	1201 70.6	79 4.6	.320	.379	.543	.962 0	19	.471	283.6	754.6
UTIL GEORGE KELL	15	881 58.7	2054 136.9	78 5.2	870 58.0	51 3.4	.306	.368	.414	.969 7	5	.377	262.2	639.2

CH J. TURNER, HARDER *PITCHERS*	YRS	W W/Y	SH SH/Y	SV SV/Y	IP	H H/IP	HR HR/IP	BB BB/IP	K K/IP	QI	WL%	PIT	GRO	ERA	CUM	AVG	PITCH #
RHP SYL JOHNSON	19	112 5.8	11 0.5	43 2.2	2165	2290 1.057	173 .079	488 .225	920 .424	.937	489	0	8.5	4.06	4.44	-149	295
LHP DAVID WELLS	19	227 11.9	12 0.6	13 0.7	3206	3337 1.041	374 .117	665 .207	2081 .649	.716	.614	7	13.2	4.06	9.14	89	1003
RFP DOOLEY WOMACK	19 5	0 3.8	24 0.0	4.8	302	253 .837	21 .069	111 .367	177 .586	.687	.514	0	8.6	2.95	5.65	-57	508

PLAYER TOTAL **7676.0** *PITCHER TOTAL* **1806** *TEAM TOTAL* **9482.0**

TEAM 4 **MGR** EARL WEAVER	YRS	R R/YR	H H/YR	HR HR/Y	RBI RBI/Y	SB SB/Y	B AV	OB AV	SG AV	FA DEF	OFF	TOT AV	GRO	PLAY #
1B LOU GEHRIG	17	1888 111.0	2721 160.0	493 29.0	1995 117.3	102 6.0	.340	.447	.601	.991 0	27	.601	423.3	1024.3
2B BILLY HERMAN	15	1163 77.5	2345 156.3	47 3.1	839 55.9	67 4.4	.304	.367	.407	.967 3	3	.295	297.2	592.2
SS MIGUEL TEJADA	9	770 85.6	1370 152.2	216 24.0	852 94.7	58 6.4	.280	.338	.477	.970 0	2	.264	362.9	626.9
3B PAUL MOLITOR	21	1782 84.9	3319 158.0	234 11.1	1307 62.2	504 24.0	.306	.372	.448	.950 0	8	.301	340.6	641.6
LF RALPH KINER	10	971 97.1	1451 145.1	369 36.9	1015 101.5	22 2.2	.279	.398	.548	.974 0	16	.565	382.8	947.8
CF DUKE SNIDER	18	1259 69.9	2116 117.5	407 22.6	1333 74.0	99 5.5	.295	.381	.540	.985 0	10	.354	289.5	643.5
RF MEL OTT	22	1859 84.5	2876 130.7	511 23.2	1860 84.5	89 4.0	.304	.414	.533	.980 0	20	.441	326.9	767.9
C ERNIE LOMBARDI	17	601 35.3	1792 105.4	190 11.1	990 58.2	8 0.4	.306	.358	.460	.979 0	1	.236	210.4	446.4
PH/DH JIMMIE FOXX	20	1751 87.5	2646 132.3	534 26.7	1922 96.1	87 4.3	.325	.428	.609	.992 3	21	.512	346.9	858.9
UTIL CHUCK KLEIN	17	1168 68.7	2076 122.1	300 17.6	1201 70.6	79 4.6	.320	.379	.543	.962 0	19	.471	283.6	754.6

CH ROARKE, CONNORS *PITCHERS*	YRS	W W/Y	SH SH/Y	SV SV/Y	IP	H H/IP	HR HR/IP	BB BB/IP	K K/IP	QI	WL%	PIT	GRO	ERA	CUM	AVG	PITCH #
RHP CHARLIE ROOT	17	201 11.8	21 1.2	40 2.4	3197	3252 1.017	187 .058	889 .278	1459 .456	.897	.557	4	15.4	3.59	11.81	-35	1146
LHP ART MAHAN	1	0 0.0	0 0.0	0 0.0	1	1 1	0 .000	0 .000	0 .000	1.000	.000	0	0.0	0.00	0.00	-333	-333
RFP DARRIN JACKSON	0 1	0 0.0	0 0.0	0.0	3 2	0 1.500	2 .000	0 1.000	.000	.000 2.500		0	9.00 0.0		-9.00	-833	-1733

PLAYER TOTAL **7304.1** *PITCHER TOTAL* **-920** *TEAM TOTAL* **6384.1**

TEAM 5

This may be the classiest Dream Team with the likes of Joe DiMaggio, Hank Greenberg, Hank Aaron, Arky Vaughan and Brooks Robinson as ambassadors. Fans may argue with Brooks' selection over George Brett for third base, but his 11 fielding titles plus 16 consecutive Gold Gloves compared to one Gold Glove for Brett is pretty persuasive. And he's no slouch with the bat.

Young Albert Pujols pushed Greenberg to leftfield. The PH/DH is Jeff Bagwell. Most of the position players are Hall of Famers. The others will most likely become members.

This powerhouse leads in RBIs (13,705), is second in hits (22,902) and third in HRs (3,345).

Lefty Billy Pierce brings some respectability to the pitching corps.

TEAM 6

By playing Stan Musial at first base, this Dream Team can add Joe Medwick to the lineup. One controversial selection is Joe Gordon over Tony Lazzari. Year after year Gordon was consistently higher in output, Lazzeri played longer adding to his numbers. Even though Tony Oliva's numbers seem better than Al Kaline's, with Oliva's bad knees, how could you not play nonpareil Kaline in right field?

Jimmy Rollins and Scott Rolen take over the left side of the infield replacing two old Red Sox: Johnny Pesky and Joe Cronin.

Fortunately for Team 6, Bob Lemon wore #6 as a third baseman/outfielder when the Indians began using him as a pitcher.

A Yankee rookie patrols center field.

TEAM 5 **MGR** DAVEY JOHNSON	YRS	R R/YR	H H/YR	HR HR/Y	RBI RBI/Y	SB SB/Y	B AV	OB AV	SG AV	FA DEF	OFF	TOT AV	GRO	PLAY #
1B ALBERT PUJOLS	5	629 125.8	982 196.4	201 40.2	621 124.2	29 5.8	.332	.416	.621	.988 0	6	.514	492.8	1006.8
2B TONY LAZZERI	14	986 70.4	1840 131.4	178 12.7	1191 85.0	148 10.5	.292	.380	.467	.967 0	0	.227	310.0	537.0
SS ARKY VAUGHAN	14	1173 83.7	2103 150.2	96 6.8	926 66.1	118 8.4	.318	.406	.453	.951 0	15	.449	315.2	764.2
3B BROOKS ROBINSON	23	1232 53.5	2848 123.8	268 11.6	1357 59.0	28 1.2	.267	.325	.401	.971 16	1	.346	249.5	595.5
LF HANK GREENBERG	13	1051 80.8	1628 125.2	331 25.4	1276 98.1	58 4.4	.313	.412	.605	.991 1	14	.496	333.9	829.9
CF JOE DIMAGGIO	13	1390 106.9	2214 170.3	361 27.7	1537 118.2	30 2.3	.325	.398	.579	.978 1	10	.429	425.9	854.9
RF HANK AARON	23	2174 94.5	3771 163.9	755 32.8	2297 99.8	240 10.4	.305	.377	.555	.980 0	23	.447	401.4	848.9
C JOHNNY BENCH	17	1091 64.1	2048 120.4	389 22.8	1376 80.9	68 4.0	.267	.345	.476	.990 10	5	.394	292.2	686.2
PH/DH JEFF BAGWELL	15	1517 101.1	2314 154.3	449 29.9	1529 101.7	202 13.5	.297	.408	.540	.993 0	8	.356	400.1	756.1
UTIL GEORGE BRETT	21	1583 75.4	3154 150.2	317 15.1	1595 76.0	201 20.0	.305	.373	.487	.951 1	15	.385	326.7	711.7

CH AMALFITANO, GRISSOM *PITCHERS*	YRS	W W/Y	SH SH/Y	SV SV/Y	IP	H H/IP	HR HR/IP	BB BB/IP	K K/IP	QI	WL%	PIT	GRO	ERA	CUM	AVG	PITCH #
RHP JOHN HUTCHINGS	6	12 2.0	3 0.5	6 1.0	471	474 1.006	36 .076	180 .382	212 .450	1.014	.400	0	3.5	3.96	-0.46	-204	-250
LHP BILLY PIERCE	18	211 11.7	38 2.1	32 1.7	3306	2989 .904	284 .085	1178 .356	1999 .604	.741	.555	8	15.5	3.27	12.23	86	1309
RFP BEN CHAPMAN	3	8 2.6	0 0.0	0 0.0	141	147 1.042	7 .049	71 .503	65 .460	1.134	.571	0	2.6	4.50	-1.80	-187	-367

PLAYER TOTAL **7591.2** *PITCHER TOTAL* **692** *TEAM TOTAL* **8283.2**

TEAM 6 **MGR** JOE TORRE	YRS	R R/YR	H H/YR	HR HR/Y	RBI RBI/Y	SB SB/Y	B AV	OB AV	SG AV	FA DEF	OFF	TOT AV	GRO	PLAY #
1B STAN MUSIAL	22	1949 88.5	3630 165.0	475 21.5	1951 88.6	78 3.5	.331	.418	.559	.984 3	46	.706	367.1	1073.1
2B JOE GORDON	11	914 83.0	1530 139.0	253 23.0	975 88.6	89 8.1	.268	.357	.466	.970 0	0	.218	341.7	559.7
SS JIMMY ROLLINS	6	503 83.8	904 150.6	59 9.8	308 51.3	171 28.5	.273	.328	.414	.981 1	4	.370	324.0	694.0
3B SCOTT ROLEN	10	805 94.2	1300 139.4	231 6.9	859 49.7	92 4.4	.284	.375	.515	.966 6	0	.356	328.3	684.3
LF DUCKY MEDWICK	17	1198 70.4	2471 145.3	205 12.0	1383 81.3	42 2.4	.324	.362	.505	.980 1	13	.402	311.4	713.4
CF MICKEY MANTLE	18	1677 93.1	2415 134.1	536 29.7	1509 83.8	153 8.5	.298	.423	.557	.992 2	25	.555	349.2	904.2
RF AL KALINE	22	1622 73.7	3007 136.6	399 18.1	1583 71.9	137 6.2	.297	.379	.480	.986 11	4	.367	306.5	673.5
C MICKEY TETTLETON	14	711 50.8	1132 80.9	245 24.6	732 52.3	23 1.6	.241	.372	.449	.991 1	1	.241	210.0	451.0
PH/DH ROCKY COLAVITO	14	971 69.3	1730 123.5	374 26.7	1159 82.7	19 2.0	.266	.362	.489	.980 1	4	.294	511.1	805.1
UTIL TONY OLIVA	15	870 58.0	1917 127.8	220 14.6	947 63.1	86 5.7	.304	.356	.476	.975 0	14	.413	269.2	682.2

CH COX, FITZSIMMONS *PITCHERS*	YRS	W W/Y	SH SH/Y	SV SV/Y	IP	H H/IP	HR HR/IP	BB BB/IP	K K/IP	QI	WL%	PIT	GRO	ERA	CUM	AVG	PITCH #
RHP BOB LEMON	13	207 15.9	31 2.3	22 1.6	2850	2559 .897	181 .063	1251 .438	1277 .448	.950	.618	15	19.8	3.23	16.57	273	1930
LHP EDDIE SMITH	10	73 7.3	8 0.8	12 1.2	1595	1554 .974	106 .066	739 463	694 .435	1.068	.392	0	9.3	3.82	5.48	-225	323
RFP CY BLANTON	9	68 7.5	14 1.5	4 0.4	1218	1243 1.020	64 .052	337 .276	611 .501	.847	.489	5	9.4	4.52	5.85	197	782

PLAYER TOTAL **7240.5** *PITCHER TOTAL* **3035** *TEAM TOTAL* **10275.5**

TEAM 7

Five out ot ten position players are Hall of Famers. Ivan Rodriguez beats out Lombardi by a nose for catcher. HOFer Chuck Klein is the PH/DH over Heinie Manush and Al Rosen.

A tougher choice was at first base where Hal Trosky, "Old Reliable" Tommy Henrich and slick-fielding Vic Power competed for the slot. Trosky showed more power as well as hitting for average more consistently. Bonds wore #7 when he broke in with the Pirates creating an awesome outfield of Bonds, Mantle and Medwick.

Future Hall hopeful, Craig Biggio, ekes out Hall of Famer George Kell for the ultility player.

A forgotten George Earnshaw leads a modest pitching staff.

TEAM 8

Nearly 80 offensive titles and 21 Gold Gloves are present on this Dream Team. A surprise for many fans may be the selection of Bill Dickey over Yogi Berra. Dickey hit for a higher average, was more selective and was a better defensive man. Although he homered less and had fewer RBI, he outslugged Berra.

This is a very team-oriented group with Willie "We Are Family" Stargell, Joe Morgan, Bob "Mr. Team" Elliott and Yaz. Clutch playing and endurance marks this team also. Many are known to play hurt when the chips are down. Ripken played every day, Dawson and Stargell have toughed it out through many injuries.

The pitching staff is comprised of old time-worn veterans: Schoolboy Rowe, Don Shaw and Bobo Newsom.

TEAM 7 **MGR** CHARLIE GRIMM	YRS	R R/YR	H H/YR	HR HR/Y	RBI RBI/Y	SB SB/Y	B AV	OB AV	SG AV	FA DEF	OFF	TOT AV	GRO	PLAY #
1B HAL TROSKY	11	835 75.9	1561 141.9	228 20.7	1012 92.0	28 2.5	.302	.371	.522	.991 0	1	.257	333.0	590.0
2B RED SCHOENDIENST	19	1223 64.3	2449 128.8	84 4.4	773 40.6	89 4.6	.289	.338	.387	.983 1	8	.297	242.7	539.7
SS HARVEY KUENN	15	951 63.4	2092 139.4	87 5.8	671 44.7	68 4.5	.303	.359	.408	.978 1	8	.333	257.8	590.8
3B EDDIE MATHEWS	17	1509 88.7	2315 136.1	512 30.1	1453 85.4	68 4.0	.271	.378	.509	.956 1	7	.325	344.3	669.3
LF DUCKY MEDWICK	17	1198 70.4	2471 145.3	205 12.0	1383 81.3	42 2.4	.324	.362	.505	.980 1	13	.402	311.4	713.4
CF MICKEY MANTLE	18	1677 93.1	2415 134.1	536 29.7	1509 83.8	153 8.5	.298	.423	.557	.992 2	25	.555	349.2	904.2
RF BARRY BONDS	20	2078 103.9	2742 137.1	708 35.4	1853 92.7	506 25.3	.300	.442	.611	.984 0	31	.581	394.2	975.2
C IVAN RODRIGUEZ	15	1085 72.3	2190 146.0	264 17.6	1050 70.0	104 6.9	.304	.343	.487	.990 11	0	.374	312.5	686.5
PH/DH CHUCK KLEIN	17	1168 68.7	2076 122.1	300 17.6	1201 70.6	79 4.6	.320	.379	.543	.962 0	19	.471	283.6	754.6
UTIL CRAIG BIGGIO	18	1697 94.3	2795 155.3	260 14.4	1063 59.1	407 22.6	.285	.370	.437	.985 5	6	.341	345.3	686.3

CH WINE, RIPKEN *PITCHERS*	YRS	W W/Y	SH SH/Y	SV SV/Y	IP	H H/IP	HR HR/IP	BB BB/IP	K K/IP	QI	WL%	PIT	GRO	ERA	CUM	AVG	PITCH #
RHP GEO. EARNSHAW	9	127 14.1	18 2.0	12 1.3	1915	1981 1.034	142 .074	809 .422	1002 .523	1.007	.577	3	17.4	4.38	13.02	-32	1270
LHP K.RAFF'NSBERGER	15	119 7.9	31 2.0	16 1.0	2151	2257 1.049	192 .089	449 .208	806 .374	.972	.436	3	10.9	3.60	7.30	-112	618
RFP JOSH TOWERS	5	38 7.6	2 0.4	1 0.2	557	659 1.183	87 .156	83 .149	276 .496	.992	.521	0	8.2	4.49	3.71	-157	214

PLAYER TOTAL **7110.0** *PITCHER TOTAL* **2102** *TEAM TOTAL* **9212.0**

TEAM 8 **MGR** YOGI BERRA	YRS	R R/YR	H H/YR	HR HR/Y	RBI RBI/Y	SB SB/Y	B AV	OB AV	SG AV	FA DEF	OFF	TOT AV	GRO	PLAY #
1B WILLIE STARGELL	21	1195 56.9	2232 106.2	475 22.6	1540 73.3	17 0.8	.282	.363	.529	.961 1	5	.291	259.8	550.8
2B JOE MORGAN	22	1650 75.0	2517 114.4	268 12.1	1133 51.5	689 31.3	.271	.395	.427	.981 3	11	.345	284.3	629.3
SS CAL RIPKEN	21	1647 78.4	3184 151.6	431 20.5	1695 80.7	36 1.7	.276	.340	.447	.977 6	3	.299	332.3	631.3
3B BOB ELLIOTT	15	1064 70.9	2061 137.4	170 11.3	1195 79.6	60 4.0	.289	.375	.440	.947 1	1	.247	303.2	550.2
LF CARL YASTRZEMSKI	23	1816 78.9	3419 148.6	452 19.6	1844 80.1	168 7.3	.285	.382	.462	.981 1	23	.434	334.5	768.5
CF ANDRE DAWSON	21	1373 65.4	2774 132.1	438 20.9	1596 75.8	314 15.0	.279	.327	.482	.983 8	3	.322	309.6	631.6
RF CHUCK KLEIN	17	1168 68.7	2076 122.1	300 17.6	1201 70.6	79 4.6	.320	.379	.543	.962 0	19	.471	283.6	754.6
C BILL DICKEY	17	930 54.7	1969 115.8	202 11,8	1209 71.1	36 2.1	.313	.382	.486	.988 4	0	.283	255.5	538.5
PH/DH ALBERT BELLE	12	974 80.3	1726 143.8	381 31.8	1239 103.3	88 7.3	.295	.369	.564	.976 0	8	.379	366.5	745.5
UTIL N. GARCIAPARRA	10	765 76.5	1395 139.5	191 19.1	740 74.0	86 8.6	.320	.367	.544	.968 0	5	.346	317.9	663.9

CH GRIMM, BUSBY *PITCHERS*	YRS	W W/Y	SH SH/Y	SV SV/Y	IP	H H/IP	HR HR/IP	BB BB/IP	K K/IP	QI	WL%	PIT	GRO	ERA	CUM	AVG	PITCH #
RHP SCH'LBOY ROWE	15	158 10.5	22 1.4	12 0.8	2219	2332 1.050	132 .059	558 .251	913 .411	.949	.610	3	12.7	3.87	8.83	-46	837
LHP DON SHAW	5	13 2.6	0 0.0	6 1.2	189	166 .878	19 .101	101 .534	123 .651	.862	.481	0	3.8	4.01	-0.21	-127	-148
RFP BOBO NEWSOM	20	211 10.5	31 1.5	21 1.0	3759	3769 1.002	206 .054	1732 .460	2082 .553	.963	.487	4	13.0	3.98	9.02	-92	810

PLAYER TOTAL **6464.2** *PITCHER TOTAL* **1499** *TEAM TOTAL* **7963.2**

TEAM 9

Occasionally, Matt Williams played shortstop—that's where he'll be used since third base is covered by Minnie Minoso. Imagine Ted Williams and Joe DiMaggio in the same outfield. Yankee and Red Sox fans might even talk to each other.

This group of sluggers has amassed over 3,300 home runs and knocked in over 13,000 runs.

Including pitcher Bob Feller, they have been selected to 89 All-Star teams.

The saddest note is that Bill Mazeroski was unable to find a spot on the club. Bobby Doerr's numbers are superior in every way and Joe Torre (556.4) ranks higher than Maz for the utility role.

Both Roger Maris (574.7) and Enos Slaughter (572.1) rank higher than Torre, but Torre is more adaptable for the utility role.

TEAM 11

This team has 53 offensive titles, but 9 are for stolen bases. Vince Coleman would have added 6 more SB titles, but without them his offensive and defensive numbers come up short. Consistent hitting by Edgar Martinez at PH/DH, and the across-the-decades outfield of Gary Sheffield, Duke Snider and Paul Waner make this an interesting group.

Second base was tough. Lazzeri, a Hall of Famer, loses out to a more constant Jeff Kent.

Kent has more power than Chuck Knoblauch who will fill the utility spot. Chuck beats out Barry Larkin by a whisker. This will prove unpopular in Cincinnati.

And finally some bona fide pitching: Hubbell and Sain and pray for Page.

TEAM 9 **MGR** JOE TORRE*	YRS	R R/YR	H H/YR	HR HR/Y	RBI RBI/Y	SB SB/Y	B AV	OB AV	SG AV	FA DEF	OFF	TOT AV	GRO	PLAY #
1B JOHN OLERUD	17	1139 67.0	2239 131.7	255 15.0	1230 72.5	11 0.6	.295	.398	.465	.995 4	3	.314	286.6	600.6
2B BOBBY DOERR	14	1094 78.1	2042 145.8	223 15.9	1247 89.0	54 3.8	.288	.362	.461	.980 4	2	.307	332.6	639.6
SS MATT WILLIAMS	17	997 58.6	1878 110.5	378 22.2	1218 71.6	53 3.1	.268	.317	.489	.964 4	2	.285	266.4	551.4
3B MINNIE MINOSO	17	1136 66.8	1963 115.4	186 10.9	1023 60.1	205 12.0	.298	.391	.459	.974 0	8	.323	265.2	588.2
LF TED WILLIAMS	19	1798 94.6	2654 139.6	521 27.4	1839 96.7	24 1.2	.344	.483	.634	.974 0	52	.839	359.5	1198.5
CF JOE DIMAGGIO	13	1390 106.9	2214 170.3	361 27.7	1537 118.2	30 2.3	.325	.398	.579	.978 1	10	.429	425.9	854.9
RF REGGIE JACKSON	21	1551 73.8	2584 123.0	563 26.8	1702 81.0	228 10.8	.262	.358	.490	.967 0	10	.317	315.4	632.4
C GABBY HARTNETT	20	867 43.3	1912 95.6	236 11.8	1179 58.9	28 1.4	.297	.370	.489	.984 6	0	.291	211.0	502.0
PH/DH RALPH KINER	10	971 97.1	1451 145.1	369 36.9	1015 101.5	22 2.2	.279	.398	.548	.974 0	16	.565	382.8	947.8
UTIL JOE TORRE*	18	996 55.3	2342 130.1	252 14.0	1185 65.8	23 1.2	.297	.367	.452	.990 2	3	.278	266.4	544.4

CH KITTELL, OATES *PITCHERS*	YRS	W W/Y	SH SH/Y	SV SV/Y	IP	H H/IP	HR HR/IP	BB BB/IP	K K/IP	QI	WL%	PIT	GRO	ERA	CUM	AVG	PITCH #
RHP BOB FELLER	18	266 14.7	44 2.4	21 1.1	3827	3271 .854	224 .058	1764 460	2561 .674	.698	.621	31	18.2	3.25	14.95	548	2043
LHP ROY WEIR	4	6 1.5	2 0.5	0 0.0	106	95 .896	4 .037	50 .471	42 396	1.008	.600	0	2.0	3.55	-1.55	-136	-291
RFP BUMP HADLEY	16	161 10.0	14 0.8	25 1.5	2945	2980 1.011	167 .056	1442 .489	1318 .447	1.109	.494	2	12.3	4.24	8.06	-163	643

PLAYING MANAGER* — *PLAYER TOTAL* **7059.8 *PITCHER TOTAL* **2395** *TEAM TOTAL* **9454.8**

TEAM 11 **MGR** SPARKY ANDSERSON	YRS	R R/YR	H H/YR	HR HR/Y	RBI RBI/Y	SB SB/Y	B AV	OB AV	SG AV	FA DEF	OFF	TOT AV	GRO	PLAY #
1B RICHIE SEXSON	9	586 65.1	979 108.7	239 26.6	737 81.9	11 1.2	.270	.352	.530	.993 0	0	.231	283.3	514.3
2B JEFF KENT	14	1139 81.4	2070 147.4	331 23.6	1312 93.7	92 6.6	.289	.354	.506	.978 0	0	.230	353.0	583.0
SS LUIS APARICIO	18	1335 74.1	2677 148.7	83 4.6	791 43.9	506 28.1	.262	.313	.343	.972 11	9	.406	299.4	705.4
3B EDDIE MATHEWS	17	1509 88.7	2315 136.1	512 30.1	1453 85.4	68 4.0	.271	.378	.509	.956 1	7	.325	344.3	669.3
LF GARY SHEFFIELD	18	1411 78.4	2345 130.3	449 24.9	1476 82.0	215 11.9	.297	.399	.527	.962 0	2	.267	327.3	594.3
CF DUKE SNIDER	18	1259 69.9	2116 117.5	407 22.6	1333 74.0	99 5.5	.295	.381	.540	.985 0	10	.354	289.5	643.5
RF PAUL WANER	20	1627 81.3	3152 157.6	113 5.6	1309 65.4	104 5.2	.333	.404	.474	.975 0	14	.382	315.1	697.1
C BILL FREEHAN	15	706 47.0	1591 106.0	200 13.3	758 50.5	24 1.6	.262	.342	.412	.993 7	0	.297	218.4	515.4
PH/DH EDGAR MARTINEZ	18	1219 67.7	2247 124.8	309 17.2	1261 70.1	49 2.7	.312	.418	.515	.952 0	9	.349	282.5	631.5
UTIL CHUCK KNOBLAUCH	12	1132 94.3	1839 153.3	98 8.2	615 51.3	407 33.9	.289	.378	.406	.982 2	2	.281	341.4	622.4

CH LEYLAND, BENGOUGH *PITCHERS*	YRS	W W/Y	SH SH/Y	SV SV/Y	IP	H H/IP	HR HR/IP	BB BB/IP	K K/IP	QI	WL%	PIT	GRO	ERA	CUM	AVG	PITCH #
RHP JOHNNY SAIN	11	139 12.6	16 1.4	51 4.6	2125	2145 1.009	180 .084	619 .291	910 .428	.956	.545	5	18.6	3.49	15.11	14	1525
LHP CARL HUBBELL	16	253 15.8	36 2.2	33 2.0	3590	3461 .964	227 .063	725 .201	1677 .467	.761	.622	21	20.0	2.98	17.02	391	2093
RFP JOE PAGE	8	57 7.1	1 0.1	76 9.5	790	727 .920	42 .053	421 .532	519 .656	.849	.538	2	16.7	3.53	13.17	-20	1297

PLAYER TOTAL **6176.2** *PITCHER TOTAL* **4915** *TEAM TOTAL* **11091.2**

TEAM 14

It was a real challenge to pick a first baseman: Kent Hrbek (530.4), Gil Hodges (542.7) and Andres Galarraga (599.4). Galarraga kept coming back his entire career. The Big Cat is a real fighter, let's pick him and move Hodges behind the plate.

With Pete Rose leading the band, this club banged out 23,608 base hits. Jim Rice was an easy pick for left field as was Larry Doby in center and Manush in right. But choosing between George Foster and Del Ennis for PH/DH was difficult. Foster helped lead 'The Big Red Machine' by winning 7 offensive titles from 1976-78, while Ennis had better numbers on the average in 6 out of 7 categories. It's Ennis.

Bob Feller and Vida Blue at their best wouldn't leave much for Dick Radatz to save.

TEAM 16

Joe Medwick, Jimmie Foxx and Billy Herman followed by Wade Boggs—an impressive start. All-Stars Edgar Renteria and Steve Finley are at shortstop and centerfield, respectively. Add Brian Downing's bat as the catcher, where he began his career.

The PH/DH is the outstanding hitter, Al Oliver. And what better utility player could you have than one who fields with unbelievable sureness and packs punch in his bat—Scott Rolen.

Add to that the power of Rocky Colavito and Jason Giambi.

A strong pitching staff of "The Chairman of the Board" Whitey Ford, "The Doctor" Dwight Gooden and Ron Perranoski as fireman rounds out the team.

EAM 14 GR LOU PINIELLA	YRS	R R/YR	H H/YR	HR HR/Y	RBI RBI/Y	SB SB/Y	B AV	OB AV	SG AV	FA DEF	OFF	TOT AV	GRO	PLAY #
B ANDRES GALARRAGA	19	1195 62.9	2333 127.8	399 21.0	1425 75.0	128 6.7	.288	.347	.499	.991 2	6	.311	288.4	599.4
B PETE ROSE	24	2165 90.2	4256 177.3	160 6.6	1314 54.7	198 8.2	.303	.377	.409	.991 5	20	.426	337.0	763.0
S ERNIE BANKS	19	1305 68.6	2583 135.9	512 26.9	1636 86.1	50 2.6	.274	.333	.500	.994 4	5	.337	320.1	657.1
B KEN BOYER	15	1104 86.7	2143 142.8	282 18.8	1141 76.0	105 7.0	.287	.351	.462	.952 7	1	.327	331.3	658.3
F JIM RICE	16	1249 78.0	2452 153.2	382 23.8	1451 90.6	58 3.6	.298	.356	.502	.980 0	9	.343	349.2	692.2
F LARRY DOBY	13	960 73.8	1515 116.5	253 19.4	970 74.6	47 3.6	.283	.387	.490	.983 0	6	.324	287.9	611.9
F HEINIE MANUSH	17	1287 75.7	2524 148.4	110 6.4	1183 69.5	114 6.7	.330	.377	.479	.979 0	6	.307	306.7	613.7
GIL HODGES	18	1105 61.3	1921 106.7	370 20.5	1274 70.7	63 3.5	.273	.361	.487	.992 5	0	.280	262.7	542.7
H/DH DEL ENNIS	14	985 70.3	2063 147.3	288 20.5	1284 91.7	45 3.2	.284	.341	.472	.969 0	1	.233	333.0	566.0
TIL BABE HERMAN	13	682 67.8	1818 139.8	181 13.9	997 76.7	94 7.2	.324	.383	.532	.961 0	1	.263	305.6	568.6

H SCIOSCIA, MENKE PITCHERS	YRS	W W/Y	SH SH/Y	SV SV/Y	IP	H H/IP	HR HR/IP	BB BB/IP	K K/IP	QI	WL%	PIT	GRO	ERA	CUM	AVG	PITCH #
HP BOB FELLER	18	266 14.7	44 2.4	21 1.1	3827	3271 .854	224 .056	1764 .460	2561 .674	.698	.621	31	18.2	3.25	14.95	548	2043
HP VIDA BLUE	17	209 12.2	37 2.1	2 0.1	3343	2939 .879	263 .078	1185 .354	2175 .650	.661	.565	4	14.4	3.27	11.13	46	1159
FP DICK RADATZ	7	52 7.4	0 0.0	122 17.4	693	532 .767	65 .101	296 .463	745 1.165	.166	.547	2	24.8	3.13	21.67	222	2389

PLAYER TOTAL **6272.9** *PITCHER TOTAL* **5591** *TEAM TOTAL* **11863.9**

TEAM 16 MGR JIM FREGOSI	YRS	R R/YR	H H/YR	HR HR/Y	RBI RBI/Y	SB SB/Y	B AV	OB AV	SG AV	FA DEF	OFF	TOT AV	GRO	PLAY #
1B JIMMIE FOXX	20	1751 87.5	2646 132.3	534 26.7	1922 96.1	87 4.3	.325	.428	.609	.992 3	21	.512	346.9	858.9
2B BILLY HERMAN	15	1163 77.5	2345 156.3	47 3.1	839 55.9	67 4.4	.304	.367	.407	.967 3	3	.295	297.2	592.2
SS EDGAR RENTERIA	10	834 83.4	1595 159.5	91 9.1	635 63.5	246 24.6	.288	.345	.399	.968 2	0	.247	340.1	587.1
3B WADE BOGGS	18	1513 84.1	3010 167.2	118 6.6	1014 56.3	24 1.3	.328	.419	.443	.962 3	18	.471	315.9	786.9
LF DUCKY MEDWICK	17	1198 70.4	2471 145.3	205 12.0	1383 81.3	42 2.4	.324	.362	.505	.980 1	13	.402	311.4	713.4
CF STEVE FINLEY	17	1368 80.5	2426 142.7	297 17.5	1125 66.2	313 18.4	.273	.334	.447	.987 6	2	.305	325.3	630.3
RF ROCKY COLAVITO	14	971 69.3	1730 123.5	374 26.7	1159 82.7	19 1.0	.266	.362	.489	.980 1	4	.294	511.1	805.1
C BRIAN DOWNING	20	1188 59.4	2099 105.0	275 13.8	1073 53.7	50 2.5	.267	.370	.425	.990 2	1	.242	234.8	476.8
PH/DH JASON GIAMBI	11	925 84.1	1526 138.7	313 28.5	1031 93.7	13 1.2	.295	.413	.539	.991 3	3	.377	346.4	723.4
UTIL SCOTT ROLEN	10	805 94.2	1300 139.4	231 6.9	859 49.7	92 4.4	.284	.375	.515	.966 6	0	.356	328.3	684.3

CH LILLIS, RETTENMUND PITCHERS	YRS	W W/Y	SH SH/Y	SV SV/Y	IP	H H/IP	HR HR/IP	BB BB/IP	K K/IP	QI	WL%	PIT	GRO	ERA	CUM	AVG	PITCH #
RHP DWIGHT GOODEN	16	194 12.1	24 1.5	3 0.2	2801	2564 .915	210 .075	954 .341	2293 .819	.512	.634	9	13.8	3.51	10.29	228	1257
LHP WHITEY FORD	16	236 14.7	45 2.8	10 0.6	3170	2766 .872	228 .071	1086 .342	1956 .617	.668	.690	14	18.1	2.75	15.35	299	1834
RFP RON PERRANOSKI	13	79 6.0	0 0.0	179 13.7	1174	1097 .934	50 .042	468 .398	687 .585	.789	516	3	19.7	2.79	16.91	-14	1677

PLAYER TOTAL **6858.4** *PITCHER TOTAL* **4768** *TEAM TOTAL* **11626.4**

TEAM 19

This is an interesting team with some recent Hall of Famers: Paul Molitor, Robin Yount and Tony Gwynn. Plus there's Joe Medwick in LF, John Olerud at 1B, and Fred Lynn in CF. Brilliant pitching by Bob Feller, Whitey Ford and Dave Righetti.

Between the three of them there are 584 wins, 283 saves (that accounts for 867 victories) and 91 shutouts. Team 34 led all pitching with this club coming in 12th. Competing for pitching slots were some pretty fair hurlers: Bob Friend, Wilber Wood, Billy Pierce, Dave McNally and Johnny Murphy to name a few.

Notable players that missed the club are Greg Luzinski, Alvin Dark, Bert Campaneris and Fred McGriff.

TEAM 21

This is a great team. It had the highest rating. Seven Hall of Famers are here: Hornsby, Carew, Vaughan, Sewell, Medwick, Clemente and Spahn. Plus Clemens, who is on his way. There were two tough choices, center field and third base. Curt Flood was the only real center fielder, but Sammy Sosa's numbers are so much better.

Both Joe Sewell and George Kell are Hall of Fame third basemen. Sewell won 3 fielding titles, Kell 7. Kell's 12 titles outweighed Sewell's 4 titles. It skewed the numbers in Kell's favor, but Sewell topped Kell in 6 of 7 categories across the board. Carew outshines Kell for the utility spot.

Very strong pitching is on Team 21. Roger Clemens (2,088), Warren Spahn (2,365) and Jeff Montgomery (2,380).

TEAM 19 **MGR** TOMMY HELMS	YRS	R R/YR	H H/YR	HR HR/Y	RBI RBI/Y	SB SB/Y	B AV	OB AV	SG AV	FA DEF	OFF	TOT AV	GRO	PLAY #
1B JOHN OLERUD	17	1139 67.0	2239 131.7	255 15.0	1230 72.5	11 0.6	.295	.398	.465	.995 4	3	.314	286.6	600.6
2B PAUL MOLITOR	21	1782 84.9	3319 158.0	234 11.1	1307 62.2	504 24.0	.306	.372	.448	.950 0	8	.301	340.6	641.6
SS ROBIN YOUNT	19	1632 81.6	3142 157.1	251 12.5	1406 70.3	271 13.5	.285	.346	.430	.967 2	6	.292	335.0	627.0
3B MIKE LOWELL	8	478 59.8	969 121.1	143 17.9	578 72.3	21 2.6	.272	.339	.461	.975 3	0	.291	273.5	564.5
LF DUCKY MEDWICK	17	1198 70.4	2471 145.3	205 12.0	1383 81.3	42 2.4	.324	.362	.505	.980 1	13	.402	311.4	713.4
CF FRED LYNN	15	1063 62.5	1960 115.2	306 18.0	1111 65.3	72 4.2	.283	.364	.484	.988 4	5	.332	265.2	597.2
RF TONY GWYNN	20	1383 69.2	3141 157.1	135 6.8	1138 56.9	319 16.0	.338	.388	.459	.987 5	16	.447	306.0	753.0
C BILL FREEHAN	15	706 47.0	1591 106.0	200 13.3	758 50.5	24 1.6	.262	.342	.412	.993 7	0	.297	218.4	515.4
PH/DH JUAN GONZALEZ	17	1061 62.4	1936 113.9	434 25.5	1404 82.6	26 1.5	.295	.343	.561	.983 0	5	.299	285.5	584.5
UTIL DANTE BICHETTE	16	934 71.8	1906 146.6	274 21.1	1141 87.8	152 11,7	.299	.336	.499	.974 0	5	.298	339.2	637.2

CH CORRIDEN, WIETELMANN *PITCHERS*	YRS	W W/Y	SH SH/Y	SV SV/Y	IP	H H/IP	HR HR/IP	BB BB/IP	K K/IP	QI	WL%	PIT	GRO	ERA	CUM	AVG	PITCH #
RHP BOB FELLER	18	266 14.7	44 2.4	21 1.1	3827	3271 .854	224 .056	1764 .460	2561 .674	.698	.621	31	18.2	3.25	14.95	548	2043
LHP WHITEY FORD	16	236 14.7	45 2.8	10 0.6	3170	2766 .872	228 .071	1086 .342	1956 .617	.668	.690	14	18.1	2.75	15.35	299	1834
RFP DAVE RIGHETTI	16	82 5.1	2 0.1	252 15.8	1404	1287 .917	95 .068	591 .421	1112 .792	.614	.509	1	21.0	3.46	17.54	-14	1740

PLAYER TOTAL **6234.4** *PITCHER TOTAL* **5617** *TEAM TOTAL* **11851.4**

TEAM 21 **MGR** MIKE HARGROVE	YRS	R R/YR	H H/YR	HR HR/Y	RBI RBI/Y	SB SB/Y	B AV	OB AV	SG AV	FA DEF	OFF	TOT AV	GRO	PLAY #
1B HAL TROSKY	11	835 75.9	1561 141.9	228 20.7	1012 92.0	28 2.5	.302	.371	.522	.991 0	1	.257	333.0	590.0
2B ROGERS HORNSBY	23	1579 68.6	2930 127.3	301 13.0	1584 68.8	135 5.8	.358	.434	.577	.965 1	49	.708	283.7	991.7
SS ARKY VAUGHAN	14	1173 83.7	2103 150.2	96 6.8	926 66.1	118 8.4	.318	.406	.453	.951 0	15	.449	315.2	764.2
3B JOE SEWELL	14	1141 81.5	2226 159.0	49 3.5	1055 75.3	74 5.2	.312	.391	.413	.951 3	1	.280	324.5	604.5
LF DUCKY MEDWICK	17	1198 70.4	2471 145.3	205 12.0	1383 81.3	42 2.4	.324	.362	.505	.980 1	13	.402	311.4	713.4
CF SAMMY SOSA	17	1422 83.6	2304 135.5	588 34.6	1575 92.6	234 13.8	.274	.345	.537	973 0	7	.231	360.9	591.9
RF ROBERTO CLEMENTE	18	1416 78.6	3000 166.6	240 14.1	1305 72.5	83 4.6	.317	.362	.475	.973 12	7	.442	336.4	778.4
C CHARLES JOHNSON	12	465 38.8	940 78.3	167 13.9	570 47.5	6 0.5	.245	.330	.433	.993 4	0	.268	179.2	447.2
PH/DH ROCKY COLAVITO	14	971 69.3	1730 123.5	374 26.7	1159 82.7	19 1.0	.266	.362	.489	.980 1	4	.294	511.1	805.1
UTIL ROD CAREW	19	1424 74.9	3053 160.6	92 4.8	1015 53.4	353 18.5	.328	.395	.429	.991 0	17	.409	312.2	721.2

CH KEANE, ROARKE *PITCHERS*	YRS	W W/Y	SH SH/Y	SV SV/Y	IP	H H/IP	HR HR/IP	BB BB/IP	K K/IP	QI	WL%	PIT	GRO	ERA	CUM	AVG	PITCH #
RHP ROGER CLEMENS	22	341 15.5	46 2.1	0 0.0	4704	3997 .850	347 .074	1520 .323	4502 .957	.290	.665	37	17.6	3.12	14.48	686	213
LHP WARREN SPAHN	21	363 17.2	63 3.0	29 1.3	5243	4830 .921	434 .082	1434 .273	2583 .492	.784	.597	37	21.5	3.09	18.41	524	236
RFP J. MONTGOMERY	13	46 3.5	0 0.0	304 23.4	869	785 .903	81 .093	296 .341	733 .843	.494	.469	1	26.9	3.27	23.63	-17	238

PLAYER TOTAL **7007.6** *PITCHER TOTAL* **6879** *TEAM TOTAL* **13886.6**

TEAM 24

Here is a team with such a great outfield that Hall of Famers Lou Brock and Earl Averill can't even break in. Bonds in LF, Mays in CF and Junior is in right. Not only has this group hit 3,560 HRs, they have stolen a remarkable 2,960 bases!

TEAM 29

This is a surprisingly strong team for an odd number. Carew and Klein are the only HOFers, but Rollins, Abreu, Foulke and Smoltz make the team contemporary. One of the leading pitching corps with Smoltz, Foulke and 1968 World Series hero lefty Mickey Lolich.

TEAM 26

These players have won 67 offensive titles and 22 defensive titles. They also have 12 batting champions. By moving Foxx to catcher we keep Joe Adcock to play first base. HOFers Wade Boggs, Billy Williams, Heinie Manush and Nellie Fox are on the squad.

A grizzled staff of Sal "The Barber," Frank Tanana and Hoyt Wilhelm does the pitching.

TEAM 32

This is the fourth highest rated team after Team 21. This is primarily due to pitching. Two Hall of Famers are on the mound: Sandy Koufax and Rollie Fingers. The great Steve Carlton is head and shoulders above everyone except Koufax.

TEAM 24 — **IGR** WALTER ALSTON

Player	YRS	R	R/YR	H	H/YR	HR	HR/Y	RBI	RBI/Y	SB	SB/Y	B AV	OB AV	SG AV	FA	DEF	OFF	TOT AV	GRO	PLAY #
B DOLPH CAMILLI	12	936	78.0	1482	123.5	239	19.9	950	79.1	60	5.0	.277	.388	.492	.990	1	5	.331	305.5	636.5
B RYNE SANDBERG	16	1318	82.4	2386	149.1	282	17.6	1061	66.3	344	21.5	.285	.347	.452	.989	9	5	.392	336.9	728.9
SS DICK GROAT	14	829	59.2	2138	152.7	39	2.7	707	50.5	14	1.0	.286	.332	.366	.961	0	2	.225	266.1	491.1
B TRAVIS FRYMAN	13	895	68.8	1776	136.6	223	17.2	1022	78.6	72	5.5	.274	.336	.443	.965	3	0	.257	306.5	563.5
F BARRY BONDS	20	2078	103.9	2742	137.1	708	35.4	1853	92.7	506	25.3	.300	.442	.611	.984	0	31	.581	394.2	975.2
F WILLIE MAYS	22	2062	93.7	3283	149.2	660	30.0	1903	86.5	338	15.3	.302	.387	.557	.981	12	23	.569	374.7	943.7
RF KEN GRIFFEY, JR.	17	1405	82.6	2304	135.5	536	31.5	1536	90.4	178	10.5	.293	.377	.561	.986	10	7	.446	350.7	796.7
C MIKE LIEBERTHAL	12	506	42.2	1080	90.0	141	11.8	573	47.8	8	0.7	.275	.339	.449	.992	1	0	.229	192.7	421.7
PH/DH MANNY RAMIREZ	13	1179	90.7	1922	147.8	435	33.5	1414	108.8	34	2.6	.314	.409	.599	.977	0	9	.403	383.8	786.8
UTIL RICKEY HENDERSON	25	2295	91.8	3055	122.2	297	11.9	1115	44.6	1406	56.2	.279	.401	.419	.979	0	23	.404	326.5	730.5

CH DEMPSEY, LAU — *PITCHERS*	YRS	W	W/Y	SH	SH/Y	SV	SV/Y	IP	H	H/IP	HR	HR/IP	BB	BB/IP	K	K/IP	QI	WL%	PIT	GRO	ERA	CUM	AVG	PITCH #
HP MORT COOPER	11	128	11.6	33	3.0	14	1.2	1840	1666	.905	85	.046	571	.310	913	.496	.765	.631	9	15.8	2.97	12.93	228	1521
HP JERRY KOOSMAN	19	222	11.6	33	1.7	17	0.8	3839	3635	.946	290	.075	1198	.312	2556	.665	.668	.515	0	14.1	3.36	10.7	-51	1023
FP GERRY STALEY	15	134	8.9	9	0.6	61	4.1	1981	2070	1.044	187	.094	529	.267	727	.366	1.039	.547	1	13.6	3.70	9.90	-142	838

PLAYER TOTAL **7074.6** *PITCHER TOTAL* **3382** *TEAM TOTAL* **10456.6**

TEAM 26 — **MGR** BURT SHOTTON

Player	YRS	R	R/YR	H	H/YR	HR	HR/Y	RBI	RBI/Y	SB	SB/Y	B AV	OB AV	SG AV	FA	DEF	OFF	TOT AV	GRO	PLAY #
1B JOE ADCOCK	17	823	48.4	1832	107.7	336	19.7	1122	66.0	20	1.1	.277	.339	.485	.994	4	0	.267	242.9	509.9
2B NELLIE FOX	19	1279	67.3	2663	140.1	35	1.8	790	41.5	76	4.0	.288	.349	.363	.984	6	5	.315	254.7	569.7
SS HARVEY KUENN	15	951	63.4	2092	139.4	87	5.8	671	44.7	68	4.5	.303	.359	.408	.978	1	8	.333	257.8	590.8
3B WADE BOGGS	18	1513	84.1	3010	167.2	118	6.6	1014	56.3	24	1.3	.328	.419	.443	.962	3	18	.471	315.9	786.9
LF HEINIE MANUSH	17	1287	75.7	2524	148.4	110	6.4	1183	69.5	114	6.7	.330	.377	.479	.979	0	6	.307	306.7	613.7
CF BOBBY BONDS	14	1258	89.8	1886	134.7	332	23.7	1024	73.1	461	32.9	.268	.356	.471	.977	3	2	.290	354.2	644.2
RF BILLY WILLIAMS	18	1410	78.3	2711	150.6	426	23.6	1475	81.9	90	5.0	.290	.364	.492	.973	0	4	.273	339.4	612.4
C JIMMIE FOXX	20	1751	87.5	2646	132.3	534	26.7	1922	96.1	87	4.3	.325	.428	.609	.992	3	21	.512	346.9	858.9
PH/DH AMOS OTIS	17	1092	64.2	2020	118.8	193	11.3	1007	59.2	341	20.0	.277	.347	.425	.991	2	3	.256	273.5	529.5
UTIL BRIAN GILES	11	863	78.5	1393	126.6	246	22.4	858	78.0	93	8.5	.299	.413	.542	.981	0	0	.251	314.6	565.6

CH WARES, HARRIS — *PITCHERS*	YRS	W	W/Y	SH	SH/Y	SV	SV/Y	IP	H	H/IP	HR	HR/IP	BB	BB/IP	K	K/IP	QI	WL%	PIT	GRO	ERA	CUM	AVG	PITCH #
RHP SAL MAGLIE	10	119	11.9	25	2.5	14	1.4	1723	1591	.923	169	.098	562	.326	862	.500	.847	.657	4	15.8	3.15	12.65	7	1272
LHP FRANK TANANA	21	240	11.4	34	1.6	1	0.0	4188	4063	.970	448	.107	1255	.300	2773	.662	.715	.504	3	13.0	3.66	9.34	-23	911
RFP HOYT WILHELM	21	143	6.8	5	0.2	227	10.8	2254	1757	.779	150	.066	778	.345	1610	.713	.476	.540	3	17.8	2.52	15.28	69	1597

PLAYER TOTAL **6281.6** *PITCHER TOTAL* **3780** *TEAM TOTAL* **10061.6**

TEAM 29 — **MGR** BURT SHOTTON

Player	YRS	R	R/YR	H	H/YR	HR	HR/Y	RBI	RBI/Y	SB	SB/Y	B AV	OB AV	SG AV	FA	DEF	OFF	TOT AV	GRO	PLAY #
1B FRED McGRIFF	19	1349	71.0	2490	131.1	493	25.9	1550	81.6	72	3.8	.284	.377	.509	.992	0	3	.266	313.0	579.0
2B ROD CAREW	19	1424	74.9	3053	160.6	92	4.8	1015	53.4	353	18.5	.328	.395	.429	.991	0	17	409	312.2	721.2
SS JIMMY ROLLINS	6	503	83.8	904	150.6	59	9.8	308	51.3	171	28.5	.273	.328	.414	.981	1	4	.370	324.0	694.0
3B TIM WALLACH	17	908	53.4	2085	122.6	260	15.3	1125	66.2	51	3.0	.257	.316	.416	.964	5	2	.280	260.7	540.7
LF JOE CARTER	16	1170	73.1	2184	136.5	396	24.8	1445	90.3	231	14.4	.259	.310	.464	.977	0	1	.219	339.3	558.3
CF BOBBY ABREU	22	853	85.3	1432	143.2	190	19.0	776	77.6	241	24.1	.303	.411	.512	.982	1	2	.285	349.4	634.4
RF CHUCK KLEIN	17	1168	68.7	2076	122.1	300	17.6	1201	70.6	79	4.6	.320	.379	.543	.962	0	19	.471	283.6	754.6
C SHERM LOLLAR	18	623	34.6	1415	78.6	155	8.6	808	44.8	20	1.1	.264	.359	.402	.992	8	0	.294	167.7	461.7
PH/DH ROCKY COLAVITO	14	971	69.3	1730	123.5	374	26.7	1159	82.7	19	2.0	.266	.362	.489	.980	1	4	.294	511.1	805.1
UTIL BRETT BOONE	14	927	66.2	1775	126.8	252	18.0	1021	72.9	94	6.7	.266	.325	.442	.986	7	1	.321	290.4	611.4

CH FLETCHER, PERRANOSKI — *PITCHERS*	YRS	W	W/Y	SH	SH/Y	SV	SV/Y	IP	H	H/IP	HR	HR/IP	BB	BB/IP	K	K/IP	QI	WL%	PIT	GRO	ERA	CUM	AVG	PITCH #
HP JOHN SMOLTZ	17	177	10.4	15	0.9	154	9.1	2929	2537	.866	234	.080	882	.301	2567	.876	.371	.580	9	20.4	3.26	17.14	246	1960
HP MICKEY LOLICH	16	217	13.5	41	2.5	11	0.6	3638	3366	.925	347	.095	1099	.302	2832	.778	.544	.532	5	16.6	3.44	13.16	100	1416
FP KEITH FOULKE	9	38	4.2	1	0.1	190	21.1	706	572	.810	78	.110	174	.246	659	.933	.233	.535	2	25.4	3.23	22.17	175	2392

PLAYER TOTAL **6326.4** *PITCHER TOTAL* **5768** *TEAM TOTAL* **12094.4**

TEAM 32 — **MGR** CASEY STENGEL

Player	YRS	R	R/YR	H	H/YR	HR	HR/Y	RBI	RBI/Y	SB	SB/Y	B AV	OB AV	SG AV	FA	DEF	OFF	TOT AV	GRO	PLAY #
1B ERIC KARROS	14	797	57.0	1724	123.1	284	20.1	1027	73.4	59	4.2	.268	.325	.454	.993	1	0	.224	277.4	501.4
2B DICK BARTELL	18	1130	62.7	2165	120.2	79	4.3	710	39.4	109	6.0	.284	.355	.391	.953	0	0	.206	232.6	438.6
SS BILL MUELLER	10	651	65.1	1202	120.2	82	8.2	478	47.8	19	1.9	.292	.373	.425	.960	1	1	.258	243.8	501.8
3B DICK ALLEN	15	1099	73.2	1848	123.2	351	23.4	1119	74.6	133	8.8	.292	.381	.534	.989	0	11	.388	303.2	691.2
LF DAVE WINFIELD	22	1669	75.9	3110	141.4	465	21.1	1833	83.3	223	10.1	.283	.355	.475	.982	7	1	.296	331.0	627.0
CF LARRY DOBY	13	960	73.8	1515	116.5	253	19.4	970	74.6	47	3.6	.283	.387	.490	.983	0	6	.324	287.9	611.9
RF ROGER MARIS	12	826	68.8	1325	110.4	275	22.9	851	70.9	21	1.7	.260	.348	.476	.982	0	5	.300	274.7	574.7
C ELSTON HOWARD	14	619	44.2	1471	105.0	167	11.9	762	54.4	9	0.6	.274	.325	.427	.993	1	0	.219	216.1	435.1
PH/DH AL SIMMONS	20	1507	75.3	2927	146.3	307	15.3	1827	91.3	84	4.3	.334	.380	.535	.982	2	7	.339	332.5	671.5
UTIL TIM RAINES	23	1571	68.3	2605	113.3	170	7.4	980	42.6	808	35.1	.294	.385	.425	.987	1	9	.308	266.3	573.3

CH MACK, COMBS — *PITCHERS*	YRS	W	W/Y	SH	SH/Y	SV	SV/Y	IP	H	H/IP	HR	HR/IP	BB	BB/IP	K	K/IP	QI	WL%	PIT	GRO	ERA	CUM	AVG	PITCH #
RHP DEREK LOWE	9	84	9.3	3	0.3	85	9.4	1312	1306	.995	108	.082	387	.295	858	.654	.718	.532	1	19.0	3.83	15.17	-25	1492
LHP SANDY KOUFAX	12	165	13.7	40	3.3	9	0.7	2324	1754	.754	204	.087	817	.351	2396	1.030	.162	.655	32	17.7	2.76	14.94	1.053	2547
RFP ROLLIE FINGERS	17	114	6.7	2	0.1	341	20.0	1701	1474	.866	123	.072	492	.289	1299	.763	.464	.491	3	26.8	2.90	23.90	68	2458

PLAYER TOTAL **5626.5** *PITCHER TOTAL* **6497** *TEAM TOTAL* **12123.5**

TEAM 10 MGR SPARKY ANDERSON	YRS	R R/YR	H H/YR	HR HR/Y	RBI RBI/Y	SB SB/Y	B AV	OB AV	SG AV	FA DEF	OFF	TOT AV	GRO	PLAY #
1B JOHNNY MIZE	15	1118 / 74.5	2011 / 134.0	359 / 23.9	1337 / 89.1	28 / 1.8	.312	.397	.562	.992 / 2	15	.480	323.3	803.3
2B RED SCHOENDIENST	19	1223 / 64.3	2449 / 128.8	84 / 4.4	773 / 40.6	89 / 4.6	.289	.338	.387	.983 / 6	3	.297	242.7	539.7
SS MIGUEL TEJADA	9	770 / 85.6	1370 / 152.2	216 / 24.0	852 / 94.7	58 / 6.4	.280	.338	.477	.970 / 0	2	.264	362.9	626.9
3B RON SANTO	15	1138 / 47.2	2254 / 150.2	352 / 22.8	1331 / 88.7	35 / 0.7	.277	.366	.464	.954 / 1	7	.327	339.8	666.8
LF CHIPPER JONES	12	1101 / 91.8	1811 / 151.4	331 / 27.6	1111 / 92.6	123 / 10.3	.303	.401	.538	.958 / 0	0	.250	373.3	623.3
CF STEVE FINLEY	17	1368 / 80.5	2426 / 142.7	297 / 17.5	1125 / 66.2	313 / 18.4	.273	.334	.447	.987 / 6	2	.305	325.3	630.3
RF ANDRE DAWSON	19	1337 / 70.3	2700 / 142.1	428 / 22.5	1540 / 81.0	314 / 16.5	.280	.321	.484	.985 / 0	3	.248	332.4	580.4
C SHERM LOLLAR	18	623 / 34.6	1415 / 78.6	155 / 8.6	808 / 44.8	20 / 1.1	.264	.359	.402	.992 / 8	0	.294	167.7	461.7
PH/DH BUCK McCORMICK	13	722 / 55.5	1711 / 131.6	128 / 9.8	951 / 73.1	27 / 2.0	.299	.348	.434	.995 / 4	5	.354	272.0	626.0
UTIL DANTE BICHETTE	16	934 / 71.8	1906 / 146.6	274 / 21.1	1141 / 87.8	152 / 11,7	.299	.336	.499	.974 / 0	5	.298	339.2	637.2

CH LARUSSA, DUNCAN *PITCHERS*	YRS	W W/Y	SH SH/Y	SV SV/Y	IP	H H/IP	HR HR/IP	BB BB/IP	K K/IP	QI	WL%	PIT	GRO	ERA	CUM	AVG	PITCH #
RHP TOMMY BRIDGES	16	194 / 12.1	33 / 2.0	10 / 0.6	2826	2675 / .946	181 / .064	1192 / .421	1674 / .592	.839	.584	5	14.7	3.57	11.13	19	1132
LHP LEFTY GROVE	17	300 / 17.6	35 / 2.0	55 / 3.2	3940	3849 / .976	162 / .041	1187 / .301	2266 / .575	.743	.680	37	22.8	3.06	19.74	704	2678
RFP GREGG OLSON	14	40 / 2.9	0 / 0.0	217 / 15.5	672	597 / .890	46 / .068	330 / .491	588 / .875	.574	.506	0	18.4	3.46	14.94	-23	1471

PLAYER TOTAL **6167.6** *PITCHER TOTAL* **5281** *TEAM TOTAL* **11448.6**

TEAM 12 MGR DUSTY BAKER	YRS	R R/YR	H H/YR	HR HR/Y	RBI RBI/Y	SB SB/Y	B AV	OB AV	SG AV	FA DEF	OFF	TOT AV	GRO	PLAY #
1B RIPPER COLLINS	9	615 / 67.8	1121 / 124.5	135 / 15.0	659 / 73.2	18 / 2.0	.296	.360	.492	.992 / 1	2	.296	282.5	578.5
2B ROBERTO ALOMAR	17	1508 / 88.7	2724 / 160.2	210 / 12.4	1134 / 66.7	474 / 27.9	.300	.371	.443	.984 / 10	1	.353	355.1	708.1
SS JACK WILSON	5	321 / 64.2	715 / 143.0	35 / 7.0	245 / 48.0	26 / 5.2	.263	.304	.368	.977 / 0	1	.225	268.0	493.0
3B WADE BOGGS	18	1513 / 84.1	3010 / 167.2	118 / 6.6	1014 / 56.3	24 / 1.3	.328	.419	.443	.962 / 3	18	.471	315.9	786.9
LF ELLIS BURKS	18	1253 / 69.6	2107 / 117.1	352 / 19.6	1206 / 67.0	181 / 10.1	.291	.363	.510	.983 / 1	2	.266	283.6	549.6
CF STEVE FINLEY	17	1368 / 80.5	2426 / 142.7	297 / 17.5	1125 / 66.2	313 / 18.4	.273	.334	.447	.987 / 6	2	.305	325.3	630.3
RF KENNY LOFTON	15	1363 / 90.9	2142 / 142.8	120 / 8.0	702 / 46.8	567 / 37.8	.299	.373	.425	.984 / 4	7	.366	326.5	692.5
C SHERM LOLLAR	18	623 / 34.6	1415 / 78.6	155 / 8.6	808 / 44.8	20 / 1.1	.264	.359	.402	.992 / 8	0	.294	167.7	461.7
PH/DH CARNEY LANSFORD	15	1007 / 67.1	2074 / 138.3	151 / 10.1	874 / 58.3	224 / 14.9	.290	.343	.411	.970 / 4	1	.276	288.3	564.3
UTIL ALFONSO SORIANO	7	505 / 72.1	912 / 130.3	162 / 23.1	465 / 66.4	169 / 24.1	.280	.320	.500	.970 / 0	3	.306	316.4	622.4

CH HANEY, DAVENPORT *PITCHERS*	YRS	W W/Y	SH SH/Y	SV SV/Y	IP	H H/IP	HR HR/IP	BB BB/IP	K K/IP	QI	WL%	PIT	GRO	ERA	CUM	AVG	PITCH #
RHP ROGER CLEMENS	22	341 / 15.5	46 / 2.1	0 / 0.0	4704	3997 / .850	347 / .074	1520 / .323	4502 / .957	.290	.665	37	17.6	3.12	14.48	686	213
LHP BILLY PIERCE	18	211 / 11.7	38 / 2.1	32 / 1.7	3306	2989 / .904	284 / .085	1178 / .356	1999 / .604	.741	.555	8	15.5	3.27	12.23	86	130
RFP DON MOSSI	12	101 / 8.4	8 / 0.6	50 / 4.1	1548	1493 / .964	156 / 100	385 / .248	932 / .602	.710	.558	0	13.1	3.43	9.67	-50	917

PLAYER TOTAL **6053.3** *PITCHER TOTAL* **4360** *TEAM TOTAL* **10413.3**

TEAM 13 MGR OZZIE GUILLEN	YRS	R R/YR	H H/YR	HR HR/Y	RBI RBI/Y	SB SB/Y	B AV	OB AV	SG AV	FA DEF	OFF	TOT AV	GRO	PLAY #
1B HAROLD BAINES	22	1299 / 59.0	2866 / 130.1	384 / 17.5	1628 / 74.0	34 / 1.5	.289	.356	.465	.978 / 0	1	.231	282.1.	513.1
2B EDGARDO ALFONZO	11	772 / 70.2	1521 / 138.3	146 / 13.3	739 / 67.2	53 / 4.8	.287	.359	.429	.977 / 2	0	.253	293.0	546.0
SS OMAR VIZQUEL	17	1195 / 70.3	2301 / 135.4	69 / 4.1	760 / 44.7	342 / 20.1	.274	.341	.358	.984 / 11	0	.325	274.0	599.0
3B ALEX RODRIGUEZ	12	1245 / 103.8	1901 / 158.4	429 / 35.8	1226 / 102.2	226 / 18.8	.307	.385	.577	.978 / 2	14	.520	419.6	939.6
LF JUAN GONZALEZ	17	1061 / 62.4	1936 / 113.9	434 / 25.5	1404 / 82.6	26 / 1.5	.295	.343	.561	.983 / 0	5	.299	285.5	584.5
CF CARL CRAWFORD	4	308 / 77.0	623 / 155.8	33 / 8.3	220 / 57.5	169 / 42.3	.289	.320	.421	.994 / 1	3	.407	340.1	747.1
RF ROBERTO CLEMENTE	18	1416 / 78.6	3000 / 166.6	240 / 14.1	1305 / 72.5	83 / 4.6	.317	.362	.475	.973 / 12	7	.442	336.4	778.4
C LANCE PARRISH	18	841 / 46.7	1755 / 97.5	320 / 17.7	1048 / 58.2	28 / 1.5	.255	.314	.445	.988 / 3	0	.236	221.6	457.6
PH/DH STEVE KEMP	11	581 / 52.8	1128 / 102.5	130 / 11.8	634 / 57.6	39 / 3.5	.278	.370	.431	.982 / 0	0	.215	228.2	443.2
UTIL DAVE CONCEPCION	19	993 / 52.2	2326 / 122.4	101 / 5.3	950 / 50.0	321 / 16.8	.267	.325	.357	.971 / 5	0	.242	246.7	488.7

CH GRIMES, FERGUSON *PITCHERS*	YRS	W W/Y	SH SH/Y	SV SV/Y	IP	H H/IP	HR HR/IP	BB BB/IP	K K/IP	QI	WL%	PIT	GRO	ERA	CUM	AVG	PITCH #
RHP MORT COOPER	11	128 / 11.6	33 / 3.0	14 / 1.2	1840	1666 / .905	85 / .046	571 / .310	913 / .496	.765	.631	9	15.8	2.97	12.93	228	1521
LHP STEVE BARBER	15	121 / 8.0	21 / 1.4	13 / 0.8	1999	1818 / .909	125 / .062	950 / .475	1309 / .654	.792	.533	1	10.2	3.36	6.84	-64	620
RFP BILLY WAGNER	11	34 / 3.1	0 / 0.0	284 / 25.8	630	409 / .649	59 / .094	217 / .344	840 / 1.333	-.246	.515	1	25.8	2.40	26.50	284	2934

PLAYER TOTAL **6097.2** *PITCHER TOTAL* **5075** *TEAM TOTAL* **11172.2**

TEAM 15 MGR DAVEY JOHNSON	YRS	R R/YR	H H/YR	HR HR/Y	RBI RBI/Y	SB SB/Y	B AV	OB AV	SG AV	FA DEF	OFF	TOT AV	GRO	PLAY #
1B JOHNNY MIZE	15	1118 / 74.5	2011 / 134.0	359 / 23.9	1337 / 89.1	28 / 1.8	.312	.397	.562	.992 / 2	15	.480	323.3	803.3
2B TONY LAZZERI	14	986 / 70.4	1840 / 131.4	178 / 12.7	1191 / 85.0	148 / 10.5	.292	.380	.467	.967 / 0	0	.227	310.0	537.0
SS BARRY LARKIN	19	1329 / 69.9	2340 / 123.2	198 / 10.4	960 / 50.5	379 / 19.9	.295	.371	.444	.975 / 3	0	.254	273.5	527.5
3B DICK ALLEN	15	1099 / 73.2	1848 / 123.2	351 / 23.4	1119 / 74.6	133 / 8.8	.292	.381	.534	.989 / 0	11	.388	303.2	691.2
LF GEORGE CASE	11	785 / 71.3	1415 / 128.6	21 / 1.9	377 / 34.2	349 / 31.7	.282	.341	.358	.970 / 0	7	.323	267.7	590.7
CF JIM EDMONDS	13	1063 / 81.8	1619 / 124.5	331 / 25.5	998 / 76.8	59 / 4.5	.291	.384	.543	.990 / 8	0	.367	313.3	680.3
RF CARLOS BELTRAN	8	699 / 87.4	1140 / 142.5	162 / 20.3	647 / 80.9	209 / 26.1	.282	.350	.479	.983 / 0	0	.223	357.2	580.2
C JOE TORRE	16	996 / 36.5	2342 / 79.7	252 / 11.1	1185 / 41.0	23 / 1.6	.297	.367	.452	.990 / 4	0	.244	169.9	413.9
PH/DH SHAWN GREEN	13	994 / 76.5	1726 / 132.8	303 / 23.3	958 / 73.7	147 / 11.3	.283	.356	.505	.989 / 1	1	.260	317.8	577.8
UTIL CRISTIAN GUZMAN	7	497 / 71.0	971 / 138.7	43 / 6.1	320 / 45.7	109 / 21.8	.260	.298	.374	.972 / 1	3	.301	283.5	584.5

CH BRENLY, McKEON *PITCHERS*	YRS	W W/Y	SH SH/Y	SV SV/Y	IP	H H/IP	HR HR/IP	BB BB/IP	K K/IP	QI	WL%	PIT	GRO	ERA	CUM	AVG	PITCH #
RHP TIM HUDSON	7	106 / 15.1	8 / 1.1	0 / 0.0	1433	1328 / .927	114 / .080	447 / .312	1014 / .708	.611	.688	4	16.2	3.33	12.87	216	1503
LHP ED LOPAT	12	166 / 13.8	27 / 2.2	3 / 0.2	2439	2464 / 1.010	179 / .073	650 / .266	859 / .352	.997	.597	3	16.2	3.21	12.99	-50	1294
RFP RICK AGUILERA	16	86 / 5.4	0 / 0.0	318 / 19.9	1291	1233 / .955	138 / .107	351 / .272	1030 / .798	.536	.515	0	25.3	3.57	21.73	-7	216

PLAYER TOTAL **5986.4** *PITCHER TOTAL* **4963** *TEAM TOTAL* **10949.4**

TEAM 17 MGR FELIPE ALOU	YRS	R R/YR	H H/YR	HR HR/Y	RBI RBI/Y	SB SB/Y	B AV	OB AV	SG AV	FA DEF	OFF	TOT AV	GRO	PLAY #
1B KEITH HERNANDEZ	17	1124 / 66.1	2182 / 128.3	162 / 9.5	1071 / 63.0	98 / 5.7	.296	.388	.436	.994 / 11	7	.436	272.6	708.6
2B FELIX MILLAN	12	699 / 58.2	1617 / 134.7	22 / 1.8	403 / 33.5	67 / 5.5	.279	.324	.343	.980 / 1	0	.205	233.7	438.7
SS TRAVIS FRYMAN	13	895 / 68.8	1776 / 136.6	223 / 17.2	1022 / 78.6	72 / 5.5	.274	.336	.443	.965 / 3	0	.257	306.5	563.5
3B SCOTT ROLEN	10	805 / 94.2	1300 / 139.4	231 / 6.9	859 / 49.7	92 / 4.4	.284	.375	.515	.966 / 6	0	.356	328.3	684.3
LF LANCE BERKMAN	7	592 / 84.6	951 / 135.9	180 / 25.7	617 / 88.1	44 / 6.3	.302	.416	.557	.985 / 0	2	.313	340.4	653.4
CF DARIN ERSTAD	10	809 / 80.9	1482 / 148.2	114 / 11.4	619 / 61.9	169 / 16.9	.287	.342	.417	.995 / 3	1	.290	319.3	609.3
RF ENOS SLAUGHTER	19	1247 / 65.6	2383 / 125.4	169 / 8.8	1304 / 68.6	71 / 3.7	.300	.382	.453	.980 / 1	6	.300	272.1	572.1
C ERNIE LOMBARDI	17	601 / 35.3	1792 / 105.4	190 / 11.1	990 / 58.2	8 / 0.4	.308	.358	.460	.979 / 0	1	.236	210.4	446.4
PH/DH SAMMY SOSA	17	1422 / 83.6	2304 / 135.5	588 / 34.6	1575 / 92.6	234 / 13.8	.274	.345	.537	.973 / 0	7	.231	360.9	591.9
UTIL BILL WHITE	13	843 / 64.8	1706 / 131.2	202 / 15.5	870 / 66.9	103 / 7.9	.286	.353	.455	.992 / 7	0	.326	286.3	612.3

CH RETTENMUND, DOBY *PITCHERS*	YRS	W W/Y	SH SH/Y	SV SV/Y	IP	H H/IP	HR HR/IP	BB BB/IP	K K/IP	QI	WL%	PIT	GRO	ERA	CUM	AVG	PITCH #
RHP DIZZY DEAN	12	150 / 12.5	26 / 2.1	30 / 2.5	1967	1919 / .975	95 / .048	453 / .230	1163 / .591	.662	.644	16	17.1	3.02	14.08	438	1846
LHP VIDA BLUE	17	209 / 12.2	37 / 2.1	2 / 0.1	3343	2939 / .879	263 / .078	1185 / .354	2175 / .650	.661	.565	4	14.4	3.27	11.13	46	1159
RFP DICK RADATZ	7	52 / 7.4	0 / 0.0	122 / 17.4	693	532 / .767	65 / .101	296 / .463	745 / 1.165	.166	.547	2	24.8	3.13	21.67	222	2389

PLAYER TOTAL **5803.5** *PITCHER TOTAL* **5394** *TEAM TOTAL* **11197.5**

TEAM 18 MGR BILL RIGNEY	YRS	R R/YR	H H/YR	HR HR/Y	RBI RBI/Y	SB SB/Y	B AV	OB AV	SG AV	FA DEF	OFF	TOT AV	GRO	PLAY #
1B KEITH HERNANDEZ	17	1124 / 66.1	2182 / 128.3	162 / 9.5	1071 / 63.0	98 / 5.7	.296	.388	.436	.994 / 11	7	.436	272.6	708.6
2B JOE MORGAN	22	1650 / 75.0	2517 / 114.4	268 / 12.1	1133 / 51.5	689 / 31.3	.271	.395	.427	.981 / 6	11	.373	284.3	657.3
SS ORLANDO CABRERA	9	510 / 56.7	1083 / 120.3	80 / 8.9	469 / 52.1	118 / 13.1	.267	.315	.403	.978 / 1	0	.219	251.3	470.3
3B BILL MADLOCK	15	920 / 61.3	2008 / 133.8	163 / 10.8	860 / 57.3	174 / 11.6	.305	.369	.442	.948 / 0	4	.276	274.8	550.8
LF JOHNNY DAMON	11	1073 / 97.5	1789 / 162.6	130 / 11.8	700 / 63.6	281 / 25.5	.290	.353	.431	.989 / 2	3	.305	361.8	666.8
CF ANDY VAN SLYKE	12	803 / 66.9	1500 / 125.0	158 / 13.1	768 / 64.0	238 / 19.8	.276	.352	.448	.989 / 5	3	.349	288.8	637.8
RF BRIAN GILES	11	863 / 78.5	1393 / 126.6	246 / 22.4	858 / 78.0	93 / 8.5	.299	.413	.542	.981 / 0	0	.251	314.6	565.6
C JASON KENDALL	16	776 / 77.6	1572 / 157.2	67 / 6.7	524 / 52.4	148 / 14.8	.302	.382	.407	.989 / 0	0	.219	308.3	527.3
PH/DH ROCKY COLAVITO	14	971 / 69.3	1730 / 123.5	374 / 26.7	1159 / 82.7	19 / 1.0	.266	.362	.489	.980 / 1	4	.294	511.1	805.1
UTIL NELLIE FOX	19	1279 / 67.3	2663 / 140.1	35 / 1.8	790 / 41.5	76 / 4.0	.288	.349	.363	.984 / 6	5	.315	254.7	569.7

CH GOMEZ, DUNCAN *PITCHERS*	YRS	W W/Y	SH SH/Y	SV SV/Y	IP	H H/IP	HR HR/IP	BB BB/IP	K K/IP	QI	WL%	PIT	GRO	ERA	CUM	AVG	PITCH #
RHP DAZZY VANCE	16	197 / 12.3	29 / 1.8	11 / 0.6	2967	2809 / .946	132 / .044	840 / .283	2045 / .689	.584	.585	25	14.7	3.24	11.46	521	1667
LHP WHITEY FORD	16	236 / 14.7	45 / 2.8	10 / 0.6	3170	2766 / .872	228 / .071	1086 / .342	1956 / .617	.668	.690	14	18.1	2.75	15.35	299	183
RFP RANDY MYERS	14	44 / 3.1	0 / 0.0	347 / 24.8	885	758 / .856	69 / .078	396 / .447	884 / .999	.319	.411	3	27.9	3.19	24.71	81	255

PLAYER TOTAL **6159.3** *PITCHER TOTAL* **6053** *TEAM TOTAL* **12212.3**

TEAM 20 MGR PIE TRAYNOR*	YRS	R R/YR	H H/YR	HR HR/Y	RBI RBI/Y	SB SB/Y	B AV	OB AV	SG AV	FA DEF	OFF	TOT AV	GRO	PLAY #
1B TED KLUSZEWSKI	15	848 / 56.5	1766 / 117.7	279 / 18.6	1028 / 68.5	20 / 1.3	.298	.354	.498	.993 / 5	3	.336	262.6	598.6
2B WILLIE RANDOLPH	18	1239 / 68.8	2210 / 122.7	54 / 3.0	687 / 38.1	271 / 15.0	.276	.375	.351	.980 / 0	1	.211	247.6	458.6
SS DICK GROAT	14	829 / 59.2	2138 / 152.7	39 / 2.7	707 / 50.5	14 / 1.0	.286	.332	.366	.961 / 0	2	.225	266.1	491.1
3B MIKE SCHMIDT	18	1506 / 83.6	2234 / 124.1	548 / 30.4	1595 / 88.6	174 / 9.6	.267	.384	.527	.955 / 10	25	.624	336.3	960.3
LF LOU BROCK	19	1610 / 84.7	3023 / 159.1	149 / 7.8	900 / 47.3	938 / 49.3	.293	.344	.410	.959 / 0	12	.335	348.2	683.2
CF GOOSE GOSLIN	18	1483 / 82.3	2735 / 151.9	248 / 13.7	1609 / 89.3	175 / 9.7	.316	.387	.500	.960 / 0	4	.285	346.9	631.9
RF FRANK ROBINSON	21	1829 / 87.0	2943 / 140.1	586 / 27.9	1812 / 86.2	204 / 9.7	.294	.392	.537	.984 / 1	13	.378	350.9	728.9
C MICKEY TETTLETON	14	711 / 50.8	1132 / 80.9	245 / 24.6	732 / 52.3	23 / 1.6	.241	.372	.449	.991 / 1	1	.241	210.0	451.0
PH/DH LUIS GONZALEZ	16	1219 / 76.2	2214 / 138.4	316 / 19.8	1251 / 78.2	121 / 7.6	.285	.369	.487	.986 / 1	1	.253	320.6	573.6
UTIL PIE TRAYNOR*	17	1183 / 69.5	2416 / 142.1	58 / 3.4	1273 / 74.8	158 / 9.2	.320	.362	.435	.947 / 1	1	.246	299.0	545.0

CH M. GRISSOM, R. JOHNSON *PITCHERS*	YRS	W W/Y	SH SH/Y	SV SV/Y	IP	H H/IP	HR HR/IP	BB BB/IP	K K/IP	QI	WL%	PIT	GRO	ERA	CUM	AVG	PITCH #
RHP PAUL DERRINGER	15	223 / 14.8	32 / 2.1	29 / 1.9	3645	3912 / 1.073	158 / .043	761 / .208	1507 / .413	.911	.513	5	18.8	3.46	15.34	-22	1512
LHP LEFTY GOMEZ	14	189 / 13.5	28 / 2.0	9 / 0.6	2503	2290 / .914	138 / .055	1095 / .437	1468 / .586	.820	.649	17	16.1	3.34	12.76	347	1623
RFP MIKE MARSHALL	14	97 / 6.9	1 / 0.0	188 / 13.4	1386	1281 / .924	79 / .056	514 / .370	880 / .634	.716	.464	3	20.3	3.14	17.16	-42	1674

PLAYING MANAGER* *PLAYER TOTAL* **6122.2 *PITCHER TOTAL* **4809** *TEAM TOTAL* **10931.2**

TEAM 22 MGR JOE TORRE	YRS	R R/YR	H H/YR	HR HR/Y	RBI RBI/Y	SB SB/Y	B AV	OB AV	SG AV	FA DEF	OFF	TOT AV	GRO	PLAY #
1B WILL CLARK	9	760 / 84.4	1406 / 156.2	189 / 21.0	789 / 87.6	57 / 6.3	.301	.379	.498	.991 / 1	4	.346	355.5	701.5
2B ROBINSON CANO	1	78 / 78.0	155 / 155.0	14 / 14.0	62 / 62.0	1 / 1.0	.297	.320	.458	.974 / 0	0	.215	310.0	525.0
SS DAVID ECKSTEIN	5	430 / 86.0	799 / 159.8	25 / 5.0	231 / 46.2	93 / 18.6	.282	.351	.362	.980 / 0	0	.208	315.6	520.6
3B MARCUS GILES	15	329 / 65.8	573 / 114.6	61 / 12.2	234 / 46.8	50 / 10.0	.292	.366	.465	.980 / 0	0	.225	249.6	474.6
LF LANCE BERKMAN	7	592 / 84.6	951 / 135.9	180 / 25.7	617 / 88.1	44 / 6.3	.302	.416	.557	.985 / 0	2	.313	340.4	653.4
CF BRETT BUTLER	17	1359 / 79.9	2375 / 139.7	54 / 3.2	578 / 34.0	558 / 32.8	.290	.379	.376	.992 / 3	8	.339	289.2	628.2
RF WALLY BERGER	11	809 / 73.5	1550 / 140.9	242 / 22.0	898 / 81.6	36 / 3.2	.300	.359	.522	.974 / 1	2	.290	321.2	611.2
C JORGE POSADA	11	588 / 53.5	1034 / 94.0	175 / 15.9	678 / 61.6	11 / 1.0	.269	.375	.469	.992 / 0	0	.223	226.4	449.4
PH/DH JUAN GONZALEZ	17	1061 / 62.4	1936 / 113.9	434 / 25.5	1404 / 82.6	26 / 1.5	.295	.343	.561	.983 / 0	5	.299	285.5	584.5
UTIL HARVEY KUENN	15	951 / 63.4	2092 / 139.4	87 / 5.8	671 / 44.7	68 / 4.5	.303	.359	.408	.978 / 1	8	.333	257.8	590.8

CH HERMAN, RETTENMUND *PITCHERS*	YRS	W W/Y	SH SH/Y	SV SV/Y	IP	H H/IP	HR HR/IP	BB BB/IP	K K/IP	QI	WL%	PIT	GRO	ERA	CUM	AVG	PITCH #
RHP ROGER CLEMENS	22	341 / 15.5	46 / 2.1	0 / 0.0	4704	3997 / .850	347 / .074	1520 / .323	4502 / .957	.290	.665	37	17.6	3.12	14.48	686	213
LHP JIMMY KEY	11	186 / 12.4	13 / 0.9	10 / 0.7	2591	2518 / .972	254 / .098	668 / .258	1538 / .594	.734	.614	5	14.0	3.51	10.49	71	112
RFP RON KLINE	17	114 / 6.7	8 / 0.4	108 / 6.3	2078	2113 / 1.016	218 / .104	731 / .351	989 / .475	.996	.442	1	13.4	3.75	9.65	-165	80

PLAYER TOTAL **5739.2** *PITCHER TOTAL* **4054** *TEAM TOTAL* **9793.2**

EAM 23
GR DICK WILLIAMS

Player	YRS	R	R/YR	H	H/YR	HR	HR/Y	RBI	RBI/Y	SB	SB/Y	B AV	OB AV	SG AV	FA	DEF	OFF	TOT AV	GRO	PLAY #
B DON MATTINGLY	14	1007	71.9	2153	153.8	222	15.9	1099	78.5	14	1.0	.307	.363	.471	.996	10	8	.485	321.3	806.3
B RYNE SANDBERG	16	1318	82.4	2386	149.1	282	17.6	1061	66.3	344	21.5	.285	.347	.452	.989	9	5	.392	336.9	728.9
S CECIL TRAVIS	12	665	55.4	1544	128.6	27	2.2	657	54.7	23	1.9	.314	.370	.416	.955	0	1	.236	242.8	478.8
B TIM WALLACH	17	908	53.4	2085	122.6	260	15.3	1125	66.2	51	3.0	.257	.316	.416	.964	5	2	.280	260.7	540.7
F DAVID JUSTICE	14	929	66.4	1571	112.2	305	21.8	1017	72.6	53	3.8	.279	.378	.500	.978	0	0	.232	276.2	508.2
F ELLIS BURKS	18	1253	69.6	2107	117.1	352	19.6	1206	67.0	181	10.1	.291	.363	.510	.983	1	2	.266	283.6	549.6
F BRIAN GILES	11	863	78.5	1393	126.6	246	22.4	858	78.0	93	8.5	.299	.413	.542	.981	0	0	.251	314.6	565.6
TED SIMMONS	21	1074	51.1	2472	117.7	248	11.8	1389	66.1	21	1.0	.285	.352	.437	.987	1	0	.224	247.7	471.7
H/DH CECIL FIELDER	13	744	57.2	1313	106.0	319	24.5	1008	77.5	2	0.2	.255	.348	.482	.992	0	6	.309	260.8	569.8
TIL MARK TEIXEIRA	3	279	93.0	484	161.3	107	35.7	340	113.3	9	3.0	.282	.362	.541	.994	1	0	.304	406.1	710.1

H J. REESE, B. HARRELSON

ITCHERS	YRS	W	W/Y	SH	SH/Y	SV	SV/Y	IP	H	H/IP	HR	HR/IP	BB	BB/IP	K	K/IP	QI	WL%	PIT	GRO	ERA	CUM	AVG	PITCH #
HP LUIS TIANT	19	229	12.0	49	2.5	15	0.7	3486	3075	.882	346	.053	1104	.316	2416	.693	.558	.571	7	15.2	3.30	11.90	127	1317
HP JOHN ANTONELLI	12	126	10.5	25	2.0	21	1.7	1992	1870	.938	185	.092	687	.344	1162	.583	.791	.534	5	14.2	3.34	10.86	53	1139
FP TIPPY MARTINEZ	14	55	3.9	0	0.0	115	8.2	834	732	.877	53	.063	425	.509	632	757	.692	.567	0	12.1	3.45	8.65	-41	824

PLAYER TOTAL **5929.7** *PITCHER TOTAL* **3280** *TEAM TOTAL* **9209.7**

TEAM 25
MGR GABBY STREET

Player	YRS	R	R/YR	H	H/YR	HR	HR/Y	RBI	RBI/Y	SB	SB/Y	B AV	OB AV	SG AV	FA	DEF	OFF	TOT AV	GRO	PLAY #
1B MARK McGWIRE	16	1167	72.9	1626	101.6	583	36.4	1414	88.4	12	0.8	.263	.394	.588	.993	1	13	.424	300.3	724.3
2B HARMON KILLEBREW	22	1283	58.3	2086	94.8	573	26.0	1584	72.0	19	0.8	.256	.379	.509	.992	0	15	.365	251.9	616.9
SS BUDDY BELL	18	1151	63.9	2514	139.6	201	11.1	1106	61.4	55	3.0	.279	.343	.406	.964	7	0	.283	279.0	562.0
3B GEORGE BRETT	21	1583	75.4	3154	150.2	317	15.1	1595	76.0	201	20.0	.305	.373	.487	.951	1	15	.385	326.7	711.7
LF BARRY BONDS	20	2078	103.9	2742	137.1	708	35.4	1853	92.7	506	25.3	.300	.442	.611	.984	0	31	.581	394.2	975.2
CF ANDRUW JONES	10	855	85.5	1408	140.8	301	30.1	894	89.4	129	12.9	.267	.342	.503	.990	8	2	.424	358.5	782.5
RF JIM EDMONDS	13	1063	81.8	1619	124.5	331	25.5	998	76.8	59	4.5	.291	.384	.543	.990	8	0	.367	313.3	680.3
C MIKE PIAZZA	14	976	69.7	1929	137.8	397	28.4	1223	87.4	17	1.2	.311	.382	.555	.989	1	0	.264	324.3	588.3
PH/DH JASON GIAMBI	11	925	84.1	1526	138.7	313	28.5	1031	93.7	13	1.2	.295	.413	.539	.991	3	3	.377	346.4	723.4
UTIL RICKEY HENDERSON	25	2295	91.8	3055	122.2	297	11.9	1115	44.6	1406	56.2	.279	.401	.419	.979	0	23	.404	326.5	730.5

CH M. RYAN, M. GONZALEZ

PITCHERS	YRS	W	W/Y	SH	SH/Y	SV	SV/Y	IP	H	H/IP	HR	HR/IP	BB	BB/IP	K	K/IP	QI	WL%	PIT	GRO	ERA	CUM	AVG	PITCH #
RHP DON NEWCOMBE	10	149	14.9	24	2.4	7	0.7	2154	2102	.975	252	.116	490	.227	1129	.524	.794	.623	7	18.0	3.56	14.44	176	1620
LHP TOMMY JOHN	26	288	11.0	46	1.7	4	0.1	4710	4783	1.015	302	.064	1259	.267	2245	.476	.476	.555	4	12.8	3.34	9.46	77	1023
RFP STU MILLER	16	105	6.5	5	0.3	154	9.6	1694	1522	.898	140	.082	600	.354	1164	.687	.647	.505	4	16.4	3.24	13.16	36	1352

PLAYER TOTAL **7095.1** *PITCHER TOTAL* **3995** *TEAM TOTAL* **11090.1**

TEAM 27
MGR WHITEY HERZOG

Player	YRS	R	R/YR	H	H/YR	HR	HR/Y	RBI	RBI/Y	SB	SB/Y	B AV	OB AV	SG AV	FA	DEF	OFF	TOT AV	GRO	PLAY #
1B DERREK LEE	9	641	71.2	1127	125.2	208	23.1	626	69.6	78	8.7	.276	.363	.501	.994	2	3	.340	297.2	637.2
2B PLACIDO POLANCO	8	491	61.4	981	122.6	59	7.4	330	41.3	49	6.1	.300	.346	.415	.988	1	0	.238	238.2	476.2
SS JOE SEWELL	14	1141	81.5	2226	159.0	49	3.5	1055	75.3	74	5.2	.312	.391	.413	.951	3	1	.280	324.5	604.5
3B SCOTT ROLEN	10	805	94.2	1300	139.4	231	6.9	859	49.7	92	4.4	.284	.375	.515	.966	6	0	.356	328.3	684.3
LF PETE REISER	10	473	47.3	786	78.6	58	5.8	368	36.8	87	8.7	.295	.380	.450	.979	0	7	.365	177.2	542.2
CF DARIN ERSTAD	10	809	80.9	1482	148.2	114	11.4	619	61.9	169	16.9	.287	.342	.417	.995	3	1	.290	319.3	609.3
RF VLADIMIR GUERRERO	10	860	86.0	1585	158.5	305	30.5	935	93.5	151	15.1	.324	.391	.587	.963	0	1	.298	372.6	670.6
C CARLTON FISK	24	1276	53.1	2356	98.1	376	15.6	1330	55.4	128	5.3	.269	.365	.457	.988	1	1	.230	227.5	457.5
PH/DH DAVID ORTIZ	9	507	56.3	877	97.4	177	19.7	626	69.6	5	0.6	.282	.366	.534	.990	0	1	.260	243.2	503.2
UTIL BOB ELLIOTT	15	1064	70.9	2061	137.4	170	11.3	1195	79.6	60	4.0	289	.375	.440	.947	1	1	.247	303.2	550.2

CH E. MACK, BENGOUGH

PITCHERS	YRS	W	W/Y	SH	SH/Y	SV	SV/Y	IP	H	H/IP	HR	HR/IP	BB	BB/IP	K	K/IP	QI	WL%	PIT	GRO	ERA	CUM	AVG	PITCH #
RHP JUAN MARICHAL	16	243	15.1	52	3.2	2	0.1	3507	3153	.899	320	.091	709	.202	2303	.656	.536	.631	12	18.4	2.89	15.51	281	1832
LHP AL BRAZLE	10	97	9.7	7	0.7	60	6.0	1377	1387	1.007	83	.060	492	.357	554	.402	1.022	.602	2	16.4	3.31	13.09	-73	1236
RFP BOB WICKMAN	13	59	4.5	1	0.1	214	16.5	955	944	.988	74	.077	398	.417	706	.739	.743	.536	0	21.1	3.62	17.48	-69	1679

PLAYER TOTAL **5735.2** *PITCHER TOTAL* **4747** *TEAM TOTAL* **10482.2**

TEAM 28
MGR WALTER JOHNSON

Player	YRS	R	R/YR	H	H/YR	HR	HR/Y	RBI	RBI/Y	SB	SB/Y	B AV	OB AV	SG AV	FA	DEF	OFF	TOT AV	GRO	PLAY #
1B DOLPH CAMILLI	12	936	78.0	1482	123.5	239	19.9	950	79.1	60	5.0	.277	.388	.492	.990	1	5	.331	305.5	636.5
2B VIC POWER	12	765	63.7	1716	143.0	126	10.5	658	54.8	45	3.7	.284	.317	.411	.994	3	1	.269	275.7	544.7
SS JAY BELL	18	1123	62.4	1963	109.1	195	10.8	860	47.8	91	5.1	.265	.343	.416	.976	2	0	.227	235.2	462.2
3B EDDIE YOST	18	1215	67.5	1863	103.5	139	7.7	683	37.9	72	4.0	.254	.395	.371	.957	2	10	.337	220.6	557.6
LF AL SIMMONS	20	1507	75.3	2927	146.3	307	11.8	1827	91.3	87	4.3	.334	.380	.535	.982	2	7	.339	332.5	671.5
CF VADA PINSON	18	1366	75.8	2757	153.1	256	14.2	1170	65.0	305	16.9	.286	.330	.442	.981	2	7	.311	325.0	636.0
RF BILLY WILLIAMS	18	1410	78.3	2711	150.6	426	23.6	1475	81.9	90	5.0	.290	.364	.492	.973	0	4	.273	339.4	612.4
C WALKER COOPER	18	573	31.8	1341	74.5	173	9.6	812	45.1	18	1.0	.285	.332	.464	.977	0	0	.216	162.0	378.0
PH/DH ORLANDO CEPEDA	17	1131	66.5	2351	138.2	379	22.2	1365	80.2	142	8.3	.297	.353	.499	.990	0	4	.276	315.4	591.4
UTIL KENNY LOFTON	15	1363	90.9	2142	142.8	120	8.0	702	46.8	567	37.8	.299	.373	.425	.984	4	7	.366	326.5	692.5

CH SCHACHT, BARTELL

PITCHERS	YRS	W	W/Y	SH	SH/Y	SV	SV/Y	IP	H	H/IP	HR	HR/IP	BB	BB/IP	K	K/IP	QI	WL%	PIT	GRO	ERA	CUM	AVG	PITCH #
RHP GAYLORD PERRY	22	314	14.2	53	2.4	11	0.5	5350	4938	.922	399	.074	1379	.257	3534	.660	.593	.542	9	17.1	3.11	13.99	119	1518
LHP VIDA BLUE	17	209	12.2	37	2.1	2	0.1	3343	2939	.879	263	.078	1185	.354	2175	.650	.661	.565	4	14.4	3.27	11.13	46	1159
RFP RANDY MYERS	14	44	3.1	0	0.0	347	24.8	885	758	.856	69	.078	396	.447	884	.999	.319	.411	3	27.9	3.19	24.71	81	2552

PLAYER TOTAL **5782.8** *PITCHER TOTAL* **5229** *TEAM TOTAL* **11011.8**

TEAM 30
MGR BILLY SOUTHWORTH

Player	YRS	R	R/YR	H	H/YR	HR	HR/Y	RBI	RBI/Y	SB	SB/Y	B AV	OB AV	SG AV	FA	DEF	OFF	TOT AV	GRO	PLAY #
1B ORLANDO CEPEDA	17	1131	66.5	2351	138.2	379	22.2	1365	80.2	142	8.3	.297	.353	.499	.990	0	4	.276	315.4	591.4
2B M. GRUDZIELANEK	11	745	67.7	1611	146.5	74	6.7	502	45.6	125	11.4	.287	.330	.391	.974	0	1	.220	277.9	497.9
SS MAURY WILLS	14	1067	76.2	2134	152.4	20	1.4	458	32.7	586	41.8	.281	.331	.331	.963	0	7	.288	304.5	592.5
3B ERIC CHAVEZ	8	593	85.6	1026	149.2	190	27.1	644	93.1	40	5.8	.275	.350	.496	.965	3	1	.320	360.4	680.4
LF TIM RAINES	23	1571	68.3	2605	113.3	170	7.4	980	42.6	808	35.1	.294	.385	.425	.987	1	9	.308	266.3	573.3
CF KEN GRIFFEY, JR.	17	1405	82.6	2304	135.5	536	31.5	1536	90.4	178	10.5	.293	.377	.561	.986	10	7	.446	350.7	796.7
RF MAGGLIO ORDONEZ	9	662	73.6	1259	139.9	195	21.7	749	83.2	82	9.1	.306	.364	.518	.988	0	0	.238	327.9	565.9
C BENITO SANTIAGO	20	755	37.8	1830	91.5	217	10.9	920	46.0	91	4.6	.263	.307	.415	.987	4	0	.237	190.8	427.8
PH/DH JACKIE JENSEN	11	810	73.6	1463	133.0	199	18.0	929	84.4	143	13.0	.279	.372	.460	.977	0	5	313	322.0	635.0
UTIL BUCK McCORMICK	13	722	55.5	1711	131.6	128	9.8	951	73.1	27	2.0	.299	.348	.434	.995	4	5	.354	272.0	626.0

CH TURNER, CORRIDEN

PITCHERS	YRS	W	W/Y	SH	SH/Y	SV	SV/Y	IP	H	H/IP	HR	HR/IP	BB	BB/IP	K	K/IP	QI	WL%	PIT	GRO	ERA	CUM	AVG	PITCH #
RHP NOLAN RYAN	27	324	12.0	61	2.2	3	0.1	5386	3923	.728	321	.058	2795	.518	5714	1.060	.244	.526	32	14.3	3.19	11.11	489	1600
LHP MARK MULDER	6	97	16.2	10	1.7	0	0.0	1208	1202	.995	118	.098	368	.305	779	.645	.753	.660	5	17.9	3.87	14.03	247	1650
RFP GREGG OLSON	14	40	2.9	0	0.0	217	15.5	672	598	.890	46	.068	330	.491	588	.875	.574	.506	0	18.4	3.46	14.94	-23	1471

PLAYER TOTAL **5986.9** *PITCHER TOTAL* **4721** *TEAM TOTAL* **10707.9**

TEAM 31
MGR CASEY STENGEL

Player	YRS	R	R/YR	H	H/YR	HR	HR/Y	RBI	RBI/Y	SB	SB/Y	B AV	OB AV	SG AV	FA	DEF	OFF	TOT AV	GRO	PLAY #
1B NORM CASH	17	1046	61.5	1820	107.0	377	22.1	1103	64.8	43	2.5	.271	.377	.488	.992	2	3	.285	257.9	542.9
2B GREG GAGNE	15	712	47.5	1440	96.0	111	7.4	604	40.3	108	7.2	.254	.304	.382	.972	1	0	.201	198.8	399.8
SS DICKIE THON	15	496	33.0	1176	78.4	71	4.7	435	29.0	167	11.1	.264	.318	.374	.965	0	1	.204	156.2	360.2
3B AUGIE GALAN	16	1004	62.7	1706	106.6	100	6.2	830	51.8	123	7.6	.287	.390	.419	.981	0	6	.294	234.9	528.9
LF PAUL WANER	20	1627	81.3	3152	157.6	113	5.6	1309	65.4	104	5.2	.333	.404	.473	.975	0	14	.382	315.1	697.1
CF TIM RAINES	23	1571	68.3	2605	113.3	170	7.4	980	42.6	808	35.1	.294	.385	.425	.987	1	9	.308	266.3	573.3
RF DAVE WINFIELD	22	1669	75.9	3110	141.4	465	21.1	1833	83.3	223	10.1	.283	.355	.475	.982	7	1	.296	331.0	627.0
C MIKE PIAZZA	14	976	69.7	1929	137.8	397	28.4	1223	87.4	17	1.2	.311	.382	.555	.989	1	0	.264	324.3	588.3
PH/DH JOSE CANSECO	17	1186	69.8	1877	110.4	462	27.2	1407	82.8	200	11.8	.266	.353	.515	.971	0	4	.273	302.8	575.8
UTIL LANCE JOHNSON	16	767	54.8	1565	111.8	34	2.4	486	34.7	327	23.4	.291	.334	.386	.983	1	7	.316	227.5	543.5

CH TURNER, SAIN

PITCHERS	YRS	W	W/Y	SH	SH/Y	SV	SV/Y	IP	H	H/IP	HR	HR/IP	BB	BB/IP	K	K/IP	QI	WL%	PIT	GRO	ERA	CUM	AVG	PITCH #
RHP GREG MADDUX	20	318	15.9	35	1.8	0	0.0	4406	4082	.926	298	.068	907	.206	3052	.693	.507	.627	27	17.7	3.01	14.69	490	1959
LHP HARRY BRECHEEN	12	133	11.0	25	2.0	18	1.5	1907	1731	.907	117	.061	536	.281	901	.472	.777	.591	7	14.5	2.92	11.58	132	1290
RFP ROBB NEN	10	45	4.5	0	0.0	314	31.4	715	607	.849	51	.071	260	.364	793	1.109	.175	.517	1	35.9	2.98	32.92	147	3439

PLAYER TOTAL **5436.8** *PITCHER TOTAL* **6688** *TEAM TOTAL* **12124.8**

TEAM 33
MGR ROGER CRAIG

Player	YRS	R	R/YR	H	H/YR	HR	HR/Y	RBI	RBI/Y	SB	SB/Y	B AV	OB AV	SG AV	FA	DEF	OFF	TOT AV	GRO	PLAY #
1B EDDIE MURRAY	21	1627	77.5	3255	155.0	504	24.0	1917	91.3	110	5.2	.287	.363	.476	.993	5	4	.310	353.8	663.8
2B ALFONSO SORIANO	7	505	72.1	912	130.3	162	23.1	465	66.4	169	24.1	.280	.320	.500	.970	0	3	.306	316.4	622.4
SS JAY BELL	18	1123	62.4	1963	109.1	195	10.8	860	47.8	91	5.1	.265	.343	.416	.976	2	0	.227	235.2	462.2
3B BILL MUELLER	10	651	65.1	1202	120.2	82	8.2	478	47.8	19	1.9	.292	.373	.425	.960	1	1	.258	243.8	501.8
LF FRANK ROBINSON	21	1829	87.0	2943	140.1	586	27.9	1812	86.2	204	9.7	.294	.392	.537	.984	1	13	.378	350.9	728.9
CF JOE CARTER	16	1170	73.1	2184	136.5	396	24.8	1445	90.3	231	14.4	.259	.310	.464	.977	0	1	.219	339.3	558.3
RF LARRY WALKER	17	1355	79.7	2160	127.1	383	22.5	1311	77.1	230	13.5	.313	.400	.565	.987	7	9	.444	319.7	763.7
C ROY CAMPANELLA	10	627	62.7	1161	116.1	242	24.2	856	85.6	25	2.5	.276	.362	.500	.988	2	1	.287	291.1	578.1
PH/DH JOSE CANSECO	17	1186	69.8	1877	110.4	462	27.2	1407	82.8	200	11.8	.266	.353	.515	.971	0	4	.273	302.8	575.8
UTIL CECIL FIELDER	13	744	57.2	1313	106.0	319	24.5	1008	77.5	2	0.2	.255	.348	.482	.992	0	6	.309	260.8	569.8

CH CUCCINELLO, HRINIAK

PITCHERS	YRS	W	W/Y	SH	SH/Y	SV	SV/Y	IP	H	H/IP	HR	HR/IP	BB	BB/IP	K	K/IP	QI	WL%	PIT	GRO	ERA	CUM	AVG	PITCH #
RHP JOHNNY SAIN	11	139	12.6	16	1.4	51	4.6	2125	2145	1.009	180	.084	619	.291	910	.428	.956	.545	5	18.6	3.49	15.11	14	1525
LHP VIDA BLUE	17	209	12.2	37	2.1	2	0.1	3343	2939	.879	263	.078	1185	.354	2175	.650	.661	.565	4	14.4	3.27	11.13	46	1159
RFP JOSE MESA	17	77	4.5	2	0.1	319	18.8	1426	1503	1,054	133	.093	590	.414	970	.680	.881	.433	1	23.4	4.29	19.11	-130	1781

PLAYER TOTAL **6024.8** *PITCHER TOTAL* **4465** *TEAM TOTAL* **10489.8**

TEAM 34
MGR BILL McKECHNIE

Player	YRS	R	R/YR	H	H/YR	HR	HR/Y	RBI	RBI/Y	SB	SB/Y	B AV	OB AV	SG AV	FA	DEF	OFF	TOT AV	GRO	PLAY #
1B DAVID ORTIZ	9	507	56.3	877	97.4	177	19.7	626	69.6	5	0.6	.282	.366	.534	.990	0	1	.260	243.2	503.2
2B BRETT BOONE	14	927	66.2	1775	126.8	252	18.0	1021	72.9	94	6.7	.266	.325	.442	.986	7	1	.321	290.4	611.4
SS ROY SMALLEY, JR.	13	745	57.3	1454	111.8	163	12.5	694	53.3	27	2.0	.257	.348	.395	.966	0	0	.200	236.9	436.9
3B BROOKS ROBINSON	23	1232	53.5	2848	123.8	268	11.6	1357	59.0	28	1.2	.267	.325	.401	.971	16	1	.346	249.5	595.5
LF AUGIE GALAN	16	1004	62.7	1706	106.6	100	6.2	830	51.8	123	7.6	.287	.390	.419	.981	0	6	.294	234.9	528.9
CF PETE REISER	10	473	47.3	786	78.6	58	5.8	368	36.8	87	8.7	.295	.380	.450	.979	0	7	.365	177.2	542.2
RF KIRBY PUCKETT	12	1071	89.3	2304	192.0	207	17.3	1085	90.4	134	11.2	.318	.363	.477	.989	6	6	.431	400.8	831.8
C KEITH MORELAND	12	511	42.5	1279	106.5	121	10.0	674	56.1	28	2.3	.279	.339	.411	.979	0	0	.205	217.4	422.4
PH/DH G, MATTHEWS, SR.	16	1083	67.6	2011	125.6	234	14.6	978	61.1	183	11.4	.281	.367	.439	.968	0	2	.242	280.3	498.7
UTIL STAN HACK	16	1239	77.4	2193	137.0	57	3.5	642	40.1	165	10.3	.301	.394	.397	.957	2	5	.305	268.3	573.3

CH COONEY, HOWSER

PITCHERS	YRS	W	W/Y	SH	SH/Y	SV	SV/Y	IP	H	H/IP	HR	HR/IP	BB	BB/IP	K	K/IP	QI	WL%	PIT	GRO	ERA	CUM	AVG	PITCH #
RHP NOLAN RYAN	27	324	12.0	61	2.2	3	0.1	5386	3923	.728	321	.058	2795	.518	5714	1.060	.244	.526	32	14.3	3.19	11.11	489	1600
LHP RANDY JOHNSON	18	263	14.6	37	2.1	2	0.1	3594	2819	.784	333	.093	1349	.375	4372	1.216	.036	.659	34	16.8	3.11	13.69	837	2206
RFP TREVOR HOFFMAN	14	49	3.5	0	0.0	436	31.1	822	627	.763	74	.090	237	.288	915	1.113	.028	.480	1	34.6	2.76	31.84	174	3358

PLAYER TOTAL **5544.3** *PITCHER TOTAL* **7164** *TEAM TOTAL* **12708.3**

TEAM 35
MGR RALPH HOUK

Player	YRS	R R/YR	H H/YR	HR HR/Y	RBI RBI/Y	SB SB/Y	B AV	OB AV	SG AV	FA DEF	OFF	TOT AV	GRO	PLAY #
1B FRANK THOMAS	16	1327 / 82.9	2136 / 133.5	448 / 28.0	1465 / 91.6	32 / 2.0	.307	.427	.568	.991 / 0	11	.398	338.4	736.4
2B PETE RUNNELS	14	876 / 62.5	1854 / 132.4	49 / 3.5	630 / 45.0	37 / 2.6	.291	.376	.378	.994 / 2	2	.265	246.0	511.0
SS RICH AURILIA	11	601 / 54.6	1220 / 110.9	146 / 13.3	585 / 53.2	19 / 1.7	.276	.330	.436	.973 / 0	0	.209	233.7	442.7
3B GRAIG NETTLES	22	1193 / 54.2	2225 / 101.1	390 / 17.7	1314 / 59.7	32 / 1.4	.248	.332	.421	.961 / 3	1	.236	234.1	470.1
LF RICKEY HENDERSON	25	2295 / 91.8	3055 / 122.2	297 / 11.9	1115 / 44.6	1406 / 56.2	.279	.401	.419	.979 / 0	23	.404	326.5	730.5
CF JEROMY BURNITZ	13	882 / 67.8	1375 / 105.8	299 / 23.0	932 / 71.7	73 / 5.6	.255	.348	.485	.977 / 0	5	.218	273.9	491.9
RF ROGER MARIS	12	826 / 68.8	1325 / 110.4	275 / 22.9	851 / 70.9	21 / 1.7	.260	.348	.476	.982 / 0	5	.300	274.7	574.7
C YOGI BERRA	19	1175 / 61.8	1150 / 113.1	358 / 18.8	1430 / 75.2	30 / 1.5	.285	.350	.482	.989 / 2	0	.244	270.4	514.4
PH/DH ERNIE LOMBARDI	17	601 / 35.3	1792 / 105.4	190 / 11.1	990 / 58.2	8 / 0.4	.306	.358	.460	.979 / 0	1	.236	210.4	446.4
UTIL KEVIN MITCHELL	13	630 / 48.5	1173 / 90.2	234 / 18.0	760 / 42.2	30 / 1.7	.284	.360	.520	.963 / 0	3	.280	200.2	480.2

CH Hon. WAGNER, HERMAN

PITCHERS	YRS	W W/Y	SH SH/Y	SV SV/Y	IP	H H/IP	HR HR/IP	BB BB/IP	K K/IP	QI	WL%	PIT	GRO	ERA	CUM	AVG	PITCH #
RHP MIKE MUSSINA	15	224 / 14.9	23 / 1.5	0 / 0.0	3013	2874 / .954	323 / .107	684 / .227	2400 / .797	.491	.638	6	16.4	3.64	12.74	182	1456
LHP DONTRELLE WILLIS	3	46 / 15.3	7 / 2.3	0 / 0.0	594	571 / .961	44 / .074	174 / .293	451 / .759	.569	.630	3	17.6	3.27	14.33	354	1787
RFP JOHN WETTELAND	12	48 / 4.0	0 / 0.0	330 / 27.5	765	616 / .805	73 / .095	252 / .329	804 / 1.051	.178	.516	1	31.5	2.93	28.57	140	2997

PLAYER TOTAL **5398.3** *PITCHER TOTAL* **6240** *TEAM TOTAL* **11638.3**

TEAM 36
MGR CASEY STENGEL

Player	YRS	R R/YR	H H/YR	HR HR/Y	RBI RBI/Y	SB SB/Y	B AV	OB AV	SG AV	FA DEF	OFF	TOT AV	GRO	PLAY #
1B JOHNNY MIZE	15	1118 / 74.5	2011 / 134.0	359 / 23.9	1337 / 89.1	28 / 1.8	.312	.397	.562	.992 / 2	15	.480	323.3	803.3
2B TIM FOLI	16	576 / 36.0	1515 / 94.6	25 / 1.5	501 / 31.3	81 / 5.0	.251	.286	.309	.973 / 2	0	.194	168.4	362.4
SS ORLANDO CABRERA	9	510 / 56.7	1083 / 120.3	80 / 8.9	469 / 52.1	118 / 13.1	.267	.315	.403	.978 / 1	0	.219	251.3	470.3
3B PINKY HIGGINS	14	930 / 66.4	1941 / 117.2	140 / 10.0	1075 / 76.7	61 / 4.3	.292	.370	.427	.935 / 0	11	.217	274.6	491.6
LF GARY MATTHEWS, SR.	16	1083 / 67.6	2011 / 125.6	234 / 14.6	978 / 61.1	183 / 11.4	.281	.367	.439	.968 / 0	2	.242	280.3	498.7
CF DWAYNE MURPHY	12	648 / 54.0	1069 / 89.1	166 / 13.8	609 / 50.8	100 / 8.3	.246	.356	.402	.987 / 6	0	.300	216.8	516.8
RF FRANK ROBINSON	21	1829 / 87.0	2943 / 140.1	586 / 27.9	1812 / 86.2	204 / 9.7	.294	.392	.537	.984 / 1	13	.378	350.9	728.9
C TERRY STEINBACH	14	638 / 45.6	1453 / 103.8	162 / 11.6	745 / 53.2	23 / 1.6	.271	.326	.420	.988 / 1	0	.218	215.6	433.6
PH/DH ALBERT BELLE	12	974 / 80.3	1726 / 143.8	381 / 31.8	1239 / 103.3	88 / 7.3	.295	.369	.564	.976 / 0	8	.379	366.5	745.5
UTIL NICK ETTEN	9	426 / 47.3	921 / 102.3	89 / 9.8	526 / 58.4	22 / 2.4	.277	.371	.423	.988 / 0	3	.280	220.2	500.2

CH CISCO, YOST

PITCHERS	YRS	W W/Y	SH SH/Y	SV SV/Y	IP	H H/IP	HR HR/IP	BB BB/IP	K K/IP	QI	WL%	PIT	GRO	ERA	CUM	AVG	PITCH #
RHP ROBIN ROBERTS	19	286 / 15.0	45 / 2.3	25 / 1.3	4688	4582 / .977	505 / .107	902 / 192	2357 / .502	.774	.539	20	18.6	3.41	15.19	272	1791
LHP SAM McDOWELL	15	141 / 9.4	23 / 1.5	14 / 0.9	2492	1948 / .781	164 / .065	1312 / .526	2453 / .984	.388	.513	10	11.8	3.17	8.63	263	112
RFP JOE NATHAN	6	32 / 5.3	0 / 0.0	88 / 14.7	409	319 / .780	44 / .108	187 / .457	383 / .936	.409	.667	0	20.0	3.44	16.56	86	1742

PLAYER TOTAL **5551.3** *PITCHER TOTAL* **4659** *TEAM TOTAL* **10210.3**

TEAM 37
MGR CASEY STENGEL

Player	YRS	R R/YR	H H/YR	HR HR/Y	RBI RBI/Y	SB SB/Y	B AV	OB AV	SG AV	FA DEF	OFF	TOT AV	GRO	PLAY #
1B KEITH HERNANDEZ	17	1124 / 66.1	2182 / 128.3	162 / 9.5	1071 / 63.0	98 / 5.7	.296	.388	.436	.994 / 11	7	.436	272.6	708.6
2B JOSE VIDRO	9	562 / 62.4	1146 / 127.3	108 / 12.0	503 / 55.9	20 / 2.2	.302	.364	.467	.983 / 0	0	.227	259.4	486.4
SS FREDDIE PATEK	14	736 / 52.5	1340 / 95.7	41 / 2.0	490 / 35.0	385 / 27.5	.242	.311	.324	.962 / 0	2	.203	212.7	415.7
3B BOB ELLIOTT	15	1064 / 70.9	2061 / 137.4	170 / 11.3	1195 / 79.6	60 / 4.0	.289	.375	.440	.947 / 1	1	.247	303.2	550.2
LF LARRY DOBY	13	716 / 55.1	1417 / 109.0	187 / 14.4	710 / 54.6	93 / 7.2	.289	.343	.472	.986 / 1	0	.236	240.5	476.5
CF LARRY DOBY	13	960 / 73.8	1515 / 116.5	253 / 19.4	970 / 74.6	47 / 3.6	.283	.387	.490	.983 / 0	6	.324	287.9	611.9
RF BABE HERMAN	13	882 / 67.8	1818 / 139.8	181 / 13.9	997 / 76.7	94 / 7.2	.324	.383	.532	.961 / 0	1	.263	305.6	568.6
C GUS NIARHOS	9	114 / 12.6	174 / 76.7	1 / 0.1	59 / 6.5	6 / 0.6	.252	.390	.308	.988 / 0	0	.190	96.5	286.5
PH/DH TONY PEREZ	23	1272 / 55.3	2732 / 118.7	379 / 16.4	1652 / 71.8	49 / 2.1	.279	.344	.463	.992 / 1	0	.225	264.3	489.3
UTIL BUCK McCORMICK	13	722 / 55.5	1711 / 131.6	128 / 9.8	951 / 73.1	27 / 2.0	.299	.348	.434	.995 / 4	5	.354	272.0	626.0

CH R. FERRELL, BUMBRY

PITCHERS	YRS	W W/Y	SH SH/Y	SV SV/Y	IP	H H/IP	HR HR/IP	BB BB/IP	K K/IP	QI	WL%	PIT	GRO	ERA	CUM	AVG	PITCH #
RHP PEDRO MARTINEZ	14	197 / 14.1	17 / 1.2	3 / 0.2	2513	1905 / .758	194 / .077	662 / .263	2861 / 1.138	-.040	.701	24	15.5	2.72	12.78	818	2096
LHP HOWIE POLLET	14	131 / 9.3	25 / 1.7	20 / 1.4	2107	2096 / .994	146 / .069	745 / .353	934 / .443	.973	.530	5	12.4	3.51	8.89	-29	860
RFP DENNIS ECKERSLEY	24	197 / 8.2	20 / 0.8	390 / 16.3	3286	3076 / .936	347 / .106	738 / .225	2401 / .731	.536	.535	3	25.3	3.50	21.80	41	2221

PLAYER TOTAL **5219.7** *PITCHER TOTAL* **5177** *TEAM TOTAL* **10396.7**

TEAM 38
MGR ROGER CRAIG

Player	YRS	R R/YR	H H/YR	HR HR/Y	RBI RBI/Y	SB SB/Y	B AV	OB AV	SG AV	FA DEF	OFF	TOT AV	GRO	PLAY #
1B NORM CASH	17	1046 / 61.5	1820 / 107.0	377 / 22.1	1103 / 64.8	43 / 2.5	.271	.377	.488	.992 / 2	3	.285	257.9	542.9
2B DANNY TARTABULL	14	756 / 54.0	1366 / 97.6	262 / 18.7	925 / 66.1	37 / 2.6	.273	.371	.496	.971 / 0	1	.242	239.2	481.2
SS RICO PETROCELLI	13	653 / 50.2	1352 / 104.0	210 / 16.1	773 / 59.4	10 / 0.7	.251	.336	.420	.969 / 3	0	.247	230.4	477.4
3B BILLY COX	11	470 / 38.2	974 / 88.5	66 / 6.0	351 / 31.9	42 / 3.8	.262	.318	.380	.965 / 1	0	.210	168.6	378.6
LF TONY OLIVA	15	870 / 58.0	1917 / 127.8	220 / 14.6	947 / 63.1	86 / 5.7	.304	356	.476	.975 / 0	14	.413	269.2	682.2
CF BILLY BRUTON	12	937 / 78.0	1651 / 137.5	94 / 7.8	545 / 45.4	207 / 17.2	.273	.329	.393	.981 / 0	6	.299	285.9	584.9
RF ROCKY COLAVITO	14	971 / 69.3	1730 / 123.5	374 / 26.7	1159 / 82.7	19 / 1.0	.266	.362	.489	.980 / 1	4	.294	511.1	805.1
C GENE TENACE	15	653 / 43.5	1060 / 70.6	201 / 13.4	674 / 44.9	36 / 2.4	.241	.391	.429	.986 / 1	2	.252	174.8	426.8
PH/DH JOSE CRUZ, SR.	19	1036 / 54.5	2251 / 118.4	165 / 8.6	1077 / 56.6	317 / 16.6	.284	.358	.420	.974 / 0	1	.222	254.7	476.7
UTIL BILL BUCKNER	22	1077 / 48.9	2715 / 123.4	174 / 7.9	1208 / 54.9	183 / 8.3	.289	.324	.408	.992 / 0	3	.231	243.4	474.4

CH McLISH, RUEL

PITCHERS	YRS	W W/Y	SH SH/Y	SV SV/Y	IP	H H/IP	HR HR/IP	BB BB/IP	K K/IP	QI	WL%	PIT	GRO	ERA	CUM	AVG	PITCH #
RHP ROBIN ROBERTS	19	286 / 15.0	45 / 2.3	25 / 1.3	4688	4582 / .977	505 / .107	902 / 192	2357 / .502	.774	.539	20	18.6	3.41	15.19	272	1791
LHP STEVE CARLTON	24	329 / 13.7	55 / 2.2	2 / 0.0	5217	4672 / .895	414 / .079	1833 / .351	4136 / .792	.533	.574	20	15.9	3.22	12.68	295	1563
RFP TODD WORRELL	11	50 / 4.5	0 / 0.0	256 / 23.3	694	608 / .876	65 / .094	247 / .356	628 / .905	.421	.490	2	27.8	3.09	24.71	84	2555

PLAYER TOTAL **5330.2** *PITCHER TOTAL* **5909** *TEAM TOTAL* **11239.2**

TEAM 39
MGR DON GUTTERIDGE

Player	YRS	R R/YR	H H/YR	HR HR/Y	RBI RBI/Y	SB SB/Y	B AV	OB AV	SG AV	FA DEF	OFF	TOT AV	GRO	PLAY #
1B GEORGE SCOTT	14	957 / 68.3	1992 / 142.2	271 / 19.3	1051 / 75.0	69 / 4.9	.268	.335	.435	.990 / 8	2	.350	309.7	659.7
2B JEFF KENT	14	1139 / 81.4	2070 / 147.9	331 / 23.6	1312 / 93.7	92 / 6.6	.289	.354	.506	.978 / 0	0	.230	353.0	583.0
SS ROY SMALLEY, JR.	13	745 / 57.3	1454 / 111.8	163 / 12.5	694 / 53.3	27 / 2.0	.257	.348	.395	.966 / 0	0	.200	236.9	436.9
3B STAN HACK	16	1239 / 77.4	2193 / 137.0	57 / 3.5	642 / 40.1	165 / 10.3	.301	.394	.397	.957 / 2	5	.305	268.3	573.3
LF MIKE GREENWELL	12	657 / 54.8	1400 / 116.7	130 / 10.8	726 / 60.5	80 / 6.7	.303	.368	.463	.981 / 0	0	.227	249.3	476.3
CF ROBERTO KELLY	14	687 / 49.1	1390 / 99.3	124 / 8.9	585 / 41.8	235 / 16.8	.290	.337	.430	.985 / 0	0	.212	215.3	427.3
RF DAVE PARKER	19	1272 / 66.9	2712 / 142.7	339 / 17.8	1493 / 78.5	154 / 8.1	.290	.342	.471	.965 / 3	8	.336	314.0	650.0
C ROY CAMPANELLA	10	627 / 62.7	1161 / 116.1	242 / 24.2	856 / 85.6	25 / 2.5	.276	.362	.500	.988 / 2	1	.287	291.1	578.1
PH/DH MONTE IRVIN	8	366 / 45.7	731 / 91.3	99 / 12.3	443 / 55.3	28 / 3.5	.293	.385	.475	.983 / 0	1	.255	208.1	463.2
UTIL GARY GAETTI	20	1130 / 56.5	2280 / 114.0	360 / 18.0	1341 / 67.1	96 / 4.8	.255	.311	.434	.965 / 7	0	.270	260.4	530.4

CH MICHAEL, CORRALES

PITCHERS	YRS	W W/Y	SH SH/Y	SV SV/Y	IP	H H/IP	HR HR/IP	BB BB/IP	K K/IP	QI	WL%	PIT	GRO	ERA	CUM	AVG	PITCH #
RHP LARRY JACKSON	14	194 / 13.8	37 / 2.6	20 / 1.4	3262	3206 / .982	259 / .079	824 / .252	1709 / .523	.790	.515	2	17.8	3.40	14.40	-44	1396
LHP BOB VEALE	13	120 / 9.2	20 / 1.5	21 / 1.6	1926	1684 / .874	91 / .047	858 / .445	1703 / .884	.482	.558	1	12.3	3.07	9.23	51	974
RFP MIKE HENNEMAN	10	57 / 5.7	0 / 0.0	193 / 19.3	733	686 / .936	47 / .064	271 / .370	533 / .727	.643	.576	0	25.0	3.21	21.79	-22	2157

PLAYER TOTAL **5378.2** *PITCHER TOTAL* **4527** *TEAM TOTAL* **9905.2**

TEAM 40
MGR BILLY SOUTHWORTH

Player	YRS	R R/YR	H H/YR	HR HR/Y	RBI RBI/Y	SB SB/Y	B AV	OB AV	SG AV	FA DEF	OFF	TOT AV	GRO	PLAY #
1B DEE FONDY	8	437 / 54.6	1000 / 125.0	69 / 8.6	373 / 46.6	84 / 10.5	.286	.326	.413	.988 / 0	2	.205	245.3	450.3
2B GEORGE SMITH	4	64 / 16.0	130 / 32.5	9 / 2.2	57 / 14.2	9 / 2.2	.205	.278	.309	.944 / 0	0	.158	67.1	225.1
SS SAM DENTE	9	205 / 22.7	585 / 65.0	4 / 0.4	214 / 23.7	9 / 1.0	.252	.303	.305	.958 / 0	0	.172	112.8	284.8
3B VERN STEPHENS	15	1001 / 66.7	1859 / 123.9	247 / 16.4	1174 / 78.2	25 / 1.6	.286	.355	.460	.960 / 1	4	.286	286.8	572.8
LF DWAYNE MURPHY	12	648 / 54.0	1069 / 89.1	166 / 13.8	609 / 50.8	100 / 8.3	.246	.356	.402	.987 / 6	0	.300	216.8	516.8
CF JACKIE JENSEN	11	810 / 73.6	1463 / 133.0	199 / 18.0	929 / 84.4	143 / 13.0	.279	.372	.460	.977 / 0	5	.313	322.0	635.0
RF DWIGHT EVANS	20	1470 / 73.5	2446 / 122.3	385 / 19.2	1384 / 69.2	78 / 3.9	.272	.373	.470	.987 / 1	5	.273	288.1	561.1
C FRAN HEALY	9	144 / 16.0	332 / 36.8	20 / 2.2	141 / 15.6	30 / 3.3	.250	.329	.350	.980 / 0	0	.185	73.9	258.9
PH/DH BOB ELLIOTT	15	1064 / 70.9	2061 / 137.4	170 / 11.3	1195 / 79.6	60 / 4.0	289	.375	.440	.947 / 1	1	.247	303.2	550.2
UTIL KEN HARRELSON	9	374 / 41.5	703 / 78.1	131 / 14.5	421 / 46.7	53 / 5.8	.239	.328	.414	.990 / 1	1	.240	186.6	426.6

CH L. HARRIS, McCRAW

PITCHERS	YRS	W W/Y	SH SH/Y	SV SV/Y	IP	H H/IP	HR HR/IP	BB BB/IP	K K/IP	QI	WL%	PIT	GRO	ERA	CUM	AVG	PITCH #
RHP BUCKY WALTERS	16	198 / 12.3	42 / 2.6	4 / 0.2	3104	2990 / .963	154 / .049	1121 / .361	1107 / .356	1.017	.553	16	15.1	3.30	11.80	178	1358
LHP FRANK TANANA	21	240 / 11.4	34 / 1.6	1 / 0.0	4188	4063 / .970	448 / .107	1255 / .300	2773 / .662	.715	.504	3	13.0	3.66	9.34	-23	911
RFP TROY PERCIVAL	11	30 / 2.7	0 / 0.0	324 / 29.5	612	412 / .673	70 / .114	264 / .431	700 / 1.144	.074	.423	0	32.2	3.10	29.10	116	3026

PLAYER TOTAL **4481.6** *PITCHER TOTAL* **5295** *TEAM TOTAL* **9776.6**

TEAM 41
MGR LOU PINIELLA

Player	YRS	R R/YR	H H/YR	HR HR/Y	RBI RBI/Y	SB SB/Y	B AV	OB AV	SG AV	FA DEF	OFF	TOT AV	GRO	PLAY #
1B DOLPH CAMILLI	12	936 / 78.0	1482 / 123.5	239 / 19.9	950 / 79.1	60 / 5.0	.277	.388	.492	.990 / 1	5	.331	305.5	636.5
2B TED SIZEMORE	12	577 / 48.0	1311 / 109.2	23 / 1.9	430 / 35.8	59 / 4.9	.262	.327	.321	.979 / 0	0	.182	199.8	381.8
SS JACKIE GUTIERREZ	6	106 / 17.6	227 / 37.8	4 / 0.6	63 / 10.5	25 / 4.1	.237	.263	.285	.945 / 0	0	.157	70.6	227.6
3B EDDIE MATHEWS	17	1509 / 88.7	2315 / 136.1	512 / 30.1	1453 / 85.4	68 / 4.0	.271	.378	.509	.956 / 1	7	.325	344.3	669.3
LF BABE HERMAN	13	882 / 67.8	1818 / 139.8	181 / 13.9	997 / 76.7	94 / 7.2	.324	.383	.532	.961 / 0	1	.263	305.6	568.6
CF IVAL GOODMAN	10	609 / 60.9	1104 / 110.4	95 / 9.5	525 / 52.5	49 / 4.9	.281	.352	.445	.975 / 0	2	.255	238.2	493.2
RF DARRELL EVANS	21	1344 / 64.0	2223 / 105.8	414 / 19.7	1354 / 64.4	98 / 4.6	.248	.364	.431	.946 / 0	3	.237	258.5	495.5
C CARLTON FISK	24	1276 / 53.1	2356 / 98.1	376 / 15.6	1330 / 55.4	128 / 5.3	.269	.365	.457	.988 / 1	1	.230	227.5	457.5
PH/DH A. GALARRAGA	19	1195 / 62.9	2333 / 127.8	399 / 21.0	1425 / 75.0	128 / 6.7	.288	.347	.499	.991 / 2	6	.311	288.4	599.4
UTIL GEORGE SCOTT	14	957 / 68.3	1992 / 142.2	271 / 19.3	1051 / 75.0	69 / 4.9	.268	.335	.435	.990 / 8	2	.350	309.7	659.7

CH COMBS, R. MILLER

PITCHERS	YRS	W W/Y	SH SH/Y	SV SV/Y	IP	H H/IP	HR HR/IP	BB BB/IP	K K/IP	QI	WL%	PIT	GRO	ERA	CUM	AVG	PITCH #
RHP TOM SEAVER	20	311 / 15.5	61 / 3.0	1 / 0.0	4782	3971 / .830	380 / .079	1390 / .290	3640 / .761	.438	.603	23	18.5	2.86	15.64	438	2002
LHP RANDY JOHNSON	18	263 / 14.6	37 / 2.1	2 / 0.1	3594	2819 / .784	333 / .093	1349 / .375	4372 / 1.216	.036	.659	34	16.8	3.11	13.69	837	2206
RFP JEFF REARDON	16	73 / 4.6	0 / 0.0	367 / 22.9	1132	1000 / .883	109 / .096	358 / .316	877 / .775	.520	.487	1	27.5	3.16	24.34	10	2444

PLAYER TOTAL **5189.1** *PITCHER TOTAL* **6652** *TEAM TOTAL* **11841.1**

TEAM 42
MGR AL LOPEZ

Player	YRS	R R/YR	H H/YR	HR HR/Y	RBI RBI/Y	SB SB/Y	B AV	OB AV	SG AV	FA DEF	OFF	TOT AV	GRO	PLAY #
1B GREG LUZINSKI	15	880 / 58.6	1795 / 119.6	307 / 20.4	1128 / 75.2	37 / 2.4	.276	.366	.478	.972 / 1	1	.250	276.2	526.2
2B JACKIE ROBINSON	10	947 / 94.7	1518 / 151.8	137 / 13.7	734 / 73.4	197 / 19.7	.311	.410	.474	.983 / 3	4	.379	373.0	752.0
SS ALAN TRAMMELL	20	1231 / 61.6	2365 / 118.3	185 / 9.3	1003 / 50.2	236 / 11.8	.285	.352	.415	.976 / 4	0	.251	251.0	502.0
3B PHIL NEVIN	11	530 / 48.2	1036 / 94.2	186 / 16.9	675 / 61.4	18 / 1.6	.273	.345	.475	.976 / 0	0	.218	222.9	440.9
LF WALT MORYN	8	324 / 40.5	667 / 83.3	101 / 12.6	354 / 44.2	7 / 0.8	.266	.338	.446	.972 / 0	0	.210	181.4	391.4
CF CURT FLOOD	15	851 / 56.7	1861 / 124.0	85 / 5.6	636 / 42.4	88 / 5.8	.293	.344	.389	.987 / 8	1	.325	234.5	559.5
RF DAVE HENDERSON	14	710 / 50.7	1324 / 94.5	197 / 14.0	708 / 50.5	50 / 3.5	.258	.320	.436	.986 / 0	0	.202	213.2	415.2
C MILT MAY	15	313 / 20.8	971 / 64.7	77 / 0.7	443 / 29.5	4 / 0.2	.263	.321	.371	.986 / 0	0	.191	115.9	306.9
PH/DH MO VAUGHN	12	861 / 71.8	1620 / 135.0	328 / 27.3	1064 / 88.7	30 / 2.5	.293	.383	.523	.988 / 0	1	.290	214.1	504.1
UTIL CASS MICHAELS	12	508 / 42.3	1142 / 95.1	53 / 4.4	501 / 41.7	64 / 5.3	.262	.349	.353	.973 / 0	0	.192	188.8	380.8

CH J. MOORE, YOST

PITCHERS	YRS	W W/Y	SH SH/Y	SV SV/Y	IP	H H/IP	HR HR/IP	BB BB/IP	K K/IP	QI	WL%	PIT	GRO	ERA	CUM	AVG	PITCH #
RHP MIKE MUSSINA	15	224 / 14.9	23 / 1.5	0 / 0.0	3013	2874 / .954	323 / .107	684 / .227	2400 / .797	.491	.638	6	16.4	3.64	12.74	182	1456
LHP HARVEY HADDIX	14	136 / 9.7	20 / 1.4	21 / 1.5	2235	2154 / .963	240 / .107	601 / .268	1575 / .704	.634	.546	2	12.6	3.63	8.97	18	915
RFP MARIANO RIVERA	11	54 / 4.9	1 / 0.1	379 / 34.5	807	630 / .781	42 / .052	215 / .266	728 / .902	.197	.607	4	39.5	2.33	37.17	258	3975

PLAYER TOTAL **4779.0** *PITCHER TOTAL* **6346** *TEAM TOTAL* **11125.0**

EAM 43
GR CITO GASTON

Player	YRS	R	R/YR	H	H/YR	HR	HR/Y	RBI	RBI/Y	SB	SB/Y	B AV	OB AV	SG AV	FA	DEF	OFF	TOT AV	GRO	PLAY #
B RICO CARTY	15	712	47.4	1677	111.8	204	13.6	890	59.3	21	1.4	.299	.372	.464	.970	0	2	.253	233.5	486.5
B SHERRY ROBERTSON	10	200	20.0	346	34.6	26	2.6	151	15.1	32	3.2	.230	.323	.342	.946	0	0	.179	75.5	254.5
S CHARLIE NEAL	8	461	57.6	858	107.2	87	10.8	391	48.8	48	6.0	.259	.331	.394	.978	1	1	.246	230.4	476.4
B DON HOAK	11	598	54.3	1144	104.0	89	8.0	498	45.2	64	5.8	.265	.347	.396	.959	2	1	.255	217.3	472.3
F RALPH KINER	10	971	97.1	1451	145.1	369	36.9	1015	101.5	22	2.2	.279	.398	.548	.974	0	16	.565	382.8	947.8
F REGGIE SANDERS	15	980	65.3	1563	104.2	292	19.5	923	61.5	297	19.8	.267	.344	.491	.980	0	0	.220	270.7	490.7
F RAUL MONDESI	13	909	69.9	1589	122.2	271	20.8	860	66.2	229	17.6	.273	.331	.485	.976	0	0	.218	296.5	514.5
JOE GINSBERG	13	168	12.9	414	31.8	20	1.5	182	14.0	7	0.5	.241	.334	.320	.983	0	0	.179	60.7	239.7
H/DH HANK SAUER	15	709	47.2	1278	85.2	288	19.2	876	58.4	11	0.7	.266	.347	.496	.974	0	2	.248	210.7	458.7
TIL BILL NICHOLSON	18	837	52.3	1484	92.7	235	14.6	948	59.2	27	1.6	.268	.365	.465	.979	1	5	.294	220.4	514.4

H HARDER, SCHOENDIENST
ITCHERS

Pitcher	YRS	W	W/Y	SH	SH/Y	SV	SV/Y	IP	H	H/IP	HR	HR/IP	BB	BB/IP	K	K/IP	QI	WL%	PIT	GRO	ERA	CUM	AVG	PITCH #
HP DEREK LOWE	9	84	9.3	3	0.3	85	9.4	1312	1306	.995	108	.082	387	.295	858	.654	.718	.532	1	19.0	3.83	15.17	-25	1492
HP JOHN ANTONELLI	12	126	10.5	25	2.0	21	1.7	1992	1870	.938	185	.092	687	.344	1162	.583	.791	.534	5	14.2	3.34	10.86	53	1139
FP DICK RADATZ	7	52	7.4	0	0.0	122	17.4	693	532	.767	65	.101	296	.463	745	1.165	.166	.547	2	24.8	3.13	21.67	222	2389

PLAYER TOTAL **4855.5** *PITCHER TOTAL* **5020** *TEAM TOTAL* **9875.5**

TEAM 44
MGR RAY MILLER

Player	YRS	R	R/YR	H	H/YR	HR	HR/Y	RBI	RBI/Y	SB	SB/Y	B AV	OB AV	SG AV	FA	DEF	OFF	TOT AV	GRO	PLAY #
1B WILLIE McCOVEY	22	1229	55.8	2211	100.5	521	23.6	1555	70.6	26	1.1	.270	.377	.515	.987	0	10	.323	251.6	574.6
2B JAY BELL	18	1123	62.4	1963	109.1	195	10.8	860	47.8	91	5.1	.265	.343	.416	.976	2	0	.227	235.2	462.2
SS ORLANDO CABRERA	9	510	56.7	1083	120.3	80	8.9	469	52.1	118	13.1	.267	.315	.403	.978	1	0	.219	251.3	470.3
3B KEN REITZ	11	366	33.2	1243	113.0	68	6.1	548	49.8	10	0.9	.260	.293	.359	.970	7	0	.310	203.0	513.0
LF REGGIE JACKSON	21	1551	73.8	2584	123.0	563	26.8	1702	81.0	228	10.8	.262	.358	.490	.967	0	10	.317	315.4	632.4
CF BEN CHAPMAN	15	1144	76.2	1958	130.5	90	6.0	977	65.1	287	19.1	.302	.383	.440	.967	0	5	.291	296.9	587.9
RF HANK AARON	23	2174	94.5	3771	163.9	755	32.8	2297	99.8	240	10.4	.305	.377	.555	.980	0	23	.447	401.4	848.9
C MIKE MATHENY	12	343	28.9	888	74.0	64	5.3	425	35.4	8	0.7	.239	.293	.344	.994	4	0	.242	144.1	386.1
PH/DH JOSE CANSECO	17	1186	69.8	1877	110.4	462	27.2	1407	82.8	200	11.8	.266	.353	.515	.971	0	4	.273	302.8	575.8
UTIL ADAM DUNN	5	420	84.0	564	112.8	158	31.6	374	74.8	41	8.2	.248	.383	.518	.977	0	0	.230	311.2	541.2

CH HEGAN, CUCCINELLO
PITCHERS

Pitcher	YRS	W	W/Y	SH	SH/Y	SV	SV/Y	IP	H	H/IP	HR	HR/IP	BB	BB/IP	K	K/IP	QI	WL%	PIT	GRO	ERA	CUM	AVG	PITCH #
RHP ROY OSWALT	5	83	16.6	4	0.8	0	0.0	981	933	.951	80	.082	225	.229	850	.866	.396	.680	2	17.4	3.07	14.33	228	1661
LHP FRANK VIOLA	15	176	11.7	16	1.1	0	0.0	2836	2827	.997	294	.104	864	.305	1844	.650	.756	.540	3	12.8	3.73	9.07	-5	902
RFP JEFF REARDON	16	73	0.0	0	0.0	367	22.9	1132	1000	.883	109	.096	358	.316	877	.775	.520	.487	1	27.5	3.16	24.34	10	2444

PLAYER TOTAL **5592.4** *PITCHER TOTAL* **5007** *TEAM TOTAL* **10599.4**

TEAM 45
MGR BILL HITCHCOCK

Player	YRS	R	R/YR	H	H/YR	HR	HR/Y	RBI	RBI/Y	SB	SB/Y	B AV	OB AV	SG AV	FA	DEF	OFF	TOT AV	GRO	PLAY #
1B CECIL FIELDER	13	744	57.2	1313	106.0	319	24.5	1008	77.5	2	0.2	.255	.348	.482	.992	0	6	.309	260.8	569.8
2B SCOTT BROSIUS	11	544	49.5	1001	91.0	141	12.8	531	48.3	57	5.2	.257	.323	.422	.962	1	2	.219	206.4	425.4
SS VINNY CASTILLA	15	876	58.4	1821	121.4	315	21.0	1078	71.9	33	2.2	.278	.324	.483	.966	1	1	.245	274.1	519.1
3B KEN BOYER	15	1104	86.7	2143	142.8	282	18.8	1141	76.0	105	7.0	.287	.351	.487	.952	7	1	.327	331.3	658.3
LF BILL WHITE	13	843	64.8	1706	131.2	202	15.5	870	66.9	103	7.9	.286	.353	.455	.992	7	0	.326	286.3	612.3
CF DIXIE WALKER	18	1037	57.6	2064	114.6	105	5.8	1023	56.8	59	3.2	.306	.383	.437	.966	0	3	.258	238.0	496.0
RF DANNY TARTABULL	14	756	54.0	1366	97.6	262	18.7	925	66.1	37	2.6	.273	.371	.496	.971	0	1	.242	239.2	481.2
C SHERM LOLLAR	18	623	34.6	1415	78.6	155	8.6	808	44.8	20	1.1	.264	.359	.402	.992	8	0	.294	167.7	461.7
PH/DH DAVE KINGMAN	16	901	56.3	1575	98.4	442	27.6	1210	75.6	85	5.3	.236	.305	.478	.957	0	3	.241	263.2	504.2
UTIL BEN OGLIVIE	16	784	49.0	1615	100.9	235	14.6	901	56.3	87	5.4	.273	.340	.450	.978	0	1	.225	226.2	451.2

CH RODGERS, TERWILLIGER
PITCHERS

Pitcher	YRS	W	W/Y	SH	SH/Y	SV	SV/Y	IP	H	H/IP	HR	HR/IP	BB	BB/IP	K	K/IP	QI	WL%	PIT	GRO	ERA	CUM	AVG	PITCH #
RHP PEDRO MARTINEZ	14	197	14.1	17	1.2	3	0.2	2513	1905	.758	194	.077	662	.263	2861	1.138	-.040	.701	24	15.5	2.72	12.78	818	2096
LHP JOHNNY PODRES	15	148	9.8	24	1.6	11	0.7	2265	2239	.988	242	.106	743	.328	1435	.633	.789	.561	4	12.1	3.68	8.42	12	854
RFP JEFF REARDON	16	73	0.0	0	0.0	367	22.9	1132	1000	.883	109	.096	358	.316	877	.775	.520	.487	1	27.5	3.16	24.34	10	2444

PLAYER TOTAL **5179.2** *PITCHER TOTAL* **5394** *TEAM TOTAL* **10573.2**

TEAM 46
MGR DALLAS GREEN

Player	YRS	R	R/YR	H	H/YR	HR	HR/Y	RBI	RBI/Y	SB	SB/Y	B AV	OB AV	SG AV	FA	DEF	OFF	TOT AV	GRO	PLAY #
1B DON MATTINGLY	14	1007	71.9	2153	153.8	222	15.9	1099	78.5	14	1.0	.307	.363	.471	.996	10	8	.485	321.3	806.3
2B JACOB BRUMFIELD	14	260	37.1	404	57.7	32	4.6	162	23.1	74	10.6	.257	.321	.393	.979	0	0	.194	132.8	326.8
SS MIKE BORDICK	14	676	48.3	1500	132.4	91	6.5	626	44.7	96	6.9	.260	.323	.362	.982	1	0	.203	213.7	416.7
3B RAY JABLONSKI	8	297	37.1	687	85.8	83	10.3	438	54.7	16	2.0	.268	.324	.423	.936	0	0	.203	189.9	392.9
LF TONY ARMAS, SR.	14	614	43.9	1302	93.0	251	17.9	815	58.2	18	1.3	.252	.290	.453	.981	0	3	.242	214.1	456.1
CF ROBERTO KELLY	14	687	49.1	1390	99.3	124	8.9	585	41.8	235	16.8	.290	.337	.430	.985	0	0	.212	215.3	427.3
RF JUAN ENCARNACION	9	501	55.7	1029	114.3	128	14.2	541	60.1	119	13.2	.268	.316	.440	.983	0	0	.205	257.7	462.7
C RICK DEMPSEY	24	525	21.8	1093	45.5	96	4.0	471	24.6	20	0.8	.233	.321	.347	.988	2	0	.196	96.7	292.7
PH/DH EDDIE ROBINSON	13	546	42.0	1146	88.1	172	13.2	723	55.6	10	0.7	.268	.354	.440	.990	1	0	.227	199.6	426.6
UTIL MIKE HEATH	14	462	33.0	1061	75.7	86	6.1	469	33.5	54	3.8	.252	.302	.367	.981	0	0	.184	152.1	336.1

CH HRINIAK, M. GRISSOM
PITCHERS

Pitcher	YRS	W	W/Y	SH	SH/Y	SV	SV/Y	IP	H	H/IP	HR	HR/IP	BB	BB/IP	K	K/IP	QI	WL%	PIT	GRO	ERA	CUM	AVG	PITCH #
RHP GAYLORD PERRY	22	314	14.2	53	2.4	11	0.5	5350	4938	.922	399	.074	1379	.257	3534	.660	.593	.542	9	17.1	3.11	13.99	119	1518
LHP JOHNNY PODRES	15	148	9.8	24	1.6	11	0.7	2265	2239	.988	242	.106	743	.328	1435	.633	.789	.561	4	12.1	3.68	8.42	12	854
RFP LEE SMITH	18	71	3.9	0	0.0	478	26.6	1289	1133	.879	89	.069	486	.377	1251	.971	.354	.436	4	30.5	3.03	27.47	101	2848

PLAYER TOTAL **4344.2** *PITCHER TOTAL* **5220** *TEAM TOTAL* **9564.2**

TEAM 47
MGR TERRY FRANCONA

Player	YRS	R	R/YR	H	H/YR	HR	HR/Y	RBI	RBI/Y	SB	SB/Y	B AV	OB AV	SG AV	FA	DEF	OFF	TOT AV	GRO	PLAY #
1B GREG BROCK	10	420	42.0	794	79.4	110	11.0	462	46.2	41	4.1	.248	.340	.399	.994	0	0	.197	182.7	379.7
2B TONY CUCCINELLO	15	730	48.6	1729	115.2	94	6.2	884	58.9	42	2.8	.280	.343	.394	.973	0	0	.203	231.7	434.7
SS ERIC McNAIR	14	592	42.2	1240	88.5	82	5.8	633	45.2	58	4.1	.274	.318	.392	.949	0	1	.211	185.8	396.8
3B KEN REITZ	11	366	33.2	1243	113.0	68	6.1	548	49.8	10	0.9	.260	.293	.359	.970	7	0	.310	203.0	513.0
LF FRANK BAUMHOLTZ	10	450	45.0	1010	101.0	25	2.5	272	27.2	30	3.0	.290	.342	.389	.980	0	0	.204	178.7	382.7
CF JUNIOR FELIX	6	309	51.5	562	93.6	55	9.1	280	46.6	49	8.1	.264	.313	.413	.970	0	0	.198	208.0	406.0
RF RUBEN SIERRA	19	1081	56.9	2147	113.0	306	16.1	1318	69.4	142	7.5	.268	.316	.450	.970	0	3	.239	262.3	501.3
C SCOTT HATTEBERG	11	423	38.5	900	81.8	83	7.5	422	38.4	1	0.1	.268	.356	.403	.991	0	0	.205	166.9	371.9
PH/DH BROOK JACOBY	11	535	48.6	1220	110.9	120	10.9	545	49.5	16	1.4	.270	.337	.405	.958	0	0	.202	211.2	413.2
UTIL JIM GANTNER	17	726	42.7	1696	99.7	47	2.7	568	33.4	137	22.4	.274	.322	.351	.985	0	0	.189	186.5	375.5

CH MYATT, RIPKEN
PITCHERS

Pitcher	YRS	W	W/Y	SH	SH/Y	SV	SV/Y	IP	H	H/IP	HR	HR/IP	BB	BB/IP	K	K/IP	QI	WL%	PIT	GRO	ERA	CUM	AVG	PITCH #
RHP A. MESSERSMITH	12	130	10.8	27	2.2	15	1.2	2230	1719	.770	174	.078	831	.372	1625	.728	.492	.568	9	14.2	2.86	11.34	275	1409
LHP TOM GLAVINE	19	275	14.5	24	1.3	0	0.0	3952	3810	.964	300	.076	1337	.338	2350	.595	.783	.599	7	15.8	3.44	12.36	61	1297
RFP LEE SMITH	18	71	3.9	0	0.0	478	26.6	1289	1133	.879	89	.069	486	.377	1251	.971	.354	.436	4	30.5	3.03	27.47	101	2848

PLAYER TOTAL **4174.8** *PITCHER TOTAL* **5554** *TEAM TOTAL* **9728.8**

TEAM 48
MGR JOE ALTOBELLI

Player	YRS	R	R/YR	H	H/YR	HR	HR/Y	RBI	RBI/Y	SB	SB/Y	B AV	OB AV	SG AV	FA	DEF	OFF	TOT AV	GRO	PLAY #
1B TRAVIS HAFNER	4	231	57.8	387	96.8	76	19.0	263	65.8	5	1.3	.293	.388	.556	.986	0	0	.248	240.5	488.5
2B ROY WHITE	15	964	64.2	1803	120.2	160	10.6	758	50.5	233	15.5	.271	.363	.404	.988	1	2	.247	261.0	508.0
SS EDDIE BRESSOUD	12	443	36.9	925	77.0	94	7.8	365	30.4	9	0.7	.252	.321	.401	.963	0	0	.194	152.8	346.8
3B JOE McEWING	8	217	27.1	443	63.3	25	3.1	158	19.8	33	4.1	.252	.303	.356	.980	0	0	.182	117.6	299.6
LF MACK JONES	10	485	48.5	778	77.8	133	13.3	415	41.5	65	6.5	.252	.349	.444	.976	0	0	.209	187.6	396.6
CF TORII HUNTER	9	492	54.7	891	99.0	133	14.8	506	56.2	96	10.7	.267	.321	.458	.991	5	0	.321	235.0	556.0
RF ANDY PAFKO	17	844	49.6	1796	105.6	213	12.5	976	57.4	38	2.2	.285	.351	.449	.984	1	0	.228	227.3	455.3
C JOE NOLAN	11	156	14.1	382	34.7	27	2.4	178	16.1	7	0.6	.263	.340	.378	.984	1	0	.214	67.9	281.9
PH/DH WILLIE HORTON	18	873	48.5	1993	110.7	325	18.0	1163	64.6	20	1.1	.273	.335	.457	.972	0	0	.213	242.9	455.9
UTIL RALPH GARR	13	717	55.1	1562	120.1	75	5.7	408	31.3	172	13.3	.306	.340	.416	.968	0	4	.273	225.5	498.5

CH HEGAN, SKINNER
PITCHERS

Pitcher	YRS	W	W/Y	SH	SH/Y	SV	SV/Y	IP	H	H/IP	HR	HR/IP	BB	BB/IP	K	K/IP	QI	WL%	PIT	GRO	ERA	CUM	AVG	PITCH #
RHP GARY NOLAN	10	110	11.0	14	1.4	0	0.0	1675	1505	.899	146	.087	413	.247	1039	.620	.613	.611	1	12.4	3.08	9.32	33	965
LHP ED LOPAT	12	166	13.8	27	2.2	3	0.2	2439	2464	1.010	179	.073	650	.266	859	.352	.997	.597	3	16.2	3.21	12.99	-50	1294
RFP LEE SMITH	18	71	3.9	0	0.0	478	26.6	1289	1133	.879	89	.069	486	.377	1251	.971	.354	.436	4	30.5	3.03	27.47	101	2848

PLAYER TOTAL **4287.1** *PITCHER TOTAL* **5107** *TEAM TOTAL* **9394.1**

TEAM 49
MGR LARRY DIERKER

Player	YRS	R	R/YR	H	H/YR	HR	HR/Y	RBI	RBI/Y	SB	SB/Y	B AV	OB AV	SG AV	FA	DEF	OFF	TOT AV	GRO	PLAY #
1B EARL WILLIAMS	8	361	45.1	756	95.6	138	17.2	457	57.1	2	0.2	.247	.321	.424	.989	0	0	.198	215.2	413.2
2B TOMMY HELMS	14	414	29.5	1342	95.8	34	2.4	477	34.0	33	2.3	.269	.303	.342	.983	3	0	.225	164.0	389.0
SS MARK BELANGER	18	676	37.5	1316	73.1	20	1.1	389	21.6	167	9.2	.228	.302	.280	.977	8	0	.251	142.5	393.5
3B BOB KENNEDY	16	514	32.1	1176	73.5	63	3.9	514	32.1	45	2.8	.254	.310	.355	.978	0	0	.183	144.4	327.4
LF WARREN CROMARTIE	10	459	45.9	1104	110.4	61	6.1	391	39.1	50	5.0	.281	.339	.402	.977	0	0	.204	206.5	410.5
CF FELIPE ALOU	17	985	57.9	2101	123.5	206	12.1	852	50.1	107	6.2	.286	.330	.433	.979	0	3	.245	249.8	494.8
RF LARRY HERNDON	14	605	43.2	1334	95.2	107	7.6	550	39.2	92	6.5	.274	.325	.409	.972	0	0	.201	191.7	392.7
C TODD HUNDLEY	14	495	35.4	883	63.1	202	14.4	599	42.8	14	1.0	.234	.320	.443	.987	0	0	.200	156.1	356.1
PH/DH STEVE BILKO	10	220	22.0	432	43.2	76	7.6	276	27.6	2	0.2	.249	.339	.444	.992	0	0	.206	100.6	306.6
UTIL MARK BELLHORN	8	296	37.0	435	54.4	61	7.6	218	27.3	30	3.8	.236	.349	.403	.972	0	0	.197	130.7	327.7

CH CLEAR, LUCCHESI
PITCHERS

Pitcher	YRS	W	W/Y	SH	SH/Y	SV	SV/Y	IP	H	H/IP	HR	HR/IP	BB	BB/IP	K	K/IP	QI	WL%	PIT	GRO	ERA	CUM	AVG	PITCH #
RHP CHARLIE ROOT	17	201	11.8	21	1.2	40	2.4	3197	3252	1.017	187	.058	889	.278	1459	.456	.897	.557	4	15.4	3.59	11.81	-35	1146
LHP RON GUIDRY	14	170	12.1	26	1.8	4	0.2	2392	2198	.918	226	.094	633	.264	1778	.743	.533	.651	11	14.1	3.29	10.81	301	1382
RFP ARMANDO BENITEZ	12	34	2.8	0	0.0	263	21.9	684	453	.662	78	.114	351	.513	849	1.241	.048	.486	1	24.7	2.92	21.78	174	2352

PLAYER TOTAL **3811.5** *PITCHER TOTAL* **4880** *TEAM TOTAL* **8691.5**

TEAM 50
MGR BUCKY HARRIS

Player	YRS	R	R/YR	H	H/YR	HR	HR/Y	RBI	RBI/Y	SB	SB/Y	B AV	OB AV	SG AV	FA	DEF	OFF	TOT AV	GRO	PLAY #
1B JIM SPENCER	15	541	36.0	1227	81.8	146	9.7	599	39.9	21	0.7	.250	.310	.387	.995	5	0	.256	168.1	424.1
2B LARRY PARRISH	15	850	56.6	1785	119.2	256	17.0	992	66.1	30	6.0	.263	.321	.439	.941	0	0	.204	260.9	464.9
SS FRANK TAVERAS	11	503	45.7	1029	93.5	2	0.1	214	19.4	300	27.2	.255	.302	.313	.953	0	1	.192	185.9	377.9
3B CHRIS SABO	9	494	54.9	898	99.8	116	12.9	426	47.3	120	13.3	.268	.326	.445	.962	2	0	.252	228.4	480.4
LF MATT LAWTON	11	751	68.3	1266	115.1	138	12.5	630	53.3	165	15.0	.267	.368	.418	.984	0	0	.210	264.8	474.8
CF BRIAN JORDAN	14	744	53.1	1433	102.4	181	12.9	811	57.9	119	8.5	.283	.334	.457	.988	0	0	.215	234.6	449.6
RF RON ROENICKE	8	141	17.6	256	32.0	17	2.1	113	14.1	24	3.0	.238	.355	.338	.989	0	0	.186	68.8	254.8
C RALPH HOUK	8	12	1.5	43	5.3	0	0.0	20	2.5	0	0.0	.272	.327	.323	.981	0	0	.184	9.3	193.3
PH/DH CHRIS CHAMBLISS	17	912	53.6	2109	124.0	185	10.8	972	57.1	40	2.3	.279	.336	.415	.993	1	0	.217	247.8	464.8
UTIL JOHN OSTROWSKI	7	73	10.4	131	18.7	14	2.0	74	10.5	7	1.0	.234	.321	.376	.950	0	0	.186	42.6	228.6

CH J. REESE, J. HEGAN
PITCHERS

Pitcher	YRS	W	W/Y	SH	SH/Y	SV	SV/Y	IP	H	H/IP	HR	HR/IP	BB	BB/IP	K	K/IP	QI	WL%	PIT	GRO	ERA	CUM	AVG	PITCH #
RHP J. R. RICHARD	10	107	10.7	19	1.9	0	0.0	1606	1227	.764	73	.045	770	.479	1493	.930	.358	.601	6	12.6	3.15	9.45	281	1226
LHP SID FERNANDEZ	15	114	7.6	9	0.6	1	0.1	1867	1421	.761	191	.102	715	.383	1743	.934	.312	.543	3	8.3	3.36	4.94	86	580
RFP TOM HENKE	14	41	2.9	0	0.0	311	22.2	790	607	.768	64	.081	255	.323	861	1.090	.082	.494	1	25.1	2.67	22.4	161	2404

PLAYER TOTAL **3813.2** *PITCHER TOTAL* **4210** *TEAM TOTAL* **8023.2**

ODD-BALLS

The dry, staccato waves of sound echoed off the green monster in old Fenway as the gravel voice of the late Sherm Feller announced new batters. This mid-September game in 1985 saw the high-flying Toronto Blue Jays coming through Boston on their way to their first divisional title.

Two veterans the Blue Jays had picked up for the pennant drive were due to bat in the inning.

Al Oliver was first.

"Nothin'," crackled Feller, "Oliver...Designated Hitter...Oliver." His voice trailed off after every word or two.

Later, big Cliff Johnson was due up.

"Double Nothin'," rattled Feller, "Johnson...First Base...Johnson."

Through the 1996 season, it's the only time in baseball history that one team had players wearing #0 and #00 the same year.

Al Oliver insisted it was an "O" for Oliver and not a zero. He was the first major leaguer to wear the digit in 1978 with the Texas Rangers. He wore it through 1981, then moved on to Montreal where he wore it for two more years. Again he had "0" in San Francisco in '84. He became the only player to wear it in both leagues the same year wearing it in Los Angeles and Toronto in '85. He also became the first player on a Canadian team to wear #0 and the first to wear it for teams in two countries in the same year. Oliver wore it for eight years with 5 teams.

Oscar Gamble wore it in his last season with the Chicago White Sox. He was the DH, but batted only .203.

Oddibe McDowell, with the Texas Rangers, wore #0 from 1985-88. He bounced around to Cleveland and Atlanta, but did not make the parent club in 1991. He worked his way back to Texas in 1994, but did not take "0." He selected #8—00 vertically?

Junior Ortiz started wearing #0 in 1989 with the Pirates. GM Andy McPhail of the Twins didn't like the idea but to keep harmony gave it to him for 1990-91. He wore it in Cleveland in 1992-93 and Texas in 1994.

Terry McDaniel wore "0" for his brief 23-game career with the New York Mets in '91. Another Met, Rey Ordonez broke in with the big club in 1996 wearing #0. He wore it for two years, but his batting dipped to .216 so he changed to #10.

Franklin Stubbs was the sixth player to wear it while he was with the Brewers in '92.

"I went through the free-agent draft last winter and was selected by only two clubs, Oakland and Cleveland, and Oakland wasn't really interested in me. Nobody really wanted me. So I figured nothing for nothing equals two zeroes," said Paul Dade when asked in 1977 why he wore #00.

Brewers coach Harvey Kuenn thought Dade was not the first to wear #00. He remembered Billy Goodman wearing it with the Red Sox.

No record has been found of Goodman wearing it and Joe Cochran, Boston's equipment manager said they never issued such numbers.

To further support Cochrane's contention, Jack Clark wore #00 with San Diego in 1990. He asked for it when he arrived in Boston the following year and it was denied.

Actually, the first use of the "00" took place in 1944 during spring training. Coach George Uhle of the Washington Senators wore it, but took #32 for the season.

Without the "0", Al Oliver batted .296, hitting over .300 four times and was an All-Star three times with the Pirates for 10 years. With the "0", he batted .311, was over .300 seven straight years, had two 200-hit seasons, led the NL in RBIs once, won a batting title and was a 4-time All-Star.

The first *player* to wear it was none other than the colorful Bobo Newsom. He wore it in 1946 and '47. Bobo toiled for 17 clubs in 20 years, among them the Senators 5 times and the hapless Browns 3 times. He was involved in 9 mid-season trades.

Joe Page, the Yankees' great reliever in the late '40s wore #11. Pittsburgh was in last place in 1954 and was desperate for some relief. They took a chance on the lefty who hadn't pitched in the majors since 1950. His #11 was not available, so he took the nearest double digit—#00. He pitched 9.2 innings in 7 games, gave up 16 hits, 4 homers, walked 7 with an ERA of 11.17. His record was 0-0. The "00" seemed appropriate. The Pirates finished last, of course.

"Bobby Bonds has always worn #25," said John Claiborne, the Cardinals General Manager in 1980 when introducing his newest player to the media. "Well, that's George's (Hendrick) number. It's being negotiated. I'm supposed to lean on George a little bit."

Bobo Newsom pitched for so many bad ball clubs, he actually did better than his career figures while he wore #00. He was 11-8 in 1946 and 4-6 the following year--a total of 15-14 with 1 save. Overall he was 211-222. He pitched in 600 games and completed 246 of them. That's 8 less than Steve Carlton who pitched in 141 more games. What a workhorse.

Bonds didn't take the "26" they offered, but wore #00.

"I'll be the first player in National League history to wear it. (Not so.) Maybe if I get hot, I'll change my name to James (as in 007 Bond, get it?)."

Jeffrey Leonard wore #00 on the Giants, Brewers and Mariners from 1987-1990.

Don Baylor with Oakland and Jerry Hairston with the White Sox both wore it in their last year of play. Baylor DHed at a .220 clip with 7 HRs, while Hairston played only 3 games, going 1 for 3.

Rudy Seanez pitched in 5 games for Cleveland, going 0-0 with 0 saves. Jim Poole did the same for Texas, but did have a save. Both wore "00" in 1991.

Buddy Bates and his cohorts in the Cardinal camp talked Omar Olivares into wearing his initials—the double 0. He had problems early in the 1993 season and was sent down. His record was 5-3 with 1 save, but he didn't pitch well. When he returned the following year, he shied away from "00" and took his old number—26.

Rookie outfielder Brandon Watson wore the #00 when he came up with the Nationals in late 2005.

Pirates pitcher Rick White wore two odd-

Jeffrey Leonard wore #00 the last four years of his career. He became the first player to wear the double digit in both leagues during the same season.

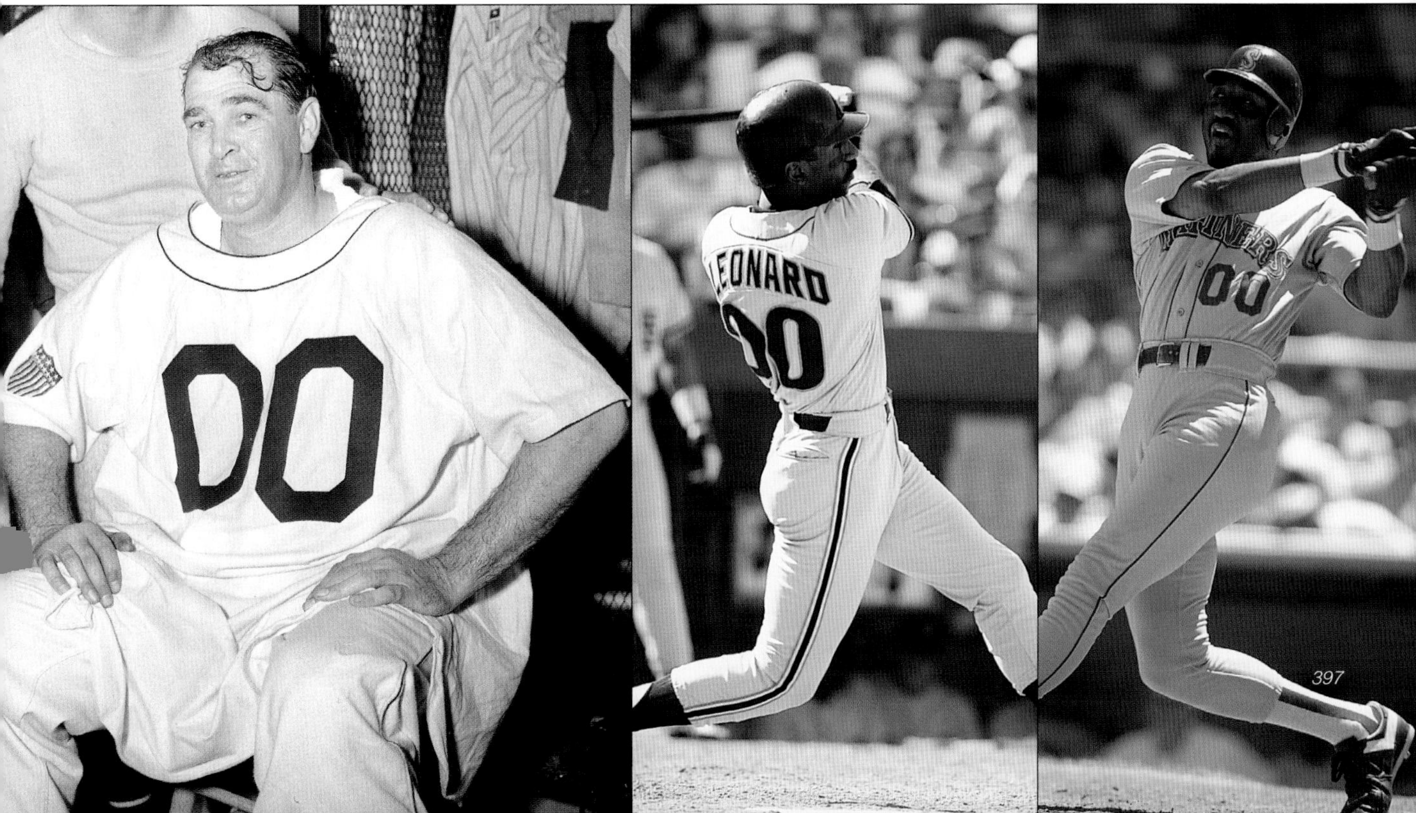

ball numbers in 2005. He switched from #88 to #00. The Mets mascot, Mr. Met, also wears a #00 on his shirt.

The 1993 season was the first time in major league baseball history that all the double digits were worn.

NUMBER	PLAYER	TEAM
00	OMAR OLIVARES	CARDINALS
11*	BARRY LARKIN	REDS
22*	JIMMY KEY	YANKEES
33*	JOSE CANSECO	RANGERS
44*	DARRYL STRAWBERRY	DODGERS
55*	OREL HERSHISER	DODGERS
66*	JUAN GUZMAN	BLUE JAYS
77	JACK ARMSTRONG	MARLINS
88*	RENE GONZALES	ANGELS
99	MITCH WILLIAMS	PHILLIES

**Worn by more than one player.*

Through 1993, Juan Guzman had the remarkable pitching percentage of .784, going 40-11 in his first three years. For the same period, Whitey Ford only managed .741. Guzman added 51-68, .429, to finish his career—a far cry from his sparkling start. Hampered by injuries, switching from #66 was fruitless.

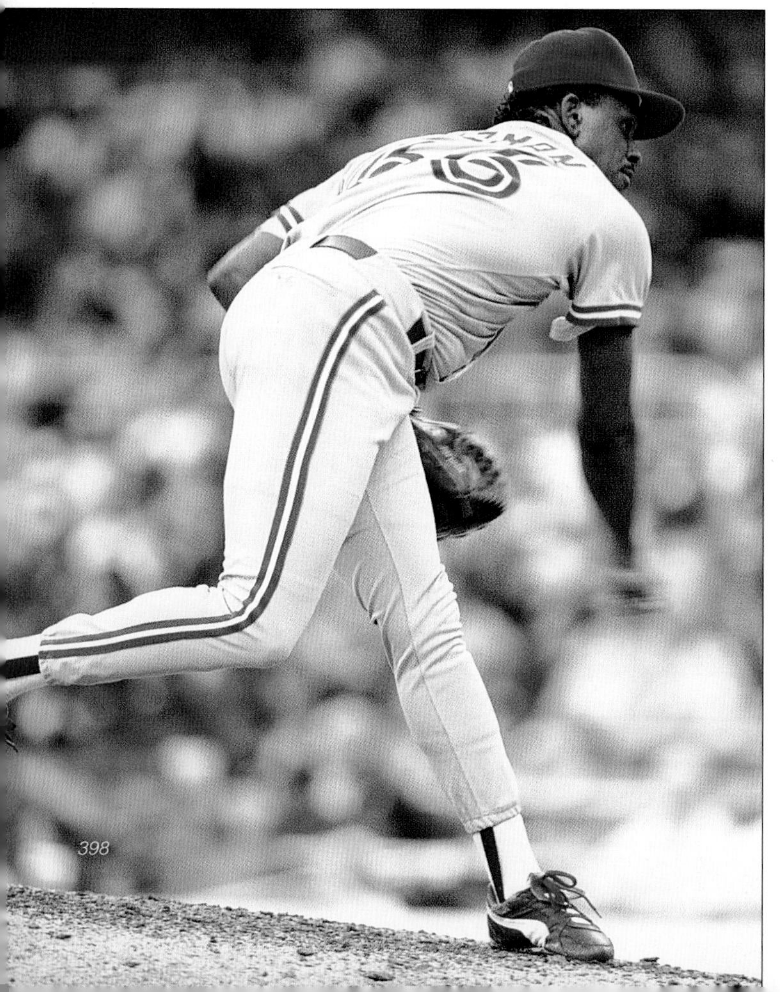

Peaches Davis, a pitcher with Cincinnati, was the first to wear #55 back in 1938. It wasn't worn again until 1953 by Coach Joe Haynes of the Washington Senators. Bob Grim, a 20-game winner in his rookie season of 1954, wore it with the Yankees for 5 years. El Tappe, a backup catcher with the Cubs wore it from 1954-56. Since 1960, the number has become quite commonplace—over 100 players have worn it.

"Croonin' Joe" Cascarella was the first to don #66. He was pitching for the Red Sox in 1935. He didn't win a game for Boston.

Juan Guzman wore different numbers in spring training with the Blue Jays before he made the roster—#52, #56. When playing Caribbean ball he wore #66 and he pitched very well. When he was called to Toronto during the season EM Jeff Ross asked if he wanted to change. "No—66!" was all he said.

The year 1993 saw three players on the same team wear #66—pitchers Blas Minor, Ben Shelton and Jeff Ballard with the Pirates.

Joe "Ducky" Medwick was a fierce competitor. Joe was a member of the famous Gashouse Gang from St. Louis. During the 1934 World Series against Detroit, Joe slid hard with spikes flashing into third, upending Marv Owen. A barrage of boos, catcalls, food and other debris greeted Medwick when he returned to his position in left field. Commissioner Landis removed Joe from the game for his own safety.

The Cards traded Ducky to the Dodgers in 1940 where he met an equally stubborn man in Coach Chuck Dressen who was wearing his beloved #7. Joe couldn't bear to take any ordinary number so he doubled his penchant for seven and took the first #77. He wore it in 1941 as well. Dressen switched with him briefly in 1940, but it didn't last long.

Hall of Famer Bob Lemon wore #77 when he managed the Yanks in 1981. Steve Balboni took it over when Lemon discarded it and wore it until 1983.

"I'm not superstitious or anything, but I was born on the seventh of March," said Jack Armstrong when joining the Indians in 1992. "When I came here all the lower numbers were taken, and when I went down the list, 77 was staring at me, so I took it. I'm going to keep it. I don't know anybody else who wears it, and hey, if it brings me some luck, I can use it," said Armstrong after a season with Cincinnati during which he was sent down. Cy Buynak was happy to give him the number, but he thought it was because Armstrong met his wife in 1977. That would have made him 12-years old. Maybe he met her at a Scout Jamboree.

Armstrong kept his word. He wore it with the Marlins and the Rangers in 1993 and 1994, respectively.

Rene Gonzales wanted to wear #8. But you can't do that in Baltimore. Cal Ripken had been wearing it since 1981. Gonzales doubled it to #88. He wore it from 1987-90 with the Orioles, 1991 in Toronto, 1992-93, 95-96 in Anaheim and with Cleveland in '94.

Paul Carey inherited it when Gonzales left the O's. "No. 8 worked for Cal Ripken," he said. "Maybe twice that is lucky for me."

"The Wild Thing," Charlie Sheen paraded in from the bullpen in the movie *Major League* wearing #99. The Phillies "Wild Thing" Mitch Williams asked EM Frank Coppenbarger in 1992 if he could wear it for real. "This was denied by our GM who thought it was a little out of line," said Frank.

A different atmosphere pervaded the Phillie clubhouse in 1993. Williams asked again for #99 and this time it seemed to fit with the zany bunch that would go on to upend the powerful Braves in the playoffs.

"I'm going to go out and try to throw every pitch 99 miles an hour," said Mitch. The Phils' and Mitch's bubble burst abruptly when Joe Carter stroked his Series-winning homerun in Game 6 off Williams. Just as abruptly, he was moved to Houston where he again took #99.

Mitch Williams was not the first major leaguer to wear that number. Back in 1977, Willie Crawford played in his last 59 games wearing #99 for the Oakland A's. He batted less than twice that number—.184.

Cardinals outfielder, So Taguchi, has worn #99 ever since joining the club in 2002. He played 10 years with Orix in Japan. His glove has lived up to his notices, but his hitting has taken several years to get used to major league pitching.

Eric Davis had been stuck on double digits for years. He wore #55 in spring training before joining the Reds and donning the familiar #44. In LA he switched to #33, which he also wore in Detroit.

Jack Armstrong was an All-Star with the Reds in 1990 wearing #40. He dominated the early goings as the Reds marched to the World Series and mowed down the powerful A's in four games. Following that season, he pitched slightly over .300 ball for the rest of his career. In his one year with Florida, he had a 9-17 record and a dubious 4.49 ERA.

You know it's spring training when you see all those crazy high numbers. Most players that are assigned a number in the 80's or 90's don't feel too confident of making the ball club, so they usually change it as quickly as they can just to feel a bit more secure.

The Oakland A's recall a minor leaguer filling in during a split squad game wearing #102. The Phillies have also gone over #100 in their combined minor league camps. None of the other teams recall using anything over #99.

Some players keep that first number: Domingo Cedeno kept #70 in 1993 for Toronto, Willie McGee continued using #51 and did pretty well with two batting titles and an MVP, Darrel Irvine kept #59 with the Red Sox and Darryl Kile kept #57 with Houston, Colorado and St. Louis.

The average number in use today is much higher than in the thirties when numbering was in its infancy. As a rule the highest number was in the mid-thirties. So, back then, when a player wore a number in the 40's or 50's, it was freakish. In 1932 Erv Brame pitched for the Pirates wearing #48.

"Dixie" Walker wore #45 and "Chilly" Chelini wore #47 for the 1936 Chicago White Sox. A pair of coaches were the first to wear numbers in the 50's: Red Corriden #51 and Johnny Schulte #56, both with the 1933 Chicago Cubs. The first players were Pirate pitcher Mace Brown (#50) in 1935 and outfielder Augie Galan with the Cubs, 1935-37 (#51).

Catcher Babe "Blimp" Phelps of the Cubs in 1934 wore #61 making him the first player to wear above #60 on his back.

When Carlton Fisk changed his Sox from Red to White and his number from #27 to #72 in 1981, he became the first player in 40 years to wear a uniform number in the 70's. Not since Joe Medwick in 1941 was it done.

Another devotee of a 70's number is Oriole reliever Alan Mills who started wearing #75 in 1992.

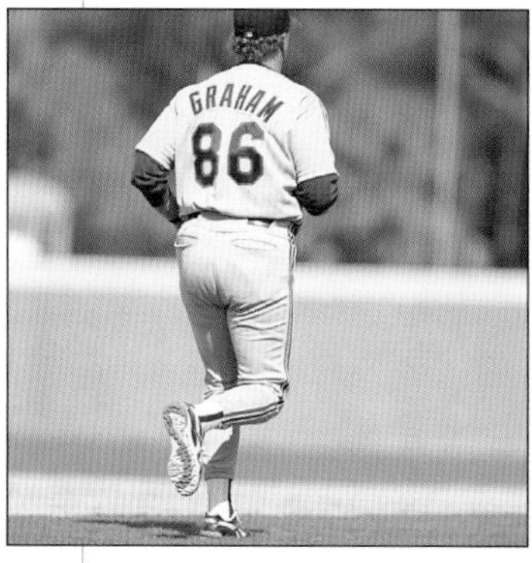

At spring training, #86 Graham, hoping to make the Indians, trotting back to rightfield (above).

John Wehner (right) kept #52 during his stints with the Pirates in 1991 and 1992. His hustle endeared him to the Pirate fans.

Fisk (far right), a Hall of Famer, played more games, had more at bats, more runs, hits, doubles, triples and batted .002 higher than Johnny Bench. He trailed in HRs by 13 and had 46 fewer RBIs. And believe it or not, he stole 60 more bases!

When Willie Crawford wore #99 on the A's in 1977, another bizarre thing happened there. Dick Allen was also finishing his career. His customary #15 was being worn by pitcher Joe Coleman. He decided to take #60 because that was the year he graduated from Wampum High in Pennsylvania. Instead of his name on the back of his shirt, he had "WAMPUM" stitched there.

Back in 1943, two Red Sox players wore unheard of numbers at the time. Pitcher Lou Lucier wore #81 and outfielder Johnny Lazor wore #82. No one seems to know the significance to the pair. The following year they took #24 and #14 respectively.

Four years later, the Boston Braves acquired pitcher Bill Voiselle from the New York Giants. Big Bill took the most talked-about number in baseball—#96. When asked what it was all about, the press discovered that he hailed from Ninety Six, South Carolina. He wore it the last four years of his career in Boston and with the Chicago Cubs.

Some strange numbering practices took place in the 1930's. It helps explain why in 1938 Peaches Davis wore #55, Hank Gowdy #66 and Hall of Famer Edd Roush #67. The fact is the entire Cincinnati Reds team wore high numbers in 1938. The lowest number was #35 worn by Ernie Lombardi and the highest was Coach Roush's #67. They did this for only one year. Was it simply to be different? Did they lose the uniforms with #1-34 on them? The Reds front office didn't have any answers.

The Pirates began numbering players in 1932. But from 1932-38, no Pirate ever wore a single digit number. That's right, no one wore numbers 1-9. Throughout that period, Lloyd Waner was #10 and Paul Waner was #11. It wasn't until 1939, did the Pirate fans see a single digit on a shirt—Oad Swigert, a pitcher, wore #5 and Eddie Yount wore #7.

The Phillies must have liked the idea, because they did the same thing from 1935-1937. No one wore #1-9 for Philly either.

Dick Allen was born and raised in Wampum, Pa. The six-time All-Star led the league in homers twice with the White Sox, RBIs once, and slugging average 3 times. He was always a dangerous hitter.

Bill Voiselle had one 21-victory season (1944) with the Giants. He also led the league in innings pitched and in strikeouts. Since his mid-year trade to the Braves in 1947 until the end of his career while sporting #96, he was 28-32. His winning percentage dropped from .469 to .466—not very significant.

The Phils did another unusual thing in 1939, the vestiges of which lasted for a time after the War. They began issuing low numbers to their pitchers.

1939	1940	1941
3 Syl Johnson	**3** Syl Johnson	**6** Bill Crouch
5 Ike Pearson	**6** Cy Blanton	**8** Rube Merton
7 Al Hollingsworth	**7** Cy Blanton	**9** Gene Lambert
8 Max Butcher	**8** Lefty Hoerst	
9 Hugh Mulcahy	**9** Hugh Mulcahy	

1942	1943	1944
7 Boom Boom Beck	**6** Al Gerheauser	**3** Rogers McKee
8 Si Johnson	**6** Andy Karl	**6** Andy Karl
8 Hilly Flitcraft		**7** Ken Raffensberger
8 Paul Masterson		
9 Gene Lambert		

1946	1948	1955
3 Eli Hodkey	**9** Jocko Thompson	**9** Saul Rogovin
8 Charlie Ripple		

Single digit pitchers were not that uncommon in the 1930s and 1940s. The more recent in time, the less frequent the occurrence. Now it is an oddity. Here's a list.

The last bona fide pitcher to wear a single digit number in the NL was Atlee Hammaker (left) with the Giants during the 1985 season. He was an All-Star in 1983. During that year he yielded a homerun every 19+ innings. Three short years later he was giving up homeruns every 7.6 innings of work. Nagging injuries prevented him from reaching his full potential. In the AL, it was Toronto's Josh Towers (right) who also wore #7 in 2003-05.

#	Pitcher	Team	Year
	American League		
2	Bob Weiland	White Sox	1931
9	Pete Daglia	White Sox	1932
1	Ed Gallagher	Red Sox	1932
9	Bump Hadley	Browns	1932
6	Johnny Welch	Red Sox	1932
8	Bots Nekola	Tigers	1933
9	Bill Trotter	Browns	1937-38
6	Gene Ford	White Sox	1938
9	Bob Feller	Indians	1939
9	Lefty Pyle	Browns	1939
6	Eddie Smith	White Sox	1939
3	Red Anderson	Senators	1940
9	Jack Wilson	Tigers	1942
7	Dewey Adkins	Senators	1943
7	Pete Center	Indians	1943
2	Chief Hogsett	Tigers	1944
3	John McGillen	Phi A's	1944
5	Jake Mooty	Tigers	1944
6	Stan Partenheimer	Red Sox	1944
3	Charlie Gassaway	Phi A's	1945
5	Billy Pierce	Tigers	1945
6	Art Houtteman	Tigers	1946
6	Bob Lemon	Indians	1946*
9	Cal Dorsett	Indians	1947
3	Lyman Linde	Indians	1947
7	Mike Garcia	Indians	1948
7	Ray Scarborough	White Sox	1950
4	Mike Fornieles	Senators	1952
5	Raul Sanchez	Senators	1952
2	Al Aber	Tigers	1953
9	George Brunet	KC A's	1956
6	Johnny Gray	Indians	1957
6	Walt Craddock	KC A's	1958
7	Al Grunwald	KC A's	1959
1	Jack Jenkins	Senators	1962
8	Bob Baird	Senators	1963
3	Dooley Womack	Oak A's	1970
5	Jim Kremmel	Rangers	1973
7	Horacio Pina	Oak A's	1973
6	Larry Harlow	Orioles	1978
3	Craig Minetto	Oak A's	1978
6	Angel Moreno	Angels	1981
1	Matt Young	Mariners	1990
7	Jeff Juden	Indians	1997
6	Rob Bell	Rangers	2001-02
7	Josh Towers	Blue Jays	2003-05

** Lemon was a converted 3B/OF but pitched to a 4-5 record.*

#	Pitcher	Team	Year
	National League		
7	George Earnshaw	Dodgers	1935-36
9	Roy Weir	Braves	1936
5	Oad Swigart	Pirates	1939
7	Newt Kimball	Cards	1940
2	Ernie White	Cards	1940
5	Ace Williams	Braves	1940
5	Johnny Hutchings	Braves	1941
7	Johnny Schmitz	Cubs	1941
8	Schoolboy Rowe	Dodgers	1942
8	Bobo Newsom	Dodgers	1942-43
5	Bill Voiselle	Giants	1943
9	Lefty Wallace	Braves	1945
9	Hal Schumacher	Giants	1946
8	Hal Gregg	Dodgers	1947
2	Al Lyons	Pirates	1947
2	Tony Jacobs	Cubs	1948
6	Murray Wall	Braves	1950
1	Tony Jacobs	Cards	1955
7	Johnny O'Brien	Pirates	1957**
8	Bob Priddy	Pirates	1962
8	Bill Monbouquette	Giants	1968
7	Atlee Hammaker	Giants	1985

*** J. O'Brien pitched 16 games while batting .314 as an infielder.*

Cleveland's Bob Lemon broke in as a third baseman. By 1946 he was playing the outfield and alternating as a pitcher. He wore #6. He played in 55 games, batted .180 and went 4-5 on the mound. The following year he pitched in 37 games, went 11-5 and only filled in occasionally in the outfield. He switched to his familiar #21. The Indians obviously made the right decision since he wound up in the Hall of Fame.

Many players have done some mop-up work in a game that had gotten out of hand, or on a team where a pitching staff had been decimated by overwork or injury. Remembering the near career-ending injury to Jose Canseco, take a look at this list and imagine some different results.

Pepper Martin (Top left) was the spirit of the Gashouse Gang. In his first outing, he gave up a hit and a run in two innings work. His second time,he gave up three runs. He was much more effective creating havoc elsewhere.

Although he began his career as a pitcher, can you imagine letting the franchise, Stan Musial (Top right), even pitch one pitch in 1952, which he did?

Scorecards in early 1946 listed Bob Lemon (Above) as a centerfielder, later that year he was listed as pitcher. He would go on to have seven 20-win seasons and rack up 2,850 innings on his way to Cooperstown.

#	Player	Team	Year
	American League		
2	Bobby Reeves-2B	Red Sox	1931
8	Doc Cramer-OF	Red Sox	1938
7	Steve Lyons-OF	Red Sox	1991
1	Lew Fonseca-1B	White Sox	1932
1	Milt Galatzer-OF	Indians	1936
6	Lefty O'Dea-OF	Indians	1944-45
6	Rocky Colavito-OF	Indians	1958
1	Jerry Terrell-UTIL	Royals	1980
9	Joe Simpson-UTIL	Royals	1983
6	Sal Bando-3B	Brewers	1979
1	John Moses-UTIL	Twins	1989-90
3	Babe Ruth-OF	Yankees	1930, 33
3	Chubby Dean-1B	Phi A's	1937
9	Mark Wagner-UTIL	Oak A's	1984
2	Vance Law-UTIL	Oak A's	1991
1	Bob Bailor-UTIL	Blue Jays	1980
	National League		
9	Kerby Farrell-1B	Braves	1943
9	Max Macon-1B/OF	Braves	1944
7	Whitey Wietelmann-2B	Braves	1945-46
9	Luis Gomez-INF	Braves	1981
6	John Russell-OF	Braves	1989
1	Dee Moore-C	Reds	1937
6	Greg Gross-OF	Astros	1989
5	Ben Chapman-OF	Dodgers	1944-45
3	Jeff Hamilton-UTIL	Dodgers	1989
9	Mickey Hatcher-UTIL	Dodgers	1989
2	Vance Law-INF	Expos	1986-87
1	Dave Martinez-OF	Expos	1990
3	Junior Noboa-UTIL	Expos	1990
7	Bud Hafey-OF	Phillies	1939
4	Art Mahan-1B	Phils	1940
4	Jimmie Foxx-INF	Phils	1945
2	Granny Hamner-SS	Phils	1956-57
9	Tomas Perez-INF	Phils	2002

Remember, these are only the players who wore single digits.

#	Player	Team	Year
	National League *(Continued)*		
6	Johnny O'Brien-INF	Pirates	1956
7	Eddie O'Brien-INF	Pirates	1956***
1	Pepper Martin-3B	Cards	1934, 36
8	Terry Moore-OF	Cards	1939
7	Erv Dusak-OF	Cards	1950
6	Stan Musial-OF	Cards	1952
8	Dane Iorg-UTIL	Padres	1986
4	Darrin Jackson-OF	Padres	1991
4	D'Angelo Jimenez-INF	Padres	2002
5	Hank Leiber	Giants	1942

****Eddie O'Brien became a bona fide pitcher in 1957 but switched his number to 16.*

Cincinnati created their "Mr. Red" logo in 1968. It included this quasi player wearing a uniform and the front office decided it should wear a number. No one was using #27 at the time, so it became incorporated in the logo. The team mascot, also "Mr. Red," wore #27 as well. The number was out of circulation for twenty years, 1968-1987. Jose Rijo joined the club in 1988 and talked them into assigning it to him. He was a mainstay of their staff wearing the number until injured.

Braves' owner Ted Turner, not one to miss a trick, signed Andy Messersmith for megabucks in 1976. Turner also owned the superstation—Channel 17. He made up a special shirt for his new star spelling out "CHANNEL 17." This was construed as "improper advertising" by the league. So he stitched "BLUTO" above the 17.

A subtler form of advertising was used by Mike Hegan in Milwaukee to open the 1977 season. For several seasons Hegan had worn #6 for the Brewers. Sal Bando joined the club and asked for his old number—6. So Hegan, playing out his last season while developing a career in the off-season as a broadcaster, gave up #6 for Sal and took #4. The 4 stood for Channel 4, his part-time employer.

Teams have taken to the practice of assigning numbers to the batboys. For many years the kids would have nothing on their shirts. Then they had "BAT BOY" stenciled or sewn on. Eventually the year was doled out to them. In the victory celebration showing the Mets players storming the mound after their 1986 win, you can see #86 being worn by batboys.

For the first time in baseball history, a totally ancillary figure was assigned a number. We've had owners, batboys, logos, and now an interpretor had been assigned a uniform number. When the Dodgers promoted Chan Ho Park (#61), a Korean pitcher, to the parent club he couldn't speak

Jubilant Mets (Left) celebrate their World Series victory in 1986. A young Kevin Mitchell is leaping above the group, Gary Carter (8) and others race to join the excitement. "Mike" the batboy (86) has his bat in the face of the other batboy (also 86). It has become the practice of teams to number the bat handlers with the particular year.

Andy Messersmith (Right) along with Dave McNally fought the powerful reserve clause virtually indenturing players to a ball club. They won their case and were declared "free agents." This gave them the right to sell their services to the highest bidder. McNally retired, but Messersmith signed on with Ted Turner's Atlanta Braves.

English very well. They signed Don Yi to serve as his interpretor and assigned him #94. Park was sent down for more seasoning shortly after the season began.

Liberties have been taken by clubs when assigning numbers as you've seen. Back in 1951, perhaps one of the funniest and certainly the most clever number assignments took place in the Northern League. The minor league franchise Fargo-Moorhead had a young second baseman named John Neves. NEVES spelled backwards is SEVEN. So he wore #7, you guessed it, backwards.

Speaking of backwards, it may have been the first time in the annals of baseball history that a player's number on the back of his shirt crossed home plate before the player did when Jimmy Piersall scored in 1963.

The occasion was Jimmy's 100th career homerun which he hit as a member of the Amazin' Mets. Jimmy bore the reputation of a flake and didn't disappoint the fans when he ran around the bases backwards to celebrate the event. One observer who didn't appreciate his antics too much was Casey Stengel, the manager. Ole Case promptly sent Piersall to the showers when he returned to the dugout.

John Neves (Above right) showing off his creation—#7 worn backwards. No records exist of any major league team allowing something like this.

Jimmy Piersall (Right) just about to score after hitting his 100th homerun for the New York Mets. Wondering how to greet his teammate is the next batter, Tim Harkness.

Backwards numbers, backwards players and perhaps the most absurd arrangement of digits of all—09. What does it mean? The "0" is a zero or an "O" as in Oliver's case. The "00" is initials as in Omar Olivares' case or it's like the double zero of a roulette table. In Benito Santiago's case it is a spacer. Used like a space bar on a typewriter or computer, it pushes the "9" to the right—out of the path of the rear strap of the chest protector. This allows the "9" to be seen. When the "9" only is used, it cannot be properly seen.

Outfielder Glenallen Hill was traded to the Indians in mid-1991. He asked for #01, but it was not allowed. Was he planning to wear a chest protector in the outfield?

"Veeck As In Wreck." That was the name of Bill Veeck's book. And it sums up his approach to the game. He was one of the most innovative men to own a ball club. He created great schemes to draw crowds to the park when his teams could not. On Sunday, September 19, 1951, in the second game of a doubleheader between the Detroit Tigers and his woeful St. Louis Browns, Veeck topped them all with this one.

It was the bottom of the first, Bob Cain was on the mound, Bob Swift was catching, the ump was Ed Hurley and Frank Saucier, a young outfielder was due up for the Browns.

Striding up to the plate came a 3' 7", 65-pound pinch-hitter dressed in a tiny uniform, and carrying a tiny bat. He was wearing the number 1/8 and announced as Eddie Gaedel.

Ira Berkow retold the story from Saucier's point of view in the *New York Times*.

Saucier: "I just laughed. I thought this was one of the greatest acts of show business I'd ever seen, and still do. But the umpire didn't. It was Ed Hurley, and he said to (Mgr. Zack) Taylor, 'You can't do this,' and Zack said, 'Yes, I can, I have the contract right here in my pocket.'"

"I remember Zack hollering to Eddie, 'Don't swing!' So Eddie bent over and his strike zone was about an inch high. He walked on four pitches, of course. As he trotted to first base, he stopped and tipped his hat to the crowd and waved and then when he got to first, Jim Delsing went out to pinch-run for him. Eddie came back to the dugout and sat down beside me. I said, 'Eddie, you were kind of showin' it up a little bit there, weren't you?'

'Man,' he said, 'I felt like Babe Root.'"

Eddie Gaedel (Above) makes baseball history as being the smallest man to ever bat in a major league ball game. Veeck told him he would live forever in baseball memory. And he was right. Gaedel was so proud of his appearance. His tiny uniform resides in the Hall of Fame in Cooperstown along with those of Babe Ruth, Lou Gehrig, Hank Aaron and all the other greats.

Benito Santiago (Right) started the 1991 season wearing #9. After the All-Star break the Padres began the second half in St. Louis where he debuted his audacious number—09.

Rawlings
PROS
09
PROS-PRY
NIKE

NIKE
24

EXTRA INNINGS

10

Trivia

Numbers. Numbers. Numbers. Wherever we turn we face numbers in our daily life. We can't get away from them. We have social security numbers, house numbers, phone numbers, bank account numbers, zip codes, area codes, PIN numbers, serial numbers, hotel reservation confirmation numbers, and if we're lucky—a winning lottery number.

But nowhere do more people know more numbers representing more things over a longer period of time than in baseball! And each year it grows. There is a fascination for the lore of the game that is not found in any other sport around the globe. If you ask any soccer fan how many goals Pele scored in Argentina or how many foul shots Michael Jordan hit in the post season of 1993? No one would know. But ask just about any baseball fan, how many homeruns Hank Greenberg hit in 1938 or how many games in a row Ripken needed to break Gehrig's record or what number the player who hit the home run that tied up the World Series at three games apiece in Boston in 1975 wore? and I would be surprised if he didn't know two out of three.

Let's take that fascination and have some fun with it. The following trivia questions provide a challenging experience for fanatic and youngster alike. The answers will be found in Chapter 13—don't peek, it's more fun. (There are clues to be found in the front of that chapter called "Stealin' Signs," if you really must take a peek.)

1. *Five players ended their careers playing over 100 games and batting over .300 since permanent numbers have been worn. We'll help you out with a couple.*

#	PLAYER	LAST YEAR	TEAM	BA
5	JOHNNY HODAPP	1933	RED SOX	.312
47	TONY CUCCINELLO	1945	WHITE SOX	.308
9	______________	1960	RED SOX	.316
1	______________	1962	METS	.306
34	______________	1995	TWINS	.314

2. *On August 20, 1947, a young pitcher wearing the #23—the first black pitcher in the major leagues—hit a homerun in his first at-bat. Who was he?*

3. *Name the only two rookies (one wearing #9, the other #25) to hit two HRs in one inning. The first did it on June 24, 1936 and the other on May 23, 1962. By the way, they were both Yankees.*

4. *What American League player wearing #23 hit the most grand slams in one season?*

5. *Who wore the lowest number ever to win a batting title? What was the number?*

TWO MONKS

THE PHILLIES HAD TWO "MONKS" WEARING #34 IN THE LATE FORTIES.

34 MONK DUBIEL, P PHILS 1948
34 MONK MEYER, P PHILS 1949

A DH supreme, Harold Baines hit over .300 six times, and led the league in slugging with .504 in 1984. The five-time All-Star hit 3 HRs in a game three times and collected nearly 2,900 hits.

6. *What individual wore the most different numbers (15) in his 17 years as a player and 4 years as a coach with 12 different teams between 1957 and 1985? He had three stints with the Mets. If you added up the different numbers he wore, it would come to 513!*

7. *What major league player had a number retired for his playing abilities though he never wore it in the field?*

8. *Name five players whose numbers were officially retired while they were still playing.*

#	PLAYER	YEAR
20	__________	1971
33	__________	1989
3	__________	1989
30	__________	1992
1	__________	1996

9. *Five teams retired numbers for two managers—which teams and who were they?*

37 **37** **14**
1 **24**
1 **2** **40** **1** **10**

10. *What player would need to double his uniform number to equal his major league-leading total bases of 18 in a game (July 31, 1954).*

11. *From 1941-60, who had the most RBIs in a season? In the American League there was a tie by two players on the same team whose uniform numbers when added together equaled the uniform number of the National League player who did it. It was done in Boston in 1949 and in Chicago in 1959.*

12. *Name the only triple crown winner to wear more than a single digit.*

13. *Who was the one and only player wearing #1 to win a homerun championship?*

14. *Only four American League players from 1929-1969 won homerun championships while not wearing a single digit uniform number. Who were they?*

#	PLAYER	TEAM
19	__________	PHILADELPHIA
14	__________	CLEVELAND (*twice*)
25	__________	BOSTON
20	__________	BALTIMORE

15. *What did Hall of Famers Joe DiMaggio, Bobby Doerr and Ted Williams have in common besides their great careers? It occurred in 1936, 1937 and 1939 respectively.*

16. *In 1963, what two brothers wore uniform numbers whose digits were the reverse of each other, while a third brother wore the two digits in between?*

17. *What three major league brothers wore consecutive numbers at some point in their careers and collectively hit 358 homeruns? You're sure.*

NUMBER 29—NEVER?

JACK O'CONNOR WAS BORN ON JUNE 2, 1958 IN TWENTY-NINE PALMS, CALIFORNIA. HE BECAME A PITCHER IN THE MAJOR LEAGUES BETWEEN 1981 AND 1987. HE NEVER WORE #29.

33 MINNESOTA TWINS 1981-84
32 MONTREAL EXPOS 1985
21 BALTIMORE ORIOLES 1987

18. *Who was the first Yankee to wear #13? A four-time All-Star, he won 20 games twice and had a lifetime W-L percentage of .717.*

19. *What major league team did not have a player wear #1 until the 1940s?*

20. *Who's the only player to wear the #0 in an All-Star game? In fact, he did it four times for two different teams in two different leagues.*

21. *Who was the first player to wear a number higher than #50 during a World Series? What Series was it and for whom did he wear it?*

22. *Only two players in the history of the game had two streaks of 500 or more games consecutively played in their careers. One wore the number 2 and the other wore #14. Who were they?*

23. *The two youngest players to win an MVP Award wore consecutive numbers. They were both 22-years old. Who were they?*

24. *Only one player in the Hall of Fame wore the number 13. Who? (He did it as a rookie.)*

25. *The Yankees never retired #6 although two Hall of Famers wore it. Can you recall who?*

26. *What rookie wore #00?*

00 00 00 00 00 00 00

27. *What two unrelated players with the same last name playing the same position wore the same number with the same team (the Mets) one year apart?*

28. *No player has ever entered the Hall of Fame as a Kansas City Athletic, but five men who are in the Hall have at one time in their careers worn their uniform. These are their KC numbers. Can you name them?*

33 **27** **9**
23 **29**

29. *What team has retired the numbers of three first basemen? And who were they? Two of the three began their careers at another position.*

30. *What 300-game winner at age 30 had fewer wins than his uniform number? The answer will amaze you and make you wonder—anything is possible.*

31. *What speedster won the American League stolen base crown six times while wearing 5 different numbers?*

10 **15**
6 **1**
7

32. *Name three National Leaguers who won the MVP Award while wearing the #24. Two of them won it twice.*

33. *While we're on #24—who was the first Hall of Famer to wear that number? Careful, it was a player who was not with his customary team and not wearing his usual number.*

34. *What's the only team through 2005 with two shortstop's numbers retired? and who were they? By the way, both are in the Hall of Fame as well.*

35. *Everybody knows that the Yankees retired the #8 twice—for Hall of Fame catchers, Yogi Berra and Bill Dickey. What other team retired the same number twice for two players?*

36. *What player had a number retired for him, yet he didn't wear it until his career was nearly half over? He's a Hall of Famer also.*

37. *Lou Gehrig's number 4 was the first number retired by any major league team—whose was the second?*

38. *Five American League homerun champions wore the #9. Can you name them?*

#	PLAYER	YEAR
9	________	1941, 42, 47, 49
9	________	1961
9	________	1968
9	________	1973, 75
9	________	1976

BIRDS OF A FEATHER

HERE'S A COUPLE OF BIRDS WITH THE SAME HAIR-DO WEARING THE SAME NUMBER IN CONSECUTIVE YEARS.

28 HAL BROWN—P BALTIMORE ORIOLES 1962
28 GEORGE BRUNET—P BALTIMORE ORIOLES 1963

39. *Ivan DeJesus did it, Freddie Patek did it, Jim Fregosi did it twice. Babe Ruth, Hank Greenberg or Roger Maris never did it. It's hard to believe but hitting for the cycle has eluded some of the game's great sluggers while some average batters accomplished the rare feat one miraculous day.*

Name three players who hit for the cycle and had their #14 retired.

#	PLAYER	DATE	OPP
14	________	JUNE 4, 1952	RED SOX
14	________	SEPT 14, 1961	CUBS
		JUNE 16, 1964	COLT .45s
14	________	JUNE 25, 1949	PIRATES

40. *What three American Leaguers won back-to-back-to-back homerun championships wearing the same uniform number? One was a Yankee and it wasn't Joe DiMaggio, he was in the service.*

41. *What National Leaguer won a homerun championship with a total that was the reverse of his uniform number? Besides the obvious pair, who else?*

IT'S A MATTER OF MATHEMATICS

DAVE ROBERTS WAS AN INFIELDER FOR THE SAN DIEGO PADRES FROM 1972-75. HE WORE #5 AND #20. THE DIFFERENCE OF WHICH IS 15.

DAVE ROBERTS WAS A PITCHER FOR THE SAN DIEGO PADRES FROM 1969-71. HE WORE #15.

42. *Who wore only one number during his entire major league career for the longest length of time? While you're at it—name the one in each league.*

43. *What infielder played in 100 games, batted more than 300 times but knocked in less runs than half his uniform number in1965? He wore number 18 that year.*

44. *Who was the first batting champion to wear #44? Hank Aaron was only 11 years old at the time.*

45. *Name the first non-Yankee with a retired number.*

46. *Who was the first player to hit a grand-slam homerun while wearing a number? It happened on May 6, 1929. And the number wasn't #3 or #4.*

47. *What brothers wore back-to-back numbers for the same team at least two years in a row? There were three pair!*

48. *Name the player in each league who played the most games on one team while wearing the same number? They both played over 3000 games.*

49. *What team had issued the highest and lowest number for a player to wear? Three National League teams did it and one American League team. Two of the NL teams issued them in the same year.*

50. *Who wore the #9 on the Padres the same year Santiago wore #09?*

09 9

51. *Six men wearing the uniform of the Kansas City A's had their numbers retired. Only one had it retired by that franchise. One other had the number he wore retired. The other four had different numbers retired by those other franchises. Can you name them?*

A's#	PLAYER	POS	TEAM/RET
33	________	OF	CARDINALS
23	________	P	DODGERS
27	________	P	A's
9	________	OF	YANKEES
5	________	M	INDIANS
44	________	CH/M	WHITE SOX

52. *What pitcher, wearing the same number as the batter, gave up one of the most famous homeruns in baseball history?*

53. *During a five-year period in the '80s, three different Cy Young Award winners wore #40. Who were they?*

54. *Since permanent numbers have been worn, Jim Bunning wearing #14, pitched a perfect game. Three other National League pitchers did it also while wearing the same number and it wasn't 14.*

55. *The last time two player-managers appeared in the same World Series, the player wearing #3 beat the player wearing #2. When? What teams and who were they?*

56. *What player, wearing a number later retired for a Hall of Famer on that same team, hit a famous World Series homerun tying up the ball game sending it into extra innings.*

57. *Who was the first pitcher for a Canadian team to wear the number 66? Try again.*

58. *What player wearing #17 was the only Blue Jay to hit for the cycle? He did it April 16, 1989 vs. the Royals.*

59. *Only one member of the Hall of Fame ever played in a Colt .45s uniform—who was it? He wore #18.*

WHAT'S IN A NAME?

ESTEL CRABTREE, OUTFIELDER (1932-33, 41-44) WITH THE REDS AND CARDINALS, WAS FROM CRABTREE, OHIO.

CHARLIE GASSAWAY, PITCHER (1944-46) WITH THE CUBS, A's, AND INDIANS, CAME FROM GASSAWAY, GEORGIA.

VINEGAR BEND MIZELL, PITCHER (1952-53, 56-62) WITH THE CARDS, PIRATES AND METS, IS FROM VINEGAR BEND, MISS.

60. *Who is the only player in ML history to win a Gold Glove while sporting the number 0?*

61. *There are two sets of brothers in the HOF. During their careers they drew their pay from Boston of the NL. One set wore numbers, the other didn't. Who were they?*

62. *Before the 1970s, most young players strove to get lower and lower numbers. But what Hall of Famer as a rookie was issued a single-digit number but switched to his more famous double digit?*

Ozzie Smith, "The Wizard," redefined the word defense. He was probably the greatest glove man that ever played the game. When he retired after the 1996 season he held or tied 17 ML and NL fielding records. His only left-handed HR came in the ninth inning of game 5 of the NLCS for the Cards against the Dodgers in 1985 setting the stage for Jack Clark's dramatic ninth inning HR in game 6 winning the Series 4-2. He was inducted into the Hall in 2002. Kids loved his backflip before ballgames.

63. *Of the three players who hit for the cycle three times, only one wore a number. And he only wore one the last time he did it in 1933. He wore #4. Who was he?*

64. *How many All-Star players have worn #9 for the St. Louis Cardinals?*

65. *In 1965, the Giants' ace starter and ace reliever had the same birthday and wore consecutive numbers. Do you remember them?*

66. *Who were the first 30-game winners in each league to wear a number?*

#	PLAYER	RECORD
10	____________	31-4 (AL)
17	____________	30-7 (NL)

67. *Who was the first pitcher wearing a number to win 20 games?*

68. *The first 20-game winner in the National League to wear a number, wore two of them—#30 and #17 en route to a 22-win season. He went on to become a major league umpire. Who was he?*

69. *What player stole the most bases while wearing the same number? He wasn't wearing #24 when he did it.*

70. *What two brothers wore the same number during the same year for different teams?*

#	PLAYER	TEAM
36	____________-P	CLEVELAND/TEXAS
36	____________-P	OAKLAND

71. *What fathers who coached, wore the same numbers as their sons?*

#	PLAYER	YEAR
24	____________	COACH 1996
56	____________	COACH 1997

72. *Incredibly, the city of Philadelphia produced two triple crown winners in the same year. On top of that, they both wore the #3. Do you know them?*

KNUCKLER AT BIRTH

DID YOU KNOW THAT HALL OF FAME 318-GAME WINNER PHIL NIEKRO WAS BORN ON APRIL FOOL'S DAY? APRIL 1, 1939. MAYBE HE WAS PREDESTINED TO BE A KNUCKLEBALL PITCHER.

73. *What number besides #3 did Babe Ruth wear?*

74. *Who's the only player to wear #0 for both Canadian teams?*

CURIOUSER AND CURIOUSER

SAM BOWENS (**#16**) WAS AN OUTFIELDER FOR THE **1966 BALTIMORE ORIOLES**. HE WAS BORN ON **MARCH 3, 1939**.

BRUCE HOWARD (**#16**) WAS A PITCHER FOR THE **1967 BALTIMORE ORIOLES**. HE WAS BORN ON **MARCH 3, 1943**.

75. *Six of the top 17 career total base hitters had their uniform number end in #4. Can you name them?*

#	PLAYER	DECADES
_4	____________	'50s-'70s
_4	____________	'50s-'70s
_4	____________	'60s-'80s
_4	____________	'80s-'00s
4	____________	'20s-'30s
4	____________	'20s-'40s

76. *Can you name the two triple crown winners who wore the #7? One did it in the 1930s and the other in the 1950s.*

77. *Who wore the highest number of any batting champion in either league? A player from each league did it twice. Another also did it once.*

78. *Who wore the lowest number in the American League while winning a batting championship? It was done by three different players—once in the '30s by a Senator, once in the '40s by a Yankee and once in the '50s by an Indian.*

79. *Tridecophobia or not? No batting champ, home-run champ, slugging % champ or RBI champ ever wore #13 during the year of accomplishment. True or false?*

80. *What Hall of Famer holds the record for most 3-HR games (6)?*

#	PLAYER	(LEAGUE) TIMES
10	____________	(NL) 4 TIMES
15	____________	(NL) 1 TIME
36	____________	(AL) 1 TIME

81. *What was the highest number worn by anyone while hitting for the cycle, done in 1984? Who wore it?*

82. *Who wore the lowest, done in 1985 by a Texas Ranger?*

83. *Can you name two pairs of brothers that wore the same number for the same team at different times? One pair did it for Cardinals in the '90s and the other pair did with the Royals in the '70s and '80s. (Three were pitchers and one an infielder.)*

84. *Pay close attention. In 1970, one not-so-famous brother of a major league trio had the same initials, first name and wore the same number for the same team as a famous brother of another major league duo did 5 years later. Who were they?*

85. *What two numbers are the most frequently worn by base stealing champs? They were worn 11 times each. One number was worn 8 times in the AL from '32-'79 and in the NL 3 times from '39-'45. The other was worn once in the AL in '54 and 10 times from '60-'84 in the NL.*

86. *On May 7, 1970, the only LA Dodger (wearing #28) to hit for the cycle accomplished it against the Mets. He was thought of as a defensive whiz.*

87. *Since 1980, the MVP award was won 9 times by a player whose number ended in 3. Name them.*

#	PLAYER	TEAM	DECADE
3	____________	YANKS	'80s
3	____________	A's	'80s
3	____________	A's	'90s
3	____________	BRAVES	'80s
3	____________	BRAVES	'80s
3	____________	CUBS	'80s
3	____________	DODGERS	'80s
3	____________	ROCKIES	'90s
3	____________	RANGERS	'00s

88. *It was the destiny of one Yankee player to wear the number of a Hall of Fame Yankee immediately before it was retired and then be the last to wear another number before another Yankee Hall of Famer-to-be was to wear it and make it famous. Who was he?*

WORLD SERIES KKKKKKKKKKKKKKKK

ON **OCTOBER 2, 1953**—CARL ERSKINE SET THE WORLD SERIES STRIKE OUT RECORD IN A GAME OF **14**.
ON **OCTOBER 2, 1963**—SANDY KOUFAX SET THE WORLD SERIES STRIKE OUT RECORD IN A GAME OF **15**.
ON **OCTOBER 2, 1968**—BOB GIBSON SET THE WORLD SERIES STRIKE OUT RECORD IN A GAME OF **17**.

Three of his first four years lefty Mark Langston led the AL in strikeouts with 204, 245 and 262. He was named AL Rookie Pitcher of the Year 1984 by The Sporting News. *In 1989, he and Mike Campbell were traded to Montreal for Brian Holman, Gene Harris and the yet-to-be "Big Unit" Randy Johnson. He pitched in his only World Series in 1998 for the Padres at the age of 37, well past his glory years.*

89. *Billy Martin wore #12 when he broke in with the Yankees. Nick Priori, the former equipment manager said, "The shirt was too big for him. You could only see the '1' anyway, so we switched him to #1."*

Can you match up these famous rookies' first number on the left, the name and their more well-known number?

ROOKIE #	PLAYER	REGULAR #
5	HANK AARON	**1**
6	DICK ALLEN	**2**
6	CLETE BOYER	**4**
9	GEORGE BRETT	**5**
9	ROBERTO CLEMENTE	**5**
9	JOE DIMAGGIO	**6**
13	BOBBY DOERR	**7**
19	BOB FELLER	**10**
24	WHITEY FORD	**15**
25	RALPH KINER	**15**
28	TONY KUBEK	**16**
32	MICKEY MANTLE	**19**
34	THURMAN MUNSON	**21**
34	RYNE SANDBERG	**23**
43	RED SCHOENDIENST	**44**

90. *Twice a club issued #0 and #00—to whom?*

91. *Two-thirds of the retired numbers from one team are managers—which team and who are they and their numbers?*

41
14 **37**

IT'S CATCHING

JACK **CROUCH** WAS A CATCHER—BROWNS 30-31, 33, REDS 33.

JOHNNIE **HEVING** WAS A CATCHER FOR THE BROWNS, RED SOX AND A's—'20s & '30s.

ELMER **KLUMPP** WAS A CATCHER—SENATORS 34, BROWNS 37.

CLYDE **KLUTTZ** WAS ALSO A CATCHER—'40s & '50s ON 6 TEAMS.

92. *What's going on here? Can you guess these great cryptic events?*

1. **44** → **27** in **12** : **+ 4** = 7-6W @WS (3-3)
2. **44** ⇒ **44** : **+ 4** = 715 on 4/8/74
3. **13** → **23** in **9** : **+ 4** w**2**= 5-4W → WS
4. **18** → **19/1/4/42/14/15/6/39/35/8** in **9** : **0 0 0** = 2-0W
5. **31** in **12** : **0 0 0**, in **13**: E**5** + S**41** + BB**44** + 2B**9** = 1-0L
6. **23** → **9** in **9** : **+ 4** = 10-9W in WS

93. *The oldest of three major league brothers at one time wore the numbers (#9 and #7) of his younger siblings. Collectively they hit 573 homeruns. Name them.*

94. *Two brothers pitched for the Yankees and both wore Jim Bouton's old number—the lefty was there in 1987 and the righty in 1990. Who were they?*

95. *Name the 3 AL players who wore #0 in 1985.*

96. *Do these uniform numbers represent AL strike-out kings or homerun kings?*

#	PLAYER	YEAR
34		1989-90
51		1992-95
21		1988, 91, 96-97
12		1984, 1986-87

97. *The first two shortstops to win an MVP Award also wore consecutive numbers. One in the NL ,one in the AL.*

98. *So did the first two third basemen to win MVP's.*

99. *Who's the only pitcher to win only 2 Cy Young Awards wearing two different uniform numbers? He did it while on the same AL team.*

100. *Nine times each the Cy Young was won by a pitcher either wearing #31 or #32. Who were they?*

#	PLAYER	YEARS	#	PLAYER	YEARS
31		'64	**32**		'60
31		'70	**32**		'63, 65-66
31		'71	**32**		'72,77,80,82
31		'83	**32**		'80
31		'85			
31		'92-95			

101. *In the American League from 1929-1940, only players wearing #3, #4, or #5 won the homerun title. There were five different players. Name them.*

#	PLAYER	YEAR
3		1929-31
3		1932-33, 35, 39
4		1931, 34, 36
5		1935, 38, 40
5		1937

102. *Who was the first HR champion to win with a lower total than his shirt number? He did it twice. It happened in the 1940s. It was done 3 more times in the NL and six times in the AL.*

103. *What player/coach/manager wore his particular number longer than anyone else in the history of the game? For over 45 years!*

104. *Only one member of the Red Sox hit for the cycle twice. Can you name him? He did it May 17, 1944 and May 13, 1947. He was not wearing #9 at the time.*

105. *What two sluggers tied for a homerun championship matching both their uniform numbers?*

106. *Number 20 was the first switch-hitter (wearing #'s) to lead the National League in RBI. Who was it?*

107. *The first AL player to score 6 runs in a 9-inning game also wore #6. It was accomplished on May 8, 1946. Who was he?*

108. *The top 9 all-time NL homerun hitters hit 5,234 between them in their league. Who among them never wore a uniform with a '4' on it?*

733 **548** 521 **503** 543

660 **512** **511** **708**

109. *What was the highest uniform number worn by a Hall of Famer during a regular season game? It occurred in the early 1940s.*

110. *What uniform number adorned more batting champs than any other? It was worn 9 times in the NL and 5 times in the AL.*

#	PLAYER	AVG.
_	____________	.368 (NL)
_	____________	.357,.365,.376,..346,.355,.336, .351 (NL)
_	____________	.344 (NL)
_	____________	.340 (AL)
_	____________	.323,.321,.337 (AL)
_	____________	.332 (AL)

111. *What famous list of uniform numbers is this:*

44, 3, 25, 24, 21, 20, 25, 3, 25, 44?

112. *Four different players wore #7 while winning batting titles—can you name them?*

#	PLAYER	AVG.
7	____________	.374 (NL)
7	____________	.390 (AL)
7	____________	.353 (AL)
7	____________	.353 (AL)

INCREDIBLE BUT TRUE

ON MAY 2, 1954—AN 8-YEAR OLD **NATE COLBERT** SAT IN THE STANDS OF OLD SPORTSMAN PARK AND WATCHED AS **#6 STAN "THE MAN" MUSIAL** WRAPPED **5 HOMERUNS** IN A DOUBLEHEADER AGAINST THE GIANTS TO SET A ML RECORD. EIGHTEEN YEARS LATER, **#17** COLBERT PLAYING FOR THE PADRES, BECAME THE ONLY OTHER PLAYER TO PERFORM THE SAME FEAT!

113. *Name the father/son combination that wore the same number 25 for the same team and accomplished the feat of being a 30-30 man. They did it an incredible 10 times combined. Who were they?*

114. *The first Hall of Famer to ever wear a Blue Jay uniform (#31) never played a game for them.*

115. *Three pitchers tied for starting the most All-Star games (5). One AL left-hander (#11)—1933-35, 37-38. And two NL right-handers (#36)—1950-51, 53-55, and (#53)—1959, 1959, 1962 (first game), 64, 68.*

*Don't feel so bad—if it was too tough you can "steal the signs" at the beginning of Chapter 13, on page 507.

Mark McGwire could hit a ball out of any park in the land. He holds the record for homers hit by a rookie in a season—49 in 1987. On June 24, 1997 he hit one 538' in Seattle, that's over a tenth of a mile. If his average homer was 430' and you put them back-to-back, they would have gone more than 31.5 miles. Nearly one-third of his hits were homeruns! Such power is spellbinding.

39

PLAYERS: BY THE NUMBERS

11

hat number did Frankie Gustine wear for the 1948 Pirates? Did Red Schoendienst ever wear #10? Which number did Ducky Schofield prefer of the six different numbers he wore? Who wore #41 for the 1962 Yanks?

Here's the argument settler. All the players that played major league baseball plus the managers and coaches since permanent numbers were worn in 1929 are listed here alphabetically.

The name most widely used during the player's career is the one listed. Common nicknames follow in parentheses.

The dominant position played follows using traditional abbreviations: SS, 2B, P and so on. Coach and manager will appear in italic after the team. Family relationships (if known) follow: F=father, S=son, GF=grandfather, GS=grandson, B=brother, U=uncle, N=nephew and C=cousin.

Teams are designated by a three-letter abbreviation followed by N (National League) or A (American League) except where a two-letter abbreviation fits more naturally such as NY, SF or SD (New York, San Francisco or San Diego).

Following the name, parentheses contain the various numbers worn with the apparent favorite in **bold**. Then begins the teams for which a player performed in light face, his **number** in bold and the years in light face.

Let's use the Boone family for example:

BOONE, AARON 3B S,B,GS
(**17**,19) CINN **17** 97-03, NYA **19** 03, CLEA **17** 05

BOONE, BOB C S,F
(**8**,2) PHIN **8** 72-81, CALA **8** 83-88, KCA **8** 89-90, CINN *CH* **8** 94, KCA *M* **2** 95, **8** 96-97, CINN *M* **8** 01-02

BOONE, BRET 2B S,B,GS
(34,5,**29**) SEAA **34** 92, **5** 93, CINN **29** 94-98, ATLN **24** 99, SDN **29** 00, SEAA **29** 01-05 MINA **21** 05

BOONE, RAY (IKE) SS/1B F,GF
(28,**8**,30,19, 39) CLEA **28** 48, **8** 49-53, DETA **8** 53-58, CHIA **8** 58-59, KCA **30** 59, MILN **19** 59-60, BOSA **39** 60

Ray is Bob's father and Bret's and Aaron's grandfather. He started as a shortstop with the Indians in 1948. He moved on to the Tigers, White Sox, A's, Braves and finished with the Red Sox. He had a preference for #8.

Son Bob also predominately wore #8 while catching for the Phils, Angels and Royals. He coached for the Reds in 1994 and managed the Royals and Reds.

Bob's son Bret, began as a second baseman with the Reds, sported three numbers in his first four years. He gained stardom with the Mariners yet prefered #29. His brother Aaron spent seven years with the Reds wearing #17. A mid-season move to the Yankees in July of 2003 set the stage for his heroic post-season homerun against the rival Red Sox to win the AL pennant.

A

AARDSMA, DAVID P
(**33**,47) SFN **33** 04, **47** 05

AARON, HANK OF B
(5,**44**) MILN **5** 54, **44** 55-65, ATLN **44** 66-74, MILA **44** 75-76

AARON, TOMMIE 1B B
(28,**18**,19,23) MILN **28** 62-63, 65, ATLN **18** 68-71, **19** 71, *CH* **23** 79-84

AASE, DON P
(45,**46**,41,49, 22) BOSA **45** 77, CALA **46** 78-84, BALA **41** 85-88, NYN **49** 89, LAN **22** 90

ABAD, ANDY 1B
(**30**,53) OAKA **30** 01, BOSA **53** 03

ABBOTT, GLENN P
(35,36,39,37, 24,**17**) OAKA **35** 73, **36** 74, **39** 74, **37** 74-76, SEAA **17** 77-83, DETA **24** 83-84, **17** 84

ABBOTT, JEFF OF/DH
(45,**25**,18) CHIA **45** 97-98, **25** 99-00, FLAN **18** 01

ABBOTT, JIM P
(**25**,52) CALA **25** 89-92, NYA **25** 93-94, CHIA **25** 95, CALA **52** 95-96, CHIA **25** 98, MILN **25** 99

ABBOTT, KURT SS
(11,**7**,20) OAKA **11** 93, FLAN **7** 94-97, OAKA **7** 98, COLN **7** 98-99, NYN **20** 00, ATLN **11** 01

ABBOTT, KYLE P
(59,44,47,39, 55) CALA **59/44** 91, PHIN **47** 92, **39** 95, CALA **55** 96

ABBOTT, PAUL P
(**37**,58,48,45, 34,40) MINA **37** 90-92, CLEA **58** 93, SEAA **48** 98-02, **45** 99, KCA **31** 03, TBA **34** 04, PHIN **40** 04

ABER, AL (LEFTY) P
(17,29,2,**22**, 16) CLEA **17** 50,*(MIL) 51-52,* **29** 53, DETA **2** 53, **22** 53-57, KCA **16** 57

ABERNATHIE, BILL P
(**48**) CLEA **48** 52

ABERNATHY, TAL (TED) P
(**37**,25) PHIA **37** 42-43, **25** 44

ABERNATHY, BRENT 2B
(**3**,14,15) TBA **3** 01-03, KCA **14** 03, MINA **15** 05

ABERNATHY, TED P
(15,11,**36**,39, 57,37,33,40) WASA **15** 55-57, **11** 60, CLEA **36** 63-64, CHIN **39** 65-66, ATLN **37/39** 66, CINN **57** 67, **33** 67-68,CHIN **37** 69-70, STLN **36/40** 70, KCA **36** 70-72

ABERNATHY, WOODY P
(**24**) NYN **24** 46-47

ABERSON, CLIFF (KIF) OF
(**11**) CHIN **11** 47-49

ABNER, SHAWN OF
(**28**,16,45) SDN **28** 87-91, CALA **16** 91, CHIA **45** 92

ABRAMS, CAL OF
(32,8,28,**18**, 25) BKNN **32** 49, **8** 50, **32** 50-52, CINN **28** 52, PITN **18** 53-54, BALA **18** 54-55, CHIA **25** 56

ABREGO, JOHNNY P
(**32**) CHIN **32** 85

ABREU, JOE INF
(**12**) CINN **12** 4

ABREU, BOBBY 2B/OF
(29,**53**) HOUN **29** 96, **53** 97, PHIN **53** 98-05

ACCARDO, JEREMY P
(**59**) SFN **59** 05

ACEVEDO, JOSE P
(**29**,30) CINN **29** 01-04, COLN **30** 05

ACEVEDO, JUAN P
(49,39,**53**,50, 57) COLN **49** 95, NYN **39** 97, STLN **53** 98-99, MILN **53** 00, COLN **50** 01, FLAN **53** 01, DETA **57** 02, NYA **57** 03, TORA **57** 03

ACHISON, SCOTT P
(**57**) SEAA **57** 04

ACKER, JIM P
(31,38,24,34) TORA **31** 83-86, ATLN **38** 86-89, TORA **24** 89, **34** 90-91, SEAA **34** 92

ACKER, TOM P
(**40**) CINN **40** 56-59

ACKLEY, FRITZ P
(**18**) CHIA **18** 63-64

ACOSTA, CY P
(**41**,31/29) CHIA **41** 72-74, PHIN **31/29** 75

ACOSTA, ED P
(46,13,**37**) PITN **46/13** 70, SDN **37** 71-72

ACOSTA, OSCAR CH
(48,46,**8**,__) CHIN *CH* **48/46** 00, **8** 01, TEXA *CH* __ 02

ACRE, MARK P
(**55**) OAKA **55** 94-97

ACTA, MANNY CH
(41,**14**,50) MONN *CH* **41** 02, **14** 03-04, NYN *CH* **50** 05

ADAIR, BILL CH/M
(3,9,34,44,46) MILN *CH* **3** 62, ATLN *CH* **9** 67, CHIA *CH,M* **34/44** 70, MONN *CH* **46** 76

ADAIR, JERRY 2B
(8,**7**,11,14,41, 25) BALA **8** 58-59, **7** 60-61, 66, CHIA **11** 66-67, BOSA **14** 67-68, KCA **14** 69-70, OAKA *CH* **41** 72-74, CALA *CH* **25** 75

ADAIR, JIMMY (CHOPPY) CH
(33,**45**,2,43, 42,3) CHIA **33** 51-52, BALA **43** 56, **45** 58-61, HOUN **2** 62-63, **42** 64, **3** 65

ADAIR, RICK CH
(**24**,35) CLEA *CH* **24** 92-93, DETA *CH* **35** 97-99

ADAMS, ACE P
(**27**) NYN **27** 41-46

ADAMS, BOB (A.) P
(**29**) PHIN **29** 32

ADAMS, BOB (M.) 1B
(**40**) DETA **40** 77

ADAMS, BOBBY 2B/3B
(**12**,25,5,7,16, 51,2) CINN **12** 46-55, CHIA **25** 55, BALA **5** 56, CHIN **7** 57, **16** 58-59, *CH* **51** 61-64, *CH* **2** 73

ADAMS, BUSTER OF
(12,8,14,5,**2**) STLN **12** 39, **8/14** 43, PHIN **5** 43-44, **2** 44-45, STLN **14** 45-46, PHIN **2** 47

ADAMS, DICK 1B/OF
(**6**) PHIA **6** 47

ADAMS, DOUG C
(**32**) CHIA **32** 69

ADAMS, GLENN OF
(43,**8**,55) SFN **43** 75-76, MINA **8** 77-81, TORA **55** 82

ADAMS, HERB OF
(2,**24**) CHIA **2** 48, **24** 49-50, *MIL* 51-52

ADAMS, MIKE OF
(25,21,30,9) MINA **25** 72-73, CHIN **21** 76, **30** 77, OAKA **9** 78

ADAMS, MIKE P
(**46**) MILN **46** 04-05

ADAMS, RED P
(15,18,**26**) CHIN **15/18** 46, LAN *CH* **26** 69-80

ADAMS, RICK SS
(48,**3**,1) CALA **48** 82, **3** 83, SFN **1**85

ADAMS, RUSS SS
(**8**) TORA **8** 04-05

ADAMS, SPARKY 3B
(**1**,10,4) STLN **1** 32-33, CINN **10** 33, **4** 34

ADAMS, TERRY P
(**51**,33) CHIN **51** 95-96, CHIN **33** 97, **51** 97-99, LAN **51** 00-01, PHIN **51** 02-03, TORA **51** 04, BOSA **51** 04, PHIN **51** 05

ADAMS, WILLIE P
(49,**40**,55) OAKA **49/40** 96, OAKA **40** 97 (-98), BOSA **55** 00

ADAMSON, JOEL P
(56,**38**) FLAN **56** 96, MILA **38** 97, ARIN **38** 98

ADAMSON, MIKE P
(**17**,47) BALA **17** 67-69, **47** 68

ADCOCK, JOE 1B
(17,21,26,**9**, 11,6) CINN **17** 50, **21** 51, **26** 52, MILN **9** 53-62, CLEA **11** 63, LAA **6** 64, CALA **6** 65-66, CLEA *M* **6** 67

ADDIS, BOB OF
(6,**16**,39) BOSN **6** 50-51, CHIN **16** 52-53, PITN **39** 53

ADDUCI, JIM 1B
(**14**,9,18) STLN **14** 83, MILA **9** 86, **14** 88, PHIN **18** 89

ADERHOLT, MORRIE UTIL
(40,__,22,**19**, 28) WASA **40** 39, __ 40, **22** 41, BKNN **19** 44-45, BOSN **28** 45

ADKINS, DEWEY P
(__,7,**17**,37) WASA __ 42, **7/17** 43, CHIN **37** 49

ADKINS, DICK SS
(__) PHIA __ 42

ADKINS, JON P
(**37**) CHIA **37** 03-05

ADKINS, STEVE P
(62,**59**) NYA **62/59** 90

ADLESH, DAVE C
(24,**8**,4,27,6) HOUN **24** 63, **8** 63-65, **27** 66-67, **4** 67, **6** 68

AFENIR, TROY C
(9,**52**,38) HOUN **9** 87, OAKA **52** 90-91, CINN **38** 92

AFFELDT, JEREMY P
(**48**) KCA **48** 02-05

AGBAYANI, BENNY OF
(39,**50**) NYN **39** 98, **50** 99-01, COLN **50** 02, BOSA **50** 02

AGEE, TOMMIE OF
(4,23,28,1,**20**, 47) CLEA **4** 62, **23** 63, **28** 64, CHIA **1** 65-67, NYN **20** 68-72, HOUN **20** 73, STL **47** 73

AGGANIS, HARRY 1B
(**6**) BOSA **6** 54-55

AGOSTO, JUAN P
(50,30,**49**,47) CHIA **50** 81-86, MINA **30** 86, HOUN **49** 87-90, STLN **49** 91-92, SEAA **47/49** 92, HOUN **49** 93

AGUAYO, LUIS INF
(**16**,33,29,23) PHIN **16** 80-88, **33** 83, NYA **29** 88, CLEA **23** 89

AGUILA, CHRIS INF/3B/OF
(16,**3**) PHIN **16** 80, FLAN **3** 04-05

AGUILERA, RICK P
(**38**,15,17) NYN **38** 85-87, **15** 87-89, **38** 89, MINA **17** 89, **38** 90-95, BOSA **38** 95, MINA **38** 96-99, CHIN **38** 99-00

AGUIRRE, HANK P
(48,28,30,**37**, 21,17,34,4) CLEA **48** 55, **28** 56-57, DETA **30** 58-59, **37** 60-63, **21** 64, **37** 64-67, LAN **17** 68, CHIN **34** 69-70, *CH* **4** 72-73, *CH* **37** 74

AHEARNE, PAT P
(**27**) DETA **27** 95, SEAA **27** 00

AIKENS, WILLIE MAYS 1B
(22,**24**) CALA **22** 77,79, KCA **24** 80-83, TORA **24** 84-85

AINGE, DANNY 2B
(**2**) TORA **2** 79-81

AINSMITH, EDDIE (DORF) C/CH
(**14**,27) STLN **14** 23, WASA *CH* **27** 32

AINSWORTH, KURT P
(**32**,22,29) SFN **32** 01-03, **22** 02, BALA **29** 03-04, (05)

AKER, JACK P
(21,23,**22**,38, 33,1) KCA **21** 64, **23** 65-67, OAKA **23** 68, SEAA **23** 69, NYA **22** 69-72, CHI N **38** 72-73, ATLN **33** 74, NYN **22** 74, CLEA *CH* **1** 85-87

AKERFELDS, DARREL P/CH
(58,47,24,**35**, 48) OAKA **58** 86, CLEA **47** 87, TEXA **24** 89, PHIN **35** 90-91, SDN *CH* **48** 01-05

AKERS, BILL (BUMP) INF
(**7**,6) DETA **7** 31, BOSN **6** 32

ALBA, GIBSON P
(**47**) STLN **47** 88

ALBANESE, JOE P
(**27**) WASA **27** 58

ALBERRO, JOSE P
(**48**) TEXA **48** 95-97

ALBERTS, BUTCH DH
(**14**) TORA **14** 78

ALBOSTA, ED (RUBE) P
(29,24) BKNN **29** 41, PITN **24** 46

ALBRECHT, ED P
(**35**) STLA **35** 49-50

ALBRIGHT, JACK SS
(**22**) PHIN **22** 47

ALBURY, VIC P
(**20**) MINA **20** 73-76

ALCALA, SANTO P
(**42**,32,33) CINN **42** 76-77, MONN **32/33** 77

ALCANTARA, IZZY OF/1B
(56,**55**) BOSA **56** 00, MILN **55** 02

ALCARAZ, LUIS 2B
(**34**,39,1) LAN **23** 67-68, KCA **39** 69, **1** 70

ALDERSON, DALE P
(**31**,47) CHIN **31** 43-44 , **47** 44

ALDRED, SCOTT P
(35,**30**,32,22, 49,57,37) DETA **35/30** 90, **30** 91-92, COLN **32** 93, MONN **22** 93, DETA **49** 96, MINA **57** 96-97, TBA **37** 98-99, **30** 99, PHIN **30** 99-00

ALDRETE, MIKE OF/1B/CH
(1,25,24,15,43, **23**,27,20,8) SFN **1** 86, **25** 87-88, MONN **24** 89-90, **25** 90, SDN **15** 91, CLEA **43** 91, OAKA **23** 93-95, CALA **27** 95-96, NYA **20** 96, SEAA *CH* **8/25** 04, ARIN *CH* **8** 05

ALDRICH, JAY P
(63,48,**33**,43, 58,46) MILA **63/48/33** 87, **33** 89 ATLN **43** 89, BALA **58/46** 90

ALDRIDGE, CORY P
(**40**) ATLN **40** 01

ALEJO, BOB CH
(50,**46**) OAKA *CH* **50** 93, *CH* **46** 97-98

ALENO, CHUCK UTIL
(**16**,28,14) CINN **16** 41-42, **28** 43, **14** 44

ALEXANDER, BOB P
(**37**,30) BALA **37** 55, CLEA **30** 57

ALEXANDER, DALE (MOOSE) 1B
(4,**15**) DETA **4** 31-32, BOSA **15** 32-33

ALEXANDER, DOYLE P
(48,24,13,52, **33**,47,37,19) LAN **48** 71, BALA **24** 72, **13** 72-76, NYA **52/13** 76, TEXA **33** 77-79, ATLN **33** 80, SFN **26/ 33** 81, NYA **52** 82-83, TORA **47** 83, **33** 84-86, ATLN **37** 86, **33** 87, DETA **19** 87-89

ALEXANDER, GARY C
(58,42,37,**35**) SFN **58** 75-76, **42** 77, OAKA **37** 78, CLEA **35** 78-80, PITN **35** 81

ALEXANDER, GERALD P
(**48**) TEXA **48** 91-92

ALEXANDER, HUGH OF
(**2**) CLEA **2** 37

ALEXANDER, MANNY SS/INF
(48,**6**,24,29, 4,20) BALA **48** 92-93, **6** 95-96, NYN **6** 97, CHIN **24** 97-99, BOSA **29** 00, TEXA **4** 04, SDN **20** 05

ALEXANDER, MATT UTIL
(29,42,31,2, 12,**36**) CHIN **29** 73, **42** 73-74, OAKA **31**75-76, **2** 77, PITN **12** 78, **36** 79-81

ALFARO, JASON SS
(**29**) HOUN **29** 04

ALFONSECA, ANTONIO P
(**57**) FLAN **57** 97-01, CHIN **57** 02-03, ATLN **57** 04, FLAN **57** 05

ALFONSO, CARLOS CH
(16,**17**) SFN *CH* **16** 92, *CH* **17** 97-99, 01-05

ALFONZO, EDGARDO 2B/3B
(**13**,12) NYN **13** 95-02, SFN **13** 03-04, **12** 05

ALICEA, LUIS 2B/UTIL
(**18**,10,12,5) STLN **18** 88, 91-94, BOSA **10** 95, STLN **12** 96, ANAA **5** 97, TEXA **10** 98-00, KCA **12** 01-02

ALLANSON, ANDY C
(**6**,10,37,28) CLEA **6** 86-89, DETA **10** 91, MILA **6** 92, SFN **37** 93, CALA **28** 95

ALLARD, BRIAN P
(24,23,12,31) TEXA **24** 79, **23/12** 80, SEAA **31** 81

ALLEN, BERNIE 2B/3B
(12,1,8,21,11, **7**,9) MINA **12** 62-63, **1** 63-64, **8** 65, **21/11** 66, WASA **7** 67-71, NYA **11** 72-73, MONN **9** 73

ALLEN, BOB (THIN MAN) P
(**41**) PHIN **41** 37

ALLEN, BOB P
(24,40,**36**) CLEA **24** 61-62, **40** 63, **36** 66-67

ALLEN, CHAD OF/DH
(**31**,9,21,13) MINA **31** 99-01, CLEA **9** 02, FLAN **21** 03, TEXA **13** 04-05

ALLEN, DICK 3B/1B B
(32,**15**,60) PHIN **32** 63-64, **15** 64-69, STLN **15** 70, LAN **15** 71, CHIA **15** 72-74, PHIN **15** 75-76, OAKA **60** 77

ALLEN, DUSTY OF/UTIL
(21,**22**) SDN **21** 00, DETA **22** 00

ALLEN, ETHAN OF
(22,24,**30**,4, 8) NYN **22** 32, STLN **24** 33, PHIN **30** 34-36, CHIN **4** 36, STLA **8** 37-38

ALLEN, HANK OF B
(17,5,6,**35**,44, 42) WASA **17** 66, **5/6** 67, **35** 67-70, MILA **44** 70, CHIA **42** 72-73

ALLEN, JAMIE 3B
(**20**) SEAA **20** 83

ALLEN, JOHNNY P
(18,**15**,30,22, 20,21) NYA **18** 32-35, CLEA **15** 36-40, STLA **30** 41, BKNN **22** 41-43, NYN **20/21** 43, **22** 44

ALLEN, KIM UTIL
(20,**2**) SEAA **20** 80, **2** 81

ALLEN, LLOYD P
(**40**,50,51,26, 37,30) CALA **40/50/51** 69, **40** 70-73, TEXA **26** 73, **30** 74, CHIA **37/40** 74, **40/26** 75

ALLEN, LUKE OF
(49,**11**) LAN **49** 02, COLN **11** 03

ALLEN, NEIL P/CH
(46,**13**,53,39, 26,33,48,27, **25**,15,57) NYN **46** 79-80, **13** 80-83, STLN **13** 83-85, NYA **53/39/ 26** 85, CHIA **33** 86-87, NYA **48** 87, **27** 88, CLEA **25/15** 89, NYA *CH* **57** 05

ALLEN, ROD OF
(18,**12**,60) SEAA **18** 83, DETA **12** 84, CLEA **60** 88

ALLEN, RON 1B B
(**16**) STLN **16** 72

ALLENSON, GARY C,CH
(28,**39**,38,32) BOSA **28** 79, **39** 79-84, TORA **38** 85, BOSA *CH* **32** 92-94, MILN *CH* **45** 00-02

ALLENSWORTH, JERMAINE OF
(**46**,23) PITN **46** 96-98, KCA **46** 98, NYN **23** 98, **46** 99

ALLEY, GENE SS
(12,**14**,22) PITN **12** 63, **14** 64-67, **22** 68-69, **14** 70-73

ALLIE, GAIR SS
(**8**) PITN **8** 54, **32** 93, MONN **22** 93

ALLIETTA, BOB C
(**18**) CALA **18** 75

ALLISON, BOB OF/1B
(15,26,**4**) WASA **15** 58, **26** 59-60, MINA **4** 61-70

ALLISON, DANA P
(**38**) OAKA **38** 91

ALLRED, BEAU OF
(**55**,37) CLEA **55** 89-90, **37** 91

ALMADA, MEL OF
(**21**,1,4,6,29) BOSA **21** 33-35, **1** 36- 37, WASA **4** 37-38, STLA **6** 38-39, BKNN **29** 39

ALMANZA, ARMANDO P
(**55**,29,34,57) FLAN **55** 99-02, **29** 03, ATL **34** 04, ARIN **57** 05

ALMANZAR, CARLOS P
(**40**,57,59) TORA **40** 97-98, SDN **40** 99-00, NYA **57** 01, CINN **59** 02, TEXA **40** 04-05

ALMON, BILL SS
(5,**6**,19,25,34, 12,2,15) SDN **5** 74-75, **6** 76-79, MONN **19** 80, NYN **25** 80, CHIA **34** 81-82, OAKA **34** 83-84, PITN **12** 85-87, NYN **2** 87, PHIN **15** 88

ALMONTE, EDWIN P
(**56**) NYN **56** 03

ALMONTE, ERICK SS
(57,**11**,60) NYA **57** 01, **11/60** 03

ALMONTE, HECTOR P
(**59**,58) FLAN **59** 99, BOSA **58** 03, MONN **59** 03

ALOMA, LUIS (WITTO) P
(**59**,11) CHIA **59** 50-52, **11** 53

ALOMAR, ROBERTO 2B S,B
(**12**,2) SDN **12** 88-90, TORA **2** 91, **12** 91-95, BALA **12** 96-98, CLEA **12** 99 -01, NYN **12** 02-03, CHIA **12** 03, ARIN **2** 04, CHIA **12** 04

ALOMAR, SANDY, JR. C/DH S,B
(4,17,**15**,25) SDN **4** 88, **17** 89, CLEA **15** 90-00, CHIA **15** 01-02, COLN **25** 02, **15** 03, CHIA **15** 04, TEXA **15** 05

ALOMAR, SANDY, SR. INF F
(16,5,11,1,4, **2**,24) MILN **16** 64-65, ATLN **16** 66, NYN **5** 67, CHIA **11** 67, **1** 68-69, CALA **4** 69-71, **2** 71-72, CALA **24** 73-74, NYA **11** 74, **2** 75-76, TEXA **2** 77-78, SDN *CH* **4** 86, **2** 87-90, CHIN *CH* **4** 00, **2** 00-02, COLN *CH* **2** 03-04, NYN *CH* **2** 05

ALOU, FELIPE OF B,F
(49,23,**29**,8, 24,48,14,16, 17) SFN **49** 58, **23** 59-63, MILN **29** 64-65, ATLN **29** 66-69, OAKA **8** 70-71, NYA **24** 71-73, MONN **48** 73, MILA **14** 74, MONN *CH* **16** 79-81, *CH* **17** 84, *CH,M* **17** 92, *M* **17** 93-01, DETA *CH* **18** 02, SFN *CH* **23** 03, *M* **23** 04-05

ALOU, JESUS OF B,U
(14,**22**,23) SFN **14** 63-68, HOUN **22** 69-73, OAKA **22** 73-74, NYN **23** 75, HOUN **22** 78-79

ALOU, MATTY OF B,U
(26,41,**18**,17, 14,2,4,32) SFN **26** 60, **41** 61-65, PITN **18** 66-70, STLN **17** 71-72, OAKA **14** 72, NYA **2** 73, STLN **4** 73, SDN **32** 74

ALOU, MOISES OF S,N
(52,**18**) PITN **52** 90, MONN **18** 90, 92-96, FLAN **18** 97, HOUN **18** 98-01, CHIN **18** 02-04, SFN **18** 05

ALSTON, DELL UTIL
(27,**13**,30) NYA **27** 77-78, OAKA **13** 78, CLEA **30** 79-80, **13** 80

ALSTON, GARVIN P
(**50**) COLN **50** 96

ALSTON, TOM 1B
(10,**22**) STLN **10** 54-55, **22** 56-57

ALSTON, WALTER (SMOKEY) 1B/M
(21,**24**) STLN **21** 36, BKNN *M* **24** 54-57, LAN *M* **24** 58-76

ALTAMIRANO, PORFI P
(**30**, 33) PHIN **57** 82, **30** 82-83, CHIN **33** 84

Bill Almon played for fifteen years because of his versatility. He played every position except pitcher. He knocked in 63 runs in 451 ABs in 1983; the following year he hit 7 HRs (his best), but only had 16 RBI in 211 ABs.

ALTMAN, GEORGE OF/1B
(**21**,26,2) CHIN **21** 59-62, STLN **26** 63, NYN **2** 64, CHIN **21** 65-67

ALTOBELLI, JOE 1B/M/CH
(45,**5**,35,6,48, 26,2) CLEA **45** 55, **5** 57,MINA **35** 61, SFN *M* **6** 77-79, NYA *CH* **48** 81-82, BALA *M* **26** 83-85, NYA *CH* **48** 86, CHIN *CH* **2** 88, *CH* **6** 88-91, *M* **6** 91

ALTROCK, NICK PH/CH
(29,28,27,23, 30,**33**,32,54) WASA **29** 31, *CH* **29** 31, **28** 32, **28** 32, **27** 33, **27** 33, **27** 34-36, **23** 35, **28** 36-40, **30** 41, **29** 42-43, **30** 43, **33** 44-49, **32** 46, **54** 50-54

ALUSIK, GEORGE OF
(35,26,**3**) DETA **35** 58, **26** 61-62, KCA **3** 62-64

ALVARADO, LUIS SS
(41,12,**1**,17,14, 15,19) BOSA **41** 68, **12** 69-70, **1** 70, CHIA **1** 71-74, STLN **1** 74, CLEA **17** 74, STLN **14** 76, DETA **15** 77, NYN **19** 77

ALVAREZ, ABE P
(**59**) BOSA **59** 04-05

ALVÁREZ, CLEMENTE C
(**15**) PHIN **15** 00

ALVÁREZ, GABE 3B/DH
(20,**25**,9) DETA **20** 98, **25** 99-00, SDN **9** 00

ALVAREZ, JOSE P
(50,**40**) ATLN **50** 81-82, **40** 88-89

ALVÁREZ, JUAN P
(**18**,51,32) ANAA **18** 99-00, TEXA **51** 02, FLAN **32** 03

ALVAREZ, ORLANDO OF
(**2**,17) LAN **2** 73-75, CALA **17** 76

ALVAREZ, OSSIE INF
(**22**,36) WASA **22** 58, DETA **36** 59

ALVÁREZ, ROGELIO 1B
(21,**11**) CINN **21** 60, **11** 62

ALVÁREZ, TAVO P
(**48**) MONN **48** 95-96

ALVÁREZ, TONY OF/3B
(**56**) PITN **56** 02, 04

ALVÁREZ, VICTOR P
(**57**) LAN **57** 02-03

ALVÁREZ, WILSON P
(43,38,**40**,47) TEXA **43** 89, CHIA **38** 91, **40** 92-97, SFN **40** 97, TBA **40** 98-02, LAN **47** 03-05

ALVIS, MAX 3B
(**10**) CLEA **10** 62-69, MILA **10** 70

ALYEA, BRANT OF
(25,3,11,7,21) WASA **25** 65, **3** 68-69, MINA **11** 70-71, OAKA **7** 72, STLN **21** 72

AMALFITANO, JOEY INF/CH/M
(12,14,11,17, **5**,6,8) NYN **12** 54-55, SFN **14** 60-61, HOUN **11** 62, SFN **14** 63, CHIN **17** 64-66, **5** 67, *CH* **5** 67-71, SFN *CH* **6** 72, **5** 72-75, SDN **5** 76-77, CHIN *CH* **5** 78-79, *M* **5** 79, *CH/M* **5** 80, *M* **5** 81, CINN *CH* **8** 82, LAN *CH* **8** 83-92, **12** 91, **8** 93-98

AMARAL, RICH UTIL
(**8**,6) SEAA **8** 91-98, BALA **6** 99-00

AMARO, RUBEN, JR. OF S
(**33**,30,20,37) CALA **30** 91, PHIN **33** 92-93, CLEA **30** 94, **20** 95, PHIN **37** 96-97, **33** 98

AMARO, RUBEN, SR. SS/CH F
(19,**20**,12,5) STLN **19** 58, PHIN **20** 60-65, NYA **12** 66-68, CALA **12** 69, PHIN *CH* **12** 80-81, CHIN *CH* **5** 83-86

AMBLER, WAYNE INF
(**4**,12,14) PHIA **4** 37, **12** 38, **14** 39

AMBRES, CHIP OF
(**18**) KCA **18** 05

AMELUNG, ED OF
(**17**,20) LAN **17** 84, **20** 86

AMEZAGA, ALFREDO SS/3B
(**5**,15,6) ANAA **5** 02-04, COLN **15** 05, PITN **6** 05

AMOR, VICENTE P
(**35**,36) CHIN **35** 55, CINN **36** 57

AMOROS, SANDY OF
(5,**15**,18,36) BKNN **5** 52, **15** 54-57, LAN **18** 59-60, DETA **36** 60

ANDERSEN, LARRY P
(42,39,**47**,40, 48,27,37) CLEA **42** 75, 77, 79, SEAA **39** 81-82, PHIN **47** 83-86, HOUN **47** 86-90, BOSA **40/48** 90, SDN **27** 91-92, **37** 92, PHIN **47** 93-94

ANDERSON, ALF SS
(**15**,37) PITN **15** 41-42, **37** 46

ANDERSON, ALLAN P
(40,**49**) MINA **40** 86, **49** 86-91

ANDERSON, ANDY INF
(**7**) STLA **7** 48-49

ANDERSON, BOB P
(27,**32**,23) CHIN **27** 57, **32** 57-62, DETA **23** 63

ANDERSON, BRADY OF
(5,16,**9**) BOSA **5** 88, BALA **16** 88, **9** 89-01, CLEA **9** 02

ANDERSON, BRIAN P
(56,**34**,31,19) CALA **56** 93-95, CLEA **34** 96-97, ARIN **34** 98-02, CLEA **31** 03, KCA **19** 03-05

ANDERSON, BRIAN OF
(**44**) CHIA **44** 05

ANDERSON, BUD P
(50,**51**) CLEA **50** 82, **51** 82-83

ANDERSON, CRAIG P
(18,**20**) STLN **18** 61, NYN **20** 62-64

ANDERSON, DAVE INF
(**10**,12) LAN **10** 83-89, SFN **10** 90-91, LAN **12** 92

ANDERSON, DWAIN INF
(**11**,19,10,14) OAKA **11** 71-72, STLN **19** 72-73, SDN **10** 73, CLEA **14** 74

ANDERSON, FERRELL (ANDY) C
(14,38) BKNN **14** 46, STLN **38** 53

ANDERSON, GARRET OF/DH
(**16**) CALA **16** 94-96, ANAA **16** 97-05

ANDERSON, HAL OF
(**36**) CHIA **36** 32

ANDERSON, HARRY OF/1B
(**9**,27) PHIN **9** 57-60, CINN **27** 60-61

ANDERSON, JASON P
(45,**17**,59,31) NYA **45** 03, NYN **17** 03, CLEA **58** 04, NYA **31** 05

ANDERSON, JIMMY P
(**55**,45,49,56) PITN **55** 99-02, CINN **45** 03, CHIN **49** 04, BOSA **56** 04

ANDERSON, JIM INF
(**14**,4,46) CALA **14** 78-79, SEAA **4** 80-81, TEXA **46** 83, **14** 84

ANDERSON, JOHN P
(33,18,35,39) PHIN **33** 58, BALA **18** 60, STLN **35** 62, HOUN **39** 62

ANDERSON, KENT INF
(**7**) CALA **7** 89-90

ANDERSON, LARRY P
(43,**45**,51) MILA **43** 74-75, **45** 75, CHIA **51** 77

ANDERSON, MARLON 2B
(16,**8**,18) PHIN **16** 98-00, **8** 01-02, TBA **8** 03, STLN **8** 04, NYN **18** 05

ANDERSON, MATT P
(51,**14**) DETA **51** 98, **14** 98-03, COLN **14** 05

ANDERSON, MIKE OF
(40,**22**,27,39) PHIN **40** 71, **22** 72-75, STLN **27** 76-77, BALA **39** 78, PHIN **22** 79

ANDERSON, RED P
(34,3,17,**18**) WASA **34** 37, **3** 40, **17** 41, **18** 41

ANDERSON, RICK (A.) P/CH
(32,**17**,40) NYN **32** 86, KCA **32** 87, **17** 87-88, MINA *CH* **40** 02-05

ANDERSON, RICK (L.) P
(19,25) NYA **19** 79, SEAA **25** 80

ANDERSON, SCOTT P
(48,52,37) TEXA **48** 87, MONN **52** 90, KCA **37** 95

ANDERSON, SPARKY 2B/CH/M
(45,**2**,10,1,11) PHIN **45/2** 59, SDN *CH* **10/1** 69, CINN *M* **10** 70-78, DETA *M* **11** 79-95

ANDINO, ROBERT INF/SS
(**4**) FLAN **4** 05

ANDRE, JOHN P
(**29**) CHIN **29** 55

ANDRES, ERNIE 3B
(**35**) BOSA **35** 46

ANDREW, KIM 2B
(**11**) BOSA **11** 75

ANDREWS, CLAYTON P
(**36**) TORA **36** 00

ANDREWS, FRED 2B
(5,26,**16**) PHIN **5/26** 76, **16** 76-77

ANDREWS, HUB P
(**38**) NYN **38** 47-48

ANDREWS, IVY (POISON) P
(22,34,28,25, 16,**18**,19,24) NYA **22** 31, **34** 31-32, **28** 32, BOSA **25** 32, **16** 33, STLA **18** 34-36, CLEA **19** 37, NYA **24** 37-38

ANDREWS, JOHN P
(31,37) STLN **31/37** 73

ANDREWS, MIKE 2B
(**2**,17) BOSA **2** 66-70, CHIA **2** 71-73, OAKA **17** 73

ANDREWS, NATE P
(29,22,12,**25**, 35,28) STLN **29** 37, **22** 39, CLEA **12** 40-41, BOSN **25** 43-45, CINN **35** 46, NYN **28** 46

ANDREWS, ROB INF
(11,**21**) HOUN **11** 75-76, SFN **21** 77-79

ANDREWS, SHANE 3B/1B/INF
(**11**,7,2) MONN **11** 95-99, CHIN **7** 99, **24** 00, BOSA **2** 02

ANDREWS, STAN (POLO) C
(29,11,**15**,32) BOSN **29** 39, **11** 40, BKNN **15** 44-45, PHIN **32** 45

ANDRUS, BILL (ANDY) 3B
(__,**26**) WASA __ 31, PHIN **26** 37

ANDUJAR, JOAQUIN (JACK) P
(52,**47**,30) HOUN **52** 76, **47** 76-81, STLN **30** 81, **47** 81-85, OAKA **47** 86-87, HOUN **47** 88

ANDUJAR, LUIS P
(**49**) CHIA **49** 95-96, TORA **49** 96-98

ANGELINI, NORM P
(**39**) KCA **39** 72-73

ANKENMAN, PAT SS
(29,33,16) STLN **29** 36, BKNN **33** 43, **16** 44

ANKIEL, RICH P
(**66**,49) STLN **66** 99-01, (02-03), **49** 04

ANTHONY, ERIC OF
(23,**21**,24,5, 9,19,29) HOUN **23** 89-90, **21** 91-92, **24** 93, SEAA **5** 94, CINN **9** 95, **19** 96, COLN **29** 96, LAN **29** 97

ANTOLICK, JOE C
(**30**) PHIN **30** 44

ANTONELLI, JOHN INF
(18,22,**2**) STLN **18** 44, **22** 45, PHIN **2** 45

ANTONELLI, JOHNNY P
(34,**43**,23) BOSN **34** 48-50, *(MIL)* 51-52, MILN **34** 53, NYN **43** 54-60, CLEA **23** 61, MILN **43** 61

ANTONELLO, BILL OF
(**32**) BKNN **32** 53

APARICIO, LUIS SS
(**11**) CHIA **11** 56-62. BALA **11** 63-67, CHIA **11** 68-70, BOSA **11** 71-73

APODACA, BOB P
(**34**,56,36) NYN **34** 73-77, *CH* **56** 96, *CH* **34** 97-99, MILN *CH* **36** 00-01, COLN *CH* **36** 03-05

APONTE, LUIS P
(**45**,38) BOSA **45** 80-83, CLEA **38** 84

APPIER, KEVIN P
(**55**,17,19,27) KCA **55** 89-95, **17** 96-99, OAKA **19** 99-00, NYN **17** 01, ANAA **27** 02-03, KCA **55** 03-04

APPLETON, PETE (JAKE) P (aka JABLONOWSKI)
(23,17,21,33, **18**,48,10,20, 36,37) CLEA **23** 30-31, **17** 32, BOSA **21** 32, NYA **33** 33, WASA **18** 36-39, CHIA **48/10** 40, **20** 41, **48** 42, STLA **27** 42, **36/37** 45, WASA __ 45,

APPLING, LUKE (OLD ACHES & PAINS) SS
(5,8,**4**,31,40, 41,44,33,55) CHIA **5** 31, **8** 32, **4** 33-50, DETA *CH* **31** 60, CLEA **40** 60-61, BALA **41** 63, KCA *CH* **44** 64-67, *M* **33** 67, CHIA *CH* **4** 70-71, ATLN *CH* **55** 84

AQUINO, GREG P
(**41**) ARIN **41** 04-05

AQUINO, LUIS P
(32,**27**,72) TORA **32** 86, KCA **27** 88-92, FLAN **27** 93-94, MONN **72** 95, SFN **72** 95

ARAGON, JACK PR
(**33**) NYN **33** 41

ARCHER, FRED (LEFTY) P
(3,**41**) PHIA **3** 36, **41** 37

ARCHER, JIM P
(**20**) KCA **20** 61-62

ARCHIE, GEORGE 1B
(35,7,52,**23**) DETA **35** 38, WASA **7** 41, STLA **52** 41, **23** 46

ARCIA, JOSE UTIL
(17,**5**) CHIN **17** 68, SDN **5** 69-70

ARDELL, DANNY 1B
(**35**) LAA **35** 61

ARDIZOIA, RUGGER P
(**14**) NYA **14** 47

ARDOIN, DANNY C
(12,**5**,55) MINA **12** 00, TEXA **5** 04, COLN **55** 05

ARFT, HANK (BOW WOW) 1B
(**3**) STLA **3** 48-52

ARIAS, ALEX SS/3B
(21,50,24,**26**) CHIN **21/50** 92, FLAN **24/26** 93, **26** 94-97, PHIN **26** 98-00, SDN **9** 01, NYA **17** 02

ARIAS, GEORGE 3B
(5,7,**14**) CALA **5** 96, ANAA **7** 97, SDN **14** 97-99

ARIAS, RUDY P
(25,49) CHIA **25/49** 59

ARLICH, DON P
(**46**) HOUN **46** 65-66

ARLIN, STEVE P
(44,27,41,**22**) SDN **44/27** 69, **41** 70-71, **22** 71-74, **41** 74

ARMAS, MARCOS UTIL
(**38**) OAKA **38** 93

ARMAS, TONY OF F
(46,11,**20**,10) PITN **46** 76, OAKA **11** 77-80, **20** 81-82, BOSA **20** 83-86, CALA **10** 87, **20** 88-89

ARMAS, TONY, JR. P S
(51,**36**) MONN **51** 99, **58** 00, **36** 00-04, WASN **36** 05

ARMBRISTER, ED OF
(**33**) CINN **33** 73-77

ARMBRUST, ORVILLE P
(**29**) WASA **29** 34

ARMSTRONG, GEORGE (DODO) C
(**33**) PHIA **33** 46

ARMSTRONG, JACK P
(**40**,77) CINN **40** 88-91, CLEA **77** 92, FLAN **77** 93, TEXA **77** 94

ARMSTRONG, MIKE P
(**36**,31,34,47) SDN **36** 80-81, KCA **31** 82-83, NYA **36** 84-86, **34** 86, CLEA **47** 87

ARNDT, LARRY INF
(**30**) OAKA **30** 89

ARNOLD, CHRIS UTIL
(31,17,15) SFN **31** 71-72, **17** 72-74, **15** 75-76

ARNOLD, JAIME P
(**52**,55) LAN **52** 99-00, CHIN **55** 00

ARNOLD, SCOTT P
(58,41) STLN **58/41** 88

ARNOLD, TONY P
(**57**) BALA **57** 86-87

ARNOVICH, MORRIE (MOE, SNOOKER) OF
(34,3,**24**,21, 22,40) PHIN **34** 36-37, **3** 38, **24** 39-40, CINN **21** 40, NYN **22** 41, **40** 46

ARNSBERG, BRAD P
(62,54,36,**28**, 38) NYA **62** 86, **54/36** 87, TEXA **28** 89-91, CLEA **36** 92, MONN *CH* **38** 00-01, FLAN *CH* **38** 02-03, TORA *CH* **38** 05

ARNTZEN, ORIE P
(**23**) PHIA **23** 43

AROCHA, RENE P
(**43**,49) STLN **43** 93-95, SFN **49/43** 97

ARRIGO, GERRY P
(**35**46,47,26, 34,30) MINA **35** 61, **46** 62-63, **35** 63-64, CINN **47** 65, CINN **35** 65-66, NYN **26/34** 66, CINN **35** 67-69, CHIA **30** 70

ARROJO, ROLANDO P
(30,17,**44**,19, 46) TBA **30** 98, **17** 99, COLN **30/44** 00, BOSA **19/46** 00, **44** 01-02

ARROYO, BRONSON P
(69,**61**) PITN **69** 00-02, BOSA **61** 03-05

ARROYO, FERNANDO P
(**36**,52,30,32, 54) DETA **36** 75,77-79, MINA **52** 80,**30** 80-82, OAKA **32** 82, **54** 86

ARROYO, LUIS (YO-YO) P
(38,35,39,**47**) STLN **38** 55, PITA **35** 56, **39** 57, CINN **47** 59, NYA **47** 60-63

ARROYO, RUDY P
(**43**) STLN **43** 71

ARSENAULT, PIERRE CH
(**67**) MONN *CH* **67** 92-01, FLAN *CH* **67** 03-05

ASADOOR, RANDY 3B/2B
(**12**) SDN **12** 86

ASBELL, JIM (BIG TRAIN) OF
(**38**) CHIN **30** 38

ASBJORNSON, CASPER (ASBY*) C
(**22**) CINN **22** 32

ASENCIO, MIGUEL P
(**53**) KCA **53** 02-03, (04)

ASHBURN, RICHIE (WHITEY) OF
(**1**) PHIN **1** 48-59, CHIN **1** 60-61, NYN **1** 62

ASHBY, ALAN C/CH
(8,**14**) CLEA **8** 73-76, TORA **8** 77-78, HOUN **14** 79-89, *CH* **8** 97

ASHBY, ANDY P
(40,**43**,48) PHIN **40** 91-92, COLN **43** 93, SDN **43** 93-99, PHIN **43** 00, ATLN **48** 00, LAN **43** 01-03, SDN **43** 04

ASHFORD, TUCKER INF
(**12**,46,29,57, 11,37) SDN **12/46** 76, **46** 77, **12** 78, TEXA **29** 80, NYA **57** 81, NYN **11** 83, KCA **37** 84

ASHLEY, BILLY OF
(**7**,21,23) LAN **7** 92-95, **21** 96-97, BOSA **23** 98

ASPROMONTE, BOB INF B
(44,34,28,**14**, 11,2) BKNN **44/34** 56, LAN **28** 60-61, HOUN **14** 62-68, ATLN **11** 69, **14** 69-70, NYN **2** 71

ASPROMONTE, KEN 2B/M B
(7,4,**2**,11,25, 15,12) BOSA **7** 57-58, WASA **4** 58-60, CLEA **2** 60, LAA **11** 61, CLEA **2** 61-62, MILN **25** 62, CHIN **15/12** 63, CLEA *M* **2** 72-74

ASSELSTINE, BRIAN OF
(18,**30**) ATLN **18** 76-77, **30** 78-81

ASSENMACHER, PAUL P
(59,30,**45**,43, 42,50) ATLN **59** 86, **30** 86-89, CHIN **30** 89, **45** 89-93, NYA **43** 93, CHIA **42/50** 94, CLEA **45** 95-99

ASTACIO, EZEQUIEL P
(**38**) HOUN **38** 05

ASTACIO, PEDRO P
(59,56,51,**34**, 39,52) LAN **59** 92, **56** 93-97, COLN **51** 97, **34** 97-01, HOUN **27** 01, NYN **34** 02-03, BOSA **39** 04, TEXA **39** 05, SDN **34** 05

ASTROTH, JOE C
(14,15,**9**,11) PHIA **14/15** 45, **14** 46, **9** 49-54, KCA **11** 55-56

ATCHISON, SCOTT P
(**27**) SEAA **27** 05

ATCHLEY, JUSTIN P
(**39**) CINN **39** 01

ATHERTON, KEITH P
(**55**,22,38) OAKA **55** 83-86, MINA **22** 86-88, CLEA **38/22** 89

ATKINS, GARRETT OF/3B
(**27**) COLN **27** 03-05

ATKINS, JIM P
(**12**,25) BOSA **12** 50, **25** 52

ATKINSON, BILL P
(52,**42**) MONN **52** 76, **42** 77-79

ATWELL, TOBY C
(**11**,39) CHIN **11** 52-53, PITN **11** 53-56, MILN **39** 56

ATWOOD, BILL C
(**11**,34,5) PHIN **11** 36-38, **34** 39, **5** 39-40

AUCOIN, DEREK P
(**66**) MONN **66** 96

AUDE, RICH 1B
(**48**) PITN **48** 93, 95-96

AUERBACH, RICK INF
(19,1,**23**,16) MILA **19** 71-73, LAN **1** 74-76, CINN **23** 77-80, SEAA **16** 81

AUFERIO, TONY CH
(**50**) STLN *CH* **50** 73

AUGUST, DON P
(**38**) MILA **38** 88-91

AUGUSTINE, DAVE OF
(**45**,27) PITN **45** 73, **27** 74

AUGUSTINE, JERRY P
(**46**) MILA **46** 75-84

AUKER, ELDON (SUBMARINE) P
(14,**13**,12,18) DETA **14** 33, **13** 34-36, **12** 37-38, BOSA **13/12** 39, STLN **18** 40-42

AULDS, DOYLE (TEX) C (**27**) BOSA **27** 47

AULT, DOUG 1B (22,**25**) TEXA **22** 76, TORA **25** 77-78, 80

AURILIA, RICH SS/3B/2B (57,**35**,21,33) SFN **57** 95-96, **35** 97-03, SEAA **35** 04, SDN **21** 04, CINN **33** 05

AUSANIO, JOE P (**54**) NYA **54** 94-95

AUSMUS, BRAD P (**11**,7,12) SDN **11** 93-96, DETA **7** 96, HOUN **11** 97-98, DETA **12** 99-00, HOUN **11** 01-05

AUST, DENNIS P (**35**) STLN **35** 65-66

AUSTIN, JEFF P (**26**) KCA **26** 01-02, CINN **51** 03

AUSTIN, JIM P (47,**42**) MILA **47** 91, **42** 92-93

AUSTIN, JIMMY (PEPPER) CH (28,37,**33**,32,) STLA *CH* **28** 31-32, CHIA *CH* **37** 33-34, **33** 35, **32** 36-37, **33** 37-40

AUSTIN, RICK P (**33**,36,43) CLEA **33** 70-71, MILA **36** 75, **43** 75-76

AUTRY, AL P (**38**) ATLN **38** 76

AVEN, BRUCE OF (36,56,**29**,37, 47,46,20) CLEA **36/56** 97, FLAN **29** 99, PITN **37** 00, LAN **47** 00, **46** 01, CLEA **20** 02

AVERILL, EARL, JR. C (15,2,**6**,31,8, 17) CLEA **15** 56, **2** 58, CHIN **6** 59-60, CHIA **31** 60, LAA **8** 61-62, PHIN **17** 63

AVERILL, EARL, SR. (ROCK) OF (**3**,24,27) CLEA **3** 30-39, DETA **24** 39, **27** 40, BOSN **3** 41

AVERY, STEVE P (42,**33**,32) ATLN **42** 90-91, **33** 91-96, BOSA **33** 97-98, CINN **33** 99, ATLN **32** 00, DETA **33** 03

AVILA, BOBBY 2B (**1**,8,12,11) CLEA **1** 49-58, BALA **8** 59, BOSA **12** 59, MILN **11** 59

AVILAS, RAMON 2B (11,**15**) BOSA **11** 77, PHIN **15** 79-81

AVREA, JIM (JAY) P (**38**) CINN **38** 50

AYALA, BENNY OF (18,15,**27**,12) NYN **18** 74, 76, STLN **15** 77, BALA **27** 79-84, CLEA **12** 85

AYALA, BOBBY P (59,**13**,31,36) CINN **59** 92-93, SEAA **13** 94-96, **31** 97-98, MONN **36** 99, CHIN **31** 99

AYALA, LUIS P (**56**) MONN **56** 03-04, WASN **56** 05

AYBAR, MANNY P (**38**,36,26,27, 40,22,50,16) STLN **38** 97-99, COLN **38** 00, CINN **36** 00, FLAN **26/27** 00, CHIN **40/38** 01, SFN **22/50** 02, **16** 03, NYN **36** 05

AYBAR, WILLY INF (**49**) LAN **49** 05

AYERS, BILL P (**39**) NYN **39** 47

AYLWARD, DICK (DANDY) C (**15**) CLEA **15** 53

AYRAULT, BOB P (**55**,50) PHIN **55** 92-93, SEAA **50** 93

AYRAULT, JOE C (**30**) ATLN **30** 96

AZCUE, JOE C (9,10,**6**,7,1,2, 31,17) CINN **9** 60, KCA **10** 62-63, CLEA **6** 63-66, 68-69, **7** 67, BOSA **1** 69, CALA **2** 69-71, **31** 72, MILA **17** 72

AZOCAR, OSCAR OF (50,**22**) NYA **50** 90, SDN **22** 91-92

B

BABCOCK, BOB P (17,**20**,46,39) TEXA **17** 79, **20** 79-80, **46** 80-81, **39** 81

BABE, LOREN (BEE BEE) 3B (39,**38**,3,36,42, 46) NYA **39** 52, **38** 52-53, PHIN **3** 53, NYA *CH* **36** 67, CHIA *CH* **42** 80-81, *CH* **46** 83-84

BABICH, JOHNNY P (26,21,**30**) BKNN **26** 34-35, BOSN **21** 36, PHIA **30** 40-41

BABITT, SHOOTY 2B (**3**) OAKA **3** 81

BACKE, BRANDON P (37,30,**41**) TBA **37** 02-03, **30** 03, HOUN **37** 04, **41** 04-05

BACKMAN, WALLY 2B (39,28,**6**,2,19, 22) NYN **39/28** 80, **6** 81-88, MINA **2** 89, PITN **19** 90, PHIA **6** 91-92, SEAA **22** 93

BACSIK, MIKE (Ja.) P (34,25,37,48 **27**) TEXA **34** 75-76, **25** 76, **37/48** 77, MINA **27** 79-80

BACSIK, MIKE (Jo.), JR. P (51,**33**) CLEA **51** 01, NYN **33** 02-03, TEXA **51** 04

BACZEWSKI, FRED (LEFTY) P (31,**46**) CHIN **31** 53, CINN **46** 53-55

BAECHT, ED P (**16**,20) CHIN **16** 32, STLA **20** 37

BAEK, CHA SEUNG P (**32**) SEAA **32** 04

BAERGA, CARLOS 2B/1B (**9**,6,8,1,10,3, 5) CLEA **9** 90-96, NYN **6** 96, **8** 97-98, SDN **1** 99, CLEA **9** 99, BOSA **10** 02, ARIN **3** 03-04, WASN **5** 05

BAEZ, BENITO P (**49**) FLAN **49** 01

BAEZ, DANYS P (**55**,28) CLEA **55** 01-03, TBA **28** 04-05

BAEZ, JOSE 2B (**14**) SEAA **14** 77-78

BAEZ, KEVIN SS (**36**,1) NYN **36** 90, 92, **1** 93, **36** 93

BAGBY, JIM, JR. P S (**17**,22,36) BOSA **17** 38-40, CLEA **17** 41-44, **22** 44-45, BOSA **17** 46, PITN **36** 47

BAGWELL, JEFF 1B (**5**) HOUN **5** 91-05

BAHNSEN, STAN P (60,**45**,39,22, 34,37) NYA **60** 66, **45** 66, 68-71, CHIA **45** 72-75, OAKA **39** 75-76, **45** 76-77, MONN **22** 77-81, CALA **34** 82, PHIN **37** 82

BAHR, ED P (46,**24**) PITN **46** 46, **24** 47

BAILES, SCOTT P (**43**,58) CLEA **43** 86-89, CALA **43** 90-92, TEXA **58** 97-98

BAILEY, BOB 3B (7,12,**3**,11,30) PITN **3** 62, **7** 63-66, LAN **12** 67, **7** 68, MONN **3** 69-75, CINN **11** 76-77, BOSA **30** 77-78

BAILEY, BUDDY CH (**43**) BOSA **43** 00

BAILEY, CORY P (**43**,39,21,58, 41,62) BOSA **43** 93-94, STLN **39** 95, **21** 96, TEXA **58** 97, SFN **41** 97-98, PITN **62** 00, KCA **58** 01 -02

BAILEY, ED C (**6**,8,9,25) CINN **6** 53-61, **8** 55, SFN **6** 61-63, MILN **9** 64, SFN **6** 65, CHIN **6** 65, CALA **25** 66

BAILEY, HOWARD P (**60**) DETA **60** 81-83

BAILEY, JIM P (**41**) CINN **41** 59

BAILEY, MARK C/CH (**6**,45,37) HOUN **6** 84-88, SFN **45** 90, **37** 92, HOUN *CH* **6** 03-05

BAILEY, ROGER P (31,38) COLN **31**95, **38** 95-96, **31** 97

BAILEY, STEVE P (**37**) CLEA **37** 67-68

BAILOR, BOB UTIL (52,21,1,4,**3**) BALA **52** 75, **21** 76, TORA **1** 77-80, NYN **4** 81-83, LAN **21** 84-85, TORA *CH* **3** 92-95

BAIN, LOREN P (**19**) NYN **19** 45

BAINES, HAROLD OF/DH/CH (**3**,13,10,33) CHIA **3** 80-89, TEXA **13/3** 89, **3** 90, OAKA **3** 90-92, BALA **3** 93-95, CHIA **3** 96-97, BALA **10** 97, **3** 97-99, CLEA **33** 99, BALA **3** 00, CHIA **3** 00-01, *CH* 04-05

BAIR, DOUG P (17,26,**40**,34, 43,52,46) PITN **17** 76, OAKA **17/26** 77 CINN **40** 78-81, STLN **43/40** 81, **40** 82-83, DETA **40** 83-85, STLN **40** 85, OAKA **52/40** 86, PHIN **34** 87, TORA **40** 88, PITN **46** 89-90

BAIRD, BOB P (17,8) WASA **17** 62, **8** 63

BAJENARU, JEFF P (**57**) CHIA **57** 04-05

BAKENHASTER, DAVE P (**43**) STLN **43** 64

BAKER, AL P (**15**) BOSA **15** 38

BAKER, BILL C (6,**1**,44,15,49) CINN **6** 40-41, PITN **1** 41-43, **44** 46, STLN **15** 48-49, CHIN *CH* **49** 50

BAKER, CHUCK INF (21,**11**,24) SDN **21/11** 78, MINA **24** 81

BAKER, DAVE 3B (**31**) TORA **31** 82

BAKER, DEL CH/M (31,**32**,27,30, 41) DETA *CH,M* **31** 33, *CH* **32** 34-38, *M* 38-42, CLEA *CH* **27** 43-44, BOSA *CH* **30** 45-48, **41** 53-54, **32** 55-60

BAKER, DOUG INF (**9**,21) DETA **9** 84-87, MINA **21** 88-90

BAKER, DUSTY OF/CH/M (**12**) ATLN **12** 68-75, LAN **12** 76-83, SFN **12** 84, OAKA **12** 85-86, SFN *CH* **12** 88-92, *M* 93-02, CHIN *M* **12** 03-05

BAKER, FLOYD INF/CH (2,1,**8**,6,29,12, 38,53) STLA **2** 43, **1** 44, CHIA **8** 45-51, WASA **6** 52-53, BOSA **29** 53, **12** 54, PHIN **38** 54-55, MINA *CH* **53** 61-64

BAKER, FRANK OF (**21**) CLEA **21** 69-70

BAKER, FRANK SS (26,**15**) NYA **26** 70-71, BALA **15** 73-74

BAKER, GENE 2B/3B/CH (**37**,23,16,47) CHIN **37** 53-57, PITN **23** 57-58, **16** 60-61, *CH* **47** 63

BAKER, JACK 1B (21,**41**) BOSA **21** 76, **41** 77

BAKER, JEFF 3B (**10**) COLN **10** 05

BAKER, SCOTT P (**38**) OAKA **38** 95

BAKER, SCOTT P (**30**) MINA **30** 05

BAKER, STEVE P (**31**,36,41) DETA **31** 78-79, OAKA **36** 82-83, STLN **41** 83

BAKER, TOM (RATTLESNAKE) P (15,22,20,12 29,**25**) BKNN **15** 35, **22** 36, **20** 37, NYN **12** 37, **29/25** 38

BAKER, TOM P (**41**) CHIN **41** 63

BAKO, PAUL C (32,6,26,**9**,18) DETA **32** 98, HOUN **6** 99-00, FLAN **26** 00, ATLN **9** 00-01, MILN **9** 02, CHIN **9** 03-04, LAN **18** 05

BALAS, MIKE SS (**26**) BOSN **26** 38

BALAZ, JOHN OF (**8**,9) CALA **8** 74-75, **9** 75

BALBONI, STEVE 1B/DH (36,66,28,18, **45**,50) NYA **36** 81-82, **66** 81-83, **28** 83, KCA **18** 84, **45** 85-88, SEAA **45** 88, NYA **50** 89, **45** 90, TEXA **36** 93

BALCENA, BOBBY OF (**24**) CINN **24** 56

BALDELLI, ROCCO OF (**5**) TBA **5** 03-04, (05)

BALDSCHUN, JACK P (**27**,47,29) PHIN **27** 61-65, CINN **47** 66, **27** 66-67, SDN **27** 69, **29** 69-70, **27** 70

BALDWIN, BILLY OF (43,**21**) DETA **43** 75, NYN **21** 76

BALDWIN, DAVE P (31,**37**,46,26) WASA **31** 66-67, **37** 67-69, MILA **46** 70, CHIA **26** 73

BALDWIN, FRANK C (5,**8**) CINN **5/8** 53

BALDWIN, JAMES P (**37**,30,33,38, 19,23,39) CHIA **37** 95-01, LAN **30** 01, SEAA **33** 02, MINA **30** 03, NYN **38** 04, BALA **19/23** 05, TEXA **39** 05, BALA **23** 05

BALDWIN, JEFF OF (**17**) HOUN **17** 90

BALDWIN, REGGIE C (**6**) HOUN **6** 78-79

BALDWIN, RICK P (**45**) NYN **45** 75-77

BALE, JOHN P (45,**49**,57) TORA **45** 99, **49** 00, BALA **49** 01, CINN **57** 03

BALES, LEE INF (11,42,12,21, 29) ATLN **11**66, HOUN **42/12/21/ 29** 67

BALFOUR, GRANT P (**19**) MINA **19** 01, 03-04, (05)

BALL, JEFF 1B (**38**) SFN **38** 98

BALLARD, JEFF P (34,**29**,66) BALA **34** 87-88, **29** 88-91, PITN **66** 93-94

BALLER, JAY P (41,**48**,37,56) PHIN **41** 82, CHIN **48** 85-87, KCA **37** 90, PHIN **56** 92

BALLINGER, MARK P (**49**) CLEA **49** 71

BALSAMO, TONY P (**39**) CHIN **39** 62

BALSLEY, DARREN CH (__,**36**) SDN *CH* __ 03, **36** 04-05

BAMBERGER, GEORGE P/CH/M (39,17,16,**31**) NYN **39** 51, **17** 52, BALA **16** 59, *CH* **31** 68-77, MILA *M* **31** 78-80, NYN *M* **31**82-83, MILA **31** 85-86

BAMBERGER, HAL (DUTCH) OF (**33**) NYN **33** 48

BANDO, CHRIS C/CH B (**23**,10,12) CLEA **23** 81-88, DETA **10** 88, OAKA **23** 89, MILA *CH* **12** 96-98

BANDO, SAL 3B B (**6**) KCA **6** 66-67, OAKA **6** 68-76, MILA **6** 77-81

BANE, EDDIE P (**18**,16) MINA **18** 73, 76, **16** 75-76

BANEY, DICK P (32,50,**44**) SEAA **32** 69, CINN **50** 73, **44** 73-74

BANISTER, JEFF PH (**28**) PITN **28** 91

BANKHEAD, DAN P (23,**43**) BKNN **23** 47, **43** 50-51

BANKHEAD, SCOTT P (49,28,**15**,50, 25,29) KCA **49/28** 86, SEAA **15** 87-91, CINN **50/25** 92, BOSA **29** 93-94, NYA **25** 95

BANKS, BRIAN UTIL (**7**,25,23,4,22) MILA **7** 96-97, **25** 98, **23** 99, FLAN **4** 02, **22** 03

BANKS, ERNIE SS/1B (**14**) CHIN **14** 53-71, *CH* 72-73

BANKS, GEORGE 3B (**11**,9,14) MINA **11** 62-64, CLEA **9** 64, **14** 65-66

BANKS, WILLIE P (60,**23**,35,27, 40,30,13,46, 17) MINA **60** 91, **23** 91-93, CHIN **35** 94, **27** 95, LAN **40** 95, FLAN **30** 95, NYA **13** 98, ARIN **46** 98, BOSA **17** 02

BANNISTER, ALAN UTIL (15,16,**7**,2,5) PHIN **15** 74-75, **16** 75, CHIA **7** 76-80, CLEA **7** 80-83, HOUN **7** 84, TEXA **2** 84-85, **5** 85

BANNISTER, FLOYD P (38,**19**,24,23, 17,22) HOUN **38** 77-78, SEAA **38** 79-81, **19** 81-82, CHIA **24** 83-85, 87, **19** 86-87, KCA **19** 88-89, CALA **23** 91, TEXA **17/22** 92

BANTA, JACK P (**11**) BKNN **11** 47-50

BAPTIST, TRAVIS P (**24**,59) MINA **24** 98, PITN **59** 00

BARAJAS, ROD C/1B (**48**,27) ARIN **48** 99-03, TEXA **27** 04-05

BARBARY, RED PH (17,**21**) WASA **17/21** 43

BARBEE, DAVE OF (**14**) PITN **14** 32

BARBER, BRIAN P (52,**44**) STLN **52** 95-96, KCA **44** 98-99

BARBER, STEVE P (59,29,**13**,18, 46,24,31,43) BALA **59/29** 60, **13** 61-67, NYA **18** 67-68, SEAA **13** 69, CHIN **46** 70, ATLN **24** 70-72, CALA **31** 72-73, SFN **43** 74

BARBER, STEVE P (**24**) MINA **24** 70-71

BARBERIE, BRET 2B (25,**8**,2,20) MONN **25** 91-92, FLAN **8** 93-94, BALA **2** 95, CHIN **20** 96

BARBIERI, JIM OF (**17**) LAN **17** 66

BARCELO, LORENZO P (**49**) CHIA **49** 00-02

BARCLAY, CURT P (**39**) NYN **39** 57, SFN **39** 58-59

BARD, JOSH C (**44**) CLEA **44** 02-05

BARE, RAY P (42,40,**21**) STLN **42** 72, **40** 74, DETA **21** 75-77

BARFIELD, JESSE OF/CH (**29,**28) TORA **29** 81-89, NYA **28** 89, **29** 89-92, HOUN *CH* **29** 95, SEAA *CH* **29** 98-99

BARFIELD, JOHN P (**27**) TEXA **27** 89-91

BARFOOT, CLYDE P (**21**) STLN **21** 23

BARGAR, GREG OF/1B (**39,**43) MONN **39** 83-84, STLN **43** 86

BARK, BRIAN P (**57**) BOSA **57** 95

BARKER, GLEN OF (**29**) HOUN **29** 99-00, **24** 01

BARKER, KEVIN 1B (**22**) HOUN **22** 00, SDN **20** 02

BARKER, LEN P (25,**39**) TEXA **25** 76, **39** 77-78, CLEA **39** 79-83, ATLN **39** 83-85, MILA **39** 87

BARKER, RAY (BUDDY) OF/1B (44,50,**42**) BALA **44** 60, CLEA **50** 65, NYA **42** 65-67

BARKER, RICHIE P (**58**) CHIN **58** 99

BARKETT, ANDY OF (**50**) PITN **50** 01

BARKLEY, BRIAN P (**59**) BOSA **59** 98, (99)

BARKLEY, JEFF P (**49**) CLEA **49** 84-85

BARKLEY, RED INF (26,37,**3**) STLA **26** 37, BOSN **37** 39 , BKNN **3** 43

BARLOW, MIKE P (24,27,39,**33**, 36,46) STLN **24/27** 75, HOUN **39** 76, CALA **33** 77-79, **36** 79, TORA **46** 80-81

BARMES, BRUCE (SQUEAKY) OF (**30**) WASA **30** 53

BARMES, CLINT SS (**12**) COLN **12** 03-05

BARNA, BABE OF (16,14,20,23, **5**,42,8) PHIA **16** 37, **14** 38, NYN **20** 41, **23** 42, **5** 43, BOSA **42/8** 43

BARNES, BRIAN P (**47**,41,52) MONN **47** 90-92, **41**93, **47** 93, CLEA **52** 94, LAN **52** 94

BARNES, FRANK (LEFTY) P (**32**) NYA **32** 30

BARNES, FRANK P (**27**) STLN **27** 57-58, 60

BARNES, JOHN INF (**40**) MINA **40** 00-01

BARNES, JUNIE (LEFTY) P (__) CINN __ 34

BARNES, LARRY 1B (37,**14**) ANAA **37** 01, LAN **14** 03

BARNES, LUTE INF (**1**) NYN **1** 72-73

BARNES, RED PH (**10**) wASA **10** 30

BARNES, RICH P (52,27) CHIA **52** 82, CLEA **27** 83

BARNES, SKEETER UTIL (15,21,17,59,**9**) CINN **15** 83, **21** 84, MONN **17** 85, STLN **59** 87, CINN **15** 89, DETA **9** 91-94

BARNETT, MIKE CH (**56**) TORA *CH* **56** 03-05

BARNEY, REX P (12,**26**) BKNN **12** 43, **26** 46-50

BARNHART, VIC SS (**17**) PITN **17** 44-46

BARNICLE, GEORGE (BARNEY) P
(20,**27**) BOSN **20** 39, **27** 40-41
BARNOWSKI, ED P
(30,**38**) BALA **30** 65, **38** 65-66
BAROJAS, SALOME P
(**30**,31) CHIA **30** 82-84, SEAA **31** 84-85, PHIN **31** 88
BARONE, DICK SS
(**48**) PITN **48** 60
BARR, BOB P
(**30**) BKNN **30** 35
BARR, JIM P
(**33**) SFN **33** 71-78, CALA **48** 79, **33** 79-80, SFN **33** 82-83
BARR, STEVE P
(**46**,35) BOSA **46** 74-75, TEXA **35** 76
BARRAGAN, CUNO C
(**9**) CHIN **9** 61-63
BARRANCA, GERMAN UTIL
(43,23,**12**) KCA **43** 79, **23** 80, CINN **12** 81-82
BARRETT, DICK (KEWPIE DICK) P
aka OLIVER, RICHARD
(20,16,38,26, **12**) PHIA **20** 33, BOSN **16** 34, CHIN **38** 43, PHIN **26** 43-44, **12** 44-45
BARRETT, FRANK (RED) P
(18,**17**,19,38) STLN **18** 39, BOSA **17** 44-45, BOSN **19** 46, PITN **38** 50
BARRETT, JOHNNY (JACK) OF
(**18**,2) PITN **18** 42-46, BOSN **2** 46
BARRETT, MARTY (BUBBLE) 2B B
(**17**,7) BOSA **17** 82-90, SDN **7** 91
BARRETT, MIKE 3B/C
(**5**,8) MONN **5** 98-03, CHIN **5** 04, **8** 04-05
BARRETT, RED P
(12,61,38,42, 19,**13**,25,38) CINN **12** 37, **61** 38, **38** 39, **42** 40, BOSN **19** 43-45, STLN **13** 45-46, BOSN **25** 47, **13** 48-49, PITN **38** 50
BARRETT, TIM P
(**50**) MONN **50** 88
BARRETT, TOM (TOMMY) 2B B
(**14**,29,33) PHIN **14** 88-89, **29** 89-90, BOSA **33** 92
BARRIOS, FRANCISCO P
(47,**46**) CHIA **47** 74, **46** 76-81
BARRIOS, JOSE 1B
(**23**) SFN **23** 82
BARRIOS, MANUEL P
(55,48,**27**) HOUN **55** 97, FLAN **48** 98, LAN **27** 98
BARRON, TONY OF
(46,**53**) MONN **46** 96, PHIN **53** 97
BARRY, JEFF OF
(18,24,**27**) NYN **18** 95, COLN **24** 98, **27** 99
BARRY, RICH OF
(**23**) PHIN **23** 69
BARTEE, KIMERA OF/DH
(39,**12**,18,23, 16) DETA **39** 96-97, **12** 98, **18** 99, CINN **23** 00, COLN **16** 01
BARTELL, DICK (ROWDY RICHARD) SS/CH
(**2**,20,5,7,14, 28) PHIN **2** 32-33, **20** 34, NYN **2** 35-38, CHIN **5** 39, DETA **7** 40-41, NYN **14** 41-43, 46, DETA *CH* **28** 49-52, CINN *CH* **2** 54-55
BARTHELSON, BOB P
(**21**) NYN **21** 44
BARTHOLOMEW, LES P
(**35**) CHIA **35** 32
BARTIROME, TONY 1B/CH
(**5**,50) PITN **5** 52, ATLN *CH* **50** 86-88
BARTLETT, JASON SS
(**18**) MINA **18** 04-05
BARTLEY, BOYD SS
(**3**) BKNN *(MIL)* **3** 43
BARTLING, IRV INF
(**24**) PHIA **24** 38
BARTON, BOB C
(43,**1**,6,26) SFN **43** 65, **1** 66-69, SDN **1** 70-72, CINN **6** 73, SDN **26** 74
BARTON, SHAWN P
(53,14,42) SEAA **53** 92, SFN **14** 95, **42** 96
BARTON, VINCE OF
(**6**) CHIN **6** 32
BARTOSCH, DAVE OF
(**8**) STLN **8** 45
BARTOSH, CLIFF P
(**56**) CLEA **56** 04, CHIN **56** 05
BASGALL, MONTY 2B/CH
(**8**,10,12,54) PITN **8** 48-49, **10** 49, **12/10** 51, LAN *CH* **54** 73-86
BASHORE, WALT UTIL
(**30**) PHIN **30** 36
BASINSKI, EDDIE (BAZOOKA) 2B
(3,27,31,**8**) BKNN **3** 44, **27/31** 45, PITN **8** 47
BASS, DICK P
(**36**) WASA **36** 39
BASS, KEVIN OF
(26,8,**17**,19, 21,20) MILA **26** 82, HOUN **8** 82-83, **17** 84-89, SFN **19** 90, **17** 90-92, NYN **21** 92, HOUN **20/17** 93-95
BASS, NORM P
(30,**22**) KCA **30** 61, **22** 62-63
BASS, RANDY 1B
(2,7,41,**5**,35) MINA **2** 77, KCA **7** 78, MONN **41** 79, SDN **5** 80-82, TEXA **35** 82
BASSLER, JOHNNY CH
(**28**,35) CLEA *CH* **28** 38-40, STLA *CH* **35** 41
BASTISTE, KEVIN OF
(**34**) TORA **34** 89

BATCHELOR, RICH P
(47,**44**,46,60) STLN **47** 93, **44** 96-97, SDN **46** 97, MINA **60** 00
BATEMAN, JOHN C
(**7**,2,6) HOUN **7** 63-68, MONN **2** 69-72, PHIN **6** 72
BATES, BILLY 2B
(**34**,12) MILA **34** 89-90, CINN **12** 90
BATES, BUD OF
(**23**) PHIN **23** 39
BATES, DEL C
(**19**) PHIN **19** 70
BATES, DICK P
(**45**) SEAA **46** 69
BATES, JASON 2B
(**6**,7) COLN **6** 95-98, ANAA **7** 00
BATHE, BILL C
(8,**18**) OAKA **8** 86, SFN **18** 89-90
BATISTA, MIGUEL P
(53,**43**,47,48, 35,25) PITN **53** 92, FLAN **43** 96, CHIN **47** 97, MONN **48** 98-00, KCA **35** 00, ARIN **43** 01-03, **25** 03, TORA **43** 04-05
BATISTA, RAFAEL 1B
(10,**20**) HOUN **10** 73, **20** 75
BATISTA, TONY INF/3B
(28,**10**,7) OAKA **28** 96-97, ARZN **10** 98-99, TORA **7** 99-01, BALA **10** 01-03, MONN **7** 04
BATISTE, KIM SS
(7,**5**,18) PHIN **7** 91, **5** 92-94, SFN **18** 96
BATTEY, EARL C
(45,35,26,14, **10**) CHIA **45/35** 55, **26** 56-59, WASA **14** 60, **10** 60, MINA **10** 61-67
BATTLE, ALLEN OF
(35,**2**,73) STLN **35** 95, OAKA **2** 96, TBA **73** 00
BATTLE, HOWARD 3B
(14,34,51,**9**) TORA **14** 95, PHIN **34** 96, ATLN **51/9** 99
BATTON, CHRIS P
(**27**) OAKA **27** 76
BATTS, MATT C
(5,**14**,10,18, 2715,6,9) BOSA **5** 47, **14** 47-51, STLA **10** 51, DETA **27/15** 52, **10** 52-54, CHIA **18** 54, CINN **6** 55, **9** 56
BAUER, HANK OF/CH/M
(25,**9**,42) NYA **25** 48-51, **9** 52-59, KCA **9** 60-61, *CH/M* **9** 61, *M* **9** 62, BALA *CH* **42** 63, *M* **42** 64-68, OAKA *M* **42** 69
BAUER, RICK P
(**30**) BALA **30** 02-05
BAUERS, RUSS P
(**51**,31,18,36) PITN **51** 36-39, **31** 40-41, CHIN **18** 46, STLA **36** 50
BAUGHMAN, JUSTIN 2B/SS
(11,**13**,8) ANAA **11** 98, **13** 98-(99), **8** 00
BAUMANN, FRANK (THE BEAU) P
(40,15,**38**,48) BOSA **40** 55-56, **15** 57-59, CHIA **38** 60-64, CHIN **48** 65
BAUMER, JIM INF
(58,**11**) CHIA **58** 49, CINN **11** 61
BAUMGARTEN, ROSS P
(41,**30**,34) CHIA **41** 78, **30** 79-81, PITN **34** 82
BAUMGARTNER, JOHN 3B
(**38**) DETA **38** 53
BAUMHOLTZ, FRANKIE OF
(21,47,**7**,16) CINN **21** 47-49, CHIN **47** 49, **7** 51-55, PHIN **16** 56-57
BAUTA, ED P
(33,**38**,19) STLN **33** 60, **38** 61-63, NYN **19** 63, **38** 64
BAUTISTA, DANNY OF
(**29**,15,14,17, 23) DETA **29** 93-96, ATLN **15/14** 96, **17** 97-98, FLAN **23** 99-00, ARIN **29** 00-04
BAUTISTA, DENNY P
(**16**,27) BALA **16** 04, KCA **27** 04-05
BAUTISTA, JOSE P
(**48**,38,33,52) BALA **48** 88-91, CHIN **38** 93-94, SFN **33/38** 95, **38** 96, DETA **52** 97, STLN **33** 97
BAUTISTA, JOSE 3B/INF
(**14**,59,27,50, 7) BALA **14** 04, TBA **59** 04, KCA **27** 04, PITN **50** 04, **7** 05
BAXES, JIM INF
(29,32) LAN **29** 59, CLEA **32** 59
BAXES, MIKE INF
(1,**11**) KCA **1** 56, **11** 58
BAY, JASON OF
(2,**38**) SDN **2** 03, PITN **38** 03-05
BAYLISS, JONAH P
(**22**) KCA **22** 05
BAYLOR, DON OF/DH/CH/M
(**25**,23,20,12, 18,00,24,23, 52) BALA **25/23** 70, **25** 71-75, OAKA **20** 76, CALA **12** 77, **25** 78-82, NYA **25** 83-85, BOSA **25** 86-87, MINA **18** 87, OAKA **12/00** 88, MILA *CH* **25** 90-91, STLN *CH* **24** 92, COLN *M* **25** 93-98, ATLN *CH* **23** 99, CHIN *M* **25** 00-02, NYN *CH* **25** 03, **52** 04, SEAA *CH* **25** 05
BAZARDO, YORMAN P
(**49**) FLAN **49** 05
BEALL, BOB 1B
(13,16,**25**,12) ATLN **13/16** 75, **25** 78-79, PITN **12** 80
BEAMON, CHARLIE P F
(**27**,43) BALA **27** 56-58, **43** 58
BEAMON, CHARLIE 1B S
(11,**12**,32) SEAA **11** 78, **12** 79, TORA **32** 81

BEAMON, TREY OF/DH
(**25**,31,37) PITN **25** 96, SDN **31** 97, DETA **37** 98
BEAN, BELVE (BILL) P
(22,**17**,31) CLEA **22** 30-31, **17** 33-35, WASA **31** 35
BEAN, BILLY OF
(**4**,40,21,31) DETA **4** 87-89, LAN **40** 89, SDN **21** 93-94, **31** 95
BEAN, COLTER P
(**58**) NYA **58** 05
BEANE, BILLY OF
(35,**20**,29,11) NYN **35** 84-85, MINA **20** 86-87, DETA **29** 88, OAKA **11** 89
BEARD, DAVE P
(59,55,**33**,50, 42) OAKA **59** 80-81, **59/55/33** 81, **33** 82-83, SEAA **33** 84, CHIN **50** 85, DETA **42** 89
BEARD, MIKE P
(27,**37**) ATLN **27** 74, **37** 75-77
BEARD, RALPH P
(**39**) STLN **39** 54
BEARD, TED OF
(**17**,13,21,16) PITN **17** 48-50, **13** 51, **21** 52, CHIA **16** 57-58
BEARDEN, GENE P
(39,17,28,**30**, 29,19,37,36) CLEA **39/17** 47, **28** 48, **30** 48-50, WASA **29** 50, **19** 51, DETA **37** 51, STLA **30** 52, CHIA **36** 53
BEARE, GARY P
(31,**29**) MILA **31** 76, **29** 77
BEARNARTH, LARRY P/CH
(**31**,29,48,**36**) NYN **31** 63-66, MILA **29** 71, MONN *CH* **48** 76, *CH* **36** 85-91, COLN *CH* **36** 93-95
BEARSE, KEVIN P
(**59**) CLEA **59** 90
BEASLEY, CHRIS P
(**36**) CALA **36** 91
BEASLEY, LEW UTIL
(**7**) TEXA **7** 77
BEATTIE, JIM P
(**45**) NYA **45** 78-79, SEAA **45** 80-86
BEATTIE, BLAINE P
(**38**) NYN **38** 89, 91
BEAUCHAMP, JIM OF/1B/CH
(17,22,20,32, 28,55,44,16, 24,**5**,26,37) STLN **17** 63, HOUN **22** 64, **20** 64-65, MILN **32** 65, ATLN **28** 67, CINN **55** 68-69, HOUN **44** 70, STLN **16** 70-71, NYN **24** 72, **5** 72-73, ATLN *CH* **26** 91, *CH* **37** 91-98
BEAZLEY, JOHNNY (NIG) P
(38,**21**,27,17) STLN **38** 41, **21** 41-42, 46, **27** 46, BOSN **27** 47, **17** 48-49
BECHLER, STEVE P
(**51**) BALA **51** 02
BECK, BOOM-BOOM P
(30,**15**,11,10, 7,23,41,20, 55) BKNN **30** 33-34, PHIN **15** 39-43, **11/10/7** 42, DETA **23** 44, CINN **41** 45,PITN **20** 45, WASA *CH* **55** 57-59
BECK, RICH P
(**23**) NYA **23** 65
BECK, ROD P
(**47**,45) SFN **47** 91-97, CHIN **47** 98-99, BOSA **47** 99-01, SDN **45** 03-04
BECKER, HEINZ (DUTCH) 1B
(24,7,**15**) CHIN **24** 43, **7** 45-46, CLEA **15** 46-47
BECKER, JOE C/CH
(8,**10**,33,4,3) CLEA **8** 36, **10** 37, BKNN *CH* **33** 55-57, LAN *CH* **33** 58-64, STLN *CH* **4** 65-66, CHIN *CH* **3** 67-70
BECKER, RICH OF
(**25**,6,18,22) MINA **25** 93-97, NYN **6** 98, BALA **18** 98, MILN **22** 99, OAKA **22** 99-00, DETA **24** 00
BECKERT, GLENN 2B
(**18**) CHIN **18** 65-73, SDN **18** 74-75
BECKETT, JOSH P
(61,**21**) FLAN **61** 01-03, **21** 03-05
BECKETT, ROBBIE P
(**41**) COLN **41** 96-97
BECKMANN, BILL P
(13,**35**,25,27) PHIA **13** 39, **35** 39-40, **25** 41-42, STLN **27** 42
BECKWITH, JOE P
(**27**,45) LAN **27** 79-83, KCA **27** 84-85, LAN **45** 86
BECQUER, JULIO 1B
(32,39,20,**29**, 19,28,40) WASA **32** 55, **39** 57, **20** 58, **29** 58-60, LAA **19** 61, MINA **28/29** 61, **40** 63
BEDARD, ERIK P
(**57**,79) BALA **57** 02, **79** 03, **45** 04-05
BEDELL, HOWIE OF/CH
(25,**37**,46,20) MILN **25** 62, PHIN **37** 68, KCA *CH* **46** 84, SEAA *CH* **20** 88
BEDROSIAN, STEVE (BEDROCK) P
(32,45,40,35, 36) ATLN **32** 81-85, PHIN **40** 86-89, SFN **45** 89, **40** 89-90, MINA **35** **/40** 91, ATLN **36** 93-95
BEECH, MATT P
(**55**) PHIN **55** 96-98, (99)
BEELER, JODIE INF
(_) CINN _ 44
BEENE, ANDY P
(64,26,**46**) MILA **64/26** 83, **26/46** 84
BEENE, FRED P
(50,33,45,**47**) BALA **50** 68, **33** 69-70, **45** 70, NYA **47** 72-74, CLEA **33** 74, **47** 74-75

BEERS, CLARENCE P
(**37**) STLN **37** 48
BEGGS, JOE (FIREMAN) P
(22,**43**,33) NYA **22** 38, CINN **43** 40-44, 46-47, NYN **33** 47-48
BEHENNA, RICK P
(49,**32**) ATLN **49** 83, CLEA **32** 83-85
BEHNEY, MEL P
(**33**) CINN **33** 70
BEHRMAN, HANK P
(31,34,**29**,18, 20,21) BKNN **31/34** 46, **29** 46-47, PITN **18** 47, BKNN **29/20** 48, NYN **21** 49
BEIMEL, JOE P
(**53**,50,97) PITN **53** 01-03, MINA **50** 04, TBA **97** 05
BEIRNE, KEVIN P
(57,**40**,58) CHIA **57** 00, TORA **40** 01, LAN **58** 02
BEJMA, OLLIE UTIL
(22,15,**28**) STLA **22** 34, **22** 35, **15** 36, CHIA **28** 39
BELANGER, MARK SS
(49,**7**,8) BALA **49** 65, **7** 66-81, LAN **8** 82
BELARDI, WAYNE 1B
(18,11,5,4,27) BKNN **18** 50-51, **11** 53, **5** 53-54, DETA **4** 54-55, **27** 56
BELCHER, KEVIN OF
(**18**) TEXA **18** 90
BELCHER, TIM P
(**49**,31,36,41) LAN **49** 87-91, CINN **31**92-93, CHIA **36** 93, DETA **41** 94, SEAA **31** 95, KCA **41** 96-98, ANAA **41** 99-00
BELINDA, STAN P
(60,**50**,43,37, 36) PITN **60** 89, **50** 90-93, KCA **43** 94, BOSA **43** 95-96, CINN **37** 97-99, COLN **37** 00, ATLN **36** 00
BELINSKY, BO P
(**36**,33,30,25, 34) LAA **36** 62-64, PHIN **33** 65-66, HOUN **30/25** 67, PITN **25** 69, CINN **34** 70
BELISLE, MATT P
(70,41,**31**) CINN **70** 03, **41** 04, **31** 05
BELITZ, TODD P
(59,**46**) OAKA **59** 00, COLN **46** 01
BELK, TIM 1B
(**39**) CHIN **39** 96
BELL, BEAU OF
(3,**10**,20,17, 23) STLA **3** 35, **10** 36-39, DETA **20** **/17** 39, CLEA **23** 40-41
BELL, BILL (DING DONG) P
(30,**20**) PITN **30** 52, **20** 55
BELL, BUDDY 3B/CH/M S,F
(9,**25**,26) CLEA **9** 72, **25** 73-78, TEXA **25** 79-85, CINN **25** 85-88, HOUN **25** 88, TEXA **25** 89, CLEA *CH* **26** 94-95, DET *M* **25** 96-98, COLN *M* **25** 00-02, CLEA *CH* **25** 03-05, KCA *M* **25** 05
BELL, DAVID INF/3B S,GS
(4,**27**,25,6,2, 28) CLEA **4** 95, STLN **27/25** 95, **27** 96-98, CLEA **6** 98, SEAA **2** 98, **25** 99-01, SFN **28** 02, PHIN **4** 03-05
BELL, DEREK OF
(**14**,4,16) TORA **14** 91-92, SDN **4** 93-94, HOUN **14** 95-99, NYN **16** 00, PITN **14** 01
BELL, ERIC P
(47,**45**,63,54) BALA **47** 85-86, **45** 87, CLEA **63** 91-92, HOUN **54** 93
BELL, FERN (DANNY) UTIL
(17,37) PITN **17** 39, **37** 40
BELL, GARY P
(**39**,45,26) CLEA **39** 58-67, BOSA **45/39** 67-68, SEAA **39** 69, CHIA **26** 69
BELL, GEORGE OF
(**11**,21) TORA **11** 81, 83-90, CHIN **11** 91, CHIA **21** 92-93
BELL, GUS OF F, GF
(21,18,7,**25**, 3,20) PITN **21** 50, **18** 50-52, **7** 52, CINN **25** 53-61,NYN **3** 62, MILN **20** 62-64
BELL, HEATH P
(**19**) NYN **19** 04-05
BELL, HI P
(16,**15**) STLN **16** 24, NYN **15** 32-34
BELL, JAY SS/INF
(16,**3**,28,33, 44) CLEA **16** 86-88, PITN **3** 89-96, KCA **28** 97, ARIN **33** 98-02, NYN **44** 03, ARIN *CH* **33** 05
BELL, JERRY P
(51,**40**) MILA **51** 71, **40** 71-74
BELL, JUAN SS
(1,11,**24**,26, 23,29) BALA **1** 89, **11** 90, **1** 91, PHIN **24** 92-93, MILA **26** 93, MONN **23** 94, BOSA **29** 95
BELL, KEVIN 3B
(**8**,'8) CHIA **8** 76-80, OAKA **8** 82
BELL, LES SS
(**11**,_) STLN **11** 23, _ 24
BELL, MIKE (A.) 1B
(**11**) ATLN **11** 90-91
BELL, MIKE (J.) INF
(**28**) CINN **28** 00
BELL, ROB P
(29,6,30,**41**) CINN **29** 00-01, TEXA **6** 01-02, **30** 02, TBA **41** 03-05
BELL, TERRY C
(**34**,11) KCA **34** 86, ATLN **11** 87
BELLA, ZEKE OF
(41,**17**) NYA **(41?)** 57, KCA **17** 59

A five-time All-Star with Cleveland and Texas, Buddy Bell had a solid 18-year career. The son of Cincinnati's Gus Bell and father of David Bell, all three wore #25 at one time. Buddy lead the league in fielding three times at third base. He drove in 100+ runs once, hit over .300 twice and wound up with 201 career home runs.

BELLE, ALBERT (JOEY) OF/DH
(36,**8**,88) CLEA **36** 89, **8** 90-96, CHIA **8** 97-98, BALA **88** 99-01, (02)

BELLHORN, MARK 2B/INF
(47,10,49,14, **28**,12,26) OAKA **47** 97, **10** 98, **49** 00, **14** 01, CHIN **28** 02-03, COLN **28** 03, BOSA **12** 04-05, NYA **26** 05

BELLIARD, RAFAEL SS
(37,38,6,**2**) PITN **37** 82-86, **38** 86, **6** 87-90, ATLN **2** 91-98

BELLIARD, RONNIE INF
(11,**10**) MILN **11** 98, **10** 99-02, COLN **10** 03, CLEA **20** 04-05

BELLINGER, CLAY INF
(**35**,12) NYA **35** 99-00, **12** 01, ANAA **35** 02

BELOIR, ROB INF
(**10**) ATLN **10** 75-78

BELTRAN, CARLOS OF/DH
(36,**15**) KCA **36** 98-99, **15** 00-04, HOUN **15** 04, NYN **15** 05

BELTRAN, FRANCIS P
(**53**,39) CHIN **53** 00, 04, MONN **39** 04

BELTRAN, RIGO P
(53,**43**,50) STLN **53** 97, NYN **43** 98-99, COLN **48** 99, MONN **50** 04

BELTRE, ADRIAN 3B
(**29**,5) LAN **29** 98-04, SEAA **5** 05

BELTRE, ESTEBAN 1B
(28,38,**6**,10, 56,62) CHIA **28** 91, **38** 92, TEXA **6** 94-95, BOSA **10** 96, TORA **56** 96, CHIA **62** 00

BENARD, MARVIN OF
(56,**7**) SFN **56** 95, **7** 96-03

BENAVIDES, FREDDIE INF/CH
(57,**12**,15,10) CINN **57** 91, **12** 92, COLN **12** 93, MONN **15** 94, CINN *CH* **10** 03

BENCH, JOHNNY C/INF
(**5**) CINN **5** 67-83

BENDER, CHIEF CH
(**32**) PHIA *CH* **32** 51-53

BENEDICT, BRUCE C/CH
(**20**) ATLN **20** 78-89, NYN *CH* **20** 97-99

BENES, ALAN P B
(40,**41**,31,35, 44) STLN **40** 95, **41** 96-97, (99), **31** 00-01, CHIN **35** 02-03, TEXA **44** 03, CHIN **35** 03

BENES, ANDY P B
(**40**) SDN **40** 89-95, SEAA **40** 95, STLN **40** 96-97, ARIN **40** 98-99, STLN **40** 00-02

BENGE, RAY P
(16,**28**,18,20, 23,46) PHIN **16** 32, BKNN **28** 33-35, BOSN **18** 36, PHIN **20/23** 36, CINN **46** 38

BENGOUGH, BENNY C/CH
(9,**10**,26,27, 11) NYA **9** 29, **10** 30, STLA **10** 31-32, WASA *CH* **26** 40, *CH* **27** 41-43, BOSN *CH* **32** 44-45, PHIN *CH* **11** 46-59

BENIQUEZ, JUAN UTIL
(20,**12**,3,26,7) BOSA **20** 71-72, 74-75, TEXA **12** 76-78, NYA **26** 79, SEAA **12** 80, CALA **3** 81, **12** 81-85, BALA **12** 86, KCA **12** 87, TORA **7** 87-88

BENITEZ, ARMANDO P
(**49**,45) BALA **49** 94-98, NYN **49** 99-03, NYA **45** 03, SEAA **49** 03, FLAN **49** 04, SFN **49** 05

BENITEZ, YAMIL OF
(1,15,39,43) MONN **1** 95, **15** 96, KCA **39** 97, ARIN **43** 98, CHIA **63** 00

BENJAMIN, MIKE SS
(26,**18**,5,28) SFN **26** 89-90, **18** 91-95, PHIN **5** 96, BOSA **28** 97-98, PITN **6** 99-02

BENJAMIN, STAN OF
(16,**7**,30,33) PHIN **16** 39, **7** 40-41, **30** 42, CLEA **33** 45

BENNETT, DAVE P B
(**59**) PHIN **59** 64

BENNETT, DENNIS P B
(23,28,38,25) PHIN **23** 62-64, BOSA **28** 65-67, NYN **38/28** 67, CALA **25** 68

BENNETT, ERIK P
(**54**,59,57) CALA **54** 95, MINN **59/57** 96

BENNETT, GARY C
(15,22,14,4,7, **29**) PHIN **15** 95, **22** 96, **14** 98-00, **4** 01, NYN **7** 01, COLN **29** 01-02, SDN **29** 03, MILN **29** 04, WASN **29** 05

BENNETT, JEFF P
(**57**) MILN **57** 04

BENNETT, JOEL P
(**28**,37) BALA **28** 98, PHIN **37** 99

BENNETT, SHAYNE P
(54,**21**) MONN **54** 97, **21** 98-99

BENOIT, JOAQUIN P
(**53**) TEXA **53** 02-05

BENSON, ALLEN (BULLET BEN) P
(**10**) WASA **10** 34

BENSON, KRIS P
(**34**) PITN **34** 99-04, NYN **34** 04-05

BENSON, VERN UTIL/CH
(14,38,36,46, 25,19,**8**,10,7) PHIA **14** 43, **38** 46, STLN **36** 51, **46/25** 52, **19** 53, *CH* **8** 61-64, CINN **10** 66-69, STLN *CH* **7** 70-71, **8** 71-75, ATLN *CH* **8** 76, *CH,M* **8** 77, SFN *CH* **8** 80, *CH* __ 81

BENTON, AL P
(21,29,27,22, **19**) PHIA **21** 34-35, DETA **29/27** 38, **22** 39, **19** 39-42, 45-48, CLEA **22** 49-50, BOSA **27** 52

BENTON, BUTCH C
(**15**,19,9) NYN **15** 78, **15/19** 80, CHIN **9** 82, CLEA **9** 85

BENTON, LARRY P
(**19**,16,28) CINN **19** 32-33, **16** 34, BOSN **28** 35

BENTZ, CHAD P
(**57**) MONN **57** 04, FLAN **57** 05

BENZINGER, TODD 1B/OF
(38,25,26,36, **14**) BOSA **38** 87-88, CINN **25** 89 91, KCA **26/38** 91, LAN **36** 92, SFN **14** 93-95

BERARDINO, DICK CH
(**33**) BOSA **33** *CH* 89-91

BERARDINO, JOHNNY (BERNIE) INF
(8,14,4,20,**2**,7, 10,12) STLA **8/14** 39, **4** 40-41, **20** 42, **4** 46-47, CLEA **2** 48-50, PITN **10** 50, STLA **7** 51, CLEA **2** 52, PITN **12** 52

BERBERET, LOU C
(49,35,10,**9**, 36,11) NYA **49** 54, **35** 55, WASA **10** 56, **9** 56-58, BOSA **36** 58, DETA **11** 59-60

BERBLINGER, JEFF INF
(**56**) STLN **56** 97

BERE, JASON P
(51,**46**,47) CHIA **51** 93, **46** 94-98, CINN **51** 98, **46** 99, MILN **47** 99-00, CLEA **46** 00, CHIN **46** 01-02

BERENGUER, JUAN P
(48,43,53,37, 52,30,44,**40**) NYN **48** 78-79, **43** 79-80, KCA **53/37** 81, TORA **52/30** 81, DETA **44** 82-85, SFN **40** 86, MINA **40** 87-90, ATLN **48** 91-92, KCA **48** 92

BERENYI, BRUCE P
(**38**,31) CINN **38** 80-84, NYN **31** 84-86

BERG, DAVE INF/UTIL
(58,13,**10**,2) FLAN **58/13** 98, **10** 99-01, TORA **2** 02-04

BERG, MOE C
(27,19,9,10, 31,**22**) CLEA **27/19** 31, WASA **9** 32, **10** 33-34, CLEA **31** 34, BOSA **19** 35, **22** 36-39, *CH* **22** 40-41

BERGAMO, AUGIE OF
(8,**17**) STLN **8** 44, **17** 44-45

BERGER, BOZE INF
(22,**2**,19,6) CLEA **22** 32, **2** 35-36, CHIA **19** 37-38, BOSA **6** 39

BERGER, BRANDON OF/DH
(**30**,24) KCA **30** 01-03, **24** 04

BERGER, WALLY OF
(**3**,4,21,62,22, 7) BOSN **3** 32-34, **4** 35-37, NYN **3** 37, **21** 38, CINN **62** 38, **22** 39-40, PHIN **7** 40

BERGERON, PETER OF
(**33**,11) MONN **33** 99-01, **11** 02, 04

BERGMAN, DAVE OF/1B
(18,54,16,**14**) NYA **18** 75, **54** 75, 77, HOUN **16** 78-81, SFN **16** 81-83, DETA **14** 84-92

BERGMAN, DUSTY P
(**65**) ANAA **65** 04

BERGMAN, SEAN P
(43,44,40,**38**) DETA **43** 93-95, SDN **44** 96, **40** 97, HOUN **38** 98-99, ATLN **38** 99, MINA **38** 00

BERGMANN, JASON P
(**57**) WASN **57** 05

BERGOLIA, WILLIAM IINF
(**27**) CINN **27** 05

BERINGER, CARROLL BPP/CH
(18,**52**,1,5) LAN *BPP* **18** 62-64, *BPP* **52** 65-66, *CH* **52** 67-72, PHIN *CH* **1** 73-77, **5** 78

BERKMAN, LANCE OF/1B
(22,**17**) HOUN **22** 99, **17** 00-05

BERLY, JACK P
(__,17,**20**) STLN __ 24, PHIN **17** 32, **20** 33

BERNAL, VIC P
(**39**) SDN **39** 77

BERNARD, DWIGHT P
(31,**28**,47,79) NYN **31** 78, **28** 78-79, MILA **47** 81-82, MILN *CH* **79** 00

BERNAZARD, TONY 2B
(7,2,**14**,16,4, 9) MONN **7** 79, **2** 80, CHIA **14** 81-83, SEAA **14** 83, CLEA **16** 84, **4** 84-87, OAKA **14** 87, DETA **9** 91

BERNERO, ADAM P
(49,26,**24**,43, 50) DETA **49** 00, **26** 01, **24** 02-03, COLN **43** 03-04, ATLN **50** 05

BERNHARDT, JUAN UTIL
(**26**) NYA **26** 76, SEAA **26** 77-79

BERNHARDT, CARLOS CH
(**45**) BALA *CH* **45** 98

BERNIER, CARLOS OF
(**17**) PITN **17** 53

BERO, JOHNNY 2B
(28,**8**) DETA **28** 48, STLA **8** 51

BERRA, DALE INF
(**4**,2) PITN **4** 77-84, NYA **2** 85-86, HOUN **4** 87

BERRA, YOGI C/CH/M
(38,35,**8**) NYA **38** 46, **35** 46-47, **8** 48-63, *CH* **8** 63, *M* **8** 64, NYN **8** 65, *CH* **8** 65-71, *M* **8** 72-75, NYA *CH* **8** 76-83, *M* **8** 84-85, HOUN *CH* **8** 86-89

BERRES, RAY C
(22,10,48,32, 12,29,8,11,9, 44,**37**) BKNN **22** 34, **10** 36, PITN **48** 37, **32** 38-39, **12** 40, BOSN **29/8** 40, **11** 41, NYN **9** 42, **10** 43, **29/9** 44-45, CHIA *CH* **44** 49-54, **37** 54-66, 68-69

BERROA, ANGEL SS
(**4**) KCA **4** 01-05

BERROA, GERONIMO OF
(18,37,35,16, **29**,10,17) ATLN **18/22** 89, **37** 90, CINN **35** 92, FLAN **16** 93, OAKA **29** 94-97, BALA **10/29** 97, CLEA **29** 98, DETA **29** 98, TORA **29** 99, LAN **17** 00

BERRY, CHARLIE C
(9,3,15,2,**10**, 29) BOSA **9** 31-32, CHIA **3** 32, **15** 33, PHIA **2** 34, **10** 35-36, *CH* **10** 36, *CH* **29** 37-40

BERRY, JOE (JITTERY JOE) P
(31,**20**,22) CHIN **31** 42, PHIA **20** 44-46, CLEA **22** 46

BERRY, KEN OF
(17,**16**,12,1) CHIA **4** 62, **17** 63-65, **16** 65-70, CALA **12** 71, **16** 72-73, MILA **16** 74, CLEA **1/17** 75

BERRY, MARK CH
(**55**,59) CINN *CH* **55** 00-02, 04, **59** 03, **55** 05

BERRY, NEIL INF
(36,**8**,34,2) DETA **36** 48, **8** 49-52, STLA **34** 53, CHIA **34** 53, BALA **2** 54

BERRY, SEAN 3B
(47,**5**,17,7,26) KCA **47** 90-91, MONN **5** 92-95, HOUN **17** 96-98, MILN **7** 99-00, BOSA **26** 00

BERRYHILL, DAMON C
(34,**9**,11,6,8) CHIN **34** 87, **9** 88-91, ATLN **49** 91, **11** 92-93, BOSA **6** 94, CINN **8** 95, SFN **8** 97

BERTAINA, FRANK P
(39,18,40,24, 23,21) BALA **39/18** 64, **40** 65-67, WASA **24** 67-69, BALA **23** 69, STLN **21** 70

BERTELL, DICK C
(9,**6**) CHIN **9** 60, **6** 61-65, SFN **6** 65, CHIN **6** 67

BERTOIA, RENO INF
(2,**16**,1,8) DETA **2** 53, **16** 54-58, WASA **1** 59-61, KCA **16** 61, DETA **8** 61-62

BERTOTTI, MIKE P
(**51**) CHIA **51** 95-97

BERTRAND, LEFTY P
(__) PHIN __ 36

BERUMEN, ANDRES P
(**55**) SDN **55** 95-96

BESANA, FRED P
(**38**) BALA **38** 56

BESSE, HERMAN P
(**20**,24) PHIA **20** 40-43, **24** 46

BESSENT, DON P
(**46**) BKNN **46** 55-57, LAN **46** 58

BEST, KARL P
(**39**,38) SEAA **39** 83-86, MINA **38** 88

BESWICK, JIM OF
(**14**) SDN **14** 78

BETANCOURT, RAFAEL P
(**63**) CLEA **63** 03-05

BETANCOURT, YUNIESKY SS
(**46**) SEAA **46** 05

BETEMIT, WILSON 3B/2B
(**24**) ATLN **24** 04-05

BETHEA, BILL (SPOT) INF
(**20**) MINA **20** 64

BETHKE, JIM P
(41,36,28,**20**) NYN **41/36/28/20** 65

BETTENCOURT, LARRY OF
(**23**) STLA **23** 31-32

BETTENDORF, JEFF P
(**52**) OAKA **52** 84

BETTS, HUCK P
(19,**18**,15) BOSN **19** 32, **18** 33, **15** 34-35

BEVACQUA, KURT UTIL
(17,25,2,14, 11,13,**7**) CLEA **17** 71, **25** 71-72, KCA **2** 73, PITN **14** 74, KCA **2** 74, MILA **2** 75, **11** 75-76, TEXA **13** 77-78, SDN **7** 79-80, PITN **11** 80-81, SDN **7** 82-85

BEVAN, HAL 3B
(**8**,3,1,9) BOSA **8** 52, PHIA **3** 52, KCA **1** 55, CINN **9** 61

BEVENS, BILL P
(29,21,**16**) NYA **29** 44, **21** 44-45, **16** 46-47

BEVERLIN, JASON P
(49,**31**) CLEA **49** 02, DETA **31** 02

BEVIL, BRIAN P
(**47**) KCA **47** 96-98

BEVIL, LOU P
(**19**) WASA **19** 42

BEVINGTON, TERRY CH/M
(**18**,35) CHIA *CH* **18** 89-95, *M* **18** 95-97, TORA *CH* **35** 99-01

BIAGINI, GREG CH
(31,**25**,24) BALA *CH* **31**92, **25** 92-93, *CH* **24** 94

BIALAS, DAVE CH
(32,**43**) SDN *CH* **32** 94, CHIN *CH* **43** 95-99, 02

BIANCALANA, BUDDY SS
(**1**,3) KCA **1** 82-87, HOUN **3** 87

BIANCO, TOMMY UTIL
(**33**) MILA **33** 75

BIASATTI, HANK 1B
(**11**) PHIA **11** 49

BIBBY, JIM P
(48,**22**,38,26) STLN **48** 72-73, TEXA **22** 73-75, CLEA **22** 75-77, PITN **38** 78, **26** 78-81, 83, TEXA **22** 84

BICHETTE, DANTE OF
(11,19,3,8,**10**) CALA **11** 88, **19** 89-90, MILA **3** 91, **8** 92, COLN **10** 93-99, CINN **9** 00, BOSA **19** 00-01

BICKFORD, VERN P
(**24**) BOSN **24** 48-52, MILN **24** 53, BALA **24** 54

BICKNELL, CHARLIE (BUD) P
(35,39) PHIN **35** 48, **39** 49

BIDDLE, ROCKY P
(**60**) CHIA **60** 00-02, MONN **60** 03-04

BIELECKI, MIKE P
(34,**36**,26) PITN **34** 84-87, CHIN **34** 88, **36** 88-91, ATLN **36** 91-92, CLEA **36** 93, ATLN **34** 94, CALA **36** 95, ATLN **26** 96-97

BIERBRODT, NICK P
(47,**32**,36,51) ARIN **47** 01, TBA **32** 01, 03, CLEA **36** 03, TEXA **51** 04

BIESER, STEVE OF
(**29**,62,60) NYN **29** 97, PITN **62** 98, STLN **60** 00

BIGBIE, LARRY OF
(**3**,34) BALA **3** 01-05, COLN **34** 05

BIGGIO, CRAIG C/2B/OF
(4,**7**) HOUN **4** 88-89, **7** 89-05

BIGGS, CHARLIE P
(**15**) CHIA **15** 32

BIITTNER, LARRY OF/1B
(4,17,**26**,33, 14) WASA **4** 70-71, TEXA **4** 72-73, MONN **17** 74-76, CHIN **26** 76-79, **33** 80, CINN **33** 81-82, TEXA **14** 83

BILARDELLO, DANN C
(9,**11**,22,7) CINN **9** 83, **11** 84-86, PITN **22** 89, 90, SDN **7** 91-92

BILBREY, JIM P
(36,**22**) STLA **36/22** 49

BILDILLI, EMIL (HILL BILLY) P
(23,**20**,__,26,) STLA **23** 37, **20** 38, __39, **26** 40, **20** 41

BILKO, STEVE 1B
(34,**5**,49,18, 33,36,29,20) STLN **34** 49, **5** 50-54, CHIN **49** 54, CINN **18** 58, LAN **33/36** 58, DETA **29** 60, LAA **20** 61-62

BILLINGHAM, JACK P
(38,42,**43**,41, 28) LAN **38** 68, HOUN **42** 69-71, CINN **43** 72-77, DETA **41** 78-80, BOSA **28** 80

BILLINGS, DICK (RICH) UTIL
(6,26,35,**8**,12, 16) WASA **6** 68, **26** 69, **35** 70, **8** 71, TEXA **8** 72-74, STLN **12** 74-75, **16** 75

BILLINGSLY, BRENT P
(**48**) FLAN **48** 99

BILLMEYER, MICK CH
(**57**) CALA *CH* **57** 96, ANAA *CH* **57** 99

BINKS, GEORGE (BINGO) OF/1B
(6,7,23,**11**,19) WASA **6** 44, **7** 45, **23** 46, PHIA **11** 47-48, STLA **19** 48

BIRAS, STEVE 2B
(**37**) CLEA **37** 44

BIRD, DOUG P
(**29**,43,47,50, 42) KCA **29** 73-78, PHIN **43** 79, NYA **43** 80-81, CHIN **50** 81, **47** 81-82, BOSA **42** 83

BIRKBECK, MIKE P
(41,**40**,50,36) MILA **41** 86, **40** 87-89, NYN **50** 92, **36** 95, *(JAP)*

BIRKOFER, RALPH (LEFTY) P
(**49**,19) PITN **49** 33-36, BKNN **19** 37

BIRRER, BABE P
(19,41,12,37, 54) DETA **19** 55, BALA **41** 56, LAN **12/37** 58, DETA *CH* **54** 67

BIRTSAS, TIM P
(49,**48**,42) OAKA **49** 85, **48** 85-86, CINN **42** 88, **48** 88-90

BISCAN, FRANK (PORKY) P
(**27**,10,22,36) STLA **27** 42, **10** 46, **22/36** 48

BISHOP, CHARLIE P
(**38**,26) PHIA **38** 52-54, KCA **26** 55

BISHOP, MAX (CAMERA EYE) 2B
(**4**,1) PHIA **4** 31-33, BOSA **1** 34-35

BISHOP, MIKE C
(**48**) NYN **48** 83

BISSONETTE, DEL 1B
(**14**,33,34) BKNN **14** 33, BOSN *CH/M* **33** 45, PITN *CH* **34** 46

BITHORN, HI P
(17,35,25,__) CHIN **17** 42, **35** 43, **25** 46, CHIA __ 47

BITKER, JOE P
(59,**44**) OAKA **59** 90, TEXA **44** 90-91

BITTIGER, JEFF P
(34,30,32,**35**) PHIN **34** 86, MINA **30** 87, CHIA **32** 88-89, **35** 89

BIVIN, JIM P
(**48**) PHIN **48** 35

BJORKMAN, GEORGE C
(**20**) HOUN **20** 83

BLACK, BILL (BUD) P/CH
(37,19,**14**,24) DETA **37/19** 52, **14** 55-56, ANAA *CH* **24** 00-05

BLACK, BUD P
(36,32,**40**,35) SEAA **36/32** 81, KCA **40** 83-88, CLEA **40** 88-90, TORA **35/40** 90, SFN **40** 91-93, CLEA **40** 95

BLACK,DON P
(**21**,35,23) PHIA **21** 43-45, CLEA **35** 46, **23** 47-48

BLACK, JOE P
(**49,**26) BKNN **49** 52-55, CINN **49** 55-56, WASA **26** 57

BLACKABY, ETHAN OF
(45,**42**) MILN **45** 62-63, **42** 64

BLACKBURN, JIM (BONES) P
(44,**33**) CINN **44** 48, **33** 51

BLACKBURN, RON P
(48,36) PITN **48** 58, **36** 59

BLACKBURN, WAYNE CH
(**54**) DETA *CH* **54** 63-64

BLACKBURNE, RUSSELL (LENA) CH
(33,**31**,28,) PHIA *CH* **33** 33, **31** 34-37, **28** 37-40, **33** 42-43, **28** 43-44

BLACKLEY, TRAVIS P
(**48**) SEAA **48** 04

BLACKWELL, EWELL (THE WHIP) P
(44,**47**,40,36) CINN **44/47** 42, **47** 42, 46-52, NYA **40** 52-53, KCA **36** 55

BLACKWELL, TIM C
(39,5,44,**9**, 17) BOSA **39** 74-75, PHIN **5** 76-77, MONN **44** 77, CHIN **9** 78-81, MONN **17** 82-83

BLADES, RAY OF/3B/CH/M
(**3**,2,7,37,34, 16,27,33,29, 41) STLN **3** 23, **2** 24, *CH* **7** 32, *M* **37** 39, *M* **34**, *CH* **37** 40, CINN *CH* **3** 42, BKNN *CH* **16** 47, *CH* **27** 47-48, STLN *CH* **33** 51, CHIN *CH* **3/29** 53, *CH* **41** 54-56

BLADT, RICK OF
(20,**24**) CHIN **20** 69, NYA **24** 75

BLAEHOLDER, GEORGE P
(**12**,41,33,16) STLA **12** 31-35, PHIA **41** 35, CLEA **33/16** 36

BLAEMIRE, RAY C
(**35**) NYN **35** 41

BLAIR, BUDDY 3B
(**6**) PHIA **6** 42

BLAIR, DENNIS
(**28**,47) MONN **28** 74-76, SDN **47** 80

BLAIR, PAUL OF
(33,**6**,2,27) BALA **33** 64-65, **6** 65-76, NYA **2** 77-79, CINN **33** 79, NYA **27** 80

BLAIR, WILLIE P
(27,39,41,**19**, 47,20,46,24) TORA **27** 90, CLEA **39** 91, HOUN **41** 92, COLN **19** 93-94, SDN **47** 95-96, DETA **20** 97, ARIN **19** 98, NYN **46** 98, DETA **20** 99-00, **24** 01

BLAKE, CASEY INF/3B/OF
(28,**38**,61,1) TORA **28** 99, MINA **38** 00-01, BALA **61** 01, MINA **38** 02, CLEA **1** 03-05

BLAKE, ED P
(**45**,21) CINN **45** 52-53, KCA **21** 57

BLAKE, SHERIFF P
(12,**27**) STLA **12** 37, STLN **27** 37

BLAKELY, LINC OF
(**12**) CINN **12** 34

BLALOCK, HANK 3B
(12,**9**) TEXA **12** 02, **9** 03-05

BLANCHARD, JOHNNY C
(**38**,14,18) NYA **38** 55, 59-65, KCA **14** 65, MILN **18** 65

BLANCHE, AL P
(**27**,36) BOSN **27** 35, **36** 36

BLANCO, ANDRES 2B
(1,3,**7**) KCA **1/3** 04, **7** 05

BLANCO, DAMIE INF
(22,**18**) SFN **22** 72, **18** 73-74

BLANCO, GIL P
(28,36,30,33) NYA **28** 65, KCA **36/30** 66, **33** 67

BLANCO, HENRY C
(54,35,**12**,20, 21,9,24) LAN **54** 97, COLN **35** 99, MILN **12** 00-01, ATLN **20** 02-03, MINA **21** 04, CHIN **9** 05, **24** 05

BLANCO, OSSIE 1B
(9,16,**18**) CHIA **9** 70, CLEA **16/18** 74

BLANCO, TONY OF
(**28**) WASN **28** 05

BLAND, NATE P
(**35**) HOUN **35** 03

BLANK, MATT P
(**50**) MONN **50** 00-01

BLANKENSHIP, KEVIN P
(50,**51**) ATLN **50** 88, CHIN **51** 88-90

BLANKENSHIP, LANCE UTIL
(30,**12**) OAKA **30** 88, **12** 89-94

BLANKS, LARVELL INF
(**4**,14,3,16) ATLN **4** 72-75, CLEA **14** 76-78, TEXA **3** 79, ATLN **16** 80

BLANTON, CY P
(43,**46**, 6,7, 14) PITN **43** 34, **46** 35-39, PHIN **6/7** 40, **14** 41-42

BLANTON, JOE P
(64,**55**) OAKA **64** 04, **55** 05

BLASINGAME, DON (BLAZER) 2B
(**3**,11,10,19, 12,1,8) STLN **3** 55-58, **11** 59, SFN **10** 60-61, CINN **19** 61-63, WASA **12** 63, **1** 64-66, KCA **8** 66

BLASINGAME, WADE P
(22,**36**,30,47, 29) MILN **22** 63, **36** 64-67, HOUN **47** 67-68, **36** 68-72, **30** 71, NYA **29** 72

BLASS, STEVE P
(23,**28**) PITN **23** 64, **28** 66-74

BLATERIC, STEVE P
(42,54,**47**) CINN **42** 71, NYA **54** 72, CALA **47** 75

BLATNIK, JOHNNY (CHIEF) OF
(**16**,35) PHIN **16** 48-50, STLN **35** 50

BLATTNER, BUDDY INF
(2,15,12,17, **7**) STLN **2** 42, NYN **15** 46, **12** 47, **17** 48, PHIN **7** 49

BLAUSER, JEFF SS
(32,**4**) ATLN **32** 87-88, **4** 89-97, CHIN **4** 98-99

BLAYLOCK, BOB P B
(**24**,16) STLN **24/16** 56, **24** 59

BLAYLOCK, GARY P/CH B
(44,22,**43**) STLN **44** 59, NYA **22** 59, KCA *CH* **43** 84-87

BLAYLOCK, MARV 1B
(10,47,**12**) NYN **10** 50, PHIN **47** 55, **12** 56-57

BLAZIER, RON P
(21,**22**) PHIN **21** 96, **22** 97

BLEFARY, CURT OF/1B
(**3**,13,39) BALA **3** 65-68, HOUN **13** 69, NYA **13** 70-71, OAKA **39** 71-72, SDN **3** 72

BLEMKER, RAY P
(**27**) KCA **27** 60

BLESSITT, IKE OF
(**22**) DETA **22** 72

BLOCK, CY 3B
(32,53,**34**) CHIN **32** 42, **53** 45, **34** 46

BLOCKER, TERRY OF
(21,29,**19**) NYN **21** 85, ATLN **29** 88, **19** 88-89

BLOMBERG, RON (BOOMER) OF/1B/DH
(**12**,10) NYA **12** 69, 71-77, CHIA **10** 78

BLOMDAHL, BEN P
(**26**) DETA **26** 95

BLOODWORTH, JIMMY 2B
(16,7,9,6,**3**, 26,11,5,37) WASA **16** 37, **7** 39, **9** 40, **6** 41, DETA **3** 42-43, **26** 46, PITN **2** 47, CINN **11** 49-50, PHIN **5/37** 50-51

BLOOMFIELD, CLYDE (BUD) INF
(19,**49**) STLN **19** 63, MINA **49** 64-65

BLOOMFIELD, JACK CH
(4,3,45) SDN *CH* **4** 74, CHIN *CH* **3** 75-76, *CH* **45** 77-78

BLOOMQUIST, WILLIE UTIL/SS/3B
(**16**) SEAA **16** 02-05

BLOSSER, GREG OF
(**47**) BOSA **47** 93-94

BLOWERS, MIKE 3B/1B
(13,21,24,14, 38, **16**,20,6, 4) NYA **13** 89, **21/24** 90, **24/14** 91, SEAA **38** 92, **16** 93-95, LAN **20** 96, SEAA **16** 97, OAKA **6** 98, SEAA **4** 99

BLUE, LU 1B
(27,**4**,26) CHIA **27** 31, **4** 32, BKNN **26** 33

BLUE, VIDA P
(21,28,17,35, **14**,33) OAKA **21/28** 69, **17** 70, **35** 70-73, **14** 73-77, SFN **14** 78-81, KCA **33** 82-83,**14** 83, SFN **14** 85-86

BLUEGE, OSSIE INF/CH/M B
(**7**,27,25,30) WASA **7** 31-35, **27** 36-39, **27** *CH* 40, *CH* **25** 41-42, *M* **25** 43, *M* **30** 44-47

BLUEGE, OTTO (SQUEAKY) INF B
(no#,**31**) CINN **no#** 32, **31** 33

BLUM, GEOFF 3B/UTIL
(50,11,**27**) MONN **50** 99, **11** 00-01, HOUN **27** 02-03, TBA **11/27** 04, SDN **27** 05, CHIA **27** 05

BLUMA, JAIME P
(**46**) KCA **46** 96

BLYLEVEN, BERT P
(**28**,22) MINA **28** 70-76, TEXA **28** 76-77, PITN **22** 78-80, CLEA **22** 81, **28** 81-85, MINA **28** 85-88, CALA **28** 89-90, 92

BLYZKA, MIKE P
(23,34) STLA **23** 53, BALA **34** 54

BELCHER, KEVIN OF
(**18**) TEXA **18** 90

BOAK, CHET 2B
(47,28) KCA **47** 60, WASA **28** 61

BOBB, RANDY C
(**6**) CHIN **6** 68-69

BOCACHICA, HIRAM UTIL/OF
(46,33,**26**,22, 44,28) LAN **46** 00-01, **33** 01, **26** 02, DETA **22** 02, **26** 03, SEAA **44** 04 OAKA **28** 05

BOCCABELLA, JOHN C
(29,22,**12**,30) CHIN **29** 63, **22** 64, **12** 65-68, MONN **12** 69-73, SFN **30** 74

BOCEK, MILT OF
(**27**,47) CHIA **27** 33, **47** 34

BOCHTE, BRUCE OF/1B
(22,**23**,20,14) CALA **22** 74-77, CLEA **23** 77, SEAA **23** 78-82, OAKA **20** 84-86, **14** 86

BOCHTLER, DOUG P
(**45**,46,39) SDN **45** 95-97, DETA **45** 98, LAN **46** 99, KCA **39** 00

BOCHY, BRUCE C
(13,9,**15**) HOUN **13** 78-80, NYN **9** 82, SDN **15** 83-87, *CH* **13** 93, *CH* **15** 94, *M* **15** 95-05

BOCKMAN, EDDIE UTIL
(**3**,2,18) NYA **3** 46, CLEA **2** 47, PITN **18** 48, **3** 49

BOCKUS, RANDY P
(26,49,**31**,41) SFN **26** 86-87, **49** 87, **31** 88, DETA **41** 89

BODDICKER, MIKE P
(**52**) BALA **52** 80-88, BOSA **52** 88-90, KCA **52** 91-92, MILA **52** 93

BOEHMER, LEN 2B
(40,**38**,25) CINN **40** 67, NYA **38** 69, **25** 71

BOEHRINGER, BRIAN P
(31,39,**41**,37, 43,71) NYA **31** 95, **39** 96, **41** 96-97, SDN **37** 98-00, NYA **41** 01, SFN **43** 01, PITN **71** 02-03, **41** 04

BOERNER, LARRY P
(**31**) BOSA **31** 32

BOEVER, JOE P
(38,36,**37**,35, 30,54,46,27, 44) STLN **38** 85, **36** 85-86, ATLN **37** 87-90, PHIN **35** 90, **30** 90-91, HOUN **54** 92, OAKA **46** 93, DETA **37** 93-95, PITN **27/44** 96

BOGAR, TIM SS
(**23**,11,27) NYN **23** 93-95, **11** 96, HOUN **27** 97-00, LAN **18** 01

BOGENER, TERRY OF
(**38**) TEXA **38** 82

BOGGS, TOMMY P
(38,47,22,50, 51,**40**) TEXA **38/47** 76, **22/38** 77, ATLN **50/51** 78-79, **40** 80-83, TEXA **40** 85

BOGGS, WADE 3B/CH
(**26**,16,12) BOSA **26** 82, **16/26** 83, **26** 84-92, NYA **12** 93-97, TBA **12** 98-99, *CH* **12** 01

BOGLE, WARREN P
(**11**) OAKA **11** 68

BOHANON, BRIAN P
(**45**,49,32,46, 57,41) TEXA **45** 90-94, DETA **49** 95, TORA **32** 96, NYN **46** 97-98, LAN **57** 98, COLN **41** 99-01

BOHNET, JOHN P
(**31**) CLEA **31** 82

BOISCLAIR, BRUCE OF
(26,**4**) NYN **26** 74, **4** 76-79

BOITANO, DANNY P
(46,**34**,45,36, 54) PHIN **46** 78, MILA **34** 79, **45/34** 80, NYN **36** 81, TEXA **54** 82

BOKELMANN, DICK P
(**25**) STLN **25** 51-53

BOKEN, BOB INF
(**25**,14) WASA **25** 33-34, CHIA **14** 34

BOKINA, JOE P
(**21**) WASA **21** 36

BOLAND, ED OF
(__,34,**3**) PHIN __ 34, **34** 35, WASA **3/17** 44

BOLEK, KEN CH
(**51**) CLEA **51** 92-93

BOLEN, STEW 1P
(**20**) PHIN **20** 32

BOLES, CARL OF
(**14**) SFN **14** 62

BOLES, JOHN MGR
(**21**) FLAN *M* **21** 96, *M* **13** 99-01

BOLEY, JOE SS
(**6**,22) PHIA **6** 31-32, CLEA **22** 32

BOLGER, JIM (DUTCH) OF
(23,30,15,**3**, 45,6) CINN **23** 50, **30** 51, **15** 54, CHIN **30** 55, **3** 57-58, CLEA **45** 59, PHIN **6** 59

BOLICK, FRANK 1B/3B
(28,55,59,**32**) MONN **28/55** 93, ANAA **59/32** 98

BOLIN, BOB (BOBBY) P
(**42**,39,26) SFN **42** 61-69, MILA **39** 70, BOSA **26** 70-73

BOLLING, FRANK 2B B
(15,24,**2**) DETA **15** 54, **24** 56-57, **2** 58-60, MILN **2** 61-65, ATLN **2** 66

BOLLING, JACK 1B
(22,6) PHIN **22** 39, BKNN **6** 44

BOLLING, MILT SS B
(18,**2**,20,23) BOSA **18** 52, **2** 53-57, WASA **20** 57, DETA **23** 58

BOLLO, GREG P
(**47**) CHIA **47** 65-66

BOLLWEG, DON 1B
(40,45,**4**,3) STLN **40** 50-51, NYA **45** 53, PHIA **4** 54, KCA **3** 55

BOLTON, CLIFF C
(10,**9**,8,18,21) WASA **10** 31, **9** 33-34, 36, **8** 35, DETA **18** 37, WASA **21** 41

BOLTON, ROD P
(**42**,86) CHIA **42** 93, 95, MILN **86** 00

BOLTON, TOM P
(**50**,49,21) BOSA **50** 87-92, CINN **50** 92, DETA **49** 93, BALA **21** 94

BOMBACK, MARK P
(**36**,28,45,17) MILA **36** 78, NYN **36/28** 80, TORA **45** 81, **17** 81-82

BOMBARD, MARC CH
(**50**,26,23) CINN *CH* **50** 96, PHIN *CH* **26** 01, **23** 05

BOND,WALT OF
(12,35,**23**,21) CLEA **12** 60-61, **35** 62, HOUN **23** 64-65, MINA **21** 67

BONDERMAN, JEREMY P
(**38**) DETA **38** 03-05

BONDS, BARRY OF S
(7,**24**,25) PITN **7** 86, **24** 86-92, SFN **25** 93-05

BONDS, BOBBY OF F
(**25**,24,00,26, 16) SFN **25** 68-74, NYA **25** 75, CALA **25** 76-77, CHIA **25** 78, TEXA **24** 78, CLEA **25** 79, STLN **00/26** 80, CHIN **25** 81, CLEA *CH* **17** 84, **25** 85-87, SFN *CH* **16** 93-96

BONES, RICKY P
(56,**25**,29,40, 38,27,49) SDN **56** 91, MILA **25** 92-96, NYA **29** 96, CINN **40** 97, KCA **38/27** 97, **49** 98, BALA **25** 99, FLAN **29** 00-01

BONETTI, JULIO P
(23,**27**,43) STLA **23** 37, **27** 38, CHIN **43** 40

BONG, JUNG P
(30,**51**) ATLN **30** 02, **51** 03, CINN **31** 04, **51** 05

BONGIOVANNI, NINO OF
(49,**27**) CINN **49** 38, **27** 39

BONHAM, BILL P S
(**33**,42) CHIN **33** 71-77, CINN **42** 78-80

BONHAM, ERNIE (TINY) P F
(**20**,35) NYA **20** 40-46, PITN **35** 47-49, **20** 49

BONIKOWSKI, JOE P
(33,48) MINA **33/48** 62

BONILLA, BOBBY (BOBBY BO) OF/3B N
(26,**25**,23,24) CHIA **26** 86, PITN **25** 86-90, **23** 91, NYN **25** 92-95, BALA **26** 95-96, FLAN **24** 97, **25** 98, LAN **25** 98, NYN **25** 99, ATLN **23** 00, STLN **24** 01

BONILLA, JUAN 2B U
(**3**,55,47,57) SDN **3** 81-83, NYA **55** 85, BALA **3** 86, NYA **47/57** 87

BONNELL, BARRY OF
(2,**9**) ATLN **2** 77-79, TORA **9** 80-83, SEAA **9** 84-86

BONNER, BOB SS
(**2**) BALA **2** 80-83

BONNESS, BILL (LEFTY) P
(**30**) CLEA **30** 44

BONURA, ZEKE 1B
(**3**,5,18) CHIA **3** 34-37, WASA **3** 38, NYN **5** 39, WASA **18/3** 40, CHIN **18** 40

BOOKER, BUDDY C
(5,**8**,6) CLEA **5/8** 66, CHIA **6** 68

BOOKER, CHRIS P
(**52**) CINN **56** 05

BOOKER, GREG P/CH
(**51**,38) SDN **51** 83-89, MINA **51** 89, SFN **51** 90, SDN *CH* **38** 97-03

BOOKER, ROD INF
(26,5,**10**,37) STLN **26/5** 87,**10** 87-89, PHIN **37** 90-91

BOONE, AARON 3B S,GS,B
(**17**,19) CINN **17** 97-03, NYA **19** 03, CLEA **17** 05

BOONE, BOB C S,F
(40,**8**,2,9) PHIN **40** 72, **8** 73-81, CALA **8** 82-88, KCA **8** 89-90, CINN *CH* **8** 94, KCA *M* **2** 95, *M* **8** 96-97, CINN *M* **9** 01-03

BOONE, BRET 2B S,GS,B
(34,5,**29**,24, 21) SEAA **34** 92, **5** 93, CINN **29** 94-98, ATLN **24** 99, SDN **29** 00, SEAA **29** 01-05, MINA **21** 05

BOONE, DAN P
(**30**,29,31,37) SDN **30** 81-82, **29** 82, HOUN **31**82, BALA **37** 90

BOONE, IKE OF
(**no#**) BKNN **no#** 32

BOONE, RAY (IKE) SS/1B F,GF
(28,**8**,30,19, 5,39) CLEA **28** 48, **8** 49-53, DETA **8** 53-58, CHIA **8** 58-59, KCA **30** 59, MILN **19** 59-60, BOSA **5/39** 60

BOOTCHECK, CHRIS P
(**51**,49) ANAA **51** 03, LAA **49** 05

BOOTY, JOSH 3B
(29,**2**) FLAN **29** 96, **2** 97-98

BOOZER, JOHN P
(29,19,28,21, 42) PHIN **29** 62-64, **19** 64-66, **28** 67-69, **21/42** 69

BORBON, PEDRO P F
(33,**34**,49) CALA **33** 69, CINN **34** 70-79, SFN **34** 79, STLN **49/34** 80

BORBON, PEDRO, JR. P S
(**51**,50,36,35, 52) ATLN **51** 92-93, 95-96, **50** 99, TORA **36** 00, **51** 00-02, HOUN **35** 02, STLN **52** 03

BORCHARD, JOE OF
(**25**) CHIA **25** 02-05

BORDAGARAY, FRENCHY OF
(34,4,14,26,27 37,19,36,33) CHIA **34** 34, BKNN **4** 35-36, STLN **14** 37-38, CINN **26** 39, NYA **27** 41, BKNN **37** 42, **19/36** 43, **33** 44-45

BORDERS, PAT C
(**10**,15,17,38, 7,29,18,26,37) TORA **10** 88-94, KCA **15** 95, HOUN **17** 95, STLN **38** 96, CALA **7** 96, CHIA **15** 96, CLEA **10** 97-99, TORA **29** 99, SEAA **18** 01, **10** 02-04, MINA **26** 04, SEAA **37** 05

BORDI, RICH P
(28,25,20,53, **42**,43,46) OAKA **28** 80-81, SEAA **25/20** 82, CHIN **42** 83-84, NYA **43** 85, BALA **53/42** 86, NYA **46** 87, OAKA **37/46** 88

BORDICK, MIKE INF
(46,**14**,17,16) OAKA **46** 90-92, **14** 93-96, BALA **14** 97-00, NYN **17** 00, BALA **14** 01-02, TORA **16** 03

BORDLEY, BILL P
(**34**) SFN **34** 80

BORGMANN, GLENN C
(24,27,**14**,38) MINA **24** 72-73, **27** 72, **14** 74-79, CHIA **38** 80

BORIS, PAUL P
(**40**) MINA **40** 82

BORK, FRANK P
(57,35,**36**) PITN **57/35/36** 64

BORKOWSKI, BOB OF/1B
(22,**24**,27) CHIN **22** 50-51, CINN **24** 52-55, BKNN **27** 55

BORKOWSKI, DAVE P
(**45**) DETA **45** 99-01, BALA **61** 04

BORLAND, TOBY P
(**42**,43,47,39, 46,33) PHIN **42** 94-96, NYN **43** 97, BOSA **47** 97, PHIN **39** 98, ANAA **46** 01, FLAN **33** 02-04

BORLAND, TOM (SPIKE) P
(21,**19**) BOSA **21** 60-61, **19** 61

BOROM, RED INF
(7,**10**,30) DETA **7** 44, **10** 45, **30** 45

BOROS, STEVE 3B/CH/M
(26,24,**1**,17, 10,14,41,22, 43) DETA **26** 57, **24** 58, **1** 61-62, CHIN **17** 63, CINN **10** 64-65, KCA *CH* **14** 75-79, MONN *CH* **41** 81, *CH* **14** 82, OAKA *M* **14** 83-84, SDN *M* **22** 86, KCA *CH* **43** 93-94, BALA *CH* **43** 95

BOROWSKI, JOE P
(77,50,52,57, **48**) BALA **77** 95, ATLN **50** 96-97, NYA **52** 97, **57** 98, CHIN **48** 01-05, TBA **48** 05

BOROWY, HANK P
(38,**15**,26,20, 24) NYA **38** 42, **15** 43-45, CHIN **26** 45-48, PHIN **20** 49-50, PITN **24** 50, DETA **15** 50-51

BOSCH, DON OF
(23,**17**,19) PITN **23** 66, NYN **17** 67-68, MONN **19** 69

BOSETTI, RICK OF
(28,29,21,**22**, 7) PHIN **28/29** 76, STLN **21** 77, TORA **22** 78-81, OAKA **7** 81-82

BOSIO, CHRIS P/CH
(**29**,25) MILA **29** 86-92, SEAA **29** 93-95, **25** 95-96, TBA *CH* **29** 03

BOSKIE, SHAWN P
(**47**,45,34,22, 32) CHIN **47** 90-94, PHIN **45** 94, SEAA **34** 94, CALA **22** 95-96, BALA **32** 97

BOSLEY, THAD OF
(32,22,**27**,20, 7,41) CALA **32** 77, CHIA **22** 78-79, **32** 80, MILA **27** 81, SEAA **20** 82, CHIN **20** 83, **27** 84-86, KCA **27** 87-88, CALA **7** 88, TEXA **32** 89-90, OAKA *CH* **41** 99-03

BOSMAN, DICK P/CH
(38,25,**27**,23, 49,32,17, 31) WASA **38/25** 66, **27** 67-69, **23** 70, **27** 70-71, TEXA **27** 72-73, CLEA **49** 73, **27** 73-75, OAKA **32** 75, **17** 75-76, CHIA *CH* **27**86-87, BALA *CH* **31** 92, *CH* **17** 92-93, *CH* **27** 94, TEXA *CH* **17** 95-00

BOSS, HARLEY (LEFTY) 1B
(__,**7**) WASA __ 30, CLEA **7** 33

BOSSER, MEL P
(**35**) CINN **35** 45

BOSTOCK, LYMAN OF
(**10**) MINA **10** 75-78

BOSTON, DARYL OF
(33,**8**,7,6,26) CHIA **33** 84, **8** 85-90, NYN **7** 90, **6** 91-92, COLN **6** 93, NYA **26** 94

BOSWELL, DAVE P
(**23**,32) MINA **23** 64-70, DETA **32** 71, BALA **32** 71

BOSWELL, KEN 2B
(24,**12**,17) NYN **24** 67, **12** 68-73, HOUN **17** 75-77

BOTELHO, DEREK P
(37,47) KCA **49/37** 82, CHIN **47** 85

BOTTALICO, RICKY P
(**52**,27,26,34, 20) PHIN **52** 94-98, STLN **52** 99, KCA **52** 00, PHIN **27** 01-02, ARIN **26** 03, NYN **34/20** 04, MILN **52** 05

BOTTARINI, JOHN C/OF
(**41**) CHIN **41** 37

BOTTENFIELD, KENT P
(**46**,14,43,45, 34,37,21,47) MONN **46** 92, **14/46** 93, COLN **46** 93-94, SFN **43** 94, CHIN **45** 96-97, **34** 97, STLN **37** 98-99, ANAA **37** 00, PHIN **21** 00, HOUN **47** 01

BOTTING, RALPH P
(43,**34**,48) CALA **79** 79, **34** 79-80, **48** 80

BOTTOMLEY, JIM (SUNNY JIM) 1B
(5,4,3,**1**,2) STLN **5** 23, **4** 24, 32, CINN **3** 33, **1** 34-35, STLA **2** 36-37

BOTTS, JASON OF/DH
(**44**) TEXA **44** 05

BOTZ, BOB P
(**22**) LAA **22** 62

BOUCHEE, ED 1B
(39,**5**,11,3) PHIN **39** 56, **5** 57-60, CHIN **11** 60-61, NYN **11/3** 62

BOUCHER, DENIS P
(35,23,49,37, **38**) TORA **35** 91, CLEA **23** 91, **49** 91-92, **37** 92, MONN **38** 93-94

BOUDREAU, LOU SS/M
(34,**5**,4,42) CLEA **34** 38, **5** 39-50, *M* **5** 42-50, BOSA **4** 51-52, *M* **4** 52-54, KCA *M* **5** 55-57, CHIN *M* **42/5** 60

BOULDIN, CARL P
(34,27,38,39, 18) WASA **34** 61, **27** 62, **38** 62, WASA **39** 63, **18** 64

BOURGEOIS, STEVE P
(**33**) SFN **33** 96

BOURJOS, CHRIS OF
(**18**) SFN **18** 80

BOURNIGAL, RAFAEL SS
(28,21,40,**26**, 2) LAN **28** 92, **21** 93-94, OAKA **40** 96, **26** 96-98, SEAA **2** 99

BOURQUE, PAT 1B
(**19**,38,10) CHIN **19** 71-73, OAKA **38** 73-74, MINA **10** 74

BOUTON, JIM P
(**56**,44,29) NYA **56** 62-68, SEAA **56** 69, HOUN **44** 69, **56** 69-70, ATLN **56** 78

BOVEE, MIKE P
(**61**) ANAA **61** 97

BOWA, LARRY SS/M/CH U
(**10**,1,2) PHIA **10** 70-81, CHIN **1** 82-85, NYN **2** 85, SDN *M* **10** 87-88, PHIN *CH* **2** 89-96, ANAA *CH* **2** 97-99, ANAA *CH* **10** 00, PHIN *M* **10** 01-04

BOWEN, ROB C
(**44**) MINA **44** 03-04

BOWEN, RYAN P
(**46**,41) HOUN **46** 91, **41/46** 92, FLAN **46** 93-95

BOWEN, SAM OF
(**29**) BOSA **29** 77-78, 80

BOWENS, SAM OF
(14,**16**,35,31) BALA **14** 63, **16** 64-67, WASA **35** 68, **31** 69

BOWERS, BILLY OF
(**12**) CHIA **12** 49

BOWERS, BRENT OF
(**30**) BALA **30** 96

BOWERS, SHANE P
(**52**) MINA **52** 97

BOWERS, STEW (DOC) P
(**23**,16,32) BOSA **23** 35-36, **16** 36, **32** 37

BOWIE, JIM 1B
(**19**) OAKA **19** 94

BOWIE, MICAH P
(43,53,**57**) ATLN **43** 99, CHIN **53** 99, OAKA **57** 02-03

BOWLER, GRANT (MOOSE) P
(19,39,**23**) CHIA **19** 31, **39/23** 32

BOWLES, BRIAN P
(**37**,26) TORA **37** 01-02, **26** 03

BOWLES, CHARLIE P
(__,35,**11**) PHIA __ 43, **35/11** 45

BOWLIN, HOSS 3B
(**10**) KCA **10** 67

BOWLING, STEVE OF/DH
(17,**3**)) MILA **17** 76, TORA **3** 77

BOWMAN, BOB P
(**26**,16,21) STLN **26** 39-40, NYN **16** 41, CHIN **21** 42

BOWMAN, BOB OF
(8,**10**) PHIN **8** 55-56, **10** 57-59

BOWMAN, ERNIE INF
(**21**) SFN **21** 61-63

BOWMAN, JOE P
(17,19,46,27, 48,**21**,28,39) PHIA **17** 32, NYN **19** 34, PHIN **46** 35-36, PITN **27** 37, **48** 38-39, **21** 40-41, BOSA **28** 44-45, CINN **39** 45

BOWMAN, ROGER P
(17,**38**,32,31) NYN **17** 49, **38** 51-52, PITN **32** 53, **31** 55

BOWSFIELD, TED P
(28,29,30,**43**) BOSA **28** 58-59, **29** 60, CLEA **30** 60, LAA **43** 61-62, KCA **43** 63-64

BOWYER, TRAVIS P
(**56**) MINA **56** 05

BOYD, BOB (THE ROPE) 1B/OF
(5,31,15,**1**,9, 10) CHIA **5** 51, **31**53-54, BALA **15** 56, **1** 56-59, **9** 60, KCA **10** 61

BOYD, GARY P
(**54**) CLEA **54** 69

BOYD, JASON P
(**60**,41,58,57, 50) PITN **60** 99, PHIN **41/60** 00, SDN **58** 02, CLEA **57** 03, PITN **50** 04

BOYD, OIL CAN P
(**23**,29) BOSA **23** 82-89, MONN **23** 90-91, TEXA **29** 91

BOYER, BLAINE P
(**48**) ATLN **48** 05

BOYER, CLETE 3B/CH B
(12,34,**6**,41, 40) KCA **12** 55-57, NYA **34** 59-61, **6** 61-66, ATLN **6** 67-71, OAKA *CH* **41** 80-85, NYA **6/40** 88, **6** 92-94

BOYER, CLOYD (JUNIOR) P B
(23,**24**,18,62, 21,48,43) STLN **23** 49, **24** 50-52, KCA **18** 55, NYA *CH* **62** 75, *CH* **21** 77, ATLN *CH* **48** 78-81, KCA *CH* **43** 82-83

BOYER, KEN 3B B
(**14**,45) STLN **14** 55-65, NYN **14** 66-67, CHIA **14** 67-68, LAN **45** 68-69, STLN *CH* **14** 71-72, *M* **14** 78-80

BOYLAND, DOE 1B
(15,5,**12**) PITN **15** 78, **5** 79, **12** 81

BOYLE, BUZZ OF
(**17**,1) BKNN **17** 33-34, **1** 35

BOYLES, HARRY (STRETCH) P
(26,**19**) CHIA **26** 38, **19** 39

BOZE, MARSHALL P
(**48**) MILA **48** 96

BRABENDER, GENE P
(**32**) BALA **32** 66-68, SEAA **32** 69, MILA **32** 70

BRACK, GIB (GIBBY) OF
(**30**,16,27) BKNN **30** 37-38, PHIN **16** 38, **27** 39

BRADEY, DON P
(**45**) HOUN **45** 64

BRADFORD, BILL P
(**14**) KCA **14** 56

BRADFORD, BUDDY OF
(53,32,19,25 29,**22**,12) CHIA **53** 66, **32** 67-68, **19** 69-70, CLEA **25** 70-71, CINN **29** 71,CHIA **22** 72-75, STLN **12** 75, CHIA **22/29** 76

BRADFORD, CHAD P
(44,**53**,54) CHIA **44** 98-00, OAKA **53** 01-03, **54** 04, **(53)** (05), BOSA **53** 05

BRADFORD, LARRY P
(30,40,38,**34**) ATLN **30** 77, **40/38** 79, **34** 79-81

BRADFORD, VIC OF
(**29**) NYN **29** 43, (46)

BRADLEY, BERT P
(**53**) OAKA **53** 83

BRADLEY, FRED P
(**39**) CHIA **39** 48-49

BRADLEY, GEORGE OF
(**22**) STLA **22** 46

BRADLEY, MARK OF
(**22**,9) LAN **22** 81-82, NYN **9** 83

BRADLEY, MILTON OF/DH
(**24**,39,21) MONN **24** 00-01, CLEA **39** 02, **24** 02, **24** 03, LAN **21** 04-05

BRADLEY, PHIL OF
(**29**,16,1,8) SEAA **29** 83-87, PHIN **29** 88, BALA **16** 89, **1**90, CHIA **8** 90

BRADLEY, SCOTT UTIL
(34,25,22,**9**, 6,47) NYA **34** 84-85, CHIA **25** 86, SEAA **22** 86, **9** 86, 88-91, **6** 92, CINN **47** 92

BRADLEY, TOM P
(49,29,24,**40**) CALA **49** 69, **29** 70, CHIA **24** 71-72, SFN **40** 73-75

BRADLEY, RYAN P
(**59**) NYA **59** 98

BRADSHAW, GEORGE C
(38,**9**) WASA **38/9** 52

BRADSHAW, TERRY OF
(**55**) STLN **55** 95-96

BRADY, BOB C
(15,23) BOSN **15** 46, **23** 47

BRADY, BRIAN OF
(**8**) CALA **8** 89

BRADY, DOUG 2B
(**33**) CHIA **33** 95

BRADY, JIM (DIAMOND JIM) P
(**26**) DETA **26** 56

BRAGAN, BOBBY (NIG) UTIL/M/CH (20,21,15,24, 2,**10**,3) PHIN **20** 40-41, **21** 42, BKNN **15** 43-44, **24** 47-48, PITN *M* **2** 56-57, CLEA *M* **2** 58, LAN *CH* **10** 60,HOUN *CH* **3** 62, MILN *M* **10** 63-66

BRAGAN, JIMMY CH (**2**,34,24) CINN *CH* **2** 67-69, MONN *CH* **34**70-72, MILA *CH* **24** 76-77

BRAGG, DARREN OF (40,34,**56**,22, 31,17,28,18, 15) SEAA **40** 94-95, **34** 95, **56** 96, BOSA **56** 96-98, STLN **22** 99, COLN **31** 00, NYN **56** 01, NYA **17** 01, ATLN **28** 02-03, SDN **18** 04, CINN **15** 04

BRAGGS, GLENN OF (36,**26**,15) MILA **36** 86, **26** 86-90, CINN **15** 90-92

BRAME, ERV P (**48**) PITN **48** 32

BRAMHALL, ART INF (**25**) PHIN **25** 35

BRAMMER, J. D. P (**64**) CLEA **64** 00

BRANCA, RALPH (HAWK) P (**13**,20,12,35 35,24,28) BKNN **13** 44-45, **20** 46-47, **13** 47-51, **12** 52, **13** 53, DETA **35** 53-54, NYA **24** 54, BKNN **28** 56

BRANCATO, AL (BRONK) INF (6,**18**,10) PHIA **6** 39, **18** 40, **10** 41, **18** 45

BRANCH, HARVEY P (**40**) STLN **40** 62

BRANCH, NORM (RED) P (**30**) NYA **30** 41-42

BRANCH, ROY P (**29**) SEAA **29** 79

BRAND, RON UTIL (16,**9**,11) PITN **16** 63, HOUN **9** 65-68, MONN **11** 69-71

BRANDENBERG, MARK P (**51**,50) TEXA **51** 95-96, BOSA **50** 96-97

BRANDON, DARRELL (BUCKY) P (**27**,57,24,32, 30) BOSA **27** 66-68, SEAA **57/27** 69, MINA **24** 69, PHIN **32** 71, **30** 72-73

BRANDT, BILL P (**24**) PITN **24** 41-43

BRANDT, ED (BIG ED) P (**11**,14,25,49) BOSN **11** 32-35, **14** 33, BKNN **25** 36, PITN **49** 37-38

BRANDT, JACKIE (FLAKEY) OF (21,**25**,22,7, 20,8) STLN **21** 56, NYN **25** 56, SFN **22** 58, **25** 59, BALA **7** 60, **25** 60-65, PHIN **20** 66-67, HOUN **8** 67

BRANSON, JEFF INF (**20**,11) CINN **20** 92-97, CLEA **11** 97-98, LAN **45** 00, **7** 01

BRANT, MARSHALL 1B/DH (61,**19**) NYA **61** 80, OAKA **19** 83

BRANTLEY, CLIFF P (**51**) PHIN **51** 91-92

BRANTLEY, JEFF P (**49**,45,44) SFN **49** 88-93, CINN **45** 94-97, STLN **44** 98, PHIN **45** 99-00, TEXA **45** 01

BRANTLEY, MICKEY OF/CH (**14**,53) SEAA **14** 86-89, NYN *CH* **53** 99, TORA *CH* **14** 05

BRANYAN, RUSS 3B (66,**33**,28,31) CLEA **66** 98, **33** 99-01, **28** 02, CINN **33** 02-03, MILN **31** 04-05

BRATCHER, JOE (GOOBERS) OF (__) STLN __ 24

BRAUN, JOHN P (**38**) MILN **38** 64

BRAUN, STEVE UTIL (**4**,2,3,11,26) MINA **4** 71-75, **2** 76, SEAA **4** 77-78, KCA **3** 78-80, TOR **11** 80, STLN **26** 81-85, *CH* **26** 90

BRAVO, ANGEL OF (1,**22**,8) CHIA **1** 69, CINN **22** 70-71, SDN **8** 71

BRAXTON, GARLAND P (20,19,25,__) WASA **20** 30, CHIA **19** 31, STLA **25** 31, __ 33

BRAY, BUSTER OF (**37**) BOSN **37** 41

BRAZELL, CRAIG P (**9**) NYN **9** 04

BRAZELTON, DEWON P (**45**) TBA **45** 01-05

BRAZLE, AL P (11,16,**27**) STLN **11** 43, **36/16** 46 **27** 46-54

BRAZOBAN, YHENCY P (**43**) LAN **43** 04-05

BREA, LESLIE P (**45**) BALA **45** 00-01

BREAM, SID 1B (33,**5**,12,31) LAN **33** 83-85, PITN **5** 85-90, ATLN **12** 91-93, HOUN **31** 94

BREAZEALE, JIM 1B (**2**,3) ATLN **2** 69,71-72, CHIA **3** 78

BRECHEEN, HARRY (THE CAT) P/CH (**31**) STLN **31** 40, 43-52, STLA **31** 53, *CH* **31**53, BALA *CH* **31** 54-67

BREDE, BRENT 1B (51,14,15) MINA **51** 96-97, ARIN **14/15** 98

BREEDEN, DANNY C (**8**,19) CINN **8** 69, CHIN **19** 71

BREEDEN, HAL OF/1B (25,**23**) CHIN **25** 71, MONN **23** 72-75

BREEDEN, JOE CH (**12**) FLAN *CH* **12** 95-96, 99-01, TORA *CH* **12** 04

BREEDEN, SCOTT CH (**2**) CINN *CH* **2** 86-89

BREEDING, MARV 2B (16,**1**,23) BALA **16** 60, **1** 60-62, WASA **1** 63, LAN **23** 63

BREINING, FRED P (**48**,19) SFN **48** 80-83, MONN **19** 84, **48** 84

BREMER, HERB C (**11**,13) STLN **11** 37-38, **13** 39

BRENLY, BOB C/UTIL/CH (**15**,9,19,14) SFN **15** 81-88, TORA **9** 89, SFN **19** 89, *CH* **14** 92, *CH* **15** 92-95, ARIN **15** 01-04

BRENNAN, BILL P (35,44) LAN **35** 88, CHIN **44** 93

BRENNAN, DON P (20,19,**28**) NYA **20** 33, CINN **19** 34, **28** 35-37, NYN **19** 37

BRENNAN, TOM P (**45**,41,59,46) CLEA **45** 81, **41** 82, **45** 82-83, CHIA **59** 84, LAN **46** 85

BRENNEMAN, JIM P (**23**) NYA **23** 65

BRENZEL, BILL C (no#,**8**) PITN **no#** 32, CLEA **8** 34-35

BRESLOW, CRAIG P (**48**) SDN **48** 05

BRESNAHAN, ROGER CH (**52**) DETA *CH* **52** 31

BRESSLER, RUBE OF (28,**24**) PHIN **28** 32, STLN **24** 32

BRESSOUD, ED (EDDIE) SS (**34**,48,16,**1**, 11) NYN **34** 56, **48** 57, SFN **16** 58-61, BOSA **1** 62-65, NYN **1** 66, STLN **11** 67

BRETT, GEORGE 3B B (25,**5**) KCA **25** 73-74, **5** 75-93

BRETT, KEN P B (36,45,15,42, 18,24,31,30, 38,50,**34**,33, 25) BOSA **36/45** 67, **15** 69, **42** 69-70, **18** 70-71, MILA **24** 72, PHIN **31** 73, PITN **30** 74-75, NYA **38** 76, CHIA **50** 76, **34** 76-77, CALA **33** 77, **34** 77-78, MINA **31** 79, LAN **34** 79, KCA **25** 80-81

BREUER, MARV (BABY FACE) P (**24**) NYA **24** 39-43

BREWER, BILLY P (29,**41**,47,49) KCA **29** 93, **41** 94-95, NYA **47** 96, OAKA **47** 97, PHIN **49** 97-99

BREWER, JACK (BUDDY) P (32,**21**) NYN **32** 44, **21** 45-46

BREWER, JIM P/CH (45,48,38,**21**, 34,2) CHIN **45** 60, **48** 61, **38** 62-63, LAN **21** 64-75, CALA **34** 75-76, **21** 76, MONN *CH* **2** 77-79

BREWER, MIKE OF (**17**) KCA **17** 86

BREWER, ROD 1B (58,**33**) STLN **58** 90-91, **33** 92-93

BREWER, TOM P (**23**) BOSA **23** 54-61

BREWER, TONY OF (**50**) LAN **50** 84-85

BREWINGTON, JAMIE P (**30**,58) SFN **30** 95, CLEA **58** 00

BREWSTER, CHARLIE INF (19,**20**,26) CINN **19** 43, PHIN **20** 43, CHIN **26** 44, CLEA **20** 46

BRICE, ALAN P (46,**30**) CHIA **46/30** 61

BRICKELL, FRED OF F (**14**) PHIN **14** 32-33

BRICKELL, FRITZIE INF S (**29**,16) NYA **29** 58-59, LAA **16** 61

BRICKNER, RALPH (BRICK) P (39,**26**) BOSA **39/26** 52

BRIDEWESER, JIM P (9,**27**,2,3,1, 40) NYA **9** 51, **27** 52-53, BALA **2** 54, CHIA **3** 55-56, DETA **1** 56, BALA **40** 57

BRIDGES, MARSHALL (SHERIFF) P (**30**,34,25,22) STLN **30** 59-60, CINN **34** 60-61, NYA **30** 62-63, WASA **25** 64, **22** 65

BRIDGES, ROCKY INF/CH (9,**14**,31,8,30, 21,22,6) BKNN **9** 51-52, CINN **14** 53-57, WASA **31** 57-58, DETA **8** 59-60, CLEA **8** 60, STLN **30** 60, LAA **21** 61, *CH* **21** 62-63, CALA *CH* **22** 68-71, SFN *CH* **6** 85

BRIDGES, TOMMY P (16,**10**) DETA **16** 31-33, **10** 33-43, 45

BRIGGS, DAN UTIL (38,4,21,23, 24,33,11) CALA **38** 75-76, **4** 76, **21** 77, CLEA **23** 78, SDN **24** 79, MONN **33** 81, CHIN **11** 82

BRIGGS, JOHNNY P (15,**16**,30,32, 27) CHIN **15** 56, **16** 56-57, **30** 58, CLEA **32** 59-60, **16** 60, KCA **27** 60

BRIGGS, JOHNNY OF/1B (58, **12**,22) PHIN **58** 64, **12** 64-71, MILA **12** 71-75, MINA **22** 75

BRIGHT, HARRY UTIL (**8**,10,11,14, 29) PITN **8** 58-60, WASA **10** 61-62, CINN **11** 63, NYA **14** 63-64, CHIN **29** 65

BRILES, NELSON (NELLIE) P (**34**,22,19,23, 55) STLN **34** 65-70, PITN **22** 71, **34** 71-73, KCA **19** 74-75, TEXA **23** 76, **34** 76-77, BALA **55** 77, **34** 78

BRILEY, GREG (PEEWEE) OF (**8**,1,20) SEAA **8** 88-90, **1** 91-92, FLAN **20** 93

BRILLHEART, JIM P (**27**) BOSA **27** 31

BRINK, BRAD P (23,**31**,49) PHIN **23** 92, **31** 92-93, SFN **49** 94

BRINKMAN, CHUCK C (10,**11**,45) CHIA **10** 69-70, **11** 71-74, PITN **45** 74

BRINKMAN, EDDIE SS (2,38,**11**,8,5, 3,20,51,37, 35) WASA **2** 61, **38** 62, **11** 63-70, DETA **8** 71-74, STLN **5** 75, TEXA **3** 75, NYA **20** 75, DETA *CH* **51** 79, SDN *CH* **37** 81, CHIA *CH* **35** 83-88

BRINKOPF, LEON SS (**43**) CHIN **43** 52

BRISCOE, JOHN P (55,**53**) OAKA **55** 91, **53** 91-96

BRISSIE, LOU P (17,**19**,12) PHIA **17** 47, **19** 48-51, CLEA **12** 51-53

BRISTOL, DAVE CH/M (**4**,1,5,2) CINN *CH* **4** 66, *M* **4** 66-69, MILA *M* **4** 70-72, MONN *CH* **1** 73, *CH* **5** 74, *CH* **1** 75, ATLN *M* **1** 76-77, SFN *CH* **1** 79, *M* **1** 79-80, PHIN *CH* **4** 82-85, *CH* **2** 88, CINN *CH* **4** 88-89, 93

BRITO, BERNARDO OF (**33**) MINA **33** 92-93, 95 *(JAP)*

BRITO, EUDE P (**58**) PHIN **58** 05

BRITO, JORGE C (**27**) COLN **27** 95-96

BRITO, JUAN C (**22**,48) KCA **22** 02, ARIN **48** 04

BRITO, TILSON INF (14,12,**8**) TORA **14** 96, **12** 97, OAKA **8** 97

BRITTAIN, GUS C (**38**,1) CINN **38** 37, *CH* **1** 37

BRITTIN, JACK P (**41**) PHIN **41** 50-51

BRITTON, JIM 1B (41,**42**,51,27) ATLN **41** 67, **42** 67-69, MONN **27** 71

BRIZZOLARA, TONY P (43,**48**) ATLN **43** 79, **48** 83-84

BROACA, JOHNNY P (26,21,20, 11,16) NYA **26/21** 34, **20** 35-37, CLEA **11/16** 39

BROBERG, PETE P (18,**40**) WASA **18** 71, TEXA **18** 72-74, **40** 74, MILA **40** 75-76, CHIN **40** 77, OAKA **40** 78

BROCAIL, DOUG P (49,46,**26**) SDN **49** 92-94, HOUN **46** 95-96 DETA **26** 97-00, HOUN **26** 01-02, TEXA **46** 04-05

BROCK, CHRIS P (49,51,**45**) ATLN **49** 97, SFN **51** 98, **45** 99, PHIN **45** 00-01, BALA **45** 02

BROCK, GREG 1B (47,17,**9**) LAN **47** 82, **17** 83, **9** 83-86, MILA **9** 87-91

BROCK, LOU OF (24,**20**) CHIN **24** 61-64, STLN **20** 64-79

BROCK, TARRIK OF (**22**) CHIN **22** 00

BRODOWSKI, DICK P (27,24,42,17, 19,**26**) BOSA **27/24** 52, **42** 55, WASA **17** 56, **19** 57, CLEA **26** 58-59

BROGLIO, ERNIE P (**32**,40) STLN **32** 59-64, CHIN **40** 64, **32** 64-66

BROGNA, RICO 1B (13,26,**2**,11) DETA **13** 92, NYN **26** 94-96, PHIN **2** 97-00, BOSA **11** 00, ATLN **2** 01

BROHAMER, JACK 2B (7,**10**,3,8) CLEA **7** 72, **10** 73-75, CHIA **10** 76-77, BOSA **3** 78-80, CLEA **8** 80

BROHAWN, ROY P (**23**) ARIN **54** 01, SFN **51** 02, LAN **54** 03

BRONDELL, KEN P (**23**) NYN **23** 44

BRONKEY, JEFF P (51,**29**) TEXA **51** 93, MILA **29** 94-95

BRONSTAD, JIM P (49,**22**) NYA **49/22** 59, WASA **39** 63, **37** 64

BROOKENS, IKE P B (**28**) DETA **28** 75

BROOKENS, TOM UTIL (**16**,12,31,10) DETA **16** 79-88, NYA **12** 89, CLEA **31/10** 90

BROOKS, BOBBY OF (**15**,17) OAKA **15** 69-70, 72, CALA **17** 73

BROOKS, FRANK P (57,**27**) PITN **57** 04, ATLN **27** 05

BROOKS, HUBIE 3B/SS/OF/DH (39,**7**,21,8, 30) NYN **39** 80, **7** 81-84, MONN **7** 85-89, LAN **21** 90, NYN **7** 91, CALA **8** 92, KCA **30** 93-94

BROOKS, JERRY OF/C/1B (**64**,35) LAN **64** 93, FLAN **35** 96

BROSIUS, SCOTT 3B (45,2,**7**,18) OAKA **45** 91-92, **2** 92, **7** 93-97, NYA **18** 98-01

BROSKIE, SIGGIE (CHOPS) C (**18**) BOSN **18** 40

BROSNAN, JIM (PROFESSOR) P (27,**42**,23,37) CHIN **27** 54, **42** 56-57, **23** 58, STLN **37** 58-59, CINN **42** 59-63, CHIA **27** 63

BROSS, TERRY P (46,37) NYN **46** 91, SFN **37** 93

BROSSEAU, FRANK P (**45**) PITN **45** 69, 71

BROUHARD, MARK OF (**29**) MILA **29** 80-85

BROUSSARD, BEN OF/1B/DH (28,**23**) CLEA **28** 02-03, **23** 04-05

BROVIA, JOE (OX) PH (**26**) CINN **26** 55

BROW, SCOTT P (**44**,27,46) TORA **44** 93-94, **27** 96, ARIN **46** 98

BROWER, BOB OF (43,**33**) TEXA **43** 86, **33** 87-88, NYA **33** 89

BROWER, JIM P (**50**,53,32,38) CLEA **50** 99-00, CINN **53** 01-02, MONN **32** 02, SFN **38** 03-05, ATLN **38** 05

BROWER, LOU INF (**7**) DETA **7** 31

BROWN, ? CH (**34**) BALA *CH* **34** 55

BROWN, ADRIAN OF (**13**,17,31) PITN **13** 97-02, BOSA **17** 03, KCA **31** 04

BROWN, ALTON (DEACON) P (**24**) WASA **24** 51

BROWN, BOB (18,17,12) BOSN **18** 32, **17** 33 **20** 34, **12** 35-36

BROWN, BOBBY (DOC) UTIL (7,**6**,9,27) NYA **7** 46, **6** 47-50, **9** 51, **6** 51-52, **27** 54

BROWN, BOBBY OF (5,22,58,13, 44,**20**) TORA **5** 79, NYA **22/58** 79, **13** 80-81, SEAA **44** 82, SDN **20** 83-85

BROWN, BRANT 1B/OF (**37**,35) CHIN **37** 96-98, PITN **37** 99, FLAN **37** 00, CHIN **35/37** 00

BROWN, CHRIS 3B (**35**) SFN **35** 84-87, SDN **35** 87-88, DETA **35** 89

BROWN, CLINT P (**16**,26,21) CLEA **16** 30-35, CHIA **26** 36-40, CLEA **21** 41-42

BROWN, CURTIS OF (**17**) MONN **17** 73

BROWN, CURT P (48,56,**52**) CALA **48** 83, NYA **56** 84, MONN **52** 86-87

BROWN, DARRELL OF/DH (34,13,**26**) DETA **34** 81, OAKA **13** 82, MINA **26** 83-84

BROWN, DERMAL (DEE) OF/DH (**27**,8) KCA **27** 98-02, **8** 03-04

BROWN, DICK C (11,20,**10**) CLEA **11** 57-59, CHIA **20** 60, DETA **10** 61-62, BALA **10** 63-65

BROWN, EMIL OF (**19**,14,17,10, 35) PITN **19** 97-99, **14** 00, **17** 01, SDN **10** 01, KCA **35** 05

BROWN, GATES OF (20,**26**) DETA **20** 63, **26** 63-75, *CH* **26** 78-84

BROWN, HAL (SKINNY) P (27,28,**29**,39,38) CHIA **27** 51-52, BOSA **27** 53-55, BALA **28** 55-62, NYA **29** 62, HOUN **38** 63-64

BROWN, IKE UTIL (**9**) DETA **9** 69-74

BROWN, JACKIE P/CH (23,17,31,28, 36,**41**) WASA **23** 70-71, TEXA **17/31** 73, **28** 74-75, CLEA **28/36** 75, **31** 75-76, MONN **31** 77, TEXA *CH* **41** 79-82, CHIA *CH* **36** 92, **41** 92-95, TBA **50** 02-03

BROWN, JAKE OF (**32**) SFN **32** 75

BROWN, JAMIE P (**52**) BOSA **52** 04

BROWN, JARVIS OF (1,**17**, 32) MINA **1** 91-92, SDN **17** 93, ATLN **17** 94, BALA **32** 95

BROWN, JIMMY INF (15,**3**,2,29) STLN **15** 37-38, **3** 39-43, PITN **2** 46, BOSN *CH* **29** 49-51

BROWN, JOPHERY P (47,**34**) CHIN **47/34** 68

BROWN, JUMBO P (19,**17**,28,24, 20) NYA **19** 32-33, **17** 35-36, CINN **17** 37, NYN **28** 37, **24** 38, **20** 39-41

BROWN, KEITH P (**38**,59) CINN **38** 88, 90-91, **59** 92

BROWN, (J.) KEVIN P
(43,41,**27**) TEXA **43** 86, **41** 88-94, BALA **41** 95, FLAN **27** 96-97, SDN **27** 98, LAN **27** 99-03, NYA **27** 04-05

BROWN, KEVIN (D.) P
(43,23,**30**,20, 16,15) NYN **43/23** 90, MILA **30** 90, **20** 91, **16** 91, SEAA **15/16** 92

BROWN, KEVIN (L.) C
(**6**,14,27,49, 38) TEXA **6** 96-97, TORA **14** 98-99, MILN **27** 00, **49** 01, BOSA **38** 02

BROWN, LARRY SS
(**16**,8,21,18) CLEA **16** 63-71, OAKA **8** 71-72, BALA **21** 73, TEXA **18** 74

BROWN, LEON OF
(**23**) NYN **23** 76

BROWN, LINDSAY (RED) SS
(**7**) BKNN **7** 37

BROWN, LLOYD (GIMPY) P
(17,14,22,26, **21**,28) WASA **17** 31, **14** 32, STLA **14** 33, BOSA **22/26** 33, CLEA **21** 34-37, PHIN **28** 40

BROWN, MACE P/CH
(50,**47**,25,28, 33) PITN **50** 35, **47** 36-39, **25** 40-41, BKNN **28/33** 41, BOSA **25** 42-43, 46, *CH* **33** 65

BROWN, MARK P
(**21**,27) BALA **21** 84, MINA **27** 85

BROWN, MARTY 3B
(**51**,28) CINN **51** 88-89, BALA **28** 90

BROWN, MIKE (C.) OF
(37,22,21,17, **4**,23) CALA **37** 83, **22/3** 84, **21** 85, PITN **17** 85, **4** 86, CALA **23** 88

BROWN, MIKE (G.) P
(**27**,37,47) BOSA **27** 82-86, SEAA **37** 86, **47** 87

BROWN, MIKE (C.orG.) CH
(**45**) CLEA *CH* **45** 02

BROWN, NORM P
(__,**31**) PHIA __ 43, **31** 46

BROWN, OLLIE (DOWNTOWN) OF
(48,**25**,26,15, 15,14,31,23) SFN **48** 65, **25** 65-68, SDN **26** 69-72, OAKA **15** 72, MILA **14** 72-73, HOUN **31** 74, PHIN **23** 74-77

BROWN, OSCAR OF
(36,**45**,20) ATLN **36** 69, **45** 70-72, **20** 73

BROWN, PAUL P
(26,23,**39**,33) PHIN **26** 61, **23** 62, **39** 62-63, **33** 68

BROWN, RANDY C
(**28**) CALA **28** 69-70

BROWN, ROOSEVELT OF
(**28**,24) CHIN **28** 99-01, **24** 02

BROWN, SCOTT P
(**53,43**) CINN **53/43** 81

BROWN, STEVE P
(**36**) CALA **36** 83-84

BROWN, TOM P
(**42**) SEAA **42** 78

BROWN, TOM 1B/OF
(**1**) WASA **1** 63

BROWN, TOMMY (BUCKSHOT) UTIL
(,9,33,**5**,37, 12) BKNN **9** 44-45, **33** 47-48, **5** 48-51, PHIN **37** 51, **5** 51-52, CHIN **12** 52-53

BROWN, WALTER P
(**36**) STLA **36** 47

BROWN, WILLARD OF
(**15**) STLA **15** 47

BROWNE, BYRON OF
(**29**,37,24) CHIN **29** 65-67, HOUN **37** 68, STLN **29** 69, PHIN **24** 70-72

BROWNE, EARL (SNITZ) OF/1B
(22,__,24,**8**) PITN **22** 35, __ 36, PHIN **24** 37, **8** 38

BROWNE, JERRY UTIL
(3,8,**14**,30) TEXA **3** 86, **8** 87-88, CLEA **14** 89-91, OAKA **30** 92-93, FLAN **14** 94-95

BROWNE, PIDGE 1B
(27,**17**) HOUN **27/17** 62

BROWNING, CAL P
(**23**) STLN **23** 60

BROWNING, TOM P
(54,**32**) CINN **54** 84, **32** 85-94, KCA **32** 95

BROWNSON, MARK P
(**32**) COLN **32** 98-99

BROXTON, JONATHAN P
(**51**) LAN **51** 05

BRUBAKER, BILL 3B
(**25**,15,23,27, 11) PITN **25** 32, **15** 33, **23** 33-34, **27** 35, **25** 36-39, **15** 40, BOSN **11** 43

BRUBAKER, BRUCE P
(**46**,31) LAN **46** 67, MILA **31** 70

BRUCE, BOB P
(20,32,**30**,42) DETA **20** 59, **32** 60-61, HOUN **30** 62-66, ATLN **42** 67

BRUCKBAUER, FRED P
(**38**) MINA **38** 61

BRUCKER, EARL, JR. C S
(**26**) PHIA **26** 48

BRUCKER, EARL, SR. C/CH F
(2,**9**,26,32,51) PHIA **2** 37, **9** 38-40, *CH* **26** 41-49, STLA *CH* **32** 50, CINN *CH/M* **51** 52

BRUETT, J. T. OF
(**26**) MINA **26** 92-93

BRUMBAUGH, CLIFF OF
(57,**35**) TEXA **57** 01, COLN **35** 01

BRUMFIELD, JACOB OF
(46,4,**5**,48,2) CINN **46** 92-93, **4** 94, PITN **5** 95-96, TORA **5** 96-97, LAN **48** 99, TORA **2** 99

BRUMLEY, DUFF P
(**39**) TEXA **39** 94

BRUMLEY, MIKE UTIL S
(17,**12**,7,10,4, 31, 36) CHIN **17** 87, DETA **12** 89, SEAA **7** 90, BOSA **10** 91-92, HOUN **4** 93, OAKA **31** 94, HOUN **36** 95

BRUMLEY, MIKE C F
(**8**) WASA **8** 64-66

BRUMMER, GLENN C
(**11**,7) STLN **11** 81-84, TEXA **7** 85

BRUMMET, GREG P
(50,57) SFN **50** 93, MINA **57** 93

BRUNANSKY, TOM (BRUNO) OF
(3,30,**24**,23, 18) CALA **3/30** 81, MINA **24** 82-88, STLN **23** 88-90, BOSA **23** 90-92, MILA **18** 93-94, BOSA **23** 94

BRUNDY, BRIAN P
(39,**30**) ARIN **39** 04, **30** 05

BRUNER, JACK P
(**49**,37) CHIA **49** 49-50, STLA **37** 50

BRUNER, ROY P
(**33**) PHIN **33** 39-40

BRUNET, GEORGE (LEFTY) P
(9,53,28,23, 30,27,31,33, 38,**43**,39,57, 34,22) KCA **9/53** 56, **28/23** 57, **30** 59, **27** 60, MILN **31** 60, **30** 60-61, HOUN **33** 62-63, BALA **28** 63, LAA **38** 64, **43** 64, CALA **43** 65-69, SEAA **39/57** 69, WASA **34** 70, PITN **22** 70, STLN **34** 71

BRUNETTE, JUSTIN P
(**56**) STLN **56** 00

BRUNEY, BRIAN P
(**30**) ARIN **30** 05

BRUNO, TOM P
(31,35,21,**49**) KCA **31/35** 76, TORA **21** 77, STLN **49** 78-79

BRUNSBERG, ARLO C
(**35**) DETA **35** 66

BRUNSON, WILL P
(**50**,58) LAN **50** 98, DETA **58** 98-99

BRUNTLETT, ERIC 2B
(**4**) HOUN **4** 03-05

BRUSKE, JIM P
(**45**,55,46,61, 88) LAN **45** 95-96, SDN **55** 97, LAN **46** 98, SDN **55** 98, NYA **61** 98, MILN **88** 00

BRUSSTAR, WARREN P
(**40**,46,41) PHIN **40** 77-82, CHIA **46** 82, CHIN **41** 83-85

BRUTON, BILLY OF
(**38**) MILN **38** 53-60, DETA **38** 61-64

BRYAN, BILLY C
(5,18,**9**,23,50, 14) KCA **5** 61, **18** 61-63, **9** 64-66, NYA **23** 66-67, **50** 67, WASA **14** 68

BRYANT, CLAY P/CH
(**18**,10,2,63,3) CHIN **18** 35-40, LAN *CH* **10** 61, CLEA *CH* **2** 67, **63** 72, **3** 74

BRYANT, DEREK OF/DH
(**23**) OAKA **23** 79

BRYANT, DON C/CH
(29,**46**) LAN **29** 85, **46** 86-87

BRYANT, RALPH OF
(35,36) PITN **35/36** 64

BRYANT, RON P
(45,49,26,34, **32**) SFN **45/49** 67, **26** 69-70, **34** 70, **32** 70-75, STLN **32** 75

BRYDEN, T. R. P
(63,**47**) CALA **63/47** 86

BRYE, STEVE OF
(37,**11**,46) MINA **37** 70-71, **11** 72-76, MILA **11** 77, PITN **46** 78

BUBELA, JAIME OF
(**62**) SEAA **62** 05

BUCHA, JOHNNY C
(24,**15**,32) STLN **24** 48, **15** 50, DETA **32** 53

BUCHANAN, BOB P
(51,**45**) CINN **51** 85, KCA **45** 89

BUCHANAN, BRIAN OF
(**30**,34,10) MINA **30** 00-02, SDN **34** 02-04, NYN **10** 04

BUCHEK, JERRY SS
(17,**11**,1) STLN **17** 61, **11** 63-66, NYN **1** 67-68

BUCHER, JIM UTIL
(**2**,30,24,5) BKNN **2** 34-37, STLN **30** 38, BOSA **24** 44, **5** 45

BUCK, JOHN C
(**2**) KCA **2** 04-05

BUCKLES, GARY P
(**59**) STLN **59** 94

BUCKLEY, KEVIN DH
(**20**) TEXA **20** 84

BUCKNER, BILL (BILLY BUCK) OF/1B/CH
(38,**22**,16,6,14) LAN **38** 69, **22** 70-76, CHIN **22** 77-84, BOSA **16** 84, **6** 85-87, CALA **6** 87-88, KCA **14** 88-89, BOSA **22** 90, CHIA *CH* **22** 96-97, *CH* __ 98

BUDASKA, MARK OF
(**17**,15) OAKA **17** 78, **15** 81

BUDDIE, MIKE P
(52,**41**,47) NYA **52** 98, **41** 99, MILN **41** 00, **47** 01-02

BUDDIN, DON SS
(**24**,1,18,8) BOSA **24** 56, 58-59, **1** 60-61, HOUN **18** 62, DETA **8** 62

BUDNICK, MIKE P
(25,40) NYN **25** 46, **40** 47

BUDZINSKI, MIKE OF
(**53**) CINN **53** 03

BUECHELE, STEVE 3B
(**22**,27,24) TEXA **22** 85-91, PITN **27** 91, **22** 91-92, CHIN **24** 92-95, TEXA **24** 95

BUEHRLE, MARK P
(**56**) CHIA **56** 00-05

BUFORD, DAMON OF S
(18,26,**2**,9) BALA **18** 93-94, **26** 95, NYN **2** 95, TEXA **2** 96-97, BOSA **2** 98-99, CHIN **9** 00-01

BUFORD, DON UTIL/CH F
(24,7,**9**,6,2,73, 13,12) CHIA **24** 63-64, **7** 65-67, BALA **9** 68-72, SFN *CH* **9** 81-83, *CH* **6** 84, BALA *CH* **2** 88, **73/13** 94, WASN *CH* **12** 05

BUHL, BOB P
(**10**,31,30) MILN **10** 53-62, CHIN **31** 62-66, PHIN **30** 66-67

BUHNER, JAY OF
(54,43,**19**) NYA **54** 87-88, SEAA **43** 88, **19** 89-01

BUICE, DEWAYNE P
(**41**,38) CALA **41** 87-88, TORA **38** 89

BUKER, CY P
(23,**19**) BKNN **23/19** 45

BUKVICH, RYAN P
(**35**) KCA **35** 02-04, TEXA **35** 05

BULGER, JASON P
(**50**) ARIN **50** 05

BULLARD, GEORGE (CURLY) SS
(**50**) DETA **50** 54

BULLETT, SCOTT OF
(47,**10**) PITN **47** 91, 93, CHIN **10** 95-96

BULLING, TERRY (BUD) C
(**11**,9) MINA **11** 77, SEAA **9** 81, **11** 82-83

BULLINGER, BRYAN P
(**60**) PITN **60** 05

BULLINGER, JIM P
(**52**,44) CHIN **52** 92-96, MONN **52** 97, SEAA **44** 98

BULLINGER, KIRK P
(38,**33**,56) MONN **38** 98, BOSA **33** 99, PHIN **33** 00, HOUN **56** 03-04

BULLOCK, ERIC OF/DH
(**9**,36,23,38, 27) HOUN **9** 85-86, MINA **36** 88, PHIN **23** 89, MONN **38** 90-91, **27** 92

BULLOCK, RED P
(**16**) PHIA **16** 36

BUMBRY, AL OF/CH
(**1**,4,37) BALA **1** 72-84, SDN **4** 85, BOSA *CH* **37** 88-93, BALA *CH* **1** 95, CLEA *CH* **1** 98, 02

BUMP, NATE P
(**40**) FLAN **40** 03-05

BUNCH, MELVIN P
(**50**,52,31) KCA **50** 95, **52** 96, SEAA **31** 99

BUNDY, LORENZO CH
(**20**,__) COLN *CH* **20** 99, ARIN __ 04

BUNKER, WALLY P
(35,**27**) BALA **35** 63, **27** 64-68, KCA **27** 69-71

BUNNING, JIM P
(15,**14**,38,17) DETA **15** 55, **41** 56, **14** 56-63, PHIN **14** 64-67, PITN **14** 68-69, LAN **38/17** 69, PHIN **14** 70-71

BURBA, DAVE P
(**34**,16,43) SEAA **34** 90-91, SFN **34** 92-95, CINN **34** 95-97, CLEA **34** 98-01, TEXA **16** 02, CLEA **34** 02, MILN **43** 03-04, SFN **43** 04

BURBACH, BILL P
(**50**) NYA **50** 69-71

BURBRINK, NELS C
(**18**) STLN **18** 55

BURCHART, LARRY P
(**36**) CLEA **36** 69

BURDA, BOB OF/1B
(24,25,31,**19**, 10,3) STLN **24** 62, SFN **25** 65, **31** 65-66, **19** 69-70, MILA **19** 70, STLN **10** 71, BOSA **3** 72

BURDETTE, FREDDIE P
(**42**) CHIN **42** 62-64

BURDETTE, LEW P/CH
(27,**33**,30,32, 5) NYA **27** 50, BOSN **33** 51-52, MILN **33** 53-63, STLN **33** 63-64, CHIN **33** 64-65, PHIN **30** 65, CALA **32** 66-67, ATLN *CH* **5** 72, *CH* **33** 73

BURGESS, SMOKY C
(4,8,11,21,7, **6**,49,2) CHIN **4/8** 49, **11** 51, PHIN **21** 52-55, CINN **7** 55-58, PITN **6** 59-64, CHIA **49** 64, **2** 65-67

BURGESS, TOM (TIM) OF/CH
(28,**15**,53,14) STLN **28** 54, LAA **15** 62, NYN *CH* **53** 77, ATLN *CH* **14** 78

BURGMEIER, TOM P/CH
(39,34,22,19, **16**,39,43) CALA **39** 68, KCA **34** 69, **22** 70-73, MINA **19** 74-77, BOSA **16** 78-82, OAKA **39** 83-84, KCA *CH* **39** 91, **43** 96, 98-00

BURGO, BILL OF
(**11**) PHIA **11** 43-44

BURGOS, AMBIORIX P
(**50**) KCA **50** 05

BURGOS, ENRIQUE P
(**51**) KCA **51** 93, SFN **51** 95

BURICH, BILL INF
(**5**,__) PHIN **5** 42, __ 46

BURK, MACK C
(**34**) PHIN **34** 56, 58

BURKART, ELMER (SWEDE) P
(__,26,14,**35**) PHIN __ 36, **26** 37, __ 38, **14/35** 39

BURKE, BOBBY (LEFTY) P
(19,17,**18**,12, 45) WASA **19** 31-32, **17** 32, **18** 33-35, **12** 35, PHIN **45** 37

BURKE, CHRIS 2B/UTIL
(**2**) HOUN **2** 04-05

BURKE, GLENN OF
(**3**,4,14) LAN **3** 76-78, OAKA **4** 78, **14** 78-79

BURKE, JAMIE C
(19,**27**) ANAA **19** 01, CHIA **27** 03-05

BURKE, JIMMY (SUNSET JIMMY) CH
(30,31) NYA *CH* **30** 30, *CH* **31** 31, *CH* **30** 32, **31** 33

BURKE, JOHN P
(**37**) COLN **37** 96-97

BURKE, LEO UTIL
(19,23,22,16, 18,**15**) BALA **19** 58, **23** 59, LAA **22** 61, **16** 62, STLN **18** 63, CHIN **15** 63-65

BURKE, STEVE P
(**39**) SEAA **39** 77-78

BURKE, TIM P
(54,**44**,41) MONN **54** 85, **44** 85-91, NYN **44** 91-92, NYA **41** 92

BURKETT, JOHN P
(40,51,32,**33**) SFN **40** 87, **51** 87-89, **32** 90, **33** 90-94, FLAN **33** 95-96, TEXA **33** 96-99, ATLN **19** 00-01, BOSA **19** 02-03

BURKHART, KEN P
(**10**,42,48) STLN **10** 45-46, **42** 46, **10** 47-48, CINN **48** 48, **48** 49

BURKHART, MORGAN DH/1B
(**54**,33) BOSA **54** 00-01, KCA **33** 03

BURKS, ELLIS OF/DH
(12,**26**,23,25) BOSA **12** 87-92, CHIA **26** 93, COLN **26** 94-98, SFN **23** 98-00, CLEVE **23** 01-03, BOSA **25** 04

BURLESON, RICK (ROOSTER) SS
(**7**,17,20,39) BOSA **7** 74-80, CALA **7** 81-86, BALA **17** 87, OAKA *CH* **20** 91, BOSA *CH* **7** 92-93, CALA *CH* **39** 95-96

BURNETT, A. J. P
(43,**34**) FLAN **43** 99-02, **34** 02-05

BURNETT, JOHNNY INF
(39,**1**,4) CLEA **39** 30, **1** 31-34, STLA **4** 35

BURNETT, SEAN P
(**61**) PITN **61** 04

BURNETTE, WALLY P
(23,**24**) KCA **23** 56-57, **24** 57-58

BURNITZ, JEROMY OF
(5,23,**20**,21, 35,3) NYN **5** 93-94, CLEA **23** 95, **20** 96, MILA **20** 96-01, NYN **20** 02-03, LAN **21** 03, COLN **35** 04, CHIN **3** 05

BURNS, BRITT P
(50,25,**40**) CHIA **50/25** 78, **40** 78-85

BURNS, GEORGE (TIOGA GEORGE) PH
(**21**) NYA **21** 29

BURNS, JACK (SLUG) 1B/CH
(**2**,29,22,31) STLA **2** 31-36, DETA **29/22** 36, BOSA *CH* **31** 55-59

BURNS, JOE 3B
(14,**22**,13) BOSN **14** 43, PHIA **22/13** 44-45

BURNS, MIKE P
(**53**) HOUN **53** 05

BURNS, TODD P
(**54**,28,41) OAKA **54** 88-91, TEXA **28** 92-93, STLN **41** 93

BURNSIDE, PETE P
(39,35,19,16, 20,18) NYN **39** 55, **35** 57, SFN **35** 58, DETA **19** 59-60, WASA **16** 61-62, BALA **20** 63, WASA **18** 63

BURNSIDE, SHELDON P
(**42**,34) DETA **42** 78-80, CINN **34** 80

BURPO, GEORGE OF
(**42**) CINN **42** 46

BURRELL, PAT OF
(33,**5**) PHIN **33** 00, **5** 01-05

BURRIGHT, LARRY (POSSUM) INF
(11,**6**) LAN **11** 62, NYN **6** 63-64

BURRIS, PAUL C
(11,**14**) BOSN **11** 48, **14** 50, **14** 52, MILN **14** 53

BURRIS, RAY P/CH
(**34**,53,36,26, 48, 20,35,50) CHIN **34** 73-79, NYA **53** 79, NYN **36** 79, **26** 79-80, **34** 80, MONN **48** 81-83, OAKA **48** 84, MILA **20/48** 85, STLN **35** 86, MILA **48** 87, *CH* **50** 90-91, TEXA *CH* **50** 92

BURROUGHS, JEFF OF
(**20**,7,5,3,44) WASA **20** 70-71, TEXA **20** 72-76, ATLN **7** 77-80, SEAA **5** 81, OAKA **3** 82-84, TORA **44** 85

BURROUGHS, SEAN 3B/2B
(21,**33**,32) SDN **21** 02, **33** 03, **32** 04, **33** 05

BURROWS, JOHN P
(31,37,**36**) PHIA **31** 43, CHIN **37** 43, **36** 43-44

BURROWS, TERRY P
(**38**,53,39,33) TEXA **38** 94-95, **53** 95, **38** 95, MILA **39** 96, SDN **33** 97

BURTON, ELLIS OF
(32,11,29,19 **21**,24) STLN **32** 58, **11** 60, CLEA **29** 63, CHIN **19** 63, **21** 63-64, **24** 65

BURTON, JIM P
(43) BOSA **43** 75, 77
BURTSCHY, MOE P
(26,**38**,33,27, 36) PHIA **26** 50, **38** 50-51, **33** 54, KCA **33** 54, **27** 55, **36** 56
BURTT, DENNIS P
(17) MINA **17** 85-86
BURWELL, BILL CH/M
(30,39,2,**41**) BOSA *CH* **30** 44, PITN *CH/M* **39** 47, *CH* **2** 48, *CH* **41** 58-62
BURWELL, DICK P
(34) CHIN **34** 60-61
BUSBY, JIM (CHOPPY) OF
(47,3,14,7,**4**, 5,31,23,33, 16,41,3,8,32) CHIA **47** 50, **3** 51-52, WASA **14** 52,**7** 53-54, **4** 55, CHIA **5** 55, CLEA **31** 56-57, BALA **23** 57, **33** 58,BOSA **7** 59-60, BALA **16** 60-61,HOUN **4** 62-64, *CH* 62-64, *CH* **4/41** 65, *CH* **5** 66, **3** 66-67, ATLN *CH* **8** 68-75, CHIA *CH* **32** 76, SEAA *CH* **33** 77-78
BUSBY, MIKE P
(57,**54**) STLN **57** 96, **54** 97-00
BUSBY, PAUL (RED) OF
(**6**,9) PHIN **6** 41, **9** 43
BUSBY, STEVE P
(40) KCA **40** 72-76, 80
BUSCH, ED SS
(2) PHIA **2** 43-45
BUSCH, MIKE 3B/OF
(25) LAN **25** 95-96
BUSCHHORN, DON P
(20) KCA **29** 65
BUSH, DAVE P
(49) TORA **49** 04-05
BUSH, DONIE M
(**22**,35) CHIA *M* **22** 31, CINN *M* **35** 33
BUSH, GUY (MISSISSIPPI MUDCAT) P
(24,14,**17**,41, 25,18,36) CHIN **24/14** 32, **17** 33-34, PITN **41** 35-36, BOSN **25** 36, **18** 37, STLN **17** 38, CINN **36** 45
BUSH, HOMER 2B/INF
(38,69,22,**18**, 8) NYA **38** 97, **69/22** 98, TORA **18** 99-02, FLAN **8** 02, NYA **18** 04
BUSH, RANDY UTIL
(25) MINA **25** 82-93
BUSHING, CHRIS P
(61) CINN **61** 93
BUSKEY, MIKE SS
(30,**43**) PHIN **30/43** 77
BUSKEY, TOM P
(29,**35**,44) NYA **29** 73-74, CLEA **35** 74-77, TORA **44** 78-80
BUSSE, RAY INF
(**16**,5) HOUN **16** 71, STLN **5** 73, HOUN **16** 73-74
BUTCHER, JOHN P
(**29**,50,32,44) TEXA **29** 80-83, **50/29** 82, MINA **32** 84-86, CLEA **44/32/38** 86
BUTCHER, MAX P
(30,15,17,24 40,8,16,**19**) BKNN **30** 36, **15** 37, **17** 38, PHIN **24** 38, **8/16** 39, PITN **40** 39, **19** 40-45
BUTCHER, MIKE P
(48,**23**) CALA **48** 92, **23** 92-95
BUTERA, SAL C
(**11**,25,33,22, 33,26) MINA **11** 80-82, DETA **25** 83, MONN **33** 84, **11** 85, CINN **22** 86-87, MINA **33** 87, TORA **33/26** 88, *CH* **22** 98
BUTKA, ED (BABE) 1B
(36,**26**) WASA **36** 43, **26** 44
BUTLAND, BILL P
(27,**28**,24,) BOSA **27/28** 40, **24** 42, **28** 46, **27** 47
BUTLER, ADAM P
(50) ATLN **50** 98
BUTLER, BILL P
(**29**,35,17,37) KCA **29** 69-71, CLEA **35** 72, MINA **17** 74-75, **37** 77
BUTLER, BRENT INF
(2,**5**) COLN **2** 01, **5** 02-03
BUTLER, BRETT OF
(**22**,2,12) ATLN **22** 81-83, CLEA **2** 84-87, SFN **2** 88-90, LAN **22** 91-94, NYN **22** 95, LAN **12/22** 95, **22** 96-97, ARIN *CH* **2** 05
BUTLER, CECIL (SLEWFOOT) P
(**22**,32) MILN **22** 62, **32** 64
BUTLER, CHARLIE P
(__) PHIN __ 33
BUTLER, JOHNNY (TROLLEY LINE) CH
(27) CHIA *CH* **27** 32
BUTLER, RICH OF B
(12,**10**) TORA **12** 97, TBA **10** 98-99
BUTLER, ROB OF B
(**2**,5,20) TORA **2** 93-94, PHIN **5** 97, TORA **20** 99
BUTTERFIELD, BRIAN CH
(55) NYA *CH* **55** 94-95, ARIN *CH* **55** 98-00, 02-03, TORA *CH* **55** 04-05
BUTTERS, TOM P
(30,36,**31**) PITN **30** 62, **36** 63-64, **31** 64-65
BUXTON, RALPH (BUCK) P
(25,**12**) PHIA **25** 38, NYA **12** 49
BUZAS, JOE SS
(12) NYA **12** 45
BUZHARDT, JOHN P
(23,38,**30**,49, 19,26,33) CHIN **23** 58, **38** 59, PHIN **23** 60-61, CHIA **30** 62-67, BALA **49/30/19** 67, HOUN **26** 67, **30/33** 68

BYERLY, BUD P
(27,38,14,40, **11**,15,36) STLN **27** 43-45, CINN **38** 50-52, WASA **14/40** 56, **11** 56-58, BOSA **15** 58, SFN **36** 59-60
BYERS, RANDY OF
(47) SDN **47** 87-88
BYNUM, FREDDIE INF
(49) OAKA **49** 05
BYNUM, MIKE P
(54) SDN **54** 02-04
BYRD, HARRY P
(36,**39**,19,24, 32,11) PHIA **36** 50, **39** 50-53, NYA **19** 54, BALA **24** 55, CHIA **24** 55, **32** 55-56, DETA **11** 57
BYRD, JEFF P
(27) TORA **27** 77
BYRD, JIM DH
(61) BOSA **61** 93
BYRD, MARLON OF
(**29**,26) PHIN **29** 02-05, WASN **26** 05
BYRD, PAUL P
(43,45,34,**36**) NYN **43** 95-96, ATLN **45** 97-98, PHIN **34** 98-01, KCA **36** 01-02, ATLN **36** 03-04, LAA **36** 05
BYRD, SAMMY (BABE RUTH'S LEGS) OF
(27,26,29,24, **25**,12, 8) NYA **27** 29, **26** 30, **29** 31, **24** 32, **25** 33-34, **12** 35, CINN **8** 36
BYRDAK, TIM P
(55,**58**,40) KCA **55** 98, **58** 99-00, BALA **40** 05
BYRNE, TOMMY (GOOFY) P
(11,39,**28**,40, 15,27,30,23) NYA **11** 43, **39** 46, **28** 46-51, STLA **40** 51, **15** 51-52, CHIA **27** 53, WASA **27/30** 53, NYA **23** 54-57
BYRNES, ERIC OF/DH
(**22**,35,15)) OAKA **22** 00-05, COLN **35** 05, BALA **15** 05
BYRNES, MILT (SKIPPY) OF
(11) STLA **11** 43-45
BYSTROM, MARTY P
(39,**50**,53) PHIN **39** 80, **50** 80-84, NYA **53** 84-85, **50** 85

C

CABALLERO, RALPH (PUTSY) 3B
(20,28,27,2, 9,**3**) PHIN **20** 44, **28** 45, **27** 47, **2** 48, **9** 49, **3** 50-52
CABELL, ENOS 1B/3B
(24,**23**,21) BALA **24** 72-74, HOUN **23** 75-80, SFN **23** 81, DETA **21** 82-83, HOUN **23** 84-85, LAN **23** 85-86
CABRERA, ALEX INF
(39) ARIN **39** 00
CABRERA, DANIEL P
(35) BALA **35** 04-05
CABRERA, FERNANDO P
(64,**56**) CLEA **64** 04, **56** 05
CABRERA, FRANCISCO 1B/C
(21,**19**) TORA **21** 89, ATLN **19** 89-93
CABRERA, JOLBERT SS/UTIL
(**6**,10,50,12) CLEA **6** 98-01, **10** 02, LAN **50** 02, **6** 03, SEAA **12** 04
CABRERA, JOSE P
(**51**,32,49) HOUN **51** 97-00, ATLN **32** 01, MILN **49** 02
CABRERA, MELKY OF
(39) NYA **39** 05
CABRERA, MIGUEL OF/3B
(20,**24**) FLAN **20** 03, **24** 04-05
CABRERA, ORLANDO SS
(2,**18**,36,44) MONN **2** 97-98, **18** 99-04, BOSA **36/44** 04, LAA **18** 05
CACEK, CRAIG 1B
(6) HOUN **6** 77
CACERES, EDGAR 2B
(46) KCA **46** 95
CADARET, GREG P
(32,**25**,31,24, 15,36) OAKA **32** 87-89, NYA **25** 89-92, CINN **25** 93, KCA **31** 93, TORA **24** 94, DETA **15** 94, ANAA **36** 97-98, TEXA **36** 98, ANAA **38** 00
CAFEGO, TOM OF
(37) STLA **37** 37
CAFFIE, JOE (RABBIT) OF
(**33**,34) CLEA **33** 56-57, **34** 57
CAGE, WAYNE DH/1B
(31) CLEA **31** 78-79
CAIN, BOB (SUGAR) P
(56,21,31,33, 16) CHIA **56** 49-51, DETA **21/31/23** 51, STLA **33** 52-53, CHIA **16** 54
CAIN, LES P
(38) DETA **38** 68, 70-72
CAIN, MATT P
(43) SFN **43** 05
CAIN, SUGAR P
(**16**,11,12,19, 17) PHIA **16** 32-35, **11** 34-35, STLA **12** 35, **19** 36, CHIA **17** 36-38
CAIRNCROSS, CAMERON P
(62) CLEA **62** 00-01
CAIRO, MIGUEL 2B/SS
(3,20,13,1,40 **41**,12) TORA **3** 96, CHIN **20** 97, TBA **20** 98, **13** 98-00, **1** 00, CHIN **40** 01, STLN **41** 01-03, **12** 03, NYA **41** 04, NYN **3** 05
CAITHAMER, GEORGE (SIDEL) C
(__) CHIA __ 34
CALDERON, IVAN OF
(13,**22**,49,27, 23) SEAA **13** 84-85, **22** 85, **49** 86, CHIA **22** 86-90, MONN **27** 91, **22** 91-92, BOSA **23** 93, CHIA **27** 93
CALDERONE, SAM C
(6,36,5,42,8) NYN **6** 50, **36/5** 53, MILN **42/8** 54

CALDWELL, BRUCE P
(no#) BKNN **no#** 32
CALDWELL, EARL (TEACH) P
(16,20,**46**,36) STLA **16** 35, **20** 36-37, CHIA **46** 45-48, BOSA **36/20** 48
CALDWELL, MIKE P
(23,37,44,**48**) SDN **23** 71-73, SFN **37** 74-76, CINN **44** 77,MILA **48** 77-84
CALERO, KIKO P
(**40**,50) STLN **40** 03-04, OAKA **50** 05
CALHOUN, JEFF P
(**49**,31) HOUN **49** 84-86, PHIN **31** 87-88
CALI, CARMEN P
(68,**54**) STLN **68** 04, **54** 05
CALIGIURI, FRED P
(23) PHIA **23** 41-42
CALLAHAN, BEN P
(48) OAKA **48** 83
CALLAHAN, JOE P
(34,**30**) BOSN **34** 39, **30** 40
CALLAWAY, MICKEY P
(61,**51**,36) TBA **61** 99, **51** 01, ANAA **51** 02-03, TEXA **36** 03-04
CALLISON, JOHNNY OF
(9,**6**,25) CHIA **9** 58-59, PHIN **6** 60-69, CHIN **6** 70-71, NYA **25** 72-73
CALLOWAY, RON OF
(53,**22**) MONN **53** 03, **22** 03-04
CALMUS, DICK P
(34,45,**35**) BKNN **34** 63, CHIN **45/35** 67
CALVERT, MARK P
(50,25,**32**) SFN **50/25** 83, **32** 83-84
CALVERT, PAUL P
(__,47,**33**,20, 31) CLEA __ 42, **47** 43, **33** 44-45, WASA **20** 49, DETA **31** 50-51
CALZADO, NAPOLEON OF
(37) BALA **37** 05
CAMACHO, ERNIE P
(53,47,40,**13**, 62) OAKA **53** 80, PITN **47** 81, CLEA **40** 83-84, **13** 84-87, HOUN **13** 88, SFN **13** 89-90, STLN **62** 90
CAMACHO, JOE CH
(40) WASA *CH* **40** 69-71, TEXA **40** 72
CAMBRIA, FRED P
(50,**36**) PITN **50/36** 70
CAMELLI, HANK C
(22,**10**) PITN **22** 43, **10** 44-46, BOSN **22** 47
CAMERON, MIKE OF
(24,**44**,9) CHIA **24** 95-96, 98, CINN **44** 99, SEAA **9** 00, **44** 00-03, NYN **44** 04-05
CAMILLI, DOLPH 1B F
(41,24,**4**,28) CHIN **41** 33-34, PHIN **24** 34, **24** 35-37, BKNN **4** 38-43, BOSA **28** 45
CAMILLI, DOUG C S
(**35**,29,21,44, 12,34) LAN **35** 60-64, WASA **29** 65, **21** 66-67, *CH* **44/12** 68, BOSA *CH* **34** 70-73
CAMILLI, LOU 3B
(17) CLEA **17** 69-72
CAMINITI, KEN 3B
(**11**,21) HOUN **11** 87-94, SDN **21** 95-98, HOUN **11** 99-00, TEXA **11** 01, ATLN **11** 01
CAMMACK, ERIC P
(29) NYN **29** 00-01
CAMP, RICK P
(33,**37**) ATLN **33** 76-78, **37** 80-85
CAMP, SHAWN P
(58) KCA **58** 05
CAMP, STEVE P
(68,**58**) KCA **68/58** 04
CAMPANELLA, ROY (CAMPY) C
(33,**39**) BKNN **33** 48, **39** 48-57, LAN **39** 58
CAMPANERIS, BERT (CAMPY) SS
(**19**,56) KCA **19** 64-67, OAKA **19** 68-76, TEXA **19** 77-79, CALA **19** 79-81, NYA **56** 83
CAMPANIS, AL 2B F
(3) BKNN **3** 43
CAMPANIS, JIM C S
(31,25,20,4) LAN **31** 66, **25** 67-68, KCA **20** 69-70, PITN **4** 73
CAMPBELL, BILL P/CH
(24,22,**39**,29, 32) MINA **24** 73-76, BOSA **22** 77-81, CHIN **39** 82-83, PHIN **29/39** 84, STLN **39** 85, DETA **39** 86, MONN **32/39** 87, MILN *CH* **39** 99
CAMPBELL, BRUCE (SOUPY) OF
(__,**9**,**4**,3,35, 23,20) CHIA __ 31, **9** 32, STLA **4** 32-33, **3** 34, CLEA **35** 35-36, **23** 37-39, DETA **20** 40-41, WASA **3** 42
CAMPBELL, CLARENCE (SOUP) OF
(34) CLEA **34** 40-41
CAMPBELL, DAVE INF
(33,**10**,18,20) DETA **33** 67-69, SDN **10** 70-73, STLN **18/10** 73, HOUN **20** 73-74
CAMPBELL, DAVE P
(32) ATLN **32** 77-78
CAMPBELL, GILLY C
(15,19,**1**,35,8) CHIN **15** 33, CINN **19** 35, **1** 36-37, **35** 37, BKNN **8** 38
CAMPBELL, JIM C
(9) HOUN **9** 62-63
CAMPBELL, JIM PH
(10) STLN **10** 70
CAMPBELL, JIM P
(57) KCA **57** 90

CAMPBELL, JOE OF
(25) CHIN **25** 67
CAMPBELL, JOHN P
(26) WASA **26** 33
CAMPBELL, KEVIN P
(55,52) OAKA **55** 91-93, MINA **52** 94-95
CAMPBELL, MIKE P
(54,**27**,24,48, 33) SEAA **54** 87, **27** 88-89, TEXA **24** 92, SDN **48** 94, CHIN **33** 96
CAMPBELL, PAUL 1B
(37,**15**,46,2) BOSA **37** 41, **15** 42, **46** 46, DETA **2** 48, **15** 49-50
CAMPBELL, RON INF
(7,15,**23**) CHIN **7** 64, **15** 65, **23** 66
CAMPER, CARDELL P
(49) CLEA **49** 77
CAMPILLO, JORGE P
(49) SEAA **49** 05
CAMPISI, SAL P
(**30**,19) STLN **30** 69-70, MINA **19** 71
CAMPOS, FRANK OF
(25) WASA **25** 51-53
CAMPUSANO, SIL OF
(**6**,11) TORA **6** 88, PHIN **6** 90, **11** 91
CANALE, GEORGE 1B
(**33**,22) MILA **33** 89-90, **22** 90-91
CANATE, WILLIAM OF
(21) TORA **21** 93
CANCEL, ROBINSON C
(50) MILN **50** 99, (00)
CANDAELE, CASEY 2B
(9,5,**1**,26) MONN **9** 86-88, **5** 88, HOUN **1** 88, 90-93, CLEA **26** 96-97
CANDELARIA, JOHN (CANDY MAN) P
(49,50,**45**,35, 48,54) PITN **49/50** 75, **45** 75-85, CALA **45** 85-87, NYN **45** 87, NYA **45** 88-89, MONN **45** 89, MINA **35/45** 90, TORA **48** 90, LAN **54** 91-92, PITN **45** 93
CANDINI, MILO P
(41,20,14,13, **19**,18) WASA **41/20** 43, **14** 44, **20** 46-47, **13** 47, **19** 48-49, PHIN **18** 50-51
CANDIOTTI, TOM P
(49) MILA **49** 83-84, CLEA **49** 86-91, TORA **49** 91, LAN **49** 92-97, OAKA **49** 98-99, CLEA **49** 99
CANEIRA, JOHN P
(39) CALA **39** 77-78
CANGELOSI, JOHN OF
(33,**44**,15,22, 27,28,23) CHIA **33** 85, **44** 86, PITN **22** 87, **44** 87-90, TEXA **15** 92, NYN **44** 94, HOUN **27** 95-96, FLAN **28** 97-98, COLN **23** 99
CANIZARO, JAY 2B
(36,**18**) SFN **36** 96, **18** 99, MINA **1** 00, (01), 02
CANNIZZARO, CHRIS C/CH
(34,**8**,5,16, 43,14,10,7,6) STLN **34** 60-61, NYN **8** 62-64, **5** 65, PITN **16** 68, SDN **8** 69-71, CHIN **43** 71, LAN **14** 72-73, SDN **10/8** 74, ATLN *CH* **7** 76, *CH* **6** 76-77, **8** 78
CANNON, JOE OF
(20,30) HOUN **20** 77-78, TORA **30** 79-80
CANO, JOSE P
(52) HOUN **52** 89
CANO, ROBINSON 2B
(14,**22**) NYA **14/22** 05
CANSECO, JOSE OF/DH B
(**33**,00,44,31) OAKA **33** 85-92, TEXA **33** 92-94, BOSA **33** 95-96, OAKA **33** 97, TORA **00/44/33** 98, TBA **33** 99-00, NYA **33** 00, CHIA **31** 01
CANSECO, OZZIE OF B
(55,46,48) OAKA **55** 90, STLN **46** 92, **48** 93
CANTU, JORGE 2B/SS
(59,**3**) TBA **59** 04, **3** 05
CANTWELL, BEN P
(15,**16**,12,19, 27) BOSN **15** 32, **16** 33-36, **12** 34, NYN **19** 37, BKNN **27** 37
CAPEL, MIKE P
(38,**35**) CHIN **38** 88, MILA **35** 90, HOUN **35** 91
CAPELLAN, JOSE P
(**34**,52) ATLN **34** 04, MILN **52** 05
CAPILLA, DOUG P
(26,**44**,35) STLN **26** 76-77, CINN **44** 77-79, CHIN **35** 79-81
CAPPS, MATT P
(62) PITN **62** 05
CAPPUZZELLO, GEORGE P
(41,52) DETA **41** 81, HOUN **52** 82
CAPRA, BUZZ P
(38,**47**) NYN **38** 71-73, ATLN **47** 74-77
CAPRA, NICK OF
(**4**,39,34,10) TEXA **4** 82-83, **39** 85, KCA **34** 88, TEXA **10** 91
CAPRI, PAT 2B
(21) BOSN **21** 44
CAPUANO, CHRIS P
(57,**39**) ARIN **57** 03, MILN **39** 04-05
CARABALLO, RAMON 2B
(15,25) ATLN **15** 93, STLN **25** 95
CARAWAY, PAT P
(16,**15**) CHIA **16** 31, **15** 32
CARBO, BERNIE OF
(25,12,**1**,7, 11,2) CINN **25** 69-72, STLN **12** 72, **1** 72-73, BOSA **1** 74-76, MILA **12** 76, BOSA **1** 77-78, CLEA **7** 78, STLN **11** 79-80, PITN **2** 80
CARDEN, JOHN P
(16) NYN **16** 46

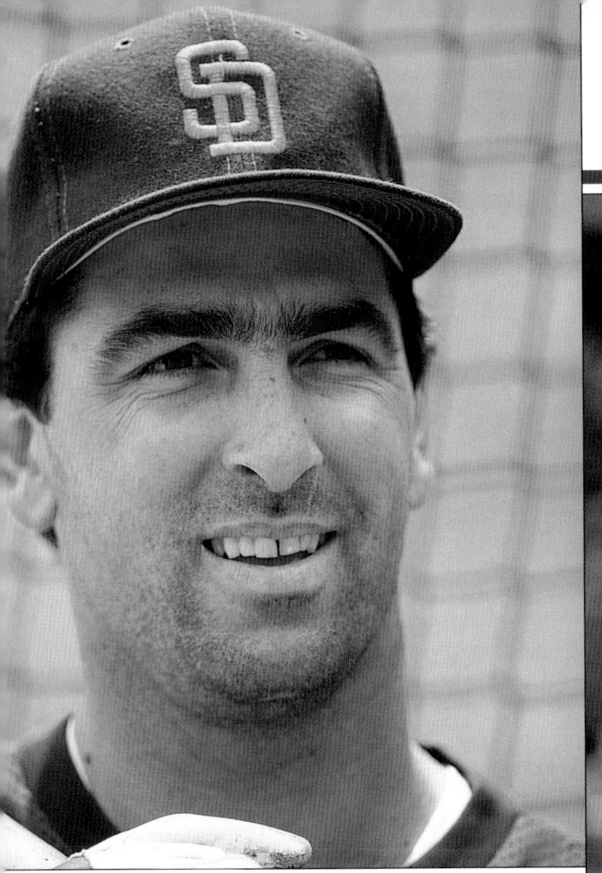

*Clark (Above) switched to #00 in San Diego where he led the league
lks for the third time. His career year was with the pennant-
ing Cardinals of 1987—35 HR, 136 BB, 106 RBI, .461 OBP and
SLG. Joe Carter (Right) led the league in RBI with 126 with the
ns. Everyone remembers his dramatic home run in the ninth
g of Game 6 to win the 1993 Series for Toronto. The quiet, efficient
r knocked in 100+ runs in 9 out of 11 years from 1986-1996. In
he missed with 98. Brett Butler (Below) scored over 100 runs in a
n 6 times, had an On Base Percentage of .400+ five times, stole
to 550 bases and bunted expertly. What a lead-off man!*

CARDENAL, JOSE OF/CH
(10,21,27,**1**,6,19, 00,8,53,7,33,2) SFN **10** 63-64, **21** 64, CALA **27** 65, **1** 66-67, CLEA **1** 68-69, STLN **1** 70-71, MILA **1** 71, CHIN **1** 72-77, PHIN **1** 78-79, NYN **6** 79-80, KCA **19** 80, CINN *CH* **00** 93, STLN *CH* **8** 94-95, NYA *CH* **53** 96-99, TBA *CH* **7** 00-01, CINN *CH* **33** 02, **2** 03

CARDENAS, LEO (CHICO) SS
(16,5,**17**,4,19) CINN **16** 67-68, MINA **5** 69-70, **17** 70-71, CALA **17** 72, CLEA **4** 73, TEXA **19** 74-75

CARDINAL, RANDY P
(**34**) HOUN **34** 63

CARDONA, JAVIER C
(53,**15**,29) DETA **53** 00-01, **15** 01, SDN **29** 02

CARDONI, BEN (BIG BEN) P
(26,**20**,25) BOSN **26** 43, **20** 44-45, **25** 45

CARDWELL, DON P
(46,**43**,30,27,29) PHIN **46** 57-60, CHIN **43** 60-62, PITN **30** 63-64, **43** 65-66, NYN **27** 67-70, ATLN **29** 70

CAREW, ROD 2B/1B /CH
(21,**29**) MINA **21** 67, **29** 67-78, CALA **29** 79-85, *CH* **29** 92-96, ANAA *CH* **29** 97-99, MINA *CH* **29** 00-01

CAREY, ANDY 3B
(54,**6**,1,7,21) NYA **54/6** 52, **6** 53-60, KCA **1** 60, **6** 61, CHIA **7** 61, LAN **21** 62

CAREY, MAX (SCOOPS) M
(**33**) BKNN *M* **33** 32-33

CAREY, PAUL 1B
(**88**) BALA **88** 93-94

CAREY, P. J. CH
(**46**) COLN **46** 97

CAREY, TOM (SCOOPS) 2B
(**14**,3) STLA **14** 35, **3** 36-37, BOSA **14** 39-42, 46

CARLETON, TEX P
(18,15,**16**,28) STLN **18** 32, **15** 33-34, CHIN **16** 35-38, BKNN **28** 40

CARLIN, JIM OF/3B
(**23**) PHIN **23** 41

CARLOS, CISCO P
(46,**30**,31,19) CHIA **46** 67, **30** 67-69, WASA **31** 69, **19** 70

CARLSEN, DON P
(16,**24**) CHIN **16** 48, PITN **24** 51-52

CARLSON, DAN P
(**29**,46,43) SFN **29** 96-97, TBA **46** 98, ARIN **43** 99

CARLTON, STEVE (LEFTY) P
(**32,**37,38) STLN **32** 65-71, PHIN **32** 72-86, SFN **32** 86, CHIA **37/32** 86, CLEA **32** 87, MINA **38** 87-88

CARLUCCI, DAVE CH
(**35**) BOSA *CH* **35** 96

CARLYLE, BUDDY P
(**58**) SDN **58** 99-00

CARMAN, DON P
(39,**42**,36,18) PHIN **39** 83-84, **42** 84-90, CINN **36** 91, TEXA **18** 92

CARMEL, DUKE OF
(**20**,43,28,1,27) STLN **20** 59, **43** 60, **28** 63, NYN **1** 63, NYA **27** 65

CARMONA, RAFAEL P
(32,**22**,26) SEAA **32/22** 95, **22** 96-97, SEAA **26** 99

CARNETT, EDDIE (LEFTY) OF/P
(20,**24**,42) BOSN **20** 41, CHIA **24** 44, CLEA **42** 45

CARNEVALE, DANNY CH
(**5**) KCA **5** 70

CARPENTER, BOB P
(22,28,12,20,33,32) NYN **22** 40, **28** 41, **12** 42, **20** 46, **33** 47, CHIN **32** 47

CARPENTER, BUBBA C
(**23**) COLN **23** 00

CARPENTER, CHRIS P
(50,**26**,29) TORA **50** 97-98, **26** 98-02, STLN (03), **29** 04-05

CARPENTER, CRIS P
(**44**,31,46,50) STLN **44** 88-92, FLAN **44** 93, TEXA **31** 93-94, MILA **46** 96

CARPENTER, LEW P
(**29**) WASA **29** 43

CARPIN, FRANK P
(20,42) PITN **20** 65, HOUN **42** 66

CARR, CHUCK OF
(1,27,43,**21**,24) NYN **1** 90, **27** 91, STLN **43** 92, FLAN **21** 93-95, MILA **24** 96-97, HOUN **21** 97

CARRARA, GIOVANNI P
(38,40,61,47,**55**,32) TORA **38** 95-96, CINN **40** 96, **61** 97, COLN **47** 00, LAN **55** 01-02, SEAA **32** 03, LAN **55** 04-05

CARRASCO, DANNY (D. J.) P
(59,**21**) KCA **59** 03-04, **21** 04-05

CARRASCO, HECTOR P
(56,**58**,24,29,48) CINN **56** 94, **58** 94-97, KCA **58** 97, MINA **24** 98, **58** 98-00, BOSA **58** 00, MINA **58** 01, BALA **29/58** 03, WASN **48** 05

CARRASQUEL, ALEX P
(14,19,**18**,58,34) WASA **14** 39-41, **19** 41, **18** 42-45, CHIA **58/34** 49

CARRASQUEL, CHICO SS
(**17**,1) CHIA **17** 50-55, CLEA **17** 56-58, KCA **1** 58, BALA **17** 59

CARRENO, AMALIO P
(**44**) PHIN **44** 91

CARREON, CAM C F
(44,**45**,7,35) CHIA **44** 59, **45** 60-64, CLEA **7** 65, BALA **35** 66

CARREON, MARK OF S
(32,**45**,15,46,4) NYN **32** 87-89, **45** 90-91, DETA **15** 92, SFN **45** 93-95, **46** 95, **45** 96, CLEA **4** 96

CARRILLO, MATIAS OF
(39,**25**) MILA **39** 91, FLAN **25** 93-94

CARRION, LEONEL CH
(**19**) MONN *CH* **19** 88

CARRITHERS, DON P
(**30**,40,18) SFN **30** 70-73, MONN **40** 74-76, **54** 75, MINA **18** 77

CARROLL, CLAY (HAWK) P
(20,**36**,33,34,48) MILN **20** 64-65, ATLN **20** 66-68, CINN **36** 68-75, CHIA **36** 76, STLN **33** 77, CHIA **34** 77, PITN **48** 78

CARROLL, JAMEY INF/2B
(**2**,5) MONN **2** 02-03, **5** 04, WASN **2** 05

CARROLL, OWNIE P
(11,17,**15**) NYA **11** 30, CINN **17** 32, BKNN **15** 33-34

CARROLL, TOM P
(**51**) CINN **51** 74-75

CARROLL, TOMMY SS
(**40**,14) NYA **40** 55-56, KCA **14** 59

CARSON, KIT OF
(**26**) CLEA **26** 34-35

CARSWELL, FRANK (WHEELS) OF
(**22**) DETA **22** 53

CARTER, ANDY P
(**50**) PHIN **50** 94-95

CARTER, ARNOLD (HOOK) P
(**33**) CINN **33** 44-45

CARTER, DICK CH
(**21**) PHIN *CH* **21** 59-60

CARTER, GARY (KID) C
(57,**8**) MONN **57** 74, **8** 75-84, NYN **8** 85-89, SFN **8** 90, LAN **8** 91, MONN **8** 92

CARTER, JEFF P
(**42**) CHIA **42** 91

CARTER, JOE OF/1B/DH
(33,30,17,**29**,43) CHIA **33** 83, CLEA **30** 84-89, SDN **17** 90, TORA **29** 91-97, **43** 97, BALA **29** 98, SFN **29** 98

CARTER, LANCE P
(53,**38**) KCA **53** 99, TBA **38** 02-05

CARTER, LARRY P
(**52**) SFN **52** 92

CARTER, SOL (BUCK) P
(**19**) PHIA **19** 31

CARTER, STEVE OF
(**42**) PITN **42** 89-90

CARTY, RICO OF/DH
(77,**43**,25,5,12,9,21,20) MILN **77** 64, **43** 64-65, ATLN **43** 66-67, ATLN **25** 69-70, 72, TEXA **5/25** 73, CHIN **43** 73, OAKA **12** 73, CLEA **9** 74-77, TORA **21** 78, OAKA **20** 78, TORA **21** 79

CARUSO, MIKE SS
(20,**17**,50) CHIA **20** 98, **17** 98-99, KCA **50** 02

CARVAJAL, MARCOS P
(**62**) COLN **62** 05

CARY, CHUCK P
(43,36,**51**,46) DETA **43** 85-86, ATLN **36** 87-88, NYA **51** 89-91, CHIA **46** 93

CARY, SCOTT P
(**23**) WASA **23** 47

CASALE, JERRY P
(**19**,40) BOSA **19** 58-60, LAA **40** 61, DETA **19** 61-62

CASANOVA, PAUL C
(32,20,22,**8**,5,15) WASA **32** 65, **20/22** 66, **8** 67-70, **5** 71, ATLN **15** 72, **5** 73-74

CASANOVA, RAUL DH/C
(**33**,25,57,31) DETA **33** 96-98, (99), MILN **25** 00-02, BALA **57** 02, CHIA **31** 05

CASCARELLA, JOE (CROONIN' JOE) P
(20,66,19,16,11,17,58) PHIA **20** 34-35, BOSA **66** 35, **19** 36, WASA **16** 36, **11**37, CINN **17** 37, **58** 38

CASE, GEORGE OF/CH
(25,6,10,**1**,15,7,41,45,46) WASA **25** 37-38, **6** 39-40, **10** 41, **1** 42-45, CLEA **15/7** 46, WASA **1** 47, *CH* **41** 61-63, *CH* **45** 65, MINA *CH* **46** 68

CASEY, HUGH P
(21,**25**,26) CHIN **21** 35, BKNN **25** 39-42, 46-48, PITN **25** 49, NYA **26** 49

CASEY, SEAN 1B
(52,**21**) CLEA **52** 97, CINN **21** 98-05

CASH, DAVE 2B/CH
(**30**,10) PITN **30** 69, **10** 70, **30** 70-73, PHIN **30** 74-76, MONN **30** 77-79, SDN **30** 80, PHIN *CH* **30** 96, BALA *CH* **30** 05

CASH, KEVIN C
(**29**,17) TORA **29** 02-04, TBA **17** 05

CASH, NORM 1B
(31,38,**25**) CHIA **31** 58, **38** 59, DETA **25** 60-74

CASH, RON UTIL
(22,**40**) DETA **22** 73, **40** 74

CASIAN, LARRY P
(19,17,**48**,51,55,45,50) MINA **19** 90, **17** 91-92, **48** 92-94, CLEA **51** 94, CHIN **55** 95-97, KCA **45** 97, CHIA **50** 98

CASIMIRO, CARLOS INF
(**36**) BALA **36** 00

CASKEY, CRAIG P
(**35**) MONN **35** 73

CASSIDY, SCOTT P
(40,**43** 75,56) TORA **40/43** 02, BOSA **57** 02, SDN **56** 05

CASSINI, JACK (GABBY) PR
(**19**) PITN **19** 49

CASTELLANO, PEDRO 3B/2B
(**15**,12) COLN **15** 93, 95, **12** 96

CASTER, GEORGE (UG) P
(__,15,20,**16**,25,27) PHIA __ 34, **15** 35, **20** 37-38, **16** 38-40, STLA **25** 41, **16** 42-45, DETA **27** 45, **25** 45-46

CASTIGLIA, JIM C
(35,**34**) PHIA **35/34** 42

CASTIGLIONE, PETE SS/3B
(**16**,29,1) PITN **16** 47 **29** 48, **16** 49-53, STLN **1** 53-54

CASTILLA, VINNY SS/3B
(45,**9**,20,19) ATLN **45** 91-92, COLN **9** 93-99, TBA **20** 00, **9** 00-01, HOUN **19** 01, ATLN **19** 02-03, COLN **9** 04, WASN **9** 05

CASTILLO, ALBERTO C
(**30**,45,50,37,7,22) NYN **30** 95-98, STLN **30** 99, TORA **30** 00-01, NYA **45** 02, SFN **50/37** 03, KCA **7** 04-05, OAKA **22** 05

CASTILLO, BOBBY P
(41,**37**,22) LAN **41** 77-79, **37** 79-81, MINA **22** 82, **37** 82-84, LAN **37** 85

CASTILLO, BRAULIO OF
(**16**) PHIN **16** 91-92

CASTILLO, CARLOS P
(61,**43**) CHIA **61** 97, **43** 97-99, BOSA **43** 01

CASTILLO, CARMEN OF/DH
(52,12,**8**,22) CLEA **52** 82, **12** 83, **8** 83-88, MINA **22** 89-91

CASTILLO, FRANK P
(**49**,48,46,37) CHIN **49** 91-93, 95-97, COLN **48** 97, DETA **46** 98, TORA **37** 00, BOSA **37** 01-02, 04, FLAN **37** 05

CASTILLO, JOSE 2B
(**14**) PITN **14** 04-05

CASTILLO, JUAN UTIL
(**3**) MILA **3** 86-89

CASTILLO, JUAN P
(**50**) NYN **50** 94

CASTILLO, LUIS 2B
(34,**1**) FLAN **34** 96, **1** 97-05

CASTILLO, MANNY UTIL
(19,**12**) KCA **19** 80, SEAA **12** 82-83

CASTILLO, MARTY UTIL
(12,**8**) DETA **12** 81-82, **8** 83-85

CASTILLO, TONY P
(27,**36**,49,44) TORA **27** 88-89, ATLN **36** 89-91, NYN **36** 91, TORA **49** 93-96, CHIA **44** 96-97, **49** 97-98

CASTILLO, TONY C
(**27**) SDN **27** 78

CASTINO, JOHN UTIL
(**2**) MINA **2** 79-84

CASTINO, VINCE 3C
(**14**) CHIA **14** 43-45

CASTLE, DON DH
(**37**) TEXA **37** 73

CASTLEMAN, FOSTER 3B
(18,**12**,8) NYN **18** 54-55, **12** 56-57, BALA **8** 58

CASTLEMAN, SLICK P
(14,33,**15**) NYN **14** 34, **33** 35, **14** 36, **15** 37-39

CASTRO, BERNIE 2B
(**64**) BALA **64** 05

CASTRO, BILL P/CH
(**35**,20,56,39) MILA **35** 74, **20** 75, **35** 75-80, NYA **56/35** 81, KCA **39** 82-83, MILA/N *CH* **35** 92-05

CASTRO, JUAN 3B/2B/SS
(60,25,**17**,12,7) LAN **60** 95-96, **25** 97-98, **17** 98-99, CINN **12** 00-01, **7** 02-04, MINA **17** 05

CASTRO, RAMON C/2B
(6,**17**,47,11) FLAN **6** 99, **17** 00-04, OAKA **47** 04, NYN **11** 05

CATALANOTTO, FRANK 2B/OF/DH
(29,**27**) DETA **29** 97-98, **27** 98-99, TEXA **27** 00-02, TORA **27** 03-05

CATER, DANNY UTIL
(10,9,**2**,5,24) PHIN **10** 64, CHIA **9** 65-66, KCA **2** 66-67, OAKA **2** 68-69, NYA **10** 70-71, BOSA **5** 72-74, STLN **24** 75

CATHER, MIKE P
(**38**) ATLN **38** 97-99

CATHEY, HARDIN (LI'L ABNER) P
(**31**) WASA **31** 42

CATO, KEEFE P
(**42**) CINN **42** 83-84

CAUDILL, BILL P
(**36**,41,37) CHIN **36** 79-81, SEAA **41** 82, **37** 82-83, OAKA **36** 84, TORA **36** 85-86 , OAKA **37** 87

CAULFIELD, JOHN (JAKE) SS/3B
(**14**) PHIA **14** 46

CAUSEY, WAYNE INF
(33,**2**,9,15,23) BALA **33** 55-57, KCA **2** 61-66, CHIA **9** 66-68, CALA **15** 68, ATLN **23** 68

CAVARRETTA, PHIL 1B/M/CH
(43,23,3,**44**,50) CHIN **43** 34-36, **23** 37-38, **3** 39-40, **44** 41-53, *M* **44** 51-53, CHIA **44** 54-55, DETA *CH* **44** 61-63, NYN *CH* **50** 75-76, 78

CECCARELLI, ART (CHIC) P
(**19**,16,41) KCA **19** 55-56, BALA **16** 57, CHIN **41** 59-60

CECENA, JOSE P
(**37**) TEXA **37** 88

CECIL, REX P
(14,**31**) BOSA **14** 44, **31** 45

CEDENO ANDUJAR SS
(17,**10**,4,15,22) HOUN **17** 90-93, **10** 93-94, SDN **4** 95, **10** 96, DETA **15** 96, HOUN **22** 96

CEDENO, CESAR OF/1B
(**28**,7) HOUN **28** 70-81, CINN **28** 82-85, STLN **7** 85, LAN **7** 86

CEDENO, DOMINGO 2B/SS
(70,**20**,34,1,26,19) TORA **70** 93, **20** 94-96, CHIA **34** 96, TEXA **1** 97-98, SEAA **26** 99, PHIN **19** 99

CEDENO, ROGER OF/SS
(27,45,**19**,14,28,32) LAN **27** 95-96, **45** 97-98, NYN **19** 99, HOUN **14** 00, DETA **19** 01, NYN **19** 02-03, STLN **28/32** 04, **19** 05

CEDENO, RONNY INF
(**11**) CHIN **11** 05

CENTER, PETE P
(**7**,40,42,29) CLEA **7** 42-43, **40/42** 45, **29** 46

CEPEDA, ORLANDO (BABY BULL, CHA CHA) 1B/DH/CH
(**30**,28,20,12,25,14) SFN **30** 58-66, STLN **28** 66, **30** 67-68, ATLN **20** 69, **30** 69-72, OAKA **12** 72, BOSA **25** 73, KCA **30** 74, CHIA *CH* **14** 80

CEPICKY, MATT OF
(22,**29**,47) MONN **22** 02, **29** 02-04, WASN **47** 05

CERDA, JAIME P
(**43**,61,56) NYN **43** 02-03, KCA **61** 04, **56** 04-05

CERONE, RICK C
(4,9,**10**,5,6,11,13) CLEA **4** 75-76, TORA **9** 77-79, NYN **10** 80-84, ATLN **5** 85, MILA **5/11** 86, NYA **6** 87, BOSA **6** 88-89, NYA **11** 90, NYN **13** 91, MONN **13** 92

CERROS, JUAN P
(**71**) CINN **71** 03

CERUTTI, JOHN P
(**55**) TORA **55** 85-90, DETA **55** 91

CERV, BOB OF
(7,34,41,33,**17**,30,27) NYA **7** 51, **34** 52, **41** 53-56, KCA **33** 57-60, NYA **17** 60, LAA **30** 61, NYA **17** 61-62, HOUN **27/17** 62

CEY, RON (PENGUIN) 3B
(**10**,11) LAN **10** 71-82, CHIN **11** 83-86, OAKA **11** 87

CHACIN, GUSTAVO P
(**39**) TORA **39** 04-05

CHACON, ELIO UTIL
(**17**,2,7) CINN **17** 60-61, NYN **2/7** 62

CHACON, SHAWN P
(56,**34**,39) COLN **56** 01, **34** 02-05, NYA **39** 05

CHADWICK, RAY P
(**48**) CALA **48** 86

CHAGNON, LEON (SHAG) P
(**46**,15) PITN **46** 32-34, NYN **15** 35

CHAKALES, BOB (CHICK) P
(29,30,20,23,28,26,**16**,40) CLEA **29** 51-52, **30** 52, **20** 53, **23** 54, BALA **20** 54, CHIA **28/26** 55, WASA **16** 55-57, BOSA **40/26** 57

CHALK, DAVE SS
(**7**,12,16) CALA **7** 73-79, TEXA **12** 79, OAKA **16** 79, KCA **7** 80-81

CHAMBERLAIN, BILL P
(**17**) CHIA **17** 32

CHAMBERLAIN, CRAIG P
(25,**28**) KCA **25** 79-80, **28** 80

CHAMBERLAIN, JOE SS/3B
(**12**) CHIA **12** 34

CHAMBERLAIN, WES OF
(31,**44**,26,32) PHIN **31** 90-91, **44** 92-94, BOSA **26** 94, **32** 95

CHAMBERS, AL OF/DH
(**47**,23) SEAA **47** 83-84, **23** 85

CHAMBERS, CLIFF (LEFTY) P
(32,23,**28**) CHIN **32** 48, PITN **23** 49-51, STLN **28** 51-53

CHAMBERS, JOHNNIE P
(**31**) STLN **31** 37

CHAMBLEE, JIM 3B
(**64**) CINN **64** 03

CHAMBLISS, CHRIS 1B/CH
(14,**10**,50,48,49) CLEA **14** 71-74, NYA **10** 74-79, ATLN **10** 80-86, NYA **50** 88, *CH* **50** 88, STLN *CH* **10** 93-95, NYA *CH* **50** 96-97, *CH* **48** 98-00, NYN **51** 02, CINN *CH* **49** 04-05

CHAMPION, BILLY P
(**31**,38,39) PHIN **31** 69-72, MILA **38** 73, **39** 74-76

CHAMPION, MIKE 2B
(18,**10**) SDN **18** 76, **10** 77-78

CHANCE, BOB OF/1B
(21,**10**,31,37) CLEA **21** 63-64, WASA **10** 65-66, **31** 67, CALA **37** 69

CHANCE, DEAN P
(41,31,**32**,41) LAA **41** 61, **31** 61-64, CALA **31** 65-66, MINA **32** 67-69, CLEA **32** 70, NYN **32** 70, DETA **14/32** 71

CHANDLER, ED P
(**39**) BKNN **39** 47

CHANDLER, SPUD P/CH
(35,24,13,**21**,27,40) NYA **35/24/13** 37, **21** 38, **27** 39, **21** 39-47, KCA *CH* **40** 57-58

CHANEY, DARREL INF
(**12**,15) CINN **12** 69-75, ATLN **15** 76-77

HANT, CHARLIE OF (24,28) OAKA 24 75, STLN 28 76
HAPIN, DARRIN P (60,41) NYA 60 91, PHIN 41 92
HAPLIN, TINY P (15) BOSN 15 36
HAPMAN, BEN OF/M (7,6,4,1,9,2, 11,44,45,5, 34,52) NYA 7 30-31, 6 32-33, 7 34-36, WASA 4 36-37, BOSA 1 37, 9 38, CLEA 2/11 39, 11/44 40, WASA 4 41, CHIA 45 41, BKNN 5 44-45, PHIN 34 45, 7 46, *M* 34 45, *M* 7 46-48, CINN *CH* 52 52
HAPMAN, CALVIN UTIL (18,14) CINN 18 35, 14 36
HAPMAN, ED P (19) WASA 19 33
HAPMAN, FRED (CHAPPIE) SS (25,11) PHIA 25 39-40, 11 41
HAPMAN, GLENN (PETE) OF/2B (20) BKNN 20 34
HAPMAN, KELVIN INF (10,11) NYN 10 79, 11 84-85
HAPMAN, SAM OF (14,10,6,4, 31) PHIA 14 38, 10 39-40, 6 41, 10 45, 4 46-51, CLEA 31 51
HAPMAN, TRAVIS 3B (23) PHIN 23 03
HAPPAS, HARRY SS (1,13) CHIA 1 78, 13 79-80
HARBONEAU, JOE OF/DH (34) CLEA 34 80-82
HARLES, ED 3B (16,24,5) KCA 16 62-67, NYN 24 67, 5 67-69
HARLES, FRANK C (56) HOUN 56 00
HARLTON, NORM (THE GENIUS) P (47,37,30) CINN 47 88, 37 88-92, SEAA 37 93, PHIN (94), 37 95, SEAA 37 95-97, BALA 37 98, ATLN 30 98, TBA 37 99, CINN 37 00, SEAA 37 01
HARTAK, MIKE OF (30,39,14,50, 10,7) NYA 30 40, 39 42, WASA 14 42, STLA 50 42, 10 42-43, 7 44
HARTON, PETE P (15) BOSA 15 64
HASE, KEN (LEFTY) P (20,21,32,11, 13,10,16) WASA 20 36, 21 37, 32 37, 11 39-41, 13 41, BOSA 10 42-43, NYN 16 43
HAVARRIA, OSSIE UTIL (59,12,10) KCA 59 66, 12 66-67, 10 67
HAVEZ, ANGEL 2B/SS (1) SFN 1 05
HAVEZ, ANTHONY P (43) ANAA 43 97
HAVEZ, ENDY OF (43,19,47) KCA 43 01, MONN 19 02-04, WASN 47 05, PHIN 47 05
HAVEZ, ERIC 3B (30,3) OAKA 30 98, 3 99-05
HAVEZ, NESTOR P (50,32,41) SFN 50/32/41 67
HAVEZ, RAUL C (12,62,72,46) MONN 12 96-97, SEAA 62 98, HOUN 72/46 00, 46 02-05
HEADLE, DAVE P (30) ATLN 30 73
HECO, ROBINSON P (40,56) BOSA 40 97-98, LAN 56 99
HELINI, ITALO (CHILLY) P (__,47,30) CHIA __ 35, 47 36, 30 36-37
HEN, BRUCE P (48,39,32,52, 31,64,27) ATLN 48 98-00, PHIN 39 00-01, NYN 32 01-02, MONN 32 02, CINN 52 02, HOUN 31 03, BOSA 52 03, BALA 64 04, 27 05
HEN, CHIN FENG OF (52) LAN 52 02-05
HENEY, TOM P (42,38,37,34, 23,20,22) STLN 42 57, (58), 38 59, PITN 37 60, 34 61, WASA 23 61-64, 20 64, 22 66
HERVINKO, PAUL C (8) BKNN 8 37-38
HESNES, BOB P (24) PITN 24 48-50
HETKOVICH, MITCH P (34) PHIN 34 45
HEVEZ, TONY P (45,35) BALA 45/35 77
HIAMPARINO, SCOTT P (43) TEXA 43 90-92
HIASSON, SCOTT P (37) CHIN 37 01-02, (03)
HIFFER, FLOYD P (39,25) SDN 39 82-83, 25 84
HILDERS, MATT P (43,28,57) MILN 43 02, ATLN 28/57 05
HILDRESS, ROCKY P (50) PHIN 50 85-88
HILES, RICH OF (29,20,12) HOUN 29 71-72, NYN 29 73, HOUN 20 76, MINA 12 77-78
HIMELIS, JOEL INF (41) SFN 41 95
HIOZZA, DINO (DYNAMO) SS B (22) PHIN 22 35
HIOZZA, LOU UTIL B (21,34,1,26) PHIN 21 34-35, 34 36, NYN 1 37, 26 38, 21 39
HIPMAN, BOB (MR. CHIPS) P (32,12,22,31, 44,14,17,16) BKNN 32 41, 12 42, 22 43, 12 44, CHIN 31 44-49, BOSN 17 50, 44/14 51, 16 52

CHIPPLE, WALT OF (6) WASA 6 45
CHISM, TOM 1B (12) BALA 12 79
CHITI, DOM CH (81,30) CLEA *CH* 81 91, *CH* 30 92-93
CHITI, HARRY C (16,32,17,8, 27,11,44) CHIN 16 50, 32 50-52, 55-56, KCA 17 58, 8 58-60, DETA 27 60, 11 61, NYN 44 62
CHITREN, STEVE P (49) OAKA 49 90-91
CHITTUM, NELSON (NELS) P (27,28) STLN 27 58, BOSA 28 59-60
CHLUPSA, BOB P (40) STLN 40 70-71
CHO, JIN HO P (61) BOSA 61 98-99
CHOATE, DON P (22) SFN 22 60
CHOATE, RANDY P (58,38,33,21) NYA 58 00-01, 38 01-03, ARIN 33 04, 21 05
CHOI, HEE SEOP 1B (19,25,5) CHIN 19 02-03, FLAN 25 04, LAN 5 04-05
CHOO, SHIN-SOO P (54) SEAA 54 05
CHOUINARD, BOBBY P (54,52,57,41, 43) OAKA 54 96, MILN 52 98, ARIN 57 98, 41 99, 43 00-01
CHOZEN, HARRY C (7) CINN 7 37
CHRIS, MIKE P (43,34,31) DETA 43 79, SFN 34 82, 31 82-83
CHRISLEY, NEIL OF (34,20,32,24, 30) WASA 34/20 57, 32 58, DETA 24 59-60, MILN 30 61
CHRISTENSEN, BRUCE SS (42,1) CALA 42/1 71
CHRISTENSEN, JOHN OF (35,7,42,20) NYN 35 84-85, 7 85, SEAA 42 87, MINA 20 88
CHRISTENSEN, McKAY OF (26,59,23) CHIA 26 99-01, LAN 59 01, NYN 23 02
CHRISTENSON, GARY P (31) KCA 31 79-80
CHRISTENSON, LARRY P (38) PHIN 38 73-83
CHRISTENSON, RYAN OF (53,28,8,6,27, 16) OAKA 53 98, 28 99-01, ARIN 8/6 01, MILN 27 02, TEXA 16 03
CHRISTIAN, BOB OF (46,15) DETA 46 68, CHIA 15 69-70
CHRISTIANSEN, CLAY P (67) NYA 67 84
CHRISTIANSEN, JASON P (41,48,40,46) PITN 41 95-00, STLN 48 00-01, SFN 40 01-05, LAA 46 05
CHRISTMAN, MARK INF (20,12,6,22, 12,24) DETA 20 38, 12 39, STLA 6 39, 43-46, WASA 22/12 47, 24 48-49
CHRISTMAN, TIM P (54) COLN 54 01
CHRISTMAS, STEVE C (4,8,58,18) CINN 4/8 83, CHIA 58 84, CHIN 18 86
CHRISTOPHER, JOE OF (23,20) PITN 23 59-61, NYN 23 62-65, BOSA 20 66
CHRISTOPHER, LOYD OF (35,32,24) BOSA 35 45, CHIN 32 45, CHIA 24 47
CHRISTOPHER, MIKE P (56,35,32,33) LAN 56 91, CLEA 35 92, 32 92-93, DETA 33 95-96
CHRISTOPHER, RUSS P (24,17,29,18) PHIA 24 42, 17 43-47, CLEA 29/18 48
CHULK, VINNY P (50) TORA 50 03-05
CHURCH, BUBBA P (23,40,41,33) PHIN 23 50-52, CINN 40 52, 41 53, CHIN 33 53, 23 54-55
CHURCH, LEN P (45) CHIN 45 66
CHURCH, RYAN OF (38,19) MONN 38 04, WASN 19 05
CHURN, CHUCK P (28,32,45) PITN 28 57, CLEA 32 58, LAN 45 59
CIAFFONE, LARRY (SYMPHONY) OF (34) STLN 34 51
CIANFROCCO, ARCHI 3B/1B (14,26,29) MONN 14 92-93, SDN 26 93-95, 29 95-98
CIARDI, MARK P (34) MILA 34 87
CIAS, DARRYL C (9) OAKA 9 83
CICERO, JOE (DODE) OF (10) PHIA 10 45
CICOTTE, AL (BOZO) P (24,21,25,20, 33,31) NYA 24 57, WASA 21 58, DETA 25 58, CLEA 20 59, STLN 33 61, HOUN 31 62
CIESLAK, TED 3B/OF (7) PHIN 7 44
CIHOCKI, AL INF (2) CLEA 2 45
CIHOCKI, ED (CY) INF (42,24) PHIA 42 32, 24 33
CIMINO, PETE P (35,31) MINA 35 65-66, CALA 31 67-68

CIMOLI, GINO OF (9,22,20,19, 4,24) BKNN 9 56-57, LAN 9 58, STLN 22 59, PITN 20 60-61, MILN 19 61, KCA 4 62-64, BALA 20 64, CALA 24 65
CIMORELLI, FRANK P (54) STLN 54 94
CINTRON, ALEX SS/INF (10,12) ARIN 10 01-05, 12 05
CIOLA, LOU P (7) PHIA 7 43
CIPRIANI, FRANK OF (25) KCA 25 61
CIRILLO, JEFF 3B (26,7,9,6) MILA/N 26 94-99, COLN 7 00-01, SEAA 9 02, 7 03, MILN 6 05
CISAR, GEORGE OF (20) BKNN 20 37
CISCO, GALEN P/CH (15,26,38,39, 40,3,9,36,54, 42,43) BOSA 15 61-62, NYN 26 62-65, BOSA 38/39/40 67, KCA 26 69, *CH* 3 71-74, 9 75, 36 75-79, MONN *CH* 36 80-84, SDN *CH* 36 85-87, TORA *CH* 54 88, 42 90-95, PHIN *CH* 42 97, 43 98-99, 40 00
CISSELL, BILL INF (1,6,4,2,22) CHIA 1 31, 6 32, CLEA 4 32-33, BOSA 2 34, PHIA 4 37, NYN 22 38
CITARELLA, RALPH P (43,14,53) STLN 43 83-84, CHIA 53/14 87
CLANCY, BUD 1B (14,23) BKNN 14 32, PHIN 23 34
CLANCY, JIM P (18,38) TORA 18 77-88, HOUN 38 89-91, ATLN 18 91
CLAPINSKI, CHRIS INF (30,2) FLAN 30 99, 2 00
CLAPP, STUBBY 2B (29) STLN 29 01
CLAREY, DOUG 2B (16) STLN 16 76
CLARK, ALLIE OF (3,31,7,18) NYA 3 47, CLEA 31 48-51, PHIA 7 51-53, CHIA 18 53
CLARK, BOBBY OF (32,25) CALA 32 79-83, MILA 25 84-85
CLARK, BRADY OF (54,22,15,27) CINN 54 00, 22 01-02, NYN 15 02, MILN 27 03-05
CLARK, BRYAN P (48,35,43,45, 40,47) SEAA 48 81-83, TORA 35 84, CLEA 43 85, CHIA 45/40 86, 47 87, SEAA 45/48 90
CLARK, CAP C (10) PHIN 10 38
CLARK, DAVE OF/DH/CH (12,25,30,26, 35,22) CLEA 12 86-88, 25 88-89, CHIN 30 90, KCA 26 91, PITN 35 92-96, LAN 35 96, CHIN 22 97-98, HOUN 35 98, PITN *CH* 35 01-02
CLARK, DOUG OF (40) SFN 40 05
CLARK, EARL OF (30,22,14) BOSN 30 32, 22 33, STLA 14 34
CLARK, GLEN PH (32) ATLN 32 67
CLARK, HOWIE UTIL/3B (11,6) BALA 11 02, TORA 6 03-04
CLARK, JACK OF/1B/DH/CH (15,22,33,6, 25,00,44) SFN 15 75-76, 22 77-84, STLN 22 85-87, NYA 33/6 88, SDN 25 89-90, 00 90, BOSA 25 91-92, LAN *CH* 44 01, 22 02-03
CLARK, JERALD OF (24,44) SDN 24 88-92, COLN 24 93, MINA 44 95
CLARK, JERMAINE INF/OF (24,17,57,4) DETA 24 01, SDN 17 03, TEXA 24 03, CINN 57 04, OAKA 4 05
CLARK, JIM SS/3B (22) WASA 22 48
CLARK, JIM (E.) OF/1B (40) CLEA 40 71
CLARK, MARK P (63,55,54,48) STLN 63 91, 55 92, CLEA 54 93-95, NYN 54 96-97, CHIN 48 97, 54 98, TEXA 54 99-00
CLARK, MEL OF (37,16,12) PHIN 37 51, 16 52-55, DETA 12 57
CLARK, MIKE P (22) STLN 22 52-53
CLARK, OTIE P (39) BOSA 39 45
CLARK, PHIL P (22,36) STLN 22 58, 36 59
CLARK, PHIL OF/3B (40,30,23) DETA 40 92, SDN 30 93-95, BOSA 23 96
CLARK, RICKEY P (44,52) CALA 44 67-69, 52 69, 44 71-72
CLARK, RON INF/CH (24,8,30,3,4, 7,5,53,6) MINA 24 66, 8 67-69, SEAA 30 69, OAKA 3 71, 4 72, MILA 7 72, PHIN 5 75, CHIA *CH* 53 88, *CH* 5 89-90, SEAA *CH* 6 91, CLEA *CH* 6 92-93
CLARK, TERRY P (42,53) CALA 42 88-89, HOUN 53 90

CLARK, TERRY P (49,36,24,52, 47,46) ATLN 49 95, BALA 36 95, KCA 24 96, HOUN 52 96, CLEA 47 97, TEXA 46 97
CLARK, TONY 1B (17,44,22,00, 52,29,34) DETA 17 95-99, 44 00-01, BOSA 22 02, NYN 00/52 03, NYA 29 04, ARIN 34 05
CLARK, WATTY (LEFTY) P/CH (12,17,10,28, 24) BKNN 12 31, 17 32-33, NYN 10 33, 28 34, BKNN 24 34, 17 35-37, *CH* 17 37
CLARK, WILL (THE THRILL) 1B (22,12,23) SFN 22 86-93, TEXA 22 94-98, BALA 12 99, BALA 23 00, STLN 22 00
CLARKE, GREY (NOISY) 3B (4) CHIA 4 44
CLARKE, HORACE 2B (20,7) NYA 20 65-74, SDN 7 74
CLARKE, STAN P (34,37) TORA 34 83-85, SEAA 37 87, KCA 34 89, STLN 61 90
CLARKE, TOMMY CH (27,31,25) NYN *CH* 27 32, 31 33-35, 25 36, 31 38
CLARKE, WEBBO P (24) WASA 24 55
CLARKSON, BUS (BUZZY) 2B/SS (40,44) BOSN 40/44 52
CLARY, ELLIS (CAT) 2B/3B (24,3,2,53) WASA 24 42-43, 3 43, STLA 2 43-45, WASA *CH* 53 55-60
CLARY, MARTY P (48) ATLN 48 87, 89-90
CLASET, GOWELL (LEFTY) P (14) PHIA 14 33
CLAUSSEN, BRANDON P (60,34) NYA 60 03, CINN 34 04-05
CLAY, DAIN (DING-A-LING) OF (20) CINN 20 43-46
CLAY, DANNY P (35) PHIN 35 88
CLAY, KEN P (50,43,16,49, 21) NYA 50 77, 43 78-79, TEXA 16 80, SEAA 49/21 81
CLAYTON, ROYCE SS (21,10,11) SFN 21 91, 10 92-95, STLN 11 96-98, TEXA 11 98-00, CHIA 10 01-02, MILN 10 03, COLN 10 04, ARIN 10 05
CLEAR, BOB CH (49) CALA *CH* 49 76-87
CLEAR, MARK P (38,25,46) CALA 38 79-80, BOSA 25 81-85, MILA 25 86-88, CALA 46 90
CLEARY, JOE (FIRE) P (14) WASA 14 45
CLEMENS, CHET OF (41,15) BOSN 41 39, 15 44
CLEMENS, DOUG OF (38,40,22,27, 17) STLN 38 60, 40 61, 22 62-64, CHIN 27 64-65, PHIN 17 66-68
CLEMENS, ROGER (THE ROCKET) P (21,12,22) BOSA 21 84-96, TORA 21 97-98, NYA 12 99, 22 99-03, HOUN 22 04-05
CLEMENSEN, BILL P (40,49,37,21, 47) PITN 40/49 39, 37/21 41, 47 46
CLEMENT, MATT P (31,21,51,30) SDN 31 98-00, 21 00, FLAN 51 01, CHIN 30 02-04, BOSA 30 05
CLEMENTE, EDGARD OF N (19,12) COLN 19 98-99, 12 99, ANAA 22 00
CLEMENTE, ROBERTO OF U (13,21) PITN 13 55, 21 55-72
CLEMENTS, PAT P (27,15,38,29) CALA 27 85, PITN 15 85-86, NYA 38 87-88, SDN 38 89-92, BALA 29 92
CLEMONS, CHRIS P (57) CHIA 57 97
CLEMONS, LANCE P (27,47,42) KCA 27 71, STLN 47 72, BOSA 42 74
CLEMONS, VERNE (STINGER)(TUBBY) C (15,__) STLN 15 23, __ 24
CLENDENON, DONN 1B (17,22,16) PITN 17 61-68, MONN 17 69, NYN 22 69-71, STLN 16 72
CLEVELAND, REGGIE P (33,22,26,47, 23,25) STLN 33 69-70, 22 70-73, BOSA 33 74, 26 74-78, TEXA 26 78, MILA 47 79, 23 79-81, 25 81
CLEVENGER, TEX P (26,11,10,14, 12,32,21) BOSA 26 54, WASA 11/10/14 56, 12 57-60, LAA 32 61, NYA 26 61-62, 21 62
CLIBURN, STAN C B (16) CALA 16 80
CLIBURN, STEW P B (33) CALA 63 84, 33 85, 88
CLIFT, HARLOND (DARKIE) 3B (7,6,31,3) STLA 7 34-39, 6 40, 7 41-43, WASA 31 43, 3 44-45
CLIFTON, FLEA INF (24,30) DETA 24 34-36, 30 37
CLINE, TY OF/1B (9,31,20,27, 19,5,17) CLEA 9 61-62, MILN 31 63-65, CHIN 20 66, ATLN 27 66-67, SFN 19 67-68, MONN 5 69-70, CINN 17 70-71

CLINES, GENE (ROADRUNNER) OF/CH
(**15**,1,16,18,3, 10,30,12,20, 2) PITN **15** 70-74, NYN **1** 75, TEXA **16** 76, CHIN **18** 77-79, *CH* **18** 79, **3** 80-81, HOUN *CH* **10** 88, SEAA *CH* **30** 89, **16** 90-92, MILA *CH* **12** 93, **15** 94, SFN *CH* **20** 97 -02, CHIN *CH* **2** 03-05

CLINTON, LU OF
(4,24,**6**,15,37, 5,20,40) BOSA **4** 60-61, **24** 61-62, **6** 62-64, LAA **15** 64-65, KCA **37/5** 65, CLEA **20** 65, NYA **40** 66-67

CLONINGER, TONY P/CH
(**40**,32,25,41) MILN **40** 61-65, ATLN **40** 66-68, CINN **32/40** 68-71, STLN **25** 72, NYA *CH* **40** 92-98, **41** 98 -99, **40** 99-00, **41** 00, **40** 01, BOSA *CH* **40** 02-03

CLONTZ, BRAD P
(**52**,30,50,49, 59) ATLN **52** 95-96, **30** 97, LAN **50** 98, NYN **49** 98, PITN **59** 99, **52** 00

CLOSSER, J. D. C
(30,**7**) COLN **30** 04, **7** 05

CLOSTER, ALAN (AL) P
(25,**50**,43) WASA **25** 66, NYA **50** 71-72, ATLN **43** 73

CLOUDE, KEN P
(27,**28**) SEAA **27** 97-98, **28** 99

CLOUGH, ED OF
(no#) STLN **no#** 24

CLUCK, BOB CH
(54,**55**,4,3) HOUN *CH* **54** 90-91, *CH* **55** 90-93, OAKA *CH* **4** 96, *CH* **3** 97, DETA *CH* **54** 03-05

CLUTTERBUCK, BRYAN P
(45,**48**) MILA **45** 86, **48** 86, 89

CLYBURN, DANNY PH
(37,**41**) BALA **37** 97, **41** 98, TBA **41** 99

CLYDE, DAVID P
(**32**) TEXA **32** 73-75, CLEA **32** 78-79

CLYDE, TOM P
(**25**) PHIA **25** 43

COACHMAN, PETE INF/DH
(**10**) CALA **10** 90

COAN, GIL OF
(22,3,30,**2**,16, 35,10,28) WASA **22** 46-47, **3** 48-49, **30** 50, **2** 51-53, BALA **16** 54-55, CHIA **35** 55, NYN **10** 55, **28** 56

COATES, JIM P
(51,**39**,28,47, 37,46) NYA **51** 56, **39** 59-62, WASA **28** 63, CINN **47** 63, CALA **37** 65, **25/50** 66, **46** 65-67

COBEL, DAVE C
(**10**) PHIN **10** 39

COCANOWER, JAIME P
(**47**) MILA **47** 83-86

COCHRANE, DAVE UTIL
(37,**43**) CHIA **37** 86, SEAA **43** 89-92

COCHRANE, MICKEY C/M/CH
(2,**3**,32) PHIA **2** 31-33, DETA **3** 34-37, *M* **3** 34-38, PHIA *CH* **32** 50

COCKRELL, ALAN OF/CH
(**44**) COLN **44** 96, *CH* 02

COCO, PASQUAL P
(54,**38**) TORA **54** 00, **38** 01-02

CODIROLI, CHRIS P
(**23**,37,34) OAKA **23** 82-87, CLEA **37** 88, KCA **34** 90

COFFEY, TODD P
(**56**) CINN **56** 05

COFFIE, IVANON INF
(**29**) BALA **29** 00

COFFMAN, DICK P
(**16**,15,14,24, 20) STLA **16** 31-32, WASA **15** 32, STLA **16** 33-35, NYN **15** 36, **14** 37-39, BOSN **24** 40, PHIN **20** 45

COFFMAN, KEVIN P
(**43**,42) ATLN **43** 87-88, CHIN **42** 90

COFFMAN, SLICK P
(**21**,25,30) DETA **21** 37-38, **25** 39, STLA **30** 40

COGAN, TONY P
(**55**) KCA **55** 01

COGGIN, DAVID P
(**48**) PHIN **48** 00-02, (03)

COGGINS, FRANK 2B
(30,**1**,17) WASA **30** 67, **1** 68, CHIN **17** 72

COGGINS, RICH OF
(**2**,26,15) BALA **2** 72-74, MONN **2** 75, NYA **26** 75-76, CHIA **15** 76

COHEN, ALTA (SCHOOLBOY) OF
(no#,**14**) BKNN **no#** 32, PHIN **14** 33

COHEN, ANDY CH/M
(**39**) PHIN *CH,M,CH* **39** 60

COHEN, HY P
(**42**) CHIN **42** 55

COHEN, SYD P
(12,**14**) WASA **12** 34, **14** 36-37

COKER, JIMMIE C
(27,10,17,2,**7**) PHIN **27** 58, **10** 60-61, **17** 62, SFN **2** 63, CINN **7** 64-67

COLANGELO, MIKE OF
(**10**,21,30) ANAA **10** 99, SDN **21** 01, OAKA **30** 02

COLAVITO, ROCKY OF/CH
(38,**6**,7,21,18 16,29,40,8) CLEA **38** 55-57, **6** 58-59, DETA **7** 60-63, KCA **7** 64, CLEA **21** 65-67, CHIA **18** 67, LAN **16** 68, NYA **29** 68, CLEA *CH* **6** 73, **7** 76, **6** 76-78, KCA *CH* **40** 82, **8** 82-83

COLBERN, MIKE C/DH
(30,**19**) CHIA **30** 78, **19** 79

COLBERT, CRAIG C/INF
(**46**) SFN **46** 92-93

COLBERT, NATE 1B
(12,22,26,**17**, 9,24,23) HOUN **12** 66, **22/26** 68, SDN **17** 69-74, DETA **9** 75, MONN **24** 75-76, OAKA **23** 76

COLBERT, VINCE P
(**44**) CLEA **44** 70-72

COLBORN, JIM P/CH
(38,**48**,45) CHIN **38** 69, **48** 69-71, MILA **48** 72-76, KCA **48** 77-78, SEAA **38/48** 78, LAN *CH* **45** 01, **48** 02-05

COLBRUNN, GREG 1B/3B/DH
(15,4,**28**,23, 39,35) MONN **15** 92-93, FLAN **4** 94-96 MINA **28** 97, ATLN **23** 97, COLN **39/28** 98, ATLN **23** 98, ARIN **28** 99-02, (03), **35** 04, TEXA (05)

COLE, ALEX OF
(**2**,36,5,1) CLEA **2** 90-92, PITN **36/5** 92, COLN **5** 93, MINA **1** 94-95, BOSA **2** 96

COLE, DAVE P
(**16**,26,29,30, 23,39,44) BOSN **16** 50-51, **26** 51, **29/30** 52, MILN **30** 53, CHIN **23/39** 5 PHIN **44** 55

COLE, DICK INF
(15,**12**,59) STLN **15** 51, PITN **12** 51, 53-56, MILN **12** 57, CHIN *CH* **59** 61

COLE, ED P
(26,**20**) STLA **26** 38, **20** 39

COLE, STU 2B/DH
(**39**) KCA **39** 91

COLE, VICTOR P
(**61**) PITN **61** 92

COLEMAN, BOB CH/M
(**31**) BOSN *CH* **31** 43, *M* **31** 44-45

COLEMAN, CHOO CHOO C
(12,**17**,20) PHIN **12** 61, NYN **12** 62, **17** 62-63, **20** 66

COLEMAN, DAVE OF
(**30**) BOSA **30** 77

COLEMAN, ED OF
(25,**9**,21) PHIA **25** 32-35, **9** 34-35, STLA **21** 35, **9** 36

COLEMAN, GORDY 1B
(45,**18**) CLEA **45** 59, CINN **18** 60-67

COLEMAN, JERRY 2B
(**42**,2) NYA **42** 49-57, SDN *M* **2** 80

COLEMAN, JOE P F
(_,36,**20**,25, 35,12) PHIA _ 42, **36** 46, **20** 47-51, **25** 53, BALA **35** 54-55, DETA **12** 55

COLEMAN, JOE P S
(36,37,20,**15**, 51,31,30,16, 40, 29,41,47) WASA **36** 65-66, WASA **37** 66, **20** 67-70, DETA **15** 71-76, CHIN **51/31**76, OAKA **30** 77, **15** 77-78, TORA **16/40** 78, SFN **29** 79, PITN **41** 79, CALA *CH* **40** 87-90, STLN *CH* **40** 91-94, CALA *CH* **47** 96, ANAA *CH* **47** 97-99

COLEMAN, MICHAEL OF
(**44**,40,13) BOSA **44** 97, 99, **40** 99, **44** 00, NYA **13** 01

COLEMAN, RAY OF
(19,11,**17**,39) STLA **19** 47-48, PHIA **11** 48, STLA **17** 50-51, CHIA **39** 51-52, STLA **17** 52

COLEMAN, RIP P
(22,30,15,36, 35) NYA **22** 55, **30** 55-56, KCA **15** 57, **36** 59, BALA **35** 59-60

COLEMAN, VINCE (VINCENT VAN GO) OF
(**29**,1,11,40, 30) STLN **29** 85-90, NYN **1** 91-92, **11** 93, KCA **29** 94, **40/29** 95, SEAA **29** 95, CINN **30** 96, DETA **29** 97

COLES, CHUCK OF
(**23**) CINN **23** 58

COLES, DARNELL UTIL
(11,**19**,7,2,33, 21,26,15,28) SEAA **11** 83, **19** 84-85, DETA **19** 86-87, PITN **7** 87-88, SEAA **2** 88-89, **33** 90, DETA **21** 90, SFN **21** 91, CINN **26** 92, TORA **11** 93-94, STLN **15** 95, COLN **28** 97

COLETTA, CHRIS OF
(**14**) CALA **14** 72

COLLIER, LOU SS/3B
(6,**16**,22,58) PITN **6** 97-98, MILN **16** 99-01, MONN **22** 02, BOSA **16** 03, PHIN **58** 04

COLLIER, ORLIN P
(**28**) DETA **28** 31

COLLINS, BOB (RIP) C
(39,11) CHIN **39** 40, NYA **11** 44

COLLINS, DAVE OF/CH
(28,5,**29**,10, 11,22,15) CALA **28** 75-76, SEAA **5** 77, CINN **29** 78-81, NYA **29** 82, TORA **10** 83-84, OAKA **11** 85, DETA **29** 86, CINN **22** 87-89, STLN **15** 90, *CH* **15** 91-93, CINN *CH* **22** 99-00, MILN *CH* **29** 02, COLN *CH* **29** 03-05

COLLINS, DON P
(**42**,47) ATLN **42** 77, CLEA **47** 80

COLLINS, EDDIE (COCKY) CH F
(**31**) PHIA **31** 31-32

COLLINS, EDDIE, JR. OF S
(26,**14**) PHIA **26** 39, **14** 41-42

COLLINS, JOE 1B
(42,41,**15**) NYA **42** 48, **41** 49-52, **15** 53-57

COLLINS, KEVIN (CASEY) INF
(10,19,16,1, 17,8,4,**44**) NYN **10** 65, **19** 67-68, **16** 68, **1** 69, MONN **17/8** 69, DETA **4** 70, **44** 71

COLLINS, PHIL (FIDGETY PHIL) P
(18,16,**40**,28) PHIN **18** 32, **16** 33, **40** 34-35, STLN **28** 35

COLLINS, RIP P
(**18**) STLA **18** 31

COLLINS, RIPPER 1B/CH
(8,**12**,3,2,55) STLN **8** 32, **12** 33-36, CHIN **3** 37-38, PITN **2** 41, CHIN *CH* **55** 61-63

COLLINS, SHANO M
(32,**31**) BOSA *M* **32** 31, *M* **31** 32

COLLINS, TERRY CH/M
(44,**2**,1,5) PITN *CH* **44** 92-93, HOUN *M* **2** 94-96, ANAA *M* **1** 97-99, FLAN *CH* **5** 01

COLLUM, JACKIE P
(21,**32**,34,15, 55,33,29) STLN **21** 51, **32** 52-53, CINN **34** 53-55, STLN **32** 56, CHIN **15** 57, BKNN **55** 57, LAN **55** 58, MINA **33** 62, CLEA **29** 62

COLMAN, FRANK OF/1B
(**23**,3,48) PITN **23** 42-46, NYA **3** 46-47, **48** 47

COLOME, JESUS P
(46,**49**) TBA **46** 01-02, **49** 03-05

COLON, BARTOLO P
(**40**,21) CLEA **40** 97-02, MONN **40** 02, CHIA **40** 03, ANAA **21** 04, LAA **40** 05

COLON, CHRIS SS
(**54**) TEXA **54** 92

COLON, RAMON P
(**40**,43) ATLN **40** 04-05, DETA **43** 05

COLPAERT, DICK P
(**36**) PITN **36** 70

COLSON, LOYD P
(**49**) NYA **49** 70

COLTON, LARRY P
(**21**) PHIN **21** 68

COLUCCIO, BOB OF/DH
(**26**,5,21) MILA **26** 73-75, CHIA **5** 75, 77, STLN **21** 78

COLYER, STEVE P
(**50**,51) LAN **50** 03, DETA **51** 04

COMBE, GEOFF P
(**48**,37) CINN **48** 80, **37** 81

COMBE, EARLE (THE KENTUCKY COLONEL) OF/CH
(**1**,30,32,41,31) NYA **1** 29-35, *CH* **30** 36-39, *CH* **32** 40-44, STLA *CH* **30** 47, BOSA *CH* **32** 48-52, *CH* **41** 52, PHIN *CH* **31** 54

COMBS, MERRILL (MERL) INF/CH
(32,24,46,**11**, 63,45) BOSA **32** 47, **24** 49-50, WASA **46** 50, CLEA **11** 51-52, TEXA *CH* **63** 74, *CH* **45** 74-75

COMBS, PAT P
(**38**,21) PHIN **38** 89-91, **21** 92

COMELLAS, JORGE (PANCHO) P
(**36**) CHIN **36** 45

COMER, STEVE P/CH
(52,28,**11**,44, 31) TEXA **52/28** 78, **11** 79-82, PHIN **44** 83, CLEA **31** 84, *CH* **31** 87

COMER, WAYNE OF
(39,27,**20**,12, 42) DETA **39** 67, **27** 68, SEAA **20** 69, MILA **20** 70, WASA **12** 70, DETA **42** 72

COMMAND, JIM (IGOR) 3B
(5,**18**) PHIN **5** 54, **18** 55

COMOROSKY, ADAM OF
(12,**14**,8) PITN **12** 32, **14** 33, CINN **8** 34, **14** 35

COMPTON, MIKE C
(**7**) PHIN **7** 70

COMPTON, CLINT P
(**34**) CHIN **34** 72

COMSTOCK, KEITH P
(21,55,36,**32**, 34) MINA **21** 84, SFN **55/36** 87, SDN **32** 87-88, SEAA **34** 89, **32** 90-91

CONATSER, CLINT (CONNIE) OF
(**19**) BOSN **19** 48-49

CONCEPCION, DAVE SS
(50,**13**) CINN **50** 70, **13** 70-88

CONCEPCION, ONIX SS
(53,**2**,29) KCA **53** 80, **2** 80--85, PITN **29** 87

CONDE, RAMON (WITO) 3B
(**9**) CHIA **9** 62

CONDREY, CLAY P
(**41**) SDN **41** 02-03

CONE, DAVID P
(13,44,17,11, 22,**36**,16) KCA **13** 86, NYN **44** 87-91, **17** 91-92, TORA **11** 92, KCA **17** 93, **22** 94, TORA **11** 95, NYA **36** 95-00, BOSA **36** 01, NYN **16** 03

CONGER, DICK P
(22,**37**,21) DETA **22** 40, PITN **37** 41-42 PHIN **21** 43

CONIGLIARO, BILLY OF B
(1,4,**40**,9,16) BOSA **4** 69, **1** 69-70, **40** 69-71, MILA **9** 72, OAKA **16** 73

CONIGLIARO, TONY (TONY C) OF B
(**25**,10,4) BOSA **25** 64-67, 69-70, CALA **10/4** 71, BOSA **25** 75

CONINE, JEFF OF/1B
(**19**,18) KCA **19** 90, 92, FLAN **19** 93-97, KCA **19** 98, BALA **18** 99-03, FLAN **18** 03-05

CONLAN, JOCKO OF
(**8**) CHIA **8** 34-35

CONLEY, BOB P
(**41**) PHIN **41** 58

CONLEY, GENE P
(56,**22**,29,18) BOSN **56** 52, MILN **22** 54-58, PHIN **29** 59-60, BOSA **18** 61-63

CONNALLY, FRITZ (FRITZIE) 3B
(26,**11**) CHIN **26** 83, BALA **11** 85

CONNALLY, SARGE P
(25,**15**) CLEA **25** 31, **15** 32-34

CONNATSER, BRUCE 1B
(**37**) CLEA **37** 31-32

CONNELLY, BILL (WILD BILL) P
(24,35,30,**26**) PHIA **24** 45, CHIA **35** 50, DETA **30** 50, NYN **26** 52-53

CONNELLY, STEVE P
(**56**) OAKA **56** 98

CONNOLLY, ED, SR. C F
(11,10,24) BOSA **11** 31, **10** 32, **24** 34

CONNOLLY, ED, JR. P S
(29,39) BOSA **29** 64, CLEA **39** 67

CONNOR, MARK CH
(**52**,53,_) NYA *CH* **52** 84-87, 90-93, ARI *CH* **52** 98-00, TORA *CH* **53** 01 02, TEXA *CH* _ 03, **52** 04-05

CONNORS, BILLY P/CH
(67,**45**,38,30, 36,28,3,22, 42,4) CHIN **67/45** 66, NYN **38/30** 67, **45** 68, KCA *CH* **36/28** 80, **36** 81, CHIN *CH* **3** 82-86, SEAA *CH* **22** 87, *CH* **36** 87-88, NYA *CH* **42** 89, *CH* **36** 89-90, CHIN *CH* **4** 92-93, NYA *CH* **36** 94-95

CONNORS, CHUCK 1B
(36,**40**) BKNN **36** 49, CHIN **40** 51

CONNORS, MERV 3B/1B
(44,**18**) CHIA **44** 37, **18** 38

CONROY, BILL C
(_,25,10,**23**) PHIA _ 35, **25** 36, **10/25** 37, BOSA **23** 42-44

CONROY, TIM P
(37,**24**,39,40) OAKA **37** 78, 82-83, **24** 83-85, STLN **39** 86, **40** 87

CONSOLO, BILLY INF/CH
(8,11,7,1,25, **6**,15,11,50) BOSA **8** 53-54, **11** 55, **7** 56-57, **1** 57-59, WASA **25** 59, **6** 59-60, MINA **6** 61, PHIN **15** 62, LAA **1** 62, KCA **6** 62, DETA *CH* **50** 79-93

CONSTABLE, JIM (SHERIFF) P
(39,46,48,37, **34**,30) NYN **39** 56, **46** 57, SFN **48** 58, CLEA **37** 58, WASA **34** 58, MILN **30** 62, SFN **34** 63

CONSUEGRA, SANDY P
(15,30,**20**,21, 49) WASA **15** 50, **30** 51-53, CHIA **20** 53-56, BALA **20** 56, **21** 57, NYN **49** 57

CONTI, GUY CH
(**56**) NYN *CH* **56** 05

CONTI, JASON OF
(13,**6**,4,29,22) ARIN **13** 00, **6** 01, TBA **4** 02, MILN **29/22** 03, TEXA **19** 04

CONTRERAS, JOSE P
(**52**) NYA **52** 03-04, CHIA **52** 04-05

CONTRERAS, NARDI P/CH
(**29**,43,54) CHIA **29** 80, NYA *CH* **43** 95, SEAA *CH* **54** 97-98, CHIA *CH* **54** 98-02, **45** 00

CONVERSE, JIM P
(41,25,32,53, 38) SEAA **41** 93, **25** 94, **32** 95, KCA **53** 95, **38** 96-97

CONWAY, JACK INF
(47,4,**7**,28) CLEA **47** 41, **4** 46, **7** 47, NYN **28** 48

CONYERS, HERB 1B
(**11**) CLEA **11** 50

COOGAN, DALE 1B
(**3**) PITN **3** 50

COOK, AARON P
(35,**28**) COLN **35** 02, **28** 03-05

COOK, ANDY P
(**34**) NYA **34** 93

COOK, CLIFF 3B
(18,19,11,15, 6,**1**) CINN **18** 59, **19** 60, **11** 61, **15** 62, NYN **6** 62, **1** 63

COOK, DENNIS P
(36,31,30,**39**, 25,27,42,21) SFN **36** 88, **31** 89, PHIN **30** 89 **39** 89-90, LAN **39** 90, **25** 90-91 CLEA **39** 92-93, CHIA **27** 94, CLEA **27** 95, TEXA **42** 95-96, FLAN **42** 97, NYN **27** 98-01, PHIN **39** 01, ANAA **21** 02

COOK, EARL P
(**34**) DETA **34** 41

COOK, GLEN P
(**33**) TEXA **33** 85

COOK, MIKE P
(**46**,36,43,33, 55) CALA **45** 86-87, **36/43** 88, MINA **33** 89, BALA **55** 93

COOK,RON P
(**41**) HOUN **41** 70-71

COOKE, DUSTY OF/CH/M
(**6**,32,7,9,42) NYA **6** 30-31, **32** 32, BOSA **7** 33, **6** 34, **9** 35-36, CINN **42** 38, PHIN *CH/M* **32** 48, *CH* **32** 49-52

COOKE, STEVE P
(**26**) PITN **26** AAA 92-97, CINN **26** 9

COOKSON, BRENT DH/OF
(48,**30**) KCA **48** 95, LAN **30** 99

COOLBAUGH, MIKE SS
(**14**,28) MILN **14** 01, STLN **28** 02

COOLBAUGH, SCOT 3B/1B
(**42**,12,53) TEXA **42** 89-90, SDN **12** 91, STLN **53** 94

COOMBS, BOBBY P
(18,**24**) PHIA **18** 33, NYN **24** 43

COOMBS, DANNY P
(41,**44**,31,46) HOUN **41** 63, **44** 64-67, **31** 67, **44** 68, **31** 68-69, SDN **46** 70-71

COOMER, RON 1B/DH
(15,**8**,6,39) MINA **15** 95, **8** 96-00, CHIN **6** 01, NYA **39** 02, LAN **8** 03

COONEY, BOB (LEFTY) P
(**20**) STLA **20** 31-32

COONEY, JIMMY (SCOOPS) SS/INF
(**8**) STLN **8** 24

COONEY, JOHNNY OF/CH
(5,15,25,34, 24,**9**,18,21, 28,34) BKNN **5** 35, **15** 36, **25** 37, BOSN **34** 38, **24** 39, **9** 40-42, BKNN **18** 43-44, NYA **21** 44, BOSN *CH* **28** 46-52, MILN *CH* **28** 53-55, CHIA *CH* **34** 57-64

COOPER, BRIAN P
(**45**,50,37,52) ANAA **45** 99-01, TORA **50** 02, SFN **37** 04, **52** 05

COOPER, CAL P
(**16**) WASA **16** 48

COOPER,CECIL 1B/DH/CH
(17,**15**,14) BOSA **17** 71-76, **15** 76, MILA **15** 77-87, MILN *CH* **14** 02, HOUN *CH* **15** 05

COOPER, DON P/CH
(**34**,36,39,50, 63,21) MINA **34** 81-82, TORA **36** 83, NYA **39** 85, CHIA *CH* **50** 95, **63** 02, **34** 03-04, **21** 05

COOPER, GARY OF/3B
(**22**,36) ATLN **22** 80, HOUN **36** 91

COOPER, MORT P
(30,25,**13**,14, 24,34) STLN **30** 38, **25** 39-40, **13** 41-42, **14/24** 42, **13** 43-45, BOSN **13** 45-47, NYN **13** 47, CHIN **34** 49

COOPER, PAT P/1B
(28,15) PHIA **28** 46, **15** 47

COOPER, SCOTT 3B/1B/DH
(45,**34**,46,16, 14) BOSA **45** 90-92, **34** 93-94, STLN **46/34** 95, KCA **16/14** 97

COOPER, WALKER (WALK) C/CH
(17,**15**,7,5,39, 28,25,30,40) STLN **17** 40, **15** 41-45, NYN **7** 46, **5** 47-49, **7** 49, CINN **7** 49-50, BOSN **39** 50-51, MILN **39** 53, PITN **28** 54, CHIN **25** 54-55, STLN **30** 56-57, KCA *CH* **40** 60

COPELAND, MAYS P
(**15**) STLN **15** 35

COPPINGER, ROCKY P
(**27**,32,56) BALA **27** 96-99, MILN **32** 99-00, **56** 01

COPPOLA, HENRY P
(22,**19**) WASA **22** 35, **19** 36

COQUILLETTE, TRACE INF
(**53**) MONN **53** 99, **28** 00

CORA, ALEX 2B/SS B
(3,**13**,12,23) LAN **3** 98-01, **13** 02-04, CLEA **12** 05, BOSA **23** 05

CORA, JOEY 2B/CH B
(4,5,21,**28**) SDN **4** 87, 89, **5** 90, CHIA **21** 91, **28** 92-94, SEAA **28** 95-98, CLEA **28** 98, CHIA *CH* **28** 05

CORBETT, DOUG P
(**23**) MINA **23** 80-82, CALA **23** 82-86, BALA **23** 87

CORBETT, GENE INF
(32,22,**23**) PHIN **32** 36, **22** 37, **23** 38

CORBETT, SHERMAN P
(23,**36**) CALA **23** 88, **36** 88-90

CORBIN, ARCHIE P
(**50**,41,43) KCA **50** 91, BALA **41** 96, FLAN **43/50** 99

CORBIN, RAY P
(41,**23**) MINA **41** 71, **23** 71-75

CORBITT, CLAUDE INF
(8,**14**) BKNN **8** 45, CINN **14** 46, 48-49

CORCORAN, ROY P
(53,**47**) MONN **53** 99, **47** 04

CORCORAN, TIM UTIL
(**25**,1,28,33, 22,27,29) DETA **25** 77-80, MINA **1** 81, PHIN **28** 83, **33** 84, **22** 84-85, NYN **27/29** 86

CORCORAN, TIM P
(**56**) TBA **56** 05

CORDERO, CHAD P
(62,**32**) MONN **62** 03, **32** 04, WASN **32** 05

CORDERO, FRANCISCO P
(43,30,**31**) DETA **43** 99, TEXA **30** 00-01, **31** 02-05

CORDERO, WIL SS/1B/OF
(**12**,1,30,26, 16,25) MONN **12** 92-96, BOSA **12** 97, CHIA **12** 98, CLEA **1** 99, PITN **12** 00, CLEA **1** 00, **30** 00-02, MONN **26** 02, **12** 03, FLAN **16** 04, WASN **25** 05

CORDOVA, FRANCISCO P
(**67**) PITN **67** 96-00, **32** 01

CORDOVA, MARTY OF
(**40**,15,46) MINA **40** 95-99, TORA **15** 00, CLEA **46** 01, BALA **40** 02-03, (04)

COREY, BRYAN P
(**49**) ARIN **49** 98, LAN **49** 02

COREY, MARK (F.) P
(**27**,44) NYN **27** 01-02, COLN **27** 02, PITN **44** 03-04

COREY, MARK (M.) OF
(**15**) BALA **15** 79-81

CORKINS, MIKE P
(30,39,**40**) SDN **30** 69-71, **39** 72, **40** 72-74

CORMIER, LANCE P
(**32**) ARIN **32** 04-05

CORMIER, RHEAL P
(52,**37**,34,13, 33) STLN **52** 91-94, **37** 94, BOSA **34** 95, MONN **37** 96, **13** 97, BOSA **37** 99-00, PHIN **33** 01, **37** 02-05

CORNEJO, MARDIE P
(47,**30**) NYN **47/30** 78

CORNEJO, NATE P
(24,**34**) DETA **24** 01, **34** 02-04

CORNELIUS, REID P
(49,47,**38**) MONN **49** 95, NYN **47** 95, FLAN **38** 99-00

CORNELL, JEFF P
(**31**) SFN **31** 84

Darren Daulton was just coming into his own when injuries began to plague him. Back-to-back 20+ HR and 100+ RBI seasons showed great promise, but in 1996 he was only able to play five games. He ended his career in 1997 on a high note. He lead all batters with a .389 BA for the World Series Champion Florida Marlins.

CORNETT, BRAD P
(58,53,22) TORA **58/53** 94, **22** 95

CORNUTT, TERRY P
(**34**) SFN **34** 77-78, **42**

CORRALES, PAT C/CH/M
(29,10,**7**,28, 45,8,18,5, 47,39) PHIN **29** 64, **10** 65, STLN **7** 66, CINN **7** 68-72, SDN **28** 72-73, **29** 73, TEXA *CH* **45** 76-78, *M* **45** 78-80, PHIN *M* **8** 82, **18/5** 83, CLEA *M* **18** 83-85, **7** 85-87, NYA *CH* **47** 89, ATLN *CH* **39** 90-05

CORREA, ED P
(56,**18**,53) CHIA **56** 85, TEXA **18** 86, **53/21 /18** 87

CORREIA, KEVIN P
(50,**53**) SFN **50** 03, **53** 03-05

CORREIA, ROD 2B
(**5**) CALA **5** 93-95

CORRELL, VIC C
(48,29,**9**) BOSA **48** 72, ATLN **29** 74-77, CINN **9** 78-80

CORRIDEN, JOHN, JR. C S
(39,49) BKNN **39/49** 46

CORRIDEN, JOHN, SR. (RED) CH/M F
(32,41,51,56, 19,**30**,31,33) CHIN *CH* **32/41** 32, *CH* **51** 33-34, *CH* **56** 36-37, *CH* **19** 37-40, BKNN *CH* **30** 41-46, NYA *CH* **31** 47-48, CHIA *M* **33** 50

CORSI, JIM P
(**41**,48,27) OAKA **41** 88-90, HOUN **41** 91, OAKA **48** 92, FLAN **41** 93, OAKA **41** 95-96, BOSA **41** 97-99, BALA **27** 99

CORT, BARRY P
(**18**) MILA **18** 77

CORTES, DAVID P
(**51**,47,50) ATLN **51** 99-00, CLEA **47** 03, COLN **50** 05

CORTEZ, FERNANDO 3B
(**2**) TBA **2** 05

CORWIN, AL P
(39,40,17,27, 41,32,**34**) NYN **39** 51, **40/17** 52, **27** 53, **41/32** 54, **34** 54-55

COSCARART, JOE 3B B
(26,22) BOSN **26** 35, **22** 36

COSCARART, PETE 2B B
(3,**5**) BKNN **3** 38-41, PITN **5** 42-46

COSEY, RAY PH
(**45**) OAKA **45** 80

COSGROVE, MIKE P
(**37**) HOUN **37** 72-76

COSMAN, JIM P
(**42**,32) STLN **42** 66-67, CHIN **32** 70

COSTA, SHANE OF
(**15**) KCA **15** 05

COSTELLO, JOHN (ELVIS) P
(**50**,45) STLN **50** 88-90, MONN **50** 90, SDN **45** 91

COSTO, TIM 1B
(57,18) CINN **57** 92, **18** 93

COTA, HUMBERTO C
(**11**) PITN **11** 01-05

COTTIER, CHUCK 2B/CH/M
(13,3,**7**,4,53, 15,5, MILN **13** 59-60, DETA **3** 61, WASA **7** 61-65, CALA **4** 68-69, NYN *CH* **53** 79-81, SEAA *CH* **15** 82-84, *M* **15** 84-86, CHIN *CH* **5** 88-91, *CH* **15** 92-93, *CH* **5** 94, BALA *CH* **15** 95, PHIN *CH* **3** 97-00

COTTO, HENRY OF/DH
(**28**,46,29) CHIN **28** 84, NYA **46** 85-87, **17/28** 87, SEAA **28** 88-93, FLAN **29** 93

COTTS, NEAL P
(38,**46**) CHIA **38** 03, **46** 04-05

COUCHEE, MIKE P
(**49**) SDN **49** 83

COUGHTRY, MARLAN 3B/2B
(2,14,30) BOSA **2** 60, LAA **14** 62, KCA **30** 62, CLEA **2** 62

COULTER, CHIP 2B
(**35**) STLN **35** 69

COUNSELL, CRAIG SS
(**4**,7,30) COLN **4** 95, **7** 97, FLAN **30** 97-99, LAN **30** 99, ARIN **4** 00-03, MILN **30** 04, ARIN **4** 05

COURTNEY, CLINT (SCRAP IRON) C/CH
(45,11,**14**,10, 22,2,6) NYA **45** 51, STLA **11** 52-53, BALA **11** 54, CHIA **11** 55, WASA **14** 55-59, BALA **10** 60, KCA **22** 61, BALA **2** 61, HOUN *CH* **6** 65

COURTRIGHT, JOHN P
(**62**) CINN **62** 95

COVINGTON, CHET P
(**10**) PHIN **10** 44

COVINGTON, WES OF
(**43**,26,14,25) MILN **43** 56-61, CHIA **26** 61, KCA **14** 61, PHIN **43** 61-65, CHIN **43** 66, LAN **25** 66

COWAN, BILLY OF
(20,3,27,24, 12,35,**14**) CHIN **20** 63-64, NYN **3** 65, MILN **27** 65, PHIN **24** 67, NYA **12** 69, CALA **35** 69, **14** 70-72

COWENS, AL OF/DH
(**18**,10,16) KCA **18** 74-79, CALA **18** 80, DETA **10** 80-81, SEAA **16** 82-86

COWLEY, JOE P
(38,**41**,40,39) ATLN **38** 82, NYN **41** 84-85, CHIA **40** 86, PHIN **39** 87

COX, BILL P
(22,66,24,**17**, 19,27,29) STLN **22** 36, CHIA **66** 37, **24** 38, STLA **17** 38, **19** 39, **27/29** 40

COX, BILLY SS/3B
(38,4,6,**3**) PITN **38** 41, **4** 46, **6** 47, BKNN **3** 48-54, BALA **3** 55

COX, BOBBY 3B/CH/M
(14,33,**6**) NYA **14** 68-69, *CH* **33** 77, ATLN *M* **6** 78-81, TORA *M* **6** 82-85, ATLN *M* **6** 90-05

COX, CASEY P
(**29**,38,39) WASA **29** 66, **38** 67, **29** 67-71, TEXA **29** 72, NYA **39** 72, **29** 73

COX, DANNY P
(**34**,57,50) STLN **34** 83-90, PHIN **34** 91-92, PITN **57** 92, TORA **50** 93-95

COX, DARRON C
(**37**) MONN **37** 99

COX, GLENN P
(8,**16**,28) KCA **8** 55, **16** 56, **28** 57, **16** 58

COX, JEFF 2B/CH
(**19**,38,17,26, __,47) OAKA **19** 80-81, KCA *CH* **38/17** 95, MONN *CH* **26** 01, FLAN *CH* __ 02, **47** 03-05

COX, JIM 2B
(56,**10**) MONN **56** 73, **10** 74-76

COX, LARRY C/CH
(**5**,6,20,9,35) PHIN **5** 73-75, SEAA **6/5** 77, CHIN **6** 78, SEAA **5** 80, TEXA **20** 81, CHIN **9** 82, *CH* **35** 88-89

COX, STEVE INF/OF
(**71**) TBA **71** 99, **28** 00-02

COX, TED UTIL
(18,**22**,10,34) BOSA **18** 77, CLEA **22** 78-79, SEAA **10** 80, TORA **34** 81

COX, TERRY P
(48,26) CALA **48/26** 70

COZART, CHARLIE P
(**21**) BOSN **21** 45

CRABTREE, ESTEL (CRABBY) OF/CH
(**3**,27,11) CINN **3** 32, STLN **27** 33, **11** 41-42, CINN **3** 43-44, *CH* **3** 44

CRABTREE, TIM P
(**37**,23,35) TORA **37** 95-97, TEXA **23** 98-00, **35** 01

CRADDOCK, WALT P
(15,6,30) KCA **15** 55-56, **6/30** 58

CRADLE, RICKY OF
(**48**) SEAA **48** 98

CRAFT, HARRY (WILDFIRE) OF/CH/M
(15,44,**23**,41, 3,53,1) CINN **15** 37, **44** 38, **23** 39-42, KCA *CH* **41** 55-57, *M* **41** 57-59, CHIN *CH* **3** 60, *CH/M* **53** 61, HOUN *M* **1** 62-64

CRAGHEAD, HOWARD (JUDGE) P
(**21**) CLEA **21** 31, 33

CRAIG, PETE P
(25,**35**) WASA **25** 64, **35** 64-66

CRAIG, ROD OF
(**19**,56,24,47) SEAA **19** 79-80, CLEA **56/24** 82, CHIA **47** 86

CRAIG, ROGER P/CH/M
(40,**38**,13,41, 37,43,35,28, 2,52,33) BKNN **40** 55-57, LAN **40** 58, **38** 59-61, NYN **38** 62-63, **13** 63, STLN **41** 64, CINN **37** 65, PHIN **43/35/28** 66, SDN *CH* **38** 69-72, HOUN *CH* **2** 74-75, SDN *CH* **38** 77, *M* **38** 78-79, DETA *CH* **52** 80, *CH* **38** 81-84, SFN *M* **33** 85-87, *M* **38** 87-92

CRAIN, JESSE P
(**28**) MINA **28** 04-05

CRAM, JERRY P
(**38**,27,49) KCA **38** 69, NYN **27** 74, **38** 74-75, KCA **49** 76

CRAMER, DOC (FLIT) OF/CH
(26,**8**,2,28) PHIA **26** 31-35, **8** 33-35, BOSA **8** 36-40, WASA **2** 41, DETA **8** 42-48, *CH* **8** 48, CHIA *CH* **28** 51-53

CRANDALL, DEL C/M/CH
(23,**1**,9,16,7) BOSN **23** 49-50, MILN **1** 53-63, SFN **9** 64, PITN **16** 65, CLEA **7** 66, MILA *M* **1** 72-75, CALA *CH* **1** 77, SEAA *M* **1** 83-84

CRANDALL, DOC CH
(**34**,32) PITN *CH* **34** 32-34, STLA *CH* **32** 53

CRAWFORD, CARL OF
(8,**13**) TBA **8** 02, **13** 03-05

CRAWFORD, CARLOS P
(**54**) PHIN **54** 96

CRAWFORD, GLENN (SHORTY) OF
(35,**28**,43) STLN **35** 45, PHIN **28** 45, **43** 46

CRAWFORD, JIM (CATFISH) P
(30,**28**) HOUN **30** 73, 75, DETA **28** 76-78

CRAWFORD, JOE P
(66,**49**) NYN **66/49** 97

CRAWFORD, LARRY P
(**41**) PHIN **41** 37

CRAWFORD, PAT 3B
(**11**) STLN **11** 33-34

CRAWFORD, PAXTON P
(**63**) BOSA **63** 00-01, (02)

CRAWFORD, RUFUS (JAKE) OF
(**21**) STLA **21** 52

CRAWFORD, STEVE P
(**28**,49) BOSA **28** 80-82, 84-87, KCA **49** 89, **28** 90-91

CRAWFORD, WILLIE OF
(43,**27**,5,21, 99) LAN **43** 64-68, **27** 69-75, STLN **5** 76, HOUN **21** 77, OAKA **99** 77

CREDE, JOE 3B
(**24**) CHIA **24** 00-05

CREEDON, CONNIE PH
(**17**) BOSN **17** 43

CREEDON, PAT (WHOOPS) 2B
(**8**) BOSA **8** 31

CREEK, DOUG P
(**37**,51,38,36, 39,52) STLN **37** 95, SFN **51**96-97, CHIN **37** 99, TBA **38** 00-02, SEAA **36** 02, TORA **39** 03, DETA **52** 05

CREEL, JACK (TEX) P
(**19**) STLN **19** 45

CREEL, KEITH P
(**21**,40,42) KCA **21** 82-83, CLEA **40** 85, TEXA **42** 87

CREGER, BERNIE SS
(**16**) STLN **16** 47

CRESPI, CREEPY 2B
(24,19,2,**7**) STLN **24** 38, **19** 39, **2** 40, **7** 41-42

CRESPO, CESAR 2B
(8,**2**,31) SDN **8** 01-02, **2** 02, BOSA **31** 04

CRESPO, FELIPE OF
(6,3,**52**) TORA **6** 96, **3** 97-98, SFN **52** 00-01, PHIN **52** 01

CRESS, WALKER (FOOTS) P
(**32**) CINN **32** 48-49

CRESSE, MARK CH
(**58**) LAN *CH* **58** 78-98

CRESSEND, JACK P
(59,**28**,27) MINA **59** 00-01, **28** 01-02, CLEA **27** 03-04

CREWS, TIM P
(**52**) LAN **52** 87-92

CRIDER, JERRY P
(27,44) MINA **27** 69, CHIA **44** 70

CRIM, CHUCK P
(**32**) MILA **32** 87-91, CALA **32** 92-93, CHIN **32** 94

CRIMIAN, JACK P
(**25**,24,19) STLN **25** 51-52, KCA **24** 56, DETA **19** 57

CRIPE, DAVE 3B
(**31**) KCA **31** 78

CRISCIONE, DAVE C
(**40**) BALA **40** 77

CRISCOLA, TONY OF
(14,**22**) STLA **14** 42-43, CINN **22** 44

CRISP, CAVELLI (COCO) OF
(**10**) CLEA **10** 02-05

CRISTANTE, LEO P
(38,27) PHIN **38** 51, DETA **27** 55

CRITZ, HUGHIE 2B
(1,**6**) NYN **1** 32, NYN **6** 33-35

CROCKER, CLAUDE P
(**27**) BKNN **27** 44-45

CROMARTIE, WARREN OF/1B
(**49**,24) MONN **49** 74, 76-83, KCA **24/49** 91

CROMER, D. T. INF
(39,12,**36**) CINN **39/12** 00, **36** 00-01

CROMER, TRIPP SS/INF
(44,**7**,41,10,3) STLN **44** 93-94, **7** 95, LAN **41** 97-98, **7** 98-99, HOUN **10** 00, **3** 03

CROMPTON, HERB (WORKHORSE) C
(**10**,16) WASA **10** 37, NYA **16** 45

CRON, CHRIS 1B
(39,**44**,57) CALA **39/44** 91, CHIA **57** 92

CRONE, RAY P
(**20**,12,44) MILN **20** 54, **12** 54-55, **20** 55-57, NYN **44** 57, SFN **44** 58

CRONIN, JOE SS/M
(**4**,6) WASA **4** 31-35, *M* **4** 33-35, BOSA **6** 36, *M* **6** 36, **4** 37-45, *M* **4** 37-47

CROON, MARC P
(**48**) COLN **48** 04

CROSBY, BOBBY SS/DH
(8,**7**) OAKA **8** 03, **7** 04-05

CROSBY, BUBBA OF
(49,**19**,18) LAN **49** 03, NYA **19** 04-05, **18** 05

CROSBY, ED INF
(**4**,17,12) STLN **4** 70, 72-73, CINN **17** 73, CLEA **12** 74-76

CROSBY, KEN P
(**39**) CHIN **39** 75-76

CROSETTI, FRANKIE (CROW) SS/CH
(5,**1**,2,) NYA **5** 32-36, **1** 37-44, **2** 45-48, *CH* **2** 47-68, SEAA *CH* **2** 69, MINA *CH* **2** 70-71

CROSS, JEFF INF
(2,35,**3**,18) STLN **2** 42, **35** 46, **3** 47-48, CHIN **18** 48

CROUCH, BILL P
(24,26,6,34, **22**) BKNN **24/26** 39, PHIN **6** 41, STLN **34** 41, **22** 45

CROUCH, JACK (ROXY) C
(**10**,25,6) STLA **10** 31, **25** 33, CINN **6** 33

CROUCH, ZACH P
(**56**) BOSA **56** 88

CROUCHER, FRANK (DINGLE) INF
(**3**,7) DETA **3** 39-41, WASA **7** 42

CROUSHORE, RICK P
(24,**44**,54,55) STLN **24** 98, **44** 99, COLN **54** 00, BOSA **55** 00

CROW, DEAN P
(**56**) DETA **56** 98, HOUN **56** 99

CROW, DON C
(**9**) LAN **9** 82

CROWDER, GENERAL P
(15,**12**,16) WASA **15** 31, **12** 32-34, DETA **16** 34-36

CROWE, GEORGE (BIG GEORGE) 1B
(37,39,**15**,18) BOSN **37** 52, MILN **37** 53, **39** 55, CINN **15** 56-58, STLN **18** 59-61

CROWELL, JIM P
(**50**,75,52) CINN **50** 97, PHIN **75** 04, FLAN **52** 05

CROWLEY, TERRY 1B/OF/CH
(37,11,17,18, 38,**10**,15,48, 55,46) BALA **37** 69-70, **11** 71-73, CINN **17** 74-75, ATLN **18** 76, BALA **38** 76, **10** 76-82, MONN **15** 83, BALA *CH* **48** 85, **10** 85-88, MINA *CH* **55** 91, **46** 91-98, BALA *CH* **48** 99-05

CROWSON, WOODY P
(**23**) PHIA **23** 45

CROZIER, ERIC DH/OF
(**17**) TORA **17** 04

CRUCETA, FRANCISCO P
(**55**) CLEA **55** 04

CRUDALE, MIKE P
(**54**,43,48) STLN **54** 02, MILN **43/48** 03

CRUMLING, GENE C
(**35**) STLN **35** 45

CRUZ, CIRILIO (TOMMY) OF B
(**17**,25) STLN **17** 73, CHIA **25** 77

CRUZ, DEIVI SS
(37,**8**,10,11, 35,4) DETA **37** 97, **8** 98-01, SDN **10/8** 02, BALA **11** 03, SFN **35** 04-05, WASN **4** 05

CRUZ, ENRIQUE SS/3B
(**9**) MILN **9** 03

CRUZ, FAUSTO SS
(**41**,48) OAKA **41** 94, **48** 95, DETA **41** 96

CRUZ, HECTOR (HEITY) OF/3B B,U
(11,25,24,9, **7**,27,30) STLN **11** 73, 75, **25** 76-77, CHIN **24** 78, SFN **9** 78-79, CHIN **7** 79-80, CHIN **27** 81, **30** 82

CRUZ, HENRY OF
(**37**,38) LAN **37** 75-76, CHIA **38** 77-78

CRUZ, IVAN 1B/DH
(47,**25**,16) NYA **47** 97, PITN **25** 99-00, STLN **16** 02

CRUZ, JACOB OF
(62,38,30,**51**, 23,44,9) SFN **62** 96, **38** 97, **30** 97-98, CLEA **51** 98-01, COLN **23** 01, DETA **44** 02, CINN **9** 04-05

CRUZ, JOSE, JR. OF S,N
(**23**,22,32) SEAA **23** 97, TORA **23** 97-02, SFN **22** 03, TBA **22** 04, ARIN **22** 05, BOSA **32** 05, LAN **22** 05

CRUZ, JOSE, SR. (CHEO) OF/CH B,F
(38,**25**,21) STLN **38** 70-74, HOUN **25** 75-87, NYA **21** 88, HOUN *CH* **25** 97-05

CRUZ, JUAN P
(**51**) CHIN **51** 01-03, ATLN **51** 04, OAKA **51** 05

CRUZ, JULIO 2B
(2,**6**,16,12) SEAA **2/6** 77, **2** 78, **6** 80-83, CHIA **16** 83-84, **12** 85-86

CRUZ, NELSON P
(60,**40**,41,35, 8) CHIA **60** 97, DETA **40** 99-00, HOUN **41** 01-02, COLN **35** 03, MILN **8** 05

CRUZ, TODD SS
(48,16,7,14, **21**,10) PHIN **48/16** 78, KCA **7** 79, CALA **14** 80, CHIA **21** 80-81, SEAA **21** 82-83, BALA **10** 83-84

CRUZ, VICTOR P
(47,27,**23**,49) TORA **47/27** 78, CLEA **47** 79, **23** 79-80, PITN **49** 81, TEXA **23** 83

CUBBAGE, MIKE INF/CH/M
(**4**,26,3,55,24, 9,39) TEXA **4** 74-76, MINA **26** 76-80, NYN **3** 81, *CH* **55** 89, **4** 90-96, *M* **4** 91, HOUN *CH* **24** 97-00, **9** 01, BOSA *CH* **39** 02-03

CUBILLAN, DARWIN P
(34,45,**31**,49) TORA **34** 00, TEXA **45** 00, MONN **31** 01, BALA **49** 04

CUCCINELLO, AL 2B/3B B
(22,**24**) NYN **22/24** 35

CUCCINELLO, TONY (COOCH, CHICK) 2B/CH B
(**5**,3,27,15,47, 51,44,33,50) BKNN **5** 32-35, BOSN **3** 36-39, **5** 40, NYN **27** 40, BOSN **15** 42-43, CHIA **47** 43-45, CINN *CH* **3** 49, **51** 50-51, CLEA *CH* **44** 52-56, CHIA *CH* **33** 57-66, DETA *CH* **50** 67-68, CHIA *CH* **33** 69

CUCCURULLO, COOKIE P
(23,**27**) PITN **23** 43, **27** 44-45

CUDDYER, MICHAEL INF/DH/OF
(**5**) MINA **5** 01-05

CUELLAR, BOBBY P/CH
(53,**24**,5,26, 46) TEXA **53/24** 77, SEAA *CH* **5** 95-96, MONN *CH* **26** 97-00, TEXA **46** 01

CUELLAR, CHARLIE P
(**49**) CHIA **49** 50

CUELLAR, MIKE P
(32,**35**) CINN **32** 59, STLN **35** 64, HOUN **35** 65-68, BALA **35** 69-76, CALA **35** 77

CUETO, BERTO P
(**16**) MINA **16** 61

CULBERSON, LEON (LEE) OF
(27,**11**,6) BOSA **27** 43, **11** 44-47, WASA **6** 48

CULLEN, JACK P
(40,**45**) NYA **40** 62, **45** 65-66

CULLEN, TIM INF
(**1**,4,6,16) WASA **1** 66-67, CHIA **4** 68, WASA **6** 68, **1** 69-71, OAKA **4/16** 72

CULLENBINE, ROY OF/1B
(19,30,8,50, 14,7,**1**,6,2) DETA **19** 38-39, BKNN **30** 40, STLA **8** 40, **50** 41-42, WASA **14** 42, NYA **7** 42, CLEA **1** 43-45, DETA **6** 45, **2** 46-47

CULLER, DICK SS
(45,28,8,**14**, 7,47) PHIA **45** 36, CHIA **28** 43, BOSN **8** 44-45, **14** 46-47, CHIN **7** 48, NYN **47** 49

CULMER, WILL OF/DH
(**25**) CLEA **25** 83

CULP, BENNY C/CH
(25,**29**,20,23, 31,2) PHIN **25** 42, **29** 43, **20/23/31/2** 44, *CH* **25** 46-47

CULP, RAY P
(37,**21**) PHIN **37** 63-66, CHIN **37** 67, BOSA **21** 68-73

CULVER, GEORGE P
(40,**39**,33,35) CLEA **40** 66-67, CINN **39** 68-69, STLN **39** 70, HOUN **39** 70, **33/39** 71, **39** 72, LAN **40** 73, PHIN **35** 73-74

CUMBERLAND, JOHN P/CH
(56,**40**,41,36, 47,52) NYA **56** 68-70, NYN **40** 70-71, **41** 72, STLN **36** 72, CALA **47** 74, BOSA *CH* **52** 99-01, KCA *CH* **47** 02-03, **52** 04

CUMMINGS, JOHN P
(47,**44**,45,41, 34,19) SEAA **47** 93, **44/45** 94, **44** 95, LAN **41** 95-96, DETA **34** 96, **19** 97

CUMMINGS, MIDRE OF
(**30**,16,29,18, 13,20,3) PITN **30** 93-97, PHIN **16** 97, BOSA **29** 98, MINA **16** 99-00, BOSA **18** 00, ARIN **13** 01, TBA **20** 04, BALA **3** 05

CUMMINGS, STEVE P
(**32**) TORA **32** 89-90

CUNNANE, WILL P
(39,**33**,49,50, 26) SDN **39** 97-99, **33** 00, MILN **33** 01, CHIN **49** 02, ATLN **50** 03, **26** 03-04

CUNNINGHAM, BILL CH
(**28**) CHIA *CH* **28** 32

CUNNINGHAM, BRUCE P
(**17**) BOSN **17** 32

CUNNINGHAM, JOE 1B
(28,**15**,5,3) STLN **28** 54, 56-58, **15** 59-61, CHIA **5** 62-64, WASA **3** 64-66

CUNNINGHAM, RAY 3B
(no#) STLN **no#** 32

CURRENCE, LAFAYETTE P
(**20**) MILA **20** 75

CURRIE, BILL P
(43,**30**) WASA **43/30** 55

CURRIN, PERRY SS
(**15**) STLA **15** 47

CURRY, STEVE P
(**53**) BOSA **53** 88

CURRY, TONY OF
(**7**,29) PHIN **7** 60-61, CLEA **29** 66

CURTIS, CHAD OF
(30,17,**9**,10, 12,28,2) CALA **30/17** 92, **9** 93-94, DETA **9** 95-96, LAN **10** 96, CLEA **12** 97, NYA **28** 97-99, TEXA **2** 00, **9** 01

CURTIS, JACK P
(**42**,10,43) CHIN **42** 61-62, MILN **10** 62, CLEA **43** 63

CURTIS, JOHN (JACK) P
(44,**22**,40,51, 28,16) BOSA **44** 70-71, **22** 71-73, STLN **22** 74-76, SFN **40** 77-79, SDN **51** 80-82, CALA **28** 82, **16** 82-84

CURTIS, VERN (TURK) P
(17,**36**) WASA **17** 43-44, **36** 46

CURTRIGHT, GUY OF
(**12**) CHIA **12** 43-46

CUSICK, JACK SS
(37,**10**) CHIN **37** 51, BOSN **10** 52

CUST, JACK OF/DH
(19,**21**,39) ARIN **19** 01, COLN **21** 02, BALA **39** 03-04

CUYLER, KIKI OF/CH
(**3**,8,4,25,38, 42,30) CHIN **3** 32-35, CINN **8** 35, **4** 36-37, BKNN **25** 38, CHIN *CH* **38** 41-42, *CH* **42** 43, BOSA *CH* **30** 49

CUYLER, MILT OF
(**22**,15,4) DETA **22** 90-95, BOSA **15** 96, TEXA **4** 98

CYR, ERIC OF
(**49**) SDN **49** 02

CZAJKOWSKI, JIM P
(**38**) COLN **38** 94

D

DAAL, OMAR P
(54,47,**37**,36, 14) LAN **54** 93-95, MONN **47** 96-97, TORA **54** 97, ARIN **37** 98-00, PHIN **37** 00-01, LAN **36** 02, BALA **14** 03, (04)

D'ACQUISTO, JOHN (THE COUNT, THE COUNT OF MONTE CRISTO) P
(**34**,43,16,12, 28,32) SFN **34** 73-76, STLN **43/34** 77, SDN **16** 77-80, MONN **12/42** 80, CALA **28** 81, OAKA **32** 82

DADE, PAUL UTIL
(29,31,**00**,21, 4) CALA **29** 75-76, CLEA **31** 77, **00**77-79, SDN **21** 79, **4** 79-80, **21** 80

DAGENHARD, JOHN P
(**42**) BOSN **42** 43

DAGLIA, PETE P
(23,**9**) CHIA **23/9** 32

DAGRES, ANGIE (JUNIOR) OF
(34,5,**20**) BALA **34/5/20** 55

DAHL, JAY P
(**42**) HOUN **42** 63

DAHLGREN, BABE 1B/CH
(8,16,28,**12**, 5,__,3,7,48) BOSA **8** 35, **16** 36, NYA **28** 37, **12** 38-40, BOSN **5** 41, CHIN **16** 41-42, STLA __ 42, BKNN **12** 42, PHIN **3** 43, PITN **7** 44-45, STLA **3** 46, KCA *CH* **48** 64

DAHLKE, JERRY (JOE) P
(**31**) CHIA **31** 56

DAIGLE, CASEY P
(**54**) ARIN **54** 04

DAILEY, BILL P
(**27**,15,32) CLEA **27** 61-62, MINA **15** 63-64, **32** 64

DAL CANTON, BRUCE P/CH
(19,**43**,27,30, 39) PITN **19** 67, **43** 68-69, **27** 70, KCA **30** 71, **43** 71-75, ATLN **43** 75, **30** 75-76, CHIA **43** 77, *CH* **43** 78, ATLN *CH* **39** 87-90

DALE, CARL P
(**51**) MILN **51** 99

DALENA, PETE DH
(**31**) CLEA **31** 89

DALESANDRO, MARK 3B/C
(**7**,59,5,66) CALA **7** 94-95, TORA **59** 98, **5** 98-99, CHIA **66** 01

DALEY, BUD P
(**28**,10,22) CLEA **28** 55-56, **10** 57, KCA **22** 58, **28** 58-61, NYA **28** 61-64

DALEY, PETE C
(24,**8**,10,22) BOSA **24** 55 , **8** 56-59, KCA **10/22** 60, WASA **8** 61

DALLESANDRO, DOM (DIM DOM) OF
(16,31,7,**46**) BOSA **16** 37, CHIN **31** 40-41, **7** 41-42, **46** 43-44, 46-47

DALLIMORE, BRIAN SS
(14,**32**,2) SFN **14** 04, **32/2** 05

DALRYMPLE, CLAY C
(**11**,3) PHIN **11** 60-68, BALA **3** 69-71

DALTON, MIKE P
(**42**) DETA **42** 91

DALY, TOM CH
(**30**,32) BOSA **30** 36-43, **32** 44-46

DAMASKA, JACK UTIL
(**19**) STLN **19** 63

D'AMICO, JEFF P
(33,**13**,56,18, 41,31) MILA **33** 96, MILN **13** 97, 99-00, KCA **56** 00, MILN **13** 01, NYN **18** 02, PITN **41** 03, CLEA **31** 04

DAMON, JOHNNY OF
(51,**18**,8) KCA **51** 95, **18** 96-00, OAKA **8** 01, BOSA **18** 02-05

DANCY, BILL CH
(**16**) PHIN *CH* **16** 05

DANEKER, PAT P
(**51**) CHIA **51** 99

DANIEL, CHUCK P
(**18**) DETA **18** 57

DANIEL, JAKE 1B
(**24**) BKNN **24** 37

DANIELS, BENNY P
(30,39,29,**21**) PITN **30** 57-58, **39** 59, **29** 60, WASA **21** 61-65

DANIELS, FRED (TONY) 2B/3B
(**6**) PHIN **6** 45

DANIELS, JACK (SOUR MASH JACK) OF
(**7**) BOSN **7** 52

DANIELS, KAL OF
(**28**) CINN **28** 86-89, LAN **28** 89-92, CHIN **28** 92

DANNING, HARRY (THE HORSE) C
(28,10,9,**8**,3) NYN **28** 33, **10** 34-35, **9** 36-38, **8** 39-40, **3** 41, **8** 42

DANTONIO, FATS C
(32,3,34) BKNN **32** 44, **3/34** 45

DAPPER, CLIFF C
(**19**) BKNN **19** 42

DARCY, PAT P
(58,**44**) CINN **58** 74, **44** 74-76

DARENSBOURG, VIC P
(**40**,20,22,45, 57,39,51) FLAN **40/20** 98, **40** 99-00, **22** 00-02, COLN **27** 03, MONN **45** 03, CHIA **57** 04, NYN **39** 04, DETA **51** 05

DARK, ALVIN (AL, BLACKIE) SS/M/CH
(23,2,19,11, 17,1,55,**5**) BOSN **23** 46, **2** 48-49, NYN **19** 50-56, STLN **11** 56-58, CHIN **17** 58-59, PHIN **1** 60, MILN **19** 60, SFN *M* **1** 61-64, CHIN *CH* **55** 65, KCA *M* **5** 66-67, CLEA *M* **5** 68-70, **1** 70-71, OAKA *M* **5** 74-75, CHIN *CH* **1/5** 77, SDN *M* **5** 77

DARLING, RON P
(44,12,15,**17**) NYN **44** 83-84, **12** 85-89, **15** 89-91, MONN **15** 91, OAKA **17** 91-95

DARNELL, BOB P
(**38**) BKNN **38** 54, 56

DARR, MIKE (C.) OF
(**26**) SDN **26** 99-01

DARR, MIKE (E.) P
(**28**) TORA **28** 77

DARROW, GEORGE P
(**41**) PHIN **41** 34

DARWIN, BOBBY OF/DH
(54,34,35,**2**, 12,42) LAN **54** 62, **34** 62, 69, **35** 71, MINA **2** 72-75, MILA **12** 75-76, BOSA **42** 76-77, CHIN **12** 77

DARWIN, DANNY P
(**44**,18,46,40, 43) TEXA **44** 78-84, MILA **18** 85-86, HOUN **44** 86-90, BOSA **46** 91, **44** 91-94, TORA **44** 95, TEXA **40/44** 95, PITN **44** 96, HOUN **44** 96, CHIA **44** 97, SFN **40** 97, **43** 97-98

DARWIN, JEFF P
(42,**48**) SEAA **42** 94, CHIA **48** 96, CHIA **48** 97

DASCENZO, DOUG OF
(**29**,17) CHIN **29** 88-92, TEXA **29** 93, SDN **17** 96

DASSO, FRANK P
(43,38) CINN **43** 45, **38** 46

DATZ, JEFF C/DH/CH
(**43**,29) DETA **43** 89, CLEA *CH* **29** 02-05

DAUBACH, BRIAN INF/DH/1B
(39,**23**,13) FLAN **39** 98, BOSA **23** 99-02, CHIA **23** 03, BOSA **23** 04, NYN **13** 05

DAUER, RICH 2B/3B/CH
(44,**25**,40,37) BALA **44** 76-77, **25** 78-85, CLEA *CH* **25** 90-91, KCA *CH* **40** 97, **37** 97-98, **25** 99-02, MILN *CH* **25** 03-05

DAUGHERTY, DOC PH
(**21**) DETA **21** 51

DAUGHERTY, JACK UTIL
(33,**8**,22,35, 21) MONN **33** 87, TEXA **8** 89-92, **22** 92, HOUN **35/22** 93, CINN **21** 93

DAUGHTERS, BOB (RED) PR
(25,**21**) BOSA **25/21** 37

DAULTON, DARREN (DUTCH) C
(29,**10**,20,25) PHIN **29** 83, **10** 83, 85-97, FLAN **20** 97, TBA **25** 01

DAVALILLO, VIC OF
(**25**,28,17,18,) 37,33) CLEA **25** 63-68, CALA **28** 68 -69, STLN **17** 69-70, PITN **18** 71-73, OAKA **37** 73-74, LAN **33** 77-80

DAVALILLO, YO-YO SS
(**15**) WASA **15** 53

DAVANON, JEFF OF/DH
(**55**,33) ANAA **55** 99-01, **33** 02, **55** 03-04, LAA **55** 05

DAVANON, JERRY INF
(36,38,46,26, 22,2,19,29, **16**) SDN **36** 69, STLN **38/26** 69, **46/ 22** 70, BALA **2** 71, CALA **19** 73, STLN **29** 74, HOUN **16** 75-76, STLN **16** 77

DAVENPORT, JIM 3B/CH/M
(**12**,34,9,2,1, 57,15) SFN **12** 58-70, *CH* **12** 70, SDN *CH* **34** 74, **12** 74-75, SFN *CH* **9** 76-77, **12** 78-83, **2** 84, *M* **1/12** 85, PHIN *CH* **2** 86-87, CLEA *CH* **12** 89, DETA *CH* **57** 91, SFN *CH* **15** 96

DAVENPORT, JOE P
(60,**23**) CHIA **60** 99, COLN **23** 01

DAVEY, MIKE P
(54,**39**) ATLN **54** 77, **39** 77-78

DAVEY, TOM P
(43,**44**,41) TORA **43** 99, SEAA **43** 99, SDN **43** 00, **44** 00-02, **41** 02

DAVIAULT, RON P
(**35**) NYN **35** 62

DAVID, ANDRE OF/DH/CH
(**21**,26) MINA **21** 84, 86, KCA *CH* **26** 05

DAVIDSON, BOBBY P
(**34**) NYA **34** 89

DAVIDSON, CLEATUS P
(**56**) MINA **56** 99

DAVIDSON, MARK OF/DH
(7,27,42, **24**, 22) MINA **7** 86, **27** 87-88, HOUN **42** 89, **24** 90, **22** 90-91

DAVIDSON, TED P
(56,**36**,32,23) CINN **56** 65-66, **36** 66-68, ATLN **32/23** 68

DAVIE, JERRY P
(**27**) DETA **27** 59

DAVIES, KYLE P
(**26**) ATLN **26** 05

DAVIS, ALVIN 1B/DH
(**21**) SEAA **21** 84-91, CALA **21** 92

DAVIS, BEN C
(25,**13**,31) SDN **25** 98-99, **13** 00-01, SEAA **13** 02-04, CHIA **31** 04

DAVIS, BILL 1B
(**12**) CLEA **12** 65-66, 69, **11** 66

DAVIS, BOB (E.) P
(24,15) KCA **24** 58, **15** 60

DAVIS, BOB (J.) C
(6,**7**,8,16) SDN **6** 73, **7** 75-78, TORA **8** 79-80, CALA **16** 81

DAVIS, BRANDY OF/CH
(**17**,2) PITN **17** 52-53, PHIN *CH* **2** 72

DAVIS, BROCK OF
(**29**,22) HOUN **29** 63-64, 66, CHIN **29** 70-71, MILA **22** 72

DAVIS, BUTCH OF/DH
(33,58,25,46, 40,**13**) KCA **33** 83-84, PITN **58** 87, BALA **25** 88, **46** 89, LAN **40** 91, TEXA **13** 93-94

DAVIS, CHILI OF/DH
(30,33,24,**44**, 45) SFN **30** 81-87, **33** 87, CALA **24** 88-90, MINA **44** 91-92, CALA **44** 93-96, KCA **44** 97, NYA **45** 98-99

DAVIS, CRASH C
(7,**12**) PHIA **7** 40, **12** 41-42

DAVIS, CURT (COONSKIN) P
(42,24,22,27, **26**) PHIN **42** 34-36, CHIN **24** 36, **22** 37, STLN **27** 38-40, BKNN **26** 40-46

DAVIS, DICK OF/DH
(56,**26**,35,28) MILA **56** 77, **26** 78-80, PHIN **26** 81-82, TORA **35** 82, PITN **28** 82

DAVIS, DOUG (P.) P
(46,**17**,48,49) TEXA **46** 99-00, **17** 01-03, TORA **48** 03, MILN **49** 03-05

DAVIS, DOUG (R.) (CRASH) C/CH
(**6**,66,23) CALA **6** 88, TEXA **66** 92, FLAN *CH* **23** 03-04

DAVIS, ERIC OF
(55,**44**,33,24) CINN **55** 84, **44** 84-91, LAN **33** 92-93, DETA **33** 93-94, CINN **44** 96, BALA **24** 97-98, STLN **24** 99-00, SFN **22** 91

DAVIS, GERRY OF
(50,28) SDN **50** 83, **28** 85

DAVIS, GLENN 1B
(**27**,37) HOUN **27** 84-90, BALA **37** 91-93, **27** 93

DAVIS, HARRY (STINKY) 1B
(**26**,27) DETA **26** 32-33, STLA **27** 37

DAVIS, J. J. OF
(**26**) PITN **26** 02-04, WASN **26** 05

DAVIS, JACKIE OF
(**17**) PHIN **17** 62

DAVIS, JASON P
(64,**50**) CLEA **64** 02, **50** 03-05

DAVIS, JIM P
(**22**,26,38) CHIN **22** 54-56, STLN **26** 57, NYN **38** 57

DAVIS, JODY C
(**7**,8) CHIN **7** 81-88, ATLN **8** 88-89, **7** 89-90

DAVIS, JOEL P
(**52**) CHIA **52** 85-88

DAVIS, JOHN (K.) P
(49,**31**,51,44) KCA **49** 87, CHIA **31** 88-89, **51** 89, SDN **44** 90

DAVIS, JOHN (H.) (RED) 3B
(**29**) NYN **29** 41

DAVIS, KANE P
(60.**37**,48,51) CLEA **60** 00, MILN **37** 00, COLN **37** 01, NYN **48** 02, MILN **51** 05

DAVIS, KIDDO OF
(1,2,4,31,7, **24**,8,48) PHIN **1** 32, NYN **2** 33, STLN **4** 34, PHIN **31** 34, NYN **7** 35, **24** 36-37, CINN **8** 37, **48** 38

DAVIS, LANCE P
(**52**) CINN **59** 01

DAVIS, MARK CH
(**13**) ARIN *CH* **13** 04-05

DAVIS, MARK (A.) OF
(**40**) CALA **40** 91

DAVIS, MARK (W.) P
(43,13,32,**48**, 45,37) PHIN **43** 80-81, SFN **13** 83-87, **32** 87, SDN **13** 87, **48** 87-89, KCA **48** 90-92, ATLN **48** 92, PHIN **48** 93, SDN **45** 93, **48** 94, MILA **37/48** 97

DAVIS, MIKE OF/DH
(**16**,37) OAKA **16** 80-87, LAN **37** 88-89 **20** 89

DAVIS, ODIE SS/3B
(**12**) TEXA **12** 78

DAVIS, OTIS (SCAT) PR
(**31**) BKNN **31** 46

DAVIS, PEACHES P
(32,18,55,37) CINN **32** 36, **18** 37, **55** 38, **37** 39

DAVIS, RON (E.) OF
(27,**22**,14,3) HOUN **27** 62, **22** 66-68, STLN **14** 68, PITN **3** 69

DAVIS, RON (G.) P
(53,**39**,34,54, 33) NYA **53** 78-79, **39** 79-81, MINA **34** 82, **39** 82-86, CHIN **39** 86-87, LAN **54** 87, SFN **33** 88

DAVIS, RUSS 3B
(**24**,18) NYA **24** 94-95, SEAA **18** 96-99, SFN **18** 00-01

DAVIS, SPUD C/CH/M
(7,**8**,24,36,4, 11,47) PHIN **7** 32, **8** 33, STLN **8** 34-36, CINN **24** 37, **36** 38, PHIN **4** 39, PITN **11** 40-41, **36** 44-45, *CH* **36** 42-46, *M* **36** 46, CHIN *CH* **47** 50-53

DAVIS, STEVE (K.) P
(**25**,37) TORA **25** 85-86, CLEA **37** 89

DAVIS, STEVE (M.) 2B/3B
(**29**) CHIN **29** 79

DAVIS, STORM P
(**34**,41,14,43, 15,48) BALA **39** 82, **34** 82-86, SDN **34** 87,OAKA **41** 87-88, **14** 88-89, KCA **14** 90-91, **43** 91, BALA **34** 92,OAKA **15** 93, DETA **48** 93-94

DAVIS, TIM P
(**47**) SEAA **47** 94-97

DAVIS, TOD INF
(**16**) PHIA **16** 49, PHIA **16** 51

DAVIS, (H.) TOMMY OF/3B/CH
(**12**,10,29,24, 36,9) LAN **12** 59-66, NYN **12** 67, CHIA **10** 68, SEAA **12** 69, HOUN **10** 69-70, CHIN **29** 70, OAKA **12** 70-71, CHIN **24** 72, BALA **36** 72, **12** 72-75, CALA **9/12** 76, KCA **10** 76, SEAA *CH* **12** 81

DAVIS, TOMMY (J.) C
(**23**) BALA **23** 99

DAVIS, TRENCH OF
(**12**,13,18) PITN **12** 85, **13** 86, ATLN **18** 87

DAVIS, WILLIE OF
(26,**3**,1,15,5, 24) LAN **26** 60, **3** 61-73, MONN **1** 74, TEXA **15/3** 75, STLN **5** 75, SDN **3** 76, CALA **24** 79

DAVIS, WOODY (BABE) P
(**35**) DETA **35** 38

DAVISON, MIKE P
(**41**) SFN **41** 69-70

DAVISON, SCOTT P
(**35**) SEAA **35** 95-96

DAWKINS, GOOKIE 2B/3B
(**3**) CINN **3** 02, KCA **1** 03

DAWKINS, TRAVIS INF
(**6**) CINN **6** 99, **26** 00

DAWLEY, BILL P
(**46**,48,43) HOUN **46** 83-85, CHIA **46** 86, STLN **48** 87, PHIN **43** 88, OAKA **46** 89

DAWLEY, JOEY P
(**33**) ATLN **33** 02, **43** 03, CLEA **58** 04

DAWSON, ANDRE OF/DH
(24,**10**,8) MONN **24** 76, **10** 77-86, CHIN **8** 87-92, BOSA **10** 93-94, FLAN **8** 95-96

DAY, BOOTS OF
(11,20,28,**8**) STLN **11** 69, CHIN **20** 70, MONN **28** 70, **8** 71-74

DAY, PEA RIDGE P
(__) STLN __ 24

DAY, ZACH P
(**54**,40,45) MONN **54** 02-04, WASN **40** 05, COLN **45** 05

DAYETT, BRIAN OF
(62,**24**) NYA **62** 83-84, CHIN **24** 85-87

DAYLEY, KEN P
(30,**46**) ATLN **30** 82-84, STLN **46** 84-90, TORA **46** 91, 93

DEAGO, ROGER P
(**58**) SDN **58** 03

DEAL, COT P/CH
(**28**,38,22,2,5, 31,42,52) BOSA **28** 47-48, STLN **38** 50, **22** 54, CINN *CH* **2** 59-60, HOUN *CH* **5** 62-64, NYA *CH* **31** 65, KCA *CH* **42** 66-67, CLEA *CH* **2** 70-71, DETA *CH* **52** 73-74, HOUN *CH* **2** 83-85

DEAL, LINDSEY OF
(**22**) BKNN **22** 39

DEAN, CHUBBY 1B/P
(28,**19**,16) PHIA **28** 36, **3** 37, **19** 38-41, CLEA **16** 41-43

DEAN, DIZZY P
(**17**,22,31) STLN **17** 32-37, CHIN **22** 38-41, STLA **31** 47

DEAN, HARRY P
(**25**) WASA **25** 41

DEAN, PAUL (DAFFY) P
(**21**,19,22) STLN **21** 34-37, **19** 38, **22** 39, NYN **21** 40-41, STLA **19** 43

DEAN, TOMMY INF
(11,**3**) LAN **11** 67, SDN **3** 69-71

de ARMAS, ROLY CH
(**56**) CHIA *CH* **56** 95-96, TORA *CH* **56** 00

DeBARR, DENNIS P
(**22**) TORA **22** 77

DEBUS, JON CH
(**44**) LAN *CH* **44** 05

DeBUSSCHERE, DAVE P
(**22**) CHIA **22** 62-64

DeCINCES, DOUG 3B/UTIL
(37,**11**,10) BALA **37** 73, **11** 74-81, CALA **11** 82-87, STLN **10** 87

DECKER, JOE P
(36,37,**21**,35) CHIN **36** 69-72, **37** 72, MINA **21** 73-76, SEAA **35** 79

DECKER, MARTY P
(**44**) SDN **44** 83

DECKER, STEVE P
(47,**35**,55,25, 29,27,37) SFN **47** 90, **35** 91-92, FLAN **55** 93, **25** 95, SFN **29** 96, COLN **27** 96, ANAA **37** 99

DEDEAUX, RAOUL (ROD) SS
(**6**) BKNN **6** 35

DEDMON, JEFF P
(**49**,50) ATLN **49** 83-87, CLEA **50** 88

DEDRICK, JIM P
(**55**) BALA **55** 95

DEER, ROB OF/1B/DH
(**45**,28,29,44 23) SFN **45** 84, **28** 85, MILA **45** 86-90, DETA **29/44** 91, **28** 92-93, BOSA **23** 93, SDN **28** 96

DEES, CHARLIE 1B
(**23**) LAA **23** 63-64, CALA **23** 65

DeFREITAS, ARTURO 1B/OF
(58,**21**) CINN **58** 78, **21** 79

DEGERICK, MIKE P
(36,47) CHIA **36** 61, **47** 62

DeHAAN, KORY OF
(**25**,18,29) SDN **25** 00, **18/29** 02

DeHART, RICK P
(**34**,58) MONN **34** 97-99, KCA **58** 03

DEIDEL, JIM C
(**43**) NYA **43** 74

DEJAN, MIKE OF
(**22**) CINN **22** 40

DeJEAN, MIKE P
(**44**,18,48,37, 47,35) COLN **44** 97-01, **18** 00, MILN **48** 01-03, STLN **37/47** 03, BALA **47** 04, NYN **35** 04-05, COLN **18** 05

DeJESUS, DAVID OF
(**9**) KCA **9** 03-05

DeJESUS, IVAN SS/3B
(14,**11**,18,26 9,30) LAN **14** 74-76, CHIN **11** 77-81, PHIN **18** 82, **11** 82-84, STLN **11** 85, NYA **26** 86, SFN **9** 87, DETA **30** 88

DeJESUS, JOSE P
(**54**,53) KCA **54** 88-89, PHIN **54** 90-91, KCA **53** 94-95

DeJOHN, MARK INF/CH
(**25**,9,34) DETA **25** 82, STLN *CH* **9** 96, **34** 96-02

DeKONING, BILL C
(**37**) NYN **37** 45

de la CRUZ, TOMMY P
(**42**) CINN **42** 44

de la HOZ, MIKE INF
(1,34,**7**,17,18) CLEA **1/34** 60, **1** 61, **7** 61-62, **17** 63, MILN **7** 64-65, ATLN **7** 66-67, CINN **18** 69

De La MAZA, ROLAND P
(**52**) KCA **52** 97

DELANCEY, BILL C
(__,**9**,15) STLN __ 32, **9** 34-35, **15** 40

DELANEY, ART (SWEDE) P
(__) STLN __ 24

DeLA ROSA, FRANCISCO P
(**58**) BALA **58** 91

De La ROSA, TOMAS INF/SS
(**29**) MONN **2** 00-01

De La ROSA, JESUS PH
(**29**) HOUN **29** 75

De La ROSA, JORGE P
(**47**) MILN **47** 04-05

DELCARMEN, MANNY P
(**57**) BOSA **57** 05

DeLEON, JOSE P
(41,25,26,**48**, 50,46) PITN **41/25** 83, **25** 85-86, CHIA **26** 86-87, STLN **48** 88-92, PHIN **48** 92, **50** 92-93, CHIA **48** 93-95, MONN **46** 95

DeLEON, LUIS P
(49,**35**,47,52) STLN **49** 81, SDN **55** 82, **35** 82-85, BALA **47** 87, SEAA **52** 89

DELGADO, ALEX C
(56,**32**) BOSA **56/32** 96

DELGADO, CARLOS C/OF/1B
(6,21,**25**) TORA **6** 93-95, **21** 96, **25** 97-04, FLAN **25** 05

DELGADO, LUIS (PUCHY) OF
(**23**) SEAA **23** 77

DELGADO, WILSON SS
(60,38,36,62, 8,14,19,4,30, **47**,17) SFN **60** 96, **38/36** 97, **62/8** 98, **62** 99, **14/62** 00, KCA **19** 00, **4** 01, STLN **30** 02, **47** 03, ANAA **47** 03, NYN **17** 04

Del GRECO, BOBBY OF
(12,8,18,9,**5**, 27,3,26,14, 29) PITN **12/8** 52, **18** 56, STLN **9** 56, CHIN **5** 57, NYA **27** 57-58, PHIN **3** 60, **26** 61, KCA **14** 61, **5** 62-63, PHIN **29** 65

DELIS, JUAN UTIL
(**34**) WASA **34** 55

DELKER, EDDIE INF
(no#,10,**11**) STLN **no#** 32, PHIN **10** 32, **11** 33

DELLAERO, JASON INF
(**34**) CHIA **34** 99

DELLUCCI, DAVID OF/DH
(26,**25**,11,22) BALA **26** 97, ARIN **25** 98-03, NYA **11** 03, TEXA **22** 04-05

DELMAS, BERT 2B
(**18**) BKNN **18** 33

DELOCK, IKE P
(29,12,**14**) BOSA **29** 52-53, **12** 53, **14** 53, 56-63, BALA **14** 63

De Los SANTOS, LUIS P
(**36**) TBA **36** 02

de los SANTOS, LUIS (M.) 1B/UTIL
(51,9,17) KCA **51** 88, **9** 89, DETA **17** 91

de los SANTOS, RAMON P
(**24**) HOUN **24** 74

De Los SANTOS, VALERIO P
(58,**28**,26) MILN **58** 98-99, **28** 00-03, PHIN **28** 03, TORA **26** 04, FLAN **26** 05

Del SAVIO, GARTON SS
(**25**) PHIN **25** 43

DELSING, JIM OF
(2,52,54,27, 18,**24**,25,6) CHIA **2** 48, NYA **52** 49, **54** 50, STLA **27** 50-51, **18** 52, DETA **24** 52-56, CHIA **25** 56, KCA **6** 60

Del TORO, MIGUEL P
(**37**) SFN **37** 99-00

DeLUCIA, RICH P
(55,53,**41**,47) SEAA **55** 90-93, CINN **53** 94-95, STLN **41** 95, SFN **41** 96-97, ANAA **41** 97-98, CLEA **47** 99

DeMAESTRI, JOE (OATS) SS/INF
(14,1,**2**,20) CHIA **14** 51, STLA **1** 52, PHIA **2** 53-54, KCA **2** 55-59, NYA **20** 60-61

DEMAREE, FRANK OF
(51,**6**,9,3,24, 20,12,17,10) CHIN **51** 32, **6** 33, 35-36, **9** 37-38, NYN **6** 39, **3** 40, **24** 41, BOSN **20** 41, **12** 42, STLN **17** 43, STLA **10** 44

DEMARIA, CHRIS P
(**52**) KCA **52** 05

DeMARS, BILLY (KID) INF/CH
(30,**1**,46,3,2, 7) PHIA **30** 48, STLA **1** 50-51, PHIN *CH* **46** 69, *CH* **3** 70-72, *CH* **2** 73-81, MONN *CH* **2** 82-84, CINN *CH* **7** 85-87

DeMERIT, JOHN (THUMPER) OF
(18,**29**) MILN **18** 57-58, **29** 58-59, 61, NYN **29** 62

DeMERRITT, MARTY CH
(38,**48**) CHIN *CH* **38/48** 99

DEMERY, LARRY P
(**44**) PITN **44** 74-77

DEMETER, DON OF/1B
(27,2,7,24, **4**,20) BKNN **27** 56, 58, **2** 58, LAN **2** 59-60, **7** 61, PHIN **24** 61-63, DETA **4** 64-66, BOSA **4** 66-67, CLEA **20** 67

DEMETER, STEVE 3B/CH
(26,**5**,32) DETA **26** 59, CLEA **5** 60, PITN *CH* **32** 85

DeMOLA, DON P
(50,**25**) MONN **50** 74, **25** 74-76

DEMPSEY, CON P
(**30**) PITN **30** 51

DEMPSEY, MARK P
(55,**40**) SFN **55** 82, **40** 82-83

DEMPSEY, RICK C/UTIL/CH
(8,38,25,46, **24**,17,14,26) MINA **8** 69, **38** 70-71, **25** 72, NYA **46** 73-76, BALA **24** 76-86, CLEA **24** 87, LAN **17** 88-90, **24** 90, MILA **14** 91, BALA **24** 92, LAN *CH* **26** 99-00, BALA *CH* **24** 02-05

DEMPSTER, RYAN P
(50,**46**,34,33) FLAN **50** 98, **46** 99-02, CINN **34** 02-03, CHIN **33** 04, **46** 05

DENBO, TOM CH
(**53**) NYA *CH* **53** 01

DENEHY, BILL P
(44,22,27) NYN **4** 67, WASA**22** 68, DETA **27** 71

DENMAN, BRIAN P
(**31**) BOSA **31** 82

DENNEY, KYLE P
(**57**) CLEA **57** 04

DENNING, OTTO (DUTCH) C/OF/1B
(**9**) CLEA **9** 42-43

DENNIS, DON P
(**29**) STLN **29** 65-66

DENNY, JOHN P
(42,36,**40**) STLN **42** 74, **48** 75, **36** 74-79, CLEA **40** 80-82, **42** 82, PHIN **40** 82-85, CINN **40** 86

DENORFIA, CHRIS OF
(**19**) CINN **19** 05

DENSON, DREW 1B
(**9**,62) ATLN **9** 89, CHIA **62** 93

DENT, BUCKY SS/MGR/CH
(30,**20**,7,21, 5) CHIA **30** 73-76, NYA **20** 77-82, TEXA **7** 82-83, KCA **21** 84, NYA *M* **30** 89-90, STLN *CH* **30** 91-94, TEXA *CH* **5** 95, *CH* **20** 96-01

DENTE, SAM (BLACKIE) INF
(17,35,1,**4**,40, 8,20,36) BOSA **17/35** 47, STLA **1** 48, WASA **4** 49, **40** 50, **4** 51, CHIA **8** 52, **20** 53, CLEA **36** 54-55

De PAULA, JORGE P
(41,**4**,61) NYA **41** 03, **43** 04, **61** 05

DePAULA, SEAN P
(**56**) CLEA **56** 99-00, 02

DePHILLIPS, TONY C
(**6**) CINN **6** 43

DERNIER, BOB SS/MGR/CH
(30,22,24,29, **20**,22) PHIN **30** 80-81, **22** 82, **24** 82-83, **29** 83, CHIN **20** 84-87, PHIN **22** 88-89

DeROSA, MARK INF/OF
(7,2,**16**) ATLN **7** 98, **2** 99-00, **16** 01-04, TEXA **7** 05

DERRICK, MIKE OF/1B
(**23**) BOSA **23** 70

DERRINGER, PAUL (DUKE) P
(20,19,21,14, 25,52,**30**) STLN **20** 32-33, **19** 33, CINN **21** 33, **14** 34, **25** 35-37, **52** 38, **30** 39-42, CHIN **30** 43-45

DERRINGTON, JIM (BLACKIE) P
(**18**) CHIA **18** 56-57

DERRY, RUSS OF
(22,27,**2**,41) NYA **22** 44, **27** 45, PHIA **2** 46, STLN **41** 49

DeSA, JOE 1B/OF/UTIL
(**4**,7,20,38) STLN **4/7** 80, CHIA **20/38** 85

DESAUTELS, GENE (RED) C
(5,25,23,**2**,4, 50,9) DETA **5** 31, **25** 32-33, BOSA **23** 37, **2** 38-40, CLEA **4** 41-43, **50** 45, PHIA **9** 46

DESHAIES, JIM P
(66,**43**,38,44, 30) NYA **66** 84, HOUN **43** 85-91, SDN **38** 92, MINA **44** 93, SFN **30** 93, MINA **44** 94, PHIN **44** 95

DeSHIELDS, DELINO 2B
(**4**,14,7,11) MONN **4** 90-93, LAN **14** 94-96, STLN **7** 97-98, BALA **11** 99-01, CHIN **16** 01-02

DeSHONG, JIMMIE P
(19,16,**15**) PHIA **19** 32, NYA **16** 34-35, WASA **15** 36-39

DeSILVA, JOHN P
(41,60,45) DETA **41** 93, LAN **60** 93, BALA **45** 95

DESSENS, ELMER P
(71,**45**,46) PITN **71** 96-98, CINN **45** 00-02, ARIN **45** 03-04, LAN **46** 04-05

DESTRADE, ORESTE 1B/DH
(61,53,2,**39**) NYA **61/53** 87, PITN **2** 88, FLAN **39** 93-94

DETHERAGE, BOBBY OF
(**4**) KCA **4** 80

DETORE, GEORGE INF/CH
(**32**,42) CLEA **32** 31, PITN *CH* **42** 59

DETTMER, JOHN P
(**21**) TEXA **21** 94-95

DETTORE, TOM P
(**32**,39,31) PITN **32** 73, CHIN **32** 74-75, **39** 75, **31** 75-76

DETWEILER, DUCKY 3B
(31,32) BOSN **31** 42, **32** 46

DEUTSCH, MEL P
(**34**) BOSA **34** 46

DEVAREZ, CESAR C
(58,**59**) BALA **58** 95, **59** 95-96

DEVENS, CHARLIE P
(20,33,**24**) NYA **20** 32, **33** 33, **24** 34

DEVEREAUX, MIKE OF/DH
(40,**12**,8,24, 10) LAN **40** 87-88, BALA **12** 89-94, CHIA **8** 95, ATLN **24** 95, BALA **10** 96, TEXA **24** 97, LAN **12** 98

DEVINE, ADRIAN P
(27,36,**35**,28, 38) ATLN **27** 73, **36** 75-76, TEXA **35** 77, ATLN **28** 78-79, **38** 79, TEXA **35** 80

DEVINE, JOEY P
(**28**) ATLN **28** 05

DEVLIN, JIM C
(**4**) CLEA **4** 44

DEVORE, DOUG OF
(**26**) ARIN **26** 04

DEWEY, MARK P
(14,43,**50**,40) SFN **14** 90, NYN **43** 92, PITN **50** 93-94, SFN **40** 95-96

DeWILLIS, JEFF C
(**27**) TORA **27** 87

DeWITT, MATT P
(**40**,49) TORA **40** 00, **49** 01, SDN **40** 02

DEWS, BOBBY CH
(10,2,22,**52**, 53) ATLN *CH* **10** 79, **2** 80-81, **22** 97, **52** 98-04, **53** 05

DIAZ, ALEX OF/DH
(18,**1**,14) MILA **18** 92, **1** 93-94, SEAA **1** 95-96, TEXA **14** 97, SFN **1** 98, TEXA **14** 98, HOUN **1** 99

DIAZ, BO C
(39,16,**6**,8) BOSA **39** 77, CLEA **16** 78-81, PHIN **6** 82-85, CINN **8** 85, **6** 86-89

DIAZ, CARLOS P
(36,48,32,**27**, 59) ATLN **36/48** 82, NYN **48/32** 82, **32/48** 83, LAN **27** 84-86, TORA **59** 90

DIAZ, EDDIE INF/DH
(**2**) MILA **2** 86, 90

DIAZ, EDDY INF
(**51**) MILA **51** 97

DIAZ, EDWIN 2B
(41,**18**,9) ARIN **41** 98, **18** 99, MONN **9** 04

DIAZ, EINAR C
(**2**,5,9,4) CLEA **2** 96-02, TEXA **5** 03, MONN **9** 04, STLN **4** 05

DIAZ, FELIX P
(**54**) CHIA **54** 04-05

DIAZ, JUAN 1B/DH
(**46**) BOSA **46** 02

DIAZ, MARIO INF
(**5**,23,34,6, 20,29) SEAA **5** 87-88, **23** 89, NYN **34** 90, TEXA **6** 91, **20** 92, **6** 93, FLAN **29** 94-95

DIAZ, MATT OF/DH
(**25**,34) TBA **25** 03-04, KCA **34** 05

DIAZ, MIKE C/UTIL
(15,10,**14**,20) CHIN **15** 83, PITN **10** 86, **14** 87-88, CHIA **20** 88

DIAZ, VICTOR OF/2B
(50,**20**) NYN **50** 04, **20** 05

DIBBLE, RON P
(**49**) CINN **49** 88-93, CHIA **49** 95, MILA **49** 95

DICKEN, PAUL PH
(**20**) CLEA **20** 64, 66

DICKERMAN, LEO P
(**19**) STLN **19** 24

DICKEY, BILL C/CH/M
(**10**,8,33) NYA **10** 29, **8** 30-46, *M* **8** 46, *CH* **33** 49-57, 60

DICKEY, GEORGE (SKEETS) C
(28,23,14,19) BOSA **28** 35, **23** 36, CHIA **14** 41-42, **19** 46-47

DICKEY, R. A. P
(51,**45**) TEXA **51** 01, **45** 03-05

DICKMAN, EMERSON P
(19,**16**) BOSA **19** 36, **16** 38-41

DICKSHOT, JOHNNY (UGLY) OF
(15,17,28,**36**) PITN **15** 36-37, **17** 38, NYN **28** 39, CHIA **36** 44-45

DICKSON, JASON P
(**19**) CALA **19** 96, ANAA **19** 97-98, (99), 00

DICKSON, JIM P
(44,34,53,22, **28**) HOUN **44/34** 63, CINN **53** 64, KCA **22** 65-66, **28** 66

DICKSON, LANCE P
(43,**33**) CHIN **43/33** 90

DICKSON, MURRY P
(32,**22**,20,36, 29,47,23,21) STLN **32** 39, **22** 40, 42-43, 46-48, PITN **22** 49-53, PHIN **20** 54-56, STLN **36** 56-57, KCA **29/47** 58, NYA **23** 58, KCA **21** 59

DIDIER, BOB C/CH
(**4**,6,36,48,45) ATLN **4** 69-72, **6** 72, DETA **36** 73, BOSA *CH* **48** 74, OAKA *CH* **45** 85-86, SEAA *CH* **6** 89-90

DIEHL, GEORGE P
(**20**) BOSN **20** 42-43

DIERING, CHUCK OF/INF
(**32**,28) STLN **32** 47-51, NYN **28** 52, BALA **32** 55-56

DIERKER, LARRY P/M
(**49**) HOUN **49** 64-76, STLN **49** 77, HOUN *M* **49** 97-01

DIETRICH, BILL (BULLFROG) P
(20,14,**18**) PHIA **20** 33, **14** 34-36, WASA **20** 36, CHIA **18** 36-46, PHIA **18** 47-48

DIETZ, DICK C/1B
(**2**,16,8,14) SFN **2** 66-71, LAN **16/8** 72, ATLN **14** 73

DIETZ, DUTCH P
(35,**22**,17) PITN **35** 40, **22** 40-43, PHIN **17** 43

DIETZEL, ROY 2B/3B
(**28**) WASA **28** 54

DIFANI, JAY 2B
(28,**27**) WASA **28** 48, **27** 49

DIFELICE, MIKE C
(49,37,**8**,26, 19,33) STLN **49** 96, **37** 97, TBA **8** 98-01, ARIN **8** 01, STLN **8** 02, KCA **26** 03, DETA **26** 04, CHIN **19** 04, NYN **33** 05

DIGGINS, BEN P
(81,**53**) MILN **81/53** 02

DIGGS, REESE (DIGGSY) P
(**22**) WASA **22** 34

DiLAURO, JACK P
(**31**) NYN **31** 69, HOUN **31** 70

DILLARD, DON OF
(38,**36**,42) CLEA **38** 59-60, **36** 61-62, MILN **42** 63, 65

DILLARD, GORDON P
(43,**50**) BALA **43** 88, PHIN **50** 89

DILLARD, STEVE INF/2B
(**3**,7,15,12) BOSA **3** 75-77, DETA **7** 78, CHIN **15** 79-81, CHIA **12** 82

DILLINGER, BOB (DUKE) 3B
(2,**6**,3,25) STLA **2** 46, **6** 47-49, PHIA **6** 50, PITN **3** 50-51, CHIA **25** 51

DILLMAN, BILL P
(**45**,17) BALA **45** 67, MONN **17** 70

DILLON, JOE INF
(**12**,22) FLAN **12/22** 05

DILLON, STEVE P
(**39**) NYN **39** 63-64

DILONE, MIGUEL OF/UTIL/DH
(37,19,32,**27**, 28,46,18,17) PITN **37** 74-77, OAKA **19** 78-79, CHIN **32** 79, CLEA **27** 80-83, CHIA **28** 83, PITN **46** 83, MONN **18** 84-85, SDN **17** 85

DiMAGGIO, DOM (THE LITTLE PROFESSOR) OF B
(**7**) BOSA **7** 40-42, 46-53

DiMAGGIO, JOE (JOLTIN' JOE, THE YANKEE CLIPPER) OF/CH B
(9,**5**) NYA **9** 36, **5** 37-42, 46-51, OAKA *CH* **5** 68-69

DiMAGGIO, VINCE OF/INF B
(6,28,21,8,37, **9**,7,34,16) BOSN **6** 37-38, CINN **28** 39, **21** 40, PITN **8/37** 40, **9** 40-44, PHIA **7** 45, **34** 46, NYN **16/9** 46

DIMICHELE, FRANK P
(**48**) CALA **48** 88

DIMMEL, MIKE OF
(**36**,21) BALA **36** 77-78, STLN **21** 79

DINARDO, LENNY P
(**55**) BOSA **55** 04-05

DINEEN, KERRY OF
(49,47,**26**) NYA **49** 75, **47** 76, PHIN **26** 78

DINGES, VANCE OF/1B
(**5**) PHIN **5** 45, **41/47** 46

DINGMAN, CRAIG P
(60,51,**57**) NYA **60** 00, COLN **51** 01, DETA **57** 04-05

DIORIO, RON P
(**21**,45) PHIN **21** 73-74, **45** 74

DiPASTINO, JOE C
(**10**) NYN **10** 03

DiPIETRO, BOB OF
(**39**) BOSA **39** 51

DiPINO, FRANK P
(49,46,11,33, **35**,31) MILA **48** 81, HOUN **46** 82-83, **11** 83-86, CHIN **33** 86-88, STLN **35** 89-92, KCA **31** 93

DiPOTO, JERRY P
(**45**) CLEA **45** 93-94, NYN **45** 95-96, COLN **45** 97-00

DISARCINA, GARY SS/INF
(4,11,**33**,9) CALA **4** 89, **11** 90-92, **33** 92-96, ANAA **9** 97-01

DISHMAN, GLENN P
(**33**,34,58) SDN **33** 95-96, PHIN **34** 96 , DETA **58** 97

DISTASO, ALEC P
(**45**) CHIN **45** 69

DISTEFANO, BENNY OF/1B/UTIL
(10,14,**30**,68) PITN **10** 84, **14/31** 86, **30** 88-89, HOUN **68** 92

DITMAR, ART P
(20,**28**) PHIA **20** 54, KCA **28** 55-56, NYA **28** 57-61, KCA **28** 61-62

DITTMER, JACK 2B
(**6**,1) BOSN **6** 52, MILN **6** 53-56, DETA **1** 57

DIXON, KEN P
(**39**,58) BALA **39** 84-86, **58/39** 87

DIXON, SONNY P
(16,**24**,21) WASA **16** 53-54, PHIA **24** 54, KCA **24** 55, NYA **21** 56

DIXON, STEVE P
(35,41) STLN **35** 93, **41** 94

DIXON, TOM P
(33,**37**,51) HOUN **33** 77, **37** 77-79, **51** 79, MONN **37** 83

DIXON, WALT CH
(**62**) CHIN *CH* **62** 64

DOAK, BILL (SPITTIN' BILL) P
(**17**,__) STLN **17** 23, __ 24

DOBBEK, DAN OF
(**22**) WASA **22** 59-60, MINA **22** 61

DOBBS, GREG 3B/1B/DH
(53,**22**) SEAA **53** 04, **22** 05

DOBERNIC, JESS P
(48,30,**17**,39) CHIA **48/30** 39, CHIN **17** 48-49, CINN **39/17** 49

DOBSON, CHUCK P
(47,**29**,50,49) KCA **47** 66, **29** 66-67, OAKA **29** 68-71,73, CALA **50/45** 74, **45/29** 75

DOBSON, JOE (BURRHEAD) P
(17,19,**15**,29, 32) CLEA **17** 39-40, BOSA **17** 41-43, **19** 43, **15** 46-50, CHIA **29** 51-53, **16** 52, BOSA **32/15** 54

DOBSON, PAT P/CH
(40,22,37,27, **36**,41,45) DETA **40** 67, **22** 68-69, SDN **37** 70, BALA **37** 71-72, ATLN **27** 73, NYA **36** 73-75, CLEA **41** 76-77, MILA *CH* **45** 82-84, SDN *CH* **36** 88-90, KCA *CH* **37** 91, BALA *CH* **37** 96

DOBY, L ARRY OF/1B/CH/M
(**14**,37,6,25, 32,17) CLEA **14** 47-48, **37** 49, **14** 50-52, **6/14** 53, **14** 54-55, CHIA **14** 56-57, CLEA **14** 58, DET **25** 59, CHIA **32** 59, MONN *CH* **17** 71, *CH* **14** 71-73, CLEA *CH* **6** 74, MONN *CH* **14** 76, CHIA *CH* **14** 77, *CH/M* **14** 78, *CH* **14** 79

DOCKINS, GEORGE (LEFTY) P
(**23**) STLN **23** 45, LAN **23** 47

DODD, ROBERT P
(**57**) PHIN **57** 98

DODD, TOM DH/3B
(**25**) BALA **25** 86

DODSON, PAT 1B
(**27**) BOSA **27** 86-88

DOERR, BOBBY 2B/CH
(9,**1**,31) BOSA **9** 37, **1** 38-44, 46-51, *CH* **31** 67-69, TORA *CH* **31** 77-81

DOHERTY, JOHN 1B/DH
(32,**5**) CALA **32** 74, **5** 74-75

DOHERTY, JOHN P
(**44**,45) DETA **44** 92-95, BOSA **45** 96

DOHMANN, SCOTT P
(**47**) COLN **47** 04-05

DOLJACK, FRANK (DOLIE) P
(6,__,9,**26**,36) DETA **6** 31, __ 32, **9** 33, **26** 34, CLEA **36** 43

DOLL, ART (MOOSE) C/P
(29,**30**) BOSN **29** 35-36, **30** 38

DOMINGUEZ, JUAN P
(**41**) TEXA **41** 03-05

DOMINIQUE, ANDY C
(**39**,56) BOSA **39** 04, TEXA **56** 05

DONAHUE, DEACON P
(__,19,**12**) PHIN __ 43, **19/12** 44

DONALD, ATLEY (SWAMPY) P
(**28**) NYA **28** 38-45

DONALDSON, JOHN 2B/INF
(22,10,**12**,2, 24) KCA **22** 66, **10/12** 67, OAKA **12** 68-69, SEAA **10** 69, OAKA **2** 70, **24** 74

DONNELLY, BLIX P
(20,**30**,11) STLN **20** 44-46, PHIA **30** 46-50, BOSN **11** 51

DONNELLY, BRENDAN P
(**53**) ANAA **53** 02-04, LAA **53** 05

DONNELLY, ED P
(**22**) CHIN **22** 59

DONNELLY, RICH CH
(37,52,**44**,46) 50,45,26,32) TEXA *CH* **37** 80, 83-85, PITN *CH* **52** 86, *CH* **45** 86-92, *CH* **46** 93, **45** 94-96, FLAN *CH* **45** 97-98, COLN *CH* **26** 99-02, MILN *CH* **45** 03-04, **32** 05

DONNELS, CHRIS 3B/INF
(23,**3**,6,18) NYN **23** 91-92, HOUN **3** 92-95, BOSA **6** 95, LAN **50** 00-01, ARIN **18** 02

DONOHUE, JIM P
(19,40) DETA **19** 61, LAA **40** 61-62, MINA **19** 62

DONOHUE, PETE P
(**35**,25) CLEA **35** 31, BOSA **25** 32

DONOHUE, TOM C
(**23**) CALA **23** 79-80

DONOSO, LINO P
(**31**) PITN **31** 55-56

DONOVAN, BILL P
(**21**) BOSN **21** 42-43

DONOVAN, DICK P
(36,20,49,31, **22**,23,30) BOSN **36** 50, **20** 50-52, DETA **49** 54, CHIA **31** 55, **22** 55-60, WASA **20** 61, CLEA **23/20** 62, **30** 63-65

DOOLAN, MICKEY CH
(**30**) CINN *CH* **30** 32

DOPSON, JOHN P
(55,54,**40**,41) MONN **55/54** 85, **54** 88, BOSA **40** 89-93, CALA **41** 94

DORAN, BILL 2B/CH
(**19**,13) HOUN **19** 82-90, CINN **19** 90-92, MILA **13** 93, CINN *CH* **19** 01, KCA *CH* **13** 05

DORANTE, LUIS CH
(**30**) FLAN *CH* **30** 05

DORISH, HARRY (FRITZ) P/CH
(20,37,35,46, **12**,23,16,29, 34,5) BOSA **20** 47-49, **37/35** 49, STLA **46** 50, CHIA **12** 51-55, BALA **23** 55-56, BOSA **16/29** 56, *CH* **34** 63, ATLN *CH* **5** 68-71

DORSETT, BRIAN C/1B
(**4**,48,56,28, 31,8,33) CLEA **4** 87, CALA **48** 88, NYA **56** 89, **28/31** 90, SDN **8** 91, CINN **33** 93-94, CHIN **4** 96

DORSETT, CAL (PREACHER) P
(43,24,33,23, **9**) CLEA **43/24** 40, **33/23** 41, **9** 47

DORSEY, JIM P
(43,**44**) CALA **43** 80, BOSA **44** 84-85

DOSTAL, BRUCE OF
(**48**) BALA **48** 94

DOSTER, DAVE 2B
(26,**15**) PHIN **26** 96, **15** 99

DOTEL, OCTAVIO P
(**29**,41,28) NYN **29** 98-99, HOUN **41** 00, **29** 01-04, OAKA **28** 04, **29** 05

DOTSON, RICH P
(49,**34**,36,35) CHIA **49** 79-83, **34** 83-87, NYA **36** 88-89, **34** 89, CHIA **34** 89, KCA **35** 90

DOTTER, GARY P
(41,27,**21**) MINA **41** 61, MINA **27** 63, **21** 64

DOTTERER, DUTCH C
(**9**,11) CINN **9** 57-60, WASA **11** 61

DOUGHERTY, JIM P (**49**,41,68) HOUN **49** 95-96, OAKA **41** 98, PITN **68** 99

DOUGLAS, JOHN 1B (**13**) BKNN **13** 45

DOUGLAS, OTIS CH (**23**) CINN *CH* **23** 62

DOUGLAS, WHAMMY P (**31**) PITN **31** 57

DOUGLASS, SEAN P (**47**,24) BALA **47** 01-03, TORA **24** 04

DOUTHIT, TAYLOR (BALLHAWK) OF (71,__,9,**11**, 31) STLN **71** 23, __ 24, CINN **9** 32, **11** 33, CHIN **31** 33

DOWELL, KEN SS (**7**) PHIN **7** 87

DOWLING, DAVE P (29,45,**46**) STLN **29** 64, CHIN **45/46** 66

DOWN, RICK CH (61,19,**48**,44) CALA *CH* **61** 87, *CH* **19** 87-88, NYA *CH* **48** 93-95, BALA *CH* **48** 96-98, LAN *CH* **44** 99-00, BOSA **48** 01, NYA **56** 02-03

DOWNING, AL P (**24**,38,36,44) NYA **24** 61-69, OAKA **38** 70, MILA **36** 70, LAN **44** 71-77

DOWNING, BRIAN C/UTIL/OF/DH (16,**5**,9,55) CHIA **16** 73-77, CALA **5** 78-90, **9** 80, TEXA **55** 91, **5** 92

DOWNS, DAVE P (**35**) PHIN **35** 72

DOWNS, KELLY P (**37**,31) SFN **37** 86-92, OAKA **31** 92-93

DOWNS, SCOTT P (**37**,31) CHIN **35/37** 00, MONN **48** 00, **37** 01, (02), 03-04

DOYLE, BRIAN INF (25,**18**) NYA **25** 78, **18** 79-80, OAKA **18** 81

DOYLE, CARL P (**18**,10,26,31, 27) PHIA •**15** 35, **18** 36, BKNN **10** , 39 **26** 40, STLN **31/27** 40

DOYLE, DANNY C (**24**) BOSA **24** 43

DOYLE, DENNY 2B (15,**5**) PHIN **15** 70-73, CALA **15** 74-75, BOSA **15** 75, **5** 75-77

DOYLE, JEFF 2B (**7**) STLN **7** 83

DOYLE, JESS P (**20**) STLA **20** 31

DOYLE, PAUL P (45,**48**,31,50) ATLN **45** 69, CALA **48** 70, SDN **31/50** 70, CALA **48** 72

DOZIER, BUZZ P (**22**,28) WASA **22** 47, **28** 49

DOZIER, D. J. OF (**7**) NYN **7** 92

DOZIER, TOM P (**59**) OAKA **59** 86

DRABEK, DOUG P (34,**15**) NYA **34** 86, PITN **15** 87-92, HOUN **15** 93-96, CHIA **15** 97, BALA **15** 98

DRABOWSKY, MOE P/CH (26,39,17,34, **25**,28,44,21, 42) CHIN **26** 56-58, **39** 59-60, MILN **17** 61, CINN **34** 62, KCA **34** 62, **25** 63-65, BALA **25** 66-68, KCA **25** 69-70, BALA **25** 70, STLN **28** 71-72, CHIA **44** 72, *CH* **21** 86, CHIN *CH* **42** 94

DRAGO, DICK P (**41**,37,40) KCA **41** 69-73, BOSA **41** 74-75, CALA **41** 76-77, BALA **37** 77, BOSA **41** 78-80, SEAA **40** 81

DRAHMAN, BRIAN P (**50**) CHIA **50** 91-93, FLAN **50** 94

DRAKE, LARRY OF (31,**14**) PHIA **31** 45, WASA **14** 48

DRAKE, SAMMY UTIL (**19**,7,12) CHIN **19** 60-61, NYN **7/12** 62

DRAKE, SOLLY OF (47,18,35) CHIN **47** 56, LAN **18** 59, PHIN **35** 59

DRAKE, TOM P (29,15) CLEA **29** 39, BKNN **15** 41

DRANSFELDT, KELLY SS (**44**,32) TEXA **44** 99-00, CHIA **32** 04

DRAPER, MIKE P (**47**) NYN **47** 93

DRAVECKY, DAVE P (**43**) SDN **43** 82-87, SFN **43** 87-89

DREES, TOM P (**42**) CHIA **42** 91

DREIFORT, DARREN P (**37**) LAN **37** 94, 96-04

DREISEWERD, CLEM (STEAMBOAT) P (29,37,**23**,35, 33) BOSA **29** 44, **37** 45, **23** 46, STLA **35** 48, NYN **33** 48

DRESCHER, BILL (DUTCH) C (20,22,36,**29**, 42) NYA **20/22** 44, **36** 45, **29** 45-46, **42** 46

DRESE, RYAN P (**57**,37,38,45) CLEA **57** 01-02, TEXA **37** 03, **38** 04-05, WASN **45** 05

DRESSEN, CHUCK 3B/M/CH (**7**,26,77,6,9) NYN **7** 33, CINN *M* **26** 34, *M* **7** 35-37, BKNN *CH* **7** 39-40, *CH* **77** 40, BKNN *CH* **7** 41-42, *CH* **6** 43, *CH* **7** 43-46, NYA *CH* **7** 47-48, BKNN *M* **7** 51-53, WASA *M* **7** 55- 57, LAN *CH* **7** 58-59, MILN *M* **7** 60-61, DETA *M* **9** 63, *M* **7** 64-66

DRESSENDORFER, KIRK P (17,**22**) OAKA **17/22** 91

DRESSLER, ROB P (25,26,**24**) SFN **25** 75-76, STLN **26** 78, SEAA **24** 79-80

DREW, CAMERON OF (**3**) HOUN **3** 88

DREW, J. D. OF B (8,**7**) STLN **8** 98, **7** 99-03, ATLN **7** 04, LAN **7** 05

DREW, TIM P B (**47**,46) CLEA **47** 00-01, MONN **47** 02-03, ATLN **46** 04

DREWS, FRANK 2B (34,**2**) BOSN **34** 44, **2** 44-45

DREWS, KARL P (26,38,19,40, 20,**22**,31,36, 53) NYA **26** 46, **38** 47, **19** 47-48, STLA **40/19** 48, **20** 49, PHIN **22** 51-54, CINN **31/36/53** 54

DREYER,STEVE P (**24**) TEXA **24** 93-94

DRIESSEN, DAN 1B/UTIL (**22**,24,25,23) CINN **22** 73-84, MONN **24** 84, **22** 85, SFN **25** 85-86, HOUN **23** 86, STLN **23** 87

DRISCOLL, JIM INF (21,22) OAKA **21** 70, TEXA **22** 72

DRISKILL, TRAVIS P (**49**,50) BALA **49** 02-03, COLN **50** 04

DROPO, WALT (MOOSE) 1B/3B (**3**,11,8,18,37, 17) BOSA **3** 49-52, DETA **11** 52, **3** 53-54, CHIA **8** 55-58, CINN **18** 58-59, BALA **37** 59, **17** 60-61

DROTT, DICK (HUMMER) P (18,**30**,36) CHIN **18** 57-58, **30** 59-61, HOUN **36** 62-63

DRUMMOND, TIM P (55,56,**54**) PITN **55/56** 87, MINA **54** 89-90

DRUMRIGHT, KEITH 2B (15,14) HOUN **15** 78, OAKA **14** 81

DRYSDALE, DON P (**53**) BKNN **53** 56-57, LAN 58-69

DUBEE, RICH CH (**31**,28) FLAN *CH* **31** 98-01, **28** 01

DUBIEL, MONK OF/DH (14,34,**26**) NYA **14** 44-45, PHIN **34** 48, CHIA **26** 49-52

DUBOIS, BRIAN P (**16**) DETA **16** 89-90

DUBOIS, JASON P (**4**,9) CHIN **4** 04-05, CLEA **9** 05

DUBOSE, ERIC P (57,**59**) DETA **57** 00, BALA **59** 02-03

DUBUC, JEAN (CHAUNCEY) CH (**43**) DETA *CH* **43** 31

DUCEY, ROB OF/DH (40,**20**,16,12, 29,25) TORA **40** 87-88, **20** 88-92, CALA **16** 92, TEXA **40** 93, **12** 94, SEAA **29** 97, **20** 98, PHIN **25** 99-00, TORA **22** 00, PHIN **25** 00, **2** 01, MONN **29** 01

DUCHSCHERER, JUSTIN P (45,**58**) TEXA **45** 01, OAKA **58** 03-05

DUCKWORTH, BRANDON P (56,**31**) PHIN **56** 01-02, **31** 03, HOUN **31** 04, **56** 05

DUCKWORTH, JIM P (**17**,31) WASA **17** 63-66, KCA **31/17** 66

DUDLEY, CLISE P (**19**,50) PHIA **19** 32, PITN **50** 33

DUDRA, JOHN INF (**15**) BOSN **15** 41

DUES, HAL P (**28**) MONN **28** 77-78, 80

DUFF, MATT P (**52**) STLN **52** 02

DUFFALO, JIM P (**45**,44) SFN **45** 61-65, CINN **44** 65

DUFFIE, JOHN P (**54**) LAN **54** 67

DUFFY, FRANK SS/INF (**15**,14,17) CINN **15** 70-71, SFN **14** 71, CLEA **15** 72-77, BOSA **17** 78-79

DUFFY, HUGH CH (**31**) BOSA *CH* **31** 39-40

DUGAN, JOE (JUMPIN' JOE) 3B (**25**) DETA **25** 31

DUGAS, GUS OF/1B (15,**4**,22) PITN **15** 32, PHIN **4** 33, WASA **22** 34

DUKES, JAN P (**22**,50,16) WASA **22** 69-70, TEXA **50/16** 72

DUKES, TOM P (48,**44**,36,15) HOUN **48** 67, **44** 67-68, SDN **44** 69-70, BALA **36** 71, CALA **15** 72

DULIBA, BOB P (24,33,34,45, 14,3`) STLN **24** 59-60, **33/34** 62, LAA **45** 63-64, BOSA **14** 65, KCA **31** 67

DUMOULIN, DAN P (53,**50**) CINN **53** 77, **50** 77-78

DUNBAR, MATT P (**27**) FLAN **27** 95

DUNBAR, TOMMY OF/DH (**13**) TEXA **13** 83-85

DUNCAN, COURTNEY P (**55**) CHIN **55** 01-02

DUNCAN, DAVE C/UTIL/CH (11,35,**10**,9, 25,4,18) KCA **11** 64, **35** 67, OAKA **10** 68-72, CLEA **11** 73-74, BALA **9** 75, **25** 76, CLEA *CH* **4** 78-81, SEAA *CH* **10** 82, CHIA *CH* **18** 83-86, OAKA *CH* **18** 86-95, STLN *CH* **18** 96-05

DUNCAN, JEFF OF (61,**10**) NYN **61** 03, **10** 04

DUNCAN, MARIANO SS/2B/UTIL (12,25,**7**,44, 77,18,24) LAN **12** 85, **25** 85-87, 89, CINN **7** 89-91, PHIN **7** 92-95, CINN **44/77** 95, NYA **18** 96-97, TORA **24** 97

DUNCAN, TAYLOR 3B/INF/DH (**16**) STLN **16** 77, OAKA **16** 78

DUNEGAN, JIMMY P (32,**34**) CHIN **32/34** 70

DUNLAP, GRANT (SNAP) OF (**10**) STLN **10** 53

DUNLOP, HARRY CH (**4**,33,2) KCA **4** 69-75, CHIN **4** 76, CINN **4** 79-82, SDN **33** 83-87, CINN *CH* **2** 98-99

DUNN, ADAM OF/1B (**44**) CINN **44** 01-05

DUNN, JIM (BILL) P (**20**) PITN **20** 52

DUNN, RON UTIL (28, **22**) CHIN **28** 74, **22** 75

DUNN, SCOTT P (**60**) AANA **60** 04

DUNN, STEVE 1B (58,**39**) MINA **58** 94, **39** 94-95

DUNN, TODD OF (**18**) MILA **18** 96-97

DUNNE, MIKE P (**41**,25,54) PITN **41** 87-89, SEAA **25/41** 89, SDN **41** 90, CHIA **54** 92

DUNNING, STEVE P (46,**27**,39,36, 24) CLEA **46** 70-73, TEXA **46** 73, **27** 73-74, CALA **39** 76, MONN **36** 76, OAKA **24** 77

DUNSTON, SHAWON SS (**12**,21,3,9,8, 23) CHIN **12** 85-95, SFN **21** 96, CHIN **12** 97, PITN **3** 97, CLEA **9** 98, SFN **8** 98, STLN **21** 99, NYN **12** 99, STLN **12** 00, SFN **23** 01-02

DUNWOODY, TODD OF (**17**,6,7,11,44) FLAN **17** 97-99, KCA **6/7** 00, CHIN **11** 01, CLEA **44** 02

DUPREE, MIKE P (**43**) SDN **43** 76

DURAN, DAN OF/1B (**21**) TEXA **21** 81

DURAN, ROBERTO P (**55**) DETA **55** 97-98

DURANT, MIKE C (**27**) MINA **27** 96

DURAZO, ERUBIEL INF/OF/DH (**44**) ARIN **44** 99-02, OAKA **44** 03-05

DURBIN, CHAD P (**33**,49,45) KCA **33** 99-02, CLEA **49** 03-04, ARIN **45** 04

DURBIN, J. D. P (**31**) MINA **31** 04

DUREN, RYNE P (36,**26**,30,18, 33,17) BALA **36** 54, KCA **26** 57, NYA **26** 58-61, LAA **30** 61-62, PHIN **18** 63-64, CINN **33** 64, PHIN **30** 65, WASA **17** 65

DURHAM, DON P (46,50,21,34, 33) STLN **46/50** 72, TEXA **21/34/33** 73

DURHAM, ED (BULL) P (25,20,**17**) BOSA **25** 31, **20** 32, CHIA **17** 33

DURHAM, JOE (POP) OF (12,27,**24**,20) BALA **12** 54, **27** (56), 57, **24** 57, STLN **20** 59

DURHAM, LEON (BULL) OF/1B (**10**,16) STLN **10** 80, CHIN **10** 81-88, CINN **10** 88, STLN **16** 89

DURHAM, RAY 2B (**5**) CHIA **5** 95-02, OAKA **5** 02, SFN **5** 03-05

DURNBAUGH, BOBBY (SCROGGY) SS (**19**) CINN **19** 57

DUROCHER, JASON P (**56**) MILN **56** 02-03

DUROCHER, LEO SS/M/CH (THE LIP) (LIPPY) (7,10,**2**,4) NYA **7** 29, CINN **10** 32-33, STLN **2** 33-37, BKNN **2** 38-41, 43, 45, *M* **2** 39-46, *M* **2** 48, NYN *M* **4** 48, *M* **2** 48-55, LAN *CH* **2** 61-64, CHIN *M* **2** 66-72, HOUN *M* **2** 72-73

DURRETT, RED OF (__,**3**) BKNN __ 44, **3** 45

DURRINGTON, TRENT INF/3B (**20**,27,22) ANAA **20** 99-00, **27** 03, MILN **22** 04

DURST, CEDRIC OF/1B (26,**27**) NYA **26** 29, **27** 30

DUSAK, ERV (FOUR SACK) OF/UTIL/P (19,17,**7**,25, 18,15) STLN **19** 41, **17** 42, **19** 46-47, **7** 47-50, **25** 51, PITN **28** 51, **15** 51-52

DUSAN, GENE CH (**56**) NYN *CH* **56** 83

DUSER, CARL P (39,15,**14**) KCA **39** 56, **15/14** 58

DUSTAL, BOB P (**35**) DETA **35** 63

DUVALL, MIKE P (**47**) TBA **47** 98-00, MINA **53** 01

DWYER, DOUBLE JOE PH (**17**) CINN **17** 37

DWYER, JIM OF/UTIL/DH (19,25,43,11, 36,1,28,**9**,5) STLN **19** 73, **25** 73-75, MONN **43** 75-76, NYN **25** 76, STLN **11** 77-78, SFN **36** 78, BOSA **1** 79-80, BALA **28** 81-84, **9** 84-88, MINA **5** 88-89, MONN **5** 89, MINA **5** 90

DYBZINZKI, JERRY INF/DH (**10**,20,17) CLEA **10** 80-82, CHIA **20** 83-84, PITN **17** 85

DYCK, JIM 3B/OF (24,27,8,33, **14**,26) STLA **24** 51-52, **27** 52, **8** 53, CLEA **33** 54, BALA **14** 55-56, CINN **26** 56

DYE, JERMAINE OF/DH (**24**,26,23) ATLN **24** 96, KCA **24** 97-01, OAKA **26** 01, **24** 01-04, CHIA **23** 05

DYER, DUFFY C/CH (**10**,5,15,8, 31,9) NYN **10** 68-74, PITN **5** 75-78, MONN **5** 79, DETA **15** 80-81, CHIN *CH* **8** 83, MILA *CH* **31** 89, *CH* **10** 89-95, *CH* **9** 96, OAKA *CH* **9** 97-98

DYER, EDDIE OF/P/M (**20**,61,30) STLN **20** 23, **61** 24, *M* **30** 46-50

DYER, MIKE P (**39**,62) MINA **39** 89, PITN **62** 94-95, MONN **39** 96

DYKES, JIMMY 3B/INF/M/CH (**5**,7,35,25,4, 42,28,40) PHIA **5** 31-32, CHIA **7** 33, **5** 34-39, *M* **7** 34-35, *M* **5** 36-46, PHIA *CH* **35** 49-50, *M* **35** 51-53, BALA *M* **25** 54, CINN *CH* **4** 55-58, *M* **4** 58, PITN *CH* **42** 59, DETA *M* **28** 59-60, CLEA *M* **35** 60-61, MILN *CH* **4** 62, KCA *CH* **40** 63-64

DYKHOFF, RADHAMES P (**28**) BALA **28** 98

DYKSTRA, LENNY (NAILS) OF (**4**) NYN **4** 85-89, PHIN **4** 89-96

E

EADDY, DON 3B (**18**) CHIN **18** 59

EARL, SCOTT 2B (**24**) DETA **24** 84

EARLEY, ARNIE P (**21**,47,50,44) BOSA **21** 60-65, CHIN **47/50** 66, HOUN **44** 67

EARLEY, BILL P (**41**) STLN **41** 86

EARLEY, TOM P (27,11,**26**,24) BOSN **27** 38, **11** 39, **26** 40-42, **24** 45

EARLY, JAKE C (9,20,11,**8**, 12) WASA **9** 39, **20** 40-41, **11** 41, **8** 41-43, 46, STLA **8** 47, WASA **11** 48, **9** 48-49, **11/12** 49

EARNSHAW, GEORGE (MOOSE) P/CH (**11**,18,7,23, 33,38) PHIA **11** 31-33, CHIA **18** 34-35, BKNN **7** 35-36, STLN **23/38** 36, PHIN *CH* **38** 49-50

EASLER, MIKE OF/DH/1B/CH (22,10,15,**24**, 7,17,34,45,4) HOUN **22** 73-75, CALA **10** 76, PITN **15** 77, **24** 79-83, BOSA **7** 84-85, NYA **17** 86, PHIN **34** 87, NYA **17** 87, MILA *CH* **22** 92, BOSA *CH* **45** 93-94, STLN *CH* **4** 99, **19** 00-01

EASLEY, DAMION INF/2B (15,1,**9**,25,2) CALA **15** 92, **1** 93-96, DETA **9** 96-02, TBA **25** 03, **2** 04, FLAN **2** 05

EASLEY, LOGAN P (42,**22**) PITN **42** 87, **22** 89

EAST, HUGH P (36,20,**32**) NYN **36** 41, **20** 42, **32** 43

EASTER, LUKE 1B/OF/CH (**9**,12) CLEA **9** 49-54, *CH* **12** 69

EASTERLING, PAUL OF (**10**) PHIA **10** 38

EASTERLY, JAMIE P (**45**,28,36,11) ATLN **45** 74-79, MILA **56** 81, **28** 81-83, CLEA **36** 83-86, **11** 87

EASTERWOOD, ROY C (**12**) CHIN **12** 44

EASTON, JOHN (GOOSE) PH (9,7,**16**) PHIN **9** 55, **7/16** 59

EASTWICK, RAWLY P (39,**49**,26,36, 35) CINN **39** 74, **49** 74-77, STLN **26** 77, NYA **36** 78, PHIN **49** 78-79, KCA **35** 80, CHIN **49** 81

EATON, ADAM P (**53**) SDN **53** 00-05

EATON, CRAIG P (**35**) KCA **35** 79

EATON, ZEB (RED) P (25,17) DETA **25** 44, **17** 45

EAVE, GARY P (**48**,37) ATLN **48** 88-89, SEAA **37** 90

EAVES, VALLIE (CHIEF) P (20,48,14,**28**, 41) PHIA **20** 35, CHIA **48/14** 39, **28** 40, CHIN **41** 41, **14** 42

EBERT, DERRIN P (**50**) ATLN **50** 99

ECHEVARRIA, ANGEL OF/1B (11,**39**,38,12) COLN **11** 96-98, **39** 99-00, MILN **38** 00, **39** 01, CHIN **12** 02

ECHOLS, JOHNNY PR (**4**) STLN **4** 39

ECKENSTAHLER, ERIC P (61,**36**) DETA **61** 02, **36** 03

ECKERSLEY, DENNIS (ECK) P (37,**43**) CLEA **37** 75-77, BOSA **43** 78-84, CHIN **43** 84-86, OAKA **43** 87-95, STLN **43** 96-97, BOSA **43** 98

ECKERT, AL (OBBIE) P (**20**) STLN **20** 35 91

ECKHARDT, OX OF (21,14) BOSN 21 32, BKNN 14 36

ECKSTEIN, DAVID SS/INF (22) ANAA 22 01-04, STLN 22 05

EDDY, CHRIS P (26) OAKA 26 95

EDDY, DON P (32) CHIA 32 70-71

EDDY, STEVE P (47/41) CALA 47/41 79

EDELEN, ED (DOC) P (31) WASA 31 32

EDELEN, JOE P (44,40) STLN 44 81, CINN 40 81-82

EDELMAN, JOHN P (30) MILN 30 55

EDEN, MIKE 2B/SS (9,65) ATLN 9 76, CHIA 65 78

EDENFIELD, KEN P (48) CALA 48 95-96

EDENS, TOM P (32,30,48,59, 46,45,33) NYN 32 87, MILA 30/48 90, MINA 59 91-92, HOUN 46 93-94, PHIN 45 94, CHIN 33 95

EDGE, BUTCH P (16) TORA 16 79

EDGERTON, BILL P (32,22,40) KCA 32 66-67, 22 67, SEAA 40 69

EDLER, DAVE 3B/UTIL (15,24,1) SEAA 15 80, 24 81, 1 82-83

EDMONDS, JIM OF/1B (25,15) CALA 25 93-96, ANAA 25 97-99, STLN 15 00-05

EDMONDSON, BRIAN P (48,20) ATLN 48 98, FLAN 20 98-00

EDMONDSON, PAUL P (41) CHIA 41 69

EDWARDS, BRUCE (BULL) C/UTIL (10,8,5,11,9) BKNN 10 46-51, CHIN 8 51-52, 5 54, WASA 11 55, CINN 9 56

EDWARDS, DAVE OF/DH/1B (33,24) MINA 33 78-80, SDN 24 81-83

EDWARDS, DOC C/1B/CH/M (25,6,10,38, 5,32) CLEA 25 62, 6 63, KCA 10 63-65, NYA 38 65, PHIN 5 70, *CH* 5 70-72, CLEA *CH* 32 86-87, *M* 32 87-89, NYN *CH* 90-91

EDWARDS, FOSTER (EDDIE) P (34) NYA 34 30

EDWARDS, HANK OF (33,32,16,24, 25,38,15) CLEA 33 41-43, 32 46-49, CHIN 16 49-50, BKNN 24 51, CINN 25 51-52, CHIA 38 52, STLA 15 53

EDWARDS, JOHNNY C (6,7) CINN 6 61-67, STLN 7 68, HOUN 7 69-74

EDWARDS, MARSHALL OF/DH (16) MILA 16 81-83

EDWARDS, MIKE OF/3B (21,25) OAKA 21 03, LAN 25 05

EDWARDS, MIKE (L.) 2B/UTIL (26,12,7) PITN 26/12 77, OAKA 7 78-80

EDWARDS, SHERMAN P (__) CINN __ 34

EDWARDS, WAYNE P (57,45) CHIA 57 89, 45 90-91,

EENHOORN, ROBERT SS/2B (50,20,11) NYA 50 94-95, 20 96, CALA 11 96, ANAA 11 97

EGAN, DICK P (41,37,52) DETA 41 63-64, CALA 41 66, LAN 37 67, TEXA *CH* 52 88-89

EGAN, TOM C/1B (30,8,10) CALA 30 65-70, CHIA 8 71-72, CALA 10 74-75

EGLOFF, BRUCE P (66,46) CLEA 66 91, 46 91-92

EICHELBERGER, JUAN P (33,13,49) SDN 33 78-80, 13 81-82, CLEA 13 83, ATLN 49/13 88

EICHHORN, MARK P (28,38,49,45, 34,48,58) TORA 28 82, 38 86-88, ATLN 49 89, CALA 45 90-92, TORA 34 92, 48 92-93, BALA 38 94, CALA 58 96

EICHRODT, FRED (IKE) OF (34) CHIA 34 31

EILAND, DAVE P (52,28,58,45, 47,38,48) NYA 52 88, 28 89-90, 58 90, 28 91, SDN 45 92-93, NYA 47 95, 38 96, TBA 48 98-00

EILERS, DAVE P (39,38,36) MILN 39 64-65, NYN 38 65-66, HOUN 36 67

EINERTSON, DARRELL P (39,38,36) NYA 56 00

EISCHEN, JOEY P (48,51,43,49, 58) MONN 48 94, LAN 51 95-96, DETA 43 96, CINN 49 97, MONN 48 01, 58 01-04, WASN 58 05

EISENHARDT, JAKE P (28) CINN 28 44

EISENREICH, JIM OF/DH/1B (4,22,8,12) MINA 4 82-84, KCA 22 87-90, 8 92, PHIN 8 93-96, FLAN 8 97-98, LAN 12 98

EISENSTAT, HARRY P (20,14,29,18, 26,24,10) BKNN 20 35, 14/29 36, 18 37, DETA 26 38, 24 39, CLEA 24 39, 10 39-42

ELARTON, SCOTT P (50,40,39) HOUN 50 98-01, COLN 40 01-03, 50 03-04, CLEA 39 04-05

ELDER, DAVE P (47,49) CLEA 47 02, 49 03

ELDER, GEORGE OF (3) STLA 3 49

ELDRED, BRAD 1B (35) PITN 35 05

ELDRED, CAL P (21,23) MILA 21 91-97, MILN 98-99, CHIA 21 00-01, STLN 23 03-05

ELIA, LEE INF/CH/M (49,19,3,4,2, 43) CHIA 49 66, CHIN 19 68, PHIN *CH* 3 80-81, CHIN *M* 4 82-83, PHIN *CH* 2 85, *CH* 4 86-87, *M* 4 87-88, NYA *CH* 43 89, SEAA *CH* 3 93, *CH* 4 94-97, TORA *CH* 3 00, SEAA *CH* 2 01-02, TBA *CH* 4 03-05

ELKO, PETE (PICCOLO PETE) 3B (52,8) CHIN 52 43-44, 8 43-44

ELLINGSON, BRUCE P (47,13) CLEA 47/13 74

ELLIOT, LARRY OF (14,5,42,17) PITN 14 62-63, 5 63, NYN 42 64, 17 66

ELLIOTT, BOB (MR. TEAM) 3B/OF/M/CH (24,37,8,3,12, 40,23,27,30) PITN 24 39, 37 40, 8 40-46, BOSN 3 47-51, NYN 37/12 52, STLA 40 53, CHIA 23/27 53, KCA *M* 30 60, LAA *CH* 3 61

ELLIOTT, DONNIE P (38) SDN 38 94-95

ELLIOTT, GLENN (LEFTY) P (37,16,18) BOSN 37 47, 16 48, 18 48-49

ELLIOTT, HAL P (20) PHIN 20 32

ELLIOTT, HARRY OF (10,11) STLN 10 53, 11 55

ELLIOTT, JIM (JUMBO JIM) P (21,17,43,18) PHIN 21 32, 17 33, 43 34, BOSN 18 34

ELLIOTT, RANDY OF/1B/DH (34,10,3,16, 4) SDN 34/10 72, 3 74, SFN 16 77, OAKA 4 80

ELLIS, DOCK P (37,40,17,36, 30,35,12) PITN 37 68, 40 68-69, 17 70-75, NYA 36 76-77, OAKA 36 77, TEXA 17 77-79, NYN 30/35 79, PITN 12 79

ELLIS, JIM P (52,34,33) CHIN 52/34 67, STLN 33 69

ELLIS, JOHNNY C/UTIL (23,7,9) NYA 23 69-72, CLEA 7 73-75, TEXA 9 76-81

ELLIS, MARK 2B/INF (14) OAKA 14 02-03, (04), 05

ELLIS, ROB OF/3B/UTIL (8) MILA 8 71, 74-75

ELLIS, ROBERT P (55) CALA 55 96, TORA 55 00, ARIN 55 01, LAN 51 02

ELLIS, SAMMY P/CH (32,58,41,46) CINN 32 62, 64-67, CALA 32 68, CHIA 32 69, NYA *CH* 58 82, *CH* 41 84, 86, CHIA *CH* 32 89, *CH* 46 90-91, CHIN *CH* 46 92, SEAA *CH* 32 93-94, BOSA *CH* 41 96, BALA *CH* 49 00

ELLISON, JASON OF (56,21) SFN 56 03-05, 21 05

ELLSWORTH, DICK P (31,37,36,50, 42,49) CHIN 31 58, CHIN 37 60-66, PHIN 37 67, BOSA 36 68-69, CLEA 50 69, 42 69-70, MILA 49 70-71

ELLSWORTH, STEVE P (28) BOSA 28 88

ELSTER, KEVIN SS (2,21,15,19, 26,3,18,10) NYN 2 86, 21 87-91, 15 92, NYA 19 94, 26 95, PHIN 3 95, TEXA 18 96, PITN 10 97, TEXA 18 98, LAN 43 00

ELSTON, DON P (33,50,36) CHIN 33 53, BKNN 50 57, CHIN 36 57-64

ELVIRA, NARCISO P (53,35) MILA 53/35 90

EMBREE, ALAN P (56,32,36,57, 41,43,46) CLEA 56 92, 95-96, ATLN 32 97, 36 98, ARIN 32 98, SFN 56 99-01, CHIA 57 01, SDN 41 02, BOSA 43 02-05, NYA 46 05

EMBREE, RED P (40,47,30,36, 22,35) CLEA 40 41, 47 42, 30 44-45, 36 46, 22 47, NYA 35 48, STLA 35 49

EMERY, CAL 1B (9) PHIN 9 63

EMMERICH, SLIM P (24,29) NYN 24 45, 29 46

ENCARNACION, ANGEL C (2,7) PITN 2 95-96, ANAA 7 97

ENCARNACION, EDWIN INF (12) CINN 12 05

ENCARNACION, JUAN OF (34,46,43) DETA 34 97-01, CINN 34 02, FLAN 46 02, 43 02-03, LAN 43 04, FLAN 43 04-05

ENCARNACION, LUIS P (34) KCA 34 90

ENCARNACION, MARIO OF (44,15) COLN 44 01, CHIN 15 02

ENDERS, TREVOR P (45) TBA 45 00

ENDICOTT, BILL OF (24) STLN 24 46

ENGLE, DAVE OF/UTIL/CH (51,20,10,4, 25) MINA 51 81, 20 81-85, DETA 10 86, MONN 4 87-88, MILA 25 89, HOUN *CH* 4 98, NYN *CH* 53 01-02

ENGLE, RICK P (51) MONN 51 81

ENGLE, STEVE P (49) CHIN 49 85

ENGLISH, CHARLIE 2B/INF (36,8,21,31) CHIA 36 32, 8 33, NYN 21 36, CINN 31 37

ENGLISH, GIL 3B/INF (23,26,24,2,4) NYN 23 32, DETA 26 36, 24 37, BOSN 2 37-38, BKNN 4 44

ENGLISH, WOODY 3B/SS/INF (14,1) CHIN 14 32, 1 32-36, BKNN 1 37-38

ENNIS, DEL OF/1B (14,7,23,3) PHIN 14 46-56, STLN 7 57-58, CINN 23 59, CHIA 3 59

ENNIS, JOHN P (45,49) ATLN 45 02, DETA 49 04

ENRIGHT, GEORGE C (29) CHIA 29 76

ENS, JEWEL CH (31,34,33,36, 3) DETA *CH* 31 32, CINN *CH* 34 33, PITN *CH* 33 35-38, *CH* 36 38, *CH* 33 39, CINN *CH* 3 41

ENSBERG, MORGAN 3B/INF (2,14) HOUN 2 00, 14 02-05

ENYART, TERRY P (55) MONN 55 74

EPPARD, JIM UTIL (12,11,26) CALA 12 87-88, 11 89, TORA 26 90

EPPERLY, AL (TUB) (PARD) P (56,11) CHIN 56 38, BKNN 11 50

EPPS, AUBREY C (37) PITN 37 35

EPPS, HAL OF (17,15,18,3) STLN 17 38, 40, STLA 15 43, 18 44, PHIA 3 44

EPSTEIN, MIKE (SUPERJEW) 1B (18,4,12,6,5, 26) BALA 18 66, 4 67, WASA 12 67-68 6 69-71, OAKA 5 71-72, TEXA 26 73, CALA 5 73-74

ERARDI, GREG P (35) SEAA 35 77

ERAUTT, EDDIE P (34,32,25) CINN 34 47-51, 53, STLN 32/25 53

ERAUTT, JOE (STUBBY) C (45) CHIA 45 50-51

ERDOS, TODD P (44,54) SDN 44 97, NYA 54 98-99, 50 00, SDN 57 00, BOSA 55 01

ERICKS, JOHN P (57) PITN 57 95-97

ERICKSON, DON P (25) PHIN 25 58

ERICKSON, HAL P (27) DETA 27 53

ERICKSON, HANK (POPEYE) C (18) CINN 18 36

ERICKSON, MATT 3B (8) MILN 8 04

ERICKSON, PAUL (LI'L ABNER) P (32,37,41,49) CHIN 32 41-42, 37 43-48, PHIN 41 48, NYN 49 48

ERICKSON, ROGER P (19,35) MINA 19 78-82, NYA 35 82-83

ERICKSON, SCOTT P (46,19,21,15) MINA 46 90, 19 91-95, BALA 21 95, 19 96-02, (03), NYN 19 04, TEXA 19 04, LAN 15 05

ERMER, CAL 2B/CH/M (__,42,43,23, 27,41) WASA __ 47, BALA *CH* 42 62, MINA *M* 43 67-68, MILA *CH* 23 70, *CH* 27 70-71, OAKA *CH* 41 77E

ERNAGA, FRANK OF (5,17) CHIN 5 57, 17 58

ERRICKSON, DICK (LIEF) P (18,19,21) BOSN 18 38-39, 19 40-42, CHIN 21 42

ERSKINE, CARL (OISK) P (17,11) BKNN 17 48-49, 11 50, 17 50-57, LAN 17 58-59

ERSTAD, DARIN OF/1B (27,17) CALA 27 96, ANAA 27 97-98, 17 99-04, LAA 17 05

ESASKY, NICK 3B/1B/UTIL (15,12,7,17) CINN 15 83, 12 83-88, BOSA 7 89, ATLN 17 90

ESCALERA, NINO P (21) CINN 21 54-55, NYN 45 95-96

ESCALONA, FELIX 2B/INF (5,3,60,29) TBA 5 02, 3 03, NYA 60 04, 29 05

ESCARREGA, CHICO P (24) CHIA 24 82

ESCHEN, LARRY SS/2B (14,16) PHIA 14/16 42

ESCOBAR, ALEX OF (25,6) NYN 25 01, CLEA 6 03-04

ESCOBAR, ANGEL SS/3B (54) SFN 54 88

ESCOBAR, JOSE INF (6) CLEA 6 91

ESCOBAR, KELVIM P (45,47) TORA 45 97-98, 47 99-00, 45 01-03, ANAA 45 04, LAA 45 05

ESHELMAN, VAUGHN P (52) BOSA 52 95-97

ESPINO, JUAN 2B (58,65,52) NYA 58 82-83, 65 83, 52 85, 5[illegible] 86-87

ESPINOSA, NINO P (42,39,35,51, 38) NYN 48 74, 39 75-78, PHIN 35 79-81, TORA 51/38 81

ESPINOZA, ALVARO SS/2B/INF/CH (40,1,47,20, 10,12,26) MINA 40 84, 1 85-86, NYA 47 88, 20 89, 12/13 90, 20 90-91, CLEA 10 93-96, NYN 12 96, SEAA 26 97, PITN *CH* 10 03-05

ESPOSITO, MIKE P (35) COLN 35 05

ESPOSITO, SAMMY INF (3,21,16,48, 14,1) CHIA 3 52, 21/16 55, 48 56-57, 14 58-63, KCA 1 63

ESPY, CECIL OF/UTIL (52,18,6,4, 56,22) LAN 52 83, TEXA 18 87-88, 6 88-90, 4 90, PITN 56 91-92, CINN 22 93

ESPY, DUANE CH (52) SDN *CH* 52 00-02, COLN *CH* 52 03-05

ESSEGIAN, CHUCK OF (37,29,10,16, 30,6) PHIN 37 58, STLN 29 59, LAN 29 59-60, BALA 10 61, KCA 16 61, CLEA 30 61-62, KCA 6 63

ESSER, MARK P (42) CHIA 42 79

ESSIAN, JIM C/UTIL/M (50,6,11,18, 16,7,17,19, 41) PHIN 50 73, 6 73-75, CHIA 11 76-77, OAKA 18 78-80, CHIA 16 81, SEAA 782, CLEA 17 83, OAKA 19 84, CHIN *M* 41 91

ESTALELLA, BOBBY 3B/OF (32,23,3,14, 4,33) WASA 32 35, 23 36, 3 39, STLA 14 41, WASA 4 42, PHIA 4 43-45, 33 49

ESTALELLA, BOBBY (M.) C (27,29,36,8, 17,20) PHIN 27 96-99, SFN 29 00-01, NYA 36 01, COLN 8 02-03, ARIN 17 04, TORA 20 04

ESTELLE, DICK P (25,28) SFN 25 64-65, 28 65

ESTES, SHAWN P (36,55) SFN 36 95-96, 55 96-01, NYN 55 02, CINN 55 02, CHIN 55 03, COLN 55 04, ARIN 55 05

ESTOCK, GEORGE P (22) BOSN 22 51

ESTRADA, CHUCK P/CH (23,47,33,43, •31) BALA 23 60-64, CHIN 47 66, NYN 33 67, TEXA *CH* 43 73, SDN *CH* 23 78-81., CLEA *CH* •31 83

ESTRADA, FRANK C (5) NYN 5 71

ESTRADA, HORACIO P (51) MILN 51 99, 48 00, COLN 27

ESTRADA, JOHNNY C (19,39,23) PHIN 19 01, 39 02, ATLN 23 03-05

ESTRELLA, LEO P (50,53) TORA 50 00, MILN 53 03, SFN 53 04

ETCHEBARREN, ANDY C (8,45,13,55) BALA 8 62, 8 65-75, CALA 8 75-77, *CH* 8 77, MILA 8 78, *CH* 45 85, *CH* 8 85-91, BALA *CH* 13 96-97, *CH* 55 97-98

ETCHISON, BUCK 1B (__,3) BOSN __ 43, 3 44

ETHERIDGE, BOBBY (LUKE) 3B/SS (17) SFN 17 67, 69

ETHERTON, SETH P (35,40,62,30) ANAA 35 00, CINN 40 01, 62 03, OAKA 30 05

ETTEN, NICK 1B (23,36,25,22, 41,5,9) PHIA 23 38, 36 39, PHIN 25 22 42, NYA 5 43-46, PHIN 36 47

ETTLES, MARK P (50) SDN 50 93

EUFEMIA, FRANK P (26) MINA 26 85

EUSEBIO, TONY C (10,20) HOUN 10 91, 20 94-01

EVANS, AL C (41,32,9,27, 11,8,10,2) WASA 41 39, 32 40-41, 9 41-42, 27 44, 11 45-46, 8 46-49, 10 50, BOSA 2 51

EVANS, ART P (14) CHIA 14 32

EVANS, BARRY INF (8,38) SDN 8 78-81, NYA 38 82

EVANS, BART P (45) KCA 45 98

EVANS, BILL P (56,25) CHIA 56 49, BOSA 25 51

EVANS, DARRELL 3B/1B/UTIL/CH (2,11,41) ATLN 2 69, 11 69-76, SFN 41 76-83, DETA 41 84-88, ATLN 11 89, NYA *CH* 41 90

EVANS, DWIGHT OF/DH/CH (28,2),6 BOSA 40 72-73, 24 73-90, BALA 24 91, COLN *CH* 24 94, BOSA *CH* 25 02

EVANS, RED P (28,22) CHIA 28 36, BKLN 22 39

EVANS, TOM 3B/INF (28,2,6) TORA 28 97, 2 98, TEXA 6 00

EVELAND, DANA P (37) MILN 37 05

EVERETT, ADAM SS (3,28) HOUN 3 01, 28 02-05

EVERETT, CARL OF/DH (3,2,27,5,8) FLAN 3 93-94, NYN 3 95-97, HOUN 3 98-99, BOSA 2 00-01, TEXA 2 02-03, CHIA 27/5 03, MONN 2 04, CHIA 8 04-05
EVERETT, LEON P (50,31) SDN 50/31 69
EVERS, WALT (HOOT) OF (17,15,14,31, 23,30) DETA 17 41, 15 46, 14 46-52, BOSA 3152-54, NYN 23 54, DETA 14 54, BALA 17 55, CLEA 30 55-56, BALA 14 56, CLEA *CH* 14 70
EVERSGERD, BRYAN P (24,26,52,21) STLN 24 94, MONN 26 95, TEXA 52 97, STLN 21 98
EWING, SAM 1B/DH/UTIL (10,19,5) CHIA 10 73, 19 76, TORA 5 77-78
EYRE, SCOTT P (36,29,49,47) CHIA 36 97-00, TORA 36 01, 29 01-02, SFN 49 02-04, 47 05
EYRICH, GEORGE P (18,21) PHIN 18/21 43
EZELL, GLENN CH (23,18,21,44, 10,55) TEXA *CH* 23 83, 18 83-85, 21 85, KCA *CH* 44 89-94, DETA *CH* 10 96, TBA *CH* 55 01-03

F

FABER, RED P/CH (18,19,23) CHIA 18 31, 33, 19 32, *CH* 23 46-48
FABREGAS, JORGE C (68,14,12,4) CALA 68 94, 14 94-96, ANAA 14 97, CHIA 12 97, ARIN 12 98, NYN 12 98, FLAN 14 99, ATLN 4 99, KCA 2 00, ANAA 6 01-02, MILN 6 02
FACE, ELROY (ROY) P (26,30,14) PITN 26 53, 55-68, DETA 30 68, MONN 14 69
FAEDO, LENNY INF/DH (21,12) MINA 21 80-81, 12 82-84
FAGAN, EVERETT P (24,38) PHIA 24 43, 38 46
FAHEY, BILL C/CH (10,12,37,14, 3,17,42) WASA 10 71, TEXA 12 72, 37 74, 14 75-77, SDN 3 79-80, DETA 17 81-83, SFN *CH* 42 86-91
FAHR, JERRY (RED) P (28) CLEA 28 51
FAIN, FERRIS (BURRHEAD) 1B (5,8,3,33) PHIA 5 47-49, 8 50-52, CHIA 8 53-54, DETA 3 55, CLEA 33 55
FAIREY, JIM OF (12,35,28) LAN 12 68, MONN 35 69-72, LAN 28 73
FAIRLY, RON (THE MULE) 1B/OF (55,8,44,6, 15,11) LAN 55 58, 8 59, 44 60, 6 61-69, MONN 6 69-74, STLN 15 75-76, OAKA 11 76, TORA 6 77, CALA 6 78
FAJARDO, HECTOR P (46,32,30) PITN 46 91, TEXA 32 91, 30 94-95
FALCONE, PETE P (56,41,33) SFN 56 75, STLN 41 76-78, NYN 33 79-82, ATLN 33 83-84
FALK, BIBB (JOCKEY) OF (5,29,20,28) CLEA 5 30, 29 31, *CH* 20 33, BOSA *CH* 28 34
FALKENBORG, BRIAN P (51,58,41) BALA 51 99, LAN 58 04, SDN 41 05
FALLENSTEIN, ED (JACK) P (24) BOSN 24 33
FALLON, BOB P (37,27) CHIA 37 84, 27 85
FALLON, GEORGE (FLASH) 2B/INF (18,7) BKNN 18 37, STLN 7 43-45
FALTEISEK, STEVE P (53,48) MONN 53 97, MILN 48 99
FANEYTE, RIKKERT OF (38,22,39,30) SFN 38 93,22 94, 39 95, TEXA 30 96
FANNIN, CLIFF (MULE) P (23,47,28,29, 20,28) STLA 23 45, 47 46, 28 47, 29 48, 22 49-51, 20/28 52
FANNING, JIM C/CH/M (48,1,4,6) CHIN 48 54, 1 55-57, ATLN *CH* 4 68, MONN *M* 6 81-82, *M* 6 84
FANOK, HARRY (FLAME THROWER) P (30) STLN 30 63-64
FANOVICH, FRANK (LEFTY) P (49,40,15) CINN 49/40 49, PHIA 15 53
FANSLER, STAN P (54) PITN 54 86
FANZONE, CARMEN 3B/UTIL (20,23) BOSA 20 70, CHIN 23 71-74
FARIES, PAUL INF (53,23,21) SDN 53 90, 23 91-92, SFN 21 93
FARISS, MONTY UTIL/OF (4) TEXA 4 91-92, FLAN 4 93
FARLEY, BOB OF/1B (18,7,26) SFN 18 61, CHIA 7 62, DETA 26 62
FARMER, ED P (47,28,43,17, 30,22,46,40) CLEA 47 71-73, DETA 28 73, PHIN 43 74, BALA 17 77, MILA 47 78, TEXA 30 79, CHIA 22 79-81, PHIN 46 82, 22 82-83, OAKA 40 83

FARMER, HOWARD P (50,49) MONN 50/49 90
FARMER, MIKE P (36) COLN 36 96
FARNSWORTH, JEFF P (52) DETA 52 02
FARNSWORTH, KYLE P (44,40) CHIN 44 99-04, DETA 44 05, ATLN 40 05
FARR, JIM P (33,35) TEXA 33/35 82
FARR, STEVE P (58,34,26,40, 41) CLEA 58/34 84, KCA 26 85-90, NYA 26 91-93, CLEA 40/26 94, BOSA 41 94
FARRELL, DICK (TURK) P (44,43,20,13, 31,32) PHIN 44 56, 43 57-61, LAN 20 61, HOUN 43 62, 13 63-67, 31 67, PHIN 39 67, 32 67-69
FARRELL, DOC INF (22) NYA 22 32-33, BOSA 22 35
FARRELL, JOHN P (52,38) CLEA 52 87-90, CALA 38 93-94, CLEA 52 95, DETA 52 96
FARRELL, KERBY 1B/P/M/CH (9,4,2,34,3) BOSN 9 43, CHIA 4 45, CLEA *M* 2 57, CHIA *CH* 34 66-69, CLEA *CH* 3 70-71
FASANO, SAL C (26,13,6,31, 9) KCA 26 96-98, 13 99, OAKA 6 00, 13 01, KCA 26 01, COLN 31 01, ANAA 9 02, BALA 26 05
FASSERO, JEFF P (39,13,14) MONN 39 91-93, 13 93-96, SEAA 13 97-99, TEXA 13 99, BOSA 31 00, CHIN 13 01-02, STLN 13 02-03, COLN 13 04, ARIN 13 04, SFN 14 05
FAST, DARCY P (38) CHIN 38 68
FASZHOLZ, JACK (PREACHER) (41) STLN 41 53
FAUL, BILL P (19,13,38) DETA 19 62, 13 63-64, CHIN 13 65-66, SFN 38 70
FAUSETT, BUCK 3B/P (18) CINN 18 44
FAZIO, ERNIE INF (19,11,7) HOUN 19 62, 11 63, KCA 7 66
FEAR, VERN P (37,30) CHIN 37/30 52
FEBLES, CARLOS 2B (43,3) KCA 43 98, 3 99-03
FEDEROFF, AL (WHITEY) 2B/SS (46,28) DETA 46 51-52, 28 52
FEHRING, BILL (DUTCH) C (__) CHIA __ 34
FEINBERG, EDDIE (ITZY) UTIL (__) PHIN __ 38-39
FELDER, MIKE OF/UTIL (16,25,28, 51) MILA 16 85-90, SFN 25 91-92, SEAA 25 93, HOUN 28/5194 9
FELDERMAN, MARV (COONIE) C (2) CHIN 2 42
FELDMAN, HARRY P (18,14) NYN 18 41-43, 14 44-46
FELDMAN, SCOTT P (39) TEXA 39 05
FELICIANO, PEDRO P (55) NYN 55 02-04
FELIX, JUNIOR OF/DH (54,47,49) TORA 54 89, 47 90, CALA 47 91-92, FLAN 47 93, DETA 49 94
FELIZ, PEDRO INF/3B/OF (39,7) SFN 39 00-03, 7 04-05
FELLER, BOB (RAPID ROBERT) P (9,14,19) CLEA 9 36, 14 37-38, 19 39-56
FELLER, JACK C (19) DETA 19 58
FELSKE, JOHN C/1B/CH/M (24,39,28,7) CHIN 24 68, MILA 39 72-73, TORA *CH* 28 80-81, PHIN *CH* 7 84, *M* 7 85-87
FELTON, TERRY P (21,37,18) MINA 21 79-80, 37 81-82, 18 82
FENNELL, MIKE CH (55?) NYA *CH* 55 87, 89
FENWICK, BOBBY INF (18) HOUN 18 72, STLN 18 73
FERENS, STAN (LEFTY) P (19,45) STLA 19 42, 45 46
FERGUSON, BOB P (39) CINN 39 44
FERGUSON, JOE C/OF/CH (13,11,41) LAN 13 70-76, STLN 13 76, HOUN 13 77-78, LAN 13 78-81, CALA 11 81, 13 82-83, TEXA *CH* 41 86, *CH* 13 86-87, LAN *CH* 13 88-89, *CH* 13 92-93
FERMIN, FELIX SS/2B (29,16,10,2) PITN 29 87-88, CLEA 16 89-93, SEAA 10 94-95, CHIN 2 96
FERMIN, RAMON P (52) OAKA 52 95
FERNANDES, ED C (38,25,27) PITN 38 40, CHIA 25/27 46
FERNANDEZ, ALEX P (32) CHIA 32 90-96, FLAN 32 97, 99 -01
FERNANDEZ, CHICO SS/INF (3,45,16,17, 9,7,1) BKNN 3 56, PHIN 45 57, 16 58, 17 58-59, DETA 9 60-63, NYN 7 63, BALA 1 68

FERNANDEZ, FRANK C/OF (38,10,39,25, 47) NYA 38 67-68, 10 69, OAKA 39 70-71, WASA 25 71, OAKA 39 71, CHIN 47 71-72
FERNANDEZ, JARED P (53,56,41) CINN 53 02, HOUN 56 03, 41 03-04
FERNANDEZ, JOSE INF/DH (14,39) MONN 14 99, ANAA 39 01
FERNANDEZ, NANNY 3B/UTIL (3,11) BOSN 3 42, 11 46-47, PITN 11 50
FERNANDEZ, OSVALDO P (22) SFN 22 96-97, CINN 43 00-01
FERNANDEZ, SID (EL SID) P (50,10) LAN 50 83, NYN 50 84-93, 10 87, BALA 50 94-95, PHIN 50 95-96, HOUN 50 97
FERNANDEZ, TONY SS/3B (1,2,8,21,6,7) TORA 1 83-90, SDN 2/8 91, 1 92, NYN 1 93, TORA 1 93, CINN 21 94, NYA 6 95, CLEA 1 97, TORA 1 98-99, MILN 7 01, TORA 1 01
FERRARA, AL (THE BULL) OF (20,9,22) LAN 20 63, 65, 9 66-68, SDN 9 69-71, CINN 22 71
FERRARESE, DON P (46,39,37,34, 28,14,36) BALA 46 55-56, 39 56-57, 37 57, CLEA 34 58-59, CHIA 28 60, PHIN 14 61-62, STLN 36 62
FERRARI, ANTHONY P (32) MONN 32 03
FERRARO, MIKE 3B/UTIL/CH/M (43,26,8,33, 2,41,34,52, 44) NYA 43 66, 26 68, SEAA 8 69, MILA 33 72, NYA *CH* 33 79, *CH* 33 79-82, CLEA *M* 2 83, KCA *CH* 41 84-86, *M* 41 86, NYA *CH* 34 87-88, *CH* 52 89, *CH* 44 90-91, BALA *CH* 43 93
FERRAZZI, BILL P (no#) PHIA no# 35
FERREIRA, TONY P (51) KCA 51 85
FERRELL, RICK C/CH B (8,9,7,2,10, 11,37,32,36) STLA 8 31-33, BOSA 9 33, 7 34-35, 2 36-37, WASA 10 37, 8 38-41, STLA 11 41, 9 42-43, WASA 8 44-45, *CH* 37 46-49, 37 47, 32 48-49, DETA *CH* 36 50-53
FERRELL, WES P B (14,12,10,25, 21,30) CLEA 14 30-33, BOSA 12 34-37, WASA 12 37, 10 38, NYA 25 38-39, BKNN 21 40, BOSN 30 41
FERRER, SERGIO INF (1,3) MINA 1 74-75, NYN 3 78, 1 79
FERRICK, TOM P/CH (34,28,38,26, 25,17,24,27, 21,3,51,33, 49) PHIA 34/28 41, CLEA 38 42, 26 46, STLA 25 46, WASA 17 47-48, STLA 24 49-50, NYA 26 50-51, WASA 26/27 51, 21 51-52, CINN *CH* 3 54-58, PHIN *CH* 51 59, DETA *CH* 33 60-63, KCA *CH* 49 64-65
FERRIS, BOB P (45) CALA 45 79-80, 44 80
FERRISS, DAVE (BOO) P/CH (38,33,) BOSA 38 45, 33 45-50, *CH* 33 55-59
FETTE, LOU P (16,18,21,23, 45) BOSN 16 37-39, 18 40, BKNN 21 40, BOSN 23 45
FETTERS, MIKE P (48,36,32,26, 37,56,39,55) CALA 48 89-91, MILA 36 92-97, OAKA 36 98, ANAA 32/26 98, BALA 37 99, LAN 56 00-01, PITN 39 01-02, ARIN 39 02, MINA 55 03, ARIN 39 04
FIALA, NEIL SS/3B (51,19) STLN 51 81, CINN 19 81
FICK, JOHN P (23) PHIN 23 44
FICK, ROB C/1B/OF (41,31,39,18, 25,5,9,29,13) DETA 41 98, 31/39 99, 18 00-01, 25 01-02, ATLN 5 03, TBA 9 04, SDN 29 04, 13 05
FIDRYCH, MARK (THE BIRD) P (20) DETA 20 76-80
FIEBER, CLARENCE (LEFTY) P (39) CHIA 39 32
FIELD, NATE P (56,55,27,57) KCA 56 02, 55/27 03, 57 04-05
FIELDER, CECIL (BIG DADDY) 1B/DH (23,45,25,33) TORA 23 85-88, DETA 45 90-96, NYA 25 96, 45 96-97, ANAA 45 98, CLEA 33 98
FIELDER, PRINCE INF (28) MILN 28 05
FIELDS, BRUCE OF/DH/CH (37,29) DETA 37 86, SEAA 29 88-89, DETA *CH* 29 03-05
FIFE, DANNY P (16) MINA 16 73-74
FIGGA, MIKE C (63,13) NYA 63 97, 13 98-99, BALA 13 99
FIGGINS, CHONE 2B/3B/OF (6,9) ANAA 6 02-03, 9 04, LAA 9 05
FIGUEROA, BIEN SS/2B (50) STLN 50 92
FIGUEROA, ED P (37,31,24,56, 32) CALA 37 74-75, NYA 31 76-80, TEXA 24 80, OAKA 56/32 81

FIGUEROA, JESUS OF (17) CHIN 17 80
FIGUEROA, LUIS 2B (25) PITN 25 80
FIGUEROA, NELSON P (56,57,52,37, 35) ARIN 56 00, PHIN 57 01, MILN 52 02, PITN 37 03, 35 04
FIKAC, JEREMY P (57,33,40) SDN 57 01-02, OAKA 33 03, MONN 40 04
FILE, BOB P (36) TORA 36 01-02, (03), 04
FILE, SAM SS/3B (6) PHIN 6 40
FILER, TOM P (50,49,39,28, 44) CHIN 50 82, TORA 49 85, MILA 39 88-89, 28 90, NYN 44 92
FILIPOWICZ, STEVE (FLIP) OF/C (34,37) NYN 34 44-45, CINN 37 48
FILLEY, MARC P (26) WASA 26 34
FILSON, PETE P (23,38,51,47, 35) MINA 23 82-86, CHIA 38/51 86, NYA 47 87, KCA 35 90
FIMPLE, JACK C/INF (31,37,13,58) LAN 31 83-84, 37 86, CALA 13 87, 58 87-88
FINCH, JOEL P (44) BOSA 44 79
FINE, TOMMY P (23,42) BOSA 23 47, STLA 42 50
FINGERS, ROLLIE P (38,32,34) OAKA 38/32 68, 34 69-76, SDN 34 77-80, MILA 34 81-82, 84-85
FINIGAN, JIM 3B/2B (15,4,5,17,33) PHIA 15 54, KCA 4 55-56, DETA 5 57, SFN 17 58, BALA 33 59
FINK, HERMAN P (68,22,18) PHIA 68 35, 22 36, 18 37
FINLEY, BOB C (15,31,9) PHIN 15 43, 31/9 44
FINLEY, CHUCK P (59,31) CALA 59 86, 31 86-96, ANAA 31 97-99, CLEA 31 00-02, STLN 31 02
FINLEY, STEVE OF (10,12,16) BALA 10 90, HOUN 12 91-94, SDN 12 95-98, ARIN 12 99-04, LAN 16/12 04, LAA 12 05
FINN, MICKEY 2B (2,7) BKNN 2 32, PHIN 7 33
FINNEY, HAL C (32) PITN 32 32-34, 36
FINNEY, LOU OF/1B (no#,7,23,8, 6,26,25,16, 31,18,12) PHIA no# 31, 7 33, 23 34-36, 8 37, 6 38-39, BOSA 26 39, 25 40, 8 41-43, 16 44, 31 45, STLA 18 45-46, PHIN 12 47
FINNVOLD, GAR P (46) BOSA 46 94
FIORE, MIKE 1B/OF (30,19,3,10,1) BALA 30 68, KCA 19 69-70, BOSA 3 70-71, STLN 10 72, SDN 1 72
FIORENTINO, JEFF OF (16) BALA 16 05
FIORIE, TONY P (36,52) TBA 36 00-01, MINA 52 01-03
FIREOVID, STEVE P (62,41,45,44, 47,29) SDN 62 81, 83, PHIN 41/44 84, CHIA 45 85, SEAA 47 86, TEXA 29 92
FIROVA, DAN C (44,31) SEAA 44 81-82, CLEA 31 88
FISCHER, BILL P/CH (27,44,20,19, 18,26,31,29, 28,21,6,34) CHIA 27 56, 44 57, 20 57-58, DETA 19 58, WASA 18 58-60, DETA 18 60, 26 61, KCA 31 61, 29 62, 28 62-63, MINA 21 64, CINN *CH* 6 79-83, BOSA *CH* 34 85-91, TBA *CH* __ 00, 54 01
FISCHER, BRAD CH (35) OAKA *CH* 35 96-05
FISCHER, CARL P (20,15,16,22, 25,29) WASA 20 31, 15 32, STLA 16 32, DETA 22 33, 15 34-35, CHIA 25 35, CLEA 29 37, WASA 16 37
FISCHER, HANK (BULLDOG) P (12,45,34,30, 38,21) MILN 12/45 62, 34 63-66, CINN 30/38 66, BOSA 38 66-67, 21 66-77
FISCHER, JEFF P (39,51) MONN 39 87, LAN 51 89
FISCHER, RUBE P (10,29,15,18) NYN 10 41, 29 43, 15 44-45, 18 46
FISCHER, TODD P (38) CALA 38 86
FISCHLIN, MIKE SS/INF (10,22,27) HOUN 10 77-78, 80, CLEA 22 81-85, NYA 22 86, ATLN 27 87
FISHEL, JOHN OF (18) HOUN 18 88
FISHER, BRIAN P (54,36,55,46) NYA 54 85-86, PITN 36/54 87, 54 88-89, HOUN 55/54 90, SEAA 46 92
FISHER, DON P (18) NYN 18 45
FISHER, EDDIE P (39,28,32,24, 34,48) SFN 39 59-61, CHIA 28 62-66, BALA 28 66-67, CLEA 32 68, CALA 24 69-72, CHIA 34 72-73, STLN 48 73

FISHER, FRITZ P
(44) DETA 44 64
FISHER, HARRY PH
(35,39,19) PITN 35/39 51, 19 52
FISHER, JACK (FAT JACK) P
(48,22,43) BALA 48 59-61, 22 62, SFN 22 63, NYN 22 64-67, CHIA 22 68, CINN 43 69
FISHER, MAURY P
(43) CINN 43 55
FISHER, SHOWBOAT OF
(__) STLA __ 32
FISHER, TOM P
(46/47) BALA 46/47 67
FISK, CARLTON (PUDGE) C/DH
(40,41,27,72) BOSA 40 69, 41 71, 27 71-80, CHIA 72 81-93
FITZGERALD, BRIAN P
(39) SEAA 39 02
FITZGERALD, ED (GOOCH) C/CH
(9,52,37,8,41, 42) PITN 9 48-53, WASA 52/37 53, 8 53-59, CLEA 8 59, *CH* 41 60, KCA *CH* 42 61, MINA *CH* 52 62-64
FITZGERALD, JOE CH
(34,29,36,52, 55) WASA *CH* 34 39, *CH* 29 44-49, *CH* 36 48-49, *CH* 52 50-56, NYN *CH* 55 73
FITZGERALD, JOHN P
(35) SFN 35 58
FITZGERALD, MIKE C/UTIL
(20,21) NYN 20 83-84, MONN 21 85, 20 85-91, CALA 20 92
FITZGERALD, MIKE 1B
(57) STLN 57 88
FITZMAURICE, SHAUN OF
(5) NYN 5 66
FITZMORRIS, AL P
(42,23,39,47, 36) KCA 42 69, 23 70-73, 39 73-76, CLEA 39 77-78, CALA 47/36 78
FITZPATRICK, JOHN CH
(40,3) PITN *CH* 40 53-56, MILN *CH* 3 58-59
FITZSIMMONS, FRED (FAT FREDDIE) P/M/CH
(11,12,10,14, 33,27,6,5,42, 3) NYN 11 32, 12 33-37, BKNN 10 37, 14 38-43, PHIN *M* 33 43-44, *M* 14 44-45, BOSN *CH* 27 48, NYN *CH* 6 49, *CH* 5 50-51, *CH* 6 51-55, CHIN *CH* 33 57-59, KCA *CH* 42 60, CHIN *CH* 3 66
FLACK, MAX OF
(1,3) STLN 1 23, 3 24
FLAGER, WALLY SS/2B
(15,33,8) CINN 15 45, PHIN 33/8 45
FLAHERTY, JOHN C
(15,12,23,6, 17) BOSA 15 92-93, DETA 12 94-96, SDN 23 96-97, TBA 23 98, 6 98-02, NYA 17 03-05
FLAIR, AL (BROADWAY) 1B
(6) BOSA 6 41
FLANAGAN, MIKE P/CH
(46) BALA 46 75-87, TORA 46 87-90, BALA 46 91-92, *CH* 46 95, *CH* 46 98
FLANIGAN, RAY P
(45,30) CLEA 45/30 46
FLANIGAN, TOM P
(39,44) CHIA 39 54, STLN 44 58
FLANNERY, JOHN INF/DH
(1) CHIA 1 77
FLANNERY, TIM 2B/INF/CH
(30,6,11,4) 20,12,17) SDN 30 79, 6 80-82, 11 83-89, *CH* 4 96, *CH* 11 97-02
FLAVIN, JOHN P
(38) CHIN 38 64
FLEITAS, ANGEL SS
(18,22) WASA 18/22 48
FLEMING, BILL P
(28,23,30,46, 36,53,32) BOSA 28 40, 23 41, CHIN 30/46 42, 36 43, 53 44, 32 44,46
FLEMING, DAVE P
(56,35,47) SEAA 56 91, 35 92-95, KCA 47 95
FLEMING, LES (MOE) 1B
(20,23,8,2) DETA 20 39, CLEA 23 41-42, 8 45-47, PITN 2 49
FLENER, HUCK P
(32,38) TORA 32 93, 38 96-97
FLETCHER, ART CH/M
(34,30,29,31) NYA *CH/M* 34 29, *CH* 30 30-31, *CH* 29 32-39, *CH* 31 40-45
FLETCHER, DARRIN C/DH
(25,24,9) LAN 25 89-90, PHIN 24 90-91, MONN 24 92-97, TORA 9 98-02
FLETCHER, ELBIE 1B
(16,23,5,3, 15,17) BOSN 16 34, 23 35, 5 37-39, PITN 16 39, 5 40, 3 40-43, 15 46, 3 47, BOSN 17 49
FLETCHER, PAUL P
(58) PHIN 58 93, 95-96
FLETCHER, SCOTT SS/INF
(20,46,1,7,12, 5,10) CHIN 20 81-82, CHIA 46 83, 1 83-85, TEXA 1 86-89, CHIA 7 89-91, MILA 12 92, BOSA 5 93-94, DETA 10 95
FLETCHER, TOM P
(31) DETA 31 62
FLETCHER, VAN P
(26) DETA 26 55
FLICK, LEW (NOISY) OF
(14) PHIA 14 43-44
FLINN, JOHN P
(37,40,57) BALA 37 78-79, MILA 40 80, BALA 57 82

FLITCRAFT, HILLY P
(16,8) PHIN 16/8 42
FLOHR, MORT (DUTCH) P
(15) PHIA 15 34
FLOOD, CURT OF
(27,14,42,21) CINN 27 56, 14 57, STLN 42 58, 21 58-69, WASA 21 71
FLORA, KEVIN 2B/DH
(38,8,30) CALA 38 91, 8 95, PHIN 30 95
FLORENCE, DON P
(36) NYN 36 95
FLORES, GIL OF/DH
(28,17) CALA 28 77, NYN 17 78-79
FLORES, JESSE P
(30,19,23) CHIN 30 42, PHIA 19 43-47, CLEA 23 50
FLORES, JOSE UTIL/SS
(30,54) OAKA 30 02, LAN 54 04
FLORES, RANDY P
(50,51,61,34) TEXA 50 02, COLN 51 02, STLN 61 04, 34 05
FLORES, RON P
(47) OAKA 47 05
FLORIE, BRYCE P
(39) SDN 39 94-96, MILA 39 96-97, DETA 39 98-99, BOSA 39 99-01
FLOWERS, BEN P
(36,25,40,37, 22) BOSA 36 51, 25 53, DETA 40 55, STLN 37 55-56, PHIN 22 56
FLOWERS, JAKE INF/UTIL/CH
(22,10,8,5, 34,29,42) STLN 22 23, 10 32, BKNN 8 33, CINN 5 34, PITN *CH* 34 40-45, BOSN *CH* 29 46, CLEA *CH* 42 51-52
FLOWERS, WES P
(20,25) BKNN 20 40, 25 44
FLOYD, BOBBY SS/INF/CH
(2,6,5,15,55, 53) BALA 2 68-70, KCA 6 70, 5 71, 15 71-74, NYN *CH* 55 01, 53 04
FLOYD, BUBBA SS
(25) DETA 25 44
FLOYD, CLIFF 1B/OF
(30,15,12) MONN 30 93-96, FLAN 15 97-99, 30 00-02, MONN 30 02, BOSA 12 02, NYN 30 03-05
FLOYD, GAVIN P
(41,34) PHIN 41 04, 34 05
FLYNN, DOUG 2B/INF
(23,21,20) CINN 23 75-77, NYN 23 77-81, TEXA 21 82, MONN 23 82-85, DETA 20 85
FLYTHE, STU P
(46) PHIA 46 36
FODGE, GENE (SUDS) P
(24) CHIN 24 58
FOILES, HANK C
(6,16,15,38, 20,12,8,10, 36,9) CINN 6 53, CLEA 16 53, 15 55-56, PITN 38 56, 20 57-59, KCA 12 60, CLEA 8 60, DETA 10 60, BALA 36 61, CINN 9 62-63, LAA 16 63-64
FOGG, JOSH P
(55,27) CHIA 55 01, PITN 27 02-05
FOLEY, MARV C/UTIL/CH
(42,17,16,30, 43,34) CHIA 42 78, 17 79-80, 16 82, TEXA 30 84, CHIN *CH* 43 94, BALA *CH* 34 99
FOLEY, TOM SS/INF/CH
(10,11,16,15, 6) CINN 10 83-85, PHIN 11 85-86, MONN 16 86-92, PITN 16 93-94, MONN 16 95, TBA *CH* 15 02-03, 16 03, 6 04-05
FOLI, TIM SS/UTIL/CH
(19,36,10,20, 2,14) NYN 19 70-71, MONN 19 72-77, SFN 36/19 77, NYN 19 78-79, PITN 10 79-81, CALA 20 82, 10 82-83, NYA 2 84, PITN 10 85, TEXA *CH* 14 86-87, MILA *CH* 14 92-95, KCA *CH* 56 96, CINN *CH* 10 01-03
FOLKERS, RICH P
(38,28,26,45) NYN 38 70, STLN 28 72-74, SDN 26 75-76, MILA 45 77
FONDY, DEE 1B
(40,3,19) CHIN 40 51-57, PITN 3 57, CINN 19 58
FONSECA, LEW 1B/UTIL/P/M
(5,7,1,12) CLEA 5 31, CHIA 7 31, 1 31, 12 32, *M* 12 32, *M* 1 33-34
FONTENOT, JOE P
(54) FLAN 54 98
FONTENOT, MIKE 2B
(29) CHIN 29 05
FONTENOT, RAY P
(57,47,31,37) NYA 57 83, 47 83-84, CHIN 31 85-86, MINA 37 86
FONVILLE, CHAD SS/UTIL
(15,22,3,50) MONN 15 95, LAN 22 95, 3 95-97, CHIA 22 97, BOSA 50 99
FOOR, JIM P
(45,32,58) DETA 45 71-72, PITN 32/58 73
FOOTE, BARRY C/CH
(54,9,8,23, 36,26) MONN 54 73-74, 9 74-77, PHIN 9 77-78, CHIN 8 79-81, NYA 23 81-82, CHIA *CH* 54 90, *CH* 36 91, NYN *CH* 26 92-93
FOPPERT, JESSE P
(34) SFN 34 03-05
FORBES, P. J. 2B/INF
(1,29) BALA 1 98, PHIN 29 01
FORD, BEN P
(50,31,48,38) ARIN 50 98, NYA 31 00, MILN 48/38 04
FORD, CURT OF
(12,27,24) STLN 12 85, 27 85-88, PHIN 24 89, 27 90

FORD, DAN OF/DH
(15) MINA 15 75-78, CALA 15 79-81, BALA 15 82-85
FORD, DAVE P
(59,21) BALA 59 78-79, 21 80-81
FORD, GENE P
(25,6) BOSN 25 36, CHIA 6 38
FORD, HOD SS/INF
(no#,24,12) STLN no# 32, BOSN 24 32, 12 33
FORD, LEW OF/DH
(20) MINA 20 03-05
FORD, MATT P
(52) MILN 52 03
FORD, TED OF
(22,3,33) CLEA 22 70-71, TEXA 3 72, CLEA 33 73
FORD, WENTY P
(45) ATLN 45 73
FORD, WHITEY (CHAIRMAN OF THE BOARD) P/CH
(18,19,16) NYA 18/19 50, 16 53-67, *CH* 16 64, 68, 74-75
FORDHAM, TOM P
(32) CHIA 32 97-98
FORDYCE, BROOK C
(5,51,6,8,26) NYN 5 95, CINN 51 96, 6 97-98, CHIA 8 99-00, BALA 26 00-03, TBA 26 04
FORNIELES, MIKE P
(4,16,25,41, 20,27) WASA 4 52, CHIA 16 53-56, BALA 25 56, 41 56-57, BOSA 20 57-63, MINA 20/27 63
FORSCH, BOB P B
(37,31) STLN 37 74, 31 74-88, HOUN 31 88-89
FORSCH, KEN P B
(43) HOUN 43 70-80, CALA 43 81-86
FORSTER, SCOTT P
(51) MONN 51 00
FORSTER, TERRY P
(51) CHIA 51 70-76, PITN 51 77, LAN 78-82, ATLN 51 83-85, CALA 51 86
FORTUGNO, TIM P
(40,55,51) CALA 40/51 92, CINN 55 94, CHIA 51 95
FORTUNATO, BARTOLOME P
(57,43) TBA 57 04, NYN 43 04, (05)
FOSNOW, JERRY P
(26) MINA 26 64-65
FOSS, LARRY P
(37,27) PITN 37 61, NYN 27 62
FOSSAS, TONY P
(46,36,48,44, 49,27) TEXA 46 88, MILA 36 89-90, BOSA 48 91-94, STLN 48 95-97, SEAA 48 98, CHIN 44 98, TEXA 49 98, NYA 27 99
FOSSE, RAY C/UTIL/DH
(8,10,38,13) CLEA 8 67-72, OAKA 10 73-75, CLEA 10 76-77, SEAA 38 77, MILA 13 79
FOSSUM, CASEY P
(59,15,23,16) BOSA 59 01, 15 02, 23 03, ARIN 16 04, TBA 15 05
FOSTER, ALAN P
(44,32,27,21) 6) LAN 44 67-70, CLEA 32 71, CALA 32 72, STLN 27 73-74, SDN 21 75-76
FOSTER, GEORGE OF/1B
(14,15,) SFN 14 69-71, CINN 15 71-81, NYN 15 82-86, CHIA 15 86
FOSTER, JOHN P
(48,40,46) ATLN 48 03, MILN 40 03, ATLN 46 05
FOSTER, KEVIN P
(57,31,32,56) PHIN 57 93, CHIN 31 94, 32 95-96, 31 97-98, TEXA 56 01
FOSTER, KRIS P
(36) BALA 36 01
FOSTER, LARRY P
(46) DETA 46 63
FOSTER, LEO SS/INF
(31,14,17,1) ATLN 31/14 71, 17 73-74, NYN 1 76-77, 19 77
FOSTER, ROY OF
(27) CLEA 27 70-72
FOSTER, STEVE P
(54) CINN 54 91-93
FOTHERGILL, BOB (FATS) OF
(35,13) CHIA 35 31, 13 32, BOSA 13 33
FOUCAULT, STEVE P
(29,40,16) TEXA 29 73-76, DETA 29 77-78, KCA 40/16 78
FOULKE, KEITH P
(38,44,29) SFN 38 97, CHIA 44 97, 29 98-02, OAKA 29 03, BOSA 29 04-05
FOWLER, ART P/CH
(51,45,24,43, 50,40,41,42) CINN 51 54-57, LAN 45 59, LAA 24 61-64, *CH* 24 64, MINA *CH* 69, DETA *CH* 50 71-73, TEXA *CH* 40 74, *CH* 41 74-75, NYA *CH* 42 77-79, OAKA *CH* 42 80-82, NYA *CH* 42 83, 88
FOWLER, DICK P
(42,32,22,,25) PHIA 42 41, 32/22 42, 25 45-52
FOWLER, JESSE (PETE) P
(__) STLN __ 24
FOWLKES, ALAN P
(29,46) SFN 29 82, CALA 46 85
FOX, ANDY 3B/INF
(26,18,6,12, 5) NYA 26 96-97, 18 97, ARIN 6 98-99, FLAN 6 00-03, MONN 12 04, TEXA 5 04

FOX, CHAD P
(40,44,49,47) ATLN 40 97, MILN 40 98-99, (00), 01-02, BOSA 44 03, FLAN 49 03, 44 04, CHIN 47 05
FOX, CHARLIE (IRISH) C/CH/M
(21,9,7,3,4) NYN 21 42, SFN *CH* 9 65-68, *M* 7 70-74, MONN *M* 3 76, CHIN *M* 4 83, NYA *CH* 52 89
FOX, ERIC OF/DH
(28,31,18) OAKA 28 92-93, 31 94, TEXA 18 95
FOX, HOWIE P
(43,37,18,21) CINN 43 44, 37 45-46, 43 48-51, PHIN 18 52, BALA 37/21 54
FOX, NELLIE 2B/CH
(28,41,18,26, 2,42) PHIA 28 47, 41 48, 18 49, CHIA 26 50-52, 2 53-63, HOUN 2 64-65, *CH* 2 65-67, WASA *CH* 42 68-71, TEXA *CH* 42 72
FOX, PETE OF
(1,12,9) DETA 1 33, 12 34, 9 35-40, BOSA 12 41-45
FOX, TERRY P
(36,18,34,19) MILN 36 60, DETA 18 61-66, PHIN 34/19 66
FOXX, JIMMIE (DOUBLE X, BEAST) 1B/C/UTIL
(3,2,16,26,1, 4) PHIA 3 31-35, 2 35, BOSA 3 36-42, CHIN 16 42, 26/1 44, *CH* 26 44, PHIN 4 45
FOY, JOE 3B/UTIL
(1,5,14) BOSA 1 66-68, KCA 1 69, NYN 5 70, WASA 14 71
FOYTACK, PAUL P
(39,36,21,49, 20) DETA 39 53, 36 55, 21 56-63, LAA 49 63, 20 64
FRAILING, KEN P
(47) CHIA 47 72-73, CHIN 47 74-76
FRANCIS, EARL P
(29,27,36) PITN 29 60, 27 60-64, STLN 36 65
FRANCIS, JEFF P
(26) COLN 26 04-05
FRANCISCO, FRANK P
(50) TEXA 50 04-05
FRANCO, JOHN P
(52,31,45) CINN 52 84, 31 84-89, NYN 31 90-98, 45 98-01, (02), 03-04, HOUN 31 05
FRANCO, JULIO SS/UTIL/DH/1B
(15,14,23,25, 18,4) PHIN 15 82, CLEA 14 83-88, TEXA 14 89-93, CHIA 14 94, CLEA 23 96-97, MILA 25 97, TBA 18 99, ATLN 4 01-02, 23 02, 14 03-05
FRANCO, MATT 1B/3B
(15,4) CHIN 15 95, NYN 15 96-00, ATLN 4 02-03
FRANCOEUR, JEFF OF
(7) ATLN 7 05
FRANCONA, TERRY OF/1B/P/DH/CH/M S
(16,10,24,30, 55,7,11,47) MONN 16 81-85, CHIN 16 86, CINN 10 87, CLEA 24 88, MILA 30 89-90, DETA *CH* 55 96, PHIN *M* 7 97-00, TEXA *CH* 11 02, OAKA *CH* 47 03, BOSA *M* 47 04-05
FRANCONA, TITO OF/1B F
(44,3,8,14,24, 23,19,11,36, 9) BALA 44 56-57, CHIA 3 58, DETA 8 58, CLEA 14 59-62, 24 63-64, STLN 23 65-66, PHIN 19 67, ATLN 11 67, 19 68-69, OAKA 36 69-70, MILA 9 70
FRANK, MIKE OF
(34) CINN 34 98
FRANKHOUSE, FRED P
(16,20,14,26, 11,12) BOSN 16 32, 20 33, 14 34-35, BKNN 26 36, 11 37-38, BOSN 12 39
FRANKLIN, JACK P
(22) BKNN 22 44
FRANKLIN, JAY P
(29,39) SDN 29/39 71
FRANKLIN, MICAH OF
(56) STLN 56 97
FRANKLIN, MURRAY (MOE) SS/INF
(28,27) DETA 28 41, 27 42
FRANKLIN, RYAN P
(45) SEAA 45 99, 45 01-05
FRANKLIN, WAYNE P
(45,53,26,36, 28,48) SEAA 45 99, HOUN 53 00-01, MILN 26 02-03, 36 02, SFN 28 04, NYA 48 05
FRANKS, CH
(55) MONN *CH* 55 95
FRANKS, HERMAN C/CH/M
(12,15,13,19, 14,3,6,37) STLN 12/15/13 39, BKNN 19 40-41, PHIA 14 47-48, NYN 3 49, *CH* 3 49-55, SFN *CH* 3 58, *CH* 6 64, *M* 3 65-68, CHIN *CH* 37 70, *M* 3 77-79
FRASCATORE, JOHN P
(50,60,52) STLN 50 94, 60 95, 50 96-98, ARIN 50 99, TORA 52 99-01
FRASER, CHICK CH ???
(33) BKNN 33 35-36
FRASER,WILLIE P
(52,46,27,44, 49) CALA 52/46 86, 27 87-90, TORA 27 91, STLN 46 91, FLAN 44 94, MONN 49 95
FRASIER, VIC P
(24,18,19,12, 16,15,45) CHIA 24 31, 18 32, 19 33, DETA 12 33, 16 34, BOSN 15 37, CHIA 45/15 39
FRASOR, JASON P
(54) TORA 54 04-05

FRAZIER, GEORGE P
(49,43,**39**,25, 21) STLN **49** 78, **43** 78-79, **39** 79-80, NYA **43** 81-83, CLEA **25** 84, CHIN **39** 84-86, MINA **21** 86-87

FRAZIER, JOE (COBRA JOE) OF/M
(36,**24**,9,2, 55) CLEA **36** 47, STLN **24** 54-56, CINN **9** 56, BALA **2** 56, NYN *M* **55** 76-77

FRAZIER, LOU OF
(**7**,4,14,54,26) MONN **7** 93-95, TEXA **4** 95, **14** 96, CHIA **54/26** 98

FREDERICK, JOHNNY OF
(**1**) BKNN **1** 32-34

FREDERICK, KEVIN P
(50,**48**) MINA **50** 02, TORA **48** 04

FREDERICKSON, SCOTT P
(**49**) COLN **49** 93

FREED, ED OF
(**30**) PHIN **30** 42

FREED, ROGER 1B/OF/C
(13,20,28,23, **7**) BALA **13** 70, PHIN **20** 71-72, CINN **28** 74, MONN **23** 76, STLN **7** 77-79

FREEHAN, BILL C/1B/UTIL
(19,**11**) DETA **19** 61, **11** 63-76

FREEL, RYAN 2B/3B
(11,3,**6**) TORA **11** 01, CINN **3** 03, **6** 03-05

FREEMAN, CHOO OF
(**21**) COLN **21** 04-05

FREEMAN, HERSH (BUSTER) P
(28,14,25,**30**, 32) BOSA **28/14** 52-53, **25** 55, CINN **30** 55-58, CHIN **32** 58

FREEMAN, JIMMY P
(24,40) ATLN **24** 72, **40** 73

FREEMAN, LaVEL DH
(**11**) MILA **11** 89

FREEMAN, MARK P
(35,45,**31**) KCA **35** 59, NYA **45** 59, CHIN **31** 60

FREEMAN, MARVIN P
(**48**,40,44,33) PHIN **48** 86, 88-90, ATLN **40** 90-93, COLN **44** 94-96, CHIA **33** 96

FREESE, GENE (AUGIE) 3B/UTIL B
(8,24,4,**12**, 18,11) PITN **8** 55-58, STLN **24** 58, PHIN **4** 59, CHIA **4** 60, CINN **21** 61-63, PITN **12** 64-65, CHIA **18** 65-66, HOUN **11** 66

FREESE, GEORGE (BUD) 3B
(15,3,8) DETA **15** 53, PITN **3** 55 CHIN **8** 61

FREGOSI, JIM SS/INF/M
(17,16,**11**,2, 17,29,18) LAA **17** 61, **16** 62, **11** 62-64, CALA **11** 65-71, NYN **2** 72-73, TEXA **17** 73-77, PITN **29** 77-78, CALA *M* **11** *78-81*, *CHIA* M **16** 86-87, *M* **16** 87,*M* **18**, PHIN *M* **11** 91-96, TORA *M* **11** 99-00

FREIBERGER, VAN 1B
(**45**) CLEA **45** 41

FREIGAU, HOWARD (TY) SS/UTIL
(61,**12**) STLN **61** 23, **12** 24

FREISLEBEN, DAVE P
(43,**14**,38,25) SDN **43** 74-75, **14** 75-78, CLEA 50,46) **38/14** 78, *TORA* **25** 79

FREITAS, TONY P
(19,**23**,26) PHIA **19** 32-33, CINN **23** 34-35, **26** 36

FRENCH, JIM C/OF
(37,28,**10**) WASA **37** 65, **28** 66, **10** 67-71

FRENCH, LARRY P
(42,**14**,20) PITN **42** 32-34, CHIN **14** 35-41, BKNN **20** 41-42

FREY, BENNY (LEFTY) P
(no#,16,28, **22**) STLN **no#** 32, CINN **16** 32-33, **28** 34, **22** 35-36

FREY, JIM CH/M
(**41**,51,8) BALA *CH* **41** 70-79, KCA *M* **41** 80-81, NYN *CH* **51** 82-83, CHIN *M* **8** 84-86

FREY, LONNY (JUNIOR) SS/2B
(**11**,8,15,47, 22,14,28) BKNN **11** 33, **8** 34-36, CHIN **15** 37, CINN **47** 38, **11** 39-43, 46, CHIN **22** 47, NYA **14** 47-48, NYN **28** 48

FREY, STEVE P
(**41**,31,46,29) MONN **41** 89-91, CALA **41** 92-93, SFN **31/46** 94, **41** 95, SEAA **41** 95, PHIN **29** 95-96

FRIAS, HANLEY SS/INF
(30,60,**2**) TEXA **30** 97, ARIN **60** 98, **2** 98-00

FRIAS, PEPE UTIL
(**38**,9,3,36) MONN **38** 73-78, ATLN **9** 79, TEXA **3** 80, LAN **36** 80-81

FRIBERG, BERNIE 2B/INF
(11,**6**) PHIN **11** 32, BOSA **6** 33

FRICANO, MARION P
(**37**,17,29) PHIA **37** 52-54, KCA **17/29** 55

FRIDLEY, JIM (BIG JIM) OF
(31,21,**17**,26) CLEA **31** 52, BALA **21/17** 54, CINN **26** 58

FRIEDRICH, BOB P
(**19**) WASA **19** 32

FRIEND, BOB (WARRIOR) P
(25,**19**,17,20) PITN **25** 51-52, **19** 53-65, NYA **19** 66, NYN **17/20** 66

FRIEND, OWEN (RED) 2B/INF/CH
(__,7,**8**,22,3, 5) STLA __ 49, **7** 50, DETA **8** 53, CLEA **8** 53, BOSA **22** 55, CHIN **3** 55-56, KCA *CH* **5** 69

FRIERE, ALEJANDRO 1B
(**23**,58) BALA **23/58** 05

FRIERSON, BUCK OF
(**7**) CLEA **7** 41

FRINK, FREDDIE OF
(**34**) PHIN **34** 34

FRISCH, FRANKIE (FORDHAM FLASH) 2B/M/CH
(**3**,35,1) STLN **3** 32-38, *M* **3** 33-38, PITN *M* **35** 40-46, NYN *CH* **1** 49, CHIN *M* **3** 49-51

FRISELLA, DANNY (BEAR) P
(29,**34**,25,31, 49,42) NYN **29** 67-69, **34** 70-72, ATLN **25** 73, **34** 73-74, SDN **34** 75, STLN **34** 76, MILA **49/31/42 /34** 76

FRITZ, CHARLIE CH ???
(**34**) DETA *CH* **34** 32 ???

FRITZ, HARRY CH ???
(**34**) DETA *CH* **34** 32 ???

FRITZ, LARRY PH
(**44**) PHIN **44** 75

FROATS, BILL P
(38,45) DETA **38/45** 55

FROBEL, DOUG OF/DH
(**51**,22,31) PITN **51** 82-85, MONN **22** 85, CLEA **31** 87

FROHWIRTH, TODD P
(**52**,49,35,28) PHIN **52** 87-90, BALA **49** 91-93, BOSA **35** 94, CALA **28** 96

FROST, DAVE P
(**37**,28) CHIA **37** 77, CALA **37** 78-81, KCA **28** 82

FRY, JERRY C
(**39**) MONN **39** 78

FRYE, CHARLIE P
(**17**) PHIN **17** 40

FRYE, JEFF 2B/INF/OF/DH
(1,**3**,6,2) TEXA **1** 92, 94-95, BOSA **3** 96-97, (98), 99-00, COLN **6/2** 00, TORA **3** 01

FRYMAN, TRAVIS 3B/SS
(**24**,17) DETA **24** 90-97, CLEA **17** 98-02

FRYMAN, WOODIE P
(22,14,**35**,38) PITN **22** 66--67, PHIN **14** 68, **22** 68-70, **35** 70-72, DETA **38** 72-74, MONN **35** 75-76, CINN **35** 77, CHIN **35** 78, MONN **35** 78-83

FUCHS, CHARLIE P
(17,12,23,**19**) DETA **17** 42, PHIN **12** 43, STLA **23** 43, BKNN **19** 44

FUENTES, BRIAN P
61,39,**40**) SEAA **61** 01, COLN **39** 02, **40** 03-05

FUENTES, MICKEY P
(**14**) SEAA **14** 69

FUENTES, MIKE OF
(**15**) MONN **25** 83, **15** 83-84

FUENTES, TITO 2B/INF
(26,**23**,29,3, 44) SFN **26** 65-66, **23** 66-67, **29** 69-70, **23** 70-74, SDN **23** 75-76, DETA **3/44** 77, OAKA **44** 78

FULGHAM, JOHN P
(**41**) STLN **41** 79-81

FULLER, JIM UTIL
(**18**,16) BALA **18** 73-74, HOUN **16** 77

FULLER, JOHN OF
(**39**) ATLN **39** 74

FULLER, VERN 2B/INF
(11,**13**) CLEA **11** 64, **13** 66-70

FULLERTON, CURT P
(**14**) BOSA **14** 33

FULLIS, CHICK OF/2B/3B
(21,**1**,31,4) NYN **21** 32, PHIN **1** 33, **31** 34, STLN **4** 34, **31** 36

FULLMER, BRAD DH/1B
(14,**20**) MONN **14** 97, **20** 98-99, TORA **20** 00-01 , ANAA **20** 02-03, TEXA **20** 04

FULTON, BILL P
(**64**) NYA **64** 87

FUNDERBURK, MARK OF/DH/UTIL
(**4**,40) MINA **4** 81, **40** 85

FULTZ, AARON P
(**38**,46) SFN **38** 00-03, MINA **38** 04, PHIN **46** 05

FULTZ, FRANK CH
(**59**) ATLN *CH* **59** 98-05

FUNK, FRANK P/CH
(**38**,32,55,56, 35,43,45,49) CLEA **38** 60-62, MILN **32** 63, SFN*CH* **55/56** 76, SEAA *CH* **35** 80-81, 83-84, KCA *CH* **43** 88-90, COLN *CH* **45** 96, *CH* **49** 97-98

FUNK, LIZ OF
(28,23,**8**) NYA **28** 29, CHIA **34** 32, **8** 33

FUNK, TOM P
(**42**) HOUN **42** 86

FURCAL, RAFAEL SS/2B
(**1**) ATLN **1** 00-05

FURILLO, CARL (SKOONJ) OF
(29,5,**6**) BKN **29/5** 46, **6** 46-57, LAN **6** 58-60

FURMANIAK, J. J. INF
(**66**) PITN **66** 05

FUSSELL, CHRIS P
(52,**49**) BALA **52** 98, KCA **49** 99-00

FUSSELMAN, LES C
(**17**) STLN **17** 52-53

FYHRIE, MIKE P
(40,**27**,31,49) NYN **40** 96, ANAA **27** 99-00, CHIN **31** 01, OAKA **49** 01-02

G

GABLER, BILL (GABE) PH
(**24**) CHIN **24** 58

GABLER, FRANK (THE GREAT GABBO) P
(25,**19**,22,45) NYN **25** 35, **19** 36-37, BOSN **22** 37, **19** 37, **27** 38, CHIA **45** 38

GABLER, JOHN (GABE) P
(**40**,26) NYA **40** 59-60, WASA **26** 61

GABLES, KEN (CORAL) P
(45,**25**) PITN **45** 45-46, **25** 47

GABRIELSON, LEN OF/1B S
(42,39,12,21, 7,6,**14**) MILN **42** 60, **39** 63-64, CHIN **12** 64-65, SFN **21** 65, **7** 65-66, CALA **6** 67, LAN **14** 67-70

GABRIELSON, LEN 1B F
(**34**) PHIN **34** 39

GADDY, JOHN (SHERIFF) P
(__) BKNN __ 38

GAEDEL, EDDIE PH
(**1/8**) STLA **1/8** 51

GAETTI, GARY 3B/DH/UTIL/CH
(39,**8**,3,4,6) MINA **39** 81, **8** 82-90, CALA **3** 91-93, KCA **4** 93, **8** 94-95, STLN **8** 96-98, CHIN **8** 98-99, BOSA **6** 00, HOUN *CH* **8** 04-05

GAFF, BRENT P
(**45**) NYN **45** 82-84

GAFFKE, FABIAN OF
(**25**,19,26,14, 46) BOSA **25** 36, **19** 37, **25** 38, **26** 39, CLEA **14** 41, **46** 42

GAGLIANO, PHIL INF/UTIL B
(**16**,19,1) STLN **16** 63-70, CHIN **19** 70, BOSA **1** 71-72, CINN **16** 73-74

GAGLIANO, RALPH PR B
(**12**) CLEA **12** 65

GAGNE, ERIC P
(48,**38**) LAN **48** 99-00, **38** 01-05

GAGNE, GREG SS
(35,31,**7**) MINA **35** 83, **31** 83-86, **7** 87-92, KCA **7** 93-95, LAN **7** 96-97

GAILLARD, EDDIE P
(54,**28**) DETA **54** 97, TBA **28** 98-99

GAINER, JAY 1B
(**37**) COLN **37** 93

GAINES, JOE OF
(22,21,**6**,27, 28,46) CINN **22** 60, **21** 61-62, BALA **6** 63-64, HOUN **22/27** 64, **28** 65, **46** 66

GAINEY, TY OF
(**24**) HOUN **24** 85-87

GAJKOWSKI, STEVE P
(**54**) SEAA **54** 98

GAKELER, DAN P
(**32**) DETA **32** 91

GALAN, AUGIE OF/INF/CH
(31,51,7,**24**, 23,29,34) CHIN **31** 34, **51** 35-36, **7** 37-41, BKNN **24** 41-46, CINN **23** 47-48, NYN **29** 49, PHIA **34** 49, *CH* **29** 54

GALANTE, MATT CH
(**48**,8) HOUN *CH* **48** 85-96, *CH* **8** 98-99-01, NYN *CH* **8** 02, **4** 03-04

GALARRAGA, ANDRES 1B/DH
(12,**14**,41) MONN **12** 85-86, **14** 87-91, STLN **41** 92, COLN **14** 93-97, ATLN **14** 98, (99), 00, TEXA **14** 01, SFN **14** 01, MONN **14** 02, SFN **14** 03, ANAA **20** 04

GALASSO, BOB P
(19,45,36,18, 13,43) SEAA **19** 77, MILA **45/36/18/ 13** 79 , SEAA **43** 81

GALATZER, MILT OF/1B
(22,35,**1**,19) CLEA **22** 33,**35** 34, **1** 35-36, CINN **19** 39

GALE, RICH P
(**38**,32,30,35) KCA **38** 78-81, SFN **32** 82, CINN **32** 83, BOSA **30** 84, *CH* **35** 92-93

GALEHOUSE, DENNY P
(24,15,36,25, 16,11,12,**22**, 30) CLEA **24** 34, **15** 35, **36/25** 36, **16** 37-38, BOSA **11**39, **12** 40, STLA **22** 41-43, **12/30** 44, **30** 46, **22** 47, BOSA **25** 47-49

GALL, JOHN 1B
(**43**) STLN **43** 05

GALLAGHER, ALAN (AL) 3B
(**10**,6) SFN **10** 70-73, CALA **6** 73

GALLAGHER, BOB OF/1B
(44,25,22) BOSA **44** 72-73, HOUN **25** 73-74, NYN **22** 75

GALLAGHER, DAVE OF/DH
(15,**17**,35,27, 8,12,18) CLEA **15** 87, CHIA **17** 88-90, BALA **35** 90, CALA **27** 91, NYN **8** 92-93, ATLN **12** 94,PHIN **17** 95, CALA **18** 95

GALLAGHER, DOUG P
(**32**) DETA **32** 62

GALLAGHER, ED P
(**1**) BOSA **1** 32

GALLEGO, MIKE 2B/INF/CH
(**9**,2,22) OAKA **9** 85-91, NYA **2** 92-94, OAKA **2** 95, STLN **22** 96-97, COLN *CH* **2** 02, 05

GALLO, MIKE P
(**45**) HOUN **45** 03-05

GAMBLE, JOHN SS
(**40**) DETA **40** 72-73

GAMBLE, LEE OF
(**25**,43) CINN **25** 35, **43** 38, **25** 39-40

GAMBLE, OSCAR P
(20,23,**17**,12, 7,0) CHIN **20** 69, PHIN **23** 70-72, CLEA **23** 73-75, NYA **23** 76, CHIA **17** 77, SDN **17** 78, TEXA **12/7** 79, NYA **17** 79-84, CHIA **0** 85

GAMBOA, TOM CH
(39,__,**21**) CHIN *CH* **39** 99, KCA *CH* __ 01, **21** 02-03

GANDARILLAS, GUS P
(**40**) MILN **53** 01

GANT, RON 2B/OF
(**5**,6,3,9) ATLN **5** 87-93, CINN **6** 95, STLN **5** 96-98, PHIN **5** 99-00, ANAA **5** 00, COLN **3** 01, OAKA **5** 01, SDN **9** 02, OAKA **5** 03

GANTENBEIN, SEP 2B/UTIL
(**12**) PHIA **12** 39-40

GANTNER, JIM 3B/2B/INF/DH/P/CH
(11,47,**17**) MILA **11** 76-77, **47** 78, **17** 78-92, *CH* **17** 96-97

GARABITO, EDDY 2B
(**25**) COLN **25** 05

GARAGIOLA, JOE C
(**17**,2,3,11,36) STLN **17** 46-51, PITN **2** 51-52, **3** 53, CHIN **11** 53-54, NYN **36** 54

GARAGOZZO, KEITH P
(**54**) MINA **54** 94

GARBARK, BOB C B
(9,**39**,15,27) CLEA **9** 34-35, CHIN **39** 37-39, PHIA **15** 44, BOSA **27** 45

GARBARK, MIKE C B
(**10**) NYA **10** 44-45

GARBER, BOB P
(**37**) PITN **37** 56

GARBER, GENE P
(31,24,36,12, 32,**26**,28) PITN **31/24** 69, **36** 70, **12** 72, KCA **32** 73-74, PHIN **26** 74-78, ATLN **26** 78-87, KCA **28** 87, **31** 88

GARBEY, BARBARO UTIL
(**27**,17) DETA **27** 84-85, TEXA **17** 88

GARBOWSKI, ALEX PR
(**19**) DETA **19** 52

GARCES, RICH P
(**41**,57,27,34) MINA **41** 90, 93, CHIN **57** 95, FLAN **27** 95, BOSA **34** 96-02

GARCIA, AMAURY INF
(**45**) FLAN **45** 99

GARCIA, CARLOS SS/2B/CH
(51,**13**,1) PITN **51** 90-92, **13** 93-96, TORA **13** 97, SDN **1** 99, SEAA *CH* **13** 05

GARCIA, CHICO 2B
(**1**) BALA **1** 54

GARCIA, DAMASO 2B/INF/DH
(23,59,**7**,18, 4) NYA **23** 78, **59** 79, TORA **7** 80-86, ATLN **18** 88, MONN **4** 89

GARCIA, DANNY (R.) OF/1B
(**45**) KCA **45** 81

GARCIA, DANNY 2B
(**12**) NYN **12** 03-04

GARCIA, DAVE CH/M
(2,3,**1**,6) SDN *CH* **2** 70-73, CLEA *CH* **3** 75, **1** 75-76, CALA *CH/M* **6** 77, *M* **1** 78, CLEA *CH/M* **1** 79, *M* **1** 80-82, MILA *CH* **1** 83-84, COLN *CH* **1** 00-02

GARCIA, FREDDY (An.) P
(**34**) SEAA **34** 99-04, CHIA **34** 04-05

GARCIA, FREDDY (Ad.) OF/3B
(**22**,14,20) PITN **22** 95, 97, **14** 98-99, ATLN **20** 99

GARCIA, GUILLERMO INF
(62,**9**) CINN **62** 98, FLAN **9** 99

GARCIA, JAIRO P
(**46**) OAKA **46** 04-05

GARCIA, JESSE INF/1B
(15,**1**,22,2,9) BALA **15** 99, **1** 99-00, ATLN **22** 01, **2** 02-04, SDN **9** 05

GARCIA, KARIM OF
(12,**24**,29,57, 50,20,28,47) LAN **12** 95-97, ARIN **24** 98, DETA **29** 99, **24** 99-00, BALA **57** 00, CLEA **50** 01, NYA **57** 02, CLEA **20** 02-03, NYA **28** 03, NYN **20** 04, BALA **47** 04

GARCIA, KIKO SS/INF
(40,**3**,23,18) BALA **40** 76, **3** 77-80, HOUN **23** 81-82, PHIN **18** 83-85

GARCIA, LEO OF
(**26**) CINN **26** 87-88

GARCIA, LUIS (C.) OF
(**9**) BALA **9** 02

GARCIA, LUIS (R.) INF
(**46**) DETA **46** 99

GARCIA, MIGUEL P
(34,28,**27**) CALA **34** 87, PITN **28** 87, **27** 88-89

GARCIA, MIKE (THE BIG BEAR) P
(7,22,**25**,19) CLEA **7/22** 48, **25** 49-59, CHIA **25** 60, WASA **19** 61

GARCIA, MIKE (R.) P
(**64**) PITN **64** 99-00

GARCIA, PETE 2B/DH
(**9**,3,38) MILA **9** 73-76, DETA **3** 76, TORA **38** 77

GARCIA, RALPH P
(47,**15**,46) SDN **47/15** 72, **46** 74

GARCIA, RAMON P
(14,22) WASA **14/22** 48

GARCIA, RAMON P
(43,51,59) CHIA **43** 91, MILA **51** 96, HOUN **59** 97

GARCIA, REYNALDO P
(**21**,57) TEXA **21** 02, **57** 03

GARCIA, ROSMAN P
(**56**) TEXA **56** 03-04

GARCIAPARRA, NOMAR SS
(**5**,8) BOSA **5** 96-04, CHIN **8** 04, **5** 04-05

GARDELLA, AL OF/1B B
(**29**) NYN **29** 45

GARDELLA, DANNY OF/1B B
(**33**,29) NYN **33** 44-45, STLN **29** 50

GARDENHIRE, RON SS/INF/CH
(**19**,35) NYN **19** 81-85, MINA *CH* **35** 91-02, *M* 03-05

GARDINER, MIKE P
(23,47,16,**46**) SEAA **23** 90, BOSA **47** 91-92, MONN **16** 93, DETA **46** 93-95

GARDNER, ART OF
(**24**,35) HOUN **24** 75, 77, SFN **35** 78

GARDNER, BILLY (SHOTGUN) INF
(15,17,**9**,12, 10,24,31,6, 42) NYN **15** 54-55, **17** 55, BALA **9** 56-59, WASA **9** 60, MINA **9** 61, NYA **12** 61-62, BOSA **10/24** 62, **15** 63, *CH* **31** 65-66, MONN *CH* **6** 77-78, MINA *CH/M* **42** 81, *M* **42** 82-85, KCA *M* **41** 87

GARDNER, CHRIS P
(**39**) HOUN **39** 91

GARDNER, GLENN P
(**15**) STLN **15** 45

GARDNER, JEFF 2B/INF
(19,41,12,**4**) NYN **19** 91, SDN **41** 92, **12** 93, MONN **4** 94

GARDNER, LEE P
(**39**,52) TBA **39** 02, **52** 05

GARDNER, MARK P/CH
(56,**28**,37,38, 26) MONN **56** 89-90, **28** 91-92, KCA **37** 93, FLAN **38** 94, **28** 95, SFN **26** 96-01, *CH* 03-05

GARDNER, ROB P
(29,33,41,38, 43,56,39,**22**) NYN **29** 65-66, CHIN **33/41** 67, CLEA **38** 68, NYA **43** 70, OAKA **56** 71, NYA **39** 71, **43** 72, OAKA **22** 73, MILA **33/22** 73

GARDNER, WES P
(27,**44**,39) NYN **27** 84-85, BOSA **44** 86-90, SDN **39** 91, KCA **39** 91

GARIBALDI, ART 3B
(**30**) STLN **30** 36

GARIBALDI, BOB P
(**28**,21,39) SFN **28** 62-63, **21** 66, **39** 69

GARIBAY, DANIEL P
(**76**) CHIN **76** 00

GARKO, RYAN C
(**25**) CLEA **25** 05

GARLAND, JON P
(52,**20**) CHIA **52** 00-02, **20** 03-05

GARLAND, LOU P
(**25**) CHIA **25** 31

GARLAND, WAYNE P
(**17**,23) BALA **17** 73-76, CLEA **23** 77, **17** 77-81

GARMAN, MIKE P
(39,38,43,44, 29) BOSA **39** 69, 71-73, **38** 73, STLN **43** 74-75, CHIN **44** 76, LAN **29** 77-78, MONN **29** 78

GARMS, DEBS (TEX) OF/3B
(__,27,15,**9**, 18) STLA __ 32, **27** 33, **15** 34-35, BOSN **9** 37-39, PITN **18** 40-41, STLN **9** 43-45

GARNER, PHIL 3B/2B/INF/CH/M
(**3**,2,29,17,20) OAKA **3** 73-74, **29** 74-76, **2/3** 76, PITN **17** 77, **3** 77-81, HOUN **3** 81-87, LAN **20** 87, SFN **20** 88, HOUN *CH* **3** 89-91, MILA *M* **3** 92-99, DETA **33** 00-03, HOUN *M* **3** 03-05

GARR, RALPH (ROADRUNNER) OF/DH
(**48**,11,28) ATLN **48** 68-75, **11** 69, CHIA **48** 76-79, CALA **28** 79, **48** 79-80

GARRELTS, SCOTT P
(52,43,54,31, **50**) SFN **52** 82, **43** 82-83, **54** 82-83, **31** 84, **50** 84-91

GARRETT, ADRIAN (PAT) OF/UTIL/CH
(18,23,58,**3**, 25,5,28,10, 41) ATLN **18** 99, CHIN **23** 70, OAKA **58** 71, **3** 72, CHIN **25** 73, **5** 73-74, **28** 75, CALA **10** 75-76, KCA *CH* **41** 88-92

GARRETT, GREG P
(43,47) CALA **43** 70, CINN **47** 71

GARRETT, WAYNE (RED) 3B/INF
(**11**) NYN **11** 69-76, MONN **11** 76-78, STLN **11** 78

GARRIDO, GIL SS/INF
(21,10,**7**) SFN **21/10** 64, ATLN **7** 68-72

GARRIOTT, RABBIT PH
(**22**) CHIN **22** 46

GARRISON, FORD (ROCKY/SNAPPER) OF/CH
(15,19,9,3,**1**, 51) BOSA **15** 43-44, **19** 44, PHIA **9** 44, **3** 45, **1** 46, CINN *CH* **51** 53

GARRISON, WEBSTER 2B/1B
(**49**) OAKA **49** 96

GARRITY, HANK C
(**12**) CHIA **12** 31

GARVER, NED P
(32,**31**) STLA **32** 48, **31** 48-52, DETA **31** 52-56, KCA **31** 57-60, LAA **31** 61

GARVEY, STEVE 1B
(**6**) LAN **6** 69-82, SDN **6** 83-87

GARVIN, JERRY P
(**36**) TORA **36** 77-82

GASPAR, ROD OF
(17,**25**,23) NYN **17** 69-70, SDN **25** 71, 74, **23** 74

GASSAWAY, CHARLIE (SHERIFF) P
(__,3,31) CHIN __ 44, PHIA **3** 45, CLEA **31** 46

GASSNER, DAVE P
(**59**) MINA **59** 05

GASTALL, TOMMY C
(**10**) BALA **10** 55-56

GASTON, CITO OF/1B/CH/M
(25,21,**43**,44) ATLN **25** 67, SDN **21** 69-74, ATLN **43** 75-78, PITN **44** 78, TORA *CH* **43** 82-89, *M* **43** 89-97, *CH* **41** 00-01

GASTON, MILT P
(19,20,26,**23**) BOSA **19/20** 31, CHIA **26** 32, **23** 33-34

GATES, BRENT 2B
(13,**8**,9,5) OAKA **13** 93-95, **8** 96, SEAA **9** 97, MINA **5** 98-99

GATES, JOE INF
(31,34,**10**) CHIA **31** 78, **34** 79, **10** 79

GATES, MIKE 2B
(**19**) MONN **19** 81-82

GATEWOOD, AUBREY P
(33,**38**,50,29) LAA **33** 63-64, **38** 64, CALA **38** 65, ATLN **50/29** 70

GATHRIGHT, JOEY OF
(43,**1**) TBA **43** 04, **1** 05

GAUDET, JIM SS/2B
(37,**13**) KCA **37** 78-79, **13** 79

GAUDIN, CHAD P
(50,**35**) TBA **50** 03-04, **35** 05

GAUTREAUX, SID (PUDGE) C
(21,**8**) BKNN **21** 36, **8** 37

GEARHART, LLOYD (GARY) OF
(**21**) NYN **21** 47

GEARY, GEOFF P
(**56**) PHIN **56** 03-05

GEARY, HUCK SS
(**4**) PITN **4** 42-43

GEBHARD, BOB P/CH
(**16**,48,40) MINA **16** 71-72, MONN **48** 74, 44) *CH* **40** 82

GEBRIAN, PETE P
(**28**) CHIA **28** 47

GEDDES, JIM P
(**55**) CHIA **55** 72-73

GEDEON, ELMER OF
(**34**) WASA **34** 39

GEDMAN, RICH C/DH
(50,**10**,2,29) BOSA **50** 80, **10** 81-90, HOUN **2** 90, STLN **29** 91-92

GEE, JOHNNY (WHIZ) P
(42,24,**26**,20, 12) PITN **42** 39, **24** 41, **26** 43-44, NYN **20** 44-45, **12** 46

GEHRIG, LOU (LARRUPIN' LOU)(THE IRON HORSE) 1B
(**4**) NYA **4** 29-39

GEHRINGER, CHARLIE (MECHANICAL MAN) 2B
(3,**2**) DETA **3** 31, **2** 32-42

GEHRMAN, PAUL (DUTCH) P
(**28**) CINN **28** 37

GEIGER, GARY OF
(31,37,**7**,**3**,19) CLEA **31** 58, BOSA **37** 59-60, **7** 60-62, **3** 63-65, ATLN **31** 66-67, HOUN **19** 69-70

GEISEL, DAVE P
(46,40,51,**35**, 37) CHIN **46** 78-79, **40** 81, TORA **51** 82, **35** 82-83, SEAA **37** 84-85

GEISHERT, VERN P
(17,48) CALA **17/48** 69

GELBERT, CHARLIE SS/INF
(11,**4**,8,30, 21,15) STLN **11** 32, **4** 35-36, CINN **8** 37, DETA **30** 37, WASA **21** 39-40, BOSA **15** 40

GELNAR,JOHN P
(38,20,35,37, **25**) PITN **38/20** 64, **35/37** 67, SEAA **25** 69, MILA **25** 70-71

GENOVESE, GEORGE PH
(**41**) WASA **41** 50

GENTILE, JIM (DIAMOND JIM) 1B
(27,52,**4**,6,12) BKNN **27** 57, LAN **27** 58, BALA **4** 60-63, KCA **6** 64, **4** 65, HOUN **52** 65, **4** 65-66, CLEA **12** 66

GENTILE, SAM PH
(**35**) BOSN **35** 43

GENTRY, GARY P
(**39**,25) NYN **39** 68-72, ATLN **39** 73, **25** 74-75

GENTRY, HARVEY PH
(**41**) NYN **41** 54

GENTRY, RUFE P
(**12**,34,24) DETA **12** 43-45, **34** 46-47, **24** 48

GEORGE, ALEX SS
(**2**) KCA **2** 55

GEORGE, CHRIS (C.) P
(53,**32**) KCA **53** 01, **32** 02-04

GEORGE, CHRIS (S.) P
(**59**) MILA **59** 91

GEORGE, GREEK C
(14,17,__,24, 12,**8**) CLEA **14** 35, **17** 36, BKNN __ 38, CHIN **24** 41, PHIA **12/8** 45

GEORGY, OSCAR P
(**18**) NYN **18** 38

GERAGHTY, BEN INF
(5,8,**2**) BKNN **5** 36, BOSN **8** 43-44, **2** 44

GERARD, DAVE (JUG) P
(31,45) CHIN **31/45** 62

GERBER, CRAIG UTIL
(**2**) CALA **2** 85

GERBERMAN, GEORGE P
(**30**) CHIN **30** 62

GEREN, BOB C/DH/CH
(58,57,52,**53**, 17) NYA **58/57/52** 88, **53** 88-91, SDN **17** 93, OAKA *CH* **52** 03-05

GERHARDT, RUSTY P
(50,**38**) SDN **50** 74, **38** 74-75

GERHART, KEN OF/DH
(**38**) BALA **38** 86-88

GERHEAUSER, AL (LEFTY) P
(6,**11**,24,40, 16,30) PHIN **6** 43, **11** 43-44, **24** 44, PITN **40** 45-46, STLA **16/30** 48

GERKIN, STEVE (SPLINTER) P
(**18**) PHIA **18** 45

GERLACH, JOHN SS/3B
(47,17,**37**) CHIA **47** 38, **17/37** 39

GERMAN, ESTEBAN 2B
(**40**,12,4) OAKA **40** 02-03, **12** 04, TEXA **4** 05

GERMAN, FRANKLYN P
(**62**) DETA **62** 02-05

GERMANO, JUSTIN P
(**47**) SDN **47** 04

GERNERT, DICK 1B/OF/CH
(14,3,**25**,12, 5,15,17,47) BOSA **14** 52, **3** 52-54, **25** 55-59, CHIN **12** 60, DETA **5** 60-61, CINN **15** 61, HOUN **17** 62, TEXA *CH* **47** 75-76

GERONIMO, CESAR OF
(34,**20**,23) HOUN **34** 69, **20** 70-71, CINN **20** 72-80, KCA **23** 81-83

GERUT, JODY OF/DH
(**9**,29) CLEA **9** 03-05, CHIN **9** 05, PITN **29** 05

GETTEL, AL P
(25,24,47,**28**, 35,36,44,31) NYA **25** 45-46, CLEA **24** 47-48, CHIA **47/24** 48, **28** 48-49, WASA **28/35/36** 49, NYN **44** 51, STLN **31** 55

GETTIS, BYRON OF
(**31**) KCA **31** 04

GHARRITY, PATSY CH
(31,26,**20**) WASA *CH* **31** 31, *CH* **26** 32, CLEA *CH* **20** 33-35

GHELFI, TONY P
(47,**35**) PHIN **47/35** 83

GIALLOMBARDO, BOB P
(**16**) LAN **16** 58

GIAMBI, JASON INF/DH B
(**16**,25) OAKA **16** 95-01, NYA **25** 02-05

GIAMBI, JEREMY OF/DH B
(15,**7**,25) KCA **15** 98-99, OAKA **7** 00-02, PHIN **7** 02, BOSA **25** 03

GIANNELLI, RAY 1B
(**19**,54) TORA **19** 91, STLN **54** 95

GIARRATANO, TONY SS
(**39**) DETA **39** 05

GIBBON, JOE P
(**22**,28,19,39, 37) PITN **22** 60-65, SFN **28** 66-69, PITN **19** 69-70, CINN **39** 71-72, HOUN **37** 72

GIBBONS, JAY INF/UTIL/OF/DH
(**25**,31) BALA **25** 01-03, **31** 04-05

GIBBONS, JOHN C/CH/M
(8,7,35,58,5) NYN **8** 84, **7/35** 86, TORA *CH* **58** 02-04, *M* 04, **5** 05

GIBBS, JAKE C/3B/CH
(**41**) NYA **41** 62-71, *CH* **41** 93

GIBRALTER, STEVE OF
(61,**33**) CINN **61** 95, **33** 96

GIBSON, BOB (HOOT) (GIBBY) P/CH
(58,31,**45**) STLN **58** 59, **31** 60, **45** 60-75, NYN *CH* **45** 81, ATLN *CH* **45** 82-84, STLN *CH* **45** 95

GIBSON, BOB P
(**40**,38) MILA **40** 83-86, NYN **38** 87

GIBSON, DERRICK OF
(**24**) COLN **24** 98-99

GIBSON, GEORGE (MOON) M
(**33**) PITN **33** 32-34

GIBSON, KIRK OF/DH/CH
(**23**,30,25,22) DETA **23** 79-87, LAN **23** 88-90, KCA **30** 91, PITN **25** 92, DETA **23** 93-95, *CH* **22** 03-05

GIBSON, PAUL P
(**48**,45,35,39) DETA **48** 88-91, NYN **45** 92-93, NYA **35** 93-94, **39** 96

GIBSON, RUSS C/1B
(35**18**) BOSA **35** 67-69, SFN **18** 70-72

GIBSON, SAM P
(__,**17**) NYA __ 30, NYN **17** 32

GICK, GEORGE P
(45,48,**30**) CHIA **45** 37, **48/30** 38

GIDEON, BRETT P
(58,**26**) PITN **58** 87, MONN **26** 89, **26** 90

GIDEON, JIM P
(**33**) TEXLA **33** 75

GIEBELL, FLOYD P
(29,22,**17**) DETA **29** 39, **22** 40, **17** 41

GIEL, PAUL P
(**31**,28,18,27) NYN **31** 54-55, SFN **31** 58, PITN **34** 59, **28** 60, MINA **18** 61, KCA **27** 61

GIGGIE, BOB P
(**32**,27,22) MILN **32** 59-60, KCA **27** 60, **22** 62

GIGON, NORM UTIL
(**15**) CHIN **15** 67

GIL, BENJI SS
(**23**) TEXA **22** 93, **23** 95-97, ANAA **10** 00-03

GIL, GERONIMO C
(60,17,**9**) BALA **60** 01, **17** 02, **9** 03-05

GIL, GUS INF
(**18**,16,22) CLEA **18** 67, SEAA **18** 69, MILA **16** 70, **22** 71

GIL, JERRY 2B/SS
(**2**) ARIN **2** 04, (05)

GILBERT, ANDY OF/CH
(**2**,42,46,8) BOSA **2** 42, **42** 46, SFN *CH* **46** 72, *CH* **8** 72-75

GILBERT, BUDDY OF
(**22**) CINN **22** 59

GILBERT, CHARLIE OF
(34,1,**4**,22,21, 3) BKNN **34/1** 40, CHIN **4** 41-42, **22** 43, 46, PHIN **21** 46, **3** 47

GILBERT, JOE P
(**42**) MONN **42** 72-73

GILBERT, MARK OF
(**44**) CHIA **44** 85

GILBERT, SHAWN SS
(**12**,47) NYN **12** 97-98, STLN **12** 98, LAN **47** 00

GILBERT, TOOKIE 1B
(15,17) NYN **15** 50, **17** 53

GILBERT, WALLY 3B
(**2**) CINN **2** 32

GILBREATH, ROD 2B/3B
(**19**) ATLN **19** 72-78

GILBRETH, BILL P
(**36**,38) DETA **36** 71-72, CALA **38** 74

GILE, DON (BEAR) C/1B
(35,**38**) BOSA **35** 59, **38** 60-62

GILES, BRIAN 2B/SS/OF B
(17,23,26,18, 29,58,22,**24**) NYN **17/15** 81, **23** 82-83, MILA **26** 85, CHIA **18** 86, SEAA **29** 90, CLEA **58** 95, **22** 96-98, PITN **24** 99-03, SDN **24** 03-05

GILES, MARCUS 2B/3B B
(20,24,**22**) ATLN **20** 01, **24** 01-02, **22** 02-05

GILFILLAN, JASON P
(**50**) KCA **50** 03

GILKEY, BERNARD OF
(**23**,28) STLN **23** 90-95, NYN **23** 96-98, ARIN **23** 98-00, BOSA **28** 00, ATLN **23** 01

GILL, GEORGE P
(**16**,19,22) DETA **16** 37-39, STLA **19/16/22** 39

GILL, JOHNNY (PATCHEYE) OF
(__,19,18,**8**) WASA __ 31, **19** 34, CHIN **18** 35, **8** 36

GILLENWATER, CARDEN OF
(28,6,18,**24**) STLN **28** 40, BKNN **6/18** 43, BOSN **4** 45, **24** 46, WASA **29** 48

GILLES, TOM P
(**46**) TORA **46** 90

GILLESPIE, BOB (BUNCH) P
(17,**36**,21,13) DETA **17** 44, CHIA **36** 47-48, BOSA **21/13** 50

GILLESPIE, PAUL C/OF
(2,24,**10**) CHIN **2** 42, **24** 44, **10** 45

GILLIAM, JIM(JUNIOR) 2B/UTIL/CH
(**19**) BKNN **19** 53-57, LAN**19** 58-66, *CH* **19** 67-78

GILLIFORD, PAUL (GORILLA) P
(**33**) BALA **33** 67

GILMORE, LEN (MEOW) P
(**17**) PITN **17** 44

GILSON, HAL (LEFTY) P
(47,54,**33**) STLN **47** 68, HOUN **54/33** 68

GINSBERG, JOE C
(1,26,2,15,9, **22**,28,24,43) DETA **1** 48, **26** 50-52, **1** 52, **2** 52-53, CLEA **15** 53-54, KCA **9** 56, BALA **22** 56-60, CHIA **28** 60-61, BOSA **24** 61, NYN **43** 62

GINTER, KEITH 2B/INF
(**1**,6) HOUN **1** 00-02, MILN **1** 02, **6** 03-04, OAKA **6** 05

GINTER, MATT P
(**58**,32,13,34) CHIA **58** 00-02, **32** 03, NYN **13** 04, DETA **34** 05

GIONFRIDDO, AL OF
(**3**,18,30) PITN **3** 44-46, **18** 47, BKNN **30** 47

GIOVANOLA, ED 2B
(30,17,**11**) ATLN **30** 95, **17** 96, **11** 96-97, SDN **17** 98-99

GIORDANO, TOMMY (T-BONE) 2B
(7,**36**) PHIA **7/36** 53

GIPSON, CHARLES INF/UTIL
(16,**1**,17,31) SEAA **16** 98, **1** 99-02, NYA **28** 03, TBA **17** 04, HOUN **31** 05

GIRARDI, JOE C
(**7**,45,25,27,8, 52) CHIN **7** 89-92, COLN **7** 93-95, NYA **45** 96, **25** 96-99, CHIN **8** 00, **27** 01-02, STLN **8** 03, NYA *CH* **52** 05

GISSELL, CHRIS P
(**59**) COLN **59** 04

GIULIANI, TONY C
(**12**,9,10,*27*, 6,38) STLA **12** 36-37, WASA **9** 38, **10** 39, BKNN **27** 40, **6/38** 41, WASA **9** 43

GIUSTI, DAVE P
(34,39,**31**,52 44) HOUN **34** 62, 64, **39** 64-68, STLN **39** 69, PITN **31** 70-76, OAKA **52/31** 77, CHIN **44** 77

GIVENS, BRIAN P
(**13**) MILA **13** 95-96

GLADD, JIM C
(**19**) NYN **19** 46

GLADDEN, DAN OF/DH
(25,**32**) SFN **25** 83-84, **32** 84-86, MINA **32** 87-91, DETA **32** 92-93

GLADDING, FRED P/CH
(11,29,20,**48**, 52) DETA **11** 61, **29** 62, **20** 63-67, HOUN **48** 68-73, DETA *CH* **52** 76-78

GLADU, ROLAND 3B/OF
(34,**27**) BOSN **34/27** 44

GLANVILLE, DOUG OF
(1,8,6,4) CHIN **1** 96-97, **8** 97, PHIN **6** 98-02, TEXA **6** 03, CHIN **4** 03, PHIN **6** 04

GLAUBER, KEITH P
(**54**,59) CINN **54** 98, **59** 00

GLAUS, TROY 3B
(12,14,**25**) ANAA **12** 98, **14** 98-99, **25** 00-04, ARIN **25** 05

GLAVIANO, TOMMY (RABBIT) 3B/INF
(**12**,11,3) STLN **12** 49-51, **11** 52, PHIN **3** 53

GLAVINE, MIKE PH
(**27**) NYN **27** 03

GLAVINE, TOM P
(**47**) ATLN **47** 87-02, NYN **47** 03-05

GLEASON, KID CH
(**30**) PHIA **30** 31-32

GLEASON, ROY PH
(**36**) LAN **36** 63

GLEATON, JERRY DON P
(**27**,28,45,15, 59,39,19,49) TEXA **27** 79-80, **15** 80, SEAA **28** 81, **27** 82, CHIA **43** 84, **46** 85, **59** 85, KCA **39** 87-89, DETA **19** 90-91, PITN **49** 92

GLEESON, JIM (GEE GEE) OF/CH
(31,**24**,21,46, 36) CLEA **31** 36, CHIN **24** 39-40, CINN **21** 41-42, KCA *CH* **46/36** 57, NYA *CH* **31** 64

GLENN, JOE (GABBY) C
(**26**,9,10) NYA **26** 32, **9** 33, **26** 35-38, STLA **26/10** 39, BOSA **26** 40

GLENN, JOHN OF
(**22**) STLN **22** 60

GLINATSIS, GEORGE P
(**26**) SEAA **26** 94

GLOAD, ROSS OF/1B
(6,**23**,26,17) CHIN **6** 00, COLN **23** 02, CHIA **26** 04, **17** 05

GLOSSOP, AL 2B/UTIL
(21,2,**27**,3,24, 20) NYN **21/2** 39, **27** 40, BOSN **3** 40, PHIN **24** 42, BKNN **20** 43, CHIN **27** 46

GLOVER, GARY P
(51,**38**,58) TORA **51** 99, CHIA **38** 01-03, ANAA **38** 03, MILN **58** 04-05

GLYNN, BILL I1B/OF
(**3**,**6**,14) PHIN **3** 49, CLEA **6** 52, **14** 53, **6** 53-54

GLYNN, ED P
(**48**,44,49) DETA **48** 75-78, NYN **48** 79-80, CLEA **44** 81, **48** 82-83, MONN **49** 85

GLYNN, GENE CH
(**2**,3,15) COLN *CH* **2** 94-98, MONN *CH* **2** 99, CHIN *CH* **3** 00-02, SFN *CH* **15** 03-05

GLYNN, RYAN P
(40,**38**,51,56) TEXA **40** 99, **38** 99-01, TORA **51** 04, OAKA **56** 05

GOBBLE, JIMMY P
(**41**) KCA **41** 03-05

GODBY, DANNY OF
(**24**) STLN **24** 74

GODDARD, JOE C
(**7**) SDN **7** 72

GOETZ, JOHN P
(**31**) CHIN **31** 60

GOFF, JERRY C
(19,57,5,**9**) MONN **19** 90, 92, PITN **57** 93-94, **5** 94, HOUN **9** 95-96

GOGGIN, CHUCK 2B/UTIL
(**12**,29,48) PITN **12** 72-73, ATLN **29** 73, BOSA **48** 74

GOGOLEWSKI, BILL P
(18,**13**,28,32) WASA **18** 70, **13** 71, TEXA **13** 72, **28** 73, CLEA **32** 74, CHIA **52/32** 75

GOHR, GREG P
(**34**,36) DETA **34** 93-96, CALA **36** 96

GOLDEN, JIM P
(41,35) LAN **41** 60-61, HOUN **35** 62-63

GOLDMAN, JONAH SS
(**7**) CLEA **7** 31

GOLDSBERRY, GORDON 1B/OF
(**25**,16,14,8) CHIA **25** 49-51, **16** 50, STLA **14** **/8** 52

GOLDSTEIN, IZZY P
(**21**) DETA **21** 32

GOLDSTEIN, LONNIE 1B
(22,**23**) CINN **22** 43, **23** 46

GOLDY, PURNAL OF
(**5**) DETA **5** 62-63

GOLETZ, STAN (STASH) PH
(__) CHIA __ 41

GOLIAT, MIKE 2B/INF
(**9**,23,6) PHIN **9** 49-51, STLA **23** 51, **6** 52

GOLTZ, DAVE P
(39,**30**,38) MINA **39** 72,**30** 72-79, LAN **38** 80-82, CALA **30** 82-83

GOMES, JONNY DH/OF
(60,**31**) TBA **60** 03-04, **31** 05

GOMES, WAYNE OF
(**61**,2) PHIN **61** 97-01, SFN **2** 01, BOSA **61** 02

GOMEZ, ALEXIS OF
(9,**43**) KCA **9** 02, **43** 04, DETA **43** 05

GOMEZ, CHILE SS/2B
(**22**,32) PHIN **22** 35-36, WASA **32** 42

GOMEZ, CHRIS SS
(35,**10**,9,8,3) DETA **35** 93-96, SDN **10** 96-01, TBA **9** 01-02, MINA **8** 03, TORA **3** 04

GOMEZ, LEFTY (GOOFY) P
(22,20,**11**,31) NYA **22** 30, **20** 31, **11** 32-42, WASA **31** 43

GOMEZ, LEO 3B/DH
(15,11,**10**,12) BALA **15** 90, **11** 91, **10** 91-95, CHIN **12** 96

GOMEZ, LUIS INF/DH/P
(**25**,11,9) MINA **25** 74-77, TORA **11** 78-79, ATLN 80-81

GOMEZ, ORLANDO CH
(**13**,6,23,25, 49) TEXA *CH* **13** 91-92, TBA *CH* **6** 98, *CH* **23** 99, **25** 00, SEAA *CH* **49** 03-04

GOMEZ, PAT P
(39,**38**,29) SDN **39** 93, SFN **38** 94-95, **29** 95

GOMEZ, PRESTON 2B/SS/CH/M
(21,31,**18**,4, 28) WASA **21** 44, LAN *CH* **31** 65, **18** 65-68, SDN *M* **16** 69-72, HOUN *CH* **4** 73, *M* **4** 74, *M* **18** 74-75, STLN *CH* **18** 76, LAN *CH* **28** 77-79, CHIN *M* **18** 80, CALA *CH* **18** 81-84

GOMEZ, RANDY C
(**37**) SFN **37** 84

GOMEZ, RUBEN P
(**28**,31,40,22, 29,33,32) NYN **28** 53-55, **31** 56, **28** 56-57, SFN **28** 58, PHIN **40** 59, **22** 59-60, CLEA **29** 62, MINA **33** 62, PHIN **22/32** 67

GONDER, JESSE C
(25,7,**12**,28, 20) NYA **25** 60-61, CINN **7** 62-63, NYN **12** 63-65, MILN **28** 65, PITN **20** 66-67

GONZALES, DAN OF/DH
(**34**) DETA **34** 79-80

GONZALES, JOE (SMOKEY) P
(**19**) BOSA **19** 37

GONZALES, JULIO P
(**16**) WASA **16** 49

GONZALES, LARRY C/1B
(**13**) CALA **13** 93

GONZALES, RENE SS/3B/INF
(19,**88**,28) MONN **19** 84, 86, BALA **88** 87-90, TORA **88** 91, CALA **88** 92-93, CLEA **88** 94, CALA **88** 95, TEXA **88** 96, COLN **28** 97

GONZALES, VINCE P
(**16**) WASA **16** 55

GONZALEZ, ADRIAN 1B/DH
(**24**) TEXA **24** 04-05

GONZALEZ, ALEX INF
(22,8,**11**) FLAN **22** 98, **8** 99, **11** 99-05

GONZALEZ, ALEX (S.) SS/2B/3B
(**8**,11,9) TORA **8** 94-01, CHIN **8** 02-04, MONN **11** 04, SDN **9** 04, TBA **8** 05

GONZALEZ, DENNY SS/UTIL
(28,24,**3**,15) PITN **28** 84, **24** 85, **28** 87, **3** 88, CLEA **15** 89

GONZALEZ, DICKY P
(**39**,43) NYN **39** 01, TBA **43** 04

GONZALEZ, EDGAR P
(**49**) ARIN **49** 03-05

GONZALEZ, FERNANDO 3B/UTIL/DH
(37,**13**,26,12) PITN **37** 72-73, KCA **13** 74, NYA **26** 74, PITN **12** 77, **13** 77-78, SDN **13** 78-79

GONZALEZ, FREDI CH
(**33**,45) FLAN *CH* **33** 00-01, ATLN *CH* **33** 03-04, **45** 05

GONZALEZ, GABE P
(**46**) FLAN **46** 98

GONZALEZ, GERMAN P
(**46**) MINA **46** 88-89

GONZALEZ, JEREMI P
(**54**,30,51,32) CHIN **54** 97, **30** 98, **54** 99, TBA **51** 03, **54** 04, BOSA **32/54** 05

GONZALEZ, JOSE OF
(36,47,**38**,5, 37) LAN **36** 85, **47** 86-87, **36** 88, **38** 89-91, PITN **5** 91, CLEA **37** 91, CALA **38** 92

GONZALEZ, JUAN OF/DH
(13,**19**,22,16) TEXA **13** 89, **19** 89-00, DETA **19** 00, CLEA **22** 01, TEXA **19** 02-03, KCA **22** 04, CLEA **16** 05

GONZALEZ, JULIO SS/2B/INF
(52,**9**,50,14, 10) HOUN **52** 77, **9** 77--80, STLN **50** 81, **14** 81-82, DETA **10** 83

GONZALEZ, LARIEL P
(**38**) COLN **38** 98

GONZALEZ, LUIS (E.) (GONZO) OF/INF
(**26**,25,28,20) HOUN **26** 90-95, CHIN **25** 95-96, HOUN **26** 97, DETA **28** 98, ARIN **20** 99-05

GONZALEZ, LUIS CH/INF
(**37**) FLAN **37** 99, *CH* **37** 99

GONZALEZ, LUIS 2B
(**4**) COLN **4** 04-05

GONZALEZ, MIKE P
(**51**) PITN **51** 03-05

GONZALEZ, MIKE (A.) C/CH
(26,**15**,25,35) STLN **26** 24, **15** 32, *CH* **25** 33-38, **35** 39-41, **25** 42-46

GONZALEZ, ORLANDO UTIL
(12,17,**4**) CLEA **12** 76, PHIN **17** 78, OAKA **4** 80

GONZALEZ, PEDRO UTIL
(42,**24**) NYA **42** 63-65, CLEA **24** 65-67

GONZALEZ, RAUL OF
(30,39,29,**21**, 45) CHIN **30** 00, CINN **39** 01, **29** 02, NYN **21** 02-03, CLEA **45** 04

GONZALEZ, TONY OF
(22,**25**,43) CINN **22** 60, PHIN **22** 60-62, **25** 62-68, SDN **25** 69, ATLN **43** 69-70, CALA **25** 70-71

GONZALEZ, WIKLENMAN (WIKI) C
(**7**,31) SDN **7** 99-03, SEAA **31** 05

GOOCH, JOHNNY C/CH
(8,**34**,37) BOSA **8** 33, PITN *CH* **34** 37-38, **37** 38, **34** 39

GOOD, ANDREW P
(**52**,50) ARIN **52** 03-04, DETA **50** 05

GOODEN, DWIGHT (DOC)(THE DOCTOR) P
(**16**,11,17) NYN **16** 84-94, NYA **11** 96-97, CLEA **16** 98-99, HOUN **16** 00, TBA **16** 00, NYA **17** 00

GOODMAN, BILLY UTIL/CH
(28,**10**,6,16, 9) BOSA **28** 47, **10** 47-57, BALA **10** 57, CHIA **6** 58-61, HOUN **16** 62, ATLN *CH* **9** 68-70

GOODMAN, IVAL (GOODIE) (VAL) OF
(10,41,**24**,51) CINN **10** 35-37, **41** 38, **24** 39-42, CHIN **51** 43-44

GOODSON, ED 1B/3B
(29,34,**21**,15) SFN **29** 70, **34** 71-72, **21** 72-75, ATLN **15** 75, LAN **21** 76-77

GOODWIN,CURTIS OF
(28,7,**00**,1, 19,17) BALA **28** 95, CINN **7**96, **00** 96-97, COLN **1** 98, CHIN **19** 99, TORA **17** 99

GOODWIN, DANNY DH/1B
(20,23,**25**,28) CALA **20** 75, 77-78, **23** 77, MINA **25** 79-81, OAKA **28** 82

GOODWIN, JIM P
(**37**) CHIA **37** 48

GOODWIN, TOM OF
(47,42,**24**,28, 8,5) LAN **47** 91-94, **42** 95-96, KCA **42** 97, TEXA **24** 97-99, COLN **24** 00, LAN **28** 00-01, SFN **8** 02, CHIN **5** 03, **24** 03-04

GOODWIN, TYRELL OF
(**1**) WASN **1** 05

GOOLSBY, RAY (OX) OF
(**39**) WASA **39** 46

GOOSSEN, GREG C/1B/OF
(20,**10**,22,34, 24) NYN **20** 65, **10** 66-68, **22** 68, SEAA **34** 69, MILA **34** 70, WASA **24** 70

GORBOUS, GLEN OF
(27,**37**,9,50) CINN **27** 55, PHIN **37** 55, **9** 56, **50** 57

GORDON, DON P
(**39**) TORA **39** 86-87, CLEA **39** 87-88

GORDON, JOE (FLASH) 2B/M
(**6**,4,33,35, 28,39) NYA **6** 38-43, 46, CLEA **4** 47-50, DETA *CH* **33** 56, CLEA *M* **35** 58-60, DETA *M* **28** 60, KCA *M* **39** 61, KCA *M* **6** 69

GORDON, KEITH OF
(**50**) CINN **50** 93

GORDON, MIKE C
(**23**) CHIN **23** 77-78

GORDON, SID OF/3B
(24,1,6,20,**4**, 30) NYN **24** 41, **1** 42-43, **6** 46, **20** 47-49, BOSN **4** 50-52, MILN **4** 53, PITN **4** 54-55, NYN **30** 55

GORDON, STEVE CH
(**60**) SEAA *CH* **60** 82

GORDON, TOM (FLASH) P
(**36**,16,45) KCA **36** 88-95, **16** 91, BOSA **36** 96-99, (00), CHIN **45** 01-02, HOUN **45** 02, CHIA **36** 03, NYA **36** 04-05

GORECKI, RICK P
(**55**) LAN **55** 97, TBA **55** 98, (99)

GORIN, CHARLIE P
(**15**) MILN **15** 54-55

GORINSKI, BOB OF/DH
(**35**) MINA **35** 77

GORMAN,HERB PH
(**38**) STLN **38** 52

GORMAN, HOWIE (LEFTY) OF/PH
(37,**21**) PHIN **37** 37, **21** 38

GORMAN, TOM (BIG TOM) P
(**15**) NYN **15** 39

GORMAN, TOM P
(24,**37**) NYA **24** 52-54, KCA **37** 55-59

GORMAN, TOM P
(32,**29**,33,39) MONN **32** 81-82, NYN **29** 82-85, PHIN **33/29** 86, SDN **39** 87

GORNICKI, HANK P
(33,20,**27**,26, 28) STLN **33** 41, CHIN **20** 41, PITN **27** 42-43, **26/28** 46

GORSICA, JOHNNY P
(34,26,**15**,35, 24) DETA **34/26** 40, **15** 41-44, **35** 46-47, **24** 47

GORYL, JOHNNY (GROUCHO) 3B/INF/CH/M
(**4**,16,8,48, 45,54,55) CHIN **4** 57-59, MINA **16** 62, **8** 63-64, *CH* **48** 68, *CH* **45** 69, 79-81, *M* **45** 80-81, CLEA *CH* **4** 82-84, *CH* **45** 84-88, *CH* **54** 97, TBA *CH* **55** 98

GORZELANNY, TOM P
(**61**) PITN **61** 05

GOSGER, JIM OF
(25,4,**21**,14, 18,42,19,5) BOSA **25** 63, **4** 65-66, KCA **21** 66-67, OAKA **21** 68, SEAA **14** 69, NYN **18** 69, MONN **42** 70-71, NYN **19** 73, **5** 74

GOSLIN, GOOSE OF
(3,5,**4**,20) WASA **3** 30, STLA **3** 31-32, WASA **5** 33, DETA **4** 34-37, WASA **20** 38

GOSLING, MIKE P
(**44**) ARIN **44** 04-05

GOSS, HOWIE OF
(5,27) PITN **5** 62, HOUN **27** 63

GOSSAGE, GOOSE P
(**54**) CHIA **54** 72-76, PITN **54** 77, NYA **54** 78-83, SDN **54** 84-87, CHIN **54** 88, SFN **54** 89, NYA **54** 89, TEXA **54** 91, OAKA **54** 92-93, SEAA **54** 94

GOTAY, JULIO INF
(27,19,16,23, 44,11,28,**17**) STLN **27** 60, **19** 61-62, PITN **16** 63, **23** 64, CALA **44** 65, HOUN **11** 66, **28** 67, **17** 68-69

GOTAY, RUBEN 2B/3B
(**30**) KCA **30** 04-05

GOTT, JIM P
(38,51,**35**,56) TORA **38** 81-82, 84, SFN **51** 85-87, PITN **35** 87-89, LAN **35** 90-94, PITN **56/38/56** 95

GOULISH, NICK PH
(28,**21**,37) PHIN **28/21** 44, **37** 45

GOWDY, HANK CH
(32,**31**,66,2,3) BOSN *CH* **32** 32,**31** 33-37, CINN *CH* **66** 38, **2** 39-42, **3** 45-46, NYN *CH* **3** 47-48

GOWELL, LARRY P
(**45**) NYA **45** 72

GOZZO, MAURO (GOOSE) P
(47,36,52,**45**) TORA **47** 89, CLEA **36** 90-91, MINA **52** 92, NYN **45** 93-94

GRABARKEWITZ, BILLY 3B/UTIL
(**1**,7,5,18,10, 8) LAN **1** 69-72, CALA **7** 73, PHIN **5** 73, **18** 74, CHIN **10** 74, OAKA **8** 75

GRABER, ROD OF
(**29**) CLEA **29** 58

GRABOW, JOHN P
(**39**) PITN **39** 03-05

GRABOWSKI, JASON OF/3B
(2,23,33,**6**) OAKA **2** 02, **23** 03, LAN **33** 04, **6** 05

GRABOWSKI, JOHNNY (NIG) C
(8,35) NYA **8** 29, DETA **35** 31

GRABOWSKI, REGGIE P
(15,28,18,**44**) PHIN **15/28** 32, **18** 33, **44** 34

GRACE, EARL C
(**30**,10) PITN **30** 32-35, PHIN **10** 36-37

GRACE, JOE OF/C
(30,3,15,9,**19**) STLA **30** 38, **3** 39, **15** 40, **9** 41, **19** 46, WASA **19** 46-47

GRACE, MARK 1B/P
(28,**17**) CHIN **28** 88, **17** 88-00, ARIN **17** 01-03

GRACE, MIKE (L.) 3B
(**17**) CINN **17** 78

GRACE, MIKE (J.) P
(**44**) PHIN **44** 95-99

GRACESQUI, FRANKLYN P
(**41**) FLAN **41** 04

GRAFF, MILT 2B/CH
(11,**4**,31) KCA **11** 57, **4** 57-58, PITN *CH* **31** 85

GRAFFANINO, TONY 2B/INF
(14,11,26,47, **17**,10) ATLN **14** 96-97, **11** 98, TBA **26** 99-00, CHIA **47** 00, **17** 01-03, KCA **14** 04-05, BOSA **10** 05

GRAHAM, BILL P
(26,46) DETA **46** 67, NYN **26** 67

GRAHAM, BRIAN CH
(**11**,24) CLEA *CH* **11** 99, BALA *CH* **24** 00

GRAHAM, DAN DH/UTIL
(**37**,41) MINA **37** 79, BALA **37** 80, **41** 81

GRAHAM, JACK 1B/OF
(9,41,28,18, **21**,11) LAN **9** 46, NYN **41/28/18/21** 46, STLA **11** 49

GRAHAM LEE OF
(**12**) BOSA **12** 83

GRAHAM, SKINNY OF
(**14**) BOSA **14** 34-35

GRAHAM, WAYNE OF/3B
(34,**4**) PHIN **34** 63, NYN **4** 64

GRAHE, JOE P
(39,44,20,**19**, 53,55,50) CALA **39** 90, **44** 90-91, **20** 91-92, **19** 92-94, COLN **53/55** 95, PHIN **50** 99

GRAMAN, ALEX P
(57,**58**) NYA **57** 04, **58** 05

GRAMLY, TOMMY P
(**44**) CLEA **44** 68

GRAMMAS, ALEX SS/INF/CH/M
(4,**10**,11,55, 5,2,6,8,51) STLN **4** 54-56, CINN **10** 56-58, STLN **10** 59-62, CHIN **11** 62-63, *CH* **55** 64, PITN*CH* **5** 65-69, CINN *CH* **2** 70-75, MILA *M* **2** 76-77, CINN *CH* **6** 78, ATLN *CH* **8** 79, DETA *CH* **51** 80-91

GRANDERSON, CURTIS OF
(26,**28**) DETA **26** 04, **28** 05

GRANGER, JEFF P
(**27**,39) KCA **27** 93-94, 96, PITN **39** 97

GRANGER,WAYNE P
(29,**37**,21,39, 44,50,47,35) STLN **29** 68, CINN **37** 69-71, MINA **21** 72, STLN **29** 73, NYA **45/39** 73, CHIA **44/50/47** 74, HOUN **35** 75, MONN **47** 76

GRANT, JIM (MUDCAT) P
(**33**,22,28,47, 19,16) CLEA **33** 58-64, MINA **33** 64-67, LAN **22** 68, MONN **22** 69, STLN **22** 69, OAKA **28** 70, PITN **22** 69, OAKA **28** 70, PITN **47** 70, **19** 71, **22** 71, OAKA **16** 71

GRANT, JIMMY 3B/2B
(20,7,**36**) CHIA **20** 42, **7** 43, CLEA **36** 43-44

GRANT, MARK P
(47,34,46,52, **55**,50) SFN **47/34** 84, **46** 86, **52** 86-87, **46/55** 87, SDN **52** 87, **55** 87-90, ATLN **55** 90, SEAA **50** 92, HOUN **47** 93, COLN **55** 93

GRANT, TOM OF
(**38**) CHIN **38** 83

GRANTHAM, GEORGE (BOOTS) 2B/INF
(**1**,22) CINN **1** 32-33, NYN **22** 34

GRAPENTHIN, DICK P
(**50**,47) MONN **50** 83-84, **47** 85

GRASMICK, LOU P
(**37**) PHIN **37** 48

GRASSO, MICKEY C
(29,**11**,15,7) NYN **29** 46, WASA **11** 50-53, CLEA **15** 54, NYN **7** 55

GRATE, DON (BUCKEYE) P
(37,**43**) PHIN **37** 45, **43** 46

GRATER, MARK P
(50,**37**) STLN **50** 91, DETA **37** 93

GRATEROL, BEIKER P
(**52**) DETA **52** 99

GRAVES, DANNY P
(35,**32**) CLEA **35** 96-97, CINN **32** 97-05, NYN **32** 05

GRAY, DAVE P
(**24**) BOSA **24** 64

GRAY, DICK 3B/UTIL
(**11**,27) LAN **11** 58-59, STLN **27** 59-60

GRAY, GARY OF/UTIL/DH
(24,35,23,49, **29**) TEXA **24** 77, **35** 78, **23** 78-79, CLEA **49** 80, SEAA **29** 81-82

GRAY, JEFF P
(43,**38**) CINN **43** 88, BOSA **38** 90-91

GRAY, JOHN (JOHNNY) P
(32,34,14,**6**, 37,38) PHIA **32/34** 54, KCA **14** 55, CLEA **6/37** 57, PHIN **38** 58

GRAY, LORENZO 3B/DH
(**27**) CHIA **27** 82-83

GRAY, MILT C
(**20**) WASA **20** 37

GRAY, PETE OF
(**14**) STLA **14** 45

GRAY, SAM (SAD SAM) P
(**15**) STLA **15** 31-33

GRAY, TED P
(**34**,30,25,14, 38) DETA **34** 46, **30** 48, **34** 48-54, CHIA **25** 55, CLEA **14** 55, NYA **38** 55, BALA **25** 55

GRBA, ELI P
(47,18,**33**) NYA **47** 59, **18** 60, LAA **33** 61-63

GREASON, BILL (BOOSTER) P
(**34**) STLN **34** 54

GREBECK, CRAIG INF/UTIL
(**14**,12,4,2) CHIA **14** 90-94, **12** 95, FLAN **14** 96, ANAA **4** 97, TORA **2** 98, **4** 98-00, BOSA **15** 01

GREEN, ANDY 2B/3B
(**1**) ARIN **1** 04-05

GREEN, CHRIS P
(62,**35**) PITN **62/35** 84

GREEN, DALLAS P/M
(**46**,35,25,27, 26,47) PHIN **46** 60-64, WASA **35** 65, NYN **25/27** 66, PHIN **26/47** 67, *M* **46** 79-81, NYA *M* **46** 89, NYN *M* **46** 93-96

GREEN, DAVID OF/1B
(**22**,18) STLN **22** 81-84, SFN **22** 85, STLN **18** 87

GREEN, DICK INF
(8,**1**) KCA **8** 63, **1** 64-67, OAKA **1** 68-74

GREEN, FRED P
(**35**,17,29) PITN **35** 59-61, WASA **17** 62, PITN **29** 64

GREEN, GARY SS/3B
(20,1,40) SDN **20** 86, 89, TEXA **57** 90, **1** 91, CINN **40** 92

GREEN, GENE OF/C
(24,**12**,1,36, 23) STLN **24** 57, **12** 58-59, **1** 59, BALA **36** 60, WASA **12** 61, CLEA **12** 62, **23** 63, CINN **9** 63

GREEN, HARVEY (BUCK) P
(**29**) BKNN **29** 35

GREEN, JASON P
(**54**) HOUN **54** 00

GREEN, LENNY OF
(21,**7**,26,6,49, 30) BALA **21** 57-59, WASA **7** 59-60, MINA **7** 61-64, LAA **26** 64, BALA **6** 64, BOSA **49** 65,**7** 65-66, DETA **30** 67-68

GREEN, NICK 2B
(**20**,18) ATLN **20** 04, TBA **18** 05

GREEN, PUMPSIE 2B/SS
(**12**,18) BOSA **12** 59-62, NYN **18** 63

GREEN, SCARBOROUGH OF
(**22**,41) STLN **22** 97, TEXA **41** 99-00

GREEN, SHAWN OF/DH/1B
(56,**15**) TORA **56** 93, **15** 94-99, LAN **15** 00-04, ARIN **15** 05

GREEN, STEVE P
(**33**) ANAA **33** 01

GREEN, TYLER P
(**28**) PHIN **28** 93, 95, 97-98, (99)

GREENBERG, ADAM OF
(**17**) CHIN **17** 05

GREENBERG, HANK (HAMMERIN' HANK) 1B/OF
(7,**5**) DETA **7** 33, **5** 34-41, 45-46, PITN **5** 47

GREENE, AL DH/OF
(**21**) DETA **21** 79

GREENE, CHARLIE C
(7,**34**,18,21) NYN **7** 96, BALA **34** 97-98, MILN **18** 99, TORA **21** 00

GREENE, KAHLIL SS
(**3**) SDN **3** 03-05

GREENE, RICK P
(**57**) CINN **57** 99

GREENE, TODD C/OF/1B
(**8**,27,43,23, 22,20) CALA **8** 96, ANAA **8** 97-99, TORA **27** 00, NYA **43** 01, TEXA **23** 02, **27/22** 03, COLN **20** 04-05

GREENE, TOMMY P
(33,**49**,54) ATLN **33** 89-90,PHIN **49** 90-95 HOUN **54** 97

GREENE,WILLIE 3B/SS
(56,**12**,11) CINN **56** 92, **12** 93-98, BALA **11** 98, TORA **12** 99, CHIN **39** 00

GREENGRASS, JIM OF
(**23**,10) CINN **23** 52-55, PHIN **10** 55, **23** 56

GREENWELL, MIKE OF/3B/DH
(**39**,37) BOSA **39** 85-96, **37** 86

GREENWOOD, BOB (GREENIE) P
(**26**) PHIN **26** 55-56

GREER, BRIAN OF
(37,**9**) SDN **37** 77, **9** 79

GREER, KENNY P
(35,36) NYN **35** 93, SFN **36** 95

GREER, RUSTY OF
(**29**) TEXA **29** 94-02, (03-04)

GREGG, HAL (SKEETS) P
(**28**,8,32,37, 20,26) BKNN **28** 43-47, **8** 47, PITN **32** 48-49, **37** 49, **20** 50, NYN **26** 52

GREGG, KEVIN P
(**63**) ANAA **63** 03-04, LAA **63** 05

GREGG, TOMMY OF/1B
(47,**16**,26,6, 19) PITN **47** 87-88, ATLN **16** 88-92, CINN **26** 93, FLAN **6** 95, ATLN **19** 97

GREGORIO, TOM C
(**3**) ANAA **3** 03

GREGORY, LEE P
(**28**) CHIN **28** 64

GREGORY, PAUL (POP) P
(45,39,**24**) CHIA **45/39** 32, **24** 33

GREGSON, GREG CH
(**33**) LAN *CH* **33** 98

GREIF, BILL P
(52,44,**27**,48, 38) HOUN **52/44** 71, SDN **27** 72-76, STLN **48/38** 76

GREINKE, ZACK P
(**23**) KCA **23** 04-05

GREISINGER, SETH P
(41,**50**,58,48) DETA **41** 98, **50** 98-99, MINA **58** 04, ATLN **48** 05

GREMP, BUDDY 1B/UTIL
(**30**,34) BOSN **30** 40, **34** 41, **30** 42

GRICH, BOBBY 2B/INF
(16,3,**4**) CALA **45** 79-80

GRIEVE, TOMMY OF/DH/UTIL F
(4,**6**,2,3,14) WASA **4** 70, TEXA **6** 72-77, NYN **2** 78, STLN **3** 79, OAKA **14** 97

GRIEVE, BEN OF/DH S
(**14**,18,12,29, 45,4) OAKA **14** 97-00, TBA **18** 01-03, MILN **12** 04, CHIN **29** 04, **45/4** 05

GRIFFEY, KEN, JR. OF/DH S
(**24**,30) SEAA **24** 89-99, CINN **30** 00-05

GRIFFEY, KEN, SR. OF/1B/DH/CH F
(**30**,6,33,22, 24) CINN **30** 73-81, NYA **6** 82, **33** 83-86, ATLN **22** 86-88, CINN **25** 88, **30** 89-90, SEAA **30** 90-91, *CH* **30** 93, COLN *CH* **24** 96, CINN *CH* **30** 97-99, **33** 00-01

GRIFFIN, ALFREDO SS/DH/UTIL/CH
(16,8,**4**,3,7) CLEA **16** 76, **8** 77-78, TORA **4** 79-84, OAKA **3** 85-87, LAN **7** 88-91, TORA **4** 92-93, *CH* **4** 96-97, ANAA *CH* **4** 00-04, LAA *CH* **4** 05

GRIFFIN, DOUG 2B/INF/DH
(33,**2**) CALA **33** 70, BOSA **2** 71-77

GRIFFIN, JOHN-FORD OF
(**24**) TORA **24** 05

GRIFFIN, MIKE P
(**52**,50,45,42, 35) NYA **52** 79-81, CHIN **50** 81, SDN **45** 82, BALA **42** 87, CINN **35** 89

GRIFFIN, TOM P
(**38**,33,43,23) HOUN **38** 69-76, SDN **33** 76-77, CALA **38** 78, SFN **43** 79-81, PITN **23** 82

GRIFFITH, DERRILL 2B
(**26**) LAN **26** 63-66

GRIFFITH, LEE P
(**31**) PHIA **31** 46

GRIFFITHS, JEREMY P
(46,**47**) NYN **46** 03, HOUN **47** 04

GRIGGS, HAL 9
(39,**24**) WASA **39** 56-57, **24** 57-58

GRILLI, GUIDO P
(37,24,**15**) BOSA **37** 66, KCA **24/15** 66

GRILLI, JASON P
(35,37,**41**,49) FLAN **35** 00, **37** 01, CHIA **41** 04, DETA **49** 05

GRILLI, STEVE P
(**49**,45) DETA **49** 75-78, TORA **45** 79

GRIM, BOB P
(**55**,34,26,46) NYA **55** 54-58, KCA **34** 58-59, CLEA **26** 60, CINN **46** 60, STLN **46** 60, KCA **34** 62

GRIMES, BURLEIGH (OL' STUBBLEBEARD)P
(18,16,21,**20**, 23,37,33,13, 43) CHIN **18/16** 32, **21** 33, STLN **20** 33-34, PITN **23/37** 34, NYA **20** 34, BKNN *M* **33** 37, *M* **13** 38, KCA *CH* **43** 55

GRIMES, ED INF
(**24**) STLA **24** 31-32

GRIMES, OSCAR INF
(31,**1**,29,12, 7,22) CLEA **31** 38, **1** 39-42, NYA **29/12** 43, **7** 44-46, PHIA **22** 46

GRIMM, CHARLIE (JOLLY CHOLLY) 1B/M
(11,6,**7**,1,38, 40,50) CHIN **11/6** 32, **7** 33-34, **8** 35, **7** 36, *M* **11/6** 32, *M* **7** 33-34, *M* **8** 35, *M* **7** 36, *M* **1** 37-38, *CH* **38** 41, *M* **40** 44-49, BOSN *M* **40** 52, MILN *M* **40** 53-56, CHIN *M* **40** 60, *CH* **50** 61-62

GRIMSLEY, JASON P
(54,48,56,**38**, 16) PHIN **54** 89-90, **48** 90-91, CLEA **48** 93-95, CALA **56** 96, NYA **38** 99-00, KCA **38** 01-04, BALA **16** 04, **38** 04-05

GRIMSLEY, ROSS, I P F
(**27**) CHIA **27** 51

GRIMSLEY, ROSS, II P S
(**48**,39) CINN **48** 71-73, BALA **39** 74-76, **48** 76-77, MONN **48** 78-80, CLEA **48** 80, BALA **48** 82

GRISSOM, LEE P B
(24,**32**,53,27, 21,10) CINN **24** 34, **32** 34-37, **53** 38, **32** 39, NYA **27** 40, BKNN **21** 40, **32** 40-41, PHIN **10** 41

GRISSOM, MARQUIS OF
(**9**,17) MONN **9** 89-94, ATLN **9** 95-96, CLEA **17** 97, MILN **9** 98-00, LAN **9** 01-02, SFN **9** 03-05

GRISSOM, MARV P B
(16,19,13,15, **42**,5,35,20, 46,24) NYN **16** 46, DETA **19** 49, CHIA **16/13** 52, BOSA **15** 53, NYN **42** 53-57, SFN **42** 58, STLN **42** 59, LAA *CH* **5** 61-66, CHIA *CH* **35** 67-68, CALA *CH* **20** 69, MINA *CH* **46** 70-71, CHIN *CH* **46** 75-76, *CH* **16** 76, CALA *CH* **24** 77-78

GROAT, DICK SS/3B/INF
(**24**,20) PITN **24** 52, 55-62, STLN **24** 63-65, PHIN **24** 66-67, SFN **20** 67

GROB, CONNIE P
(41,**38**) WASA **41/38** 56

GRODZICKI, JOHNNY (GROD) P
(34,**33**,52) STLN **34** 41, **33** 46-47, DETA *CH* **52** 79

GROMEK, STEVE P
(36,25,**27**,18) CLEA **36** 41-42, **25** 43-47, **27** 48-53, DETA **18** 53-57

GROOM, BUDDY P
(**42**,50,24,29, 27,38,28) DETA **42** 92-95, FLAN **50** 95, OAKA **42** 96-97, **24** 97, **29** 98-99, BALA **27** 00-04, NYA **38** 05, ARIN **28** 05

GROSKLOSS, HOWDIE SS
(**26**) PITN **26** 32

GROSS, DON P
(**31**,38,37) CINN **31** 55-57, PITN **38** 58, **37** 59, **38** 59-60

GROSS, GABE OF
(21,**18**) TORA **21** 04, **18** 05

GROSS, GREG OF/1B/P/CH
(**21**,23,6,8) HOUN **21** 73-76, CHIN **21** 77-78, PHIN **23** 79-82, **21** 82-88, HOUN **6** 89,PHIN *CH* **21** 01-03, **8** 04

GROSS, KEVIN P
(48,**46**,45,44) PHIN **48** 83, **46** 83-88, MONN **46** 89-90, LAN **45** 91, **46** 92-96, ANAA **44** 97

GROSS, KIP P
(59,36,**57**,27, 56) CINN **59** 90-91, **36** 91, LAN **57** 92-93, BOSA **27** 99, HOUN **56** 00

GROSS, WAYNE 3B/1B/UTIL
(**10**,6,14,11) OAKA **10** 76-83, BALA **6** 84, **14** 84-85, OAKA **11** 86

GROSSMAN, HARLEY P
(**15**) WASA **15** 52

GROTE, JERRY C/3B/UTIL
(8,**15**,9) HOUN **8** 63-64, NYN **15** 66-77, LAN **9** 77-78, KCA **15** 81, LAN **9** 81

GROTEWOLD, JEFF UTIL
(48,**14**) PHIN **48** 92, KCA **14** 95

GROTH, ERNIE P
(29,26,**28**,36) CLEA **29** 47, **26/28** 48, CHIA **36** 49

GROTH, JOHNNY OF
(24,**3**,5,4,39) DETA **24** 46-48, **3** 49-52, STLA **3** 53, CHIA **5** 54-55, WASA **4** 55, KCA **39** 56-57, DETA **3** 57-60

GROTT, MATT P
(**65**) CINN **65** 75

GROVE, LEFTY P
(**10**) PHIA **10** 31-33, BOSA **10** 34-41

GROVE, ORVAL P
(**45**,11,22) CHIA **45/11** 40, **22** 41, **45** 41-49

GRUBB, JOHNNY OF/3B/DH
(**1**,2,21,6,30) SDN **1** 72-74, **2** 74-76, CLEA **21** 77, **1** 77-78, TEXA **6** 78-82, DETA **30** 83-87

GRUBE, FRANK (HANS) C
(**9**,1,14,35,6) CHIA **9** 31, **1** 32, **14** 33, STLA **9** 34-35, CHIA **35** 35-36, STLA **6** 41

GRUBER, KELLY 3B/UTIL/DH
(**17**) TORA **17** 84-92, CALA **17** 93

GRUDZIELANEK, MARK SS/2B
(**4**,30,16,8,11, 12) MONN **4** 96-98, LAN **30/16** 98, **8** 99-02, CHIN **11** 03-04, STLN **12** 05

GRUNDT, KEN P
(**57**,59) BOSA **57** 96, **59** 97

GRUNWALD, AL (STRETCH) P
(**37**,7) PITN **37** 55, KCA **7** 59

GRYBOSKI, KEVIN P
(**49**,48) ATLN **49** 02-05, TEXA **48** 05

GRYSKA, SIG SS
(__,**4**) STLA __ 38, **4** 39

GRZANICH, MIKE P
(**23**) HOUN **23** 98

GRZENDA, JOE P
(46,36,17,35, 48,43,33,**31**) DETA **46** 61, KCA **36** 64, **17/35** 66, NYN **48/43** 67, MINA **33/17** 69, WASA **19** 70, **31** 70-71, STLN **31** 72

GUANTE, CECILIO P
(**47**,54,51,38) PITN **47** 82-86, NYA **54** 87, **51** 87-88, TEXA **51** 88-89, CLEA **38** 90

GUARDADO, EDDIE P
(**18**) MINA **18** 93-03, SEAA **18** 04-05

GUBANICH, CREIGHTON C
(**39**) BOSA **39** 99

GUBICZA, MARK P
(**23**) KCA **23** 84-96, ANAA **23** 97

GUDAT, MARV OF/1B
(22,**24**) CHIN **22/24** 32

GUERRA, MIKE (MICKEY) C
(38,**9**,37,8,15) WASA **38** 37, **9** 44-46, PHIA **9** 47-48, **37** 49-50, BOSA **8** 51, WASA **15** 51

GUERRERO, JUAN UTIL
(**19**) HOUN **19** 92

GUERRERO, MARIO (MIKE)(MICKEY) SS/INF
(41,18,19,11, **3**) BOSA **41** 73, **18** 73-74, STLN **19** 75, CALA **11** 76-77, OAKA **3** 78-80

GUERRERO, PEDRO (PETE) OF/1B/UTIL
(57,**28**) LAN **57** 78-79, **28** 80-88, STLN **28** 88-92

GUERRERO, VLADIMIR OF B
(**27**) MONN **27** 96-03, ANAA **27** 04, LAA **27** 05

GUERRERO, WILTON 2B/INF B
(30,**4**,6,1) LAN **30** 96-98, MONN **4** 98-00, CINN **6** 01-02, MONN **4** 02, KC **1** 04

GUERRIER, MATT P
(**54**) MINA **54** 04-05

GUETTERMAN, LEE P
(36,34,**35**,51, 48) SEAA **36** 84, 86, **34** 87, NYA **35** 88-92, NYN **35** 92, STLN **51** 93, SEAA **48** 95-96

GUEVARA, GIOMAR 2B/DH
(34,59,**4**) SEAA **34** 97, **59** 98, **4** 98-99

GUIDRY, RON (LUOISIANA LIGHTNIN') P
(54,**49**) NYA **54** 75, **49** 75-88

GUIEL, AARON OF/DH
(**45**) KCA **45** 02-05

GUILLEN, CARLOS 2B/SS/INF/DH
(11,5,**8**,**9**) PITN **11** 97, SEAA **5** 98, **8** 99-03, DETA **9** 04-05

GUILLEN, JOSE OF/DH
(11,30,**6**) PITN **11** 97-99, TBA **30** 99-01, ARIN **11** 02, CINN **6** 02-03, OAKA **6** 03, ANAA **6** 04, WASN **6** 05

GUILLEN, OZZIE SS/DH/M
(**13**) CHIA **13** 85-97, BALA **13** 98, ATLN **13** 98-99, TBA **13** 00, MONN *CH* **13** 01, FLAN *CH* **13** 02-03, CHIA *M* **13** 04-05

GUINDON, BOBBY 1B/OF
(**51**) BOSA **51** 64

GUINN, SKIP P
(37,**35**) ATLN **37** 68, HOUN **35** 69, 71

GUINTINI, BEN OF
(49,**3**) PITN **49** 46, PHIA **3** 50

GUISE, WITT (LEFTY) P
(**25**) CINN **25** 40

GULAN, MIKE 3B
(**21**,**27**) STLN **21** 97, FLAN **27** 01

GULDEN, BRAD C
(40,**27**,19,6, 33,4,10) LAN **40** 78, NYA **27** 79-80, **19/6** 80, SEAA **27** 81, MONN **33** 82, CIN/N **4** 84, SFN **10** 86

GULLETT, DON P/CH
(56,**35**) CINN **56** 70, **35** 70-76, NYA **35** 77-78, CINN *CH* **35** 93-05

GULLIC, TED UTIL
(**26**) STLA **26** 33

GULLICKSON, BILL P
(**34**,45,36) MONN **34** 79-85, CINN **34** 86-87, NYA **39/45** 87, HOUN **36** 90, DETA **36** 91-94

GULLIVER, GLENN 3B
(**11**) BALA **11** 82-83

GUMBERT, HARRY (GUNBOAT) P
(15,**10**,42,19, 37,41) NYN **15** 35, **10** 36-41, STLN **42** 41, **19** 42-44, CINN **37** 44, **41** 44, 46-49, PITN **37** 49-50

GUMPERT, DAVE (GUMP) P
(43,**45**,30) DETA **43** 82-83, CHIN **45** 85-86, KCA **30** 87

GUMPERT, RANDY P/CH
(20,14,19,26, **18**,24,33) PHIA **20** 36, **14/19** 36, **31/ 26** 38, NYA **18** 46-48, CHIA **24** 48, **18** 48-51, BOSA **24** 52, WASA 52, NYA *CH* **33** 57

GUNDERSON, ERIC P
(**53**,40,28,39) SFN **53** 90-91, NYN **40** 94-95, BOSA **28** 95-96, TEXA **53** 97-99, TORA **39** 00

GURA, LARRY P
(40,42,39,37, **32**) CHIN **40** 70-73, NYA **42** 74, **39** 74-75, KCA **37** 76-78, **32** 78-85, CHIN **32** 85

GUSTINE, FRANKIE 3B/INF
(22,**16**,6,31) PITN **22** 39, **16** 40-48, CHIN **6** 49, STLA **6** 50, PITN *CH* **31** 50

GUTH, BUCKY SS
(25/**27**) MINA **25/27** 72

GUTHRIE, JEREMY P
(53,**36**) CLEA **53** 04, **36** 05

GUTHRIE, MARK P
(**53**,52,44,40, 30,36,38,19, 31) MINA **53** 89-95, LAN **52** 95, **44** 96-98, BOSA **40** 99, CHIN **30** 99-00, TBA **36** 00, TORA **38** 00, OAKA **19** 01, NYN **53** 02, CHIN **31** 03

GUTIERREZ, CESAR (COCA) SS/INF
(17,31,**7**) SFN **17** 67, **31** 69, DETA **7** 69-71

GUTIERREZ, FRANKLIN OF
(**38**) CLEA **38** 05

GUTIERREZ, JACKIE SS/INF
(41,**11**,15) BOSA **41** 83-85, BALA **11** 86-87, PHIN **15** 88

GUTIERREZ, RICKY SS/UTIL
(7,**12**,6,16) SDN **7** 93-94, HOUN **12** 95-99, CHIN **12** 00-01, CLEA **12** 02-03, NYN **6** 04, BOSA **16** 04

GUTTIEREZ, ??? CH
(**55**) TORA *CH* **55** 02

GUTTERIDGE, DON (FIRPO) 3B/INF/CH/M
(22,5,**4**,10, 29,**39**) STLN **22** 36, **5** 37-40, STLA **4** 42-45, BOSA **10** 46-47, PITN **29** 48, CHIA *CH* **39** 55-66, **39** 68-69, *M* **39** 69-70

GUZMAN, CRISTIAN INF
(**15**) MINA **15** 99-04, WASN **15** 05

GUZMAN, DOMINGO P
(**46**,43) SDN **46** 99, **43** 00

GUZMAN, EDWARDS 3B
(**2**,9,13,35) SFN **2** 99, **9/13** 01, MONN **35** 03

GUZMAN, FREDDY OF
(**7**) SDN **7** 04, (05)

GUZMAN, GERALDO P
(**50**) ARIN **50** 00-01

GUZMAN, JOHNNY P
(45,**41**) OAKA **45** 91, **41** 92

GUZMAN, JOSE P
(29,**23**) TEXA **29** 85, **23** 85-88, 90-92, CHIN **29** 93-94

GUZMAN, JUAN P
(66,**57**) TORA **66** 91-95, **57** 96-98, BALA **57** 98-99, CINN **57** 99, TBA **57** 00-01

GUZMAN, SANTIAGO P
(46,50,**36**) STLN **46** 69, **50** 69-70, **36** 70-72

GWOSDZ, DOUG C
(**10**) SDN **10** 81-84

GWYNN, CHRIS OF B
(45,15,29,14, **10**,9) LAN **45** 87-89, **15** 89-91, KCA **29** 92, **14** 93, LAN **10** 94-95, SDN **9** 96

GWYNN, TONY OF B
(**19**) SDN **19** 82-01

GYSELMAN, DICK INF
(**27**,24) BOSN **27** 33, **24** 34

H

HAAD, YAMID C
(31,**8**) PITN **31** 99, SFN **8** 05

HAAS, BERT OF/1B/UTIL
(4,28,**18**,3, 39,5) BKNN **4** 37, **28** 38-39, CINN **18** 42-43, 46-47, PHIN **3** 48-49, NYN **39** 49, CHIA **5** 51

HAAS, DAVE P
(**16**,18) DETA **16** 91-93, **18** 93

HAAS, EDDIE OF/CH/M
(37,40,**11**,1,5, 36,22) CHIN **37** 57, MILN **40** 58, **11** 58, 60, ATLN CH **1** 75, CH **5** 76-77, CH **36** 84, M **22** 85

HAAS, MOOSE P
(**30**) MILA **30** 76-85, OAKA **30** 86-87

HAAS, MULE OF/DH
(8,**6**,30,**22**) PHIA **8** 31-32, CHIA **6** 33-37, PHIA **30** 38, CHIA CH **22** 40-46

HABENICHT, BOB (HOBBY) P
(**22**,39,35) STLN **22** 51, STLA **39/35** 53

HABYAN, JOHN P
(54,27,50,60, 61,57,42,41, **32**, 48) BALA **54** 85-88, **27** 88, NYA **50/60/61** 90, **57** 91, **42** 91-93, KCA **41**93, STLN **32** 94-95, CALA **32** 95, COLN **48** 96

HACK, STAN (SMILIN' SAM) 3B/1B/M/CH
(1,31,49,34, 39,**6**,20,25, 35) CHIN **1/31** 32, **49** 33, **34** 34, **39** 35-36, **6** 37-42, **20** 43, **25** 44, **6** 45-47, M **6** 54-56, STLN CH **35** 57-58

HACKER, RICH SS/CH
(**20**,**7**) MONN **20** 71, STLN CH **7** 86-90, TORA CH **7** 91-93

HACKER, WARREN P
(**18**,36,16,49, 28) CHIN **18** 48-56, CINN **36** 57, PHIN **16** 57, **49** 57-58, CHIA **28**

HACKMAN, LUTHER P
(51,**63**,47,58, 16) COLN **51** 99, STLN **63** 00-02, **47** 02, SDN **58/16** 03

HADDIX, HARVEY (THE KITTEN) P
(42,20,32,**31**, 30,52,33,2, 57) STLN **42** 52-56, PHIN **20** 56-57, CINN **32** 58, PITN **31** 59-63, BALA **30** 64-65, NYN *CH* **52** 66-67, CINN *CH* **31** 69, BOSA *CH* **33** 71, CLEA *CH* **2** 75-78, PITN *CH* **57** 79-80, **31** 81-84

HADLEY, BUMP P
(16,24,9,17, 18,**14**,32) WASA **16** 31, CHIA **24** 32, STLA **9** 32, **17** 33, WASA **18** 35, NYA **14** 36-40, NYN **18** 41, PHIA **32/17** 41

HADLEY, KENT 1B
(**18**,25) KCA **18** 58-59, NYA **25** 60

HAEFNER, MICKEY P
(28,19,10,**16**, 12,18,22) WASA **28/19** 43, **10** 44-46, **16** 46-49, CHIA **12** 49-50, **18** 50, BOSN **22** 50

HAFEY, BUD OF
(__,**12**,36,7) CHIA __ 35, PITN **47** 35, **12** 36, CINN **36** 39, PHIN **7** 39

HAFEY, CHICK OF
(__,6,4,9,11, 14) STLN __ 24, CINN **6** 32, **4** 33, **9** 34, **11** 35, **14** 37

HAFEY, TOM (HEAVE-O)(THE ARM) 3B
(**19**,17) NYN **19** 39, STLA **17** 44

HAFNER, TRAVIS 1B/DH
(6,32,**48**) TEXA **6** 02, CLEA **32** 03, **48** 04-05

HAGEN, KEVIN P
(**35**) STLN **35** 83-84

HAGUE, JOE 1B/OF
(**12**,25) STLN **12** 68-72, CINN **25** 72-73

HAHN, DICK C
(**29**) WASA **29** 40

HAHN, DON OF
(43,**25**,29,6) MONN **43** 69-70, NYN **25** 71-74, PHIN **25** 75, STLN **29** 75, SDN **6** 75

HAHN, FRED P
(**41**) STLN **41** 52

HAID, HAL P
(**24**) CHIA **24** 33

HAINES, JESSE (POP) P/CH
(31,18,**16**,32) STLN **31** 23, **18** 24, **16** 32-37, BKNN *CH* **32** 38

HAIRSTON, JERRY, JR. UTIL S,GS,GGS
(39,13,**15**) BALA **39/13** 98, **15** 99-04, CHIN **15** 05

HAIRSTON, JERRY OF/DH F,S,GS
(2,22,25,**17**, 15) CHIA **2** 73-75, **22** 75-76, **25** 77, PITN **22** 77, CHIA **17** 81-88, **15** 89

HAIRSTON, JOHNNY C/OF S,F,GF
(**43**) CHIN **43** 69

HAIRSTON, SAMMY C/CH F,GF,GGF
(**27**,57) CHIA **27** 51, *CH* **57** 78

HAIRSTON, SCOTT 2B
(5,**9**) ARIN **5** 04, **9** 05

HAJDUK, CHET PH
(**42**) CHIA **42** 41

HAJEK, DAVE 2B
(21,30,**4**) HOUN **21** 95, **30/4** 96

HALAMA, JOHN P
(**54**,52) HOUN **54** 98, SEAA **54** 99-02, OAKA **54** 03, TBA **52** 04, BOSA **54** 05, WASN **54** 05

HALE, BOB 1B
(**6**,20,10,8,9, 34) BALA **6** 55-57, **20** 58, **10** 59, CLEA **8** 60, **9** 60-61, NYA **34** 61

HALE, CHIP 3B/UTIL
(58,**4**,12,5) MINA **58** 89, **4** 90, 93-95, **12** 96, LAN **5** 97

HALE, DeMARLO CH
(**20**,16) TEXA *CH* **20** 02-03, **16** 04-05

HALE, JOHN OF/CH
(**43**,44,20) LAN **43** 74-77, SEAA **44** 78, **43** 79, KCA *CH* **20** 02

HALE, ODELL (BAD NEWS) 2B/3B
(7,25,34,**4**,6, 26) CLEA **7** 31, **25** 33, **34** 34-36, **4** 37-40, BOSA **6** 41, NYN **26** 41

HALICKI, ED P
(**28**) SFN **28** 74-80, CALA **28** 80

HALL, ALBERT OF
(31,2,**1**,19) ATLN **31** 81-82, **2** 82-86, **1** 86-88, PITN **19** 89

HALL, BILL SS/3B/INF
(**2**) MILN **2** 02-05

HALL, BILL (L.) C
(46,31,**11**) PITN **46** 54, **31** 56, **11** 58

HALL, BOB P
(25,**36**) BOSN **25** 49-50, PITN **36** 53

HALL, DARREN P
(36,**52**) TORA **36** 94-95, LAN **52** 96-98, CHIA **52** 99

HALL, DICK OF/INF/P
(7,5,17,38,30, 24,**29**,35,27) PITN **7** 52, **5** 53, **17** 54, **38** 55, **30** 55-57, 59, KCA **24** 60, BALA **29** 61-66, PHIN **35** 67, **27** 67-68, BALA **29** 69-71

HALL, DREW P
(**44**,45) CHIN **44** 86-88, TEXA **44** 89, MONN **45** 90

HALL, IRV 2B/INF
(**6**) PHIA **6** 43-46

HALL, JIMMIE OF/1B
(30,**7**,9,20, 26,23,19) MINA **30** 63-64, **7** 64-66, CALA **9** 67-68, CLEA **20** 68-69, NYA **26** 69, CHIN **23** 69-70, ATLN **23/19** 70

HALL, JOE OF
(**26**,28,44,43) CHIA **26** 94, DETA **28** 95, **44/43** 97

HALL, JOHNNY P
(23,**45**) BKNN **23/45** 48

HALL, JOSH P
(**58**) CINN **58** 03, (04)

HALL, MEL OF/CH
(32,**27**,2) CHIN **32** 81-82, **27** 82-84, CLEA **27** 84-88, NYA **27** 89-92, SFN **2** 96

HALL, TOBY C
(55,**44**) TBA **55** 00-01, **44** 01-05

HALL, TOM P
(**21**,42,19) MINA **21** 68-71, CINN **21** 72-75, NYN **42** 75, **19** 75-76, KCA **42** 76-77

HALLADAY, ROY P
(52,**32**) TORA **52** 98, **32** 99-05

HALLAHAN, BILL (WILD BILL) P
(**22**,24,21,19) STLN **22** 32-36, CINN **24** 36, **21** 37, **19** 38

HALLER, TOM C/OF/CH
(51,**5**,15,14, 8) SFN **51** 61, **5** 62-67, LAN **15** 68-70, **14** 71, DETA **14** 72, SFN *CH* **8** 77-78, *CH* **5** 78-79

HALLETT, JACK P
(28,**40**,39) CHIA **28** 40, **28** 41, PITN **40** 42, **40** 43, **39** 46, NYN **40** 48

HALSEY, BRAD P
(57,61,**37**) NYA **57/61** 04, ARIN **37** 05

HALTER, SHANE 2B/OF
(43,4,11,39, **17**,18) KCA **43** 97, **4** 98, NYN **11** 99, DETA **39** 00, **17** 00-03, ANAA **18** 04

HAMBRIGHT, ROGER P
(**46**) NYA **46** 71

HAMELIN, BOB 1B/DH
(48,**3**,41,30) KCA **48** 93, **3** 94-96, DETA **41** 97, MILN **30** 98

HAMILTON, DARRYL OF/DH
(18,**24**,4,5, 27,12) MILA **18** 88, 90, **24** 90-95, TEXA **4** 96, SFN **5** 97-98, COLN **27** 98, **12** 98-99, NYN **18** 99-01

HAMILTON, DAVE P
(**33**,26,30,25) OAKA **33** 72-75, CHIA **26** 75-77, STLN **26** 78, PITN **30** 78, OAKA **33** 79-80, **25** 80

HAMILTON, JACK P
(48,31,**32**,50, 24) PHIN **48** 62-63, DETA **48** 64, **31** 65, NYN **32** 66-67, CALA **50** 67, **24** 67-68, CLEA **32** 69, CHIA **50/32** 69

HAMILTON, JEFF 3B/SS/INF
(33,**3**) LAN **33** 86-88, **3** 88, 90-91

HAMILTON, JOEY P
(**50**,54) SDN **50** 94-98, TORA **50** 99-01, CINN **50** 01-02, **54** 03

HAMILTON, STEVE P/CH
(27,28,**39**,45, 29,38,37,52) CLEA **27** 61, WASA **28** 62-63, NYA **39** 63-70, CHIA **45/29** 70, SFN **38** 71, CHIN **37** 72, DETA *CH* **52** 75

HAMILTON, TOM (HAM) 1B/OF
(**4**) PHIA **4** 52-53

HAMLIN, KEN SS/INF
(31,2,12,5,**7**) PITN **31** 57, 59, KCA **2** 60, LAA **12** 61, WASA **5** 62, **7** 65-66

HAMLIN, LUKE (HOT POTATO) P
(20,29,**12**,13, 31) DETA **20** 33, **29/20** 34, BKNN **12** 37-41, PITN **13** 42, PHIA **31** 44

HAMM, PETE P
(34,**24**,33) MINA **34/24** 70, **33/34/24** 71

HAMMAKER, ATLEE P
(33,17,**14**,7, 34) KCA **33** 81, SFN **17** 82-83, **14** 83-84, **7** 85, **14** 87-90, SDN **14** 90-91, CHIA **34** 94-95

HAMMOCK, ROBBY C/3B
(**7**) ARIN **7** 03-04

HAMMOND, CHRIS P B
(52,45,38,**11**, 32,40,36,39, 29) CINN **52/45** 90-92, FLAN **38** 93, **11** 93-96, BOSA **32** 97, FLAN **40** 98, ATLN **36** 02, NYA **39** 03, OAKA **29** 04, SDN **29** 05

HAMMOND, STEVE OF/DH B
(**27**) KCA **27** 82

HAMMONDS, JEFFREY OF/DH
(**11**,4,41,51, 16,12) BALA **11** 93-98, CINN **4** 98-99, COLN **4** 00, MILN **41** 01-03, SFN **51/16** 03, **12** 04, WASN **11** 05

HAMNER, GARVIN INF B
(**8**) PHIN **8** 45

HAMNER, GRANNY SS/INF/P B
(21,6,37,35, 1,17,33,**2**,7, 36) PHIN **21** 44, **6** 45, **37** 46, **35** 47, **1/17/33** 48, **2** 49-59, CLEA **7** 59, KCA **36** 62

HAMNER, RALPH (BRUZ) P
(26,8,**35**) CHIA **26/8** 46, CHIN **22** 47, **35** 48-49

HAMPTON, IKE UTIL
(20,**15**) NYN **20** 74, CALA **15** 75-78, **20** 79

HAMPTON, MIKE P
(46,38,**10**,32) SEAA **46** 93, HOUN **38** 94, **10** 95-99, NYN **32** 00, COLN **10** 01-02, ATLN **32** 03-05

HAMRIC, BERT PH
(51,**20**) BKNN **51** 55, BALA **20** 58

HAMRICK, RAY INF
(**20**,21) PHIN **20** 43-44, **21** 44

HAMULACK, TIM P
(**46**) NYN **46** 05

HANCKEN, BUDDY C/CH
(22,**39**,4) PHIA **22/39** 40,HOUN *CH* **4** 68-72

HANCOCK, FRED UTIL
(59,**26**) CHIA **59/26** 49

HANCOCK, GARRY OF/DH/UTIL
(38,**37**,9,11) BOSA **38** 78, **37** 80-82, OAKA **9** 83-84, **11** 83-84

HANCOCK, JOSH P
(53,**50**,43) BOSA **53** 02, PHIN **50** 03-04, CINN **43** 04-05

HANCOCK, LEE P
(**42**) PITN **42** 95-96

HANCOCK, RYAN P
(**60**) CALA **60** 96

HAND, RICH P
(45,**25**,47) CLEA **45** 70-71, TEXA **25** 72-73, CALA **47/25** 73

HANDLEY, GENE 2B/INF
(15,**2**) PHIN **15** 46, **2** 47

HANDLEY, LEE (JEEP) 3B/INF
(15,22,20,4, **6**,35) CINN **15** 36, PITN **22** 37, **20** 38-39, **4** 40, **6** 40-42, 44-46, PHIN **35** 47

HANDRAHAN, VERN P
(19,37,26) KCA **19** 64, **37/26** 66

HANDS, BILL P
(32,27,**49**,17, 34) SFN **32** 65, CHIN **27** 66, **49** 66-72, MINA **17** 73-74, **49** 74, TEXA **49** 74, **34/49** 75, SDN **1** 72

HANEBRINK, HARRY 2B/3B/UTIL
(2,**26**,6,20) MILN **2** 53, MILN **26** 57-58, **6** 57-58, PHIN **20** 59

HANEY, CHRIS P
(42,**33**,44,48, 56) MONN **42** 91-92, KCA **33** 92-98, CHIN **44** 98, CLEA **48** 99-00, BOSA **56** 02

HANEY, FRED (PUDGE) MGR
(32,26,34,**2**) STLA *M* **32/26** 39, *M* **34** 40-41 PITN *M* **2** 53-55, MILN **2** 56-59

HANEY, LARRY C/INF/CH
(34,10,**12**,3, 15,7) BALA **34** 66-68, SEAA **10** 69, OAKA **12** 69-70, **3** 72, **15** 73, STLN **7** 73, **12** 73, OAKA **12** 74-76, MILA **12** 77-78, *CH* **12** 78-91

HANEY, TODD 2B/OF
(1,20,**24**,18) MONN **1** 92, CHIN **20** 94, **24** 95-96, NYN **18** 98

HANKINS, JAY OF
(21,**9**) KCA **21** 61, **9** 63

HANNA, PRESTON P
(24,39,34,**49**, 55) ATLN **24/39** 75,**34** 76, **49** 77-82, OAKA **55/49** 82

HANNAHS, GERRY (ARK) P
(12,35,**29**) MONN **12** 76,**35** 77, **29** 78-79

HANNAN, JIM P
(**19**,26,16,34) WASA **19** 62, **26** 63, **19** 64-70, DETA **16** 71, MILA **34** 71

HANNING, LOY P
(__,**24**) STLA __ 39, **24** 42

HANSELL, GREG P
(52,**19**,53,57) LAN **52** 95, MINA **19** 96, MILA **53** 97, PITN **57** 99

HANSEN, ANDY (SWEDE) P
(24,28,**44**,20) NYN **24** 44, **28** 45, **44** 47-50, PHIN **20** 51-53

HANSEN, BOB DH/1B
(14,**17**) MILA **14** 74, **17** 76

HANSEN, CRAIG P
(**56**) BOSA **56** 05

HANSEN, DAVE 3B/1B/UTIL
(43,15,5,**25**, 27,10) LAN **43** 90-91, **15** 92-94, **5** 94--96, CHIN **25** 97, LAN **25** 99-02, SDN **25** 03, SEAA **25** 04, SDN **27** 04, SEAA **10** 05

HANSEN, DOUG PR
(**2**) CLEA **2** 51

HANSEN, GUY CH
(43,46,**55**,37) KCA *CH* **43** 92, **46** 92-93, **55** 96-98, **37/55** 05

HANSEN, JED 2B
(**2**) KCA **2** 97-99

HANSEN, ROGER CH
(**25**) SEAA *CH* **25** 92

HANSEN, RON SS/INF/CH
(3,**4**,6,28,2, 18,26) BALA **3** 58-62, CHIA **4** 63-67, WASA **6** 68, CHIA **4** 68-69, NYA **28** 70-71, KCA **2** 72, MILA *CH* **18** 80-83, MONN *CH* **26** 85-87, *CH* **18** 87-89

HANSEN, SNIPE P
(22,19,**45**,25) PHIN **22** 32, **19** 33-34, **45** 34-35, STLA **25** 35

HANSKI, DON 1B/P
(**34**) CHIA **34** 43-44

HANSON, ERIK P
(**39**,40) SEAA **39** 88-93,CINN **39** 94, BOSA **40** 95, TORA **39** 96-98

HANYZEWSKI, ED P
(45,**34**) CHIN **45** 42, **34** 43-46

HARANG, AARON P
(56,**39**) OAKA **56** 02-03, CINN **39** 03-05

HARDEN, RICH P
(16,**40**) OAKA **16** 03, **40** 04-05

HARDER, MEL (CHIEF) P/CH/M
(**18**,43,2,53, 59,3) CLEA **18** 31-47, *CH* **43** 48-62, *M* **43** 61, *CH* **2** 63, NYN *CH* **53** 64, CHIN *CH* **59** 65, CINN *CH* **3** 66-68, KCA *CH* **3** 69

HARDIN, BUD SS/2B
(**41**) CHIN **41** 52

HARDIN, JIM P
(**44**,29,27) BALA **44** 67-71, NYA **29** 71, ATLN **27** 72

HARDTKE, JASON 2B
(**19**) NYN **19** 96-97, CHIN **19** 98

HARDY, CARROLL OF
(**30**,16,26,20) CLEA **30** 58-60, BOSA **16** 60-62, HOUN **26** 63, **20** 64, MINA **30** 67

HARDY, J. J. SS
(**7**) MILN **7** 05

HARDY, JACK P
(45,**27**) CHIA **45/27** 89

HARDY, LARRY P/CH
(**25**,42,53) SDN **25** 74-75, HOUN **42/53** 76, TEXA *CH* **25** 95-98, **48** 98-01

HARDY, RED P
(**38**) NYN **38** 51

HARE, SHAWN OF/DH/1B
(**25**,19,45) DETA **25** 91-92, **10** 92, NYN **19** 94, TEXA **45** 95

HAREN, DANNY P
(50,**55**,24) STLN **50** 03, **55** 04, OAKA **24** 05

HARGAN, STEVE P
(**34**,26,50) CLEA **34** 65-72, TEXA **26** 74-76, TORA **26** 77, TEXA **26** TEXA **26** 77, ATLN **50** 77

HARGESHEIMER, ALAN P
(**40**,50) SFN **40** 80-81, CHIN **50** 83, KCA **50** 86

HARGIS, GARY PR
(**2**) PITN **2** 79

HARGRAVE, BUBBLES C B
(**9**) NYA **9** 30

HARGRAVE, PINKY C B
(__,**9**,23) WASA __ 30, **9** 31, BOSN **9** 32, **23** 33

HARGROVE, MIKE 1B/OF/UTIL/CH/M
(**21**,12,30) TEXA **21** 74-78, SDN **21** 79, CLEA **21** 79-85, *CH* **12** 90-91, *M* **12** 91, *M* **21** 92-98, *M* **30** 98-99, BALA *M* **30** 00, 02, **21** 01,03 SEAA *M* **21** 05

HARIKKALA, TIM P
(**39**,56,46,49) SEAA **39** 95-96, BOSA **56** 99, COLN **46** 04, OAKA **49** 05

HARKEY, MIKE P
(48,**22**,27,32, 19,34,50) CHIN **48** 88, **22** 90-93, COLN **27/32** 94, OAKA **19** 95, CALA **34** 95, LAN **50** 97

HARKNESS, TIM 1B
(15,**3**) LAN **15** 61-62, NYN **3** 63-64

HARLOW, LARRY (HAWK) OF/P/UTIL
(51,36,6,**20**) BALA **51** 75, **34** 77, **6** 78-79, CALA **20** 79-81

HARMAN, BILL C/P
(**30**) PHIN **30** 41

HARMON, CHUCK 3B/UTIL
(**10**,24,27,50) CINN **10** 54-56, STLN **24** 56, **27** 57, PHIN **50** 57-58

HARMON, TERRY INF
(34,19,**17**) PHIN **34** 67, **19** 69, **17** 70-77

HARMON, TOM CH
(**8**) CHIN *CH* **8** 82

HARNISCH, PETE P
(42,**27**,31,38) BALA **42** 88-90, **17** 90, HOUN **27** 91-94, NYN **27** 95-97, MILA **31** 97, CINN **38** 98-01, (02)

HARPER, BRIAN OF/DH/C/UTIL
(7,3,12,25, 32,31) CALA 7 79, 3/12 81, PITN 12 83-84, STLN 25 85, DETA 32 86, OAKA 31 87, MINA 12 88-93, MILA 12 94, OAKA 12 95

HARPER, TERRY OF
(19,17) ATLN 19 80-86, DETA 17 87, PITN 19 87

HARPER, TOMMY 3B/OF/UTIL/CH
(14,17,21,4, 20,31,12,32, 1,51,35) CINN 14 62, 17 63-67, CLEA 21 68,SEAA 21 69,MILA 21 70-71, BOSA 4 72-74, CALA 20/31 75, OAKA 21 75, BALA 12 76, BOSA CH 32 80-84, MONN CH 21 90-96, 1 97-99, BOSA 51 00, 35 00-01, 51 02

HARPER, TRAVIS P
(58) TBA 58 00-05

HARRAH, TOBY SS/3B/UTIL/CH/M
(17,11,10) WASA 17 69, 11 71, TEXA 11 72-78, CLEA 11 79-83, NYA 11 84, TEXA 11 85-86, CH 11 89-92, M 11 92, CLEA CH 11 96, DETA CH 10 98, COLN CH 11 00-02

HARRELL, BILLY SS/INF
(57,37,6,38, 10) CLEA 57 55,37/6 57, 38 58, BOSA 10 61

HARRELL, JOHN C
(9) SFN 9 69

HARRELL, RAY (COWBOY) P
(20,28,16,12, 27,18) STLN 20 35, 28 37-38, CHIN 16 39, PHIN 12 39, PITN 27 40, NYN 18 45

HARRELSON, BILL P
(17) CALA 17 68

HARRELSON, BUD SS/INF/CH/M
(3,14,15,7, 53,23) NYN 3 65-77, PHIN 14 78, 15 79, TEXA 7 80, NYN CH 53 82, CH 23 85-88, CH 3 88-90, M 3 90-91

HARRELSON, KEN (HAWK) IB/OF
(12,4,6,3,40) KCA 12 63-64, 4 64, 6 65-66, 4 66, WASA 3 66-67, KCA 6 67, BOSA 40 67-69, CLEA 40 69-71

HARRIGER, DENNY P
(41) DETA 41 98

HARRINGTON, BILL P
(18,41,26,14) PHIA 18/41 53, KCA 26 55-56, 14 56

HARRINGTON, MICKEY PR
(9) PHIN 9 63

HARRIS, ALONZO PH
(29) HOUN 29 67

HARRIS, BILL P
(44,11,20) PITN 44 32-34, BOSA 11/20 38

HARRIS, BILL P
(21) BKNN 21 57, LAN 21 59

HARRIS, BILLY INF/2B
(15,38) CLEA 15 68, KCA 38/15 69

HARRIS, BOB P
(14,26,12,19, 24,20,25) DETA 14 38, 26 39, STLA 12/ 24/20 39, 24 40-41, 20 42, PHIA 25 42

HARRIS, BRENDAN 2B/3B
(19,12,54) CHIN 19 04, MONN 12 04, WASN 54 05

HARRIS, BUCKY 2B/M
(34,32,27,30, 28, 24,37,50) DETA 34 31, M 32 31-33, BOSA 27 34, WASA M 35 35, 30 36-40, M 28 41-42, PHIN M 24 43, NYA M 37 47-48, WASA M 50 50-54, DETA M 32 55-56

HARRIS, BUDDY P
(46) HOUN 46 70-71

HARRIS, CHARLIE (BUBBA) P
(17,18) PHIA 17 48-49, 51, CLEA 18 51

HARRIS, DAVE (SHERIFF) OF/UTIL
(26,24) WASA 26 31, 24 32-34

HARRIS, DONALD OF/DH
(33,18) TEXA 33 91-92, 18 92-93

HARRIS, GAIL 1B
(15,14,5) NYN 15 55-56, 14 57, DETA 5 58-60

HARRIS, GENE P
(61,41,47,33, 38,29) MONN 61 89, SEAA 41 89, 47 89-92, SDN 33 92-94, DETA 38 94, PHIN 33 95, BALA 29 95

HARRIS, GREG A. P
(20,37,33,42, 27,34,29) NYN 20 81, CINN 37/33 82-83, MONN 20 84, SDN 42 84, TEXA 27 85-87, PHIN 33 88-89, BOSA 42 89, 27 89-94, NYA 34 94, MONN 29 95

HARRIS, GREG W. P
(46,27,31,23) SDN 46 88-93, COLN 27 93, 31/46 94, MINA 23 95

HARRIS, HERB (HUB)(LEFTY) P
(43) PHIN 43 36

HARRIS, JEFF P
(58) SEAA 58 05

HARRIS, JOHN 1B
(9,13) CALA 9 79-80, 13 81

HARRIS, LENNY 3B/UTIL
(56,7,29,28, 19,16,18,10) CINN 56 88, 7 88-89, LAN 29 89-93, CINN 28 94-98, NYN 19 98, COLN 28 99, ARIN 29 99-00, NYN 19 00-01, MILN 16 02, CHIN 29 03, FLAN 18 03, 10 03 -05

HARRIS, LUM P/CH/M
(18,12,40,26, 6) PHIA 18 41-44, 46, WASA 12 47, CHIA CH 40 51-54, BALA CH 26 55-61, M 26 61, HOUN CH 6 62-64, M 6 64, M 26 65, ATLN M 26 68-72

HARRIS, MICKEY P
(20,19,14,34, 35,17,20) BOSA 20 40, 19 41, 46-49, WASA 14/34/35 49, 17 50-52, CLEA 20 52

HARRIS, NED OF
(24,28,26) DETA 24 41, 28 42, 26 42-43, 46

HARRIS, PEP P
(48) CALA 48 96, ANAA 48 97-99

HARRIS, REGGIE P
(57,32,23,40, 44,45) OAKA 57 90, 32 91, BOSA 23 96, PHIN 40 97, HOUN 44 98, MILN 45 99

HARRIS, VIC 2B/SS/UTIL
(7,4,20,28) TEXA 7 72-73, CHIN 4 74-75, STLN 4 76, SFN 20 77-78, MILA 28 80

HARRIS, WILLIE OF/2B
(40,12,13) BALA 40 01, CHIA 12 02-03, 13 03, 1 04-05

HARRISON, BOB P
(47) BALA 47 55-56

HARRISON, CHUCK 1B
(35,22,17,7) HOUN 35/22 65, 17 66-67, KCA 7 69, 71

HARRISON, RORIC P
(44,24,27,37) BALA 44 72, ATLN 24 73-75, CLEA 27 75, MINA 37 78

HARRISON, TOM P
(35,23) KCA 35/2365

HARRIST, EARL (IRISH) P
(18,49,28,35, 39) CINN 18 45, CHIA 49 47-48, WASA 49/28 48, STLA 35 52, CHIA 35 53, DETA 35/39 53

HARSHANY, SAM C
(__,4,21,9,8) STLA __ 37, 4 38, 21/9 39, 8 40

HARSHMAN, JACK 1B/P
(8,15,29,39, 23) NYN 8 48, 15 50, 29 52, CHIA 29 54-57, BALA 29 58-59, BOSA 39 59,CLEA 23 59-60

HART, BILL 3B/SS/INF
(9,6) BKNN 9 43, 6 44-45

HART, BO 2B
(31) STLN 31 03-04

HART, COREY OF
(1) MILN 1 04-05

HART, JASON 1B
(16) TEXA 16 02

HART, JIM RAY 3B/OF/DH
(16,43) SFN 16 63-73, NYA 43 73-74

HART, JOHN CH/M
(47,__) CLEA CH 47 88, M __ 89

HART, MIKE OF
(30,31,36) TEXA 30 80, MINA 31 84, BALA 36 87

HARTENSTEIN, CHUCK (TWIGGY) P/CH
(42,22,50,26, 44,20,23,24, 2) CHIN 42 65-68, PITN 42 69, 22 70, STLN 50/26/22 70, BOSA 44/20/23 70, TORA 24 77, CLEA CH 2 79, MILA CH 24 87-90

HARTGRAVES, DEAN P
(58,34,45) HOUN 58 95-96, ATLN 34 96, SFN 45 98

HARTJE, CHRIS C
(23) BKNN 23 39

HARTLEY, GROVER (SLICK) CH
(35,33,34) PITN CH 35 32-33, STLA 27 34-36, NYN 33/34 46

HARTLEY, MIKE P
(43,46,42,49, 39) LAN 43 89, 46 90-91, PHIN 42 91-92, MINA 49 93, BOSA 49 95, BALA 39 95

HARTMAN, BOB P
(34,31,26) MILN 34/31 59, CLEA 26 62

HARTMAN, J. C. SS
(18) HOUN 18 62-63

HARTNETT, GABBY C/1B/M/CH
(9,7,2,48) CHIN 9/7 32, 9 33-36, 2 37-40, M 2 38-40, NYN 9 41, KCA CH 48 65

HARTS, GREG PH
(6) NYN 6 73

HARTSFIELD, ROY (SPEC) 2B/CH/M
(12,7) BOSN 12 50-52, LAN CH 7 69-72, ATLN CH 7 73, TORA M 7 77-79

HARTSOCK, JEFF P
(44) CHIN 44 92

HARTUNG, CLINT (THE HONDO HURRICANE) (HONDO) P/OF
(23,36,26,33) NYN 23 47-48, 36 49-50, 26 51, 33 52

HARTZELL, PAUL P
(58,45,18,28, 39) CALA 58 76, 45 76-78, MINA 18 79, BALA 28 80, MILA 39 84

HARVEY, BRYAN P
(38,34) CALA 38 87, 34 88-92, FLAN 34 93-95

HARVEY, KEN 1B/DH
(28) KCA 28 01, 03-05

HARVILLE, CHAD P
(56,32,31,43) OAKA 56 99, 32 01, 03-04, 31 04, HOUN 43 04-05, BOSA 43 05

HASEGAWA, SHIGETOSHI P
(21,17) ANAA 21 97-01, SEAA 17 02-05

HASELMAN, BILL C/DH/UTIL
(33,15,37) TEXA 33 90, SEAA 15 92, 33 93-94, BOSA 37 95-97, TEXA 37 98, DETA 37 99, TEXA 33 00-02, BOSA CH 37 05

HASENMAYER, DON 3B/2B
(21,40) PHIN 21 45, 40 46

HASH, HERB P
(26,29,24) BOSA 26/29 40, 24 41

HASLIN, MICKEY 2B/INF
(18,5,22,42, 25,6,21,19, 27) PHIN 18/5 33, 22 34, 42 35, 25 36, BOSN 6 36, NYN 21 37, 19/27 38

HASSETT, BUDDY 1B/OF
(6,22,2,34) BKNN 6 36-37, 22 38, BOSN 6 39, 2 40-41, NYA 34 42

HASSEY, RON C/UTIL/DH/CH
(9,15,12,25, 24,27,29,28) CLEA 9 78-84, CHIN 15 84, NYA 12 85-86, 34 86, CHIA 25 86-87, OAKA 24 88-89, 27 89-90, MONN 24 91, COLN CH 29 93-95, STLN CH 28 96, SEAA CH 9 05

HASSLER, ANDY P
(42,43,16,48, 31,50,44,41, 47) CALA 42 71, 73-76, KCA 43 76, 16 76-78, BOSA 48 78, 31 78-79, NYN 50/44 79, PITN 41 80, CALA 47 80, 41 80-83, STLN 44 84-85, 41 85

HASSON, GENE 1B
(35,5) PHIA 35 37, 5 38

HATCHER, BILLY OF/CH
(22,28,29,3 14,2) CHIN 22 84-85, HOUN 28 86-89, PITN 29 89, CINN 22 90-92, BOSA 22 92-94, PHIN 3 94, TEXA 14 95, TBA CH 22 98-03, 2 03-04, 20 05

HATCHER, CHRIS OF
(51) KCA 51 98

HATCHER, MICKEY OF/3B/UTIL/CH
(44,9,43,7) LAN 44 79-80, MINA 44 81, 9 81-86, LAN 9 87-90, TEXA CH 43 93-94, LAN CH 9 98, ANAA CH 7 00-04, LAA CH 7 05

HATFIELD, FRED 3B/INF/CH
(39,27,1,2,3, 7,33,51) BOSA 39 50, 27 51, 1 52, DETA 2 52, 1 52-56, CHIA 3 56-57, CLEA 7 58, CINN 33 58, DETA CH 51 77-78

HATHAWAY, HILLY P
(48) CALA 48 92-93

HATHAWAY, RAY P/CH
(22,61) BKNN 22 45, CLEA CH 61 72

HATTEBERG, SCOTT C/1B/DH
(30,47,10) BOSA 30 95, 47 96, 10 97-01, OAKA 10 02-05

HATTEN, JOE P
(19,53) BKNN 19 46-51, CHIN 53 51, 19 52

HATTER, CLYDE P
(12,21) DETA 12 35, 21 37

HATTON, GRADY 3B/INF/M/CH
(15,3,1,28, 5,20) CINN 15 46-54, CHIA 3 54, BOSA 1 54-56, STLN 28 56, BALA 5 56, CHIN 20 60, HOUN M 1 66-68, CH 1 73-74

HAUGHEY, CHRIS (BUD) P
(14) BKNN 14 43

HAUGHT, GARY P
(49) OAKA 49 97

HAUGSTAD, PHIL P
(20,45) BKNN 20 47-48, 51, CINN 45 52

HAUSMAN, TOM P
(38,25,18,32 34) MILA 38/25/38 75, 18 75-76, NYN 32 78-82, ATLN 34 82

HAUSMANN, CLEM P
(21,34) BOSA 21 44-45, PHIA 34 49

HAUSMANN, GEORGE 2B
(12) NYN 12 44-45, 49

HAVENS, BRAD P
(27,31,47,41, 22,55) MINA 27 81-83, BALA 31 85-86, 47 86, LAN 41 87-88, CLEA 22 88-89, DETA 55 89

HAWBLITZEL, RYAN P
(13) COLN 13 96

HAWES, ROY 1B
(26) WASA 26 51

HAWKINS, ANDY P
(40,56) SDN 63 82, 40 82-88, NYA 40 89-91, OAKA 56/41 91

HAWKINS, LA TROY P
(32) MINA 32 95-03, CHIN 32 04-05, SFN 32 05

HAWKINS, WYNN (HAWK) P
(34) CLEA 34 60-62

HAWPE, BRAD OF
(11) COLN 11 04-05

HAYDEL, HAL P
(30) MINA 30 70-71

HAYDEN, GENE (LEFTY) P
(31) CINN 31 58

HAYES, BEN P
(50,45) CINN 50 82, 45 82-83

HAYES, BILL C/CH
(16,50) CHIN 16 80-81, COLN CH 50 98

HAYES, CHARLIE 3B/INF
(26,8,28,13, 17,33,14) SFN 26 88-89, PHIN 8 89-91, NYA 28 92, COLN 13 93-94, PHIN 13 95, PITN 17 96, NYA 33 96, 13 97, SFN 13 98-99, MILN 14 00, HOUN 14 01

HAYES, FRANKIE (BLIMP) C
(no#,28,2,1, 8,11,26,25) PHIA no# 33, 28 34, 2 36, 1 37, 8 38-42, STLA 8 42-43, PHIA 8 44-45, CLEA 11 45-46, CHIA 26/8 46, BOSA 25 47

HAYES, JACKIE 2B/INF
(22,5,2,37) WASA 22 31, CHIA 5 32, 2 33-35, 37 36-39, 2 40

HAYES, JIM (WHITEY) P
(14) WASA 14 35

HAYES, VON OF/IB/UTIL
(8,26,9) CLEA 8 81-82, PHIN 26 83, 9 83-91, CALA 9 92

HAYNES, HEATH P
(41) MONN 41 94

HAYNES, JIMMY P
(60,50,51,43) BALA 60 95, 50 96, OAKA 51 97-99, MILN 51 00-01, CINN 43 02-04

HAYNES, JOE P/CH
(19,23,35,26, 18,55) WASA 19 39-40, CHIA 23 41, 35 41-48, WASA 26 49-50, 18 50-52, CH 55 53-56

HAYWARD, RAY P
(32) TEXA 32 88

HAYWOOD, BILL P
(21) WASA 21 68

HAYWOOD, RAY P
(58,25) SDN 58 86, 25 87

HAYWORTH, RAY C/CH
(9,23,__,10, 14,32,46) DETA 9 31, 23 32-38, BKNN __ 38, 10 39, NYN 14 39, STLA 10 42, BKNN 32 44-45, CH 32 45, CHIN CH 46 55

HAYWORTH, RED C
(9) STLA 9 44-45

HAZEWOOD, DRUNGO P
(41) BALA 41 80

HAZLE, BOB (HURRICANE) OF
(26,12,27) CINN 26 55, MILN 12 57-58, DETA 27 58

HEAD, ED P
(23,19) BKNN 23 40-43, 19 44, 23 46

HEALY, FRAN C/DH
(45,5,6,16, 40) KCA 45 69, SFN 5 71-72, 6 72, KCA 16 73-76, NYA 40 76-78

HEALY, FRANCIS C/UTIL
(24,27) NYN 24 32, STLN 27 34

HEARD, JAY P
(38) BALA 38 54-55

HEARN, ED CH
(49,7) NYN 49 86, KCA 7 87-88

HEARN, JIM P
(34,21,22) STLN 34 47-50, NYN 34 50, 21 50-56, PHIN 22 57-59

HEARRON, JEFF C
(54) TORA 54 85-86

HEATH, BILL C
(34,8,38,19) CHIA 34 65, HOUN 8 66-67, DETA 38 67, CHIN 19 69

HEATH, JEFF OF
(21,24,4,33,3, 18,20) CLEA 21 36, 24 37-44, 4 45, 33 40, WASA 3 46, STLA 18 46, 20 47, BOSN 4 48-49

HEATH, KELLY 2B
(45) KCA 45 82

HEATH, MICKEY 1B
(no#) CINN no# 32

HEATH, MIKE C/UTIL
(46,48,2,5,8) NYA 46 78, OAKA 48 79-80, 2 81-85, STLN 5 86, DETA 8 86-90, ATLN 8 91

HEATH, TOMMY C
(9,19) STLA 9 35, 19 37, 9 38

HEATHCOCK, JEFF P
(31,41) HOUN 3183, 85, 87-88, 41 88

HEATHCOTE, CLIFF 1B
(no#,15) CINN no# 32, PHIN 15 32

HEATHCOTT, MIKE P
(66) CHIA 66 98

HEATON, NEAL P
(44,32,26,41, 46,27,53) CLEA 44 82-86, MINA 32 86, MONN 41 87, 26 87-88, PITN 26 89-91, KCA 46/26 92, MILA 27 92, NYA 53 93

HEAVERLO, DAVE P
(60,33) SFN 6075-77, OAKA 33 78, 60 78-79, SEAA 60 80, OAKA 60 81

HEBERT, WALLY (PREACHER) P
(27,19,21) STLA 27 31, 19 32-33, PITN 21 43

HEBNER, RICHIE 3B/1B/UTIL/CH
(20,3,18,2, 10,32,7) PITN 20 68-71, 3 72-76, PHIN 18 77-78, NYN 3 79, DETA 2 80-82, PITN 10 82-83, CHIN 18 84-85, BOSA CH 32 89-91, PHIN CH 7 01

HEBSON, BRYAN P
(59) MONN 59 03

HEDLUND, MIKE (RED) P
(41,36,32) CLEA 41 65, 36 68, KCA 32 69-72

HEEP, DANNY OF/1B/UTIL/P
(20,24,25,12, 29,17) HOUN 20 79-80, 24 81-82, NYN 25 83-86, LAN 12 87-88, BOSA 29 89-90, ATLN 17 91

HEFFERNAN, BERT C
(6) SEAA 6 92

HEFFNER, BOB P
(20,37) BOSA 20 63-65, CLEA 37 66, CALA 37 68

HEFFNER, DON (JEEP) 2B/UTIL/CH
(10,1,22,5,39, 31,52,23) NYA 10 34-37, STLA 1 38-43, PHIA 22 43, DETA 5 44, KCA CH 39 58-60, DETA CH 31 61, NYN CH 52 64-65, CINN M 10 66, CALA CH 23 67-68

HEFLIN, BRONSON P
(43) PHIN 43 96

HEFLIN, RANDY (WHALE) P
(41,19,26) BOSA 41/19 45, 26 46

HEGAN, JIM C/CH F
(30,14,10,4, 15,38,27,41, 9,44,50,48) CLEA 30 41, 40 42, 14 46, 10 47-50, 4 51-57, DETA 15 58, PHIN 38 58-59, SFN 27 59, CHIN 41 60, 9 60, NYA CH 44 60-73, DETA CH 50 74-78, NYA CH 48 79-80

HEGAN, MIKE 1B/OF/UTIL S
(12,34,8,20, 18,6,4) NYA 12 64, 34 66-67, SEAA 8 69, MILA 8 70-71, OAKA 20 71-73, NYA 18 73-74, MILA 6 74-76, 4 77,

HEGMAN, BOB 2B
(61) KCA 61 85

HEIDEMANN, JACK SS/INF/DH
(**18**,17,11,12,8) CLEA **18** 69-72, **17** 74, STLN **11** 74, NYN **12** 75-76, MILA **8** 76-77

HEILMANN, AARON P
(**48**) NYN **48** 03-05

HEILMANN, HARRY (SLUG) 1B
(**no#**) CINN **no#** 32

HEIM, VAL OF
(**2**) CHIA **2** 42

HEIMACH, FRED (LEFTY) P
(17,**18**) NYA **17** 29, BKNN **18** 32-33

HEIMUELLER, GORMAN P
(**13**) OAKA **13** 83-84

HEINKLE, DON P
(17,**30**) DETA **17** 88, STLN **30** 89

HEINTZ, CHRIS C
(**41**) MINA **41** 05

HEINTZELMAN, KEN P
(44,53,32,20,**27**) PITN **44** 37, **53** 38-39, **32** 40-42, **20** 46-47, PHIN **27** 47-52

HEINTZELMAN, TOM 2B/INF
(**5**,32,34) STLN **5** 73-74, SFN **32** 77-78, **34** 78

HEISE, BOB INF
(23,29,17,**2**,28,9,12,6) NYN **23** 67-68, **28** 69, SFN **17** 70-71, MILA **2** 71-73, STLN **29** 74, CALA **9** 74, BOSA **12** 75-76, KCA **6** 77

HEISE, CLARENCE (LEFTY) P
(**27**) STLN **27** 34

HEISE, JIM P
(**34**) WASA **34** 57

HEISER, ROY P
(**47**) WASA **47** 61

HEISERMAN, RICK INF
(**48**,62) STLN **48/62** 99

HEIST, AL OF/CH
(18,**22**,6,19) CHIN **18** 60, **22** 61, HOUN **22** 62, *CH* **6** 66-67, SDN *CH* **19** 80

HELD, MEL (COUNTRY) P
(**40**) BALA **40** 56

HELD, WOODIE SS/UTIL
(27,38,5,3,**12**,15,9) NYA **27** 54, 57, KCA **38** 57, **5** 58, CLEA **3** 58-62, **12** 63-64, WASA **12** 65, BALA **12** 66-67, CALA **15** 67-68, CHIA **9** 68-69

HELF, HANK C
(10,40,11) CLEA **10** 38, **40** 40, STLA **11** 46

HELFAND, ERIC C
(48,**6**) OAKA **48** 93-94, **6** 95

HELLING, RICK P
(**32**,33,35,38) TEXA **32** 94-96, FLAN **33** 96-97, TEXA **32** 97-01, ARIN **32** 02, BALA **35** 03, FLAN **38** 03, MILN **30** 05

HELMS, TOMMY 2B/UTIL/CH/M
(**19**,15,24,49,12,37) CINN **19** 64-71, HOUN **19** 72-75, PITN **15** 76-77, **24** 77, BOSA **49/12** 77, TEXA *CH* **37** 81, *CH* **19** 81-82, CINN *CH* **19** 83-89, *M* **19** 89

HELMS, WES 3B/1B
(9,**18**) ATLN **9** 98, **18** 00-02, MILN **18** 03-05

HELTON, TODD OF/1B
(**17**) COLN **17** 97-05

HELTZEL, HEINIE 3B/SS
(**8**,21) BOSN **8** 43, PHIN **21** 44

HEMAN, RUSS P
(**20**,46) CLEA **20** 61, LAA **46** 61

HEMOND, SCOTT 3B/UTIL
(31,16,36,**2**,26) OAKA **31** 89-92, **16** 92, CHIA **36** 92, OAKA **2** 93-94, STLN **26** 95

HEMPHILL, BRENT C
(**4**) ANAA **4** 99

HENDERSON, DAVE OF/DH
(**42**,40,41) SEAA **42** 81-86, BOSA **40** 86, **42** 87, SFN **41** 87, OAKA **42** 88-93, KCA **42** 94

HENDERSON, JOE P
(40,**53**,50) CHIA **40** 74,CINN **53/50** 76-77

HENDERSON, KEN OF/DH
(23,43,**15**,24,28,7,20,10,19) SFN **23** 65, **43** 66, **15** 67-72, CHIA, **24** 73-75, ATLN **28/7** 76, TEXA**20** 77, NYN **20/10** 78**,** CINN **19** 78-79, CHIN **24** 79-80

HENDERSON, RAMON CH
(**59**,31) PHIN *CH* **59** 99-03, **31** 04-05

HENDERSON, RICKEY OF/DH
(35,**24**,14,25) OAKA **35** 79-84, NYA **24** 85-89, OAKA **24** 89-93, TORA **14/24** 93, OAKA **24** 94-95, SDN **24** 96 -97, ANAA **24** 97, OAKA **24** 98, NYN **24** 99-00, SEAA **35** 00, SDN **24** 01, BOSA **35** 02, LAN **25** 03

HENDERSON, ROD P
(20,**53**) MONN **20** 94, MILN **53** 98-99

HENDERSON, STEVE OF/DH/CH
(**5**,28,55) NYN **5** 77-80, CHIN **28** 81-82, SEAA **5** 83-84, OAKA **5** 85-86, **24** 87, HOUN **5** 88, *CH* **55** 94-96, TBA *CH* **5** 98

HENDLEY, BOB P
(36,38,**33**) MILN **36** 61-63, SFN **38** 64-65, CHIN **33** 65-67, NYN **33** 67

HENDRICK, GEORGE OF/DH/CH
(31,**25**,20,1,21,15,24,22) OAKA **31** 71, **25** 71-72, CLEA **20** 73-74, **21** 75-76, **1** 76, SDN **20** 77, **25** 77-78, STLN **27** 78, **25** 78-84, PITN **15** 85, CALA **25** 85-88, STLN *CH* **25** 96-97, ANAA *CH* **24** 98-99, LAN *CH* **22** 03

HENDRICK, HARVEY (GINK) 3B/1B/UTIL
(no#,**4**,8,32) STLN **no#** 32, CINN **4** 32, CHIN **8** 33, PHIN **32** 34

HENDRICKS, ELROD (ELLIE) C/UTIL/CH
(**10**,39,18,44) BALA **10** 68-72, CHIN **39** 72, BALA **10** 73-76, NYA **18** 76-77, BALA **44** 78-79, BALA *CH* **44** 78-05

HENDRICKSON, BEN P
(**40**) MILN **40** 04

HENDRICKSON, DON P
(24,35,**34**) BOSN **24** 45, **35/34** 46

HENDRICKSON, MARK P
(**43**,30) TORA **43** 02-03, TBA **30** 04-05

HENGEL, DAVE OF/DH
(**38**,20,16) SEAA **38** 86, **20** 87, **16** 88, CLEA **38** 89

HENKE, TOM P
(35,**50**) TEXA **35** 82-84, TORA **50** 85-92, TEXA **50** 93-94, STLN **50** 95

HENLEY, BOB C
(54,**13**) MONN **54** 98, **13** 98-99

HENLEY, GAIL OF
(**26**) PITN **26** 54

HENLINE, BUTCH C
(**12**) CHIA **12** 31

HENN, SEAN P
(**58**) NYA **58** 05

HENNEMAN, MIKE P
(**39**) DETA **39** 87-95, HOUN **39** 95, TEXA **39** 96

HENNESSEY, BRAD P
(**41**) SFN **41** 04-05

HENNESSEY, GEORGE (THREE-STAR) P
(**25**,31,27) STLA **25** 37, PHIN **31** 42, CHIN **27** 45

HENNIGAN, PHIL P
(**38**,34) CLEA **38** 69-72, NYN **34** 73

HENNINGER, RICK P
(22,**35**) TEXA **22/35** 73

HENNIS, RANDY P
(**54**) HOUN **54** 90

HENRICH, BOBBY UTIL/INF
(**17**) CINN **17** 57-59

HENRICH, TOMMY (OLD RELIABLE)(THE CLUTCH) OF/1B/CH
(22,17,7,**15**,2,31) NYA **22** 37, **17** 38-39, **7** 39-42, **15** 46-50, *CH* **15** 51, NYN *CH* **2/7** 57, DETA *CH* **31** 58-59

HENRIQUEZ, OSCAR P
(54,**41**) HOUN **54** 97, FLAN **41** 98, DETA **41** 02

HENRY, BILL (F.) P
(**29**) NYA **29** 66

HENRY, BILL (R.) P
(26,28,29,19,37,**44**,45,46,31,41) BOSA **26** 52, **28** 53-54, **29** 54-55, CHIN **19** 58, **37** 59, CINN **44** 60-65, SFN **45** 65-67, **46** 67, **45** 68, PITN **31** 68, HOUN **41** 69

HENRY, BUTCH P
(50,**27**) HOUN **50** 92, COLN **27** 93, MONN **27** 93-95, BOSA **27** 96-98, SEAA **27** 99

HENRY, DOUG P
(**28**,35,57,43,19) MILA **28** 91-94, NYN **35** 95-96, SFN **57** 97, HOUN **43** 98, **19** 98 -00, SFN **57** 00, KCA **19** 01

HENRY, DWAYNE P
(36,**45**,46,47,48,22,38) TEXA **36** 84, **45** 84-88, ATLN **46** 89-90, HOUN **47** 91, CINN **48** 92-93, SEAA **48/22** 93, DETA **38** 95

HENRY, EARL (HOOK) P
(**34**) CLEA **34** 44-45

HENRY, JIM P
(**21**,12) BOSA **21** 36-37, PHIN **12** 39

HENRY, RON C/1B
(11,12) MINA **11** 61, **12** 64

HENSHAW, ROY (KID) P
(34,**22**,31,21,18) CHIN **34** 33, **22** 35-36, BKNN **22** 37, STLN **31** 38, DETA **21** 42, **18** 43-44

HENSIEK, PHIL (SID) P
(**12**) WASA **12** 35

HENSLEY, CHUCK P
(**26**) SFN **26** 86

HENSLEY, CLAY P
(**52**) SDN **52** 05

HENSLEY, MATT P
(**52**) ANAA **52** 04, LAA **(52)** (05)

HENSON, DREW DH/3B
(57,**38**) NYA **57** 02, **38** 03

HENTGEN, PAT P
(**41**) TORA **41** 91-99, STLN **41** 00, BALA **41** 01-03, TORA **41** 04

HEPLER, BILL P
(46,**28**) NYN **46/28** 66

HERBEL, RON P
(**34**,31,29) SFN **34** 63-69, SDN **34** 70, NYN **31** 70, ATLN **29** 71

HERBERT, RAY P
(24,30,20,45,17,38,**21**) DETA **24/30** 50, **20** 51, **45** 53, **20** 53-54, KCA **17** 55, **38** 58-61, CHIA **21** 61-64, PHIN **21** 65-66

HEREDIA, FELIX P
(24,**49**,35,94,45,46) FLAN **24** 96, **49** 97-98, CHIN **35** 98, **49** 98-00, **94** 01, TORA **49** 02, CINN **49** 03, NYA **45** 03-04, NYN **46** 05

HEREDIA, GIL P
(36,52,**34**,37,31) SFN **36** 91-92, MONN **52** 92, **34** 93-95, TEXA **37** 96, OAKA **31** 98-01

HEREDIA, UBALDO P
(**35**) MONN **35** 87

HEREDIA, WILSON P
(55,**48**) TEXA **55** 95, **48** 97

HERGES, MATT P
(**49**) LAN **49** 99-01, MONN **49** 02, SDN **52** 03, SFN **48** 03-05, ARIN **31** 05

HERMAN, BABE OF/1B/CH
(5,**4**,14,11,6,37,32,3,41) CHIN **5** 32, **4** 33-34, PITN **14** 35, CINN **11** 35, **6** 36, DETA **27** 37, BKNN **32/4/3** 45, PITN *CH* **41** 51

HERMAN, BILLY 2B/INF/M/CH
(2,**4**,16,20,11,22,8,35) CHIN **2** 32-36, **4** 37-41, BKNN **16** 41-43, 46, BOSN **20** 46, PITN **11** 47, *M* **11** 47, BKNN *CH* **22** 52-57, MILN *CH* **8** 58-59, BOSA *CH* **35** 60-64, *M* **35** 64-66, CALA *CH* **22** 67, SDN *CH* **22** 78-79

HERMANSEN, CHAD OF
(**3**,31,41,33) PITN **3** 99-01, **31** 02, CHIN **3** 02, LAN **41** 03, TORA **33** 04

HERMANSKI, GENE OF
(14,**22**,48,7) BKNN **14** 43, **22** 46-51, CHIN **48** 51, **22** 52-53, PITN **7** 53

HERMANSON, DUSTIN P
(48,**30**,31,32) SDN **48** 95-96, MONN **30** 97-00, STLN **30** 01 BOSA **31** 02 , STLN **32** 03, SFN **32** 03-04, CHIA **32** 05

HERMIDA, JEREMY OF
(**27**) FLAN **27** 05

HERMOSO, ANGEL (REMY) SS/2B/INF
(16,**37**,4) ATLN **16** 67, MONN **37** 69-70, CLEA **4** 74

HERNAIZ, JESUS P
(**47**) PHIN **47** 74

HERNANDEZ, ADRIAN (EL DUQUECITO) P
(**65**,31) NYA **65** 01-02, MILN **31** 04

HERNANDEZ, ALEX 1B/OF
(19,**27**) PITN **19** 00, **27** 01

HERNANDEZ, ANDERSON INF
(**1**) NYN **1** 05

HERNANDEZ, CARLOS (A.) C
(41,26,65,**9**,8) LAN **41** 90-93, **26** 94-96, SDN **65** 97, **9** 97-98, (99), 00, STLN **8** 00, (01)

HERNANDEZ, CARLOS (Ed.) SS
(**4**,20) HOUN **4** 99, SEAA **20** 00

HERNANDEZ, CARLOS (E.) P
(55,**27**) HOUN **55** 01-02, (03), **27** 04

HERNANDEZ, CESAR OF
(**58**) CINN **58** 92-93

HERNANDEZ, CHICO C
(9,12) CHIN **9** 42, **12** 43

HERNANDEZ, CHUCK CH
(73,**55**) CALA *CH* **73** 92, NYN *CH* **55** 93-96, TBA *CH* **55** 04-05

HERNANDEZ, ENZO SS
(**11**,3) SDN **11** 71-77, LAN **3** 78

HERNANDEZ, EVELIO P
(29,**34**) WASA **29** 56, **34** 57

HERNANDEZ, FELIX P
(**59**) SEAA **59** 05

HERNANDEZ, FERNANDO P
(**42**) DETA **42** 97

HERNANDEZ, JACKIE SS/3B/UTIL
(12,**24**,2) CALA **12** 65-66, MINA **24** 67-68, KCA **24** 69-70, PITN **2** 71-73

HERNANDEZ, JEREMY P
(**50**,53,42) SDN **50** 91-93, CLEA **53** 93, FLAN **42** 94-95

HERNANDEZ, JOSE SS/3B/2B
(3,2,**18**,16,15,11) TEXA **3** 91, CLEA **2** 92, CHIN **18** 94-99, ATLN **16** 99, MILN **18** 00-02, COLN **18** 03, CHIN **15** 03, PITN **16** 03, LAN **18** 04, CLEA **11** 05

HERNANDEZ, KEITH (MEX) 1B
(18,37,**17**) STLN **18** 74-75, **37** 76-83, NYN **17** 83-89, CLEA **17** 90

HERNANDEZ, LEO 3B/UTIL
(**3**,38) BALA **3** 82-83, 85, NYA **38** 86

HERNANDEZ, LIVAN P B
(**61**) FLAN **61** 96-99, SFN **61** 99-02, MONN **61** 03-04, WASN **61** 05

HERNANDEZ, MANNY P
(**38**,36) HOUN **38** 86-87, NYN **36** 89

HERNANDEZ, MICHEL C
(**57**) NYA **57** 03

HERNANDEZ, ORLANDO (EL DUQUE) P B
(**26**) NYA **26** 98-02, 04, CHIA **26** 05

HERNANDEZ, PEDRO UTIL
(**29**,39) TORA **29** 79, **39** 82

HERNANDEZ, RAMON P
(24,47,33,51,**36**,29) ATLN **24/47** 67, CHIN **33** 68, PITN **51** 71, **36** 71-76, CHIN **36** 76-77, BOSA **29** 77

HERNANDEZ, RAMON (J.) C
(**55**) OAKA **55** 99-03, SDN **55** 04-05

HERNANDEZ, ROBERTO P
(**39**,34,35) CHIA **39** 91-97, SFN **39** 97, TBA **39** 98-00, KCA **39** 01-02, ATLN **34** 03, PHIN **35** 04, NYN **39** 05

HERNANDEZ, RUDY P
(11,23) WASA **11** 60, **23** 61

HERNANDEZ, RUDY SS
(**19**) CHIA **19** 72

HERNANDEZ, RUNELVIS P
(**40**) KCA **40** 02-03, (04), 05

HERNANDEZ, TOBY C
(**1**) TORA **1** 84

HERNANDEZ, WILLIE P
(**38**,48,21) CHIN **38** 77-83, PHIN **48** 83, DETA **21** 84-89

HERNANDEZ, XAVIER P
(42,**31**,37,41) TORA **42** 89, HOUN **31** 90-93, NYA **31** 93-94, CINN **37** 95-96, HOUN **41/31** 96, TEXA **31** 97-98

HERNDON, JUNIOR P
(**59**) SDN **59** 01

HERNDON, LARRY OF
(49,**31**,54) STLN **49** 74, SFN **31** 76-81, DETA **31** 82-88, *CH* **54** 92, *CH* **31** 92-98

HERR, TOMMY 2B/UTIL
(**28**,33) STLN **28** 79-88, MINA **33** 88, PHIN **28** 89-90, NYN **28** 90-91, SFN **28** 91

HERRERA, ALEX P
(**49**,59) CLEA **49** 02, **59** 03

HERRERA, JOE (LOCO) OF/UTIL
(34,22,38,**37**) HOUN **34** 67, **22** 68, MONN **38/37** 69-70

HERRERA, JOSE P
(**44**) OAKA **44** 95-96

HERRERA, PANCHO 3B/1B/INF
(**18**,7) PHIN **18** 58, 60, **7** 61

HERRERA, TITO (BOBBY) P
(**25**) STLA **25** 51

HERRIAGE, TROY (DUTCH) P
(**17**) KCA **17** 56

HERRIN, TOM P
(24,29) BOSA **24/29** 54

HERRING, ART (RED) (SANDY) P
(41,**18**,29,17,3,16,21,27) DETA **41** 31, **18** 32-33, BKNN **29** 34, CHIA **17** 39, BKNN **3** 44, **16** 45, **21** 46, PITN **27** 47

HERRMANN, ED C/DH
(42,**12**,45,8,34) CHIA **42** 67, **12** 69-74, NYA **45** 75, CALA **12** 76, HOUN **8** 76-78, MONN **34** 78

HERRMANN, LEROY P
(**23**,21,20) CHIN **23** 32, **21** 33, CINN **20** 35

HERRNSTEIN, JOHN OF/1B
(21,44,**22**,7,26) PHIN **21** 62, **44** 63-64, **22** 64-66, CHIN **7** 66, ATLN **26** 66

HERRSCHER, RICK UTIL
(**6**) NYN **6** 62

HERSCH, EARL OF
(**28**) MILN **28** 56

HERSHBERGER, MIKE OF
(40,**3**,6,15) CHIA **40** 61-64, KCA **3** 65-67, OAKA **3** 68-69, MILA **6** 70, CHIA **15** 71

HERSHBERGER, WILLARD (BILL) C/2B
(50,**5**) CINN **50** 38, **5** 39-40

HERSHISER, OREL P/CH
(**55**,53) LAN **55** 83-94, CLEA **55** 95-97, SFN **53** 98, NYN **55** 99, LAN **55** 00, TEXA *CH* **55** 02-05

HERTWECK, NEAL 1B
(**40**) STLN **40** 52

HERTZ, STEVE 3B
(**17**) HOUN **17** 64

HERZOG, WHITEY (THE WHITE RAT) OF/1B/CH/M
(30,22,**6**,4,40,54,23,24,3,27) WASA **30** 56-58, KCA **22** 58-59, **6** 60,BALA **6** 61-62, DETA **4** 63, KCA *CH* **40** 65, NYN *CH* **54** 66, TEXA *M* **40** 73, CALA *CH* **23** 74, *M* **23** 74, *M* **24** 74, *CH* **24** 74-75, KCA *M* **24** 75-79, STLN *M* **3** 80, *M* **27** 81, *M* **24** 81-90

HESKETH, JOE P
(**38**,28,55) MONN **38** 84-90, ATLN **38/28** 90, BOSA **55** 90-94

HESSMAN, MIKE 3B
(12,**15**) ATLN **12** 03, **15** 04

HETKI, JOHNNY P
(42,**40**,33,24,29) CINN **42** 45, **40** 47-48, **33** 50, STLA **24** 52, PITN **29** 53-54

HETZEL, ERIC P
(**31**) BOSA **31** 89-90

HEUSSER, ED (THE WILD ELK OF THE WASATCH) P
(32,14,21,**34**) STLN **32** 35, **14** 36, PHIN **21** 38, PHIA **21** 40, CINN **34** 43-46, PHIN **21** 48

HEVING, JOE P B
(25,17,19,**11**,12) CHIA **25** 33-35, CLEA **17** 37-38, BOSA **19** 38-40, CLEA **11** 41-44, BOSN **12** 45

HEVING, JOHNNIE C B
(**20**) PHIA **20** 31-32

HEYDERMAN, GREG P
(**29**) LAN **29** 73

HIATT, JACK C/1B/UTIL/CH
(16,2,**7**,22,21,8,4) LAA **16** 64, SFN **2** 65-66, **29** 66, **7** 67-69, MONN **22** 70, CHIN **21** 70, HOUN **8** 71-72, CALA **8** 72, CHIN **4** 81

HIATT, PHIL 3B/DH/UTIL
(**25**,8,44) KCA **25** 93, 95, DETA **8** 96, LAN **44** 01

HIBBARD, GREG P
(54,**27**,34,37) CHIA **52/54** 89, **27** 89-92, CHIN **37** 93, SEAA **34/37** 94

HIBBARD, JACK CH
(**7**) STLN *CH* **7** 93

HIBBS, JIM PH
(51,**47**) CALA **51/47** 67

HICKERSON, BRYAN P
(**41**,47) SFN **41** 91-94, CHIN **41** 95 COLN **47** 95

HICKEY, JIM (SID) P
(24,**17**) BOSN **24** 42, **17** 44

HICKEY, JIM CH
(**48**) HOUN *CH* **48** 04-05

HICKEY, KEVIN P
(**45**) CHIA **45** 81-83, BALA **23** 89, **45** 89-91

HICKMAN, JESSE P
(11,22,29,**31**) KCA **11** 65-66, **22/29/31** 66

HICKMAN, JIM OF/UTIL/P
(9,27,6,35,41,**28**,24) NYN **9** 62-65, **27** 66, **6** 66, LAN **35/41** 67, CHIN **28** 68-73, STLN **24** 74

HICKS, BUDDY INF
(**12**) DETA **12** 56

A ten-time All-Star, Rickey Henderson (left), was an awesome mixture of speed and power. He hit the most leadoff HRs—70 and stole the most bases—1,406 in the history of the game. He stole more bases (326) than any other Yankee. But as an Oakland Athletic, he has the most steals—867, the most runs—1,270, the most hits—1,768, the most doubles—289, and the highest BA (with 4000+ AB)—.288. In 1982, he stole 130 bases, but got caught 42 times—both records. To put things in perspective, Minnesota stole 38 bases that year. Teddy Higuera's (above) first four years showed great promise, winning 69, losing 38 (.645). His best year was 1986 (20-11 and 2.79 ERA). Shoulder trouble plagued the rest of his career. Kent Hrbek (below) was a hero in Minnesota, they retired his uniform #14 in 1985. His entire career was played in a Twins uniform, a rarity today. He scored 903 runs, had 1,749 hits, 838 walks, 312 doubles, 293 homeruns, 1,086 RBIs, batted .282, but slugged .481. A big man, 6'4" and 245 lbs., he was a surprisingly graceful fielder.

HICKS, JIM OF/1B (44,24,5) CHIA 44 64-66, STLN 24 69, CALA 5 69-70

HICKS, JOE OF (28,32,31,22) CHIA 28 59, 32 60, WASA 32 61, 31 62, NYN 22 63

HIDALGO, RICHARD OF (15,16,51) HOUN 15 97, 16 98, 15 98-04, NYN 15 04, TEXA 51 05

HIETPAS, JOE C (10) NYN 10 04

HIGBE, KIRBY P (49,29,25,14, 15,13,30) CHIN 49 37, 29 38, 25 38-39, PHIN 14 39-40, BKNN 15 41, 13 41-43, 46-47, PITN 13 47-49, NYN 30 49-50

HIGDON, BILL OF (59) CHIA 59 49

HIGGINS, DENNY P (41,28,35,37) CHIA 41 66-67, WASA 28 68-69, CLEA 35 70, STLN 37 71-72

HIGGINS, KEVIN C/UTIL (25) SDN 25 93

HIGGINS, MARK 1B (66) CLEA 66 89

HIGGINS, MIKE (PINKY) 3B/M (5,6,36) PHIA 5 33-36, BOSA 5 37-38, DETA 6 39-44, 46, BOSA 36 46, M 5 55-62

HIGGINSON, BOBBY OF (4) DETA 4 95-05

HIGH, ANDY (HANDY ANDY) 3B/2B/CH (23,31) CINN 23 32-33, PHIN 23 34, BKNN CH 31 37-38

HIGUERA, TEDDY P (55,49) MILA 55 85, 49 85-91, 93-94

HILCHER, WHITEY P (21,30,31) CINN 21 32, 30 35, 31 36

HILDEBRAND, ORAL P (26,19,18,20) CLEA 26 31, 19 32-36, STLA 18 37-38, NYA 20 39-40

HILGENDORF, TOM P (19,35,40) STLN 19 69-70, CLEA 35 72, 40 72-74, PHIN 35 75

HILJUS, ERIK P (55,35,41,37) DETA 55/35 99, 41 00, OAKA 37 01-02

HILL, AARON INF/DH (2) TORA 2 05

HILL, BOBBY 2B (17) CHIN 17 02-03, PITN 17 03-05

HILL, DAVE P (12) KCA 12 57

HILL, DONNIE SS/UTIL/P (25,15,18,2) OAKA 25 83-86, CHIA 15 85-88, CALA 18 90-91, MINA 2 92

HILL, GARRY P (22) ATLN 22 69

HILL, GLENALLEN OF/DH (29,24,1,22, 34,4,6) TORA 29 89, 24 90-91, CLEA 24 91, 1 92, 22 93, CHIN 42/34 93, 4 94, SFN 1 95-96, 34 97,SEAA 1 98, CHIN 6 98-00, NYA 31 00, ANAA 31 01

HILL, HERM OF (19) MINA 19 69-70

HILL, JEREMY P (52) KCA 52 02-03

HILL, JESSE OF (25,3,15) NYA 25 35, WASA 3 36, 25 37, PHIA 15 37

HILL, KEN P (56,43,44) STLN 56 88, 43 88-91, MONN 44 92-94, STLN 44 95, CLEA 44 95, TEXA 44 96-97, ANAA 44 97-00, CHIA 44 00, TBA 44 01

HILL, KOYIE C (55,15,5) LAN 55 03, ARIN 15 04, 5 05

HILL, MARC C/1B/INF/CH (16,2,21,7,8, 54,47) STLN 16 73-74, SFN 2 75-80, SEAA 21 80, CHIA 7 81-86, 8 82, HOUN CH 54 88, NYA CH 47 90-91

HILL, MILT P (39,49,41) CINN 39 91-93, ATLN 49 94, SEAA 41 94

HILL, OLIVER PH (28) BOSN 28 39

HILL, PERRY CH (6,47,49,13, 19,7,16) TEXA CH 6 92, 47 93, 49 94, DETA CH 13 97-98, 19 99, MONN CH 7 00-01, FLAN CH 7 02, 16 03, 7 04-05

HILL, RICH P (53) CHIN 53 05

HILL, SHAWN P (49) MONN 49 04

HILLEGAS, SHAWN P (57,45,42,38, 36) LAN 57 87-88, CHIA 45 88-89, 57 90, CLEA 42/38 91, NYA 36 92, OAKA 57 92-93

HILLENBRAND, SHEA 3B/1B/DH (29,28) BOSA 29 01-03, ARIN 28 03-04, TORA 29 05

HILLER, CHUCK 2B/UTIL/CH (26,2,18,41, 4,23) SFN 26 61-65, NYN 2 65-67, PHIN 18 67, PITN 2 68, TEXA CH 41 73, KCA CH 4 76-79, STLN CH 4 81-83, SFN CH 2 85, NYN CH 23 90

HILLER, FRANK (DUTCH) P (43,38,39,45, 30,41,42) NYA 43/38 46, 39 48-49, CHIN 45 50, 30 50-51, CINN 41 52, NYN 42 53

HILLER, JOHN P (39,18) DETA 39 65-66, 18 67-70, 73-80

HILLMAN, DAVE P (53,21,31,17, 38,34,27) CHIN 53 55-57, 21 58, 31 59, BOSA 17 60-61, CINN 38 62, NYN 34/27 62

HILLMAN, ERIC P (53) NYN 53 92-94

HILTON, DAVE 3B/2B/CH (18,8,10) SDN 18 72-73, 8 74, 10 74-75, MILA CH 1087-88

HILTON, HOWARD P (62) STLN 62 90

HIMSL, VEDIE CH/M (4,54) CHIN CH 4 60, M 54 61-64, CH 54 62-64

HINCH, A. J. C (23,7,40,2) OAKA 23 98-00, KCA 7 01-02, DETA 40 03, PHIN 2 04

HINCHLIFFE, BRETT P (32,53) SEAA 32 99, ANAA 53 00, NYN 32 01

HINDS, SAM P (40) MILA 40 77

HINES, BEN CH (36,35,37,56) SEAA CH 36 84, LAN CH 36 86, CH 35 89, CH 37 90-93, HOUN CH 56 94-95

HINES, BRUCE CH (38,19) CALA 38/19 91

HINKLE, GORDIE C/CH (9,17,33) BOSA 9 34, DETA CH 17 39, CH 33 39-40

HINRICKS, PAUL (HERKY) P (24) BOSA 24 51

HINSHAW,GEORGE OF (11,22) SDN 11 82, 22 83

HINSKE, ERIC 3B/1B (11) TORA 11 02-05

HINSLEY, JERRY P (24,43,40) NYN 24 64, 43/40 67

HINTON, CHUCK OF/UTIL (32,23,26) WASA 32 61-64, CLEA 23 65-67, CALA 26 68, CLEA 23 69-71

HINTON, RICH P (50,45,35,15, 44,36,47,37) CHIA 50 71, NYA 45 72, TEXA 35/15 72, CHIA 44 75, CINN 36 76, CHIA 47 78-79, SEAA 37 79

HINZO, TOMMY 2B/INF/DH (1) CLEA 1 87, 89

HIPPAUF, HERB P (24) ATLN 24 66

HISER, GENE OF (16,21) CHIN 16 71-72, 21 72-75

HISLE, LARRY OF/DH/CH (24,4,22,9, 39) PHIN 24 68, 4 69, 22 70-71, MINA 9 73-77, MILA 9 78-82, TORA CH 39 92-95

HISNER, HARLEY P (24) BOSA 24 51

HITCHCOCK, BILLY SS/INF/CH/M (7,23,39,27, 2,11,17,34, 45,8) DETA 7 42, 23 46, WASA 39/27 46, STLA 2 47, BOSA 11 48-49, PHIA 11 50-52, DETA 17 53, CH 34 55-60, M 34 60, BALA M 45 62-63, ATLN CH 8 66, M 8 66-67

HITCHCOCK, JIM SS/2B (29) BOSN 29 38

HITCHCOCK, STERLING P (54,34,41) NYA 54 92, 34 93,41 94-95, SEAA 41 96, SDN 41 97-01, NYA 41 01-03, STLN 41 03, SDN 41 04

HITTLE, LLOYD (RED) P (37,19) WASA 37 49, 19 50

HOAG, MYRIL OF/INF/P (28,27,9,15, 4,14,8,28,17) NYA 28 31, 27 32, 28 34-36, 9 37-38, STLA 15/4 39, 14 40, 15 41, CHIA 2441, 8 42, 28 44, CLEA 17 44-45

HOAK, DON (TIGER) 3B/INF/CH (43,7,12,3) BKNN 43 54-55, CHIN 7 56, CINN 12 57-58, PITN 12 59-62, PHIN 12 63-64, CH 3 67

HOBAUGH, ED P (18,36) WASA 18 61-62, 36 63

HOBBIE, GLEN P (28,40) CHIN 28 57-58, 40 59-64, STLN 40 64

HOBBS, JACK P (40) MINA 40 81-82

HOBSON, BUTCH 3B/DH/INF/M (51,4,10,24, 35,17) BOSA 51 75, 4 76-80, CALA 10 81, NYA 24/35 82, BOSA M 17 92-94

HOCKENBERY, CHUCK P (46) CALA 46 75

HOCKETT, ORIS (BROWN) OF (17,28,__,34, 25) BKNN 17 38, 2839, CLEA __ 41, 34 42-44, CHIA 25 45

HOCKETTE, GEORGE (LEFTY) P (__,28) BOSA __ 34, 28 35

HOCKING, DENNY SS/2B/3B/UTIL (7,16,1) MINA 7 93-03, COLN 16 04, KCA 1 05

HODAPP, JOHNNY 2B/UTIL (4,6,5) CLEA 4 31-32, CHIA 6 32, BOSA 5 33

HODERLEIN, MEL 2B/INF (2,28) BOSA 2 51, WASA 28 52-54

HODGE, BERT 3B (25) PHIN 25 42

HODGE, ED P (17) MINA 17 84

HODGE, HAROLD (GOMER) INF (10) CLEA 10 71

HODGES, GIL C/1B/UTIL/M (4,14,) BKNN 4 43, 14 47-57, LAN 14 58-61, NYN 14 62-63, WASA M 14 63-67, NYN M 14 68-71

HODGES, KEVIN P (58) SEAA 58 00

HODGES, RON C (42) NYN 42 73-84

HODGES, TREY P (45) ATLN 45 02-03

HODGIN, RALPH OF/3B (25,24) BOSN 25 39, CHIA 25 43-44, 24 46, 25 47-48

HODGSON, PAUL OF/DH (49) TORA 49 80

HODKEY, ELI P (12,3) PHIN 12/3 46

HOEFT, BILL P (44,39,29,20, 26,40,30 DETA 44 52-59, BOSA 39 59 BALA 29 59, 20 60-62, SFN 20 63, MILN 26 64, CHIN 40 65-66, SFN 30 66

HOERNER, JOE P (44,43,39,27, 40) HOUN 44 63-64, STLN 43 66 69, PHIN 43 70-72, ATLN 39/43 72, 43 73, KCA 27 73-74, PHIN 43 75, TEXA 43 76, CINN 42/40 77

HOERST, FRANK (LEFTY) P (8,11,14,22, 34) PHIN 8 40, 11 41, 14 42, 22 46, 34 47

HOFFERTH, STEW C (29,21,9,27) BOSN 29 44, 21/9 45, 27 46

HOFFMAN, BILL P (28) PHIN 28 39

HOFFMAN, GLENN 3B/SS/INF/DH/M/CH B (18,37,9,22, 35) BOSA 18 80-87, LAN 37 87, CALA 9 89, LAN M 22 98, CH 35 99-05

HOFFMAN, GUY P (36,47,50,30, 42,43) CHIA 36 79-80, 47 83, CHIN 50 86, CINN 50/30 87, TEXA 42/43 88

HOFFMAN, JOHN (PORK CHOP) C (9,57) HOUN 9 64, 57 65

HOFFMAN, RAY 3B/CH? (6,36) WASA 6 42, STLA CH? 36 51

HOFFMAN, TREVOR P B (51,34) FLAN 51 93, SDN 34 93, 51 94-05

HOFMAN, BOBBY INF/C/CH (26,14,23,40, 4,43,6) NYN 26 49, 14 52-56, 23 57, KCA CH 40 66-67, CH 4 67, WASA CH 43 68, OAKA CH 43 69-70, CLEA CH 6 71-72, OAKA CH 43 74-75, 78

HOFMANN, FRED (BOOTNOSE) CH (28,35,33,30) STLA 28 38-39, 35 39, 33 40-49, 30 43

HOGAN, SHANTY C (7,8,31) NYN 7 32, BOSN 8 33-35, WASA 31 36, 8 37

HOGG, BERT (SONNY) 3B (__) BKNN __ 34

HOGSETT, CHIEF P (18,17,16,14, 2) DETA 18 31, 17 32-36, STLA 16 36-37, WASA 14 38, DETA 2 44

HOGUE, BOBBY P (37,18,40,24) BOSN 37 48-51, STLA 18 51, NYA 40 51-52, STLA 24 52

HOGUE, CAL P (36,32,25) PITN 36 52, 32 53, 25 54

HOILES, CHRIS 3B/INF/M/CH (17,23) BALA 17 89-90, 23 91-96, 98

HOLBERT, AARON 2B/SS B (13,7) STLN 13 96, CINN 7 05

HOLBERT, RAY SS/2B B (12,18,30,36, 32,4) SDN 12 94, 18 95, ATLN 30 98, MONN 36 98, KCA 32 99, 4 00

HOLBOROW, WALT (WALLY) P (19,18) WASA 19 44-45, PHIA 18 48,

HOLBROOK, SAMMY C (9) WASA 9 35

HOLCOMBE, KEN P (19,48,34,58, 17,14) NYA 19 45, CINN 48 48, CHIA 58 50, 34 50-52, STLA 17 52, BOSA 14 53

HOLDEN, JOE (SOCKS) C (10,__) PHIN 10 34-35, __ 36

HOLDRIDGE, DAVID P (59) SEAA 59 98

HOLDSWORTH, FRED P (20,41,38,16, 47) DETA 20 72-74, 41 73, BALA 38 76-77, MONN 16 77-78, MILA 47 80

HOLKE, WALTER CH (32) STLA CH 32 40

HOLLAND, AL P (46,31,19,35, 56,53,36,29) PITN 46/31 77, SFN 19 79-82, PHIN 19 83-85, PITN 35 85, CALA 19 85, NYA 56/53/36 86, 58/29 87

HOLLAND, BILL (DUTCH) P (38) WASA 38 39

HOLLAND, DUTCH OF (28,10,35) BOSN 28 32, 10 33, CLEA 35 34

HOLLANDSWORTH, TODD OF (28,27,21,14, 20) LAN 28 95-00, COLN 27 00-02, TEXA 21 02, FLAN 14 03, CHIN 28 04-05, ATLN 20 05

HOLLE, GARY 1B (39) TEXA 39 79

HOLLEY, ED P (24,21,46,44) PHIN 24 32, 21 33, 46 34, PITN 44 34

HOLLIDAY, MATT OF (5) COLN 5 05

HOLLINGSWORTH, AL (BOOTS) P/CH (26,19,56,17, 24,35,25,59, 33) CINN 26 35, 19 36-37, 56 38, PHIN 17 38-39, BKNN 24 39, WASA 35 40, STLA 25 42-46, CHIA 59 46, STLN CH 33 57-58

HOLLINS, DAMON OF (16,70,20,27) ATLN 16 98, LAN 70 98, ATLN 20 04, TBA 27 05

HOLLINS, DAVE 3B/1B/DH (15,27,10,17, 20) PHIN 15 90-95, BOSA 27 95, MINA 15 96, SEAA 10 96, ANAA 10 97-98, TORA 17 99, CLEA 20 01, PHIN 15 02

HOLLINS, JESSIE P (32) CHIN 32 92

HOLLMIG, STAN (HONDO) OF (17) PHIN 17 49-51

HOLLOMAN, BOBO P (24) STLA 24 53

HOLLOWAY, KEN P (32) NYA 32 30

HOLLY, JEFF P (32,36,21) MINA 32 77, 36 77-79, 21 79

HOLM, BILLY C (12,10,23) CHIN 12 43, 10 44, BOSA 23 45

HOLM, WATTIE OF (71,24) STLN 71 24, 24 32

HOLMAN, BRAD P (38) SEAA 38 93

HOLMAN, BRIAN P (59,36) MONN 59 88-89, SEAA 36 89-91

HOLMAN, GARY 1B/OF (5) WASA 5 68-69

HOLMAN, SCOTT P (46,26,28) NYN 46/26 80, 28 82-83

HOLMAN, SHAWN P (38) DETA 38 89

HOLMBERG, DENNIS CH (46) TORA CH 46 94-95

HOLMES, DARREN P (20,40,41,46) LAN 20 90, MILA 40 91-92, COLN 40 93-97, NYA 41/40 98, ARIN 46 99, 40 00, STLN 37 00, BALA 36 00, ARIN 40 00, 02-03

HOLMES, TOMMY (KELLY) OF/M (1,29) BOSN 1 42-51, M 1 51-52, BKNN 29 52

HOLMQUIST, DOUG CH (42) NYA CH 42 84-85

HOLT, CHRIS P (45,44,41) HOUN 45 96-97, 99, 44 99-00, DETA 41 01

HOLT, GOLDIE CH (19,31,57) PITN CH 19 48, CH 31 49-50, CHIN CH 57 61-64

HOLT, JIM OF/1B/DH (45,26,38) MINA 45 68, 26 69-74, OAKA 38 74-76

HOLT, ROGER 2B (55) NYA 55 80

HOLTGRAVE, VERN (WOODY) P (19) DETA 19 65

HOLTON, BRIAN P (50,51,37) LAN 50 85, 51 86-88, BALA 37 89, 51 89-90

HOLTZ, MIKE P (65,31,58) CALA 65 96, ANAA 65 97-01, OAKA 31 02, SDN 58 02

HOLTZMAN, KEN P (30,53) CHIN 30 65-71, OAKA 30 72-75, BALA 30 76, NYA 53 76-78, CHIN 30 78-79

HOLZEMER, MARK P (42,59,28,46) CALA 42 93, 95-96, SEAA 59 97 OAKA 28 98, PHIN 46 00

HONEYCUTT, RICK P (40,22,23,47, 32) SEAA 40 77-80, TEXA 22 81, 40 81-83, LAN 23 83, 40 83-87, OAKA 40 87-93, TEXA 40 94, OAKA 40 95, NYA 47 95, STLN 32 96-97

HOOD, DON P (44,52,32,46, 26,48) BALA 44 73,52/44 74, CLEA 32 75-77, 44 77-79, NYA 46 79, STLN 26 80, KCA 48 82, 48 83

HOOD, WALLY P (39) NYA 39 49

HOOK, CHRIS P (61,37) SFN 61 95, 37 95-96

HOOK, JAY P (36,47) CINN 36 57, 47 57-61, NYN 47 62-64

HOOKS, ALEX 1B (3) PHIA 3 35

HOOPER, BOB P (23,26,37) PHIA 23 50-52, CLEA 26 53-54, CINN 37 55

HOOPER, KEVIN 2B (49) DETA 49 05

HOOTEN, LEON P (20) OAKA 20 74

HOOTEN, BURT P/CH (44,46,48) CHIN 44 71-75, LAN 46 75-84, TEXA 46 85, HOUN CH 48 01-04

HOOVER, DICK P (30) BOSN 30 52

HOOVER, JOE SS/2B (7,24) DETA 7 43, 24 44, 7 45

HOOVER, JOHN P (44) TEXA 44 90

HOOVER, PAUL C (15) TBA 15 01-02

HOPE, JOHN P (56,29) PITN 56 93-95, 29 96

HOPKINS, DON OF/DH
(**1**) OAKA **1** 75-76

HOPKINS, GAIL 1B/UTIL/DH
(**18**,16) CHIA **18** 68-70, KCA **18** 71-73, LAN **16** 74

HOPKINS, MARTY 3B/2B
(23,**27**) PHIN **23** 34, CHIA **27** 34-35

HOPP, JOHNNY (HIPPITY) 1B/OF/CH
(19,**12**,35,38, 32,36,40) STLN **19** 39, **12** 40-45, BOSN **12** 46-47, PITN **12** 48-49, BKNN **35** 49, PITN **12** 49-50, NYA **38** 50-52, DETA **32** 52, *CH* **36** 54, STLN *CH* **40** 56

HOPPER, JIM P
(**42**) PITN **42** 46

HORGAN, JOE P
(59,**39**) MONN **59** 04, WASN **39** 05

HORLEN, JOE P
(**20**,22) CHIA **20** 61-71, OAKA **22** 72

HORN, SAM DH/1B
(**30**,15,38,1) BOSA **30** 87-89, BALA **15** 90-92, **38** 92, CLEA **1** 93, TEXA **30** 95

HORNER, BOB 3B/1B
(**5**,11) ATLN **5** 78-84, **11** 85-86, STLN **5** 88

HORNSBY, ROGERS (RAJAH) 2B/UTIL/M/CH
(**4**,**6**,21,16,11, 42,50,57,35, 53) STLN **4** 23, **6** 24, CHIN **21** 32, STLN **4** 33, STLA *M* **16** 33, *M* **11** 34-35, *M* **4** 36-37, *M* **42** 52, CINN *M* **50** 52-53, CHIN *CH* **57** 58, *CH* **35** 58-59, NYN *CH* **53** 62

HORSMAN, VINCE P
(**26**,57) TORA **26** 91, OAKA **26** 92-94, MINA **57** 95

HORTON, RICKY P
(**49**,26,29) STLN **49** 84-87, CHIA **26** 88, LAN **29** 88-89, STLN **49** 89-90

HORTON, TONY OF/1B
(30,**11**) BOSA **30** 64-67, CLEA **11** 67-70

HORTON, WILLIE OF/3B/DH/CH
(48,**23**,53) DETA **48** 63, **23** 64-77, TEXA **23** 77, CLEA **23** 78, OAKA **23** 78, TORA **48** 78, SEAA **53** 79-80, NYA *CH* **48** 85, CHIA *CH* **48** 86

HOSCHEIT, VERN CH
(41,**44**,24,51) BALA *CH* **41** 68, OAKA *CH* **44** 69-74, CALA *CH* **24** 76, NYN *CH* **51** 84-87

HOSEY, DWAYNE OF
(52,**46**) KCA **52** 94, BOSA **46** 95-96

HOSEY, STEVE OF
(**29**) SFN **29** 92-93

HOSKINS, DAVE P
(52,51,**22**) CLEA **52/51** 53, **22** 53-54

HOSLEY, TIM C/UTIL/DH
(34,15,6,**30**, 25) DETA **34** 70-71, OAKA **15** 73, **23** 74, CHIN **6** 75-76, OAKA **30** 76, 78, **25** 77-78, 81

HOST, GENE (TWINKLES)(SLICK) P
(33,**28**) DETA **33** 56, KCA **28** 57

HOSTETLER, CHUCK OF
(**26**) DETA **26** 44-45

HOSTETLER, DAVE 1B/DH/C
(55,**12**) MONN **55** 81, TEXA **12** 82-84, PITN **55** 88

HOTTMAN, KEN OF
(**16**) CHIA **16** 71

HOUGH, CHARLIE P/CH
(31,**49**,54) LAN **31** 70, **49** 70-80, TEXA **49** 80-90, CHIA **49** 91-92, FLAN **49** 93-94, LAN *CH* **49** 98-99, NYN *CH* **54** 01-02

HOUK, RALPH (MAJOR) C/CH/M
(50,**32**,35) NYA **50** 47, **32** 47-54, *CH* **32** 54, *CH* **35** 58-60, *M* **35** 61-63, 66-73, DETA *M* **35** 74-78, BOSA *M* **35** 81-84

HOULTON, DENNIS (D. J.) P
(**27**) LAN **27** 05

HOUSE, CRAIG P
(**48**) COLN **48** 00

HOUSE, FRANK (PIG) C
(35,**2**,36,12, 8,5) DETA **35** 50-52, **2** 54-57, KCA **36** 58, **12** 58-59, CINN **8** 60, DETA **5** 61

HOUSE, J. R. PH
(**30**) PITN **30** 03-04

HOUSE, PAT P
(42,50,**43**) HOUN **42** 67, **50/43** 68

HOUSE, TOM P/CH
(39,26,**29**,35) ATLN **39** 71-72, **26** 73-75, BOSA **29** 76-77, SEAA **29** 77-78, TEXA *CH* **35** 85-92

HOUSEHOLDER, PAUL OF/DH
(56,**21**,7,37, 26) CINN **56** 80, **21** 81-83, **7** 84, STLN **37** 84, MILA **7** 85-86, HOUN **26** 87

HOUSIE, WAYNE OF/DH
(**17**,2) BOSA **17** 91, NYN **2** 93

HOUSTON, TYLER 1B/C
(5,**7**,29,2) ATLN **5** 96, CHIN **7** 96-99, CLEA **29** 99, MILN **2** 00-02, LAN **5** 02, PHIN **2** 03

HOUTTEMAN, ART P
(21,6,15,12, 41,29,**11**) DETA **21** 45, **6** 46, **15** 47-49, **21** 48, **12** 49-50, **21** 52-53, CLEA **41/29** 53, **11** 53-57, BALA **21** 57

HOVLEY, STEVE OF/1B/DH
(36,23,28, **30**) SEAA **36** 69, MILA **36** 70, OAKA **23** 70, **28** 71, KCA **30** 72-73

HOWARD, BEN P
(36,**39**) SDN **36** 02, **39** 03, FLAN **39** 04

HOWARD, BRUCE P
(**19**,16,18) CHIA **19** 63-67, BALA **16** 68

HOWARD, CHRIS H. C
(**45**) SEAA **45** 91-95

HOWARD, CHRIS P
(58,31,41) CHIA **58** 93, BOSA **31** 94, TEXA **41** 95

HOWARD, DAVID SS/OF/UTIL
(31,13,**6**,29) KCA **31** 91-92, **13** 92, **6** 93-97, STLN **13** 98, **29** 98-99

HOWARD, DOUG UTIL
(**4**,44,14,37, 27) CALA **4** 72-73, **44/14** 74, STLN **37** 75, CLEA **27** 76

HOWARD, ELSTON (ELLIE) C/UTIL/CH
(**32**,18) NYA **32** 55-67, BOSA **18** 67-68, NYA *CH* **32** 69-79

HOWARD, FRANK (THE CAPITOL PUNISHER) (HONDO) OF/1B/DH/CH/M
(**25**,9,33) LAN **25** 58-64, WASA **9** 65-68, **33** 69-71, TEXA **33** 72, DETA **33** 72-73, MILA *CH* **33** 77-80, SDN *M* **33** 81, NYN *CH* **55** 82-84, *M* **55** 83, MILA *CH* **33** 85-SEAA *CH* **33** 88, NYA *CH* **48** 89, *CH* **46** 91-93, NYN *CH* **55** 94-96, TBA *CH* **33** 98, **25** 99

HOWARD, FRED P
(**41**) CHIA **41** 79

HOWARD, LARRY C/UTIL
(**10**,24,25) HOUN **10** 70-73, ATLN **24/25** 73

HOWARD, LEE P
(**11**,__) PITN **11** 46, __47

HOWARD, MATT 2B
(**38**) NYA **38** 96

HOWARD, MIKE OF/2B
(15,**5**) NYN **15** 81, **5** 81-83

HOWARD, RYAN 1B
(12,**6**) PHIN **12** 04, **6** 05

HOWARD, STEVE OF/DH
(**48**) OAKA **48** 90

HOWARD, THOMAS OF/DH
(**33**,22,5) SDN **33** 90-92, CLEA **33** 92-93, CINN **22** 93-96, HOUN **22** 97, LAN **22** 98, STLN **5** 99-00

HOWARD, WILBUR OF/DH/UTIL
(28,**26**) MILA **28** 73, HOUN **26** 74-78

HOWARTH, JIM OF/1B
(37,**19**) SFN **37** 71, **19** 72-74

HOWE, ART 3B/INF/CH/M
(14,**18**,7,10, 16,41) PITN **14** 74-75, HOUN **18** 76-82, STLN **7** 84-85, TEXA *CH* **10** 85-88, **16** 88, HOUN *M* **18** 89-93, COLN *CH* **41** 95, OAKA *M* **18** 96-02, NYN *M* **18** 03-04

HOWE, CAL P
(**43**) CHIN **43** 52

HOWE, STEVE P
(**57**,29,30) LAN **57** 80-83, **57** 85, MINA **29/30** 85, TEXA **57** 87, NYA **57** 91-96

HOWELL, DIXIE (HOMER) C
(1,**6**,9,54) PITN **1** 47, CINN **6** 49-52, BKNN **9** 53, **54** 55-56

HOWELL, DIXIE (MILLARD) P
(35,39,**28**) CLEA **35** 40, CINN **39**49, CHIA **28** 55-58

HOWELL, J. P. P
(**53**) KCA **53** 05

HOWELL, JACK 3B/UTIL
(**16**,28,32,36) CALA **16** 85-91, SDN **28** 91, CALA **32** 96, ANAA **32** 97, HOUN **36** 98-99

HOWELL, JAY P
(43,45,53,**50**, 52) CINN **43** 80, CHIN **45** 81, NYA **53** 82-83, **50** 83-84, OAKA **50** 85-87, LAN **50** 88-92, ATLN **52** 93, TEXA **52** 94

HOWELL, KEN P
(**43**) LAN **43** 84-88, PHIN **43** 89-90

HOWELL, PAT OF
(**38**) NYN **38** 92

HOWELL, RED (PORKY) PH
(45,**35**) CLEA **45/35** 41

HOWELL, ROY 1B
(27,**13**) TEXA **27** 74-75, **13** 75-77, TORA **13** 77-80, MILA **13** 81-84

HOWERTON, BILL (HOPALONG) OF
(36,**8**) STLN **36** 49-51, PITN **8** 51-52, NYN **8** 52

HOWITT, DANN OF/1B/UTIL/DH
(51,**23**,44,34) OAKA **51** 89-90, **23** 91-92, SEAA **23** 92, **44** 92-93, CHIA **34** 94

HOWLEY, DAN (HOWLING DAN)(DAPPER DAN) M
(**31**) CINN **31** 32

HOWRY, BOBBY P
(62,**46**) CHIA **62** 98, **46** 99-02, BOSA **46** 02-03, CLEA **62** 04, **46** 05

HOWSER, DICK SS/INF/CH/M
(1,18,**10**,34, 21) KCA **1** 61-63, CLEA **18** 63-66, NYA **10** 67-68, *CH* **34** 69-78, *M* **34** 78, 80, KCA *M* **21** 81, *M* **10** 82-86

HOY, PETER P
(57,**31**) BOSA **57/31** 92

HOYLE, TEX P
(**18**) PHIA **18** 52

HOYT, LAMARR P
(50,**31**) CHIA **50** 79-80, **31** 80-84, SDN **31** 85-86

HOYT, WAITE (SCHOOLBOY) P
(12,11,14,28, no#,19,**48**, 34,32,15) NYA **12** 29, **11** 30, DETA **14** 31, PHIA **28** 31, BKNN **no#** 32, NYN **19** 32, PITN **48** 33-37, BKNN **34** 37, **15** 38

HRABOSKY, AL (THE MAD HUNGARIAN) P
(**39**) STLN **39** 70-77, KCA **39** 78-79, ATLN **39** 80-82

HRBEK, KENT 1B/DH
(26,**14**) MINA **26** 81, **14** 82-94 **37** 36-39, **2** 40

HRINIAK, WALT C/CH
(39,24,34,46, **33**,6) ATLN **39** 68-69, SDN **24/34** 69, MONN *CH* **46** 74-75, BOSA *CH* **33** 77-88, CHIA *CH* **6** 89-95

HUBBARD, GLENN OF/IB/UTIL/CH
(**17**) ATLN **17** 78-87, OAKA **17** 88-89, ATLN *CH* **17** 99-05

HUBBARD, JACK CH
(__) TORA *CH* __ 98

HUBBARD, MIKE C
(**6**,3,27,36) CHIN **6** 95-97, MONN **3** 98, ATLN **27** 00, TEXA **36** 01

HUBBARD, TRENIDAD OF
(1,7,14,30,47, 27,23,28,12, 45) COLN **1** 94-95, **7** 96, SFN **14** 96, CLEA **30** 97, LAN **47** 98-99, ATLN **27** 00, BALA **23/27** 00, KCA **28** 01, SDN **12** 02, CHIN **45** 03

HUBBELL, CARL (KING CARL)(THE MEAL TICKET) P
(10,**11**) NYN **10** 32, **11** 33-43

HUBBS, KEN 2B
(33,**16**) CHIN **33** 61, **16** 62-63

HUBER, JUSTIN 1B
(**16**) KCA **16** 05

HUBER, OTTO 2B/3B
(25,**2**) BOSN **25/2** 39

HUCKABY, KEN C
(45,**20**,9,15) ARIN **45** 01, TORA **20** 02-03, BALA **9** 04, TEXA **15** 04, TORA **20** 05

HUCKLEBERRY, EARL P
(**24**) PHIA **24** 35

HUDEK, JOHN P
(**35**,43,33,26, 28,43) HOUN **35** 94-97, NYN **43** 98, CINN **33** 98, **26** 99, ATLN **28** 99, TORA **43** 99

HUDGENS, DAVE 1B/DH/CH
(**51**,45,48) OAKA **51** 83, *CH* **45** 99, **48** 03-05

HUDGENS, JIMMY 1B/2B
(**10**) STLN **10** 23

HUDLER, REX 2B/UTIL
(56,1,25,**10**, 14) NYA **56** 84-85, BALA **1** 86, MONN **25** 88-90, STLN **10** 90-92, CALA **10** 94-96, PHIN **14** 97-98

HUDLIN, WILLIS (ACE) P
(**12**,34,18,19, 22,27,33) CLEA **12** 31-40, WASA **34/18** 40, STLA **19** 40, NYN **22** 40, STLA **27** 44, DETA *CH* **33** 57-59

HUDSON, CHARLES P
(43,**49**,41,27) PHIN **43** 83, **49** 83-86, NYA **41** 87-88, DETA **27** 89

HUDSON, CHARLIE P
(30,49,14,41) STLN **30** 72, TEXA **49/14** 73, CALA **41** 75

HUDSON, HAL (BUD)(LEFTY) P
(24,**34**) STLA **34** 52, CHIA **24** 52, **34** 53

HUDSON, JESSE P
(**38**) NYN **38** 69

HUDSON, JOHNNY (MR. CHIPS) INF
(7,**6**,12) BKNN **7** 36-37, **6** 38-40, CHIN **12** 41, NYN **7** 45

HUDSON, JOE P
(**54**,43) BOSA **54** 95-97, MILN **43** 98

HUDSON, LUKE P
(**54**) CINN **54** 02, 04-05

HUDSON, ORLANDO 2B
(3,**1**) TORA **3** 02-03, **1** 04-05

HUDSON, REX P
(**40**) LAN **40** 74

HUDSON, SID 2B
(15,14,13,**20**, 40,41,54) WASA **15** 40-42, **14** 46, **13** 46-47, **20** 48, **15** 49, **20** 50-52, BOSA **20** 52-54, WASA *CH* **40** 61-65, **41** 68-71, TEXA **41** 72, **54** 76-78

HUDSON, TIM P
(52,**15**) OAKA **52** 99, **15** 00-04, ATLN **15** 05

HUFF, AUBREY 3B/INF/DH
(21,**19**) TBA **21** 00, **19** 01-05

HUFF, MIKE OF/2B/DH
(45,44,12,10, **26**) LAN **45** 89, CLEA **44** 91, CHIA **12** 91, **10** 92, **12** 93, TORA **26** 94-95

HUFFMAN, BEN C
(**28**) STLA **28** 37

HUFFMAN, PHIL P
(47,**21**) TORA **47** 79, BALA **21** 85

HUGGINS, MILLER (MIGHTY MITE)(HUG) M
(**no#**) NYA *M* **no#** 29

HUGHES, ??? CH
(**39**) CINN **39** 37

HUGHES, BOBBY C
(33,**31**) MILN **33** 98, **31** 99

HUGHES, DICK P
(**31**) STLN **31** 66-68

HUGHES, JIM P
(**18**,50,25,32) BKNN **18** 52-56, **13** 55, CHIN **50/25** 56, CHIA **32** 57

HUGHES, JIM P
(37,**31**) MINA **37** 74, **31** 74-77

HUGHES, KEITH OF/DH
(27,19,35,12, 45) NYA **27** 87, PHIN **19** 87, BALA **35** 88, NYN **12** 90, CINN **45** 93

HUGHES, ROY (JEEP)(SAGE) 2B/INF
(**29**,5,11,16, **28**,23,6) CLEA **29** 35, **5** 36-37, STLA **11** 38-39, PHIN **16** 39, **28** 39-41, **5** 44, **23** 44-45, PHIN **6** 46

HUGHES, TERRY 3B/OF/DH
(17,14,38) CHIN **17** 70, STLN **14** 73, BOSA **38** 74

HUGHES, TOM P
(**38**) STLN **38** 59

HUGHES, TOMMY P
(15,**28**,44) PHIN **15** 42, **28** 46-47, CINN **44** 48

HUGHES, TRAVIS P
(57,**34**) TEXA **57** 04, WASN **34** 05

HUGHSON, TEX P
(29,15,**21**,27) BOSA **29** 41, **15** 41-42, **21** 42-44, **21** 46-49

HUISMAN, JUSTIN P
(**37**) KCA **37** 04

HUISMAN, RICK P
(**37**) KCA **37** 95-96

HUISMANN, MARK P
(**38**,28,27,37, 52,41) KCA **38** 83-86, SEAA **28** 86, **27** 87, CLEA **37** 87, DETA **27** 88, BALA **52** 89, PITN **41** 90, **27** 91

HULETT, TIM 2B/INF/DH
(32,**36**,25) CHIA **32** 83-87, **23** 86, BALA **36** 89-94, STLN **25** 95

HULSE, DAVID OF/DH
(**15**) TEXA **15** 92-94, MILA **15** 95-96

HULSWITT, RUDY CH
(33,32,**31**) BOSA *CH* **33** 31, **32** 32, **31** 33

HUME, TOM P/CH
(**47**,37,41,49) CINN **47** 77-85, PHIN **37** 86, **41** 86-87, **41** 87, CINN **41** 87, *CH* **47/49** 96, **47** 97, 99-05

HUMMEL, TIM 3B
(**60**) CINN **60** 03-04

HUMPHREY, BILL P
(**19**) BOSA **19** 38

HUMPHREY, TERRY C/INF
(22,47,**9**) MONN **22** 71-74, DETA **47** 75, CALA **9** 76-79

HUMPHREYS, BOB P
(46,47,36,18, **23**,50) DETA **46** 62, STLN **47** 63-64, CHIN **36** 65, WASA **18** 66, **23** 66-70, MILA **50/47** 70

HUMPHREYS, MIKE OF/DH/UTIL
(36,31,34,**29**) NYA **36** 91, **31/34** 92, **29** 93

HUMPHRIES, JOHN (JOHNNY) P
(21,**26**,40) CLEA **21** 38-40, CHIA **26** 41-45, PHIN **40** 46

HUNDLEY, RANDY C/CH F
(39,1,**9**,15,4, 5) SFN **39** 64, **1** 65, CHIN **9** 66-73, MINA **15** 74, SDN **4** 75, CHIN **5** 76, **4** 77, *CH* **4** 77

HUNDLEY, TODD C S
(49,**9**,99) NYN **49** 90-91, **9** 92-98, LAN **9** 99-00, CHIN **99** 01, **9** 01-02, LAN **9** 03, (04)

HUNNEFIELD, BILL (WILD BILL) SS/2B
(**35**) CLEA **35** 31

HUNT, JOEL (JODIE) OF
(**no#**) STLN **no#** 32

HUNT, KEN OF/UTIL
(44,**26**,20,6, 12) NYA **44** 59-60, LAA **26** 61-63, WASA **20** 63, **6/12** 64

HUNT, KEN P
(**41**) CINN **41** 61

HUNT, RANDY C
(**10**,47) STLN **10** 85, MONN **47** 86

HUNT, RON 2B
(**33**,32) NYN **33** 63-66, LAN **33** 67, SFN **33** 68-70, MONN **33** 71-74, STLN **32** 74

HUNTER, BILLY SS/INF/CH/M
(6,20,1,7,55,5) STLA **6** 53, BALA **6** 54, NYA **20** 55-56, KCA **1** 57-58, CLEA **7** 58, BALA *CH* **55** 64-77, TEXA *M* **5** 77-78

HUNTER, BRIAN (L.) OF
(19,**21**,22,12, 44) HOUN **19** 94-96, DETA **21** 97-99, SEAA **22** 99, COLN **12** 00, CINN **44** 00, PHIN **12** 01, HOUN **21** 02-03

HUNTER, BRIAN (R.) 1B/OF
(**14**,30,34,21, 19) ATLN **14** 91-93, PITN **14** 94, CINN **30** 94-95, SEAA **34** 96, STLN **21** 98, ATLN **19** 99-00, PHIN **19** 00

HUNTER, BUDDY 2B/INF/DH
(**38**,5) BOSA **38** 71, 73, **5** 75

HUNTER, EDDIE 3B
(__) CINN __33

HUNTER, JIM (CATFISH) P
(**27**,29) KCA **27** 65-67, OAKA **27** 68-74, NYA **29** 75-79

HUNTER, JIM P
(**43**) MILA **43** 91

HUNTER, NEWT CH
(26,**27**) PHIN *CH* **26/27** 33

HUNTER, RICH P
(**39**) PHIN **39** 96

HUNTER, TORII OF/DH
(**48**) MINA **48** 98-05

HUNTER, WILLARD P
(**34**) CLEA **34** 60-62

HUNTZ, STEVE 2B/INF
(**14**,25,19,18) STLN **14** 67-68, SDN **25** 70, CHIA **19** 71, SDN **18** 75

HUPPERT, DAVE C
(**32**,19,42,37) BALA **32/19** 83, MILA **42** 85, WASN *CH* **37** 05

HURD, TOM (WHITEY) P
(**28**) BOSA **28** 54-56

HURDLE, CLINT OF/UTIL/CH
(**10**,9,30,33,13,7,14) KCA **10** 77, **9** 77-79, **10** 79-81, CINN **30** 82, NYN **33** 83, **13** 85, STLN **13** 86, NYN **7** 87, COLN *CH* **13** 97-02, *M* 02-03, **14** 04, **13** 04-05

HURST, BILL P
(**50**) FLAN **50** 96

HURST, BRUCE (LEFTY) P
(**47**) BOSA **47** 80-88, SDN **47** 89-93, COLN **47** 93, TEXA **47** 94

HURST, DON 1B
(4,**15**,24,41) PHIN **4** 32, **15** 32, **24** 34, CHIN **41** 34

HURST, JAMES P
(61,**25**) TEXA **61/25** 94

HURST, JIMMY OF
(**53**) DETA **53** 97

HURST, JONATHAN P
(37,**13**) MONN **37** 92, NYN **13** 94

HURTADO, EDWIN P
(**32**,39) TORA **32** 95-96, SEAA **39** 97

HUSKEY, BUTCH 3B
(10,**42**,44,35) NYN **10** 93, **42** 95-98, SEAA **42** 99, BOSA **44** 99, MINA **42** 00, COLN **35** 00

HUSON, JEFF UTIL
(15,**9**,30,5,29) MONN **15** 88-89, TEXA **9** 90-93, BALA **30** 95-96, MILA **15** 97, SEAA **9** 98, ANAA **5** 99, CHIN **29** 00

HUSTON, WARREN INF
(10,**15**) PHIA **10** 37, BOSN **15** 44

HUTCHESON, JOE (SLUG)(POODLE) OF
(**14**) BKNN **14** 33

HUTCHINGS, JOHNNY P
(40,38,5,30,**17**) CINN **40** 40, **38** 41, BOSN **5** 41, **17** 42, **30** 44, **17** 44-46

HUTCHINSON, CHAD P
(**65**) STLN **65** 01

HUTCHINSON, FRED P/M
(18,**29**,1) DETA **18** 39-40, **29 41,**46-53, *M* **29** 52-54, STLN *M* **29** 56-58, CINN *M* **1** 59-64

HUTCHINSON, IRA P
(34,20,19,17,**30**,43,11) CHIA **34** 33, BOSN **20** 37-38, BKNN **19** 39, STLN **17** 40, **30** 40-41, BOSN **43/30** 44, **11/19** 45

HUTSON, HERB P
(**40**) CHIN **40** 74

HUTTO, JIM UTIL/C
(**20**,33) PHIN **20** 70, BALA **33** 75

HUTTON, MARK P
(53,**52**,45) NYA **53** 93, **52** 94, 96, FLAN **52** 96-97, COLN **53** 97, CINN **45** 98

HUTTON, TOMMY 1B/OF/UTIL/P
(4,**14**,37) LAN **4** 66, 69, PHIN **14** 72-77, TORA **14** 78, MONN **37** 78, **14** 79-81

HYDE, DICK P
(32,**35**,38) WASA **32** 55, **35** 57-60, BALA **38** 61

HYERS, TIM OF/1B
(**17**,7,26) SDN **17** 94-95, DETA **7** 96, FLAN **26** 99

HYZDU, ADAM OF/1B
(27,**38**,37,14,25) PITN **27** 00, **38** 01-03, BOSA **37** 04, SDN **14** 05, BOSA **25** 05

I

IBANEZ, RAUL OF/1B/DH
(26,38,5,23,**18**,28) SEAA **26** 96, **38** 98, **5** 99, **23** 00, KCA **18** 01-03, SEAA **28** 04-05

IGNASIAK, GARY P F
(**45**) DETA **45** 73

IGNASIAK, MIKE P S
(53,**40**) MILA **53** 91, **40** 93-95

IGUCHI, TADAHITO 2B
(**15**) CHIA **15** 05

ILSLEY, BLAISE P
(**51**) CHIN **51** 94

INCAVIGLIA, PETE OF/DH
(5,**29**,8,28,22,9,55,26,52,37,20,22) TEXA **5** 86, **29** 86-90, DETA **8/29** 91, HOUN **28** 92, PHIN **22** 93-94, **9** 96, BALA **55** 96, **26/29** 97, NYA **52** 97, DETA **37/20** 98, HOUN **22** 98

INFANTE, ALEX UTIL
(**14**,6,8) TORA **14** 87

INFANTE, OMAR SS/2B
(**20**) DETA **20** 02-05

INGE, BRANDON C/UTIL
(12,**15**) DETA **12** 02, **15** 03-05

INGRAM, GAREY 2B
(**33**,56) LAN **33** 94-95, **56** 97

INGRAM, RICCARDO OF/DH
(17,24) DETA **17** 94, MINA **24** 95

INNIS, JEFF P
(**40**) NYN **40** 87-93

IORG, DANE 1B/OF/UTIL B
(22,**19**,9,8) PHIN **22** 77, STLN **19** 77-84, KCA **9** 84-85, SDN **8** 86

IORG, GARTH 2B/UTIL/DH/CH
(29,**16**) TORA **29** 78, **16** 80-87, *CH* **16** 01-02

IOTT, CLARENCE (HOOKS) P
(26,31,30,**35**) STLA **26** 41, **31**47, NYN **30/35** 47

IRABU, HIDEKI P
(35,**14**,45) NYA **35** 97, **14** 98-99, MONN **14** 00-01, TEXA **45** 02

IRELAND, TIM 1B/UTIL
(33,17,15) KCA **33/17** 81, **15** 82

IRVIN, MONTE OF/1B
(7,**20**,39) NYN **7** 49, **20** 50-55, CHIN **39** 56

IRVINE, DARYL P
(**59**,57) BOSA **59** 90, **57/59** 91, **59** 92

IRWIN, TOMMY SS
(**32**) CLEA **32** 38

ISAAC, LUIS CH
(**7**,13,6,4) CLEA *CH* **7** 88-90, *CH* **13** 90-91, *CH* **6** 94-96, *CH* **4** 97-05

ISALES, ORLANDO OF
(29,**28**) PHIN **29/28** 80

ISHII, KAZUHISA P
(**17**,23) LAN **17** 02-04, NYN **23** 05

ISRINGHAUSEN, JASON (IZZY) P
(**44**,48) NYN **44** 95-97, 99, OAKA **48** 99, **44** 00-01, STLN **44** 02-05

IVIE, MIKE C/UTIL/1B
(27,28,17,**15**) SDN **28** 71, **15** 74-77, SFN **15** 78-81, HOUN **15** 81-82, DETA **15** 82-83

IZQUIERDO, HANK CH/C
(45,21) CLEA *CH* **45** 62, MINA **21** 67

IZQUIERDO, HANSEL P
(**62**) FLAN **62** 02

IZTURIS, CESAR SS B
(2,**3**) TORA **2** 01, LAN **3** 02-05

IZTURIS, MAICER 2B B
(2,**6**) MONN **2** 04, LAA **6** 05

J

JABLONSKI, RAY (JABBO) 3B/UTIL
(11,15,**12**,46,10,16,4) STLN **11** 53-54, CINN **15** 55, **12** 55-56, NYN **46** 57, **10** 57-58, STLN **16** 59, KCA **4** 59-60

JACHYM, ?? CH
(**16**) DETA *CH* **16** 39

JACKSON, AL (LITTLE AL) P
(**38**,25,15,44,32,31,54) PITN **38** 59, **25** 61, NYN **15** 62-65, STLN **38** 66-67, NYN **38** 68-69, CINN **44** 69, BOSA *CH* **32** 77-79, BALA *CH* **31** 89-91, NYN *CH* **54** 99-00

JACKSON, BO OF/DH
(**16**,8,22) KCA **16** 86-90, CHIA **8** 91, 93, CALA **22** 94

JACKSON, CHUCK UTIL
(**23**,11) HOUN **23** 87-88, TEXA **11** 94

JACKSON, CONOR 1B/OF
(**16**) ARIN **16** 05

JACKSON, DAMIAN SS/INF
(9,11,4,**2**,12,19,1) CLEA **9** 96, **11** 97, CINN **4/12** 97-98, SDN **2** 99-01, DETA **12** 02, BOSA **2** 03, CHIN **19** 04, KCA **1** 04, SDN **2** 05

JACKSON, DANNY P
(45,**25**,15,20,32,34,27,29) KCA **45** 83-84, **25** 84-87, **15** 87, CINN **20** 88-90, CHIN **32** 91-92, PITN **34** 92, PHIN **27** 93-94, STLN **29** 95-97, SDN **34** 97

JACKSON, DARRELL P
(40,**31**) MINA **40** 78, **31** 78-82

JACKSON, DARRIN (D.J.) OF/P
(30,22,**4**,14,3,15,24) CHIN **30** 85-89, SDN **22** 89, **4** 90-92, TORA **14** 93, NYN **3** 93, CHIA **22** 94, MINA **15** 97, MILA **24** 97, MILN **24** 98, CHIA **22** 99

JACKSON, EDWIN P
(36,**22**,58) LAN **36** 03, **22** 04, **58** 05

JACKSON, GRANT (BUCK) P/CH
(29,**23**,25,35,19,36,35,3) PHIN **29** 65-70, BALA **23** 71-76, NYA **25** 76, PITN **35** 77, **23** 77-81, MONN **19** 81, KCA **36** 82, PITN **35** 82, *CH* **23** 84-85, CINN *CH* **3** 94-95

JACKSON, JOHN P
(**28**) PHIN **28** 33

JACKSON, KEN SS
(**7**) PHIN **7** 87

JACKSON, LARRY P
(39,**46**) STLN **39** 55-62, CHIN **46** 63-66, PHIN **46** 66-69

JACKSON, LOU OF
(**22**,42,44) CHIN **22** 58, **42** 59, BALA **44** 64

JACKSON, MIKE (R.) P
(33,38,**42**) PHIN **33** 86-87, SEAA **38** 88-91, SFN **42** 92-94, CINN **42** 95-96 CLEA **42** 97-99, PHIN **42** 00, HOUN **38** 01, MINA **42** 02, CHIA **38** 04

JACKSON, MIKE (W.) P
(33,46,15,**25**) PHIN **33** 70, STLN **46** 71, KCA **15** 72, **25** 72-73, CLEA **46** 73

JACKSON, RANDY (HANDSOME RANSOM) 3B
(**2**,16) CHIN **2** 50-55, BKNN **2** 56-57, LAN **2** 58, CLEA **2** 58-59, CHIN **16** 59

JACKSON, REGGIE (MR. OCTOBER) OF/DH/CH
(31,9,**44**) KCA **31** 67, OAKA **9** 68-75, BALA, **9** 76, NYA **44** 77-81, CALA **44** 82-86, OAKA **44** 87, *CH* **44** 91-92

JACKSON, RON (H.) 1B
(42,**4**,5) CHIA **42** 54-56, **4** 57-59, BOSA **5** 60

JACKSON, RON (D.) (PAPA JACK) 1B/3B/CH
(2,32,16,**15**,11,52,28,30,22) CALA **2** 75, **32** 75-76, **16** 76-78, MINA **15** 79-81, DETA **15** 81, CALA **15** 82-84, BALA **11** 84, CHIA *CH* **52** 95-97, *CH* **28** 98, MILN *CH* **30** 99, BOSA *CH* **22** 03-05

JACKSON, ROY LEE P
(31,**25**,39,23) NYN **31** 77-80, TORA **25** 81-84, SDN **39** 85, MINA **23** 86

JACKSON, RYAN OF/1B
(3,37,57,**20**) FLAN **3** 98, SEAA **37** 99, DETA **57** 01, **20** 01-02

JACKSON, SONNY SS/UTIL/CH
(29,19,**16**,36,57,15) HOUN **29** 63-64, **19** 65, **16** 66-67, ATLN **16** 68-74, *CH* **36** 82, *CH* **57/36** 83, SFN *CH* **15** 97-99, **16** 00-02, **15** 01-02

JACKSON, TRAVIS (STONEWALL) SS/3B/CH
(6,**5**,31,1) NYN **6** 32, **5** 33-35, **6** 36, *CH* **31** 38-40, *CH* **1** 47-48

JACOBS, ART P
(**14**) CINN **14** 39

JACOBS, BUCKY P
(**20**,17) WASA **20** 37, 39, **17** 40

JACOBS, LAMAR (JAKE) PH
(**4**,25) WASA **4** 60, MINA **25** 61

JACOBS, MIKE C/1B
(**27**) NYN **27** 05

JACOBS, SPOOK 2B
(**6**,27) PHIA **6** 54, KCA **6** 55-56, PITN **27** 56

JACOBS, TONY P
(2,**1**) CHIN **2** 48, STLN **1** 55

JACOBSON, BUCKY 1B/DH
(**33**) SEAA **33** 04

JACOBY, BROOK 3B/1B/UTIL/DH
(47,**26**) ATLN **47** 81, 83, CLEA **26** 84-91, OAKA **26** 91, CLEA **26** 92

JACOME, JASON P
(47,**45**,46) NYN **47** 94-95, KCA **45** 95-97, CLEA **46** 97-98

JACQUEZ, PAT P
(**44**) CHIA **44** 71

JACQUEZ, THOMAS P
(**43**) PHIN **43** 00

JAECKEL, PAUL (JAKE) P
(**39**) CHIN **39** 64

JAHA, JOHN 1B/UTIL/DH
(**32**,5) MILA **32** 92-97, MILN **32** 98, OAKA **5** 99-01

JAKUCKI, SIG (JACK) P
(23,**22**) STLA **23** 36, **22** 44-45

JAMES, ART OF
(**42**) DETA **42** 75-76

JAMES, BERNIE INF
(**24**) NYN **24** 33

JAMES, BOB P
(20,24,42,**43**) MONN **20** 78-79, 82, DETA **24** 82-83, MONN **42** 83-84, CHIA **43** 85-87

JAMES, CHARLIE OF
(**23**,26) STLN **23** 60-64, CINN **26** 65

JAMES, CHRIS OF/3B/DH
(34,26,**18**,7,14,30,16,4,22) PHIN **34** 86, **26** 86-88, **18** 87-89, SDN **18** 89, CLEA **18** 90, **7** 91, SFN **14/30** 92, HOUN **16** 93, TEXA **4** 93-94, KCA **26** 95, BOSA **22** 95

JAMES, CHUCK P
(**36**) ATLN **36** 05

JAMES, CLEO OF/3B
(30,41,**24**,29) LAN **30** 68, CHIN **41**70, **24** 70-71, 73, **29** 73

JAMES, DELVIN P
(**48**) TBA **48** 02

JAMES, DION OF/DH/UTIL
(14,**10**,20,19,39) MILA **14** 83-85, ATLN **10** 87-89, CLEA **20** 89-90, NYA **19** 92-93, **39** 95-96

JAMES, JEFF (JESSE) P
(**30**) PHIN **30** 68-69

JAMES, JOHNNY P
(27,**53**,22) NYA **27** 58, **53** 60-61, LAA **22** 61

JAMES, MIKE P
(**46**,49,48) CALA **46** 95-95, ANAA **46** 97-98, (99), STLN **49** 00-01, COLN **48** 02

JAMES, RICK P
(48,**38**) CHIN **48/38** 67

JAMES, SKIP 1B
(**36**) SFN **36** 77-78

JAMIESON, CHARLIE (CUCKOO) OF
(**28**) CLEA **28** 31-32

JANESKI, JERRY P
(**26**) CHIA **26** 70, WASA **26** 71, TEXA **26** 72

JANOWICZ, VIC C/3B/0F
(**31**) PITN **31** 53-54

JANSEN, LARRY P/CH
(**46**,43,3) NYN **46** 47-54, *CH* **46** 54, CINN **43** 56, SFN *CH* **46** 61-71, CHIN *CH* **3** 72-73

JANZEN, MARTY P
(**36**) TORA **36** 96-97

JARAMILLO, RUDY CH
(**42**,8) HOUN *CH* **42** 90-93, TEXA *CH* **8** 95-05

JARVIS, KEVIN P
(42,**32**,26,46,20,38) CINN **42** 94-95, **32** 95-97, MINA **26** 97, DETA **46** 97, OAKA **20** 99, COLN **32** 00, SDN **32** 01-03, SEAA **32** 04, COLN **38** 04, STLN **32** 05

JARVIS, PAT P
(**33**,34) ATLN **33** 66-72, MONN **34** 73

JARVIS, RAY P
(**17**,26) BOSA **17** 69-70, **26** 70

JARVIS, ROY C
(34,**31**) BKNN **34** 44, PITN **31** 46-47

JASTER, LARRY P
(**39**,21,29,23) STLN **39** 65-68, MONN **21** 69, ATLN **29** 70, **23** 72

JATA, PAUL UTIL
(**31**) DETA **31** 72

JAUSS, DAVE CH
(**48**,43) BOSA *CH* **48** 97-98, **43** 99

JAVERY, AL (BEARTRACKS) P
(**18**,21) BOSN **34** 40, **18** 41-45, **21** 46

JAVIER, AL OF
(**29**) HOUN **29** 76

JAVIER, JULIAN (HOOLIE)(THE PHANTOM) 2B/INF F
(**25**,17) STLN **25** 60-71, CINN **17** 72

JAVIER, STAN OF/DH/1B S
(55,30,**28**,5,22,25,38,16) NYA **55** 84, OAKA **30** 86, **28** 87-90, LAN **5** 90-92, PHIN **22** 92, CALA **25** 93, OAKA **28** 94-95, SFN **28** 96-99, HOUN **38** 99, SEAA **16** 00, **28** 00-01

JAY, JOEY P
(**47**,42,30,34) MILA **47** 53-55, **42** 57, **47** 57-60, CINN **30** 61-66, ATLN **34/42** 66

JEAN, DOMINGO P
(**42**) NYA **42** 93

JEFFCOAT, GEORGE P F
(**23**,42,26) BKNN **23** 36-38, **42** 39, BOSN **26** 43

JEFFCOAT, HAL P
(19,**4**,3,42,36) CHIN **19** 48-49, **4** 49-53, **3** 53, **19** 54-55, CINN **42** 56-59, STLN **36** 59

JEFFCOAT, MIKE P
(54,46,33,**30**,37) CLEA **54** 83-84, **46** 84-85, SFN **33/46** 85, TEXA **30** 87-92, FLAN **37** 94

JEFFERIES, GREGG 3B/INF/OF
(9,**25**,12,21) NYN **9** 87-91, KCA **9** 92, STLN **25** 93-94, PHIN **25** 95-98, ANAA **12** 98, DETA **25** 99, **21** 99-00

JEFFERSON, JESSE P
(38,25,**34**,51) BALA **38** 73-75, CHIA **38** 75, **25** 75-76, TORA **34** 77-80, PITN **51** 80, CALA **34** 81

JEFFERSON, REGGIE 1B/DH
(42,24,44,**18**) CINN **42** 91, CLEA **24** 91, **44** 92-93, SEAA **18** 94, BOSA **18** 95-99

JEFFERSON, STAN OF/DH
(32,27,**22**,26,49,24,42) NYN **32/27** 86, SDN **22** 87-88, NYA **26** 89, BALA **49** 89-90, CLEA **24** 90, CINN **42** 91

JEFFRIES, IRV INF
(28,34,**25**) CHIA **28** 31, PHIN **34/25** 34

JELIC, CHRIS OF
(**46**) NYN **46** 90

JELINICH, FRANK (JELLY) OF
(**21**) CHIN **21** 41

JELKS, GREG UTIL
(**45**) PHIN **45** 87

JELTZ, STEVE SS/UTIL
(15,**30**,2) PHIN **15** 83-84, **30** 84-89, KCA **2** 90

JENKINS, FERGUSON (FERGIE) P/CH
(46,30,**31**,19) PHIN **46** 65, **30** 66, CHIN **31** 66-73, TEXA **19** 74, **31** 74-75, BOSA **31** 76-77, TEXA **31** 78-81, CHIN **31** 82-83, *CH* **31** 95-96

JENKINS, GEOFF OF
(**5**) ANAA **5** 98, MILN **5** 99-05

JENKINS, JACK P
(1,**22**,29) WASA **1** 62, **22** 63, LAN **29** 69

JENKINS, TOM (TUT) OF
(**26**) STLA **26** 31-32

JENKS, BOBBY P
(**45**) CHIA **45** 05

JENNINGS, BILL SS
(**6**) STLA **6** 51

JENNINGS, DOUG OF/UTIL
(48,**21**,2,13,53) OAKA **48** 88, **21** 88-89, **2** 90, **13** 91, CHIN **53** 93

JENNINGS, JASON P
(57,**32**) COLN **57** 01, **32** 02-05

JENNINGS, ROBIN OF
(39,**29**,30,31,26) CHIN **39** 96, **29** 97, 99, OAKA **30** 01, COLN **31** 01, CINN **26** 01

JENSEN, JACKIE OF
(40,27,25,8,**4**,30) NYA **40** 50-51, **27** 51, **25** 52, WASA **8** 52, **4** 53, BOSA **30** 54, **4** 55-59, 61

JENSEN, MARCUS C
(**30**,10,23,59,28,57,26)) SFN **30** 96-97, DETA **10** 97, MILN **23** 98, STLN **59** 99, MINA **28** 00, BOSA **28** 01, TEXA **57** 01, MINA **26** 02

JENSEN, RYAN P
(**43**,15,38) SFN **43** 01, **15** 01-02, **43** 02-03, KCA **38** 05

JENSEN, WOODY OF
(**16**) PITN **16** 32-39

JERZENBECK, MIKE P
(**58**) NYA **58** 98, (99)

JESTADT, GARRY SS/INF
(41,16,**12**) MONN **41** 69, CHIN **16** 71, SDN **12** 71-72

JESTER, VIRGIL P
(40,**22**) BOSN **40/22** 52, MILN **22** 53

JETER, DEREK SS
(**2**) NYA **2** 95-05

JETER, JOHNNY OF/DH F
(14,25,**8**,20,27,42) PITN **14** 69, **25** 70, SDN **8** 71-72, CHIA **20/27** 73, CLEA **42** 74

JETER, SHAWN OF/DH S
(**10**) CHIA **10** 92

JETHROE, SAM (JET) OF
(**5**,20) BOSN **5** 50-52, PITN **20** 54

JEWETT, TRENT CH
(**26**) PITN *CH* **26** 00, **44** 01-02

JIMENEZ, D'ANGELO INF/SS/P
(**59**,4,28,5,3) NYA **59** 99, SDN **4** 01-02, CHIA **28** 02, **5** 03, CINN **3** 03-05

JIMENEZ, ELVIO OF
(**48**) NYA **48** 64

JIMENEZ, GERMAN P
(**49**) ATLN **49** 88

JIMENEZ, HOUSTON SS/INF
(**1**,19,4) MINA **1** 83-84, PITN **19** 87, CLEA **4** 88

JIMENEZ, JASON P
(**54**,63) TBA **54** 02, DETA **63** 02

JIMENEZ, JOSE P
(52,49,**16**) STLN **52** 98, **49** 99, COLN **49** 00 -01, **16** 02-03, CLEA **36** 04

JIMENEZ, JUAN P
(**56**) PITN **56** 74

JIMENEZ, MANNY OF
(**12**,20,21,24, 23) KCA **12** 62-63, **20** 63-64, **12** 64, **21** 66, PITN **24** 67-68, CHIN **23** 69

JIMENEZ, MIGUEL P
(**47**) OAKA **47** 93-94

JIMERSON, CHARLTON OF
(**52**) HOUN **52** 05

JODIE, BRETT P
(62,**58**) NYA **62** 01, SDN **58** 01

JOHN, TOMMY (T.J.) P
(37,**25**,35) CLEA **37** 63-64, CHIA **25** 65-71, LAN **25** 72-78, NYA **25** 79-82, CALA **35** 82-83, **25** 83-85, OAKA **25** 85, NYA **25** 86-89

JOHNS, DOUG P
(51,**55**) OAKA **51** 95-96, BALA **55** 98-99

JOHNS, KEITH 2B
(**51**) BOSA **51** 98

JOHNSON, ADAM P
(37,**38**) MINA **37** 01, **38** 03

JOHNSON, ALEX OF/DH
(60,26,12,29, 17,20,15,23, 33) PHIN **60** 64, **26** 64-65, STLN **12** 66-67, CINN **29** 68-69, CALA **17** 70-71, CLEA **20** 72, TEXA **15** 73-74, NYA **23** 74-75, DETA **33** 76

JOHNSON, ART (LEFTY) P
(**29**) BOSN **12** 40, **29** 41-42

JOHNSON, BART P
(32,42,**21**,24) CHIA **32** 69, **42** 69-71, **21** 71-74, 76, **24** 77

JOHNSON, BEN P
(**45**) CHIN **45** 59-60

JOHNSON, BEN OF
(**4**) SDN **4** 05

JOHNSON, BILL P
(**37**) CHIN **37** 83-84

JOHNSON, BILLY (THE BULL) 3B/INF
(7,**24**,1) NYA **7** 43, **24** 46-51, STLN **1** 51 -53

JOHNSON, BOB (INDIAN BOB) OF/INF
(26,7,**4**,30,8) PHIA **26** 33, **7** 34-37, **4** 38-42, WASA **30/4** 43, BOSA **8** 44-45

JOHNSON, BOB (D.) P
(29,30,**27**,32, 50) NYN **29** 69, KCA **30** 70, PITN **27** 71-73, CLEA **32** 74, ATLN **50** 77

JOHNSON, BOBBY (E.) C/1B
(**8**,9) TEXA **8** 81, **9** 82, **8** 82-83

JOHNSON, BOB (W.) INF/UTIL
(5,29,**2**,6,14, 32) KCA **5** 60, WASA **29** 61-62, BALA **2** 63-67, NYN **6** 67, CINN **6** 68, ATLN **14** 68, STLN **29** 69, OAKA **32** 69-70

JOHNSON, BRIAN C
(28,**25**,10,18, 29,19,26) SDN **28** 94, **25** 95-96, DETA **10** 97, SFN **18** 97-98, CINN **29** 99, KCA **19** 00, LAN **26** 01

JOHNSON, C. CH
(**36**) ATLN *CH* **36** 48-49

JOHNSON, CHARLES C
(**23**,26,21,8, 24) FLAN **23** 94-98, LAN **26** 98, BALA **21** 99-00, CHIA **8** 00, FLAN **23** 01-02, COLN **23** 03-04, TBA **24** 05

JOHNSON, CHET (CHESTY CHET) P
(**39**) STLA **39** 46

JOHNSON, CLIFF C/1B/UTIL/DH
(6,9,41,**44**, 7,00) HOUN **6** 72-77, **9** 77, NYA **41** 77-79, CLEA **44** 79-80, CHIN **7** 80, OAKA **44** 81-82, TORA **44** 83-84, TEXA **44** 85-86, TORA **00** 85-86

JOHNSON, CONNIE P
(24,45,18,46, 44,**36**) CHIA **24/45/18** 53, **45/46** 54, **44** 55-56, BALA **36** 56-58

JOHNSON, DAN 1B
(**11**) OAKA **11** 05

JOHNSON, DANE P
(38,**50**,59) CHIA **38** 94, TORA **50** 96, OAKA **59** 97

JOHNSON, DARRELL C/CH/M
(40,47,39,**22**, 8,10,9,5,36, 33,3,15) STLA **40** 52, CHIA **47** 52, NYA **39** 57, **22** 58, STLN **8** 60, *CH* **8** 60-61, PHIN **10** 61, CINN **9** 61, **5** 62, BALA **36** 62, *CH* **36** 62, BOSA *CH* **33** 67-69, *M* **22** 74-76, *M* **3** 75, SEAA *M* **22** 77-80, TEXA *CH* **40** 81, *CH* **22** 81-82, *M* **22** 82, NYN*CH* **15** 93

JOHNSON, DAVE (C.) P
(45,**27**) BALA **45** 74-75, MINA **27** 77-78

JOHNSON, DAVE (W.) P
(56,35,**27**,40) PITN **56** 87, BALA **35** 89, **27** 89 -91, DETA **40** 93

JOHNSON, DAVEY 2B/INF/M
(6,27,40,**15**, 31,5,18) BALA **6** 65, **15** 65-72, ATLN **6** 73-75, PHIN **15** 77-78, CHIN **31** 78, NYN *M* **5** 84-90, CINN *M* **15** 93, *M* **18** 95, *M* **15** 95, BALA *M* **15** 96-97, LAN *M* **15** 99, **5** 00

JOHNSON, DERON 3B/OF/INF/DH
(43,6,**11**,7,3, 15,30,12,27, 51,2,8,54) NYA **43** 60, **6** 61, KCA **6** 61-62, CINN **11** 64-67, ATLN **11** 68, PHIN **11** 69-73, OAKA **7** 73-74, MILA **3** 74, BOSA **30** 74, CHIA **12** 75, BOSA **15** 75, **30** 75-76, CALA *CH* **27** 79, *CH* **6** 79-80, NYN *CH* **51** 81, PHIN *CH* **2** 82-84, SEAA *CH* **8** 85-86, CHIA *CH* **54** 87, CALA *CH* **2** 89-91

JOHNSON, DICK (FOOTER)(TREADS) PH
(**12**) CHIN **12** 58

JOHNSON, DON (PEP) 2B/3B
(**20**,9) CHIN **20** 43, **9** 44, **20** 44-48

JOHNSON, DON (R.) P
(**26**,22,37,24, 19,44) NYA **26** 47, 50, STLA **22** 50-51, **26** 50-51, WASA **37** 51, **24** 51-52, CHIA **26** 54, BALA **19** 55, SFN **44** 58

JOHNSON, EARL (LEFTY) P
(20,**12**,18) BOSA **20** 40-41, **12** 46-50, DETA **18** 51

JOHNSON, ERIK 2B/INF
(36,**31**) SFN **36** 93, **31** 94

JOHNSON, ERNIE P
(19,**32**,46) BOSN **19** 50, **32** 52, MILN **32** 53-58, BALA **46** 59

JOHNSON, FRANK OF/1B/UTIL
(47,19,**20**,37) SFN **47** 66, **19** 67, **20** 68-69, **37** 70-71

JOHNSON, FRED (DEACON)(CACTUS) P
(**16**) STLA **16** 38-39

JOHNSON, GARY OF
(**46**) ANAA **46** 03

JOHNSON, HANK P
(15,**14**,17,18, 16,12) NYA **15** 29, **14** 30-31, **17** 32, BOSA **18** 33, **16** 34-35, PHIA **12** 36, CINN **14** 39

JOHNSON, HOWARD (HOJO) 3B/OF/UTIL
(5,**20**) DETA **5** 82, **20** 83-84, NYN **20** 85-93, COLN **20** 94, CHIN **20** 95

JOHNSON, JASON P
(36,**41**,16,21) PITNN **36** 97, TBA **41** 98, BALA **41** 99-00, **16** 01-03, DETA **21** 04-05

JOHNSON, JEFF P
(**43**,49) NYA **43** 91-92, **49** 92, **43** 93

JOHNSON, JERRY P
(48,33,21,35, **28**,32,47,40, 44) PHIN **48** 68, **33** 68-69, STLN **21** 70, SFN **35** 70, **28** 71-72, CLEA **32** 73, HOUN **47** 74, SDN **40** 75-76, TORA **44** 77

JOHNSON, JIM P
(49,**30**) SFN **49/30** 70

JOHNSON, JOE P
(55,38,**33**) ATLN **55** 85, **38** 85-86, TORA **33** 86-87

JOHNSON, JOHN HENRY P
(**38**,48,34) OAKA **38** 78-79, TEXA **38** 79-81, BOSA **48** 83-84, MILA **34** 86, **38** 87

JOHNSON, JOHNNY (SWEDE) P
(18,23) NYA **18** 44, CHIA **23** 45

JOHNSON, JONATHAN P
(45,**50**,17,41) TEXA **45** 98, **50** 99-01, SDN **17** 02, HOUN **41** 03

JOHNSON, JOSH P
(**55**) FLAN **55** 05

JOHNSON, KEITH 1B
(**1**) ANAA **1** 00

JOHNSON, KELLY OF
(**27**) ATLN **27** 05

JOHNSON, KEN (HOOK) P
(**35**,16,39,26) STLN **35** 47-50, PHIN **16** 50, **39** 51, DETA **26** 52

JOHNSON, KEN P
(27,35,17,36, 40,**30**,54,50, 46) KCA **27** 58, **35** 59, **17** 60-61, CINN **40** 61, HOUN **36** 62, **40** 62-65, MILN **30** 66-69, NYA **54** 69, CHIN **50/46** 69, MONN **30** 70

JOHNSON, LAMAR 1B/DH/CH
(48,12,**23**,6, 27,28,33) CHIA **48** 74, **12** 75, **23** 76-81, TEXA **6/27** 82, MILA *CH* **28** 95-97, MILN *CH* **23** 98, KCA *CH* **23** 99-01, SEAA *CH* **33** 03

JOHNSON, LANCE OF/DH
(21,**1**,31) STLN **21** 87, CHIA **1** 88-95, NYN **1** 96-97, CHIN **1** 97-99, NYA **31** 00

JOHNSON, LARRY DOBY C/DH
(52,**9**,53,47, 54) CLEA **52** 72, **9** 74, MONN **53** 75, **47** 76, CHIA **54** 78

JOHNSON, LLOYD (EPPA) P
(**50**) PITN **50** 34

JOHNSON, LOU (SLICK) OF
(24,27,18,**41**, 22,26) CHIN **24** 60, LAA **27** 61, MILN **18** 62-63, LAN **41** 65-67, CHIN **41** 68, CLEA **22** 68, CALA **26** 69

JOHNSON, MARK (J.) P
(**46**) DETA **46** 00

JOHNSON, MARK (L.) C
(64,57,10,**8**,7) CHIA **64/57** 98, **10** 99-00, **8** 01-02, OAKA **7** 03, MILN **8** 04

JOHNSON, MARK (P.) 1B
(**36**,32,5,20) PITN **36** 95-97, ANAA **32** 98, JAP 99, NYN **5** 00, **20** 01, **5** 02

JOHNSON, MIKE (K.) P
(55,39,**47**) BALA **55/39** 97, MONN **47** 97-00, **31** 01

JOHNSON, MIKE (N.) P
(38,**22**) SDN **38/22** 74

JOHNSON, NICK 1B/DH N
(60,36,**24**) NYA **60** 01, **36** 02-03, MONN **24** 04, WASN **24** 05

JOHNSON, RANDY (D.) (THE BIG UNIT) P
(57,**51**,34,41) MONN **57** 88, **51** 88-89, SEAA **51** 89-92, **34** 93, **51** 93-98, HOUN **51** 98, ARIN **51** 99-04, NYA **41** 05

JOHNSON, RANDY (G.) 3B/2B
(**6**) ATLN **6** 82-84

JOHNSON, RANDY (S.) OF/UTIL
(**7**,22) CHIA **7** 80, MINA **22** 82

JOHNSON, RANKIN, JR. P
(**15**) PHIA **15** 41

JOHNSON, REED OF
(37,**3**) TORA **37** 03-04, **3** 05

JOHNSON, RON 1B/C/OF
(27,**35**) KCA **27** 82, **35** 83, MONN **35** 84

JOHNSON, RONDIN 2B
(**36**) KCA **36** 86

JOHNSON, RONTREZ OF
(**25**) KCA **25** 03

JOHNSON, ROY (C.) OF/3B
(22,**1**,18,3,4, 12) DETA **22** 31, **1** 32, BOSA **18** 32, **3** 33, **4** 34, **3** 35, NYA **1** 36, **22** 37, BOSN **12** 37-38

JOHNSON, ROY (E.) OF
(**27**) MONN **27** 82, 84-85

JOHNSON, ROY (J.) (HARDROCK) CH/M
(61,20,**42**) CHIN *CH* **61** 35-37, *CH* **20** 37-39, *CH* **42** 44-53, *M* **42** 44

JOHNSON, RUSS 3B/SS
(19,**9**),10,25, 14) HOUN **19** 97, **9** 98-00, TBA **10** 00, **25** 01-02, NYA **14** 05

JOHNSON, SI P/CH
(14,15,21,24, 18,12,**34**,8, 16,10,20,36) CINN **14** 32-33, **15** 34, **21** 35, **24** 36, STLN **18** 36, **12** 37-38, PHIN **34** 40-41, **8/16** 42, **10** 43, **20** 46, BOSN **34/36** 46-47, *CH* **36** 48

JOHNSON, STAN OF
(**40**,22) CHIA **40** 60, KCA **22** 61

JOHNSON, SYL P
(23,30,20,**47**, 22,3) STLN **23** 22, **30** 33, CINN **20** 34, PHIN **47** 34-37, **22** 38, **3** 39-40

JOHNSON, TIM SS/UTIL/CH
(4,**1**,17) MILA **4** 73-76, **1** 77-78, TORA **17** 78-79, MONN *CH* **1** 93-94, BOSA *CH* **17** 95-96, TORA *CH* **17** 98

JOHNSON, TOM P
(32,**21**) MINA **32** 74-75, **21** 76-78

JOHNSON, TONY OF/DH
(42,**45**) MONN **42** 81, TORA **45** 82

JOHNSON, TYLER P
(**61**) STLN **61** 05

JOHNSON, VIC P
(16,34,22) BOSA **16** 44, **34** 45, CLEA **22** 46

JOHNSON, WALLACE 2B/1B/CH
(62,1,5,37,**6**, 18) MONN **62** 81, **1** 82-83, SFN **5** 83, MONN **37** 84, **6** 86-90, CHIA *CH* **18** 98-02

JOHNSON, WALTER (THE BIG TRAIN) (BARNEY) M
(28,25,**10**) WASA *M* **28** 31, *M* **25** 32, CLEA *M* **10** 33-35

JOHNSTON, GREG OF
(23,18,21) SFN **23** 79, MINA **18** 80, **21** 81

JOHNSTON, JOEL P
(58,37,**64**,45) KCA **58** 91, **37** 92, PITN **64** 93-94, BOSA **45** 95

JOHNSTON, LEN CH
(**62**) CLEA *CH* **62** 72

JOHNSTON, MIKE P
(**37**) PITN **37** 04-05

JOHNSTON, REX OF
(**4**) PITN **4** 64

JOHNSTONE, JAY (MOON MAN) OF/UTIL/1B
(10,3,**21**,27, 37,4,12,59) CALA **10** 66-70, CHIA **10** 71-72, OAKA **3** 73, PHIN **21** 74-78, NYA **21** 78, **27** 78-79, SDN **37/4** 79, **21** 79, LAN **21** 80-82, CHIN **21** 82-84, LAN **12** 85

JOHNSTONE, JOHN P
(**40**,39,41,37 53,49) FLAN **40** 93-94, HOUN **39** 96, SFN **41/37** 97, OAKA **53** 97, SFN **49** 98-00, (01)

JOINER, ROY (POP) P
(21,23,19) CHIN **21** 34, **23** 35, NYN **19** 40

JOK, STAN (TUCKER) 3B/OF
(12,32,**21**) PHIN **12** 54, CHIA **32** 54, **21** 55

JOLLEY, SMEAD (GUINEA)(SMUDGE) OF/C
(**4**,3,9) CHIA **4** 31, **3** 32, BOSA **9** 32, **4** 33

JOLLY, DAVE (GABBY) P
(**16**,17) MILN **16** 53-57, **17** 54

JONES, A. CH
(**45**) CLEA **45** 61

JONES, AL P
(**49**) CHIA **49** 83-85

JONES, ANDRUW OF
(**25**) ATLN **25** 96-05

JONES, ART P
(**no#**) BKNN **no#** 32

JONES, BARRY P
(**50**,38,46) PITN **50** 86-88, CHIA **38** 88-89, **50** 89-90, MONN **50** 91, PHIN **50** 92, NYN **46** 92, CHIA **50** 93

JONES, BOBBY (J.) P
(**28**) NYN **28** 93-00, SDN **28** 01-02

JONES, BOBBY (M.) P
(**36**,21,39) COLN **36** 97-99, NYN **21** 00, (01), 02, SDN **39** 02, BOSA **36** 04

JONES, BOBBY (O.) OF/DH/UTIL/CH
(8,9,18,27,**6**, 31) TEXA **8** 74-75, CALA **9** 76, **18** 76-77, TEXA **27** 81, **6** 83-86, *CH* **31** 01

JONES, CALVIN P
(**52**) SEAA **52** 91-92

JONES, CHIPPER SS/3B/OF
(16,**10**) ATLN **16** 93, **10** 95-05

JONES, CHRIS (C.) OF
(20,24,33,**5**, 18,2,39) CINN **20** 91, HOUN **24** 92, COLN **33** 93-94, NYN **5** 95-96, SDN **20** 97, ARIN **18** 98, SFN **2** 98, MILN **39** 00

JONES, CHRIS (D.) OF
(22,**12**) HOUN **22** 85, SFN **12** 86

JONES, CLARENCE CH
(21,29,54,**28**, 38,9) CHIN *CH* **21/27** 67, **29** 68, ATLN *CH* **54** 88-89, *CH* **18** 89 *CH* **28** 90, *CH* **38** 91, *CH* **28** 91-98, CLEA *CH* **9** 99, **28** 99-01

JONES, CLEON OF/1B
(34,12,**21**,14) NYN **34** 63, 65, **12** 65, **21** 66-75, CHIA **14** 76

JONES, DALE (NUBS) P
(**33**) PHIN **33** 41

JONES, DALTON 2B/INF/UTIL
(39,**3**,2,14) BOSA **39** 64-65, **3** 66-69, DETA **2** 70-72, TEXA **14** 72

JONES, DARRYL DH/OF
(2,**27**) NYA **2/27** 79

JONES, DAX OF
(**52**) SFN **52** 96

JONES, DEACON 1B/CH
(**50**,4,29) CHIA **50** 62-63, 66, HOUN *CH* **4** 76-82, SDN *CH* **29** 84-87

JONES, DOUG P
(45,54,39,46, **11**,23,31,27, 43,24) MILA **45/54** 82, CLEA **39** 86, **46** 87-88, **11** 88-91, HOUN **23** 92-93, PHIN **23** 94, BALA **31** 95, CHIN **27** 96, MILA **43** 96-97, MILN **43** 98, CLEA **43** 98, OAKA **24** 99-00

JONES, EARL (LEFTY) P
(35,**17**) STLA **35/17** 45

JONES, GARY P/CH
(**39**,11) NYA **39** 70-71, OAKA *CH* **11** 98

JONES, GORDON P/CH
(**45**,47,38,19, 34,46,3,5) STLN **45** 54-56, NYN **47** 57, SFN **38** 58-59, BALA **19** 60-61, KCA **34** 62, HOUN **34** 64, **46** 65, *CH* **3** 66, *CH* **5** 66-67

JONES, GREG P
(58,**37**) ANAA **58** 03, (04), LAA **37** 05

JONES, HAL 1B
(7,**15**) CLEA **7** 61, **15** 62

JONES, JACK CH
(**45**) PITN *CH* **45** 97

JONES, JACQUE OF/DH
(**11**) MINA **11** 99-05

JONES, JAKE 1B
(__,**3**) CHIA __ 41-42, **3** 46-47, BOSA **3** 47-48

JONES, JASON OF/DH
(**21**) TEXA **21** 03

JONES, JEFF (A.) P
(**38**) OAKA **38** 80-84

JONES, JEFF (R.) OF/1B/CH
(23,**54**) CINN **23** 83, DETA *CH* **54** 95, 98-99

JONES, JIMMY P
(**45**,26,37,38) SDN **45** 86-88, NYA **26** 89-90, HOUN **37** 91-92, MONN **38** 93

JONES, JOE CH
(41,43,**37**,18) KCA *CH* **41** 87, *CH* **43** 92, PITN *CH* **37** 97-98, **27** 99-00, KCA *CH* **18** 05

JONES, JOHN (SKINS) OF
(**23**) PHIA **23** 32

JONES, LYNN OF/DH/CH
(**35**) DETA **35** 79-83, KCA **35** 84-86, *CH* **35** 91-92, FLAN *CH* **35** 01, BOSA *CH* **35** 04-05

JONES, MACK (MACK THE KNIFE) OF/1B
(30,48,12,**9**) MILN **30** 61-63, **48** 65, ATLN **48** 66-67, CINN **12** 68, MONN **9** 69-71

JONES, MARCUS P
(**22**) OAKA **22** 00

JONES, MIKE P
(50,28,40,**17**) KCA **50/28** 80, **40** 81, **17** 84-85

JONES, NIPPY 2B/OF/1B
(7,19,**3**,9,25) STLN **7** 46-47, **19** 47-48, **3** 48-51, PHIN **9** 52, MILN **25** 57

JONES, ODELL P
(50,**36**,22,21, 13,28) PITN **50** 75, **36** 77-78, SEAA **36** 79, PITN **22** 81, TEXA **21** 83-84, BALA **13** 86, MILA **28** 88

JONES, RANDY P
(**35**,25) SDN **35** 73-80, NYN **25** 81, **35** 81-82

JONES, RED OF
(**19**) STLN **19** 40

JONES, RICK P
(**46**) BOSA **46** 76, SEAA **46** 77-78

JONES, RICKY 2B/3B
(**30**) BALA **30** 86

JONES, RON OF
(**26**,20) PHIN **26** 88-89, **20** 90, **26** 91

JONES, ROSS SS/INF/DH
(21,**2**,3) NYN **21** 84, SEAA **2** 86, KCA **3** 87

JONES, RUPPERT OF/DH
(30,**9**,22,28,32,19,13) KCA **30** 76, SEAA **9** 77-79, NYA **22** 80, SDN **28** 81, **22** 81-82, **9** 83, DETA **32** 84, CALA **19** 85, **13** 85-86, **9** 87

JONES, SAD SAM P
(14,25,**28**,17) WASA **14** 31, CHIA **25** 32, **28** 33-34, **17** 35

JONES, SAM (TOOTHPICK SAM) P
(36,22,27,23,**19**,35) CLEA **36** 51, **22** 51-52, CHIN **27** 55-56, STLN **23** 57-58, SFN **19** 59-61, DETA **23** 62, STLN **35** 63, BALA **35** 64

JONES, SHELDON (AVAILABLE) P
(28,39,**37**,11,26) NYN **28** 46, **39** 47, **37** 48-51, BOSN **11** 52, CHIN **26** 53

JONES, SHERMAN (ROADBLOCK) P
(**36**,34,28) SFN **36** 60, CINN **34** 61, NYN **36/28** 62

JONES, STACY P
(51,**49**) BALA **51** 91, CHIA **49** 96

JONES, STEVE P
(39,34,37,46) CHIA **39** 67, WASA **34** 68, KCA **37/46** 69

JONES, TERRY OF
(**1**,9,16) COLN **1** 96, MONN **9** 98-99, **1** 00, **16** 01

JONES, TIM (B.) P
(48,**32**) PITN **48/32** 77

JONES, (W.) TIM INF/UTIL
(22,**8**) STLN **22** 88-89, **8** 90-93

JONES, TODD P
(**59**,50) HOUN **59** 93-96, DETA **59** 97-01, MINA **59** 01, COLN **59** 02-03, BOSA **59** 03, CINN **59** 04, PHIN **59** 04, FLAN **50** 05

JONES, TOMMY CH
(**17**) ARIN *CH* **17** 04

JONES, TRACY OF/DH
(29,24,**25**,15) CINN **29** 86-88, MONN **24** 88, SFN **25** 89, DETA **15** 89-90, SEAA **25** 90-91

JONES, WILLIE (PUDDIN' HEAD) 3B/INF
(12,37,**6**,23,14) PHIN **12** 47, **37**48, **6** 49-59, CLEA **12** 59, CINN **23** 59, **14** 59-61

JONNARD, BUBBER C/CH
(**10**,30) PHIN **10** 35, NYN *CH* **30** 42-46

JOOST, EDDIE SS/INF/M
(17,22,2,9,27,**1**,20) CINN **17** 36, **22** 37, **17** 39-42, BOSN **2** 43, **27/9** 45, PHIA **1** 47-54, *M* **1** 54, BOSA **20** 55

JORDAN, BRIAN OF/DH
(50,**3**,33) STLN **50** 92, **3** 92-98, ATLN **33** 99-01, LAN **33** 02-03, TEXA **33** 04, ATLN **33** 05

JORDAN, BUCK 1B/UTIL
(27,**5**,12,34,45,8) WASA **27** 31, BOSN **5** 32-36, **12** 37, CINN **34** 37, **45** 38, PHIN **8** 38

JORDAN, JIMMY (LORD) INF
(24,**12**) BKNN **24** 33, **12** 34-36

JORDAN, KEVIN 1B
(**23**) PHIN **23** 95-01

JORDAN, MILT P
(**35**) DETA **35** 53

JORDAN, NILES P
(41,25,**40**) PHIN **41** 51, CINN **25** 52, **40** 52

JORDAN, RICARDO (RICK) P
(**48**) TORA **48** 95, PHIN **48** 96, NYN **48** 97, CINN **48** 98

JORDAN, RICKY 1B
(**17**,29) PHIN **17** 88-94, SEAA **29** 96

JORDAN, SCOTT OF
(**68**) CLEA **68** 88

JORDAN, TOM C
(17,**26**,8) CHIA **17** 44, **26** 46, CLEA **26** 46, STLA **8** 48

JORGENS, ART C B
(32,15,28,10,**9**,18) NYA **32/15** 29, **28** 30, **10** 31, **9** 32-35, **18** 36-39

JORGENS, ORVILLE P B
(32,**44**) PHIN **32** 35, **44** 35-37

JORGENSEN, MIKE 1B/OF/UTIL/M
(10,**16**,18,35,2,22,11,19) NYN **10** 68, **16** 70-71, MONN **16** 72-77, OAKA **18** 77, TEXA **35** 78-79, N YN **22** 80-83, ATLN **11** 83-84, STLN **19** 84-85, *M* **22** 95

JORGENSEN, PINKY OF
(**29**) CINN **29** 37

JORGENSEN, JOHNNY (SPIDER) 3B/OF
(**21**,10,27) BKNN **21** 47-50, NYN **10** 50, **27** 51

JORGENSEN, RYAN C
(**22**) FLAN **22** 05

JORGENSEN, TERRY 3B/INF
(56,**27**) MINA **56** 89, **27** 92-93

JOSE, FELIX OF/DH
(6,5,**34**,45,8) OAKA **6** 88-90, STLN **5** 90-91, **34** 91-92, KCA **34** 93-95, NYA **45** 00, ARIN **8** 02-03

JOSEPH, KEVIN P
(**58**) STLN **58** 02

JOSEPH, RICK 1B/3B/UTIL
(23,20,**18**) KCA **23** 64, PHIN **20** 67-68, **18** 69-70

JOSEPHSON, DUANE C/1B
(46,**5**,24) CHIA **46** 65-66, **5** 67-70, BOSA **24** 71-73

JOSHUA, VON OF/DH/1B/CH
(**12**,19,14,28,22,48) LAN **12** 69-74, SFN **19** 75-76, MILA **14** 76, **28** 76-77, LAN **14** 79, SDN **22** 80, CHIA *CH* **48** 98-01

JOURNELL, JIMMY P
(**77**) STLN **77** 03, 05

JOYCE, BOB P
(15,**24**) PHIA **15** 39, NYN **24** 46

JOYCE, DICK P
(**34**) KCA **34** 65

JOYCE, MIKE P
(**23**) CHIA **23** 62-63

JOYNER, WALLY 1B
(**21**,12,22,24,5) CALA **21** 86-91, KCA **12** 92-95, SDN **22** 96-99, ATLN **24** 00, ANAA **5** 01

JUDD, MICHAEL P
(**60**,50,58) LAN **60** 97-00, TBA **50** 01, TEXA **58** 01

JUDD, OSCAR (OSSIE) P
(15,**29**,17) BOSA **15** 41, **29** 42-45, PHIN **29** 45, **17** 46-48

JUDEN, JEFF P
(44,37,43,**14**,12,7,33,57) HOUN **44** 91, 93, PHIN **37** 94, **43** 94-95, SFN **14** 96, MONN **14** 96-97, CLEA **12/7** 97, MILN **14** 98, ANAA **33** 98, NYA **57** 99

JUDGE, JOE 1B/CH
(5,**6**,2,23,25,38,31,33) WASA **5** 31, **6** 32, BKNN **2** 33, BOSA **23** 33, **25** 34, WASA *CH* **38/31** 45, *CH* **33** 46

JUDNICH, WALT (WALLY) OF/1B
(**12**,17,18,35,14) STLA **12** 40-42, **17** 46, **18** 47, CLEA **35** 48, PITN **14** 49

JUDSON, HOWIE P
(**48**,47) CHIA **48** 48-52, CINN **47** 53-54

JUDY, LYLE (PUNCH) 2B
(**10**) STLN **10** 35

JUELICH, JACK (RED) 2B/3B
(**22**) PITN **22** 39

JULIO, JORGE P
(59,**50**) BALA **59** 01, **50** 02-05

JUMONVILLE, GEORGE SS/3B
(7,**16**) PHIN **7** 40, **16** 41

JUNGE, ERIC P
(**28**) PHIN **28** 02-03, (04)

JUNGELS, KEN (CURLY) P
(24,19,**33**,43,36,24) CLEA **24** 37, **19** 38, **33** 40-41, **43/36** 41, PITN **24** 42

JURAK, ED (R.) P
(**22**,27,8) BOSA **22** 82-85, OAKA **27** 88, SFN **8** 89

JUREWICZ, MIKE P
(**29**) NYA **29** 65

JURGES, BILLY SS/INF/CH/M
(12,11,8,5,**7**,45,54,16) CHIN **12** 32, **11** 32-33, **8** 34, **11** 35-36, **5** 37-38, NYN **7** 39, **2** 40-41, **7** 42-45, **16** 45, CHIN **45** 46, *CH* **45** 47-48, WASA *CH* **54** 56-59, BOSA *M* **16** 59-60

JURISICH, AL P
(**29**,38) STLN **29** 44-45, PHIN **38** 46-47

JUST, JOE C
(**5**) CINN **5** 44-45

JUSTICE, DAVID OF/1B
(**23**,33,28) ATLN **23** 89-96, CLEA **33** 97, **23** 97-00, NYA **28** 00-01, OAKA **23** 02

JUTZE, SKIP C
(18,26,**9**,3) STLN **18** 72, HOUN **26** 73-74, **9** 75-76, SEAA **3** 77

K

KAAT, JIM (KITTY) P/CH
(21,**36**,39,47,45) WASA **21**59-60,**36** 60, MINA **36** 61-73, CHIA **36** 73-75, PHIN **39** 76-79, NYA **47** 79, **36** 79-80, STLN **36** 80-83, CINN *CH* **45** 84-85

KAHLE, BOB PH
(**22**) BOSN **22** 38

KAHN, LOU CH
(**27**) STLN *CH* **27** 55

KAINER, DON P
(33,**43**) TEXA **33/43** 80

KAISER, BOB P
(**51**) CLEA **51** 71

KAISER, DON (TIGER) P
(**45**) CHIN **45** 55-57

KAISER, JEFF P
(40,48,47,**46**,49,56) OAKA **40** 85, CLEA **48** 87, **47** 88, **46** 89-90, DETA **49** 91, CINN **56** 93, NYN **56** 93

KALFASS, BILL (LEFTY) P
(**61**) PHIA **61** 37

KALIN, FRANK (FATS) OF
(23,**36**) PITN **23** 40, CHIA **36** 43

KALINE, AL OF/3B/1B/DH
(25,**6**) DETA **25** 53-54, **6** 54-74

KAMIENIECKI, SCOTT P
(40,22,28,**30**,50) NYA **40** 91, **22** 92, **28** 93-96, BALA **30** 97-99, CLEA **30** 00, ATLN **50** 00

KAMM, WILLIE 3B
(7,**5**) CHIA **7** 31, CLEA **5** 31-35

KAMMEYER, BOB P
(40,53) NYA **40** 78, **53** 79

KAMPOURIS, ALEX 2B/UTIL
(30,**3**,38,26,7,22,31,15) CINN **30** 34, **3** 35-37, **38** 38, NYN **26/7** 38, **22** 39, BKNN **31** 41, **3** 42-43, WASA **15** 43

KANE, TOM (SUGAR) 2B
(**29**) BOSN **29** 38

KANEHL, ROD (HOT ROD) UTIL
(**10**) NYN **10** 62-64

KAPLER, GABE OF
(51,23,**19**,18,29,44) DETA **51** 98, **23** 99, TEXA **23** 00, **19** 01, **18** 02, COLN **19** 02-03, BOSA **29** 03, **19** 04, **44** 05

KARCHNER, MATT P
(60,**47**,52) CHIA **60** 95, **47** 96-98, CHIN **52** 98-00

KARDOW, PAUL (TEX) P
(**17**) CLEA **17** 36

KARKOVICE, RON C/DH
(53,5,**20**) CHIA **53** 86-87, **5** 87-88, **20** 89-97

KARL, ANDY P
(19,**24**,6,28,3,23,11,33,44,24,18) BOSA **19/24** 43, PHIN **6** 43, **28 /3** 44, **23/11** 45, **33** 45-46, **44** 46, BOSN **24/18** 47

KARL, SCOTT P
(**42**,19,33) MILA **42** 95-97, MILN **42** 98-99, COLN **19** 00, ANAA **33** 00

KARLON, BILL (HANK) OF
(**32**) NYA **32** 30

KARNUTH, JASON P
(41,**39**) STLN **41** 01, DETA **39** 05

KARP, RYAN P
(52,**57**) PHIN **52** 95, **57** 96

KARPEL, HERB (LEFTY) P
(**37**) NYA **37** 46

KARROS, ERIC 1B
(**23**,32,18) LAN **23** 91-02, CHIN **32** 03, OAKA **18/32** 04

KARSAY, STEVE P
(50,**20**,36,31,21) OAKA **50** 93, **20** 94, 97-01, ATLN **36/20** 01, NYA **31** 02, (03), 04-05, TEXA **21** 05

KASHIWADA, TAKASHI P
(**18**) NYN **18** 97

KASKO, EDDIE INF/M
(**10**,11,12,2,30) STLN **10** 57-58, CINN **10** 59-63, HOUN **11** 64-65, BOSA **12/2** 66, *M* **30** 70-73

KATA, MATT OF/INF
(**11**,8,27) ARIN **11** 03, **8** 04, **11** 05, PHIN **27** 05

KATT, RAY C/CH
(**8**,15,5,21,9,40) NYN **8** 52-56, STLN **15** 56, NYN **5** 57, STLN **21** 58, **9** 59, *CH* **9** 59-60, CLEA *CH* **40** 62

KATZ, BOB P
(**35**) CINN **35** 44

KAUFMAN, CURT P
(38,47,55,48) NYA **38/47** 82-83, CALA **48** 84

KAUFMANN, TONY P/CH
(20,**25**) STLN **20** 35, *CH* **25** 47-50

KAYE, JUSTIN P
(**36**) SEAA **36** 02

KAZAK, EDDIE 3B/INF
(12,21,**1**,3,10) STLN **12** 48, **21** 49-50, **1** 51-52, **3** 52, CINN **10** 52

KAZANSKI, TED SS/INF
(**7**) PHIN **7** 53-58

KAZMIR, SCOTT P
(57,**26**) TBA **57** 04, **26** 05

KEAGLE, GREG P
(**57**) DETA **57** 96-98

KEALEY, STEVE P
(48,31,39,**23**) CALA **48** 68, **31** 68-70, **39** 70, CHIA **23** 71-73

KEANE, JOHNNY CH/M
(**5**,21) STLN *CH* **5** 59-61, *M* **5** 61-64, NYA *M* **21**65-66

KEARNEY, BOB C/DH
(30,32,**11**) SFN **30** 79, OAKA **32** 81, **30** 82-83, SEAA **11** 84-87

KEARNS, AUSTIN OF
(**28**) CINN **28** 02-05

KEARSE, ED (TRUCK) C
(**25**) NYA **25** 42

KEATLEY, GREG C
(**39**) KCA **39** 81

KEEDY, PAT 3B/OF/UTIL
(36,38,**33**) CALA **36** 85, CHIA **38** 87, CLEA **33** 89

KEEFE, DAVE CH
(32,31,**29**) PHIA *CH* **32** 39-40, *CH* **31** 41-43, *CH* **29** 43-50

KEEGAN, BOB (SMILEY) P
(**15**) CHIA **15** 53-58

KEEGAN, ED P
(**50**,36) PHIN **50** 59, KCA **36** 61, PHIN **50** 62

KEELY, BOB C/CH
(**2**,18,9,35) STLN **2** 44-45, **18** 45, BOSN *CH* **9** 46, *CH* **35** 47-52, MILN **35** 53-57

KEENER, JEFF P
(**44**) STLN **44** 82-83

KEENER, JOE P
(**56**) MONN **56** 76

KEETON, RICKEY (BUSTER) P
(50,**45**) MILA **50** 80, **45** 80-81

KEHN, CHET P
(**33**) BKNN **33** 42

KEISLER, RANDY P
(63,58,**57**) NYA **63** 00, **58** 01, SDN **57** 03, CINN **57** 05

KEKICH, MIKE P
(37,**18**,24,41) LAN **37** 65, 68, NYA **18** 69-73, CLEA **18** 73, TEXA **24/18** 75, SEAA **41/37** 77

KELL, GEORGE 3B/1B/UTIL B
(**7**,21,15,1,4,3) PHIA **7** 43-46, DETA **21** 46-48, **15** 48, **21** 49-50, **7** 51-52, BOSA **1** 52-54, CHIA **1** 54-56, BALA **4** 56, **3** 56-57

KELL, SKEETER 2B B
(**2**) PHIA **2** 52

KELLEHER, FRANKIE OF
(28,**22**) CINN **28** 42, **22** 43

KELLEHER, HAL P
(11,**43**,24) PHIN **11** 35, **43** 36-37, **24** 38

KELLEHER, MICK INF/CH
(25,9,28,**20**,18,2,19) STLN **25** 72-73, HOUN **9** 74, STLN **28** 75, CHIN **20** 76-80, DETA **18** 81-82, CALA **2** 82, PITN *CH* **19** 86, DETA *CH* **18** 03-05

KELLER, CHARLIE (KING KONG) OF/CH
(**9**,15,12,27,28,33) NYA **9** 39-43, 45, **15** 45, **12** 45-48, **9**49, DETA **27** 50-51, NYA **28** 52, *CH* **33** 57

KELLER, HAL C
(37,17,14,33,**9**) WASA **37/17** 49, **14/33** 50, **9** 52

KELLER, KRIS P
(30,**18**) DETA **30** 02

KELLER, RON P
(30,**18**) MINA **30** 66, **18** 68

KELLERT, FRANK 1B
(2,15,**7**,12,5) STLA **2** 53, BALA **15/7** 54, BKNN **12** 55, CHIN **5** 56

KELLETT, DON (RED) INF
(**8**) BOSA **8** 34

KELLEY, DICK P
(**22**,20,42) MILN **22** 64-65, **20** 65, ATLN **22** 66-69, SDN **42** 71

KELLEY, HARRY P
(19,16,15,**22**) PHIA **19** 36, **16** 37, **15** 38, WASA **22** 38-39

KELLEY, TOM P
(**45**,47,36) CLEA **45** 64-67, ATLN **47** 71, **36** 71-73

KELLNER, ALEX P B
(22,**20**,41,34) PHIA **22** 48-54, KCA **20** 55-58, CINN **41** 58, STLN **34** 59

KELLNER, WALT P B
(**21**) PHIA **21** 52-53

KELLY, BOB P
(18,**33**,45,37) CHIN **18** 51, **33** 51-53, CINN **33** 53, **45** 58, CLEA **37** 58

KELLY, BRYAN P
(**45**) DETA **45** 86-87

KELLY, GEORGE (HIGHPOCKETS) 1B/CH
(**14**,33,30,32,2) BKNN **14** 32,CINN *CH* **33** 35, **30** 36-37, BOSN *CH* **32** 38-39, **33** 40-43, CINN *CH* **2** 47-48

KELLY, KENNY OF
(**15**,29,39) TBA **15** 00, CINN **29** 05, WASN **39** 05

KELLY, MIKE (B.) CH
(56,33,36) CHIA *CH* **33** 31, CHIN *CH* **56** 34, BOSN *CH* **33** 38-39, PITN *CH* **36** 40-41

KELLY, MIKE (R.) OF
(**25**,15,24,27) ATLN **25** 94-95, CINN **15** 96-97 TBA **24** 98, COLN **27** 99

KELLY, PAT (D.) C
(**6**) TORA **6** 80

KELLY, PAT (F.) 2B/3B
(**14**,12,7) NYA **14** 91-97, STLN **12** 98, TORA **7** 99

KELLY, PAT (H.) OF/DH
(25,30,**18**) MINA **25** 67, **30** 68, KCA **18** 69-70,CHIA **18** 71-76, BALA **18** 77-80, CLEA **25** 81

KELLY, ROBERTO (BOBBY)(DON'T CALL ME BOBBY) OF
(59,46,**39**,30,14,28,21,5,10,19) NYA **59/46** 87, **39** 87-92, CINN **30** 93-94, ATLN **14** 94, MONN **28** 95, LAN **21** 95, MINA **5** 96-97, SEAA **10** 97, TEXA **39** 98-99, NYA **19** 00

KELLY, TOM (JAY) 1B/OF/CH/M
(**16**,41,10) MINA **16** 75,*CH* **41** 83-86, *M* **41** 86, *M* **10** 87-01

KELLY, VAN 3B/2B
(**16**,36) SDN **16/36** 69, **16** 70

KELSO, BILL P
(22,41,**26**) LAA **22** 64, CALA **22** 66, **41** 66-67, CINN **41/26** 68

KELTNER, KEN (BUTCH) 3B/1B
(35,25,8,9,**6**,4) CLEA **35** 37, **25** 38-41, **8** 41-44, **9** 46, **6** 47-49, BOSA **4** 50

KELTON, DAVE 3B/OF
(24,28,**27**) CHIN **24/28** 03, **27** 04

KEMMERER, RUSS (RUSTY)(DUTCH) P
(24,40,28,**16**,31,44,39) BOSA **24** 54, **40** 55, **28** 57, WASA **16** 57-60, CHIA **31** 60, **44** 60-62, HOUN **39** 62-63

KEMP, STEVE OF/DH
(43,**33**,22,21,13,24) DETA **43** 77, **33** 77-81, CHIA **22** 82, NYA **21** 83-84, PITN **13** 85, **23** 86, TEXA **24** 88

KENDALL, FRED C/INF/DH/CH F
(36,**16**,18,5) SDN **36** 69, **16** 70-76, CLEA **16** 77, BOSA **18** 78, SDN **5** 79-80, DETA *CH* **18** 96-98, COLN *CH* **16** 00-02, **18** 02

KENDALL, JASON C S
(**18**) PITN **18** 96-04, OAKA **18** 05

KENDERS, AL C
(**10**) PHIN **10** 61

KENNEDY, ADAM SS/2B
(8,**2**) STLN **8** 99, ANAA **2** 00-04, LAA **2** 05

KENNEDY, BILL (A,) (LEFTY) P
(29,38,26,**30**,46,37,15,18,43,19) CLEA **29** 48, STLA **38** 48, **26** 48-49, **30** 49-50, **46** 51, CHIA **37/15** 52, BOSA **18** 53, CINN **43** 56, **19** 57

KENNEDY, BILL (G.) P
(21,20,**38**,51) WASA **21** 42, **20** 46, **38** 46, **51** 47

KENNEDY, BOB 3B/OF/UTIL/M/CH F
(2,36,25,5,24,**33**,40,30,3,16,49,61,4) CHIA **2** 39, **36** 40-41, **25** 42, **36** 46, **5** 46-48, CLEA **24** 48, **33** 49-54, BALA **40** 54-55, **33** 55, CHIA **24** 55, **30** 55-56, DETA **3** 56, CHIA **16** 57, BKNN **49** 57, CHIN *M* **61** 63-65, ATLN *CH* **4** 67, OAKA *M* **33** 68

KENNEDY, JIM INF
(**24**) STLN **24** 70

KENNEDY, JOE P (50,17,37) TBA 50 01, 17 02-03, COLN 37 04-05, OAKA 37 05

KENNEDY, JOHN 3B/INF/DH (8,34,2,11,26,12) PHIN 8 57, WASA 34 62, 2 63-64, LAN 11 65-66, NYA 26 67, SEAA 11 69, MILA 11 70, BOSA 12 70-74

KENNEDY, JUNIOR 2B/INF (11,26,15) CINN 11 74, 26 78-81, CHIN 15 82-83

KENNEDY, KEVIN M/CH (31,44) MONN *CH* 3192, BOSA *M* 44 94-96

KENNEDY, MONTE P (36,23,32) NYN 36/23 46, 32 47-53

KENNEDY, TERRY C/1B S (16,15) STLN 16 78-80, SDN 16 81-86, BALA 15 87-88, SFN 16 89-91

KENNEDY, VERN P (24,11,33,23,27,17,22,12,19,36) CHIA 24 34-37, DETA 11 38-39, STLA 11/24/33 39, 23 40, 27 41, WASA 17/22/33 41, CLEA 12 42-44, PHIN 11 44, 19 45, CINN 36 45

KENNEY, ART P (11) BOSN 11 38

KENNEY, JERRY SS/UTIL (14,2,9) NYA 14 67, 2 69-72, CLEA 9 73

KENSING, LOGAN P (54) FLAN 54 04-05

KENT, JEFF 2B/INF (11,39,12,2,21) TORA 11 92,NYN 39 92, 12 93-96, CLEA 2/12 96, SFN 21 97-02, HOUN 12 03-04, LAN 12 05

KENT, STEVE P (51) TBA 51 02

KENWORTHY, DICK 3B/2B (46,23,26,2) CHIA 46 62, 23 64, 26 66-67, 2 68

KEOUGH, JOE OF/1B B (16,46,29) OAKA 16 68, KCA 16 69-72, CHIA 46/29 73

KEOUGH, MARTY OF/1B B (20,41,2,15,9,25,11,28) BOSA 20 56, 41 57, 2 58-60, CLEA 15 60, WASA 9 61, CINN 25 62-65, ATLN 11 66, CHIN 28 66

KEOUGH, MATT P B (27,34,33,48,46) OAKA 27 77-83, NYA 34 83, STLN 33 85, CHIN 33 86, HOUN 48/46 86

KEPPINGER, JEFF 2B/SS (6) NYN 6 04

KEPSHIRE, KURT P (50) STLN 50 84-86

KERFELD, CHARLEY P (37,40) HOUN 37 85-87, 90, ATLN 40 90

KERIAZAKOS, GUS P (35,16,27) CHIA 35 50, WASA 16 54, KCA 27 55

KERN, BILL OF (38) KCA 38 62

KERN, JIM P (34,67,37,21,31,42,46) CLEA 34 74-78, TEXA 34 79-81, CINN 34 82, CHIA 67 82-83, PHIN 37 84, MILA 21/31 84, 42/37 85, CLEA 46 86

KERNEK, GEORGE 1B (30,14) STLN 30 65, 14 66

KERNS, RUSS PH (29) DETA 29 45

KERR, BUDDY SS/INF (18,10) NYN 18 43, 10 44-49, BOSN 10 50-51

KERR, JOHN 2B/INF/CH (29,23) CHIA 29 31, WASA 23 32-34, CHIA *CH* 29 35

KERRIGAN, JOE P/CH (18,32,26,40,45,16) MONN 18 76-77, BALA 32 78, 26 80, MONN *CH* 40 83-85, 18 86, 45 92-94, 32 95-96, BOSA *CH* 16 97-01, *M* 16 01, PHIN *CH* 16 03-04

KERSHNER, JASON P (46,23) SDN 46 02, TORA 46 02-03, 23 04

KERSIECK, BILL P (11) PHIN 11 39

KESSINGER, DON SS/M F (11,30) CHIN 11 64-75, STLN 11 76-77, CHIA 30 77-78, 11 78-79, *M* 11 79

KESSINGER, KEITH SS S (62) CINN 62 93

KESTER, RICK P (37,53,27) ATLN 37 68-69, 53/27 70

KEY, JIMMY P (27,22,21) TORA 27 84, 22 84-92, NYA 22 93-96, BALA 21 97-98

KEYSER, BRIAN P (26) CHIA 26 95-96

KHALIFA, SAMMY SS/2B (27) PITN 27 85-87

KIDA, MASAO P (41,60) DETA 41 99-00, LAN 60 03-04, SEAA 35 04-05

KIECKER, DANA P (19) BOSA 19 90-91

KIEFER, MARK P (43) MILA 43 93-96

KIEFER, STEVE UTIL (28,30,26) OAKA 28 84-85, MILA 30 86-88, NYA 26 89

KIELTY, BOBBY OF/1B/DH (23,24) MINA 23 01-03, TORA 24 03, OAKA 23 04-05

KIELY, JOHN P (46) DETA 46 91-93

KIELY, LEO (KIKI) P (25,19,17,32,34) BOSA 25 51, 19 54-56, 17 58-59, KCA 32/34 60

KIESCHNICK, BROOKS OF/INF/P (19,46,55) CHIN 19 96-97, CINN 46 00, COLN 55 01, MILN 55 03-04

KILE, DARRYL P (57) HOUN 57 91-97, COLN 57 98-99, STLN 57 00-02

KILGUS, PAUL P (39,17,41,47,36) TEXA 39 87-88, CHIN 39 89, TORA 39 90, BALA 17/41/47 91, STLN 36 93

KILKENNY, MIKE P (35,33,25,42) DETA 35 69-72, OAKA 33 72, SDN 25 72, CLEA 42 72-73

KILLEBREW, HARMON (KILLER) 3B/1B/UTIL/DH (25,12,3) WASA 25 54, 12 55-56, 3 57-60, MINA 3 61-74, KCA 3 75

KILLEEN, EVANS P (36) KCA 36 59

KILLIFER, BILL M/CH (33,31,2) STLA 33 31-33, BKNN 31 39, PHIN *CH* 2 42

KIM, BYUNG-HYUN P (49,51) ARIN 49 99-03, BOSA 51 03-04, COLN 49 05

KIM, SUN WOO (SUNNY) P (62,47,31,51) BOSA 62 01, 47 02, MONN 31 02-04, WASN 31 05, COLN 51 05

KIM, WENDELL CH (20,31,12,7,3) SFN *CH* 20 89-96, BOSA *CH* 31 97, 12 98-00, MONN *CH* 7 02-03, CHIN *CH* 3 03-04

KIMBALL, NEWT P (43,26,32,33,7,21,27) CHIN 43 37, 26/32 38, BKNN 33 40, STLN 7 40, BKNN 21 41-43, PHIN 27 43

KIMBERLIN, HARRY (MURPHY)(MULE TRADER) P (14,23,25,27,21) STLA 14 36-37, 23 38, 25/27/21 39

KIMBLE, DICK SS (11,4) WASA 11/4 45

KIMM, BRUCE C/DH/CH (46,11,7,6,4,36,34,12,10) DETA 46 76, 11 77, CHIN 7 79, CHIA 11 80, CINN *CH* 6 84-85, 4 86-88, PITN *CH* 36 89-90, SDN CH 34 90-92, FLAN *CH* 12 97-98, COLN *CH* 6 99, CHIN *M* 10 02, *CH* 10 03

KIMSEY, CHAD P (17,35,29,12) STLA 17 31-32, CHIA 35 32, 29 33, DETA 12 36

KINDALL, JERRY SS/INF (23,16,1,14) CHIN 23 56-58, 16 60-61, CLEA 1 62, 14 63-64, MINA 16 64-65

KINDER, ELLIS (OLD FOLKS) P (21,26,16,27) STLA 21 46, 26 47, BOSA 16 48-55, STLN 16 56, CHIA 27 56-57

KINER, RALPH OF/1B (43,4,9) PITN 43 46, 4 47-53, CHIN 4 53-54, CLEA 9 55

KING, CHARLIE (CHICK) OF (21,3,20,25) DETA 21 54-55, 3 56, CHIN 20 58-59, STLN 25 59

KING, CLYDE P/CH/M (18,29,21,16,23,37,2,6,14,48,50,42,40) BKNN 18 44, 29 45, 21 47, 16 47-48, 23 51-52, CINN 37 53, *CH* 2 59, PITN *CH* 6 65-67, SFN *M* 23 69-70, ATLN *M* 14 74-75, NYA *CH* 48 78, 50 81, 42 81-82, *M* 42 82, *CH* 40 88

KING, CURTIS P (57) STLN 57 97-99

KING, ERIC P (25,36,40) DETA 25 86-88, CHIA 36 89-90, CLEA 40 91, DETA 25 92

KING, HAL C (5,8,15,6) HOUN 5 67, 8 68, ATLN 15 70-71, TEXA 15 72, CINN 6 73-74

KING, JEFF 3B/UTIL (7) PITN 7 89-96, KCA 7 97-99

KING, JIM OF/C (48,9,22,30,18,21) CHIN 48 55-56, STLN 9 57,SFN 22 58, WASA 30 61-67, CHIA 18 67, CLEA 21 67

KING, KEVIN P (50) SEAA 50 93-95

KING, LYNN (DIG) OF (24,5,17) STLN 14 35, 5 36, 17 39

KING, NELLIE P (30,29) PITN 30 54-55, 29 56-57

KING, RAY P (56,46) CHIN 56 99, MILN 46 00-02, ATLN 46 03, STLN 56 04-05

KINGDON, WES 3B/SS (19) WASA 19 32

KINGERY, MIKE OF (27,7,26,12,11) KCA 27 86, SEAA 7 87-89, SFN 26 90-91, OAKA 7 92, COLN 12 94-95, PITN 11 96

KINGMAN, BRIAN P (50,25) OAKA 50 79-82, 29 81-82, SFN 25 83

KINGMAN, DAVE OF/UTIL/P/1B/DH (45,26,10,48) SFN 45 71-72, 26 72-74, NYN 26 75-77, SDN 26 77, CALA 10 77, NYA 48 77, CHIN 10 78-80, NYN 26 81-83, OAKA 10 84-86, 26 86

KINGSALE, EUGENE OF (40,38,18,43) BALA 40 96, 98, 38 99, 40 00-01, SEAA 18 02, SDN 18 02, DETA 43 03

KINKADE, MIKE INF/OF (33,39,17,7) NYN 33 98-00, BALA 39 00, 17 01, LAN 7 02-03

KINNEY, DENNIS P (51,48,21,56,47) CLEA 51 78, SDN 48 78-80, DETA 21 81, OAKA 56/47 82

KINNEY, MATT P (51,50,52,38) MINA 51 00-02, 50 03, MILN 50 04, KCA 52 04, SFN 38 05

KINNUNEN, MIKE P (35,48) MINA 35 80, BALA 48 86-87

KINZER, MATT P (59,43) STLN 59 89, DETA 43 90

KINZY, HARRY (SLIM) P (17) CHIA 17 34

KIPP, FRED P (26,18) BKNN 26 57, LAN 26 58-59, NYA 18 60

KIPPER, BOB P/CH (36,51,16,50) CALA 36 85, PITN 51 85-87, 16 87-91, MINA 50/16 92, BOSA *CH* 16 02

KIPPER, THORNTON P (34) PHIN 34 53-55

KIRBY, CLAY P (43,31) SDN 43 69-73, CINN 31 74-75, MONN 31 76

KIRBY, JIM PH (36) CHIN 36 49

KIRBY, WAYNE OF/DH (73,35,55,11) CLEA 73 91, 35 92-96, LAN 55 96, 35 97, NYN 11 98

KIRK, BILL P (29) KCA 29 61

KIRK, TOM PH (30) PHIA 30 47

KIRKLAND, WILLIE OF (29,8,27,3,31,6) SFN 29 58-60, CLEA 8 61-62, 27 63, BALA 3 64, WASA 31 64, 6 64-66

KIRKPATRICK, ED C/UTIL (39,8,23,18,3) LAA 39 62, 8 63-64, CALA 8 65-68, KCA 8 69-73, PITN 23 74-77, TEXA 18 77, MILA 3 77

KIRKWOOD, DON P (52,33,32) CALA 52 74-75, 33 75-77, CHIA 33 77, TORA 32 78

KIRRENE, JOE 3B (15,33) CHIA 15 50, 33 54

KISER, GARLAND 2B/INF (58) CLEA 58 91

KISH, ERNIE OF (12) PHIA 12 45

KISON, BRUCE P/CH (37,25,24,29,42,__,54) PITN 37 71, 25 71-79, CALA 24 80-84, BOSA 29 85, KCA *CH* 42 92-93, *CH*__ 94, *CH* 42 95, *CH* 54 95-98, BALA *CH* 54 99

KISSELL, GEORGE CH (3) STLN *CH* 3 69-75

KITSOS, CHRIS SS (12) CHIN 12 54

KITTLE, HUB CH (3,9) HOUN 3 71-75, STLN 9 81-83,

KITTLE, RON OF/DH (42,33,35) CHIA 42 82-86, NYA 33 86-87, CLEA 33 88, CHIA 42 89-90, BALA 35 90, CHIA 42 91

KLAERNER, HUGO (DUTCH) P (19) CHIA 19 34

KLAGES, FRED P (27) CHIA 27 66-67

KLASSEN, DANNY SS (7) ARIN 7 98-99, 3 00, 7 02, DETA 49 03

KLAUS, BILLY SS/INF/UTIL B (2,35,6,32) BOSN 2 52, MILN 2 53, BOSA 35 55-58, BALA 6 59-60, WASA 6 61, PHIN 32 62-63

KLAUS, BOBBY INF B (12,6) CINN 12 64, NYN 6 64-65

KLAWITTER, TOM P (35) MINA 35 85

KLEIN, CHUCK OF/CH (3,6,4,32,36,1,26,29,8) PHIN 3 32-33, CHIN 6 34, 4 35-36, PHIN 32 36, 36 36-37, 1 38, 26 39, PITN 14 39, PHIN 29 40-42, *CH* 3 42, 8 43-44, *CH* 26 44-45

KLEIN, LOU 2B/INF/CH/M (2,7,29,6,60) STLN 2 43,45, 7 46, 29 49, CLEA 2 51, PHIA 6 51, CHIN *CH* 3 60, 60 61-65, *M* 60 61-62, 65

KLEINE, HAL P (16,15,35) CLEA 16 44, 15 44-45, 35 45

KLEINHANS, TED P (47,20,25,23,59) PHIN 47 34, CINN 20 34, NYA 25 36, CINN 23 37, 59 38

KLEINKE, NUBS P (24) STLN 24 35, 24 37

KLESKO, RYAN OF/1B (18,30) ATLN 18 92-99, SDN 30 00-05

KLEVEN, JAY C (22) NYN 22 76

KLIEMAN, ED (SPECS)(BABE) P (39,33,37,16,14,35,28) CLEA 39 43-45, 33/37 46, 16 47-48, WASA 14 49, CHIA 35/39 49, PHIA 28 50

KLIMCHOCK, LOU 2B/UTIL (4,18,34,16,11,6,29) KCA 4 58-61, MILN 18 62, WASA 34 63, MILN 16 63, 11 63-65, NYN 6 66, CLEA 29 68-70

KLIMKOWSKI, BRIAN C (51,24,17,22) NYA 51 69, 24 70, OAKA 17 71, NYA 22 72

KLINE, BOB (JUNIOR) P (28,24,16,30,20) BOSA 28 31, 24 32-33, PHIA 16 34, WASA 30/20 34

KLINE, BOBBY INF/P (25) WASA 25 55

KLINE, RON P (20,22,44,41,11,27,28,26) PITN 20 52, 22 55-59, STLN 44 60, LAA 41 61, DETA 11 61, 22 61-62, WASA 27 63-66, MINA 27 67, PITN 27 68-69, SFN 28 69, BOSA 26 69, ATLN 27 70

KLINE, STEVE (JACK) P (38) NYA 38 70-74, CLEA 38 74, ATLN 38 77

KLINE, STEVE (JAMES) P (52,44,49,34,41) CLEA 52 97, MONN 44 97-00, STLN 44 01, 49 02-03, 34 04, BALA 41 05

KLINGENBECK, SCOTT P (55,52,56) BALA 55 94-95, MINA 52 95-96, CINN 56 98

KLINGER, BOB P (41,20,37) PITN 41 38-39, 20 40-43, BOSA 37 46-47

KLINK, JOE P (46,58,40) MINA 46 87, OAKA 58 90-91, FLAN 58 93, SEAA 40 96

KLIPPSTEIN, JOHNNY P (36,35,17,47,45,27,30) CHIN 36 50-54, CINN 35 55-58, LAN 35 58-59, CLEA 17 60, WASA 17 61, CINN 47 62, PHIN 45 63-64, MINA 27 64-66, DETA 30 67

KLOPP, STAN (BETZ) P (34) BOSN 34 44

KLOZA, NAP OF (__,25) STLA __ 31, 25 32

KLUMPP, ELMER C (21,34) WASA 21 34, BKNN 34 37

KLUSZEWSKI, TED (BIG KLU) 1B/CH (20,18,3,8,15) CINN 20 47, 18 48-57, PITN 3 58-59, CHIA 8 59-60, LAA 15 61, CINN *CH* 18 70-78

KLUTTS, MICKEY SS/3B/DH (20,39,24,12,9,27) NYA 20 76, 39 77, 24 78, OAKA 12 79-81, 9 81-82, TORA 27 83

KLUTTZ, CLYDE C (11,12,9,23,39,10) BOSN 11 42, 12 43, 11 44-45, NYN 23 45, 9 46, STLN 9/39 46, PITN 10 47-48, STLA 11 51, WASA 10 51-52

KMAK, JOE C (27,7) MILA 27 93, CHIN 7 95

KNACKERT, BRENT P (27,59) SEAA 27 95, BOSA 59 96

KNAPP, CHRIS P (45,42) CHIA 45 75-77, CALA 42 78-80

KNAPP, RICK CH (67) MINA 67 99

KNEPPER, BOB P (39,28) SFN 39 76-80, HOUN 39 81-89, SFN 28 89, 39 90

KNERR, LOU P (30,14) PHIA 30 45-46, WASA 14 47

KNICELY, ALAN 1B/C/UTIL (11,4,34,6,23) HOUN 11 79-82, CINN 11 83, 4 83, 34 84-85, PHIN 6 85, STLN 23 86

KNICKERBOCKER, AUSTIN OF (30,15) PHIA 30/15 47

KNICKERBOCKER, BILL SS/INF (26,4,1,10,2,12) CLEA 26 33, 4 34-36, STLA 1 37, NYA 10 38-40, CHIA 2/12 41, PHIA 2 42

KNIFFIN, CHUCK CH (50) ARIN *CH* 50 02-04

KNIGHT, BRANDON P (62,48) NYA 62 01, 48 02

KNIGHT, RAY 3B/UTIL/CH/M (25,22,9,4) CINN 25 74, 77-81, HOUN 22 82-84, NYN 22 84-86, BALA 25 87, DETA 9/22 88, CINN *CH* 4 93, *CH* 25 94-95, *M* 25 96-97, *CH* 25 02-03

KNOBLAUCH, CHUCK 2B/UTIL (11) MINA 11 91-97, NYA 11 98-01, KCA 11 02

KNOEDLER, JUSTIN C (52,33) SFN 52 04, 33 05

KNOOP, BOBBY 2B/3B/CH (29,19,1,2) LAA 29 64, CALA 29 65-69, CHIA 29 69-70, KCA 19 71-72, CHIA *CH* 29 77-78, CALA *CH* 1 79-92, *CH* 2 93-96, TORA *CH* 29 00

KNORR, RANDY C (49,54,27,9,4,17,55,15) TORA 49/54 91, 27 92-95, HOUN 9 96-97, FLAN 4 98, HOUN 17 99, TEXA 55 00, MONN 15 01

KNOTHE, FRITZ 3B/INF B (7,5) BOSN 7 32-33, PHIN 5 33

KNOTHE, GEORGE 2B B (23) PHIN 23 32

KNOTT, ERIC P (57,41) ARIN 57 01, MONN 41 03

KNOTT, JACK P (18,24,17,16,35) STLA 18 33, 24 34-35, 17 36-38, CHIA 24 38-40, PHIA 16 41-42, 35 42, 46

KNOTT, JON 1B/OF (10) SDN 10 04

Brock stole more bases in one World Series than Terry Kennedy did is entire career (6). Not a speedster, he excelled in his handling of hing staffs. A four-time All-Star, he helped San Diego (1984) and Francisco (1989) both get to the World Series. His best years were in adres uniform where he hit 38 HRs and had 195 RBI in '82 and '83.

KNOTTS, GARY P
(56,**35**) FLAN **56** 01, **35** 02, DETA **35** 03-04

KNOWLES, DAROLD P/CH
(43,**32**,22,31, 51,34,3,33) BALA **43** 65, PHIN **32** 66, WASA **32** 67-71, OAKA **22** 71, **32** 71-74, CHIN **31** 75, **32** 75-76, TEXA **32** 77, MONN **32** 78, STLN **51**79, **34** 79-80, *CH* **23** 83, PHIN *CH* **3** 89-90, *CH* **33** 90

KNOX, JOHN 2B/INF/DH
(44,**2**) DETA **44** 72-73, **2** 74-75

KNUDSEN, KURT P
(**27**) DETA **27** 92-94

KNUDSON, MARK P
(**41**) HOUN **41** 85-86, MILA **41** 86-91, COLN **41** 93

KOBACK, NICK C
(**9**) PITN **9** 53-55

KOBEL, KEVIN P
(34,29,**49**) MILA **34** 73-74, 76, NYN **29/49** 78-80

KOCH, ALAN P
(**42**,26) DETA **42** 63-64, WASA **26** 64

KOCH, BARNEY 2B/SS
(**16**) BKNN **16** 44

KOCH, BILLY P
(**44**,88) TORA **44** 99-01, OAKA **44** 02, CHIA **44** 03-04, FLAN **88** 04

KOECHER, DICK (HIGHPOCKETS) P
(__,**26**) PHIN __ 46, **26** 47-48

KOEGEL, PETE OF/C/UTIL
(17,**12**) MILA **17** 70-71, PHIN **12** 71-72

KOELLING, BRIAN 2B/SS
(**60**) CINN **60** 93

KOENECKE, LEN OF
(2,**18**) NYN **2** 32, BKNN **18** 34-35

KOENIG, FRED CH
(20,8,9,**47**) CALA *CH* **20** 70-71, STLN *CH* **8** 76, TEXA *CH* **47** 77-82, CHIN *CH* **9** 83, CLEA *CH* **47** 86

KOENIG, MARK SS/INF/P
(**2**,27,9,12,3, 23,22) NYA **2** 29-30, DETA **27** 31, CHIN **9** 32, **12** 33, CINN **3** 34, NYN **23** 35, **22** 36

KOHLMAN, JOE (BLACKIE) P
(35,32,33,**20**) WASA **35** 37, **32/33/20** 38

KOHLMEIER, RYAN P
(50,**30**) BALA **50** 00, **30** 01

KOKOS, DICK OF
(**19**) STLA **19** 48-50, 53, BALA **19** 54

KOLB, BRANDON P
(**47**) SDN **47** 00, MILN **38** 01

KOLB, DANNY P
(52,**41**,51) TEXA **52** 99-02, MILN **41** 03-04, ATLN **51** 05

KOLB, GARY OF/UTIL/C
(22,20,**27**,18, 10) STLN **22** 60, 62, STLN **20** 62-63, MILN **27** 64-65, NYN **18** 65, PITN **10** 68-69

KOLLOWAY, DON (BUTCH)(CAB) 2B/INF
(**47**,17,11) CHIA **47** 40-43, 46-49, DETA **17** 49-52, PHIA **11** 53

KOLP, RAY (JOCKEY) P
(**15**,21) CINN **15** 32-33, **21** 34

KOLSTAD, HAL OF/1B/UTIL
(42,**28**) BOSA **42** 62, **28** 62-63

KOMIYAMA, SATORU P
(**17**) NYN **17** 02

KOMMINSK, BRAD OF/3B/DH
(7,**36**,66,45, 32,49,29,48) ATLN **7** 83-84, **36** 85-86, MILA **36** 87, CLEA **66/45** 89, SFN **45 /32**90, BALA **49/29** 90, OAKA **48** 91

KONERKO, PAUL 1B/INF/DH
(66,7,28,**14**) LAN **66** 97, **7** 98, CINN **28** 98, CHIA **14** 99-05

KONIECZNY, DOUG P
(**46**) HOUN **46** 73-75, 77

KONIKOWSKI, ALEX (WHITEY) P
(36,**38**) NYN **36** 48, **38** 51-(52), 54

KONOPKA, BRUCE 1B/OF
(**11**,14,36) PHIA **11** 42-43, **14** 43, **36** 46

KONSTANTY, JIM P
(**35**,38,21, 26) CINN **35** 44, BOSN **38** 46, PHIN **26** 48, **35** 49-54, NYA **21** 54-56, STLN **25** 56

KONUSZEWSKI, DENNIS P
(**50**) PITN **50** 95

KOO, DAE-SUNG P
(**17**) NYN **17** 05

KOONCE, CAL P
(**34**,17) CHIN **34** 62-67, NYN **34** 67-70, BOSA **17** 70-71

KOONCE, GRAHAM 1B
(**18**) OAKA **18** 03

KOOSMAN, JERRY P
(47,**36**,27,24) NYN **47** 67, **36** 67-78, MINA **27** 79, **36** 79-81, CHIA **36** 81-83, PHIN **24** 84-85

KOPACZ, GEORGE (SONNY) 1B
(9,6,**10**) ATLN **9** 66, PITN **6/10** 70

KOPLITZ, HOWIE P
(45,16,**31**) DETA **45** 61-62, WASA **16** 64, **31** 65-66

KOPLOVE, MIKE P
(58,**22**,76) ARIN **58** 01-03, **22** 04, **76** 05

KOPPE, JOE SS/INF/UTIL
(11,15,**1**) MILN **11** 58, PHIN **15** 59-61, LAA **1** 61-64, CALA **1** 65

KOPSHAW, GEORGE PH
(__) STLN __ 23

KORCHECK, STEVE (HOSS) C
(31,29,**10**) WASA **31** 54, **29** 55, **10** 58-59

KORINCE, GEORGE (MOOSE) P
(49,**19**) DETA **49** 66, **19** 67

KORONKA, JOHN P
(**49**) CHIN **49** 05

KOSCO, ANDY OF/1B/UTIL
(8,24,28,**9**, 10,29,44,23) MINA **8** 65-66, **24** 67, NYA **28** 68, LAN **9** 69-70, M ILA **10** 71, CALA **29** 72, BOSA **44** 72, CINN **23** 73-74

KOSHOREK, CLEM (SCOOTER) INF
(26,**37**) PITN **26** 52, **37** 53

KOSKI, BILL (T-BONE) P
(**26**) PITN **26** 51

KOSKIE, COREY 3B
(**47**) MINA **47** 98-05

KOSLO, DAVE (SONNY) 1B
(33,21,22,**31**, 20) NYN **33** 41, **21** 42, **22** 46, **31** 47-53, BALA **22** 54, MILN **20** 54-55

KOSLOFSKI, KEVIN OF/DH
(**40**,18) KCA **40** 92-94, MILA **18** 96

KOSMAN, MIKE PR
(**26**) CINN **26** 44

KOSTRO, FRANK 3B/UTIL
(24,14,11,16, **2**) DETA **24** 62-63, LAA **14** 63, MINA **11** 64-65, **16** 67, **2** 68-69

KOTCHMAN, CASEY 1B
(**35**) ANAA **35** 04, LAA **35** 05

KOTSAY, MARK OF
(4,**7**,14,21) FLAN **4** 97-98, **7** 98-00, SDN **14** 01-03, OAKA **21** 04-05

KOUFAX, SANDY P
(**32**) BKNN **32** 55-57, LAN **32** 58-66

KOUPAL, LOU P
(**22**) STLA **22** 37

KOWALIK, FABIAN P
(23,**24**,42,__) CHIA **23** 32, CHIN **24** 35-36, PHIN **42** 36, BOSN __ 36

KOWITZ, BRIAN OF
(**15**) ATLN **15** 95

KOY, ERNIE (CHIEF) OF
(33,**20**,19,25) BKNN **33** 38, **20** 38-40, STLN **19** 40-41, CINN **25** 41-42, PHIN **12** 42

KOZAR, AL 2B/3B
(**2**,1,42) WASA **2** 48, **1** 49, **42** 50, CHIA **2** 50

KOZLOWSKI, BEN P
(**56**) TEXA **56** 02

KRACHER, JOE (JUG) C
(**7**) PHIN **7** 39

KRAEMER, JOE P
(**43**) CHIN **43** 89-90

KRAKAUSKAS, JOE P
(36,**12**,15,30) WASA **36** 37, **12** 38-40, CLEA **15** 41-42, **30** 46

KRALICK, JACK P
(45,37,38,15, **31**) WASA **45/37** 59, **38/15** 60, MINA **15** 61-63, CLEA **31** 63-67

KRALY, STEVE P
(**35**) NYA **35** 53

KRAMER, JACK P
(30,**19**,27,35, 21,18,33) STLA **30** 39, **19** 40-41, **27** 43, **19** 44-45, **35** 46, **21** 47, BOSA **18** 48-49, NYN **33** 50-51, NYA **18** 51

KRAMER, RANDY P
(60,**28**,38,22, 54) PITN **60** 88-89, **28** 89-90, CHIN **38** 90, SEAA **22** 92, **54** 93

KRAMER, TOM P
(64,**29**) CLEA **64** 91,93, **29** 93

KRANEPOOL, ED 1B/OF
(21,**7**) NYN **21** 62-64, **7** 65-79

KRANITZ, RICK A-CH
(**63**,36) CHIN *A-CH* **63** 98, *A-CH* **63** 01, *CH* **36** 02

KRAUS, JACK (TEX)(TEXAS JACK) P
(16,19,14) PHIN **16** 43, **19** 45, NYN **14** 46

KRAUSE, HARRY (HAL) CH
(**21**) NYN **21** 38

KRAUSSE, LEW, JR. P S
(24,31,21,25, **20**,30,18,29, 36) KCA **24** 61, **31** 64, **21** 64-65, **25** 65, **29** 66, **20** 66-67, OAKA **20** 68-69, MILA **30** 70, **24** 70-71,BOSA **18** 72, STLN **29** 73, ATLN **36** 74

KRAUSSE, LEW, SR. P F
(**18**) PHIA **18** 31-32

KRAVEC, KEN P
(**27**,37) CHIA **27** 75-80, CHIN **37** 81-82

KRAVITZ, DANNY (DUSTY)(BEAK) C/3B
(17,28,**10**,12) PITN **17** 56-57, **28** 58, **10** 59 -60, KCA **12** 60

KRAWCZYK, RAY P
(61,**46**,59,43, 36) PITN **61** 84, **46** 85-86, CALA **59/43** 88, MILA **36** 89

KREEVICH, MIKE OF/3B
(__,**8**,1,12, 32,6) CHIA __ 35, **8** 36-41, PHIA **1** 42, STLA **12** 43-45, WASA **32/6** 45

KREITNER, MICKEY C
(**11**) CHIN **11** 43-44

KREMER, RAY (WIZ) P
(**40**) PITN **40** 32-33

KREMERS, JIMMY C
(**17**) ATLN **17** 90

KREMMEL, JIM P
(5,**49**) TEXA **5** 73, CHIN **49** 74

KRENCHICKI, WAYNE 3B/2B/UTIL
(45,6,19,12, **15**) BALA **45/12** 79, **6** 80-81, CINN **19** 82, **12/15** 83, DETA **15** 83, CINN **15** 84-85, MONN **15** 86

KRESS, CHARLIE (CHUCK) 1B/OF
(17,**25**,4,5) CINN **17** 47, 49, CHIA **25** 49-50, DETA **4** 54, BKNN **5** 54

KRESS, RED 3B/UTIL/P/CH
(4,24,**3**,25,14, 26,23,31,2,7, 5,42,48) STLA **4** 31-32, CHIA **24** 32, **3** 33, **14** 34, WASA **25** 34, **26** 35, **25** 36, STLA **3** 38-39, DETA **23** 39, **26** 40, *CH* **26** 40, NYN **31** 46, *CH* **31** 46, *CH* **2** 47-48, *CH* **7** 48-49, *CH* **5** 49, CLEA *CH* **42** 53-60, LAA *CH* **2** 61, NYN *CH* **48** 62

KRETLOW, LOU (LENA) P
(35,**23**,36,25, 28,22,18, 33) DETA **35** 46, **23** 48, **36** 49, STLA **25** 50, CHIA **28** 50, **23** 51-53, STLA **22** 53, BALA **23** 54-55, KCA **18/23/33** 56

KREUGER, RICK P
(**21**,46) BOSA **21** 75-77, CLEA **46** 78

KREUTER, CHAD C/DH/UTIL
(**7**,19,18,12, 6,15,4,21) TEXA **7** 88-91, DETA **19** 92-94, SEAA **18** 95, CHIA **12** 96-97, ANAA **6** 97, CHIA **12/15** 98, ANAA **4** 98, KCA **19** 99, LAN **21** 00-02, TEXA **12** 03

KREUTZER, FRANK P
(29,49,**18**,32, 30,22) CHIA **29** 62, **49** 62-64, **29** 64, WASA **18** 64-66, **32/30** 66, **22** 69

KRIEGER, KURT (DUTCH) P
(24,**30**,42) STLN **24** 49, **30/42** 51

KRIST, HOWIE (SPUD) P
(22,33,26,**29**, 35) STLN **22** 37, **33** 38, **26** 41, **29** 42-43, **35** 43, **29** 46

KRIVDA, RICK P
(62,37,**38**,30, 48) BALA **62/37** 95, **38** 96-97, CLEA **30** 98, CINN **48** 98

KROEGER, JOSH OF
(**43**) ARIN **43** 04

KROL, JACK CH/M
(8,**34**) STLN *CH* **8** 77-80, *M* **8** 78, 80, SDN *CH* **34** 81-86

KROLL, GARY P
(55,**25**,31,37) PHIN **55** 64, NYN **25** 64-65, HOUN **31** 66, CLEA **37** 69

KRONER, JOHN 3B/INF
(__,26,22,**2**) BOSA __ 35, **26** 36, CLEA **22** 37, **2** 38

KROON, MARC P
(54,**32**,33) SDN **54** 95, **32** 97-98, CINN **33** 98

KRSNICH, MIKE OF/UTIL B
(42,**39**) MILA **42** 60, **39** 62

KRSNICH, ROCKY 2B/3B B
(58,24,**6**) CHIA **58/24** 49, **6** 52-53

KRUEGER, BILL P
(64,**32**,59,41, 47,44,22,42, 30,33,48) OAKA **64** 83, **32** 83-87, LAN **59** 87, **41** 88, MILA **47** 89-90, SEAA **44** 91, MINA **22/47** 92, MONN **42** 92, DETA **30** 93-94, SDN **33** 94, **48/33** 95, SEAA **44** 95

KRUG, CHRIS C
(25,26,24) CHIN **25** 65-66, SDN **26/24** 69

KRUG, GARY (GENE) PH
(**47**) CHIN **47** 81

KRUK, JOHN (JOHNNY) OF/1B/DH
(8,11,19,28, **29**) SDN **8** 86-89, PHIN **11** 89-90, **19/28** 90, PHIN **29** 91-94, CHIA **29** 95

KRUKOW, MIKE P
(40,**39**,34) CHIN **40** 76, **39** 77-81, PHIN **39** 82, SFN **34** 83, **39** 83-89

KRYHOSKI, DICK 1B
(23,19,30,9, 16,**8**) NYA **23** 49, DETA **19** 50, **30** 50-51, STLA **9** 52, **16** 53, BALA **8** 54, KCA **8** 55

KRYNZEL, DAVE OF
(**10**) MILN **10** 04-05

KUBEK, TONY SS/UTIL
(34,**10**) NYA **34** 57, **10** 58-65

KUBEL, JASON OF
(**1**) MINA **1** 04, (05)

KUBENKO, JEFF P
(67,**45**) LAN **67** 98, **45** 99

KUBIAK, TED INF
(14,1,7,**11**,8) KCA **14** 67, OAKA **14** 68-69, MILA **1** 70-71, STLN **1** 71, TEXA **7** 72, OAKA **11** 72-75, SDN **8** 75-76

KUBINSKI, TIM P
(**58**) OAKA **58** 97, 99

KUBISZYN, JACK INF
(6,**2**) CLEA **6** 61, **2** 62

KUBSKI, GIL OF
(**22**) CALA **22** 80

KUCAB, JOHNNY P
(17,**37**) PHIA **17** 50, **37** 51-52

KUCEK, JACK P
(**55**,34,32) CHIA **55** 74-79, PHIN **34** 79, TORA **32** 80

KUCKS, JOHNNY P
(**53**,26) NYA **53** 55-59, KCA **26** 59-60

KUCYZNSKI, BERT P
(**14**) PHIA **14** 43

KUCZEK, STEVE PH
(**16**) BOSN **16** 49

KUEHL, KARL M/CH
(6,**41**) MONN *M* **6** 76, MINA *CH* **41** 77-82

KUENN, HARVEY SS/OF/UTIL/CH/M
(26,**7**,6,22, 31,32) DETA **26** 52-54, **7** 54-59, CLEA **6/7** 60, SFN **7** 61-65, CHIN **7** 65-66, PHIN **22** 66, MILA *CH* **31** 71-74, *CH* **32** 74-82, *M* **32** 75, 82-83

KUHAULUA, FRED P
(**31**,51,41) CALA **31** 77, SDN **51/41** 81

KUHEL, JOE 1B/3B/M
(23,21,2,5,6, 7,**3**,26,14, 40) WASA **23** 31, **21** 32, **2** 33, **5** 34-35, **6** 35, **7** 36-37, CHIA **3** 38-43, WASA **5** 44-45, **26** 46, CHIA **14** 46-47, WASA *M* **40** 48-49

KUHN, KENNY SS/INF
(**8**) CLEA **8** 55-57

KUIPER, DUANE 2B/DH/UTIL
(**18**) CLEA **18** 74-81, SFN **18** 82-85

KUME, MIKE P
(**29**) KCA **29** 55

KUNKEL, BILL P F
(32,25,**20**) KCA **32** 61, **25** 62, NYA **20** 63

KUNKEL, JEFF SS/DH/UTIL/P S
(**20**,11) TEXA **20** 84-91, CHIN **11** 92

KUNTZ, RUSTY OF/DH/CH
(**47**,11,15,22, 48) CHIA **47** 79-83, MINA **11** 83, DETA **15** 84-85, SEAA *CH* **22** 89-92, FLAN *CH* **22** 95-96, 99-00, PITN *CH* **48** 03, **15** 04-05

KUO, HONG-CHIH P
(**56**) LAN **56** 05

KUROSAKI, RYAN P
(**40**) STLN **40** 75

KUROWSKI, WHITEY 3B
(5,**1**) STLN **5** 41, **1** 42-49

KURTZ, HAL (BUD) P
(**46**) CLEA **46** 68

KUSH, EMIL P
(20,22,**29**) CHIN **20** 41, **22** 42, **29** 46-49

KUSICK, CRAIG UTIL/1B/DH/P
(**22**,10,5) MINA **22** 73, **10** 74, **22** 74-79, TORA **5** 79

KUSNYER, ART C/CH
(30,39,**15**,10, 21,51,5,53) CHIA **30** 70, CALA **39** 71-73, **15** 73, MILA **10** 76, KCA **21** 78, CHIA *CH* **15** 80-86, *CH* **51** 87, OAKA *CH* **5** 89-95, CHIA *CH* **53** 97-05

KUTCHER, RANDY UTIL
(9,19,55,**5**) SFN **9** 86-87, **19** 87, BOSA **55** 88, **5** 88-90

KUTYNA, MARTY P
(36,**22**) KCA **36** 59-60, WASA **22** 61-62

KUTZLER, JERRY 2B/3B
(**52**) CHIA **52** 90

KUZAVA, BOB (SARGE) P
(20,26,46,25, **21**,15,12,37, 46) CLEA **20** 46-47, **26** 47, CHIA **46** 49-50, WASA **25** 50, **21** 51, NYA **21** 51-54, BALA **15** 54-55, PHIN **12** 55, PITN **37** 57, STLN **46** 57

KVASNAK, AL OF
(**34**) WASA **34** 42

L

LAABS, CHET OF
(6,25,3,17,8, 10,**28**,12) DETA **6** 37, **25/3** 38, **17** 39, STLA **8** 39, **10** 40, **28** 41-45, **12** 45-46, PHIA **28** 47

LABANDEIRA, JOSH SS
(**1**) MONN **1** 04

LABINE, CLEM P
(**41**,23,29,28) BKNN **41** 50-57, LAN **41** 58-60, DETA **23** 60, PITN **29** 60-61, NYN **28** 62

LABOY, COCO 3B/INF
(**39**) MONN **39** 69-73

LACEY, BOB P
(46,**34**,35,33, 17) OAKA **46** 77-78, **34** 77-80, CLEA **35** 81, TEXA **35** 81, CALA **33** 83, SFN **17** 84

LACHEMANN, BILL CH B
(**38**) CALA *CH* **38** 95-96

LACHEMANN, MARCEL P/CH/M B
(**16**,24,14,51, 53) OAKA **16/24** 69, **14** 70, **16** 70-71, CALA *CH* **51** 84-86, *CH* **53** 86-92, FLAN *CH* **53** 93-94, CALA *M* **53** 94-96, ANAA *CH* **53** 97-98, COLN *CH* **53** 00-01

LACHEMANN, RENE C/M/CH B
(11,**18**,15,4, 9,36,43,5) KCA **11** 65, **18** 66, OAKA **18** 68, SEAA *M* **15** 81, *M* **4** 82-83, MILA *M* **9** 84, BOSA *CH* **36** 85-86, OAKA *CH* **43** 87, *CH* **15** 87- 88-92, FLAN *M* **15** 93-96, STLN *CH* **15** 97-99, CHIN *CH* **5** 00-02, *M* **5** 02, SEAA *CH* **9** 03, **15** 04, OAKA *CH* **15** 05

LACHOWICZ, AL P
(**51**) TEXA **51** 83

LACKEY, JOHN P
(**41**) ANAA **41** 02-04, LAA **41** 05

LaCOCK, PETE OF/1B/DH
(24,25,23,**8**) CHIN **24** 72, **25** 73-74, **23** 75-76, KCA **8** 77-80

LaCORTE, FRANK P
(40,25,26,42, **31**,27) ATLN **40** 75, **25** 75-76, **26** 76-78, **42** 78-79, HOUN **31** 79-82, **27** 82-83, CALA **27/31** 84

LaCOSS, MIKE P
(**51**,30,42,29) CINN **51** 78-81, HOUN **51** 82-84, KCA **30** 85, SFN **42** 86, **29** 86-91

LACY, KERRY P
(**53**) BOSA **53** 96-97

LACY, LEE 2B/OF/UTIL/DH
(**34**,17,27) LAN **34** 72-75, ATLN **34** 76, LAN **34** 76-78, PITN **17** 79-84, BALA **27** 85-87

LADD, PETE P
(42,39,**27**,46) HOUN **42/39** 79, MILA **27** 82-85, SEAA **46** 86

LADE, DOYLE (PORKY) P
(19,**23**) CHIN **19** 46, **23** 47-50

LAFATA, JOE OF/1B
(**24**,26) NYN **24** 47, **26** 48, **24** 49

LaFOREST, PETE DH/C
(**39**) TBA **39** 03, 05

LaFOREST, TY 3B/OF
(**18**) BOSA **18** 45

LaFRANCOIS, ROGER C
(**54**) BOSA **54** 82

LAGA, MIKE 1B/DH
(**4**,35,8,21,39) DETA **4** 82-86, STLN **35** 86-88, SFN **8** 89, **21/39** 90

LAGGER, ED P
(**19**) PHIA **19** 34

LaGROW, LERRIN P
(**30**,44,36,50, **37**,39) DETA **30** 70, 72-75, STLN **44** 76, CHIA **36** 77-79, LAN **50/37/36** 79, PHIN **39** 80

LAHOUD, JOE OF/DH
(24,15,14,**3**,4, 35,10) BOSA **24/15** 68, **14** 69-71, MILA **3** 72-73, CALA **4** 74-76, TEXA **3** 76, KCA **35** 77, **10** 77-78

LAHTI, JEFF P
(50,**32**) STLN **50** 82, **32** 82-86

LAIRD, GERALD C
(51,**6**) TEXA **51** 03, **6** 04-05

LAJESKIE, DICK 2B
(**21**) NYN **21** 46

LAKE, EDDIE (SPARKY) SS/INF/P
(4,1,**7**) STLN **4** 39, **1** 40-41, BOSA **7** 43-45, DETA **7** 46-50

LAKE, STEVE C
(16,**25**,30,10) CHIN **16** 83-86, STLN **25** 86-88, PHIN **25** 89-91, **30** 92, CHIN **10** 93

LAKEMAN, AL (MOOSE) OF/C/P/UTIL/CH
(**4**,26,36,25, 14,50,33,34) CINN **4** 42-47, PHIN **26/36** 47, **25** 48, BOSN **14** 49, DETA **50/14** 54, BOSA *CH* **33** 63-64, *CH* **34** 67-69

LAKER, TIM C
(53,**19**,37,26, 16,27,63,45, 15,36) MONN **53** 92, **19** 93, 95, BALA **37** 97, TBA **26/16** 98, PITN **27** 98, **63** 99, CLEA **45** 01, **15** 03-04, TBA **36** 05

LAMABE, JACK P
(**36**,31,34,45, 47,28,23,40) PITN **36** 62, BOSA **36** 63-65, HOUN **31** 65, CHIA **45** 66, **36** 66-67, NYN **34/45** 67, STLN **47/28/23** 67, CHIN **40** 68

LaMACCHIA, AL P
(19,23,31,**44**) STLA **19** 43, **23** 44,**31** 45, **44** 46, WASA **44** 46

LaMANNA, FRANK (HANK) P
(31,**24**) BOSN **31** 40, **24** 41-42

LAMANNO, RAY C
(9,**5**) CINN **9** 41-42, **5** 46-48

LAMANSKE, FRANK (LEFTY) P
(**14**) BKNN **14** 35

LaMASTER, WAYNE P
(45,21,23) PHIN **45** 37, **21** 38, BKNN **23** 38

LAMB, DAVID INF
(**15**,26,44) TBA **15** 99, NYN **26** 00, MINA **44** 02

LAMB, JOHN P
(**24**,44,48) PITN **24** 70-71, **44/48** 73

LAMB, MIKE INF/UTIL
(**13**,26) TEXA **13** 00-03, HOUN **26** 04-05

LAMB, RAY P
(42,34,**30**) LAN **42** 69, **34** 70, CLEA **30** 71-73

LAMBERT, CLAY P
(**32**) CINN **32** 46-47

LAMBERT, GENE P
(**9**) PHIN **9** 41-42

LAMONT, GENE C/CH/M
(33,**10**,32,7, 23,31,38) DETA **33** 70-72, **10** 74-75, PITN *CH* **32** 86-91, CHIA *M* **7** 92, *M* **33** 92-95, PITN *CH* **23** 96, *M* **32** 97-00, BOSA *CH* **31** 01, HOUN *CH* **38** 02-04

LAMP, DENNIS P
(45,47,43,**53**, 49,15,26) CHIN **45** 77, **47** 77-80, CHIA **43** 81, **53** 81-83, TORA **53** 84-86, OAKA **49** 87, BOSA **49** 88, **15** 88-91, PITN **26** 92

LAMPARD, KEITH OF/1B
(**26**) HOUN **26** 69-70

LAMPKIN, TOM C
(17,**25**,22,49) CLEA **17** 88, SDN **25** 90-92, MILA **22** 93, SFN **49** 95-96, STLN **49** 97-98, SEAA **17** 99-01, SDN **25** 02

LANAHAN, DICK P
(12,20,33,17, **28**) WASA **12** 35, **20/33** 37, PITN **17** 40, **28** 40-41

LANCASTER, LES P
(**50**,48,26) CHIN **50** 87-91, DETA **48** 92, STLN **26/50** 93

LANCE, GARY P
(**39**) KCA **39** 77

LANCELLOTTI, RICK 1B/OF
(20,31,**9**,10) SDN **20** 82, SFN **31/9** 86, BOSA **10** 90

LANDENBERGER, KEN (RED) 1B
(**34**) CHIA **34** 52

LANDESTOY, RAFAEL 2B/SS/UTIL/CH
(56,**17**,7,8,53, 50) LAN **56** 77, HOUN **17** 78-81, CINN **7** 81-82, **8** 83, LAN **17** 83-84, MONN *CH* **17** 89, 91, NYN *CH* **53** 96, DETA *CH* **50** 03

LANDIS, BILL P
(34,**29**) KCA **34** 63, BOSA **29** 67-69

LANDIS, JIM OF
(**1**,7,26,4,20) CHIA **1** 57-64, KCA **7** 65, CLEA **26** 66, DETA **4** 67, BOSA **4** 67, HOUN **20** 67

LANDREAUX, KEN OF/DH
(19,**44**) CALA **19** 77-78, MINA **44** 79-80, LAN **44** 81-87

LANDRETH, LARRY P
(57,**21**) MONN **57** 76, **21** 77

LANDRITH, HOBIE C/CH
(**5**,8,10,3,15, 16,30,44) CINN **5** 50-52, **8** 50, **10** 52, **3** 53, **5** 53-55, CHIN **15** 56, STLN **16** 57-58, SFN **5** 59-61, NYN **5** 62, BALA **30** 62-63, WASA **5** 63, *CH* **44** 64

LANDRUM, BILL P
(**43**,47,34,40) CINN **43** 86-87, CHIN **47** 88, PITN **43** 89-91, MONN **34/40** 92, CINN **43** 93

LANDRUM, CED OF
(28,26) CHIN **28** 91, N YN **26** 93

LANDRUM, DON OF/2B
(3,24,**27**,20, 43) PHIN **3** 57, STLN **24** 60-62, CHIN **27** 62-64, **20** 65, SFN **43** 66

LANDRUM, JESSE 2B
(**28**) CHIA **28** 38

LANDRUM, JOE P
(11,**19**) BKNN **11** 50, **19** 52

LANDRUM, TITO (TERRY) OF/DH
(**21**,39,27,30) STLN **21** 80-83, BALA **39** 83, STLN **21** 84-87, LAN **27** 87, BALA **30** 88

LANE, DICK UTIL
(**12**) CHIA **12** 49

LANE, JASON OF
(24,**16**) HOUN **24** 02-05, **16** 05

LANE, JERRY P
(25,36,**31**) WASA **25** 53, CINN **36** 54, **31** 55

LANE, MARVIN OF/DH
(46,43,**21**,34) DETA **46** 71, **43** 72, **21** 73-74, **34** 76

LANFRANCONI, WALT P
(3,**34**) CHIN **3** 41, BOSN **34** 47

LANG, CHIP P
(**33**) MONN **33** 75-76

LANG, DON 3B/INF
(51,46,**29**) CINN **51/46** 38, STLN **29** 48

LANGE, DICK P
(**35**,49) CALA **35** 72, **49** 73, **35** 73-75

LANGERHANS, RYAN OF
(28,**18**) ATLN **28** 02, **18** 03, 05

LANGFORD, RICK P
(30,**22**) PITN **30** 76, OAKA **22** 77-86, TORA *CH* **22** 00

LANGSTON, MARK P
(**12**,24,22) SEAA **12** 84-89, MONN **12** 89, CALA **12** 90-96, ANAA **12** 97, SDN **24** 98, CLEA **22** 99

LANIER, HAL 2B/SS/INF/CH/M S
(**22**,36,8) SFN **22** 64-71, NYA **36** 72, **22** 73, STLN *CH* **8** 81-85, HOUN *M* **22** 86-88, PHIN *CH* **22** 90-91

LANIER, LORENZO (RIMP) OF
(48,**3**) PITN **48/3** 71

LANIER, MAX P F
(32,30,**23**,21, 42,37,17) STLN **32** 38, **30** 39-40, **23** 40-43, **21** 43-46, **23** 49-51, NYN **42** 52, **37** 52-53, STLA **17** 53

LANKFORD, FRANK P
(**49**) LAN **49** 98

LANKFORD, RAY OF
(**16**,12) STLN **16** 90-01, SDN **16** 01-02, STLN **12** 04

LANNING, JOHNNY (TOBACCO CHEWIN' JOHNNY) P B
(**17**,29,25,24) BOSN **17** 36-39, PITN **29** 40-43, **25** 45-46, BOSN **24** 47

LANNING, TOM P B
(__) PHIN __ 38

LANSFORD, CARNEY 3B/UTIL/DH/CH B
(12,**4**,5) CALA **12** 78-80, **5** 80, BOSA **4** 81-82, OAKA **5** 83, **4** 83-92, *CH* **4** 94-95, STLN *CH* **4** 97-98

LANSFORD, JODY 1B B
(**21**) SDN **21** 82-83

LANSING, MIKE 2B/INF
(59,**3**) MONN **59** 93, **3** 93-97, COLN **3** 98-00, BOSA **3** 00-01

LaPALME, PAUL (LEFTY) P
(**24**,32,35,36, 31) PITN **24** 51, **32** 52, **24** 53-54, STLN **35** 55-56, CINN **36** 56, CHIA **31** 56-57

LAPIHUSKA, ANDY (APPLES) P
(10,**21**) PHIN **10** 42, **21** 43

LaPOINT, DAVE P
(62,42,47,**39**, 40,49,24,38, 50,29) MILA **62/42** 80, STLN **47** 81, **39** 82-84, SFN **40** 85, DETA **40** 86, SDN **49/24** 86, STLN **39** 87, CHIA **38** 88, PITN **50** 88, NYA **29** 89, **42** 89-90, PHIN **42** 91

LaPOINTE, RALPH SS/INF
(23,22,**16**) PHIN **23/22** 47, STLN **16** 48

LARA, YOVANNY P
(**57**) MONN **57** 00

LARKER, NORM OF/1B
(**5**,10,9,16) LAN **5** 58-61, HOUN **10** 62, MILN **9** 63, SFN **16** 63

LARKIN, ANDY P
(**36**),52,54) FLAN **36** 96, 98, CINN **52** 00, KCA **54** 00

LARKIN, BARRY SS/2B B
(15,**11**) CINN **15** 86-87, **11** 88-04

LARKIN, GENE 1B/DH/UTIL
(**9**) MINA **9** 87-93

LARKIN, PAT P
(**25**) SFN **25** 83

LARKIN, STEPHEN 1B B
(**0**) CINN **0** 98

LARKIN, STEVE P
(**19**) DETA **19** 34

LaROCCA, GREG 3B/INF
(20,**62**) SDN **20** 00, CLEA **62** 02-03

LaROCHE, ADAM 1B S
(**19**) ATLN **19** 04-05

LaROCHE, DAVE P/CH F
(37,16,**17**,43, 34,53,28) CALA **37** 70, **16** 71, MINA **17** 72, CHIN **37** 73, **17** 73-74, CLEA **43** 75, **17** 75-77, CALA **17** 77-80, NYA **34** 81-83, **38** 83, CHIA *CH* **53** 89-90, *CH* **53** 89-90, *CH* **17** 90-91, NYN *CH* **28** 92-93

LaROSE, JOHN P
(**28**) BOSA **28** 78

LaROSE, VIC 2B/SS
(**22**) CHIN **22** 68

LaROSE, JOHN P
(**26**) BOSA **26** 78

LaROSE, VIC 2B/SS
(**22**) CHIN **22** 68

LARSEN, DON P
(27,**18**,26,31, 40) STLA **27** 53, BALA **27** 54, NYA **18** 55-59, KCA **18** 60-61, CHIA **26** 61, SFN **18** 62-64, HOUN **31** 64-65, BALA **18** 65, CHIN **40** 67

LARSEN, SWEDE 2B
(**20**) BOSN **20** 36

LARSON, BRANDON OF/UTIL
(4,**16**) CINN **4** 01, **16** 02-04

LARSON, DAN P
(34,48,50,**49**, 32) HOUN **34** 76-77, PHIL **48** 78-79, **50** 79, **49** 80-81, CHIN **32** 82

LaRUE, JASON C
(26,2,**23**) CINN **26** 99, **2** 00, **23** 01-05

La RUSSA, TONY INF/M
(29,**10**,11,22, 42,6,42) KCA **29** 63, OAKA **10** 68, **11** 69, **22** 70, **42** 71, ATLN **6** 71, CHIN **42** 73, CHIA *M* **10** 79-86, OAKA *M* **10** 86, *M* **10** 87-95, STLN *M* **10** 96-05

LARY, AL P B
(**31**,46) CHIN **31** 54-55, **46** 62

LARY, FRANK (THE YANKEE KILLER)(MULE) P B
(30,**17**,40) DETA **30** 54, **17** 55-64, NYN **17** 64, MILN **17** 64, NYN **17** 65, CHIA **40/17** 65

LARY, LYN (BROADWAY) SS/UTIL
(24,**2**,22,21, 28,1,11,26,3) NYA **24** 29-30, **2** 30-34, **22** 34, BOSA **21** 34, WASA **28** 35, STLA **1** 35-36, CLEA **1** 37-38, **11** 39, BKNN **26** 39, STLN **2** 39, STLA **3** 40

LASHER, FRED P
(33,**15**,36,30) MINA **33** 63, DETA **15** 67-70, CLEA **36** 70, CALA **30** 71

LASKEY, BILL P
(45,**19**,17) SFN **45** 82, **19** 83-85, MONN **19** 85, SFN **45/19** 86, CLEA **17** 88

LASORDA, TOM P/CH/M
(29,**27**,23,52, 2) BKNN **29** 54, **27** 54-55, KCA **23** 56, LAN *CH* **52** 73-76, *M* **2** 77-96

LASSETER, DON OF
(**46**) STLN **46** 57

LATHAM, BILL P
(64,33,**44**,35) NYN **64/33/44** 85, MINA **35** 86

LATHAM, CHRIS OF
(59,**28**,27) MINA **59** 97, **28** 98-99, TORA **27** 01, NYA **28** 03

LATMAN, BARRY P
(27,**18**,24,32, 34,45,48) CHIA **27** 57, **18** 58-59, CLEA **27/24** 60, **18** 60-62, **32** 63, LAA **34** 64, CALA **34** 65, HOUN **45** 66, **48** 66-67

LAU, CHARLIE C/CH
(12,6,42,**44**,8, 14,10,41,24, 27,40) DETA **12** 56, 58-59, MILA **6** 60-61, BALA **42** 61, **44** 62-63, KCA **8** 63, **14** 63-64, BALA **44** 64-67, ATLN **10** 67, BALA *CH* **41** 69, OAKA *CH* **41** 70, KCA *CH* **24** 71-74, *CH* **27** 75-78, NYA *CH* **40** 79-81, CHIA *CH* **6** 82-84

LAUDNER, TIM C/DH/1B/UTIL
(**15**) MINA **15** 81-89

LAUZERIQUE, GEORGE P
(42,**28**,49) KCA **42** 67, OAKA **28** 68-69, MILA **49** 70

LAVAGETTO, COOKIE 2B/3B/CH/M
(22,**5**,27,51, 8) PITN **22** 34-36, BKNN **5** 37-41, 46-47, *CH* **27** 51-53, WASA *CH* **51** 55-57, *M* **51** 57-60, MINA *M* **51** 61, NYN *CH* **51** 62-63, SFN *CH* **8** 64-67

LaVALLIERE, MIKE (SPANKY) C
(10,11,4,**12**) PHIN **10** 84, STLN **10** 85-86, **11** 86, PITN **4** 87, **12** 87-93, CHIA **10** 93-95

LAVAN, DOC INF
(**8**,no#) STLN **8** 23, **no#** 24

LAVELLE, GARY P
(**46**) SFN **46** 74-84, TORA **46** 85, 87, OAKA **46** 87

LAW, RON P
(**41**) CLEA **41** 69

LAW, RUDY 1B
(3,**11**,23,7) LAN **3** 78, 80, CHIA **11** 82-84, **23** 84-85, KCA **7** 86

LAW, VANCE INF/UTIL/P S
(**2**,5,24) PITN **2** 80-81, CHIA **5** 82-84, MONN **2** 85-87, CHIN **24** 88, **2** 88-89, OAKA **2** 91

LAW, VERN (DEACON) P F
(20,**32**) PITN **20** 50-51, **32** 54-67, *CH* **32** 68-69

LAWING, GARLAND (KNOBBY) OF
(28,**29**) CINN **28** 46, NYN **29** 46

LAWLESS, TOM 2B/INF/UTIL
(17,20,**12**,18) CINN **17** 82, 84 MONN **20** 84, STLN **12** 85-88, TORA **18** 89-90

LAWRENCE, BILL OF
(**7**) DETA **7** 32

LAWRENCE, BRIAN P
(**50**) SDN **50** 01-05

LAWRENCE, BROOKS (BULL) P
(31,**46**) STLN **31** 54-55, CINN **46** 56-60

LAWRENCE, JIM C
(**5**) CLEA **5** 63

LAWRENCE, JOE 2B
(**6**) TORA **6** 02

LAWRENCE, SEAN P
(**48**) PITN **48** 98

LAWSON, ROXIE P
(24,__,26,**15**, 23,12,17) CLEA **24** 31, DETA __ 33, **26** 35, **15** 36-38, **23** 39, STLA **23/12** 39, **17** 39-40

LAWSON, STEVE P
(**24**) TEXA **24** 72

LAWTON, MARCUS OF/DH
(24,28) NYA **24/28**

LAWTON, MATT OF/DH
(**50**,23,11) MINA **50** 95-01, NYN **23** 01, CLEA **11** 02-04, PITN **50** 05, CHIN **50** 05, NYA **50** 05

LAXTON, BILL P
(45,48,41,36, 27,**38**) PHIN **45** 70, SDN **48/41** 71, **41/36** 74, DETA **27** 76, SEAA **38** 77, CLEA **38** 77

LAXTON, BRETT P
(58,**32**) OAKA **58** 99, KCA **32** 00

LAYANA, TIM P
(**43**,36) CINN **43** 90-91, SFN **36** 93

LAYDON, PETE OF
(**20**) STLA **20** 48

LAYNE, HILLY (TONY) 3B/2B
(34,**22**) WASA **34** 41, **22** 44-45

LAYTON, LES OF
(**21**) NYN **21** 48

LAZAR, DAN P
(**40**) CHIA **40** 68-69

LAZOR, JOHNNY OF/C
(82,**14**,29) BOSA **82** 43, **14** 44-45, **29** 46

LAZORKO, JACK P
(41,33,46,36, 47,**17**) MILA **41/33** 84, SEAA **46** 85, DETA **36** 86, CALA **47** 87, **17** 87-88

LAZZERI, TONY (POOSH'EM UP) 2B/UTIL
(**6**,5,23,7,15, 11,19) NYA **6** 29, **5** 30-31, **23** 32, **7** 33, **6** 34-37, CHIN **15** 38, BKNN **11** 39, NYN **19** 39

LEA, CHARLIE P
(47,**53**) MONN **47** 80,**53** 80-84, 87, MINA **53** 88

LEACH, FREDDY OF
(**22**) BOSN **22** 32

LEACH, JALAL (JAY) OF
(**18**) SFN **18** 01

LEACH, RICK UTIL/P
(7,**9**,25) DETA **7** 81-83, TORA **9** 84-88, TEXA **9** 89, SFN **25** 90

LEACH, TERRY P
(43,**26**,38,30, 34) NYN **43** 81-82, **26** 85-89, KCA **38** 89, MINA **30** 90-91, CHIA **34** 92-93

LEAGUE, BRANDON P
(35,**22**) TORA **35** 04, **22** 05

LEAK, GENE 3B/SS/UTIL
(7,**14**) CLEA **7** 59, LAA **14** 61-62

LEAL, LUIS P
(**48**) TORA **48** 80-85

LEARY, TIM P
(38,39,23,**54**, 28,36) NYN **38** 81, 83-84, MILA **39** 85-86, LAN **23** 87, **54** 88-89, CINN **54** 89, NYA **28** 90, **54** 90-92, SEAA **54** 92-93, TEXA **36** 94

LeCROY, MATT C/1B/DH
(**24**) MINA **24** 00-05

LEDEE, RICKY OF
(38,17,23,12, **33**) NYA **38** 98, **17** 99-00, CLEA **23** 00, TEXA **12** 00-01, PHIN **33** 02-04, SFN **33** 04, LAN **33** 05

LEDESMA, AARON SS/3B/INF
(11,6,**4**,2) NYN **11** 95, BALA **6** 97, TBA **4** 98-99, COLN **2** 00

LEDEZMA, WILFREDO P
(**41**) DETA **41** 03-05

LEE, BILL (BIG BILL) P
(19,15,**11**,31, 38,25,17,26, 24) CHIN **19** 34, **15** 35-36, **11** 37-42, **31** 43, PHIN **38/25** 43, **17** 44-45, BOSN **26** 45-46, CHIN **24** 47

LEE, BILL (SPACEMAN) P
(**37**) BOSA **37** 69-78, MONN **37** 79-82

LEE, BOB (MOOSE)(HORSE) P
(**39**,48) LAA **39** 64, CALA **39** 65-66, LAN **39** 67, CINN **39** 67, **48** 67-68

LEE, CARLOS OF
(**45**) CHIA **45** 99-04, MILN **45** 05

LEE, CLIFF P
(65,34,**31**) CLEA **65** 02-03, **34** 03-04, **31** 05

LEE, COREY P
(**37**) TEXA **37** 99

LEE, DAVID P
(43,54,51,**36**, 47) COLN **43/54** 99, **51** 00, SDN **36** 01, CLEA **47** 03-04

LEE, DEREK OF
(**52**) MINA **52** 93

LEE, DERREK 1B
(27,**25**) SDN **27** 97, FLAN **27** 98, **25** 98-03, CHIN **25** 04-05

LEE, DON P
(41,20,**48**,40, 43) DETA **41** 57, **20** 58, WASA **20** 60,MINA **20** 61-62, LAA **48** 62-64, CALA **48** 65, HOUN **40/48** 65, **43** 66, CHIN **43** 66

LEE, HAL (SHERIFF) OF/2B
(6,14,**10**) PHIN **6** 32-33, BOSN **14** 33, **10** 34-36

LEE, LERON OF/DH
(37,**24**,22,9) STLN **37** 69-71, SDN **24** 71-73, CLEA **22** 74-75, LAN **9** 75-76

LEE, MANNY INF/DH/UTIL
(**4**,2,18) TORA **4** 85-91, **2** 92, TEXA **2** 93-94, STLN **18** 95

LEE, MARK P
(42,46,35,50, **34**,52) SDN **42** 78-79, PITN **46** 80-81, KCA **35** 88, MILA **50** 90, **34** 90-91, BALA **52** 95

LEE, MIKE P
(20,30) CLEA **20** 60, LAA **30** 63

LEE, ROY P
(**22**) NYN **22** 45

LEE, SANG HOON P
(**40**) BOSA **40** 00

LEE, TERRY 1B
(**26**) CINN **26** 90-91

LEE, THORNTON (LEFTY) P
(30,22,28,**27**, 49) CLEA **30** 33, **22** 34,**28** 35, **22** 36, CHIA **27** 37-47, NYN **49** 48

LEE, TRAVIS 1B
(**16**,10,38) ARIN **16** 98-00, PHIN **10** 00, **16** 01-02, TBA **16** 03, NYA **38** 04, TBA **16** 05

LEEPER, DAVE OF/DH
(58,**36**) KCA **58** 84, **36** 85

LeFEBVRE, BILL (LEFTY) P
(19,**15**,12,20) BOSA **19** 38, **15** 39, WASA **12** 43, **20** 44

LEFEBVRE, JIM (FRENCHY) 2B/UTIL/CH/M
(**5**,45,6,11,29, 4) LAN **5** 65-72, *CH* **45** 78-79, SFN *CH* **5** 80-82, OAKA *CH* **5** 87-88, SEAA *M* **5** 89-91, CHIN *M* **5** 92-93, OAKA *CH* **6** 94, *CH* **11** 94-95, MILN *CH* **29** 98-99, *M* 99, CINN *CH* **4** 02

LEFEBVRE, JOE OF/UTIL/CH
(46,18,**23**,16) NYA **46** 80, SDN **18** 81-83, PHIN **23** 83-84, 86, SFN *CH* **18** 02-04, **16** 05

LEFFERTS, CRAIG P
(60,37,32,**11**, 31,21) CHIN **60/32** 83, SDN **37** 84-87, SFN **32** 87-89, SDN **11** 90-92, BALA **31** 92, TEXA **11** 93, CALA **21** 94

LeFLORE, RON OF/DH
(42,**8**,7) DETA **42** 74, **8** 75-79, MONN **7** 80, CHIA **8** 81-82

LEFTWICH, PHIL P
(21,**45**) CALA **21** 93, **45** 93-94, 96

LEGETT, LOU (DOC) C
(21,28,**24**) BOSA **21** 33, **28** 34, **24** 34-35

LEGG, GREG 2B/SS/INF
(**11**) PHIN **11** 86-88

LEHENY, REGIS P
(**25**) BOSA **25** 32

LEHEW, JIM P
(39,**38**) BALA **39** 61, **38** 62

LEHMAN, KEN P
(**16**,40,39,25) BKNN **16** 52, 56-57, BALA **40** 57, **39** 57-58, PHIN **25** 61

LEHNER, PAUL (PEANUTS)(GULLIVER) OF/1B
(19,**17**,5,15, 38) STLA **19** 46, **17** 47-49, PHIA **5** 50-51, CHIA **15** 51, STLA **1** 51, CLEA **38** 51,BOSA **37** 52

LEHR, JUSTIN P
(57,**43**) OAKA **57** 04, MILN **43** 05

LEIBER, HANK OF/1B/P
(27,16,5,4,3, 26, **9**) NYN **27** 33-34, **16** 35, **5** 36, **4/3/26** 37,**5** 38, CHIN **9** 39-41, NYN **5** 42

LEIBRANDT, CHARLIE P
(44,**37**,32,45) CINN **44** 79-82, KCA **37** 84-89, ATLN **45** 90, **32** 90-92, TEXA **32** 93

LEICESTER, JON P
(**51**) CHIN **51** 04-05

LEIP, ED 2B
(**10**,2,6) WASA **10** 39, PITN **2** 40, **10** 41, **6** 42

LEIPER, DAVE P
(**52**,43) OAKA **52** 84, 86-87, SDN **43** 87-88, **52** 88-89, OAKA **52** 94-95, MONN **52** 95, PHIN **43** 96, MONN **52** 96

LEISTER, JOHN P
(**22**,38) BOSA **22** 87, **38** 90

LEITER, AL P B
(56,**28**,25,22) NYA **56** 87, **28** 88-89, TORA **28** 89-95, FLAN **25** 96-97, NYN **22** 98-04, FLAN **22** 05, NYA **19** 05

LEITER, MARK P B
(56,23,13,27, **31**) NYA **56** 90, DETA **23** 91-92, **13** 93, CALA **27** 94, SFN **31** 95-96, MONN **31** 96, PHIN **31** 97-98, SEAA **23** 99, MILN **23** 01

LEIUS, SCOTT P
(**31**,30,8) MINA **31** 90-95, CLEA **30** 96, KCA **8** 98-99

LEJA, FRANK 1B
(**51**,2) NYA **51** 54-55, LAA **2** 62

LeJOHN, DON 3B
(**31**) LAN **31** 65

LEMANCZYK, DAVE P
(35,19,**23**,45) DETA **35** 73, **19** 74-76, TORA **23** 77-80, CALA **45** 80

LEMASTER, DENNY P
(**23**) MILN **23** 62-65, ATLN **23** 66-67, HOUN **23** 68-71, MONN **23** 72

LeMASTER, JOHNNIE SS/INF/DH
(**10**,11,27) SFN **10** 75-85, CLEA **11** 85, PITN **27/10** 85, OAKA **11** 87

LeMAY, DICK P
(**39**,30) SFN **39** 61-62, CHIN **30** 63

LEMBO, STEVE C
(**7**,18) BKNN **7** 50, **18** 52

LEMKE, MARK 2B/3B
(17,**20**,15) ATLN **17** 88-89, **20** 90-97, BOSA **15** 98

LEMON, BOB 3B/OF/P/CH/M B
(38,42,6,**21**, 2,20,33,66) CLEA **38** 41, **42** 42, **6** 46, **21** 47-58,*CH* **21** 59-60, PHIN *CH* **2** 61, CALA *CH* **20** 67-68, KCA *CH* **2** 70, *M* **2** 70, *M* **21** 71-72, NYA *CH* **21/33** 76, CHIA *M* **21** 77-78, NYA *M* **21** 78-79, 81-82

LEMON, CHET OF/DH
(2,44,**34**) CHIA **2** 75, **44** 76-81, DETA **34** 82-90

LEMON, JIM OF/1B/CH/M B
(30,17,14,**23**, 21,25,52,40, 44) CLEA **30** 50, **17** 53, WASA **14** 54-55, **23** 56-60, MINA **23** 61-63, PHIN **21** 63, CHIA **25** 63, MINA *CH* **52** 65-67, WASA *M* **40** 68, MINA *CH* **44** 81-84

LEMONGELLO, MARK P
(51,**42**,40) HOUN **51** 76, **42** 77-78, TORA **40** 79

LEMONDS, DAVE P
(48,**43**) CHIN **48** 69, CHIA **43** 72

LENHARDT, DON (FOOTSIE) OF/1B/CH
(**14**,6,31,23, 32,3) STLA **14** 50-51, CHIA **6** 51, BOSA **31** 52, DETA **14** 52, STLA **23** 52, **14** 53, BALA **14** 54, BOSA **32** 54, *CH* **31** 70-73

LENNON, PAT DH/OF
(26,33,46,23, 20) SEAA **26** 91, **33** 92, KCA **46** 96, OAKA **23** 97, TORA **20** 98-99

LENNON, BOB (ARCH) OF
(36,**30**,9) NYN **36** 54, 56, **30** 56, CHIN **9** 57

LENTINE, JIM OF/DH
(**21**,27) STLN **21** 78-80, DETA **27** 80

LEON, DANNY P
(**49**) TEXA **49** 92

LEON, EDDIE SS/INF/DH
(**24**,11,3,20) CLEA **24** 68-71, **11** 72, CHIA **3** 73-74, NYA **20** 75

LEON, IZZY P
(**31**) PHIN **31** 45

LEON, JOSE UTIL
(**31**,14) BALA **31** 02-03, **14** 04

LEON, MAX P
(32,50,**31**) ATLN **32** 73, **50** 74, **31** 74-78

LEONARD, DENNIS P
(**22**) KCA **22** 74-83, 85-86

LEONARD, DUTCH P/CH
(27,**16**,20,32) BKNN **27** 33-36, WASA **16** 38-46, PHIN **20** 47-48, CHIN **32** 49, **20** 49-53, *CH* **20** 54-56

LEONARD, JEFFREY OF/1B/DH
(51,46,30,26, 20,**00**) LAN **51** 77, HOUN **46** 78, **30** 79-81, SFN **26** 81-84, **20** 85-86, **00** 87-88, MILA **00** 88, SEAA **00** 89-90

LEONARD, MARK OF/DH
(21,**1**,38,2) SFN **21** 90, **1** 91-92, BALA **38** 93, SFN **21** 94, **2** 95

LEONE, JUSTIN 3B
(**26**) SEAA **26** 04, (05)

LEONHARD, DAVE P
(46,**40**) BALA **24/46** 67, **40** 68-72

LEOVICH, JOHN C
(**33**) PHIA **33** 41

LEPCIO, TED 2B/INF
(**12**,5,22,4, 36,6) BOSA **12** 52, **5** 53-54, **12** 55-59, DETA **22** 59, PHIN **4** 60, CHIA **36** 61, MINA **6** 61

LEPPERT, DON (TIGER) 2B/C/CH
(9,2,**10**,6,43, 3) BALA **9** 55, PITN **2** 61-62, WASA **10** 63-64, PITN *CH* **6** 68-69, *CH* **43** 70-79, HOUN *CH* **3** 80-81, *CH* **43** 81-85

LERCH, RANDY P
(**47**,35,29,35) PHIN **47** 75-80, MILA **35** 81, PHIN **47** 81, MILA **35** 82, MONN **47** 82-83, SFN **29** 83-84, PHIN **35** 86

LERCHEN, GEORGE OF
(32,**20**) DETA **32** 52, CINN **20** 53

LEREW, ANTHONY P
(**50**) ATLN **50** 05

LeROY, JOHN P
(**50**) ATLN **50** 97

LERSCH, BARRY P
(**34**,15) PHIN **34** 69-73, STLN **15** 74

LESHER, BRIAN OF
(24,5,20,65, **31**) OAKA **24** 96, **5** 97, **20** 98, SEAA **65/31** 00, TORA **31** 02

LESHNOCK, DON P
(**48**) DETA **48** 72

LESKANIC, CURTIS P
(45,**16**,39,00, 33,30) COLN **45** 93-94, **16** 95-99, MILN **39** 00, **00** 00-01, (02), **33** 03, KCA **33** 03 -04, BOSA **30** 04

LESLEY, BRAD P
(**50**,37) CINN **50** 82-84, MILA **37** 85

LESLIE, SAM (SAMBO) 1B
(20,22,**6**,26) NYN **20** 32, **22** 33, BKNN **6** 33-35, NYN **26** 36, **20** 37-38

LETCHAS, CHARLIE C/INF
(10,36,1,**6**,23) PHIN **10** 39, WASA **36** 41, PHIN **1/6** 44, **23** 46

LETT, JIM CH
(79,**3**,55,10, 17,18) CINN *CH* **79** 86, **3** 87-89, *CH* **55** 96, TORA *CH* **10** 97-99, LAN *CH* **17** 01, **18** 02-05

LEVAN, JESSE 3B/1B
(__,**35**) PHIN __ 47, WASA **35** 54-55

LEVEY, JIM SS
(**1**) STLN **1** 31-33

LEVINE, ALAN P
(54,**43**,40,33) CHIA **54** 96-97, TEXA **43** 98, ANAA **43** 99-02, TBA **40** 03, KCA **43** 03, DETA **43** 04, SFN **33** 05

LEVIS, JESSE C/DH
(68,**12**,16,26) CLEA **68** 92, **12** 92, 94-95, MILA **16** 96-97, MILN **16** 98, CLEA **26** 99, MILN **50** 01

LEVRAULT, ALLEN P
(**55**,44) MILN **55** 00-01, FLAN **44** 03

LEVY, ED 1B/OF
(8,17,**9**) PHIN **8** 40, NYA **17** 42, **9** 44

LEVY, LENNY C/CH
(27,35,42,**45**) PITN **27** 48, *CH* **27** 48, *CH* **35** 50, *CH* **42** 57-58, *CH* **45** 59-64

LEWALLYN, DENNIS P/CH
(**35**,21,28,41, __) LAN **35** 75-78, **21** 78-79, TEXA **28** 80, CLEA **41** 81-82, ARIN *CH* __ 04

LEWANDOWSKI, DAN P
(**34**) STLN **34** 51

LEWIS, ALLAN (PANAMANIAN EXPRESS) OF
(10,16,8,**15**, 32,24) KCA **10/16** 67, OAKA **8** 68, **15** 69, **32** 70, **24** 72-73

LEWIS, BILL (BUDDY) C
(31,22,8) STLN **31** 33, BOSN **22** 35, **8** 36

LEWIS, BUDDY 3B/OF
(33,**2**,3) WASA **33** 35, **2** 36-40, **3** 41, **2** 45-49

LEWIS, COLBY P
(**48**) TEXA **48** 02-04

LEWIS, DARREN OF/DH
(16,**2**,7,10,20, 6) OAKA **16** 90, SFN **2** 91-95, CINN **7** 95, CHIA **10** 96-97, LAN **20** 97, BOSA **20** 98-01, CHIN **6** 02

LEWIS, DUFFY CH
(33,**32**) BOSN *CH* **33** 32, *CH* **32** 33-35

LEWIS, JIM P
(26,61,21,34, 39) SEAA **26** 79, NYA **61** 82, MINA **21** 83, SEAA **34** 85, SDN **39** 91

LEWIS, JOHNNY OF/CH
(28,**24**,30,48,9) STLN **28** 64, NYN **24** 65-67, STLN *CH* **30** 73-76, *CH* **48** 84-85, *CH* **8** 86-89

LEWIS, MARK 2B/INF
(10,**20**,17,14,5,28,1) CLEA **10** 91-92, **20** 93-94, CINN **17** 95, DETA **14** 96, SFN **14** 97, PHIN **5** 98, CINN **28** 99-00, BALA **10** 00, CLEA **1** 01

LEWIS, RICHIE P
(55,26,**24**,51,44,58,38) BALA **55** 92, FLAN **26** 93, **24** 93-95, DETA **43/51** 96, OAKA **51/44** 97, CINN **58** 97, BALA **38** 98

LEWIS, SCOTT P
(46,**18**) CALA **46** 90-91, **18** 92-94

LEY, TERRY P
(**43**) NYA **43** 71

LEYLAND, JIM CH/M
(28,21,31,14,**10**,11) CHIA *CH* **28** 82, *CH* **21** 82-85, PITN *M* **31/14** 86, *M* **10** 87-96, FLAN *M* **11** 97-98, COLN *M* **11** 99

LEYRITZ, JIM C/UTIL/DH
(12,**13**,31,18) NYA **12** 90-92, **13** 93-96, ANAA **13** 97, TEXA **13** 97, BOSA **31** 98, SDN **13** 98-99, NYA **13** 99-00, LAN **18** 00

LEYVA, NICK CH/M
(**16**,45) STLN *CH* **16** 84-88, PHIN *M* **16** 89-91, TORA *CH* **45** 93, *CH* **16** 94-97

LEZCANO, CARLOS OF
(**30**) CHIN **30** 80-81

LEZCANO, SIXTO OF/DH
(37,**16**,14,43,28) MILA **37** 74, **16** 75-80, STLN **16** 81, SDN **14** 82-83, PHIN **43** 83, **28** 83-85

LIBKE, AL OF/P/1B
(**22**) CINN **22** 45-46

LIBRAN, FRANKIE SS
(31,**29**) SDN **31/29** 69

LICKERT, JOHN C
(**29**) BOSA **29** 81

LIDDELL, DAVE C
(**36**) NYN **36** 90

LIDDLE, DON P
(43,15,**37**,21) MILN **43/15** 53, NYN **37** 54-56, STLN **21** 56

LIDDLE, STEVE CH
(66,**9**) MINA *CH* **66** 99, **9** 02-05

LIDGE, BRAD P
(**54**,27) HOUN **54** 02-05

LIDLE, CORY P
(11,27,**21**,15,30) NYN **11** 97, TBA **27** 99-00, OAKA **21** 01-02, TORA **21** 03, CINN **15** 04, PHIN **30** 04-05

LIEBER, DUTCH P
(**16**) PHIA **16** 35-36

LIEBER, JON P
(**47**,32,22,21) PITN **47** 94-98, CHIN **32** 99-02, NYA **22** 04, PHIN **21** 05

LIEBERTHAL, MIKE C
(**24**) PHIN **24** 94-05

LIEBHARDT, GLENN (SANDY) P
(22,**20**) STLA **22** 36, **20** 38

LIEFER, JEFF OF/1B/3B
(**39**,45,3,9,8) CHIA **39** 99-02, MONN **45** 03, TBA **3** 03, MILN **9** 04, CLEA **8** 05

LIGTENBERG, KERRY P
(**46**,36) ATLN **46** 97-02, BALA **46** 03, TORA **46** 04, ARIN **36** 05

LILLARD, BILL SS/2B B
(**3**) PHIA **3** 39-40

LILLARD, GENE SS/3B/P B
(**3,**27,31) CHIN **3** 36, **27** 39, STLN **31** 40

LILLIQUIST, DEREK (THE GEORGIA BULLDOG) P
(24,26,**28**,37) ATLN **24** 89-90, SDN **26** 90-91, CLEA **28** 92-94, BOSA **28** 95, CINN **37** 96

LILLIS, BOB (FLEA) SS/INF/CH/M
(11,30,35,**15**,16,4,5) LAN **11** 58, **30** 58-59, **11** 59-61, STLN **35** 81, HOUN **15** 62-67, *CH* **16** 73, **4** 74, **5** 73-82, *M* **5** 82-85, SFN *CH* **5** 86-96

LILLY, TED P
(28,56,61,43,**31**) MONN **28** 99, NYA **56** 00, **61** 01-02, **43** 02, OAKA **31** 02-03, TORA **31** 04-05

LIMA, JOSE P
(32,**42**,25,27,33) DETA **32** 94-96, HOUN **42** 97-01, DETA **42** 01-02, KCA **25** 03 , LAN **27** 04, KCA **33** 05

LIMMER, LOU 1B
(**3**,48,14) PHIA **3** 51, **48/14** 54

LINARES, JULIO CH
(**1**) HOUN **1** 94-96

LINARES, RUFINO OF
(**25**,11,24) ATLN **25** 81-82, **11** 84, **24** 85

LINCOLN, MIKE P
(19,**57**33,36) MINA **19** 99-00, PITN **57** 01-03, STLN **33/36** 04, (05)

LIND, JACK SS/2B/CH
(2,**8**,45) MILA **2** 74, **8** 75, PITN *CH* **45** 98-00

LIND, JOSE (CHICO) 2B
(**13**) PITN **13** 87-92, KCA **13** 93-95, ANAA **13** 95

LINDBECK, EM P
(**23**) DETA **23** 60

LINDBLAD, PAUL P
(32,**25**,46,24,36) KCA **32** 65, **46** 66, **25** 66-67, **24** 67,OAKA **25** 68-71, WASA **32** 71, TEXA **32** 72, OAKA **25** 73-76, TEXA **24** 77, **25** 77-78, NYA **36/40** 78

LINDE, LYMAN P
(3,**20**) CLEA **3** 47, **20** 48

LINDELL, JOHNNY P/OF/1B
(16,18,8,**27**,5,28) NYA **16** 41, **18** 42-43, **8** 44-45, **27** 46-50, STLN **5** 50, PITN **28** 53, **18** 53-54

LINDEMAN, JIM OF/1B
(**15**,33,19,29) STLN **15** 86-89, DETA **33** 90, PHIN **19** 91-92, HOUN **19** 93, NYN **29** 94

LINDEN, TODD OF
(50,**39**) SFN **50** 03, **39** 05

LINDEN, WALT C
(**22**) BOSN **22** 50

LINDQUIST, CARL P
(**21**) BOSN **21** 43-44

LINDSEY, BILL C
(**20**) CHIA **20** 87

LINDSEY, DOUG C
(57,35,68) PHIN **57** 91, **35** 93, CHIA **68** 93

LINDSEY, JIM P
(**19**,20,24,31) STLN **19** 32, **20** 33, CINN **24** 34, STLN **31** 34, BKNN **19** 37

LINDSEY, RODNEY OF
(**54**) DETA **54** 00

LINDSTROM, CHUCK C S
(**31**) CHIA **31** 58

LINDSTROM, FREDDY OF/3B
(3,**12**,7,1) NYN **3** 32, PITN **12** 33-34, CHIN **7** 35, BKNN **1** 36

LINEBRINK, SCOTT P
(41,**36**,38) SFN **41** 00, HOUN **41** 00, **36** 00-03, SDN **38** 03-05

LINES, DICK P
(**18**) WASA **18** 66-67

LINHART, CARL PH
(**15**) DETA **15** 52

LINIAK, COLE INF
(**18**) CHIN **18** 99-00

LINKE, ED (BABE) P
(20,**29**,19,33,14,22) WASA **20** 33, **29** 34-36, **19** 35, **33/14** 36, **19** 37, STLA **22** 38

LINT, ROYCE P
(**25**) STLN **25** 54

LINTON, DOUG P
(**26**,35,30,49) TORA **26** 92-93, CALA **35** 93, NYN **30** 94, KCA **49** 95-96, BALA **49** 99, TORA **30** 03

LINTZ, LARRY 2B/SS/UTIL
(51,**12**,25,45,21,30) MONN **51** 73, **12** 74-75, STLN **25** 75, OAKA **45** 76, **21** 76-77, CLEA **30** 78

LINZ, PHIL UTIL/SS
(34,12,18,**2**) NYA **34** 62-64, **12** 65, PHIN **18** 66-67, NYN **2** 67-68

LINZY, FRANK P
(36,**35**,25,31) SFN **36** 63, **35** 65-70, STLN **35** 70-71, MILA **25** 72-73, PHIN **31** 74

LiPETRI, ANGELO P
(45,50) PHIN **45** 56, **50** 58

LIPON, JOHNNY (SKIDS) SS/INF/CH
(7,37,26,**2**,6,34,15,4) DETA **7** 42, **37** 46, **26** 48, **2** 49-52, BOSA **6** 52-53, STLA **34** 53, CINN **15** 54, CLEA *CH* **4** 68-71

LIPSCOMB, JERRY (NIG) INF/P
(**15**) STLA **15** 37

LIPSKI, BOB C
(**7**) CLEA **7** 63

LIRA, FELIPE P
(**40**,41,43) DETA **40** 95-97, SEAA **41** 97-98, DETA **40** 99, MONN **43** 00-0

LIRIANO, FRANCISCO P
(**47**) MINA **47** 05

LIRIANO, NELSON 2B/INF/DH
(**2**,4,16,46,22) TORA **2** 87-90, MINA **2** 90, KCA **2** 91, COLN **4** 93-94, PITN **16** 95-96, LAN **46** 97, COLN **22** 98

LIRIANO, PEDRO P
(**48**) MILN **48** 04, PHIN **48** 05

LIS, JOE OF/1B/UTIL/DH
(46,25,10,**30**,18) PHIN **46** 70-71, **25** 71-72, MINA **10** 73-74, CLEA **30** 74-76, SEAA **18** 77

LISENBEE, HOD P
(**24**,22,29,42) BOSA **24** 31, **22** 32, PHIA **29** 36, CINN **42** 45

LISI, RICK OF
(**24**) TEXA **24** 81

LISKA, AD P
(18,30,**22**) WASA **18** 31, PHIN **30** 32, **22** 33

LISTACH, PAT SS/2B/UTIL
(**16**,4,29) MILA **16** 92-95, **4** 96, HOUN **4** 97

Dennis Lamp had one of those miraculous years in 1985 for Toronto. He didn't lose. Lamp had a perfect 11-0 record with two saves. The Jays played in their first post-season against the Royals and Lamp was brilliant—one walk and 10 strikeouts in 9.1 innings. His ERA was 0.00. His short stay in Oakland was undistinguished, 1-3, 5.08 ERA.

A five-time All-Star, Kenny Lofton led the American League in stolen bases each of his first five full seasons. He is the top base stealer in Indians history with 450. He holds the AL rookie stolen base record—66 in 1992. He was generally conceded to be the premier leadoff hitter in the game during the 1990s, wresting the mantle from Brett Butler.

LITTELL, MARK P
(27,**17**,32,34) KCA **27** 73, **17** 75-77, STLN **32** 78-80, **34** 81-82

LITTLE, BRYAN (TWIG) 2B/SS/INF/CH
(**3**,47,26,59 20) MONN **3** 82-84, CHIA **47** 85-86, NYA **26** 86, CHIA *CH* **59** 98, **20** 98-00

LITTLE, GRADY CH
(20,35,9,**3**) SDN *CH* **20** 96, BOSA *CH* **35** 97-99, CLEA *CH* **9** 00-01, BOSA *M* **3** 02-03

LITTLE, JEFF P
(43,45,**36**) STLN **43** 80, MINA **45/36** 82

LITTLE, MARK OF
(58,**19**,21,11, 31) STLN **58** 98, COLN **19** 01-02, NYN **21** 02, ARIN **11** 02, CLEA **31** 04

LITTLE, SCOTT OF
(38,**41**) PITN **38/41** 89

LITTLEFIELD, DICK P
(34,39,38,18, **27**,45,30,25) BOSA **34** 50, CHIA **39** 51, DETA **38** 52, STLA **38** 52, **18** 52-53, BALA **18** 54, PITN **27** 54-56, STLN **45** 56, NYN **30** 56, CHIN **34** 57, MILN **25** 58

LITTLEFIELD, JOHN P
(48,**50**) STLN **48/50** 80, SDN **50** 81

LITTLEJOHN, DENNIS C
(**35**,47) SFN **35** 78, **47** 79, **35** 80

LITTLETON, LARRY OF
(**32**) CLEA **32** 81

LITTON, GREG UTIL/ALL*
(**15**,29,17,28) SFN **15** 89-92, **29/17** 92, SEAA **15** 93, BOSA **28** 94

LITTRELL, JACK SS/3B/INF
(16,3,**9**,39,6) PHIA **16** 52, **3** 54, KCA **9** 55, CHIN **39/6** 57

LITWHILER, DANNY OF/3B
(28,**4**,11,7,31, 8,42,22,52) PHIN **28** 40, **4** 40-41, **11/7/31** 42, **4** 43, STLN **8** 43-44, **42** 46, BOSN **22** 46, **4** 46-48, CINN **28** 48-51, **52** 51

LIVELY, BUD (RED) P
(**37**) CINN **37** 47-49

LIVENGOOD, WES P
(**36**) CINN **36** 39

LIVINGSTON, MICKEY C
(21,3,6,7,38, **11**,8,10) WASA **21** 38, PHIN **3** 41, **6** 42, **7** 43, CHIN **38** 43, **11** 45-47, NYN **8** 47-49, BOSN **10** 49, BKNN **11** 51

LIVINGSTON, SCOTT 3B/1B/DH
(21,**7**,9,8,29, 24) DETA **21** 91, **7** 92-94, SDN **9** 94-95, **8** 95-97, STLN **29** 97, MONN **24** 98

LLENAS, WINSTON 3B/UTIL/CH
(15,14,**12**,57) CALA **15** 68-69, **14** 69, **12** 72-75, TORA *CH* **57** 88

LLOYD, GRAEME P
(**37**,27,47,17) MILA **37** 93-96, NYA **27** 96-98, TORA **37** 99, MONN (00), **47** 01-02, FLAN **47** 02, NYN **17** 03, KCA **37** 03

LOAIZA, ESTEBAN P
(34,54,25,28, **21**) PITN **34** 95-98, TEXA **54/25** 98, **28** 99-00, TORA **21** 00-02, CHIA **21** 03-04, NYA **28** 04, WASN **21** 05

LOANE, BOBBY OF
(**17**) WASA **17** 39, BOSN **17** 40

LOBE, BILL CH
(31,40) CLEA *CH* **31** 39, *CH* **40** 51-57

LOBERT, HANS CH/M
(50,25,**2**,1) PHIN *CH* **50** 34-37, *CH* **25** 38, *M* **25** 38, *CH* **2** 39-41, *M* **2/1** 42, CINN *CH* **2** 43-44

LOCK, DON OF/1B
(25,**4**,23,18) WASA **25** 62, **4** 63-66, PHIN **23** 67-69, BOSA **18** 69

LOCKE, BOBBY P
(23,29,36,14, **34**,39,47,48) CLEA **23** 59, **29** 59-61, STLN **36** 62, PHIN **14** 62, **34** 63-64, CINN **39** 65, CALA **47** 67-68, **48/34** 68

LOCKE, CHARLIE (CHUCK) P
(**43**) BALA **43** 55

LOCKE, RON P
(**45**) NYN **45** 64

LOCKER, BOB P
(23,27,50,**36**, 39) CHIA **23** 65-69, SEAA **27** 69, MILA **27/23** 70, OAKA **50** 70, **36** 70-72, CHIN **36** 73, 75

LOCKHART, KEITH 3B/2B/DH
(2,43,4,1,**7**, 18) SDN **2** 94, KCA **43** 95, **4** 96, ATLN **1** 97-98, **7** 99-02, SDN **18** 03

LOCKLEAR, GENE OF
(27,5,**32**,46) CINN **27** 73, SDN **5** 73-74, **32** 74-76, NYA **46** 76-77

LOCKLIN, STU OF
(**32**) CLEA **32** 55-56

LOCKMAN, WHITEY OF/1B/UTIL/CH/M
(22,28,**25**,2, 34,19,6,3,5, 16) NYN **22** 45, **28** 47, **25** 47-56, STLN **2** 56, NYN **25** 57, SFN **25** 58, BALA **34/25** 59, CINN **19** 59-60, SFN *CH* **6** 61, *CH* **3** 61-64, CHIN *CH* **5** 66, *M* **16** 72-74

LOCKWOOD, SKIP 3B/P
(8,42,41,**38**) KCA **8** 65, SEAA **42** 69, MILA **42** 70-73, CALA **41** 74, NYN **38** 75-79, BOSA **38** 80

LODIGIANI, DARIO 2B/3B/CH
(**7**,37,39,40) PHIA **7** 38, **37** 40, CHIA **7** 41-42, **39** 46, KCA *CH* **40** 61-62

Lo DUCA, PAUL C/1B/OF
(64,**16**,14) LAN **64** 98, **16** 99-04, FLAN **14** 04, **16** 05

LOE, KAMERON P
(44,**43**) TEXA **44** 04, **43** 05

LOES, BILLY P
(38,**30**,18,28) BKNN **38** 50, **30** 52-56, BALA **38** 56, **18** 57-59, SFN **28** 60-61

LOEPP, GEORGE OF
(**11**) WASA **11** 30

LOEWER, CARLTON P
(**46**,37) PHIN **46** 98-99, SDN (00), **46** 01, (02), **37** 03

LOFTON, KENNY OF
(28,**7**,1,12) HOUN **28** 91, CLEA **7** 92-96, ATLN **7** 97, CLEA **7** 98-01, CHIA **1** 02, SFN **1** 02, PITN **1** 03, CHIN **1/7** 03, NYA **12** 04, PHIN **7** 05

LOGAN, BOB (LEFTY) P
(15,17,39,41, 40,20) BKNN **15** 35, DETA **17** 37, CHIN **39** 37, **41** 38, CINN **40** 41, BOSN **20** 45

LOGAN, JOHNNY (YATCHA) SS/3B
(**23**,16) BOSN **23** 51-52, MILN **23** 53-61, PITN **16** 61-62, **23** 63

LOGAN, NOOK OF
(40,**19**) DETA **40** 04, **19** 05

LOHRKE, JACK (LUCKY) 3B/INF
(16,**17**,7) NYN **16** 47-48, **17** 49-51, PHIN **7** 52-53

LOHRMAN, BILL P
(49,24,**12**,34, 22,32,43) PHIN **49** 34, NYN **24** 37, **12** 38-41, STLN **34** 42, NYN **22** 42-43, BKNN **32** 43, **22** 44, CINN **43** 44

LOHSE, KYLE P
(**49**) MINA **49** 01-05

LOIS, ALBERTO OF
(37,**11**) PITN **37** 78, **11** 79

LOISELLE, RICH P
(75,**51**) PITN **75** 96, **51** 97-01

LOLICH, MICKEY P
(**29**) DETA **29** 63-75, NYN **29** 76, SDN **29** 78-79

LOLICH, RON OF
(19,23,**22**) CHIA **19** 71, CLEA **23** 72, **22** 73

LOLLAR, SHERM C/1B/CH
(12,29,9,45, **10**,41,42) CLEA **12** 46, NYA **29** 47-48, STLA **9** 49-51, CHIA **45** 52, **10** 53-63, BALA *CH* **41** 64-67, OAKA *CH* **42** 68

LOLLAR, TIM P
(53,**48**,46) NYA **53** 80, SDN **48** 81-84, CHIA **46** 85, BOSA **48** 85-86

LOMAN, DOUG OF
(**5**) MILA **5** 84-85

LOMASNEY, STEVE C
(**56**) BOSA **56** 99

LOMBARD, GEORGE OF
(**26**,30,24) ATLN **26** 98-00, (01), 02, DETA **30** 02, TBA **24** 03

LOMBARDI, ERNIE (SCHNOZZ)(BOCCI) C
(7,27,17,2, 35,**4**,5,9,8,6) CINN **7** 32-33, **27** 34, **17** 35, **2** 36-37, **35** 38, **4** 39-41, BOSN **5** 42, NYN **9** 43, **8** 44-46, **6** 47

LOMBARDI, PHIL OF/C/1B
(36,50,61,39) NYA **36/50** 86, **61** 87, NYN **39** 89

LOMBARDI, VIC P
(**18**,28) BKNN **18** 45-47, PITN **28** 48-50

LOMBARDO, LOU P
(**35**) NYN **35** 48

LOMBARDOZZI, STEVE 2B/INF
(49,**4**) MINA **49** 85, **4** 85-88, HOUN **4** 89

LOMON, KEVIN P
(44,**32**) NYN **44** 95, ATLN **32** 96

LONBORG, JIM P
(**16**,27,29,41) BOSA **16** 65-71, MILA **27/29** 72, PHIN **41** 73-79

LONG, BILL P
(36,46,**47**,37 48) CHIA **36** 85, **46** 87-88, **47** 88-90, CHIN **37** 90, MONN **48** 91

LONG, BOB P
(57,34,50) PITN **57/34** 81, SEAA **50** 85

LONG, DALE 1B/OF/C/CH
(2,24,29,3,27, 8,20,7,**25**, 26) PITN **2** 51, STLA **24** 51, PITN **29** 55, **3** 56-57, CHIN **27** 57, **8** 58-59, SFN **20/7** 60, NYA **25** 60, WASA **25** 61, WASA **25** 62, NYA **26** 62-63, *CH* **26** 63

LONG, JEOFF OF/1B
(**10**,18) STLN **10** 63-64, CHIA **18** 64

LONG, JOEY P
(**52**) SDN **52** 97

LONG, RYAN OF
(**36**) KCA **36** 97

LONG, TERRANCE OF
(26,37,**12**,14, 3) NYN **26** 99, OAKA **37** 00, **12** 01-03, SDN **14** 04, KCA **3** 05

LONGMIRE, TONY OF
(**16**) PHIN **16** 93-95

LONNETT, JOE C/CH
(35,8,**7**,37,44, 41,3,32) PHIN **35** 56-57, **8** 58, **7** 59, CHIA *CH* **37** 71-75, OAKA *CH* **44/41** 76, PITN *CH* **3/35** 77, **32** 78-84

LOOK, BRUCE C
(**25**) MINA **25** 68

LOOK, DEAN OF
(**30**) CHIA **30** 61

LOONEY, BRIAN P
(53,**35**,51) MONN **53** 93, **35** 94, BOSA **51** 95

LOOPER, AARON P
(**46**) SEAA **46** 03

LOOPER, BRADEN P
(55,**41**,40) STLN **55** 98, FLAN **41** 99-03, NYN **40** 04-05

LOPAT, ED (STEADY EDDIE) P/CH/M
(48,**30**,15,36, 52,37) CHIA **48** 44-47, NYA **30** 48-55, BALA **15** 55, NYA *CH* **36** 60, MINA *CH* **52** 61, KCA *CH* **37** 62, *M* **37** 63, *M* **30** 63-64, *CH* **30** 65

LOPATA, STAN (STASH) C/1B
(41,**29**,6,15) PHIN **41** 48, **29** 49-58, MILN **6** 59, **15** 60

LOPATKA, ART P
(24,32) STLN **24** 45, PHIN **32** 46

LOPES, DAVEY 2B/UTIL/OF/CH
(**15**,12,11,14, 42,30,24,25) LAN **15** 72-81, OAKA **15** 82-84, CHIN **12** 84, **15** 85-86, HOUN **11** 86-87, **15** 87, TEXA *CH* **14** 88, **15** 88-91, BALA *CH* **42** 92, **15** 92-94, SDN *CH* **14** 95, **42** 95-98, **30** 98-99, MILN *CH* **30** 00-02, SDN *CH* **24** 03, **25** 04-05

LOPEZ, AL C/INF/M
(10,7,8,**12**, 42) BKNN **10** 32-35, BOSN **7** 36-39, **8** 40, PITN **12** 40-46, CLEA **12** 47, *M* **10** 51-56, CHIA *M* **42** 57-63, *M* **10** 64-65, 69, *M* **42** 68-69

LOPEZ, ALBIE P
(59,**32**,31) CLEA **59** 93-97, TBA **32** 98-01, ARIN **32** 01, ATLN **32** 02, KCA **31** 03

LOPEZ, AQUILINO P
(**44**,51,33) TORA **44** 03-04, COLN **51** 05, PHIN **33** 05

LOPEZ, ART OF
(**57**) NYA **57** 65

LOPEZ, AURELIO P
(38,39,**29**,35) KCA **38** 74, STLN **39** 78, DETA **29** 79-85, HOUN **35** 86-87

LOPEZ, CARLOS OF/DH
(15,32,**8**,9) CALA **15/32** 76, SEAA **8** 77, BALA **9** 78

LOPEZ, FELIPE 3B/INF
(**7**,12,2) TORA **7** 01-02, CINN **12** 03, **2** 04-05

LOPEZ, HECTOR 3B/2B/OF/UTIL
(1,10,**11**) KCA **1** 55, **10** 55-59, NYA **11** 59-66

LOPEZ, JAVIER P
(**45**,39) COLN **45** 03-05, ARIN **39** 05

LOPEZ, JAVY C
(**8**,18) ATLN **8** 92-03, BALA **18** 04-05

LOPEZ, JOSE SS/2B
(22,**4**) SEAA **22** 04-05, **4** 05

LOPEZ, JUAN CH
(**59**) SFN *CH* **59** 98-02, CHIN *CH* **59** 03-05

LOPEZ, LUIS, JR. 1B
(**12**) TORA **12** 01

LOPEZ, LUIS (A.) 1B/UTIL
(12,**22**,37) LAN **12** 90, CLEA **22** 91

LOPEZ, LUIS 1B
(**37**) MONN **37** 04

LOPEZ, LUIS (M.) 2B/UTIL
(**1**,17,9,26,15) SDN **1** 93-94, 96, NYN **17** 98-99, MILN **1** 00-02, BALA **9** 02, **26** 04, CINN **15** 05

LOPEZ, MARCELINO P
(**33**,29,46,32, 38,43) CALA **33** 65-67, BALA **29/46** 67, **32** 69-70, MILA **38** 71, CLEA **43** 72

LOPEZ, MATT 1B
(**17**) NYN **17** 97

LOPEZ, MENDY SS/3B/1B
(32,14,9,22, **25**,17,7) KCA **32** 98, **14** 99, FLAN **9** 00, HOUN **22** 01, PITN **25** 01, **17** 02, KCA **7** 03-04

LOPEZ, MICKEY 2B/DH
(**30**) SEAA **30** 04

LOPEZ, PEDRO INF
(**62**) CHIA **62** 05

LOPEZ, RAMON P
(**25**) CALA **25** 66

LOPEZ, RODRIGUEZ P
(**19**) BALA **19** 04

LOPEZ, RODRIGO P
(44,**13**,19) SDN **44** 00, BALA **13** 02-03, **19** 04-05, **13** 05

LORETTA, MARK SS/2B/INF
(**8**) MILA **8** 95-02, HOUN **8** 02, SDN **8** 03-05

LORRAINE, ANDREW P
(35,34,49,62, **55**,63,23) CALA **35** 94, CHIA **34** 95, OAKA **49** 97, SEAA **62** 98, CHIN **55** 99-00, CLEA **63** 00, MILN **23** 02

LOUCKS, SCOTT OF
(22,**26**,17) HOUN **22** 80-81, **26** 82-83, PITN **17** 85

LOUGHLIN, LARRY P
(47,**30**) PHIN **47/30** 67

LOUN, DON P
(**16**) WASA **16** 64

LOUX, SHANE P
(**58**) DETA **58** 02-03

LOVELACE, VANCE P
(**45**,42) CALA **45** 88-89, SEAA **42** 90

LOVRICH, PETE P
(**32**) KCA **32** 63

LOVULLO, TOREY INF
(**23**,12,13,43 10,27,6,9,4) DETA **23** 88-89, NYA **12/13/43** 91, CALA **10** 93, SEAA **27** 94, OAKA **6** 96, CLEA **9** 98, PHIN **4** 99

LOWE, DEREK P
(36,43,**32**,23) SEAA **36** 97, BOSA **43** 97, **32** 98-04, LAN **23** 05

LOWE, Q. V. CH
(**5**) CHIN *CH* **5** 72

LOWE, SEAN P
(34,48,**50**,52, 39) STLN **34** 97, **48** 98, CHIA **50** 99-01, PITN **48** 02, COLN **52** 02, KCA **39** 03

LOWELL, MIKE 3B/DH
(60,28,**19**) NYA **60** 98, FLAN **28** 99, **19** 00-05

LOWERY, TERRELL OF
(**10**,50,14) CHIN **10** 97-98, TBA **50** 99, SFN **14** 00

LOWENSTEIN, JOHN (STEINER) OF/UTIL/DH
(29,30,34,**38**) CLEA **29** 70-76, **30** 77, TEXA **34** 78, BALA **38** 79-85

LOWN, TURK P
(35,31,45,48, **27**) CHIN **35** 51-54, **31** 56-58, CINN **45/48** 58, CHIA **27** 58-62

LOWREY, HARRY (PEANUTS) OF/UTIL/CH
(43,**47**,21,37, 3,6,33,7,22,2) CHIN **43** 42, **47** 43, 45-49, CINN **21** 49-50, STLN **29** 50, **37** 50-54, PHIN **3** 55, *CH* **21** 60, *CH* **3** 61-66, SFN *CH* **6** 67-68, MONN *CH* **33** 69, CHIN *CH* **7** 70-71, CALA *CH* **22** 72, CHIN *CH* **2** 77-79, 81

LOWRY, DWIGHT C/UTIL
(25,,**12**,39) DETA **25** 84, **12** 86-87, MINA **39** 88

LOWRY, NOAH P
(60,**51**) SFN **60** 03, **51** 04-05

LOWRY, SAM P
(__,**22**) PHIA __ 42, **22** 43

LOYND, MIKE P
(50,**46**) TEXA **50** 86, **46** 86-87

LOZADO, WILLIE INF/DH
(**26**) MILA **26** 84

LUBRATICH, STEVE 3B/INF
(23,**28**) CALA **23** 81, **28** 83

LUBY, HUGH (HAL) P
(27,**2**) PHIA **27** 36, NYN **2** 44

LUCADELLO, JOHNNY 3B/2B/UTIL
(23,__,3,5, **7**, 29,52) STLA **23** 38, __ 39, **3** 40, **5** 41, **7** 46, NYA **29/52** 47

LUCARELLI, VITO CH
(__) SEAA *CH* __ 81

LUCAS, FRED (FRITZ) OF
(**34**) PHIN **34** 35

LUCAS, GARY P
(43,**25**,36) SDN **43** 80-81, **25** 81-83, MONN **25** 84-85, CALA **36** 86-87

LUCAS, JOHNNY (BUSTER) OF
(31,**16**) BOSA **31** 31, **16** 32

LUCAS, RAY (LUKE) P
(39,**26**) BKNN **39** 33, **26** 34

LUCAS, RED (THE NASHVILLE NARCISSUS) P
(12,**40**) CINN **12** 32-33, PITN **40** 34-38

LUCCHESI, FRANK M/CH
(1,49,**44**,48) PHIN *M* **1** 70-72, TEXA *CH* **49** 74, *CH* **44** 74-75, *M* **44** 75-77, *CH* **48** 79-80

LUCIER, LOU P
(81,15,24,36, **16**) BOSA **81/15** 43, **24** 44, PHIN **36?** 44, **16** 45

LUDWICK, ERIC P
(**57**,41,43,40) STLN **57** 96-97, OAKA **41** 97, FLAN **43** 98, TORA **40** 99

LUDWICK, RYAN OF
(**15**,38) TEXA **15** 02-03, CLEA **38** 03-05

LUEBBER, STEVE P
(**32**,34,23,46, 25,36) MINA **32** 71-72, **34/23** 76, TORA **46/25** 79, BALA **36** 81

LUEBBERS, LARRY P
(**52**,63,53) CINN **52** 93, STLN **63** 99, CINN **53** 00

LUEBKE, DICK P
(**26**) BALA **26** 62

LUECKEN, RICK P
(40,49,**38**) KCA **40** 89, ATLN **49** 90, TORA **38** 90

LUGO, JULIO INF/SS
(**4**,23) HOUN **4** 00-03, TBA **23** 03-05

LUGO, URBANO P
(**18**,59,43,20) CALA **18** 85-88, MONN **59/43** 89, DETA **20** 90

LUKACHYK, ROB PH
(**16**) MONN **16** 96

LUKASIEWICZ, MARK P
(**47**) ANAA **47** 01-02

LUKE, MATT OF
(**39**,40,33) NYA **39** 96, LAN **40** 98, CLEA **33** 98, LAN **40** 98, ANAA **33** 99

LUKON, EDDIE (MONGOOSE) OF
(**27**,26,15) CINN **27/26** 41, **15** 45, **27** 46-47

LUM, MIKE OF/1B/CH
(**28**,21,33) ATLN **28** 67-75, CINN **21** 76-78, ATLN **28** 79-81, CHIN **33** 81, CHIA *CH* **28** 85, KCA *CH* **28** 88-89

LUMENTI, RALPH P
(36,**27**,15) WASA **36** 57, **27** 58, **15** 59

LUMPE, JERRY SS/3B/INF/CH
(**11**,9,41) NYA **11** 56-59, KCA **11** 59-63, DETA **9** 64-67, OAKA *CH* **41** 71

LUNA, HECTOR 2B/SS/OF
(**7**) STLN **7** 04-05

LUNA, MEMO P
(**40**) STLN **40** 54

LUNAR, FERNANDO C
(20,**51**) ATLN **20** 00, BALA **51** 00-02

LUND, DON OF/CH
(25,40,17,8, 12,**30**,32) BKNN **25** 45, **40/17** 47, **8** 48, STLA **12** 48, DETA **30** 49, 52-54, *CH* **32** 57-58

LUND, GORDY SS/INF
(**14**) CLEA **14** 67, SEAA **14** 69

LUNDQUIST, DAVID P
(**49**,47) CHIA **49** 99, SDN **49** 01, **47** 02

LUNDSTEDT, TOM C/DH
(**8**,13) CHIN **8** 73-74, MINA **8** 75

LUNSFORD, TREY C
(**52**) SFN **52** 03

LUPIEN, TONY 1B
(32,16,**3**,29, 20) BOSA **32** 40, **16** 42, **3** 43, PHIN **29** 44, **20** 45, CHIA **3** 48

LUPLOW, AL OF
(32,**22**,18,20) CLEA **32** 61-62, **22** 63-65, NYN **18** 66-67, PITN **20** 67

LUQUE, DOLF (THE PRIDE OF HAVANA) P/CH
(16,**20**,30,31) NYN **16** 32, **20** 33-35, *CH* **30** 36, *CH* **31** 37-38, 41-45

LUSADER, SCOTT OF/DH
(24,**7**,17) DETA **24** 87-88, **7** 88-90, NYA **17** 91

LUTTRELL, LYLE SS
(**22**,31) WASA **22** 56, 58, **31** 57

LUTZ, JOE 1B/CH
(**18**,3) STLA **18** 51, CLEA *CH* **3** 72-73

LUUBA, KEITH SS
(**39**) ANAA **39** 00

LUZINSKI, GREG 1B/OF/DH/CH
(42,**19**) PHIN **42** 70-71, **19** 71-80, CHIA **19** 81-84, KCA *CH* **19** 95-97

LYDEN, MITCH C
(**52**) FLAN **52** 93

LYDY, SCOTT OF/DH
(**49**) OAKA **49** 93

LYLE, SPARKY OF/DH
(**28**,39,) BOSA **15** 67, **28** 67-71, NYA **28** 72-78, TEXA **28** 79-80, PHIN **39** 80-81, **28** 81-82, CHIA **28** 82

LYNCH, DANNY (DUMMY) 2B
(**20**) CHIN **20** 48

LYNCH, ED P
(50,35,34,31, **36**,37) NYN **50** 80, **35** 80-81, **34/31** 81, **36** 82-86, CHIN **37** 86-87

LYNCH, JERRY OF/C
(14,18,**24**) PITN **14** 54, **18** 55, **14** 56, CINN **24** 57-63, PITN **24** 63-66

LYNN, FRED OF/DH
(**19**,8,9) BOSA **19** 74-80, CALA **8** 81, **19** 82-84, BALA **19** 85-88, DETA **9** 88-89, SDN **8** 90

LYNN, JERRY 2B
(__) WASA __ 37

LYNN, RED P
(27,26,**14**,39) DETA **27** 39, NYN **26/19** 39, **14** 40, CHIN **39** 44

LYON, BRANDON P
(**28**,38) TORA **28** 01-02, BOSA **38** 03, ARIN **38** 05

LYON, ROSS C
(**38**) CLEA **38** 44

LYONS, AL P/OF
(24,19,**36**,2, 25) NYA **24/19** 44, **36** 46-47, PITN **2** 47, BOSN **25** 48

LYONS, BARRY C/1B
(**33**,40,41,54) NYN **33** 86-90, LAN **40** 90-91, CALA **41** 91, CHIA **54** 95

LYONS, BILLY INF
(**30**) STLN **30** 83-84

LYONS, CURT P
(**59**) CINN **59** 96

LYONS, EDDIE (MOUSE) 2B/CH
(**25**,41) WASA **25** 47, MINA *CH* **41** 76

LYONS, HERSH P
(**42**) STLN **42** 41

LYONS, STEVE OF/UTIL/P
(**12**,10,7,18,3, 19,30) BOSA **12** 85-86, CHIA **10** 86, **12** 87-90, BOSA **7** 91, ATLN **18** 92, MONN **3/18** 92, BOSA **19** 92, **30** 93

LYONS, TED P/M/CH
(14,**16**,*33*) CHIA **14** 31, **16** 32-42, 46, *M* **16** 46-48, DETA *CH* **33** 49-53, BKNN *CH* **33** 54

LYSANDER, RICK P
(29,**19**) OAKA **29** 80, MINA **19** 83-85

LYTTLE, JIM OF
(21,27,26,**2**, 20,41) NYA **21** 69, **27** 70-71, CHIA **26** 72, MONN **2** 73-74, **20** 75-76, LAN **41** 76

M

MAAS, DUKE P
(47,23,34,**24**, 29) DETA **47** 55-56, **23** 57, KCA **34** 58, NYA **24** 58-60, **29** 61

MAAS, KEVIN 1B/DH
(21,**24**,14) NYA **21/24** 90, **14** 91, **24** 91-93, MINA **24** 95

MABE, BOB P
(32,35,30) STLN **32** 58, CINN **35** 59, BALA **30** 60

MABRY, JOHN OF/1B/3B
(**47**,17,7) STLN **47** 94-98, SEAA **47** 99-00, SDN **17** 00, STLN **47** 01, FLAN **47** 01, PHIN **7** 02, OAKA **7/47** 02, SEAA **47** 03, STLN **47** 04-05

MacCORMACK, FRANK P
(29,24) DETA **29** 76, SEAA **24** 77

MacDONALD, BILL P
(**25**) PITN **25** 50, 53

MacDONALD, BOB (ROB) P
(**45**,38,34,49) TORA **45** 90-92, DETA **38** 93, NYA **34** 95, NYN **49** 96

MacDOUGAL, MIKE P
(**54**) KCA **54** 01-05

MacFARLAND, ??? CH
(**32**) PHIA *CH* **32** 36

MACFARLANE, MIKE C/DH
(28,8,**15**,5) KCA **28** 87, **8** 88, **15** 89-94, BOSA **15** 95, KCA **15** 96-98, OAKA **5** 98, **15** 99

MacFAYDEN, DANNY (DEACON DANNY) P
(21,18,17,24, **14**,22,36) BOSA **21** 31, **18** 32, NYA **17** 32-34, CINN **24** 35, BOSN **21** 35, BOSN **14** 36-39, PITN **22** 40, WASA **17** 41, BOSN **36** 43

MACHA, KEN C/UTIL/CH B
(34,29,30,**31**, 8,39) PITN **34** 74, **29** 77, **30** 77-78, **29** 78, MONN **31** 79-80, TORA **8** 81, MONN *CH* **31** 86-91, CALA *CH* **39** 92-94, OAKA *CH* **39** 00-02, *M* **39** 03-05

MACHA, MIKE 3B/C B
(31,**11**) ATLN **31** 79, TORA**11** 80

MACHADO, ALEJANDRO INF
(**40**) BOSA **40** 05

MACHADO, ANDERSON SS
(12,**19**,43,1) PHIN **12** 03, CINN **43** 04, **19** 04-05, COLN **1** 05

MACHADO, JULIO P
(31,48,14,**18**) NYN **31** 89, **48** 90, MILA **14** 90, **48/14/18** 91

MACHADO, ROBERT C
(55,38,39,**72**) CHIA **55** 96-98, MONN **55/38** 99, SEAA **39** 00, CHIN **29** 01, **72** 01-02, MILN **72** 02, BALA **38** 03, **72** 03-04

MACHEMEHL, CHARLES P
(**50**) CLEA **50** 71

MACHEMER, DAVE UTIL
(35,**9**) CALA **35** 78, DETA **9** 79

MACIAS, JOSE 2B/UTIL
(48,39,2,**1**) DETA **48** 99, **39** 00-02, MONN **2** 02, **1** 02-03, CHIN **1** 04-05

MACK, CONNIE (THE TALL TACTICIAN) M F
(NONE) PHIA **( )** 31-50

MACK, CONNIE, Jr. CH S,B
(**32**) PHIA *CH* **32** 35

MACK, EARLE CH S,B
(32,30,**27**) PHIA **32** 31-37, **30** 33, 35-36, **27** 37-50

MACK, JOE 1B
(**3**) BOSN **3** 45

MACK, QUINN OF
(**34**) SEAA **34** 94

MACK, RAY 2B/3B
(36,**6**,38,2, 25,49) CLEA **36** 38, **6** 39-43, **38** 44, **2** 46, NYA **25** 47, CHIN **49** 47

MACK, SHANE OF/DH
(23,24,**15**,5, 31) SDN **23** 87-88, MINA **24** 90-94, BOSA **24/15** 97, OAKA **15/5** 98, KCA **31** 98

MACK, TONY P
(**17**) CALA **17** 85

MACKANIN, PETE SS/INF/UTIL/CH/M
(**24**,5,17,14, 25) TEXA **24** 73-74, MONN **5** 75-77, PHIN **24** 78-79, **17** 79, MINA **14** 80-81, MONN *CH* **25** 97-00, PITN *CH* **25** 03-05, *M* 05

MacKENZIE, ERIC C
(**10**) KCA **10** 55

MacKENZIE, GORDY C/CH
(**16**,43,5,8, 55) KCA **16** 61, *CH* **43** 80-81, CHIN *CH* **5** 82, SFN *CH* **8** 86, **43** 86-87, **55** 87-88

MacKENZIE, KEN P
(36,**19**,28,37, 34) MILA **36** 60-61, NYN **19** 62-63, STLN **28** 63, SFN **37** 64, HOUN **34** 65

MACKIEWICZ, FELIX (MAC) OF
(32,7,**19**,41, 17,35,51) PHIA **32** 41, **19** 41-43, **7** 43, CLEA **41** 45, **17** 46, **35** 47, WASA **51** 47

MACKINSON, JOHNNY P
(40,36,41,28) PHIA **40/36/41** 53, STLN **28** 55

MACKO, JOE CH
(**64**) CHIN *CH* **64** 64

MACKO, STEVE (LI'L MAC) 2B/3B/INF
(**12**) CHIN **12** 79-81

MACKOWIAK, ROB 2B/UTIL
(**59**,3) PITN **59** 01-04, **3** 05

MacLEOD, BILLY P
(**47**) BOSA **47** 62

MACLIN, LONNIE OF
(**55**) STLN **55** 93

MACON, MAX P
(16,36,**28**,9, 20) STLN **16** 38, BKNN **36** 40, **28** 42-43, BOSN **9** 44, **20** 47

MacPHERSON, HARRY P
(**26**) BOSN **26** 44

MacRAE, SCOTT P
(**26**) CINN **51** 01

MacWHORTER, KEITH P
(**31**) BOSA **31** 80

MADDEN, MIKE P
(**53**) HOUN **53** 83-86

MADDEN, MORRIS P
(42,**59**) DETA **42** 87, PITN **59** 88-89

MADDERN, CLARENCE OF/1B
(54,**22**,20) CHIN **54** 46, **22** 48-49, CLEA **20** 51

MADDON, JOE CH
(**70**) CALA *CH* **70** 95-96, ANAA *CH* **70** 97-04, LAA *CH* **70** 05

MADDOX, ELLIOTT OF/INF/DH
(41,37,23,**27**, 21) DETA **41** 70, WASA **37** 71, TEXA **23** 72-73, NYA **27** 74-76, BALA **21** 77, NYN **21** 78-80

MADDOX, GARRY OF
(**31**,29) SFN **31** 72-75, PHIN **29** 75, **31** 75-86

MADDOX, JERRY 3B
(**12**) ATLN **12** 78

MADDUX, GREG P B
(**31**) CHIN **31** 86-92, ATLN **31** 93-03, CHIN **31** 04-05

MADDUX, MIKE P/CH B
(44,54,**51**,60, 19,20) PHIN **44** 86-89, LAN **54** 90, SDN **51** 91-92, NYN **51** 93-94, PITN **60** 95, BOSA **19** 95-96, SEAA **20** 97, MONN **51** 98-99, LAN **51** 99, HOUN **36** 00, MILN *CH* **36** 03-05

MADISON, DAVE P
(46,18,26,**14**) NYA **46/18** 50, STLA **26** 52, DETA **14** 52-53

MADISON, SCOTTI DH/C/3B/UTIL
(19,18,**38**,28) DETA **19** 85, **18** 86, KCA **38** 87-88, CINN **28** 89

MADJESKI, ED C
(**21**,1,25) PHIA **21** 32-34, **22** 33, CHIA **1** 34, NYN **25** 37

MADLOCK, BILL (MAD DOG) 3B/INF/DH/CH
(38,18,**5**,52, 12,7,48) TEXA **38** 73, CHIN **18** 74-76, SFN **18** 77-79, PITN **5** 79-85, LAN **52** 85, **12** 86-87, DETA **7** 87, *CH* **48** 00-01

MADRID, ALEX P
(61,31,**34**) MILA **61/31** 87, PHIN **34** 88-89

MADRID, SAL SS
(**21**) CHIN **21** 47

MADRITSCH, BOBBY P
(**56**) SEAA **56** 04-05

MADSON, RYAN P
(57,**63**) PHIN **57** 03, **63** 04-05

MADURO, CALVIN P
(56,50,**12**) PHIN **56** 96, **50** 97, BALA **12** 00-02

MAESTRI, HECTOR P
(39,**24**) WASA **39** 60, **24** 61

MAGADAN, DAVE 1B/3B/CH
(29,10,**18**,22, 16,17,12) NYN **29** 86-89, **10** 89-91, **29** 92, FLAN **18** 93, SEAA **18** 93, FLAN **18** 94, HOUN **18/22** 95, CHIN **16** 96, OAKA **17** 97-98, SDN **12** 99-01, *CH* **12** 03-05

MAGALLANES, EVER SS
(**6**) CLEA **6** 91

MAGEE, WENDELL,JR. OF
(**29**) PHIN **29** 96-99, DETA **29** 00-02

MAGGERT, HARL OF/3B
(**21**) BOSN **21** 38

MAGLIE, SAL (THE BARBER) P/CH
(19,21,**35**,26, 43,33) NYN **19** 45, **35** 50-55, CLEA **26** 55-56, BKNN **35** 56-57, NYA **21** 57-58, STLN **43** 58, BOSA *CH* **33** 60-62, 66-67

MAGNANTE, MIKE P
(57,**52**) KCA **57** 91-96, HOUN **52** 97-98, ANAA **52** 99, OAKA **52** 00-02

MAGNUSON, JIM P
(**40**,39) CHIA **40** 70-71, NYA **39** 73

MAGRANE, JOE P
(41,**32**,**34**) STLN **41** 87-88, **32** 88-93, CALA **32** 93-94, CHIA **34** 96

MAGRANN, TOM C
(**76**) CLEA **76** 89

MAGRINI, PETE P
(45,36) BOSA **45/36** 66

MAGRUDER, CHRIS OF
(11,**30**,24) TEXA **11** 01, CLEA **30** 02-03, MILN **24** 04-05

MAGUIRE, JACK OF/1B/UTIL
(**24**,12) NYN **24** 50-51, PITN **12** 51, STLA **12** 51

MAHAFFEY, ART P
(**28**,30) PHIN **28** 60-65, STLN **30** 66

MAHAFFEY, ROY (POPEYE) P
(**15**,17,23) PHIA **15** 31-35, **17** 34-35, STLA **23** 36

MAHAN, ART 1B/P
(**4**) PHIN **4** 40

MAHAY, RON P
(46,57,**17**,47, 54,32) BOSA **46** 95, **57** 97-98, OAKA **17** 99-00, FLAN **47** 00, CHIN **54** 01-02, TEXA **32** 03-05

MAHLBERG, GREG C
(43,**30**) TEXA **43** 78, **30** 79

MAHLER, MICKEY P B
(**24**,30,49,22, 48,42,50,40) ATLN **24** 77-79, PITN **30** 80, CALA **49** 81, **22** 81-82, MONN **48/24** 85, DETA **42** 85, TEXA **50/42** 86, TORA **40** 86

MAHLER, RICK P B
(39,**42**,26) ATLN **39** 79, **42** 80-88, **26** 88, CINN **42** 89-90, MONN **42** 91, ATLN **42** 91

MAHOLM, PAUL P
(**30**) PITN **30** 05

MAHOMES, PAT P
(21,**20**,59,23, 52,39) MINA **21** 92, **20** 92-96, BOSA **20** 96, **59** 96-97, NYN **23** 99-00, TEXA **23** 01, CHIN **52** 02, PITN **39** 03

MAHONEY, BOB P
(16,25,**23**) CHIA **16** 51, STLA **25** 51, **23** 52

MAHONEY, JIM (MOE) SS/2B/INF/CH
(1,29,16,**7**, 25,31,6) BOSA **1** 59, WASA **29** 61, CLEA **16/7** 62, HOUN **25** 65, CHIA *CH* **31** 72-76, SEAA *CH* **6** 85-86

MAHONEY, MIKE C
(58,**46**) CHIN **58** 00, 02, STLN **46** 05

MAIER, BOB 3B/OF
(**22**) DETA **22** 45

MAILHO, EMIL (LEFTY) OF
(**26**) PHIA **26** 36

MAIN, WOODY P
(36,30,39,**35**) PITN **33** 48, **30/39** 50, **35** 52-53

MAINE, JOHN P
(49,**61**) BALA **49** 04, **61** 05

MAINS, BUD P
(**25**) PHIA **25** 43

MAIRENA, OSWALDO P
(**40**,45,46) CHIN **40** 00, FLAN **45/46** 02

MAJESKI, HANK (HEENEY)(HEINE) 3B/INF
(2,14,28,3,**5**) BOSN **2** 39, **14** 40-41, NYA **28** 46, PHIA **3** 46-49, CHIA **5** 50-51, PHIA **5** 51-52, CLEA **5** 52-55, BALA **5** 55

MAJEWSKI, GARY P
(50,**38**) MONN **50** 04, WASN **38** 05

MAJEWSKI, VAL P
(**63**) BALA **63** 04, (05)

MAJTYKA, ROY CH
(11,26) ATLN *CH* **11** 88-89, *CH* **26** 89-90

MAKOSKI, FRANK P
(34,**23**,28) NYA **34/23/28** 37

MAKOWSKI, COOKIE 2B/3B/CH/M
(**37**) DETA **37** 75

MAKSUDIAN, MIKE 1B
(21,59,**7**) TORA **21** 92, MINA **59** 93, CHIN **7** 94

MALASKA, MARK P
(**46**) TBA **46** 03, BOSA **46** 04

MALAVE, JOSE OF
(**38**) BOSA **38** 96-97

MALAY, JOE 1B
(27,**22**) NYN **27** 33, **22** 35

MALDONADO, CANDY OF/3B/DH
(47,20,29,**21**, 22,23,25,0) LAN **47** 81, **20** 82-85, SFN **29** 86, **21** 86-89, CLEA **22** 90, MILA **22** 91, TORA **23** 91-92, CHIN **25** 93, CLEA **22** 93-94, TORA **0/23** 95, TEXA **21** 95

MALDONADO, CARLOS P
(**59**,52,48) KCA **59** 90-91, MILA **52/48** 93

MALER, JIM 1B/DH
(11,**33**) SEAA **11** 81, **33** 82-83

MALINOSKY, TONY INF
(**4**) BKNN **4** 37

MALIS, CY P
(**49**) PHIN **49** 34

MALKMUS, BOBBY INF
(29,**7**,2,19) MILN **29** 57, WASA **7** 58-59, PHIN **2** 60, **19** 61-62

MALLETT, JERRY OF
(**39**) BOSA **39** 59

MALLETTE, BRIAN P
(**59**) MILN **59** 02

MALLETTE, MAL P
(**35**) BKNN **35** 50

MALLICOAT, ROB P
(**56**) HOUN **56** 87, 91-92

MALLON, LES 2B/3B/UTIL
(12,30,**20**) PHIN **12** 32, BOSN **30** 34, **20** 35

MALLORY, JIM (SUNNY JIM) OF
(21,18,**3**) WASA **21** 40, STLN **18** 45, NYN **3** 45

MALLORY, SHELDON UTIL
(**19**) OAKA **19** 77

MALLOY, BOB P
(**38**,44,30) CINN **38** 43-44, 46, **44** 46-47, STLA **30** 49

MALLOY, BOB P
(**16**,42) TEXA **16** 87, MONN **42** 90

MALLOY, MARTY INF
(**20**,2) ATLN **20** 98-99, FLAN **2** 02

MALMBERG, HARRY (SWEDE) 2B/CH
(**25**,*32*) DETA **25** 55, BOSA *CH* **32** 63-64

MALONE, CHUCK P
(**53**) PHIN **53** 90

MALONE, EDDIE C
(58,**28**) CHIA **58** 49, **28** 49-50

MALONE, PAT P
(17,15,18,**21**) CHIN **17/15** 32, **18** 33-34, NYA **21** 35-37

MALONEY, JIM P
(**46**,43) CINN **46** 60-70, CALA **43** 71

MALONEY, SEAN P
(**46**,58) MILA **46** 97, LAN **58** 98

MALOOF, JACK CH
(**16**) SDN *CH* **16** 90, FLAN *CH* **16** 99-01

MALTZBERGER, GORDON (MALTZY) P/CH
(**37**,38,54) CHIA **37** 43-44, 47, **38** 44, 46, MINA *CH* **54** 62-64

MALZONE, FRANK 3B
(**11**,15) BOSA **11** 55-65, CALA **15** 66

MANCUSO, FRANK C B
(**8**,44,9) STLA **8** 44-46, **44** 46, WASA **9** 47

MANCUSO, GUS (BLACKIE) C/CH B
(14,**8**,12,10, 24,9,52) STLN **14** 32, NYN **8** 33-38, CHIN **12** 39, BKNN **10** 40, STLN **14** 41-42, NYN **24** 42, **8** 43, **9** 44, PHIN **9** 45, CINN *CH* **52** 50

MANDERS, HAL P
(**24**,12,13) DETA **24** 41, **12** 42, **24** 46, CHIN **13** 46

MANGAN, JIM C
(29,20,**33**) PITN **29** 52, **20** 54, NYN **33** 56

MANGUAL, ANGEL OF/UTIL/DH B
(31,**2**) PITN **31** 69, OAKA **2** 71-76

MANGUAL, PEPE OF
(**11**) MONN **11** 72-76, NYN **11** 76-77

MANGUM, LEO (BLACKIE) P
(27,**21**) BOSN **27** 32, **21** 33-35

MANION, CLYDE (PETE) C
(11,24,**25**) CINN **11** 32, **24** 33, **25** 34

MANKOWSKI, PHIL 3B/2B/DH
(**2**,19,8) DETA **2** 76-79, NYN **19/2** 80, **8** 82

MANN, BEN (RED) PR
(38,**45**) CHIN **38/45** 44

MANN, JIM P
(39,**58**,48) NYN **39** 00, HOUN **58** 01-02, PITN **48** 03

MANN, KELLY C
(**38**) ATLN **38** 89-90

MANN, LES OF
(**12**) STLN **12** 23

MANNING, DAVID P
(**33**) MILN **33** 03

MANNING, JIM P
(**42**) MINA **42** 62

MANNING, RICK OF/DH
(**28**,20) CLEA **28** 75-81, **20** 81-83, MILA **28** 83-87

MANNO, DON OF/UTIL
(**17**,35) BOSN **17** 40, **35** 41

MANON, JULIO P
(**44**) MONN **44** 03

MANON, RAMON P
(**51**) TEXA **51** 90

MANRIQUE, FRED (FREDDIE) INF/UTIL/DH
(**2**,6,5,10,14, 17) TORA **2** 81, 84, MONN **6** 85, STLN **5** 86, CHIA **10** 87-88, **14** 89, TEXA **17** 89, MINA **17** 90, OAKA **14** 91

MANSOLINO, DOUG CH
(**17**,27,38,36, 32,29) CHIA *CH* **17** 92-94, **27** 95, **17** 95-96, MILN *CH* **38** 98, **36** 99, DETA *CH* **32** 00-01, HOUN *CH* **29** 05

MANTEI, MATT P
(18,33,**31**) FLAN **18** 95-96, **33** 98-99, ARIN **31** 99-04, BOSA **31** 05

MANTILLA, FELIX SS/3B/UTIL
(5,**18**,12,25) MILN **5** 56-58, **18** 59-61, NYN **18** 62, BOSA **12** 63-65, HOUN **25** 66

MANTLE, MICKEY (MICK)(THE COMMERCE COMET) OF/1B/CH
(6,**7**) NYA **6** 51, **7** 51-68, *CH* **7** 70

MANTO, JEFF 1B/3B/UTIL
(44,45,30,12, 48,10,2,20, 26,23 CLEA **44** 90, **45** 90-91, PHIN **30** 93, BALA **12** 95, BOSA **48** 96, SEAA **10** 96, BOSA **2** 96, CLEA **44** 97, **12** 97-98, DETA **20** 98, CLEA **26** 98-99, NYA **13** 99, CLEA **16** 99, COLN **23** 00

MANUEL, BARRY P
(**44**,26,39) TEXA **44** 91-92, NYN **26** 97, ARIN **39** 98

MANUEL, CHARLIE (CHUCK) OF/CH/M
(**9**,46,16,4,42, 32,48,41) MINA **9** 69-72, LAN **46** 74, **16** 75, CLEA *CH* **9** 88, **4** 89, **42** 94 96, **32/48** 97, **32** 98-99, *M* **32** 00-02, PHIN *M* **41** 05

MANUEL, JERRY 2B/INF/DH/CH/M
(40,**1**,43,11, 6,17, 7,53) DETA **40** 75, **1** 75-76, MONN **43** 80-81, SDN **11** 82, MONN *CH* **6** 91-96, FLAN *CH* **17/6** 97 CHIA *M* **7** 98-03, NYN *CH* **53** 05

MANUSH, HEINIE OF/CH
(**3**,2,7,26,36, 14,51) WASA **3** 31, **2** 32, **3** 33-35, BOSA **7** 36, BKNN **26** 37-38, PITN **36** 38, **14** 39, WASA *CH* **51** 53-54

MANVILLE, DICK P
(**39**,19) BOSN **39** 50, CHIN **19** 52

MANWARING, KIRT C/3B
(17,19,**8**,3) SFN **17** 87-90, **19** 90, **8** 91-96, HOUN **3** 96, COLN **8** 97-99

MANZANILLO, JOSIAS P B
(51,**39**,38,41, 49) BOSA **51** 91, MILA **51** 93, NYN **39** 93-95, NYA **38** 95, SEAA **41** 97, NYN **39** 98-99, PITN **49** 00-02, CINN **39** 03, FLAN **38** 04

MANZANILLO, RAVELO (RAVIOLI) P B
(56,**59**) CHIA **56** 88, PITN **59** 94-95

MAPES, CLIFF OF
(3,13,**7**,46,5) NYA **3/13** 48, **7** 49-51, STLA **46** 51, DETA **5** 52

MAPLE, HOWIE (MAPE) C
(**10**) WASA **10** 32

MARAK, PAUL P
(**34**) ATLN **34** 90

MARANDA, GEORGES P
(35,**47**) SFN **35** 60, MINA **47** 62-63

MARANVILLE, RABBIT 2B
(**1**) BOSN **1** 32-33, 35

MARBERRY, FIRPO P
(12,**11**,19,16, 20) WASA **12** 31, **11** 32, DETA **19** 33, **11** 34-35, NYN **16** 36, WASA **20** 36

MARCHILDON, PHIL (BABE) P
(23,**21**,10,36, 26) PHIA **23** 40, **21** 41-42, **10** 42, **36** 45, **23** 45-46, **21** 47-49, BOSA **26** 50

MARCUM, JOHNNY (FOOTSIE) P
(46,12,**11**,14, 34) PHIA **46** 33, **12** 34-35, BOSA **11** 36-37, **12** 38, STLA **14/34** 39, CHIA **34** 39

MARCUM, SHAUN P
(**28**) TORA **28** 05

MARENTETTE, LEO P
(46,**22**) DETA **46** 65, MONN **22** 69

MARGONERI, JOE P
(**38**) NYN **38** 56-57

MARICHAL, JUAN (MANITO) P
(**27**,21,46) SFN **27** 60-73, BOSA **21** 74, LAN **46** 75

MARION, MARTY (SLATS)(MR. SHORTSTOP) (THE OCTOPUS) SS/M/CH B
(**4**,28) STLN **4** 40-50, *M* **4** 51, STLA **4** 52, **4** 53, *M* **4** 52, *M* **4** 53, CHIA *CH/M* **28** 54, *M* **4** 55-56

MARION, RED OF B
(**10**,36,32) WASA **10** 35, **36/32** 43

MARIS, ROGER OF
(32,5,35,3,**9**) CLEA **32** 57, **5** 58, KCA **35** 58, **3** 59, NYA **9** 60-66, STLN **9** 67-68

MARKELL, DUKE P
(**28**) STLA **28** 51

MARKLAND, GENE (MOUSEY) 2B
(**14**) PHIA **14** 50

MARLOWE, DICK P
(**37**,24) DETA **37** 51-56, CHIA **24** 56

MARNIE, HAL P
(18,24,**9**,15) PHIN **18** 40, **24/9** 41, **15** 42

MAROLEWSKI, FRED (FRITZ) 1B
(**15**) STLN **15** 53

MARONE, LOU P
(**29**) PITN **29** 69-70

MAROTH, MIKE P
(**46**) DETA **46** 02-05

MARQUARDT, OLLIE 2B/INF
(**7**) BOSA **7** 31

MARQUEZ, GONZALO 1B
(12,**19**) CHIN **12** 72-73, **19** 73-74

MARQUEZ, ISIDRO P
(**47**) CHIA **47** 95

MARQUEZ, LUIS (CANENA) OF
(18,48,**44**) BOSN **18** 51, CHIN **48** 54, PITN **44** 54

MARQUIS, BOB OF
(**20**) CINN **20** 53

MARQUIS, JASON P
(51,**38**,21) ATLN **51** 00, **38** 01-03, STLN **21** 04-05

MARQUIS, ROGER (NOONIE) OF
(**24**) BALA **24** 55

MARRERO, CONNIE P
(21,**22**) WASA **21** 50, **22** 51-54

MARRERO, ELI C/OF/UTIL
(**26**,8,11,16) STLN **26** 97-03, ATLN **8** 04, KCA **11** 05, BALA **16** 05

MARRERO, ORESTE P
(**46**,62) MONN **46** 93, LAN **62** 96

MARROW, BUCK P
(29,**24**) DETA **29** 32, BKNN **24** 37-38

MARSH, FREDDIE 3B/INF/OF
(15,2,7,**25**) CLEA **15** 49, STLA **2** 51-52, WASA **7** 52, CHIA **25** 53-54, BALA **2** 55-56

MARSH, TOM OF
(9,**21**) PHIN **9** 92, **21** 94-95

MARSHALL, BILL 2B
(**7**,31) BOSA **7** 31, CINN **31** 34

MARSHALL, CHARLIE C
(**33**) STLN **33** 41

MARSHALL, CUDDLES P
(14,40,21,**19** 36,29) NYA **14** 46, **40/21** 48, **19** 49, STLA **36/29** 50

MARSHALL, DAVE OF
(**18**,8) SFN **18** 67-69, NYN **18** 70-72, SDN **8** 73

MARSHALL, ED SS
(**24**) NYN **24** 32

MARSHALL, JIM 1B/OF/CH/M
(44,27,12,**25**, 6,14,2,1) BALA **44** 58, CHIN **27** 58, **12** 59, SFN **25** 60-61, NYN **6** 62, PITN **14** 62, CHIN *CH* **2** 74, *M* **25** 74-76, OAKA *M* **1/25** 79

MARSHALL, KEITH OF
(**42**) KCA **42** 73

MARSHALL, MAX OF
(**21**) CINN **21** 42-44

MARSHALL, MIKE OF/1B/UTIL
(**5**,6,22,41) LAN **5** 81-89, NYN **6** 90, BOSA **22** 90-91, CALA **41** 91

MARSHALL, MIKE (IRON MIKE) P
(**28**,53,20,31) DETA **28** 67, SEAA **28** 69, HOUN **53** 70, MONN **23** 70, **28** 70-73, LAN **28** 74-76, ATLN **50** 76, **20** 76-77, TEXA **31** 77, MINA **33** 78, **28** 78-80, NYN **28** 81

MARSHALL, WILLARD OF
(2,35,**27**,22) NYN **2** 42, **35** 46, **27** 47-49, BOSN **27** 50-52, CINN **22** 52-53, CHIA **27** 54-55

MARSONEK, SAM P
(**60**) NYA **60** 04

MARTE, ANDY INF
(**11**) ATLN **11** 05

MARTE, DAMASO P
(37,46,**43**) SEAA **37** 99, PITN **46** 01, CHIA **43** 02-05

MARTIN, ALBERT (AL) OF
(**28**,20,18,23, 9) PITN **28** 92-99, SDN **20** 00, SEAA **18** 00, **23** 01, TBA **9** 03

MARTIN, BABE C
(10,18,**34**,32) STLA **10** 44, **18** 45, **10** 46, BOSA **34** 48-49, STLA **32** 53

MARTIN, BARNEY P
(**48**) CINN **48** 53

MARTIN, BILLY (THE KID) 2B/3B/UTIL/CH/M
(12,**1**,4,3) NYA **12** 50, **1** 51-57, KCA **4** 57, DETA **1** 58, CLEA **1** 59, CINN **12** 60, MILN **3** 61, MINA **1** 61, *CH* **1** 65-68, *M* **1** 69, DETA *M* **1** 71-73, TEXA *M* **1** 73-75, NYA *M* **1** 75-79, OAKA *M* **1** 80-82, NYA *M* **1** 83, 85, 88

MARTIN, FRED P
(**34**,36,39,58, 31) STLN **34** 46, **36** 49, **39** 49-50, CHIN *CH* **58** 61-64, CHIA *CH* **31**79

MARTIN, GENE OF
(**22**) WASA **22** 68

MARTIN, HERSH OF
(30,2,25,19, **9**) PHIN **30** 37, **2** 38, **25** 39-40, NYA **19** 44, **9** 44-45

MARTIN, J.C. 3B/1B/UTIL/C/CH
(32,**12**,10,9, 6) CHIA **32** 59, **12** 60-65, **10** 66-67, NYN **9** 68-69, CHIN **12** 70-72, *CH* **6** 74

MARTIN, JERRY OF/1B/DH
(11,**25**,28,9) PHIN **11** 74-75, **25** 75-78, CHIN **28** 79-80, SFN **25** 81, KCA **25** 82-83, NYN **9** 84

MARTIN, JOE (SMOKEY JOE) 3B
(**20**,45) NYN **20** 36, CHIA **45** 38

MARTIN, JOHN P
(40,**33**) STLN **40** 80, **33** 80-83, DETA **33** 83

MARTIN, MIKE C
(**41**) CHIN **41** 86

MARTIN, MORRIE (LEFTY) P
(16,**26**,36,19, 25,32,45) BKNN **16** 49, PHIA **26** 51-54, CHIA **36** 54-56, BALA **19** 56, STLN **25** 57-58, CLEA **32** 58, CHIN **45** 59

MARTIN, NORBERTO (PACO) 2B/3B/DH
(53,**7**,3) CHIA **53** 93, **7** 94-97, ANAA **7** 98, TORA **3** 99

MARTIN, PAUL P
(**28**) PITN **28** 55

MARTIN, PEPPER (THE WILD HORSE OF THE OSAGE) OF/3B/P/CH
(2,28,**1**,11,10, 19) STLN **2** 32, **28** 33, **1** 34-38, **11** 39-40, **10** 44, CHIN *CH* **19** 56

MARTIN, RAY P
(35,38,**11**) BOSN **35** 43, **38** 47, 49, **11** 47-48

MARTIN, RENIE P
(**27**,39,17,37) KCA **27** 79-81, SFN **39** 82-83, **17** 84, PHIN **37** 84

MARTIN, STU 2B/INF
(**6**,4,22) STLN **6** 36-40, PITN **4** 41-42, CHIN **22** 43

MARTIN, TOM P
(41,**36**,34,52, 51,38) HOUN **41** 97, CLEA **36** 98-00, NYN **34** 01, TBA **52** 02, LAN **51** 03-04, ATLN **38** 04-05

MARTINEZ, ANASTACIO P
(**67**) BOSA **67** 04

MARTINEZ, ANGEL (SANDY) C
(53,35,8,**15**, 14,16,2,58) TORA **53** 95-96, **35** 96-97, CHIN **8** 98, **15** 98-99, FLAN **14** 00, MONN **16** 01, CLEA **2** 04, BOSA **58** 04

MARTINEZ, BUCK C/P/DH/M
(**21**,6,13) KCA **21** 69, **6** 70-71, **21** 74-77, MILA **21** 78-80, TORA **13** 81-86, *M* **13** 01-02

MARTINEZ, CARLOS 3B/UTIL/DH
(28,**24**,22,42, 9) CHIA **28** 88, **24** 89-90, CLEA **22** 91, **42** 92-93, CALA **9** 95

MARTINEZ, CARMELO 1B/OF/UTIL
(12,**14**,24,35, 28,13,25) CHIN **12** 83, SDN **14** 84-89, PHIN **24** 90, PITN **35** 90, **28** 91, KCA **13** 91, CINN **25** 91

MARTINEZ, CHITO OF/DH/UTIL
(**14**) BALA **14** 91-93

MARTINEZ, DAVE OF/P/1B
(**1**,3,30,17, 14) CHIN **1** 86-88, MONN **3** 88, **1** 89-91, CINN **30** 92, SFN **17** 93, **1** 93-94, CHIA **14** 95-97, TBA **14** 98-00, CHIN **1** 00, TEXA **1** 00, TORA **14** 00, ATLN **14** 01, (02)

MARTINEZ, DENNIS (EL PRESIDENTE) P
(61,30,**32**) BALA **61** 76, **30** 77-86, MONN **32** 86-93, CLEA **32** 94-96, SEAA **32** 97, ATLN **32** 98

MARTINEZ, DOMINGO 1B/3B
(19,**5**) TORA **19** 92, **5** 93

MARTINEZ, EDGAR 1B/3B/DH
(**11**) SEAA **11** 87-04

MARTINEZ, FELIX SS/2B
(14,26,**16**) KCA **14** 98, **26** 99, TBA **16** 00-01

MARTINEZ, FREDDIE P
(**27**) CALA **27** 80-81

MARTINEZ, GREG OF
(**50**) MILN **50** 98

MARTINEZ, HECTOR OF
(17,**9**) KCA **17** 62, **9** 63

MARTINEZ, JAVIER P
(**36**) PITN **36** 98

MARTINEZ, JESUS P B
(**47**) LAN **47** 96

MARTINEZ, JOSE UTIL/CH
(**15**,42,3) PITN **15** 69-70, KCA *CH* **42** 80-87, CHIN *CH* **3** 88-94

MARTINEZ, JOSE P
(**47**) SDN **47** 94

MARTINEZ, LUIS P
(**31**) MILN **31** 03

MARTINEZ, MANNY OF
(40,**34**,30,31) SEAA **40** 96, PHIN **34** 96, PITN **30** 98, MONN **31** 99

MARTINEZ, MARTY SS/3B/UTIL/P/CH/M
(38,2,**14**,11, 10,43) MINA **38** 62-63, ATLN **2** 67-68, HOUN **14** 69-71, STLN **11** 72, OAKA **11** 72, TEXA **10** 72, SEAA *CH* **43** 84, *CH* **10** 85-86, *CH* **14** 92

MARTINEZ, MATA SS
(**36**) KCA **36** 97

MARTINEZ, PABLO PH
(**5**) ATLN **5** 96

MARTINEZ, PEDRO (A.) P
(**42**,41,48,39, 53) SDN **42** 93-94, HOUN **41** 95, **42** 95, NYN **48** 96, CINN **39** 96, **53** 97

MARTINEZ, PEDRO (J.) P
(**45**,37) LAN **45** 92-93, MONN **37** 94, **45** 94-95, **37** 95, **45** 96-97, BOSA **45** 98-04, NYN **45** 05

MARTINEZ, RAMON (E.) 2B/SS/INF
(**34**,7,6,14, 12) SFN **34** 98-02, CHIN **7** 03, **6** 03-04, DETA **14** 05, PHIN **12** 05

MARTINEZ, RAMON (J.) P B
(**48**,38) LAN **48** 88-98, BOSA **48** 99-00, PITN **38** 01

MARTINEZ, ROGELIO (LIMONAR) P
(**19**) WASA **19** 50

MARTINEZ, SYLVIO P
(47,**35**) CHIA **47** 77, STLN **35** 78-81

MARTINEZ, TEDDY 2B/SS/UTIL
(17,**23**,19,32) NYN **17** 70-73, **23** 74, STLN **19** 75, OAKA **32** 75, LAN **23** 77-79

MARTINEZ, TINO 1B/DH
(14,23,**24**,21) SEAA **14** 90-91, **23** 92-95, NYA **24** 96-01, STLN **21** 02-03, TBA **24** 04, NYA **24** 05

MARTINEZ, TIPPY P
(40,18,36,**23**, 57) NYA **40** 74-76, **18** 76, BALA **36** 76, **23** 76-87, MINA **57** 88

MARTINEZ, TONY SS/2B
(16,**14**,22) CLEA **16** 63, **14** 64-65, **22** 66

MARTINEZ, WILLIE P
(**66**) CLEA **66** 00

MARTINEZ, VICTOR C/DH
(63,20,**41**) CLEA **63** 02, **20** 03, **41** 04-05

MARTINI, WEDO (SOUTHERN) P
(**20**) PHIA **20** 35

MARTY, JOE OF/P
(8,**35**) CHIN **8** 37-39, PHIN **35** 39-41

MARTYN, BOB OF
(**32**) KCA **32** 57-59

MARTZ, GARY OF
(**12**) KCA **12** 75

MARTZ, RANDY P
(**34**,33) CHIN **34** 80-82, CHIA **33** 83

MARZANO, JOHN C
(37,**20**,14,17) BOSA **37** 87, **20** 88-92, TEXA **14** 95, SEAA **17** 96-98

MASAOKA, ONAN P
(70,55,**40**) LAN **70/55** 99, **40** 00

MASHORE, CLYDE OF/3B/2B
(21,**5**) CINN **21** 69, MONN **5** 70-73

MASHORE, DAMON OF
(**33**,31,22) OAKA **33** 96, **31** 97, ANAA **22** 98

MASI, PHIL C/UTIL
(**10**,17,38) BOSN **10** 39-49, PITN **17** 49, CHIA **38** 50-52

MASON, DON 2B/3B/INF
(41,21,**6**) SFN **41** 66-67, **21** 68-70, SDN **6** 71-73

MASON, HANK P
(19,**37**) PHIN **19** 58, **37** 60

MASON, JIM SS/INF/DH
(14,**2**,22,10, 3,12) WASA **14** 71-72, TEXA **2** 72-73, NYA **22** 74-76, TORA **10** 77, TEXA **3** 77-78, MONN **12** 79

MASON, MARTY CH
(**38**) STLN *CH* **38** 00-05

MASON, MIKE P/CH
(**16**,41,20,39) TEXA **16** 82-87, CHIN **41** 87, MINA **20** 88, KCA *CH* **39** 04

MASON, ROGER P
(**48**,19,45,67, 22) DETA **48** 84, SFN **19** 85-86, **45** 86, **48** 86-87, **19** 88, HOUN **67 /22** 89, PITN **48** 91-92, SDN **48** 93, PHIN **48** 93-94, NYN **48** 94

MASSA, GORDON (MOOSE)(DUKE) C
(**9**,22) CHIN **9** 57, **22** 58

MASTERS, WALT P
(**18**,49,20) WASA **18** 31, PHIN **49** 37, PHIA **20** 39

MASTELLER, DON 1B
(**16**) MINA **16** 95

MASTERSON, PAUL (LEFTY) P
(27,23,**8**) PHIN **27** 40, **23** 41, **8** 42

MASTERSON, WALT P
(33,22,14,34, 35,**20**,16,29) WASA **33** 39, **22** 40, **14** 41-42, **34** 42, **35** 45-49, BOSA **35** 49, **20** 49-52, WASA **20** 52-53, DETA **16/29** 56

MATA, VIC OF
(55,**17**) NYA **55** 84-85, **17** 85

MATARAZZO, LEN P
(**36**) PHIA **36** 52

MATCHICK, TOM SS/INF
(43,**2**,3,19,32) DETA **43** 67, **2** 68-69, BOSA **3** 70, KCA **19** 70, M ILA **19** 71, BALA **32** 72

MATEO, HENRY 2B/UTIL
(59,29,**4**) MONN **59** 01, **29** 02, **4** 03-04, WASN **4** 05

MATEO, JULIO P
(**40**) SEAA **40** 02-05

MATEO, RUBEN OF
(38,**21**,15) TEXA **38** 99, **21** 99-01, CINN **15** 02-03, PITN **24** 04, KCA **24** 04

MATHENY, MIKE C
(15,22,44) MILA 15 94, 22 94-97, MILN 22 98, TORA 22 99, STLN 44 00, 22 00-04, SFN 22 05

MATHEWS, EDDIE 3B/OF/1B/CH/M
(41,11,7) BOSN 41 52, MILN 41 53-65, ATLN 41 66, HOUN 11 67, DETA 7 67-68, ATLN CH 41 71-72, M 41 72-74

MATHEWS, NELSON OF
(12,23,5) CHIN 12 60, 23 61-63, KCA 5 64-65

MATHEWS, RICK CH
(37,53) COLN CH 37 95, 53 03-05

MATHEWS, T. J. P
(51,33,29,37, 39) STLN 51 95, 33 96-97, OAKA 29 97, 33 98-01, STLN 37 01, HOUN 39 02

MATHEWS, TERRY P
(32,38,51,39) TEXA 32 91, 38 91-92, FLAN 51 94-96, BALA 51 96-98, KCA 39 99

MATHIAS, CARL (STUBBY) P
(32,30,24) CLEA 32/30 60, WASA 24 61

MATHIS, JEFF C
(44) LAA 44 05

MATHIS, RON P
(42,13) HOUN 42 85, 13 87

MATIAS, JOHN OF/1B
(8) CHIA 8 70

MATLACK, JON P
(35,32,54) NYN 35 71, 32 71-77, TEXA 32 78-83, DETA CH 54 96

MATOS, FRANCISCO 2B
(37) OAKA 37 94

MATOS, JULIUS UTIL
(10,23) SDN 10 02, KCA 23 03

MATOS, LUIS OF/DH
(32) BALA 32 00-05

MATOS, PASQUAL C
(11) ATLN 11 99

MATRANGA, DAVID SS
(1,5) HOUN 1 03, LAA 5 05

MATSUI, HIDEKI (GODZILLA) OF
(55) NYA 55 03-05

MATSUI, KAZUO (KAZ) SS/2B
(25) NYN 25 04-05

MATTES, TROY P
(56) MONN 56 01

MATTHEWS, GARY, JR. OF/DH
(21,51,19,22, 25,36,13,14) SDN 21 99, CHIN 51 00, 19 01, PITN 22 01, NYN 25 02, BALA 36 02-03, SDN 13 03, TEXA 14 04-05

MATTHEWS, GARY, SR. (SARGE) OF/DH/CH
(36,34) SFN 36 72-76, ATLN 36 77-80, PHIN 34 81-83, CHIN 36 84-87, SEAA 36 87, TORA CH 36 98-99, MILN CH 36 02, CHIN CH 36 03-05

MATTHEWS, MIKE P
(50,60,48,30, 49,33,27) STLN 50 00, 60 01, 48 02, MILN 30 02, SDN 49 03, CINN 33 04, NYN 27 05

MATTHEWSON, DALE P
(12,20) PHIN 12 43, 20 44

MATTICK, BOBBY SS/3B/INF/M
(29,15,3) CHIN 29 38, 15 39-40, CINN 15 41-42, TORA M 3 80-81

MATTINGLY, DON 1B/OF/DH
(46,23) NYA 46 82-84, 23 84-95, CH 23 04-05

MATULA, RICK P
(54,29) ATLN 54 79, 29 79-81

MATUSZEK, LEN 1B/3B/UTIL
(26,24,12,25, 17) PHIN 26 81, 24 82, 12 82-84, TORA 25 85, LAN 17 85-87

MATUZAK, HARRY (MATTY) P
(19,37) PHIA 19 34, 37 36

MAUCH, GENE (SKIP) SS/2B/INF/M
(3,42,29,44, 33,2,24,36 32,4) BKNN 3 44, PITN 42 47, BKNN 29/44 48, CHIN 33 48-49, BOSN 2 50-51, STLN 36 52, BOSA 24 56-57, PHIN M 32 60, M 4 61-68, MONN M 4 69-75, MINA M 4 76-80, CALA M 3 81-82, 85-87, M 4 87

MAUER, JOE C
(7) MINA 7 04-05

MAULDIN, MARK 3B
(36) CHIA 36 34

MAUNEY, DIC K P
(15) PHIN 15 45-47

MAURER, DAVE P
(54,50,51) SDN 54 00-01, CLEA 50 02, TORA 51 04

MAURER, ROB 1B/DH
(39) TEXA 39 91-92

MAURIELLO, RALPH (TAMI) P
(29) LAN 29 58

MAURO, CARMEN OF/3B
(41,48,20,6) CHIN 41 48, 50-51, BKNN 48/20 53, WASA 6 53, PHIA 6 53

MAUSER, TIM P
(52) PHIN 52 91, 93, SDN 52 93-95

MAVIS, BOB PR
(32) DETA 32 49

MAXCY, BRIAN P
(15) DETA 15 95-9684,

MAXIE, LARRY P
(23) ATLN 23 69

MAVIS, BOB PR
(32) DETA 32 49

MAXVILL, DAL (MAX)(MAXIE) SS/INF/CH
(27,21,11,16, 45,53) STLN 27 62-72, OAKA 21 72-73, PITN 11 73-74, OAKA 16 74, CH 41/45 75, NYN CH 53 78, STLN CH 27 79-80, ATLN CH 53 82-85

MAXWELL, CHARLIE (SMOKEY) OF/1B
(37,26,35,34, 4,7) BOSA 37 50, 26 51, 37 52, 35 54, BALA 34 55, DETA 4 55-62, CHIA 7 62-64

MAXWELL, JASON INF
(50) CHIN 50 98, MINA 9 00-01

MAY, CARLOS OF/1B/UTIL/DH
(17,38,44) CHIA 17 68-76, NYA 38 76-77, CALA 44 77

MAY, DARRELL P
(34,61,21,22, 31,34,36) ATLN 34 95, PITN 61 96, CALA 21 96, ANAA 22 97, KCA 31 02, 34 03-04, SDN 34 05, NYA 46 05

MAY, DAVE OF/DH
(12,11,27,16, 49) BALA 12 67-70, MILA 11 70-74, ATLN 27 75-76, TEXA 16 77, MILA 11 78, PITN 49 78

MAY, DERRICK OF/DH
(27,12,16,34, 14,29) CHIN 27 90-94, MILA 12 95, HOUN 16 95-96, PHIN 34 97, MONN 14 98, BALA 29 99

MAY, JAKIE P
(26,19) CHIN 26/19 32

MAY, JERRY C
(5,4,12,30,20) PITN 5/4 64, 12 65-70, KCA 12 71-73, NYN 30/20 73

MAY, LEE 1B/OF/DH/CH
(23,14,45,7, 35,47) CINN 23 65-71, HOUN 23 72-74, BALA 14 75-80, KCA 14 81-82, CH 14 84-86, CINN CH 23 88-89, KCA CH 45 92-94, BALA CH 14 95, TBA CH 7 01, 35 02, 47 02-03

MAY, MILT C/CH
(29,8,12,5,42, 7,14,39,29, 35) PITN 29 70-73, HOUN 8 74-75, DETA 12 76-79, CHIA 5 79, SFN 42 80, 7 80-83, PITN 14 83-84, CH 39 87-96, FLAN CH 29 97-98, COLN 29 99, TBA CH 35 03

MAY, PINKY 3B/SS
(19,26,2) PHIN 19 39-41, 26 42, 2 43

MAY, RUDY P
(40,34,36,43, 45) CALA 40 65-67, 34 69-74, NYA 43 74-76, BALA 43 76-77, MONN 36 78, 43 78-79, NYA 45 80-83

MAY, SCOTT P
(48,39) TEXA 48 88, CHIN 39 91

MAYBERRY, JOHN 1B/DH/CH
(00,33,7,10, 28,12) HOUN 00 68, 33 69-71, KCA 7 72-77, TORA 10 78-82, NYA 28/12 82, KCA CH 7 89-90

MAYE, LEE OF/3B/INF
(24,20,26,5, 21) MILN 24 59-65, HOUN 20 65-66, CLEA 26 67-69, WASA 5 69-70, CHIA 21 70-71

MAYER, ED P
(40,20) CHIN 40 57, 20 58

MAYNARD, BUSTER OF/UTIL
(24,26,6,41) NYN 24 40, 26 42, 6 43, 41 46

MAYNE, BRENT C/3B/DH
(49,24,17,6, 9,8,2) KCA 49 90-91, 24 91-95, NYN 17 96, OAKA 6 97, SFN 9 98-99, COLN 8 00-01, KCA 2 01-03, ARIN 6 04, LAN 6 04

MAYO, EDDIE (HOTSHOT) 3B/2B/INF/CH
(20,29,2,3, 33,32) NYN 20 36, BOSN 29 37-38, PHIA 2 43, DETA 3 44-48, BOSA CH 33 51, PHIN CH 32 52-54

MAYO, JACKIE (BUTCH) OF
(18,15) PHIN 18 48, 15 49-53

MAYS, JOE P
(53,25) MINA 53 99-00, 25 01-03, (04), 05

MAYS, WILLIE (SAY HEY) OF/1B/CH
(24) NYN 24 51-57, SFN 24 58-72, NYN 24 72-73, CH 24 74-79

MAYSEY, MATT P
(36,50) MONN 36 92, MILA 50 93

MAZEROSKI, BILL (MAZ) 2B/3B/CH
(9,51,30) PITN 9 56-72, CH 9 73, SEAA CH 51 78, CH 30 79, CH 9 80

MAZZERA, MEL (MIKE) OF
(8,20,29,14, 18) PHIN 8 40, STLA 20 35, 29 37, 14 38, 18 39

MAZZILLI, LEE OF/1B/DH/CH/M
(12,16,24,11, 13,54,53) NYN 12 76, 16 76-81, TEXA 16 82, NYA 24 82, PITN 11 83-84, 16 84-86, NYN 13 86-89, TORA 13 89, NYA CH 54 00-01, 13 02, 53 03, BALA M 13 04-05, 12 05

MAZZONE, LEO CH
(52,54) ATLN CH 52 85 CH, 54 90-05

McAFEE, BILL P
(17,19,20) WASA 17 32, 19 33, STLA 20 34

McANALLY, ERNIE P
(49,21) MONN 49 71, 21 71-74

McANANY, JIM OF
(48,3,20,22) CHIA 48 58, 3 59-60, CHIN 20 61, 22 62

McANDREW, JAMIE P
(49,31,33) MILA 49/31 95, 33 97

McANDREW, JIM P
(43,36) NYN 43 68-73, SDN 36 74

McANULTY, PAUL INF
(18) SDN 18 05

McAULIFFE, DICK SS/3B/INF/DH
(3) DETA 3 60-73, BOSA 3 74-75

McAVOY, TOM P
(25) WASA 25 59

McBEAN, AL P
(34,54,31,36) PITN 34 61-68, SDN 34 69, LAN 54 69, 31 69-70, PITN 36 70

McBRIDE, BAKE OF/DH
(21,22,26) STLN 21 73-77, PHIN 22 77-78, 21 78-81, CLEA 26 82-83

McBRIDE, KEN P/CH
(15,37) CHIA 15 59-60, LAA 37 61-64, CALA 37 65, MILA CH 37 75

McBRIDE, MACAY P
(49) ATLN 49 05

McBRIDE, TOM OF/1B/3B
(42,25,18,32, 25) BOSA 42 43, 25 44-45, 18 46-47, WASA 32 47-48, 25 48

McCABE, JOE C
(12,48,31) MINA 12/48 64, WASA 31 65

McCABE, RALPH (MACK) P
(33) CLEA 33 46

McCAHAN, BILL P
(40,23) PHIA 40 46, 23 47-49

McCALL, BRIAN (BAM) OF
(8,16) CHIA 8 62, 16 63

McCALL, DUTCH P
(27) CHIN 27 48

McCALL, LARRY P
(51,53,40,37) NYA 51 77, 53/51/40 78, TEXA 37 79

McCALL, WINDY P
(35,40) BOSA 35 48-49, PITN 40 50, NYN 40 54-57

McCAMENT, RANDY P
(36) SFN 36 89-90

McCANN, BRIAN C
(16) ATLN 16 05

McCARDELL, ROGER C
(8) SFN 8 59

McCARTHY, BRANDON P
(41) CHIA 41 05

McCARTHY, GREG P
(40,39) SEAA 40 96-97, 39 97-98

McCARTHY, JERRY 1B
(12) STLA 12 48

McCARTHY, JOE (MARSE JOE) M
(no#) NYA no# 32-46, BOSA no# 48-50

McCARTHY, JOHNNY SS/1B/OF/P
(7,23,25,6,18, 34,3,14) BKNN 7 34, 23 35, NYN 25 36, 6 37-38, 23 39, 18 40, 34 41, BOSN 3 43, 46, NYN 14 48

McCARTHY, TOM P
(43,57,49) BOSA 43 85, CHIA 57 88, 49 89

McCARTY, DAVID UTIL/1B/OF
(8,22,10,23, 6,20,18) MINA 8 93-95, SFN 22 95, 10 96, SEAA 23 98, KCA 6 00-01, TBA 20 02, OAKA 18 03, BOSA 10 03-05

McCARVER, TIM OF/UTIL/P
(51,9,20,15,6, 2,33,11) STLN 51 59, 9 60, 20 61, 15 63-69, PHIN 6 70-72, MONN 2 72, STLN 15 73-74, BOSA 33 74-75, PHIN 11 75-80

McCASKILL, KIRK P
(15,26,25) CALA 15 85-91, CHIA 26 92, 25 92-94, 15 95-96

McCATTY, STEVE P
(37,54) OAKA 37 77, 54 78-85, DETA CH 54 02

McCLAIN, JOE P
(27) WASA 27 61-62

McCLAIN, SCOTT 1B/3B
(20,9) TBA 20 98, CHIN 9 05

McCLELLAN, PAUL P
(52,28,48) SFN 28 90, 52 90-91, 48 91

McCLENDON, LLOYD UTIL/OF/1B/CH
(23,30,10,22) CINN 23 87, 30 88, CHIN 10 89-90, PITN 30 90-91, 22 91, 23 92-94, CH 23 97-00, M 23 01-05

McCLOSKY, JIM (IRISH) P
(27,40) BOSN 27/40 36

McCLUNG, SETH P
(37) TBA 37 03, 05

McCLURE, BOB P
(10,32,48,40, 22,7,27,37, 33) KCA 10 75, 32 76, MILA 48 77, 10 77-86, MONN 40 86, 22 86-88, NYN 7/27 88, CALA 37 89, 33 89-91, STLN 22 91-92, FLAN 10 93

McCOLL, ALEX (RED) P
(26) WASA 26 33-34

McCOOL, BILLY P
(42,43) CINN 42 64-68, SDN 42 69, STLN 43 70

McCONNELL, SAM P
(28) ATLN 28 04

McCORMACK, DON C
(17) PHIN 17 80-81

McCORMICK, FRANK (BUCK) 1B/UTIL/CH
(10,30,12,37, 26,6,2) CINN 10 34, 30/12 37, 37 38, 10 39-45, PHIN 26 46, 10 47, BOSN 6 47-48, CINN CH 2 56-57

McCORMICK, MIKE OF
(20,23,31,7, 21,2,12) CINN 20 40-42, 23 46, BOSN 31 46-48, BKNN 7 49, NYN 21 50, CHIA 2 50, WASA 12 51

McCORMICK, MIKE P
(29,40,16,56, 25) NYN 29 56-57, SFN 40 58-62, BALA 40 63-64, WASA 16 65-66, SFN 40 67-70, NYA 56/29 70, KCA 25 71

McCOSKY, BARNEY OF
(21,7,26,32) DETA 21 39-42, 46, PHIA 7 46-48, 50-51, CINN 26 51, CLEA 32 51-53

McCOVEY, WILLIE (STRETCH) 1B/OF/DH
(44) SFN 44 59-73, SDN 44 74-76, OAKA 44 76, SFN 44 77-80

McCOY, BENNY 2B/INF
(24,27,2) DETA 24 38-39, 27 39, PHIA 2 40-41

McCRABB, LES (BUSTER) P/CH
(31,29) PHIA 31 39-40, 29 41-42, 31 50, CH 31 49-54

McCRACKEN, QUINTON OF/DH
(3,8,6,9,4) COLN 3 95-97, TBA 3 98-00, MINA 8 01, ARIN 6 02-03, SEAA 9 04, ARIN 4 04, 6 05

McCRAW, TOMMY 1B/OF/UTIL/C/CH
(14,24,6,3,22, 36,12,21,47, 40,27,10,16, 17) CHIA 14 63-64, 24 65-68, 6 69-70, WASA 3 71, CLEA 22 72, CALA 22 73-74, CLEA 14 74-75, CH 14 75, 79-82, SFN CH 36 83, 12 83-84, 21 84-85, BALA CH 47 89, 40 90-91, NYN CH 27 92-94, 10 95-96, HOUN CH 16 97-99, 22 00, MONN CH 17 02-04, WASN CH 17 05

McCRAY, RODNEY OF/DH
(28,26,13) CHIA 28 90, 26 91, NYN 13 92

McCULLERS, LANCE P
(50,41,18,46) SDN 50 85, 41 86-88, NYA 41 89-90, DETA 18 90, TEXA 46 92

McCULLOUGH, CLYDE C/1B/3B/CH
(21,5,10,9,8, 3,55,54) CHIN 21 40-41, 5 41-42, 10 43, 9 45*-48, PITN 8 49-51, 3 51-52, CHIN 8 53-56, WASA CH 55 60, MINA CH 55 61, NYN CH 54 63

McCULLOUGH, PHIL P
(21) WASA 21 42

McCURDY, HARRY (HANK) C/1B
(16,8,9,22) STLN 16 23, PHIN 8 32, 9 33, CINN 22 34

McCURRY, JEFF P
(53,43,38,47) PITN 53 95 , DETA 43 96, COLN, 38 97, PITN 53 98, HOUN 47 99

McDANIEL, LINDY P B
(41,43,39,40) STLN 41 55-62, CHIN 43 63-65, SFN 39 66-68, NYA 40 68-73, KCA 41 74-75

McDANIEL, TERRY OF
(0) NYN 0 91

McDANIEL, VON P
(45) STLN 45 57-58

McDAVID, RAY OF
(20) SDN 20 94-95

McDERMOTT, MICKEY (MAURY) P/CH
(35,36,19,21, 22,20,38,27, 48) BOSA 35 48, 36 48-49, 19 49-53, WASA 21 54-55, NYA 22 56, KCA 19 57, DETA 20 58, STLN 38 61, KCA 27 61, CALA CH 48 67-68

McDERMOTT, TERRY 1B
(9) LAN 9 72

McDEVITT, DANNY P
(16,24,18,47, 29) BKNN 16 57-58, LAN 16 59-60, NYA 24 61, MINA 24/18 61, KCA 47 62, 29 62

McDILL, ALLEN P
(56,55,49,46) KCA 56 97, 55 98, DETA 49 00, BOSA 46 01

McDONALD, BEN P
(19,40) BALA 19 89-95, MILA 40 95, 97

McDONALD, DARNELL OF
(11,41,39) BALA 11/41/39 04

McDONALD, DAVE 1B/OF
(55,17) NYA 55 69, MONN 17 71

McDONALD, DONZELL OF
(59,19) NYA 59 01, KCA 19 02

McDONALD, HANK OF
(16,21,30) PHIA 16 31, 21 33, STLA 30 33

McDONALD, JASON OF
(2) OAKA 2 97-99, TEXA 2 00

McDONALD, JIM (HOT ROD) P
(26,24,18,25, 36) BOSA 24/26 50, STLA 24 51, NYA 18 52-54, BALA 25 55, CHIA 36 56-58

McDONALD, JOHN INF
(8,6,36) CLEA 8 99-04, TORA 6 05, DETA 36 05

McDONALD, KEITH C
(32) STLN 32 00-01

McDONNELL, JIM C
(22,29,14) CLEA 22 43, 29 44, 14 45

McDONNELL, ROBERT (MAJE) CH
(40) PHIN 40 49-57

McDOUGALD, GIL 3B/2B/INF
(12) NYA 12 51-60

McDOUGALL, MARSHALL 3B/INF
(25,20) TEXA 25/20 05

McDOWELL, JACK (BLACKJACK) P
(40,29,72) CHIA 40 87-88, 90, 29 90-94, NYA 19 95, CLEA 29 96-97, ANAA 72 98-99

McDOWELL, ODDIBE OF/DH/
(0,20,1,8) TEXA 0 85-88, CLEA 20 89, ATLN 1 89-90, TEXA 8 94

McDOWELL, ROGER (BUBBLES) P
(42,13,17,31) NYN 42 85-89, PHIN 13 89-91, LAN 13 91, 31 92, 17 93-94, TEXA 31 95, BALA 31 96

McDOWELL, SAM (SUDDEN SAM) P
(17,34,48,36, 29) CLEA 17 61-62, 34 63, 48 64-71, SFN 36 72, 48 72-73, NYA 29 73, 48 73-74, PITN 48 75

McELROY, CHUCK P
(51,35,31,17, 26,23,34,47, 43) PHIN 51 89-90, CHIN 35 91-93, CINN 31 94-96, CALA 17 96, ANAA 17 97, CHIA 26 97, COLN 23 98-99, NYN 34 99, BALA 47 00-01, SDN 43 01

McELYEA, FRANK OF
(20) BOSN 20 42

McENANEY, WILL P
(37,20,44,24 16,47) CINN 37 74-76, MONN 20 77, PITN 44/24/16 78, STLN 47 79

McEVOY, LOU P
(29,18,34) NYA 29/18 30, 34 31

**McCullough only played in the World Series in 1945 having just returned from Military Service.*

McEWING, JOE (LITTLE MAC) INF/UTIL
(48,**47**,11,8) STLN **48** 98, **47** 99, NYN **47** 00-02, **11** 03-04, KCA **8** 05

McFADDEN, LEON SS/OF
(**20**) HOUN **20** 68-70

McFARLAND, HOWIE OF
(**6**,32) WASA **6/32** 45

McFARLAND, ??? CH
(**32**) PHIA *CH* **32** 36

McFARLANE, ORLANDO C/OF
(3,47,5,34, 38,**12**) PITN **3** 62, **47/5** 64, DETA **34/38** 66, CALA **12** 67-68

McGAFFIGAN, ANDY P
(58,28,37,**27**, 26,38) NYA **58** 81, SFN **28** 82-83, MONN **37** 84, CINN **37** 84-85, MONN **27** 86-89, SFN **26** 90, KCA **38** 90-91

McGAH, ED C
(38,**2**) BOSA **38** 46, **2** 47

McGAHA, MEL CH/M
(42,41,**3**) CLEA CH **42** 61, *M* **42** 62, KCA *CH* **41** 63-64, *M* **41** 64-65, HOUN *CH* **3** 68-70

McGEE, BILL (FIDDLER BILL) P
(19,24,**29**,21, 10) STLN **19** 35, **24** 36-37, **29** 38-41, NYN **21** 41, **10** 42

McGEE, DAN SS
(**23**) BOSN **23** 34

McGEE, WILLIE OF/DH
(**51**) STLN **51** 82-90, OAKA **51** 90, SFN **51** 91-94, BOSA **51** 95, STLN **51** 96-99

McGEHEE, KEVIN P
(**48**) BALA **48** 93

McGHEE, BILL (FIBBER) 1B/OF
(11,**14**) PHIA **11** 44, **14** 45

McGHEE, ED OF
(14,16,3,35,**6**) CHIA **14** 50, PHIA **16** 53-54, CHIA **3** 54, **35/6** 55,

McGILBERRY, RANDY P
(**31**,17,28) KCA **31** 77-78, **17/28** 78

McGILLEN, JOHN P
(3,**32**) PHIA **3/32** 44

McGINN, DAN P
(31,**25**,30) CINN **31** 68, MONN **25** 69-71, CHIN **30** 72

McGINNIS, RUSS 1B/UTIL
(57,**37**) TEXA **57** 92, KCA **37** 95

McGLINCHY, KEVIN P
(**30**) ATLN **30** 99-00

McGLOTHEN, LYNN P
(16,36,**47**,40, 27,50) BOSA **16** 72, **36** 72-73, STLN **47** 74-76, SFN **47** 77-78, CHIN **40** 78-81, CHIA **27** 81, NYA **50** 82

McGLOTHIN, PAT P
(**23**) BKNN **23** 49-50

McGLOTHLIN, JIM (RED) P
(50,45,**31**,40) CALA **50** 65, **45** 66-69, CINN **31** 70-73, CHIA **40** 73

McGOWAN, BEAUTY OF
(**19**) BOSN **19** 37

McGOWAN, DUSTIN P
(**40**) TORA **40** 05

McGOWAN, MICKEY P/M/CH
(**36**) NYN **36** 48

McGRAW, JOHN (LITTLE NAPOLEON) (MUGGSY) M
(no#) NYN **no#** 32

McGRAW, TOM P
(**61**) STLN **61** 97

McGRAW, TUG P
(**45**) NYN **45** 65-67, 69-74, PHIN **45** 75-84

McGREGOR, SCOTT P
(39,**16**) BALA **39** 76-77, **16** 78-88

McGRIFF, FRED 1B/DH
(19,**29**,27,28) TORA **19** 86-90, SDN **29** 91-93, ATLN **27** 93-97, TBA **29** 98-01, CHIN **29** 01-02, LAN **28** 03, TBA **29** 04

McGRIFF, TERRY C
(**8**,9,50,54,7) CINN **8** 87-90, HOUN **8/9** 90, FLAN **50** 93, STLN **54/7** 94

McGUIRE, BILL C
(**35**) SEAA **35** 88-89

McGUIRE, MICKEY SS/2B
(34,**2**) BALA **34** 62, **2** 67

McGUIRE, RYAN 1B/OF
(**9**,6,40,28) MONN **9** 97-98, **6** 98-99, NYN **40** 00, FLAN **9** 01, BALA **28** 02

McGWIRE, MARK 3B/1B/UTIL/DH
(**25**) OAKA **25** 86-97, STLN **25** 97-01

McHALE, JOHN 1B
(27,**25**,12,23) DETA **27** 43, **25** 44-45, **12** 45, **23** 47-48

McHENRY, VANCE SS/DH
(8,**26**) SEAA **8** 81, **26** 82 **15** 95, KCA **15** 96

McILWAIN, STOVER (SMOKEY) P
(**6**,28) CHIA **6** 57, **28** 58

McINTOSH, JOE P
(**24**) SDN **24** 74-75

McINTOSH, TIM C/OF/UTIL
(**26**,35,60) MILA **26** 90-93, MONN **35** 93, NYA **60** 96

McKAIN, ARCHIE (HAPPY) P
(29,20,14,**28**, 30,36) BOSA **29/20** 37, **14** 38, DETA **28** 39-41, STLA **30** 41, **36** 43

McKAIN, HAL P
(17,**23**) CHIA **17** 31, **23** 32

McKAY, CODY C/P/3B
(**26**) OAKA **26** 02, STLN **26** 04

McKAY, DAVE 3B/UTIL/DH/CH
(7,**39**,46,44, 31,8,33) MINA **7** 75-76, TORA **39** 77-79, OAKA **39** 80-82, *CH* **46** 84-85, *CH* **39** 85-87, **44** 88, **31** 88-89, **8** 89-95, STLN *CH* **39** 96-97, **33** 98, **39** 99-05

McKECHNIE, BILL (DEACON) M/CH
(34,33,30,65, **1**,41,40) BOSN *M* **34** 32, *M* **33** 33-36, *M* **30** 37, CINN *M* **65** 38, *M* **1** 39-46, CLEA *CH* **41** 47-49, BOSA *CH* **40** 52-53

McKEE, JIM P
(49,39,**46**) PITN **49** 72, **39** 72-73, **46** 73

McKEE, J. R. CH
(**37**) PITN **37** 47

McKEE, ROGERS P
(17,**3**) PHIN **17** 43, **3** 44

McKEEL, WALT C
(**45**,26) BOSA **45** 96-97, COLN **26** 02

McKEITHAN, TIM P
(**24**) PHIA **24** 32-34

McKEON, JACK M
(**31**,1,15) KCA *M* **31** 73-75, OAKA *M* **1** 77-78, **42** 78, SDN *M* **15** 88-90, CINN *M* **31** 97, **15** 98, **31** 99-00, FLAN *M* **15** 03-05

McKEON, JOEL P
(61,**50**) CHIA **61** 86, **50** 86-87

McKINNEY, RICH P
(1,26,27,5,**21**, 9) CHIA **1** 70, **26** 71, NYA **27** 72, OAKA **5** 73, **21** 74-75, **9** 77

McKNIGHT, JEFF 2B/INF/UTIL S
(**15**,13,38,5, 17,18) NYN **15** 89, BALA **13** 90, **38** 91, NYN **5/15** 92, **7/17** 93, **18** 94

McKNIGHT, JIM 2B/OF/UTIL F
(6,**15**) CHIN **6** 60, **15** 62

McKNIGHT, TONY P
(**59**,45) HOUN **59** 00-01, PITN **45** 01

McLAIN, DENNY P
(34,**17**,30) DETA **34** 63-64, **17** 65-70, WASA **17** 71, OAKA **17** 72, ATLN **30** 72

McLAREN, JOHN CH
(24,**7**,36,8) TORA *CH* **24** 86-88, *CH* **7** 88-90, BOSA *CH* **36** 91, CINN *CH* **8** 92, SEAA *CH* **7** 93-02, TBA *CH* **7** 03-05

McLARNEY, ART SS
(**28**) NYN **28** 32

McLAUGHLIN, BYRON P
(**30**,27,54) SEAA **30** 77-78, **27** 79, **54** 80, **27** 80, 83

McLAUGHLIN, BO P
(**39**,32,43) HOUN **39** 76-79, ATLN **32** 79, OAKA **34** 81-82

McLAUGHLIN, JIM 3B
(**22**) STLA **22** 32

McLAUGHLIN, JOEY P
(37,48,46, **50**, 53) ATLN **37/48** 77, **46/50** 79, TORA **46** 80, **50** 80-84, TEXA **53** 84

McLAUGHLIN, JUD P
(30,16,**21**) BOSA **30** 31, **16** 32, **21** 33

McLAUGHLIN, PAT P
(22,17,33,26, **20**) DETA **22/17** 37, PHIA **33** 40, DETA **26/20** 45

McLEAN, AL (ELROD) P
(**12**) WASA **12** 35

McLEARY, MARTY P
(**54**) SDN **54** 04

McLELAND, WAYNE (NUBBIN') P
(19,31,**23**) DETA **19** 51, **31/23** 52

McLEMORE, MARK 2B/INF/OF/UTIL
(28,10,6,63, 20,2,**3**,**4**) CALA **28** 86-88, **10** 89-90, CLEA **6** 90, HOUN **63/20** 91, BALA **2** 92-94, TEXA **3** 95-99, SEAA **4** 00-03, OAKA **2** 04

McLEOD, JIM SS/3B
(20,**7**) WASA **20** 32, PHIN **7** 33

McLEOD, RALPH OF
(**12**) BOSN **12** 38

McLISH, CAL (BUSTER) P/CH
(34,35,40,38, 25,12,27,33, **22**,15,26,2, 32,38) BKNN **34** 44, **35** 46, PITN **40** 47, **38/25** 48, CHIN **12** 49, **27** 51, CLEA **33** 56, **22** 56-59, CINN **40** 60, CHIA **15** 61, PHIN **26** 62-64, *CH* **2** 65-66, MONN *CH* **32** 69-75, MILA *CH* **38** 76-82

McLOUTH, NATE OF
(**59**) PITN **59** 05

McMAHAN, JACK P
(25,**14**) PITN **25** 56, KCA **14** 56

McMAHON, DON P
(20,31,44,**47**, 42,13) MILN **20** 57-62, HOUN **31** 62-63, CLEA **44** 64-66, BOSA **44** 66-67, CHIA **44** 67-68, DETA **47** 68-69, SFN **47** 69-74, *CH* **47** 73-75, MINA *CH* **42** 76-77, SFN *CH* **47** 80-82, CLEA **47** 83-85, LAN *CH* **13** 86

McMANUS, JIM 1B
(**48**) KCA **48** 60

McMANUS, MARTY 3B/INF/M
(5,28,3,**2**) DETA **5** 31, BOSA **28** 31, **3** 32, *M* **3** 32, **2** 33, *M* **2** 33, BOSN **28** 34

McMATH, JIMMY OF
(**24**) CHIN **24** 68

McMICHAEL, GREG P
(**38**,36,35,49) ATLN **38** 93-96, NYN **36** 97-98, LAN **35** 98, NYN **36** 98-99, OAKA **49** 99, ATLN **38** 00

McMILLAN, ROY SS/INF/CH/M
(**11**,26,51) CINN **11** 51-60, MILN **11** 61-64, NYN **11** 64-66, MILA *CH* **26** 70-72, *M* **26** 72, NYN *CH* **51** 73-76, *M* **51** 75

McMILLAN, TOM SS
(**21**) SEAA **21** 77

McMULLEN, KEN (POSSUM) OF/3B/UTIL/DH
(14,11,**2**,7,4, 3,5,35,17) LAN **14** 62, **11** 63-64, WASA **2** 65-70, CALA **7** 70-71, **4/3** 72, LAN **5** 73-75, OAKA **35** 76, MILA **17** 77

McMILLON, BILLY OF
(**40**,41,74,43, 49,13) FLAN **40** 96-97, PHIN **41** 97, DETA **74** 00, **43** 00-01, OAKA **49** 01, **13** 01, 03-04

McMURTRY, CRAIG P
(29,39,**38**) ATLN **29** 83-86, **39** 86, TEXA **38** 88-90, HOUN **38** 95

McNABB, CARL (SKINNY) PH
(39,**29**) DETA **39/29** 45

McNAIR, ERIC (BOOB) SS/INF
(**22**,6,4,47,7, 9,14) PHIA **22** 31-35, **6** 33-35, BOSA **4** 36, **6** 37-38, CHIA **47** 39, **7** 40, DETA **9** 41-42, PHIA **14** 42

McNALLY, DAVE P
(**19**,20,26) BALA **19** 62-74, MONN **20/26** 75

McNAMARA, BOB INF
(23,**3**) PHIA **23/3** 39

McNAMARA, JIM C
(55,**30**) MINA **55** 64, WASA **30** 65

McNAMARA, JOHN CH/M
(41,11,**1**,2,3) OAKA *CH* **41** 68-69, *M* **41** 69, *M* **11** 70, SFN *CH* **1** 71-73, SDN *M* **2** 74, *M* **1** 75-77, CALA *CH* **2** 78, CINN *M* **3** 79-82, CALA *M* **2** 83-84, BOSA *M* **1** 85-88, CLEA *M* **1** 90-91, CALA *M* **1** 96

McNEALY, RUSTY DH/OF
(**47**) OAKA **47** 83

McNEELY, EARL OF/CH
(**22**,29) STLA **22** 31, WASA *CH* **29** 36-37

McNEELY, JEFF OF/DH
(58,**50**) BOSA **58/50** 93

McNERTNEY, JERRY C
(**15**,11,43,32) CHIA **15** 64, 66-68, SEAA **15** 69, MILA **15** 70, STLN **15** 71-72, PITN **11** 73, NYA *CH* **43** 84, BOSA *CH* **32** 88

McNICHOL, BRIAN P
(**33**) CHIN **33** 99

McNOUGHTON, GORDON P
(**16**) BOSA **16** 32

McNULTY, BILL OF/3B
(37,**18**) OAKA **37** 69, **18** 72

McQUAIG, JERRY OF
(**10**) PHIA **10** 34

McQUEEN, MIKE P
(**22**,47) ATLN **22** 69-72, **47** 74

McQUILLEN, GLENN (RED) OF
(4,**15**) STLA **4** 38, **15** 41-42, 46-47

McQUINN, GEORGE (MAC) 1B
(11,5,**3**,9) CINN **11** 36, STLA **5** 38-40, **3** 41-45, PHIA **5** 46, NYA **9** 47-48

McPHERSON, DALLAS 3B
(**23**) ANAA **23** 04, LAA **23** 05

McRAE, BRIAN OF S
(**56**) KCA **56** 90-94, CHIN **56** 95-97, NYN **56** 97-99, COLN **56** 99, TORA **56** 99

McRAE, HAL 2B/OF/INF/DH/UTIL/CH/M F
(**11**,17,12,4, 56,8) CINN **11** 68, 70-72, KCA **11** 73-87, *CH* **11** 87, MONN *CH* **17** 90, *CH* **12** 90-91, KCA *M* **11** 91-94, CINN *CH* **4** 95-96, PHIN *CH* **56** 97-00, TBA *CH/M* **56** 01, *M* **11** 02, STLN *CH* **8** 05

McRAE, NORM P
(**36**) DETA **36** 69-70

McREYNOLDS, KEVIN OF/DH
(18,**22**) SDN **18** 83-86, NYN **22** 87-91, KCA **22** 92-93, NYN **22** 94

McWILLIAMS, BILL PH
(**27**) BOSA **27** 31

McWILLIAMS, LARRY P
(27,**49**,**49**,25, 46,34) ATLN **27** 78-82, PITN **49** 82-86, ATLN **25** 87, STLN **49** 88, PHIN **46** 89, KCA **34** 89-90

MEACHAM, BOBBY SS/INF/DH
(**20**) NYA **20** 83-88

MEACHAM, RUSTY P
(41,**28**,38,37) DETA **41** 91, KCA **28** 92-95, HOUN **38** 00, TBA **37** 01

MEAD, CHARLIE OF
(22,24,**3**) NYN **22** 43, **24** 44, **3** 45

MEADOWS, BRIAN P
(**34**,59,31,46) FLAN **34** 98-99, SDN **34** 00, KCA **59** 00, **31** 01, PITN **46** 02-05

MEADOWS, LOUIE OF/1B
(**26**,29) HOUN **26** 86, 88-90, PHIN **29** 90

MEADS, DAVE P
(**53**) HOUN **53** 87-88

MEARES, PAT SS
(**2**) MINA **2** 93-98, PITN **2** 99-01

MEARS, CHRIS P
(**45**) DETA **45** 03

MECHE, GIL P
(**55**) SEAA **55** 99-00, (01-02), 03-05

MECIR, JIM P
(42,54,**45**) SEAA **42** 95, NYA **54** 96-97, TBA **45** 98-00, OAKA **48** 00, **45** 00-04, FLAN **45** 05

MEDDERS, BRANDON P
(**52**) ARIN **52** 05

MEDEIROS, RAY (PEP) PR
(**18**) CINN **18** 45

MEDICH, DOC P
(50,42,**33**,32, 34,53,41,22, 27) NYA **50** 72, **42** 72-73, **33** 74-75, PITN **32/34** 76, OAKA **53/33** 77, SEAA **41** 77, NYN **22** 77, TEXA **27** 78, **42** 78-80, **33** 80-82, MILA **33** 82

MEDINA, LUIS 1B/UTIL/DH
(**29**,23) CLEA **29** 88-89, **23** 90-91

MEDINA, RAFAEL P
(**47**) FLAN **47** 98-99

MEDLINGER, IRV P
(18,**26**) STLA **18** 49, **26** 51

MEDVIN, SCOTT P
(**55**,53) PITN **55** 88-89, SEAA **53** 90

MEDWICK, JOE (DUCKY)(MUSCLES) OF/1B
(28,**7**,77,6,19, 3,16,21) STLN **28** 32, **7** 33-40, BKNN **77** 40-41, **7** 40, 43, **6** 41-42, NYN **19** 43, **3** 44-45, BOSN **5/3** 45, BKNN **16** 46, STLN **21** 47-48

MEECHAM, RUSTY P
(**43**) SEAA **43** 96

MEEKS, SAMMY SS/2B
(22,**14**) WASA **22** 48, CINN **14** 49-51

MEELER, PHIL P
(**47**) DETA **47** 72

MEERS, RUSS (BABE) P
(27,**17**) CHIN **27** 41, **17** 46-47

MEIER, DAVE UTIL/OF/3B/DH
(**7**,51,20) MINA **7** 84-85, TEXA **51** 87, CHIN **20** 88

MEINE, HEINIE (COUNT OF LUXEMBURG) P
(**41**) PITN **41** 32-34

MEJIA, MIGUEL OF
(**35**) STLN **35** 96

MEJIA, ROBERTO 2B
(**8**,38,67) COLN **8** 93-95, STLN **38/67** 97

MEJIAS, ROMAN OF
(25,**15**,4) PITN **25** 55, 58-59, **15** 59-61, HOUN **25** 62, BOSA **4** 63-64, PITN **25** 57

MEJIAS, SAM (SAMMY) OF/P/CH
(7,14,32,**28**, 49,40,16) STLN **7** 76, MONN **14** 77-78, CHIN **32** 79, CINN **28** 79-81, SEAA *CH* **49** 93-95, **40/49** 96, **49** 97-98, **16** 99

MELE, DUTCH OF
(**37**) CINN **37** 37

MELE, SAM OF/1B/CH/M
(**14**,4,27,31, 5,15,7,24,36, 54) BOSA **14** 47, **4** 48-49, WASA **27** 49, **31** 50, **14** 51-52, CHIA **14** 52, **5** 53, BALA **15** 54, BOSA **31** 54, **7** 55, CINN **24** 55, CLEA **36** 56, WASA *CH* **54** 59-60, MINA *CH* **54/14** 61, *M* **14** 61-67

MELENDEZ, FRANCISCO 1B/OF
(52,**18**,35) PHIN **52** 84, **18** 86, SFN **18** 87-88, BALA **43/35** 89

MELENDEZ, JOSE P
(54,48,46,**19**) SEAA **54** 90, SDN **48** 91-92, BOSA **46** 93, **19** 93-94

MELENDEZ, LUIS OF
(**26**,25,2) STLN **26** 70-76, SDN **25** 76-77, **2** 77

MELHUSE, ADAM 1B/INF/C
(45,30,21,**17**) LAN **45** 00, COLN **30/21** 00, OAKA **17** 03-05

MELILLO, SKI (SPINACH) 2B/INF/CH
(**5**,24,29,27, 40,41,42) STLA **5** 31-35, BOSA **5** 35, **24** 35-37, STLA *CH* **29** 38, CLEA *CH* **27** 39-40,42,45-46, *CH* **40** 47-48, *CH* **41** 50, BOSA *CH* **42** 52-53, KCA *CH* **42** 55-56

MELO, JUAN INF
(**28**) SFN **28** 00

MELTON, BILL 3B/OF/INF/DH
(**14**,11) CHIA **14** 68-75, CALA **14** 76, CLEA **11** 77

MELTON,CLIFF (MICKEY MOUSE) (MOUNTAIN MUSIC) P
(**16**,15) NYN **16** 37-39, 44, **15** 40-43

MELTON, DAVE OF
(31,35,**3**) KCA **31** 56, **35/3** 58

MELTON, RUBE P
(8,17,12,32, 14,**37**) PHIN **8** 41, **17** 42, BKNN **12/32** 43, **14** 44, **37** 46-47

MELUSKEY, MITCH C
(4,**21**,2) HOUN **4** 98, **21** 99-00, DETA **21** (01), 02, HOUN **2** 03

MELVIN, BOB C/3B/1B/UTIL/DH/CH
(18,7,9,36,**2**, 3,43,49,12, 15) DETA **18** 85, SFN **18** 86, **7** 86-88, **9** 88, BALA **36** 89, **2** 89-91, KCA **2** 92, BOSA **3** 93, NYA **43** 94, CHIA **49** 94, MILN *CH* **12** 99, DETA *CH* **15** 00-01, ARIN *CH* **3** 01-02, SEAA *M* **3** 03-04, ARIN *M* **3** 05

MENCH, KEVIN OF/DH
(**28**) TEXA **28** 02-05

MENDEZ, CARLOS DH
(71,**53**) BALA **71/53** 03

MENDEZ, DONALDO SS
(**17**) SDN **17** 01, 03

MENDOZA, CARLOS OF
(**6**,29) NYN **6** 97, COLN **29** 00

MENDOZA, MARIO SS/3B/INF/P
(**11**,14) PITN **11** 74-78, SEAA **11** 79-80, TEXA **14** 81-82

MENDOZA, MIKE P
(**54**) HOUN **54** 79

MENDOZA, MINNIE 3B/2B/CH
(**27**,40) MINA **27** 70, BALA **40** 88

MENDOZA, RAMIRO P
(**55**,57,26,38) NYA **55/57** 96, **55** 97-02, BOSA **55** 03, **26** 03-04, NYA **38** 05

MENECHINO, FRANK INF
(7,**11**,4) OAKA **7** 99, **11** 00-04, TORA **4** 04-05

MENENDEZ, TONY P
(52,67,**36**) CINN **52** 92, PITN **67** 93, SFN **36** 94

MENHART, PAUL P
(55,**16**,54) TORA **55** 95, SEAA **16** 96, SDN **54** 97

MENKE, DENIS SS/INF/UTIL/CH
(29,19,**11**,16, 14,15,4) MILN **29** 62, **19** 63-65, ATLN **19** 66-67, HOUN **11** 68-71, CINN **16** 72, **11** 73, HOUN **11** 74, TORA *CH* **14** 80-81, HOUN *CH* **15** 83-88, *CH* **16/11** 87, PHIN *CH* **4** 89,*CH* **14** 89-96, CINN *CH* **19** 97-00

MEOLA, MIKE P
(23,24,**16**) BOSA **23** 33, STLA **24** 36, BOSA **16** 36

MEOLI, RUDY P
(15,**3**,12,18) CALA **15** 71, **3** 73-75, CHIN **12** 78, PHIN **18** 79

MERCADO, HECTOR P
(39,52,**54**) CINN **39** 00, **52** 01, PHIN **54** 02-03

MERCADO, ORLANDO C/CH
(**2**,7,24,48,3, 4,35,15) SEAA **2** 82-84, TEXA **7** 86, DETA **24/7** 87, LAN **48** 87, OAKA **3** 88, MINA **4** 89, NYN **35** 90, MONN **15** 90, LAA *CH* **48** 05

MERCED, ORLANDO OF/C/1B/UTIL
(19,54,**6**,9,26, 25,7,16) PITN **19/54** 90, **6** 91-96, TORA **6** 97, MINA **9** 98, BOSA **26** 98, CHIN **25** 98, MONN **7** 99, HOUN **16** 01-03

MERCEDES, HENRY C/DH
(**39**,15,36,10) OAKA **39** 92-93, KCA **15** 95, **36** 96, TEXA **10** 97

MERCEDES, JOSE P
(**41**,31,50) MILA **41** 94-97, MILN **41** 98, BALA **31** 00-01, MONN **50** 03

MERCEDES, LUIS OF/DH
(51,**11**,17) BALA **51** 91, **11** 91-93, SFN **17** 93

MERCER, MARK P
(**53**) TEXA **53** 81

MERCHANT, ANDY C
(**50**) BOSA **50** 75-76

MERCKER, KENT P
(**50**,21,39,38, 43,41,47,54) ATLN **50** 89-95, BALA **21** 96, CLEA **39** 96, CINN **38** 97, STLN **43** 98-99, BOSA **41** 99, ANAA **47** 00, COLN **54** 02, CINN **50** 03, ATLN **50** 03, CHIN **50** 04, CINN **50** 05

MERENA, SPIKE P
(__) BOSA __ 34

MERIDITH, CLA P
(**51**) BOSA **51** 05

MERIDITH, RON P
(**38**) CHIN **38** 84-85, TEXA **38** 86-87

MERLONI, LOU 2B/INF/UTIL
(50,**26**,28,13, 12,21) BOSA **50** 98, **26** 99-02, SDN **28** 03, BOSA **13** 03, CLEA **12** 04, LAA **21** 05

MERRICKS, MATTHEW P
(**60**) COLN **60** 05

MERRILL, STUMP CH/M
(**42**,41,46,22) NYA *CH* **42** 85-87, *M* **41/46** 90, *M* **22** 91

MERRIMAN, BRETT P
(**47**) MINA **47** 93-94

MERRIMAN, LLOYD (CITATION) 0F
(**20**,30,28) CINN **20** 49-51, 54, CHIA **30** 55, CHIN **28** 55

MERRITT, JIM P
(**26**,17,30,16) MINA **26** 65-66, **17** 67-68, **26** 67-68, CINN **30** 69-72, TEXA **16** 73-75

MERRITT, LLOYD P
(**43**) STLN **43** 57

MERSON, JACK 2B/3B
(**10**,12) PITN **10** 51-52, BOSA **12** 53

MERTZ, JIM P
(10,**14**) WASA **10/14** 43

MERULLO, LENNY SS/INF F
(35,**21**) CHIN **35** 41-42, **21** 43-47

MERULLO, MATT C/UTIL/DH S
(7,**5**,2,12) CHIA **7** 89, **5** 91-93, CLEA **2** 94, MINA **12** 95

MESA, JOSE P
(51,52,**49**,33, 47) CHIA **51** 87, BALA **52** 90-92, CLEA **49** 92-98, **33** 93, SFN **47** 98, SEAA **49** 99-00, PHIN **49** 01-03, PITN **49** 04-05

MESNER, STEVE SS/3B/INF
(28,21,15,5, **16**) CHIN **28/21** 38, **15** 39, STLN **5** 41, CINN **16** 43-45

MESSENGER, RANDY P
(**23**) FLAN **23** 05

MESSERSMITH, ANDY P
(**47**,17,27) CALA **47** 68-72, LAN **47** 73-75, ATLN **17** 76-77, **27** 77, NYA **47** 78, LAN **47** 79

METCALF, TOM P
(**29**) NYA **29** 63

METCALFE, MIKE INF/OF
(62,**45**) LAN **62** 98, **45** 00

METHA, SCAT 2B/3B
(**33**) DETA **33** 40

METHENY, BUD OF
(**3**) NYA **3** 43-46

METKOVICH, GEORGE (CATFISH) OF/1B
(**2**,31,47,36, 11,44,22,27) BOSA **2** 43-46, CLEA **31** 47, CHIA **47/36** 49, PITN **11** 51, **44** 52-53, CHIN **22** 53, MILN **27** 54

METRO, CHARLIE OF/UTIL/CH/M
(**21**,14,15,63, 36,46) DETA **21** 43-44, PHIA **14** 44, **15** 45, CHIN *CH* **63** 62, *M* **63** 62, CHIA *CH* **36** 65, KCA *M* **36** 70, OAKA *CH* **46** 82

METZGER, BUTCH P
(48,**36**,34,45) SFN **48** 74, SDN **36** 75-76, STLN **34** 77, NYN **45** 78

METZGER, ROGER SS/2B/INF
(16,15,**14**) CHIN **16** 70, HOUN **15** 71, **14** 72-78, SFN **16** 78-80

METZIG, BILL 2B
(**29**) CHIA **29** 44

MEULENS, HENSLEY (BAM-BAM) 3B/OF
(28,58,57,**31**, 59,29) NYA **28/58/57** 89, **31** 90-91, **59** 92, **31** 93, MONN **31** 97, ARIN **29** 98

MEUSEL, BOB (LONG BOB) OF B
(**5**) NYA **5** 29

MEYER, BILLY M
(**1**) PITN **1** 48-52

MEYER, BOB P
(49,41,30,**38**) NYA **49** 64, LAA **41** 64, KCA **30** 64, SEAA **38** 69, MILA **38** 70

MEYER, BRIAN P
(**35**) HOUN **35** 88-90

MEYER, DAN OF/1B/UTIL/DH
(37,25,**7**,4,9) DETA **37** 74, **25** 74-76, SEAA **7** 77-81, OAKA **4** 82-83, **7** 83-84, **9** 85

MEYER, DAN P
(**45**) ATLN **45** 04

MEYER, DUTCH 2B
(43,33,**9**,26, 24,3) CHIN **43** 37, DETA **33** 40, **9** 41, **26** 42, CLEA **24** 45, **3** 46

MEYER, GEORGE 2B
(**17**) CHIA **17** 38

MEYER, JACK P
(**42**) PHIN **42** 55-61

MEYER, JOEY DH/1B
(**23**) MILA **23** 88-89

MEYER, RUSS (MONK)(THE MAD MONK) (ROWDY) P/CH
(38,28,**34**,48, 26,20) CHIN **38** 46, **28** 47-48, PHIN **34** 49-52, BKNN **48** 53, **34** 53-55, CHIN **34** 56, CINN **26** 56, BOSA **20** 57, KCA **20** 59, NYA *CH* **48** 92

MEYER, SCOTT C
(**26**) OAKA **26** 78

MEYERS, CHAD OF/DH
(**20**,30) CHIN **20** 99-01, SEAA **30** 03

MIADICH, BART P
(**52**) ANAA **52** 01, 03

MICELI, DAN P
(**32**,33,34,43, 40,58) PITN **32** 93-96, DETA **32** 97, SDN **33** 98-99, FLAN **34** 00-01, COLN **32** 01, TEXA **32** 02, COLN **43** 03, CLEA **34** 03, NYA **40** 03, HOUN **40** 03, **58** 03-04, COLN **58** 05

MICELOTTA, MICKEY SS
(**5**) PHIA **5** 54-55

MICHAEL, GENE (STICK) SS/INF/P/CH/M
(45,26,**17**,16, 39,33,11,40, 1,4,48,43) PITN **45** 66, LAN **26** 67, NYA **17** 68-74, DETA **16** 75, NYA *CH* **39** 76, *CH* **33** 78, *M* **11** 81-82, *CH* **40** 84-86, *CH* **1** 86, CHIN *M* **4** 86-87, NYA *CH* **48** 88, *CH* **43** 89

MICHAELS, CASS 3B/SS/2B/UTIL
(29,28,**7**,42, 27,6,5) CHIA **29** 43-44, **28** 44-46, **7** 46-50, WASA **42** 50-51, **7** 51, STLA **27/6** 52, PHIA **5** 52-53, CHIA **6** 54

MICHAELS, JASON OF/3B
(**22**) PHIN **22** 01-05

MICHAELS, JOHN P
(**27**) BOSA **27** 32

MICHALAK, CHRIS P
(48,**17**,55,54) ARIN **48** 98, TORA **17** 01, TEXA **55** 01, **54** 02

MICKELSON, ED 1B
(34,**9**,46) STLN **34** 50, STLA **9** 53, CHIN **46** 57

MICKENS, GLENN P
(**46**) BKNN **46** 53

MIDDLEBROOK, JASON P
(54,**27**) SDN **54** 01-02, NYN **54** 01, **27** 02-03

MIDDLEIFF, DICK P
(**27**) BOSA **27** 38

MIDKIFF, DICK P
(**27**) BOSA **27** 38

MIELKE, GARY P
(**50**) TEXA **50** 87, 89-90

MIENTKIEWICZ, DOUG 1B
(51,25,**16**,13) MINA **51** 98, **25** 99-00, **16** 01-03, BOSA **13** 04, NYN **16** 05

MIERKOWICZ, ED (BUTCH)(MOUSE) OF
(2,**12**,40) DETA **2** 45, **12** 47-48, STLN **40** 50

MIESKE, MATT OF
(**30**,20,23) MILA **30** 93-97, CHIN **20** 98, SEAA **20** 99, HOUN **23** 99-00, ARIN **23** 00

MIGGINS, LARRY (IRISH) OF
(41,**23**) STLN **41** 48, **23** 52

MIHALIC, JOHN SS/2B
(34,**24**) WASA **34** 35, **24** 36-37

MIKKELSEN, PETE P
(51,19,40,**46**) NYA **51** 64-65, PITN **19** 66-67, CHIN **51** 67, **40** 67-68, STLN **46** 68, LAN **46** 69-72

MIKLOS, HANK P
(38,**39**) CHIN **38/39** 44

MIKSIS, EDDIE 3B/INF/UTIL
(16,**34**,21,4, 6,28) BKNN **16** 44, **34** 46-51, CHIN **21** 51-56, STLN **4** 57, BALA **16** 57, **6** 58, CINN **28** 58

MILACKI, BOB P
(52,**18**,49,38, 53) BALA **52** 88-89, **18** 89-92, CLEA **49** 93, KCA **38** 94, SEAA **53** 96

MILAN, CLYDE (DEERFOOT) CH
(29,26,**31**,51) WASA *CH* **29** 38-40, *CH* **26** 41-43, *CH* **31** 44-49, *CH* **51** 50-52

MILBOURNE, LARRY 2B/SS/UTIL/DH
(**10**,2,18,7, 17,15,39,8) HOUN **10** 74-76, SEAA **10** 77-79, **2** 80, NYA **18** 81-82, MINA **7** 82, CLEA **17** 82, PHIN **15** 83, NYA **39** 83, SEAA **8** 84

MILCHIN, MIKE P
(51,**21**) MINA **51** 96, BALA **21** 96

MILES, AARON 2B
(39,**6**) CHIA **39** 03, COLN **6** 04-05

MILES, CARL P
(**14**) PHIA **14** 40

MILES, DEE OF
(31,24,11,**7**,2) WASA **31** 35, **24** 36, PHIA **11** 39-40, **7** 41-42, BOSA **2** 43

MILES, DON OF
(**45**) LAN **45** 58

MILES, JIM P
(31,21,**24**) WASA **31** 68, **21/24** 69

MILEY, DAVE CH/M
(2,**12**) CINN *CH* **2** 93, *M* **12** 03-05

MILEY, MIKE SS
(**21**) CALA **21** 75-76

MILITELLO, SAM P
(43,**34**) NYA **43** 92, **34** 93

MILLAN, FELIX 2B/INF
(18,11,**17**,16) ATLN **18** 66, **11** 66-67, **17** 67-72, NYN **16** 73, **17** 74-77

MILLAR, KEVIN 1B/INF/OF/DH
(18,**15**) FLAN **18** 98-99, **15** 00-02, BOSA **15** 03-05

MILLER, BILL (WILD BILL) P
(**25**) STLA **25** 37

MILLER, BILL (LEFTY)(HOOKS) P
(**23**,13) NYA **23** 52-54, BALA **13** 55

MILLER, BING OF/1B/CH
(**9**,25,27,31, 33) PHIA **9** 31-34, **27** 34, BOSA **25** 35, **27** 36, *CH* **27** 37, DETA *CH* **31** 38-41, CHIA *CH* **33** 42-49, PHIA *CH* **33** 50-53

MILLER, BOB (G.) P
(**28**,13,39,36) DETA **28** 53-56, **13** 56, CINN **39** 62, NYN **36** 62

MILLER, BOB (J.) P
(41,**19**) PHIN **41** 49, **19** 50-58

MILLER, BOB (L.) P/CH
(26,49,35,36, 24,**15**,21,33, 23,45,37,32, 42,30,17,48) STLN **26** 57, **49** 59, **35** 60, **36** 60-61, NYN **24** 62, LAN **15** 63-67, MINA **21** 68, **49** 68-69, CLEA **33** 70, CHIA **23** 70, CHIN **45** 70-71, SDN **37** 71, PITN **32** 71-72, SDN **42/37** 73, NYN **30** 73, DETA **17** 73, NYN **30** 74, TORA *CH* **15** 77-79, SFN *CH* **48** 85

MILLER, BRUCE INF
(**29**) SFN **29** 73-76

MILLER, CORKY C
(37,**22**,51) CINN **37** 01-02, **22** 03-04, MINA **51** 05

MILLER, DAMIAN C
(39,**26**,27) MINA **39** 97, ARIN **26** 98-02, CHIN **27** 03, OAKA **26** 04, MILN **26** 05

MILLER, DARRELL 1B/OF/UTIL
(**32**) CALA **32** 84-88

MILLER, DYAR P/CH
(37,**41**,46,56, 49) BALA **37** 75-77, CALA **41** 77-79, TORA **46** 79, NYN **56** 80, **49** 80-81, CHIA *CH* **49** 87-88

MILLER, EDDIE (EPPIE) SS/INF
(13,33,1,**7**,15, 11,14,5,3) CINN **13** 36, **33** 37, BOSN **1** 39, **7** 40-42, CINN **15** 43, **11** 44-45, **13** 46-47, **14** 47, PHIN **5** 48-49, **3** 49, STLN **33** 50

MILLER, EDDIE OF/DH
(30,17,**14**,45, 27,39) TEXA **30** 77, ATLN **17** 78, **14** 79-80, **45** 81, DETA **27** 82, SDN **39** 84

MILLER, HACK C
(22,23,**31**) DETA **22** 44, **23/31** 45

MILLER, JAKE P
(**15**,38) CLEA **15** 31, CHIA **38** 33

MILLER, JOHN (A.) 1B/OF/UTIL
(26,43) NYA **26** 66, LAN **43** 69

MILLER, JOHN (E.) P
(**17**,35) BALA **17** 62-63, **35** 65, **17** 66-67

MILLER, JUSTIN P
(**34**) TORA **34** 02, (03), 04-05

MILLER, (N.) KEITH UTIL
(11,37) PHIN **11** 88, **37** 89

MILLER, KEITH (A.) OF/2B/UTIL
(**25**,16) NYN **25** 87-91, KCA **16** 92-95

MILLER, KEN (WHITEY) P
(**21**) NYN **21** 44

MILLER, KURT P
(**53**,35) FLAN **53** 94, 96, **35** 97, CHIN **53** 98-99

MILLER, LARRY P
(41,20,16,**35**) LAN **41/20** 64, NYN **16** 65, **35** 65-66

MILLER, LEMMIE OF
(**51**) LAN **51** 84

MILLER, MATT P
(57,**58**,46,59) DETA **57** 01, **58** 01-02, COLN **46** 03, CLEA **59** 04-05

MILLER, NORM OF/3B/C
(54,34,**21**,42) HOUN **54** 65, **34** 65-66, **21** 67-73, ATLN **42** 73-74

MILLER, ORLANDO SS
(**24**,14) HOUN **24** 94-96, DETA **14** 97

MILLER, OTTO 3B/2B
(5,**8**) BOSA **5** 31, **8** 32

MILLER, (L.) OTTO (MOONIE) CH
(**32**,37) BKNN **32** 32-37, **37** 38

MILLER, OX P
(17,36,**37**,24) WASA **17** 43, STLA **36** 43, 45, **37** 46, CHIN **24** 47

MILLER, PAUL P
(64,**53**) PITN **64** 91-92, **53** 93

MILLER, RANDY P
(35,**47**) BALA **35** 77, MONN **47** 78

MILLER, RAY CH/M
(41,**31**,44,34) TEXA *CH* **41** 78, BALA *CH* **31** 78-85, MINA *M* **44** 85-86, PITN *CH* **31** 87-96, BALA *CH* **31** 97, *M* **31** 98-99, *CH* **34** 04-05

MILLER, RICK OF/DH/UTIL
(35,16,**3**) BOSA **35** 71-72, **16** 72-77, CALA **3** 78-80, BOSA **3** 81-85

MILLER, ROD PH
(**50**) BKNN **50** 57

MILLER, ROGER P
(**27**) MILA **27** 74

MILLER, RONNIE P
(**17**) WASA **17** 41

MILLER, STU P
(36,25,23,**37**, 47) STLN **36** 52-54, 56, PHIN **25** 56, NYN **23** 57, SFN **37** 58-62, BALA **37** 63-67, ATLN **47/23** 68

MILLER, TRAVIS P
(59,**20**) MINA **59** 96, **20** 97-02

MILLER, TREVER P
(37,**46**,51) DETA **37** 96, HOUN **46** 98-99, LAN **46** 00, PHIN **46** 00, TORA **51** 03, TBA **51** 04-05

MILLER, WADE P
(**52**) HOUN **52** 99-04, BOSA **52** 05

MILLETTE, JOE INF/SS/3B
(27,**24**) PHIN **27** 92, **24** 93

MILLIARD, RALPH 2B/INF
(37,**21**,26) FLAN **37** 96, **21** 97, NYN **26** 98

MILLIES, WALLY C
(14,10,9,8,**23**) BKNN **14** 34, WASA **10** 36, **9** 37, PHIN **8** 39, **23** 39-41

MILLIGAN, JOHN P
(**30**) WASA **30** 34

MILLIGAN, RANDY (MOOSE) 1B/OF/DH
(27,47,**39**,19, 40) NYN **27** 87, PITN **47** 88, BALA **39** 89-92, CINN **19** 93, CLEA **40** 93, MONN **39** 94

MILLIKEN, BOB (BOBO) P/CH
(25,46,**8**,33) BKNN **25** 53-54, STLN **8** 65-70, **33** 76

MILLS, ALAN P
(69,64,28,45, 50,**75**) NYA **69/64/28** 90, **45/50** 91, BALA **75** 92-98, LAN **75** 99-00, BALA **75** 00-01

MILLS, ART CH
(**31**) DETA *CH* **28** 44, *CH* **31** 44-48

MILLS, BILL C
(22,**23**) PHIA **22/23** 44

MILLS, BRAD 3B/2B/1B/CH
(2,7,**24**,9,7) MONN **2** 80-81, **7** 82, **24** 82-83, PHIN *CH* **9** 97-00, MONN *CH* **7** 03-04, BOSA *CH* **2** 04-05

MILLS, BUSTER (BUS) OF/CH/M
(10,21,7,15, 27,14,24,**22**, 52,40) STLN **10** 34, BKNN **21** 35, BOSA **7** 37, STLA **15** 38, NYA **27** 40, CLEA **14** 42, **24** 46, *CH* **24** 46, CHIA *CH* **22** 46-50, CINN *CH* **52** 53, *M* **52** 53, BOSA *CH* **40** 54

MILLS, DICK P
(**36**) BOSA **36** 70

MILLS, LEFTY P
(**25**,27,20,22) STLA **25** 34, 37-38, **27/25/20** 39, **22** 40

MILLWOOD, KEVIN P
(**34**) ATLN **34** 97-02, PHIN **34** 03-04, CLEA **34** 05

MILNAR, AL (HAPPY) P
(24,17,**20**,15 ,30,40,39) CLEA **24/17** 36, **20** 38-43, STLA **15/30** 43, **40** 46, PHIN **39** 46

MILNE, PETE OF
(39,9,16,**26**) NYN **39** 48, **9/16** 49, **26** 50

MILNER, BRIAN C
(**3**) TORA **3** 78

MILNER, EDDIE OF
(57,**20**,00,9) CINN **57** 80, **20** 81-86, SFN **20** 87, CINN **00/9** 88

MILNER, JOHN (THE HAMMER) OF/1B
(**28**,16,34,5, 14) NYN **28** 71-77, PITN **16** 78, **34** 78-81, MONN **5** 81-82, PITN **14** 82

MILOSEVICH, MIKE (MOLLIE) SS
(12,26) NYA **12** 44, **26** 45

MILTON, ERIC P
(41,**21**,22) MINA **41** 98-99, **21** 00-04, CINN **22** 05

MIMBS, MICHAEL P
(45,**47**) PHIN **45** 95, **47** 96-97

MINARCIN, RUDY (BUSTER) P
(54,36,**29**) CINN **54/36** 55, BOSA **29** 56-57

MINCHER, DON 1B/OF
(32,28,**5**,30,6, 4) WASA **32** 60, MINA **28** 60-61, **5** 62-66, CALA **5** 67-68, SEAA **5** 69, OAKA **30/5** 70-71, WASA **6** 71, TEXA **6/5** 72, OAKA **4** 72

MINCHEY, NATE P
(**57**,58,47) BOSA **57** 93-94, **58** 96, COLN **47** 97

MINETTO, CRAIG P
(**32**) OAKA **3** 78, **32** 78-81

MINGORI, STEVE P
(31,33,**23**) CLEA **31** 70-73, KCA **33** 73, **23** 73-79

MINNER, PAUL (LEFTY) P
(38,**24**) BKNN **38** 46, **38** 48-49, CHIN **24** 50-56

MINNICK, DON P
(**32**) WASA **32** 57-58

MINOR, BLAS P
(66,**55**,34,23, 43) PITN **66** 92-93, **55** 93-94, NYN **55** 95, **34** 95-96, SEAA **23** 96, HOUN **43** 97

MINOR, DAMON 3B/INF
(22,**37**,1) SFN **22** 00, **37** 01-02, **1** 04

MINOR, RYAN 3B/INF
(**10**,25,4) BALA **10** 98-99, **25** 00, MONN **4** 01

MINOSO, MINNIE OF/3B/INF/DH/CH
(18,6,**9**) CLEA **18** 49, **6** 51, CHIA **9** 51-57, CLEA **9** 58-59, CHIA **9** 60-61, STLN **9** 62, WASA **9** 63, CHIA **9** 64, 76, 80, *CH* **9** 76-81

MINSHALL, JIM P
(46,29) PITN **46** 74-75, **29** 75

MINTON, GREG P
(41,42,**38**) SFN **41** 75-76, **38** 78-87, CALA **38** 87-90

MINTZ, STEVE P
(**26**,46) SFN **26** 95, ANAA **46** 99

MINUTELLI, GINO P
(**33**,36) CINN **33** 90-91, SFN **36** 93

MIRABELLA, PAUL P
(16,36,50,55, 42, 34,39,52, **27**) TEXA **16** 78, NYA **36/50/55** 79, TORA **42** 80-81, **51** 81,TEXA **34** 82, BALA **39** 83, SEAA **52** 84-86, MILA **27** 87-90

MIRABELLI, DOUG C/DH
(66,2,29,1,19, 15,6,**28**) SFN **66** 96, **2** 97, **29/1** 98, **19** 98-99, **15** 00, TEXA **6** 01, BOSA **28** 01-05

MIRANDA, ANGEL P
(**38**,25) MILA **38** 93-96, **25** 97

MIRANDA, WILLIE 2B/SS/INF
(16,49,34,1, 38,20,**7**) WASA **16** 51, CHIA **49** 52,STLA **34** 52, CHIA **49** 52, STLA **1** 53, NYA **38** 53, **20** 53-54, BALA **7** 55-59

MISURACA, MIKE P
(**52**) MILA **52** 97

MITCHELL, BOBBY OF/DH
(23,46,**17**) MILA **23** 71, NYA **46** 70, MILA **17** 73-75

MITCHELL, BOBBY OF
(17,**10**) LAN **17** 80-81, MINA **10** 82-83

MITCHELL, CHARLIE P
(**38**) BOSA **38** 84-85

MITCHELL, CLARENCE P/CH
(**25**) NYN **25** 32, *CH* **25** 32

MITCHELL, CRAIG P
(**20**,29) OAKA **20** 75-76, **29** 77

MITCHELL, DALE OF/1B
(46,33,34,**3**, 8) CLEA **46** 46, **33** 47, **34** 48-50, **3** 51-56, BKNN **8** 56

MITCHELL, JOHN P
(66,**43**,24) NYN **66** 86, **43** 86-89, BALA **24** 90

MITCHELL, KEITH OF/DH
(**17**,52,30) ATLA **17** 91, SEAA **17** 94, CINN **52** 96, BOSA **30** 98

MITCHELL, KEVIN 3B/OF/1B/DH
(32,35,**7**,9,24, 44,31) NYN **32** 84, **35/7** 86, SDN **7** 87, SFN **9** 87-88, **7** 88-91, SEAA **7** 92, CINN **7** 93-94, BOSA **7** 96, CINN **24** 96, CLEA **44** 97, OAKA **31/7** 98

MITCHELL, LARRY P
(**57**) PHIN **57** 96

MITCHELL, PAUL P
(36,36,24,**34**, 43) BALA **36** 75, OAKA **36** 76-77, **24** 77, SEAA **34** 77-79, MILA **43** 79-80

MITRE, SERGIO P
(**52**) CHIN **52** 03-05

MITTERWALD, GEORGE C/OF/DH/1B/CH
(29,34,**15**,44, 40,48) MINA **29** 66, **34** 68, **15** 69-73, CHIN **15** 74-77, OAKA *CH* **44** 79-80, *CH* **40** 81-82, NYA *CH* **48** 88

MIZE, JOHNNY (THE BIG CAT)(BIG JAWN) (BIG JOHN) 1B/CH
(**10**,3,15,36, 44,39) STLN **10** 36-41, NYN **3** 42, 46, **15** 47-49, NYA **36** 49-53, KCA *CH* **44/39** 61

MIZELL, VINEGAR BEND P
(**33**,17,30,26) STLN **33** 52-53, **17** 56-58, **33** 59-60, PITN **30** 60-62, NYN **26** 62

MIZEROCK, JOHN C
(**4**,8,13) HOUN **4** 83, 85-86, ATLN **8** 89, KCA *M* **13** 02, *CH* **13** 03-04

MLICKI, DAVE P
(36,37,23,**38**, 30,43) CLEA **36/37** 92, **23** 93, NYN **38** 95-98, LAN **38** 98-99, DETA **30** 99-01, HOUN **43** 01, **23** 01-02

MMAHAT, KEVIN P
(**45**) NYA **45** 89

MOATES, DAVE OF/DH
(**30**) TEXA **30** 74-76

MODAK, MIKE P
(**35**) CINN **35** 45

MOEHLER, BRIAN P
(**38**,39,36) DETA **38** 96-02, CINN **38** 02, HOUN **39** 03, FLAN **36** 05

MOELLER, CHAD C
(39,**16**,21) MINA **39** 00, ARIN **39** 01, **16** 02 -03, MILN **21** 04-05

MOELLER, DENNIS P
(53,**24**) KCA **53** 92, PITN **24** 93

MOELLER, JOE P
(38,27,**25**) LAN **38** 62, 64, 66-67, **27** 68, **25** 69-71

MOELLER, RON (THE KID) P
(**32**,40,39,45, 16) BALA **32** 56-57, **40** 58, LAA **39** 61, **45** 63, WASA **16** 63

MOFFITT, RANDY P
(39,**17**) SFN **39** 72-75, **17** 75-81, HOUN **17** 82, TORA **17** 83

MOFORD, HERB P
(40,37,35,42, **26**) STLN **40** 55, DETA **37** 58, BOSA **35/42** 59, NYN **26** 62

MOHLER, MIKE P
(58,**32**,22,52) OAKA **58** 93-95, **32** 96-98, STLN **32** 99-00, CLEA **22** 00, ARIN **52** 01

MOHORCIC, DALE P
(**34**,67,51,54, 28) TEXA **34** 86-88, NYA **67/51** 88, **54** 88-89, **28** 89, MONN **54** 90

MOHR, DUSTAN OF/DH
(**17**,22) MINA **17** 01-03, SFN **22** 04, COLN **22** 05

MOISAN, BILL P
(**26**) CHIN **26** 53

MOLE, FENTON (MUSCLES) 1B
(18,**23**) NYA **18/23** 49

MOLINA, BENGIE C B
(38,63,5,**1**) ANAA **38** 98, **63** 99, **5** 00, **1** 00-04, LAA **1** 05

MOLINA, IZZY C
(21,**13**,31) OAKA **21** 96 , **13** 97-98, BALA **31** 02

MOLINA, GABE P
(45,**56**) BALA **45** 99-00, ATLN **56** 00, STLN **56** 02-03

MOLINA, JOSE C B
(19,**28**) CHIN **19** 99-00, ANAA **28** 01-04, LAA **28** 05

MOLINA, YADIER C B
(**41**) STLN **41** 04-05

MOLINARO, BOB OF/DH
(34,,**5**,9,29, 18,25,26) DETA **34** 75, 77, CHIA **5** 77-78, BALA **9** 79, CHIA **5** 80-81, CHIN **29** 82, PHIN **18** 82, **25** 83, DETA **37** 83

MOLITOR, PAUL (MOLLIE) 2B/3B/UTIL/DH/CH
(**4**,19) MILA **4** 78-92, TORA **19** 93-95, MINA **4** 96-98, *CH* **4** 00-01, SEAA *CH* **4** 04

MOLONEY, RICHIE P
(**48**) CHIA **48** 70

MONACO, BLAS 2B
(24,**7**) CLEA **24** 37, **7** 46

MONAHAN, RINTY P
(**34**) PHIA **34** 53

MONAHAN, SHANE OF
(**12**) SEAA **12** 98-99

MONBOUQUETTE, BILL (MOMBO) P/CH
(**27**,40,8,39, 56,28) BOSA **27** 58-65, DETA **27** 66-67, NYA **40** 67-68, SFN **8/39** 68, NYN *CH* **56** 82, NYA *CH* **28** 85

MONCHAK, AL SS/2B/CH
(**25**,35,43,42, 52) PHIN **25** 40, CHIA *CH* **35** 71-75, OAKA *CH* **43** 76, PITN *CH* **42** 77-84, ATLN *CH* **52** 86-88

MONDAY, RICK OF/1B
(28,**7**,16) KCA **28** 66-67, **7** 67, OAKA **7** 68-71, CHIN **7** 72-76, LAN **16** 77-84

MONDESI, RAUL OF
(**43**) LAN **43** 93-99, TORA **43** 00-02, NYA **43** 02-03, ARIN **43** 03, PITN **43** 04, ANAA **43** 04, ATLN **43** 05

MONEY, DON (BROOKS) SS/3B/UTIL
(5,16,**7**) PHIN **5** 68-69, **16** 70-72, MILA **7** 73-83

MONGE, SID P
(**43**,21,49,42, 45) CALA **43** 75-77, CLEA **43** 77-81, PHIN **21** 82, **49** 82-83, SDN **49** 83, **42** 83-84, DETA **42** 84

MONROE, CRAIG OF/DH
(**21**,27) TEXA **21** 01, DETA **27** 03-05

MONROE, LARRY P
(**41**) CHIA **41** 76

MONROE, ZACH P
(**55**) NYA **55** 58-59

MONTAGUE, ED SS/3B
(35,**7**) CLEA **35** 31, **7** 32

MONTAGUE, JOHN P
(53,**25**,24,39) MONN **53** 73-75, PHIN **25/24** 75, SEAA **25** 77-79, CALA **39** 79-80

MONTALVO, RAFAEL P
(**51**) HOUN **51** 86

MONTANEZ, WILLIE 1B/OF/DH
(10,33,27,22, **25**,24,5,14) CALA **10** 66, PHIN **33** 70, **27** 71-75, SFN **22** 75-76, ATLN **25** 76-77, NYN **25** 78-79, TEXA **24** 79, SDN **25** 80, MONN **5** 80-81, PITN **14** 81-82, PHIN **25** 82

MONTEAGUDO, AURELIO P S
(31,14,**34**,37, 45,17,21,41) KCA **31** 63-64, **14** 65, **34** 66, HOUN **37/34** 66, CHIA **45/17** 67, KCA **21** 70, CALA **41** 73

MONTEAGUDO, RENE P F
(__,**25**,17,22) WASA __ 38, **25** 40, **17** 44, PHIN **22** 45

MONTEFUSCO, JOHN (THE COUNT) P
(50,**26**,24,27) SFN **50** 74-75, **26** 75-80, ATLN **24**81, SDN **54** 82, **27** 82-83, NYA **24** 83-84, **26** 85-86

MONTEJO, MANNY P
(**24**) DETA **24** 61

MONTELEONE, RICH P
(19,44,**55**,45, 43,52) SEAA **19** 87, CALA **44** 88-89, NYA **55** 90, **45** 91, **55** 91-93, SFN **55** 94, CALA **43** 95-96, NYA *CH* **52** 02-04

MONTEMAYOR, FELIPE (MONTY) OF
(**14**) PITN **14** 53, 55

MONTGOMERY, AL C
(**27**) BOSN **27** 41

MONTGOMERY, BOB C/DH/UTIL
(39,**10**) BOSA **39** 70, **10** 70-79

MONTGOMERY, JEFF P
(40,**21**) CINN **40** 87, KCA **21** 88-99

MONTGOMERY, MONTY P
(43,**20**) KCA **43** 71, **20** 71-72

MONTGOMERY, RAY OF
(**21**,39) HOUN **21** 96 , **39** 97-98

MONTGOMERY, STEVE P
(**37**,53,57,27) OAKA **37** 96, **53** 97, PHIN **57** 99, SDN **27** 00

MONTOYA, CHARLIE 2B
(**25**) MONN **25** 93

MONTREUIL, AL 2B
(**29**) CHIN **29** 72

MONZANT, RAY P
(34,**41**) NYN **34** 54, **41** 55-57, SFN **41** 58-60

MONZON, DAN UTIL
(**14**) MINA **14** 72-73

MOOCK, JOE 3B
(**18**) NYN **18** 67

MOODY, ERIC P
(**45**) TEXA **45** 97

MOON, LEO (LEFTY) P
(**21**) CLEA **21** 32

MOON, WALLY OF/1B/CH
(20,**9**,6) STLN **20** 54-58, LAN **9** 59-65, SDN *CH* **6** 69

MOONEY, JIM P
(14,**21**,28) NYN **14** 32, STLN **21** 33, **28** 34

MOONEYHAM, BILL P
(**35**) OAKA **35** 86

MOORE, ALVIN (JUNIOR) UTIL
(17,**34**) CHIA **17** 78, **34** 79-80

MOORE, ANSE OF
(**20**) DETA **20** 46

MOORE, ARCHIE OF/1B
(**26**) NYA **26** 64-65

MOORE, BALOR P
(**15**,35,38) MONN **15** 70, 72-74, CALA **35** 77, TORA **38** 78-80

MOORE, BARRY P
(17,**25**,31,19) WASA **17** 65, **25** 66-69, CLEA **31** 70, CHIA **19** 70

MOORE, BILLY 1B/OF
(**14**) MONN **14** 86

Paul Molitor, with his short powerful swing, quietly and efficiently drove his statistics toward the Hall of Fame. He led the AL in runs scored three times, in hits three times, doubles once, triples once, had over 200 hits in a season four times and bypassed the coveted 3,000-hit plateau in 1996. He batted over .300 11 times with .353 in 1987 being his best.

MOORE, BOBBY P
(**34**) SFN **34** 85

MOORE, BOBBY OF
(**9**) KCA **9** 91

MOORE, BRAD P
(37,48,**46**) PHIN **37** 88, **48/46** 90

MOORE, CARLOS P
(**25**) WASA **25** 30

MOORE, CHARLIE C/UTIL/DH
(**22**,21) MILA **22** 73-86, TORA **21** 87

MOORE, CY P
(24,**23**,48) BKNN **24** 32, PHIN **23** 33, **48** 34

MOORE, DEE P/C/UTIL
(27,**1**,10.46) CINN **27** 36, **1** 37, BKNN **27** 43, PHIN **10** 43, **46** 46

MOORE, DONNIE P
(49,33,26,27, 31,**37**) CHIN **49** 75, 77-79, STLN **33** 80, MILA **26/27** 81, ATLN **33/31** 82-84, CALA **37** 85-88

MOORE, EDDIE INF
(**3**,26) NYN **3** 32, CLEA **26** 34

MOORE, EUEL (CHIEF) P
(**43**,15,45) PHIN **43** 34-35, NYN **15** 35, PHIN **45** 36

MOORE, GARY OF/1B
(**31**) LAN **31** 70

MOORE, GENE (ROWDY) OF/1B
(21,24,10,**1**, 31,3,8,44,__, 15) STLN **21** 33, **24** 34, **10** 35, BOSN **1** 36-38, BKNN **1** 39, **31** 40, BOSN **3** 40, **8** 40-41, WASA __ 42, **44/24** 43, STLA **15** 44-45

MOORE, JACKIE C/CH/M
(**35**,24,30,42, 43,45,4,47) DETA **35** 65, MILA *CH* **24** 70, *CH* **30** 70-72, TEXA *CH* **42** 73-76,TORA *CH* **42** 77-79, TEXA *CH* **43** 80, OAKA *CH* **45** 81-82, *CH* **42** 83-84, *M* **42** 84-86, MONN*CH* **42** 87-89, CINN *CH* **4** 90-92, TEXA *CH* **42** 93-94, COLN *CH* **47** 96-97, *CH* **4** 98

MOORE, JIM P
(**23**,46) CHIA **23** 31, **46** 32

MOORE, JIMMY OF
(**25**) PHIA **25** 31

MOORE, JO-JO (THE GAUSE GHOST) OF
(2,**1**,5,3,21) NYN **2** 32, **1** 33-36, **5** 37, **1** 38, **3** 39, **1** 40, **23** 41

MOORE, JOHNNY OF
(4,5,10,**33**,38) CHIN **4/5** 32, CINN **5** 33, **10** 34, PHIN **33** 34-37, CHIN **38** 45

MOORE, JUNIOR UTIL
(48,**14**) ATLN **48** 76, **14** 77

MOORE, KELVIN 1B
(24,**25**) OAKA **24** 81, **25** 82-83

MOORE, KERWIN OF
(**45**) OAKA **45** 96

MOORE, MARCUS P
(54,**53**) COLN **54** 93-94, CINN **53** 96

MOORE, MIKE P
(25,23,**21**) SEAA **25** 82-88, OAKA **23** 89, **21** 89-92, DETA **21** 93-95

MOORE, RANDY OF/1B/C/UTIL
(20,4,**7**,24,10, 22) BOSN **20** 32, **4** 33-34, **7** 35, BKNN **24** 36, **10** 37, STLN **22** 37

MOORE, RAY (FARMER) P
(45,48,**29**,21) BKNN **45** 52, **48** 53, BALA **29** 55-57, CHIA **29** 58-60, WASA **21** 60, MINA **21** 61-63

MOORE, TERRY OF/PCH/M
(11,2,**8**,34) STLN **11** 35-37, **2** 38, **8** 39-42, 46-48, *CH* **8** 50-52, PHIN *M* **8** 54, STLN *CH* **34** 56-58

MOORE, TOMMY P
(40,39,**27**,19 28,20) NYN **40/19** 72, **39** 73, STLN **27** 75, TEXA **27/28** 75, SEAA **20** 77

MOORE, TREY P
(**29**) MONN **29** 98, (99), ATLN **50** 00

MOORE, WHITEY P
(**35**,36,60) CINN **35** 36, **36** 37, **60** 38, **35** 39-42, STLN **35** 42

MOORE, WILCY (CY) P
(18,26,31,19, **16**) NYA **18** 29, BOSA **26/31** 31, **19** 32, NYA **16** 32-33

MOORHEAD, BOB P
(22,**21**) NYN **22** 62, **21** 65

MOOSE, BOB P
(**38**) PITN **38** 67-76

MOOTY, JAKE P
(39,26,**25**,33, 5) CINN **39** 36, **26** 37, CHIN **25** 40-42, **33** 43, DETA **5** 44

MORA, ANDRES DH/OF/UTIL
(**27**,26) BALA **27** 76-78, CLEA **26** 80

MORA, MELVIN 3B
(**6**) NYN **6** 99-00, BALA **6** 00-05

MORAGA, DAVID P
(**6**) MONN **48** 00, COLN **31** 00

MORALES, JERRY OF/3B/CH
(32,**24**,25,27, 28) SDN **32** 69-73, CHIN **24** 74-77, STLN **25** 78, DETA **27** 79, NYN **25** 80, CHIN **24** 81-83, MONN *CH* **28** 02-04

MORALES, JOSE DH/C/UTIL/1B/CH
(35,58,**34**,43, 28,32) OAKA **35** 73, MONN **58** 73-74, **34** 74-77, MINA **34** 78-80, BALA **34** 81-82, LAN **43** 82-84, SFN *CH* **28** 86-88, CLEA *CH* **32** 90, *CH* **34** 90-93, FLAN *CH* **43** 95, FLAN *CH* **34** 96

MORALES, RICH SS/2B/INF/CH
(**17**,2,**30**,6, 55) CHIA **17** 67, **2** 68-70, **30** 71-73, SDN **6** 73-74, ATLN *CH* **55** 86-87

MORALES, WILLIE C
(**13**), BALA **13** 00

MORAN, AL SS/3B
(**40**) NYN **40** 63-64

MORAN, BILL (BUGS) P
(**34**) CHIA **34** 74

MORAN, BILLY 2B/SS/INF
(16,18,**12**,11) CLEA **16** 58 , **18** 59, LAA **12** 61-64, CLEA **11** 64-65

MORAN, HIKER P
(**26**) BOSN **26** 38-39

MORANDINI, MICKEY 2B
(**12** ,1) PHIN **12** 90-97, CHIN **12** 98-99, PHIN **12** 00, TORA **1** 00

MORBAN, JOSE INF
(**12**) BALA **12** 03

MORDECAI, MIKE SS/OF
(19,**16**,15,12) ATLN **19** 94, **16** 95-97, MONN **15** 98, **12** 99-02, FLAN **12** 02-05

MOREHEAD, DAVE (MOE) P
(23,37,**17**) BOSA **23** 63-66, **37** 67-68, **17** 67-68, KCA **17** 69-70

MOREHEAD, SETH (MOE) P
(**44**,38,19) PHIN **44** 57-59, CHIN **38** 59-60, MILN **19** 61

MOREJON, DAN OF
(**45**) CINN **45** 58

MOREL, RAMON P
(**55**,33) PITN **55** 95-97, CHIN **33** 97

MORELAND, KEITH (ZONK) C/OF/INF/DH
(34,24,**6**,7,30) PHIN **34** 78-79, **24** 79-80, **6** 80-81, CHIN **6** 82-87, SDN **6/7** 88, DETA **30** 89, BALA **6** 89

MORENO, ANGEL P
(47,6,**21**) CALA **47/6** 81, **21** 81-82

MORENO, JOSE 2B/3B/0F/DH
(**22**,14,31) NYN **22** 80, SDN **14** 81, CALA **31** 82

MORENO, JUAN P
(**45**) TEXA **52/41** 01, SDN **43** 02

MORENO, JULIO P
(33,19,**23**) WASA **19/33** 50, **23** 51-53

MORENO, OMAR OF/DH
(24,**18**,22,28) PITN **24** 75, **18** 76-82, HOUN **24** 83, NYA **22** 83-85, KCA **28** 85, ATLN **18** 86

MORENO, ORBER P
(45,**49**) KCA **45** 99, (00), **49** 03, NYN **49** 04

MORET, ROGER P
(**29**,46,14,42) BOSA **29** 70-75, ATLN **46/14** 76, TEXA **42** 77, **29** 77-78

MORGAN, BOBBY 3B/SS/INF
(**2**,4,42,3,12) BKNN **2** 50, 52-53, PHIN **4** 54-56, STLN **42** 56, PHIN **3** 57, CHIN **12** 57-58

MORGAN, CHET (CHICK) OF
(27,**25**) DETA **27** 35, **25** 38

MORGAN, ED 1B
(**33**,3) CLEA **33** 31-33, BOSA **3** 34

MORGAN, EDDIE (PEPPER) OF/1B
(30,27,31) STLN **30** 36, BKNN **27** 37, **31** 38

MORGAN, JOE 2B/OF/3B/DH
(12,35,28,**8**) HOUN **12** 63, **35** 64, **18** 65-71, CINN **8** 72-79, HOUN **8** 80, SFN **8** 81-82, PHIN **8** 83, OAKA **8** 84

MORGAN, JOE 2B/3B/OF/CH/M
(19,10,1,**4**,45, 35) MILN **19** 59, KCA **10** 59, PHIN **1** 60, CLEA **4** 60-61, STLN **10** 64, PITN *CH* **45** 72, BOSA *CH* **35** 85-88, *M* **35** 88-91

MORGAN, KEVIN 3B
(**10**) NYN **10** 97

MORGAN, MIKE P
(15,63,39,30, 35,16,14,12, **36**,31,38) OAKA **15** 78-79, NYA **63/39** 82, TORA **30** 83, SEAA **35** 85-86, **16** 87, BALA **14/12** 88, LAN **36** 89-91, CHIN **36** 92-95, STLN **36** 95-96, CINN **31** 96, **36** 97, MINA **30** 98, CHIN **38** 98, TEXA **36** 99, ARIN **36** 00-02

MORGAN, TOM (PLOWBOY) P
(52,**28**,17,18, 47,27,29,42) NYA **52** 51, **28** 51-52, 54-56, KCA **17** 57, DETA **18** 58-60, WASA **18** 60, LAA **47** 61-63, *INSTR* **47** 64, CALA *CH* **27** 72-74, SDN *CH* **29** 75, NYA *CH* **42** 79, CALA *CH* **47** 81-83

MORGAN, VERN 3B/CH
(30,**5**,44) CHIN **30** 54, **5** 55, MINA *CH* **44** 69-75

MORHARDT, MOE 1B
(25,**11**) CHIN **25** 61, **11** 62

MORIARTY, ED 2B
(__,**30**) BOSN __ 35, **30** 36

MORIARTY, MIKE INF
(**11**) BALA **11** 02

MORLAN, JOHN P
(32,**12**) PITN **32** 73, **12** 73-74

MORMAN, ALVIN P
(**51**,52) HOUN **51** 96, CLEA **51** 97-98, SFN **52** 98, KCA **51** 99

MORMAN, RUSS 1B/UTIL
(14,**45**,43) CHIA **14** 86, 88-89, **26** 89, KCA **45** 90-91, FLAN **43** 94, **45** 95-96, **43** 97

MORNEAU, JUSTIN DH/1B
(**27**) MINA **27** 03-05

MOROGIELLO, DAN P
(**21**) BALA **21** 83

MORONKO, JEFF 3B/UTIL/DH
(11,36) CLEA **11** 84, NYA **36** 87

MORRIS, DANNY P
(**27**,24) MINA **27** 68, **24** 69

MORRIS, DOYT OF
(**10**) PHIA **10** 37

MORRIS, ED (BIG ED) P
(**23**) BOSA **23** 31

MORRIS, HAL OF/DH/1B
(62,38,28,22, **23**,9) NYA **62/38** 88, **28/22/21** 89, CINN **23** 90-97, KCA **23** 98, CINN **9** 99, **23** 00, DETA **25** 00

MORRIS, JACK P
(**47**) DETA **47** 77-90, MINA **47** 91, TORA **47** 92-93, CLEA **47** 94

MORRIS, JIM P
(**63**) TBA **63** 99-00

MORRIS, JOHN P
(27,37,**35**,38, 42,43), PHIN **27** 66, BALA **37** 68, SEAA **35** 69, MILA **35** 70-71, SFN **38/42** 72, **43** 73-74

MORRIS, JOHN OF
(**33**) STLN **33** 86-90, PHIN **33** 91, CALA **33** 92

MORRIS, MATT P
(**35**) STLN **35** 97-98, (99), 01-05

MORRIS, WARREN 2B
(**30**,36,24) PITN **30** 99 -01, MINA **36** 02, DETA **24** 03

MORRISON, JIM 3B/INF/UTIL/DH/P
(15,30,16,12, **2**,9,17,27) PHIN **15** 77, **30** 77-78, **16/15** 78, CHIA **12** 79-82, PITN **2** 82-87, DETA **9** 87, **17** 87-88, ATLN **27** 88

MORRISSEY, JO-JO 2B/INF/UTIL
(**2**,27) CINN **24** 32, **2** 33, CHIA **27** 36

MORSE, MIKE SS
(**12**) SEAA **12** 05

MORTON, BUBBA OF/1B/3B
(40,31,10,**27**) DETA **40** 61-63, MILA **31** 63, CALA **10** 66, **27** 67-69

MORTON, CARL P
(**44**,49) MONN **44** 69-72, ATLN **49** 73-76

MORTON, GUY (MOOSE) PH S
(**39**) BOSA **39** 54

MORTON, KEVIN P
(**43**) BOSA **43** 91

MORYN, WALT (MOOSE) OF
(40,43,**7**,42, 28,20) BKNN **40** 54-55, CHIN **43** 56-58, **7** 58-60, STLN **42** 60, **28** 60-61, PITN **20** 61

MOSCHITTO, ROSS OF
(**53**) NYA **53** 65, 67

MOSEBY, LLOYD OF/DH/CH
(**15**,17,16) TORA **15** 80-89, DETA **17** 90, **15** 90-91, TORA *CH* **16** 99

MOSER, ARNIE PH
(**26**) CINN **26** 37

MOSES, JERRY C/OF/1B/DH
(41,**10**,19,23, 12,17,11) BOSA **41** 65, **10** 68-70, CALA **19/10** 71, CLEA **10** 72, NYA **23** 73, DETA **12** 74, SDN **17** 75, CHIA **11** 75

MOSES, JOHN 1B/DH/OF/UTIL/P/CH
(**26**,1,**8**,6,25) SEAA **26** 82-87, MINA **1** 88-90, DETA **8** 91, SEAA **6** 92, *CH* **25** 97-98, **12** 00-03, CINN *CH* **32** 05

MOSES, WALLY OF/CH
(19,9,**1**,24,2, 28,32,3,36, 51) PHIA **19** 35, **9** 36-37, **1** 38-41, CHIA **9** 42-46, BOSA **24** 46-48, PHIA **2** 49-51, *CH* **28** 52-54, PHIN *CH* **32** 55-58, CINN *CH* **3** 59-60, NYA *CH* **36** 61-62, 66, DETA *CH* **51** 67-70

MOSKAU, PAUL P
(**31**,41,37) CINN **31** 77-81, PITN **41** 82, CHIN **37** 83

MOSOLF, JIM OF
(**31**) CHIN **31** 33

MOSQUERA, JULIO C
(**46**,29) TORA **46** 96-97, MILN **29** 05

MOSS, CHARLIE C
(10,27,**12**) PHIA **10** 34, **27** 35, **12** 36

MOSS, DAMIAN P
(61,**27**,28) ATLN **61** 01, **27** 01-02, SFN **28** 03, BALA **28** 03

MOSS, HOWIE OF/3B
(19,21,40,**8**) NYN **19** 42, CINN **21** 46, CLEA **40/8** 46

MOSS, LES C/CH/M
(23,**10**,14,12, 33,35,28,6, 55) STLA **23** 46, **10** 47-51, BOSA **14** 51, STLA **10** 52-53, BALA **10** 54-55, CHIA **12** 55-58, *CH* **33** 67-68, *M* **33** 68, *CH* **35** 69-70, DETA *M* **28** 79, CHIN *CH* **6** 81, HOUN *CH* **55** 82-89

MOSSI, DON (THE SPHINX) P
(**12**,15,41,43) CLEA **12** 54-58, DETA **15** 59-63, CHIA **41** 64, KCA **43** 65

MOSSOR, EARL P
(**16**) BKNN **16** 51

MOTA, ANDY 2B S,B
(**23**) HOUN **23** 91

MOTA, DANNY P
(**52**) MINA **52** 00

MOTA, GUILLERMO P
(40,**59**) MONN **40** 99-01, LAN **59** 02-04, FLAN **59** 04-05

MOTA, JOSE 2B/SS S,B
(15,**40**) SDN **15** 91, KCA **40** 95

MOTA, MANNY OF/UTIL/PH/CH F
(38,15,**11**) SFN **38** 62, PITN **15** 63-68, MONN **15** 69, LAN **11** 69-80, 8[illegible] -83, *CH* **11** 80-89, 92-93, 96-05

MOTLEY, DARRYL OF/DH
(4,49,**24**,6) KCA **4** 81, **49** 83, **24** 84-86, ATLN **6** 86-87

MOTT, BITSY SS/INF
(**1**) PHIN **1** 45

MOTTOLA, CHAD OF
(54,15,**22**,27, 39) CINN **54** 96, TORA **15/22** 00, FLAN **27** 01, BALA **39** 04

MOTTON, CURT OF/DH/CH
(**21**,6,43,47) BALA **21** 67-71, MILA **21** 72, CALA **6** 72, BALA **43** 73-74, **21** 74, *CH* **47** 90-91

MOULDER, GLEN P
(__,**23**,38) BKNN __ 46, STLA **23** 47, CHIA **38** 48

MOUNCE, TONY P
(47,**43**) TEXA **47/43** 03

MOUTON, JAMES OF
(18,**6**,7,24) HOUN **18** 94-95, **6** 95-97, SDN **7** 98, MONN **24** 99, MILN **24** 0[illegible] -01

MOUTON, LYLE OF
(**28**,32,34) CHIA **28** 95-97, BALA **32** 98, MILN **34** 99, **33** 00, FLAN **4** 01

MOWRY, JOE OF/2B
(**10**,23,19) BOSN **10** 33, **23** 34, **19/10** 35

MOYER, JAMIE P
(49,39,41,51, **50**) CHIN **49** 86-88, TEXA **39** 89-90 STLN **41** 91, BALA **51** 93-95 BOSA **50** 96, SEAA **50** 96-05

MOZZALLI, MO CH
(**4**) STLN *CH* **4** 77-78

MR. RED LOGO
(**27**) CINN **27** 68-87

MROZINSKI, RON P
(**27**) PHIN **27** 54-55

MUDROCK, PAUL P
(**33**) CHIN **33** 63

MUELLER, BILL (HAWK) OF
(12,**34**) CHIA **12** 42, **34** 45

MUELLER, BILL 3B/2B
(**32**,33,11) SFN **32** 96-00, CHIN **33** 01-02, SFN **32** 02, BOSA **11** 03-05

MUELLER, DON (MANDRAKE THE MAGICIAN OF
(**22**,32) NYN **22** 48-57, CHIA **32** 58-59

MUELLER, EMMETT (HEINIE) 2B/3B/UTIL
(9,21,**31**) PHIN **9** 38, **21** 39-40, **31** 40-41 **21** 41

MUELLER, GORDIE P
(**25**) BOSA **25** 50

MUELLER, HEINIE 1B/OF
(9,**20**) STLN **9** 23, **7** 24, STLA **20** 35

MUELLER, LES P
(27,**15**) DETA **27** 41, **15** 45

MUELLER, RAY (IRON MAN) C/CH
(22,20,10,30, 14,**7**,8,1,9,2, 5) BOSN **22** 35, **20** 36, **10** 37-38, PITN **30** 39, **14** 40, CINN **7** 43-44, 46-49, NYN **8** 49, **7** 50, PITN **9** 50, BOSN **8/1** 51, NYN*CH* **2** 56, CHIN *CH* **22** 57, CLEA *CH* **5** 66

MUELLER, WILLIE P
(40,49,51,**42**) MILN **40/49** 78, **51/42** 81

MUFFETT, BILLY (MUFF) P/CH
(38,22,**36**,4, 66,26,24,52) STLN **38** 57-58, **22** 58, SFN **36** 59, BOSA **36** 60-62, STLN *CH* **4** 67-70, CALA *CH* **66** 74, **26** 74-76, *CH* **24** 77, DETA *CH* **52** 85, **56** 85-94

MUIR, JOE P
(31,**30**) PITN **31** 51, **30** 52

MULCAHY, HUGH (LOSING PITCHER) P
(40,42,15,**9**, 17,48,19,33) PHIN **42** 35, **40** 36, **42** 37, **15** 38, **9** 39-40, **17** 45, **48** 46, PITN **19** 47, CHIA *CH* **33** 70

MULDER, MARK P
(**20**,30) OAKA **20** 00-04, STLN **30** 05

MULHOLLAND, TERRY P
(52,**45**,40,46) SFN **52/45** 86, **45** 88-89, PHIN **40** 89, **45** 89-93, NYA **46** 94, SFN **46/45** 95, PHIN **45** 96, SEAA **45** 96, CHIN **45** 97, SFN **45** 97, CHIN **45** 98-99, ATLN **43** 99, **45** 99-00, PITN **45** 01, LAN **45** 01-02, CLEA **45** 02-03, MINA **46** 04, **45** 04-05

MULL, JACK CH
(**42**) SFN *CH* **42** 85

MULLEAVY, GREG (MOE) 2B/CH
(35,49,**2**,51, 31) CHIA **35/49** 32, BOSA **2** 33, BKNN *CH* **51** 57, LAN *CH* **31** 5[illegible] -60, 62-64

MULLEN, MOON 2B/UTIL
(17,**1**) PHIN **17/1** 44

MULLEN, SCOTT P
(**57**,49) KCA **57** 00-03, LAN **49** 03

MULLER, FREDDIE 2B/3B
(23,**21**) BOSA **23** 33, **21** 34

MULLIGAN, DICK P
(__,10,31,**32**) WASA __ 41, PHIN **10** 46, BOSN **31** 46, **32** 47

MULLIGAN, JOE (BIG JOE) P
(**14**) BOSA **14** 34

MULLIGAN, SEAN C
(**59**) SDN **59** 96

MULLIN, PAT OF/CH
(17,27,18,33, **6**,34,52,4,58, 39) DETA **17** 40, **27/18** 41, **33** 46, **6** 47-53, *CH* **52** 62, *CH* **34** 63, *CH* **52** 64-66, CLEA *CH* **4** 67, MONN *CH* **58** 79, *CH* **39** 80-81

MULLINIKS, RANCE SS/INF/UTIL/DH
(18,**5**) CALA **18** 77-79, KCA **18** 80-81, TORA **5** 82-92

MULLINS, FRAN 3B/INF/UTIL
(26,16,**22**) CHIA **26** 80, SFN **16** 84, CLEA **22** 86

MULLINS, GREGORY P
(**57**) MILN **57** 98

MUMPHREY, JERRY OF
(48,29,28,**22**) STLN **48** 74, **29** 74-79, SDN **28** 80, NYA **22** 81-83, HOUN **28** 83-85, CHIN **22** 86-88

MUNCRIEF, BOB P
(__,13,**29**,44, 25,40,27,11, 18) STLA __ 37, **13** 39, **29** 41-42, **29** 43-46, **44** 47, CLEA **25** 48, PITN **40/27** 49, CHIN **11** 49, NYA **18** 51

MUNGER, GEORGE (RED) P
(18,39,**20**,19) STLN **18** 43-44, **39** 46-47, **20** 46-49, **39** 49, **20** 50-52, PITN **19** 52, **20** 56

MUNGO, VAN LINGLE P/CH
(**16**,20,17) BKNN **16** 32-41, *CH* **16** 40-41, NYN **20** 42, **17** 43, **16** 45

MUNIZ, MANNY P
(**29**) PHIN **29** 71

MUNNINGHOFF, SCOTT P
(**34**) PHIN **34** 80

MUNNS, LES (BIG ED) (NEMO) P
(**25**,24) BKNN **25** 34-35, STLN **24** 36

MUNOZ, ARNIE P
(**49**) CHIA **49** 04

MUNOZ, BOBBY P
(54,**35**,32,46) NYA **54** 93, PHIN **35** 94-97, BALA **32** 98, MONN **46** 01

MUNOZ, JOSE 2B
(**71**) CHIA **71** 96-97

MUNOZ, MIKE P
(56,**43**,51) LAN **56** 89-90, DETA **43** 91-93, COLN **43** 93-98, TEXA **51** 99

MUNOZ, NOE C
(45,**36**) COLN **45/36** 95

MUNOZ, OSCAR P
(99,**55**) MINA **99/55** 95

MUNOZ, PEDRO OF/DH
(**5**) MINA **5** 90-96

MUNRO, PETER P
(69,**13**,53) TORA **69** 99, **13** 99-00, HOUN **53** 02-04

MUNSON, ERIC 1B/C/DH
(35,50,33,**31**, 24) DETA **35** 00, **50** 01, **33** 02, **31** 03-04, TBA **24** 05

MUNSON, THURMAN C/OF/UTIL/DH
(**15**) NYA **15** 69-79

MUNTER, SCOTT P
(**54**) SFN **54** 05

MURA, STEVE P
(59,**27**,38,43, 36) SDN **59** 78-79, **27** 79-81, STLN **38** 82, CHIA **43** 83, OAKA **36** 85

MURAKAMI, MASANORI P
(10,37) SFN **10** 64, **37** 65

MURCER, BOBBY SS/OF/3B/DH
(17,**1**,20,7,2, 39) NYA **17** 65-66, **1** 69-74, SFN **20** 75-76, CHIN **7** 77-79, NYA **2** 79-83, *CH* **39** 87

MURFF, RED P
(**19**) MILN **19** 56-57

MURPHY, BILLY OF
(**23**) NYN **23** 66

MURPHY, DALE C/1B/OF
(**3**) ATLN **3** 76-90, PHIN **3** 90-92, COLN **3** 93

MURPHY, DAN P
(**39**) SDN **39** 89

MURPHY, DANNY OF/P
(20,42,**27**,24) CHIN **20/42** 60, **27** 61-62, CHIA **24** 69-70

MURPHY, DICK PH
(**19**) CINN **19** 54-55

MURPHY, DONNIE 2B
(**31**) KCA **31** 04-05

MURPHY, DWAYNE OF/DH/UTIL/CH
(36,**21**,40,6) OAKA **36** 78-79, **21** 79-87, DETA **40** 88, PHIN **6** 89, ARIN *CH* **21** 98-03

MURPHY, ED 1B
(**14**) PHIN **14** 42

MURPHY, JOHNNY (GRANDMA)(FIREMAN) (FORDHAM JOHNNY) P
(20,**19**,29,38) NYA **20** 32, **19** 34-43, **29/19** 46, BOSA **38** 47

MURPHY, ROB P
(54,**46**,47,34, 44) CINN **54** 85, **46** 85-88, BOSA **47** 89-90, SEAA **46** 91, HOUN **47** 92, STLN **46** 93-94, NYA **34** 94, LAN **46** 95, FLAN **44** 95

MURPHY, TOM P
(49,46,**41**,29, 34,36,42,47, 45) 77, CALA **49/46/41** 68, **41** 69-72, KCA **29** 72, STLN **34/36** 73, MILA **42** 74-76, BOSA **47** 76-77, TORA **45** 77-79

MURPHY, WALTER P
(**29**) BOSA **29** 31

MURRAY, AMBY P
(**26**) BOSN **26** 36

MURRAY, CALVIN OF
(**8**,21,17) SFN **8** 99-02, TEXA **21** 02, CHIN **17** 04

MURRAY, DALE P
(**27**,37,22,29, 33,48,31) MONN **27** 74-76, CINN **37** 77-78, NYN **22** 78-79, MONN **29** 79-80, TORA **33** 81-82, NYA **48** 83-85, TEXA **31** 85

MURRAY, DAN P
(**48**,57) NYN **48** 99, KCA **57** 99, **36** 00

MURRAY, EDDIE 1B/DH/UTIL/CH
(**33**) BALA **33** 77-88, LAN **33** 89-91, NYN **33** 92-93, CLEA **33** 94-96, BALA **33** 96, ANAA **33** 97, LAN **33** 97, CLEA *CH* **33** 02-05

MURRAY, GEORGE (SMILER) P
(**35**) CHIA **35** 33

MURRAY, GLENN OF
(**7**) PHIN **7** 96

MURRAY, HEATH P
(48,**27**,35,18, 58) SDN **48** 97, **27** 99, DETA **35/18** 01, CLEA **58** 02

MURRAY, JOE P
(**21**) PHIA **21** 50

MURRAY, LARRY OF/UTIL
(18,52,47,**20**) NYA **18** 74, **52** 75, **47** 76, OAKA **20** 78-79

MURRAY, MATT P
(**34**,45) ATLN **34** 95, BOSA **45** 95

MURRAY, RAY (DEACON) C
(15,35,12,**14**, 9) CLEA **15** 48, **35** 50, **12** 50-51, PHIA **14** 51-53, BALA **9/14** 54

MURRAY, RICH 1B
(**29**,25) SFN **29** 80, **25** 83

MURRELL, IVAN OF/1B
(23,25,**20**,14, 18) HOUN **23** 63, **25** 64, **20** 67-68, SDN **20** 69-72, **14** 73, ATLN **18** 74

MURTAUGH, DANNY 2B/SS/INF/CH/M
(16,27,1,9,15, **7**,40) PHIN **16** 41, **27** 42, **1** 43, **9** 46, BOSN **15** 47, PITN **7** 48-51, *CH* **40** 56-57, *M* **40** 57-64, 67, 70-71, 73-76

MURTON, MATT OF
(**19**) CHIN **19** 05

MUSER, TONY 1B/OF/UTIL/DH/CH/M
(43,5,**25**,34, 16,35,40) BOSA **43** 69, CHIA **5** 71-72, **25** 73-75, BALA **34** 75, **16** 75-77, MILA **5** 78, *CH* **35** 85-89, CHIN *CH* **40** 93-97, KCA *M* **40** 97-99, 02, SDN *CH* **40** 03-05

MUSGRAVES, DENNIS P
(41,36,**34**) NYN **41/36/34** 65

MUSIAL, STAN (THE MAN)(STASH) OF/1B/P
(**6**) STLN **6** 41-44, 46-63

MUSSELMAN, JEFF P
(35,**13**) TORA **35** 86-87, **13** 87-89, NYN **13** 89-90

MUSSELMAN, RON P
(35,**30**) SEAA **35** 82, TORA **30** 84-85

MUSSER, DANNY 3B
(__) WASA __ 32

MUSSILL, BARNEY P
(29,**27**) PHIN **29/27** 44

MUSSINA, MIKE (MOOSE) P
(42,**35**) BALA **42** 91, **35** 92-00, NYA **35** 01-05

MUSTAIKIS, ALEX P
(**28**) BOSA **28** 40

MUTIS, JEFF P
(**50**,36,47) CLEA **50** 91-93, **36** 93, FLAN **47** 94

MYATT, GEORGE (MERCURY)(FOGHORN) (STUD) SS/3B/INF/UTIL/CH/M
(7,19,1,43,28, **24**,53,34,52, 8,1,47,2) NYN **7** 38, **19/1** 39, WASA **43/28** 43, **24** 44-47, *CH* **53** 50-54, CHIA *CH* **34** 55-56, CHIN *CH* **52** 57-58, *CH* **34** 58-59, MILN *CH* **8** 60-61, DETA *CH* **34** 62-63, PHIN *CH* **1** 64-68, *M* **1** 68, *CH/M* **47** 69, *CH* **2** 70-72

MYATT, GLENN C
(**9**,16) CLEA **9** 31-35, NYN **9** 35, DETA **16** 36

MYER, BUDDY 2B/OF
(**1**) WASA **1** 31-41

MYERS, BILLY SS/2B
(**5**,39,12,10) CINN **5** 35-37, **39** 38, **12** 39-40, CHIN **5/10** 41

MYERS, BRETT P
(41,**39**) PHIN **41** 02, **39** 03-05

MYERS, DAVE CH
(**31**) SEAA *CH* **31** 01-04

MYERS, GREG C/DH
(52,16,21,**11**, 24,48,20,28) TORA **52** 87, **16** 89, **21** 90-92, CALA **21** 92, **11** 93-95, MINA **24** 96-97, ATLN **48** 97, SDN **20** 98-99, ATLN **28** 99, BALA **37** 00-01, OAKA **24** 01, **28** 01-02, TORA **28** 03-05

MYERS, HY OF
(7,**9**) STLN **7** 23, **9** 24

MYERS, JIMMY P
(48,**46**) BALA **48** 95, **46** 96

MYERS, LYNN SS/INF
(22,**1**) STLN **22** 38, **1** 39

MYERS, MIKE P
(32,27,**28**,35, 53,36) FLAN **32** 95, DETA **27** 95-97, MILN **28** 98-99, COLN **28** 00-01, ARIN **35** 02-03, SEAA **53** 04, BOSA **36** 04-05

MYERS, RANDY P
(48,**28**,18) NYN **48** 85-89, CINN **28** 90-91, SDN **28** 92, CHIN **28** 93-96, BALA **28** 97, TORA **28** 98, SDN **18** 98, **48** (99-00)

MYERS, RICHIE PH
(**10**) CHIN **10** 56

MYERS, ROD OF
(58,**31**) KCA **58** 96, **31** 97

MYERS, RODNEY P
(59,66,**46**,58) CHIN **59** 96-99, SDN **66** 00-01, **46** 02, LAN **58** 03, **46** 04

MYETT, AARON P
(62,**38**,39) CHIA **62** 99, **38** 00, TEXA **39** 01, **38** 02, CLEA **38** 03, CINN **56** 04

MYRICK, BOB P
(**44**) NYN **44** 76-78

MYROW, BRIAN INF
(**52**) LAN **52** 05

N

NABHOLZ, CHRIS P
(**43**,49,53) MONN **43** 90-93, CLEA **43** 94, BOSA **49** 94, CHIN **53** 95

NADY, XAVIER 3B/OF/1B
(**22**) SDN **22** 00, 03-05

NAEHRING, TIM 3B/INF/UTIL/DH
(**11**) BOSA **11** 90-97

NAGEL, BILL INF/P
(34,24,9,**7**) PHIA **34** 39, PHIN **24/9** 41, CHIA **7** 45

NAGELSON, RUSS OF/1B
(**25**,31) CLEA **25** 68-70, DETA **31** 70

NAGEOTTE, CLINT P
(**37**) SEAA **37** 04-05

NAGY, CHARLES P
(**41**) CLEA **41** 90-02, SDN **39** 03

NAGY, MIKE P
(**15**,49,45,31) BOSA **15** 69-72, STLN **49** 73, HOUN **45/31** 74

NAGY, STEVE P
(28,**22**) PITN **28** 47, WASA **22** 50

NAHEM, SAM (SUBWAY SAM) P
(__,37,**18**) BKNN __ 38, STLN **37** 41, PHIN **18** 42, **18** 48

NAHORODNY, BILL C/1B/UTIL/DH
(9,20,**15**,18, 6) PHIN **9** 76, CHIA **20** 77, **15** 78-79, ATLN **15** 80-81, CLEA **15** 82, DETA **18** 83, SEAA **6** 84

NAKAMURA, MIKE P
(59,**57**,53) MINA **59/57** 03, TORA **53** 04

NAKAMURA, NORIHIRO 3B
(**66**) LAN **66** 05

NAKTENIS, PETE P
(**15**,38) PHIA **15** 36, CINN **38** 39

NANCE, SHANE P
(**47**) MILN **47** 02-03, ARIN **40** 04

NAPLES, AL SS
(**3**) STLA **3** 49

NAPOLEON, DANNY OF/3B
(**16**) NYN **16** 65-66

NAPOLEON, ED CH
(**1**,46,5,50,12) CLEA *CH* **1** 83-85, KCA *CH* **46** 87-88, HOUN *CH* **5** 89-90, NYA *CH* **50** 92-93, TEXA *CH* **12** 95-00

NARAGON, HAL (BO) C/CH
(23,**18**,8,51, 52) CLEA **23** 51, **18** 54-59, WASA **8** 59-60, MINA **8** 61-62, *CH* **51** 63-66, DETA *CH* **52** 67-69

NARANJO, CHOLLY P
(**27**) PITA **26** 56

NARLESKI, RAY P
(**20**,16) CLEA **20** 54-58, DETA **16** 59

NARRON, JERRY C/1B/UTIL/DH/CH/M
(38,3,**34**,31, 11,5,41,50) NYA **38** 79, SEAA **3** 80-81, CALA **34** 83-86, SEAA **38** 87, BALA *CH* **31** 93-94, *CH* **34** 94, TEXA *CH* **11** 95, **5** 95-02, *M* **5** 02, BOSA *CH* **41** 03, CINN *CH* **50** 04, **41** 05, *M* **41** 05

NARRON, SAM C/CH
(33,**32**,43) STLN **33** 35, **32** 42-43, PITN *CH* **43** 51-64

NARRON, SAM P
(**49**) TEXA **49** 04

NARUM, BUSTER P
(35,34,**20**,28, 38) BALA **35** 63, WASA **35/34** 64, **20** 65-66, **28/38** 67

NASH, COTTON 1B/OF
(50,34,**40**) CHIA **50** 67, MINA **34** 69, **40** 70

NASH, JIM P
(33,30,24,**23**, 42) KCA **33** 66, **30** 67, OAKA **30** 68-69, ATLN **24** 70, **23** 70-72, PHIN **42/23** 72

NATAL, BOB C/CH
(**13**,16) MONN **13** 92, FLAN **13** 93-97, MONN *CH* **13** 02-04, WASN *CH* **16** 05

NATHAN, JOE P
(**36**) SFN **36** 99-00, 02-03, MINA **36** 04-05

NATION, JOEY P
(**36**) CHIN **52** 00

NATON, PETE C
(**57**) PITN **57** 53

NATSU, PHIL P
(**25**,23,34) SFN **25/23** 78-79, **34/23** 80

NAULTY, DAN P
(**31**) MINA **31** 96-98, NYA **31** 99

NAVARRO, DIONER C
(68,**41**) NYA **68** 04, LAN **41** 05

NAVARRO, JAIME P
(51,**31**,38,37) MILA **51** 89, **31** 89-94, CHIN **38** 95-97, CHIA **38** 98-99, MILN **38** 00, CLEA **37** 00

NAVARRO, JULIO (WHIPLASH) P
(**35**,33,42,36) LAA **35** 62-64, DETA **33** 64, **42** 64-66, ATLN **36** 70

NAVARRO, TITO SS
(**36**) NYN **36** 93

NAYLOR, EARL OF/1B/P
(32,5,**10**) PHIN **32** 42, **5** 43, BKNN **10** 46

NAYMICK, MIKE P
(**30**,31,32) CLEA **30** 39-40, **31** 43-44, STLN **32** 44

NEAGLE, DENNY P
(58,32,**15**,12) MINA **58** 91, PITN **32** 92-93, **15** 93-96, ATLN **15** 96-98, CINN **15** 99-00, NYA **12** 00, COLN **15** 01-03, (04)

NEAL, BLAINE P
(54,**39**,59) FLAN **54** 01-02, **39** 03, SDN **39** 04, BOSA **59** 05, COLN **39** 05

NEAL, CHARLIE 2B/SS/INF
(**43**,4,19) BKNN **43** 56-57, LAN **43** 58-61, NYN **4** 62-63, CINN **19** 63

NECCIAI, RON P
(**21**) PITN **21** 52

NEEL, TROY 1B/DH/UTIL
(29,**16**) OAKA **29** 92, **16** 93-94

NEEMAN, CAL C
(30,**11**,5,10, 23,3) CHIN **30** 57, **11** 58-60, PHIN **5** 60, **10** 61, PITN **23** 62, CLEA **5** 63, WASA **3** 63

NEGRAY, RON P
(34,**38**) BKNN **34** 52, PHIN **38** 55-56, LAN **38** 58

NEIBAUER, GARY P
(**31**,43,36) ATLN **31** 69-72, PHIN **43/36** 72, ATLN **31** 73

NEIDLINGER, JIM P
(**31**) LAN **31** 90-91

NEIGER, AL P
(**44**) PHIN **44** 60

NEIGHBORS, BOB SS
(__) STLA __ 39

NEILL, MIKE OF
(**54**) OAKA **54** 98

NEILL, TOMMY OF
(3,**2**) BOSN **3** 46, **2** 47

NEKOLA, BOTS P
(30,**8**) NYA **30** 29, DETA **8** 33

NELSON, BOB (TEX)(BABE) OF/1B
(**37**) BALA **37** 55-57

NELSON, BRYANT 2B/UTIL
(**58**) BOSA **58** 02

NELSON, DAVE 2B/SS/OF/INF/DH/CH
(**14**,15,1,5,3, 38,17,8) CLEA **14** 68-69, WASA **14** 70-71, **15** 71, TEXA **1** 72-73, **5** 74-75, KCA **3** 76-77, CHIA *CH* **38** 81-84, CLEA *CH* **17** 92, *CH* **14** 93-94, *CH* **1** 94-96, *CH* **8** 97, MILN *CH* **14** 03-05

NELSON, EMMETT (RAMROD) P
(29,31,**27**) CINN **29** 35, **31/27** 36

NELSON, GENE P
(46,21,43,24, 30,**19**,16,23) NYA **46** 81, SEAA **21/43** 82, **24** 82-83, CHIA **30** 84-86, OAKA **19** 87-92, CALA **16** 93, TEXA **23** 93

NELSON, JAMIE C
(**6**) SEAA **6** 83

NELSON, JEFF P
(40,**43**) SEAA **40** 92-93, **43** 93-95, NYA **43** 96-00, SEAA **43** 01-03, NYA **43** 03, TEXA **43** 04, SEAA **43** 05

NELSON, JIM P
(24,**32**) PITN **24** 70, **32** 71

NELSON, JOE P
(**40**) ATLN **40** 01, BOSA **57** 04

NELSON, LYNN (LINE DRIVE) P
(23,11,**22**,25) CHIN **23** 33-34, PHIA **11** 37, **22** 38-39, DETA **25** 40

NELSON, MEL P
(35,43,29,26, **47**,35) STLN **35** 60, LAA **43** 63, MINA **29** 65, **26** 67, STLN **47** 68-69, **35** 69

NELSON, RICKY OF/DH
(**10**,28,16) SEAA **10** 83-84, **28** 85, **16** 86

NELSON, ROB 1B/DH
(49,40,**7**) OAKA **49** 86-87, **40** 87, SDN **7** 87-90

NELSON, ROCKY 1B/OF
(19,6,37,32, 21,8,7,**14**) STLN **19** 49, **19** 50-51, PITN **6** 51, CHIA **37** 51, LAN **32/21** 52, CLEA **37** 54, BKNN **8** 56, STLN **7** 56, PITN **14** 59-61

NELSON, ROGER (SPIDER) P
(48,**35**,45) CHIA **48** 67, BALA **35** 68, KCA **35** 69-72, CINN **45** 73-74, KCA **35** 76

NELSON, TOM (TOMMY) 3B/2B
(5,**11**) BOSN **5/11** 45

NEN, DICK 1B/OF F
(**5**,15,4) LAN **5** 63, WASA **5** 65-67, CHIN **15** 68, WASA **4** 70

NEN, ROBB P S
(**31**) TEXA **31** 93, FLAN **31** 93-97, SFN **31** 98-03, (04)

NETTLES, GRAIG 3B/OF/DH/INF/CH B
(35,2,12,**9**,19, 41,8) MINA **35** 67, **28** 68, **2** 69, CLEA **12** 70-72, NYA **9** 73-83, SDN **9** 84-86, ATLN **19** 87, MONN **9** 88, NYA *CH* **2/41** 91, SDN *CH* **8/9** 95

NETTLES, JIM OF/1B/DH B
(34,39,**7**,28, 29) MINA **34** 70, **39** 71, **7** 71-72, DETA **28** 74, KCA **28** 79, OAKA **29** 81

NETTLES, MORRIS OF/DH
(14,**16**) CALA **14** 74, **16** 74-75

NEU, MIKE P
(**32**) OAKA **49** 03, FLAN **39** 04

NEUGEBAUER, NICK P
(**32**) MILN **32** 01-03

NEUMEIER, DAN P
(38,**39**) CHIA **38/39** 72

NEUN, JOHNNY CH/M
(**32**,1) NYA *CH* **32** 44-46, *M* **32** 46, CINN *M* **1** 47-48

NEVEL, ERNIE P
(20,26,**46**) NYA **20** 50, **26** 51, CINN **46** 53

NEVIN, PHIL 3B/OF/DH/C/1B
(21,42,12,20, **23**,25) HOUN **21** 95, DETA **42** 95, **12** 96-97, ANAA **20** 98, SDN **23** 99-05, TEXA **25** 05

NEWCOMBE, DON (NEWK) P
(**36**,30,25) BKNN **36** 49-51, 54-57, LAN **36** 58, CINN **30** 58, **36** 58-60, CLEA **25** 60

NEWELL, TOM P
(**50**) PHIN **50** 87

NEWFIELD, MARC OF/DH
(28,27,**14**,10) SEAA **28** 93-94, **27** 95, SDN **14** 95-96, MILA **10** 96-97, MILN **10** 98

NEWHAN, DAVID INF/DH/OF
(**24**,11) SDN **24** 99, **14** 00, PHIN **27** 00, **9** 01, BALA **11** 04-05

NEWHAUSER, DON P
(**28**) BOSA **28** 72-74

NEWHOUSER, HAL (PRINCE) P
(**16**) DETA **16** 39-53, CLEA **16** 54-55

NEWKIRK, FLOYD (THREE-FINGER) P
(20,**23**) NYA **20/23** 34

NEWLIN, MAURY P
(19,**23**) STLA **19** 40, **23** 41

NEWMAN, ALAN P
(4,**26**,8,46) TBA **46** 99, CLEA **59** 00

NEWMAN, AL 2B/SS/UTIL/DH/CH
(4,**26**,8,46,62) MONN **4** 85-86, MINA **26** 87-91, TEXA **8** 92, TBA *CH* **46** 99, MINA *CH* **62** 02-05

NEWMAN, FRED P
(42,**17**) LAA **42** 62, **17** 62-64, CALA **17** 65-67

NEWMAN, JEFF C/UTIL/1B/DH/CH/M
(**5**,46,55,29, 16,15) OAKA **5** 76-82, BOSA **5** 83-84, OAKA *CH* **46** 86, *M* **46** 86, CLEA *CH* **55** 92-95, **29** 95, **16** 96-97, **55** 98-99, BALA *CH* **55** 00, SEAA *CH* **15** 05

NEWMAN, RAY P
(54,45,**49**) CHIN **54/45** 71, MILA **49** 72-73, **43** 72

NEWSOM, BOBO (BUCK) P
(27,21,**12**,18, 8,33,15,00, 16,34,48,20, 29) CHIN **27** 32, STLA **21** 34-35, WASA **21** 35, **12** 36-37, BOSA **12** 37, STLA **12** 38-39, DETA **18** 39, **12** 39-41, WASA **12** 42, BKNN **8** 42-43, STLA **33/15** 43, WASA **00** 43, PHIA **16** 44-46, WASA **00** 46-47, NYA **34** 47, NYN **48** 48, WASA **12** 52, PHIA **20** 52-53, **29** 53

NEWSOME, DICK P
(**28**) BOSA **28** 41-43

NEWSOME, SKEETER SS/UTIL
(28,**6**,2,26, 29) PHIA **28** 35, **6** 36-37, **2** 38-39, BOSA **26** 41-44, **6** 45, PHIN **29** 46, **6** 47

NEWSON, WARREN OF/DH
(**24**,29,26,21) CHIA **24** 91-95, SEAA **29/26** 95, TEXA **21** 96-98

NIARHOS, GUS C/CH
(24,37,**38**,11, 25,42) NYA **24/37** 46, **38** 48-50, CHIA **24** 50-51, BOSA **11** 52-53, PHIN **25** 54-55, KCA *CH* **42** 62-65

NICHOLAS, DON PH
(56,25,**37**) CHIA **56/25** 52, **37** 54

NICHOLS, CARL C/OF/UTIL
(25,26,**28**) BALA **25** 86, **26** 87-88, HOUN **28** 89-91

NICHOLS, CHET, Sr. (NICK) P F
(**18**) PHIN **18** 32

NICHOLS, CHET, Jr. P S
(17,16,**31**,34) BOSN **17** 51, MILN **16** 54, **17** 54-56, BOSA **31** 60-64, CINN **34** 64

NICHOLS, DOLAN (NICK) P
(**27**) CHIN **27** 58

NICHOLS, REID, OF/DH/UTIL/CH
(**51**,13,20,5) BOSA **51** 80-84, **13** 85, CHIA **20** 85-86, MONN **5** 87

NICHOLS, ROD P
(57,**54**,40) CLEA **57** 88, **54** 89-92, LAN **57** 93, ATLN **40** 95

NICHOLS, ROY 2B/3B
(**32**) NYN **32** 44

NICHOLSON, BILL (SWISH) OF F
(21,8,**43**,12) PHIA **21** 36, CHIN **8** 39-42, **43** 43-48, PHIN **12** 49-53

NICHOLSON, DAVE OF S
(33,**11**,21,18) BALA **33** 60, 62, CHIA **11** 63-65, HOUN **21** 66, ATLN **18** 67

NICHOLSON, KEVIN INF
(**16**) SDN **16** 00

NICHTING, CHRIS P
(54,67,57,**47**) TEXA **54** 95, CLEA **67** 00, CINN **57** 01, COLN **47** 02

NICKLE, DOUG P
(**51**,43) PHIN **51** 00-02, SDN **43** 02

NICOSIA, STEVE C/OF/1B
(**16**,7,6,38) PITN **16** 78-83, SFN **7** 83-84, MONN **6** 85, TORA **38** 85

NIEBERGALL, CHARLIE C
(14,**17**) STLN **14** 23, **17** 24

NIED, DAVID P
(38,**17**) ATLN **38** 92, COLN **17** 93-96

NIEDENFUER, TOM P
(42,**49**,41) LAN **49** 81-87, BALA **42** 87, **49** 87-88, SEAA **49** 89, STLN **41** 90

NIEKRO, JOE P B,F
(48,47,37,19, 40,**36**,32,26, 39) CHIN **48** 67-69, SDN **47/37** 69, DETA **19** 70-72, ATLN **40/36** 73, **32/36** 74, HOUN **36** 75-85, NYA **26** 85-86, **39** 86-87, MINA **39** 87, **36** 87-88

NIEKRO, LANCE 1B S,N
(**28**) SFN **28** 03, 05

NIEKRO, PHIL P/CH B,U
(**35**) MILN **35** 64-65, ATLN **35** 66-83, NYA **35** 84-85, CLEA **35** 86-87, TORA **35** 87, ATLN **35** 87, PHIN *CH* **35** 90

NIELSEN, JERRY P
(34,36) NYA **34** 92, CALA **36** 93 STLN **34** 77, NYN **45** 78

NIELSEN, MILT OF
(17,**32**) CLEA **17** 49, **32** 51

NIELSEN, SCOTT P
(**41**,38,47,55, 33) NYA **41** 86, CHIA **41** 87, NYA **38/47** 88, **55/33** 89

NIEMAN, BOB OF
(19,5,18,3,**4**, 20) STLA **19** 51-52, DETA **5** 53-54, CHIA **18** 55-56, BALA **3** 56, **4** 56-59, STLN **4** 60-61, CLEA **4** 61-62, SFN **20** 62

NIEMAN, BUTCH OF
(29,**16**) BOSN **29** 43, **16** 44-45

NIEMANN, RANDY P/CH
(**46**,23,48,28, 45,40,19,52) HOUN **46** 79-80, PITN **23** 82-83, CHIA **48/28** 84, NYN **45/46** 85, **40** 86, MINA **19** 87-88, NYN *CH* **45** 97-98, **48** 98-99, **52** 01-02

NIEMES, JACK P
(**29**) CINN **29** 43

NIEMIEC, AL 2B/SS
(__,**27**) BOSA __34, PHIA **27** 36

NIESON, CHUCK P
(**29**) MINA **29** 64

NIETO, TOM C
(23,34,**11**,19) STLN **23** 84-85, MONN **34** 86, MINA **11** 87-88, PHIN **19** 89, **11** 90

NIEVES, JOSE SS
(**11**,8) CHIN **11** 98-00, ANAA **8** 01-02

NIEVES, JUAN P
(**20**,10) MILA **20** 86-88, **10** 86

NIEVES, MELVIN OF
(7,10,**3**,30,46) ATLN **7** 92, SDN **10** 93, **3** 94-95, TEXA **30** 96, DETA **30** 97, CINN **46** 98

NIEVES, WIL C
(47,**33**,60) SDN **47/33** 02, NYA **60** 05

NIGGELING, JOHNNY P
(25,36,**21**,12, 32) BOSN **25** 38, CINN **36** 39, STLA **21** 40-43, WASA **10** 43, **12** 44-46, BOSN **32** 46

NILSSON, DAVE C/1B/UTIL/OF
(13,11,**14**,7) MILA **13** 92, **11** 92-95, **14** 96-97, MILN **7** 98, **14** 99

NIPPER, AL P/CH
(**49**,45,42,47, 35) BOSA **49** 83-87, CHIN **45** 88, CLEA **42** 90, BOSA *CH* **47** 95-96, KCA *CH* **35** 01-02

NIPPERT, DUSTIN P
(**57**) ARIN **57** 05

NIPPERT, MERLIN P
(19,**15**) BOSA **19/15** 62

NISCHWITZ, RON P
(32,29,42,27) DETA **32** 61, **29** 62, CLEA **42** 63, DETA **32/27** 65

NITCHOLAS, OTTO (NICK) P
(**25**) BKNN **25** 45

NITKOWSKI, C. J. 3B/SS/2B/UTIL
(**49**,36,48,47, 27,40,50) CINN **49** 95, DETA **36** 95, **48** 96, HOUN **47** 98, DETA **49** 99, **27** 00-01, NYN **40** 01, TEXA **50** 02-03, ATLN **40** 04, NYA **40** 04, WASN **47** 05

NIVAR, RAMON OF
(**2**,15) TEXA **2** 03-04, BALA **15** 05

NIX, LAYNCE OF
(**17**) TEXA **17** 03-05

NIXON, DONELL OF/DH
(6,**30**,52,21) SEAA **6** 87, SFN **30** 88-89, BALA **52/21** 90

NIXON, OTIS 0F/DH/SS/CH
(52,39,20,35, 1,**2**,10) NYA **52/39** 83, CLEA **20** 84-87, MONN **35** 88-90, ATLN **1** 91-93, BOSA **2** 94, TEXA **2** 95, TORA **2** 96-97, LAN **10** 97, MINA **1** 98, ATLN **1** 99, *CH* __ 03

NIXON, RUSS C/CH/M
(15,22,**5**,20,2, 7,12,9,53) CLEA **15** 57-60, BOSA **22** 60-62, **5** 63-65, MINA **20** 66-67, **5** 67, BOSA **15** 68, CINN *CH* **2** 76-82, *M* **7** 83, MONN *CH* **12** 84, *CH* **9** 85, ATLN *CH* **53** 86, *CH* **2** 86-87, *M* **2** 88-90, SEAA *CH* **5** 92

NIXON, TROT OF
(**7**) BOSA **7** 96, 98-05

NIXON, WILLARD P
(**21**,15) BOSA **21** 50-54, **15** 55-56, **21** 57-58

NOBLE, RAY C
(6,5,**8**) NYN **6** 51, **5** 51-52, **8** 53

NOBOA, JUNIOR 2B/UTIL,DH,P
(17,9,**3**,46) CLEA **17** 84, 87, CALA **9** 88, MONN **3** 89-91, NYN **3** 92, OAKA **9** 94, PITN **46** 94

NOCE, PAUL P
(**16**,12) CHIN **16** 87, CINN **12** 90

NOKES, MATT C/UTIL/DH
(26,**33**,38,24, 11) SFN **26** 85, DETA **33** 86-90, NYA **38** 90-94, BALA **24** 95, COLN **11** 95

NOLAN,GARY P
(**38**,48) CINN **38** 67-73, **38** 76-77, CALA **48/38** 77

NOLAN, JOE C
(48,35,20,58, 11,**17**) NYN **48/35** 72, ATLN **20** 75, **58** 77, **11** 77-80, CINN **17** 80-81, BALA **17** 82-85

NOLD, DICK P
(38,22) WASA **38/22** 67

NOLES, DICKIE P
(**48**,36,47,27, 37,60) PHIN **48** 79-81, CHIN **48** 82-84, TEXA **36** 84-85, CLEA **48** 86, CHIN **47** 87, DETA **27** 87, BALA **37** 88, PHIN **60** 90

NOLTE, ERIC P
(**37**,42) SDN **37** 87-89, 91, TEXA **42** 91

NOMO, HIDEO P
(**16**,11,23,10) LAN **16** 95-98, NYN **16** 98, MILN **11** 99, DETA **23** 00, BOSA **11** 01, LAN **10** 02-04, TBA **11** 05

NOMURA, TAKAHITO P
(**95**) MILN **95** 02

NONNENKAMP, RED OF/1B
(40,**24**) PITN **40** 33, BOSA **24** 38-40

NORDBROOK, TIM SS/2B/UTIL/DH
(43,8,38,**1**,16) BALA **43** 74-75, **8** 75-76, CALA **38** 76, CHIA **1** 77, TORA **16** 77-78, MILA **1** 78-79

NORDHAGEN, WAYNE UTIL/P/OF/DH
(15,**20**,3,30, 28) CHIA **15** 76-77, **20** 78-81, TORA **3/30** 82, PITN **28** 82, CHIN **20** 83

NOREN, IRV OF/1B/CH
(32,8,**25**,11, 20,15,43,5) WASA **32** 50-51, **8** 51-52, NYA **25** 52-56, KCA **11** 57, STLN **8** 57-59, **25** 59, CHIN **20** 59-60, LAN **15** 60, OAKA *CH* **43** 71-74, CHIN *CH* **5** 75

NORIEGA, JOHN P
(44,**42**) CINN **44** 69, **42** 70

NORMAN, BILL 2B/INF/OF/CH/M
(34,**27**,47,29) CHIA **34** 31, **27** 32, STLA *CH* **47** 52-53, DETA *M* **29** 58-59

NORMAN, DAN OF
(33,**8**,44) NYN **33** 77-78, **8** 79-80, MONN **44** 82

NORMAN, FRED P
(36,27,45,41, 35,47,**32**) KCA **36** 62, **27** 63, CHIN **45** 64, **41** 66-67, LAN **35** 70, STLN **47** 70-71, SDN **35** 71-73, CINN **32** 73-79, MONN **32** 80

NORMAN, LES OF
(16,25) KCA **16** 95, **25** 96

NORMAN, NELSON SS/INF/CH
(**4**,25,33) TEXA **4** 78-81, PITN **25** 82, MONN **33** 87, BOSA *CH* **58** 01

NORRIS, JIM OF/1B/UTIL/DH
(**27**,19) CLEA **27** 77-79, TEXA **19** 80

NORRIS, LEO SS/2B
(**21**) PHIN **21** 36-37

NORRIS, MIKE P
(16,**17**) OAKA **16** 75-78, **17** 78-83, 90

NORTH, BILLY OF/DH
(25,**4**,36) CHIN **25** 71-72, OAKA **4** 73-78, LAN **4** 78, SFN **36** 79-81

NORTH, LOU P
(**51**,no#) STLN **51** 23, **no#** 24

NORTHEY, RON (ROLLO)(ROUND MAN) OF/CH F
(33,14,4,30, **5**,10,23,6,32, 26,42) PHIN **33** 42, **14** 42-44, **4** 44, **30** 46, **4** 46-47, STLN **5** 47-49, CHIN **10** 50, CINN **23** 50, CHIN **10** 52, CHIA **6** 55-56, **32** 56-57, PHIN **26** 57, PITN *CH* **42** 61-63

NORTHEY, SCOTT OF
(**44**) KCA **44** 69

NORTHRUP, JIM OF/1B/DH
(30,**5**,2,28) DETA **30** 64-66, **5** 67-74, MONN **2** 74, BALA **28** 74, **2** 75

NORTON, GREG 3B/UTIL/DH
(31,**14**,28) CHIA **31** 96-00, COLN **14** 01-03, DETA **28** 04

NORTON, PHIL P
(**50**,66,51) CHIN **50** 00, 03, CINN **66** 03, **51** 04

NORTON, TOM P
(41,**22**) MINA **41/22** 72

NORWOOD, WILLIE OF/DH
(**24**) MINA **24** 77-80

NOSEK, RANDY P
(**37**) DETA **37** 89-90

NOSSEK, JOE OF/CH
(16,**24**,11,32, 40,4,41,14, 15,21,23,26) MINA **16** 64, **24** 65-66, KCA **24** 66-67, OAKA **24** 69, STLN **24** 69, **11** 70, MILA *CH* **24** 73-74, **32** 73-74, **24** 75, MINA *CH* **40** 76, CLEA *CH* **4** 77, **24** 78-81, KCA *CH* **41** 82- 83, CHIA *CH* **14** 84-85, **2** 86, **15** 91-94, **21** 95-99, **23** 00-02, **26** 03, **23** 04

NOTTEBART, DON P
(32,**43**,23,38, 48) MILN **32** 60-62, HOUN **43** 63-67, NYA **23** 69, CHIN **38/48** 69

NOTTLE, ED CH
(**44**) OAKA *CH* **44** 83

NOVIKOFF, LOU (THE MAD RUSSIAN) OF
(26,19,**14**,45, 39) CHIN **26** 41, **19** 41-42, **14** 42-43, **45** 43-44, PHIN **39** 46

NOVOA, RAFAEL P
(36,**39**) SFN **36** 90, MILA **39** 93

NOVOA, ROBERTO P
(51,**44**) DETA **51** 04, CHIN **44** 05

NOVOTNEY, RUBE C
(**9**) CHIN **9** 49

NUNEZ, ABRAHAM OF
(**27**,38) FLAN **27** 02-04, KCA **38** 04

NUNEZ, ABRAHAM O. SS/INF
(48,**10**,6,7,3) PITN **48** 97, **10** 98-02, **6** 03, **7** 04, STLN **3** 05

NUNEZ, EDWIN P
(**30**,45,41,29, 52) SEAA **30** 82-88, NYN **45** 88, DETA **41** 89-90, MILA **45** 91-92, **41** 92, TEXA **29** 92, OAKA **52** 93-94

NUNEZ, FRANKLIN P
(**47**) TBA **47** 04-05

NUNEZ, JOSE P
(**45**,39) TORA **45** 87-89, CHIN **39** 90

NUNEZ, JOSE A. P
(62,**37**) LAN **62** 01, SDN **37** 01-02

NUNEZ, LEO P
(**43**) KCA **43** 05

NUNEZ, VLADIMIR P
(67,48,39,**36**, 24) ARIN **67** 98, **48** 99, FLAN **39** 99, **36** 99-03, COLN **24** 04

NUNN, HOWIE P
(57,**38** 43) STLN **57** 59, CINN **38** 61-62, **43** 62

NUNNALLY, JON OF
(29,**22**) KCA **29** 95, **22** 95-97, CINN **22** 97-98, BOSA **29** 99, NYN **26** 00

NUNNARI, TALMADGE INF
(**56**) MONN **56** 00

NUXHALL, JOE P
(43,**39**,33,41) CINN **43** 44, **39** 52-60, KCA **33** 61, LAA **39** 62, CINN **41** 62-66

NYE, RICH P
(**32**,22) CHIN **32** 66-69, STLN **22** 70, MONN **22** 70

NYE, RYAN P
(**35**,39) PHIN **35** 97, **39** 98

NYMAN, CHRIS 1B/OF/DH
(**23**) CHIA **23** 82-83

NYMAN, JERRY P
(**49**,31,24) CHIA **49** 68-69, SDN **31/24** 70

NYMAN, NYLS OF/DH
(**20**) CHIA **20** 74-77

O

OANA, PRINCE OF/P
(33,36,**14**) PHIN **33** 34, DETA **14** 43, **36** 45

OATES, JOHNNY C/CH/M
(38,12,15,6,**5**, 26,9,46,26) BALA **38** 70, **12** 70, 72, ATLN **15** 73-75, PHIN **6** 75-76, LAN **5** 77-79, NYA **26** 80-81, CHIN *CH* **9** 84-87, BALA *CH* **46** 89-90, *CH* **26** 89-91, *M* **26** 91-94, TEXA *M* **26** 95-01

OBANDO, SHERMAN DH/OF
(42,**29**) BALA **42** 93, 95, MONN **29** 96-97

OBERKFELL, KEN (OBIE) 2B/3B
(24,**10**,14,5) STLN **24** 77-81, **10** 81-84, ATLN **24** 84-88, PITN **14** 88-89, SFN **10** 89, HOUN **10** 90-91, CALA **5** 92

OBERMUELLER, WES P
(43,30,**33**) KCA **43** 02, **30** 03, MILN **33** 04-05

O'BERRY, MIKE C/3B
(50,6,**9**,3,58, 18) BOSA **50** 79, CHIN **6** 80, CINN **9** 81-82, CALA **3** 83, NYA **58** 84, MONN **18** 85

OBRADOVICH, JIM 1B
(**19**) HOUN **19** 78

O'BRIEN, BOB P
(**50**) LAN **50** 71

O'BRIEN, CHARLIE C
(7,11,**22**,33, 5,12,21) OAKA **7** 85, MILA **11** 87-88, **22** 88-90, NYN **33** 90, **5** 91, **22** 92-93, ATLN **11** 94-95, TORA **22** 96-97, CHIA **22** 98, ANAA **12** 98, **22** 98-99, MONN **21** 00

O'BRIEN, DAN P
(**34**) STLN **34** 78-79

O'BRIEN, EDDIE SS/UTIL/P B
(27,7,**16**,6) PITN **27** 53, **7** 55, **16** 57-58, SEAA *CH* **6** 69

O'BRIEN, JOHNNY 2B/SS/P B
(30,**6**,19,11) PITN **30** 53, **6** 55-58, STLN **19** 58, MILN **11** 59

O'BRIEN, PETE UTIL/1B/DH/OF
(23,**9**,12) TEXA **23** 82, **9** 83-88, CLEA **9** 89, SEAA **12** 90-92, **9** 93

O'BRIEN, SYD INF/UTIL/3B/2B
(19,**7**,8) BOSA **19** 69, CHIA **7** 70, CALA **8** 71-72, MILA **7** 72

O'BRIEN, TOMMY (OBIE) OF/3B
(26,**11**,23,35) PITN **26** 43, **11** 43-45, BOSA **23** 49-50, WASA **35** 50

OCEAK, FRANK (FEZ) CH
(**44**,5) PITN *CH* **44** 58-64, CINN *CH* **5** 65, PITN *CH* **44** 70-72

OCHOA, ALEX SS/OF
(**22**,25,24,7, 3,23,18) NYN **22** 95-97, MINA **25** 98, MILN **24** 99, CINN **7** 00-01, COLN **3** 01, MILN **23** 02, ANAA **18** 02

OCK, WHITEY C
(__) BKNN __ 35

OCKEY, WALTER (FOOTIE) P
(**20**) NYN **20** 44

O'CONNELL, DANNY SS/3B/INF/CH
(11,10,**4**,27,2, 19,22,41) PITN **11** 50, **10** 53, MILN **4** 54, **27** 55, **4** 55-57, NYN **2** 57, SFN **19** 58, **22** 58-59, WASA **4** 61-62, *CH* **41** 63-64

O'CONNOR, BRIAN P
(**58**) PITN **58** 00

O'CONNOR, JACK P
(**33**,42,32,21) MINA **33** 81-84, **42** 82, MONN **32** 85, BALA **21** 87

O'DEA, KEN C
(41,12,9,8, **16**,27) CHIN **41** 35-36, **12** 37-38, NYN **9** 39-40, **8** 41, STLN **16** 42-46, BOSN **27** 46

O'DEA, PAUL (LEFTY) UTIL/OF/P
(**6**) CLEA **6** 44-45

O'DELL, BILLY P
(24,18,38,41, **31**,33,29) BALA **24** 54, **18** 56, **38** 57, **41**58-59, SFN **31** 60-64, MILN **33** 65, ATLN **33** 66, PITN **29/31** 66-67

ODOM, BLUE MOON P
(**13**) KCA **13** 64-67, OAKA **13** 68-75, CLEA **13** 75, ATLN **13** 75, CHIA **13** 76

ODOM, DAVE (BLIMP)(PORKY) P
(**34**) BOSN **34** 43

O'DONNELL, GEORGE P
(**23**) PITN **23** 54

O'DONOGHUE, JOHN P
(35,26,32,28, 43,23,46) KCA **35** 63, **26** 64-65, CLEA **32** 66-67, BALA **28** 68, SEAA **43** 69, MILA **43** 70, MONN **23** 70-71, BALA **46** 93

O'DOUL, LEFTY OF
(**6**,16) BKNN **6** 32-33, NYN **16** 33-34

OELKERS, BRYAN P
(**17**,33) MINA **17** 83, CLEA **33** 86

OERTEL, CHUCK (DUCKY)(SNUFFY) OF
(**40**) BALA **40** 58

OESTER, RON SS/INF/2B/CH
(**16**,3,19,0,7) CINN **16** 78-90, *CH* **3** 93, DETA *CH* **19/16** 96, CINN *CH* **0** 97-98, **7** 98, **16** 99-01

O'FARRELL, BOB C/M
(9,8,26,12,29) NYN **9** 32, STLN **8** 33, CINN **26** 34, *M* **26** 34, CHIN **12** 34, STLN **29** 35

OFFERMANN, JOSE SS/1B/INF
(**30**,33,35) LAN **30** 90-95, KCA **30** 96-98, BOSA **30** 99-02, SEAA **30** 02, MINA **30** 04, PHIN **33** 05, NYN **35** 05

OFFICE, ROWLAND OF/1B
(18,**22**,25,20) ATLN **18** 72, **22** 74-79, MONN **25** 80-82, NYA **20** 83

OGDEN, JACK P
(**20**) CINN **20** 32

OGEA, CHAD P
(**37**,33) CLEA **37** 94-98, PHIN **33** 99

OGLESBY, JIM 1B
(**3**) PHIA **3** 36

OGLIVIE, BEN OF/DH/UTIL/CH
(45,4,14,22, **24**) BOSA **45/4** 71, **14** 72-73, DETA **22** 74-77, MILA **24** 78-86, SDN *CH* **24** 78

OGRODOWSKI, BRUCE (BRUSIE) C
(**9**) STLN **9** 36-37

O'HALLORAN, GREG 1B
(**16**) FLAN **16** 94

OHKA, TOMO P
(53, 18,24,**34**, 55) BOSA **53** 99-00, **18** 01, MONN **24** 01-03, **34** 04, WASN **34** 05, MILN **55** 05

OHMAN, WILL P
(**35**,50,45) CHIN **35** 00-01, (03), **50/45** 05

OHME, KEVIN P
(**43**) STLN **43** 03

OJALA, KIRT P
(33,**24**) FLAN **33** 97, **24** 98-99

OJEDA, AUGIE INF
(57,**1**,4) CHIN **57** 00, **1** 01-03, MINA **4** 04

OJEDA, BOB (BOBBY O) P
(28,46,**19**,17) BOSA **28** 80, **19** 81-85, NYN **46** 86, **19** 86-90, LAN **17** 91-92, CLEA **17** 93, NYA **19** 94

OJEDA, MIGUEL C
(**20**,2) SDN **20** 03-05, SEAA **2** 05

OKRIE, LEN C
(9,**12**,10,33, 32,34,52) WASA **9** 48, **12** 50, **10** 51, BOSA **33** 52, *CH* **32** 61-62, *CH* **34** 65-66, DETA *CH* **52** 70

OLANDER, JIM OF/DH
(**18**) MILA **18** 91

OLDHAM, JOHN PR
(**36**) CINN **36** 56

OLDIS, BOB C/CH
(**10**,9,2,34,5) WASA **10** 53, **9** 54-55, PITN **2** 60-61, PHIN **10** 62-63, *CH* **34** 64, *CH* **5** 64-66, MINA *CH* **5** 68, MONN *CH* **34** 69

O'LEARY, CHARLEY CH/PH
(**33**,31,42,26) NYA *CH* **33** 29, **31** 30, CHIN *CH* **33/42** 32, **33** 33, STLA *CH* **26** 34-37

O'LEARY, TROY OF
(33,**25**) MILA **33** 93-94, BOSA **25** 95-01, MONN **25** 02, CHIN **25** 03

OLERUD, JOHN 1B/DH
(**9**,5,18,19) TORA **9** 89-96, NYN **5** 97-99, SEAA **5** 00-04, NYA **18** 04, BOSA **19** 05

OLIN, STEVE P
(50,**31**) CLEA **50** 89, **31** 90-92

OLIVA, JOSE 3B
(**45**,42) ATLN **45** 94-95, STLN **42** 95

OLIVA, TONY OF/DH/CH
(37,**6**) MINA **37** 62-64, **6** 64-76, *CH* **6** 77-78, 85-91

OLIVARES, ED 2B/OF
(**17**,24) STLN **17** 60, **24** 61

OLIVARES, OMAR P
(**26**,00,47,28, 27,39,40,31) STLN **55** 90, **26** 90-92, **00** 93, **26** 94, COLN **47** 95, PHIN **00** 95, DETA**28** 96-97, SEAA **27/26** 97, ANAA **39** 98-99, OAKA **40** 99-00, PITN **31** 01

OLIVER, AL OF/1B/DH F
(29,16,**0**) PITN **29** 68-69, **16** 69-77, TEXA **0** 78-81, MONN **0** 82-83, SFN **0** 84, PHIN **0** 84, LAN **0** 85, TORA **0** 85

OLIVER, BOB OF/1B/3B/UTIL/DH
(27,**33**,42) PITN **27** 65, KCA **33** 69-72, CALA **33** 72-74, BALA **33** 74, NYA **42** 75

OLIVER, DARREN P S
(**28**,32,33,14, 36,37) TEXA **28** 93-98, STLN **32** 98, **33** 99, TEXA **14** 00, **28** 01, BOSA **36** 02, COLN **37** 03, FLAN **37** 04, HOUN **37** 04

OLIVER, DAVE 2B/CH
(**26**,16) CLEA **26** 77, TEXA *CH* **26** 87-94, BOSA *CH* **16** 95-96

OLIVER, DICK (KEWPIE DICK) P
(a.k.a. Dick Barrett)
(**16**) BOSN **16** 34

OLIVER, GENE UTIL/C/OF/1B
(29,**12**,9,22) STLN **29** 59,61-63, MILN **12** 63-65, ATLN **12** 66-67, PHIN **9** 67, BOSA **22** 68, CHIN **12** 68-69

OLIVER, JOE C/1B/UTIL
(**9**,7,17,18, 14) CINN **9** 89-94, MILA **9** 95, CINN **9** 96, **7** 97, DETA **7** 98, SEAA **9** 98, PITN **17** 99, SEAA **18/9** 00, NYA **14** 01

OLIVER, NATE (PEEWEE) NF
(**29**,17,21,15) LAN **29** 63-66, **17** 67, SFN **29** 68, NYA **21** 69, CHIN **15** 69

OLIVER, TOM (REBEL) OF/CH
(14,**12**,29) BOSA **14** 31-32, **12** 33, PHIA *CH* **29** 51-54

OLIVERAS, FRANCISCO P
(30,**45**) MINA **30** 89, SFN **45** 90-92

OLIVERAS, MAX (MAKO) P/CH
(**72**,3,2) CALA **72** 94, CHIN *CH* **3** 95-96, *CH* **2** 97

OLIVO, CHI-CHI P
(40,**30**,38) MILN **40** 61, **30** 64-65, **38** 65, ATLN **38** 66

OLIVO, DIOMEDES (CATFISH) OF/1B
(**38**,41) PITN **38** 60, 62, STLN **41** 63

OLIVO, MIGUEL C
(61,**8**,7,14) CHIA **61** 02, **8** 03-04, SEAA **7** 04, **8** 04-05, SDN **14** 05

OLLOM, JIM P
(30,**18**) MINA **30** 66, **18** 67

OLMEDA, RAINIER (RAY) INF/SS
(**4**) CINN **4** 03-05

OLMO, LUIS OF/UTIL
(**21**,37,15) BKNN **21** 43-45, **37** 49, BOSN **15** 50-51

OLMSTED, AL P
(**47**) STLN **47** 80

OLSEN, BARNEY OF
(29,**19**) CHIN **29/19** 41

OLSEN, KEVIN P
(**56**) FLAN **56** 01-03

OLSEN, SCOTT P
(**48**) FLAN **48** 05

OLSEN, VERN P
(**23**) CHIN **23** 39-42, 46

OLSON, GREG C/3B
(11,**10**) MINA **11** 89, ATLN **10** 90-93

OLSON, GREGG P
(**30**,40,10,37, 48) BALA **30** 88-93, ATLN **40/10** 94,CLEA **30** 95, KCA **30** 95, DETA **37** 96, HOUN **30** 96, MINA **30** 97, KCA **48** 97, ARIN **30** 98-01

OLSON, IVY CH
(**26**) NYN *CH* **26** 32

OLSON, KARL (OLE) OF
(28,**34**,21,3, 30) BOSA **28** 51, **34** 53-54, **21** 55, WASA **3** 56-57, DETA **30** 57

OLSON, MARV (SPARKY) 2B/3B
(10,5,**14**) BOSA **10** 31, **5** 32, **14** 33

OLSON, TED P
(23,28,**12**) BOSA **23** 36, **28** 37, **12** 38

OLSON, TIM 3B/SS
(**14**,48) ARIN **14** 04, COLN **48** 05

OLWINE, ED P
(**31**) ATLN **31** 86-88

O'MALLEY, TOM 3B/INF
(**35**,26,17,41, 23,27) SFN **35** 82-84, CHIA **26** 84, BALA **17** 85-86, TEXA **41** 87, MONN **23** 88, NYN **27** 89-90

O'NEAL, RANDY P
(**49**,37,39,27, 55) DETA **49** 84-86, ATLN **37** 87, STLN **39** 87-88, PHIN **27** 89, SFN **55** 90

O'NEIL, JOHN (BUCK) CH
(**53**) CHIN **53** 62, 64

O'NEIL, JOHN SS
(**27**) PHIN **27** 46

O'NEILL, EMMETT (PINKY) P
(**15**,19,38) BOSA **15** 43-45, CHIN **19** 46, CHIA **38** 46

O'NEILL, HARRY C
(36,**30**) PHIA **36/30** 39

O'NEILL, PAUL OF/DH/1B/P
(**21**) CINN **21** 85-92, NYA **21** 93-01

O'NEILL, STEVE CH/M
(30,26,33,**32**, 45,24) CLEA *CH/M* **30** 35, *M* **30** 36, **26** 37, DETA *CH* **33** 41, *M* **32** 43-48, CLEA *CH* **45** 49, BOSA *M* **30** 50-51, PHIN *M* **24** 52-54

ONIS, CURLY C
(**22**) BKNN **22** 35

ONSLOW, JACK CH/M
(27,26,**23**) PHIN *CH* **27** 32, BOSA *CH* **26** 34, CHIA *M* **23** 49-50

ONTIVEROS, STEVE P
(**53**,41,52,50) OAKA **53** 85-88, PHIN **41** 89-90, SEAA **52** 93, OAKA **50** 94-95, BOSA **41** 00

ONTIVEROS, STEVE 1B/OF/3B/UTIL
(**16**) SFN **16** 73-76, CHIN **16** 77-80

OQUENDO, JOSE SS,INF/UTIL/2B/P/C/ALL/CH
(2,5,**11**) NYN **2** 83-84, STLN **5** 86, **11** 86-95, *CH* **11** 99-05

OQUIST, MIKE P
(**56**,40,45,44) BALA **56** 93-95, SDN **40** 96, OAKA **45** 97, **44** 98-99

ORAVETZ, ERNIE OF
(**37**) WASA **37** 55-56

ORDAZ, LUIS SS/INF
(52,23,11,13, 8,**1**) STLN **52** 97-98, **23/11** 98, **13** 99, KCA **8** 00-01, **1** 02

ORDENANA, TONY (MOSQUITO) C
(**2**) PITN **2** 43

ORDOÑEZ, MAGGLIO OF
(**30**) CHIA **30** 97-04, DETA **30** 05

ORDOÑEZ, REY SS
(0,**10**,29,13) NYN **0** 96-97, **10** 98-02, TBA **10** 03, CHIN **29/13** 04

ORENGO, JOE SS/INF
(**4**,18,6,26,28, 22,3) STLN **4** 39, **18** 40, NYN **6** 41, **26/28** 43, BKNN **4** 43, DETA **22** 44, CHIA **3** 45

ORIE, KEVIN 3B
(**15**,27) CHIN **15** 97-98, FLAN **27** 98-99, CHIN **15** 02

O'RILEY, DON P
(23,**32**) KCA **23** 69, **32** 70

OROPESA, EDDIE P
(65,**54**,47,40, 43) PHIN **65/54** 01, ARIN **47** 02, **40 /54** 03, SDN **43** 04

OROSCO, JESSE P
(61,**47**,50) NYN **61/47** 79, **47** 81-87, LAN **47** 88, CLEA **47** 89-91, MILA **47** 92-94, BALA **47** 95-99, STLN **47** 00, LAN **47** 01-02, SDN **47** 03, NYA **47** 03, MINA **50** 03

O'ROURKE, CHARLIE PH
(**25**) STLN **25** 59

O'ROURKE, FRANK (BLACKIE) SS/1B
(**21**) STLA **21** 31

ORR, PETE SS
(**4**) ATLN **4** 05

ORRELL, JOE OF/UTIL/CH/M
(**14**) DETA **14** 43-45

ORSATTI, ERNIE OF
(**5**,6) STLN **5** 32, **6** 33, **5** 34-35

ORSINO, JOHN (HORSE) C/1B
(34,**12**,3) SFN **34** 61-62, BALA **12** 63-65, WASA **12** 66, **3** 67

ORSULAK, JOE OF/DH/1B
(16,11,**6**,19) PITN **16** 83-84, **11** 84-86, BALA **6** 88-92, NYN **6** 93-95, FLAN **6** 96, MONN **19** 97

ORTA, JORGE INF/UTIL/DH/OF
(**6**,31,33,3) CHIA **6** 72-79, CLEA **6** 80-81, LAN **31**82, TORA **33** 83, KCA **3** 84-87

ORTEGA, BILL OF
(**28**) STLN **28** 01

ORTEGA, PHIL (KEMO) P
(**17**,26,31) LAN **17** 60-64, WASA **26** 65-68, CALA **31** 69

ORTENZIO, FRANK OF
(**17**) KCA **17** 73

ORTIZ, BABY P
(**17**) WASA **17** 44

ORTIZ, DAVID (BIG PAPI) 1B/DH
(**27**,34) MINA **27** 97-02, BOSA **34** 03-05

ORTIZ, HECTOR C
(52,**22**) KCA **52** 98, **22** 00-01, TEXA **22** 02

ORTIZ, JAVIER OF
(**29**) HOUN **29** 90-91

ORTIZ, JOSE (D.) INF
(**2**,12) OAKA **2** 00-01, COLN **12** 01-02, **2** 02

ORTIZ, JOSE (L.) OF
(23,15,**20**) CHIA **23** 69, **15** 70, CHIN **20** 71

ORTIZ, JUNIOR C/DH
(36,34,26,**0**) PITN **36** 82-83, NYN **34** 83-84, PITN **26** 85-89, **0** 89, MINA **0** 90-91, CLEA **0** 92-93, TEXA **0** 94

ORTIZ, LUIS 3B/DH
(51,**9**) BOSA **51** 93-94, TEXA **9** 95-96

ORTIZ, ROBERTO OF
(**4**,24,__,35, 33,28) WASA **4** 41, **24** 42, __ 43, **4** 44, **35** 49, **33** 50, PHIA **28** 50

ORTIZ, RAMON P
(**36**,45) ANAA **36** 99-03, **45** 03, **36** 04, CINN **36** 05

ORTIZ, RUSS P
(**48**) SFN **48** 98-02, ATLN **48** 03-04, ARIN **48** 05

ORTMEIER, DANIEL OF
(**34**) SFN **34** 05

ORTON, JOHN C/DH
(**14**) CALA **14** 89-93

ORVELLA, CHAD P
(**54**) TBA **54** 05

OSBORN, DON CH
(41,**42**,51) PITN *CH* **41** 63-64, *CH* **42** 70-72, 74-76, *CH* **51** 79

OSBORN, OZZIE (DANNY) P
(50,**46**) CHIA **50/46** 75

OSBORN, PAT P
(46,49) CINN **46** 74, MILA **49** 75

OSBORN, BOBO OF/1B/3B/UTIL
(1,47,32,**28**, 25) DETA **1** 57, **47** 58, **32** 59, **28** 61-62, WASA **25** 63

OSBORNE, DONOVAN P
(**31**,46) STLN **31** 92-93, 95-99, CHIN **31** 02, NYA **46** 04

OSBORNE, WAYNE (OSSIE)(FISH HOOK) P
(52,**20**) PITN **52** 35, BOSN **20** 36

OSGOOD, CHARLIE P
(**20**) BKNN **20** 44

OSIK, KEITH C
(63,**15**,21,40, 55) PITN **63** 96, **15** 97-02, MILN **21** 03, BALA **40** 04, WASN **55** 05

OSINSKI, DAN P
(31,**40**,26,19, 37,21,39,43) KCA **31** 62, LAA **40** 62-64, MILN **26** 65, BOSA **19** 66, **37** 67, CHIA **21** 69, HOUN **39/43** 70

OSORIA, FRANQUELIS P
(**57**) LAN **57** 05

OSTEEN, CLAUDE P/CH
(34,30,32,24,**23**, 50,41,18,3, 48,38) CINN **34** 57, **32** 59-61, WASA **34** 61-62, **24** 62-64, LAN **23** 65-73, HOUN **24** 74, STLN **50** 74, CHIA **41** 75, STLN *CH* **18** 77-80, PHIN *CH* **3** 82-88, TEXA *CH* **48** 93-94, LAN *CH* **38** 99-00

OSTEEN, DARRELL P
(**54**,39,35,37) CINN **54** 65-67, **39** 67, OAKA **35/37** 70

OSTER, BILL P
(**17**) PHIA **17** 54

OSTERMUELLER, FRITZ P
(19,14,**21**,16, 23,27) BOSA **19** 34, **14** 35-38, **21** 38-40, STLA **16** 41, **23** 42-43, BKNN **27** 43-44, PITN **21** 44-48

OSTING, JIMMY P
(40,**30**) SDN **40** 01, MILN **30** 02

OSTROSSER, BRIAN SS
(**19**) NYN **19** 73

OSTROWSKI, JOE (PROFESSOR)(SPECS) P
(39,30,21,**35**) STLA **39/30** 48, **21** 49-50, NYA **35** 50-52

OSTROWSKI, JOHNNY OF/3B/2B
(47,50,**27**,2, 35) CHIN **47** 43, **50** 44-46, **27** 46, BOSA **27** 48, CHIA **2** 49-50, WASA **35** 50

OSUNA, AL P
(52,**29**,45,35) HOUN **52** 90-92, **29** 92-93, LAN **45** 94, SDN **35** 96

OSUNA, ANTONIO P
(50,**13**) LAN **50** 95, **13** 95-00, CHIA **13** 01-02, NYA **13** 03, SDN **13** 04, WASN **13** 05

OSWALT, ROY P
(**44**) HOUN **44** 01-05

OTANEZ, WILLIS OF
(52,24,**21**) BALA **52** 98, **24** 99, TORA **21** 99

OTERO, REGGIE 1B/CH
(**51**,4) CHIN **51** 45, CINN *CH* **4** 59-65, CLEA *CH* **4** 66

OTERO, RICKY OF
(**1**,15) NYN **1** 95, PHIN **15** 96-97

OTIS, AMOS OF/3B/DH/CH
(25,**26**) NYN **25** 67, 69, KCA **26** 70-83, PITN **26** 84, SDN *CH* **26** 88-90, COLN *CH* **26** 93

O'TOOLE, DENNY P
(42,47,**52**) CHIA **42** 69, **47** 69-70, **52** 70-73

O'TOOLE, JIM P
(**31**,21) CINN **31** 58-66, CHIA **21** 67

OTSUKA, AKINORI P
(**16**) SDN **16** 04-05

OTT, BILLY OF
(20,**28**) CHIN **20** 62, **28** 64

OTT, ED C/OF/CH
(27,26,**14**,24, 56) PITN **27** 74, **26** 74-75, **32** 75, **14** 76-80, CALA **14** 81, HOUN *CH* **24** 89, *CH* **14** 90-93, DETA *CH* **56** 01

OTT, MEL (MASTER MELVIN) OF/3B/M
(5,**4**,3) NYN **5** 32, **4** 33-47, **3** 37, *M* **4** 42-48

OTTEN, JIM P
(**38**,34,40) CHIA **38** 74-76, STLN **34** 80, **40** 80-81

OTTO, DAVE DH/OF/P
(**38**,27,48,53) OAKA **38** 87-90, CLEA **27** 91-92, PITN **48** 93, CHIN **53** 94

OUELLETTE, PHIL C
(**12**) SFN **12** 86

OULLIBER, JOHNNY OF
(**29**) CLEA **29** 33

OUTEN, CHICK C
(**19**) BKNN **19** 33

OUTLAW, JIMMY 3B/OF
(6,51,22,**27**) CINN **6** 37, **51** 38, BOSN **22** 39, DETA **27** 43-49

OVERBAY, LYLE INF/1B
(61,23,**11**) ARIN **61** 01, **23** 02-03, MILN **11** 04-05

OVERMIRE, STUBBY P/CH
(19,**18**,40,24, 25,41,53) DETA **19** 43-44, **18** 45-49, STLA **40** 50-51, NYA **24** 51, STLA **25** 52, DETA *CH* **41** 63, *CH* **53** 63-66

OVERY, MIKE P
(45,**44**) CALA **45/44** 76

OWCHINKO, BOB P
(**44**,42,27,53, 51,28,32,43) SDN **44** 76-79, CLEA **42/27** 80, OAKA **53** 81, **51** 81-82, PITN **28** 83, CINN **32** 84, MONN **43** 86

OWEN, DAVE SS/3B/INF
(**19**,2) CHIN **19** 83-85, KCA **2** 88

OWEN, LARRY C
(12,**24**,8) ATLN **12** 81, **24** 82-83, **8** 85, KCA **24** 87-88

OWEN, MARV (FRECK) 3B/INF/1B
(29,**8**,2,6) DETA **29** 31,**15** 33, **8** 34-37, CHIA **2** 38-39, BOSA **6** 40

OWEN, MICKEY C/CH
(8,14,**10**,9, 16,12,11,30) STLN **8** 37-38, **14** 39-40, BKNN **10** 41-45, CHIN **9/16** 49, **12** 50-51, BOSA **11** 54, *CH* **30** 55-56

OWEN, SPIKE SS/DH/3B
(**7**,1,5,11,17) SEAA **7** 83-86, **1** 86 BOSA **5** 86, **7** 87-88, MONN **11** 89-92, NYA **17** 93, CALA **17** 94-95

OWENS, ERIC 3B/OF
(51,18,39,3, **8**,7,4,16) CINN **51** 95, **18** 96-97, MILN **39** 98, SDN **3** 99, **8** 00, FLAN **7/ 4** 01, **16** 02, ANAA **8** 03

OWENS, JACK C
(__) PHIA __ 35

OWENS, JAYHAWK C
(32,**34**) COLN **32** 93, **34** 94-96

OWENS, JIM (BEAR) P/CH
(18,39,49,48, **33**,***5***) PHIN **18** 55, **39** 56, **49** 59-62, CINN **48** 63, HOUN **33** 64-67, *CH* **33** 67, *CH* **5** 68-72

OWENS, PAUL M
(8,**5**) PHIN *M* **8** 72, *M* **5** 83-84

OWNBEY, RICK P
(20,**40**) NYN **20** 82-83, STLN **40** 84, 86

OXSPRING, CHRIS P
(**58**) SDN **58** 05

OYLER, RAY INF/SS/3B
(**1**,42) DETA **1** 65-68, SEAA **1** 69, CALA **42/1** 70

OZARK, DANNY CH/M
(**33**,22,8,3,1) LAN *CH* **33** 65-66, *CH* **22** 67, *CH* **8** 68,*CH* **33** 69-72, PHIN *M* **3** 73-79, LAN *CH* **33** 80-82, SFN *CH* **3/1** 83, *CH/M* **1** 84

OZUNA, PABLO INF/UTIL
(**3**,1,38) FLAN **3** 00-02, COLN **1** 03, CHIA **38** 05

P

PACELLA, JOHN (JOHNNY) P
(**20**,50,19,41, 43,27) NYN **20** 77, 79-80, NYA **50** 82, MINA **19** 82, BALA **41** 84, DETA **43/27** 86

PACHECO, ALEX P
(**59**) MONN **59** 96

PACHECO, TONY CH
(21,**3**,56) CLEA *CH* **21** 74, HOUN *CH* **3** 76-79, *CH* **56** 82

PACILLO, PAT P
(**35**) CINN **35** 87-88

PACIOREK, JIM UTIL B
(**14**) MILA **14** 87

PACIOREK, JOHN OF B
(**22**) HOUN **22** 63

PACIOREK, TOM OF/1B/UTIL B
(17,12,14,**44**, 34) LAN **17** 71-75, ATLN **12** 76-78, SEAA **14** 78-81, CHIA **44** 82-85, NYN **44** 85, TEXA **34** 86, **44** 86-87

PACK, FRANKIE PH
(**3**) STLA **3** 49

PACTWA, JOE P
(39,**44**) CALA **39/44** 75

PADDEN, TOM C
(**31**,18,29) PITN **31** 32-37, PHIN **18** 43, WASA **29** 43

PADGETT, DON C/OF/1B
(4,**16**,33,6,8, 22) STLN **4** 37-38, **16** 39-41, BKNN **33** 46, BOSN **6** 46, PHIN **8** 47-48, **22** 48

PADILLA, JUAN P
(61,60,**28**) NYA **61** 04, CINN **60** 04, NYN **28** 05

PADILLA, VICENTE P
(**45**) ARIN **45** 99-00, PHIN **44** 00-05

PAEPKE, DENNIS C/OF
(28,**17**) KCA **28** 69, **17** 71-72, 74

PAEPKE, JACK CH
(48,**3**,20) LAA *CH* **48** 61, *CH* **3** 62-64, CALA *CH* **20** 65-66

PAFKO, ANDY (HANDY ANDY)(PRUSCHKA) OF/3B/CH
(33,**48**,22,) CHIN **33** 43, **48** 44-51, BKNN **22** 51, **48** 52, MILN **48** 53-59, *CH* **48** 60-62

PAGAN, DAVE P
(50,18,**53**,30, 55) NYA **50/18** 73, **53** 74-76, BALA **30/53** 76, SEAA **30** 77, PITN **55** 77

PAGAN, JOSE INF/SS/3B/UTIL/CH
(10,15,**11**,16, 2) SFN **10** 59, **15** 60-65, PITN **11** 65-72, PHIN **16** 73, PITN *CH* **2** 74-78

PAGE, JOE (FIREMAN) P
(16,**11**,00) NYA **16** 44, **11** 45-50, PITN **00** 54

PAGE, MIKE OF
(**43**) ATLN **43** 68

PAGE, MITCHELL OF/DH/CH
(**6**,39,12) OAKA **6** 77-83, PITN **39** 84-85 KCA *CH* **39** 95-97, STLN *CH* **12** 01-04

PAGE, PHIL P/CH
(**21**,3,4,53) BKNN **21** 34, CINN *CH* **3** 47-48, *CH* **4** 49, *CH* **53** 49-52

PAGE, SAM P
(**20**) PHIA **20** 39

PAGE, VANCE P
(**41**) CHIN **41** 38-41

PAGEL, KARL 1B/DH/OF
(45,23,**30**) CHIN **45** 78, **23** 79, **45** 79-80, CLEA **30** 81-83

PAGLIARONI, JIM (PAG) C
(22,8,29,3,10, **17**) BOSA **22** 55, **8** 60, **29** 60-62, PITN **3** 63-64, **10** 65-67, OAKA **17** 68-69, SEAA **17** 69

PAGLIARULO, MIKE (PAGS) 3B/1B/DH,2B
(46,6,**13**) NYA **46** 84, **6** 85, **13** 86-89, SDN **13** 89-90, MINA **13** 91-93, BALA **6/13** 93, TEXA **13** 95

PAGNOZZI, TOM C/1B
(**19**) STLN **19** 87-98

PAIGE, SATCHEL P/CH
(31,**29**,65) CLEA **31** 48, **29** 48-49, STLA **47/22** 51, **29** 51-53, KCA **29** 65, ATLN *CH* **65** 68-69

PAINE, PHIL (FLIP) P
(**11**,24,44) BOSN **11** 51, (52), MILN **11** 54-56, **24** 57, STLN **44** 58

PAINTER, LANCE P
(47,**28**,27) COLN **47** 93, **28** 93-96, STLN **28** 97-99, TORA **28** 00-01, MILN **27** 01, STLN **28** 03

PALACIOS, REY UTIL
(**29**) KCA **29** 88-90

PALACIOS, VICENTE P
(38,**58**) PITN **38** 87-88, **58** 90-92, STLN **58** 94-95

PALAGYI, MIKE SS/INF
(**35**) WASA **35** 39

PALICA, ERV C/UTIL/DH S
(40,**12**,23,16) BKNN **40** 47-48, **12** 48-51, **23** 53, **12** 54, BALA **16** 55-56

PALL, DONN P
(25,30,**22**,39, 47,46,44) CHIA **25** 88, **30** 89-90, **22** 91-93, PHIN **39** 93, NYA **39** 94, CHIN **47** 94, FLAN **46** 96, **44** 97-98

PALM, MIKE SS/3B/INF
(**20**) BOSA **20** 48

PALMEIRO, ORLANDO OF
(**3**,16,19) CALA **3** 95-96, ANAA **3** 97-02, STLN **16** 03, HOUN **19** 04-05

PALMEIRO, RAFAEL OF/1B/DH
(**25**,3) CHIN **25** 86-88, TEXA **3** 89, **25** 89-93, BALA **25** 94-98, TEXA **25** 99-03, BALA **25** 04-05

PALMER, DAVID P
(**46**,45,16) MONN **46** 78-80, 82, 84-85, ATLN **46** 86-87, PHIN **45** 88, DETA **16** 89

PALMER, DEAN UTIL/3B/SS
(**16**,7) TEXA **16** 89, 91-97, KCA **16** 97-98, DETA **7** 99-03

PALMER, JIM P
(**22**) BALA **22** 65-67, 69-84

PALMER, LOWELL P
(26,**40**,44,33, 29) PHIN **26** 69-70, **40** 70-71, STLN **44** 72, CLEA **33** 72, SDN **29** 74

PALMISANO, JOE C/2B
(**21**) PHIA **21** 31

PALMQUIST, ED P
(**23**,24) LAN **23** 60-61, MINA **24** 61

PALYS, STAN OF/1B
(**23**,15) PHIN **23** 53, **15** 54-55, CINN **23** 55-56

PANIAGUA, JOSE P
(**36**,30,22,50) MONN **36** 96-97, SEAA **30** 98-99, **36** 00-01, DETA **22** 02, CHIA **50** 03

PANKOVITS, JIM UTIL/INF/2B
(**20**,42) HOUN **20** 84-88, BOSA **42** 90

PANTHER, JIM P
(20,31,22) OAKA **20** 71, TEXA **31** 72, ATLN **22/20** 73

PAPA, JOHN P
(**39**) BALA **39** 61-62

PAPAI, AL P
(36,29,34, 41,24) STLN **36** 48, STLA **37/29** 49, BOSA **34** 50, STLN **41** 50, CHIA **24** 55

PAPE, KEN INF/DH
(**5**) TEXA **5** 76

PAPELBON, JONATHAN P
(**58**) BOSA **58** 05

PAPI, STAN INF/UTIL/3B
(29,**12**,9) STLN **29** 74, MONN **12** 77-78, BOSA **12** 79-80, DETA **9** 80-81

PAPISH, FRANK (PAP) P
(**17**,26,30) CHIA **17** 45-48, CLEA **26** 49, PITN **30** 50

PAPPAS, ERIK C/UTIL
(37,1,**12**) CHIN **37/1** 91, STLN **12** 93-94

PAPPAS, MILT (GIMPY) P
(23,**32**,34) BALA **23** 57, **32** 58-65, CINN **34** 66-67, **32** 68, ATLN **23** 68, **32** 68-70, CHIN **32** 70-73

PAQUETTE, CRAIG 3B/UTIL/OF
(3,12,18,**21**, 8) OAKA **3** 93-95, KCA **12** 96-97, NYN **18** 98, STLN **21** 99-01, DETA **8** 02, **21** 03

PARDO, AL C/DH
(**26**,35,31) BALA **26** 85-86, PHIN **35** 88, **31** 89

PAREDES, JOHNNY 2B/OF/UTIL
(**5**,18,34) MONN **5** 88, DETA **18** 90, MONN **5** 90, DETA **34** 91

PARENT, MARK C/DH
(**27**,10,13,6, 8,14,24) SDN **27** 86-90, TEXA **10** 91, BALA **27** 92-93, **6** 93, CHIN **8** 94, PITN **14** 95, CHIN **8** 95, DETA **8** 96, BALA **24** 96, PHIN **8** 97-98

PARIS, KELLY INF/2B/DH
(35,17,**21**,28) STLN **35** 82, CINN **17** 83, BALA **21** 85-86, CHIA **28** 88

PARISSE, TONY C
(**10**) PHIA **10** 43-44

PARK, CHAN HO P
(**61**) LAN **61** 94, 96-01, TEXA **61** 02-04-05, SDN **61** 05

PARKER, ACE UTIL
(26,31,17,**25**) PHIA **26/31/17** 37, **25** 38

PARKER, BILLY 2B/SS/UTIL
(**18**) CALA **18** 71-73

PARKER, CHRISTIAN P
(**71**) NYA **71** 01

PARKER, CLAY P
(27,**38**,37,17, 59,32) SEAA **27** 87, NYA **38** 89-90, DETA **37/17** 90, SEAA **59/32** 92

PARKER, DAVE 0F/1B/2B/DH/CH
(**39**) PITN **39** 73-83, CINN **39** 84-87, OAKA **39** 88-89, MILA **39** 90, CALA **39** 91, TORA **39** 91, ANAA *CH* **39** 97, STLN *CH* **39** 98

PARKER, HARRY P
(**31**,34,40) STLN **31** 70-71, NYN **31** 73-75, STLN **34** 75, CLEA **40** 76

PARKER, RICK UTIL/OF
(32,30,11,46) SFN **32** 90-91, HOUN **30** 93, NYN **11** 94, LAN **46** 95, **40** 96

PARKER, SALTY SS/1B/CH/M
(**24**,2,41,21, 54,1) DETA **24** 36, SFN *CH* **2** 58-61, CLEA *CH* **41** 62, LAA *CH* **21** 64, CALA *CH* **21** 65-66, NYN *CH/M* **54** 67, HOUN *CH* **2** 68-72, *CH* **1** 72, CALA *CH* **21** 73-74

PARKER, WES OF/1B
(**28**) LAN **28** 64-72

PARKS, ART OF
(28,32,**8**) BKNN **28** 37, **32/8** 39

PARKS, DEREK C
(**16**) MINA **16** 92-94

PARMELEE, ROY (TARZAN) P
(35,**18**,15,24, 21) NYN **35** 32, **18** 33-35, STLN **15** 36, CHIN **24** 37, PHIA **21** 39

PARNELL, MEL (DUSTY) P
(**17**) BOSA **17** 47-56

PARONTO, CHAD P
(39,**16**) BALA **39** 01, CLEA **16** 02-03

PARQUE, JIM P
(**40**,28) CHIA **40** 98-02, TBA **28** 03

PARRA, JOSE P
(65,**45**,56,60 52,46) LAN **65/45** 95, MINA **56** 95-96, PITN **60** 00, ARIN **52** 02, NYN **46** 04

PARRETT, JEFF P
(**49**,33,38) MONN **49** 86-88, PHIN **49** 89-90, ATLN **33** 90, **49** 91, OAKA **38**92, COLN **38** 93, STLN **49** 95-96, PHIN **49** 96

PARRILLA, SAM OF
(**27**) PHIN **27** 70

PARRIS, STEVE P
(55,60,27,58, **39**) PITN**55/60** 95, **27** 96, CINN **58** 98-00, TORA **39** 01-02, TBA **39** 03

PARRISH, JOHN P
(53,**36**) BALA **53** 00-01, **36** 03-05

PARRISH, LANCE C/UTIL/DH/OF/1B/CH B
(**13**,3,5) DETA **13** 77-86, PHIN **13** 87-88, CALA **13** 89-92, SEAA **3** 92, CLEA **13** 93, PITN **5** 94, TORA **13** 95, DETA *CH* **13** 99-01, 03-05

PARRISH, LARRY 3B/INF/OF/DH/CH/M B
(50,**15**,9,25) MONN **50** 74-75, **15** 75-81, TEXA **9** 82, **15** 82-88, BOSA **25** 88, DETA *CH* **15** 97-98, *M* **15** 98-99

PARROTT, MIKE P
(32,**20**) BALA **32** 77, SEAA **20** 78-81

PARSONS, BILL P
(**52**,50,23,39) MILA **52** 71-73, OAKA **50/23/ 39** 74

PARSONS, CASEY OF/1B/DH/UTIL
(27,14,**23**,15) SEAA **27** 81, CHIA **14** 83, **23** 84, CLEA **15** 87

PARSONS, DIXIE C
(8,**23**) DETA **8** 39, **23** 42-43

PARSONS, TOM P
(16,47,**27**) PITN **16** 63, NYN **47** 64, **27** 64-65

PARTEE, ROY C
(**6**,16,12,11) BOSA **6** 43-44, **16** 46-47, STLA **12/11** 48

PARTENHEIMER, STAN (PARTY) P
(**17**,32) BOSA **17** 44, STLN **32** 45

PASCHAL, BEN OF
(**25**) NYA **25** 29

PASCHALL, BILL P
(28,43,42) KCA **28/43** 78, **42** 79, **28** 81

PASCUAL, CAMILO (LITTLE POTATO) P/CH
(27,**17**,33,36, 35,42) WASA **27** 54-56, **17** 57-60, MINA **17** 61-69, CINN **33** 69, LAN **17** 70, CLEA **36/35** 71, MINA *CH* **42** 78-80

PASCUAL, CARLOS P
(**13**) WASA **13** 50

PASCUCCI, VAL OF
(**35**) MONN **35** 04

PASEK, JOHNNY C
(**5**,8) DETA **5** 33, CHIA **8** 34

PASHNICK, LARRY P
(**22**,58,19) DETA **22** 82-83, MINA **58/19** 84

PASLEY, KEVIN C
(**4**,18) LAN **4** 74, 76-77, SEAA **18** 77-78

PASQUA, DAN OF/DH/UTIL/1B
(21,23,**44**) NYA **21** 85-87, CHIA **23** 88, **44** 88-94

PASSEAU, CLAUDE P
(12,48,**13**) PITN **12** 35, PHIN **48** 36, **48** 37, **13** 38-39, CHIN **13** 39-47

PASTORE, FRANK P
(53,**35**,33) CINN **53** 79, **35** 79-85, MINA **33** 86

PASTORNICKY, CLIFF 3B
(**3**) KCA **3** 83

PATE, BOB OF
(**24**) MONN **24** 80-81

PATEK, FREDDIE (THE FLEA) SS/DH/UTIL
(**2**,37) PITN **2** 68-70, KCA **37** 71-75, **2** 71, 75-79, CALA **2** 80-81

PATKIN, MAX CH
(**11**,0) CLEA *CH* **11** 46, STLA *CH* **0** 51

PATRICK, BOB OF
(34,**24**) DETA **34** 41, **24** 42

PATRICK, BRONSWELL P
(**31**,39) MILN **31** 98, SFN **39** 99

PATTERSON, BOB P
(46,30,**38**,28, 37,35) SDN **46** 85, PITN **30** 86-87, **38** 89-92, TEXA **38** 93, CALA **28** 94, **37** 95, CHIN **35** 96-98

PATTERSON, COREY OF
(27,**20**) CHIN **27** 00, **20** 01-05

PATTERSON, DANNY P
(56,**28**,17) TEXA **56** 96-99, DETA **28** 00-03, **17** 04

PATTERSON, DARYL P
(**43**,58,48,45, 32) DETA **43** 68-71, OAKA **58** 71, STLN **48** 71, PITN **45/32** 74

PATTERSON, DAVE P
(**56**) LAN **56** 79

PATTERSON, GIL P
(**22**,54,47) NYA **22/54** 77, TORA *CH* **47** 01-04

PATTERSON, HANK C
(**11**) BOSA **11** 32

PATTERSON, JARROD 3B
(**43**) DETA **43** 01

PATTERSON, JEFF P
(**38**) NYA **38** 95

PATTERSON, JOHN A. 2B/OF
(**7**) SFN **7** 92-95

PATTERSON, JOHN P
(**24**,21,22) ARIN **24** 02-03, MONN **21** 04, WASN **22** 05

PATTERSON, KEN P
(**34**,38,47) CHIA **34** 88, **38** 89, **34** 89-91, CHIN **34** 92, CALA **47** 93-94

PATTERSON, MIKE OF/DH
(14,47,56,**18**) OAKA **14/47** 81, NYA **56** 81-82, **18** 82

PATTERSON, REGGIE P
(51,**52**) CHIA **51** 81, CHIN **52** 83-85

PATTIN, MARTY P/CH
(**33**,25,56) CALA **33** 68, SEAA **33** 69, MILA **33** 70-71, BOSA **25** 72, **33** 72-73, KCA **33** 74-80, *CH* **56** 89

PATTON, BILL C
(**67**) PHIA **67** 35

PATTON, GENE PR
(**12**) BOSN **12** 44

PATTON, TOM C
(**10**) BALA **10** 57

PAUL, JOSH C
(15,**27**,29,8) CHIA **15** 99-00, **27** 01-03, CHIN **29** 03, ANAA **8** 04, LAA **8** 05

PAUL, MIKE P/CH
(**39**,30,35,45, 20) CLEA **39** 68-71, TEXA **30** 72-73, CHIN **35** 73-74, OAKA *CH* **45** 87-88, SEA *CH* **20** 89-91

PAULA, CARLOS OF
(23,**31**) WASA **23** 54, **31** 55-56

PAULINO, RONNY C
(**56**) PITN **56** 05

PAVANO, CARL P
(**45**) MONN **45** 98-02, FLAN **46** 02, **45** 02-04, NYA **45** 05

PAVLAS, DAVE P
(**46**,56,47) CHIN **46** 90-91, NYA **56** 95, **47** 96

PAVLETICH, DON 1B/C/INF
(**8**,7,19) CINN **8** 57, 59, 62-68, CHIA **7** 69, BOSA **19** 70-71

PAVLICK, GREG CH
(**52**) NYN *CH* **52** 85-86, 88-91, 94-96

PAVLIK, ROGER P
(**59**) TEXA **59** 92-98

PAWELEK, TED (PORKY) C
(**32**) CHIN **32** 46

PAWLOSKI, STAN 2B
(**35**) CLEA **35** 55

PAWLOWSKI, JOHN P
(47,**48**) CHIA **47** 87, **48** 87-88

PAXTON, MIKE P
(**48**) BOSA **48** 77, CLEA **48** 78-80

PAYNE, MIKE P
(**47**) ATLA **47** 84

PAYTON, JAY OF
(25,**44**,27,24, 17,16) NYN **25** 98, **44** 99-02, COLN **27** 02, **24** 03, SDN **17** 04, BOSA **44** 05, OAKA **16** 05

PAZIK, MIKE P/CH
(54,18,40,26, **33**,25) MINA **54/41/18** 75, **40/26** 76, **33** 77, CHIA *CH* **25** 95, *CH* **25** 96-98

PEACOCK, JOHNNY C/2B/UTIL
(__,23,**11**,9, 19,10,5) BOSA __ 37, **23** 38-40, **11** 41-43, **9** 44, PHIN **19** 44, **10** 45, BKNN **5** 45

PEARCE, FRANK P
(25,**49**) PHIN **25** 33, **49** 34-35

PEARCE, JIM P
(19,24,49,54 **32**) WASA **19** 49, **24** 50, **49** 53, CINN **54**54, **32** 55

PEARCE, JOSH P
(**60**,54) STLN **60** 02-03, **54** 04

PEARSON, ALBIE OF
(6,21,**28**) WASA **6** 58-59, BALA **21** 59-60, LAA **28** 61-64, CALA **28** 65-66

PEARSON, IKE P
(5,**12**,21,38, 19) PHIN **5** 39, **12** 40-41, **19** 42, **21** 46, CHIA **38/19** 48

PEARSON, JASON P
(59,**53**) SDN **59** 02, STLN **53** 03

PEARSON, MONTE (HOOT) P
(24,33,30,**16**, 32) CLEA **24** 32, **33** 33-35, **30** 35, NYA **16** 36-40, CINN **32** 41

PEARSON, TERRY P
(**45**) DETA **45** 02

PEAVY, JAKE P
(**44**) SDN **44** 02-05

PECK, HAL OF
(6,__,1,3,34, **36**) BKNN **6** 43, PHIA __ 44, **1** 45, **3** 46, CLEA **34** 47, **36** 48-49

PECKINPAUGH, ROGER (PECK) M
(**10**,27) CLEA *M* **10** 31-33, *M* **27** 41

PECOTA, BILL INF/UTIL/DH
(**32**) KCA **32** 86-91, NYN **32** 92, ATLA **32** 93-94

PEDEN, LES (GOOCH) C
(**8**) WASA **8** 53

PEDERSON, STU OF
(**57**) LAN **57** 85-86

PEDRE, JORGE C/1B
(**53**) KCA **53** 91, CHIN **53** 92

PEDRIQUE, AL SS/INF/CH/M
(25,**22**,17,__) NYN **25** 87, PITN **22** 87-88, DETA **17** 89, ARIN *CH* __ 04, *M* 04

PEEK, STEVE P
(**18**) NYA **18** 41

PEEL, HOMER OF
(**26**) NYN **26** 33-34

PEERSON, JACK SS
(no#,**45**) PHIA **no#** 35, **45** 36

PEETE, CHARLIE (MULE) OF
(**38**) STLN **38** 56

PEGUERO, JULIO OF
(**37**) PHIN **37** 92

PEGUES, STEVE OF
(26,**25**) CINN **26** 94, PITN **25** 94-95

PELAEZ, ALEX INF
(**24**) SDN **24** 02

PELLAGRINI, EDDIE 3B/SS/INF
(39,4,**13**) BOSA **39** 46-47, STLA **4** 48-49, PHIN **13** 51, CINN **13** 52, PITN **13** 53-54

PELLOW, KIT 3B/1B
(**19**) KCA **19** 02, COLN **19** 03-04

PELTIER, DAN OF/1B
(53,**17**,30) TEXA **53** 92, **17** 92-93, SFN **30** 96

PEMBER, DAVE P
(**13**) MILN **13** 02, (03)

PEMBERTON, BROCK 1B
(**2**) NYN **2** 74-75

PEMBERTON, RUDY OF/DH
(**18**,57,44) DETA **18** 95, BOSA **57** 96, **44** 97

PENA, ALEJANDRO P
(**26**,34,44,32) LAN **26** 81-89, NYN **26** 90-91, ATLN **26** 91-92, PITN **34** 94, BOSA **26** 95, FLAN **44/32** 95, ATLN **26** 95, FLAN **32** 96

PENA, ANGEL C
(63,**36**) LAN **63** 98, **36** 99, 01

PENA, BERT SS/INF
(**1**) HOUN **1** 81, 83-87

PENA, BRAYAN C
(**8**) ATLN **8** 05

PENA, CARLOS 1B
(15,2,43,**12**) TEXA **15** 01, OAKA **2** 02, DETA **43** 02, **12** 03-05

PENA, ELVIS INF/2B
(23,**9**) COLN **23** 00, MILN **9** 01

PENA, GERONIMO 2B
(60,7,**21**,27) STLN **60** 90, **7** 91-92, **21** 93-95, CLEA **27** 96

PENA, HIPOLITO P
(**16**,49,60,46) PITN **16** 86-87, **49** 87, NYA **60/46** 88

PENA, JESUS P
(**61**) CHIA **61** 99-00, BOSA **38** 00

PENA, JIM P
(**31**) SFN **31** 92

PENA, JOSE P
(34,49,**29**) CINN **34** 69, LAN **49** 70, **29** 71-72

PENA, JUAN P
(**57**) BOSA **57** 99

PENA, ORLANDO P
(43,19,22,24, **28**,31,36,46, 27,34,51) CINN **43** 58-60, KCA **19** 62-63, **22** 64, **24** 64-65, DETA **28** 66-67, CLEA **31** 67, PITN **22/36/46** 70, BALA **27** 71, 73, STLN **34** 73, **36** 73-74, CALA **51** 74-75, **28** 75

PENA, RAMON P
(**18**) DETA **18** 89

PENA, ROBERTO (BABY) SS/INF
(7,**28**,34,11, 14,17) CHIN **7** 65, **28** 66, PHIN **34** 68, SDN **11** 69, OAKA **14/17** 70, MILA **28** 70-71

PENA, TONY C/1B
(11,**6**,26,17, 29,4) PITN **11** 80, **6** 80-86, STLN **26** 87-89, BOSA **6** 90-93, CLEA **17** 94-96, CHIA **29** 97, HOUN **4** 97, *CH* **6** 02, KCA *M* **6** 02-05

PENA, WILY MO OF
(**26**) CINN **26** 02-05

PENDLETON, JIM OF/SS/INF/UTIL
(**3**,11,12,23) MILN **3** 53-56, **11** 56, PITN **12** 57-58, CINN **12** 59, HOUN **23** 62

PENDLETON, TERRY 3B
(**9**,5,6) STLN **9** 84-90, ATLN **9** 91-94, FLAN **9** 95-96, ATLN **5** 96, CINN **9** 97, KCA **6** 98, ATLN *CH* **9** 02-05

PENN, HAYDEN P
(**49**) BALA **49** 05

PENN, SHANNON 2B
(**7**,42) DETA **7** 95, **42** 96

PENNINGTON, BRAD P
(47,**29**,41,31, 21,57) BALA **47** 93, **29** 94-95, CINN **41**95, BOSA **31** 96, CALA **21** 96, TBA **57**98

PENNOCK, HERB (THE KNIGHT OF KENNETT SQUARE) P
(11,16,**12**,17, 31) NYA **11** 29, **16** 30-31, **12** 32-33, BOSA **17** 34, *CH* **31** 36-39

PENNY, BRAD P
(28,**31**,30) FLAN **28** 00-01, **31** 01-04, LAN **30** 04, **31** 05

PENNYFEATHER, WILL OF
(**25**) PITN **25** 92-94

PENSON, PAUL P
(**44**) PHIN **44** 54

PENTLAND, JEFF CH
(**2**,4,__,22,26) CHIN *CH* **2** 98-00, **4** 00-02, KCA *CH* __ 02, **22** 03, **26** 04-05

PENTZ, GENE P
(39,**30**) DETA **39** 75, HOUN **30** 76-78

PEPITONE, JOE (PEPI) OF/1B/CH
(**25**,9,8,7,46) NYA **25** 62-69, HOUN **9** 70, CHIN **8** 70-73, ATLN **7** 73, NYA *CH* **46** 82

PEPPER, DON 1B
(**32**) DETA **32** 66

PEPPER, LAURIN P
(18,**23**,31) PITN **18** 54, **23** 55-56, **31** 57

PEPPER, RAY OF
(no#,29,**8**) STLN **no#** 32, **29** 33, STLA **8** 34-36

PERALTA, JHONNY SS/3B
(60,16,**2**) CLEA **60** 03, **16** 04, **2** 05

PERALTA, JOEL P
(**58**) LAA **58** 05

PERAZA, LOU P
(**28**) PHIN **28** 69

PERAZA, OSWALD P
(**23**) BALA **23** 88

PERCIVAL, TROY P
(**40**) CALA **40** 95-96, ANAA **40** 97-04, DETA **40** 05

PERCONTE, JACK 2B
(45,16,**14**,42) LAN **45** 80-81, CLEA **16** 82-83, SEAA **14** 84-85, CHIA **42** 86

PEREZ, ANTONIO SS
(**1**,26) TBA **1** 03, LAN **26** 04-05

PEREZ, CARLOS P
(**33**) MONN **33** 95, 97-98, LAN **33** 98-00, (01)

PEREZ, DANNY PH
(**7**) MILA **7** 96

PEREZ, EDDIE C
(**12**,38) ATLN **12** 95-01, CLEA **38** 02, MILN **12** 03, ATLN **12** 04-05

PEREZ, EDUARDO 3B/1B/DH/OF S
(45,21,24,30, 39,48,**33**) CALA **45/21** 93, **24** 94-95, CINN **30** 96, **39** 97-98, STLN **48** 99, **33** 00, 02-03, TBA **33** 04-05

PEREZ, GEORGE P
(**47**) PITN **47** 58

PEREZ, MARTY SS/2B/INF
(42,**9**,1,27,7, 17) CALA **42** 69-70, ATLN **9** 71-76, SFN **1** 76, NYA **27** 77, OAKA **7** 77, OAKA **17** 78

PEREZ, MELIDO P B
(31,**33**) KCA **31** 87, CHIA **33** 88-91, NYA **33** 92-95

PEREZ, MIGUEL C
(**29**) CINN **29** 05

PEREZ, MIKE P
(**42**,47,52) STLN **63** 90, **42** 90-94, CHIN **47** 95-96, KCA **52** 97

PEREZ, NEIFI 2B/SS
(**5**,17,8,1,10, 13) COLN **5** 96-01, KCA **17** 01, **8** 02, SFN **1** 03, **10** 04, CHIN **13** 04-05

PEREZ, ODALIS P
(**45**,43) ATLN **45** 98-99, **43** 99-00, **45** 01, LAN **43** 02, **45** 02-05

PEREZ, OLIVER P
(**59**,48) SDN **59** 02-03, PITN **48** 03-05

PEREZ, PASCUAL P B
(25,50,27,**34**) PITN **25** 80-81, **50** 81, ATLN **27** 82-85, MONN **34** 87-89, NYA **34** 90-91

PEREZ, ROBERT OF
(**17**,30,12,48, 9) TORA **17** 94-97, SEAA **30** 98, MONN **12** 98, NYA **48** 01, MILN **9** 01

PEREZ, SANTIAGO INF
(38,**1**) MILN **38** 00, SDN **1** 01

PEREZ, TIMO OF
(**6**,7) NYN **6** 00-03, CHIA **7** 04-05

PEREZ, TOMAS SS/2B/OF/P
(1,13,**9**) TORA **1** 95-97, **13** 98, PHIN **13** 98, 00-01, **9** 01-05

PEREZ, TONY 1B/INF/DH/CH/M F
(**24**,5,37) CINN **24** 64-76, MONN **24** 77-79, BOSA **5** 80-82, PHIN **37/24** 83, CINN **24** 84-86, *CH* **24** 87-92, *M* **24** 93, FLAN *M* **24** 01

PEREZ, YORKIS P
(33,**58**,25,45, 48,46,39) CHIN **33** 91, FLAN **58** 94-96, NYN **25** 97, PHIN **45** 98, **48** 99, HOUN **46** 00, BALA **39** 02

PEREZCHICA, TONY 2B/SS/INF/DH
(**1**,28,39,21, 44,20) SFN **1** 88, **28** 90, **39/21** 91, CLEA **44** 91, **20** 92

PERISHO, MATT P
(62,**40**,46) ANAA **62** 97, TEXA **40** 98-00, DETA **40** 01-02, FLAN **46** 04-05, BOSA **46** 05

PERKINS, BRODERICK 1B/OF/UTIL/DH
(**15**) SDN **15** 78-82, CLEA **15** 83-84

PERKINS, CECIL P
(**48**) NYA **48** 67

PERKINS, CHARLIE (LEFTY) P
(**23**) BKNN **23** 34

PERKINS, CY C/PH/CH
(**9**,31,30) NYA **9** 31, *CH* **31** 32, *CH* **30** 33, DETA **31** 34-37, *CH* **31** 34-37, PHIA *CH* **31** 46-53

PERKINS, DAN P
(**49**) MINA **49** 99

PERKOVICH, JOHN (PERKY) P
(**57**) CHIA **57** 50

PERKOWSKI, HARRY P
(**35**,43) CINN **35** 47, 49-54, CHIN **43** 55

PERLMAN, JON P
(35,46,44) CHIN **35** 85, SFN **46** 87, CLEA **44** 88

PERLOZZO, SAM 2B/3B/CH/M
(**36**,40,34,2) MINA **36** 77, SDN **40** 79, NYN *CH* **34** 87-89, CINN *CH* **2** 90-92, SEAA *CH* **2** 93-95, BALA *CH* **2** 96-05, *M* **2** 05

PERME, LEN P
(**34**) CHIA **34** 42, 46

PERRANOSKI, RON P/CH
(**16**,45,29) LAN **16** 61-67, MINA **16** 68-71, DETA **16** 71-72, LAN **16** 72, CALA **45** 73, LAN *CH* **29** 81-84, *CH* **16** 85-94, SFN *CH* **16** 97-99

PERRIN, BILL (LEFTY) P
(__) CLEA __ 34

PERRY, BOB OF
(**25**) LAA **25** 63-64

PERRY, BOYD SS/2B
(**7**) DETA **7** 41

PERRY, CHAN OF
(61,**43**) CLEA **61** 00, KCA **43** 02

PERRY, GAYLORD P B
(28,22,35,**36**, 46) SFN **28/22** 62, **35** 63, **36** 63-71, CLEA **35** 72, **36** 72-75, TEXA **36** 75-77, SDN **36** 78-79, TEXA **36** 80, NYA **36** 80, ATLN **46/36** 81, SEAA **36** 82-83, KCA **36** 83

PERRY, GERALD 1B/OF/DH/CH
(36,**28**,17,21, 29,27) ATLN **36** 83, **28** 83-89, KCA **17** 90, STLN **21** 91-92, **28** 93-95, SEAA *CH* **29** 00, **27** 01-02, PITN *CH* **28** 03-05

PERRY, HERBERT 3B/1B/DH
(36,**35**,43) CLEA **36** 94-96, TBA **35** 99-00, CHIA **43** 00-01, TEXA **35** 02-04

PERRY, JIM P B
(**31**,36) CLEA **31** 59-63, MINA **31** 63-72, DETA **31** 73, CLEA **31** 74-75, OAKA **36** 75

PERRY, PAT P
(**37**,38,26) STLN **37** 85-87, CINN **38** 87-88, CHIN **37** 88-89, LAN **26** 90

PERSON, ROBERT P
(29,**31**) NYN **29** 95-96, TORA **31** 97-99, PHIN **31** 99-02, BOSA **31** 03

PERTICA, BILL P
(no#) STLN **no#** 23

PERZANOWSKI, STAN P
(44,46,**18**,39) CHIA **44** 71, **46** 71, 74, TEXA **18** 75-76, MINA **39** 78

PESKY, JOHNNY SS/3B/INF/M/CH
(**6**,7,11,22,4, 35) BOSA **6** 42, 46-52, DETA **7** 52-54, WASA **11** 54, BOSA *M* **22** 63-64, PITN *CH* **4** 65-67, BOSA *CH* **35** 75-80, *M* **35** 80, *CH* **6** 81-84

PETAGINE, ROBERTO 1B
(29,24,**20**,10, 57,13) HOUN **29** 94, SDN **24** 95, NYN **20** 96, **10** 97, CINN **57** 98, BOSA **13** 05

PETEREK, JEFF P
(**28**) MILA **28** 89

PETERMAN, BILL C
(**12**) PHIN **12** 42

PETERS, CHRIS P
(**38**,31,48) PITN **38** 96-99, **31** 00, MONN **48** 01

PETERS, GARY P
(12,23,**43**) CHIA **12** 59, **23** 60-62, **43** 63-69, BOSA **43** 70-72, MILA **23** 70

PETERS, RAY P
(**41**) MILA **41** 70

PETERS, RICKEY OF/UTIL/DH
(**32**,8,31) DETA **32** 79-81, OAKA **8** 83, **31** 86

PETERS, RUSTY 2B/INF/UTIL
(29,12,11,**3**,) PHIA **29** 36, **12** 37, **11** 38, CLEA **3** 40-44, **12** 46, STLA **3** 47

PETERS, STEVE P
(**36**) STLN **36** 87-88

PETERSEN, CHRIS SS
(**2**) COLN **2** 99

PETERSON, ADAM P
(42,**43**,32) CHIA **42** 87-88, **43** 87, 89-90, SDN **32** 91

PETERSON, ADAM P
(**59**) TORA **59** 04

PETERSON, BUDDY SS
(11,**8**) CHIA **11** 55, BALA **8** 57

PETERSON, CAP SS/OF/INF/UTIL
(**17**,4,20) SFN **17** 62-66, WASA **4** 67-68, CLEA **20** 69

PETERSON, FRITZ P
(52,**19**,30,16) NYA **52** 66, **19** 67-74, CLEA **30** 74, **16** 74-76, TEXA **19** 76

PETERSON, HARDY C
(**17**,20) PITN **17** 55, 57-58, **20** 59

PETERSON, JARROD DH
(**19**) KCA **19** 03

PETERSON, JIM P
(17,**27**,24) PHIA **17** 31, **27** 33, BKNN **24** 37

PETERSON, KENT (PETE) P
(39,**30**,38,33, 27) CINN **39/30** 44, **38** 47-48, **30** 49-51, PHIN **33** 52, **27** 53

PETERSON, KYLE P
(41,**26**) MILN **41** 99, (00), **26** 01

PETERSON, RICK CH
(**55**,47,46,51) PITN *CH* **55** 84-85, CHIA *CH* **55** 95, OAKA *CH* **47** 98-02, **46** 03, NYN **51** 04-05

PETERSON, SID P
(**31**) STLA **31** 43

PETKOVSEK, MARK P
(56,65,**46**,34) TEXA **56** 91, PITN **65** 93, STLN **46** 95-98, ANAA **34** 99-00, TEXA **46** 01

PETOSKEY, TED OF
(2,**11**) CINN **2** 34, **11** 35

PETRALLI, GENO C/3B/UTIL/DH
(14,**12**) TORA **14** 82-84, TEXA **12** 85-93

PETRICK, BEN C/OF
(15,**6**,30) COLN **15** 99-00, **6** 01-03, DETA **30** 03

PETROCELLI, RICO SS/3B/1B/UTIL/DH
(38,**6**) BOSA **38** 63, 65, **6** 66-76

PETRY, DAN P
(**46**,23) DETA **46** 79-87, CALA **46** 88-89, DETA **23** 90, **46** 91, ATLN **46** 91, BOSA **46** 91

PETTIBONE, JAY P
(**35**) MINA **35** 83

PETTINI, JOE SS/3B/INF
(**2**,24) SFN **2** 80-83, STLN *CH* **24** 02-05

PETTIS, GARY OF/DH/CH
(30,20,**24**,22, 8,18,2) CALA **30** 82, **20** 83-86, **24** 86-87, DETA **22** 88, **24** 88-89, TEXA **24** 90-91, SDN **8** 92, DETA **18** 92, CHIA *CH* **20** 01-02, NYN *CH* **2** 03-04

PETTIT, LEON (LEFTY) P
(**20**,__) WASA **20** 35, PHIN __ 37

PETTIT, PAUL (LEFTY) P
(23,**20**) PITN **23** 51, **20** 53

PETTITTE, ANDY P
(**46**,21) NYA **46** 95-03, HOUN **21** 04-05

PETTYJOHN, ADAM P
(**46**) NYA **46** 95

PEVEY, MARTY C/OF/CH
(**49**,30) MONN **49** 89, TORA *CH* **30** 99

PEZZULLO, PRETZEL P
(**41**) PHIN **41** 35-36

PFEFFER, JEFF P
(**18**,49) STLN **18** 23, **49** 24

PFEIL, BOBBY UTIL
(1,28,**18**) NYN **1** 69, PHIN **28/18** 71

PFISTER, DAN P
(43,**27**,14) KCA **43** 61, **27** 62-64, **14** 64

PFISTER, GEORGE C/CH
(**47**) BKNN **47** 41, *CH* **47** 52

PFUND, LEE P
(**14**) BKNN **14** 45

PHEBUS, BILL P
(**19**,21,11) WASA **19** 36, **21/11** 37, **19** 38

PHELPS, BABE (BLIMP) C
(__,61,19,**9**, 10) WASA __ 31, CHIN **61** 33-34, BKNN **19** 35-36, **9** 37-41, PITN **10** 42

PHELPS, JOSH C/DH/1B
(19,**17**,45) TORA **19** 00, **17** 01-04, CLEA **45** 04, TBA **21** 05

PHELPS, KEN 1B/DH
(52,6,42,**44**, 46,21) KCA **52** 80, **16** 81, MONN **42** 82, SEAA **44** 83-88, NYA **46** 88, **21** 88-89, OAKA **44** 89-90, CLEA **44** 90

PHELPS, RAY P
(**19**,29) BKNN **19** 32, CHIA **29** 35-36

PHELPS, TOMMY P
(**57**,41) FLAN **57** 03-04, MILN **41** 05

PHELPS, TRAVIS P
(**61**,50) TBA **61** 01-02, MILN **50** 04

PHILLEY, DAVE 0F/3B1B/UTIL (49,38,**9**,5,17, 4,6,12,32,22, 19) CHIA **49** 41, **38** 46, **9** 46-51, PHIA **5** 51, **17** 51-53, CLEA **17** 54-55, BALA **4** 55-56, CHIA **6** 56-57, DETA **9** 57, PHIN **12** 58-60, SFN **32** 60, BALA **22** 60-61, BOSA **19** 62

PHILLIPS, ADOLFO OF (54,23,41,**20**, 28) PHIN **54** 64, **23** 65-66, CHIN **41** 66, **20** 66-69, MONN **20** 69-70, CLEA **28** 72

PHILLIPS, ANDY INF (39,18,**14**) NYA **39** 04, **18/14** 05

PHILLIPS, BRANDON 2B (49,**27**) CLEA **61** 02-03, **7** 03-05

PHILLIPS, BUBBA OF/3B/UTIL (**5**,7,1) CHIA **5** 56-59, CLEA **7** 60, **5** 60-62, DETA **1** 63-64

PHILLIPS, DAMON (DEE) SS/3B (16,2,**5**,__) CINN **16** 42, BOSN **2/5** 44, __ 46

PHILLIPS, DICK 1B/3B/INF/CH (14,**29**,22,37) SFN **14** 62, WASA **29** 63-64, **22** 66, SDN *CH* **37** 80

PHILLIPS, ED P (49,**27**) BOSA **49/27** 70

PHILLIPS, EDDIE C (32,**15**) NYA **32** 32, WASA **32** 34, CLEA **15** 35

PHILLIPS, EDDIE PR (**20**) STLN **20** 53

PHILLIPS, J. M. (BUBBA) OF/3B (**11**) DETA **11** 55

PHILLIPS, J. R. 1B (31,13,**17**,29) SFN **31** 93, **13** 94-95, **17** 95-96, PHIN **17** 96, HOUN **29** 97-98, COLN **31** 99

PHILLIPS, JACK (STRETCH) 1B/3B/P/UTIL (36,34,**5**,30) NYA **36** 47-49, **34** 48, PITN **5** 49-52, DETA **30** 55-57

PHILLIPS, JASON C. P (**26**) PITN **26** 99, CLEA **59** 02-03

PHILLIPS, JASON L. C/1B (26,7,**23**,9) NYN **26** 01, **7** 02, **23** 03-04, LAN **9** 05

PHILLIPS, JOHN (JACK) P (__) NYN __ 45

PHILLIPS, LEFTY CH/M (**36**) LAN *CH* **36** 65-68, CALA *M* **36** 69-71

PHILLIPS, MIKE INF (10,**5**,12) SFN **10** 73-75, NYN **5** 75-77, STLN **5** 77-80, SDN **10** 81, MONN **12** 81-83

PHILLIPS, PAUL C (3,**11**) KCA **3** 04, **11** 05

PHILLIPS, RED P (19,**28**) DETA **19** 34, **28** 36

PHILLIPS, TAYLOR (TAY) P (17,**29**,41,44) MILN **17** 56-57, CHIN **29** 58, **41** 59, PHIN **44** 59-60, CHIA **29** 63

PHILLIPS, TONY SS/2B/OF/UTIL (18,2,4,19,8, 73,12,**6**) OAKA **18** 82-86, **2** 86-89, DETA **4** 90-94, CALA **19** 95, CHIA **8** 96, **73** 97, ANAA **73** 97, TORA **12** 98, NYN **6** 98, OAKA **6** 99

PHOEBUS, TOM P (**36**) BALA **36** 66-70, SDN **36** 71-72, CHIN **36** 72

PHOENIX, STEVE P (**38**) OAKA **38** 94-95

PIATT, ADAM OF/1B/DH (58,**48**) OAKA **36** 00, **6** 01-02, **8** 03, TBA **3/32** 03

PIATT, DOUG P (58,**48**) MONN **58/48** 91

PIAZZA, MIKE C/1B (25,**31**) LAN **25** 92, **31** 93-98, FLAN **31** 98, NYN **31** 98-05

PICCIOLO, ROB SS/INF/UTIL/DH/CH (**8**,10,23,5) OAKA **8** 77-82, MILA **8** 82-83, CALA **10** 84, OAKA **8** 85, SDN *CH* **23** 90, *CH* **5** 91-05

PICCIUTO, NICK 3B/2B (**7**) PHIN **7** 45

PICHARDO, HIPOLITO P (58,**35**) KCA **58** 92, **35** 93-98, (99), BOSA **35** 00-01, HOUN **35** 02

PICHE, RON P/CH (35,**38**,23,37, 41) MILN **35** 60-62, **38** 63, CALA **23** 65, STLN **37** 66, MONN *CH* **41** 76

PICINICH, VAL C/CH (**12**,23,30) BKNN **12** 32-33, PITN **23** 33, CINN *CH* **30** 34

PICKERING, CALVIN 1B/DH (**6**,39,34,57) BALA **6** 98, **39** 99 , CINN **34** 01, BOSA **57** 01, (02), KCA **36** 04-05

PICKERING, URBANE (PICK) 3B/2B/C (8,**7**) BOSA **8** 31, **7** 32

PICKETT, RICKY P (**57**) ARIN **57** 98

PICKFORD, KEVIN P (**57**) SDN **43** 02

PICKREL, CLARENCE P (18,**26**) PHIN **18** 33, BOSN **26** 34

PICO, JEFF P (51,**41**) CHIN **51** 88, **41** 88-90

PICONE, MARIO (BABE) P (37,24,**36**) NYN **37** 47, **24** 52, **36** 54, CINN **36** 54

PIECHOTA, AL (PIE) P (**28**) BOSN **28** 40-41

PIEDRA, JORGE OF (**3**) COLN **3** 04-05

PIERCE, BILLY P (5,20,10,**19**) DETA **5/12/20** 45, **10** 48, CHIA **19** 49-61, SFN **19** 62-64

PIERCE, ED P (**54**) KCA **54** 92

PIERCE, JACK 1B (**18**,27) ATLN **18** 73-74, DETA **27** 75

PIERCE, JEFF P (**56**) BOSA **56** 95

PIERCE, TONY P (**32**) KCA **32** 67, OAKA **32** 68

PIERETTI, MARINO (CHICK) P (**15**,49,14,47, 18,28) WASA **15** 45-48, CHIA **49** 48, **14** 48-49, CLEA **47/18/28** 50

PIERRE, JUAN OF (6,**9**) COLN **6** 00, **9** 01-02, FLAN **9** 03-05

PIERRO, BILL (WILD BILL) P (21,**13**) PITN **21/13** 50

PIERSALL, JIMMY OF/3B/UTIL (26,24,2,34, **37**,4) BOSA **26/24** 50, **2** 52, **34** 53, **37** 53-58, CLEA **37** 59-61, WASA **37** 62-63, NYN **34** 63, LAA **4** 63-64, CALA **4** 65-67

PIERSOLL, CHRIS P (**60**) CINN **60** 01

PIERZYNSKI, A. J. C (9,**26**,36,12) MINA **9** 98-99, **26** 00-03, SFN **36** 04, CHIA **12** 05

PIET, TONY 2B/3B/OF (22,**2**,8,37,27) PITN **22** 32-33, CINN **2** 34, **8** 35, CHIA **37** 35, **2** 36-37, DETA **27** 38

PIGNATANO, JOE C/3B/CH (**58**,12,2,5, 44,52) BKNN **58** 57, LAN **58** 58-60, KCA **12** 61, SFN **2/5** 62, WASA *CH* **44** 65-67, NYN *CH* **52** 68-81, ATLN *CH* **52** 82-84

PIKE, JESS OF (**39**) NYN **39** 46

PIKTUZIS, GEORGE P (**50**) CHIN **50** 56

PILARCIK, AL OF (6,**2**,14,29) KCA **6** 56, BALA **2** 57-60, KCA **14** 61, CHIA **29** 61

PILLETTE, DUANE (DEE) P (**35**,21,12,28, 33) NYA **35** 49-50, STLA **35** 50, **21** 50-51, **12** 52-53, **21** 53, BALA **28** 54-55, PHIN **33** 56

PILNEY, ANDY PH (**19**) BOSN **19** 36

PINA, HORACIO P B (31,**28**,7,36, 34,35) CLEA **31** 68-69, WASA **28** 70-71, TEXA **28** 72, OAKA **7/28** 73, CHIN **36** 74, CALA **34** 74, PHIN **35** 78

PINEDA, LUIS P (30,**49**) DETA **30** 01, CINN **49** 02

PINEIRO, JOEL P (**19**) SEAA **38** 00-05

PINIELLA, LOU (SWEET LOU) OF/1B/DH/CH/M (24,23,9, **14**, 41) BALA **24** 64, CLEA **23** 68, KCA **9** 69-73, NYA **14** 74-84, *CH* **14** 85, *M* **14** 86-88, CINN *M* **41** 90-92, SEAA *M* **14** 93-02, TBA *M* **14** 03-05

PINKUS, ? CH (**5**) CHIN *CH* **5** 77

PINSON, VADA OF/1B/UTIL/CH (**28**) CINN **28** 58-68, STLN **28** 69, CLEA **28** 70-71, CALA **28** 72-73, KCA **28** 74-75, SEAA *CH* **28** 77-80, CHIA *CH* **28** 81, SEAA *CH* **28** 82-83, DETA *CH* **28** 86-91, FLAN *CH* **28** 93-94

PIPGRAS, ED P (**24**) BKNN **24** 32

PIPGRAS, GEORGE P (14,12,10,11, 35) NYA **14** 29, **12** 30-31, **10** 32-33, BOSA **11** 33, **14** 34, **35** 35

PIPPEN, COTTON P (20,25,26,17, **11**) STLN **20** 36, PHIA **25** 39, DETA **26** 39, **17** 40, **11** 40

PIRKL, GREG 1B/DH (**20**,45) SEAA **20** 93-96, BOSA **45** 96

PIRTLE, GERRY P (**18**) MONN **18** 78

PISCIOTTA, MARC P (**41**,34) CHIN **41** 97-98, KCA **34** 99

PISONI, JIM OF (__,36,32,24, **15**) STLA __ 53, KCA **36** 56, **32** 57, MILN **24** 59, NYA **15** 59-60

PITKO, ALEX (SPUNK) OF (__,**36**) PHIN __ 38, WASA **36** 39

PITLER, JAKE CH (**31**) BKNN **31** 47-57

PITLOCK, SKIP P (38,**26**) SFN **38** 70, CHIA **26** 74-75

PITTARO, CHRIS INF/2B/SS/DH (12,**2**) DETA **12** 85, MINA **2** 86-87

PITTMAN, JOE 2B/3B/OF/INF (**9**,8,2) HOUN **9** 81-82, SDN **8** 82, SFN **2** 84

PITTS, GAYLEN INF/CH (**23**,4) OAKS **23** 74-75, STLN **4** 91-95

PITTSLEY, JIM P (51,**34**,43) KCA **51** 95, **34** 96-99, MILN **43** 99

PITULA, BOB OF (30,**34**) CLEA **30/34** 57

PIZARRO, JUAN P (34,**32**,29,26, 24,49,43,42, 11,50,46,51, 39) MILN **34** 57-60, CHIA **32** 61-66, PITN **29** 67-68, BOSA **26** 68-69, **24** 68-69, CLEA **49/43** 69, OAKA **42/11** 69, CHIN **50/42** 70, **46** 70-73, HOUN **51/39** 73, PITN **49** 74

PLADSON, GORDY P (34,26,**44**) HOUN **34** 79, **26** 80-81, **33** 80, **44** 81-82

PLANK, ED P (**37**) SFN **37** 78-79

PLANTENBERG, ERIK P (32,34,**12**,41) SEAA **32/34** 93, **12** 94, PHIN **41** 97

PLANTIER, PHIL OF (55,7,29,**24**, 17, 23) BOSA **55/7** 90, **29** 91-92, SDN **24** 93-94, HOUN **17** 95, SDN **7** 95, OAKA **23** 96, SDN **7** 97, STLN **23** 97

PLARSKI, DON OF (**6**) KCA **6** 55

PLASKETT, ELMO C/3B (3,**2**) PITN **3** 62, **2** 63

PLATT, WHITEY OF/1B (48,23,**5**) CHIN **48** 42-43, CHIA **23** 46, STLA **5** 46, 48-49

PLAZA, RON CH (7,**11**,43) SEAA *CH* **7** 69, CINN *CH* **11** 78-83, OAKA *CH* **43** 86

PLEIS, BILL P (40,**19**) MINA **40** 61, **19** 62-66

PLESAC, DAN P (**37**,32,19) MILA **37** 86-92, CHIN **32** 93, **37** 94, PITN **19** 95-96, TORA **19** 97-99, ARIN **19** 99-00, TORA **19** 01-02, PHIN **19** 02-03

PLESS, RANCE 1B/3B (**8**) KCA **8** 56

PLEWS, HERB 2B/3B/INF (**25**,1) WASA **25** 56-59, BOSA **1**59

PLODINEC, TIM P (**56**) STLN **56** 72

PLUMMER, BILL C/3B/INF/CH/M (8,**9**,3,41) CHIN **8** 68, CINN **9** 70-77, SEAA **3** 78, *BPP* **9** 78, 83, *CH* **3** 88-91, *M* **9** 92, COLN *CH* **41** 94

PLUNK, ERIC P (51,33,**38**,39) OAKA **51** 86-89, NYA **33** 89-91, CLEA **38** 92-98, MILN **39** 98, **38** 99

PLYMPTON, JEFF P (**54**) BOSA **54** 91

POAT, RAY P (35,**30**,27) CLEA **35** 42-44, NYN **30** 47-49, PITN **27** 49

POCOROBA, BIFF C/3B (**42**,4) ATLN **42** 75-76, **4** 77-84

PODBIELAN, BUD P (40,**38**,23) BKNN **40** 49-52, CINN **38** 52-55, 57, **34** 57, CLEA **23** 59

PODGAJNY, JOHNNY (SPECS) P (22,**17**,20,39, 31) PHIN **22** 40, **17** 41, **20** 42, **17** 43, PITN **39** 43, CLEA **31** 46

PODRES, JOHNNY P/CH (45,**22**,34,46) BKNN **45** 53-55, 57, LAN **22** 58-66, DETA **22** 66-67, SDN **34** 69, **45** 69, *CH* **45** 73, BOSA *CH* **34** 80, MINA *CH* **46** 81-85, PHIN *CH* **46** 91-96

PODSEDNIK, SCOTT OF/DH (**20**,22) SEAA **20** 01-03, MILN **20** 04, CHIA **22** 05

POEPPING, MIKE OF (**26**) MINA **26** 75

POFAHL, JIMMY SS/2B (7,12,**23**) WASA **7** 40, **12** 41, **23** 42

POFF, JOHN OF/1B/UTIL (26,**8**) PHIN **26** 79, MILA **8** 80

POFFENBERGER, BOOTS P (24,**17**,32) DETA **24** 37, **17** 38, BKNN **32** 39

POHOLSKI, TOM P (10,29,**23**) STLN **10** 50, **29** 51, **23** 54-56, CHIN **29** 57

POINDEXTER, JENNINGS (JINX) P (20,11,**23**) BOSA **20** 36, PHIN **11/23** 39

POINTER, AARON (HAWK) OF (17,28,**23**) HOUN **17** 63, **28** 66-67, **23** 67

POLANCO, PLACIDO INF (67,**27**,23,14) STLN **67** 98, **27** 98-02, PHIN **23** 02, **27** 03-05, DETA **14** 05

POLAND, HUGH C (9,16,14,18, 34,**6**) NYN **9** 43, BOSN **16** 43, **14** 44, **18/9** 46, PHIN **34** 47, CINN **6** 47-48

POLCOVICH, KEVIN SS (**2**) PITN **2** 97-98

POLDBERG, BRIAN CH (**25**,49) KCA *CH* **25** 04-05, **49** 05

POLE, DICK P/CH (**45**,13,34,48, __,38,46,39) BOSA **45** 73-76, SEAA **45** 77-78, **13** 78, CHIN *CH* **34** 88-91, SFN *CH* **48** 93-97, BOSA *CH* __ 98, ANAA *CH* **38** 99, CLEA *CH* **38** 00, CHIN *CH* **46** 03-04, **39** 05

POLIDOR, GUS SS/OF/INF/UTIL/DH (56,12,**14**,10) CALA **56** 85, **12** 86, **14** 87-88, MILA **10** 89, **14** 89-90, FLAN **14** 93

POLITTE, CLIFF P (40,**35**,19) STLN **40** 98, PHIN **35** 99-02, TORA **19** 02-03, CHIA **18** 04-05

POLIVKA, KEN (SOUP) P (**42**) CINN **42** 47

POLLET, HOWIE P/CH (37,27,**11**,30, 16,24,4,26, 5) STLN **37** 41, **27** 42, **11** 42-43, 46-51, PITN **30** 51, **11** 52-53, CHIN **16** 53-55, CHIA **24** 56, PITN **11** 56, STLN *CH* **4** 59, *CH* **26** 60-62, *CH* **4** 63-64, HOUN *CH* **5** 65

POLLEY, DAVE P (**56**) NYA **56** 96

POLLI, LOU (CRIP) P (21,26) STLA **21** 32, NYN **26** 44

POLLY, NICK 3B (21,**19**) BKNN **21** 37, BOSA **19** 45

POLONI, JOHN P (**27**) TEXA **27** 77

POLONIA, LUIS OF/DH (**22**,17,29,1, 46,19) OAKA **22** 87-89, NYA **22** 89-90, CALA **22** 90-93, NYA **17** 94-95, ATLN **17** 95, BALA **29** 96, ATLN **1/17** 96, DETA **46/29** 99, **22** 00, NYA **19** 00

POMORSKI, JOHN P (**28**) CHIA **28** 34

PONCE, CARLOS UTIL (**36**) MILA **36** 85

POND, SIMON OF/DH (**18**) TORA **18** 04

PONSON, SIDNEY P (**43**) BALA **43** 98-03, SFN **43** 03, BALA **43** 04-05

POOL, HARLIN (SAMSON) OF (10,**15**) CINN **10** 34, **15** 35

POOLE, JIM P (54,31,52,**45**, 62,19,41,37, 48) LAN **54/31** 90, TEXA **52** 91, BALA **45** 91-94, CLEA **62** 95-96, SFN **19** 96-98, CLEA **62** 98, PHIN **41** 99, CLEA **62** 99, DETA **37** 00, MONN **48** 00

POOLE, RAY PH (35,**31**) PHIA **35** 41, **31** 47

POPE, DAVE OF (6,**34**,3) CLEA **6** 52, **34** 54-55, BALA **3** 55-56, CLEA **34** 56

POPOVICH, PAUL 2B/INF/UTIL (11,**22**,26,24) CHIN **11** 64, **22** 66-67, LAN **26** 68, **22** 69, CHIN **22** 69-73, PITN **24** 74-75

POPOWSKI, EDDIE CH/M (**32**,54,36) BOSA *CH* **32** 67-74, *M* **32** 69, *CH* **54** 75, *CH* **36** 75-76

POQUETTE, TOM OF/DH (44,**25**,17,16, 3,__,38) KCA **44** 73, **25** 76-79, BOSA **17** 79, 81, TEXA **16** 81, KCA **3** 82, KCA *CH* __ 96, *CH* **38** 98

PORTER, BO OF (35,21,**16**) CHIN **35** 99, OAKA **21** 00, TEXA **16** 01

PORTER, BOB OF/1B (22,**7**) ATLN **22** 81, **7** 82

PORTER, CHUCK P (**43**) MILA **43** 81-85

PORTER, COLIN OF (1,**9**,28) HOUN **1/9** 03, STLN **28** 04

PORTER, DAN OF (**29**) WASA **29** 51

PORTER, DARRELL C/DH/UTIL (**15**,25,17) MILA **15** 71-76, KCA **15** 77-80, STLN **15** 81-85, TEXA **25** 86, **17** 86-87

PORTER, DICK (WIGGLES)(TWITCHES) OF/2B (**2**,23) CLEA **2** 31-34, BOSA **23** 34

PORTER, JAY (J. W.) OF/1B/C/UTIL (22,9,23,**15**,4, 44) STLA **22** 52, DETA **9** 55, **23** 56, **15** 56-57, CLEA **4** 58, WASA **9** 59, STLN **44** 59

PORTERFIELD, BOB P (18,23,29,**19**, 16,20,43) NYA **18** 48-50, **23** 50-51, WASA **29** 51, **19** 51-55, BOSA **16/20** 56, **19** 57-58, PITN **16** 58-59, CHIN **43** 59

PORTO, AL (LEFTY) P (**36**) PHIN **36** 48

PORTOCARRERO, ARNIE P (**25**,24) PHIA **25** 54, KCA **25** 55-57, BALA **24** 58-60

PORTUGAL, MARK P (45,36,51,19, **21**,31) MINA **45** 85, **36** 85-87, **51/19** 88, HOUN **51** 89-93, SFN **19** 94-95, CINN **21** 95-96, PHIN **21** 97-98, BOSA **31** 99

PORZIO, MIKE P (53,**41**) COLN **53** 99, CHIA **53** 02, **41** 02-03

POSADA, JORGE C (62,41,55,**20**, 22) NYA **62** 95, **41/55** 96, **20/22** 97, **20** 98-05

POSADA, LEO OF (37,**19**) KCA **37** 60, **19** 61-62

POSE, SCOTT OF (**2**,26,38) FLAN **2** 93, NYA **26/38** 97, KCA **38** 99-00

POSEDEL, BILL (BARNACLE BILL)(SAILOR BILL) P/CH (**21**,20,17,25, 32,42,33,31, 1,40,9) BKNN **21** 38, BOSN **21** 39-40, **20** 40, **17** 41, **25** 46, PITN *CH* **32** 49-50, *CH* **42** 51-52, STLN *CH* **33** 54-57, PHIN *CH* **31** 58, SFN *CH* **1** 59- 60, OAKA *CH* **40** 68-72, SDN *CH* **9** 74

POSER, BOB P (37,35,29,**20**) CHIA **37/35/29** 32, STLA **20** 35

POSSEHL, LOU P (39,29,**12**,16, 41) PHIN **39** 46, **29** 47, **12** 48, **16** 51, **41** 52

POST, WALLY OF
(29,25,**28**,14, 20) CINN **29** 49, **25** 51, **28** 52-57, PHIN **14** 58-60, CINN **29** 60-63, MINA **29** 63, CLEA **20** 64

POTE, LOU P
(**58**,57) ANAA **58** 99-02, CLEA **57** 04

POTTER, DYKES P
(**36**) BKNN **36** 38

POTTER, MIKE P
(**40**) STLN **40** 76-77

POTTER, NELSON (NELS)(NELLIE) P
(20,**24**,27,22) STLN **20** 36, PHIA **24** 38-41, BOSA **24** 41, STLN **24** 43-45, **27** 46-48, PHIA **22** 48, BOSN **22** 48-49

POTTS, MIKE P
(**49**) MILA **49** 96

POULSEN, KEN 3B/SS
(**17**) BOSA **17** 67

POWELL, ALONZO OF/UTIL
(21,**7**) MONN **21** 87, SEAA **7** 91

POWELL, BOOG 1B/OF/DH
(30,16,**26**,8 22) BALA **30** 61, **16** 62, **26** 63, **8** 64, **26** 64-74, CLEA **26** 75-76, LAN **22** 77

POWELL, BRIAN P
(36,**45**,40,51) DETA **36** 98, HOUN **45** 00-01, DETA **40** 02, SFN **51** 03, PHIN **51** 04

POWELL, DANTE OF
(23,30,**4**,56) SFN **23** 97, **30** 98, ARIN **4** 99, SFN **56** 01

POWELL, DENNIS P
(**48**,34) LAN **48** 85-86, SEAA **48** 87-90, MILA **34** 90, SEAA **48** 92-93,

POWELL, GROVER P
(**41**) NYN **41** 63

POWELL, HOSKEN OF/DH
(**10**,22) MINA **10** 78-81, TORA **22** 82-83

POWELL, JAKE OF/3B/2B
(9,24,4,**7**,17, 22,23,36) WASA **9** 34, **24** 35, **4** 36, NYA **7** 36-39, **17** 39-40, WASA **22** 43, **23** 44, **4** 45, PHIN **36** 45

POWELL, JAY P
(59,**39**,43) FLAN **59** 96, **39** 96-98, HOUN **39** 98-01, COLN **39** 01, TEXA **39** 02-04, ATLN **43** 05

POWELL, JEREMY OF
(**49**) MONN **49** 98-00

POWELL, LEROY PR
(21,**17**) CHIA **21** 55, **17** 57

POWELL, PAUL OF/C
(**7**,2,12) MINA **7** 71, LAN **2** 73, **71/12** 75

POWELL, ROSS P
(55,**52**,49) CINN **55** 93, HOUN **52** 94-95, PITN **49** 95

POWER, TED P
(25,**48**,43,42) LAN **25** 81-82, CINN **48** 83-87, KCA **48** 88, DETA **43** 88, STLN **42** 89, PITN **48** 90, CINN **48** 91, CLEA **48** 92-93, SEAA **42/48** 93

POWER, VIC 1B/UTIL/INF
(5,**7**,10,28,14, 62) PHIA **5** 54, KCA **7** 55-58, CLEA **10** 58-61, MINA **28** 62-64 LAA **14** 64, PHIN **62** 64, CALA **14** 65

POWERS, JOHNNY OF/2B
(**14**,27,20,8) PITN **14** 55-58, CINN **27** 59, BALA **20** 60, CLEA **8** 60

POWERS, LES 1B
(**28**,16) NYN **28** 38, PHIN **16** 39

POWERS, MIKE OF
(31,**27**) CLEA **31** 32, **27** 33

POWIS, CARL (JUG) OF
(**42**) BALA **42** 57

POZO, ARQUIMEDEZ 2B/3B
(41,48,29) SEAA **41** 95, BOSA **48** 96, **29** 97

PRALL, WILLIE P
(38,**37**) CHIN **38/37** 75

PRAMESA, JOHNNY C
(**9**,25) CINN **9** 49-51, CHIN **25** 52

PRATT, ANDY P
(**26**,29) ATLN **26** 02, CHIN **29** 04

PRATT, TODD C/1B
(23,3,6,8,43, **7**,3) PHIN **23** 92-93, **3/6** 94, CHIN **8** 95, NYN **43** 97, **7** 98-01, PHIN **3** 01-05

PREGENZER, JOHN P
(40,**18**) SFN **40** 63, **18** 64

PREIBISCH, MEL (PRIMO) OF
(14,**36**) BOSN **14** 40, **36** 41

PRENDERGAST, JIM P
(**38**) BOSN **38** 48

PRESCOTT, BOBBY OF
(**22**) KCA **22** 61

PRESKO, JOE (LITTLE JOE) P
(21,**32**,41,27) STLN **21** 51-53, **32** 53-54, DETA **41** 57, **27** 58

PRESLEY, JIM 3B/1B/UTIL/DH/CH
(**17**,18) SEAA **17** 84-89, ATLN **18** 90, SDN **18** 91, ARIN *CH* **17** 98-00

PRESSNELL, TOT P
(**18**,40) BKNN **18** 38-40, CHIN **40** 41-42

PRICE, BRYAN CH
(**35**,32,34) SEAA *CH* **35** 00, **32** 01-02, **35** 03-04, **34** 05

PRICE, JACKIE (JOHNNY) SS
(**35**) CLEA **35** 46

PRICE, JIM C
(34,**12**) DETA **34** 67, **12** 68-71

PRICE, JOE P
(**49**,47,23) CINN **49** 80-86, SFN **47** 87-89, BOSA **49** 89, BALA **23** 90

PRICHARD, BOB 1B
(**17**) WASA **17** 39

PRIDDY, BOB P
(8,**37**,31,47, 38,16,39,26, 40,46,) PITN **8** 62, **37/31** 64, SFN **47** 65, **38** 65-66, WASA **16** 67, CHIA **39** 68, **26** 69, CALA **40** 69, ATLN **46** 69, **37** 69-71

PRIDDY, JERRY 2B/SS/INF
(14,6,2,**4**) NYA **14** 41-42, WASA **6** 43, 46-47, STLA **2** 48-49, DETA **4** 50-53

PRIDE, CURTIS OF/DH
(16,15,36,2, 19,**11**,28) MONN **16** 93, **15** 95, DETA **36** 96-97, BOSA **2** 97, ATLN **19** 98, BOSA **11** 00, MONN **28** 01, NYA **11** 03, ANAA **19** 04, LAA **19** 05

PRIEST, EDDIE OF
(**51**) CINN **51** 98

PRIETO, ALEX SS/2B
(**46**) MINA **46** 03, **17** 04

PRIETO, ARIEL P
(**48**) OAKA **48** 95-98, (99), **30** 00, TBA **48** 01

PRIETO, CHRIS OF
(**38**) LAA **38** 05

PRIM, RAY (POP) P
(30,45,**39**) WASA **30** 33-34, PHIN **45** 35, CHIN **39** 43, 45-46

PRINCE, DON P/BPP
(**47**,48) CHIN **47** 62, *BPP* **48** 65

PRINCE, TOM C/1B/3B
(44,46,14,**15**, 12,22,11) PITN **44** 87, **46** 87-90, **14** 90-93, LAN **15** 94-98, PHIN **12** 99, **22** 00, MINA **12** 01-03, KCA **11** 03

PRINZ, BRET P
(**41**,38,47,64) ARIN **41** 01-03, NYA **38** 03, **47** 04, LAA **64** 05

PRIOR, MARK P
(**22**) CHIN **22** 02-05

PRITCHARD, BUDDY SS/2B
(**5**) PITN **5** 57

PRITCHETT, CHRIS 1B
(**28**) CALA **28** 96, ANAA **28** 98-99, PHIN **28** 00

PROCTOR, JIM P
(**37**) DETA **37** 59

PROCTOR, SCOTT P
(56,57,**43**) NYA **56/57** 04, **43** 05

PROKOPEC, LUKE P
(**37**) LAN **57** 00-01, TORA **44** 02

PROLY, MIKE P
(46,**24**,30,36) STLN **46** 76, CHIA **24** 78-80, PHIN **30** 81, CHIN **36** 82-83

PROTHRO, DOC M
(**1**) PHIN *M* **1** 39-41

PRUETT, HUB (SHUCKS) P
(**21**) BOSN **21** 32

PRUETT, JIM C
(__**9**) PHIA __ 44, **9** 45

PRUITT, RON C/OF/UTIL
(35,**13**,7,18, 25,14) TEXA **35** 75, CLEA **13** 76-77, **7** 78, **13** 78-80, CHIA **18** 80, CLEA **13** 81, SFN **25** 82, **14** 83

PRYOR, GREG SS/INF/DH
(15,16,11,**4**) TEXA **15** 76, CHIA **16** 78-80, **11** 80-81, KCA **4** 82-86

PUCCINELLI, GEORGE (POOCH)(COUNT) OF
(30,4,**8**) STLN **30** 32, STLA **4** 34, PHIA **8** 36

PUCKETT, KIRBY OF/DH/UTIL
(**34**) MINA **34** 84-95

PUENTE, MIGUEL P
(**41**) SFN **41** 70

PUFFER, BRANDON P
(**59**,58,38) HOUN **59** 02-03, SDN **58** 04, SFN **38** 05

PUGH, TIM P
(55,**40**,46,53, 50) CINN **55** 92-93, **40** 93-96, KCA **46** 96, CINN **53** 96, DETA **50** 97

PUHL, TERRY OF/1B/DH
(**21**,26) HOUN **21** 77-90, KCA **26** 91

PUIG, RICH 2B/3B
(**6**) NYN **6** 74

PUJOLS, ALBERT 3B/1B/OF
(**5**) STLN **5** 01-05

PUJOLS, LUIS C/1B/3B/CH
(53,8,**6**,49,31, 55,56) HOUN **53** 77, **8** 78-79, **6** 80-83, KCA **49** 84, TEXA **8** 85, MONN *CH* **31** 93, **55** 94-96, **56** 96, **55** 97-00, DETA *M* **53** 02, SFN *CH* **55** 03-05

PULEO, CHARLIE P
(**25**,45) NYN **25** 81-82, CINN **25** 83-84, ATLN **45** 86-89

PULIDO, ALFONSO P
(**58**,47) PITN **58** 83-85, **26** 84, NYA **47** 86

PULIDO, CARLOS P
(**22**,51) MINA **22** 94, **51** 03-04

PULLIAM, HARVEY OF
(51,**26**,24,29) KCA **51** 91-92, **26** 93, COLN **24** 95, **29** 96, **24** 97

PULSIPHER, BILL P
(**21**,46,25,41 36,40) NYN **21** 95, 98, MILN **46** 98-99, NYN **25** 00, BOSA **46/41** 01, CHIA **36** 01, STLN **40** 05

PUNTO, NICK SS/2B
(34,**8**) PHIN **34** 01-02, **8** 03, MINA **8** 04-05

PURDIN, JOHN P
(47,**35**) LAN **47** 64, **35** 65, 68-69

PURKEY, BOB P
(34,**37**,28) PITN **34** 54-57, CINN **37** 58-64, STLN **28** 65, PITN **37** 66

PUTNAM, ED C/1B/UTIL
(**8**,17,12) CHIN **8** 76, **17** 78, DETA **12** 79

PUTNAM, PAT 1B/OF/UTIL/DH
(**18**,23,35) TEXA **18** 77-82, SEAA **23** 83-84, MINA **35** 84

PUTZ, J. J. P
(**20**) SEAA **20** 03-05

PYBURN, JIM 3B/OF/C
(**8**) BALA **8** 55-57

PYE, EDDIE SS
(60,**3**) LAN **60** 94, **3** 95

PYECHA, JOHN P
(**34**) CHIN **34** 54

PYLE, EWALD (LEFTY) P
(9,23,21,12, **18**,15) STLA **9** 39, **23** 42, WASA **21/12** 43, NYN **18** 44-45, BOSN **15** 45

PYTLAK, FRANKIE C/1B
(**11**,8,2,29,24) CLEA **11** 32-36, **8** 37-40, BOSA **2** 41, **29** 45, **24** 46

PYZNARSKI, TIM 1B
(**17**) SDN **17** 86

Q

QUADE, MIKE CH
(45,**48**) OAKA *CH* **45** 00, **48** 01-02

QUALLS, CHAD P
(**50**) HOUN **50** 04-05

QUALLS, JIM OF/2B
(42,**19**) CHIN **42** 69, MONN **19** 70, CHIA **19** 72

QUALTERS, TOM (MONEYBAGS) P
(**33**,36,31) PHIN **33** 53, 57-58, CHIA **36/31** 58

QUANTRILL, PAUL P
(49,**48**,46) BOSA **49** 92-94, PHIN **48** 94-95, TORA **48** 96-01, LAN **46** 02-03, NYA **48** 04-05, SDN **46** 05, FLAN **48** 05

QUEEN, BILLY (DOC) OF
(**7**) MILN **7** 54

QUEEN, MEL, JR. OF/P/CH S
(**22**,46,6,34) CINN **22** 64-69, CALA **46** 70-72, CLEA *CH* **6** 82, TORA *CH* **34** 96-99

QUEEN, MEL P F
(36,16,38,**17**, 23,27) NYA **36** 42, **16** 44, **38** 46, **17** 46-47, PITN **23** 47-48, **27** 50, **36** 51-52

QUELICH, GEORGE OF
(**37**) DETA **37** 31

QUEVEDO, RUBEN P
(48,**37**) CHIN **48** 00, MILN **37** 01-03

QUICK, HAL (BLONDIE) SS
(**39**) WASA **39** 39

QUILICI, FRANK (GUIDO) 2B/SS/INF/CH/M
(11,**7**,43) MINA **11** 65, **7** 67-70, *CH* **43** 71-72, *M* **43** 72-75

QUILRICO, RAFAEL P
(**43**) PHIN **43** 96

QUINLAN, ROBB 1B/3B
(**39**) ANAA **39** 03-04, LAA **39** 05

QUINLAN, TOM 3B
(**16**,30,23) TORA **16** 90, 92, PHIN **30** 94, MINA **23** 96

QUINN, FRANK P
(**26**) BOSA **26** 49-50

QUINN, JACK P
(**22**,29) BKNN **22** 32, CINN **29** 33

QUINN, MARK OF/DH
(52,**14**) KCA **52** 99, **14** 00-02

QUINN, WIMPY P
(18,**16**) CHIN **18/16** 41

QUINONES, LUIS INF/DH
(52,11,2,28, 9,**10**,49) OAKA **52/11** 83, SFN **2** 86, CHIN **28** 87, CINN **9** 88-89, **10** 89-91, MINA **49** 92

QUINONES, REY SS/DH
(**51**) BOSA **51** 86, SEAA **51** 86-89, PITN **51** 89

QUINTANA, CARLOS OF/1B/UTIL/DH
(**18**) BOSA **18** 88-93

QUINTANA, LUIS P
(**44**) CALA **44** 74-75

QUINTANILLA, OMAR SS/2B
(**8**) COLN **8** 05

QUINTERO, HUMBERTO C
(**11**,9) SDN **11** 03-04, HOUN **9** 05

QUIRK, ART P
(**27**,22) BALA **27** 62, WASA **22** 63

QUIRK, JAMIE INF/C/UTIL/OF/CH
(30,**9**,5,10,16, 13,18,27,3, 15,6,8) KCA **30** 75, **9** 75-76, MILA **5** 77, KCA **10** 78, **9** 79-82, STLN **16** 83, *CH* **9** 84, CHIA **13** 84, CLEA **9** 84, KCA **18** 85-86, **9** 86-88, NYA **27** 89, OAKA **3** 89, BALA **15** 89, OAKA **3** 90, **6** 90-91, **9** 92, KCA *CH* **9** 94-01, TEXA *CH* **9** 02, COLN *CH* **9** 03, **8** 04, **9** 05

QUIROZ, GUILLERMO C
(**16**) TORA **16** 04-05

QUISENBERRY, DAN (QUIZ) P
(**29**,28,40,47) KCA **29** 79-88, STLN **28** 88, **40** 88-89, SFN **47** 90

R

RAABE, BRIAN 2B
(26,30,**12**) MINA **26** 95-96, SEAA **30** 97, COLN **12** 97

RABB, JOHN (JOHNNY) OF/UTIL
(3,**5**,31,30) SFN **3** 82, **5** 83-84, ATLN **31** 85, SEAA **30** 88

RABE, CHARLIE P
(34,**31**) CINN **34** 57, **31** 58

RABURN, RYAN 3B
(**55**) DETA **55** 04

RACHUNOK, STEVE (THE MAD RUSSIAN) P
(**18**) BKNN **18** 40

RACKLEY, MARV OF
(**35**,17,25) BKNN **35** 47-49, PITN **17** 49, CINN **25** 50

RACZKA, MIKE P
(**52**) OAKA **52** 92

RADATZ, DICK (THE MONSTER) P
(**17**,46,43,14, 22) BOSA **17** 62-66, CLEA **46** 66-67, CHIN **43/46** 67, DETA **14** 69, MONN **17/22** 69

RADCLIFF, RIP OF/1B
(**9**,11,18,5) CHIA **9** 34-39, STLA **11** 40-41, DETA **18** 41, **5** 42-43

RADER, DAVE C/DH B
(6,8,**14**,9,15) SFN **6/8** 71, **14** 72-76, STLN **14** 77, CHIN **9** 78, PHIN **6** 79, BOSA **15** 80

RADER, DOUG (THE RED ROOSTER)(ROJO) 1B/3B/UTIL/CH/M B
(**12**,17,10,4, 11,5,28) HOUN **12** 67-75, SDN **17** 76, **12** 76-77, TORA **10** 77, SDN *CH* **4** 78, *CH* **12** 79, TEXA *M* **11** 83-85, **5** 85, CHIA *CH* **28** 86-87, *M* **28** 86, CALA *M* **12** 89, *M* **4** 90-91, OAKA *CH* **11** 92, FLAN *CH* **12** 93-94, CHIA *CH* **17** 97-98, **12** 98

RADINSKY, SCOTT P
(56,31,**36**) CHIA **56** 90, **31** 90-93, 95, LAN **36** 96-98, STLN **36** 99-00, CLEA **36** 01

RADISON, DAN CH
(**22**,42,3) SDN *CH* **22** 93-94, CHIN *CH* **42** 95-97, *CH* **3** 97-99

RADKE, BRAD P
(59,**22**) MINA **59** 95, **22** 95-05

RADLOSKY, ROB P
(**51**) MINA **51** 99

RADMANOVICH, RYAN OF
(**33**) SEAA **33** 98

RADTKE, JACK INF
(**5**) BKNN **5** 36

RAETHER, HAL (BUD) P
(36,**34**) PHIA **36** 54, KCA **34** 57

RAFFENSBERGER, KEN P
(23,16,14,15, 7,**36**) STLN **23** 39, CHIN **16** 40-41, **14** 41, PHIN **15** 43, **7** 44, **15** 44-45, **16** 46-47, CINN **36** 47-54

RAFFO, AL P
(**25**) PHIN **25** 69

RAGAZZO, DICK CH
(**57**) CALA *CH* **57** 88

RAGGIO, BRADY P
(**64**,38,58,36) STLN **64/38/64** 97, **58** 98, ARIN **36** 03

RAGLAND, FRANK P
(18,**4**) WASA **18** 32, PHIN **4** 33

RAGLAND, TOM 2B/SS/INF
(15,**21**,16) WASA **15/21** 71, TEXA **21** 72, CLEA **16** 73

RAICH, ERIC P
(**33**) CLEA **33** 75-76

RAIN, STEVE P
(**41**) CHIN **41** 99-00

RAINES, LARRY UTIL
(**9**) CLEA **9** 57

RAINES, TIM, JR. OF S
(63,**38**,16) BALA **63** 01, **38** 03-04, **16** 04

RAINES, TIM, SR. (ROCK) 2B/OF/DH/CH F
(**30**,31,32) MONN **30** 79-90, CHIA **30** 91-95, NYA **31** 96-98, OAKA **30** 99, MONN **30** 01, BALA **11** 01, FLAN **32/30** 02, MONN *CH* **30** 04, CHIA *CH* **30** 05

RAINEY, CHUCK P
(**42**,30) BOSA **42** 79-82, CHIN **30** 83-84, OAKA **30** 84

RAJSICH, DAVE P B
(52,36,**26**) NYA **52/36** 78, TEXA **26** 79-80

RAJSICH, GARY OF/1B B
(**21**,33,26) NYN **21** 82-83, STLN **33** 84, SFN **26** 85

RAKERS, AARON P
(**47**) BALA **47** 05

RAKERS, JASON P
(**59**,31) CLEA **59** 98, KCA **31** 00

RAKOW, ED (ROCK) P
(**21**,15,35,19, 27) LAN **21/15** 60, KCA **35** 61, **21** 62-63, DETA **19** 64-65, ATLN **27** 67

RAMAZZOTTI, BOB 3B/2B/INF
(38,17,9,**5**) BKNN **38** 46, **17** 46, 48, **9** 49, CHIN **5** 49-53

RAMBERT, PEP P
(**23**) PITN **23** 39-40

RAMIREZ, ALEX OF
(**61**) CLEA **61** 98-00, PITN **61** 00

RAMIREZ, ALLAN P
(**36**) BALA **36** 83

RAMIREZ, ARAMIS 3B
(**16**) PITN **16** 98-03, CHIN **16** 03-05

RAMIREZ, ELIZARDO P
(**46**,67) PHIN **46** 04, CINN **67** 05

RAMIREZ, ERASMO P
(**54**) TEXA **54** 03-05

RAMIREZ, HANLEY INF
(**60**) BOSA **60** 05

RAMIREZ, HECTOR P
(**54**) MILN **54** 99, **58** 00

RAMIREZ, HORACIO P
(**30**) ATLN **30** 03-05

RAMIREZ, JULIO OF
(37,28,39,**43**, 57) FLAN **37** 99, CHIA **28** 01, ANAA **39** 02, **43** 03, SFN **57** 05

RAMIREZ, MANNY OF/DH
(**24**) CLEA **24** 93-00, BOSA **24** 01-05

RAMIREZ, MARIO SS/3B/INF
(3,**12**) NYN **3** 80, SDN **12** 81-85

RAMIREZ, MILT INF
(**41**,31) STLN **41** 70-71, OAKA **31** 79

RAMIREZ, ORLANDO SS/UTIL/DH
(**1**,14,2) CALA **1** 74-76, **14** 77, **2** 79

RAMIREZ, RAFAEL SS/3B/INF/UTIL
(47,**16**) ATLN **47** 80, **16** 81-87, HOUN **16** 88-92

RAMIREZ, ROBERTO P
(**32**,49) SDN **32** 98, COLN **49** 99

RAMOS, BOBBY C/CH
(**44**,57) MONN **44** 78, 80-81, NYA **57** 82, MONN **44** 83-84, ANAA *CH* **13** 01-02

RAMOS, CHUCHO OF
(**24**) CINN **24** 44

RAMOS, DOMINGO SS/INF/DH
(26,17,2,**3**,4, 6,15) NYA **26** 78, TORA **17** 80, SEAA **2** 82, **3** 83-87, CLEA **4** 88, CALA **6** 88,CHIN **15** 89-90

RAMOS, EDGAR P
(**49**) PHIN **49** 97

RAMOS, JOHN C/DH
(**48**) NYA **48** 91

RAMOS, KEN OF
(**29**) HOUN **29** 97

RAMOS, MARIO P
(**40**) TEXA **40** 03

RAMOS, PEDRO (PETE) P
(28,**14**,40,35, 21,29,34,17) WASA **28** 55-60, **14** 60, MINA **28/14** 61, CLEA **28/40** 62, **35** 63-64, NYA **14** 64-66, PHIN **21/ 28** 67, PITN **29** 69, CINN **34** 69, WASA **17** 70

RAMSAY, ROBERT P
(23,**37**) SEAA **23** 99, **37** 00

RAMSDELL, WILLIE (THE KNUCK) P
(32,33,**40**,30) BKNN **32** 47-48, **33** 48, 50, CINN **40** 50-51, CHIN **30** 52

RAMSEY, BILL (SQUARE JAW) OF
(29,**14**) BOSN **29/14** 45

RAMSEY, FERNANDO OF
(**39**) CHIN **39** 92

RAMSEY, MIKE OF
(88,56,**37**) LAN **88/56/37** 87

RAMSEY, MIKE (SUPER SUB) SS/INF/2B
(50,4,**5**,37, 48) STLN **50** 78, **4** 80, **5** 81-84, MONN **4** 84, LAN **37/48** 85

RAND, DICK C
(**16**,10) STLN **16** 53, 55, PITN **10** 57

RANDA, JOE 2B/3B/DH
(18,**16**,19,28) KCA **18** 95, **16** 96, PITN **16** 97, DETA **19** 98, KCA **16** 99-04, CINN **16** 05, SDN **28** 05

RANDALL, BOB 2B/UTIL
(**32**) MINA **32** 76-80

RANDALL, SAP UTIL
(**30**) CHIA **30** 88

RANDALL, SCOTT P
(**65**) CINN **65** 03

RANDLE, LENNY 2B/3B/UTIL
(2,21,33,**7**,11, 34,1) WASA **2** 71, TEXA **2** 72, **21** 73, **33** 74-75, **7** 74-76, NYN **11** 77-78, NYA **34** 79, CHIN **21** 80, SEAA **1** 81-82

RANDOLPH, STEPHEN P
(54,**34**) ARIN **54** 03, **34** 03-04<None>

RANDOLPH, WILLIE 2B/3B/DH/CH/M
(18,12,25,**30**, 20) PITN **18** 75, NYA **25** 76, **30** 76-88, LAN **20** 89, **12** 89-90, OAKA **30** 90, MILA **30** 91, NYN **12** 92, NYA *CH* **30** 94-04, NYN *M* **12** 05

RANEW, MERRITT C/1B/UTIL
(**7**,8,19,26) HOUN **7** 62, CHIN **7** 63-64, MILN **8** 64, CALA **19** 65, SEAA **26** 69

RANEY, RIBS P
(29,**46**) STLA **29** 49, **46** 50

RANSOM, CODY SS
(1,**2**) SFN **1** 01, **2** 02-04

RANSOM, JEFF C
(16,3,**37**) SFN **16** 81, **3** 82, **37** 83

RAPP, EARL OF
(32,26,27,17, **7**) DETA **32** 49, CHIA **26** 49, NYN **27** 51, STLA **17** 51-52, WASA **7** 52

RAPP, PAT P
(**48**,49,28) SFN **48** 92, FLAN **48** 93-97, SFN **49** 97, KCA **28** 98, BOSA **28** 99, BALA **34** 00, ANAA **34** 01

RAPP, VERN M/CH
(**9**,3) STLN *M* **9** 77-78, MONN *CH* **3** 79, *CH* **9** 79-83, CINN *M* **9** 84

RASCHI, VIC (THE SPRINGFIELD RIFLE) P
(42,43,19,**17**, 16) NYA **42** 46, **43/19** 47, **17** 47-53, STLN **17** 54-55, KCA **16** 55

RASMUSSEN, DENNIS P
(47,27,**45**,43, 48,37) SDN **47/27** 83, NYA **45** 84-87, CINN **45** 87-88, SDN **43** 88-91, CHIN **48** 92, KCA **47** 92-93, **37** 95

RASMUSSEN, ERIC (a.k.a. HARRY) P
(**42**,41,34,28) STLN **42** 75-78, SDN **41** 78-80, STLN **34** 82-83, KCA **28** 83

RASNER, DARRELL P
(**31**) WASN **31** 05

RATH, FRED P
(**45**,53) CHIA **45** 68-69, COLN **53** 98

RATH, GARY P
(**49**,57) LAN **49** 98, MINA **57** 99

RATLIFF, GENE PH
(**27**) HOUN **27** 65

RATLIFF, PAUL C
(24,**8**,5,17) MINA **24** 63, **8** 70-71, MILA **5** 71, **17** 72

RATZER, STEVE P
(52,**47**) MONN **52** 80, **47**80-81

RAU, DOUG P
(**31**,48) LAN **31** 72-79, CALA **48** 81

RAUCH, BOB P
(**44**) NYN **44** 72

RAUCH, JON P
(**51**) CHIA **51** 02, 04, MONN **51** 04, WASN **51** 05

RAUDMAN, BOB (SHORTY) OF
(**27**) CHIN **27** 66-67

RAUTZHAN, LANCE P
(60,**38**,29) LAN **60** 77, **38** 77-79, MILA **29** 79

RAWLEY, SHANE P
(41,46,**26**,48, 28,18) SEAA **41** 78-81, NYA **46** 82, **26** 82-84, PHIN **48** 84-86, **28** 86-88, MINA **18** 89

RAY, CHRIS P
(**37**) BALA **37** 05

RAY, JIM (STING) P
(21,35,43,38, **45**,36) HOUN **21** 65, **35** 65, **43/38** 66, **45** 68-73, DETA **36** 74

RAY, JOHNNY 2B/DH/UTIL
(**3**) PITN **3** 81-87, CALA **3** 87-90

RAY, KEN P
(**57**) KCA **57** 99

RAY, LARRY OF
(**37**) HOUN **37** 82

RAYDON, CURT P
(**34**) PITN **34** 58

RAYFORD, FLOYD 3B/UTIL
(9,12,**6**) BALA **9** 80, 82, STLN **12** 83, BALA **6** 84-87

RAYMOND, CLAUDE (FRENCHY) P/CH
(28,35,**36**,16) CHIA **28** 59, MILN **35** 61-63, HOUN **36** 64-67, ATLN **36** 67-69, MONN **16** 69-71, *CH* **16** 69

RAZIANO, BARRY P
(20,31) KCA **20** 73, CALA **31** 74

READY, RANDY 3B/UTIL/DH
(**2**,5,23,20,39, 31) MILA **2** 83-86, SDN **5** 86-89, PHIN **23** 89-91, OAKA **20/2** 92, MONN **39** 93, PHIN **31** 94-95, **23** 95

REAMES, BRITT P
(68,**34**,37) STLN **68** 00, MONN **34** 01-03, OAKA **37** 05

REAMS, LEROY PH
(**23**) PHIN **23** 69

REARDON, JEFF P
(45,44,31,**41**, 54) NYN **45** 79-80, **44** 81, MONN **31** 81, **41** 82-86, MINA **41** 87-89, BOSA **41** 90-92, ATLN **31** 92, CINN **41** 93, NYA **54** 94

REBEL, ART OF
(4,**8**) PHIN **4** 38 , STLN **8** 45

REBERGER, FRANK (CRANE) P/CH
(54,37,46,**39**, 41,51,33) CHIN **54/37** 68, SDN **46** 69, SFN **39** 70-71, **41** 72, CALA *CH* **51** 91, FLAN *CH* **33** 93-94

REBOULET, JEFF SS/2B/UTIL
(**17**,36,14,49) MINA **17** 92-96, BALA **36** 97-99, KCA **17** 00, LAN **14** 01-02, PITN **49** 03

REDDING, TIM P
(**51**,39,29) HOUN **51** 01-04, SDN **39** 05, NYA **29** 05

REDER, JOHNNY 1B/3B
(**28**) BOSA **28** 32

REDFERN, PETE (RED) P
(**17**) MINA **17** 76-82

REDFIELD, JOE 3B
(**6**,36) CALA **6** 88, PITN **36** 91

REDMAN, MARK P
(**55**,18) MINA **55** 99-01, DETA **55** 01-02, FLAN **55** 03, OAKA **55/18** 04, PITN **55** 05

REDMAN, PRENTICE OF
(**20**) NYN **20** 03

REDMAN, TIKE OF
(**5**) PITN **5** 00-01, 03-05

REDMON, GLENN 2B
(**20**) SFN **20** 74

REDMOND, JACK (RED) C
(**10**) WASA **10** 35

REDMOND, MIKE C
(**52**,55) FLAN **52** 98-04, MINA **55** 05

REDMOND, WAYNE OF
(**32**,31) DETA **32** 65, **31** 69

REDUS, GARY OF/DH/1B/UTIL
(61,**2**,22,21, 19,5) CINN **61** 82, **2** 83-85, PHIN **22** 86, CHIA **21** 87-88, PITN **19** 88, **2** 89-92, TEXA **5** 93-94

REDYS, ? CH
(**44**) STLA **44** 51

REECE, BOB C
(**9**) MONN **9** 78

REED, BILL 2B
(**6**) BOSN **6** 52

REED, BOB P
(**20**) DETA **20** 69-70

REED, DARREN OF
(6,**5**,18) NYN **6** 90, MONN **5** 92, MINA **18** 92

REED, HOWIE (DIZ) P
(16,20,**39**,41, 25,19,29) KCA **16** 58-60, **20** 59, LAN **39** 64-66, CALA **41/25** 66, HOUN **19** 67, MONN **29** 69-71

REED, JACK OF
(15,**27**) NYA **15** 61, **27** 62-63

REED, JEFF C
(21,10,24,**34**, 52,15,16) MINA **21** 84, **10** 85-86, MONN **24** 87-88, CINN **34** 88-92, SFN **52** 93-95, COLN **15** 96-99, CHIN **16** 99-00

REED, JEREMY OF
(58,**7**) SEAA **58** 04, **7** 05

REED, JERRY P
(35,**31**,45) PHIN **35** 81-82, CLEA **31** 82, **35** 83, 85, SEAA **31** 86-90, BOSA **45** 90

REED, JODY INF/SS/2B
(52,**3**,8,2,7) BOSA **52** 87, **3** 88-92, LAN **3** 93, MILA **8** 94, SDN **2** 95, **3** 96, DETA **7** 97

REED, KEITH OF
(**28**) BALA **28** 05

REED, RICK P
(34,38,39,48, **35**,31) PITN **34** 88-91, KCA **38** 92-93, TEXA **39** 93-94, CINN **48** 95, NYN **35** 97-01, MINA **36** 01, **31** 02-03

REED, RON P
(28,**38**,42,36) ATLN **28** 66, **38** 67-75, STLN **42/38** 75, PHIN **42** 76-83, CHIA **36** 84

REED, STEVE P
(36,**39**,50) SFN **36** 92, COLN **39** 93-97, SFN **39** 98, CLEA **39** 98-01, ATLN **50/36** 01, SDN **39** 02, NYN **39** 02, COLN **39** 03-04, BALA **39** 05

REEDER, BILL P
(40,**33**) STLN **40/33** 49

REESE, JIMMIE 2B/3B/CH
(25,26,**9**,63, 23,50) NYA **25** 30, **26** 31, STLN **9** 32, CALA *CH* **63** 68, *CH* **23** 72-73, *CH* **50** 74-94

REESE, KEVIN OF
(**39**) NYA **39** 05

REESE, PEEWEE (THE KENTUCKY COLONEL) SS/3B/CH
(**1**) BKNN **1** 40-42, 46-57, LAN **1** 58, *CH* **1** 58

REESE, POKEY SS/3B/INF
(**3**) CINN **3** 97-01, PITN **3** 02-03, BOSA **3** 04, (05)

REESE, RICH 1B/OF
(24,13,5,**20**,7, 1) MINA **24** 64, **13** 65-66, **5** 67, **20** 67-72, DETA **7** 73, **20** 73, MINA **1** 73

REEVES, BOBBY (GUNNER) 2B/P
(**2**) BOSA **2** 31

REGALADO, RUDY 3B/2B
(**8**,17) CLEA **8** 54-55, **17** 56

REGAN, PHIL (THE VULTURE) P/CH
(16,**27**,38) DETA **16** 60-65, LAN **27** 66-68, CHIN **27** 68-72, CHIA **38** 72, SEAA *CH* **27** 84-86, CLEA *CH* **27** 94, BALA *CH* **27** 95, CHIN *CH* **27** 97-98, CLEA *CH* **38** 99

REGILIO, NICK P
(**57**) TEXA **57** 04-05

REIBER, FRANK (TUBBY) C
(9,**21**) DETA **9** 33, **21** 34-36

REICH, HERM OF/1B
(28,**9**,22) WASA **28** 49, CLEA **9** 49, CHIN **22** 49

REICHARDT, RICK OF
(20,**3**,12,48) LAA **20** 64, CALA **3** 65-70, WASA **3** 70, CHIA **48** 71-73, KCA **12** 73, **48** 74

REICHERT, DAN P
(54,**41**) KCA **54** 99, **41** 00-01, TORA **54** 03

REID, EARL P
(22,**23**) BOSN **22/23** 46

REID, JESSIE OF
(**26**) SFN **26** 87-88

REID, SCOTT OF
(**25**) PHIN **25** 69-70

REIMER, KEVIN OF/DH
(**47**,29) TEXA **47** 88-92, MILA **29** 93

REINBACH, MIKE OF/DH
(**9**) BALA **9** 74

REIS, BOBBY 3B/UTIL/P
(no#,**24**) BKNN **no#** 32, **24** 35-38

REIS, TOMMY P
(**16**,25) PHIN **16** 38, BOSN **25** 38

REISER, PETE (PISTOL PETE) OF/3B/UTIL/CH
(34,**27**,7,11, 23,6) BKNN **34** 40, **27** 41-42, 46-48, BOSA **11** 49-50, PITN **27** 51, CLEA **38/23** 52, LAN *CH* **27** 60-64, CHIN *CH* **7** 66-69, CALA **27** 70-71, CHIN *CH* **6** 72-73, *CH* **27** 73

REISS, AL SS
(**24**) PHIA **24** 32

REITH, BRIAN P
(50,**52**) CINN **50** 01, **52** 03-04

REITSMA, CHRIS P
(**41**,37) CINN **41** 01-03, ATLN **37** 04-05

REITZ, KEN 3B/SS
(47,**44**,21,33, 10) STLA **47**72, **44** 73-75, SFN **21** 76, STLN **33** 77, **44** 78-80, CHIN **44** 81, PITN **10** 82

REKAR, BRYAN P
(56,38,23,**35**, 47) COLN **56/38** 95, **23** 96-97, TBA **56** 98-00, **35** 00-01, KCA **47** 02

RELAFORD, DESI OF/SS/2B
(17,30,**8**,14, 25,12) PHIN **17** 96, **30** 97-98, **8** 99-00, SDN **14** 00, NYN **8** 01, SEAA **25** 02, KCA **12** 03-04, COLN **8** 05

REMLINGER, MIKE P
(14,**43**,38) SFN **14** 91, NYN **43** 94-95, CINN **38** 95, **43** 96-98, ATLN **37** 99-02, CHIN **37** 03-05, BOSA **37** 05

REMMERSWAAL, WIN P
(**49**) BOSA **49** 79-81

REMY, JERRY 2B/3B/UTIL/DH
(**2**) CALA **2** 75-77, BOSA **2** 78-84

RENFROE, LADDIE P
(**39**) CHIN **39** 91

RENFROE, MARSHALL P
(**28**) SFN **28** 59

RENICK, RICK SS/UTIL/OF/CH
(**10**,46,35,44, 40) MINA **10** 68-72, *CH* **46** 81, MONN *CH* **35** 85-86, MINA *CH* **46** 81, *CH* **44** 87-90, PITN *CH* **44** 97-00, MONN *CH* **44** 01, FLAN *CH* **40** 02

RENIFF, HAL (PORKY) P
(**18**,32) NYA **18** 61-67, NYN **32** 67

RENINGER, JIM P
(30,**21**) PHIA **30** 38-39, **21** 39

RENKO, STEVE P
(22,**18**,50,28, 25,45) MONN **22** 69, **18** 69-76, CHIN **50** 76-77, CHIA **50** 77, OAKA **28** 78, BOSA **25** 79-80, CALA **45** 81-82, KCA **18** 83

RENNA, BILL (BIG BILL) OF
(28,8,**34**,30) NYA **28** 53, PHIA **8** 54, KCA **34** 55-56, BOSA **30** 58-59

RENSA, TONY (PUG) C
(10,**35**) NYA **10** 33, CHIA **35** 37-39

RENTERIA, EDGAR SS
(16,**3**) FLAN **16** 96, **3** 97, **16** 97-98, STLN **3** 99-04, BOSA **16/3** 05

RENTERIA, RICH 2B/UTIL
(56,1,6,**16**) PITN **56** 86, SEAA **1** 87-88, FLAN **6** 93-94, **16** 96

REPASS, BOB 2B/INF
(23,**6**) STLN **23** 39, WASA **6** 42

REPKO, JASON OF
(**17**) LAN **17** 05

REPLOGLE, ANDY P
(49,**27**,50) MILA **49** 78, **27** 78-79, **50** 79

REPOZ, ROGER OF/1B
(43,9,**6**) NYA **43** 64-66, KCA **9** 66-67, CALA **6** 67-72

REPULSKI, RIP OF
(**8**,14,15,20, 28) STLN **8** 53-56, PHIN **14** 57, **15** 58, LAN **20** 59-60, BOSA **28** 60-61

RESCIGNO, XAVIER (MR. X) P
(**41**) PITN **41** 43-45

RESINGER, GROVER CH
(6,37,50,27) ATLN *CH* **6** 66, CHIA *CH* **37** 67-68, DETA *CH* **50** 69-70, CALA *CH* **27** 75-76

RESOP, CHRIS P
(**51**) FLAN **51** 05

RESTELLI, DINO (DINGO) OF/1B
(**14**,21) PITN **14** 49, **21** 51

RESTOVICH, MICHAEL OF
(**41**,25,34) MINA **41** 02-04, COLN **25** 05, PITN **34** 05

RETTENMUND, MERV OF/3B/DH/CH
(47,**14**,26,17, 8,7,22,29,45, 16,28,19) BALA **47** 68, **14** 68-73, CINN **26** 74-75, SDN **17** 76-77, CALA **8** 78-80, *CH* **7** 80, *CH* **14** 81, *CH* **17** 81-82, TEXA *CH* **22** 83-85, **29** 84, OAKA *CH* **45** 89-90, SDN *CH* **16** 90-98, **8** 99, ATLN **28** 00-01, DETA **19** 02

RETZER, KEN C
(9,6,**20**) WASA **9** 62, **6** 63, **20** 64

REUSCHEL, PAUL P B
(**43**,41) CHIN **43** 75-78, CLEA **41** 78-79

REUSCHEL, RICK P
(39,43,**48**,36, 47) CHIN **39/43** 72, **48** 72-81, NYA **36/48** 81, CHIN **47** 83-84, **48** 84, PITN **48** 85-87, SFN **48** 87-91

REUSS, JERRY P
(49,47,**41**,25, 21,44) STLN **49** 69-71, HOUN **47** 72-73, PITN **41** 74-78, LAN **25/21** 79, **41** 79-87, CINN **41** 87, CALA **44** 87, CHIA **44** 88, **41** 88-89, MILA **21** 89, PITN **47** 90

REVENIG, TODD P/CH
(**56**,__) OAKA **56** 92, ARIN *CH* __ 00

REVERING, DAVE 1B/DH
(24,**13**,12,10, 5) OAKA **24** 78-79, **13** 80-81, NYA **12** 81-82, TORA **10** 82, SEAA **5** 82

REYES, AL P
(**47**,32,52,39) MILA **47** 95-99, BALA **32** 99-00, LAN **52** 00-01, PITN **39** 02, NYA **47** 03, STLN **52** 04-05

REYES, ANTHONY P
(**26**) STLN **26** 05

In 1981, Dave Righetti led the league with a 2.05 ERA and opponents hit only .196 against him. On July 4, 1983, "Rags" pitched a no-hitter against the Red Sox, winning 4-0. Three years later he led the American League in saves with 46. Much criticism was aimed at the Yankee brass when he was converted to a closer, but he went on to save 252 games in his career. He appeared in more games as a Yankee pitcher overall (522) and in a season (74) in both 1985 and 1986 plus he finished more games—68 in 1986, that is, until Mariano Rivera came along.

REYES, CANANEA CH
(**10**) SEAA *CH* **10** 81

REYES, CARLOS P
(40,37,**17**,56, 55,44) OAKA **40** 94, **37** 95, **17** 96, **37** 97, SDN **56** 98, BOSA **55** 98, SDN **44** 99, PHIN **44** 00, SDN **39** 00, TBA **57** 03

REYES, DENNYS P
(57,**49**,46,44, 40) LAN **57** 97-98, CINN **49** 98-01, COLN **49** 02, TEXA **46** 02, PITN **44** 03, ARIN **40** 03, KCA **49** 04, SDN **49** 05

REYES, GIL C
(**15**,2,6) LAN **15** 83-85, 87-88, MONN **2** 89, 91

REYES, JOSE SS
(**7**) NYN **7** 03-05

REYES, NAP 1B/3B/UTIL
(21,**6**,20) NYN **21** 43, **6** 44-45, **20** 50

REYES, RENE OF
(3,**7**) COLN **3** 03, **7** 04

REYNOLDS, ALLIE (SUPERCHIEF)(CHIEF) (WAHOO) P
(__,21,**22**) CLEA __ 42, **21** 43-46, NYA **22** 47-54

REYNOLDS, ARCHIE P
(**39**,46,35,49) CHIN **39** 68, **46** 69, **39** 70, CALA **35** 71, MILA **49** 72

REYNOLDS, BOB P
(42,37,50,25, **34**,40,39) MONN **42** 69, STLN **37** 71, MILA **50/25** 71, BALA **34** 72-75, DETA **34** 75, CLEA **40/39** 75

REYNOLDS, CARL OF
(3,2,5,6,8,**43**) CHIA **3/2** 31, WASA **5** 32, STLA **3** 33, BOSA **5** 34, **6** 35, WASA **8** 36, CHIN **43** 37-39

REYNOLDS, CRAIG SS/2B/UTIL/P
(18,**12**) PITN **18** 75, **12** 75-76, SEAA **12** 77-78, HOUN **12** 79-89

REYNOLDS, DANNY (SQUIRREL) SS/2B
(**2**) CHIA **2** 45

REYNOLDS, DON OF
(**26**) SDN**26** 78-79

REYNOLDS, HAROLD 2B/DH
(18,24,19,**4**, 6,25,3) SEAA **18** 83, **24** 84-86, **19** 86, **4** 87-92, BALA **6/25** 93, CALA **3** 94

REYNOLDS, KEN P
(47,42,46,**24**, 34) PHIN **47** 70-72, **42** 71, MILA **46** 73, STLN **24** 75, SDN **34/24** 76

REYNOLDS, R. J. OF
(**23**,39) LAN **23** 83-85, PITN **39** 85-86, **23** 86-90

REYNOLDS, RONN C
(**8**,29,30,54) NYN **8** 82-83, 85, PHIN **29** 86, HOUN **30** 87, SDN **54** 90

REYNOLDS, SHANE P
(38,30,**37**) HOUN **38/30** 92, **37** 93-02, ATLN **37** 03, ARIN **37** 04

REYNOLDS, TOMMIE OF/3B/UTIL/CH
(9,35,12,16, **5**,19,10,47, 15) KCA **9** 63, **35** 64, **12** 65, NYN **16** 67, OAKA **35** 69, CALA **5** 70 -71, MILA **10** 72, OAKA *CH* **47** 89-94, *CH* **15** 94-96

REYNOSO, ARMANDO P
(**42**,40,27) ATLN **42** 91-92, COLN **42** 93-96, NYN **40** 97-98, ARIN **27** 99-02

RHAWN, BOBBY (ROCKY) 2B/3B/SS
(14,22,**12**,17, 2) NYN **14** 47, **22** 48, **12** 48-49, PITN **17** 49, CHIA **2** 49

RHEM, FLINT (SHAD) P
(__,no#,**24**,31, 29,13,19) STLN __ 24, **no#** 32, PHIN **24** 32-33, STLN **31** 34, BOSN **29** 34, **13** 35, STLN **19** 36

RHIEL, BILLY UTIL/OF
(**5**) DETA **5** 32-33

RHODEN, RICK P
(36,41,44,**29**, 26) LAN **36** 74-78, PITN **41/44** 79, **29** 80-86, NYA **26** 87-88, HOUN **36** 89

RHODES, ARTHUR P
(**53**) BALA **53** 91-99, SEAA **53** 00-03, OAKA **53** 04, CLEA **53** 05

RHODES, DUSTY OF
(38,**26**) NYN **38** 52-53, **26** 54-57, SFN **26** 59

RHODES, GORDON (DUSTY) P
(30,21,19,16, 17,**11**) NYA **30** 29, **21** 29-31, **19** 30-31, **16** 32, BOSA **19** 32, **17** 33, **11** 34-35, PHIA **11** 36

RHODES, KARL (TUFFY) OF
(**4**, 25,29) HOUN **4** 90-93, CHIN **25** 93-95, BOSA **29** 95

RHOMBERG, KEVIN OF/DH/UTIL
(54,18,**12**) CLEA **54** 82-83, **18** 83, **12** 83-84

RHYNE, HAL SS/INF
(6,4,**12**) BOSA **6** 31, **4** 32, CHIA **12** 33

RIBANT, DENNIS P
(17,18,**30**,36, 14,19,35,42) NYN **17** 64, **18** 64-65, **30** 65-66, PITN **36** 67, DETA **14** 68, CHIA**19** 68, STLN **35** 69, CINN **42** 69

RICCELLI, FRANK P
(**45**) SFN **45** 76, HOUN **45** 78-79

RICCI, CHUCK P
(**37**) PHIN **37** 95

RICE, DEL C/CH/M
(11,**18**,7,9, 29,35,9,5) STLN **11** 45, **18** 46-55, MILN **7** 55-59, CHIN **9** 60, STLN **29** 60, BALA **35** 60, LAA **9** 61, *CH* **9** 62-64, CALA **9** 65-66, CLEA *CH* **5** 67, CALA *M* **7** 72

RICE, HAL (HOOT) OF
(21,16,1,**39**, 44,28) STLN **21** 48, **16** 49, **1** 50, **39** 51-53, PITN **44** 53-54, CHIN **28** 54

RICE, HARRY OF/3B/INF
(19,25,**9**) NYA **19** 30, WASA **25** 31, CINN **9** 33

RICE, JIM OF/DH/CH
(**14**) BOSA **14** 74-89, *CH* **14** 95-00

RICE, LEN P
(**6**,8) CINN **6** 44, CHIN **8** 45

RICE, PAT P
(**23**) SEAA **23** 91

RICE, SAM OF
(**2**,22,29) WASA **2** 31, **22** 32-33, CLEA **29** 34

RICH, WOODY P
(**15**,28) BOSA **15** 39-41, BOSN **28** 44

RICHARD, CHRIS 1B/OF
(8,**38**,21) STLN **8** 00, BALA **38** 00-02, COLN **21** 03

RICHARD, J.R. P
(**50**) HOUN **50** 71-80

RICHARD, LEE (BEE BEE) SS/OF/UTIL/DH
(**9**,3) CHIA **9** 71-72, 74-75, STLN **3** 76

RICHARDS, DUANE P
(__) CINN __ 60

RICHARDS, FRED (FUZZY) 1B
(**6**) CHIN **6** 51

RICHARDS, GENE OF/1B
(29,9,19,**17**, 25) SDN **29** 77, **9/19** 78, **17** 79-83, SFN **25** 84

RICHARDS, PAUL C/M
(no#,**9**,27,22, 12) BKNN **no#** 32, NYN **9** 33-35, PHIA **27** 35, DETA **9** 43-46, CHIA *M* **22** 51-54, BALA *M* **12** 55-61, CHIA *M* **12** 76

RICHARDS, RUSTY P
(**52**) ATLN **52** 89-90

RICHARDSON, BOBBY 2B/SS/INF
(17,29,**1**) NYA **17** 55-56, **29** 57, **1** 58-66

RICHARDSON, GORDIE P
(22,40,**41**) STLN **22** 64, **40/41** 65-66

RICHARDSON, JEFF SS/3B/P/INF/DH
(15,37,36,**20**) CINN **15** 89, CALA **37** 90, PITN **36** 91, BOSA **20** 93

RICHARDSON, KEN 2B/UTIL
(11,**2**) PHIA **11/2** 42, PHIN **2** 46

RICHARDSON, NOLEN 3B/SS
(29,**8**,5,45,14) DETA **29** 31, **8** 32, NYA **5** 35, CINN **45** 38, **14** 39

RICHARDT, MIKE 2B/UTIL/DH
(**2**,30) TEXA **2** 80, 82-84, HOUN **30** 84

RICHBOURG, LANCE OF
(**8**) CHIN **8** 32

RICHERT, PETE P
(45,**24**,46,34) LAN **45** 62-64, WASA **24** 65-67, BALA **46** 67, **24** 67-71, LAN **45** 72-73, STLN **34** 74, PHIN **45** 74

RICHIE, ROB OF/DH
(**10**) DETA **10** 89

RICHMOND, BERYL P
(**42**,__) CHIN **42** 33, CINN __ 34

RICHMOND, DON 3B/2B
(35,41,**14**,38) PHIA **35** 41, **41** 46, **14** 47, STLN **38** 51

RICHTER, AL SS
(**34**,35) BOSA **34** 51, **35** 53

RICKERT, MARV (TWITCH) OF/1B
(46,**35**,28,20, 4, 31,13,3) CHIN **46** 42, **35** 46-47, CINN **28** 48, BOSN **20/4** 48, **31** 49, PITN **13** 50, CHIA **3** 50

RICKETTS, DAVE C/CH B
(38,**10**,5,14, 15,3) STLN **38** 63, **10** 65, 67-69, PITN **5** 70, *CH* **5** 70-73, STLN *CH* **14** 74-75, 78, *CH* **15** 78-80, *CH* **3** 81-91

RICKETTS, DICK P B
(**47**) STLN **47** 59

RICKEY, BRANCH M
(no#) STLN *M* **no#** 23

RICO, FRED OF/3B
(**46**) KCA **46** 69

RIDDLE, ELMER P
(**41**,38,48,37, 21) CINN **41** 39-44, **38** 45, **48** 47, PITN **37** 48-49, **21** 49

RIDDLE, JOHNNY (MUTT) C/CH
(__,4,19,7,**6**, 3,34,29,8,2, 39) WASA __ 37, BOSN **4** 37, **19** 38, CINN **7** 41, **6** 44-45, PITN **3** 48, *CH* **3** 48-50, *CH* **34** 49-50, STLN *CH* **29** 52-55, MILN *CH* **8** 56, *CH* **3** 56-57, CINN *CH* **2** 58, PHIN *CH* **39** 59

RIDDLEBERGER, DENNY P
(34,**19**,37) WASA **34** 70, **19** 71, CLEA **37** 72

RIDDOCH, GREG CH/M
(38,**3**,7) SDN *CH* **38** 87, *CH* **3** 88-90, *M* **3** 90-92, TBA *CH* **7** 98-99

RIDZIK, STEVE P
(20,**37**,33,44, 35,28,42,27) PHIN **20** 50, **37** 52-55, CINN **33** 55, NYN **44** 56-57, CLEA **35** 58, WASA **28** 63-65, PHIN **42** 66, **27** 66

RIEBE, HANK C
(9,**25**) DETA **9** 42, **25** 47-49

RIEDLING, JOHN P
(52,**46**,41) CINN **52** 00, **46** 03-04, FLAN **41** 05

RIESGO, NIKCO OF
(**6**) MONN **6** 91

RIGBY, BRAD P
(**57**,30,22,31) OAKA **57** 97, 99, KCA **30** 99, **22** 00, MONN **31** 00

RIGDON, PAUL P
(46,**31**) CLEA **46** 00, MILN **31** 00-01, (02)

RIGGAN, JERROD P
(34,38,**51**) NYN **34** 00, **38** 01, CLEA **51** 02-03

RIGGINS, MARK CH
(**12**) STLN *CH* **12** 95

RIGGLEMAN, JIM CH/M
(16,**5**,8,28,25) STLN *CH* **16** 89, *CH* **5** 89-90, SDN *M* **8** 92-94, CHIN *M* **5** 95-99, CLEA *CH* **16** 00, LAN *CH* **5** 01-02, **28** 02, **25** 03, LAN *CH* **56** 04

RIGGS, ADAM 2B
(51,16,9,**10**) LAN **51** 97, SDN **16** 01, ANAA **9** 03, **10** 04

RIGGS, LEW 3B/INF
(29,9,40,**15**, 18,10) STLN **29** 34, CINN **9** 35-37, **40** 38, **15** 39-40, BKNN **18** 41-42, **10/15** 46

RIGHETTI, DAVE (RAGS) P/CH
(56,**19**,24) NYA **56** 79, **19** 81-90, SFN **19** 91-93, OAKA **19** 94, TORA **24** 94, SFN *CH* **19** 00-05

RIGHTNOWAR, RON P
(**33**) MILA **33** 95

RIGNEY, BILL (SPECS)(THE CRICKET) 2B/3B/INF/M/CH
(1,**18**,3) NYN **1** 46, **18** 47-53, *M* **18** 56-57, SFN *M* **18** 58-60, LAA *M* **18** 61-64, CALA *M* **18** 65-69, MINA *M* **18** 70-72, SDN *CH* **3** 75, SFN *M* **18** 76

RIGNEY, JOHNNY P
(**29**) CHIA **29** 37-42, 46-47

RIGOLI, JOE CH
(**59**) PHIN *CH* **59** 97-98

RIJO, JOSE P
(38,**27**) NYA **38** 84, OAKA **38** 85-87, **27** 87, CINN **27** 88-95, 01-02

RIKARD, CULLEY OF
(40,17,**12**) PITN **40/17** 41, **40** 42, **12** 47

RILES, ERNEST SS/3B/INF/UTIL/DH
(58,**1**,11,10, 13,12) MILA **58** 85, **1** 85-88, SFN **1** 88-90, OAKA **11** 91, HOUN **10/13** 92, BOSA **12** 93

RILEY, GEORGE P
(33,**37**,51,46) CHIN **33** 79, **37** 80, SFN **51** 84, MONN **46** 86

RILEY, LEE OF
(**23**) PHIN **23** 44

RILEY, MATT P
(25,35,**12**,48) BALA **25** 99, **35** 03, **12** 04, TEXA **48** 05

RINCON, ANDY P
(**46**) CHIA **46** 80-82

RINCON, JUAN P
(**39**) MINA **39** 01-05

RINCON, RICARDO (RICKY) P
(**73**) PITN **73** 97-98, CLEA **73** 99-02, OAKA **73** 02-05

RINEER, JEFF P
(27,**43**) SDN **27/43** 79

RING, ROYCE P
(**22**) NYN **22** 05

RINKER, BOB C
(**38**) PHIA **38** 50

RIOS, ALEXIS OF
(**15**) TORA **15** 04-05

RIOS, ARMANDO OF
(**1**,17,7,28) SFN **1** 98-01, PITN **17** 01, **7** 02, CHIA **28** 03

RIOS, DANNY P
(63,**52**,51) NYA **63/52** 97, KCA **51** 98

RIOS, JUAN INF
(**12**) KCA **12** 69

RIPKEN, BILLY 2B/INF/UTIL/DH S,B
(**3**,7,16,9,14) BALA **3** 87-92, **7** 88, TEXA **3** 93-94, CLEA **16** 95, BALA **3** 96, TEXA **9** 97, DETA **14** 98

RIPKEN, CAL, Jr. SS/3B S,B
(**8**) BALA **8** 81-01

RIPKEN, CAL, Sr. CH/M F
(47,**7**) BALA *CH* **47** 76-85, *M* **47/7** 85, *CH* **7** 86, *M* **7** 87-88, *CH* **7** 89-92

RIPLEY, ALLEN P
(28,**33**,45) BOSA **28** 78-79, SFN **33** 80-81, **45** 81, CHIN **33** 82

RIPLEY, WALT P
(**18**) BOSA **18** 35

RIPPLE, CHARLIE (ROCKY) 2B/3B/SS
(10,35,**8**) PHIN **10** 44, **35** 45, **8** 46

RIPPLE, JIMMY OF
(23,3,24,17, 32,**22**,12) NYN **23** 36-37, **3** 38, **24** 39, BKNN **17** 39, **32** 40, CINN **22** 40-41, PHIA **12** 43

RIPPLEMEYER, RAY P/CH
(**20**,4) WASA **20** 62, PHIN *CH* **4** 70-78

RISKE, DAVE P
(**54**) CLEA **54** 99-05

RISLEY, BILL P
(50,**55**) MONN **50** 92-93, SEAA **55** 94-95, TORA **55** 96-98

RITCHIE, JAY P
(**19**,26,30) BOSA **19** 64-65, ATLN **26** 66-67, CINN **30** 68

RITCHIE, TODD P
(23,**48**,46) MINA **23** 97-98, PITN **48** 99-01, CHIA **48** 02, MILN **46** 03, TBA **31** 04

RITCHIE, WALLY P
(38,**39**) PHIN **38** 87-88, **39** 91-92

RITTER, REGGIE P
(53,**44**) CLEA **53** 86-87, **44** 87

RITTWAGE, JIM P
(**42**) CLEA **42** 70

RITZ, KEVIN P
(31,**30**) DETA **31** 89-92, COLN **30** 94-98, (99)

RIVAS, LUIS INF/2B
(**2**) MINA **2** 00-05

RIVERA, BEN P
(51,**34**) ATLN **51** 92, PHIN **34** 92-94

RIVERA, BOMBO OF/DH
(44,**9**,38) MONN **44** 75-76, MINA **9** 78-80, KCA **38** 82

RIVERA, CARLOS 1B
(**55**) PITN **55** 03-04

RIVERA, GERMAN 3B
(**25**,23) LAN **25** 83-84, HOUN **23** 85

RIVERA, JIM (JUNGLE JIM) OF/1B
(**7**,39,10) STLA **7** 52, CHIA **39** 52, **7** 53-61, KCA **10** 61

RIVERA, JUAN OF/DH
(56,59,53,**20**) NYA **56** 01, **59** 02-03, MONN **53** 03, LAA **20** 05

RIVERA, LUIS SS/INF/UTIL/DH
(17,12,**2**,7,3, 1) MONN **17** 86, **12** 87-88, BOSA **2** 89, **7** 90, **2** 90-93, NYN **3** 94, HOUN **2** 97, KCA **1/3** 98

RIVERA, LUIS G. P
(**36**,60) ATLN **36** 00, BALA **60** 00, (01)

RIVERA, MARIANO P C
(**42**) NYA **42** 95-05

RIVERA, MIKE C
(**49**,10) DETA **49** 01-02, SDN **10** 03

RIVERA, RENE C
(59,**30**) SEAA **59** 04-05, **30** 05

RIVERA, ROBERTO P
(41,**32**) CHIN **41** 95, SDN **32** 99

RIVERA, RUBEN OF C
(17,47,**28**,24, 21) NYA **17** 95, **47/28** 96, SDN **28** 97-00, CINN **28** 01, TEXA **24** 02, SFN **21** 03

RIVERS, MICKEY OF/DH
(3,5,**17**) CALA **3** 70-71, **5** 71-73, **17** 74-75, NYA **17** 76-79, TEXA **17** 79-84

RIXEY, EPPA (JEPTHA) P
(**18**) CINN **18** 32-33

RIZZO, JOHNNY OF/3B
(12,**7**,21,33, 5,32) PITN **12** 38-39, **7** 40, CINN **21** 40, PHIN **33** 40, **5** 41, BKNN **32** 42

RIZZO, TODD P
(**52**) CHIA **52** 98-99

RIZZUTO, PHIL (SCOOTER) SS/2B
(**10**) NYA **10** 41-42, 46-56

ROA, JOE P
(47,**37**,35,51, 71) CLEA **47** 95-96, SFN **37** 97, PHIN **35** 02-03, COLN **51** 03, SDN **37** 03, MINA **71** 04-05

ROACH, JASON P
(29,26,14,**12**, NYN **57** 03

ROACH, MEL 2B/1B/UTIL/
(29,26,14,**12**, 31) MILN **29/26** 53, **14** 54, **29** 57-58, **12** 58-61, CHIN **12** 61, PHIN **31** 62

ROARK, MIKE C/CH
(**12**,21,53,4, 36,33) DETA **12** 61-64, *CH* **12** 65-66, CALA *CH* **21** 67-69, DETA *CH* **53** 70, CHIN *CH* **4** 78-80, STLN *CH* **4** 84-90, SDN *CH* **36** 90-93, BOSA *CH* **33** 94

ROBBINS, BRUCE P
(48,**44**) DETA **48** 79-80, **44** 80

ROBBINS, JAKE P
(**49**) CLEA **49** 04

ROBELLO, TOMMY (TONY) 2B/3B
(27,**23**) CINN **27** 33, **23** 34

ROBERGE, BERT P
(**42**,40,53) HOUN **42** 79-80, 82, CHIA **53** 84, MONN **42** 85-86, **40** 86

ROBERGE, SKIPPY 3B/INF
(3,14,20) BOSN **3** 41, **14** 42, **20** 46

ROBERSON, KEVIN OF
(**19**,18) CHIN **19** 93-95, NYN **18** 96

ROBERSON, SID P
(**51**) MILA **51** 95

ROBERTS, BIP 2B/INF/UTIL
(2,**10**,1,3) SDN **2** 86, **10** 88-91, CINN **10** 92-93, SDN **10** 94-95, KCA **1** 96-97, CLEA **6** 97, DETA **10** 98, OAKA **3** 98

ROBERTS, BRIAN SS/2B/DH
(**1**) BALA **1** 01-05

ROBERTS, CURT 2B
(**7**,9) PITN **7** 54-55, **9** 56

ROBERTS, DALE (MOUNTAIN MAN) P
(**43**) NYA **43** 67

ROBERTS, DAVE (A.) P
(31,**15**,17,41, 25,48,49,34) SDN **31** 69, **15** 69-71, HOUN **15** 72-75, DETA **17** 76-77, CHIN **41** 77-78, **17** 77, SFN **25/48** 79, PITN **49** 79-80, SEAA **49** 80, NYN **34/15** 81

ROBERTS, DAVE (L.) OF/1B
(**24**,26,45) HOUN **24** 62, **26** 64, PITN **45** 66

ROBERTS, DAVE (R.) OF
(52,10,**30**) CLEA **52** 99, **10** 00-01, LAN **30** 02-04, BOSA **31** 04, SDN **10** 05

ROBERTS, DAVE (W.) 3B/UTIL/INF/C/CH
(**20**,3,14,8,19, 10,4) SDN **20** 72-75, **3** 77-78, TEXA **14** 79-80, HOUN **8** 81, PHIN **19/10** 82, CLEA *CH*B **4** 87

ROBERTS, GRANT P
(**36**) NYN **36** 00-04

ROBERTS, LEON OF/UTIL/DH/P/CH
(39,44,22,**8**, 16,7,3,5) DETA **39** 74, **44** 74-75, HOUN **22** 76-77, SEAA **8** 78-80, TEXA **16** 81, **7** 81-82, TORA **3** 82, KCA **16** 83-84, TBA *CH* **5** 99-00

ROBERTS, MEL CH
(**26**) PHIN *CH* **26** 92-95

ROBERTS, RED SS/3B
(38,29,**21**) WASA **38/29/21** 43

ROBERTS, ROBIN P
(**36**, 38) PHIN **36** 48-61, BALA **38** 62-65, HOUN **38** 66, *CH* **38** 66, CHIN **36** 66

ROBERTS, WILLIS P
(58,**37**,43) DETA **58** 99, BALA **37** 01-03, PITN **43** 04

ROBERTSON, ANDRE SS/2B/INF
(55,**18**,56) NYA **55** 81-83, **18** 82, **56** 82, **18** 83-85

ROBERTSON, BOB 1B/UTIL/DH
(3,25,27,6,**7**, 5) PITN **3** 67-(68), **25/27** 69, **6** 70, **7** 70-76, SEAA **6** 78, TORA **5** 79

ROBERTSON, DARYL SS/3B
(**19**) CHIN **19** 62

ROBERTSON, DON OF
(**52**) CHIN **52** 54

ROBERTSON, GENE 3B
(**22**) NYA **22** 29

ROBERTSON, JERIOME P
(60,62,**53**) HOUN **60** 02-03, **62** 03, CLEA **53** 04

ROBERTSON, JERRY P
(**27**,29) MONN **27** 69, DETA **29** 70

ROBERTSON, JIM C
(**18**,33) PHIA **18** 54, KCA **33** 55

ROBERTSON, MIKE 1B/OF
(43,**34**,51) CHIA **43** 96, PHIN **34** 97, ARIN **51** 98

ROBERTSON, NATE P
(32,59,**37**) FLAN **32** 02, DETA **59** 03, **37** 04-05

ROBERTSON, RICH (P.) P
(49,43,**45**) SFN **49** 66, **43** 67-68, **45** 69-71

ROBERTSON, RICH (W.) P
(58,63,**47**,23) PITN **58** 93, **63** 94, MINA **47** 95-97, ANAA **23** 98

ROBERTSON, SHERRY SS/3B/INF/OF/UTIL/CH
(28,40,23,1,3, **5**,43,16,47) WASA **28** 40-41, **40/23** 43, **1** 46, **3** 46-47, **5** 48-49, **43** 50-51, **5** 51-52, PHIA **16** 52, MINA *CH* **47** 70

ROBIDOUX, BILLY JO UTIL/1B/OF/DH
(9,**13**,28) MILA **9** 85, **13** 86-88, CHIA **28** 89, BOSA **13** 90

ROBINSON, AARON C
(25,8,7,35,18, **1**,28) NYA **25** 43, **8** 45, **7** 46, **35** 46, **8** 47, CHIA **18** 48, DETA **1** 49-51, BOSA **28** 51

ROBINSON, BILL OF/1B/3B/UTIL/CH
(24,11,21,**28**, 26) ATLN **24** 66, NYA **11** 67-69, PHIN **21** 72, **24** 72-74, PITN **28** 75-82, PHIN **26** 82, **28** 83, NYN *CH* **26** 84, *CH* **28** 84-89, FLAN *CH* **28** 02-05

ROBINSON, BROOKS (THE VACCUUM CLEANER) 3B/INF/CH
(21,34,**5**) BALA **21** 55, **34** 56-57, **5** 57-77, *CH* **5** 77

ROBINSON, BRUCE C
(48,58,**47**) OAKA **48** 78, NYA **58** 79, **47** 79-80

ROBINSON, CRAIG SS/2B/INF
(**18**,10,1,16) PHIN **18** 72-73, ATLN **10** 74-75, SFN **18** 75, **1** 76, ATLN **16** 76-77

ROBINSON, DAVE OF
(**34**) SDN **34** 70-71

ROBINSON, DEWEY P/CH
(32,**35**,55) CHIA **32** 79, **35** 80-81, *CH* **55** 93-94

ROBINSON, DON P
(**43**,48,40,31, 35) PITN **43** 78-87, SFN **48** 87, **40** 87-89, **31** 89-91, CALA **40** 92, PHIN **40/35** 92

ROBINSON, EARL 3B/OF
(61,**14**,34) LAN **61** 58, BALA **14** 61-62, **34** 64

ROBINSON, EDDIE 1B/DH
(31,34,**3**,25, 44,46,8,36, 11,6,37) CLEA **31** 42, **34** 46, **3** 47-48, WASA **25** 49, **44** 50, CHIA **46** 50-52, PHIA **8** 53, NYA **36** 54-56, KCA **25** 56, DETA **11** 57, CLEA **6** 57, BALA **37** 57, *CH* **37** 57-59

ROBINSON, FLOYD OF
(**3**,25,15,11) CHIA **3** 60-66, CINN **25** 67, OAKA **15** 68, BOSA **11** 68

ROBINSON, FRANK (ROBBY) F/1B/3B/UTIL/DH/M/CH
(**20**,36,33) CINN **20** 56-65, BALA **20** 66-71, LAN **36** 72, CALA **20** 73-74, CLEA **33** 74, **20** 75-76, *M* **20** 75-77, CALA *CH* **20** 77, BALA *CH* **20** 79-80, SFN *M* **20** 81-84, BALA *C H* **20** 85-87, *M* **20** 88-91, MONN *M* **20** 02-04, WASN *M* **20** 05

ROBINSON, HUMBERTO P
(**49**,29,34) MILA **49** 55-56, 58, CLEA **29** 59, PHIN **34** 59-60

ROBINSON, JACKIE (ROBBY) 1B/2B/INF/OF
(**42**) BKNN **42** 47-56

ROBINSON, JACK P
(**44**) BOSA **44** 49

ROBINSON, JEFF (D.) P
(**49**,52,43,38) SFN **49** 84-87, PITN **52** 87, **43** 87-88, **49** 87-89, NYA **43** 90, CALA **49** 91, CHIN **38** 92

ROBINSON, JEFF (M.) P
(**44**,34,20,26) DETA **44** 87-90, BALA **34** 91, TEXA **20** 92, PITN **26** 92

ROBINSON, KEN P
(**44**,50,52) TORA **44** 95, KCA **50** 96, TORA **52** 97

ROBINSON, KERRY OF
(15,00,**13**,0,2) TBA **15** 498, CINN **00** 99, STLN **13** 01-02, **0** 02-03, SDN **2** 04

ROBINSON, RON P
(58,**33**,38) CINN **58** 84, **33** 84-90, MILA **38** 90, **33** 90-92

ROBINSON, SHERIFF CH
(54,**53**,55) NYN *CH* **54** 64, *CH* **53** 65-67, *CH* **55** 72

ROBLES, OSCAR 3B
(**13**) LAN **13** 05

ROBLES, RAFAEL SS/3B
(35,49,6,**31**) SDN **35/31** 69, **49/6** 70, **31** 72

ROBLES, SERGIO C
(**10**,30,55) BALA **10** 72, **30** 73, LAN **55** 76

ROBSON, TOM 1B/DH/CH
(**38**,31,53,51, 57) TEXA **38** 74-75, *CH* **31** 86-92, NYN *CH* **53** 97-00, **51** 02, CINN *CH* **57** 03

ROCCO, MICKEY (MIKE) 1B
(9,**10**) CLEA **9** 43-44, **10** 45-46

ROCHE, ARMANDO P
(**32**) WASA **32** 45

ROCHELLI, LOU 2B
(**18**) BKNN **18** 44

ROCHFORD, MIKE P
(**54**) BOSA **54** 88-90

ROCK, LES 1B
(**19**) CHIA **19** 36

ROCKER, JOHN P
(**49**,48) ATLN **49** 98-01, CLEA **49** 01, TEXA **49** 02, TBA **48** 03

ROCKETT, PAT SS
(34,**9**) ATLN **34** 76, **9** 77-78

RODAS, RICH P
(**56**) LAN **56** 83-85

RODGERS, ANDRE (ANDY) SS/3B/UTIL
(15,17,**18**,30, 16,7)) NYN **15** 57, SFN **15** 58-59, **17** 59-60, CHIN **18** 61-64, PITN **30** 65, **16** 66-67, **7** 67

RODGERS, BILL OF
(**3**) PITN **3** 44-45

RODGERS, BOB (BUCK) C/CH/M
(**7**,45,8,37) LAA **7** 61-64, CALA **7** 65-69, MINA *CH* **45** 70-74, SFN *CH* **8** 76, MILA *CH* **37** 78-80, *M* **37** 80-82, MONN *M* **37** 85-91, CALA *M* **7** 91-94, *M* **37** 91

RODIN, ERIC OF
(**5**) NYN **5** 54

RODNEY, FERNANDO P
(**56**) DETA **56** 02-03, (04), 05

RODRIGUEZ, ALEX (A-ROD) SS
(**3**,13) SEAA **3** 94-00, TEXA **3** 01-03, NYA **13** 04-05

RODRIGUEZ, AURELIO 3B/2B/SS/INF/DH
(47,12,1,2,**4**, 27,20,6,22) CALA **47/12** 67, **1** 68-70, WASA **2** 70, DETA **4** 71-79, SDN **4** 80, NYA **27** 80-81, CHIA **20** 82, BALA **6** 83, CHIA **22** 83

RODRIGUEZ, CARLOS SS/2B
(12,**3**) NYA **12** 91, BOSA **3** 94-95

RODRIGUEZ, EDUARDO SS/2B/UTIL/P
(**23**,41,21) MILA **23** 73-78, **41** 74, KCA **21** 79

RODRIGUEZ, EDDIE 2B/INF/CH
(20,36,**10**,7, 14) NYA **20** 82, SDN **36** 83, **10** 85, TORA *CH* **7** 98, ARIN *CH* **14** 01-03, MONN *CH* **45** 04, WASN *CH* **14** 05

RODRIGUEZ, ELLIE C/DH/
(23,11,**6**,2) NYA **23** 68, KCA **11** 69-70, MILA **6** 71-73, CALA **6** 74-75, LAN **2** 76

RODRIGUEZ, FELIX P
(50,67,**47**,49) LAN **50** 95-96, CINN **67** 97, ARIN **47** 98, SFN **47** 99-04, PHIN **49/47** 04, NYA **47** 05

RODRIGUEZ, FRANCISCO P
(**57**) ANAA **57** 02-04, LAA **57** 05

RODRIGUEZ, FRANKIE P
(30,**33**) BOSA **33** 95, MINA **33** 95-98, SEAA **33** 99-00, CINN **58** 01

RODRIGUEZ FREDDY P
(**22**,41) CHIN **22** 58, PHIN **41** 59

RODRIGUEZ, HECTOR 3B
(**36**) CHIA **36** 52

RODRIGUEZ, HENRY OF/1B
(26,**40**,45) LAN **26** 92-93, **40** 94-95, MONN **40** 95-97, CHIN **40** 98-99-00, FLAN **40** 00, NYA **45** 01, MONN **40** 02

RODRIGUEZ, IVAN (PUDGE) C/DH
(**7**) TEXA **7** 91-02, FLAN **7** 03, DETA **7** 04-05

RODRIGUEZ, JON OF
(**53**) STLN **53** 05

RODRIGUEZ, JOSE P
(52,58**20**) STLN **52** 00, **58** 02, MINA **20** 02

RODRIGUEZ, LIU INF
(**55**) CHIA **55** 99

RODRIGUEZ, LUIS 3B
(**38**) MINA **38** 05

RODRIGUEZ, NERIO P
(63,**39**,49,52) BALA **63** 96, **39** 96-98, TORA **39** 98-99, CLEA **49** 02, STLN **52** 02

RODRIGUEZ, RICARDO P
(46,56,**30**) CLEA **46** 02, **56** 03, TEXA **30** 04-05

RODRIGUEZ, RICH P (42,**33**,46,44,18) SDN **42** 90-93, FLAN **42** 93, STLN **33** 94-95, 97, SFN **33** 98-99, NYN **46** 00, CLEA **44** 01, TEXA **44** 02, ANAA **18** 03

RODRIGUEZ, RICK P (**27**,12,36,59) OAKA **27** 86-87, **12** 87, CLEA **36** 88, SFN **59** 90

RODRIGUEZ, ROSARIO P (**56**,30) CINN **56** 89-90, PITN **30** 91

RODRIGUEZ, RUBEN C (7,**3**) PITN **7/3** 88

RODRIGUEZ, STEVE SS/2B (**7**,41) BOSA **7** 95, DETA **41/7** 95

RODRIGUEZ, TONY SS (**31**) BOSA **31** 96

RODRIGUEZ, VIC 2B/3B/DH (**18**,20) BALA **18** 84, MINA **20** 89

RODRIQUEZ, ROBERTO P (16,17,45,31,50,43) KCA **16/17** 67, OAKA **45/23** 70, SDN **31** 70, CHIN **50/43** 70

RODRIGUEZ, WANDY P (**51**) HOUN **51** 05

RODRIGUEZ, WILFREDO P (**45**) HOUN **45** 01

ROE, PREACHER P (19,29,**28**) STLN **19** 38, PITN **29** 44-47, BKNN **28** 48-54

ROEBUCK, ED P (**37**,54,17,27) BKNN **37** 55-57, LAN **37** 58, 60-63, WASA **37** 63-64, PHIN **54** 64, **17** 64-65, **27** 66

ROENICKE, GARY OF/1B/UTIL/DH B (29,**35**,11,15) MONN **29** 76, BALA **35** 78-85, NYA **11** 86, ATLN **15** 87-88

ROENICKE, RON OF/UTIL/CH B (50,40,21,41 10,**17**,39,12) LAN **50** 81, **40** 82-83, SEAA **21** 83, SDN **41** 84, SFN **10** 85, PHIN **17** 86-87, CINN **39** 88, ANAA *CH* **12** 01-04, LAA **10** 05

ROESLER, MIKE P (55,**58**) CINN **55** 89, PITN **58** 90

ROESSLER, PAT CH (**6**) MONN *CH* **6** 00-01

ROETTGER, OSCAR (OKKIE) 1B B (**23**) PHIA **23** 32

ROETTGER, WALLY OF B (**8**,14) CINN **8** 32-33, PITN **14** 34

ROGALSKI, JOE P (**34**) DETA **34** 38

ROGELL, BILLY SS/3B/INF (**7**,6,5) DETA **7** 31, **6** 32-33, **7** 34-39, CHIN **5** 40

ROGERS, BUCK (LEFTY) P (**14**) WASA **14** 35

ROGERS, ED 2B/SS (**11**,67) BALA **11** 02, **67** 05

ROGERS, JIMMY P (**47**) TORA **47** 95

ROGERS, KENNY P (**37**,17,73) TEXA **37** 89-95, NYA **17** 96-97, OAKA **37** 98-99, NYN **73** 99, TEXA **37** 00-02, MINA **37** 03, TEXA **37** 04-05

ROGERS, KEVIN P (58,21,**28**) SFN **58/21** 92, **28** 93-94

ROGERS, LEE (BUCK) P (**15**,24) BOSA **15** 38, BKNN **24** 38

ROGERS, PACKY UTIL (1,**7**) BKNN **1/7** 38

ROGERS, STEVE P (**45**) MONN **45** 73-85

ROGGENBURK, GARRY (DUCK) P (32,**30**,18,17,44,37,46,39) MINA **32** 63, **30** 65-66, BOSA **18** 66, **17/26** 68, **44** 68, **37** 69, SEAA **46/44/39** 69

ROGODZINZKI, MIKE OF (29,**28**) PHIN **29** 73, **28** 73-75

ROGOVIN, SAUL P (23,**35**,14,27,9,26) DETA **23** 49-51, CHIA **35** 51-53, **14** 53, BALA **27** 55, PHIN **9** 55, **26** 56-57

ROHDE, DAVE INF/3B (**6**,22) HOUN **6** 90-91, CLEA **22** 92

ROHN, DAN 2B/SS/INF (**17**,15) CHIN **17** 83-84, CLEA **15** 86

ROHR, BILLY P (46,17,**15**,38) BOSA **46/17/15** 67, CLEA **38** 68

ROHR, LES P (42,**31**,33) NYN **42** 67, **31** 67-68, **33** 69

ROHRMEIER, DAN DH (**35**) SEAA **35** 97

ROIG, TONY 2B/SS/INF (29,36,**4**) WASA **29** 53, **36** 55, **4** 56

ROJAS, COOKIE 2B/3B/UTIL/C/DH/CH/M (17,16,11,**1**,2,4,8) CINN **17** 62, PHIN **16** 63-69, STLN **11** 70, KCA **1** 70-77, CHIN *CH* **1** 78-81, CALA *M* **2** 88, FLAN *CH* **1** 93-96, NYN *CH* **4** 97-98, **8** 99-00, TORA *CH* **1** 01, **4** 01-02

ROJAS, EUCLIDES CH (**54**) BOSA *CH* **54** 03-04

ROJAS, MEL P (**51**,27) MONN **51** 90-92, **27** 93, PHIN **51** 93-96, CHIN **51** 97, NYN **51** 97-98, LAN **51** 99, DETA **51** 99, MONN **51** 99

ROJAS, MINNIE P (22,**19**) CALA **22** 66, **19** 66-68

ROJEK, STAN SS/2B/INF (3,**6**,19,28) BKNN **3** 42, 46-47 PITN **6** 48-51, STLN **19** 51, STLA **28** 52

ROLAND, JIM P (44,34,25,32,39,19,**33**,54) MINA **44** 62, **34** 63, **25** 64, **44** 64-65, **32/39** 66, **19** 67-68, OAKA **33** 69-72, NYA **54** 72, TEXA **34** 72

ROLEN, SCOTT 3B (6,**17**,16,27) PHIN **6** 96, PHIN **17** 97-02, STLN **16** 02, **27** 02-05

ROLFE, RED 3B/SS/CH/M (**2**,31,10) NYA **2** 31, 34-42, *CH* **31** 46, DETA *M* **10** 49-52

ROLISON, NATE INF (**26**) FLAN **26** 00

ROLLINS, RICH (RED) 2B/3B/UTIL (**9**,10) MINA **9** 61-68, SEAA **9** 69, MILA **9** 70, CLEA **10** 70

ROLLINS, JIMMY INF/SS (29,**11**,6) PHIN **29** 00, **11** 01-02, **6** 03, **11** 04-05

ROLLS, DAMIAN INF/OF/3B/UTIL (71,**33**,10) TBA **71** 00, **33** 01-03, **10** 04

ROMAN, BILL 1B (37, **27**) DETA **37** 64, **27** 65

ROMAN, JOSE P (65,31,**34**) CLEA **65** 84, **31** 85, **34** 86

ROMANICK, RON P (37,**10**) CALA **37** 84, **10** 85-86

ROMANO, JASON OF/UTIL (**4**,3,5,8,33,7) TEXA **4** 02, COLN **3** 02, LAN **5** 03, TBA **8** 04, CINN **33** 04, **7** 05

ROMANO, JIM P (**33**) BKNN **33** 50

ROMANO, JOHNNY (HONEY) C/1B/UTIL (20,11,9,**7**,5,1) CHIA **20** 58-59, CLEA **11** 60-62, **9** 63, **7** 64, CHIA **5** 65-66, STLN **1** 67

ROMANO, MIKE P (**46**) TORA **46** 99

ROMANO, TOM OF (**41**) MONN **41** 87

ROMBERGER, DUTCH P (**49**) PHIA **49** 54

ROMERO, ED SS/INF/UTIL/DH (31,34,**11**,25,3,7,19,15,12) MILA **31** 77, **34** 80, **11** 81-85, BOSA **25/3/7** 86, **11** 87-89, ATLN **19** 89, MILA **15** 89, DETA **12** 90

ROMERO, J. C. P (**33**) MINA **33** 99-05

ROMERO, MANDY C (**3**,54,6) SDN **3** 97-98, BOSA **54** 98, COLN **6** 03

ROMERO, RAMON P (**50**) CLEA **50** 84-85

ROMINE, KEVIN OF/DH (50,**16**) BOSA **50** 85, **16** 85-91

ROMMEL, EDDIE P/CH (**14**,32) PHIA **14** 31-32, *CH* **32** 34

ROMO, ENRIQUE P (43,**15**) SEAA **43** 77-78, PITN **15** 79-82

ROMO, VICENTE (HUEVO) P (47,43,24,27,44,**45**) LAN **47** 68, CLEA **43** 68-69, BOSA **24** 69-70, CHIA **27** 71-72, SDN **44** 73, **45** 74, LAN **45** 82

ROMONOSKY, JOHN P (39,21,38,**34**) STLN **39** 53, WASA **21** 58, **38/34** 59

RONAN, DEL C (**29**) STLN **29** 93

RONDON, GIL P (**45**,55) HOUN **45** 76, CHIA **55** 79

RONEY, MATT P (**52**) DETA **52** 03

ROOF, GENE OF/CH B (**29**,47,52) STLN **29** 81-83, MONN **47** 83, DETA *CH* **52** 92-95

ROOF, PHIL C/1B/CH B (40,17,16,7,6,4,5,**8**,9,24,48,68) MILN **40** 61, **17** 64, CALA **16** 65, CLEA **7** 65, KCA **6** 66, **4** 66-67, OAKA **4** 68-69, MILA **5** 70-71, MINA **8** 71-76, CHIA **17** 76, TORA **4** 77, SDN *CH* **40/4** 78, SEAA *BPP* **9** 83, *CH* **4** 84-85, *CH* **24** 86-88, CHIN *CH* **48** 90-91, MINA *CH* **68** 00

ROOKER, JIM P (34,22,13,14,25,**19**) DETA **34** 68, KCA **22** 69, **13** 69-70, **14** 71, **25** 72, PITN **19** 73-80

ROOMES, ROLANDO OF (27,**36**) CHIN **27** 88, CINN **36** 89-90, MONN **27** 90

ROONEY, PAT OF (**56**) MONN **56** 81

ROOT, CHARLIE (CHINSKI) P/CH (15,12,19,14,**17**,49,31,4) CHIN **15/12** 32, **19** 33, **14** 34, **17** 35-41, *CH* **49** 51-53, MILN *CH* **31** 56-57, CHIN *CH* **4** 60

ROPER, JOHN P (**44**,41,42) CINN **44** 93, **41** 94, **44** 94-95, SFN **42** 95

ROQUE, JORGE OF (**24**,21,17) STLN **24** 70, **21** 71-72, **24** 72, MONN **17** 73

ROQUE, RAFAEL P (**52**) MILN **52** 98-00

ROSADO, JOSE P (**50**) KCA **50** 96-00, (01)

ROSADO, LUIS 1B/C (**35**,58) NYN **35** 77, **58** 80

ROSAR, BUDDY C (26,12,2,11,9,**8**) NYA **26** 39-40, **12** 41-42, CLEA **2** 43-44, PHIA **11/9** 45, **8** 46-49, BOSA **11** 50-51

ROSARIO, JIMMY OF/DH (**43**,22,11) SFN **43** 71-72, **22** 72, MILA **11** 76

ROSARIO, MEL C (**50**) BALA **50** 97

ROSARIO, RODRIGO P (**60**) HOUN **60** 03

ROSARIO, SANTIAGO 1B/OF (**21**) KCA **21** 65

ROSARIO, VICTOR SS/2B (**8**) ATLN **8** 90

ROSE, BOBBY 2B/3B/UTIL (**6**) CALA **6** 89-92

ROSE, BRIAN P (**19**,40,23,52) BOSA **19** 97-00, COLN **40** 00, NYN **23** 01, TBA **52** 01

ROSE, DON P (31,45,**41**) NYN **31** 71, CALA **45/41** 72, SFN **41** 74

ROSE, MIKE C (**6**,54) OAKA **6** 04, LAN **54** 05

ROSE, PETE (CHARLIE HUSTLE) 2B/OF/3B/1B/INF/UTIL/M (**14**) CINN **14** 63-78, PHIN **14** 79-83, MONN **14** 84, CINN **14** 84-86, *M* **14** 84-89

ROSE, PETE, Jr. 3B (**14**) CINN **14** 97

ROSEBORO, JOHNNY C/1B/3B/CH (**8**,44,10,13,2) BKNN **8** 57, LAN **8** 58, **44** 59-60, **8** 60-67, MINA **10** 68, **13** 68-69, WASA **13** 70, *CH* **13** 70, CALA *CH* **13** 72, *CH* **2** 73-74

ROSELLI, BOB 2B/3B/SS (**24**,25,31) MILN **24** 55-56, 58, **25** 58, CHIA **31** 61-62

ROSELLO, DAVE SS/2B/INF/DH (**17**,29,12) CHIN **17** 72-73, **29** 73-75, **17** 75-77, CLEA **12** 79-81

ROSEN, AL (FLIP) 3B/OF/INF (17,**7**) CLEA **17** 47, **7** 48-56

ROSEN, GOODY OF (32,**27**,35) BKNN **32** 37, **27** 38-39, **35** 44, **35** 45-46, NYN **27** 46

ROSENBAUM, GLEN CH (36,**39**) CHIA **36** 72-73, **39** 73-75, 87-89

ROSENBERG, STEVE P (61,46,**47**,32,41) CHIA **61** 88, **46** 88-89, **47/32** 90, SDN **41** 91

ROSENFELD, MAX OF (**25**) BKNN **25** 32-33

ROSENTHAL, LARRY OF/1B (**12**,14,19) CHIA **12** 36-41, CLEA **14** 41, NYA **19** 44, PHIA **12** 44-45

ROSENTHAL, WAYNE P/CH (**52**,26) TEXA **52** 91-92, FLAN *CH* **26** 03-04

ROSER, STEVE P (**26**,24,17) NYA **26** 44, **24** 45, **26** 46, BOSN **17** 46

ROSKOS, JOHN INF (**19**,22) FLAN **19** 98-99, SDN **22** 00

ROSS, BOB P (19,29,**30**) WASA **19** 50, **29** 51, PHIA **30** 56

ROSS, BUCK P (**17**,19) PHIA **17** 36-41, CHIA **19** 41-45

ROSS, CHET OF (38,**6**,28) BOSN **38** 39, **6** 40-44, **28** 44

ROSS, CLIFF P (**31**) CINN **31** 54

ROSS, CODY OF (**26**,49) DETA **26** 03, LAN **49** 05

ROSS, DAMIAN P (**32**) TBA **32** 04

ROSS, DAVID C (**40**,29,9) LAN **40** 02-04, PITN **29** 05, SDN **9** 05

ROSS, DON 3B/OF/INF (6,33,**20**,2,1) DETA **6** 38, BKNN **33** 40, DETA **20** 42, **2** 45, CLEA **1** 45-46

ROSS, GARY P (**33**,48,47) CHIN **33** 68-69, SDN **48** 69, **33** 69-74, CALA **47** 75-77

ROSS, MARK P (**47**,53,21,29,30) HOUN **47** 82, 84-85, PITN **53** 87, TORA **21** 88, PITN **29/30** 90

ROSSELLI, JOE P (**53**) SFN **53** 95

ROSSI, JOE C (**9**) CINN **9** 52

ROSSO, FRANK P (**36**) NYN **36** 44

ROSSY, RICO 3B/INF (34,**32**,44) ATLN **34** 91, KCA **32** 92-93, SEAA **44** 98

ROTBLATT, MARV (ROTTY) P (37,**49**) CHIA **37** 48, **49** 50-51

ROTHEL, BOB 3B (**3**) CLEA **3** 45

ROTHROCK, JACK OF/2B/INF/UTIL (3,12,14,**6**,23) BOSA **3** 31, **12** 32, CHIA **14** 32, STLN **6** 34-35, PHIA **23** 37

ROTHSCHILD, LARRY P/CH/M (**42**,3,47,11,41) DETA **42** 81-82, CINN *CH* **3** 90-92, FLAN *CH* **47** 95-97, TBA *M* **11** 98-01, CHIN *CH* **47** 02-03, **41** 04-05

ROUNSAVILLE, GENE P (**47**) CHIA **47** 70

ROUSH, EDD CH (**67**) CINN *CH* **67** 38

ROWAND, AARON OF (44,**33**) CHIA **44** 01-02, **33** 03-05

ROWDON, WADE SS/3B/UTIL (56,**17**,18,11) CINN **56** 84-85, **17** 85-86, CHIN **18** 87-88, BALA **11** 88

ROWE, DON P/CH (**29**,54,45) NYN **29** 63, CHIA *CH* **54** 88, MILA *CH* **45** 92-98

ROWE, KEN P/CH (39,17,**35**,42,31) LAN **39** 63, BALA **17** 64, **35** 65, *CH* **42** 85-86, *CH* **31** 85-86

ROWE, RALPH CH (42,54) MINA *CH* **42** 72-75, BALA *CH* **54** 81-84

ROWE, SCHOOLBOY P/CH (24,**14**,8,22,19,33) DETA **24** 33, **14** 34-42, BKNN **8** 42, PHIN **22**43, **19** 46-49, DETA *CH* **33** 54-55

ROWELL, BAMA OF/2B/UTIL (1,16,4,**5**,15) BOSN **1** 39, **16** 40-41, **4** 46, **5** 46-47, PHIN **15** 48

ROWLAND, MIKE P (35,**28**) SFN **35** 80, **28** 80-81

ROWLAND, RICH C/UTIL/DH (**12**,18) DETA **12** 90-93, BOSA **18** 94, **12** 95

ROY, EMILE P (no#) PHIA **no#** 33

ROY, JEAN PIERRE P (**34**) BKNN **34** 46

ROY, NORM (JUMBO)(NORMIE) P (**26**) BOSN **26** 50

ROYER, STAN OF/3B/1B (55,**5**,27) STLN **55** 91, **5** 92-94, BOSA **27** 94

ROYSTER, JERRY INF/UTIL/CH (8,4,13,**1**,3,5,28,46) LAN **8** 73-75, ATLN **4** 76, **13** 77, **1** 78-84, SDN **3** 85-86, CHIA **5/1** 87, NYA **28/46** 87, ATLN **4** 88, COLN *CH* **1/3/1** 93, MILN *CH* **3** 00-02, *M* **3** 02

ROYSTER, WILLIE C (**59**) BALA **59** 81

ROZEK, DICK P (**26**,23,49) CLEA **26** 50-52, PHIA **23** 53-54, **49** 54

ROZEMA, DAVE P (**19**,30) DETA **19** 77-84, TEXA **30** 85-86

ROZNOVSKY, VIC C (**8**,23,7) CHIN **8** 64-65, BALA **23** 66-67, PHIN **7** 69

RUAN, WILKIN OF (**26**) LAN **26** 02-03

RUBELING, AL 3B/2B (34,39,**4**) PHIA **34** 40, **39** 41, PITN **4** 43-44

RUBERTO, SONNY C/CH (**10**,7,3) SDN **10** 69, CINN **7** 72, STLN *CH* **3** 77-78

RUBIO, JORGE P (57,46,41,**37**) CALA **57/46/41** 66, **37** 67

RUBLE, ART (SPEEDY) OF (**34**) PHIN **34** 34

RUCKER, DAVE P (49,18,**36**,39,51) DETA **49** 81-83, **18** 83, STLN **36** 83-84, PHIN **39** 85-86, PITN **51/36** 88

RUCKER, JOHNNY OF (26,**1**,3,37) NYN **26** 40-41, **1** 41, **3** 43, **1** 44-45, **37** 46

RUDI, JOE OF/1B/UTIL/DH/CH (15,8,**26**,46) KCA **45/15** 67, OAKA **8** 68, **26** 69-76, CALA **26** 77-80, BOSA **26** 81, OAKA **26** 82, *CH* **46** 86-88, *CH* **26** 87

RUDOPLH, DON P (26,27,15,47,**33**) CHIA **26** 57, **27** 58-59,**15** 59, CINN **47** 59, CLEA **26** 62, WASA **26** 62, **33** 62-64

RUDOPLH, ERNIE P (**10**) BKNN **10** 45

RUDOPLH, KEN C/OF (50,8,**15**,2,9,14,12) CHIN **50** 69, **8** 69-70, **15** 70-73, SFN **2** 74, STLN **9** 75-76, SFN **14** 77, BALA **12** 77

RUEBEL, MATT P (**49**,36,53) PITN **49** 96-97, TBA **36/53** 98

RUEL, MUDDY C/CH/M (10,8.**9**,49,38,51,42) BOSA **10** 31, DETA **8** 31, **9** 32, STLA **9** 33, CHIA **49** 34, *CH* **38** 35-45, STLA *M* **51** 47, CLEA *CH* **42** 48-50

RUETER, KIRK P (**42**,45,46) MONN **42** 93-96, SFN **42** 96-97, **45** 97, **46** 97-05

RUFER, RUDY SS (28,**14**) NYN **28** 49, **14** 50

RUFFCORN, SCOTT P (45,**36**,42,33) CHIA **45** 93, **36** 94-95, **42** 96, PHIN **33** 97

RUFFIN, BRUCE P (**47**,30,18) PHIN **47** 86-91, MILA **30** 92, COLN **18** 93-97

RUFFIN, JOHNNY P (58,47,**26**) CINN **58** 93, **47** 94, **26** 95-96, ARIN **56/47** 00, FLAN **48** 01

RUFFING, RED P/CH (18,**15**,22,34,44,54) NYA **21** 30, **18** 31, **15** 32-42, **22** 45-46, CHIA **34** 47, CLEA *CH* **44** 51, NYN *CH* **54** 62

RUHLE, VERN P/CH (31,**48**,43,46,53,58) DETA **31** 74-77, HOUN **48** 78-84, CLEA **48** 85, CALA **43** 86, HOUN *CH* **48** 97-00, PHIN *CH* **46** 01-02, NYN *CH* **53** 03, CINN *CH* **58** 05

RUIZ, CHICO (Hiraldo) 3B/2B/SS/UTIL (**15**,12) CINN **15** 64-69, CALA **12** 70, **15** 70-71

RUIZ, CHICO (Manuel) 2B/3B/INF (**16**,14) ATLN **16** 78, **14** 80

RULLO, JOE 2B/1B (**12**) PHIA **12** 43-44

RUNGE, PAUL SS/2B/INF (15,**12**) ATLN **15** 81-82, **12** 83-88

RUNNELLS, TOM SS/2B/INF/CH/M (**10**,19) CINN **10** 85-86, MONN *CH* **19** 90, *CH* **10** 90-91, *M* **10** 91-92

RUNNELS, PETE SS/2B/1B/INF/UTIL/CH/M (35,5,**3**,32) WASA **35** 51-53, **5** 54-57, BOSA **3** 58-62, HOUN **3** 63-64, BOSA *CH* **32** 65-66, *M* **32** 66

RUNYAN, SEAN P (**44**,55,49) DETA **44** 98-99, **55/49** 00

RUPE, JOSH P (**59**) TEXA **59** 05

RUPE, RYAN P (**24**,30) TBA **24** 99-02, BOSA **30** 03

RUSCH, GLENDON P (53,**48**,39) KCA **53** 97-99, NYN **48** 99-01, MILN **39** 02-03, CHIN **33** 04-05

RUSH, BOB P (30,**17**,29) CHIN **30** 48-49, **17** 49-57, MILN **17** 58-60, CHIA **29** 60

RUSHFORD, JIM OF (**33**) MILN **33** 02

RUSKIN, SCOTT P (56,**34**,28) PITN **56** 90, MONN **34** 90-91, CINN **28** 92-93

RUSSELL, BILL OF/SS/UTIL/CH/M (**18**) LAN **18** 69-86, *CH* **18** 87-91, 94-95, *M* **18** 96-98, TBA *CH* **18** 00

RUSSELL, JACK P (22,21,**17**,16,26,28) BOSA **22** 31, **21** 32, CLEA **17** 32, WASA **17** 33-36, **16** 36, BOSA **17** 36, DETA **26** 37, CHIN **28** 38-39, STLN **28** 40

RUSSELL, JEFF P (46,**40**,23,25,29) CINN **46** 83-84, TEXA **40** 85-92, OAKA **23** 92, BOSA **25** 93-94, CLEA **29/40** 94, TEXA **40** 95-96

RUSSELL, JIM OF/1B (**32**,17,5,37) PITN **32** 42-47, **17** 47, BOSN **5** 48-49, BKNN **37** 50-51

RUSSELL, JOHN OF/C/1B/UTIL/P/CH (37,29,**6**,3,8,13) PHIN **37** 84, **29** 84-85, **6** 86-88, ATLN **6** 89, TEXA **17** 90-91, **3** 92, **8** 93, PITN *CH* **13** 03-05

RUSSELL, LLOYD PR (**35**) CLEA **35** 38

RUSSELL, RIP 1B/3B/UTIL (32,**12**,5) CHIN **32** 39, **12** 40-42, BOSA **5** 46-47

RUSSO, MARIUS (LEFTY) P (38,25,**22**,26) NYA **38/30/25** 39, **22** 39-43, **26** 46

RUSTECK, DICK P (49,43,**40**) NYN **49/43/40** 66

RUSZKOWSKI, HANK C (**16**,11) CLEA **16** 44-45, **11** 47

RUTH, BABE (BAMBINO)(THE SULTAN OF SWAT)(GIDGE) OF/P/1B/CH (**3**,35) NYA **3** 29-34, BOSN **3** 35, BKNN *CH* **35** 38

RUTHERFORD, JOHNNY (DOC) P (**15**) BKNN **15** 52

RUTHVEN, DICK P (40,**44**) PHIN **40** 73-75, ATLN **40** 76-78, PHIN **44** 78-83, CHIN **44** 83-86

RUTNER, MICKEY 3B (**31**) PHIA **31** 47

RYAL, MARK OF/1B/UTIL (36,0,**6**,7,31,27) KCA **36** 82, CHIA **0** 85, CALA **6** 86-87, **7** 87, PHIN **31** 89, PITN **27** 90

RYAN, B. J. P (43,**52**) CINN **43** 99, BALA **52** 99-05

RYAN, BLONDY SS/INF (23,**22**,27) NYN **23** 33-34, PHIN **22** 35, NYA **27** 35, NYN **22** 37-38

RYAN, CONNIE 2B/3B/INF/UTIL/CH/M (6,30,**8**,16,3,19,1,41) NYN **6** 42, BOSN **30** 43, **8** 44, 46-50, CINN **16** 50-51, PHIN **8** 52-53, CHIA **3** 53, CINN **19** 54, MILN *CH* **8** 57, ATLN *CH* **10** 71, *CH* **1** 73-74, *M* **6** 75, TEXA *CH* **41**77, *M* **41** 77, *CH* **8** 77-79

RYAN, JASON P (**54**) MINA **54** 99-00

RYAN, KEN P (**50**,51) BOSA **50** 92-95, PHIN **51** 96-99

RYAN, MIKE J. C/CH (40,22,**9**,5,25) BOSA **40** 64-65, **22** 66-67, PHIN **9** 68-73, PITN **5** 74, PHIN *CH* **5** 80-83, *CH* **25** 83-84, *CH* **5** 85-89, *CH* **25** 92, *CH* **9** 93-95

RYAN, MIKE S. OF (**54**,12) MINA **54** 02-03, **12** 04-05

RYAN, NOLAN P (**34**,**30**) NYN **34** 66, **30** 68-71, CALA **30** 72-79, HOUN **34** 80-88, TEXA **34** 89-93

RYAN, ROB OF (**15**) ARIN **15** 99-00, **8** 01, OAKA **26** 01

RYAN, ROSY P (35,**22**) BKNN **35/22** 33

RYBA, MIKE P/CH (19,25,**20**,35) STLN **19** 35-38, BOSA **25** 41-42, **20** 42-46, STLN *CH* **35** 51-54

RYE, GENE (HALF-PINT) OF (**16**) BOSA **16** 31

RYERSON, GARY P (**43**) MILA **43** 72-73

S

SAARLOOS, KIRK P (50,**23**,31) HOUN **50** 02, **23** 03, OAKA **31** 04-05

SABATHIA, C. C. P (**52**) CLEA **52** 01-05

SABEL, ERIK P (**36**) ARIN **36** 99, **56** 01, DETA **58** 02

SABERHAGEN, BRET P (31,**18**,17) KCA **31** 84-87, **18** 87-91, NYN **18** 92-95, COLN **38/31** 95, BOSA **17** 97-99, (00), 01

SABO, ALEX (GIZ) C (22,**26**) WASA **22** 36, **26** 37

SABO, CHRIS 3B/SS/1B/DH (**17**,18) CINN **17** 88-93, BALA **17** 94, CHIA **17** 95, STLN **18** 95, CINN **17** 96

SACKA, FRANK C (25,**10**) WASA **25** 51, **10** 53

SACKINSKY, BRIAN P (**57**) BALA **57** 96

SADECKI, RAY P (**37**,33,34,43,27) STLN **37** 60-66, SFN **37** 66-69, NYN **33** 70-74, STLN **37** 75, ATLN **34** 75, KCA **43** 75, **37** 76, MILA **34/27** 76, NYN **33** 77

SADEK, MIKE C/OF (**3**) SFN **3** 73, 75-81

SADLER, CARL P (**53**) CLEA **53** 02-03

SADLER, DONNIE 2B/INF/SS (62,**52**) BOSA **62/52** 98, **15** 99-00, CINN **15** 01, KCA **30** 01, **1** 02, TEXA **4** 02, ARIN **4** 04

SADLER, RAY OF (**43**) PITN **43** 05

SADOWSKI, BOB (SID) 2B/3B/OF (19,5,**15**) STLN **19** 60, PHIN **5** 61, CHIA **15** 62, LAA **15** 63

SADOWSKI, BOB P B (**37**,21) MILN **37** 63-65, BOSA **21** 66

SADOWSKI, ED C B (8,**6**,45) BOSA **8** 60, LAA **6** 61-63, ATLN **45** 66

SADOWSKI, JIM P B (**32**) PITN **32** 74

SADOWSKI, TED P B (35,**16**,45) WASA **35** 60, MINA **35/16** 61, **45** 62

SAENZ, CHRIS P (**38**) MILN **38** 04

SAENZ, OLMEDO 3B/INF/1B (8,**9**) CHIA **8** 94, OAKA **9** 99-02, LAN **8** 04-05

SAFFELL, TOM OF (18,21,17,**16**,3) PITN **18** 49-50, **21** 50, **17** 51, **16** 55, KCA **3** 55

SAGER, A. J. P (44,48,49) SDN **44** 94, COLN **48** 95, DETA **49** 96-98

SAGMOEN, MARC OF (**37**) TEXA **37** 97

SAIN, JOHNNY P/CH (28,**33**,11,15,40,31,53,23) BOSN **28** 42, **33** 46-51, NYA **11** 51-55, KCA **15** 55, *CH* **40** 59, NYA *CH* **31** 61-63, MINA *CH* **53** 65-66, DETA *CH* **53** 67-69, CHIA *CH* **33** 71-75, ATLN *CH* **23** 77, *CH* **33** 85-87

ST. CLAIRE, EBBA C F (**7**,42) BOSN **7** 51, **42** 52, MILN **42** 53, NYN **7** 54

ST. CLAIRE, RANDY P S (**51**,35,38,46,37,49) MONN **51** 84-88, CINN **51/35** 88, MINA **38** 89, ATLN **46** 91-92, TORA **37** 94, MONN *CH* **49** 03-04, WASN *CH* **46** 05

SAIPE, MIKE P (**20**) COLN **20** 98

SAKATA, LENN 2B/SS/INF/DH (21,2,**12**,17,11) MILA **21** 77, **2** 78-79, BALA **12** 80-85, OAKA **17** 86, NYA **11** 87

SALAS, MARK OF/C/UTIL/DH/CH (55,**12**,27,8,10,58) STLN **55** 84, MINA **12** 85-87, NYA **12/27** 87, CHIA **27** 88, CLEA **8** 89, DETA **10** 90, **27** 91, CHIA *CH* **58** 96-99

SALAZAR, ANGEL SS/2B/INF (51,6,11,**2**,18) MONN **51** 83, **6** 83-84, **11** 84, KCA **2** 86-87, CHIN **18** 88

SALAZAR, LUIS 3B/OF/UTIL/P/CH (24,**4**,5,12,11,10,43) SDN **24** 80, **4** 81-84, CHIA **5** 85, SDN **24** 87, DETA **12** 88, SDN **4** 89, CHIN **11** 89-90, **10** 91-92, MILN *CH* **43** 01

SALAZAR, OSCAR INF (**40**) DETA **40** 02

SALKELD, BILL C (1,**15**) PITN **1** 45-47, BOSN **15** 48-49, CHIA **15** 50

SALKELD, ROGER P (**42**,22) SEAA **42** 93, **22** 94, CINN **42** 96

SALMON, CHICO INF/UTIL (26,**17**,30) CLEA **26** 64, **17** 64-68, BALA **30** 69-72

SALMON, TIM OF/DH (**15**) CALA **15** 92-96, ANAA **15** 97-04, LAA **(15)** (05)

SALTZGAVER, JACK 2B/3B/1B/INF (7,**12**,4) NYA **7** 32, **12** 34-37, PITN **4** 45

SALVERSON, JACK P (25,28,**44**,48,38,30) NYN **25** 33-34, **28** 34, PITN **44** 35, CHIA **48** 35, CLEA **38** 43, **35/30/44** 45

SALVO, MANNY (GYP) P (18,31,**23**,24,__) NYN **18** 39, BOSN **31** 40, **23** 40-42, **24** 43, PHIN __ 43

SAMBITO, JOE P (**35**,43) HOUN **35** 76-82, 84, NYN **35** 85, BOSA **43** 86-87

SAMCOFF, EDDIE 2B (**6**) PHIA **6** 51

SAMFORD, RON 2B/SS/INF (17,37,**27**,32) NYN **17** 54, DETA **37** 55, **27** 57, WASA **32** 59

SAMPEN, BILL P (**55**,50,36) MONN **55** 90-92, KCA **50** 92-93, CALA **36** 94

SAMPLE, BILLY OF/DH (7,**5**,11,6) TEXA **7** 78, **5** 79-84, NYA **11** 85, ATLN **6/5** 86

SAMPSON, BENJ P (53,**23**) MINA **53** 98, **23** 99

SAMUEL, AMADO SS/2B/INF (**27**,7) MILN **27** 62-63, NYN **7** 64

SAMUEL, JUAN (SAMMY) 2B/OF/UTIL/DH/CH (9,16,**8**,7,10,17,27,11) PHIN **9/16** 83, **8** 84-89, NYN **7** 89, LAN **10** 90-92, KCA **17** 92, CINN **8** 93, DETA **8** 94-95, KCA **27** 95, TORA **11** 96-98, DETA *CH* **10** 99-04, **8** 04-05

SAMUELS, ROGER P (**58**) SFN **58** 88, PITN **58** 89

SANCHEZ, ALEX (ALEJANDRO) OF/DH (**27**,33,32,18,24) PHIN **27** 82-83, SFN **33** 84, DETA **32** 85, MINA **18** 86, OAKA **24** 87, TORA **33** 89

SANCHEZ, ALEX (ALEXIS) OF (7,**22**,19,2,21) MILN **7** 01, **22** 02-03, DETA **19** 03-04, TBA **2** 05, SFN **21** 05

SANCHEZ, CELARANO 3B/UTIL (**10**) NYA **10** 72-73

SANCHEZ, DUANER P (52,**45**,50) ARIN **52** 02, PITN **45** 02-03, LAN **50** 04-05

SANCHEZ, FELIX P (**62**) CHIN **62** 03

SANCHEZ, FREDDY UTIL/SS/3B (52,26,**12**) BOSA **52** 02, **26** 03, PITN **12** 04-05

SANCHEZ, ISRAEL P (**31**) KCA **31** 88, 90

SANCHEZ, JESUS P (**21**,41,55) FLAN **21** 98-01, CHIN **41** 02, COLN **55** 03, CINN **41** 04

SANCHEZ, LUIS P (**40**) CALA **40** 81-85

SANCHEZ, ORLANDO C (**23**,49,41) STLN **23** 81-83, KCA **49** 84, BALA **41** 84

SANCHEZ, RAUL P (33,37,**13**32,35) WASA **33/37/13** 52, CINN **32** 57, **35** 60

SANCHEZ, REY SS/2B (15,6,**11**,26,14,1,2,13,10) CHIN **15** 91, **6** 92, **11** 93-97, NYA **26** 97, SFN **14** 98, KCA **1** 99-01, ATLN **2** 01, BOSA **13** 02, NYN **10** 03, SEAA **1** 03, TBA **1** 04, NYA **26** 05

SANDBERG, JARED 3B/UTIL (24,**23**) TBA **10** 01-02, **26** 03

SANDBERG, RYNE (RYNO) 2B/SS (24,**23**) PHIN **24** 81, CHIN **23** 82-94, 96-97

SANDERS, ANTHONY OF (27,13,**10**) TORA **27** 99, SEAA **13** 00, **10** 01

SANDERS, DAVID P (**52**,65) CHIA **52** 03, **65** 05

SANDERS, DEE P (**23**) STLA **23** 45

SANDERS, DEION (NEON DEION) (**24**,21,12,2) NYA **24** 89, **21**90, ATLN **24** 91-94, CINN **12** 94, **21** 95, SFN **21** 95, CINN **21** 97, **2** 01

SANDERS, JOHN PR (36,**15**) KCA **36/15** 65

SANDERS, KEN (DAFFY) P (27,29,34,32,**20**,33,47,39,28) KCA **27** 64, BOSA **29** 66, KCA **34** 66, OAKA **32** 68, MILA **20** 70-73, CLEA **33** 73, **47** 73-74, CALA **47/39** 74, NYN **33** 75-76, KCA **28** 76

SANDERS, RAY 1B (**5**,4,6) STLN **5** 42-45, BOSN **5/4** 46, **5** 48, **6** 49

SANDERS, REGGIE 1B/DH (**43**) DETA **43** 74

SANDERS, REGGIE OF (53,**16**,19) CINN **53** 91, **16** 91-98, SDN **16** 99, ATLN **16** 00, ARIN **16** 01, SFN **16** 02, PITN **19** 03, STLN **16** 04-05

SANDERS, SCOTT P (**27**,28,26) SDN **27** 93-96, SEAA **27** 97, DETA **28** 97, **27** 98, SDN **26** 98, CHIN **27** 99

SANDERSON, SCOTT P (**21**,24,40,22,29) MONN **40** 78, **21** 78-83, CHIN **24** 84, **21** 85-89, OAKA **22** 90, NYA **21** 91-92, CALA **21** 93, SFN **29** 93, CHIA **21** 94, CALA **21** 95-96

SANDLOCK, MIKE P (19,1,**4**,6) BOSN **19** 42, **6** 44, BKNN **1** 45, **4** 46, PITN **6** 53

SANDOVAL, DANNY SS (**29**) PHIN **29** 05

SANDS, CHARLIE C/DH (68,49,4,**19**,7) NYA **68/49** 67, PITN **4** 71-72, CALA **19** 73-74, OAKA **7** 75

SANDT, TOMMY 2B/INF/CH (**13**,37,46) OAKA **13** 75-76, PITN *CH* **37** 87-96, FLAN *CH* **37** 97-98, COLN *CH* **37** 99, PITN *CH* **46** 00, **37** 01-02

SANFORD, CHANCE INF (70,**31**,54) PITN **70/31** 98, LAN **54** 99

SANFORD, FRED P (27,41,25,**21**,18,28) STLA **27** 43, **41** 46, **25** 47-48, NYA **21** 49-51, WASA **27/21** 51, STLA **18/28** 51

SANFORD, JACK 1B (35,**27**) WASA **35** 40, **27** 41, 46

SANFORD, JACK P/CH (48,39,**33**,23,49,2) PHIN **48** 56, **39** 57-58, SFN **33** 59-65, CALA **23** 65, **49** 65-67, KCA **33** 67, CLEA *CH* **2** 68-69

SANFORD, MO P (52,**34**,54) CINN **52** 91, COLN **34** 93, MINA **54** 95

SANGUILLEN, MANNY C/OF/1B/UTIL (**35**) PITN **35** 67, 69-76, OAKA **35** 77, PITN **35** 78-80

SANICKI, ED (BUTCH) OF (33,**15**) PHIN **33** 49, **15** 51

SANTANA, ANDRES SS (**35**) SFN **35** 90

SANTANA, ERVIN P (**54**) LAA **54** 05

SANTANA, JOHAN P (**57**) MINA **57** 00-05

SANTANA, JULIO P (**60**,54,48) TEXA **60** 97-98, TBA **60** 98-99, MONN **54** 00, DETA **48** 02, MILN **48** 05

SANTANA, MARINO P (**52**,62) DETA **52** 98, BOSA **62** 99

SANTANA, PEDRO 2B (**49**) DETA **49** 01

SANTANA, RAFAEL SS/2B/IN/CH (14,**3**,17,2.1) STLN **14** 83, NYN **3** 84-87, NYA **17** 88, CLEA **2** 90, CHIA *CH* **1** 03

SANTANGELO, F. P. OF (**7**,14,2) MONN **7** 95-98, SFN **14** 99, LAN **14** 00, OAKA **2** 01

SANTIAGO, BENITO C/OF (10,9,**09**,18,6,33,30,34) SDN **10** 86, **9** 87-91, **09** 91-92, FLAN **09** 93-94, CINN **18** 95, PHIN **18** 96, TORA **18** 97-98, CHIN **9** 99, CINN **6** 00, SFN **33** 01-03, KCA **30** 04, PITN **34** 05

SANTIAGO, JOSE P (49,**46**,40,48,33) KCA **49** 97, **46** 98-01, PHIN **40** 01-02, CLEA **48** 03, NYN **33** 05

SANTIAGO, JOSE (G.) (PANTS) P (38,51,34,26) CLEA **38** 54, **51/34** 55, KCA **26** 56

SANTIAGO, JOSE (R.) P (22,21,29,**30**,36) KCA **22** 63-64, **21** 64, **29** 65, BOSA **30** 66-69, **36** 70

SANTIAGO, RAMON SS/3B (**39**,1) DETA **39** 02-03, SEAA **1** 04-05

SANTO DOMINGO, RAFAEL PH (**21**) CINN **21** 79

SANTO, RON 3B/SS/UTIL/DH (**10**) CHIN **10** 60-73, CHIA **10** 74

SANTORINI, AL P (43,24,**23**,34) ATLN **43/24** 68, SDN **23** 69-71, STLN **34** 71-73

SANTOS, ANGEL 2B/2B (**53**,56) BOSA **53** 01, CLEA **56** 03

SANTOS, FRANCISCO 1B (**53**,56) SFN **60** 03

SANTOS, VICTOR P (**22**,45,49.53) DETA **22** 01, COLN **45** 02, TEXA **49** 03, MILN **53** 04-05

SANTOVENIA, NELSON C/1B (47,**22**,48,53,26) MONN **47** 87-88, **22** 89-91, CHIA **48** 92, KCA **53** 93, **26** 94

SARDINHA, DANE C (67,**59**) CINN **67** 03, **59** 05

SARMIENTO, MANNY P (**45**,44,38) CINN **45** 76-79, SEAA **44** 80, PITN **38** 82-83

SARNI, BILL C/CH (16,**15**,8) STLN **16** 51-52, **15** 54-56, NYN **15/8** 56, *CH* **8** 57

SASAKI, KAZUHIRO P (**22**) SEAA **22** 00-03

SASSER, MACKEY C/UTIL (10,17,**2**,4,15) NYN **10/17** 87, PITN **2** 87, NYN **2** 88-92, SEAA **4** 94, **15** 94, PITN **17** 95

SASSER, ROB 3B (**14**) TEXA **14** 98

SATRIANO, TOM P (29,**2**,4) LAA **29** 61-63, **2** 64, CALA **2** 65-69, BOSA **4** 69-70

SATURRIA, LUIS OF (13,**23**) STLN **13** 00, **23** 01

SAUCIER, FRANK OF (**16**) STLA **16** 51

SAUCIER, KEVIN P
(**33**,31) PHIN **33** 78-80, DETA **31** 81-82, **33** 82

SAUER, ED (HORN) OF/3B B
(24,49,**2**,45, 10,14) CHIN **24** 43, **49** 44, **2** 44, **45** 45, STLN **10** 49, BOSN **14** 49

SAUER, HANK OF/1B B
(29,28,43,**9**, 10,6) CINN **29** 41-42, **28** 44-45, **29** 48-49, CHIN **43** 49, **9** 50-55, STLN **10** 56, NYN **6** 57, SFN **6** 58-59

SAUERBECK, SCOTT P
(**47**,48) PITN **47** 99-03, BOSA **48/47** 03, CLEA **47** 05

SAUL, JIM CH
(**2**,42) CHIN *CH* **2** 75-76, OAKA *CH* **42** 79

SAUNDERS, DENNIS P
(**46**) DETA **46** 70

SAUNDERS, DOUG INF
(**2**) NYN **2** 93

SAUNDERS, JOE P
(**68**) LAA **68** 05

SAUNDERS, TONY P
(41,**31**) FLAN **41** 97, TBA **31** 98-99, (00)

SAUVEUR, RICH P
(36,39,26,**70**, 56) PITN **36** 86, MONN **39** 88, NYN **39** 91, KCA **26** 92, CHIA **70** 96-97, OAKA **56** 00

SAVAGE, BOB P
(29,37,**16**,27) PHIA **29** 42, **37** 46, **16** 47-48, STLA **27** 49

SAVAGE, DON 3B/OF
(**6**) NYA **6** 44-45

SAVAGE, JACK P
(50,**20**) LAN **50** 87, MINA **20** 90

SAVAGE, TED OF/3B/INF
(14,7,**2**,22, 31,20,5) PHIN **14/7** 62, PITN **2/14** 63, STLN **22** 65-67, CHIN **25** 67-68, LAN **31** 68, CINN **20** 69, MILA **2** 70-71, KCA **5/7** 71

SAVARINE, BOB (RABBIT) 2B/SS/OF/UTIL
(33,2,**1**,15) BALA **33** 59, **2** 62, **1** 63-64, WASA **15** 66-67

SAVRANSKY, MOE P
(**42**) CINN **42** 54

SAWATSKI, CARL (SWATS) C/OF
(18,11,15,14, 47,**1**) CHIN **18** 48, **11** 50, **15** 53, CHIA **14** 54, MILN **15** 57-58, PHIN **47** 58-59, STLN **1** 60-63

SAWYER, EDDIE M
(7,**24**) PHIN *M* **7** 48, *M* **24** 49-52, *M* **24** 58-60

SAWYER, RICK P
(40,45,41,**27**) NYA **40** 74, **41** 75, SDN **27** 76-77

SAX, DAVE C/OF/1B B
(23,22,**16**,50, 12) LAN **23** 82-83, **22** 83, BOSA **16** 85-86, **50** 86, **12** 87

SAX, STEVE 2B/3B/UTIL B
(52,**3**,6,7) LAN **52** 81, **3** 82-88, NYA **6** 89-91, CHIA **7** 92-93, OAKA **6** 94

SAYLES, BILL P
(17,**20**,22) BOSA **17** 39, NYN **20** 43, BKNN **22** 43

SCALA, JERRY OF
(14,**2**,36,39) CHIA **14** 48, **2** 49, **36/39** 50

SCALZI, SKEETER SS/3B
(**1**) NYN **1** 39

SCANLAN, BOB P
(**30**,39,38,24, 43,50,26) CHIN **30** 91-93, MILA **39** 94-95, DETA **38** 96, KCA **24** 96, HOUN **43** 98, MILN **50** 00, MONN **26** 01

SCANLON, PAT 3B/1B/UTIL
(**42**,8) MONN **42** 74-76, SDN **8** 77

SCANTLEBURY, PAT P
(**48**) CINN **48** 56

SCARBERY, RANDY P
(**26**) CHIA **26** 79-80

SCARBOROUGH, RAY P/CH
(66,**10**,34,21, 25,46,7,18, 19,48) WASA **66** 42, **10** 42-43, **34** 43, **21** 46-47, **10** 48-49, **25** 50, CHIA **46/7** 50, BOSA **18** 51-52, NYA **19** 52-53, DETA **19** 53, BALA *CH* **48** 68

SCARCE, MAC P
(**44**,28) PHIN **44** 72-74, NYN **44** 75, MINA **28** 78

SCARRITT, RUSS OF
(**12**,25) BOSA **12** 31, PHIN **25** 32

SCARSELLA, LES 1B/OF
(24,**11**,16,3) CINN **24** 35, **11** 36-37, **16** 39, BOSN **3** 40

SCARSONE, STEVE 2B/3B/INF
(31,27,38,**23**, 6) PHIN **31** 92, BALA **27** 92, SFN **38** 93, **23** 93-96, STLN **38** 97, KCA **6** 99

SCHAAL, PAUL 2B/3B/INF
(42,**10**,9) LAA **42** 64, CALA **42** 65-68, KCA **10** 69-74, CALA **9** 74

SCHACHT, AL (THE CLOWN PRINCE OF BASEBALL) CH
(30,29,**28**,26, 32) WASA *CH* **30** 31, *CH* **29** 32, *CH* **28** 33-34, BOSA *CH* **26** 35, *CH* **32** 36

SCHACHT, SID P
(27,42,37,**11**) STLA **27** 50, **42** 51, BOSN **37/11** 51

SCHACKER, HAL P
(**26**) BOSN **26** 45

SCHAEFER, BOB CH/M
(**42**),44) KCA *CH* **42** 88-91, *M* **42** 91, *CH* **44** 02-05

SCHAEFER, JEFF INF/DH
(15,**2**,42) CHIA **15** 89, SEAA **2** 90-92, OAKA **42** 94

SCHAEFFER, HARRY (LEFTY) P
(34,**39**) NYA **34/39** 52

SCHAEFFER, MARK P
(44,**46**) SDN **44/46** 72

SCHAFFER, JIMMIE C/CH
(**4**,5,18,17,34, 21,25,42,46, 44) STLN **4** 61-62, CHIN **5** 63-64, CHIA **18** 65, NYN **17** 65, PHIN **34** 66 **21** 67, CINN **25** 68, TEXA *CH* **42/46** 78, KCA *CH* **44** 80-88

SCHAFFERNOTH, JOE P
(**46**,23) CHIN **46** 59-61, CLEA **23** 61

SCHALK, ROY 2B/SS
(__,7,**6**) NYA __ 32, CHIA **7** 44, **6** 44-45

SCHALL, GENE 1B
(**6**,5) PHIN **6** 95-96, **5** 96

SCHALLOCK, ART P
(26,**20**,38,19) NYA **26/20** 51-52, **38** 53, **20** 53, **19** 54, **38** 54-55, BALA **20** 55

SCHANG, WALLY C/CH
(8,**27**) DETA **8** 31, CLEA *CH* **27** 37-38

SCHANZ, CHARLEY P
(22,16,**18**) PHIN **22** 44, **16** 44-45, **18** 46-47, BOSA **18** 50

SCHAREIN, ART (SCOOP) 3B/INF B
(__,7,**4**) STLA __ 32, **7** 33, **4** 34

SCHAREIN, GEORGE (TOM) SS/INF B
(20,6,**18**) PHIN **20** 37, **6** 38, **18** 39-40

SCHATTINGER, JEFF P
(**31**) KCA **31** 81

SCHATZEDER, DAN P
(**43**,36,35,31, 37,20) MONN **43** 77-78, **36** 78-79, DETA **36** 80-81, SFN **36** 82, MONN **43** 82-86, PHIN **35** 86-87, **43** 87, MINA **31** 87, CLEA **31** 88, MINA **37/31** 88, HOUN **20** 89-90, NYN **43** 90, KCA **43** 91

SCHEETZ, OWEN P
(15,**12**) WASA **15/12** 43

SCHEFFING, BOB C/CH/M
(33,**10**,7,30, 44,46,25,3, 27) CHIN **33** 41-42, **10** 46-50, CINN **7** 50-51, STLN **30** 51, STLA *CH* **44** 52-53, CHIN *CH* **46** 54-55, *M* **25** 57-59, MILN *CH* **3** 60, DETA *M* **27** 61-63

SCHEIB, CARL P/OF
(14,**24**,31) PHIA **14** 43, **24** 44-45, 47-54, STLN **31** 54

SCHEID, RICH P
(**49**,37) HOUN **49** 92, FLAN **37** 94-95

SCHEINBLUM, RICHIE OF/DH
(24,**28**,39,5, 26,9,30,19) CLEA **24** 65, **28** 67-69, WASA **35/39** 71, TEXA **39** 72, KCA **5** 72, CINN **26** 73, CALA **9** 73-74, KCA **30/5** 74, STLN **19** 74

SCHELL, DANNY OF
(**10**) PHIN **10** 54-55

SCHELLE, JIM P
(**21**) PHIA **21** 39

SCHEMER, MIKE (LEFTY) 1B
(35,**38**) NYN **35** 45, **38** 46

SCHENZ, HANK 3B/2B/INF
(17,**5**,2,10) CHIN **17** 46, **5** 47-49, PITN **2** 50 **10** 51, NYN **10** 51

SCHERBARTH, BOB C
(**39**) BOSA **39** 50

SCHERGER, GEORGE CH
(**3**) CINN *CH* **3** 70-78, 82-86

SCHERMAN, FRED P
(**39**,44,21) DETA **39** 69-73, HOUN **44** 74-75, MONN **21** 75-76, **55/44** 75

SCHERRER, BILL P
(34,**17**,37) CINN **34** 82-84, DETA **17** 84-86, CINN **37** 87, BALA **37** 88, PHIN **34** 88

SCHIAVE, JOHNNY 2B/3B
(29,9,37,**6**) WASA **29** 58, **9** 59, **37** 60, **6** 62-63

SCHILLING, CHUCK 2B
(**2**) BOSA **2** 61-65

SCHILLING, CURT P
(43,45,19,**38**) BALA **43** 88-90, **45** 90, HOUN **19** 91, PHIN **38** 92-00, ARIN **38** 00-03, BOSA **38** 04-05

SCHIRALDI, CALVIN P
(40,55,31,38, **32**) NYN **40** 84-85, BOSA **55** 86, **31** 86-87, CHIN **32** 88-89, SDN **32** 89-90, TEXA **38/32** 91

SCHLESINGER, RUDY PH
(**4**) BOSA **4** 65

SCHLUETER, JAY OF
(**17**) HOUN **17** 71

SCHLUETER, NORM (DUKE) C
(36,**4**) CHIA **36** 38-39, CLEA **4** 44

SCHMACK, BRIAN P
(**53**) DETA **53** 03

SCHMEES, GEORGE (ROCKY) OF/1B/UTIL/P
(21,**37**) STLA **21** 52, BOSA **37** 52

SCHMELZ, AL P
(**44**) NYN **44** 67

SCHMIDT, BOB C
(27,**9**,6,12,47) SFN **27** 58, **9** 59-61, CINN **6** 61, WASA **12** 62-63, NYA **47** 65

SCHMIDT, CURT P
(63,**43**) MONN **63/43** 95

SCHMIDT, DAVE (F.) C
(**50**) BOSA **50** 81

SCHMIDT, DAVE (J.) P
(**24**,28,26,15) TEXA **24** 81-85, CHIA **24** 86, BALA **24** 87-89, MONN **28** 90, **26** 91, SEAA **15** 92

SCHMIDT, FREDDY P
(11,**37**,29,23, 33,34) STLN **11** 44, **37** 46, **29** 47, PHIN **23/33/34** 47, CHIN **34** 47

SCHMIDT, JASON P
(46,42,22,**29**) ATLN **46** 95-96, PITN **42** 96-97 **22** 98-01, SFN **29** 01-05

SCHMIDT, JEFF P
(**37**) CALA **37** 96

SCHMIDT, MIKE 3B/1B/INF
(**20**) PHIN **20** 72-89

SCHMIDT, WILLARD P
(**44**,47,43,10) STLN **44** 52, **47** 53, **44** 55-57, CINN **43** 58, **44** 58-59, **10** 59

SCHMITZ, JOHNNY (BEAR TRACKS) P
(7,31,**53**,19, 40,45,35,31, 37,20,21) CHIN **7** 41, **31** 41-42, **53** 46-51, BKNN **19** 51-52, NYA **40** 52, CINN **45** 52, NYA **35** 53, WASA **31/37** 53, **20** 54-55, BOSA **21** 56, BALA **40** 56

SCHMOLL, STEVE P
(**40**) LAN **40** 05

SCHMULBACH, HANK PR
(__) STLA __ 43

SCHNECK, DAVE P
(23,**16**) NYN **23** 72-73, **16** 74

SCHNEIDER, BRIAN C/OF/1B
(**39**,23) MONN **39** 00-04, WASN **23** 05

SCHNEIDER, DAN P
(**25**,46,41) MILN **25** 63-64, 66, HOUN **46** 67, **58/41** 69

SCHNEIDER, JEFF P
(57,**36**) BALA **57/36** 81

SCHOEN, GERRY P
(**19**) WASA **19** 68

SCHOENDIENST, RED 2B/OF/INF/CH/M
(6,**2**,10,7,4, 43) STLN **6** 45, **2** 46-56, NYN **10** 56, **7** 57, MILN **4** 57-60, STLN **2** 61-63, *CH* **2** 62-64, *M* **2** 65-76, OAKA *CH* **43** 77, *CH* **2** 78, STLN *CH* **2** 79-95, *M* **2** 80, 90

SCHOENEWEIS, SCOTT P
(**60**) ANAA **60** 99-03, CHIA **60** 03-04, TORA **60** 05

SCHOFIELD, DICK (DUCKY) SS/3B/UTIL F
(19,6,**11**,15, 27,2,9) STLN **19** 53-58, PITN **6** 58, **11** 59-65, SFN **15** 65-66, NYA **27** 66, LAN **2** 66-67, STLN **11** 68, BOSA **11** 69-70, STLN **11** 71, MILA **9** 71

SCHOFIELD, DICK SS/3B/INF S
(30,**22**,17,11, 4,9) CALA **30** 83-84, **22** 84-89, **17** 90-92, NYN **11** 92, TORA **22** 93, **4** 94, LAN **22** 95, CALA **9** 95-96

SCHOOLER, MIKE P
(**40**,29,23) SEAA **40** 88-91, **29** 92, TEXA **23** 93

SCHOONMAKER, JERRY OF
(**29**) WASA **29** 55, 57

SCHOTT, GENE P
(27,**20**,54,34) CINN **27** 35, **20** 36-37, **54** 38, PHIN **34** 39, BKNN **34** 39

SCHOUREK, PETE P
(48,**46**,41,51) NYN **48** 91-93, CINN **46** 94-97, HOUN **41** 98, BOSA **51** 98, PITN **46** 99, BOSA **50** 00-01

SCHRAMKA, PAUL OF
(**14**) CHIN **14** 53

SCHREIBER, PAUL (VON) P/CH
(**35**,31,45,34) NYA **35** 45, BOSA *CH* **31** 47-52, *CH* **45** 52-54, *CH* **34** 55-58

SCHREIBER, TED INF
(**43**) NYN **43** 63

SCHRENK, STEVE P
(**52**) PHIN **52** 99-00

SCHRODER, BOB 2B/3B/INF
(**10**,15) SFN **10** 65, **15** 66, **10** 66-68

SCHROEDER, BILL C/1B/UTIL
(39,**21**,14,23) MILA **39** 83, **21** 84-88, CALA **14** 89, **23** 89-90

SCHROLL, AL (BULL) P
(29,33,30,**43**) BOSA **29** 58, PHIN **33** 59, BOSA **30** 59, CHIN **43** 60, MINA **43** 61

SCHROM, KEN P
(21,**18**) TORA **21** 80, 82, MINA **18** 83-85, CLEA **18** 86-87

SCHU, RICK 3B/1B/UTIL/P/CH
(53,**15**,25,13, 35,60,20,27, 16,9) PHIN **53** 84, **15** 85-87, BALA **25** 88, **13** 88-89, DETA **35** 89, CALA **60/20** 90, PHIN **27** 91, MONN **16** 96, ARIN *CH* **9** 04

SCHUBLE, HEINIE 3B/SS/INF
(33,**22**,30) DETA **33** 32-33, **22** 34-35, STLN **30** 36

SCHUELER, RON P/CH
(**37**,34,43,45) ATLN **37** 72-73, PHIN **37** 74-76, MINA **34** 77, CHIA **37** 78-79, *CH* **37** 79-82, OAKA *CH* **43** 83, **37** 84, PITN *CH* **45/37** 86

SCHULER, DAVE P
(**41**,47,61,23) CALA **41** 79-80, **47** 80, ATLN **61/23** 85

SCHULLSTROM, ERIK P
(**58**) MINA **58** 94-95

SCHULMERICH, WES OF
(4,11,14,**6**, 35,7) BOSN **4** 32, **11/14** 33, PHIN **6** 33, **35** 34, CINN **7** 34

SCHULT, ART (DUTCH) OF/1B
(**43**,37,27,19, 23) NYA **43** 53, CINN **37** 56, **27** 57, WASA **19** 57, CHIN **43** 59-60, **23** 60

SCHULTE, FRED (FRITZ) OF/1B
(**6**,2,14) STLA **6** 31-32, WASA **6** 33-34, **2** 35, PITN **14** 36-37

SCHULTE, HAM 2B/SS
(**10**) PHIN **10** 40

SCHULTE, JOHNNY C/CH
(27,**18**,23,56, 21,31,33,29) STLA **27/18** 32, BOSN **23** 32, CHIN *CH* **56** 33, NYA *CH* **21** 34, *CH* **31** 35-39, *CH* **33** 40-48, *CH* **31** 43, BOSA *CH* **29** 49-50

SCHULTE, LEN 2B/3B/INF
(18,**1**) STLA **18** 44, **1** 45-46

SCHULTZ, BARNEY P/CH F
(43,20,41,36, **33**,6) STLN **43** 55, DETA **20** 59, CHIN **41** 61-63, STLN **36** 63-64, **33** 64-65, *CH* **33** 71-75, CHIN *CH* **6** 77

SCHULTZ, BOB P
(32,10,**34**,9, 19) CHIN **32** 51, **10** 52, **34** 52-53, PITN **9** 53, DETA **19** 55

SCHULTZ, BUDDY P S
(35,**22**) CHIN **35** 75-76, STLN **22** 77-79

SCHULTZ, HOWIE (STRETCH)(STEEPLE) (HIGH POCKETS) 1B
(**8**,26,10,12, 19) BKNN **8** 43-47, PHIN **26/10** 47, **12** 48, CINN **19** 48

SCHULTZ, JOE (DODE) C/CH/M
(38,20,**7**,9,11, 32,3,51) PITN **38** 39-41, STLA **20** 43, **7** 44-45, **9** 46, **11** 47-48, **9** 48, *CH* **32** 49, STLN *CH* **3** 63-68, SEAA *M* **3** 69, KCA *CH* **3** 70, DETA *CH* **51** 71-76

SCHULTZ, JOE (GERMANY) PH
(**no#**) STLN **no#** 23-24

SCHULTZ, MIKE P
(**35**) CINN **35** 47

SCHULZ, JEFF OF/DH
(**24**,47) KCA **24** 89-90, PITN **47** 91

SCHULZE, DON P
(43,**37**,49,34, 51) CHIN **43** 83-84, CLEA **37** 84-86, NYN **49** 87, NYA **34** 89, SDN **51** 89

SCHUMACHER, HAL (PRINCE HAL) P
(18,**17**,9,13) NYN **18** 32,**17** 33-42, **9/13** 46

SCHUMAKER, SKIP OF
(**55**) STLN **55** 05

SCHURR, WAYNE P
(**30**) CHIN **30** 64

SCHUSTER, BILL (BROADWAY BILL) SS/INF
(32,36,21,**22**, 7) PITN **32** 37, BOSN **36** 39, CHIN **21** 43, **22** 44, **7** 44, **22** 45

SCHUTZ, CARL P
(**49**) ATLN **49** 96

SCHWABE, MIKE P
(**46**) DETA **46** 89-90

SCHWALL, DON P
(33,**37**,29) BOSA **37** 61-62, PITN **29** 63-66, ATLN **33** 66, **37** 66-67

SCHWAMB, BLACKIE P
(**20**) STLA **20** 48

SCHWARTZ, RANDY 1B
(38,**31**) KCA **38** 65, **31** 66

SCHWARZ, JEFF P
(**49**,36) CHIA **49** 93-94, CALA **36** 94

SCHYPINSKI, JERRY SS/2B
(**6**) KCA **6** 55

SCIOSCIA, MIKE C/CH/M
(**14**) LAN **14** 80-92, *CH* **14** 97-98, ANAA *M* **14** 00-04, LAA *M* **14** 05

SCOFFIC, LOU (WEASER) OF
(**31**) STLN **31** 36

SCONIERS, DARYL 1B/UTIL/DH
(21,**6**) CALA **21** 81, **6** 82-85

SCORE, HERB P
(**27**,18) CLEA **27** 55-59, CHIA **18** 60

SCOTT, DARRYL P
(**43**) CALA **43** 93

SCOTT, DICK (E.) SS
(**3**) OAKA **3** 89

SCOTT, DICK (L.) P
(**20**,38) LAN **20** 63, CHIN **38** 64

SCOTT, DONNIE C
(**43**,2,6) TEXA **43** 83-84, SEAA **2** 85, CINN **6** 91

SCOTT, GARY 3B/SS
(**25**) CHIN **25** 91-92

SCOTT, GEORGE (BOOMER) 1B/DH
(39,**5**,15,0, 41) BOSA **39** 66, **5** 66-71, MILA **5** 72-76, BOSA **15** 77-79, **5** 79, KCA **0** 79, NYA **41** 79

SCOTT, JOHN OF/DH
(12,34,**6**,11) SDN **12/34** 74, **6** 75, TORA **11** 77

SCOTT, LE GRANT OF
(**28**) PHIN **28** 39

SCOTT, LEFTY P
(**36**) PHIN **36** 45

SCOTT, LUKE OF
(**30**) HOUN **30** 05

SCOTT, MICKEY P
(43,16,50,25, **19**) BALA **43** 72, **16** 72-73, MONN **50/25** 73, CALA **19** 75-77

SCOTT, MIKE P
(30,**33**) NYN **30** 79-82, HOUN **33** 83-91

SCOTT, RODNEY 2B/SS/UTIL/DH
(44,25,12,30, **3**,32,19,18) KCA **44/25** 75, MONN **12/30** 76, OAKA **3** 77, CHIN **32** 78, MONN **19** 79, **3** 79-82, NYA **18** 82

SCOTT, TIM P
(**54**,32) SDN **54** 91-93, MONN **54** 93-96, SFN **54** 96, SDN **32** 97, COLN **54** 97

SCOTT, TONY OF
(52,**30**,1) MONN **52** 73-75, **30** 75, STLN **30** 77-81, HOUN **30** 81-84, MONN **1** 84, PHIN *CH* **30** 01-03

SCRANTON, JIM SS/3B
(50,**16**) KCA **50** 84, **16** 85

SCRIVENER, CHUCK 3B/SS/INF
(**9**) DETA **9** 75-77

SCRUGGS, TONY OF
(**18**) TEXA **18** 91

SCUDDER, SCOTT P
(56,**47**) CINN **56** 89, **47** 89-91, CLEA **47** 92-93

SCURRY, ROD P
(31,**19**,47,28,41) PITN **31** 80, **19** 81-85, NYA **47** 85, **28** 86,SEAA **41/19** 88

SCUTARO, MARCO UTIL/INF
(**26**,49,19) NYN **26** 02-03, OAKA **49** 04, **19** 05

SEABOL, SCOTT OF
(48,**28**) NYA **48** 01, STLN **28** 05

SEALE, JOHNNIE (DURANGO KID) P
(**39**) DETA **39** 64-65

SEAMAN, KIM P
(48,**50**) STLN **48** 79-80, **50** 80

SEANEZ, RUDY P
(64,32,54,57,**40**,47,48,17,43,37) CLEA **64** 89, **32** 90-91, SDN **54** 93, LAN **57** 94-95, ATLN **40** 98-00, SDN **47** 01, ATLN **48** 01, TEXA **40** 02, BOSA **17** 03, KCA **43** 04, FLAN **37** 04, SDN **37** 05

SEARAGE, RAY P
(44,**41**,36,59) NYN **44** 81, MILA **41** 84-86, CHIA **36** 86-87, LAN **59** 89-90

SEARCY, STEVE P
(**49**,50,24) DETA **49** 88-91, PHIN **50** 91, **24** 92

SEARS, KEN (ZIGGY) C
(**26**,12) NYA **26** 43, STLA **12** 46

SEARS, TODD 1B
(**58**,9) MINA **58** 02-03, SDN **9** 03

SEATS, TOM P
(24,**17**) DETA **24** 40, BKNN **17** 45

SEAVER, TOM (TOM TERRIFIC) P
(**41**) NYN **41** 67-77, CINN **41** 77-82, NYN **41** 83, CHIA **41** 84-86, BOSA **41** 86

SEAY, BOBBY P
(27,**46**) TBA **27** 01, 03, **46** 04, COLN **46** 05

SEBRA, BOB P
(28,48,**37**,45,30) TEXA **28** 85, MONN **48** 86-87, PHIN **37** 88-89, CINN **45** 89, MILA **30** 90

SECORY, FRANK OF
(__,29,**49**) DETA __ 40, CINN **29** 42, CHIN **49** 45-46

SECRIST, DON P
(**27**) CHIA **27** 69-70

SEDLACEK, SHAWN P
(**56**) KCA **56** 02

SEE, LARRY 1B/UTIL
(20,**13**) LAN **20** 86, TEXA **13** 88

SEEDS, BOB (SUITCASE BOB) 1B/OF/3B
(**31**,37,10,23,2,44,22,19,25,29) CLEA **31** 31-32, CHIA **37** 32, BOSA **10** 33, **23** 34, CLEA **2** 34, NYA **44/22** 36, NYN **19** 38, **25** 39, **29** 40

SEELBACH, CHRIS P
(**37**) ATLN **58** 00, **51** 01

SEELBACH, CHUCK P
(**37**) DETA **37** 71-74

SEEREY, PAT OF
(**23**,30,5) CLEA **23** 43-46, **30** 47-48, CHIA **5** 48-49

SEFCIK, KEVIN 3B
(31,**11**) PHIN **31** 95-96, **11** 97-00, COLN **16** 01

SEGELKE, HERMAN P
(**43**) CHIN **43** 82

SEGRIST, KAL 2B/3B/INF
(19,34,8,**4**) NYA **19/34** 52, BALA **8/4** 55

SEGUI, DAVID 1B/OF/DH
(**21**,10,25,19,24,23) BALA **21** 90-93, NYN **10** 94, **21** 94-95, MONN **25** 95, **21** 96-97, SEAA **21** 98-99, TORA **19** 99, TEXA **24** 00, CLEA **23** 00, BALA **23** 01-04

SEGUI, DIEGO P
(**24**,23,17,32,26,35,36,28,27) KCA **24** 62, **23** 63, **17** 64-65, WASA **32** 66, KCA **26** 67, OAKA **24/26** 68, SEAA **24** 69, OAKA **24** 70-72, STLN **35** 72-73, BOSA **36** 74-75, **28** 75, SEAA **27** 77

SEGUIGNOL, FERNANDO OF/INF
(33,**19**,48) MONN **33** 98, **19** 99-01, NYA **48** 03

SEGURA, JOSE P
(58,**36**,54,46) CHIA **58/36** 88, **54** 89, SFN **46** 91

SEIBEL, PHIL P
(**53**) BOSA **53** 04

SEIBURT, KURT 2B
(**17**) CHIN **17** 79

SEIBOLD, SOCKS P
(12,**19**) BOSN **12** 32, **19** 33

SEIFRIED, GORDON P
(**43**) CLEA **43** 63-64

SEILHEIMER, RICKY C
(**6**) CHIA **6** 80

SEITZER, KEVIN 3B/UTIL/DH/P
(33,2,**20**) KCA **33** 86-87, **2** 88, **33** 88-91, MILA **20** 92, OAKA **20** 93, MILA **20** 93-96, CLEA **20** 96-97

SELBY, BILL 3B/OF/UTIL
(29,60,54,**36**) BOSA **29** 96, CLEA **60** 00, CINN **54** 01, CLEA **36** 02-03

SELE, AARON P
(36,26,**30**,34) BOSA **36** 93-95, **26** 96-97, TEXA **30** 98-99, SEAA **30** 00-01, ANAA **34** 02-04, SEAA **30** 05

SELF, TODD OF
(**37**) HOUN **37** 05

SELKIRK, GEORGE (TWINKLETOES) OF
(1,**3**) NYA **1** 34, **3** 35-42

SELL, EPP P
(__) STLN __ 23

SELLERS, JEFF P
(50,**19**) BOSA **50** 85, **19** 86-88

SELLS, DAVE P
(46,**29**,41) CALA **46** 72-73, CALA **29** 73-75, LAN **41** 75

SELMA, DICK P
(**39**,34,30,50,*27*,50,35) NYN **39** 65-66, **34** 66, **30** 67, **39** 67-68, SDN **39** 69, CHIN **50/39** 69, PHIN **27** 70, **39** 70-73, CALA **39** 74, MILA **50/35** 74

SELPH, CAREY 3B/2B
(**7**) CHIA **7** 32

SEMBER, MIKE 2B/INF
(10,**15**) CHIN **10** 77, **15** 78

SEMBERA, CARROLL 3B/2B
(**41**,28) HOUN **41** 65-67, MONN **28** 69-70

SEMINARA, FRANK P
(**44**,34) SDN **44** 92-93, NYN **34** 94

SEMINICK, ANDY C/OF/CH
(15,24,**21**,7,2,48) PHIN **15** 43-44, **24** 44-48, **21** 49-51, CINN **7** 52-55, PHIN **21** 55-57, *CH* **21** 57-58, *CH* **2** 67-68, *CH* **48** 69

SEMPROCH, RAY (BABY) P
(**48**,16,35) PHIN **48** 58-59, DETA **16** 60, LAA **35** 61

SENERCHIA, SONNY 3B
(**14**) PITN **14** 52

SENTENEY, STEVE P
(**34**) TORA **34** 82

SEO, JAE P
(38,40,**26**) NYN **38** 02, **40** 03, **26** 04-05

SEOANE, MANNY P
(35,37) PHIN **35** 77, **37** 78

SEPKOWSKI, TED 2B/3B/OF
(15,39,36,**14**) CLEA **15** 42, **39** 46, **36** 47, NYA **14** 47

SERAFINI, DAN P
(22,**16**,33,50) MINA **22** 96, **16** 97-98, CHIN **33** 99, SDN **55** 00, PITN **45** 00, CINN **50** 03

SERENA, BILL 3B/2B
(27,**6**,1) CHIN **27** 49, **6** 50-53, **1** 54

SERNA, PAUL 22/2B/UTIL
(38,**3**) SEAA **38** 81, **3** 82

SERRANO, JIMMY P
(**50**) KCA **50** 04

SERRANO, WESCAR P
(**39**) SDN **39** 01

SERUM, GARY P
(**20**) MINA **20** 77-79

SERVAIS, SCOTT C
(**9**,29,21) HOUN **9** 91-95, CHIN **9** 95-98, SFN **29** 99, COLN **29** 00, SFN **9** 00, HOUN **21** 01

SERVICE, SCOTT P
(39,36,**34**,50,46,48,26,53) PHIN **39** 88, MONN **36** 92, COLN **34** 93, CINN **34** 93-94, SFN **34** 95, CINN **36** 96, **50** 97, KCA **46** 97, **48** 98-99, OAKA **26** 00, ARIN **36** 03, TORA **53** 03, ARIN **36** 04

SESSI, WALTER (WATSIE) C
(29,**38**) STLN **29** 41, **38** 46

SEVCIK, JOHN C
(41,25,**20**) MINA **41/25/20** 65

SEVERINSON, AL P
(18,44,**42**) BALA **18** 69, SDN **44** 71-72, **42** 72

SEVERSON, RICH SS/2B/INF
(**15**) KCA **15** 70-71

SEWARD, FRANK P
(28,**19**) NYN **28** 43, **19** 44

SEWELL, JOE 3B/2B/INF/CH B
(27,**21**,30) NYA **27** 31, **21** 32-33, *CH* **30** 34-35

SEWELL, LUKE C/1B/CH B
(**8**,14,10,16,32,2,50) CLEA **8** 31-32, WASA **8** 33-34, CHIA **14** 35-38, CLEA **10** 39, *CH* **10/2** 39, *CH* **16** 40-41, STLA *M* **32** 41-46, CINN *CH* **2** 49, *M* **50** 49-52

SEWELL, RIP P
(22,18,44,**30**) DETA **22/18** 32, PITN **44** 38-39, **30** 40-49

SEXAUER, ELMER P
(**20**) BKNN **20** 48

SEXSON, RICHIE 1B
(44,**11**) CLEA **44** 97-00, MILN **11** 00-03, ARIN **11** 04, SEAA **44** 05

SEXTON, CHRIS OF/INF
(**4**) COLN **4** 99, CINN **26** 00

SEXTON, JIMMY SS/3B/INF/DH
(20,**24**,15,19,21) SEAA **20** 77, HOUN **24** 78-79, OAKA **15** 81, **19** 82, STLN **21** 83

SHABALA, ADAM OF
(**1**) SFN **1** 05

SHACKLEFORD, BRIAN P
(**37**) CINN **37** 05

SHAMSKY, ART OF/1B
(12,**24**,7) CINN **12** 65-67, NYN **24** 68-71, CHIN **24** 72, OAKA **7** 72

SHANAHAN, GREG P
(**41**) LAN **41** 73-74

SHANK, HARVEY P
(**68**) CALA **68** 70

SHANKS, HOWIE (HANK) CH
(**20**) CLEA *CH* **20** 31-32

SHANNON, MIKE (MOONMAN) OF/3B
(28,**18**) STLN **28** 62, **18** 63-70

SHANNON, WALLY INF
(**25**) STLN **25** 59-60

SHANTZ, BILLY C B
(11,22,47) PHIA **11** 54, KCA **22** 55, NYA **47** 60

SHANTZ, BOBBY P B
(**30**,21,28,42,34,45,53,35) PHIA **30** 49-54, KCA **21** 55-56, NYA **30** 57-60, PITN **28** 61, HOUN **42** 62, STLN **34** 62-64, CHIN **45** 64, PHIN **53/35** 64

SHARON, DICK OF
(**27**,13) DETA **27** 73-74, SDN **13** 75

SHARP, BILL OF/DH
(**5**,26) CHIA **5** 73-75, MILA **26** 75-76

SHARPERSON, MIKE C B
(10,60,**27**,26) TORA **10** 87, LAN **60** 87, **27** 88-93, ATLN **26** 95

SHAUTE, JOE (LEFTY) P
(**21**,22) BKNN **21** 32-33, CINN **22** 34

SHAVE, JON SS/2B
(**10**,15) TEXA **10** 93, MINA **15** 98, TEXA **15** 99

SHAVER, JEFF SS/2B
(**52**) OAKA **52** 88

SHAW, BOB P/CH
(25,32,35,**26**,29,47,33,18,10) DETA **25** 57-58, CHIA **32** 58, **35** 58-61, KCA **26** 61, MILN **26** 62-63, SFN **29** 64-66, NYN **26** 66-67, CHIN **47/33** 67, MILA *CH* **18/10** 73

SHAW, DON P
(35,46,23,**44**,8,14) NYN **35** 67-68, **46** 67-68, MONN **23** 69, STLN **44** 71-72, OAKA **8/14** 72

SHAW, JEFF P
(57,42,31,48,**41**) CLEA **57** 90-92, MONN **42** 93, **31** 93-95, CHIA **48** 95, CINN **41** 96-98, LAN **41** 98-01

SHAWKEY, BOB CH/M
(**29**) NYA *CH* **29** 29, *M* **29** 30

SHEA, FRANK (SPECS)(THE NAUGATUCK NUGGET) P
(**20**,19,32,17) NYA **20** 47-49, **19** 51, WASA **32** 52, **17** 52-55

SHEA, MERV C/CH
(9,8,**15**,26,28,30,25,45) BOSA **9** 33, STLA **8** 33, CHIA **15** 34-37, BKNN **26/28** 38, DETA **30** 39, *CH* **30** 39-42, PHIN **9** 44, *CH* **9** 44, *CH* **25** 44-45, CHIN *CH* **45** 49

SHEA, STEVE P
(51,42,46,**20**) HOUN **51/42** 68, MONN **46/20** 69

SHEAFFER, DANNY C/UTIL
(29,34,**16**,5,4,12) BOSA **29** 87, CLEA **34** 89, COLN **16** 93-94, STLN **5** 95, **4** 96, **12** 97

SHEALY, RYAN 1B
(**38**) COLN **38** 05

SHEARER, RAY OF
(**56**) MILN **56** 57

SHEEHAN, JIM (BIG JIM) C
(__) NYN __ 36

SHEEHAN, TOM CH/M
(31,**29**,33,6) CINN *CH* **31** 35, **29** 36-37, BKNN *CH* **29** 38, BOSN *CH* **33** 44, SFN *M* **6** 60

SHEELY, BUD C S
(45,15,**6**,30) CHIA **45** 51, **15/6** 52, **30** 53

SHEERIN, CHARLIE (CHUCK) INF
(**20**) PHIN **20** 36

SHEETS, ANDY SS/INF
(30,12,2,3,7,18,**26**) SEAA **30** 96, **12** 97, SDN **2/3** 98, ANAA **7** 99, BOSA **18** 00, TBA **26** 01-02

SHEETS, BEN P
(**15**) MILN **15** 01-05

SHEETS, LARRY OF/UTIL/DH
(**18**,19,9,40) BALA **18** 84-88, **19** 89, DETA **9** 90, SEAA **40** 93

SHEFFIELD, GARY SS/3B/OF/DH
(1,11,**10**) MILA **1** 88-89, **11** 90-91, SDN **10** 92-93, FLAN **10** 93-98, LAN **5** 98, **10** 98-01, ATLN **11** 02-03, NYA **11** 04-05

SHELBY, JOHN (T-BONE) OF/UTIL/DH/CH
(39,**37**,31,25,30) BALA **39** 81, **37** 81-87, LAN **31** 87-90, DETA **25** 90-91, LAN *CH* **31** 98-05, **30** 05

SHELDON, BOBBY 2B/DH
(**2**,21) MILA **2** 74-75, **21** 77

SHELDON, ROLLIE P
(**45**,15,40) NYA **45** 61-62, 64-65, KCA **15** 65-66, BOSA **40** 66

SHELDON, SCOTT SS/INF
(51,8,14,**4**) OAKA **51/8** 97, TEXA **14** 98, **4** 99-01

SHELLENBACK, FRANK CH
(29,31,30,14,**1**) STLA *CH* **29** 39, BOSA *CH* **31** 40-44, DETA *CH* **30** 46-47, NYN *CH* **14** 49, *CH* **1** 50-55

SHELLENBACK, JIM P/CH
(38,19,21,**16**,25,50,28,45) PITN **38** 66-67, **19** 69, WASA **21** 69-70, **16** 71, TEXA **16** 72-73, **25** 74, MINA **50/28** 77, *CH* **45** 83

SHELLEY, HUGH OF
(**15**) DETA **15** 35

SHELTON, BEN OF/1B
(66,**44**) PITN **66/44** 93

SHELTON, CHRIS C/1B
(30,**31**) DETA **30** 04, **31** 05

SHELTON, DEREK CH
(__) CLEA *CH* __ 05

SHEMO, STEVE 2B/3B/INF
(14,**28**) BOSN **14** 44, **28** 45

SHEPARD, BERT P
(**34**) WASA **34** 45

SHEPARD, JACK C/1B
(**10**) PITN **10** 53-56

SHEPARD, LARRY CH/M
(5,7,**4**,8) PHIN *CH* **5** 67, PITN *M* **7** 68, **4** 68-69, CINN *CH* **4** 70-78, SFN *CH* **8** 79

SHEPHERD, ? CH
(**13**) BALA *CH* **13** 94

SHEPHERD, KEITH P
(52,30,54,45,27) PHIN **52** 92, COLN **30** 93, BOSA **54** 95, BALA **45/27** 96

SHEPHERD, RON OF/DH
(20,**21**) TORA **20** 84, **21** 85-86

SHEPHERDSON, RAY C
(no#) STLN **no#** 24

SHERDEL, BILL (WEE WILLIE) P
(23,**24**,no#) STLN **23** 23-24, BOSN **24** 32, STLN **no#** 32

SHERID, ROY P
(31,**15**) NYA **31** 29, **15** 30-31

SHERIDAN, NEILL (WILD HORSE) PH
(**23**) BOSA **23** 48

SHERIDAN, PAT OF/DH
(37,**15**,17) KCA **37** 81, **15** 83-85, DETA **15** 86-89, SFN **25** 89, NYA **17** 91

SHERLOCK, GLENN CH
(**53**) NYA *CH* **53** 92,*BPC* **53** 94-95, ARIN *CH* **53** 98-99, 01-05

SHERLOCK, VINCE (BALDY) 2B
(**22**) BKNN **22** 35

SHERMAN, DARRELL OF
(**3**) SDN **3** 93

SHERRILL, DENNY INF/DH
(**18**,57,47) NYA **18** 78, **57/47** 80

SHERRILL, GEORGE P
(**52**) SEAA **52** 04-05

SHERRILL, TIM P
(**56**) STLN **56** 90-91

SHERRY, LARRY P/CH B
(35,**51**,15,31,37,50,43) LAN **35** 58, **51** 58-63, DETA **15** 64-67, HOUN **31/37/50** 67, CALA **31** 68, PITN *CH* **43** 77, *CH* **51** 78, CALA *CH* **51** 79-80

SHERRY, NORM C/CH/M B
(**34**,5,21,37,40,46) LAN **34** 59-62, NYN **5** 63, CALA *CH* **21** 70-71, *CH* **37** 76, *M* **37** 76-77, MONN *CH* **40** 78-81, SDN *CH* **46** 82-84, SFN *CH* **34** 86-91

SHETRONE, BARRY OF
(**40**,2) BALA **40** 59-62, WASA **2** 63

SHEVLIN, JIMMY 1B
(no#,**12**) CINN **no#** 32, **12** 34

SHIELDS, SCOT P
(**62**) ANAA **62** 01-04, LAA **62** 05

SHIELDS, STEVE P
(57,43,38,**40**,33,36) ATLN **57** 85, **43** 85-86, KCA **38** 86, SEAA **40** 87, NYA **33/40** 88, MINA **36** 89

SHIELDS, TOMMY UTIL
(**1**) CHIN **1** 93

SHIELDS, VINCE P
(no#) STLN **no#** 24

SHIELL, JASON P
(**46**,57) SDN **46** 02, BOSA **57** 03, (04)

SHIFFLETT, GARLAND (DUCK) P
(**24**,21) WASA **24** 57, MINA **21** 64

SHIFFLETT, STEVE P
(**49**) KCA **49** 92

SHILLING, JIM 2B/SS/OF
(32,**20**) CLEA **32** 39, PHIN **20** 39

SHINALL, ZAK P
(**40**) SEAA **40** 93

SHINES, RAZOR (RAY) OF/1B/3B
(**31**,47) MONN **31** 83-85, **47** 87

SHINJO, TSUYOSHI OF
(**5**) NYN **5** 01, SFN **5** 02, NYN **5** 03

SHIPANOFF, DAVE P
(**33**) PHIN **33** 85

SHIPLEY, CRAIG SS/3B/INF/OF
(38,35,**18**,16,5) LAN **38** 86-87, NYN **35** 89, SDN **18** 91-94, HOUN **16** 95, **18** 95-96, SDN **18** 97, ANAA **5** 98

SHIPLEY, JOE (MOSES) P
(38,**42**,19) SFN **38** 58, **42** 59-60, CHIA **19** 63

SHIRES, ART (ART THE GREAT) 1B
(**5**) BOSN **5** 32

SHIRLEY, BART 3B/SS/2B
(23,**2**,6,11) LAN **23** 64, **2** 66, NYN **6** 67, LAN **11** 68

SHIRLEY, BOB P
(47,**32**,29,31) SDN **47** 77-78, **32** 78-80, STLN **32** 81, CINN **32** 82, NYA **29** 83-87, KCA **31** 87

SHIRLEY, STEVE P
(**36**) LAN **36** 82

SHIRLEY, TEX P
(17,**21**,28) PHIA **17** 41-42, STLA **21** 44-45, **28** 46

SHIVER, IVEY (CHICK) OF
(26,**11**) DETA **26** 31, CINN **11** 34

SHOCKLEY, COSTEN 1B/OF
(17,31,34,**12**) PHIN **17/31/34** 64, CALA **12** 65

SHOEMAKER, CHARLIE 2B
(45,17,**14**) KCA **45** 61, **17** 62, **14** 64

SHOFFNER, MILT P
(17,22,**15**,37) CLEA **17** 31, BOSN **22** 37, **15** 38-39, CINN **37** 39-40

SHOFNER, STRICK 3B
(**29**) BOSA **29** 47

SHOKES, EDDIE 1B
(19,**17**) CINN **19** 41, **17** 46

SHOOP, RON C
(**25**) DETA **25** 59

SHOPAY, TOM OF/UTIL/C/DH
(27,**28**) NYA **27** 67, 69, BALA **28** 71-72, 76-77

SHOPPACH, KELLY C
(**48**) BOSA **48** 05

SHORE, RAY P/CH
(16,37,29,34, **36**,13) STLA **16** 46, **37/29** 48, **34** 49, CINN *BPP* **36** 63-66, *CH* **36/13** 66, *BPP* **13** 66-67

SHORES, BILL P
(13,22,**14**,29) PHIA **13** 31, NYN **22/14** 33, CHIA **29** 36

SHORT, BILL P
(46,30,24,15, 37,42) NYA **46** 60, BALA **30** 62, **24** 66, BOSA **15** 66, PITN **37** 67, NYN **40** 68, CINN **42** 69

SHORT, CHRIS P
(18,**41**,21,27) PHIN **18** 59, **41** 60-72, MILA **21/27** 73

SHORT, DAVE OF
(__,**23**) CHIA __ 40, **23** 41

SHORT, RICK 3B
(**35**) WASN **35** 05

SHOTTON, BURT (BARNEY) PR/M/CH
(**24**,26,27,29, no#) STLN **24** 23, PHIN *M* **26** 32-33, *M* **27** 33, CINN *CH* **29** 34, *M* **29** 34, CLEA *CH* **26** 42-45, BKNN *M* **no#** 47-50

SHOUN, CLYDE (HARDROCK) P
(23,21,36,**24**, 35,29,26,45) CHIN **23** 35-36, **21** 37, STLN **36** 38, **24** 39-42, CINN **35** 42-43, **29** 44, **36** 44, 46-47, BOSN **26** 47-49, CHIA **45** 49

SHOUSE, BRIAN P
(42,55,52,**58**) PITN **42** 93, BOSA **55** 98, KCA **52** 02, TEXA **58** 03-05

SHOW, ERIC P
(44,**30**) SDN **44** 81-82, **30** 82-90, OAKA **30** 91

SHOWALTER, BUCK CH/M
(48,**11**) NYA *CH* **48** 90-91, *CH* **11** 91, *M* **11** 92-95, ARIN *M* **11** 98-00, TEXA *M* **11** 03-05

SHUBA, GEORGE (SHOTGUN) OF
(**8**) BKNN **8** 48-50, 52-55

SHUEY, PAUL P
(**53**,44) CLEA **53** 94-02, LAN **44** 02-03, (04)

SHUMAKER, ANTHONY P
(**37**) PHIN **37** 99

SHUMAN, HARRY P
(**25**,10) PITN **25** 42-43, PHIN **10** 44

SHUMPERT, TERRY 2B/SS/INF/DH
(50,3,4,2,15, 26,28,**22**) KCA **50** 90, **3** 91-93, **4** 94, BOSA **2** 95, CHIN **15** 96, SDN **26** 97, COLN **28** 98, **22** 99-02, TBA **22** 03

SHUPE, VINCE 1B
(**5**) BOSN **5** 45

SIDDALL, JOE C/UTIL
(26,28,29,**30**) MONN **26** 93, **28** 95, FLAN **29** 96, DETA **30** 98

SIEBERN, NORM OF/1B
(36,25,**7**,4,16, 29) NYA **36** 56, **25** 58-59, KCA **7** 60-63, BALA **4** 64-65, CALA **16** 66, SFN **29** 67, BOSA **4** 67-68

SIEBERT, DICK 1B/OF
(38,18,22,10 **5**) BKNN **38** 32, **18** 36, STLN **22** 37-38, PHIA **10** 38, **5** 39-45

SIEBERT, PAUL P
(**31**,40,46,43) HOUN **31** 74-76, SDN **40/46** 77, NYN **46** 77, **43** 77-78

SIEBERT, SONNY P/CH
(**42**,27,19,40, 35,34,44) CLEA **42** 64-69, BOSA **27** 69-70, **42** 70-73, TEXA **19** 73, STLN **40/42** 74, SDN **40** 75, OAKA **35** 75, SDN *CH* **34** 94, *CH* **44** 95

SIEBLER,DWIGHT P
(34,**25**) MINA **34** 63-65, **25** 65-67

SIERRA, CANDY P
(**53**,45) SDN **53** 88, CINN **45** 88

SIERRA, RUBEN OF/DH
(47,3,**21**,29, 25,22,14,44, 16,28,24) TEXA **47** 86, **3** 86-87, **21** 87-92, OAKA **29** 92, **21** 93-95, NYA **25** 95-96, DETA **21** 96, CINN **22** 97, TORA **14** 97, CHIA **44** 98, TEXA **16/28** 00, **24** 01, SEAA **21** 02-03, NYA **24** 03-04, **28** 05

SIEVERS, ROY (SQUIRREL) OF/3B/1B/INF/CH
(15,7,**2**,26,5, 12,9,25) STLA **15** 49-51, **7** 52-53, WASA **2** 54-59, CHIA **26** 60, **5** 60-61, PHIN **5** 62-64, WASA **12** 64, **9** 64, **25** 65, CINN *CH* **2** 66

SIGNER, WALTER P
(50,**27**) CHIN **50** 43, **27** 45

SIKORSKY, BRIAN P
(55,**49**) HOUN **55** 98, TEXA **49** 00

SILBER, EDDIE OF
(**20**,__) STLA **20** 37, __ 39

SILVA, CARLOS P
(**52**) PHIN **52** 02-03, MINA **52** 04-05

SILVA, JOSE P
(45,**56**,39) TORA **45** 96, PITN **56** 97-01, CINN **39** 02

SILVERA, AL OF
(**27**) CINN **27** 55-56

SILVERA, CHARLIE (SWEDE) C/3B/CH
(46,**29**,8,52, 47,43) NYA **46/40** 48, **29** 50-56, CHIN **8** 57, MINA *CH* **26** 69, DETA *CH* **52** 71-73, TEXA *CH* **47** 74, *CH* **43** 74-75

SILVERIO, LUIS OF/DH/CH
(**17**,__,13) KCA **17** 78, *CH* __ 02, **17** 03-04, **13/17** 05

SILVERIO, TOMMY OF/1B/INF
(45,**33**) CALA **45** 70-71, **33** 71-72

SILVESTRI, DAVE SS/3B/INF/DH
(56,36,47,43, **9**,14,17,4) NYA **56/36** 92, **47** 93-94, **43** 95, MONN **9** 95-96, TEXA **14** 97 TBA **17** 98, ANAA **4** 99

SILVESTRI, KEN (HAWK) C/2B/CH/M
(14,26,34,**25**, 31,3,33) CHIA **14** 39-40, NYA **26** 41, **34** 46-47, PHIN **25** 49-51, *CH* **31** 59-60, MILN *CH* **3** 63-65, ATLN *CH* **3** 66-67, *M* **3** 67, *CH* **3** 68-75, CHIA *CH* **33** 76

SIMA, AL P
(28,**36**,26) WASA **28** 50-51, **36** 53, CHIA **36** 54, PHIA **26** 54

SIMAS, BILL P
(**41**) CHIA **41** 95-00, (01)

SIMMONS, AL (BUCKETFOOT AL) OF/1B/CH
(**7**,5,6,3,20, 38,28,10,8, 32,44) PHIA **7** 31-32, CHIA **5** 33, **7** 34-35, DETA **6** 36, WASA **3** 37, **7** 38, BOSN **20** 39, CINN **38** 39, PHIA **6** 40, *CH* **6** 40, **28** 41, *CH* **28** 41-42, BOSA **10/8** 43, PHIA *CH* **28** 43, **32** 44-45, *CH* **32** 44-49, CLEA *CH* **44** 50-51

SIMMONS, BRIAN OF
(**27**,22) CHIA **27** 98-99, (00), TORA **22** 01

SIMMONS, CURT P
(32,**28**,31,39, 46,49) PHIN **32** 47, **28** 48-50, 52-60, STLN **31** 60-66, CHIN **39** 66-67, CALA **46/49/32** 67

SIMMONS, JOHN OF
(**23**) WASA **23** 49

SIMMONS, NELSON OF/DH
(**37**,42) DETA **37** 84-85, BALA **42** 87

SIMMONS, TED (SIMBA) C/1B/UTIL/DH
(**23**) STLN **23** 68-80, MILA **23** 81-85, ATLN **23** 86-88

SIMMS, MIKE OF/1B/DH
(30,22,23,18, **16**) HOUN **30** 90-91, **22** 92, 94-95, **23** 95-96, TEXA **18** 97, **16** 98-99

SIMON, RANDALL 1B
(33,**15**) ATLN **33** 97-98, **15** 99, DETA **35** 01-02, PITN **35** 03, CHIN **35** 03, PITN **35** 04, TBA **35** 04

SIMONTACCHI, JASON P
(**46**) STLN **46** 02-04

SIMONS, DOUG P
(65,43,41,45) NYN **65/43** 91, MONN **41/45** 92

SIMONS, MEL (BUTCH) OF
(**2**,34) CHIA **2** 31, **34** 32

SIMPSON, ALLAN P
(**51**,46) COLN **51** 04-05, CINN **46** 05

SIMPSON, DICK OF
(38,**10**,20,12, 37,9,16) LAA **38/10** 62, **10** 64, CALA **10** 65, CINN **20** 66-67, STLN **12** 68, HOUN **37** 68, NYA **9** 69, SEAA **16** 69

SIMPSON, DUKE P
(**30**) CHIN **30** 53

SIMPSON, HARRY (SUITCASE)(GOODY) OF/1B
(35,37,38,36, **5**,8,23) CLEA **35** 51-53, **37** 55, KCA **38** 55-57, NYA **36** 57-58, KCA **5** 58-59, CHIA **8** 59, PITN **23** 59

SIMPSON, JOE OF/1B/DH
(17,**18**,9) LAN **17** 75-78, SEAA **18** 79-82, KCA **9** 83

SIMPSON, STEVE P
(**36**) SDN **36** 72

SIMPSON, WAYNE P
(**45**,44,42,46) CINN **45** 70-72, KCA **45** 73, PHIN **44** 75, CALA **42/46** 77

SIMS, DUKE C/OF/UTIL/DH
(32,**9**,8,12,50, 41,2) CLEA **32** 64, **9** 65-70, LAN **8** 71-72, DETA **12** 72-73, NYA **50** 73, **41** 74, TEXA **2** 74

SIMS, GREG OF
(**22**) HOUN **22** 66

SINATRO, MATT C/CH
(14,11,52,**17**, 15,22) ATLN **14** 81-84, OAKA **11** 87-88, DETA **52** 89, SEAA **17** 90-92, *CH* **17** 95, *CH* **15** 95-02, TBA *CH* **15** 03-04, **22** 05

SINCLAIR, STEVE P
(**53**) TORA **53** 98, **46** 99, SEAA **41** 99

SINGER, BILL (THE SINGER THROWING MACHINE) P
(**40**,48,18) LAN **40** 64-72, CALA **48** 73-75, TEXA **48** 76, MINA **48/18** 76, TORA **48** 77

SINGLETON, CHRIS OF
(**12**,29,2,10) CHIA **12** 99-01, BALA **29** 02, OAKA **2** 03, TBA **10** 05

SINGLETON, DUANE OF
(18,**15**) MILA **18** 94-95, DETA **15** 96

SINGLETON, ELMER (SMOKY) P
(22,15,26,20, 42) BOSN **22** 45, **15** 46, PITN **26** 47-48, WASA **22** 50, CHIN **20** 57-58, **42** 59

SINGLETON, KEN OF/DH
(**29**) NYN **29** 70-71, MONN **29** 72-74, BALA **29** 75-84

SINGTON, FRED OF
(6,25,19,**31**, 37,28) WASA **6** 34, **25** 35, **19** 36, **31** 37, BKNN **37** 38, **28** 39

SIPEK, DICK OF
(**21**) CINN **21** 45

SIPIN, JOHN 2B
(37,**2**) SDN **37/2** 69

SIROTKA, MIKE P
(38,**33**) CHIA **38** 95-96, **33** 97-00

SISCO, ANDY P
(**51**) KCA **51** 05

SISCO, STEVE OF
(**11**) ATLN **11** 00

SISK, DOUG P
(**39**,43) NYN **39** 82-87, BALA **39** 88, ATLN **43** 90-91

SISK, TOMMIE P
(29,37,**25**,16, 23) PITN **29/37** 62, **25** 63-68, SDN **25/16** 69, CHIA **23** 70

SISLER, DAVE P S,B
(**39**,41,30,15, 40) BOSA **39** 56-59, DETA **41** 59, **30** 59-60, WASA **15** 61, CINN **40** 62

SISLER, DICK 1B/OF/CH/M S,B
(**15**,6,8,23,2, 5,51) STLN **15** 46-47, PHIN **6** 48, **8** 49-51, CINN **23** 52, STLN **15** 52-53, CINN *CH* **2** 61-64, *M* **2** 64-65, STLN *CH* **5** 66-70, SDN *CH* **9** 75-76, NYN *CH* **51** 79-80

SISTI, SIBBY (RABBIT) 2B/SS/OF/UTIL
(25,5,1,2,3,**7**, 13) BOSN **25/5** 39, **1** 40-41, **2** 42, **3** 46, **7** 47-51, MILN **13** 51-54, SEAA *CH* **31** 69

SIVESS, PETE P
(41,**20**) PHIN **41** 36-37, **20** 38

SIWY, JIM P
(**54**) CHIA **54** 82, 84

SIZEMORE, GRADY OF
(**24**) CLEA **24** 04-05

SIZEMORE, TED 2B/C/UTIL
(**41**,29,5,6,11) LAN **41** 69-70, STLN **29** 71, **41** 71-75, LAN **5** 76, PHIN **6** 77-78, CHIN **6** 79, BOSA **11** 79-80

SKAFF, FRANK 3B/INF/CH/M
(14,**10**,30,55, 53) BKNN **14** 35, PHIA **10** 43, BALA *CH* **30** 54, DETA *CH* **55** 65-66, *M* **55** 66, *CH* **53** 71

SKAGGS, DAVE C
(49,**8**) BALA **49** 77, **8** 77-80, CALA **8** 80

SKALSKI, JOE P
(67,**27**) CLEA **67/27** 89

SKAUGSTAD, DAVE P
(**45**) CINN **45** 57

SKETCHLEY, BUD OF
(**12**) CHIA **12** 42

SKIDMORE, ROE PH
(**38**) CHIN **38** 70

SKINNER, BOB 1B/OF/INF/M/CH F
(3,**4**,24,19,1) PITN **3** 54, **4** 56-63, CINN **24** 63-64, STLN **19** 64-66, PHIN *M* **19** 68, *M* **1** 69, SDN *CH* **4** 70-73, PITN *CH* **4** 74-76, SDN *CH* **4** 77, *M* **4** 77, CALA *CH* **48** 78, PITN *CH* **48** 79-85, *CH* **4** 85, ATLN *CH* **4** 86-88

SKINNER, JOEL C/CH/M S
(**12**,22,4) CHIA **12** 83-84, **22** 85-86, NYA **12** 86-88, CLEA **13** 89, **4** 90-91, CLEA *CH* **35** 01-05, *M* **35** 02

SKIZAS, LOU (THE NERVOUS GREEK) OF/3B
(45,**35**,22,20, 3) NYA **45** 56, KCA **35** 56-57, DETA **22/20** 58, CHIA **3** 59

SKOK, CRAIG P
(49,33,**40**) BOSA **49** 73, TEXA **33** 76, ATLN **40** 78-79

SKOWRON, BILL (MOOSE) 1B/3B
(53,**14**,3,5) NYA **53** 54, **14** 55-62, LAN **14** 63, WASA **3** 64, CHIA **5** 64, **14** 65-67, CALA **14** 67

SKRMETTA, MATT P
(**53**,64) MONN **53** 00, PITN **64** 00

SKUBE, BOB OF/UTIL/DH
(**26**) MILA **26** 82-83

SLADE, GORDON (OSKIE) SS/2B/INF/UTIL
(8,14,**6**) BKNN **8** 32, STLN **14** 33, CINN **6** 34-35

SLAGLE, ROGER P
(52,**50**) NYA **52/50** 79

SLATON, JIM P/CH
(67,**41**,29,21, 47,40,20) MILA **67** 71, **41** 71-77, **29** 74, DETA **21** 78, MILA **41** 79-83, CALA **47** 84, **41** 84-86, DETA **40/20** 86, SEAA *CH* **41** 05

SLAUGHT, DON C
(7,4,**11**,29, 14) KCA **7** 82-84, TEXA **4** 85-87, NYA **11** 88-89, PITN **11** 90-95, CALA **11** 96, CHIA **29** 96, SDN **14** 97

SLAUGHTER, ENOS (COUNTRY)
(**9**,17,33,25) STLN **9** 38-42, 46-53, NYA **17** 54-55, KCA **33** 55-56, NYA **17** 56-59, MILN **25** 59

SLAUGHTER, STERLING P
(**41**) CHIN **41** 64

SLAYBACK, BILL P
(44,**14**) DETA **44** 72, **14** 73-74

SLEATER, LOU OF/1B B
(22,39,25,31, 34,36,**19**) STLA **22** 50, **39** 51, **25** 52, WASA **31/34** 52, KCA **31** 55, MILN **36** 56, DETA **19** 57-58, BALA **19** 58

SLEDGE, TERRMEL OF
(48,**18**) MONN **48** 04, WASN **18** 05

SLIDER, RAC CH
(**36**) BOSA *CH* **36** 87-90

SLOAN, BRUCE (FATSO) OF
(**25**) NYN **25** 44

SLOAT, DWAIN (LEFTY) P
(30,**20**) BKNN **30** 48, CHIN **20** 49

SLOCUM, RON INF/C
(45,**12**) SDN **45** 69, **12** 69-71

SLOCUMB, HEATHCLIFF (HEATH) P
(**51**,52,58) CHIN **51** 91-93, CLEA **51** 93, PHIN **51** 94-95, BOSA **51** 96-97, SEAA **52** 97-98, BALA **51** 99, STLN **58** 99-00, SDN **58** 00

SLUSARSKI, JOE P
(**37**,48,58) OAKA **37** 91-93, MILA **48** 95, HOUN **58** 99-00, ATLN **36** 01, HOUN **58** 01

SMAJSTRIA, CRAIG 2B
(**29**) HOUN **29** 88

SMALL, AARON P
(38,37,**30**,31, 50) TORA **38** 94, FLAN **37** 95, OAKA **30** 96-98, ARIN **31** 98, ATLN **30** 02, DETA **50** 04, NYA **31** 05

SMALL, HANK 1B
(**12**) ATLN **12** 78

SMALL, JIM OF
(**20**,35) DETA **20** 55-57, KCA **35** 58

SMALL, MARK P
(**36**) HOUN **36** 96

SMALLEY, ROY, JR. SS/1B/UTIL/DH S
(15,**5**,34,39, 55,12) TEXA **15** 75-76, MINA **5** 76-82, NYA **34/39/55** 82, **12** 83, CHIA **12** 84, NYA **12** 84, MINA **5** 85-87

SMALLEY, ROY, SR. SS/INF
(**39**,30,17) CHIN **39** 48-53, MILN **30** 54, PHIN **17** 55-58

SMART, J. D. P
(56,**44**) MONN **56** 99, TEXA **44** 01

SMAZA, JOE OF
(__) CHIA __ 46

SMILEY, JOHN P
(**57**) PITN **57** 86-91, MINA **57** 92, CINN **57** 93-97, CLEA **57** 97

SMITH, AL (E.) (FUZZY) OF/3B/INF
(32,**16**,9,28) CLEA **32** 53-55, **16** 55-57, CHIA **9** 58, **16** 58-62, BALA **16** 63, CLEA **28** 64, BOSA **28** 64

SMITH, AL (J.) P
(21,18,14,**32**, 22) NYN **21** 33-35, *CH* **21** 33, **18** 36-37, PHIN **18** 38-39, **14** 39, CLEA **32** 40-45, **22** 41

SMITH, ART P
(**36**) CHIA **36** 32

SMITH, BERNIE OF
(**22**) MILA **22** 70-71

SMITH, BILL P
(**30**,47) STLN **30** 58-59, PHIN **47** 62

SMITH, BILLY (E.) INF/2B/SS/DH
(14,16,12,**2**, 21) CALA **14** 75, **16** 76, BALA **12** 77, **2** 77-79, SFN **21** 81

SMITH, BILLY (F.) CH
(**42**) TORA *CH* **42** 84-88

SMITH, BILLY (L.) P
(**27**) HOUN **27** 81

SMITH, BOB (E.) P
(28,18,27,**12**, 17,32,25) CHIN **28/18** 32, CINN **27** 33, BOSN **12** 33, **17** 34-35, **32** 36, **25** 37

SMITH, BOB (G.) P
(39,45,**37**,26) BOSA **39** 55, STLN **45** 57, PITN **37** 57-59, DETA **26** 59

SMITH, BOBBY 3B/INF
(**9**) TBA **9** 98-00, **20** 00-02

SMITH, BOBBY GENE OF/3B
(15,24,**16**,23, 35) STLN **15** 57-58, **24** 59, PHIN **16** 60-62, CHIN **23** 62, STLN **35** 62, CALA **24** 65

SMITH, BRIAN P
(**26**) PITN **26** 00

SMITH, BRICK 1B/DH
(**35**) SEAA **35** 87-88

SMITH, BRYN P
(66,38,**28**,36) MONN **66** 81, **38** 82, **28** 83-89, STLN **36** 90-92, COLN **28** 93

SMITH, BUD P
(**35**) STLN **51** 01, **52** 01-02

SMITH, CHARLEY 3B/SS/INF/UTIL
(18,15,9,27 **1**,6,19) LAN **18** 60-61, PHIN **15** 61, CHIA **9** 62-63, **27** 64, NYN **1** 64-65, STLN **1** 66, NYA **6** 67-68, CHIN **19** 69

SMITH, CHRIS 2B/UTIL
(6,**5**,32,31) MONN **6** 81, **5** 82, SFN **32/31** 83

SMITH, CHUCK P
(**30**,29) FLAN **23** 00, **45** 00-01

SMITH, CLAY P
(**30**,29) CLEA **30** 38, DETA **29** 40

SMITH, DAN P
(42,**35**) TEXA **42** 92, **35** 94

SMITH, DAN C. P
(**43**,41) MONN **43** 99, BOSA **41** 00, MONN **43** 02-03, (04)

SMITH, DARYL P
(**40**) KCA **40** 90

SMITH, DAVE (M.) P
(**11**,31) PHIA **11** 38, **31/23** 39

SMITH, DAVE (S.) P/CH
(**45**,42) HOUN **45** 80-90, CHIN **42** 91-92, SDN *CH* **45** 99-01

SMITH, DAVE (W.) (D. W.) P
(**35**) CALA **35** 84-85

SMITH, DICK 3B/SS/INF/OF/1B
(7,31,**6**,32, 16,25,14) PITN **7** 51, **31/6/32** 52, **7** 53, **6** 54-55, NYN **16** 63-64, LAN **25** 65, WASA **14** 69

SMITH, DWIGHT OF
(**18**,35,30,7) CHIN **18** 89-93, CALA **35** 94, BALA **30** 94, ATLN **7** 95-96

SMITH, EARL OF
(**21**) PITN **21** 55

SMITH, EDDIE P
(no#,22,**18**,6, 23,46,21,49) PHIA **no#** 36, **22** 37, **18** 38-39, CHIA **6/23** 39, **46/23** 40, **21** 41, **46** 41-43, **49** 46, **18** 46-47, BOSA **18** 47

SMITH, FRANK P
(**32**,25) CINN **32** 50-54, STLN **25** 55, CINN **32** 56

SMITH, GEORGE 2B/SS/INF
(**40**,14) DETA **40** 63-65, BOSA **14** 66

SMITH, GREG 2B/SS/OF
(**16**,12) CHIN **16** 89-90, LAN **12** 91

SMITH, HAL (L.) P
(**47**) PITN **47** 32-35

SMITH, HAL (R.) (CURA) C/CH
(18,**2**,9,37) STLN **18** 56-58, **2** 59-60, **9** 61, *CH* **18** 62, PITN **2** 65, *CH* **2** 65-67, CINN *CH* **9** 68-69, MILA *CH* **37** 76-77

SMITH, HAL (W.) C
(22,**9**,5,8) BALA **22** 55-56, KCA **9** 56-59, PITN **5** 60-61, HOUN **8** 62, **9** 62-64, CINN **9** 64

SMITH, JACK OF
(2,**1**) STLN **2** 23, **1** 24

SMITH, JACK (H.) P
(**41**,53,45) LAN **41** 62-63, MILN **53/45** 64

SMITH, JASON SS/UTIL/3B
(56,29,**3**,44, 17) CHIN **56** 01, TBA **29** 02, **3** 03, DETA **44** 04, **17** 05

SMITH, JIM INF
(**11**) PITN **11** 82

SMITH, JOHN 1B
(**9**) BOSA **9** 31

SMITH, KEITH (L.) OF
(26,3,**11**) TEXA **26** 77, STLN **3** 79-80, **11** 80

SMITH, (P.) KEITH SS
(**13**) NYA **13** 84-85

SMITH, KEN 1B/OF
(**11**) ATLN **11** 81-83

SMITH, LEE P
(46,48,**47**,31, 49) CHIN **33** 80, **46** 81-87, BOSA **48** 88-90, STLN **47** 90-93, NYA **47** 93, BALA **47** 94, CALA **47** 95-96, CINN **31/47** 96, MONN **49** 97

SMITH, LONNIE (SKATES) OF/DH
(**27**,21,6,39) PHIN **27** 78-81, STLN **27** 82-85, KCA **21** 85-87, ATLN **6** 88, **27** 89-92, PITN **27** 93, BALA **27** 93, **39** 94

SMITH, MARK (C.) P
(**49**) OAKA **49** 83

SMITH, MARK (E.) OF
(14,34,**25**,18, 29) BALA **14** 94, **34** 94-96, PITN **25** 97-98, FLAN **18** 00, MONN **25** 01, MILN **29** 03

SMITH, MAYO OF/M
(**24**,1,10) PHIA **10** 45, PHIN *M* **24** 55-58, CINN *M* **1** 59, DETA *M* **10** 67-70

SMITH, MIKE P
(**53**) TORA **53** 02-03

SMITH, MIKE P
(**37**,53,34,43, 41) CINN **37** 84, **53** 84-85, **34** 85, **37** 86, MONN **43** 88, PITN **41** 89

SMITH, MIKE P
(34,41,**31**) BALA **34** 89, **41** 89-90, **31** 90

SMITH, MILT 3B/2B
(**12**) CINN **12** 55

SMITH, NATE C
(**27**) BALA **27** 62

SMITH, OZZIE (THE WIZARD)
(**1**) SDN **1** 78-81, STLN **1** 82-96

SMITH, PAUL 1B/OF
(21,**11**,19) PITN **21** 53, **11** 57-58, CHIN **19** 58

SMITH, PETE (J.) P
(**25**,32,34,47, 56,26) ATLN **25** 87-93, NYN **32** 94, CINN **34** 95, SDN **47** 97-98, BALA **56/26** 98

SMITH, PETE (L.) P
(49,**23**) BOSA **49/23** 62

SMITH, RAY C
(18,5,**1**) MINA **18** 81-82, **18/5/1** 83

SMITH, RED CH
(**52**) CHIN *CH* **52** 46-48

SMITH, REGGIE OF/1B/UTIL/CH
(41,**7**,8,14,9) BOSA **41** 66, **7** 67-73, STLN **7** 74-76, LAN **8** 76-81, SFN **14** 82, LAN *CH* **9** 94-98

SMITH, RIVERBOAT (BOB) P
(**28**,43) BOSA **28** 58, CLEA **28** 59, CHIN **43** 59

SMITH, ROY (L.) P
(33,51,**23**,43) CLEA **33** 84-85, MINA **51/19** 86, **23** 87-90, BALA **43** 91

SMITH, (W.) ROY P
(33,51,**23**,43) CLEA **48** 01-02

SMITH, STEVE CH
(**2**,10,1) SEAA *CH* **2** 96-97, *CH* **10** 98-99, TEXA *CH* **1** 02-05

SMITH, TOMMY OF/DH
(26,**11**) CLEA **26** 73-74, **11** 75-76, SEAA **11** 77

SMITH, TRAVIS P
(**52**,53,43,32) MILN **52** 98, STLN **53** 02, ATLN **43** 04, FLAN **32** 05

SMITH, VINNIE C
(**28**) PITN **28** 41, 46

SMITH, WILLIE P/OF/1B
(40,33,35,22, **25**,20) DETA **40/33** 63, LAA **35** 64, CALA **35** 65-66, CLEA **22** 67-68, CHIN **25** 68-70, CINN **20** 71

SMITH, WILLIE P
(**57**) STLN **57** 94

SMITH, ZANE P
(**34**,23,41,48, 24) ATLN **34** 84-89, MONN **23** 89, **34** 90, PITN **41** 90-94, BOSA **48** 95, PITN **24** 96

SMITHBERG, ROGER P
(**51**) OAKA **51** 93-94

SMITHERMAN, STEPHEN OF
(**37**) CINN **37** 03

SMITHSON, MIKE P
(**48**,34,41) TEXA **48** 82-83, MINA **34** 84, **48** 84-87, BOSA **41** 88-89

SMOLL, LEFTY P
(**16**) PHIN **16** 40

SMOLTZ, JOHN P
(57,**29**) ATLN **57** 88, **29** 88-05

SMYRES, CLANCY PH
(**5**) BKNN **5** 44

SMYTH, STEVE P
(**39**) CHIN **39** 02-03

SMYTHE, HARRY P
(**20**,21) NYA **20** 34, BKNN **21** 34

SNARE, RYAN P
(**49**) TEXA **49** 04

SNEAD, ESIX OF
(23,**1**) NYN **23** 02, **1** 04

SNELL, IAN P
(**53**) PITN **53** 04-05

SNELL, NATE P
(**36**,49) BALA **36** 84-86, DETA **49/36** 87

SNELLING, CHRIS OF
(39,**32**) SEAA **39** 02, **32** 05

SNIDER, DUKE (THE SILVER FOX) OF/CH
(**4**,11,28) BKNN **4** 47-57, LAN **4** 58-62, NYN **11/4** 63, SFN **28** 64, SDN *CH* **4** 69

SNIDER, VAN OF
(57,**26**) CINN **57** 88, **26** 88-89

SNITKER, BRIAN CH
(50,**55**,56) ATLN *CH* **50** 85, **55** 88-90, **56** 03

SNOOK, FRANK P
(**42**) SDN **42** 73

SNOPEK, CHRIS 3B
(**27**,10,26) CHIA **27** 95-97, **10** 98, BOSA **26** 98

SNOW, J. T. 1B/DH
(60,**6**) NYA **60** 92, CALA **6** 93-96, SFN **6** 97-05

SNYDER, BERNIE 2B/SS
(**70**) PHIA **70** 35

SNYDER, BRIAN P
(**33**,53) SEAA **33** 85, OAKA **53** 89

SNYDER, CHRIS C
(**19**) ARIN **19** 04-05

SNYDER, CORY OF/SS/UTIL/DH
(**28**,27) CLEA **28** 86-90, CHIA **28** 91, TORA **27** 91, SFN **28** 92, LAN **28** 93-94

SNYDER, EARL 1B/3B
(**37**) CLEA **37** 02, BOSA **37** 04

SNYDER, FRANK (PANCHO) CH
(**32**) NYN *CH* **32** 33-41

SNYDER, GENE P
(**37**) LAN **37** 59

SNYDER, JERRY 2B/SS/INF
(27,**6**,34) WASA **27** 52, **6** 53-57, **34** 58

SNYDER, JIM 2B/1B/CH/M
(**6**,21,5,8,29, 17) MINA **6** 61-62, **21** 64, CHIN *CH* **5** 87, SEAA *M* **6** 88, *CH* **8** 88, SDN *CH* **29** 90, *CH* **17** 91-92

SNYDER, JOHN P
(**59**) CHIA **59** 98-99, MILN **59** 00

SNYDER, KYLE P
(36,**39**) KCA **36** 03, **39** 05

SNYDER, RUSS OF/1B
(14,**9**,7,27) KCA **14** 59-60, BALA **9** 61-67, CHIA **7** 68, CLEA **27** 68-69, MILA **7** 70

SOBKOWIAK, SCOTT P
(**64**) ATLN **64** P

SODD, BILL OF
(**29**) CLEA **29** 37

SODERHOLM, ERIC 3B/SS/UTIL/DH
(48,1,**12**,21) MINA **48** 71, **1** 71-73, **12** 75, CHIA **12** 77-79, TEXA **12** 79, NYA **21** 80

SODERSTROM, STEVE 1B/UTIL
(65,**39**) SFN **65** 96, **39** 98

SODOWSKY, CLINT P
(**46**,63,36) DETA **46** 95-96, PITN **63** 97, ARIN **36** 98 , STLN **50** 99

SOFF, RAY P
(**47**) STLN **47** 86-87

SOFIELD, RICK OF/DH
(25,**12**) MINA **25** 79, **12** 80-81

SOJO, LUIS 2B/UTIL/INF/CH
(6,10,2,9,**19**, 14,53) TORA **6** 90, CALA **10** 91-92, TORA **2** 93, SEAA **9** 94-96, NYA **19** 96-99, PITN **19** 00, NYA **14** 00, **19** 01, *CH* **53** 04-05

SOLAITA, TONY 1B/C/UTIL/DH
(51,8,**27**,25) NYA **51** 68, KCA **8** 74-76, CALA **27** 76-78, MONN **25** 79, TORA **27** 79

SOLANO, JULIO P
(**52**,37) HOUN **52** 83-87, SEAA **37** 88-89

SOLIS, MARCELINO P
(**20**) CHIN **20** 58

SOLOMON, EDDIE (BUDDY) P
(50,40,49,48, 24,34,37,**44**, 27) LAN **50** 73-74, CHIN **50/40** 75, STLN **49/48/24** 76, ATLN **34/37** 77-79, PITN **44** 80-82, CHIA **27** 82

SOLTERS, MOOSE (LEMONS) OF
(22,5,**6**,19,9) BOSA **22** 34, **5** 35, STLA **5** 35-36, CLEA **6** 37-39, STLA **19** 39, CHIA **9** 40-41, **6** 43

SOMMERS, BILL 3B/2B
(**8**) STLA **8** 50

SOMMERS, DENNY CH
(51,2,**6**,34,58) NYN *CH* **51** 77-78, CLEA *CH* **2** 80-82, *CH* **6** 83-85, SDN *CH* **34** 88-90, SFN *CH* **58** 94

SORENSEN, LARY P
(49,**39**,38,40, 27,42,19) MILA **49** 77, **39** 77-80, STLN **39** 81, CLEA **38** 82-83, OAKA **40/38/27** 84, CHIN **42** 85, MONN **40/42** 87, SFN **19** 88

SORENSEN, ZACH INF
(**2**,51) CLEA **2** 03, LAA **51** 05

SORIANO, ALFONSO DH/SS/2B
(58,53,33,**12**) NYA **58** 99, **53** 00, **33** 01, **12** 02-03, TEXA **12** 04-05

SORIANO, RAFAEL P
(**39**) SEAA **39** 02-05

SORRELL, BILL 3B/OF/UTIL
(24,18,**7**) PHIN **24** 65, SFN **18** 67, KCA **7** 70

SORRELL, VIC P
(12,11,**18**) DETA **12** 31, **11** 32-33, **18** 35-37

SORRENTO, PAUL 1B/UTIL/DH
(55,18,**11**,44) MINA **55** 89-90 **18** 91, CLEA **11** 92-95, SEAA **44** 96-97, TBA **44** 98-99

SOSA, ELIAS P
(**38**,27,33,36, 29,39) SFN **38** 72-74, STLN **38** 75, ATLN **38** 75-76, LAN **38** 76, **27** 76-77, OAKA **33** 78, MONN **27** 79-81, DETA **36** 82, SDN **29/39** 83

SOSA, JORGE P
(**59**,36,34) TBA **59** 02-03, **36** 04, ATLN **34** 05

SOSA, JOSE P
(**44**) HOUN **44** 75-76

SOSA, JUAN OF
(**2**) COLN **2** 99, ARIN **2** 01

SOSA, SAMMY OF/DH
(17,25,**21**) TEXA **17** 89, CHIA **25** 89-91, CHIN **21** 92-04, BALA **21** 05

SOTHORON, ALLEN CH/M
(**51**,29) STLN **51** 24, STLA *CH* **29** 32-33, *M* **29** 33

SOTO, GEOVANY C
(**58**) CHIN **58** 05

SOTO, LUIS INF
(**27**) NYA **27** 03

SOTO, MARIO P
(30,**36**) CINN **30** 77, **36** 77-88

SOUCHOCK, STEVE (BUD) 1B/OF/UTIL
(29,41,3,**12**) NYA **29** 46, **41** 46, 48, CHIA **3** 49, DETA **12** 51-55

SOUTHWORTH, BILL 3B
(**47**) MILN **47** 64

SOUTHWORTH, BILLY M
(36,40,**30**) STLN *M* **36** 40, *M* **40** 40-41, *M* **30** 42-45, BOSN *M* **30** 46-51

SOUZA, MARK P
(**58**) OAKA **58** 80

SPAHN, WARREN P/CH
(16,**21**) BOSN **16** 42, **21** 46-52, MILN **21** 53-64, NYN **21** 65, *CH* **21** 65, SFN **21** 65, CLEA *CH* **21** 72-73

SPALDING, DICK CH
(51,**37**,41) PHIN *CH* **51** 34-36, CHIN *CH* **37** 41-42, *CH* **41** 43

SPANGLER, AL OF/CH
(25,**21**,26,20, 3) MILN **25** 59-61, HOUN **21** 62-65, CALA **26** 65-66, CHIN **21** 67-69, **20** 70, *CH* **20** 70, **3** 71, *CH* **3** 71, 74

SPANSWICK, BILL P
(**14**) BOSA **14** 64

SPARKS, JEFF P
(**62**) TBA **62** 99-00

SPARKS, JOE CH
(3,8,52,19,46) CHIA *CH* **3** 79, CINN *CH* **8** 84, MONN *CH* **52** 88, *CH* **19** 89, NYA *CH* **46** 90

SPARKS, STEVE (L.) P
(**57**) PITN **57** 00

SPARKS, STEVE (W.) P
(50,23,**37**) MILA **50** 95-96, ANAA **23** 98-99, DETA **37** 00-03, OAKA **37** 03, ARIN **23** 04

SPARMA, JOE P
(47,**21**) DETA **47** 64, **21** 65-70

SPEAKE, BOB (SPOOK) OF/1B
(**11**,23,26) CHIN **11** 55, 57, SFN **23** 58, **26** 58-59

SPEAKER, TRIS (THE GREY EAGLE) CH
(**43**) CLEA *CH* **43** 47

SPECK, CLIFF P
(**39**) ATLN **39** 86

SPEED, HORACE OF/DH
(38,**20**) SFN **38** 75, CLEA **20** 78-79

SPEER, FLOYD P
(29,**39**) CHIA **29** 43, **39** 44

SPEHR, TIM C
(7,**2**,9,33,12) KCA **7** 91, MONN **2** 93-96, KCA **2** 97, ATLN **9** 97, NYN **33** 98, KCA **12** 98-99

SPEIER, CHRIS SS/2B/3B/INF/CH F
(35,**4**,5,28,2, 43,46) SFN **35** 71-77, MONN **4** 77-84, STLN **5** 84, MINA **4** 84, CHIN **28** 85-86, SFN **2** 87, **35** 88-89, MILN *CH* **43** 00, ARIN *CH* **35** 01, OAKA *CH* **46** 04, CHIN *CH* **35** 05

SPEIER, JUSTIN P S
(56,51,32,45 **30**) CHIN **56** 98, FLAN **51** 98, ATLN **32** 99, CLEA **45** 00-01, COLN **30** 01-03, TORA **30** 04-05

SPEIER, RYAN P
(**23**) COLN **23** 05

SPENCE, BOB 1B
(**22**) CHIA **22** 69-71

SPENCE, STAN OF/1B
(24,21,**2**,5,8) BOSA **24** 40, **21** 41, WASA **2** 42-44, **5** 46-47, BOSA **2** 48-49, STLA **8** 49

SPENCER, DARYL (BIG DEE) SS/3B/INF
(30,12,**20**,7, 9) NYN **30** 52, **12** 53, **20** 56-57, SFN **20** 58-59, STLN **20** 60-61, LAN **7** 61, **20** 62-63, CINN **9** 63

SPENCER, GEORGE P
(**30**,24,31) NYN **21** 50-55, DETA **24** 58, **31** 60

SPENCER, GLENN P
(47,**19**) PITN **47** 32, NYN **19** 33

SPENCER, JIM 1B/OF/DH
(**9**,3,12) CALA **9** 68-73, TEXA **3** 73-75, **9** 75, CHIA **3** 76-77, NYA **12** 78-81, OAKA **12** 81-82

SPENCER, ROY C
(**8**,21,14,10) WASA **8** 31-32, CLEA **8** 33-34, NYN **21** 36, BKNN **14** 37, **10** 38

SPENCER, SEAN P
(**48**) SEAA **48** 99, MONN **53** 00

SPENCER, SHANE OF
(26,**47**,48,43) NYA **26** 98, **47** 98-02, CLEA **48** 03, TEXA **47** 03, NYN **43** 04

SPENCER, STAN P
(58,34,**32**) SDN **58** 98, **34** 99, **32** 00

SPENCER, TOM OF/DH/CH
(49,25,2,51, 52) CHIA **49/25** 78, CLEA *CH* **2** 88-89, NYN *CH* **51** 91, HOUN *CH* **52** 92-93

SPERRING, ROB 2B/SS/INF/UTIL
(**16**,11) CHIN **16** 74-76, HOUN **11** 77

SPERRY, STAN 2B
(23,20,**7**) PHIN **23/20** 36, PHIA **7** 38

SPICER, BOB P
(**29**) KCA **29** 55-56

SPIERS, BILL SS/2B/3B/1B/INF/UTIL
(6,9,19,**28**) MILA **6** 89-91, **9** 92-94, NYN **19** 95, HOUN **28** 96-01

SPIEZIO, ED 3B/OF F
(26,**7**,5) STLN **26** 64-68, SDN **7** 69-72, CHIA **5** 72

SPIEZIO, SCOTT 3B/2B/1B/UTIL S
(13,21,**23**) OAKA **13** 96, **21** 97-99, ANAA **23** 00-03, SEAA **23** 04-05

SPIKES, CHARLIE OF/DH
(42,**24**,34,46) NYA **42** 72, CLEA **24** 73-77, DETA **34** 78, ATLN **46** 79-80

SPILBORGHS, RYAN OF
(**19**) COLN **19** 05

SPILLNER, DAN P
(48,**37**) SDN **48** 74-78, CLEA **37** 78-84, CHIA **37** 84-85

SPILMAN, HARRY 1B/3B/C/UTIL/CH
(56,12,**16**,23, 27,6,10) CINN **56** 78, **12** 78-81, HOUN **16** 81-85, DETA **23/27** 86, SFN **16** 86-88, HOUN **6** 88, **10** 89, *CH* **2** 99, **12** 01-02, **8** 03-04

SPINDEL, HAL C
(31,25,10,**23**) STLA **31/25** 39, PHIN **10** 45, **23** 46

SPINKS, SCIPIO P
(**37**,24) HOUN **37** 69-72, STLN **24** 72-73

SPIVEY, JUNIOR 2B
(**37**,11) ARIN **37** 01-03, MILN **37** 04-05, WASN **11** 05

SPLITTORFF, PAUL P
(25,**34**) KCA **25** 70-71, **34** 71-84

SPOGNARDI, ANDY INF
(**2**) BOSA **2** 32

SPOHRER, AL C
(8,**9**) BOSN **8** 32, **9** 33-35

SPOLJARIC, PAUL P
(45,**24**,23,34, 50,40) TORA **45** 94, **24** 96-97, SEAA **23** 97-98, **34** 98, PHIN **50** 99, TORA **40** 99, KCA **28** 00

SPOONER, KARL P
(**48**) BKNN **48** 54-55

SPOONEYBARGER, TIM P
(**43**,91) ATLN **43** 01-02, FLAN **91** 03, (04-05)

SPRADLIN, JERRY P
(**48**,43,37) CINN **48** 93-94, 96, PHIN **48** 97-98, CLEA **48** 99, SFN **43** 99, KCA **48** 00, CHIN **37** 00

SPRAGINS, HOMER P
(**37**) PHIN **37** 47

SPRAGUE, ED, JR. 3B/UTIL S
(**33**,8,5,4,44, 10) TORA **33** 92-98, OAKA **8** 98, PITN **5** 99, SDN **4** 00, BOSA **44** 00, SDN **4** 00, SEAA **10** 01

SPRAGUE, ED, SR. P F
(17,22,44,48, **29**,25) OAKA **17** 68, **22** 68-69, CINN **44** 71-73, STLN **48** 73, MILA **29** 73, **25** 74, **29** 74-76

SPRIGGS, GEORGE OF
(**23**,30,6,12) PITN **23** 65-67, KCA **30** 69, **6/12** 70

SPRING, JACK P
(45,36,11,**41**, 33,22,49) PHIN **45** 55, BOSA **36** 57, WASA **11** 58, LAA **41** 61-64, CHIN **33** 64, STLN **22** 64, CLEA **49** 65

SPRINGER, DENNIS P
(47,**35**,49,46, 45,56) PHIN **47** 95, CALA **35** 96, ANAA **35** 97, TBA **35** 98, FLAN **49** 99, ARIN **46** 00, LAN **45** 01, **56** 01-02

SPRINGER, RUSS P
(36,41,40,**43**, 33,31,46,48) NYA **36/41** 92, CALA **40** 93, **43** 94-95, PHIN **33** 95-96, HOUN **31** 97, ARIN **31** 98, ATLN **36** 98-99, ARIN **46** 01, STLN **48** 03, HOUN **36** 04-05

SPRINGER, STEVE 3B/2B/DH
(2,**13**) CLEA **2** 90, NYN **13** 92

SPRINGMAN, BILL CH
(**64**) MINA **64** 00

SPRINZ, JOE (MULE) C
(**11**,31) CLEA **11** 31, STLN **31** 33

SPROULL, CHARLIE P
(**18**) PHIN **18** 45

SPROUT, BOB P
(**34**) LAA **34** 61

SPROWL, BOBBY P
(47,**41**) BOSA **47** 78, HOUN **41** 79-81, **40** 80

SPURGEON, JAY P
(**29**) BALA **29** 00

SPURLING, CHRIS P
(**29**) DETA **48** 03, (04), 05

SQUIRES, MIKE 1B/OF/C/UTIL/P/CH
(19,**25**,6,26) CHIA **19** 75, 77-78, **25** 79-85, *CH* **25** 85, TORA *CH* **25** 90-91, *CH* **6** 91, CHIA *CH* **26** 92

STABLEIN, GEORGE P
(**42**) SDN **42** 80

STAEHLE, MARV 2B/SS/3B
(29,**14**) CHIA **29** 64-67, MONN **14** 69-70, ATLN **14** 71

STAFFORD, BILL P
(**22**,28) NYA **22** 60-65, KCA **28** 66, **22** 67

STAGGS, STEVE 2B/INF/DH
(**2**,31) TORA **2** 77, OAKA **31** 78

STAHL, LARRY OF/1B
(**14**,24,25,29) KCA **14** 64, **24** 65, **14** 66, NYN **25** 67-68, SDN **14** 69-72, CINN **29** 73

STAHOVIAK, SCOTT 3B/1B
(**37**) MINA **37** 93, 95-98

STAIGER, ROY 3B/SS
(35,**2**,57) NYN **35** 75, **2** 76-77, NYA **57** 79

STAINBACK, TUCK OF/3B
(42,**5**,34,16, 30,23,16,9,1, 18) CHIN **42** 34, **5** 35, **42** 37, STLN **34** 38, PHIN **16** 38, BKNN **30** 38-39, DETA **23** 40-41, NYA **16** 42-43, **9/1** 44, **18** 45, PHIA **1** 46

STAIRS, MATT OF/DH
(59,3,25,35, **12**,24,30,11) MONN **59/3** 92, **25** 93, BOSA **12**,24,30,11) **35** 95, OAKA **12** 96-00, CHIN **24/30** 01, MILN **12** 02, PITN **12** 03, KCA **11** 04, **12** 05

STALEY, GERRY P
(**14**,42,24,66, 44,21,38,20) STLN **14** 47-54, CINN **42** 55, NYA **24** 55-56, CHIA **66/44/24 /21** 56-61, KCA **38** 61, DETA **38/20** 61

STALLARD, TRACY P
(**39**,36,40) BOSA **39** 60-62, NYN **36** 63-64, STLN **40** 65-66

STALLCUP, VIRGIL (RED) SS
(**10**,3) CINN **10** 47-52, STLN **3** 52-53

STALLER, GEORGE (STOPPER) OF/CH
(__,41,**48**) PHIA __ 43, BALA *CH* **41** 62, *CH* **48** 68-75

STANCEAU, CHARLEY P
(**17**,16,29,42) NYA **17** 41, **16/29** 46, PHIN **42** 46

STANDRIDGE, JASON P
(**53**),44,35) TBA **53** 01-04, TEXA **44** 05, CINN **35** 05

STANEK, AL (LEFTY) P
(**48**) SFN **48** 63

STANFIELD, KEVIN P
(**40**) MINA **40** 79

STANFORD, JASON P
(**61**) CLEA **61** 03-04

STANGE, LEE P/CH
(18,39,**20**,43, 37,45,33,35, 42,41,34) MINA **18** 61, **39** 61-63, **20** 63-64, CLEA **43** 64-66, BOSA **37** 66, **20** 67-70, CHIA **45** 70, BOSA *CH* **33** 72, *CH* **35** 72-74, MINA *CH* **45** 75, OAKA *CH* **42** 77, *CH* **41** 78-79, BOSA *CH* **34** 81-84

STANHOUSE, DON P
(17,50,36,27, 48,**26**,22,29) TEXA **17** 72-73, **50/36/27** 74, MONN **26** 75-77, BALA **48** 78, **26** 78-79, LAN **22/29** 80, BALA **26** 82

STANICEK, PETE INF/OF/UTIL/DH B
(**12**) BALA **12** 87-88, **17** 88

STANICEK, STEVE P B
(**22**,33) MILA **22** 87, PHIN **33** 89

STANIFER, ROB P
(**38**,26) FLAN **38** 97-98, BOSA **26** 00

STANKA, JOE P
(**36**) CHIA **36** 59

STANKIEWICZ, ANDY (STANKY) SS/2B/DH
(17,35,28,4, **5**) NYA **17** 92, **35/28** 93, HOUN **4** 94-95, MONN **5** 96-97, ARIN **5** 98

STANKY, EDDIE (THE BRAT)(MUGGSY) 2B/INF/M/CH
(25,**12**,44,__) CHIN **25** 43-44, BKNN **12** 44-47, BOSN **12** 48-49, NYN **12** 50-51, STLN *M* **12** 52-55, CLEA *CH* **44** 57-58, CHIA *M* **12** 66-68, TEXA *M* __ 77

STANLEY, BOB P
(**46**) BOSA **46** 77-89

STANLEY, FRED (CHICKEN) SS/2B/INF/UTIL/CH
(22,45,16,6, **11**,13) SEAA **22** 69 , MILA **45** 70, CLEA **16** 71-72, SDN **6** 72, NYA **11** 73 -80, OAKA **11** 81-82, MILA *CH* **13** 91

STANLEY, MICKEY OF/1B/INF/UTIL
(49,**24**) DETA **49** 64-65, **24** 66-78

STANLEY, MIKE C/UTIL/1B/DH/CH
(5,**20**,22,18, 24) TEXA **5** 86-91, NYA **20** 92-95, BOSA **22** 96, **20** 97, NYA **18/ 20** 97, TORA **20** 98, BOSA **24** 98-00, OAKA **10** 00, BOSA *CH* **20** 02

STANTON, LEROY (LEE) OF/DH
(44,23,**36**) NYN **44** 70, **23** 71, CALA **36** 72-76, SEAA **36** 77-78

STANTON, MIKE (T.) P
(48,**46**) HOUN **48** 75, CLEA **46** 80-81, SEAA **46** 82-85, CHIA **48** 85

STANTON, MIKE (W.) P
(**30**,32,29,37) ATLN **30** 89-95, BOSA **32** 95-96, TEXA **32** 96, NYA **29** 97-02, NYN **32** 03-04, NYA**29** 05, WASN **30** 05, BOSA **37** 05

STAPLETON, DAVE 1B/INF/UTIL/DH
(26,**11**) BOSA **26** 80, **11** 80-86

STAPLETON, DAVE P
(**43**) MILA **43** 87-88

STARGELL, WILLIE OF/1B/CH
(**8**) PITN **8** 62-82, *CH* **8** 85, ATLN *CH* **8** 86-88

STARK, DENNIS P
(56,67,**41**) SEAA **56** 99, **67** 01, COLN **41** 02-04

STARK, MATT C/DH
(47,**21**) TORA **47** 87, CHIA **21** 90

STARR, CHICK C
(15,**22**) WASA **15** 35, **22** 36

STARR, DICK P
(36,19,**28**,31) NYA **30** 47, **36** 48, **19** 48, STLA **28** 49-51, WASA **31** 51

STARR, RAY (IRON MAN) P
(__,16,26,**37**, 20,38,32) STLN __ 32, NYN **16** 33, BOSN **26** 33, CINN **37** 41-43, PITN **20** 44-45, CHIN **26/38/32** 45

STARRETTE, HERM P/CH
(**24**,23,4,38, 3,31,40) BALA **24** 63-65, ATLN *CH* **23** 74 -76, SFN *CH* **23** 77-78, PHIN *CH* **4** 79-81, SFN *CH* **23** 83-84, MILA *CH* **38** 85-86, CHIN *CH* **3** 87, BALA *CH* **31** 88, BOSA *CH* **23** 95, 97, *CH* **40** 97

STATON, DAVE 1B S
(28,**31**) SDN **28** 93, **31** 94

STATON, JOE 1B F
(**42**) DETA **42** 72-73

STAUB, RUSTY (LE GRAND ORANGE) OF/1B/DH
(**10**,4,6,20) HOUN **10** 63-68, MONN **10** 69-71, NYN **4** 72-75, DETA **10** 76-79, MONN **6** 79, TEXA **20** 80, NYN **10** 81-85

STAUFFER, TIM P
(**47**) SDN **47** 05

STEARNS, JOHN C/1B/3B/INF/UTIL/CH
(9,16,**12**,44, 18) PHIN **9** 74, NYN **16** 75-76, **12** 76-84, NYA *CH* **44** 89, BALA *CH* **18** 96-98, NYN *CH* **12** 00-01

STECHSCHULTE, GENE P
(67,**36**) STLN **67** 00-01, **36** 01-02, (03)

STEELS, JIM OF/1B/UTIL
(52,**21**,27,19) SDN **52/21** 87, TEXA **27** 88, SFN **19** 89

STEENSTRA, KENNIE P
(**49**) CHIN **49** 98

STEEVENS, MORRIE P
(35,**23**,47) CHIN **35** 62, PHIN **58** 64, **23** 65, **47** 65

STEFERO, JOHN C/2B
(9,**21**,19) BALA **9** 83, **21** 86, MONN **19** 86

STEGMAN, DAVE OF/DH
(**22**,38,8) DETA **22** 78-80, NYA **38** 82, CHIA **8** 83-84

STEIN, BILL 3B/OF/INF/UTIL/DH
(32,**1**,13) STLN **32** 72-73, CHIA **1** 74-76, SEAA **1** 77-80, TEXA **13** 81, **1** 82-85

STEIN, BLAKE P
(59,41,**34**) OAKA **59** 98-99, KCA **41** 99, **34** 00-02

STEIN, IRV P
(**17**) PHIA **17** 32

STEIN, JUSTIN (OTT) 3B/2B/SS
(**8**,45) PHIN **8** 38, CINN **45** 38

STEIN, RANDY P
(40,43,33,**26**, 50) MILA **40/43** 78, SEAA **33** 79, **26** 81, CHIN **50/43** 82

STEINBACH, TERRY C/1B/UTIL
(**36**) OAKA **36** 86-96, MINA **36** 97-99

STEINBACHER, HANK OF
(**46**) CHIA **46** 37-39

STEINER, BEN 2B/3B
(1,**44**,26) BOSA **1** 45, **44** 46, DETA **26** 47

STEINER, RED C
(**12**,40) CLEA **12** 45, BOSA **40** 45

STEIRER, RICK P
(**42**) CALA **42** 82-84

STELMASZEK, RICK C/CH
(34,32,**8**,43) WASA **34** 71, TEXA **32** 73, CALA **8** 73, CHIN **8** 74, MINA *CH* **43** 81-05

STEMBER, JEFF P
(**50**) SFN **50** 80

STEMLE, STEVE P
(**37**) KCA **37** 05

STENGEL, CASEY (THE OLD PROFESSOR) CH/M
(31,36,32,**37**) BKNN *CH* **31** 32-33, *M* **31** 34-36, *M* **36** 36, BOSN *M* **31** 38-39, *M* **32** 40-43, NYA *M* **37** 49-60, NYN *M* **37** 62-65

STENHOUSE, DAVE P F
(**15**) WASA **15** 62-64

STENHOUSE, MIKE OF/1B/UTIL S
(**32**,33,37) MONN **32** 82-84, MINA **33** 85, BOSA **37** 86

STENNETT, RENNIE 2B/SS/OF/3B/UTIL
(**6**) PITN **6** 71-79, SFN **6** 80-81

STENSON, DERNELL OF
(**63**) CINN **63** 03

STEPHEN, BUZZ P
(**17**) MINA **17** 68

STEPHENS, BRYAN P
(28,29,31,**21**) CLEA **28/29** 47, STLA **31/21** 48

STEPHENS, GENE OF
(38,36,**10**,8, 3,26) BOSA **38** 52, **36** 53, **38** 55-59, **10** 59-60, BALA **8** 60-61, KCA **3** 61-62, CHIA **26** 63-64

STEPHENS, JOHN P
(**28**) BALA **28** 02

STEPHENS, RAY C
(54,**24**) STLN **54** 90-91, TEXA **24** 92

STEPHENS, VERN (BUSTER)(JUNIOR) SS/3B
(6,**5**,3,40,4, 35) STLA **6** 41, **5** 42-47 BOSA **5** 48-52, CHIA **3** 53, STLA **40** 53, BALA **4** 54-55, CHIA **35** 55

STEPHENSON, BOB INF
(**21**) STLN **21** 55

STEPHENSON, EARL P
(37,35,38,52) CHIN **37** 71, MILA **35/38** 72, BALA **52** 77-78

STEPHENSON, GARRETT P
(52,54,**55**) BALA **52** 96, PHIN **54** 96-98, STLN **55** 99-00, (01), 02-03

STEPHENSON, JERRY P S
(29,18,**38**,41, 40,45)) BOSA **29** 63, **18** 65-67, **38** 67-68, SEAA **41/40** 69, LAN **45** 70

STEPHENSON, JOE C F
(**25**,50,26) NYN **25** 43, CHIN **50** 44, CHIA **26** 47

STEPHENSON, JOHNNY 3B/OF/C
(49,19,12,6, 10,5,37,**11**) NYN **49** 64-65, **19** 65, **12** 66, CHIN **6** 67-68, SFN **10** 69, **5** 70, CALA **37** 71-72, **11** 73

STEPHENSON, PHIL OF/1B
(11,**21**) CHIN **11** 89, SDN **21** 89-92

STEPHENSON, RIGGS (OLD HOSS) OF
(7,4,**5**) CHIN **7/4** 32, **5** 33-34

STEPHENSON, WALTER (TARZAN) C
(**42**,47,22) CHIN **42** 35-36, PHIN **47/22** 37

STERLING, RANDY P
(**35**) NYN **35** 74

STERN, ADAM OF
(**39**) BOSA **39** 05

STEVENS, CHUCK 1B
(10,24,**3**) STLA **10** 41, **24** 46, **3** 48

STEVENS, DAVE P
(**41**,40,48,33, 56) MINA **41** 94-97, CHIN **40** 97, **48** 98, CLEA **33** 99, ATLN **56** 00

STEVENS, ED (BIG ED) 1B
(8,36,**5**,37) BKNN **8** 45, **36** 46-47, PITN **5** 48-49, **37** 50, DETA *BPCH* **36**61

STEVENS, LEE 1B/OF
(**9**,23,11) CALA **9** 90-92, **23** 92, TEXA **11** 96-98, **9** 98-99, MONN **9** 00-02, CLEA **9** 02

STEVENS, R. C. 1B
(**7**,28,2) PITN **7** 58, **28** 59, **7** 60, WASA **2** 61

STEVERSON, TODD PH
(**13**) DETA **13** 95, SDN **13** 96

STEWART, ANDY C
(**63**) KCA **63** 97

STEWART, BILL OF
(38,**31**) KCA **38/31** 55

STEWART, EDDIE (BUD) OF/UTIL
(14,42,6,34, 7,**21**) PITN **14** 41-42, NYA **42** 48, WASA **6** 48-49, **34** 50, CHIA **7** 51-52, **21** 53-54

STEWART, BUNKY P
(34,14,38,23, **24**) WASA **34/14** 52, **38/23** 53, **24** 54-56

STEWART, DAVE P/CH
(48,31,43,38, **34**,35) LAN **48** 78, 81-83, TEXA **31** 83-84, **43/48** 85, PHIN **38** 85-86, OAKA **34** 86-92, TORA **34** 93-94, OAKA **35** 95, SDN *CH* **34** 98, MILN *CH* **43** 02

STEWART, GLEN (GABBY) 3B/SS/INF/UTIL
(23,**19**,8) NYN **23** 40,PHIN **19** 43-44, **8** 44

STEWART, JIMMY SS/2B/OF/UTIL
(**19**,11,16) CHIN **19** 63-67, CHIA **11** 67, CINN **16** 69-71, HOUN **11** 72-73

STEWART, JOSH P
(**48**) CHIA **48** 03-04

STEWART, LEFTY P
(**14**,24) STLA **14** 31-32, WASA **14** 33-35, CLEA **24** 35

STEWART, MACK P
(**38**) CHIN **38** 44-45

STEWART, NEB OF
(**25**) PHIN **25** 40

STEWART, SAMMY P
(**53**) BALA **53** 78-85, BOSA **53** 86, CLEA **53** 87

STEWART, SCOTT P
(**51**,55,57) MONN **51** 01-03, CLEA **55** 04, LAN **57** 04

STEWART, SHANNON OF/DH
(7,**24**,23) TORA **7** 95-97, **24** 98-03, MINA **23** 03-05

STIDHAM, PHIL P
(**10**) DETA **10** 94

STIEB, DAVE P
(**37**,10) TORA **37** 79-92, CHIA **10** 93, TORA **37** 98

STIELY, FRED (LEFTY) P
(**20**) STLA **20** 31

STIGMAN, DICK P
(22,**18**,36,42) CLEA **22** 60-61, MINA **18** 62-65, BOSA **36/42** 66

STILES, ROLLIE (LENA) P
(19,**22**) STLA **19** 31, **22** 33

STILLMAN, ROYLE OF/1B/UTIL/DH
(**15**,18) BALA **15** 75-76, CHIA **18** 77

STILLWELL, KURT SS/2B/INF S
(11,**1**,15,3) CINN **11** 86-87, KCA **1** 88-91, SDN **15** 92-93, CALA **3** 93, TEXA **1** 96

STILLWELL, RON SS/2B F
(29,**8**) WASA **29** 61, **8** 62

STIMAC, CRAIG C/3B
(**7**) SDN **7** 80-81

STINE, LEE P
(27,25,21,33, **13**) CHIA **27** 34, **25** 35, CINN **21** 36, NYA **33/13** 38

STINNETT, KELLY C
(33,11,5,**35**, 31) NYN **33** 94-95, MILA **11** 96, **5** 97, ARIN **35** 98-00, CINN **31** 01-03, PHIN **35** 03, KCA **18** 04, ARIN **35** 05

STINSON, BOB C/OF/3B/UTIL/DH
(8,19,9,7,**15**) LAN **8** 69-70, STLN **19** 71, HOUN **9** 72, MONN **7** 73-74, KCA **15** 75-76, SEAA **15** 77-80

STIRNWEISS, SNUFFY 2B,SS,3B,INF
(2,**1**,5) NYA **2** 43-44, **1** 45-50, STLA **2** 50, CLEA **5** 51-52

STOBBS, CHUCK P
(22,**18**,38,27) BOSA **42** 47, **22** 47-51, CHIA **18** 52, WASA **18** 53-58, STLN **38** 58, WASA **27** 59-61

STOCK, MILT 3B/CH
(**6**,41,27,40) STLN **6** 23, CHIN *CH* **41** 44-48, BKNN *CH* **27** 49-50, PITN *CH* **40** 51-52

STOCK, WES P/CH
(27,**18**,15,3, 42,40,32,44) BALA **27** 59, **18** 60-64, KCA **18** 64-65, **15** 66, **18** 66-67, *CH* **18** 67, MILA *CH* **18** 70-72, OAKA *CH* **3/42** 73, *CH* **40** 73-74, *CH* **42** 74-76, SEAA *CH* **32** 77-81, OAKA *CH* **44** 85-86

STOCKER, KEVIN SS
(**19**,38,1) PHIN **19** 93-97, TBA **19** 98-00, ANAA **38/1** 00

STODDARD, BOB P
(**34**,48,47,19) SEAA **34** 81-84, DETA **48** 85, SDN **47** 86, KCA **19** 87

STODDARD, TIM P
(42,**49**,33,43, 36) CHIA **42** 75, BALA **49** 78-83, CHIN **49** 84, SDN **49** 85-86, NYA **33** 86, **43** 86-88, CLEA **36** 89

STONE, DEAN P
(31,32,**26**,28, 45,33,44,22) WASA **31/32** 53, **26** 54-57, BOSA **28** 57, STLN **45** 59, HOUN **33** 62, CHIA **44** 62, BALA **22** 63

STONE, DICK P
(**21**) WASA **21** 45

STONE, GENE 1B
(**10**) PHIN **10** 69

STONE, GEORGE P
(32,**40**) ATLN **32** 67-68, **40** 68-72, NYN **40** 73-75

STONE, JEFF OF
(23,26,**14**,1, 19,28) PHIN **23** 83, **26** 83-86, **14** 86-87, BALA **1** 88, TEXA **19** 89, BOSA **28** 89-90

STONE, JOHN (ROCKY) OF
(24,3,2,4,**6**) DETA **24** 31, **3** 32-33, WASA **2** 34-35, **4** 35, **6** 36-38

STONE, RICKY P
(35,**20**,52) HOUN **35** 01-02, **20** 02-04, SDN **52** 04, CINN **52** 05

STONE, ROCKY P
(**39**) CINN **39** 43

STONE, RON OF/1B
(51,1,3,**21**) KCA **51/11** 66, PHIN **3** 69, **21** 70-72

STONE, STEVE P
(33,29,**32**,30, 21) SFN **33/35** 71, **29** 72, CHIA **32** 73, CHIN **30** 74-76, CHIA **32** 77-78, BALA **21** 79, **32** 79-81

STONE, TIGE OF/P
(**12**) STLN **12** 23

STONEHAM, JOHN OF
(**17**) CHIA **17** 33

STONEMAN, BILL P
(50,36,**26**) CHIN **50** 67,**36** 67-68, MONN **26** 69-73, CALA **26** 74

STOOPS, JIM P
(**39**) COLN **39** 98

STORIE, HOWIE (SPONGE) C
(19,**11**) BOSA **16/19** 31, **11** 32

STORTI, LIN 3B/2B
(**7**,24) STLA **7** 31-32, **24** 33

STOTTLEMYRE, MEL, JR. P
(**52**) KCA **52** 90

STOTTLEMYRE, MEL, SR. P/CH
(**30**,48,34) NYA **30** 64-74, NYN *CH* **48** 84, **30** 84-93, HOUN *CH* **30** 94-95, NYA *CH* **34** 96-05

STOTTLEMYRE, TODD P
(16,**30**,44,32) TORA **16** 88, **30** 89-94, OAKA **30** 95, STLN **30** 96-98, TEXA **44** 98, ARIN **32** 99, **30** 00, (01), 02

STOUT, ALLYN (FISH HOOK) P
(**21**,23,11,18, 14,36) STLN **21** 32-33, **23** 33, CINN **11** 33, **18** 34, NYN **14** 35, BOSN **36** 43

STOVALL, DaROND OF
(**50**) MONN **50** 98

STOVIAK, RAY OF
(**4**) PHIN **4** 38

STOWE, HAL P
(**29**) NYA **29** 60

STOWERS, CHRIS OF
(**34**) MONN **34** 99

STRAHLER, MIKE P
(**37**,34) LAN **37** 70-72, DETA **34** 73

STRAHS, DICK P
(**35**) CHIA **35** 54

STRAIN, JOE 2B/3B/INF
(**20**) SFN **20** 79-80, CHIN **20** 81

STRAKER, LES P
(**17**) MINA **17** 87-88

STRAMPE, BOB P
(**46**) DETA **46** 72

STRANGE, ALAN (INKY) SS/2B/INF
(1,28,**2**) STLA **1** 34-35, WASA **28** 35, STLA **2** 40-42

STRANGE, DOUG 3B/2B/INF
(20,1,**12**,15, 17) DETA **20** 89, CHIN **1** 91-92, TEXA **20** 93-94, SEAA **12** 95-96, MONN **15** 97, PITN **17** 98,(99)

STRANGE, PAT P
(**38**) NYN **38** 02-03

STRATTON, MONTY (GANDER) P/CH
(24,36,**25**) CHIA **24** 34, **36** 35, **25** 36-38, *CH* **25** 39-41

STRAWBERRY, DARRYL (STRAW) OF/DH
(**18**,44,17,26, 39) NYN **18** 83-90, LAN **44** 91-94, SFN **17** 94, NYA **26** 95, **39** 96-99

STREET, GABBY (OLD SARGE) M
(**25**,31,13) STLN *M* **25** 32-33, STLA *M* **31/ 13** 38

STREET, HUSTON P
(**20**) OAKA **20** 05

STREULI, WALT 3B/UTIL/DH/P
(19,40,**39**) DETA **19** 54, **40** 55, **39** 56

STRICKLAND, BILL P
(**14**) STLA **14** 37

STRICKLAND, GEORGE (BO) 2B/3B/SS/INF/CH/M
(14,**2**,3,4,51, 5,11) PITN **14** 50-52, CLEA **2** 52-56, **3** 57, **4** 59-60, MINA *CH* **51** 62, CLEA *CH* **3** 63-69, *M* **3** 64, 66, KCA *CH* **14** 70, *CH* **5** 71, *CH* **11** 71-72

STRICKLAND, JIM P
(53,**19**,44) MINA **53** 71, **19** 71-73, CLEA **44** 75

STRICKLAND, SCOTT P
(52,20,**25**,28, 43) MONN **52** 99, **20** 00-01, **25** 02, NYN **25** 02, **28** 03, (04), HOUN **43** 05

STRIKER, JAKE P
(**23**,31) CLEA **23** 59, CHIA **31** 60

STRINCEVICH, NICK (JUMBO) P
(25,**22**,36) BOSN **25** 40-41, PITN **25** 41-42, **22** 44-48, PHIN **36** 48

STRINGER, LOU 2B/SS/INF
(15,12,**27**) CHIN **15** 41-42, **12** 46, BOSA **27** 48-50

STRIPP, JOE (JERSEY JOE) 3B/1B/INF
(**3**,17,11) BKNN **3** 32-37, STLN **17** 38, BOSN **11** 38

STRITTMATTER, MARK C
(**22**) COLN **22** 98

STROHMAYER, JOHN P
(**36**,30,34,39) MONN **36** 70-73, NYN **30/34** 73, **39** 73-74

STROM, BRENT P/CH
(40,34,**22**,42, 30) NYN **40** 72, CLEA **34** 73, SDN **22** 75-77, HOUN *CH* **42** 96, KCA *CH* **30** 00-01

STROMME, FLOYD (ROCK) P
(10,**31**) CLEA **10/31** 39

STRONG, JAMAL DH
(**36**) SEAA **36** 03, 05

STRONG, JOE P
(**50**) FLAN **50** 00-01

STROUD, ED OF
(40,**36**,6) CHIA **40** 66-67, WASA **36** 67-70, CHIA **6** 71

STROUGHTER, STEVE OF/DH
(**14**) SEAA **14** 82

STRUSS, STEAMBOAT P
(__) PITN __ 34

STUART, DICK (DR. STRANGEGLOVE) 1B/OF/3B
(**7**,17,5) PITN **7** 58-62, BOSA **7** 63-64, PHIN **7** 65, NYN **17** 66, LAN **7** 66, CALA **5** 69

STUART, JOHNNY (STUD) P
(**19**,41) STLN **19** 23, **41** 24

STUART, MARLIN P
(24,**26**,40,27) DETA **24** 49-52, **26** 50, STLA **40/24/26** 52, **26** 53, BALA **26** 54, NYA **27** 54

STUBBS, FRANKLIN 1B/OF/UTIL
(**22**,24,28,0, 19) LAN **22** 84-89, HOUN **24/22** 90, MILA **28** 91, **0** 92, DETA **19** 95

STUBING, MOOSE PH/CH/M
(**17**,47) CALA **17** 67, *CH* **47** 85-90, *M* **47** 88

STUFFEL, PAUL (STU) P
(39,41,**34**) PHIN **39** 50, **41** 52, **34** 53

STULL, EVERETT P
(**38**,56) MONN **38** 97, ATLN **56** 99, MILN **41** 00, **50** 02

STUMP, JIM P
(31,**20**) DETA **31** 57, **20** 59

STUMPF, GEORGE OF
(30,23,17,**25**, 7) BOSA **30/23** 31, **17** 32, **25** 33, CHIA **7** 36

STUPER, JOHN P
(**48**,42) STLN **48** 82-84, CINN **42** 85

STURDIVANT, TOM (SNAKE) P
(**47**,32,15,35, 22,20,18) NYA **47** 55-59, KCA **32** 59, BOSA **15** 60, WASA **35/47** 61, PITN **15** 61-63, DETA **22** 63, KCA **20** 63, **18** 63-64, NYN **47** 64

STURGEON, BOBBY SS/2B/INF
(**28**,38,7,14) CHIN **28** 40-42, **38** 46, **7** 46-47, BOSN **14** 48

STURM, JOHNNY 1B
(**34**) NYA **34** 41

STURTZE, TANYON P
(34,47,**49**,31, 56) CHIN **34** 95-96, TEXA **47** 97, CHIA **47** 99-00, TBA **49** 00-02, TORA **31** 03, NYA **56** 04-05

STYNES, CHRIS 2B/3B
(38,**14**,20,23, 3) KCA **38** 95, **14** 96, CINN **20** 97, **23** 98, **12** 99, **4** 00, BOSA **12** 01, CHIN **11** 02, COLN **7** 03, PITN **3** 04

SUAREZ, KEN C/UTIL
(8,17,**7**,12,10) KCA **35** 66, **8** 66-67, **17** 67, CLEA **7** 68-69, 71, TEXA **12** 72, **10** 73

SUAREZ, LUIS 3B
(**6**) WASA **6** 44

SUCH, DICK P/CH
(**18**,52,42,44) WASA **18** 70, TEXA *CH* **52** 83-85, MINA *CH* **42** 85-97, *CH* **44** 98-01

SUCHE, CHARLEY P
(__) CLEA __ 38

SUCHECKI, JIM P
(37,21,42,**27**) BOSA **37/21** 50, STLA **42** 51, PITN **27** 52

SUDAKIS, BILL (SUDS) 3B/1B/C/UTIL
(**16**,9,21,44, 4) LAN **16** 68-71, NYN **9** 72, TEXA **21** 73, NYA **44** 74, CALA **9** 75, CLEA **4** 75

SUDER, PETE (PECKY) 3B/SS/2B/INF/UTIL
(3,**12**) PHIA **3** 41-43, **12** 46-54, KCA **12** 55

SUERO, WILLIAM 2B/SS/3B
(**2**) MILA **2** 92-93

SUGDEN, JOE CH
(**25**) STLN *CH* **25** 23

SUHR, GUS 1B/OF
(**24**,6) PITN **24** 32-39, PHIN **6** 39-40

SUKEFORTH, CLYDE (SUKEY) C/CH/M
(**11**,35,34,__, 40,15,41) BKNN **11** 32-34, *CH* **35** 43-44, **34** 45, *CH* **34** 45, __ 46, *CH* **40** 47, *M* **15** 47, *CH* **15** 48-51, PITN *CH* **41** 52-57

SUKLA, ED P
(51,**23**) LAA **51** 64, CALA **51** 65, **23** 65-66

SULARZ, GUY 2B/3B/SS/INF
(**21**) SFN **21** 80-83

SULIK, ERNIE (DAVE) OF
(37,**32**) PHIN **37/32** 36

SULLIVAN, BILLY 3B/1B/C/INF/UTIL
(26,49,36,29, 14,**9**,2,8,42) CHIA **26** 31, **49** 32, **36** 33, CINN **29** 35, CLEA **14** 36, **9** 37, STLA **2** 38-39, DETA **8** 40-41, BKNN **9** 42, PITN **42/14** 47

SULLIVAN, CHARLIE P
(**19**) DETA **19** 31

SULLIVAN, CORY OF
(**31**) COLN **31** 05

SULLIVAN, FRANK P
(30,**18**,29,20) BOSA **30** 53, **18** 53-60, PHIN **29** 61, **18** 62, MINA **20** 62-63

SULLIVAN, HAYWOOD C/1B/UTIL/M
(41,16,30,**8**, 41) BOSA **41** 55, **16** 57, 59, **30** 60, KCA **8** 61-63, *M* **41** 65

SULLIVAN, JACK 2B
(**18**) DETA **18** 44

SULLIVAN, JOE P
(**19**,21,26) DETA **19** 35-36, BOSN **19** 39, **21** 40-41, PITN **26** 41

SULLIVAN, JOHN (PAUL) SS/2B/INF
(32,7,11,**1**) WASA **32** 42-43, **7** 43-44, **11** 47, **1** 48, STLA **1** 49

SULLIVAN, JOHN (PETER) C/CH
(**36**,20,37,16, 8) DETA **36** 63-65, NYN **20** 67, PHIN **37** 68, KCA *CH* **16** 79, ATLN *CH* **8** 80-81, TORA *CH* **8** 82-93

SULLIVAN, LEFTY P
(**30**) CLEA **30** 39

SULLIVAN, MARC C
(**15**) BOSA **15** 82, 84-87

SULLIVAN, RUSS OF
(18,38,**19**) DETA **18** 51, **38/18** 52, **19** 52-53

SULLIVAN, SCOTT P
(47,**56**,31,47) CINN **47** 95, **56** 96-97, **31** 98, **56** 99-03, CHIA **47** 03, KCA **47** 04, (05)

SUMMERS, CHAMP OF/3B/1B/UTIL/DH/CH
(**28**,27,24,6, 47) OAKA **28** 74, CHIN **27** 75-76, CINN **28** 77-79, DETA **24** 79-81, SFN **6** 82-83, SDN **24** 84, NYA *CH* **47** 89-90

SUNDBERG, JIM C/OF/DH
(**10**,8,11) TEXA **10** 74-83, MILA **8** 84, KCA **8** 85-86, CHIN **11** 87-88, TEXA **10** 88-89

SUNDIN, GORDIE P
(**42**) BALA **42** 56

SUNDRA, STEVE (SMOKEY) P
(24,32,25,**17**, 31) NYA **24** 36, **32** 38-39, **23**, **25** 40, WASA **32** 41, **17** 42, STLA **17** 42-44, **31** 46

SUNKEL, TOM (LEFTY) P
(21,28,26,**16**, 19) STLN **21** 37, **28** 39, NYN **26** 41, **16** 42-43, BKNN **19** 44

SUPLIZIO, SAM CH
(__) ANAA __ 99

SUPPAN, JEFF P
(55,20,**37**,35) BOSA **55** 95-97, ARIN **20** 98, KCA **37** 98-02, PITN **37** 03, BOSA **35** 03, STLN **37** 04-05

SURHOFF, B. J. C/3B/1B/UTIL/OF B
(**5**,17,15) MILA **5** 87-95, BALA **17** 96-00, ATLN **15** 00-02, BALA **17** 03-05

SURHOFF, RICK P B
(56,**44**) PHIN **56** 85, TEXA **44** 85

SURKONT, MAX P
(16,**36**,35,25) CHIA **16** 49, BOSN **36** 50-52, MILN **36** 53, PITN **35** 54-56, STLN **25** 56, NYN **36** 56-57

SUSCE, GEORGE (C.) (GOOD KID) C/CH F
(24,31,9,**28**, 42,44,36,43, 40,35) DETA **24** 32, PITN **31** 39, STLA **9** 40, CLEA **28** 41-45, *CH* **28** 43-46, *CH* **42** 47, *CH* **44** 49, BOSA *CH* **36** 50, *CH* **42** 51-52, *CH* **43** 52-54, KCA *CH* **40** 55-56, MILN *CH* **35** 58-59, WASA *CH* **43** 61-67, 69-71, TEXA **43** 72

SUSCE, GEORGE (D.) P S
(41,**27**,26) BOSA **45** 55, **27** 55-58, DETA **26** 58-59

SUSKO, PETE 1B
(19,**22**) WASA **19/22** 34

SUTCLIFFE, BUTCH C
(**25**) BOSN **25** 38

SUTCLIFFE, RICK P
(48,44,43,**40**) LAN **48** 76-77, **43** 78-81, CLEA **44** 82, **43** 82-84, CHIN **40** 84-91, BALA **40** 92-93, STLN **40** 94

SUTHERLAND, DARRELL P
(47,**43**,40)) NYN **47** 64, **43** 65-66, **45** 66, CLEA **40** 68

SUTHERLAND, DIZZY P
(**11**) WASA **11** 49

SUTHERLAND, GARY SS/OF/2B/3B/INF/UTIL
(32,23,35,**1**, 8,3,9,21) PHIN **32/23** 66, **35** 67-68, MONN **1** 69-71, HOUN **8** 72-73, DETA **3** 74-76, MILA **9** 76, SDN **21** 77, STLN **21** 78

SUTHERLAND, LEO OF
(**48**) CHIA **48** 80-81

SUTKO,GLENN C
(**55**) CINN **55** 90-91

SUTTER, BRUCE P
(**42**,40) CHIN **42** 76-80, STLN **42** 81-84, ATLN **40** 85-86, **40/42** 88

SUTTON, DON P
(**20**,21,27) LAN **20** 66-80, HOUN **20** 81, MILA **21** 82-83, **20** 83-84, OAKA **27/20** 85, CALA **20** 85, **27** 85-86, **20** 86-87, LAN **20** 88

SUTTON, JOHN (JOHNNY)(IKE) P
(35,40,**41**) STLN **35** 77, MINA **40/41** 78

SUTTON, LARRY 1B/INF/OF
(**22**,28,19,29) KCA **22** 97-99, STLN **28** 00-01, OAKA **19** 02, FLAN **29** 04

SUZUKI, ICHIRO OF
(**51**) SEAA **51** 01-05

SUZUKI, MAC P
(96,41,55,**17**, 16,52) SEAA **96** 96, **41** 98-99, KCA **55** 99, **17** 00-01, COLN **16** 01, MILN **52** 01, KCA **17** 02

SVEUM, DALE SS/2B/3B/INF/UTIL/DH/CH
(27,**7**,9,8,42, 6,36,17,11, 41) MILA **27** 86, **7** 87-88, 90-91, PHIN **9/8** 92, CHIA **42** 92, OAKA **6** 93, SEAA **36** 94, PITN **17** 96-97, NYA **17** 98, PITN **11** 99, BOSA *CH* **41** 04-05

SWAGGERTY, BILL P
(**32**) BALA **32** 83-86

SWAN, CRAIG P
(46,**27**) NYN **46** 73, **27** 73-84, CALA **27** 84

SWAN, RUSS P
(52,33,59,**37**, 17,44) SFN **52/33** 89, **59** 90, SEAA **37** 90-92, **17** 93, CLEA **44** 94

SWANN, PEDRO OF/DH
(**57**,8) ATLN **57** 00, TORA **8** 02, BALA **57** 03

SWANSON, EVAR OF
(25,**9**) CHIA **25** 32, **9** 33-34

SWANSON, RED P
(20,13,**17**,35) PITN **20** 55, **13/17** 56, **35** 57

SWANSON, STAN OF
(50,**37**) MONN **50/37** 71

SWARTZ, BUD P
(**31**) STLA **31** 47

SWARTZBAUGH, DAVE P
(**36**,38) CHIN **36** 95-96, **38** 97

SWEENEY, BILL 1B/CH
(**1**,33) BOSA **1** 31, DETA *CH* **33** 47-48

SWEENEY, BRIAN P
(**59**) SEAA **59** 03, SDN **37** 04

SWEENEY, HANK 1B
(__) PITN __ 44

SWEENEY, MARK 1B/OF
(30,**23**,8,7, 23,25,11) STLN **30** 95, **23** 96-97, SDN **8** 97-98, CINN **7** 99, MILN **23** 00, **33** 01, SDN **33** 02, COLN **25** 03-04, SDN **11** 05

SWEENEY, MIKE C/1B/DH
(**29**) KCA **29** 95-05

SWEET, RICK C/CH
(45,2,**8**,18) SDN **45/2** 78, NYN **8** 82, SEAA **8** 82-83, *CH* **18** 84, HOUN *CH* **18** 96

SWETONIC, STEVE P
(43,**15**) PITN **43** 32-33, **15** 35

SWIFT, BILL (C.) P
(**18**,26,20) SEAA **18** 85-86, 88-91, SFN **26** 92-94, COLN **20** 95-97, SEAA **26** 98

SWIFT, BILL (V.) P
(**45**,23,22,48, 16) PITN **45** 32-39, BOSN **23** 40, BKNN **22** 41, CHIA **48/16** 43

SWIFT, BOB C
(7,8,1,12,**9**, 42,52,35,51) STLA **7** 40 **8** 41-42, PHIA **8** 42-43, DETA **1** 44-45, **12** 46, **9** 47-53, *CH* **9** 53-54, KCA *CH* **42** 57-59, WASA *CH* **52** 60, DETA *CH* **35** 63, *CH* **51** 63-66, *M* **51** 65, 66

SWIGART, OAD P
(5,**26**) PITN **5** 39, **26** 40

SWINDELL, GREG P
(**21**,29,41,12, 17,37) CLEA **21** 86-91, CINN **29** 92, HOUN **21** 93-95, **41** 95, **21** 96, CLEA **12** 96, MINA **21** 97, **17** 97-98, BOSA **37** 98, ARIN **22** 99-02

SWINGLE, PAUL P
(**20**) CALA **20** 93, (94)

SWISHER, NICK OF S
(25,**33**) OAKA **25** 04, **33** 05

SWISHER, STEVE C/CH F
(**9**,2,8) CHIN **9** 74-77, STLN **2** 78, **9** 79-80, SDN **9** 81-82, NYN *CH* **8** 94, 96

SWITZER, JON P
(43,**48**) TBA **43** 03, **48** 05

SWOBODA, RON (ROCKY) OF/1B/DH
(14,**4**) NYN **14** 65, **4** 66-70, MONN **14** 71, NYA **14** 71-73

SYKES, BOB P
(**27**,42,38) DETA **27** 77-78, STLN **42** 79-80, **38** 81

SZEKELY, JOE OF
(**27**) CINN **27** 53

SZOTKIEWICZ, KEN SS
(**42**) DETA **42** 70

SZUMINSKI, JASON P
(**27**) SDN **58** 04

T

TABAKA, JEFF P
(63,46,**31**,41, 51,49) PITN **63** 94, SDN **46** 94-95, MINA **31** 95, HOUN **31/41** 96, CINN **51** 97, PITN **49** 98, STLN **46** 01

TABB, JERRY 1B/DH
(**12**,14) CHIN **12** 76, OAKA **12** 77, **14** 78

TABLER, PAT 2B/3B/OF/1B/UTIL/DH
(19,**10**,30,35, 15) CHIN **19** 81-82, CLEA **10** 83-88, KCA **30** 88-90, NYN **35** 90, TORA **15** 91-92

TABOR, GREG 2B/DH
(**3**) TEXA **3** 87

TABOR, JIM (RAWHIDE) 3B/SS/OF
(26,**5**) BOSA **26** 38, **5** 39-44, PHIN **5** 46-47

TACKETT, JEFF C/3B/P
(49,**41**) BALA **49** 91, **41** 91-94

TADANO, KAZUHITO P
(**32**) CLEA **32** 04-05

TAGUCHI, SO OF
(**99**) STLN **99** 02-05

(Far top) Lonnie Smith played in five World Series with four teams. An offensive-minded player, with the Cards he had most runs (6) and doubles (4) in the '82 WS, most doubles (3) in the '85 WS with KC, most HR (3) in '91 WS and most RBI (5) in '92 with Atlanta. (Far bottom) Bill Swift broke in with Seattle in 1985, but his best year was in 1993 with the Giants going 21-8. He had a no-decision in the only playoff game the Rockies won in 1995, leaving in the 7th with a 5-4 lead.

(Above) A Texas Longhorn with Roger Clemens, Greg Swindell never quite reached expectations. The second pick overall in the 1986 free-agent draft, he hovered around the .500 mark. In 1988 he was 18-14 for the Indians, his best year. An All-Star the following year, he again broke down with elbow problems.

TAITT, DOUG (POCO) PH
(no#) PHIN **no#** 32
TAKATSU, SHINGO P
(**10**) CHIA **10** 04-05, NYN **10** 05
TALBOT, DALE (BOB) OF
(**10**) CHIN **10** 53-54
TALBOT, FRED (BUBBY) P
(35,28,**22**,23, 17,46) CHIA **35** 63-64, KCA **28** 65-66, NYA **22** 66-69, SEAA **23** 69, OAKA **17** 69-70, **46** 70
TALCOTT, ROY P
(**28**) BOSN **28** 43
TALLET, BRIAN P
(60,**30**) CLEA **60** 02, **30** 03, (04), 05
TALTON, TIM C/1B
(**11**) KCA **11** 66-67
TAM, JEFF P
(36,38,46,**29**, 33) NYN **36/38** 98, CLEA **46** 99, NYN **38** 99, OAKA **29** 00-02, TORA **33** 03
TAMARGO, JOHN C/CH
(**12**,30,26,11) STLN **12** 76-78, SFN **30** 78-79, MONN **26** 79-80, **11** 80, HOUN *CH* **30** 99-04
TAMULIS, VITO P
(22,20,10,**15**) NYA **22** 34-35, STLA **20** 38, BKNN **15** 38-40, PHIN **10** 41, BKNN **15** 41
TANANA, FRANK P
(**40**,28,26,29, 31) CALA **40** 73-80, BOSA **40** 81, TEXA **28** 83-85, DETA **26** 85-92, NYN **29** 93, NYA **31** 93
TANKERSLEY, DENNIS P
(**45**,49) SDN **45** 02-03, **49** 04
TANNER, BRUCE P/CH S
(**31**,52) CHIA **31** 85, PITN *CH* **52** 01-05
TANNER, CHUCK OF/M F
(**18**,39,6,43, 11,31,7,4,52) MILN **18** 55-57, CHIN **39** 57, **6** 58, CLEA **43** 59, **6** 60, LAA **11** 61-62, CHIA *M* **31** 70, *M* **7** 71-75, OAKA *M* **7** 76, PITN *M* **4** 77, *M* **7** 77-85, ATLN *M* **7** 86-88, MILA *CH* **7** 97, PITN *CH* **52** 05
TAPANI, KEVIN P
(26,**36**,46,60) NYN **26** 89, MINA **36** 89-95, LAN **46** 95, CHIA **36** 96-98, CHIN **36** 99-01
TAPPE, EL C/CH/M
(55,**10**,2,52) CHIN **55** 54-56, **10** 58, *CH* **10** 59, **2** 60, *CH* **2** 60, *CH* **52** 61, 62, *M* **52** 61-62, **52** 62
TAPPE, TED P
(2,26,**4**) CINN **2** 50, **26** 51, CHIN **4** 55
TARASCO, TONY OF/1B
(26,44,**1**,3,43, 45) ATLN **26** 93-94, MONN **44** 95, BALA **1** 96, **3/43** 97, CINN **45** 98, NYA **22** 99, NYN **40** 02
TARTABULL, DANNY SS.2B/3B/OF/UTIL/DH S
(38,4,**45**) SEAA **38** 84-86, **4** 86, KCA **4** 87-91, NYA **45** 92-95, OAKA **45** 95, CHIA **45** 96, PHIN **45** 97
TARTABULL, JOSE OF F
(**15**,10,12,31) KCA **15** 62-64, **10** 65-66, BOSA **12** 66-68, OAKA **31** 69-70
TARVER, LA SCHELLE OF
(**55**) BOSA **55** 86-87
TASBY, WILLIE OF/3B/2B
(**44**,10,1,6,28) BALA **44** 58-60, BOSA **10** 60, WASA **1** 61-62, CLEA **6** 62, **28** 63
TASCHNER, JACK P
(**37**) SFN **37** 05
TATE, AL P
(**11**) PITN **11** 46
TATE, BENNIE C
(14,8,**2**,11) WASA **14** 30, CHIA **8** 31, **2** 32, BOSA **8** 32, CHIN **11** 34
TATE, LEE (SKEETER) SS/INF
(36,**19**) STLN **36** 58, **19** 59
TATE, RANDY P
(**48**) NYN **48** 75
TATE, STU P
(**53**) SFN **53** 89
TATIS, FERNANDO 3B
(4,11,**23**,21) TEXA **4** 97-98, STLN **11** 98, **23** 98-00, MONN **21** 02-03
TATIS, RAMON P
(**52**) CHIN **52** 97, TBA **52** 98
TATUM, JARVIS OF
(35,**8**) CALA **35** 68, **8** 69-70
TATUM, JIM 3B/1B/UTIL
(39,20,19,48, **2**,19) MILA **39** 92, COLN **20** 93, **19** 95, BOSA **48** 96, SDN **2** 96, NYN **19** 98
TATUM, KEN P
(**19**,25,41) CALA **19** 69-70, BOSA **25/41** 71, **19** 72-74
TATUM, TOMMY P
(24,**17**) BKNN **24** 41, **17** 47, CINN **24** 47
TAUBENSEE, EDDIE C
(56,6,**10**,16) CLEA **56** 91, HOUN **6** 92-94, CINN **10** 94-00, CLEA **16** 01
TAUBY, FRED OF
(45,**37**) CHIA **45** 35, PHIN **37** 37
TAUSCHER, WALT P
(**21**) WASA **21** 31
TAUSSIG, DON P
(14,27,20) SFN **14** 58, STLN **27** 61 HOUN **20** 62
TAVAREZ, JESUS OF
(**20**,30,32) FLAN **20** 94-96, BOSA **30** 97, BALA **32** 98
TAVAREZ, JULIAN P
(**50**,52) CLEA **50** 93-96, SFN **52** 97, **50** 98, SFN **50** 99, COLN **50** 00, CHIN **50** 01, FLAN **50** 02, PITN **50** 03, STLN **50** 04-05
TAVERAS, ALEX SS/2B/INF
(15,**37**) HOUN **15** 76, LAN **37** 82-83
TAVERAS, FRANK SS/2B
(50,37,**10**,11) PITN **50/37** 71, **10** 72, 74-79, NYN **11** 79-81, MONN **11** 82
TAVERAS, WILLY OF
(**1**) HOUN **1** 04-05
TAYLOR, AARON P
(52,**54**) SEAA **52** 02, **54** 03-04
TAYLOR, BENNIE 1B
(8,30,**19**) STLA **8** 51, DETA **30** 52, MILN **19** 55
TAYLOR, BILL OF
(**27**,21,29) NYN **27** 54-56, **21** 57, DETA **29** 57-58
TAYLOR, BILLY P
(**22**,26,37,36) OAKA **22** 94, 96-99, NYN **26** 99, TBA **37** 00, PITN **36** 01
TAYLOR, BOB OF/C
(**31**) SFN **31** 70
TAYLOR, BRUCE P
(**32**) DETA **32** 78-79
TAYLOR, CARL C/OF/1B/UTIL
(36,44,45,11, **14**) PITN **36** 68-69, **44** 69, STLN **44** 70, PITN **45** 71, KCA **44** 71, **14** 72-73
TAYLOR, CHUCK P
(**42**,30,36,21) STLN **42** 69-71, NYN **42** 72, MILA **30** 72, MONN **36** 73-75, **21** 76
TAYLOR, DANNY OF
(5,**9**) CHIN **5** 32,BKNN **9** 32-36
TAYLOR, DORN P
(**52**,46) PITN **52** 87, 89, BALA **46** 90
TAYLOR, DWIGHT OF/DH
(**15**) KCA **15** 86
TAYLOR, FRED 1B
(46,36,**34**) WASA **46** 50-51, **36** 51, **36/34** 52
TAYLOR, GARY P
(**47**) DETA **47** 69
TAYLOR, HARRY (E.) P
(**15**) KCA **15** 57
TAYLOR, HARRY (W.) 1B
(**19**) CHIN **32** 32
TAYLOR, (J.) HARRY P
(38,**41**,36,12, 23) BKNN **38** 46, **41** 47-49, BOSA **36/35** 50, **12** 51, **23** 52
TAYLOR, HAWK C/OF/1B
(**19**,15,26,29, 17,16,31) MILN **19** 57-58, **15** 58, **26** 61, **29** 62-63, NYN **19** 64-67, **17** 67, CALA **16** 67, KCA **31** 69-70
TAYLOR, JOE (CASH) OF
(20,**27**,21,22) PHIA **20** 54, CINN **27** 57, STLN **21/22** 58, BALA **27** 58-59
TAYLOR, KERRY
(**37**) SDN **37** 93-94
TAYLOR, PETE P
(**23**) STLA **23** 52
TAYLOR, REGGIE OF
(28,**19**) PHIN **28** 00-01, CINN **19** 02-03, TBA **29** 05
TAYLOR, RON P
(20,22,39,46, 40,**42**) CLEA **20/22** 62, **39** 63-65, HOUN **46** 65, **40** 65-66, NYN **42** 67-71, SDN **42** 67-71, SDN **42** 72
TAYLOR, SAMMY C
(15,7,16,**5**) CHIN **15** 58-59, **7** 61-62, NYN **16** 62-63, CINN **7** 63, CLEA **5** 63
TAYLOR, SCOTT P
(**56**,26) BOSA **56** 92-93, TEXA **57** 95
TAYLOR, TERRY P
(50,**44**) SEAA **50/44** 88
TAYLOR, TONY 2B/3B/SS/INF/UTIL/CH
(5,**8**,10,12) CHIN **5** 58-60, PHIN **8** 60-71, DETA **10** 71-73, PHIN **12** 74-76, *CH* **12** 77-79, 88-89, FLAN *CH* **8** 99-01, 04
TAYLOR, WADE P
(**41**) NYA **41** 91
TAYLOR, ZACK C/CH/M
(23,**34**,14,27, 20,36,38) CHIN **23/34** 32, **14** 33, NYA **27** 34, BKNN **20** 35, *CH* **20** 36, STLA *CH* **36** 41, *CH* **34** 42-46, *M* **34** 46, PITN *CH* **38** 47, STLA *M* **38** 48-51
TEACHOUT, BUD P
(no#) STLN **no#** 32
TEAHEN, MARK 3B
(**24**) KCA **24** 05
TEBBETTS, BIRDIE C/M
(16,28,**1**,8,15, 6) DETA **16** 36, **28** 37-38, **1** 39-42, 46-47, BOSA **8** 47-50, CLEA **15** 51-52, CINN *M* **1** 54-58, MILN *M* **6** 61-62, CLEA *M* **1** 63-66
TEED, DICK PH
(**9**) BKNN **9** 53
TEIXEIRA, MARK 1B/DH
(**23**) TEXA **23** 03-05
TEJADA, MIGUEL SS
(**4**,10) OAKA **4** 97-03, BALA **10** 04-05
TEJADA, WIL C
(55,**11**) MONN **55** 86, **11** 88
TEJEDA, ROB P
(**50**) PHIN **50** 05
TEJERA, MICHAEL P
(**58**,56) FLAN **58** 99, (00), 02-04, TEXA **56** 04-05
TEKULVE, KENT P
(32,**27**,43) PITN **32** 74, **27** 75-85, PHIN **27** 85-88, CINN **43** 89
TELEMACO, AMAURY P
(44,**47**,57) CHIN **44** 96-98, ARIN **44** 98-99, PHIN **47** 99-01, 03-04, **57** 04-05
TELFORD, ANTHONY P
(21,**50**,32) BALA **21** 90, **50** 90-91, 93, MONN **32** 97-01, TEXA **32** 02
TELGHEDER, DAVE P
(38,40,**50**) NYN **38** 93-94, **40** 95, OAKA **50** 96-98
TELLMANN, TOM P
(49,**42**,34) SDN **49** 79-80, MILA **42** 83-84, OAKA **34** 85
TEMPLE, JOHNNY 2B/OF/1B/3B/CH
(**16**,1,2,5) CINN **16** 52-59, CLEA **1** 60, **16** 60-61, BALA **2** 62, HOUN **26** 62, **16** 63, CINN *CH* **5** 64
TEMPLE, LEW CH
(__) SEAA __ 81
TEMPLETON, CHUCK P
(18,49,**28**) BKNN **18** 55, **49** 56, **28** 55-56
TEMPLETON, GARRY SS/3B/UTIL
(**1**,11) STLN **19** 76, **1** 77-81, SDN **1** 82-91, NYN **11** 91
TENACE, GENE C/OF/1B/UTIL/CH
(24,38,**18**,15, 14) OAKA **24** 69, **38** 70-72, **18** 73-76, SDN **18** 77-80, STLN **18** 81-82, PITN **18** 83, HOUN *CH* **18** 86-87, TOR *CH* **15** 90, *CH* **18** 91-96, *CH* **14** 97
TEPEDINO, FRANK 1B/OF/INF
(70,47,46,21, **7**,41) NYA **70/47** 67, **46** 69, **21** 70-71, MILA **7** 71, NYA **41** 72, ATLN **7** 73-75
TEPSIC, JOE OF
(**32**) BKNN **32** 46
TERLECKI, BOB P
(**38**) PHIN **38** 72
TERLECKY, GREG P
(**35**) STLN **35** 75
TERPKO, JEFF P
(**46**,48) TEXA **46** 74-76, MONN **48** 77
TERRELL, JERRY UTIL/INF/P
(35,7,**1**) MINA **35** 73, **7** 73-75, **1** 75-77, KCA **1** 78-80
TERRELL, WALT P
(49,**35**,34) NYN **49** 82-84, DETA **35** 85-88, SDN **35** 89, NYA **34** 89, PITN **35** 90, DETA **35** 90-92
TERRERO, LUIS OF
(**27**) ARIN **27** 03-05
TERRY, BILL (MEMPHIS BILL) 1B/M
(4,**3**,30) NYN **4** 32, *M* **4** 32, **3** 33-36, *M* **3** 33-36, *M* **30** 37-41
TERRY, RALPH P
(21,26,**23**,32, 46,25,38,29) NYA **21** 56-57, KCA **26** 57-59, NYA **23** 59-64, CLEA **32** 65, KCA **26** 66, NYN **46/25** 66, **38** 66-67, **29** 67
TERRY, SCOTT P
(59,38,**37**) CINN **59/38** 86, STLN **37** 87-91
TERRY, YANK P
(27,**18**) BOSA **27** 40, **18** 42-45
TERWILLIGER, DICK P
(**31**) STLN **31** 32
TERWILLIGER, WAYNE (TWIG) 2B/3B/INF/UTIL/CH
(6,21,34,12, 10,**1**,44,42, 45) CHIN **6** 49, **21** 50-51, BKNN **34** 51, WASA **12** 53-54, NYN **34** 55, **10** 56, KCA **1** 59-60, WASA *CH* **44** 69-71, TEXA *CH* **44** 72, *CH* **42** 81-85, MINA *CH* **45** 86-94
TESSMER, JAY P
(**62**) NYA **62** 98, **57** 99, **62** 00, **48** 02
TESTA, NICK C/CH
(**47**,45) SFN **47** 58, *CH* **45** 58
TETTLEBACH, DICK (TUT) OF
(44,34,32,**4**) NYA **44** 55, WASA **34** 56, **32** 56, **4/32** 57
TETTLETON, MICKEY C/UTIL/DH
(6,14,**20**,15) OAKA **6** 84-87, BALA **14** 88-90, DETA **20** 91-94, TEXA **15** 95-97
TEUFEL, TIM 2B/1B/3B/INF/UTIL
(34,5,**11**,20) MINA **34/5** 83, **11** 84-85, NYN **11** 86-91, SDN **20** 91-93
TEUT, NATE P
(**62**) FLAN **53** 02
TEWKSBURY, BOB P
(35,42,**39**,31, 19) NYA **35** 86-87, CHIN **42** 87-88, STLN **39** 89-94, TEXA **39** 95, SDN **31** 96, MINA **19** 97, **39** 98
THACKER, MOE C
(19,23,22,25, **8**,29) CHIN **19/23** 58, **22** 60, **25** 61, **8** 61-62, STLN **29** 63
THAMES, MARCUS OF/DH
(18.27,**33**) NYA **18** 02, TEXA **27** 03, DETA **33** 04-05
THAYER, GREG P
(**18**) MINA **18** 78
THEISS, DUANE P
(52,**34**) ATLN **52** 77, **34** 77-78
THEOBALD, RON 2B/INF
(**16**) MILA **16** 71-72
THEODORE, GEORGE OF/1B
(18,**9**) NYN **18** 73, **9** 73-74
THEODORE, GEORGE OF/1B
(18,**9**) NYN **18** 73, **9** 73-74
THERIOT, RYAN 2B
(**55**) CHIN **55** 05
THESENGA, JUG P
(**11**) WASA **11** 44
THEVENOW, TOMMY SS/3B/INF
(__,**25**,17,32, 22) STLN __ 24, PITN **25** 32-35, CINN **17** 36, BOSN **32** 37, PITN **22** 38
THEIL, BERT P
(**22**) BOSN **22** 52
THIES, DAVE P
(**25**) KCA **25** 63
THIES, JAKE P
(**39**) PITN **39** 54-55
THIGPEN, BOBBY P
(58,**37**,31) CHIA **58** 86, **37** 87-93, PHIN **37** 93, SEAA **31** 94
THOBE, J. J. P
(**39**) MONN **39** 95
THOBE, TOM P
(**49**) ATLN **49** 95-96
THOENEN, DICK P
(**43**) PHIN **43** 67
THOMAS, ANDRES SS/3B
(**14**) ATLN **14** 85-90
THOMAS, BRAD P
(**56**) MINA **56** 01, 03-04
THOMAS, BUD (J.) SS
(**4**) STLA **4** 51
THOMAS, BUD (L.) P
(17,**21**,20,31, 11,22) WASA **17** 32, **21** 33, PHIA **21** 37-38, **20** 38-39, WASA **31** 39, DETA **11** 39-40, **17** 40, **22** 41
THOMAS, CARL P
(**25**) CLEA **25** 60
THOMAS, CHARLES OF
(**26**) CLEA **26** 04, OAKA **26** 05
THOMAS, DANNY OF/DH
(39,**20**) MILA **39** 76-77, **20** 77
THOMAS, DERREL 2B/SS/OF/UTIL
(19,**30**,34,1, 13,15,18) HOUN **19** 71, SDN **30** 72-74, SFN **30** 75-77, SDN **30** 78, LAN **34/1** 79, **30** 80-83, MONN **13** 84, CALA **15/30** 84, PHIN **18** 85
THOMAS, FAY (SCOW) P
(25,26,**17**) CLEA **25** 31, BKNN **26** 32, STLA **17** 35
THOMAS, FRANK (E.) (THE BIG HURT) 1B/DH
(**35**) CHIA **35** 90-05
THOMAS, FRANK (J.) OF/3B/1B/UTIL
(27,28,**15**,25, 12,45,24,31, 39) PITN **27** 51, **28** 52, **15** 53-58, CINN **15** 59, CHIN **25** 60-61, MILN **12** 61, NYN **25** 62-64, PHIN **45** 64, **24** 65, HOUN **31** 65, MILN **39** 65, CHIN __ 66
THOMAS, GEORGE 3B/OF/SS/INF/UTIL
(28,15,**24**,17, 4, 22) DETA **28** 57, **15** 58, **24** 61, LAA **4** 61-63, DETA **24** 63-65, BOSA **24** 66-67, **17** 68, **22** 69-71, MINA **24** 71
THOMAS, GORMAN OF/UTIL/DH
(44,3,**20**) MILA **44** 73-74, **3** 75-6, **20** 78-83, CLEA **20** 83, SEAA **20** 84-86, MILA **20** 86
THOMAS, KITE OF/C
(**6**,26) PHIA **6** 52-53, WASA **26** 53
THOMAS, LARRY P
(**50**) CHIA **50** 95-97
THOMAS, LEE OF/'B/CH
(17,**32**,6,9,8, 28,50) NYA **17** 61, LAA **32** 61-64, BOSA **6** 64-65, ATLN **9** 66, CHIN **8** 66-67, HOUN **28** 68, STLN *CH* **50** 71-72
THOMAS, LEO (TOMMY) 3B/INF
(2,8,**3**) STLA **2** 50, **8** 52, CHIA **3** 52
THOMAS, MIKE P
(**53**) MILA **53** 95
THOMAS, MYLES P
(**20**) NYA **20** 29
THOMAS, RAY C
(**7**) BKNN **7** 38
THOMAS, ROY P
(45,42,43,**49**) HOUN **45** 77, STLN **42** 78, **43** 79-80, SEAA **49** 83-85, 87
THOMAS, STAN P
(**23**,52,36) TEXA **23** 74-75, CLEA **23** 76, SEAA **23** 77, NYA **52/36/23** 77
THOMAS, TOMMY P
(**15**,17,20,__, 25,32) CHIA **15** 31, **17** 32, WASA **20** 32-33, **15** 33-35, PHIN __ 35, STLA **25** 36-37, BOSA **32** 37
THOMAS, VALMY C/3B
(16,7,8,41,15) NYN **16** 57, SFN **7** 58, PHIN **8** 59, BALA **41** 60, CLEA **15** 61
THOMASON, ERSKINE P
(**48**) PHIN **48** 74
THOMASSON, GARY OF/1B/DH
(**12**,24,9) SFN **12** 72-77, OAKA **12** 78, NYA **24** 78, LAN **9** 6979-80
THOME, JIM 3B/1B
(6,**25**) CLEA **6** 91, **25** 92-02, PHIN **25** 03-05
THOMPSON, ANDY OF
(**12**) TORA **16** 00, **15** 01
THOMPSON, BOBBY OF/DH
(48,**20**) TEXA **48/20** 78
THOMPSON, BRAD P
(**48**) STLN **48** 05
THOMPSON, DANNY 2B/SS/3B/INF/UTIL
(**5**,4) MINA **5** 70-76, TEXA **4** 76
THOMPSON, DON OF
(23,**29**) BOSN **23** 49, BKNN **29** 51, 53-54
THOMPSON, DEREK P
(**56**) LAN **56** 05
THOMPSON, FORREST P
(**12**) WASA **12** 48-49
THOMPSON, FRESCO (TOMMY) INF
(no#,**24**) BKNN **no#** 32 , NYN **24** 34
THOMPSON, HANK 2B/3B/OF/UTIL
(7,**16**) STLA **7** 47, NYN **16** 49-56

THOMPSON, JASON (D.) 1B/DH
(30,22,24,35) DETA 30 76-80, CALA 22 80, PITN 30 81-85, MONN 24 86

THOMPSON, JASON (M.) 1B
(35) SDN 35 96

THOMPSON, JOCKO P
(9,37,33) PHIN 9 48, 37 49, 33 50-51

THOMPSON, JUNIOR P
(39,42,35) CINN 39 39-42, NYN 42 46, 35 47

THOMPSON, JUSTIN P
(22,38) DETA 22 96-99, TEXA 38 05

THOMPSON, MARK P
(47,32,29,43, 46) COLN 47 94, 32 95-98, 29 98, STLN 43 99, 46 00

THOMPSON, MIKE P
(24,46,41,33) WASA 24 71, STLN 46 73-74, ATLN 41 74, 33 75

THOMPSON, MILT OF/CH
(30,28,24,25, 29,27,15) ATLN 30 84-85, PHIN 28 86, 24 86-88, STLN 25 89-92, PHIN 25 93-94, HOUN 28 94-95, LAN 29 96, COLN 27 96, PHIN *CH* 15 04-05

THOMPSON, RICH P
(41,48) CLEA 41 85, MONN 48 89-90

THOMPSON, RICH OF
(24) KCA 24 04

THOMPSON, ROBBY 2B/SS/CH
(6,5) SFN 6 86-96, *CH* 5 00-01, CLEA *CH* 6 02, 05

THOMPSON, RYAN OF
(44,20,46,35, 88,33,45,14, 38) NYN 44 92-93, 20 94-95, CLEA 46 96, HOUN 35 99, NYA 88/33/45 00, FLAN 14 01, MILN 38 02

THOMPSON, SCOT OF/1B
(25,29,18,41, 24) CHIN 25 78-81, 29 81, 18 82-83, SFN 41 84-85, MONN 24 85

THOMPSON, TIM C/OF
(21,22,12) BKNN 21 54, KCA 22 56-57, DETA 12 58

THOMPSON, TOMMY OF/1B
(18,25,13,6, 33) BOSN 22 33, 18 34, 25 35, 13 36, CHIA 6 38-39, STLA 33 39

THOMSON, BOBBY (THE FLYING SCOT)(THE STATEN ISLAND SCOT) 3B/OF/2B/1B
(23,19,34,25, 21,9,35) NYN 23 46, 19 47-48, 23 49-53, MILN 34 54-55, 25 56-57, NYN 21 57, CHIN 9 58-59, BOSA 25 60, BALA 35 60

THOMSON, JOHN P
(52,50,46) COLN 52 97-99, (00), 01-02, NYN 50 02, TEXA 46 03, ATLN 52 04-05

THON, DICKIE SS/INF/DH
(31,10,21,8) CALA 31 79-80, HOUN 10 81-87, SDN 21 88, PHIN 21 89-91, TEXA 10 92, MILA 8 93

THORMODSGARD, PAUL P
(23) MINA 23 77-79

THORNTON, ANDRE (ANDY) OF/1B/3B/DH
(12,1729) CHIN 12 73-76, MONN 17 76, CLEA 29 77-79, 81-87

THORNTON, LOU OF/DH
(28,4,1) TORA 28 85, 87-88, NYN 4 89, 1 90

THORNTON, MATT P
(43,54,53) SEAA 43 04, 54/53 05

THORNTON, OTIS C
(9) HOUN 9 73

THORPE, BOB OF
(8,18) BOSN 8 51, 18 52, MILN 18 53

THORPE, BOB P
(26) CHIN 26 55

THRONEBERRY, FAYE OF B
(37,2,26,4,30, 29) BOSA 37/2 52, 26 55-57, WASA 4 57, 30 58-60, LAA 29 61

THRONEBERRY, MARV (MARVELOUS MARV) 1B/OF B
(41,20,3,8,2) NYA 41 55, 20 58-59, KCA 3 60-61, BALA 8 61-62, NYN 2 62-63

THROOP, GEORGE P
(42,35,33) KCA 42/35 75, 35 77-79, HOUN 33 79

THUMAN, LOU P
(41,__) WASA 41 39, __ 40

THURMAN, BOB OF
(22) CINN 22 55-59

THURMAN, COREY CH
(22) TORA *CH* 35 02-03

THURMAN, GARY OF/DH
(53,25,15,32, 10) KCA 53 87, 25 87-92, DETA 15 93, SEAA 32 95, NYN 10 97

THURMAN, MIKE P
(51,35,53) MONN 51 97, 35 98-01, NYA 53 02

THURMOND, MARK P
(58,38,40,57, 53,21,30) SDN 58 83, 38 83-86, DETA 38 86, 40 86-87, BALA 57/53 88, 21 88-89, SFN 30 90

THURSTON, JOE 2B
(41,49) LAN 41 02, 49 03-04

THURSTON, SLOPPY P
(20) BKNN 20 32-33

TIANT, LUIS P
(33,23,38) CLEA 33 64-69, MINA 33 70, BOSA 23 71-78, NYA 23 79-80, PITN 38 81, CALA 23/33 82

TIBBS, JAY P
(38,39,50,53, 30) CINN 38 84-85, MONN 39 86, 50 87, BALA 53 88-89, 50 89-90, PITN 30 90

TIDROW, DICK P
(41,19,32) CLEA 41 72-74, NYA 19 74-79, CHIN 41 79-82, CHIA 41 83, NYN 32 84

TIEFENAUER, BOBBY P/CH
(44,34,28,43, 18,29,36,38, 22,5) STLN 44 52, 34 55, CLEA 28 60, STLN 43 61, HOUN 44 62, MILN 18 63-65, NYA 29 65, CLEA 36 65, 41 67, CHIN 38/22 68, PHIN *CH* 5 79

TIEFENTHALER, VERLE P
(41) CHIA 41 62

TIETJE, LES (TOOTS) P
(35,38,21,19, 17) CHIA 35 33, 38/21 34, 19 35, 17 36, STLA 19 36-38

TIFFEE, TERRY 3B/1B
(30,10,23) MINA 32 04-05

TIGHE, JACK CH/M
(31,35) DETA *CH* 31 42, *CH* 35 55-56, *M* 35 57-58

TILLMAN, BOB C
(30,10,23) BOSA 30 62, 10 63-67, NYA 23 67, ATLN 10 68-70

TILLMAN, RUSTY OF
(34,24,30) NYN 34 82, OAKA 24 86, SFN 30 88

TILLOTSON, THAD P
(54) NYA 54 67-68

TIMBERLAKE, GARY C
(45) SEAA 45 69

TIMLIN, MIKE P
(40,50) TORA 40 91-97, SEAA 40 97-98, BALA 40 99-00, STLN 50 00-02, PHIN 50 02, BOSA 50 03-05

TIMMERMANN, TOM P
(28,31,39) DETA 28 69-73, CLEA 31 73-74, 39 74

TIMMONS, OZZIE OF
(30,31) CHIN 30 95-96, CINN 31 97, SEAA 40 99, TBA 44 00

TINCUP, BEN CH
(22) BKNN *CH* 22 40

TINGLEY, RON C
(5,18,32,24, 22,43,55,25) SDN 5 82, CLEA 18 88, CALA 32 89-90, 24 91-93, FLAN 22/43 94, CHIA 55 94, DETA 25 95

TINNING, BUD P
(29,21,22,19) CHIN 29/21 32, 22 33-34, STLN 19 35

TINSLEY, LEE OF/DH
(27,38,26,47, 10,5) SEAA 27 93, BOSA 38 94-95, 26 95, PHIN 26 96, BOSA 47/10 96, SEAA 5 97

TIPTON, ERIC (BLUE DEVIL)(DUKIE) OF
(18,40,38,23) PHIA 18 39, 40 40, 38 41, CINN 23 42-45

TIPTON, JOE C
(12,15,18,10) CLEA 12 48, CHIA 15 49, PHIA 15 50-52, CLEA 18 52-53, WASA 10 54

TISCHINSKI, TOM C
(22) MINA 22 69-71

TISING, JACK P
(44) PITN 44 36

TOBIK, DAVE P
(38,45,41) DETA 38 78-80, 45 81-82, TEXA 41 83-84, SEAA 41 85

TOBIN, JACK CH
(25,33) STLA *CH* 25 49, *CH* 33 50-51

TOBIN, JIM (ABBA DABBA) P B
(50,22,14) PITN 50 37-39, BOSN 22 40-45, DETA 12/14/22 45

TOBIN, JOHNNY (TIP) PH
(30) NYN 30 32

TOBIN, JOHNNY (JACKIE) 3B/UTIL B
(3) BOSA 3 45

TOBIN, PAT P
(24) PHIA 24 41

TOCA, JORGE 1B
(30) NYN 30 99-01, (02)

TODD, AL C/OF
(9,10,11,30, 2) PHIN 9 32, 10 33, 11 34-35, PITN 30 36-38, BKNN 21 39, CHIN 10 40, 2 41, 11 43

TODD, JACKSON P
(30,40) NYN 30 77, TORA 32 79, 40 80-81

TODD, JIM P
(39,50,22,31, 27,28) CHIN 39 74, OAKA 39/50 75, 22 75-76, CHIN 31 77, SEAA 27 78, OAKA 28 79

TODT, PHIL (HOOK) 1B
(24) PHIA 24 31

TOENES, HAL P
(19) WASA 19 47

TOLAN, BOBBY OF/1B/CH
(17,28,24,13, 22) STLN 17 65-68, CINN 28 69-70, 72-73, SDN 28 74-75, PHIN 28 76-77, PITN 24 77, SDN 13 79, *CH* 13 80, 22 81, 28 81-83, SEAA *CH* 28 87

TOLAR, KEVIN P
(52,51) DETA 52 00-01, BOSA 51 03

TOLENTINO, JOSE 1B/OF
(20) HOUN 20 91

TOLIVER, FREDDIE P
(59,30,43,31, 41,61) CINN 59/30 84, PHIN 43 85-87, MINA 31 88-89, SDN 41 89, PITN 61 93

TOLLBERG, BRIAN P
(20) SDN 55 00-03

TOLLESON, WAYNE 3B/SS/INF/UTIL/DH
(3,1,2) TEXA 3 81-85, CHIA 1 86, NYA 2 86-90

TOLMAN, TIM OF/1B/UTIL/DH
(38,18) HOUN 38 81-84, 18 84-85, DETA 38 86-87

TOMANEK, DICK (BONES) P
(28,29,39,15) CLEA 28 53-54, 29 57-58, KCA 39 58, 15 58-59

TOMASIC, ANDY P
(48) NYN 48 49

TOMBERLIN, ANDY OF
(59,30,33) PITN 59 93, BOSA 30 94, OAKA 33 95-96, NYN 33 97, DETA 30 98

TOMKO, BRETT P
(40,20,30,50, 35) CINN 40 97-99, SEAA 40 00-01, SDN 20 02, STLN 30 03, SFN 50 04-05, 35 05

TOMLIN, DAVE P
(49,37,43,34 35,24) CINN 49 72-73, SDN 37 74-77, CINN 43 78, 37 78-80, MONN 37 82, PITN 34 83, 35 85, MONN 24 86

TOMLIN, RANDY P
(29) PITN 29 91-94

TOMPKINS, RON (STRETCH) P
(46,38) KCA 46 65, CHIN 38 71

TOMS, TOMMY P
(40,51) SFN 40 75, 51 76-77

TONEY, FRED P
(49) STLN 49 23

TONIS, MIKE C
(3) KCA 3 04

TOPORCER, SPECS INF
(26,11) STLN 26 23, 11 23-24

TOPPIN, RUPE 1B/UTIL
(31) KCA 31 62

TORBORG, JEFF C/CH/M
(10,3,6,7,31, 47,41,11,44, 1) LAN 10 64-70, CALA 3 71, 10 72-73, CLEA *CH* 6 75-76, *CH* 7 76-77, *M* 7 77, *M* 10 77-79, NYA *CH* 31/47 79, *CH* 41 80-83, *CH* 11 83, *CH* 44 84-88, CHIA *M* 10 89-91, NYN *M* 10 92-93, MONN *M* 1 01, FLAN *M* 10 02-03

TORCATO, TONY OF
(14,20,51,21) SFN 14 02, 20/51 03, 21 04-05

TORCHIA, TONY CH
(32) BOSA *CH* 32 85

TORGESON, EARL (THE EARL OF SNOHOMISH) 1B/OF
(9,17,29) BOSN 9 47-52, PHIN 9 53-55, DETA 9 55-57, CHIA 17 57-61, NYA 29 61

TORRE, FRANK 1B
(14,30,16) MILN 14 56-60, PHIN 30/16 62, 14 63

TORRE, JOE C/1B/3B/UTIL/M
(15,9,22,6) MILN 15 60-65, ATLN 15 66-68, STLN 9 69-74, NYN 9 75-77, *M* 9 77-81, ATLN *M* 9 82-84, STLN *M* 22 90, *M* 9 91-95, NYA *M* 6 96-05

TORREALBA, PABLO P
(39,36,28,35) ATLN 39/36 75, 28 76, OAKA 28 77, CHIA 35 78-79

TORREALBA, STEVE C
(39,36,28,35) ATLN 50 02

TORREALBA, YORVIT C
(9,8) SFN 9 01-02, 8 03-05, SEAA 8 05

TORRES, ANDRES OF
(44,2) DETA 44 02-04, TEXA 2 05

TORRES, ANGEL P
(36,38,46) CINN 36/38/46 77

TORRES, DILSON P
(52) KCA 52 95

TORRES, FELIX 3B/1B
(19) LAA 19 62-64

TORRES, GIL P/3B/INF
(34,25) WASA 34 40, 25 44-46

TORRES, HECTOR SS/2B/INF/UTIL/P/CH
(15,21,25,17, 30,29,56) HOUN 15 68-70, CHIN 21 71, MONN 25 72, HOUN 17 73, SDN 30 75-76, TORA 29 77, *CH* 56 91

TORRES, RUSTY OF/UTIL/DH
(21,28,3,2) NYA 21 71-72, CLEA 28 73-74, CALA 3 76-77, CHIA 21 78-79, KCA 2 80

TORRES, SALOMON P
(35,38,44,31, 16) SFN 35 93-95, SEAA 38 95-97, MONN 44 97, PITN 31 02-03, 16 04-05

TORREZ, MIKE P
(48,24,36,21, 30,33) STLN 48 67-71, MONN 24 71-74, BALA 24 75, OAKA 24 76-77, NYA 48/36/24 77, BOSA 21 78-82, NYN 30 83-84, OAKA 33 84

TORVE, KELVIN 1B/OF/DH
(18,39) MINA 18 88, NYN 39 90-91

TOSCA, CARLOS CH/M
(14) ARIN *CH* 14 98-00, TORA *CH* 14 02, *M* 14 02-04, ARIN *CH* 14 05

TOST, LOU P
(27,23) BOSN 27 42-43, PITN 23 47

TOTH, PAUL P
(42,39) STLN 42 62, CHIN 39 62-64

TOUCHSTONE, CLAY P
(37) CHIA 37 45

TOVAR, CESAR (PEPITO) OF/INF/UTIL/DH
(12,7,3,2,26) MINA 12 65-72, PHIN 12 73, TEXA 7 74, 12 74-75, OAKA 3 75-76, 2 76,NYA 26 76

TOWERS, JOSH P
(35,7) BALA 35 01-02, 7 03, TORA 7 04-05

TRABER, BILLY P
(40) CLEA 40 03

TRABER, JIM 1B/UTIL/DH
(28) BALA 28 84, 86, 88-89

TRACEWSKI, DICK SS/2B/INF/CH
(44,53) LAN 44 62-65, DETA 44 66-69, *CH* 53 72-95

TRACHSEL, STEVE P
(46,29) CHIN 46 93-99, TBA 46 00, TORA 46 00, NYN 29 01-05

TRACY, ANDY INF/1B
(46,22,18) MONN 46 00, 22 01, COLN 18 04

TRACY, CHAD 3B
(18) ARIN 18 04-05

TRACY, JIM (TRACE) OF/1B/CH/M
(23,12,16) CHIN 23 80-81, MONN *CH* 23 95-98, LAN *CH* 12 99-00, *M* 12 01-04, 16 04-05

TRAMBACK, RED OF
(2) NYN 2 40

TRAMMELL, ALAN SS/C/UTIL/DH/CH/M
(42,3) DETA 42 77, 3 78-96, *CH* 3 99, SDN *CH* 3 00-02, DETA *M* 3 03-05

TRAMMELL, BUBBA OF
(43,44,21,33, 27,29) DETA 43/44 97, TBA 21 98-00, NYN 33 00, SDN 27 01-02, NYN 29 03

TRAUTWEIN, JOHN P
(45,42) BOSA 45/42 88

TRAVERS, BILL P
(46,25,26,35) MILA 46 74-75, 25 74-80, CALA 26 81, 35/26 83

TRAVIS, CECIL 3B/SS/OF/UTIL
(26,31,20,5, 23,7) WASA 26/31 33, 20 34, 5 35-41, 23 45, 7 46-47

TRAXLER, BRIAN 1B
(20) LAN 20 90

TRAYNOR, PIE 3B/1B/M
(20,34,35) PITN 20 32-35, 37, *M* 20 34-37, *M* 34 38, *M* 35 38-39

TREADWAY, JEFF 2B/3B/INF/DH
(58,15,27,12, 14) CINN 58 87, 15 88, ATLN 15 89-92, CLEA 27 93, LAN 12 94-95, MONN 14 95

TREADWAY, RAY 3B
(__) WASA __ 30

TREADWAY, RED OF
(26,2) NYN 26 44, 2 45

TREANOR, MATT C
(6) FLAN 6 04-05

TREBELHORN, TOM CH/M
(35,42,41,55, 49) MILA *CH* 35 84, *M* 42 86-91, CHIN *CH* 41 92-93, *M* 41 94, BALA *CH* 55 01, 49 02, 55 02-03, 49 04, 55 04-05

TRECHOCK, FRANK SS
(40) WASA 40 37

TREMARK, NICK OF
(11,28) BKNN 11 34-35, 28 36

TREMEL, BILL (MUMBLES) P
(33) CHIN 33 54-56

TREMIE, CHRIS C
(53,18,66,59) CHIA 53 95 , TEXA 18 98, PITN 66 99, HOUN 59 04

TRESH, MIKE C F
(15,11) CHIA 15 38-48, CLEA 11 49

TRESH, TOM SS/OF/3B/UTIL S
(15,4) NYA 15 61-69, DETA 4 69

TREUEL, RALPH CH
(51) DETA *CH* 51 95

TREVINO, ALEX C/3B/1B/UTIL B
(29,25,6,9,8) NYN 29 78-81, CINN 29 82-84, ATLN 25 84, SFN 29 85, LAN 29 86-87, HOUN 9 88-90, NYN 6 90, CINN 8 90

TREVINO, BOBBY OF B
(12) CALA 12 68

TRIANDOS, GUS C/1B/UTIL
(26,11,10,9,7) NYA 26 53-54, BALA 11 55-62, DETA 10 63, PHIN 9 64-65, HOUN 7 65

TRICE, BOB P
(23) PHIA 23 53-54, KCA 23 55

TRILLO, MANNY 2B/SS/3B/INF
(8,19,9,17,10) OAKA 8 73-74, CHIN 19 75-78, PHIN 9 79-82, CLEA 8 83, MONN 17 83, SFN 9 84-85, CHIN 19 86-88, CINN 10 89

TRIMBLE, JOE P
(44,36,16) BOSA 44 55, PITN 36/16 57

TRINKLE, KEN P
(19,26,34,22) NYN 19 43, 26 46, 34 47-48, PHIN 22 49

TRIPLETT, COAKER OF
(32,20,4,5,27) CHIN 32 38, STLN 20 41-43, PHIN 4 43-44, 5 44, 27 45

TRLICEK, RICK P
(35,36,15,34, 43,50) TORA 35 92, LAN 36 93, BOSA 15 94, NYN 34 96, BOSA 43 97, NYN 50 97

TROEDSON, RICH P
(47) SDN 47 73-74

TROMBLEY, MIKE P
(20,21,28,40, 19) MINA 20 92, 21 92-99, BALA 28 00-01, LAN 40 01, MINA 19 02

TROSKY, HAL, SR. 1B
(21,7,6) CLEA 25 33, 7 34-41, CHIA 6/7 44, 7 46

TROSKY, HAL, JR. (HOOT) P
(3) CHIA 3 58

TROTTER, BILL P
(9,22,17,14) STLA 9 37-38, 22 39, 17 39-42, WASA 17 42, STLN 14 44

TROUPPE, QUINCY C
(16) CLEA 16 52

TROUT, DIZZY P F
(15,**11**,25,24) DETA **15** 39-40, **11** 41-52, BOSA **25** 52, BALA **24** 57

TROUT, STEVE P S
(33,**34**,35) CHIA **33** 78-82, CHIN **34** 83-87, NYA **35** 87, SEAA **34** 88-89

TROWBRIDGE, BOB P
(**30**,37) MILN **30** 56-59, KCA **37** 60

TRUBY, CHRIS INF/3B
(**6**,26,27,35) HOUN **6** 00-01, MONN **26** 02, DETA **27** 02, TBA **35** 03

TRUCKS, VIRGIL (FIRE) P/CH
(17,**22**,35,23, 11, 21,10) DETA **17** 41, **22** 42-43, **35** 45, **22** 46-52, STLA **22** 53, CHIA **27** 53, **23** 53-55, DETA **23/11** 56, KCA **23** 57-58, NYA **21** 58, PITN *CH* **10** 62-63

TRUJILLO, J. J. P
(**58**) SDN **58** 02

TRUJILLO, MIKE P
(45,**43**,36) BOSA **45** 85-86, SEAA **43** 86 -87, DETA **36** 88, **43** 89

TSAMIS, GEORGE P
(**22**) MINA **22** 93

TSAO, CHIN-HUI P
(**71**) COLN **71** 03-05

TSITOURIS, JOHN P
(12,20,11,**38**, 37) DETA **12** 57, KCA **20** 58-60, **11** 59, CINN **38** 62-67, **37** 68

TUBBS, GREG OF
(**51**) CINN **51** 93

TUCKER, EDDIE (SCOOTER) C
(20,**36**,31,16) HOUN **20** 92, **36** 93, **31/36** 95, CLEA **16** 95

TUCKER, MICHAEL OF/DH
(31,**24**,34,11, 29) KCA **31** 95-96, ATLN **24** 97-98, CINN **34** 99-01, CHIN **11/24** 01, KCA **24** 02-03, SFN **20** 04-05, PHIN **29** 05

TUCKER, THURMAN (JOE E.) OF
(__,8,2,**38**) CHIA __ 42, **8** 43-44, **2** 46-47, CLEA **38** 48-51

TUCKER, T. J. P
(**52**) MONN **52** 00, 02-04, WASN **52** 05

TUDOR, JOHN P
(**30**,24,48) BOSA **30** 79-83, PITN **24** 84, STLN **48** 85, **30** 85-88, LAN **30** 88-89, STLN **30** 90

TUFTS, BOB (BUCK) P
(50,17,27,36) SFN **50/17** 81, KCA **27** 82, **36** 82-83

TUNNELL, LEE P
(**22**,42,27) PITN **22** 82-85, STLN **42** 87, MINA **27** 89

TURANG, BRIAN UTIL
(**1**) SEAA **1** 93-94

TURBEVILLE, GEORGE P
(66,20,18,**24**) PHIA **66/20/18** 35, **20** 36, **24** 37

TURCHIN, EDDIE (SMILEY) 3B/SS
(**14**) CLEA **14** 43

TURLEY, BOB (BULLET BOB) P/CH
(26,24,33,**19**, 39,29,34) STLA **26** 51, **24** 53, BALA **33** 54, NYA **19** 55-62, LAA **39** 63, BOSA **29** 63, *CH* **34** 64

TURNBOW, DERRICK P
(**54**,59) ANAA **54** 00, 03-04, MILN **59** 05

TURNER, CHRIS C
(53,**20**,15,9, 25) CALA **53** 93, **20** 94-96, ANAA **20** 97, KCA **15** 98, CLEA **9** 99, NYA **25** 00

TURNER, EARL C
(31,**10**) PITN **31** 48, **10** 50

TURNER, JERRY OF/DH
(42,2,**20**,24) SDN **42** 74-76, **2** 77, **20** 77-81, CHIA **24** 81, DETA **20** 82, SDN **20** 83

TURNER, JIM (MILKMAN JIM) P/CH
(23,34,**30**,31, 3) BOSN **23** 37-39, CINN **34** 40-42, NYA **30** 42-45, *CH* **31** 49-59, CINN *CH* **3** 61-65, NYA *CH* **31** 66-73

TURNER, JOE OF
(**20**) SDN **20** 83

TURNER, KEN P
(51,**39**) CALA **51/39** 67

TURNER, MATT P
(54,**34**) FLAN **54** 93, CLEA **34** 94

TURNER, RICK CH
(**57**) CALA **57** 91-93

TURNER, SHANE 3B/SS/2B/DH
(25,28,**20**) PHIN **25** 88, BALA **28** 91, SEAA **20** 92

TURNER, TED M (TNT)
(__) ATLN *M* __ 77

TURNER, TOM C
(**17**) CHIA **17** 40-44, STLA **17** 44

TURNER, TUCK CH
(__) STLN *CH* __ 24

TUTTLE, BILL OF/3B/UTIL
(20,17,5,**13**) DETA **20** 52, **17** 54, **5** 55-56, **13** 56-57, KCA **13** 58-61, MINA **13** 61-63

TWITCHELL, WAYNE P
(48,**33**,36,35) MILA **48** 70, PHIN **33** 71-77, MONN **33** 77-78, NYN **36** 79, SEAA **35** 79

TWITTY, JEFF P
(54,**21**) KCA **54/21** 80

TYACK, JIM OF
(**12**) PHIA **12** 43

TYLER, JOHNNIE (TY TY)(KATZ) OF
(23,**24**) BOSN **23** 34, **24** 35

TYNER, JASON OF
(**11**,14,21) NYN **11** 00, TBA **14** 00-02, **11** 03, MINA **21** 05

TYRIVER, DAVE P
(**26**) CLEA **26** 62

TYRONE, JIM OF/3B/UTIL
(**27**,29,26) CHIN **27** 72, 74-75, **29** 75, OAKA **26** 77

TYRONE, WAYNE UTIL
(**22**) CHIN **22** 76

TYSON, MIKE 2B
(**10**,4,2,18) STLN **10** 72-78, **4** 79, CHIN **2** 80, **18** 81

TYSON, TURKEY (SLIM) PH
(**22**) PHIN **22** 44

U

UECKER, BOB (UKE) C
(8,**9**,12) MILN **8** 62-63, STLN **9** 64-65, PHIN **9** 66-67, ATLN **12** 67

UGUETO, LUIS DH/INF
(**23**) SEAA **23** 02-03

UHALT, FRENCHY OF
(**36**) CHIA **36** 34

UHL, BOB (LEFTY) P
(47,**22**,25) CHIA **47/22** 38, DETA **25** 40

UHLAENDER, TED (SLIM) OF/CH
(34,16,**11**,26, 26,22) MINA **34** 65-66, **16** 66-67, **11** 67-69, CLEA **26** 70-71, **11** 71, CINN **22** 72, CLEA *CH* **11** 00-01

UHLE, GEORGE (THE BULL) P/CH
(15,**14**,28,26, 10,20,32) DETA **15** 31, **14** 32-33, NYN **28** 33, NYA **26** 33-34, CLEA **10** 36, CHIN *CH* **20** 40, WASA *CH* **32** 44

UHLIR, CHARLIE OF
(**34**) CHIA **34** 34

UJDUR, JERRY P
(**28**,43) DETA **28** 80-83, CLEA **43** 84

ULISNEY, MIKE (SLUGS) C
(**29**) BOSN **29** 45

ULLGER, SCOTT UTIL/CH
(**7**,45,46) MINA **7** 83,*CH* **45** 95-04, **46** 04-05

ULLRICH, SANDY P
(19,28) WASA **19** 44, **28** 45

UMBACH, ARNIE P
(46,**32**) MILN **46** 64, ATLN **32** 66

UMBARGER, JIM P
(**40**,30,23) TEXA **40** 75-76, OAKA **30/23** 77, TEXA **40** 77-78

UMBRICHT, JIM P
(37,45,**32**) PITN **37** 59-61, HOUN **45** 62, **32** 62-63

UMPHLETT, TOMMY OF
(38,4,**22**) BOSA **38** 53, WASA **4** 54, **22** 55

UNDERWOOD, PAT P B
(**40**) DETA **40** 79-80, 82-83

UNDERWOOD, TOM P B
(**34**,40,24,38, 31,42) PHIN **34** 74-77, STLN **40** 77, TORA **24** 78-79, NYA **38** 80-81, OAKA **31** 81-83, BALA **42** 84

UNROE, TIM 1B
(8,**9**,36,20) MILA **8** 95, **9** 96-97, ANAA **36** 99, ATLN **20** 00

UNSER, AL C/2B F
(31,**30**,5) DETA **31** 42, **30** 43-44, CINN **5** 45

UNSER, DEL OF/1B/CH S
(30,1,**25**) WASA **30** 68-71, CLEA **1** 72, PHIN **25** 73-74, NYN **25** 75-76, MONN **25** 76-78, PHIN **25** 79-82, *CH* **25** 85-88

UPCHURCH, WOODY P
(**9**,21) PHIA **9** 35, **21** 36

UPHAM, JOHN P/OF
(45,**37**) CHIN **45** 67, **37** 68

UPRIGHT, DIXIE PH
(**36**) STLA **36** 53

UPSHAW, CECIL 3B/UTIL/DH/P
(**34**,35,38,42) ATLN **52** 66, **34** 66-73, HOUN **34** 73, CLEA **35** 74, NYA **38** 74, CHIA **42/34** 75

UPSHAW, WILLIE 1B/UTIL/DH/CH
(**26**,20,46,28) TORA **26** 78, 80-87, CLEA **20** 88, TEXA *CH* **46** 93-94, TORA *CH* **28** 96, *CH* **26** 97

UPTON, B. J. SS/DH/3B
(35,**9**) PHIA **35** 04, **9** 04-05

UPTON, BILL P
(**17**) PHIA **17** 54

UPTON, TOM (MUSCLES) SS/INF
(**4**) STLA **4** 50-51, WASA **4** 52

URBAN, JACK P
(**21**,24) KCA **21** 57-58, STLN **24** 59

URBANI, TOM P
(41,**34**,24,42) STLN **41** 93, **34** 93-95, **24** 95-96, DETA **42** 96

URBANSKI, BILLY (BUMP) SS/3B
(10,6,**2**) BOSN **10** 32, **6** 33, **2** 34-37

URBINA, UGUETH P
(59,41,**74**) MONN **59** 95, **41** 95-01, BOSA **41** 01-02, TEXA **41** 03, FLAN **74** 03, DETA **74** 04-05, PHIN **74** 05

URDANETA, LINO P
(**45**) COLN **45** 04

URIBE, JOSE SS/2B/INF
(7,5,**23**,28) STLN **7/5** 84, SFN **23** 85-92, HOUN **28** 93

URIBE, JUAN SS/2B
(4,**5**) COLN **4** 01-03, **5** 04, CHIA **5** 05

URREA, JOHN P
(**38**) STLN **38** 77-80, SDN **38** 81

USHER, BOB OF/3B
(19,**24**,12,35, 21) CINN **19** 46, **24** 47, 50-51, CHIN **12** 52, CLEA **35** 57, WASA **21** 57

UTLEY, CHASE 2B
(**26**) PHIN **26** 03-05

V

VAIL, MIKE OF/3B/1B/UTIL/DH
(6,35,**27**,23, 32,33) NYN **31** 75, **6** 76-77, CLEA **35** 78, CHIN **27** 78-80, CINN **23** 81-82, SFN **32** 83, MONN **33** 83, LAN **37** 84

VALDERRAMA, CARLOS OF
(**21**) SFN **21** 03

VALDES, MARC P
(44,**18**,16,43) FLAN **44** 95-96, MONN **18** 97-98, HOUN **16** 00, ATLN **43** 01

VALDES, PEDRO OF
(**28**,9) CHIN **28** 96, 98, TEXA **9** 00

VALDES, ROY PH
(**27**) WASA **27** 44

VALDESPINO, SANDY OF
(47,**28**,48,5) MINA **47** 65, **28** 65-67, ATLN **48** 68, HOUN **28** 69, SEAA **28** 69, MILA **28** 70, KCA **5** 71

VALDEZ, CARLOS P
(**35**,65) SFN **35** 95, BOSA **65** 98

VALDEZ, EFRAIN P
(**33**,58) CLEA **33** 90-91, ARIN **58** 98

VALDEZ, ISMAEL P
(**59**),14,47,31) LAN **59** 94-99, CHIN **59** 00, LAN **59** 00, ANAA **59** 01, TEXA **14** 02, SEAA **47** 02, TEXA **14** 03, SDN **59** 04, FLAN **31** 04-05

VALDEZ, JULIO SS/UTIL/DH
(15,**12**) BOSA **15** 80, **12** 80-83

VALDEZ, MARIO 3B/1B
(34,50,**23**) CHIA **34** 97, OAKA **50** 00, **23** 01, (02)

VALDEZ, MERKIN P
(**37**) SFN **37** 04

VALDEZ, RAFAEL P
(35,**41**) SDN **35/41** 90

VALDEZ, RENE P
(**49**) BKNN **49** 57

VALDEZ, SERGIO P
(50,34,30,**26**, 40,41) MONN **50** 86, ATLN **34** 89-90, CLEA **30** 90-91, MONN **26** 92-93, BOSA **40** 94, SFN **41** 95

VALDEZ, WILSON SS
(**39**,12) CHIA **39** 04, SEAA **12** 05, SDN **39** 05

VALDIVIELSO, JOSE (JOSIE) SS/INF
(36,22,**5**) WASA **36** 55, **22** 56, **36** 59, **5** 60, MINA **5** 61

VALENT, ERIC OF/1B
(15,12,68,**57**) PHIN **15** 01, **12** 02, CINN **68** 03, NYN **57** 04-05

VALENTIN, JAVIER C
(**26**,8,20,17) MINA **26** 97-99, **8** 02, TBA **20** 03, CINN **17** 04-05

VALENTIN, JOHN SS/2B
(**13**,4) BOSA **13** 92-01, NYN **4** 02

VALENTIN, JOSE SS/2B/3B
(54,**2**,22,10) MILA **54**92, **2** 93-99, CHIA **22** 00 -04, LAN **10** 05

VALENTINE, BOBBY SS/OF/1B/UTIL/CH/M
(**2**,13,11,33,1, 53,22,26,3) LAN **2** 69, 71-72, CALA **13** 73-74, **11** 75, SDN **33** 75-76, **13** 77, NYN **1** 77-78, SEAA **2** 79, NYN *CH* **53** 83, *CH* **22/28** 84, *CH* **26** 84-85, *CH* **2** 85, TEXA *M* **2** 85-92, CINN *CH* **3** 93, NYN *M* **2** 96-02

VALENTINE, CORKY P
(**49**) CINN **49** 54-55

VALENTINE, ELLIS OF/DH
(54,22,**17**) MONN **54** 75, **22** 76, **17** 77-81, NYN **17** 81-82, CALA **17** 83, TEXA **17** 85

VALENTINE, FRED (SQUEAKY) OF/1B
(27,20,5,**34**, 16) BALA **27** 59, **20** 63, WASA **5** 64, **34** 64, 66-68, BALA **16** 68

VALENTINE, JOE P
(**48**) CINN **48** 03-05

VALENTINETTI, VITO P
(33,57,26,28, **11**,15) CHIA **33** 54, CHIN **57** 56-57, CLEA **26** 57, DETA **28** 58, WASA **11** 58-59, **15** 59

VALENZUELA, BENNY (PAPELERO) 3B
(**24**) STLN **24** 58

VALENZUELA, FERNANDO P
(**34**,36,33) LAN **34** 80-90, CALA **36** 91, BALA **34** 93, PHIN **33** 94, SDN **34** 95-97, STLN **34** 97

VALERA, JULIO P
(**34**,44,51) NYN **34** 90-91, CALA **44** 92, **34** 93, KCA **51** 96-97

VALERA, YOHANNY C
(**58**) MONN **58** 00

VALLE, DAVE C/1B/UTIL
(41,5,**10**,23, 18) SEAA **41** 84, **5** 85-86, **10** 87-93, BOSA **23** 94, MILA **18** 94, TEXA **10** 95-96

VALLE, HECTOR (HEC) C
(**17**) LAN **17** 65

VALLONE, GAR P
(**99**) ANAA **99** 98

VALO, ELMER OF/CH
(38,15,21,**10**, 35,3,17,32, 18,4) PHIA **38** 40, **15** 41-43, **21** 46, **10** 47-54, KCA **35** 55-56, PHIN **15** 56, BKNN **3** 57, LAN **3** 58, CLEA **17** 59, NYA **17** 60, WASA **32** 60, MINA **32** 61, PHIN **18** 61, CLEA *CH* **4** 63-64

VALVERDE, JOSE P
(**47**) ARIN **47** 03-05

VAN ATTA, RUSS (SHERIFF) P
(14,19,**21**) NYA **14** 33-35, STLA **19** 35, **21** 36-39

VAN BENSCHOTEN, JOHN P
(**47**) PITN **47** 04, (05)

VAN BRABANT, OZZIE P
(42,**15**) PHIA **42** 54, KCA **15** 55

VAN BUREN, JERMAINE P
(**37**) CHIN **37** 05

VAN BURKLEO, TY 1B
(46,**27**) CALA **46** 93, COLN **27** 94

VAN CAMP, AL OF/1B
(17,**1**) BOSA **17** 31, **1** 32

VANCE, CORY P
(53,**47**) COLN **53** 02, **47** 03

VANCE, DAZZY P
(**15**,18,17,19, 21) BKNN **15** 32, STLN **18** 33, CINN **17** 34 STLN **19** 34, BKNN **21** 35

VANCE, JOE (SANDY) P
(20,**25**) CHIA **20** 35, NYA **25** 37-38

VANCE, SANDY P
(**38**) LAN **38** 70-71

VAN CUYK, CHRIS P B
(**25**) BKNN **25** 50-52

VAN CUYK, JOHNNY P B
(43,**37**) BKNN **43** 47, **37** 48-49

VANDE BERG, ED P
(**32**,31,44,36, 43) SEAA **32** 82-85, LAN **31** 86, CLEA **44/36** 87, TEXA **43** 88

VANDENBERG, HY P
(23,27,18,**22**, 35) BOSA **23** 35, NYN **27** 37, **18** 38, **27** 39, **22** 40, CHIN **35** 44, **35** 45

VANDER MEER, JOHNNY (DOUBLE NO-HIT) (THE DUTCH MASTER)(VANDY) P
(27,31,57,**33**, 34,22) CINN **27/31** 37, **57** 38, **33** 39-43, 46-49, CHIN **34** 50, CLEA **22** 51

VANDER WAL, JOHN OF/1B
(23,35,44,29, **28**,24,25) MONN **23** 91-93, COLN **35** 94-98, SDN **44** 98, **29** 99, PITN **28** 00-01, SFN **28** 01, NYA **28** 02, MILN **24** 03, SDN **24** 03, CINN **25** 04

VAN DUSEN, FRED PH
(**45**) PHIN **45** 55

VANEGMOND, TIM P
(**53**,31,34) BOSA **53** 94-95, MILA **31/34** 96

VAN GORDER, DAVE C/1B
(24,**23**,14) CINN **24** 82-83, **23** 84-86, BALA **14** 87

VAN HEKKEN, ANDY P
(**50**) DETA **50** 02

VAN LANDINGHAM, BILL P
(**50**) SFN **50** 94-97

VAN NOY, JAY OF
(**36**) STLN **36** 51

VAN ORNUM, JOHN CH
(**42**) SFN *CH* **42** 80-84

VAN POPPEL, TODD P
(59,29,51,57, **47**,45) OAKA **59** 91, 93-96, DETA **59/29** 96, TEXA **51** 98, PITN **57** 98, CHIN **47** 00-01, TEXA **47** 02-03, CINN **45** 03-04

VAN ROBAYS, MAURICE (BOMBER) OF/3B/1B
(18,**17**,19,7) PITN **18** 39, **28** 40, **17** 40-43, **19/7** 46

VANRYN, BEN P
(**17**58,49,50) CALA **17** 96, CHIN **58** 98, SDN **49** 98, TORA **50** 98

VAN SLYKE, ANDY (SLICK) OF/1B
(**18**,7,34) STLN **18** 83-86, PITN **7** 87, **18** 87-94, BALA **18** 95, PHIN **34/18** 95

VARGA, ANDY P
(**33**) CHIN **33** 50-51

VARGAS, CLAUDIO P
(**33**,45,29) MONN **33** 03-04, WASN **45** 05, ARIN **45/29** 05

VARGAS, HEDI (EDDIE) 1B
(**50**) PITN **50** 82, 84

VARGAS, JASON P
(**56**) FLAN **56** 05

VARGAS, ROBERTO P
(**29**) MILN **29** 55

VARITEK, JASON C
(47,**33**) BOSA **47** 97-99, **33** 99-05

VARNER, BUCK OF
(**15**) WASA **15** 52

VARNEY, PETE C/DH
(**8**,32) CHIA **8** 73-76, ATLN **32** 76

VARSHO, GARY OF/1B/CH
(24,**42**,22,5, 25,7,19) CHIN **24** 88-90, PITN **42** 91-92, CINN **42** 93, PITN **22** 94, PHIN **5** 95, *CH* **25** 02, **7** 03-04, **19** 05

VASQUEZ, JORGE P
(59,**36**) KCA **59** 04, ATLN **36** 05

VASQUEZ, RAFAEL P
(**21**) SEAA **21** 79

VATCHER, JIM OF
(31,24,**2**) PHIN **31** 90, ATLN **31/24** 90, SDN **2** 91-92

VAUGHAN, ARKY SS/OF/3B/INF
(**21**,3,5,9) PITN **21** 32-39, **3** 40, **5** 40-41, BKNN **5** 42-43, **9** 47-48

VAUGHAN, CHARLIE P
(**34**,43) ATLN **34** 66, **43** 69

VAUGHAN, GLENN (SPARKY) SS/3B
(**4** HOUN **4** 63

VAUGHAN, PORTER (LEFTY) P
(**22**,28) PHIA **22** 40-41, **28** 46

VAUGHN, DeWAYNE P
(**54**) TEXA **54** 88

VAUGHN, FRED (MUSCLES) 2B/3B
(3,20) WASA 3 44, 20 45

VAUGHN, GREG OF/DH
(11,23,7,25, 20) MILA 11 89, 23 90-96, SDN 7 96, 25 97, 23 98, CINN 23 99, TBA 23 00-02, COLN 20 03

VAUGHN, MO 1B/DH
(42) BOSA 42 91-98, ANAA 42 99-01, NYN 42 02-03, (04)

VAUGHN, ROY P
(16) PHIA 16 34

VAZQUEZ, JAVIER P
(28,23,33) MONN 28 98, 23 99-03, NYA 33 04, ARIN 23 05

VAZQUEZ, RAMON SS/2B/INF
(13,1,23,15) SEAA 13 01, SDN 1 02-04, BOSA 23 05, CLEA 15 05

VEACH, AL P
(__) PHIA __ 35

VEAL, COOT SS/INF
(23,8,5,25,28) DETA 23 58-59, 8 60, WASA 5 61, PITN 25 62, DETA 28 63

VEALE, BOB P
(39,55) PITN 39 62-72, BOSA 55 72-74

VEGA, JESUS 1B/UTIL/DH
(37,1) MINA 37 79, 1 80, 82

VEIGEL, AL P
(27) BOSN 27 39

VELANDIA, JORGE 2B/SS
(13,45,11) SDN 13 97, OAKA 45 98, 13 99-00, NYN 11 00-01, 13 03

VELARDE, RANDY SS/3B/2B/INF/UTIL
(28,29,46,18) NYA 28 87-88, 29 87-88, 46 88, 8,25) 18 89-95, CALA 18 96, ANAA 18 97-99, OAKA 8 99-00, TEXA 18 01, NYA 25 01, OAKA 8 02

VELASQUEZ, GUILLERMO 1B
(43,23) SDN 43 92, 23 93

VELAZQUEZ, CARLOS P
(33) MILA 33 73

VELAZQUEZ, FREDDIE C
(30,18) SEAA 30 69, ATLN 18 73

VELEZ, OTTO OF/1B/UTIL/DH
(24,19,32) NYA 24 73-76, TORA 19 77-82, CLEA 32 83

VELTMAN, PAT C
(29,35) NYN 29 32, PITN 35 34

VENABLE, MAX OF/DH
(49,9,8) SFN 49 79-83, MONN 49 84, CINN 9 85-87, CALA 8 89-91

VENAFRO, MICHAEL P
(43,46,41) TEXA 43 99-01, OAKA 46 02, TBA 43 03, LAN 41 04

VENTRO, MIKE OF
(58) NYA 58 05

VENTURA, ROBIN 3B/1B
(23,4,19) CHIA 23 89-98, NYN 4 99-01, NYA 19 02-03, LAN 23 03-04

VENTURA, VINCE OF
(35) WASA 35 45

VERAS, DARIO P
(53,31) SDN 53 96-97, BOSA 31 98

VERAS, QUILVIO 2B
(3,4) FLAN 3 95-96, SDN 4 97-99, ATLN 4 00-01

VERAS, WILTON INF
(38) BOSA 38 99-00

VERBAN, EMIL (DUTCH)(ANTELOPE) 2B
(3,50,9,7,18) STLN 3 44-46, PHIN 50 46, 9 46-48, CHIN 7 48-50, BOSN 18 50

VERBANIC, JOE P
(26,52) PHIN 26 66, NYA 52 67-68, 70

VERBLE, GENE (SATCHEL) SS/INF
(6,15) WASA 6 51, 15 53

VERDEL, AL (STUMPY) P
(30,18) PHIN 30/18 44

VERDI, FRANK SS
(44) NYA 44 53

VERES, DAVE P
(43,47) HOUN 43 94-95, MONN 43 96-97, COLN 47 98-99, STLN 43 00-02, CHIN 43 03

VERES, RANDY P
(43,45,52,42) MILA 43 89-90, CHIN 45 94, FLAN 52 95, DETA 42 96

VERGEZ, JOHNNY 3B/SS
(8,44,7,23,30) NYN 8 32, 44 33, 7 33-34, PHIN 23 35-36, STLN 30 36

VERHOEVEN, JOHN P
(42,48,51,50, 22) CALA 42 76, 48 76-77, CHIA 51 77, MINA 50 80, 22 80-81

VERLANDER, JUSTIN P
(59) DETA 59 05

VERNON, MICKEY 1B/OF/CH/M
(34,29,5,4,3, 44,6,8,15,42, 7,40) WASA 34 39-40, 29 41, 5 42-43, 4 46-48, CLEA 3 49-50, WASA 44 50-51, 3 51-55, BOSA 6 56-57, CLEA 8 58, MILN 15 59, PITN 42 60, CH 42 60, WASA M 3 61-63, PITN CH 42 64, STLN CH 7 65, MONN CH 3 77-78, NYA CH 40 82

VERSAILLES, ZOILO (ZORRO) SS/INF
(5,2,17,15,18) WASA 5 59-60, MINA 2 61-67, LAN 2 68, CLEA 17 69, WASA 15 69, ATLN 18 71

VERYZER, TOM SS/2B/3B/INF
(7,21,15,11, 29) DETA 7 73-77, CLEA 21 78-79, 15 79-81, NYN 11 82, CHIN 29 83-84

VESELIC, BOB P
(39,37,20,35) MINA 39/37/20 80, 20/35 81

VICK, ERNIE C
(20) STLN 20 24

VICO, GEORGE (SAM) 1B
(5) DETA 5 48-49

VICTORINO, SHANE OF
(3,8) SDN 3 03, PHIN 8 05

VIDAL, JOSE (PAPITO) OF/1B
(22,29,31) CLEA 22 66, 29 67-68, SEAA 31 69

VIDRO, JOSE 2B
(37,3) MONN 37 97-98, 3 99-04, WASN 3 05

VILLACIS, EDUARDO P
(59) KCA 59 04

VILLAFUERTE, BRANDON P
(56,50,47,43) DETA 56 00, TEXA 50 01, SDN 47 02, 43 03, ARIN 43 04

VILLANUEVA, HECTOR C/1B
(32,19,29) CHIN 32 90, 19 91-92, STLN 29 93

VILLARREAL, OSCAR P
(56) ARIN 56 03-05

VILLEGAS, ISRAEL P
(70) ATLN 70 00

VILLONE, RON P
(33,49,47,41, 29,39,28,31) SEAA 33 95, SDN 49 95-96, MILA 49 96-97, CLEA 47 98, CINN 41 99-00, COLN 29 01, HOUN 39 01, PITN 28 02, HOUN 31 03, SEAA 47 04-05, FLAN 49 05

VINA, FERNANDO INF/2B/DH
(6,1,4,10) SEAA 6 93, NYN 1 94, MILA 1 95-97, MILN 1 98-99, STLN 4 00-03, DETA 10 04, (05)

VINCENT, AL CH
(31,30,1,41) DETA CH 31 43-44, BALA CH 30 55-59, PHIN CH 1 61-63, KCA CH 41 66-67

VINES, BOB P
(no#) STLN no# 24

VINING, KEN P
(61) CHIA 61 01

VINYARD, DAVE P
(20) BALA 20 64

VINSON, CHUCK 1B
(14) CALA 14 66

VIOLA, FRANK P
(16,29,44,19) MINA 16 82-89, NYN 29 89-91, BOSA 16 92-94, CINN 44 95, TORA 19 96

VIRDON, BILL OF/CH/M
(9,18,4,7,41, 21,19) STLN 9 55-56, PITN 18 56-65, 4/7 68, CH 7 68-69, CH 41 70-71, M 41 72-73, NYA M 21 74-75, HOUN M 7 75-82, MONN 7 83-84, PITN CH 18 86, CH 19 93-94, CH 18 95, HOUN CH 18 97-98, PITN CH 19 01-02

VIRGIL, OZZIE, JR. C/DH S
(24,11,17,9, 21,26) PHIN 24 80, 11 80-82, 17 82-85, ATLN 9 86-88, TORA 21 89, 26 90

VIRGIL, OZZIE, SR. C/3B/2B/UTIL/CH F
(17,22,8,16, 4,34,28,40, 3,1,32) NYN 17 56-57, DETA 22 58, 60, 8 61, KCA 16/4 61, BALA 34 62, PITN 28 65, SFN 40 66, CH 3 69-72, CH 1 74-75, MONN CH 1 76-81, SDN CH 32 82-85, SEAA CH 32 86-88

VITELLI, JOE P/PR
(25) PITN 25 44-45

VITIELLO, JOE DH/1B/INF
(44,32,27,31, 24) KCA 44 95-96, 32 97, 27/32 98, 31 99, SDN 24 00, MONN 32 03

VITKO, JOE P
(49) NYN 49 92

VITT, OSSIE M
(26) CLEA M 26 38-40

VIZCAINO, JOSE SS/2B/INF
(44,16,15,10, 5,7,13) LAN 44 89-90, CHIN 16 91-93, NYN 15 94-96, CLEA 10 96, SFN 10 97-98, LAN 10 98, 5 98-99, 7 00, NYA 13 00, HOUN 10 01-05

VIZCAINO, LUIS P
(61,51) OAKA 61 99-00, 51 01, MILN 51 02-04, CHIA 51 05

VIZQUEL, OMAR SS
(13) SEAA 13 89-93, CLEA 13 94-04, SFN 13 05

VOGELSONG, RYAN P
(51,14,32,28, 22) SFN 51 00, 14/32 01, PITN 28 01, (02) 22 03-05

VOIGT, JACK UTIL
(28,21,24) BALA 28 93-95, TEXA 21 95, 24 96, MILA 28 97, OAKA 28 98

VOISELLE, BILL (BIG BILL)(NINETY-SIX) P
(19,5,17,30, 96) NYN 19 42, 5 43, 17 44-46, 30 47, BOSN 96 47-49, CHIN 96 50

VOLLMER, CLYDE OF
(29,46,28,25, __,22,35,23, 30,24,15) CINN 29 42, CINN 46/28 46, 25 47-48, WASA __ 48, 22 49, 35 50, BOSA 23 50-51, 30 52-53, WASA 24 53, 15 54

VOLQUEZ, EDISON P
(40) TEXA 40 05

VON HOFF, BRUCE P
(42,45,38,31) HOUN 42 65, 45/38/31 67

VON OHLEN, DAVE P
(38,57) STLN 38 83-84, CLEA 38 85, OAKA 57 86-87

VOSBERG, ED P
(50,28,57,52, 38) SDN 50 86, SFN 28 90, OAKA 57 94, TEXA 52 95-97, FLAN 52 97, (98), SDN 52 99, ARIN 50 99, PHIN 50 00-01, MONN 38 02

VOSMIK, JOE OF
(6,5,7,8) CLEA 6 31-36, STLA 5 37, BOSA 7 38-39, BKNN 8 40-41, WASA 6 44

VOSS, BILL OF/1B
(40,17,32,24) CHIA 40 65-66, 17 66-68, CALA 32 69-70, MILA 32 71-72, OAKA 24 72, STLN 17 72

VOYLES, BRAD P
(46) KCA 46 01-03

VUCKOVICH, PETE P/CH
(40,30,46,50) CHIA 40 75-76, TORA 30 77, STLN 46 78-80, 40 80, MILA 50 81-83, 85-86, PITN CH 50 97-00

VUKOVICH, GEORGE OF
(29,24) PHIN 29 80-82, CLEA 24 83-85

VUKOVICH, JOHN SS/3B/INF/CH/M
(30,26,21,16, 22,28,18,2, 7,3) PHIN 30 70-71, 26 71, MILA 21 73-74, CINN 16 75, PHIN 22 76, 28 77, 18 79-81, CHIN CH 2 82-87, M 2 86, CH 22 86-87, PHIN CH 7 88-89, M 7 88, CH 18 90-95, CH 3 96, CH 18 97-04

W

WADDELL, TOM P
(46,54) CLEA 46 84, 54 84-85, 87

WADDEY, FRANK OF
(25) STLA 25 31

WADE, BEN P
(24,46,10,28) CHIN 24 48, BKNN 46 52-54, STLN 10 54, PITN 28 55

WADE, GALE OF
(3,2) CHIN 3 55, 2 56

WADE, JAKE (WHISTLING JAKE) P
(21,29,18,12, 28, 24,46,36, 6,34) DETA 21 36, 29 36-37, 18 38, BOSA 12 39, STLA 28 39-40, CHIA 24 42-43, 46 44, NYA 36 46, WASA 6/34 46

WADE, TERRELL P
(36) ATLN 36 95-97, TBA 36 98

WAECHTER, DOUG P
(40) TBA 40 03-05

WAGNER, BILLY P
(13) HOUN 13 95-03, PHIN 13 04-05

WAGNER, CHARLIE (BROADWAY) P/CH
(25,27,33) BOSA 11 38, 25 39-40, 27 40-42, 46, CH 33 70

WAGNER, GARY P
(64,31,36,35) PHIN 64 65, 31 65-69, BOSA 36 69, 35 70

WAGNER, HAL C
(__,19,26,9, 8,1,17) PHIA __ 37, 19 38, 26 38-40, 9 41-44, BOSA 19/9 44, 8 46-47, DETA 1 47-48, PHIA 17 48, 26 49

WAGNER, HECTOR P
(58,34) KCA 58 90, 34 91

WAGNER, HONUS (THE FLYING DUTCHMAN) CH
(36,35,33) PITN CH 36 33-37, CH 35 38, CH 36 38-39, CH 33 40-51

WAGNER, LEON (DADDY WAGS) OF
(39,21,22,27, 7,38) SFN 39 58, 21 59, STLN 22 60, LAA 27 61-63, CLEA 27 64-68, CHIA 7 68, SFN 38 69

WAGNER, MARK SS/2B/INF/OF/DH
(5,30,9) DETA 5 76-80, TEXA 30 81-83, OAKA 9 84

WAGNER, MATT P
(52) SEAA 52 96

WAGNER, PAUL P
(43,46,37) PITN 43 92-97, MILA 46 97, MILN 46 98, CLEA 37 99

WAGNER, RYAN P
(38) CINN 38 03-05

WAHL, KERMIT 3B/INF
(12,19,18,23) CINN 12 44-45, 19 47, PHIA 18 50-51, STLA 23 51

WAINHOUSE, DAVE P
(40,26,53,41, 43,44,88) MONN 40 91, SEAA 26 93, PITN 53 96-97, COLN 41 98, 43 99, STLN 44/88 00

WAINWRIGHT, ADAM P
(60) STLN 60 05

WAITKUS, EDDIE 1B/OF
(27,36,4,3,44) CHIN 27 41, 36 46-48, PHIN 4 49-53, BALA 3 54, 9 55, PHIN 44 55

WAITS, RICK P/CH
(39,30,36,20, 52) TEXA 39 73, CLEA 30 75, 36 75-83, MILA 36 83-85, 20 85, NYN CH 52 03-04

WAKAMATSU, DON C/CH
(47,18) CHIA 47 91, TEXA CH 18 03-05

WAKEFIELD, BILL P
(43) NYN 43 64

WAKEFIELD, DICK OF
(26,24,2,4,9, 26) DETA 26/24 41, 2 43-44, 4 46-49, NYA 9 50, NYN 26 52

WAKEFIELD, TIM P
(49) PITN 49 92-93, BOSA 49 95-05

WAKELAND, CHRIS OF
(43) DETA 43 01

WALBECK, MATT C
(9,23,8,6,4, 45) CHIN 9 93, MINA 23 94, 9 95-96, DETA 8 97, ANAA 6 98-00, PHIN 4 01, DETA 45 02, 8 03

WALBERG, RUBE P
(12,15) PHIA 12 31-33, BOSA 15 34-37

WALCZAK, ED (HUSKY) 2B/SS
(8) PHIN 8 45

WALEWANDER, JIM INF/UTIL/DH
(32,63,3) DETA 32 87-88, NYA 63 90, CALA 3 93

WALK, BOB P
(41,50,43,18, 17) PHIN 41 80, ATLN 50/41 81, 43 81-83, PITN 18 84-85, 17 86-93

WALKER, BILL P
(12,10,18,21) NYN 12 32, STLN 10 33, 18 34-36, 21 36

WALKER, CHICO 2B/OF/UTIL/DH
(3,1,30,29,9, 10,24,34) BOSA 3 80, 1 81-84, CHIN 30 85, 29 86-87, CALA 9/10 88, CHIN 24 91-92, NYN 34 92-93

WALKER, DIXIE (THE PEOPLE'S CHERCE) OF/CH B
(35,27,45,7,8, 11,30,6) NYA 35 31-32, 27 33-36, CHIA 45 36, 7 36-37, DETA 8 38-39, BKNN 11 39-47, PITN 11 48-49, STLN CH 30 53, 55, MILN CH 6 63-65

WALKER, DUANE OF/1B/DH
(26,59,21) CINN 26 82-85, TEXA 59/21 85, STLN 21 88

WALKER, GEE (MUTT) OF/3B/CH
(2,27,6,11,7, 4) DETA 2 31, 27 32-33, 6 34-35, 11 36-37, CHIA 7 38-39, WASA 4 40, CLEA 2 41, CINN 27 42-45, CH 6 46

WALKER, GREG 1B/DH/CH
(27,29,35) CHIA 27 82, 29 82-90, BALA 35 90, CHIA CH 29 03-05

WALKER, HARRY (THE HAT) OF/1B/M/CH B
(42,10,5,4,43, 29,1,38,3,25) STLN 42 40, 6 41, 10 42-43, 5 46-47, 10 47, PHIN 4 47-48, CHIN 43 49, CINN 29 49, STLN 1 50, 38 51, 5 55, M 5 55, CH 3 59-62, PITN M 3 65-67, HOUN M 25 68-72

WALKER, HUB OF/2B/UTIL
(1,30,16,34) DETA 1 31, 30 35, CINN 16 36-37, DETA 30/34 45

WALKER, JAMIE P
(57,32) KCA 57 97-98, DETA 32 02-05

WALKER, JERRY P/CH
(41,38,23,48, 34,42,54) BALA 41 57, 38 58-60, KCA 23 61-62, CLEA 48 63-64, 34 64, NYA CH 53 81, 42 82, HOUN CH 54 83-85

WALKER, KEVIN P
(56),54,58) SDN 56 00-03, 54 04, CHIA 58 05

WALKER, LARRY OF/1B
(33) MONN 33 89-94, COLN 33 95-04, STLN 33 04-05

WALKER, LUKE P
(31,27,23,17) PITN 31 65-66, 27 66, 23 68-73, DETA 17 74

WALKER, MIKE (A.) P
(47) SEAA 47 92

WALKER, MIKE (C.) P
(75,48,39,21) CLEA 75 88, 48 90-91, CHIN 39 95, DETA 21 96

WALKER, PETE P
(49,39,71,54, 43,41) NYN 49 95, SDN 39 96, COLN 71/54 00, NYN 43 01-02, TORA 41 02-03, 05

WALKER, RUBE C/CH
(8,10,41,54) CHIN 8 48-51, BKNN 10 51-57, LAN 10 58, CH 10 58, WASA CH 41 65-67, NYN CH 54 68-81, ATLN CH 54 82-84

WALKER, SPEED PH
(__) STLN __ 23

WALKER, TODD 3B/2B
(13,12,14,2, 7) MINA 13 96, 12 97-00, COLN 14 00, 12 01, CINN 2 01, 12 02, BOSA 12 03, CHIN 7 04-05

WALKER, TOM P
(20,32,34,16, 43) MONN 20 72-74, DETA 32 75, STLN 34 76, MONN 16 77, CALA 43 77

WALKER, TONY OF
(30) HOUN 30 86-87

WALKER, TYLER P
(46,45) NYN 46 02, SFN 45 04-05

WALKER, VERLON (RUBE) CH
(56,4) CHIN CH 56 61-65, CH 4 66-71

WALKUP, JIM P
(14,15,22,24, 26) STLA 14 34, 15 35, 22 36, 24 37-39, DETA 26 39

WALL, DONNE P
(56,36,33,18) HOUN 56 95-97, SDN 36 98-00, NYN 33 01, ANAA 18 02

WALL, MURRAY P
(6,26) BOSN 6 50, BOSA 26 57-59, WASA 26 59

WALL, STAN P
(45) LAN 45 75-77

WALLACE, BOBBY CH/M
(33,__) CINN CH 33 32, M __ 37

WALLACE, DAVE P
(39,49,46,17, 52,37,35) PHIN 39 73, 49 74, TORA 46 78, LAN CH 17 95-98, NYN CH 52 99-00, BOSA CH 37/35 03, 17 04-05

WALLACE, DEREK P
(47,34) NYN 47 96, (97), KCA 34 99

WALLACE, DON INF
(34) CALA 34 67

WALLACE, JEFF P
(39) PITN 39 97, (98), 99-00, TBA 51 01, BOSA (02)

WALLACE, LEFTY P
(16,34,19) BOSN 16 42, 9/15 45, 34 46, 19 46

WALLACE, MIKE P
(49,41,32,24, 27) PHIN 49 73-74, NYA 41 74-75, STLN 32 75-76, TEXA 24/27 77

WALLACH, TIM OF/1B/3B/INF/P
(29,25,23) MONN 29 80-92, LAN 25 93, 29 94-95, CALA 23 96, LAN 29 96, LAN CH 25 04-05

WALLAESA, JACK SS/OF/UTIL
(41,25,10,**12**) PHIA **41/25** 40, **10** 42, 46, CHIA **12** 47-48

WALLEN, NORM 3B
(**12**) BOSN **12** 45

WALLER, TY 3B/OF/UTIL
(40,12,**21**,29, 30) STLN **40/12** 80, CHIN **21** 81-82, **29** 82, HOUN **30** 87

WALLING, DENNY OF/1B/UTIL/3B/CH
(7,5,**29**,21,3, 25,15) OAKA **7** 75, **5** 76, HOUN **29** 77-88, STLN **21** 88-90, TEXA **3** 91, HOUN **25** 92, OAKA *CH* **15** 96-98, NYN *CH* **15** 03-04

WALLIS, JOE OF/DH
(28,27,**9**) CHIN **28** 75-76, **27** 77-78, OAKA **9** 78-79

WALLS, LEE OF/3B/1B/UTIL/C/CH
(6,16,2,27, 9,**7**,43) PITN **6** 52, **16** 56-57, CHIN **2** 57-59, CINN **27** 60, PHIN **9** 60-61, LAN **7** 62-64, OAKA *CH* **43** 79-81

WALROND, LES P
(**56**) KCA **56** 03

WALSH, DAVE P
(**51**) LAN **51** 90

WALSH, ED P
(**18**) CHIA **18** 32

WALSH, JOE (TWEET) SS
(**29**) BOSN **29** 38

WALSH, JUNIOR P
(27,34,**29**) PITN **27** 46, **34** 48, **29** 49-51, **34** 51

WALTER, GENE P
(48,**31**,32) SDN **48** 85-86, NYN **31** 87-88, SEAA **32** 88

WALTERS, BUCKY 3B/2B/P/M/CH
(9,6,8,35,20, 40,46,17,56, **31**,1,3) BOSN **9** 32, BOSA **6** 33, **8** 34, PHIN **35** 34, **20** 35-36, **40** 36-37, **46** 37, **17** 38, CINN **56** 38, **31** 39-49, *M* **31** 48-49, *M* **1** 49, BOSN **31** 50, *CH* **31** 50-52, MILN *CH* **31** 53-55, NYN *CH* **3** 56-57

WALTERS, CHARLEY P
(56,**27**) MINA **56/27** 69

WALTERS, DAN C
(58,**11**) SDN **58** 92, **11** 93

WALTERS, FRED (WHALE) C
(**26**) BOSA **26** 45

WALTERS, KEN OF/1B/INF
(**17**,21) PHIA **17** 60-61, CINN **21** 63

WALTERS, MIKE P
(**30**) MINA **30** 83-84

WALTON, BRUCE P/CH
(50,**53**,52) OAKA **50** 91-92, MONN **53** 93, COLN **53** 94, TORA *CH* **52** 02-05

WALTON, DANNY (MICKEY) OF/3B/1B/UTIL
(50,**12**,7,11, 39,48,31,8) HOUN **50** 68, SEAA **12** 69, MILA **12** 70, **7** 71, NYA **11** 71, MINA **12** 73, **39** 73, **7** 75, LAN **48** 76, HOUN **31** 77, TEXA **8** 80

WALTON, JEROME OF/DH
(**20**,19,1,37, 27) CHIN **20** 89-92, CALA **20** 93, CINN **19** 94-95, ATLN **19** 96, BALA **1/37** 97, TBA **27** 98

WALTON, JIM CH
(**30**) MILA *CH* **30** 73-75

WALTON, REGGIE OF/DH
(26,**33**,46) SEAA **26** 80, **33** 81, PITN **46** 82

WANER, LLOYD (LITTLE POISON) OF/3B B
(**10**,37,27,34, 9,15) PITN **10** 32-41, BOSN **37** 41, CINN **27** 41, PHIN **34** 42, BKNN **9** 44, PITN **15** 44-45

WANER, PAUL (BIG POISON) OF/1B B
(**11**,9,24,31, 8,1,22) PITN **11** 32-39, **9** 40, BKNN **24** 41, BOSN **31** 41, **8** 42, BKNN **1** 43-44, NYA **24** 44, **22** 45

WANG, CHIEN-MING P
(**40**) NYA **40** 05

WANTZ, DICK P
(25,**41**) CALA **25/41** 65

WAPNICK, STEVE P
(43,51) DETA **43** 90, CHIA **51** 91

WARD, BRYAN P
(**56**) CHIA **56** 98-99, PHIN **37** 00, ANAA **39** 00

WARD, CHRIS OF/1B
(**20**) CHIN **20** 72, 74

WARD, COLBY P
(**50**) CLEA **50** 90

WARD, COLIN P
(**43**) SFN **43** 85

WARD, DARYLE INF/OF
(**31**,36) HOUN **31** 98-02, LAN **36** 03, PITN **31** 04-05

WARD, DICK P
(15,10,**27**) CHIN **15** 34, STLN **10/27** 35

WARD, DUANE P
(56,48,**31**) ATLN **56/48** 86, TORA **31** 86-93, 95

WARD, GARY OF/UTIL/DH/CH
(35,**32**,22,47) MINA **35** 79, **32** 80-83, TEXA **32** 84-86, NYA **22** 87-89, DETA **32** 89-90, CHIA *CH* **47** 02-03

WARD, JAY 3B/OF/2B/INF/CH
(**26**,17,50,35) MINA **26** 63-64, CINN **17** 70, NYA *CH* **50** 87, MONN *CH* **35** 91-92

WARD, KEVIN OF
(**30**) SDN **30** 91-92

WARD, PETE OF/3B/UTIL/CH
(28,**8**,25,23) BALA **28** 62, CHIA **8** 63-69, NYA **25** 70, ATLN *CH* **23** 78

WARD, PRESTON 1B/OF/3B/UTIL
(52,36,29,**5**, 26,7) BKNN **52/36** 48, CHIN **29** 50, 53, PITN **5** 53-56, CLEA **26** 56-58, KCA **7** 58-59

WARD, TURNER OF/1B/DH
(68,20,**24**,16, 27,12,10,25) CLEA **68** 90, **20** 91, TORA **24** 91-93, **16** 93, MILA **27** 94-96, PITN **12** 97-99, ARIN **10** 99-00, PHIN **25** 01

WARDEN, JON (WARBLER) P
(**39**) DETA **39** 68

WARDLE, CURT P
(36,55,39,**31**) MINA **36** 84-85, CLEA **55/39/31** 85

WARE, JEFF P
(**52**) TORA **52** 95-96

WARES, BUZZY CH
(**26**,23,36) STLN *CH* **26** 32-35, **23** 36, **26** 36-38, **36** 39-41, **26** 42-52

WARNEKE, LON (THE ARKANSAS HUMMING-BIRD) P
(30,17,16,12, **18**,21,19,32, 36) CHIN **30/17** 32, **16** 33-34, **12** 35-36, STLN **18** 37-38, **21** 39-41, **18** 41-42, CHIN **19** 42, **32** 43, **36** 45

WARNER, HARRY CH
(**41**,36) TORA *CH* **41** 77-79, MILA *CH* **36** 81-82

WARNER, JACK P
(38,32,30,34, **40**) CHIN **38/32** 62, **30/33/32** 63, **34/38** 64, **40** 64-65

WARNER, JACK 2B/INF
(**12**) PHIN **12** 33

WARNER, JACKIE OF
(37,**26**) CALA **37/26** 66

WARNOCK, HAL OF
(**25**) STLA **25** 35

WARREN, BENNIE C/1B
(**26**,24,5,36, 9) PHIN **26** 39-41, **24/5** 42, NYN **36** 46, **9** 47

WARREN, MIKE P
(46,**43**) OAKA **46** 83, **43** 83-85

WARREN, TOMMY P
(13,**20**) BKNN **13/20** 44

WARSTLER, RABBIT (BUDDY) 2B/SS/3B
(4,2,1,22,30, **8**,12,43) BOSA **4** 31, **2** 32, **1** 33, PHIA **22** 34-35, **4** 36, BOSN **30** 36, **8** 37-39, **12** 40, CHIN **43** 40

WARTHEN, DAN P/CH
(**39**,33,31,49, 37) MONN **39** 75-77, PHIN **33** 77, HOUN **31** 78, SEAA *CH* **49** 91-92, SDN *CH* **37** 96-97, DETA *CH* **31** 99-02

WARWICK, CARL OF/1B
(54,24,27,16, 20,**17**,23) LAN **54** 61, STLN **24** 61, **27** 62, HOUN **16** 62, **20** 62-63, STLN **17** 64-65, BALA **23** 65, CHIN **23** 66

WASDELL, JIMMY 1B/OF
(26,24,19,7, **3**,29,8,11,28, 10,1) WASA **26** 37, **24/19** 38, **7** 39, **3** 40, BKNN **29** 40-41, **8** 41, PITN **11** 42-43, PHIN **28** 43-44, **3** 44-46, CLEA **10** 46, **1** 47

WASDIN, JOHN P
(31,**46**,45,38, 47) OAKA **31** 95-96, BOSA **46** 97-99-00, COLN **46** 00-01, BALA **45** 01, TORA **38** 03, TEXA **47** 04-05

WASEM, LINK C
(**22**) BOSN **22** 37

WASHBURN, GEORGE P
(**29**) NYA **29** 41

WASHBURN, GREG P
(51,**23**) CALA **51/23** 69

WASHBURN, JARROD P
(**56**) ANAA **56** 98-04, LAA **56** 05

WASHBURN, RAY P
(**44**,39) STLN **44** 61-69, CINN **39** 70

WASHINGTON, CLAUDELL OF/DH
(**15**,16,18,33, 7,17) OAKA **15** 74-76, TEXA **16** 77, **15** 77-78, CHIA **18** 78-80, NYN **15** 80, ATLN **18** 81-82, **15** 82-86, NYA **33** 86, **18** 86-88, CALA **7** 89, **18** 89-90, NYA **17** 90

WASHINGTON, GEORGE (VERN) OF
(**12**) CHIA **12** 35-36

WASHINGTON, HERB PR
(2,**3**) OAKA **2** 74, **3** 74-75

WASHINGTON, LA RUE 2B/UTIL/DH
(**15**) TEXA **15** 78-79

WASHINGTON, RON SS/INF/OF/UTIL/DH/CH
(44,**38**,24,37, 15) LAN **44** 77, MINA **38** 81, **24** 82, **38** 83-86, BALA **37** 87, CLEA **15** 88, HOUN **15** 89, OAKA *CH* **38** 96-05

WASHINGTON, U. L. SS/INF/DH
(**30**,1,0,28,3) KCA **30** 77-84, MONN **1** 85, PITN **0/28** 86, **3** 87

WASINGER, MARK 3B/2B/INF
(**12**,33) SDN **12** 86, SFN **12** 87, **33** 88

WASLEWSKI, GARY P
(47,**19**,54,17) BOSA **47** 67, **19** 67-68, STLN **19** 69, MONN **47** 69-70, NYA **54** 70-71, OAKA **17** 72

WASZGLS, B. J. C
(**39**) TEXA **39** 00

WATERBURY, STEVE P
(**48**) STLN **48** 76

WATERS, FRED P
(34,**35**) PITN **34** 55, **35** 56

WATHAN, DUSTY C
(**17**) KCA **17** 02

WATHAN, JOHN (DUKE) C/1B/UTIL/M/CH
(**12**,37) KCA **12** 76-85, *CH* **12** 86, *M* **12** 87-91, CALA *CH* **37** 92-93, BOSA *CH* **12** 94

WATKINS, BOB P
(**47**) HOUN **47** 69

WATKINS, DAVE UTIL
(**2**) PHIN **2** 69

WATKINS, GEORGE (WATTY) OF
(6,5,2,**31**,37, 11) STLN **6** 32, **5** 33, NYN **2** 34, PHIN **31** 35, **37** 36, BKNN **11** 36

WATKINS, PAT 3B/OF
(44,**9**) CINN **44** 97, **9** 98, COLN **22** 99

WATKINS, SCOTT P
(**51**) MINA **51** 95

WATKINS, STEVE P
(**58**) SDN **58** 04

WATLINGTON, NEIL C
(45,**11**) PHIA **45/11** 53

WATSON, ALLEN P
(38,**34**,30,41, 27) STLN **38** 93-95, SFN **34** 96, ANAA **34** 97-98, NYN **30** 99, SEAA **41** 99, NYA **27** 99-01

WATSON, BOB (BULL) 1B/OF/UTIL/DH/CH
(38,11,26,**27**, 5,28,8,55) HOUN **38** 66, **11** 67, **26** 68, **27** 68-79, BOSA **5** 79, NYA **28** 80-82, ATLN **8** 82-84, OAKA *CH* **55** 87-88

WATSON, BRANDON OF
(**00**) WASN **00** 05

WATSON, MARK P
(59,**26**,61) CLEA **59** 00, SEAA **26** 02, CINN **61** 03

WATSON, MATT OF
(50,**12**) NYN **50** 03, OAKA **12** 05

WATT, EDDIE P
(**39**,49) BALA **39** 66-73, PHIN **39** 74, CHIN **49/39** 75

WATWOOD, JOHNNY (LEFTY) OF/1B
(6,14,12,**7**,5) CHIA **6** 31, **14** 32, BOSA **12** 32, **7** 33, PHIN **5** 39

WAUGH, JIM P
(**23**) PITN **23** 52-53

WAYNE, GARY P
(**47**,48,53) MINA **47** 89-90, **48** 91-92, **47** 92, COLN **53** 93, LAN **47** 94

WAYNE, JUSTIN P
(**48**) FLAN **48** 02-04

WEAFER, HAL (AL) P
(**28**) BOSN **28** 36

WEATHERLY, ROY (STORMY) OF/3B
(23,2,**22**,10, 40,3,39) CLEA **23** 36, **2** 37, **22** 38-42, NYA **10** 43, **40/3** 46, NYN **39** 50

WEATHERS, DAVID P
(53,**35**,28,52, 50,49,41,25) TORA **53** 91-92, FLAN **35** 93-96, NYA **28** 96, **52** 96-97, CLEA **50** 97, CINN **49** 98, MILN **49** 98-01, CHIN **41/49** 01, NYN **35** 02-04, HOUN **35** 04, FLAN **25** 04, CINN **25** 05

WEAVER, EARL CH/M
(**4**) BALA *CH* **4** 68, *M* **4**68-82, 85-86

WEAVER, ERIC P
(**56**) LAN **56** 98, SEAA **52** 99, ANAA **28** 00

WEAVER, FLOYD P
(23,35,41,49, 37) CLEA **23** 62, **35** 65, CHIA **41** 70, MILA **49** 71

WEAVER, JEFF P
(**36**,18) DETA **36** 99-02, NYA **18** 02-03, LAN **36** 04-05

WEAVER, JIM (BIG JIM) P
(24,23,12,15, **43**,16,63,34) NYA **24** 31, STLA **23** 34, CHIN **12/15** 34, PITN **43** 35-37, STLA **16** 38, CINN **63** 38, **34** 39

WEAVER, JIM (FLUFF) P
(50,47,**35**) CALA **50/47** 67, **35** 67-68

WEAVER, JIM OF/DH
(**20**,46,45) DETA **20** 85, SEAA **46** 87, SFN **45** 89

WEAVER, MONTE (PROF) P
(__,16,**17**,25) WASA __ 31, **16** 32-36, **17** 36-38, BOSA **25** 39

WEAVER, ROGER P
(44,**48**) DETA **44/48** 80

WEBB, BILL P
(**20**) PHIN **20** 43

WEBB, BILLY CH
(2,**22**) CHIA *CH* **2** 35,*CH* **22** 35-39

WEBB, BRANDON P
(55,**17**) ARIN **55** 03-04, **17** 05

WEBB, EARL OF/1B
(15,**4**,34) BOSA **15** 31-32, DETA **4** 32-33, CHIA **34** 33

WEBB, HANK P
(42,30,22,**29**, 44,37) NYN **42** 72, **30** 73, **22** 74, **29** 74-75, **30** 76, LAN **44/37** 77

WEBB, JOHN P
(29,**38**) TBA **53** 04-05

WEBB, RED P
(29,**38**) NYN **29** 48, **38** 49

WEBB, SKEETER SS/2B/IN
(1,5,37,**2**,28) STLN **1** 32, CLEA **5** 38-39, CHIA **37** 40-42, **2** 43-44, DETA **28** 45-47, PHIA **2** 48

WEBBER, LES P
(**31**,32,44,33, 28) BKNN **31** 42-45, **32** 45-46, CLEA **44/33** 46, **28** 48

WEBER, BEN P
(57,**77**) SFN **57** 00, ANAA **57** 00, **77** 01-04, CINN **77** 05

WEBER, NEIL P
(**66**) ARIN **66** 98

WEBSTER, LENNY C/DH
(52,**15**,25,27, 42,38) MINA **52** 89-90, **15** 91-93, MONN **25** 94, PHIN **27** 95, MONN **25** 96, BALA **42** 97-99, BOSA **38** 99, MONN **15** 00

WEBSTER, MITCH OF/1B/UTIL/DH
(**23**,28,33,20, 53) TORA **23** 83-85, MONN **23** 85-88, CHIN **28** 88, **33** 89, CLEA **23** 90-91, LAN **20** 91, PITN **53** 91, LAN **20** 92-95

WEBSTER, RAMON (RAY) 1B/OF
(34,31,**23**,11, 29,13,52) KCA **34** 67, OAKA **31** 68, **23** 69, SDN **11** 70, **29/13** 71, OAKA **52** 71, CHIN **23** 71

WEBSTER, RAY 2B/3B
(**5**,31) CLEA **5** 59, BOSA **31** 60

WEDGE, ERIC C/DH/M
(**22**,36) BOSA **22** 91, **36** 92, COLN **22** 93, BOSA **22** 94, CLEA *M* **22** 03-05

WEEKLY, JOHNNY OF
(24,**26**) HOUN **24** 62, **26** 63-64

WEEKS, RICKIE 2B
(**23**) MILN **23** 03, 05

WEGENER, MIKE P
(**24**) MONN **24** 69-70

WEGMAN, BILL P
(**46**) MILA **46** 85-95

WEHDE, BIGGS P
(**25**) CHIA **25** 31

WEHMEIER, HERM P
(19,45,**31**,22, 37,20) CINN **19** 45, **45** 47-49, **31** 49-54, PHIN **22** 54-56, STLN **37** 56-58, DETA **20** 58

WEHNER, JOHN 3B/OF/UTIL
(52,22,**12**,14, 7) PITN **52** 91-92, **22** 92-93, **12** 94-96, FLAN **14** 97-98, PITN **7** 99, **12** 00, **7** 01

WEHRMEISTER, DAVE P
(**24**,58,56,33, 51) SDN **24** 76-78, NYA **58** 81, PHIN **56/33** 84, CHIA **51** 85

WEIGEL, RALPH (WIG) C/OF
(42,33,26,**11**) CLEA **42/33** 46, CHIA **26** 48, WASA **11** 49

WEIK, DICK (LEGS) P/PR
(18,27,48,31, 28,37,**21**,30) WASA **18** 48-49, **27** 50, CLEA **48/31/28** 50, **37** 53, DETA **21** 53-54, **30** 54

WEILAND, BOB (LEFTY) P B
(2,26,19,12, 14,25,**20**) CHIA **2** 31, BOSA **26** 32, **19** 33, **12** 34, CLEA **14** 34, STLA **25** 35, STLN **20** 37-40

WEILAND, ED P B
(19,**39**) CHIA **19** 40, **39** 42

WEINERT, LEFTY P
(**19**) NYA **19** 31

WEINGARTNER, ELMER (DUTCH) SS
(**34**) CLEA **34** 45

WEINTRAUB, PHIL (MICKEY) OF/1B
(14,22,27,15, 15,**5**) NYN **14** 33-34, **22** 34, **27** 35, CINN **15** 37, NYN **15** 37, PHIN **14** 38, NYN **5** 44-45

WEIR, ROY P
(9,**11**,40) BOSN **9** 36, **11** 37-38, **40** 39

WEIS, AL SS/2B/INF/UTIL
(**6**) CHIA **6** 62-67, NYN **6** 68-71

WEISS, GARY SS
(**1**) LAN **1** 80-81

WEISS, WALT SS
(17,7,**22**) OAKA **17** 87, **7** 88-91, **22** 92, FLAN **22** 92, COLN **22** 94-97, ATLN **22** 98-00

WELAJ, JOHNNY OF
(**24**,11) WASA **24** 39-41, PHIA **11** 43

WELCH, BOB P/CH
(**35**,32) LAN **35** 78-87, OAKA **35** 88-94, ARIN *CH* **32** 01

WELCH, JOHNNY P
(6,20,18,**17**, 51) BOSA **6** 32, **20** 33, **18** 34, **17** 35-36, PITN **51** 36

WELCH, MIKE P
(**47**) PHIN **47** 98

WELCH, MILT C
(**23**) DETA **23** 45

WELCHEL, DON P
(**51**) BALA **51** 82-83

WELLEMEYER, TODD P
(**40**) CHIN **40** 03-05

WELLMAN, BOB 1B/OF
(56,**38**) PHIA **56** 48, **38** 50-51

WELLMAN, BRAD 2B/SS/INF/DH
(**36**,8,56,3) SFN **36** 82, **8** 83, **36** 84-86, LAN **56** 87, KCA **3** 88-89

WELLS, BOB P
(56,**46**) PHIN **56** 94, SEAA **46** 94-98, MINA **46** 99-02

WELLS, DAVID P
(36,16,**33**,3) TORA **36** 87-92, DETA **16** 93-95, CINN **36** 95, BALA **36** 96, NYA **33** 97-98, TORA **33** 99-00, CHIA **33** 01, NYA **33** 02-03, SDN **33** 04, BOSA **3/16** 05

WELLS, ED (SATCHEL) P
(19,**17**,14,28) NYA **19** 29, **17** 30-31, **14** 32, STLA **28** 33, **19** 34

WELLS, GREG (BOOMER) 1B/DH
(43,**7**) TORA **43** 81, MINA **7** 82

WELLS, JOHN P
(__) BKNN __ 44

WELLS, KIP P
(**32**) CHIA **32** 99-01, PITN **32** 02-05

WELLS, LEO SS/3B
(36,37) CHIA **36** 42, **37** 46

WELLS, TERRY P
(40,**51**) LAN **40/51** 90

WELLS, VERNON OF
(3,**10**) TORA **3** 99, **10** 00-05

WELSH, CHRIS P
(**26**,41,45) SDN **26** 81-83, MONN **26** 83, TEXA **41** 85, CINN **45** 86

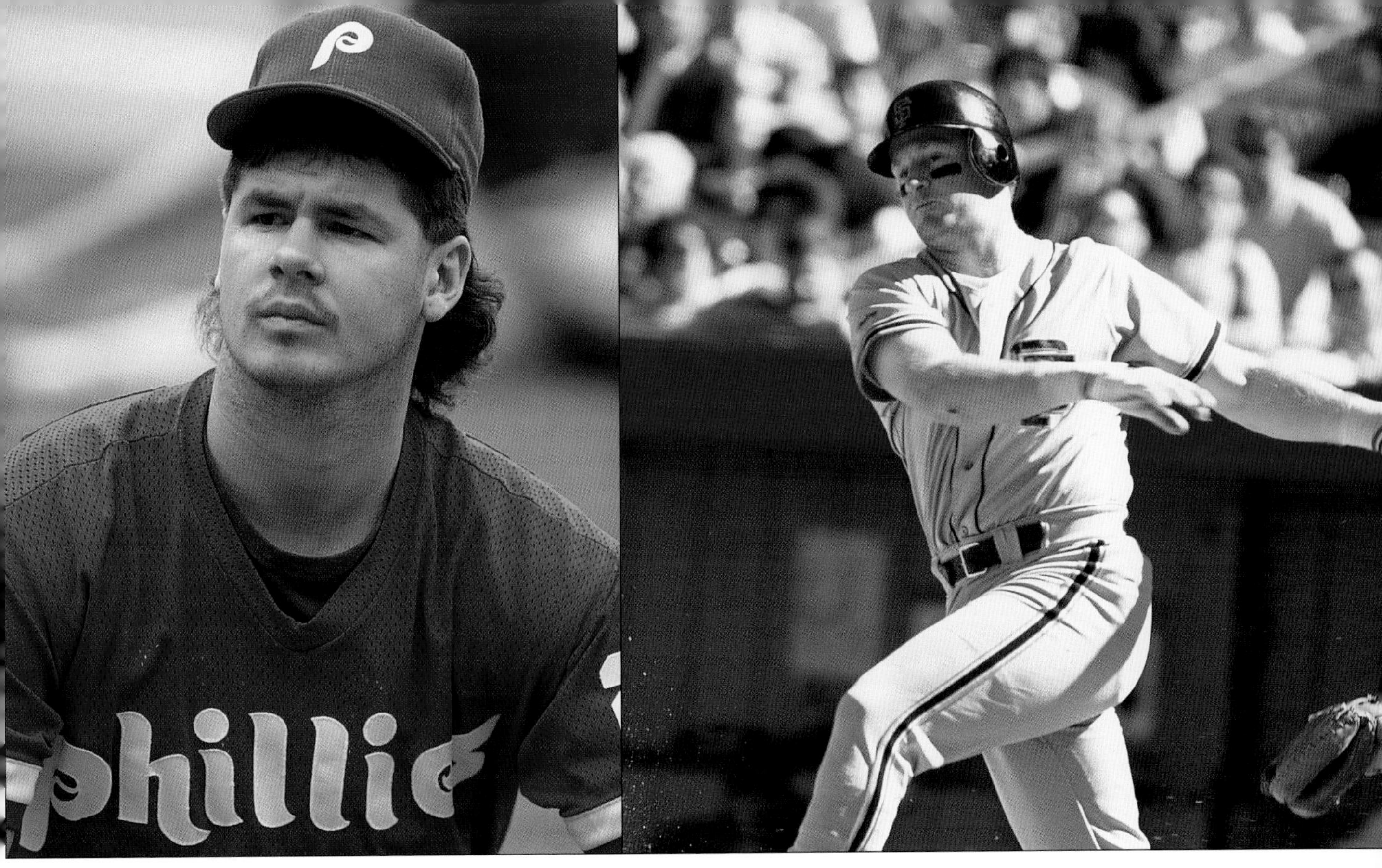

(Above, left) "Wild Thing" was an appropriate nickname for Mitch Williams. Starting pitchers would duck under towels when Mitch came in, managers got grey hairs. He would often walk the bases full before striking out the side. He's most remembered for giving up the series-ending HR to Toronto's Joe Carter in 1993, ironically his best year with 43 saves. (Above, right) Matt Williams was a solid all-around ballplayer. He led the NL in HRs with 43 in 1994 and RBIs with 122 in 1990 while winning 4 Gold Gloves for his play at third base.

WELTEROTH, DICK P
(36,**21**,28) WASA **36** 48, **21** 48-49, **28** 50

WENDELL, TURK P
(**13**,99) CHIN **13** 93-97, NYN **99** 97-01, PHIN **99** 01, **13** 01, (02), 03, COLN **99** 04

WENGERT, DON P
(**56**,26,33,41, 50,38) OAKA **56** 95-97, SDN **26** 98, CHIN **33** 98, KCA **41** 99, ATLN **50** 00, PITN **38** 01

WENSLOFF, CHARLEY (BUTCH) P
(17,14,25,**42**) CLEA **17** 48, NYA **14** 43, **25/42** 47

WENTZEL, STAN OF
(**4**) BOSN **4** 45

WENZ, FRED (FIREBALL) P
(24,**26**,32) BOSA **24** 68, **26** 69, PHIN **32** 70

WERA, JULIE 3B
(**20**) NYA **20** 29

WERBER, BILLY SS/3B/INF/OF/UTIL
(20,24,22, 2,5,3,**18**,1) NYA **20** 30, **24** 33, BOSA **22** 33, **20** 34, **2** 35, **5** 36, PHIA **5** 37, **3** 38, CINN **18** 39-41, NYN **1** 42

WERHAS, JOHNNY (PEACHES) 3B/UTIL
(**14**,44,25) LAN **14** 64-65, 67, CALA **25** 67

WERLE, BILL (BUGS) P/CH
(29,20,**19**,22, 28,14,26,46) PITN **29/20** 49, **19** 49-51, **22/20** 52, STLN **20** 52, BOSA **28** 53, **14/26** 54, SFN *CH* **46** 66

WERLEY, GEORGE P
(**15**) BALA **15** 56

WERNER, DON C/DH
(**7**,19,20) CINN **7** 75-78, **19** 80, TEXA **20** 81-82

WERT, DON 3B/SS/INF
(**8**,2) DETA **8** 63-70, WASA **2** 71

WERTH, DENNIS 1B/C/UTIL
(**24**,16) NYA **24** 79-81, KCA **16** 82

WERTH, JAYSON OF
(54,13,**28**) TORA **54** 02, **13** 03, LAN **28** 04-05

WERTZ, BILL P
(**46**) CLEA **46** 93-94

WERTZ, VIC OF/1B
(**20**,5,23,6) DETA **20** 47-50, **5** 50-52, **20** 52, STLA **20** 52-53, BALA **20** 54, CLEA **23** 54-58, BOSA **6** 59-61, DETA **20** 61-63, MINA **6** 63

WESSINGER, JIM 2B
(**16**) ATLN **16** 79

WESSON, BARRY OF
(**45**) HOUN **45** 02, ANAA **45** 03

WEST, DAVID P
(46,50,39,**40**) NYN **46** 88-89, MINA **50** 89-91, **39** 91-92, PHIN **40** 93-96, BOSA **39** 98

WEST, DICK OF/C
(59,38,**5**) CINN **59** 38, **38** 39, **5** 40-43

WEST, LEFTY P
(**20**) STLA **20** 44-45

WEST, MAX OF/1B
(**4**,24,14) BOSN **4** 38-42, 46, CINN **24** 46, PITN **14** 48

WEST, SAMMY OF/1B/CH
(6,3,4,**23**,34) WASA **6** 31, **3** 32, STLA **6** 33-38, WASA **4** 38, **23** 39-41, CHIA **34** 42, WASA *CH* **34** 47-49

WESTBROOK, JAKE P
(57,**37**) NYA **57** 00, CLEA **37** 01-05

WESTLAKE, JIM PH B
(**48**) PHIN **48** 55

WESTLAKE, WALLY OF/3B B
(**15**,17,23,31, 14) PITN **15** 47, **15** 48-51, STLN **17** 51, **15** 52, CINN **23** 52, CLEA **31** 52-55, BALA **14** 55, PHIN **15** 56

WESTON, MICKEY P
(**34**,26,52,43) BALA **34** 89-90, TORA **26** 91, PHIN **52** 92,NYN **43** 93

WESTRUM, WES C/CH
(40,6,**9**,3,51, 5) NYN **40** 47, **6** 48, **9** 49-57, SFN *CH* **9** 58,*CH* **3** 59-61, *CH* **9** 61-63, NYN *CH* **51** 64-65, *M* **51** 65-66, *M* **9** 66-67, SFN *CH* **38** 68, *CH* **5** 68-69, *CH* **9** 69-71, *M* **9** 74-75

WETHERBY, JEFF OF
(**12**) ATLN **12** 89

WETTELAND, JOHN P
(**57**,35) LAN **57** 89-91, MONN **57** 92-95, NYA **35** 95-96, TEXA **35** 97-00

WEVER, STEFAN P
(**25**) NYA **25** 82

WHEAT, LEE P
(40,**16**) PHIA **40** 54, KCA **16** 55

WHEATON, WOODY OF/P
(**30**) PHIA **30** 43-44

WHEELER, DAN P
(**34**,39,35) TBA **34** 99-01, NYN **39** 03-04, HOUN **35** 04-05

WHEELER, DON (SCOTT) C
(**38**) CHIA **38** 49

WHEELER, ED INF
(**7**) CLEA **7** 45

WHEELOCK, GARY P
(52,**16**) CALA **52** 76, SEAA **16** 77, 80

WHILLOCK, JACK P
(**43**) DETA **43** 71

WHISENANT, PETE OF/2BUTIL/C/CH
(8,10,30,**29**, 27,16,24) BOSN **8** 52, STLN **10** 55, CHIN **30** 56, CINN **29** 57-60, CLEA **27** 60, WASA **16** 60, MINA **24** 61, CINN **27** 61-62

WHISENANT, MATT P
(30,**56**,50) FLAN **30** 97, KCA **56** 97-99, SDN **50** 99-00

WHISENTON, LARRY OF
(20,**18**,28) ATLN **20** 77-78, **18** 78-79, **28** 81-82

WHISLER, RANDY CH
(**53**) CINN *CH* **53** 04-05

WHITAKER, LOU 2B
(**1**) DETA **1** 77-95

WHITAKER, STEVE OF
(28,**9**,19,37) NYA **28** 66-67, **9** 68, SEAA **19** 69, SFN **37** 70

WHITBY, BILL P
(**58**) MINA **58** 64

WHITCHER, BOB P
(**15**) BOSN **15** 45

WHITE, ABE P
(**22**) STLN **22** 37

WHITE, BARNEY INF
(**9**) BKNN **9** 45

WHITE, BILL 1B/OF
(45,17,**12**,26, 10,7) NYN **45** 56, **17** 58, STLN **26** 59, **12** 59-65, PHIN **10** 66-68, STLN **7** 69

WHITE, CHARLIE C
(**24**) MILN **24** 54-55

WHITE, DERRICK 1B
(**14**,20,25,19) MONN **14** 93, DETA **20** 95, CHIN **25** 98, COLN **19** 98

WHITE, DEVON OF/DH
(**30**,19,25,2, 22) CALA **30** 85-90, TORA **19** 91, **25** 91-95, FLAN **2** 96, **22** 97, ARIN **22** 98, LAN **22** 99-00, MILN **22** 01

WHITE, DON OF/3B
(**15**) PHIA **15** 48-49

WHITE, ED OF
(**27**) CHIA **27** 55

WHITE, ELDER SS/2B
(**19**) CHIN **19** 62

WHITE, ERNIE P/CH
(30,**28**,18,29, 53) STLN **2/30** 40, **28** 41-43, BOSN **18** 46, **29** 47-48, NYN *CH* **53** 63

WHITE, FRANK 2B/SS/INF/UTIL/DH/CH
(19,**20**) KCA **19** 73, **20** 74-90, BOSA *CH* **20** 94-96, KCA *CH* **20** 98-01

WHITE, FUZZ OF
(29,**28**) STLA **29** 40, NYN **28** 47

WHITE, GABE P
(47,48,**36**,40 53) MONN **47** 94-95, CINN **48** 97, **36** 98-00, COLN **36** 00-01, CINN **36** 02-03, NYA **40** 03-04, CINN **36** 04, STLN **53** 05

WHITE, HAL (RED) P
(**25**,17,26) DETA **25** 41-43, **17** 46-49, **26** 49, **25** 50-52, STLA **25** 53, STLN **26** 53-54

WHITE, JERRY OF/CH
(**37**,32,18,25, 48,13) MONN **37** 74-78, CHIN **32** 78, MONN **32** 79, **18** 79-83, STLN **25** 86, MINA *CH* **48** 89, DETA *CH* **48** 97-98, MINA *CH* **13** 99-05

WHITE, JO-JO OF/SS/CH/M
(28,**25**,22,1, 21,40,41,4,2) DETA **28** 32-33, **25** 34-37, **22** 38, PHIA **1** 43-44, CINN **21** 44, CLEA *CH* **40** 58-60, *M* **40** 60, DETA *CH* **40** 60, KCA *CH* **41** 61-62, MILN *CH* **4** 63-65, ATLN *CH* **4** 66, KCA *CH* **2** 69

WHITE, LARRY P
(**47**) LAN **47** 83-84

WHITE, MATT P
(**59**,47) BOSA **59** 03, SEAA **59** 03, WASN **47** 05

WHITE, MIKE 2B/3B/UTIL
(**16**) HOUN **16** 63-65

WHITE, MYRON OF
(**52**) LAN **52** 78

WHITE, RICK P
(44,**51**,27,50, 24,00,88) PITN **44** 94-95, TBA **51/27** 98, **51** 99-00, NYN **51** 00-01, COLN **51** 02, STLN **50** 02, CHIA **50** 03, HOUN **50** 03, CLEA **24/00** 04, PITN **88/00** 05

WHITE, RONDELL OF/DH
(37,**22**,27,14, 24) MONN **37** 93, **22** 94-00, CHIN **22** 00-01, NYN **27** 02, SDN **27** 03, KCA **14** 03, DETA **24** 04-05

WHITE, ROY OF/2B/3B/UTIL/DH/CH
(48,21,**6**) NYA **48** 65-68, **21** 68, **6** 69-79, *CH* **6** 83-84, 86, **54** 04-05

WHITE, SAMMY C
(38,**22**,8,9) BOSA **38** 51, **22** 52-54, **8** 55, **22** 56-59, MILN **22** 61, PHIN **9** 62

WHITED, ED 3B/1B
(15,**10**) ATLN **15/10** 89

WHITEHEAD, BURGESS (WHITEY) 2B/INF
(14,**7**,2,9) STLN **14** 33, **14** 34-35, NYN **7** 36-38, **2** 39, **7** 40-41, PITN **9** 46

WHITEHEAD, JOHN (SILENT JOHN) P
(11,**34**,20,28, 14,25,26) CHIA **11/34** 35, **20/34** 36, **28** 37, 39, **34** 37-39, STLA **14/28/11** 39, **25** 40, **26** 42

WHITEHILL, EARL P/CH
(**11**,15,31,23) DETA **11** 31, **15** 32, WASA **11** 33-36, CLEA **11** 37-38, CHIN **31** 39, PHIN *CH* **23** 43

WHITEHOUSE, LEN P
(15,12,**22**) TEXA **15/12** 81, MINA **22** 83-85

WHITEHURST, WALLY P
(**47**,41,55) NYN **47** 89-92, SDN **41** 93-94, NYA **55** 96

WHITEN, MARK OF/DH
(40,23,**22**,27, 25,20,12,29) TORA **40** 90, **23** 91, CLEA **23** 91-92, STLN **22** 93-94, BOSA **27** 95, PHIN **22** 95-96, ATLN **25** 96, SEAA **20** 96, NYA **22** 97, CLEA **12** 98, **29** 99-00

WHITESIDE, ELI C
(15,**77**) BALA **15/77** 05

WHITESIDE, MATT P
(46,**27**,37,49, 48) TEXA **46** 92, TEXA **27** 93-97, PHILS **37** 98, SDN **49** 99-00, ATLN **48** 01, TORA **48** 05

WHITESIDE, SEAN P
(**30**) DETA **30** 95

WHITFIELD, FRED 1B
(17,**15**,23) STLN **17** 62, CLEA **15** 63-67, CINN **17** 68-69, MONN **23** 70

(Above) "Teddy Ballgame," "Thumper," "The Splendid Splinter." This was perhaps the best pure hitter the game has ever seen. The legendary slugger lead the league in runs scored (6 times), in doubles (2 times), Homeruns (4 times), RBI (4 times), walks (8 times), batting titles (7 times), on base percentage (12 times), and slugging (9 times). The most he ever struck out in a season was 64, his rookie year. He was the last .400 hitter with .406 in 1941. A lifetime .344 BA with 1,978 runs scored, 1,839 RBI, 521 HR, 525 2B, and he missed the better part of four years in the military! It's worth viewing old films or tapes just to see him swing—it's a thing of beauty.

WHITFIELD, TERRY OF
(51,44,**45**) NYA **51** 74, **44** 75-76, SFN **45** 77-80, LAN **45** 84-86

WHITMAN, DICK OF
(31,15,14,**18**, 37) BKNN **31/15** 46, **14** 47, **18** 48-49, PHIN **37** 50-51

WHITMAN, FRANK (HOOKER) SS
(**34**,__) CHIA **34** 46, __ 48

WHITMER, DAN C/CH
(36,**6**,59) CALA **36** 80, TORA **6** 81, DETA *CH* **59** 92-94

WHITMORE, DARRELL OF
(**17**) FLAN **17** 93-95

WHITNEY, PINKY 3B/2B/INF
(**5**,7,25,20) PHIN **5** 32-33, BOSN **7** 33, **6** 34-36, PHIN **25** 36-37, **5** 38, **20** 39

WHITSON, ED P
(47,**31**,29,32, 31,38) PITN **47/46** 77, **31** 78-79, SFN **29** 79, **32** 79-81, CLEA **32** 82, SDN **31** 83-84, NYA **38** 85-86, SDN **38/32** 86-87, **31** 87-91

WHITT, ERNIE C/DH/CH
(22,**12**,28) BOSA **22** 76, TORA **12** 77-78, 80-89, ATLN **12** 90, BALA **28/11** 91, TORA *CH* **12** 05

WICKANDER, KEVIN P
(**53**,45,38,52) CLEA **53** 89-90, 92-93, CINN **45/53** 93, DETA **38** 95, MILA **52** 95-96

WICKER, FLOYD OF
(35,36,40,19) STLN **35** 68, MONN **36** 69, MILA **40** 70-71, SFN **19** 71

WICKER, KEMP P
(25,**20**) NYA **25** 36-37, **20** 37-38, BKNN **20** 41

WICKERSHAM, DAVE P
(45,27,26,**14**, 40) KCA **45** 60, **27** 61, **26** 62-63, DETA **14** 64-67, PITN **40** 68-69

WICKMAN, BOB P
(31,**27**,37,26) NYA **31** 92, **27** 93-96, MILA **37** 96, **27** 97, MILN **27** 98-00, CLEA **26** 00-02, (03), 04-05

WIDGER, CHRIS C
(36,**16**,11,50, 32) SEAA **36** 95-96, MONN **16** 97-00, SEAA **16** 00, (01), NYA **11** 02, STLN **50/32** 03, CHIA **36** 05

WIDMAR, AL P/CH
(32,24,**20**,37, 2,3,49,18,41) BOSA **32** 47, STLA **24** 48, **20** 50-51, CHIA **47/37** 52, PHIN *CH* **2** 62-64, *CH* **3** 67, *CH* **49** 69, MILA *CH* **18** 73-74, TORA *CH* **41** 80-89

WIEAND, TED P
(33,35,**34**) CINN **33/35** 58, **34** 60

WIEDERMEYER, CHICK (CHARLIE) P
(**11**) CHIN **11** 34

WIEDENBAUER, TOM OF
(**33**) HOUN **33** 79

WIEGHAUS, TOM C
(50,**11**,13) MONN **50** 81, **11** 83, HOUN **13** 84

WIESLER, BOB P
(40,39,**21**) NYA **40** 51, **39** 54-55, WASA **21** 56-58

WIETELMANN, WHITEY 22/2B/INF/P/CH
(15,25,**7**,68, 9,19) BOSN **15** 39-41, **25** 42, **7** 43-46, PITN **7** 47, CINN *CH* **68** 66, *CH* **9** 66-67, SDN *CH* **19** 69-78, *CH* **9** 78-79, *CH* **19** 79

WIGGINGTON, TY UTIL/3B
(**9**,19) NYN **9** 02-04, PITN **19** 04-05

WIGGINS, ALAN OF/2B/1B/UTIL/DH
(**2**) SDN **2** 81-85, BALA **2** 85-87

WIGGINS, SCOTT OF/2B/1B/UTIL/DH
(**2**) TORA **57** 02

WIGHT, BILL (LEFTY) P
(30,29,15,18, 27,**17**,47,45) NYA **30** 46, **28** 47, CHIA **29** 48-50, BOSA **15** 51-52, DETA **18** 52-53, CLEA **27** 53, **30** 55, BALA **17** 55-57, CINN **47** 58, STLN **45** 58

WIGINGTON, FRED P
(__) STLN __ 23

WIHTOL, SANDY P
(56,42,**25**) CLEA **56** 79-80, **42** 79, **25** 82

WILBER, DEL (BABE) C/1B/CH/M
(23,40,10,**33**, 14,45,__) STLN **23** 46-48, **40** 47, 49, **10** 49, PHIN **10** 51-52, BOSA **33** 52-54, CHIA *CH* **14** 55, *CH* **33** 56, WASA *CH* **45** 70, TEXA *M* __ 73

WILBORN, CLAUDE OF
(**31**) BOSN **31** 40

WILBORN, TED OF/DH
(**37**,59,56) TORA **37** 79, NYA **59/56** 80

WILCOX, MILT P
(43,32,42,**39**, 34) CINN **43** 70-71, CLEA **32** 72, **43** 73-74, CHIN **42** 75, DETA **39** 77-85, SEAA **34** 86

WILES, RANDY P
(**52**) CHIA **52** 77

WILEY, MARK P/CH
(**18**,27,21,31, 35,28,34,38) MINA **18/27** 75, SDN **27** 78, TORA **21** 78, BALA *CH* **31** 87, CLEA *CH* **35** 88-91, *CH* **28** 95-98, KCA *CH* **28** 99, BALA *CH* **34** 01-04, FLAN *CH* **38** 05

WILFONG, ROB 2B/OF/UTIL/DH
(7,**9**) MINA **7** 77-82, CALA **9** 82-86, SFN **9** 87

WILHELM, HOYT P
(49,25,26,15, **31**,39,47) NYN **49** 52-56, STLN **25** 57, CLEA **26** 57-58, BALA **15** 58-62, CHIA **31** 63-68, CALA **39** 69, ATLN **47** 69, **39** 69-70, CHIN **39** 70, ATLN **39** 71, LAN **31** 71-72

WILHELM, JIM OF
(**25**) SDN **25** 78-79

WILHELM, SPIDER SS
(**7**) PHIA **7** 53

WILKERSON, BRAD OF/1B
(48,**6**) MONN **48** 01, **6** 02-04, WASN **7** 05

WILKERSON, CURTIS P
(**19**,30,26) TEXA **19** 83-88, CHIN **19** 89-90, PITN **19** 91, KCA **30/26** 92, **19** 93

WILKIE, LEFTY P
(**39**,31) PITN **39** 41-42, **31** 46

WILKINS, BOBBY SS
(23,**22**) PHIA **23** 44, **22** 45

WILKINS, DEAN P
(**38**,36) CHIN **38** 89-90, HOUN **36** 91

WILKINS, ERIC P
(**33**) CLEA **33** 79

WILKINS, MARC P
(62,**35**) PITN **62** 96, **35** 97-00, **50** 01

WILKINS, RICK C
(**2**,3,43,39) CHIN **2** 91-95, HOUN **3** 95-96, SFN **2** 96-97, SEAA **43** 97, SEAA **2** 98, NYN **39** 98, LAN **46** 99, STLN **29** 00, SDN **20** 01

WILKINSON, BILL P
(51,**13**) SEAA **51** 85, **13** 85, 88

WILKS, TED (CORK) P/CH
(**28**,36,29,45, 37) STLN **28** 44-51, PITN **28** 51-52, CLEA **36/29** 52, **28** 53, *CH* **45** 60, KCA *CH* **37** 61

WILL, BOB (BUTCH) OF/1B
(16,**28**) CHIN **16** 57-58, **28** 60-63

WILLARD, JERRY C/1B/UTIL/DH
(53,16,54,7, 26,**31**,2) CLEA **53** 84, **16** 84-85, OAKA **54** 86, **7** 86-87, CHIA **26** 90, ATLN **31** 91-92, MONN **2** 93, SEAA **31** 94

WILLEY, CARL P
(**16**,28) MILN **16** 58-62, NYN **28** 63-65

WILLHITE, NICK P
(28,37,22,**45**, 24,32,29) LAN **28** 63, **37** 64, WASA **22** 65, LAN **45** 65-66, CALA **24** 67, NYN **32/29** 67

WILLIAMS, ACE P
(5,18,**23**) BOSN **5** 40, **18/23** 46

WILLIAMS, AL (ALMON) P
(25,19,**21**) PHIA **25/19** 37, **21** 38

WILLIAMS, AL (ALBERT) P
(27,**28**) MINA **27** 80, **28** 80-84

WILLIAMS, BERNIE OF
(**20**,23) SFN **20** 70-72, SDN **23** 74

WILLIAMS, BERNIE OF/DH
(**51**) NYA **51** 91-05

WILLIAMS, BILLY (L.) OF/1B/DH/CH
(4,41,**26**,7,28, 51) CHIN **4** 59, **41** 60, **26** 61-74, OAKA **7** 75, **28** 75-76, CHIN *CH* **26** 80-82, OAKA *CH* **28** 83, *CH* **26** 84-85, CHIN *CH* **26** 86-87, CLEA *CH* **51** 90-91, CHIN *CH* **26** 92-01

WILLIAMS, BILLY OF
(**51**) SEAA **51** 69

WILLIAMS, BRIAN P
(**53**,26,55,51, 57) HOUN **53** 91-94, SDN **26** 95, DETA **26** 96, BALA **55** 97, HOUN **53** 99, CHIN **51** 00, CLEA **57** 00

WILLIAMS, CHARLIE P
(47,35,**49**) NYN **47/35** 71, SFN **49** 72-78, **47** 76

WILLIAMS, DALLAS OF/CH
(39,**30**,20) BALA **39** 81, CINN **30** 83, COLN *CH* **20** 00-02, BOSA *CH* **20** 03

WILLIAMS, DAN CH
(**43**) CLEA *CH* **43** 96-00

WILLIAMS, DANA OF/DH
(**19**) BOSA **19** 89

WILLIAMS, DAVE P
(**58**) PITN **58** 01-02, (03), 04-05

WILLIAMS, DAVEY 2B/CH
(26,14,**10**,1) NYN **26** 49, **14** 51, **10** 52-55, *CH* **1** 56-57

WILLIAMS, DEWEY (DEE) C
(**12**,6,8) CHIN **12** 44-45, **6** 46, **12** 47, CINN **8** 48

WILLIAMS, DIB SS/2B/INF/UTIL
(23,**6**,4,27) PHIA **23** 31, **6** 32-33, **23** 33, **4** 34-35, BOSA **27** 35

WILLIAMS, DICK OF/UTIL/3B/M/CH
(38,**23**,36,10, 16,33) BKNN **38** 51-54, 56, BALA **23** 56-57, CLEA **36** 57, BALA **23** 58, KCA **23** 59-60, BALA **10** 61-62, BOSA **16** 63-64, *M* **23** 67-69, MONN *CH* **33** 70, OAKA *M* **23** 71-73, CALA *M* **23** 74-76, MONN *M* **23** 77-81, SDN *M* **23** 82-85, SEAA *M* **23** 86-88

WILLIAMS, DON (E.) CH
(**28**,29,39) SDN *CH* **28** 77-79, *CH* **29/39** 80

WILLIAMS, DON (F.) P
(**35**,34,22) PITN **35** 58-59, **34** 59, KCA **22** 62

WILLIAMS, DON (R.) (DINO) P
(**43**) MINA **43** 63

WILLIAMS, EARL 1B/3B/C/INF/UTIL
(**32**,18) ATLN **32** 70-72, BALA **32** 73-74, ATLN **18** 75, **32** 75- 76, MONN **32** 76, OAKA **32** 77

WILLIAMS, EDDIE OF/3B/1B
(24,**34**,22,23, 20,26,30) CLEA **24** 86-87, **34** 87-88, CHIA **34/25** 89, SDN **22** 90, **23** 94-95, DETA **20** 96, LAN **26** 97, PITN **30** 97, SDN **25** 98

WILLIAMS, FRANK P
(**47**,36) SFN **47** 84-86, CINN **47** 87-88, DETA **36** 89

WILLIAMS, GEORGE 2B/UTIL
(5,19,**8**) PHIN **5** 61, HOUN **19** 62, KCA **8** 64

WILLIAMS, GEORGE C
(42,**19**,77,39) OAKA **42** 95, **19** 95-97, SDN **77/39** 00

WILLIAMS, GERALD (ICE) OF/DH
(13,36,**29**,27, 4,17) NYA **13** 92, **36** 93, **29** 94-96, MILA **29** 96-97, ATLN **27** 98-99, TBA **4** 00-01, NYA **17** 01-02, FLAN **4** 03, NYN **21** 04-05

WILLIAMS, GLENN 2B
(**16**) MINA **16** 05

WILLIAMS, JEFF P
(**54**) LAN **54** 99-02

WILLIAMS, JEROME P
(59,**57**,32) SFN **59** 03, **57** 04-05, CHIN **32** 05

WILLIAMS, JIM OF
(**39**,24) SDN **39** 69-70, **24** 70

WILLIAMS, JIMMY CH
(4,**40**) HOUN *CH* **4** 75, BALA *CH* **40** 81-87

WILLIAMS, JIMY SS/INF/CH/M
(**24**,3,22) STLN **24** 66-67, TORA *CH* **24** 80-83, *CH* **3** 84-85, *M* **3** 86-89, ATLN *CH* **22** 91-96, BOSA *M* **22** 97-01, HOUN **22** 02-04

WILLIAMS, KEITH P
(**42**) SFN **42** 96

WILLIAMS, KENNY OF/UTIL/DH
(16,1,**7**,25, 12,13,44) CHIA **16** 86, **1** 86-87, **7** 87-88, DETA **25** 89-90, TORA **12** 90-91, **13** 91, MONN **44/12** 91

WILLIAMS, MARK OF
(**27**) OAKA **27** 77

WILLIAMS, MATT (D.) SS/3B/C
(60,10,**9**) SFN **60** 87, **10** 87-88, **9** 89-96, CLEA **9** 97, ARIN **9** 98-03

WILLIAMS, MATT (E.) P
(45,**29**) TORA **45** 83, TEXA **29** 85

WILLIAMS, MATT (T.) P
(**41**) MILN **41** 00

WILLIAMS, MIKE P
(**41**,46,64,43) PHIN **41** 92-96, KCA **46** 97, PITN **64** 98, **43** 99-01, HOUN **43** 01, PITN **43** 02-03, PHIN **41** 03

WILLIAMS, MITCH (WILD THING) P
(**28**,99,49) TEXN **28** 86-88, CHIN **28** 89-90, PHIN **28** 91-92, **99** 93, HOUN **99** 94, CALA **99** 95, KCA **49** 97

WILLIAMS, POP (PAPA) P
(**9**) CLEA **9** 45

WILLIAMS, RANDY P
(**41**,57,54) SEAA **41** 04, SDN **57** 05, COLN **54** 05

WILLIAMS, REGGIE (B.) OF
(11,**41**) CALA **11** 92, LAN **41** 95, ANAA **55** 98, **12** 99

WILLIAMS, REGGIE (D.) OF
(51,**21**,36,55) LAN **51** 85-86, **21** 86-87, CLEA **36** 88, ANAA **55** 98

WILLIAMS, RICK P/CH
(**34**,38,33,65, 30) HOUN **34** 78, **65/38** 79, *CH* **38** 80, FLAN *CH* **33** 95, *CH* **30** 96, TBA *CH* **38** 98-00

WILLIAMS, SHAD P
(**59**) CALA **59** 96, ANAA **59** 97

WILLIAMS, SPIN CH
(**54**) PITN *CH* **54** 94-05

WILLIAMS, STAN P/CH
(**40**,19,35,21, 50,25,32,31, 42) LAN **40** 58-62, NYA **19** 63-64, CLEA **40** 65, **35** 67-69, MINA **35** 70-71, STLN **21** 71, BOSA **50/25** 72, *CH* **32** 75-76, CHIA *CH* **31** 77-78, NYA *CH* **42** 80-82, CINN *CH* **40** 84, **40** 87, *CH* **42** 88, CINN *CH* **35** 90-91, SEAA *CH* **35** 98-99

WILLIAMS, TED (THE SPLENDID SPLINTER) (THUMPER)(TEDDY BALL GAME) OF/P/M
(**9**) BOSA **9** 39-42, 46-60, WASA *M* **9** 69-71, TEXA *M* **9** 72

WILLIAMS, TODD P
(66,**53**,31,56) LAN **66** 95, CINN **53** 98, SEAA **31** 99, NYA **56** 01, BALA **53** 04-05

WILLIAMS, WALT (NO-NECK) OF/3B/UTIL/DH/CH
(28,**3**,13,51) HOUN **28** 64, CHIA **3** 67-72, CLEA **13** 73, NYA **13** 74-75, CHIA *CH* **51** 88

WILLIAMS, WOODY SS/3B/INF/2B
(7,**17**) BKNN **7** 38, CINN **17** 43-45

WILLIAMS, WOODY P
(54,20,30,18, **19**,17) TORA **54** 93-97, **20** 97, **30** 97-98, SDN **18** 99-01, STLN **19** 01-04, SDN **17** 05

WILLIAMSON, ANTONE 1B
(**11**) MILA **11** 97

WILLIAMSON, MARK P
(64,**32**) BALA **64** 87, **32** 87-94

WILLIAMSON, SCOTT P
(**48**) CINN **48** 99-03, BOSA **48** 03-04, CHIN **48** 05

WILLINGHAM, HUGH PH
(no#,**31**) PHIN **no#** 32, **31** 33

WILLINGHAM, JOSH OF
(**14**) FLAN **14** 04-05

WILLIS, CARL P/CH
(28,40,42,45, **51**,57) DETA **28** 84, CINN **40** 84-86, **42** 86, CHIA **45** 88, MINA **51** 91-95, CLEA *CH* **57** 03-05

WILLIS, DALE P
(20,**24**) KCA **20/24** 63

WILLIS, DONTRELL P
(**35**) PITN **35** 03-05

WILLIS, JIM P
(**28**) CHIN **28** 53-54

WILLIS, LES (WIMPY)(LEFTY) P
(29,**15**) CLEA **29/15** 47

WILLIS, MIKE P
(**33**,23) TORA **33** 77-80, **23** 80-81

WILLIS, RON P
(**36**,50,43,22) STLN **36** 66-69, HOUN **50/43** 69, SDN **22** 70

WILLOUGHBY, JIM P
(50,19,42,**38**, 26,34) SFN **50** 71, **19** 71-72, **42** 72-74, BOSA **33** 75, **38** 75-77, CHIA **38/26/34** 78

WILLS, BUMP 2B/UTIL/DH S
(**1**,17) TEXA **1** 77-81, CHIN **17** 82

WILLS, FRANK P
(19,43,45,22, **44**) KCA **19** 83-84, SEAA **43** 85, CLEA **44/45** 86, **22/44** 87, TORA **44** 88-91

WILLS, MAURY SS/3B/2B/M F
(**30**) LAN **30** 59-66, PITN **30** 67-68, MONN **30** 69, LAN **30** 69-72, SEAA *M* **30** 80-81

WILLS, TED P
(28,36,**25**,39, 26) BOSA **28** 59, **36** 60, **25** 60-62, CINN **39** 62, CHIA **26** 65

WILMET, PAUL P
(**54**) TEXA **54** 89

WILSHERE, WHITEY P
(26,73,**24**) PHIA **26** 34, **73** 35, **24** 35-36

WILSHUSEN, TERRY P
(**47**) CALA **47** 73

WILSON, ARCHIE P
(23,**15**,26,32) NYA **23** 51, **15** 52, WASA **26** 52, BOSA **32** 52

WILSON, ARTIE INF
(**15**) NYN **15** 51

WILSON, BILL OF/P
(34,**38**,40,32) CHIA **34** 50, **38** 53-54, PHIA **40** 54, KCA **32** 55

WILSON, BILLY P
(24,**37**) PHIN **24** 69-70, **37** 70-73

WILSON, BOB OF
(**16**) LAN **16** 58

WILSON, CHARLIE (SWAMP BABY) SS/3B
(24,**2**,33) STLN **24** 32, **2** 33, **33** 35

WILSON, C. J. P
(**36**) TEXA **36** 05

WILSON, CRAIG 3B/UTIL
(**12**,8) STLN **12** 89-92, KCA **8** 93

WILSON, CRAIG (A.) C/1B/OF
(**36**) PITN **36** 01-05

WILSON, CRAIG (F.) 3B/UTIL
(**28**) CHIA **28** 98-00

WILSON, DAN C/1B
(**6**) CINN **6** 92-93, SEAA **6** 94-05

WILSON, DESI 1B
(**8**) SFN **8** 96

WILSON, DON P
(23,**40**) HOUN **23** 66-67, **40** 67-74

WILSON, DUANE P
(**15**) BOSA **15** 58

WILSON, EARL P
(**26**,16,42) BOSA **26** 59-60, 62-66, DETA **16** 66-70, SDN **42** 70

WILSON, EDDIE OF
(31,28,**23**) BKNN **31** 36, **28/23** 37

WILSON, ENRIQUE SS/2B/INF/DH
(35,25,**14**,19) CLEA **35** 97-00, PITN **25** 00-01, NYA **14** 01-04, CHIN **19** 05

WILSON, GARY P
(**46**) PITN **46** 95

WILSON, GARY (S.) P
(**41**) HOUN **41** 79

WILSON, GEORGE (TEDDY) OF/1B
(57,5,**40**,29, 39) CHIA **57/5** 52, NYN **40** 52-53, **29** 56, NYA **39** 56

WILSON, GLENN OF/3B/
(**12**,27,22,11, 13,53) DETA **12** 82-83, PHIN **27** 84, **12** 85-87, SEAA **22** 88, PITN **11** 88-89, HOUN **13** 89-90, PITN **53** 93

WILSON, GRADY SS
(**17**) PITN **17** 48

WILSON, HACK OF
(**4**,34) BKNN **4** 32-34, PHIN **34** 34

WILSON, ICEHOUSE PH
(**19**) DETA **19** 34

WILSON, JACK (BLACK JACK) P
(__,16,20,**18**, 19,9,24) PHIA __ 34, BOSA **16/20** 35, **18** 36-41, WASA **19** 42, DETA **9/24** 42

WILSON, JACK (E.) SS
(12,**2**) PITN **12** 01-02, **2** 03-05

WILSON, JIM P
(16,10,28,19, 36,**30**) BOSA **16** 45-46, **10** 46, STLA **28** 48, PHIA **28** 49, BOSN **19** 51-52, MILN **19** 53-54, BALA **36** 55-56, CHIA **30** 56-58

WILSON, JIM 1B/DH
(58,54) CLEA **58** 85, SEAA **54** 89

WILSON, JIMMIE (ACE) C/INF/M/CH
(**12**,9,3,1 40,2) STLN **12** 32, **9** 33, PHIN **12** 34, **12** 35-38, *M* **12** 34-38, CINN **3** 39-40, *CH* **3** 39-40, CHIN *M* **1** 41-42, *M* **40** 43-44, CINN *CH* **2** 45-46

WILSON, JOSH INF
(**20**) FLAN **20** 05

WILSON, KRIS P
(24,**19**) KCA **51** 00-03

WILSON, MAXIE P
(24,**19**) PHIN **24** 40, WASA **19** 46

WILSON, MOOKIE OF/DH/CH F
(**1**,3,51) NYN **1** 80-89, TORA **3** 89-91, NYN *CH* **51**97, *CH* **1** 97-02

WILSON, NEIL C
(**6**) SFN **6** 60

WILSON, NIGEL C/OF
(30,49,**48**) FLAN **30** 93, CINN **49** 95, CLEA **48** 96

WILSON, PAUL P
(32,**41**,40) NYN **32** 96, TBA **41** 00-02, CINN **40** 03-05

WILSON, PRESTON OF/1B S
(11,8,**44**) NYN **11** 98, FLAN **8** 98, **44** 99-02, COLN **44** 03-05, WASN **44** 05

WILSON, RED C
(16,__,26,18, **10**,27) CHIA **16** 51, __ 52, **26** 53, **18** 54, DETA **10** 54-60, CLEA **27** 60

WILSON, STEVE P
(34,**44**,38,50) TEXA **34** 88, CHIN **44** 89-91, LAN **38** 91-92, **50** 93,

WILSON, TACK OF/DH
(**12**,2) MINA **12** 83, CALA **2** 87

WILSON, TOM C/DH/1B
(17,15,**9**,6,7) OAKA **17** 01, TORA **15** 02, **9** 03, NYN **6** 04, LAN **7** 04

WILSON, TREVOR P
(41,**32**,17) SFN **41** 88-91, **32** 91-93, ANAA **17** 98

WILSON, VANCE C/1B
(**3**) NYN **3** 98-04, DETA **26** 05

WILSON, WALTER P
(**24**) DETA **24** 45

WILSON, WILLIE OF/DH
(19,32,**6**,16) KCA **19** 76-77, **32** 77, **6** 78-90, OAKA **16** 91, **6** 92, CHIN **6** 93-94

WINCENIAK, ED 3B/2B/INF
(**12**) CHIN **12** 56-57

WINCHESTER, SCOTT P
(52,**44**,__,37) CINN **52** 97, **44** 98, (99), __ 00, **37** 01

WINDHORN, GORDIE OF
(51,**23**,35) NYA **51** 59, LAN **23** 61, KCA **35** 62, LAA **35** 62

WINE, BOBBY SS/3B/1B/OF/INF/CH/M
(1,42,**7**,13, 9) PHIN **1** 60, **42** 62, **7** 63-64, **13** 65, **7** 66-68, MONN **7** 69-72, PHIN *CH* **7** 73-83, ATLN *CH/M* **7** 85, *CH* **7** 88-89, *CH* **9** 89-90, NYN *CH* **7** 93-96

WINE, ROBBIE C
(**7**) HOUN **7** 86-87

WINEGARNER, RALPH P/UTIL/CH
(21,**23**,32,26, 40,34) CLEA **21** 32, **23** 34-36, STLA *CH* **32** 48, **26** 49, *CH* **40** 49, *CH* **34** 50-51

WINFIELD, DAVE OF/1B/UTIL/DH
(**31**,32) SDN **31** 73-80, NYA **31** 81-88, 90, CALA **32** 90-91, TORA **32** 92, MINA **32** 93-94, CLEA **31** 95

WINFORD, JIM (COWBOY) P
(__,19,**27**) STLN __ 32, **19** 34, **27** 35-37, BKNN __ 38

WINGO, IVEY CH
(**12**) CINN **12** 36-37

WINKELSAS, JOE P
(**51**) ATLN **51** 99

WINKLES, BOBBY CH/M
(21,**1**,43,44,5) CALA *CH* **21** 72, *M* **1** 73-74, OAKA *CH* **43** 74, 75, *CH* **44** 74-75, SFN *CH* **5** 76-77, OAKA *M* **1** 77-78, SFN *CH* **5** 78, CHIA *CH* **1** 79-81, MONN *CH* **1** 86-88

WINN, JIM P
(44,**41**,40,48) PITN **44** 83, **41** 84-86, CHIA **40** 87, MINA **48** 88

WINN, RANDY OF/DH
(**2**) TBA **2** 98-03, SEAA **2** 04-05, SFN **2** 05

WINNINGHAM, HERM OF/SS
(21,**3**,29,5) NYN **21** 84, MONN **3** 85-88, CINN **29** 88-91, BOSA **5** 92

WINSETT, TOM (LONG TOM) OF
(12,11,9,34, **29**) BOSA **12** 31, **11** 33, STLN **34** 35, BKNN **9** 36, **29** 37-38

WINSTON, DARRIN P
(**58**) PHIN **58** 97-98

WINSTON, HANK P
(no#,**34**) PHIA **no#** 33, BKNN **34** 36

WINTERS, MATT OF/DH
(**17**) KCA **17** 89

WIRTH, ALAN P
(52,45,**30**) OAKA **52** 78, **45** 78, **30** 78-80

WISE, ARCHIE P
(**15**) CHIA **15** 32

WISE, CASEY 2B/SS/INF
(**7**,27,19,22) CHIN **7** 57, MILN **27** 58, **19** 59, DETA **22** 60

WISE, DEWAYNE OF/DH
(55,**16**,11) TORA **55** 00, **16** 02, ATLN **11** 04

WISE, MATT P
(**32**,26,38) ANAA **32** 00-03, MILN **26** 04, **38** 05

WISE, RICK P
(62,18,28,**40**) PHIN **62/18** 64, **28** 66, **38** 66-71, STLN **40** 72-73, BOSA **40** 74-77, CLEA **40** 78-79, SDN **40** 80-82

WISE, ROY P
(**15**) PITN **15** 44

WISSMAN, DAVE OF
(61,**2**) PITN **61/2** 64

WISTERT, WHITEY P
(**19**) CINN **19** 34

WITASICK, JAY P
(30,**52**,47,28, 34,45,26,46, 41) OAKA **30** 96, **52** 96-98, KCA **47** 99, **28** 00, SDN **34** 00-01, NYA **45** 01, SFN **26** 02, SDN **46** 03-04, COLN **41** 05, OAKA **45** 05

WITEK, MICKEY SS/2B/3B
(6,25,**2**,17,35) NYN **6** 40, **25** 41-42, **2** 43, 46, **17** 47, NYA **35** 49

WITHEM, SHANNON P
(**58**) TORA **58** 98

WITHROW, CORKY OF
(**29**) STLN **29** 63

WITMEYER, RON 1B
(**57**) OAKA **57** 91

WITT, BOBBY P
(48,**36**,32,53, 37,40) TEXA **48** 86, **36** 87-92, OAKA **32** 92-94, FLAN **36** 95, TEXA **36** 95-98, STLN **36** 98, TBA **53** 99, CLEA **37** 00, ARIN **40** 01

WITT, GEORGE (RED) P
(38,29,30,**39**, 48,36) PITN **38** 57, **29** 58, **30** 59-60, **39** 60-61, LAA **48** 62, HOUN **36** 62

WITT, KEVIN 1B/DH
(**6**,18,21) TORA **6** 98-99, SDN **18** 01, DETA **21** 03

WITT, MIKE P
(**39**,22,36) CALA **44** 81, **39** 81-90, NYA **22** 90, **36** 91, **39** 93

WITTE, JERRY 1B
(37,**7**) STLA **37** 46, **7** 47

WITTIG, JOHNNIE (HANS) P
(23,**19**,29,12, 35) NYN **23** 38, **29** 39, **19** 39, 41, **12** 43, BOSA **35** 49

WOCKENFUSS, JOHN C/OF/1B/3B/UTIL/DH
(45,**14**,15) DETA **45** 74-76, **14** 77-83, PHIN **15** 84, **14** 85

WOHLERS, MARK P
(**43**,39,51,57, 34) ATLN **43** 91-99, CINN **39/43** 99, **51** 00-01, NYA **57/39** 01, CLEA **34** 02, **39** 03

WOHLFORD, JIM 2B/OF/3B/DH
(**6**,14,9,1,5) KCA **6** 72-76, MILA **14** 77-79, SFN **9** 80, **1** 81-82, MONN **5** 83-86

WOJCIECHOWSKI, STEVE P
(**39**) OAKA **39** 95-97

WOJCIK, JOHN OF
(**17**,4) KCA **17** 62-63, **4** 64

WOJEY, PETE P
(27,35,**29**) BKNN **27/35** 54, DETA **29** 56-57

WOJNA, ED P
(**26**,50,34) SDN **26** 85-87, CLEA **50/34** 89

WOLCOTT, BOB P
(**33**,29) SEAA **33** 95-97, ARIN **29** 98, BOSA **29** 99

WOLF, RANDY P
(54,**43**) PHIN **54** 99-00, **43** 01-05

WOLF, WALLY P
(**39**) CALA **39** 69-70

WOLFE, ED P
(**34**) PITN **34** 52

WOLFE, LARRY 3B/SS/UTIL/DH
(39,1,**20**) MINA **39** 77, **1** 78, BOSA **20** 79-80

WOLFF, ROGER (ROO) P
(16,30,19,15, **17**,20,32) PHIA **16** 41, **30/19** 42, **30/16** 43, WASA **15** 44, **17** 45-46, CLEA **20** 47, PITN **32** 47

WOLGAMOT, EARL CH
(**30**) CLEA *CH* **37** 31, *CH* **30** 32-34

WOMACK, DOOLEY P
(**58**,37,41,3, 16) NYA **58** 66-68, HOUN **37** 69, SEAA **41** 69, OAKA **3/16** 70

WOMACK, TONY SS/2B/OF
(51,**5**,4,12) PITN **51** 93, 96, **5** 97-98, ARIN **5** 99-03, COLN **5** 03, CHIN **5** 03, STLN **4** 04, NYA **12** 05

WOOD, JAKE 2B/3B/INF/OF/UTIL
(**2**,45) DETA **2** 61-67, CINN **45** 67-68

WOOD, JASON SS/INF
(**39**,43) OAKA **39** 98, DETA **43** 98, **32** 99

WOOD, JOE (LITTLE JOE, J. P.) 2B/3B
(**24**) DETA **24** 43

WOOD, JOE P
(**17**) BOSA **17** 44

WOOD, KEN OF
(**12**,32,36,26) STLA **12** 48-51, BOSA **32** 52, WASA **36** 52, **26** 52-53

WOOD, KERRY P
(**34**) CHIN **34** 98, (99), 00-05

WOOD, MIKE P
(**51**,46) OAKA **51** 03, KCA **46** 04-05

WOOD, TED OF
(39,**11**) SFN **39** 91-92, MONN **11** 93

WOOD, WILBUR P
(**28**,41,19,16, 35) BOSA **28** 61, **41** 62, **19** 63-64, PITN **16** 64, **35** 65, CHIA **28** 67-78

WOODALL, BRAD P
(49,**48**,63,31) ATLN **49** 94, **48** 95-96, MILN **63 /48** 98, CHIN **31** 99

WOODALL, LARRY CH
(**22**,29) BOSA **22** 42-47, **29** 48

WOODARD, DARRELL INF/DH
(**44**) OAKA **44** 78

WOODARD, MIKE 2B/INF/DH
(**41**,20) SFN **41** 85-87, CHIA **20** 88

WOODARD, STEVE P
(48,**37**,29,43, 47) MILA **48** 97, **37** 97-00, CLEA **29** 00-01, TEXA **43** 02, BOSA **47** 03

WOODEND, GEORGE P
(**35**) BOSN **35** 44

WOODESHICK, HAL P
(25,28,19,20, **46**) DETA **25** 56, CLEA **28** 58, WASA **19** 59-61, DETA **20** 61, HOUN **46** 62-65, STLN **46** 65-67

WOODLING, GENE OF/CH
(46,16,**14**,31, 11) CLEA **46** 43, **16** 46, PITN **14** 47, NYA **14** 49-54, BALA **14** 55, CLEA **31** 55-56, **14** 56-57, BALA **14** 58-60, WASA **14** 61-62, NYN **11** 62, BALA *CH* **14** 64-67

WOODS, AL OF/DH
(**20**,11) TORA **20** 77-82, MINA **11** 86
WOODS, GARY OF/2B
(46,35,15,22, **25**) OAKA **46** 76, TORA **35** 77-78, HOUN **15** 80, **22** 81, CHIN **25** 82-85
WOODS, JAKE P
(**34**) LAA **34** 05
WOODS, JIM (WOODY) 3B
(**15**,30) CHIN **15** 57, PHIN **30** 60-61
WOODS, PINKY P
(**10**) BOSA **10** 43-45
WOODS, RON OF
(27,9,**43**) DETA **27** 69, NYA **9** 69-71, MONN **43** 71-74
WOODSON, DICK P
(35,18,32,**13**, 29) MINA **35/18** 69, **32** 70, **13** 72-74, NYA **29** 74
WOODSON, KERRY P/CH
(**42**) SEAA **42** 92, ARIN *CH* __ 00
WOODSON, TRACY 3B/1B
(7,**21**,54) LAN **7** 87, **21** 88-89, STLN **54** 92-93
WOODWARD, CHRIS SS/2B/UTIL
(42,**5**,4) TORA **31** 99-00, **5** 01-04, NYN **4** 05
WOODWARD, ROB P
(42,**45**) BOSA **42** 85-86, **45** 87-89
WOODWARD, WOODY SS/2B/INF
(**14**,6) MILN **14** 63-65, ATLN **14** 66-68, CINN **6** 68-71
WOODYARD, MARK P
(**50**) DETA **50** 05
WOOLDRIDGE, FLOYD P
(37,**41**) STLN **37/41** 55
WOOTEN, EARL (JUNIOR) OF/1B/P
(32,**23**) WASA **32** 47, **23** 47-48
WOOTEN, SHAWN C/DH/UTIL
(76,**44**,23,10) ANAA **76** 00, **44** 01-03, PHIN **23** 04, BOSA **10** 05
WORKMAN, CHUCK OF/INF/3B
(33,38,**4**,6,41, 11) CLEA **33** 38, **38** 41, BOSN **4** 43-44, **6** 45-46, PITN **41/11** 46
WORKMAN, HANK 1B
(**9**) NYA **9** 50
WORRELL, TIM P B
(58,**36**,33,30, 45,38) SDN **58** 93, **36** 94-97, DETA **36** 98, CLEA **33** 98, OAKA **30** 98, **36** 99, BALA **36** 00, CHIN **45** 00, SFN **45** 01-03, PHIN **38** 04-05, ARIN **45** 05
WORRELL, TODD P B
(**38**) STLN **38** 85-89, 92, LAN **38** 93-97
WORTHAM, RICH P
(52,**28**,45) CHIA **52** 78, **28** 79-80, OAKA **45** 83
WORTHINGTON, AL (RED) P/CH
(26,33,32,39, 36,**15**,19,46) NYN **26** 53, **33** 54, **32** 56-59, BOSA **39** 60, CHIA **36** 60, CINN **33** 63-64, MINA **15** 64-68, **19** 69, *CH* **46** 72-73
WORTHINGTON, CRAIG 3B/DH
(3,11,**25**,12, 39,24) BALA **3** 88, **11** 89, **25** 90-91, CLEA **12** 92, CINN **39** 95, TEXA **24** 95-96
WORTHINGTON, RED OF
(**2**,7,31) BOSN **2** 32-33, **7** 34, STLN **31** 34
WOTUS, RON SS/3B/CH
(**15**,10) PITN **15** 83-84, SFN *CH* **10** 98-05
WRIGHT, AB OF
(31,**5**) CLEA **31** 35, BOSN **5** 44
WRIGHT, AL (A-1) 2B
(**26**) BOSN **26** 33
WRIGHT, CLYDE P F
(**38**,52,25) CALA **38** 66, **52** 67, **38** 67-73, MILA **38** 74, TEXA **25/38** 75
WRIGHT, DAN P
(62,**36**,46) CHIA **62** 01, **36** 02, **46** 03, **36** 04
WRIGHT, DAVID 3B
(**5**) NYN **5** 04-05
WRIGHT, ED P
(14,**16**,34) BOSN **14** 45, **16** 46-48, PHIA **34** 52
WRIGHT, GEORGE OF/DH
(**26**,25) TEXA **26** 82-86, MONN **25** 86
WRIGHT, GLENN (BUCKSHOT) SS/2B
(**7**,28) BKNN **7** 32-33, CHIA **28** 35
WRIGHT, JAMEY P
(19,**21**,23,49) COLN **19** 96-97, **21** 98-99, MILN **21** 00-02, STLN **23** 02, KCA **49** 03, COLN **16** 04-05
WRIGHT, JARET P S
(**27**),21,33) CLEA **27** 97-02, SDN **21** 03, ATLN **27** 03-04, NYA **33** 05
WRIGHT, JIM P/CH
(45,50,**35**58, 55) BOSA **45** 78-79, KCA **50** 80, **35** 81-82, PHIN *CH* **58** 96, COLN *CH* **55** 02
WRIGHT, KEN P
(48,**28**,42) KCA **48** 70, **28** 70-73, NYA **42** 74
WRIGHT, MEL P/CH
(39,**17**,2,45, __,59,1,42, 31,22) STLN **39** 54, **17** 55, MILN *CH* **2** 55, CHIN **45** 60-61, *CH* __ 63, **59** 64, *CH* **1** 71, PITN *CH* **42** 73, NYA *CH* **31** 74-75, HOUN *CH* **2** 76-82, MONN *CH* **22** 83
WRIGHT, RICKY P
(37,21,**38**,24) LAN **37** 82, **21** 82-83, TEXA **38** 83-86, **24** 86
WRIGHT, RON DH
(**26**) SEAA **26** 02
WRIGHT, ROY P
(**31**) NYN **31** 56

WRIGHT, TAFT (TAFFY) OF
(23,4,**6**) WASA **23** 38, **4** 39, CHIA **6** 40-42, 46-48, PHIA **6** 49
WRIGHT, TOM OF
(23,**28**,22,5, 32,29,41) BOSA **23** 48, **28** 48-51, STLA **22** 52, CHIA **5** 52, **32** 53, WASA **29** 54-55, **41** 56
WRONA, RICK C/1B
(**1**,7,27,42) CHIN **1** 88-90, CINN **7** 92, CHIA **27** 93, MILA **42** 94
WUERTZ, MICHAEL P
(**43**) CHIN **43** 04-05
WUESTLING, YATS SS/3B
(**2**) NYA **2** 30
WUNSCH, KELLY P
(**65**,59) CHIA **65** 00-04, LAN **59** 05
WURM, FRANK P
(**22**) BKNN **22** 44
WYATT, JOHN P
(27,**33**,26,51, 37,35,11) KCA **27** 61, **33** 62-66, BOSA **26** 66-68, NYA **51** 68, DETA **37** 68, OAKA **35/11** 69
WYATT, WHIT P/CH
(**17**,12,19,23, 20,11,31,5) DETA **17** 31, **12** 32-33, CHIA **19** 33-34, **23** 35, **19** 36, CLEA **20** 37, BKNN **17** 39-44, PHIN **11** 45, *CH* **31** 55-58, MILN *CH* **31** 58, *CH* **5** 59-65, ATLN *CH* **5** 66-67
WYNEGAR, BUTCH C/3B/DH/CH
(**16**,27,35) MINA **16** 76-82, NYA **27** 82-86, CALA **35** 87-88, MILN *CH* **16** 03-05
WYNN, EARLY (GUS) P/CH
(44,20,11,26, **24**,32,38,2, 47) WASA **44** 39, **20** 41, **11** 42-44, **26** 46-48, CLEA **24** 49-57, CHIA **32** 58, **24** 58-62, CLEA **38** 63, *CH* **2** 64-66, MINA *CH* **53** 67, *CH* **47** 67-69
WYNN, JIMMY (THE TOY CANNON) OF/DH
(18,**24**,23,8) HOUN **18** 63, **24** 64-73, LAN **23** 74-75, ATLN **24** 76, NYA **24** 77, MILA **8** 77
WYNNE, BILLY P
(35,**46**,45) NYN **35** 67, CHIA **46** 68-70, CALA **45** 71
WYNNE, MARVELL OF
(36,7,**16**,25) PITN **36** 83-85, SDN **7** 86, **16** 87-89, CHIN **25** 89-90
WYROSTEK, JOHNNY OF/1B/UTIL
(23,14,**22**,1, 17) PITN **23** 42, **14** 43, PHIN **1** 46-47, CINN **22** 48-52, PHIN **17** 52-54
WYSE, HANK (HOOKS) P
(45,**33**,36,19) CHIN **45** 42-43, **33** 43-47, PHIA PHIA **36** 50-51, WASA **19** 51
WYSONG, BIFF P
(no#) CINN **no#** 32

Y

YABU, KEIICHI P
(**13**) OAKA **13** 05
YAN, ESTEBAN P
(**43**,56,59) BALA **43** 96, **56** 97, TBA **43** 98-02, TEXA **43** 03, STLN **43** 03, DETA **59** 04, LAA **59** 05
YANCY, HUGH 3B/2B/DH
(34,19,**14**) CHIA **34** 72, **19** 74, **14** 76
YANKOWSKI, GEORGE C
(**11**,58) PHIA **11** 42, CHIA **58** 49
YARNELL, ED P
(**9**) NYA **52** 99, **41** 00
YASTRZEMSKI, CARL (YAZ) OF/3B/1B/DH
(**8**) BOSA **8** 61-83
YATES, AL OF
(**9**) MILA **9** 71
YATES, TYLER P
(**33**) NYN **33** 04
YEAGER, STEVE C
(41,**7**) LAN **41** 72, **7** 73-85, SEAA **7** 86
YELDING, ERIC SS/OF/INF/UTIL
(**15**,20) HOUN **15** 89-92, CHIN **20** 93
YELLEN, LARRY P
(37,**47**) HOUN **37** 63-64, **47** 63-64
YERKES, CARROLL (LEFTY) P
(**41**) CHIN **41** 32-33
YETT, RICH P
(37,**42**,41) MINA **37** 85, CLEA **42** 86-89, MINA **41** 90
YEWCIC, TOM (KIBBY) C
(**12**) DETA **12** 57
YI, DON INTERPRETER
(**94**) LAN **94** 94
YOCHIM, LEN P B
(**38**) PITN **38** 51, **38** 54
YOCHIM, RAY P B
(__,**39**) STLN __ 48, **39** 49
YORK, JIM P
(40,**42**,43) KCA **40** 70-71, HOUN **42** 72-75, NYA **43** 76
YORK, MIKE P
(53,56) PITN **53** 90, CLEA **56** 91
YORK, RUDY C/3B/1B/CH/M
(19,20,**4**,3,6, 34) DETA **19** 34, **20** 37, **4** 38-45, BOSA **3** 46-47, CHIA **3** 47, PHIA **6** 48, BOSA *CH* **34** 59-62, *M* **34** 59
YORK, TONY SS/3B
(4,**24**) CHIN **4/24** 44
YOSHII, MASATO P
(29,**21**,55) NYN **29** 98, **21** 98-99, COLN **21** 00, MONN **55** 01-02

YOST, EDDIE (THE WALKING MAN) 3B/SS/OF/1B/2B/UTIL/CH F
(6,28,7,45,**1**, 10,23,42,53, 36) WASA **6** 44, **28** 46-48, **7** 48-49, **45** 50-51, **1** 51-58, DETA **1** 59-60, LAA **10** 61-62, **23** 62, WASA *CH* **42** 63-67, NYN *CH* **53** 68-76, BOSA *CH* **36** 77-84
YOST, NED C/DH/CH/M
(56,**5**,10,14, 52,53,42,3) MILA **56** 80, **5** 81-83, TEXA **10** , 84 MONN **14** 85, ATLN *CH* **52** 91-92, *CH* **42** 93-98, **5** 99-02, MILN *M* **3** 03-05
YOUKILIS, KEVIN 3B/2B
(**20**) BOSA **20** 04-05
YOUMANS, FLOYD P
(33,**17**,15) MONN **33** 85-86, **17** 87-88, PHIN **15** 89
YOUNG, ANTHONY P
(33,19,**16**,22) NYN **33** 91, **19** 92-93, CHIN **16** 94-95, HOUN **22** 96
YOUNG, BABE 1B/OF
(__,21,**5**,28, 14,17,10) NYN __ 36, **21** 39, **5** 40-41, **28** 42, **5** 46, **14** 47, CINN **17** 47-48, STLN **10** 48
YOUNG, BOBBY 1B/2B/3B
(3,**5**,37) STLN **3** 48, STLA **5** 51-53, BALA **5** 54-55, CLEA **5** 55-56, PHIN **37** 58
YOUNG, CHRIS P
(**49**) TEXA **49** 04-05
YOUNG, CLIFF P
(**35**,43) CALA **35** 90-91, CLEA **43** 93
YOUNG, CURT P/CH
(**29**,40,35) OAKA **29** 83-91, KCA **40** 92, NYA **35** 92, OAKA **29** 93, *CH* **41** 04-05
YOUNG, DANNY P
(**35**) CHIN **35** 00
YOUNG, DEL 2B/SS
(23,7,**17**) PHIN **23** 37, **7** 38, **17** 39-40
YOUNG, DICK 2B
(9,**5**) PHIN **9** 51, **5** 52
YOUNG, DMITRI 1B/OF/DH/3B
(24,**25**,26) STLN **24** 96-97, CINN **25** 98-01, DETA **26** 02, **25** 03-05
YOUNG, DON OF
(23,**29**) CHIN **23** 65, **29** 69
YOUNG, ERIC 2B/OF/INF/UTIL
(**21**,26,7) LAN **21** 92, COLN **21** 93-97, LAN **26** 97, **21** 98-99, CHIN **7** 00-01, MILN **7** 02-03, SFN **21** 03, TEXA **7** 04, SDN **7** 05
YOUNG ERNIE OF
(9,**11**,12,47, 30,36) OAKA **9** 94-95, **11** 96-97, KCA **12** 98, ARIN **47** 99, DETA **30** 03, CLEA **36** 04
YOUNG, GERALD OF
(**2**,15) HOUN **2** 87-92, COLN **2** 93, STLN **15** 94
YOUNG, JASON P
(29,**49**) COLN **29** 03, **49** 04
YOUNG, JOHN 1B
(**41**) DETA **41** 71
YOUNG, KEVIN 3B/1B/OF
(36,**29**,32) PITN **36** 92-94, **29** 95, KCA **32** 96, PITN **29** 97-03
YOUNG, KIP P
(44,**37**) DETA **44/37** 78-79
YOUNG, MATT P
(**40**,36,20,1, 30) SEAA **40** 83-86, LAN **36** 87, OAKA **20** 88-89, SEAA **1/30** 90, BOSA **30** 91-92, CLEA **40** 93
YOUNG, MICHAEL (B.) 2B/INF/SS
(2,**10**) TEXA **2** 00-01, **10** 02-05
YOUNG, MIKE (D.) OF/DH
(**43**,19,2,44) BALA **43** 82-87, PHIN **19** 88, MILA **2** 88, CLEA **44** 89
YOUNG, PEP 2B/SS/INF/UTIL
(**26**,6,4,17,7) PITN **26** 33-39, **6/4** 40, CINN **17** 41, STLN **6** 41, **7** 45
YOUNG, PETE P
(**20**) MONN **20** 92-93
YOUNG, RUSS C
(**9**) STLA **9** 31
YOUNG, TIM P
(**43**,59) MONN **43** 98, BOSA **59** 00

YOUNG, WALTER 1B
(**75**) BALA **75** 05
YOUNGBLOOD, JOEL OF/3B/INF/UTIL/CH
(19,**18**,25,8, 12,2,36) CINN **19** 76, STLN **19** 77, NYN **18** 77-82, MONN **25** 82, SFN **8** 83-88, CINN **12** 89, *CH* **2** 94-97, MILN *CH* **36** 98
YOUNT, EDDIE OF
(**8**,7) PHIA **8** 37, PITN **7** 39
YOUNT, LARRY P B
(**31**) HOUN **31** 71
YOUNT, ROBIN SS/OF/UTIL/DH B
(**19**) MILA **19** 74-93, ARIN *CH* **19** 02-04
YUHAS, EDDIE P
(**43**) STLN **43** 52-53
YURAK, JEFF OF
(**11**) MILA **11** 78
YVARS, SAL C
(**7**,45,48,17, 21) NYN **7** 47, **45** 48, **48** 49, **7** 50-53, STLN **17** 53, **21** 54

Z

ZABALA, ADRIAN P
(28,**29**) NYN **28** 45, **29** 49
ZACHARY, CHINK P
(**38**) BKNN **38** 44-45
ZACHARY, CHRIS P
(44,**37**,27,42, 40,36,35,49) HOUN **44** 63, **37** 64-67, **27** 67, KCA **42/40** 69, STLN **36** 71, DETA **35** 72, PITN **49** 73
ZACHARY, TOM P
(**16**,18,14,15, **14** 34,41) NYA **16** 29-30, **18** 30, BOSN 32, **15** 33, **16** 34, BKNN **34** 34-36, PHIN **41** 36
ZACHRY, PAT P
(**40**,38) CINN **40** 76-77, NYN **40** 77-82, LAN **38** 83-84, PHIN **38** 85
ZAHN, GEOFF P
(**38**,35) LAN **38** 73-75, CHIN **35** 75, **38** 75-76, MINA **38** 77-80, CALA **38** 81-85
ZAK, FRANKIE SS/2B
(**14**) PITN **14** 44-46
ZAMBRANO, CARLOS P
(**38**) CHIN **38** 01-05
ZAMBRANO, EDDIE OF/1B
(39,**22**) CHIN **39** 93, **22** 94
ZAMBRANO, VICTOR P
(60,47,**38**) TBA **60** 01-02, **47** 03-04, NYN **38** 04-05
ZAMORA, OSCAR P
(**45**,51,44) CHIN **45** 74-76, HOUN **51/44** 78
ZANNI, DOM P
(51,34,19,**43**, 33) SFN **51** 58, **34** 59, 61, CHIA **19** 62-63, CINN **43** 63, **33** 65-66
ZAPUSTUS, JOE OF
(**no#**) PHIA **no#** 33
ZARDON, JOSE (GUINEO) OF
(**27**) WASA **27** 45
ZARILLA, AL (ZEKE) OF/CH
(**14**,20,2,32, 45) STLA **14** 43-44, **20** 46, **14** 46-49, BOSA **2** 49-50, CHIA **2** 51-52, STLA **14** 52, BOSA **32** 52-53, WASA *CH* **45** 71
ZASKE, JEFF P
(53,**44**) PITN **53** 84, **44** 85
ZAUCHIN, NORM 1B
(35,**3**,5) BOSA **35** 51, **3** 55-57, WASA **5** 58-59
ZAUN, GREGG C
(48,24,**9**,6, 44,8,2,31 BALA **48** 95, **24** 95-96, FLAN **9** 96-98, TEXA **6** 99, KCA **44** 00-01, HOUN **8** 02, **2** 02-03, COLN **31** 03, TORA **9** 04-05
ZAVARAS, CLINT P
(**41**) SEAA **41** 89
ZDEB, JOE OF/UTIL
(46,**19**) KCA **46** 77, **19** 77-79
ZEBER, GEORGE 2B/INF/DH
(**25**) NYA **25** 77-7

ZEILE, TODD C/3B/1B
(58,**27**,14,25, 9,7) STLN **58** 89, **27** 89-95, CHIN **27** 95, PHIN **27** 96, BALA **14** 96, LAN **27** 97-98, FLAN **25/27** 98, TEXA **27** 98-99, NYN **9** 00-01, COLN **7** 02, MONN **7** 03, NYN **27** 04

ZELLER, BART C/CH
(**29**) STLN **29** 70, *CH* **29** 70

ZEPP, BILL P
(19,**25**,21) MINA **19** 69, **25** 69-70, DETA **21** 71

ZERBE, CHAD P
(**38**) SFN **41** 00-03

ZERNIAL, GUS (OZARK IKE)(ZEKE) OF/1B
(6,**19**,30,9) CHIA **6** 49-51, PHIA **6** 51, **19** 51-54, KCA **30** 55-57, DETA **9** 58-59

ZICK, BOB P
(**38**) CHIN **38** 54

ZIEM, STEVE P
(59,**29**) ATLN **59/29** 87

ZIENTARA, BENNY 2B/3B/INF
(12,**16**) CINN **12** 41, **16** 46-48

ZIMMER, DON (POPEYE) SS/INF/UTIL/CH/M
(**23**,17,14,34, 30,9,40,4,1, 48,5052,53, 54) BKNN **23** 54-57, LAN **23** 58-59, CHIN **17** 60-61, NYN **17** 62, CINN **14** 62, LAN **23** 63, WASA **34** 63, **23** 64-65, MONN *CH* **30** 71-72, SDN *M* **9** 72-73, BOSA *CH* **34** 74-76, *M* **34** 76-80, TEXA *M* **23** 81-82, NYA *CH* **40/23** 83, CHIN *CH* **4** 84-86, NYA *CH* **40** 86, SFN *CH* **1** 87, CHIN *M* **4** 88-91, BOSA *CH* **34** 92, COLN *CH* **23** 93-95, NYA *CH* **48** 96-97, **50** 98-00, **52** 01, **53/54** 02-03

ZIMMER, TOM CH
(**50**) STLN **50** 76

ZIMMERMAN, JEFF P
(**59**) TEXA **59** 99-01

ZIMMERMAN, JERRY (PIG)(ZIM) C/CH
(8,**22**,31,43) CINN **8** 61, MINA **22** 62-68, MONN *CH* **31** 69-75, MINA *CH* **43** 76-80

ZIMMERMAN, JORDAN P
(**46**) SEAA **46** 99

ZIMMERMAN, ROY 1B/OF
(**5**) NYN **5** 45

ZIMMERMAN, RYAN INF
(**25**) WASN **25** 05

ZINSER, BILL P
(**41**) WASA **41** 44

ZINTER, ALAN 1B/C
(**43**) HOUN **43** 02, ARIN **25** 04

ZIPFEL, BUD 1B/OF
(**11**) WASA **11** 61-62

ZISK, RICHIE OF/DH
(10,**22**) PITN **10** 71, **22** 71-76, CHIA **22** 77, TEXA **22** 78-80, SEAA **22** 81-83

ZITO, BARRY P
(53,**75**) OAKA **53** 00, **75** 01-05

ZOCCOLILLO, PETE OF
(**57**) MILN **57** 03

ZOLDAK, SAM (SAD SAM) P
(**26**,24,20,30, 21) STLA **26** 44-46, **24** 47, **26** 48, CLEA **30/26** 48, **20** 48-50, PHIA **21** 51-52

ZOSKY, EDDIE SS
(**1**,16,47,45, 23) TORA **1** 91-92, FLAN **16** 95, MILN **47/45** 99, HOUN **23** 00

ZUBER, BILL (GOOBER) P
(31,19,14,20, **17**,44,26) CLEA **31** 36, **19** 38, **14** 39-40, WASA **31** 41, **20** 42, NYA **17** 43-46, BOSA **44** 46, **26** 46-47

ZUBER, JON P
(21,43,**40**) PHIN **21** 96, **43** 96, **40** 98

ZULETA, JULIO INF/1B
(21,43,**40**) CHIN **15** 00-01

ZUPCIC, BOB OF/DH
(16,**28**,43) BOSA **16** 91, **28** 92-94, CHIA **43** 94

ZUPO, FRANK (NOODLES) C
(**42**) BALA **42** 57-58, 61

ZUVELLA, PAUL SS/2B/INF/DH/CH
(**18**,26,17,29 12,10,17,46) ATLN **18** 82-85, NYA **26** 86-87, **17/29** 87, CLEA **12** 88, **10** 88-89, KCA **17** 91, COLN *CH* **46** 96

ZUVERINK, GEORGE P
(17,53,38,15, **35**) CLEA **17** 51-52, CINN **53** 54, DETA **50/38** 54, **15** 55, BALA **35** 55-59

ZWILLING, DUTCH CH
(**12**) CLEA *CH* **12** 41

Todd Zeile (Opposite) hung them up at the end of 2004 as a Met. He requested to catch his last game since that's how he began his MLB career with the Cardinals. He finished with 2004 hits, 253 HRs, 1,110 RBIs, batting .265. He played on 10 different teams in his 16 years, but wore only 6 numbers, most often ending in a 7.

The Mets finally have found a third baseman—David Wright (Below). He looks like the real McCoy. His first full year showed a very good line: 99 runs, 176 hits, 42 doubles, 27 homers, 102 runs knocked in, and 72 walks adding up to a .306 BA, a .388 On base percentage and an impressive .523 slugging percentage. As good a year as a lot of #5's have had.

Fernando Valenzuela (Below) captured the imagination of the press with his unusual eye-rotating delivery and his effective screwball. He was jointly named Rookie of the Year and Cy Young Award winner in 1981. The six-time All-Star had accomplished a most unusual feat by 1990—he completed more than one-third of his starts—107 of 320. He completed only 6 of 104 thereafter. He won 173, lost 153.

Garagiola getting the scoop from Evans

Numbers, Italian-style (in Florence)

Retired numbers in Shea

Spring Training

On the lines in Fenway

Varying points of view

Lasorda hobnobbing

INTO THE SUNSET

12

Numbers are out of sight. They have jumped by leaps and bounds in terms of prevalence and importance. They not only have become part of a player's career but a major force in his life. Orel Hershiser kidded on seeking his #55 upon joining the Giants in 1998, "It's not a big deal other than all the jewelry my wife has with the No. 55 and the room that we have shaped like the No. 55 and hardwood floor that I had designed and the swimming pool and all the different things we have with 55, all the engraved glass and the baccarat crystal glasses, other than that, it's fine."

Shawn Estes, wearing it at the time, considered giving it up, but Hershiser said he didn't want to appear to be bullying a teammate. He picked Drysdale's old number—53.

"I've always said if I couldn't wear No. 55, I'd wear No. 53 as a tribute to Don," Hershisher said.

As time passes, teams have made increasingly more roster moves, retired more numbers, and have larger field staffs—all contributing to higher and higher numbers being used. In the Thirties a team had a manager and one or two coaches. Today, they have a manager (or two, or three) six coaches, bullpen catchers, batting pracitce pitchers, instructors, interpretors—all wearing numbers. The average high numbers have elevated significantly through the years.

AVERAGE HIGH NUMBER

	AL	NL
1930s	**34**	**41**
1940s	**39**	**45**
1950s	**47**	**50**
1960s	**51**	**52**
1970s	**52**	**52**
1980s	**57**	**56**
1990s	**64**	**61**
2000s	**66**	**68**

The figure is the average of all the highest numbers taken from each team for each year during each decade.

In the early years players liked the lowest numbers for it gave a sense of value by the team and in many cases reflected the power slots in the batting order. Generally speaking, a single digit player was a starter. Today, many players avoid a single digit on his shirt like the plague. That notion got a big boost from Hank Aaron who opted for #44 rather than the #5 originally issued to him.

Second and third generation major leaguers are more prevalent with each new season. Here's the Boone family taken at the 2003 All-Star game in Chicago. Both boys were selected to the their respective teams —Aaron (Reds) for the National League and Bret (Mariners) for the American League.

Aaron Boone is on the left, Grandfather Ray (who wore #8) is next, then Bret, followed by Father Bob (who also wore #8). Neither boy ever wore their elders' favorite number during their playing careers.

The pervasion of uniform numbers has reached new heights. In addition to the countless number of items already mentioned, now stuffed teddy bears have players' names and numbers embroidered on their backs. Celebrities go out of their way to get involved with teams. Garth Brooks wearing #77 participated in spring training with the Padres in 1999. This connection probably started in Los Angeles with the affable Tommy Lasorda hobnobbing with all the Hollywood stars. It's very common now to see actors and politicians surrounding the home dugouts.

The Pro-Am golf tournaments and softball games promote this as well.

Fans and collectors have vanity plates—Yanks 5 (for DiMaggio) and 23 Yank (for Mattingly) have been spotted in the New York area. Players autograph numbered shirts with the same number included in the signature.

A page torn from an Upper Deck catalog showing Mickey Mantle's rookie shirt with #6 and the Mick also signed it with No. 6.

Madonna's uniform worn in the movie "A League of Their Own" was auctioned off for $9000 while John Goodman's worn in "The Babe" brought in $1600.

Fathers search high and wide for Little Leaguers to have the beloved idol's number. Ray Knight wore the odd #41 for his idol Eddie Mathews when his Dad finally found one such shirt.

A cartoon showing astronauts circling the earth which had a huge "19" consuming the globe—one astronaut says, "I guess Yount finally retired!"

In California, the Padres Class A team moved from San Bernardino to Rancho Cucamonga. A contest was held to name the team. The winner of the 2000 entries was the "Quakes." The club's owner, Hank Stickney, said the clean-up hitter would wear #7.3 referring to the Richter scale.

Peter Prince, of Fairlawn, NJ, composed a song to commemorate Tom Seaver's induction into the Hall of Fame. He called it "#41." A folksy kind of ballad, Prince donated it to the museum at Cooperstown for which he received a lifetime pass.

Novelist Stephen King, a die-hard fan who can be seen at many a Red Sox game, got into the act with his book, *The Girl Who Loved Tom Gordon*. The back cover copy has a blurb that states "...wearing her blue Red Sox batting practice jersey (the one with 36 GORDON on the back..."

John Elway, the ex-Denver Bronco Super-Bowl-winning quarterback, has inserted his old #7 in the "O" of JOHN in his new company logo.

David Cone was a teammate of Daryl Strawberry on both the Mets and later the Yankees. When Strawberry was diagnosed with colon cancer, Cone embroidered Daryl's #39 on his hat to show his support for his friend's ordeal. Even Red Sox opponents Mo Vaughn and Nomar Garciaparra did it at the time for Strawberry.

Steve Lyons on ESPN talked about Jose Lima while he was an Astros pitcher, "Jose Lima wears the numbers of just about everybody in the league on his hat. They don't let him do it anymore though—it's against league regulations."

In the movie "The Fan," Robert De Niro played a homocidal maniac who stabbed an up-and-coming star playing with San Francisco because he took the #11 of the injured and fading star, Bobby Rayburn.

The Durham Bulls of the Class A Carolina League decided to retire the number of Joe Morgan many years after he passed through on his way to the big leagues and the Hall of Fame. They retired the #18 in his honor. A skeptical fan showed up with a vintage roster to prove they had retired the wrong number. Joe wore #8 as he did later with the Cincinnati Reds.

In the HBO film "Soul of the Game" on the integration of Major League Baseball, Blair Underwood played Jackie Robinson. While portraying Robinson's days with the Kansas City Monarchs, he was wearing #42. The truth is, Robinson only wore #42 on the Dodgers, not anytime before. It turns out the filmmakers insisted that Underwood wear the wrong number because "the public associated it with Robinson." Perception outweighed reality.

Billy Crystal is also a huge Yankee fan. In a recent interview with Michael Kay on the YES network, he talked about his part ownership of the Arizona Diamondbacks. While watching the 2001 World Series where his team was playing the Yankees, he turned to his wife and said, "We're beating us!"

Crystal achieved a lifelong goal when he filmed the story he held close to his heart for many years—the story of Roger Maris and Mickey Mantle, "61*." It aired to great success.

One of the clips shown on the interview was of Crystal throwing out a first ball while wearing the Yankee shirt with the number 61* on it.

In a further moment of absurdity, a major publishing firm in New York City retired the phone extension #8605 to honor a revered employee who left the company because of a family move.

The Yankees have so many numbers retired that only two single digit numbers remain, #2 and #6. Derek Jeter wears #2 and when Joe Torre became manager he took the only remaining one. "I usually wear #9," he said, "but now I wear #6. When I go out to the mound to make a pitching change, I'll just walk on my hands."

The practice of hanging a jersey in the dugout during the season to inspire the team has come into vogue. On June 15, 1999 the Astros hung Larry Dierker's #49 shirt to bolster their manager during his brain surgery. They finished in first place in the NL Central but lost to Atlanta in the NLDS. Dierker returned to manage for two more seasons.

The Cardinals' starting pitcher Darryl Kile died suddenly in his hotel room in Chicago, June 2001. The Cards hung his #57 jersey in their dugout for the remainder of the season. They went on to win the Wild Card in the NL only to have their dream season come to an end in the NLDS in Arizona, losing 3 of 5.

When Joe DiMaggio died, the entire Yankee scoreboard lit up with the #5. There's Cooperstown, there's individual Halls of Fame in many cities and there's Monument Park in centerfield of Yankee Stadium where his plaque hangs.

At Joe's memorial service in St. Patrick's Cathedral in New York, Bobby Brown, a former Yankee teammate, an AL President, and post-baseball medical doctor addressed those present, "I know Joe is in heaven. I suspect there's a committee up there right now trying to determine when to retire his number."

Millions of baseball fans watched Mickey Mantle's memorial service on TV. The camera showed a row of heads from above and to the rear. It moved slowly forward and took in another row and then another, quietly moving toward the voice in the front of the chapel. Bob Costas spoke on as the camera ever so slowly panned to the floral arrangement shaping the Mick's famous number seven.

His words describing the truth, warmth and courage of the man drifted around the peaceful seven in sharp contrast to the images playing through the minds of the listeners—Mickey crashing a titanic homerun; Mickey flashing across the grass to the out-of-reach white dot easily disappearing into his glove; Mickey's powerful speed bursting into second

The Mick and The Yankee Clipper at a ceremony in Yankee Stadium well after their glory days had gone.

on a routine single to left; and Mickey's winged homerun-gait coming around third again and again and again.

A hero was gone. A figure that loomed ever larger when his playing days were over. It was the stuff of baseball legends. The deeds grew larger. The abilities increased. His homeruns were monumental. His fabled speed unmatched.

Only near death did Mantle fully realize the power of his magnitude. And he put on the role of responsibility with simple dignity. He asked that we support his charities and told us that a life such as his disregarded the body and the loved ones around him.

Several generations of kids that trotted around diamonds everywhere with a graceful limp, elbows stabbing the air, with head bowed slightly to the left, buried this hero deep in their hearts.

All walked away with the warm feeling for a friend who touched us with his exciting performances and with a sense of pride that he got it right at the end, dissolving the dark years of pathos endured between.

Wherever Mantle went during and after his playing days, an idolizing crowd swarmed. The giants of any sport do this. Michael Jordan certainly, Tiger Woods, Jean Claude Killy in France, Peggy Fleming and Pele throughout the world, all have this allure.

But there is something about the nature of baseball—something that has been with us longer, perhaps. Something that builds the folklore in our national psyche. That number 7 will be the only number 7 for millions. It goes far beyond Yankee fans, beyond baseball fans to people who cherish fairness, truth and friendship.

I thought Harry Caray's singing of "Take Me Out to the Ballgame" during the seventh inning stretch of the Cubs' games was a little bit hokey until I found myself in Chicago at old Wrigley Field.

Everyone seemed to be anticipating the moment and when his loud, rough call crackled through the speakers—"TAKE..."—they cheered and broke right in, "...ME OUT TO THE BALLGAME..."

I was surprised to find my throat tighten a little and my eyes watery. It was a happy moment transcending singing a song, it connected me with Gabby Hartnett, Connie Mack, Babe Ruth and other moments of other people being part of this great game.

They don't use a number to remember Caray in Chicago, there is a caricature with an enormous pair of horn-rimmed glasses everywhere.

But, alas, it is a business. A business where the numbers of the bottom line and salary limitations play a big part. Smaller market teams such as Oakland have resorted to numbers of a different sort. In *Moneyball* by Michael Lewis, we see GM Billy Beane hiring statistical wizards and computer experts to crunch the performance numbers of collegians, minor league players and secondary players on other franchises to spotlight unusual attributes.

He strives to isolate those players on all levels that fly under other teams' radar and who quietly perform well in those categories that he thinks are extraordinary. He looks at on base percentage, walks, seeing more pitches in an at-bat and for pitchers: first pitch strikes, walks, and deception. He tends to avoid the obvious power hitters. "Good hitters develop power. Power hitters don't become good hitters," says Beane.

He has a limited amount of time to develop and benefit from young players before they become eligible to file for free agency and the big bucks that Oakland can't afford to pay. Giambi, Tejada, Damon, Mulder, Hudson and Isringhausen have all gone. Others may leave soon. But the draft choices the A's have gotten in return have given them a chance to develop new players for a time.

Rick Peterson, another such guru, has moved over to the Mets as pitching coach in 2004. The veterans on the staff were extremely skeptical. One by one he slowly won them over with his computer models showing specific deliveries in key situations revealing tendencies that could be modified and monitored for improvement.

Turk Wendell, a Mets pitcher well before Peterson showed up, had other numbers on the brain. The superstitious reliever wore #99 and signed a three-year contract with incentives that was worth $9,999,999.99 in 2000.

To most of us, it is *the* game of numbers. One of the great closers in history, Lee Smith, had already amassed 398 of his 478 saves by the time he joined the Yankees at the tail-end of the 1993 season. When asked what number he would get, he quipped, "They have retired so many numbers, I might be wearing No. 105."

Baseball has become a favorite sport in Japan. They have already had players wearing over 100 during the season. Isn't it ironic that they use the arabic digits that we use and not numbers from their own heritage.

JAPANESE #
1 一
2 二
3 三
4 四
5 五
6 六
7 七
8 八
9 九
10 十

The Japanese use the Chinese numbers primarily. Ordinarilly they would write them vertically, but have begun writing numerals in a horizontal fashion. Imagine a player with the number '57.' It would look like this:

五十七

No wonder they use the Arabic system.

In Williamsport, Pa. this past summer, the US team from the South had Dante Bichette, Jr. pitching. He wore his father, the former major leaguer's number—19. Unfortunately it didn't help the youngster since his team went on to lose before reaching the finals.

The Packanack Lake, NJ, champion softball team 'KLORPZ' posed for a team picture showing off their most distinctive feature—their numbers.

Here's a playful look at the future of numbers in the Numbers Game of Baseball. The author's grandson, Jack Ryan Looney proudly shows off his All-star uniform with myriad possibilities for adornment with numbers.

Since the Klorpz were the champs of their league, perhaps teams in the Major Leagues might benefit by adapting their numbering system to improve their karma. (The author is kneeling, third from the right, # .)

FOR GRAMMIE'S BIRTHDAY
FOR THE SICK PUPPY
GR
K-9
GUESSING NEW BABY'S ARRIVAL DATE
FOR SISTER'S BIRTHDAY
MOMMY'S BIRTHDAY
YEAR OF GRADUATION
HONORING FLINT RHEM'S SCOREBOARD NUMBER IN 1932
611
7
135
17
18
ALL-STARS
DAD'S OLD COLLEGE NUMBER
2
8
LAST YEAR'S FAVORITE NUMBER
GLOVE BELONGS TO UNCLE DOUG
3/5
44
FOR BIRTHDAY-GOING TO ZOO
HONORING HANK AARON—THE RECORD HE WANTS TO BREAK
FOR RETIREMENT AGE
165
4
BORROWED MATT'S BAT
PLAYER WITH THE HARDEST HEAD
6

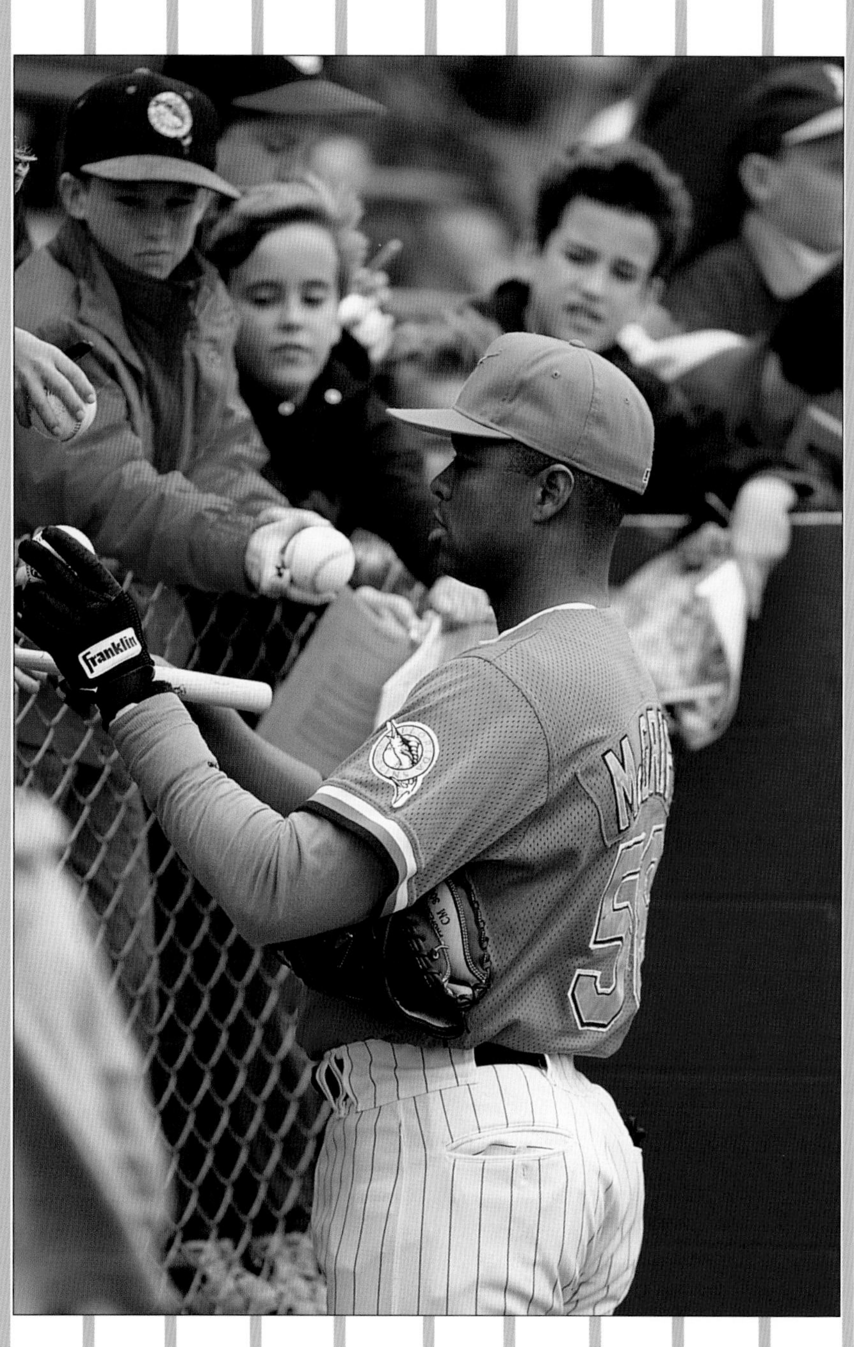
Franklin

THE ANSWERS

13

STEALIN' SIGNS (Clues)

If the Extra Innings (Chapter 10) were too tough for you and you need a few clues, we're going to steal a few signs to help you out before you go to the answers. Pause here a while and check these hints to see if it helps trigger a new response. This midi-section is designed to prolong the fun.

If you're still in the dark at the end of your trials, the answers follow immediately after this section.

1. *The #9 is a Hall of Famer who hit a homerun in his last ML at-bat. The #1 was recently inducted into the Hall and was a Phillie announcer until his death. Number 34 was diagnosed with a serious health condition and was forced to retire.*

2. *He beat Joe Black and Don Newcombe to Brooklyn.*

3. *The #9 is a decoy, he wore #5 after his rookie year The #25 was a rather colorful first baseman.*

4. *He was a Gold Glove first baseman.*

5. *The player who wore it said it was his initial, not his number.*

6. *He was a pitcher. There were three pitchers of the same name that wore numbers.*

7. *The Pirates retired the number he wore as a coach.*

8. *The #20 and #33 were retired by the Orioles, the #3 by the White Sox, the #30 by the Angels and the #1 by the Cardinals.*

9. *The Mets: #37 + #14; the Yanks: #37 + #1; the Dodgers: #24 + #2; the Pirates: #40 + #1; and the Reds: #1 + #10.*

10. *He was a first baseman who wore #9 for the Milwaukee Braves.*

11. *The Red Sox players were a Hall of Fame outfielder and a power-hitting shortstop. The Cub was a Hall of Fame shortstop.*

12. *He was an Oriole—#20, a Hall of Famer.*

13. *A Boston Braves outfielder and it was 1945.*

14. *Number 19 was traded to the A's from the White Sox during the season (1951); the Indians retired his number 14; #25 had reached the 100 HR plateau at the youngest age in 1967; and here's that Oriole again.*

15. *Williams wore his number his entire career. The other two wore the number as rookies.*

16. *In 1963, the brothers played in San Francisco.*

17. *The numbers were 15, 16 and 17. The last name began with an A and it wasn't Aaron.*

18. *He was 109-43. He was a 30-year old rookie.*

19. *One NL club began their numbering sequence with #10 until 1939.*

20. *He did it for Montreal and Texas.*

21. *He wore the number because he came from a town of that name.*

22. *They were around for a long time: #14 played 3,562 games for the Reds, Phils and Expos; the #2 played 2,323 games for the Tigers.*

23. *One 22-year old played his whole career with St. Louis, the other with the Reds.*

24. *A Pirate in 1955.*

25. *A second baseman who wore several numbers and a rookie outfielder who retired another number.*

26. *It wasn't Oddibe McDowell, it wasn't Omar Olivares or Cliff Johnson. In fact...*

27. *They were both pitchers for the Mets wearing #42.*

28. *KC A's: #33—outfield, Hall of Fame as a Cardinal; #23—pitcher turned manager, HOF as a Dodger; #27—HOF pitcher, but with Oakland; #9—outfielder, HOF as Yankee; #29—pitcher, HOF, Negro Leagues.*

29. *The numbers were for a third baseman turned first baseman (#3) and a second baseman turned first baseman (#29) and a bona fide first baseman (#14).*

30. *He pitched till he was 48-years-old while wearing #35 the whole time.*

31. *He wore #6 in 1939 and '40, #10 in '41, #1 in '42-'43—all for Washington and #15 and #7 in 1946 for Cleveland.*

32. *The obvious two played for the Giants and the Pirates. The other one also was a Pirate.*

33. *A Tiger outfielder—but he was better known as an Indian wearing #3.*

34. *One wore #11 his entire career for several teams, the other #4, but did coach and manage with various numbers. Both strictly American Leaguers.*

35. *Eh, it was a Canadian team.*

36. *He wore the #9 for this West Coast team. He won two HR titles while wearing it for them.*

37. *And another Yankee.*

38. *Five American League homerun champions wore the #9. Can you name them?*

#	NICKNAME	YEAR
9	THUMPER	1941, 42, 47, 49
9	(YANKS)	1961
9	HONDO	1968
9	MR. OCTOBER	1973, 75
9	(YANKS)	1976

39. *The first #14 (HOF) listed did it for Cleveland. The one that did it twice played third base for the Cards, and the last one played for the Dodgers but his number wasn't retired until he became a manager elsewhere.*

#	PLAYER	DATE	OPP
14	____________	JUNE 4, 1952	RED SOX
14	____________	SEPT 14, 1961	CUBS
		JUNE 16, 1964	COLT .45s
14	____________	JUNE 25, 1949	PIRATES

40. *The number was 5 and it was around WWII—a Yankee, Brownie and Tiger, respectively.*

41. *The obvious pair wore #44, but a hint to the real answer would be #14.*

42. *AL= #8; NL= #14.*

43. *He batted in only 6 runs. He went on to manage successfully, but sadly died of a brain tumor.*

44. *The year was 1945 on a pennant winner.*

45. *An American League fireballer.*

46. *It was #5—the guy that batted after Ruth and Gehrig.*

47. *A pair of outfielders in the 1930s, and two pairs of pitchers—one in the '70s, the other in the '90s.*

48. *AL = #8, NL = #6.*

49. *Is #00 lower than #0?*
- *One team issued #0 in 1984 and #99 in 1993.*
- *Another issued #00 in 1988 and #99 in 1977.*
- *Still another issued both #0 and #99 in 1997, yet another did that in 2002 and 2003.*

50. *Santiago didn't wear #09 till after the All-Star break.*

51. *Six men wearing the uniform of the Kansas City A's had their numbers retired. Only one had it retired by that franchise. One other had the number he wore retired. The other four had different numbers retired by those other franchises. Can you name them?*

A's#	PLAYER	POS	TEAM/RET	# RETIRED
33	____________	OF	CARDINALS	**9**
23	____________	P	DODGERS	**2**
27	____________	P	A's	**27**
9	____________	OF	YANKEES	**44**
5	____________	M	INDIANS	**5**
44	____________	CH/M	WHITE SOX	**4**

52. *It happened in Atlanta before the home crowd.*

53.
- *In 1983, a Phillies pitcher*
- *In 1984, a Cubs pitcher*
- *In 1987, another Phillies pitcher*

54.
- *A Dodgers pitcher in 1965*
- *A Reds pitcher in 1988*
- *An Expos pitcher in 1991*

55. *1934.*

56. *It was in Boston in 1975.*

57. *It wasn't Juan Guzman. In fact, it was an Expo.*

58. *He played for Toronto from 1984-92. He only wore #17 for his entire career.*

59. *He later wore a lower number for 'The Big Red Machine.'*

60. *A shortstop did it in 1997.*

61. *They all began with the letter 'W.' The first two were in 1876-1881. The other twosome were in 1941 and they were still a bit poisonous.*

62. *He was first issued his birthday digit—#5, then switched to his famous #44.*

63. *The first two times he did it numberless for the 1931 Dodgers. Then wearing #4 he did it again for the Cubs.*

64. *There were six:*
- *OF—1938-42, 46-53*
- *OF—1955-56*
- *OF—1962*
- *OF—1967-68*
- *3B/1B—1969-74*
- *3B—1984-90*

65. •*The reliever wore #35 and had 21 saves. He was born on September 15, 1940.*
•*The starter wore #36 and was 8-12. He was born on September 15, 1938.*

66. *The pitcher wearing #10 did it in 1931 for the A's. The other pitcher, #17, did it in 1934 for the Cardinals.*

67. *It was not a Yankee nor a 1930 Senator. Therefore, 1931 was the first year all the AL teams wore numbers permanently. There were several 20-game winners, but don't you think the 30-game winner got there first?*

68. *In 1932, he was 22-6 for the Cubs. He umpired 1949-55 in the National League.*

69. *He was wearing #20 while stealing 888 bases from 1964-79.*

70. *The year was 1975. And they were both pitchers. One made it to the Hall of Fame.*

71. *They both had illustrious careers. In fact one actually played the outfield with his son. There are four different teams involved: Mariners, Reds, Mets and Phillies.*

72. *Both were Hall of Famers.*

	BA	HR	RBI
#3 A's	.356	48	163
#3 PHILLIES	.368	28	120

73. *Remember, he was a coach with the Dodgers in 1938.*

74. *He was a 7-time All-Star and a batting champion.*

75. *Six of the top 17 career total base hitters had their uniform number end in #4. Can you name them?*

#	PLAYER	YEARS	TOTAL BASES
_4	______________	1954-76	6856
_4	______________	1951-73	6066
_4	______________	1963-86	5752
_4	______________	1986-	5584
4	______________	1923-39	5060
4	______________	1926-47	5041

76. *A Cardinal in 1937 and a Yankee in 1956.*

77. *One batted .353 in 1985 and .335 in 1990. Another hit .350 in 2001 and .372 in 2004. The solo player hit .339 in 1998. They all wore #51.*

78. *No batting champ in the AL wore a number below 1.*
- *A Senator in 1935*
- *A Yankee in 1945*
- *A Indian in 1954*

79. *Clemente only wore it in his rookie year.*

80. *He did it as a Cardinal, a Giant and a Yankee.*

81. *He was with the White Sox at the time.*

82. *And it wasn't Al Oliver this time.*

83. *The two Cardinal pitchers had the same initials. The other pair of siblings was a third baseman and a well-traveled pitcher.*

84. *The number was #44—and you have the initials, right? HA, HA!*

85. *First number: The three times in the NL were:*
- *1938-39—Cubs*
- *1945—Cardinals*

The eight times in the AL were:
- *1932-33—Yankees*
- *1939-40—Senators*
- *1947-49—Browns*
- *1979—Royals*

Second number: Once in the AL:
- *1954—Red Sox*

And ten times in the NL:
- *1960-65—Dodgers*
- *1981-84—Expos*

86. *He was a first baseman. Remember,* ***LA***.

87. *In the AL:* *1985 Yankees*
1988 A's
1992 A's
2003 Rangers

In the NL: *1982 Braves*
1983 Braves
1984 Cubs
1988 Dodgers
1997 Rockies

88. *The first number (#3) was retired right off his back for someone else in 1948. He switched to another number (#7) in 1951, just prior to another Yankee Hall of Famer wearing it and retiring it.*

89. *We'll give you a couple: Aaron's first number was 5, then he switched to his famous #44. Red Schoendienst began with #6 then moved to his #2. Some other hints have been touched upon earlier.*

ROOKIE #	PLAYER	REGULAR #
5 ←	HANK AARON →	1
6	DICK ALLEN	2
6	CLETE BOYER	4
9	GEORGE BRETT	5
9	ROBERTO CLEMENTE	5
9	JOE DIMAGGIO	6
13	BOBBY DOERR	7
19	BOB FELLER	10
24	WHITEY FORD	15
25	RALPH KINER	15
28	TONY KUBEK	16
32	MICKEY MANTLE	19
34	THURMAN MUNSON	21
34	RYNE SANDBERG	23
43	RED SCHOENDIENST	44

90. *In 1985, this northern city did it for two players; in 1997 another team had a player and a coach.*

91. *The other was a Hall of Fame pitcher.*

92. *1. The pitcher (#44) pitched to the batter (#27) in the 12th inning who hit a homerun (4) meant a 7-6 win in a World Series game tying the series at three each.*
2. Pitcher to batter who hit a HR (his 715th, 4/18/74).
3. Pitcher to batter in the 9th inning who homered with two men on to win game 5-4 and send team to WS.
4. Pitcher mowed down the line-up in 9, winning 2-0. It was a very special game.
5. Pitcher in 12 innings and then what happened?
6. Another famous World Series feat.

93. *Three outfielders, not the Alous. One was much traveled while the other two each played for one team.*

94. *Later, one pitched a no-hitter for the Marlins.*

95. *AL: with Toronto; with Chicago; &Texas.*

96. *The #12 is the turning point.*

97. *In the NL, #4 in 1944 & in the AL , #5 in 1948.*

98. *In the AL, #7 in 1953 & in the NL, #8 in 1947.*

99. *He did it with the Royals in the '80s.*

100. *Nine times each the Cy Young Award was won by a pitcher either wearing the #31 or #32. Who were they?*

#	TEAM	YEARS	#	TEAM	YEARS
31	ANGELS	'64	32	PIRATES	'60
31	TWINS	'70	32	DODGERS	'63, 65-66
31	CUBS	'71	32	PHILLIES	'72,77,80,82
31	WHITE SOX	'83	32	ORIOLES	'80
31	ROYALS	'85			
31	CUBS/BRAVES	'92-95			

101. *Here's their teams. Does that help?*

#	TEAM	YEAR
3	YANKEES	1929-31
3	A's/RED SOX	1932-33, 35, 39
4	YANKEES	1931, 34, 36
5	TIGERS	1935, 38, 40
5	YANKEES	1937

102. *It was in 1943 when #43 hit 29 HRs for the Cubs. In 1944 he did it again—33 HRs.*

AL: *#44 hit 41 in '80*
#24 hit 22 in '81
#33 hit 22 in '81
#44 hit 39 in '82
#41 hit 40 in '85
#45 hit 44 in '91

NL: *#43 hit 23 in '46*
#44 hit 39 in '67
#44 hit 36 in '68

103. *Think the color red!*

104. *He wore #9 as a rookie, but he switched to the number retired for him. His career spanned 1937-51.*

105. *NL, one was a Giant, the other a Brave—in 1963.*

106. *Remember, the NL—and it was in New York.*

107. *He lead off for the Red Sox. He had 200 hits or more in his first three seasons.*

108. *One played in Philadelphia, the other in Chicago.*

109. *Traded to the Dodgers, his favorite number (#7) was taken. A pure hitter who played the outfield.*

110. *It was almost #19 where Tony Gwynn single-handedly did it 8 times.*

AL	NL
TIGERS .340 in 1955	DODGERS .368 in 1932
TWINS .323 in 1964	CARDINALS .357 in 1943
TWINS .321 in 1965	CARDINALS .365 in 1946
TWINS .337 in 1971	CARDINALS .376 in 1948
ROYALS .332 in 1982	CARDINALS .346 in 1950
	CARDINALS .355 in 1951
	CARDINALS .336 in 1952
	DODGERS .344 in 1953
	CARDINALS .351 in 1957

111. *They sure aren't stolen base champs!*

44, 3, 25, 24, 21, 20, 25, 3, 25, 44.

112. *Here's the teams and the years.*

#	PLAYER	AVG.	YEAR
7	CARDINALS	.374 (NL)	1937
7	A's	.390 (AL)	1931
7	YANKEES	.353 (AL)	1956
7	TIGERS	.353 (AL)	1959

113. *The father did it 5 times, the son 5 times. He even did 40-40 with a second near miss.*

114. *He was a coach who wore one of those digits in his Hall of Fame career in Beantown.*

115. *The AL left-hander (#11)—1933-35, 37-38 was a Yankee. The NL right-handers (#36)—1950-51, 53-55 was a Phillie and the other was a Dodger, (#53)—1959, 1959, 1962 (first game), 64, 68.*

The remarkable Tony Gwynn's a Hall of Famer. He's an eight-time batting champion with a career .340 average, a 5-time Gold Glove winner, selected to 13 All-Star teams and has led the NL in singles (7) and in hits (7). In 1997, he drove in over one hundred runs (119) for the first time in his career. He holds most of the all-time offensive records for the Padres—most runs (1,383), most hits (3,141), most doubles (543), most triples (85), highest BA (.338), most RBI (1,138), and most stolen bases (319).

ANSWERS

Let's hope that by the time you get here, you are not totally frustrated. Finally these are the complete answers. We hope that you have had fun and have come up with many questions to stump your friends. Extra Innings (Chapter 10) could have gone on endlessly since baseball is so rich with anecdotes, comparisons and numbers, numbers, numbers.

1. *Five players ended their careers playing over 100 games and batting over .300 since permanent numbers have been worn. Here they are:*

#	PLAYER	LAST YEAR	TEAM	BA
5	JOHNNY HODAPP	1933	RED SOX	.312
47	TONY CUCCINELLO	1945	WHITE SOX	.308
9	TED WILLIAMS	1960	RED SOX	.316
1	RICHIE ASHBURN	1962	METS	.306
34	KIRBY PUCKETT	1995	TWINS	.314

2. *The first black pitcher in the major leagues, hitting a homerun in his first at-bat was Dan Bankhead (#23) of the Brooklyn Dodgers. He pitched three years going 9-5.*

3. *Joe DiMaggio wore #9 as a rookie in 1936. The other Yankee was Joe Pepitone, #25. Other players hit two HRs in one inning, but they were the only rookies to do it.*

4. *Don Mattingly hit 6 grand slams in one 162-game season in 1987.*

5. *In 1982, playing for the Montreal Expos, Al Oliver won the title with a .331 while wearing #0. He claimed it was an 'O' for Oliver, not a zero.*

6. *Robert L. (Bob) Miller wore the most different numbers (15) in his 17 years as a player and 4 years as a coach. He had three stints with the Mets including the expansion club of 1962. He won 69 and lost 81. The Dodgers used him a league-leading 74 times one year. His best year was 1971 where he won 8 and saved 10. Ironically it was with three different teams.*

7. *Honus Wagner never wore a number when he played. The Pirates retired #33 which he wore coaching.*

8. *Name five players whose numbers were officially retired while they were still playing.*

#	PLAYER	YEAR
20	FRANK ROBINSON	1971
33	EDDIE MURRAY	1989
3	HAROLD BAINES	1989
30	NOLAN RYAN	1992
1	OZZIE SMITH	1996

9. *The retired managers:*

YANKS: #**1** BILLY MARTIN
#**37** CASEY STENGEL

METS: #**14** GIL HODGES
#**37** CASEY STENGEL

DODGERS: #**2** TOMMY LASORDA
#**24** WALTER ALSTON

PIRATES: #**1** BILLY MEYER
#**40** DAN MURTAUGH

REDS: #**1** FRED HUTCHINSON
#**10** SPARKY ANDERSON

10. *Joe Adcock, #9, of the Milwaukee Braves on July 31, 1954 had 4 homeruns and a double against the Dodgers at Ebbetts Field in Brooklyn.*

11. *The two AL RBI leaders played for the Red Sox in 1949. Ted Williams (#9) and Vern Stephens (#5) each had 159 RBIs. By adding their shirt numbers together you get 14 which was the number worn by Ernie Banks of the Cubs who led the NL in RBIs with143 in 1959.*

12. *The only triple crown winner so far who wore double digits was Frank Robinson, #20, who did it for Baltimore in 1966—.316-49-122.*

13. *Tommy Holmes did it for the Boston Braves in 1945 with a total of 28 homeruns.*

14. *Only four American League players from 1929-1969 won homerun championships while not wearing a single digit uniform number. Who were they?*

#	PLAYER	TEAM
19	ZEKE ZERNIAL	PHILADELPHIA
14	LARRY DOBY	CLEVELAND *(twice)*
25	TONY CONIGLIARO	BOSTON
20	FRANK ROBINSON	BALTIMORE

15. *Hall of Famers Joe DiMaggio, Bobby Doerr and Ted Williams all began their careers wearing the #9. Only Williams kept it for his career.*

16. *In San Francisco during 1963,
Jesus Alou wore #14, Matty Alou wore #41,
Felipe Alou wore #23.*

17.

#**15**	DICK ALLEN	351 HRs
#**16**	RON ALLEN	1 HR
#**17**	HANK ALLEN	6 HRs
		358 HRs

18. *The first Yankee to wear #13 was a four-time All-Star, he won 20 games twice and had a lifetime W-L percentage of .717—Spud Chandler in 1937.*

19. *The Pittsburgh Pirates did not issue a single digit uniform number until the 1939, #1—not until 1940.*

20. *The only player to wear the #0 in an All-Star game was Al Oliver. He did it for Texas in 1980-81 and for Montreal in 1982-83.*

21. *Bill Voiselle was from Ninety Six, S.C. He wore that number in the 1948 World Series for the Boston Braves. He wore it four years for the Braves and the Cubs.*

22. *Charlie Gehringer (#2) had streaks of 504 and 511 consecutive games in his career with the Tigers. Pete Rose (#14) had two streaks of 678 and 745 games played in a row.*

23. *The two 22-year olds wore #5 and #6. Johnny Bench won the MVP in 1980 for the Reds, and Stan Musial won it for the Cardinals in 1943.*

24. *The Hall of Fame outfielder wore #13 as a rookie—the Pirates' Roberto Clemente.*

25. *Mickey Mantle wore #6 in his rookie year—1951. And Tony Lazzeri wore it in 1929, 34-37.*

27. *What rookie wore #00? Brandon Watson—OF, Nationals in 2005.*

27.

#42 RON TAYLOR—P METS 1971
#42 CHUCK TAYLOR—P METS 1972

28. *No **player** has ever entered the Hall of Fame as a Kansas City Athletic, but five men who are in the Hall have at one time in their **playing** careers worn their uniform. These are their KC numbers.*

33 ENOS SLAUGHTER—OF
27 CATFISH HUNTER—P
9 REGGIE JACKSON—OF
23 TOMMY LASORDA—P
29 SATCHEL PAIGE—P

29. *The three first basemen played for the Twins: #3 Harmon Killebrew ('75), #29 Rod Carew ('87), and #14 Kent Hrbek ('95).*

30. *Phil Niekro, #35, had only 31 wins at age 30. He had only 197 wins at 40. Imagine that—over 100 wins after age 40! (Gaylord Perry had 76 wins at 30; Early Wynn had 83 by the time he reached 30.*

31. *The AL stolen base champ won six times with 5 different numbers: George Case.*

6 WASHINGTON—1939 (51 SB), 1940 (35 SB)
10 WASHINGTON—1941 (33 SB)
1 WASHINGTON—1942 (44 SB), 1943 (61 SB)
15/7 CLEVELAND —1946 (28 SB)

32. *Willie Mays #24, MVP—1954, '65; Barry Bonds #24, MVP—1990, '92; Dick Groat #24, MVP—1960.*

33. *Earl Averill wore #24 for the 1939-40 Tigers.*

34. *The only team with numbers retired for two shortstops through 2005 was the Chicago White Sox—*
#4 Luke Appling—SS
#11 Luis Aparicio—SS

35. *The other team to retire one number twice was the Montreal Expos: #10*
Rusty Staub #10
Andre Dawson #10

36. *Reggie Jackson wore #9 for 10 years in KC, Oakland and Baltimore, then switched to #44 with the Yankees who retired it for "Mr. October."*

37. *Babe Ruth's #3 was retired in 1948. No numbers were retired between Gehrig's in 1939 and the Babe's.*

38. *Five American League homerun champions wore the #9. Here they are:*

#	PLAYER	YEAR
9	TED WILLIAMS	1941, 42, 47, 49
9	ROGER MARIS	1961
9	FRANK HOWARD	1968
9	REGGIE JACKSON	1973, 75
9	GRAIG NETTLES	1976

39. *Ivan DeJesus did it, Freddie Patek did it, Jim Fregosi did it twice. Babe Ruth, Hank Greenberg or Roger Maris never did it. It's hard to believe but hitting for the cycle has eluded some of the game's great sluggers while some average batters accomplished the rare feat one miraculous day. Here's the three players who hit for the cycle and had their #14 retired. Hodges #14 was retired by Mets as their manager after his sudden death.*

#	PLAYER	DATE	OPP
14	LARRY DOBY	JUNE 4, 1952	RED SOX
14	KEN BOYER	SEPT 14, 1961	CUBS
		JUNE 16, 1964	COLT .45s
14	GIL HODGES	JUNE 25, 1949	PIRATES

40. *It was during WWII and many players were away.*

1944 **5** NICK ETTEN—YANKEES 22 HRs
1945 **5** VERN STEPHENS—BROWNS 24 HRs
1946 **5** HANK GREENBERG—TIGERS 44 HRs

41. *If 44 is opposite: Hank Aaron hit 44 homers 4 times winning three titles, sharing one with Willie McCovey #44 also. But Ernie Banks wore #14 when he won the 1960 HR crown with 41 homers.*

42. *The longest careers with the same number belong to Pete Rose #14—24 years, 1963-86 with three teams. In the AL it's Carl Yastrzemski #8 for 23 years, 1961-83.*

43. *Dick Howser knocked in just 6 runs for the Indians in 1965 in 307 AB. He wore #18.*

44. *Phil Cavarretta playing with the NL Champion Cubs in 1945, batted .355 while wearing #44.*

45. *The first non-Yankee to have a number retired for him was Cleveland fireballer Bob Feller—#19 in 1957.*

46. *It happened on May 6, 1929. It wouldn't be surprising if Combs, Ruth and Gehrig were on base when #5 Bob Meusel of the Yankees hit the first Grand Slam while numbers were being permanently worn.*

47. *The Niekro brothers, Phil #35 and Joe #36 did it for the Braves in 1973-74. Before that, Lloyd Waner #10 and Paul Waner #11 did it for the Pirates for the 1930s, and Andy Benes #40 and Alan Benes #41 did it while with the Cardinals in 1996-97. The O'Brien twins did it (#6, #7) only one year (1955) with the Pirates.*

48. *The player in each league who played the most games on* ***one*** *team while wearing the same number was Carl Yastrzemski #8 for the Red Sox in the AL, 23 years or 3308 games, and Stan Musial #6 for the Cardinals, 22 years or 3026 games.*

49.

TEAM	#	PLAYER	YEAR	#	PLAYER	YEAR
PHILLIES	**0**	AL OLIVER	1984	**99**	MITCH WILLIAMS	1993
A's	**00**	DON BAYLOR	1988	**99**	WILLIE CRAWFORD	1977
METS	**0**	REY ORDONEZ	1996-7	**99**	TURK WENDELL	1997
CARDS	**0**	KERRY ROBINSON	2002-3	**99**	SO TAGUCHI	2002-5

50. *Who wore the #9 on the Padres the same year Santiago wore #09? This is a trick question. Santiago did. He wore #9 the first half of the season and #09 the rest.*

51. *The six men wearing the uniform of the Kansas City A's who had their numbers retired are listed below:*

A's#	PLAYER	POS	TEAM/RET	#/RET
33	ENOS SLAUGHTER	OF	CARDINALS	**9**
23	TOM LASORDA	P	DODGERS	**2**
27	CATFISH HUNTER	P	A's	**27**
9	REGGIE JACKSON	OF	YANKEES	**44**
5	LOU BOUDREAU	M	INDIANS	**5**
44	LUKE APPLING	CH/M	WHITE SOX	**4**

52. *Anybody who saw the event probably will remember Al Downing (#44) of the Dodgers serving up the 715th homerun ball of Hank Aaron's (#44) career in Atlanta.*

53. *The three Cy Young winners wore #40.*

#	PLAYER	TEAM	YEAR
40	JOHN DENNY	PHILLIES	1983
40	RICK SUTCLIFFE	CUBS	1984
40	STEVE BEDROSIAN	PHILLIES	1987

54. *Three National League pitchers pitched perfect games while wearing the same number and it wasn't 14. The number was 32.*

#	PLAYER	TEAM	YEAR	OPP
32	SANDY KOUFAX	DODGERS	1965	CUBS
32	TOM BROWNING	REDS	1988	DODGERS
32	DENNIS MARTINEZ	EXPOS	1991	DODGERS

55. *1934. The Cardinals vs. the Tigers—Frankie Frisch wore #3, the manager/2B for the Cards beat Mickey Cochrane, #2, the manager/C for the Tigers, 4 games to 3.*

56. *Bernie Carbo wore Bobby Doerr's #1 when he pinch-hit a 3-run HR for the Red Sox in the 8th inning of Game 6 to tie Cincinnati setting the stage for Carlton Fisk to win the game with his famous foul-pole home run.*

57. *It wasn't Guzman. It was Montreal Expo pitcher Bryn Smith #66 in 1981, ten years before Guzman.*

58. *The only Blue Jay to hit for the cycle was Kelly Gruber, #17. He did it on April 16, 1989 vs. the Royals.*

59. *The only Hall of Fame to ever play in a Colt .45s uniform was second baseman Joe Morgan. He wore #18.*

60. *The Gold Glover wearing number 0 was shortstop Rey Ordoñez of the Mets in 1997.*

61. *Brothers George Wright (1876-78, 80-81) and Harry Wright (1876-81) with Boston of the NL never wore numbers but Lloyd (1941) and Paul Waner (1941-42) while with the old Braves did wear them.*

62. *Hank Aaron was issued #5 (his birthday), but switched to #44 for his second season.*

63. *Babe Herman hit for the cycle twice with the Dodgers before they wore numbers, then on Sept. 30,1933 he did it again for the Cubs wearing #4.*

64. *All-Star players who have worn #9 for the Cards?*

9 ENOS SLAUGHTER—OF 1938-42, 46-53
9 BILL VIRDON—OF 1955-56
9 MINNIE MINOSO—OF 1962
9 ROGER MARIS—OF 1967-68
9 JOE TORRE—3B/1B 1969-74
9 TERRY PENDLETON—3B 1984-90

65. *In 1965, the Giants' ace starter and ace reliever: Both were born on September 15th—#35 Frank Linzy, the reliever was 2 years younger than Gaylord Perry #36.*

66. *Who were the first 30-game winners in each league to wear a number?*

YEAR	#	PLAYER	RECORD	TEAM
1931	**10**	LEFTY GROVE	31-4 (AL)	PHILDELPHIA A's
1934	**17**	DIZZY DEAN	30-7 (NL)	ST. LOUIS CARDINALS

67. *Grove reached 20 that same year before anyone else accomplished it. No Yankee did the previous 2 years, nor any Senator in 1930.*

68. *The first 20-game winner in the NL wore two numbers—#30 and #17 en route to a 22-win season and became a major league umpire. He was Lon Warneke, "The Arkansas Hummingbird," Cubs, in 1932.*

69. *The player who stole the most bases with the* ***same*** *number was Lou Brock, 17 more than Henderson.*

#	PLAYER	SB	TEAM	YEARS
20	LOU BROCK	888	STLN	1964-79
35	RICKEY HENDERSON	532	OAKA,SEAA,BOSA	1979-84,00,02
24	RICKEY HENDERSON	871	NYA,OAKA,TORA, SDN,ANAA,NYN	1985-2001
30	TIM RAINES	777	MONN,CHIA	1979-95
19	BERT CAMPANERIS	649	KCA,OAKA,TEXA CALA,NYA	1964-83

70. *What two brothers wore the same number during the same year for different teams?*

#	PLAYER	TEAM	YEAR
36	GAYLORD PERRY-P	CLEVELAND/TEXAS	1975
36	JIM PERRY -P	OAKLAND	1975

71. *What fathers who coached, wore the same numbers as their sons?*

#	PLAYER		TEAM	YEAR	#	PLAYER		TEAM
24	KEN GRIFFEY, SR.	CH	COLN	1996	**24**	KEN GRIFFEY, JR.	OF	SEAA
56	HAL McRAE	CH	PHIN	1997	**56**	BRIAN McRAE	OF	CHIN/PHIN

72. *The two triple crown winners in Philadelphia were:*

1933	**3**	JIMMIE FOXX	A's	.356	48	163
1933	**3**	CHUCK KLEIN	PHILLIES	.368	28	120

73. *Babe wore #35 as a coach for the Brooklyn Dodgers in 1938. Ironically, rookie second baseman Pete Coscarart wore #3 and batted .152 without a HR.*

74. *Al Oliver wore #0 for Montreal, 1982-83, and for Toronto in 1985.*

75. *Six of the top 17 career total base hitters had their most famous uniform number end in the digit 4.*

#	PLAYER	TB	YEARS
44	HANK AARON	6856	1954-76 (WORE #5 IN 1954)
24	WILLIE MAYS	6066	1951-73
14	PETE ROSE	5752	1963-86
24	BARRY BONDS	5584	1986- (WORE #24—1986-92)
4	LOU GEHRIG	5060	1923-39
4	MEL OTT	5041	1926-47 (WORE #5 IN 1932)

76. *The two triple crown winners who wore the #7:*

7	DUCKY MEDWICK	CARDS	1937	.374	31	154
7	MICKEY MANTLE	YANKS	1956	.353	52	130

77. *The batting champs with the highest number:*

51	WILLIE McGEE	CARDS	.353	1985
51	WILLIE McGEE	CARDS/A's	.335	1990
51	BERNIE WILLIAMS	YANKS	.339	1998
51	ICHIRO SUZUKI	MARINERS	.350	2001
51	ICHIRO SUZUKI	MARINERS	.372	2004

78. *The lowest number in the American League while winning a batting championship:*

1	BUDDY MYER	SENATORS	.349	1935
1	SNUFFY STIRNWEISS	YANKS	.309	1945
1	BOBBY AVILA	INDIANS	.341	1954

79. *True. Roberto Clemente wore #13 in his rookie season, but did not lead the league in anything.*

80. *The Hall of Famer with the most 3-HR games (6):*

#	PLAYER	TEAM	TIMES
10	JOHNNY MIZE	CARDS	4 (7/13 & 7/20/38; 5/13 & 9/8/40)
15	JOHNNY MIZE	GIANTS	1 (4/24/47)
36	JOHNNY MIZE	YANKEES	1 (9/15/50)

81. *Carlton Fisk #72, wore the highest hitting for the cycle on May 16, 1984 for the White Sox vs. the Royals.*

82. *Oddibe McDowell #0, did it for the Rangers on July 23, 1985 vs. the Indians.*

83. *The Royals pair: George Brett #25, KC 1973-75*
Ken Brett #25, KC 1980-81
The Cardinals pair: Alan Benes #40, St. Louis 1995
Andy Benes #40, St. Louis 1996-97

84. *In 1970, one not-so-famous brother* ***(Hank Allen)*** *of a major league trio* ***(Dick, Ron)*** *had the same initials,* ***(H.A.)*** *first name* ***(Hank)*** *and wore the same number* ***(#44)*** *for the same team* ***(Brewers)*** *as a famous brother* ***(Hank Aaron)*** *of another major league duo* ***(Hank, Tommy)*** *did 5 years later.*

44	HANK ALLEN	BREWERS	1970 (BROTHER OF DICK & RON)
44	HANK AARON	BREWERS	1975-76 (BROTHER OF TOMMY)

85. *The 2 most frequently worn numbers of base stealing champs:*

#	NAME	TEAM	SB	YEARS
6	BEN CHAPMAN	YANKS	38,27	1932-33
6	GEORGE CASE	SENATORS	51,35	1939-40
6	BOB DILLINGER	BROWNS	34,28,20	1947-49
6	WILLIE WILSON	ROYALS	83	1979
6	STAN HACK	CUBS	16, 17	1938-39
6	RED SCHOENDIENST	CARDS	26	1945
30	JACKIE JENSEN	RED SOX	22	1954
30	MAURY WILLS	DODGERS	50,35,104, 40,53,94	1960-65
30	TIM RAINES	EXPOS	71,78,90, 75	1981-84

86. *On May 7, 1970, Wes Parker #28, the only LA Dodger to hit for the cycle accomplished it against the Mets.*

87. *Since 1980, the MVP award was won 9 times by a player whose number ended in 3:*

	#	PLAYER	TEAM	YEAR
AL	**23**	DON MATTINGLY	YANKS	1985
	33	JOSE CANSECO	A's	1988
	43	DENNIS ECKERSLEY	A's	1992
	3	ALEX RODRIGUEZ	RANGERS	2003
NL	**3**	DALE MURPHY	BRAVES	1982
	3	DALE MURPHY	BRAVES	1983
	23	RYNE SANDBERG	CUBS	1984
	23	KIRK GIBSON	DODGERS	1988
	33	LARRY WALKER	ROCKIES	1997

88. *Cliff Mapes wore Babe Ruth's #3 until it was retired in 1948. Then he wore Mickey Mantle's #7 for three years, 1949-51, until he was traded to the Browns mid-season. The Mick then picked it up.*

89. *Matching up these famous rookies' first number on the left, the name and their more well-known number:*

ROOKIE #	PLAYER	REGULAR #
5	HANK AARON	**44**
32	DICK ALLEN	**15**
34	CLETE BOYER	**6**
25	GEORGE BRETT	**5**
13	ROBERTO CLEMENTE	**21**
9	JOE DIMAGGIO	**5**
9	BOBBY DOERR	**1**
9	BOB FELLER	**19**
19	WHITEY FORD	**16**
43	RALPH KINER	**4**
34	TONY KUBEK	**10**
6	MICKEY MANTLE	**7**
28	THURMAN MUNSON	**15**
24	RYNE SANDBERG	**23**
6	RED SCHOENDIENST	**2**

90. *In 1985, Toronto issued #0 and #00. Al Oliver wore #0 and Cliff Johnson wore #00. In 1997, the Reds had #0 Ron Oester, coach and #00 Curtis Goodwin-OF.*

91. *Two-thirds of the Mets retired numbers are managers—Casey Stengel #37, Gil Hodges #14 and the only other one is Tom Seaver #41, their great pitcher.*

92. *What's going on here? Can you guess these great cryptic events?*

1. **44** ⟶ **27** in **12** : **+ 4** = 7-6W @WS (3-3)
[PAT DARCY **#44** pitches to CARLTON FISK **#27** in the 12th inning, he homers to win 7-6 tying the 1975 Series at 3 games apiece.]

2. **44** ⟶ **44** : **+ 4** = 715 on 4/8/74
[AL DOWNING **#44** pitches to HANK AARON **#44**, his homer is #715 of his career on April 8, 1974.]

3. **13** ⟶ **23** in **9** : **+ 4** w**2**= 5-4W ⟶ WS
[RALPH BRANCA **#13** pitches to BOBBY THOMSON **#23** in the bottom of the 9th, he homers with 2 on and Giants win 5-4. They go to the 1951 Series.]

4. **18** ⟶ **19/1/4/42/14/15/6/39/35/8** in **9** : **0 0 0** = 2-0W
[DON LARSEN **#18** mows down the Dodgers line-up in 9 innings, no hits, no runs, no errors—a perfect game and a 2-0 win in the 1955 World Series.]

5. **31** in **12** : **0 0 0**, in **13**: E**5** + S**41** + BB**44** + 2B**9** = 1-0L
[HARVEY HADDIX **#31** in 12 innings is perfect, but in the 13th—Hoak at third makes an error, MATHEWS **#41** Sacrifices Mantilla to second, Aaron **#44** walks, Adcock **#9** doubles to the wall, Mantilla scores—Haddix loses 1-0.]

6. **23** ⟶ **9** in **9**: **+ 4**= 10-9W in WS. [RALPH TERRY **#23** pitches to BILL MAZEROSKI **#9** who hits HR in **9**th inning of Game 7 as Bucs win WS 10-9 in 1960.]

93. *The brothers DiMaggio:*

#	PLAYER	TEAM	YEAR	CAREER HR
9	VINCE DIMAGGIO	PIRATES	1940-44	125
7	VINCE DIMAGGIO	PHILLIES	1944-45	
9	JOE DIMAGGIO	YANKEES	1936	361
7	DOM DIMAGGIO	RED SOX	1940-42, 46-53	87

94. *Lefty Al Leiter #56 on the 1987 Yankees and righty Mark Leiter #56 in 1990.*

95. *The 3 AL players who wore #0 in 1985:*

0 AL OLIVER—DODGERS, BLUE JAYS
0 OSCAR GAMBLE—WHITE SOX
0 ODDIBE McDOWELL—RANGERS

96. *Do these uniform numbers represent AL strike-out kings or homerun kings?*

#	PLAYER	Ks	YEAR
34	NOLAN RYAN	301,232	1989-90*
51	RANDY JOHNSON	241,308,204,294	1992-95
21	ROGER CLEMENS	291,241,257,292	1988, 91, 96-97
12	MARK LANGSTON	204,245,262	1984, 1986-87

**Ryan, of course, won many more titles*

97. *Marty Marion #4, for St. Louis in 1944 and Lou Boudreau #5 for Cleveland in 1948.*

98. *Al Rosen #7 for Cleveland in 1953 and in the NL Bob Elliott #8 for Boston in 1947.*

99. *Bret Saberhagen wore #31 when he won in 1985 and #18 in 1989—both times with the Royals.*

100. *Nine times each the Cy Young Award was won by a pitcher either wearing the #31 or #32. Who were they?*

#	PLAYER	YRS	#	PLAYER	YEARS
31	DEAN CHANCE—LAA	'64	32	VERN LAW—PITN	'60
31	JIM PERRY—MINA	'70	32	SANDY KOUFAX—LAN	'63, 65-66
31	FERGY JENKINS—CHIN	'71	32	STEVE CARLTON—PHIN	'72,77, '80,82
31	LAMARR HOYT—CHIA	'83			
31	BRET SABERHAGEN—KCA	'85	32	STEVE STONE—BALA	'80
31	GREG MADDUX—CHIN,ATLN	'92-95			

101. *In the American League from 1929-1940, only players wearing #3, #4, or #5 won the homerun title:*

#	PLAYER	YEARS
3	BABE RUTH—YANKS	1929-31
3	JIMMIE FOXX—A's, RED SOX	1932-33, 35, 39
4	LOU GEHRIG—YANKS	1931, 34, 36
5	HANK GREENBERG—TIGERS	1935, 38, 40
5	JOE DIMAGGIO—YANKS	1937

102. *HR champions to win with a lower total than their shirt number:*

#	PLAYER	HR YR	#	PLAYER	HR YR
44	REGGIE JACKSON, NYA	41 '80	43	BILL NICHOLSON, CHIN	29 '43
24	DWIGHT EVANS, BOSA	22 '81	43	BILL NICHOLSON, CHIN	33 '44
33	EDDIE MURRAY, BALA	22 '81	43	RALPH KINER, PITN	23 '46
44	REGGIE JACKSON, NYA	39 '82	44	HANK AARON, ATLN	39 '67
41	DARRELL EVANS, DETA	40 '85	44	HANK AARON, ATLN	36 '68
45	CECIL FIELDER, DETA	44 '91			

103. *Red Schoendienst wore his beloved #2 for over 45 years with the St. Louis Cardinals.*

104. *The Red Sox who hit for the cycle twice was #1, Bobby Doerr. He did it May 17, 1944 and May 13, 1947.*

105. *Willie McCovey #44, Giants, and Hank Aaron #44, Braves, each hit 44 HRs, tying for HR lead. Aaron hit 44 homeruns 4 times—3 times winning homerun titles.*

106. *The first switch-hitter to lead the NL in RBI was Howard Johnson as a Met in 1991 with 117. (He led in homers too with 38.)*

107. *The first AL player to score 6 runs in a 9-inning game also wore #6. It was accomplished on May 8, 1946. Johnny Pesky. He also started his career with three 200-hit, league-leading seasons, 102 more than Pete Rose.*

108. *The top 9 all-time NL HR hitters hit 5,234 of them in their league. Who among them never wore a uniform with a '4' on it? Mike Schmidt, #20, and Sammy Sosa #21*

#	NAME	TEAM	NL HR
5/44	HANK AARON	BRAVES	733
24/25	BARRY BONDS	PIRATES, GIANTS	708
24	WILLIE MAYS	GIANTS, METS	660
20	MIKE SCHMIDT	PHILLIES	548
21	SAMMY SOSA	CUBS	543
44	WILLIE McCOVEY	GIANTS,PADRES	521
14	ERNIE BANKS	CUBS	512
5/4	MEL OTT	GIANTS	511
41/11	EDDIE MATHEWS	BRAVES, ASTROS	503

109. *The highest uniform number worn by a Hall of Famer during a regular season game was #77 by Ducky Medwick of the Brooklyn Dodgers in 1940-41.*

110. *The uniform number adorning more batting champs than any other was #6.*

	#	PLAYER	AVG/YEAR
NL	6	LEFTY O'DOUL, BKNN	.368 1932
	6	STAN MUSIAL, STLN	.357,.365,.376,.346,.355,.336,.351 1943,46,48,50-52,57
	6	CARL FURILLO, BKNN	.344 1953
AL	6	AL KALINE, DETA	.340 1955
	6	TONY OLIVA, MINA	.323,.321,.337 1964-65,71
	6	WILLIE WILSON, KCA	.332 1982

111. *What famous list of uniform numbers is this:* **44, 3, 25, 24, 21, 20, 25, 3, 25, 44?** *The All-Time HR list.*

#	NAME	YEARS	HR
44	HANK AARON	1953-76	755
3	BABE RUTH	1914-35	714
25	BARRY BONDS	1986-	708
24	WILLIE MAYS	1951-73	660
21	SAMMY SOSA	1989-	588
20	FRANK ROBINSON	1956-76	586
25	MARK MCGWIRE	1986-01	583
3	HARMON KILLEBREW	1954-75	573
25	RAFAEL PALMEIRO	1986-	569
44	REGGIE JACKSON	1967-87	563

112. *Four different players wore #7 while winning batting titles—can you name them?*

#	PLAYER	AVG.	YEAR
7	JOE MEDWICK, CARDS	.374	1937
7	AL SIMMONS, A's	.390	1931
7	MICKEY MANTLE, YANKS	.353	1956
7	HARVEY KUENN, TIGERS	.353	1959

113. *Bobby Bonds and Barry Bonds. Barry wore #24 in Pittsburgh where he did it twice. In San Francisco, they both wore #25. Barry did it three more times.*

	#	NAME/TEAM	HR	SB	YEAR
	25	BOBBY BONDS, GIANTS	32	45	1969
	25	BOBBY BONDS, GIANTS	39	43	1973
	25	BOBBY BONDS, YANKS	32	30	1975
	25	BOBBY BONDS, ANGELS	37	41	1977
	25	BOBBY BONDS, WH. SOX	2	6	1978
	25	BOBBY BONDS, RANGERS	29	37	1978
			31	43	1978
	24	BARRY BONDS, PIRATES	33	52	1990
	24	BARRY BONDS, PIRATES	34	39	1992
	25	BARRY BONDS, GIANTS	33	31	1995
	25	BARRY BONDS, GIANTS	42	40	1996
	25	BARRY BONDS, GIANTS	40	37	1997
Close:	**25**	BARRY BONDS, GIANTS	46	29	1993
	25	BARRY BONDS, GIANTS	37	29	1994

114. *Bobby Doerr wore #31 as the Blue Jay hitting coach from their inception in 1977 to 1981.*

115. *Most All-Star starts (5):*

#	NAME/TEAM	YEAR
11	LEFTY GOMEZ, YANKEES	1933-35, 37-38
36	ROBIN ROBERTS, PHILLIES	1950-51, 53-55
53	DON DRYSDALE, DODGERS	1959, 59*, 62 (1st G)*, 64, 68

**Drysdale pitched during the period of two All-Star Games a year.*

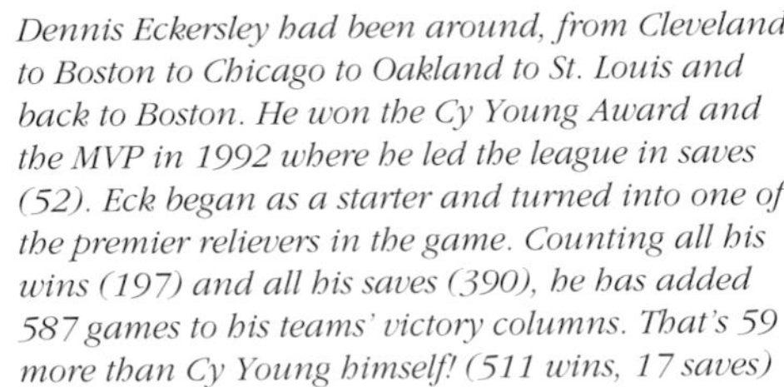

Dennis Eckersley had been around, from Cleveland to Boston to Chicago to Oakland to St. Louis and back to Boston. He won the Cy Young Award and the MVP in 1992 where he led the league in saves (52). Eck began as a starter and turned into one of the premier relievers in the game. Counting all his wins (197) and all his saves (390), he has added 587 games to his teams' victory columns. That's 59 more than Cy Young himself! (511 wins, 17 saves)

Tim Teufel (Far left) played for the Twins, Mets and Padres, 1983-93. He had 86 career homeruns and batted .308 in 1987.

Jim Gott (Left) was converted into a closer in Pittsburgh where in one season he collected more than one-third of his saves—34 of 91 in 1988. He also saved 25 games for the Dodgers in 1993.

NATIONAL
AMERICAN
WELCOME TO
RAIN CHECK
Enter Gate D
FIELD LEVEL BOX
YANKEE STADIUM
GAME TIME
BUDWEISER
RYAN FREEL
MADE HIS LAST 32 STARTS
BATTING IN THE LEADOFF
POSITION.
"A life is not important except in the impact it has on other lives."
-Jackie Robinson

GROUND RULES

Only players who have actually played in a major league game are included in this book. Many players join a team roster in spring, during the season as injury-protection or at September call-up when rosters are expanded.

Some of these players never enter a major league ball game. These players and their numbers will not be here.

Rostered players who have played and miss a season due to injury or illness will be carried with a notation (INJ) or (ILL) until they either return or it's clear that they can't come back and are released by the club.

To gather the rosters and numbers in Chapter 7, *Team Rosters* and the individual's numbers in Chapter 11, *Players: By the Numbers*, many sources were used. The complete roster of every team using numbers since 1916 was verified in *The Sports Encyclopedia—Baseball.* Then individual player's records were cross-checked in *Total Baseball* to ensure accuracy and completeness.

Other sources used were: *Baseball Digest*, the *Black Book*, the *American League Red Book*, the *National League Green Book*, *Spalding's Baseball Guide*, *Who's Who in Baseball*, *The Sporting News*, *The Sporting News Baseball Yearbook*, *USA Today's Sports Weekly*, *MLB.Com*, each team's official web-site and team year books, media guides and hundreds and hundreds of game score cards.

Every major league franchise was contacted by phone, letter, questionnaire or in person over the course of the project with varying degrees of success.

The National Baseball Hall of Fame Library was exhausted of material as well as many libraries around the country.

Chapter 3, *The Caretakers*, was the result of many hours of travel at Spring Training interviewing equipment managers for many of the clubs.

The "Dream Teams" of Chapter 8 were compiled from the tables on the following pages. The position players and pitchers who had a conceivable chance of being the best at a position while wearing a particular number are included in their respective listings.

Judging which players were to be selected above others wasn't as easy as it appears. When looking at existing methods of evaluation, I didn't feel that the best players would be chosen. A "Dream Team" should be comprised of all the players at the peak of their playing ability at the same time. The best way was to average their career stats, as batting average, slugging percentage, on-base percentage and also mixing in a cross-section of what each did on a year-in, year-out basis.

The formulae used to arrive at the PLAYER NUMBER and the PITCHER NUMBER are below:

POSITION PLAYER FORMULA

1. RUNS/YR + HITS/YR + HR/YR + RBI/YR + SB/YR = GROSS # (GRO)

2. B AV + OB AV + SLG AV + DEF TITLES*/YR + OFF TITLES**/YR ÷ 5 = TOTAL AVERAGES (TOT AV)

3. (TOT AV x 1000) + GROSS = PLAYER #

PITCHER FORMULA

1. WINS/YR + SHUTOUTS/YR + SAVES/YR = GROSS # (GRO)

2. H/IP + HR/IP + BB/IP - K/IP =QUALITY INNING (QI)

3. GROSS - ERA = CUMULATIVE # (CUM)

4. W/L% + P TITLES§/YR - QI ÷ 3 = AVERAGING (AVG)

5. (CUM x 100) + (AVG x 1000) = PITCHER #

**Defensive Title included is fielding percentage and/or Gold Glove. (Without duplication)*

***Offensive Titles included are: runs, hits, 2B, 3B, HR, RBI, BB, B AV, OB AV, SLG AV and SB.*

§Pitching Titles included are: wins, shutouts, saves, innings, complete games, W/L %, strikeouts, ERA, Opp B AV, and Opp OnBase AV.

Not Hornsby, Ruth, Gehrig, Williams, Boggs nor even Rose had the most average hits per year with more than 5 years playing experience since the wearing of uniform numbers. Believe it or not, it's Kirby Puckett retiring in 1995 with 192 base hits per year. Two players are fast on his heels—Ichiro Suzuki is well ahead with 226 hits per year and Albert Pujols with 196.4 hits per year. Suzuki (#51) won't be on a "Dream Team."

POSITION PLAYERS

NAME	YRS	RUNS YR	HITS YR	HR YR	RBI YR	SB YR	B AV	OB AV	SG AV	D TIT	D AV	O TIT	O AV	TOT AV	GROSS	PLAY #
AARON, HANK*	23	94.5	163.9	32.8	99.8	10.4	.305	.377	.555	0	.000	23	1.000	.4470	401.4	848.9
ABREU. BOBBY	10	85.3	143.2	19.0	77.6	24.1	.303	.411	.512	1	.100	2	.200	.2852	349.2	634.4
ADAIR, JERRY	13	29.0	78.6	4.3	28.1	2.2	.254	.294	.347	2	.153	0	.000	.2090	142.2	351.2
ADCOCK, JOE	17	48.4	107.7	19.7	66.0	1.1	.277	.339	.485	4	.235	0	.000	.2670	242.9	509.9
ALFONZO, EDGARDO	11	70.2	138.3	13.3	67.2	4.8	.287	.363	.429	2	.182	0	.000	.2522	293.8	546.0
ALLEN, DICK	15	73.2	123.2	23.4	74.6	8.8	.292	.381	.534	0	.000	11	.733	.3880	303.2	691.2
ALLEY, GENE	11	40.1	90.8	5.0	31.0	5.7	.254	.312	.354	2	.182	0	.000	.2200	172.6	392.6
ALMON, BILL	15	26.0	56.4	2.4	19.7	8.5	.254	.307	.343	0	.000	0	.000	.1800	113.0	293.0
ALOMAR, ROBERTO	17	88.7	160.2	12.4	66.7	27.9	.300	.371	.443	10	.588	1	.059	.3522	355.9	708.1
ALOMAR, SANDY	18	28.4	66.8	6.2	31.7	1.4	.273	.312	.408	0	.000	0	.000	.1986	134.5	333.1
ALOU, FELIPE	17	57.9	123.5	12.1	50.1	6.2	.286	.330	.433	0	.000	3	.176	.2450	249.8	494.8
ALOU, JESUS	15	29.8	81.0	2.1	25.1	2.0	.280	.307	.353	0	.000	0	.000	.1880	140.0	328.0
ALOU, MATTY	15	52.0	118.4	2.0	28.4	10.4	.307	.346	.381	0	.000	3	.200	.2460	211.2	457.2
ALOU, MOISES	14	71.6	135.8	21.2	82.5	7.1	.301	.373	.513	0	.000	0	.000	.2374	318.2	555.6
ANDERSON, BRADY	15	70.8	110.7	14.0	50.7	21.0	.256	.362	.425	0	.000	0	.000	.2086	267.2	475.8
ANDERSON, GARRET	12	69.0	160.8	18.7	87.0	5.8	.298	.327	.473	2	.167	0	.000	.2530	341.3	594.3
APARICIO, LUIS*	18	74.1	148.7	4.6	43.9	28.1	.262	.313	.343	11	.611	9	.500	.4060	299.4	705.4
APPLING, LUKE*	20	65.9	137.4	2.2	55.8	8.9	.310	.399	.398	0	.000	3	.190	.2590	270.2	529.2
ARMAS, TONY, SR.	14	43.9	93.0	17.9	58.2	1.3	.252	.290	.453	0	.000	3	.214	.2418	214.3	456.1
ASHBURN, RICHIE*	15	88.1	171.6	1.9	39.0	15.8	.308	.397	.382	0	.000	16	1.066	.4300	316.4	746.4
ASPROMONTE, BOB	13	29.7	84.8	4.6	35.2	1.5	.252	.310	.336	2	.154	0	.000	.2104	155.8	366.2
AURILIA, RICH	11	54.6	110.9	13.3	53.2	1.7	.276	.333	.436	0	.000	0	.000	.2090	233.7	442.7
AUSMUS, BRAD	13	47.3	100.5	5.5	39.1	7.1	.255	.328	.353	3	.231	0	.000	.2334	199.5	432.9
AVERILL, EARL*	13	94.1	155.3	18.3	89.5	5.3	.318	.395	.534	0	.000	2	.153	.2800	362.5	642.5
AVILA, BOBBY	11	65.9	117.8	7.2	42.4	7.0	.281	.360	.388	1	.090	1	.090	.2410	240.3	481.3
BACKMAN, WALLY	14	34.4	63.7	0.7	17.1	8.3	.275	.339	.339	1	.071	0	.000	.2040	124.2	328.2
BAERGA, CARLOS	14	52.2	113.1	9.6	55.3	4.2	.291	.332	.423	0	.000	0	.000	.2092	234.4	443.6
BAGWELL, JEFF	15	101.1	154.3	29.9	101.7	13.5	.297	.408	.540	0	.000	8	.533	.3556	400.5	756.1
BAINES, HAROLD	22	59.0	130.1	17.5	74.0	1.5	.289	.356	.465	0	.000	1	.045	.2310	282.1	513.1
BAKER, DUSTY	19	50.7	104.2	12.7	53.3	7.2	.278	.351	.432	1	.053	0	.000	.2230	228.1	451.1
BALBONI, STEVE	11	31.9	64.9	16.4	45.0	0.0	.229	.290	.451	0	.000	0	.000	.1940	158.2	352.2
BANDO, SAL	16	61.3	111.8	15.1	64.9	4.6	.254	.355	.408	0	.000	1	.062	.2150	257.7	472.7
BANKS, ERNIE*	19	68.6	135.9	26.9	86.1	2.6	.274	.333	.500	4	.210	5	.263	.3370	320.1	657.1
BARFIELD, JESSE	12	59.6	101.6	20.1	59.7	5.5	.256	.338	.466	2	.167	1	.083	.2620	246.5	508.5
BARRETT, MICHAEL	8	37.9	88.0	8.8	39.9	1.1	.263	.322	.420	0	.000	0	.000	.2010	175.7	376.7
BARTELL, DICK	18	62.7	120.2	4.3	39.4	6.0	.284	.355	.391	0	.000	0	.000	.2060	232.6	438.6
BATTEY, EARL	13	30.2	74.5	8.0	34.5	1.0	.270	.351	.409	3	.231	0	.000	.2520	148.2	400.2
BAUER, HANK	14	59.5	101.7	11.7	50.2	3.5	.277	.347	.439	0	.000	1	.071	.2260	226.6	452.6
BAUMHOLTZ, F.	10	45.0	101.0	2.5	27.2	3.0	.290	.342	.389	0	.000	0	.000	.2040	178.7	382.7
BAYLOR, DON	19	65.0	112.3	17.7	67.1	15.0	.260	.346	.436	0	.000	2	.105	.2290	277.1	506.1
BECKERT, GLENN	11	62.2	133.9	2.0	32.7	4.4	.283	.319	.345	1	.091	1	.091	.2260	235.2	461.2
BELANGER, MARK	18	37.5	73.1	1.1	21.6	9.2	.228	.302	.280	8	.444	0	. 000	.2510	142.5	393.5
BELL, BUDDY	18	63.9	139.6	11.1	61.4	3.0	.279	.343	.406	7	.389	0	.000	.2830	279.0	562.0
BELL, DAVID	11	47.9	100.3	10.3	47.8	1.5	.255	.321	.396	0	.000	0	.000	.1944	207.8	402.2
DEREK BELL	11	58.4	114.7	12.2	60.7	15.5	.276	.336	.421	0	.000	0	.000	.2066	261.5	468.1
BELL, GEORGE	11	70.7	146.6	22.9	85.2	6.0	.282	.325	.477	0	.000	1	.090	.2340	331.4	565.4
BELL, GUS	15	48.0	121.5	13.7	62.8	2.0	281	.333	.445	2	.133	1	.066	.2510	248.0	499.0
BELL, JAY	18	62.4	109.1	10.8	47.8	5.1	.265	.343	.416	2	.111	0	.000	.2270	235.2	462.2
BELLE, ALBERT	12	80.3	143.8	31.8	103.3	7.3	.295	.369	.564	0	.000	8	.667	.3790	366.5	745.5
BELLHORN, MARK	8	37.0	54.4	7.6	27.3	3.8	.236	.349	.403	0	.000	0	.000	.1976	130.1	327.7
BELTRAN, CARLOS	8	87.4	142.5	20.3	80.9	26.1	.282	.354	.479	0	.000	0	.000	.2230	357.2	580.2
BELTRE, ADRIAN	8	65.6	137.9	20.8	74.6	8.1	.271	.287	.455	0	.000	1	.125	.2276	307.0	534.6
BENCH, JOHNNY*	17	64.1	120.4	22.8	80.9	4.0	.267	.345	.476	10	.588	5	.294	.3920	292.2	684.2
BERGER, WALLY	11	73.5	140.9	22.0	81.6	3.2	.300	.359	.522	1	.090	2	.181	.2900	321.2	611.2
BERKMAN, LANCE	7	84.6	135.9	25.7	88.1	6.3	.302	.419	.557	0	.000	2	.286	.3128	340.6	653.4
BERRA, YOGI*	19	61.8	113.1	18.8	75.2	1.5	.285	.350	.482	2	.105	0	.000	.2440	270.4	514.4
BICHETTE, DANTE	13	71.8	146.6	21.1	87.5	11.7	.299	.336	.499	0	.000	5	.357	.2982	339.0	637.2
BIGGIO, CRAIG	18	94.3	155.3	14.4	59.1	22.6	.285	.370	.437	5	.278	6	.333	.3406	345.7	686.3
BILKO, STEVE	10	22.0	43.2	7.6	27.6	0.2	.249	.339	.444	0	.000	0	.000	.2060	100.6	306.6
BLAIR, PAUL	17	45.6	89.0	7.8	36.4	10.0	.250	.305	.382	8	.471	1	.058	.2930	188.8	481.8
BLANCHARD, JOHN	8	17.1	35.6	8.3	25.0	0.2	.239	.320	.441	0	.000	0	.000	.2000	86.2	286.2
BLASINGAME, DON	12	60.9	114.0	1.7	25.6	8.7	.258	.330	.327	0	.000	0	.000	.1830	210.9	393.9
BLEFARY, CURT	8	49.2	87.3	14.0	47.7	3.0	.237	.345	.400	0	.000	0	.000	.1960	201.2	397.2
BLUEGE, OSSIE	18	49.0	97.2	2.3	47.1	7.7	.272	.352	.356	1	.055	0	.000	.2070	203.3	410.3

*HALL OF FAME

LEGEND: **YRS**=CAREER YEARS, **RUNS YR**=RUNS PER YEAR, **HITS YR**=HITS PER YEAR, **HR YR**=HOMERUNS PER YEAR, **RBI YR**=RUNS BATTED IN PER YEAR, **SB YR**=STOLEN BASES PER YEAR, **B AV**=CAREER BATTING AVERAGE, **OB AV**=CAREER ON-BASE AVERAGE, **SG AV**=CAREER SLUGGING AVERAGE, **D TIT**=DEFENSIVE TITLES, **D AV**=AVERAGE OF DEFENSIVE TITLES PER YEAR FOR CAREER, **O TIT**=OFFENSIVE TITLES, **O AV**=AVERAGE OF OFFENSIVE TITLES PER YEAR FOR CAREER, **TOT AV**=TOTAL AVERAGES (THE SUM OF THE FIVE AVERAGES DIVIDED BY 5), **GROSS**=GROSS NUMBER (THE SUM OF THE 5 YEARLY OFFENSIVE NUMBERS), **PLAY #**=PLAYER NUMBER (THE SUM OF THE TOTAL AVERAGES TIMES 1000 AND THE GROSS NUMBER.

NAME	YRS	RUNS YR	HITS YR	HR YR	RBI YR	SB YR	B AV	OB AV	SG AV	D TIT	D AV	O TIT	O AV	TOT AV	GROSS	PLAY #
BOGGS, WADE*	18	84.1	167.2	6.6	56.3	1.3	.328	.419	.443	3	.167	18	1.000	.4714	315.5	786.9
BONDS, BARRY	20	103.9	137.1	35.4	92.7	25.3	.300	.443	.611	0	.000	31	1.550	.5808	394.4	975.2
BONDS, BOBBY	14	89.8	134.7	23.7	73.1	32.9	.268	.356	.471	3	.214	2	.142	.2900	354.2	644.2
BONILLA, BOBBY	16	67.8	125.6	17.9	73.3	2.8	.279	.358	.472	0	.000	1	.063	.2344	287.4	521.8
BOONE, AARON	8	52.4	102.3	13.5	56.6	12.5	.265	.327	.436	0	.000	0	.000	.2056	237.3	442.9
BOONE,BOB	19	35.7	96.7	5.5	43.4	2.0	.254	.318	.346	7	.368	0	.000	.2570	183.3	440.3
BOONE, BRET	14	66.2	126.8	18.0	72.9	6.7	.266	.325	.442	7	.500	1	.071	.3208	290.6	611.4
BOONE, RAY	13	49.6	96.9	11.6	56.6	1.6	.275	.363	.429	0	.000	1	.076	.2280	216.3	444.3
BORDAGARAY, FRENC.	11	37.2	67.7	1.2	24.5	6.0	.283	.331	.366	0	.000	0	.000	.2000	136.6	336.6
BORDICK, MIKE	14	48.3	107.1	6.5	44.7	6.9	.260	.323	.362	1	.071	0	.000	.2032	213.5	416.7
BOTTOMLEY, JIM*	16	73.5	144.5	13.6	88.8	3.6	.310	.369	.500	0	.000	7	.437	.3230	324.0	647.0
BOUDREAU, LOU*	15	57.4	118.6	4.5	52.6	3.4	.295	.380	.415	8	.533	4	.266	.3770	236.5	613.5
BOWA, LARRY	16	61.6	136.9	0.9	32.8	19.8	.260	.301	.320	6	.375	1	.062	.2630	252.0	515.0
BOYER, CLETE	16	56.0	87.2	10.1	40.8	2.5	.242	.301	.372	2	.125	0	.000	.2080	196.6	404.6
BOYER, KEN	15	86.7	142.8	18.8	76.0	7.0	.287	.351	.462	7	.467	1	.066	.3270	331.3	658.3
BREAM, SID	12	29.2	68.2	7.5	37.9	4.1	.264	.339	.420	0	.000	0	.000	.2040	146.9	350.9
BRESSOUD, ED	12	36.9	77.0	7.8	30.4	0.7	.252	.321	.401	0	.000	0	.000	.1940	152.8	346.8
BRETT, GEORGE*	21	75.4	150.2	15.1	76.0	9.6	.305	.373	.487	1	.048	15	.714	.3854	326.3	711.7
BRIGGS, JOHNNY	12	50.0	86.7	11.5	42.2	5.3	.253	.357	.416	0	.000	0	.000	.2050	195.7	400.7
BRINKMAN, EDDIE	15	36.6	90.3	5.0	30.7	2.0	.224	.282	.300	2	.133	0	.000	.1870	164.6	351.6
BROCK, GREG	10	42.0	79.4	11.0	46.2	4.1	.248	.340	.399	0	.000	0	.000	.1970	182.7	379.7
BROCK, LOU*	19	84.7	159.1	7.8	47.3	49.3	.293	.344	.410	0	.000	12	.631	.3350	348.2	683.2
BROOKS, HUBIE	15	43.7	107.2	9.9	54.9	4.8	.269	.314	.403	0	.000	0	.000	.1970	220.5	417.5
BROSIUS, SCOTT	11	49.5	91.0	12.8	48.3	5.2	.257	.323	.422	1	.091	0	.000	.2186	206.8	425.4
BROWN, OLLIE	13	31.0	74.1	7.8	34.9	2.3	.265	.326	.394	0	.000	0	.000	.1970	150.1	347.1
BRUMFIELD, JACOB	7	37.1	57.7	4.6	23.1	10.6	.257	.321	.393	0	.000	0	.000	.1942	132.6	326.8
BRUNANSKY, TOM	14	57.4	110.2	19.3	65.6	4.9	.245	.327	.433	1	.071	0	.000	.2150	257.4	472.4
BRUTON, BILL	12	78.0	137.5	7.8	45.4	17.2	.273	.329	.393	0	.000	6	.500	.2990	285.9	584.9
BUCKNER, BILL	22	48.9	123.4	7.9	54.9	8.3	.289	.324	.408	0	.000	3	.136	.2310	243.4	474.4
BUFORD, DON	10	71.8	120.3	9.3	41.8	20.0	.264	.364	.379	0	.000	1	.100	.2214	263.2	484.6
BUHNER, JAY	15	53.2	84.9	20.7	64.3	0.4	.254	.359	.494	2	.133	0	.000	.2480	223.5	471.5
BURGESS, SMOKY	18	26.9	73.2	7.0	37.3	0.7	.295	.364	.446	3	.166	0	.000	.2540	145.1	399.1
BURKS, ELLIS	18	69.6	117.1	19.6	67.0	10.1	.291	.363	.510	1	.056	2	. 111	.2662	283.4	549.6
BURLESON, RICK	13	50.5	107.8	3.8	34.5	5.5	.273	.331	.361	1	.077	0	.000	.2084	202.1	410.5
BURNITZ, JEROMY	13	62.8	105.8	23.0	71.7	5.6	.255	.350	.485	0	.000	0	.000	.2180	273.9	491.9
BURRELL, PAT	6	70.7	132.0	26.5	91.5	0.8	.258	.360	.476	0	.000	0	.000	.2188	321.5	540.3
BURROUGHS, JEFF	16	45.0	90.1	15.0	55.1	1.0	.261	.359	.439	0	.000	3	.187	.2490	206.2	455.2
BUTLER, BRETT	17	79.9	139.7	3.2	34.0	32.8	.290	.379	.376	3	.176	8	.471	.3384	289.6	628.0
CABELL, ENOS	15	50.2	109.8	4.0	39.7	15.8	.277	.309	.370	0	.000	0	.000	.1910	219.5	410.5
CABRERA, MIGUEL	3	82.0	153.0	26.0	96.7	2.0	.300	.387	.523	0	.000	0	.000	.2420	359.7	601.7
CABRERA, ORLANDO	9	56.7	120.3	8.9	52.1	13.1	.267	.315	.403	1	.111	0	.000	.2192	251.1	470.3
CALLISON, JOHN	16	57.8	109.8	14.1	52.5	4.6	.264	.333	.441	1	.062	3	.187	.2570	238.8	495.8
CAMERON, MIKE	11	62.7	92.9	15.7	56.8	20.8	.249	.343	.442	2	.182	0	.000	.2432	248.9	492.1
CAMILLI, DOLPH	12	78.0	123.5	19.9	79.1	5.0	.277	.388	.492	1	.083	5	.416	.3310	305.5	636.5
CAMINITI, KEN	15	59.6	114.0	15.9	65.5	5.9	.272	.347	.447	3	.200	0	.000	.2532	260.9	514.1
CAMPANELLA, ROY*	10	62.7	116.1	24.2	85.6	2.5	.276	.362	.500	2	.200	1	.100	.2870	291.1	578.1
CAMPANERIS, BERT	19	62.1	118.3	4.1	34.0	34.1	.259	.313	.342	0	.000	8	.421	.2670	252.6	519.6
CANO, ROBINSON	1	78.0	155.0	14.0	62.0	1.0	.297	.320	.458	0	.000	0	.000	.2150	310.0	525.0
CANSECO, JOSE	17	69.8	110.4	27.2	82.8	11.8	.266	.353	.515	0	.000	4	.235	.2738	302.0	575.8
CARDENAL, JOSE	18	52.0	106.2	7.6	43.0	18.2	.275	.335	.395	0	.000	0	.000	.2010	227.0	428.0
CARDENAS, LEO	16	41.3	107.8	7.3	43.0	2.4	.257	.313	.367	3	.187	0	.000	.2240	201.8	425.8
CAREW, ROD*	19	74.9	160.6	4.8	53.4	18.5	.328	.395	.429	0	.000	17	.894	.4090	312.2	721.2
CARR, CHUCK	8	31.8	54.4	1.6	15.4	18.0	.254	.316	.332	0	.000	1	.125	.2054	121.2	326.6
CARRASQUEL, CHICO	10	56.8	119.9	5.5	47.4	3.1	.258	.334	.342	3	.300	0	.000	.2460	232.7	478.7
CARTER, GARY*	19	53.9	110.1	17.0	64.4	2.0	.262	.338	.439	4	.211	1	.052	.2640	247.4	511.4
CARTER, JOE	16	73.1	136.5	24.8	90.3	14.4	.259	.306	.464	0	.000	1	.063	.2184	339.1	557.5
CARTY, RICO	15	47.4	111.8	13.6	59.3	1.4	.299	.372	.464	0	.000	2	.133	.2530	233.5	486.5
CASE, GEORGE	11	71.3	128.6	1.9	34.2	31.7	.282	.341	.358	0	.000	7	.636	.3230	267.7	590.7
CASEY, SEAN	9	65.4	136.1	13.1	67.2	1.7	.305	.373	.462	0	.000	0	.000	.2280	283.5	511.5
CASH, DAVE	12	61.0	130.9	1.7	35.5	10.0	.283	.336	.358	2	.166	1	.083	.2450	239.1	484.1
CASH, NORM	17	61.5	107.0	22.1	64.8	2.5	.271	.377	.488	2	.117	3	.176	.2850	257.9	542.9
CASTILLA, VINNY	15	58.4	121.4	21.0	71.9	2.2	.278	.326	.483	1	.067	1	.067	.2442	274.9	519.1
CAVARRETTA, PHIL	22	45.0	89.8	4.3	41.8	2.9	.293	.372	.416	0	.000	3	.136	.2430	183.8	426.8
CEDENO, CESAR	17	63.7	122.7	11.7	57.4	32.3	.285	.350	.443	6	.353	2	.117	.3100	287.8	597.8
CEPEDA, ORLANDO*	17	66.5	138.2	22.2	80.2	8.3	.297	.353	.499	0	.000	4	.235	.2760	315.4	591.4
CERONE, RICK	18	21.8	55.4	3.2	24.2	0.3	.245	.304	.343	2	.111	0	.000	.2000	104.9	304.9
CERV, BOB	12	26.6	52.0	8.7	31.1	1.0	.276	.343	.481	0	.000	0	.000	.2200	119.4	339.4
CEY, RON	17	57.4	109.8	18.5	67.0	1.4	.261	.357	.445	2	.117	0	.000	.2360	254.1	490.1
CHAMBLISS, CHRIS	17	53.6	124.0	10.8	57.1	2.3	.279	.336	.415	1	.058	0	.000	.2170	247.8	464.8
CHAPMAN, BEN	15	76.2	130.5	6.0	65.1	19.1	.302	.383	.440	0	.000	5	.333	.2910	296.9	587.9
CHAVEZ, ERIC	8	85.6	149.2	27.1	93.1	5.8	.275	.341	.482	3	.375	1	.125	.3196	360.8	680.4

NAME	YRS	RUNS YR	HITS YR	HR YR	RBI YR	SB YR	B AV	OB AV	SG AV	D TIT	D AV	O TIT	O AV	TOT AV	GROSS	PLAY #
CIMOLI, GINO	10	37.0	80.8	4.4	32.1	2.1	.265	.317	.383	0	.000	1	.100	.2130	156.4	369.4
CIRILLO, JEFF	12	61.9	122.2	8.9	56.4	5.0	.297	.371	.433	1	.083	0	.000	.2362	254.4	490.6
CLARK, JACK	18	62.1	101.4	18.8	65.5	4.2	.267	.383	.476	0	.000	5	.277	.2800	252.0	532.0
CLARK, TONY	11	51.5	96.5	20.1	65.6	0.5	.268	.345	.494	0	.000	0	.000	.2202	234.2	454.4
CLARK, WILL	15	79.1	145.1	18.9	80.3	4.5	.303	.384	.497	1	.067	4	.267	.3036	327.9	631.5
CLAYTON, ROYCE	15	57.5	115.9	7.1	44.7	14.3	.258	.316	.370	1	.067	0	.000	.2022	239.5	441.7
CLEMENTE, R.*	18	78.6	166.6	14.1	72.5	4.6	.317	.362	.475	12	.667	7	.388	.4420	336.4	778.4
CLENDENON, DONN	12	49.5	106.0	13.2	56.8	7.5	.274	.331	.442	0	.000	0	.000	.2090	233.0	442.0
CLIFT, HARLOND	12	89.1	129.8	14.8	69.0	5.7	.272	.390	.441	2	.166	1	.083	.2700	308.4	578.4
COCHRANE, MICKEY*	13	80.0	127.0	9.1	64.0	4.9	.366	.433	.512	2	.153	1	.076	.3080	284.7	592.7
COLAVITO, ROCKY	14	69.3	123.5	26.7	82.7	1.0	.266	.362	.489	1	.071	4	.285	.2940	511.1	805.1
COLBERT, NATE	10	48.1	83.3	17.3	52.0	5.2	.243	.324	.451	0	.000	0	.000	.2030	205.9	408.9
COLEMAN, JERRY	9	29.6	62.0	1.7	24.1	2.4	.263	.341	.339	1	.111	0	.000	.2100	119.8	329.8
COLEMAN, VINCE	13	65.3	109.6	2.2	26.6	57.8	.264	.324	.345	0	.000	6	.462	.2790	196.2	475.2
COLLINS, DAVE	16	41.6	83.4	2.0	23.3	24.6	.272	.340	.351	0	.000	1	.062	.2050	174.6	379.9
COLLINS, JOE	10	40.4	59.6	8.6	32.9	2.7	.256	.351	.421	0	.000	0	.000	.2050	144.2	349.2
COLLINS, RIPPER	9	67.8	124.5	15.0	73.2	2.0	.296	.360	.492	1	.111	2	.222	.2960	282.5	578.5
COMBS, EARLE*	12	98.8	155.5	4.8	52.6	8.0	.325	.397	.462	0	.000	4	.333	.3030	319.8	622.8
CONCEPCION, DAVE	19	52.2	122.4	5.3	50.0	16.8	.267	.325	.357	5	.263	0	.000	.2420	246.7	488.7
CONIGLIARO, TONY	8	58.0	106.1	20.7	65.7	2.5	.264	.330	.476	0	.000	1	.125	.2390	253.0	492.0
CONINE, JEFF	15	52.7	119.1	13.2	64.5	3.1	.288	.354	.449	0	.000	0	.000	.2182	252.6	470.8
COOPER, CECIL	17	59.5	128.9	14.1	66.1	5.2	.298	.340	.466	2	.116	4	.235	.2910	273.8	564.8
COOPER, WALKER	18	31.8	74.5	9.6	45.1	1.0	.285	.332	.464	0	.000	0	.000	.2160	162.0	378.0
CORA, JOEY	11	56.7	94.1	2.7	26.7	10.6	.277	.348	.369	0	.000	0	.000	.1988	190.8	389.6
COTTO, HENRY	10	29.6	56.9	4.3	21.0	13.0	.261	.296	.369	0	.000	0	.000	.1850	124.8	309.8
COVINGTON, WES	11	32.2	75.6	11.9	45.3	0.6	.279	.339	.466	0	.000	0	.000	.2160	165.6	381.6
COX, BILLY	11	38.2	88.5	6.0	31.9	3.8	.262	.318	.380	1	.091	0	.000	.2102	168.4	378.6
CRANDALL, DEL	16	36.5	79.7	11.1	41.0	1.6	.254	.315	.404	5	.313	0	.000	.2570	169.9	426.9
CRAWFORD, CARL	4	77.0	155.8	8.3	57.5	42.3	.289	.321	.421	1	.250	3	.750	.4062	340.9	747.1
CRAWFORD, WILLIE	14	36.2	65.7	6.1	29.9	3.3	.268	.351	.408	0	.000	0	.000	.2050	141.2	346.2
CRISP, COCO	4	58.8	116.8	8.8	44.0	13.5	.287	.334	.424	0	.000	0	.000	.2090	241.9	450.9
CROMARTIE, WARREN	10	45.9	110.4	6.1	39.1	5.0	.281	.339	.402	0	.000	0	.000	.2040	206.5	410.5
CRONIN, JOE*	20	61.6	114.2	8.5	71.2	4.3	.301	.390	.468	2	.100	3	.150	.2810	259.8	540.8
CROSETTI, FRANK	17	59.1	90.6	5.7	38.1	6.6	.245	.341	.354	1	.058	1	.05	.2110	200.1	411.1
CRUZ, JOSE, JR.	9	70.7	116.6	21.4	65.0	11.3	.250	.338	.456	1	.111	0	.000	.2310	285.0	516.0
CRUZ, JOSE, SR.	19	54.5	118.4	8.6	56.6	16.6	.284	.358	.420	0	.000	1	.052	.2220	254.7	476.7
CUCCINELLO, TONY	15	48.6	115.2	6.2	58.9	2.8	.280	.343	.394	0	.000	0	.000	.2030	231.7	434.7
CUNNINGHAM, JOE	12	43.7	81.6	5.3	36.3	1.3	.291	.406	.417	1	.083	1	.083	.2560	168.2	424.2
CUYLER, KIKI*	18	71.9	127.7	7.1	59.1	18.2	.321	.386	.474	0	.000	8	.444	.3250	284.0	609.0
DAMON, JOHNNY	11	97.5	162.6	11.8	63.6	25.5	.290	.353	.431	2	.182	3	.273	.3258	361.0	666.8
DARK, ALVIN	14	76.0	149.2	9.0	54.0	4.2	.289	.334	.411	0	. 000	1	.071	.2210	292.4	513.4
DAUER, RICH	10	44.8	98.4	4.3	37.2	0.6	.257	.313	.343	1	.100	0	.000	.2020	185.3	387.3
DAULTON, DARREN	14	36.5	59.4	9.8	42.0	3.6	.245	.357	.427	0	.000	1	.071	.2200	151.3	371.3
DAVENPORT, JIM	13	42.2	87.8	5.9	35.0	1.2	.258	.320	.367	4	.308	0	.000	.2510	172.1	423.1
DAVIS, CHILI	19	65.3	125.3	18.4	72.2	7.5	.274	.360	.451	0	.000	0	.000	.2170	288.7	505.7
DAVIS, ERIC	17	55.2	84.1	16.6	54.9	20.5	.269	.359	.482	3	.176	0	.000	.2572	231.3	488.5
DAVIS, GLENN	10	51.0	96.5	19.0	60.3	2.8	.259	.326	.467	1	.100	0	.000	.2300	229.6	459.6
DAVIS, MIKE	10	41.9	77.8	9.1	37.1	13.4	.259	.316	.415	0	.000	0	.000	.1980	179.3	377.3
DAVIS, SPUD	16	24.2	82.0	4.8	40.4	0.3	.308	.369	.430	2	.125	0	.000	.2460	151.7	397.7
DAVIS, TOMMY	18	45.0	117.8	8.5	58.4	7.5	.294	.332	.405	0	.000	4	.222	.2500	237.2	487.2
DAVIS, WILLIE	18	67.6	142.2	10.1	58.5	22.1	.279	.314	.412	3	.167	2	.111	.2570	300.5	557.5
DAWSON, ANDRE	21	65.4	132.1	20.9	75.8	15.0	.279	.327	.482	8	.381	3	.143	.3224	309.2	631.6
DEER, ROB	11	52.5	77.5	20.9	54.5	3.9	.220	.324	.442	0	.000	0	.000	.1972	209.3	406.5
DEJESUS, IVAN	15	39.6	77.8	1.4	21.6	12.9	.254	.324	.326	0	.000	1	.066	.1940	153.3	347.3
DELGADO, CARLOS	13	74.6	120.8	28.4	90.2	0.7	.284	.393	.559	0	.000	2	.154	.2780	314.7	592.7
DEMPSEY, RICK	24	21.8	45.5	4.0	24.6	0.8	.233	.321	.347	2	.083	0	.000	.1960	96.7	292.7
DENT, BUCKY	12	37.5	92.8	3.3	35.2	1.4	.247	.300	.321	3	.250	0	.000	.2230	170.2	393.2
DENTE, SAM	9	22.7	65.0	0.4	23.7	1.0	.252	.303	.305	0	.000	0	.000	.1720	112.8	284.8
DESHIELDS, DELINO	13	67.1	119.1	6.2	43.2	35.6	.268	.352	.377	0	.000	1	.077	.2148	271.2	486.0
DIAZ, BO	13	25.1	64.1	6.6	34.7	0.6	.255	.300	.387	0	.000	0	.000	.1880	131.1	319.1
DICKEY, BILL*	17	54.7	115.8	11.8	71.1	2.1	.313	.382	.486	4	.235	0	.000	.2830	255.5	538.5
DILLINGER, BOB	6	66.8	148.0	1.6	35.5	17.6	.306	.363	.391	0	.000	4	.666	.3450	269.5	614.5
DIMAGGIO, DOM	11	95.0	152.2	7.9	56.1	9.0	.298	383	.419	0	.000	4	.363	.2920	320.2	612.2
DIMAGGIO, JOE*	13	106.9	170.3	27.7	118.2	2.3	.325	.398	.579	1	.076	10	.769	.4290	425.9	854.9
DIMAGGIO, VINCE	10	49.1	95.9	12.5	58.4	7.9	.249	.324	.413	0	.000	0	.000	.1970	223.8	420.8
DOBY, LARRY*	13	73.8	116.5	19.4	74.6	3.6	.283	.387	.490	0	.000	6	.461	.3240	287.9	611.9
DOERR, BOBBY*	14	78.1	145.8	15.9	89.0	3.8	.288	.362	.461	4	.285	2	.142	.3070	332.6	639.6
DORAN, BILL	12	60.5	113.8	7.0	41.4	17.4	.266	.355	.373	2	.166	0	.000	.2320	240.1	472.1
DOWNING, BRIAN	20	59.4	108.0	13.8	53.7	2.5	.267	.370	.425	2	.100	1	.050	.2424	234.4	476.8
DREW, J. D.	8	65.1	95.6	17.8	51.1	9.0	.287	.395	.514	0	.000	0	.000	.2392	238.3	477.5
DRIESSEN, DAN	15	49.7	97.6	10.2	50.8	10.2	.267	.359	.411	3	.200	1	.066	.2600	218.5	478.5

NAME	YRS	RUNS YR	HITS YR	HR YR	RBI YR	SB YR	B AV	OB AV	SG AV	D TIT	D AV	O TIT	O AV	TOT AV	GROSS	PLAY #
DROPO, WALT	13	36.7	85.6	11.6	54.1	0.3	.270	.327	.432	1	.076	1	.076	.2360	188.3	424.3
DUNCAN, MARIANO	9	51.6	103.9	7.3	40.9	14.5	.267	.300	.388	0	.000	1	.083	.2076	218.2	425.8
DUNN, ADAM	5	84.0	112.8	31.6	74.8	8.2	.248	383	.518	0	.000	0	000	.2298	311.4	541.2
DUNSTON, SHAWON	18	40.9	88.7	8.3	37.1	11.8	.269	.296	.416	0	.000	0	.000	.1962	186.8	383.0
DURHAM, RAY	11	95.5	154.5	13.5	60.5	22,5	.280	.357	.435	0	.000	0	.000	.2144	346.5	560.9
DUROCHER, LEO*	17	33.8	77.6	1.4	33.3	1.8	.247	.299	.320	3	.176	0	.000	.2080	147.9	355.9
DYE, JERMAINE	10	63.9	118.2	19.2	69.7	3.4	.272	.336	.469	1	.100	0	.000	.2354	274.4	509.8
DYKES, JIMMY	22	50.3	102.5	4.9	48.6	3.1	.280	.365	.399	1	.045	0	.000	.2170	209.4	426.4
DYKSTRA, LENNY	12	50.2	108.2	6.8	33.7	23.8	.285	.375	.419	0	.000	4	.333	.3954	222.7	618.1
EASLEY, DAMIAN	14	46.7	85.9	9.9	41.9	8.1	.251	.328	.403	2	.143	0	.000	.2950	192.5	417.5
ECKSTEIN, DAVID	5	86.0	159.8	5.0	46.2	18.6	.282	.363	.395	0	.000	0	.000	.2080	315.6	520.6
EDMONDS, JIM	13	81.8	124.5	25.5	76.8	4.5	.291	.387	.543	8	.615	0	.000	.3672	313.1	680.3
EDWARDS, JOHNNY	14	30.7	79.0	5.8	37.4	1.1	.242	.314	.353	5	.357	0	.000	.2532	154.0	407.2
ELLIOTT, BOB	15	70.9	137.4	11.3	79.6	4.0	.289	.375	.440	1	.066	1	066	.2470	303.2	550.2
ENCARNACION, JUAN	9	55.7	114.3	14.2	60.1	13.2	.268	.318	.440	0	.000	0	.000	.2052	257.5	462.7
ENNIS, DEL	14	70.3	147.3	20.5	91.7	3.2	.284	.341	.472	0	.000	1	.071	.2330	333.0	566.0
ENSBERG, MORGAN	5	44.0	81.6	14.8	49.2	4.2	.279	.366	.493	0	.000	0	.000	.2276	193.8	421.4
ERSTAD, DARIN	10	81.0	148.4	11.4	62.0	16.9	.287	.344	.417	3	.300	1	.100	.2896	319.7	609.3
ETTEN, NICK	9	47.3	102.3	9.8	58.4	2.4	.277	.371	.423	0	.000	3	.333	.2800	220.2	500.2
EVANS, DARRELL	21	64.0	105.8	19.7	64.4	4.6	.248	.364	.431	0	.000	3	.142	.2370	258.5	495.5
EVANS, DWIGHT	20	73.5	122.3	19.2	69.2	3.9	.272	.373	.470	8	.400	5	.200	.3430	288.1	631.1
EVERETT, CARL	13	51.5	94.9	14.7	58.4	8.2	.274	.346	.469	0	000	0	.000	.2178	222.7	440.5
EVERS, HOOT	12	46.3	87.9	8.1	47.0	3.7	.278	.353	.426	1	.083	1	.083	.2440	193.0	437.0
FAIN, FERRIS	9	66.1	126.5	5.3	63.3	5.1	.290	.425	.396	0	.000	4	.444	.3110	266.3	577.3
FAIRLY, RON	21	44.3	91.0	10.2	49.7	1.6	.266	.363	.408	1	.047	0	.000	.2160	196.8	412.8
FELIX, JUNIOR	6	51.5	93.6	9.1	46.6	8.1	.264	.313	.413	0	.000	0	.000	.1980	208.0	406.9
FERGUSON, JOE	14	29.0	51.3	0.7	31.7	1.5	.240	.361	.409	1	.071	0	.000	.2160	114.2	330.2
FERNANDEZ, TONY	16	65.4	140.0	5.8	51.8	15.3	.288	.350	.399	5	.313	1	.063	.2826	278.3	560.9
FERRELL, RICK*	18	38.1	94.0	1.5	40.7	1.6	281	.378	.363	1	.055	0	.000	.2150	175.9	390.0
FIELDER, CECIL	13	57.2	101.0	24.5	77.5	0.2	.255	.348	.482	0	.000	6	.462	.3094	260.4	569.8
FINLEY, STEVE	17	80.5	142.7	17.5	66.2	18.4	.273	.334	.447	6	.353	2	.118	.3050	325.3	630.3
FISK, CARLTON*	24	53.1	98.1	15.6	55.4	5.3	.270	.344	.458	1	.041	1	.041	.2300	227.5	457.5
FLETCHER, ELBIE	12	60.2	110.2	6.5	51.3	2.6	.271	.384	.390	1	.083	5	.416	.3080	230.8	538.8
FLOOD, CURT	15	56.7	124.0	5.6	42.4	5.8	.293	.344	.389	8	.533	1	.066	.3250	234.5	559.5
FLOYD, CLIFF	13	54.4	96.2	15.5	56.7	10.8	.281	.363	.494	0	.000	0	.000	.2276	233.6	461.2
FOLI, TIM	16	36.0	94.6	1.5	31.3	5.0	.251	.286	.309	2	.125	0	.000	.1940	168.4	362.4
FONDY, DEE	8	54.6	125.0	8.6	46.6	10.5	.286	.326	.413	0	.000	0	.000	.2050	245.3	450.3
FONSECA, LEW	12	43.2	89.6	2.6	40.4	5.3	.316	.355	.432	0	.000	1	.083	.2372	181.1	418.3
FOSTER, GEORGE	18	54.7	106.9	19.3	68.8	2.8	.274	.341	.480	1	.055	7	.388	.3070	252.5	559.5
FOX, NELLIE*	19	67.3	140.1	1.8	41.5	4.0	.288	.349	.363	8	.421	5	.263	.3370	254.7	591.7
FOX, PETE	13	68.8	129.0	5.0	53.3	12.1	.298	.347	.415	1	.076	0	.000	.2270	256.1	483.1
FOXX, JIMMIE*	20	87.5	132.3	26.7	96.1	4.3	.325	.428	.609	3	.150	21	1.050	.5120	346.9	858.9
FRANCO, JULIO	21	60.1	120.0	8.1	54.9	13,0	.299	.366	.419	0	.000	1	.048	.2264	256.1	482.5
FRANCONA, TITO	15	43.3	93.0	8.3	43.7	3.0	.272	.346	.403	0	.000	1	.066	.2170	191.3	408.3
FREEHAN, BILL	15	47.0	106.0	13.3	50.5	1.6	.262	.342	.412	7	.467	0	.000	.2970	218.4	515.4
FREGOSI, JIM	18	46.8	95.8	8.3	39.2	4.2	.265	.340	.398	1	.056	1	.055	.2230	194.3	417.3
FREY, LONNY	14	60.5	105.8	4.3	39.2	7.5	.269	.359	.374	2	.142	0	.000	.2280	217.3	445.3
FRISCH, FRANKIE*	19	80.6	151.5	5.5	65.4	22.0	.316	.369	.432	3	.157	5	.263	.3070	325.0	632.0
FRYMAN, TRAVIS	13	68.8	136.6	17.2	78.6	5.5	.274	.336	.443	3	231	0	.000	.2568	306.7	563.5
FUENTES, TITO	13	46.9	114.6	3.4	33.6	6.1	.268	.309	.347	1	.076	0	.000	.2000	204.6	404.6
FULLMER, BRAD	8	49.4	97.3	14.3	92.1	4.0	.279	.336	.486	0	.000	0	.000	.2202	257.1	477.3
FURCAL, RAFAEL	6	92.3	154.0	9.5	48.7	31.5	.284	.350	.409	0	.000	1	.167	.2420	336.0	578.0
FURILLO, CARL	15	59.6	127.3	12.8	70.5	3.2	.299	.356	.458	0	.000	1	.066	.2350	273.4	508.4
GAETTI, GARY	20	56.5	114.0	18.0	67.1	4.8	.255	.311	.434	7	.350	0	.000	.2700	260.4	530.4
GAGNE, GREG	15	47.5	96.0	7.4	40.3	7.2	.254	.304	.382	1	.067	0	.000	.2014	198.4	399.8
GALAN, AUGIE	16	62.7	106.6	6.2	51.8	7.6	.287	.390	.419	0	.000	6	.375	.2940	234.9	528.9
GALARRAGA, ANDRES	19	62.9	127.8	21.0	75.0	6.7	.288	.347	.499	2	.105	6	.316	.3110	288.4	599.4
GANT, RON	16	67.5	103.2	20.1	63.0	15.2	.256	.336	.468	0	.000	0	.000	.2120	269.0	481.0
GANTNER, JIM	17	42.7	99.7	2.7	33.4	8.0	.274	.322	.351	0	.000	0	.000	.1890	186.5	375.5
GARCIAPARRA, N.	10	76.5	139.5	19.1	74.0	8.6	.320	.387	.544	0	.000	5	.500	.3462	317.7	663.9
GARNER, PHIL	16	48.7	99.6	6.8	46.1	14.0	.260	.326	.389	0	.000	0	.000	.1950	215.2	410.2
GARR, RALPH	13	55.1	120.1	5.7	31.3	13.3	.306	.340	.416	0	.000	4	.307	.2730	225.5	498.5
GARVEY, STEVE	19	60.1	136.7	14.3	68.8	4.3	.294	.333	.446	6	.316	2	.105	.2990	284.2	583.2
GEHRIG, LOU*	17	111.0	160.0	29.0	117.3	6.0	.340	.447	.632	0	.000	27	1.588	.6010	423.3	1024.3
GEHRINGER, CHAS.*	19	93.3	149.4	9.6	75.1	9.5	.320	.404	.480	7	.368	9	.473	.4090	336.9	745.9
GENTILE, JIM	9	48.2	84.3	19.9	61.0	0.3	.260	.372	.486	1	.111	0	.000	.2458	213.7	459.5
GIAMBI, JASON	11	84.1	138.7	28.5	93.7	1.2	.295	.416	.539	0	.000	7	.636	.3772	346.2	723.4
GIBSON, KIRK	17	57.9	91.4	15.0	51.2	16.7	.268	.355	.463	0	.000	0	.000	.2172	232.2	449.4
GILES, BRIAN	11	78.5	126.6	22.4	78.0	8.5	.299	.417	.542	0	.000	0	.000	.2516	314.0	565.6
GILES, MARCUS	5	65.8	114.6	12.2	46.8	10.0	.292	.369	.465	0	.000	0	.000	.2252	249.4	474.6

NAME	YRS	RUNS YR	HITS YR	HR YR	RBI YR	SB YR	B AV	OB AV	SG AV	D TIT	D AV	O TIT	O AV	TOT AV	GROSS	PLAY #
GILKEY, BERNARD	10	50.5	92.9	9.8	45.5	9.6	.275	.352	.434	0	.000	0	.000	.2122	208.3	420.5
GILLIAM, JUNIOR	14	83.0	133.5	4.6	39.8	14.5	.265	.361	.355	1	.071	1	.071	.2240	275.4	499.4
GINSBERG, JOE	13	12.9	31.8	1.5	14.0	0.5	.241	.334	.320	0	.000	0	.000	.1790	60.7	239.7
GLADDEN, DON	11	60.3	110.5	6.7	40.5	20.2	.270	.324	.382	0	.000	0	.000	.1952	238.2	433.4
GLAUS, TROY	8	75.1	110.9	27.3	76.5	6.6	.253	.359	.501	0	.000	1	.125	.2476	296.4	544.0
GONZALEZ, JUAN	17	62.4	113.9	25.5	82.6	1.5	.295	.343	.561	0	.000	5	.294	.2986	285.9	584.5
GONZALEZ, LUIS	16	76.2	138.4	19.8	78.2	7.6	.285	.369	.487	1	.063	1	.063	.2534	320.2	573.6
GONZALEZ, TONY	12	57.5	123.7	8.5	51.2	6.5	.286	.353	.413	3	.250	0	.000	.2600	247.4	507.4
GOODMAN, BILLY	16	50.4	105.6	1.1	36.9	2.3	.300	.377	.378	1	.062	1	.062	.2350	196.3	431.3
GOODMAN, IVAL	10	60.9	110.4	9.5	52.5	4.9	.281	.352	.445	0	.000	2	.200	.2550	238.2	493.2
GORDON, JOE	11	83.0	139.0	23.0	88.6	8.1	.268	.357	.466	0	.000	0	.000	.2180	341.7	559.7
GORDON, SID	13	56.5	108.8	15.5	61.9	1.4	.283	.377	.466	2	.153	0	.000	.2550	244.1	499.1
GOSLIN, GOOSE*	18	82.3	151.9	13.7	89.3	9.7	.316	.387	.500	0	.000	4	.222	.2850	346.9	631.9
GRACE,MARK	16	73.7	152.8	10.8	71.6	4.4	.303	.383	.442	6	.375	1	.063	.3132	313.3	626.5
GREEN, SHAWN	13	76.5	132.8	23.3	73.7	11.3	.283	.359	.505	1	.077	1	.077	.2602	317.6	577.8
GREENBERG, HANK.*	13	80.8	125.2	25.4	98.1	4.4	.313	.412	.605	1	.076	14	1.076	.4960	333.9	829.9
GREENWELL, MIKE	12	54.8	116.7	10.8	60.5	6.7	.303	.368	.463	0	.000	0	.000	.2268	249.5	476.3
GREER, RUSTY	9	71.4	129.6	13.2	68.2	3.4	.305	.387	.478	0	.000	0	.000	.2340	258.8	492.8
GRICH, BOBBY	17	60.7	107.8	13.1	50.8	6.1	.266	.373	.424	5	.294	2	.117	.2990	238.5	537.5
GRIFFEY, KEN, JR.	17	82.6	135.5	31.5	90.4	10.5	.293	.377	.561	10	.588	7	.412	4462	350.5	796.7
GRIFFEY, KEN,SR.	19	59.4	112.7	8.0	45.2	10.5	.296	.361	.431	0	.000	0	.000	.2170	235.8	452.8
GRIFFIN, ALFREDO	18	42.4	93.8	1.3	27.7	10.7	.249	.287	.319	1	.056	1	.056	.1934	175.9	369.3
GRIMM, CHARLIE	20	45.4	114.9	3.9	53.9	2.8	.290	.341	.397	7	.350	0	.000	.2750	220.9	495.9
GRISSOM, MARQUIS	17	69.8	132.4	13.4	56.9	25.2	.272	.318	.415	6	.353	2	.118	.2952	297.7	592.9
GROAT, DICK	14	59.2	152.7	2.7	50.5	1.0	.286	.332	.366	0	.000	2	.142	.2250	266.1	491.1
GROTH, JOHNNY	15	32.0	70.9	4.0	32.4	1.2	.279	.353	.395	1	.066	0	.000	.2180	140.5	358.5
GRUBER, KELLY	10	43.1	81.8	11.7	44.3	8.0	.259	.302	.432	1	.100	0	.000	.2190	188.9	407.9
GRUDZIELANEK, M.	11	67.7	146.5	6.7	45.6	11.4	.287	.331	.391	0	.000	1	.091	.2200	277.9	497.9
GUERRERO, PEDRO	15	48.6	107.8	14.3	59.8	6.4	.300	.374	.480	0	.000	3	.200	.2700	236.9	506.9
GUERRERO, VLADIMIR	10	86.0	158.6	19.1	93.6	15.1	.324	.393	.574	0	.000	2	.200	.2982	372.4	670.6
GUILLEN, JOSE	9	53.9	111.8	14.9	59.3	2.3	.276	.324	.448	0	.000	0	.000	.2096	242.2	451.8
GUILLEN, OZZIE	16	48.3	110.3	1.8	38.7	10.6	.264	.290	.338	2	.125	0	.000	.2034	209.7	413.1
GUTIERREZ, JACK	6	17.6	37.8	0.6	10.5	4.1	.237	.263	.285	0	.000	0	.000	.1570	70.6	227.6
GUZMAN, CRISTIAN	7	71.0	138.7	6.1	45.7	21.8	.260	.300	.374	1	.143	3	.429	.3012	283.3	584.5
GWYNN, TONY*	20	69.2	157.1	6.8	56.9	16.0	.328	.388	.459	5	.250	16	.800	.4470	306.0	753.0
HACK, STAN	16	77.4	137.0	3.5	40.1	10.3	.301	.394	.397	2	.125	5	.312	.3050	268.3	573.3
HAFEY, CHICK*	13	59.7	112.7	12.6	64.0	5.3	.317	.372	.526	0	.000	2	.153	.2730	254.3	527.3
HAFNER, TRAVIS	4	57.8	96.8	19.0	65.8	1.3	.293	.390	.556	0	.000	0	.000	.2478	240.7	488.5
HALL, MEL	13	43.7	91.0	10.3	47.7	2.4	.276	.322	.437	0	.000	0	.000	.2070	194.2	401.2
HAMNER, GRANNY	17	41.8	89.9	6.1	41.6	2.0	.262	.304	.383	0	.000	0	.000	.1890	181.4	370.4
HARGROVE, MIKE	12	65.2	134.5	6.6	57.1	2.0	.290	.400	.391	0	.000	3	.250	.2660	265.4	531.4
HARPER, TOMMY	15	64.8	107.2	9.7	37.8	27.2	.257	.340	.379	0	.000	3	.200	.2350	246.7	481.7
HARRAH, TOBY	17	65.5	114.9	8.5	54.0	14.0	.264	.368	.395	1	.058	1	.058	.2280	256.9	484.9
HARRELSON, BUD	16	33.6	70.0	0.4	16.6	7.9	.236	.329	.288	1	.063	0	.000	.1830	128.5	311.5
HARRELSON, KEN	9	41.5	78.1	14.5	46.7	5.8	.239	.328	.414	1	.111	1	.111	.2400	186.6	426.6
HARRIS, BUCKY	12	60.1	108.0	0.7	42.1	13.8	.274	.352	.354	1	.083	0	.000	.2120	224.7	436.7
HARRIS, LENNY	18	25.6	58.6	2.1	20.5	7.3	.269	.320	.349	0	.000	0	.000	.1876	114.1	301.7
HART, JIM RAY	12	43.1	87.6	14.1	48.1	1.4	.278	.348	.467	0	.000	0	.000	.2180	194.3	412.3
HARTNETT, GABBY*	20	43.3	95.6	11.8	58.9	1.4	.297	.370	.489	6	.300	0	.000	.2910	211.0	502.0
HATTEBERG, SCOTT	11	38.5	81.8	7.5	38.4	0.1	.268	.357	.403	0	.000	0	.000	.2056	166.3	371.9
HATTON, GRADY	12	46.8	89.0	7.5	44.4	3.5	.254	.355	.374	3	.250	0	.000	.2460	191.2	437.2
HAYES, VON	12	63.9	116.8	11.9	58.0	21.0	.267	.357	.416	0	.000	2	.166	.2410	271.6	512.6
HEALY, FRAN	9	16.0	36.8	2.2	15.6	3.3	.250	.329	.350	0	.000	0	.000	.1850	73.9	258.9
HEATH, JEFF	14	55.5	103.3	13.8	63.3	4.0	293	.370	.509	1	.071	2	.142	.2770	239.9	516.9
HEBNER, RICHIE	18	48.0	94.1	11.2	49.4	2.1	.276	.356	.438	0	.000	0	.000	.2140	204.7	418.7
HEGAN, JIM	17	32.3	63.9	5.4	30.8	0.8	.228	.296	.344	2	117	0	.000	.1970	133.2	330.2
HELMS, TOMMY	14	29.5	95.8	2.4	34.0	2.3	.269	.303	.342	4	.286	0	.000	.2400	164.0	404.0
HELTON, TODD	9	102.7	170.6	30.1	101.7	3.7	.337	.436	.607	3	.333	6	.667	.4760	408.8	884.8
HENDERSON, D.	14	50.7	94.5	14.0	50.5	3.5	.258	.320	.436	0	.000	0	.000	.2020	213.2	415.2
HENDERSON, R.	25	91.8	122.2	11.9	44.6	56.2	.279	. 401	.419	0	.000	23	.920	.4038	326.7	730.5
HENDRICK, GEORGE	18	52.2	110.0	14.8	61.7	3.2	.278	.333	.446	0	.000	0	.000	.2110	241.9	452.9
HENDRICKS, ELLIE	12	17.0	34.5	5.1	19.1	0.0	.220	.308	.361	2	.166	0	.000	.2110	75.7	286.7
HENRICH, TOMMY	11	81.9	117.9	16.6	72.2	3.3	.282	.382	.491	0	.000	3	.272	.2850	292.5	577.5
HERMAN, BABE	13	67.8	139.8	13.9	76.7	7.2	.324	.383	.532	0	.000	1	.077	.2632	305.4	568.6
HERMAN, BILLY*	15	77.5	156.3	3.1	55.9	4.4	.304	.367	.407	3	.200	3	.200	.2950	297.2	592.2
HERNANDEZ, KEITH	17	66.1	128.3	9.5	63.0	5.7	.296	.388	.436	11	.647	7	.411	.4360	272.6	708.6
HERNDON, LARRY	14	43.2	95.2	7.6	39.2	6.5	.274	.325	.409	0	.000	0	.000	.2010	191.7	392.7
HERR, TOMMY	13	52.0	111.5	2.1	44.1	14.4	.271	.350	.350	1	.076	0	.000	.2090	224.1	433.1
HIGGINS, PINKY	14	66.4	117.2	10.0	76.7	4.3	.292	.370	.427	0	.000	0	.000	.2170	274.6	491.6
HIGGINSON, BOBBY	11	66.9	121.5	17.0	64.5	8.3	.272	.303	.385	0	.000	0	.000	.1920	278.2	470.2
HILL, GLENALLEN	13	40.6	77.3	14.3	45.1	7.4	.271	.321	.482	0	.000	0	.000	.2148	184.7	399.5

NAME	YRS	RUNS YR	HITS YR	HR YR	RBI YR	SB YR	B AV	OB AV	SG AV	D TIT	D AV	O TIT	O AV	TOT AV	GROSS	PLAY #
HILL, MARC	14	10.4	28.8	2.4	14.1	0.0	.223	.298	.317	0	.000	0	.000	.1670	55.7	222.7
HILLENBRAND, SHEA	5	73.0	160.0	16.6	78.2	3.0	.288	.327	.448	0	.000	0	.000	.2126	330.8	543.4
HISLE, LARRY	14	46.5	81.8	11.8	48.1	9.1	.273	.350	.452	0	.000	1	.071	.2290	197.3	426.3
HOAG, MYRIL	13	29.5	65.6	2.1	30.8	4.5	.271	.328	.364	0	.000	0	.000	.1920	132.5	324.5
HOAK, DON	11	54.3	104.0	8.0	45.2	5.8	.265	.347	.396	2	.181	1	.090	.2550	217.3	472.3
HODGES, GIL	18	61.3	106.7	20.5	70.7	3.5	.273	.361	.487	5	.278	0	.000	.2800	262.7	542.7
HOLMES, TOMMY	11	63.4	37.0	8.0	52.8	3.6	.302	.366	.432	0	.000	5	.454	.3100	264.8	574.8
HOPP, JOHNNY	14	49.8	90.1	3.2	32.7	9.1	.296	.368	.414	1	.071	0	.000	.2290	184.9	413.9
HORNER, BOB	10	56.0	104.7	21.8	68.5	1.4	.277	.344	.499	0	.000	0	.000	.2240	252.4	476.4
HORNSBY, ROGERS*	23	68.6	127.3	13.0	68.8	5.8	.358	.434	.577	1	.043	49	2.130	.7080	283.7	991.7
HORTON, WILLIE	18	48.5	110.7	18.0	64.6	1.1	.273	.335	.457	0	.000	0	.000	.2130	242.9	455.9
HOUK, RALPH	8	1.5	5.3	0.0	2.5	0.0	.272	.327	.323	0	.000	0	.000	.1840	9.3	193.3
HOWARD, ELSTON	14	44.2	105.0	11.9	54.4	0.6	.274	.325	.427	1	.071	0	.000	.2190	216.1	435.1
HOWARD, FRANK	16	54.0	110.8	23.8	69.9	0.5	.273	.355	.499	0	.000	5	.312	.2870	259.0	546.0
HRBEK, KENT	14	64.5	124.9	20.9	77.5	2.6	.282	.368	.481	1	.071	0	.000	.2400	290.4	530.4
HUBBS, KEN	3	49.3	103.3	4.6	32.6	3.6	.247	.292	.336	0	.000	0	.000	.1750	193.4	368.4
HUNDLEY, TODD	14	35.4	63.1	14.4	42.8	1.0	.234	.320	.443	0	.000	0	.000	.1680	113.6	281.6
HUNT, RON	12	62.0	119.0	3.2	30.8	5.4	.273	.369	.347	0	.000	0	.000	.1970	220.4	417.4
HUNTER, TORII	9	54.7	99.0	14.8	56.2	10.7	.267	.322	.458	5	.556	0	.000	.3206	235.4	556.0
INCAVIGLIA, PETE	12	45.5	86.9	17.2	54.6	2.8	.246	.310	.448	0	.000	0	.000	.2008	207.0	407.8
IRVIN, MONTE*	8	45.7	91.3	12.3	55.3	3.5	.293	.385	.475	0	.000	1	.125	.2550	208.1	463.1
IZTURIS, CESAR	5	49.4	117.0	2.0	34.6	11.6	.261	.295	.338	1	.200	0	.000	.2188	214.6	433.4
JABLONSKI, RAY	8	37.1	85.8	10.3	54.7	2.0	.268	.324	.423	0	.000	0	.000	.2030	189.9	392.9
JACKSON, REGGIE*	21	73.8	123.0	26.8	81.0	10.8	.262	.358	.490	0	.000	10	.476	.3170	315.4	632.4
JACKSON, TRAVIS*	15	55.5	117.8	9.0	61.9	4.7	.291	.337	.433	2	.133	0	.000	.2380	248.9	486.9
JACOBY, BROOK	11	48.6	110.9	10.9	49.5	1.4	.270	.337	.405	0	.000	0	.000	.2020	211.2	413.2
JAVIER, JULIAN	13	55.5	113.0	6.0	38.9	10.3	.257	.298	.355	0	.000	0	.000	.1820	223.7	405.7
JEFFERIES, GREGG	14	54.4	113.8	9.0	47.4	14.0	.289	.344	.421	0	.000	1	.071	.2250	238.6	463.6
JENKINS, GEOFF	8	69.3	122.9	21.8	71.3	3.1	.281	.349	.508	1	.125	0	.000	.2526	288.4	541.0
JENSEN, JACKIE	11	73.6	133.0	18.0	84.4	13.0	.279	.372	.460	0	.000	5	.454	.3130	322.0	635.0
JETER, DEREK	11	105.4	176.0	15.4	69.4	19.5	.314	.396	.461	2	.182	2	.182	.2980	385.7	683.7
JOHNSON, ALEX	13	42.3	102.3	6.0	40.3	8.6	.288	.329	.392	0	.000	1	.076	.2170	199.5	416.5
JOHNSON, BILLY	9	46.5	98.0	6.7	54.1	1.4	.271	.346	.391	1	.111	0	.000	.2010	206.7	407.7
JOHNSON, BOB	13	95.3	157.7	22.1	98.6	7.3	.296	.393	.506	0	.000	1	.076	.2540	381.0	635.0
JOHNSON, CHARLES	12	38.8	78.3	13.9	47.5	0.5	.245	.330	.433	4	.333	0	.000	.2682	179.0	447.2
JOHNSON, CLIFF	15	35.9	67.7	13.0	46.6	0.6	.258	.358	.459	0	.000	0	.000	.2150	163.8	378.8
JOHNSON, DAVEY	13	43.3	96.3	10.4	46.8	2.5	.261	.343	.404	4	.308	0	.000	.2630	199.3	462.3
JOHNSON, HOWARD	14	54.3	87.8	16.3	54.3	16.5	.269	.343	.446	0	.000	3	.214	.2544	229.2	483.6
JOHNSON, LANCE	14	54.8	111.8	2.4	34.7	23.4	.291	.334	.386	1	.071	7	.500	.3164	227.1	543.5
JOHNSON, ROY	10	71.7	129.2	5.8	55.6	13.5	.296	.369	.437	0	.000	2	.200	.2600	275.8	535.8
JONES, ANDRUW	10	85.5	140.8	30.1	89.4	12.9	.267	.344	.508	8	.800	2	.200	.4238	358.7	782.5
JONES, CHIPPER	12	91.8	151.4	27.6	92.6	10.3	.303	.406	.539	0	.000	0	.000	.2496	373.7	623.3
JONES, CLEON	13	43.4	92.0	7.1	40.3	7.0	.281	.342	.404	0	.000	0	.000	.3420	189.8	531.8
JONES, JACQUE	7	70.1	139.1	18.9	68.0	9.6	.279	.328	.455	0	.000	0	.000	.2124	302.7	515.1
JONES, MACK	10	48.5	77.8	13.3	41.5	6.5	.252	.349	.444	0	.000	0	.000	.2090	187.6	396.6
JONES, RUPPERT	12	53.5	91.9	12.2	48.2	11.9	.250	.332	.416	0	.000	0	.000	.1990	217.7	416.7
JONES, WILLIE	15	52.4	100.1	12.6	54.1	6.8	.258	.345	.410	6	.400	0	.000	.2820	229.0	511.0
JOOST, EDDIE	17	51.4	78.7	7.8	35.3	3.5	.239	.361	.366	0	.000	0	.000	.1930	176.7	369.7
JORDAN, BRIAN	14	53.1	102.4	12.9	57.9	8.5	.283	.334	.457	0	.000	0	.000	.2148	234.8	449.6
JOYNER, WALLY	16	60.8	128.8	12.8	69.5	3.8	.289	.362	.440	4	.250	0	.000	.2682	275.7	543.9
JURGES, BILLY	17	42.4	94.8	2.5	38.5	2.1	.258	.325	.335	4	.235	0	.000	.2300	180.3	410.3
JUSTICE, DAVID	14	66.4	112.2	21.8	72.6	3.8	.279	.378	.500	0	.000	0	.000	.2314	276.8	508.2
KALINE, AL*	22	73.7	136.6	18.1	71.9	6.2	.297	.379	.480	11	.500	4	.181	.3674	306.5	673.9
KAMM, WILLIE	13	61.7	126.4	2.2	63.5	9.7	.281	.372	.384	8	.615	1	.077	.3458	263.5	609.3
KARROS, ERIC	14	57.0	123.1	20.1	73.4	4.2	.268	.325	.454	1	.071	0	.000	.2236	277.8	501.4
KEARNS, AUSTIN	4	48.8	84.3	13.8	71.0	3.3	.266	.359	.461	0	.000	0	.000	.1640	221.2	385.2
KELL, GEORGE*	15	58.7	136.9	5.2	58.0	3.4	.306	.368	.414	7	.466	5	.333	.3770	262.2	639.2
KELLER, CHARLIE	13	55.7	83.4	14.5	58.4	3.4	.286	.410	.518	0	.000	2	.153	.2730	215.4	488.4
KELLY, ROBERTO	14	49.1	99.3	8.9	41.8	16.8	.290	.337	.430	0	.000	0	.000	.2114	215.9	427.3
KELTNER, KEN	13	56.6	120.7	12.5	65.5	3.0	.276	.338	.441	3	.230	0	.000	.2570	258.3	515.3
KEMP, STEVE	11	52.8	102.5	11.8	57.6	3.5	.278	.370	.431	0	.000	0	.000	.2150	228.2	443.2
KENDALL, JASON	10	77.6	157.2	6.7	52.4	14.8	.302	.384	.407	0	.000	0	.000	.2238	288.9	512.9
KENNEDY, ADAM	7	56.7	119.9	6.9	44.9	15.3	.281	.336	.401	0	.000	0	.000	.2036	243.7	447.3
KENNEDY, BOB	16	32.1	73.5	3.9	32.1	2.8	.254	.310	.355	0	.000	0	.000	.1830	144.4	327.4
KENNEDY, TERRY	14	33.8	93.7	8.0	44.8	0.4	.264	.316	.386	0	.000	0	.000	.1930	180.7	373.7
KENT, JEFF	14	81.4	147.9	23.6	93.7	6.6	.289	.354	.506	0	.000	0	.000	.2298	353.2	583.0
KERR, BUDDY	9	42.0	100.3	3.4	37.0	4.2	.249	.312	.328	1	.111	0	.000	.2000	186.9	386.9
KESSINGER, DON	16	56.1	120.6	0.8	32.9	6.3	.252	.316	.312	2	.124	0	.000	.2010	216.7	417.7
KILLEBREW, HARMON*	22	58.3	94.8	26.0	72.0	0.8	.256	.379	.509	0	.000	15	.681	.3650	251.9	616.9
KINER, RALPH*	10	97.1	145.1	36.9	101.5	2.2	.279	.398	.548	0	.000	16	1.600	.5650	382.8	947.8

NAME	YRS	RUNS YR	HITS YR	HR YR	RBI YR	SB YR	B AV	OB AV	SG AV	D TIT	D AV	O TIT	O AV	TOT AV	GROSS	PLAY #
KINGMAN, DAVE	16	56.3	98.4	27.6	75.6	5.3	.236	.305	.478	0	.000	3	.187	.2410	263.2	504.2
KITTLE, RON	10	35.6	64.8	17.6	46.0	1.6	.239	.309	.473	0	.000	0	.000	.2040	165.6	369.6
KLEIN, CHUCK*	17	68.7	122.1	17.6	70.6	4.6	.320	.379	.543	0	.000	19	1.117	.4710	283.6	754.6
KLESKO, RYAN	14	58.8	104.8	19.4	67.2	6.1	.280	.375	.507	0	.000	0	.000	.2324	256.3	488.7
KLUSZEWSKI, TED	15	56.5	117.7	18.6	68.5	1.3	.298	.354	.498	5	.333	3	.200	.3360	262.6	598.6
KNIGHT, RAY	13	37.6	100.8	6.4	45.7	1.0	.271	.325	.390	0	.000	0	.000	.1970	191.5	388.5
KNOBLAUCH, CHUCK	12	94.3	153.3	8.2	51.3	33.9	.289	.378	.406	2	.167	2	.167	.2814	341.0	622.4
KONERKO, PAUL	9	64.4	123.9	23.3	76.9	0.4	.279	.352	.488	0	.000	0	.000	.2238	288.9	512.9
KRANEPOOL, ED	18	29.8	78.8	6.6	34.1	0.8	.261	.319	.377	1	.056	0	.000	.2026	150.1	352.7
KREEVICH, MIKE	12	56.3	110.0	3.7	42.8	9.5	.283	.346	.391	2	.166	1	.083	.2530	222.3	475.3
KRESS, RED	14	49.3	103.8	6.3	57.0	3.3	.286	.347	.420	2	.142	0	.000	.2390	219.7	458.7
KRUK, JOHNNY	10	58.2	117.0	10.0	59.2	5.8	.300	.397	.446	0	.000	0	.000	2286	250.2	478.8
KUBEK, TONY	9	58.0	123.2	6.3	41.4	3.2	.266	.305	.364	0	.000	0	.000	.1870	232.1	419.1
KUENN, HARVEY	15	63.4	139.4	5.8	44.7	4.5	.303	.359	.408	1	.066	8	.533	.3330	257.8	590.8
KUHEL, JOE	18	68.6	122.8	7.2	58.2	9.8	.277	.359	.406	1	.055	0	.000	.2190	266.6	485.6
KUROWSKI, WHITEY	9	57.5	102.7	11.7	58.7	2.1	.286	.366	.455	2	.222	0	.000	.2650	232.7	497.7
LACY, LEE	16	40.6	81.4	5.6	28.6	11.5	.286	.342	.410	1	.062	0	.000	.2200	167.6	387.7
LANDREAUX, KEN	11	47.5	99.9	8.3	43.5	13.2	.268	.317	.400	1	.091	0	.000	.2152	212.4	427.7
LANDRITH, HOBIE	14	12.7	32.1	2.4	14.5	0.3	.233	.323	.327	0	.000	0	.000	.1760	62.0	238.0
LANKFORD, RAY	14	69.1	111.5	17.0	62.4	18.4	.272	.364	.477	1	.071	1	.071	.2510	278.4	529.4
LANSFORD, CARNEY	15	67.1	138.2	10.1	58.3	14.9	.290	.343	.411	4	.267	1	.067	.2756	288.7	564.3
LANSING, MIKE	9	61.6	124.9	9.3	48.9	13.2	.271	.324	.401	0	.000	0	.000	.1992	257.9	457.1
LARKIN, BARRY	19	69.9	123.2	10.4	50.5	19.9	.295	.371	.444	3	.158	0	.000	.2536	273.9	527.5
LaRUSSA, TONY	6	2.5	5.8	0.0	1.1	0.0	.199	.295	.250	0	.000	0	.000	.1480	9.4	157.4
LARY, LYN	12	67.0	103.2	3.1	43.8	13.5	.269	.369	.372	1	.083	1	.083	.2350	230.6	465.6
LAWTON, MATT	11	68.3	115.1	12.5	53.3	15.0	.267	.368	.418	0	.000	0	.000	.2106	264.2	474.8
LAZZERI, TONY*	14	70.4	131.4	12.7	85.0	10.5	.292	.380	.467	0	.000	0	.000	.2270	310.0	537.0
LEE, CARLOS	7	88.3	160.1	26.3	95.1	11.0	.284	.341	.488	2	.286	0	.000	.2798	358.8	638.6
LEE, DERREK	9	71.2	125.2	23.1	69.6	8.7	.276	.365	.501	2	.222	3	.333	.3394	297.8	637.2
LeFLORE, RON	9	81.2	142.5	6.5	39.2	50.5	.288	.344	.392	0	.000	3	.333	.2710	319.9	590.9
LEMON, CHET	16	60.8	117.1	13.4	55.2	3.6	.273	.357	.442	0	.000	1	.062	.2260	250.4	476.4
LEMON, JIM	12	37.1	75.0	13.6	44.0	1.0	.262	.335	.460	0	.000	1	.083	.2280	170.7	398.7
LEONARD, JEFFREY	14	43.8	95.8	10.2	51.6	11.6	.266	.316	.411	0	.000	0	.000	.1980	213.0	411.0
LEWIS, BUDDY	11	75.4	142.0	6.4	55.1	7.5	.297	.368	.420	0	.000	1	.090	.2350	286.4	521.4
LIEBERTHAL, MIKE	12	42.2	90.0	11.8	47.8	0.7	.275	.339	.449	1	.083	0	.000	.2292	192.5	421.7
LIND, JOSE	9	40.9	103.9	1.0	36.0	6.9	.254	.297	.316	2	.222	0	.000	.2178	188.7	406.5
LINDSTROM, FRED*	13	68.8	134.3	7.9	59.9	6.4	.311	.351	.449	1	.076	1	.076	.2520	277.3	529.3
LOCKMAN, WHITEY	15	55.7	110.5	7.6	37.5	2.8	.279	.342	.391	0	.000	0	.000	.2020	214.1	416.1
LO DUCA, PAUL	8	42.6	98.3	8.3	45.4	1.8	.285	.342	.417	0	.000	0	.000	.2088	196.4	405.2
LOFTON, KENNY	15	90.9	142.8	8.0	46.8	37.8	.299	.373	.425	4	.267	7	.463	.3662	326.3	692.5
LOGAN, JOHNNY	13	50.0	108.2	7.1	42.0	1.4	.268	.331	.378	3	.230	1	.076	.2560	208.7	464.7
LOLLAR, SHERM	18	34.6	78.6	8.6	44.8	1.1	.264	.359	.402	8	.444	0	.000	.2940	167.7	461.7
LOMBARDI, ERNIE*	17	35.3	105.4	11.1	58.2	0.4	.306	.358	.460	0	.000	1	.058	.2360	210.4	446.4
LOPATA, STAN	13	28.8	50.8	8.9	30.5	1.3	.254	.354	.452	0	.000	0	.000	.2120	120.3	332.3
LOPES, DAVEY	16	63.9	104.4	9.6	38.3	34.8	.263	.351	.388	1	.063	2	.125	.2380	251.0	489.0
LOPEZ, AL*	19	32.2	81.4	2.6	34.3	2.4	.261	.326	.337	4	.210	0	.000	.2260	152.9	378.9
LOPEZ, JAVY	14	45.6	102.9	18.0	59.2	0.6	.290	.342	.500	1	.071	0	.000	.2406	226.3	466.9
LORETTA, MARK	11	54.1	116.8	5.7	42.4	3.7	,301	.369	.408	1	.091	0	.000	.2338	222.7	456.5
LOWELL, MIKE	8	59.8	121.1	17.9	72.3	2.6	.272	.344	.461	3	.375	0	.000	.2908	273.7	564.5
LUZINSKI, GREG	15	58.6	119.6	20.4	75.2	2.4	.276	.366	.478	1	.066	1	.066	.2500	276.2	526.2
LYNCH, JERRY	13	28.0	61.3	8.8	36.1	0.9	.277	.331	.463	0	.000	0	.000	.2140	135.1	349.1
LYNN, FRED	17	62.5	115.2	18.0	65.3	4.2	.283	.364	.484	4	.235	5	.294	.3320	265.2	597.2
MACK, SHANE	9	48.4	94.8	8.9	44.2	10.0	.299	.364	.456	0	.000	0	.000	.2238	206.3	430.1
MADDOX, GARRY	15	51.8	120.1	7.8	50.2	16.5	.285	.323	.413	8	.533	0	.000	.3110	246.4	557.4
MADLOCK, BILL	15	61.3	133.8	10.8	57.3	11.6	.305	.369	.442	0	.000	4	.266	.2760	274.8	550.8
MAJESKI, HANK	13	31.0	73.5	4.3	38.5	0.7	.279	.342	.398	2	.153	0	.000	.2340	148.0	382.0
MALZONE, FRANK	12	53.9	123.8	11.0	60.6	1.1	.274	.318	.399	3	.250	0	.000	.2480	250.4	498.4
MANNING, RICK	13	51.0	103.7	4.3	35.2	12.9	.257	.319	.341	0	.000	0	.000	.1830	207.1	390.1
MANTLE, MICKEY*	18	93.1	134.1	29.7	83.8	8.5	.298	.423	.557	2	.111	25	1.388	.5550	349.2	904.2
MANUSH, HEINIE*	17	75.7	148.4	6.4	69.5	6.7	.330	.377	.479	0	.000	6	.352	.3070	306.7	613.7
MARANVILLE, RABBIT*	23	54.5	113.2	1.2	38.4	12.6	.258	.318	.340	5	.217	0	.000	.2260	219.9	445.9
MARION, MARTY	13	46.3	111.3	2.7	48.0	2.6	.263	.323	.345	3	.230	1	.076	.2550	210.9	465.9
MARIS, ROGER	12	68.8	110.4	22.9	70.9	1.7	.260	.348	.476	0	.000	5	.416	.3000	274.7	574.7
MARSHALL, MIKE	11	39.3	88.2	13.4	48.1	2.3	.270	.324	.446	0	.000	0	.000	.2080	191.3	399.3
MARSHALL, WILLARD	11	53.0	105.4	11.8	54.9	1.2	.274	.347	.423	1	.090	0	.000	.2260	226.3	452.3
MARTIN, AL	11	60.4	106.5	12.0	44.1	15.7	.276	.339	.444	0	.000	0	.000	.2118	238.7	450.5
MARTIN, PEPPER	13	58.0	94.3	4.5	38.5	11.2	.298	.358	.443	0	.000	4	.307	.2810	206.5	432.5
MARTINEZ, EDGAR	18	67.7	124.8	17.2	70.1	2.7	.312	.418	.515	0	.000	9	.500	.3490	282.5	631.5
MARTINEZ, TINO	16	63.0	120.3	21.2	79.4	1.7	.271	.347	.471	1	.063	0	.000	.2304	285.6	516.0
MASI, PHIL	14	30.0	65.5	3.3	29.7	3.2	.264	.344	.370	3	.214	0	.000	.2380	131.7	369.7
MATHENY, MIKE	12	28.9	74.0	5.3	35.4	0.7	.239	.293	.344	4	.333	0	.000	.2418	144.3	386.1

NAME	YRS	RUNS YR	HITS YR	HR YR	RBI YR	SB YR	B AV	OB AV	SG AV	D TIT	D AV	O TIT	O AV	TOT AV	GROSS	PLAY #
MATHEWS, EDDIE*	17	88.7	136.1	30.1	85.4	4.0	.271	.378	.509	1	.058	7	.411	.3250	344.3	669.3
MATTHEWS, GARY,SR.	16	67.6	125.6	14.6	61.1	11.4	.281	.367	.439	0	.000	2	.125	.2420	280.3	522.3
MATTINGLY, DON	14	71.9	153.8	15.9	78.5	1.0	.307	.363	.471	10	.714	8	.571	.4852	321.1	806.3
MAY, LEE	18	53.2	112.8	19.6	69.1	2.1	.267	.315	.459	0	.000	1	.055	.2190	256.8	475.8
MAY, MILT	15	20.8	64.7	0.7	29.5	0.2	.263	.321	.371	1	.066	0	.000	.1910	115.9	306.9
MAY, PINKY	5	42.0	122.0	0.8	43.0	2.6	.275	.354	.337	3	.600	0	.000	.3130	210.4	523.4
MAYBERRY, JOHN	15	48.8	91.9	17.0	58.6	2.8	.253	.363	.439	2	.133	3	.200	.2770	219.1	496.1
MAYS, WILLIE*	22	93.7	149.2	30.0	86.5	15.3	.302	.387	.557	12	.545	23	1.045	.5690	374.7	943.7
MAZEROSKI, BILL*	17	45.2	118.5	8.1	50.1	1.5	.260	.302	.367	8	.471	0	.000	.2800	223.4	503.4
MAZZILLI, LEE	14	40.7	76.2	6.6	32.8	14.0	.259	.361	.385	0	.000	0	.000	.2010	170.3	371.3
McAULIFFE, DICK	16	55.5	95.6	12.3	43.5	3.9	.247	.344	.403	0	.000	1	.062	.2110	210.8	421.8
McBRIDE, BAKE	11	49.8	104.8	5.7	39.0	16.6	.299	.348	.420	1	.090	0	.000	.2310	215.9	446.9
McCARVER, TIM	21	28.0	68.2	4.4	29.3	2.7	.271	.340	.388	2	.090	1	.045	.2260	132.6	358.6
McCORMICK, FRANK	13	55.5	131.6	9.8	73.1	2.0	.299	.348	.434	4	.307	5	.384	.3540	272.0	626.0
McCOVEY, WILLIE*	22	55.8	100.5	23.6	70.6	1.1	.270	.377	.515	0	.000	10	.454	.3230	251.6	574.6
McDOUGALD, GIL	10	69.7	129.1	11.2	57.6	4.5	.276	.358	.410	1	.100	1	.100	.2480	272.1	520.1
McEWING, JOE	8	27.1	63.3	3.1	19.8	4.1	.252	.303	.356	0	.000	0	.000	.1822	117.4	299.6
McGEE, WILLIE	18	56.1	125.2	4.4	47.6	19.6	.295	.335	.396	3	.167	4	.222	.2830	252.9	535.9
McGRIFF, FRED	19	71.0	131.1	25.9	81.6	3.8	.284	.377	.509	1	.053	2	.105	.2656	313.4	579.0
McGWIRE, MARK	16	72.9	101.6	36.4	88.4	0.8	.263	.394	.588	1	.063	13	.813	.4242	300.1	724.3
McMANUS, MARTY	15	67.2	128.4	8.0	66.4	8.4	.289	.357	.430	1	.066	2	.133	.2550	278.4	533.4
McMILLAN, ROY	16	46.1	102.4	4.2	37.1	2.5	.243	.316	.321	6	.375	0	.000	.2510	192.3	443.3
McNAIR, ERIC	14	42.2	88.5	5.8	45.2	4.1	.274	.318	.392	0	.000	1	.071	.2110	185.8	396.8
McQUINN, GEORGE	12	69.3	132.3	11.2	66.1	2.6	.276	.357	.424	3	.250	0	.000	.2610	281.5	542.5
McRAE, HAL	19	49.4	110.0	10.0	57.7	5.7	.290	.355	.454	0	.000	4	.210	.2610	232.8	493.8
McREYNOLDS, KEVIN	12	60.5	119.9	17.5	67.2	7.7	.265	.330	.447	0	.000	0	.000	.2080	272.8	480.8
MEDWICK, JOE*	17	70.4	145.3	12.0	81.3	2.4	.324	.362	.505	1	.058	13	.764	.4020	311.4	713.4
MELE, SAM	10	40.6	91.6	8.0	54.4	1.5	.267	.329	.408	0	.000	1	.100	.2200	196.1	416.1
MEUSEL, BOB	11	75.0	153.9	14.1	97.0	12.6	.309	.356	.497	0	.000	2	.181	.2680	352.6	620.6
MICHAELS, CASS	12	42.3	95.1	4.4	41.7	5.3	.262	.349	.353	0	.000	0	.000	.1920	188.8	380.8
MIENTKIEWICZ, DOUG	8	40.3	84.9	6.9	38.1	1.4	.268	.359	.405	2	.250	0	.000	.2564	171.6	428.0
MILLAN, FELIX	12	58.2	134.7	1.8	33.5	5.5	.279	.324	.343	1	.083	0	.000	.2050	233.7	438.7
MILLAR, KEVIN	8	52.4	108.3	13.9	58.9	0.6	.289	.368	.477	0	.000	0	.000	.2268	234.1	460.9
MILLER, EDDIE	14	38.5	90.7	6.9	45.7	4.5	.238	.290	.352	5	.357	1	.071	.2610	186.3	447.3
MINOSO, MINNIE	17	66.8	115.4	10.9	60.1	12.0	.298	.391	.459	0	.000	8	.470	.3230	265.2	588.2
MITCHELL, DALE	11	50.4	113.0	3.7	36.6	4.0	.312	.368	.416	2	.181	2	.181	.2910	207.7	498.7
MITCHELL, KEVIN	13	48.5	90.2	18.0	42.2	1.7	.284	.363	.520	0	.000	3	.231	.2796	200.6	480.2
MIZE, JOHNNY*	15	74.5	134.0	23.9	89.1	1.8	.312	.397	.562	2	.133	15	1.000	.4800	323.3	803.3
MOLINA, BENGIE	8	31.3	84.8	8.1	45.3	0.3	.273	.313	.370	2	.250	0	.000	.2412	169.8	411.0
MOLITOR, PAUL*	21	84.9	158.0	11.1	62.2	24.0	.306	.372	.448	0	.000	8	.381	.3014	340.2	641.6
MONDAY, RICK	19	50.0	85.2	12.6	40.7	5.1	.264	.362	.443	1	.052	0	.000	.2240	193.6	417.6
MONDESI, RAUL	13	69.9	122.2	20.8	66.2	17.6	.273	.331	.485	0	.000	0	.000	.2178	296.7	514.5
MONEY, DON	16	49.8	101.4	11.0	45.5	5.0	.261	.330	.406	3	.187	0	.000	.2360	212.7	448.7
MONTANEZ, WILLIE	14	46.0	114.5	9.9	57.2	2.2	.275	.331	.402	0	.000	1	.071	.2150	229.8	444.8
MOON, WALLY	12	61.4	116.5	11.8	55.0	7.4	.289	.374	.445	0	.000	2	.166	.2540	252.1	506.1
MOORE, JO-JO	12	67.4	134.5	6.5	42.7	3.8	.298	.344	.408	0	.000	0	.000	.2100	254.9	464.9
MOORE, TERRY	11	65.3	119.8	7.2	46.6	7.4	.280	.340	.399	1	.090	0	.000	.2210	246.3	467.3
MORA, MELVIN	7	66.6	117.4	14.7	57.1	9.3	.281	.365	.486	0	.000	1	.143	.2550	265.1	520.1
MORANDINI, MICKEY	11	54.3	111.1	2.9	31.9	11.2	.268	.340	.359	1	.091	0	.000	.2116	211.4	423.0
MORELAND, KEITH	12	42.5	106.5	10.0	56.1	2.3	.279	.339	.411	0	.000	0	.000	.2050	217.4	422.4
MORENO, OMAR	12	58.2	104.7	3.0	32.1	40.5	.252	.308	.343	0	.000	1	.083	.1970	238.5	435.5
MORGAN, JOE*	22	75.0	114.4	12.1	51.5	31.3	.271	.395	.427	3	.136	11	.500	.3450	284.3	629.3
MORRIS, HAL	13	41.2	93.5	5.8	39.5	3.5	.304	.361	.433	1	.077	0	.000	.2350	183.5	418.5
MORYN, WALT	8	40.5	83.3	12.6	44.2	0.8	.266	.338	.446	0	.000	0	.000	.2100	181.4	391.4
MOSES, WALLY	17	66.1	125.7	5.2	39.9	10.2	.291	.364	.416	0	.000	2	.117	.2370	247.1	484.1
MOTA, MANNY	20	24.8	57.4	1.5	21.9	2.5	.304	.358	.389	0	.000	0	.000	.2100	108.1	318.1
MUELLER, BILL	10	65.1	120.2	8.2	47.8	1.9	.292	.376	.425	1	.100	1	.100	.2586	243.2	501.8
MUELLER, DON	12	41.5	107.6	5.4	43.3	0.9	.296	.324	.390	0	.000	1	.083	.2180	198.7	416.7
MUMPHREY, JERRY	15	44.0	96.1	4.6	38.3	11.6	.289	.351	.396	0	.000	0	.000	.2070	194.6	401.6
MUNSON, THURMAN	11	63.2	141.6	10.2	63.7	4.3	.292	.350	.410	1	.090	0	.000	.2280	283.0	511.0
MURCER, BOBBY	17	57.1	109.5	14.8	61.3	7.4	.277	.361	.445	0	.000	2	.117	.2400	250.1	490.1
MURPHY, DALE	18	66.5	117.2	22.1	70.3	8.9	.265	.360	.469	0	.000	8	.444	.3070	285.0	592.0
MURPHY, DWAYNE	12	54.0	89.1	13.8	50.8	8.3	.246	.356	.402	6	.500	0	.000	.3008	216.0	516.8
MURRAY, EDDIE*	21	77.5	155.0	24.0	91.3	5.2	.287	.363	.476	5	.238	4	.190	.3108	353.0	663.8
MUSIAL, STAN*	22	88.5	165.0	21.5	88.6	3.5	.331	.418	.559	3	.136	46	2.090	.7060	367.1	1073.1
MYER, BUDDY	17	69.0	125.3	2.2	50.0	9.1	.303	.389	.406	2.	117	2	.117	.2660	255.6	521.6
NEAL, CHARLIE	8	57.6	107.2	10.8	48.8	6.0	.259	.331	.394	1	.125	1	.125	.2468	230.4	477.2
NETTLES, GRAIG	22	54.2	101.1	17.7	59.7	1.4	.248	.332	.421	3	.136	1	.045	.2364	234.1	470.5
NEVIN, PHIL	11	48.2	94.2	16.9	61.4	1.6	.273	.345	.475	0	.000	0	.000	.2186	222.3	440.9
NIARHOS, GUS	9	12.6	76.7	0.1	6.5	0.6	.252	.390	.308	0	.000	0	.000	.1900	96.5	286.5
NICHOLSON, BILL	18	52.3	92.7	14.6	59.2	1.6	.268	.365	.465	1	.062	5	.312	.2940	220.4	514.4

NAME	YRS	RUNS YR	HITS YR	HR YR	RBI YR	SB YR	B AV	OB AV	SG AV	D TIT	D AV	O TIT	O AV	TOT AV	GROSS	PLAY #
NIXON, TROT	9	54.2	90.0	13.9	52.3	3.2	.279	.370	.489	0	.000	0	.000	.2276	213.6	441.2
NOKES, MATT	11	28.2	63.2	12.4	38.4	0.7	.254	.311	.441	0	.000	0	.000	.2012	142.9	344.1
NOLAN, JOE	11	14.1	34.7	2.4	16.1	0.6	.263	.340	.378	1	.090	0	.000	.2140	67.9	281.9
NOREN, IRV	11	40.2	77.9	5.9	41.1	3.0	.275	.349	.410	0	.000	0	.000	.2060	168.1	374.1
NORTH, BILLY	11	58.1	92.3	1.8	20.9	35.9	.261	.366	.323	0	.000	2	.181	.2260	209.0	435.0
OBERKFELL, KEN	16	34.8	84.6	1.8	27.8	3.8	.278	.353	.362	3	.187	0	.000	.2360	152.8	388.8
O'DOUL, LEFTY	11	56.7	103.6	10.2	49.2	3.2	.349	.413	.532	0	.000	4	.363	.3310	222.9	553.9
OFFERMAN, JOSE	15	56.0	103.4	3.8	35.8	11.5	.273	.360	.373	0	.000	2	.133	.2278	210.5	438.3
OGLIVIE, BEN	16	49.0	100.9	14.6	56.3	5.4	.273	.340	.450	0	.000	1	.062	.2250	226.2	451.2
OLERUD, JOHN	17	67.0	131.7	15.0	72.5	0.6	.295	.398	.465	4	.235	3	.176	.3138	286.8	600.6
OLIVA, TONY	15	58.0	127.8	14.6	63.1	5.7	.304	.356	.476	0	.000	14	.933	.4130	269.2	682.2
OLIVER, AL	18	66.0	152.3	12.1	73.6	4.6	.303	.348	.451	0	.000	5	.277	.2750	308.6	583.6
O'NEILL, PAUL	16	60.3	123.1	16.3	74.9	7.4	.289	.369	.471	2	.125	1	.063	.2634	282.0	545.0
ORDONEZ, MAGGLIO	9	73.6	139.9	21.7	83.2	9.1	.306	.368	.518	0	.000	0	.000	.2384	327.5	565.9
ORTIZ, DAVID	9	56.3	97.4	19.7	69.6	0.6	.282	.371	.534	0	.000	1	.111	.2596	243.6	503.2
OSTROWSKI, JOHNNY	7	10.4	18.7	2.0	10.5	1.0	.234	.321	.376	0	.000	0	.000	.1860	42.6	228.6
OTIS, AMOS, SR.	17	64.2	118.8	11.3	59.2	20.0	.277	.347	.425	5	.294	3	.176	.3040	273.5	577.5
OTT, MEL*	22	84.5	130.7	23.2	84.5	4.0	.304	.414	.533	1	.045	20	.909	.4410	326.9	767.9
OVERBAY, LYLE	5	37.2	78.8	7.8	37.6	0.8	.285	.374	.450	0	.000	1	.200	.2618	167.2	424.0
OWEN, MARV	9	52.5	115.5	3.4	55.2	3.3	.275	.339	.367	1	.111	0	.000	.2180	229.9	447.9
PAFKO, ANDY	17	49.6	105.6	12.5	57.4	2.2	.285	.351	.449	1	.058	0	.000	.2280	227.3	455.3
PALMEIRO, RAFAEL	20	83.2	151.0	28.5	91.8	4.9	.288	.374	.515	3	.150	3	.150	.2954	359.4	654.8
PALMER, DEAN	14	52.4	87.8	19.6	60.6	3.4	.251	.324	.472	0	.000	0	.000	.2094	223.8	433.2
PARKER, DAVE	19	66.9	142.7	17.8	78.6	8.1	.290	.339	.471	3	.158	8	.421	.3358	314.1	649.9
PARKER, WES	9	60.8	123.3	7.1	52.2	6.6	.267	.353	.375	8	.889	1	.111	.3990	250.0	649.0
PARRISH, LANCE	18	46.7	97.5	17.7	58.2	1.5	.255	.314	.445	3	.167	0	.000	.2362	221.6	457.8
PARRISH, LARRY	15	56.6	119.2	17.0	66.1	2.0	.263	.321	.439	0	.000	0	.000	.2040	260.9	464.9
PATEK, FREDDIE	14	52.5	95.7	2.0	35.0	27.5	.242	.311	.324	0	.000	2	.142	.2030	212.7	415.7
PATTERSON, COREY	6	48.8	91.5	11.7	38.5	14.3	.252	.293	.414	1	.167	0	.000	.2252	204.8	430.0
PAYTON, JAY	8	48.9	98.4	11.9	45.4	3.1	.282	.330	.443	1	.125	0	.000	.2360	207.7	443.7
PEARSON, ALBIE	9	53.8	92.3	3.1	23.7	8.5	.270	.370	.355	0	.000	1	.111	.2210	181.4	402.4
PENA, TONY	18	37.1	93.7	5.9	39.3	4.4	.260	.311	.364	5	.278	0	.000	.2426	180.4	423.0
PENDLETON, TERRY	15	56.7	126.5	9.3	60.1	8.5	.270	.318	.391	3	.200	3	.200	.2758	261.1	536.9
PEPITONE, JOE	12	50.5	109.5	18.2	60.0	3.4	.258	.303	.432	3	.250	0	.000	.2480	241.6	489.6
PEREZ, NEIFI	10	60.4	128.6	6.1	45.4	5.6	.270	.301	.380	1	.100	1	.100	.2302	246.1	476.3
PEREZ, TONY*	23	55.3	118.7	16.4	71.8	2.1	.279	.344	.463	1	.043	0	.000	.2250	264.3	489.3
PESKY, JOHNNY	10	86.7	145.5	1.7	40.4	5.3	.307	.394	.386	0	.000	3	.250	.2670	279.6	546.6
PETROCELLI, RICO	13	50.2	104.0	16.1	59.4	0.7	.251	.336	.420	3	.230	0	.000	.2470	230.4	477.4
PETTIS, GARY	11	51.6	77.7	1.9	23.5	32.1	.236	.333	.310	5	.455	0	.000	.2670	186.8	453.8
PHILLIPS, TONY	13	65.8	109.2	7.2	43.6	9.6	.266	.368	.376	0	.000	2	.153	.2320	235.4	467.4
PIAZZA, MIKE	14	69.7	137.8	28.4	87.4	1.2	.311	.382	.555	1	.071	0	.000	.2638	324.5	588.3
PIERRE, JUAN	6	86.7	173.3	1.5	41.1	44.5	.305	.355	.375	2	.333	4	.667	.4070	347.1	754.1
PIERSALL, JIM	17	47.7	94.3	6.1	34.7	6.7	.272	.334	.386	4	.235	1	.058	.2570	189.5	446.5
PINSON, VADA	18	75.8	153.1	14.2	65.0	16.9	.286	.330	.442	3	.167	7	.388	.3230	325.0	648.0
PODSEDNIK, SCOTT	5	53.6	96.6	4.4	26.0	34.4	.279	.346	.385	0	.000	1	.200	.2420	215.0	457.0
POLANCO, PLACIDO	8	61.4	122.6	7.4	41.3	6.1	.300	.347	.415	1	.125	0	.000	.2374	238.8	476.2
POSADA, JORGE	11	53.5	94.0	15.9	61.6	1.0	.269	.379	.469	0	.000	0	.000	.2234	226.0	449.4
POWELL, BOOG	17	52.2	104.4	19.9	69.8	1.1	.266	.364	.462	1	.058	1	.058	.2300	247.4	477.4
POWER, VIC	12	63.7	143.0	10.5	54.8	3.7	.284	.317	.411	8	.667	1	.083	.3520	275.7	627.7
PUCKETT, KIRBY*	12	89.3	192.0	17.3	90.4	11.2	.318	.363	.477	6	.500	6	.500	.4316	400.2	831.8
PUHL, TERRY	15	45.1	90.7	4.1	29.0	14.5	.280	.349	.388	2	.133	0	.000	.2300	183.4	413.4
PUJOLS, ALBERT	5	125.8	196.4	40.2	124.2	5.8	.332	.419	.621	0	.000	6	1.200	.5144	492.4	1006.8
RAINES, TIM	23	68.3	113.3	7.4	42.6	35.1	.296	.385	.425	1	.043	9	.391	.3076	266.7	574.3
RAMIREZ, ARAMIS	8	53.0	114.5	19.8	68.8	0.1	.277	.332	.481	0	.000	0	.000	.2076	256.2	463.8
RAMIREZ, MANNY	13	90.7	147.8	33.5	108.8	7.6	.314	.412	.599	0	.000	9	.692	.4034	383.4	786.8
RANDA, JOE	11	61.3	135.3	10.8	64.6	3.8	.285	.344	.427	1	.091	0	.000	.2294	275.8	505.2
RANDOLPH, WILLIE	18	68.8	122.7	3.0	38.1	15.0	.276	.375	.351	0	.000	1	.055	.2110	247.6	458.6
REESE, PEE WEE*	16	83.6	135.6	7.8	55.3	14.5	.269	.366	.377	1	.062	3	.187	.2520	296.8	548.8
REESE, POKEY	8	45.8	88.0	5.5	30.3	18.0	.248	.307	.352	2	.250	0	.000	.2314	187.6	419.0
REISER, PETE	10	47.3	78.6	5.8	36.8	8.7	.295	.380	.450	0	.000	7	.700	.3650	177.2	542.2
REITZ, KEN	11	33.2	113.0	6.1	49.8	0.9	.260	.293	.359	7	.636	0	.000	.3100	203.0	513.0
RENTERIA, EDGAR	10	83.4	159.5	9.1	63.5	24.6	.288	.348	.399	2	.200	0	.000	.2470	340.1	587.1
REPULSKI, RIP	9	45.2	92.2	11.7	46.2	2.7	.269	.322	.436	0	.000	0	.000	.2050	198.0	403.0
REYES, JOSE	3	59.7	110.0	4.7	34.7	30.7	.277	.303	.395	0	.000	2	.667	.3284	239.8	568.2
REYNOLDS, HAROLD	12	53.3	102.7	1.7	29.4	20.8	.258	.326	.341	3	.250	1	.083	.2520	207.9	459.9
RICE, JIM	16	78.0	153.2	23.8	90.6	3.6	.298	.356	.502	0	.000	9	.562	.3430	349.2	692.2
RICE, SAM*	20	75.7	149.3	1.7	53.9	17.5	.322	.374	.427	0	.000	4	.200	.2640	298.1	562.1
RICHARDSON, BOBBY	12	53.5	119.3	2.8	32.5	6.0	.266	.301	.335	5	.417	1	.083	.2800	214.1	494.1
RIPKEN, CAL	21	78.4	151.6	20.5	80.7	1.7	.276	.340	.447	6	.286	3	.143	.2984	332.9	631.3
RIVERS, MICKEY	15	52.3	110.6	4.0	33.2	17.8	.295	.329	.397	0	.000	3	.200	.2440	217.9	461.9

NAME	YRS	RUNS YR	HITS YR	HR YR	RBI YR	SB YR	B AV	OB AV	SG AV	D TIT	D AV	O TIT	O AV	TOT AV	GROSS	PLAY #
RIZZUTO, PHIL*	13	67.4	122.1	2.9	43.3	11.4	.273	.351	.355	2	.153	0	.000	.2260	247.1	473.1
ROBERTS, BRIAN	5	64.8	114.6	6.0	39.0	20.0	.278	.311	.357	0	.000	1	.200	.2292	244.4	473.6
ROBERTSON, SHERRY	10	20.0	34.6	2.6	15.1	3.2	.230	.323	.342	0	.000	0	.000	.1790	75.5	254.5
ROBINSON, BROOKS*	23	53.5	123.8	11.6	59.0	1.2	.267	.325	.401	16	.696	1	.043	.3464	249.1	595.5
ROBINSON, EDDIE	13	42.0	88.1	13.2	55.6	0.7	.268	.354	.440	1	.076	0	.000	.2270	199.6	426.6
ROBINSON, FRANK*	21	87.0	140.1	27.9	86.2	9.7	.294	.392	.537	1	.048	13	.619	.3780	350.9	728.9
ROBINSON, JACKIE*	10	94.7	151.8	13.7	73.4	19.7	.311	.410	.474	3	.300	4	.400	.3790	373.0	752.0
RODRIGUEZ, ALEX	12	103.8	158.4	35.8	102.2	18.8	.307	.385	.577	2	.167	14	1.167	.5206	419.0	939.6
RODRIGUEZ, IVAN	15	72.3	146.0	17.6	70.0	6.9	.304	.346	.487	11	.733	0	.000	.3740	312.5	868.5
ROENICKE, RON	8	17.6	32.0	2.1	14.1	3.0	.238	.355	.338	0	.000	0	.000	.1860	68.8	254.8
ROGELL, BILLY	14	53.9	98.2	3.0	43.5	5.8	.267	.351	.370	3	.214	0	.000	.2400	204.4	444.4
ROLEN, SCOTT	10	80.5	130.0	23.1	85.9	9.2	.284	.379	.515	6	.600	0	.000	.3556	328.7	684.3
ROLFE, RED	10	94.2	139.4	6.9	49.7	4.4	.289	.360	.413	2	.200	4	.400	.3320	294.6	626.6
ROLLINS, JIMMY	6	83.8	150.6	9.8	51.3	28.5	.273	.329	.414	1	.167	4	.667	.3700	324.0	694.0
ROMANO, JOHNNY	10	35.5	70.6	12.9	41.7	0.7	.255	.358	.443	0	.000	0	.000	.2110	161.4	372.4
ROSAR, BUDDY	13	25.7	64.3	1.3	28.2	1.3	.261	.330	.334	4	.307	0	.000	.2460	120.8	366.8
ROSE, PETE	24	90.2	177.3	6.6	54.7	8.2	.303	.377	.409	5	.208	20	.833	.4260	337.0	763.0
ROSEBORO, JOHNNY	14	36.5	86.1	7.4	39.1	4.7	.249	.329	.371	2	.143	0	.000	.2180	173.8	391.8
ROSEN, AL	10	60.3	106.3	19.2	71.7	3.9	.285	.386	.495	0	.000	6	.600	.3530	261.4	614.6
ROSEN, GOODY	6	51.6	92.8	3.6	32.8	2.0	.291	.364	.398	1	.166	0	.000	.2430	182.8	425.8
ROWAND, AARON	5	51.0	93.2	10.8	42.2	7.6	.283	.333	.451	0	.000	0	.000	.2134	204.8	418.2
RUDI, JOE	16	42.7	91.7	11.1	50.6	1.5	.264	.314	.427	3	.188	3	.188	.2760	197.6	473.6
RUNNELS, PETE	14	62.5	132.4	3.5	45.0	2.6	.291	.376	.378	2	.142	2	.142	.2650	246.0	511.0
RUSSELL, BILL	18	44.2	107.0	2.5	34.8	9.2	.263	.312	.338	0	.000	0	.000	.1820	197.7	397.7
RUTH, BABE*	22	98.8	130.5	32.4	100.5	5.5	.342	.474	.690	1	.045	60	2.727	.8550	367.7	1222.7
SABO, CHRIS	9	54.9	99.8	12.9	47.3	13.3	.268	.326	.445	2	.222	0	.000	.2522	228.2	480.4
SALMON, TIM	13	73.5	124.5	22.3	76.1	3.7	.386	.500	.283	0	.000	0	.000	.2338	300.1	533.9
SAMUEL, JUAN	16	54.6	98.6	10.1	43.9	24.8	.259	.317	.420	0	.000	2	.125	.2242	232.0	456.2
SANDBERG, RYNE*	16	82.4	149.1	17.6	66.3	21.5	.285	.347	.452	9	.563	5	.313	.3920	336.9	728.9
SANDERS, RAY	7	45.8	85.2	6.0	47.0	1.1	.274	.370	.401	1	.142	0	.000	.2370	185.1	422.1
SANDERS, REGGIE	15	65.3	104.2	19.5	61.5	19.8	.267	.344	.491	0	.000	0	.000	.2204	270.3	490.7
SANGUILLEN, MANNY	13	43.5	115.3	5.0	45.0	2.6	.296	.329	.398	0	.000	0	.000	.2040	211.4	415.4
SANTIAGO, BENITO	20	37.8	91.5	10.9	46.0	4.6	.263	.307	.415	4	.200	0	.000	.2370	190.8	427.8
SANTO, RON	15	75.8	150.2	22.8	88.7	2.3	.277	.366	.464	5	.333	7	.466	.3850	339.8	724.8
SAUER, HANK	15	47.2	85.2	19.2	58.4	0.7	.266	.347	.496	0	.000	2	.133	.2480	210.7	458.7
SAX, STEVE	14	65.2	139.2	3.8	39.2	31.7	.281	.334	.358	1	.071	0	.000	.2080	279.1	487.1
SCHMIDT, MIKE*	18	83.6	124.1	30.4	88.6	9.6	.267	.384	.527	10	.555	25	1.388	.6240	336.3	960.3
SCHOENDIENST, RED*	19	64.3	128.8	4.4	40.6	4.6	.289	.338	.387	6	.315	3	.157	.2970	242.7	539.7
SCHOFIELD, DICK,JR.	12	41.7	81.5	4.6	29.2	9.9	.230	.301	.317	4	.333	0	.000	.2360	166.9	402.9
SCOTT, GEORGE	14	68.3	142.2	19.3	75.0	4.9	.268	.335	.435	8	.571	2	.142	.3500	309.7	659.7
SEGUI, DAVID	15	45.5	94.1	9.3	45.6	1.1	.291	.359	.443	2	.133	0	.000	.2452	195.6	440.8
SEITZER, KEVIN	12	61.6	129.8	6.2	51.1	6.7	.295	.375	.404	1	.083	1	.083	.2480	255.4	503.4
SELKIRK, GEORGE	9	55.8	90.0	12.0	64.0	5.4	.290	.400	.483	1	.111	0	.000	.2560	227.2	483.2
SEMINICK, ANDY	15	33.0	63.5	10.9	37.0	1.5	.243	.347	.417	1	.066	0	.000	.2140	145.9	359.9
SEWELL, JOE*	14	81.5	159.0	3.5	75.3	5.2	.312	.391	.413	3	.214	1	.071	.2800	324.5	604.5
SEXSON, RICHIE	9	65.1	108.7	26.6	81.9	1.2	.270	.354	.530	0	.000	0	.000	.2308	283.5	514.3
SHEFFIELD, GARY	18	78.4	130.3	24.9	82.0	11.9	.297	.399	.527	0	.000	2	.111	.2668	327.5	594.3
SIEBERN, NORM	12	55.1	101.4	11.0	53.0	1.5	.272	.372	.423	0	.000	1	.083	.2300	222.0	452.0
SIERRA, RUBEN	19	56.9	113.0	16.1	69.4	7.5	.268	.316	.450	0	.000	3	.158	.2384	262.9	501.3
SIEVERS, ROY	17	55.5	100.1	18.7	67.4	0.8	.267	.357	.475	0	.000	2	.117	.2430	242.5	485.5
SIMMONS, AL*	20	75.3	146.3	15.3	91.3	4.3	.334	.380	.535	2	.100	7	.350	.3390	332.5	671.5
SIMMONS, TED	21	51.1	117.7	11.8	66.1	1.0	.285	.352	.437	1	.047	0	.000	.2240	247.7	471.7
SINGLETON, KEN	15	65.6	135.2	16.4	71.0	1.4	.282	.391	.436	1	.066	1	.066	.2480	289.6	537.6
SIZEMORE, GRADY	2	63.0	109.5	13.0	56.5	12.0	.281	.345	.470	0	.000	0	.000	.2192	250.0	469.2
SIZEMORE, TED	12	48.0	109.2	1.9	35.8	4.9	.262	.327	.321	0	.000	0	.000	.1820	199.8	381.8
SKOWRON, MOOSE	14	48.6	111.8	15.0	63.4	1.1	.282	.335	.459	1	.071	0	.000	.2290	239.9	468.9
SLAUGHTER, ENOS*	19	65.6	125.4	8.8	68.6	3.7	.300	.382	.453	1	.052	6	.315	.3000	272.1	572.1
SMALLEY, ROY, JR.	13	57.3	111.8	12.5	53.3	2.0	.257	.348	.395	0	.000	0	.000	.2000	236.9	436.9
SMITH, AL	12	70.2	121.5	13.6	56.3	5.5	.272	.360	.429	0	.000	1	.083	.2280	267.1	495.1
SMITH, LONNIE	17	53.4	87.5	5.7	31.3	21.7	.288	.364	.420	0	.000	2	.117	.2370	199.6	436.6
SMITH, OZZIE*	19	66.2	129.5	1.5	41.7	30.5	.262	.339	.328	14	.737	0	.000	.3332	269.4	602.6
SMITH, REGGIE	17	66.0	118.8	18.4	64.2	8.0	.287	.370	.489	0	.000	1	.058	.2400	275.4	515.4
SNIDER, DUKE*	18	69.9	117.5	22.6	74.0	5.5	.295	.381	.540	0	.000	10	.555	.3540	289.5	643.5
SNOW, J. T.	14	56.6	107.1	13.5	62.4	1.4	.268	.361	.428	6	.429	0	.000	.2972	241.0	538.2
SNYDER, CORY	9	48.7	100.2	16.5	54.2	3.1	.247	.291	.425	1	.111	0	.000	.2140	222.7	436.7
SORIANO, ALFONSO	7	72.1	130.3	23.1	66.4	24.1	.280	.323	.500	0	.000	3	.429	.3064	316.0	622.4
SOSA, SAMMY	17	83.6	135.5	34.6	92.6	13.8	.274	.348	.537	0	.000	7	.412	.2318	360.1	591.9
SPENCER, DARYL	10	45.7	90.1	10.5	42.8	1.3	.244	.329	.380	0	.000	0	.000	.1900	190.4	380.4
SPENCER, JIM	15	36.0	81.8	9.7	39.9	0.7	.250	.310	.387	5	.333	0	.000	.2560	168.1	424.1
SPIEZIO, SCOTT	10	44.2	86.1	10.2	46.6	3.2	.253	.324	.414	3	.300	0	.000	.2582	190.3	448.5
STAIRS, MATT	13	45.5	79.9	15.9	53.8	1.9	.267	.361	.489	0	.000	0	.000	.2234	197.0	420.4

NAME	YRS	RUNS YR	HITS YR	HR YR	RBI YR	SB YR	B AV	OB AV	SG AV	D TIT	D AV	O TIT	O AV	TOT AV	GROSS	PLAY #
STANKY, EDDIE	11	73.7	104.9	2.6	33.0	4.3	.268	.410	.348	1	.090	5	.454	.3140	218.5	532.5
STARGELL, WILLIE*	21	56.9	106.2	22.6	73.3	0.8	.282	.363	.529	1	.047	5	.238	.2910	259.8	550.8
STAUB, RUSTY	23	51.6	118.0	12.6	63.7	2.0	.279	.366	.431	0	.000	1	.043	.2230	247.9	470.9
STEINBACH, TERRY	14	45.6	103.8	11.6	53.2	1.6	.271	.326	.420	1	.072	0	.000	.2178	215.8	433.6
STEPHENS, VERN	15	66.7	123.9	16.4	78.2	1.6	.286	.355	.460	1	.066	4	.266	.2860	286.8	572.8
STEPHENSON, RIGGS	14	51.0	108.2	4.5	55.2	3.8	.336	.407	.473	0	.000	1	.071	.2570	222.7	479.7
STEWART, SHANNON	11	67.2	126.6	9.1	45.2	16.3	.300	.364	.441	0	.000	0	.000	.2210	264.4	485.4
STIRNWEISS, SNUFFY	10	60.4	98.9	2.9	28.1	13.4	.268	.362	.371	2	.200	8	.800	.4000	203.7	603.7
STONE, JOHN	11	67.1	126.4	7.0	64.2	4.0	.310	.376	.467	0	.000	0	.000	.2300	268.7	498.7
STRAWBERRY, D.	17	52.2	82.4	19.7	58.8	13.0	.259	.360	.505	0	.000	3	.176	.2600	226.1	486.1
STRIPP, JOE	11	52.2	112.5	2.1	42.1	4.5	.294	.340	.384	2	.181	0	.000	.2390	213.4	452.4
STUART, DICK	10	50.6	105.5	22.8	74.3	0.2	.264	.319	.489	0	.000	1	.100	.2340	253.4	487.4
SUDER, PETE	13	36.0	97.5	3.7	41.6	1.4	.249	.291	.337	2	.153	0	.000	.2060	180.2	386.2
SUHR, GUS	11	64.9	131.4	7.6	74.3	4.8	.279	.368	.428	1	.090	0	.000	.2330	283.0	516.0
SUNDBERG, JIM	16	38.8	93.3	5.9	39.0	1.2	.248	.328	.348	8	.500	0	.000	.2840	178.2	462.2
SURHOFF, B. J.	19	55.9	122.4	9.9	60.7	7.4	.282	.336	.413	1	.053	0	.000	.2168	256.3	473.1
SWEENEY, MIKE	11	59.2	115.6	16.5	69.6	4.1	.304	.374	.500	0	.000	0	.000	.2356	265.0	500.6
TARTABULL, DANNY	14	54.0	97.6	18.7	66.1	2.6	.273	.371	.496	0	.000	1	.071	.2422	239.0	481.2
TAUBENSEE, ED	11	31.9	71.3	8.5	38.1	1.0	.273	.331	.430	0	.000	0	.000	.2068	150.8	357.6
TAVERAS, FRANK	11	45.7	93.5	0.1	19.4	27.2	.255	.302	.313	0	.000	1	.090	.1920	185.9	377.9
TEBBETTS, BIRDIE	14	25.5	71.4	2.7	33.5	2.0	.270	.341	.358	0	.000	0	.000	.1930	135.1	328.1
TEIXEIRA, MARK	3	93.0	161.3	35.7	113.3	3.0	.282	.363	.541	1	.333	0	.000	.3038	406.3	710.1
TEJADA, MIGUEL	9	85.6	152.2	24.0	94.7	6.4	.280	.341	.477	0	.000	2	.222	.2640	362.9	626.9
TEMPLE, JOHNNY	13	55.3	114.1	1.6	30.3	10.7	.284	.365	.350	0	.000	1	.076	.2150	212.0	427.0
TEMPLETON, GARRY	16	55.8	131.0	4.3	45.5	15.1	.271	.306	.369	0	.000	4	.250	.2390	251.7	490.7
TENACE, GENE	15	43.5	70.6	13.4	44.9	2.4	.241	.391	.429	1	.066	2	.133	.2520	174.8	426.8
TERRY, BILL*	14	80.0	156.6	11.0	77.0	4.0	.341	.393	.506	2	.142	4	.285	.3330	328.6	661.6
TERWILLIGER, WAYNE	9	30.1	55.6	2.4	18.0	3.4	.240	.323	.325	0	.000	0	.000	.1770	109.5	286.5
TETTLETON, MICKEY	14	50.8	80.9	24.6	52.3	1.6	.241	.372	.449	1	.071	1	.071	.2408	210.2	451.0
THOMAS, FRANK E.	16	82.9	133.5	28.0	91.6	2.0	.307	.429	.568	0	.000	11	.688	.3984	338.0	736.4
THOMAS, FRANK J.	16	49.5	104.4	17.8	60.1	0.9	.266	.323	.454	0	.000	0	.000	.2080	232.7	440.7
THOMAS, GORMAN	13	52.3	80.8	20.6	60.1	3.8	.225	.328	.448	0	.000	2	.153	.2300	217.6	447.6
THOMAS, LEE	8	50.6	105.8	13.2	53.5	3.1	.255	.328	.397	0	.000	0	.000	.1960	226.2	422.2
THOME, JIM	15	76.7	111.0	28.7	79.5	1.2	.281	.408	.562	1	.067	5	.333	.3302	297.1	627.3
THON, DICKIE	15	33.0	78.4	4.7	29.0	11.1	.264	.318	.374	0	.000	1	.066	.2040	156.2	360.2
THORNTON, ANDRE	14	56.5	95.8	18.0	63.9	3.4	.254	.364	.452	0	.000	0	.000	.2140	237.6	451.6
TOLAN, BOBBY	13	44.0	86.2	6.6	38.2	14.8	.265	.317	.382	0	.000	1	.076	.2080	190.1	398.1
TORGESON, EARL	15	56.5	87.8	9.9	49.3	8.8	.265	.387	.417	0	.000	1	.066	.2270	212.3	439.3
TORRE, JOE	18	55.3	130.1	14.0	65.8	1.2	.297	.367	.452	3	.166	3	.166	.2900	266.4	556.4
TOVAR, CESAR	12	69.5	128.8	3.8	36.2	18.8	.278	.337	.368	0	.000	3	.250	.2460	257.1	503.1
TRACEWSKI, DICK	8	18.5	32.7	1.0	11.3	1.8	.213	.291	.272	0	.000	0	.000	.1550	65.3	220.3
TRAMMELL, ALAN	20	61.6	118.3	9.3	50.2	11.8	.285	.354	.415	4	.200	0	.000	.2508	250.2	502.0
TRAVIS, CECIL	12	55.4	128.6	2.2	54.7	1.9	.314	.370	.416	0	.000	1	.083	.2360	242.8	478.8
TRAYNOR, PIE*	17	69.5	142.1	3.4	74.8	9.2	.320	.362	.435	1	.058	1	.058	.2460	299.0	545.0
TRIANDOS, GUS	13	29.9	73.3	12.8	46.7	0.0	.244	.324	.413	1	.076	0	.000	.2110	162.7	373.7
TRILLO, MANNY	17	35.1	91.8	3.5	33.5	3.2	.263	.318	.345	1	.058	0	.000	.1960	167.1	363.1
TROSKY, HAL	11	75.9	141.9	20.7	92.0	2.5	.302	.371	.522	0	.000	1	.090	.2570	333.0	590.0
TUTTLE, BILL	11	52.5	100.4	6.0	40.2	3.4	.259	.336	.363	0	.000	0	.000	.1910	202.5	393.5
UPSHAW, WILLIE	10	59.6	110.3	12.3	52.8	8.8	.262	.335	.419	0	.000	0	.000	.2032	243.8	447.0
URIBE, JOSE	10	30.7	73.8	1.9	21.9	7.4	.241	.300	.314	0	.000	0	.000	.1710	135.7	306.7
URIBE, JUAN	5	57.2	112.2	12.6	56.0	6.4	.262	.305	.432	0	.000	0	.000	.1998	244.4	444.2
UTLEY, CHASE	3	47.3	87.0	14.3	61.0	7.3	.276	.351	.496	0	.000	0	.000	.2246	216.9	441.5
VALENTIN, JOHN	11	55.8	99.4	11.3	50.7	4.3	.279	.360	.454	0	.000	1	.091	.2368	221.5	458.3
VALENTINE, ELLIS	10	38.0	88.1	12.3	47.4	5.9	.278	.319	.458	1	.100	0	.000	.2310	191.7	422.7
VALO, ELMER	20	38.4	71.0	2.9	30.0	5.5	.282	.399	.391	0	.000	0	.000	.2140	147.8	361.8
VAN SLYKE, ANDY	13	64.2	120.2	12.6	60.9	18.9	.274	.349	.443	5	.385	3	.231	.3364	276.7	613.1
VARITEK, JASON	9	48.1	96.1	13.2	54.2	2.6	.272	.350	.456	1	.111	0	.000	.2378	214.2	452.0
VAUGHAN, ARKY*	14	83.7	150.2	6.8	66.1	8.4	.318	.406	.453	0	.000	15	1.071	.4490	315.2	764.2
VAUGHN, GREG	15	67.8	98.3	23.7	71.5	8.1	.242	.337	.470	0	.000	0	.000	.2098	269.4	479.2
VAUGHN, MO	12	71.8	135.0	27.3	88.7	2.5	.293	.383	.523	0	.000	1	.083	.2564	325.3	581.7
VENTURA, ROBIN	16	62.9	117.8	18.4	73.9	1.5	.267	.362	.444	6	.375	0	.000	.2896	214.5	504.1
VERAS, QUILVIO	7	67.0	107.1	4.6	34.1	26.1	.270	.372	.362	0	.000	1	.143	.2294	238.9	468.3
VERNON, MICKEY	20	59.8	124.7	8.6	65.5	6.8	.286	.359	.428	4	.200	5	.250	.3040	265.4	569.4
VERSALLES, ZOILO	12	54.1	103.8	7.9	39.2	8.0	.242	.292	.367	0	.000	5	.416	.2630	213.0	476.0
VIDRO, JOSE	9	62.4	127.3	12.0	55.9	2.2	.302	.364	.467	0	.000	0	.000	.2266	259.8	486.4
VINA, FERNANDO	13	52.3	99.7	3.3	28.6	9.7	.282	.348	.379	3	.230	0	.000	.2478	193.6	441.4
VIRDON, BILL	12	61.2	133.0	7.5	41.8	3.9	.267	.318	.379	0	.000	1	.083	.2090	247.4	456.4
VIRGIL, OZZIE, SR.	9	8.3	19.3	1.5	8.1	0.6	.231	.264	.331	0	.000	0	.000	.1650	37.8	202.8
VIZCAINO, JOSE	17	36.1	83.5	2.0	27.8	4.4	.271	.318	.346	1	.059	0	.000	.1988	153.8	352.6
VIZQUEL, OMAR	17	70.3	135.4	4.1	44.7	20.1	.274	.343	.358	11	.647	0	.000	.3244	274.6	599.0

NAME	YRS	RUNS YR	HITS YR	HR YR	RBI YR	SB YR	B AV	OB AV	SG AV	D TIT	D AV	O TIT	O AV	TOT AV	GROSS	PLAY #
VOLLMER, CLYDE	10	28.3	50.8	6.9	33.9	0.7	.251	.335	.402	0	.000	0	.000	.1970	120.6	317.6
VOSMIK, JOE	13	62.9	129.3	5.0	67.2	1.7	.307	.369	.438	1	.076	4	.307	.2990	266.1	565.1
WAGNER, LEON	12	53.0	100.1	17.5	55.7	4.5	.272	.343	.455	0	.000	0	.000	.2140	230.8	444.8
WAITKUS, EDDIE	11	48.0	110.3	2.1	33.9	2.5	.285	.344	.374	0	.000	0	.000	.2000	196.8	396.8
WAKEFIELD, DICK	9	37.1	69.4	6.2	35.0	1.1	.293	.396	.447	0	.000	2	.222	.2710	148.8	419.8
WALKER, DIXIE	18	57.6	114.6	5.8	56.8	3.2	.306	.383	.437	0	.000	3	.166	.2580	238.0	496.0
WALKER, HARRY	11	35.0	71.4	0.9	19.4	3.8	.296	.358	.383	0	.000	2	.181	.2430	130.5	373.5
WALKER, LARRY	17	79.7	127.1	22.5	77.1	13.5	.313	.400	.565	7	.412	9	.529	.4438	319.9	763.7
WALKER, TODD	10	58.6	118.0	9.8	48.8	6.4	.290	.351	.441	1	.100	0	.000	.2364	241.6	478.0
WALLACH, TIM	17	53.4	122.6	15.3	66.2	3.0	.257	.316	.416	5	.294	2	.118	.2802	260.5	540.7
WANER, LLOYD*	18	66.7	136.6	1.5	33.2	3.7	.316	.353	.393	0	.000	3	.166	.2450	241.7	486.7
WANER, PAUL*	20	81.3	157.6	5.6	65.4	5.2	.333	.404	.473	0	.000	14	.700	.3820	315.1	697.1
WARD, GARY	12	49.5	103.0	10.8	49.7	6.9	.276	.330	.425	0	.000	0	.000	.2060	219.9	425.9
WASHINGTON, CLAUD.	17	54.4	110.8	9.6	48.4	18.3	.278	.328	.420	0	.000	0	.000	.2050	241.5	446.5
WATSON, BOB	19	42.2	96.1	9.6	52.0	1.4	.295	.367	.447	0	.000	0	.000	.2210	201.3	422.3
WEATHERLY, ROY	10	41.5	79.4	4.3	29.0	4.2	.286	.331	.418	0	.000	0	.000	.2070	158.4	365.4
WEISS, WALT	14	44.5	86.2	1.8	27.6	6.9	.258	.351	.326	0	.000	0	.000	.1870	167.0	354.0
WELLS, VERNON	7	55.3	106.9	15.6	56.4	5.1	.285	.333	.481	2	.286	2	.286	.3342	239.3	573.5
WERBER, BILLY	11	79.5	123.9	7.0	49.0	19.5	.271	.364	.392	1	.090	4	.363	.2960	278.9	574.9
WERTZ, VIC	17	51.0	99.5	15.6	69.2	0.5	.277	.366	.469	0	.000	0	.000	.2220	235.8	457.8
WEST, SAM	16	58.3	114.8	4.6	52.3	3.3	.299	.371	.425	2	.125	0	.000	.2440	233.3	477.3
WESTLAKE, WALLY	10	47.4	84.8	12.7	53.9	1.9	.272	.346	.450	1	.100	0	.000	.2330	200.7	433.7
WHEAT, ZACK*	19	67.8	151.7	6.9	65.6	10.7	.317	.367	.450	1	.052	2	.105	.2580	302.7	560.7
WHITAKER, LOU	19	72.9	124.7	12.8	57.1	7.5	.276	.366	.426	5	.263	0	.000	.2662	275.0	541.2
WHITE, BILL	13	64.8	131.2	15.5	66.9	7.9	.286	.353	.455	2	.153	0	.000	.2490	286.3	535.3
WHITE, DEVON	17	66.2	113.8	12.2	49.8	20.4	.263	.319	.419	7	.412	0	.000	.2826	262.4	545.0
WHITE, FRANK	18	50.6	111.4	8.8	49.2	9.8	.255	.295	.383	3	.166	0	.000	.2190	229.8	448.8
WHITE, JO-JO	9	50.6	75.3	0.8	25.4	10.1	.256	.353	.328	0	.000	0	.000	.1870	162.2	349.2
WHITE, RONDELL	13	55.1	109.0	14.4	54.6	7..2	.289	.343	.472	1	.077	0	.000	.2362	240.3	476.5
WHITE, ROY	15	64.2	120.2	10.6	50.5	15.5	.271	.363	.404	1	.066	2	.133	.2470	261.0	508.0
WHITE, SAMMY	11	29.4	83.2	6.0	38.2	1.2	.262	.307	.377	0	.000	0	.000	.1890	158.0	347.0
WHITNEY, PINKY	12	58.0	41.7	7.7	77.3	3.7	.295	.343	.415	3	.250	0	.000	.2600	288.4	548.4
WILBER, DEL	8	8.3	21.7	2.3	14.3	0.1	.242	.287	.389	0	.000	0	.000	.1830	46.7	229.7
WILKERSON, BRAD	5	73.8	116.0	16.6	53.0	8.6	.256	.366	.452	0	.000	0	.000	.2148	268.0	482.8
WILLIAMS, BERNIE	15	86.7	147.9	18.3	79.7	9.7	.298	.386	.480	5	.333	1	.067	.3128	342.3	655.1
WILLIAMS, BILLY*	18	78.3	150.6	23.6	81.9	5.0	.290	.364	.492	0	.000	4	.222	.2730	339.4	612.4
WILLIAMS, EARL	8	45.1	95.6	17.2	57.1	0.2	.247	.321	.424	0	.000	0	.000	.1980	215.2	413.2
WILLIAMS, MATT	17	58.6	110.5	22.2	71.6	3.1	.268	.317	.489	4	.235	2	.118	.2854	266.0	551.4
WILLIAMS, TED*	19	94.6	139.6	27.4	96.7	1.2	.344	.483	.634	0	.000	52	2.736	.8390	359.5	1198.5
WILLS, MAURY	14	76.2	152.4	1.4	32.7	41.8	.281	.331	.331	0	.000	7	.500	.2880	304.5	592.5
WILSON, GLENN	10	45.1	109.8	9.8	52.1	2.7	.265	.307	.398	0	.000	0	.000	.1940	219.5	413.5
WILSON, HACK*	12	73.6	121.7	20.3	88.5	4.3	.307	.395	.545	0	.000	10	.833	.4160	308.4	724.4
WILSON, JACK	5	64.2	143.0	7.0	48.0	5.2	.263	.305	.355	0	.000	1	.200	.2246	268.4	493.0
WILSON, JIMMIE	18	32.2	75.4	1.7	34.5	4.7	.284	.336	.370	0	.000	0	.000	.1980	148.5	346.5
WILSON, MOOKIE	12	60.9	116.4	5.6	36.5	27.3	.274	.314	.386	0	.000	0	.000	.1948	246.7	441.5
WILSON, PRESTON	8	63.6	113.6	21.4	73.9	13.6	.264	.334	.478	0	.000	1	.125	.2402	286.1	526.3
WILSON, WILLIE	19	61.5	116.1	2.1	30.7	35.1	.285	.323	.376	1	.052	9	.473	.3010	245.5	546.5
WINE, BOBBY	12	20.7	56.8	2.5	22.3	0.5	.215	.265	.286	1	.083	0	.000	.1690	102.8	271.8
WINFIELD, DAVE*	22	75.9	141.0	21.1	83.3	10.1	.283	.355	.475	7	.318	1	.045	.2952	331.8	627.0
WINN, RANDY	8	67.0	132.3	8.6	50.1	17.9	.288	.349	.425	0	.000	0	.000	.2124	275.9	488.3
WOMACK, TONY	12	61.0	111.3	2.9	30.3	30.2	.273	.318	.356	0	.000	4	. 333	.2560	235.7	491.7
WOODLING, GENE	17	48.8	93.2	8.6	48.8	1.7	.284	.388	.431	2	.117	1	.058	.2550	201.1	456.1
WRIGHT, DAVID	2	70.0	126.5	20.5	71.0	11.5	.302	.372	.524	0	.000	0	.000	.2396	299.5	539.1
WYNN, JIM	15	73.6	111.0	19.4	64.2	15.0	.250	.369	.436	0	.000	2	.133	.2370	283.2	520.2
YASTRZEMSKI, CARL*	23	78.9	148.6	19.6	80.1	7.3	.285	.382	.462	1	.043	23	1.000	.4340	334.5	768.5
YORK, RUDY	13	67.3	124.6	21.3	88.6	2.9	.275	.362	.483	1	.076	3	.230	.2850	304.7	589.7
YOST, EDDIE	18	67.5	103.5	7.7	37.9	4.0	.254	.395	.371	2	.111	10	.555	.3370	220.6	557.6
YOUNG, BOBBY	8	30.5	76.1	1.8	17.1	2.2	.249	.308	.318	0	.000	0	.000	.1750	127.7	302.7
YOUNG, DMITRI	10	55.7	115.7	14.7	57.6	2.4	.291	.350	.479	0	.000	0	.000	.2240	246.1	470.1
YOUNG, ERIC	14	69.7	121.6	5.4	37.7	32.6	.285	.361	.392	0	.000	2	.143	.2362	267.0	503.2
YOUNG, MICHAEL	6	78.0	147.8	13.3	62.2	6.5	.297	.344	.451	0	.000	2	.333	.2850	307.8	592.8
YOUNT, ROBIN*	20	81.6	157.1	12.5	70.3	13.5	.285	.346	.430	2	.100	6	.300	.2920	335.0	627.0
ZARILLA, ZEKE	10	50.7	97.5	6.1	45.6	3.3	.276	.357	.405	0	.000	0	.000	.2070	203.2	410.2
ZEILE, TODD	16	61.6	125.3	15.8	69.4	3.3	.265	.346	.423	0	.000	0	.000	.2068	275.4	482.2
ZERNIAL, GUS	11	52.0	99.3	21.5	70.5	1.3	.265	.331	.486	0	.000	2	.181	.2520	244.6	496.6
ZISK, RICHIE	13	52.3	113.6	15.9	60.9	0.6	.287	.355	.466	0	.000	0	.000	.2210	243.3	464.3

Remember, the ratings range from one to fifty. Consequently there will be some outstanding pitchers missing. Don Drysdale (#53) and Johan Santana (#57) come to mind.

Lefty Grove led all starting pitchers with a Pitcher's Number of 2678 by dint of copping 37 pitching titles placing him well above the competition of his time.

Among the relievers, Mariano Rivera had the highest Pitcher's Number of 3975. He averaged an amazing 34.5 saves a year for his entire career. That coupled with his 4.9 wins a year add up to 38.9 games in the win column each year for the Yankees.

The best Quality Inning belongs to none other than Billy Wagner (-.246). Of course, he only pitched 630 innings careerwise while starter Pedro Martinez pitched 2,513 innings with a QI of -.040 and Nolan Ryan threw 5,387 innings with a QI of .244.

A remarkable statistic is that Babe Ruth's ERA for his pitching career was 2.28. That's better than any pitcher that ever wore a number. While Ruth himself wore his famous #3 and pitched, his ERA ballooned to 4.00, but his W/L % was 1.000 (2-0).

The three highest ratios of strikeouts per inning for starters are Randy Johnson (1.216), Mark Prior (1.173) and Kerry Wood (1.160).

Ron Dibble had the highest ratio for relievers whiffing 1.352 batters each frame. Three relievers following him were: Billy Wagner (1.333), Armando Benitez (1.241) and B. J. Ryan (1.220).

PITCHERS

NAME	YRS	W YR	SH YR	SV YR	IP	H IP	HR IP	BB IP	K IP	QI	WL %	P TIT	PT AV	GROSS	ERA	CUM	RESULTS OF AVERAGING SHOWN HERE AVG	PITCH
AASE, DON R	13	5.0	0.3	6.3	1109	.978	.080	.412	.577	.893	.524	0	.000	11.6	3.80	7.80	-123	657
ABER, AL L	6	4.0	0	2.3	389	1.023	.074	.411	.434	1.074	.490	0	.000	6.3	4.18	2.12	-194	18
ABBOTT, JIM L	10	8.7	0.6	0	1674	1.063	.092	.370	.530	.995	.446	0	.000	9.3	4.25	5.05	-183	322
ABERNATHY, TED R	14	4.5	0.1	10.5	1147	.880	.061	.516	.666	.791	.477	2	.143	15.1	3.46	11.64	-57	1107
AGUILERA, RICK R	16	5.4	0	19.9	1291	.955	.107	.272	.798	.536	.515	0	.000	25.3	3.57	21.73	-7	2166
AGUIRRE, HANK L	16	4.6	0.5	2.0	1375	.884	.089	.348	.622	.699	.510	3	.187	7.1	3.24	3.86	0	386
ALEXANDER, DOYLE R	19	10.2	0.9	0.1	3367	1.002	.096	.290	.453	.935	.527	1	.052	11.2	3.76	7.44	-118	626
ALFONSECA, ANTONIO R	9	3.3	0	13.4	547	1.077	.090	.395	.678	.884	.462	2	.222	16.7	3.95	12.75	-67	1208
ALLEN, JOHNNY R	13	10.9	1.3	1.3	1950	.948	.053	.378	.548	.831	.654	3	.230	13.5	3.75	9.75	17	992
ALLEN, NEIL R	11	5.2	0.5	6.8	988	.996	.073	.422	.618	.873	.453	0	.000	12.5	3.88	8.62	-140	722
ALVAREZ, WILSON L	14	7.3	0.4	0.3	1748	.929	.109	.461	.761	.738	.526	0	.000	8.0	3.96	4.04	-71	333
ANDUJAR, JOAQUIN R	13	9.7	1.4	0.6	2153	.936	.071	.339	.479	.867	.518	3	.230	11.7	3.58	8.12	-39	773
ANTONELLI, JOHNNY L	12	10.5	2.0	1.7	1992	.938	.092	.344	.583	.791	.534	5	.416	14.2	3.34	10.86	53	1139
APPIER, KEVIN R	16	10.6	0.8	0	2595	.934	.089	.360	.768	.615	.552	0	.000	11.4	3.74	7.66	-21	745
ARROYO, LUIS L	8	5.0	0.1	5.5	531	.986	.109	.391	.632	.854	.556	1	.125	10.6	3.93	6.67	-58	609
ASSENMACHER, PAUL L	14	4.4	0	4.0	856	.954	.085	.368	.943	.464	.581	0	.000	8.4	3.53	4.87	39	526
ASTACIO, PEDRO R	14	8.9	0.8	0	2106	1.037	.132	.330	.770	.729	.510	0	.000	9.7	4.61	5.09	-73	436
AUKER, ELDON R	10	13.0	1.4	0.2	1963	1.136	.065	.359	.302	1.258	.563	1	.100	14.6	4.42	10.18	-198	820
AVERY, STEVE L	11	8.7	0.6	0	1555	.983	.095	.366	.630	.814	.536	0	.000	9.3	4.19	5.11	-93	418
BAGBY, JIM R	10	9.7	1.3	0.9	1666	1.089	.058	.364	.258	1.253	.503	1	.100	11.9	3.96	7.94	-216	578
BAHNSEN, STAN R	16	9.1	1.0	1.2	2529	.964	.088	.365	.537	.880	.495	0	.000	11.3	3.60	7.70	-128	642
BANNISTER, FLOYD L	15	8.9	1.0	0	2388	.971	.121	.354	.721	.725	.484	1	.066	9.9	4.06	5.84	-58	526
BARBER, STEVE L	15	8.0	1.4	0.8	1999	.909	.062	.475	.654	.792	.533	1	.066	10.2	3.36	6.84	-64	620
BARR, JIM R	12	8.4	1.6	1.0	2065	1.050	.077	.227	.358	.996	.474	0	.000	11.0	3.56	7.44	-174	570
BECK, ROD R	13	2.9	0	22.0	768	.915	.126	.249	.839	.451	.458	0	.000	24.9	3.30	21.60	2	2162
BECKETT, JOSH R	5	8.2	0.4	0	609	.869	.090	.366	.997	.328	.547	1	.200	8.6	3.46	514	140	654
BEDROSIAN, STEVE R	14	5.4	0	13.1	1191	.861	.096	.435	.773	.619	.490	1	.071	18.5	3.38	15.12	-19	1493
BELCHER, TIM R	14	10.4	1.3	0.4	2443	.992	.108	.352	.622	.830	.510	2	.143	12.1	4.16	7.94	-59	735
BELL, GARY R	12	10.0	0.7	4.2	2015	.890	.102	.417	.683	.726	.508	0	.000	14.9	3.68	11.22	-72	1050
BENES, ANDY R	14	11.1	0.6	0.1	2505	.949	.115	.363	.798	.629	.527	0	.000	11.8	3.97	7.83	-34	749
BENITEZ, ARMANDO R	12	2.8	0	21.9	684	.662	.114	.513	1.241	.048	.486	1	.083	24.7	2.92	21.78	174	2352
BENSON, KRIS R	6	9.5	0.3	0	1024	1.018	.108	.356	.683	.799	.483	0	.000	9.8	4.25	5.55	-105	450
BENTON, AL R	14	7.0	0.7	4.7	1688	.991	.063	.434	.413	1.075	.527	2	.143	12.4	3.66	8.74	-135	739
BERENGUER, JUAN R	15	4.4	0.1	2.1	1205	.858	.096	.501	.809	.646	.519	0	.000	6.6	3.90	2.70	-42	228
BIBBY, JIM R	12	9.2	1.5	0.6	1722	.908	.076	.419	.626	.777	.524	2	.166	11.3	3.76	7.54	-29	725
BLACK, BUD L	15	8.1	0.8	0.7	2053	.963	.106	.303	.506	.866	.511	1	.067	9.6	3.84	5.76	-96	480
BLACKWELL, EWELL R	10	8.2	1.5	1.0	1321	.870	.050	.425	.635	.710	.512	5	.500	10.7	3.30	7.40	100	840
BLANTON, CY R	9	7.5	1.5	0.4	1218	1.020	.052	.276	.501	.847	.489	5	.555	9.4	3.55	5.85	.197	782
BLASS, STEVE R	10	10.3	1.6	0.2	1597	.975	.080	.373	.561	.867	.575	2	.200	12.1	3.63	8.47	-30	817
BLUE, VIDA L	17	12.2	2.1	0.1	3343	.879	.078	.354	.650	.661	.565	4	.235	14.4	3.27	11.13	.046	1159

*HALL OF FAME **L** OR **R** FOLLOWING THE PITCHER'S NAME=LEFTY OR RIGHTY
LEGEND: **YRS**=CAREER YEARS, **W YR**=WINS PER YEAR, **SH YR**=SHUTOUTS PER YEAR, **SV YR**=SAVES PER YEAR, **IP**=INNINGS PITCHED,CAREER, **H IP**=HITS PER INNING, **CAREER**, **HR IP**=HOMERUNS PER INNING, **CAREER**, **BB IP**=WALKS PER INNING, **CAREER**, **K IP**=STRIKEOUTS PER INNING, **CAREER**, **QI**=QUALITY INNING (Ks ARE SUBTRACTED FROM HITS, HRs, and BBs; THE LOWER THE QI, THE BETTER), **WL %**=WON/LOST PERCENTAGE, CAREER, **P TIT**=PITCHING TITLES, CAREER, **PT AV**=AVERAGE OF PITCHING TITLES PER YEAR FOR CAREER, **GROSS**=THE SUM OF WINS, SHUTOUTS AND SAVES, **ERA**=CAREER EARNED RUN AVERAGE, **CUM**=CUMULATIVE NUMBER, GROSS NUMBER MINUS ERA (THE BETTER THE ERA, THE HIGHER THE CUM #), **AVG**=AVERAGING, W/L% + P TITLES/YR-QI DIVIDED BY 3 (THE LOWER THE QI, THE LESS IT DETRACTS FROM THE OTHER AVERAGES), **PITCH #**=(CUM X 100) + (AVG X 1000) PITCHER'S NUMBER.

NAME	YRS	W YR	SH YR	SV YR	IP	H IP	HR IP	BB IP	K IP	QI	WL %	P TIT	PT AV	GROSS	ERA	CUM	AVG	PITCH
BLYLEVEN, BERT R	22	13.0	2.7	0	4970	.931	.086	.265	.744	.538	.534	7	.318	15.7	3.31	12.39	104	1343
BORBON, PEDRO R	12	5.7	0	6.6	1026	1.070	.061	.244	.398	.977	.639	0	.000	12.3	3.52	8.78	-112	766
BOROWY, HANK R	10	10.8	1.6	0.7	1717	.967	.063	.363	.402	.991	.568	1	.100	13.1	3.50	9.63	-108	855
BOTTALICO, RICKY R	12	2.8	0	9.7	628	.893	.113	.503	.916	.593	.440	0	.000	12.5	3.99	8.51	-51	800
BRANCA, RALPH R	12	7.3	1.0	1.5	1484	.924	.100	.446	.558	.912	.564	0	.000	9.8	3.79	6.01	-116	485
BRANTLEY, JEFF R	14	3.1	0	12.3	859	.878	.122	.426	.847	.579	.483	1	.071	15.4	3.39	12.01	-8	1193
BRAZLE, AL L	10	9.7	0.7	6.0	1377	1.007	.060	.357	.402	1.022	.602	2	.200	16.4	3.31	13.09	-73	1236
BRECHEEN, HARRY L	12	11.0	2.0	1.5	1907	.907	.061	.281	.472	.777	.591	7	.583	14.5	2.92	11.58	132	1290
BRIDGES, TOMMY R	16	12.1	2.0	0.6	2826	.946	.064	.421	.592	.839	.584	5	.312	14.7	3.57	11.13	19	1132
BROWN, KEVIN R	19	11.1	0.9	0	3256	.946	.639	.277	.736	1.126	.594	7	.368	12.0	3.28	8.72	-55	817
BROWN, MACE R	10	7.6	0.2	4.8	1075	1.047	.041	.361	.405	1.044	.571	2	.200	12.6	3.46	9.14	-91	823
BROWNING, TOM L	12	10.3	1.0	0	1921	1.005	.123	.266	.521	.873	.577	0	.000	11.3	3.94	7.36	-99	637
BUHL, BOB R	15	11.0	1.3	0.4	2587	.945	.091	.427	.490	.973	.557	2	.133	12.7	3.55	9.15	-94	821
BUNNING, JIM* R	17	13.1	2.3	0.9	3760	.913	.098	.265	.759	.517	.549	8	.470	16.3	3.27	13.03	167	1470
BURDETTE, LEW R	18	11.2	1.8	1.7	3067	1.038	.094	.204	.350	.986	.585	7	.388	14.7	3.66	11.04	-4	1100
BURKE, TIM R	8	6.1	0	12.7	699	.892	.070	.313	.635	.640	.598	0	.000	18.8	2.72	16.08	-14	1594
BURNETT, A. J. R	7	7.0	1.1	0	854	.842	.077	.441	.882	.478	.495	1	.143	8.1	3.73	4.37	53	490
BUSBY, STEVE R	8	8.7	0.8	0	1060	.946	.068	.408	.621	.801	.565	0	.000	9.5	3.72	5.78	-78	500
BUSH, GUY R	17	10.4	0.9	2.0	2722	1.084	.558	.316	.312	1.646	,564	2	.118	3.3	3.86	9.44	-321	623
BUTCHER, MAX R	10	9.5	1.4	0.9	1786	1.083	.055	.326	.271	1.193	.473	0	.000	11.8	3.73	8.07	-240	567
CALDWELL, MIKE L	14	9.7	1.6	1.2	2408	1.071	.090	.247	.389	1.019	.513	2	.142	12.5	3.81	8.69	-121	748
CANDELARIA, JOHN L	19	9.3	0.6	1.5	2526	.949	.096	.198	.662	.581	.592	2	.105	11.4	3.33	8.07	38	845
CANDIOTTI, TOM R	16	9.4	0.7	0	2725	.977	.092	.324	.637	.765	.479	0	.000	10.1	3.73	6.37	-92	545
CARLTON, STEVE* L	24	13.7	2.2	0	5217	.895	.079	.351	.792	.533	.574	20	.833	15.9	3.22	12.68	295	1563
CARPENTER, CHRIS R	8	10.6	1.1	0	1294	1.049	.118	.325	.755	.737	.586	1	.125	11.7	4.26	7.44	-9	735
CARROLL, CLAY R	15	6.4	0	9.5	1353	.957	.049	.326	.503	.829	.568	1	.067	15.9	2.94	12.96	-65	1231
CASEY, HUGH R	9	8.3	0.3	6.1	939	.995	.061	.341	.371	1.026	.641	2	.222	14.7	3.45	11.25	-54	1071
CHANCE, DEAN R	11	11.6	3.0	2.0	2147	.868	.056	.344	.714	.554	.527	7	.636	16.6	2.92	13.68	203	1571
CHANDLER, SPUD R	11	9.9	2.3	0.5	1485	.893	.043	.311	.413	.834	.717	6	.545	12.7	2.84	9.86	142	1128
CHAPMAN, BEN R	3	2.6	0	0	141	1.042	.049	.503	.460	1.134	.571	0	.000	2.6	4.40	-1.80	-187	-367
CHARLTON, NORM L	13	3.9	0.1	7.5	899	.888	.078	.455	.899	.522	.486	1	.077	11.5	3.71	7.79	14	793
CLANCY, JIM R	15	9.3	0.7	0.6	2517	.998	.096	.376	.564	.906	.456	0	.000	10.6	4.23	6.37	-150	487
CLEMENS, ROGER R	22	15.5	2.1	0	4704	.850	.074	.323	.957	.290	.665	37	1.682	17.6	3.12	14.48	686	2134
CLEMENT, MATT R	8	10.3	0.4	0	1347	.927	.101	.454	.872	.610	.503	0	.000	10.7	4.37	6.33	-36	597
CLONINGER, TONY R	12	9.4	1.0	0.5	1767	.929	.101	.451	.633	.848	.538	0	.000	10.9	4.07	6.83	-103	580
COLON, BARTOLO R	9	15.4	0.8	0	1820	.963	.116	.351	.788	.642	.629	2	.222	16.2	3.94	12.26	70	1296
CONE, DAVID R	17	11.4	1.3	0.1	2898	.864	.089	.392	.921	.424	.606	6	.353	12.8	3.46	9.34	178	1112
CONTRERAS, JOSE R	3	11.7	0	0	446	.886	.130	.424	.843	.597	.660	1	.333	11.7	4.28	7.42	132	874
COOPER, MORT R	11	11.6	3.0	1.3	1841	.905	.046	.310	.496	.765	.631	9	.818	15.9	2.97	12.93	228	1521
CORDERO, CHAD R	3	3.3	0	24.0	168	.756	.107	.375	.929	.309	.588	1	.333	24.0	2.36	21.64	204	2368
CUELLAR, MIKE L	15	12.3	2.4	0.7	2808	.903	.079	.292	.581	.693	.587	5	.333	15.4	3.14	12.26	.075	1301
DARLING, RON R	13	10.5	1.0	0	2360	.951	.101	.384	.674	.762	.540	0	.000	11.5	3.87	7.63	-74	689
DARWIN, DANNY R	21	8.1	0.4	1.5	3017	.966	.106	.290	.644	.718	.484	3	.143	10.0	3.84	6.16	-30	586
DAVIS, CURT R	13	12.1	1.8	2.5	2325	1.057	.061	.206	.294	1.030	.547	0	.000	16.4	3.42	12.98	-161	1137
DAVIS, MARK L	15	3.4	0.1	6.4	1145	.933	.113	.466	.879	.633	.378	1	.067	9.9	4.17	5.73	-63	510
DAVIS, RON R	11	4.2	0	11.8	746	.985	.109	.402	.800	.696	.470	0	.000	16.0	4.05	11.95	-75	1120
DAVIS, STORM R	13	8.7	0.4	0.8	1780	1.007	.076	.386	.589	.880	.541	0	.000	9.9	4.02	5.88	-113	475
DEAN, DIZZY* R	12	12.5	2.1	2.5	1967	.975	.048	.230	.591	.662	.644	16	1.333	17.1	3.02	14.08	438	1846
DELOCK, IKE R	11	7.6	0.5	2.8	1238	.998	.113	.428	.542	.997	.528	0	.000	10.9	4.03	6.87	-156	531
DENNY, JOHN R	13	9.4	1.3	0	2148	.974	.063	.362	.534	.865	.532	3	.230	10.7	3.59	7.11	-34	677
DERRINGER, PAUL R	15	14.8	2.1	1.9	3645	1.073	.043	.208	.413	.911	.513	5	.333	18.8	3.46	15.34	-22	1512
DIBBLE, RON R	7	3.9	0	12.7	477	.696	.057	.499	1.352	-.100	.519	0	.000	16.6	2.98	13.62	206	1568
DICKSON, MURRY R	18	9.5	1.5	1.2	3052	.992	.098	.346	.419	1.017	.487	1	.055	12.2	3.66	8.54	-158	696
DIERKER, LARRY R	14	9.9	1.7	0	2333	.912	.078	.304	.639	.728	.531	1	.071	11.6	3.31	8.29	-41	787
DOBSON, JOE R	14	9.7	1.5	1.2	2170	.943	.063	.392	.457	.941	.571	1	.071	12.4	3.62	8.78	-99	779
DONALD, ATLEY R	8	8.1	0.7	0.1	932	.973	.070	.395	.395	1.043	.663	0	.000	9.7	3.52	6.18	-126	492
DONNELLY, BRENDAN R	4	4.3	0	1.0	231	.784	.078	.333	1.048	.147	.680	0	.000	5.3	2.57	2.73	178	451
DONOVAN, DICK R	15	8.1	1.6	0.3	2017	.985	.098	.245	.436	.892	.552	5	.333	10.0	3.67	6.33	-2	631
DOTEL, OCTAVIO R	7	5.3	0	10.1	600	.773	.123	.432	1.208	.120	.544	0	.000	15.4	3.63	11.77	141	1318
DOWNING, AL L	17	7.2	1.4	0.1	2268	.858	.078	.411	.722	.625	.535	3	.176	8.7	3.22	5.48	28	576
DRABEK, DOUG R	13	11.9	1.6	0	2535	.966	.097	.278	.629	.712	.536	2	.154	13.5	3.73	9.77	-7	970
DRAGO, DICK R	13	8.3	0.7	4.4	1875	1.013	.083	.297	.526	.867	.480	0	.000	13.4	3.62	9.78	-129	849
DRAVECKY, DAVE L	8	8.0	1.1	1.2	1062	.911	.091	.296	.525	.773	.529	0	.000	10.3	3.13	7.17	-81	636
DUREN, RYNE R	10	2.7	0.1	5.7	589	.752	.067	.665	1.069	.415	.380	1	.100	8.5	3.83	4.67	21	488
EARNSHAW, GEORGE R	9	14.1	2.0	1.3	1915	1.034	.074	.422	.523	1.007	0.577	3	.333	17.4	4.38	13.02	-32	1270
EASTWICK, RAWLY R	8	3.5	0	8.5	525	.988	.072	.297	.561	.796	.509	2	.250	12.0	3.31	8.69	-12	857
ECKERSLEY, DENNIS* R	24	8.2	0.8	16.3	3286	.936	.106	.225	.731	.536	.535	3	.125	25.3	3.50	21.64	41	2221
ELLIS, DOCK R	12	11.5	1.1	0	2127	.971	.065	.316	.534	.818	.537	0	.000	12.6	3.46	9.14	-93	821
ELLIS, SAMMY R	7	9.0	0.4	2.5	1004	.963	.117	.376	.674	.782	.521	0	.000	11.9	4.15	7.75	-87	688
ERICKSON, SCOTT R	14	10.1	1.2	0	2349	1.095	.096	.365	.532	1.024	.511	5	.357	11.3	4.57	6.73	-52	621
ERSKINE, CARL R	12	10.1	1.1	1.0	1718	.952	.115	.376	.571	.872	.610	1	.083	12.2	4.00	8.20	-59	761

NAME	YRS	W YR	SH YR	SV YR	IP	H IP	HR IP	BB IP	K IP	QI	WL %	P TIT	PT AV	GROSS	ERA	CUM	AVG	PITCH
FABER, RED* R	20	12.7	1.5	0.1	4087	1.005	.027	.297	.360	1.689	.544	9	.450	14.3	3.15	11.15	-232	883
FACE, ROY R	16	6.5	0	12.0	1375	.979	.102	.263	.637	.707	.523	3	.188	18.5	3.48	15.02	1	1503
FELLER, BOB* R	18	14.7	2.4	1.1	3827	.854	.058	.460	.674	.698	.621	31	1.722	18.2	3.25	14.95	548	2043
FERNANDEZ, SID L	15	7.6	0.6	0.1	1867	.761	.102	.383	.934	.312	.543	3	.200	8.3	3.36	4.94	86	580
FERRELL, WES R	15	12.8	1.1	0.8	2623	1.084	.050	.396	.375	1.155	.601	8	.533	14.7	4.04	10.66	-7	1059
FERRISS, BOO R	6	10.8	2.0	1.3	880	1.038	.047	.356	.336	1.105	.684	1	.166	14.1	3.64	10.46	-85	961
FIDRYCH, MARK R	5	5.8	1.0	0	412	.963	.055	.240	.412	.846	.604	2	.400	6.8	3.10	3.70	.052	422
FIGUEROA, ED R	8	10.0	1.5	0.1	1309	.992	.068	.338	.436	.962	.544	0	.000	11.6	3.51	8.09	-139	670
FINGERS, ROLLIE* R	17	6.7	0.1	20.0	1701	.866	.072	.289	.763	.464	.491	3	.176	26.8	2.90	23.90	68	2458
FINLEY, CHUCK L	17	11.8	0.9	0	3197	.960	.095	.417	.816	.656	.536	2	.118	12.7	3.85	8.85	- 1	884
FISHER, EDDIE R	15	5.6	0.1	5.4	1538	.908	.096	.284	.527	.761	.548	0	.000	11.1	3.41	7.69	-71	698
FITZSIMMONS, FRED R	19	11.4	1.6	0.7	3224	1.034	.058	.262	.270	1.084	.598	3	.158	13.7	3.51	10.19	-109	910
FLANAGAN, MIKE L	18	9.2	1.0	0.2	2770	1.012	.090	.321	.538	.885	.539	2	.111	10.4	3.90	6.50	-78	572
FONSECA, LEW R	1	0	0	0	1	.000	.000	.000	.000	.000	.000	0	.000	0.0	0.00	0.00	0	0
FORD, WHITEY* L	16	14.7	2.8	0.6	3170	.872	.071	.342	.617	.668	.690	14	.875	18.1	2.75	15.35	299	1834
FORSCH, BOB R	16	10.5	1.1	0.1	2794	.992	.077	.297	.405	.961	.553	0	.000	11.7	3.76	7.94	-136	658
FORSCH, KEN R	16	7.1	1.1	3.1	2127	.973	.072	.275	.492	.828	.502	2	.125	11.3	3.37	7.93	-67	726
FORSTER, TERRY L	16	3.4	0	7.9	1106	.935	.046	.413	.715	.679	.454	1	.063	11.3	3.23	8.07	-54	753
FOULKE, KEITH R	9	4.2	0.1	21.1	706	.810	.110	.246	.933	.233	.535	2	.222	25.4	3.23	22.17	175	2392
FRANCO, JOHN L	21	4.3	0	20.2	1246	.936	.065	.397	.783	.615	.508	3	.143	24.5	2.89	21.61	12	2173
FRIEND, BOB R	16	14.3	2.2	0.6	3611	1.044	.079	.247	.480	.890	.461	5	.312	17.1	3.58	13.52	-39	1313
FRYMAN, WOODIE L	18	7.8	1.5	3.2	2411	.981	.077	.369	.658	.769	.476	0	.000	12.5	3.77	8.73	-97	776
GAGNE, ERIC R	7	3.6	0	22.9	543	.799	.114	.335	1.153	.075	.543	1	143	26.5	3.28	23.22	204	2526
GARBER, GENE R	19	5.0	0	11.4	1510	.969	.081	.294	.622	.722	.459	0	.000	16.4	3.34	13.06	-88	1218
GARCIA, FREDDY R	7	14.1	0.6	0	1427	.950	.111	.337	.748	.650	.615	3	.429	14.7	3.93	10.77	131	1208
GARCIA, MIKE R	14	10.1	1.9	1.6	2174	.988	.056	.330	.513	.861	.594	5	.357	13.6	3.27	10.33	30	1063
GARLAND, JON R	6	10.7	0.7	0.2	1009	1.007	.136	.372	.546	.969	.512	1	.167	11.6	4.42	7.18	-97	621
GARVER, NED R	14	9.2	1.2	0.8	2477	.991	.085	.353	.353	1.076	.451	2	.142	11.2	3.73	7.47	-161	586
GIBSON, BOB* R	17	14.7	3.2	0.3	3884	.844	.066	.343	.802	.451	.591	11	.647	18.2	2.91	15.29	262	1791
GIUSTI, DAVE R	15	6.6	0.6	9.6	1716	.963	.073	.332	.642	.726	.518	1	.066	16.8	3.60	13.20	.047	1273
GLAVINE, TOM L	19	14.5	1.3	0	3952	.964	.076	.338	.595	.783	.599	7	.368	15.8	3.44	12.36	61	1297
GOMEZ, LEFTY* L	14	13.5	2.0	0.6	2503	.914	.055	.437	.586	.820	.649	17	1.214	16.1	3.34	12.76	347	1623
GOODEN, DWIGHT R	16	12.1	1.5	0.2	2801	.915	.075	.341	.819	.512	.634	9	.562	13.8	3.51	10.29	228	1257
GORDON, TOM R	17	7.5	0.2	6.8	1977	.891	.079	.466	.911	.525	.525	1	.059	14.5	3.93	10.57	20	1077
GOTT, JIM R	13	4.1	0.2	6.7	1089	.957	.076	.416	.751	.698	.435	0	.000	11.0	3.80	7.20	-87	633
GRANGER, WAYNE R	9	3.8	0	12.0	638	.990	.073	.315	.474	.904	.500	1	.111	15.8	3.14	12.66	-98	1168
GRANT, MUDCAT R	14	10.3	1.2	3.7	2441	.938	.119	.347	.519	.885	.549	3	.214	15.2	3.63	11.57	-40	1117
GRAVES, DANNY R	10	4.1	0.1	18.2	794	1.057	.117	.335	.537	.972	.488	0	.000	22.4	4.02	18.38	-161	1677
GRIM, BOB R	8	7.6	0.5	4.6	759	.932	.065	.434	.583	.848	.598	1	.125	12.7	3.61	9.09	-41	868
GRIMES, BURLEIGH* R	19	14.2	1.8	0.9	4179	1.055	.035	.309	.361	1.038	.560	12	.632	16.9	3.53	13.37	51	1388
GRISSOM, MARV R	10	4.7	0.3	5.8	810	.951	.080	.423	.566	.888	.511	0	.000	10.8	3.41	7.39	-125	614
GROVE, LEFTY* L	17	17.6	2.0	3.2	3940	.976	.041	.301	.575	.743	.680	37	2.176	22.8	3.06	19.74	704	2678
GUARDADO, EDDIE L	13	3.1	0.1	13.1	799	.932	.143	.371	.874	.572	.435	1	.077	16.3	4.28	12.02	-20	1182
GUBICZA, MARK R	14	9.4	1.1	0.1	2223	1.007	.070	.354	.617	.814	.493	0	.000	10.6	3.96	6.64	-107	557
GUIDRY, RON L	14	12.1	1.8	0.2	2392	.918	.094	.264	.743	.533	.651	11	.785	14.1	3.29	10.81	301	1382
GULLETT, DON L	9	12.1	1.5	1.2	1390	.866	.082	.360	.662	.646	.686	2	.222	14.8	3.11	11.69	87	1256
GULLICKSON, BILL R	14	11.6	0.8	0	2560	1.039	.110	.243	.500	.892	.544	1	.071	12.4	3.93	8.47	-92	755
GUMBERT, HARRY R	15	9.5	0.9	3.2	2156	1.014	.056	.334	.329	1.075	.559	1	.067	13.6	3.68	9.92	-150	842
GURA, LARRY L	16	7.8	1.0	0.8	2047	.986	.099	.293	.391	.987	.565	0	.000	9.6	3.76	5.84	-140	444
HADDIX, HARVEY L	14	9.7	1.4	1.5	2235	.963	.107	.268	.704	.634	.546	2	.143	12.6	3.63	8.97	18	915
HADLEY, BUMP R	16	10.0	0.8	1.5	2945	1.011	.056	.489	.447	1.109	.494	2	.125	12.3	4.24	8.06	- 163	643
HAEFNER, MICKEY L	8	9.7	0.3	0.3	1466	.964	.051	.393	.346	1.062	.462	0	.000	10.3	3.50	6.80	-200	480
HAINES, JESSE* R	19	11.0	1.2	0.5	3208	1.078	.051	.271	.305	1.095	.571	3	.158	12.7	3.64	9.06	-122	784
HALLADAY, ROY R	8	9.9	1.0	0.1	1116	.988	.088	.268	.726	.618	.648	6	.750	11.0	3.70	7.30	26	756
HALLAHAN, BILL R	12	8.5	1.1	0.6	1740	1.056	.040	.447	.491	1.052	.520	3	.250	10.2	4.03	6.17	-94	523
HAMLIN, LUKE R	9	8.1	1.3	1.0	1405	1.026	.075	.251	.400	.952	.490	0	.000	10.4	3.77	6.63	-154	509
HAMMAKER, ATLEE L	12	4.9	0.5	0.4	1077	.974	.087	.266	.570	.757	.468	2	.167	5.8	3.66	2.14	-41	173
HAMPTON, MIKE L	13	10.6	0.7	0.1	2074	1.040	.085	.398	.613	.910	.577	2	.154	11.4	3.97	7.34	-60	683
HANDS, BILL R	11	10.0	1.5	1.2	1951	.971	.085	.252	.578	.730	.502	0	.000	12.7	3.35	9.35	-76	859
HARDER, MEL R	20	11.1	1.2	1.1	3426	1.081	.046	.326	.338	1.115	.545	1	.050	13.4	3.80	9.60	-173	787
HARNISCH, PETE R	14	8.7	0.8	0	1041	.884	.089	.407	.754	.626	.525	3	.214	9.5	3.73	5.77	.36	613
HAWKINS, LA TROY R	11	4.6	0	6.8	956	1.136	,128	.343	.674	.933	.425	0	.000	11.4	4.77	6.63	-169	494
HENKE, TOM R	14	2.9	0	22.2	790	.768	.081	.323	1.090	.082	.494	1	.076	25.1	2.67	22.43	161	2404
HENNEMAN, MIKE R	10	5.7	0	19.3	733	.936	.064	.370	.727	.643	.576	0	.000	25.0	3.21	21.79	-22	2157
HENTGEN, PAT R	14	9.4	0.7	0.1	2075	1.017	.130	.373	.622	.898	.539	6	.429	10.2	4.32	5.88	23	611
HERNANDEZ, LIVAN R	10	11.0	0.7	0	1951	1.054	.107	.345	.681	.825	.514	5	.500	11.7	4.11	7.59	63	822
HERNANDEZ, WILLIE L	13	5.3	0	11.3	1044	.911	.092	.334	.754	.583	.526	0	.000	16.6	3.38	13.22	-19	1303
HIGBE, KIRBY R	12	9.8	0.9	2.0	1952	.910	.060	.502	.497	.975	.539	2	.167	12.7	3.69	9.01	-90	811
HIGUERA, TED L	9	10.3	1.3	0	1380	.914	.094	.320	.783	.545	.592	1	.111	11.6	3.61	7.99	52	851
HILLER, JOHN L	15	5.8	0.4	8.3	1242	.837	.088	.430	.834	.521	.534	1	.067	14.5	2.83	11.67	27	1194
HOERNER, JOE L	14	2.7	0	7.0	562	.901	.086	.314	.715	.586	.534	0	.000	9.7	2.99	6.71	-17	654

NAME	YRS	W YR	SH YR	SV YR	IP	H IP	HR IP	BB IP	K IP	QI	WL %	P TIT	PT AV	GROSS	ERA	CUM	AVG	PITCH
HOFFMAN, TREVOR R	14	3.5	0	31.1	822	.763	.090	.288	1.113	.028	.480	1	.071	34.6	2.76	31.84	174	3358
HOGSETT, CHIEF L	11	5.7	0.1	3.0	1222	1.236	.069	.409	.360	1.354	.420	0	.000	8.8	5.02	3.78	-311	67
HOLLAND, AL L	10	3.4	0.0	7.8	646	.848	.085	.359	.794	.498	.531	0	.000	11.2	2.98	8.22	11	833
HOLTZMAN, KEN L	15	11.6	2.0	0.2	2867	.972	.086	.317	.558	.817	.537	0	.000	13.8	3.49	10.31	-93	938
HOOTON, BURT R	15	10.0	1.9	0.4	2652	.941	.072	.301	.562	.752	.526	0	.000	12.3	3.38	8.92	-75	817
HORLEN, JOE R	12	9.6	1.5	0.3	2002	.913	.072	.276	.531	.730	.498	6	.500	11.4	3.11	8.29	89	918
HOUGH, CHARLIE R	25	8.6	0.5	2.4	3801	.863	.100	.438	.621	.780	.500	2	.080	11.5	3.74	7.76	-66	710
HOWE, STEVE L	12	3.9	0	7.6	606	.967	.053	.229	.541	.708	.534	0	.000	11.5	3.03	8.47	-58	789
HOYT, LA MARR R	8	12.2	1.0	1.2	1311	1.001	.106	.212	.519	.800	.590	3	.375	14.4	3.99	10.41	55	1096
HOYT, WAITE* R	21	11.2	1.2	2.4	3762	1.073	.040	.266	.320	1.059	.566	3	.142	14.8	3.59	11.21	-117	1004
HROBOSKY, AL L	13	4.9	0	7.4	722	.857	.069	.436	.759	.603	.646	1	.076	12.3	3.10	9.20	39	959
HUBBELL, CARL* L	16	15.8	2.2	2.0	3590	.964	.063	.201	.467	.761	.622	21	1.312	20.0	2.98	17.02	.391	2093
HUDSON, SID R	12	8.6	0.9	1.0	2181	1.093	.062	.382	.336	1.201	.406	0	.000	10.5	4.28	6.22	-265	357
HUDSON, TIM R	7	15.1	1.1	0	1433	.927	.080	.312	.708	.611	.688	4	.571	16.2	3.33	12.87	216	1503
HUGHSON, TEX R	8	12.0	2.3	2.1	1375	.923	.056	.270	.504	.745	.640	7	.875	16.4	2.94	13.46	.256	1602
HUME, TOM R	11	5.1	0	8.3	1086	1.018	.081	.353	.493	.959	.445	0	.000	13.4	3.85	9.55	-171	784
HUNTER, CATFISH* R	15	14.9	2.8	0	3449	.857	.108	.276	.583	.658	.574	10	.666	17.7	3.26	14.44	194	1638
HURST, BRUCE L	15	9.7	1.5	0	2417	1.019	.107	.306	.699	.733	.562	2	.142	11.2	3.92	7.28	-35	693
HUTCHINGS, JOHNNY R	6	2.0	0.5	1.0	471	1.006	.076	.382	.450	1.014	.400	0	.000	3.5	3.96	-46	-204	-250
HUTCHINSON, FRED R	10	9.5	1.3	0.7	1464	1.015	.086	.265	.403	.963	.572	2	.200	11.5	3.73	7.77	-63	714
ISRINGHAUSEN, JASON R	10	3.6	0.1	21.6	741	.915	.072	.406	.819	.574	.500	2	.200	25.3	3.60	21.70	42	2212
JACKSON, AL L	10	6.7	1.4	1.0	1389	1.043	.082	.293	.531	.887	.404	0	.000	9.1	3.98	5.12	-161	351
JACKSON, DANNY L	15	7.5	1.0	0.1	2073	1.018	.064	.394	.591	.885	.461	2	.133	8.6	4.01	4.59	-97	362
JACKSON, DARRIN R	1	0	0	0	2	1.500	.000	1.000	.000	2.500	.000	0	.000	0.0	9.00	-9.00	-833	-1733
JACKSON, GRANT L	18	4.7	0.2	4.3	1358	.936	.080	.376	.654	.738	.534	0	.000	9.2	3.46	5.74	-68	506
JACKSON, LARRY R	14	13.8	2.6	1.4	3262	.982	.079	.252	.523	.790	.515	2	.142	17.8	3.40	14.40	-44	1396
JANSEN, LARRY R	9	13.5	1.8	1.1	1765	.992	.108	.232	.477	.855	.578	4	.444	16.4	3.58	12.82	55	1337
JAY, JOEY R	13	7.6	1.2	0.5	1546	.944	.098	.392	.646	.788	.521	2	.153	9.3	3.77	5.53	-38	515
JENKINS, FERGIE* R	19	14.9	2.5	0.3	4500	.920	.107	.221	.709	.539	.557	9	.473	17.7	3.34	14.36	163	1599
JOHN, TOMMY L	26	11.0	1.7	0.1	4710	1.015	.064	.267	.476	.476	.555	4	.153	12.8	3.34	9.46	77	1023
JOHNSON, RANDY L	18	14.6	2.1	0.1	3594	.784	.093	.375	1.216	.036	.659	34	1.889	16.8	3.11	13.69	837	2206
JOHNSON, SYL R	19	5.8	0.5	2.2	2165	1.057	.079	.225	.424	.937	.489	0	.000	8.5	4.06	4.44	-149	295
JONES, RANDY L	10	10.0	1.9	0.2	1933	.990	.066	.260	.380	.936	.448	5	.500	12.1	3.42	8.68	4	872
JONES, SAM R	12	8.5	1.4	0.7	1643	.853	.091	.500	.837	.607	.502	8	.666	10.6	3.59	7.01	187	888
KAAT, JIM L	25	11.3	1.2	0.7	4530	1.019	.087	.239	.543	.802	.544	4	.160	13.2	3.45	9.75	-32	943
KERN, JIM R	13	4.0	0	6.7	793	.844	.044	.559	.820	.627	.482	0	.000	10.7	3.32	7.38	-48	690
KEY, JIMMY L	15	12.4	0.9	0.7	2591	.972	.098	.258	.594	.734	.614	5	.333	14.0	3.51	10.49	71	1120
KIM, BYUNG-HYUN R	7	5.1	0	12.3	568	.829	.099	.435	1.004	.359	.474	1	.143	17.4	3.76	13.64	86	1450
KINDER, ELLIS R	12	8.5	0.8	8.5	1479	.960	.079	.364	.506	.897	.590	4	.333	17.8	3.43	14.37	9	1446
KISON, BRUCE R	15	7.6	0.5	0.8	1809	.935	.082	.365	.593	.789	.567	0	.000	8.9	3.66	5.24	-74	450
KLINE, RON R	17	6.7	0.4	6.3	2078	1.016	.104	.351	.475	.996	.442	1	.058	13.4	3.75	9.65	-165	800
KNOWLES, DAROLD L	16	4.1	0	8.9	1092	.921	.059	.439	.623	.796	.471	0	.000	13.0	3.12	9.88	-108	880
KONSTANTY, JIM R	11	6.0	0.1	6.7	945	1.012	.093	.284	.283	1.106	.579	1	.091	12.8	3.46	9.34	-145	789
KOOSMAN, JERRY L	19	11.6	1.7	0.8	3839	.946	.075	.312	.665	.668	.515	0	.000	14.1	3.36	10.74	-51	1023
KOUFAX, SANDY* L	12	13.7	3.3	0.7	2324	.754	.087	.351	1.030	.162	.655	32	2.666	17.7	2.76	14.94	1053	2547
LABINE, CLEM R	13	5.9	0.2	7.4	1080	.966	.075	.367	.510	.898	.579	2	.154	13.5	3.63	9.87	-55	932
LACKEY, JOHN R	4	11.8	0.8	0	720	1.054	.106	.319	.782	.697	.553	1	.250	12.6	4.15	8.45	35	880
LANGSTON, MARK L	16	11.2	1.1	0	2963	.919	.105	.435	.832	.627	.531	3	.188	12.3	3.97	8.33	31	864
LANIER, MAX L	14	7.7	1.5	1.2	1619	.920	.040	.377	.507	.830	.568	0	.000	10.4	3.01	7.39	-87	652
LAROCHE, DAVE L	14	4.6	0	9.8	1049	.876	.090	.438	.781	.623	.528	0	.000	13.6	3.53	10.07	-32	975
LARY, FRANK R	12	10.7	1.8	0.9	2162	.982	.091	.285	.508	.850	.525	7	.583	13.4	3.49	9.91	86	1077
LAW, VERN R	16	10.1	1.8	0.8	2672	1.060	.100	.223	.409	.974	.524	0	.000	12.7	3.77	8.93	-150	743
LEE, BILL L	14	8.5	0.7	1.3	1944	1.091	.090	.273	.366	1.088	.569	0	.000	10.5	3.62	6.88	-173	515
LEE, BILL R	14	12.0	2.0	0.9	2864	1.031	.048	.311	.348	1.042	.518	6	.428	14.9	3.54	11.36	-32	1104
LEE, CLIFF L	4	8.8	0	0	444	.966	.133	.363	.797	.665	.673	1	.250	8.8	4.38	4.42	86	528
LEITER, AL L	19	8.5	0.5	0.1	2391	.900	.083	.486	.826	.643	.551	1	.053	9.1	3.80	5.30	-13	517
LEMON, BOB* R	13	15.9	2.3	1.6	2850	.897	.063	.438	.448	.950	.618	15	1.153	19.8	3.23	16.57	273	1930
LEONARD, DENNIS R	12	12.0	1.9	0	2187	.977	.092	.284	.604	.749	.576	3	.250	13.9	3.70	10.20	25	1045
LEONARD, DUTCH R	20	9.5	1.5	2.2	3218	1.026	.049	.229	.363	.941	.513	2	.100	13.2	3.25	9.95	-109	886
LIEBER, JON R	11	10.6	0.3	0.2	1905	1.072	.127	.194	.720	.673	.529	1	.091	11.1	4.20	6.90	-18	672
LINZY, FRANK R	11	5.6	0	10.0	816	.968	.042	.345	.438	.917	.521	0	.000	15.6	2.85	12.75	-132	1143
LITTELL, MARK R	9	3.5	0	6.2	532	.781	.052	.571	.875	.529	.508	0	.000	9.7	3.32	6.38	-7	631
LOCKWOOD, SKIP R	12	4.7	0.4	5.6	1236	.914	.079	.396	.670	.719	.370	0	.000	10.7	3.55	7.15	-116	599
LOES, BILLY R	11	7.2	0.8	2.9	1190	.953	.099	.353	.542	.863	.559	0	.000	10.9	3.89	7.01	-92	609
LOLICH, MICKEY L	16	13.5	2.5	0.6	3638	.925	.095	.302	.778	.544	.532	5	.312	16.6	3.44	13.16	100	1416
LONBORG, JIM R	15	10.4	1.0	0.2	2464	.974	.094	.334	.598	.804	.534	2	.133	11.6	3.86	7.74	-45	729
LOPAT, ED L	12	13.8	2.2	0.2	2439	1.010	.073	.266	.352	.997	.597	3	.250	16.2	3.21	12.99	-50	1294
LOPEZ, AURELIO R	11	5.6	0	8.4	910	.862	.112	.403	.697	.680	.633	0	.000	14.0	3.56	10.44	-15	1029
LOWE, DEREK R	9	9.3	0.3	9.4	1312	.995	.082	.295	.654	.718	.532	1	.111	19.0	3.83	15.17	-25	1492
LYLE, SPARKY L	16	6.1	0	14.8	1390	.929	.060	.346	.628	.707	.566	3	.187	20.9	2.88	18.02	15	1817

NAME	YRS	W YR	SH YR	SV YR	IP	H IP	HR IP	BB IP	K IP	QI	WL %	P TIT	PT AV	GROSS	ERA	CUM	AVG	PITCH
LYONS, TED* R	21	12.3	1.2	1.0	4161	1.078	.053	.269	.257	1.143	.531	10	.476	14.5	3.67	10.83	-45	1038
MADDUX, GREG R	20	15.9	1.8	0	4406	.926	.068	.206	.693	.507	.627	27	1.350	17.7	3.01	14.69	490	1959
MAGLIE, SAL R	10	11.9	2.5	1.4	1723	.923	.098	.326	.500	.847	.657	4	.400	15.8	3.15	12.65	7	1272
MAHAN, ART L	1	0	0	0	1	1.000	.000	.000	.000	1.000	.000	0	.000	0.0	0.00	0.00	-333	-333
MALONEY, JIM R	12	11.1	2.5	0.3	1849	.820	.074	.438	.868	.464	.615	1	.083	13.9	3.19	10.71	78	1149
MARBERRY, FIRPO R	14	10.6	0.5	7.2	2067	.991	.046	.332	.398	.971	.627	7	.500	18.3	3.63	14.67	52	1519
MARICHAL, JUAN* R	16	15.1	3.2	0.1	3507	.899	.091	.202	.656	.536	.631	12	.750	18.4	2.89	15.51	281	1832
MARSHALL, MIKE R	14	6.9	0	13.4	1386	.924	.056	.370	.634	.716	.464	3	.214	20.3	3.14	17.16	-42	1674
MARTINEZ, DENNIS R	23	10.7	1.3	0.3	4000	.974	.093	.291	.537	.821	.559	6	.261	12.3	3.70	8.60	0	860
MARTINEZ, PEDRO R	14	14.1	1.2	0.2	2513	.758	.077	.263	1.138	-.040	.701	24	1.714	15.5	2.72	12.78	818	2096
MARTINEZ, TIPPY R	14	3.9	0	8.2	834	.877	.063	.509	.757	.692	.567	0	.000	12.1	3.45	8.65	-41	824
MAY, RUDY L	16	9.5	1.5	0.7	2622	.882	.075	.365	.671	.651	.494	2	.125	11.7	3.46	8.24	-10	814
McCASKILL, KIRK R	12	8.8	0.9	0.6	1729	1.011	.089	.385	.580	.905	.495	0	.000	10.3	4.12	6.18	-137	481
McCORMICK, MIKE L	16	8.3	1.4	0.7	2380	.958	.107	.334	.555	.844	.511	2	.125	10.4	3.73	6.67	-69	598
McDANIEL, LINDY R	21	6.7	0	8.1	2139	.981	.080	.291	.636	.716	.542	3	.142	14.8	3.45	11.35	-10	1125
McDOWELL, JACK R	12	10.6	1.1	0	1889	.981	.092	.321	.694	.700	.593	5	.417	11.7	3.85	7.85	103	888
McDOWELL, ROGER R	12	5.8	0	13.3	1050	.995	.048	.390	.499	.934	.500	0	.000	19.1	3.30	15.80	-145	1435
McDOWELL, SAM L	15	9.4	1.5	0.9	2492	.781	.065	.526	.984	.388	.513	10	.666	11.8	3.17	8.63	263	1126
McGLOTHLIN, JIM R	9	7.4	1.2	0.3	1300	.959	.096	.321	.545	.831	.465	1	.111	8.9	3.61	5.29	-85	444
McGRAW, TUG L	19	5.0	0	9.4	1514	.870	.071	.384	.732	.593	.511	0	.000	14.4	3.14	11.26	-27	1099
McGREGOR, SCOTT L	13	10.6	1.7	0.3	2140	1.049	.109	.242	.422	.978	.561	1	.076	12.6	3.99	8.61	-113	748
McLAIN, DENNY R	10	13.1	2.9	0.2	1886	.872	.128	.290	.679	.611	.590	7	.700	16.2	3.39	12.81	226	1507
McMAHON, DON R	18	5.0	0	8.5	1310	.804	.080	.441	.765	.560	.570	1	.055	13.5	2.96	10.54	21	1075
McNALLY, DAVE L	14	13.1	2.3	0.1	2730	.911	.084	.302	.553	.744	.607	2	.142	15.5	3.24	12.26	1	1227
MESA, JOSE R	17	4.5	0.1	18.8	1426	1.054	.093	.414	.680	.881	.433	1	.059	23.4	4.29	19.11	-130	1781
MESSERSMITH, ANDY R	12	10.8	2.2	1.2	2230	.770	.078	.372	.728	.492	.568	9	.750	14.2	2.86	11.34	275	1409
MILLER, STU R	16	6.5	0.3	9.6	1694	.898	.082	.354	.687	.647	.505	4	.250	16.4	3.24	13.16	36	1352
MILLWOOD, KEVIN R	9	11.9	0.6	0	1559	.934	.101	.304	.821	.518	.588	4	.444	12.5	3.76	8.74	171	1045
MONBOUQUETTE, BILL R	11	10.3	1.6	0.2	1961	1.017	.107	.235	.572	.787	.504	0	.000	12.1	3.68	8.42	-94	748
MONGE, SID R	10	4.9	0	5.6	764	.927	.103	.466	.616	.880	.551	0	.000	10.5	3.53	6.97	-110	587
MONTGOMERY, JEFF R	13	3.5	0	23.4	869	.903	.093	.341	.843	.494	.469	1	.077	26.9	3.27	23.63	17	2380
MOORE, DEE R	1	0	0	0	7	.428	.000	.285	.428	.285	.000	0	.000	0.0	0.00	0.00	-95	-95
MOORE, MIKE R	14	11.5	1.1	0.1	2832	1.009	.103	.408	.589	.931	.478	0	.000	12.7	4.39	8.31	-151	680
MOOSE, BOB R	10	7.6	1.3	1.9	1304	1.003	.057	.296	.634	.722	.517	0	.000	10.8	3.50	7.30	-68	662
MORRIS, JACK R	18	14.1	1.5	0	3824	.932	.101	.363	.648	.748	.577	6	.333	15.6	3.90	11.70	54	1224
MORRIS, MATT R	8	12.6	1.0	0.5	1377	.993	.094	.275	.716	.646	.620	2	.250	14.1	3.61	10.49	75	1124
MORTON, CARL R	8	10.8	1.6	0.1	1648	1.063	.072	.342	.394	1.083	.486	0	.000	12.5	3.73	8.77	-199	678
MOSSI, DON L	12	8.4	0.6	4.1	1548	.964	.100	.248	.602	.710	.558	0	.000	13.1	3.43	9.67	-50	917
MOYER, JAMIE L	19	10.8	0.4	0	3140	1.028	.121	.285	.600	.834	.574	0	.000	11.2	4.16	7.04	-87	617
MULDER, MARK L	6	16.2	1.7	0	1208	.995	.098	.305	.645	.753	.660	5	.833	17.9	3.87	14.03	247	1650
MUNGO, VAN R	14	8.6	1.4	1.1	2113	.926	.042	.411	.588	.791	.511	5	.357	11.1	3.47	7.63	26	789
MURPHY, JOHNNY R	13	7.1	0	8.2	1045	.942	.049	.424	.361	1.054	.637	4	.307	15.3	3.50	11.80	-36	1144
MUSSINA, MIKE R	15	14.9	1.5	0	3013	.954	.107	.227	.797	.491	.638	6	.400	16.4	3.64	12.74	182	1456
MYERS, RANDY L	14	3.1	0	24.8	885	.856	.078	.447	.999	.382	.411	3	.214	27.9	3.19	24.71	81	2552
NARLESKI, RAY R	6	7.1	0.1	9.6	702	.863	.113	.477	.646	.807	.566	1	.166	16.8	3.60	13.20	-25	1295
NATHAN, JOE R	6	5.3	0	14.7	409	.780	.108	.457	.936	.409	.667	0	.000	20.0	3.44	16.56	86	1742
NEAGLE, DENNY L	13	9.5	0.5	0.2	1890	.998	.132	.314	.749	.695	.574	2	.154	10.2	4.24	5.96	11	607
NEN, ROBB R	10	4.5	0	31.4	715	.849	.071	.364	1.109	.175	.517	1	.100	35.9	2.98	32.92	147	3439
NEWCOMBE, DON R	10	14.9	2.4	0.7	2154	.975	.116	.227	.524	.794	.623	7	.700	18.0	3.56	14.44	176	1620
NEWHOUSER, HAL* L	17	12.1	1.9	1.5	2993	.893	.045	.417	.600	.755	.580	17	1.000	15.5	3.06	12.44	275	1519
NEWSOM, BOBO R	20	10.5	1.5	1.0	3759	1.002	.054	.460	.553	.963	.487	4	.200	13.0	3.98	9.02	-92	810
NIEDENFUER, TOM R	10	3.6	0	9.7	653	.920	.091	.346	.725	.632	.439	0	.000	13.3	3.29	10.01	-64	937
NIEKRO, JOE R	22	10.0	1.3	0.7	3584	.967	.077	.352	.487	.909	.520	2	.090	12.0	3.59	8.41	-99	742
NIEKRO, PHIL* R	24	13.3	1.8	1.2	5404	.933	.089	.334	.618	.738	.537	13	.541	16.3	3.35	12.95	113	1408
NOLAN, GARY R	10	11.0	1.4	0	1675	.899	.087	.247	.620	.613	.033	1	.100	12.4	3.08	9.32	33	965
NOMO, HIDEO R	11	11.2	0.8	0	1972	.891	.126	.458	.971	.504	.530	4	.364	12.0	4.21	7.79	13	7 92
OJEDA, BOBBY L	15	7.6	1.0	0	1884	.972	.079	.358	.598	.811	.540	2	.133	8.6	3.65	4.95	-46	449
OLSON, GREGG R	14	2.9	0	15.5	672	.890	.068	.491	.875	.574	.506	0	.000	18.4	3.46	14.94	-23	1471
OROSCO, JESSE L	24	3.6	0	6.0	1295	.815	.087	.449	.910	.441	.521	0	.000	9.6	3.16	6.44	27	671
ORTIZ, RUSS R	8	13.5	0.4	0	1457	.940	.102	.513	.721	.834	.603	2	.250	13.9	4.32	9.58	6	964
OSTEEN, CLAUDE L	18	10.8	2.2	0	3460	1.003	.071	.271	.465	.880	.501	0	.000	13.0	3.30	9.70	-126	844
OSWALT, ROY R	5	16.6	0.8	0	981	.951	.082	.229	.866	.396	.680	2	.400	17.4	3.07	14.33	228	1661
PAGE, JOE L	8	7.1	0.1	9.5	790	.920	.053	.532	.656	.849	.538	2	.250	16.7	3.53	13.17	-20	1297
PAIGE, SATCHEL* R	6	4.6	0.6	5.3	476	.901	.060	.384	.609	.736	.475	0	.000	10.5	3.29	7.21	-87	634
PALMER, JIM* R	19	14.1	2.7	0.2	3948	.848	.076	.332	.560	.696	.638	15	.789	17.0	2.86	14.14	243	1657
PAPPAS, MILT R	17	12.2	2.5	0.2	3186	.956	.093	.269	.542	.776	.560	1	.058	14.9	3.40	11.50	-52	1098
PARK, CHAN HO R	12	8.8	0.2	0	1610	.916	.113	.482	.876	.635	.570	0	.000	9.0	4.33	4.67	-22	445
PARNELL, MEL L	10	12.3	2.0	1.0	1752	.978	.059	.432	.417	1.052	.621	3	.300	15.3	3.50	11.80	-43	1137
PASCUAL, CAMILO R	18	9.7	2.0	0.6	2931	.926	.087	.365	.739	.639	.506	9	.500	12.3	3.63	8.67	122	989
PASSEAU, CLAUDE R	13	12.4	2.0	1.6	2719	1.050	.038	.267	.406	.949	.519	3	.230	16.0	3.32	12.68	-66	1202

NAME	YRS	W YR	SH YR	SV YR	IP	H IP	HR IP	BB IP	K IP	QI	WL %	P TIT	PT AV	GROSS	ERA	CUM	AVG	PITCH
PEARSON, MONTE R	10	10.0	0.5	0.4	1429	974	.057	.517	.491	1.057	.621	3	.300	10.9	4.00	6.90	-45	645
PEAVY, JOSH R	4	11.5	0.8	0	662	.887	.113	.329	.959	,370	.597	2	.500	12.3	3.33	8.97	242	1139
PENA, ALEJANDRO R	15	3.7	0.5	4.9	1058	.906	.071	.313	.793	.497	.519	2	.133	9.1	3.11	5.99	52	651
PENNOCK, HERB* L	22	10.9	1.5	1.5	3571	1.092	.035	.256	.343	1.040	.597	5	.227	13.9	3.60	10.30	-72	958
PENNY, BRAD R	6	9.3	0.3	0	969	.992	.099	.316	.720	.687	.514	0	.000	9.6	4.00	5.60	-58	502
PERCIVAL, TROY R	11	2.7	0	29.5	612	.673	.114	.431	1.144	.074	.423	0	.000	32.2	3.10	29.10	116	3026
PERRANOSKI, RON L	13	6.0	0	13.7	1174	.934	.042	.398	.585	.789	.516	3	.231	19.7	2.79	16.91	-14	1677
PERRY, GAYLORD* R	22	14.2	2.4	0.5	5350	.922	.074	.257	.660	.593	.542	9	.409	17.1	3.11	13.99	119	1518
PERRY, JIM R	17	12.6	1.8	0.5	3285	.951	.093	.303	.479	.868	.553	4	.235	14.9	3.45	11.45	-26	1119
PETERS, GARY L	14	8.8	1.6	0.3	2081	.910	.075	.339	.682	.642	.546	5	.357	10.7	3.25	7.45	116	861
PETRY, DAN R	13	9.6	0.8	0.0	2080	.953	.104	.409	.511	.955	.546	0	.000	10.4	3.95	6.45	-136	509
PIERCE, BILLY L	18	11.7	2.1	1.7	3306	.904	.085	.356	.604	.741	.555	8	.444	15.5	3.27	12.23	86	1309
PODRES, JOHNNY L	15	9.8	1.6	0.7	2265	.988	.106	.328	.633	.789	.561	4	.266	12.1	3.68	8.42	12	854
POLLET, HOWIE L	14	9.3	1.7	1.4	2107	.994	.069	.353	.443	.973	.530	5	.357	12.4	3.51	8.89	-29	860
PORTERFIELD, BOB R	12	7.2	1.9	0.6	1567	1.002	.072	.352	.365	1.061	.473	4	.333	9.7	3.79	5.91	-85	506
PRIOR, MARK R	4	10.3	0.3	0	613	.874	.111	.318	1.173	.013	.641	0	.000	10.6	3.24	7.36	209	945
PURKEY, BOB R	13	9.9	1.0	0.6	2114	1.026	.092	.241	.375	.984	.529	1	.076	11.5	3.79	7.71	-126	645
QUISENBERRY, DAN R	12	4.6	0	20.3	1043	1.020	.056	.155	.363	.868	.549	5	.417	24.9	2.76	22.14	33	2247
RADATZ, DICK R	7	7.4	0	17.4	693	.767	.101	.463	1.165	.166	.547	2	.286	24.8	3.13	21.67	222	2389
RADKE, BRAD R	11	12.4	0.9	0	2289	1.069	.132	.180	.605	.776	.511	0	.000	13.3	4.22	9.08	-88	820
RAFFENSBERGER, KEN L	15	7.9	2.0	1.0	2151	1.049	.089	.208	.374	.972	.436	3	.200	10.9	3.60	7.30	-112	618
RASCHI, VIC R	10	13.2	2.6	0.3	1819	.915	.076	.399	.518	.872	.667	3	.300	16.1	3.72	12.38	31	1269
RAWLEY, SHANE L	12	9.2	0.5	3.3	1871	1.033	.081	.392	.529	.977	.485	0	.000	13.0	4.02	8.98	-164	734
REARDON, JEFF R	16	4.6	0	22.9	1132	.883	.096	.316	.775	.520	.487	1	.062	27.4	3.16	24.24	10	2434
REEVES, BOBBY R	1	0	0	0	7	.857	.000	.142	.000	.999	.000	0	.000	0.0	3.68	-3.68	-333	-701
REGAN, PHIL R	13	7.3	0	7.0	1372	1.014	.109	.325	.541	.907	.542	2	.153	14.3	3.84	10.46	-70	976
RENKO, STEVE R	15	8.9	0.9	0.4	2494	.977	.099	.404	.583	.897	.479	0	.000	10.2	3.99	6.21	-139	482
REUSCHEL, RICK R	19	11.2	1.3	0.2	3548	1.011	.062	.263	.567	.769	.528	2	.105	12.7	3.37	9.33	-45	888
REUSS, JERRY L	22	10.0	1.7	0.5	3669	1.017	.066	.307	.519	.871	.535	1	.045	12.2	3.64	8.56	-97	759
REYNOLDS, ALLIE R	13	14.0	2.7	3.7	2492	.880	.053	.506	.571	.868	.630	8	.615	20.4	3.30	17.10	125	1835
RHODEN, RICK R	16	9.4	1.0	0	2593	1.005	.076	.308	.547	.842	.547	0	.000	10.4	3.59	6.81	-98	583
RICHARD, J. R. R	10	10.7	1.9	0	1606	.764	.045	.479	.930	.358	.601	6	.600	12.6	3.15	9.45	281	1226
RIGHETTI, DAVE L	16	5.1	0.1	15.8	1404	.917	.068	.421	.792	.614	.509	1	.063	22.1	3.44	18.66	-14	1852
RIJO, JOSE R	12	9.3	0.3	0.3	1786	.897	.074	.355	.871	.455	.561	3	.250	9.9	3.16	6.74	119	793
RIVERA, MARIANO R	11	4.9	0.1	34.5	807	.781	.052	.266	.902	.197	.607	4	.364	39.5	2.33	37.17	258	3975
ROBERTS, ROBIN* R	19	15.0	2.3	1.3	4688	.977	.107	.192	.502	.774	.539	20	1.052	18.6	3.41	15.19	272	1791
ROE, PREACHER L	12	10.5	1.4	0.8	1914	.996	.103	.263	.499	.863	.602	3	.250	12.7	3.43	9.27	-3	924
ROGERS, KENNY L	17	11.2	0.5	1.6	2862	1.043	.100	.355	.612	.886	.592	0	.000	13.3	4.21	9.09	-98	811
ROGERS, STEVE R	13	12.1	2.8	0.1	2837	.923	.053	.308	.571	.713	.510	4	.307	15.0	3.17	11.83	34	1217
ROOT, CHARLIE R	17	11.8	1.2	2.4	3197	1.017	.058	.278	.456	.897	.557	4	.235	15.4	3.59	11.81	-35	1146
ROWE, SCHOOLBOY R	15	10.5	1.4	0.8	2219	1.050	.059	.251	.411	.949	.610	3	.200	12.7	3.87	8.83	-46	837
RUETER, KIRK L	13	10.0	0.1	0	1918	1.091	.115	.303	.426	1.083	.586	1	.077	10.1	4.27	5.83	-140	443
RUFFING, RED* R	22	12.4	2.0	0.7	4344	.986	.058	.354	.457	.941	.548	6	.272	15.1	3.80	11.3	-40	1090
RUTH, BABE L (ALL)	10	9.4	1.7	0.4	1221	.797	.008	.361	.399	.767	.671	4	.400	11.5	2.28	9.22	101	1023
RUTH, BABE L (POST#)	2	1.0	0	0	18	1.277	.000	.277	.166	1.388	1.000	0	.000	1.0	4.00	-3.00	-129	-429
RYAN, B. J. L	7	2.3	0	6.0	381	.806	.076	.512	1.220	.174	.457	0	.000	8.3	3.54	4.76	94	570
RYAN, NOLAN* R	27	12.0	2.2	0.1	5387	.728	.058	.518	1.060	.244	.526	32	1.185	14.3	3.19	11.11	489	1600
SABERHAGEN, BRET R	16	10.4	1.0	0.1	2563	.957	.085	.184	.669	.557	.588	8	.500	11.5	3.34	8.16	177	993
SADECKI, RAY L	18	7.5	1.1	0.3	2500	.982	.096	.368	.645	.801	.508	0	.000	8.9	3.78	5.12	-97	415
SAIN, JOHNNY R	11	12.6	1.4	4.6	2125	1.009	.084	.291	.428	.956	.545	5	.454	18.6	3.49	15.11	14	1525
SAMBITO, JOE L	11	3.3	0	7.6	629	.893	.076	.310	.777	.502	.493	0	.000	10.9	3.03	7.87	-3	784
SCHILLING, CURT R	18	10.7	1.1	1.2	2906	.899	.103	.227	.975	.254	.594	12	.667	13.0	3.40	9.60	336	1296
SCHMIDT, JASON R	11	10.5	0.7	0	1740	.925	.091	.394	.890	.520	.589	6	.545	11.2	3.95	7.25	205	930
SCHMITZ, JOHNNY L	13	7.1	1.2	1.6	1812	.974	.053	.417	.411	1.033	.449	3	.230	9.9	3.55	6.35	-118	517
SCHUMACHER, HAL R	13	12.1	2.0	0.5	2482	.976	.056	.363	.365	1.030	.566	1	.076	14.6	3.36	11.24	-129	995
SCORE, HERB L	8	6.8	1.3	0.3	858	.709	.092	.667	.975	.493	.545	5	.625	8.4	3.36	5.04	225	729
SCOTT, MIKE R	13	9.5	1.6	0.2	2068	.898	.083	.303	.710	.574	.534	8	.615	11.3	3.54	7.76	191	967
SEAVER, TOM* R	20	15.5	3.0	0	4782	.830	.079	.290	.761	.438	.603	23	1.150	18.5	2.86	15.64	438	2002
SEWELL, RIP R	13	11.0	1.5	1.1	2119	.991	.054	.352	.300	1.097	.596	2	.153	13.6	3.48	10.12	-116	896
SHANTZ, BOBBY L	16	7.4	0.9	3.0	1935	.927	.078	.332	.554	.783	.546	4	.250	11.3	3.38	7.92	4	796
SHAW, DON L	5	2.6	0	1.2	189	.878	.101	.534	.651	.862	.481	0	.000	3.8	4.01	-0.21	-127	-148
SHEA, FRANK R	8	7.0	1.5	0.6	943	.900	.069	.527	.382	1.114	.549	2	.250	9.1	3.80	5.30	-105	425
SHEETS, BEN R	5	11.0	0.2	0	982	.996	.119	.222	.844	.493	.470	0	.000	11.2	3.83	7.37	-8	729
SHORT, CHRIS L	15	9.0	1.6	1.2	2325	.952	.078	.346	.700	.676	.506	0	.000	11.8	3.43	8.37	-56	781
SIMMONS, CURT L	20	9.6	1.8	0.2	3348	.989	.076	.317	.506	.876	.513	1	.050	11.6	3.54	8.06	-104	702
SMITH, EDDIE L	10	7.3	0.8	1.2	1595	.974	.066	.463	.435	1.068	.392	0	.000	9.3	3.82	5.48	-225	323
SMITH, LEE R	18	3.9	0	26.6	1289	.879	.069	.377	.971	.354	.436	4	.222	30.5	3.03	27.47	101	2848
SMITH, ZANE L	13	7.7	1.2	0.2	1919	1.032	.064	.309	.527	.878	.465	0	.000	9.1	3.74	5.36	-138	398
SMOLTZ, JOHN R	17	10.4	0.9	9.1	2929	.866	.080	.301	.876	.371	.580	9	.529	20.4	3.26	17.14	246	1960
SOTO, MARIO R	12	8.3	1.0	0.3	1730	.806	.099	.379	.837	.447	.521	4	.333	9.6	3.47	6.13	135	748

NAME	YRS	W YR	SH YR	SV YR	IP	H IP	HR IP	BB IP	K IP	QI	WL %	P TIT	PT AV	GROSS	ERA	CUM	AVG	PITCH
SPAHN, WARREN* L	21	17.2	3.0	1.3	5243	.921	.082	.273	.492	.784	.597	37	1.761	21.5	3.09	18.41	524	2365
SPLITTORFF, PAUL L	15	11.0	1.1	0	2554	1.035	.075	.305	.413	1.002	.537	1	.067	12.1	3.81	8.29	-133	696
STALEY, GERRY R	15	8.9	0.6	4.0	1981	1.044	.094	.267	.366	1.039	.547	1	.067	13.5	3.70	9.80	-142	838
STEWART, DAVE R	16	10.5	0.6	1.2	2630	.950	.100	.393	.662	.781	.566	6	.375	12.3	3.95	8.35	53	888
STIEB, DAVE R	16	11.0	1.9	0.2	2895	.888	.078	.357	.577	.746	.562	7	.438	13.1	3.44	9.66	80	1046
STOTTLEMYRE, MEL SR.R	11	14.9	3.6	0	2661	.915	.064	.304	.472	.811	.541	3	.272	18.5	2.97	15.53	0	1553
STRATTON, MONTY R	5	7.2	1.0	0.4	487	1.004	.065	.305	.402	.972	.610	1	.200	8.6	3.71	4.89	-54	435
STURDIVANT, TOM R	10	5.9	0.7	1.7	1137	.905	.094	.394	.619	.774	.536	2	.200	8.3	3.74	4.56	-12	444
SUTCLIFFE, RICK R	18	9.5	1.0	0.3	2698	.986	.087	.400	.622	.851	.551	4	.222	10.8	4.08	6.72	-26	646
SUTTER, BRUCE R	12	5.6	0	25.0	1042	.843	.073	.296	.826	.386	.489	5	.416	30.6	2.83	27.77	173	2950
SUTTON, DON* R	23	14.0	2.5	0.2	5282	.888	.089	.254	.676	.555	.559	7	.304	16.7	3.26	13.44	102	1446
SWIFT, BILL C. R	13	7.2	0.3	2.1	1600	1.055	.073	.317	.479	.966	.547	1	.111	9.6	3.95	5.65	-114	451
SWIFT, BILL V. R	11	8.6	0.6	1.8	1637	1.027	.062	.214	.388	.915	.537	0	.000	11.6	3.58	7.42	-126	616
SWINDELL, GREG L	17	7.2	0.7	0.4	2233	1.036	.117	.224	.691	.686	.502	0	.000	8.3	3.86	4.44	-61	383
TANANA, FRANK L	21	11.4	1.6	0	4188	.970	.107	.300	.662	.715	.504	3	.143	13.0	3.66	9.34	-23	911
TEKULVE, KENT R	16	5.8	0	11.5	1436	.908	.043	.341	.542	.750	.511	0	.000	17.3	2.85	14.45	-80	1365
TERRY, RALPH R	12	8.9	1.6	0.9	1849	.945	.116	.241	.540	.762	.519	3	.250	11.4	3.62	7.78	2	780
TEWKSBURY, BOB R	13	8.5	0.5	0.1	1807	1.131	.079	.162	.449	.923	.519	1	.077	9.1	3.92	5.18	-109	409
THIGPEN, BOBBY R	9	3.4	0	22.3	568	.945	.098	.419	.661	.801	.463	1	.111	25.7	3.44	22.26	-76	2150
TIANT, LUIS R	19	12.0	2.5	0.7	3486	.882	.053	.316	.693	.558	.571	7	.368	15.2	3.30	11.90	127	1317
TIMLIN, MIKE R	15	4.2	0	8.7	1036	.950	.092	.316	.752	.606	.504	1	.067	12.9	3.50	9.40	-12	928
TORREZ, MIKE R	18	10.2	0.8	0	3044	.999	.073	.450	.461	1.061	.536	1	.055	11.0	3.96	7.04	-156	548
TOWERS, JOSH R	5	7.6	0.4	0.2	557	1.183	.156	.149	.496	.992	.521	0	.000	8.2	4.49	3.71	-157	214
TRACHSEL, STEVE R	13	9.2	0.5	0	2139	1.016	.138	.356	.673	.837	.469	0	.000	9.7	4.23	5.47	-123	424
TROUT, DIZZY R	15	11.3	1.8	2.3	2725	.969	.041	.383	.460	.933	.514	6	.400	15.4	3.23	12.17	-6	1211
TRUCKS, FIRE R	17	10.4	1.9	1.7	2682	.900	.070	.405	.571	.804	.567	3	.176	14.0	3.39	10.61	-20	1041
TUDOR, JOHN L	12	9.7	1.3	0	1797	.933	.086	.264	.549	.734	.619	2	.166	11.0	3.12	7.88	17	805
TURLEY, BOB R	12	8.4	2.0	1.0	1712	.797	.081	.623	.738	.763	.543	8	.666	11.4	3.64	7.76	148	924
UPSHAW, CECIL R	9	3.7	0	9.5	563	.968	.065	.314	.573	.774	.486	0	.000	13.2	3.13	10.07	-96	911
URBINA, UGUETH R	11	4.0	0	21.5	697	.846	.123	.440	1.168	.241	.473	1	.091	25.5	3.45	22.05	108	2313
VALENZUELA, FERN'DO L	17	10.2	1.8	0.1	2930	.928	.077	.393	.708	.690	.531	7	.412	12.1	3.54	8.56	84	940
VANCE, DAZZY* R	16	12.3	1.8	0.6	2967	.946	.044	.283	.689	.584	.585	25	1.562	14.7	3.24	11.46	521	1667
VANDER MEER, JOHN L	13	9.1	2.2	0.1	2104	.855	.047	.538	.615	.825	.496	4	.307	11.4	3.44	7.96	-7	789
VAZQUEZ, JAVIER R	8	11.1	0.9	0	1643	1.013	.136	.266	.863	552	.489	1	.125	12.0	4.28	7.72	21	793
VEALE, BOB L	13	9.2	1.5	1.6	1926	.874	.047	.445	.884	482	.558	1	.077	12.3	3.07	9.23	51	974
VIOLA, FRANK L	15	11.7	1.1	0	2836	.997	.104	.308	.650	.756	.540	3	.230	14.6	3.67	10.93	11	1104
VUCKOVICH, PETE R	11	8.4	0.7	0.9	1455	.999	.073	.374	.606	.840	.574	3	.272	10.0	3.66	6.34	2	636
WAGNER, BILLY L	11	3.1	0	25.8	630	.649	.094	.344	1.333	-.246	.515	1	.091	28.9	2.40	26.50	284	2934
WAKEFIELD, TIM R	13	11.1	0.5	1.7	2292	.968	.129	.391	.694	.794	.539	0	.000	13.3	4.28	9.02	-85	817
WALTERS, BUCKY R	16	12.3	2.6	0.2	3104	.963	.049	.361	.356	1.017	.553	16	1.000	15.1	3.30	11.80	178	1358
WARD, DUANE R	9	3.6	0	13.4	667	.826	.048	.429	1.018	.285	.464	1	.111	17.0	3.28	13.72	23	1395
WARNEKE, LON R	15	12.8	2.0	0.8	2782	.979	.062	.265	.409	.897	.613	6	.400	15.6	3.18	12.42	38	1280
WASHBURN, RAY R	10	7.2	1.0	0.5	1209	.999	.088	.292	.578	.801	.529	0	.000	8.7	3.53	5.17	-90	427
WATT, EDDIE R	10	3.8	0	8.0	659	.804	.056	.385	.701	.544	.514	0	.000	11.8	2.91	8.89	-10	879
WEAVER, JEFF R	7	11.1	0.7	0.3	1396	1.045	.113	.273	.671	.760	.473	1	.143	12.1	4.44	7.66	-48	718
WEIR, ROY L	4	1.5	0.5	0	106	.896	.037	.471	.396	1.008	.600	0	.000	2.0	3.55	-1.55	-136	-291
WELCH, BOB R	17	12.4	1.6	0.4	3092	.935	.086	.334	.636	.719	.591	3	.176	14.4	3.47	10.93	16	1109
WELLS, DAVID L	19	11.9	0.6	0.7	3206	1.041	.117	.207	.649	.716	.614	7	.368	13.2	4.06	9.14	89	1003
WETTELAND, JOHN R	12	4.0	0	27.5	765	.805	.095	.329	1.051	.178	.516	1	.083	31.5	2.93	28.57	140	2997
WICKMAN, BOB R	13	4.5	0.1	16.5	955	.988	.077	.417	.739	.743	.536	0	.000	21.1	3.62	17.48	-69	1679
WILHELM, HOYT* R	21	6.8	0.2	10.8	2254	.779	.066	.345	.714	.476	.540	3	.143	17.8	2.52	15.28	69	1597
WILKS, TED R	10	5.9	0.5	4.6	913	.911	.083	.309	.441	.862	.663	4	.400	11.0	3.26	7.74	67	841
WILLIAMS, MITCH L	11	5.3	0	23.2	654	.752	.064	.752	.948	.620	.476	0	.000	28.5	3.39	25.11	-48	2463
WILLIAMS, STAN R	14	7.7	0.7	3.0	1764	.865	.090	.424	.739	.640	.537	0	.000	11.4	3.48	7.92	-34	758
WILLIS, DONTRELL L	3	15.3	2.3	0	594	.961	.074	.293	.759	.569	.630	3	1.000	17.6	3.27	14.33	354	1787
WILSON, DON R	9	11.5	2.2	0.2	1748	.846	.068	.366	.733	.547	.531	1	.111	13.9	3.15	10.75	31	1106
WILSON, EARL R	11	11.0	1.1	0	2051	.908	.115	.388	.707	.704	.526	1	.090	12.1	3.69	8.41	-29	812
WISE, RICK R	18	10.4	1.6	0	3127	1.031	.083	.257	.526	.845	.509	0	.000	12.0	3.69	8.31	-112	724
WITT, MIKE R	12	9.8	0.9	0.5	2108	.980	.087	.338	.651	.754	.502	0	.000	11.2	3.83	7.37	-84	653
WOLF, RANDY L	7	9.3	1.0	0	1118	.953	.129	.361	.829	.614	.520	0	.000	10.3	4.14	6.16	-31	585
WOMACK, DOOLEY R	5	3.8	0	4.8	302	.837	.069	.367	.586	.687	.514	0	.000	8.6	2.95	5.65	-57	508
WOOD, KERRY R	7	10.0	0.7	0	1109	.772	.111	.485	1.160	.208	.565	4	.571	10.7	3.67	7.03	309	1012
WOOD, WILBUR R	17	9.6	1.4	3.3	2684	.961	.077	.269	.525	.782	.512	4	.235	14.3	3.24	11.06	-12	1094
WOODESHICK, HAL L	11	4.0	0	5.5	847	.963	.047	.459	.571	.898	.415	1	.090	9.5	3.56	5.94	-131	463
WORRELL, TODD R	11	4.5	0	23.3	694	.876	.094	.356	.905	.421	.490	2	.182	27.8	3.09	24.71	84	2555
WORTHINGTON, AL R	14	5.3	0.2	7.8	1246	.906	.084	.422	.669	.743	.478	1	.071	13.3	3.39	9.91	-64	926
WYATT, WHIT R	16	6.6	1.0	0.8	1761	.956	.055	.364	.495	.880	.527	7	.437	8.4	3.79	4.61	28	489
WYNN, EARLY* R	23	13.0	2.1	0.6	4564	.940	.074	.388	.511	891	.551	11	.478	15.7	3.54	12.16	46	1262
YOUNG, MATT L	10	5.5	0.5	2.5	1190	1.014	.083	.474	.720	.851	.367	0	.000	8.5	4.40	4.10	-161	249
ZITO, BARRY L	6	14.3	0.7	0	1209	.841	.100	.381	.782	.540	.619	1	.167	15.0	3.50	11.50	82	1232

BIBLIOGRAPHY

BOOKS

Baseball America, *Baseball America 2001 Directory,* Durham, NC, 2001
Blake, Mike, *The Incomplete Book or Baseball Superstitions, Rituals and Oddities,* New York, Wynwood Press, 1991
Broeg, Bob, *Stan Musial: "The Man's" Own Story,* New York, Doubleday, 1964
Broeg, Bob and Jerry Vickery, *The St. Louis Cardinals Encyclopedia,* Chicago, Master's Press, 1998
Carter, Craig, Editor, *The Complete Baseball Record Book,* St. Louis, The Sporting News, 1986
Charlton, James, Editor, *The Baseball Chronology,* New York, Macmillan Publishing Co., 1991
Connor Floyd and John Snyder, *Day By Day in Cincinnati Reds History,* New York, Leisure Press, 1983
Dickson, Paul, *The Joy of Keeping Score,* New York, Walker and Company, 1996
Flynn, George L., *Great Moments in Baseball,* New York, Gallery Books, 1987
Garber III, Angus G., *Baseball Legends,* Philadelphia, Courage Books, 1993
Golenbock, Peter, *Number 1,* New York, Dell, 1981
Graham, Frank, *The New York Yankees,* New York, Putnam & Sons, 1958
Gutman, Bill, *The Golden Age of Baseball 1941-1963,* New York, Gallery Books, 1989
Hawkins, John C., *This Date in Baltimore Orioles and St. Louis Browns History,* New York, Stein and Day, 1983
Honig, Donald, *The St. Louis Cardinals, An Illustrated History,* New York, Prentice Hall Press, 1991
James, Bill, *The Bill James Baseball Abstract, New York, Ballantine Books, 1983*
James, Bill, *The Baseball Book 1990, New York, Villard Books, 1990*
Kubik, Richard S., *Baseball Trades and Acquisitions 1950-1979,* Smithtown, NY, Exposition Press, 1981
Leptich, John and Dave Baranowski, *This Date in St. Louis Cardinals History,* New York, Stein and Day, 1983
Leventhal, Josh, *Take Me Out to the Ballpark,* New York, Black Dog and Leventhal, 2000
Lewis, Michael, *Moneyball:The Art of Winning an Unfair Game,* New York, W. W. Norton & Co., 2003
Loverro, Thom, *The Encyclopedia of Negro League Baseball,* New York, Checkmark Books, 2003
Mann, Steve, *The Bseball Superstats 1989,* New York, McGraw-Hill, 1989
Mead, William B., *Even the Browns,* Chicago, Contemporary Books, 1978
Mote, James, *Everything Baseball,* New York, Prentice Hall Press, 1989
Nash, Bruce and Allan Zullo, *Believe It or Else!,* New York, Dell Publishing, 1992
National Baseball Hall of Fame and Museum, The National Baseball Library and Gerald Astor, *The Baseball Hall of Fame 50th Anniversary Book,* New York, Prentice Hall Press, 1988
Neft, David S., Richard M. Cohen and Michael L. Neft, *The Sports Encyclopedia: Baseball,* New York, St, Martin's Griffin, 2003
Nemec, David., *Great Baseball Feats, Facts and Firsts,* New York, Signet, NAL, 1990
Nemec, David, et al, *20th Century Baseball Chronicle,* New York, Beekman House, 1991
Neuman, Jeffrey, *The Cardinals,* New York, Collier Books, 1983
Obojski, Robert, *Baseball Bloopers and Diamond Oddities,* New York, Sterling Publishing, 1989
Okkonen, Marc, *Baseball Uniforms of the 20th Century,* New York, Sterling Publishing, 1991
Okrent, Daniel, and Harris Lewine, *The Ultimate Baseball Book,* Boston, Houghton Mifflin Co. 1981
Raycraft, M. Donald, *Value Guide to Baseball Collectibles,* Paducah, KY, Collector Books, 1992
Reidenbaugh, Lowell, *Baseball's Hall of Fame Cooperstown,* New York, Gramercy Books, 1999
Roberts, Brendan, Editor, *The Official Major League Baseball Fact Book,* St. Louis, The Sporting News, 2000
Robinson, Jackie, and Alfred Duckett, *I Never Had It Made,* New York, Harper Collins, 1995
Siwoff, Seymour, Steve Hirdt and Peter Hirdt, *The 1986 Elias Baseball Analyst,* New York, Collier Books, 1986
Solomon, Burt, *The Baseball Timeline,* New York, Dorling Kindersley, 2001
Spalding, A. G., *Spalding's Base Ball Guide 1883,* Chicago, A. G. Spalding & Bros., 1883
Spalding, A. G., *Spalding's Base Ball Guide 1888,* Chicago, A. G. Spalding & Bros., 1888
Stang, Mark and Linda Harkness, *Baseball By the Numbers,* Lanham, MD, Scarecrow Press, 1996
Sugar, Bert Randolph, *Baseballistics,* New York, St. Martin's Press, 1990
Sporting News, The, *Baseball Guide,* St. Louis, The Sporting News, 1986-2005
Sporting News, The, *Baseball Register,* St. Louis, The Sporting News, 1985-2005
Sporting News, The, *The American League Red Book,* St. Louis, The Sporting News, 1996
Sporting News, The, *The National League Green Book,* St. Louis, The Sporting News, 1996
Thorn, John, *Treasures of the Baseball Hall of Fame,* New York, Villard, 1998
Thorn, John, Pete Palmer, et al, *Complete Baseball, Kingston,* NY, Total Sports Publications, 2001
Veeck, Bill with Ed Linn, *Veeck As in Wreck,* New York, Putnam's, 1962
Wheeler, Lonnie and John Baskin, *The Cincinnati Game,* Wilmington, OH, Orange Frazer Press
Wolf, George D., *Yankees By the Numbers 1929-1991,* New York, George D. Wolf, 1991
Zminda, Don, *From Abba Dabba to Zorro,* Morton Grove, IL, Stats Publishing, 1999

MAGAZINES

Baseball Digest, Evanston, IL, 1943-1992
Sporting Life, Philadelphia, July 8, 1916
Sports Collectors Digest, Iola, WI, Krause Publications Inc., 1992-2002
Sports Illustrated, New York, Time Inc., 12/27/93-1/ 2/94

NEWSPAPERS

The Bergen Record, Hackensack, NJ, 1991-present
The Cincinnati Commercial Gazette, Cincinnati, OH, 1883-1899
The Cincinnati Enquirer, Cincinnati, OH, 1883-present
The Cleveland Plain-Dealer, Cleveland, OH, 1916-1933
The Cleveland Press, Cleveland, OH, 1916-1924
The New York Daily News, New York, 1916-present
The New York Times, New York, 1883-present
The Sporting News, St. Louis, 1886-present
USA Today, Baseball Weekly, McLean, VA, Gannett Co., Inc., 1992-2001
USA Today, Sports Weekly, McLean, VA, Gannett Co., Inc., 2002-present
The Washington Post, Washington DC, 1916-1933

VIDEO

World Series Videos 1943-present, Charlottesville, VA, Baseball Direct 1995

WEBSITES

baseball-almanac.com
BaseballLibrary.com
ignarski.tripod.com (Kasey's Cubs Page)
MLB.COM
Official MLB Team Websites of each team
retrosheet.org
sportingnews.com

OTHER

Many teams published their own scorecards other than Stevens.
Stevens, Harry M., Official Daily Scorecards of MLB games
Television: ABC, CBS, ESPN, ESPN2, FOX Sports, NBC, TBS, WPIX, YES Network

PHOTO CREDITS

All illustrations by Jack Looney.

AP Wide World Photos: pp. 3, 6, 7 (left), 26, 39, 44, 45, 90, 93 (bottom, left), 95 (bottom right), 30, 32, 33, 35, 40, 62 (left), 103 (right), 109 (bottom), 121 (right), 172, 236, 238, 251, 295, 395, 396, 397, 402, 403, 496, 497 (left), 500.

Jack Looney: pp. iii, vi, x (bottom left & right), 4, 9 (bottom right), 12, 42 (background), 68, 98, 353, 498, 504, 520.

John Tremmel: pp. i, x (top), 0, 2, 7 (right), 8, 31, 38, 42, 46, 47, 48, 49, 50, 51, 52, 53, 54, 55, 57, 58, 59, 60, 61, 62, 63, 64, 66, 67, 80, 9 3(right), 100, 101, 102, 103 (left), 104, 105, 106, 107, 108, 110, 116, 117 (bottom), 118, 119, 120, 121 (left), 122, 123, 138, 149, 189, 231, 245, 249, 262, 273, 284, 312, 319, 330, 371, 377, 398, 399, 400, 407, 408, 410, 43, 415, 417, 418, 421, 425, 431, 435, 450, 457, 460, 467, 477, 487, 493, 497(right), 498, 502, 506, 512, 519, 521, 522.

National Baseball Hall of Fame Library Cooperstown, N.Y.: 10, 34, 95, 403 (top, left, bottom).

Transcendental Graphics: pp. 5, 11, 23, 24, 28, 29, 30, 32, 33, 35, 40, 62 (left), 65, 70, 71, 81, 83, 84, 85, 95, 96, 97, 103 (center), 109 (top), 113, 117 (top), 401, 406.

INDEX